THE UNION ARMY

1861–1865

Organization and Operations

VOLUME II: THE WESTERN THEATER

THE UNION ARMY

1861–1865

★ ★ ★ ★

Organization and Operations
VOLUME II: THE WESTERN THEATER

By Frank J. Welcher

INDIANA UNIVERSITY PRESS

BLOOMINGTON AND INDIANAPOLIS

The author wishes to thank Dr. Richard J. Sommers for reading the manuscript of this volume and for his many helpful suggestions, which contributed greatly to an improvement in the quality of the text.

The paper used in this publication meets the minimum requirements of American National Standard for Information Sciences—Permanence of Paper for Printed Library Materials, ANSI Z39.48-1984.

Manufactured in the United States of America

Library of Congress Cataloging-in-Publication Data
(Revised for vol. 2)

Welcher, Frank Johnson, date.
The Union Army, 1861–1865 : organizations and operations.

Includes index.
Contents: v. 1. The Eastern theater — v. 2. The Western theater.
1. United States. Army—History—Civil War, 1861–1865.
2. United States. Army—Organization—History—19th century.
3. United States—History—Civil War, 1861–1865—Campaigns. I. Title.
E491.W43   1989   973.7'41   88-45749
ISBN 0-253-36453-1 (v. 1)
ISBN 0-253-36454-X (v. 2)
1 2 3 4 5 96 95 94 93

VOLUME II: THE WESTERN THEATER

CONTENTS

✰✰✰✰

FIELD ARMIES 157

ARMY CORPS 236

MISCELLANEOUS ORGANIZATIONS 374

BATTLES AND CAMPAIGNS 401

THE UNION ARMY

1861–1865

Organization and Operations

VOLUME II: THE WESTERN THEATER

MILITARY DIVISIONS
OF THE ARMY

✮✮✮✮

MILITARY DIVISION
OF THE GULF

In the reorganization of the military divisions and departments of the army June 27, 1865, the Military Division of the Gulf was created to include the Department of Florida, the Department of Mississippi, and the Department of Louisiana and Texas. Philip H. Sheridan was assigned command, with headquarters at New Orleans. Henry W. Slocum was assigned command of the Department of Mississippi, with headquarters at Vicksburg; Edward R. S. Canby was assigned command of the Department of Louisiana and Texas, with headquarters at New Orleans; and John G. Foster was assigned command of the Department of Florida, with headquarters at Tallahassee. Sheridan assumed command of the Military Division of the Gulf July 17, 1865.

For additional information, see Department of Mississippi, June 27, 1865–August 6, 1866; Department of Louisiana and Texas; and Department of Florida, June 27, 1865–August 6, 1866. The Department of Florida is included in Volume I.

MILITARY DIVISION
OF THE MISSISSIPPI

In October 1863 the War Department recognized that a unified command in the West was necessary and, in an order dated October 16, 1863, created the Military Division of the Mississippi to include the Department of the Cumberland, the Department of the Tennessee, and the Department of the Ohio. Ulysses S. Grant assumed command October 18 (assigned October 16).

Grant's first important task was assembling a force for the relief of the Army of the Cumberland, which was then under siege at Chattanooga, Tennessee by Braxton Bragg's Confederate Army of Tennessee. Grant assumed personal command of the troops of the Military Division of the Mississippi that he had brought together near Chattanooga in late October and early November 1863 and began to prepare for the campaign that was to end with the relief of Chattanooga and the defeat of Bragg's army. For details of this operation, see Chattanooga-Ringgold Campaign (Battles of Lookout Mountain and Missionary Ridge, Tennessee).

March 18, 1864, Grant was called east to Washington, where he was assigned as general in chief to the command of all armies of the United States, and he was succeeded in command of the Military Division of the Mississippi by William T. Sherman. In the spring of 1864, Sherman assembled the Army of the Cumberland, the Army of the Tennessee, and the Army of the Ohio near Chattanooga, Tennessee and Dalton, Georgia and exercised personal command of the combined armies in the ensuing campaign, which resulted in the capture of Atlanta, Georgia. For details, see Atlanta, Georgia Campaign.

As Sherman approached Atlanta with his army, he created the District of Marietta, Military Division of the Mississippi, on the west side of the Chattahoochee, for the administration of affairs in the rear of the army. The district was to include Kennesaw, Marietta, Roswell, and the west bank of the Chattahoochee and Sweetwater rivers in Georgia. John McArthur was assigned command of the district August 5, 1864 and was relieved by William Vandever, who was assigned by an order of September 27, 1864. Vandever was in turn relieved November 6, 1864 by Giles A. Smith who, in addition to command of the district, retained command of his Fourth Division, Seventeenth Corps, Army of the Tennessee.

After the capture of Atlanta in September 1864, John B. Hood, then commanding the Confederate Army of Tennessee, moved north from the vicinity of Lovejoy's Station through Georgia and Alabama toward Tennessee. Sherman followed Hood as far as the Georgia-Alabama line. There he detached Fourth Corps and Twenty-Third Corps from his army and sent them to George H. Thomas, who was then organizing the forces assembling in Middle Tennessee for the defense of the state against Hood. After their departure, Sherman marched back with the rest of the army toward Atlanta.

On November 9, 1864, in preparation for a contemplated march through Georgia, Sherman reorganized the remaining four corps of his army into a Right Wing under the command of Oliver O. Howard and a Left Wing under Henry W. Slocum. Howard's wing consisted of Fifteenth Corps and Seventeenth Corps of the Army of the Tennessee and Slocum's wing of Fourteenth Corps and Twentieth Corps of the Army of the Cumberland. Sherman left Atlanta November 15 and occupied Savannah December 21. For details, see Savannah Campaign (Sherman's March through Georgia), in Volume I.

In January 1865 Sherman left Savannah on his march northward through South Carolina and North Carolina. For details, see Carolinas Campaign, in Volume I. January 12, 1865, John G. Foster's Department of the South was placed under the orders and control of Sherman, as commander of the Military Division of the Mississippi. January 31, 1865, the state of North Carolina was detached from the Department of the South and constituted as the Department of North Carolina, and John M. Schofield was assigned command. Schofield's department was also placed under Sherman's control.

When Sherman reached Goldsboro, North Carolina March 23–24, 1865, he was joined by Schofield's Army of the Ohio, which had been sent east from Tennessee. The Army of the Ohio was then reorganized to consist of the newly organized Tenth Corps and Twenty-Third Corps. These two corps, under the command of Schofield, were designated as the Center of Sherman's army, and they were to retain that designation while operating with Howard's Right Wing and Slocum's Left Wing against Joseph E. Johnston's army in North Carolina. This arrangement was not in effect for long, however, because Johnston surrendered his army in North Carolina to Sherman April 26, 1865, and a short time later Sherman's Right Wing (Army of the Tennessee) and Slocum's Left Wing (Army of Georgia) marched northward from North Carolina toward Washington, D.C. While at Goldsboro, Slocum's Left Wing had been officially constituted as the Army of Georgia by a presidential order of March 28, 1865. The Army of the Ohio was left behind to occupy North Carolina.

An organization designated as Cavalry Corps, Military Division of the Mississippi was created in Tennessee October 24, 1864, and James H. Wilson was assigned command. Wilson assumed command October 29 and led the corps during the rest of the war. For details of the organization and activities of Wilson's command, see Cavalry Corps, Military Division of the Mississippi.

When the Military Division of the Mississippi was created, Grant's headquarters was in the field. When Sherman assumed command, his headquarters was also in the field, but he established a general and business office at Nashville, Tennessee, where it remained until December 27, 1864, and then it was moved to Savannah, Georgia.

In the reorganization of the military divisions and departments of the army June 27, 1865, the Military Division of the Mississippi was reorganized to consist of the Department of Arkansas, the Department of the Missouri, and the Department of the Ohio. William T. Sherman was assigned command, with headquarters at Saint Louis, Missouri.

For additional information, see the following: Department of the Cumberland, October 24, 1862–

June 27, 1865; Department of the Tennessee, October 16, 1862–November 28, 1864; Department of the Ohio, August 19, 1862–January 17, 1865; and Army of Georgia (in Volume I).

MILITARY DIVISION OF THE MISSOURI

In order to provide a better coordination of the operations of the army against the Indians and guerrillas in the territory included in the Department of Kansas, the Department of the Missouri, and the Department of the Northwest, there were some organizational changes ordered January 30, 1865. The Department of Kansas was merged into the Department of the Missouri, and on that same date, the Military Division of the Missouri was created to include the newly reorganized Department of the Missouri and the Department of the Northwest. John Pope was assigned command (assumed command February 3, 1865), with headquarters at Saint Louis.

February 17, 1865 the Military Division of the Missouri was redefined to consist of the states of Missouri, Kansas, Wisconsin, Iowa, and the territories of Utah, Nebraska, Colorado (except Fort Garland), and Dakota. The territory of Utah, part of which was in the Department of the Pacific, was transferred to the Department of the Missouri.

March 21, 1865, the Department of Arkansas and also the Indian Territory were transferred from the Military Division of West Mississippi to the Military Division of the Missouri. At that time, Grenville M. Dodge commanded the Department of the Missouri, with headquarters at Saint Louis; Samuel R. Curtis commanded the Department of the Northwest, with headquarters at Milwaukee, Wisconsin; and Joseph J. Reynolds commanded the Department of Arkansas, with headquarters at Little Rock, Arkansas.

In the reorganization of the military divisions and departments of the army June 27, 1865, the Department of the Missouri was extended so as to include all the territory originally belonging to the Military Division of the Missouri, except the state of Arkansas and the Indian Territory. Pope was assigned command of the newly organized Department of the Missouri. Also on June 27, 1865, the Military Division of the Mississippi was created to consist of the new Department of the Missouri, the Department of the Ohio, and the Department of Arkansas. William T. Sherman was assigned command of the Military Division of the Missouri, with headquarters at Saint Louis. He assumed command July 10. Edward O. C. Ord commanded the Department of the Ohio, with headquarters at Detroit, Michigan; and Joseph J. Reynolds commanded the Department of Arkansas, with headquarters at Little Rock. Thus, on June 27, 1865, the Military Division of the Missouri was discontinued.

For additional information, refer to the various departments that were included in the Military Division of the Missouri.

MILITARY DIVISION OF THE PACIFIC

In the reorganization of the military divisions and departments of the army June 27, 1865, the Military Division of the Pacific was created to consist of the Department of the Columbia and the Department of California. Henry W. Halleck was assigned command, with headquarters at San Francisco, California. Irvin McDowell commanded the Department of California, with headquarters at San Francisco; and Horatio G. Wright commanded the Department of the Columbia, with headquarters at Fort Vancouver, Washington. For additional information, see Department of the Columbia and Department of California.

MILITARY DIVISION OF THE SOUTHWEST

May 17, 1865, Philip H. Sheridan was relieved from command of the Middle Military Division in the East, and was assigned command of the territory west of the Mississippi River and south of the Arkansas River. On May 29, Sheridan's command was designated as the Military Division of the Southwest. Sheridan's mission was to restore to the Union as quickly as possible the state of Texas and that part of Louisiana that was held by the enemy. On June 2, E. Kirby Smith surrendered the Confederate forces in the Trans-Mississippi region (the agreement was reached May 26), and Sheridan was then free to proceed with his reconstruction efforts.

June 3, 1865, Gordon Granger, with that part of Thirteenth Corps then at Mobile Bay, Alabama, was ordered to report to Sheridan. On June 17, Granger assumed command of all Federal troops in Texas, as commander of the District of Texas, but he was relieved from this command July 19.

July 7, 1865, Christopher C. Andrews was assigned command of the District of Houston (a subdistrict of the District of Texas), which included the posts of Galveston, Houston, Millican, Columbus, and intermediate points.

The Military Division of the Southwest was discontinued July 17, 1865, and the territory was merged into the new Military Division of the Gulf. Sheridan was assigned command of this new military division.

MILITARY DIVISION OF THE TENNESSEE

The Military Division of the Tennessee was created June 20, 1865, to consist of the Department of Kentucky, Department of the Tennessee, Department of Georgia, Department of Alabama, and Department of Florida. George H. Thomas was assigned command, with headquarters at Nashville, Tennessee. John M. Palmer commanded the Department of Kentucky, with headquarters at Louisville; George Stoneman commanded the Department of Tennessee, with headquarters at Knoxville; James B. Steedman commanded the Department of Georgia, with headquarters at Augusta; Charles R. Woods commanded the Department of Alabama, with headquarters at Mobile; and Andrew A. Humphreys commanded the Department of Florida (the state of Florida and the District of Key West), with headquarters at Tallahassee.

The order creating the Military Division of the Tennessee was corrected June 22, 1865 by the secretary of war, Edwin M. Stanton, to include also the state of Mississippi (Department of Mississippi), which was omitted in the original order through error. This correction was announced by Thomas June 23, and Henry W. Slocum was assigned command of the Department of Mississippi.

The orders annexing the Department of Florida, the Department of Mississippi, and the District of Key West were revoked June 30, 1865, and thereafter the military division consisted of the Department of Alabama, Department of Kentucky, Department of Georgia, and Department of the Tennessee.

For additional information, see the various departments included in the Military Division of the Tennessee.

MILITARY DIVISION OF WEST MISSISSIPPI

The failure of Nathaniel P. Banks' Red River Campaign in the Department of the Gulf in April 1864 was attributed to a lack of ability on the part of Banks, commander of the Department of the Gulf, and also poor cooperation between Banks and Frederick Steele, commander of the Department of Arkansas. Accordingly, on May 7, 1864, the Military Division of West Mississippi was created to consist of the Department of the Gulf and the Department of Arkansas. Edward R. S. Canby was assigned command of the military division, and he was also authorized to employ, in case of necessity, troops on the east bank of the Mississippi River that belonged to James B. McPherson's Department and Army of the Tennessee. Canby's headquarters was not fixed at the time, but was at Vicksburg and Natchez, Mississippi until June 8, and was then moved to New Orleans.

There were several changes in the composition of the Military Division of West Mississippi before it was abolished in May 1865. These were as follows:

May 27, 1864, the Department of the Missouri was assigned to the Military Division of West Mississippi.

November 7, 1864, the Federal posts on the east bank of the Mississippi were added to Canby's command, and at the same time the organizations of Sixteenth Corps and Nineteenth Corps in the Military Division of West Mississippi were discontinued.

November 28, 1864, the Department of Mississippi was created and assigned to the Military Division of West Mississippi.

February 10, 1865, the Department of the Gulf was reduced in size to include only the states of Louisiana and Texas. From that date, the District of West Florida and South Alabama and the District of Key West and Tortugas, formerly belonging to the Department of the Gulf, reported directly to Headquarters, Military Division of West Mississippi.

March 21, 1865, the Department of Arkansas and the Indian Territory were transferred from the Military Division of West Mississippi to the Military Division of the Missouri.

The Military Division of West Mississippi was abolished May 17, 1865. Canby commanded the division during the entire period of its existence, except for a time in November 1864, when he was disabled and Joseph J. Reynolds was in temporary command.

Districts in the Military Division of West Mississippi. November 7, 1864, the Federal posts on the east bank of the Mississippi River were placed under the command of Canby, and at the same time Sixteenth Corps was discontinued. Thus, the troops formerly belonging to the Department and Army of the Tennessee in the District of West Tennessee and at Vicksburg were assigned to the Military Division of West Mississippi. October 18, 1864, the posts of Vicksburg and Natchez had been designated as separate brigades. On November 20, the District of West Tennessee and the District of Vicksburg were formed into a single command, which was designated as the District of West Tennessee and Vicksburg, Military Division of West Mississippi. Napoleon J. T. Dana was assigned command of the new district, with headquarters at Memphis, Tennessee.

November 28, 1864, the Department of Mississippi was created and the District of West Tennessee and Vicksburg was merged into the new department. February 10, 1865, the Department of Mississippi was defined to include so much of the state of Mississippi as might be occupied by troops of the Military Division of the Mississippi that were on the river.

When the Department of the Gulf was reduced in size February 10, 1865, to include only the states of Louisiana and Texas, the military districts on the Gulf of Mexico were dropped from the rosters of the Department of the Gulf, and they then reported directly to Headquarters, Military Division of West Mississippi. In order that the continuity of the descriptions of these districts can be maintained, they are included with the districts of the Department of the Gulf. They were: District of Key West and Tortugas, District of South Alabama, District of West Florida, and District of West Florida and South Alabama. For details, see Department of the Gulf, Districts in the Department of the Gulf.

Troops in the Military Division of West Mississippi. At the time the Military Division of West Mississippi was created, the troops in the Department of Arkansas were organized as Seventh Corps, and the troops in the Department of the Gulf belonged to Thirteenth Corps and Nineteenth Corps. Thirteenth Corps was temporarily discontinued June 11, 1864, and early in the following month two divisions of Nineteenth Corps were sent north from New Orleans to Virginia. November 25, 1864, the Reserve Corps, Military Division of West Mississippi was created from the troops of Nineteenth Corps remaining within the limits of the Military Division of West Mississippi.

February 18, 1865, Thirteenth Corps was re-created from the Reserve Corps, Military Division of West Mississippi, and Sixteenth Corps was re-created from troops under the command of Andrew J. Smith arriving at New Orleans from the Department of the Cumberland. When the Department of the Gulf was redefined February 10, 1865, to consist only of the states of Louisiana and Texas, the districts on the Gulf of Mexico that formerly belonged to the Department of the Gulf were ordered to report directly to Headquarters, Military Division of West Mississippi. Thus, the newly created Thirteenth

Corps and Sixteenth Corps that later engaged in operations against Mobile, Alabama were designated as Thirteenth Corps, Military Division of West Mississippi and Sixteenth Corps, Military Division of West Mississippi.

During March and April 1865, the troops in the Military Division of West Mississippi consisted of the following: troops of the Department of the Gulf, Department of Mississippi, Department of Arkansas (until March 21, 1865), and troops of Canby's Army of West Mississippi that were operating against Mobile. The latter consisted of Thirteenth Corps; Sixteenth Corps; cavalry forces of the Department of the Gulf; First Division, United States Colored Troops; and the Engineer Brigade. For details, see Department of Arkansas; Department of Mississippi, November 28, 1864–May 17, 1865; Thirteenth Corps, Military Division of West Mississippi; Sixteenth Corps, Military Division of West Mississippi; and a cavalry command consisting of two divisions. In addition to the above, there were the troops of the District of South Alabama, the District of West Florida, and the District of Key West and Tortugas. For details of the organization of these troops, see Land Operations against Mobile Bay and Mobile, Alabama.

The Military Division of West Mississippi was abolished May 17, 1865, and the troops were transferred to the newly constituted Department of the Gulf.

DEPARTMENTS OF THE ARMY

☆ ☆ ☆ ☆

DEPARTMENT OF ALABAMA

In the reorganization of the military divisions and departments of the army June 27, 1865, the Department of Alabama was created to consist of the state of Alabama. Charles R. Woods was assigned command, but he did not assume command until July 18. Headquarters of the department was at Mobile. The Department of Alabama was included in the newly created Military Division of the Tennessee.

DEPARTMENT OF ARKANSAS

On August 10, 1863, Frederick Steele, commanding an expedition, left Helena, Arkansas, and advanced toward Little Rock, which he occupied September 10. He established his headquarters at Little Rock and remained there with his army to occupy the territory. After leaving Helena, Steele was operating within the boundaries of the Department of the Missouri, and he then reported to John M. Schofield, commander of that department, until January 6, 1864. For details, see Little Rock, Arkansas Expedition (Steele).

On January 6, 1864, the Department of Arkansas was created by General Order No. 14 of the War Department, which also designated the troops under Steele's command as Seventh Corps. The new Department of Arkansas consisted of the state of Arkansas, except Fort Smith. Fort Smith and the Indian Territory were transferred from the Department of Kansas to the Department of Arkansas April 17, 1864.

May 7, 1864, the Department of Arkansas was included in Edward R. S. Canby's Military Division of West Mississippi, and it remained a part of that organization until transferred to John Pope's Military Division of the Missouri March 21, 1865.

In the reorganizations of the military divisions and departments of the army June 27, 1865, the Department of Arkansas was reconstituted to consist of the state of Arkansas and the Indian Territory, and it was assigned to William T. Sherman's Military Division of the Mississippi. Headquarters of the department remained at Little Rock.

The Department of Arkansas was discontinued August 1, 1865.

COMMANDERS OF THE DEPARTMENT OF ARKANSAS

Frederick Steele   January 6, 1864 to December 22, 1864
Joseph J. Reynolds   December 22, 1864 to August 1, 1865

Note. Steele officially assumed command of the Department of Arkansas January 30, 1864 and at the same time announced the formation of Seventh Corps.

DISTRICTS IN THE DEPARTMENT OF ARKANSAS

On May 11, 1864, the Department of Arkansas was divided into three districts as follows:

District of Eastern Arkansas. The District of Eastern Arkansas was in existence when the Department of Arkansas was created January 6, 1864, and when the department was districted May 11, 1864, it was defined as consisting of the post of Helena and such other points in the eastern tier of counties of the state that were, or might later be, occupied by troops of the department. Headquarters of the district was at Helena.

The District of Eastern Arkansas was designated as a Separate Brigade November 26, 1864 and was discontinued August 1, 1865. The troops in the district consisted of unbrigaded regiments.

The commanders of the district were as follows:

Napoleon B. Buford	January 6, 1864 to August 6, 1864
William Crooks	August 6, 1864 to September 28, 1864
Napoleon B. Buford	September 28, 1864 to October 7, 1864
William Crooks	October 7, 1864 to October 10, 1864
Napoleon B. Buford	October 10, 1864 to March 9, 1865
Alexander McD. McCook	March 9, 1865 to April 27, 1865
Charles Bentzoni	April 27, 1865 to May 13, 1865
John M. Thayer	May 13, 1865 to June 5, 1865

District of the Frontier. The District of the Frontier was in existence in the Department of the Missouri January 6, 1864, when it became a part of the Department of Arkansas. The original limits included the western tier of counties in the state of Arkansas. When the Department of Arkansas was divided into districts May 11, 1864, the District of the Frontier was redefined to include that part of the state of Arkansas west of Dardenelle, and the Indian Territory. John M. Thayer was assigned command, with headquarters at Fort Smith. Thayer remained in command of the district, but William R. Judson commanded temporarily on several occasions when Thayer was absent.

The district was designated as a Separate Brigade November 26, 1864.

A Frontier Division was organized from troops of the district in March 1864 in preparation for Steele's expedition to Camden, Arkansas. For the organization of this division, see below, Troops in the Department of Arkansas and Operations in the Department of Arkansas.

The principal posts in the district were Van Buren, Fort Smith, and Roseville, all in Arkansas.

The District of the Frontier was discontinued February 1, 1865 (ordered December 30, 1864).

For details of the organization of the troops in the District of the Frontier, see the following: Department of the Missouri, District of the Frontier; and Department of Kansas, District of the Frontier. See also, below, Troops in the Department of Arkansas, and Operations in the Department of Arkansas, Camden, Arkansas Expedition (Steele).

District of Northeastern Arkansas. The District of Northeastern Arkansas was in existence as a district in the Department of the Missouri when the Department of Arkansas was created January 6, 1864. When the district was originally constituted in November 1863, its limits were not defined except that it was to include all of that part of northeastern Arkansas that was not occupied by troops of Frederick Steele's command. Robert R. Livingston was assigned command of the district, with headquarters at Batesville, Arkansas. The designation of his command was changed to Independent Brigade (Livingston's Brigade), Devall's Bluff, in May 1864, but it was discontinued about June 1, 1864. The principal post of the district was Batesville.

District of Little Rock. The District of Little Rock was constituted May 11, 1864, to include the line of posts from Pine Bluff to Dardenelle, and along the railroad from Little Rock to Devall's Bluff. Eugene A. Carr was assigned command of the district, with headquarters at Little Rock. The district was discontinued in December 1864. Carr was the only commander of the district.

The principal posts in the district were Little Rock, Lewisburg, and Pine Bluff, all in Arkansas.

The troops in the district consisted of Frederick Salomon's First Division, Seventh Corps; Joseph R. West's Second Division, Seventh Corps; Robert R. Livingston's Independent Brigade from the District of Northeastern Arkansas; and Powell Clayton's Cavalry Brigade. For details of the organization of these troops, see below, Troops in the Department of Arkansas.

District of South Kansas. April 22, 1865, the District of South Kansas, Department of the Missouri was extended to include the Indian country west of Arkansas, except the posts of Fort Smith, Fort Scott, and Paola, and it was then transferred to the Department of Arkansas. James G. Blunt was assigned command, with headquarters at Fort Gibson. Blunt was relieved from duty in the department June 3, 1865, when his services there were no longer needed.

TROOPS IN THE DEPARTMENT OF ARKANSAS

The first Federal troops to advance into Arkansas belonged to Frederick Steele's Little Rock Expedition, and at the end of December 1863, Steele's command, known as the Army of Arkansas, was organized as follows:

ARMY OF ARKANSAS, Frederick Steele

First (Cavalry) Division, John W. Davidson
    First Brigade, Cyrus Bussey
    Second Brigade, Lewis Merrill
    Third Brigade, Daniel Anderson
    Artillery
        Battery D, 2nd Missouri Light Artillery, Charles Schaerff
        Battery E, 2nd Missouri Light Artillery, Gustave Stange
        25th Battery, Ohio Light Artillery, Edward B. Hubbard

Second Division, Eugene A. Carr
    Second Brigade, Adolph Engelmann
    Third Brigade, William H. Graves
    Artillery
        Vaughn's Battery, Illinois Light Artillery, Thomas F. Vaughn

Third Division, Frederick Salomon
    First Brigade, William E. McLean
    Second Brigade, James M. Lewis
    Artillery
        3rd Battery, Iowa Light Artillery, Melvil C. Wright

Battery K, 1st Missouri Light Artillery, Stillman O. Fish

Independent Cavalry Brigade, Powell Clayton

Post of Little Rock

Seventh Corps, Department of Arkansas was organized from these troops, and other troops in Arkansas, January 6, 1864. At the end of the month the corps was organized as follows:

SEVENTH CORPS, Frederick Steele

First Division (or Cavalry Division), John W. Davidson
    First Brigade, John F. Ritter
    Second Brigade, Washington F. Geiger
    Third Brigade, Daniel Anderson
        Artillery
        Battery D, 2nd Missouri Light Artillery, Charles Schaerff
        Battery E, 2nd Missouri Light Artillery, Gustave Stange

Note. First Division was at Little Rock, with detachments at Brownsville and Devall's Bluff.

Second Division, Eugene A. Carr
    Second Brigade, Adolph Engelmann
    Third Brigade, Greenville M. Mitchell
    Vaughn's Battery, Illinois Light Artillery, Edward B. Stillings

Note. Second Division was at Little Rock.

Third Division, Frederick Salomon
    First Brigade, William E. McLean
    Second Brigade, James M. Lewis
    Artillery
        3rd Battery, Iowa Light Artillery, Melvil C. Wright
        Battery K, 1st Missouri Light Artillery, Stillman O. Fish

Note. Third Division was at Little Rock.

District of Eastern Arkansas, Napoleon B. Buford

District of Northeastern Arkansas, Robert R. Livingston

District of the Frontier, William R. Judson
    Second Brigade, John Edwards
    Third Brigade, Thomas M. Bowen
    Clarksville, Arkansas, Gideon M. Waugh

Roseville, Arkansas, James M. Williams

Note. In January 1864, William A. Phillips' First (or Indian) Brigade was at Fort Gibson, Indian Territory, and John Edwards commanded the troops at Fort Smith, both in the District of the Frontier, Department of Kansas. Thus, it appears that Second Brigade was also in the Department of Kansas.

Pine Bluff, Arkansas, Powell Clayton

There were some changes of the division commanders in Seventh Corps during the next few months. Nathan Kimball relieved Eugene A. Carr in command of Second Division February 13, 1864, and that same day Carr relieved John W. Davidson in command of First Division. Joseph R. West relieved Kimball in command of Second Division April 25, 1864, and Kimball was relieved from duty in the Department of Arkansas.

For some time there had been pressure in the North for an invasion of Texas, and early in March 1864 preparations were begun for an expedition against Shreveport, Louisiana, which was a major Confederate supply depot for the area and was also the gateway to eastern Texas. The plan finally adopted called for a land force under Nathaniel P. Banks, commander of the Department of the Gulf, and a naval force commanded by David D. Porter to move up the Red River to Shreveport, where it would be joined by a force under Frederick Steele marching down from Little Rock. The combined force was then to attack and occupy the town. Steele's force was to consist of Frederick Salomon's Third Division, a cavalry division commanded by Eugene A. Carr, and a division under John M. Thayer from the District of the Frontier, all from the Department of Arkansas.

There was extensive reorganization of the troops in the District of the Frontier in preparation for this expedition. First Brigade was reorganized by transfer of the regiments of Second Brigade, which was thus discontinued. Second Brigade was then reorganized from unattached regiments of the District of the Frontier. Third Brigade, which had been discontinued in January 1864 by the transfer of troops, was reorganized in March 1864 as Third (or Cavalry) Brigade, from three Kansas cavalry regiments, and was assigned to Owen A. Bassett. These three brigades were assigned to the Frontier Division, which was organized for the expedition toward Shreveport, and placed under the command of John M. Thayer. William R. Judson was assigned command of the Frontier District March 24, 1864 and was to command during the absence of Thayer. Carr's Cavalry Division was also organized for this expedition from cavalry regiments of the department. It consisted of a First Brigade, commanded by John F. Ritter, and a Second Brigade, commanded by Daniel Anderson.

For the organization and operations of Steele's Camden Expedition, see below, Operations in the Department of Arkansas.

By an order of May 11, 1864, the same day on which the districts were constituted in the Department of Arkansas, the infantry, cavalry, and artillery then serving within the limits of the District of Little Rock were organized into two divisions. The former First Division, Seventh Corps was broken up, and the regiments were reassigned. First Division, District of Little Rock was then organized from the regiments of the former Third Division, Seventh Corps, and Third Division was thus discontinued. Frederick Salomon was assigned command of the new First Division.

The designation of the former Second Division, Seventh Corps was changed to Second Division, District of Little Rock, and Joseph R. West was assigned command.

At the end of June 1864 the Department of Arkansas, Seventh Corps was organized as follows:

DISTRICT OF LITTLE ROCK, Eugene A. Carr

First Division, Frederick Salomon
    First Brigade, Charles E. Salomon
    Second Brigade, Adolph Engelmann
    Third (or Cavalry) Brigade, Cyrus Bussey
    Artillery, Gustave Stange
        Battery A, 3rd Illinois Light Artillery, Thomas F. Vaughn
        3rd Battery, Iowa Light Artillery, Melvil C. Wright
        Battery E, 2nd Missouri Light Artillery, Anthony Boedicker
        25th Battery, Ohio Light Artillery, Julius L. Hadley

Note. First Division was known as Third Division, Seventh Corps until May 11, 1864.

Second Division, Christopher C. Andrews
    First Brigade, William H. Graves
    Second Brigade, Oliver Wood

Third (or Cavalry) Brigade, Washington F. Geiger
Artillery
    Battery K, 1st Missouri Light Artillery, James Marr
    Battery D, 2nd Missouri Light Artillery, Charles
      Schaerff
    5th Battery, Ohio Light Artillery, Theophilus Kates
    11th Battery, Ohio Light Artillery, Fletcher E.
      Armstrong

*Note. Second Division was reorganized May 11,
1864. The troops were at Brownsville, Devall's Bluff,
Huntersville, Lewisburg, Little Rock, and Pine Bluff.*

Cavalry Brigade (at Pine Bluff), Powell Clayton

DISTRICT OF EASTERN ARKANSAS, Napoleon B.
  Buford

*Note. The troops of the District of Eastern Arkansas
were at Helena, and consisted of ten unbrigaded infantry
regiments (or detachments of regiments), a detachment
of cavalry, and one battery.*

DISTRICT OF THE FRONTIER, John M. Thayer

First Brigade (at Fort Smith), John Edwards
Second Brigade (at Fort Smith), James M. Williams
Third Brigade (at Fort Smith), Edward Lynde
Post of Fort Smith, Arkansas, William R. Judson
Fayetteville, Arkansas, M. La Rue Harrison
Indian Brigade (at Fort Gibson), William A. Phillips
Van Buren, Arkansas, Benjamin F. Goss
Mackey's Salt Works, Indian Territory, John Ritchie

There were some organizational and command
changes during the remainder of the year. September 15, 1864, the cavalry serving in the District of
Little Rock was organized into a cavalry division of
four brigades, and Joseph R. West was assigned
command. First Brigade was commanded by Albert
Erskine, Second Brigade by Cyrus Bussey, Third
Brigade by Washington F. Geiger, and Fourth Brigade by John K. Mizner. Another significant change
occurred when the District of Little Rock and the
District of the Frontier were discontinued December 30, 1864.

In September and October 1864, Second Division and Third Division of Joseph J. Reynolds'
Nineteenth Corps were sent to Arkansas from the
Department of the Gulf as reinforcements for Seventh Corps during Sterling Price's expedition into
Missouri in September. These two divisions were in
the Department of Arkansas when Nineteenth Corps

was discontinued in the Department of the Gulf
November 7. These troops were then organized into
the Reserve Corps, Military Division of West Mississippi on November 25. Eventually most of the
troops of the Reserve Corps assembled at Memphis,
Tennessee and at the mouth of the White River and
later left the Department of Arkansas. Some troops,
however, were transferred to Seventh Corps. For
additional information about these troops, see Nineteenth Corps, Department of the Gulf, and Reserve
Corps, Military Division of West Mississippi.

There were two significant changes in command
during December 1864. On December 22, Frederick
Steele was relieved from command of the Department of Arkansas and Seventh Corps, and he was
succeeded in command by Joseph J. Reynolds.
Christopher C. Andrews was relieved from duty in
the Department of Arkansas by an order of December 5, and was succeeded in command of Second
Division, District of Little Rock by Alexander
Shaler on December 27.

The organization of Joseph J. Reynolds' Department of Arkansas, Seventh Corps at the end of
December 1864 was as follows:

DISTRICT OF LITTLE ROCK, Eugene A. Carr

First Division, Frederick Salomon
  First Brigade, Cyrus H. Mackey
  Second Brigade, John A. Garrett
  Artillery
    Battery A, 3rd Illinois Light Artillery, Thomas F.
      Vaughn
    3rd Battery, Iowa Light Artillery, Melvil C. Wright
    Battery E, 2nd Missouri Light Artillery, William
      Jackson
    25th Battery, Ohio Light Artillery, Julius L. Hadley

Second Division, Alexander Shaler
  First Brigade, Hans Mattson
  Second Brigade, James M. True
  Artillery
    Battery K, 1st Missouri Light Artillery, Charles
      Green
    Battery D, 2nd Missouri Light Artillery, Charles
      Schaerff
    5th Battery, Ohio Light Artillery, Theophilus Kates

Cavalry Division, Joseph R. West
  First Brigade, Albert Erskine
  Second Brigade, Cyrus Bussey

Third Brigade, Washington F. Geiger
Fourth Brigade, John K. Mizner

DISTRICT OF EASTERN ARKANSAS, Napoleon B. Buford

DISTRICT OF THE FRONTIER, John M. Thayer

Frontier Division, John Edwards
　First Brigade, Charles W. Adams
　Second Brigade, James M. Williams
　Third Brigade, William R. Judson
　Indian Brigade, William A. Phillips

Fort Smith, Arkansas, William R. Judson

Van Buren, Arkansas, Thomas M. Bowen

January 20, 1865, a brigade known as Detached Brigade was organized from First Brigade, First Division, Seventh Corps and two regiments of Second Brigade, First Division, and Eugene A. Carr was assigned command.

Both the infantry and cavalry of Seventh Corps were reorganized February 1, 1865. By an order of January 24, 1865, the organization of the Cavalry Division was to be discontinued January 31, and the regiments were to be reassigned February 1. The cavalry at the post of Little Rock was to consist of a brigade commanded by Cyrus Bussey, and cavalry units were assigned to the following posts: Devall's Bluff, Pine Bluff, Lewisburg, Brownsville Station, Saint Charles, White River, Helena, and the Cavalry Depot. In addition, a Cavalry Division consisting of two brigades was to be formed under the command of Joseph R. West, whose headquarters was to be at Little Rock.

The infantry of Seventh Corps was also reorganized February 1, 1865, to consist of three divisions as follows: First Division, to be commanded by Frederick Salomon, with headquarters at Little Rock; Second Division, to be commanded by Alexander Shaler, with headquarters at Devall's Bluff; and Third Division, to be commanded by John M. Thayer, with headquarters at Fort Smith. Thayer was assigned to the command of the post of Saint Charles, Arkansas February 27, 1865, and Cyrus Bussey assumed command of Third Division. Eugene A. Carr's Detached Brigade was assigned to Third Division, but Carr, with his brigade, was ordered to New Orleans February 1. Before Carr departed, however, Reynolds relieved him because of drunkenness, and on February 8 assigned James C. Veatch to command the brigade. Veatch then took the brigade to New Orleans.

The organization of Joseph J. Reynolds' Department of Arkansas, Seventh Corps at the end of February 1865 was as follows:

First Division, Frederick Salomon
　First Brigade, Adolph Dengler
　Second Brigade, James M. Williams
　Artillery
　　Battery A, 3rd Illinois Light Artillery, Thomas F. Vaughn
　　Company A, 1st Indiana Heavy Artillery, Merritt C. Skinner
　　Battery K, 1st Missouri Light Artillery, James Marr
　　Battery E, 2nd Missouri Light Artillery, Gustave Stange
　　3rd Battery, Iowa Light Artillery, Orlo H. Lyon
　　5th Battery, Ohio Light Artillery, Theophilus Kates

Note. Second Brigade was composed of regiments of United States Colored Troops.

Post of Little Rock, Frederick Salomon
　Cavalry Brigade, Matthew M. Trumbull

Second Division, Alexander Shaler
　First Brigade, William H. Graves
　Second Brigade, James M. True
　Artillery
　　1st Battery, Delaware Light Artillery, Thomas A. Porter

Third Division, Cyrus Bussey
　First Brigade, John Edwards
　Third (or Indian) Brigade, William A. Phillips

Note 1. A Second Brigade was organized February 1, 1865, but it was discontinued February 18, 1865, when its regiments were reassigned.
Note 2. William Mayes' 1st Battery, Arkansas Light Artillery and Andrew G. Clark's 2nd Battery, Kansas Light Artillery were attached to First Brigade.

Cavalry Division, Joseph R. West
　First Brigade, John K. Mizner
　Second Brigade, Washington F. Geiger
　Artillery
　　25th Battery, Ohio Light Artillery, Julius L. Hadley

Note. The Cavalry Division was organized for field service February 1, 1865, but it was later dismounted to provide horses for the remainder of the cavalry in the department.

District of Eastern Arkansas, Napoleon B. Buford
United States Forces Mouth of White River, George F. McGinnis
Post of Saint Charles, Arkansas, John M. Thayer
Post of Pine Bluff, Arkansas, Powell Clayton
Post of Lewisburg, Arkansas, Abraham H. Ryan

There was little further change in the organization of the Department of Arkansas during the war.

OPERATIONS IN THE DEPARTMENT OF ARKANSAS

Camden, Arkansas Expedition (Steele) March 23, 1864–May 3, 1864

From the time of the organization of the Department of Arkansas, the troops of Seventh Corps were engaged almost constantly in skirmishing with the enemy and conducting scouts and expeditions into various parts of the state, but with one important exception there were no major campaigns or battles. The one major campaign occurred during the period March 23, 1864–May 3, 1864, when Frederick Steele led an army composed of troops of Seventh Corps on an expedition toward Shreveport, Louisiana. The purpose of this expedition was to join a force under the command of Nathaniel P. Banks, which was then advancing up the Red River, and with him attempt to drive Confederate forces from the town and thus open the way to Texas. For information on the genesis of the plan to move into Texas, and for details of Banks' expedition toward Shreveport, see Department of the Gulf, Operations in the Department of the Gulf, Texas Expeditions; and see also Red River, Louisiana Campaign.

Steele had been asked to begin his movement by March 5, 1864, but for valid reasons he was unable to get away until March 23. That day, he left Little Rock with Frederick Salomon's Third Division, Seventh Corps and two brigades of Eugene A. Carr's Cavalry Division and took the road leading to Benton and Rockport. The next day, the advance of Steele's column camped on the Saline River,

twenty-six miles from Little Rock, and by March 26, the entire command was encamped in and around Rockport, a town on the east side of the Ouachita (Washita) River. Three days later, the army was at Arkadelphia.

On March 17, 1864, Steele had ordered John M. Thayer, commanding at Fort Smith, Arkansas, to march with his newly organized Frontier Division and join the main column at Arkadelphia April 1. Thayer left Fort Smith March 21 but experienced considerable difficulty on the march, and he did not arrive at Arkadelphia at the expected time. Steele waited for Thayer until April 1, and then marched out on the Washington road to Spoonville (Hollywood or Witherspoonville). On the march that day William E. McLean's Second Brigade of Salomon's division was in the lead, and it was followed in turn by Adolph Engelmann's Third Brigade and Samuel A. Rice's First Brigade. While on the march, Joseph O. Shelby's brigade of John S. Marmaduke's Confederate Cavalry Division attacked the rear of Steele's column near Gentry's Creek, but it was driven off by Rice's brigade. Rice then moved on toward Okolona and, after another sharp engagement, reached that place about 10:00 P.M. On the evening of April 2, the cavalry and McLean's brigade were sent forward to seize the crossing of the Little Missouri River at Elkin's Ferry (or Ford), about four miles beyond Okolona, and by 9:00 P.M. they had gained possession of the crossing.

On the morning of April 3, 1864, Engelmann's brigade, reinforced by a regiment of McLean's brigade, was left at Okolona with orders to move back with John F. Ritter's First Brigade of Carr's Cavalry Division, both under Engelmann, as far as Spoonville, and attempt to communicate with Thayer. Rice's brigade moved on to Elkin's Ferry, and camped there on the left bank of the Little Missouri River. Engelmann was attacked by Shelby near Okolona, before Ritter arrived, but drove him back. Then, when Ritter arrived, Engelmann proceeded on to Spoonville, where he arrived April 4. Engelmann then returned with his command and rejoined the division near Elkin's Ferry on the evening of April 5. He reported to Steele that he had not heard from Thayer.

Steele remained at Elkin's Ferry until the morning of April 6, and then moved on. He soon learned that Thayer had been seen at Rockport and decided to wait for him at the Widow Cornelius' place, about three and a half miles from the Ferry. The three days that Steele remained there were spent in foraging and in repairing the roads to the rear to facilitate Thayer's march.

Thayer finally came up, and on April 10, the entire command marched for Prairie D'Ane. Steele soon found enemy cavalry commanded by Sterling Price in position on his front. Steele was advancing on the road to Spring Hill, which intersected the Washington-Camden road on the prairie at nearly a right angle. Price held a position in front of the intersection of the two roads. That evening, after a severe skirmish, Salomon's division drove back the enemy and occupied a high ridge on the prairie. Engelmann, with Vaughn's battery, was on the right, and Rice, with Martin Voegele's battery, was on the left. McLean's brigade was in reserve, guarding the trains.

On April 12, Salomon advanced to within a mile of the enemy works. Rice was on the right, Engelmann on the left, McLean in reserve, and the cavalry on both flanks. Rice then outflanked the works, and Price retired on the Washington road. Salomon then marched on the road to Camden, crossed the prairie through Moscow, and camped for the night at the edge of the prairie. At noon the next day Salomon moved forward over bad roads through low ground and camped near Cypress Bayou. Toward evening on April 14, Rice, with Stange's battery, moved on in advance and, reporting to Carr, camped for the night near White Oak Creek, eighteen miles from Camden. The rest of the division camped about six miles back with the trains. At sunrise April 15, Rice moved forward, skirmishing with the enemy, until within about two miles of the junction of the Camden road, on which he was marching, and the Middle Washington road. Then, after an artillery engagement of about two hours, the infantry moved on, and Rice entered Camden shortly after sundown. Engelmann halted about a mile and a half back to wait for McLean's brigade, which was guarding the trains. The rest of the division had come in by midnight.

After arriving in Camden, Steele learned of Banks' defeat in Louisiana, and realized that there was no further reason for continuing the advance toward Louisiana. His position at that time was not encouraging. He was far from his supply bases at Little Rock and Pine Bluff, and for some time his army had been traveling on reduced rations and was then depending on foraging for corn for bread and forage for the animals.

On the morning of April 17, 1864, James M. Williams left Camden on a foraging expedition. He took with him about 200 empty wagons and a force consisting of 438 men of his 1st Kansas Colored Infantry, about 250 troopers of the 2nd Kansas Cavalry, 6th Kansas Cavalry, and 14th Kansas Cavalry, and two guns of William W. Haines' 2nd Battery, Indiana Light Artillery.

Williams marched out about fourteen miles on the Camden and Prairie D'Ane road and went into camp. From there he sent about 100 wagons six miles farther out to collect corn; they completed their mission and returned safely to camp about midnight.

Early the next morning, Williams started his return to Camden. He continued to load his wagons with corn as he moved along the road. After marching four miles to the east, he encountered about 500 men belonging to the 18th Iowa Infantry, 2nd Kansas Cavalry, 6th Kansas Cavalry, and 14th Kansas Cavalry, and also two mountain howitzers from the 6th Kansas Cavalry. Williams' command, thus reinforced, was increased to 1,170 men.

John S. Marmaduke, commanding a Confederate cavalry division, soon learned of Williams' expedition, and he marched with Colton Greene's brigade of his division and William Crawford's brigade and William L. Cabell's brigade of James F. Fagan's division toward the Lee plantation, ten miles from Camden. While on the march, Marmaduke learned that Williams' advance had reached a place on the road called Poison Spring, and he dismounted about 1,700 of his men and put them in position across the road. About 9:30 that morning, Samuel B. Maxey arrived with his cavalry division, consisting of the brigades of Charles De Morse and Tandy Walker, bringing the total Confederate strength to about 3,300 men. Maxey placed his men on the left side of the road and parallel to it.

Williams deployed his 1st Kansas Colored Infantry in line of battle and covered both flanks with his cavalry. Firing began at 10:00 A.M., and at 10:45 the enemy launched a vigorous attack. Williams counterattacked and forced back a part of the enemy line, creating a gap, but before he could take advantage of this break in the line, Greene attacked and halted the Union advance. Williams' men fought with great determination for about three-fourths of an hour as they attempted to save the train, but then the enemy charged against their rear and at the same time opened with a deadly artillery fire. This was too much for the 1st Kansas Colored Infantry, which broke and fled to the rear, but Williams' men rallied and remained fighting long enough for all the men, and the wounded who were still able to walk, to reach a nearby swamp, where they found some protection.

The fighting ended at about 2:00 P.M., and then the scattered survivors of the expedition made their way back to Camden. The entire wagon train and the four Union guns, however, were captured and carried off by the enemy.

Total Union losses were reported as 204 killed and 97 wounded, but for the black soldiers, the numbers were 117 killed and 65 wounded. Therefore, of the 438 black soldiers present, 117 were killed, and of the 732 white soldiers engaged, only 87 were killed. Because of the far higher death rate of blacks compared to whites, there were Union claims, as there were on other occasions where blacks were engaged, that Confederate troops ruthlessly murdered black soldiers, but this claim was vigorously denied by the enemy.

A supply train arrived at Camden April 20 with rations for ten days, and Steele immediately ordered it back for more supplies. The train left Camden April 23. It was protected by William E. McLean's Second Brigade (commanded by Francis M. Drake) of Salomon's division, four hundred cavalry, and four pieces of artillery. Two days later, the column was attacked at Marks' Mills, eight miles east of the Saline River on the road from Camden to Pine Bluff, by Confederate cavalry commanded by Joseph O. Shelby and James F. Fagan. After three hours of hard fighting, the train and artillery, together with the greater part of the infantry and cavalry, were captured. About three hundred men escaped to Little Rock and Pine Bluff.

Upon receipt of this information, Steele reconsidered his situation. He had heard that the enemy had been reinforced. He knew that his line of commu-nications had been effectually interrupted and that the line of the Arkansas was threatened by a large enemy force. He therefore decided to evacuate Camden and return to Little Rock. During the day of April 26, the trains and artillery crossed the Ouachita River, and at nightfall the infantry began to follow. At daylight April 27, the army was well out on the road to Princeton, where it camped the following night.

Engagement at Jenkins' Ferry, Arkansas, April 30, 1864. At 2:00 P.M. April 29, 1864, Steele's column arrived at Jenkins' Ferry on the Saline River, from which point a direct road ran to Little Rock. The engineers laid a pontoon bridge, and at 4:15 P.M. the troops began to cross. All the cavalry and many of the wagons were over before dark. After crossing, the artillery and wagons were parked on high ground about two and a half miles from the bridge. When the cavalry had crossed, Carr was ordered to move with nearly all of his effective force, as rapidly as possible, to Little Rock to intercept any Confederate force that might be moving in that direction.

The rain that had begun about noon April 29 continued all that afternoon and night, and the road, which ran along the low ground to the river, became almost impassable because of the mud and swollen streams.

Jenkins' Ferry was located near the center of the low bottom land that extended for about two miles on each side of the river to the ridges that bordered the valley. As the road from Princeton ran up toward Jenkins' Ferry, it reached the crest of the bluff at the edge of the valley and then dropped down the slope to the level of the bottom land. It then ran across the low ground for about two miles to Jenkins' Ferry on the river. On the south side of the road, as it crossed the bottom, were two fields that were to become significant during the fighting on April 30, 1864. The first field, which began at the base of the bluff, was about one-fourth mile square; the second field was farther on and was of about the same size. The two fields were separated by a strip of woods about one-fourth mile in width, and the fields were bounded on the south and east, all the way to the river, by heavy woods and swampy ground. Immediately to the north of the road, and parallel to it, was a creek or bayou with deep, impassable sides, which were covered on the north with cane and undergrowth. This creek has been referred to in some reports as Toxie Creek, but the correct name was probably Cox's Creek.

Thayer's division led the infantry on the road toward the ferry April 29, and it was followed by Rice's brigade of Salomon's division. During the afternoon both had moved down from the high ground onto the bottom land and marched toward the river. Engelmann's brigade covered the rear of the column, and the 40th Iowa, which was at the rear of the brigade, was engaged in slight skirmishing with the pursuing enemy during the afternoon.

On arriving at the bluff above the Saline bottom, Engelmann left the 43rd Illinois and a section of artillery as a picket at that point and moved on down the slope and into the first field. He had not proceeded beyond the field when the enemy attacked the picket on the ridge above. Engelmann then formed the 40th Iowa in the field as a support to the 43rd Illinois. Some fighting ensued, and at nightfall Rice sent the 33rd Iowa of his brigade to report to Engelmann, who sent the regiment to relieve the 43rd Illinois. The latter regiment withdrew under the brow of the bluff, where it remained in support of the 33rd Iowa.

About 3:00 A.M. April 30, Salomon ordered the withdrawal of his troops to a line beyond the effective range of the Confederate artillery on the bluff. Earlier that morning, at 2:00, he had ordered Engelmann to withdraw all regiments from the picket line except one, which was to be deployed in rear of the field at the foot of the bluff. The 33rd Iowa of Rice's brigade was assigned to the picket duty. Soon after daybreak, Rice ordered the 33rd Iowa to retire, but before it could be brought back the enemy attacked, and Rice sent up the 50th Indiana, which formed on the left of the 33rd Iowa.

Engelmann sent the 27th Wisconsin up to relieve the 33rd Iowa, but by that time the engagement had become quite severe. Rice then formed a second line about a half-mile in rear of the first line with some of his troops. This was done to hold the enemy in check while the 43rd Illinois and 40th Iowa of Engelmann's brigade and the 43rd Iowa of Rice's brigade, who had suffered from fatigue and expo-

sure during the preceding night, could get some rest. Rice formed his new line at the second field with the 9th Wisconsin and 29th Iowa. This position was protected on the right by the bayou mentioned above (Toxie Creek), and the left rested on swampy ground and was somewhat refused. To strengthen this line, Rice placed the 50th Indiana en echelon on the extreme left and sent the detachment of Second Brigade (troops that did not accompany McLean's brigade to Marks' Mills) and two companies of the 29th Iowa over the bayou (or creek) on his right.

When Rice's new line was completed, the 27th Wisconsin was withdrawn from its advanced position, and Engelmann's brigade moved back to a position in the edge of woods on the last field, on the road to the bridge. The 33rd Iowa of Rice's brigade also moved back into the same field. They were, however, not to remain in this position very long because they were needed elsewhere.

A short time after Rice's line was formed the enemy attacked, first on the Federal right and then on the left. At 8:00 A.M. Thomas J. Churchill, commanding the Arkansas Division of Price's command, ordered James C. Tappan to move forward with his brigade and attack Rice's line, and he then sent up Alexander T. Hawthorn's brigade in support. He held Lucien C. Gause's brigade in reserve. When the attack started, Rice sent the 33rd Iowa to the left of the 50th Indiana, but that flank was soon turned and the 33rd Iowa was driven back about 250 yards. The 12th Kansas of Charles W. Adams' Second Brigade, Thayer's Frontier Division was then sent to the left of 33rd Iowa, and it succeeded in driving the enemy back. Salomon's entire line then advanced about 250 yards.

Meantime, Mosby M. Parsons' Missouri Division of Price's command had arrived on the field, and about 10:00 A.M., when Churchill's two brigades were hard-pressed, Parsons went into action. He advanced Simon P. Burns' Second Brigade of the division and placed it on the right of Gause's brigade, and he then formed John B. Clark's First Brigade on the left of Gause. When this new line was formed, Price sent it forward to support Tappan and Hawthorn, who were fighting on its front.

When the enemy moved against the right of Rice's line they threw a force across the creek that covered Rice's right and advanced through a thick woods. At that time, Samuel J. Crawford's 2nd Kansas (colored) of Adams' brigade, Thayer's division came up and was placed in advance of the 9th Wisconsin and 29th Iowa, whose ammunition was nearly exhausted. The 43rd Illinois was also sent up to support the troops across the creek. At about the same time, the 27th Wisconsin was moved up to support Rice's left. The enemy renewed the attack from an open field in front of Rice's right, but after some hard fighting it was repulsed, and then the 2nd Kansas and the 29th Iowa advanced and captured their guns.

At about that time, John G. Walker's Confederate division arrived, and Price directed Churchill to support Walker. After a brief pause, both divisions attacked. The first movement was a feint against the Federal right, and this was followed immediately by an assault on the left. John A. Garrett, with four companies of his 40th Iowa, was ordered to form on the extreme left of the line, and also the detachment of Second Brigade was moved from the right to the left of the line. These troops, and also the 50th Indiana, the 12th Kansas, and the 33rd Iowa, opened with a very heavy fire on the advancing enemy. When the companies of the 40th Iowa became hard-pressed, the 1st Arkansas of Adams' brigade, Thayer's division, then coming up, was sent to support them. The fighting continued for about forty-five minutes, and finally the enemy withdrew about noon. Rice was wounded during that part of the fighting, and Charles E. Salomon succeeded him in command of the brigade.

Meantime, the 43rd Illinois had moved up to the center of the line, just as the 33rd Iowa had exhausted its ammunition for the second time. The 43rd Illinois then took its place in front and drove the enemy about a half-mile to the foot of the bluff.

The Federal artillery was not used during the engagement that day because of the swampy nature of the ground on which the fighting took place.

Shortly after noon, the Federal troops were recalled and the march was resumed toward Little Rock, where Steele arrived May 3, 1864.

The organization of the expeditionary forces commanded by Frederick Steele during the Camden, Arkansas Campaign was as follows:

Third Division, Seventh Corps, Frederick Salomon
First Brigade, Samuel A. Rice, to April 30, 1864, wounded
Charles E. Salomon
50th Indiana, Samuel T. Wells; 29th Iowa, Thomas H. Benton, Jr.; 33rd Iowa, Hiram D. Gibson; 9th Wisconsin, Charles E. Salomon
Second Brigade, William E. McLean
43rd Indiana, Wesley W. Norris; 36th Iowa, Charles W. Kittredge; 77th Ohio, William B. Mason
Third Brigade, Adolph Engelmann
43rd Illinois, Adolph Dengler; 40th Iowa, John A. Garrett; 27th Wisconsin, Conrad Krez

Note. Third Division was reorganized as given above for the expedition. Engelmann's brigade was temporarily attached to Third Division March 19, 1864.

Artillery
Battery E, 2nd Missouri Light Artillery, Charles Peetz
Battery A, 3rd Illinois Light Artillery, Thomas F. Vaughn
Wisconsin Battery, Martin Voegele

Frontier Division, John M. Thayer
First Brigade, John Edwards
1st Arkansas, Elhanon J. Searle; 2nd Arkansas (eight companies), Marshall L. Stephenson; 18th Iowa, William M. Duncan; 2nd Battery, Indiana Light Artillery, Hugh Espey
Second Brigade, Charles W. Adams
1st Kansas (Colored), James M. Williams; 2nd Kansas (Colored), Samuel J. Crawford; 12th Kansas, Josiah E. Hayes; 1st Battery, Arkansas Light Artillery, Denton D. Stark
Third (or Cavalry) Brigade, Owen A. Bassett
2nd Kansas Cavalry, Julius G. Fisk; 6th Kansas Cavalry, William T. Campbell; 14th Kansas Cavalry, John G. Brown

Cavalry Division, Eugene A. Carr
First Brigade, John F. Ritter
3rd Arkansas (four companies), George F. Lovejoy
13th Illinois (Company B), Adolph Bechand
3rd Iowa (detachment), Franz W. Arnim
1st Missouri (eight companies), Miles Kehoe
2nd Missouri, William H. Higdon
Third Brigade, Daniel Anderson
10th Illinois, James Stuart
1st Iowa, Joseph W. Caldwell
3rd Missouri, John A. Lennon

DEPARTMENT OF CALIFORNIA

The Department of California was created September 13, 1858, to include the territory of the United States west of the Rocky Mountains and south of Oregon and Washington territories, except that part of Utah lying east of the 117th degree of west longitude, and of New Mexico lying east of the 110th degree of west longitude. In addition, the Rouge River and Umpqua districts in southwestern Oregon were included in the Department of California.

On January 1, 1861, the department was commanded by Benjamin L. Beall, who had assumed command by seniority on the death of Newman S. Clarke October 17, 1860. The troops under Beall's command at the outbreak of war consisted of five companies of the 1st United States Dragoons, nine companies of the 4th United States Infantry, nine companies of the 6th United States Infantry, one company of the 9th United States Infantry, and eight companies of the 3rd United States Artillery. These troops were stationed at the following posts: Fort Crook, Fort Ter-Waw, Fort Humboldt, Fort Gaston, Fort Bragg, Benicia Barracks, Benicia Arsenal, Presidio of San Francisco, Alcatraz Island, Fort Tejon, New San Diego, and Fort Yuma, all in California; Fort Umpqua in Oregon; Fort Mojave in New Mexico; and Fort Churchill in Nevada Territory.

By an order of January 1, 1861, the Department of Oregon and the Department of California were merged into the Department of the Pacific, and Albert Sidney Johnston was assigned command. He arrived at San Francisco January 15 and assumed command, and on that date he announced that the departments of Oregon and California were officially merged.

In the reorganization of the military divisions and departments of the army June 27, 1865, the Department of California was re-created to consist of the states of California and Nevada and the territories of Colorado, New Mexico, and Utah. Irvin McDowell was assigned command, with headquarters at San Francisco, but he did not assume command until July 27. The new Department of California was included in the Military Division of the Pacific, which was commanded by Henry W. Halleck.

DEPARTMENT OF THE COLUMBIA

In the reorganization of the military divisions and departments of the army June 27, 1865, the Department of the Columbia was created to consist of the state of Oregon and the territories of Washington and Idaho. Horatio G. Wright was assigned command, with headquarters at Fort Vancouver. The department was included in the Military Division of the Pacific. The first commander of the department was George B. Currey of the 1st Oregon Infantry, who assumed command August 8, 1865, when he learned of the creation of the department. He established headquarters at Fort Vancouver, Washington Territory.

DEPARTMENT OF THE CUMBERLAND AUGUST 15, 1861– NOVEMBER 9, 1861

The Department of the Cumberland was organized August 15, 1861, to consist of the states of Kentucky and Tennessee. Robert Anderson was assigned command, with headquarters at Cincinnati, Ohio. Headquarters was moved to Louisville, Kentucky September 7, 1861.

September 19, 1861, that part of Kentucky lying within fifteen miles of Cincinnati was transferred to the Department of the Ohio. In a further change, the Federal forces operating near the junction of the Ohio, Cumberland, and Tennessee rivers and near the junction of the Ohio and Mississippi rivers were announced as belonging to the Western Department.

The department was discontinued November 9, 1861, and its territory was assigned as follows: that part of Kentucky west of the Cumberland River was assigned to the Department of the Missouri, and that part of Kentucky east of the Cumberland River and the state of Tennessee were assigned to the Department of the Ohio.

The commanders of the Department of the Cumberland during this period were as follows: Robert

Anderson from September 24, 1861 to October 8, 1861, and William T. Sherman from October 8, 1861 to November 15, 1861. Anderson officially assumed command of the department September 24, 1861, but the records show that he was exercising command as early as September 4, 1861.

TROOPS IN THE DEPARTMENT OF THE CUMBERLAND

The organization and distribution of the troops in the Department of the Cumberland early in November 1861 are given here in some detail because many of the regimental commanders moved up to higher command during the war.

Camp Nevin at Nolin River, Kentucky, Alexander McD. McCook
First Brigade, Lovell H. Rousseau
6th Indiana, Thomas T. Crittenden; 5th Kentucky, Harvey M. Buckley; 6th Kentucky, Walter C. Whitaker; 2nd Kentucky Cavalry, Buckner Board; four companies of United States Regulars; and David C. Stone's Battery A, Kentucky Light Artillery
Second Brigade, Thomas J. Wood
29th Indiana, John F. Miller; 30th Indiana, Sion S. Bass; 38th Indiana, Benjamin F. Scribner; 39th Indiana, Thomas J. Harrison
Third Brigade, Richard W. Johnson
34th Illinois, Edward N. Kirk; 32nd Indiana, August Willich; 15th Ohio, Moses R. Dickey; 49th Ohio, William H. Gibson
Fourth Brigade, James S. Negley
77th Pennsylvania, Frederick S. Stumbaugh; 78th Pennsylvania, William Sirwell; 79th Pennsylvania, Henry A. Hambright; Michael Mueller's 6th Battery, Indiana Light Artillery; and Charles S. Cotter's Battery A, 1st Ohio Light Artillery

Camp Dick Robinson, George H. Thomas
1st Kentucky, Thomas E. Bramlette; 4th Kentucky, Speed S. Fry; 1st Kentucky Cavalry, Francis M. Wolford; 14th Ohio, James B. Steedman; 31st Ohio, Moses B. Walker; 1st Tennessee, Robert K. Byrd; and 2nd Tennessee, Samuel P. Carter

Note. The Kentucky regiments were organized as the "Kentucky Brigade," and the Tennessee regiments as the "Tennessee Brigade."

Bardstown, Kentucky
10th Indiana, Mahlon D. Manson

Crab Orchard, Kentucky
33rd Indiana, John Coburn

Jeffersonville, Indiana
34th Indiana, Asbury Steele; 36th Indiana, William Grose; 1st Wisconsin, John C. Starkweather

Mouth of Salt River, Kentucky
37th Indiana, George W. Hazzard; 9th Michigan, William W. Duffield

Lebanon Junction, Kentucky
2nd Minnesota, Horatio P. Van Cleve

Olympian Springs, Kentucky
2nd Ohio, Leonard A. Harris

Cynthiana, Kentucky
35th Ohio, Ferdinand Van Derveer

Nicholasville, Kentucky
21st Ohio, Jesse S. Norton; 38th Ohio, Edwin D. Bradley

Big Hill, Kentucky
17th Ohio, John M. Connell

Colesburg, Kentucky
24th Illinois, Frederick Hecker

Elizabethtown, Kentucky
19th Illinois, John B. Turchin

Owensboro, Kentucky
31st Indiana, Charles Cruft

It should be noted here that the designations of some of the above regiments were later changed to conform to those officially recognized by the United States government.

In addition to the above, other regiments were in the process of formation in Kentucky by the following officers: Theophilus T. Garrard at Rockcastle; Jeremiah T. Boyle at Harrodsburg; Sidney M. Barnes at Irvine; David R. Haggard at Burkeville; and William A. Hoskins at Somerset.

DEPARTMENT OF THE CUMBERLAND OCTOBER 24, 1862– JUNE 27, 1865

The Department of the Cumberland was re-created October 24, 1862 to consist of that part of the state of Tennessee east of the Tennessee River (excluding Fort Henry and Fort Donelson and the country around Cumberland Gap), and such parts of Alabama and Georgia as might be occupied by United States forces. William S. Rosecrans assumed command of the department at Louisville, Kentucky October 30, 1862 (assigned October 24).

There were several changes in the limits of the department during the period of its existence. These were as follows:

January 25, 1863, Fort Henry and Fort Donelson were transferred from the Department of the Tennessee to the Department of the Cumberland, and later Fort Heiman was also transferred.

The Military Division of the Mississippi was created October 16, 1863, to consist of the Department of the Cumberland, the Department of the Tennessee, and the Department of the Ohio.

November 16, 1863, that part of East Tennessee that was then occupied by troops of the Army of the Ohio was excluded from the Department of the Cumberland.

January 17, 1865, the Department of the Ohio was merged into the Department of the Cumberland, which then consisted of the state of Kentucky; Tennessee east of the Tennessee River; and such parts of Alabama, Georgia, and Mississippi as were occupied by forces commanded by George H. Thomas.

February 10, 1865, the Department of Kentucky was created to consist of the state of Kentucky, and the latter was thus removed from the Department of the Cumberland. Also on February 10, that part of Tennessee west of the Tennessee River, known as the District of West Tennessee, was transferred from the Department of Mississippi to the Department of the Cumberland, and by this action the entire state of Tennessee became a part of the Department of the Cumberland.

May 27, 1865, northern Mississippi was added to the District of West Tennessee, Department of the Cumberland.

In the reorganization of the military divisions and departments of the army June 27, 1865, the Department of the Cumberland was discontinued, and the Department of Tennessee was constituted to consist of the state of Tennessee. On the same date, the Military Division of the Tennessee was constituted, to include the departments of Tennessee, Georgia, Kentucky, and Alabama. The Military Division of the Tennessee was organized June 20, 1865.

COMMANDERS OF THE DEPARTMENT OF THE CUMBERLAND

William S. Rosecrans   October 30, 1862 to October 20, 1863
George H. Thomas   October 20, 1863 to June 27, 1865

POSTS IN THE DEPARTMENT OF THE CUMBERLAND

After the Battle of Perryville, Kentucky October 8, 1862, the Army of the Ohio was concentrated at Glasgow and Bowling Green, Kentucky. When the Department of the Cumberland was created by the order of October 24, 1862, the same order designated the troops under Rosecrans' command, which consisted largely of Don Carlos Buell's former Army of the Ohio, as Fourteenth Corps, Department of the Cumberland. Although the troops of the Department of the Cumberland were officially designated as Fourteenth Corps, they were commonly called the Army of the Cumberland.

On October 24, 1862, the only Union troops in Tennessee, within the limits of the new department, were those of the garrison of Nashville. At that time the post was commanded by James S. Negley. During the early part of November 1862 the Army of the Cumberland advanced to Nashville, and during the month a number of posts were established in the department. These were:

Post of Nashville, Tennessee. As noted, this post had already been established by the Army of the Ohio, and James S. Negley had been assigned command in September 1862. Negley remained in command of the post until December 1862, when he advanced with his division at the beginning of the Stones River Campaign. He was then succeeded by Robert B. Mitchell.

Post of Gallatin, Tennessee. This post was established in November 1862 and consisted of troops guarding the Louisville and Nashville Railroad. Eleazer A. Paine was assigned command.

Post of Bowling Green, Kentucky. When the Army of the Cumberland moved to Nashville in November 1862, Mahlon D. Manson was left in command of the troops that remained at Bowling Green.

Post of Clarksville, Tennessee. Clarksville, Tennessee was occupied by a force commanded by Sanders D. Bruce in November 1862, and the Post of Clarksville was established the following month.

DISTRICTS IN THE DEPARTMENT OF THE CUMBERLAND

For better administrative control of the territory within the limits of the Department of the Cumberland, the department was divided into a number of districts as follows: District of Nashville, District of Tennessee, District of Northern Alabama, District of the Etowah, District of Kentucky, and District of East Tennessee. In February 1865, the entire state of Tennessee was included in the Department of the Cumberland, and the department was redistricted February 28 as follows: District of West Tennessee, District of Middle Tennessee, District of East Tennessee, and District of the Etowah.

The descriptions of the above-mentioned districts are given in the following sections.

District of Nashville

The District of Nashville was created November 10, 1863, to consist of the defenses of the Louisville and Nashville Railroad from Nashville to the Kentucky line; the Nashville and Northwestern Railroad to the Tennessee River; the Nashville and Chattanooga Railroad to the Duck River; the Nashville and Columbia Railroad (Tennessee and Alabama Railroad) to Columbia, Tennessee; and the posts of Nashville, Clarksville, McMinnville, and Fort Donelson. Lovell H. Rousseau was assigned command of the district, with headquarters at Nashville. He remained in command until May 30, 1864, when the district was merged into the District of Tennessee (see below).

The posts eventually established in the district were as follows: Clarksville, Columbia, Fort Donelson, Gallatin, La Vergne, McMinnville, Murfreesboro, and Nashville, all in Tennessee, and Bridgeport, Alabama.

Troops in the District of Nashville. The troops in the district were stationed generally along the railroads and at the various posts in the district. The troops of the post of Nashville were known as Granger's Division, and were commanded by Robert S. Granger. The division consisted of Ward's Brigade, commanded by William T. Ward, and unassigned regiments. Horatio P. Van Cleve commanded the troops at Murfreesboro, which consisted of Coburn's Brigade, commanded by John Coburn, and unassigned regiments. Coburn's Brigade served as an unassigned brigade at Tullahoma, Tennessee during October and November 1863. Eleazer A. Paine commanded the equivalent of a brigade at Gallatin, and Alvan C. Gillem commanded the equivalent of a brigade on the Nashville and Northwestern Railroad.

A new division was formed in the District of Nashville January 2, 1864 and was designated as First Division, Eleventh Corps. It was organized as follows:

First Division, Eleventh Corps, William T. Ward

First Brigade, Benjamin Harrison
Second Brigade, John Coburn

Note. First Brigade was formerly Ward's Brigade.

February 23, 1864, Harrison's brigade left Nashville for Tullahoma, and later moved on to Wauhatchie, Tennessee. The troops of Coburn's brigade were posted at Nashville, La Vergne, and McMinnville.

By an order of January 2, 1864, Granger's division in the District of Nashville was reorganized, and this division, together with the posts in the district, was assigned to Rousseau. The new division was assigned to Twelfth Corps, but it remained in the District of Nashville, and did not join the corps. It was organized as follows:

First Brigade, Robert S. Granger
Second Brigade, Horatio P. Van Cleve
Third Brigade, James G. Spears

Note. Third Brigade, which belonged to the post of Chattanooga, was serving in East Tennessee at that time.

On April 14, 1864 (ordered April 4, 1864), Eleventh Corps and Twelfth Corps, Department of the Cumberland were consolidated to form a new Twentieth Corps. Rousseau was assigned command of Fourth Division, Twentieth Corps, which consisted of Robert S. Granger's First Brigade and unassigned regiments. Fourth Division was detached for post and garrison duty in the District of Nashville (and later in the District of Tennessee), and did not join Twentieth Corps. In April 1864, the garrison of Bridgeport, Alabama, formerly belonging to Eleventh Corps, was assigned to Fourth Division, Twentieth Corps, District of Nashville. It was the equivalent of a brigade in strength, and was commanded by Albert Von Steinhausen.

At the end of May 1864, the troops in the District of Nashville consisted of the following:

District of Nashville, Lovell H. Rousseau
    First Brigade, Fourth Division, Twentieth Corps,
      Robert S. Granger
    Post of Nashville, Robert S. Granger
    Garrison Artillery, Josiah W. Church
    Artillery Reserve, James Barnett
      First Division (Regulars), Edmund C. Bainbridge
      Second Division (Volunteers), John J. Ely

Nashville and Northwestern Railroad, Alvan C.
    Gillem
Murfreesboro, Horatio P. Van Cleve

There were also troops at the posts of Clarksville, Columbia, Fort Donelson, and Gallatin in Tennessee, and at Bridgeport, Alabama. In addition, unassigned regiments of Fourth Division, Twentieth Corps were stationed at Clarksville, Duck River Bridge, Elk River Bridge, Fort Donelson, McMinnville, and Murfreesboro in Tennessee, and at Bridgeport in Alabama.

District of Tennessee

May 30, 1864, the designation of the District of Nashville (see above) was changed to the District of Tennessee, and Lovell H. Rousseau was assigned command. This district continued in existence until the state was redistricted February 28, 1865. It was organized as follows:

Defenses of the Nashville and Chattanooga Railroad. May 22, 1864, Robert H. Milroy was assigned the task of organizing the forces guarding the railroad from Nashville, Tennessee to Bridgeport, Alabama into two brigades, one of which was to be stationed at Tullahoma, Tennessee and the other at Bridgeport. In July 1864, this command was reported as the Defenses of the Nashville and Chattanooga Railroad and, as finally organized, consisted of three brigades as follows: Horatio P. Van Cleve's First Brigade at Murfreesboro, Edward J. Robinson's Second Brigade at Tullahoma, and Wladimir Krzyzanowski's Third Brigade at Bridgeport. There was also a post at Stevenson, Alabama. Second Brigade was discontinued in September 1864 and was designated as Post of Tullahoma.

Nashville and Northwestern Railroad. Alvan C. Gillem commanded the troops along the Nashville and Northwestern Railroad in the district from May 30, 1864 to August 1864, when he was transferred to East Tennessee. He was succeeded by Charles R. Thompson, who remained in command until the state was redistricted February 28, 1865. Headquarters of the command was at Nashville, but Springfield, Tennessee was an important post.

Post and Garrison of Nashville. John F. Miller commanded the Post and Garrison of Nashville from May 30, 1864 until February 28, 1865, when the state was redistricted. The troops of Miller's command consisted largely of unassigned regiments, but there was also the garrison artillery under Josiah W. Church and the Reserve Artillery under James Barnett. The latter consisted of a First Division of regular artillery and a Second Division of volunteer artillery commanded by John J. Ely.

Fourth Division, Twentieth Corps. This division was organized April 14, 1864 in the District of Nashville (see above). It continued to serve on post and garrison duty in the District of Tennessee, detached from the corps. When first formed, Fourth Division consisted of a First Brigade under Robert S. Granger, which was posted at Decatur, Alabama, and also some unassigned regiments. When Granger was assigned command of the District of Northern Alabama May 30, 1864, he was succeeded in command of First Brigade by Charles C. Doolittle. Doolittle was relieved by William P. Lyon in November 1864. Edwin C. Mason was assigned command of a new Second Brigade, Fourth Division, which was organized from unassigned regiments.

District of Northern Alabama

On May 30, 1864, the date on which the District of Tennessee was created, Robert S. Granger was assigned command of the railroad from Nashville to Decatur, Huntsville, and Stevenson in Alabama, and to the command of the garrisons of the posts along the railroad. Granger's command was designated as the District of Northern Alabama. Its commander reported directly to Headquarters, District of Tennessee, and it was, in effect, a sub-district of the District of Tennessee. Granger was in command of the district from June 2, 1864 to September 10, 1865, with headquarters at Decatur, Alabama.

The principal posts of the district were Brownsboro, Decatur, Huntsville, and Larkinsville in Alabama, and Pulaski, Tennessee. Charles C. Doolittle's First Brigade, Fourth Division, Twenti-

eth Corps and Jacob M. Thornburgh's First Brigade, Fourth Cavalry Division were at Decatur, and John C. Starkweather commanded the equivalent of a brigade at Pulaski.

When the Department of the Cumberland was redistricted February 28, 1865, the District of Northern Alabama became a sub-district of the newly created District of Middle Tennessee, and was defined as follows: It included the line of the Memphis and Charleston Railroad from Decatur, Alabama to, and including, the blockhouse at Widow's Creek, near Bridgeport, Alabama; the line of the Tennessee and Alabama Railroad from Huntsville, Alabama to, and including, the post of Athens, Alabama; and the line of the Tennessee River from Bridgeport to Waterloo, at the foot of Mussel Shoals. Robert S. Granger was assigned command of the district, with headquarters at Decatur.

For a time, Stevenson, Alabama was in the First Sub-district of the District of Middle Tennessee, but April 8, 1865 the post and adjacent country were transferred to the District of Northern Alabama.

District of the Etowah

The District of the Etowah was created June 10, 1864, to include the country along the route from Bridgeport, Alabama to Allatoona, Georgia, including Cleveland, Tennessee and Rome, Georgia, and the country to the east as far as controlled by United States forces. The district was created to protect the line of supply south from Chattanooga to William T. Sherman's army, which was then advancing into Georgia toward Atlanta. James B. Steedman was assigned command of the district June 15, 1864, with headquarters at Chattanooga.

When the Department of the Cumberland was redistricted February 28, 1865, the District of the Etowah was redefined to include the line of the Nashville and Chattanooga Railroad from, and including, Bridgeport, Alabama to Chattanooga, Tennessee; the Western and Atlantic Railroad as far south as garrisoned by United States forces; and the East Tennessee and Georgia Railroad from Chattanooga to the Hiawassee River. Steedman was assigned command, with headquarters at

Chattanooga. The principal posts in the district were Chattanooga, Cleveland, Lookout Mountain, and Whiteside in Tennessee, and Allatoona and Rome in Georgia.

The commanders of the district were as follows:

James B. Steedman	June 15, 1864 to November 29, 1864
Thomas F. Meagher	November 29, 1864 to January 5, 1865
James B. Steedman	January 5, 1865 to June 20, 1865

Troops in the District of the Etowah. The post of Chattanooga was established in October 1863, after the Battle of Chickamauga, and the troops of the post consisted of James G. Spears' Brigade, James B. Steedman's First Separate Brigade, the Regular Brigade, and the artillery at Chattanooga. Spears' Brigade was sent to East Tennessee in December 1863, where it became the First East Tennessee Brigade. The other organizations remained at Chattanooga, and later became a part of the District of the Etowah. When Steedman assumed command of the district, First Separate Brigade, which he had commanded, was assigned to Timothy R. Stanley. John R. Edie commanded the Regular Brigade. There were other troops at various posts in the district.

October 31, 1864, Charles Cruft was assigned command of the convalescents of Fourteenth Corps, Fifteenth Corps, Seventeenth Corps, and Twentieth Corps, who had arrived from the north and who were unable to rejoin their commands in Georgia. Cruft was directed to organize convalescents into brigades, each brigade to consist of troops of the corps to which they belonged. November 12, 1864, these brigades were assigned to a newly created First Separate Division (see below).

By an order of November 12, 1864, the garrisons at Lookout Mountain, Chattanooga, and Whiteside in Tennessee, and Bridgeport in Alabama were organized into a new First Separate Division, Army of the Cumberland, under the command of Steedman. It consisted of a First Brigade under John H. King, a Second Brigade under Caleb L. Carlton, unassigned regiments of the district, and the garrison artillery. Second Brigade was officially created January 14, 1865, and was assigned to Charles H. Grosvenor, the senior colonel.

November 25, 1864, Charles Cruft's command of convalescents was divided, and Thomas F. Meagher was assigned command of all officers and men of Fifteenth Corps and Seventeenth Corps that were then in the District of the Etowah and any that might arrive later. These were to be organized into two or more brigades, and the organization was to be known as the Provisional Division of the Army of the Tennessee. Meagher was assigned the task of guarding the Chattanooga and Nashville Railroad as far as Loudon, and the railroad from Chattanooga to Atlanta to its terminus. Charles Cruft was assigned command of all officers and men belonging to Fourteenth Corps and Twentieth Corps that were then in the district, and his command was designated as Provisional Division of the Army of the Cumberland. Cruft was to garrison Bridgeport with a part of his command and to hold the rest in reserve.

In early January 1865, Meagher was ordered with his command to join William T. Sherman's Army of the Military Division of the Mississippi, which was then beginning its march northward from Savannah, Georgia through the Carolinas. Meagher moved his command to Nashville and left there for the East January 18–19, 1865. He later joined Sherman in North Carolina. Cruft followed with his command to join Sherman March 13, 1865.

An unattached command, known as First Colored Brigade, Army of the Cumberland, was organized in December 1864 by Thomas J. Morgan. The brigade was discontinued the following month but was reorganized in March 1865.

Second Separate Division, Army of the Cumberland was organized March 15, 1865. It consisted of a First Brigade commanded by Henry M. Judah and a Second Brigade commanded by Felix Prince Salm. A Third Brigade commanded by Heber Le Favour was added to the division in April 1865.

After February 28, 1865, the troops in the District of the Etowah were known as Second Division, Department of the Cumberland.

Steedman commanded a Provisional Detachment (or Division), District of the Etowah that moved to reinforce George H. Thomas' command at Nashville during John B. Hood's Confederate invasion of Tennessee November 29, 1864–January 13, 1865. Thomas F. Meagher commanded the district during Steedman's absence. For additional information, see below, Troops in the Department of the

Cumberland, United States Forces under Thomas; and see also Franklin and Nashville Campaign (Hood's Invasion of Tennessee).

District of Kentucky

August 7, 1864, the state of Kentucky was constituted as a separate district, which was designated as the District of Kentucky, Department of the Ohio. The organization of the district was essentially unchanged until January 17, 1865, when the Department of the Ohio was annexed to the Department of the Cumberland. The designation of the district was then changed to District of Kentucky, Department of the Cumberland. February 10, 1865, the Department of Kentucky was created to consist of the state of Kentucky, and the district then passed into that department. For details of the organization of the District of Kentucky, see Department of the Ohio, August 19, 1862–January 17, 1865, Posts and Districts in the Department of the Ohio.

District of East Tennessee

East Tennessee was first occupied by troops of the Department of the Ohio in September 1863. Jacob Ammen's Fourth Division, Twenty-Third Corps, which occupied the area in January 1865, was also designated as the District of East Tennessee, Department of the Ohio. Davis Tillson relieved Ammen in command of the district January 14, 1865 and was in command when the Department of the Ohio was merged into the Department of the Cumberland three days later. Tillson remained in command of the district until relieved by George Stoneman March 9, 1865 (ordered February 14, 1865).

The District of East Tennessee, Department of the Cumberland was officially constituted February 28, 1865 to consist of East Tennessee, and the line of the East Tennessee and Georgia Railroad and the line of the Tennessee and Virginia Railroad as far as it was garrisoned by United States troops. Headquarters of the district was at Knoxville, Tennessee.

March 17, 1865, the infantry of the district was designated as Fourth Division, Department of the Cumberland, and the cavalry of the district was organized as Cavalry Division, District of East Tennessee. The troops of the district were then organized as follows:

Fourth Division, Department of the Cumberland, Davis Tillson
  First Brigade, Chauncey G. Hawley
  Second Brigade, Horatio G. Gibson

Cavalry Division, District of East Tennessee, Alvan C. Gillem
  First Brigade, William J. Palmer
  Second Brigade, Simeon B. Brown
  Third Brigade, John K. Miller

District of West Tennessee

February 10, 1865, that part of Tennessee west of the Tennessee River was transferred as the District of West Tennessee from the Department of Mississippi to the Department of the Cumberland, and the transfer was completed March 1. At that time, the district, then under the command of Benjamin S. Roberts, was organized as follows:

Post and Defenses of Memphis, Augustus L. Chetlain
  Second Brigade, Frank A. Kendrick
  Fort Pickering, Ignatz G. Kappner
Post of Columbus, Kentucky
Enrolled Militia

Note 1. At the end of February 1865, Second Brigade was en route to New Orleans.
Note 2. Fort Pickering was manned by regiments of United States Colored Troops.
Note 3. The Enrolled Militia was disbanded May 8, 1865.

When the Department of the Cumberland was redistricted February 28, 1865, the District of West Tennessee was defined as consisting of all of the state of Tennessee west of the Tennessee River. Cadwallader C. Washburn assumed command of the district March 4, with headquarters at Memphis.

The troops in the district were designated as Third Division, Department of the Cumberland by the order of February 28, 1865.

In April 1865, the district was organized as follows:

District of West Tennessee, Cadwallader C. Washburn

Post and Defenses of Memphis, Augustus L. Chetlain
   Fort Pickering, Ignatz G. Kappner
   Unassigned Regiments

Cavalry Division, Embury D. Osband
   First Brigade, John E. Phelps
   Second Brigade, William Thompson
   Third Brigade, Otto Funke

Note. In March 1865, Osband's Cavalry Division of the Department of Mississippi moved into the District of West Tennessee, Department of the Cumberland.

Artillery, Raphael G. Rombauer

May 27, 1865, northern Mississippi was included in the District of West Tennessee.

For additional information, see Department of Mississippi, November 28, 1864–May 17, 1865, Districts in the Department of Mississippi, District of West Tennessee.

District of Middle Tennessee

The District of Middle Tennessee was constituted February 28, 1865 to consist of Middle Tennessee and northern Alabama as far as Widow's Creek, near Bridgeport, on the Nashville and Chattanooga Railroad; and also all lines of railroad and water communications lying within this region. Lovell H. Rousseau was assigned command of the district, with headquarters at Nashville. On that date, Fourth Division, Twentieth Corps, District of Tennessee was discontinued, and the troops within the District of Middle Tennessee were organized as First Division, Department of the Cumberland.

The District of Middle Tennessee was divided into sub-districts as follows:

First Sub-district, District of Middle Tennessee. This sub-district was constituted February 28, 1865, to consist of the line of the Nashville and Chattanooga Railroad and the adjacent country as far south as, but not including, Stevenson, Alabama. Stevenson was later transferred to the First Sub-district, but on April 8 the post and adjacent country were transferred to the District of Northern Alabama. Robert H. Milroy was assigned command of the First Sub-district, with headquarters at Tullahoma, Tennessee.

The troops in the sub-district were organized into brigades as follows: First Brigade, March 13, 1865, under the command of Horatio P. Van Cleve, with headquarters at Murfreesboro; Second Brigade, March 11, 1865, under Nathan A. M. Dudley, with headquarters at Tullahoma; and Third Brigade, April 23, 1865, under Amasa Cobb, with headquarters at Decherd.

July 11, 1865, Milroy was ordered home for muster out, and Horatio P. Van Cleve assumed command of the First Sub-district. Headquarters was then moved to Murfreesboro.

Second Sub-district, District of Middle Tennessee. This sub-district was constituted February 28, 1865, to include the Tennessee and Alabama Railroad and the adjacent country from Nashville to, but not including, Athens, Alabama. Richard W. Johnson was assigned command, with headquarters at Pulaski, Tennessee.

Third Sub-district, District of Middle Tennessee. This sub-district was constituted February 28, 1865 to include the Nashville and Northwestern Railroad, Johnsonville, and the adjacent country. Charles R. Thompson was assigned command, with headquarters at Kingston Springs, Tennessee.

Fourth Sub-district, District of Middle Tennessee. The Fourth Sub-district was constituted February 28, 1865 to include the Louisville and Nashville Railroad from Nashville northward to the Kentucky state line, and the Cumberland River above Nashville, including Hartsville, Carthage, and the adjacent country. James Gilfillan was assigned command, with headquarters at Gallatin, Tennessee.

Fifth Sub-district, District of Middle Tennessee. This sub-district was constituted February 28, 1865 to consist of the garrisons of Clarksville and Fort Donelson, the line of the Edgefield and Clarksville Railroad, and the adjacent country. Arthur A. Smith was assigned command, with headquarters at Clarksville, Tennessee.

District of Northern Alabama, District of Middle Tennessee. When the Department of the Cumberland was redistricted February 28, 1865, the District of Northern Alabama was constituted as a sub-district of the District of Middle Tennessee. For details of the organization of this district, see above, District of Northern Alabama, Department of the Cumberland.

Post and Garrison of Nashville, District of Middle Tennessee. John F. Miller commanded the forces of the Post of Nashville, which consisted of Edwin C. Mason's First Brigade, First Division, Department of the Cumberland; John J. Ely's garrison artillery; and unassigned regiments.

TROOPS IN THE DEPARTMENT OF THE CUMBERLAND

In addition to the many organizations that belonged to the various districts of the Department of the Cumberland, and that have already been described, there were other organizations, two of them of army size, that were formed and operated within the limits of the Department of the Cumberland. These were as follows:

Army of the Cumberland. The large mobile force of the department was the Army of the Cumberland. There were two armies of the Cumberland organized during the war, but it was the second of these, commanded by William S. Rosecrans, that is referred to here. This army fought at the Battle of Murfreesboro, took part in the Tullahoma Campaign, and was engaged at Chickamauga. Under the command of George H. Thomas, it took part in the battles around Chattanooga, and then was with William T. Sherman's army as the Center, Army of Invasion of Georgia during the Atlanta Campaign. For details of the organization and operations of this army, see Army of the Cumberland, October 24, 1862–November 14, 1864.

United States Forces under Thomas. The other major force in the Department of the Cumberland was the army that was assembled in Middle Tennessee in November and December 1864 under George H. Thomas, when John B. Hood threatened the invasion of the state with his Confederate Army of Tennessee. September 18, 1864, after the fall of Atlanta, Hood's army moved northward from Lovejoy's Station, Georgia, along Sherman's supply line to Dalton. There it turned to the west and marched across Georgia and northern Alabama to Tuscumbia, on the Tennessee River, where it was in position to cross the river and march into Tennessee. Sherman followed Hood to the Georgia-Alabama line, and then sent Thomas to Nashville, where he was to establish headquarters and organize for the defense of Tennessee. Thomas arrived at Nashville October 3.

When it became clear that the state was threatened with invasion, Sherman detached David S. Stanley's Fourth Corps from his army and October 26 ordered it to join Thomas. Four days later, John M. Schofield's Twenty-Third Corps, Army of the Ohio was also sent back to Tennessee. Both corps became a part of the force organized by Thomas, which was known as United States Forces under Thomas, Department of the Cumberland.

In addition to the infantry forces, James H. Wilson's Cavalry Corps of the Military Division of the Mississippi, which had been operating with Fourth Corps and Twenty-Third Corps during their retreat to Nashville, also moved back and went into camp across the Cumberland River from Nashville at Edgefield. Wilson's command consisted of John T. Croxton's First Brigade of First Cavalry Division, Edward Hatch's Fifth Division, Richard W. Johnson's Sixth Division, and Joseph F. Knipe's Seventh Division.

There was a further addition to Thomas' command when Andrew J. Smith arrived at Nashville December 5, 1864 with a force known as Right Wing, Sixteenth Corps. Earlier, while returning from Nathaniel P. Banks' ill-fated Red River, Louisiana expedition, Smith's command was ordered to proceed on to Missouri during Sterling Price's invasion of that state. Then, when Hood threatened in Tennessee, Smith was ordered with his command to Nashville. After its arrival there, the designation of Smith's command was changed to Detachment, Army of the Tennessee.

James B. Steedman also joined Thomas with a Provisional Detachment from his District of the Etowah.

For the complete organization of the United States forces under Thomas, see Franklin and Nashville Campaign (Hood's Invasion of Tennessee).

Thomas defeated Hood in front of Nashville December 15–16, 1864, and a short time later, after Hood's Army of Tennessee had been driven from the state, Thomas' command was broken up. Twenty-Third Corps was ordered to North Carolina to cooperate with William T. Sherman's Army of the Military Division of West Tennessee, which was then beginning its march northward from Savannah, Georgia through the Carolinas. Twenty-Third Corps left the Department of the Cumberland January 15, 1865 and did not return. For additional information, see Twenty-Third Corps, Army of the Ohio (in the Department of North Carolina); Carolinas Campaign; and Department of North Carolina, January 31, 1865–May 19, 1866, all in Volume I.

February 7–8, 1865, Smith's Detachment, Army of the Tennessee embarked for New Orleans, where it arrived February 20–21. It was then transferred to the reorganized Sixteenth Corps, Military Division of West Mississippi, and it took part in the campaign against Mobile, Alabama. For additional information, see Sixteenth Corps, Military Division of West Mississippi; and also see Land Operations against Mobile Bay and Mobile, Alabama.

Cavalry Forces (Cavalry Corps). For the organization of the cavalry in the department, see Cavalry Corps, Army of the Cumberland.

Engineer Troops (Pioneer Brigade and Engineer Brigade). The Pioneer Brigade, Army of the Cumberland was organized in December 1862 under the command of James St. Clair Morton, chief engineer of Fourteenth Corps. In addition, the 1st Michigan Engineers (Engineers and Mechanics), which was commanded by William P. Innes and was unassigned, served as engineers. Commanders of the Pioneer Brigade were as follows: James St. Clair Morton from December 1862 to August 1863; Patrick O'Connell from August 1863 to October 1863; George P. Buell from October 1863 to June 17, 1864; and Patrick O'Connell from June 17, 1864 to September 10, 1864. The Pioneer Brigade was disbanded September 10, 1864.

In November 1863, William F. Smith commanded the engineer troops at Chattanooga, which consisted of five regiments of engineers and George P. Buell's Pioneer Brigade. January 18, 1864, these troops were organized as the Engineer Brigade, and Timothy R. Stanley was assigned command. The 1st Michigan Engineers (Engineers and Mechanics) was added in March 1864, and the engineer troops then consisted of Stanley's Engineer Brigade, Buell's Pioneer Brigade, and Innes' 1st Michigan Engineers. This was essentially the organization of the engineer troops until the Pioneer Brigade was disbanded September 10, 1864. These troops were stationed at, or near, Chattanooga from October 1863.

The commanders of the Engineer Brigade were: Timothy R. Stanley from January 18, 1864 to April 1864; William B. McCreery from April 1864 to September 10, 1864. Joshua B. Culver commanded temporarily in July 1864.

Artillery Reserve. An Artillery Reserve was organized October 15, 1863, under the command of John M. Brannan. It consisted of the following:

First Division, James Barnett
    First Brigade
    Second Brigade

Second Division
    First Brigade, Josiah W. Church
    Second Brigade, Arnold Sutermeister

Note. The commanders of First Brigade and Second Brigade, First Division, and of Second Division are not of record.

Governor's Guard. The Governor's Guard was a special organization under the control of Governor Andrew Johnson of Tennessee.

Reserve Brigade. The Reserve Brigade was organized in April 1864 and commanded by John F. Burke until he was mustered out May 27, 1864. Heber Le Favour then commanded the brigade until it was discontinued March 31, 1865.

DEPARTMENT OF THE GULF

The Department of the Gulf was constituted February 23, 1862 to consist of all of the coast of the Gulf of Mexico west of Pensacola Harbor, and that part of the Gulf states that might be occupied by United States forces commanded by Benjamin F. Butler. Butler's command, which consisted of regiments raised in New England, was then en route to Louisiana. Butler assumed command of the department at Ship Island in the Gulf of Mexico March 20, 1862.

A Union fleet under David G. Farragut, preceding Butler's land force on transports, moved up the Mississippi River, passed Fort Jackson and Fort Saint Philip, and captured New Orleans April 25, 1862. Butler, who followed the fleet with his command, occupied New Orleans May 1 and established headquarters of the department in the city that day. George F. Shepley was assigned as military governor of Louisiana on June 3. For details of Butler's expedition see below, Troops in the Department of the Gulf, Ship Island, Mississippi Expedition, and Butler's Gulf Expedition (New Orleans).

The department was enlarged August 8, 1862 when that part of Florida west of the Appalachicola River was transferred from the Department of the South to the Department of the Gulf. Lewis G. Arnold was in command of the troops in West Florida, with headquarters at Pensacola.

On November 8, 1862, Nathaniel P. Banks was assigned command of the Department of the Gulf, including Texas, and he was ordered to organize an expedition in the New England states with which to reinforce the troops with Butler in Louisiana. When this task was completed, he sailed for the Gulf of Mexico. Upon arriving at New Orleans, he assumed command of the Department of the Gulf, including Texas, on December 17, relieving Butler. For details of Banks' expedition, see below, Troops in the Department of the Gulf, Banks' Expedition to the Department of the Gulf (or Banks' Southern Expedition).

The Department of the Gulf was further enlarged March 16, 1863 when Key West and Tortugas, Florida were transferred from the Department of the South to the Department of the Gulf.

The Military Division of West Mississippi was created May 7, 1864 to include the Department of Arkansas and the Department of the Gulf, and Edward R. S. Canby was assigned command of the military division.

Stephen A. Hurlbut assumed temporary command of the Department of the Gulf September 23, 1864 while Banks was on leave. Banks resumed command of the department April 22, 1865.

February 10, 1865, the Department of the Gulf was defined to include only the states of Louisiana and Texas. The military districts on the Gulf of Mexico in Alabama and Florida were ordered to report directly to Headquarters, Military Division of West Mississippi. By this order, Key West, the Tortugas, West Florida, and South Alabama were transferred from the Department of the Gulf to the Military Division of West Mississippi. Also on February 10, the Federal troops on the west bank of the Mississippi River in the District of Natchez and the District of Vicksburg were transferred from the Department of Mississippi to the Department of the Gulf.

May 17, 1865, the Military Division of West Mississippi was abolished, and the Department of the Gulf was constituted from the states of Alabama, Florida, Louisiana, and Mississippi, and also the District of Key West and Tortugas. Canby was assigned command of the Department of the Gulf, and he assumed command June 3. Also on May 17, the Military Division of the Southwest was constituted to consist of the territory west of the Mississippi River and south of the Arkansas River. Philip H. Sheridan assumed command of the Military Division of the Southwest May 29, with headquarters at New Orleans.

In the order of June 27, 1865 that reorganized the military divisions and departments of the army, the Department of the Gulf was discontinued, and its territory was assigned to the Department of Louisiana and Texas, the Department of Mississippi, and the Department of Florida, all of which constituted Sheridan's Military Division of the Gulf, and the Department of Alabama, which was assigned to George H. Thomas' Military Division of the Tennessee.

The Military Division of the Southwest was discontinued July 17, 1865 (ordered June 27, 1865), and Sheridan assumed command of the Military Division of the Gulf.

COMMANDERS OF THE DEPARTMENT OF THE GULF

Benjamin F. Butler   March 20, 1862 to December 17, 1862

Nathaniel P. Banks	December 17, 1862 to September 23, 1864
Stephen A. Hurlbut	September 23, 1864 to April 22, 1865
Nathaniel P. Banks	April 22, 1865 to June 3, 1865
Edward R. S. Canby	June 3, 1865 to June 27, 1865

DISTRICTS IN THE DEPARTMENT OF THE GULF

During the period of its existence, the following districts were organized in the Department of the Gulf:

District of Alabama

The Military Division of West Mississippi was abolished May 17, 1865, and the Department of the Gulf was reconstituted on the same date to include the states of Alabama, Florida, Louisiana, and Mississippi, and the District of Key West and Tortugas. On June 3, Edward R. S. Canby assumed command of the department and then divided it into four districts, each state constituting a district. Andrew J. Smith was assigned command of the District of Alabama, with headquarters at Montgomery. The Department of the Gulf was discontinued June 27, 1865, and the Department of Alabama was constituted to consist of the state of Alabama.

Post and District of Baton Rouge

The first land forces to occupy Baton Rouge belonged to Thomas Williams' Second Brigade, Department of the Gulf. Soon after the occupation of New Orleans, Williams' brigade accompanied David G. Farragut's fleet up the Mississippi River to Vicksburg, but the combined force was too weak to capture the post, and Williams' brigade returned to Baton Rouge May 29, 1862. Williams was reinforced by three regiments sent up from New Orleans, and then, leaving two regiments at Baton Rouge, Williams again returned to Vicksburg with

Farragut. This expedition was also unsuccessful, and on July 26, Williams once more returned to Baton Rouge and occupied the town.

Williams was strongly attacked at Baton Rouge August 5, 1862 but succeeded in driving off the enemy and retaining possession of the town. Williams was killed during the battle, and was succeeded in command of the post by Halbert E. Paine. On August 21, the United States forces at Baton Rouge were transferred to Carrollton, Louisiana, and the post was abandoned. For details of the Battle of Baton Rouge, see below, Operations in the Department of the Gulf, Battle of Baton Rouge, Louisiana.

On December 17, 1862, Cuvier Grover, with 11,000 men, reoccupied Baton Rouge, and on December 30 these troops were organized into Grover's Division, Department of the Gulf. This division later became Fourth Division, Nineteenth Corps.

The post of Baton Rouge was occupied by Union forces during the remainder of the war.

October 8, 1863, Philip St. George Cooke was assigned command of the troops at Baton Rouge and in the surrounding country and from Baton Rouge to the neighborhood of Donaldsonville. This command was designated as the District of Baton Rouge. On October 28, the country west of the Mississippi River and between the Mississippi River and Bayou Plaquemine and Grosse Tete as far as Lobdell's Landing was assigned to the District of Baton Rouge.

In May 1864 the District of Baton Rouge was included in the Defenses of New Orleans, which was commanded by Joseph J. Reynolds.

August 6, 1864, the Military District of Baton Rouge and Port Hudson was created to include the District of Baton Rouge and the post of Port Hudson. Francis J. Herron was assigned command of the new district, with headquarters at Baton Rouge. From August 6, 1864 to February 9, 1865, the District of Baton Rouge was a sub-district of the District of Baton Rouge and Port Hudson.

August 13, 1864, the Bayou Manchac was announced as the dividing line between the District of Carrollton and the District of Baton Rouge. On August 20, the Bayou Manchac was announced as the boundary between the District of Baton Rouge and the Defenses of New Orleans. This order was revoked August 22, and the boundary east of the Mississippi River was defined as a line from Frenier Station on Lake Ponchartrain to the post of Bonnet Carre. The Union forces at Frenier Station, and at points north on the railroad to Jackson, reported to Herron at Baton Rouge.

February 9, 1865, the Northern Division of Louisiana was constituted to include the District of Baton Rouge and Port Hudson, and the post of Morganza. Thereafter, the forces at Baton Rouge, Port Hudson, and Morganza were designated, respectively, as the District of Baton Rouge, District of Port Hudson, and District of Morganza, all belonging to the Northern Division of Louisiana.

May 29,1865, the District of Baton Rouge, the District of Port Hudson, and the post of Clinton, Louisiana were consolidated and designated as the District of East Louisiana.

The principal posts of the District of Baton Rouge were Baton Rouge, Plaquemine, Gaines' Landing, Pass Manchac, and De Sair.

The commanders of the district were as follows:

Philip St. G. Cooke	October 8, 1863 to May 2, 1864
Henry W. Birge	May 2, 1864 to May 24, 1864
Fitz Henry Warren	May 24, 1864 to June 13, 1864
William P. Benton	June 13, 1864 to October 3, 1864
William J. Landram	October 3, 1864 to December 3, 1864
Joseph Bailey	December 3, 1864 to March 11, 1865
Edmund J. Davis	March 11, 1865 to March 18, 1865
John G. Fonda	March 18, 1865 to March 23, 1865
Michael K. Lawler	March 23, 1865 to May 30, 1865
John G. Fonda	May 30, 1865 to July 1865

Troops of the Post and District of Baton Rouge.
The first land forces to occupy Baton Rouge belonged to Thomas Williams' Second Brigade, Department of the Gulf, which disembarked there in May 1862 during David G. Farragut's operations on the Mississippi River against Vicksburg.

The troops at Baton Rouge were reinforced by regiments from New Orleans, and December 30, 1862 they were organized into a division under Cuvier Grover and designated as Grover's Division. Later the designation was changed to Fourth Division, Nineteenth Corps.

On January 3, 1863, a division was organized under William H. Emory, and Emory was ordered to assume command of that part of the division that was then at Carrollton, Louisiana and to concentrate the entire division at Baton Rouge as soon as possible. This division was known as Emory's Division and was later designated as Third Division, Nineteenth Corps.

On January 12, 1863, a division known as Augur's Division was organized under Christopher C. Augur, and later this was designated as First Division, Nineteenth Corps. The Third Brigade of this division was at Baton Rouge, and the other brigades were at Carrollton, but later they were also transferred to Baton Rouge. Augur assumed command at Baton Rouge.

Nineteenth Corps, Department of the Gulf was constituted by an order of January 6, 1863, and the designations of the above divisions were changed as indicated.

In March 1863 the divisions of Augur, Emory, and Grover were assembled at Baton Rouge. Grover's division then left for operations in western Louisiana March 26, and Emory's division followed April 1. Augur's division remained at Baton Rouge until it joined Banks' army at Port Hudson May 23. During the siege of Port Hudson, only a few regiments under the command of Charles W. Drew occupied Baton Rouge.

After the surrender of Port Hudson, Nineteenth Corps remained near Baton Rouge through August 1863, but it then departed in September, leaving only Jacob Sharpe's Second Brigade, First Division there. Oliver P. Gooding commanded the United States Forces at Baton Rouge from the time of the capture of Port Hudson until October 1863.

The District of Baton Rouge was created October 8, 1863, and Sharpe's brigade of First Division remained in the district until February 1864. In the reorganization of Nineteenth Corps February 15, 1864, the designation of Sharpe's brigade was changed to Third Brigade, Second Division, Nineteenth Corps.

Thirteenth Corps, Army of the Tennessee was transferred from Vicksburg and Natchez, Mississippi to the Department of the Gulf August 10–26, 1863, and in November it began to leave the department for Texas. Before it left, however, a detachment of four infantry regiments taken from Third

Brigade and Fourth Brigade, First Division was sent to Plaquemine in the District of Baton Rouge under the command of Lionel A. Sheldon.

At the end of May 1864, after Banks' Red River, Louisiana Campaign, Frederick W. Moore's Fourth Division, Detachment Thirteenth Corps was sent to Baton Rouge, and in June, the division was reorganized as Third Brigade, Third Division, Nineteenth Corps.

Generally thereafter, until the end of the war, only unassigned regiments were in the district. A Cavalry Brigade was organized in February 1865, under the command of Webster P. Moore (later commanded by John G. Fonda), and a Provisional Brigade was formed in the district in April 1865.

District of Baton Rouge and Port Hudson

The District of Baton Rouge and Port Hudson was created August 6, 1864 to consist of the District of Baton Rouge and the post of Port Hudson. Francis J. Herron was assigned command, with headquarters at Baton Rouge. The district was organized as follows:

District of Baton Rouge, William P. Benton
United States Forces at Port Hudson, George L. Andrews

The principal posts in the district were Baton Rouge, Plaquemine, Gaines' Landing, Pass Manchac, De Sair, and Port Hudson.

February 9, 1865, the District of Baton Rouge and Port Hudson was included in the newly created Northern Division of Louisiana, and the District of Baton Rouge and the District of Port Hudson were established as separate districts.

The commanders of the district were as follows:

Francis J. Herron	August 6, 1864 to October 3, 1864
William P. Benton	October 3, 1864 to December 26, 1864
George L. Andrews	December 26, 1864 to February 13, 1865

District of Bonnet Carre

The post of Bonnet Carre was occupied by United States Forces of the Defenses of New Or-

leans from the summer of 1863 to February 11, 1865, at which time the Defenses of New Orleans became the Southern Division of Louisiana. Then, on March 27, the country between Bayou Manchac and Kennerville (or Kenner), Louisiana was designated as the District of Bonnet Carre, Southern Division of Louisiana. The district was continued in existence after the war. Charles Everett and James Byrne were the commanders of the district.

District of Carrollton

Carrollton, Louisiana and nearby Camp Parapet were occupied by United States troops from the time of the occupation of New Orleans in 1862. The District of Carrollton, Defenses of New Orleans was organized in May 1864, and Nelson B. Bartram was assigned command, with headquarters at Carrollton. August 13, 1864, the Bayou Manchac was announced as the dividing line between the District of Carrollton and the District of Baton Rouge.

February 11, 1865, the designation of the Defenses of New Orleans was changed to the Southern Division of Louisiana, and the District of Carrollton became the District of Carrollton, Southern Division of Louisiana.

The principal posts in the district were Carrollton, Camp Parapet, De Sair, Fort Banks, Kennerville, Jeffersonville, and Pass Manchac.

Nelson Viall relieved Bartram in command of the district in October 1864, and William S. Mudgett relieved Viall in April 1865.

District of East Louisiana

Headquarters of the Northern Division of Louisiana was moved from Baton Rouge to Shreveport June 3, 1865 (ordered May 29), and May 29, 1865 the District of Baton Rouge and Port Hudson and the post of Clinton, Louisiana were organized into a new district known as the District of East Louisiana. Michael K. Lawler was assigned command of the district. The commander of the district reported directly to Headquarters, Department of the Gulf. The Department of the Gulf was discontinued June 27, 1865, and the state of Louisiana was included in the newly created Department of Louisiana and Texas.

District of Florida

The Military Division of West Mississippi was abolished May 17, 1865, and the Department of the Gulf was reconstituted on the same date to include the states of Alabama, Florida, Louisiana, and Mississippi and the District of Key West and Tortugas. On June 3, Edward R. S. Canby assumed command of the department. He divided it into four districts, each state constituting a district. Alexander Asboth was assigned command of the District of Florida, with headquarters at Tallahassee.

The Department of the Gulf was discontinued June 27, 1865, and the Department of Florida was created to consist of the state of Florida.

Post of Fort Jackson

Fort Jackson was occupied by United States troops from the time of its surrender April 28, 1862, and it was included in the Defenses of New Orleans.

December 13, 1863, the post of Fort Jackson was established as a separate command that reported directly to Headquarters, Department of the Gulf. William Dwight was assigned command, with headquarters at Fort Jackson. Fort Jackson was again included in the Defenses of New Orleans in February 1864. In May 1864, Fort Jackson and Fort Saint Philip constituted a single command in the Defenses of New Orleans, with Jonathan Tarbell in command.

February 11, 1865, Fort Jackson became a separate command in the newly constituted Southern Division of Louisiana.

District of Key West and Tortugas

Key West and Tortugas, Florida were transferred from the Department of the South to the Department of the Gulf March 16, 1863, and they were then designated as the District of Key West and Tortugas.

Daniel P. Woodbury was assigned command, with headquarters at Key West. In an order of April 29, 1864, the District of Key West and Tortugas was assigned to the Defenses of New Orleans, but it does not appear that this transfer was carried out.

February 10, 1865, the Department of the Gulf was reduced in size to include only the states of Louisiana and Texas, and thereafter the commander of the District of Key West and Tortugas was ordered to report directly to Headquarters, Military Division of West Mississippi.

The Military Division of West Mississippi was abolished May 17, 1865, and the Department of the Gulf was reconstituted on the same date to include the states of Alabama, Florida, Louisiana, and Mississippi, and the District of Key West and Tortugas. On June 3, Edward R. S. Canby assumed command of the Department of the Gulf and divided it into four districts, with each state constituting a district. The District of Key West and Tortugas was thus merged into the District of Florida, Department of the Gulf.

The principal posts of the district were Key West, Fort Jefferson, Cedar Keys, and Fort Myers.

The commanders of the district were as follows:

Daniel P. Woodbury	March 16, 1863 to September 13, 1864
Charles Hamilton	September 13, 1864 to October 15, 1864
John Newton	October 15, 1864 to July 1865

Note. Hamilton was in temporary command of the district in December 1864.

District of La Fourche

An organization known as Reserve Brigade, Department of the Gulf was organized September 16, 1862 at Carrollton, Louisiana under the command of Godfrey Weitzel. Late in October 1862, Weitzel moved with his brigade to Donaldsonville, on the west bank of the Mississippi, and then marched to the south and occupied Thibodeaux (present-day Thibodaux) on the Bayou La Fourche October 27. The purpose of this expedition was to disperse enemy forces belonging to Richard Taylor's command in western Louisiana that were operating in the area.

In an order of November 2, 1862, Benjamin F. Butler, commander of the Department of the Gulf, announced the organization of the District of the Teche, which was to consist of that part of Louisiana west of the Mississippi River, and assigned Weitzel to command. The Teche country, however, was not occupied by troops of Weitzel's command, and for that reason the name of the district was changed to the District of La Fourche on November 9. The district was defined as consisting of all territory in the state of Louisiana west of the Mississippi River, except the parishes of Plaquemine and Jefferson.

January 3, 1863, the Reserve Brigade was designated as Second Brigade, First Division, Nineteenth Corps, and as such it took part in Nathaniel P. Banks' operations in west Louisiana in April and May 1863. It then left the district to take part in the siege of Port Hudson, Louisiana May 23–July 8.

The District of La Fourche was reconstituted August 11, 1863, to consist of all of that part of the La Fourche country lying south of Napoleonville and west of the Bayou Des Allemands. Henry W. Birge was assigned command. On the same date, the Defenses of New Orleans was redefined to include Donaldsonville, and the boundary was to extend from that point down the Bayou La Fourche to Napoleonville and the canal running from Bayou La Fourche to Lake Venet, and from Algiers, Louisiana westward to Bayou Des Allemands. The District of La Fourche was thus included in the Defenses of New Orleans.

The organization of the district appears not to have been carried out, although the District of La Fourche was mentioned during August and September 1863. The troops in the district during this period belonged to Henry W. Birge's First Brigade, Fourth Division, Nineteenth Corps of the Defenses of New Orleans.

The District of La Fourche was again constituted October 8, 1863 as a separate command under Birge. The boundary of the district was defined as follows: the Bayou La Fourche from its mouth to Thibodeaux; then north to the Mississippi River, and along the west bank to Donaldsonville and its immediate vicinity; then west to Grand River and from there down the river to Grand Lake; then down the Atchafalaya River to the Gulf of Mexico; and from there to the mouth of the La Fourche.

October 28, 1863, the district was extended to include all troops stationed on the New Orleans, Opelousas, and Great Western Railroad as far as the Bayou Des Allemands.

About January 1, 1864, Edward L. Molineux succeeded Birge in command of First Brigade, Fourth Division, Nineteenth Corps and of the District of La Fourche. Molineux's brigade was withdrawn in March to take part in Banks' Red River Campaign as Second Brigade, Second Division, Nineteenth Corps. The troops remaining in the district were commanded by Nicholas W. Day until May 4, 1864. On that date, the District of La Fourche was again included in the Defenses of New Orleans, with John McNeil in command of the district.

In June 1864, James R. Slack's Brigade, formerly Second Brigade, Third Division, Thirteenth Corps, was in the district at Thibodeaux. Slack was nominally in command of Third Division, but the other two brigades were detached.

February 11, 1865, the District of La Fourche became a part of the newly constituted Southern Division of Louisiana.

The Department of the Gulf was discontinued June 27, 1865, and the state of Louisiana was included in the newly created Department of Louisiana and Texas.

The principal posts in the district were Bayou Boeuf, Bayou Des Allemands, Brashear City, Donaldsonville, Napoleonville, Terre Bonne, Thibodeaux, Tigerville, and along the New Orleans, Opelousas, and Great Western Railroad.

The commanders of the district were as follows:

Godfrey Weitzel	November 9, 1862 to April 1863
Henry W. Birge	August 30, 1863 to about January 1, 1864
Edward L. Molineux	January 1864 to the latter part of March 1864
Nicholas W. Day	March 1864 to May 4, 1864
John McNeil	May 4, 1864 to June 9, 1864
Robert A. Cameron	June 9, 1864 to July 1865

District of Louisiana

The Military Division of West Mississippi was abolished May 17, 1865, and the Department of the Gulf was reconstituted on that date to include the states of Alabama, Florida, Louisiana, and Mississippi, and the District of Key West and Tortugas. June 3, 1865, Edward R. S. Canby assumed command of the department and divided it into four districts, each state constituting a district. Louisiana became the District of Louisiana, Department of the Gulf.

The Department of the Gulf was discontinued June 27, 1865, and the state of Louisiana was included in the newly constituted Department of Louisiana and Texas.

District of Mississippi

The Military Division of West Mississippi was abolished May 17, 1865, and the Department of the Gulf was reconstituted on the same date to include the states of Alabama, Florida, Louisiana, and Mississippi, and the District of Key West and Tortugas. On June 3, Edward R. S. Canby assumed command of the department and divided it into four districts, each state constituting a district. Peter J. Osterhaus was assigned command of the District of Mississippi, with headquarters at Jackson.

On June 13, 1865, the state was divided into five sub-districts as follows:

Sub-district of Southwest Mississippi. This sub-district consisted of the counties in the southwestern part of the state and terminated on the north and the east with the counties of Issaquena, Yazoo, Madison, Rankin, Simpson, Lawrence, and Pike. John W. Davidson was assigned command, with headquarters at Vicksburg.

Sub-district of Northwest Mississippi. This sub-district consisted of the counties north of the Sub-district of Southwest Mississippi and terminated on the east with the counties of Marshall, Fayette, Calhoun, Choctaw, and Attala. Morgan L. Smith was assigned command, with headquarters at Grenada.

Sub-district of Northeast Mississippi. This sub-district consisted of the counties east of the Sub-district of Northwest Mississippi and terminated on the south with the counties of Oktibbeha and Lowndes.

Jasper A. Maltby was assigned command, with headquarters at Okolona.

Sub-district of East Mississippi. This sub-district consisted of the counties east and south of the sub-districts described above, and terminated with the counties of Covington, Jones, and Wayne. William L. McMillen was assigned command, with headquarters at Meridian.

Sub-district of Southeast Mississippi. This sub-district consisted of the counties in the southeastern part of the state that were not included in the other sub-districts.

The District of Mississippi was announced as a separate brigade June 16, 1865.

The Department of the Gulf was discontinued June 27, 1865, and the Department of Mississippi was created to consist of the state of Mississippi.

District of Mobile

Mobile, Alabama was occupied by Union forces April 12, 1865, and on April 27 the District of Mobile, Military Division of West Mississippi was created. It was defined to consist of the post of Mobile and the outposts of Spring Hill and Whistler and such other posts on the west shore of Mobile Bay and the Alabama River as might later be attached. James C. Veatch, commander of First Division, Thirteenth Corps, was assigned command of the post and district, in addition to his division. Christopher C. Andrews, commander of Second Division, Thirteenth Corps, relieved Veatch in command of the district about May 19, 1865.

The Military Division of West Mississippi was abolished May 17, 1865, and the Department of the Gulf was reconstituted on the same date to include the states of Alabama, Florida, Louisiana, and Mississippi, and also the District of Key West and Tortugas. On June 3, Edward R. S. Canby assumed command of the department and divided it into four districts, each state constituting a district. By this order, the District of Mobile became a sub-district of the District of Alabama, Department of the Gulf.

June 12, 1865, T. Kilby Smith relieved Andrews in command of the district of Mobile, and Fort Gaines, Fort Morgan, and their dependencies were attached to the district.

The Department of the Gulf was discontinued June 27, 1865, and the Department of Alabama was created to consist of the state of Alabama.

Post and District of Morganza

After Banks' army had returned to Alexandria from its ill-fated Red River Campaign, Thirteenth Corps, Nineteenth Corps, First Brigade, First Division, United States Colored Troops (First Brigade, First Division, Corps d'Afrique until April 19, 1864), and Edmund J. Davis' cavalry command moved to Morganza, Louisiana, where they arrived May 22. Most of these forces remained at Morganza for some time to cover the approaches from the direction of the Red River, and also to provide a suitable place for assembling troops for service west of the Mississippi River. Morganza remained an important post in the Department of the Gulf to the end of the war.

February 9, 1865, the Northern Division of Louisiana was constituted to include the District of Baton Rouge and Port Hudson and the post of Morganza. Thereafter, the United States forces at Morganza were designated as the District of Morganza, Northern Division of Louisiana.

The district was discontinued May 29, 1865, and the troops were transferred to Port Hudson.

The commanders of the post and district were as follows:

William H. Emory	May 22, 1864 to June 16, 1864
Joseph J. Reynolds	June 16, 1864 to July 5, 1864
Michael K. Lawler	July 5, 1864 to November 23, 1864
Daniel Ullmann	November 23, 1864 to February 26, 1865
Henry W. Fuller	February 26, 1865 to February 27, 1865
Edmund J. Davis	February 27, 1865 to March 3, 1865
Thomas J. McKean	March 3, 1865 to April 27, 1865
William H. Dickey	April 27, 1865 to May 29, 1865

Note. George F. McGinnis commanded temporarily, beginning October 30, 1864.

Troops of the Post and District of Morganza. After the close of the Red River Campaign on May 22, 1864, the following troops of Banks' army arrived at Morganza: First Division and Second Division of Nineteenth Corps and First Division, Third Division, and Fourth Division of Thirteenth Corps, both corps commanded by William H. Emory; First Brigade, First Division, United States Colored Troops; the engineer troops of Thirteenth Corps; and Edmund J. Davis' cavalry command. Fourth Division, Thirteenth Corps was sent on to Baton Rouge, but the other troops remained at Morganza for some time. For the organization of these troops, see Thirteenth Corps, Department of the Gulf and Nineteenth Corps, Department of the Gulf.

Thirteenth Corps, Department of the Gulf was discontinued June 11, 1864, and on June 27, Nineteenth Corps was reorganized into a corps of three divisions. For details of the reorganization, see Nineteenth Corps, Department of the Gulf. The new First Division and Second Division of Nineteenth Corps were then sent down the Mississippi to New Orleans, and on July 1–2 they embarked for Virginia.

July 30, 1864, Elias S. Dennis arrived at Morganza from Vicksburg with First Division, Seventeenth Corps, and in August James R. Slack was at Morganza in command of a Provisional Division (consisting of only one brigade) that had arrived from Thibodeaux in the District of La Fourche.

August 18, 1864, Nineteenth Corps was reorganized at Morganza, and Dennis' division was assigned to the corps as Second Division. On August 22, Joshua J. Guppey's Third Brigade, Second Division, Nineteenth Corps was sent to Mobile Bay as a part of the land forces cooperating with David G. Farragut in his operations against the enemy forts at the entrance to the bay. The brigade returned to Morganza in September.

On August 29, 1864, Sterling Price began an advance from Arkansas into Missouri, and reinforcements were sent from Morganza to report to Frederick Steele, commander of the Department of Arkansas. Dennis' Second Division, Nineteenth Corps was ordered to the mouth of the White River on August 31 (departed September 3). A part of

Third Division, Nineteenth Corps was also sent in October.

At the end of October 1864, the only troops remaining at Morganza were William T. Spicely's Second Brigade and Albert H. Brown's Third Brigade of Third Division, Nineteenth Corps, and Daniel Ullmann's First Division, United States Colored Troops, which consisted of Henry N. Frisbie's First Brigade and Alonzo J. Edgerton's Second Brigade.

Third Brigade, Third Division, Nineteenth Corps was sent to the mouth of the White River early in November 1864. George F. McGinnis, who was commanding at Morganza during the absence of Michael K. Lawler, was ordered to join Third Brigade, Third Division on November 6, and to assume command of the troops at the Mouth of White River. In December, only Ullmann's division of United States Colored Troops remained at Morganza. William H. Dickey commanded First Brigade, and Alonzo J. Edgerton commanded Second Brigade.

United States Colored Troops at Morganza. The first colored troops to arrive at Morganza, May 22, 1864, belonged to William H. Dickey's First Brigade, First Division, United States Colored Troops. This brigade had taken part in Banks' Red River, Louisiana Campaign.

In June 1864, a Provisional Brigade, United States Colored Troops, commanded by Theodore H. Barrett, was attached to the district, and Daniel Ullmann was assigned command of all colored troops at Morganza. In August 1864, the designation of Provisional Brigade was changed to Second Brigade, First Division, United States Colored Troops. There was no change in the organization of the colored troops at Morganza until February 1865, and then the designation of First Brigade was changed to Second Brigade, and the designation of Second Brigade was changed to First Brigade.

From March 1865 to May 1865, the United States Colored Troops at Morganza were designated as United States Forces, Post of Morganza.

Cavalry at Morganza. At the end of May 1864, the cavalry at Morganza belonged to Edmund J. Davis' command, which consisted of John M. Crebs' Third Brigade and Edmund J. Davis' Fourth Brigade of the Cavalry Division, Department of the Gulf. In June 1864, it consisted of Crebs' Third Brigade, and four unbrigaded regiments under Davis. Thereafter, no cavalry organization of brigade strength appears on the rosters for Morganza.

Defenses of New Orleans

After the occupation of New Orleans May 1, 1862, Henry W. Birge's Third Brigade, Department of the Gulf (formerly commanded by George F. Shepley) remained in and near the city. Birge was in command of the forces in New Orleans until relieved by Lewis G. Arnold on September 22. While Arnold was in command, the designation of his troops was changed to United States Forces at New Orleans. Thomas W. Cahill relieved Arnold on November 10, and in December the designation of this command was changed to Defenses of New Orleans. It should be noted, however, that the troops of Third Brigade, Department of the Gulf had been referred to as the Defenses of New Orleans as early as September 1862.

On May 4, 1862, soon after the occupation of New Orleans by forces of Benjamin F. Butler's Expedition, John W. Phelps was ordered to Carrollton with his First Brigade, Department of the Gulf. Additional regiments arrived in the department from the East, and when Baton Rouge was evacuated on August 21, Halbert E. Paine's Second Brigade, Department of the Gulf (formerly commanded by Thomas Williams) was transferred to Carrollton. Thomas W. Sherman was assigned command of the United States Forces at Carrollton September 18, and from that date until December his command was known as First Division, Department of the Gulf or as Sherman's Division. In December 1862, Sherman's command was designated as United States Forces at Carrollton. January 9, 1863, Sherman was assigned command of all troops in and near New Orleans and its immediate defenses. The next day his command was merged into the Defenses of New Orleans, and he was assigned command of the defenses.

January 13, 1863, a new division, known as Sherman's Division, was organized from regiments at Carrollton, Chalmette, New Orleans, and Bonnet Carre. The Second Brigade of this division was stationed in New Orleans. On January 14 this division became Second Division, Nineteenth Corps. For a more detailed description of these troops, see below, Troops in the Department of the Gulf.

The principal posts in the Defenses of New Orleans during the spring and summer of 1863 were Bonnet Carre, Brashear (or Brashear City), Donaldsonville, Fort Jackson, Fort Saint Philip, Fort Macomb, Fort Pike, New Orleans, Pass Manchac, Ship Island, and Thibodeaux.

August 11, 1863, the District of La Fourche was added to the Defenses of New Orleans. Donaldsonville was still included in the defenses, and the boundary was extended from that point down the La Fourche to Napoleonville and the canal running from the Bayou La Fourche at that point to Lake Venet, and from Algiers west to the Bayou Des Allemands.

In December 1863, the post of Fort Jackson was established as a separate command, but in February 1864 it was returned to the Defenses of New Orleans.

Posts added after the first of the year were Kennerville, Madisonville, Lakeport, and Englishtown.

The Defenses of New Orleans were reorganized April 29, 1864 by Joseph J. Reynolds to consist of the following: District of Baton Rouge, District of Carrollton, District of La Fourche, District of West Florida, Fort Jackson and Fort Saint Philip, and other posts mentioned above. In an order from Headquarters, Department of the Gulf, dated April 29, 1864, the District of Key West and Tortugas was assigned to the Defenses of New Orleans, but later rosters do not show the district as a part of the Defenses of New Orleans. In June 1864, the District of Bonnet Carre was added to the Defenses of New Orleans, and in August Robert B. Jones' troops at Lakeport on Lake Ponchartrain were also added.

August 20, 1864, Bayou Manchac was announced as the dividing line between the Defenses of New Orleans and the District of Baton Rouge. This order was revoked two days later, and the boundary east of the Mississippi River was announced as a line from Frenier Station on Lake Ponchartrain to the post of Bonnet Carre. Forces at Bonnet Carre reported to Headquarters, Defenses of New Orleans, and the forces at Frenier Station and at points north on the railroad to Jackson reported to Francis J. Herron at Baton Rouge.

On January 9, 1865, the boundaries of the Defenses of New Orleans were defined as follows: Beginning at North Pass Manchac, the line ran west along the southern shore of Lake Maurepas to the Amite River; thence through Bayou Manchac to the Mississippi River; then through Bayou Plaquemine to Grand River and on to Berwick Bay; from there to the Gulf of Mexico, and then east to Ship Island; thence through Mississippi Sound, the Rigolets, and Lake Ponchartrain to North Pass Manchac.

Regularly garrisoned posts in the district were New Orleans, Algiers, Camp Parapet, Carrollton, Greensville, Kennerville (or Kenner), Lakeport, Proctorville, Ship Island, Fort Jackson, Fort Saint Philip, Plaquemine, Fort Pike, Fort Macomb, Fort Livingston, Donaldsonville, Napoleonville, Thibodeaux, Brashear City, Bonnet Carre, and Terre Bonne.

On February 9, 1865, the Defenses of New Orleans was designated as the Southern Division of Louisiana, to date from February 11.

The commanders of the Defenses of New Orleans were as follows:

Thomas W. Cahill	December 16, 1862 to January 10, 1863
Thomas W. Sherman	January 10, 1863 to May 21, 1863
William H. Emory	May 21, 1863 to August 25, 1863
Edward G. Beckwith	August 25, 1863 to January 6, 1864
Joseph J. Reynolds	January 6, 1864 to June 16, 1864
Thomas W. Sherman	June 16, 1864 to February 9, 1865

Troops in the Defenses of New Orleans. January 13, 1863, Sherman's Division, Department of the Gulf was organized as follows: First Brigade from regiments at Carrollton and Chalmette; Second Brigade from regiments at Customs House Barracks in New Orleans; and Third Brigade from regiments at Bonnet Carre and Carrollton. On January 14, the designation of Sherman's Division was changed to Second Division, Nineteenth Corps.

During the winter and early spring of 1863, Second Division, Nineteenth Corps remained at New Orleans during Banks' campaign in the Teche country, but it moved to Port Hudson in late March. Only unbrigaded regiments were left in the Defenses of New Orleans.

August 15, 1863, Third Brigade, First Division (formerly Second Brigade, First Division) was assigned as Reserve Brigade, Defenses of New Orleans.

In September 1863, Henry W. Birge's First Brigade and Thomas W. Cahill's Second Brigade of Fourth Division, Nineteenth Corps and some unbrigaded regiments constituted the troops in the Defenses of New Orleans. Cahill's brigade remained there during October and November.

In January 1864, George F. McGinnis' Third Division, Thirteenth Corps was at Madisonville, Louisiana, north of Lake Ponchartrain. It had been brought to New Orleans for embarkation for Texas, but it was not included in the Rio Grande Expedition and remained in Louisiana.

In February 1864, Cuvier Grover's Second Division, Nineteenth Corps (less Third Brigade) was also at Madisonville, and Joseph J. Reynolds' Third Division, Nineteenth Corps was in the Defenses of New Orleans. First Brigade, Second Division, Nineteenth Corps was in the defenses in March, and Third Division, Nineteenth Corps in April. For troops in the defenses after April 1864, see districts of the Department of the Gulf that were included in the Defenses of New Orleans.

For the purpose of better administration, a Provisional Division was organized by an order from Banks, dated August 25, 1864. It consisted of three brigades as follows: First Brigade, which was in the Defenses of New Orleans and largely in the District of La Fourche; Second Brigade, which was Henry Bertram's Second Brigade and was at Mobile Bay; and Third Brigade, which consisted of scattered regiments. Thomas W. Sherman was assigned command September 12, and the regiments reported through their district commanders to Sherman, the commander of the Defenses of New Orleans.

For a description of the troops in and around New Orleans prior to the organization of the Defenses of New Orleans, see below, Troops in the Department of the Gulf.

Northern Division of Louisiana

The Northern Division of Louisiana was created February 9, 1865, to consist of the District of Baton Rouge and Port Hudson, the post of Morganza, and all territory in the Department of the Gulf north of the Defenses of New Orleans on both banks of the Mississippi River. Francis J. Herron was assigned command (assumed command February 14, 1865), with headquarters at Baton Rouge. Baton Rouge, Port Hudson, and Morganza were designated as districts of the Northern Division of Louisiana. Joseph Bailey was assigned command of the District of Baton Rouge, Cyrus Hamlin of the District of Port Hudson, and Henry W. Fuller of the District of Morganza.

February 28, 1865, the Bayou Plaquemine and the Grand River were established as the boundary between the Northern Division of Louisiana and the Southern Division of Louisiana on the west side of the Mississippi River.

March 7, 1865, the Division of Northern Louisiana was defined as a Division of Troops.

By an order of May 29, 1865 that transferred headquarters of the Northern Division of Louisiana from Baton Rouge to Shreveport (completed June 3), the District of Baton Rouge, the District of Port Hudson, and the post of Clinton, Louisiana were consolidated to form a new district, known as the District of East Louisiana. This district reported directly to Headquarters, Department of the Gulf. The District of Morganza was discontinued May 29, and the troops there were transferred to Port Hudson.

The Department of the Gulf was discontinued June 27, 1865, and the state of Louisiana became a part of the Department of Louisiana and Texas. The Northern Division of Louisiana was merged into the Western District of Louisiana in July.

District of Pensacola

For information about the District of Pensacola, see District of West Florida.

Post and District of Port Hudson

July 9, 1863, the day after the surrender of Port Hudson, George L. Andrews was assigned command of the post of Port Hudson, and he assumed command the next day. On August 6, the District of Baton Rouge and the post of Port Hudson were consolidated to constitute the new District of Baton Rouge and Port Hudson. Port Hudson remained as a post in this district until February 9, 1865, when the Northern Division of Louisiana was formed to include the District of Baton Rouge and Port Hudson and the post of Morganza. Thereafter, the forces at Port Hudson were designated as the District of Port Hudson, Northern Division of Louisiana.

May 29, 1865, the District of Baton Rouge, the District of Port Hudson, and the post of Clinton, Louisiana were consolidated to form the District of East Louisiana.

The United States Forces at Port Hudson consisted primarily of regiments of Corps d'Afrique and later of United States Colored Troops. For additional information, see below, Troops in the Department of the Gulf.

July 24–25, 1863, Francis J. Herron's Division (formerly Army of the Frontier) was transferred from Vicksburg, Mississippi to Port Hudson. It did not remain there long, however, but in August moved on to Carrollton, Louisiana. On August 14 it was designated as Second Division, Thirteenth Corps.

The commanders of the Post and District of Port Hudson were as follows:

George L. Andrews	July 10, 1863 to April 22, 1864
Daniel Ullmann	April 22, 1864 to June 23, 1864
John McNeil	June 23, 1864 to August 6, 1864
George L. Andrews	August 6, 1864 to December 26, 1864
Charles W. Drew	December 26, 1864 to February 20, 1865
Cyrus Hamlin	February 20, 1865 to June 1865

Note. Ullmann commanded the district temporarily in January 1864 during the absence of Andrews.

District of South Alabama

For information about the District of South Alabama, see below, District of West Florida and South Alabama, and see also Land Operations against Mobile Bay and Mobile, Alabama.

Southern Division of Louisiana

On February 11, 1865, the designation of the Defenses of New Orleans was changed to the Southern Division of Louisiana. Thomas W. Sherman, who was in command of the Defenses of New Orleans, was assigned command, with headquarters at New Orleans.

February 28, 1865, the Bayou Plaquemine and Grand River were established as the boundary between the Northern and Southern divisions of Louisiana on the west side of the Mississippi River.

When organized, the Southern Division of Louisiana consisted of the following:

District of Carrollton, Nelson Viall
District of La Fourche, Robert A. Cameron
Forces at Lake Ponchartrain, Henry Street
Forces at Ship Island, Mississippi, Ernest W. Holmstedt

Troops reporting directly to New Orleans were at the following posts: Algiers, Bonnet Carre, Pass Manchac and De Sair, Fort Macomb, Fort Pike, Fort Jackson, Fort Saint Philip, Fort Livingston, Kennerville, New Orleans, and Hermitage Plantation.

March 7, 1865, the Southern Division of Louisiana was defined as a Division of Troops.

March 27, 1865, the country between Bayou Manchac and Kennerville was designated as the District of Bonnet Carre.

The Department of the Gulf was discontinued June 27, 1865, and the state of Louisiana was included in the newly created Department of Louisiana and Texas.

District of the Teche

For information see above, District of La Fourche.

District of West Florida

West Florida was transferred from the Department of the South to the Department of the Gulf

August 8, 1862 as the District of Pensacola (sometimes called the District of West Florida). Lewis G. Arnold was assigned command, with headquarters at Pensacola, Florida. This command was called the District of Pensacola until February 1864, at which time it became the District of West Florida.

In May 1864, the district was included in the Defenses of New Orleans.

September 11, 1864, the commander of the district was directed to report to Headquarters, Department of the Gulf through the United States Forces at Mobile Bay. The next day, however, the District of West Florida and South Alabama was constituted to include the District of West Florida and the United States Forces on Mobile Bay (United States Forces, Dauphin Island, and United States Forces, Mobile Point). The District of West Florida thus became a sub-district of the District of West Florida and South Alabama.

February 10, 1865, the Department of the Gulf was reduced in size to include only the states of Louisiana and Texas, and on March 1, the District of West Florida and South Alabama was transferred from the Department of the Gulf to the Military Division of West Mississippi. Then, on March 17, the District of South Alabama and the District of West Florida were organized as separate districts.

May 17, 1865, the Military Division of West Mississippi was abolished, and on the same day the Department of the Gulf was reconstituted to include the states of Alabama, Florida, Louisiana, and Mississippi. On June 3, Edward R. S. Canby assumed command of the department, and the state of Florida was then organized as the District of Florida, Department of the Gulf.

The principal posts of the district were Fort Barrancas, Camp Barrancas, Fort Pickens, Pensacola, Camp Asboth, and Camp Roberts.

The commanders of the District of Pensacola and the District of West Florida were as follows:

Lewis G. Arnold	August 8, 1862 to September 22, 1862
William Wilson	September 22, 1862 to October 2, 1862
Neal Dow	October 2, 1862 to January 24, 1863
Isaac Dyer	January 24, 1863 to April 21, 1863
William C. Holbrook	April 21, 1863 to May 21, 1863
Isaac Dyer	May 21, 1863 to June 18, 1863
William C. Holbrook	June 18, 1863 to November 9, 1863
Alexander Asboth	November 9, 1863 to October 2, 1864
Joseph Bailey	October 2, 1864 to November 25, 1864
Thomas J. McKean	November 25, 1864 to February 15, 1865
Alexander Asboth	February 15, 1865 to June 3, 1865

Note 1. Neal Dow was assigned command October 2, 1862 but assumed command sometime later.

Note 2. Asboth was wounded September 27, 1864 at Marianna, Florida, and Bailey assumed command sometime thereafter.

Troops in the District of West Florida. Until the spring of 1864, the troops in the District of West Florida consisted only of a few unbrigaded regiments. A First Brigade, District of West Florida was organized in October 1864 from troops of the United States Colored Troops, and William C. Holbrook was assigned command. Later, Ladislas L. Zulavsky assumed command. When the United States Colored Troops were organized into divisions on October 18, the regiments of First Brigade, District of West Florida were included in First Brigade, Third Division, United States Colored Troops. Also in October 1864, a Second Brigade, consisting of two cavalry regiments, was organized in the district under the command of Ephraim W. Woodman.

January 23, 1865, a Third Brigade, District of West Florida was organized by the consolidation of First Brigade and Second Brigade, and Woodman was assigned command.

In preparation for Edward R. S. Canby's movement against Mobile, Alabama in March and April 1865, additional troops were sent to West Florida. January 24–28, 1865, Christopher C. Andrews' Third Brigade, Reserve Corps, Military Division of West Mississippi was transferred from New Orleans to Barrancas, and Charles Black's Fourth Brigade, First Division, Reserve Corps followed on February 17.

On February 18, 1865, Thirteenth Corps was reorganized from the Reserve Corps, and the two brigades in the District of West Florida and Henry Bertram's brigade at Mobile Point were constituted as Second Division, Thirteenth Corps under the command of Andrews. The division was organized as follows:

Second Division, Christopher C. Andrews
    First Brigade, Henry Bertram
    Second Brigade, William T. Spicely
    Third Brigade, Charles Black

Note. First Brigade was at Mobile Point, Alabama.

First Division, United States Colored Troops was organized under John P. Hawkins in New Orleans February 23, 1865 and was assigned to a command to be organized in the District of West Florida by Frederick Steele. Embarkation began for Florida that same day.

On February 26, 1865, Steele was assigned command of troops that were to operate from Pensacola in a campaign against Mobile, Alabama, and he was ordered to Barrancas to complete the organization and preparation of this column. When organized, Steele's command consisted of Hawkins' First Division, United States Colored Troops; Second Brigade and Third Brigade, Second Division, Thirteenth Corps under Andrews; and a Separate Cavalry Brigade (organized February 8 under Thomas J. Lucas). On March 29, Lucas' command was organized as a cavalry division.

Steele's column left Pensacola March 20, 1865, and moved out of the District of West Florida. For additional information, see Land Operations against Mobile Bay and Mobile, Alabama.

District of West Florida and South Alabama

This district was constituted September 12, 1864 to include the District of West Florida and the United States Forces on Mobile Bay (United States Forces on Dauphin Island and United States Forces on Mobile Point). Gordon Granger was assigned command, with headquarters at Fort Gaines.

In December 1864, the United States Forces on Dauphin Island and on Mobile Point were designated as the District of South Alabama, and Henry Bertram was assigned command. It appears that the

district was officially constituted by an order of February 9, 1865, and Elias S. Dennis was assigned command.

On February 21, 1865, the District of South Alabama was suspended, and the District of West Florida and South Alabama again consisted of the District of West Florida, the United States Forces on Dauphin Island, and the United States Forces on Mobile Point.

March 1, 1865, the District of West Florida and South Alabama was transferred from the Department of the Gulf to the Military Division of West Mississippi.

March 17, 1865, the District of West Florida and the District of South Alabama were separated. Alexander Asboth continued in command of the District of West Florida, and T. Kilby Smith was assigned command of the District of South Alabama (assumed command March 19). Smith was relieved from command on May 27.

May 27, 1865, the Military Division of West Mississippi was abolished, and on that same date the Department of the Gulf was reconstituted to include the states of Alabama, Florida, Louisiana, and Mississippi. On June 3, Edward R. S. Canby assumed command of the Department of the Gulf and divided it into four districts, each state constituting a district. Thus, the state of Florida became the District of Florida, and the state of Alabama became the District of Alabama.

For additional information, see Land Operations against Mobile Bay and Mobile, Alabama.

TROOPS IN THE DEPARTMENT OF THE GULF

On November 15, 1861, Federal authorities in Washington approved a plan submitted by David D. Porter of the navy for a joint army-navy operation to capture New Orleans and open the Mississippi River. Captain David G. Farragut was selected to lead the entire expedition, and George B. McClellan, then general in chief of the army, assigned Benjamin F. Butler to lead the land forces.

In September 1861, Butler had gone to New England to raise, organize. and equip a force for an expedition along the eastern coast, but with the decision to move on New Orleans, the destination of Butler's command was changed to the Gulf of Mexico. On November 23, the first of Butler's troops embarked for Ship Island, off the Gulf Coast of Mississippi, where his force was to assemble. For additional information about Butler's command, see Department of New England, in Volume I. Farragut assembled his fleet in the Gulf of Mexico and then proceeded to Ship Island, where he arrived February 20, 1862. He then assumed command as flag officer of the West Gulf Blockading Squadron. On March 20, Butler formally assumed command of the Department of the Gulf at Ship Island. For additional information, see following sections.

Ship Island, Mississippi Expedition, November-December 1861. The first of the New England regiments (26th Massachusetts, 9th Connecticut, and 4th Battery, Massachusetts Light Artillery), under the command of Edward F. Jones of the 26th Massachusetts, sailed from Portland, Maine and Boston, Massachusetts in late November 1861 for Ship Island in the Gulf of Mexico. On November 27, 1861, the expedition stopped briefly at Fort Monroe, Virginia, where John W. Phelps joined and assumed command, relieving Jones. The voyage was then resumed, and the expedition arrived and occupied Ship Island December 3, 1861.

Butler's Gulf Expedition (New Orleans). The Department of the Gulf was created by an order of February 23, 1862, and Butler was assigned command. On the same date, Butler was assigned command of the land forces that were to cooperate with the navy in an operation against New Orleans. His force consisted of thirteen New England regiments, and the 21st Indiana, 6th Michigan, and 4th Wisconsin, which were taken from the Defenses of Baltimore.

The primary objective of this expedition was the capture of New Orleans, but in addition Butler was instructed to reduce the enemy posts at Baton Rouge, Berwick Bay, and Fort Livingston (on Grand Terre Island, Barataria Bay). He was further directed to open communications by way of the Mississippi River with the United States Forces at Vicksburg, Mississippi. A feint toward Galveston, Texas was also suggested.

Phelps remained in command at Ship Island until

March 20, 1862, when Butler arrived and assumed command of the Department of the Gulf. A short time later he organized his force (four regiments had not yet arrived) for the expedition against New Orleans. This force was called Butler's Expeditionary Corps, and it consisted of three brigades as follows:

Butler's Expeditionary Corps, Benjamin F. Butler
    First Brigade, John W. Phelps
    Second Brigade, Thomas Williams
    Third Brigade, George F. Shepley

Note 1. Williams was assigned command of Second Brigade February 20, 1862.
Note 2. The three western regiments formed a part of Williams' brigade.

The brigades of Phelps and Williams embarked at Ship Island April 10, 1862 for the mouth of the Mississippi River. Shepley remained on the island with his brigade until April 30, and was then ordered to join Butler.

Phelps' and Williams' brigades were present with David G. Farragut's fleet at the passage of Fort Jackson and Fort Saint Philip, but they were not engaged. When the forts surrendered, however, they were occupied by troops of Phelps' brigade.

New Orleans was surrendered to Farragut April 25, 1862, and was occupied by Butler's forces May 1. Shepley was assigned as military governor of Louisiana. Shepley's Third Brigade remained near New Orleans, and on May 4, Phelps' First Brigade was sent to Camp Parapet near Carrollton.

Williams' Second Brigade accompanied Farragut up the Mississippi River to Vicksburg, but after a short stay returned to Baton Rouge May 29, 1862. After being reinforced with three regiments from New Orleans, Williams returned to Vicksburg with Farragut's fleet for the purpose of cutting a canal across the bend of the Mississippi at Burey's Point, opposite the town. Failing in this, Williams returned to Baton Rouge on July 26.

On August 5, 1862, Union troops under Williams' command repulsed a strong enemy attack at the Battle of Baton Rouge (see below, Operations in the Department of the Gulf, Battle of Baton Rouge, Louisiana). Williams was killed during the battle, and was succeeded in command at Baton Rouge by Halbert E. Paine. The town was evacuated on August 21, and the troops there were transferred to Carrollton.

The forces at Camp Parapet and Carrollton under Phelps were organized August 22, 1862 and placed in position as follows: A Left Wing under Thomas W. Cahill was on a line from the bank of the Mississippi River to the New Orleans, Jackson, and Great Northern Railroad; a Right Wing under Nathan A. M. Dudley was at Camp Parapet (Metairie Ridge); and a reserve under Halbert E. Paine was at Carrollton. The reserve was formed from the troops that had just arrived from Baton Rouge.

Thomas W. Sherman relieved Phelps in command of the forces near Carrollton September 18, 1862, and his command was designated as First Division, Department of the Gulf (or simply Sherman's Division). This division consisted of Halbert E. Paine's First Brigade and Nathan A. M. Dudley's Second Brigade. The Second Brigade dated from October 1862. This organization was retained until December 1862.

A Reserve Brigade, Department of the Gulf was organized at Carrollton September 27, 1862, and Godfrey Weitzel was assigned command. Weitzel moved his brigade to the western bank of the Mississippi River in late October, and occupied the newly constituted District of La Fourche, Department of the Gulf.

In September 1862, the Third Brigade of Butler's force, then commanded by Henry W. Birge, became United States Forces at New Orleans and Algiers.

Back on August 8, 1862, West Florida had been transferred from the Department of the South to the Department of the Gulf. Lewis G. Arnold was in command of the troops in West Florida, which were stationed at Pensacola, Fort Barrancas, Fort Pickens, and on Santa Rosa Island.

Banks' Expedition to the Department of the Gulf (or Banks' Southern Expedition), November-December 1862. On October 28, 1862, Nathaniel P. Banks established headquarters in New York City for the purpose of organizing an expedition to the Department of the Gulf. The objectives of this expedition were to open the Mississippi River and to gain control of Mobile Bay. On November 8, 1862, Banks was assigned command of the Department of the Gulf, with orders to assume command when he arrived with his expedition in Louisiana.

The troops for Banks' expedition were assembled in New York and at Fort Monroe. Michael Corcoran's Brigade (Irish Legion) was ordered from New York to Fort Monroe October 31, 1862 to join the expedition, but after arriving there it remained in Virginia and did not accompany Banks to the Gulf.

In late September 1862, William H. Emory was in command of eight regiments, in the Middle Department, Eighth Corps, that were designated as Troops Guarding Baltimore, Maryland (or Emory's Brigade, Defenses of Baltimore). With five of these regiments, Emory proceeded to Fort Monroe in November 1862, and upon arrival there he assumed command of the troops assigned to Banks' expedition.

Emory's command, called Emory's Division, sailed for the Gulf early in December 1862 and by mid-December had arrived at Ship Island. The troops that were assembled in New York sailed December 2–4. Banks, in person, departed December 4. When Banks arrived in New Orleans, he took command of the Department of the Gulf on December 15 and relieved Butler, but he did not issue the formal order until December 17.

Immediately upon assuming command of the department, Banks ordered Cuvier Grover to take all serviceable troops then at New Orleans to Baton Rouge, under protection of the fleet, and place them in camp. The advance of Grover's command, which consisted of twelve regiments of infantry, three batteries, and two troops of cavalry, left New Orleans on the morning of December 16, 1862 and arrived at Baton Rouge the next day. Christopher C. Augur, who had supervised the embarkation of the troops, then went upriver and assumed command.

When Banks assumed command of the Department of the Gulf, not all of his troops from New York had arrived, and the last did not come in until February 11, 1863. The troops in the department were then stationed as follows: on the lower Mississippi River at Fort Jackson, Fort Saint Philip, and English Bend; upriver at New Orleans, Bonnet Carre, Donaldsonville, Plaquemine, and Baton Rouge; at Fort Pike and Fort Macomb on the passages from the Gulf of Mexico to Lake Ponchartrain; and at Berwick Bay, Key West, Pensacola, and Ship Island.

Organization of Nineteenth Corps, Late December 1862–Early January 1863. In late December 1862 and early January 1863, Banks reorganized the troops of the Gulf so as to form a field force for operations in the department, and also to provide troops for the occupation of the country. The main body of troops was organized into four divisions of three brigades each, and the garrison troops of the defenses and the permanent detachments for guard and provost duties were kept separate. At that time, the former brigade and division organizations of the department were discontinued.

The four divisions were organized as follows:

Grover's Division, Cuvier Grover
    First Brigade, William Dwight
    Second Brigade, Thomas W. Cahill
    Third Brigade, Oliver P. Gooding

Note. This division was organized December 30, 1862 from troops at Baton Rouge.

Emory's Division, William H. Emory
    First Brigade, George L. Andrews
    Second Brigade, Halbert E. Paine
    Third Brigade, Henry W. Birge

Note. This division was organized January 3, 1863 and was under orders to concentrate at Baton Rouge.

Augur's Division, Christopher C. Augur
    First Brigade, Edward P. Chapin
    Second Brigade, Godfrey Weitzel
    Third Brigade, Nathan A. M. Dudley

Note 1. This division was organized January 12, 1863.
Note 2. First Brigade was originally assigned to Michael Corcoran, but Corcoran's brigade was detained in Virginia and did not join Banks in the Department of the Gulf.
Note 3. Weitzel's Reserve Brigade, serving in the District of La Fourche, was nominally assigned to Augur's division as Second Brigade.
Note 4. Third Brigade of this division was at Baton Rouge.

Sherman's Division, Thomas W. Sherman
    First Brigade, Neal Dow
    Second Brigade, Alpha B. Farr
    Third Brigade, Frank S. Nickerson

Note 1. This division was organized January 13, 1863.
Note 2. Third Brigade of this division was in and near New Orleans.

George L. Andrews, who had been left in New York to bring up the rear of Banks' Expedition, was made Banks' chief of staff March 6, 1863.

Nineteenth Corps was organized under an order dated January 5, 1863 to consist of all troops in the Department of the Gulf. The order was made retroactive to December 14, 1862.

On January 14, 1863, the divisions of Nineteenth Corps were numbered as follows:

Augur's Division became First Division, Nineteenth Corps
Sherman's Division became Second Division, Nineteenth Corps
Emory's Division became Third Division, Nineteenth Corps
Grover's Division became Fourth Division, Nineteenth Corps

For a detailed description of the various reorganizations and the operations of Nineteenth Corps, see Nineteenth Corps, Department of the Gulf.

Early in July 1864, First Division and Second Division of Nineteenth Corps embarked at New Orleans for Virginia as Detachment Nineteenth Corps. These troops were under the command of William H. Emory, and they did not return to the Department of the Gulf. The remaining troops of Nineteenth Corps were reorganized and remained in the department until November 7, 1864, when Nineteenth Corps was discontinued as a corps in the Department of the Gulf. For details of the organization of the corps during this period, see Nineteenth Corps, Department of the Gulf.

November 25, 1864, the Reserve Corps, Military Division of West Mississippi was created to consist of troops formerly belonging to Nineteenth Corps that were within the limits of the Military Division of West Mississippi. The Reserve Corps was discontinued February 15, 1865, when it was merged into the newly reorganized Thirteenth Corps. For additional information, see Reserve Corps, Military Division of West Mississippi.

Thirteenth Corps, Department of the Gulf. In July and August 1863, Banks' forces were seriously depleted by the departure of twenty-one nine-month regiments for home and muster out, and troops were needed to replace them. A further need for more troops arose in July when Henry W. Halleck proposed that Banks organize an expedition for the purpose of establishing United States forces in Texas. Supplying the needed troops was difficult until the Mississippi River was finally opened by the capture of Port Hudson in July. Then Ulysses S. Grant sent troops down the river from Vicksburg to report to Banks. The first to leave belonged to Francis J. Herron's Division (formerly Army of the Frontier), which moved to Port Hudson July 24–25. Herron remained there only a short time, however, and then moved on to Carrollton during the early part of August. On August 14, Herron's Division was assigned to Thirteenth Corps as Second Division.

On August 7, 1863, Edward O. C. Ord's Thirteenth Corps, Department of the Tennessee was assigned to the Department of the Gulf, and on that same date Ord, who was ill, was relieved by Cadwallader C. Washburn. Then, during the period August 10–26, the corps was transferred from Vicksburg and Natchez to Carrollton.

September 3, 1863, Washburn's First Division, Thirteenth Corps was ordered to Brashear City and the Atchafalaya River to drive out enemy forces reported to be in the vicinity. Having accomplished this mission, Herron moved to Morganza on September 20. September 26, Napoleon J. T. Dana assumed command of Second Division when Herron departed on leave. During the latter part of September, George F. McGinnis' Third Division moved to Brashear City, and on October 3, Stephen G. Burbridge's Fourth Division followed McGinnis from Carrollton.

Beginning on October 3, 1863, a Union force commanded by William B. Franklin left Berwick Bay and New Iberia on an expedition up the Teche River. This force consisted of two divisions of Nineteenth Corps, and a detachment of Thirteenth Corps under Washburn, consisting of First Division, Third Division, and Fourth Division. Franklin's command reached Opelousas at the end of the month and then returned to New Iberia November 1–17. For additional information, see below, Operations in the Department of the Gulf, Operations in the Teche Country.

At the beginning of the operations on the Teche, Dana's Second Division, Thirteenth Corps remained at Morganza to watch the Atchafalaya, but it was then ordered to New Orleans to embark for the mouth of the Rio Grande River in Texas. It left October 26, 1863. Washburn's First Division moved to New Orleans, and during the period November 21–December 10, it embarked at Algiers for Matagorda Island, Texas. During November, Third Division and Fourth Division remained under Franklin at New Iberia. Then, in December, Fourth Division marched to Brashear City and from there by rail to Algiers, where it embarked for Decros' (Decrow's) Point, Texas. The transfer was completed by January 2, 1864. Third Division moved to Algiers, and on January 15 was assigned to duty in the Defenses of New Orleans. It remained there until it joined Banks' Red River, Louisiana Campaign in March.

Fourth Division was relieved from duty in Texas February 10, 1864, and was transferred from Texas to Berwick Bay February 24–28 to take part in Banks' Red River Campaign. First Division and Second Division remained in Texas during the Red River Campaign, except Michael K. Lawler's Second Brigade, First Division, which was transferred to Alexandria April 18–26. The rest of First Division arrived near Fort De Russey, on the Red River, in May.

After Banks returned to Alexandria from his unsuccessful attempt to reach Shreveport, Third Division and Fourth Division of Thirteenth Corps marched to Morganza, where they arrived May 22, 1864. Fourth Division moved to Baton Rouge two days later, and Thirteenth Corps was discontinued June 11.

For additional information about Thirteenth Corps during its stay in the Department of the Gulf, see Thirteenth Corps, Army of the Tennessee and Thirteenth Corps, Department of the Gulf. Also see below, Operations in the Department of the Gulf, Rio Grande Expedition and Operations on the Coast of Texas.

In preparation for Edward R. S. Canby's operations against Mobile, Alabama in the spring of 1865, Thirteenth Corps was reorganized from the Reserve Corps, Military Division of West Mississippi February 18, 1865. For additional information, see Thirteenth Corps, Military Division of West Mississippi, and also see Land Operations against Mobile Bay and Mobile, Alabama.

Detachment Army of the Tennessee (Banks' Red River, Louisiana Campaign). On March 10, 1864, a detachment of the Army of the Tennessee under Andrew J. Smith embarked at Vicksburg to join Banks in an expedition up the Red River toward Shreveport, Louisiana. Smith's detachment consisted of First Division and Third Division of Sixteenth Corps, both under the command of Joseph A. Mower, and a Provisional Division, Seventeenth Corps, commanded by T. Kilby Smith. The detachment accompanied Banks during the Red River Campaign, but then left the department for Vicksburg May 21–22, when it reembarked near the mouth of Red River. For additional information, see Red River, Louisiana Campaign.

Detachment Army of the Tennessee, and Sixteenth Corps. To provide reinforcements for Canby's operations against Mobile, Alabama in the spring of 1865, Andrew J. Smith's Detachment Army of the Tennessee (formerly Right Wing, Sixteenth Corps) was ordered from the Department of the Cumberland to New Orleans. Smith's command had taken part in the Battle of Nashville December 15–16, 1864, and in late January 1865, it was at Eastport in northern Mississippi. It departed for New Orleans February 5–8, and upon arriving there on February 18, it was reorganized as Sixteenth Corps, Military Division of West Mississippi. Sixteenth Corps embarked for the Mobile area March 6–19, and there it took part in the operations that resulted in the capture of the city. For details, see Sixteenth Corps, Army of the Tennessee; and also see Land Operations against Mobile Bay and Mobile, Alabama.

United States Colored Troops (USCT) in the Department of the Gulf. An organization known as Native Guards (free colored) was established April 23, 1861, when free colored people of New Orleans were legally enrolled as a part of the militia of the state of Louisiana. Its officers were commissioned by Governor Thomas O. Moore, who also commanded the State Militia. The ancestors of many of these people had fought with Andrew Jackson at the Battle of New Orleans in 1815, and they had organized, although not wholeheartedly, under the Confederate governor of the state. When Federal troops

under Benjamin F. Butler occupied New Orleans, the Native Guards immediately offered their services to Butler.

As early as July 3, 1862, John W. Phelps, commanding at Carrollton, Louisiana, proposed that three regiments of colored troops be raised in the Department of the Gulf, but then, as a matter of principle, he resigned when Butler used blacks as laborers on the fortifications instead of as soldiers. Butler changed his mind, however, and soon thereafter began the organization of colored regiments. He believed that the Native Guards and all other free colored people were loyal to the United States, and he decided to enlist them in the volunteer forces of the United States and issued a proclamation to that effect. The first regiment of Louisiana Volunteers, designated as the 1st Native Guards Infantry, was organized August 22, 1862, and the 2nd regiment, 3rd regiment, and 4th regiment of Native Guards were organized as soon as their enrollment could be completed. The 1st Regiment of Engineers was organized early the next year.

By General Order No. 40, Headquarters, Department of the Gulf, issued May 1, 1863, Banks proposed the organization of a corps of colored troops to be designated as Corps d'Afrique. The organization of the regiments of the Corps d'Afrique at Port Hudson was announced by General Order No. 47 June 6, 1863. By this order, the 1st, 2nd, 3rd, and 4th regiments of infantry, Louisiana Native Guards became 1st, 2nd, 3rd, and 4th regiments of infantry, Corps d'Afrique. The 5th Regiment, then organizing in the District of Pensacola, was designated 5th Regiment of Infantry, Corps d'Afrique.

In February 1863, Daniel Ullmann was ordered to organize a brigade of five regiments of colored troops to serve with Nineteenth Corps in the Department of the Gulf. The officers for these regiments were mustered in at New York City in February and March, but the regiments were not fully organized at Port Hudson until August and September of that year.

During the early part of the organization of this brigade, the regiments were designated as 1st, 2nd, 3rd, and 4th regiments of Ullmann's Brigade. By the above-mentioned order of June 6, 1863, however, the regiments listed in that order were designated as 6th, 7th, 8th, 9th, and 10th regiments,

Corps d'Afrique. Ullmann's Brigade was carried on the roster for May 1863, but it was not fully organized at that time. On July 10, 1863, Ullmann was assigned command of the brigade, but John F. Appleton was in command at the end of July, and Samuel B. Jones at the end of August.

George L. Andrews assumed command of the Corps d'Afrique, as well as of the post of Port Hudson, July 9, 1863. By August 15, there were nineteen regiments of infantry and two regiments of engineers composed of colored troops.

An engineer brigade was organized in August 1863 that consisted of the 1st, 2nd, and 3rd regiments of the Corps d'Afrique, and David C. Houston was assigned command. Houston remained in command of the brigade until August 1864, and then Peter C. Hains assumed command. The brigade was discontinued in October 1864. During Banks' Red River Campaign, George D. Robinson commanded an Engineer Brigade that was composed of troops of the Corps d'Afrique.

An order of September 16, 1863 directed that the first twenty regiments of infantry of the Corps d'Afrique be organized into two divisions of two brigades each, and the following organization was announced on September 22:

CORPS D'AFRIQUE, George L. Andrews

First Division, Daniel Ullmann
    First Brigade, Chauncey J. Bassett
    Second Brigade, Cyrus Hamlin

Second Division
    First Brigade, Charles W. Drew
    Second Brigade, Samuel B. Jones

Note 1. The commander of Second Division is not of record.
Note 2. Second Brigade was broken up in December 1863.

On April 19, 1864, all regiments of colored troops in the Department of the Gulf were designated as regiments of United States Colored Troops, or simply as USCT. More specifically, they were known as United States Colored Infantry, United States Colored Cavalry, United States Colored Heavy Artillery, and United States Colored Light Artillery. With this change in designation, the 1st Regiment, Corps d'Afrique became 73rd United States Colored Infantry (73rd USCT), the 2nd Regiment, Corps d'Afrique became 74th United States Colored Troops, and so on until the 26th Regiment, Corps d'Afrique, and the last of the infantry regiments, became 94th Regiment of United States Colored Troops. Also by the order of April 19, 1864, the colored engineer regiments were designated as infantry. Thus, for example, the 1st Regiment of Engineers, Corps d'Afrique became 95th United States Colored Infantry.

The United States Colored Troops of the Department of the Gulf were reorganized October 18, 1864 as follows:

UNITED STATES COLORED TROOPS, DEPARTMENT OF THE GULF, George L. Andrews

First Division, Daniel Ullmann
    First Brigade, Henry N. Frisbie
    Second Brigade, Alonzo J. Edgerton

Note. First Division was at Morganza in October 1864.

Second Division, Charles W. Drew
    First Brigade, Senior Colonel
    Second Brigade, Samuel B. Jones

Third Division, Cyrus Hamlin
    First Brigade, John C. Cobb
    Second Brigade, Simon Jones
    Third Brigade, Charles A. Hartwell

The above makes it appear that the organization of United States Colored Troops was a compact one, but actually the brigades and divisions were rather widely scattered in the Department of the Gulf. In November 1864, the headquarters of the various units were reported as follows: Headquarters, United States Colored Troops, Department of the Gulf was at Port Hudson; of First Division at Morganza; of Second Division at Port Hudson; of Third Division at New Orleans; of First Brigade, Third Division at Mobile Point, Alabama; of Second Brigade, Third Division at Berwick City; and of Third Brigade, Third Division at Fort Saint Philip.

In preparation for Canby's operations against Mobile in early 1865, the United States Colored Troops under John P. Hawkins at Vicksburg, in the Department of Mississippi, were sent downriver to

New Orleans February 8. There, on February 23, these troops were organized into a division of colored infantry under Hawkins. This division, which reported directly to Headquarters, Military Division of West Mississippi, was organized as follows:

First Division, USCT, Military Division of West Missis-
  sippi, John P. Hawkins
  First Brigade, William A. Pile
  Second Brigade, Hiram Scofield
  Third Brigade, Charles W. Drew

Note. Pile and Drew were assigned to their commands February 25, 1865.

Hawkins' division was assigned to Frederick Steele's Column, which was forming at Pensacola, Florida, and Hawkins' troops began embarking at Algiers, Louisiana February 23, 1865.

In addition to the above, there was a Provisional Brigade of United States Colored Troops in the District of Morganza, and also First Brigade, District of West Florida that was composed of regiments of United States Colored Troops. The latter was commanded by William C. Holbrook and later by Ladislas L. Zulavsky.

Cavalry Forces in the Department of the Gulf. The units of the cavalry forces in the Department of the Gulf during the first year of its existence consisted generally only of companies, battalions, and detachments that were assigned to various posts in the department.

On April 17, 1863, Benjamin H. Grierson left La Grange, Mississippi with First Brigade, Cavalry Division, Sixteenth Corps, Department of the Tennessee, and moved southward on a raid through Mississippi and Louisiana. He arrived at Baton Rouge May 2, and there came under the orders of Nathaniel P. Banks, commander of the Department of the Gulf. For details, see Grierson's Raid, April 17, 1863–May 2, 1863. Because of a shortage of cavalry in the Department of the Gulf, Banks retained Grierson and his command for service in the department until after the surrender of Port Hudson July 8. In May 1863 Grierson was assigned command of First Cavalry Brigade, Department of the Gulf, which consisted of Grierson's 6th and 7th Illinois cavalry regiments, the 2nd Massachusetts Cavalry, and detachments of other regiments, some of mounted infantry from the Department of the Gulf.

Grierson's brigade was with Banks' army during the siege of Port Hudson, but on July 18, 1863 Grierson was ordered, with his Illinois regiments, to Vicksburg in the Department of the Tennessee.

August 14, 1863, a Separate Cavalry Brigade, Thirteenth Corps was organized at Vicksburg, and John J. Mudd was assigned command. On the same day Mudd was ordered to take his brigade to Carrollton, Louisiana.

September 15, 1863, the mounted forces of the Department of the Gulf were organized into a Cavalry Division, and Albert L. Lee, chief of cavalry of the department, was assigned command. That same day, Mudd's brigade was assigned to Cavalry Division, Department of the Gulf as Second Brigade, with Mudd remaining in command. Lee's division was organized as follows:

Cavalry Division, Department of the Gulf, Albert L. Lee
  First Brigade, Edmund J. Davis
  Second Brigade, John J. Mudd

On November 7, 1863, the cavalry division was reorganized to consist of three brigades as follows:

Cavalry Division, Department of the Gulf, Albert L. Lee
  First Brigade, Thomas J. Lucas
  Second Brigade, John G. Fonda
  Third Brigade, Charles J. Paine

Note. In addition to the above cavalry organization, there were four unbrigaded regiments and some companies of cavalry in the field.

A Fourth Brigade of the Cavalry Division was organized in December 1863 at New Orleans, and Nathan A. M. Dudley was assigned command.

In December 1863, division headquarters of the cavalry was at New Orleans, but the brigades were somewhat scattered. First Brigade and Third Brigade, both under Thomas J. Lucas, were near New Iberia, Louisiana, and Second Brigade was at Donaldsonville, but the latter moved to Port Hudson in January 1864. The unassigned cavalry troops were largely at New Orleans.

In December 1863, the cavalry with Thirteenth Corps in Texas was organized into a cavalry brigade under Edmund J. Davis. For additional information, see below, Operations in the Department of the

Gulf, Rio Grande Expedition and Operations on the Coast of Texas.

In February 1864, Lucas commanded a Provisional Division of five cavalry brigades. James H. Redfield's First Brigade and Harai Robinson's Third Brigade were at Franklin, Louisiana; John G. Fonda's Second Brigade was at Port Hudson; Nathan A. M. Dudley's Fourth Brigade and Oliver P. Gooding's Fifth Brigade were at New Orleans. Division headquarters was also at New Orleans.

The Cavalry Division accompanied Banks' army on the Red River, Louisiana Campaign and was engaged at Mansfield (or Sabine Cross Roads) and at Pleasant Hill April 8–9, 1864. The division was organized as follows:

Cavalry Division, Department of the Gulf, Albert L. Lee, to April 18, 1864
    Richard Arnold
    First Brigade, Thomas J. Lucas
    Third Brigade, Harai Robinson, to April 8, 1864, wounded
        John M. Crebs
    Fourth Brigade, Nathan A. M. Dudley
        Edmund J. Davis
    Fifth Brigade, Oliver P. Gooding

Note. John G. Fonda's Second Brigade was at Port Hudson.

In May 1864, after the Red River Campaign, Crebs' Third Brigade and Davis' Fourth Brigade were at Morganza, both under the command of Davis; Lucas' First Brigade and Gooding's Fifth Brigade were at Donaldsonville, both under the command of Lucas; and Fonda's Second Brigade was at Port Hudson.

June 25, 1864, John P. Sherburne, chief of cavalry, Department of the Gulf relieved Arnold in command of the cavalry division, and at the end of the month the division was organized as follows:

Cavalry Division, John P. Sherburne
    First Brigade, Charles Everett
    Second Brigade, John G. Fonda
    Third Brigade, John M. Crebs
    Fourth Brigade, Morgan H. Chrysler

Note. Fifth Brigade was discontinued in June 1864.

First Brigade was at Greenville, Louisiana, Second Brigade was at Port Hudson, and Third Brigade

and Fourth Brigade were at Morganza. In addition to the above, unbrigaded cavalry troops were at Greenville, under William J. Landram, and Morganza, under Edmund J. Davis, and regiments and companies were distributed at the posts of Baton Rouge, Camp Parapet, Hermitage Landing, Napoleonville, New Orleans, Carrollton, Kennerville, and Thibodeaux in Louisiana, and at Barrancas, Florida and Brownsville, Texas.

When Thirteenth Corps was discontinued June 11, 1864, the Cavalry Brigade, Thirteenth Corps in Texas became Cavalry Brigade, United States Forces in Texas, and was under the command of Edward J. Noyes.

June 30, 1864, Nathan A. M. Dudley was assigned command of First Brigade, Cavalry Forces, Department of the Gulf in the field, and was ordered to Baton Rouge to organize the brigade.

August 22, 1864, Sherburne, chief of cavalry, reported the following organization of the cavalry of the department: Albert L. Lee was again in command of the Cavalry Division (assigned August 18), and John G. Fonda's First Brigade and William J. Landram's Second Brigade were designated as Cavalry Division, Department of the Gulf. These two brigades were at Baton Rouge. Third Brigade was at Morganza with Nineteenth Corps. On August 22, Third Brigade was assigned to Nineteenth Corps, and was dropped from the brigade organization of the Cavalry Forces, Department of the Gulf. Two days later, it became Separate Cavalry Brigade, Nineteenth Corps at Morganza, and was commanded by John M. Crebs. Fourth Brigade was in the District of La Fourche, and Fifth Brigade was at Barrancas, Florida. It should be noted, however, that in the roster for August 1864, the regiments assigned to Fourth Brigade in the order of August 22 were in the District of La Fourche, but were not designated as Fourth Brigade. The regiments assigned to Fifth Brigade were at Barrancas, and were carried on the roster as Fourth Brigade, Cavalry Forces of the Department of the Gulf.

September 23, 1864, the cavalry division was reorganized to consist of three brigades by the formation of a new Third Brigade. The organization was then as follows:

Cavalry Division, Albert L. Lee
    First Brigade, Oliver P. Gooding

Second Brigade, John G. Fonda
Third Brigade, Hasbrouck Davis

After September 1864, there were numerous changes in the organization of the cavalry in the Department of the Gulf. These are given as follows:

In October 1864, a cavalry brigade, designated as Second Brigade, District of West Florida, was organized and assigned to Ephraim W. Woodman. This brigade was discontinued January 23, 1865, when it was merged with First Brigade to form a new Third Brigade under Woodman.

October 27, 1864, Benjamin S. Roberts assumed his duties as chief of cavalry, Department of the Gulf.

In November 1864, Lee's Cavalry Division was still at Baton Rouge, with the same brigade commanders, except that Abraham Bassford commanded First Brigade.

November 20, 1864, John W. Davidson was assigned command of the Cavalry Forces of the Military Division of West Mississippi, and on November 23 he also assumed personal command of the Cavalry Division when Lee became ill. The following organizational changes were then announced:

1. Lee's Cavalry Division was designated as First Division, and John P. Sherburne was assigned command of First Brigade;
2. Second Separate Cavalry Brigade was organized at Morganza, and was assigned to Abraham Bassford;
3. John M. Crebs' Separate Brigade and Abraham Bassford's Second Separate Brigade, both at Morganza, were organized as Second Cavalry Division, which was assigned to Edmund J. Davis.

Second Separate Brigade was discontinued December 17, 1864, and the regiments of the separate brigades were organized as Separate Cavalry Brigade, Reserve Corps, Military Division of West Mississippi under the command of Edmund J. Davis. The cavalry forces of the Reserve Corps were transferred to the Department of the Gulf January 3, 1865.

Joseph Bailey was assigned command of the Cavalry Division December 17, 1864 and assumed command December 28.

December 29, 1864, the chiefs of cavalry at head-quarters of the departments of the Military Division of West Mississippi were relieved for other duty.

A Separate Brigade, District of West Florida was organized February 8, 1865, under the command of Thomas J. Lucas. On March 29, the designation of this brigade was changed to First Brigade, Lucas' Cavalry Division, United States Forces Operating from Pensacola (or Frederick Steele's Column from Pensacola). For additional information, see Mobile Bay and Mobile, Alabama, Land Operations against.

A Cavalry Brigade, District of Baton Rouge was organized February 15, 1865, and it remained in the district until July. It was commanded by Edmund J. Davis to February 27, Webster P. Moore to March 18, and John G. Fonda to May 30.

The Cavalry Division, Department of the Gulf was discontinued February 9, 1865.

The commanders of the Cavalry Division, Department of the Gulf were as follows:

Albert L. Lee	September 14, 1863 to April 18, 1864
Richard Arnold	April 18, 1864 to June 25, 1864
John P. Sherburne	June 25, 1864 to August 18, 1864
Albert L. Lee	August 18,1864 to October 27, 1864
Oliver P. Gooding	October 27, 1864 to November 11, 1864
John W. Davidson	November 11, 1864 to December 28, 1864
Joseph Bailey	December 28, 1864 to February 9, 1865

United States Forces in Texas. On June 11, 1864, Thirteenth Corps was discontinued, and Herron's troops at Brownsville and Brazos Santiago were designated as United States Forces in Texas. Herron's command consisted of the following:

First Brigade, William McE. Dye
Second Brigade, John McNulta
Colored Brigade, Justin Hodge
Cavalry Brigade, Edward J. Noyes
Artillery, Martin Welfley
   Battery B, 1st Missouri Light Artillery, Martin Welfley
   Provisional Battery

Note. First Brigade and Second Brigade were carried

on the original returns as Second Division, Thirteenth Corps.

Henry Bertram was assigned command of a brigade, designated as Second Brigade, which was composed of regiments from the former Second Division, Thirteenth Corps, and early in August 1864, it was transferred by way of New Orleans to Dauphin Island, Mobile Bay. There it joined Gordon Granger's command that was besieging Fort Gaines and Fort Morgan at the entrance to Mobile Bay. See Land Operations against Mobile Bay and Mobile, Alabama.

After August 1864, United States forces in Texas were reported as only of brigade strength (but apparently not as an organized brigade) at Brazos Santiago, and they remained essentially unchanged to the end of the war. Commanders of the post were Henry M. Day, William A. Pile, Robert B. Jones, and Theodore H. Barrett.

OPERATIONS IN THE DEPARTMENT OF THE GULF

Troops of the Department of the Gulf were engaged in a number of operations during the war, and most of these were undertaken primarily for the purpose of establishing United States forces in Texas. There were also two attempts to eliminate the Confederate fortifications on the Mississippi River at Port Hudson, and the second of these was successful. Finally, late in the war, there was an expedition against Mobile and Mobile Bay that resulted in the occupation of the city. The first serious engagement in the department, however, which was related to none of the above, was the successful defense of Baton Rouge against an attack by a Confederate force commanded by John C. Breckinridge. These operations are described in the following sections.

Battle of Baton Rouge, Louisiana, August 5, 1862. In May 1862, after the capture of New Orleans, David G. Farragut moved up the Mississippi River with a combined naval and land force to attempt the capture of Vicksburg, Mississippi. An attempt to dig a canal across the peninsula opposite

Vicksburg and a prolonged bombardment of the enemy positions failed to force the surrender of the town, and on July 26, Farragut abandoned his efforts and started down the river toward New Orleans.

After his departure, Earl Van Dorn, commander of the Confederate District of Vicksburg, ordered John C. Breckinridge to lead an expedition against Baton Rouge, then held by Union forces. The capture of that important city would open up the Red River to the Confederates and enable them to obtain much-needed supplies from western Louisiana and Texas by that route.

Breckinridge left Vicksburg July 27, 1862 with about 4,000 men, and moved by rail to Camp Moore, near Tangipahoa, Louisiana, where he arrived the next day. There he joined Daniel Ruggles, who was already at Camp Moore with a small force. Breckinridge then organized his command into two divisions as follows: a First Division under Charles Clark, which consisted of Thomas H. Hunt's Second Brigade and Thomas B. Smith's Fourth Brigade, and a Second Division commanded by Daniel Ruggles, which consisted of Albert P. Thompson's First Brigade and Henry Watkins Allen's Second Brigade.

Breckinridge then waited for the ram *Arkansas,* which was on its way downriver from Vicksburg to cooperate with the land force in the attack on Baton Rouge. When Breckinridge learned that the ram was on its way, he advanced with his force to Greenwell Springs on the Comite River in preparation for his attack.

At that time, the United States forces at Baton Rouge consisted of Thomas Williams' Second Brigade, Department of the Gulf, which, on the day of the battle, was organized as follows:

Second Brigade, Department of the Gulf, Thomas Williams
   9th Connecticut, Thomas W. Cahill
   21st Indiana, John A. Keith
   14th Maine, Frank S. Nickerson
   30th Massachusetts, Nathan A. M. Dudley
   6th Michigan, Charles E. Clarke
   7th Vermont, George T. Roberts
   4th Wisconsin, Sidney A. Bean
   2nd Battery, Massachusetts Light Artillery (Nims' Battery), George G. Trull

4th Battery, Massachusetts Light Artillery, Charles H. Manning

6th Battery, Massachusetts Light Artillery (Everett's Battery), William W. Carruth

Note. In addition to the above artillery, James H. Brown commanded a section of artillery that the 21st Indiana had captured from the enemy and which had been attached to that regiment with an improvised crew.

Williams expected the enemy attack and believed that it would be made against his left flank under the cover of the *Arkansas,* which he knew was approaching the city. He further believed that the attack would be made across the open fields of the Dougherty plantation in an attempt to gain possession of the arsenal grounds. With this in mind, Williams had placed his troops in position as follows:

On the far left, and to the north of the city, two pieces of Manning's battery were in position on the elevated right bank of the Bayou Grosse, and across the bayou, to the east and south of Manning's guns, was the 4th Wisconsin near the penitentiary grounds.

The 9th Connecticut was on the right of 4th Wisconsin, with the remaining four guns of Manning's battery between the 4th Wisconsin and the 9th Connecticut, in the Government Cemetery.

The 14th Maine was to the west of the Bayou Sara road and to the north of the Greenwell Springs road, and not far from the intersection of the two roads.

The 21st Indiana was in rear of Magnolia Cemetery, and four pieces of Everett's battery were on the left of the 21st Indiana and on the right of the Greenwell Springs road. The 21st Indiana supported these guns when the battle began. The camps of both the 14th Maine and the 21st Indiana were located in front of their lines of battle.

The camp of the 6th Michigan was on the extreme right near the junction of the Perkins road and the Clay Cut road, and to the west of the Catholic Church and the Race Course. The regiment was posted across the country road on the right of Magnolia Cemetery and from there on to the right across the Clay Cut road. The left of the 6th Michigan supported two guns of Everett's Battery, which were posted on the country road just south of Magnolia Cemetery.

The 7th Vermont was in rear of 21st Indiana and 6th Michigan, on the right of the Catholic Cemetery, to strengthen their position.

The 30th Massachusetts was in reserve on the right, and was posted about a half-mile east of the State House, where it supported Nims' battery.

Federal gunboats on the river supported the right of Williams' line.

When the battle began, Williams assigned Nathan A. M. Dudley, colonel of the 30th Massachusetts, to command the Right Wing of the brigade. Dudley's command consisted of 6th Michigan, 7th Vermont, 30th Massachusetts (then commanded by Horace O. Whittemore), and also the batteries of Nims, Manning, and Everett, and Brown's artillery. When Williams was killed during the battle, Cahill assumed command of Second Brigade, and Nickerson assumed command of the Left Wing of the brigade. Nickerson then had under his control the 9th Connecticut, 21st Indiana, 14th Maine, and 4th Wisconsin.

When Breckinridge approached Baton Rouge on the Greenwell Springs road, he deployed Clark's division on the Confederate right of the road, with Hunt's brigade on the left, next to the road, and Smith's brigade on the right of Hunt; he placed Ruggles' division on the left of the road, with Thompson's brigade on the right, next to the road, and Allen's brigade on the left of Thompson.

At 4:00 A.M. August 5, 1862, Clark's division advanced, in a dense fog, between the Greenwell Springs road and the Clinton road toward the line of the 14th Maine. At the same time, Thompson's brigade of Ruggles' division advanced on the left side of the road through Magnolia Cemetery. It came under a heavy fire from the 21st Indiana and Nims' battery but pushed on and soon was seriously engaged in a lively struggle with the Indiana troops. Keith was wounded and was succeeded in command of the regiment by James Grimsley. During the fighting along the Greenwell Springs road, a portion of Clark's division retreated, and Thompson's brigade also fell back a short distance. The 21st Indiana followed but was soon stopped.

Under the pressure of Clark's attack, the 14th Maine moved to the left and formed on the opposite side of the road, and the 21st Indiana then fell back and took position with the 14th Maine. Both regiments were formed in rear of the camp of the 21st Indiana and soon were engaged in some of the heaviest fighting of the day. Hunt's brigade pushed the 14th Maine back from its second position, through the camp of the 7th Vermont, and into a ravine on the south side of the penitentiary grounds. Hunt was wounded in this attack and was succeeded in command by John A. Buckner. There was then a pause in the fighting, and 14th Maine started back toward its second position. Clark was wounded in this attack, and his men then retired to the shelter of a ravine. There they rallied and drove the 14th Maine back toward the camp of 7th Vermont.

Thompson's brigade finally drove the 21st Indiana from its camp back to the line of 7th Vermont. During the fighting in this area, the Federal troops were forced to retire about one-fourth mile to a line near the penitentiary, and for a time the enemy occupied the camps of the 14th Maine, 21st Indiana, and 7th Vermont.

When Williams was certain of the direction of Breckinridge's main attack, he ordered up the 9th Connecticut, the 4th Wisconsin, and a section of Manning's battery to support the left of the 21st Indiana, and he also ordered the 30th Massachusetts and two sections of Nims' battery to support the right of the regiment. The 30th Massachusetts took position in front of the camp of the 7th Vermont, directly in rear of the camp of 21st Indiana, which was then occupied by the enemy. Nims' battery was posted on the right of 30th Massachusetts, and 7th Vermont on the left.

There was heavy fighting around the camp of the 7th Vermont, and for almost an hour the 21st Indiana, the 7th Vermont, and a part of the 9th Connecticut held up the Confederate advance. Williams was killed during that time, and Thomas W. Cahill assumed command of Second Brigade.

On the Confederate left, Allen's brigade of Ruggles' division advanced steadily for a time but was halted by a battery that was supported by some infantry. Allen resumed the advance, however, and soon arrived in front of Nims' battery, which was supported by the 6th Michigan. The Michigan regiment, as already noted, was on the extreme right of Williams' line between Magnolia Cemetery and the Race Course. Allen attacked at once, but his line was met with a devastating fire from both infantry and artillery and was driven back in disorder with heavy losses. Allen was wounded during the attack, and his troops could not be rallied for any further effort.

It was then 10:00 A.M., and the battle was over. Breckinridge waited for some time, expecting the arrival of the *Arkansas,* but at 4:00 P.M. he learned that the ram had been destroyed by its own crew about four miles above Baton Rouge when its engines failed. Then, knowing that he would receive no further support, Breckinridge began to withdraw his troops about dark.

Although Breckinridge was unable to take Baton Rouge, he did accomplish the primary objective of his expedition, which was to gain possession of a point on the Mississippi below the mouth of Red River. Instead of returning to Camp Moore, he marched north about thirty miles miles from Baton Rouge to Port Hudson and there began the construction of heavy batteries. He left Ruggles with a force to garrison these works and marched with the rest of his command to join Van Dorn at Jackson, Mississippi.

Texas Expeditions

As early as 1861, there were strong political and economic pressures for the occupation of Texas by United States forces. There was a shortage of cotton in New England, and Texas was seen as a source for this important commodity. There was also an interest in settling on the vacant lands in the state among immigrants from the North. Federal occupation would cut Confederate trade with Mexico, and also with Europe by way of Mexico. Militarily, however, the importance of opening the Mississippi River forced the postponement of any expedition to Texas until after this could be accomplished.

When Banks took his expedition to the Gulf of Mexico in 1862, he was specifically ordered to assist in clearing the Mississippi before undertaking any other operations. To appease some former Texans, however, he ordered a small token force to go by sea to Galveston and occupy the city. This operation ended in failure when the naval force in the harbor was defeated and the land forces were forced to surrender.

The Mississippi River was finally opened in July 1863, by the surrender of Vicksburg and Port Hudson, and then the administration seriously considered the problem of sending United States troops to Texas. On August 6, Henry W. Halleck directed Banks to prepare an expedition for that purpose, and on September 8, William B. Franklin attempted to land, with the help of the navy, a force consisting of troops from Nineteenth Corps at Sabine Pass, Texas. From there he intended to move overland by way of Beaumont to Houston. This expedition failed when, after a short naval engagement, Franklin did not attempt to land his troops, and the expedition returned to New Orleans September 12.

After the failure at Sabine Pass, Banks organized another attempt to reach northern Texas by way of the Bayou Teche. Franklin, with an expedition composed of troops of Thirteenth Corps and Nineteenth Corps, left Fort Bisland and Berwick Bay October 3, 1863 and moved up the Teche. The column reached Opelousas, Louisiana October 21, but Banks decided to proceed no farther, and the expedition returned to New Iberia November 1–7.

The second effort to land troops on the Gulf Coast of Texas was made by troops of Thirteenth Corps under the personal command of Banks. The expedition left New Orleans October 26, 1863 and landed near the mouth of the Rio Grande River early in November. This force was known as the Rio Grande Expedition. Banks' troops occupied Brownsville and Point Isabel, Texas, near the mouth of the Rio Grande, and then established garrisons at the posts of Fort Esperanza, Pass Cavallo, Indianola, and Decros' (Decrow's) Point near Corpus Christi. Banks' troops, however, were unable to move into the interior of the state. While the expedition was not altogether a failure, its principal purpose was not accomplished.

As early as 1862, Halleck had recommended the Red River as the preferred jumping-off place for an advance on Texas, but nevertheless he had accepted the earlier plans. Then, after Banks' Expedition was stalled on the coast of Texas, Halleck insisted on an advance up the Red River as a base of operations for a movement on Texas. On January 23, 1864, Banks finally accepted the Red River route. He was prompted to do this for several reasons: because of political considerations, because Halleck was insistent, and also because there were large quantities of cotton owned by the Confederate government in the Red River country. Banks' Expedition got under way in March 1864, and by the end of May it had ended in complete failure.

For details of the above-mentioned expeditions, see the following sections.

Attempt to Occupy Galveston, Texas, December 21, 1862–January 1, 1863. The harbor at Galveston, Texas had been occupied October 5, 1862 by a Union fleet commanded by William B. Renshaw, and the vessels were still there when Banks' Expedition arrived at New Orleans in December. Andrew J. Hamilton, a former Texan who had been appointed military governor of Texas November 14, and other Texas refugees had accompanied the expedition. To appease their anger upon learning that Louisiana and not Texas was the destination of the expedition, and also to aid in the recruiting of Texas refugees, Banks ordered that a token force be sent to Galveston, which was reported to be threatened by an enemy force. Selected for this purpose was Isaac S. Burrell's 42nd Massachusetts Regiment.

Burrell sailed from New Orleans with companies D, G, and I of the regiment and arrived at Galveston on the evening of December 24, 1862. He had intended to land at Pelican Spit, where there were United States barracks, but acting upon the advice of the naval officers, Burrell's troops occupied Kuhn's Wharf, where they were under the protection of the gunboats. Patrols were sent through the city during the day, but at night they withdrew to the wharf for greater security. A barricade was constructed across the head of the wharf, and some of the planking was taken up.

John B. Magruder, commanding the Confederate District of Texas, New Mexico, and Arizona, had for some time been aware of the defenseless condition of the coast, and had prepared an expedition to advance on Galveston. His command consisted of the brigades of William R. Scurry and Henry Hopkins Sibley, a regiment of heavy artillery, a light battery, and also two armed steamboats. During the night of December 30, 1862, Magruder's troops entered the town, and between 2:00 and 3:00 A.M. January 1, 1863, they opened with artillery fire. The Federal gunboats quickly returned the fire. After the artillery had been firing for about an hour, the enemy attacked the wharf in two infantry columns, but they were repulsed and at daylight withdrew. Then the enemy gunboats appeared and engaged the Union fleet. After losing two ships, the rest of the Union fleet steamed out of the harbor. Without further help from the navy, Burrell was forced to surrender. The transports returned to New Orleans, and the gunboats remained to blockade the harbor.

Sabine Pass, Texas Expedition, September 4–11, 1863. In August 1863 Banks began the organization of another Texas expedition under the command of William B. Franklin. Franklin was to proceed by sea to Sabine Pass, Texas, where he was to land and advance into Texas by way of Beaumont to Houston and Galveston. Franklin's command consisted of George M. Love's First Brigade and Robert B. Merritt's Third (or Reserve) Brigade of Godfrey Weitzel's First Division, Nineteenth Corps, and William H. Emory's Third Division, Nineteenth Corps. William P. Benton's First Division and Francis J. Herron's Second Division of Thirteenth Corps were to assemble at Berwick Bay and were to follow after the troops of Nineteenth Corps had landed.

Weitzel sailed from New Orleans September 4, 1863, accompanied by a naval escort, and Franklin followed close behind. The expedition entered the Sabine River early on the morning of September 8. About one-half mile below Sabine City, the channel was divided into two parts by an oyster reef, and there the enemy had constructed an earthwork mounting six guns. This work was called Fort Griffin and was commanded by Richard W. Dowling. Upon reaching that point, the gunboats steamed up both the eastern (or Louisiana) channel and the western (or Texas) channel, and they soon came under fire from Fort Griffin and another fort farther upriver near Sabine City. Three gunboats were soon disabled, and, without attempting to land the infantry, Franklin started back toward New Orleans. The expedition landed at Algiers September 11.

Operations in the Teche Country, Louisiana, October 3, 1863–November 30, 1863. After the return of Franklin's expedition from Sabine Pass, Banks, mindful of his instructions from Halleck, began to prepare for another expedition into Texas. This time he proposed to make an overland movement up the Bayou Teche as far as Vermillionville (present-day Lafayette) and from there march across the plains of western Louisiana by way of Niblett's Bluff into Texas. During the latter part of September 1863, Banks moved Godfrey Weitzel's First Division and William H. Emory's Third Division of Nineteenth Corps from their camps at Algiers to Brashear City, and from there to Fort Bisland on the lower Teche. On September 17, Emory went north on sick leave, and James W. McMillan assumed temporary command of Third Division. Then, on October 6, after turning over the command of Fourth Division, Nineteenth Corps to Edward G. Beckwith, Cuvier Grover assumed command of Third Division.

Around the first of September 1863, Edward O. C. Ord's Thirteenth Corps was in camp at Carrollton, Louisiana. A few days later, however, Francis J. Herron's Second Division was sent to Morganza to prevent Confederate troops from operating on the upper Atchafalaya, and Cadwallader C. Washburn's First Division was sent to Brashear City. During September George F. McGinnis' Third Division moved to Berwick. Stephen G. Burbridge's Fourth Division remained at Carrollton but later joined Ord in time for the advance up the Teche. At the end of the month the two divisions of Nineteenth Corps were near Fort Bisland, in readiness to march, and they were supported by the divisions of Thirteenth Corps. Albert L. Lee's Cavalry Division covered the front toward New Iberia.

October 3, 1863, Franklin, who was in command of Nineteenth Corps, began his advance from Fort Bisland toward Opelousas. At the same time Ord, reinforced by Burbridge's division, set out from Berwick and followed Ord at an interval of a day's march. Nineteenth Corps arrived near New Iberia October 5 and reached Vermillion Bayou October 8. That day Banks and his staff joined the army from New Orleans. He then decided that the march across western Louisiana was impracticable because of a lack of water and subsistence along the route. Banks remained with the army until October 11, at which time it was near Carrion Crow (Carencro) Bayou, and then returned to New Orleans to begin preparations for an expedition to the coast of Texas. When

Banks departed, he left Franklin in command of all the forces in western Louisiana.

On October 20, 1863, Ord became ill, and Washburn replaced him in command of the three divisions of Thirteenth Corps. Michael K. Lawler assumed command of Washburn's First Division, Thirteenth Corps.

Franklin began to encounter more resistance as he advanced, but he reached Opelousas October 21, 1863. He remained there until October 27, and then began to withdraw toward New Iberia. Lawler's division marched first, and it was followed on November 1 by the divisions of McGinnis, Grover, and Weitzel, and John G. Fonda's First Brigade, Cavalry Division. Burbridge, followed by John J. Mudd's Second Brigade, Cavalry Division, took the Teche road by Grand Coteau.

During the night of November 2, 1863, Richard Owen's First Brigade of Burbridge's division was encamped about three miles south of Carrion Crow Bayou, near Grand Coteau. Early the next morning, Burbridge's outposts were driven in, alerting his troops to a possible attack, but a short time later the enemy withdrew. Then, about 12:30 P.M., Fonda, who was out in front with his 118th Illinois Mounted Infantry, reported that a heavy force of the enemy was approaching, and Burbridge immediately formed the brigade for the impending attack. He ordered the 67th Indiana, one section of Ormand F. Nims' 2nd Battery, Massachusetts Light Artillery, and one section of Charles S. Rice's 17th Battery, Ohio Light Artillery to take position on the left. He also posted a detachment of cavalry on the left of this force to guard against an attack on the left and rear of the line. He formed the 60th Indiana, the 96th Ohio, the 23rd Wisconsin, and four pieces of the 17th Ohio Battery to meet the Confederate infantry that was approaching from the direction of Opelousas. Finally, he placed Fonda's mounted infantry to protect his right.

A short time later, the enemy launched a vigorous attack, overwhelming and capturing the greater part of Theodore E. Buehler's 67th Indiana and one gun of Rice's battery and scattering many of the men of the other regiments. Burbridge was forced to fall back, but then the 83rd Indiana, which had been guarding a foraging train, and Robert A. Cameron, temporarily commanding McGinnis' Third Division, came up, and after some further firing, the enemy withdrew. The fighting, which began about 12:30 P.M., ended at about 3:00 P.M., and Burbridge fell back to Carrion Crow Bayou. The march was then resumed, and by November 17, 1863, Franklin's army was at New Iberia.

The organization of the troops under Franklin's immediate command during the operations on the Teche, October 30, 1863, was as follows:

THIRTEENTH CORPS (DETACHMENT), Cadwallader C. Washburn

First Division, Michael K. Lawler
    First Brigade, Henry D. Washburn
    Second Brigade, Charles L. Harris
    Third Brigade, Lionel A. Sheldon
    Artillery
        Battery A, 2nd Illinois Light Artillery, Herman Borris
        1st Battery, Indiana Light Artillery, Lawrence Jacoby (at Carrollton)
        Battery G, 1st Michigan Light Artillery, George L. Stillman (at Carrollton)
        1st Battery, Wisconsin Light Artillery, Daniel Webster

Note 1. Cadwallader C. Washburn assumed command of Thirteenth Corps October 20, 1863, when Ord became ill. At about the same time, William B. Franklin assumed command of the combined forces of Thirteenth Corps and Nineteenth Corps. On October 26, 1863, Napoleon J. T. Dana assumed command of Thirteenth Corps, but Washburn remained in command of Detachment Thirteenth Corps.

Note 2. Henry D. Washburn succeeded David Shunk in command of First Brigade October 12, 1863.

Note 3. Third Brigade was formed by the consolidation of Third Brigade and Fourth Brigade September 23, 1863. Michael K. Lawler assumed command of the new Third Brigade, but Lionel A. Sheldon assumed command of the brigade October 19, when Lawler assumed command of the division.

Third Division, George F. McGinnis
    First Brigade, Robert A. Cameron
    Second Brigade, James R. Slack
    Battery A, 1st Missouri Light Artillery, Charles M. Callahan

Note 1. McGinnis assumed command of Third Division September 13, 1863.

Note 2. Cameron was assigned command of First Brigade October 8, 1863.

Note 3. Three other batteries reported as belonging to the division were not with the division on the Teche.

Fourth Division, Stephen G. Burbridge
  First Brigade, Richard Owen
  Second Brigade, William J. Landram
  Artillery
    Chicago Mercantile Battery, Illinois Light Artillery, Patrick H. White
    17th Battery, Ohio Light Artillery, Charles S. Rice

Note. Burbridge was assigned command of Fourth Division September 18, 1863, when Michael K. Lawler was transferred to First Division.

NINETEENTH CORPS, William B. Franklin

First Division, Godfrey Weitzel
  First Brigade, George M. Love
  Third Brigade, Robert B. Merritt
  Artillery
    1st Battery, Maine Light Artillery, Albert W. Bradbury
    6th Battery, Massachusetts Light Artillery, Edward K. Russell

Note. Oliver P. Gooding's Second Brigade was at Baton Rouge.

Third Division, Cuvier Grover
  First Brigade, Lewis Benedict
  Second Brigade, James W. McMillan
  Artillery
    4th Battery, Massachusetts Light Artillery, George G. Trull
    Battery F, 1st United States Artillery, Hardman P. Norris

Note. September 17, 1863, McMillan relieved William H. Emory, who departed on sick leave, in command of Third Division. McMillan was succeeded by Grover on October 6.

Artillery Reserve, Henry W. Closson
  25th Battery, New York Light Artillery, John A. Grow
  Battery L, 1st United States Artillery, Henry W. Closson

Cavalry Division, Albert L. Lee
  First Brigade, John G. Fonda
  Second Brigade, John J. Mudd
  87th Illinois Mounted Infantry, John M. Crebs
  16th Indiana Mounted Infantry, Thomas J. Lucas
  2nd Louisiana Mounted Infantry, Charles J. Paine
  2nd Battery, Massachusetts Light Artillery, Ormand F. Nims

Note. The cavalry division was organized September 14, 1863, and Lee was assigned command.

Rio Grande Expedition and Operations on the Coast of Texas, November-December 1863. While Franklin's operations on the Bayou Teche were in progress, Banks became convinced that an overland march across the barren and waterless plains of western Louisiana was impossible, and he then decided on an attempt to occupy the country at the mouth of the Rio Grande River, a plan that he had proposed as early as September 12, 1863. He proceeded to organize an expedition, which sailed from New Orleans under his personal command on October 26. It consisted of Napoleon J. T. Dana's Second Division, Thirteenth Corps, which had been brought down from Morganza and to which were added the 13th Maine and 15th Maine, the 1st Texas Cavalry, and the 1st and 16th regiments of the Corps d'Afrique. On the day of sailing, Dana was assigned command of Thirteenth Corps. Second Division, Thirteenth Corps was organized as follows:

Second Division, Thirteenth Corps, Napoleon J. T. Dana
  First Brigade, William Vandever
  Second Brigade, William McE. Dye

Note. 13th Maine and 15th Maine were attached to Second Division.

After long delays and bad weather, the expedition landed at Brazos Santiago November 3–5, 1863, and November 6 occupied Brownsville and Point Isabel on the mainland. Having thus gained a foothold on the coast of Texas, Banks then attempted to occupy successively all the passes or inlets that gave access from the Gulf of Mexico to the sounds that ran along the coast from the Rio Grande to the Sabine River.

On November 14, 1863, Thomas E. G. Ransom was placed in command of a force consisting of five regiments of Second Division, and two days later he sailed from Brazos Santiago Island. He landed on Mustang Island, near Corpus Christi, and then captured the enemy works that commanded Aransas Pass.

Cadwallader C. Washburn arrived at Aransas Pass with his First Division, Thirteenth Corps November 21, 1863, and the next day was ordered to assume command of an expedition against Fort Esperanza, Pass Cavallo. Washburn's command was organized as follows:

Washburn's Command, Cadwallader C. Washburn
    First Brigade, First Division, Thirteenth Corps, Henry
      D. Washburn
    Ransom's Brigade, Thomas E. G. Ransom

*Note. Ransom's five regiments were organized as
Third Brigade, Second Division, Thirteenth Corps December 3, 1863.*

Washburn's command crossed Aransas Pass and
began the siege of Fort Esperanza at the entrance of
Matagorda Bay November 27–29, 1863. The fort
was evacuated November 30 and was occupied by
Washburn's troops the same day.

Meantime, Second Division, Thirteenth Corps,
except Ransom's detachment and a regiment at
Aransas, continued to occupy Brownsville.

At the end of November 1863, the divisions of
Thirteenth Corps were located as follows:
Washburn's First Division was at Matagorda Is-
land; Dana's Second Division was at Brownsville;
and George F. McGinnis' Third Division and Ste-
phen G. Burbridge's Fourth Division were at New
Iberia, Louisiana, under Franklin. During Decem-
ber 1863, Fourth Division, then commanded by
William J. Landram, moved from New Iberia to
Algiers, where it embarked for Decros' (Decrow's)
Point, Texas. The first troops arrived in mid-De-
cember, and the transfer had been completed by
January 2, 1864.

Third Division, Thirteenth Corps was at Algiers
in December 1863 and was then assigned to duty in
the Defenses of New Orleans January 15, 1864.
Only two regiments were transferred to Texas. The
first arrived at Pass Cavallo in December 1863, and
the second during the following month. Both were
recalled to New Orleans February 20–23, 1864.

The organization of the troops of Thirteenth
Corps in Texas at the end of December 1863 was as
follows:

WASHBURN'S COMMAND, Cadwallader C. Wash-
    burn (headquarters at Decros' Point)

First Division, Thirteenth Corps, William P. Benton
    (headquarters at Matagorda Island)
    First Brigade, Fitz Henry Warren (at Indianola)
    Second Brigade, Charles L. Harris (at Decros' Point)
    Third Brigade, James Keigwin (at Decros' Point)
    Battery G, 1st Michigan Light Artillery, George L.
      Stillman

*Note 1. Warren was assigned to duty with Thirteenth
Corps November 14, 1863, and Benton assumed command of First Division, relieving Washburn, December
15.*
*Note 2. Keigwin assumed command of Third Brigade
in December 1863.*

Second Division, Thirteenth Corps
    Third Brigade, Thomas E. G. Ransom

Fourth Division, Thirteenth Corps, William J. Landram
    First Brigade, John Cowan
    Second Brigade, Memoir V. Hotchkiss
    Artillery
        Chicago Mercantile Battery, Illinois Light Artil-
          lery, Patrick H. White
        17th Battery, Ohio Light Artillery, Charles S. Rice

*Note 1. Landram relieved Stephen G. Burbridge, who
had departed on leave December 9, 1863.*
*Note 2. On December 31, 1863, troops of Fourth
Division were reported both as en route and as at
Decros' Point.*
*Note 3. David P. Grier was ordered north on recruit-
ing service, and December 5, 1863 Hotchkiss was as-
signed command of Second Brigade.*

Company L, 1st Indiana Heavy Artillery, Isaac C. Hen-
    dricks
Independent Company (Kentucky) Pioneer Corps, Wil-
    liam F. Patterson
19th Infantry, Corps d'Afrique, Charles E. Bostwick
23rd Iowa Infantry, Samuel L. Glasgow

FORCES AT BROWNSVILLE AND POINT ISABEL,
    Napoleon J. T. Dana

Second Division, Thirteenth Corps, Napoleon J. T. Dana
    First Brigade, John Charles Black
    Second Brigade, William McE. Dye
    Artillery
        Battery B, 1st Missouri Light Artillery, Martin
          Welfley
        Battery E, 1st Missouri Light Artillery, Joseph B.
          Atwater
        Battery F, 1st Missouri Light Artillery, Joseph
          Foust

*Note 1. Dana assumed command of Second Division
September 28, 1863.*
*Note 2. Ransom's Third Brigade was with
Washburn's command on Matagorda Island.*
*Note 3. William Vandever was relieved from com-
mand of First Brigade, at his own request, November 11,
1863 and was ordered to the Department of the Tennes-
see.*

Cavalry, Edmund J. Davis
　1st Texas Cavalry
　2nd Texas Cavalry, Clemente Zapata

Detachments at Brownsville, E. Manville Hamilton
Troops at Point Isabel (Corps d'Afrique), Justin Hodge

December 24, 1863, Francis J. Herron was ordered to Brownsville to report to Dana and to take command of the Rio Grande Frontier of Texas, and January 3, 1864, Dana was ordered to Fort Esperanza, Pass Cavallo to assume command of the United States troops on the coast of Texas. On January 4, Ransom was assigned command of Fourth Division, Thirteenth Corps at Decros' Point.

Banks was unable to advance inland from the coast because of the strong fortifications at the mouth of the Brazos and at Galveston. Banks believed that these could be taken from the land side, but he did not believe that his force was strong enough to accomplish this. Halleck was unwilling to send reinforcements to Texas, but he again suggested that Banks attempt to reach northern Texas by way of the Red River. Banks agreed and began preparations for still another Texas expedition.

To provide the necessary troops for this movement, Banks began to withdraw Third Division and Fourth Division of Thirteenth Corps from Texas to Louisiana. He left as garrisons in Texas First Division and attached troops at Pass Cavallo under Dana, and Second Division and attached troops at Brownsville and Brazos Santiago under Herron.

During the period April 18–26, 1864, Michael K. Lawler's Second Brigade, First Division, Thirteenth Corps was transferred to Alexandria, Louisiana, and on April 17, Fitz Henry Warren was directed to take the remainder of First Division, Thirteenth Corps to the Red River. This transfer was carried out in May.

After January 1864, Second Division, Thirteenth Corps was designated as United States Forces on the Rio Grande, Department of the Gulf, under the command of Herron. The troops on the Gulf Coast of Texas were first designated as United States Forces Pass Cavallo, Texas, under Dana, and then as United States Forces Matagorda Peninsula, Department of the Gulf, still under Dana. The designation of Second Division, Thirteenth Corps was continued in use, however, until Thirteenth Corps was discontinued June 11, 1864.

On May 1, 1864, Herron assumed command of all United States forces on the Rio Grande Frontier of Texas and on the coast of Texas. On May 5, on Herron's orders, William McE. Dye assumed command of the troops on the Rio Grande.

On June 11, 1864, Thirteenth Corps was discontinued, and Herron's troops at Brownsville and Brazos Santiago were designated as United States Forces in Texas. For additional information, see above, Troops in the Department of the Gulf.

Red River, Louisiana Campaign, March 10, 1864–May 22, 1864. The final effort to establish United States troops in Texas was made by way of the Red River in the spring of 1864. In this undertaking, Banks was to move up the Teche River with 17,000 men of Thirteenth Corps and Nineteenth Corps to Alexandria, where he was to be joined by Andrew J. Smith with 10,000 men of Sixteenth Corps and Seventeenth Corps from the Army of the Tennessee at Vicksburg. Banks was then to assume command of the combined forces and advance up the Red River toward Shreveport.

At the same time, Frederick Steele, commanding the Department of Arkansas, was to move south from Little Rock with 15,000 men of his Seventh Corps and join Banks at Alexandria, Natchitoches, or Shreveport as circumstances might dictate. Steele was unable to advance farther than Camden, Arkansas, however, and he then turned back without having made any significant contribution to the outcome of Banks' campaign.

Smith's Detachment Army of the Tennessee arrived at Alexandria March 15, 1864, and Banks' command of the Department of the Gulf joined him there March 20–25. Banks then left Cuvier Grover's Second Division, Nineteenth Corps at Alexandria and with the rest of his combined force, accompanied by Rear Admiral David D. Porter's gunboats on the river, departed from Alexandria March 26–28 and marched up the Red River toward Shreveport. At Sabine Cross Roads, on April 8, Banks was attacked and defeated by a Confederate force under Richard Taylor and that night withdrew to Pleasant Hill. Taylor followed and attacked again the next day but was repulsed.

Despite his success at Pleasant Hill, Banks was in a difficult position. He had learned that he could expect no help from Steele, and there was also a further complication. According to Grant's orders, Smith's Detachment Army of the Tennessee was to return to Vicksburg no later than April 15, 1864. Therefore, Banks was compelled to abandon his attempt to capture Shreveport, and he began his return march to Alexandria. He arrived there April 25, and on May 13 resumed his retreat toward the Mississippi River. On May 21–22, Smith embarked his command for Vicksburg, and by May 26 Banks had reached Donaldsonville. For details of this campaign, see Red River, Louisiana Campaign.

Operations against Port Hudson, Louisiana

When Banks arrived in Louisiana in mid-December 1862, his primary instructions were to cooperate with the forces under Ulysses S. Grant at Vicksburg in opening the Mississippi River. Banks' part in this undertaking would later become the elimination of the Confederate batteries blocking the river at Port Hudson. Banks, however, did not have sufficient troops, after garrisoning all the posts in the department, to make a direct attack on Port Hudson. He was, therefore, forced to consider methods for removing this obstacle other than by direct assault.

On January 18, 1863, Godfrey Weitzel, who was then in command on the La Fourche, proposed that an expedition be sent up the Atchafalaya River to turn the enemy position at Port Hudson. He believed that by so doing, a proper force could clear out the Atchafalaya, the Red River, and the Black River and thus cut off the supplies for both Vicksburg and Port Hudson, which were drawn mainly from western Louisiana and Texas by way of the Red River. Banks generally accepted this idea, but to avoid the longer route from Berwick Bay by way of the Teche, he sent Emory with his division west from the Mississippi at Plaquemine to find a shorter route through a bayou into the Atchafalaya River. Banks intended that Weitzel move northward from Berwick Bay and join Emory at Butte-a-la-Rose, and then, after capturing the fort there, the combined force was to move on to the Red River.

For several weeks in February 1863, Emory remained near the head of Bayou Plaquemine, with his headquarters at Indian Village, while he attempted to find a navigable waterway to the Atchafalaya River. He had been unable to find such a route, however, and then his efforts were cut short when David G. Farragut learned that the Confederates had gained control of the Mississippi between Vicksburg and Port Hudson. Farragut then decided that it would be necessary to patrol the river above Port Hudson, and asked Banks to make a demonstration against that post while he passed the enemy batteries there with his fleet. Banks agreed and immediately recalled Emory from the west side of the river. He also brought up all available forces from New Orleans to Baton Rouge.

Farragut arrived at Baton Rouge with his fleet March 13, 1863, and that same day Banks began to move his infantry toward Port Hudson. Grover's division moved first, and it was followed the next day by the divisions of Emory and Augur. Banks then placed his troops on the roads east of Port Hudson, but they were not needed because Farragut passed the batteries unaided on the night of March 14. Banks returned to Baton Rouge with his divisions, and then turned his attention to his original plan for an advance along the Atchafalaya.

Operations in West Louisiana, April 9, 1863– May 14, 1863. Banks returned to New Orleans March 24, 1863 and the next day issued orders for the assembly of the troops for an expedition up the Bayou Teche. Grover was instructed to move with his Fourth Division by transports to Donaldsonville and from there to march along the Bayou La Fourche to Thibodeaux. Emory's Third Division was to move by transports from Baton Rouge to Algiers and from there by rail to Berwick Bay. Augur was to remain at Baton Rouge with his First Division (less Weitzel's Second Brigade, which was near Brashear City), three regiments of Colored Troops, three batteries, and two companies of cavalry.

At that time the Confederate forces in western Louisiana consisted of about 4,000 men under Richard Taylor, commander of the Confederate District of Western Louisiana. The principal post in the district was Alexandria, but outposts had been established as far south as the New Orleans, Opelousas, and Great Western Railroad, which ran from New Orleans to Brashear City. Below Alexandria, near Marksville, was an earthwork on the Red River known as Fort De Russy. On the Bayou

Teche, not far from Pattersonville, was another earthwork known as Fort Bisland, and there was still another work on the Atchafalaya River at Butte-a-la-Rose, about twenty miles north of Grand Lake. These fortifications had been constructed to defend the only two routes by which a Union army could advance from southern Louisiana to the Red River. One was a road that ran northward along the west bank of the Bayou Teche from Brashear City, by way of Opelousas, to Alexandria, and the other was a water route. During periods of high water, the Bayou Teche was navigable as far up as Opelousas, and the Atchafalaya River was navigable all the way to the Red River.

Banks arrived at Brashear City April 8, 1863 and found his troops ready to move. By that date, Weitzel had reoccupied his former position on Berwick Bay; Emory's division was in bivouac at Bayou Ramos, about five miles in rear of Weitzel; and Grover's division was on Bayou Boeuf, about four miles behind Emory. Banks' plan was for his main force to advance against the Confederate fortifications at Fort (or Camp) Bisland, below Franklin, while Grover moved with his division on transports through Grand Lake to Indian Bend (or Indian Village) near Franklin. Grover was then to disembark and move against the rear of Fort Bisland while Banks attacked the position from the front.

On the morning of April 9, 1863, Emory advanced from his camp and closed up on the rear of Weitzel. Grover also advanced from Bayou Boeuf at 9:00 A.M., just as Emory was arriving at Brashear City. Weitzel began to cross Berwick Bay at 10:00 A.M., and Emory followed as soon as the boats were available. That night the four brigades bivouacked near the landing place.

Grover was to have embarked his troops as soon as the boats used by Weitzel and Emory were available, but not all was ready until the night of April 11, 1863. Then, however, because of a heavy fog, the start up the lake was delayed until 9:00 A.M. April 12. Banks did not wait until Grover was ready but started forward with his main column at noon April 11, with Weitzel's brigade in the lead. Skirmishing began almost at once and continued during the day. That evening, Weitzel halted a short distance above Pattersonville, and Emory came up and bivouacked on his left. Banks had started late that day and had marched slowly because he did not wish to engage the enemy until Grover had arrived on the rear of their line.

Engagement at Fort Bisland, Louisiana, April 12–13, 1863. On the road ahead of Banks' column, the enemy had constructed an earthwork between Pattersonville and Franklin called Fort (or Camp) Bisland. This consisted of a single line of entrenchments along a narrow strip of dry land that extended out from both sides of the Bayou Teche. There were redoubts on both sides of the bayou, which ran through the right-center of the line, and the flanks were protected by impenetrable swamps and canebrakes. Alfred Mouton's Confederate brigade of Richard Taylor's command was on the left (or north) bank of the Teche, and Henry Hopkins Sibley's brigade was on the right bank.

Until 11:00 A.M. April 12, 1863, there was skirmishing along the front, and then, when Banks learned that Grover was on his way, he continued the advance until he came under fire from Fort Bisland about 4:00 P.M. The line of march led up the right bank of the Atchafalaya River to the mouth of Bayou Teche and then up the Teche. The main force advanced on the right bank of the bayou, and a smaller force on the left bank. At first, Banks advanced with Weitzel's brigade on the right and Emory's division on the left of the line. Then as they approached a great bend in the bayou, the front narrowed, and the change in direction of the bayou made necessary some changes in troop dispositions. Weitzel took ground to the left in two lines, while Emory advanced Halbert E. Paine's brigade into the front line, on the right of Weitzel. Timothy Ingraham's brigade formed a second line, and Gooding's brigade a third line.

When Emory observed the enemy across the Teche, he sent the 175th New York of Gooding's brigade and a section of the 1st Battery, Maine Light Artillery under Eben D. Haley to the left bank of the bayou.

The artillery opened about 5:30 P.M., and the firing continued until dark. Then Emory sent forward the 4th Wisconsin of Paine's brigade to hold a grove of trees near the bayou, some distance in front of the right of the main line.

Early on the morning of April 13, 1863, Banks advanced his line, which was in much the same order as the night before, to within short musket range of the enemy works. There were some enemy demonstrations against Banks' advanced troops, and Emory sent forward the remaining regiments of Paine's brigade (8th New Hampshire, 133rd New York, and 173rd New York) to support the 4th Wisconsin in the grove of trees. At the same time, Banks ordered Emory to send the other regiments of Gooding's brigade (31st, 38th, and 53rd Massachusetts and the 156th New York) and the other two sections of the 1st Battery, Maine Light Artillery to join the 175th New York on the left bank of the Teche.

When these dispositions had been completed, Banks continued his advance, and by noon the last of the enemy troops had retired within their works. Banks' troops on the right bank of the Teche were formed in two lines, with Paine's brigade on the right and Weitzel's brigade on the left. Ingraham's brigade, in column of companies, advanced in support of both. Richard C. Duryea's Battery F, 1st United States Artillery was in advance of the center, between Paine and Weitzel. Edmund C. Bainbridge's Battery A, 1st United States Artillery and William W. Carruth's 6th Battery, Massachusetts Light Artillery were in battery near the left flank. During the advance, Gooding, on the left bank, conformed to the movements of the main force across the bayou.

As Banks advanced, the firing became heavy, and Weitzel sent the 75th New York out to the left in an attempt to turn the enemy right flank, which was protected by a dense canebrake. He then sent the 114th New York to support the 75th New York, but they were unable to drive the enemy.

As on the day before, Banks was not aggressive because he was primarily interested in holding the enemy in their positions until the arrival of Grover on the road to their rear. Toward evening, however, Banks became fearful that the enemy would escape from the trap that he was preparing, and he gave Emory and Weitzel discretionary orders to attack if they thought that the situation was favorable. They did decide to attack, but before they could do so, Banks received information that Grover had landed his division and was then on the march to join him. Banks then called off the attack for that evening and issued orders for an attack the next morning.

At 9:00 that night, however, Taylor also learned of Grover's approach and promptly sent William G. Vincent with his 2nd Louisiana Cavalry and a section of Florian O. Cornay's battery to watch and retard Grover. Taylor then sent the trains ahead on the road to the rear and marched rapidly from his lines at Fort Bisland toward Franklin. He left Thomas Green of the 5th Texas Mounted Volunteers in command of the rear guard. The next morning, Banks began the pursuit, with Weitzel's brigade in the lead.

Engagement at Irish Bend, Louisiana, April 14, 1863. Meantime, Grover had arrived on the shore of Grand Lake beyond Magee's Point, and after daylight April 13, 1863 the troops of his division began to disembark. It was not until 4:00 P.M., however, that all were ashore and assembled on the plantation of Duncan McWilliams, near the lake. The Bayou Teche, at the upper reaches of Irish Bend, was only about four miles to the south. Irish Bend was the name given to a great loop in the Bayou Teche, which began at a point about three miles north of Franklin. There the bayou, coming down from the north, made an abrupt turn and flowed to the east and north for about five miles, then turned again at a right angle and flowed south for about two miles, and finally turned and flowed back to the west for another four miles to Franklin. It thus flowed around three sides of a rectangle.

By noon April 13, 1863, William Dwight, whose brigade had landed first, had moved out and seized the bridge over the Teche on the road that led to Madame Porter's plantation from the north, and also the Porter Bridge on the road that came in from the east. Grover, however, did not leave the landing area with the brigades of Henry W. Birge and William K. Kimball until 6:00 P.M., but he crossed the Teche that evening and bivouacked on the Porter plantation. He then called in Dwight's brigade to rejoin the division.

When Taylor reached Franklin from Fort Bisland, he took James Reily's 4th Texas Regiment and marched about a mile to the north and east on the road along the Bayou Teche, on which Grover's division was approaching. There he joined Vincent, who was still watching Grover. Also at that time, Franklin H. Clack's Louisiana Battalion, which had just arrived from New Iberia, joined Taylor.

Taylor then formed his troops on the McKerrall plantation. Along the western boundary of the plantation was a wooded area known as Nearson's (or Nerson's) Woods. Here, among the trees along the eastern edge of the woods, and behind a fence, Taylor deployed his troops in line of battle, facing east. Clack's battalion was south of the Teche with two pieces of Cornay's battery; Reily's troops were north of the Teche, on the left of Clack, and they held the ground between the bayou and the Franklin road; Vincent was on the left of Reily, with his right extending across the road; and two of Cornay's guns were on the left of Vincent, next to an impenetrable swamp. It was the difficult task of these troops to delay Grover's advance until the main body of Taylor's command had passed through Franklin, after which they were to withdraw and follow the main column northward.

Early on the morning of April 14, 1863, Grover resumed his march from the Porter plantation toward Franklin. From the bridge over the Bayou Teche at the McWilliams plantation to Franklin, the road ran close along the right bank of the bayou. From the bridge, the bayou flowed east for a short distance, then south for about two miles, and then almost due west for about a mile until it passed through Taylor's line. From that point, it ran to the southwest for about a mile to Franklin.

Birge's brigade took the lead that morning, with John I. Rodgers' Battery C, 2nd United States Artillery; Dwight's brigade, with Henry W. Closson's Battery L, 1st United States Artillery followed; and Kimball's brigade, with Ormand F. Nims' 2nd Battery, Massachusetts Light Artillery, brought up the rear.

After advancing about two miles to the big bend at the southeast corner of the loop of the Teche, Birge encountered enemy skirmishers, but he pushed them back and moved up close to Taylor's position. The 25th Connecticut, which was in the lead, moved well to the right of the road and formed in line of battle. As the other regiments came up, they also were placed in line as follows: the 26th Maine was on the left and a little to the rear of the 25th Connecticut, with its left near the road; the 159th New York was moved out some distance in front of the interval between the 25th Connecticut and the 26th Maine, with Theodore Bradley's section of Rodgers' battery on its right; and Edward L. Molineux's 13th Connecticut advanced on the left, between the bayou and the road, and halted some distance in front and to the left of the 26th Maine.

Molineux was wounded in the advance, and Alexander Warner assumed command of the regiment.

At 7:00 that morning Henry Gray arrived with his 28th Louisiana Regiment and reported to Taylor, and he also informed Taylor that the main Confederate column was near Franklin and that it was in no difficulty. Gray's regiment was then sent to the Confederate left, where it took position overlapping Grover's right. Taylor ordered an attack to gain time until the rest of his army was secure, and then Gray moved out of the woods beyond the right and to the rear of the 159th New York and forced it back. In retreating, it passed over the positions of the 25th Connecticut and the 26th Maine and carried these regiments back with it. Bradley and Rodgers did good service with their guns in slowing the enemy advance. The regiments of Birge's brigade fell back to the rear of Dwight's brigade, which was then getting into position, and re-formed in rear of it.

Meantime, while the enemy was attacking on the right of Birge, the 13th Connecticut again advanced on the left and drove back Clack's battalion, and with it Cornay's guns. The 13th Connecticut was called back, however, and directed to form on the new brigade line.

As Birge's right was driven back, Dwight deployed his brigade in two lines. The 6th and 91st New York regiments were in front, and these were supported by 22nd Maine, 1st Louisiana, and 131st New York. Dwight then advanced against Taylor's left, which he overlapped, and drove it back into the woods. At about the same time that he ordered the 13th Connecticut to draw back, Birge again advanced in two lines on the left of Dwight. Kimball, whose brigade was in reserve, brought up the 12th Maine to support the 13th Connecticut. Finally, Grover's entire division advanced and drove the enemy out of Nearson's Woods and into the open fields beyond. When Grover found the enemy again, in line on a knoll to which they had just retired, he did not press forward but halted his line while he reconnoitered their position.

Meantime, the main enemy column had been steadily moving northward. By 9:30 A.M. all the wagons, and the troops that were following, had passed through Franklin and had moved out on the cutoff road across the base of Irish Bend toward New Iberia. Weitzel entered the town a short time later with his brigade. Mouton, then commanding the troops that had been with Taylor at Irish Bend, marched across country to the cutoff road at a point beyond the northern outskirts of Franklin and then followed the rest of the army.

Grover did not renew his advance until 2:00 P.M., and he then marched down the bayou road toward Franklin. Before proceeding very far, he met the head of Emory's division. Banks then put his weary troops in camp early in the afternoon. Grover remained on the battlefield of that morning, Emory halted on the road between the battlefield and Franklin, and Weitzel bivouacked on the cutoff road north of Franklin.

* * * * * * * * *

Taylor continued his retreat northward through Cypremort and Jeannerette (Jeanerette) and reached New Iberia April 15, 1863. From there he marched on by way of Vermillionville (present-day Lafayette), Opelousas, and Washington to Alexandria. He remained at Alexandria until driven out by Banks in May 1863 and then moved on to Natchitoches.

Banks began the pursuit of Taylor on the morning of April 15, 1863. Weitzel took the lead on the cutoff road and was followed by Emory's division, but Grover's division took the long way, following the bayou road along the Teche. When Grover finally reached the junction with the cutoff road, he fell in behind the main column. On the following afternoon Banks entered New Iberia. From there, Banks marched with Weitzel and Emory on a road to the right to Saint Martinsville on the Teche, and Grover marched to the left on the direct road to Opelousas, but he was forced to halt at the Vermillion Bayou to rebuild a bridge that had been destroyed.

On the evening of April 17, 1863, Banks passed through Saint Martinsville and halted at Cote Gelee, about four miles in rear of Grover. The next day, Weitzel moved up to support Grover, who was rebuilding the bridge, but Banks, with Emory, remained at Cote Gelee to wait for its completion.

April 19, 1863, Banks' army crossed Vermillion Bayou and Carrion Crow (Carencro) Bayou and marched to Grand Coteau, and on the following day arrived at Opelousas. Three days later, Dwight's brigade was moved forward to Washington, four miles farther on toward Alexandria.

April 25, 1863, Banks turned over the command of his column to Emory and returned to New Orleans to look after the affairs of the department. He returned, however, and resumed command May 1.

On May 4, 1863, the army started toward Alexandria. Dwight's brigade marched from Washington, Weitzel's brigade from Opelousas, and Paine's brigade from Barre's Landing. That day Emory left for New Orleans because of a severe illness, and his division was placed temporarily under the command of Weitzel, whose brigade had meantime been ordered to report to Dwight. Emory's division marched from Opelousas toward Alexandria on May 5, and Grover's division marched from Barre's Landing the same day. At 10:00 P.M. May 7, the first troops under Weitzel arrived at Alexandria, and the rest of the army soon followed. Taylor's broken command then retired to Shreveport. Weitzel followed with his division to a point about seventy miles north of Alexandria.

Banks remained at Alexandria for a week, and while there, he and Grant attempted to work out some means of cooperation in opening the Mississippi River, but Grant had already crossed the Mississippi and begun his successful campaign in the rear of Vicksburg. Banks then decided to move his army to Port Hudson and attempt the capture of the Confederate batteries that had been constructed there.

The organization of Banks' Detachment Nineteenth Corps during its advance from Brashear City to Alexandria was as follows:

DETACHMENT NINETEENTH CORPS, Nathaniel P. Banks

First Division
    Second Brigade, Godfrey Weitzel

Third Division, William H. Emory
    First Brigade, Timothy Ingraham
    Second Brigade, Halbert E. Paine
    Third Brigade, Oliver P. Gooding

    Artillery
        4th Battery, Massachusetts Light Artillery, George G. Trull
        Battery F, 1st United States Artillery, Richard C. Duryea

2nd Battery, Vermont Light Artillery, Pythagoras E. Holcomb

Fourth Division, Cuvier Grover
  First Brigade, William Dwight
  Second Brigade, William K. Kimball
  Third Brigade, Henry W. Birge

Artillery
  2nd Battery, Massachusetts Light Artillery, Ormand F. Nims
  Battery L, 1st United States Artillery, Henry W. Closson
  Battery C, 2nd United States Artillery, John I. Rodgers

Capture of Port Hudson, Louisiana, May 21, 1863–July 8, 1863. Early in May 1863, Banks arrived at Alexandria with the divisions of Cuvier Grover and William H. Emory (later commanded by Halbert E. Paine) of Nineteenth Corps, after an advance up the Bayou Teche. For details, see preceding section, Operations in West Louisiana, April 9, 1863–May 14, 1863. He then learned that Grant had crossed the Mississippi River below Vicksburg, and was then moving to the rear of the city. Realizing that it was no longer feasible to cooperate with Grant in the advance on Vicksburg, Banks decided to attempt the capture of Port Hudson. On May 14, he started his two divisions toward Simsport (Simmsport), on the way to Port Hudson. On May 18, he placed Emory in command of the Defenses of New Orleans and directed Thomas W. Sherman to move upriver with the brigades of Neal Dow and Frank S. Nickerson of his Second Division, Nineteenth Corps and join Christopher C. Augur at Port Hudson.

Meantime, on May 13, Augur, then commanding First Division, Nineteenth Corps at Baton Rouge, had sent Benjamin H. Grierson's cavalry and Nathan A. M. Dudley's infantry brigade to a point near the junction of the Springfield Landing and Bayou Sara roads to observe the enemy movements near Port Hudson. Then on May 20, Augur moved with the remainder of his division to join Dudley and cover the landing of Sherman's division at Springfield. Sherman arrived in front of Port Hudson May 22.

On May 21, 1863, Banks arrived at Simsport, where his divisions were assembled, and ordered them to proceed to Bayou Sara. The next day, Grover's division began to disembark at Bayou Sara, and Paine's division followed close behind. Both divisions then marched toward Port Hudson, and by the night of May 22, the Confederate garrison at Port Hudson was practically hemmed in.

Banks then attempted to capture the enemy works by direct assault, and on the morning of May 27, 1863 he launched an attack, which was repulsed with heavy losses. He succeeded in capturing some outposts June 11, but on June 14, Grover's division made an unsuccessful attack on a part of the enemy works known as the Priest Cap. Banks then resorted to siege operations that lasted until July 8, when Port Hudson finally surrendered.

For details of the siege and the assaults on Port Hudson, see Port Hudson, Louisiana Campaign.

Operations in Louisiana, West of the Mississippi River, June 7, 1863–July 13, 1863. In April 1863 Nathaniel P. Banks led an expedition along the Bayou Teche toward the Red River in an attempt to gain the rear of the Confederate works at Port Hudson. For details of this campaign, see above, Operations in the Department of the Gulf, Operations against Port Hudson, Louisiana, Operations in West Louisiana, April 9, 1863–May 14, 1863. During Banks' advance, Richard Taylor, commanding the Confederate forces in western Louisiana, fell back to Alexandria, and when Banks' troops entered the city on May 7, Taylor continued his retreat to Natchitoches.

On April 30, 1863, Ulysses S. Grant's army near Vicksburg began crossing to the east bank of the Mississippi River at the beginning of its movement to the rear of the city. John C. Pemberton, commanding the Confederate forces at Vicksburg, asked E. Kirby Smith, commander of the Confederate Trans-Mississippi Department, to send troops to attempt to relieve some of the pressure on his command. In response, Smith sent Taylor, who was joined by John G. Walker's division from Arkansas May 24, on a movement toward New Carthage by way of the New River and the Tensas River. Taylor and Walker arrived on the river opposite Vicksburg and attacked fortified camps at Richmond and near Young's Point, but their presence had little influence on the results of Grant's campaign.

After remaining near Vicksburg for a short time,

Taylor left Walker's division in northern Louisiana and returned with his command to Alexandria, where he arrived June 10, 1863. Meantime, Banks had moved from Alexandria to Port Hudson, and was then investing the town.

Taylor immediately began preparations for a campaign that he had proposed earlier. His plan was designed to afford some relief for the Confederate forces east of the Mississippi by moving south in Louisiana, capturing the Federal fortifications at Berwick Bay, then occupying the La Fourche country and interrupting Banks' communications with New Orleans. He recruited additional troops, and reorganized his force of about 3,000 men into two detachments that were to move south by different routes. Alfred Mouton, who was in command of the Confederate Forces South of the Red River, was to command the main column, which included Thomas Green's First Brigade, Texas Cavalry and was to move by boats down the Bayou Teche and the Atchafalaya River and attack Brashear (or Brashear City). James P. Major, with his Second Brigade, Texas Cavalry, was to constitute the second column, and he was to move by way of Morgan's Ferry on the Atchafalaya to Plaquemine, then down the west bank of the Mississippi toward Donaldsonville, and later join Mouton at Brashear.

Major surprised and captured a small Federal detachment at Plaquemine on the morning of June 18, 1863, and then marched the next day by Bayou Goula toward Donaldsonville. Before arriving at Donaldsonville, however, he moved off to the right and crossed over to the La Fourche road, which he reached at a point about six miles from the town, and then proceeded on his way toward Thibodeaux (present-day Thibodaux) and Brashear.

On June 20, 1863, William H. Emory, commanding the Defenses of New Orleans, learned of Major's movement, and he notified Albert Stickney, who was in command at Brashear. He also directed Stickney to provide for the protection of Brashear and Bayou Boeuf, and to move to La Fourche Crossing with whatever other troops were available. Emory also directed Thomas W. Cahill, commanding the Second Brigade of William Dwight's Second Division, Nineteenth Corps at New Orleans, to collect what men he could and go to the support of Stickney.

Troops of Major's command arrived at Thibodeaux at 3:30 A.M. June 21, 1863, and the next day set out in a driving rain for La Fourche Crossing, four miles away. Meantime, Stickney had been reinforced by the 26th Massachusetts from New Orleans, and he then had at La Fourche Crossing about 800 men belonging to the following regiments: 23rd Connecticut, 176th New York, 42nd Massachusetts, 26th Maine, 26th Massachusetts, 1st Louisiana Cavalry, some artillerymen of the 1st Indiana Heavy Artillery (also called the 21st Indiana), and a section of John A. Grow's 25th Battery, New York Light Artillery. These troops were in position behind the levee of the Bayou La Fourche; behind the embankment of the New Orleans, Opelousas, and Great Western Railroad; and in rifle pits.

At 7:00 P.M. June 21, 1863, Charles L. Pyron, commanding the 2nd Texas Cavalry Regiment, charged against Stickney's position but was repulsed. Pyron made two more unsuccessful attacks, and Major then ended the fight and marched off toward Brashear to join Green's cavalry brigade.

The next day, June 21, 1863, the 15th Maine Regiment from Pensacola, Florida reported to Emory at New Orleans and was immediately sent on to join Cahill, who was moving toward Brashear. At 11:00 that morning, Cahill arrived at La Fourche Crossing with the 9th Connecticut, a detachment of the 26th Massachusetts, and the rest of Grow's battery. Cahill then assumed command at La Fourche Crossing, and sent troops to occupy Thibodeaux.

Meantime, Mouton had collected forty to fifty rowboats, and at nightfall June 22, 1863, Sherod Hunter, with about 325 men, started out from near the mouth of the Teche and rowed down the bayou and the Atchafalaya, landing the next morning in rear of the Federal defenses at Brashear. At that time the garrison consisted of only about 400 men, including some Indiana troops, four companies of the 23rd Connecticut, two companies of the 176th New York, and one company of the 42nd Massachusetts. In addition, there were 300 convalescents at the post. In command at Brashear was Robert C. Anthony of the 2nd Rhode Island Cavalry.

While Hunter was getting in position in rear of Brashear, Green, with two regiments and one battalion and two batteries of his command, moved into the ruins of Berwick. He then advanced into some woods on the west bank of Berwick Bay to attract the attention of the Federal garrison at Brashear.

Just before dawn June 23, 1863, Green opened fire with his artillery and, under the cover of this fire, Hunter's men moved up close to the rear of Brashear and then attacked in two columns. The left column charged against the fort and a camp to the left of the depot, and the right column attacked the fort and a sugarhouse above and to the right of the depot. The two columns were to join at the railroad buildings. Hunter's attack completely surprised Anthony's troops, and by 10:00 A.M. the fighting ended with the surrender of the garrison.

Banks had intended that the large depot of military stores at Brashear be broken up and that all regimental baggage and other property that had been left at Brashear and Bayou Boeuf, both before and after the Teche Campaign, be sent for storage to New Orleans or Algiers. For some reason, however, this had not been done, and all these stores fell into enemy hands.

On June 23, 1863, Green crossed Berwick Bay with a part of his command and pushed forward to Bayou Ramos. He skirmished for a time with the Federal troops of the post, who were in position on the east bank of the bayou, but when they were outflanked by Green they retreated to Bayou Boeuf. Meantime, as noted above, Major had been advancing from La Fourche Crossing to join Green at Brashear. He started out at nightfall June 22 and, marching all night, passed by Chacahoula Station just before dawn and arrived near Bayou Boeuf about 4:30 P.M. June 23. He then occupied the east bank of the bayou, opposite the troops of the Federal garrison who were in position on the other side.

Augustin J. H. Dugann, commanding the post of Bayou Boeuf, was then in a difficult situation. Major's brigade was to his rear on the road back to New Orleans, and Green's brigade was only a few miles away and was approaching from the west. That night Dugann decided to surrender, and at daylight June 24, 1863 he offered to do so to a small party of scouts from Green's brigade. After the surrender was completed, Green and Major then joined forces and moved toward Thibodeaux.

On June 24, 1863, Cahill learned that Green and Major were approaching La Fourche Crossing and Thibodeaux from Bayou Boeuf, and he was alarmed by the exaggerated reports of the strength of the enemy force. Cahill immediately ordered his command to Raceland Station on the railroad, and a short time later he moved on toward New Orleans. By July 1, his troops were back at Algiers. Enemy cavalry under Pyron and Edward Waller followed Cahill as far as Boutte Station, where it finally halted only twenty miles from New Orleans.

On June 24, 1863, Taylor came down to Brashear with Mouton's men, and upon arrival, he turned over the immediate command of his force to Mouton and hurried back to Alexandria to bring down Walker's division to help hold and extend the country then occupied by the Confederates in southern Louisiana.

On June 26, 1863, Mouton ordered Green and Major to march to Donaldsonville and capture the post. The principal fortification there was Fort Butler, which was a strong earthwork that was protected on one side by the Mississippi River and on the other by the Bayou La Fourche, and it was also surrounded by a moat. This work was further strengthened on the sides along the river and the bayou by strong stockades of logs that extended from the levee to the water. The fort was commanded by Joseph D. Bullen, and he had with him only two companies of the 28th Maine and a number of convalescents from several regiments.

On the night of June 27, 1863, Green, with his own brigade, Major's brigade, and a battery, arrived within a mile and a half of Donaldsonville and demanded the surrender of the fort. Bullen refused, and Green prepared to attack. He sent a part of his command around to the left, and shortly after midnight on the morning of June 28, these troops moved down the Mississippi levee toward Fort Butler. Some attacked at the stockade on the flank of the works, and others moved around the end of the stockade, through the shallow water, and into the outer part of the fort.

Green began his main attack at 2:00 A.M. One regiment surrounded the fort and moved forward; one regiment flanked the two end ditches and fired on the gunners and sharpshooters on the parapet; and another regiment became lost and did not join in the action. On both flanks enemy troops succeeded in getting through and around the stockades between the levee and the river, but they were unable to cross the deep ditch that they found inside the levee, and which separated them from the main works.

While the fighting was going on, a Federal gunboat came up and shelled the attackers. Toward daylight two more gunboats arrived and also engaged the enemy.

A short time after dawn, after suffering severe losses, Green called off the attack. He then left three regiments to watch Fort Butler, and ordered Major's brigade and several batteries to the Mississippi River, where they were to prevent the passage of Federal vessels between Port Hudson and New Orleans. Major placed his cavalry and artillery along about twenty miles of the river, and from July 3, 1863 to the fall of Port Hudson, they seriously interfered with shipping on the river. Major's batteries were placed at Gaudet's plantation, opposite White Hall Point, opposite College Point, and at Fifty-Five Mile Point.

The interruption of traffic on the river and the proximity of Confederate troops to New Orleans caused Banks at Port Hudson serious concern, but nevertheless he decided to continue with the siege. In response to a request by Bullen for reinforcements, Banks relieved the 1st Louisiana Regiment on the lines at Port Hudson and sent it to Donaldsonville, and Emory sent two companies of the 28th Maine from New Orleans. Two sections of Henry W. Closson's Battery L, 1st United States Artillery, commanded by Franck E. Taylor, were also sent to Donaldsonville.

With the surrender of Port Hudson, Banks moved quickly to deal with Mouton's force between him and New Orleans. At Port Hudson, Christopher C. Augur, who had been ill for some time, turned over the command of his First Division, Nineteenth Corps to Godfrey Weitzel and went north. He did not return to the Department of the Gulf. On the evening of July 9, 1863, the day of the ceremony of the surrender of Port Hudson, Weitzel left Port Hudson with his division and moved downriver on transports to Donaldsonville, where he arrived the next morning.

Cuvier Grover's Fourth Division, Nineteenth Corps followed Weitzel to Donaldsonville. Joseph S. Morgan, with Grover's First Brigade, and Ormand F. Nims' 2nd Battery, Massachusetts Light Artillery of Fourth Division, left Port Hudson at midnight July10, 1863, and Grover with his other two brigades followed the next day. Grover, as the senior officer, assumed command of both divisions at Donaldsonville; he placed his own division, temporarily under the command of Henry W. Birge, on the east side of the Bayou La Fourche and sent Weitzel's division to the west side of the bayou.

Facing Grover when he arrived at Donaldsonville was Green's cavalry brigade, which was on the west bank of the bayou, with its pickets out within a mile or two of Donaldsonville. Major's cavalry brigade and the artillery were then withdrawn from their positions on the Mississippi and placed on the east side of the bayou. This movement was completed July 11.

On the morning of July 13, Grover sent out a part of his command on a foraging expedition along both banks of the La Fourche. Nathan A. M. Dudley's Third Brigade, First Division, Nineteenth Corps, two sections of William W. Carruth's 6th Battery, Massachusetts Light Artillery (commanded by John F. Phelps), and Richard Barrett's troop of 1st Louisiana Cavalry advanced on the west bank; and Charles J. Paine's First Brigade, with Eben D. Haley's 1st Battery, Maine Light Artillery, followed in support. Joseph S. Morgan's First Brigade of Birge's division moved along the east bank of Bayou La Fourche, keeping in line with Dudley's brigade on the opposite bank.

After advancing about a mile, Dudley's skirmishers encountered Green's pickets, and after a brief skirmish continued their advance toward the Cox (also spelled Koch and Kock) plantation, which was about six miles from Donaldsonville. When Dudley's brigade came up abreast of the Cox house, he formed his troops in line of battle along a lane facing a field about 100 yards wide, and which extended from the bayou to a swamp on the west.

Green deployed his command and advanced through the field against Dudley's line. Struck on both flanks and in front, all Federal troops on the west bank of the bayou were driven back. They made several attempts to halt the enemy advance, but they were steadily pushed back for several miles until they were joined by Paine's brigade. Together, the two brigades made a more determined stand.

Simultaneously with the attack on Dudley, a small force under Major advanced against Morgan's force on the east bank. Inexplicably, Morgan's men broke in panic and rapidly retreated along the bayou. Weitzel then came up and ordered both columns to return to Donaldsonville and re-form under the protection of the guns at Fort Butler.

The fighting was not resumed, and Mouton then ordered Green and Major to move back to Berwick Bay, where his command could be assembled. Two Federal gunboats were sent to Berwick Bay, however, and when Mouton learned of their approach, he moved his force up the Bayou Teche to Franklin and went into camp. Weitzel then transferred his divisions from Donaldsonville to Thibodeaux and Brashear and allowed his men to rest for the next few weeks.

Mobile, Alabama Campaign
March 17, 1865–May 4, 1865

On August 3, 1864, a Federal force under Gordon Granger landed on Dauphin Island, Alabama, and the next day invested Fort Gaines. Two days later, Rear Admiral David G. Farragut ran past the forts at the entrance to Mobile Bay with his fleet and entered the bay. On August 8, Fort Gaines surrendered, and Granger then moved with his command against Fort Morgan, which surrendered August 23. Federal naval forces then controlled the waters of the bay, and Granger's troops were firmly established at Fort Morgan and on Dauphin Island. Granger, however, did not have a sufficient force to attempt the capture of Mobile.

Early in 1865, strong reinforcements were sent to Mobile Bay and to Pensacola, Florida, and that spring Edward R. S. Canby, commander of the Military Division of West Mississippi, undertook the capture of Mobile. The movement against the city was made in two columns: one column consisted of Andrew J. Smith's Sixteenth Corps and Gordon Granger's Thirteenth Corps, both under the personal direction of Canby; and the other consisted of troops assembled at Pensacola, Florida under Frederick Steele. On March 17, 1865, Sixteenth Corps moved by water from Fort Gaines, and Thirteenth Corps marched from Fort Morgan, and the two corps joined at Danley's Ferry. They then advanced and laid siege to Spanish Fort. Steele's column marched from Pensacola on March 20 and arrived near Blakely, Alabama April 1. It promptly began

the siege of Fort Blakely, the Confederate fortification in front of the town. Canby occupied Spanish Fort on April 8, and then joined Steele's column at Blakely. In a general assault on April 9, Canby captured Fort Blakely. Confederate forces evacuated Mobile April 11, and Canby's troops occupied the city the next day.

For details of the operations around Mobile from March 17, 1865 to May 4, 1865, see Land Operations against Mobile Bay and Mobile, Alabama.

DEPARTMENT OF KANSAS
NOVEMBER 16, 1861– MARCH 11, 1862

The Department of Kansas was created November 9, 1861 from territory of the Western Department. It consisted of the state of Kansas, the Indian Territory west of Arkansas, and the territories of Colorado, Dakota, and Nebraska. This included the present-day states of Colorado, Kansas, Montana, Nebraska, North Dakota, Oklahoma, South Dakota, and Wyoming. David Hunter was assigned command of the department, with headquarters at Fort Leavenworth, Kansas.

Fort Garland, Colorado Territory was transferred to the Department of New Mexico February 14, 1862, and on March 11, the Department of Kansas was merged into the Department of the Mississippi.

In August 1861, Senator James H. Lane, with vague authority, assumed command of the Kansas forces at Fort Scott. His command was known as the Kansas Brigade and also as Lane's Brigade, Western Department. This brigade consisted of William Weer's 4th Kansas Infantry and James Montgomery's 3rd Kansas Infantry. Charles R. Jennison commanded a cavalry force that later became the 7th Kansas Cavalry, and which was commonly known as "Jennison's Jayhawkers." Lane's and Jennison's commands represented the Union military forces along the Kansas border during the summer and fall of 1861 and also 1862. In November 1861, the designation of this force was changed to Troops in Kansas, Department of the Missouri.

December 2, 1861, James W. Denver was assigned command of all troops in Kansas, with headquarters at Fort Leavenworth. These consisted essentially of Montgomery's 3rd Kansas Infantry at Fort Scott, and Charles R. Jennison's cavalry regiment and Henry W. Wessells' 8th Kansas Infantry, both at West Point, Missouri. Denver's command was designated as Troops in Kansas, Department of Kansas.

February 1, 1862, George W. Deitzler was ordered to Fort Scott to assume command of the newly organized 1st Kansas Brigade, which consisted of the 1st, 5th, and 6th Kansas Infantry. On February 15, Charles Doubleday was assigned command of a brigade consisting of Doubleday's 2nd Ohio Cavalry and the 9th and 12th Wisconsin Infantry. These were the only brigade organizations in the Department of Kansas until it merged into the Department of the Mississippi March 11, 1862.

DEPARTMENT OF KANSAS
MAY 2, 1862–
SEPTEMBER 19, 1862

The Department of Kansas was re-created May 2, 1862, to have the same boundaries as described for the Department of Kansas, November 16, 1861–March 11, 1862. James G. Blunt was assigned command, with headquarters at Fort Leavenworth, Kansas.

September 19, 1862, the department was merged into the re-created Department of the Missouri, except Colorado Territory, which was included in the Department of the Missouri on October 11.

TROOPS AND OPERATIONS IN THE DEPARTMENT OF KANSAS

When the Department of Kansas was re-created May 2, 1862, most of the troops within its boundaries were at Fort Riley and Fort Scott in Kansas, and the rest were scattered over the department at a number of posts.

Robert B. Mitchell was in command at Fort Riley, where the following regiments were stationed: 1st Kansas Infantry, 2nd and 7th Kansas Cavalry, 12th

and 13th Wisconsin Infantry, and two batteries. During the period May 18–June 2, 1862, all of these except the 2nd Kansas Cavalry were sent to Columbus, Kentucky, and they then became a part of the District of Mississippi (also called District of the Mississippi), Department of the Mississippi. For additional information, see Department of the Mississippi (Halleck), District of Mississippi.

At Fort Scott, Frederick Salomon commanded the equivalent of a brigade, and his troops consisted of Charles Doubleday's 2nd Ohio Cavalry, Salomon's own 9th Wisconsin Infantry, and Matthias K. Haines' 2nd Battery, Indiana Light Artillery. John A. Thompson was at Fort Kearny with detachments of the 8th Kansas Infantry, and the 4th and 6th United States Cavalry. William E. Prince was at Fort Leavenworth with detachments of the 8th Kansas and the 1st United States Infantry and two batteries. Other posts occupied by smaller bodies of Union troops were Fort Laramie and Fort Randall in Nebraska Territory; Fort Larned, Leavenworth, Ohio City, and Paola in Kansas; Fort Wise, Colorado Territory; and Springfield, Missouri.

Troops on the Overland Mail Route. On April 16, 1862, James Craig was assigned command of the troops on the Overland Mail Route, District of Kansas, Department of the Mississippi. Craig's command extended from the eastern terminus of the Mail Route to the western boundary of the district. His headquarters was at Fort Leavenworth, Kansas, but this was moved to Fort Laramie, Nebraska Territory in May 1862. When the Department of Kansas was re-created May 2, 1862, Craig's force became a part of the Department of Kansas. On November 2, Craig was assigned command of the District of Nebraska Territory, which included the Overland Mail Route.

Expedition to the Indian Territory (Weer, Salomon), June 28, 1862–July 1862. As early as the fall of 1861, Senator James H. Lane had proposed an invasion of the Indian Territory for the purpose of isolating it from the rest of the Confederacy, and also of freeing the thousands of slaves owned by the Confederate Indian tribes. It was not until June 1862 that the expedition was approved, and James G. Blunt, commander of the Department of Kansas, appointed William Weer to lead the expedition. Weer arrived at Fort Scott, Kansas on June 5 and assumed command of the Indian Expedition. This consisted of a First Brigade, commanded by Frederick Salomon, and a Second Brigade, commanded by Charles Doubleday. Later in the month William R. Judson succeeded Doubleday in command of Second Brigade.

When preparations were completed, Weer left Baxter Springs, Kansas June 28, 1862 to join Salomon. He moved down the Grand River. The only Confederate troops in the area that were in position to oppose Weer's advance were the regiments of John Drew and Stand Watie and a battalion of Missouri troops under James J. Clarkson.

A Federal vanguard of about 1,000 men under Doubleday surprised Watie at his camp at Cowskin Prairie and drove him back to Spavina (or Spavinaw) Creek. Thomas C. Hindman, commanding the Confederate Trans-Mississippi Department, ordered Albert Pike to move from Fort McCulloch and support Watie. Pike refused, but ordered Douglas H. Cooper to take command of the Indian troops in the field and go to the aid of Watie.

Weer sent a detachment of cavalry down the east side of the Grand River to engage Watie on Spavina Creek, and with the rest of his command moved against Clarkson at Locust Grove. Watie and Drew were again surprised at Spavina Creek and defeated, and a part of Weer's cavalry overran Clarkson's command, drove it from the area, and captured Clarkson.

After the victories at Cowskin Prairie June 6, Spavina Creek July 3, and Locust Grove July 3, Weer pushed on farther south toward Fort Gibson and nearby Fort Davis. He halted his command on the Grand River about ten miles from the forts and sent out reconnoitering parties to determine the strength and dispositions of the enemy forces ahead.

Weer then moved on and captured Fort Gibson on July 14, and a small force proceeded to the home of Chief John Ross of the Cherokees and persuaded him to surrender. By this act, the Cherokees were relieved from their alliance with the Confederate forces.

By mid-July 1862, all effective opposition to the Indian Expedition had been driven back, but by that time Blunt had become seriously concerned about Weer's command, which was operating deep in hostile territory and far from its base. Accordingly,

Blunt warned Weer that he might be cut off by the enemy and asked him to return to Kansas. Blunt's warning caused concern among Weer's subordinate officers. This was especially true of Salomon, his second-in-command, and on July 18, Salomon, doubting Weer's competence, put him in arrest.

Salomon then assumed command of the expedition and ordered its withdrawal, which was to begin the following morning. Robert W. Ratliff, as senior officer, assumed command of Salomon's First Brigade.

Salomon issued no orders for the withdrawal of the Indian regiments that were with the expedition, and they were left to hold and protect the captured territory. Robert W. Furnas, commanding the 1st Indian Regiment, consulted with the other two regimental commanders, and they concluded that they would be more secure if they consolidated the three regiments into a brigade. This was done, and Furnas assumed command of the First Indian Brigade.

Furnas put his brigade in camp on the Verdigris River, but his situation soon deteriorated, and he marched northward with his command toward Kansas. Meantime, Salomon had halted at Camp Quapaw in the northeastern corner of the Cherokee Nation, where he would be closer to his supply depot at Fort Scott. Salomon then ordered Furnas to join him there, and he transferred to the Indian Brigade a section of artillery, a small detachment of infantry, and some supplies. Furnas then established Camp Wattles on Horse Creek for his brigade.

With the Indian Expedition thus divided into two commands, Salomon moved with his white regiments to Hudson's Crossing on the Grand River, and Furnas' Indian Brigade remained in camp about forty-five miles farther south. Later, Salomon marched back into Kansas and halted at Fort Scott. This left the Indian Brigade isolated and unsupported deep in enemy territory, and then it too marched north to within supporting distance of the main body and encamped at Baxter Springs.

Army of Kansas. On August 8, 1862, Blunt, at Fort Scott, Kansas, organized the troops in southeast Kansas into a field force of three brigades, and marched into western Missouri to cooperate with troops in Missouri in driving out of the state the many bands of enemy troops that infested the area. Blunt's command was called the Army of Kansas.

When most of the enemy troops had been driven south into Arkansas, Blunt returned to Fort Scott. For additional information about the organization and movements of Blunt's command, see Army of Kansas.

DEPARTMENT OF KANSAS
JANUARY 1, 1864–
JANUARY 30, 1865

The Department of Kansas was again created January 1, 1864, and was to consist of the state of Kansas, the territories of Colorado and Nebraska, and the Indian Territory, as well as the post of Fort Smith. Samuel R. Curtis was assigned command, with headquarters at Fort Leavenworth, Kansas.

Fort Smith and the Indian Territory were transferred to the Department of Arkansas April 17, 1864 (see below, District of the Frontier).

In December 1864 the boundaries of the department were described as follows: the eastern boundary ran along the Missouri River down to Kansas City, and from there it extended southward along the Kansas-Missouri border; the southern boundary was the border with the Indian Territory and New Mexico; the western boundary ran northward along the western border of Colorado Territory (the 109th meridian), then east along the present northern border of Colorado, and then north along the crest of the Rocky Mountains; and the northern boundary ran eastward from the Rocky Mountains along the 43rd parallel to the Keya Paha River, then along the river to its junction with the Niobrara River, and along that river to its junction with the Missouri River.

The Department of Kansas was merged into the Department of the Missouri January 30, 1865.

DISTRICTS IN THE DEPARTMENT
OF KANSAS

District of Colorado Territory. This district was in existence as a district in the Department of the Missouri. On February 28, 1864, it was constituted as the District of Colorado Territory, Department of Kansas, and consisted of the Colorado Territory. John M. Chivington was assigned command January 1, 1864, and he was succeeded by Thomas Moonlight January 4, 1865.

The principal posts in the district were as follows: Bent's Old Fort, Camp Evans, Camp Fillmore, Camp Wild, Denver, Fort Garland, and Fort Lyon. The post of Fort Lyon and vicinity was transferred from the District of Upper Arkansas, Department of Kansas to the District of Colorado Territory January 15, 1865.

District of the Frontier. This district was in existence as a district of the Department of the Missouri.

The troops in the district at the end of December 1863 were as follows:

First Brigade (or Indian Brigade), William A. Phillips
Second Brigade, John Edwards
Third Brigade, Thomas M. Bowen
Post of Roseville, Arkansas, James M. Williams
Post of Van Buren, Arkansas, Henry Goodsell

Note. First Brigade was at Fort Gibson, Indian Territory; Second Brigade was at Fort Smith, Arkansas; and Third Brigade was at Van Buren, Arkansas.

On January 6, 1864, the Department of Arkansas was constituted to consist of the state of Arkansas, except Fort Smith. A part of the territory of the District of the Frontier was included in the newly created Department of Arkansas. Almost immediately there was some uncertainty concerning to which department the troops at Fort Smith belonged. According to the order creating the Department of Arkansas, the forces at Fort Smith belonged to the Department of Kansas, but they were claimed by the commander of the Department of Arkansas. The roster for January 31, 1864 gives the troops in the District of the Frontier, which were commanded by William R. Judson, as consisting of John Edwards' Second Brigade at Waldron and Thomas M. Bowen's Third Brigade at Van Buren. On the other hand, the tri-monthly report for January 31, 1864 shows that Second Brigade was at Fort Smith. If this report is correct, then Second Brigade and First (or Indian) Brigade had been assigned to the Department of Kansas.

On February 22, 1864, Frederick Steele, commanding the Department of Arkansas, informed John M. Thayer, commanding at Fort Smith, that his post was included in the Department of Arkansas, and that according to this order, Phillips' Indian Brigade at Fort Gibson was the only Federal force in the District of the Frontier, Department of Kansas.

February 23, 1864, James G. Blunt was assigned command of that part of the old District of the Frontier remaining in the Department of Kansas, and he assumed command March 12.

February 28, 1864, the District of the Frontier was constituted as a district of the Department of Kansas, and was defined as consisting of that part of the Department of Kansas lying south of the state of Kansas. Blunt was assigned command, with headquarters at Fort Gibson, Indian Territory.

The controversy over the control of the troops at Fort Smith was terminated April 17, 1864, when Fort Smith and the Indian Territory were formally assigned to the Department of Arkansas.

District of Nebraska Territory. This district was in existence as a part of the Department of the Missouri. February 28, 1864, it was constituted as a district in the Department of Kansas, and it was defined to include all of Nebraska Territory. Thomas J. McKean was in command of the district from January 1 to February 28, 1864, and then Robert B. Mitchell assumed command (assigned February 16).

On March 21, 1864, all of the Department of Kansas lying north of the 40th parallel was assigned to the District of Nebraska Territory.

September 29, 1864, the district was divided into sub-districts as follows:

Eastern Sub-district. That part of the District of Nebraska Territory east of Julesburg, Colorado Territory, and south of Omaha was designated as the Eastern Sub-district. Julesburg was included in the sub-district but Omaha was not. Robert R. Livingston was assigned command, with headquarters at Fort Kearny.

The posts in the sub-district were as follows: Alkali Station, Columbus, Post Cottonwood (later Fort McPherson), Fort Kearny, and Plum Creek, all in Nebraska Territory, and Julesburg in Colorado Territory.

Western Sub-district. All of the District of Nebraska

Territory west of and excluding Julesburg was designated as the Western Sub-district. William O. Collins was assigned command of the sub-district, with headquarters at Fort Laramie.

The posts in the district were as follows: Camp Collins, Colorado Territory, and Camp Mitchell, Fort Halleck, Fort Laramie, and Platte Bridge, all in Idaho Territory.

District of North Kansas. The District of North Kansas was constituted February 28, 1864 to include all of the state of Kansas north of the Kansas River and its tributary, the Smoky Hill Fork. Thomas A. Davies was assigned command, with headquarters at Fort Leavenworth. The principal posts in the district were Fort Leavenworth, Fort Riley, and Wyandotte Bridge.

District of South Kansas. The District of South Kansas was constituted February 28, 1864 to include all of the state of Kansas lying south of the Kansas River and its tributary, the Smoky Hill Fork. Thomas J. McKean was assigned command, with headquarters at Paola, Kansas.

The commanders of the District of South Kansas were as follows:

Thomas J. McKean	February 28, 1864 to September 1, 1864
George Sykes	September 1, 1864 to October 10, 1864
James G. Blunt	October 10, 1864 to October 31, 1864
Thomas A. Davies	October 31, 1864 to November 22, 1864
James G. Blunt	November 22, 1864 to January 30, 1865

Note. Davies was in temporary command of the district, while Blunt was in command in the field during Sterling Price's Missouri Expedition.

Troops in the District of South Kansas. On April 1, 1864, the troops in the District of South Kansas were organized into two brigades, which were designated as First Brigade, District of South Kansas and Second Brigade, District of South Kansas.

First Brigade was organized from troops at Fort Scott, under the command of Charles W. Blair. The troops were stationed by detachments at the following posts: Fort Scott and Humboldt in Kansas, and

Halltown, Camp Hamer, Camp Insley, Dry Wood, Osage Mission, Pawnee Creek, and Pleasant Grove, all in Missouri.

Second Brigade was organized under the command of Thomas Moonlight, whose headquarters was at Mound City, Kansas. The troops of the brigade were stationed at the following posts: Aubery, Coldwater Grove, Lawrence, Mound City, Olathe, Osawatomie, Oxford, Paola, Potosi, Rockville, Shawnee Mission, and Trading Post, all in Kansas.

In addition to the territory occupied by these two brigades, important posts held by other troops of the district were Fort Larned, Council Grove, and Topeka, all in Kansas.

The brigade organization was discontinued August 1, 1864, and the district was divided into sub-districts as follows:

Sub-district No. 1. This sub-district consisted of the counties of Linn, Anderson, Coffey, Lyon, Greenwood, Woodson, and Allen, and the territory of the District of South Kansas lying south of the three last-named counties. Charles R. Jennison was in command of the sub-district, with headquarters at Mound City, Kansas.

Fort Scott (later Sub-district of Fort Scott). This sub-district consisted of the county of Bourbon and the outposts to the south and east. Charles W. Blair commanded the sub-district, with headquarters at Fort Scott.

Sub-district No. 3. This sub-district consisted of the counties of Miami, Johnson, Douglas, Shawnee, Wabaunsee, Osage, and Franklin. Thomas Moonlight was assigned command of the sub-district, with headquarters at Paola.

On September 19, 1864, some changes in the District of South Kansas resulted in a change in the sub-districts. Headquarters of the district were moved from Paola to Lawrence, and the Sub-district of Fort Scott was discontinued. The district was then organized as follows:

Sub-district No 1. This sub-district consisted of the counties of Linn, Anderson, Coffee, Greenwood, Woodson, Allen, Bourbon, and the tier of counties of the District of South Kansas lying south of the four last-named counties. Charles R. Jennison was

assigned command of the sub-district, with headquarters at Mound City.

Sub-district No 2. This sub-district consisted of the counties of Miami, Johnson, Franklin, Douglas, Osage, Shawnee, Lyon, and Wabaunsee. Thomas Moonlight was assigned command of the sub-district, with headquarters at Paola.

Again, on December 6, 1864, the sub-districts of the District of South Kansas were reorganized as follows:

Sub-district No. 1. This sub-district consisted of the counties of Linn, Anderson, Coffee, Lyon, and Osage. Charles R. Jennison was assigned command, with headquarters at Mound City.

Sub-district No. 2. This sub-district consisted of the counties of Bourbon, Allen, Woodson, Greenwood, and Butler, and all territory south of the southern boundary of Kansas, and the military outposts of Fort Scott. Charles W. Blair was assigned command, with headquarters at Fort Scott.

Sub-district No. 3. This sub-district consisted of the counties of Miami, Franklin, Johnson, Douglas, Shawnee, and Wabaunsee. Thomas Moonlight was assigned command, with headquarters at Paola.

There was still another change when on December 27, 1864, Sub-district No. 1 was attached to Sub-district No. 2, which was commanded by Charles W. Blair.

District of the Upper Arkansas. The District of the Upper Arkansas was created July 25, 1864, and it included roughly the territory of the Department of Kansas that extended westward from Fort Riley to a north-south line west of Fort Lyon, Colorado Territory, and north of the Indian Territory. Particularly, it included the posts on the Santa Fe Trail. James G. Blunt was assigned command, with headquarters at Fort Riley, Kansas. He assumed command on August 2.

The principal posts in the district, all in Kansas, were as follows: Cottonwood Crossing, Council Grove, Fort Ellsworth, Fort Larned, Fort Lyon, Fort Riley, Salina, and Fort Zarah.

On January 15, 1865, Fort Lyon was transferred to the District of Colorado.

Commanders of the District of the Upper Arkansas were as follows:

James G. Blunt	August 2, 1864 to October 14, 1864
Benjamin S. Henning	October 14, 1864 to December 22, 1864
James H. Ford	December 22, 1864 to January, 30, 1865

DEPARTMENT OF KENTUCKY MAY 28, 1861–AUGUST 15, 1861

The Department of Kentucky was constituted May 28, 1861 to include all of the state of Kentucky lying within 100 miles of the Ohio River. Robert Anderson was assigned command, with headquarters at Cincinnati, Ohio.

The principal activities in the department at this early stage of the war were generally related to receiving volunteer regiments that reported in the state and then organizing and training the troops for field service. As a part of this effort, Naval Lieutenant William Nelson established Camp Dick Robinson near Danville, Kentucky for the assembly of Union volunteers, and Lovell H. Rousseau established Camp Joe Holt between New Albany and Jeffersonville, Indiana for the same purpose.

August 15, 1861, the Department of Kentucky was merged into the newly created Department of the Cumberland. It should be mentioned that during this period of existence of the Department of Kentucky, the state was officially "neutral," but this ended September 3, 1861 when Confederate forces commanded by Gideon J. Pillow, acting under orders from Leonidas Polk, entered Kentucky as they marched toward Hickman and Columbus on the Mississippi River.

DEPARTMENT OF KENTUCKY FEBRUARY 10, 1865–JUNE 5, 1866

The Department of Kentucky was re-created February 10, 1865 from the District of Kentucky, Department of the Cumberland, and it consisted of the state of Kentucky. John M. Palmer was assigned command, with headquarters at Louisville. Palmer assumed command February 22, 1865, at which time he relieved Stephen G. Burbridge from command of the District of Kentucky.

March 24, 1865, Jeffersonville and New Albany in Indiana were included in the Department of Kentucky.

In the post-war reorganization of the military divisions and departments of the army on June 27, 1865, the Department of Kentucky was reaffirmed. It was to have the same boundaries, and John M. Palmer was assigned command. On the same date, the Department of Kentucky was assigned to the Military Division of the Tennessee.

The Department of Kentucky was discontinued June 5, 1866, when it was merged into the Department of the Cumberland.

COMMANDERS OF THE DEPARTMENT OF KENTUCKY

John M. Palmer	February 18, 1865 to June 21, 1865
Edward H. Hobson	June 21, 1865 to June 27, 1865
John M. Palmer	June 27, 1865 to April 13, 1866
Jefferson C. Davis	April 13, 1866 to June 5, 1866

TROOPS IN THE DEPARTMENT OF KENTUCKY

When the Department of Kentucky was constituted in February 1865, the troops within its limits were organized as follows:

First Division, Edward H. Hobson
Second Division, Hugh Ewing
Newport Barracks, Sidney Burbank
District of Western Kentucky, Solomon Meredith

The troops of First Division were not organized as a field force, but were assigned at the following posts: Campbellsville, Camp Nelson, Covington, Frankfort, Lexington, Louisa, Mount Sterling, New

Castle, and Paris. James F. Wade was in temporary command of the division while Hobson was in command of the department.

Second Division consisted of a Second Brigade, commanded by Walter S. Babcock, and many unbrigaded troops, largely of the United States Veteran Reserve Corps. The posts occupied by troops of Second Division were as follows: Bowling Green, Hopkinsville, Louisville, Owensboro, and, later, New Albany, Indiana. Jeffersonville, Indiana was included in the post of Louisville after March 24, 1865. Eli H. Murray relieved Ewing in command of the division March 2, 1865.

The troops in the District of Western Kentucky were principally stationed at the following posts: Columbus (commanded by Stephen G. Hicks), Paducah (commanded by Joshua J. Guppey), and Smithland. Caleb L. Carlton relieved Meredith in command of the district May 21, 1865; and he, in turn, was relieved by Stephen G. Hicks June 15, 1865.

On March 2, 1865, the Second Military District was created in the Department of Kentucky. Eli H. Murray assumed command March 3, relieving Hugh Ewing. The district was organized March 9 from the Second Division, Department of Kentucky as follows:

Eastern Division, Second Military District. This division consisted of the counties of Warren, Muhlenberg, Todd, and Logan, and that part of Simpson County lying west of the Louisville and Nashville Railroad. Oliver H. P. Carey was assigned command, with headquarters at Bowling Green. Troops in the division were responsible for the protection of the Memphis Branch of the Louisville and Nashville Railroad.

Western Division, Second Military District. This division consisted of the counties on the Ohio River from the mouth of the Salt River to the mouth of the Cumberland River. John H. Ward was assigned command, with headquarters at Owensboro.

Southern Division, Second Military District. This division consisted of the counties of Christian, Hopkins, Caldwell, and those parts of the counties of Lyon and Trigg lying east of the Cumberland River.

Lewis Wolfley was assigned command, with headquarters at Hopkinsville.

Walter S. Babcock, whose headquarters was at Bowling Green, was assigned command of the Defenses of the Louisville and Nashville Railroad, which extended from Louisville to the boundary between Simpson and Warren counties, about fifteen miles south of Bowling Green.

On April 8, 1865, the organization of the Second Military District was changed as follows: The designation of Carey's Eastern Division was changed to First Brigade, Second Division, Department of Kentucky; the designation of Wolfley's Southern Division was changed to Second Brigade, Second Division, Department of Kentucky; and the designation of Ward's Western Division was changed to Third Brigade, Second Division, Department of Kentucky. On April 27, the counties of Edmonson and Butler were added to First Brigade, Second Division.

DEPARTMENT OF LOUISIANA AND TEXAS

In the reorganization of the military divisions and departments of the army June 27, 1865, the Department of Louisiana and Texas was created to consist of the states of Louisiana and Texas. Edward R. S. Canby was assigned command, with headquarters at New Orleans. The department was included in the Military Division of the Gulf.

On July 20, 1865, the department was divided into districts as follows:

Eastern District of Louisiana. This district consisted of that part of the state of Louisiana east of the Mississippi River; that part of the state included between the Mississippi River and the Atchafalaya River; and the posts along the line from Brashear City by way of New Iberia to Washington. Thomas W. Sherman was assigned command, with headquarters at New Orleans.

Western District of Louisiana. This district consisted of the remainder of the state, and the posts in northeastern Texas that were held by troops from western Louisiana. John P. Hawkins was assigned command, with headquarters at Alexandria.

Eastern District of Texas. The Eastern District of Texas was defined as consisting of that part of the state of Texas east of the Brazos River and the Navasota River; and of the meridian of the town of Springfield, on the Navasota River, except the posts included in the Western District of Louisiana. Joseph A. Mower was assigned command, with headquarters at Houston.

Central District of Texas. The Central District of Texas consisted of that part of the state between the Nueces River and the western boundary of the Eastern District of Texas, as defined above. David S. Stanley was assigned command, with headquarters at Victoria.

Western District of Texas. This district consisted of that part of Texas lying between the Rio Grande River and the Nueces River. Frederick Steele was assigned command, with headquarters at Brownsville, Texas.

In the latter part of 1863, troops of Thirteenth Corps, Department of the Gulf arrived near the mouth of the Rio Grande River, and then established posts on the coast of Texas. When Thirteenth Corps was discontinued July 20, 1865, the remaining troops were formed into a division and assigned to Frederick Steele for service in the Western District of Texas.

During May and June 1865, Twenty-Fifth Corps, under the command of Godfrey Weitzel, was transferred from City Point, Virginia to Texas, where it joined the Federal Army of Occupation. It was stationed at Indianola, Brazos Santiago, Corpus Christi, and other points in Texas.

see, which included the Combined Districts of West Tennessee and Vicksburg. Then, on November 7, 1864, Sixteenth Corps was discontinued, and the troops on the east bank of the Mississippi River were detached from their various corps and departments and directed to report to Edward R. S. Canby, commander of the Military Division of West Mississippi.

The Department of Mississippi was created November 28, 1864, to consist of the state of Mississippi and that part of Tennessee west of the Tennessee River. Napoleon J. T. Dana assumed command December 8 (assigned November 28). When the Department of Mississippi was created, it was assigned to the Military Division of West Mississippi.

January 17, 1865, the department was redefined to consist of the state of Mississippi, except such part of the state as might be occupied by troops of George H. Thomas' Department of the Cumberland, and that part of Tennessee west of the Tennessee River.

The department was again redefined February 10, 1865, and was to include that part of Mississippi occupied by United States troops of the Military Division of West Mississippi on the Mississippi River. On March 1, headquarters of the department was established at Vicksburg (ordered February 10).

May 14, 1865, Gouverneur K. Warren assumed command of the Department of Mississippi (assigned May 1).

The Military Division of West Mississippi was abolished May 17, 1865, and the Department of the Gulf was constituted to consist of the states of Louisiana, Mississippi, Alabama, Florida, and the District of Key West and Tortugas. On June 3, 1865, the state of Mississippi became the District of Mississippi, Department of the Gulf. Peter J. Osterhaus was assigned command of the district, with headquarters at Jackson.

DEPARTMENT OF MISSISSIPPI
NOVEMBER 28, 1864–
MAY 17, 1865

October 15, 1864, Napoleon J. T. Dana assumed command of Sixteenth Corps, Army of the Tennes-

COMMANDERS OF THE
DEPARTMENT OF MISSISSIPPI

| Napoleon J. T. Dana | December 8, 1864 to May 14, 1865 |

Gouverneur K. Warren   May 14, 1865 to May 17, 1865

DISTRICTS IN THE DEPARTMENT OF MISSISSIPPI

District of Natchez. The post and defenses of Natchez were included in the District of Vicksburg, Department of Mississippi until January 3, 1865. At that time the District of Natchez was constituted to include the country east and west of the Mississippi River south of the thirty-second degree of latitude and north of the mouth of the Red River. John W. Davidson was assigned command, with headquarters at Natchez. Davidson remained in command until June 3, 1865.

January 6, 1865, Mason Brayman was assigned command of that part of the District of Natchez west of the Mississippi River. Brayman's headquarters was at Vidalia, Louisiana, and his command was designated as the Sub-district of Vidalia, District of Natchez. Willard C. Earle succeeded Brayman in command of the sub-district on March 3 (assigned February 26).

The principal posts in the district were Natchez, Fort McPherson (at Natchez), and Rodney in Mississippi, and Vidalia and Bullitt's Bayou in Louisiana.

In addition to a number of unassigned regiments in the district, a Provisional Brigade, District of Natchez was organized January 7, 1865. Commanders of the brigade were as follows: Frederick W. Moore, January 7–January 27, 1865; Simon M. Preston, January 27–March 3, 1865; Joseph Karge, March 3–March 6, 1865; and Bernard G. Farrar. Farrar commanded the post of Natchez, in addition to the Provisional Brigade.

District of Vicksburg. The District of Vicksburg was created in the Department of the Tennessee April 12, 1864. At that time the troops in the district belonged to Seventeenth Corps, Army of the Tennessee, and for a time the district was reported as a part of Seventeenth Corps. On October 15, Napoleon J. T. Dana assumed command of Sixteenth Corps, Army of the Tennessee, which included the Combined Districts of West Tennessee and Vicks-

burg. Sixteenth Corps was discontinued November 7, and the troops on the east bank of the Mississippi River were detached from their various corps and departments and were ordered to report to Edward R. S. Canby, commander of the Military Division of West Mississippi. Then, on November 28, the District of Vicksburg was transferred to the newly created Department of Mississippi.

Dana remained in command of the Combined Districts of West Tennessee and Vicksburg until December 8, 1864, and then assumed command of the Department of Mississippi. Cadwallader C. Washburn was assigned command of the post and district of Vicksburg November 20, 1864. By an order of February 6, 1865, Washburn was relieved from duty in the Department of Mississippi, and on February 11, he relinquished command of the District of Vicksburg to Morgan L. Smith. On February 22, Washburn was ordered to report to George H. Thomas, commander of the Department of the Cumberland, for assignment to the District of Vicksburg. Then, on February 27, Washburn again turned over the command of the district to Morgan L. Smith. Smith remained in command of the District of Vicksburg until June 22, 1865.

The principal posts in the district were Vicksburg, Natchez, and Davis Bend. The District of Natchez, however, was constituted January 3, 1865, and this removed the post of Natchez from the District of Vicksburg.

When Morgan L. Smith assumed command of the post and defenses of Vicksburg, the troops of his command consisted of the following:

First Division, District of Vicksburg, John P. Hawkins
  First Brigade, Frederick M. Crandall
  Second Brigade, Hiram Scofield

Note. Hawkins' division consisted of regiments of United States Colored Troops.

Maltby's Brigade, Jasper A. Maltby
Reserve Artillery, William H. Bolton
Enrolled Militia, George C. McKee
Post and Defenses of Natchez, Mason Brayman

Note. The troops under Brayman's command consisted of six unbrigaded infantry regiments, three of which were regiments of United States Colored Troops; six companies of the 5th Illinois Cavalry; one battery of heavy artillery; and one battery of light artillery. January 3, 1865, the post of Natchez was transferred to the

District of Natchez, which was constituted on that date (see above).

February 8, 1865, Hawkins left Vicksburg with his division for New Orleans, where he reported to Edward R. S. Canby, commander of the Military Division of West Mississippi, and later joined the land force that conducted operations against Mobile and Mobile Bay.

March 28, 1865, George W. Jackson was assigned command of the cavalry force of the District of Vicksburg, which consisted of three regiments.

District of West Tennessee. The District of West Tennessee was constituted in the Department of the Tennessee January 15, 1863, and it remained in existence until October 15, 1864, when Napoleon J. T. Dana assumed command of Sixteenth Corps, which included the Combined Districts of West Tennessee and Vicksburg. Sixteenth Corps was discontinued November 7, 1864, and all troops on the east bank of the Mississippi were detached from their various departments and corps and ordered to report to Edward R. S. Canby, commander of the Military Division of West Mississippi.

The Department of Mississippi was created November 28, 1864, and on that date the District of West Tennessee was transferred to the Department of Mississippi. Headquarters of the district was at Memphis, Tennessee. By an order of February 10, 1865, that part of Tennessee west of the Tennessee River was transferred from the Department of the Mississippi to the Department of the Cumberland. On the same date, the Department of Kentucky was constituted, and the state of Kentucky was transferred to that department.

The principal posts in the district were Memphis, Tennessee; Columbus, Kentucky; and Cairo, Illinois.

In December 1864 the forces in the District of West Tennessee consisted of the following:

Post and Defenses of Memphis, James C. Veatch
   First Brigade, George B. Hoge
   First Brigade, United States Colored Troops, Frank A. Kendrick
   Fort Pickering (United States Colored Troops), Ignatz G. Kappner

Post of Columbus, Kentucky, James N. McArthur
Post of Cairo, Illinois, Ezra T. Sprague
Enrolled Militia, Charles W. Dustan
Light Artillery, Raphael G. Rombauer

Cavalry Division, Benjamin H. Grierson

Note. For additional information about the cavalry in the District of West Tennessee, see below, Cavalry Forces of the Department of Mississippi.

January 7, 1865, the post and defenses of Memphis were reorganized as follows:

First Brigade, George B. Hoge
Second Brigade, Frank A. Kendrick
Garrison of Fort Pickering, Ignatz G. Kappner

In February 1865, the District of West Tennessee was reorganized as follows:

Post and Defenses of Memphis, Augustus L. Chetlain
   Second Brigade, Frank A. Kendrick
   Fort Pickering, Ignatz G. Kappner
   Unassigned regiments

Note 1. First Brigade was broken up in February 1865, and the regiments were then listed as unassigned.
Note 2. In late February 1865, Second Brigade was en route to New Orleans.

Post of Columbus, James N. McArthur
Enrolled Militia, Milton T. Williamson
Light Artillery, Raphael G. Rombauer

The commanders of the District of West Tennessee were as follows:

Napoleon J. T. Dana	November 20, 1864 to December 8, 1864
James C. Veatch	December 8, 1864 to February 3, 1865
Benjamin S. Roberts	February 3, 1865 to March 4, 1865

Note. Dana assumed command of the Department of Mississippi December 8, 1864.

CAVALRY FORCES OF THE DEPARTMENT OF MISSISSIPPI

By an order of November 9, 1864, the Cavalry Corps, Military Division of the Mississippi was organized into eight divisions. First Division, Cavalry Corps, District of West Tennessee, Department of the Tennessee was designated as Fifth Division, Cavalry Corps, Military Division of the Mississippi and was placed under the command of Edward Hatch. This division was then ordered to join the corps in Middle Tennessee and left the District of West Tennessee.

Second Division, Cavalry Corps, District of West Tennessee, commanded by Edward F. Winslow, was designated as Fourth Division, Cavalry Corps, Military Division of the Mississippi, and was assigned to Benjamin F. Grierson. In October 1864, Winslow, with his division, had been ordered to Missouri during Sterling Price's Missouri Expedition, and he was still on that mission when assigned to Wilson's Cavalry Corps. Only a part of Winslow's force returned to West Tennessee and reported to Grierson. December 13, 1864, Grierson was relieved from command by Emory Upton, who was ordered to collect the scattered regiments of Fourth Division and take them to Louisville, Kentucky. The cavalry forces remaining in West Tennessee during the period December 1864–March 1, 1865 were designated as Cavalry Division, District of West Tennessee but were also referred to as Cavalry Division, Department of Mississippi.

December 21, 1864, Grierson left Memphis in command of an expedition to destroy the Mobile and Ohio Railroad. He marched eastward to threaten Corinth, Mississippi, then moved south along the railroad through Tupelo to Verona, where he surprised a camp of Nathan B. Forrest's dismounted cavalry on Christmas night. Grierson quickly dispersed this force and destroyed 300 army wagons, 4,000 new carbines, two trains of cars, large amounts of ammunition, and quartermaster and commissary stores before moving on.

Grierson then passed through Okolona, destroying the track as he went, and arrived at Egypt Station on the morning of December 28, 1864. There he found a considerable force of the enemy and immediately attacked. At that time, two trains loaded with infantry under the command of Franklin Gardner were approaching the station, but Grierson threw out a part of his command to prevent Gardner's troops from joining the garrison. After a fight of about two hours, the Union troopers carried the stockade by assault and captured about 500 men. Confederate General Samuel J. Gholson was killed in the attack. Grierson then destroyed a train of fourteen cars, and marched on with his prisoners to the southwest to Winona and Grenada on the Mis-

sissippi Central Railroad. After destroying a portion of this railroad, he arrived at Vicksburg January 5, 1865. He returned with his command to Memphis four days later. The organization of Grierson's command on this expedition was as follows:

Cavalry Division, Department of Mississippi, Benjamin H. Grierson
First Brigade, Joseph Karge
Second Brigade, Edward F. Winslow
Third Brigade, Embury D. Osband

Grierson was relieved from duty in the Department of Mississippi, and January 15, 1864, Osband was assigned command of the Cavalry Division.

January 25, 1865, the Cavalry Division was reorganized as follows:

Cavalry Division, Department of Mississippi, Embury D. Osband
First Brigade, John P. C. Shanks
Second Brigade, Hamilton B. Dox
Third Brigade, Otto Funke

Note 1. Shanks commanded the division temporarily in January 1865.
Note 2. Hasbrouck Davis succeeded Dox in command of Second Brigade in February 1865.

Osband received orders to move out on an expedition to drive off guerrilla and partisan bands that were operating in the upper parishes of Louisiana and in southeastern Arkansas between the Mississippi River and the Washita River. These forces were commanded by Isaac F. Harrison and a Captain Lee. The expedition left Memphis on transports during the evening of January 26, 1865, and on the morning of January 28 landed at Eunice, Arkansas. The cavalry then scoured the country as far as the Washita and drove the enemy bands beyond the river. Osband then marched back to Gaines' Landing, Arkansas, where he reembarked his command and returned to Memphis on February 11.

After the District of West Tennessee, to which Osband's Cavalry Division then belonged, was transferred to the Department of the Cumberland March 1, 1865, the cavalry of the Department of Mississippi consisted only of George W. Jackson's Cavalry Brigade of the Post and Defenses of Vicksburg, District of Vicksburg. Jackson was assigned command March 28.

DEPARTMENT OF MISSISSIPPI
JUNE 27, 1865–
AUGUST 6, 1866

In the reorganization of the military divisions and departments of the army June 27, 1865, the Department of Mississippi was re-created to consist of the state of Mississippi. On the same date, the department was assigned to the newly created Military Division of the Gulf. On July 14, Henry W. Slocum assumed command of the department (assigned June 27), with headquarters at Vicksburg, Mississippi.

July 17, 1865, the department was divided into districts as follows:

Western District of Mississippi. The Western District of Mississippi included the following counties of the state: Bolivar, Sunflower, Washington, Yazoo, Issaquena, and Warren. Jasper A. Maltby was assigned command of the district, with headquarters at Vicksburg. The Western District was designated as a separate brigade.

Southern District of Mississippi. The Southern District of Mississippi included all of that part of the state of Mississippi south of the northern line of the following counties: Claiborne, Copiah, Lawrence, Covington, Jones, and Wayne. John W. Davidson was assigned command of the district, with headquarters at Natchez. The Southern District was designated as a division.

Northern District of Mississippi. The Northern District of Mississippi consisted of all of that part of the state of Mississippi that was not included in the Western and Southern districts. Peter J. Osterhaus was assigned command of the district, with headquarters at Jackson. The Northern District was designated as a division.

DEPARTMENT OF THE
MISSISSIPPI (HALLECK)

The Department of the Mississippi was created March 11, 1862 to secure better cooperation among Don Carlos Buell's Army of the Ohio; Ulysses S. Grant's Army of the District of West Tennessee, then operating along the Tennessee River; and John Pope's Army of the Mississippi, operating on the Mississippi near New Madrid, Missouri. The department was in existence during the Battle of Shiloh and the subsequent advance of Halleck's army on Corinth, Mississippi.

When created, the Department of the Mississippi consisted of the territory of David Hunter's former Department of Kansas, Halleck's Department of the Missouri, and that part of the Department of the Ohio lying west of a north-south line through Knoxville, Tennessee. Halleck assumed command of the department March 13, 1862 (assigned April 11), with headquarters at Saint Louis, Missouri. The Department of Kansas was re-created May 2, 1862, and this removed from the Department of the Mississippi the state of Kansas, the Indian Territory west of Arkansas, and the territories of Nebraska, Colorado, and Dakota.

On June 8, 1862, that part of Kentucky and Tennessee east of the north-south line through Knoxville was added to the Department of the Mississippi. At that time the department consisted of the states of Missouri, Minnesota, Iowa, Wisconsin, Indiana, Illinois, Kentucky, Tennessee, Arkansas, and all of the states of Michigan and Ohio lying west of a north-south line through Knoxville, Tennessee.

On July 16, 1862, Halleck was called to Washington, D.C., as general in chief of the army, but no one was officially assigned to command the Department of the Mississippi. Grant, as the senior officer in the department and commander of the District of West Tennessee, became, in a practical sense, commander of the department and reported directly to Halleck.

Also on July 16, 1862, the District of the Ohio, Department of the Mississippi (see below, Districts in the Department of the Mississippi) was removed from control of the Department of the Mississippi when Halleck became general in chief of the army, and thereafter was under direct orders from Halleck. The department was reduced in size August 19, 1862 when the Department of the Ohio was re-created, and the following territory was transferred from the Department of the Mississippi to the Department of the Ohio: the states of Illinois, Indiana, and Wisconsin; that part of Ohio and Michigan west of a north-south line through Knoxville; and that part of Kentucky east of the Tennessee River, including Cumberland Gap and the troops operating in the vicinity. The department then consisted of the states of Missouri, Minnesota, Iowa, and Arkansas; all of Kentucky west of the Tennessee River; and all of Tennessee, excluding Cumberland Gap and the troops operating in the vicinity.

When the Department of the Northwest was created September 6, 1862, Iowa and Minnesota were transferred from the Department of the Mississippi and included in the Department of the Northwest. The Department of the Mississippi then consisted of the states of Missouri and Arkansas, all of Kentucky west of the Tennessee River, and the state of Tennessee.

The Department of the Mississippi was discontinued September 19, 1862, and the states of Arkansas and Missouri were transferred to the newly created Department of the Missouri. The parts of Kentucky and Tennessee formerly belonging to the Department of the Mississippi remained in Buell's District of the Ohio, which then belonged to no department.

DISTRICTS IN THE DEPARTMENT OF THE MISSISSIPPI

District of Arkansas. The Army of the Southwest, which was operating in eastern Arkansas under Samuel R. Curtis and Frederick Steele during the period July–September 1862, was sometimes called the District of Arkansas, Department of the Mississippi. Headquarters of the district was at Helena, Arkansas. For additional information, see Army of the Southwest.

District of Cairo. The troops which Ulysses S. Grant organized and led against Fort Henry and Fort Donelson in February 1862 were from the District of Cairo, Department of the Missouri. For additional information, see Department of the Missouri, November 9, 1861–March 11, 1862, Districts in the Department of the Missouri, District of Cairo.

When the Department of the Mississippi was created March 11, 1862, the District of Cairo became a district in that department. Mississippi County in Missouri was attached to the District of Cairo June 1, 1862. William K. Strong commanded the district from March 21 to August 12, 1862.

July 15, 1862, the District of Cairo was included in the District of West Tennessee. For further information, see District of West Tennessee, District of Cairo, under Miscellaneous Organizations.

The principal posts in the district were Cairo in Illinois and Paducah, Columbus, and Hickman in Kentucky.

District of Central Missouri. This district was in existence in the Department of the Missouri, and was under the command of James Totten. On June 1, 1862, the District of Missouri, Department of the Mississippi was created to consist of most of the state of Missouri, and the District of Central Mississippi was included within its limits. For additional information, see below, District of Missouri.

District of Columbus. Columbus, Kentucky was evacuated by Confederate troops soon after Grant captured Fort Donelson, and on March 4, 1862 it was occupied by United States forces from William T. Sherman's command at Paducah, Kentucky. These belonged to the District of Cairo, Department of the Missouri. On March 11, when the Department of the Mississippi was created, the post of Columbus became a part of the District of Cairo. During April and May 1862 the troops at Columbus were known as United States Forces at Columbus, and also as the District of Columbus, and Isaac F. Quinby was in command.

The counties of New Madrid and Pemiscot in Missouri were attached to the District of Columbus June 1, 1862, and soon thereafter the district was merged into the District of Mississippi. For further information, see below, District of Mississippi.

District of Jackson. For information about the District of Jackson, see District of West Tennessee, District of Jackson, under Miscellaneous Organizations.

District of Kansas. The District of Kansas was constituted March 19, 1862 and included the territory that before the creation of the Department of the Mississippi belonged to the Department of Kansas. An exception was the troops in the field under George W. Deitzler at Fort Scott, near the southwestern frontier of Missouri, which were ordered to report to Samuel R. Curtis in Arkansas. James W. Denver was assigned command of the district March 19 and assumed command April 1, with headquarters at Fort Leavenworth, Kansas. Samuel D. Sturgis relieved Denver April 10, and remained in command of the district until May 5.

April 16, 1862, James Craig was assigned command of the Overland Mail Route that ran across the district. Craig's headquarters was at Fort Leavenworth, but was moved to Laramie, Nebraska Territory in May 1862.

The District of Kansas was merged into the Department of Kansas when the latter was re-created May 2, 1862.

District of Mississippi (also called District of the Mississippi). This district was in existence as the District of the Mississippi in the Department of the Missouri, and it consisted of that part of the state of Missouri lying between the Saint Francis River and the Mississippi River. John Pope was in command of the district.

The forces in the district consisted of Pope's Army of the Mississippi, which was operating against New Madrid and Island No. 10 during the period February 28–April 8, 1862. After the capture of Island No. 10, Pope moved with his army to Hamburg, Tennessee, where he arrived April 21. He then joined Halleck's forces for an advance against Corinth, Mississippi.

When Pope left the Mississippi River with his army, he left James R. Slack with his First Brigade, Third Division to garrison Island No. 10, Tiptonville, and New Madrid. Slack's command was designated as the District of New Madrid.

The counties of New Madrid and Pemiscot in Missouri were attached to the District of Columbus, Department of the Mississippi June 1, 1862, and shortly thereafter the District of Columbus was merged into the District of Mississippi. Isaac F. Quinby was assigned command of the District of Mississippi, with headquarters at Columbus, Kentucky. Quinby also assumed responsibility for New Madrid in Missouri; Island No. 10 in the Mississippi River; and Humboldt in Tennessee.

The District of Mississippi was included in the District of West Tennessee July 16, 1862. For further information, see District of West Tennessee, under Miscellaneous Organizations.

Troops in the District of Mississippi. The troops in the District of Mississippi consisted essentially of the following: the 54th and 62nd Illinois regiments from the District of Cairo; 2nd Illinois Cavalry and five companies of 6th Illinois Cavalry from the District of Cairo; Slack's First Brigade, Third Division, Army of the Mississippi; the 5th Missouri Infantry from the Department of the Missouri; and the 1st Kansas and 12th Kansas regiments, and the 13th Wisconsin Regiment from the Department of Kansas.

In May 1862, Robert B. Mitchell was in command at Fort Riley in the Department of Kansas, with the following troops: 1st Kansas, 12th Wisconsin, and 13th Wisconsin infantry regiments; the 7th Kansas Cavalry; and Stephen J. Carpenter's 8th Battery, Wisconsin Light Artillery, and George S. Hollister's Kansas Battery. Mitchell and his command were transferred to Columbus, Kentucky May 18–June 2, 1862, and George W. Deitzler, commanding the forces in southeastern Kansas, was also transferred to Columbus.

It is difficult to determine the exact organization of the troops in the District of Mississippi. From June 1862, many of the troops were on the line of the Mobile and Ohio Railroad, and they appear to have been concentrated at Trenton, Tennessee. Some of the correspondence bears the heading "Central Army of the Mississippi," and this appears to have been the designation of the forces in the District of Mississippi, and which later became the "Central Division" of the district. Isaac F. Quinby commanded the district and presumably also the Central Division. From the correspondence and orders of the period, it is known that Robert B. Mitchell commanded First Brigade, First Division and George W. Deitzler commanded Second Brigade, First Division of the district, but no commander of First Division is given (possibly Quinby). Deitzler, whose command was known as United States Forces at Trenton, Tennessee, has also been noted as commanding First Brigade, Second Division of the district. It is also known that brigade commanders reported directly to Quinby.

In June 1862, the troops at Columbus, Kentucky became the Central Division of the Mississippi, and Grenville M. Dodge was assigned command, with headquarters at Trenton. For additional information, see District of West Tennessee, under Miscellaneous Organizations.

District of Missouri. The District of Missouri was created June 1, 1862 to consist of the state of Missouri, except the county of Mississippi, which was in the District of Cairo, and the counties of New Madrid and Pemiscot, which were in the District of Columbus. John M. Schofield was assigned command, with headquarters at Saint Louis. Schofield remained in command until September 26, 1862.

On June 4, 1862, the district was organized into divisions as follows:

Central Division. The Central Division consisted of that part of the state of Missouri lying south of the Missouri River, west of the Gasconade River, and north of the northern line of Dallas County. James Totten was assigned command of the division, with headquarters at Jefferson City. Ben Loan relieved Totten in command August 25, 1862, and remained in command until November 2.

Northeastern Division. The Northeastern Division was created by a change in designation of the District of Northeast Missouri. For a description of the district, see below, District of Northeast Missouri. John McNeil was assigned command of the district, with headquarters at Palmyra, Missouri.

On August 2, 1862, that part of the Saint Louis Division north of the Missouri River was added to the Northeastern Division, and Lewis Merrill was assigned command. Merrill remained in command until November 2.

Northwestern Division. The Northwestern Division was created by a change in designation of the District of Northwest Missouri. For a description of the district, see below, District of Northwest Missouri. Ben Loan was assigned command, and he was succeeded by Willard P. Hall August 25, 1862.

Southwestern Division. The Southwestern Division consisted of that part of the state of Missouri lying south of the northern line of Dallas County and west of the Gasconade River and of the Big North Fork or White River. Egbert B. Brown was assigned command, with headquarters at Springfield. He was succeeded by James Totten August 27, 1862.

The Southwestern Division became the Fourth Brigade, Missouri State Militia in August 1862.

Saint Louis Division. The Saint Louis Division consisted of the territory of the District of Missouri not included in the above-mentioned divisions, except the Camp of Instruction at Benton Barracks. Lewis Merrill was assigned command of the district, with headquarters at Saint Louis.

On August 7, 1862, that part of the Saint Louis Division north of the Missouri River was transferred to the Northeastern Division. Merrill was assigned command of the Northeastern Division, and was succeeded in command of the Saint Louis Division by John W. Davidson August 7.

Rolla Division. In July 1862, John M. Glover was in command of a small force of the District of Missouri consisting of infantry, artillery, and cavalry. Glover's command was known as the Rolla Division, and his headquarters was at Rolla.

District of New Madrid. For information about this district, see District of Mississippi, above.

District of North Missouri. The District of North Missouri was in existence as a district of the Department of the Missouri (see Department of the Missouri, November 9, 1861–March 11, 1862, District of North Missouri). On March 12, 1862, the day after the order creating the Department of the Mississippi was issued, the District of North Missouri was divided to form the District of Northwest Missouri and the District of Northeast Missouri. For information about these two districts, see below.

District of Northeast Missouri. The District of Northeast Missouri was formed March 12, 1862 from a part of the former District of North Missouri. It consisted of that part of the state of Missouri north of the northern boundary of Randolph County and east of the eastern boundary of Linn County. John M. Glover was assigned command, with headquarters at Palmyra. June 1, 1862, the District of Missouri was created, and on June 4, the District of

Northeast Missouri was redesignated as Northeastern Division, District of Missouri.

District of Northwest Missouri. The District of Northwest Missouri was formed March 12, 1862 from a part of the former District of North Missouri. It consisted of that part of the state of Missouri north of the Missouri River and west of the eastern boundary of Linn County. Ben Loan was assigned command, with headquarters at Saint Joseph.

June 1, 1862 the District of Missouri was created, and on June 4 the District of West Missouri was designated as Northwestern Division, District of Missouri.

District of the Ohio. The District of the Ohio was created March 19, 1862 to consist of that part of the Department of the Ohio that was included in the Department of the Mississippi. Don Carlos Buell, commander of the Army of the Ohio, was assigned command.

The district was redefined June 12, 1862 as consisting of those parts of the states of Kentucky and Tennessee east of the Tennessee River, excepting Forts Henry and Donelson, and such portions of northern Alabama and Georgia that might be occupied by troops of the Department of the Mississippi.

On July 16, 1862, when Halleck departed for Washington to become general in chief of the army, the District of the Ohio was removed from the control of the commander of the Department of the Mississippi, and then Buell reported directly to Halleck in Washington. Buell remained in command of the district until October 24, 1862. For further information, see District of the Ohio, under Miscellaneous Organizations.

District of Saint Louis. The District of Saint Louis was originally created as a district of the Department of the Missouri, and it was commanded by John M. Schofield. The territory included in the district was increased March 12, 1862 by the order creating the districts of Northeastern and Northwestern Missouri from the Northern District of Missouri. The transfer to the District of Saint Louis consisted of that part of the Northern District of Missouri south of the northern boundary of Randolph County and east of the eastern boundary of Linn County.

The District of Missouri was created June 1, 1862, and on June 4, the designation of the District of Saint Louis was changed to Saint Louis Division, District of Missouri. Schofield remained in command of the district until April 10, 1862 and was then relieved by Lewis Merrill.

District of Southeast Missouri. The District of Southeast Missouri was originally formed as a part of the Department of the Missouri, and was under the command of Frederick Steele. On June 4, 1862, when the designation of the Saint Louis District was changed to the Saint Louis Division, District of the Missouri, the District of Southeast Missouri was included in the Saint Louis Division. Steele was in command of the district from March 11 to June 4, 1862, but on May 2 he was placed under the orders of Samuel R. Curtis, commander of the Army of the Southwest. For additional information, see Army of the Southwest.

District of Southwest Missouri. The District of Southwest Missouri was originally formed as a part of the Department of the Missouri, and was under the command of Samuel R. Curtis. June 4, 1862, the designation of the District of Southwest Missouri was changed to Southwestern Division, District of Missouri.

District of West Tennessee. When the District of West Tennessee was first formed, it was not a part of any department until it was included in the Department of the Mississippi March 11, 1862. For a description of the district, see District of West Tennessee, under Miscellaneous Organizations.

TROOPS AND OPERATIONS IN THE DEPARTMENT OF THE MISSISSIPPI

When the Department of the Mississippi was constituted March 11, 1862, there were four armies operating within the limits of the department: Don Carlos Buell's Army of the Ohio, which was then near Nashville, Tennessee; Ulysses S. Grant's Army of the District of West Tennessee River (temporarily under Charles F. Smith), which was at that time moving up the Tennessee River from Fort Henry toward Savannah and Pittsburg Landing; John Pope's Army of the District of Mississippi (or Army of the Mississippi), which was on the Mississippi River near New Madrid, Missouri and Island No. 10; and Samuel R. Curtis' Army of the Southwest, which was in northwestern Arkansas, following its victory at Pea Ridge March 6–8. For details of the organization of these armies, see the respective armies.

The divisions of Grant's army were assembled around Pittsburg Landing early in April 1862, and were engaged at the Battle of Shiloh April 6–7. Buell's army, which had been ordered to march from Nashville to Savannah, Tennessee, arrived at Pittsburg Landing, above Savannah, in time to join Grant's army during the second day of the Battle of Shiloh. For details, see Battle of Shiloh, Tennessee.

After the capture of Island No. 10 April 7, 1862, Pope moved his army to Fort Pillow, above Memphis, Tennessee, and upon arriving there he received orders from Halleck on April 17 to proceed to Pittsburg Landing, where he arrived April 21. For details of Pope's operations on the Mississippi River, see Capture of New Madrid, Missouri and Island No. 10, Mississippi River. Thus toward the end of April 1862, the three armies were assembled in the vicinity of Pittsburg Landing.

Halleck, the commander of the Department of the Mississippi, arrived at Pittsburg Landing from Saint Louis April 12, 1862 and assumed personal command of the combined forces, which are generally referred to simply as Halleck's Army or Army of the Department of the Mississippi.

On April 28, 1862, Halleck issued an order for the reorganization of his army in preparation for an advance on Corinth, Mississippi. By this order, the troops under Grant, Buell, and Pope would retain their organizations as three distinct army corps, and were assigned as follows: The Army Corps of the Tennessee, under Grant, was constituted as the Right Wing of the army; the Army Corps of the Ohio, under Buell, was constituted as the Center of the army; and the Army Corps of the Mississippi, under Pope, was constituted as the Left Wing of the army. A Reserve was also formed from detachments of the three corps.

Halleck's order of April 28, 1862 was modified somewhat two days later, when George H. Thomas' First Division was transferred from the Army of the Ohio to the Army of the Tennessee as Seventh Division, and Thomas was assigned command of the Right Wing of the Army. Grant retained command of the District of West Tennessee, including the Army Corps of the Tennessee, but in the ensuing advance on Corinth he was assigned as second-in-command to Halleck.

The Army of the Department of the Mississippi was organized as follows:

RIGHT WING, George H. Thomas

Second Division, Army of the Tennessee, Thomas A. Davies
Fourth Division, Army of the Tennessee, Stephen A. Hurlbut
Fifth Division, Army of the Tennessee, William T. Sherman
Sixth Division, Army of the Tennessee, Thomas J. McKean
Seventh Division, Army of the Tennessee, Thomas W. Sherman

Note. Seventh Division was formerly Thomas' First Division, Army of the Ohio.

CENTER, Don Carlos Buell

Second Division, Army of the Ohio, Alexander McD. McCook
Fourth Division, Army of the Ohio, William Nelson
Fifth Division, Army of the Ohio, Thomas L. Crittenden
Sixth Division, Army of the Ohio, Thomas J. Wood

LEFT WING, John Pope

First Division, Army of the Mississippi, Eleazer A. Paine
Second Division, Army of the Mississippi, David S. Stanley
Third Division, Army of the Mississippi, Schuyler Hamilton
Cavalry Division, Army of the Mississippi, Gordon Granger

RESERVE, John A. McClernand

First Division, Army of the Tennessee, Henry M. Judah
Third Division, Army of the Tennessee, Lewis Wallace
Fifth Division, Army of the Ohio, Thomas L. Crittenden

Note. In the reorganization of Halleck's army after the Battle of Shiloh, Crittenden's division was nominally assigned to McClernand's Reserve. It did not join the

Reserve, however, but served with Buell's army during the advance on Corinth.

After a slow advance of only twenty-two miles in one month, Halleck's army finally arrived before Corinth, Mississippi, which was then evacuated by the Confederates during the night of May 29–30, 1862. Then, on June 10, when the object of Halleck's advance had been accomplished, the order that divided the army into wings was revoked, and Grant, Buell, and Pope resumed command of the armies of the Tennessee, the Ohio, and the Mississippi, respectively. For further information, see Army of the Tennessee, District of West Tennessee; Army of the Ohio (Buell); and Army of the Mississippi (Pope, Rosecrans). For details of the advance on Corinth, see Halleck's Advance on Corinth, Mississippi.

DEPARTMENT OF THE MISSOURI
NOVEMBER 9, 1861–
MARCH 11, 1862

The Department of the Missouri was created November 9, 1861 to consist of the states of Missouri, Iowa, Minnesota, Wisconsin, Illinois, Arkansas, and that part of Kentucky west of the Cumberland River. Henry W. Halleck assumed command November 19 (ordered November 9), with headquarters at Saint Louis, Missouri.

The department was merged into the newly created Department of the Mississippi March 11, 1862, during the movement of Ulysses S. Grant's Army of the District of West Tennessee (temporarily commanded by Charles F. Smith) up the Tennessee River toward Savannah, Tennessee.

DISTRICTS IN THE DEPARTMENT
OF THE MISSOURI

District of Cairo. The District of Southeast Missouri, Department of the Missouri (see below) was redesignated as the District of Cairo, Department of the Missouri December 23, 1861. Ulysses S. Grant was assigned command, with headquarters at Cairo, Illinois. The district consisted of the southern part of Illinois, that part of Kentucky west of the Cumberland River, and the southern counties of Missouri south of Cape Girardeau.

Early in February 1862, Grant left Cairo with an army to attempt the capture of Fort Henry and Fort Donelson, and on February 14, William T. Sherman relieved Grant in command of the district.

February 27, 1862, the Mississippi District (see below) was constituted to include that part of Missouri between the Mississippi River and the Saint Francis River, and thus removed the counties in Missouri from the District of Cairo.

The Department of the Mississippi was created March 11, 1862, and the District of Cairo was not again in the Department of the Missouri.

The principal posts in the district were as follows: Bird's Point and Cape Girardeau in Missouri; Cairo, Mound City, and Shawneetown in Illinois; and Fort Holt, Paducah, and Smithland in Kentucky.

Troops in the District of Cairo. On October 14, 1861, the troops in the District of Southeast Missouri, Western Department were organized into brigades as follows:

First Brigade, John A. McClernand, at Cairo and Mound City, Illinois
Second Brigade, Richard J. Oglesby, at Bird's Point, Missouri
Third Brigade, William H. L. Wallace, at Bird's Point, Missouri
Fourth Brigade, John Cook, at Fort Holt, Kentucky
Fifth Brigade, Joseph B. Plummer, at Cape Girardeau, Missouri

This brigade organization was continued when the District of Southeastern Missouri was merged into the District of Cairo, Department of the Missouri December 23, 1861, although the designations were changed. January 1, 1862, the United States forces at Bird's Point were organized as Second Brigade, under the command of Eleazer A. Paine; the forces at Fort Holt under Cook were designated as Third Brigade; and the forces at Cape Girardeau were designated as Fourth Brigade, under Leonard

F. Ross. Paine was transferred from Paducah, Kentucky to Cairo December 20, 1861, and was assigned command of the United States forces at Bird's Point December 23.

The infantry regiments present in the District of Cairo at the end of December 1861 are given here because many of the regimental commanders rose to higher command later in the war, and their names became well known in the army.

At Bird's Point, Missouri
    8th Illinois, Richard J. Oglesby
    11th Illinois, William H. L. Wallace
    20th Illinois, C. Carroll Marsh
    22nd Illinois, Henry Dougherty
    10th Iowa, Nicholas Perczel

At Cairo, Illinois
    18th Illinois, Michael K. Lawler
    27th Illinois, Napoleon B. Buford
    29th Illinois, James Rearden
    30th Illinois, Philip B. Fouke
    31st Illinois, John A. Logan
    48th Illinois, Isham N. Haynie

At Cape Girardeau, Missouri
    17th Illinois, Leonard F. Ross
    11th Missouri, Joseph B. Plummer

At Fort Holt, Kentucky
    7th Illinois, John Cook
    28th Illinois, Amory K. Johnson

At Mound City, Illinois
    10th Illinois, James D. Morgan

On January 31, 1862, in preparation for an advance against Fort Henry, Tennessee, Grant ordered Charles F. Smith to organize a Second Division from troops at Paducah, Fort Holt, and Smithland. This division was organized as follows:

Second Division, District of Cairo, Charles F. Smith
    First Brigade, John McArthur
    Third Brigade, John Cook
    Fourth Brigade, Jacob G. Lauman

A Third Division of the army was organized under the command of Lewis Wallace during operations at Fort Donelson, but this was composed largely of regiments sent to Grant from Missouri and Kentucky. It was organized as follows:

Third Division, Lewis Wallace
    First Brigade, Charles Cruft
    Second Brigade (attached to Third Brigade)
    Third Brigade, John M. Thayer

In addition to the above, a Third Brigade, District of Cairo, under Eleazer A. Paine, was at Cairo and Mound City; and a Fourth Brigade, District of Cairo, under James D. Morgan, was at Bird's Point.

For details of the organization and operations of the army that Grant led at Fort Henry and Fort Donelson February 6–16, 1862, and which later became the Army of the District of West Tennessee, and still later the Army of the Tennessee, see Capture of Fort Henry and Fort Donelson, Tennessee; and see also Army of the Tennessee, District of West Tennessee.

District of Central Missouri. The District of Central Missouri, Department of the Missouri was created December 3, 1861 to consist of all United States forces serving between the Missouri River and the Osage River. John Pope was assigned command of the district, and remained in command until February 12, 1862, when he was ordered to Commerce, Missouri to organize and command an expedition against New Madrid, Missouri and Island No. 10 in the Mississippi River. James Totten then assumed command of the District of Central Missouri.

The district was discontinued March 11, 1862 when the Department of the Missouri was merged into the Department of the Mississippi.

The principal posts in the district were La Mine Crossing, Jefferson City, Otterville, Sedalia, Boonville, and Lexington. Frederick Steele commanded at Sedalia, Missouri from December 3, 1861 to March 1, 1862, when he was ordered to Pilot Knob, Missouri.

Pope's forces in the District of Central Missouri were sometimes called the Army of Western Missouri, but this generally consisted of the regiments assigned to the various posts of the district. These were frequently formed into brigades, or commands of brigade strength, for various expeditions or other movements. Thus, an expedition to Blackwater Creek December 15–20, 1861 consisted of a First Brigade commanded by Jefferson C. Davis and a Second Brigade commanded by Frederick Steele. January 29, 1862, William H. Worthington was ordered with three regiments from Syracuse and La Mine to Boonville, Missouri; and John M. Thayer, with four regiments from Sedalia and Smithton, was ordered to Jefferson City. February 5, 1862, Alvin P. Hovey led a column of three regiments from Otterville to Jefferson City.

Mississippi District. The Mississippi District was constituted February 27, 1862 to consist of that part of Missouri lying between the Saint Francis River and the Mississippi River. John Pope was assigned command, with headquarters at Commerce. The Department of the Missouri was merged into the Department of the Mississippi March 11, 1862; thus the district was transferred to the latter department.

When Pope arrived at Commerce, he proceeded to organize an army, which he led to New Madrid, and with it and the cooperation of the navy he forced the surrender of New Madrid and Island No. 10 during the period February 28–April 8, 1862. For details of the organization of Pope's army, see Army of the Mississippi (Pope, Rosecrans).

District of North Missouri (also District of Northern Missouri). The District of North Missouri was constituted November 26, 1861 to consist of that part of the state of Missouri north of the Missouri River. Benjamin M. Prentiss, who on September 17 had been assigned command along the Hannibal and Saint Joseph Railroad and the territory to the north of it, was assigned command of the district. His responsibility was to protect the Hannibal and Saint Joseph Railroad and the Northern Missouri Railroad. Prentiss established his headquarters at Quincy, Illinois, and later at Palmyra, Missouri. On December 26, John M. Schofield assumed command along the Northern Missouri Railroad, with headquarters at Warrenton and Wellsville, Missouri. The troops in the district consisted of regiments stationed along the railroads at Macon and Palmyra and at important bridges along the line.

District of Saint Louis. The District of Saint Louis was constituted January 6, 1862 to include the territory bounded by the Missouri River, the Mississippi River, and the Meramec River, including the line of the railroad from Pacific to Rolla as far as Lindsey's Station and a line drawn through that point from the mouth of the Osage River, just west of Jefferson City, to the Meramec River. The Camp of Instruction at Benton Barracks was not included in the district, but was transferred to it on March 6. Schuyler Hamilton was assigned command of the district January 6, 1862, with headquarters at Saint Louis.

The District of Southeastern Missouri was added to the District of Saint Louis March 8, 1862.

The Department of the Missouri was merged into the Department of the Mississippi March 11, 1862, and the District of Saint Louis became a part of the latter department.

District of Southeast Missouri (District of Southeastern Missouri). The District of Southeast Missouri was already in existence as a district in the Western Department when the Department of the Missouri was created. It included the United States forces at Ironton, Jefferson City, and Cape Girardeau in Missouri, and at Cairo, Illinois. On November 9, 1861, when the Department of the Missouri was created, the designation of the district was changed to District of Southeast Missouri, Department of the Missouri. Ulysses S. Grant was assigned command, with headquarters at Cairo.

December 17, 1861, William P. Carlin was assigned command of that part of the state of Missouri east of the Meramec River, exclusive of Bird's Point, which was under Grant's command at Cairo. The District of Cairo was organized from the District of Southeast Missouri on December 23.

The District of Southeastern Missouri was constituted March 1, 1862 to consist of all troops in southeastern Missouri west of the Saint Francis River. Frederick Steele was assigned command, with headquarters at Pilot Knob.

The District of Southeastern Missouri was attached to the District of Saint Louis March 8, 1862, but this change did not interfere with Steele's command.

The principal posts in the district were Cape

Girardeau, New Madrid, Pilot Knob, Fredericktown, Patterson, Ironton, and Centerville.

District of Southwest Missouri (Southwestern District of Missouri). The Southwestern District of Missouri was constituted December 25, 1861 to include that part of the state of Missouri south of the Osage River and west of the Meramec River. Samuel R. Curtis assumed command December 28 (assigned December 25), with headquarters at Rolla, Missouri.

The district was modified January 8, 1862 to conform with the limits set for the District of Saint Louis. The western limit of the District of Saint Louis was defined as a line beginning at the mouth of the Osage River, just west of Jefferson City, and passing through Lindsey's Station on the railroad from Pacific to Rolla, and then on to the Meramec River.

The district was discontinued March 11, 1862, when the Department of the Missouri was merged into the Department of the Mississippi, and the district was thus transferred to the latter department.

The troops commanded by Curtis in the Southwestern District of Missouri were called the Army of the Southwest, and it was this army that fought at the Battle of Pea Ridge, Arkansas March 6–8, 1862. For details, see Army of the Southwest; and see also Battle of Pea Ridge (or Elkhorn Tavern), Arkansas.

District of West Tennessee. On February 1, 1862, the Army of the District of Cairo was organized under Grant for a campaign against Fort Henry and Fort Donelson, which took place February 6–16. On February 14, the District of West Tennessee was constituted, and Grant was assigned command. The geographical limits of the new district were not defined, but it consisted of the troops operating with Grant on the Tennessee River. The district was organized February 17, after the surrender of Fort Donelson, with headquarters at Fort Donelson.

The District of West Tennessee remained in the Department of the Missouri only until March 11, 1862, at which time the department was merged into the newly created Department of the Mississippi. For additional information, see Capture of Fort Henry and Fort Donelson, Tennessee; District of West Tennessee, in section on Miscellaneous Organizations; and also Army of the Tennessee, District of West Tennessee.

TROOPS AND OPERATIONS IN THE DEPARTMENT OF THE MISSOURI

In addition to the troops in the various districts of the Department of the Missouri, there were three major armies organized in the department during this period of its existence, and each took part in an important and successful campaign. These were:

Army of the District of Cairo. This army, which later became the Army of the District of West Tennessee, and then the Army of the Tennessee, has already been noted in the description of the District of Cairo. In February 1862, Ulysses S. Grant led this army against Fort Henry and Fort Donelson, and in April 1862 it was engaged at the Battle of Shiloh. For details of its organization and operations while still in the Department of the Missouri, see Capture of Fort Henry and Donelson, Tennessee.

Army of the Mississippi. In February 1862, John Pope was ordered to Commerce, Missouri to organize an army for the purpose of capturing New Madrid, Missouri and Island No. 10 in the Mississippi River. The army was still operating in the Department of the Missouri when it arrived before New Madrid on March 4, but the department was discontinued March 11, and the army was a part of the Department of the Mississippi when Island No. 10 was captured on April 8. For details, see Capture of New Madrid, Missouri and Island No. 10, Mississippi River.

Army of the Southwest. The Army of the Southwest was organized in the Southwestern District of Missouri in February 1862 under Samuel R. Curtis, and it then marched into Arkansas and defeated a Confederate army at Pea Ridge, or Elkhorn Tavern, March 6–8, 1862, just before the Department of the Missouri was merged into the Department of the Mississippi. For details, see Battle of Pea Ridge (or Elkhorn Tavern), Arkansas.

DEPARTMENT OF THE MISSOURI SEPTEMBER 19, 1862– MAY 27, 1865

The Department of the Missouri was re-created September 19, 1862 to meet a threatened invasion of Missouri by a Confederate army under Thomas C. Hindman. The department consisted of the states of Missouri, Arkansas, and Kansas and the bordering Indian Territory. Alton, Illinois was attached to the Department of the Missouri by an order of the same date. Samuel R. Curtis assumed command September 24 (assigned September 19), with headquarters at Saint Louis.

The territories of Colorado and Nebraska were added to the department October 11, 1862. The northern boundary of Nebraska Territory, which was slightly different from that of the present-day state of Nebraska, ran east on the present-day border of Nebraska to its intersection with the Keya Paha River, then along the Keya Paha River to the Niobrara River, and then eastward along the Niobrara River to the Missouri River.

On January 22, 1863, that part of eastern Arkansas that was occupied by Union troops that were within reach of orders of Ulysses S. Grant, commanding the Department of the Tennessee, was attached to the Department of the Tennessee.

May 13, 1863, John M. Schofield was assigned command of the Department of the Missouri, and he assumed command May 24.

The Department of Kansas was re-created January 1, 1864, and the state of Kansas, the territories of Nebraska and Colorado, the Indian Territory, and the post of Fort Smith, Arkansas were transferred from the Department of the Missouri to the Department of Kansas. The Department of the Missouri then consisted of the states of Missouri and Arkansas, except Fort Smith, and Alton, Illinois.

The department was further reduced January 6, 1864, when the Department of Arkansas was created to consist of the state of Arkansas, and this left only the state of Missouri and the city of Alton, Illinois in the Department of the Missouri.

January 12, 1864, the Northern Department was created, and it included the state of Illinois within its boundaries. Thus, Alton, Illinois was transferred to the Northern Department.

January 30, 1864, William S. Rosecrans assumed command of the Department of the Missouri (assigned January 22). February 15, 1864, Alton, Illinois was again assigned to the Department of the Missouri.

On May 27, 1864, the Department of the Missouri was included in the Military Division of West Mississippi. At that time the department consisted only of the state of Missouri and Alton, Illinois.

December 9, 1864, Grenville M. Dodge assumed command of the Department of the Missouri (assigned December 24), relieving Rosecrans.

The Military Division of the Missouri was created January 30, 1865 to consist of the Department of the Missouri and the Department of the Northwest, and on that date the Department of the Missouri was expanded by the addition of the territory of the former Department of Kansas. The Department of the Missouri then consisted of the states of Missouri and Kansas; Alton, Illinois; and the territories of Nebraska and Colorado, except Fort Garland.

February 17, 1865, the Utah Territory and that part of the Nebraska Territory lying west of the 104th degree west longitude were added to the Department of the Missouri, which then consisted of the states of Missouri and Kansas; Alton, Illinois; Colorado Territory, except Fort Garland; Utah Territory; Nebraska Territory; all of present-day Wyoming, except a small area in the western part; and all of Dakota Territory west of the 104th degree west longitude. Part of Utah was taken from the Department of the Pacific, and the part of Dakota described above was taken from the Department of the Northwest.

In the reorganization of the military divisions and departments of the army June 27, 1865, the Department of the Missouri was redefined to consist of the states of Wisconsin, Minnesota, Iowa, Missouri, and Kansas, and the territories of Nebraska, Dakota, and Montana. The same order assigned the Department of the Missouri to the newly created Military Division of the Mississippi. John Pope was assigned command of the department, with headquarters at

Fort Leavenworth. Pope assume command July 21, 1865, but his headquarters remained at Saint Louis until May 9, 1866.

COMMANDERS OF THE DEPARTMENT OF THE MISSOURI

Samuel R. Curtis	September 24, 1862 to May 24, 1863
John M. Schofield	May 24, 1863 to January 30, 1864
William S. Rosecrans	January 30, 1864 to December 9, 1864
Grenville M. Dodge	December 9, 1864 to July 21, 1865
John Pope	July 21, 1865 to August 20, 1866

The department was continued in existence long after the war, with different boundaries and different commanders.

DISTRICTS IN THE DEPARTMENT OF THE MISSOURI

Numbered Districts. On November 2, 1862, Samuel R. Curtis, the department commander, announced the districts within the department, assigning to each a numbered district designation. These were, with the corresponding name designation, as follows:

1st District	District of Saint Louis
2nd District	District of Rolla
3rd District	District of Southwestern Missouri
4th District	Central District of Missouri
5th District	District of Northwest Missouri
6th District	District of Northeast Missouri
7th District	District of Eastern Arkansas
8th District	District of Western Arkansas
9th District	District of Indian Territory
10th District	District of Kansas
11th District	District of Colorado Territory
12th District	District of Nebraska Territory

District of the Border. The District of the Border was created June 9, 1863 from First Division, Army of the Frontier (see Army of the Frontier). It consisted of the state of Kansas north of the 38th parallel and the two western tiers of counties in Missouri north of the 38th parallel and south of the Missouri River. The counties in Missouri were Jackson, Cass, Bates, Lafayette, Johnson, Henry, and Saint Clair, and the northern part of Vernon. Thomas Ewing, Jr. was assigned command, with headquarters at Kansas City.

On September 23, 1863, the district was reduced in size when the counties of Lafayette, Johnson, and Henry were transferred to the District of Central Missouri.

The entire state of Kansas was included in the district October 19, 1863, but on January 1, 1864 it was transferred to the re-created Department of Kansas.

January 14, 1864, the counties of Bates, Cass, and Jackson and the northern part of Vernon were transferred to the District of Central Missouri, and the District of the Border was discontinued.

The principal posts in the district were as follows: in Kansas, Fort Leavenworth, Fort Larned, Fort Riley, Fort Scott, Lawrence, Olathe, and Humboldt; in Missouri, Kansas City, Pleasant Hill, Westport, Balltown, Drywood, and Warrensburg; and in Colorado Territory, Fort Lyon.

The troops in the district consisted primarily of the garrisons of the posts, but in addition Edward Lynde was in command of a force consisting of the 9th, 11th, and 15th Kansas Cavalry, which was designated as Troops on the Border.

District of Central Missouri (Central District of Missouri). When the Department of the Mississippi was created March 11, 1862, the District of Central Missouri became a district of that department. On June 1, 1862 the District of Missouri, Department of the Mississippi was created, and on June 4 the designation of the District of Central Missouri was changed to Central Division, District of Missouri. The Central Division consisted of that part of Missouri lying south of the Missouri River, west of the Gasconade River, and north of the northern boundary of Dallas County, Missouri, and it was in existence when the Department of the Missouri was re-created September 19, 1862. On September 26, 1862, the designation of Central Division, District of Missouri was changed to District of Central Missouri, Department of the Missouri. The boundaries remained the same as for the Central Division.

June 9, 1863, the two western tiers of counties of Missouri north of the 38th degree north latitude and south of the Missouri River (Jackson, Cass, Bates, Lafayette, Johnson, Henry, and Saint Clair, and the northern part of Vernon) were transferred to the newly created District of the Border (see above).

The counties of Lafayette, Johnson, and Henry, of the District of the Border, were transferred to the District of Central Missouri September 23, 1863, and the counties of Cass, Jackson, and Bates and the northern part of Vernon, also of the District of the Border, were transferred to the District of Central Missouri January 14, 1864.

December 26, 1864, the northern boundary of the District of Southwest Missouri was moved northward to the Osage River, and the southern boundary of the District of Central Missouri then became the Osage River instead of the 38th parallel.

The district was continued in existence until July 10, 1865, and on that date the District of Central Missouri, the District of Saint Louis, the District of Southwest Missouri, and the District of Rolla were consolidated to form the District of Missouri.

The principal posts in the district were Calhoun, Harrisonville, Independence, Jefferson City, Kansas City, Lexington, Osage City, Pleasant Hill, Sedalia, Tipton, and Warrensburg.

The commanders of the District of Central Missouri were as follows:

Benjamin F. Loan	September 26, 1862 to June 9, 1863
Egbert B. Brown	June 9, 1863 to July 24, 1864
Alfred Pleasonton	July 24, 1864 to September 3, 1864
Egbert B. Brown	September 3, 1864 to November 3, 1864
John F. Philips	November 3, 1864 to February 27, 1865
John McNeil	February 27, 1865 to April 24, 1865
Chester Harding, Jr.	April 24, 1865 to June 26, 1865
John L. Beveridge	June 26, 1865 to July 10, 1865

At various times during the period of its existence, the District of Central Missouri was divided into sub-districts. On January 14, 1864, all old sub-districts were discontinued, and the following new sub-districts were defined:

First Sub-district. This sub-district consisted of that part of the district lying east of the Second Sub-district, with headquarters at Jefferson City.

Second Sub-district. This sub-district consisted of the counties in Missouri of Saline, Pettis, and Benton, and that part of Hickory lying north of the northern boundary of Dallas County, with headquarters at Sedalia.

Third Sub-district. This sub-district consisted of the counties of Lafayette, Johnson, Henry, and Saint Clair, with headquarters at Warrensburg.

Fourth Sub-district. This sub-district consisted of the counties in Missouri of Jackson, Cass, and Bates, and the northern part of Vernon County, with headquarters at Kansas City.

In February 1864 there were six sub-districts, described as follows:

First Sub-district. This sub-district consisted of the counties in Missouri of Osage, Cole, Miller, and Camden, and that part of the district east of these counties, with headquarters at Jefferson City.

Second Sub-district. This sub-district consisted of the counties in Missouri of Morgan, Moniteau, and Cooper, with headquarters at Tipton.

Third Sub-district. This sub-district consisted of the counties in Missouri of Saline, Pettis, Benton, and Hickory, with headquarters at Sedalia.

Fourth Sub-district. This sub-district consisted of the counties in Missouri of Johnson and Lafayette, with headquarters at Warrensburg.

Fifth Sub-district. This sub-district consisted of the counties in Missouri of Jackson and Cass, with headquarters at Kansas City.

Sixth Sub-district. This sub-district consisted of the counties in Missouri of Henry, Bates, and Saint Clair, with headquarters at Clinton.

On July 27, 1864, all of the above sub-districts were discontinued, except the Fourth Sub-district, and the District of Central Missouri was again sub-districted, as follows:

First Sub-district. This sub-district was to consist of all of that part of the district lying south of Saline County and east of the eastern line of Johnson, Henry, and Saint Clair counties in Missouri, with headquarters at Jefferson City.

Second Sub-district. This sub-district was to consist of the counties in Missouri of Saline and Lafayette, with headquarters at Lexington.

Third Sub-district. This sub-district was to consist of the counties in Missouri of Johnson, Henry, and Saint Clair, with headquarters at Warrensburg.

Fourth Sub-district. This sub-district was to consist of the counties in Missouri of Jackson, Cass, and Bates, and the northern part of Vernon County, with headquarters at Kansas City.

On January 10, 1865, the District of Central Missouri was again sub-districted, as follows:

First Sub-district. This sub-district was to consist of that part of the district lying east of the counties in Missouri of Saline, Pettis, and Benton, with headquarters at Jefferson City.

Second Sub-district. This sub-district was to consist of the counties of Saline and Pettis, and that part of Benton north of the Osage River, with headquarters at Sedalia.

Third Sub-district. This sub-district was to consist of the counties in Missouri of Lafayette, Johnson, and Henry, and that part of Saint Clair County north of the Osage River, with headquarters at Warrensburg.

Fourth Sub-district. This sub-district was to consist of the counties in Missouri of Jackson, Cass, and Bates, and that part of Vernon County north of the Osage River, with headquarters at Kansas City. On March 27, 1865, the Fourth Sub-district was extended to include Lafayette County, with headquarters transferred to Lexington.

After the war ended, on May 13, 1865, the District of Central Missouri was divided into three sub-districts as follows:

First Sub-district. This sub-district consisted of the counties in Missouri of Pettis, Cooper, Moniteau, Morgan, and Cole, and all of Miller, Camden, and Benton counties that were north of the Osage River, with headquarters at Jefferson City.

Second Sub-district. This sub-district consisted of the counties in Missouri of Jackson, Lafayette, and Saline, with headquarters at Lexington.

Third Sub-district. This sub-district consisted of the counties in Missouri of Bates, Henry, and Johnson, and all of Saint Clair and Vernon counties north of the Osage River, with headquarters at Pleasant Hill.

Central Division, District of Missouri. See above, District of Central Missouri.

District of Colorado Territory (District of Colorado). Colorado Territory was included in the Department of the Missouri October 11, 1862, and on November 2 it was constituted as the District of Colorado Territory. John M. Chivington was assigned command, with headquarters at Denver.

The territory of the district was increased July 19, 1863 by the transfer of that part of the District of Nebraska lying west of the 104th degree west longitude (present-day western border of the state of Nebraska). This consisted of that part of the Idaho Territory that formerly belonged to the Nebraska Territory.

Colorado Territory was transferred to the newly created Department of Kansas January 1, 1864, and it remained in that department until January 30, 1865. It then again became a part of the Department of the Missouri. Thomas Moonlight was assigned command, with headquarters at Denver.

February 15, 1865, the District of Colorado was defined as consisting of the Colorado Territory, except the post of Julesburg.

The district was merged into the District of the Plains March 28, 1865, with P. Edward Connor commanding.

The principal posts in the district were Camp Collins, Camp Fillmore, Colorado City, Denver, Fort Garland, Fort Lyon, and Junction Station.

District of Eastern Arkansas. The District of Eastern Arkansas, in the Department of the Missouri, was constituted November 2, 1862 to consist of that part of eastern Arkansas that was under the control of United States troops. Alvin P. Hovey was assigned command, with headquarters at Helena. The principal post in the district was Helena.

On November 2, 1862, the Army of the Southwest (see Army of the Southwest) was merged into the District of Eastern Arkansas.

January 21, 1863, Ulysses S. Grant, commanding the Army and Department of the Tennessee, was directed to assume control of all troops in Arkansas that were within reach of his orders, and that part of Arkansas that was occupied by such troops was temporarily attached to the Department of the Tennessee. Grant assumed command of the troops in this region on January 22.

The Department of Arkansas was created January 6, 1864 to include the state of Arkansas.

Before the creation of the District of Eastern Arkansas, the United States troops in the area that it was to include belonged to the Army of the Southwest, and in December 1862, after the district was organized, the following troops were present:

First Division, Frederick Steele
  First Brigade, Peter J. Osterhaus
  Second Brigade, John M. Thayer
  Third Brigade, Senior Colonel

Second Division, Alvin P. Hovey
  First Brigade, James R. Slack
  Second Brigade, Peter Kinney
  Third Brigade, George F. McGinnis

Third Division (Cavalry), Cadwallader C. Washburn
  First Brigade, Conrad Baker
  Second Brigade, Cyrus Bussey

Steele's division was transferred to the Department of the Tennessee, and organized into the Eleventh Division, Thirteenth Corps in December 1862. It was then designated as Fourth Division of William T. Sherman's Yazoo River Expedition against Vicksburg, and later in the month it left the district for the Yazoo River. See Operations against Vicksburg, Mississippi, 1861–1863, Early Attempts to Capture Vicksburg, Yazoo River, Mississippi Expedition (William T. Sherman)Battle of Chickasaw Bayou (or Walnut Hills).

The commanders of the post of Helena and District of Eastern Arkansas were as follows:

Post of Helena
  Frederick Steele   August 29, 1862 to October 7, 1862
  Eugene A. Carr   October 7, 1862 to October 1862
  Alvin P. Hovey   October 1862 to November 2, 1862

District of Eastern Arkansas, Department of the Missouri
  Alvin P. Hovey   November 2, 1862 to December 3, 1862
  Willis A. Gorman   December 3, 1862 to February 14, 1863

Note. On February 14, 1863, Benjamin M. Prentiss was assigned command of the District of Eastern Arkansas, Department of the Tennessee.

District of the Frontier. The District of the Frontier was constituted June 9, 1863 to consist of the Indian Territory, the state of Kansas south of the 38th parallel, the western tier of counties in Missouri, and the western tier of counties in Arkansas. The counties in Missouri were as follows: Vernon, Barton, Jasper, Newton, McDonald, Cedar, Dade, Lawrence, and Barry. The counties in Arkansas were Benton, Washington, Crawford, Sebastian, Scott, Polk, Sevier, and Little River. James G. Blunt was assigned command of the district, with headquarters at Fort Scott or in the field.

In the formation of the District of the Frontier, the District of Northwestern Arkansas was merged into that district June 9, 1862.

July 15, 1863, the western tier of counties of Missouri, which were within the limits of the District of the Frontier, were transferred to the District of Southwest Missouri.

October 19, 1863, the entire state of Kansas was placed in the District of the Border. The District of the Frontier was then unchanged until it was merged into the Department of Kansas January 1, 1864.

The important posts in the District of the Frontier were as follows: in Missouri, Kansas City and Westport; in Kansas, Fort Scott, Fort Larned, Fort Leavenworth, Fort Riley, Drywood, Humboldt, Baxter Springs, and Paola; and in the Indian Territory, Fort Blunt.

July 15, 1863, the posts in Missouri were transferred to the District of Southwest Missouri, and on October 19, the posts in Kansas were transferred to the District of the Border. After that date, the principal posts in the District of the Frontier were Fort Smith, Van Buren, and Roseville in Arkansas, and Fort Blunt and Fort Gibson in the Indian Territory.

When the District of the Frontier was organized, the troops in the district were stationed as regiments or detachments at the various posts in Missouri, Kansas, and the Indian Territory. Forces of brigade strength, however, were organized in the district. The troops at Fort Gibson, Indian Territory consisted of Third Brigade, First Division, Army of the Frontier (see Army of the Frontier) under the command of William A. Phillips, and a command, which was the equivalent of a small brigade, was stationed at Fort Scott, Kansas under Charles W. Blair.

By October 1863, the forces in the district had been organized as follows:

First Brigade, John Ritchie
Second Brigade, William F. Cloud
Third Brigade, Thomas M. Bowen

First Brigade was in the field in the Indian Territory, and was later at Fort Gibson under William A. Phillips. Second Brigade was at Fort Smith, Arkansas, and was later commanded by John Edwards. Third Brigade was at Van Buren, Arkansas.

There was no further change in organization until the district was merged into the Department of Kansas January 1, 1864.

District of Indian Territory. For details of this district, see below, District of Northwestern Arkansas.

District of Kansas. The District of Kansas was constituted November 2, 1862 to consist of the state of Kansas, and James G. Blunt was assigned command, with headquarters in the field.

The district was modified March 30, 1863 as follows: It was extended southward to the Arkansas River, and its eastern border was changed to run southward from the Missouri River along the eastern border of the western tier of counties in Missouri (Jackson, Cass, Bates, Vernon, Barton, Jasper, Newton, and McDonald), and then along this line prolonged to the southern boundary.

The district was merged into the District of the Border and the District of the Frontier June 9, 1863.

The principal posts in the district were Fort Leavenworth, Fort Scott, Fort Larned, Fort Riley, Old Trading Post, Paola, and Wyandotte in Kansas, and Westport in Missouri.

The District of Kansas was re-formed June 28, 1865 by the consolidation of the District of North Kansas and the District of South Kansas, and Robert B. Mitchell was assigned command.

District of Missouri. July 10, 1865, the District of Saint Louis, District of Central Missouri, District of Southwest Missouri, and District of Rolla were consolidated to form the District of Missouri. James A. Williamson was assigned command, with headquarters at Saint Louis. Williamson was relieved from command of the district by Thomas C. H. Smith on July 21. On August 22, the District of Missouri was reestablished to consist of the state of Missouri, and Smith was assigned command.

District of Nebraska. The District of Nebraska was constituted November 2, 1862 to include the Nebraska Territory. James Craig was assigned command, with headquarters at Omaha.

The district was modified July 19, 1863 by the transfer of that part of its territory lying west of the 104th degree west longitude (the western boundary of the present-day state of Nebraska) to the District of Colorado. This included that part of Idaho Territory that formerly belonged to the Nebraska Territory.

January 1, 1864, Nebraska Territory was included in the re-created Department of Kansas.

The District of Nebraska was again in the Department of the Missouri from January 30, 1865 until

March 28, 1865, and then the District of the Plains was formed by the consolidation of the districts of Nebraska, Colorado, and Utah.

The District of Nebraska was announced as a separate brigade February 15, 1865.

The principal posts in the district during the period November 2, 1862–January 1, 1864 were Fort Kearny, Omaha, Cottonwood Springs, and Dakota in Nebraska Territory, and Fort Halleck and Fort Laramie in Idaho Territory.

On September 29, 1864, the District of Nebraska, Department of Kansas was divided into sub-districts as follows:

Eastern Sub-district. The Eastern Sub-district consisted of all territory of the district that was west and south of Omaha and east of Julesburg, Colorado Territory, excluding the post of Omaha and including Julesburg. Robert R. Livingston was assigned command, with headquarters at Fort Kearny, Nebraska Territory.

The principal posts in the sub-district were Alkali Station, Cottonwood Springs, Fort Kearny, and Plum Creek in Nebraska Territory and Julesburg in Colorado Territory.

Western Sub-district. The Western Sub-district consisted of all territory of the district lying west of, and excluding, Julesburg. This included the present-day state of Wyoming and a part of Idaho. William O. Collins was assigned command, with headquarters at Camp Collins, Colorado Territory.

The principal posts in the sub-district were Camp Collins, Colorado Territory, and Deer Creek, Fort Halleck, Fort Laramie, Scott's Bluff, and Sweetwater Bridge in Idaho Territory.

These sub-districts were continued when the District of Nebraska was included in the Department of the Missouri January 30, 1865, with Robert B. Mitchell in command of the Eastern Sub-district and William O. Collins in command of the Western Sub-district.

The commanders of the District of Nebraska were as follows:

James Craig	November 2, 1862 to May 1863
William F. Sapp	May 1863 to June 4, 1863
Thomas J. McKean	June 4, 1863 to January 1, 1864

Robert B. Mitchell	January 30, 1865 to March 28, 1865

District of North Kansas. The District of North Kansas was in existence as a district in the Department of Kansas when the latter was merged into the Department of the Missouri January 30, 1865. As defined in the Department of Kansas, the district included that part of Kansas north of the Kansas River and its tributary, the Smoky Hill Fork. Thomas A. Davies was assigned command, with headquarters at Fort Leavenworth. Robert B. Mitchell assumed command of the district April 11, 1865 (assigned March 28).

The District of Kansas was formed by the consolidation of the District of North Kansas and the District of South Kansas June 28, 1865, and Robert B. Mitchell was assigned command.

District of North Missouri (also District of Northern Missouri). The District of North Missouri was constituted in the Western Department July 29, 1861, under the command of John Pope, and it consisted of all troops in Missouri north of the Missouri River. It was continued in the Department of the Missouri when the latter was constituted November 9, 1861. The Department of the Missouri was merged into the Department of the Mississippi March 11, 1862, and the next day the District of North Missouri was divided into two districts, designated as the District of Northeast Missouri and the District of Northwest Missouri, Department of the Mississippi.

On June 4, 1862, the designations of the two districts were changed as follows: The Northeast District became the Northeastern Division, District of Missouri, Department of the Mississippi; and the Northwest District became the Northwestern Division, District of Missouri, Department of the Mississippi. These designations were still in use when the Department of the Missouri was re-created September 19, 1862.

On November 2, 1862, the designation of of the Northeastern Division was changed to the District of Northeast Missouri, Department of the Missouri, and the designation of the Northwestern Division was changed to the District of Northwest Missouri, Department of the Missouri. On July 6, 1863, these districts were merged into a new District of Northern Missouri, which was to include that part of the state of Missouri north of the Missouri River. Odon Guitar was assigned command, with headquarters at Macon City.

The name of the district was changed to the District of North Missouri in January 1864. Headquarters of the district was moved to Saint Joseph, Missouri April 8, 1864.

The principal posts in the district were Columbia, Glasgow, Hannibal, Macon, Mexico, Saint Joseph, and Savannah.

Beginning in June 1864, the district was divided into sub-districts as follows:

Sub-district of Saint Joseph. This sub-district was formed June 20, 1864, to consist of the following counties: Buchanan, Platte, Clay, Clinton, De Kalb, Andrew, Holt, Gentry, Worth, Nodaway, and Atchison. Although a sub-district, this command was designated as the Saint Joseph District (see below).

Sub-district of Macon. This sub-district was formed July 30, 1864, to consist of the following counties: Putnam, Schuyler, Sullivan, Adair, Linn, Macon, and Chariton.

Sub-district of Mexico. This sub-district was formed July 30, 1864, to consist of the following counties: Randolph, Howard, Monroe, Pike, Audrain, Boone, Callaway, Montgomery, Warren, Saint Charles, and Lincoln. On March 31, 1865, the counties of Howard, Randolph, and Chariton, which were added to the sub-district March 16, 1865, were formed into the new Sub-district of Howard.

Sub-district of Hannibal. This sub-district was formed July 30, 1864, to consist of the following counties: Ralls, Marion, Lewis, Clark, Scotland, Knox, and Shelby.

Sub-district of Howard. This sub-district was formed March 31, 1865, to consist of the counties of Randolph, Howard, and Chariton, which were taken from the Sub-district of Mexico.

The District of North Missouri was discontinued by an order of June 24, 1865, but it remained in existence until July while public property and stores were being removed to Saint Louis.

The commanders of the District of North Missouri were as follows:

Odon Guitar	July 10, 1863 to April 6, 1864
Clinton B. Fisk	April 6, 1864 to May 28, 1865
George Spalding	May 28, 1865 to July 1865

District of Northeastern Arkansas. The District of Northeastern Arkansas was constituted November 30, 1863, but without any defined limits other than that it included all of northeastern Arkansas not occupied by troops of Frederick Steele's Arkansas Expedition (see Little Rock, Arkansas Expedition [Steele]). Robert R. Livingston was assigned command, with headquarters at Batesville. The district was merged into the newly created Department of Arkansas January 6, 1864.

District of Northeast Missouri. The District of Northeast Missouri was organized in the Department of the Mississippi March 12, 1862, and on June 4, the District of Northeast Missouri was designated as the Northeastern Division, District of Missouri, Department of the Mississippi. This organization was in effect September 19, 1862, when the Department of the Missouri was re-created, and on September 27, the designation was again changed to the District of Northeast Missouri, Department of the Missouri.

The district was defined November 2, 1862 as consisting of the following counties in northeastern Missouri: Scotland, Schuyler, Adair, Marion, Randolph, Audrain, Shelby, Boone, Howard, Saint Charles, Callaway, Lincoln, Montgomery, Macon, Lewis, Knox, Clarke, Sullivan, Ralls, and Pike.

Lewis Merrill was assigned command, with headquarters at Macon City, and later at Palmyra and Warrenton. Thomas J. McKean relieved Merrill January 29, 1863 and remained in command until July 6.

The principal posts in the district were Sturgeon, Fayette, Paris, Canton, Kirkesville, Macon, Palmyra, Columbia, Fulton, Hannibal, and Warrenton.

The District of Northeast Missouri was discontinued July 6, 1863, when it was combined with the District of Northwest Missouri to form the District of North Missouri.

100 DEPARTMENTS OF THE ARMY

Northeastern Division, District of Missouri. See above, District of Northeast Missouri.

District of Northwestern Arkansas. The District of Western Arkansas (8th District, Department of the Missouri) and the District of the Indian Territory (9th District, Department of the Missouri) were constituted November 2, 1862. January 13, 1863, William A. Phillips, commanding Third Brigade, First Division, Army of the Frontier (see Army of the Frontier), was assigned command of the two districts, and from that time Phillips' command was reported as the District of Northwestern Arkansas. Headquarters of the district was at Fort Gibson, Indian Territory.

The principal posts in the district were Pomeroy and Fayetteville in Arkansas, and Fort Blunt and Fort Gibson in Indian Territory. The troops in the district consisted of Phillips' brigade.

District of Northwest Missouri. The District of Northwest Missouri was organized in the Department of the Mississippi March 12, 1862, and on June 4, the designation of the district was changed to Northwestern Division, District of Missouri, Department of the Mississippi. This organization was in effect when the Department of the Missouri was re-created September 19, 1862. The designation was again changed September 27, 1862, to the District of Northwest Missouri, Department of the Mississippi.

On November 2, 1862, the district was defined as consisting of the following counties in northwestern Missouri: Mercer, Grundy, Livingston, Carroll, Harrison, Davies, Caldwell, Ray, Worth, Gentry, De Kalb, Clinton, Clay, Nodaway, Andrew, Buchanan, Platte, Atchison, and Holt. Willard P. Hall was assigned command, with headquarters at Saint Joseph.

Despite the fact that the district was constituted by an order of November 2, 1862, it does not appear to have been organized until March 1863, when Chester Harding, Jr. assumed command.

The troops in the district consisted of Missouri Enrolled Militia, and the commanders were officers of the Missouri Enrolled Militia. Harding remained in command until June 1863, and then Hall resumed command.

The District of Northwestern Missouri was dis-

continued July 6, 1863 when it was combined with the District of Northeastern Missouri to form the District of Northern Missouri.

Northwestern Division, District of Missouri. See above, District of Northwest Missouri.

District of the Plains. The District of the Plains was formed March 28, 1865 from the District of Utah, District of Colorado, and District of Nebraska, and it was organized to aid in the protection of overland commerce, the telegraph line, and mail transportation. P. Edward Connor was assigned command, with headquarters at Denver, Colorado Territory. Headquarters was moved to Julesburg, Colorado Territory May 1, 1865.

Fort Lyon, Colorado Territory was transferred from the District of the Plains to the District of the Upper Arkansas April 22, 1865. Connor was still in command of the District of the Plains in July 1865, with headquarters at Fort Laramie, Dakota Territory.

On April 8, 1865, the district was divided into sub-districts as follows:

South Sub-district of the Plains. This sub-district consisted of the Colorado Territory, except the posts of Julesburg and Fort Halleck, Dakota Territory. Guy V. Henry was assigned command, with headquarters at Denver.

The principal posts in the sub-district were Camp Collins, Denver, Camp Fillmore, Fort Garland, Junction Station, Camp Robbins, and Fort Halleck.

East Sub-district of the Plains. This sub-district consisted of the Territory of Nebraska. Robert R. Livingston was assigned command, with headquarters at Fort Kearny.

The principal posts in the sub-district were Cottonwood Springs, Fort Kearny, Omaha, Plum Creek, and Midway Station.

North Sub-district of the Plains. This sub-district consisted of the post of Julesburg and that part of Dakota Territory, except Fort Halleck, lying west of the 104th degree west longitude, which was formerly included in the District of Nebraska. Thomas Moonlight was assigned command, with headquarters at Fort Laramie.

The principal posts in the district were Fort Laramie, Julesburg, Camp Marshall, Platte Bridge, Camp Mitchell in Dakota Territory, and Fort Rankin in Colorado Territory.

West Sub-district of the Plains. This sub-district consisted of Utah Territory. Milo George was assigned command, with headquarters at Camp Douglas. The principal posts in the district were Fort Bridger, Camp Douglas, and Camp Connor.

District of Rolla. The District of Rolla was constituted November 2, 1862, but the limits of the district were not defined until March 30, 1863, when the boundaries were defined as follows: the boundary on the east was the 91st degree west longitude from its intersection with the northern line of Washington County to the southern boundary of Missouri; on the south it was the Missouri-Arkansas state line; on the north it was the northern line of Washington County extended westward to the Gasconade River; and on the west it was the Gasconade River southward to the western line of Pulaski County, and from there along a line southward to the Missouri-Arkansas state line.

As thus described, the District of Rolla included all of the counties of Crawford, Phelps, Texas, Howell, Oregon, Shannon, and Dent; the eastern parts of the counties of La Clede, Wright, Douglas, and Ozark; the western parts of the counties of Washington, Iron, Reynolds, Carter, and Ripley; Pulaski County south of the Gasconade; and the southeastern part of Maries County. John M. Glover was assigned command, with headquarters at Rolla. The principal posts in the district were Rolla, Salem, Huston, and Waynesville.

In June 1863 John W. Davidson organized a First Cavalry Division, District of Southeastern Missouri, and in July 1863 it moved into the District of Rolla at Arcadia. It was organized as follows:

First Division (Cavalry), John W. Davidson
    First Brigade, Lewis Merrill
    Second Brigade, John M. Glover
    Reserve Brigade, Henry C. Caldwell

This division left the District of Rolla and joined Frederick Steele's Arkansas Expedition in August 1863. For further information, see Little Rock, Arkansas Expedition (Steele). The only brigade organization in the district, other than the brigades of Davidson's cavalry division, was First Brigade, District of Rolla, commanded by John T. Burris.

The District of Rolla was discontinued July 10, 1865, when it was combined with the District of Central Missouri, the Saint Louis District, and the District of Southwest Missouri to form the District of Missouri.

The commanders of the District of Rolla were as follows:

John M. Glover	November 2, 1862 to March 13, 1863
Sempronius H. Boyd	Temporarily in March 1863
Thomas A. Davies	March 13, 1863 to March 25, 1864
Odon Guitar	March 25, 1864 to July 17, 1864
Albert Sigel	July 17, 1864 to August 28, 1864
John McNeil	August 28, 1864 to October 4, 1864
Albert Sigel	October 4, 1864 to November 15, 1864
John McNeil	November 15, 1864 to November 28, 1864
Albert Sigel	November 28, 1864 to December 2, 1864
Edwin C. Catherwood	December 2, 1864 to January 5, 1865
Egbert B. Brown	January 5, 1865 to March 8, 1865
Edwin C. Catherwood	March 8, 1865 to March 17, 1865
John Morrill	March 17, 1865 to July 10, 1865

Saint Joseph District. On June 20, 1864, Clinton B. Fisk, commander of the District of North Missouri, announced the formation of the Saint Joseph District, which was to consist of the counties of Buchanan, Platte, Clay, Clinton, De Kalb, Andrew, Holt, Gentry, Worth, Nodaway, and Atchison. Daniel M. Draper was assigned command. This district was in fact a sub-district of the District of North Missouri.

District of Saint Louis. The District of Saint Louis was formed in the Department of the Missouri January 5, 1862, and was continued in the Department of the Mississippi when the latter was created March 11, 1862. In a reorganization of that department June 4, 1862, the Saint Louis District became the Saint Louis Division, District of Missouri, Department of the Mississippi.

The Department of the Missouri was re-created September 19, 1862, and on September 27, the designation of the Saint Louis Division was changed to District of Saint Louis, Department of the Missouri.

The District of Saint Louis was constituted November 2, 1862 to have the same limits as previously defined and all of the territory in the Department of the Missouri to the south of it. John W. Davidson was assigned command, with headquarters at Saint Louis.

The territory of the District of Saint Louis was reduced March 30, 1863 when the eastern border of the District of Rolla (see above) was defined as the 91st degree west longitude from the northern line of Washington County, south through the counties of Washington, Iron, Reynolds, Center, and Ripley to the southern border of Missouri.

The district was further reduced June 16, 1863 when the District of Southeastern Missouri was reconstituted, but on November 30, the latter was again added to the District of Saint Louis.

Benton Barracks was removed from the district in October 1863, but it was again reported in the district in August 1864.

July 10, 1865, the District of Saint Louis was consolidated with the District of Central Missouri, the District of Southwest Missouri, and the District of Rolla to form the District of Missouri, Department of the Missouri.

The principal posts in the district were Barnesville, Benton Barracks, Bloomfield, Cape Girardeau, De Soto, Franklin, Jackson, New Madrid, Pacific, Pilot Knob, Potosi, and Saint Louis.

Most of the troops in the district were regiments and detachments at the various posts in the district, and some commands were of brigade size, but in addition there were several brigade and some divisional organizations.

September 30, 1862, John W. Davidson, commander of the district, ordered the organization of two infantry brigades and one cavalry brigade from regiments in the district. These were as follows:

First Brigade, Thomas C. Fletcher
Second Brigade, Chester Harding, Jr.
Cavalry Brigade, Bazel F. Lazear

In October 1862, John W. Davidson was relieved from command of the District of Saint Louis, and he was then assigned to the command of the troops in the field in southeastern Missouri, which he designated as the Army of Southeastern Missouri. For additional information, see Army of Southeastern Missouri.

In December 1862, a brigade in the District of Saint Louis under Clinton B. Fisk was sent to Columbus, Kentucky during Nathan B. Forrest's expedition into western Tennessee. The brigade arrived at Columbus on December 26, but January 8–9, 1863 it departed for Helena, Arkansas.

In July 1864 the District of Saint Louis was divided into sub-districts as follows:

First Sub-district. This sub-district included the counties of Saint Louis (except Benton Barracks), Jefferson, and Franklin, and those parts of the counties of Gasconade, Osage, and Maries lying east of the Gasconade River and north of the northern boundary of Washington County extended westward. The principal post in the sub-district was Saint Louis.

Jefferson County and the line of the Iron Mountain Railroad were transferred from the First Sub-district to the Third Sub-district October 5, 1864.

Commanders of the sub-district were James H. Baker, Hugo Wangelin, and Joseph Weydemeyer.

Two special forces were organized in the sub-district September 28, 1864 during Sterling Price's invasion of Missouri. These were:

First Brigade (or Illinois Brigade), District of Saint Louis, Hugo Wangelin

Pike's Division, Enrolled Militia of Saint Louis, Edward C. Pike
First Brigade, Madison Miller
Second Brigade, David C. Coleman
Third Brigade, Joseph S. Gage

Second Sub-district. This sub-district was formed from the post of Cape Girardeau and consisted of the counties of Perry, Bollinger, Cape Girardeau, Scott, Stoddard, Mississippi, New Madrid, Pemiscot, and

Dunklin. The commanders of the sub-district were John B. Rogers, Hiram M. Hiller, and James C. Thomson.

On April 11, 1865, the Second Sub-district was consolidated with the Third Sub-district.

Third Sub-district. This sub-district included the counties of Sainte Genevieve, Saint Francois, Madison, Wayne, and Butler, and the eastern parts of the counties of Washington, Iron, Reynolds, Carter, and Ripley. The principal posts were Ironton, Patterson, Pilot Knob, Sainte Genevieve, and Potosi; headquarters of the sub-district was at Pilot Knob.

April 11, 1865, the Third Sub-district was consolidated with the Second Sub-district.

Saint Louis Division. See above, Saint Louis District.

District of South Kansas. This district was in existence in the Department of Kansas, and it was defined as including that part of Kansas lying south of the Kansas River and its tributary, the Smoky Hill Fork. James G. Blunt was in command of the district, with headquarters at Paola, Kansas. On January 30, 1865, when Kansas was included in the Department of the Missouri, the District of South Kansas was transferred to the Department of the Missouri, with Blunt still in command.

On April 22, 1865, the District of South Kansas was extended to include the Indian country west of Arkansas, except the posts of Fort Smith, Fort Scott, and Paola, and then the district was transferred to the Department of Arkansas.

The principal posts in the district were as follows: in Kansas, Fort Scott, Humboldt, Mound City, Osage Mission, Pawnee Station, Trading Post, Paola, and Olathe; and in Missouri, Fort Curtis and Fort Insley.

The District of South Kansas, Department of the Missouri retained the same sub-districts that were assigned in the Department of Kansas, except that on December 27, 1864, while still in the Department of Kansas, Sub-district No. 1 was attached to Sub-district No. 2. The two remaining sub-districts, which were transferred to the Department of the Missouri, were as follows:

Sub-district No. 2. This sub-district included the counties in Kansas of Bourbon, Allen, Woodson, Greenwood, and Butler, and all of the territory south of the southern border of Kansas and the post of Fort Scott. Charles W. Blair was assigned command, with headquarters at Fort Scott.

Sub-district No. 3. This sub-district included the counties in Kansas of Miami, Franklin, Johnson, Douglas, Shawnee, and Wabaunsee.

On April 20, 1865, all of that part of the District of South Kansas south of the Kansas River was designated as First Sub-district, and was commanded by Charles W. Blair, with headquarters at Fort Scott.

District of Southeastern Missouri. When the Department of the Missouri was re-created September 19, 1862, the territory of southeastern Missouri was included in the Saint Louis Division, and on November 2, the District of Saint Louis was announced as including all of the state of Missouri to the south of Saint Louis. The troops in this district were organized as the Army of Southeastern Missouri. For additional information, see Army of Southeastern Missouri.

The District of Southeastern Missouri was reconstituted June 16, 1863 from territory taken from the District of Saint Louis. The southern boundary of the District of Saint Louis was then to be a line running east through Steeleville, in Crawford County, and the former territory of the District of Saint Louis south of this line was to constitute the District of Southeastern Missouri. John W. Davidson was assigned command of the district, with headquarters at Pilot Knob.

The principal posts in the district were Cape Girardeau, Centerville, Fredericktown, Ironton, New Madrid, Patterson, and Pilot Knob.

The District of Southeastern Missouri was made a part of the District of Saint Louis November 30, 1863.

The First Cavalry Division, District of Southeastern Missouri was organized by John W. Davidson in June 1862. It initially consisted of a First Brigade commanded by Lewis Merrill and a Second Brigade commanded by John M. Glover, but a Reserve Brigade under Henry C. Caldwell was added later. The division moved into the District of Rolla in July

1863. Clinton B. Fisk relieved Davidson in command of the district July 20, 1863, and the latter marched south with his cavalry division to join Frederick Steele's Arkansas expedition early in August. For further information, see Little Rock, Arkansas Expedition (Steele).

District of Southwest Missouri. The District of Southwestern Missouri was organized in the Department of the Missouri December 25, 1861, and March 11, 1862 the district was transferred to the newly organized Department of the Mississippi. On June 4, 1862, the designation of the District of Southwestern Missouri was changed to Southwestern Division, District of Missouri, Department of the Mississippi. The Southwestern Division was defined as that part of Missouri lying south of the north line of Dallas County and west of the Gasconade River and of the Big North Fork of White River.

The Department of the Missouri was re-created September 19, 1862, and on September 27, the designation of the Southwestern Division was changed to District of Southwest Missouri, Department of the Missouri, and its territory was unchanged. On November 2, 1862, the district was defined as consisting of the following counties in Missouri: Vernon, Barton, Jasper, Newton, McDonald, Cedar, Dade, Lawrence, Barry, Polk, Green, Christian, Stone, Taney, Ozark, Douglas, Webster, Wright, and La Clede, and parts of Hickory and Saint Clair.

March 30, 1863, the district was extended southward to the Arkansas River.

The district was reduced in size June 9, 1863 when the western tier of counties (Vernon, Barton, Jasper, Newton, and McDonald) were transferred to the new District of the Frontier. These counties were again included in the District of Southwest Missouri July 15, 1863.

The limits of the district were again changed August 18, 1864, when the Missouri-Arkansas state line was fixed as the southern boundary, and again on December 26, 1864, when the Osage River was made the northern boundary.

The District of Southwest Missouri was discontinued July 10, 1865, when it was consolidated with the District of Saint Louis, the District of Central Missouri, and the District of Rolla to form the District of Missouri, Department of the Missouri.

The commanders of the District of Southwestern Missouri were as follows:

John M. Schofield	November 2, 1862 to November 10, 1862
Egbert B. Brown	November 10, 1862 to March 30, 1863
John M. Schofield	March 30, 1863 to May 24, 1863
William F. Cloud	May 24, 1863 to July 15, 1863
John McNeil	July 15, 1863 to October 19, 1863
John B. Sanborn	October 19, 1863 to December 9, 1864
Joseph J. Gravely	December 9, 1864 to January 9, 1865
John B. Sanborn	January 9, 1865 to June 10, 1865
John D. Allen	June 10, 1865 to June 19, 1865
Thomas J. McKean	June 19, 1865 to July 10, 1865

In October 1862, John M. Schofield commanded a force in southwestern Missouri called the Army of Southwestern Missouri (see Army of Southwestern Missouri), and on October 12, the designation of this command was changed to Army of the Frontier. For details, see Army of Southwestern Missouri; and see also Army of the Frontier.

In October 1864 the troops in the District of Southwest Missouri, then commanded by John B. Sanborn, were organized into brigades during Sterling Price's invasion of Missouri (August 29–December 2, 1864). These were as follows:

First Brigade, John F. Philips
Second Brigade, John L. Beveridge
Third Brigade, Joseph J. Gravely

For additional information, see Price's Missouri Expedition.

Southwestern Division, District of Missouri. See above, District of Southwest Missouri.

District of the Upper Arkansas. The District of the Upper Arkansas was created July 25, 1864 in the Department of Kansas, and was in existence when the Department of Kansas was merged into the Department of the Missouri January 30, 1865. James H. Ford was assigned command, with headquarters at Fort Riley, Kansas.

When created, the district was bounded on the east by a north-south line through Fort Riley, Kansas; on the west by a north-south line through Fort Lyon, Colorado Territory, including Fort Lyon; on the south by the Indian Territory; and on the north by the 2nd Standard Parallel (Gunn and Mitchell, New Map of Kansas). This included the territory through which the Santa Fe Trail passed. Fort Lyon, which had been in the District of the Plains, was transferred to the District of the Upper Arkansas April 22, 1865. The district was continued in existence after the war, with Ford still in command.

The principal posts in the district were Fort Riley, Fort Ellsworth, Fort Larned, Fort Zarah, Fort Dodge, and Salina, all in Kansas; and Fort Lyon, Colorado Territory. On June 13, 1865, the district was sub-divided as follows:

Sub-district No. 1. This sub-district included the posts of Fort Riley, Ellsworth, and the stations of Salina and Lake Sibley. Headquarters of the sub-district was at Fort Riley.

Sub-district No. 2. This sub-district consisted of that part of the Santa Fe Trail from Council Grove, Kansas to Fort Zarah, inclusive. Headquarters of the sub-district was at Council Grove.

Sub-district No. 3. This sub-district included that part of the Santa Fe Trail from Fort Zarah to Fort Lyon, including Fort Lyon. Headquarters of the sub-district was at Fort Larned.

District of Utah. The District of Utah was in existence in the Department of the Pacific, and it included the Utah Territory, Camp Ruby, the Nevada Territory, and the post of Soda Springs in Idaho Territory. P. Edward Connor was in command, with headquarters at Camp Douglas, Utah Territory.

The Utah Territory was added to the Department of the Missouri February 17, 1865, and was merged into the District of the Plains on March 28, when the latter was created from the districts of Utah, Colorado, and Nebraska.

District of Western Arkansas. See District of Northwestern Arkansas.

District of Western Arkansas and Indian Territory. See District of Northwestern Arkansas.

POSTS AND SPECIAL COMMANDS IN THE DEPARTMENT OF THE MISSOURI

There were several posts and special commands in the Department of the Missouri during the period of its existence, and the most important of these were as follows:

Prisoner of War Camp at Alton, Illinois. Commanders were Jesse Hildebrand, William B. Mason, George W. Kinkead, William Weer, Joseph T. Copeland, and Roy Stone.

Benton Barracks. Commanders were Benjamin L. E. Bonneville, William A. Pile, and Pitcairn Morrison.

United States Colored Troops at Benton Barracks. These troops were commanded by William A. Pile from January 1864 to May 1864.

Cavalry Depot at Benton Barracks. The depot was commanded by John P. Hatch and John W. Davidson.

Schofield Barracks. Schofield Barracks was commanded by James Clifford from December 1863 to June 1864.

Draft Rendezvous at Benton Barracks. The Draft Rendezvous was commanded by Pitcairn Morrison from December 1864 to August 1865.

Jefferson Barracks. Jefferson Barracks was commanded by James H. Corns and Donald C. McVean.

TROOPS IN THE DEPARTMENT OF THE MISSOURI

During the period of its existence, there were several armies operating in the Department of the Missouri. Some of these were officially designated armies, and others were simply so-called by their commanding officers. These were:

Army of Arkansas
Army of the Border
Army of the District of Cairo (also called the Army of the District of West Tennessee and Army of the Tennessee in the Department of the Mississippi)
Army of the Frontier
Army of Kansas
Army of the Mississippi (Pope)
Army of the Department of the Missouri
Army of North Missouri (Prentiss)
Army of Southeastern Missouri
Army of the Southwest
Army of Southwestern Missouri
Army of Western Missouri (also Pope's Army in the Field)

For additional information about the armies listed above, see the respective armies.

In addition to the various armies in the department, brigades and divisions were organized in some of the districts of the department, and they are reported in the descriptions of the districts, which are given above.

There were other commands that were organized or operated in the Department of the Missouri during the war. The more important of these are given in the following sections.

Detachment Sixteenth Corps. First Division and Third Division, Sixteenth Corps under Andrew J. Smith were sent from the Army of the Tennessee to Missouri when Sterling Price invaded the state with an army in September 1864. At that time, Smith and his command were en route on transports from Memphis, Tennessee to join William T. Sherman's army, then operating in Georgia. On September 6, when the transports were passing Cairo, Illinois on the way to Nashville, Tennessee, Smith was halted, and on September 9 he was ordered to take his command to Missouri. He arrived at Jefferson Barracks below Saint Louis September 13 and joined in the pursuit of Price across the state. After Price had left Missouri, Smith's command was transferred to Nashville November 1–30, 1864, where it was engaged under George H. Thomas at the Battle of Nashville in December. For additional information, see Price's Missouri Expedition.

Smith's command was organized as follows:

SIXTEENTH CORPS (DETACHMENT), Andrew J. Smith

First Division, Joseph J. Woods
First Brigade, William L. McMillen
Second Brigade, Lucius F. Hubbard
Third Brigade, Sylvester G. Hill

Third Division, David Moore
First Brigade, Thomas J. Kinney
Second Brigade, James I. Gilbert
Third Brigade, Edward H. Wolfe

Kansas Division. September 19, 1862, when the Department of Kansas was merged into the Department of the Missouri, James G. Blunt was in command of the Army of Kansas, which consisted of three brigades as follows:

First Brigade, Frederick Salomon
Second Brigade, William Weer
Third Brigade, William F. Cloud

On September 19, 1862, Blunt was ordered to take his division and join a force commanded by John M. Schofield in southwest Missouri. The designation of Blunt's force was then changed to Kansas Division, and it retained this designation until October 12, 1862, when it became Blunt's First Division in Schofield's Army of the Frontier. For additional information, see Army of the Frontier.

Fisk's Brigade. This command was also known as Fisk's Division; as Second Brigade, United States Volunteers; and later as Left Wing, United States Forces at Columbus, Kentucky. This brigade was formed in the District of Saint Louis under Clinton B. Fisk, and was then sent to Columbus, Kentucky during Nathan B. Forrest's raid into western Tennessee. The brigade arrived at Columbus December 26, 1862 and in January moved to Helena, Arkansas. During the period February to June 1863, Fisk's brigade was organized as Second Brigade, Thirteenth Division, Thirteenth Corps, Army of the Tennessee. In July the brigade returned to the Department of the Missouri, and until November it served in the District of Southeastern Missouri.

Missouri State Militia. Shortly after he was elected governor of Missouri, on July 20, 1861, Hamilton R. Gamble asked President Abraham Lincoln for authority to raise a special force of State Militia. These troops were to be employed only for the defense of the state, but they were to be paid, equipped, and supplied by the United States government. This force was to be organized in conformity with the Militia Laws of Missouri. It was to be under the exclusive control of the governor except when, by his orders, he placed it under the command of a United States officer. This organization was to be known as the Missouri State Militia, and was limited by the president to 10,000 men.

By an order of November 27, 1861, John M. Schofield was assigned command of all militia in the state, and was directed to raise and organize this force. The organization was completed by mid-April 1862, and it consisted of fourteen regiments of cavalry (mounted infantry) and one infantry regiment. These troops were enrolled largely in the districts where their services were required, but they were put in the field with United States troops to improve their discipline and to provide the necessary instruction. The militia regiments were employed largely in opposing the numerous guerrilla bands that infested the state.

On May 29, 1863, the militia was placed under the control of Schofield, who was then in command of the Department of the Missouri. On July 22, Schofield ordered the immediate organization of all militia in Missouri, and on September 28, the governor placed all militia of the state under Schofield's command.

Winslow's Cavalry Division. Edward F. Winslow was in command of Second Division, Cavalry Corps in the District of West Tennessee in August 1864, and on September 2 he was ordered with a detachment of his division to Missouri during Sterling Price's invasion of the state. The command that Winslow took to Missouri was organized as follows:

Second Division, Cavalry Corps (detachment), Edward F. Winslow
First Brigade (detachment), Joseph Karge
Second Brigade (detachment), George Duffield

Winslow's command remained in Missouri as a brigade in Alfred Pleasonton's Cavalry Division until Price left the state, and it then transferred from the department. For additional information, see Price's Missouri Expedition.

Army of the Border. The Army of the Border was another force that entered Missouri briefly during Price's invasion of Missouri. It was formed in Kansas under James G. Blunt, and served only in the western part of Missouri. For additional information, see Price's Missouri Expedition; and see also Army of the Border.

DEPARTMENT OF NEW MEXICO

The Territory of New Mexico was constituted September 9, 1850 to have the following boundaries: Beginning at a point where the Colorado River crosses the Mexican border, the southern boundary ran eastward along the border to the Rio Grande at El Paso; then northward along the Rio Grande to the parallel of the 32nd degree north latitude; then east along the 32nd parallel (the present-day southern border of New Mexico) to its intersection with the 103rd degree west longitude (which is essentially the eastern border of New Mexico); then north on the 103rd degree to the parallel of the 38th degree north latitude; then west along the 38th parallel to the Continental Divide near Cochetopa Pass, about fifteen miles northeast of present-day Creede, Colorado; then south along the crest of the mountains to the 37th parallel north latitude (present-day northern boundary of Arizona and New Mexico); then west along that parallel to the California state line; then south along the state line to the point of its beginning at the Mexican border. On February 28, 1861, the northeastern part of New Mexico north of the 37th parallel was transferred from the Territory of New Mexico to the newly created Colorado Territory.

On October 31, 1853, the Department of New Mexico was created to consist of that part of the

Territory of New Mexico lying east of the 110th degree west longitude. The department was still in existence, with the same boundaries, at the beginning of the war. On July 3, 1861, however, the department was merged into John C. Fremont's Western Department, but it was re-created under Edward R. S. Canby November 9, 1861, and was then continued in existence until the end of the war.

In order to preserve continuity in the description of affairs in the Territory of New Mexico during the war, the period July 3–November 9, 1861, during which the Department of New Mexico was not in existence, is included in the description of the organization of the troops and their operations in the department. Particularly, it should be noted that for this reason Baylor's invasion of southern New Mexico in July 1861 is included under Troops and Operations in the Department of New Mexico.

DEPARTMENT OF NEW MEXICO
OCTOBER 31, 1853–
JULY 3, 1861

The Department of New Mexico was in existence at the beginning of the war, and in 1861 it consisted of that part of the Territory of New Mexico east of the 110th degree west longitude, which passes just east of Holbrook, Tombstone, and Bisbee in present-day Arizona.

The Colorado Territory was organized February 28, 1861, and that part of the Department of New Mexico north of the 37th parallel became a part of that territory.

William W. Loring assumed command of the Department of New Mexico March 23, 1861, but on June 11 he left Santa Fe, and Edward R. S. Canby was placed in general charge of affairs in the department. On June 23, Loring left the department and joined the Confederacy, and Canby was assigned command of the Department of New Mexico.

July 3, 1861, the Department of New Mexico was merged into the newly created Western Department. John C. Fremont was assigned command of the new department, but he did not assume command until July 25.

DEPARTMENT OF NEW MEXICO
NOVEMBER 9, 1861–
AUGUST 14, 1865

The Department of New Mexico was re-created November 9, 1861 to consist of the entire Territory of New Mexico, which consisted of the present-day states of New Mexico and Arizona, and that part of Nevada lying south of the northern border of Arizona prolonged westward to the California state line. Edward R. S. Canby was assigned command, with headquarters at Santa Fe.

On February 14, 1862, Fort Garland, Colorado Territory was transferred from the Department of Kansas to the Department of New Mexico.

July 21, 1862, that part of the Department of New Mexico west of a north-south line passing through Apache Pass, and from that point to Mesilla, was transferred to the Department of the Pacific as the District of Western Arizona

January 14, 1863, the District of Western Arizona, Department of the Pacific was transferred to the Department of New Mexico.

An order from the War Department dated January 20, 1865 transferred the Territory of Arizona to the Department of the Pacific. Some time elapsed before the order was received by James H. Carleton, commanding the Department of New Mexico, and then he announced the transfer on March 7. Thereafter, the Department of New Mexico consisted of the present-day state of New Mexico and Fort Garland, Colorado.

In the reorganization of the military divisions and departments of the army June 27, 1865, the Territory of New Mexico was assigned to the Department of California, Military Division of the Pacific. Pending the completion of the reorganization required by the June 27 order, the Department of New Mexico continued in existence until August 14, and on that date Carleton's command was designated as the District of New Mexico, Department of California.

Canby remained in command of the Department of New Mexico from November 9, 1861 until September 18, 1862, and then he was succeeded by James H. Carleton, who had arrived from California with his Column from California. For additional information, see below, Expedition from California, through Arizona, to New Mexico and Northwestern Texas (Column from California). Carleton remained in command until the department was discontinued August 14, 1865.

DISTRICTS IN THE DEPARTMENT OF NEW MEXICO

District of Arizona. June 20, 1862 John M. Chivington, commanding the Southern District of New Mexico, was ordered by Canby to be prepared to move in the direction of Mesilla Valley to support James H. Carleton and his Column from California when they approached from Tucson, Arizona. The country south of Santa Barbara when occupied was to be constituted as the District of Arizona.

The leading troops of Carleton's command arrived on the Rio Grande near Fort Thorn July 4, 1862, and Carleton in person arrived August 7. During the remainder of the month the California troops occupied Las Cruces, Fort Fillmore, and Mesilla in New Mexico, and Fort Bliss, Fort Quitman, and Fort Davis in Texas.

The District of Arizona was constituted August 30, 1862 to consist of all territory from Fort Thorn, New Mexico, along the Rio Grande to Fort Quitman, Texas. Carleton assumed command of the district and established his headquarters at Mesilla. It should be noted, however, that Carleton referred to his command as the District of Arizona as early as mid-August 1862.

The name Arizona may be confusing to the present-day reader, because it did not have the same meaning during the Civil War period as it does today. Until Arizona was organized as a territory, in Confederate usage, and also in de facto usage in the Southwest until 1863, "Arizona" meant that part of the Territory of New Mexico south of the 34th parallel, which passes just south of Socorro, New Mexico, and about thirty-five miles north of Phoenix in present-day Arizona. There is also some confusion about the proper meaning of the designation Territory of Arizona. In a proclamation issued June 8, 1862, Carleton announced that Congress had set apart a portion of the Territory of New Mexico and organized it into the Territory of Arizona. At that time the Territory of Arizona comprised all of the country eastward from the Colorado River that was occupied by the Column from California, and the limits were to be extended eastward as Carleton advanced toward the Rio Grande. Because there was no civil government in this territory, Carleton proclaimed martial law and assumed control as military governor. The territory was officially organized February 24, 1863, with the eastern border established as 109 degrees west longitude.

September 5, 1862, the limits of the District of Arizona were defined as consisting of all the Territory of Arizona and that part of New Mexico south of an east-west line through Fort Thorn, and also the territory occupied by Union troops in northwest Texas.

September 18, 1862, Carleton succeeded Canby in command of the Department of New Mexico, and Joseph R. West assumed command of an enlarged District of Arizona, which included all of New Mexico south of the Jornada del Muerto, and the country westward to the Colorado River. Fort McRae was transferred from the District of Arizona to the District of Fort Craig October 23, 1862.

Headquarters of the district was moved to Franklin (El Paso), Texas in the spring of 1863.

The District of Arizona was abolished December 8, 1864.

Commanders of the District of Arizona were as follows:

James H. Carleton	August 30, 1862 to September 5, 1862
Joseph R. West	September 5, 1862 to January 29, 1864
George W. Bowie	January 29, 1864 to November 1864
Joseph Smith	November 1864 to December 8, 1864

The principal posts in the District of Arizona were as follows: in New Mexico, Camp Mimbres, Fort Cummings, Fort Fillmore, Las Cruces, and Mesilla; in Arizona Territory, Fort Bowie, Fort Goodwin, Tubac, and Tucson; and in Texas, Fort Quitman and Franklin (El Paso).

The troops in the District of Arizona belonged to the Column from California. For details of this organization, see below, Troops and Operations in the Department of New Mexico, Expedition from Southern California, through Arizona, to New Mexico and Northwestern Texas (Column from California).

Central District of New Mexico. The Central District of New Mexico consisted generally of the territory in New Mexico between the Northern District and the Southern District, and west of the Eastern District. Following Henry Hopkins Sibley's withdrawal from Santa Fe and Albuquerque April 16, 1862 (see below, Troops and Operations in the Department of New Mexico, Sibley's Invasion of New Mexico), Benjamin S. Roberts was assigned command of the territory included in the former Northern and Central districts of New Mexico and the Santa Fe District.

Central, Santa Fe, and Northern District (Combined District of Central, Santa Fe, and Northern Districts of New Mexico). Henry Hopkins Sibley occupied Albuquerque and Santa Fe March 2–4, 1862 and remained in the area until April 12. On April 16, after the Confederate withdrawal, Benjamin S. Roberts was assigned command of that part of New Mexico that was formerly included in the Central and Northern districts of New Mexico and the Santa Fe District. He was instructed to establish garrisons, secure the public property, and restore order in that part of New Mexico. A short time later, Roberts was ordered east and there served as John Pope's inspector general and chief of staff during the Northern Virginia Campaign.

Eastern District of New Mexico. The Eastern District of New Mexico generally included the territory east of the Santa Fe District, and especially the road leading to Kansas. The principal post was Fort Union, near present-day Watrous, New Mexico. William Chapman was in command of the district, with headquarters at Fort Union, but he was succeeded by Gabriel R. Paul early in January 1862. Paul remained in command until April 16, 1862, when he was assigned command of the First Column of Canby's Army of New Mexico during its pursuit of Sibley. Commanders at Fort Union during the remainder of the war were Peter W. L. Plympton, William McMullen, Francisco P. Abreu, and Henry R. Selden.

District of Fort Craig. Early in 1863, Edwin A. Rigg was assigned command at Fort Craig, and his command was designated as the District of Fort Craig. Rigg remained in command of the district until he departed on the Apache Expedition of May 16, 1864. He resumed command of the district briefly in August 1864, and other commanders of the district were Clarence E. Bennett and Oscar M. Brown.

Fort McRae was transferred from the District of Arizona to the District of Fort Craig October 23, 1862.

The District of Fort Craig was abolished November 23, 1864.

District of Northern Arizona. The District of Northern Arizona was constituted October 23, 1863 to include all the Territory of Arizona lying north of the Gila River, and that part of the territory west of the Colorado River, except that occupied by Fort Mojave, which was in the Department of the Pacific. Edward B. Willis, with two companies of the 1st California Infantry and troops of the 1st California Cavalry, was ordered into the district to establish Fort Whipple, near Prescott, Arizona. He arrived in late December 1863, and remained there in command of the district. The district was created to protect from the Indians the mines and miners in the newly discovered gold fields near the San Francisco Mountains, and to provide for the general security of the region.

The district was transferred to the Department of the Pacific January 20, 1865.

Northern District of New Mexico. The Northern District of New Mexico included the territory of the northern part of New Mexico. William W. Loring commanded the district, with headquarters at Santa Fe, until he resigned June 11, 1861 and left the department. Canby was left in charge of the department, and also in command of the Northern District.

When Sibley evacuated Santa Fe and Albuquerque April 16, 1862, Benjamin S. Roberts was assigned command of all territory formerly included in the Northern and Central districts of New Mexico and the Santa Fe District.

District of Santa Fe. James L. Donaldson, chief quartermaster of the Department of New Mexico, was in command of the District of Santa Fe until it was evacuated March 2–4, 1862 during Sibley's invasion of New Mexico. When the Confederate forces evacuated Santa Fe and Albuquerque April 16, 1862, Benjamin S. Roberts was assigned command of the combined Northern and Central districts of New Mexico and the District of Santa Fe.

Southern District of New Mexico. The Southern District of New Mexico included the territory and posts in the southern part of New Mexico. At the outbreak of war, Isaac Lynde was in command of the district, with headquarters at Fort Fillmore, four miles south of Mesilla. Lynde surrendered his command, consisting of seven companies of the 7th United States Infantry and three companies of Mounted Rifles, to John R. Baylor at San Augustine Springs (or San Augustine Pass) July 27, 1861. Lynde was succeeded in command of the district by Benjamin S. Roberts on August 8, and at the same time the Southern District of New Mexico was extended to include all country south of, and including, Albuquerque.

During Sibley's invasion of New Mexico, Roberts, with most of his command (known as the Southern Division), was engaged with the enemy at Valverde, and he then returned to Fort Craig. When Sibley evacuated Santa Fe and Albuquerque April 16, 1862 and withdrew to the south, Roberts was assigned command of that part of New Mexico that was formerly included in the Northern and Central districts of New Mexico and the District of Santa Fe.

On April 16, 1862, Canby reorganized his Army of New Mexico for the pursuit of Sibley, and he assigned Gabriel R. Paul to the command of the First Column and John M. Chivington to the command of the Second Column. On April 23, Paul was assigned command of the field force operating in the neighborhood of Fort Craig, and on May 1 he was in command of the Southern District of New Mexico. Paul was succeeded by Chivington in June 1862, and he in turn was relieved by Marshall S. Howe on July 4.

On August 30, 1862, after the arrival of the Column from California, the southern part of the Southern District of New Mexico became the District of Arizona.

Early in 1863 the area about Fort Craig was designated as the District of Fort Craig, with Edwin A. Rigg in command.

District of Western Arizona. The District of Western Arizona, Department of the Pacific was created by an order of James H. Carleton, commanding the Column from California, July 21, 1862. The district was defined as consisting of all of that part of the Territory of New Mexico west of a north-south line through Apache Pass, and from that point to Mesilla, New Mexico. David Fergusson was placed in command of the district, as well as of the post and town of Tucson, where he established his headquarters.

January 14, 1863, the District of Western Arizona was transferred to the Department of New Mexico, and it remained in that department until the Territory of Arizona was annexed to the Department of the Pacific by an order of January 20, 1865. The transfer was not effected, however, until March 7, 1865.

For additional information, see Department of the Pacific, Districts in the Department of the Pacific, District of Western Arizona; and see also below, Troops and Operations in the Department of New Mexico, Expedition from Southern California, through Arizona, to New Mexico and Northwestern Texas (Column from California).

TROOPS AND OPERATIONS IN THE DEPARTMENT OF NEW MEXICO

The troops in the Department of New Mexico at the outbreak of war consisted of regulars of the 5th United States Infantry, the 7th United States Infantry, two companies of the 10th United States Infantry, and the Regiment of Mounted Rifles (later redesignated the 3rd United States Cavalry). These regiments were scattered as companies at the various posts of the department to protect the settlements and the travel routes from Indian raiders.

The principal posts were Fort Marcy, Fort Garland, Fort Union, Fort Craig, Fort McLane, Fort Stanton, Fort Breckinridge, Fort Buchanan, Fort Fillmore, Albuquerque, Cubero, Abo Pass, Hatch's Ranch, and Camp Connelly. Posts were frequently changed, however, as circumstances required.

After the firing on Fort Sumter, the regulars from posts throughout the West, including those in the Department of New Mexico, were ordered east to be incorporated into the Union armies being assembled to suppress the rebellion. On May 17, 1861, the regulars of the Department of New Mexico were ordered to march to Fort Leavenworth, Kansas as soon as possible (the order was repeated on August 13), and the regulars were to be replaced by New Mexico Volunteers. This order was later modified, and the 5th United States Infantry and a few other companies remained in the department throughout the war.

Baylor's Invasion of Southern New Mexico, July 1861. During the first week of July 1861, John R. Baylor, with his battalion of John S. Ford's 2nd Regiment of Texas Mounted Volunteers, reached the southern border of New Mexico from Fort Brown and occupied Fort Bliss, which had been abandoned by United States troops. Baylor then moved up the Rio Grande July 23, crossed the river, and occupied Mesilla, New Mexico two days later. Baylor then decided to attack Fort Fillmore, three miles from Mesilla, but at 1:00 A.M. July 27, Isaac Lynde, commanding the Southern District of New Mexico at Fort Fillmore, abandoned the fort, and with seven companies of the 7th United States Infantry and three companies of Mounted Rifles marched toward Fort Stanton, New Mexico. Later that day, Lynde and his entire command were captured without resistance by Baylor at San Augustine Springs, about twenty miles east of Fort Fillmore.

Baylor's forces then occupied that part of New Mexico lying south of the Jornada del Muerto (south of Las Cruces). Forts McLane, Breckinridge, Buchanan, Fillmore, and Stanton were all abandoned, and Edward R. S. Canby, commanding United States troops in the territory (then a part of the Western Department), concentrated his forces at Santa Fe.

In a proclamation dated August 1, 1861, Baylor, as commander of the Confederate troops in the territory, organized the Territory of Arizona as a military government, and took possession in the name of the Confederate States of America. He defined the territory as comprising all that part of New Mexico lying south of the 34th parallel north latitude. To avoid confusion, it must be remembered that the territory of New Mexico at that time included all of the present-day state of Arizona.

Sibley's Invasion of New Mexico, February 7, 1862– April 22, 1862

July 9, 1861, Henry Hopkins Sibley was authorized to raise troops in Texas and to march with them into New Mexico and establish a military government. Sibley mustered his command at San Antonio during the period August-November 1861, and, beginning on October 22, his troops began the long march across western Texas toward El Paso. The last of his command arrived there in mid-December, and he went into quarters at Fort Bliss. Sibley's command was known as the Confederate Army of New Mexico, but it comprised only one brigade and some artillery. It consisted of John Ford's 2nd Regiment of Texas Mounted Volunteers, James Reily's 4th Regiment of Texas Mounted Volunteers, Thomas Green's 5th Regiment of Texas Mounted Volunteers, William Steele's 7th Regiment of Texas Mounted Volunteers, and Trevanion T. Teel's artillery. On January 4, 1862, William R. Scurry relieved Reily in command of the 4th Regiment of Texas Mounted Volunteers.

On December 14, 1861, Sibley assumed command of all Confederate forces on the Rio Grande at and above Fort Quitman, Texas, and designated his command as the Army of New Mexico. He established his headquarters at Fort Bliss. John R. Baylor, although he lost the command of his troops in the territory, continued with his duties as civil and military governor of Arizona.

Sibley moved with his command to Mesilla January 11, 1862, and there he joined with Baylor's battalion. A few days later he advanced and occupied Fort Thorn, which was a short distance north of present-day Hatch, New Mexico.

When Sibley moved into southern New Mexico, Canby concentrated his forces at Fort Craig, about twenty miles south of San Antonio, New Mexico. These consisted of the following: five companies of the 5th United States Infantry; three companies of the 7th United States Infantry; three companies of the 10th United States Infantry; two companies of the 1st United States Cavalry; five companies of the 3rd United States Cavalry; Alexander McRae's and Robert H. Hall's batteries; William Dodd's company of Colorado Volunteers; the 1st New Mexico

Infantry; seven companies of the 2nd New Mexico Infantry; seven companies of the 3rd New Mexico Infantry; one company of the 4th New Mexico Infantry; two companies of the 5th New Mexico Infantry; and Graydon's Independent New Mexico Spy Company (cavalry).

February 14, 1862, Canby organized his command into columns for field service as follows:

First Column
Henry R. Selden

Company D, 1st United States Cavalry
1st Battalion, Benjamin Wingate
   Companies B, D, F, and I, 5th United States Infantry
2nd Battalion, Peter W. L. Plympton
   Companies C and F, 7th United States Infantry
   Companies A and H, 10th United States Infantry
   Dodd's Company, Colorado Volunteers
McRae's Battery, Alexander McRae
Hall's Battery, Robert H. Hall

Note. McRae's provisional battery was composed of Company G, 2nd United States Cavalry and Company I, 3rd United States Cavalry. Hall's Battery of the 10th United States Infantry consisted of two howitzers.

Second Column
Benjamin S. Roberts

Companies C, D, G, and K, 3rd United States Cavalry, Thomas Duncan
Barriento's Company, 5th New Mexico Volunteers
New Mexico Mounted Militia

Third Column
Christopher (Kit) Carson

1st Battalion (four companies), 1st New Mexico Volunteers
2nd Battalion (four companies), 1st New Mexico Volunteers

Fourth Column
Miguel E. Pino

1st Battalion (four companies), 2nd New Mexico Volunteers
2nd Battalion (two companies), 2nd and 3rd New Mexico Volunteers

Fifth Column

1st New Mexico Militia (six companies)
2nd New Mexico Militia (four companies)

Engagement at Valverde, New Mexico, February 21, 1862. Sibley left Fort Thorn February 7, 1862 and marched up the Rio Grande toward Fort Craig. His force consisted of Scurry's 4th Regiment of Texas Volunteers; Green's 5th Regiment of Texas Volunteers; most of Baylor's battalion of the 2nd Regiment of Texas Volunteers, under Charles L. Pyron; J. S. Sutton's battalion of the 7th Regiment of Texas Volunteers; some Arizona Volunteers; and Teel's artillery battalion.

On February 12, 1862, Sibley arrived at a point about five miles below Fort Craig, and on February 16, he pushed a reconnaissance up to within a mile of the fort. An examination of the works, however, convinced him that they could not be successfully attacked, and he returned to his camp. Sibley then decided to cross to the east side of the Rio Grande, march northward under the cover of a range of hills that ended at the Mesa de la Contadera, recross the river at the ford at Valverde, and there place his army on the road between Canby's army and Albuquerque and Santa Fe to the north.

Because of a dust storm, the Confederate army did not move until February 20, and then Green, who was in temporary command because of the illness of Sibley, started the army northward. That day Green arrived at a point opposite Fort Craig, but he was unable to move closer to the fort. When Canby learned of the enemy's movement that day, he sent James Graydon's Spy Company and 500 mounted militia under Pino and Robert H. Stapleton to the east side of the river to watch the enemy and to impede their movements as much as possible. They were strongly posted on the hills between Green and the river.

The next morning, the Confederate army, with Sibley again in command, resumed its march northward toward the ford of the Rio Grande, about six miles above Fort Craig. Canby then detached Benjamin S. Roberts with one company of the 1st United States Cavalry, three companies of the 3rd United States Cavalry, and four companies of the New Mexico Mounted Volunteers, commanded by José M. Valdez, and sent them upstream to observe Sibley's movement. Immediately afterward, Canby sent two sections of McRae's Battery and Hall's two howitzers, David H. Brotherton's company of the 5th United States Infantry, Charles H. Ingraham's company of the 7th United States Infantry, and two companies of New Mexico Volunteers to follow Roberts.

When Canby was certain that Sibley was moving toward the ford at Valverde, he recalled Henry R. Selden's battalion of regular infantry, which had been sent to the east side of the river, and sent it to reinforce Roberts. Christopher (Kit) Carson's eight companies of the 1st New Mexico Volunteers followed Selden. Finally, Canby left two companies of New Mexico Volunteers, a regiment of New Mexico Militia under Manuel Armijo, and a detachment of regulars to garrison Fort Craig, and he ordered Miguel E. Pino's 2nd New Mexico Volunteers back from the opposite bank of the river. When he had completed this business, he set out for the ford with Company G, 1st United States Cavalry and the remaining section of McRae's Battery.

When Roberts reached the crossing, near the foot of the Mesa de la Cantadora, he found that a part of Sibley's command had arrived before him, and had taken position in a large, thick bosque (or grove) on the opposite bank, near the ford. Thomas Duncan, who was in charge of the immediate advance, crossed his troopers of the 3rd United States Cavalry and, fighting dismounted, pushed the enemy back from the river. In doing so he enabled Roberts to establish his batteries so as to drive the enemy out of the bosque, and this was finally accomplished after about two hours of fighting.

At noon Selden arrived at the ford. Under Roberts' direction, he crossed the river and forced the enemy back from their second position. The artillery then crossed and, aided by Duncan's and Selden's troops, drove the enemy back to a new position behind a sand ridge about 600 yards from the river, and nearly parallel to it. By this time the enemy had been strongly reinforced by the arrival of the rest of Sibley's column. At 1:30 P.M. Sibley, claiming that he was too sick to continue (some say that he was drunk), again turned over the command to Green.

Canby arrived on the field at 2:45 P.M. and decided to launch an attack on the enemy's left flank. For this purpose, he began to form his command as follows: he placed McRae's Battery, supported by New Mexico Volunteers, on the left near the river; he assigned Selden's regular infantry and Carson's 1st New Mexico Volunteers to the center of the line; and he sent Hall's Battery and its infantry supports

and Duncan's dismounted cavalry to the left. He held in reserve Pino's volunteers, a squadron of the 1st United States Cavalry, and Valdez's volunteers. Carson's regiment, which had been held on the west bank of the river, was ordered to cross and take its place in line.

After issuing the order for the above disposition of his troops, Canby made some additional changes in their positions. He directed Richard S. C. Lord to unite his company of the 1st United States Cavalry with Ira W. Claflin's Company G, 1st United States Cavalry and report to Canby as a reserve. He increased the support for McRae's Battery by ordering up Peter W. L. Plympton's battalion, consisting of four companies of regulars and Dodd's company of Colorado Volunteers. He also ordered Pino's regiment, which was then coming up from Fort Craig, to cross the river as a reserve.

When Canby's line was finally completed, the troops were in line, from left to right, as follows: Dodd, McRae's Battery, Selden, and Carson, and Lord's cavalry near the ford. Then about a mile to the south were Duncan and Hall's Battery. This gap was to have been filled by Pino's New Mexico Volunteers, but when ordered up they mutinied and remained west of the river.

While the above movements were in progress, a large body of enemy cavalry charged Hall's Battery on the Union right and quickly became engaged with Duncan's 3rd United States Cavalry. Canby then sent Ingraham's Company F, 7th United States Infantry, and then Benjamin Wingate's battalion to support Duncan. The enemy attack was repulsed, and Carson's 1st New Mexico Volunteers, which was then coming up, joined in the pursuit of the retreating Texans.

The enemy then launched a heavy attack on McRae's Battery and its supports. The volunteer supports quickly gave way and fled through Plympton's regulars, which were to the rear, and carried some of these troops with them, but the rest of the regulars attempted manfully to halt the enemy advance. Finally, however, they were overwhelmed and driven to the rear. Wingate's battalion then arrived from the right, but it was unable to restore the line. McRae's Battery was captured, and McRae was killed. Wingate was wounded during the fighting that afternoon and later died of his wound.

Finally, Canby withdrew his command across the

Rio Grande and, with Selden's regulars covering the retreat, returned to Fort Craig.

Skirmish at Apache Canyon, New Mexico, March 26, 1862. After his victory at Valverde, Sibley moved on northward along the Rio Grande by way of Socorro to Albuquerque and then to Santa Fe, which were abandoned by Federal troops March 2 and March 4, 1862, respectively. The supplies at these two posts had been removed to Fort Union, which was about twenty-five miles northeast of Las Vegas, New Mexico, near the present-day town of Watrous.

At that time Gabriel R. Paul was in command of the Eastern District of New Mexico, with headquarters at Fort Union. Upon the approach of Sibley's army, Paul asked Governor William Gilpin of Colorado for help, and Gilpin responded by sending the 1st Colorado Volunteers under John P. Slough to New Mexico. Slough arrived with his regiment at Fort Union on March 11.

When Slough arrived at Fort Union, Paul had already completed arrangements for putting a column in the field to oppose Sibley. As the senior officer, however, Slough assumed command of the troops at the post, and organized a column from his own 1st Colorado Infantry and the regulars and New Mexico Volunteers at Fort Union. This new organization was called the Northern Division, Department of New Mexico (Canby's troops at Fort Craig were called the Southern Division). The Northern Division consisted of the following:

1st Colorado Infantry, John P. Slough

Lewis' Battalion, 5th United States Infantry, William H. Lewis

Ford's Independent Company of Colorado Volunteers, James H. Ford

Howland's Cavalry Detachment of 1st and 3rd United States Cavalry, George W. Howland

Ritter's Battery, John F. Ritter

Claflin's Battery, Ira W. Claflin

Note. Ford's Independent Company of Colorado Volunteers was a part of the garrison at Santa Fe and was later mustered in as Company A, 2nd Colorado Volunteers. Dodd's Independent Company of Colorado Volunteers was mustered in as Company B, 2nd Colorado Volunteers.

Slough left Fort Union March 23, 1862 and marched toward Santa Fe on a road that generally followed the route of present-day Interstate 85. Marching by way of Las Vegas, he arrived at Bernal Springs (near present-day Soham, New Mexico) on March 25, forty-five miles from Fort Union. He was then about one day's march from the important mountain pass at Glorieta, through which the Santa Fe Trail passed toward Santa Fe.

The pass at Glorieta, at the southern end of the Sangre de Cristo Mountains, is several miles in length, and about one-fourth mile wide near the center, but it narrows at both ends where it runs through the hills. The western end of the valley, which is quite narrow, was sometimes called Apache Canyon.

March 25, 1862, John M. Chivington, of the 1st Colorado Volunteers, left Bernal Springs at 3:00 A.M. and moved on toward Santa Fe. With him were about 200 cavalry, consisting of troopers of the 3rd United States Cavalry and Samuel H. Cook's Company F of the 1st Regiment of Cavalry, Colorado Volunteers, and 180 infantry taken from companies A, E, and D of the 1st Colorado Volunteers. Chivington's column camped that evening at Kozlowski's Ranch, near the eastern end of Glorieta Pass. At 2:00 the next morning, Chivington sent a small party into the pass, and near the eastern end of Apache Canyon, at Pigeon's Ranch (a place owned by Alexander Valle that served as a hotel for travelers on the Santa Fe Trail), these troops captured a few of the enemy. When this was reported to Chivington, he broke camp at 8:00 A.M. on March 26 and marched into the pass and entered the upper end of Apache Canyon. About 2:00 P.M. Chivington encountered the advance of Sibley's column under Charles L. Pyron, which was headed for Fort Union. During the rest of the afternoon, with constant fighting, Chivington advanced and drove the enemy back to Johnson's farm at the western end of Apache Canyon. Chivington camped that night at Pigeon's Ranch, but he moved back to Kozlowski's Ranch the next morning and rejoined Slough's command.

Engagement at Glorieta (or Pigeon's Ranch), New Mexico, March 28, 1862. Slough left Bernal Springs at noon March 27, 1862, and by 2:00 the next morning had his entire force assembled at Kozlowski's Ranch. Before dawn he divided his

Northern Division into two columns in preparation for the day's march. He assigned Chivington to the command of an infantry force consisting of the following: Lewis' battalion, which was composed of companies A and G of the 5th United States Infantry; Company B of the 1st Colorado Volunteers; James H. Ford's Company A of the 2nd Colorado Volunteers; and Edward W. Wynkoop's battalion, which was composed of companies A, E, and H of the 1st Colorado Volunteers. Chivington was directed to advance on the Galisteo road to the left of Apache Canyon, and then cross the mountain and march toward Johnson's Ranch at the western end of the canyon, where spies had reported that Sibley's train was parked.

The troops remaining with Slough consisted of the rest of the Colorado Volunteers, two batteries, and two companies of cavalry, totaling 600 men. That morning, March 28, Samuel F. Tappan was assigned immediate command of a battalion of infantry consisting of companies C, D, G, I, and K of the 1st Colorado Volunteers, and the batteries of John F. Ritter and Ira W. Claflin were attached to Tappan's command.

Slough left Kozlowski's Ranch at 8:30 A.M., with George W. Howland's cavalry in advance, and marched toward Santa Fe. After advancing about five miles, Slough arrived at Glorieta, near Pigeon's Ranch, and there the Federal pickets reported that the enemy was advancing in force less than one-half mile away.

Sibley was in nominal command of the Army of New Mexico, but William R. Scurry, as the senior officer, was in immediate command that day. He had advanced from Johnson's Ranch that morning with nine companies of the 4th Texas, four companies of the 5th Texas, four companies of the 7th Texas, and a detachment of the 2nd Texas, and had placed his command in position across the canyon from wall to wall. Charles L. Pyron was in command on the right, Henry W. Raguet on the center, and Scurry, in person, on the left.

When the enemy appeared, Slough brought forward the artillery, posted companies C and K in support, and advanced companies D and I as skirmishers. He held Company G in reserve. He then formed his command across the canyon as follows: Ritter's Battery was on the right of the Santa Fe

Trail, a short distance beyond Pigeon's Ranch, and Richard Sopris' Company C was immediately in rear of the battery; Charles Kleber's Company I (commanded by Charles Mailie) was to the right of Sopris; Hall's Battery was on the left of the Santa Fe Trail, across from Ritter's Battery, and Samuel M. Robbins' Company K was in rear of Hall, on the left of Sopris; Jacob Downing's Company D was on the left of Robbins; and Charles J. Walker's troopers of the 2nd United States Cavalry were on the left of Downing. Samuel H. Cook's Company F was in position across the road at Pigeon's Ranch, and William F. Wilder's Company G was with the wagons some distance to the rear.

The Confederates attacked about 11:00 A.M., and the fighting soon became general and determined. Because of the absence of a part of his troops with Chivington, Slough was outnumbered, and he was compelled to fight on the defensive during the day. He was subjected to steady frontal attacks and was forced to give ground, and after about half an hour he withdrew to a position in front of and near the Pigeon house. At that point, Company G was brought up from reserve and placed in line. Finally, after about five hours of fighting, Slough withdrew about two miles to a new position, where the fighting finally ended at 5:00 P.M.

Meantime, Chivington had left camp at Kozlowski's Ranch with Slough but, after marching about two miles on the road toward Santa Fe, turned off to the left on the road (merely a trail) leading to Galisteo. He continued on this road for eight miles, then turned off and marched eight miles across the mountain, and about 1:30 P.M. reached a point on the cliffs overlooking Johnson's Ranch. There he discovered the enemy wagon train parked and protected by only a small guard. Chivington's column then descended the mountain and, after driving off the guard, destroyed the train, which consisted of eighty wagons loaded with ammunition, clothing, subsistence, forage, baggage, and medical stores. Chivington then returned to camp at Kozlowski's Ranch that evening.

Although Slough's force at Pigeon Ranch had been driven back during the day, the destruction of the enemy's wagon train was a serious loss, and it resulted in the withdrawal of Sibley's army to Santa Fe, and eventually from New Mexico.

* * * * * * * * * *

At 2:00 P.M. March 29, 1862, after caring for the wounded and burying the dead, Slough left Kozlowski's Ranch for San Jose. He continued on toward Fort Union March 31, arriving there April 2. On April 5, however, Canby ordered Slough to move southward with his regiment and join the troops with Canby, who was then moving north from Fort Craig. The troops, under the immediate command of Benjamin S. Roberts, were known as the Southern Division, Department of New Mexico.

Paul, who had resumed command of the regulars and New Mexico troops in the Eastern District of New Mexico when Slough departed for Glorieta, learned that Canby had left Fort Craig April 1, and on April 6 he left Fort Union with a column with the intention of effecting a junction with Canby near Albuquerque. When Sibley learned of the Federal advance, he withdrew from Santa Fe and concentrated his forces at Albuquerque.

Canby arrived before the town April 8, where he demonstrated for a time, and then moved on April 9–10 by way of Carnuel Canyon to the village of San Antonio, east of Albuquerque. There he was joined by Paul with his command from Fort Union. Canby continued on to Tijeras, and there on April 12–13 he was joined by the 1st Colorado Volunteers. Before joining Canby, on April 12, Slough resigned and departed for Denver. Before leaving he placed Samuel F. Tappan in command of the regiment, but, acting on the request of the officers of the regiment, Canby assigned Chivington to the command.

Sibley began the evacuation of Albuquerque April 12, 1862, and then retreated southward along the Rio Grande toward Texas. On April 14, both Canby and Sibley were in camp, only a few miles apart, near Peralta, thirty-six miles south of Albuquerque. Canby's troops skirmished with the enemy at Peralta, during the evening of April 15, but during the night Sibley pulled out and continued his retreat.

At Peralta, on April 16, Canby reorganized his command as follows: Gabriel R. Paul was assigned command of the First Column and John M. Chivington was assigned command of the Second Column of the Union Army of New Mexico. Benjamin S. Roberts was assigned command of that part

of New Mexico formerly included in the Northern and Central districts of New Mexico and the Santa Fe District. Robert M. Morris was assigned command of all cavalry forces with Canby's command, except Graydon's Spy Company.

Canby then moved down the east side of the Rio Grande with Paul's and Chivington's columns, while Sibley moved in the same direction across the river. Near La Joya, north of Fort Craig, Sibley marched inland to the southwest to bypass Fort Craig, and he later returned to the river near Fort Thorn. He ended his retreat at Mesilla. Canby followed Sibley as far as Fort Craig, and there he ended the pursuit April 22.

The Confederates did not again attempt an invasion of New Mexico, and from May 1862 until the end of the war, the Union troops in the Department of New Mexico were employed on the Indian frontier and in guarding the roads in the department from attacks by bands of Indians.

By mid-1862, volunteer regiments of New Mexico troops had largely replaced the regulars in the department, who had departed for the East. Advance elements of James H. Carleton's Column from California, under the command of Edward E. Eyre, arrived on the Rio Grande at abandoned Fort Thorn July 4, 1862, and by early August of that year the greater part of Carleton's command, totaling about 1,800 men, had arrived in southern New Mexico. For information about Carleton's Column from California, see the following section.

Expedition from California, through Arizona, to New Mexico and Northwestern Texas (Column from California)

On January 31, 1862, George Wright, commander of the Department of the Pacific, assigned James H. Carleton to the command of an expedition that was to move eastward from the southeastern part of the state into Arizona and New Mexico. The object of this expedition was to recapture the forts that had been lost in Arizona and New Mexico, and to capture or drive from the country any Confederate forces operating there. In addition it was to open the southern mail route.

This operation had been under consideration for some time, and as early as November 3, 1861, Joseph R. West, with companies B, H, and I of his own 1st Infantry, California Volunteers, had arrived at Fort Yuma on the Arizona border to relieve George Andrews' regulars of the 6th United States Infantry, which had been ordered east. West in turn was relieved at Fort Yuma by Edwin A. Rigg November 26.

The troops assigned to Carleton's expedition, except for the artillery, consisted of California Volunteers, and these were mobilized at Camp Drum (Drum Barracks) at Wilmington, California, and at Camp Wright near Oak Grove, on the Overland Stage Route in eastern San Diego County.

Carleton with his command marched eastward April 13, 1862 and arrived at Fort Yuma May 1. There, on May 15, he designated his command as the Column from California. It consisted of the following:

1st California Infantry (nine companies), Joseph R. West
5th California Infantry (companies A, B, E, and G), Theodore A. Coult
1st California Cavalry (five companies), Edward B. Eyre
2nd California Cavalry (company B), John C. Cremony
Battery B, 3rd United States Artillery, John B. Shinn

Note. Eyre commanded all cavalry with the expedition.

For additional information, see Department of the Pacific, Districts in the Department of the Pacific, District of Southern California, Column from California.

Meantime, California troops had already been sent forward into Arizona. Late in February 1862, William A. McCleave, with a small detachment of the 1st California Cavalry, was ordered out on a scout up the Gila River, and he had reached White's Mill near the Pima Villages when he was captured by the Confederates. The Pima Villages were near Maricopa Wells, south of present-day Phoenix, Arizona. A column under William P. Calloway, consisting of companies A and D of the 1st California Cavalry, Company I and a detachment of Company K of the 1st California Cavalry, and two howitzers,

was then sent to rescue McCleave, and to open the road to Tucson. Calloway reached the Pima Villages April 12, 1862, and there he learned that McCleave had been sent to Mesilla. He then sent a small detachment of his cavalry under James Barrett on toward Tucson, and on April 14, the rest of Calloway's battalion followed. On April 15, Barrett's small command was engaged in a skirmish at Picacho Pass, and Barrett and two of his men were killed. Calloway then fell back to the Pima Villages and established a fortified position. Picacho Pass was the most westerly land combat between the North and South during the war.

While Calloway was thus occupied, a second contingent of the Column from California under Joseph R. West was approaching from Yuma. West's command, consisting of two companies of cavalry and five companies of infantry, joined Calloway April 29 and established a post, which was named Fort Barrett, near the Pima Villages.

On May 4, the Confederates, recognizing the hopelessness of their situation, evacuated Tucson.

On May 14, West advanced with Company B, 1st California Cavalry, companies C, I, and K of the 1st California Infantry, and companies B and G of the 5th California Infantry, and he arrived at Tucson and occupied the town May 20. By early June all of the troops of the Column from California were near Tucson, except for a part of the 5th California Infantry that was left to garrison Fort Yuma and Fort Barrett. Carleton remained at Yuma until mid-May, when he turned over the command of the post to George W. Bowie of the 5th California Infantry, and he then joined his command at Tucson.

Upon arrival at Tucson, Carleton declared martial law, and on June 8 he announced himself as military governor of the Territory of Arizona. This done, Carleton began preparations for the movement on to New Mexico.

June 21, 1862, Edward E. Eyre left Tucson with the 1st California Cavalry on a reconnaissance toward the Rio Grande arriving on the river near Fort Thorn July 4.

On July 10, Thomas L. Roberts left Tucson with a detachment to scout the country in advance of the column and to look for Indians. His command consisted of his own Company E, 1st California Infantry; a detachment of Company H of the same regiment under Alexander B. MacGowan; Company B of the 2nd California Cavalry under John C. Cremony; and a battery commanded by William A. Thompson. Roberts reached Apache Pass July 15 and was under attack by Indians that day and the next, but on July 17, he continued on to join the column at Rio de Sauz.

Back in Mesilla, Henry Hopkins Sibley left William Steele with 400 men to hold the town, and with the rest of his brigade departed June 17 for San Antonio, Texas. Finally, Steele evacuated Mesilla July 8 and El Paso July 12 and followed Sibley south.

The remainder of the Column from California left Tucson in three columns July 20–23, 1862. West marched out July 20 with companies B, C, and K of his 1st California Infantry and Company G of the 5th California Infantry, and he was joined at Rio de Sauz by Company E, 1st California Infantry and Thompson's battery. July 21, the second column, consisting of John B. Shinn's Battery B, 3rd United States Artillery, Company A, 1st California Infantry, and Company B, 5th California Infantry, left Tucson, and it was followed on July 23 by the third column under Edwin A. Rigg, which consisted of companies D, F, H, and I of the 1st California Infantry.

Company D, 1st California Cavalry, which was at Tubac at the beginning of the march, was ordered to move directly to the crossing of the San Pedro River, and thereafter to move ahead of the column as an advance guard.

On July 21, Carleton, before leaving Tucson, organized the territory through which the Column from California was operating as the District of Western Arizona, Department of the Pacific, and he assigned David Fergusson of the 1st California Cavalry as commander of the district, and also of the post and town of Tucson. Carleton remained at Tucson until July 23, while forwarding troops and supplies, and then left with Riggs' third column. From the San Pedro River, he led the column toward New Mexico.

On July 31, a wagon train loaded with supplies for the entire command left Tucson, escorted by Company A, 1st California Cavalry and Company A, 5th California Infantry.

Because of the hostility of the Chiricahua Apaches, Carleton established a post (Fort Bowie) at Apache Pass and left Theodore A. Coult in command with detachments of two companies of the 5th California Infantry.

The head of Carleton's column arrived on the Rio Grande near Fort Thorn August 7, 1862, and by August 27, the California troops had occupied Fort Thorn, Las Cruces, Fort Fillmore, and Mesilla in New Mexico and Fort Bliss, Fort Davis, Fort Quitman, and Franklin (El Paso) in Texas. The territory occupied by troops of the Column from California was organized August 30 as the District of Arizona (see above, Districts in the Department of New Mexico).

The entry of Carleton's command into the Department of New Mexico created a command problem. Carleton succeeded Canby in command of the department September 18, 1862, and Joseph R. West was assigned command of the Column from California and of the District of Arizona. Although West continued to report to Carleton, the Column from California remained on the rolls of the Department of the Pacific, and some of its troops actually served in the District of Western Arizona, which was a part of the Department of the Pacific. This arrangement resulted from a ruling of March 22, 1862 by the adjutant general of the army, Lorenzo Thomas. Thomas stated that in changes recently made in the boundaries of departmental commands, troops belonging to one department might either be in, or move into, another department. In such cases, the troops so situated would continue under the command of the general officer under whom they had been operating. Carleton had been operating under orders from Headquarters, Department of the Pacific.

To complicate matters further, Carleton had created his own District of Arizona, embracing the Mesilla Valley and some territory on both sides of it, and had assigned West to command the district. Acting on Carleton's request, the War Department eliminated these difficulties January 14, 1863 by transferring the Column from California and the District of Western Arizona to the Department of New Mexico.

From the time that Carleton assumed command of the Department of New Mexico until the end of the war, and even thereafter, his principal concern was the control of the hostile Indians, especially the Mescalero Apaches, the Navajos, and the Comanches. His first step was to repair and garrison the old posts and to build new ones so that he could distribute his troops effectively for the protection of the territory of the department. Then, from that time on, the troops of the Department of New Mexico were occupied with garrison duty, expeditions against the Indians, and patrolling the main routes of travel through the department.

The posts occupied by troops of the Department of New Mexico during the period of Carleton's command, from 1862 to the end of the war, were as follows: Fort Union, Fort Marcy, Fort Craig, Fort Sumner, Fort Stanton, Albuquerque, Los Pino, Fort Wingate, Las Cruces, Fort McRae, Fort Bascom, and Fort Cummings, all in New Mexico, and Franklin (El Paso) in Texas. Other posts were as follows: in Arizona Territory, Tucson (January 1863–August 1864), Fort Bowie (January 1863–February 1865), Reventon (April 1864–May 1864), Tubac (June 1864–February 1865), Fort Goodwin (August 1864–February 1865), and Fort Whipple (December 1864–February 1865); and in New Mexico, Camp Easton (May 1863–June 1863), Fort West (May 1863–December 1863), Fort Canby (September 1863–September 1864), Mesilla (November 1863–January 1864), Valles Grande (Las Valles) (November 1863–March 1864), Camp Mimbres (November 1863–August 1864), and Fort Selden (May 1865).

NORTHERN DEPARTMENT

The Northern Department was constituted January 12, 1864, to consist of the states of Illinois, Indiana, Michigan, and Ohio, and Samuel P. Heintzelman was assigned command, with headquarters at Columbus, Ohio. Heintzelman assumed command January 20, 1864, and the department was organized during the following month.

On February 8, 1864, Jeffersonville, Indiana was transferred to the Department of the Ohio, and Cairo, Illinois was transferred to the Department of the Tennessee.

When the Northern Department was constituted, Alton, Illinois, which had been attached to the Department of the Missouri September 19, 1862, was included within its limits. On February 15, 1864, however, Alton was again assigned to the Department of the Missouri.

The city of Cincinnati, Ohio was within the territorial limits of the Northern Department, but the cities of Covington and Newport in Kentucky, and the fortifications surrounding them, which were intended primarily for the defense of Cincinnati, were in the Department of the Ohio. To remedy this situation, Covington and the country around it within a radius of ten miles were added to the Northern Department June 25, 1864. Joseph Hooker assumed command of the Northern Department October 1, 1864 (assigned September 28), and on October 6 he established headquarters at Cincinnati.

November 28, 1864, the Department of the Tennessee was largely broken up, and as a consequence, Cairo, Illinois was again included in the Northern Department.

February 10, 1865, Jeffersonville, Indiana was transferred from the Department of the Cumberland to the Northern Department, and Covington, Kentucky and the surrounding country were taken from the Northern Department and included in the Department of Kentucky.

March 24, 1865, Jeffersonville and New Albany in Indiana were transferred to the Department of Kentucky.

The Northern Department was discontinued June 27, 1865 when it was merged into the Department of the Ohio.

COMMANDERS OF THE NORTHERN DEPARTMENT

Samuel P. Heintzelman	January 20, 1864 to October 1, 1864
Joseph Hooker	October 1, 1864 to June 27, 1865

DISTRICTS IN THE NORTHERN DEPARTMENT

District of Illinois. From November 16, 1863 to

January 12, 1864, the entire state of Illinois, except the posts of Cairo and Alton, was not included in any department. When the Northern Department was created January 12, 1864, however, the state of Illinois was included within its limits. Then, by an order of August 7, 1864, the state was constituted as the District of Illinois, Northern Department. Halbert E. Paine was assigned command of the district, and on August 12 was ordered to Springfield to establish his headquarters.

The post of Alton was transferred to the Department of the Missouri February 15, 1864.

When Hooker assumed command of the department October 1, 1864, Illinois was already constituted as a military district, and this was reaffirmed as a district of the Northern Department by an order of the same date.

The principal posts of the district were as follows: Camp Butler (Charles M. Prevost) at Springfield, Camp Douglas (Benjamin J. Sweet) at Chicago, Cairo (Ezra T. Sprague), Quincy (Henry H. Dean), and Rock Island (Andrew J. Johnson). (The commanders of the posts are given as of December 31, 1864.)

Commanders of the District of Illinois were as follows:

Halbert E. Paine	August 12, 1864 to September 30, 1864
John Cook	September 30, 1864 to June 27, 1865

District of Indiana. Indiana was a district in the Department of the Ohio until November 16, 1863, and then was in no department until January 12, 1864, when the Northern Department was created. John S. Simonson was in command in Indiana during this interval. When Joseph Hooker assumed command of the Northern Department October 1, 1864, Indiana, which had already been constituted as a military district, was redesignated as the District of Indiana, Northern Department.

The principal posts of the district were Burnside Barracks, Evansville, Indianapolis, Madison, and New Albany.

The commanders of the District of Indiana were as follows:

John S. Simonson	January 12, 1864 to May 23, 1864
Henry B. Carrington	May 23, 1864 to August 25, 1864
Alvin P. Hovey	August 25, 1864 to June 27, 1865

District of Michigan. The state of Michigan was not in any department from November 16, 1863 until January 12, 1864, when it was included in the newly created Northern Department. While Heintzelman was in command of the Northern Department, he exercised personal command of the states of Michigan and Ohio. When Hooker assumed command of the department on October 1, 1864, he designated the state of Michigan as the District of Michigan, Northern Department. Bennett H. Hill was assigned command of the district, with headquarters at Detroit.

The principal posts in the district were Detroit, and Lysander Cutler's Draft and Recruiting Rendezvous at Jackson.

District of Ohio. From November 16, 1863 until January 12, 1864, that part of the state of Ohio that had previously belonged to the Department of the Ohio (see Department of the Ohio, August 19, 1862–January 17, 1865) was in no department. The remainder of the state was divided between the Department of the Monongahela and the Department of West Virginia. On January 12, 1864, the entire state was included in the Northern Department. During the time that Heintzelman was in command of the Northern Department he exercised direct control over the state of Ohio. When Hooker assumed command October 1, 1864, he designated the state of Ohio as the District of Ohio, Northern Department.

The principal posts in the district were as follows: Camp Chase, near Columbus (William P. Richardson); Camp Thomas, near Columbus (James N. Caldwell and James Van Voast); Camp Dennison, near Miamisville, Hamilton County (Edward F. Noyes, William Von Doehn, and Darius B. Warner); Cincinnati (August Willich); Sandusky and Johnson's Island (Charles W. Hill); Camp Cleveland (Charles C. Smith); and Gallipolis (Lyman Allen). (Commanders of the posts are given as of December 31, 1864.)

Hooker appears to have commanded the District of Ohio as well as the Northern Department. Until the close of the war, the troops in the district were reported as posts, and the post commanders appear to have reported directly to Hooker.

DEPARTMENT OF THE NORTHWEST

The Department of the Northwest was created September 6, 1862, following the Sioux uprising in mid-August of that year. It included the states of Wisconsin, Minnesota, and Iowa, and the territories of Dakota and Nebraska. John Pope was assigned command, with headquarters at Saint Paul, Minnesota.

The department was reduced in size October 11, 1862 when Nebraska Territory was transferred to the Department of the Missouri.

Headquarters of the department was moved to Madison, Wisconsin November 23, 1862, and then to Milwaukee, Wisconsin February 7, 1863.

The Military Division of the Missouri was created January 30, 1865 to include the Department of the Northwest and the Department of the Missouri. Pope was assigned to command the military division, and Samuel R. Curtis was assigned to succeed Pope in command of the Department of the Northwest February 13, 1865.

April 9, 1865, the boundary of the Department of the Northwest was changed. Originally the southern boundary in the west ran along the 43rd parallel to the crest of the Rocky Mountains, but it was changed to run along the 43rd parallel westward from the Keya Paha River to the eastern boundary of the present state of Wyoming (104th degree west longitude); then northward to the northern border of the present state of Wyoming (45th parallel); then westward to the western border of Wyoming (111th degree west longitude); then south along the western border of Wyoming to the parallel of 44 degrees 30 minutes; and then westward to the crest of the Rocky Mountains.

In the reorganization of the military divisions and departments of the army June 27, 1865, the territory comprising the Department of the Northwest was included in the newly constituted Department of the Missouri, to which Pope was assigned command.

COMMANDERS OF THE DEPARTMENT OF THE NORTHWEST

John Pope	September 16, 1862 to November 28, 1862
Washington L. Elliott	November 28, 1862 to February 13, 1863
John Pope	February 13, 1863 to February 13, 1865
Samuel R. Curtis	February 13, 1865 to June 27, 1865

Note. Alfred Sully commanded the department temporarily for some time after November 23, 1864, while Pope was absent in Washington, D.C.

DISTRICTS IN THE DEPARTMENT OF THE NORTHWEST

First Military District. The First Military District was created in November 1862 to include that part of the Department of the Northwest west of the Red River Valley. It consisted of the state of Iowa and Dakota Territory. John Cook was assigned command, with headquarters at Sioux City, Iowa.

May 21, 1863, Alfred Sully was ordered to Sioux City to relieve Cook in command of the district, and to assume command of the Indian Expedition (see below, Troops in the Department of the Northwest). Sully assumed command about June 1, and was carried on the June 1863 roster as commander of the District of Dakota (see below). The designation of the First Military District was not officially changed to District of Dakota, however, until August 24, 1863.

June 8, 1863, Benjamin S. Roberts was assigned command of the District of Iowa (see below), and was ordered to assume command with headquarters at Davenport, Iowa. The state of Iowa was thus removed from the First Military District.

Second Military District. The Second Military District was created November 17, 1862 to include the territory between the Mississippi River and a line drawn south and east from Sauk Center, Minnesota, including the post of Sauk Center. Henry Hastings Sibley was assigned command, with headquarters at Fort Snelling, Minnesota.

November 23, 1862, the Second, Third, and Fourth military districts were consolidated to form the District of Minnesota (see below).

Third Military District. The Third Military District was created November 17, 1862 to include the territory north of a line drawn east through Sauk Center, Minnesota to the Mississippi River. Minor T. Thomas was assigned command, with headquarters at Fort Ripley, Minnesota.

November 23, 1862, the Second, Third, and Fourth military districts were consolidated to form the District of Minnesota (see below).

Fourth Military District. The Fourth Military District was created November 17, 1862 to include the Red River Valley and the route between Fort Abercrombie and Sauk Center, Minnesota. Francis Peteler was assigned command, with headquarters at Fort Abercrombie, Dakota Territory.

November 23, 1862, the Second, Third, and Fourth military districts were consolidated to form the District of Minnesota (see below).

District of Dakota. Sully arrived at Sioux City, Iowa about June 1, 1863 and assumed command of the expedition against the Sioux Indians in Dakota Territory. He relieved John Cook in command of the First Military District, Department of the Northwest. The June 1863 roster, however, gives Sully's command as the District of Dakota. On August 24, 1863, the District of Dakota was officially constituted from the First Military District (see above). Headquarters of the district was at Fort Randall, Dakota Territory. Sully remained in command until the district was discontinued December 4, 1863.

August 24, 1863, the following counties in the state of Iowa were detached from the District of Iowa (see below) and assigned to the District of Dakota: Calhoun, Sac, Ida, Woodbury, Plymouth, Cherokee, Buena Vista, Pocahontas, Palo Alto, Clay, O'Brien, Sioux, Buncombe (Lyon), Osceola, Dickerson, and Emmett. These counties were in the northwestern corner of the state and west of the Des Moines River.

The District of Dakota was discontinued December 4, 1863, when it was merged into the District of Iowa.

District of Iowa. June 8, 1863, Benjamin S. Roberts was assigned command of the District of Iowa, and was ordered to Davenport to assume command.

December 4, 1863, a new order constituted the District of Iowa to include the state of Iowa and Dakota Territory. The district was formed by the consolidation of the former District of Iowa and the District of Dakota. Alfred Sully was assigned command, with headquarters for the winter at Davenport. On November 23, 1864, headquarters was moved to Dubuque, Iowa.

Sully was in the field with the Northwestern Indian Expedition during the summer of 1864, and Edward P. Ten Broeck was in charge of district headquarters.

The District of Iowa was designated as a Separate Brigade November 12, 1864, to date from October 25.

The principal posts in the district were as follows: in Iowa, Davenport, Sioux City, Dubuque, Fort Berthold, Crow Creek, and Spirit Lake; in Dakota Territory, Farm Island, Fort Randall, Yankton, Vermillion, Fort Rice, Fort Sully, and Fort Union.

District of Minnesota. The District of Minnesota was created November 23, 1862 by the consolidation of the Second, Third, and Fourth military districts of the Department of the Northwest (see above). Henry Hastings Sibley was assigned command, with headquarters at Saint Paul, Minnesota.

The district was extended March 4, 1864 to include all territory east of a line drawn from the head of the Pembina River to the western extremity of Devil's Lake; then to the head of James River; from there along the course of James River south to the forty-fourth parallel of latitude; then east along the forty-fourth parallel to the Big Sioux River; and finally along that river to the northern boundary of the state of Iowa.

The principal centers of command in the district were Fort Snelling, Fort Ridgely, and Fort Abercrombie.

In April 1864 the District of Minnesota was sub-districted as follows:

First Sub-district of Minnesota. The following were the principal posts of the sub-district: Fort Snelling (headquarters), Fort Ripley, Chengwatona, Princeton, and Sauk Center.

Second Sub-district of Minnesota. The principal posts of this sub-district were Saint Peter (headquarters until June 1862) and Fort Ridgely (headquarters after June 1864).

Third Sub-district of Minnesota. The principal posts of this sub-district were as follows: Fort Abercrombie (headquarters) and Fort Wadsworth in Dakota Territory and Princeton, Minnesota.

The commanders of the headquarters posts were also commanders of the sub-districts.

October 25, 1864, the District of Minnesota was designated as a Separate Brigade.

District of Wisconsin. After the Department of the Northwest was created in September 1862, Washington L. Elliott was assigned command of the troops in the state of Wisconsin. These were stationed at Madison, under Daniel J. Dill; Racine, under Isaac E. Messmore; Bayfield, under Harvey Fairchild; and Superior, under J. L. Dickson. Later the state of Wisconsin was designated as the District of Wisconsin.

Elliott was relieved from duty in the Department of the Northwest February 16, 1863, and Thomas C. H. Smith assumed command of the District of Wisconsin, with headquarters at Milwaukee. In Late October 1864, Smith was on detached service at Keokuk, Iowa, and Joseph McC. Bell was in temporary command of the district. Charles T. Campbell was in temporary command of the district from November 7 to November 17, 1864. Smith then returned to the district and resumed command, but in December he departed on leave of absence, and Bell was again in temporary command of the district. Thomas A. Davies was assigned command of the district April 17, 1865, and remained in command until the Department of the Northwest was merged into the Department of the Missouri.

TROOPS AND OPERATIONS IN THE DEPARTMENT OF THE NORTHWEST

The troops in the Department of the Northwest were generally assigned as regiments, or parts of regiments, at the various posts in the department. In October 1862 these were as follows:

Fort Snelling, Benjamin F. Smith
Fort Ripley, Francis Hall
Fort Ridgely, Edwin A. Folsom
Fort Kearny, Edmund B. Alexander
Camp near Fort Ridgely, William R. Marshall
New Ulm, Milton Montgomery
Troops en route to Crow Wing, James I. Gilbert
Glencoe, Joseph Weinmann
Saint Cloud, George G. McCoy
Saint Peter, Asgrim K. Skaro

For additional posts, and at later dates, see Districts in the Department of the Northwest.

Larger organizations were formed for the several Indian expeditions that were carried out by troops of the department. These were as follows:

Sibley's Expedition to Wood Lake, Minnesota after Little Crow, September 1862. On September 19, 1862, Henry Hastings Sibley left camp at Fort Ridgely, Minnesota and marched toward Wood Lake. He arrived on the lake, near Yellow Medicine, early in the afternoon of September 22. At 7:00 the next morning Sibley's command was attacked by about 300 Indians under Little Crow, but after an engagement of about two hours, the Indians were repulsed.

The troops of Sibley's Expedition consisted of the following:

3rd Minnesota, A. Edward Welch
6th Minnesota, John T. Averill
7th Minnesota (five companies), William R. Marshall
9th Minnesota (one company), attached to 7th Minnesota
10th Minnesota (detachment), James Gorman
Renville Rangers (or Guard), J. R. Sterrett
Battery of Light Artillery, Mark Hendricks

Sibley's and Sully's Sioux Expeditions, Summer of 1863. In the summer of 1863, two cooperating expeditions were planned against the Sioux Indians. One of these, commanded by Henry Hastings Sibley, left Fort Ridgely June 16; the other, commanded by Alfred Sully, left Sioux City, Iowa about June 20. Plans called for the two columns to meet near Devil's Lake, Dakota Territory. Circumstances prevented the junction of the two columns as planned, but both remained in the field until September 1863.

On September 3, 1863, Sully gained an important victory over the Indians in an engagement at White Stone Hill, Dakota Territory, so-called because that was the name of a prominent hill near the scene of the action. That day Sully was encamped on a lake in what is now North Dakota, not far from the present-day town of Ellendale. He sent out Major Albert E. House with a battalion of the 6th Iowa Cavalry, and Frank La Framboise as a guide, to attack and capture any small parties of Indians, and to observe and hold any larger body until help could come up from the main column.

About 3:00 P.M. House found an Indian camp of at least 400 lodges after traveling about ten miles. He immediately sent word back to Sully for help and prepared to attack. House began his attack before help arrived in order to prevent the Indians' removal of their families and supplies. When Sully came up, he ordered Robert W. Furnas to charge on the right of the camp with his 2nd Nebraska Cavalry, and David S. Wilson to charge on the left with his 6th Iowa Cavalry. Sully, with two companies of the 6th and one company of the 7th Iowa Cavalry, followed by a battery, charged through the center of the camp.

Fighting continued until dark. The Indians were completely routed and driven from their camps, with the loss of many killed, wounded, and prisoners. In addition, Sully's men destroyed practically all tents and belongings of the Indians, including large quantities of buffalo meat. This was one of the most serious defeats suffered by the Indians since the uprising in the Minnesota Valley in 1862.

Sibley's command, sometimes called Sibley's Sioux Expedition, consisted of the following:

1st Minnesota Mounted Rangers, Samuel McPhaill
6th Minnesota Infantry, William Crooks
7th Minnesota Infantry, William R. Marshall

10th Minnesota Infantry, James H. Baker

Sully's force consisted of the following:

6th Iowa Cavalry, David S. Wilson
2nd Nebraska Cavalry, Robert W. Furnas

Sully's Northwestern Indian Expedition, July 1864–October 1864. Pope's plans for operations for 1864 were designed to provide for two basic necessities in the area: the protection of the Minnesota border, and the protection of the settlers who were arriving in increasing numbers along the Missouri River and its tributaries. Another matter also required attention—gold was discovered in northern Idaho and along the Salmon River, and consequently it became necessary to protect the mining area and the route leading to it.

According to Pope's plan, he intended to build and hold four forts that were to be so located as to dominate the Indian country, and three of these were to be built along the trail to the gold region in the Northern Rockies. In addition, he was to send out a strong mobile column for the purpose of demonstrating to the Sioux Indians his firm intention to prevent attacks on settlers and travelers in the area, and also of punishing those guilty of such attacks.

For this expedition, Alfred Sully, commander of the District of Iowa, was placed in command of a force, designated as Northwestern Expedition, which consisted of a brigade of Iowa and Wisconsin troops and a brigade of Minnesota troops from Henry Hastings Sibley's District of Minnesota. These brigades were organized as follows:

First Brigade, Samuel M. Pollock
   6th Iowa Cavalry (eleven companies), Samuel M. Pollock
   7th Iowa Cavalry (3rd Battalion), John Pattee
   Dakota Cavalry (1st Battalion), Nelson Miner
   Brackett's Minnesota Battalion of Cavalry, Alfred B. Brackett
   Prairie Battery, Nathaniel Pope
   Scouts (seventy)

Second Brigade, Minor T. Thomas
   8th Minnesota Infantry (ten companies), Henry C. Rogers
   2nd Minnesota Cavalry (six companies), Robert N. McLaren

3rd Minnesota Battery (two sections), John Jones Scouts (forty)

Sibley ordered the troops assigned to Second Brigade (also called the Minnesota Brigade) to assemble at Fort Ridgely May 28, 1864, and Thomas then moved out from Fort Ridgely June 5 and marched westward toward the Missouri River, with orders to join Sully and his First Brigade (or Iowa Brigade) at Swan Lake, Dakota Territory.

Sully left Sioux City, Iowa and moved up the Missouri River toward Swan Lake. He reached Yankton Agency June 9; Fort Randall, Dakota Territory, near the Nebraska border June 12; Fort Pierre (present-day Pierre, South Dakota) June 20; and joined Thomas' Minnesota Brigade at Swan Lake June 28.

On July 3, Sully left Swan Lake with both brigades. He reached the site of present-day Bismarck, North Dakota July 7. Upon arrival there he began the construction of Fort Rice on the Missouri River. As soon as the work was started, Sully's brigades were ferried across the river; they moved up the Cannonball River July 19 and reached the Heart River July 23. With Sully on this march was a large emigrant train bound for the gold country in Idaho, which had joined the column from Fort Ridgely, Minnesota.

At Heart River, Sully learned that Indians were in the Knife River region, and he then left the emigrant train and his wagons, with a cavalry force under William Tripp to protect them, and at 3:00 P.M. July 26 left Heart River and moved ahead with his unencumbered command. About fifteen miles out, his scouts found a large party of Sioux, and Sully set out to follow them to their main camp, which was located on a group of high hills, known as Killdeer Mountain (Mountains). Sully then marched eighty miles in forty-three hours and arrived near the Indian camp at 10:00 A.M. July 28.

Sully deployed his force, with First Brigade on the right and Second Brigade on the left, and he then advanced toward the mountain. After driving the Indians back to the mountain and into the wooded ravines that separated the hills, the troops dismounted and advanced on foot.

Six companies of the 6th Iowa Cavalry and three companies of the 8th Minnesota Infantry formed the front line, and Pope's Prairie Battery was placed in the center with a guard of two companies of cavalry. Brackett's Minnesota Battalion was in support on the right, and the 2nd Minnesota Cavalry was in support on the left. Jones' battery, with four companies of cavalry, was in reserve.

When Sully's line neared the base of the mountain, the Indians launched an attack on both flanks. The 2nd Minnesota Cavalry easily drove back the attackers on the left, and Brackett's Battalion repulsed the attack on the right. Brackett then advanced to the base of the mountain, where he was vigorously assailed, but with the help of Jones' battery he succeeded in driving the Indians back.

The artillery then opened fire on the parties of Indians on the hills and in the ravines, and then four companies of the 8th Minnesota under George A. Camp advanced and drove the last of the warriors from Killdeer Mountain. The Indians departed during the night, and the next day Sully completely destroyed their camp and all supplies.

Sully then marched on through the Badlands to the Yellowstone River, where he arrived August 12. He obtained supplies from two steamers that had arrived on the Yellowstone, but he decided to abandon the pursuit of the Indians. He then marched down the Yellowstone River to the Missouri River, and then down the Missouri to Fort Berthold.

DEPARTMENT OF THE OHIO
MAY 3, 1861–MARCH 11, 1862

The Department of the Ohio was created by an order of May 3, 1861 and consisted of the states of Ohio, Indiana, and Illinois. George B. McClellan, commander of the Ohio Volunteer Militia, was assigned command, with headquarters at Cincinnati, Ohio. McClellan assumed command of the department May 13.

The department limits were extended May 9, 1861 to include parts of Western Virginia and Pennsylvania as follows: all territory in the two states lying north of the Great Kanawha River, north and west of the Greenbrier River, and of a line that ran northward to the southwest corner of Maryland, then along the western Maryland line to the Pennsylvania line, and from that point northward to the northeast corner of McKean County in Pennsylvania.

The department was further extended by an order of June 6, 1861 to include the state of Missouri. This order was not put into effect, however, and Missouri remained in the Department of the West until the creation of the Western Department July 3, 1861. On that date Illinois and Missouri were transferred to the Western Department.

July 23, 1861, William S. Rosecrans assumed command of the Department of the Ohio, and two days later the department was redefined as consisting of the states of Indiana and Ohio and that part of Western Virginia lying north of the Great Kanawha River, north and west of the Greenbrier River, and of a line that ran northward to the southwest corner of Maryland. The territory in western Pennsylvania that was formerly a part of the Department of the Ohio was transferred to the Department of Pennsylvania.

The department was reorganized September 19, 1861 to include the states of Indiana and Ohio, and that part of Kentucky lying within fifteen miles of Cincinnati, Ohio. Ormsby M. Mitchel assumed command of the department September 21, 1861 (assigned command September 19), with headquarters at Cincinnati.

In a further reorganization November 9, 1861, the Department of the Ohio was defined as consisting of the states of Ohio, Michigan, Indiana, Tennessee, and that part of Kentucky lying east of the Cumberland River. It should be noted that, following the capture of Fort Henry and Fort Donelson, the forces under Ulysses S. Grant from the Department of the Missouri soon controlled the western part of Kentucky and Tennessee.

November 15, 1861, Don Carlos Buell assumed command of the Department of the Ohio (assigned November 9), with headquarters at Louisville, Kentucky.

The Department of the Ohio was abolished March 11, 1862, when it was merged into the Mountain Department and the Department of the Mississippi. That part of the Department of the Ohio east of a north-south line through Knoxville, Tennessee became a part of the Mountain Department, and that part of the department west of the same line became a part of the Department of the Mississippi.

DISTRICTS IN THE DEPARTMENT OF THE OHIO

Cheat River District. The Cheat River District was created July 25, 1861 to include the region within the Department of the Ohio that was watered by the lower Tygart's Valley and the Cheat River. James J. Biddle was assigned command, but on August 8, 1861 he was assigned to the Department of the Shenandoah. On August 20, 1863, Henry W. Benham was assigned command of Third Brigade, Army of Occupation of Western Virginia, and he also commanded the Cheat River District.

On September 19, 1861, the Cheat River District was transferred to the Department of Western Virginia.

Cheat Mountain (or Cheat Mountain District). On July 24, 1861, Joseph J. Reynolds was assigned command of First Brigade, Army of Occupation of Western Virginia, and in September he was ordered to Cheat Mountain, Virginia to relieve Newton Schleich in command there. The district was discontinued in the Department of the Ohio when its territory was transferred to the Department of Western Virginia.

District of Grafton. The District of Grafton was constituted August 3, 1861 to consist of the line of the Baltimore and Ohio Railroad from Cumberland, Maryland to Wheeling, West Virginia, and the Northwestern Virginia Railroad from Grafton west to Parkersburg. The district also included all posts and stations along the lines. Benjamin F. Kelley was assigned command of the district.

September 19, 1861, the Department of Western Virginia was created, and its territory included the District of Grafton, which then became a district of the new department.

TROOPS AND OPERATIONS IN THE DEPARTMENT OF THE OHIO

During the first few months of the existence of the Department of the Ohio, the principal task of its commander was the raising and organizing of troops to serve at the front. The first troops were sent to Western Virginia, where they were later organized as the Army of Occupation of Western Virginia, Department of the Ohio. For details of its organization and operations, see Volume I, Western (West) Virginia Operations, May 26–October 11, 1861.

Many regiments from the Department of the Ohio were also sent to Kentucky, and in August 1861 they were included in the newly organized Department of the Cumberland. For details of the organization of the troops in Kentucky during the period August-November 1861, see Army of the Cumberland, August 15, 1861–November 9, 1861, and see also Department of the Cumberland, August 15, 1861–November 9, 1861.

On November 9, 1861, the Department of the Cumberland was discontinued, and that part of Kentucky lying east of the Cumberland River was assigned to the Department of the Ohio. For the organization of the troops in Kentucky at that time, see Department of the Cumberland, August 15, 1861–November 9, 1861.

Don Carlos Buell assumed command of the Department of the Ohio November 15, 1861, and on December 2 reorganized the troops of the department into brigades and divisions and called his new organization the Army of the Ohio. For details of this organization, see Army of the Ohio (Buell).

For some time Felix K. Zollicoffer, commanding the Confederate forces in eastern Kentucky, had been active in that region. In November 1861 he moved westward through northern Tennessee, and December 5–8 he crossed the Cumberland River into Kentucky at Mill Springs. When George H. Thomas, commanding First Division, Army of the Ohio, learned of Zollicoffer's approach, he concentrated his division near Somerset, Kentucky. On December 13, George B. Crittenden was ordered to Kentucky to assume command of all forces then commanded by Zollicoffer, and he moved to Mill Springs, where he assumed command. Then, on January 19, 1862, he moved forward, north of the river, and attacked Thomas' division, but he was defeated at the Engagement of Mill Springs and driven from the state. Zollicoffer, commanding a brigade in Crittenden's division, was killed. For details, see Engagement at Mill Springs (or Logan's

Cross Roads, Fishing Creek, Beech Grove), Kentucky.

On February 16, 1862, Fort Donelson on the Cumberland River was surrendered to Ulysses S. Grant, and this resulted in the collapse of the first Confederate defensive in Kentucky, including Columbus and Bowling Green. Buell was then ordered to advance with his Army of the Ohio and occupy Nashville, Tennessee. His first troops entered the city February 26, and the rest of the army arrived March 2–4.

DEPARTMENT OF THE OHIO AUGUST 19, 1862–JANUARY 17, 1865

The Department of the Ohio was re-created August 19, 1862 when Confederate forces under Braxton Bragg and E. Kirby Smith threatened invasion of Kentucky. The department was defined as consisting of the states of Illinois, Indiana, Michigan, Ohio, Wisconsin, and that part of Kentucky east of the Tennessee River, including Cumberland Gap and the troops operating in its vicinity. Horatio G. Wright was assigned command, with headquarters at Cincinnati, Ohio.

There were many changes in the boundaries of the department during the period of its existence. These were as follows:

September 6, 1862, Wisconsin became a part of the newly created Department of the Northwest.

September 19, 1862, the post of Alton, Illinois was transferred to the Department of the Missouri.

September 19, 1862, all of Western Virginia became a part of the Department of the Ohio.

October 16, 1862, the post of Cairo, Illinois was annexed to the Department of the Tennessee.

March 16, 1863, all of Western Virginia was transferred to the Middle Department.

June 9, 1863 (ordered May 15, 1863), Gallipolis,

Ohio and the Ohio shore opposite the mouth of the Kanawha River were assigned to the Middle Department.

June 9, 1863, the counties of Columbiana, Jefferson, and Belmont in Ohio became a part of the Department of the Monongahela.

June 24, 1863, the counties of Monroe, Athens, Washington, Meigs, Gallia, and Lawrence in Ohio were assigned to the Middle Department.

The Military Division of the Mississippi was created October 16, 1863 to consist of the Department of the Ohio, the Department of the Cumberland, and the Department of the Tennessee. Ulysses S. Grant assumed command October 18.

November 16, 1863, the Department of the Ohio was reorganized to consist of that part of the state of Kentucky east of the Tennessee River and such part of East Tennessee as might be occupied by troops of the Army of the Ohio. The states of Illinois, Indiana, Michigan, and Ohio were in no department until January 12, 1864, when they were assigned to the newly created Northern Department.

February 8, 1864, Jeffersonville, Indiana was annexed to the Department of the Ohio.

June 25, 1864, the town of Covington, Kentucky and the country around within a radius of fifteen miles was annexed to the Northern Department.

On January 17, 1865, the Department of the Ohio was discontinued when it was united with George H. Thomas' Department of the Cumberland.

COMMANDERS OF THE DEPARTMENT OF THE OHIO

Horatio G. Wright	August 23, 1862 to March 25, 1863
Ambrose E. Burnside	March 25, 1863 to December 11, 1863
John G. Foster	December 11, 1863 to February 9, 1864
John M. Schofield	February 9, 1864 to November 17, 1864
George Stoneman	November 17, 1864 to January 17, 1865

Note. Stoneman was assigned to duty as second in command to Schofield, who was absent in the field with the Army of the Ohio or Twenty-Third Corps. Stoneman, whose headquarters was at Louisville, Kentucky, was authorized to exercise the duties of department commander during Schofield's absence. Schofield remained in command of the department until it was discontinued January 17, 1865.

POSTS AND DISTRICTS IN THE DEPARTMENT OF THE OHIO

Post of Cairo, Illinois. The state of Illinois was included in the Department of the Mississippi until August 19, 1862, and it was then transferred to the newly created Department of the Ohio. The Post of Cairo remained in the Department of the Ohio until transferred to the Department of the Tennessee October 16, 1862. James M. Tuttle commanded the post during this period.

District of Central Kentucky. On November 17, 1862, the state of Kentucky was divided into three districts: the District of Eastern Kentucky, the District of Central Kentucky, and the District of Western Kentucky. The territory of the District of Central Kentucky consisted of that part of the state not included in the District of Western Kentucky (see below) and the District of Eastern Kentucky (also see below). Gordon Granger, commander of the Army of Kentucky, was assigned command of the district, with headquarters at Lexington.

The troops in the district were designated as the Army of Kentucky (see Army of Kentucky [Granger]) until January 20, 1863. First Division, Army of Kentucky, under Andrew J. Smith, was transferred to Memphis, Tennessee in the Department of the Tennessee November 13, 1862.

On January 20, 1863, Quincy A. Gillmore was assigned command of the District of Central Kentucky, and Granger was ordered to Louisville, where he organized a new division, which he took to Nashville, Tennessee in the Department of the

Cumberland. On January 25, Gillmore organized the troops remaining in the district into brigades as follows:

First Brigade, Samuel A. Gilbert (at Frankfort, Kentucky)

Second Brigade, Benjamin P. Runkle (at Danville, Kentucky)

Third Brigade, Charles C. Doolittle (at Lexington, Kentucky)

On March 18, 1863, Samuel P. Carter was placed in command of all United States forces in and near Lexington. Meantime, Ninth Corps had been transferred from Newport News, Virginia to Kentucky March 9–13, and on March 27 Benjamin C. Christ was ordered with his Second Brigade, First Division, Ninth Corps to report to Gillmore at Lexington. Upon arrival there, Christ was assigned to Carter's command.

First Division and Second Division of Ninth Corps were also sent to Central Kentucky, and on April 10 Orlando B. Willcox, commanding First Division, relieved Gillmore in command of the District of Central Kentucky.

During April and May 1863, the forces in the District of Central Kentucky consisted of the following: Thomas Welsh's First Division, Ninth Corps, which was at Middleburg; Samuel D. Sturgis' Second Division, Ninth Corps at Lexington and Mount Sterling; and Samuel P. Carter's Fourth Division, Ninth Corps, which was at Monticello. There were also troops stationed at Cynthiana, Frankfort, Nicholasville, and Paris in Kentucky.

Fourth Division seems to have been a temporary arrangement, with Christ's brigade retaining its original designation of Second Brigade, First Division. This brigade was transferred from Carter's command June 4 and was sent to Vicksburg with Ninth Corps.

On April 27, 1863, all troops stationed in Kentucky, exclusive of Ninth Corps, were designated as Twenty-Third Corps, Department of the Ohio. The corps was organized May 22, and George L. Hartsuff was assigned command. For additional information, see Twenty-Third Corps, Army of the Ohio.

On June 3, troops of Ninth Corps began embarkation for Vicksburg, Mississippi, where they joined Ulysses S. Grant's Army of the Tennessee in its attempts to capture the city.

On June 4, Samuel D. Sturgis was assigned command of all troops in the District of Central Kentucky, including those under Samuel P. Carter. Sturgis' command was the District of Central Kentucky, but it was also designated as First Division, Twenty-Third Corps. After the organization of Twenty-Third Corps in May 1863, the use of the designation "District of Central Kentucky" was generally discontinued.

The principal posts in the district were as follows: Columbia, Cynthiana, Danville, Frankfort, Lexington, Middleburg, Monticello, Mount Sterling, Nicholasville, Paris, Somerset, Stanford, and Winchester.

The commanders of the District of Central Kentucky were as follows:

Gordon Granger	November 17, 1862 to January 20, 1863
Quincy A. Gillmore	January 20, 1863 to April 10, 1863
Orlando B. Willcox	April 10, 1863 to June 4, 1863
Samuel D. Sturgis	June 4, 1863 to July 4, 1863

Note. On July 19, 1863, after the departure of Sturgis, Samuel P. Carter was assigned command of First Division, Twenty-Third Corps.

Cheat Mountain District. On September 24, 1862, Robert H. Milroy's brigade of Eleventh Corps, Defenses of Washington was detached and sent to Western Virginia. Milroy moved to Clarksburg October 18, and during the remainder of the month and in early November he operated in the Cheat Mountain District, Department of the Ohio, which included the country from Clarksburg to Sutton and extended to the front as far as Beverly and the mountain summits.

On November 13, Milroy was ordered to report to Benjamin F. Kelley, commander of the Railroad Division in the District of Western Virginia, Middle Department. Milroy then moved with his command, at that time called the Cheat Mountain Division, to New Creek, Western Virginia and out of the district.

District of the Clinch. Orlando B. Willcox, commanding the Left Wing Forces in East Tennessee, Army of the Ohio, moved with his command to Cumberland Gap about November 21, 1863. Early in January 1864, the area about the gap, and the forces therein, were designated as the District of the Clinch. Theophilus T. Garrard relieved Willcox in command of the district January 17, 1864 (assigned January 11), and on January 19, Willcox assumed command of Ninth Corps, which was then in East Tennessee.

The district was discontinued April 10, 1864, when its territory became a part of the District of East Tennessee (see following section), and the troops of the district became First Brigade of Jacob Ammen's Fourth Division, Twenty-Third Corps. Garrard was assigned command of the brigade. For additional information, see Knoxville, Tennessee Campaign; and see also, in section on Miscellaneous Organizations, Left Wing Forces in East Tennessee (Willcox).

District of East Tennessee. The District of East Tennessee was constituted April 10, 1864 to consist of that part of East Tennessee occupied by Fourth Division, Twenty-Third Corps, including the District of the Clinch. The designations of Fourth Division, Twenty-Third Corps and District of East Tennessee were frequently used synonymously. Jacob Ammen, commanding Fourth Division, Twenty-Third Corps, was assigned command of the district.

At the end of April 1864, Fourth Division was organized as follows:

Fourth Division, Jacob Ammen
   First Brigade, John Mehringer
   Second Brigade, Davis Tillson
   Third Brigade, Silas A. Strickland

Note. Second Brigade was a brigade of Reserve Artillery.

For additional information, see Twenty-Third Corps, Army of the Ohio.

The principal posts of the district were as follows: Cumberland Gap, Knoxville, and Loudon.

On January 17, 1865, the territory of the Department of the Ohio was annexed to the Department of the Cumberland.

District of Eastern Kentucky. The District of Eastern Kentucky was constituted November 17, 1862, at the same time that the District of Central Kentucky and the District of Western Kentucky were constituted. The district consisted of the following counties in Kentucky: Boyd, Carter, Floyd, Greenup, Johnson, Lawrence, Lewis, Magoffin, and Pike. Jonathan Cranor was assigned command, with headquarters in the field. Julius White succeeded Cranor in command of the district in February 1863.

The troops were stationed at various points in the district, but principally at Louisa, Catlettsburg, and Paintsville.

In June 1863 the United States Forces in the district were organized into Fourth Division, Twenty-Third Corps, with White in command. Twenty-Third Corps was reorganized August 6, in preparation for Ambrose E. Burnside's East Tennessee Campaign, and Samuel P. Carter was assigned command of Fourth Division. In mid-August, Carter withdrew from the area for the transfer of his division to East Tennessee, and George W. Gallup assumed command of the troops remaining in the District of Eastern Kentucky, with headquarters at Louisa.

After November 6, 1863, the District of Eastern Kentucky was a sub-district of the District of Kentucky, or First Division, Twenty-Third Corps.

The District of Eastern Kentucky remained in existence until April 10, 1864, when Twenty-Third Corps was reorganized. At that time, Gallup's command became First Brigade of Edward H. Hobson's First Division, District of Kentucky.

District of Illinois. The District of Illinois was constituted April 7, 1863 to consist of the state of Illinois. Jacob Ammen was assigned command, with headquarters at Springfield, Illinois. The principal posts in the district were Camp Butler, near Springfield; Camp Douglas, near Chicago; and Quincy, Illinois.

In a reorganization of the Department of the Ohio November 16, 1863, the state of Illinois was detached from the department, and until January 12, 1864 it was not a part of any department. On that date the Northern Department was organized to include the state of Illinois.

District of Indiana. The District of Indiana was created March 23, 1863 to consist of the state of Indiana, and Henry B. Carrington was assigned command, with headquarters at Indianapolis. Milo S. Hascall relieved Carrington on April 15 and remained in command until June 5. On that date, the District of Michigan was attached to the District of Indiana to form the District of Indiana and Michigan, and Orlando B. Willcox was assigned command, with headquarters at Indianapolis. Willcox was relieved of command September 11 and was ordered to Kentucky. The District of Indiana and Michigan was then discontinued, and the District of Indiana remained a separate district in the Department of the Ohio under John S. Simonson.

In the reorganization of the Department of the Ohio November 16, 1863, the state of Indiana was detached from the department, and until the creation of the Northern Department January 12, 1864, the state of Indiana was not in any department.

District of Indiana and Michigan. The District of Indiana and Michigan was formed by an order of June 5, 1863, which attached the District of Michigan to the District of Indiana. Orlando B. Willcox was assigned command of the district, with headquarters at Indianapolis, Indiana. Willcox was relieved of command September 11 and ordered to Kentucky. The District of Indiana and Michigan was then broken up, and the District of Indiana remained as a separate district in the Department of the Ohio under the command of John S. Simonson.

Jeffersonville, Indiana. The town of Jeffersonville, Indiana was annexed to the Department of the Ohio February 8, 1864, and it then became a part of the District of Kentucky March 23.

District of the Kanawha. The District of the Kanawha was constituted in the Department of Western Virginia in December 1861. When the Mountain Department was created March 11, 1862, the District of the Kanawha was defined as consisting of all valleys of the Kanawha River and the Guyandotte River and the mouth of the Big Sandy River. Jacob D. Cox was assigned command of the district, and the troops in the district were organized into four brigades as follows:

Lightburn's Brigade, Joseph A. J. Lightburn
Crook's Brigade, George Crook
Scammon's Brigade, Eliakim P. Scammon
Moor's Brigade, Augustus Moor

On June 26, 1862, the Mountain Department was

organized into First Corps of John Pope's Army of Virginia. In August Cox was ordered East with the brigades of Scammon and Moor to join Pope near Washington, D.C. Cox's force was known as the Kanawha Division. It was attached to Ninth Corps and served with the Army of the Potomac at South Mountain and Antietam during the Maryland Campaign.

When Western Virginia was transferred to the Department of the Ohio September 19, 1862, the District of the Kanawha was included as a sub-district of the District of Western Virginia (see below). Joseph A. J. Lightburn was assigned command of the District of the Kanawha, with headquarters at Gauley, Western Virginia.

The troops in the district were organized as Lightburn's Division, which was organized as follows:

Lightburn's Division, Joseph A. J. Lightburn
  Siber's Brigade, Edward Siber
  Gilbert's Brigade, Samuel A. Gilbert
  Toland's Brigade, John T. Toland

Scammon relieved Lightburn in command of the district in October 1862 and commanded the district in the Department of the Ohio until Western Virginia was transferred to the Middle Department March 16, 1863.

District of Kentucky. In the organization of Twenty-Third Corps May 22, 1863 (ordered April 27), the District of Kentucky was constituted to consist of the state of Kentucky. Jeremiah T. Boyle was assigned command, with headquarters at Louisville. In June Boyle's command was reported as Second Division, Twenty-Third Corps, which was organized as follows:

Second Division, Twenty-Third Corps, Jeremiah T. Boyle
  First Brigade, James M. Shackelford
  Bowling Green, Kentucky, Cicero Maxwell
  Munfordville, Charles D. Pennebaker
  Louisville, Kentucky, commander not given
  Lebanon, Kentucky, commander not given

In a reorganization of Twenty-Third Corps August 6, 1863, Boyle's command was designated as First Division, Twenty-Third Corps, and on August

31, the troops were distributed about the state as follows:

Bowling Green, commander not given
Camp Nelson, commander not given
Eminence, Richard T. Jacob
Frankfort, Thomas B. Allard
Glasgow, William Y. Dillard
Hopkinsville, Eli H. Murray
Lexington, Joshua K. Sigfried
Louisa, George W. Gallup
Louisville, commander not given
Mount Sterling, Ralph R. Maltby
Muldraugh's Hill, Silas A. Strickland
Munfordville, Charles D. Pennebaker
New Haven, James McManomy
Russellville, Benjamin H. Bristow
Smithland, Jonathan Belt

On November 6, 1863, the District of Kentucky (or First Division, Twenty-Third Corps) was organized into the following districts:

District of Southwestern Kentucky, Cicero Maxwell (headquarters at Bowling Green)
District of Southern Central Kentucky, Edward H. Hobson (headquarters at Munfordville)
District of Eastern Kentucky, George W. Gallup (headquarters at Louisa)
District of Northern Central Kentucky, Speed S. Fry (headquarters at Camp Nelson)
District of Somerset, Theophilus T. Garrard (headquarters at Somerset)

In December 1863, Boyle's division was ordered to East Tennessee, and Jacob Ammen was assigned command of the District of Kentucky, which remained sub-districted as described above. On February 15, 1864 Stephen G. Burbridge was assigned temporary command of the district during the absence of Ammen, and on March 25, Burbridge was assigned permanent command.

On March 23, 1864, Jeffersonville, Indiana was transferred to the District of Kentucky.

Twenty-Third Corps was again reorganized April 10, 1864, and all troops belonging to the District of Kentucky were designated as Fifth Division, Twenty-Third Corps. Stephen G. Burbridge was assigned command, with headquarters at Louisville, Kentucky. Despite the designation of Fifth Division, the troops in the District of Kentucky were organized into two divisions as follows:

First Division, District of Kentucky, Edward H. Hobson
First Brigade, George W. Gallup
Second Brigade, Clinton J. True
Third Brigade, Charles S. Hanson
Fourth Brigade, John M. Brown

Second Division, District of Kentucky, Hugh Ewing
First Brigade, Sanders D. Bruce
Second Brigade, Cicero Maxwell

On August 7, 1864, that part of Kentucky west of the Cumberland River was transferred from the Department of the Tennessee to the Department of the Ohio, and the state of Kentucky was constituted as a separate district. The newly acquired portion of the state was designated as the District of Western Kentucky (see below). At the end of August 1864, the troops in the District of Kentucky (or Fifth Division) were organized as follows:

District of Kentucky (or Fifth Division), Stephen G. Burbridge

First Division, District of Kentucky, Nathaniel C. McLean
First Brigade, Edward H. Hobson
Second Brigade, John M. Brown
Third Brigade, Charles S. Hanson
Fourth Brigade, Robert W. Ratliff
Camp Nelson, Kentucky, Speed S. Fry

Note. In addition to Fourth Brigade, Ratliff also commanded the post of Lebanon, Kentucky.

Second Division, District of Kentucky, Hugh Ewing
First Brigade, Thomas B. Fairleigh
Second Brigade, Cicero Maxwell
Unbrigaded regiments

The organization of the District of Kentucky remained essentially unchanged until it was transferred to the Department of the Cumberland January 17, 1865.

The commanders of the District of Kentucky were as follows:

Jeremiah T. Boyle	May 22, 1863 to December 1863
Jacob Ammen	December 1863 to February 15, 1864

Stephen G. Burbridge	February 15, 1864 to April 1, 1864
Edward H. Hobson	April 1, 1864 to April 10, 1864
Stephen G. Burbridge	April 10, 1864 to January 17, 1865

District of Louisville. During the threat of invasion of Kentucky in the late summer of 1862 by Confederate forces commanded by Braxton Bragg and E. Kirby Smith, Jeremiah T. Boyle was assigned command of the United States troops in and about Louisville August 24, and in October this command was known as the District of Louisville. The principal posts were Louisville, Bowling Green, Munfordville, and West Point. The district was merged into the District of Western Kentucky on November 17.

District of Michigan. The District of Michigan was constituted June 2, 1863 to consist of the state of Michigan. Jacob D. Cox, commanding the District of Ohio, was also assigned temporary command of the District of Michigan, with headquarters at Columbus, Ohio. By an order of June 5, 1863, the District of Michigan was attached to the District of Indiana to form the District of Indiana and Michigan (see above).

District of Middle Tennessee. The District of Middle Tennessee was constituted December 16, 1863 to consist of that part of Tennessee and Kentucky lying south of the Cumberland River and between the roads running from Carthage, Tennessee to Clinton, Tennessee, and from Clinton to Point Isabel, Kentucky, including the garrisons and depots at Camp Talbott, Point Isabel, and Carthage. Jacob Ammen was assigned command, with headquarters at Camp Talbott. The order establishing the district was rescinded February 14, 1864.

District of Northern (North) Central Kentucky. The District of Northern (North) Central Kentucky was created as a sub-district of the District of Kentucky November 6, 1863. See District of Kentucky (above).

District of Ohio. The District of Ohio was constituted April 6, 1863 to consist of the state of Ohio. John S. Mason was assigned command, but on April 14 Jacob D. Cox was assigned command, with headquarters at Cincinnati, Ohio.

When the District of Michigan was constituted June 2, 1863, it was attached to the District of Ohio, and Cox commanded both districts, with headquarters at Columbus, Ohio. On June 5, the District of Michigan was attached to the District of Indiana as the District of Indiana and Michigan.

On June 9, 1863 (ordered May 15), the counties of Columbiana, Jefferson, and Belmont were transferred to the Department of the Monongahela, where they remained until the formation of the Northern Department January 12, 1864. On the same date, Gallipolis, Ohio, and the Ohio shore opposite the mouth of the Kanawha River were transferred to the Middle Department, and from June 24, 1863 to January 12, 1864, the counties of Monroe, Washington, Athens, Meigs, Gallia, and Lawrence were in the Department of West Virginia.

In a reorganization of the Department of the Ohio November 16, 1863, that part of the state of Ohio in the Department of the Ohio was detached and was not a part of any department until January 12, 1864, when it was included in the newly created Northern Department.

The principal posts in the District of Ohio in October 1863 were as follows:

Camp Dennison, Mason Brayman
Cincinnati, Seth Eastman
Columbus, John S. Mason
Covington, Kentucky, Chauncey G. Hawley

Note. Mason's command included Columbus, Camp Chase, and Camp Thomas.

District of Somerset. The District of Somerset was constituted November 6, 1863 as a sub-district of the District of Kentucky (see above). The district consisted of the troops at Barboursville, London, Point Isabel, Somerset, and Stanford, all in Kentucky. Theophilus T. Garrard commanded the district from October 1863 to December 1863.

District of Southern Central Kentucky. The District of Southern Central Kentucky was constituted November 6, 1863 as a sub-district of the District of Kentucky (see above).

District of Southwest Kentucky. The District of

Southwest Kentucky was constituted November 6, 1863 as a sub-district of the District of Kentucky (see above).

District of Western Kentucky, November 17, 1862–May 22, 1863. The District of Western Kentucky was constituted November 17, 1862 to consist of that part of Kentucky lying west of the counties of La Grange, Shelby, Spencer, Washington, Marion, Taylor, Adair, Russell, and Clinton. Jeremiah T. Boyle was assigned command, with headquarters at Louisville.

The troops in the district were at the following posts:

Thirty-Fourth Brigade, William P. Reid, at Hopkinsville, Kentucky
Munfordville, Kentucky, Edward H. Hobson
Lebanon, Kentucky, William A. Hoskins
Bowling Green, Kentucky, Mahlon D. Manson
Henderson, Kentucky, commander not given
Clarksville, Tennessee, Sanders D. Bruce

On May 22, 1863, the District of Western Kentucky was merged into the District of Kentucky.

District of Western Kentucky, August 7, 1864–January 17, 1865. On August 7, 1864, that part of Kentucky west of the Cumberland River was transferred from the Department of the Tennessee to the Department of the Ohio as the District of Western Kentucky, a sub-district of the District of Kentucky. Eleazer A. Paine was assigned command, with headquarters at Paducah. Solomon Meredith succeeded Paine in command of the district September 11, 1864.

The troops in the district were posted as follows:

Paducah, Kentucky, Henry W. Barry
Cairo, Illinois, Solomon Meredith
Columbus, Kentucky, James N. McArthur
Mayfield, Kentucky, commander not given
Smithland, Kentucky, commander not given

The district was transferred to the Department of the Cumberland January 17, 1865.

District of Western Virginia. Western Virginia was transferred to the Department of the Ohio by an order of September 19, 1862, and it was, together with the counties in Ohio bordering on it, designated as the District of Western Virginia, Department of the Ohio. Quincy A. Gillmore was assigned temporary command September 28, with headquarters at Point Pleasant, Ohio. Jacob D. Cox was assigned permanent command of the district October 4, and he assumed command October 13, with headquarters at Gallipolis, Ohio.

The district remained in the Department of the Ohio until March 16, 1863, when its territory, except the counties of Hancock, Brooke, and Ohio, was transferred to the Middle Department. The counties of Hancock, Brooke, and Ohio were transferred to the Department of the Monongahela June 9, 1863.

During the period September-December 1862, there were several organized commands in the District of Western Virginia. The most important of these were as follows:

Railroad Division. Benjamin F. Kelley's forces that were guarding the Baltimore and Ohio Railroad in Western Virginia were attached to John E. Wool's Middle Department June 27, 1862, the day John Pope assumed command of the newly created Army of Virginia. Kelley was still in command September 19, 1862 when the District of Western Virginia, Department of the Ohio was constituted. Kelley's command, which was known as the Railroad Division, did not operate as a unit, but the troops were scattered along and in front of the railroad west of, and including, Cumberland, Maryland. The principal posts in Western Virginia in October 1862 were as follows: Beverly, commanded by Moses S. Hall; Bulltown, commanded by Thomas M. Harris; Parkersburg, commanded by Benjamin F. Smith; Weston, commanded by John H. Showalter; Buckhannon, commanded by John B. Klunk; Clarksburg, commanded by Nathan Wilkinson; New Creek Station, commanded by Edward C. James; Rowlesburg, commanded by William Hall; and West Union, commanded by John Carroll. Robert Bruce commanded the post of Cumberland.

The Railroad Division was transferred to the Middle Department December 17, 1862.

Lightburn's Division, District of the Kanawha. Joseph A. J. Lightburn assumed command of the District of the Kanawha, Army of Virginia August 17,

1862 when Jacob D. Cox was ordered East with the Kanawha Division to join John Pope's Army of Virginia. When the District of Western Virginia was constituted September 19, 1862, the District of the Kanawha became a sub-district of the former.

The troops in the District of the Kanawha commanded by Lightburn were as follows:

District of the Kanawha, Joseph A. J. Lightburn
    First Brigade, Edward Siber
        34th Ohio, John T. Toland
        37th Ohio, Louis Von Blessingh
    Second Brigade, Samuel A. Gilbert
        44th Ohio, Ackber O. Mitchell
        47th Ohio, Lyman S. Elliott
        4th Virginia [West], William H. H. Russell
    Unbrigaded Regiments
        8th Virginia [West], John H. Oley
        9th Virginia [West], Leonard Skinner

Headquarters of the district was at Gauley Bridge until mid-September 1862, when Lightburn was forced to retire to Point Pleasant on the Ohio River.

In October 1862, Samuel A. Gilbert's brigade was transferred to the Army of Kentucky, and John T. Toland was assigned command of a new brigade.

Early in December, Lightburn's Division was designated as Second Kanawha Division under the command of Eliakim P. Scammon.

Cumberland Division. The Seventh Division, Army of the Ohio, commanded by George W. Morgan, evacuated Cumberland Gap September 17, 1862 and marched to Greenup, Kentucky on the Ohio River, where it arrived October 3. Morgan's division was then transferred to Charleston, Western Virginia in the Department of the Ohio. In mid-November it was sent to Memphis, Tennessee, where it became a part of the Army of the Tennessee. While in Western Virginia, the division was organized as follows:

Cumberland Division, George W. Morgan
    First Brigade, James G. Spears
    Third Brigade, Samuel P. Carter
    Fourth Brigade, John F. De Courcy

Kanawha Division. Following the Battle of Antietam, the Kanawha Division, which had been attached to Ninth Corps, Army of the Potomac during George B. McClellan's Maryland Campaign, was ordered back to Western Virginia, where it had been organized. Jacob D. Cox, formerly commander of the Kanawha Division, assumed command of the District of Western Virginia October 13, 1862, and George Crook assumed command of the Kanawha Division. In October 1862 the division was organized as follows:

Kanawha Division, George Crook
    First Brigade, Eliakim P. Scammon
    Second Brigade, Ebenezer B. Andrews
    Third Brigade, Jonathan Cranor

In December 1862, the designation of the division was changed to First Kanawha Division.

Crook's division was discontinued January 21, 1863, and Crook was ordered with a brigade of four regiments to report to Horatio G. Wright, commander of the Department of the Ohio, at Cincinnati. This brigade then became a part of Gordon Granger's Army of Kentucky (see Army of Kentucky [Granger]).

Cheat Mountain Division. Robert H. Milroy, who was in command of a division of troops at Cheat Mountain in Western Virginia, was ordered with his command to New Creek in Western Virginia and instructed to cooperate with Benjamin F. Kelley in the protection of the Baltimore and Ohio Railroad. Milroy's command was known as the Cheat Mountain Division, and in November 1862 it was organized as follows:

Cheat Mountain Division, Robert H. Milroy
    First Brigade, Gustave P. Cluseret
    Second Brigade, James Washburn

On December 17, 1862, both Kelley's Railroad Division and Milroy's Cheat Mountain Division were transferred to the Middle Department.

* * * * * * * * * *

On December 28, 1862, a brigade consisting of the 30th, 37th, and 47th Ohio and the 4th West Virginia regiments, and commanded by Hugh Ewing, was ordered to report to Ulysses S. Grant's command on the Mississippi River, and upon arrival there it was assigned to Fifteenth Corps.

In January 1863, Augustus Moor was assigned command of a new brigade at Buckhannon in Western Virginia, and his mission was to protect the Baltimore and Ohio Railroad west of New Creek and the frontier from Grafton south to Sutton. This brigade was designated as the Northern Brigade.

TROOPS IN THE DEPARTMENT OF THE OHIO

In addition to the troops in the districts of the Department of the Ohio that have already been described, there were also several armies and army corps that at one time or another operated in the department. The armies were Don Carlos Buell's Army of the Ohio (known during a part of its existence as the Army of the District of the Ohio); Ambrose E. Burnside's Army of the Ohio; John M. Schofield's Army of the Ohio; the Army of Occupation of Western Virginia; and the Army of Kentucky. For details of their organizations and operations, see the respective armies.

There were also the following army corps that were in the Department of the Ohio: First Corps, Second Corps, and Third Corps, Army of the Ohio; Ninth Corps; Twenty-Third Corps, Army of the Ohio; and Cavalry Corps, Army of the Ohio. For additional information, refer to these corps.

DEPARTMENT OF THE OHIO JUNE 27, 1865– AUGUST 6, 1866

In the reorganization of the military divisions and departments of the army June 27, 1865, the Department of the Ohio was re-created to consist of the states of Illinois, Michigan, Ohio, and Indiana, except Jeffersonville and New Albany. Edward O. C. Ord was assigned command, with headquarters at Detroit, Michigan. Ord assumed command July 5. The department was included in the newly created Military Division of the Mississippi.

On October 30, 1865, the state of Wisconsin was added to the Department of the Ohio by transfer from the Department of the Missouri.

December 26, 1865, Orlando B. Willcox assumed temporary command of the department by seniority, but in mid-January 1866, Ord resumed command.

June 5, 1866, the Department of Kentucky was discontinued, and Jeffersonville and New Albany in Indiana were added to the Department of the Ohio.

The Department of the Ohio was discontinued August 6, 1866, when it was merged into the Department of the Lakes.

DEPARTMENT OF OREGON

The Department of Oregon was created September 13, 1858, to include the territories of Washington and Oregon, except the Rogue River and Umpqua districts in southwestern Oregon. William S. Harney commanded the department until July 5, 1860, with headquarters at Fort Vancouver, Washington Territory. He was relieved on that date by George Wright (assigned command June 8). The troops in Wright's department were stationed at the following posts: Fort Vancouver, Vancouver Depot, Fort Colville, Camp Pickett on San Juan Island, Fort Steilacoom, Fort Walla Walla, Fort Cascades, Camp Chehalis, and Fort Townsend, all in Washington Territory; and Fort Dalles, Fort Yamhill, and Fort Hoskins in Oregon Territory.

By an order of January 1, 1861, the Department of California and the Department of Oregon were merged into the Department of the Pacific. Albert Sidney Johnston was assigned command of the Department of the Pacific, and on January 15 he arrived in San Francisco and assumed command. On that date, the departments of Oregon and California were officially merged. Both of the former departments became districts in the Department of the Pacific.

At the outbreak of the Civil War, the troops serving in the District of Oregon were as follows: four companies of the 1st United States Dragoons, two companies of the 4th United States Infantry, nine companies of the 9th United States Infantry, and two companies of the 3rd United States Artillery.

DEPARTMENT OF THE PACIFIC

The Department of California was created September 13, 1858 to include the territory west of the Rocky Mountains and south of Oregon, except that part of Utah lying east of 117 degrees west longitude and of New Mexico lying east of 110 degrees west longitude. The department also included the Rogue River and Umpqua districts in southwestern Oregon. The department was commanded January 1, 1861 by Benjamin L. Beall, who had assumed command by seniority on the death of Newman S. Clarke October 17, 1860.

The Department of Oregon was also created September 13, 1858 to include the territories of Washington and Oregon, except the Rogue River and Umpqua districts in southwestern Oregon. George Wright was assigned command June 8, 1860, and he was still in command January 1, 1861.

The Department of California and the Department of Oregon were merged into the Department of the Pacific by an order of January 1, 1861. Albert Sidney Johnston was assigned command, with headquarters at San Francisco, California. Johnston arrived in San Francisco January 15, and it was on that date that he announced that the departments of California and Oregon were merged into the Department of the Pacific.

July 3, 1861, the boundary was modified, and the department then consisted of the country west of the Rocky Mountains except New Mexico and that part of Utah lying east of 117 degrees west longitude. Thus the part of New Mexico that was formerly in the Department of the Pacific was transferred to the Western Department. July 27, 1861, Fort Crittenden (formerly Camp Floyd), which was located about forty miles southwest of Salt Lake City, was abandoned by United States forces under Philip St. G. Cooke, and the territory of Utah was then transferred to the Department of the Pacific. It was not until late August 1862, however, that troops from California under P. Edward Connor moved into Utah (see District of Utah, below).

On November 9, 1861, all of present-day Arizona, and that part of Nevada south of the 37th parallel and east of the California border, were transferred to the Department of New Mexico.

The Department of the Pacific was extended somewhat in the early part of 1863, when the eastern border along the Rocky Mountains was extended southward to the northern border of Colorado, and from there back to the west to conform to the northern boundary of Utah.

In an order of January 20, 1865, Arizona Territory was transferred to the Department of the Pacific, but the transfer was not announced until March 7. Thus the territory south of the 37th parallel and west of 109 degrees west longitude became a part of the Department of the Pacific.

February 17, 1865, Utah Territory and that part of Nebraska west of 104 degrees west longitude were transferred to the Department of the Missouri. At that time, the western boundary of Utah Territory was along 114 degrees west longitude.

In the reorganization of the military divisions and departments of the army June 27, 1865, the Military Division of the Pacific was created to consist of the newly created Department of California and the Department of Columbia. The Department of California consisted of the states of California and Nevada, and the territories of Utah, New Mexico, and Colorado. The Department of Columbia consisted of the state of Oregon and the territories of Washington and Idaho.

COMMANDERS OF THE DEPARTMENT OF THE PACIFIC

Albert Sidney Johnston	January 15, 1861 to April 25, 1861
Edwin V. Sumner	April 25, 1861 to October 20, 1861
George Wright	October 20, 1861 to July 1, 1864
Irvin McDowell	July 1, 1864 to June 27, 1865

Note. Wright assumed command by seniority October 20, 1861, and was formally assigned November 19.

DISTRICTS IN THE DEPARTMENT OF THE PACIFIC

District of Arizona. In June 1862, the troops of the Column from California under James H. Carleton, then stationed at Fort Barrett and Tucson, Arizona Territory, and those en route to those places, were designated as the District of Arizona. Although operating in the Department of New Mexico, Carleton's command was subject to orders from Headquarters, Department of the Pacific. For additional information, see District of Southern California, below.

Before leaving Tucson for the Rio Grande, Carleton announced the formation of the District of Western Arizona (see below) as consisting of all of Arizona Territory west of a north-south line through Apache Pass, and from there to Mesilla, New Mexico. The District of Western Arizona was transferred to the Department of New Mexico January 14, 1863.

When the Column from California arrived on the Rio Grande in August 1862, Carleton organized the District of Arizona to consist of all the territory from Fort Thorn, New Mexico along the Rio Grande River to Fort Quitman, Texas. For additional information, see Department of New Mexico, Districts in the Department of New Mexico, District of Arizona.

In an order dated January 20, 1865, Arizona Territory was transferred from the Department of New Mexico to the Department of the Pacific, but this transfer was not announced until March 7. On March 10, the District of Arizona, Department of the Pacific was constituted to include all of Arizona and that part of California lying within the watershed of the Colorado River.

The principal posts in the district were as follows: Fort Yuma, California and Fort Mojave, Fort Bowie, Fort Goodwin, Fort Whipple, and Fort Tubac in Arizona Territory.

The troops present in the District of Arizona that was constituted in June 1862 and reconstituted August 30, 1863 belonged to the Column from California. The troops serving in the District of Arizona that was constituted March 10, 1865 were as follows: 7th California Infantry, one company of the 4th California Infantry, three companies of the 1st California Cavalry, two companies of the 1st New Mexico Infantry, one company of the 1st New Mexico Cavalry, and one company of the 5th United States infantry.

The commanders of the District of Arizona were as follows:

James H. Carleton	June 1862 to July 1862
James H. Carleton	August 30, 1862 to September 5, 1862
Joseph R. West	September 5, 1862 to January 29, 1864
George W. Bowie	January 29, 1864 to November 1864
Joseph Smith	November 1864 to December 8, 1864
John S. Mason	March 7, 1865 to June 27, 1865

District of California. There were no districts in the state of California until the District of Southern California was constituted September 25, 1861 and the District of Humboldt December 12, 1861. The troops in Central California and in the northeastern part of the state were known simply as Troops in California until late in 1863, when that part of the state lying north of the District of Southern California and east of the District of Humboldt was called the District of California. George Wright, commander of the Department of the Pacific, also commanded the District of California. When Irvin McDowell assumed command of the Department of the Pacific July 1, 1864, he assigned Wright to the command of the District of California. Headquarters of the district was established at Sacramento.

March 3, 1865, the limits of the District of California were extended to include all posts and troops in the state of Nevada.

March 14, 1865, Camp Wright, Round Valley, was detached from the District of Humboldt and annexed to the District of California.

In the reorganization of the military divisions and departments of the army June 27, 1865, the District of California was merged into the Department of California.

The principal posts in the district were as follows: in California, Fort Point, San Francisco Harbor; Camp Reynolds, Angel Island; Presidio of San Francisco; Alcatraz Island, San Francisco Harbor; Benicia Barracks; Benicia Arsenal; Fort Crook, in Shasta County; Fort Wright, in Round Valley; Camp Union, near Sacramento; Camp Babbit, at Visalia; Camp (or Fort) Bidwell, Modock County; Point San Jose (Black Point), later to become Fort Macon, at San Francisco, on the harbor; Fort Miller, on the San Joaquin River; Monterey Barracks; and Camp Independence, in Owens River Valley; in Nevada, Camp

Nye, near Carson City, and Fort Ruby, in Ruby Valley; and in Oregon, Fort Klamath, at present-day Klamath Falls. In the spring of 1861, the troops in California and Nevada Territory consisted of four companies of the 1st United States Dragoons, the 4th United States Infantry, the 6th United States Infantry, one company of the 9th United States Infantry, and seven batteries of the 3rd United States Artillery. Upon the outbreak of war, these Regulars were ordered East; by late 1861 only three batteries of the 3rd United States Artillery remained, but the 9th United States Infantry had been increased to six companies. The rest had been replaced by the 3rd California Infantry, the 5th California Infantry, the 2nd California Cavalry, and parts of the 1st and 4th California Cavalry. Other troops that served in the district were the following: 6th California Infantry, seven companies of the 8th California Infantry, three companies of the 1st Washington Territory Infantry, one company of the 1st Oregon Cavalry, two companies of the Native California Cavalry Battalion, four companies of the 1st Nevada Infantry, and four companies of the 1st Nevada Cavalry.

November 15, 1864, the troops in the District of California were designated as a Separate Brigade.

The commanders of the troops in California and in the District of California were as follows:

Albert Sidney Johnston	January 15, 1861 to April 25, 1861
Edwin V. Sumner	April 25, 1861 to October 20, 1861
George Wright	October 26, 1861 to June 27, 1865

Note. Wright was formally assigned command of the District of California July 1, 1864.

District of Humboldt. The District of Humboldt was constituted December 12, 1861 to consist of the counties of Sonoma, Napa, Mendocino, Trinity, Humboldt, Klamath, and Del Norte in northwestern California. The district generally included that part of California west of the Coast Range and from its northern border south to San Francisco Bay. Francis J. Lippitt was assigned command, with headquarters at Fort Humboldt, near present-day Eureka, on Humboldt Bay. Headquarters was transferred temporarily to Fort Gaston in Hoopa Valley December 22, 1863.

Camp Wright, Round Valley, was transferred from the District of Humboldt to the District of California March 14, 1865.

The District of Humboldt was continued in existence until the general reorganization of the military divisions and departments of the army June 27, 1865.

The principal posts in the district were Fort Humboldt; Camp Lincoln, near Crescent City; Fort Gaston; Fort Bragg; Fort Wright; and Camp Iaqua, in Humboldt County.

The first troops in the District of Humboldt were the 2nd California Infantry, two companies of the 3rd California Infantry, and two companies of the 2nd California Cavalry. Later the 2nd California Infantry was reinforced by the 1st Battalion, California Mountaineers, a few companies of the 4th California Infantry, and the 6th California Infantry.

The commanders of the District of Humboldt were as follows:

Francis J. Lippitt	December 12, 1861 to July 13, 1863
Stephen G. Whipple	July 13, 1863 to February 6, 1864
Henry M. Black	February 6, 1864 to July 1864
Stephen G. Whipple	July 1864 to May 1, 1865
John C. Schmidt	May 1, 1865 to June 27, 1865

Nevada (Sub-district of Nevada). In 1861, Utah Territory was divided at 114 degrees west longitude, and the western part was called Nevada. On October 31, 1864, Nevada was admitted to the Union as a state, and it remained in the Department of the Pacific throughout the war. Fort Churchill, on the Carson River in Churchill County, was the most important post in the territory. The commander of this post reported directly to Headquarters, Department of the Pacific until August 6, 1862. On that date, at Fort Churchill, P. Edward Connor assumed command of the District of Utah, which included the territories of Utah and Nevada. Fort Churchill then became a part of Connor's command.

In September 1862, after Connor's departure for Salt Lake City, Fort Churchill again reported to Headquarters, Department of the Pacific.

February 17, 1865, Utah Territory was transferred to the Department of the Missouri. On March 3, the limits of the District of California were extended to include the state of Nevada, which then became a sub-district of the District of California. Headquarters of the sub-district was at Fort Churchill.

The state of Nevada was included in the Department of California in the general reorganization of the military divisions and departments of the army June 27, 1865.

The principal posts in Nevada were Fort Churchill; Camp Nye, near Carson City; Fort Ruby, in Ruby Valley (established in the fall of 1862 by Connor); and Owens River (established in October 1864 near Carson City).

At the outbreak of war, one company of the 1st United States Dragoons and three companies of the 6th United States Infantry were stationed at Fort Churchill, Nevada Territory under George A. H. Blake. The Regulars left for the East November 2, 1861, and they were replaced by troops of the 2nd California Cavalry. One company of the 1st Nevada Infantry and two companies of the 1st Nevada Cavalry also served in Nevada. Later, two companies of the 6th California Infantry were added to the forces there. The troops were employed principally in guarding the Overland Mail Route, and in protecting the settlers and Indians.

The commanders of the troops in Nevada were as follows:

George A. H. Blake	January 15, 1861 to November 2, 1861
Edwin A. Rowe	November 2, 1861 to late March 1862
Charles McDermit	Late March 1862 to June 27, 1865

Note 1. Michael O'Brien commanded temporarily in June 1865.

Note 2. McDermit was in command of the post of Fort Churchill, and after March 3, 1865 he also commanded the Sub-district of Nevada.

District of Oregon. The creation of the District of Oregon was announced January 15, 1861, on the same date that the Department of the Pacific was organized. It consisted of the state of Oregon and Washington Territory, except the Rogue River and Umpqua districts in southwestern Oregon. George Wright was assigned command.

At that time Washington Territory consisted of all the country west of the Rocky Mountains and north of the forty-second parallel, except Oregon. Idaho Territory was created March 4, 1863, with its western boundary generally along 117 west longitude. That part of Idaho Territory that was originally in Washington Territory remained under the control of the commander of the District of Oregon. The post of Soda Springs, Idaho Territory was included in the District of Utah August 20, 1863.

March 14, 1865, the limits of the District of Oregon were extended to include the entire state of Oregon.

The principal posts in the District of Oregon were as follows: in Washington Territory, Fort Vancouver, Vancouver Arsenal, Fort Colville, Camp Pickett (San Juan Island), Fort Walla Walla, and Fort Steilacoom; in Oregon, Fort Dalles, Fort Yamhill (Yam Hill), Fort Hoskins, Fort Umpqua, Fort Klamath, Fort Stevens, and Camp Watson; and in Idaho Territory, Camp Lapwai and Fort Boise.

At the outbreak of war, the troops in the District of Oregon consisted of the 9th United States Infantry, four companies of the 1st United States Dragoons, two companies of the 4th United States Infantry, and units of the 3rd United States Artillery. Most of these soon left for the East, and by the end of 1861 only two companies of the 9th United States Infantry and Battery D, 3rd United States Artillery remained. The Regulars that had departed were replaced by four companies of the 2nd California Infantry and five companies of the 4th California Infantry. Other troops that later served in the District of Oregon were the 1st Washington Territory Infantry, the 1st Oregon Infantry, and the 1st Oregon Cavalry. The companies of the 9th United States Infantry remained in the district until the end of the war.

November 15, 1864, the troops in the District of Oregon were designated as a Separate Brigade.

The commanders of the District of Oregon were as follows:

George W. Wright	January 15, 1861 to September 13, 1861
Benjamin L. Beall	September 13, 1861 to October 23, 1861
Albemarle Cady	October 23, 1861 to May 5, 1862
Justus Steinberger	May 5, 1862 to July 7, 1862
Benjamin Alvord	July 7, 1862 to March 23, 1865
Reuben F. Maury	March 23, 1865 to June 27, 1865

District of Southern California. The District of Southern California was created September 25, 1861 to consist of the counties of San Luis Obispo, Buena Vista, Tulare, Santa Barbara, Los Angeles, San Bernardino, and San Diego. The district was continued in existence until the general reorganization of the military divisions and departments of the army June 27, 1865.

The principal posts in the district were as follows: Fort Yuma; San Diego; Camp Drum, near San Pedro; Camp Independence, in Owens River Valley; Camp Babbitt, at Visalia; Camp Morris, at San Bernardino; Fort Tejon, near Tejon Pass; Santa Barbara; and Fort Mojave.

At the outbreak of war, the troops in Southern California were: one company of the 4th United States Infantry at San Diego; one company of the 4th United States Infantry and one company of the 6th United States Infantry at Fort Yuma; and two companies of the 1st United States Dragoons and two companies of the 6th United States Infantry at Los Angeles. These troops were soon ordered East, and they were replaced by the 1st California Infantry. During the winter of 1861, the troops of the 1st California were stationed at Camp Wright, near Oak Grove; Camp Latham, near Los Angeles; Camp Carleton, near San Bernardino; and San Diego and Fort Yuma.

The 1st California Infantry left the state in May 1862 with the Column from California (see below). At that time, a part of the 5th California Infantry and the 1st California Cavalry were in the district, but they too left with the Column from California.

During the remainder of the war, the 4th California Infantry and 2nd California Cavalry and companies of the 1st California Cavalry and 2nd California Infantry served in the district.

Column from California. During the winter of 1861, preparations were made for an expedition to march from California into Arizona, and then on across New Mexico to the Rio Grande. The purpose of this expedition was to open the Southern Mail Route, to recapture the forts and posts in Arizona and New Mexico, and to capture or drive from the country any Confederate troops found there.

November 3, 1861, Joseph R. West arrived with three companies of the 1st California Infantry at Fort Yuma, on the Arizona border, and there he relieved George Andrews, who had been ordered East. West was succeeded in command by Edwin A. Rigg November 26, 1861.

The main force of the California Volunteers were mobilized at Camp Drum and at Camp Wright. James H. Carleton was assigned command of the expedition January 31, 1862, and on April 13 he left Camp Drum for Fort Yuma, where he arrived May 1. There, on May 15, his command was designated as the Column from California. It consisted of the following: the 1st California Infantry; four companies of the 5th California Infantry; five companies of the 1st California Cavalry; Battery A, 3rd United States Artillery; and Company B, 2nd California Cavalry.

From that time, the Column from California operated outside the District of Southern California, but it did continue under the orders of the commander of the Department of the Pacific even though it was operating in the Department of New Mexico. Further, the District of Western Arizona was constituted under Carleton and, because it consisted of territory occupied by troops of the Column from California, the district was also under the direction of the commander of the Department of the Pacific, although its territory belonged to the Department of New Mexico. This created a command problem, but it was resolved January 14, 1863 when the District of Western Arizona and the Column from California were transferred to the Department of New Mexico. For additional information, see Department of New Mexico, Troops and Operations in the Department of New Mexico, Expedition from Southern California, through Arizona, to New Mexico and Northwestern Texas (Column from California).

The commanders of the District of Southern California were as follows:

George Wright	October 4, 1861 to October 14, 1861
James H. Carleton	October 14, 1861 to January 12, 1862
Joseph R. West	January 12, 1862 to February 5, 1862
James H. Carleton	February 5, 1862 to May 15, 1862
George W. Bowie	May 17, 1862 to February 7, 1863
Harvey Lee	February 7, 1863 to April 10, 1863

Ferris Foreman	April 10, 1863 to July 7, 1863
James F. Curtis	July 7, 1863 to June 27, 1865

Note. Wright was assigned command of the district September 14, 1861, but he did not assume command until October 4.

District of Utah. At the outbreak of war, Philip St. George Cooke commanded the Union Department of Utah. At Fort Crittenden (formerly Camp Floyd), about forty miles south and a little west of Salt Lake City in Cedar Valley, were two companies of the 2nd United States Cavalry, two companies of the 10th United States Infantry, and two companies of the 4th United States Artillery; and at Fort Bridger, northwest of Salt Lake City, were two companies of the 10th United States Infantry.

Cooke abandoned Fort Crittenden July 27, 1861, and marched eastward with his command to Fort Leavenworth, Kansas, picking up the troops at Fort Bridger on the way. Troops from California were to occupy the territory after Cooke departed.

P. Edward Connor assumed command of the District of Utah, Department of the Pacific August 6, 1862 at Fort Churchill, Nevada Territory. He defined his command as consisting of the territories of Nevada and Utah. Connor left Fort Churchill in mid-August and then marched eastward for two weeks along the Overland Mail Route to Ruby Valley, where he established Fort Ruby. He then moved on to Salt Lake City, where he arrived about the first of October, and then established Camp Douglas, east of the city.

August 20, 1863, the District of Utah was defined as consisting of the Utah Territory; Camp Ruby, Nevada Territory; and the post of Soda Springs, Idaho Territory.

February 17, 1865, Utah Territory and that part of Nebraska west of 104 degrees west longitude were transferred to the Department of the Missouri.

The principal posts in the District of Utah were Camp Douglas and Fort Bridger in Utah Territory; Fort Ruby and Fort Churchill in Nevada Territory; and Camp Connor in Idaho Territory.

The troops that served in the District of Utah consisted of the 3rd California Infantry, five companies of the 2nd California Cavalry, and the 1st Nevada Cavalry.

P. Edward Connor was in command of the district from August 6, 1862 to February 17, 1865.

District of Western Arizona. The District of Western Arizona was created July 21, 1862 to include all of Arizona Territory west of a north-south line through Apache Pass, and thence to Mesilla, New Mexico. David Fergusson was assigned command, with headquarters at Tucson. The troops in the district consisted of the Column from California, commanded by James H. Carleton. During the period July 20–23, these troops began their march eastward from Tucson toward the Rio Grande. Fergusson remained in the district with three companies of the 5th California Infantry and one company of the 1st California Cavalry.

Although the District of Western Arizona was within the limits of the Department of New Mexico, Fergusson and his troops were subject to orders from Headquarters, Department of the Pacific. The District of Western Arizona and the Column from California were transferred to the Department of New Mexico January 14, 1863. For additional information, see above, District of Southern California, Column from California, and see also Department of New Mexico, Troops and Operations in the Department of New Mexico, Expedition from Southern California, through Arizona, to New Mexico and Northwestern Texas (Column from California).

The principal posts in the district were Fort Bowie, in Apache Pass, and Tucson.

The commanders of the District of Western Arizona were as follows:

David Fergusson	July 21, 1862 to September 5, 1862
Theodore A. Coult	September 5, 1862 to January 14, 1863

DEPARTMENT OF THE TENNESSEE
OCTOBER 16, 1862– NOVEMBER 28, 1864

The Department of the Tennessee was created October 16, 1862 to include the post of Cairo, Illinois; Fort Henry and Fort Donelson in Tennessee; northern Mississippi; and the portions of Kentucky and Tennessee west of the Tennessee River. Ulysses S. Grant assumed command on October 25 (assigned October 16).

On October 24, 1862 the troops in the Department of the Tennessee under Grant's command were designated as Thirteenth Corps.

Earlier, on September 24, 1862, the troops in the District of West Tennessee had been organized into four divisions (see District of West Tennessee, in section on Miscellaneous Organizations), and on October 26, these divisions were designated as districts in the Department of the Tennessee as follows:

First Division became District of Memphis, under the command of William T. Sherman.

Second Division became District of Jackson, commanded by Stephen A. Hurlbut.

Third Division became District of Corinth, under the command of Charles S. Hamilton.

Fourth Division became District of Columbus, under the command of Thomas A. Davies.

The following changes occurred in the department during the period of its existence:

January 25, 1863, Fort Henry and Fort Donelson were transferred to the Department of the Cumberland, and Fort Heiman was similarly transferred a short time later.

The Military Division of the Mississippi was created October 16, 1863 to consist of the Department of the Tennessee, the Department of the Ohio, and the Department of the Cumberland. Grant assumed command of the Military Division of the Mississippi on October 24, and William T. Sherman assumed command of the Army and Department of the Tennessee.

January 12, 1864, Cairo, Illinois was transferred to the Northern Department, but on February 8 it was returned to the Department of the Tennessee.

March 26, 1864, James B. McPherson assumed command of the Department of the Tennessee (assigned March 12).

July 22, 1864, McPherson was killed at the Battle of Atlanta, and John A. Logan was assigned temporary command. On July 27, Oliver O. Howard assumed command of the department.

August 7, 1864, that part of Kentucky west of the Tennessee River was transferred to the Department of the Ohio, and Cairo was transferred to the Northern Department.

October 27, 1864, Headquarters, Department of the Tennessee was established at Memphis, Tennessee.

November 7, 1864, Sixteenth Corps, Department of the Tennessee was abolished, and all troops on the east bank of the Mississippi River were detached from their several corps and departments and ordered to report to Headquarters, Military Division of West Mississippi. On November 8, however, the Department of the Tennessee was defined as including the Tennessee River and that part of Alabama and Mississippi that might be occupied by troops of the Army of the Tennessee.

The Department of Mississippi was created November 28, 1864 to include the state of Mississippi and that part of Tennessee west of the Tennessee River. At the same time Cairo was transferred to the Northern Department, and Fort Henry and Fort Donelson to the Department of the Cumberland. This left no territory defined as the Department of the Tennessee. The designation "Army and Department of the Tennessee" was, however, continued in use until the Army of the Tennessee, which formed a part of Sherman's Army of the Military Division of the Mississippi, arrived in North Carolina after its march northward from Savannah, Georgia. Then, on March 31, 1865, Howard ordered the word "Department" be discontinued, but the "Army of the Tennessee," commanded by Howard, and by Logan after May 23, 1865, continued in existence until disbanded July 13, 1865.

In the reorganization of the military divisions and departments of the army June 27, 1865, the Department of the Tennessee was re-created to consist of the state of Tennessee. George Stoneman was assigned command, with headquarters at Knoxville. The department was included in the Military Division of the Tennessee. The department was merged into the Department of the Cumberland June 5, 1866.

COMMANDERS OF THE DEPARTMENT OF THE TENNESSEE

Ulysses S. Grant	October 25, 1862 to October 24, 1863
William T. Sherman	October 24, 1863 to March 26, 1864
James B. McPherson	March 26, 1864 to July 22, 1864
John A. Logan	July 22, 1864 to July 27, 1864
Oliver O. Howard	July 27, 1864 to May 23, 1865
John A. Logan	May 23, 1865 to July 13, 1865

DISTRICTS IN THE DEPARTMENT OF THE TENNESSEE

District of Cairo. Cairo, Illinois was in the Department of the Tennessee during the period of its existence except for a brief time, January 12 to February 8, 1864, when it was in the Northern Department.

In the reorganization of Sixteenth Corps, Army of the Tennessee January 24, 1864, Sixth Division (or District of Columbus) was discontinued. A new Third Division, Sixteenth Corps, commanded by Andrew J. Smith, was organized from troops of the District of Columbus, and the troops remaining were designated as the District of Cairo, Sixteenth Corps. Hugh T. Reid was assigned command of the District of Cairo January 25, 1864.

Cadwallader C. Washburn relieved Stephen A. Hurlbut in command of the District of West Tennessee April 23, 1864, and the designation of the district was then changed to District of Cairo, District of West Tennessee, Department of the Tennessee.

Henry Prince arrived April 27, 1864 to assume command of the District of Cairo, and the designation was again changed to District of Columbus, District of West Tennessee. Prince's command was defined May 2 as consisting of all troops in the Department of the Tennessee north of New Madrid, Missouri.

It should be noted that there is some confusion about the designation of the District of Cairo. On April 29, 1864, Washburn refers to the District of Columbus, but the army rosters continue to include the District of Cairo through April 1864.

The principal posts in the district were Cairo, Illinois; Paducah and Columbus in Kentucky; and Island No. 10 in the Mississippi River.

The commanders of the District of Cairo were as follows:

Hugh T. Reid	January 25, 1864 to March 19, 1864
Mason Brayman	March 19, 1864 to April 29, 1864
Henry Prince	April 29, 1864 to May 1864

District of Columbus. In an order of September 24, 1862, which divided the forces in the District of West Tennessee into four divisions, the Fourth Division, District of West Tennessee was defined as consisting of what was then known as the districts of Cairo and of the Mississippi, including Fort Henry and Fort Donelson, and excluding that part of the district lying along the railroads in the state of Tennessee.

On October 26, 1862, Fourth Division was designated as the District of Columbus, Thirteenth Corps, Department of the Tennessee, and Thomas A. Davies was assigned command.

The district was later defined to include Paducah, Kentucky and all of Kentucky and Tennessee west of the Tennessee River and north of a line running from Big Sandy west through Paris, Tennessee to the Obion River, and then along that river to the Mississippi River.

When Sixteenth Corps was organized December 22, 1862, the forces in the District of Columbus were included in Sixteenth Corps as the District of Columbus, Sixteenth Corps, Department of the Tennessee.

The District of West Tennessee, Department of the Tennessee was constituted January 15, 1863 under the command of Charles S. Hamilton, and the District of Columbus became a sub-district of the District of West Tennessee. February 11, 1863, Stephen A. Hurlbut assumed command of the District of West Tennessee, and the forces therein were attached to Sixteenth Corps.

In a reorganization of Sixteenth Corps April 16, 1863, the designation of the District of Columbus was changed to Sixth Division (or District of Columbus), Sixteenth Corps.

January 24, 1864, a new Third Division, Sixteenth Corps was organized by Andrew J. Smith from the District of Columbus, and the next day the district was discontinued as Sixth Division and redesignated as the District of Cairo (see above).

April 23, 1864, Cadwallader C. Washburn assumed command of the District of West Tennessee, Department of the Tennessee, and the District of Columbus was revived on April 29 as the District of Columbus, District of West Tennessee, Department of the Tennessee. Henry Prince was assigned command April 29, and the district was defined as including all troops in the Department of the Tennessee north of New Madrid, Missouri.

Early in July 1864, the District of Columbus was discontinued when its designation was changed to the District of Western Kentucky.

The principal posts in the district were Columbus, Clinton, and Hickman in Kentucky: Cairo, Illinois; Fort Pillow and Fort Heiman in Tennessee; and Island No. 10 in the Mississippi River.

The commanders of the District of Columbus were as follows:

Thomas A. Davies	November 1, 1862 to January 11, 1863
Alexander Asboth	January 11, 1863 to August 5, 1863
Andrew J. Smith	August 5, 1863 to January 25, 1864
Henry Prince	April 29, 1864 to July 1864

The forces in the District of Columbus belonged principally to Thirteenth Corps and Sixteenth Corps of the Army of the Tennessee. For details of the organization of these troops in the District of Columbus, see Thirteenth Corps, Army of the Tennessee, October 24, 1862–January 14, 1863; Thirteenth Corps, Army of the Tennessee, January 14, 1863–August 7, 1863; Sixteenth Corps, Army of the Tennessee; and Army of the Tennessee, Department of the Tennessee. See also District of West Tennessee, below.

Two other organizations should be mentioned. In November 1862, troops formerly of the District of Cairo, Department of the Mississippi under the command of James M. Tuttle were designated as the Cairo Division, Department of the Tennessee. Tuttle commanded this division until January 19, 1863, and was then succeeded by Napoleon B. Buford. In July 1863 the designation of this organization was changed to Post of Cairo. The other organization was a brigade commanded by Clinton B. Fisk (Fisk's Brigade, or Second Brigade, United States Volunteers). This brigade was sent from the District of Saint Louis, Department of the Missouri for temporary duty in the District of Columbus during Nathan B. Forrest's Raid into western Tennessee in December 1862. Fisk arrived at Columbus, Kentucky on December 26, and then departed for Helena, Arkansas January 9–10, 1863.

District of Corinth. In the order of September 24, 1862 that divided the forces in the District of West Tennessee into four divisions, the Third Division, District of West Tennessee was described as consisting of all territory occupied by William S. Rosecrans' Army of the Mississippi, and the forces of the post of Corinth, Mississippi that were commanded by Edward O. C. Ord. On October 26, the designation of Third Division, District of West Tennessee was changed to District of Corinth, Thirteenth Corps, Department of the Tennessee. Charles S. Hamilton was assigned command, with headquarters at Corinth.

By an order of December 22, 1862, four new army corps were created in the Department of the Tennessee, and the District of Corinth was made a part of Seventeenth Corps.

The District of West Tennessee was constituted January 15, 1863 under Charles S. Hamilton, and the District of Corinth became a sub-district of the District of West Tennessee. On January 20, the District of Corinth was transferred to Sixteenth Corps as the District of Corinth, Left Wing, Sixteenth Corps.

February 11, 1863, Stephen A. Hurlbut assumed command of the District of West Tennessee, and the District of Jackson was attached to Sixteenth Corps. On February 17, Charles S. Hamilton was assigned command of the troops in the districts of Corinth and Jackson, and these districts, together with James W. Denver's First Division of Sixteenth Corps, which was assigned to Hamilton's command, and Benjamin H. Grierson's Cavalry Brigade were assigned as the Left Wing, Sixteenth Corps.

Hamilton was relieved of his command March 23, 1863, and there was no commander of the Left Wing, Sixteenth Corps until Richard J. Oglesby was assigned on April 8. The same order that assigned Oglesby to command also defined his Left Wing, Sixteenth Corps as including the districts of Corinth and Jackson.In the reorganization of Sixteenth Corps April 16, 1863, the troops of Grenville M. Dodge's District of Corinth were designated as Second Division (or District of Corinth), Sixteenth Corps. Dodge took the Second Division, Sixteenth Corps to Pulaski, Tennessee in the early part of November 1863, and during the following month the district was again reorganized. It was finally discontinued in the reorganization of Sixteenth Corps January 24, 1864.

The principal posts in the District of Corinth were Corinth, Glendale, and Danville in Mississippi; Bethel in Tennessee; and Tuscumbia in Alabama.

For the organization of the troops in the District of Corinth, see Thirteenth Corps, Army of the Tennessee, October 24, 1862–January 14, 1863; Thirteenth Corps, Army of the Tennessee, January 14, 1863–August 7, 1863; Sixteenth Corps, Army of the Tennessee; and Seventeenth Corps, Army of the Tennessee.

District of Eastern Arkansas. The troops in eastern Arkansas during October and November 1862 belonged to the Army of the Southwest, Department of the Missouri, and on November 2, that part of eastern Arkansas under the control of United States troops was designated as the District of Eastern Arkansas, Department of the Missouri.

On January 21, 1863, Ulysses S. Grant was assigned command of all troops in Arkansas that were within reach of his orders. This included the troops of the District of Eastern Arkansas, Department of the Missouri, and accordingly the District of Eastern Arkansas, then commanded by Willis A. Gorman, was attached to the Department of the Tennessee. On January 22, the district was attached to Thirteenth Corps, Department of the Tennessee. Headquarters of the district was at Helena, which was the principal post. On July 29, 1863 the District of Eastern Arkansas was transferred to Sixteenth Corps, Department of the Tennessee. For additional information, see Thirteenth Corps, Army of the Tennessee, January 14, 1863–August 7, 1863; and Sixteenth Corps, Army of the Tennessee.

The District of Eastern Arkansas was discontinued in the Department of the Tennessee when it was transferred to the newly created Department of Arkansas (Seventh Corps), January 6, 1864.

Commanders of the District of Eastern Arkansas were as follows:

Willis A. Gorman	December 22, 1862 to February 8, 1863
Benjamin M. Prentiss	February 8, 1863 to August 3, 1863
Frederick Salomon	August 3, 1863 to September 1863
Napoleon B. Buford	September 1863 to January 6, 1864

For the organization of the troops in the District of Eastern Arkansas, see Army of the Southwest; Thirteenth Corps, Army of the Tennessee, January 14, 1863–August 7, 1863; Sixteenth Corps, Army of the Tennessee; and Little Rock, Arkansas Expedition (Steele).

District of Jackson. In the order of September 24, 1862 that divided the United States forces in the District of West Tennessee into four divisions, Second Division was described as including all territory in the District of West Tennessee south of the Kentucky state line to the Hatchie River on the west and Bethel Station on the east, including Bolivar, Tennessee. On October 26, Second Division was designated as the District of Jackson, Department of the Tennessee, and Stephen A. Hurlbut was assigned command.

When Sixteenth Corps, Department of the Tennessee was organized December 22, 1862, the forces in the district were included in Sixteenth Corps as the District of Jackson, Sixteenth Corps, Department of the Tennessee.

January 15, 1863, the District of West Tennessee, Department of the Tennessee was constituted under Charles S. Hamilton, and the District of Jackson became a sub-district of the District of West Tennessee.

Stephen A. Hurlbut assumed command of the District of West Tennessee, and the District of Jackson was attached to Sixteenth Corps.

On February 17, 1863, Hamilton was assigned command of the troops in the districts of Jackson and Corinth, and these districts, together with James

W. Denver's First Division of Sixteenth Corps, which was assigned to Hamilton's command, and Benjamin F. Grierson's Cavalry Brigade, were organized as Left Wing, Sixteenth Corps. Hamilton was relieved from command on March 23, and there was no commander of the Left Wing until Richard J. Oglesby was assigned command April 8. The same order that assigned Oglesby to command the Left Wing, Sixteenth Corps also assigned the districts of Jackson and Corinth to the Left Wing, Sixteenth Corps.

In the reorganization of Sixteenth Corps April 16, 1863, the designation of the District of Jackson was changed to Third Division (or District of Jackson), Sixteenth Corps.

The District of Jackson was discontinued in May 1863 when the Third Division, except James M. True's Third Brigade, was sent to Vicksburg as Nathan Kimball's Provisional Division of Cadwallader C. Washburn's Detachment Sixteenth Corps.

The principal posts in the district were Jackson, Union City, Bolivar, Grand Junction, La Grange, Trenton, and Humboldt, all in Tennessee.

The commanders of the District of Jackson were as follows:

Stephen A. Hurlbut	October 26, 1862 to November 19, 1862
Jeremiah C. Sullivan	November 19, 1862 to March 20, 1863
Nathan Kimball	March 20, 1863 to May 1863

For details of the organization of the troops in the District of Jackson, see Thirteenth Corps, Army of the Tennessee, October 24, 1862–January 14, 1863; and Sixteenth Corps, Army of the Tennessee.

District of Memphis. In the order of September 24, 1862 that divided the District of West Tennessee into four divisions, the First Division, District of West Tennessee was defined as consisting of all territory of the District of West Tennessee south of the Hatchie River and west of Bolivar, Tennessee that was occupied by United States troops.

October 26, 1862, First Division was designated as the District of Memphis, Thirteenth Corps, Department of the Tennessee. William T. Sherman was assigned command, with headquarters at Memphis, Tennessee.

When Fifteenth Corps, Department of the Tennessee was created December 22, 1862, the District of Memphis was included in its organization as District of Memphis, Fifteenth Corps.

The District of West Tennessee, Department of the Tennessee was constituted January 15, 1863 under the command of Charles S. Hamilton, and the District of Memphis became a sub-district of the District of West Tennessee.

Stephen A. Hurlbut was assigned command of the District of West Tennessee February 11, 1863, and the District of Memphis was attached to Sixteenth Corps

In the reorganization of Sixteenth Corps April 16, 1863, the District of Memphis was designated as Fifth Division, Sixteenth Corps, but it was still referred to as the District of Memphis.

Sixteenth Corps was again reorganized January 24, 1864, and the designation of the district was again changed to the District of Memphis, Sixteenth Corps.

April 23, 1864, Cadwallader C. Washburn assumed command of the District of West Tennessee, Department of the Tennessee, relieving Stephen A. Hurlbut. On May 2, Hurlbut was relieved from command in Sixteenth Corps, and no successor was named. At that time the district was designated as District of Memphis, District of West Tennessee, Department of the Tennessee.

In October 1864, Napoleon J. T. Dana was assigned command of Sixteenth Corps, and once more the designation was changed to the District of Memphis, District of West Tennessee, Sixteenth Corps.

The district was transferred to the Department of Mississippi November 28, 1864 as Post and Defenses of Memphis, District of West Tennessee.

The principal posts were Memphis, Fort Pickering, near Memphis, and Fort Pillow.

The commanders of the District of Memphis were as follows:

William T. Sherman	October 26, 1862 to November 25, 1862
Stephen A. Hurlbut	November 25, 1862 to January 6, 1863
James C. Veatch	January 6, 1863 to January 25, 1864
Ralph P. Buckland	January 25, 1864 to November 1864

The troops in the District of Memphis generally belonged to Thirteenth Corps (old), Fifteenth Corps, and Sixteenth Corps. In addition, the First Brigade, Tennessee Enrolled Militia, commanded by C. McDonald and Charles W. Dustan, was in the district from January 1864 to December 1864. For details of the organization of the troops in the district, see Thirteenth Corps, Army of the Tennessee, October 24, 1862–January 14, 1863; Fifteenth Corps, Army of the Tennessee; and Sixteenth Corps, Army of the Tennessee.

District of Northeastern Louisiana. In May 1863, when Fifteenth Corps departed from Milliken's Bend and Young's Point, Louisiana at the beginning of Ulysses S. Grant's advance to the rear of Vicksburg, Mississippi, Isaac F. Shepard's African Brigade occupied the area. On May 28, that part of the state of Louisiana then occupied by troops of the Army of the Tennessee was constituted as the District of Northeastern Louisiana. Jeremiah C. Sullivan was assigned command, and during the absence of John P. Hawkins the colored troops were under the immediate command of Shepard.

In late January 1864, the troops in the district were designated as First Brigade, United States Colored Troops, Post of Vicksburg, and later they became First Brigade, First Division, United States Colored Troops, District of Vicksburg. For additional information, see below, District of Vicksburg.

The principal posts in the district were Milliken's Bend, Young's Point, Goodrich's Landing, Lake Providence, and Transylvania.

The commanders of the District of Northeastern Louisiana were as follows:

Jeremiah C. Sullivan May 28, 1863 to early June 1863
Elias S. Dennis Early June 1863 to July 28, 1863
Isaac F. Shepard July 28, 1863 to August 18, 1863
John P. Hawkins August 18, 1863 to January 1864

Note. Shepard commanded the district during the absence of Hawkins, who was sick.

District of the Tallahatchie. During Ulysses S. Grant's advance into northern Mississippi in his campaign against Vicksburg in November and December 1862, C. Carroll Marsh is noted as commanding the District of the Tallahatchie. This appears to have been a temporary command of only short duration.

District of Vicksburg. In the spring of 1864, when headquarters of both Seventeenth Corps and the Department and Army of the Tennessee were moving toward northern Georgia in preparation for William T. Sherman's advance on Atlanta, the proper administration of affairs at and near Vicksburg became increasingly difficult. To remedy this situation, on April 12, 1864 the District of Vicksburg was created to extend southward from the mouth of the Arkansas River on the west bank of the Mississippi River, and the mouth of the Tallahatchie River on the east side down to the Department of the Gulf. Henry W. Slocum assumed command of the district April 20, with headquarters at Vicksburg.

The troops at Vicksburg at that time belonged to Seventeenth Corps, and for a time the District of Vicksburg was reported as a part of Seventeenth Corps. The district, however, reported directly to Headquarters, Department and Army of the Tennessee.

In April 1864 the District of Vicksburg was organized as follows:

DISTRICT OF VICKSBURG, Henry W. Slocum

First Division, Seventeenth Corps, Elias S. Dennis
    First Brigade, Frederick A. Starring
    Second Brigade, James H. Coates
    Artillery, William H. Bolton
        Battery L, 2nd Illinois Light Artillery, William H. Bolton
        Battery M, 1st Missouri Light Artillery, John H. Tiemeyer
        7th Battery, Ohio Light Artillery, Harlow P. McNaughton
    Second Brigade, Fourth Division, Benjamin Dornblaser
    Mississippi Marine Brigade, Alfred W. Ellet
    Maltby's Brigade, Jasper A. Maltby

Note. James F. Putnam's 8th Battery, Ohio Light Artillery and Theobold D. Yost's 26th Battery, Ohio Light Artillery were attached to Maltby's Brigade.

Cavalry Brigade, Horace P. Mumford

Note 1. July 28, 1864, First Division, Seventeenth Corps moved from the District of Vicksburg to

Morganza, Louisiana in the Department of the Gulf. The designation of this command was retained until a reorganization of Nineteenth Corps was ordered on August 18, and then First Division, Seventeenth Corps was merged into Second Division, Nineteenth Corps, and Dennis was assigned command of Second Division. First Brigade, First Division was in the District of Vicksburg until October 1864.

Note 2. The Mississippi Marine Brigade was ordered discontinued August 3, 1864.

Note 3. In October 1864, First Brigade, First Division, Seventeenth Corps was merged into Maltby's Brigade.

First Division, United States Colored Troops, John P. Hawkins
First Brigade, Isaac F. Shepard
Second Brigade, Hiram Scofield
Forces at Vicksburg
United States Forces at Milliken's Bend and Goodrich's Landing, A. Watson Webber

Note 1. In January 1864, troops in the District of Northeastern Louisiana were designated as First Brigade, United States Colored Troops, Post of Vicksburg, and in March 1864 these troops were designated as First Brigade, First Division, United States Colored Troops. The Colored Brigade at Vicksburg under Hiram Scofield became Second Brigade, First Division, United States Colored Troops.

Note 2. In October 1864, First Division, United States Colored Troops became Fourth Division, Sixteenth Corps.

Note 3. First Brigade consisted of the 46th, 48th, 49th, and 53rd United States Colored Troops; Second Brigade consisted of the 47th, 50th, and 53rd United States Colored Troops; the Forces at Vicksburg consisted of the 3rd United States Colored Cavalry, 2nd United States Colored Artillery (Battery A), and 4th United States Colored Heavy Artillery; and the troops at Milliken's Bend and Goodrich's Landing consisted of the 51st and 66th United States Colored Troops, and 2nd United States Colored Light Artillery (Battery B).

Defenses and Post of Natchez, James M. Tuttle

On October 15, 1864, Napoleon J. T. Dana assumed command of Sixteenth Corps (assigned September 17), which included the Combined Districts of West Tennessee and Vicksburg.

The organization of the District of Vicksburg in October 1864 was as follows:

DISTRICT OF VICKSBURG, SIXTEENTH CORPS, Napoleon J. T. Dana

Garrison of Vicksburg
Maltby's Brigade, Jasper A. Maltby

5th United States Colored Heavy Artillery, Herman Lieb
64th United States Colored Troops, Samuel Thomas

Note. James F. Putnam's 8th Battery, Ohio Light Artillery and Theobold D. Yost's 26th Battery, Ohio Light Artillery were attached to Maltby's Brigade.

Cavalry Forces, Embury D. Osband

Artillery at Vicksburg, Charles Mann
Battery L, 2nd Illinois Light Artillery, Charles H. Felton
7th Battery, Ohio Light Artillery, Silas A. Burnap

Post and Defenses of Natchez, Mason Brayman

Fourth Division, Sixteenth Corps, John P. Hawkins
First Brigade, Van E. Young
Second Brigade, Hiram Scofield
Goodrich's Landing, A. Watson Webber
Milliken's Bend, Julian E. Bryant

Note 1. Fourth Division, Sixteenth Corps was formerly First Division, United States Colored Troops.

Note 2. William M. Pratt's Battery D, Second United States Colored Light Artillery was at Goodrich's Landing; and Robert Ranney's Battery C, 2nd United States Colored Light Artillery was at Milliken's Bend.

Sixteenth Corps was discontinued November 7, 1864, and all troops on the east bank of the Mississippi River were detached from their several departments and corps and ordered to report to Edward R. S. Canby, commander of the Military Division of West Mississippi.

The District of Vicksburg was transferred to the Department of Mississippi November 28, 1864.

The principal posts in the district were Vicksburg and Natchez in Mississippi, and Goodrich's Landing, Milliken's Bend, and Davis' Bend in Louisiana.

The commanders of the District of Vicksburg, Department of the Tennessee were as follows:

Henry W. Slocum   April 20, 1864 to August 19, 1864
Napoleon J. T. Dana   August 19, 1864 to November 28, 1864

Note 1. Slocum left Vicksburg August 19, 1864 to assume command of Twentieth Corps, Army of the Cumberland, which was with William T. Sherman's army in Georgia.

Note 2. Cadwallader C. Washburn was assigned com-

mand of the District of Vicksburg, in addition to the District of West Tennessee, August 4, 1864, but Slocum remained in command until August 19.

Note 3. Napoleon J. T. Dana continued in command of the District of Vicksburg after it was transferred to the Department of Mississippi November 28, 1864, and remained in command until May 14, 1865.

District of West Tennessee. The District of West Tennessee was first organized February 17, 1862 under Ulysses S. Grant, and it remained in existence, with Grant in command, until October 16, 1862, when it became a part of the newly created Department of the Tennessee. At that time there were four divisions in the District of West Tennessee (see District of West Tennessee in section on Miscellaneous Organizations), and these were transferred to the Department of the Tennessee as the districts of Columbus, Corinth, Jackson, and Memphis.

On December 22, 1862, Thirteenth Corps, Fifteenth Corps, Sixteenth Corps, and Seventeenth Corps were created, the districts of Columbus and Jackson were assigned to Sixteenth Corps, and the district of Corinth and Memphis was assigned to Seventeenth Corps.

Early in January 1863, Thirteenth Corps and Fifteenth Corps were operating to the south along the Mississippi River, and Seventeenth Corps was under orders to join them in preparation for Grant's campaign against Vicksburg. Sixteenth Corps was left to occupy western Kentucky, western Tennessee, and northern Mississippi.

Charles S. Hamilton was assigned command of Sixteenth Corps January 10, 1863 during the temporary absence of Stephen A. Hurlbut, who was ill. Then on January 15, Hamilton was assigned command of the districts of Columbus, Corinth, Jackson, and Memphis, and his command was to be known as the District of West Tennessee, Department of the Tennessee. He assumed command of the district the next day.

February 5, 1863, Hurlbut assumed command of Sixteenth Corps, and on February 7 his command was extended to include the districts of Columbus, Jackson, Memphis, and Corinth. From that date these districts were designated as follows:

District of Columbus, Sixteenth Corps
District of Corinth, Sixteenth Corps
District of Jackson, Sixteenth Corps
District of Memphis, Sixteenth Corps

The District of Jackson was discontinued in May 1863, and the District of Corinth was discontinued in January 1864.

Following Nathan B. Forrest's raid into western Kentucky and western Tennessee March 16–April 14, 1864, Cadwallader C. Washburn was ordered to Memphis on April 17 to relieve Hurlbut in command of the District of West Tennessee. Then on May 2, Hurlbut was relieved of all command in Sixteenth Corps, and the troops in western Kentucky, in western Tennessee, and on the Mississippi River were included in the District of West Tennessee, Department of the Tennessee.

During 1864 the District of West Tennessee was divided into sub-districts as follows:

April 1864	District of Cairo and District of Memphis
May–June 1864	District of Columbus and District of Memphis
July–August 1864	District of Memphis and District of Western Kentucky
September–October 1864	District of Memphis

For additional information, see the respective districts.

Napoleon J. T. Dana assumed command of Sixteenth Corps October 15, 1864 (assigned September 27), which included the Combined Districts of West Tennessee and Vicksburg. The designation of the district was then changed to District of West Tennessee and Vicksburg.

Sixteenth Corps was discontinued November 7, 1864, and all the United States troops on the east bank of the Mississippi River were detached from their respective departments and corps and were ordered to report directly to Edward R. S. Canby, commander of the Military Division of West Mississippi. The District of West Tennessee and Vicksburg was transferred to the Department of Mississippi on November 28.

The commanders of the District of West Tennessee were as follows:

Charles S. Hamilton	January 15, 1863 to February 11, 1863

Stephen A. Hurlbut	February 11, 1863 to April 17, 1864
Cadwallader C. Washburn	April 17, 1864 to November 28, 1864

District of Western Kentucky, District of West Tennessee. The District of Western Kentucky, District of West Tennessee was created early in July 1864 from the District of Columbus, District of West Tennessee. Eleazer A. Paine was assigned command, with headquarters at Paducah, Kentucky.

The District of Western Kentucky was transferred to the Department of the Ohio August 7, 1864.

The troops in the district consisted of regiments stationed at the various posts as follows: Paducah, Kentucky, commanded by Henry W. Barry; Cairo, Illinois, commanded by Solomon Meredith; Columbus, Kentucky, commanded by James N. McArthur; and Mayfield, Kentucky, commanded by John C. Bigelow.

TROOPS AND OPERATIONS IN THE DEPARTMENT OF THE TENNESSEE

In addition to the troops assigned to the many districts and posts of the department, the principal field force was the Army of the Tennessee. For details of its organization and operations, see Army of the Tennessee, Department of the Tennessee.

DEPARTMENT OF THE TENNESSEE
JUNE 27, 1865–JUNE 5, 1866

In the reorganization of the military divisions and departments of the army June 27, 1865, the Department of the Tennessee was re-created to consist of the state of Tennessee. On that date, the Department of the Tennessee was assigned to the Military Division of the Tennessee. On July 1, George Stoneman assumed command of the department, with headquarters at Knoxville, Tennessee. On January 3, 1866, headquarters was moved to Memphis, Tennessee. The department was discontinued June 5,

1866 when it was merged into the Department of the Cumberland.

DEPARTMENT OF TEXAS
OCTOBER 31, 1853– FEBRUARY 1862

The Department of Texas was in existence long before the beginning of the war, and from December 8, 1860 it consisted only of the state of Texas. David E. Twiggs was in command of the department, with headquarters at San Antonio. On February 18, 1861, Twiggs surrendered all Federal posts and property to the state authorities, and then resigned his commission in the United States Army and joined the Confederacy. Carlos A. Waite was assigned command of the department by an order of January 28, 1861, but he did not assume command until February 19.

The order of February 23, 1862 which created the Federal Department of the Gulf did not specifically include the state of Texas within its limits, but on November 8, 1862, the limits of the department were formally extended to include Texas.

DEPARTMENT OF TEXAS
JUNE 27, 1865– AUGUST 6, 1866

In the order of June 27, 1865 that reorganized the military divisions and departments of the army, the Department of Texas was constituted to consist of the state of Texas. By the same order, the department was attached to the Military Division of the Gulf. Horatio G. Wright was assigned command of the department, but he did not assume command until August 6. He then established headquarters at Galveston. On August 6, 1866, the Department of Texas was merged into the Department of the Gulf.

DEPARTMENT OF UTAH

The Department of Utah was in existence at the beginning of the Civil War, and it consisted of that part of the Territory of Utah east of 117 degrees west longitude. When it was created January 1, 1858, the Territory of Utah was bounded on the north by the 42nd degree north latitude, on the south by the 37th degree north latitude, and it extended westward from the Rocky Mountains to the eastern boundary of California. Headquarters of the department, and the principal post in the department, was Camp Floyd (later Fort Crittenden), which was about forty miles southwest of Salt Lake City in Cedar Valley. Philip St. G. Cooke, who was in command of the department at the outbreak of the Civil War, was assigned command August 20, 1860.

The troops in the Department of Utah at Fort Crittenden consisted of the following: companies B, E, and H of the 2nd United States Dragoons; companies E and I of the 10th United States Infantry; and batteries A, B, and C of the 4th United States Artillery. In addition, companies B and G of the 10th United States Infantry were at Fort Bridger.

On July 27, 1861, Fort Crittenden was abandoned, and Cooke marched eastward with his command to Fort Leavenworth, Kansas. From there his troops were moved on to Washington.

On the same day that Fort Crittenden was abandoned, the Territory of Utah was attached to the Department of the Pacific as the District of Utah. It was not until August 6, 1862, however, that California Volunteers under the command of P. Edward O'Connor moved in to occupy the district. By that time the Territory of Utah had been greatly reduced in size by the creation of the Territory of Nevada and the Territory of Colorado.

DEPARTMENT OF THE WEST

The Department of the West was in existence at the beginning of the war and was under the command of William S. Harney. At that time it included all of the territory of the United States from the Rocky Mountains to the Mississippi River, except Texas and New Mexico. Thus it included the present-day states of Arkansas, Iowa, Kansas, Louisiana, Minnesota, Missouri, Montana, Nebraska, North Dakota, Oklahoma, South Dakota, and parts of Colorado and Wyoming. The area of the department was reduced when Louisiana seceded from the Union January 26, 1861, and again when Arkansas seceded May 6, 1861.

Harney relinquished command of the department April 23, 1861 and resumed command May 11. No one was assigned as department commander during his absence, but Seth Williams of Harney's staff was at headquarters, and on April 29, Williams notified Colonel Edmund B. Alexander, 10th United States Infantry at Fort Laramie, who was the senior officer in the department, that he was in command of the Department of the West. Nathaniel Lyon assumed command of the department May 31, by right of seniority. Headquarters of the department was at Saint Louis, Missouri until June 6, 1861, but on that date the state of Missouri was included in the Department of the Ohio, and headquarters was moved to Fort Leavenworth, Kansas.

On July 3, 1861, the Department of the West was merged into the newly organized Western Department.

TROOPS IN THE DEPARTMENT OF THE WEST

At the outbreak of war, the troops in the Department of the West consisted of regulars, who were scattered in small units at the various posts in the department. In Missouri, where military activities began early and increased rapidly, the principal forces were at the Saint Louis Arsenal and at Jefferson Barracks, ten miles below Saint Louis. There were at Saint Louis about 430 men, consisting of a detachment of ordnance; James Totten's Company F, 2nd United States Artillery, which had arrived from Little Rock, Arkansas; Nathaniel Lyon's Company B, 2nd United States Infantry; and some recruits.

On March 13, 1861, Lyon was assigned, as the senior officer present, to the command of the troops and defenses of Saint Louis Arsenal.

At Fort Leavenworth, Kansas, William Steele, of the 2nd Dragoons, was in command of a small force, but this was soon increased by the arrival of troops from other posts in the department. On April 17, 1861, William H. Emory of the 1st United States Cavalry, at Fort Washita, Indian Territory, was ordered to assemble the troops at Fort Washita, Fort Cobb, and Fort Arbuckle, all in the Indian Territory, and march with them to Fort Leavenworth. Emory's column consisted of two companies of regular cavalry and five companies of regular infantry.

On April 23, 1861, Samuel D. Sturgis of the 1st United States Cavalry evacuated Fort Smith, Arkansas and joined Emory's column, which arrived at Fort Leavenworth May 31. At that time the column consisted of eleven companies of United States troops, or about 750 men. Emory then turned over his command to Delos B. Sacket of the 1st Cavalry and departed for the East.

On April 10, 1861, Dixon S. Miles, colonel of the 2nd United States Infantry, was ordered to move from Fort Kearny, Nebraska Territory to Fort Leavenworth with companies E and F of his regiment. Upon arriving there on April 29, Miles assumed command of the post, but a short time later was ordered East.

On June 12, 1861, the Regiment of Mounted Riflemen (Rifles), two companies of the First Dragoons, and two companies of the 2nd Dragoons were ordered from New Mexico to Fort Leavenworth.

On April 21, 1861, Nathaniel Lyon began enrolling volunteers at the Saint Louis Arsenal, with authority to muster four regiments, and by the end of the week the 1st Regiment was filled and the others were nearing completion. On April 29, he was authorized to increase his force to 10,000 men.

Lyon succeeded William S. Harney in command of the Department of the West May 31, 1861, and on June 1 he announced the organization of the First Brigade, Missouri Volunteers as follows:

First Brigade, Missouri Volunteers, Nathaniel Lyon
  1st Missouri Volunteers, Frank P. Blair, Jr.
  2nd Missouri Volunteers, Henry Boernstein
  3rd Missouri Volunteers, Franz Sigel
  4th Missouri Volunteers, Nicholas Schuettner
  5th Missouri Volunteers, Charles E. Salomon

Lyon also announced the organization of five regiments of the United States Reserve Corps, which were also called regiments of Missouri Home Guards (or simply Home Guards). These were:

1st Regiment Home Guards, Henry Almstedt
2nd Regiment Home Guards, Herman Kallman
3rd Regiment Home Guards, John McNeil
4th Regiment Home Guards, B. Gratz Brown
5th Regiment Home Guards, Charles A. Stifel

For further information about the organization and operations of the troops in the Department of the West, see Operations in Missouri in 1861.

WESTERN DEPARTMENT

The Western Department was constituted July 3, 1861 to consist of the state of Illinois and the states and territories west of the Mississippi River and east of the Rocky Mountains, including New Mexico. John C. Fremont assumed command July 25, 1861 (assigned July 3), with headquarters at Saint Louis, Missouri. David Hunter succeeded Fremont in command November 2, 1861, and remained in command until the department was discontinued on November 9.

November 9, 1861, the Department of Kansas, the Department of the Missouri, and the Department of New Mexico were created from the territory of the Western Department, which was then discontinued.

DISTRICTS IN THE WESTERN DEPARTMENT

District of Ironton. The District of Ironton was created to consist of the post of Ironton and the surrounding country. It was merged into the Southeast District of Missouri September 1, 1861. Commanders of the district were as follows: B. Gratz Brown, to August 8, 1861; Ulysses S. Grant, August 8, 1861 to August 15, 1861; and Benjamin M. Prentiss, August 15, 1861 to September 1, 1861.

District of North Missouri. The District of North Missouri was constituted July 29, 1861, when John Pope assumed command of all troops in the state of Missouri north of Saint Louis. Pope established his headquarters at Mexico, Missouri.

On the same day that Pope assumed command of the district, Stephen A. Hurlbut was assigned command of all Union forces along the line of the Hannibal and Saint Joseph Railroad, from Quincy, Illinois and Hannibal, Missouri to Saint Joseph, Missouri. Also on July 29, 1861, the following assignments were made: Ulysses S. Grant, with his 21st Illinois Regiment, to the post of Mexico; Leonard F. Ross, with his 17th Illinois, to Warrenton, Missouri; and John M. Palmer, with his 14th Illinois, to Renick and Sturgeon, with his headquarters at Renick.

On August 2, 1861, William H. Worthington, who was in command of Iowa troops at Keokuk, Iowa, was ordered to move with his command into northeastern Missouri. Worthington's troops consisted of the 5th and 6th Iowa regiments, and cavalry under Cyrus Bussey and John McNulta. A part of these troops were ordered to march by way of Memphis in Scotland County to Edina in Knox County, and the rest were to go by way of Monticello in Lewis County and join the rest of the command at Edina.

September 17, 1861, Benjamin M. Prentiss was assigned command of that part of Missouri bordering on, and lying north of, the Hannibal and Saint Joseph Railroad, with headquarters at Mason City.

The Department of the Missouri was created November 9, 1861, and the District of North Missouri became a part of that department.

Southeast District of Missouri (later called District of Southeast Missouri). The Southeast District of Missouri was formed September 1, 1861 when Ulysses S. Grant assumed command of all Union troops in southeastern Missouri. The district was enlarged on September 4 with the addition of Cairo, Illinois. The command at Cairo also included the troops at Bird's Point, Missouri and Mound City, Illinois. Troops from Cairo under the command of Charles F. Smith also occupied Paducah, Kentucky September 6, 1861. Headquarters of the Southeast District of Missouri was established at Cairo.

The principal posts in the district were Bird's Point and Cape Girardeau in Missouri, Cairo and Mound City in Illinois, and Fort Holt and Paducah in Kentucky.

On October 14, 1861, Grant organized the troops of the district into brigades as follows:

First Brigade, John A. McClernand, at Cairo and Mound City

Second Brigade, Richard J. Oglesby, at Bird's Point

Third Brigade, William H. L. Wallace, at Bird's Point

Fourth Brigade, John Cook, at Fort Holt

Fifth Brigade, Joseph B. Plummer, at Cape Girardeau

OPERATIONS IN THE WESTERN DEPARTMENT

Baylor's Invasion of New Mexico, July 1861–August 1861. A Confederate force from Texas under John R. Baylor reached the southern border of New Mexico during the first week of July 1861 and occupied Fort Bliss. Baylor advanced to Mesilla on July 25 and later occupied that part of New Mexico lying south of the Jornado del Muerto, including Las Cruces. He then organized temporarily the Territory of Arizona under a military government and took possession in the name of the Confederate States Government. This territory included all of the state of New Mexico south of the 34th degree of north latitude. Baylor served as civil and military governor of Arizona. For additional information, see Department of New Mexico, Troops and Operations in the Department of New Mexico, Baylor's Invasion of Southern New Mexico.

Engagement at Belmont, Missouri, November 7, 1861. Ulysses S. Grant was assigned command of the District of Southeastern Missouri, in John C. Fremont's Western Department, August 28, 1861 (he assumed command September 1), and he established headquarters at Cairo, Illinois. On October 14 he organized the troops of the district into five brigades, commanded by John A. McClernand, Richard J. Oglesby, William H. L. Wallace, John Cook, and Joseph B. Plummer.

November 5, 1861, Grant received information from department headquarters that Confederate troops were being sent from Columbus, Kentucky to reinforce Sterling Price's army in southwestern Missouri, and he was ordered to make a demonstration against Columbus in an attempt to stop this movement.

On the evening of November 6, Grant left Cairo on transports with about 3,100 men consisting of

McClernand's First Brigade, District of Southeastern Missouri, and Henry Dougherty's 22nd Illinois Infantry and Jacob G. Lauman's 7th Iowa Infantry. Also with the expedition were two companies of cavalry and a six-gun battery. Preceded by the gunboats *Tyler* (Captain Henry Walke) and *Lexington* (Captain Roger N. Stembel), the transports moved downstream about nine miles to the foot of Island No. 1, and tied up for the night against the Kentucky shore.

Later that night, Grant received further information that enemy forces had been crossing the Mississippi River from Columbus to intercept a force under Richard J. Oglesby, which was then operating on the Missouri side of the river toward Bloomfield, and which was under orders to proceed toward New Madrid, Missouri. This information caused Grant to change his plans, because it was then necessary to protect Oglesby's column. Instead of a demonstration against Columbus, Grant decided to attack a Confederate force at the small village of Belmont, Missouri, directly across the river from Columbus. He also made a change in the organization of his command by assigning Dougherty to the command of a small brigade consisting of his own 22nd Illinois and Lauman's 7th Iowa.

The next morning, November 7, 1861, the gunboats and transports moved on downstream, and the troops disembarked on the Missouri shore at 8:30, about three miles above the enemy encampment at Belmont, and out of range of the enemy's batteries at Columbus. The gunboats then dropped downriver and soon engaged the batteries at Columbus.

The troops marched out in column about one mile and formed in line of battle along the eastern side of a cornfield, facing southeast. The regiments were in line, from right to left, as follows: 27th Illinois, 30th Illinois, 31st Illinois, 7th Iowa, and 22nd Illinois. The line then moved to the right and front, and the skirmishers became engaged about 9:00 A.M.

James C. Tappan's 13th Arkansas Regiment was encamped at Belmont when Grant's troops landed, but Gideon J. Pillow soon arrived from Columbus with four regiments of his First Division. Pillow then assumed command of all Confederate troops at Belmont, and it was this force that was in front of Grant's advancing line. The engagement proper began at 10:30 A.M., and, despite stiff resistance, Grant's troops continued to move forward, finally driving the enemy from their camp and the village of Belmont and forcing them to take shelter under the river bank. Federal troops then occupied the enemy camp at Belmont, and they proceeded to burn, or otherwise destroy, the tents, blankets, camp equipage, and transportation. When this work was completed, Grant ordered his command to retire to the transports and reembark.

Meantime, the strongly reinforced Confederates had moved up the river bank to a point above the camp, and then into a position in rear of Grant's command. A vigorous charge drove the enemy back, and the troops then continued on to the landing where, with the exception of the 27th Illinois and James J. Dollins' cavalry, they reembarked without further difficulty. The enemy appeared on the river bank and opened fire on the transports as they were pulling out. The troops returned the fire from the decks of the steamers, and the gunboats soon cleared the bank of the enemy. The fighting ended about sunset. The 27th Illinois and the cavalry were later picked up from the river bank, and the expedition returned to Cairo.

The gunboats rendered valuable service during the day by engaging the enemy batteries and protecting the transports.

The organization of Grant's command at the Engagement of Belmont November 7, 1861 was as follows:

First Brigade, John A. McClernand
    27th Illinois, Napoleon B. Buford
    30th Illinois, Philip B. Fouke
    31st Illinois, John A. Logan

Second Brigade, Henry Dougherty, wounded
    22nd Illinois, Harrison E. Hart
    7th Iowa, Jacob G. Lauman, wounded

Dollins' Company, Illinois Cavalry, James J. Dollins
Delano's Company, Illinois Cavalry, James K. Catlin

Battery B, 1st Illinois Light Artillery, Ezra Taylor

For additional information, see above, Districts in the Western Department, Southeast District of Missouri.

FIELD ARMIES

☆☆☆☆

ARMY OF ARKANSAS

July 27, 1863, Frederick Steele was assigned by Ulysses S. Grant, commander of the Department of the Tennessee, to organize and command a force at Helena, Arkansas for the purpose of advancing into the interior toward Little Rock. Steele arrived at Helena July 31 and proceeded to organize his command. It consisted of two infantry divisions and one cavalry division, and was called the Army of Arkansas. Steele left Helena on August 10 and occupied Little Rock one month later. For details of the organization and operations of the Army of Arkansas, see Little Rock, Arkansas Expedition (Steele).

ARMY OF THE BORDER

On September 19, 1864, a Confederate army under Sterling Price entered southeastern Missouri from Arkansas and approached Saint Louis. Without attacking the city, however, it marched west past Jefferson City, through Boonville, and arrived near Lexington on October 17. To oppose this threat of an invasion of the state of Kansas, Samuel R. Curtis, commander of the Department of Kansas, persuaded the governor to call out the Kansas State Militia, and he then proceeded to organize a force called the Army of the Border from troops then serving in the department.

On October 13, 1864, James G. Blunt, commander of the District of South Kansas, was ordered to move to Hickman Mills, Missouri with all of this cavalry and artillery, and on October 15 he organized his command as First Division, Army of the Border as follows:

First Division, Army of the Border, James G. Blunt
　　First Brigade, Charles R. Jennison
　　Second Brigade, Thomas Moonlight
　　Third Brigade, Charles W. Blair

A Fourth Brigade commanded by James H. Ford joined the division on October 21.

In addition to the regiments of Blunt's command, George W. Deitzler assembled eleven unassigned regiments of the Kansas State Militia near Kansas City. These and Kersey Coates' Kansas City Home Guards were also under Curtis' command.

The Army of the Border was engaged at Lexington, at Little Blue River, at Byram's Ford on the Big Blue River, and at Westport, and it then joined in the pursuit of Price's retreating army through southwestern Missouri and into Arkansas. Curtis arrived on the Arkansas River November 8, the day after Price had crossed, and he then abandoned the pursuit. The Army of the Border was then broken up, and the brigades returned to Kansas by different routes.

For details of the organization and operations of the Army of the Border, see Price's Missouri Expedition.

ARMY OF THE CUMBERLAND
AUGUST 15, 1861–NOVEMBER 9, 1861

When the Department of the Cumberland was

created August 15, 1861, the troops within its limits consisted of regiments organized in Kentucky and regiments sent there from the northern states. On September 10, 1861, George H. Thomas was assigned command at Camp Dick Robinson, Kentucky, succeeding William Nelson, and a short time later he organized the First Kentucky Brigade. This was the first brigade organized in Kentucky. It was later designated as First Brigade, Army of the Cumberland. Later Thomas organized from regiments of his command Second Brigade, Army of the Cumberland, under Mahlon D. Manson, and Third Brigade under Robert L. McCook.

While Robert Anderson was in command of the Department of the Cumberland, William T. Sherman was in charge of the troops on the Louisville and Nashville Railroad near Elizabethtown, Kentucky. When Sherman was assigned command of the department October 7, 1861, Lovell H. Rousseau succeeded him in command of the troops along the railroad. Rousseau then moved the troops of Sherman's former force to Nolin, Kentucky, and established Camp Nevin. This post became the assembly point and training center for new regiments arriving in Kentucky from the North.

Alexander McD. McCook relieved Rousseau in command at Camp Nevin October 18, 1861, and he then organized the regiments at the camp into three brigades. That same day, he announced the organization of the "Central Division" (a provisional division of the Department of the Cumberland) from these three brigades.

Central Division, Alexander McD. McCook
    Fourth Brigade, Lovell H. Rousseau
    Fifth Brigade, Thomas J. Wood
    Sixth Brigade, Richard W. Johnson

Back in Pittsburgh, Pennsylvania, James S. Negley was in charge of forming a brigade from regiments organized there during September and October 1861, and when this was completed, the brigade was sent to McCook at Camp Nevin. Upon arrival there, it was designated as Seventh Brigade, Department of the Cumberland, with Negley in command.

In a report of November 10, 1861, Sherman listed McCook's command at Camp Nevin as First Division, Department of the Cumberland, and Thomas' command at Camp Dick Robinson as Second Division, Department of the Cumberland. These designations, however, were not commonly used. When the Army of the Ohio was organized December 2, 1862 by Don Carlos Buell, McCook's division became Second Division, Army of the Ohio and Thomas' division became First Division, Army of the Ohio.

The Department of the Cumberland was not divided into districts during the first period of its existence, and the troops serving in the department were distributed among the various posts of the department. In early November 1861, these were as follows:

McCook's forces at Camp Nevin, Nolin, Kentucky
Thomas' forces at Camp Dick Robinson, Kentucky
Nelson's Brigade in Eastern Kentucky, William Nelson
Ward's Brigade at Campbellsville, Kentucky, William T. Ward
Bardstown, Kentucky, Mahlon D. Manson
Colesburg, Kentucky, Frederick Hecker
Elizabethtown, Kentucky, John B. Turchin
Lebanon Junction, Kentucky, Horatio P. Van Cleve
Big Hill, Kentucky, John M. Connell
Owensboro (or Henderson), Kentucky, Charles Cruft
Jeffersonville, Indiana, John C. Starkweather
Crab Orchard, Kentucky, John Coburn
Cynthiana, Kentucky, Ferdinand Van Derveer
Mouth of Salt River, Kentucky
Paris, Kentucky

The forces at the above-mentioned posts were designated as Sherman's Army of the Cumberland, and they later became Buell's Army of the Ohio. For details, see Army of the Ohio (Buell).

The commanders of the Army of the Cumberland during the period August-November 1861 were as follows:

Robert Anderson	August 15, 1861 to October 8, 1861
William T. Sherman	October 8, 1861 to November 15, 1861

Although the Department of the Cumberland was discontinued by an order of November 9, 1861, Sherman remained in command until November 15,

1861, when Buell assumed command of the Department of the Ohio.

Buell's former Army of the Ohio at Bowling Green, Kentucky on November 1.

ARMY OF THE CUMBERLAND OCTOBER 24, 1862– NOVEMBER 14, 1864

When the western departments of the Army were reorganized in November 1861, the states of Kentucky and Tennessee were included in the Department of the Ohio, and the Department of the Cumberland was discontinued. Don Carlos Buell assumed command of the Department of the Ohio November 15, 1861, and on December 2 he announced the organization of the Army of the Ohio, which included the troops of the former Army of the Cumberland. This was the Army of the Ohio that fought at the Battle of Shiloh April 6–7, 1862 and at the Battle of Perryville October 8, 1862.

After the Battle of Perryville, the Department of the Cumberland was re-created by an order of October 24, 1862, and William S. Rosecrans was assigned command. The same order designated the troops of Rosecrans' command, which consisted largely of Buell's former Army of the Ohio, as Fourteenth Corps, Department of the Cumberland. For the organization of the army at that time, see Army of the Ohio (Buell).

Although the official designation of the army of the Department of the Cumberland was Fourteenth Corps, Department of the Cumberland, it was commonly called the Army of the Cumberland, as it had been when commanded by Robert Anderson and William T. Sherman. It should be noted, however, that Fourteenth Corps was a much larger organization than the former Army of the Cumberland. There was no real distinction between Fourteenth Corps, Department of the Cumberland and the Army of the Cumberland from October 24, 1862 to January 9, 1863, at which time three new army corps were created from the troops of Fourteenth Corps.

Rosecrans assumed command of the Department of the Cumberland and Fourteenth Corps at Louisville, Kentucky October 30, 1862, and then joined

REORGANIZATION OF THE ARMY, NOVEMBER 5, 1862

By an order of November 5, 1862, Rosecrans divided Fourteenth Corps, which included the entire army, into a Right Wing, Center, and Left Wing as follows:

Right Wing, Fourteenth Corps. The Right Wing consisted of Philip H. Sheridan's Eleventh Division, Army of the Ohio; William E. Woodruff's Ninth Division, Army of the Ohio; and Joshua W. Sill's Second Division, Army of the Ohio. Alexander McD. McCook was assigned command of the Right Wing. On November 5, 1862, Jefferson C. Davis resumed command of Ninth Division, relieving Woodruff, and on December 9, Richard W. Johnson relieved Sill in command of Second Division.

Center, Fourteenth Corps. The Center consisted of Lovell H. Rousseau's Third Division, Army of the Ohio; Ebenezer Dumont's Twelfth Division, Army of the Ohio; Speed S. Fry's First Division, Army of the Ohio; James S. Negley's Eighth Division, Army of the Ohio; and John M. Palmer's Thirteenth Division, Army of the Ohio (organized from First Division, Army of the Mississippi in September 1862). George H. Thomas was assigned command of the Center. The divisions of Negley and Palmer were at Nashville, Tennessee and were regarded as detached, and therefore reported directly to Headquarters, Fourteenth Corps instead of to Thomas. December 10, 1862, Palmer was assigned command of William Sooy Smith's Fourth Division of the Left Wing, and Robert B. Mitchell assumed command of Palmer's division. On December 11, Joseph J. Reynolds assumed command of Twelfth Division, relieving Dumont, who was sick.

Left Wing, Fourteenth Corps. The Left Wing consisted of Thomas J. Wood's Sixth Division, Army of the Ohio; William Sooy Smith's Fourth Division, Army of the Ohio; and Horatio P. Van Cleve's Fifth Division, Army of the Ohio. John M. Palmer relieved Smith in command of Fourth Division December 10, 1862.

In addition to the above, there were also garrison troops at Nashville under Robert B. Mitchell and at Bowling Green under Mahlon D. Manson, and also a reserve force consisting of a Regular brigade and unassigned regiments.

STONES RIVER (OR MURFREES-BORO) CAMPAIGN, DECEMBER 26, 1862–JANUARY 5, 1863

During November 1862, Rosecrans concentrated the Right Wing, the Left Wing, part of the Center, and John Kennett's Cavalry Division at Nashville, where he prepared for offensive operations against the enemy forces in Middle Tennessee. The rest of Thomas' Center was stationed along the Louisville and Nashville Railroad to protect the line.

The numbers used to designate the divisions and brigades of the army, which were carried over from the Army of the Ohio, were generally assigned in the order of the dates of their organization. This was a cumbersome system, however, and tended to cause some confusion. By an order of December 19, 1862, Rosecrans renumbered the brigades and divisions in the wings of the army to the more conventional method in which they were numbered from right to left as First, Second, Third, etc. The relationship of the old to the new designations is shown in the following roster of the army for December 26, 1862, just before the Battle of Murfreesboro.

ARMY OF THE CUMBERLAND
William S. Rosecrans

RIGHT WING, Alexander McD. McCook

First Division (former Ninth Division), Jefferson C. Davis
    First Brigade (former Thirtieth Brigade), P. Sidney Post
    Second Brigade (former Thirty-First Brigade), William P. Carlin

    Third Brigade (former Thirty-Second Brigade), William E. Woodruff

Note. Oscar F. Pinney's 5th Battery, Wisconsin Light Artillery was attached to First Brigade; William A. Hotchkiss' 2nd Battery, Minnesota Light Artillery was attached to Second Brigade; and Stephen J. Carpenter's 8th Battery, Wisconsin Light Artillery was attached to Third Brigade.

Second Division (former Second Division), Richard W. Johnson
    First Brigade (former Sixth Brigade), August Willich
    Second Brigade (former Fifth Brigade), Edward N. Kirk
    Third Brigade (former Fourth Brigade), Philemon P. Baldwin

Note. Edmund B. Belding's Battery A, 1st Ohio Light Artillery was attached to First Brigade; Warren P. Edgarton's Battery E, 1st Ohio Light Artillery to Second Brigade; and Peter Simonson's 5th Battery, Indiana Light Artillery to Third Brigade.

Third Division (former Eleventh Division), Philip H. Sheridan
    First Brigade (former Thirty-Seventh Brigade), Joshua W. Sill
    Second Brigade (former Thirty-Fifth Brigade), Frederick Schaefer
    Third Brigade (former First Brigade, Thirteenth Division), George W. Roberts

Note. Asahel K. Bush's 4th Battery, Indiana Light Artillery was attached to First Brigade; Henry Hescock's Battery G, 1st Missouri Light Artillery was assigned to Second Brigade; and Charles Houghtaling's Battery C, 1st Illinois Light Artillery was assigned to Third Brigade.

CENTER, George H. Thomas

First Division (former Third Division), Lovell H. Rousseau
    First Brigade (former Ninth Brigade), Benjamin F. Scribner
    Second Brigade (former Seventeenth Brigade), John Beatty
    Third Brigade (former Twenty-Eighth Brigade), John C. Starkweather

Note. George W. Van Pelt's 1st Battery, Michigan Light Artillery was attached to Second Brigade; David C. Stone's Battery A, Kentucky Light Artillery was attached to Third Brigade; and Francis L. Guenther's Battery H, 5th United States Artillery was attached to Fourth Brigade.

Second Division (former Eighth Division), James S. Negley
   First Brigade (former Twenty-Fifth Brigade), James G. Spears
   Second Brigade (former Twenty-Ninth Brigade), Timothy R. Stanley
   Third Brigade (former Seventh Brigade), John F. Miller
   Artillery
      Battery B, Kentucky Light Artillery, Alban A. Ellsworth
      Battery G, 1st Ohio Light Artillery, Alexander Marshall
      Battery M, 1st Ohio Light Artillery, Frederick Schultz

Note. Schultz's battery was attached to Second Brigade.

Third Division (former First Division), Speed S. Fry
   First Brigade, Moses B. Walker
   Second Brigade, John M. Harlan
   Third Brigade, James B. Steedman
   Artillery
      4th Battery, Michigan Light Artillery, Josiah W. Church
      Battery C, 1st Ohio Light Artillery, Daniel K. Southwick
      Battery I, 4th United States Artillery, Frank G. Smith

Fourth Division (former Thirteenth Division), Robert B. Mitchell
   First Brigade (former Second Brigade, Thirteenth Division), James D. Morgan
   Second Brigade (former Thirty-Sixth Brigade), Daniel McCook
   Artillery
      Battery I, 2nd Illinois Light Artillery, Charles M. Barnett
      10th Battery, Wisconsin Light Artillery, Yates V. Beebe
   Cavalry (three regiments)
   Unattached Infantry (two regiments)
   Artillery Reserve
      11th Battery, Indiana Light Artillery, Arnold Sutermeister
      12th Battery, Indiana Light Artillery, James A. Dunwoody
      5th Battery, Michigan Light Artillery, John J. Ely

Fifth Division (former Twelfth Division), Joseph J. Reynolds

First Brigade (former Thirty-Third Brigade), Albert S. Hall
Second Brigade (former Fortieth Brigade), Abram O. Miller
Artillery
   18th Battery, Indiana Light Artillery, Eli Lilly
   19th Battery, Indiana Light Artillery, Samuel J. Harris

LEFT WING, Thomas L. Crittenden

First Division (former Sixth Division), Thomas J. Wood
   First Brigade (former Fifteenth Brigade), Milo S. Hascall
   Second Brigade (former Twenty-First Brigade), George D. Wagner
   Third Brigade (former Twentieth Brigade), Charles G. Harker
   Artillery, Seymour Race
      8th Battery, Indiana Light Artillery, George Estep
      10th Battery, Indiana Light Artillery, Jerome B. Cox
      6th Battery, Ohio Light Artillery, Cullen Bradley

Note. Estep's battery was assigned to First Brigade, Cox's battery to Second Brigade, and Bradley's battery to Third Brigade.

Second Division (former Fourth Division), John M. Palmer
   First Brigade (former Twenty-Second Brigade), Charles Cruft
   Second Brigade (former Nineteenth Brigade), William B. Hazen
   Third Brigade (former Tenth Brigade), William Grose
   Artillery, William E. Standart
      Battery B, 1st Ohio Light Artillery, William E. Standart
      Battery F, 1st Ohio Light Artillery, Daniel T. Cockerill
      Batteries H and M, 4th United States Artillery, Charles C. Parsons

Third Division (former Fifth Division), Horatio P. Van Cleve
   First Brigade (former Eleventh Brigade), Samuel Beatty
   Second Brigade (former Fourteenth Brigade), James P. Fyffe
   Third Brigade (former Twenty-Third Brigade), Samuel W. Price
   Artillery, George R. Swallow
      7th Battery, Indiana Light Artillery, George R. Swallow

Battery B (26th), Pennsylvania Light Artillery, Alanson J. Stevens

3rd Battery, Wisconsin Light Artillery, Cortland Livingston

CAVALRY, David S. Stanley

Cavalry Division, John Kennett
  First Brigade, Robert H. G. Minty
  Second Brigade, Lewis Zahm
  Battery D (section), 1st Ohio Light Artillery, Nathaniel M. Newell

Reserve Cavalry

Note. Stanley, Chief of Cavalry of the department, relieved Kennett in command of the cavalry of the army November 24, 1863. The Reserve Cavalry was under the direct command of Stanley.

MISCELLANEOUS COMMANDS

Pioneer Brigade, James St. Clair Morton
Engineers and Mechanics (1st Michigan), William P. Innes
Post of Gallatin, Tennessee, Eleazer A. Paine
  Ward's Brigade, William T. Ward
Cavalry (three regiments of Kentucky Cavalry)

December 26, 1862, the Army of the Cumberland marched out of Nashville on different roads toward Murfreesboro, Tennessee, where it was engaged with Braxton Bragg's Army of Tennessee at the Battle of Stones River (or Murfreesboro) December 31, 1862–January 2, 1863. For details of the advance and the ensuing battle, and the organization of the troops that were engaged, see Stones River (or Murfreesboro), Tennessee Campaign.

AT MURFREESBORO, JANUARY 1863–JUNE 1863

After the Battle of Stones River, the Army of the Cumberland and the Confederate Army of Tennessee remained in position on the battlefield until the night of January 3–4, 1863, and then Bragg withdrew to a strong position in front of Tullahoma. His line extended along the Duck River from Shelbyville, through Wartrace, to Fairfield, Tennessee.

After Bragg's withdrawal, Rosecrans occupied Murfreesboro. He was relatively inactive there and in the vicinity until June 1863 while he prepared for a campaign designed to drive Bragg out of Middle Tennessee. During this period, however, Rosecrans sent out numerous expeditions, reconnaissances, and scouts into the surrounding country to the east, south, and west of Murfreesboro, and these resulted in a great many skirmishes and engagements. In some of these, units as large as brigades and divisions were involved. The principal movements were to or toward Auburn, Bradyville, Carthage, Eagleville, Franklin, Lebanon, Liberty, McMinnville, Middleton, Rover, Unionville, Versailles, and Woodbury. One expedition was also sent south on the Columbia Turnpike from Franklin to act in conjunction with another column moving out from Murfreesboro, but this had an unhappy ending. March 5, 1863, after a sharp engagement with Earl Van Dorn's Confederate First Cavalry Corps at Thompson's Station, about nine miles south of Franklin, John Coburn's brigade of the Army of Kentucky, then a part of the Army of the Cumberland, was forced to surrender. For details, see Engagement at Thompson's Station, Tennessee, and also Army of Kentucky (Granger).

Another expedition that resulted in the capture of a Union brigade was Abel D. Streight's raid against the Western and Atlantic Railroad in Georgia. Streight, in command of a Provisional Brigade that was composed of regiments detached from Fourteenth Corps, left Nashville April 10, 1863 and traveled by transport on the Cumberland and Tennessee rivers to Eastport, Mississippi. He then moved to Tuscumbia, Alabama. There he mounted his command on mules and marched across northern Alabama toward Rome, Georgia. He was closely followed by a Confederate cavalry force under Nathan B. Forrest and on May 3 was forced to surrender, short of his goal, at Cedar Bluff, Alabama. For details, see Streight's Raid from Tuscumbia, Alabama toward Rome, Georgia.

Reorganization of the Army, January 1863. January 9, 1863, the Army of the Cumberland, Fourteenth Corps was reorganized into three corps as follows: A new, and smaller, Fourteenth Corps was organized from George H. Thomas' former Center, Fourteenth Corps; a new Twentieth Corps was organized from Alexander McD. McCook's former

Right Wing, Fourteenth Corps; and a new Twenty-First Corps was organized from Thomas L. Crittenden's former Left Wing, Fourteenth Corps. The reorganization was not effected for some time, but when it was completed, the army was organized as follows:

ARMY OF THE CUMBERLAND
William S. Rosecrans

FOURTEENTH CORPS, George H. Thomas

First Division, Lovell H. Rousseau, to January 17, 1863
  Robert S. Granger
  First Brigade, Benjamin F. Scribner
  Second Brigade, John Beatty
  Third Brigade, John C. Starkweather
  Fourth Brigade, Oliver L. Shepherd
  Artillery
    1st Battery, Michigan Light Artillery, George W. Van Pelt
    Battery A, Kentucky Light Artillery, David C. Stone
    Battery H, 5th United States Artillery, Francis L. Guenther

Second Division, James S. Negley
  First Brigade, James G. Spears
  Second Brigade, Timothy R. Stanley
  Third Brigade, John F. Miller
  Artillery
    Battery B, Kentucky Light Artillery, Alban A. Ellsworth
    Battery G, 1st Ohio Light Artillery, Alexander Marshall
    Battery M, 1st Ohio Light Artillery, Frederick Schultz

Third Division, Speed S. Fry, to January 28, 1863
  James B. Steedman
  First Brigade, Moses B. Walker
  Second Brigade, John M. Harlan
  Third Brigade, James B. Steedman, to January 28, 1863
    Ferdinand Van Derveer
  Artillery
    4th Battery, Michigan Light Artillery, Josiah W. Church
    Battery C, 1st Ohio Light Artillery, Daniel K. Southwick
    Battery I, 4th United States Artillery, Frank G. Smith

Fourth Division, James D. Morgan, to January 27, 1863
  Robert B. Mitchell
  First Brigade, Robert F. Smith, to January 27, 1863
    James D. Morgan
  Second Brigade, Daniel McCook
  Artillery
    Battery I, 2nd Illinois Light Artillery, Charles M. Barnett
    10th Battery, Wisconsin Light Artillery, Yates V. Beebe

Fifth Division, Joseph J. Reynolds
  First Brigade, Albert S. Hall
  Second Brigade, Abram O. Miller
  Artillery
    18th Battery, Indiana Light Artillery, Eli Lilly
    19th Battery, Indiana Light Artillery, Samuel J. Harris

TWENTIETH CORPS, Alexander McD. McCook

First Division, Jefferson C. Davis
  First Brigade, P. Sidney Post
  Second Brigade, William P. Carlin
  Third Brigade, William E. Woodruff
  Artillery
    5th Battery, Wisconsin Light Artillery, Charles B. Humphrey
    8th Battery, Wisconsin Light Artillery, Henry E. Stiles
    2nd Battery, Minnesota Light Artillery, William A. Hotchkiss

Second Division, Richard W. Johnson
  First Brigade, William H. Gibson
  Second Brigade, Joseph B. Dodge
  Third Brigade, Philemon P. Baldwin
  Artillery
    Battery A, 1st Ohio Light Artillery, Edmund B. Belding
    Battery E, 1st Ohio Light Artillery, Warren P. Edgarton
    5th Battery, Indiana Light Artillery, Peter Simonson

Third Division, Philip H. Sheridan
  First Brigade, Nicholas Greusel
  Second Brigade, Bernard Laiboldt
  Third Brigade, Luther P. Bradley
  Artillery
    Battery C, 1st Illinois Light Artillery, Charles Houghtaling

4th Battery, Indiana Light Artillery, Asahel K. Bush

Battery G, 1st Missouri Light Artillery, Henry Hescock

TWENTY-FIRST CORPS, Thomas L. Crittenden

First Division, Thomas J. Wood
  First Brigade, Milo S. Hascall
  Second Brigade, George D. Wagner
  Third Brigade, Charles G. Harker
  Artillery, Seymour Race
    8th Battery, Indiana Light Artillery, George Estep
    10th Battery, Indiana Light Artillery, Jerome B. Cox
    6th Battery, Ohio Light Artillery, Cullen Bradley

Second Division, John M. Palmer
  First Brigade, Charles Cruft
  Second Brigade, William B. Hazen
  Third Brigade, William Grose
  Artillery, William E. Standart
    Battery B, 1st Ohio Light Artillery, William E. Standart
    Battery F, 1st Ohio Light Artillery, Norval Osburn
    Batteries H and M, 4th United States Artillery, Charles C. Parsons

Third Division, Samuel Beatty
  First Brigade, Benjamin C. Grider
  Second Brigade, James P. Fyffe
  Third Brigade, Samuel W. Price
  Artillery, George R. Swallow
    7th Battery, Indiana Light Artillery, George R. Swallow
    Battery B, Pennsylvania Light Artillery, Alanson J. Stevens
    3rd Battery, Wisconsin Light Artillery, Cortland Livingston

CAVALRY, David S. Stanley

Cavalry Division, John Kennett
  First Brigade, Robert H. G. Minty
  Second Brigade, Lewis Zahm

Note. A new Third Brigade, commanded by Ebenezer Gay, was later added to the division.

Reserve Cavalry

Note. The Reserve Cavalry consisted of three regiments, and was under the immediate command of Stanley, Chief of Cavalry.

Organization of the Cavalry Corps, Army of the Cumberland, May 1863. David S. Stanley's cavalry command consisted of three brigades until May 1863, and it was then reorganized into two divisions, and designated unofficially as Cavalry Corps, Department of the Cumberland. At the end of May 1863, it was organized as follows:

CAVALRY CORPS, ARMY OF THE CUMBERLAND, David S. Stanley

First Cavalry Division, Robert B. Mitchell
  First Brigade, Archibald P. Campbell
  Second Brigade, Edward M. McCook

Second Cavalry Division, John B. Turchin
  First Brigade, Robert H. G. Minty
  Second Brigade, Eli Long

For additional information, see Cavalry Corps, Army of the Cumberland.

Organization of the Reserve Corps, Army of the Cumberland, June 1863. In February 1863, the Army of Kentucky (or Baird's Division), commanded by Gordon Granger, was transferred from Louisville, Kentucky to Nashville, Tennessee, where it became a part of the Army of the Cumberland. On June 8, 1863 a new corps, designated as Reserve Corps, Army of the Cumberland, was organized from the following: Army of Kentucky (Granger); Fourth Division, Fourteenth Corps; and troops at Fort Henry, Fort Donelson, and Gallatin, Tennessee. Granger was assigned command of the corps, which was organized as follows:

RESERVE CORPS, ARMY OF THE CUMBERLAND, Gordon Granger

First Division, Absalom Baird
  First Brigade, Smith D. Atkins
  Second Brigade, William P. Reid
  Third Brigade, William L. Utley

Second Division, James D. Morgan
  First Brigade, Robert F. Smith
  Second Brigade, Daniel McCook
  Third Brigade, Charles C. Doolittle

Third Division, Robert S. Granger
  First Brigade, William P. Lyon

Second Brigade, William T. Ward
Third Brigade, James G. Spears

For additional information, see Army of Kentucky (Granger); Fourteenth Corps, Army of the Cumberland, January 9, 1863–November 14, 1864; and Reserve Corps, Army of the Cumberland.

In June 1863, when these reorganizations were completed, the Army of the Cumberland consisted of Fourteenth Corps, Twentieth Corps, Twenty-First Corps, the Reserve Corps, and the Cavalry Corps.

TULLAHOMA (OR MIDDLE TENNESSEE) CAMPAIGN, JUNE 23, 1863–JULY 7, 1863

On the morning of June 23, 1863, Gordon Granger, commanding the Union forces at Triune, Tennessee, sent Robert B. Mitchell's First Cavalry Division of Stanley's Cavalry Corps south from Triune to threaten the left of Bragg's line at Shelbyville, and a short time later Granger moved with Absalom Baird's First Division of the Reserve Corps and John M. Brannan's Third Division of Fourteenth Corps to Salem, Tennessee, which was on the road to Versailles. Early the next morning, McCook's Twentieth Corps and Thomas' Fourteenth Corps left Murfreesboro on different roads to seize the gaps in the hills to the south and southeast. Thomas, with the three divisions remaining with him, marched out on the Manchester Pike toward Hoover's Gap, with Joseph J. Reynolds' Fourth Division in the lead. Reynolds, with help from Lovell H. Rousseau's First Division, drove the enemy from the gap. To the right of Thomas, McCook's Twentieth Corps gained possession of Liberty Gap.

When Bragg learned that Thomas had turned his right flank at Hoover's Gap and that the way to his rear was open, he withdrew his army to a new position at Tullahoma. Then, on June 26, 1863, Thomas again attacked, drove the enemy from their positions beyond Hoover's Gap, and thus cleared the way to Manchester, which he occupied the next day. The rest of the army followed toward Manchester as rapidly as the poor conditions of the road would permit. On June 30, when Bragg received the news that Rosecrans had a large force at Manches-

ter, and was beginning once again to move around his right flank, he fell back with his army from Tullahoma and took position on the south side of Elk River, near Dechard. He then withdrew to Cowan, and formed another defensive line at the foot of the mountain. Finally, he crossed the Cumberland Mountains and marched back to Chattanooga, where his army encamped July 7.

After Bragg had departed, the Army of the Cumberland encamped in South-Central Tennessee while Rosecrans made preparations for a further advance toward Chattanooga. For details of the operations and organization of the Army of the Cumberland during the last week of June and the first week of July 1863, see Tullahoma (or Middle Tennessee) Campaign.

CHICKAMAUGA, GEORGIA CAMPAIGN, AUGUST 16, 1863– SEPTEMBER 22, 1863

Five weeks passed before Rosecrans was ready to resume his advance. On August 16, 1863, the Army of the Cumberland again began to move forward toward Chattanooga. It crossed the Cumberland Mountains and the Tennessee River and then moved to the east and southeast on a broad front. Crittenden's Twenty-First Corps occupied Chattanooga, and Thomas' Fourteenth Corps and McCook's Twentieth Corps, with Stanley's cavalry, marched to the south and east toward La Fayette and Rome in Georgia. There they would be in position to intercept Bragg if he decided to retreat. Bragg did not retreat, however, and after considerable marching and countermarching, Rosecrans concentrated the Army of the Cumberland on Chickamauga Creek, south of Chattanooga. It was engaged there at the Battle of Chickamauga September 19–20. The army suffered a decisive defeat, and during the night of September 20 and the next day, it retreated toward Chattanooga. Upon arriving there on September 22, it began the preparation of an entrenched defensive position in and around the town and awaited the arrival of the enemy. Bragg's army followed and occupied Missionary Ridge and Lookout Mountain, but it made no further offensive effort. Instead, Bragg decided to prepare for the siege of Chattanooga. For details of the troop movements and the battle, and also of the organization of the army at the time of battle, see Chickamauga, Georgia Campaign.

SIEGE OF CHATTANOOGA, TENNESSEE, SEPTEMBER 23, 1863–OCTOBER 30, 1863

Reinforcements for the Army of the Cumberland. When the investment of Chattanooga was complete, Confederate troops on Raccoon Mountain and along the south bank of the Tennessee River blocked the direct road through Whiteside to Brigeport, Alabama, and also the road that ran along the north side of the river to the same place. The only road to the rear that was open, and over which supplies could be brought to the army, ran over Walden's Ridge and along the Sequatchie Valley to Bridgeport, a distance of about sixty miles. This was a long and difficult route, and in a short time the army was suffering from a lack of food and supplies. It was faced with possible starvation if it remained in Chattanooga and the siege was not broken.

Both President Lincoln and Secretary of War Edwin M. Stanton believed that the occupation of Chattanooga was vital to the Union cause, and to prevent its loss, they immediately ordered reinforcements to the army of the Cumberland. On September 25, Eleventh Corps and Twelfth Corps were detached from the Army of the Potomac in Virginia and, under the command of Joseph Hooker, were started west by rail from Washington, D.C. Eleventh Corps arrived at Bridgeport September 30–October 2. Twelfth Corps followed as far as Nashville and was then retained along the Nashville and Chattanooga Railroad. Later in the month, John W. Geary's Second Division, Twelfth Corps was sent forward to join Eleventh Corps at Bridgeport.

The organization of Hooker's two corps at the end of October 1863 was as follows:

ELEVENTH CORPS, Oliver O. Howard

Second Division, Adolph Von Steinwehr

First Brigade, Adolphus Buschbeck
Second Brigade, Orland Smith

Third Division, Carl Schurz
First Brigade, Hector Tyndale
Second Brigade, Wladimir Krzyzanowski
Third Brigade, Frederick Hecker

Artillery, Thomas W. Osborn
Battery I, 1st New York Light Artillery, Michael Wiedrich
13th Battery, New York Light Artillery, William Wheeler
Battery I, 1st Ohio Light Artillery, Hubert Dilger
Battery K, 1st Ohio Light Artillery, Nicholas Sahm
Battery G, 4th United States Artillery, Eugene A. Bancroft

TWELFTH CORPS, Henry W. Slocum

First Division, Alpheus S. Williams
First Brigade, Joseph F. Knipe
Third Brigade, Thomas H. Ruger

Second Division, John W. Geary
First Brigade, Charles Candy
Second Brigade, George A. Cobham, Jr.
Third Brigade, David Ireland

Artillery, John A. Reynolds
Battery M, 1st New York Light Artillery, John D. Woodbury
Battery E, Pennsylvania Light Artillery, James A. Dunlevy
Battery F, 4th United States Artillery, Edward D. Muhlenberg
Battery K, 5th United States Artillery, Edmund C. Bainbridge

In an order dated September 13, 1863, a short time before the Battle of Chickamauga, Henry W. Halleck, general in chief of the armies, had directed Ulysses S. Grant, commanding the Department of the Tennessee, to send all available troops of the Army of the Tennessee, then on the Mississippi River, to cooperate with Rosecrans, whose Army of the Cumberland was then advancing against Bragg's army. It was not until September 25, however, that William T. Sherman left Vicksburg, Mississippi with three divisions of his Fifteenth Corps for Chattanooga. On the way he was joined by a division of Seventeenth Corps from Helena, Arkansas.

When the first division arrived at Memphis, Tennessee, it was sent eastward along the Memphis and Charleston Railroad to Corinth, Mississippi, and the remaining divisions followed as soon as they came up. Progress was very slow at first because Sherman had been given orders to repair the railroad as he advanced. Sherman did not arrive at Iuka, Mississippi and establish headquarters there until October 19, although Peter J. Osterhaus had been there for some time and had established an advance guard at Eastport, Mississippi.

At that time Sherman's command consisted of the following:

DETACHMENT ARMY OF THE TENNESSEE, William T. Sherman

First Division, Fifteenth Corps, Peter J. Osterhaus
Second Division, Fifteenth Corps, Morgan L. Smith
Fourth Division, Fifteenth Corps, John M. Corse
Second Division, Seventeenth Corps, John E. Smith

Note 1. Sherman referred to John E. Smith's division as Third Division of his command, although it belonged to Seventeenth Corps.
Note 2. Hugh Ewing resumed command of Fourth Division, Fifteenth Corps October 16, 1863.
Note 3. Frank P. Blair, Jr. joined Sherman at Memphis, and was sent to Corinth to assume command of the advance of Sherman's troops. Blair was designated as second in command to Sherman October 16, 1863, and the next day he was sent to Iuka to assume command of First Division and Second Division of Fifteenth Corps.

Reorganization of the Army of the Cumberland, October 9, 1863. While Sherman was moving slowly eastward, the Army of the Cumberland was reorganized October 9, 1863 at Chattanooga. By a presidential order of September 28, 1863, Twentieth Corps and Twenty-First Corps were consolidated to form a new Fourth Corps, Army of the Cumberland. For details of its organization, see Fourth Corps, Army of the Cumberland. Gordon Granger, formerly commander of the Reserve Corps, was assigned command of Fourth Corps, and Alexander McD. McCook and Thomas L. Crittenden, former commanders of Twentieth Corps and Twenty-First Corps, respectively, were relieved from further duty with the Army of the Cumberland. At the same time, the Reserve Corps, Army of the Cumberland was discontinued, and its troops were assigned to Fourth Corps and Fourteenth Corps.

Another important organizational change in the army, which was ordered October 16, 1863, was to affect in an important way the future operations about Chattanooga and also thereafter. In order to secure better cooperation among the various Union commands in the West, the Military Division of the Mississippi was created to consist of the Department of the Cumberland, the Department of the Tennessee, and the Department of the Ohio. Ulysses S. Grant was assigned command.

The same order that created the Military Division of the Mississippi also relieved Rosecrans from command of the Army and Department of the Cumberland and assigned George H. Thomas to succeed him. Grant assumed command of the Military Division of the Mississippi October 18, 1863, and the next day Thomas assumed command of the Army of the Cumberland (his formal order of assumption was issued October 20). On October 19, as commander of the Military Division of the Mississippi, Grant assigned William T. Sherman to succeed him in command of the Army and Department of the Tennessee, and this assignment was confirmed by the president on October 27. Sherman assumed command at Iuka October 24, and Frank P. Blair, Jr. succeeded him in command of Fifteenth Corps October 29. Grant's order assigning Sherman to the command of the Army and Department of the Tennessee also instructed him to retain command of the army in the field.

Grant proceeded to Chattanooga October 23 to determine the state of affairs there, and a short time later he issued orders for the movements that were to result in the reopening of the Tennessee River and thus end the siege of Chattanooga. On October 27, he ordered Sherman to stop all work on the railroad and to move with his command as rapidly as possible to Bridgeport, Alabama.

Reopening of the Tennessee River, October 23–30, 1863. After Grant had assumed command of the Military Division of the Mississippi, his first concern was opening the Tennessee River so that adequate supplies could be forwarded to the Army of the Cumberland. When he arrived at Chattanooga on October 23, he met with William F. Smith, chief engineer of the Army of the Cumberland, and, after examining the ground, approved a plan prepared by the latter for opening a shorter supply line from Kelley's Ferry on the Tennessee, by way of Brown's Ferry, to Chattanooga. For this to be successful, it was necessary to capture Brown's Ferry, drive the enemy from Raccoon Mountain and Lookout Valley, and secure the road and river line eastward from Bridgeport.

On October 25, Smith was assigned command of a force with which he was to move to Brown's Ferry, drive away the enemy troops posted there, and then occupy the south bank of the river at that point. The troops selected for this expedition consisted of William B. Hazen's Second Brigade, Third Division, Fourth Corps and John B. Turchin's First Brigade, Third Division, Fourteenth Corps. Hazen's brigade was assigned the task of capturing the ferry, and Turchin's brigade was to act in support.

Early the next morning, Turchin crossed the Tennessee River from Chattanooga and marched to the vicinity of Brown's Ferry, where he bivouacked for the night. At 3:00 A.M. on October 27, Hazen embarked about 1,700 men in pontoons at Chattanooga, and started them down the river. The remainder of his brigade followed Turchin toward Brown's Ferry and camped nearby.

Also on October 27, other troops were brought up to act as a reserve for Smith. Walter C. Whitaker's Second Brigade, First Division, Fourth Corps, which had been on duty along the Tennessee River from Williams' Island to Lookout Mountain during October 1863, was ordered to Brown's Ferry. A brigade commanded by John G. Mitchell, which was composed of four regiments of James G. Spears' Second Brigade, Second Division, Fourteenth Corps, was directed to the same place.

Hazen's boats arrived near Brown's Ferry at 5:00 A.M. on October 27, and, after landing his troops on the south bank of the river, he quickly drove off the small enemy force posted there. The rest of Hazen's men then crossed the river, and they were followed by Turchin's brigade. Smith formed a defensive line across the road leading up to Brown's Ferry, with Hazen's brigade on the left of the road and Turchin's brigade on the right.

Meantime, early on the morning of October 25, John M. Palmer had left Chattanooga with Charles Cruft's First Brigade and William Grose's Second Brigade (commanded by P. Sidney Post because of the illness of Grose) of his First Division, Fourth Corps and marched northward toward Rankin's Ferry, which was about midway between Shellmound and Whiteside. Joseph Hooker was also under orders to march eastward from Bridgeport toward Lookout Valley with Oliver O. Howard's Eleventh Corps and John W. Geary's Second Division, Twelfth Corps. His mission was to clear the road south of the Tennessee River and take position near Brown's Ferry. Upon arriving at Rankin's Ferry, Palmer was to cross to the south side of the river and hold the road in rear of Hooker after the latter had passed.

Hooker left Bridgeport October 27 and arrived the next day at Wauhatchie, Tennessee, in Lookout Valley. He left Geary's division there to guard the road to Kelley's Ferry and with Eleventh Corps moved on about three miles and camped near Brown's Ferry.

Meantime, Palmer had marched northward across Walden's Ridge and arrived in the Sequatchie Valley on the same day that Hooker arrived at Wauhatchie. While there, Palmer, who was suffering from the effects of an earlier wound, was relieved in command of the division by Charles Cruft, and Thomas D. Sedgwick assumed command of Cruft's First Brigade. Cruft continued on with his command and arrived at Rankin's Ferry after Hooker had passed. He then crossed to the south side of the Tennessee River at Shellmound and occupied that post, and also Whiteside, with his two brigades. Whitaker's brigade of Cruft's division, which was with Smith at Brown's Ferry, was sent forward to join Cruft, and it arrived at Shellmound on November 2. Cruft's three brigades were then posted on the Nashville and Chattanooga Railroad, in rear of Hooker, as follows: Sedgwick's First Brigade was at Bridgeport, Whitaker's Second Brigade at Shellmound, and Post's Third Brigade at Whiteside. Grose returned to duty November 5 and resumed command of Third Brigade.

Engagement at Wauhatchie, Tennessee, October 29, 1863. Very early on the morning of October 29, 1863, Geary's division was strongly attacked by Micah Jenkins' brigade (commanded by John Bratton) of John B. Hood's division of James Longstreet's corps. The heaviest blow was sustained by the three Pennsylvania regiments (29th,

109th, and 111th) of George A. Cobham's Second Brigade, the 137th New York Regiment of George S. Greene's Third Brigade, and two sections of Joseph M. Knap's Battery E, Pennsylvania Light Artillery, commanded by Charles A. Atwell. The other two regiments of Cobham's brigade were also engaged during a part of the fighting. Candy's First Brigade was approaching on the road from Bridgeport, but it did not arrive until late on the night of October 31.

The exact positions of Geary's troops are difficult to determine, because the fighting was done in darkness, and the commanders of the various units involved were generally uncertain as to where they were at all times. The best evidence indicates that Cobham's regiments were formed north of Wauhatchie on a line perpendicular to and west of the railroad, and that Greene's brigade was parallel to the railroad and on the right of Cobham. Some changes, however, were made in the positions of the regiments during the engagement. Geary held his position for about three hours, and then the enemy withdrew. Greene was badly wounded during the action, and he was succeeded in command of Third Brigade by David Ireland.

While Jenkins was engaged at Wauhatchie, Evander McI. Law's Confederate brigade was in position to the north, on some high ground just east of the Brown's Ferry road, and it was supported by the brigades of Jerome B. Robertson and Henry L. Benning.

Hooker and Howard, who were near Brown's Ferry that night, heard the firing at Wauhatchie and took prompt measures to reinforce Geary. Carl Schurz's Third Division, Eleventh Corps, with Hector Tyndale's First Brigade in the lead, marched toward Wauhatchie. Adolph Von Steinwehr's Second Division of Eleventh Corps, with Orland Smith's Second Brigade in the lead, followed Schurz. These two divisions soon came under fire from Law's brigade on the high ground to their left, and Tyndale and Orland Smith were sent to dislodge Law. While these two brigades were engaged in this mission, Wladimir Krzyzanowski's Second Brigade and Frederick Hecker's Third Brigade of Schurz's division halted on the road for a time to await developments and then pushed on to Wauhatchie. Hecker arrived at daylight and Krzyzanowski about 7:00 A.M., long after Geary's battle had ended.

These two brigades remained in line with Geary's division until relieved October 31, and they then rejoined Eleventh Corps.

In addition to the troops of Eleventh Corps, John G. Mitchell's brigade advanced from Brown's Ferry early on the morning of October 29 and arrived at Wauhatchie at 8:00 A.M.

* * * * * * * * * *

At the end of October 1863, the organization of the Army of the Cumberland was as follows:

ARMY OF THE CUMBERLAND
George H. Thomas

FOURTH CORPS. Gordon Granger

First Division, Charles Cruft
    First Brigade, Thomas D. Sedgwick
    Second Brigade, Walter C. Whitaker
    Third Brigade, William Grose
    Artillery, Peter Simonson
        5th Battery, Indiana Light Artillery, Peter Simonson
        Battery H, 4th United States Artillery, Harry C. Cushing
        Battery M, 4th United States Artillery, Francis L. D. Russell

Second Division, Philip H. Sheridan
    First Brigade, Francis T. Sherman
    Second Brigade, George D. Wagner
    Third Brigade, Charles G. Harker
    Artillery, William A. Naylor
        Battery M, 1st Illinois Light Artillery, George W. Spencer
        10th Battery, Indiana Light Artillery, William A. Naylor
        Battery G, 1st Missouri Light Artillery, Gustavus Schueler

Third Division, Thomas J. Wood
    First Brigade, August Willich
    Second Brigade, William B. Hazen
    Third Brigade, Samuel Beatty
    Artillery, Cullen Bradley
        Bridges' (Illinois) Battery, Lyman Bridges
        6th Battery, Ohio Light Artillery, Oliver H. P. Ayres
        Battery B, Pennsylvania Light Artillery, Samuel M. McDowell

ELEVENTH AND TWELFTH CORPS, Joseph Hooker

ELEVENTH CORPS, Oliver O. Howard

Second Division, Adolph Von Steinwehr
First Brigade, Adolphus Buschbeck
Second Brigade, Orland Smith

Third Division, Carl Schurz
First Brigade, Hector Tyndale
Second Brigade, Wladimir Krzyzanowski
Third Brigade, Frederick Hecker

Artillery, Thomas W. Osborn
Battery I, 1st New York Light Artillery, Michael Wiedrich
13th Battery, New York Light Artillery, William Wheeler
Battery I, 1st Ohio Light Artillery, Hubert Dilger
Battery K, 1st Ohio Light Artillery, Nicholas Sahm
Battery G, 4th United States Artillery, Eugene A. Bancroft

TWELFTH CORPS, Henry W. Slocum

First Division, Alpheus S. Williams
First Brigade, Joseph F. Knipe
Second Brigade, Thomas H. Ruger

Second Division, John W. Geary
First Brigade, Charles Candy
Second Brigade, George A. Cobham, Jr.
Third Brigade, David Ireland

Artillery, John A. Reynolds
Battery M, 1st New York Light Artillery, John D. Woodbury
Battery E, Pennsylvania Light Artillery, James A. Dunlevy
Battery F, 4th United States Artillery, Edward D. Muhlenberg
Battery K, 5th United States Artillery, Edmund C. Bainbridge

FOURTEENTH CORPS, John M. Palmer

First Division, Lovell H. Rousseau
First Brigade, William P. Carlin
Second Brigade, Marshall F. Moore
Third Brigade, William Sirwell
Artillery, Mark H. Prescott

Battery C, 1st Illinois Light Artillery, Mark H. Prescott
Battery A, 1st Michigan Light Artillery, Francis E. Hale
Battery H, 5th United States Artillery, Edmund D. Spooner

Second Division, Jefferson C. Davis
First Brigade, Robert F. Smith
Second Brigade, James G. Spears
Third Brigade, Daniel McCook
Artillery, William A. Hotchkiss
Battery I, 2nd Illinois Light Artillery, Charles M. Barnett
2nd Battery, Minnesota Light Artillery, Richard L. Dawley
5th Battery, Wisconsin Light Artillery, Joseph McKnight

Third Division, Absalom Baird
First Brigade, John B. Turchin
Second Brigade, James George
Third Brigade, Edward H. Phelps
Artillery, George R. Swallow
7th Battery, Indiana Light Artillery, Otho H. Morgan
19th Battery, Indiana Light Artillery, Samuel J. Harris
Battery I, 4th United States Artillery, Frank G. Smith

UNATTACHED

Coburn's Brigade, John Coburn

ARTILLERY RESERVE, John M. Brannan

First Division, James Barnett
First Brigade
Battery A, 1st Ohio Light Artillery, Wilbur F. Goodspeed
Battery B, 1st Ohio Light Artillery, Norman A. Baldwin
Battery C, 1st Ohio Light Artillery, Marco B. Gary
Battery F, 1st Ohio Light Artillery, Giles J. Cockerill
Second Brigade
Battery G, 1st Ohio Light Artillery, Alexander Marshall
Battery M, 1st Ohio Light Artillery, Frederick Schultz
18th Battery, Ohio Light Artillery, Charles C. Aleshire

20th Battery, Ohio Light Artillery, John Otto

Note. The brigade commanders are not of record.

Second Division
First Brigade, Josiah W. Church
Battery D, 1st Michigan Light Artillery, Josiah W. Church
Battery A, 1st Tennessee Light Artillery, Ephraim P. Abbott
3rd Battery, Wisconsin Light Artillery, Hiram F. Hubbard
8th Battery, Wisconsin Light Artillery, John D. McLean
Second Brigade, Arnold Sutermeister
4th Battery, Indiana Light Artillery, Willis H. Pettit
8th Battery, Indiana Light Artillery, Jeremiah Voris
11th Battery, Indiana Light Artillery, Arnold Sutermeister
21st Battery, Indiana Light Artillery, William E. Chess

Note. The commander of Second Division is not of record.

CAVALRY CORPS, David S. Stanley

First Division, Washington L. Elliott
First Brigade, Archibald P. Campbell
Second Brigade, Edward M. McCook
Third Brigade, Louis D. Watkins

Second Division, George Crook
First Brigade, Robert H. G. Minty
Second Brigade, Eli Long
Third Brigade, William W. Lowe

Artillery
Chicago (Illinois) Board of Trade Battery, George I. Robinson

Mounted Infantry Brigade, John T. Wilder

Note. Eli Lilly's 18th Battery, Indiana Light Artillery was attached to Wilder's brigade.

In addition to the above troops, Arthur A. Smith commanded a force at Clarksville; Elijah C. Brott at Fort Donelson; Eleazer A. Paine at Gallatin; and Robert S. Granger at Nashville. Granger's command consisted of William T. Ward's brigade and unattached troops. Nine infantry regiments, one cavalry regiment, and five batteries were distributed at the following points: Anderson's Cross Roads,

Chattanooga, Dallas, Elk River, Murfreesboro, Stevenson, Sullivan's Branch, Tullahoma, and Walden's Ridge.

CHATTANOOGA-RINGGOLD CAMPAIGN (BATTLES OF LOOKOUT MOUNTAIN AND MISSIONARY RIDGE), NOVEMBER 23–28, 1863

During the three weeks following the opening of Thomas' supply line to Bridgeport, the Army of the Cumberland was relatively quiet at Chattanooga while it received much-needed food and supplies and awaited the arrival of Sherman's Detachment Army of the Tennessee.

On November 4, 1863, Longstreet's corps was detached from Bragg's army at Chattanooga, and was sent to attempt the recapture of Knoxville and the expulsion of Ambrose E. Burnside's forces from East Tennessee. Longstreet soon appeared in front of Knoxville and laid siege to the town. On November 15, Halleck urged Grant to send troops to reinforce Burnside, but Grant had already completed plans for an attack on Bragg's army. This attack was scheduled to begin November 15, and Grant was forced to delay aid to Burnside until after the issue at Chattanooga had been resolved.

The head of Sherman's column reached Bridgeport November 15, and Grant began the assembly of the troops for the battles around Chattanooga. Then, on November 23, Gordon Granger, with Thomas J. Wood's Third Division and Philip H. Sheridan's Second Division of Fourth Corps, advanced and captured Orchard Knob, an elevation about midway between the Union lines at Chattanooga and Missionary Ridge.

The next day, Hooker assembled the following troops for an attack on the enemy positions on Lookout Mountain: John W. Geary's Second Division, Twelfth Corps; Walter C. Whitaker's Second Brigade and William Grose's Third Brigade of Charles Cruft's First Division, Fourth Corps; and Peter J. Osterhaus' First Division, Fifteenth Corps (commanded that day by Charles R. Woods). Later in the day, William P. Carlin's First Brigade, First Division, Fourteenth Corps came up to support

Hooker. The attack was successful, and after stubborn fighting, Hooker's troops drove the enemy from Lookout Mountain and by that night had gained possession of that important position.

On November 25, Sherman attacked the right flank of Bragg's line on Missionary Ridge with Morgan L. Smith's Second Division and Hugh Ewing's Fourth Division of Fifteenth Corps and John E. Smith's Second Division of Seventeenth Corps, but they made little progress.

On November 25, Hooker advanced from Lookout Mountain to Rossville with the divisions of Geary, Osterhaus, and Cruft and moved against the left flank of the enemy line on Missionary Ridge. Hooker was advancing along the ridge that afternoon when Thomas launched an attack against the center of the enemy line on the ridge. Joining in this attack were Philip H. Sheridan's Second Division and Thomas J. Wood's Third Division of Fourth Corps, and Richard W. Johnson's First Division and Absalom Baird's Third Division of Fourteenth Corps, all of the Army of the Cumberland. Thomas' attack was completely successful, and the enemy was driven in confusion from Missionary Ridge. During the next two days, Thomas and Sherman pursued Bragg's defeated army into Georgia, where Bragg finally halted at Dalton. For details of the organization of the Army of the Cumberland and its part in the fighting around Chattanooga and the pursuit that followed, see Chattanooga-Ringgold Campaign (Battles of Lookout Mountain and Missionary Ridge, Tennessee).

RELIEF OF KNOXVILLE, TENNESSEE, NOVEMBER 27, 1863– DECEMBER 6, 1863

November 27, 1863, Gordon Granger was ordered to proceed to Knoxville, Tennessee with the divisions of Thomas J. Wood and Philip H. Sheridan and relieve Burnside, who was under siege by Longstreet's corps. The next day Grant organized an expedition under William T. Sherman for the relief of Knoxville. Sherman's command consisted of Granger's two divisions of Fourth Corps, Oliver O. Howard's Eleventh Corps, Jefferson C. Davis'

Second Division of Fourteenth Corps, all of the Army of the Cumberland, and Morgan L. Smith's Second Division and Hugh Ewing's Fourth Division of Frank P. Blair's Fifteenth Corps. As Sherman approached Knoxville, Longstreet abandoned the siege December 3 and moved on to the east. Sherman then assembled all of his command at Marysville except the two divisions with Granger, who moved on to Knoxville and reported to Burnside. On December 6, Sherman's troops at Maryville began to withdraw toward Chattanooga. For additional information, see Relief of Knoxville, Tennessee (William T. Sherman).

WINTER OF 1863–1864

After Sherman's Expedition for the Relief of Knoxville had been broken up in December 1863, the Army of the Cumberland passed the rest of the winter in relative quiet in their various encampments. In December, Second Division and Third Division of Fourth Corps remained in East Tennessee, with corps headquarters at Blain's Cross Roads. Second Division was stationed at Loudon until April 1864, and then moved to Cleveland. Third Division moved more frequently. It was at Blain's Cross Roads in December 1863; at Maryville in January 1864; at New Market in February 1864; at Powder Spring Gap in March 1864; and at McDonald's Station in April 1864. First Division was at Bridgeport, Alabama in December 1863; in January 1864, it moved to Tyner's Station; and in February it moved to Blue Springs, remaining there until April.

Headquarters, Eleventh Corps was established in Lookout Valley in December 1863, and it remained there until April 5, 1864. Second Division was in Lookout Valley from December 1863 until April 1864, and Third Division was at Shellmound during the same period. A new First Division, Eleventh Corps was organized in the District of Nashville January 2, 1864, but it moved to Wauhatchie in February and remained there until April.

In December 1863, Henry W. Slocum, commanding Twelfth Corps, was in command of all troops guarding the Nashville and Chattanooga Railroad, with headquarters at Tullahoma. First Division was at Tullahoma from January to April 1864, and Second Division was at Bridgeport during the same period. A Third Division, Twelfth Corps was organized January 2, 1864 from troops in the District of Nashville. Lovell H. Rousseau was assigned command, and he remained with his division near Nashville.

By an order of April 4, 1864, Eleventh Corps and Twelfth Corps were consolidated to form a new Twentieth Corps, which was assigned to the command of Joseph Hooker. The same order relieved Gordon Granger from command of Fourth Corps and assigned Oliver O. Howard in his place. Howard assumed command April 8.

The new Twentieth Corps was organized as follows:

TWENTIETH CORPS, Joseph Hooker

First Division, Alpheus S. Williams
    First Brigade, Joseph F. Knipe
    Second Brigade, Thomas H. Ruger
    Third Brigade, Hector Tyndale
    Artillery, John D. Woodbury
        Battery I, 1st New York Light Artillery, Christian Stock
        Battery M, 1st New York Light Artillery, John D. Woodbury

Second Division, John W. Geary
    First Brigade, Charles Candy
    Second Brigade, Adolphus Buschbeck
    Third Brigade, David Ireland
    Artillery, William Wheeler
        13th Battery, New York Light Artillery, William Wheeler
        Battery E, Pennsylvania Light Artillery, James D. McGill

Third Division, Daniel Butterfield
    First Brigade, William T. Ward
    Second Brigade, Samuel Ross
    Third Brigade, James Wood, Jr.
    Artillery, Marco B. Gary
        Battery I, 1st Michigan Light Artillery, Luther R. Smith
        Battery C, 1st Ohio Light Artillery, Marco B. Gary

Fourth Division, Robert S. Granger

Note 1. For details of the consolidation, see Twentieth

Corps, Army of the Cumberland, April 14, 1864–November 14, 1864.

Note 2. The organization of Fourth Division was not complete. Its troops served in the District of Nashville, which was commanded by Lovell H. Rousseau, and were not present with the corps. First Brigade, Fourth Division was composed of the white regiments of infantry of Robert S. Granger's Post of Nashville. In addition, four regiments at Bridgeport, Alabama, one regiment from Clarksville, Tennessee, one regiment at Fort Donelson, and two regiments at Gallatin, Tennessee were assigned to Fourth Division.

Corps headquarters was in Lookout Valley. First Division was in the field in April 1864, Second Division was at Bridgeport, Third Division was in Lookout Valley, and Fourth Division was at Nashville.

Headquarters, Fourteenth Corps was at Chattanooga during the winter. In December 1863 and January 1864, First Division was at Chattanooga; in February it was at Tyner's Station, Tennessee; and in March and April it was at Graysville, Georgia. Second Division was near Rossville from December 1863 through March 1864, and it then moved to a point near Ringgold, Georgia. Third Division was at Chattanooga in December 1863 and January 1864, and it then moved to Ringgold, where it remained until April.

Headquarters of the cavalry of the Army of the Cumberland was at Talbott's Station, Tennessee in December 1863, but in January 1864 it was moved to Chattanooga, where it remained through April. First Division was at Talbott's Station in December 1863, in East Tennessee in January and February 1864, and then at Cleveland, Tennessee in March and April. Second Division was at Pulaski, Tennessee in December 1863. Headquarters, Second Division was at Huntsville, Alabama in February and March 1864, with troopers of the division at Bridgeport and Huntsville in Alabama, Rossville in Georgia, and Calhoun, Colliersville, Columbus, Nashville, and Pulaski in Tennessee.

The Cavalry Corps was reorganized by an order of April 2, 1864 (to take effect April 1), as follows:

CAVALRY CORPS, Washington L. Elliott

First Division, Edward M. McCook
    First Brigade, Joseph B. Dorr
    Second Brigade, Oscar H. La Grange

Third Brigade, Louis D. Watkins
18th Battery, Indiana Light Artillery, William B. Rippetoe

Second Division, Kenner Garrard
First Brigade, Robert H. G. Minty
Second Brigade, Eli Long
Third Brigade (Mounted Infantry), John T. Wilder
Chicago (Illinois) Board of Trade Battery, George I. Robinson

Third Division, Robert H. G. Minty, to April 17, 1864
Eli H. Murray, to April 26, 1864
Judson Kilpatrick
First Brigade, William W. Lowe
Second Brigade, Charles C. Smith
Third Brigade, Eli H. Murray

Fourth Division, Alvan C. Gillem
First Brigade, Duff G. Thornburgh
Second Brigade, George Spalding
Third Brigade, John K. Miller

Note. Gillem was also in command of the troops along the Nashville and Northwestern Railroad.

For additional information, see Cavalry Corps, Army of the Cumberland.

ATLANTA, GEORGIA CAMPAIGN, MAY 1, 1864–SEPTEMBER 8, 1864

Early in May 1864, the Army of the Cumberland advanced with William T. Sherman's army into Georgia at the beginning of the Atlanta Campaign. For the next four months it was engaged in marching and fighting, and finally, on September 2, Federal forces occupied Atlanta. During this time the Army of the Cumberland was engaged at Rocky Face Ridge May 5–9, Resaca May 13–16, Dallas (Pumpkin Vine Creek, New Hope Church, and Pickett's Mill) May 25–June 4, Kennesaw Mountain June 9–30, Peach Tree Creek July 20, and the siege of Atlanta July 28–September 2; Fourteenth Corps, Army of the Cumberland was at Jonesboro August 31–September 1. For details of the organization of the Army of the Cumberland and of its operations during this period, see Atlanta, Georgia Campaign.

AFTER THE ATLANTA CAMPAIGN, SEPTEMBER 9, 1864– NOVEMBER 9, 1864

After the Battle of Jonesboro and the evacuation of Atlanta, Hood withdrew with his army southward to Lovejoy's Station, Georgia. On September 18, 1864, Hood left his camps there and moved northward along the Western and Atlantic Railroad, which was Sherman's line of communications with the north.

On October 3, Sherman's army started in pursuit. Twentieth Corps was left behind to hold Atlanta and the crossing of the Chattahoochee River railroad bridge, and the other two corps of the Army of the Cumberland accompanied Sherman on his march back along the railroad.

Sherman followed Hood to Dalton, Georgia and then continued the pursuit westward toward Alabama. On October 20 he reached Gaylesville, Alabama, where he halted to await developments. He finally decided that Hood's objective was Tennessee, and on October 26 he detached Fourth Corps from the Army of the Cumberland and sent it to reinforce George H. Thomas, who was in command of the Federal troops in Tennessee. Fourth Corps did not rejoin the Army of the Cumberland, which was thus reduced to only Fourteenth Corps and Twentieth Corps. Later Sherman also sent Twenty-Third Corps to Tennessee.

Shortly after Fourth Corps left to join Thomas, Sherman began to draw back the rest of the army toward Atlanta, and on November 9, 1864, while at Kingston, Georgia, he reorganized his army into two wings as follows: a Left Wing, commanded by Henry W. Slocum, which consisted of Jefferson C. Davis' Fourteenth Corps and Alpheus S. Williams' Twentieth Corps of the Army of the Cumberland; and a Right Wing, commanded by Oliver O. Howard, which consisted of Peter J. Osterhaus' Fifteenth Corps and Frank P. Blair's Seventeenth Corps of the Army of the Tennessee. Slocum's command was designated as Left Wing, Army of Georgia, and it was commonly known as the Army of Georgia.

Finally, on November 15, when all preparations had been completed, Sherman's army began to leave Atlanta on its march across Georgia toward Savannah.

Although the Army of the Cumberland was not

officially discontinued by the reorganization of November 9, 1864, it was not again referred to by that name after the beginning of the Savannah Campaign.

For additional information about the Army of the Cumberland after the occupation of Atlanta, see Franklin and Nashville Campaign (Hood's Invasion of Tennessee), and also Savannah Campaign (Sherman's March through Georgia), the latter in Volume I.

ARMY OF THE DEPARTMENT OF THE MISSISSIPPI

After the Battle of Shiloh, Henry W. Halleck, commander of the Department of the Mississippi, moved his headquarters from Saint Louis to Pittsburg Landing on the Tennessee River, and he then assumed personal command of Ulysses S. Grant's Army of the Tennessee, John Pope's Army of the Mississippi, and Don Carlos Buell's Army of the Ohio, all of which were assembled in the area.

Halleck then reorganized the combined armies into a Right Wing, Center, Left Wing, and Reserve and with this command advanced during the month of May 1862 toward Corinth, Mississippi. He occupied the town May 30. On June 10 he abolished the wing organization, and on that date Grant, Pope, and Buell resumed command of their respective armies.

There appears to have been no official designation of Halleck's army in May 1862 as the Army of the Department of the Mississippi, but this name properly applies to the command with which Halleck forced the evacuation of Corinth. For additional information, see Department of the Mississippi (Halleck); Halleck's Advance on Corinth, Mississippi; and also Army of the Mississippi (Pope, Rosecrans); Army of the Tennessee, District of West Tennessee; and Army of the Ohio (Buell).

ARMY OF THE DEPARTMENT OF THE MISSOURI

September 19, 1864, Sterling Price led a Confederate army from Arkansas into Missouri, and on September 29 an order was issued directing that all unorganized troops within the limits of the Department of the Missouri be formed into provisional brigades during the emergency.

When Jefferson City was threatened by Price's approach, John B. Sanborn, commanding the District of Southwest Missouri; Egbert B. Brown, commanding the District of Central Missouri; and John McNeil, commanding the District of Rolla marched with troops from their respective districts to protect the capital. Brown, as the senior officer, assumed command at Jefferson City. He organized his troops into three brigades, commanded by Sanborn, McNeil, and Franklin W. Hickox, and placed them in the fortifications about the city. Price decided not to attack the fortifications at Jefferson City, however, and marched on with his army toward Boonville, Missouri.

Alfred Pleasonton arrived at Jefferson City on October 8. He placed Sanborn in command of a cavalry division, and directed him to go in pursuit of Price. Sanborn organized his division as follows:

Provisional Cavalry Division, John B. Sanborn
   First Brigade, John F. Philips
   Second Brigade, John L. Beveridge
   Third Brigade, Joseph J. Gravely

Pleasonton remained behind in command at Jefferson City when Sanborn led his division westward after Price. Pleasonton joined the division near Dunksburg, Missouri October 20 and assumed personal command. He then reorganized the division as follows:

Provisional Cavalry Division, Alfred Pleasonton
   First Brigade, John B. Sanborn
   Second Brigade, Egbert B. Brown
   Third Brigade, John McNeil
   Fourth Brigade, Edward F. Winslow

Winslow had been sent into Arkansas with his Second Division, Cavalry Corps, District of West Tennessee about the first of September 1864 when Price became active in that state, but he was then sent on to Missouri, where he joined Pleasonton's division near Dunksburg with a cavalry brigade.

The Provisional Cavalry Division was sometimes referred to as the Army of the Department of the Missouri.

For additional information, see Price's Missouri Expedition.

ARMY OF THE DISTRICT OF CAIRO

The army organized by Ulysses S. Grant, commander of the District of Cairo, for the campaign against Fort Henry and Fort Donelson February 6–16, 1862 was sometimes called the Army of the District of Cairo. After the capture of Fort Donelson, however, it became known as the Army of the District of West Tennessee, and a short time later as the Army of the Tennessee. For the organization and operations of this army, see Department of the Missouri, November 9, 1861–March 11, 1862, Districts in the Department of the Missouri, District of Cairo, Troops in the District of Cairo; and see also Capture of Fort Henry and Fort Donelson, Tennessee.

ARMY OF THE DISTRICT OF MISSISSIPPI

Army of the District of Mississippi is a name sometimes used for the Army of the Mississippi that was organized by John Pope February 21–March 3, 1862 in Missouri for an expedition against New Madrid, Missouri and Island No. 10 in the Mississippi River. For details of its organization and operations, see Army of the Mississippi (Pope, Rosecrans).

ARMY OF THE DISTRICT OF THE OHIO

The District of the Ohio was constituted March 19, 1862 as a district in Henry W. Halleck's Department of the Mississippi, and it consisted of that part of the Department of the Ohio that was transferred to the newly created Department of the Mississippi. Don Carlos Buell, former commander of the De-partment of the Ohio, assumed command of the district, and also retained command of the Army of the Ohio, although it was then in the Department of the Mississippi, and Buell was subject to Halleck's orders. On July 16, 1862, Halleck departed from headquarters at Corinth, Mississippi for Washington, D.C. to become the general in chief of the army. After that date the District of the Ohio was not a part of any department, but was under the direct control of Halleck in Washington, D.C. Buell commanded the army in the field, which was then, in effect, the Army of the District of the Ohio. The army, however, was still called the Army of the Ohio during the remainder of its period of existence. For additional information, see Army of the Ohio (Buell); District of the Ohio, under Miscellaneous Organizations; and Department of the Mississippi (Halleck).

ARMY OF THE DISTRICT OF WEST TENNESSEE

The army commanded by Ulysses S. Grant from the time of the surrender of Fort Donelson until the creation of the Department of the Tennessee operated in the District of West Tennessee, and was properly called the Army of the District of West Tennessee. At Savannah, Tennessee, however, shortly before the Battle of Shiloh, Grant began calling his army the Army of the Tennessee, and thereafter it was known by that name, and was officially so designated April 21, 1862. The Department of the Tennessee was created by an order dated October 16, 1862, and then the Army of the Tennessee, District of West Tennessee became the Army of the Tennessee, Department of the Tennessee. For details of the organization of Grant's army prior to October 16, 1862, see Army of the Tennessee, District of West Tennessee.

ARMY OF THE FRONTIER

On August 12, 1862, Theophilus H. Holmes was assigned command of the Confederate Trans-Mississippi District, with headquarters at Little Rock, Arkansas, relieving Thomas C. Hindman. Holmes then ordered Hindman to move with the greater part of the force that he had assembled to a point near Fort Smith, and there organize it for an expedition into Missouri. On August 24, Hindman assumed command at Fort Smith, Arkansas, and he then advanced his troops from Fort Smith and Fort Gibson to a line along the northern border of western Arkansas.

On September 10, Hindman was recalled to Little Rock to help in organizing the troops there, and he turned over the command of his army to James S. Rains, instructing him not to become engaged unless attacked.

A Confederate brigade under Joseph O. Shelby then crossed the border into Missouri and moved to the vicinity of Newtonia, where he was joined by Douglas H. Cooper with a force of about 3,000 Indian troops on the evening of September 26, 1862. Cooper assumed command of the combined force that evening, and occupied Newtonia the next day.

In late August 1862, John M. Schofield, commanding the District of Missouri, Department of the Mississippi, learned that Hindman was preparing for an invasion of Missouri, and he called for help. On September 24, Samuel R. Curtis assumed command of the re-created Department of the Missouri. Two days later he relieved Schofield, who was then at Springfield, from the command of the District of Missouri and assigned him to the command of all Union troops in the field in southwestern Missouri. At the same time he ordered James G. Blunt, commanding the District of Kansas, Department of the Missouri, to move with his Army of Kansas (see Army of Kansas) and join Schofield. At that time Schofield was at Springfield, Missouri with the divisions of James Totten and Francis J. Herron.

Everything was quiet in southwestern Missouri until September 30, and then Frederick Salomon with his First Brigade of Blunt's Army of Kansas approached Newtonia. Shelby and Cooper attacked Salomon and drove him back to Sarcoxie on the rest of the division. On October 1, the combined force under Schofield's command was designated as the Army of Southwestern Missouri. On October 3, Blunt's and Totten's divisions were camped at Sarcoxie, and Herron's division was on the Cassville Road.

The next day Blunt's and Totten's divisions advanced on Newtonia, and the enemy withdrew toward the mountains of northwestern Arkansas. Cooper retreated to the south toward Indian Territory, and Rains withdrew to Huntsville, Arkansas.

On October 12, Schofield advanced to Cassville with the divisions of Totten and Herron, and Blunt's division was at Keetsville. That day the combined Kansas and Missouri troops then commanded by Schofield were designated as the Army of the Frontier.

On October 15, Hindman returned to Fort Smith from Little Rock. He then hastened to the front, where he removed Rains and assumed personal command of the troops in the field. Hindman decided to take up a strong position at Fayetteville and await expected reinforcements.

Schofield then sent Blunt in pursuit of Cooper, and Blunt caught up with him at Old Fort Wayne, near Maysville, October 22. In a sharp fight, Cooper's force was completely routed and driven back into the Indian Territory.

On October 27, Schofield advanced Totten's division toward Fayetteville, and Hindman then fell back to the Arkansas River. With the enemy thus driven south of the Boston Mountains, Schofield, believing that the object of his advance had been accomplished, retired with the divisions of Totten and Herron to Springfield. Blunt's division was in camp at Lindsey's Prairie, fifteen miles south of Maysville. Then Schofield, who had been in poor health and believed that active operations had ended for the winter, turned over the command of the Army of the Frontier to Blunt, and on November 20 departed for Saint Louis.

In November 1862 the army was organized as follows:

ARMY OF THE FRONTIER, John M. Schofield

First Division, James G. Blunt
  First Brigade, Frederick Salomon
  Second Brigade, William Weer
  Third Brigade, William F. Cloud

Second Division, James Totten
  First Brigade, Daniel Huston, Jr.
  Second Brigade, William McE. Dye
  Third Brigade, Egbert B. Brown

Note 1. Herman Borris' Battery A, 2nd Illinois Light Artillery (Peoria Battery) was assigned to First Brigade; and Joseph Foust's Battery F, 1st Missouri Light Artillery was assigned to Second Brigade.

Note 2. Third Brigade did not accompany the army in the field, but remained at Springfield.

Third Division, Francis J. Herron
   First Brigade, Bertine Pinkney
   Second Brigade, Benjamin Crabb

Note. Frank Backof's Battery L, 1st Missouri Light Artillery was attached to First Brigade.

In late November 1862, John S. Marmaduke marched northward to Cane Hill, Arkansas with a division of cavalry, and when Blunt, who was at Lindsey's Prairie, learned of this, he marched on November 27 to meet him. There was skirmishing about Newburg, then on November 28, Blunt finally attacked and forced Marmaduke to withdraw to the vicinity of Van Buren. Blunt then took position with his division on Cane Hill.

Hindman decided to make another effort to regain control of northwestern Arkansas, and on December 3 he left Van Buren and advanced with his army toward Cane Hill. When Blunt learned that Hindman was approaching, he ordered Herron to move at once with Second Division and Third Division of the Army of the Frontier from Springfield to join him at Cane Hill. Herron left at once, and the head of his column arrived at Fayetteville during the night of December 6.

Hindman drove in Blunt's pickets on the evening of December 6, and was preparing to attack him the next morning when he learned of Herron's approach. He then decided to march and intercept Herron and defeat him before Blunt could come to his support, and then to turn on Blunt.

Herron attacked Hindman at Prairie Grove the next day, and Blunt's division joined Herron during the battle. All attacks on the enemy line were repulsed, and the fighting did not end until dark. During the night, Hindman withdrew toward the Arkansas River, leaving Blunt in possession of the field.

The organization of the Army of the Frontier at the Battle of Prairie Grove was as follows:

ARMY OF THE FRONTIER, James G. Blunt

First Division, James G. Blunt

First Brigade, Frederick Salomon
Second Brigade, William Weer
Third Brigade, William F. Cloud
Artillery
   1st Battery, Kansas Light Artillery, Marcus D. Tenney (with Second Brigade)
   2nd Battery, Indiana Light Artillery, John W. Rabb (with Third Brigade)
   2nd Battery, Kansas Light Artillery, Henry Hopkins (with Third Brigade)

Second Division, Daniel Huston, Jr.
   First Brigade, John G. Clark
   Second Brigade, William McE. Dye
   Artillery
      Battery A, 2nd Illinois Light Artillery, Herman Borris (with First Brigade)
      Battery F, 1st Missouri Light Artillery, David Murphy (with Second Brigade)

Third Division, Francis J. Herron
   First Brigade, Henry Bertram
   Second Brigade, William W. Orme
   Artillery
      Battery L, 1st Missouri Light Artillery, Frank Backof (with First Brigade)
      Battery E, 1st Missouri Light Artillery, Joseph Foust (with Second Brigade)

Schofield returned to the army December 29, 1862 and assumed command of the Army of the Frontier. Early in January 1863, Blunt returned to Fort Leavenworth to look after the business affairs of the District of Kansas, and William Weer assumed command of First Division of the army.

At the end of January 1863, Weer was in command of First Division; John G. Clark was in command of Second Division during the absence of Totten; and James O. Gower was in command of Third Division. Headquarters was at Springfield, Missouri.

At the end of February, the Army of the Frontier was organized as follows:

ARMY OF THE FRONTIER, John M. Schofield

First Division, William Weer
   First Brigade, William R. Judson
   Second Brigade

Note. The regiments of Second Brigade were scattered on detached service.

Second Division, James Totten
   First Brigade, John G. Clark
   Second Brigade, William McE. Dye

Third Division (Herron's), Washington F. Geiger
   First Brigade, Henry Bertram
   Second Brigade, John McNulta

Headquarters of the army was at Springfield.

The Army of the Frontier remained in southwest Missouri and northwestern Arkansas until March 1863, and then James Totten's Second Division and Third Division, then commanded by Washington F. Geiger, moved to southeastern Missouri to meet a threatened invasion of Missouri from Batesville by John S. Marmaduke's cavalry division, which was guarding the northeastern frontier of Arkansas.

On March 30, 1863, Herron assumed command of the Army of the Frontier when Schofield was assigned to the command of the District of Southwestern Missouri. At that time Weer's First Division was at Carrollton, Arkansas; Second Division, then commanded by Dudley Wickersham, was at Elk Creek, Missouri; and Geiger's Third Division was at Rolla, Missouri. Headquarters of the army was at Rolla.

Beginning on April 18, 1863, Marmaduke did lead an expedition into southeastern Missouri. His division reached Patterson on the evening of April 20, and he then moved through Bloomfield and Fredericktown. He remained in the area for several days, pushing out columns in different directions, including a strong force toward Cape Girardeau. William Vandever, who had assumed command of Second Division, Army of the Frontier April 9, advanced to Pilot Knob April 23, then moved on to Fredericktown April 25. Vandever came up with Marmaduke at Jackson at 9:00 on the evening of April 26, and drove his command beyond the town. He then pursued the enemy through Bloomfield to Chalk Bluff on the Saint Francis River before turning back.

At the end of April 1863, Weer's First Division was at Houston, Missouri; Second Division, then commanded by William Vandever, was at Pilot Knob, Missouri; and Third Division, commanded by William W. Orme, was at Lake Spring, Missouri. Headquarters of the Army of the Frontier was at Rolla.

On May 13, 1863, Thomas Ewing, Jr. assumed command of First Division, Army of the Frontier at Salem, Missouri (ordered April 26), with orders to take the Kansas regiments back to Kansas.

At the end of May 1863, Thomas Ewing, Jr. was in command of First Division, William Vandever of Second Division, and Washington Geiger of Third Division.

On June 2, Herron was ordered to move to Vicksburg with six infantry regiments and three batteries to join Ulysses S. Grant's army at Vicksburg. The 37th Illinois, 26th Indiana, and 20th Iowa of the Second Division, Army of the Frontier were organized as a brigade under William Vandever; and the 94th Illinois, 19th Iowa, and 20th Wisconsin of the Third Division were organized into a brigade under William W. Orme, and on June 6 they departed for Saint Louis for transfer to Vicksburg. Nelson Cole's Battery E, 1st Missouri Light Artillery and Joseph Foust's Battery F, 1st Missouri Light Artillery accompanied First Brigade, and Martin Welfley's Battery B, 1st Missouri Light Artillery was assigned to Second Brigade, but Welfley's battery was retained in Missouri. These six regiments were the only infantry regiments then with Second Division and Third Division, and with their departure the two divisions were discontinued. Herron's brigades arrived at Vicksburg June 11, and they were designated as Herron's Division. On July 28, the designation of Herron's Division was changed to Second Division, Thirteenth Corps, Army of the Tennessee.

On June 9 there was some reorganization in the Department of the Missouri. James G. Blunt was assigned to the newly created District of the Frontier, and Ewing's First Division, Army of the Frontier was assigned to the newly created District of the Border. Ewing was assigned command of the district.

With the three former divisions of the Army of the Frontier thus reassigned, the army was discontinued.

ARMY OF THE GULF

The Army of the Gulf was the name given to the forces of the Department of the Gulf commanded by Nathaniel P. Banks during the Red River Campaign in Louisiana, March 10–May 22, 1864. For details of the organization and operations of this army, see Red River, Louisiana Campaign.

ARMY OF THE INVASION OF GEORGIA

The Army of the Invasion of Georgia was the name sometimes used for the combined armies of the Tennessee, the Ohio, and the Cumberland, which were assembled near Chattanooga, Tennessee and Dalton, Georgia in the spring of 1864 in preparation for an advance into Georgia toward Atlanta. The army was under the command of William T. Sherman, commander of the Military Division of the Mississippi. For details of its organization and operations, see Atlanta, Georgia Campaign.

ARMY OF KANSAS

In the summer of 1862, southwestern Missouri was infested with bands of enemy troops commanded by such men as D. C. Hunter, John C. Tracy, Sidney D. Jackman, Jeremiah V. Cockrell, Charles Quantrill, J. T. Hughes, L. M. Harris, and J. T. Coffee, and Federal authorities decided to destroy them or drive them out of the state. In August, James G. Blunt, commander of the Department of Kansas, organized at Fort Scott the troops in southeast Kansas into a field force with which to move into Missouri. There he was to cooperate with John M. Schofield, who commanded the Union troops in southwest Missouri, in moving against the enemy. Blunt's command, which was known as the Army of Kansas, was organized as follows:

Army of Kansas, James G. Blunt
  First Brigade, Frederick Salomon
  Second Brigade, William Weer
  Third Brigade, William F. Cloud

Also present with the army were the 1st and 2nd batteries of Kansas Light Artillery; Stockton's Light Battery; and David G. Rabb's 2nd Battery, Indiana Light Artillery.

When preparations were completed, Blunt led his command to the northeast into Missouri. On the morning of August 16, 1862, an enemy force of about 4,000 men, consisting of troops under Coffee, Hunter, Tracy, Jackman, and Cockrell, attacked and defeated Emory S. Foster's 7th Cavalry, Missouri State Militia at Lone Jack, Missouri, about thirty miles southeast of Kansas City. Blunt, who was then approaching, arrived at Lone Jack about 7:00 P.M. August 17 and found Fitz Henry Warren, with a command consisting of men of the 1st Missouri Cavalry and the 1st Iowa Cavalry, threatened with an immediate attack by the entire enemy force. When the enemy learned of Blunt's approach, however, they withdrew during the night, crossed to the south side of the Osage River, and continued on toward the Arkansas border.

Blunt immediately started out in pursuit, with Cloud's brigade in advance. Blunt arrived at Fayetteville, Missouri at 2:00 A.M. August 20, and moved on toward Greenfield that day. He was unable, however, to come up with the enemy, who left the state and marched into Arkansas. Blunt's advance followed the enemy as far as Carthage, Missouri, and the main force halted at Montevallo. Finally, when it appeared that all enemy forces south of the Missouri River had left the state, Blunt began his return march toward Fort Scott. He was not interrupted except for a brief skirmish August 24, about eight miles south of Lamar, Missouri, and a short time later he was back in Fort Scott.

On September 19, the Department of Kansas was merged into the Department of the Missouri, and Blunt was ordered to join his command with that of Schofield in southwest Missouri. Schofield assumed command of the combined force, which was designated as the Army of Southwestern Missouri. Blunt's former Army of Kansas was then designated as the Kansas Division, Army of Southwestern Missouri. On October 12, the designation of the Army of Southwestern Missouri was changed to the Army of the Frontier, and the former Army of Kansas became First Division, Army of the Frontier. For additional information, see Army of Southwestern Missouri; and see also Army of the Frontier.

ARMY OF KENTUCKY (NELSON)
AUGUST 24, 1862–AUGUST 30, 1862

In late August 1862, E. Kirby Smith invaded Kentucky with an army from East Tennessee. Lewis Wallace, who was then at Cincinnati, Ohio, was ordered on August 20 to Lexington, Kentucky to assume command of the Federal troops assembled there. There were at that time six Indiana regiments at Lexington, but additional troops, mostly new regiments from Indiana and Ohio, were quickly sent to report to Wallace.

Meantime, however, William Nelson had been relieved from command of the Fourth Division of Don Carlos Buell's Army of the Ohio, which was then in Tennessee, and had been ordered back to Kentucky to assume command. Nelson arrived at Lexington on August 24 and relieved Wallace, and the next day he organized the regiments of his command, which he called the Army of Kentucky, into a First Division, Army of Kentucky. It was organized as follows:

First Division, Army of Kentucky, William Nelson
    First Brigade, Mahlon D. Manson
    Second Brigade, Charles Cruft
    Cavalry Brigade, James S. Jackson

On August 29–30, 1862, the two infantry brigades of Nelson's division, both under the immediate command of Manson, were engaged at Richmond, Kentucky with two Confederate divisions under E. Kirby Smith. Nelson was at Lexington at the beginning of the battle, but he arrived on the field during the afternoon and assumed command. Nelson was wounded and Manson was captured, and the two brigades were virtually destroyed. Cruft reorganized the remnants of the division and led them back to Louisville, Kentucky. Jackson's Cavalry Brigade was near the field at the close of the battle, but it was not engaged.

For details of the Battle of Richmond, the only battle in which Nelson's Army of Kentucky was engaged, see Invasion of Kentucky and Tennessee (E. Kirby Smith and Braxton Bragg), Battle of Richmond, Kentucky.

ARMY OF KENTUCKY (GRANGER)
OCTOBER 7, 1862–JUNE 8, 1863

After Lewis Wallace was relieved of command at Lexington, Kentucky by William Nelson, a short time before the Battle of Richmond, he was assigned command of the defenses of Cincinnati, Ohio and of Covington and Newport in Kentucky. Wallace assumed command September 2, 1862. A number of general officers were sent to the area and assigned to a force that was being formed to oppose Henry Heth, who was approaching Cincinnati through Kentucky with his Second Division of E. Kirby Smith's Confederate Department of East Tennessee. Among the officers reporting to Wallace was Gordon Granger, who had recently been transferred from the Army of the Mississippi (see Army of the Mississippi [Pope-Rosecrans]), and he was assigned command at Covington, Kentucky.

On October 7, Granger was assigned command of all United States forces in Kentucky operating on the line of the Licking River and extending southward from the Ohio River toward Lexington. This command was called the Army of Kentucky, and was composed largely of new regiments. On October 16, these were organized into brigades and divisions as follows:

ARMY OF KENTUCKY, Gordon Granger

First Division, Stephen G. Burbridge
    Second Brigade, Peter T. Swaine
    Third Brigade, Charles C. Doolittle

    Note. Ambrose A. Blount's 17th Battery, Ohio Light Artillery was attached to Third Brigade.

Second Division, Green Clay Smith
    First Brigade, Frederick W. Moore
    Second Brigade, Joseph W. Vance

Note. Josiah H. Burton's Battery F, 1st Illinois Light Artillery was attached to Second Brigade.

Third Division, Absalom Baird
No brigade organization given
Artillery
　　5th Battery, Kentucky Light Artillery, N. P. Shaler
　　19th Battery, Ohio Light Artillery, Joseph C. Shields

On October 27, Granger established his headquarters at Lexington and reorganized the army, which on October 31 consisted of the following:

ARMY OF KENTUCKY, Gordon Granger

First Division, Andrew J. Smith
First Brigade, Stephen G. Burbridge
Second Brigade, William J. Landram

Second Division, Quincy A. Gillmore
First Brigade, Green Clay Smith
Second Brigade, Samuel A. Gilbert

Third Division, Absalom Baird
First Brigade, John Coburn
Second Brigade, Peter T. Swaine

Artillery
　　21st Battery, Indiana Light Artillery, William W. Andrew
　　9th Battery, Ohio Light Artillery, Henry S. Wetmore
　　17th Battery, Ohio Light Artillery, Ambrose A. Blount
　　18th Battery, Ohio Light Artillery, Charles C. Aleshire
　　19th Battery, Ohio Light Artillery, Joseph C. Shields

Note. The unbrigaded artillery was at Lexington, Kentucky.

Unbrigaded troops were also posted at Lexington, Paris, Covington, and Nicholasville in Kentucky.

On November 17, 1862, Granger, as commander of the Army of Kentucky, was also assigned command of the District of Central Kentucky. For additional information, see Department of the Ohio, August 19, 1862–January 17, 1865, Posts and Districts in the Department of the Ohio.

Andrew J. Smith, who had been assigned command of First Division, Army of Kentucky October 31, 1862, was ordered on November 13 to take his division to Memphis, Tennessee. Upon arrival there, the designation of the division was changed to Tenth Division, Thirteenth Corps. For additional information, see Thirteenth Corps, Army of the Tennessee, October 24, 1862–January 14, 1863. The designation of Smith's division was again changed in December 1862, when it became First Division, Right Wing, Thirteenth Corps of William T. Sherman's Yazoo Expedition. For details of this operation, see Operations against Vicksburg, Mississippi, 1861–1863, Early Attempts to Capture Vicksburg, Yazoo River Expedition (William T. Sherman)—Battle of Chickasaw Bayou (or Walnut Hills).

After the departure of Smith's First Division, the Army of Kentucky consisted of only Gillmore's Second Division and Baird's Third Division. Then on January 20, 1863, Gillmore was assigned command of the District of Central Kentucky, relieving Granger, and Granger was ordered to Louisville to assume command of a force that was to be assembled there for transfer to Nashville, Tennessee in the Department of the Cumberland. Granger's new command was called the Army of Kentucky, and also Baird's Division, and it was organized into four brigades as follows:

Army of Kentucky (or Baird's Division), Absalom Baird
First Brigade, John Coburn
Second Brigade, Smith D. Atkins
Third Brigade, William P. Reid
Fourth Brigade, George Crook

Note 1. First Brigade was organized from First Brigade, Third Division, Army of Kentucky.
Note 2. Second Brigade was organized from Second Brigade, Third Division, Army of Kentucky.
Note 3. Third Brigade was organized from Reid's Brigade, District of Western Kentucky, Department of the Ohio.
Note 4. Fourth Brigade was organized from regiments brought from Western Virginia by George Crook.

Granger's troops, under the immediate command of Baird, Crook, and Charles C. Gilbert, arrived at Nashville by way of the Ohio and Cumberland rivers during February 1863, and they then took position in and around the city as a part of the Army of the Cumberland. Baird's and Granger's headquarters were at Nashville; Gilbert occupied Franklin,

Tennessee on February 12; and later in the month Crook's brigade moved to Carthage, Tennessee.

March 4, 1863, Coburn's brigade, with some cavalry, left Franklin on the Columbia Pike on a reconnaissance toward Spring Hill, and the next day most of the infantry was surrounded and captured at Thompson's Station on the Tennessee and Alabama Railroad. For details, see Engagement at Thompson's Station, Tennessee.

On June 8, 1863, a new corps, called Reserve Corps, Army of the Cumberland, was organized, and Granger was assigned command. Baird's Division (or Army of Kentucky) of Granger's former command was assigned as First Division, Reserve Corps under the command of Baird. The brigades of Baird's Division were assigned to First Division, Reserve Corps as follows: Atkins' Second Brigade became First Brigade, First Division; Reid's Third Brigade became Second Brigade, First Division; and Coburn's First Brigade became Third Brigade, First Division. Crook's Fourth Brigade was transferred to Fourteenth Corps and was assigned as Third Brigade, Fourth Division. Fourth Division, Fourteenth Corps, under James D. Morgan, was then transferred to the Reserve Corps as Second Division. Third Division, Reserve Corps, under the command of Robert S. Granger, was composed of regiments from Fort Henry, Fort Donelson, and Gallatin, Tennessee. For additional information, see Reserve Corps, Army of the Cumberland.

The Reserve Corps was sometimes called unofficially the Army of Kentucky, because most of the troops of First Division were originally from that organization.

ARMY OF THE MILITARY DIVISION OF THE MISSISSIPPI (SHERMAN)

When Ulysses S. Grant was called east in March 1864 to assume command of all armies of the United States, he was succeeded in command of the Military Division of the Mississippi by William T. Sherman. In late April 1864, Sherman began to assemble the Army of the Tennessee, the Army of the Cumberland, and the Army of the Ohio near Chattanooga, Tennessee and Dalton, Georgia in preparation for his campaign against Atlanta. The name given the forces commanded by Sherman was the Army of Invasion of Georgia, and on April 25, James B. McPherson's Army of the Tennessee was designated as the Right Wing; George H. Thomas' Army of the Cumberland as the Center; and John M. Schofield's Army of the Ohio as the Left Wing.

These three armies were not generally referred to as the Army of Invasion of Georgia, but were generally called the Army in the Field, Military Division of the Mississippi or, more simply, Sherman's Army.

In November 1864 Sherman reorganized his army in preparation for a march through Georgia to Savannah, and, in effect, he organized the troops of the Military Division of the Mississippi into two armies—one was near Atlanta, Georgia, and was commanded by Sherman; and the other was in Central Tennessee, and was commanded by George H. Thomas. For details, see Savannah Campaign (Sherman's March through Georgia) in Volume I.

On November 9, Sherman organized the four corps that were under his personal direction into wings as follows: a Right Wing under Oliver O. Howard, which consisted of Fifteenth Corps and Seventeenth Corps of the Army of the Tennessee; and a Left Wing under Henry W. Slocum, which consisted of Fourteenth Corps and Twentieth Corps of the Army of the Cumberland. During the march through Georgia and, later, the march through the Carolinas, Slocum's Left Wing was commonly called the Army of Georgia. The army which Sherman led through Georgia, and then northward through the Carolinas to Goldsboro, North Carolina, was usually simply called Sherman's Army, but it is better defined by using the designation Sherman's Army of the Military Division of the Mississippi, although this does not appear to have been officially approved. Sherman's orders and official communications, however, were issued under the heading Headquarters, Military Division of the Mississippi.

Sherman's army remained in existence until after the Grand Review in Washington May 24, 1865, but it was discontinued soon thereafter as the troops were mustered out of service.

For details of the organization and operations of the forces of the Military Division of the Mississippi while under Sherman's command, see the following: Atlanta, Georgia Campaign; Franklin and Nashville Campaign (Hood's Invasion of Tennessee); Savannah Campaign (Sherman's March through Georgia), in Volume I; and Carolinas Campaign, also in Volume I.

ARMY OF THE MISSISSIPPI (McCLERNAND)

During the latter part of December 1862, William T. Sherman made an attempt to capture Vicksburg, Mississippi by way of the Yazoo River, but when this ended in failure, he withdrew with his army to Milliken's Bend. There, on January 4, 1863, John A. McClernand, who had arrived from the north, relieved Sherman of his command. That same day, McClernand reorganized Sherman's former Yazoo Expedition, which he then designated as the Army of the Mississippi. He did this in preparation for an attack on Arkansas Post (or Fort Hindman) on the Red River. McClernand's new army consisted of a First Corps, commanded by George W. Morgan, and a Second Corps, commanded by Sherman. McClernand then moved his army by way of the Mississippi River and the Red River to Arkansas Post, which he captured January 11. The next day he completed a reorganization that had been ordered in the Department of the Tennessee December 22, 1862. The designation of First Corps, Army of the Mississippi was changed to Thirteenth Corps, Army of the Tennessee, and the designation of Second Corps, Army of the Mississippi was changed to Fifteenth Corps, Army of the Tennessee. With this reorganization, McClernand's Army of the Mississippi was discontinued.

For details of the organization and operations of McClernand's Army of the Mississippi, see Operations against Vicksburg, Mississippi, 1861–1863, Yazoo River, Mississippi Expedition (William T. Sherman), and see also Operations against Vicksburg, Mississippi, 1861–1863, Expedition against Arkansas Post (or Fort Hindman), Arkansas.

ARMY OF THE MISSISSIPPI (POPE, ROSECRANS)

In July 1861, Leonidas Polk was in Memphis, Tennessee in command of Confederate Department No. 2, which included West Tennessee and the state of Mississippi. On July 27, he ordered Gideon J. Pillow to move with about 6,000 men of his so-called Army of Liberation from Memphis to New Madrid, Missouri, and there, on the last day of August, he began the construction of fortifications at the town and on Island No. 10 in the Mississippi River. When the first Confederate defensive line in Kentucky was broken in February 1862 by the fall of Fort Henry and Fort Donelson, Columbus, Kentucky was evacuated, and New Madrid and Island No. 10 became the next defensive position on the Mississippi. Leonidas Polk, commanding the First Corps of the Confederate Army of the Mississippi, sent John P. McCown with his division of about 5,000 men to reinforce the approximately 2,000 men already there.

The defenses on the river consisted of a redoubt and land batteries at New Madrid, land batteries and a floating battery at Island No. 10, and land batteries and a redoubt on the Tennessee shore to the south and east of Island No. 10. McCown's troops at New Madrid and Island No. 10 during the latter part of February 1862 consisted of four brigades, commanded by Edward W. Gantt, Rufus P. Neely, Samuel F. Marks, and Alexander P. Stewart.

Organization of the Army, February 21, 1862– March 3, 1862. On February 18, 1862, Henry W. Halleck, commanding the Union Department of the Missouri, directed John Pope to organize and command a force for the reduction of these Confederate fortifications. Polk proceeded to Commerce, Missouri on February 21 and, with the assistance of Schuyler Hamilton, David S. Stanley, John M. Palmer, and Gordon Granger, began the organization of the regiments that arrived from Cairo, Cincinnati, and Saint Louis into brigades and divisions. Pope's command was first organized temporarily into two divisions as follows:

First Division, Schuyler Hamilton
  First Brigade, John Groesbeck

Second Brigade, Joseph B. Plummer

Note. First Division was constituted February 25, 1862 and organized February 27, 1862.

Second Division, John M. Palmer
First Brigade, James R. Slack
Second Brigade, William H. Worthington

Note. Second Division was constituted February 23, 1862, and Worthington was assigned command of Second Brigade on February 25.

On February 28, 1862, Gordon Granger, colonel of the 2nd Michigan Cavalry, was assigned command of cavalry in Pope's army, which ultimately consisted of the 2nd Michigan Cavalry, 3rd Michigan Cavalry, 7th Illinois Cavalry, and 2nd Iowa Cavalry.

The Mississippi District, Department of the Missouri was constituted February 27, 1862 to include the country in which Pope's army was to operate, and accordingly his command was first called the Army of the District of Mississippi. Later, however, it was called the Army of the Mississippi.

Pope began his advance from Commerce on February 28 and, marching by way of Sikeston, arrived before New Madrid March 3 and invested the town. The next day Pope announced a new organization of the army, as follows:

First Division, David S. Stanley
First Brigade, John Groesbeck
Second Brigade, J. L. Kirby Smith

Second Division, Schuyler Hamilton
First Brigade, William H. Worthington
Second Brigade, Joseph B. Plummer

Third Division, John M. Palmer
First Brigade, commander not of record
Second Brigade, commander not of record

On the Mississippi River (New Madrid, Missouri and Island No. 10). The siege of New Madrid began March 3, 1862, and it was continued until the town was surrendered March 14. There was an engagement at Point Pleasant, Missouri March 7, and then Pope began operations against Island No. 10. March 15, Flag Officer Andrew H. Foote arrived above Island No. 10 with six gunboats and ten mortarboats, and he brought with him on transports

a brigade of infantry under Napoleon B. Buford called the Flotilla Brigade. This brigade remained on the east bank of the Mississippi River, but it was placed under Pope's orders and thus became a part of the Army of the Mississippi.

On the night of April 4, and again on the night of April 6, gunboats ran downriver past the batteries at Island No. 10, and then assisted in the crossing of Pope's army from New Madrid to the east bank of the river to a position in rear of the enemy works. The navy captured Island No. 10 on April 7, and the river at this point was thus opened to traffic. All enemy forces surrendered the next day. For additional information, see Capture of New Madrid, Missouri and Island No. 10, Mississippi River.

There were some changes in the organization of the Army of the Mississippi during the operations at New Madrid and Island No. 10, but it was finally organized as follows:

ARMY OF THE MISSISSIPPI, John Pope

First Division, David S. Stanley
First Brigade, John Groesbeck
Second Brigade, J. L. Kirby Smith

Second Division, Schuyler Hamilton
First Brigade, William H. Worthington
Second Brigade, Nicholas Perczel

Third Division, John M. Palmer
First Brigade, James R. Slack
Second Brigade, Graham N. Fitch

Fourth Division, Eleazer A. Paine
First Brigade, James D. Morgan
Second Brigade, Gilbert W. Cumming

Fifth Division, Joseph B. Plummer
First Brigade, John Bryner
Second Brigade, John M. Loomis

Cavalry Division, Gordon Granger
2nd Michigan Cavalry, John C. Godley
3rd Michigan Cavalry, Francis W. Kellogg
7th Illinois Cavalry, John M. Graham
2nd Iowa Cavalry, Washington L. Elliott

Artillery Division, Warren L. Lothrop
Battery G, 1st Missouri Light Artillery, Henry Hescock

Battery M, 1st Missouri Light Artillery, Albert M. Powell

Battery C, 1st Illinois Light Artillery, Charles Houghtaling

Battery F, 2nd United States Artillery, John A. Darling

11th Battery, Ohio Light Artillery, Frank C. Sands

3rd Battery, Michigan Light Artillery, Alexander W. Dees

2nd Battery, Iowa Light Artillery, Nelson T. Spoor

Flotilla Brigade, Napoleon B. Buford
  27th Illinois Infantry, Fazilo A. Harrington
  42nd Illinois Infantry, George W. Roberts
  15th Wisconsin Infantry, Hans C. Heg
  Battery G, 1st Illinois Light Artillery, Arthur O'Leary
  Battery I, 2nd Illinois Light Artillery, Frederick Sparrestrom

Flotilla Brigade, Army of the Mississippi. The Flotilla Brigade, as a special force, requires some description. When Pope was assigned the task of capturing New Madrid and Island No. 10, he was to be aided by Flag Officer Andrew H. Foote, commanding the Naval Forces Western Waters, but Foote was delayed in joining Pope while the damage suffered by his gunboats at Fort Donelson was being repaired.

Finally Foote left Cairo March 14, 1862 with six ironclad gunboats and ten mortarboats and steamed down the Tennessee River. That day he was joined at Columbus, Kentucky by transports carrying a mixed force known as the Flotilla Brigade. This brigade was commanded by Napoleon B. Buford and consisted of the 27th Illinois, 42nd Illinois, 15th Wisconsin Infantry, Battery G, 1st Illinois Light Artillery, and Battery I, 2nd Illinois Light Artillery, all from the District of Cairo.

Foote's naval force and the Flotilla Brigade arrived at Hickman, Kentucky on the evening of March 15, and the next day moved on to the vicinity of Island No. 10.

The Flotilla Brigade was not originally a part of the Army of the Mississippi, but Pope was authorized to issue orders to Buford if that became necessary, and for this reason, in effect, the Flotilla Brigade became a part of the army. Buford, with his brigade, remained on the opposite side of the Mississippi River from the Army of the Mississippi and did not join it at that time. During the operations

around New Madrid and Island No. 10, Buford led an expedition from Hickman to Union City, Tennessee March 30–31, destroying an enemy camp at Union City before returning to Hickman.

After the capture of New Madrid and Island No. 10, when Pope's army was ordered to join Halleck at Pittsburg Landing, Pope took the Flotilla Brigade with him, and in the reorganization of the Army of the Mississippi at Hamburg, Tennessee April 24, the Flotilla Brigade was discontinued. The 27th Illinois and 42nd Illinois were assigned to First Brigade, First Division (the 15th Wisconsin was left to garrison Island No. 10, but later joined the army), and the batteries were assigned to the Artillery Division, Army of the Mississippi. Buford was assigned command of First Brigade, Third Division.

* * * * * * * * *

After the capture of New Madrid and Island No. 10, the Army of the Mississippi was ordered downriver to reduce Fort Pillow. Then, leaving James R. Slack's First Brigade of Palmer's Third Division as garrison of New Madrid, Pope's army embarked on transports April 12, 1862 and two days later landed about four miles from Fort Pillow. Pope then began preparations for an attack on the fort.

Transfer of the Army from the Mississippi River to Pittsburg Landing, Tennessee, April 16, 1862– April 28, 1862. Halleck, then commanding the Department of the Mississippi, who had arrived at Pittsburg Landing after the Battle of Shiloh, wanted Pope's army to join him there for an advance with the Army of the Tennessee and the Army of the Ohio against Corinth, Mississippi, and on April 15, 1862 he sent Pope an order (received April 16) to move with his army to Pittsburg Landing. He also directed Pope to leave a sufficient force to occupy Fort Pillow, which was under bombardment by the navy, if it should be evacuated. Pope immediately moved up the Mississippi, into the Ohio River, and then up the Tennessee River and arrived at Pittsburg Landing April 21. The troops did not go ashore there, but proceeded on upriver about four miles to Hamburg, where they disembarked the next day. Pope then took position on the Farmington road, with his right connecting with Don Carlos Buell's

Army of the Ohio on Lick Creek, and his left covered by Chester Creek.

On April 24, the Army of the Mississippi was reorganized to consist of three infantry divisions and a cavalry division, and at the end of April the army was organized as follows:

ARMY OF THE MISSISSIPPI, John Pope

First Division, Eleazer A. Paine
    First Brigade, John M. Palmer
    Second Brigade, James D. Morgan

Note. Henry Hescock's Battery G, 1st Missouri Light Artillery was assigned to First Brigade; and Charles Houghtaling's Battery C, 1st Illinois Light Artillery was assigned to Second Brigade.

Second Division, David S. Stanley
    First Brigade, John Groesbeck, to May 1, 1862
        Daniel Tyler
    Second Brigade, Joseph B. Plummer

Note. Alexander W. Dees' 3rd Battery, Michigan Light Artillery and Thomas D. Maurice's Battery F, 2nd United States Artillery were attached to First Brigade, and Nelson T. Spoor's 2nd Battery, Iowa Light Artillery was attached to Second Brigade.

Third Division, Schuyler Hamilton
    First Brigade, Napoleon B. Buford
    Second Brigade, Nicholas Perczel

Note 1. Frank C. Sands' 11th Battery, Ohio Light Artillery was assigned to First Brigade.
Note 2. Second Brigade was not yet formed at the end of April, and Perczel was not assigned command until May 6.

Cavalry Division, Gordon Granger
    First Brigade, William P. Kellogg
        7th Illinois Cavalry, William P. Kellogg
        3rd Michigan Cavalry, John K. Mizner
    Second Brigade, Washington L. Elliott
        2nd Iowa Cavalry, Edward Hatch
        2nd Michigan Cavalry, Selden H. Gorham

Artillery Brigade, Warren L. Lothrop
    Battery I, 2nd Illinois Light Artillery, Charles M. Barnett
    Battery M, 1st Missouri Light Artillery, Albert M. Powell
    5th Battery, Wisconsin Light Artillery, Oscar F. Pinney

First Division and Second Division were formed as a "Battle Corps," and Third Division served as a reserve.

The Flotilla Brigade accompanied Pope's Army of the Mississippi to Pittsburg Landing, but in the reorganization of April 24, 1862 it was discontinued, and the regiments were reassigned.

Advance on Corinth, Mississippi, April 29, 1862–May 30, 1862. Halleck had assumed personal command of the combined armies of the Tennessee, Ohio, and Mississippi near Pittsburg Landing April 12, 1862, and on April 29 he began his advance from Pittsburg Landing and Hamburg toward Corinth, Mississippi. The next day he announced the reorganization of his command into a Right Wing, Center, Left Wing, and Reserve. The Army of the Mississippi, which was then on the left of the Army at Hamburg, was designated as the Left Wing. It carried this designation in May 1862 during the advance on Corinth and until the wing organization was discontinued on June 10. For details of this reorganization, and the movements of the army during the advance on Corinth, see Department of the Mississippi (Halleck), and see also Halleck's Advance on Corinth, Mississippi.

On May 29, 1862, the Army of the Mississippi was divided into wings as follows:

Right Wing, William S. Rosecrans
    First Division, Right Wing, Eleazer A. Paine
    Second Division, Right Wing, David S. Stanley

Left Wing, Schuyler Hamilton
    First Division, Left Wing, Joseph B. Plummer
    Second Division, Left Wing, Jefferson C. Davis

Note 1. First Division, Left Wing was formerly Schuyler Hamilton's Third Division, Army of the Mississippi, to which Joseph B. Plummer was assigned command.
Note 2. Davis' Second Division, Left Wing was a new division. It consisted of the brigades of Jefferson C. Davis and Alexander Asboth, which had arrived at Hamburg from Samuel R. Curtis' Army of the Southwest May 25–26, 1862. For additional information, see Army of the Southwest.

A brigade commanded by William P. Carlin was also transferred to the Army of the Mississippi from

Missouri, and this was constituted as a reserve to report directly to Pope.

During the night of May 29–30, the enemy evacuated Corinth, and the next morning Federal troops occupied the town. For details of the operations of the Army of the Mississippi during the month of May 1862, see Halleck's Advance on Corinth, Mississippi.

In Northern Mississippi, June 1862–October 1862. The day after the evacuation of Corinth, Pope was reinforced temporarily by the addition of Thomas W. Sherman's Seventh Division, Army of the Tennessee (George H. Thomas' First Division, Army of the Ohio) and Thomas A. Davies' Second Division, Army of the Tennessee, which supported him on the left. As soon as it was definitely determined that the enemy had retreated southward, Pope, with his reinforced army, was sent in pursuit.

On June 1, 1862, because of the reinforcements received, the Army of the Mississippi was again reorganized. The Right Wing and Left Wing were essentially unchanged, but the divisions of Davies and Thomas W. Sherman were organized into a Center of the army, with Sherman in command. Asboth's brigade was detached from Davis' division of the Left Wing and designated as a reserve to report directly to Pope. The two regiments of Carlin's brigade, formerly of the reserve, were added to Davis' division.

By June 2, one of Rosecrans' divisions was near Baldwyn, and one was near Booneville; one division of Hamilton's command was at Rienzi, and one was beyond Danville; and Thomas W. Sherman, with his own and Davies' divisions, was on Tuscumbia Creek. The cavalry was out in front of the infantry.

The enemy finally ended its retreat at Tupelo, Mississippi, and on June 9 Pope was ordered to take up a suitable defensive position between Corinth and Baldwyn, Mississippi and to remain in observation south of Corinth. Thomas W. Sherman's division of the Army of the Ohio returned to Corinth that day, and the temporary Center of Pope's Army was discontinued.

On June 11, Washington L. Elliott was appointed by Pope as his chief of staff, and Philip H. Sheridan, as senior officer, assumed command of Second Brigade of the cavalry division. Sheridan was a new-comer to the Army of the Mississippi, having arrived at Pittsburg Landing from Saint Louis just a little over a week after the Battle of Shiloh. He was soon made commissary of subsistence at Halleck's headquarters, and held that position when appointed colonel of the 2nd Michigan Cavalry on May 25.

On June 26, Pope left for the East to assume command of the newly created Army of Virginia, and he was succeeded in command of the Army of the Mississippi by William S. Rosecrans.

Action at Booneville, Mississippi, July 1, 1862. Toward the end of June 1862, Sheridan's cavalry brigade, which consisted of 2nd Michigan and 2nd Iowa cavalry, encamped just north of Booneville, about twenty miles south of the army and covering its front. Booneville was a station on the Mobile and Ohio Railroad and was also the center for a number of radiating roads that ran out in various directions. Braxton Bragg, who had relieved Pierre G. T. Beauregard in command of the Confederate Army of the Mississippi on June 17, held a position covering Tupelo and Guntown some fifteen miles to the south.

The activities of Federal cavalry in the area between Booneville and Tupelo were a source of annoyance to Bragg, and on July 1 he sent James R. Chalmers with his cavalry division toward Booneville to destroy Sheridan's command or drive it back. Chalmers advanced on two converging roads that joined about one-half mile from the town. His main command approached from the west on the Blackland-Booneville road, and the remainder came up on the converging road that ran in from the southwest from the direction of Baldwyn.

On the Blackland road, about three and one-half miles west of Booneville, and just west of Osburn's Creek, Chalmers' advance encountered the pickets of the 2nd Michigan Cavalry, commanded by Leonidas S. Scranton. Scranton's small command fought a skillful delaying action for a time, and then made a strong stand in the woods at the junction of the two roads on which Chalmers was advancing. Here Scranton was reinforced by four companies of the 2nd Michigan under Archibald P. Campbell; fighting dismounted, the Federal troopers held their ground.

While Chalmers was deploying his command, Sheridan ordered Edward Hatch with his 2nd Iowa to take position in rear of Campbell's line. When finally ready, Chalmers launched an attack on Sheridan's line across an open field but was repulsed. He then advanced again, but was driven back after hand-to-hand fighting when Hatch arrived and joined in the fighting.

Chalmers launched a third attack, and Sheridan's situation became critical. Sheridan then sent Russell A. Alger of the 2nd Michigan with two companies of each of the two regiments around the left flank of Chalmers' line and toward the rear of the enemy position. Alger marched by a trail that ran through the woods to the north of the Blackland road, and roughly parallel to it, until it joined the road near the crossing of Osburn's Creek.

When Alger reached the Blackland road, he turned back to the east toward Chalmers' position. He quickly captured the Confederate headquarters, then continued on at a gallop and struck the rear of the enemy line. At the same time, Sheridan attacked from the front. The enemy was thrown into confusion by the two attacks and, believing that they were surrounded and that Sheridan had been reinforced, they broke and fled from the field.

The action at Booneville was a comparatively minor one, but Sheridan's victory, although he was greatly outnumbered by the enemy, attracted the attention of his superiors, and this resulted in his rapid rise to higher command.

* * * * * * * * *

July 8, 1862, Rosecrans ordered that the wing organization of the Army of the Mississippi be discontinued, and he announced a new organization of the army as follows:

ARMY OF THE MISSISSIPPI, William S. Rosecrans

First Division, Eleazer A. Paine
Second Division, David S. Stanley
Third Division (formerly Plummer's First Division, Left Wing), Charles S. Hamilton
Fourth Division (formerly Second Division, Left Wing), Jefferson C. Davis
Fifth Division (formerly Reserve), Alexander Asboth
Cavalry Division, Gordon Granger

Note. On July 30, 1862, Granger assumed command of Fifth Division, to which the cavalry regiments were added.

July 16, 1862, Ulysses S. Grant's District of West Tennessee was redefined to include the District of Cairo, the District of Mississippi, that part of the state of Mississippi occupied by Federal troops, and that part of Alabama that might be occupied by the troops of the Department of the Mississippi, including the Army of the Mississippi. Grant assumed command of the reorganized District of West Tennessee July 17, and the commander of the Army of the Mississippi was then subject to his orders.

At that time Rosecrans' army held a front of about thirty-five miles, with its left at Cherokee, Alabama and its right in front of Corinth. The principal concentration was at Jacinto, Mississippi, where Davis' Fourth Division and Granger's Fifth Division were located.

At the end of July 1862, the Army of the Mississippi was organized as follows:

ARMY OF THE MISSISSIPPI, William S. Rosecrans

First Division, James D. Morgan
   First Brigade, John M. Palmer
   Second Brigade, James D. Morgan
   Artillery
      Battery C, 1st Illinois Light Artillery, Charles Houghtaling
      Battery G, 1st Missouri Light Artillery, Henry Hescock
      Battery M, 1st Missouri Light Artillery, Junius W. MacMurray
      10th Battery, Wisconsin Light Artillery, Yates V. Beebe

Note. Morgan was in command of First Division during the temporary absence of Eleazer A. Paine.

Second Division, David S. Stanley
   First Brigade, J. L. Kirby Smith
   Second Brigade, Robert C. Murphy

Note. Carl A. Lamberg's 3rd Battery, Michigan Light Artillery and Thomas D. Maurice's Battery F, 2nd United States Artillery were attached to First Brigade.

Third Division, Charles S. Hamilton
   First Brigade, Napoleon B. Buford
   Second Brigade, Jeremiah C. Sullivan

Note. Frank C. Sands' 11th Battery, Ohio Light Artillery was attached to First Brigade, and Henry Hopkins' (Kansas) Battery (later 3rd Battery, Kansas Light Artillery) and William A. Pile's Battery I, 1st Missouri Light Artillery were attached to Second Brigade.

Fourth Division, Jefferson C. Davis
First Brigade, Robert B. Mitchell
Second Brigade, William P. Carlin
Artillery
5th Battery, Wisconsin Light Artillery, Oscar F. Pinney
8th Battery, Wisconsin Light Artillery, Stephen J. Carpenter

Fifth Division, Gordon Granger
First Brigade, Nicholas Greusel
Second Brigade, Bernard Laiboldt
Artillery
Battery I, 2nd Illinois Light Artillery, Charles M. Barnett
2nd Battery, Iowa Light Artillery, Nelson T. Spoor
6th Battery, Wisconsin Light Artillery, Henry Dillon

Note. The following cavalry regiments were with the Fifth Division: Horatio C. Nelson's 7th Illinois Cavalry; Edward Hatch's 2nd Iowa Cavalry; Albert L. Lee's 7th Kansas Cavalry; Philip H. Sheridan's 2nd Michigan Cavalry; John K. Mizner's 3rd Michigan Cavalry; James Clifford's Company F, 1st Missouri Cavalry; and Alfred Borcherdt's Company C, 5th Missouri Cavalry.

In mid-August 1862, the divisions of the Army of the Mississippi were in position as follows: First Division was at Tuscumbia, Second Division at Camp Clear Creek, Third Division at Jacinto, Fourth Division on the roads between Tuscumbia and Corinth, and Fifth Division at Rienzi.

During the early part of August, Paine's First Division and Jefferson C. Davis' Fourth Division (commanded since August 12 by Robert B. Mitchell during the absence of Davis on sick leave) were guarding the Memphis and Charleston Railroad east of Corinth, and on August 14, Grant ordered these two divisions to Decatur, Alabama, where they were to be subject to the orders of Don Carlos Buell, commander of the Army of the Ohio.

During the latter part of August 1862, E. Kirby Smith marched into eastern Kentucky from Knoxville, Tennessee, and Braxton Bragg, with his Confederate Army of the Mississippi, crossed the Tennessee River at Chattanooga and moved northward into Central Tennessee.

On August 30, Stanley's Second Division was ordered to relieve Paine's division, which was then guarding the railroad from Iuka to Decatur, and Paine's First Division and Mitchell's Fourth Division were ordered to Tennessee to reinforce Buell. Also on August 30, John M. Palmer was ordered to relieve Eleazer A. Paine, who was sick, in command of First Division.

Mitchell's division arrived at Murfreesboro on September 1, and retreated with Buell's army to Louisville, Kentucky. There, on September 29, its designation was changed to Ninth Division, Army of the Ohio, and that day it was assigned to Charles C. Gilbert's newly organized Third Corps, Army of the Ohio. It fought with Gilbert's corps at the Battle of Perryville, Kentucky October 8.

Palmer's First Division arrived at Nashville September 12 and formed a part of the garrison of that post during Bragg's invasion of Tennessee and Kentucky. On September 29 it was reorganized as Thirteenth Division, Army of the Ohio.

September 4, Granger was ordered to move with his Fifth Division, Philip H. Sheridan's 2nd Michigan Cavalry, Henry Hescock's Battery G, 1st Missouri Light Artillery, and Charles M. Barnett's Battery I, 2nd Illinois Light Artillery to Louisville. The infantry of Granger's division consisted of four regiments brought to the Army of the Mississippi from Samuel R. Curtis' Army of the Southwest in Arkansas by Jefferson C. Davis and Alexander Asboth and was known as the Pea Ridge Brigade. Sheridan was given the command of the Pea Ridge Brigade, and his own 2nd Michigan Cavalry. Sheridan moved with his command to Columbus, Kentucky by rail, and from there on transports to Louisville, where the division arrived September 14. There Sheridan assumed command of the Pea Ridge Brigade, which consisted of the 2nd Missouri, 15th Missouri, 36th Illinois, 44th Illinois, and such other regiments as might be sent to him prior to the arrival of Buell's army. On September 29, Sheridan's command was organized as Eleventh Division, Army of the Ohio, and Sheridan was assigned command. That same day Eleventh Division was assigned to Gilbert's Third Corps, Army of the Ohio, and fought with that corps at the Battle of Perryville, Kentucky October 8. Sheridan's Pea Ridge Brigade became Bernard Laiboldt's 35th Brigade of Sheridan's Eleventh Division.

On September 17, Granger was assigned to duty in Horatio G. Wright's Department of the Ohio, and on October 7 he was assigned command of the Army of Kentucky, Department of the Ohio.

With the departure of the three divisions to join the Army of the Ohio, Rosecrans' Army of the Mississippi was reduced to two divisions, as follows:

ARMY OF THE MISSISSIPPI, William S. Rosecrans

Second Division, David S. Stanley
    First Brigade, John W. Fuller
    Second Brigade, Joseph A. Mower

Note. Albert M. Powell's Battery M, 1st Missouri Light Artillery; John D. McLean's 8th Battery, Wisconsin Light Artillery (one section); and Thomas D. Maurice's Battery F, 2nd United States Artillery were attached to First Brigade. Nelson T. Spoor's 2nd Battery, Iowa Light Artillery and Alexander W. Dees' 3rd Battery, Michigan Light Artillery were attached to Second Brigade.

Third Division, Charles S. Hamilton
    First Brigade, John B. Sanborn
    Second Brigade, Jeremiah C. Sullivan

Note. Cyrus Sears' 11th Battery, Ohio Light Artillery was attached to First Brigade, and Lorenzo D. Immell's 12th Battery, Wisconsin Light Artillery was attached to Second Brigade.

Cavalry Division, John K. Mizner
    First Brigade, Edward Hatch
    Second Brigade, Albert L. Lee

Note. When Granger departed with his division for Louisville, Mizner assumed command of the Cavalry Division, and when Sheridan departed, Albert L. Lee assumed command of Second Brigade.

Engagement at Iuka, Mississippi, September 19, 1862. In September 1862, Sterling Price advanced with a Confederate army from Tupelo to Iuka, Mississippi, and there on September 19 he attacked the two divisions of Rosecrans' Army of the Mississippi. The fighting ended at dark, and that night Price withdrew to the south to join a force commanded by Earl Van Dorn. The organization of the army given above was the same as that of Rosecrans' command at the Engagement of Iuka. For details of the battle, see Engagement at Iuka, Mississippi.

* * * * * * * * *

On September 24, 1862, the District of West Tennessee, which at that time was not a part of any department, was reorganized into four divisions, designated as First Division, Second Division, Third Division, and Fourth Division, all of the District of West Tennessee. For details of this reorganization, see District of West Tennessee. All territory occupied by the Army of the Mississippi, and the forces commanded by Edward O. C. Ord at Corinth, was designated at Third Division, District of West Tennessee, and Rosecrans was assigned command.

Battle of Corinth, Mississippi, October 3–4, 1862. After the Engagement at Iuka, Price joined Van Dorn, who advanced with the combined forces on Corinth, Mississippi. Rosecrans called in all of his command at Corinth, which consisted of the Army of the Mississippi and Thomas A. Davies' Second Division and Thomas J. McKean's Sixth Division of the Army of the Tennessee. On October 3, 1862, Van Dorn launched a violent and unsuccessful assault on the works in front of the town, and renewed the attack the next day. Despite the desperate attempts to gain possession of the town, Van Dorn was forced to abandon the effort and withdraw. For details of the battle, see Battle of Corinth, Mississippi. The Army of the Mississippi had the same organization at Corinth as at Iuka, except that Napoleon B. Buford commanded First Brigade, Third Division. Jeremiah C. Sullivan was disabled during the battle, and Samuel A. Holmes assumed command of Second Brigade, Third Division. At the Battle of Corinth, John K. Mizner's Cavalry Division was organized into two brigades: Edward Hatch commanded the First Brigade, and Albert L. Lee commanded the Second Brigade.

* * * * * * * * *

The District of West Tennessee was merged into the newly constituted Department of the Tennessee October 16, 1862, and on October 26 the designation of Third Division, District of West Tennessee was changed to District of Corinth, Department of the Tennessee. On that date the Army of the Mississippi was discontinued. October 23, Rosecrans was ordered to Cincinnati, Ohio, where he was assigned command of the newly created Department of the Cumberland (ordered October 24). Charles S. Hamilton was assigned command of the District of Corinth.

ARMY OF NEW MEXICO

Army of New Mexico is the name sometimes applied to the Union troops under Edward R. S. Canby, commander of the Department of New Mexico, during Henry Hopkins Sibley's invasion of New Mexico with his brigade of Texans in 1862. For details, see Department of New Mexico, Troops and Operations in the Department of New Mexico, Sibley's Invasion of New Mexico.

ARMY OF NORTH MISSOURI

The Army of North Missouri is the name given by Benjamin M. Prentiss to the forces under his command in the District of North Missouri, Department of the Missouri. For additional information, see Department of the Missouri, November 9, 1861–March 11, 1862, District of North Missouri.

ARMY OF THE OHIO (BUELL) DECEMBER 2, 1861–OCTOBER 24, 1862

Organization of the Army. The Army of the Ohio dates from November 9, 1861, although it was not so designated until December 2. The first troops organized in the state of Kentucky, and which later became a part of the Army of the Ohio, belonged to the Department of the Cumberland. These were seven brigades that were organized under George H. Thomas at Camp Dick Robinson, Kentucky, and under Alexander McD. McCook at Nolin River (or Camp Nevin), Kentucky. These were as follows:

Camp Dick Robinson, Kentucky, George H. Thomas
    First Brigade, Albin Schoepf
    Second Brigade, Mahlon D. Manson
    Third Brigade, Robert L. McCook

Nolin River, Kentucky, Alexander McD. McCook
    Fourth Brigade, Lovell H. Rousseau
    Fifth Brigade, Thomas J. Wood

Sixth Brigade, Richard W. Johnson
Seventh Brigade, James S. Negley

In a reorganization of November 9, 1861, the Department of the Cumberland was discontinued, and that part of Kentucky lying east of the Cumberland River was included in the Department of the Ohio, to which Don Carlos Buell was assigned command.

During November 1861, the troops of the Department of the Ohio were organized into sixteen brigades, including the seven listed above. The nine new brigades were as follows:

Eighth Brigade, John B. Turchin
Ninth Brigade, Joshua W. Sill
Tenth Brigade, Jacob Ammen
Eleventh Brigade, Jeremiah T. Boyle
Twelfth Brigade, Samuel P. Carter
Thirteenth Brigade, Charles Cruft
Fourteenth Brigade, James G. Jones
Fifteenth Brigade, Milo S. Hascall
Sixteenth Brigade, William T. Ward

By an order of December 2, 1861, Buell designated the troops under his command as the Army of the Ohio, and organized the brigades of the department into divisions. Because these divisions were the basic organizations of the Army of the Ohio, and later of the Army of the Cumberland, a description of each is given here in some detail:

First Division, George H. Thomas
    First Brigade, Albin Schoepf
    Second Brigade, Mahlon D. Manson, to March 22, 1862
        Speed S. Fry
    Third Brigade, Robert L. McCook
    Eleventh Brigade, Jeremiah T. Boyle
    Twelfth Brigade, Samuel P. Carter
    Artillery
        Battery B, 1st Ohio Light Artillery, William E. Standart
        Battery C, 1st Ohio Light Artillery, Dennis Kenny, Jr.
        Battery B, 1st Kentucky Light Artillery, John M. Hewett
    1st Kentucky Cavalry, Frank Wolford

Note 1. First Division was organized from troops at Camp Dick Robinson, and Thomas assumed command December 6, 1861.

Note 2. Twelfth Brigade was detached from First

Division December 5, 1861 and ordered to report directly to Headquarters, Army of the Ohio.

Note 3. Eleventh Brigade was assigned to First Division December 5, 1861, and was then transferred to Fifth Division March 9, 1862.

Note 4. First Division was engaged under Thomas at Mill Springs (or Logan's Cross Roads) January 19, 1861. For details, see Engagement at Mill Springs (Logan's Cross Roads, Fishing Creek, or Beech Grove), Kentucky.

Second Division, Alexander McD. McCook
  Fourth Brigade, Lovell H. Rousseau
  Fifth Brigade, Thomas J. Wood, to December 24, 1861
    Edward N. Kirk
  Sixth Brigade, Richard W. Johnson
  Seventh Brigade, James S. Negley
  Artillery
    Battery A, 1st Ohio Light Artillery, Charles S. Cotter
    Battery A, 1st Kentucky Light Artillery, David C. Stone
    Battery B, Pennsylvania Light Artillery, Charles F. Mueller
  2nd Kentucky Cavalry, Buckner Board

Note 1. Second Division was originally First Division, Department of the Cumberland. October 18, 1861, McCook announced the organization of a "Central Division," which was composed of Fourth Brigade, Fifth Brigade, and Sixth Brigade. When James S. Negley arrived at Nolin River with his brigade from Pittsburgh, Pennsylvania, it was designated as Seventh Brigade. When Buell organized the Army of the Ohio December 2, 1861, McCook's division became Second Division, Army of the Ohio, and this was announced December 3.

Note 2. Seventh Brigade was detached March 15, 1862 and designated as an Independent Brigade. It remained at Columbia, Tennessee when the Army of the Ohio marched to Savannah, Tennessee to take part in the Battle of Shiloh. It was then ordered to join Ormsby M. Mitchel, commanding Third Division, Army of the Ohio, in northern Alabama and Middle Tennessee in May 1862.

Third Division, Ormsby M. Mitchel
  Eighth Brigade, John B. Turchin
  Ninth Brigade, Joshua W. Sill
  Seventeenth Brigade, William H. Lytle, to December 22, 1861
    Ebenezer Dumont, to March 21, 1862
    William H. Lytle
  Artillery, Cyrus O. Loomis
    Battery E, 1st Ohio Light Artillery, Warren P. Edgarton

5th Battery, Indiana Light Artillery, Peter Simonson

1st Battery, Michigan Light Artillery, Cyrus O. Loomis

Note 1. Mitchel was relieved from command at Cincinnati, Ohio November 19, 1861 and was assigned command at Camp Jenkins, near Louisville, Kentucky. A short time later he was ordered to Camp John Quincy Adams at Bacon Creek, Kentucky for the purpose of organizing and training the troops assembling there. These troops were organized as Third Division, Army of the Ohio, and Mitchel was assigned command December 3.

Note 2. Eighth Brigade was discontinued in July 1862.

Note 3. Seventeenth Brigade was organized in December 1861, with orders to assemble at Elizabethtown, Kentucky.

Note 4. John C. Starkweather's Twenty-Eighth Brigade was attached to Third Division in August 1862.

Fourth Division, William Nelson
  Tenth Brigade, Jacob Ammen
  Fifteenth Brigade, Milo S. Hascall
  Nineteenth Brigade, William B. Hazen
  Artillery
    Battery D, 1st Ohio Light Artillery, Andrew J. Konkle
    10th Battery, Indiana Light Artillery, Jerome B. Cox
    7th Battery, Indiana Light Artillery, Samuel J. Harris
  2nd Indiana Cavalry, Edward M. McCook

Note 1. Nelson, who was in command at Louisville, Kentucky, was assigned command of Fourth Division December 3, 1861. The division was immediately transferred to Camp Wickliffe at New Haven, Kentucky. It was then ordered to Nashville, Tennessee, and it arrived there February 28, 1862.

Note 2. Nineteenth Brigade was assigned to Fourth Division December 2, 1861, but it was not organized until January 3, 1862.

Note 3. Twenty-Second Brigade, commanded by Sanders D. Bruce, was organized January 18, 1862 and was assigned to Fourth Division February 11.

Note 4. Fifteenth Brigade was transferred to Sixth Division March 9, 1862.

Fifth Division, Thomas L. Crittenden
  Thirteenth Brigade, Charles Cruft
  Fourteenth Brigade, William Sooy Smith
  Artillery
    Battery G, 1st Ohio Light Artillery, Joseph Bartlett
    Battery M, 4th United States Artillery, John Mendenhall

Note 1. Crittenden was assigned command of the troops organizing at Owensboro and Henderson, Kentucky early in October 1861. These troops were designated as Fifth Division December 3, 1861, and Crittenden was assigned command.

Note 2. Jeremiah T. Boyle's Eleventh Brigade was transferred from First Division to Fifth Division March 9, 1862.

Note 3. Twenty-Third Brigade was organized as an Independent Brigade under William W. Duffield March 8, 1862, and it was attached to Fifth Division in August 1862.

Note 4. Early in February 1862, Cruft, with his Thirteenth Brigade, was ordered to join Ulysses S. Grant's Army of the District of Cairo, Department of the Missouri at Fort Henry, Tennessee. Then, after the capture of Fort Henry and Fort Donelson, Cruft's brigade was transferred to Henry W. Halleck's command as First Brigade, Third Division, Army of the Tennessee.

Sixth Division, Thomas J. Wood
    Twentieth Brigade, James W. Forsyth
        Charles G. Harker
    Twenty-First Brigade, George D. Wagner
    Fifteenth Brigade, Milo S. Hascall
    Artillery
        6th Battery, Ohio Light Artillery, Cullen Bradley
        8th Battery, Indiana Light Artillery, George Estep
        10th Battery, Indiana Light Artillery, Jerome B. Cox

Note 1. On December 24, 1861, Wood was relieved from the command of Fifth Brigade, Second Division and was ordered to Bardstown, Kentucky to establish a Camp of Instruction for the troops assembling at that place. These troops were organized into Sixth Division January 15, 1862, and Wood was assigned command.

Note 2. Twentieth Brigade and Twenty-First Brigade were organized January 8, 1862.

Note 3. Fifteenth Brigade was transferred to Sixth Division from Fourth Division March 9, 1862.

In addition to the six divisions of the army, two brigades were organized in the department but were not assigned to a division. These were as follows:

Sixteenth Brigade was organized in November 1861 under William T. Ward, and on January 8, 1862 Ward was assigned command of Sixteenth Brigade and other troops that had been posted to guard the front of Louisville. Ward's headquarters was at Elizabethtown, Kentucky. When the Army of the Ohio moved into Tennessee, Sixteenth Brigade remained in Kentucky and was posted at the Camp of Instruction at Bardstown during the Shiloh Campaign.

Eighteenth Brigade was organized December 17, 1861 for duty in eastern Kentucky under James A. Garfield. This brigade was broken up by an order of April 18, 1862, after the Battle of Shiloh.

December 1861–February 1862—Advance of the Army to Nashville, Tennessee.

During the period November 1861–January 1862, Buell was occupied principally in organizing and outfitting his army for field service, and he did not attempt any offensive movements. There were, however, some changes in the positions of the divisions of the army during this period. One of the more significant of these occurred in December 1861, when Buell decided to advance a part of his army toward the enemy position at Bowling Green, Kentucky, and he then began some preliminary movements.

In early February 1862, Henry W. Halleck, commander of the Department of the Missouri, approved a plan proposed by Ulysses S. Grant, commanding the District of Cairo, to lead an army against Fort Henry on the Tennessee River and Fort Donelson on the Cumberland River. This movement, which resulted in the capture of Fort Henry February 6 and Fort Donelson February 16, was to have a decided effect on the operations of Buell's Army of the Ohio. The capture of Fort Donelson was followed by the complete collapse of the first Confederate line of defense in Kentucky and resulted in the evacuation of Columbus, Clarksville, Bowling Green, and Nashville. Buell's Army of the Ohio and Grant's Army of the District of West Tennessee then advanced into Tennessee to occupy Bowling Green and Nashville.

To assist the reader's understanding of the participation of the Army of the Ohio in this advance, the movements of the divisions during the period November 1861–February 1862 are briefly described here as follows:

Alexander McD. McCook's Second Division remained at Camp Nevin on Nolin River until December 7, 1861, and it was then ordered forward to Bacon Creek (Camp Wood), about six miles north of Munfordville on the road to Elizabethtown. McCook remained in the vicinity of Munfordville until the evacuation of Bowling Green February 11, 1862, and he then followed Mitchel's division to

Nashville, where it arrived at the Cumberland River on the night of March 1.

On December 17, 1861, Ormsby M. Mitchel, commanding Third Division at Elizabethtown, was directed to send a brigade to Bacon Creek, and to follow with the rest of his division as soon as convenient. He was ordered to make a demonstration against Bowling Green to prevent the transfer of enemy troops to Fort Donelson, but the enemy evacuated the town February 11, 1862, before his arrival, and Mitchel occupied Bowling Green without opposition February 15. Buell then advanced toward Nashville with Mitchel's division. Nashville was evacuated February 23, and Mitchel arrived across the river from the city the next day. Buell occupied Nashville February 25. All land movements of the army were slow at that time because of the terrible conditions of the roads.

On December 24, 1861, Thomas J. Wood was ordered to Bardstown to command a Camp of Instruction to be established there, and by January 15, 1862 he had fully organized a new Sixth Division, to which he was assigned command. The next day he was ordered to Lebanon, Kentucky, where he remained with his division until February 12. From there he moved toward Munfordville and joined the other troops on Bacon Creek February 14. Wood then followed Mitchel and McCook toward Nashville.

Soon after William Nelson had been relieved in command of Camp Dick Robinson in September 1861 by George H. Thomas, he was ordered to Maysville, Kentucky to organize a force to operate in the eastern part of the state. After driving the enemy from eastern Kentucky, Nelson returned to Louisville in late November. He was then assigned command of Fourth Division, which he immediately moved to Camp Wickliffe near New Haven, Kentucky, about thirteen miles east of Elizabethtown. On February 13, 1862, he was ordered to Louisville, where he embarked his division February 16, the day Fort Donelson was surrendered, to reinforce Grant. Nelson then proceeded by way of the Ohio and Cumberland rivers to Nashville, where he arrived February 25.

December 3, 1861, Thomas L. Crittenden was assigned command of Fifth Division, which was organized at Henderson and Owensboro, Kentucky. About mid-January 1862, Crittenden moved his division to Calhoun, Kentucky, about eighteen miles south and a little west of Owensboro on Green River, and he then occupied South Carrollton, about twenty miles farther upriver from Calhoun. He remained there protecting navigation on the river until the end of the month, then returned to Calhoun before continuing on to Owensboro. Early in February, Charles Cruft was sent with his Thirteenth Brigade, Fifth Division to join Grant's army at Fort Henry. He arrived there February 14, after the surrender of Fort Henry, and his brigade then became First Brigade, Third Division, District of Cairo, Department of the Missouri. On February 15, Crittenden was ordered to embark at Owensboro with the rest of his division (the Fourteenth Brigade and Eleventh Brigade), and he then followed Nelson's division to Nashville.

George H. Thomas' First Division, which had remained near Somerset, Kentucky after the Battle of Mill Springs, was ordered to Lebanon February 6, 1862 to join in Buell's movement toward Munfordville. Progress was very slow because of the terrible condition of the roads, and on February 19 the division was halted at Bardstown. By that time Fort Donelson had surrendered, and on February 21, Thomas was ordered to march with his division to Louisville, where it was to embark for Nashville by way of the Ohio and Cumberland rivers. Thomas arrived at Nashville March 2.

March of the Army to Savannah, Tennessee, March 15, 1862–April 7, 1862. On February 14, 1862, Grant was assigned command of the newly created District of West Tennessee, and on February 17, after the surrender of Fort Donelson, he assumed command. His army then became the Army of the District of West Tennessee, and later the Army of the Tennessee.

On March 1, 1862, Halleck ordered Grant with his army to move up the Tennessee River to Savannah, and from there to send troops to Eastport, Mississippi to destroy the Bear Creek bridge on the Memphis and Charleston Railroad.

For some time Halleck had sought control over Buell's Army of the Ohio to secure better cooperation in his projected operations on the Tennessee River, and finally, on March 11, 1862, he was assigned command of the newly created Department of the Mississippi, which included Grant's Army of the District of West Tennessee, Buell's Army of the Ohio, and John Pope's Army of the Mississippi. On that date the Department of the Ohio was discontinued, but a new District of the Ohio was constituted March 19 as a district in the Department of the Mississippi. This district included the territory of that part of the Department of the Ohio that was included in the Department of the Mississippi. Buell was assigned command of the District of the Ohio, and thus came under Halleck's orders. Although no longer operating in the Department of the Ohio, Buell's army was still called the Army of the Ohio, and it fought under this designation at Shiloh and later, in October 1862, at Perryville, Kentucky. For additional information, see Department of the Mississippi (Halleck), and see also District of the Ohio, under Miscellaneous Organizations.

On March 15, 1862, Halleck directed Buell to march with his Army of the Ohio from Nashville to Savannah, where the advance of Grant's forces had arrived March 5, 1862. While in Nashville, before the army marched for Savannah, Buell issued orders that led to the following changes in the organization and disposition of the troops in the Army of the Ohio:

Seventh Division, Army of the Ohio. March 26, 1862, Buell ordered the formation of a new Seventh Division under George W. Morgan from troops then serving under Samuel P. Carter at Cumberland Ford, Kentucky; from regiments of the Eighteenth Brigade recently withdrawn from eastern Kentucky; and from additional regiments in Kentucky. The division was organized as follows:

Seventh Division, George W. Morgan
    Twenty-Fourth Brigade, Samuel P. Carter
    Twenty-Fifth Briagade, James G. Spears
    Twenty-Sixth Brigade, John F. De Courcy
    Twenty-Seventh Brigade, John Coburn, to April 12, 1862
        Absalom Baird

Morgan captured Cumberland Gap June 18, 1862, and occupied the position until E. Kirby Smith's advance into Kentucky from East Tennessee forced its abandonment September 17. Morgan then retreated northward to the Ohio River and arrived at Greenup, Kentucky on October 3. He then moved with his division up the Kanawha River to Charleston in Western Virginia. While there its designation was changed from Seventh Division, Army of the Ohio to Cumberland Division, District of Western Virginia, Department of the Ohio.

November 10, 1862, Morgan and two brigades of the Cumberland Division were transferred from the Department of the Ohio and sent to Memphis in the District of West Tennessee (after October 16, 1862 in the Department of the Tennessee). In November 1862 the designation of the division was again changed to Ninth Division, Thirteenth Corps. As Third Division, Right Wing, Thirteenth Corps, it took part in William T. Sherman's Yazoo River Expedition in December 1862. For additional information, see Operations against Vicksburg, Mississippi, 1861–1863, Yazoo River, Mississippi Expedition (William T. Sherman).

Third Division, Army of the Ohio. Ormsby M. Mitchel's Third Division, Army of the Ohio did not accompany the army to Savannah, and in mid-March 1862 it left Nashville for Murfreesboro, Tennessee, where it remained until relieved by William W. Duffield's Twenty-Third Brigade (see below). It then moved through Shelbyville and Fayetteville to Huntsville, Alabama, on the Memphis and Charleston Railroad, where it arrived April 11.

May 10, 1862, Mitchel was assigned command of all troops between Nashville and Huntsville, and this order placed James S. Negley's Twenty-Seventh Brigade, which was at Columbia, Tennessee, under Mitchel's command.

Mitchel's forces soon established control of the Memphis and Charleston Railroad and all of Alabama north of the Tennessee River. Third Division remained in the area until it was joined by Buell's army as it moved eastward from Corinth, Mississippi in June 1862. For additional information, see Invasion of Kentucky and Tennessee (E. Kirby Smith and Braxton Bragg).

Seventh Brigade, Army of the Ohio. James S. Negley's Seventh Brigade was detached from Second Division, Army of the Ohio March 15, 1862 as an Independent Brigade, and it was left at Columbia, Tennessee when Buell's army marched toward Savannah, Tennessee to join Grant's army. The brigade was ordered to join Mitchel's Third Division on May 10. Negley was assigned command of a new Eighth Division September 14, 1862, and his brigade, under the command of John F. Miller, was assigned to that division.

Sixteenth Brigade, Army of the Ohio. William T. Ward's Sixteenth Brigade was ordered to the Camp of Instruction at Bardstown when Buell's army marched to Savannah, and it remained there during the Shiloh Campaign. The regiments of the brigade were largely transferred to Twenty-Third Brigade (see below) in March 1862.

Twenty-Third Brigade, Army of the Ohio. This brigade was organized under the command of William W. Duffield March 8, 1862 and was ordered from Kentucky to Murfreesboro, Tennessee to protect the road from La Vergne to Shelbyville, and to be in position to reinforce either Buell or Mitchel if needed. Most of the brigade was captured at Murfreesboro July 13, 1862 when Nathan B. Forrest captured the town (see below, Action at, and Surrender of, Murfreesboro, Tennessee). Stanley Matthews commanded Twenty-Third Brigade until it was attached to Fifth Division, Army of the Ohio in August 1862.

Forces at Nashville, Army of the Ohio. When Buell's army left for Savannah, Tennessee, Ebenezer Dumont was assigned command at Nashville March 20, 1862. In early May, however, Dumont left Nashville in command of an expedition to Lebanon, Kentucky, and Stanley Matthews was assigned temporary command of the post. John F. Miller commanded at Nashville from July to August, and he was then assigned command of a newly formed "Light Brigade" (see below). He was succeeded in command at Nashville by Lovell H. Rousseau. George H. Thomas commanded for a time during the Confederate invasion of Kentucky and Tennessee August-October 1862. James S. Negley assumed command September 15. For additional information about Negley's command, see Invasion of Kentucky and Tennessee (E. Kirby Smith and Braxton Bragg).

Light Brigade, Army of the Ohio. August 27, 1862, John F. Miller, commanding at Nashville, was assigned command of a brigade composed of infantry and cavalry and was directed to concentrate his troops at Murfreesboro and protect the lines of communications running out of Nashville south of the Cumberland River. This brigade was known as the Light Brigade, and it was broken up on September 14 when the infantry regiments were assigned to Negley's Eighth Division, Army of the Ohio.

* * * * * * * * *

For the movement to Savannah, Buell took with him George H. Thomas' First Division, Alexander McD. McCook's Second Division, William Nelson's Fourth Division, Thomas L. Crittenden's Fifth Division, and Thomas J. Wood's Sixth Division. The army left Nashville March 15–20, 1862 and moved by way of Franklin to Columbia, where it was delayed until late in the month while building bridges. It then moved on by way of Mount Pleasant, Ashland, and Waynesboro, and Nelson's leading division arrived at Savannah April 5, on the eve of the Battle of Shiloh.

Battle of Shiloh, Tennessee, April 6–7, 1862. Early on the morning of April 6, 1862, Albert Sidney Johnston's Confederate Army of the Mississippi attacked Grant's Army of the Tennessee, which was then encamped near Pittsburg Landing on the Tennessee River, about nine miles above Savannah. Nelson was ordered to march with his division upriver to a point opposite Pittsburg Landing, and at about 5:00 P.M. on the first day of the battle, Jacob Ammen's leading Tenth Brigade crossed the river, joining Grant near the end of the day's battle. The rest of Buell's army, except Thomas' division and one brigade of Wood's division, arrived at Pittsburg Landing in time to take part in the second day's fighting and to aid in defeating Johnston's army. Johnston was killed during the battle of April 6, and he was succeeded in command of the army by Pierre G. T. Beauregard. After stubborn fighting on the morning of April 7, the enemy finally withdrew to Corinth, Mississippi.

For details of the organization of the troops of the Army of the Ohio, and their participation in the Battle of Shiloh, see Battle of Shiloh (or Pittsburg Landing), Tennessee.

Advance of Halleck's Army on Corinth, Mississippi, May 1862. After the Battle of Shiloh, Halleck ordered Pope's Army of the Mississippi to join the Army of the Tennessee and the Army of the Ohio at Pittsburg Landing. Halleck then moved his headquarters from Saint Louis to Pittsburg Landing, where he arrived April 12, 1862 and assumed personal command of the three armies. He then began preparations for an advance on Corinth.

The organization of the divisions of Buell's Army of the Ohio April 30, 1862 was as follows:

First Division, George H. Thomas
   First Brigade, Albin Schoepf
   Second Brigade, Speed S. Fry
   Third Brigade, Robert L. McCook
   Artillery
      4th Battery, Michigan Light Artillery, Alonzo F. Bidwell
      Battery C, 1st Ohio Light Artillery, Dennis Kenny. Jr.
      Battery I, 4th United States Artillery, Oscar A. Mack

Second Division, Alexander McD. McCook
   Fourth Brigade, Lovell H. Rousseau
   Fifth Brigade, Edward N. Kirk
   Sixth Brigade, Richard W. Johnson
   Artillery
      Battery A, Kentucky Light Artillery, David C. Stone
      Battery A, 1st Ohio Light Artillery, Wilbur F. Goodspeed
      Battery B, Pennsylvania Light Artillery, Charles F. Mueller
      Battery H, 5th United States Artillery, William R. Terrill
   Unattached
      3rd Indiana Cavalry, Alfred Gaddis
      2nd Kentucky Cavalry, Buckner Board
      1st Michigan Engineers (detachment), William P. Innes

Third Division, Ormsby M. Mitchel
   Eighth Brigade, John B. Turchin
   Ninth Brigade, Joshua W. Sill
   Seventeenth Brigade, William H. Lytle

Artillery
      5th Battery, Indiana Light Artillery, Peter Simonson
      1st Battery, Michigan Light Artillery, Cyrus O. Loomis
      Battery E, 1st Ohio Light Artillery, Warren P. Edgarton
   Unattached
      4th Ohio Cavalry, John Kennett
      1st Michigan Engineers (two companies), John B. Yates

Note. Third Division was in northern Alabama.

Fourth Division, William Nelson
   Tenth Brigade, Jacob Ammen
   Nineteenth Brigade, William B. Hazen
   Twenty-Second Brigade, Sanders D. Bruce
   Artillery
      7th Battery, Indiana Light Artillery, Samuel J. Harris
      10th Battery, Indiana Light Artillery, Jerome B. Cox
      Battery D, 1st Ohio Light Artillery, Andrew J. Konkle
   Unattached
      2nd Indiana Cavalry, Edward M. McCook
      3rd Indiana Cavalry (one company)

Fifth Division, Thomas L. Crittenden
   Eleventh Brigade, Jeremiah T. Boyle
   Fourteenth Brigade, Horatio P. Van Cleve
   Artillery
      6th Battery, Indiana Light Artillery (Morton Battery), William Mussman
      7th Battery, Michigan Light Artillery, John J. Dennis
      Battery G, 1st Ohio Light Artillery, Joseph Bartlett
      Battery M, 4th United States Artillery, John Mendenhall
      Battery H, 4th United States Artillery, Charles C. Parsons
   Cavalry
      3rd Kentucky Cavalry, James S. Jackson

Sixth Division, Thomas J. Wood
   Fifteenth Brigade, Milo S. Hascall
   Twentieth Brigade, James A. Garfield
   Twenty-First Brigade, George D. Wagner

Seventh Division, George W. Morgan
   Twenty-Fourth Brigade, Samuel P. Carter
   Twenty-Fifth Brigade, James G. Spears
   Twenty-Sixth Brigade, John F. De Courcy

Twenty-Seventh Brigade, Absalom Baird
Artillery
    7th Battery, Michigan Light Artillery. Charles H. Lanphere
    9th Battery, Ohio Light Artillery, Henry S. Wetmore
    1st Battery, Wisconsin Light Artillery, Jacob T. Foster
Unattached
    1st Kentucky Battalion Cavalry, Ruben Munday
    Engineer Company, William F. Patterson

Note. Seventh Division was operating against Cumberland Gap.

Unassigned to Divisions
    18th Kentucky Infantry, William A. Warner
    4th Battery, Indiana Light Artillery, Asahel K. Bush
    11th Battery, Indiana Light Artillery, Arnold Sutermeister
    12th Battery, Indiana Light Artillery, George W. Sterling
    6th Battery, Ohio Light Artillery, Cullen Bradley
    3rd Battery, Wisconsin Light Artillery, Lucius H. Drury

April 30, 1862, Halleck reorganized his command, which was the Army of the Department of the Mississippi, for the advance on Corinth, Mississippi. As reorganized, it consisted of a Right Wing, Center, Left Wing, and Reserve. Thomas was assigned command of the Right Wing, and his First Division was assigned to the Right Wing as Seventh Division under the command of Thomas W. Sherman. The other divisions of Thomas' Right Wing belonged to Grant's Army of the Tennessee. Grant was assigned as second-in-command to Halleck. Buell was assigned command of the Center, which consisted of McCook's Second Division, Nelson's Fourth Division, and Wood's Sixth Division, all of the Army of the Ohio. Crittenden's Fifth Division, Army of the Ohio was nominally assigned to the Reserve, which was commanded by John A. McClernand, but actually it remained in Buell's army and never joined McClernand.

During May 1862, Halleck's army advanced slowly on Corinth, and finally, on the night of May 29–30, Beauregard's Confederate Army of the Mississippi evacuated the town and retreated southward toward Tupelo, Mississippi. Federal troops occupied the town the next day. For details of the organization of Halleck's army and its advance on Corinth, see Department of the Mississippi (Halleck), Troops and Operations in the Department of the Mississippi, and see also Halleck's Advance on Corinth, Mississippi.

June 4, 1862, Buell, with the divisions of Nelson and Crittenden, moved south to Boonville, Mississippi to support Pope's Army of the Mississippi, which was pursuing the enemy toward Tupelo. The next day, Thomas was assigned command of the troops at Corinth, which consisted of McCook's Second Division, Army of the Ohio and John B. S. Todd's Sixth Division of the Army of the Tennessee.

Return of the Army of the Ohio from Corinth, Mississippi to Tennessee, June 11, 1862–August 1862. On June 9, 1862, Buell was directed to return to Tennessee with his Army of the Ohio by marching eastward through northern Alabama toward Chattanooga. He was also ordered to repair the Memphis and Charleston Railroad as he advanced. That same day Thomas W. Sherman's Seventh Division, Right Wing of Halleck's army (Thomas' First Division, Army of the Ohio) was ordered to Corinth to replace McCook's division there.

On June 10, 1862, Halleck revoked the order dividing his army into wings, and on that date Buell resumed command of the Army of the Ohio, and Thomas resumed command of his First Division, Army of the Ohio. Thomas' division, however, was posted in Corinth as a part of the Army of the Tennessee, and it did not rejoin the Army of the Ohio until the end of July 1862.

The troops in Buell's District of the Ohio June 10, 1862 were organized as follows:

Second Division, Alexander McD. McCook
    Fourth Brigade, Lovell H. Rousseau, to July 11, 1862
        Harvey M. Buckley, to August 10, 1862
        Joshua W. Sill
    Fifth Brigade, Frederick S. Stumbaugh
    Sixth Brigade, Richard W. Johnson, to July 24, 1862
        William H. Gibson, to August 10, 1862
        August Willich
    Artillery
        Battery A, Kentucky Light Artillery, David C. Stone
        Battery A, 1st Ohio Light Artillery, Wilbur F. Goodspeed
        Battery H, 5th United States Artillery, William R. Terrill

Third Division, Ormsby M. Mitchel, to July 2, 1862
  William Sooy Smith, to July 11, 1862
  Lovell H. Rousseau
  Eighth Brigade, John B. Turchin, to July 2, 1862
  Ninth Brigade, Joshua W. Sill, to August 10, 1862
    Leonard A. Harris
  Seventeenth Brigade, William H. Lytle
  Artillery
    5th Battery, Indiana Light Artillery, Peter Simonson
    1st Battery, Michigan Light Artillery, Cyrus O. Loomis
    Battery E, 1st Ohio Light Artillery, Warren P. Edgarton
  Cavalry
    4th Ohio Cavalry, John Kennett

Note 1. Mitchel was ordered to Washington, D.C. July 2, 1862, and was later assigned to the Department of the South, where he died October 30, 1862.
Note 2. Eighth Brigade was discontinued July 2, 1862, and the regiments served as unattached Railroad Guards, Army of the Ohio.
Note 3. A Twenty-Eighth Brigade under John C. Starkweather was organized in August 1862 and was assigned to Third Division.

Fourth Division, William Nelson, to August 16, 1862
  Jacob Ammen
  Tenth Brigade, Jacob Ammen, to August 16, 1862
    William Grose
  Nineteenth Brigade, William Grose, to July 10, 1862
    William B. Hazen
  Twenty-Second Brigade, Mahlon D. Manson, to August 16, 1862
    Sanders D. Bruce
  Artillery
    10th Battery, Indiana Light Artillery, Jerome B. Cox
    Battery D, 1st Ohio Light Artillery, Andrew J. Konkle
    Battery M, 4th United States Artillery, John Mendenhall

Fifth Division, Thomas L. Crittenden
  Eleventh Brigade, Jeremiah T. Boyle, to May 27, 1862
    Samuel Beatty
  Fourteenth Brigade, Horatio P. Van Cleve
  Artillery
    Battery B, Pennsylvania Light Artillery, Charles F. Mueller
    3rd Battery, Wisconsin Light Artillery, Lucius H. Drury

Note. Twenty-Third Brigade under Stanley Matthews was assigned to Fifth Division in August 1862.

Sixth Division, Thomas J. Wood
  Fifteenth Brigade, Milo S. Hascall
  Twentieth Brigade, James A. Garfield, to July 7, 1862
    Charles G. Harker
  Twenty-First Brigade, George D. Wagner
  Artillery, Seymour Race
    8th Battery, Indiana Light Artillery, George T. Cochran
    6th Battery, Ohio Light Artillery, Cullen Bradley
    Battery F, 1st Ohio Light Artillery, Daniel T. Cockerill

Seventh Division, George W. Morgan
  Twenty-Fourth Brigade, Samuel P. Carter
  Twenty-Fifth Brigade, James G. Spears
  Twenty-Sixth Brigade, John F. De Courcy
  Twenty-Seventh Brigade, Absalom Baird
  Artillery, Jacob T. Foster
    7th Battery, Michigan Light Artillery, Charles H. Lanphere
    9th Battery, Ohio Light Artillery, Leonard P. Barrows
    1st Battery, Wisconsin Light Artillery, John D. Anderson

Independent Brigades
  Seventh Brigade, James S. Negley
  Twenty-Third Brigade, Henry C. Lester
  Dumont's Brigade, Ebenezer Dumont

Artillery Reserve, James Barnett
  4th Battery, Indiana Light Artillery, Asahel K. Bush
  5th Battery, Michigan Light Artillery, John J. Dennis
  Battery G, 1st Ohio Light Artillery, Joseph Bartlett
  Battery M, 1st Ohio Light Artillery, Frederick Schultz

Cavalry Brigade
  2nd Indiana Cavalry, Edward M. McCook
  3rd Indiana Cavalry (three companies), Robert Klein
  3rd Kentucky Cavalry, James S. Jackson
  3rd Ohio Cavalry, Lewis Zahm

Unattached Infantry (seven regiments)

Unattached Cavalry (five regiments and one troop)

Unattached Artillery
  11th Battery, Indiana Light Artillery, Arnold Sutermeister
  Battery B, Kentucky Light Artillery, John M. Hewett

Battery B, 1st Ohio Light Artillery, William E. Standart

George H. Thomas' First Division was assigned to the Army of the Tennessee April 30, 1862 in preparation for the advance of Halleck's army on Corinth, and it did not rejoin the Army of the Ohio until the end of July. On June 10 it was organized as follows:

First Division, George H. Thomas
First Brigade, Albin Schoepf
Second Brigade, Speed S. Fry
Third Brigade, Robert L. McCook, to August 6, 1862, killed
Ferdinand Van Derveer

The Army of the Ohio began its march toward Chattanooga June 11, 1862. Wood's Sixth Division was sent out first to repair the railroad from Corinth to Decatur, Alabama; McCook's Second Division marched from Corinth; Crittenden's Fifth Division from Baldwyn, Mississippi; and Nelson's Fourth Division from Boonville, Mississippi. All these divisions took the road from Iuka, Mississippi to Decatur, Alabama, and Wood's division moved on to Decatur.

On June 12, 1862, the District of the Ohio was redefined, and Buell was assigned command. From that time on Buell's army was, in fact, the Army of the District of the Ohio, but it continued to be known as the Army of the Ohio. Buell received orders from Halleck, as commander of the Department of the Mississippi, until July 12, when the latter was ordered to Washington, D.C. and was appointed as general in chief. Thereafter, Buell was not subject to the orders of any department commander, but received orders directly from Halleck. Although the Army of the Ohio operated in the Department of the Ohio during E. Kirby Smith's and Braxton Bragg's invasion of Kentucky and Tennessee August 14–October 19, 1862, Buell was not subject to the orders of Horatio G. Wright, the department commander. For additional information, see District of the Ohio, under Miscellaneous Organizations.

Buell's progress was slow as he moved across northern Alabama, and by mid-July his divisions had reached the following places: Crittenden and McCook were at Battle Creek, near Jasper, Tennes-

see, at the lower end of the Sequatchie Valley; Nelson was at Athens, Alabama, guarding the Tennessee and Alabama Railroad from Reynolds (or Reynolds' Station), about nine miles north of Pulaski, Tennessee; Wood was at Mooresville, near Decatur, until July 13; and Thomas was in the rear, on the railroad between Iuka and Decatur. On July 15, Thomas was ordered to rejoin the Army of the Ohio with his division, and by the end of the month he had advanced to Athens and Huntsville. Lovell H. Rousseau, who had succeeded Ormsby M. Mitchel in command of Third Division in northern Alabama July 2, had his troops on the Nashville and Decatur Railroad (Tennessee and Alabama Railroad).

Action at, and Surrender of, Murfreesboro, Tennessee, July 13, 1862.. On March 8, 1862, the Twenty-Third Brigade, Army of the Ohio was organized under William W. Duffield and sent to Murfreesboro to protect the road from LaVergne to Shelbyville. Duffield's command consisted of his own 9th Michigan, commanded by John G. Parkhurst; Henry C. Lester's 3rd Minnesota; two sections of John M. Hewett's Battery B, Kentucky Light Artillery; and James J. Seibert's cavalry command, consisting of the 3rd Battalion of the 7th Pennsylvania Cavalry and the 1st Squadron of the 4th Kentucky Cavalry under Levi Chilson.

On May 9, 1862, Duffield was sent to Louisville to command all troops in the state of Kentucky (except Seventh Division at Cumberland Gap), and Lester assumed command of Twenty-Third Brigade. On June 26, Lester divided his command and established his troops in three rather widely separated camps in and about the town. The 3rd Minnesota and Hewett's battery were sent out to a camp about one and one-half miles north of Murfreesboro on the east side of Stones River. Five companies of the 9th Michigan and Levi Chilson's squadron of the 4th Kentucky Cavalry occupied the old camp about three-fourths of a mile east of Murfreesboro on the Liberty Pike. One company of the 9th Michigan held the court house, and other troops occupied the jail, inn, and other buildings in the central part of town. Three companies of the 9th Michigan had been sent to Tullahoma.

On the afternoon of July 11, Duffield, who had been relieved from duty in Kentucky, returned to

Murfreesboro. With him came Thomas T. Crittenden, who had been assigned as commander of the troops at Murfreesboro July 8. Neither assumed command that day, but on July 12, Crittenden assumed command of the post, with headquarters in the town, and Duffield assumed command of Twenty-Third Brigade, with his headquarters with the 9th Michigan. Lester resumed command of the 3rd Minnesota.

Meantime, Nathan B. Forrest had been assigned command of a new cavalry brigade, which he organized at Chattanooga. This consisted of John A. Wharton's Texas Rangers (8th Texas Cavalry); Winburn J. Lawton's 2nd Georgia Cavalry; and the 2nd Georgia Battalion, commanded by James J. Morrison.

From his scouts, Forrest had learned of the Federal regiments at Murfreesboro, and on July 9 he left Chattanooga to attempt the capture of these troops. On the night of July 11, he was joined by reinforcements at McMinnville, and he then marched toward Murfreesboro. He arrived near the town at 4:30 A.M. July 13, and immediately attacked. The action that followed developed into three separate contests.

Wharton charged into the town with two companies of his Texas Rangers, but this force was too small to expel the Federal troops. Morrison was then ordered up with a portion of his command to storm the court house, and the rest of the Texas Rangers came up to attack the buildings occupied by troops near the center of the town. After about two or three hours, the troops in the court house surrendered to Morrison, and the private buildings were soon cleared. Crittenden and his staff also surrendered.

A force of Texas Rangers was sent back to attack the camp of the 9th Michigan east of town, but the force was too small, and several attacks were repulsed. Duffield was wounded during the fighting, but Parkhust continued to resist until 11:30 A.M., and then, when he had received no support, he surrendered.

Forrest also sent a column to attack the camp of the 3rd Minnesota and the artillery. They resisted for several hours, while repulsing three attacks, but finally Lester surrendered at 3:30 P.M.

Forrest was reported to have captured about 1,700 men, four guns, 600 horses and mules, and large quantities of stores. In addition he destroyed great amounts of supplies that he was unable to carry away.

* * * * * * * * * *

On July 17, 1862, Nelson's division was ordered to move by rail from Reynolds on the Tennessee and Alabama Railroad to Murfreesboro, where he arrived a short time later and occupied the town. On July 13, Wood was also ordered from near Decatur, Alabama toward Murfreesboro. Wood advanced with his division through Stevenson, Huntsville, and Fayetteville, and arrived at Shelbyville July 16. The division remained there for a few days and then continued on through Winchester to Dechard, where it arrived July 27. It remained there until mid-August.

On July 27, Nelson was ordered to leave one brigade and a battery at Murfreesboro and to proceed with the rest of his Fourth Division to McMinnville, where he arrived August 5. Left at Murfreesboro were William B. Hazen's Nineteenth Brigade, Fourth Division and Jerome B. Cox's 10th Battery, Indiana Light Artillery.

On July 24, after the departure of Nelson's division for Murfreesboro, Richard W. Johnson was assigned command of a cavalry brigade on the line of the Tennessee and Alabama Railroad between Franklin and Reynolds, Tennessee. This brigade consisted of the 2nd Indiana Cavalry and the 2nd Kentucky Cavalry, and it was to be used against any enemy force in the vicinity.

Action on the Hartsville Road, near Gallatin, Tennessee, August 21, 1862. After his raid on Murfreesboro, Forrest continued his raids on Federal communications south of Nashville, while John H. Morgan was conducting raids on the Louisville and Nashville Railroad. Finally, as a result of this activity, Buell was compelled to organize his cavalry into larger units to provide for a more effective defense against these raiders. On August 18, Buell assigned Johnson to the command of a cavalry brigade (to be formed from the 2nd, 4th, and 5th Kentucky and 7th Pennsylvania cavalry) and ordered him to make his rendezvous at Murfreesboro. His responsibility was to protect the lines of communication with Nashville, protect Nashville, and destroy the enemy cavalry and guerrilla bands in the area. Johnson was also informed that Hazen's Nineteenth Brigade, Fourth Division and Cox's 10th Battery, Indiana Light Artillery (which had been left at Murfreesboro by Nelson when his division advanced to McMinnville) were assigned to his command.

On August 11, Buell sent Johnson out from McMinnville against Morgan, who was then operating around Gallatin, Tennessee. Johnson took with him detachments from Edward M. McCook's 2nd Indiana Cavalry (commanded by Robert R. Stewart during the absence of McCook on special duty), George C. Wynkoop's 7th Pennsylvania Cavalry, Levi Chilson's 4th Kentucky Cavalry, and David R. Haggard's 5th Kentucky Cavalry (commanded by Thomas C. Winfrey during the temporary absence of Haggard). Johnson also took with him three infantry regiments and a battery, but these were soon sent back to McMinnville.

Johnson marched by way of Liberty to Caney Fork, where Morgan had been reported some time earlier. Upon arrival there he learned that Morgan had gone to Kentucky, and he returned to Liberty and then marched to Cookville to await Morgan's return. At Cookville Johnson heard that Morgan was encamped near Hartsville, but upon arriving there he found that Morgan had gone to Gallatin. At Hartsville Johnson also heard that Forrest was approaching his rear, and he decided to move to Gallatin and join the Federal force there before Forrest arrived. On approaching Gallatin, however, Johnson found that Morgan had captured the town and its garrison.

Johnson then ordered an immediate attack on Morgan. Stewart and Winfrey led the attack, and Wynkoop and Chilson brought up their commands and joined in the action. A short time later, however, some confusion began to develop in Johnson's ranks, and the 5th Kentucky broke and fled in disorder, carrying other troops with them. Johnson ordered a withdrawal and attempted to form a second line. This line also broke and fled, and the troopers fell back about three miles and once more attempted to hold their position. Finally, Johnson led his command toward Cairo on the Cumberland River, closely followed by the enemy. He succeeded in forming a line with the 2nd Indiana and 5th Kentucky, but once again the 5th Kentucky fled.

Johnson then decided to surrender, but before he did, Stewart led a part of the 2nd Indiana from the field, and Wynkoop broke through the enemy troops and also escaped. Johnson surrendered the rest of his command to Morgan, and the survivors made their way to Nashville.

Confederate Invasion of Kentucky and Tennessee, August 1862–October 1862. Meantime, while the Army of the Ohio was moving eastward across northern Alabama, the enemy had also become active. On June 27, 1862, Braxton Bragg relieved Beauregard in command of the Confederate Army of the Mississippi, and July 21 he ordered the transfer of the army to Chattanooga, Tennessee. Bragg, in person, arrived at Chattanooga July 30, and with E. Kirby Smith, commander of the Confederate forces in East Tennessee, prepared plans for an invasion of Kentucky and Tennessee.

An organizational change was made August 16, when the Department of the Ohio was re-created, and Horatio G. Wright was assigned command.

Also on August 16, Nelson was relieved from command of his Fourth Division and was ordered to Kentucky to take charge of affairs in the state and to organize the troops that were assembling there for the defense of the state against an army commanded by E. Kirby Smith, which had left Knoxville for Kentucky August 14. Jacob Ammen assumed temporary command of Nelson's division, which was at McMinnville at that time.

Thomas was relieved temporarily from command of his division, and was ordered to McMinnville, where, on August 19, he assumed command of Ammen's Fourth Division and Wood's Sixth Division, which had moved to McMinnville. Albin Schoepf assumed temporary command of Thomas' First Division.

Bragg's army arrived at Chattanooga during the first two weeks of August, and on August 19, some troops crossed to the north side of the Tennessee River. When this movement was reported to Buell, he concentrated the Army of the Ohio at Murfreesboro and then moved on to Nashville.

On August 28, Bragg completed the crossing of the Tennessee River and began his march up the Sequatchie Valley into Tennessee. On September 5, the same day that Buell arrived at Murfreesboro, Bragg's troops marched into Sparta, Tennessee.

Meantime, in response to a request for help from Buell, Grant had sent three divisions from William S. Rosecrans' Army of the Mississippi to Tennessee. Jefferson C. Davis' Fourth Division, under the command of Robert B. Mitchell, arrived at Murfreesboro September 1, and Eleazer A. Paine's First Division, under John M. Palmer, arrived at Nashville September 12. Philip H. Sheridan, with the infantry of Gordon Granger's Fifth Division (the Pea Ridge Brigade) and his own 2nd Michigan Cavalry, arrived at Louisville September 14, but did not join Buell's army until the end of the month.

On September 7, Thomas was assigned command at Nashville, and the troops there consisted of his own First Division, Army of the Ohio; Palmer's First Division, Army of the Mississippi; and the forces at Nashville under James S. Negley. Negley's command was organized September 14 as Eighth Division, Army of the Ohio. The troops at Nashville then consisted of the following:

Eighth Division, James S. Negley
   Seventh Brigade, John F. Miller
   Twenty-Ninth Brigade, Timothy R. Stanley

Note 1. Eighth Division remained at Nashville as a part of the garrison during Bragg's invasion of Kentucky.
Note 2. Seventh Brigade and Twenty-Ninth Brigade were organized from unattached Railroad Guards, Army of the Ohio.

Thirteenth Division, Army of the Ohio, John M. Palmer
   First Brigade, George W. Roberts
   Second Brigade, James D. Morgan

Note 1. Thirteenth Division, Army of the Ohio was organized from First Division, Army of the Mississippi in September 1862.
Note 2. Palmer's division remained at Nashville during Bragg's invasion of Kentucky.

After thus providing for the safety of Nashville, Buell, with the rest of the Army of the Ohio and Mitchel's Fourth Division, Army of the Mississippi, marched on toward Bowling Green, Kentucky.

Meantime, Bragg's army had continued its march northward from Sparta, through Carthage in Tennessee and Tompkinsville and Glasgow in Kentucky, and September 14–16 arrived before the Union fortifications at Munfordville, Kentucky. When John T. Wilder, who commanded the troops

and defenses at Munfordville, learned that he was confronted by Bragg's entire army, he realized that further resistance was futile, and he surrendered the post September 17. As a result, Bragg had gained a position that placed his army on the road between Buell's army and Louisville. For additional information, see Invasion of Kentucky and Tennessee (E. Kirby Smith and Braxton Bragg).

On September 15, as Bragg's army was arriving at Munfordville, Negley was assigned command at Nashville, and Thomas was ordered to march with his First Division and join the rest of the army, which had gone on ahead. He came up with Buell September 20 at Prewitt's Knob, south of Munfordville.

Bragg remained near Munfordville until Buell approached from the south, and then, beginning on September 19, he marched to the northeast toward Bardstown. In so doing, he turned away from the road to Louisville and left it open for the passage of Buell's army. By September 29, the Army of the Ohio had arrived safely at Louisville.

On August 30, E. Kirby Smith's army, which had arrived in Kentucky from East Tennessee, had defeated and scattered William Nelson's small Army of Kentucky at Richmond. The remnants of Nelson's command retreated to Louisville, which was then under the command of Charles C. Gilbert. Nelson relieved Gilbert and immediately began the organization of the defenses of the city. When Buell arrived there with his army at the end of September, Nelson had assembled about forty regiments, largely composed of new troops, but on September 29, Nelson was killed by Brigadier General Jefferson C. Davis.

Battle of Perryville, Kentucky, October 8, 1862. Buell at once began the reorganization of the army in preparation for an offensive movement against the forces of Bragg and Kirby Smith. New regiments were incorporated into veteran divisions, and two new divisions were organized as divisions of the Army of the Ohio. In addition, the three divisions of the Army of the Mississippi were organized into divisions of the Army of the Ohio. One of these, Sheridan's Eleventh Division, also consisted of some new regiments.

The new divisions were organized as follows:

Ninth Division, Robert B. Mitchell
    Thirtieth Brigade, Michael Gooding
    Thirty-First Brigade, William P. Carlin
    Thirty-Second Brigade, William W. Caldwell

Note 1. Oscar F. Pinney's 5th Battery, Wisconsin Light Artillery was attached to Thirtieth Brigade; William A. Hotchkiss' 2nd Battery, Minnesota Light Artillery to Thirty-First Brigade; and Stephen J. Carpenter's 8th Battery, Wisconsin Light Artillery to Thirty-Second Brigade.
Note 2. Ninth Division was organized from Jefferson C. Davis' Fourth Division, Army of the Mississippi.

Tenth Division, James S. Jackson
    Thirty-Third Brigade, William R. Terrill
    Thirty-Fourth Brigade, George Webster

Note 1. Charles C. Parson's improvised battery was attached to Thirty-Third Brigade, and Samuel J. Harris' 19th Battery, Indiana Light Artillery was attached to Thirty-Fourth Brigade.
Note 2. Tenth Division was organized from new regiments.

Eleventh Division, Philip H. Sheridan
    Thirty-Fifth Brigade, Bernard Laiboldt
    Thirty-Sixth Brigade, Daniel McCook
    Thirty-Seventh Brigade, Nicholas Greusel
    Artillery
        Battery I, 2nd Illinois Light Artillery, Charles M. Barnett
        Battery G, 1st Missouri Light Artillery, Henry Hescock

Note. Eleventh Division was organized from the infantry of Gordon Granger's Fifth Division, Army of the Mississippi and new regiments.

Twelfth Division, Ebenezer Dumont
    Thirty-Eighth Brigade, Marshal W. Chapin
    Thirty-Ninth Brigade, George T. Limberg
    Fortieth Brigade, Abram O. Miller
    Ward's Brigade, William T. Ward
    Artillery
        Stokes' Battery, Illinois Light Artillery, James H. Stokes
        13th Battery, Indiana Light Artillery, Benjamin S. Nicklin
        18th Battery, Indiana Light Artillery, Eli Lilly

Note 1. All brigades except Ward's were organized from new regiments.
Note 2. In the reorganization of September 29, 1862, Twelfth Division was not assigned to an army corps. During the Perryville Campaign, it operated toward

Frankfort, Kentucky with Joshua W. Sill's Second Division of McCook's First Corps.
Note 3. Thirty-Eighth Brigade, then under the command of Robert S. Granger, was ordered to take post at Bowling Green, Kentucky October 23, 1862.

Thirteenth Division, John M. Palmer
    First Brigade, George W. Roberts
    Second Brigade, James D. Morgan

Note 1. Yates V. Beebe's 10th Battery, Wisconsin Light Artillery was attached to First Brigade, and Charles Houghtaling's Battery C, 1st Illinois Light Artillery was attached to Second Brigade.
Note 2. Thirteenth Division was organized from First Division, Army of the Mississippi, formerly commanded by Eleazer A. Paine. This division remained at Nashville with Negley's Eighth Division during the Perryville Campaign.

In addition to the new infantry divisions, a Cavalry Division, Army of the Ohio was organized September 5, 1862 and was assigned to John Kennett. It was organized as follows:

Cavalry Division, John Kennett
    First Brigade, Edward M. McCook
    Second Brigade, Lewis Zahm
    Third Brigade, Ebenezer Gay

At Louisville on September 29, 1862, Buell announced the reorganization of the Army of the Ohio into three army corps as follows:

First Corps, Alexander McD. McCook
    Third Division, Lovell H. Rousseau
    Tenth Division, James S. Jackson
    Second Division, Joshua W. Sill

Second Corps, Thomas L. Crittenden
    Fourth Division, William Sooy Smith
    Fifth Division, Horatio P. VanCleve
    Sixth Division, Thomas J. Wood

Third Corps, Charles C. Gilbert
    First Division, Albin Schoepf
    Ninth Division, Robert B. Mitchell
    Eleventh Division, Philip H. Sheridan

For additional information about this reorganization, see First Corps, Second Corps, and Third Corps, Army of the Ohio (Buell), and see also Invasion of Kentucky and Tennessee (E. Kirby Smith and Braxton Bragg), Battle of Perryville (or Chaplin Hills), Kentucky.

October 1, 1862, George H. Thomas was announced as second-in-command of the Army of the Ohio, under Buell. He served in this capacity during the Perryville Campaign, and accompanied Crittenden's corps at that time.

On October 1, the reorganized Army of the Ohio began its advance against the armies of Smith and Bragg. Sill's division of McCook's corps and Dumont's unattached division marched toward Frankfort, Kentucky, and Buell, with the rest of the army, moved out toward Bragg's army at Bardstown. Leonidas Polk, then in temporary command of the Confederate forces at Bardstown, withdrew to Perryville, Kentucky, closely followed by the corps of Gilbert, McCook, and Crittenden.

Gilbert arrived in front of Perryville on the evening of October 7, and most troops of the other two corps were up and in position by about noon the next day. During the morning of October 8, a part of Gilbert's corps was engaged on the right of Buell's line, and at 2:00 P.M. Bragg launched a vigorous attack on McCook's corps, on the left of the line, and drove it back for about a mile before darkness ended the fighting.

* * * * * * * * * *

Bragg withdrew that night and soon joined E. Kirby Smith's army, and then the combined forces began the march back toward East Tennessee. Buell followed as far as Crab Orchard and London in Kentucky, and then turned back and marched to Bowling Green and Glasgow, where he arrived at the end of October. For additional information about the Battle of Perryville and Buell's pursuit, see Invasion of Kentucky and Tennessee (E. Kirby Smith and Braxton Bragg).

The Department of the Cumberland was re-created October 24, 1862, and William S. Rosecrans was assigned command. The troops of the Army of the Ohio were thus transferred to the Department of the Cumberland and were officially designated as Fourteenth Corps, Department of the Cumberland. From that time, however, they were commonly known as the Army of the Cumberland. For further information, see Army of the Cumberland, October 24, 1862–November 14, 1862.

ARMY OF THE OHIO (BURNSIDE) APRIL 11, 1863– APRIL 4, 1864

Following the Battle of Fredericksburg, Virginia in December 1862, Ninth Corps remained with the Army of the Potomac near Falmouth, Virginia until February 4, 1863. It then embarked at Fort Monroe and, under the command of William F. Smith, moved to Newport News, Virginia.

On March 16, 1863, Ambrose E. Burnside, then in Washington, D.C., was ordered to resume command of Ninth Corps, and he also was directed to go west and relieve Horatio G. Wright in command of the Department of the Ohio. He was further instructed to take with him two divisions of Ninth Corps to reinforce the troops in his new command.

Burnside assumed command of Ninth Corps March 17, and two days later he ordered John G. Parke to Newport News to take command of Orlando B. Willcox's First Division and Samuel D. Sturgis' Second Division of Ninth Corps and move with them to the Department of the Ohio. During the period March 19–30, the two divisions were transferred to Cincinnati, Ohio, and from there to Kentucky. George W. Getty's Third Division, Ninth Corps was ordered to Suffolk, Virginia, and it did not again join Ninth Corps.

At the time of their transfer to Kentucky, the two divisions of Ninth Corps were organized as follows:

First Division, Orlando B. Willcox
    First Brigade, David Morrison
    Second Brigade, Benjamin C. Christ
    Third Brigade, Daniel Leasure

Second Division, Samuel D. Sturgis
    First Brigade, James Nagle
    Second Brigade, Edward Ferrero

Burnside arrived at Cincinnati and assumed command of the Department of the Ohio March 25, 1863. Parke, who had directed the transfer of Ninth Corps from Virginia to Cincinnati, reported to Burnside's headquarters at Cincinnati March 28 and was assigned to duty in that city.

On April 10, Willcox assumed command of the District of Central Kentucky, relieving Quincy A.

Gillmore, and Thomas Welsh assumed command of First Division, Ninth Corps. During April 1863 both divisions of Ninth Corps were in the District of Central Kentucky, with Welsh's First Division at Columbia and Samuel D. Sturgis' Second Division at Winchester. Thus, as commander of the District of Central Kentucky, Willcox was in command of Ninth Corps.

In April 1863 Samuel P. Carter was in command of a division in the District of Central Kentucky, and on April 29, the division was reorganized and designated as Fourth Division, Ninth Corps. It was organized as follows:

Fourth Division, Ninth Corps, Samuel P. Carter
  First Brigade, James W. Reilly
  Second Brigade, Benjamin P. Runkle
  Third Brigade, August V. Kautz

On April 11, Burnside designated the troops serving in the Department of the Ohio as the Army of the Ohio. These included the two divisions of Ninth Corps and the numerous regiments and batteries that were serving at the various posts in Kentucky. Then, on April 27, Burnside designated the troops serving in Kentucky, except those belonging to Ninth Corps, as Twenty-Third Corps, Army of the Ohio, and he assigned George L. Hartsuff to command the corps. Twenty-Third Corps was not organized until May 22, and at that time Hartsuff assumed command. Thus, Burnside's Army of the Ohio consisted of Ninth Corps and Twenty-Third Corps.

Upon being sent to the Department of the Ohio, Burnside was instructed to move as soon as possible with an army to occupy East Tennessee and provide protection for the inhabitants of the area, who were staunchly loyal to the United States. There were many important affairs in the department that required his attention after he assumed command, and before he could begin his advance toward Knoxville, Ninth Corps was ordered to Vicksburg, Mississippi to reinforce Ulysses S. Grant's army, which was attempting to capture the city.

There were some changes in command in Ninth Corps before it departed for Vicksburg. On May 21, John F. Hartranft relieved Sturgis in command of Second Division, and on June 5, Hartranft was relieved by Robert B. Potter, who commanded the division at Vicksburg; Simon G. Griffin relieved James Nagle in command of First Brigade, Second Division May 21; and on June 5, Parke resumed command of Ninth Corps. On June 3, Samuel P. Carter's Fourth Division, Ninth Corps (also called Fourth Corps, District of Central Kentucky) was assigned to Twenty-Third Corps.

On June 4, Sturgis was assigned command of all troops within the limits of the District of Central Tennessee, including Carter's division, relieving Willcox, who was sent to Indianapolis, Indiana to assume command of the District of Indiana, Department of the Ohio.

During the period June 3–30, Parke moved his Ninth Corps from Kentucky to Vicksburg. With the departure of Ninth Corps, the Army of the Ohio consisted only of Twenty-Third Corps, which, at the end of June 1863, was organized as follows:

TWENTY-THIRD CORPS, George L. Hartsuff

First Division, Samuel D. Sturgis
  First Brigade, Samuel P. Carter
  Second Brigade, Samuel A. Gilbert
  Third Brigade, August V. Kautz
  Unassigned
    2nd Maryland, Thomas B. Allard
    21st Massachusetts, George P. Hawkes
    7th Ohio Cavalry, Israel Garrard
    Battery D, 1st Rhode Island Light Artillery, William W. Buckley

Note. R. Clay Crawford's 1st Battery, East Tennessee Light Artillery was attached to First Brigade; Wilder's Battery, Indiana Light Artillery, commanded by Casper W. McLaughlin, was attached to Second Brigade; and Jesse S. Law's Mountain Howitzer Battery was attached to Third Brigade.

Second Division, Jeremiah T. Boyle
  First Brigade, James M. Shackelford
  Munfordville, Kentucky, Charles D. Pennebaker
  Bowling Green, Kentucky, Cicero Maxwell
  Lebanon, Kentucky, Silas A. Strickland, as senior officer

Third Division, Henry M. Judah
  First Brigade, Mahlon D. Manson
  Second Brigade, Edward H. Hobson
  Third Brigade, Joseph A. Cooper

Note. Andrew M. Wood's Elgin Battery (also called Renwick's Battery), Illinois Light Artillery and Edward

C. Henshaw's Battery, Illinois Light Artillery were attached to First Brigade; Joseph A. Sims' 24th Battery, Indiana Light Artillery was attached to Second Brigade. A detachment manning two pieces of artillery, commanded by Judge R. Clingan, was attached to Third Brigade.

Fourth Division, Julius White
   First Brigade, Daniel Cameron
   Second Brigade, Samuel R. Mott

Note. John C. Phillips' Battery M (2nd Section), 2nd Illinois Light Artillery and William C. G. L. Stevenson's Battery M (1st Section), 2nd Illinois Light Artillery were attached to First Brigade; and John C. H. Von Sehlen's 15th Battery, Indiana Light Artillery and Joseph C. Shields' 19th Battery, Ohio Light Artillery were attached to Second Brigade.

Morgan's Raid into Indiana and Kentucky, July 2, 1863–July 26, 1863. In June 1863, Burnside prepared for a second effort to move into East Tennessee with the available troops of Twenty-Third Corps, but once again he was diverted from that purpose when John H. Morgan moved forward into Kentucky from Tennessee on a raid into Indiana and Ohio. On July 2, Morgan's cavalry division crossed the Cumberland River at Burkesville, Kentucky, moved northward through Kentucky, crossed the Ohio River at Brandenburg, Kentucky, and then moved northward into Indiana. Burnside immediately sent his available cavalry and some infantry in pursuit. The cavalry, under the command of Edward H. Hobson, followed Morgan into Indiana, then eastward across the southern part of the state, and into Ohio. There other forces joined in the chase, and Morgan and the remnants of his command were finally captured near New Lisbon, Ohio July 26. Then all Federal forces that had joined in the pursuit of Morgan returned to their proper commands in Kentucky. For details, see Morgan's Raid into Indiana and Ohio.

East Tennessee Campaign, August 16, 1863–October 19, 1863. Finally, on August 17, 1863, after all preparations had been completed, Burnside began his long-delayed advance toward East Tennessee with three divisions of George L. Hartsuff's Twenty-Third Corps. With little opposition, he occupied Knoxville September 2 and captured the Confederate forces at Cumberland Gap September 9. Burnside's command was reinforced in late September when Potter's Ninth Corps, which had returned to Kentucky from Vicksburg in mid-August, arrived in East Tennessee. Burnside was further reinforced October 4, when Orlando B. Willcox arrived with a new division consisting of four Indiana regiments and an Ohio battery. By mid-October Burnside's forces had established Federal control over the greater part of East Tennessee. For details, see East Tennessee Campaign (Burnside).

Knoxville, Tennessee Campaign, November 4, 1863–December 23, 1863. On November 4, 1863, James Longstreet's Confederate corps was detached from Braxton Bragg's Army of Tennessee, which was then besieging Chattanooga, and was sent into East Tennessee in an attempt to drive Burnside's army from Knoxville and recover that part of the state for the Confederacy.

Longstreet moved with his command to Sweet Water, Tennessee, and from there he advanced toward Knoxville on November 13. Burnside, who did not intend to make a stand south of the city, withdrew Potter's Ninth Corps and Marshal W. Chapin's Second Brigade of Julius White's Second Division, Twenty-Third Corps from their positions along the Tennessee River and started them toward Knoxville. They fought a delaying action at Campbell's Station November 16, and then retired with the rest of the army into the defenses of Knoxville.

Longstreet's troops appeared in front of the defenses November 18, and soon began the siege of the city. On the morning of November 29, the enemy launched an assault on Fort Sanders, but it was quickly repulsed. Longstreet made no further attack, and on the afternoon of December 5, he abandoned the siege and withdrew his command toward Rogersville in East Tennessee. Burnside pursued for a time, and then directed his troops to go into camp.

During the operations in East Tennessee, Burnside was reinforced by troops from the Army of the Cumberland. On November 27, a short time after the Union victory at Missionary Ridge, Ulysses S. Grant ordered Gordon Granger to move from Chattanooga with Philip H. Sheridan's Second Division and Thomas J. Wood's Third Division of his Fourth Corps, Army of the Cumberland and go to the relief of Burnside at Knoxville. The next day Grant ordered William T. Sherman, who was then leading the forces pursuing Bragg's defeated army toward Dalton, Georgia, to march to Knoxville with the following troops: Eleventh Corps, Army of the Cumberland; Second Division, Fourteenth Corps, Army of the Cumberland; a part of Fifteenth Corps, Army of the Tennessee; and Eli Long's Second Brigade, Second Cavalry Division, Army of the Cumberland.

Granger's two divisions joined Sherman's column en route, and they arrived at Maryville, Tennessee on December 5. There Sherman learned that Longstreet had abandoned the siege of Knoxville, and had moved off to the east of the city. Sherman then ordered Granger to continue on with his corps to Knoxville and report to Burnside, but he marched back to Chattanooga with the rest of his command. James G. Spears' East Tennessee Brigade (officially Second Brigade, Second Division, Fourteenth Corps) was placed under Granger's orders as he moved toward Knoxville, and it too remained in East Tennessee. For additional information, see Relief of Knoxville, Tennessee (William T. Sherman).

A cavalry reinforcement was also sent to Burnside. On November 27, Washington L. Elliott, commanding the Cavalry Corps, Army of the Cumberland, was ordered to move eastward from Murfreesboro with Archibald P. Campbell's First Brigade and Oscar H. La Grange's Second Brigade of Edward M. McCook's First Cavalry Division. Eli Lilly's 18th Battery, Indiana Light Artillery also accompanied the column. Elliott arrived at Kingston, Tennessee December 11, then moved on to Knoxville. McCook's division remained in East Tennessee during the winter of 1863–1864.

John G. Foster relieved Burnside in command of the Department of the Ohio December 11, 1863.

Winter of 1863–1864. At the end of December 1863, when active operations had virtually ended for the season, the Army of the Ohio and attached troops were in camp in East Tennessee as follows: Jacob D. Cox, who had assumed command of Twenty-Third Corps December 21, with Milo S. Hascall's Third Division and Chapin's Second Brigade of Mahlon D. Manson's Second Division, was at Strawberry Plains; and Samuel R. Mott's First Brigade, Second Division was at Mossy Creek. Potter's Ninth Corps and Granger's Fourth Corps

were at Blain's Cross Roads; Willcox's Left Wing Forces in East Tennessee was near Maynardville; and Sturgis, with his Cavalry Corps, Army of the Ohio and McCook's First Cavalry Division, Army of the Cumberland, was at Mossy Creek and Talbott's Station.

Operations about Dandridge, Tennessee, January 16–17, 1864. By early January 1864, Foster's army in East Tennessee had exhausted all grain and forage for a distance of twenty miles in all directions, and he then decided to move a part of his command to Dandridge to occupy the country south of the French Broad River, where grain and forage were reported to be abundant.

On January 14, Frank Wolford's First Cavalry Division and Israel Garrard's Second Division of the Cavalry Corps, Army of the Ohio moved from Mossy Creek to Dandridge, and the next day Granger's Fourth Corps and Cox's Twenty-Third Corps, both under the direction of John G. Parke, started toward Dandridge. Granger, with his Fourth Corps, and Cox, with Chapin's Second Brigade of Manson's Second Division, arrived at Dandridge January 15, and Daniel Cameron's Second Brigade of Hascall's Third Division arrived there the next day. Mott's First Brigade, Second Division marched to Strawberry Plains and remained there until January 20.

Potter's Ninth Corps remained at Blain's Cross Roads until January 16, then marched to Strawberry Plains, eight miles in the direction of Knoxville.

On January 16, the enemy strongly attacked Wolford's and Garrard's cavalry and drove them back, and McCook's cavalry division was ordered up in support. Campbell was in command of the division that day, because of the illness of McCook, and Thomas J. Jordan was in command of Campbell's First Brigade. La Grange was in command of First Brigade of the division.

The entire command was strongly attacked again January 17, and the fighting continued until dark, when the enemy advance was finally halted. At 10:00 that night, Elliott, with McCook's division, marched toward New Market. He crossed the Holston River at McKinney's Ford and moved on to Strawberry Plains the next day. Garrard and Wolford fell back to Mossy Creek that night, and then moved to Strawberry Plains January 18.

The infantry that had arrived at Dandridge were under orders to cross the French Broad River and occupy the country to the south, but when the cavalry was attacked, and when problems arose in attempting to cross the river, Parke decided to withdraw to Strawberry Plains. The movement was started on the night of January 17, and was completed by January 19.

On January 18, Potter departed on leave of absence for thirty days, and Willcox was assigned command of Ninth Corps. Second Division, Ninth Corps was temporarily attached to Edward Ferrero's First Division.

* * * * * * * * *

After the failure at Dandridge, Foster ordered all of his cavalry to march back through Knoxville and then out on the road to Sevierville, and he also directed Parke to move with the infantry at Strawberry Plains and follow the cavalry toward Sevierville. Elliott, with McCook's cavalry division, left Strawberry Plains January 19, 1864 and marched to Knoxville, then twelve miles out on the road to Sevierville. Sturgis, who had assumed command of the Cavalry Corps, Army of the Ohio December 15, moved with the divisions of Wolford and Garrard to Knoxville that same day. Elliott's cavalry moved to Sevierville on January 20, and two days later moved on to Fair Garden.

On January 20, Granger's Fourth Corps was ordered to march by way of Knoxville to Sevierville. The next day Granger passed through Knoxville and then moved out on the Sevierville road. Before Granger had moved more than five miles beyond the Holston River, however, Foster learned from the cavalry that the reports of large quantities of grain and forage south of the French Broad River had been greatly exaggerated, and that there was barely enough to support the cavalry. This report, combined with the fact that Foster was apprehensive of an attack by Longstreet, caused Foster to change his plans.

Foster decided to place Twenty-Third Corps in position around Knoxville, and to send Willcox, who had assumed command of Ninth Corps January 19, to a position a few miles south of the town, where it would be within supporting distance. He also ordered one division of Fourth Corps to guard the railroad south of Knoxville, including Loudon and Kingston, and he directed the other division to move to Maryville to collect grain and forage from the surrounding country. He also ordered the cavalry to hold the country as far up the French Broad River as possible and to obtain their subsistence there.

In conforming with this plan, Manson's Second Division of Twenty-Third Corps marched from Strawberry Plains January 20 and moved slowly toward Knoxville, arriving there January 24. Hascall's Third Division of Twenty-Third Corps followed from Strawberry Plains, and encamped near Knoxville until the end of the month.

On January 22, Ninth Corps moved to its assigned position and formed in line of battle about three miles from Knoxville. It remained there until January 24, when the enemy which had been threatening Knoxville retired to Strawberry Plains, and the corps then moved to Erin's Station, about five and one-half miles southwest of Knoxville.

On January 23, two brigades of Sheridan's Second Division, Fourth Corps were ordered to Loudon, and one brigade was sent to Kingston. Also on January 23, two brigades of Wood's Third Division, Fourth Corps were sent to Maryville, and one brigade to Lenoir's Station.

Meantime, on January 21, there were two changes in the command arrangement of Foster's army. Elliott was relieved from duty in the Department of the Ohio that day, and he was ordered to report in person to George H. Thomas, commanding the Army of the Cumberland. McCook's First Cavalry Division, Army of the Cumberland remained in East Tennessee under the direction of Sturgis. Spears' East Tennessee Brigade, which had been under Granger's orders since it arrived in East Tennessee, was assigned to Twenty-Third Corps January 21.

Engagement near Fair Garden, Tennessee, January 26–27, 1864. On July 26, 1864, Sturgis' cavalry was in position in the general vicinity of Sevierville. Garrard's division was picketing all fords and ferries on the French Broad River below Tom Evans' Ford. Wolford's division was posted on the Flat Creek road near the Fowler house, about six miles from Sevierville. Campbell's brigade of McCook's division was in position on the main road from

Sevierville to Newport, four miles east of Sevierville. La Grange's brigade of McCook's division was on the same road, in rear of Campbell and about a mile and a half from Sevierville.

William T. Martin's Confederate Cavalry Corps crossed the French Broad River at Swann's Island, and in the afternoon advanced against the Union cavalry. Frank C. Armstrong's cavalry division attacked Wolford's division on the Flat Creek road and drove it back to within about two miles of Sevierville. John T. Morgan's cavalry division advanced from the direction of Fair Garden and attacked Campbell's brigade on the Sevierville and Newport road, which ran through Fair Garden, but Campbell was able to hold the enemy in check.

Sturgis learned that the enemy had concentrated on the road near Fair Garden, and he ordered McCook to attack at daylight January 27. Campbell attacked in a heavy fog that morning and drove the enemy back on the main road a couple of miles, and McCook then sent La Grange's brigade forward on a by-road in an attempt to reach the rear of the enemy's position. This road turned off to the left from the main road at the Dickey house and ran nearly parallel to the main road to Eastport, which it rejoined at the Walker house about two and one-half miles from Fair Garden. Campbell drove the enemy back to the junction of the main road with the road used by La Grange, and then about 4:00 P.M. he charged dismounted, while La Grange, coming in on the enemy's right, charged with the saber. As a result of the combined attack, Martin's men were completely routed, and they fled with a loss of about 200 men killed, wounded, and captured.

* * * * * * * * *

On the morning of January 28, 1864, Sturgis advanced with his entire command toward the French Broad River, on the direct road from Fair Garden to Dandridge. Sturgis found the enemy cavalry in position, and was preparing to attack when he learned that infantry was crossing the river in support. Wolford, supported by La Grange, attacked and made some progress, but Sturgis ordered the withdrawal of his command at dark. Sturgis then marched back by way of Fair Garden, Trotter's Bridge, and Wear's Cove to Maryville, where he

went into camp. He sent Garrard's Second Cavalry Division out to Miller's Cove to picket the country twenty miles to the east of Maryville.

On January 26, the following command changes were made in Foster's Army in East Tennessee: Henry M. Judah was assigned command of Second Division, Twenty-Third Corps, relieving Manson; and John G. Parke was assigned command of Ninth Corps, relieving Orlando B. Willcox. At the same time, Second Division, Ninth Corps was relieved from duty with Ferrero's First Division, and Willcox was assigned command of Second Division.

On January 28, the brigades of David S. Stanley's First Division, Fourth Corps broke camp at Bridgeport, Alabama, and Shellmound and Whiteside in Tennessee and moved toward Chattanooga on their way to rejoin the corps. Stanley's division arrived and took position near Tyner's Station January 29–30.

At the end of January 1864, Foster's troops in East Tennessee were in camp as follows: headquarters of Parke's Ninth Corps was near Knoxville; Ferrero's First Division was near Erin's Station; and Willcox's Second Division was at Miller's Cove, Tennessee. Headquarters of Cox's Twenty-Third Corps, with Judah's Second Division and Hascall's Third Division of the corps, was at Knoxville, and Spears' East Tennessee Brigade was at Love's Mill. Headquarters of Granger's Fourth Corps and Sheridan's Second Division of the corps were at Loudon; Stanley's First Division was at Tyner's Station; and Wood's Third Division (temporarily commanded by August Willich) was at Maryville. Headquarters of Sturgis' Cavalry Corps and Wolford's First Cavalry Division were at Maryville; and Garrard's Second Cavalry Division was at Miller's Cove, Tennessee. McCook's First Cavalry Division, Army of the Cumberland was also with Sturgis, near Maryville.

The cavalry of the Army of the Ohio had been in the field almost continuously during December 1863 and January 1864, and by early February 1864 the men and animals were so reduced in numbers and were in such poor physical condition that Foster realized that they needed rest if the cavalry was to be of service during the spring campaign. Accordingly, on February 3, Sturgis was ordered to dismount one of his divisions and to turn over the horses to the divisions of Garrard and McCook. This was done, and by February 11, Sturgis was on his way to Mount Sterling, Kentucky with Wolford's division, which was to be remounted, reorganized, and reequipped for field service. On March 10, Wolford was placed in arrest because of a speech that he delivered, while in service, criticizing President Lincoln. He was tried by court martial, and on March 24 he was dishonorably discharged from the army.

On February 15, Garrard's cavalry division was sent to Clinton to guard the roads between the Holston River and the Clinch River, and McCook's cavalry division was moved to the headwaters of the Little Tennessee River to watch the passes in that area. On February 17, McCook's division was attached to Granger's Fourth Corps.

On February 5, Stanley's First Division, Fourth Corps broke camp at Tyner's Station, and the next day it moved to Blue Springs. David A. Enyart's First Brigade remained there during the month guarding the railroad, while Sidney M. Barnes' Second Brigade and John E. Bennett's Third Brigade conducted reconnaissances toward Dalton, Georgia. Stanley departed on leave February 13, and Charles Cruft was in temporary command during his absence.

Sheridan's Second Division was in camp near Loudon during the month. Sheridan departed on leave February 24, and George D. Wagner assumed command during his absence. Wood's Third Division was at Maryville during the early part of February, and it was commanded by Willich until February 12, when Wood returned from leave and resumed command.

On February 9, John M. Schofield relieved John G. Foster in command of the Army and Department of the Ohio (assigned January 28), and on February 10, George Stoneman assumed command of Twenty-Third Corps (assigned January 28, and again on February 4), relieving Jacob D. Cox. Cox then served as acting chief of staff to Schofield.

On February 10, Longstreet's infantry became active when he ordered Micah Jenkins to advance with his division to Strawberry Plains. Troops were also sent to Bull's Gap and Blain's Cross Roads. Jenkins took pontoons for bridging the Holston River, and he also sent out some of his cavalry in observation toward Knoxville.

In response to this threat, Ferrero's First Division of Ninth Corps moved to Knoxville and camped at Fort Sanders, and Willcox's Second Division, Ninth Corps moved up to the Clinton road near the city. Wood's Third Division, Fourth Corps was ordered to concentrate at Knoxville, and on February 15, the division marched from Maryville. Wood reported to Schofield the next day.

On February 6, Spears was placed in arrest, and William Cross assumed command of the First East Tennessee Brigade. The brigade remained at Love's Mill until Longstreet's advance, and it then moved to Knoxville.

Longstreet did not attempt an advance on Knoxville, but on February 22 he began to withdraw his troops eastward from Strawberry Plains. Schofield immediately sent a part of his command in pursuit. Ninth Corps advanced through Strawberry Plains and Mossy Creek and arrived at Morristown February 29. Wood's Third Division, Fourth Corps moved forward to Flat Creek and on to Strawberry Plains February 27, and arrived at New Market the next day. Twenty-Third Corps, which had been at Knoxville during the month, also joined in the pursuit. Judah's Second Division advanced to Strawberry Plains February 24. It crossed the Holston River February 28 and marched to New Market the next day. Hascall's Third Division, Twenty-Third Corps advanced to Strawberry Plains at the end of the month. Spears' brigade, under Cross, moved to Strawberry Plains February 23, then moved on to New Market February 29.

At the end of February 1864, Ninth Corps was at Morristown; Second Division, Twenty-Third Corps was at Strawberry Plains, and Third Division was at Knoxville; Cruft's First Division, Fourth Corps was at Blue Springs, Wagner's Second Division was at Loudon, and Wood's Third Division was at New Market. Headquarters of Sturgis' Cavalry Corps and Wolford's First Division were at Mount Sterling, Kentucky, and McCook's and Garrard's cavalry divisions were in East Tennessee.

During March 1864, Fourth Corps was comparatively inactive. First Brigade, First Division was at Ooltewah, and Second Brigade and Third Brigade were at Blue Springs. Second Division was at Loudon, where it assisted in building the railroad bridge over the Tennessee River and in guarding stores. On March 19, Third Division marched to Strawberry Plains and then, leaving First Brigade as garrison of that place, moved on to Rutledge. On March 24 it marched to Powder Springs Gap. On

March 7, McCook's cavalry division, then attached to Fourth Corps, was ordered to Cleveland, Tennessee.

During March 1864, Ninth Corps ended its association with the Army of the Ohio. On March 2, the corps moved from Morristown to Mossy Creek, and then March 12–13, it moved back to Morristown in preparation for a possible advance against Longstreet's army. While there, however, on March 14, the corps was ordered east to Annapolis, Maryland. On March 16, Willcox relieved Parke in command of Ninth Corps, and March 17–19, the corps marched back to Knoxville. On March 21 it left there for Camp Nelson, Kentucky, where it arrived March 31. It then moved on to Annapolis.

On March 1, Judah's Second Division, Twenty-Third Corps was at Mossy Creek. First Brigade of Hascall's Third Division was at Knoxville, and Second Brigade, Third Division was at Strawberry Plains. On March 10, First Brigade joined Second Brigade at Strawberry Plains, and Third Division then marched to Mossy Creek that day and joined Second Division. Both divisions marched to Morristown March 12, to take part in the movement against Longstreet's army, but with the departure of Ninth Corps, both divisions returned to Mossy Creek March 18 and went into camp.

On April 9, John M. Schofield assumed command of Twenty-Third Corps (assigned April 4), relieving George Stoneman. On April 9, Stoneman relieved Sturgis in command of the cavalry of the Army of the Ohio and was directed to organize and command a special cavalry force to be formed under the orders of the commander of the Army of the Ohio. Schofield remained in East Tennessee with his Army of the Ohio, which consisted of only Twenty-Third Corps, until late in April, then marched to join William T. Sherman's army for its movement into Georgia toward Atlanta. For further information, see Army of the Ohio (Schofield), and see also Atlanta, Georgia Campaign.

ARMY OF THE OHIO (SCHOFIELD) APRIL 9, 1864–AUGUST 1, 1865

On April 9, 1864, John M. Schofield assumed command of Twenty-Third Corps, Department of the Ohio (assigned April 4), relieving George Stoneman. At that time only Twenty-Third Corps, Army of the Ohio and Gordon Granger's Fourth Corps, with Edward M. McCook's First Cavalry Division, of the Army of the Cumberland remained in East Tennessee. Ninth Corps, which had been serving with the Army of the Ohio, was en route to Annapolis, Maryland, and Samuel D. Sturgis' cavalry was at Mount Sterling, Kentucky.

Fourth Corps remained in East Tennessee during April 1864, but late in the month it moved in the direction of Chattanooga, preparatory to rejoining the Army of the Cumberland for William T. Sherman's advance toward Atlanta, Georgia. There were two important changes of command in Fourth Corps during the month. On April 10, Oliver O. Howard relieved Granger in command of the corps, and after Philip H. Sheridan had been ordered east to assume command of the Cavalry Corps, Army of the Potomac, John Newton assumed command of Second Division April 16.

David S. Stanley's First Division, Fourth Corps remained at Blue Springs during the month, except Charles Cruft's First Brigade, which moved to Cleveland, Tennessee. Newton's Second Division remained at Loudon until April 15, and then it moved to Cleveland. Thomas J. Wood's Third Division was at Strawberry Plains April 1, but it then moved to McDonald's Station and remained there during the rest of the month. McCook's cavalry division was also at Cleveland.

At the end of March 1864, Henry M. Judah's Second Division and Jacob D. Cox's Third Division of Twenty-Third Corps were at Mossy Creek. On April 1, Cox's division moved to Morristown to watch James Longstreet's Confederate Army, which was still in East Tennessee (See Knoxville, Tennessee Campaign), and the next day it moved on to Bull's Gap. Cox remained there until Longstreet left East Tennessee in April 1864 to rejoin the Army of Northern Virginia, and on April 29, Cox marched toward Charleston, Tennessee. Judah's division remained at Mossy Creek until April 26, and it then marched by way of Knoxville to Calhoun.

On April 3, Alvin P. Hovey left Nashville, Tennessee with six new Indiana regiments to join Twenty-Third Corps in East Tennessee. He passed through Chattanooga April 20 and reached Charleston April 24. Upon arrival there, his command joined Twenty-Third Corps as First Division. At the end of the month, Hovey's and Judah's divisions were at Charleston, and Cox's division was nearby.

On April 30, 1864, Twenty-Third Corps, which was also known as the Army of the Ohio during the Atlanta Campaign, was organized as follows:

TWENTY-THIRD CORPS, John M. Schofield

First Division, Alvin P. Hovey
First Brigade, Richard F. Barter
Second Brigade, John C. McQuiston
Artillery
23rd Battery, Indiana Light Artillery, Luther S. Houghton
24th Battery, Indiana Light Artillery, Henry W. Shafer

Second Division, Henry M. Judah
First Brigade, Joseph A. Cooper
Second Brigade, Milo S. Hascall
Artillery
Battery F, 1st Michigan Light Artillery, Byron D. Paddock
19th Battery, Ohio Light Artillery, Joseph C. Shields

Third Division, Jacob D. Cox
First Brigade, James W. Reilly
Second Brigade, Mahlon D. Manson

Fourth Division, Jacob Ammen
First Brigade, John Mehringer
Second Brigade, Davis Tillson
Third Brigade, Silas A. Strickland

Note. Fourth Division was at Knoxville and did not accompany the corps on the Atlanta Campaign.

District of Kentucky, Stephen G. Burbridge

First Division, Edward H. Hobson
First Brigade, George W. Gallup
Second Brigade, Clinton J. True
Third Brigade, Charles S. Hanson
Fourth Brigade, John M. Brown

Second Division, Hugh Ewing
First Brigade, Sanders D. Bruce
Second Brigade, Cicero Maxwell

Note 1. The District of Kentucky was also called Fifth Division, Twenty-Third Corps, but the troops of this division did not accompany the corps on the Atlanta Campaign.

Note 2. Headquarters, First Division, District of Kentucky was at Lexington, Kentucky. Gallup's brigade was at Louisa; True's brigade was at Mount Sterling; Hanson's brigade was at Irvine; and Brown's brigade was at Lexington.

Note 3. Headquarters of Second Division was at Munfordville, Kentucky. Bruce's brigade was at Louisville, and Maxwell's brigade was at Bowling Green.

Schofield's Army of the Ohio (or Twenty-Third Corps) marched with William T. Sherman's Army of the Military Division of the Mississippi at the beginning of its advance into Georgia, and it took an active part in all of the operations that led to the Federal occupation of Atlanta September 2, 1864. Twenty-Third Corps joined in the pursuit of John B. Hood's Army of Tennessee to Lovejoy's Station after the Battle of Jonesboro August 31–September 1, and then moved to Decatur, Georgia, where it remained in camp during the rest of September. For details of the organization and operations of the Army of the Ohio during the period May 3–September 8, 1864, see Atlanta, Georgia Campaign.

When Hood left Lovejoy's Station in September 1864 to move on Sherman's line of communications, Sherman's army, including the Army of the Ohio, followed in pursuit. Hood marched northward along the Western and Atlantic Railroad as far as Dalton, Georgia, and there he turned westward and moved into Alabama. He then advanced to the Tennessee River, where he threatened an invasion of Middle Tennessee.

Sherman followed Hood as far as Gaylesville, Alabama and then abandoned the pursuit. He sent Fourth Corps, Army of the Cumberland, then commanded by David S. Stanley, and Schofield's Army of the Ohio to reinforce George H. Thomas, who was in command in Middle Tennessee. That done, Sherman marched back with the rest of his army to Atlanta, and from there he began his march eastward across Georgia toward Savannah November 15.

On November 21–22, Hood advanced from Florence, Alabama toward Columbia, Tennessee. At that time Twenty-Third Corps was near Pulaski, Tennessee, and as Hood advanced farther into the state, the corps was engaged at Columbia November 24–27, at the Battle of Franklin November 30, and at the Battle of Nashville December 15–16. For details of the organization and operations of the Army of the Ohio (Twenty-Third Corps) during this period, see Franklin and Nashville campaign (Hood's Invasion of Tennessee).

Schofield's Twenty-Third Corps moved southward with the rest of Thomas' army in pursuit of Hood's defeated army after the Battle of Nashville, and it then halted at Columbia, Tennessee. While there, on January 14, 1865, Schofield was ordered to take his corps eastward to North Carolina. It embarked at Clifton, Tennessee January 15–19 and moved on transports on the Tennessee and Ohio rivers by way of Louisville and Cincinnati to Pittsburgh, then by rail to Washington, D.C. It then moved by sea from Alexandria, Virginia to Fort Fisher, North Carolina, where it arrived during the period February 8–23.

On February 9, Schofield assumed command of the Department of North Carolina, and thereafter the designation of his command was Department of North Carolina, Army of the Ohio.

Troops of Schofield's Army of the Ohio were present at the occupation of Wilmington, North Carolina February 22, 1865; at the Battle of Kinston (or Wise's Forks), North Carolina March 8–10, 1865; and at the occupation of Goldsboro, North Carolina March 21, 1865.

Sherman's Army of the Military Division of the Mississippi arrived at Goldsboro after its march through the Carolinas from Savannah, Georgia March 23–24, and it was joined there by Schofield's army.

On March 31, Jacob D. Cox was assigned by the president to the permanent command of Twenty-Third Corps, and on April 1, in preparation for further operations against Joseph E. Johnston's army in North Carolina, Sherman designated Cox's Twenty-Third Corps and Alfred H. Terry's Tenth Corps as the Center of his army. Schofield was assigned command of the Center, which was to continue in existence as long as it was operating with Sherman's army.

Johnston surrendered his army to Sherman April 26, and the war in the East was over. Sherman's army then marched northward to Washington, D.C., but the troops of Twenty-Third Corps remained in North Carolina until the corps was discontinued, to date from August 1, 1865. For additional information, see Twenty-Third Corps, Army of the Ohio.

For details of the organization and operations of the Army of the Ohio while in North Carolina, see Department of North Carolina, January 31, 1865–May 19, 1866, in Volume I; and see also Twenty-Third Corps, Army of the Ohio.

SHERMAN'S ARMY OF OBSERVATION AT VICKSBURG, MISSISSIPPI

In June 1863, while Ulysses S. Grant's Army of the Tennessee was besieging Vicksburg, Joseph E. Johnston, commanding all Confederate forces in Mississippi, assembled an army of four infantry divisions and one cavalry division east of the Big Black River for the purpose of relieving the beleaguered city. Two of the infantry divisions were at Vernon, one was at Jackson, and the other was southwest of Livingston. The cavalry division was active in scouting and patrolling the country in the area.

Johnston made no attempt to advance to the relief of Vicksburg, however, but the presence of his army and the activity of his cavalry prompted Grant to order the formation of a special force to take position west of the Big Black River and guard the rear of his investing lines. William T. Sherman was placed in command of all troops designated to prevent the approach of Johnston's Army of Relief, and this force was known as Sherman's Army of Observation. It remained in position guarding the crossings of the Big Black River until the surrender of Vicksburg July 4, 1863.

For details of the organization of the Army of Observation and the positions that it occupied during the siege of Vicksburg, see Operations against Vicksburg, Mississippi, 1861–1863, Grant's Operations against Vicksburg, Siege of Vicksburg, Mississippi, Sherman's Exterior Line at Vicksburg—Sherman's Army of Observation; and see also Jackson, Mississippi Campaign (William T. Sherman).

ARMY OF SOUTHEASTERN MISSOURI

On September 30, 1862, John W. Davidson, commander of the District of Saint Louis, Department of the Missouri, ordered the formation of two infantry brigades and one cavalry brigade in the district. These were organized as follows:

First Infantry Brigade, Thomas C. Fletcher
Second Infantry Brigade, Chester Harding, Jr.
Cavalry Brigade, Bazel F. Lazear

On December 3, 1862 Eugene A. Carr relieved Davidson in command of the District of Saint Louis, and Davidson then assumed command of the army of the field. This was designated as the Army of Southeastern Missouri, and it was formed from troops of the Army of the Southwest and from the District of Saint Louis. In December 1862 it was organized as follows:

ARMY OF SOUTHEASTERN MISSOURI, John W. Davidson

First Division, William P. Benton
    First Brigade, Charles L. Harris
    Second Brigade, David Shunk
    Unattached artillery
        1st Battery, Indiana Light Artillery, Martin Klauss

Note. First Division was organized from regiments of Benton's First Division, Army of the Southwest.

Second Division, Sempronius H. Boyd
    First Brigade, Chester Harding, Jr.
    Second Brigade, Robert R. Livingston
    Artillery
        Battery B, 1st Missouri Light Artillery, Martin Welfley
        Battery M, 2nd Missouri Light Artillery, Gustave Stange

Note 1. Second Division was organized principally from regiments of the infantry brigades of the District of Saint Louis.
Note 2. Harding commanded Second Division in January 1863, and Eugene A. Carr in February 1863.

Cavalry Brigade, George E. Waring

Note. The regiments of the cavalry brigade were taken from the District of Saint Louis.

The Army of Southeastern Missouri was discontinued when William P. Benton's First Division and William M. Stone's Second Brigade, Second Division were transferred March 13–26, 1863 from Saint Genevieve, Missouri, by way of Cairo, Illinois and Memphis, Tennessee, to Ulysses S. Grant's Army of the Tennessee at Vicksburg. On March 28, Carr's command was reorganized as Fourteenth Division, Thirteenth Corps as follows:

Fourteenth Division, Thirteenth Corps, Eugene A. Carr
    First Brigade, William P. Benton
    Second Brigade, William M. Stone, to May 2, 1863
        Michael K. Lawler

First Brigade, Second Division remained in southeastern Missouri.

For additional information, see Department of the Missouri, September 19, 1862–May 27, 1865, Districts in the Department of the Missouri, District of Saint Louis; and see also Army of the Southwest.

ARMY OF THE SOUTHWEST

Following the Battle of Wilson's Creek, Sterling Price moved north through Missouri to Lexington, which he besieged and captured September 18–20, 1861. For details, see Operations in Missouri in 1861, Siege and Capture of Lexington, Missouri. Then, on September 21, Fremont, commanding the Western Department, issued an order for the organization of the Union troops in Missouri into five divisions to deal with Price. When organized early in October, these divisions were as follows:

First Division, David Hunter, to November 2, 1861
    Thomas J. Turner

Note 1. Hunter was assigned command of the division September 22, 1861, and relieved Fremont in command of the Western Department November 2 (assigned October 24).
Note 2. The original organization of First Division is not given.

Second Division, John Pope
    First Brigade, Jefferson C. Davis
    Second Brigade, John C. Kelton

Note 1. Pope assumed command and announced the organization of Second Division at Jefferson City September 28, 1861.

Third Division, Franz Sigel
    First Brigade
    Second Brigade, Peter J. Osterhaus

Note. Second Brigade was organized and Osterhaus was assigned command October 4, 1861.

Fourth Division, Alexander Asboth
    First Brigade, Anselm Albert
    Second Brigade, Eugene A. Carr

Note. Albert and Carr were assigned command October 10, 1861.

Fifth Division, Justus McKinstry, to November 7, 1861
    Samuel D. Sturgis
    Brigade, James Totten
    Brigade, Frederick Steele

Headquarters of the divisions were as follows: Fremont's First Division was at Versailles, Second Division at Boonville, Third Division at Sedalia, Fourth Division at the terminus of the Pacific Railroad at Tipton, and Fifth Division at Syracuse, all in Missouri, and all in communication with one another.

In addition to the above, James H. Lane's Kansas Brigade and a force under Samuel D. Sturgis, totaling about 5,000 men, were along the Kansas-Missouri border.

From his headquarters at Tipton, Fremont ordered his five divisions to move forward to Springfield, Missouri in pursuit of Price, and to follow routes that would enable them to consolidate within twenty-four hours if they met with strong enemy resistance. They crossed the Osage River below the remains of Osceola, which had been destroyed by artillery fire September 22, when Lane arrived at the town, and on October 24, Fremont had arrived within sixty miles of Springfield.

At 8:30 that night, Charles Zagonyi rode south of camp with Fremont's Bodyguard, with orders to pick up Frank J. White's squadron of United States Prairie Scouts, which were scouting out in front, and attempt to capture Springfield. At 3:00 P.M. October 25, Zagonyi arrived at Springfield and after a spirited engagement entered and cleared the town. It was then nearly dark, and he decided to withdraw

and rejoin the army. At Three Mounds Prairie to the north, he met Eugene A. Carr with eight troops of cavalry that had been sent out to relieve him.

Fremont, whose army had been moving forward, arrived at Springfield October 26–27 and occupied the town. He was joined there by Lane's and Sturgis' commands from Kansas. At that time Sterling Price's army was at Neosho, eighty miles away.

On November 2, all of Fremont's divisions were at Springfield except Hunter's division. That day, by an order from Headquarters of the Army in Washington, dated October 24, Fremont relinquished command of the Western Department and of the army at Springfield, and that evening Hunter arrived and assumed command.

Shortly after assuming command, Hunter ordered the withdrawal of the army from Springfield in three columns: one under Franz Sigel marched back to Rolla; another under John Pope marched to Sedalia; and the third under Lane and Sturgis moved northward along the Missouri-Kansas border.

The Department of the Missouri was constituted November 9, 1861 to consist of the states of Missouri, Iowa, Minnesota, Wisconsin, Illinois, Arkansas, and that part of Kentucky west of the Cumberland River; Henry W. Halleck was assigned command of the department (assumed command November 19).

The divisions organized by Fremont in the Western Department were retained in the new department, and at the end of November 1861 they were commanded as follows: First Division, Thomas J. Turner; Second Division, Jefferson C. Davis; Third Division, Peter J. Osterhaus; Fourth Division, Alexander Asboth; and Fifth Division, Frederick Steele.

In December, Halleck learned that Price had again moved northward in Missouri, and that on December 16 his army was near Osceola. Halleck then decided to drive the enemy from the state, and on December 25, he assigned Samuel R. Curtis to the command of the newly created District of Southwestern Missouri, which included the country south of the Osage River and west of the Meramec River. Curtis was directed to organize an army and advance with it against Price, who was at that time at Springfield. Curtis assumed command of the district December 28 and established headquarters at Rolla. On December 24, prior to Curtis' arrival, Sigel was assigned command of all troops at Rolla, which consisted of Sigel's own Third Division, commanded by Osterhaus, and Asboth's Fourth Division; and December 28, Eugene A. Carr was assigned command of a cavalry brigade at Rolla.

It should be noted here that the reporting of troops in the District of Southwestern Missouri at the time of its organization was confusing because the old brigade organization was retained, while at the same time officers as acting major generals were reported as commanding divisions, as has been noted above. Thus the troops reported in the district for January 1862 were as follows:

First Brigade, Grenville M. Dodge
Second Brigade, Peter J. Osterhaus
Third Brigade (cavalry), Eugene A. Carr
Fourth Brigade, Franz Sigel
Fifth Brigade, Alexander Asboth

On December 28, 1861, Carr was assigned command of a Cavalry Expedition consisting of twenty-four companies, and the next day he left Rolla and advanced on the road toward Springfield. By January 8, 1862, his advance had arrived within eight miles of Springfield, and he then learned that Price occupied the town in force. Carr moved his command to Lebanon, about sixty miles southwest of Rolla, and Osterhaus was sent out to join him.

Curtis then decided to establish a forward base at Lebanon and ordered Asboth and Sigel to march to that place. Asboth's division, consisting of Anselm Albert's First Brigade (temporarily commanded by Francis J. Joliat) and Carr's Second Brigade (temporarily commanded by Frederick Schaefer), arrived at Lebanon February 6.

Meantime, on January 25, by Halleck's orders, Jefferson C. Davis marched with his Second Division from Otterville, Missouri in John Pope's District of Central Missouri, to join Curtis at Lebanon, and that same day Curtis, in person, left Rolla for Lebanon to take command of the army assembling there.

By February 7, all of Curtis' troops of the District of Southwestern Missouri had arrived at Lebanon, and on February 9 they were organized into divisions of the Army of the Southwest. In this reorganization, Sigel's old Third Division was redesignated as First Division; Davis' old Second Division became Third Division; Asboth's old

Fourth Division was redesignated as Second Division; and a new Fourth Division was created from Dodge's old brigade and a new brigade under William Vandever, and this division was assigned to Carr. The Army of the Southwest was then organized as follows:

ARMY OF THE SOUTHWEST, Samuel R. Curtis

First Division, Franz Sigel, to May 9, 1862
    Frederick Steele
    First Brigade, Peter J. Osterhaus
    Second Brigade, Nicholas Greusel
    Artillery
        Welfley's Missouri Battery, Martin Welfley
        4th Battery, Ohio Light Artillery, Louis Hoffmann

Note 1. Sigel was assigned command of both First Division and Second Division.
Note 2. Welfley's Battery was later designated as Battery B, 1st Missouri Light Artillery.

Second Division, Alexander Asboth
    First Brigade, Frederick Schaefer
    Artillery
        1st Missouri Horse Battery, Gustavus M. Elbert
        2nd Battery, Ohio Light Artillery, William B. Chapman

Third Division, Jefferson C. Davis
    First Brigade, Thomas Pattison
    Second Brigade, Julius White
    Artillery
        Peoria Battery, 2nd Illinois Light Artillery, Peter Davidson

Fourth Division, Eugene A. Carr
    First Brigade, Grenville M. Dodge
    Second Brigade, William Vandever

Note. Junius A. Jones' 1st Battery, Iowa Light Artillery was attached to First Brigade; and Third Battery (Dubuque Battery), Iowa Light Artillery was attached to Second Brigade.

On February 10, 1862, the Army of the Southwest began its march toward Springfield, and on February 13 Carr's division entered the town, which had been evacuated by the enemy. The next day Curtis marched out of Springfield in two columns in pursuit of Price. Price did not intend to make a stand and retired into Arkansas. Curtis followed and occupied Bentonville February 18, Cross Hollows

February 22, and Fayetteville February 23. Curtis then learned that the enemy were concentrating their forces to move against him, and he began to withdraw his army, which was rather widely scattered, northward toward the state line. A short time later, March 6–8, Curtis' Army of the Southwest was engaged at the Battle of Pea Ridge or Elkhorn Tavern with Southern forces commanded by Earl Van Dorn. For details of the organization of the Army of the Southwest and its operations before and during the battle, see Battle of Pea Ridge (or Elkhorn Tavern), Arkansas.

After the Battle of Pea Ridge, the Army of the Southwest remained in northwestern Arkansas until April 4. From there it marched eastward through southern Missouri and then turned south toward Batesville, Arkansas, where it arrived early in May.

On May 9, Asboth's Second Division and Davis' Third Division were discontinued when Davis, with four regiments of his division, and Asboth, with four regiments of his division, marched toward Cape Girardeau, Missouri for transfer to John Pope's Army of the Mississippi, then near Corinth, Mississippi. For additional information, see Army of the Mississippi (Pope, Rosecrans).

While at Batesville, on May 13, the Army of the Southwest was reorganized into three divisions. The record of the brigade commanders from the time of the reorganization until the Army of the Southwest was merged into the District of Eastern Arkansas is difficult to determine, but the following organization, without dates of command, is informative.

First Division, Frederick Steele
    First Brigade, William P. Benton
    Second Brigade, Charles E. Hovey
    Fourth Brigade, Conrad Baker

Second Division, Eugene A. Carr
    Brigade, John B. Wyman
    Brigade, William Vandever

Third Division, Peter J. Osterhaus
    First Brigade, Francis Hassendeubel
    Second Brigade, Robert J. Rombauer

The Army of the Southwest remained near Batesville until the end of June 1862, and then early in July moved to Helena, Arkansas.

On July 22, Alvin P. Hovey was ordered to move from Memphis, Tennessee with his Third Division, Army of the Tennessee (formerly commanded by Lewis Wallace) to Helena to join the Army of the Southwest. Upon arrival there, Hovey's division was redesignated as Fourth Division, Army of the Southwest.

Frederick Steele succeeded Curtis in command of the Army of the Southwest August 29, and he remained in command until October 7, when he was relieved by Eugene A. Carr. Carr retained command of his Second Division. Alvin P. Hovey was in command of the army briefly in late October 1862.

The Army of the Southwest was merged into the District of Eastern Arkansas, Department of the Missouri November 2, 1862, and in December 1862 the District of Eastern Arkansas was organized as follows:

DISTRICT OF EASTERN ARKANSAS, Willis A. Gorman

First Division, Frederick Steele
    First Brigade, Peter J. Osterhaus
    Second Brigade, John M. Thayer
    Third Brigade

Note. In preparation for William T. Sherman's expedition to the Yazoo River, a division was organized at Helena under Steele, and on December 21, 1862 it left the district as Fourth Division of Sherman's Yazoo River Expedition. For details, see Operations against Vicksburg, Mississippi, 1861–1863, Early Attempts to Capture Vicksburg, Yazoo River Expedition (William T. Sherman)—Battle of Chickasaw Bayou (or Walnut Hills).

Second Division, Alvin P. Hovey
    First Brigade, James R. Slack
        Charles E. Hovey
    Second Brigade, Peter Kinney
    Third Brigade, George F. McGinnis

Cavalry Division, Cadwallader C. Washburn
    First Brigade, Conrad Baker
    Second Brigade, Cyrus Bussey

Note. The Cavalry Division was also called Third Division.

By an order of the president, dated January 21, 1863, Union troops in Arkansas that were within reach of orders from Ulysses S. Grant were temporarily attached to the Army of the Tennessee. For further information, see Army of the Tennessee, Department of the Tennessee.

ARMY OF SOUTHWESTERN MISSOURI

When the Department of the Missouri was re-created September 19, 1862, the state of Kansas became a part of that department as the District of Kansas. At that time, James G. Blunt, commander of the district, was in the field with his Army of Kansas near Fort Scott, Kansas. When Samuel R. Curtis, commanding the Department of the Missouri, learned that Thomas C. Hindman, commanding a Confederate army in northwestern Arkansas, was marching toward Springfield, Missouri, he ordered Blunt on September 27 to report with his army, which was of division strength, to John M. Schofield, who was then in command of all Union forces in the field in southwest Missouri.

On October 1, Blunt's division was near Carthage, Missouri; Schofield, with Totten's First Division, was near Osage Spring, Arkansas; and Francis J. Herron's division was somewhere in the vicinity. Herron's division was a new one that had been formed from regiments brought to Springfield from Saint Louis by Herron during the latter part of September. On October 1, these three divisions were constituted as the Army of Southwestern Missouri, and Schofield was assigned command. At that time Blunt's division was designated as the Kansas Division.

The organization of Schofield's command was as follows:

Army of Southwestern Missouri, John M. Schofield
    First Division, James Totten
    Herron's Division, Francis J. Herron
    Kansas Division, James G. Blunt

On October 12, the designation of the Army of Southwestern Missouri was changed to Army of the Frontier, and Schofield was assigned command. Blunt's division became First Division, Army of the Frontier; Totten's First Division became Second Division, Army of the Frontier; and Herron's Division became Third Division, Army of the Frontier.

For additional information about the organization and operations of, the Army of Southwestern Missouri, see Army of Kansas, and see also Army of the Frontier.

ARMY OF THE TENNESSEE, DEPARTMENT OF THE TENNESSEE

When the Department of the Tennessee was created from the District of West Tennessee October 16, 1862, the troops in the new department consisted of First Division, Second Division, Third Division, and Fourth Division of the District of West Tennessee, and these consisted largely of troops of John Pope's Army of the Mississippi and the Army of the Tennessee, District of West Tennessee. For additional information, see Army of the Tennessee, District of West Tennessee, and also Army of the Mississippi (Pope, Rosecrans).

Thirteenth Corps, Department of the Tennessee was created by an order of October 24, 1862 to consist of the troops under Ulysses S. Grant in the new Department of the Tennessee. Grant assumed command of the Department of the Tennessee and of Thirteenth Corps October 25, and on October 26 the former divisions of the District of West Tennessee were transferred to the Department of the Tennessee as districts with the following designations:

First Division as the District of Memphis, Thirteenth Corps, under the command of William T. Sherman.

Second Division as the District of Jackson, Thirteenth Corps, under the command of Stephen A. Hurlbut.

Third Division as the District of Corinth, Thirteenth Corps, under the command of Charles S. Hamilton.

Fourth Division as the District of Columbus, Thirteenth Corps, under the command of Thomas A. Davies.

During November and December 1862, the

troops in the districts of Memphis, Jackson, and Corinth were organized into divisions of Thirteenth Corps, or Army of the Tennessee, as follows:

First Division, in the District of Memphis, commanded by James W. Denver

Second Division, in the District of Memphis, commanded by Morgan L. Smith

Third Division, in the District of Jackson, commanded by John A. Logan

Fourth Division, in the District of Jackson, commanded by Grenville M. Dodge

Fifth Division, in the District of Memphis, commanded by William T. Sherman

Sixth Division, in the District of Corinth, commanded by John McArthur

Seventh Division, in the District of Corinth, commanded by Isaac F. Quinby

Eighth Division, in the District of Corinth, commanded by David S. Stanley

Ninth Division, in the District of Memphis, commanded by George W. Morgan

Tenth Division, in the District of Memphis, commanded by Andrew J. Smith

Eleventh Division, at Helena Arkansas, commanded by Frederick Steele

Note. Fifth Division was later reorganized into First Division and Second Division in the District of Memphis.

Until December 18, 1862, the date on which an order was issued dividing Thirteenth Corps into four new corps, the Army of the Tennessee was synonymous with Thirteenth Corps. Actually, however, Thirteenth Corps was operational for some time after that date, until the organization of the new corps could be completed. For details of the organization of the Army of the Tennessee from October 25, 1862 to mid-January 1863, see Thirteenth Corps, Army of the Tennessee, October 24, 1862–January 14, 1863.

The reorganizational order of December 18, 1862 created a new, and smaller, Thirteenth Corps, Fifteenth Corps, Sixteenth Corps, and Seventeenth Corps, which were to be formed from troops in the Department of the Tennessee, including those troops of the Army of the Mississippi that were operating on the Mississippi River. The organizations of the four corps were announced December 22, 1862, although they were not completed on that date, but when they were organized, this gave the general form to the Army of the Tennessee that

fought at Vicksburg, and was with William T. Sherman during the Atlanta Campaign and on his march through Georgia and the Carolinas.

Sixteenth Corps was constituted December 22, 1862 to consist of John McArthur's Sixth Division, Isaac F. Quinby's Seventh Division, and Eighth Division, then commanded by John E. Smith. Stephen A. Hurlbut was assigned command. Because of Grant's operations in northern Mississippi in late December 1862, Sixteenth Corps was not fully organized until January 10, 1863, and at that time the corps was in the District of West Tennessee.

Seventeenth Corps was constituted December 22, 1862 to consist of James W. Denver's First Division, John A. Logan's Third Division, and Fourth Division, then commanded by Jacob G. Lauman. In addition, Benjamin H. Grierson's cavalry brigade and the forces in the District of Corinth commanded by Grenville M. Dodge were also assigned to Seventeenth Corps. James B. McPherson was assigned command of the corps, but he did not assume command until January 11, 1863.

Thirteenth Corps and Fifteenth Corps were not organized until later because the troops assigned to these two corps were absent with William T. Sherman on his expedition to the Yazoo River.

On December 20, 1862, Sherman left Memphis on transports with Andrew J. Smith's Tenth Division (redesignated as First Division, Right Wing, Thirteenth Corps for the expedition), Morgan L. Smith's Second Division, and George W. Morgan's Ninth Division (redesignated as Third Division, Right Wing, Thirteenth Corps) and steamed down the Mississippi River to Helena, Arkansas, where he arrived the next day. There he picked up Frederick Steele's Eleventh Division (redesignated as Fourth Division, Right Wing, Thirteenth Corps), arriving at Johnson's plantation on the Yazoo River on December 26. Sherman's command was designated as the Right Wing, Thirteenth Corps, and was also called Sherman's Yazoo River Expedition.

Sherman attempted to drive the enemy forces from Walnut Hills and advance on Vicksburg from the north, but when the assault of December 29, 1862 at Chickasaw Bayou (or Walnut Hills) was unsuccessful, he withdrew his troops to the Mississippi River January 2, 1863. For details of the organization and operations of Sherman's troops at Chickasaw Bayou, see Operations against Vicksburg, Mississippi, 1861–1863, Early Attempts to Capture Vicksburg, Yazoo River, Mississippi Expedition (William T. Sherman)—Battle of Chickasaw Bayou (or Walnut Hills).

John A. McClernand joined Sherman's army at the mouth of the Yazoo River, and January 4, 1863 assumed command, relieving Sherman. McClernand reorganized his new command into a First Corps, commanded by George W. Morgan, and a Second Corps, commanded by William T. Sherman, and called it the Army of the Mississippi. He then moved the army on transports up the Mississippi and Arkansas rivers to Arkansas Post or Fort Hindman, which he captured January 11. For the organization and operations of McClernand's Army of the Mississippi, see Operations against Vicksburg, Mississippi, 1861–1863, Early Attempts to Capture Vicksburg, Engagement at Arkansas Post (or Fort Hindman), Arkansas.

On January 12, McClernand proceeded to execute a part of the long-delayed order of December 22, 1862, which had directed the organization of four new army corps of the Army of the Tennessee. On January 12, the designation of George W. Morgan's First Corps, Army of the Mississippi was changed to Thirteenth Corps, Army of the Tennessee, and the designation of Sherman's Second Corps, Army of the Mississippi was changed to Fifteenth Corps, Army of the Tennessee. For the organizations of the two corps, see Thirteenth Corps, Army of the Tennessee, January 14, 1863–August 7, 1863, and Fifteenth Corps, Army of the Tennessee.

After the capture of Arkansas Post, McClernand was ordered to take Thirteenth Corps and Fifteenth Corps down the Mississippi to Vicksburg, and by the end of January 1863 he had them assembled at Milliken's Bend and Young's Point in Louisiana, opposite Vicksburg.

Grant transferred his headquarters to Young's Point, and on January 30, as senior officer, he assumed personal command of the Vicksburg expedition. McClernand then assumed command of Thirteenth Corps.

Seventeenth Corps was sent downriver from Memphis to Lake Providence to attempt to open a route through the bayous to the river below Vicksburg, but when this effort failed, it was ordered to join the other two corps at Vicksburg, and by April 20 it was concentrated at Milliken's Bend.

Grant's army was kept active during the late winter and early spring of 1863 in the so-called Bayou Expeditions above Vicksburg, and in digging a canal across the De Soto peninsula. Then, on April 20, Grant moved out with the army at the beginning of his campaign to the rear of Vicksburg.

On April 30, Grant's army began crossing the Mississippi River below Grand Gulf and moving eastward away from the river, first toward Edwards Station, and then toward Jackson, Mississippi. During this movement the army was divided into three wings as follows: the Right Wing consisted of McClernand's Thirteenth Corps; the Left Wing consisted of Sherman's Fifteenth Corps; and the Center consisted of McPherson's Seventeenth Corps.

On May 1, McClernand's Thirteenth Corps and Logan's Third Division of Seventeenth Corps were engaged at the Battle of Port Gibson; on May 12, Logan's Third Division, Seventeenth Corps was engaged at Raymond; and on May 14, James M. Tuttle's Third Division of Sherman's Fifteenth Corps and Marcellus M. Crocker's Seventh Division of Seventeenth Corps were engaged at Jackson, Mississippi. From Jackson, Grant's army turned back and marched westward toward Vicksburg, and May 16, McClernand's Thirteenth Corps and McPherson's Seventeenth Corps were heavily engaged at the Battle of Champion Hill. Following their defeat at Champion Hill, the Confederate forces fell back to the Big Black River, and there, on May 17, McClernand's Thirteenth Corps attacked and drove them back into the fortifications of Vicksburg. Grant followed with his army and, after two unsuccessful assaults on May 19 and May 22, settled down to a siege of the city.

During the siege of Vicksburg, Grant's Army of the Tennessee was heavily reinforced. During the period June 14–17, 1863, John G. Parke's Ninth Corps arrived at Vicksburg by way of the Mississippi River from the Department of the Ohio. Parke's command was organized as follows:

NINTH CORPS, John G. Parke

First Division, Thomas Welsh
　First Brigade, Henry Bowman

Second Brigade, Daniel Leasure

Second Division, Robert B. Potter
   First Brigade, Simon G. Griffin
   Second Brigade, Edward Ferrero
   Third Brigade, Benjamin C. Christ

In late May and the early part of June 1863, some troops of Sixteenth Corps were sent from Tennessee to Vicksburg. Jacob G. Lauman's Fourth Division joined Grant from Memphis during the period May 13–20; a Provisional Division under Nathan Kimball arrived from Memphis June 3; and William Sooy Smith's First Division arrived June 12 from La Grange. These troops were designated Detachment Sixteenth Corps, and Cadwallader C. Washburn was assigned command. Washburn's troops were organized as follows:

DETACHMENT SIXTEENTH CORPS, Cadwallader
   C. Washburn

First Division, William Sooy Smith
   First Brigade, John M. Loomis
   Second Brigade, Stephen G. Hicks
   Third Brigade, Joseph R. Cockerill
   Fourth Brigade, William W. Sanford

Fourth Division, Jacob G. Lauman
   First Brigade, Isaac C. Pugh
   Second Brigade, Cyrus Hall
   Third Brigade, George E. Bryant, to June 9, 1863
      Amory K. Johnson

Provisional Division, Nathan Kimball
   Engelmann's Brigade, Adolph Engelmann
   Richmond's Brigade, Jonathan Richmond
   Montgomery's Brigade, Milton Montgomery

On June 11, 1863, a division commanded by Francis J. Herron arrived at Vicksburg from the Department of the Missouri. It was organized as follows:

Herron's Division, Francis J. Herron
   First Brigade, William Vandever
   Second Brigade, William W. Orme

Also in June 1863, Cyrus Bussey, with an unattached cavalry brigade, arrived at Vicksburg from the District of Eastern Arkansas.

For details of the organization and operations of the Army of the Tennessee during the Vicksburg Campaign, see Operations against Vicksburg, Mississippi, 1861–1863.

Immediately after the surrender of Vicksburg July 4, 1863, Sherman led a large part of Grant's army to Jackson, Mississippi to drive back or destroy an army that had been assembled by Joseph E. Johnston for the relief of Vicksburg, and to destroy Jackson as a rail and supply center for Confederate forces operating in the area. Sherman left the Big Black River for Jackson July 5, and after completing his mission returned to Vicksburg July 25. His army consisted of Parke's Ninth Corps, to which William Sooy Smith's First Division, Sixteenth Corps was temporarily attached; Thirteenth Corps, then commanded by Edward O. C. Ord, to which Lauman's Fourth Division, Sixteenth Corps was temporarily attached; and Sherman's Fifteenth Corps, temporarily commanded by Frederick Steele. For details of this operation, see Jackson, Mississippi Campaign (William T. Sherman).

In the weeks following the capture of Vicksburg, Grant's army was gradually broken up. On July 24, Ninth Corps was ordered to return to the Department of the Ohio, and by mid-August the last troops were on their way to Kentucky.

On July 27, Frederick Steele was assigned command of an expedition to capture Little Rock, Arkansas, and August 27–30, Nathan Kimball's Provisional Division was sent to Helena, Arkansas to join this expedition. Steele organized his command at Helena, in the Department of the Tennessee, from Frederick Salomon's Thirteenth Division, Sixteenth Corps, Kimball's Provisional Division, and John W. Davidson's Cavalry Division from the Department of the Missouri. Steele left Helena with his command August 10–11, and thereafter operated in the Department of the Missouri and reported to John M. Schofield, commander of that department. The troops of Sixteenth Corps with the expedition, however, were carried on the rolls of the Department of the Tennessee as detached. For details of Steele's expedition, see Little Rock, Arkansas Expedition (Steele).

August 7, 1863, Thirteenth Corps was sent downriver to the Department of the Gulf, and upon arrival there was sent to Carrollton, near New Orleans. For further information, see Department of the Gulf, Troops in the Department of the Gulf; and see also Thirteenth Corps, Department of the Gulf.

September 25–28, 1863, Sherman, with First Division, Second Division, and Fourth Division of his Fifteenth Corps, left Vicksburg for Memphis, en route to Chattanooga, Tennessee, where William S. Rosecrans' Army of the Cumberland was besieged by Braxton Bragg. Third Division, Fifteenth Corps was left at Vicksburg. Second Division, Seventeenth Corps joined Sherman and his Fifteenth Corps at Memphis October 8, and together they marched toward Chattanooga, where they arrived November 20. Sherman's command then participated in the Battle of Missionary Ridge November 23–25, 1863. For additional information, see Chattanooga-Ringgold Campaign (Battles of Lookout Mountain and Missionary Ridge, Tennessee). On October 24, Grant assumed command of the newly created Military Division of the Mississippi, and was succeeded by Sherman in command of the Army of the Tennessee.

In the early part of November 1863, Grenville M. Dodge with the Left Wing, Sixteenth Corps (Second Division, Sixteenth Corps) moved from Corinth, Mississippi to Pulaski, Tennessee, and remained there during the winter of 1863–1864. He was engaged in guarding and repairing the Tennessee and Alabama Railroad during this time.

Following the Union victories at Chattanooga in November 1863, Fifteenth Corps marched with Sherman's column for the relief of Knoxville, Tennessee, and arrived there December 6. James Longstreet, who had been threatening the town, then withdrew to the east, and Fifteenth Corps returned to Chattanooga. It spent the rest of the winter along the Memphis and Charleston Railroad in northern Alabama. For additional information, see Relief of Knoxville, Tennessee (William T. Sherman).

Seventeenth Corps, less Second Division, spent the winter at and near Vicksburg, Mississippi.

In February 1864, Sherman led an expedition eastward from Vicksburg to Meridian, Mississippi for the purpose of destroying the railroads and facilities of this important rail center. His command consisted of the following troops of Sixteenth Corps that Stephen A. Hurlbut had brought down from Memphis on transports: James M. Tuttle's First Division, Andrew J. Smith's Third Division, a detach-

ment of James C. Veatch's Fourth Division, and the following troops of James B. McPherson's Seventeenth Corps: Alexander Chambers' First Brigade, First Division; Mortimer D. Leggett's Third Division; and Marcellus M. Crocker's Fourth Division. In addition, William Sooy Smith, chief of cavalry of the Military Division of the Mississippi, commanded a cooperating column consisting of Benjamin H. Grierson's cavalry division of Sixteenth Corps. The expedition, except Tuttle's division, which was left on the Big Black River, left Vicksburg February 3 and, after completing its mission, returned to Vicksburg March 6. For details of the organization of operations of Sherman's force, see Meridian, Mississippi Expedition.

March 6, 1864, Veatch was ordered with his Fourth Division, Sixteenth Corps, then at Vicksburg, to move by way of Cairo, Illinois and report to Dodge, who was still at Pulaski, Tennessee with his Left Wing, Sixteenth Corps guarding the Tennessee and Alabama Railroad. Veatch arrived at Decatur, Alabama early in April, and Dodge then assembled his Second Division and Veatch's Fourth Division at Huntsville, Alabama May 2.

In March 1864 a detachment from the Army of the Tennessee was temporarily assigned to the Department of the Gulf to take part in Nathaniel P. Banks' Red River Campaign in Louisiana. This detachment, commanded by Andrew J. Smith, left Vicksburg March 10 for the Red River, and was organized as follows:

DETACHMENT ARMY OF THE TENNESSEE, Andrew J. Smith

First Division, Sixteenth Corps, Joseph A. Mower
    Second Brigade, Lucius F. Hubbard
    Third Brigade, Sylvester G. Hill

    Note 1. Mower was in command of both First Division and Third Division.
    Note 2. First Brigade was at Memphis, Tennessee.

Third Division, Sixteenth Corps
    First Brigade, William F. Lynch
    Second Brigade, William T. Shaw
    Third Brigade, Risdon M. Moore

    Note. Andrew J. Smith was the commander of Third Division, but during the Red River Campaign, Mower was in charge of both First Division and Third Division.

Provisional Division, Seventeenth Corps, T. Kilby Smith
    First Brigade, Jonathan B. Moore
    Second Brigade, Lyman M. Ward

Note. The Provisional Division was organized from First Brigade, Fourth Division, Seventeenth Corps, and was also known as the Red River Division.

Andrew J. Smith's Detachment Army of the Tennessee was engaged at the Battle of Pleasant Hill, Louisiana April 9, 1864, and at the unsuccessful conclusion of the Red River Campaign, Smith's command returned to Vicksburg May 23. On June 1, it was ordered to Memphis in the District of West Tennessee, and was then stationed at La Grange, Tennessee on the Memphis and Charleston Railroad. From that time Smith's command, then consisting of First Division and Third Division of Sixteenth Corps, was called Right Wing, Sixteenth Corps. For details of the participation of troops of the Army of the Tennessee in the Red River Campaign, see Red River, Louisiana Campaign.

Meantime, on April 17, 1864, Cadwallader C. Washburn was ordered to Memphis to relieve Stephen A. Hurlbut in command of the District of West Tennessee, and on May 2 Hurlbut was relieved of all command in Sixteenth Corps. No commander was assigned to succeed him. For the organization of the troops in West Tennessee at that time, see Department of the Tennessee, October 16, 1862–November 28, 1864, District of West Tennessee.

Meantime, preparations were continuing elsewhere for Sherman's spring campaign in northern Georgia. Fifteenth Corps left its winter quarters in northern Alabama May 1, 1864 and joined the army that Sherman was assembling in northern Georgia for the Atlanta Campaign May 8. Dodge, with his two divisions of Sixteenth Corps, joined Sherman's army in northern Georgia May 9. The rest of Sixteenth Corps was at Memphis, Tennessee; Columbus, Kentucky; Cairo, Illinois; Paducah, Kentucky, and, as noted above, with Banks' army on the Red River in the Department of the Gulf.

At the beginning of the Atlanta Campaign, the Army of the Tennessee was designated as the Right Wing, Army of Invasion of Georgia.

In March and April 1864, many of the regiments of Third Division and Fourth Division of Seventeenth Corps were in the North on veterans' furlough, and were under orders to rendezvous at Cairo, Illinois. Frank P. Blair, Jr. assumed command of Seventeenth Corps at Cairo May 4, then moved with the regiments that had assembled there to Huntsville, Alabama, where he arrived May 23. Seventeenth Corps was reorganized at Huntsville, and it then marched on to join Sherman's army at Acworth, Georgia June 8. First Division, Seventeenth Corps remained at Vicksburg, and did not participate in the Atlanta Campaign. Thus, in early June 1864 the Army of the Tennessee, then under the command of McPherson, and consisting of Fifteenth Corps; Left Wing, Sixteenth Corps; and Seventeenth Corps (less First Division), was assembled for the advance on Atlanta.

On March 18, 1864, Sherman had assumed command of the Military Division of the Mississippi, and on March 26 he had been succeeded by James B. McPherson in command of the Army of the Tennessee. McPherson was killed at the Battle of Atlanta July 22, and John A. Logan was then in temporary command until Oliver O. Howard assumed command July 27. Howard remained in command of the Army of the Tennessee until the end of the war.

During the Atlanta Campaign, the troops of the Army of the Tennessee were engaged as follows: Fifteenth Corps and Sixteenth Corps (Left Wing, Sixteenth Corps) at Rocky Face Ridge, May 5–9; Fifteenth Corps and Sixteenth Corps at Resaca, May 13–16; Fifteenth Corps and Sixteenth Corps at Dallas (New Hope Church, Pumpkin Vine Creek, and Pickett's Mill), May 25–June 4; Army of the Tennessee at Kennesaw Mountain, June 9–30 (assault of June 27); Army of the Tennessee at the Battle of Atlanta, July 22; Army of the Tennessee at the Battle of Ezra Church, July 28; Army of the Tennessee at the Siege of Atlanta, July 28–September 2; and Army of the Tennessee at Jonesboro August 31–September 1.

John B. Hood, then commanding the Confederate Army of Tennessee, evacuated Atlanta September 1, 1864. After the Battle of Jonesboro, he retreated southward to Lovejoy's Station, and Sherman's troops occupied Atlanta.

For details of the organization and operations of the Army of the Tennessee during the Atlanta Campaign, May 3–September 8, 1864, see Atlanta, Georgia Campaign.

During the Atlanta Campaign, Nathan B.

Forrest's Confederate cavalry was a constant threat to Sherman's supply line from the North, and to destroy his command or, failing that, to keep him occupied in northern Mississippi, three expeditions consisting of troops of the Army and Department of the Tennessee were sent out from Memphis during June, July, and August 1864. The first of these was Samuel D. Sturgis' Expedition from Memphis into Mississippi, June 1–13, with William L. McMillen's First Infantry Division of Sixteenth Corps and Benjamin H. Grierson's Cavalry Division, Sixteenth Corps. This expedition ended in defeat at Brice's Cross Roads, Mississippi. For details, see Sturgis' Expedition from Memphis, Tennessee into Mississippi (Battle of Brice's Cross Roads). The second was Andrew J. Smith's Expedition to Tupelo, Mississippi with his Right Wing, Sixteenth Corps and Grierson's Cavalry Division, District of West Tennessee. This expedition ended with a Union victory at Harrisburg, near Tupelo. For details, see Tupelo, Mississippi Expedition (Andrew J. Smith). The third expedition was to Oxford, Mississippi, August 1–30, and was also carried out by Andrew J. Smith's Right Wing, Sixteenth Corps and Grierson's Cavalry Division. For details, see Oxford, Mississippi Expedition (Andrew J. Smith).

In late August and early September 1864, Andrew J. Smith's Right Wing, Sixteenth Corps, consisting of First Division and Third Division, was relieved from duty in the District of West Tennessee, and was ordered to join Sherman's army in Georgia. Upon arrival at Cairo, Illinois, on the way to Nashville, Tennessee, however, Smith was directed to take his command to Saint Louis, Missouri to reinforce the troops of the Department of the Missouri, who were then confronted with a Confederate army under Sterling Price that had invaded the state from Arkansas. Smith's troops did not again return to the Department of the Tennessee. For information about their service in Missouri, see Price's Missouri Expedition.

In November 1864, after Price had been driven from the state, Smith's command was transferred to Nashville, Tennessee, in the Department of the Cumberland, which was then threatened by Hood's Confederate Army of Tennessee. On December 8, Sixteenth Corps as a corps organization having been discontinued, Smith's command, previously known as Right Wing, Sixteenth Corps, was redesignated as Detachment Army of the Tennessee.

Smith's Detachment Army of the Tennessee was engaged at the Battle of Nashville December 15–16, and in February 1865 it was sent to New Orleans, where on February 18 it was reorganized as Sixteenth Corps, Military Division of West Mississippi.

September 27, 1864, Napoleon J. T. Dana was assigned command of Sixteenth Corps, including the Combined Districts of West Tennessee and Vicksburg. Dana assumed command October 15, but on November 7, Sixteenth Corps was abolished. From that time on, the only troops of the Department and Army of the Tennessee were with Sherman in Georgia and later in the Carolinas, or with A. J. Smith.

For a description of the troops of Seventeenth Corps that were left at Vicksburg during the Atlanta Campaign, see Department of the Tennessee, October 16, 1862–November 28, 1864, District of Vicksburg.

The Left Wing, Sixteenth Corps with Sherman's army, commonly called Sixteenth Corps, consisted of only two divisions, and on September 22, 1864, Second Division, Sixteenth Corps was transferred to Fifteenth Corps as Fourth Division, Fifteenth Corps, and Fourth Division, Sixteenth Corps was transferred to Seventeenth Corps as First Division, Seventeenth Corps. On that date Sixteenth Corps was discontinued.

On September 28, Hood left Lovejoy's Station with his army and moved northward against the Western and Atlantic Railroad in an effort to destroy Sherman's supply line with the North. When he reached Dalton, Georgia, he turned westward toward Gadsden, Alabama. Sherman followed with his army, including the Army of the Tennessee, as far as Gaylesville, Alabama, near the Alabama state line, where he arrived on October 20. Hood moved on through northern Alabama to Decatur and Florence, where he arrived at the end of October. Later he began his invasion of Tennessee, which ended with his defeat at the Battle of Nashville December 15–16. Sherman remained near Gaylesville until October 28, and then began his return toward Atlanta.

On November 1, 1864, Fifteenth Corps and Seventeenth Corps of the Army of the Tennessee marched back from Cave Spring, twelve miles southwest of Rome, Georgia, by way of Kingston, and arrived at Smyrna Camp Ground, about midway between Marietta and the Chattahoochee River, November 5–8. The two corps remained there until November 13.

On November 9, in preparation for his march through Georgia, Sherman reorganized his field army, then consisting of four corps, into two wings as follows: Fifteenth Corps and Seventeenth Corps, Army of the Tennessee were designated as the Right Wing, under the command of Oliver O. Howard; and Fourteenth Corps and Twentieth Corps, Army of the Cumberland were designated as the Left Wing, under the command of Henry W. Slocum.

On November 11, Slocum's command was designated as the Left Wing, Army of Georgia (Slocum said Left Wing of the Army of Georgia). This seems to imply that there was a Right Wing, Army of Georgia, and if so, that should have been the designation of Howard's command. Howard seems to have recognized no such arrangement, and during the Savannah Campaign and the Carolinas Campaign, he signed his orders and official communications using the heading "Headquarters, Army of the Tennessee." Fifteenth Corps and Seventeenth Corps were commonly referred to as the Right Wing of Sherman's army in describing operations, but the designation Army of the Tennessee was used until the corps were discontinued August 1, 1865.

As the Right Wing of Sherman's army, the Army of the Tennessee marched through Georgia from Atlanta to Savannah during November and December 1864. It left Atlanta November 15 and marched generally by way of McDonough, Jackson, Hillsboro, Clinton, Gordon, Irwinton, Summerville, and Statesboro, arriving near the Atlantic Coast December 10–11. For details of the march through Georgia, see Savannah Campaign (Sherman's March through Georgia), in Volume I.

When Sherman's army left Atlanta on the march through Georgia, many officers and men belonging to Fifteenth Corps and Seventeenth Corps were left behind at Chattanooga (in the District of the Etowah), and were then unable to rejoin their proper commands. These were convalescents and others absent from the army for other reasons. On November 25, 1864, Thomas F. Meagher was assigned command of these troops, which were designated Provisional Division, Army of the Tennessee. These troops were taken to New Berne, North Carolina by Meagher, and from there they were sent to rejoin

Sherman's army when it arrived from Savannah. In February 1865 these troops became a part of the District of North Carolina, Department of North Carolina.

After the capture of Savannah December 21, 1864, Sherman prepared to march northward through the Carolinas with his army and join Grant and the Army of the Potomac in Virginia. Early in January 1865, Howard's Army of the Tennessee (or Right Wing of Sherman's Army) was transferred by sea to Beaufort, South Carolina. February 1 it marched from the vicinity of Pocotaligo, South Carolina by way of Bamberg, Orangeburg, Columbia, and Cheraw, all in South Carolina, arriving at Fayetteville, North Carolina March 11–12. From Fayetteville the Army of the Tennessee marched on toward Goldsboro without serious opposition.

At the same time, Slocum's Left Wing of Sherman's army was marching on roads to the left of the Army of the Tennessee toward Goldsboro, and was engaged at Averasboro March 16 and at Bentonville March 19. On March 20, Howard's march was interrupted when he turned aside with his two corps to help Slocum at Bentonville, but the Army of the Tennessee resumed its advance March 23 and reached Goldsboro the next day.

On April 10, 1865, the Army of the Tennessee again advanced toward Raleigh, North Carolina with the rest of Sherman's army, which had been reinforced with John M. Schofield's Army of the Ohio from the Department of North Carolina. It arrived there about April 13. Then, on April 26, Joseph E. Johnston surrendered his army to Sherman at Durham Station, North Carolina, and the war in the East was ended.

For details of the organization and operations of the Army of the Tennessee during the period January-April 1865, see Carolinas Campaign, in Volume I, and see also Fifteenth Corps, Army of the Tennessee and Seventeenth Corps, Army of the Tennessee.

April 29, 1865, the Army of the Tennessee left Raleigh for Washington, D.C. The line of march was generally by way of Jones' Springs and Macon to Robinson's Ferry on the Roanoke River; then by way of Lawrenceville and the Boydton Plank Road to Petersburg, Virginia; and finally on through Richmond, Fredericksburg, Dumfries, and Fairfax Court House to Alexandria, Virginia, where it arrived May 19.

On May 7, Howard, while at Petersburg, was ordered to Washington to report to the secretary of war. The commanders of Fifteenth Corps and Seventeenth Corps were directed to bring their corps on to Washington. On May 12, Howard was assigned to duty in the War Department as commissioner of the Bureau of Refugees, Freedmen, and Abandoned Lands. May 19, John A. Logan was assigned command of the Army of the Tennessee, and he assumed command May 23, relieving Howard.

The Army of the Tennessee marched in the Grand Review in Washington May 24, 1865, and was then ordered to Louisville, Kentucky for muster out. Fifteenth Corps left Washington June 1–2 and arrived at Louisville June 7–8. Seventeenth Corps left Washington and arrived at Louisville June 10–12.

There were two additions to the Army of the Tennessee in June 1865. The Army of Georgia was broken up early in the month, when Twentieth Corps was discontinued, and June 9–12, Fourteenth Corps, which then consisted only of western regiments, left Washington for Louisville. Upon arrival there, Fourteenth Corps was attached to the Army of the Tennessee.

On June 5, ten western regiments belonging to Second Corps and Fifth Corps, Army of the Potomac were detached and ordered to Louisville under the command of Henry A. Morrow, commander of First Brigade, Third Division, Fifth Corps. Upon arrival at Louisville, Morrow reported to Logan, and on June 28, the regiments of his command were organized into a provisional division, designated as Provisional Division, Army of the Tennessee. It was organized as follows:

Provisional Division, Henry A. Morrow
  First Brigade, John Pulford
  Second Brigade, John A. Kellogg

The regiments of this division were mustered out July 5–15, 1865.

The last regiments of the Army of the Tennessee were mustered out July 28, 1865, and the army was officially discontinued August 1.

For details of the organization and movements of the Army of the Tennessee during the period April 27–July 1865, see Fourteenth Corps, Army of the Cumberland; and see also Fifteenth Corps, Army of the Tennessee and Seventeenth Corps, Army of the Tennessee.

COMMANDERS OF THE ARMY OF THE TENNESSEE, DEPARTMENT OF THE TENNESSEE

Ulysses S. Grant	October 25, 1862 to October 24, 1863
William T. Sherman	October 24, 1863 to March 26, 1864
James B. McPherson	March 26, 1864 to July 22, 1864
John A. Logan	July 22, 1864 to July 27, 1864
Oliver O. Howard	July 27, 1864 to May 23, 1865
John A. Logan	May 23, 1865 to August 1, 1865

Note. March 18, 1864, Grant left for the East to assume command of the Armies of the United States, and Sherman assumed command of the Military Division of the Mississippi. McPherson did not arrive from Vicksburg and assume command of the Department and Army of the Tennessee until March 26.

ARMY OF THE TENNESSEE, DISTRICT OF WEST TENNESSEE FEBRUARY 17, 1862– OCTOBER 16, 1862

In February 1862, Ulysses S. Grant organized the troops in the District of Cairo, Department of the Missouri into three divisions, which he led in his successful campaign against Fort Henry and Fort Donelson February 6–16. At that time the designation of Grant's command was Army in the Field, District of Cairo, Department of the Missouri, and its organization at Fort Donelson was as follows:

ARMY IN THE FIELD, DISTRICT OF CAIRO, Ulysses S. Grant

First Division, John A. McClernand
  First Brigade, Richard J. Oglesby
    8th Illinois, Frank L. Rhoads
    18th Illinois, Michael K. Lawler
    29th Illinois, James S. Rearden
    30th Illinois, Elias S. Dennis

31st Illinois, John A. Logan
Artillery
  Battery D, 2nd Illinois Light Artillery, Jasper M. Dresser
  Battery E, 2nd Illinois Light Artillery, George C. Gumbart
Cavalry
  Companies A and B, 2nd Illinois Cavalry, John R. Hotaling
    Thomas J. Larison
  Company C, 2nd United States Cavalry, James Powell
  Company I, 4th United States Cavalry, James Powell
  Carmichael's Illinois Cavalry, Eagleton Carmichael
  Dollins' Illinois Cavalry, James J. Dollins
  O'Harnett's Illinois Cavalry, Morrison J. O'Harnett
  Stewart's Illinois Cavalry, Ezra King

Second Brigade, William H. L. Wallace
  11th Illinois, Thomas E. G. Ransom
  20th Illinois, C. Carroll Marsh
  45th Illinois, John E. Smith
  48th Illinois, Isham N. Haynie
  Battery B, 1st Illinois Light Artillery, Ezra Taylor
  Battery D, 1st Illinois Light Artillery, Edward McAllister
  4th Illinois Cavalry, T. Lyle Dickey

Third Brigade, William R. Morrison
  Leonard F. Ross
  17th Illinois, Francis M. Smith
    Henry H. Bush
  49th Illinois, Phineas Pease

Second Division, Charles F. Smith
  First Brigade, John McArthur
    9th Illinois, Jesse J. Phillips
    12th Illinois, Augustus L. Chetlain
    41st Illinois, Isaac C. Pugh
  Third Brigade, John Cook
    7th Illinois, Andrew J. Babcock
    50th Illinois, Moses M. Bane
    52nd Indiana, James M. Smith
    12th Iowa, Joseph J. Woods
    13th Missouri, Crafts J. Wright
    Battery D, 1st Missouri Light Artillery, Henry Richardson
    Battery H, 1st Missouri Light Artillery, Frederick Welker
    Battery K, 1st Missouri Light Artillery, George H. Stone

Fourth Brigade, Jacob G. Lauman
  25th Indiana, James C. Veatch
  2nd Iowa, James M. Tuttle
  7th Iowa, James C. Parrott
  14th Iowa, William T. Shaw
  Birge's Missouri Sharpshooters
Fifth Brigade, Morgan L. Smith
  11th Indiana George F. McGinnis
  8th Missouri, John McDonald

Third Division, Lewis Wallace
  First Brigade, Charles Cruft
    31st Indiana, John Osborn
    44th Indiana, Hugh B. Reed
    17th Kentucky, John H. McHenry, Jr.
    25th Kentucky, James M. Shackelford
  Second Brigade (attached to Third Brigade)
    46th Illinois, John A. Davis
    57th Illinois, Silas D. Baldwin
    58th Illinois, William F. Lynch
    20th Ohio, Charles Whittlesey
  Third Brigade, John M. Thayer
    1st Nebraska, William D. McCord
    58th Ohio, Ferdinand F. Remple
    68th Ohio, Samuel H. Steedman
    76th Ohio, William B. Woods
  Unattached
    Battery A, 1st Illinois Light Artillery, Peter P. Wood
    Company A, 32nd Illinois, Henry Davidson

Note. Cruft's First Brigade was formerly Thirteenth Brigade, Fifth Division, Army of the Ohio at Owensboro, Kentucky. Early in February 1862, Cruft was ordered to embark with his brigade, move down the Ohio River, and join Grant's army from the District of Cairo. Cruft joined Grant at Fort Henry after its capture by the navy, and he then joined Grant's column when it moved to Fort Donelson.

For details of the operations at Fort Henry and Fort Donelson, see Capture of Fort Henry and Fort Donelson, Tennessee.

February 14, 1862, Grant was assigned command of the newly created District of West Tennessee, Department of the Missouri. He assumed command February 17, with headquarters at Fort Donelson, which had just been surrendered to his army. The limits of the district were not defined, but it consisted of the United States forces that were to operate with him on the Tennessee River.

Also on February 14, when Halleck assigned

Grant to the command of the District of West Tennessee, he assigned William T. Sherman to command the District of Cairo in place of Grant. On February 25, Sherman moved to Paducah, Kentucky, where he began to organize a First Division, District of Cairo from new regiments at the post.

On February 21, the Army of the District of West Tennessee was reorganized into a force of four divisions. First Division and Third Division remained essentially the same as they were at Fort Donelson, but Jacob G. Lauman's Fourth Brigade of Second Division was transferred to a newly organized Fourth Division. This division, commanded by Stephen A. Hurlbut, was organized at Fort Donelson immediately after the surrender, and it consisted of new regiments that had arrived at Fort Donelson, and also of Lauman's brigade, which was redesignated as Third Brigade, Fourth Division. Fourth Division was organized as follows:

Fourth Division, Stephen A. Hurlbut
  First Brigade, Nelson G. Williams
    28th Illinois, Amory K. Johnson
    32nd Illinois, John Logan (not John A. Logan)
    41st Illinois, Isaac C. Pugh
    3rd Iowa, William M. Stone
  Second Brigade, James C. Veatch
    14th Illinois, Cyrus Hall
    15th Illinois, Edward F. W. Ellis
    46th Illinois, John A. Davis
    25th Indiana, William H. Morgan
  Third Brigade, Jacob G. Lauman
    31st Indiana, Charles Cruft
    44th Indiana, Hugh B. Reed
    17th Kentucky, John H. McHenry, Jr.
    25th Kentucky, Benjamin H. Bristow

Note. Lauman's Third Brigade, Fourth Division was formerly First Brigade of Lewis Wallace's Third Division, and it fought with that division at Fort Donelson before it was reassigned.

  Cavalry
    5th Ohio Cavalry (1st and 2nd Battalions), William H. H. Taylor

  Artillery
    2nd Battery, Michigan Light Artillery, Cuthbert W. Laing
    Mann's Missouri Battery, Edward Brotzmann
    13th Battery, Ohio Light Artillery, John B. Myers

On March 1, 1862, Halleck ordered Grant to move with his army up the Tennessee River for the purpose of destroying the Memphis and Charleston Railroad bridge over Bear Creek, near Eastport, Mississippi, and also of disrupting railroad communications at Corinth, Mississippi and Jackson and Humboldt in Tennessee, if practicable. Halleck then became dissatisfied with Grant for his alleged failure to forward reports as ordered, and for an unauthorized trip to Clarksville and Nashville, Tennessee, and on March 5 he replaced him in command of the expedition with Charles F. Smith. William H. L. Wallace assumed command of Smith's Second Division.

On March 4, 1862, Grant's forces at Fort Donelson marched to Fort Henry in preparation for the advance up the Tennessee River to Savannah, and March 7–8, Sherman embarked his division at Paducah for Fort Henry, where he joined the four divisions of Grant's army (then commanded by Charles F. Smith). The organization of Sherman's division at that time was as follows:

First Division, William T. Sherman
  First Brigade, Stephen G. Hicks
    40th Illinois, Stephen G. Hicks
    46th Ohio, Thomas Worthington
    Morton's Battery (6th Battery), Indiana Light Artillery, Frederick Behr
  Second Brigade, David Stuart
    55th Illinois, David Stuart
    71st Ohio, Rodney Mason
    54th Ohio, T. Kilby Smith
  Third Brigade, Jesse Hildebrand
    77th Ohio, Jesse Hildebrand
    57th Ohio, William Mungen
    53rd Ohio, Jesse J. Appler
  Fourth Brigade, Ralph P. Buckland
    72nd Ohio, Ralph P. Buckland
    48th Ohio, Peter J. Sullivan
    70th Ohio, Joseph R. Cockerill

The army moved upriver on transports from the landings near Fort Henry, and Sherman occupied Savannah March 8, 1862. By March 11, the rest of Smith's divisions had arrived.

Also on March 11, the Department of the Missouri was merged into the newly created Department of the Mississippi, under Halleck, and the District of West Tennessee and the Army of the District of West Tennessee became a part of Halleck's new department.

On the night of March 12, Lewis Wallace's Third Division moved upriver on transports, and in the morning it disembarked at Crump's Landing, about four miles above Savannah. Wallace then occupied the area around the landing with his infantry, and sent his cavalry on an expedition to destroy the Mobile and Ohio Railroad above Purdy.

From Savannah, on March 14, Sherman moved with his division on up the Tennessee to the mouth of Yellow Creek, where he landed and attempted to reach the Bear Creek bridge on the Memphis and Charleston Railroad. He was forced to abandon the movement because of rain and high water, and he then withdrew downstream to Pittsburg Landing, where he disembarked March 16 and went into camp. Hurlbut's Fourth Division was at Pittsburg Landing when Sherman arrived, and William H. L. Wallace's Second Division arrived within a few days. Lewis Wallace's Third Division was still encamped near Crump's Landing, and John A. McClernand's First Division had disembarked and occupied Savannah and the surrounding country. On March 20, however, McClernand was ordered with his division to Pittsburg Landing.

Grant resumed command of the army March 17, 1862, and headquarters was moved to Savannah. At about that time, Grant first referred to his Army of the District of West Tennessee as the Army of the Tennessee. It was not, however, until April 21, after the Battle of Shiloh, that the army was formally designated as the Army of the Tennessee.

Since Sherman had organized his division at Paducah, he continued to refer to it as First Division, Expeditionary Corps, although McClernand's Division at Savannah was also designated as First Division. When McClernand's First Division, Army of the Tennessee joined Grant's army at Pittsburg Landing on April 2, the designation of Sherman's division was changed to Fifth Division, Army of the Tennessee.

March 26, 1862, Benjamin M. Prentiss was assigned command of the unattached troops at Pittsburg Landing. As these troops arrived, they were formed into brigades, which were then organized into a new Sixth Division, Army of the Tennessee under the command of Prentiss. This division was organized as follows:

Sixth Division, Benjamin M. Prentiss

First Brigade, Everett Peabody
  12th Michigan, Francis Quinn
  21st Missouri, David Moore
  25th Missouri, Robert T. Van Horn
  16th Wisconsin, Benjamin Allen
Second Brigade, Madison Miller
  61st Illinois, Jacob Fry
  16th Iowa, Alexander Chambers
  18th Missouri, Isaac V. Pratt
  11th Illinois Cavalry (eight companies), Robert G. Ingersoll
  1st Battery, Minnesota Light Artillery, Emil Munch
  5th Battery, Ohio Light Artillery, Andrew Hickenlooper

With the organization of Prentiss' division, Grant's Army of the Tennessee, which was encamped near Pittsburg Landing, consisted of six divisions.

On the morning of April 6, 1862, Albert Sidney Johnston's Confederate Army of the Mississippi, which had advanced from Corinth, Mississippi, launched a surprise attack on Grant's divisions near Pittsburg Landing, driving them from their camps and during the day pushing them back to a final position near the Tennessee River. Don Carlos Buell's Army of the Ohio arrived that night, after a march from Nashville, Tennessee, and the next morning both armies advanced and, after stubborn fighting, forced the enemy to withdraw to Corinth. For details of the Battle of Shiloh, and the organization of the Army of the Tennessee at that time, see Battle of Shiloh (or Pittsburg Landing), Tennessee.

After the Battle of Shiloh, Halleck ordered John Pope to bring his Army of the Mississippi from near Fort Pillow on the Mississippi River and join the Army of the Tennessee and the Army of the Ohio at Pittsburg Landing. Halleck arrived at Pittsburg Landing April 12 and assumed personal command of Grant's and Buell's armies. Pope's army arrived at Pittsburg Landing on transports April 21 and the next day disembarked at Hamburg, Tennessee, above Pittsburg Landing.

Halleck then decided to advance on Corinth with his combined armies and, in preparation for this movement, reorganized his new Army of the Department of the Mississippi into a Right Wing, Center, Left Wing, and Reserve. In this reorganization, the Army of the Tennessee was partially broken up.

George H. Thomas, commander of First Division, Army of the Ohio, was assigned command of the Right Wing, which consisted of Second Division, Fourth Division, Fifth Division, and Sixth Division of Grant's Army of the Tennessee, and First Division, Army of the Ohio. First Division and Third Division of the Army of the Tennessee were assigned to the Reserve. Grant was made second-in-command to Halleck and was virtually without command during the advance on Corinth.

When Thomas' First Division, Army of the Ohio, then commanded by Thomas W. Sherman, was assigned to the Right Wing, its designation was changed to Seventh Division, Army of the Tennessee, and it retained that designation until the Army of the Ohio left Corinth in June 1862 on its return to Tennessee.

During May 1862, Halleck advanced very slowly toward Corinth, which was evacuated by the enemy May 30. The wing organization of the army was then discontinued, and on June 10, Grant resumed command of the restored Army of the Tennessee. The Army of the Tennessee, District of West Tennessee, however, did not again operate as a unit in the field.

Because of the loss of many officers and men at the Battle of Shiloh, there were many changes in the commanders of brigades and divisions during April and May 1862, and there were also some reorganizations in the army. These are described for each of the divisions as follows:

First Division

First Division, John A. McClernand, to May 2, 1862
  John A. Logan, to May 4, 1862
  Henry M. Judah, to June 2, 1862
  John B. S. Todd
  First Brigade, Marcellus M. Crocker, to April 19, 1862
    John A. Logan, to May 2, 1862
    Michael K. Lawler, to May 4, 1862
    John A. Logan
  Second Brigade, C. Carroll Marsh, to May 11, 1862
    Leonard F. Ross
  Third Brigade, Enos P. Wood
    C. Carroll Marsh
    John E. Smith, to May 4, 1862
    Michael K. Lawler

Artillery
  Battery D, 1st Illinois Light Artillery, George J. Wood
  Battery E, 2nd Illinois Light Artillery, George L. Nispel

Note 1. John A. Logan commanded the division temporarily when McClernand was assigned command of the Reserve of Halleck's army.
Note 2. C. Carroll Marsh commanded both Second Brigade and Third Brigade during the Battle of Shiloh.
Note 3. John E. Smith assumed temporary command of Third Brigade during the absence of Marsh on sick leave.

Second Division

Second Division, James M. Tuttle, to April 9, 1862
  John McArthur, to April 14, 1862
  Thomas A. Davies
  First Brigade, James M. Tuttle
  Second Brigade, Thomas Morton, to April 15, 1862
    Richard J. Oglesby
  Third Brigade, Silas D. Baldwin
  2nd Battalion, 1st Missouri Light Artillery, John S. Cavender

Third Division

Third Division, Lewis Wallace
  First Brigade, Morgan L. Smith, to mid-May 1862
    Alvin P. Hovey
  Second Brigade, John M. Thayer
  Third Brigade, Charles Whittlesey, to May 1862
    Charles R. Woods
  Artillery
    Battery A, 1st Illinois Light Artillery, Peter P. Wood
    Battery F, 1st Illinois Light Artillery, John T. Cheney
    Cogswell's Independent Battery, Illinois Light Artillery, William Cogswell
    9th Battery, Indiana Light Artillery, Noah S. Thompson
    8th Battery, Ohio Light Artillery, Louis Markgraf

Fourth Division

Fourth Division, Stephen A. Hurlbut
  First Brigade, Isaac C. Pugh, to April 1862

Jacob G. Lauman
Second Brigade, James C. Veatch
Third Brigade, Jacob G. Lauman
Artillery
    Battery L, 2nd Illinois Light Artillery, William H. Bolton
    Battery C, 1st Missouri Light Artillery, Charles Mann
    15th Battery, Ohio Light Artillery, Edward Spear

Note. Lauman's Third Brigade (which had originally been Charles Cruft's Thirteenth Brigade) was returned to the Army of the Ohio after the Battle of Shiloh, and it was then broken up and the regiments were reassigned. Lauman did not accompany the brigade when it departed; he was assigned command of First Brigade, Fourth Division.

Fifth Division

Fifth Division, William T. Sherman
    First Brigade, John A. McDowell, to May 15, 1862
        Morgan L. Smith
    Second Brigade, T. Kilby Smith
        David Stuart, to May 15, 1862
        John A. McDowell
    Third Brigade, Jesse Hildebrand, to May 15, 1862
        Ralph P. Buckland, to May 16, 1862
        James W. Denver
    Fourth Brigade, Ralph P. Buckland, to May 15, 1862
    Artillery, Ezra Taylor
        Battery B, 1st Illinois Light Artillery, Samuel E. Barrett
        Battery E, 1st Illinois Light Artillery, John A. Fitch
        Battery H, 1st Illinois Light Artillery, Axel Silfversparre
        Battery I, 1st Illinois Light Artillery, Edward Bouton
        6th Battery, Indiana Light Artillery, William Mussman

On May 15, 1862, Fifth Division was completely reorganized because of the reduced strength of the brigades. The new division consisted of three brigades of four regiments each. The two regiments of the original Second Brigade; the 8th Missouri, which had just been assigned to the division; and the 57th Ohio of the original Third Brigade were transferred to the new First Brigade, which was commanded by Morgan L. Smith. The three regiments of the original First Brigade (including John A. McDowell's 6th Iowa) and the 77th Ohio of the original Third Brigade were transferred to the new Second Brigade, which was commanded by McDowell. The three regiments of the original Fourth Brigade (including Ralph P. Buckland's 72nd Ohio) and the 53rd Ohio of the original Third Brigade were assigned to the new Third Brigade. Buckland was assigned command of the new Third Brigade, but on May 16, James W. Denver assumed command.

Sixth Division

Sixth Division suffered heavy losses in the Battle of Shiloh, including many that were taken prisoner, and among the latter were Benjamin M. Prentiss, the division commander, and Everett Peabody and Madison Miller, the two brigade commanders. As a result, it was necessary to reorganize the division. Thomas J. McKean was assigned as the new commander of the division, which was then reorganized into three brigades. The new First Brigade consisted of three regiments of the original First Brigade and John L. Doran's 17th Wisconsin. The new Second Brigade consisted of 18th Missouri of the original Second Brigade, and two unassigned regiments, including John M. Oliver's 15th Michigan. The new Third Brigade consisted of two regiments of First Brigade, First Division, Army of the Tennessee, including Marcellus M. Crocker's 13th Iowa; one regiment from the original Second Brigade; and one unassigned regiment.

The new Sixth Division was organized as follows:

Sixth Division, Thomas J. McKean
    First Brigade, John L. Doran, to May 23, 1862
        John McArthur
    Second Brigade, John M. Oliver
    Third Brigade, Ralph P. Buckland, to May 16, 1862
        Marcellus M. Crocker
    Artillery, Andrew Hickenlooper
        Battery F, 2nd Illinois Light Artillery, Christian D. Bliss
        1st Battery, Minnesota Light Artillery, William Pfaender
        3rd Battery, Ohio Light Artillery, William S. Williams
        5th Battery, Ohio Light Artillery, Lewis C. Sawyer
        10th Battery, Ohio Light Artillery, Hamilton B. White

* * * * * * * * * *

After the Confederates evacuated Corinth May 30, 1862, the divisions of the Army of the Tennessee were dispersed in West Tennessee to repair and guard the railroads in the area. On June 2, John A. McClernand's Reserve, Army of the Department of the Mississippi, which consisted of First Division and Third Division, Army of the Tennessee, was near Corinth. That day McClernand was ordered to move with his command toward Jackson and Bolivar, Tennessee. Lewis Wallace's Third Division arrived at Memphis June 18, and troops of his division also occupied Bolivar until June 24. John A. Logan's First Division arrived at Jackson on June 21.

The wings of the army were discontinued June 10, 1862, and on that date Grant resumed command of the Army of the Tennessee and the District of West Tennessee.

The Reserve was discontinued June 24, 1862, and that day McClernand was assigned command of the newly created District of Jackson, District of West Tennessee. First Division, Army of the Tennessee then became First Division, District of Jackson.

July 22, 1862, Wallace's Third Division, then commanded by Alvin P. Hovey while Wallace was on leave, was ordered to Helena, Arkansas to join Samuel R. Curtis' Army of the Southwest, which was moving toward Helena from northwestern Arkansas. Third Division thus left the District of West Tennessee and the Army of the Tennessee.

June 11, 1862, William T. Sherman led his own Fifth Division and Hurlbut's Fourth Division of the Army of the Tennessee from Chewalla, Tennessee, near Corinth, toward Grand Junction, Tennessee to cover the rebuilding of the Memphis Railroad. Fifth Division arrived at La Grange, Tennessee on June 14 and remained there until June 22. It then moved to Moscow, Tennessee, on the railroad, where it arrived June 25, then moved on to Memphis July 18. Sherman assumed command at Memphis July 21.

Hurlbut remained near La Grange until ordered to Moscow July 14, 1862, and from there he joined Sherman at Memphis. Hurlbut's division then left Memphis September 6 as an independent command, arriving at Bolivar, Tennessee, in the District of Jackson, September 13, where it remained through October.

In June 1862, Edward O. C. Ord relieved Thomas A. Davies in command of Second Division, and this division and Thomas J. McKean's Sixth Division of the Army of the Tennessee were assigned to the garrison of Corinth, where they remained during the rest of the summer and into the fall. There were some changes in command of Second Division during this period. On August 5, Ord was relieved from command of Second Division and the town of Corinth, and George Cadwalader assumed command. On August 13, however, Cadwalader was relieved from this command by Thomas A. Davies.

The Battle of Iuka, Mississippi was fought September 19, 1862, primarily by William S. Rosecrans' Army of the Mississippi. Ord, with three divisions of the Army of the Tennessee, was near the battlefield but was not engaged. During the battle, Sixth Division, then commanded by John McArthur, and Leonard F. Ross' Second Division, District of Jackson were near Iuka; and Thomas A. Davies' Second Division was near Burnsville. For additional information, see Engagement at Iuka, Mississippi.

The Department of the Mississippi was discontinued September 19, 1862, and on September 24, the District of West Tennessee, then in no department, was reorganized into four divisions as follows:

Sherman's command (Fifth Division, Army of the Tennessee) at Memphis became the First Division, District of West Tennessee, and Sherman was assigned command. His headquarters was at Memphis.

The District of Jackson, including First Division and Fourth Division of the Army of the Tennessee, became Second Division, District of West Tennessee, and Edward O. C. Ord was assigned command, with headquarters at Jackson or Bolivar.

The garrison at Corinth, which included Second Division and Sixth Division of the Army of the Tennessee and the Army of the Mississippi, became Third Division, District of West Tennessee. William S. Rosecrans was assigned command, with headquarters at Corinth.

Fourth Division, District of West Tennessee was

formed from the former districts of Cairo and Mississippi in the Department of the Mississippi, but it included no troops of the Army of the Tennessee. It did include Grenville M. Dodge's Central Division at Trenton, Tennessee, and Dodge was assigned command of the new Fourth Division.

For more detailed information about the organization of the troops in western Tennessee, see District of West Tennessee, under Miscellaneous Organizations. Second Division and Sixth Division, Army of the Tennessee fought with the Army of the Mississippi at the Battle of Corinth October 3–4, 1862. For details of the battle, see Battle of Corinth, Mississippi.

By an order of October 16, 1862, the Department of the Tennessee was created, and Grant was assigned command. Then, on October 24, the troops under Grant's command were designated as Thirteenth Corps, and the Army of the Tennessee, District of West Tennessee was discontinued.

ARMY OF THE WEST (LYON)

On July 13, 1862, Nathaniel Lyon arrived at Springfield, Missouri with a small army consisting of his own command from Boonville, Missouri and a force that Samuel D. Sturgis had brought from Fort Leavenworth, Kansas. At Springfield Lyon joined Thomas W. Sweeny's Southwestern Column, which had arrived there from Saint Louis, Missouri. Lyon immediately assumed command of all forces in the field, and on July 15 he called his command the Army of the West. On July 24 he reorganized his army as follows:

Army of the West, Nathaniel Lyon
    First Brigade, Samuel D. Sturgis
    Second Brigade, Franz Sigel
    Third Brigade, George L. Andrews
    Fourth Brigade, George W. Deitzler

This is the army that Lyon led at the Battle of Wilson's Creek August 10, 1861, although it was organized somewhat differently on that date. Lyon was killed at Wilson's Creek, and his army was defeated, and then Sturgis led the Army of the West

back to Saint Louis, where it was discontinued August 19, 1861.

For more detailed information, see Operations in Missouri in 1861.

ARMY OF WEST MISSISSIPPI

The forces commanded by Edward R. S. Canby that participated in the campaign against Mobile, Alabama March 17–April 12, 1865 were known as the Army of West Mississippi. They consisted of Thirteenth Corps, Military Division of West Mississippi; Sixteenth Corps, Military Division of West Mississippi; Frederick Steele's Column from Pensacola; and Benjamin H. Grierson's Cavalry Command. For details of the organization and operations of this army, see Land Operations against Mobile Bay and Mobile, Alabama.

ARMY OF WEST TENNESSEE

The District of West Tennessee was organized February 17, 1862, after the surrender of Fort Donelson, to include Ulysses S. Grant's forces operating on the Tennessee River. Grant's command was properly the Army of the District of West Tennessee, but it was sometimes called the Army of West Tennessee. Later, while Grant was at Savannah, Tennessee in March 1862, he began calling his army the Army of the Tennessee, and this designation was officially confirmed April 21, 1862. For further information, see Army of the Tennessee, District of West Tennessee.

ARMY OF WESTERN MISSOURI

The Army of Western Missouri is the name sometimes used to designate the troops commanded by John Pope in the District of Central Missouri, Department of the Missouri. For additional information, see Department of the Missouri, November 9, 1861–March 11, 1862, District of Central Missouri.

ARMY CORPS

★ ★ ★ ★

FIRST CORPS, ARMY OF THE MISSISSIPPI (McCLERNAND)

After William T. Sherman's unsuccessful expedition against Vicksburg, Mississippi by way of the Yazoo River, he returned with his army to Milliken's Bend, and there, on January 4, 1863, John A. McClernand relieved Sherman in command. McClernand then changed the designation of Sherman's Yazoo Expedition to Army of the Mississippi, which he organized into two corps. This was done in preparation for an expedition that McClernand proposed to lead against Arkansas Post (or Fort Hindman).

George W. Morgan's First Corps, Army of the Mississippi (McClernand) was organized January 4, 1863 from First Division and Third Division of Sherman's Yazoo Expedition. Andrew J. Smith's First Division, First Corps was organized from Smith's former First Division of the Yazoo Expedition, and Peter J. Osterhaus' Second Division, First Corps was organized from George W. Morgan's former Third Division of the Yazoo Expedition.

First Corps was engaged at Arkansas Post January 9–11, 1863, but on January 12, after the capture of Arkansas Post, the Army of the Mississippi was discontinued, and the designation of First Corps, Army of the Mississippi was changed to Thirteenth Corps, Army of the Tennessee, which had been constituted by an order of December 22, 1862.

For details of the organization and operations of First Corps, Army of the Mississippi (McClernand), see Operations against Vicksburg, Mississippi, 1861–1863, Early Attempts to Capture Vicksburg, Yazoo River, Mississippi Expedition (William T. Sherman)—Battle of Chickasaw Bayou (or Walnut Hills); and see also Engagement at Arkansas Post (or Fort Hindman), Arkansas.

FIRST CORPS, ARMY OF THE OHIO (BUELL)

In August 1862, E. Kirby Smith marched with an army from Knoxville, Tennessee into Kentucky, and Braxton Bragg with another army advanced from Chattanooga into Central Tennessee and then continued on northward into Kentucky to join Smith. At the beginning of Bragg's march, Don Carlos Buell, with his Army of the Ohio, was in South-Central Tennessee, but then Buell marched northward, first to Nashville and then on toward Louisville, where he arrived September 24–27. At Louisville, on September 29, Buell announced the reorganization of the Army of the Ohio into three corps, designated as First Corps, Second Corps, and Third Corps, Army of the Ohio. These corps were formed from the troops of the Army of the Ohio, two divisions recently arrived from the Army of the Mississippi, and many new regiments. For additional information, see Army of the Ohio (Buell), and see also Invasion of Kentucky and Tennessee (E. Kirby Smith and Braxton Bragg).

Alexander McD. McCook was assigned command of First Corps, which was organized as follows:

FIRST CORPS, ARMY OF THE OHIO, Alexander McD. McCook

Second Division, Joshua W. Sill
Fourth Brigade, Harvey M. Buckley
Fifth Brigade, Edward N. Kirk
Sixth Brigade, William H. Gibson
Artillery
    Battery A, 1st Ohio Light Artillery, Wilbur F. Goodspeed
    Battery E, 1st Ohio Light Artillery, Warren P. Edgarton
    Battery H, 5th United States Artillery, Francis L. Guenther

Third Division, Lovell H. Rousseau
Ninth Brigade, Leonard A. Harris
Seventeenth Brigade, William H. Lytle, to October 8, 1862, captured
    Curran Pope
Twenty-Eighth Brigade, John C. Starkweather

Note. Peter Simonson's 5th Battery, Indiana Light Artillery was attached to Ninth Brigade; Cyrus O. Loomis' 1st Battery, Michigan Light Artillery was attached to Seventeenth Brigade; and David C. Stone's Battery A, Kentucky Light Artillery was attached to Twenty-Eighth Brigade.

Tenth Division, James S. Jackson, to October 8, 1862, killed
    Albert S. Hall
Thirty-Third Brigade, William R. Terrill, to October 8, 1862, killed
    Albert S. Hall
    Thomas G. Allen
Thirty-Fourth Brigade, George Webster, to October 8, 1862, killed
    William P. Reid

Note. Parsons' Battery (improvised), commanded by Charles C. Parsons, was attached to Thirty-Third Brigade; and Samuel J. Harris' 19th Battery, Indiana Light Artillery was attached to Thirty-Fourth Brigade.

During the Perryville Campaign, Sill's division advanced from Louisville toward Frankfort to demonstrate in that direction, and it was not present at the Battle of Perryville. McCook, however, with the divisions of Rousseau and Jackson, bore the brunt of the enemy attack on the afternoon of October 8, 1862. Sill's division rejoined the corps after the battle, and the entire corps joined in the pursuit of the armies of Bragg and E. Kirby Smith as they

retreated toward East Tennessee. First Corps halted at Crab Orchard, however, then turned back, and toward the end of October marched to Bowling Green, Kentucky. For details of the activities of First Corps during the Perryville Campaign, see Invasion of Kentucky and Tennessee (E. Kirby Smith and Braxton Bragg), Battle of Perryville (or Chaplin Hills, Kentucky).

On October 23, 1862, Rousseau's Third Division and Jackson's Tenth Division were relieved from duty with First Corps, and Sheridan's Eleventh Division and Robert B. Mitchell's Ninth Division of Third Corps were transferred to First Corps. McCook's corps then consisted of Sill's Second Division, Mitchell's Ninth Division, and Sheridan's Eleventh Division. Charles C. Gilbert, formerly commander of Third Corps, Army of the Ohio, was assigned command of Jackson's former Tenth Division, which was detached from the corps, and also all troops on the lines of the railroad from Louisville to Munfordville and Lebanon, Kentucky. Thirty-Third Brigade of Tenth Division was stationed at Munfordville, and Thirty-Fourth Brigade of the same division was at Lebanon.

The Department of the Cumberland was re-created October 24, 1862, and the designation of Buell's Army of the Ohio was changed to Fourteenth Corps, Department of the Cumberland or, as it was more commonly known, the Army of the Cumberland.

On November 5, 1862, First Corps was discontinued and reassigned as the Right Wing, Fourteenth Corps (or Army of the Cumberland).

For further information, see Fourteenth Corps, Army of the Cumberland, October 24, 1862–January 9, 1863, and see also Army of the Cumberland, October 24, 1862–November 14, 1864, Reorganization of the Army, November 5, 1862.

SECOND CORPS, ARMY OF THE MISSISSIPPI (McCLERNAND)

After William T. Sherman's unsuccessful expedition against Vicksburg, Mississippi by way of the Yazoo River, he returned with his army to Milliken's Bend, and there, on January 4, 1863,

John A. McClernand relieved Sherman in command. McClernand then changed the designation of Sherman's Yazoo Expedition to Army of the Mississippi, which he organized to consist of two corps. This was done in preparation for an expedition that McClernand proposed to lead against Arkansas Post (or Fort Hindman). William T. Sherman's Second Corps, Army of the Mississippi (McClernand) was organized January 4, 1863 from Second Division and Fourth Division of the Yazoo Expedition. Frederick Steele's First Division, Second Corps was organized from Steele's former Fourth Division, and David Stuart's Second Division, Second Corps was organized from Morgan L. Smith's former Second Division.

Second Corps was engaged at Arkansas Post January 9–11, 1863, but on January 12, after the capture of Arkansas Post, the Army of the Mississippi was discontinued, and the designation of Second Corps, Army of the Mississippi was officially changed to Fifteenth Corps, Army of the Tennessee, which had been constituted by an order of December 22, 1862.

For details of the organization and operations of Second Corps, Army of the Mississippi (McClernand), see Operations against Vicksburg, Mississippi, 1861–1863, Early Attempts to Capture Vicksburg, Yazoo River, Mississippi Expedition (William T. Sherman)—Battle of Chickasaw Bayou (or Walnut Hills); and also Engagement at Arkansas Post (or Fort Hindman), Arkansas.

SECOND CORPS, ARMY OF THE OHIO (BUELL)

In August 1862, Braxton Bragg and E. Kirby Smith planned an invasion of Kentucky and Tennessee, with an army under Smith marching into Kentucky from Knoxville, Tennessee, and Bragg with his Army of the Mississippi marching northward into Central Tennessee and then into Kentucky to join Smith. At the beginning of Bragg's march, Don Carlos Buell was in South-Central Tennessee with his Army of the Ohio, but he then moved northward, keeping pace with Bragg, first to Nashville, and then on to Louisville, where he arrived September 24–27. At Louisville, on September 29, Buell reorganized the Army of the Ohio to consist of three corps, which were designated as First Corps, Second Corps, and Third Corps, Army of the Ohio. These corps were formed from troops of the Army of the Ohio, two divisions from the Army of the Mississippi, and many new regiments. For additional information about this reorganization, see Army of the Ohio (Buell), and see also Invasion of Kentucky and Tennessee (E. Kirby Smith and Braxton Bragg).

Thomas L. Crittenden was assigned command of Second Corps, which was organized as follows:

SECOND CORPS, Thomas L. Crittenden

Fourth Division, William Sooy Smith
   Tenth Brigade, William Grose
   Nineteenth Brigade, William B. Hazen
   Twenty-Second Brigade, Charles Cruft

Note. John Mendenhall's Battery M, 4th United States Artillery was attached to Smith's brigade; Daniel T. Cockerill's Battery F, 1st Ohio Light Artillery was attached to Hazen's brigade; and William E. Standart's Battery B, 1st Ohio Light Artillery was attached to Cruft's brigade.

Fifth Division, Horatio P. Van Cleve
   Eleventh Brigade, Samuel Beatty
   Fourteenth Brigade, Pierce B. Hawkins
   Twenty-Third Brigade, Stanley Matthews
   Artillery
      7th Battery, Indiana Light Artillery, George R. Swallow
      Battery B, Pennsylvania Light Artillery, Alanson J. Stevens
      3rd Battery, Wisconsin Light Artillery, Lucius H. Drury

Sixth Division, Thomas J. Wood
   Fifteenth Brigade, Milo S. Hascall
   Twentieth Brigade, Charles G. Harker
   Twenty-First Brigade, George D. Wagner

Note. George Estep's 8th Battery, Indiana Light Artillery was attached to Hascall's brigade; Cullen Bradley's 6th Battery, Ohio Light Artillery was attached to Harker's brigade; and Jerome B. Cox's 10th Battery, Indiana Light Artillery was attached to Wagner's brigade.

Second Corps marched with the army to Perryville and during the afternoon of October 8, 1862 formed on the right of Buell's line, south of the

Springfield Pike. It was on the field during the battle, but with the exception of Wagner's brigade of Wood's division, it was not engaged. Wagner's brigade was ordered forward late in the afternoon, when the enemy attacked Charles C. Gilbert's Third Corps, and was slightly engaged. Harker's brigade of Wood's division was ordered forward in support of Wagner, but it did not join in the fighting.

Second Corps joined in the pursuit of Braxton Bragg's army after the Battle of Perryville, following as far as Crab Orchard before turning back. The corps then marched back to Glasgow, Kentucky and arrived there near the end of October.

The Department of the Cumberland was re-created October 24, 1862, and the designation of Buell's Army of the Ohio was changed to Fourteenth Corps, Department of the Cumberland or, as it was commonly known, the Army of the Cumberland. On November 5, 1862, Second Corps was discontinued and was reassigned as Left Wing, Fourteenth Corps, Department of the Cumberland. For additional information, see Invasion of Kentucky and Tennessee (E. Kirby Smith and Braxton Bragg), and see also Fourteenth Corps, Army of the Cumberland, October 24, 1862–January 9, 1863, and Army of the Cumberland, October 24, 1862–November 14, 1864, Reorganization of the Army, November 5, 1862.

THIRD CORPS, ARMY OF THE OHIO (BUELL)

In August 1862, E. Kirby Smith advanced with an army from Knoxville, Tennessee into Kentucky, and Braxton Bragg marched northward with his Army of the Mississippi from Chattanooga into Central Tennessee, and then on into Kentucky to join Smith. At the beginning of Bragg's march, Don Carlos Buell, with his Army of the Ohio, was in South-Central Tennessee, but when Bragg continued his march toward Kentucky, Buell moved northward, keeping pace with Bragg, first to Nashville and then on to Louisville, where he arrived September 24–27. At Louisville, on September 29, Buell reorganized the Army of the Ohio to consist of three corps, which were designated as First Corps, Second Corps, and Third Corps, Army of the

Ohio. These corps were formed from troops of the Army of the Ohio, two divisions from the Army of the Mississippi, and many new regiments. For additional information, see Invasion of Kentucky and Tennessee (E. Kirby Smith and Braxton Bragg).

Charles C. Gilbert was assigned command of Third Corps, which was organized as follows:

THIRD CORPS, Charles C. Gilbert

First Division, Albin Schoepf
  First Brigade, Moses B. Walker
  Second Brigade, Speed S. Fry, to October 18, 1862, sick
  John M. Harlan
  Third Brigade, James B. Steedman
  Artillery
    4th Battery, Michigan Light Artillery, Josiah W. Church
    Battery C, 1st Ohio Light Artillery, Daniel K. Southwick
    Battery I, 4th United States Artillery, Frank G. Smith

Ninth Division, Robert B. Mitchell, to about October 21, 1862
  William E. Woodruff
  Thirtieth Brigade, Michael Gooding, to October 8, 1862, captured
  P. Sidney Post
  Thirty-First Brigade, William P. Carlin
  Thirty-Second Brigade, William W. Caldwell

Note 1. Ninth Division was organized from Jefferson C. Davis' Fourth Division, Army of the Mississippi.
Note 2. Oscar F. Pinney's 5th Battery, Wisconsin Light Artillery was assigned to Gooding's brigade; William A. Hotchkiss' 2nd Battery, Minnesota Light Artillery was assigned to Carlin's brigade; and Stephen J. Carpenter's 8th Battery, Wisconsin Light Artillery was assigned to Caldwell's brigade.

Eleventh Division, Philip H. Sheridan
  Thirty-Fifth Brigade, Bernard Laiboldt
  Thirty-Sixth Brigade, Daniel McCook
  Thirty-Seventh Brigade, Nicholas Greusel
  Artillery
    Battery I, 2nd Illinois Light Artillery, Charles M. Barnett
    Battery G, 1st Missouri Light Artillery, Henry Hescock

Note. Eleventh Division was organized from Gordon Granger's Fifth Division, Army of the Mississippi.

Third Corps marched with the Army of the Ohio to Perryville, and troops of Mitchell's and Sheridan's divisions were engaged in heavy fighting. Schoepf's division was on the field and was under fire, but it was not seriously engaged.

After the battle, Third Corps joined in the pursuit of Braxton Bragg's army on its return march toward East Tennessee. The corps halted at London, Kentucky and then marched back to Glasgow, Kentucky, where it arrived near the end of October.

On October 23, 1862, Third Corps was broken up by the transfer of Mitchell's Ninth Division and Sheridan's Eleventh Division to First Corps, Army of the Ohio. That same day Gilbert, former commander of Third Corps, was assigned command of 10th Division (formerly commanded by Jackson), which was detached from First Corps and consisted of Albert S. Hall's Thirty-Third Brigade, Silas A. Strickland's Thirty-Fourth Brigade, and a detachment of three infantry regiments and a company of cavalry commanded by William H. Benneson. Hall's brigade was at Munfordville, and Strickland's brigade at Lebanon. Gilbert's command was assigned to guard the Louisville and Nashville Railroad from Munfordville to Louisville, and the Lebanon Branch Railroad from Lebanon to Lebanon Junction.

The Department of the Cumberland was re-created October 24, 1862, and the designation of Buell's Army of the Ohio was changed to Fourteenth Corps, Department of the Cumberland or, as it was more commonly known, Army of the Cumberland. Tenth Division, the remaining division of Third Corps, was transferred to the newly organized Center, Fourteenth Corps (or Army of the Cumberland) November 5, 1862. For further information, see Fourteenth Corps, Army of the Cumberland, October 24, 1862–January 9, 1863, and see also Army of the Cumberland, October 24, 1862–November 14, 1864.

FOURTH CORPS, ARMY OF THE CUMBERLAND

By a presidential order dated September 28, 1863, Twentieth Corps and Twenty-First Corps of the Army of the Cumberland were consolidated to form a new Fourth Corps, Army of the Cumberland. The same order assigned Gordon Granger to the command of the corps, which he assumed October 10, with headquarters at Chattanooga, Tennessee. The organization of the corps was announced October 9, 1863 as follows:

FOURTH CORPS, Gordon Granger

First Division, John M. Palmer, to October 27, 1863
  Charles Cruft
  First Brigade, Charles Cruft
    Thomas D. Sedgwick
  Second Brigade, Walter C. Whitaker
  Third Brigade, William Grose
  Artillery, Peter Simonson
    5th Battery, Indiana Light Artillery, Peter Simonson
    Battery H, 4th United States Artillery, Harry C. Cushing
    Battery M, 4th United States Artillery, Francis L. D. Russell

Note 1. Palmer was assigned command of Fourteenth Corps October 27, 1863.
Note 2. First Brigade was formed by the consolidation of Second Brigade, First Division, Twentieth Corps and First Brigade, Second Division, Twenty-First Corps.
Note 3. Second Brigade was organized from First Brigade, First Division, Reserve Corps.
Note 4. Third Brigade was formed from the following unassigned regiments: 59th, 75th, and 84th Illinois; 9th, 30th, and 36th Indiana; 24th Ohio; and 77th Pennsylvania.
Note 5. Grose was assigned command of Third Brigade October 10, 1863.

Second Division, Philip H. Sheridan
  First Brigade, James B. Steedman
  Second Brigade, George D. Wagner
  Third Brigade, Charles G. Harker
  Artillery, William A. Naylor
    Battery M, 1st Illinois Light Artillery, George W. Spencer
    10th Battery, Indiana Light Artillery, William A. Naylor
    Battery G, 1st Missouri Light Artillery, Gustavus Schueler

Note 1. First Brigade was organized from First Brigade, Third Division, Twentieth Corps and Second Brigade, Third Division, Twentieth Corps.
Note 2. Second Brigade was organized from First Brigade, First Division, Twenty-First Corps and Second Brigade, First Division, Twentieth Corps.

Note 3. Third Brigade was organized from Third Brigade, First Division, Twenty-First Corps and from Third Brigade, Third Division, Twentieth Corps.

Note 4. Wagner's Second Brigade served at the post of Chattanooga, Tennessee until ordered to report to Granger and Fourth Corps November 6, 1863.

Third Division, Thomas J. Wood
First Brigade, August Willich
Second Brigade, William B. Hazen
Third Brigade, Samuel Beatty
Artillery, Cullen Bradley
Bridges' Battery, Illinois Light Artillery, Lyman Bridges
6th Battery, Ohio Light Artillery, Oliver H. P. Ayres
Battery B, Pennsylvania Light Artillery, Samuel M. McDowell

Note 1. First Brigade was organized from First Brigade, Second Division, Twentieth Corps and Third Brigade, First Division, Twentieth Corps.

Note 2. Second Brigade was organized from Second Brigade, Second Division, Twenty-First Corps and Third Brigade, Second Division, Twentieth Corps.

Note 3. Third Brigade was formed from First Brigade, Third Division, Twenty-First Corps and Second Brigade, Third Division, Twenty-First Corps.

It should be noted that in the above reorganization, some brigades were not reassigned intact, and in some instances regiments were added to an existing brigade.

During the battles around Chattanooga in November 1863, Charles Cruft's First Division, Fourth Corps, which was a part of the force commanded by Joseph Hooker, was engaged at the Battle of Lookout Mountain November 24, and on the afternoon of November 25, Philip H. Sheridan's Second Division and Thomas J. Wood's Third Division took part in the Battle of Missionary Ridge. At that time, First Brigade, First Division, Fourth Corps was at Bridgeport, Alabama; two regiments of Second Brigade, First Division were at Shellmound, Tennessee; and two regiments of Third Brigade, First Division were at Whiteside, Tennessee. At the end of November and during December, First Division, then under David S. Stanley, was at Bridgeport.

In late November, following the Battle of Missionary Ridge, Granger, with Second Division and Third Division, Fourth Corps, marched with a force commanded by William T. Sherman to the relief of

Ambrose E. Burnside, who was besieged by James Longstreet's corps at Knoxville, Tennessee. When Sherman arrived at Maryville, Tennessee, he learned that Longstreet had left the front of Knoxville and had marched away to the east. Sherman returned to Chattanooga with a part of his force, but he left Granger with his two divisions in East Tennessee as a reinforcement for Burnside. For additional information, see Relief of Knoxville, Tennessee (William T. Sherman). First Division joined the corps in East Tennessee in January 1864.

Headquarters, Fourth Corps was established at Blain's Cross Roads in December 1863, and it was then moved to Loudon, Tennessee, where it remained until preparations were begun for the Atlanta Campaign. Headquarters was then moved to Cleveland, Tennessee in April 1864.

In February 1864, First Division, under the temporary command of Charles Cruft, took part in George H. Thomas' demonstration before Dalton, Georgia. First Brigade, First Division, temporarily commanded by David A. Enyart while Cruft commanded the division, remained at Ooltewah, Tennessee, and its place was taken in the demonstration by Charles L. Matthies' brigade of Fifteenth Corps, which was commanded by Willard A. Dickerman. During the demonstration, this brigade was designated as First Brigade, First Division, but the assignment was not permanent. It was ordered to rejoin Fifteenth Corps March 1, 1864. The organization of First Division for the demonstration was as follows:

First Division, Charles Cruft
First Brigade, Willard A. Dickerman
Second Brigade, Thomas E. Champion
Third Brigade, William Grose

For details of Thomas' demonstration, see Demonstration on Dalton, Georgia.

Fourth Corps rejoined the Army of the Cumberland for the Atlanta Campaign May 3–September 8, 1864. It was most heavily engaged at Pickett's Mills and at Kennesaw Mountain, but it was also engaged at Rocky Face Ridge, Resaca, Dallas and New Hope Church, Peach Tree Creek, the Siege of Atlanta, and Jonesboro. For details of the operations of Fourth Corps during the Atlanta Campaign, see Atlanta, Georgia Campaign.

The organization of Fourth Corps during the Atlanta Campaign was as follows:

FOURTH CORPS, Oliver O. Howard, to July 27, 1864
  David S. Stanley

First Division, David S. Stanley, to July 27, 1864
  William Grose, to August 4, 1864
  Nathan Kimball
  First Brigade, Charles Cruft, to June 10, 1864, sick
    Isaac M. Kirby
  Second Brigade, Walter C. Whitaker, to June 30, 1864, sick
    Jacob E. Taylor
  Third Brigade, William Grose, to July 27, 1864
    P. Sidney Post, to August 4, 1864
    William Grose, to September 4, 1864
    John E. Bennett
  Artillery, Peter Simonson, to June 16, 1864, killed
    Samuel M. McDowell, to June 27, 1864, killed
    Theodore S. Thomasson
    5th Battery, Indiana Light Artillery, Alfred Morrison
    Battery B, Pennsylvania Light Artillery, Samuel M. McDowell
    Jacob Ziegler

Note 1. Howard assumed command of the Army of the Tennessee July 27, 1864.
Note 2. The artillery of the division was merged into the Artillery Brigade of the corps July 26, 1864.

Second Division, John Newton
  First Brigade, Francis T. Sherman, to May 22, 1864
    Nathan Kimball, to August 4, 1864
    Emerson Opdyke
  Second Brigade, George D. Wagner, to July 10, 1864, sick
    John W. Blake, to July 25, 1864
    George D. Wagner
  Third Brigade, Charles G. Harker, to June 27, 1864, killed
    Luther P. Bradley
  Artillery, Charles C. Aleshire, to June 24, 1864
    Wilbur F. Goodspeed
    Battery M, 1st Illinois Light Artillery, George W. Spencer
    Battery A, 1st Ohio Light Artillery, Wilbur F. Goodspeed
    Charles W. Scovill

Note 1. Newton was assigned command of Second Division, Fourth Corps April 16, 1864, relieving Philip H. Sheridan. Sheridan was assigned command of the Cavalry Corps, Army of the Potomac by an order dated April 4, 1864.

Note 2. The division artillery was merged into the Artillery Brigade of the corps July 26, 1864.

Third Division, Thomas J. Wood, to September 2, 1864, wounded
  P. Sidney Post, temporarily
  Thomas J. Wood
  First Brigade, August Willich, to May 15, wounded
    William H. Gibson
    Richard H. Nodine, left for muster out August 1, 1864
    William H. Gibson, left for muster out August 25, 1864
    Charles T. Hotchkiss
  Second Brigade, William B. Hazen, to August 17, 1864
    Oliver H. Payne, to August 19, 1864
    P. Sidney Post
  Third Brigade, Samuel Beatty, to May 23, 1864, sick
    Frederick Knefler
  Artillery, Cullen Bradley
    Bridges' Battery, Illinois Light Artillery, Lyman Bridges, to May 23, 1864
    Morris D. Temple, to June 8, 1864
    Lyman A. White
    6th Battery, Ohio Light Artillery, Oliver H. P. Ayres, to May 30, 1864
    Lorenzo D. Immell, to June 28, 1864
    Oliver H. P. Ayres, to July 6, 1864, wounded
    Lorenzo D. Immell

Note. William B. Hazen was transferred to the Army of the Tennessee August 17, 1864.

Artillery Brigade, Thomas W. Osborn, July 26, 1864 to July 30, 1864
  Lyman Bridges
  Battery M, 1st Illinois Light Artillery, George W. Spencer
  Bridges' Battery, Illinois Light Artillery, Lyman A. White
  5th Battery, Indiana Light Artillery, Alfred Morrison
  George H. Briggs
  Battery A, 1st Ohio Light Artillery, Wilbur F. Goodspeed
  Battery M, 1st Ohio Light Artillery, Frederick Schultz
  6th Battery, Ohio Light Artillery, Lorenzo D. Immell, to August 1, 1864
  Cullen Bradley
  Battery B, Pennsylvania Light Artillery, Jacob Ziegler

Note. The Artillery Brigade of Fourth Corps was organized July 26, 1864.

In late September 1864, after the capture of Atlanta, John B. Hood, in command of the Confederate Army of Tennessee, moved northward from Lovejoy's Station along the Western and Atlantic Railroad to interrupt Sherman's communications with the North and to threaten the invasion of Tennessee. Hood moved northward as far as Dalton, Georgia, then turned west toward Alabama and arrived at Decatur on October 26. Sherman followed with his army from near Atlanta until he reached Gaylesville, Alabama, and there he halted. As a precautionary measure against a possible Confederate invasion of Tennessee, Sherman sent George H. Thomas to Nashville to take command in the state, and he then sent David S. Stanley's Fourth Corps and John M. Schofield's Twenty-Third Corps to reinforce the troops under Thomas in Tennessee. For additional information about the movement of Fourth Corps to Tennessee, see Franklin and Nashville Campaign (Hood's Invasion of Tennessee).

At the end of October 1864, Fourth Corps was organized as follows:

FOURTH CORPS, David S. Stanley

First Division, Walter C. Whitaker
    First Brigade, Isaac M. Kirby
    Second Brigade, James C. Evans
    Third Brigade, Louis H. Waters

Second Division, George D. Wagner
    First Brigade, Emerson Opdyke
    Second Brigade, William Grose
    Third Brigade, Luther P. Bradley

Third Division, Thomas J. Wood
    First Brigade, John A. Martin
    Second Brigade, P. Sidney Post
    Third Brigade, Frederick Knefler

Artillery Brigade, Lyman Bridges
    Bridges' Battery, Illinois Light Artillery, Lyman A. White
    Battery A, 1st Ohio Light Artillery, Charles W. Scovill
    6th Battery, Ohio Light Artillery, Cullen Bradley
    Battery B, Pennsylvania Light Artillery, Jacob Ziegler

Fourth Corps was concentrated at Pulaski, Tennessee between November 1 and November 5, 1864, except First Brigade, First Division, which was guarding the trains and did not arrive until November 25. On October 29, 1864, Hood's army marched northward into Tennessee from Decatur, Alabama; John M. Schofield, commanding both Fourth Corps and Twenty-Third Corps, was forced to fall back to Columbia, Tennessee November 23–24. Hood followed, then crossed the Duck River above Columbia and marched toward Spring Hill, where he hoped to cut Schofield's line of retreat to Nashville. On November 29–30, Fourth Corps and Twenty-Third Corps marched by Spring Hill to Franklin, Tennessee, and that evening both corps were engaged in the bloody Battle of Franklin.

The organization of Fourth Corps November 30, 1864 was as follows:

FOURTH CORPS, David S. Stanley

First Division, Nathan Kimball
    First Brigade, Isaac M. Kirby
    Second Brigade, Walter C. Whitaker
    Third Brigade, William Grose

    Note. Kimball rejoined the division and resumed command November 25, 1864.

Second Division, George D. Wagner
    First Brigade, Emerson Opdyke
    Second Brigade, John Q. Lane
    Third Brigade, Joseph Conrad

    Note. Luther P. Bradley was wounded at Spring Hill November 29, 1864, and he was succeeded in command of Third Brigade by Joseph Conrad.

Third Division, Thomas J. Wood
    First Brigade, Abel D. Streight
    Second Brigade, P. Sidney Post
    Third Brigade, Samuel Beatty

Artillery Brigade, Lyman Bridges
    Bridges' Battery, Illinois Light Artillery, Lyman A. White
    1st Battery, Kentucky Light Artillery, Theodore S. Thomasson
    Battery A, 1st Ohio Light Artillery, Charles W. Scovill
    Battery G, 1st Ohio Light Artillery, Alexander Marshall
    6th Battery, Ohio Light Artillery, Aaron P. Baldwin
    20th Battery, Ohio Light Artillery, John S. Burdick
    Battery B, Pennsylvania Light Artillery, Jacob Ziegler
    Battery M, 4th United States Light Artillery, Samuel Canby

For details of the march from Columbia to Franklin and the Battle of Franklin, see Franklin and Nashville Campaign (Hood's Invasion of Tennessee).

Soon after the Battle of Franklin ended, Fourth Corps and Twenty-Third Corps marched toward Nashville, where they arrived December 1, 1864 and became a part of the United States Forces under Thomas. Hood followed and formed his army in a fortified position south of Nashville. A number of command changes occurred at Nashville December 2. Stanley, who had been wounded at Franklin November 30, was relieved from command of Fourth Corps by Thomas J. Wood. In turn, Samuel Beatty assumed command of Wood's Third Division, and Frederick Knefler assumed command of Beatty's Third Brigade. Also on December 2, George D. Wagner was relieved from command of Second Division, and he was succeeded by Washington L. Elliott. The two armies remained quietly confronting one another for about two weeks, during which there was some very bad weather that halted all troop movements, but when this had ended, Thomas advanced and attacked Hood's army. In the Battle of Nashville December 15–16, 1864, he decisively defeated Hood and drove his army from the state. The organization of Fourth Corps at Nashville was as follows:

FOURTH CORPS, Thomas J. Wood

First Division, Nathan Kimball
    First Brigade, Isaac M. Kirby
    Second Brigade, Walter C. Whitaker
    Third Brigade, William Grose

Second Division, Washington L. Elliott
    First Brigade, Emerson Opdyke
    Second Brigade, John Q. Lane
    Third Brigade, Joseph Conrad

Third Division, Samuel Beatty
    First Brigade, Abel D. Streight
    Second Brigade, P. Sidney Post, to December 16, 1864, wounded
        Robert L. Kimberly
    Third Brigade, Frederick Knefler

Artillery Brigade, Wilbur F. Goodspeed
    25th Battery, Indiana Light Artillery, Frederick C. Sturm

1st Battery, Kentucky Light Artillery, Theodore S. Thomasson
Battery E, 1st Michigan Light Artillery, Peter De Vries
Battery G, 1st Ohio Light Artillery, Alexander Marshall
6th Battery, Ohio Light Artillery, Aaron P. Baldwin
Battery B, Pennsylvania Light Artillery, Jacob Ziegler
Battery M, 4th United States Artillery, Samuel Canby

For details of the operations of Fourth Corps at the Battle of Nashville, see Franklin and Nashville Campaign (Hood's Invasion of Tennessee).

The Battle of Nashville was the last battle in which Fourth Corps was engaged. After the battle, the corps joined in the pursuit of Hood's defeated army until January 5, 1865, when it arrived at Huntsville, Alabama. Fourth Corps remained at Huntsville through February and into early March. At the end of February it was organized as follows:

FOURTH CORPS, David S. Stanley

First Division, William Grose
    First Brigade, Isaac M. Kirby
    Second Brigade, Jesse H. Moore
    Third Brigade, John E. Bennett

Note. Stanley resumed command of Fourth Corps January 31, 1865.

Second Division, Washington L. Elliott
    First Brigade, John Russell
    Second Brigade, Ferdinand Van Derveer
    Third Brigade, Joseph Conrad

Third Division, Samuel Beatty
    First Brigade, Abel D. Streight
    Second Brigade, Henry K. McConnell
    Third Brigade, George F. Dick

Note. Beatty was in temporary command of Third Division during the absence of Thomas J. Wood.

Artillery Brigade, Alexander Marshall
    1st Battery, Kentucky Light Artillery, Theodore S. Thomasson
    Battery G, 1st Ohio Light Artillery, Nathaniel M. Newell
    6th Battery, Ohio Light Artillery, Aaron P. Baldwin
    Battery B, Pennsylvania Light Artillery, Jacob Ziegler

On March 12, 1865, Fourth Corps received orders to move to East Tennessee to prevent a possible attempt to escape by Robert E. Lee's Army of Northern Virginia in Virginia and Joseph E. Johnston's army in North Carolina. Both armies were hard-pressed, and it was feared that they might escape into the interior. First Division, Fourth Corps left Huntsville March 13–14, and Third Division followed March 15. Second Division remained at Huntsville. On April 17, Fourth Corps was ordered to begin its withdrawal from East Tennessee and move to Nashville. On April 26, Headquarters, Fourth Corps was established at Nashville.

May 30, 1865, Fourth Corps was ordered from the Department of the Cumberland to the Military Division of the Southwest. For further information, see Fourth Corps, Military Division of the Southwest.

COMMANDERS OF FOURTH CORPS, ARMY OF THE CUMBERLAND

Gordon Granger	October 10, 1863 to April 10, 1864, relieved
Oliver O. Howard	April 10, 1864 to July 27, 1864
David S. Stanley	July 27, 1864 to December 2, 1864
Thomas J. Wood	December 2, 1864 to January 31, 1865
David S. Stanley	January 31, 1865 to May 30, 1865

FOURTH CORPS, MILITARY DIVISION OF THE SOUTHWEST

In March 1865, Fourth Corps, Army of the Cumberland was ordered to move from Huntsville, Alabama, where it was then encamped, to East Tennessee. The purpose of this movement was to guard the passes in the mountains and prevent a possible attempt by Robert E. Lee's army in Virginia and Joseph E. Johnston's army in North Carolina to escape the advancing Union armies in the East and to retire into the interior. On April 17, when no longer required in East Tennessee, Fourth Corps

was ordered to Nashville, Tennessee, where it remained until the end of May. On May 30, the corps was ordered from the Department of the Cumberland to the Military Division of the Southwest. For the operations and organization of Fourth Corps, Army of the Cumberland, see Fourth Corps, Army of the Cumberland.

On June 5, that part of Fourth Corps that consisted of veterans was ordered to New Orleans to report to Edward R. S. Canby. On the same day, an order was issued from Headquarters, Department of the Cumberland for the reorganization of Fourth Corps. This was the first reorganization of the corps since its formation. The following organization was announced June 7, 1865:

FOURTH CORPS, David S. Stanley

First Division, Nathan Kimball
    First Brigade, Thomas E. Rose
    Second Brigade, Isaac C. B. Suman

Second Division, Washington L. Elliott
    First Brigade, Emerson Opdyke
    Second Brigade, Luther P. Bradley

Third Division, Thomas J. Wood
    First Brigade, August Willich
    Second Brigade, Samuel Beatty

Ferdinand Van Derveer, formerly commanding Second Brigade, Second Division, was assigned command of the men of Fourth Corps who were to be mustered out after the remainder of Fourth Corps had departed. On June 9, 1865, William Grose, formerly commander of Third Brigade, First Division, was relieved from duty in Fourth Corps.

On June 15, Second Division, Fourth Corps was ordered from Nashville to New Orleans, and Third Division followed two days later. All three divisions had arrived at New Orleans by June 29. On June 24, while the movement was in progress, Emerson Opdyke relieved Washington L. Elliott in command of Second Division.

During the first two weeks of July 1865, the three divisions embarked for Indianola, Texas. Stanley's headquarters was at Victoria until October, and was then moved to San Antonio. At about that time, the first troops of the regiments to be mustered out were sent home. Fourth Corps was officially discontinued by an order of August 1, 1865. Some troops of the former Fourth Corps remained in Texas during the rest of the year as a part of Philip H. Sheridan's Army of Occupation, but most regiments were mustered out in December.

David S. Stanley commanded Fourth Corps, Military Division of the Southwest from the time it left Nashville for Texas until it was discontinued August 1, 1865.

SEVENTH CORPS, DEPARTMENT OF ARKANSAS

On September 10, 1863, Frederick Steele captured Little Rock, Arkansas and established Federal control in that part of the state. Then, on January 6, 1864, the Department of Arkansas was constituted to consist of the state of Arkansas, except Fort Smith, and Steele was assigned command. On the same date, the troops in the Department of Arkansas were designated as Seventh Corps. Steele assumed command January 20. For details of the organization of Seventh Corps, see Department of Arkansas.

NINTH CORPS

A general description of the service of Ninth Corps in the Department of the Ohio and at Vicksburg in the Department of the Tennessee has been included under Ninth Corps in Volume I. For additional information about Ninth Corps in Kentucky and East Tennessee that is covered in Volume II, see Army of the Ohio (Burnside), April 11, 1863–April 4, 1864, and see also East Tennessee Campaign (Burnside). For information about Ninth Corps at Vicksburg, Mississippi in the Department of the Tennessee, see Operations against Vicksburg, Mississippi, 1861–1863, Siege of Vicksburg, Mississippi, May 23, 1863–July 4, 1863, and see also Jackson, Mississippi Campaign (William T. Sherman).

ELEVENTH CORPS, ARMY OF THE CUMBERLAND

When the secretary of war, Edwin M. Stanton, learned of William S. Rosecrans' defeat at the Battle of Chickamauga in September 1863, he became concerned at the possible loss of Chattanooga, and on the night of September 23 he called a meeting at the War Department to which President Abraham Lincoln was invited. It was then decided to send two corps from the Army of the Potomac to reinforce the Army of the Cumberland, and the next morning the president directed that Eleventh Corps and Twelfth Corps be sent to Tennessee under the command of Joseph Hooker.

In September 1863, the Eleventh Corps in Virginia consisted of only two divisions, the First Division having been sent to the Department of the South, and it was organized as follows:

ELEVENTH CORPS, Oliver O. Howard

Second Division, Adolph Von Steinwehr
    First Brigade, Adolphus Buschbeck
    Second Brigade, Orland Smith

Third Division, Carl Schurz
    First Brigade, George Von Amsberg
    Second Brigade, Wladimir Krzyzanowski

Artillery, Thomas W. Osborn
    Battery I, 1st New York Light Artillery, Michael Wiedrich
    13th Battery, New York Light Artillery, William Wheeler
    Battery I, 1st Ohio Light Artillery, Hubert Dilger
    Battery K, 1st Ohio Light Artillery, Columbus Rodamour
    Battery G, 4th United States Artillery, Eugene A. Bancroft

Eleventh Corps was already encamped along the Orange and Alexandria Railroad when it received the order, and it moved first. On September 25, the troops entrained at Bristoe Station and Manassas Junction and traveled to Washington, D.C. From there they moved west by the Baltimore and Ohio Railroad to Benwood, West Virginia.

By 9:15 A.M. September 27, 12,600 men, 33 cars

of artillery, and 21 cars of baggage had left Washington, and the first train had arrived at Benwood. At that time Twelfth Corps began embarking at Bealeton Station on the Orange and Alexandria Railroad to follow Eleventh Corps west.

After crossing the Ohio River to Bellaire, Ohio, Eleventh Corps continued on by way of the Central Ohio and Indiana Central railroads through Columbus, Ohio to Indianapolis, Indiana. The first train reached Indianapolis on the afternoon of September 28, and at the same time the last troops of Twelfth Corps were leaving Bealeton Station in Virginia.

From Indianapolis, Eleventh Corps proceeded on to Jeffersonville, Indiana, then crossed the Ohio River to Louisville, Kentucky. From there it continued on to Nashville, Tennessee by the Louisville and Nashville Railroad, and the men then boarded the cars of the Nashville and Chattanooga Railroad for Stevenson and Bridgeport in Alabama. The first four trains arrived at Bridgeport September 30, but they could go no farther because the bridge over the Tennessee River had been destroyed. On September 30, the last troop trains reached Benwood, and on October 2, the last troops of Eleventh Corps arrived at Bridgeport. Some regiments of Twelfth Corps also joined them there.

The next day, October 3, Hooker arrived at Stevenson, Alabama and established his headquarters of Eleventh Corps and Twelfth Corps. Oliver O. Howard, commanding Eleventh Corps, joined the corps at Bridgeport October 4.

By October 8, 1863, the troop movement was completed. The baggage of the two corps, including horses, wagons, ambulances, and commissary, followed over the same route during the first two weeks of October.

During the period September 3–October 17, 1863, Philip D. Roddey and Joseph Wheeler were conducting cavalry raids in Tennessee on Rosecrans' lines of communications, and on October 4, Eleventh Corps was assigned to guard the railroad from Bridgeport, Alabama to Tantalon, Tennessee, a short distance south of Cowan. Orland Smith's Second Brigade, Second Division was posted at Tantalon, Anderson, Stevenson, and Widow's Creek, and the rest of the corps remained at Bridgeport. For additional information about the protection of the railroad north of Tantalon, see Twelfth Corps, Army of the Cumberland. The organization of Eleventh Corps during this period was as follows:

ELEVENTH CORPS, Oliver O. Howard

Second Division, Adolph Von Steinwehr
    First Brigade, Adolphus Buschbeck
    Second Brigade, Orland Smith

Third Division, Carl Schurz
    First Brigade, Frederick Hecker, to October 19, 1863
        Stephen J. McGroarty, temporarily
        Hector Tyndale
    Second Brigade, Wladimir Krzyzanowski
    Third Brigade, Frederick Hecker

Note. Third Brigade was organized October 19, 1863 from three regiments taken from Second Division and Third Division of Eleventh Corps and one regiment from Fourteenth Corps.

October 16, 1863, Ulysses S. Grant was assigned command of the newly created Military Division of the Mississippi, and he immediately began preparations for the relief of the Army of the Cumberland, which was under siege at Chattanooga. John W. Geary's Second Division of Twelfth Corps was ordered to Bridgeport October 23 to join Eleventh Corps for an advance into Lookout Valley.

Hooker's advance began on October 27, with Adolph Von Steinwehr's Second Division of Eleventh Corps in the lead, and it was followed by Carl Schurz's Third Division of Eleventh Corps and then by John W. Geary's Second Division of Twelfth Corps. Hooker's column marched along the railroad, passing through Whiteside, and arrived at Brown's Ferry on the Tennessee River during the afternoon of October 28. Geary's division camped that night at Wauhatchie, about three miles from the encampments of Eleventh Corps. Hooker accompanied Geary on the march that day but joined Schurz's division that night.

Shortly after midnight on October 29, Geary was attacked at Wauhatchie by troops of John B. Hood's Confederate division, and Schurz was sent with his division to support him. A short time later Von Steinwehr's division followed Schurz. Hector Tyndale's First Brigade, which was leading Schurz's division, and Orland Smith's Second Brigade, which was leading Von Steinwehr's division, encountered some resistance during the advance, and Frederick Hecker's Third Brigade and Wladimir Krzyzanowski's Second Brigade of Schurz's Third Division halted until the way was clear. They then moved on. Hecker's brigade finally arrived at Wauhatchie at daybreak, about two hours after the fighting had ended, and it was placed in line near the railroad. Krzyzanowski's brigade arrived about 7:00 A.M. and was placed on the extreme right of Geary's line. The latter two brigades returned to their proper commands on the afternoon of October 31. For details of the Battle of Wauhatchie, see Army of the Cumberland, October 24, 1862–November 14, 1864, Siege of Chattanooga, Tennessee, Reopening of the Tennessee River, Engagement at Wauhatchie, Tennessee.

In preparation for its part in the battles that were to drive Bragg's army from its positions at Chattanooga, Howard's Eleventh Corps marched from its camps in Lookout Valley at 2:00 P.M. November 22, 1863 and crossed the Tennessee River at Brown's Ferry. It then took the direct road to Chattanooga, recrossed the river there, and camped near Fort Wood,

Eleventh Corps took no part in the Battle of Lookout Mountain, and only a minor part in the Battle of Missionary Ridge, where it was attached to William T. Sherman's command of the Army of the Tennessee. Only Buschbeck's brigade was seriously engaged.

On November 26, 1863, Eleventh Corps marched with Sherman in pursuit of Bragg's retreating army and advanced as far as Graysville, Georgia. The next morning it moved on toward the railroad between Dalton, Georgia and Cleveland, Tennessee. For additional information about the operations of Eleventh Corps during this period, see Chattanooga-Ringgold Campaign (Battles of Lookout Mountain and Missionary Ridge, Tennessee).

The organization of Eleventh Corps during the battle around Chattanooga in late November 1863 was as follows:

ELEVENTH CORPS, Oliver O. Howard

Second Division, Adolph von Steinwehr
    First Brigade, Adolphus Buschbeck
    Second Brigade, Orland Smith

Third Division, Carl Schurz
    First Brigade, Hector Tyndale
    Second Brigade, Wladimir Krzyzanowski
    Third Brigade, Frederick Hecker

Artillery, Thomas W. Osborn
    Battery I, 1st New York Light Artillery, Michael Wiedrich
    13th Battery, New York Light Artillery, William Wheeler
    Battery I, 1st Ohio Light Artillery, Hubert Dilger
    Battery K, 1st Ohio Light Artillery, Nicholas Sahm
    Battery G, 4th United States Artillery, Christopher F. Merkle

Note. Dilger's and Merkle's batteries were temporarily attached to Second Division, Fourth Corps, Army of the Cumberland.

Eleventh Corps was at Parker's Gap, near Red Clay, Georgia, on November 28, when William T. Sherman was ordered with his command to Knoxville, Tennessee, where Ambrose E. Burnside was under siege by a Confederate force commanded by James Longstreet. The relief column reached Maryville, Tennessee December 5, and there Sherman learned that Longstreet had given up the siege and had withdrawn from in front of Knoxville and moved off to the east. Sherman then sent Gordon Granger's Fourth Corps to reinforce Burnside's forces in East Tennessee, and he returned with his command, including Eleventh Corps, to Chattanooga. By December 17, Eleventh Corps had returned to its old camps in Lookout Valley. For additional information, see Relief of Knoxville, Tennessee (William T. Sherman).

On January 25, 1864, Schurz's Third Division left Lookout Valley and took positions for guarding the Nashville and Chattanooga Railroad. First Brigade was posted opposite Bridgeport, Alabama; Second Brigade at Shellmound, Tennessee; and Third Brigade at Whiteside, Tennessee. Third Division remained generally along the railroad during February and March 1864.

On January 2, 1864, a new division was organized from William T. Ward's brigade at Nashville and John Coburn's brigade at Murfreesboro. Ward was assigned command of the division, with headquarters at Nashville, and Benjamin Harrison was assigned command of Ward's brigade. On January 16, this division was designated as First Division, Eleventh Corps, and it was organized as follows:

First Division, Eleventh Corps, William T. Ward
  First Brigade, Benjamin Harrison
  Second Brigade, John Coburn

Ward's division remained at Nashville until February 23, 1864, and then Harrison's First Brigade moved to Tullahoma, where it arrived February 29. Harrison's brigade, with Division Headquarters, left Tullahoma on March 2 and arrived at Wauhatchie March 10.

On March 24, Third Division, Eleventh Corps was reduced to two brigades when its Third Brigade was discontinued.

On April 14, (ordered April 4), Eleventh Corps was discontinued when it was consolidated with Twelfth Corps to form a reorganized Twentieth Corps, Army of the Cumberland. For details of the reorganization, see Twentieth Corps, Army of the Cumberland, April 14, 1864–November 14, 1864.

TWELFTH CORPS, ARMY OF THE CUMBERLAND

On September 24, 1863, Eleventh Corps and Twelfth Corps were detached from the Army of the Potomac and ordered to Tennessee as a reinforcement for William S. Rosecrans' Army of the Cumberland, which was then under siege by Braxton Bragg's Confederate Army of Tennessee at Chattanooga. On the same day, Joseph Hooker was assigned command of the two corps.

The organization of Twelfth Corps in Virginia in September 1863 was as follows:

TWELFTH CORPS, Henry W. Slocum

First Division, Alpheus S. Williams
  First Brigade, Joseph F. Knipe
  Second Brigade, Thomas H. Ruger

Second Division, John W. Geary
  First Brigade, Charles Candy
  Second Brigade, George A. Cobham, Jr.
  Third Brigade, George S. Greene

Artillery, John A. Reynolds

Battery M, 1st New York Light Artillery, Charles E. Winegar
Battery E, Pennsylvania Light Artillery, Charles A. Atwell
Battery F, 4th United States Artillery, Edward D. Muhlenberg
Battery K, 5th United States Artillery, David H. Kinzie

On the afternoon of September 24, 1863, Henry W. Slocum's Twelfth Corps was relieved from duty along the Rapidan River by John Newton's First Corps, Army of the Potomac, and at 5:30 P.M. it marched for Brandy Station on the Orange and Alexandria Railroad to entrain for Washington, D.C. The corps arrived at Brandy Station the next day but, finding no cars there, it moved on that evening to Bealeton Station. It then departed for Washington September 27–28, following Eleventh Corps, which had started September 25. It then moved westward by rail through Columbus, Ohio, Indianapolis, Indiana, and Louisville, Kentucky to Nashville, Tennessee. For additional information about the route followed, see Eleventh Corps, Army of the Cumberland.

A few regiments of Twelfth Corps arrived at Bridgeport, Alabama with Eleventh Corps about October 1, 1863, but the corps proper did not arrive at Nashville until the next day. On October 3, Hooker arrived at Stevenson, Alabama and established headquarters there for his command of Eleventh Corps and Twelfth Corps.

Also on October 3, Slocum, the commander of Twelfth Corps, and Oliver O. Howard, commander of Eleventh Corps, were informed by Rosecrans that Confederate cavalry under Philip D. Roddey and Joseph Wheeler were raiding on his lines of communications in Tennessee, and that the Nashville and Chattanooga Railroad was probably one of their objectives. Eleventh Corps was already safely at Bridgeport, but Slocum was directed to stop his corps on the railroad and place one division at Wartrace and one division at Decherd. The next day Twelfth Corps was assigned to guard the railroad from Wartrace south to Tantalon, a short distance south of Cowan. This order was not immediately complied with, however, as the troops were for a time shifted about in an effort to prevent the destruction of the railroad by the enemy cavalry.

On October 4, 1863, Wheeler's cavalry approached Murfreesboro from McMinnville, and troops of Twelfth Corps were ordered to Murfreesboro to protect the railroad between that point and Wartrace. Part of the corps was also guarding the railroad between Cowan and Bridgeport. October 5–6, Wheeler's cavalry destroyed trestles and bridges between Murfreesboro and Wartrace, then moved on and captured Shelbyville, Tennessee.

On October 6, most of the troops of Twelfth Corps had arrived at Nashville from the east, and Slocum was also there attending to the supplies and corps property that were then in transit. That day, Hooker, who was then at Stevenson, Alabama, ordered Daniel Butterfield, his chief of staff, to assume command of the troops of Twelfth Corps that were below the break in the line of the railroad caused by Wheeler and to advance northward toward Murfreesboro and restore communications. Butterfield relinquished his temporary command to Slocum October 9 at Murfreesboro.

On October 10, Alpheus S. Williams moved the headquarters of his First Division, Twelfth Corps from Murfreesboro to Decherd, and John W. Geary established headquarters of his Second Division at Murfreesboro. On October 13, Slocum formally assumed command of all United States troops that were along the Nashville and Chattanooga Railroad from Murfreesboro to Tantalon, and he established his headquarters at Wartrace.

On October 16, Ulysses S. Grant was assigned command of the newly created Military Division of the Mississippi (assumed command October 18), and he immediately began preparations for the relief of the Army of the Cumberland at Chattanooga. The same order of October 16, 1863 that assigned Grant to the command of the Military Division of the Mississippi also assigned George H. Thomas to the command of the Army of the Cumberland, relieving Rosecrans. Thomas assumed command October 19.

On October 23, Williams was assigned to guard the railroad from Murfreesboro to Bridgeport, and Geary was ordered to move with his Second Division to Bridgeport, where he was to join Hooker and the Eleventh Corps for an advance along the south side of the Tennessee River toward Chattanooga.

Slocum then established headquarters of Twelfth Corps at Wartrace; Williams moved his headquarters of First Division, Twelfth Corp to Tullahoma;

and Hooker's headquarters of Eleventh Corps and Twelfth Corps was at Stevenson, Alabama.

Hooker's command left Bridgeport October 27, 1863 and advanced along the Nashville and Chattanooga Railroad toward Lookout Valley. Geary's division, which followed Eleventh Corps, arrived at Wauhatchie, Tennessee during the afternoon of October 28 and camped for the night. At about the same time, Eleventh Corps reached Brown's Ferry on the Tennessee River, about three miles from Wauhatchie, and it also went into camp.

Shortly after midnight, Geary's division was strongly attacked by a brigade of John B. Hood's Confederate division, but it was able to hold its position for about three hours until the enemy withdrew. For details of this engagement, see Army of the Cumberland, October 24, 1862–November 14, 1864, Siege of Chattanooga, Tennessee, Reopening of the Tennessee River, Engagement at Wauhatchie, Tennessee. George S. Greene, commanding the Third Brigade of Geary's division, was seriously wounded during the fighting, and he was succeeded in command of the brigade by David Ireland.

On October 31, Hooker changed his position at Wauhatchie to a range of hills about a mile and a half from the railroad in the direction of Kelley's Ferry. The line ran diagonally across Lookout Valley, with Geary's division on the right near Raccoon Mountain.

On the afternoon of November 22, Howard's Eleventh Corps marched into Chattanooga and left Geary's division to cover the entire front. The opening movements to drive Bragg's army from Chattanooga began the next day. During the battles of Lookout Mountain and Missionary Ridge, and during the pursuit of Bragg's army to Ringgold, Georgia, Geary's Second Division was the only part of either Eleventh Corps or Twelfth Corps that was under Hooker's immediate command. The temporary command to which Geary's division was attached during these operations, and which was under Hooker's direct control, consisted of Charles Cruft's First Division, Fourth Corps; John W. Geary's Second Division, Twelfth Corps; and Peter J. Osterhaus' First Division, Fifteenth Corps of the Army of the Tennessee.

Geary's division took part in the Battle of Lookout Mountain November 24, 1863, and the next day it advanced across the valley of Chattanooga Creek to Missionary Ridge, but it was not seriously engaged. On November 26, it marched in pursuit of Bragg's army through Graysville, arriving at Ringgold, Georgia November 27. That day Geary's and Osterhaus' divisions were engaged at Ringgold Gap in Taylor's Ridge. The organization of Geary's division during the operations about Chattanooga was as follows:

Second Division, Twelfth Corps, John W. Geary
    First Brigade, Charles Candy, to November 24, 1863, disabled
        William R. Creighton, to November 27, 1863, killed
        Thomas J. Ahl
    Second Brigade, George A. Cobham, Jr.
    Third Brigade, David Ireland

Note. Candy later resumed command of First Brigade.

For details of the operations around Chattanooga and the pursuit of Bragg, see Chattanooga-Ringgold Campaign (Battles of Lookout Mountain and Missionary Ridge, Tennessee).

Geary's division remained at Ringgold until December 1, 1863, then returned to its camps at Wauhatchie. During the remainder of its period of existence, Twelfth Corps was engaged in garrison duty and in guarding the Nashville and Chattanooga Railroad. Williams' First Division, which in October 1863 was assigned to guard the railroad from Wartrace to Bridgeport, continued in this duty until the corps was discontinued April 14, 1864.

On December 23, 1863, First Brigade of Geary's Second Division, then commanded by John H. Patrick, was ordered to Bridgeport, and Cobham's Second Brigade was sent to Tantalon. The next day Ireland's Third Brigade was ordered to Stevenson. Headquarters of Geary's division was established at Bridgeport.

By an order of January 2, 1864, Robert S. Granger's division in the District of Nashville, Department of the Cumberland was reorganized, and this division, together with the posts within the district, was assigned to Lovell H. Rousseau. Rousseau's division was assigned to Twelfth Corps, but it remained in the District of Nashville and did not join the corps. It was organized as follows:

Rousseau's Division, Lovell H. Rousseau

First Brigade, Robert S. Granger
Second Brigade, Horatio P. Van Cleve
Third Brigade, James G. Spears, to February 6, 1864
    William Cross, to March 7, 1864
    Joseph A. Cooper

Note. Third Brigade belonged to the post of Chattanooga, but was serving in East Tennessee.

Twelfth Corps was discontinued April 14, 1864 (ordered April 4) by the consolidation of Eleventh Corps and Twelfth Corps to form a new Twentieth Corps under the command of Joseph Hooker. For details of the consolidation, see Twentieth Corps, Army of the Cumberland, April 14, 1864–November 14, 1864.

THIRTEENTH CORPS, ARMY OF THE TENNESSEE OCTOBER 24, 1862– JANUARY 14, 1863

The Department of the Tennessee was created October 16, 1862 to include the territory previously belonging to the District of West Tennessee, and Ulysses S. Grant was assigned command. On October 24, 1862, Thirteenth Corps was constituted to consist of the troops in the Department of the Tennessee under the command of Grant. Although the official designation was Thirteenth Corps, it was commonly called the Army of the Tennessee. Grant assumed command of the department and Thirteenth Corps October 25, 1862.

At the time the District of West Tennessee was merged into the Department of the Tennessee, the troops present in the district were organized as four divisions, but on October 26, 1862 these divisions were redesignated as districts of the Department of the Tennessee as follows:

First Division, District of West Tennessee became the District of Memphis, under the command of William T. Sherman.

Second Division, District of West Tennessee became the District of Jackson, under the command of Stephen A. Hurlbut.

Third Division, District of West Tennessee became the District of Corinth, under the command of Charles S. Hamilton.

Fourth Division, District of West Tennessee became the District of Columbus, under the command of Thomas A. Davies.

DIVISIONS OF THIRTEENTH CORPS

During November and December 1862, the troops in the districts of Memphis, Corinth, and Jackson were organized into divisions of Thirteenth Corps (or Army of the Tennessee), and because Thirteenth Corps included all troops in the Department of the Tennessee, its original organization was fairly complex. Then on December 18, 1862, a new Thirteenth Corps, a Fifteenth Corps, a Sixteenth Corps, and a Seventeenth Corps were created to consist of the troops of the former Thirteenth Corps. Considerable confusion results when attempting to understand the organizations of the new corps, and also the changes in organization that resulted from the numerous assignments and reassignments in the following months. For this reason, a brief summary of the organization of each of the original divisions of Thirteenth Corps and their assignments among the four new corps of the army are given here.

First Division. First Division was organized November 12, 1862 in the District of Memphis, in part from regiments of William T. Sherman's former Fifth Division of the District of Memphis, and it was assigned to the Right Wing, Army in the Field, Thirteenth Corps as First Division. It was assigned to Seventeenth Corps December 22, 1862 and to Sixteenth Corps January 20, 1863. It was then transferred to Fifteenth Corps July 28 and designated as Fourth Division, Fifteenth Corps.

The commanders of the division were as follows:

James W. Denver	November 12, 1862 to December 9, 1863
James B. McPherson	December 9, 1863 to December 18, 1863
James W. Denver	December 18, 1863

Second Division. Second Division was organized in the District of Memphis, in part from troops of Sherman's former Fifth Division, District of Memphis. It was designated as Second Division, Right Wing, Thirteenth Corps of Sherman's Yazoo Expedition in late December 1862. It then became Second Division, Second Corps of John A. McClernand's Army of the Mississippi during the expedition against Arkansas Post. On January 12, 1863, it was designated as Second Division, Fifteenth Corps.

The commanders of the division were as follows:

Morgan L. Smith	November 12, 1862 to December 28, 1862
David Stuart	December 28, 1862

Third Division. Third Division, Thirteenth Corps was organized November 1, 1862 in the District of Jackson, and it was assigned to the Right Wing, Army in the Field, Thirteenth Corps during Ulysses S. Grant's operations in northern Mississippi. John A. Logan was assigned command of the division. On December 22, 1862, Third Division was assigned to Seventeenth Corps.

To avoid confusion, it should be noted that a Third Division, District of Memphis was organized at Memphis, Tennessee November 23, 1862 under the command of Jacob G. Lauman. This division accompanied William T. Sherman to Oxford, Mississippi during Grant's operations in northern Mississippi, but it was broken up December 10, 1862.

Fourth Division. Fourth Division was organized in November 1862 in the District of Jackson, and it was assigned to the Right Wing, Army in the Field, Thirteenth Corps during Ulysses S. Grant's operations in northern Mississippi. Fourth Division was assigned to Seventeenth Corps December 22, 1862, but on January 20, 1863 it was assigned to Sixteenth Corps. Then on June 24, 1863 it was temporarily attached to Thirteenth Corps, and this was made a permanent assignment on July 28. Finally, on August 7, 1863, the division was transferred to Seventeenth Corps as Fourth Division, Seventeenth Corps.

The commanders of Fourth Division were as follows:

| Thomas J. McKean | November 11, 1862 to December 9, 1862 |
| Jacob G. Lauman | December 9, 1862 |

Fifth Division. There was no Fifth Division in Thirteenth Corps, and the Fifth Division referred to in this section was formerly William T. Sherman's Fifth Division, District of Memphis, Army of the Tennessee. In October 1862, this division, together with some new regiments and regiments from other organizations, was reorganized into five brigades in the District of Memphis. Then on November 12, these brigades were organized into a First Division and a Second Division, District of Memphis, Thirteenth Corps. The troops of the former Fifth Division were assigned to Fifteenth Corps December 22, 1862.

Sixth Division. Sixth Division was organized in the District of Corinth early in November 1862, and it was assigned to the Left Wing, Army in the Field, Thirteenth Corps during Grant's operations in northern Mississippi. John McArthur was assigned command of the division. On December 22, Sixth Division was assigned to Sixteenth Corps, and on January 20, 1863 it was assigned to Seventeenth Corps. The division was discontinued as Sixth Division September 14, 1863, and was redesignated as First Division, Sevent   h Corps.

Seventh Division. Seventh Division was organized from Third Division, Army of the Mississippi in the District of Corinth in November 1862, and it was assigned to the Left Wing, Army in the Field, Thirteenth Corps during Grant's operations in northern Mississippi. Isaac F. Quinby was assigned command of the division. For additional information, see Army of the Mississippi (Pope, Rosecrans). Seventh Division was assigned to Sixteenth Corps December 22, 1862, and then to Seventeenth Corps January 20, 1863. The division was discontinued as Seventh Division, and was redesignated as Second Division, Seventeenth Corps September 14, 1863.

Eighth Division. Eighth Division was organized in the District of Corinth November 1, 1862 from Second Division, Army of the Mississippi, and it was assigned to the Left Wing, Army in the Field, Thirteenth Corps during Grant's operations in northern Mississippi. The division was assigned to Sixteenth Corps December 22, 1862, and to Fifteenth Corps April 1, 1863. On April 3, 1863, the designation of the division was changed to Third Division, Fifteenth Corps.

The commanders of Eighth Division were as follows:

David S. Stanley	November 1, 1862 to November 11, 1862
Leonard F. Ross	November 11, 1862 to December 26, 1862
John E. Smith	December 26, 1862

Ninth Division. Ninth Division was formerly Seventh Division, Army of the Ohio, and it was transferred to Memphis, Tennessee in November 1862 as the Cumberland Division, District of Western Virginia, Department of the Ohio. Upon arrival at Memphis, it was redesignated as Ninth Division, Thirteenth Corps. It was assigned to the newly constituted Thirteenth Corps December 22, 1862, and later in the month it was designated as Third Division, Right Wing of Thirteenth Corps, in William T. Sherman's Yazoo Expedition.

January 4, 1863, the division was redesignated as Second Division, First Corps, Army of the Mississippi, which John A. McClernand led against Arkansas Post and Fort Hindman. On January 12, the designation was changed to Ninth Division of the newly organized Thirteenth Corps. On July 30, 1863, Ninth Division was consolidated with Fourteenth Division, and the designation became First Division, Thirteenth Corps.

The commanders of the division were as follows:

| George W. Morgan | November 1862 to January 4, 1863 |
| Peter J. Osterhaus | January 4, 1863 |

Tenth Division. Tenth Division was formerly First Division, Army of Kentucky, which was ordered to Memphis, Tennessee November 13, 1862. It was then redesignated as Tenth Division, Thirteenth Corps under the command of Andrew J. Smith, and in late December it was designated as First Division, Right Wing, Thirteenth Corps, Sherman's Yazoo Expedition. On December 22, Tenth Division was assigned to Thirteenth Corps, which was reconstituted by a presidential order of December

18, 1862, but this order was not immediately put into effect. On January 4, 1863, the designation of the division was changed to First Division, First Corps of John A. McClernand's newly organized Army of the Mississippi, but on January 14, the designation was again changed to Tenth Division, of the reconstituted Thirteenth Corps.

On August 7, 1863, Thirteenth Corps was transferred to the Department of the Gulf, and on August 14, the designation of Smith's division became Fourth Division, Thirteenth Corps, Department of the Gulf.

Eleventh Division. Eleventh Division was organized in December 1862 at Helena, Arkansas from Frederick Steele's Division, District of Eastern Arkansas, and Steele was assigned command. Later in the month it was designated as Fourth Division, Right Wing, Thirteenth Corps, Sherman's Yazoo Expedition, and then on January 4, 1863 it became First Division, Second Corps of John A. McClernand's Army of the Mississippi. It had been assigned to Fifteenth Corps December 22, 1862, but because of operations then in progress, this change was not effected until January 12, 1863, and the division was then designated as First Division, Fifteenth Corps.

ORGANIZATION OF THIRTEENTH CORPS

In late October 1862, Ulysses S. Grant planned an advance southward from West Tennessee into northern Mississippi, and by this movement he hoped to force the evacuation of Vicksburg and Port Hudson and thus open the Mississippi River for Union traffic. For this purpose, Grant organized an Army in the Field from forces at Bolivar, Tennessee and Corinth Mississippi, and by November 4, 1862, these were concentrated at Grand Junction and La Grange, Tennessee. This army was organized as follows:

ARMY IN THE FIELD
Ulysses S. Grant

RIGHT WING, James B. McPherson

Third Division, John A. Logan
    First Brigade, C. Carroll Marsh
    Second Brigade, Mortimer D. Leggett
    Fourth Brigade, John D. Stevenson
    Artillery, George C. Gumbart
        Battery D, 1st Illinois Light Artillery, James A. Borland
        Batteries E and F, 2nd Illinois Light Artillery, Henry R. Henning
        8th Battery, Michigan Light Artillery, Samuel De Golyer
        3rd Battery, Ohio Light Artillery, William S. Williams

Note 1. The Right Wing, Army in the Field was organized from the District of Jackson. It was also called Right Wing, Thirteenth Corps, and Right Wing, Army of the Tennessee.
Note 2. Third Division consisted of the division lately commanded by Leonard F. Ross at Bolivar, Tennessee, plus four additional regiments.
Note 3. Michael K. Lawler's Third Brigade remained at Jackson, Tennessee.

Fourth Division, Jacob G. Lauman
    First Brigade, Isaac C. Pugh
    Second Brigade, James C. Veatch
    Third Brigade, Amory K. Johnson
    Artillery
        Battery L, 2nd Illinois Light Artillery, William H. Bolton
        9th Battery, Indiana Light Artillery, George R. Brown
        Battery C, 1st Missouri Light Artillery, Edward Brotzmann
        7th Battery, Ohio Light Artillery, Silas A. Burnap
        15th Battery, Ohio Light Artillery, Edward Spear, Jr.

Note 1. Fourth Division was from the District of Jackson.
Note 2. Thomas J. McKean was assigned command of Fourth Division November 11, 1862, when Lauman was assigned to duty in the District of Memphis.

LEFT WING, Charles S. Hamilton

Sixth Division, John McArthur
    First Brigade, George W. Deitzler
    Second Brigade, Gabriel Bouck
    Third Brigade, Hugh T. Reid, to November 11, 1863
        Marcellus M. Crocker

Note 1. The Left Wing, Army in the Field was organized from troops in the District of Corinth. It was also known as Left Wing, Thirteenth Corps, and Left Wing, Army of the Tennessee.

Seventh Division, Isaac F. Quinby
First Brigade, John B. Sanborn
Second Brigade, Ephraim R. Eckley
Third Brigade, George B. Boomer

Eighth Division, David S. Stanley, to November 11, 1863
Leonard F. Ross
First Brigade, John W. Fuller
Second Brigade, John M. Loomis, to December 16, 1863
Joseph A. Mower

Note. Ross was assigned command of Eighth Division November 11, 1863 when Stanley was transferred to the Department of the Cumberland.

ARTILLERY

Battery F, 2nd Illinois Light Artillery, Joseph W. Mitchell
3rd Battery, Michigan Light Artillery, Alexander W. Dees
1st Battery, Minnesota Light Artillery, William Z. Clayton
Battery M, 1st Missouri Light Artillery, Junius W. MacMurray
5th Battery, Ohio Light Artillery, Charles J. Marsh
10th Battery, Ohio Light Artillery, Edward Grosskopff
11th Battery, Ohio Light Artillery, Frank C. Sands
Battery F, 2nd United States Artillery, Albert J. S. Molinard
6th Battery, Wisconsin Light Artillery, Henry Dillon
12th Battery, Wisconsin Light Artillery, Lorenzo D. Immell

Note. The assignment of the batteries to the divisions of the Left Wing is not given in the original returns.

In addition to the troops belonging to the Army in the Field, there were others that remained in the various districts of the Department of the Tennessee. These are described briefly in the following sections:

District of Columbus. The troops remaining in the District of Columbus under the command of Thomas A. Davies consisted of James M. Tuttle's Division of Cairo and some unbrigaded regiments. During Nathan B. Forrest's expedition into West Tennessee December 15, 1862–January 3, 1863, Clinton B. Fisk's Second Brigade, United States Volunteers was sent from the Department of the Missouri to the District of Columbus. The brigade arrived at Columbus December 26, 1862, but was then transferred to Helena, Arkansas January 11, 1863.

During the time of Forrest's expedition, the troops of the District of Columbus were organized into a Left Wing under Fisk, and a Right Wing under Tuttle.

District of Corinth. The troops of the District of Corinth, which was commanded by Isaac F. Quinby until November 11, 1862, and then by Grenville M. Dodge, consisted of three brigades as follows:

First Brigade, District of Corinth, Thomas W. Sweeny
Second Brigade, District of Corinth, August Mersey
Third Brigade, District of Corinth, Moses M. Bane

These troops formerly belonged to Thomas A. Davies' Second Division, Army of the Tennessee, District of West Tennessee.

The artillery in the district consisted of four batteries of the 1st Missouri Light Artillery under the command of George H. Stone

District of Jackson. Third Division, Thirteenth Corps was organized from the troops in the District of Jackson early in November 1862, and Michael K. Lawler's Third Brigade remained in the District of Jackson when the rest of Third Division departed to join Grant's Army in the Field. Mason Brayman commanded the post of Bolivar, which consisted of the 42nd Illinois, 61st Illinois, 109th Illinois, and 12th Michigan regiments.

December 18, 1862, during Forrest's expedition into West Tennessee, John W. Fuller's First Brigade, Eighth Division of Thirteenth Corps was sent to Jackson. It was then ordered to Corinth January 5, 1863.

District of Memphis. During the early part of November 1862, the troops in William T. Sherman's District of Memphis were organized into six brigades as follows:

First Brigade, Morgan L. Smith
Second Brigade, James W. Denver, to November 12, 1862

John A. McDowell
Third Brigade, Joseph R. Cockerill
Fourth Brigade, David Stuart
Fifth Brigade, Ralph P. Buckland
Reserve Brigade, Risdon M. Moore

On November 12, 1862, the first five of these brigades were organized into two divisions as follows:

First Division, James W. Denver
  Second Brigade, John A. McDowell
  Third Brigade, Joseph R. Cockerill
  Fifth Brigade, Ralph P. Buckland

Second Division, Morgan L. Smith
  First Brigade, Giles A. Smith
  Fourth Brigade, David Stuart

On November 23, 1862, Sherman organized a Third Division, District of Memphis under Jacob G. Lauman from a new Sixth Brigade and the Fifth Brigade, which was transferred from First Division.

As a part of Grant's plan for the invasion of northern Mississippi, Sherman was to march from Memphis and join the Army in the Field near Oxford. Sherman received his orders to march November 25, 1862, and he joined Grant December 5 with the following force:

First Division, James W. Denver
  Second Brigade, John A. McDowell
  Third Brigade, Joseph R. Cockerill

Second Division, Morgan L. Smith
  First Brigade, Giles A. Smith
  Fourth Brigade, David Stuart

Third Division, Jacob G. Lauman
  Fifth Brigade, Ralph P. Buckland
  Sixth Brigade, Jacob G. Lauman

With the arrival of Sherman's divisions, the wing designations of the Army in the Field were changed as follows: Sherman's command became the Right Wing, McPherson's command the Center, and Hamilton's command the Left Wing.

A Cavalry Division was organized under T. Lyle Dickey November 26, 1862 as follows:

Cavalry Division, T. Lyle Dickey

First Brigade, Albert L. Lee
Second Brigade, Edward Hatch
Third Brigade, Benjamin H. Grierson

Lee's First Brigade was assigned to the Left Wing, Hatch's Second Brigade to the Center, and Grierson's Third Brigade to the Right Wing.

In a change in plan, Grant decided to send Sherman down the Mississippi River in command of an expedition to attempt the capture of Vicksburg. Accordingly, a short time after his arrival at Oxford, Sherman was ordered to return to Memphis with Morgan L. Smith's Second Division to organize the expedition, and move with it to the Yazoo River, north of Vicksburg.

Sherman left Oxford with Smith's division December 9, 1862, leaving Denver's First Division and Lauman's Third Division with Grant's army. Denver's division was assigned to McPherson's Right Wing as First Division, and Lauman's division was broken up. Buckland's brigade of Lauman's division was assigned to Leonard F. Ross' Eighth Division on December 10, and Lauman relieved McKean in command of Fourth Division of McPherson's Right Wing.

When Sherman arrived in Memphis, he organized a force of four divisions for his expedition. This force was designated as Right Wing, Thirteenth Corps, but it was commonly known as Sherman's Yazoo Expedition. Sherman moved with this army down the Mississippi and landed at Johnson's plantation on the Yazoo River December 26, 1862. He made several unsuccessful attempts at Chickasaw Bayou, with a major attack December 29, to reach the high ground north of Vicksburg, and then on January 2, 1863 he withdrew with his command to the mouth of the Yazoo River. There he was joined by John A. McClernand, who assumed command of Sherman's expedition on January 4. That same day, McClernand announced the organization of the Army of the Mississippi from Sherman's former command, and he then began a movement up the Arkansas River to capture Arkansas Post and Fort Hindman. McClernand captured Arkansas Post January 11, then moved his command to the mouth of the Arkansas River, where he completed the reorganization of the Army of the Tennessee, ordered December 22, 1862, by formally announcing the organization of the new Thirteenth Corps and Fifteenth Corps January 14, 1863.

For details of the organization and operations of the troops of Thirteenth Corps that were under the command of William T. Sherman and John A. McClernand in late December 1862 and early January 1863, see Operations against Vicksburg, Mississippi, 1861–1863, Early Attempts to Capture Vicksburg, Yazoo River, Mississippi Expedition (William T. Sherman)—Battle of Chickasaw Bayou (or Walnut Hills), and also Engagement at Arkansas Post (or Fort Hindman), Arkansas.

The organization of the wings of Thirteenth Corps during this period may be somewhat confusing. Sherman continued to refer to his command during the Yazoo Expedition as Right Wing, Thirteenth Corps until January 4, 1863, when the designation was changed to McClernand's Army of the Mississippi. McPherson also used the designation Right Wing, Thirteenth Corps for his command in Grant's army in northern Mississippi after Sherman's departure for the Yazoo River. Properly, however, McPherson's command was Right Wing, Army in the Field, Thirteenth Corps.

After the departure from Memphis of Sherman's Yazoo Expedition, Grant's army in northern Mississippi and West Tennessee consisted of the following:

RIGHT WING, THIRTEENTH CORPS, James B. McPherson

First Division, James W. Denver
    Second Brigade, John A. McDowell
    Third Brigade, Joseph R. Cockerill
    Artillery, William Cogswell
        Battery F, 1st Illinois Light Artillery, John T. Cheney
        Battery I, 1st Illinois Light Artillery, Edward Bouton
        Battery M, 1st Illinois Light Artillery, William Cogswell
        6th Battery, Indiana Light Artillery, Michael Mueller

Note. Cogswell's battery was officially known as Cogswell's Independent Battery.

Third Division, John A. Logan
    First Brigade, C. Carroll Marsh
    Second Brigade, Mortimer D. Leggett

    Fourth Brigade, John D. Stevenson
    Artillery, Charles J. Stolbrand
        Battery D, 1st Illinois Light Artillery, Henry A. Rogers
        Battery G, 2nd Illinois Light Artillery, Frederick Sparrestrom
        Battery L, 2nd Illinois Light Artillery, William H. Bolton
        8th Battery, Michigan Light Artillery, Samuel De Golyer
        3rd Battery, Ohio Light Artillery, William S. Williams

Fourth Division, Jacob G. Lauman
    First Brigade, Isaac C. Pugh
    Second Brigade, Cyrus Hall
    Third Brigade, Amory K. Johnson
    Artillery, George C. Gumbart
        Battery E, 2nd Illinois Light Artillery, Martin Mann
        Battery K, 2nd Illinois Light Artillery, Benjamin F. Rodgers
        9th Battery, Indiana Light Artillery, George R. Brown
        5th Battery, Ohio Light Artillery, Anthony B. Burton
        7th Battery, Ohio Light Artillery, Silas A. Burnap
        15th Battery, Ohio Light Artillery, Edward Spear, Jr.

LEFT WING, THIRTEENTH CORPS, Charles S. Hamilton

Sixth Division, John McArthur
    First Brigade, George W. Deitzler
    Second Brigade, Thomas E. G. Ransom
    Third Brigade, Marcellus M. Crocker

Note. Joseph W. Mitchell's Battery F, 2nd Illinois Light Artillery was attached to First Brigade; Edward Brotzmann's Battery C, 1st Missouri Light Artillery was attached to Second Brigade; Hamilton B. White's 10th Battery, Ohio Light Artillery was attached to Third Brigade; and William Z. Clayton's 1st Battery, Minnesota Light Artillery of the division was unassigned.

Seventh Division, Isaac F. Quinby
    First Brigade, Jesse I. Alexander
    Second Brigade, Ephraim R. Eckley
    Third Brigade, George B. Boomer
    Artillery, Albert M. Powell
        Battery M, 1st Missouri Light Artillery, Junius W. MacMurray
        11th Battery, Ohio Light Artillery, Frank C. Sands

6th Battery, Wisconsin Light Artillery, Henry Dillon

12th Battery, Wisconsin Light Artillery, William Zickerick

Eighth Division, Leonard F. Ross
First Brigade, John W. Fuller
Second Brigade, John M. Loomis

Note 1. Daniel P. Walling's 2nd Battery, Iowa Light Artillery was attached to Second Brigade.

Note 2. First Brigade was sent to Jackson, Tennessee December 18, 1862 during Nathan B. Forrest's expedition in West Tennessee, and on January 5, 1863 it was sent to Corinth, Mississippi.

Note 3. On December 10, 1862, after Sherman left for Memphis, Ralph P. Buckland's brigade of his division was assigned to Ross' Eighth Division.

Grant's planned advance down the Mississippi Central Railroad was seriously compromised December 20, 1862 when Earl Van Dorn with his Confederate cavalry captured the Union supply base of the army at Holly Springs, Mississippi. Facing a difficult supply problem, Grant began the withdrawal of his forces during the last week of December. Some troops were sent back to the vicinity of Grand Junction to guard the railroad from Memphis to Corinth, Mississippi, but Grant remained at Holly Springs with Lauman's Fourth Division (formerly Thomas J. McKean's). December 25, Quinby's Seventh Division, Left Wing was ordered from near Waterford, Mississippi to Memphis as guard for a supply train of the army. Quinby arrived at Memphis December, 1862. For additional information, see Operations against Vicksburg, Mississippi, 1861–1863, Early Attempts to Capture Vicksburg, Grant's Northern Mississippi Campaign (Operations on the Mississippi Central Railroad from Bolivar, Tennessee to Coffeeville, Mississippi).

It has already been explained that originally Thirteenth Corps included all forces in the Department of the Tennessee. The efficient administration of such a large command was difficult, and this situation was improved by dividing the corps into wings. Then, by a presidential order of December 18, 1862, the troops in the Department of the Tennessee and those in the Department of the Missouri operating on the Mississippi River were to be divided into four corps, which were to be designated as Thirteenth

Corps, Fifteenth Corps, Sixteenth Corps, and Seventeenth Corps. The Army of the Tennessee was to consist of these four corps.

The four corps were formally constituted by an order of December 22, 1862 from Headquarters, Army of the Tennessee to consist of the following:

ARMY OF THE TENNESSEE
Ulysses S. Grant

THIRTEENTH CORPS, John A. McClernand

Ninth Division, George W. Morgan
Tenth Division, Andrew J. Smith
All troops operating on the Mississippi River below Memphis not included in Fifteenth Corps

FIFTEENTH CORPS, William T. Sherman

Fifth Division, Morgan L. Smith
Frederick Steele's division from Helena, Arkansas
Forces in the District of Memphis

SIXTEENTH CORPS, Stephen A. Hurlbut

Sixth Division, John McArthur
Seventh Division, Isaac F. Quinby
Eighth Division, Leonard F. Ross
Second Cavalry Brigade, Albert L. Lee
Troops in the District of Columbus under Thomas A. Davies
Troops in the District of Jackson under Jeremiah C. Sullivan

Note. January 20, 1863, Denver's First Division and Lauman's Fourth Division were transferred from Seventeenth Corps to Sixteenth Corps, and McArthur's Sixth Division and Quinby's Seventh Division were transferred from Sixteenth Corps to Seventeenth Corps.

SEVENTEENTH CORPS, James B. McPherson

First Division, James W. Denver
Third Division, John A. Logan
Fourth Division, Jacob G. Lauman
First Cavalry Brigade, Benjamin H. Grierson
Troops in the District of Corinth under Grenville M. Dodge

Note. See above note under Sixteenth Corps.

Because of operations in progress in northern Mississippi, in West Tennessee, and near Vicksburg in late December 1862, the above organization was not put into effect until January 1863. For details of this organization, see the four army corps involved.

December 30, 1862, the cavalry of the army was reorganized into two brigades as follows:

First Brigade, Benjamin H. Grierson
Second Brigade, Albert L. Lee

First Brigade was assigned to the newly constituted Seventeenth Corps and Second Brigade to the Sixteenth Corps.

Henry W. Halleck, general in chief of the army, learned of Sherman's repulse at Chickasaw Bayou, and on January 8, 1863 ordered Grant to take all of his disposable force in Mississippi and West Tennessee and reinforce the Vicksburg expedition, which was then under the command of John A. McClernand. Grant then left Holly Springs, arriving at Memphis January 10. On January 12, Halleck authorized Grant to relieve McClernand in command of the Vicksburg expedition if he wished to do so. Grant then went down the Mississippi River to Young's Point, Louisiana, where he assumed personal command of the Vicksburg expedition on January 30.

Following Grant's withdrawal from northern Mississippi, there was a transition period in which the Army of the Tennessee was reorganized and the corps organization ordered December 22, 1862 became operative. The divisions sent downriver with Sherman's Yazoo Expedition in December 1862, and which later were called by McClernand the Army of the Mississippi, were formally designated as Thirteenth Corps (under George W. Morgan) January 14, 1863 and Fifteenth Corps (under William T. Sherman) January 12, 1863. Stephen A. Hurlbut had assumed command of Sixteenth Corps January 6, but had been relieved by Charles S. Hamilton January 10, when he departed on leave of absence. McPherson assumed command of Seventeenth Corps on January 11.

On January 22, the Federal troops at Helena, in eastern Arkansas, were placed under Grant's orders, and they were assigned to the new Thirteenth Corps.

For further information about the troops of the former Thirteenth Corps, see Thirteenth Corps, Army of the Tennessee, January 14, 1863–August 7, 1863; Fifteenth Corps, Army of the Tennessee; Sixteenth Corps, Army of the Tennessee; and Seventeenth Corps, Army of the Tennessee; and see also Operations against Vicksburg, Mississippi, 1861–1863.

THIRTEENTH CORPS, ARMY OF THE TENNESSEE JANUARY 14, 1863– AUGUST 7, 1863

A new Thirteenth Corps was created by a presidential order of December 18, 1862, and by an order of December 22, 1862 from Headquarters, Army of the Tennessee, it was constituted to consist of George W. Morgan's Ninth Division and Andrew J. Smith's Tenth Division of the Army of the Tennessee and all troops operating on the Mississippi River that were not included in the newly created Fifteenth Corps. John A. McClernand was assigned command of Thirteenth Corps by the order of December 18.

The corps was not organized at that time because the troops that were assigned to it were preparing to embark at Memphis, Tennessee for active operations against Vicksburg. George W. Morgan's Ninth Division and Andrew J. Smith's Tenth Division were temporarily redesignated as Third Division and First Division, respectively, of William T. Sherman's Yazoo Expedition, and they retained that designation from December 18, 1862 to January 4, 1863. On that date, McClernand relieved Sherman in command of the expedition, changing its designation to Army of the Mississippi, which he organized into two corps. Smith's First Division (formerly Tenth Division, Thirteenth Corps) was assigned to George W. Morgan's First Corps, Army of the Mississippi as First Division; and Morgan's Third Division (formerly Ninth Division, Thirteenth Corps), then commanded by Peter J. Osterhaus, was also assigned to First Corps, Army of the Mississippi as Second Division.

As First Corps, Army of the Mississippi, these two divisions took part in McClernand's expedition against Arkansas Post, which surrendered January 11, 1863. McClernand then moved back with his command to the mouth of the Arkansas River, and on January 14 he announced the change in designation of First Corps, Army of the Mississippi to Thirteenth Corps, Army of the Tennessee, and of William T. Sherman's Second Corps, Army of the Mississippi to Fifteenth Corps, Army of the Tennessee. George W. Morgan was in command of Thirteenth Corps until January 31, while McClernand was in command of the two corps. During the latter part of January 1863, McClernand moved with Morgan's Thirteenth Corps and Sherman's Fifteenth Corps to Young's Point, Louisiana, where they were encamped at the end of the month. McClernand assumed command of Thirteenth Corps January 31, relieving Morgan.

For additional information, see Operations against Vicksburg, Mississippi, 1861–1863, Early Attempts to Capture Vicksburg, Yazoo River, Mississippi Expedition (William T. Sherman)—Battle of Chickasaw Bayou (or Walnut Hills), and also Engagement at Arkansas Post (or Fort Hindman), Arkansas.

The organization of Thirteenth Corps January 31, 1863 was as follows:

THIRTEENTH CORPS, John A. McClernand

Ninth Division, Peter J. Osterhaus
First Brigade, William Vandever
Second Brigade, Daniel W. Lindsey
Third Brigade, John F. De Courcy
Artillery
    7th Battery, Michigan Light Artillery, Robert M. Wilder
    1st Battery, Wisconsin Light Artillery, Jacob T. Foster

Tenth Division, Andrew J. Smith
First Brigade, Stephen G. Burbridge
Second Brigade, William J. Landram
Artillery
    Chicago Mercantile Battery, Illinois Light Artillery, Charles G. Cooley
    17th Battery, Ohio Light Artillery, Ambrose A. Blount

Note 1. George W. Morgan was in command of the corps from January 4 until January 31, 1863, when he was relieved by McClernand.
Note 2. On January 22, 1863, the forces at Helena, Arkansas became a part of Thirteenth Corps as the District of Eastern Arkansas. Willis A. Gorman was

assigned command, but Benjamin F. Prentiss relieved Gorman in command of the district February 14, 1863.

On February 8, 1863, the following organization was announced for the District of Eastern Arkansas, Thirteenth Corps:

DISTRICT OF EASTERN ARKANSAS, Willis A. Gorman, to February 14, 1863
Benjamin M. Prentiss

Twelfth Division, Alvin P. Hovey
First Brigade, James R. Slack
Second Brigade, Peter Kinney
Third Brigade, George F. McGinnis
Artillery
    Battery A, 2nd Illinois Light Artillery, Jacob C. Hansel
    3rd Battery, Iowa Light Artillery, Mortimer M. Hayden
    2nd Battery, Ohio Light Artillery, Newton J. Smith
    16th Battery, Ohio Light Artillery, Russell P. Twist

Note. Twelfth Division was organized February 8, 1863. It was reorganized later in the month by the redesignation of Third Brigade as First Brigade, and Third Brigade was thus discontinued. The regiments of the former First Brigade were reassigned, and Slack was assigned command of Second Brigade.

Thirteenth Division, Clinton B. Fisk, to second week in February 1863
Leonard F. Ross
First Brigade, Charles W. Kittredge
Second Brigade, James M. Lewis
Artillery
    Battery A, 1st Missouri Light Artillery, George W. Schofield

Note 1. Thirteenth Division was organized February 8, 1863, and was transferred to Sixteenth Corps July 28, 1863.
Note 2. Second Brigade was formerly Clinton B. Fisk's Second Brigade, United States Volunteers, which had been transferred from the Department of the Missouri to Columbus, Kentucky and Memphis, Tennessee January 11, 1863.

CAVALRY DIVISION, Cadwallader C. Washburn

First Brigade, Conrad Baker
Second Brigade, Cyrus Bussey

Note. On February 8, 1863, the cavalry of Thirteenth Corps in the District of Eastern Arkansas was organized as the Second Cavalry Division, Army of the Tennessee, and Washburn was assigned command.

During the period March 13–26, 1863, First Division and Second Brigade, Second Division of the Army of Southeastern Missouri, under the command of Eugene A. Carr, were transferred to Milliken's Bend, Louisiana, where on March 28 they were organized as Fourteenth Division, Thirteenth Corps. The troops transferred from Missouri consisted of the following:

First Division, William P. Benton
    First Brigade, Charles L. Harris
    Second Brigade, David Shunk

Second Division
    Second Brigade, Robert R. Livingston

Note. Livingston did not accompany the brigade to Milliken's Bend.

For additional information, see Army of Southeastern Missouri.

On March 28, 1863, Carr's command was reorganized by consolidating First Brigade and Second Brigade of First Division to form a new First Brigade, Fourteenth Division, and the new Fourteenth Division was organized as follows:

Fourteenth Division, Eugene A. Carr
    First Brigade, William P. Benton
    Second Brigade, Michael K. Lawler
    Artillery
        1st Battery, Indiana Light Artillery, Martin Klauss

At the beginning of the Vicksburg Campaign in March 1863, Thirteenth Corps was composed of five divisions, only four of which were eventually engaged in active operations. Thirteenth Division remained in the District of Eastern Arkansas. The other divisions of Thirteenth Corps were designated as the Right of Ulysses S. Grant's army during the Vicksburg Campaign.

Thirteenth Division, under Leonard F. Ross, took part in the Yazoo Pass Expedition February 23–April 5, 1863, and under Frederick Salomon fought at the Battle of Helena, Arkansas July 4, 1863. For details, see Operations against Vicksburg, Mississippi, 1861–1862, Grant's Operations against

Vicksburg, Bayou Expeditions, Yazoo Pass, Mississippi Expedition; and see also Attack on Helena, Arkansas.

The cavalry of the District of Eastern Arkansas, Thirteenth Corps was reorganized in May 1863 into two brigades. Powell Clayton's Second Brigade of Cyrus Bussey's Second Cavalry Division remained in the district under the command of Clayton, and the other brigade, under the command of Cyrus Bussey, joined Grant's army at Vicksburg in June 1863. For additional information, see Cavalry Forces of the Army of the Tennessee.

Thirteenth Corps advanced with the Army of the Tennessee at the beginning of Grant's movement to the rear of Vicksburg. The Battle of Port Gibson (May 1, 1863) and the Engagement at Big Black River Bridge (May 17, 1863) were fought largely by Thirteenth Corps. The corps was also engaged at Champion Hill May 16, 1863, and it participated in the assaults at Vicksburg May 19 and May 22. It then took part in the siege of Vicksburg until its surrender July 4, 1863.

On June 19, 1863, during the siege of Vicksburg, Edward O. C. Ord relieved McClernand in command of Thirteenth Corps.

For details of the Vicksburg Campaign, see Operations against Vicksburg, Mississippi, 1861–1863, Grant's Operations against Vicksburg.

The organization of Thirteenth Corps during the Vicksburg Campaign was as follows:

THIRTEENTH CORPS, John A. McClernand, to June
    19, 1863
    Edward O. C. Ord

Ninth Division, Peter J. Osterhaus, to May 17, 1863,
    wounded
    Albert L. Lee, temporarily May 17–18, 1863
    Peter J. Osterhaus
    First Brigade, Theophilus T. Garrard, to May 18, 1863
        Albert L. Lee, May 18–19, 1863, wounded
        James Keigwin
    Second Brigade, Lionel A. Sheldon, to May 1, 1863,
        sick
        Daniel W. Lindsey
    Artillery, Jacob T. Foster
        7th Battery, Michigan Light Artillery, Charles H.
            Lanphere
        1st Battery, Wisconsin Light Artillery, Charles B.
            Kimball
            Oscar F. Nutting

Tenth Division, Andrew J. Smith
First Brigade, Stephen G. Burbridge
Second Brigade, William J. Landram
Artillery
Chicago Mercantile Battery, Illinois Light Artillery, Patrick H. White
17th Battery, Ohio Light Artillery, Ambrose A. Blount
Charles S. Rice

Twelfth Division, Alvin P. Hovey
First Brigade, George F. McGinnis
Second Brigade, James R. Slack
Artillery
Battery A, 1st Missouri Light Artillery, George W. Schofield
2nd Battery, Ohio Light Artillery, Augustus Beach
16th Battery, Ohio Light Artillery, Russell P. Twist

Fourteenth Division, Eugene A. Carr
First Brigade, William P. Benton, to May 31, 1863
Henry D. Washburn, to June 27, 1863
David Shunk

Second Brigade, Charles L. Harris, to April 30, sick
William M. Stone, to May 2, 1863
Michael K. Lawler
Artillery
Battery A, 2nd Illinois Light Artillery, Frank B. Fenton
Peter Davidson
1st Battery, Indiana Light Artillery, Martin Klauss

June 24, 1863, Fourth Division, Sixteenth Corps, which had joined Grant's army at Vicksburg, was attached to Thirteenth Corps. This division was organized as follows:

Fourth Division, Jacob G. Lauman
First Brigade, Isaac C. Pugh
Second Brigade, Cyrus Hall
Third Brigade, Amory K. Johnson
Artillery, George C. Gumbart
Battery E, 2nd Illinois Light Artillery, George L. Nispel
Battery K, 2nd Illinois Light Artillery, Benjamin F. Rodgers
5th Battery, Ohio Light Artillery, Anthony B. Burton
7th Battery, Ohio Light Artillery, Silas A. Burnap
15th Battery, Ohio Light Artillery, Edward Spear, Jr.

Note. Fourth Division, then under the command of

Marcellus M. Crocker, was transferred to Seventeenth Corps August 7, 1863.

After the surrender of Vicksburg July 4, 1863, Ord's Thirteenth Corps formed a part of the command of William T. Sherman that marched to Jackson, Mississippi to drive back or destroy the Confederate army that Joseph E. Johnston had assembled for the relief of Vicksburg. In the operations around Jackson, Jacob G. Lauman, commanding the Fourth Division, Sixteenth Corps, which was attached to Thirteenth Corps, performed badly; he was relieved of his command July 12, 1863 by Alvin P. Hovey. This was done by attaching Lauman's division to Hovey's Twelfth Division, Thirteenth Corps, and the three brigades of Fourth Division were temporarily redesignated as Third Brigade, Fourth Brigade, and Fifth Brigade of Twelfth Division. Johnston evacuated Jackson July 16, 1863, and Thirteenth Corps returned to Vicksburg with the rest of Sherman's army. For details of this operation, see Jackson, Mississippi Campaign (William T. Sherman).

July 30, 1863, Ninth Division and Fourteenth Division were consolidated and designated as First Division, Thirteenth Corps. Cadwallader C. Washburn was assigned command of the new First Division, which was organized as follows:

First Division, Cadwallader C. Washburn
First Brigade, William P. Benton
Second Brigade, William M. Stone
Third Brigade, James Keigwin
Fourth Brigade, Daniel W. Lindsey

On June 11, 1863, Francis J. Herron's division, formerly known as the Army of the Frontier, joined Grant's army at Vicksburg from the Department of the Missouri. It was then designated as the Left, Investing Forces, and was organized as follows:

Herron's Division, Francis J. Herron
First Brigade, William Vandever
Second Brigade, William W. Orme

For additional information, see Army of the Frontier, and see also Operations against Vicksburg, Mississippi, 1861–1863, Grant's Operations against Vicksburg, Siege of Vicksburg, Mississippi.

This division was transferred from Vicksburg to

Port Hudson, Louisiana July 24–25, 1863, and it then moved on to Carrollton, Louisiana early in August. On August 7, Herron's division was assigned to Thirteenth Corps.

During the period August 10–26, 1863, Thirteenth Corps was transferred from Vicksburg to Carrollton in the Department of the Gulf. For further information about Thirteenth Corps, see Thirteenth Corps, Department of the Gulf.

THIRTEENTH CORPS, DEPARTMENT OF THE GULF AUGUST 7, 1863– JUNE 11, 1864

Thirteenth Corps, Army of the Tennessee took part in the Vicksburg, Mississippi Campaign April 1, 1863–July 4, 1864 and the Siege of Jackson, July 10–16, 1863, after which it returned to the vicinity of Vicksburg. The Thirteenth Division of Thirteenth Corps was not with the corps during these operations but remained in eastern Arkansas, where it had been serving. The organization of the troops of Thirteenth Corps at Vicksburg in July 1863 was as follows:

THIRTEENTH CORPS, Edward O. C. Ord

Ninth Division, Peter J. Osterhaus
First Brigade, James Keigwin
Second Brigade, Daniel W. Lindsey
Artillery, Jacob T. Foster
    7th Battery, Michigan Light Artillery, Charles H. Lanphere
    1st Battery, Wisconsin Light Artillery, Oscar F. Nutting

Tenth Division, Andrew J. Smith
First Brigade, Stephen G. Burbridge
Second Brigade, William J. Landram
Artillery
    Chicago Mercantile Battery, Illinois Light Artillery, Patrick H. White
    17th Battery, Ohio Light Artillery, Charles S. Rice

Twelfth Division, Alvin P. Hovey

First Brigade, George F. McGinnis
Second Brigade, James R. Slack
Artillery
    Battery A, 1st Missouri Light Artillery, George W. Schofield
    2nd Battery, Ohio Light Artillery, Augustus Beach
    16th Battery, Ohio Light Artillery, Russell P. Twist

Fourteenth Division, Eugene A. Carr
First Brigade, David Shunk
Second Brigade, Michael K. Lawler
Artillery
    Battery A, 2nd Illinois Light Artillery, Peter Davidson
    1st Battery, Indiana Light Artillery, Martin Klauss

On July 28, 1863, Fourth Division, Sixteenth Corps (formerly Jacob G. Lauman's, and then under Marcellus M. Crocker) was transferred to Thirteenth Corps, but it was assigned to Seventeenth Corps on August 7 and did not accompany the corps to Louisiana. On July 30, 1863, Ninth Division and Fourteenth Division were consolidated and designated as First Division, Thirteenth Corps, and Cadwallader C. Washburn was assigned command. First Brigade, Fourteenth Division became First Brigade, First Division; Second Brigade, Fourteenth Division became Second Brigade, First Division; First Brigade, Ninth Division became Third Brigade, First Division; and Second Brigade, Ninth Division became Fourth Brigade, First Division.

Francis J. Herron's Division, formerly known as the Army of the Frontier, joined Ulysses S. Grant's army at Vicksburg from the Department of the Missouri June 11, 1863, and later became a part of Thirteenth Corps, Department of the Gulf. It was organized as follows:

Herron's Division, Francis J. Herron
First Brigade, William Vandever
Second Brigade, William W. Orme

Note. Nelson Cole's Battery E, 1st Missouri Light Artillery and Joseph Foust's Battery F, 1st Missouri Light Artillery were attached to First Brigade, and Martin Welfley's Battery B, 1st Missouri Light Artillery was attached to Second Brigade.

In July and August 1863, Nathaniel P. Banks' forces of the Department of the Gulf were seriously depleted by the departure of twenty-one nine-month regiments for home and muster out. A further need for more troops arose when, in July 1863, Henry W. Halleck proposed that Banks organize an expedition for the purpose of establishing United States forces in Texas. Providing the needed troops was difficult until the Mississippi River was finally opened by the capture of Port Hudson in July 1863. Then Ulysses S. Grant sent reinforcements down the river from Vicksburg to report to Banks in Louisiana. The first troops to leave belonged to Herron's Division, which moved to Port Hudson July 24–26. Herron remained there only a short time and then moved on to Carrollton during the early part of August. On August 7, Edward O. C. Ord's Thirteenth Corps was assigned to the Department of the Gulf. Ord, who was ill, departed on sick leave August 7, and Cadwallader C. Washburn assumed command of Thirteenth Corps. Also on August 7, Herron's Division was assigned to Thirteenth Corps.

Thirteenth Corps, Army of the Tennessee, under the command of Washburn, was transferred from Vicksburg to Carrollton during the period August 10–26, 1863. On August 14, the corps was reorganized, largely by a change in designations of the divisions, as follows: Ninth Division and Fourteenth Division had already been consolidated July 30 to form First Division, Thirteenth Corps; Herron's Division was designated as Second Division, Thirteenth Corps; Twelfth Division was designated as Third Division, Thirteenth Corps; and Tenth Division was designated as Fourth Division, Thirteenth Corps.

At the end of August, when the reorganization had been completed, the corps was organized as follows:

THIRTEENTH CORPS, DEPARTMENT OF THE GULF, Cadwallader C. Washburn

First Division, William P. Benton
    First Brigade, David Shunk
    Second Brigade, Samuel L. Glasgow
    Third Brigade, Thomas W. Bennett
    Fourth Brigade, Daniel W. Lindsey

Note 1. Fourth Brigade was consolidated with Third Brigade September 23, 1863, and Michael K. Lawler was assigned command of the new Third Brigade. When Lawler assumed command of First Division October 19, 1863, Lionel A. Sheldon assumed command of Third Brigade.

Note 2. Jacob Mann's 1st Battery, Indiana Light Artillery was assigned to First Brigade; Peter Davidson's Battery A, 2nd Illinois Light Artillery was assigned to Second Brigade; Charles H. Lanphere's 7th Battery, Michigan Light Artillery was assigned to Third Brigade; and Oscar F. Nutting's 1st Battery, Wisconsin Light Artillery was assigned to Fourth Brigade.

Second Division, Francis J. Herron
    First Brigade, William McE. Dye
    Second Brigade, Henry M. Day

Note 1. William Vandever, commander of First Brigade, was on detached service, and William W. Orme, commander of Second Brigade, was on sick leave.

Note 2. Joseph B. Atwater's Battery E, 1st Missouri Light Artillery and Joseph Foust's Battery F, 1st Missouri Light Artillery were attached to First Brigade; and Martin Welfley's Battery B, 1st Missouri Light Artillery was assigned to Second Brigade.

Third Division, Albert L. Lee
    First Brigade, George F. McGinnis
    Second Brigade, James R. Slack

Note. Emil Steger's Battery E, 2nd Illinois Light Artillery and Russell P. Twist's 16th Battery, Ohio Light Artillery were assigned to First Brigade; and Charles M. Callahan's Battery A, 1st Missouri Light Artillery and Augustus Beach's 2nd Battery, Ohio Light Artillery were attached to Second Brigade.

Fourth Division, Michael K. Lawler
    First Brigade, Thomas J. Lucas
    Second Brigade, John Cowan

Note 1. Andrew J. Smith, former commander of Fourth Division, was assigned command of the District of Columbus, Sixteenth Corps August 15, 1863.

Note 2. Stephen G. Burbridge, commander of First Brigade, was on sick leave.

Note 3. William Hunt, Jr.'s 17th Battery, Ohio Light Artillery was assigned to First Brigade; and Patrick H. White's Chicago Mercantile Battery, Illinois Light Artillery was assigned to Second Brigade.

Cavalry Brigade, John J. Mudd

Note. The Cavalry Brigade was organized August 14, 1863, and was transferred to the Department of the Gulf September 14, 1863.

At the end of September 1863, Washburn's First Division was at Brashear City; Napoleon J. T. Dana's Second Division was at Morganza (Dana relieved Herron in command of Second Division September 24); McGinnis' Third Division was at

Berwick; and Burbridge's Fourth Division was at Carrollton, all in Louisiana.

Beginning October 3, 1863, Nathaniel P. Banks led an expedition up the Bayou Teche with the intention of turning west at Vermillionville (present-day Lafayette) and moving into northern Texas. His command consisted of Cadwallader C. Washburn's First Division, George F. McGinnis' Third Division, and Stephen G. Burbridge's Fourth Division of Thirteenth Corps, all under the command of Edward O. C. Ord; and Godfrey Weitzel's First Division and Cuvier Grover's Third Division of Nineteenth Corps, under the command of William B. Franklin. Ord became ill, and Washburn was in command of Detachment Thirteenth Corps after October 20. Michael K. Lawler assumed command of First Division October 19. Also on or about October 20, Franklin assumed command of the combined forces of Thirteenth Corps and Nineteenth Corps. The route selected for the advance into Texas proved impracticable, however, and after advancing as far as Opelousas, the expedition returned to New Iberia during the latter part of November. For additional information, see Department of the Gulf, Operations in the Department of the Gulf, Texas Expeditions, Operations in the Teche Country, Louisiana, October 3, 1863–November 30, 1863.

On October 26, 1863, Napoleon J. T. Dana assumed command of Thirteenth Corps, but Washburn continued in command of the detachment in the Teche country.

Also on October 26, Banks sailed from New Orleans in command of an expedition for the mouth of the Rio Grande. He took with him Dana's Second Division, Thirteenth Corps and arrived at Brazos Santiago Island November 2. Banks then proceeded to establish his command at various posts on the coast of Texas.

November 21, 1863, Henry D. Washburn's First Brigade, First Division, Thirteenth Corps arrived in Texas from Louisiana, and by December 10, the last troops of First Division had left Algiers for Texas, except four regiments of Third Brigade that were at Plaquemine, Louisiana under the command of Lionel A. Sheldon.

During November 1863, Third Division and Fourth Division of Thirteenth Corps were near New Iberia, as a part of Franklin's command in western Louisiana. During December, however, Fourth Di-

vision marched to Algiers, where it embarked for Texas. The first troops had arrived at Decros' (Decrow's) Point by mid-December 1863, and by January 2, 1864, the rest of the division had joined them there.

Third Division, Thirteenth Corps was at Algiers in December 1863, and it was then assigned to duty in the Defenses of New Orleans January 15, 1864. The division remained near New Orleans until it joined the Red River Expedition in March 1864. Only two of its regiments were transferred to Texas—the first arrived at Pass Cavallo in December 1863, and the second followed in January 1864. Both regiments were recalled to New Orleans February 20–23, 1864.

For additional information about Thirteenth Corps in Texas, see Department of the Gulf, Operations in the Department of the Gulf, Texas Expeditions, Rio Grande Expedition and Operations on the Coast of Texas.

The organization of Thirteenth Corps at the end of December 1863 was as follows:

THIRTEENTH CORPS, Napoleon J. T. Dana

First Division, William P. Benton
    First Brigade, Fitz Henry Warren (at Indianola, Texas)
    Second Brigade, Charles L. Harris (at Decros' Point, Texas)
    Third Brigade, James Keigwin (at Decros' Point, Texas)
    Artillery
        Battery G, 1st Michigan Light Artillery, George L. Stillman

Note 1. Dana was in command of the United States Forces in Texas. Edward O. C. Ord resumed command of Thirteenth Corps January 9, 1864, with headquarters at New Orleans.
Note 2. Benton was assigned command of First Division December 15, 1863.
Note 3. Keigwin assumed command of Third Brigade December 23, 1863.

Second Division, Napoleon J. T. Dana (at Brownsville, Texas)
    First Brigade, John Charles Black
    Second Brigade, William McE. Dye
    Third Brigade, Thomas E. G. Ransom
    Artillery
        Battery B, 1st Missouri Light Artillery, Martin Welfley

Battery E, 1st Missouri Light Artillery, Joseph B. Atwater

Battery F, 1st Missouri Light Artillery, Joseph Foust

Cavalry Brigade, Edmund J. Davis

Troops at Point Isabel, Texas, Justin Hodge

Note 1. Francis J. Herron was assigned command of all United States forces on the Rio Grande January 3, 1864, and these included Second Division, Thirteenth Corps.

Note 2. Third Brigade, Second Division was organized December 3, 1863, and was assigned to Second Brigade, Fourth Division, Thirteenth Corps January 4, 1864.

Note 3. Henry Bertram succeeded Dye in command of Second Brigade in January 1864.

Third Division, George F. McGinnis
First Brigade, Daniel Macauley
Second Brigade, William H. Raynor
Artillery
Battery A, 1st Missouri Light Artillery, Elisha Cole

Note 1. Third Division was at Algiers, Louisiana, but it was assigned to the Defenses of New Orleans January 15, 1864 and moved to Madisonville, north of Lake Ponchartrain. Two regiments of Third Division were sent to Texas in December 1863, but they were ordered to return to Louisiana February 15, 1864.

Note 2. McCauley commanded First Brigade while Robert A. Cameron was detached on special service.

Fourth Division, William J. Landram, to January 4, 1864
(at Decros' Point, Texas)
Thomas E. G. Ransom
First Brigade, John Cowan, to January 4, 1864
William J. Landram
Second Brigade, Memoir V. Hotchkiss
Artillery
Chicago Mercantile Battery, Illinois Light Artillery, Patrick H. White
17th Battery, Ohio Light Artillery, Charles S. Rice

Note 1. The infantry of Fourth Division was reorganized November 21, 1863, as reported above.

Note 2. Fourth Division was transferred from Texas to Berwick Bay, Louisiana February 24–28, 1864.

Note 3. Hotchkiss was assigned command of Second Brigade December 5, 1863, in place of David P. Grier, who was ordered north on recruiting service. Hotchkiss was succeeded by Henry Rust, Jr. in January 1864.

Note 4. A Provisional Brigade was formed January 13, 1864 from the 13th Maine, 15th Maine, 20th Iowa, and 34th Iowa, and was assigned to Fourth Division. This organization was formerly Ransom's Third Brigade, Second Division, Thirteenth Corps.

John A. McClernand returned to Thirteenth Corps and resumed command February 23, 1864, with headquarters at New Orleans.

Third Division and Fourth Division, Thirteenth Corps accompanied Banks on his Red River Campaign March–May 1864; at the end of March 1864, they were at Natchitoches on the Cane River. These two divisions were designated as Detachment Thirteenth Corps, which at that time was organized as follows:

DETACHMENT THIRTEENTH CORPS, Thomas E. G. Ransom

Third Division, Robert A. Cameron
First Brigade, Aaron M. Flory
Second Brigade, William H. Raynor
Artillery
Battery A, 1st Missouri Light Artillery, Elisha Cole
2nd Battery, Ohio Light Artillery, William H. Harper

Note 1. Ransom relieved McClernand in command of Detachment Thirteenth Corps March 15, 1864.

Note 2. Cameron assumed command of Third Division March 3, 1864.

Fourth Division, William J. Landram
First Brigade, Frank Emerson
Second Brigade, Joseph W. Vance
Artillery
1st Battery, Indiana Light Artillery, Martin Klauss
Chicago Mercantile Battery, Illinois Light Artillery, Pinckney S. Cone

First Division, Thirteenth Corps, which was in Texas, was reorganized March 10, 1864. Third Brigade was discontinued and consolidated with Second Brigade under the command of Michael K. Lawler. A Provisional Brigade was also formed from attached troops of the Corps d'Afrique and 1st Battalion, Rhode Island Heavy Artillery. The new organization of First Division was as follows:

First Division, Napoleon J. T. Dana
First Brigade, Fitz Henry Warren
Second Brigade, Michael K. Lawler
Provisional Brigade, John C. Cobb

Note. Warren succeeded Dana in command of First Division April 4, 1864.

First Division and Second Division remained in

Texas during the greater part of Banks' Red River Campaign. Lawler's Second Brigade, First Division was transferred from Pass Cavallo to Alexandria, Louisiana April 18–26, 1864, and on April 17, Warren was ordered to take the remainder of First Division to the Red River as soon as practicable. Warren arrived with First Brigade, First Division near Fort De Russy in May 1864.

Third Division and Fourth Division, Thirteenth Corps were engaged at Sabine Cross Roads (or Mansfield), Louisiana April 8, 1864, where Ransom was wounded, and Robert A. Cameron assumed command of Detachment Thirteenth Corps. The two divisions were also in action at Monett's Ferry (or Cane River Crossing) on April 23. For details of the operations of Thirteenth Corps during the Red River Campaign, see Red River, Louisiana Campaign.

At the end of April 1864, Third Division, Fourth Division, and Second Brigade, First Division were at Alexandria; and Warren's First Brigade, First Division was under orders to join them from Texas. Detachment Thirteenth Corps then moved with William H. Emory's Nineteenth Corps toward Morganza, Louisiana, where it arrived May 22.

Lawler was assigned command of First Division, Thirteenth Corps May 19, 1864. William P. Benton assumed command of Thirteenth Corps at Morganza May 22. On May 24, Landram's Fourth Division was ordered to Baton Rouge under the command of Fitz Henry Warren, and upon arrival there, Warren assumed command of the District of Baton Rouge.

On June 11, 1864, Thirteenth Corps was temporarily discontinued, and the troops were reassigned by Edward R. S. Canby, commander of the Military Division of West Mississippi. First Division, Thirteenth Corps, which was somewhat scattered at that time, was attached to Nineteenth Corps at Morganza. Second Division, Thirteenth Corps was redesignated as United States Forces in Texas under Francis J. Herron.

In the reorganization of Nineteenth Corps June 27, 1864, First Division, Thirteenth Corps became Third Division, Nineteenth Corps under Michael K. Lawler. Third Brigade, Third Division, Nineteenth Corps was organized from regiments of Fourth Division, Thirteenth Corps that were serving in the

District of Baton Rouge. Other regiments of Fourth Division, Thirteenth Corps were assigned to the Defenses of New Orleans, and to Second Brigade, First Division, Nineteenth Corps. Third Division, Thirteenth Corps was broken up, and the regiments of Second Brigade were assigned to the Defenses of New Orleans and the District of La Fourche as Slack's Brigade, commanded by James R. Slack.

Finally, by an order of June 21, 1864, the troops of Thirteenth Corps not included in the reorganized Nineteenth Corps were to be organized into brigades and divisions, which were to report directly to the commander of the Department of the Gulf.

COMMANDERS OF THIRTEENTH CORPS, DEPARTMENT OF THE GULF

Cadwallader C. Washburn	August 7, 1863 to September 15, 1863
Edward O. C. Ord	September 15, 1863 to October 20, 1863
Cadwallader C. Washburn	October 20, 1863 to October 26, 1863
Napoleon J. T. Dana	October 26, 1863 to January 9, 1864
Edward O. C. Ord	January 9, 1864 to February 23, 1864
John A. McClernand	February 23, 1864 to March 15, 1864
Thomas E. G. Ransom	March 15, 1864 to April 8, 1864
Robert A. Cameron	April 8, 1864 to April 27, 1864
John A. McClernand	April 27, 1864 to May 5, 1864
Michael K. Lawler	May 5, 1864 to May 9, 1864
William P. Benton	May 22, 1864 to June 11, 1864

Note 1. Ransom, and the succeeding commanders, actually commanded Detachment Thirteenth Corps in the field, although this was commonly called Thirteenth Corps.

Note 2. Cameron assumed temporary command April 8, 1864 when Ransom was wounded, and he officially assumed command on April 12.

Note 3. Lawler assumed temporary command May 1, 1864 when McClernand became ill, and he officially assumed command on May 10.

THIRTEENTH CORPS, MILITARY DIVISION OF WEST MISSISSIPPI

January 18, 1865, Ulysses S. Grant ordered Edward R. S. Canby, commander of the Military Division of West Mississippi, to begin operations against Mobile, Montgomery, and Selma, Alabama; and Canby began to reinforce the United States forces in South Alabama and West Florida for this purpose. Among the first troops to be sent from New Orleans were those belonging to the Reserve Corps, Military Division of West Mississippi. The Reserve Corps was reorganized February 3, 1865 from the brigades of the corps and additional regiments, and Gordon Granger was assigned command. This reorganization was not fully completed when, by an order of February 18, 1865, Thirteenth Corps, Military Division of West Mississippi was created to consist of the troops of the Reserve Corps. For details of the organization and operations of Thirteenth Corps, Military Division of West Mississippi, see Land Operations against Mobile Bay and Mobile, Alabama.

FOURTEENTH CORPS, ARMY OF THE CUMBERLAND OCTOBER 24, 1862– JANUARY 9, 1863

The Department of the Cumberland was created by a presidential order dated October 24, 1862, and William S. Rosecrans was assigned command. The same order directed that the troops assigned to Rosecrans in the new department be designated as Fourteenth Corps. At that time the troops in the Department of the Cumberland consisted of twelve divisions and, like Thirteenth Corps, which was created at the same time, it embraced an entire army. The troops assigned to Fourteenth Corps were essentially the same as those that had previously been known as the Army of the Ohio under Don Carlos Buell, and which had fought at Shiloh

April 6–7, 1862 and at Perryville, Kentucky October 8, 1862.

Rosecrans assumed command of the Department of the Cumberland and of Fourteenth Corps October 30, 1862. He immediately began preparations for an advance from Kentucky to Nashville, Tennessee, and a movement against Braxton Bragg's Army of the Mississippi, which was then in Central Tennessee.

When first organized, Fourteenth Corps consisted of eleven divisions and consequently was difficult to control. Because of this, on November 7, 1862, Rosecrans divided the army into three parts: a Right Wing of three divisions, commanded by Alexander McD. McCook; a Center of five divisions, commanded by George H. Thomas; and a Left Wing of three divisions, commanded by Thomas L. Crittenden. For details of the organization of Fourteenth Corps at that time, see Army of the Cumberland, October 24, 1862–November 14, 1864.

On December 26, 1862, Rosecrans left three divisions of Thomas' Center to garrison Nashville and to protect the army's line of communications through Nashville to Louisville, and with the remaining eight divisions of Fourteenth Corps marched against Bragg's army, which was then at Murfreesboro, Tennessee. The Army of the Cumberland, or Fourteenth Corps, was engaged at the Battle of Stones River (or Murfreesboro) December 31, 1862–January 3, 1863, and after the enemy had withdrawn, it encamped at Murfreesboro. For details of the organization of Fourteenth Corps at the Battle of Stones River, and of its advance to Murfreesboro, see Stones River (or Murfreesboro), Tennessee Campaign.

On January 9, 1863, while Fourteenth Corps (or Army of the Cumberland) was at Murfreesboro, it was reorganized to consist of three corps as follows: McCook's Right Wing was redesignated as Twentieth Corps; Thomas' Center was redesignated as a new, and smaller, Fourteenth Corps; and Crittenden's Left Wing was redesignated as Twenty-First Corps. The old Fourteenth Corps was thus discontinued. For details of the organization and operations of the new Fourteenth Corps, see Fourteenth Corps, Army of the Cumberland, January 9, 1863–November 14, 1864.

FOURTEENTH CORPS, ARMY OF THE CUMBERLAND JANUARY 9, 1863– NOVEMBER 14, 1864

On January 9, 1863, while William S. Rosecrans' Army of the Cumberland was at Murfreesboro, Tennessee, following the Battle of Stones River, it was reorganized to consist of three corps as follows: the Right Wing was to be redesignated as Twentieth Corps, Army of the Cumberland, and was to be commanded by Alexander McD. McCook; the Center was to be redesignated as Fourteenth Corps, and was to be commanded by George H. Thomas; and the Left Wing was redesignated as Twenty-First Corps, and was to be commanded by Thomas L. Crittenden. Whereas prior to January 9 the Army of the Cumberland consisted of only a single corps, the Fourteenth Corps, after the reorganization it consisted of three corps.

The new Fourteenth Corps was limited to the five divisions commanded by Thomas, and on January 10, 1863, these were as follows: Lovell H. Rousseau's First Division, James S. Negley's Second Division, Speed S. Fry's Third Division, James D. Morgan's Fourth Division, and Joseph J. Reynolds' Fifth Division. Morgan's division was at Nashville, and the other four divisions were near Murfreesboro.

On January 9, 1863, the day on which the order reorganizing the Army of the Cumberland was issued, the Center, Fourteenth Corps was organized as follows:

CENTER, FOURTEENTH CORPS, George H. Thomas

First Division, Lovell H. Rousseau
  First Brigade, Benjamin F. Scribner
  Second Brigade, John Beatty
  Third Brigade, John C. Starkweather
  Fourth Brigade, Oliver L. Shepherd
  Artillery
    Battery A, Kentucky Light Artillery, David C. Stone
    1st Battery, Michigan Light Artillery, George W. Van Pelt
    Battery H, 5th United States Artillery, Francis L. Guenther

Second Division, James S. Negley
  First Brigade, James G. Spears
  Second Brigade, Timothy R. Stanley
  Third Brigade, John F. Miller
  Artillery
    Battery B, Kentucky Light Artillery, Alban A. Ellsworth
    Battery G, 1st Ohio Light Artillery, Alexander Marshall
    Battery M, 1st Ohio Light Artillery, Frederick Schultz

Third Division, Speed S. Fry
  First Brigade, Moses B. Walker
  Second Brigade, John M. Harlan
  Third Brigade, James B. Steedman
  Artillery
    4th Battery, Michigan Light Artillery, Josiah W. Church
    Battery C, 1st Ohio Light Artillery, Daniel K. Southwick
    Battery I, 4th United States Artillery, Frank G. Smith

Fourth Division, Robert B. Mitchell
  First Brigade, James D. Morgan
  Second Brigade, Daniel McCook
  Cavalry
    5th Kentucky, John Q. Owsley
    3rd Tennessee, William C. Pickens
    2nd Indiana, Company A, John G. Kessler
  Artillery
    Battery I, 2nd Illinois Light Artillery, Charles M. Barnett
    10th Battery, Wisconsin Light Artillery, Yates V. Beebe
  Artillery Reserve
    11th Battery, Indiana Light Artillery, Arnold Sutermeister
    12th Battery, Indiana Light Artillery, James A. Dunwoody
    5th Battery, Michigan Light Artillery, John J. Ely

Fifth Division, Joseph J. Reynolds
  First Brigade, Albert S. Hall
  Second Brigade, Abram O. Miller
  Artillery
    18th Battery, Indiana Light Artillery, Eli Lilly
    19th Battery, Indiana Light Artillery, Samuel J. Harris

The new Fourteenth Corps retained the same organization as that given above until April 17, 1863, when it was reorganized as follows:

FOURTEENTH CORPS, George H. Thomas

First Division, Lovell H. Rousseau
First Brigade, Benjamin F. Scribner
Second Brigade, Henry A. Hambright
Third Brigade, Robert S. Granger

Note 1. First Brigade, Second Division was discontinued April 17, 1863, when the regiments were transferred to the District of Central Kentucky, Department of the Ohio. First Brigade, Second Division was then reorganized the same day by the transfer of Second Brigade, First Division to Second Division.
Note 2. Second Brigade, First Division was reorganized April 17, 1863 from the regiments of Third Brigade, First Division, and Third Brigade was reorganized from the regiments of Fourth Brigade, First Division. Fourth Brigade was then discontinued.

Second Division, James S. Negley
First Brigade, John Beatty
Second Brigade, John B. Turchin
Third Brigade, John F. Miller

Note 1. Turchin was assigned command of Second Brigade April 17, 1863.
Note 2. As noted above, First Brigade was formerly Second Brigade, First Division.

Third Division, John M. Schofield
First Brigade, Moses B. Walker
Second Brigade, Charles W. Chapman
Third Brigade, Ferdinand Van Derveer

Note. Schofield was assigned command of Third Division April 17, 1863.

Fourth Division, James D. Morgan
First Brigade, Robert F. Smith
Second Brigade, Daniel McCook
Third Brigade, George Crook

Note. Third Brigade was organized June 8, 1863 from five regiments brought to Tennessee from the Army of Kentucky by George Crook.

Fifth Division, Joseph J. Reynolds
First Brigade, John T. Wilder
Second Brigade, Albert S. Hall

A provisional brigade was organized in April 1863 under the command of Abel D. Streight and was designated as Streight's Provisional Brigade. For details of its organization and operations, see Streight's Raid from Tuscumbia, Alabama toward Rome, Georgia.

The Army of the Cumberland was again reorganized June 8, 1863, with the creation of the Reserve Corps, Army of the Cumberland under Gordon Granger, and the troops composing Fourth Division, Fourteenth Corps were transferred to Granger's command. That same day, Fourth Division was re-created by the change of designation of Fifth Division to Fourth Division, and Fifth Division was thus discontinued. A new Third Brigade, Fourth Division was organized on June 8 from five regiments brought to Tennessee from the Army of Kentucky by George Crook. Crook's command had served as an independent brigade at Carthage, Tennessee until June 8. On June 23, Rosecrans began his advance from Murfreesboro with the Army of the Cumberland at the beginning of the Tullahoma Campaign, which was to result in the retreat of Braxton Bragg with his Confederate Army of Tennessee from Middle Tennessee to Chattanooga and was to culminate in the Battle of Chickamauga, Georgia September 19–20, 1863.

June 24, 1863, Thomas' Fourteenth Corps advanced from Murfreesboro on the Manchester Pike to Hoover's Gap. Joseph J. Reynolds' Fourth Division was in the lead, and it was followed by Lovell H. Rousseau's First Division and James S. Negley's Second Division. John M. Brannan's Third Division, which at that time was at Triune, Tennessee, accompanied Granger's command in its advance for a time, but it joined Thomas and the other three divisions of the corps on June 25. Thomas attacked and captured Hoover's Gap June 24, where Reynolds' division did most of the fighting, but received support from John H. King's Third Brigade of Rousseau's division.

Fourteenth Corps moved on toward Manchester, Tennessee, which it occupied June 27, 1863. Fourteenth Corps then advanced with the rest of the Army of the Cumberland and occupied Tullahoma on July 1. As the army advanced beyond Tullahoma and Manchester, Bragg's army fell back, finally crossing the Tennessee River and retiring to Chattanooga, where it arrived July 7.

Rosecrans did not follow at once, but halted his army until supplies could be brought up and preparations made for a further advance. At the end of

July 1863, the divisions of Fourteenth Corps were encamped as follows: First Division and Second Division were at Cowan, Tennessee; Third Division was near Winchester, Tennessee; and Fourth Division was near Decherd, Tennessee.

For details of the operations of Fourteenth Corps during the Tullahoma Campaign, see Tullahoma (or Middle Tennessee) Campaign.

The organization of Fourteenth Corps at the end of June 1863 was as follows:

FOURTEENTH CORPS, George H. Thomas

First Division, Lovell H. Rousseau
  First Brigade, Benjamin F. Scribner
  Second Brigade, Henry A. Hambright
  Third Brigade, John H. King
  Artillery, Cyrus O. Loomis
    4th Battery, Indiana Light Artillery, David Flansburg
    1st Battery, Michigan Light Artillery, George W. Van Pelt
    Battery H, 5th United States Artillery, George A. Kensel

Second Division, James S. Negley
  First Brigade, John Beatty
  Second Brigade, William L. Stoughton
  Third Brigade, William Sirwell
  Artillery, Frederick Schultz
    2nd Battery, Kentucky Light Artillery, John M. Hewett
    Battery G, 1st Ohio Light Artillery, Alexander Marshall
    Battery M, 1st Ohio Light Artillery, Frederick Schultz

Third Division, John M. Brannan
  First Brigade, Moses B. Walker
  Second Brigade, James B. Steedman
  Third Brigade, Ferdinand Van Derveer
  Artillery
    4th Battery, Michigan Light Artillery, Josiah W. Church
    Battery C, 1st Ohio Light Artillery, Daniel K. Southwick
    Battery I, 4th United States Artillery, Frank G. Smith

Fourth Division, Joseph J. Reynolds
  First Brigade, John T. Wilder
  Second Brigade, Albert S. Hall

Third Brigade, George Crook
  Artillery
    18th Battery, Indiana Light Artillery, Eli Lilly
    19th Battery, Indiana Light Artillery, Samuel J. Harris
    21st Battery, Indiana Light Artillery, William W. Andrew

There were some changes in command and organization during July 1863, and at the end of the month the organization of Fourteenth Corps was as follows:

FOURTEENTH CORPS, George H. Thomas

First Division, John H. King
  First Brigade, Benjamin F. Scribner
  Second Brigade, John C. Starkweather
  Third Brigade, Samuel K. Dawson

  Note. Almerick W. Wilbur's 1st Battery, Michigan Light Artillery was attached to First Brigade; David Flansburg's 4th Battery, Indiana Light Artillery was attached to Second Brigade; and Francis L. Guenther's Battery H, 5th United States Artillery was attached to Third Brigade.

Second Division, James S. Negley
  First Brigade, John Beatty
  Second Brigade, Timothy R. Stanley
  Third Brigade, William Sirwell

  Note. John M. Hewett's 2nd Battery, Kentucky Light Artillery was attached to First Brigade; Frederick Schultz's Battery M, 1st Ohio Light Artillery was attached to Second Brigade; and Alexander Marshall's Battery G, 1st Ohio Light Artillery was attached to Third Brigade.

Third Division, John M. Brannan
  First Brigade, John M. Connell
  Second Brigade, James B. Steedman
  Third Brigade, Ferdinand Van Derveer

  Note. Josiah W. Church's 4th Battery, Michigan Light Artillery was attached to First Brigade; Daniel K. Southwick's Battery C, 1st Ohio Light Artillery was attached to Second Brigade; and Frank G. Smith's Battery I, 4th United States Artillery was attached to Third Brigade.

Fourth Division, Joseph J. Reynolds
  First Brigade, Abram O. Miller
  Second Brigade, Milton S. Robinson
  Third Brigade, John B. Turchin

  Note. Eli Lilly's 18th Battery, Indiana Light Artillery

was attached to First Brigade; Samuel J. Harris' 19th Battery, Indiana Light Artillery was attached to Second Brigade; and William W. Andrew's 21st Battery, Indiana Light Artillery was attached to Third Brigade.

About July 26, 1863, Lovell H. Rousseau was sent to Washington on army business, and John H. King assumed temporary command of First Division. He was relieved, also temporarily, by Walter C. Whitaker on August 10, and a few days later he was relieved by John C. Starkweather. Absalom Baird was relieved from duty with the Reserve Corps, Army of the Cumberland on August 11, and on August 19 assumed command of First Division, Fourteenth Corps.

On August 16, 1863, the Army of the Cumberland once again moved forward toward Bragg's army at Chattanooga. Fourteenth Corps moved forward to the Tennessee River, where Negley's and Johnson's divisions crossed at Caperton's Ferry near Stevenson, Alabama; Brannan's division crossed at Battle Creek; and Reynolds' division crossed at Shellmound. Baird's division, followed by Negley's division, crossed Sand Mountain into Lookout Valley, then marched by way of Trenton and occupied Stevens' Gap in Lookout Mountain, twenty-six miles south of Chattanooga. Reynolds' division crossed Raccoon Mountain into Lookout Valley and moved to Stevens' Gap. Brannan's division followed Reynolds from the Battle Creek crossing.

Bragg then left Chattanooga and marched southward with his army to La Fayette, Georgia, and Crittenden's Twenty-First Corps moved up and occupied Chattanooga, on the left of Thomas, who was at Stevens' Gap. McCook's Twentieth Corps marched up Lookout Valley to Winston's Gap, far to the right of Stevens' Gap.

From Stevens' Gap, Thomas sent Negley's division on a reconnaissance into McLemore's Cove in the direction of La Fayette, Georgia, but it encountered troops of Bragg's army in front of Dug Gap in Pigeon Mountain. Thomas sent forward Baird's division in support, but both divisions withdrew and rejoined the corps near Stevens' Gap on the evening of September 11, 1863.

When Rosecrans learned that Bragg was not retreating beyond La Fayette, he assembled the corps of his army south of Chattanooga along Chickamauga Creek, and there he was attacked by Bragg's army on the morning of September 19, 1863, at the beginning of the Battle of Chickamauga. Fourteenth Corps was on the left of Rosecrans' line of battle and, reinforced strongly by troops of Twentieth and Twenty-First Corps, held the line east of the Chattanooga La Fayette road during the first day's fighting. When the Union line was broken during the fighting of September 20, Thomas assumed command of the troops that assembled on Horseshoe Ridge, including some men of Fourteenth Corps, and held the position until dark. Fourteenth Corps then retreated with the Army of the Cumberland to Chattanooga, remaining there under siege by Bragg's army until late November. For details of the operations of Fourteenth Corps during the Chickamauga Campaign, see Chickamauga, Georgia Campaign.

The organization of Fourteenth Corps at the Battle of Chickamauga September 19–20, 1863 was as follows:

FOURTEENTH CORPS, George H. Thomas

First Division, Absalom Baird
    First Brigade, Benjamin F. Scribner
    Second Brigade, John C. Starkweather
    Third Brigade, John H. King

Note. George W. Van Pelt's Battery A, 1st Michigan Light Artillery was attached to First Bri_ ·de; David Flansburg's 4th Battery, Indiana Light Artillery was attached to Second Brigade; and Howard M. Burnham's Battery H, 5th United States Artillery was attached to Third Brigade.

Second Division, James S. Negley
    First Brigade, John Beatty
    Second Brigade, Timothy R. Stanley, to September 20, 1863, wounded
        William L. Stoughton
    Third Brigade, William Sirwell

Note. Lyman Bridges' Battery, Illinois Light Artillery was attached to First Brigade; Frederick Schultz's Battery M, 1st Ohio Light Artillery was attached to Second Brigade; and Alexander Marshall's Battery G, 1st Ohio Light Artillery was attached to Third Brigade.

Third Division, John M. Brannan
    First Brigade, John M. Connell
    Second Brigade, John T. Croxton, to September 20, wounded
        William H. Hays

Third Brigade, Ferdinand Van Derveer

Note. Josiah W. Church's Battery D, 1st Michigan Light Artillery was attached to First Brigade; Marco B. Gary's Battery C, 1st Ohio Light Artillery was attached to Second Brigade; and Frank G. Smith's Battery I, 4th United States Artillery was attached to Third Brigade.

Fourth Division, Joseph J. Reynolds
First Brigade, John T. Wilder
Second Brigade, Edward A. King, to September 20, 1863, killed
   Milton S. Robinson
Third Brigade, John B. Turchin

Note 1. Wilder's brigade was detached from the division and was serving as mounted infantry.
Note 2. Eli Lilly's 18th Battery, Indiana Light Artillery was attached to First Brigade; Samuel J. Harris' 19th Battery, Indiana Light Artillery was attached to Second Brigade; and William W. Andrew's 21st Battery, Indiana Light Artillery was attached to Third Brigade.

Another reorganization of the Army of the Cumberland was announced October 9, 1863, while the army was at Chattanooga. By a presidential order dated September 28, 1863, Twentieth Corps and Twenty-First Corps were consolidated to form a new Fourth Corps, Army of the Cumberland. The Reserve Corps was discontinued, and its troops were assigned to Fourth Corps and Fourteenth Corps. Also on October 9, Fourteenth Corps was reorganized as follows:

FOURTEENTH CORPS, George H. Thomas, to October 28, 1863
John M. Palmer

First Division, Lovell H. Rousseau
First Brigade, William P. Carlin
Second Brigade, John H. King, to October 13, 1863
   Jesse H. Moore
Third Brigade, John C. Starkweather

Note 1. First Brigade was organized from First Brigade, First Division and First Brigade, Second Division, Fourteenth Corps.
Note 2. Second Brigade was organized from Third Brigade, First Division and Second Brigade, Second Division, Fourteenth Corps
Note 3. Third Brigade was organized from Second Brigade, First Division and Third Brigade, Second Division, Fourteenth Corps.
Note 4. At the time the organization of the corps was announced, Starkweather was absent from the division

and William Sirwell assumed command of Third Brigade.

Second Division, Absalom Baird
First Brigade, John B. Turchin
Second Brigade, James George
Third Brigade, Edward H. Phelps

Note 1. First Brigade was organized from Third Brigade, Fourth Division and First Brigade, Third Division, Fourteenth Corps.
Note 2. Second Brigade was organized from Second Brigade, Fourth Division and Third Brigade, Third Division, Fourteenth Corps.
Note 3. Third Brigade was organized from Second Brigade, Third Division, Fourteenth Corps.
Note 4. Special Field Orders, Department of the Cumberland, dated October 9, 1863, announcing the reorganization of Fourteenth Corps given here were amended on October 10 to number the division commanded by Baird as Third Division and the division command by Davis (see below) as Second Division.

Third Division, Jefferson C. Davis
First Brigade, James D. Morgan
Second Brigade, John Beatty
Third Brigade, Daniel McCook

Note 1. First Brigade was organized from First Brigade, Second Division, Reserve Corps.
Note 2. Second Brigade was organized from Second Brigade, First Division, Reserve Corps.
Note 3. Third Brigade was organized from Second Brigade, Second Division, Reserve Corps.
Note 4. The number of Third Division was changed to Second Division by an order of October 10, 1863. See Note 4, Second Division, above.

On October 31, 1863, after the reorganization had been completed, Fourteenth Corps was organized as follows:

FOURTEENTH CORPS, John M. Palmer

First Division, Lovell H. Rousseau
First Brigade, William P. Carlin
Second Brigade, Marshall F. Moore
Third Brigade, William Sirwell
Artillery, Mark H. Prescott
   Battery C, 1st Illinois Light Artillery, Mark H. Prescott
   Battery A, 1st Michigan Light Artillery, Francis E. Hale
   Battery H, 5th United States Artillery, Edmund D. Spooner

Second Division, Jefferson C. Davis
 First Brigade, Robert F. Smith
 Second Brigade, James G. Spears
 Third Brigade, Daniel McCook
 Artillery, William A. Hotchkiss
  Battery I, 2nd Illinois Light Artillery, Charles M. Barnett
  2nd Battery, Minnesota Light Artillery, Richard L. Dawley
  5th Battery, Wisconsin Light Artillery, Joseph McKnight

Note. The 78th Illinois and 98th, 13th, and 121st Ohio regiments were on detached duty under the command of John G. Mitchell.

Third Division, Absalom Baird
 First Brigade, John B. Turchin
 Second Brigade, James George
 Third Brigade, Edward H. Phelps
 Artillery, George R. Swallow
  7th Battery, Indiana Light Artillery, Otho H. Morgan
  19th Battery, Indiana Light Artillery, Samuel J. Harris
  Battery 1, 4th United States Artillery, Frank G. Smith

The Military Division of the Mississippi was constituted October 16, 1863, and Ulysses S. Grant assumed command on October 18. He then began preparations for opening the Tennessee River and thus enabling the Army of the Cumberland to obtain greatly needed supplies from Bridgeport, Alabama and the North. He also assigned George H. Thomas to the command of the Department of the Cumberland, to relieve William S. Rosecrans. On October 28, John M. Palmer relieved Thomas in command of Fourteenth Corps.

The Tennessee River was opened October 27, 1863 with the capture of Brown's Ferry, and then Grant began preparations for driving Bragg's army from its positions on Missionary Ridge and Lookout Mountain, where it had held the Army of the Cumberland under virtual siege since the Battle of Chickamauga. To aid Grant in this undertaking, Eleventh Corps and Twelfth Corps of the Army of the Potomac were sent from Virginia to Tennessee, and Grant also ordered William T. Sherman, with four divisions of the Army of the Tennessee, to march toward Chattanooga. For details of the siege of Chattanooga and the opening of the Tennessee River, see Army of the Cumberland, October 24, 1862–November 14, 1864, Siege of Chattanooga, Tennessee. During the first three weeks of November 1863, Richard W. Johnson's First Division and Absalom Baird's Third Division of Fourteenth Corps were encamped within the fortifications of Chattanooga, and Jefferson C. Davis' Second Division was deployed on the north bank of the Tennessee River, to the east of Chattanooga, guarding the fords and ferries in the area. Then on November 23, in preparation for the battles that were to begin the next day, Johnson, with William P. Carlin's First Brigade and Marshall F. Moore's Second Brigade of his First Division, and Baird's Third Division moved out and formed in line of battle in front of Missionary Ridge. John C. Starkweather's Third Brigade, First Division remained in line of battle in the trenches at Chattanooga. Davis concentrated his Second Division at Caldwell's Ford on the Tennessee River, and was joined there by Sherman and his three divisions. Davis then reported to Sherman, crossing the river with him and taking position at the northern end of Missionary Ridge.

On November 24, 1863, Joseph Hooker, in command of a mixed Union force, successfully attacked Lookout Mountain. Late in the afternoon of that day, William P. Carlin's First Brigade, First Division, Fourteenth Corps joined Hooker in the attack, but it later returned to its division.

On November 25, First Brigade and Second Brigade of First Division and Third Division of Fourteenth Corps took part, together with Fourth Corps, in the successful attack on Missionary Ridge, and Fourteenth Corps took part in the pursuit of Bragg's defeated army toward Dalton, Georgia.

For details of the operations of Fourteenth Corps in late November 1863, see Chattanooga-Ringgold Campaign (Battles of Lookout Mountain and Missionary Ridge, Tennessee).

The organization of Fourteenth Corps at the battles of Lookout Mountain and Missionary Ridge was as follows:

FOURTEENTH CORPS, John M. Palmer

First Division, Richard W. Johnson
 First Brigade, William P. Carlin
 Second Brigade, Marshall F. Moore
  William L. Stoughton

Third Brigade, John C. Starkweather
Artillery
  Battery C, 1st Illinois Light Artillery, Mark H. Prescott
  Battery A, 1st Michigan Light Artillery, Francis E. Hale
  Battery H, 5th United States Artillery, Francis L. Guenther

Note 1. Johnson was assigned command of First Division November 12, 1863, after Rousseau was assigned command of the District of Nashville.

Note 2. Guenther's battery was temporarily attached to Second Division, Fourth Corps during the battles about Chattanooga.

Second Division, Jefferson C. Davis
  First Brigade, James D. Morgan
  Second Brigade, John Beatty
  Third Brigade, Daniel McCook
  Artillery, William A. Hotchkiss
    Battery I, 2nd Illinois Light Artillery, Henry B. Plant
    2nd Battery, Minnesota Light Artillery, Richard L. Dawley
    5th Battery, Wisconsin Light Artillery, George Q. Gardner

Third Division, Absalom Baird
  First Brigade, John B. Turchin
  Second Brigade, Ferdinand Van Derveer
  Third Brigade, Edward H. Phelps
    William H. Hays
  Artillery, George R. Swallow
    7th Battery, Indiana Light Artillery, Otho H. Morgan
    19th Battery, Indiana Light Artillery, Robert G. Lackey
    Battery I, 4th United States Artillery, Frank G. Smith

On November 30, 1863, Davis' Second Division, Fourteenth Corps accompanied a force commanded by William T. Sherman that marched to the relief of Ambrose E. Burnside's army, which was threatened by James Longstreet's Confederate corps at Knoxville, Tennessee. Upon the approach of Sherman's forces, however, Longstreet withdrew into eastern Tennessee, and Davis' division returned to Chattanooga December 19, 1863. For additional information, see Relief of Knoxville, Tennessee (William T. Sherman).

Headquarters, Fourteenth Corps was at Chatta-nooga during the winter of 1863–1864. First Division was at Chattanooga during December and January, then moved to Tyner's Station in February; it was at Graysville, Georgia during March and April. Second Division was encamped near Rossville, Georgia from December to March, and it then moved to Ringgold, Georgia. Third Division was at Chattanooga during December and January, then moved to Ringgold.

On May 6, 1864, in preparation for the advance of Sherman's army of the Military Division of the Mississippi toward Atlanta, Georgia, the divisions of Palmer's Fourteenth Corps were assembled at Stone Church, about three miles south of Ringgold. The next day the corps advanced to Tunnel Hill, then moved up to Rocky Face Ridge, where it was engaged in skirmishing May 8–11. It then withdrew and moved to Snake Creek Gap to support the Army of the Tennessee.

Fourteenth Corps was engaged at the Battle of Resaca May 14–15, 1864, then moved south by different routes; on May 26, First Division was at Burnt Hickory, Second Division was near Dallas, and Third Division was at Raccoon Ford. The corps was with the army while it was in position along the Pumpkin Vine Creek, but was largely engaged in guarding the trains and in reserve.

From there the corps moved to Pine Mountain June 6, 1864, and then to the front of Kennesaw Mountain June 19. During the fighting at Kennesaw Mountain June 27, Davis' Second Division, supported by Baird's Third Division, attacked at Cheatham's Hill, south of the mountain.

The enemy retired from their lines at Kennesaw Mountain on the night of July 2, 1864, and a week later crossed the Chattahoochee River. Fourteenth Corps advanced with the rest of the army in pursuit, arriving on the river bank on July 10. It then crossed at Pace's Ferry July 17 and advanced to Peach Tree Creek, where it was engaged at the Battle of Peach Tree Creek July 20. From there it advanced to within two and a half miles of Atlanta and entrenched. It remained on the siege lines until August 29, then marched toward Jonesboro. All divisions of Fourteenth Corps were engaged at the Battle of Jonesboro August 31–September 1, and the corps then returned to Atlanta September 8, at the end of the Atlanta Campaign. It remained there during the rest of the month. On August 6, Richard W. Johnson relieved Palmer in command of Fourteenth Corps, and he in turn was relieved by Jefferson C. Davis on August 22.

For details of the operations of Fourteenth Corps during the period May–September 1864, see Atlanta, Georgia Campaign.

The organization of Fourteenth Corps during the period May 3–September 8, 1864 was as follows:

FOURTEENTH CORPS, John M. Palmer, to August 7, 1864
 Richard W. Johnson, temporarily to August 22, 1864
 Jefferson C. Davis

First Division, Richard W. Johnson, to May 29, 1864, disabled
 John H. King, to June 6, 1864
 Richard W. Johnson, to June 13, 1864, on leave
 John H. King, to July 13, 1864
 Richard W. Johnson, to August 7, 1864
 John H. King, to August 17, 1864
 William P. Carlin
 First Brigade, William P. Carlin, to July 2, 1864, on leave
  Anson G. McCook, to July 27, 1864
  Marion C. Taylor, to August 3, 1864
  William P. Carlin, to August 17, 1864
  Marion C. Taylor
 Second Brigade, John H. King, to June 6, 1864
  William L. Stoughton, to July 4, 1864, wounded
  Marshall F. Moore, to July 13, 1864
  John H. King, to August 7, 1864
  John R. Edie
 Third Brigade, Benjamin F. Scribner, to July 5, 1864, sick
  Josiah Given, to July 15, 1864
  Marshall F. Moore
 Artillery, Lucius H. Drury
  Battery C, 1st Illinois Light Artillery, Mark H. Prescott
  Battery I, 1st Ohio Light Artillery, Hubert Dilger

Note 1. Johnson was disabled and absent May 29–June 6 and June 13–July 13.
Note 2. The divisional artillery was assigned to the Artillery Brigade of the corps July 24, 1864.

Second Division, Jefferson C. Davis, to July 28, 1864, sick
 James D. Morgan, temporarily to August 25, 1864
 James D. Morgan
 First Brigade, James D. Morgan

  Robert F. Smith, temporarily
  James D. Morgan, to August 23, 1864
  Charles M. Lum
 Second Brigade, John G. Mitchell
 Third Brigade, Daniel McCook, to June 27, 1864, mortally wounded
  Oscar F. Harmon, June 27, 1864, mortally wounded
  Caleb J. Dilworth, to September 1, 1864, wounded
  James W. Langley
 Artillery, Charles M. Barnett
  Battery I, 2nd Illinois Light Artillery, Alonzo W. Coe
  5th Battery, Wisconsin Light Artillery, George Q. Gardner

Note 1. James D. Morgan was in temporary command of the active operations of Second Division until August 25, 1864 and was then assigned command of the division when Davis was assigned command of Fourteenth Corps. Morgan also commanded First Brigade, as well as Second Division, during the illness of Davis July 28–August 23.
Note 2. The divisional artillery was assigned to the Artillery Brigade of the corps July 24, 1864.

Third Division, Absalom Baird
 First Brigade, John B. Turchin, to July 15, 1864, sick
  Moses B. Walker
 Second Brigade, Ferdinand Van Derveer, to July 27, 1864, sick
  Newell Gleason
 Third Brigade, George P. Este
 Artillery, George Estep
  7th Battery, Indiana Light Artillery, Otho H. Morgan
  19th Battery, Indiana Light Artillery, William P. Stackhouse

Note. The divisional artillery was assigned to the Artillery Brigade of the corps July 24, 1864.

Artillery Brigade, Charles Houghtaling
 Battery C, 1st Illinois Light Artillery, Mark H. Prescott
 Battery I, 2nd Illinois Light Artillery, Charles M. Barnett
 7th Battery, Indiana Light Artillery, Otho H. Morgan
 19th Battery, Indiana Light Artillery, William P. Stackhouse
 20th Battery, Indiana Light Artillery, Milton A. Osborne

Battery I, 1st Ohio Light Artillery, Hubert Dilger

5th Battery, Wisconsin Light Artillery, George Q. Gardner, to July 28, 1864, sick

Joseph McKnight

Note. The Artillery Brigade was organized July 24, 1864, and was reorganized into three battalions on August 27 as follows: First Battalion, commanded by Mark H. Prescott, consisted of Battery C, 1st Illinois Light Artillery and 19th Battery, Indiana Light Artillery; Second Battalion, commanded by Charles M. Barnett, consisted of Battery I, 2nd Illinois Light Artillery and 5th Battery, Wisconsin Light Artillery; and Third Battalion, commanded by Milton A. Osborne, consisted of the 7th Battery, Indiana Light Artillery and 20th Battery, Indiana Light Artillery.

In late September 1864, John B. Hood, who had retired with his army to Lovejoy's Station after the Battle of Jonesboro, again became active. He marched northward for the purpose of destroying the Western and Atlantic Railroad and interrupting Sherman's communications with the North, and also of threatening the invasion of Tennessee. Sherman followed with his army, including Fourteenth Corps, as far north as Dalton, Georgia, then westward to Gaylesville, Alabama, where he halted to await the further movements of Hood's army. When Hood moved on to Florence and Decatur, Alabama, Sherman sent Fourth Corps and Twenty-Third Corps to reinforce George H. Thomas, who was assembling an army in Tennessee to oppose Hood, and then marched back toward Atlanta with the rest of his army. On November 1–2, the divisions of Fourteenth Corps were at Rome and Kingston. For details of the operation of Fourteenth Corps in October 1864, see Franklin and Nashville Campaign (Hood's Invasion of Tennessee).

The organization of Fourteenth Corps at the first of November 1864 was as follows:

FOURTEENTH CORPS, Jefferson C. Davis

First Division, William P. Carlin

First Brigade, Douglas Hapeman

Third Brigade, Henry A. Hambright

Note. Second Brigade was discontinued September 24, 1864 when John R. Edie and the Regular Infantry regiments were assigned to the post and garrison of Chattanooga. The two volunteer regiments of the brigade were reassigned.

Second Division, James D. Morgan

First Brigade, Robert F. Smith

Second Brigade, John S. Pearce

Third Brigade, James W. Langley

Third Division, Absalom Baird

First Brigade, Morton C. Hunter

Second Brigade, Newell Gleason

Third Brigade, Hubbard K. Milward

Artillery Brigade, Charles Houghtaling

Battery C, 1st Illinois Light Artillery, Mark H. Prescott

Battery I, 2nd Illinois Light Artillery, Charles M. Barnett

19th Battery, Indiana Light Artillery, William P. Stackhouse

5th Battery, Wisconsin Light Artillery, George Q. Gardner

Sherman established his headquarters at Kingston and began preparations for a march through Georgia to Savannah. On November 8, 1864, James D. Morgan's Second Division was sent to Cartersville, and by November 12 the entire corps had assembled there for the purpose of destroying the railroad from the Etowah River to Big Shanty, thus cutting Sherman's communications with the North. Two days later, with that work completed, Fourteenth Corps advanced to the Chattahoochee River, where it went into camp.

On November 9, 1864, while at Kingston, Sherman announced the reorganization of his army into two wings as follows: the Left Wing, commanded by Henry W. Slocum, which consisted of Fourteenth Corps and Twentieth Corps of the Army of the Cumberland (the Left Wing was unofficially called the Army of Georgia); and the Right Wing, commanded by Oliver O. Howard, which consisted of Fifteenth Corps and Seventeenth Corps of the Army of the Tennessee. Sherman left Atlanta November 15 on his march across Georgia, and from that time Fourteenth Corps was not carried on the rosters of the Army of the Cumberland, but was included in the rosters of the Military Division of the Mississippi. For further information, see Fourteenth Corps, Army of Georgia; and see also Savannah Campaign (Sherman's March through Georgia), in Volume I.

COMMANDERS OF FOURTEENTH CORPS, ARMY OF THE CUMBERLAND

George H. Thomas   January 9, 1863 to October 28, 1863

John M. Palmer   October 28, 1863 to August 7, 1864

Richard W. Johnson   August 7, 1864 to August 24, 1864

Jefferson C. Davis   August 24, 1864 to November 14, 1864

FOURTEENTH CORPS, ARMY OF GEORGIA NOVEMBER 14, 1864– AUGUST 1, 1865

Following the evacuation of Atlanta, Georgia by the Confederates September 1, 1864, John B. Hood withdrew with his Army of Tennessee to Lovejoy's Station, where he remained until near the end of the month. He then moved northward toward Tennessee in an attempt to force Sherman to draw back from Atlanta and out of Georgia. Sherman left Twentieth Corps of the Army of the Cumberland to garrison Atlanta, then followed in pursuit of Hood as far as Gaylesville, Alabama. When Hood moved on to Florence, Alabama, Sherman sent two corps to reinforce the forces that George H. Thomas was gathering for the defense of Tennessee, and with the rest of his army marched back toward Atlanta. For details of the operations during this period, see Franklin and Nashville Campaign (Hood's Invasion of Tennessee).

Sherman then established headquarters at Kingston, Georgia and began preparations for a march through Georgia from Atlanta to Savannah. As a part of his preparations, Sherman announced on November 9, 1864 the reorganization of his Army of the Military Division of the Mississippi into two wings as follows: a Left Wing, commanded by Henry W. Slocum, which consisted of Fourteenth Corps and Twentieth Corps of the Army of the Cumberland; and a Right Wing, commanded by

Oliver O. Howard, which consisted of Fifteenth Corps and Seventeenth Corps of the Army of the Tennessee. The Left Wing was unofficially called the Army of Georgia, and when Fourteenth Corps was assigned to the Left Wing, it became, also unofficially, Fourteenth Corps, Army of Georgia. Thereafter, Fourteenth Corps was dropped from the rosters of the Army and Department of the Cumberland.

When Sherman's army began its march through Georgia, Fourteenth Corps left Atlanta November 16, 1864 and, passing through Decatur, Milledgeville, Sandersville, and Louisville, arrived in front of Savannah in mid-December. The enemy evacuated Savannah December 20, and Sherman moved up with his forces and encamped in and around the city. For details of the operations of Fourteenth Corps during this period, see Savannah Campaign (Sherman's March through Georgia), in Volume I.

The organization of Fourteenth Corps during the Savannah Campaign was as follows:

FOURTEENTH CORPS, Jefferson C. Davis

First Division, William P. Carlin
    First Brigade, Harrison C. Hobart
    Second Brigade, Joseph H. Brigham, to January 17, 1865
        George P. Buell
    Third Brigade, Henry A. Hambright, to November 18, 1864, sick
        David Miles

Note. Second Brigade was reorganized under Joseph H. Brigham November 13, 1864 from the 13th Michigan and 21st Michigan infantry regiments of the Engineer Troops of the army and the 59th Ohio of the earlier Second Brigade.

Second Division, James D. Morgan
    First Brigade, Robert F. Smith
    Second Brigade, John S. Pearce
    Third Brigade, James W. Langley

Third Division, Absalom Baird
    First Brigade, Morton C. Hunter
    Second Brigade, Newell Gleason
    Third Brigade, George P. Este

Artillery Brigade, Charles Houghtaling
    Battery C, 1st Illinois Light Artillery, Joseph R. Channel

Battery I, 2nd Illinois Light Artillery, Alonzo W. Coe

19th Battery, Indiana Light Artillery, William P. Stackhouse

5th Battery, Wisconsin Light Artillery, Joseph McKnight

After arriving at Savannah, Sherman began preparing his army for a march northward through the Carolinas to join Grant's armies in Virginia. The movement was delayed by high waters and muddy roads, and Slocum's Left Wing (Army of Georgia) was unable to advance until late January 1865.

Jefferson C. Davis' Fourteenth Corps left Savannah January 20, 1865 and marched to Sister's Ferry on the Savannah River. It crossed the river there February 3, then marched by way of Robertsville, Lexington, Winnsboro, and Cheraw, South Carolina to Fayetteville, North Carolina, where it arrived March 11. Alpheus S. Williams' Twentieth Corps of the Left Wing marched generally by roads parallel to those used by Fourteenth Corps.

March 15, 1865, Davis left Fayetteville with William P. Carlin's First Division and James D. Morgan's Second Division of Fourteenth Corps and followed Williams' Twentieth Corps along the Cape Fear River toward Averasboro, North Carolina. Absalom Baird's Third Division accompanied the trains by roads to the right of the other divisions toward Goldsboro.

On March 16, Judson Kilpatrick's cavalry and Twentieth Corps were engaged with William J. Hardee's Confederate corps near Averasboro, and Davis' two divisions were moved up in support. Fighting continued near Averasboro during the afternoon, but Fourteenth Corps was not heavily engaged. During the night the enemy withdrew, and the next day the Left Wing, with Fourteenth Corps in the lead, marched toward Bentonville on the road toward Goldsboro.

Two days later, on March 19, 1865, Carlin's and Morgan's divisions were strongly attacked on the road just south of Bentonville by Joseph E. Johnston's entire army. Twentieth Corps was quickly brought up, and together the two corps repulsed the final enemy attacks that evening. Baird's division rejoined the corps early on the morning of March 20, and Howard's Right Wing (Army of the Tennessee) also came up in support. The Union and Confederate armies remained in position, with heavy skirmishing and some severe fighting, through March 21, and then the enemy withdrew to the north. The next day Fourteenth Corps, with the rest of the army, moved on toward Goldsboro, where it arrived March 23.

After resting and refitting near Goldsboro, Sherman moved forward with his army toward Johnston's forces, which were then near Smithfield, North Carolina. When Johnston withdrew, Sherman moved on toward Raleigh, and Fourteenth Corps arrived near the town April 13. Fourteenth Corps and Twentieth were then sent on in the direction of Charlotte, North Carolina to head off Johnston's army, which was believed to be retreating in that direction.

On April 14, Fourteenth Corps arrived near Martha's Vineyard, not far from the Cape Fear River. It was preparing to cross, when all movements of the army were suspended while Sherman and Johnston met near Durham's Station to discuss terms for ending hostilities. Johnston surrendered his army April 26, 1865, thus ending the war in the East. The next day orders were issued for Sherman's army to march to Washington, D.C.

For details of the operations of Fourteenth Corps during the march through the Carolinas, see Carolinas Campaign, in Volume I.

The organization of Fourteenth Corps during the march through the Carolinas was as follows:

FOURTEENTH CORPS, Jefferson C. Davis

First Division, William P. Carlin, to March 28, 1865
    George P. Buell, to April 4, 1865
    Charles C. Walcutt
    First Brigade, Harrison C. Hobart
    Second Brigade, George P. Buell, to March 28, 1865
        Michael H. Fitch
        George P. Buell
    Third Brigade, David Miles, to March 19, 1865, wounded
        Arnold McMahan, to March 28, 1865
        Henry A. Hambright

Second Division, James D. Morgan
    First Brigade, William Vandever
    Second Brigade, John S. Pearce, to February 7, 1865
        John G. Mitchell
    Third Brigade, Benjamin D. Fearing, to March 19, 1865, wounded

James W. Langley

Third Division, Absalom Baird
  First Brigade, Morton C. Hunter
  Second Brigade, Thomas Doan, to April 3, 1865
    Newell Gleason
  Third Brigade, George P. Este, to March 29, 1865
    Hubbard K. Milward, to April 9, 1865
    George S. Greene

Note. George S. Greene had previously been in command of a Provisional Division consisting of men of the Army of the Cumberland that had been unable to join their proper commands while Sherman was marching through Georgia. These men had been brought to North Carolina from Chattanooga by Thomas F. Meagher to rejoin their proper commands. See Department of North Carolina, January 31, 1865–May 19, 1866, Troops in the Department of North Carolina, in Volume I.

Artillery Brigade, Charles Houghtaling
  Battery C, 1st Illinois Light Artillery, Joseph R. Channel
    Palmer F. Scovel
  Battery I, 2nd Illinois Light Artillery, Judson Rich
  19th Battery, Indiana Light Artillery, Samuel D. Webb
    Clinton Keeler
  5th Battery, Wisconsin Light Artillery, Joseph McKnight
    Elijah Booth, Jr.

Fourteenth Corps remained near Martha's Vineyard until April 28, 1865, and two days later moved back to Raleigh. It left Raleigh April 30–May 1 and marched through Oxford, North Carolina to the Roanoke River at Taylor's Ferry. It crossed the river there May 3 and marched by way of Boydton, Greensboro, and Lewiston to Nottaway Court House, Virginia, where it arrived two days later. It then continued on by way of Swift Creek and arrived at Manchester, Virginia, opposite Richmond, on May 7.

The corps remained in camp at Manchester until May 11, and then resumed the march northward. It passed through Richmond, Hanover Court House, and Chilesburg, and crossed the Rapidan river at Raccoon Ford on May 16. From there it marched through Stevensburg, Rappahannock Station, Centreville, and Annandale and arrived at Cloud's Mill, near Alexandria, on May 18.

Fourteenth Corps marched with Sherman's army in the Grand Review in Washington, D.C. May 24,

1865, then camped in the vicinity until ordered to Louisville, Kentucky. While it was in camp near Washington, there were some organizational changes in Fourteenth Corps. On June 7, 1865, First Division was reduced to two brigades by the muster out of five regiments in First Brigade and Second Brigade, and Third Brigade was discontinued by the assignment of its regiments to First Brigade and Second Brigade. First Division was then organized as follows:

First Division, Fourteenth Corps, Charles C. Walcutt
  First Brigade, Henry A. Hambright
  Second Brigade, George P. Buell

Second Division was also reduced to two brigades when Third Brigade was discontinued by the muster out of its regiments. Second Division was then organized as follows:

Second Division, Fourteenth Corps, James D. Morgan
  First Brigade, William Vandever
  Second Brigade, John G. Mitchell

Third Brigade, Third Division was also discontinued in June 1865 by the transfer and muster out of regiments.

In addition to the above changes, a Temporary Division, Fourteenth Corps was organized June 7, 1865 that was composed of western regiments transferred from Twentieth Corps, which had been discontinued on June 4. This division was organized as follows:

Temporary Division, Fourteenth Corps, Alpheus S. Williams
  First Brigade, James S. Robinson or Stephen J. McGroarty
  Second Brigade, William Hawley

Note. Williams formerly commanded Twentieth Corps; Robinson commanded Third Brigade, First Division, Twentieth Corps; and Hawley commanded Second Brigade, First Division, Twentieth Corps.

The troops of Fourteenth Corps left Washington June 9–12, 1865 and traveled by rail to Parkersburg, West Virginia, and from there by steamer on the Ohio River to Louisville, where they arrived June 14–20. Upon arrival there, Fourteenth Corps was attached to John A. Logan's Army of the Tennessee.

On July 18, 1865, the brigade organization of Fourteenth Corps was discontinued, and the regimental commanders reported directly to the commanders of the divisions to which they were attached.

Fourteenth Corps was discontinued July 28, 1865, to date from August 1.

The organization of Fourteenth Corps from April 27 to August 1, 1865 was as follows:

FOURTEENTH CORPS, Jefferson C. Davis, to July 31, 1865

First Division, William P. Carlin, to May 2, 1865, on leave
   Charles C. Walcutt, to June 17, 1865
   George P. Buell, to June 27, 1865
   Charles C. Walcutt, to July 30, 1865
   First Brigade, Harrison C. Hobart, to June 8, 1865, muster out
      Henry A. Hambright, to June 18, 1865
   Second Brigade, George P. Buell
   Third Brigade, Henry A. Hambright, to June 7, 1865

Note. Third Brigade was discontinued June 7, 1865.

Second Division, James D. Morgan, to June 23, 1865
   William Vandever, temporarily to about July 1, 1865
   James D. Morgan, to July 30, 1865
   First Brigade, William Vandever
      George W. Grummond, to July 18, 1865
   Second Brigade, John G. Mitchell, to June 20, 1865
      James E. Burton
      Peter Ege, to July 18, 1865
   Third Brigade, James W. Langley, to June 9, 1865

Note. Third Brigade was discontinued June 9, 1865.

Third Division, Absalom Baird, to June 9, 1865
   Newell Gleason, commanded a few days
   Absalom Baird, to July 20, 1865
   First Brigade, Morton C. Hunter, to June 9, 1865
      Judson W. Bishop
      Hubbard K. Milward, to July 18, 1865
   Second Brigade, Newell Gleason, to June 9, 1865
      George P. Este, to July 7, 1865
      Benjamin H. Showers, to July 18, 1865
   Third Brigade, George S. Greene, to June 6, 1865

Note. Third Brigade was discontinued June 6, 1865.

Temporary Division, Alpheus S. Williams, to July 27, 1865

First Brigade, James S. Robinson, to July 24, 1865
Second Brigade, William Hawley, to July 27, 1865

FIFTEENTH CORPS, ARMY OF THE TENNESSEE

Fifteenth Corps was created by a presidential order of December 18, 1862 and was constituted December 22, 1862 to consist of the troops of William T. Sherman's former Fifth Division, Army of the Tennessee, the forces in the District of Memphis, and Frederick Steele's division at Helena, Arkansas. William T. Sherman was assigned command of the corps. At that time, however, Sherman was at Memphis organizing his Yazoo Expedition for a movement against Vicksburg, and two of the divisions that were to become a part of Fifteenth Corps accompanied Sherman's expedition to Chickasaw Bayou near Vicksburg. These were Morgan L. Smith's Second Division, Right Wing, Thirteenth Corps, and Frederick Steele's Fourth Division, Right Wing, Thirteenth Corps.

Sherman's attempt to reach Vicksburg by way of the Yazoo River was unsuccessful, and he withdrew his command to the Mississippi River. There on January 4, 1863, John A. McClernand relieved Sherman in command of the expedition, changing its designation to Army of the Mississippi. For additional information, see Operations against Vicksburg, Mississippi, 1861–1863, Early Attempts to Capture Vicksburg, Yazoo River, Mississippi Expedition (William T. Sherman)—Battle of Chickasaw Bayou (or Walnut Hills).

McClernand then organized his command into two corps commanded by Sherman and George W. Morgan. Sherman was assigned command of Second Corps, Army of the Mississippi, which consisted of Steele's division, designated as First Division, Second Corps, and Morgan L. Smith's division, then commanded by David Stuart, and designated as Fourth Division, Second Corps.

McClernand took the Army of the Mississippi up the Arkansas River to Arkansas Post, which he captured January 11, 1863. For details, see Operations against Vicksburg, Mississippi, 1861–1863, Early Attempts to Capture Vicksburg, Engagement at Arkansas Post (or Fort Hindman), Arkansas. The next day the designation of Sherman's command was officially changed from Second Corps, Army of the Mississippi to Fifteenth Corps, Army of the Tennessee. It should be noted here that Sherman's command in the Army of the Mississippi had for some time been called Fifteenth Corps, and in fact Sherman had assumed command of Fifteenth Corps January 5. On January 14, George W. Morgan's First Corps, Army of the Mississippi was designated as Thirteenth Corps.

On January 17, McClernand began moving his two corps down the Mississippi River to Young's Point and Milliken's Bend near Vicksburg, and they remained there until the beginning of Ulysses S. Grant's movement of the Army of the Tennessee to the rear of Vicksburg.

At the end of January 1863, Fifteenth Corps was in camp across the river from Vicksburg, and it was organized as follows:

FIFTEENTH CORPS, William T. Sherman

First Division, Frederick Steele
    First Brigade, Frank P. Blair, Jr.
    Second Brigade, Charles E. Hovey
    Third Brigade, John M. Thayer
    Artillery
        1st Battery, Iowa Light Artillery, Henry H. Griffiths
        Battery F, 2nd Missouri Light Artillery, Clemens Landgraeber
        4th Battery, Ohio Light Artillery, Louis Hoffmann

Note. First Division, Fifteenth Corps was formerly Eleventh Division, Army of the Tennessee.

Second Division, David Stuart
    First Brigade, Giles A. Smith
    Second Brigade, T. Kilby Smith
    Third Brigade, Hugh Ewing
    Artillery
        Battery A, 1st Illinois Light Artillery, Peter P. Wood
        Battery B, 1st Illinois Light Artillery, Samuel E. Barrett
        Battery H, 1st Illinois Light Artillery, Levi W. Hart
        8th Battery, Ohio Light Artillery, Albert Cudney

Note 1. Second Division, Fifteenth Corps was formerly Fifth Division, Army of the Tennessee, and more recently Second Division of the original Thirteenth Corps.
Note 2. Ewing's Third Brigade was ordered from the

District of Western Virginia to Kentucky December 28, 1862. Then on January 8, 1863, it was ordered to join Grant's army on the Mississippi, where it was assigned to Fifth Division, Army of the Tennessee. It joined Fifteenth Corps January 16, 1863 and was assigned to Second Division.

Note 3. Morgan L. Smith was wounded at Chickasaw Bayou, and he was succeeded by David Stuart, who commanded Second Division at Arkansas Post. Frank P. Blair, Jr. relieved Stuart in command of the division April 4, 1863.

A third division joined Fifteenth Corps in April 1863. This was the former Eighth Division, Army of the Tennessee. James M. Tuttle was assigned command on April 1, and the designation was changed April 3 to Third Division, Fifteenth Corps. The division was organized as follows:

Third Division, Fifteenth Corps, James M. Tuttle
    First Brigade, Ralph P. Buckland
    Second Brigade, Joseph A. Mower
    Third Brigade, Joseph J. Woods
    Artillery, Nelson T. Spoor
        Battery E, 1st Illinois Light Artillery, Allen C. Waterhouse
        2nd Battery, Iowa Light Artillery, Joseph R. Reed

At the beginning of Grant's campaign to the rear of Vicksburg, Thirteenth Corps and then Seventeenth Corps left their camps and marched downriver before crossing to the east bank at Bruinsburg April 30, 1863. On April 20, for this campaign, Sherman's Fifteenth Corps was designated as the Left of the army, McClernand's Thirteenth Corps as the Right, and James B. McPherson's Seventeenth Corps as the Center.

Fifteenth Corps remained near Vicksburg until April 29, 1863, at which time Steele's First Division and Tuttle's Third Division were ordered to join Grant's army east of the Mississippi River. The two divisions crossed near Grand Gulf May 6–7, and on May 8 arrived near Hankinson's Ferry on the Big Black River. Blair's Second Division remained as the garrison at Milliken's Bend until May 7, and then Giles A. Smith's First Brigade and T. Kilby Smith's Second Brigade were ordered to join Grant. These two brigades rejoined the corps near Vicksburg May 18, and Ewing's Third Brigade, which started later, joined the same day.

The only battle during the campaign in rear of

Vicksburg in which Fifteenth Corps participated was at Jackson, Mississippi, and only Tuttle's division was engaged. Steele's division was in reserve, and Blair's division did not join until after the battle. Fifteenth Corps took part in the assaults at Vicksburg May 19 and May 22, then served on the siege lines until the surrender of Vicksburg on July 4. In late June, Tuttle's division was moved east of the town to become a part of Sherman's Exterior Line (or Army of Observation), which was formed to prevent Joseph E. Johnston's Confederate army from relieving Vicksburg.

For details of the operations of Fifteenth Corps during Grant's campaign at Vicksburg, see Operations against Vicksburg, Mississippi, 1861–1863, Grant's Operations against Vicksburg.

The organization of Fifteenth Corps at Vicksburg during the period March 18, 1863–July 4, 1863 was as follows:

FIFTEENTH CORPS, William T. Sherman

First Division, Frederick Steele
    First Brigade, Francis H. Manter, to June 13, 1863
      Bernard G. Farrar
    Second Brigade, Charles R. Woods
    Third Brigade, John M. Thayer
    Artillery, Ezra Taylor
      1st Battery, Iowa Light Artillery, Henry H. Griffiths
      Battery F, 2nd Missouri Light Artillery, Clemens Landgraeber
      4th Battery, Ohio Light Artillery, Louis Hoffmann

Note 1. Steele was assigned command of the Little Rock, Arkansas Expedition July 27, 1863, and John M. Thayer commanded First Division temporarily until July 28, when Elias S. Dennis assumed command. Peter J. Osterhaus was assigned to Fifteenth Corps August 24, and about a week later relieved Dennis in command of First Division.

Note 2. Third Brigade was discontinued September 15, 1863.

Second Division, Frank P. Blair, Jr.
    First Brigade, Giles A. Smith
    Second Brigade, T. Kilby Smith, to May 24, 1863
      Joseph A. J. Lightburn
    Third Brigade, Hugh Ewing
    Artillery
      Battery A, 1st Illinois Light Artillery, Peter P. Wood

      Battery B, 1st Illinois Light Artillery, Samuel E. Barrett
      Israel P. Rumsey
      Battery H, 1st Illinois Light Artillery, Levi W. Hart
      8th Battery, Ohio Light Artillery, James F. Putnam

Note 1. Blair departed on leave July 26, 1863, and Lightburn assumed command of Second Division.

Note 2. Third Brigade was discontinued October 19, 1863, and the regiments were transferred to Second Brigade.

Third Division, James M. Tuttle
    First Brigade, Ralph P. Buckland, to June 22, 1863
      William L. McMillen
    Second Brigade, Joseph A. Mower
    Third Brigade, Charles L. Matthies, to June 1, 1863
      Joseph J. Woods
    Artillery, Nelson T. Spoor
      Battery E, 1st Illinois Light Artillery, Allen C. Waterhouse
      2nd Battery, Iowa Light Artillery, Joseph R. Reed

After the surrender of Vicksburg July 4, 1863, Fifteenth Corps, temporarily commanded by Frederick Steele, took part in William T. Sherman's Jackson, Mississippi Campaign July 5–25 against Joseph E. Johnston's Confederate army. After the evacuation of Jackson on July 16, Fifteenth Corps returned to the Big Black River, where it went into camp. For details, see Jackson, Mississippi Campaign (William T. Sherman).

William Sooy Smith's First Division, Sixteenth Corps, which had been attached to Ninth Corps during the siege of Vicksburg, and which had been under the command of Hugh Ewing since July 20, 1863, was transferred to Fifteenth Corps on July 28 and redesignated as Fourth Division, Fifteenth Corps. It was organized as follows:

Fourth Division, Fifteenth Corps, Hugh Ewing
    First Brigade, John M. Loomis
    Second Brigade, Stephen G. Hicks
    Third Brigade, Joseph R. Cockerill
    Fourth Brigade, William W. Sanford, to August 27, 1863
      John M. Corse
    Artillery, William Cogswell
      Battery F, 1st Illinois Light Artillery, John T. Cheney
      Battery I, 1st Illinois Light Artillery, William N. Lansing

Cogswell's Battery, Illinois Light Artillery, Henry G. Eddy

8th Battery, Indiana Light Artillery, Michael Mueller

Note. Fourth Brigade was discontinued September 1, 1863.

On August 6, 1863, at Vicksburg, Edward F. Winslow was assigned command of a cavalry brigade that consisted of the 3rd and 4th Iowa Cavalry and the 5th Illinois Cavalry, and this brigade was later attached to Fifteenth Corps at Vicksburg. After the departure of Sherman with the First Division, Second Division, and Fourth Division for Chattanooga, Tennessee in late September, Winslow's brigade was attached to Tuttle's Third Division, which remained near Vicksburg until November 8 and then moved upriver to West Tennessee. Winslow's brigade was then transferred to Seventeenth Corps and remained near Hebron and Natchez, Mississippi.

On September 22, 1863, John E. Smith, commanding Second Division, Seventeenth Corps (formerly Seventh Division, Army of the Tennessee), was ordered with his division to Chattanooga, Tennessee to reinforce the Army of the Cumberland. At that time, Smith's division was at Helena, Arkansas, where it had halted on its way from Vicksburg to reinforce Frederick Steele's army in Arkansas. Smith promptly moved to Memphis, Tennessee, where he joined Sherman's Fifteenth Corps, and marched with that corps to Chattanooga. Thereafter, Sherman referred to Smith's division as Third Division, Fifteenth Corps, because he considered it a replacement for Tuttle's Third Division, Fifteenth Corps, which was left at Vicksburg. Officially, however, Smith's division was Second Division, Seventeenth Corps until December 20, 1863, when it was changed to Third Division, Fifteenth Corps. John E. Smith's Second Division, Seventeenth Corps was organized as follows:

Second Division, Seventeenth Corps, John E. Smith
First Brigade, Jesse I. Alexander
Second Brigade, Green B. Raum
Third Brigade, Charles L. Matthies

September 23, 1863, Grant ordered Sherman to move with his Fifteenth Corps to the relief of the Army of the Cumberland, which was then besieged in Chattanooga. He was to move by transports to Memphis, then eastward by rail and by road to Chattanooga. His orders were to repair the Memphis and Charleston Railroad as he advanced, as far as Athens, Alabama, and to draw supplies by that route.

Osterhaus' First Division left Vicksburg first, and upon reaching Memphis it moved by rail to Corinth, Mississippi. John E. Smith's division of Seventeenth Corps had already arrived at Memphis, and it began moving eastward along the railroad October 2, 1863. That day Sherman arrived with his Second Division, Fifteenth Corps, then commanded by Giles A. Smith. Fourth Division, temporarily commanded by John M. Corse, arrived a day or two later.

Tuttle's Third Division, Fifteenth Corps remained at Vicksburg until November 8, and then returned to West Tennessee. Tuttle's division was carried on the roster of Fifteenth Corps as Third Division until January 4, 1864, when it was transferred to Sixteenth Corps as First Division. This transfer had been ordered September 20, 1863.

Second Division, Fifteenth Corps left Memphis by rail October 9, 1863, and, because of a shortage of transportation, Fourth Division was ordered to march on the main road. Sherman, accompanied by Hugh Ewing, proper commander of Fourth Division, and some other officers and a few troops, started for Corinth by rail October 11. A short time later, Sherman's train was halted at Collierville, Tennessee, where the post was under enemy attack. Upon the approach of Corse's division, however, the Confederate force withdrew, and Sherman proceeded on to Corinth. He then moved on to Iuka, Mississippi on October 19.

On October 18, 1863, Ulysses S. Grant, commanding the Army of the Tennessee, assumed command of the newly created Military Division of the Mississippi (ordered October 16), and at Iuka, Mississippi Sherman assumed command of the Army of the Tennessee on October 24. On October 27, John A. Logan was assigned command of Sherman's former Fifteenth Corps, but he did not arrive and assume command until December 11. Meantime, on October 29, Frank P. Blair, Jr., who was on beyond Iuka with the divisions of Osterhaus and John E. Smith, assumed temporary command of Fifteenth Corps, and he remained in command until relieved by Logan.

On October 24, 1863, Sherman ordered Fourth Division to cross the Tennessee River at Eastport, Mississippi and, with the aid of two gunboats, move to Florence, Alabama. On October 27, Sherman was ordered to halt his repairs on the Memphis and Charleston Railroad and hurry forward toward Chattanooga. Upon receiving this order, Sherman moved on to Eastport with his remaining three divisions, crossed the Tennessee River there, and pushed on to the east. Sherman, in person, crossed the river November 1 and rode on to Florence, where he overtook Fourth Division, then commanded by Hugh Ewing. The other divisions of his command followed on the road.

Sherman decided that crossing the Elk River east of Florence would be too time-consuming, and he then moved by a route along the north bank of the river by way of Elkton, Fayetteville, and Winchester to Decherd. He reached Bridgeport on the night of November 13, 1863, and his troops followed, marching on several roads.

Grant delayed his effort to drive back Braxton Bragg's Confederate army from in front of Chattanooga until Sherman arrived with his four divisions from Memphis, and then on November 24, 1863, Peter J. Osterhaus' First Division, Fifteenth Corps was engaged at the Battle of Lookout Mountain under the direction of Joseph Hooker. The next day Sherman attacked unsuccessfully at the northern end of Missionary Ridge with Morgan L. Smith's Second Division and Hugh Ewing's Fourth Division of Fifteenth Corps. For details of the battles of Lookout Mountain and Missionary Ridge, see Chattanooga-Ringgold Campaign (Battles of Lookout Mountain and Missionary Ridge, Tennessee).

The organization of Fifteenth Corps during the Chattanooga-Ringgold Campaign November 23–27, 1863 was as follows:

FIFTEENTH CORPS, Frank P. Blair, Jr.

First Division, Peter J. Osterhaus
  First Brigade, Charles R. Woods
  Second Brigade, James A. Williamson
  Artillery, Henry H. Griffiths
    1st Battery, Iowa Light Artillery, James M. Williams
    Battery F, 2nd Missouri Light Artillery, Clemens Landgraeber
    4th Battery, Ohio Light Artillery, George Froehlich

Note. Osterhaus assumed command of First Division July 27, 1863 when Frederick Steele assumed command of the Little Rock, Arkansas Expedition at Helena.

Second Division, Morgan L. Smith
  First Brigade, Giles A. Smith, to November 24, 1863, wounded
  Nathan W. Tupper
  Second Brigade, Joseph A. J. Lightburn
  Artillery
    Battery A, 1st Illinois Light Artillery, Peter P. Wood
    Battery B, 1st Illinois Light Artillery, Israel P. Rumsey
    Battery H, 1st Illinois Light Artillery, Francis De Gress

Third Division, James M. Tuttle
  First Brigade, William L. McMillen
  Second Brigade, Joseph A. Mower
  Third Brigade, James L. Geddes
  Cavalry Brigade, Edward F. Winslow
  Artillery, Nelson T. Spoor
    Battery E, 1st Illinois Light Artillery, John A. Fitch
    6th Battery, Indiana Light Artillery, Michael Mueller
    2nd Battery, Iowa Light Artillery, Joseph R. Reed

Note 1. The organization given above for Third Division is for October 31, 1863.
Note 2. Third Division was detached from Fifteenth Corps, and the troops were at Memphis, La Grange, and Pocahontas, Tennessee during the Chattanooga-Ringgold Campaign. The division did not rejoin the corps, but was transferred to Sixteenth Corps January 4, 1864.

Fourth Division, Hugh Ewing
  First Brigade, John M. Loomis
  Second Brigade, John M. Corse, to November 25, wounded
    Charles C. Walcutt
  Third Brigade, Joseph R. Cockerill
  Artillery, Henry Richardson
    Battery F, 1st Illinois Light Artillery, John T. Cheney
    Battery I, 1st Illinois Light Artillery, Josiah H. Burton
    Battery D, 1st Missouri Light Artillery, Byron M. Callender

SEVENTEENTH CORPS

Second Division, John E. Smith
  First Brigade, Jesse I. Alexander

Second Brigade, Green B. Raum, to November 25, 1863, wounded

Francis C. Deimling, temporarily November 25, 1863

Clark R. Wever

Third Brigade, Charles L. Matthies, to November 25, 1863, wounded

Benjamin D. Dean, November 25, 1863

Jabez Banbury

Artillery, Henry Dillon

Cogswell's Battery, Illinois Light Artillery, William Cogswell

6th Battery, Wisconsin Light Artillery, Samuel F. Clark

12th Battery, Wisconsin Light Artillery, William Zickerick

Note. Second Division, Seventeenth Corps served with Fifteenth Corps from early October until December 20, 1863, when it was officially assigned to Fifteenth Corps as Third Division.

After the Battle of Missionary Ridge, Fifteenth Corps joined in the pursuit of Bragg's defeated army into Georgia, and then it marched with a force commanded by Sherman to the relief of an army commanded by Ambrose E. Burnside, which was besieged by James Longstreet's Confederate corps at Knoxville, Tennessee. Sherman had arrived at Maryville, Tennessee December 5, 1863 when he learned that Longstreet had lifted the siege of Knoxville two days earlier and had marched eastward toward Rogersville, Tennessee.For additional information, see Relief of Knoxville, Tennessee (William T. Sherman).

Fifteenth Corps then moved back into northern Alabama, where it went into winter quarters along the Memphis and Charleston Railroad at Huntsville, Woodville, Larkin's Landing, and Scottsburg. It remained in these positions until April 1864.

There were numerous leaves granted to officers during the winter, and this resulted in many temporary changes in command in the army. On January 31, 1864, Fifteenth Corps was organized as follows:

FIFTEENTH CORPS, John A. Logan

First Division, Charles R. Woods

First Brigade, Milo Smith

Second Brigade, Jeremiah W. Jenkins

Third Brigade, George A. Stone

Artillery, George Froehlich

1st Battery, Iowa Light Artillery, William H. Gay

Battery F, 2nd Missouri Light Artillery, Louis Voelkner

4th Battery, Ohio Light Artillery, Louis Zimmerer

Second Division, Morgan L. Smith

First Brigade, David C. Coleman

Second Brigade, Theodore Jones

Artillery, Peter P. Wood

Battery A, 1st Illinois Light Artillery, Peter P. Wood

Battery B, 1st Illinois Light Artillery, Israel P. Rumsey

Battery H, 1st Illinois Light Artillery, Francis De Gress

Third Division, John E. Smith

First Brigade, Jesse I. Alexander

Second Brigade, Clark R. Wever

Third Brigade, Jabez Banbury

Artillery, Henry Dillon

Cogswell's Battery, Illinois Light Artillery, William Cogswell

6th Battery, Wisconsin Light Artillery, James G. Simpson

12th Battery, Wisconsin Light Artillery, Edward G. Harlow

Fourth Division, Hugh Ewing

First Brigade, Reuben Williams

Second Brigade, Charles C. Walcutt

Third Brigade, Alexander Fowler

Artillery, Albert Cudney

Battery F, 1st Illinois Light Artillery, Samuel S. Smyth

Battery I, 1st Illinois Light Artillery, Albert Cudney

Battery D, 1st Missouri Light Artillery, Frank White

Note. William Harrow succeeded Ewing in command of Fourth Division February 8, 1864.

February 10, 1864, Charles L. Matthies of Third Division, Fifteenth Corps was assigned command of an expedition to move to Chattanooga and there join with other forces for a movement into East Tennessee to reinforce John M. Schofield for an advance against Confederate forces under James Longstreet. Schofield had relieved John G. Foster in command of the Department and Army of the Ohio on February 9. Matthies' command, which consisted of six regiments selected from the four divisions of Fifteenth Corps, which were along the Memphis and Charleston Railroad, departed the next day and arrived at Chattanooga February 13. The movement into East Tennessee, however, was delayed, and on February 16 it was canceled. Instead, the expedition was sent to Cleveland, Tennessee as a reserve. This command at Cleveland was called Detachment Fifteenth Corps, also known as Matthies' Brigade. This brigade, under the command of Willard A. Dickerman, was sent to reinforce Charles Cruft's First Division, Fourth Corps, Army of the Cumberland during the demonstration on Dalton, Georgia February 22–27. It was assigned to Cruft's division as First Brigade during the demonstration because the proper First Brigade, commanded by David A. Enyart, had remained at Ooltewah, Tennessee. Matthies' Brigade was ordered to rejoin Fifteenth Corps March 1. For additional information, see Demonstration on Dalton, Georgia.

In the spring of 1864, Congress created the grade of lieutenant general, and on March 9, in Washington, D.C., Grant received his commission of that rank. He was also assigned command of the Armies of the United States. Grant assumed this command March 12, and on that same date William T. Sherman was assigned command of the Military Division of the Mississippi (he assumed command March 18). James B. McPherson was assigned command of the Department and Army of the Tennessee.

Grant's plan for the spring campaign of 1864 called for the concerted action of all armies of the United States against the two principal armies of the Confederacy. In the East, Grant was to move with George G. Meade's Army of the Potomac against Robert E. Lee's Army of Northern Virginia; and in the West, Sherman was to advance with the Army of the Cumberland, the Army of the Tennessee, and the Army of the Ohio against Joseph E. Johnston's Confederate Army of Tennessee, which was then encamped near Dalton, Georgia, and drive it back toward Atlanta.

During March and April 1864, Fifteenth Corps was in northern Alabama, with headquarters at Huntsville; Osterhaus' First Division at Woodville; Morgan L. Smith's Second Division at Larkinsville; John E. Smith's Third Division at Hunstville; William Harrow's Fourth Division at Scottsboro; and

Thomas T. Heath's cavalry at Huntsville. Dodge's Left Wing, Sixteenth Corps was also in northern Alabama at Decatur and Athens.

Sherman fixed the date for the general advance of his armies as May 5, 1864, and at that time McPherson had under his immediate command of the Army of the Tennessee only John A. Logan's Fifteenth Corps and Grenville M. Dodge's Left Wing of Sixteenth Corps. McPherson began his march toward Chattanooga on May 1, in preparation for the advance into Georgia. Logan left John E. Smith's division to guard the Memphis and Charleston Railroad and with his other three divisions marched with McPherson, arriving at Chattanooga May 4. Two days later, McPherson's two corps moved to Lee and Gordon's Mill, and on May 7 they marched by way of Villanow toward Resaca, Georgia, where they arrived west of the town May 9. Fifteenth Corps was engaged at the Battle of Resaca May 13–16. It then crossed the Oostanaula at Lay's Ferry, near the mouth of Snake Creek, and marched with the Army of the Tennessee on the left of Sherman's army to the southwest to Hermitage, about nine miles northeast of Rome. There it turned to the southeast and moved to a point near Kingston, Georgia.

When Johnston withdrew across the Etowah River, and Sherman began his flanking movement to the right, the Army of the Tennessee crossed the Etowah at Wooley's Bridge and marched by way of Swaintown and Van Wert to Dallas, where it arrived May 26, 1864. Fifteenth Corps was engaged at Dallas May 28, then moved with Sherman's army back to the Western and Atlantic Railroad at Acworth, where it arrived on June 7. The next day, Frank P. Blair's Seventeenth Corps joined the army in Georgia. The Army of the Tennessee, then consisting of three corps, was on the left of Sherman's line.

On June 10, 1864, Fifteenth Corps advanced on the Acworth-Marietta road, through Big Shanty, until it encountered the enemy in position at Brush Mountain. The corps took part in the general assault at Kennesaw (also spelled Kenesaw) Mountain June 27, and when Johnston withdrew across the Chattahoochee River on July 9, McPherson's Army of the Tennessee advanced on the right of Sherman's army to the river at Turner's Ferry, where it demonstrated while Federal troops crossed the river to the north. Fifteenth Corps marched north with the Army of the

Tennessee to Roswell, where it crossed the Chattahoochee on July 17, and then marched on the left of Sherman's army to Decatur on the Georgia Railroad, where it arrived the following afternoon. It then turned to the west and advanced along the railroad toward Atlanta. It was heavily engaged at the Battle of Atlanta July 22, and at Ezra Church (or Chapel) July 27, and then took part in the siege of Atlanta. It then moved south to Jonesboro, and was engaged at the Battle of Jonesboro August 31–September 1. John B. Hood, then commanding the Army of Tennessee, evacuated Atlanta September 1 and moved south to Lovejoy's Station, and the campaign for Atlanta was ended. For details of the operations of Fifteenth Corps during the Atlanta Campaign, see Atlanta, Georgia Campaign.

The organization of Fifteenth Corps during the Atlanta Campaign was as follows:

FIFTEENTH CORPS, John A. Logan, to July 22, 1864
    Morgan L. Smith, to July 27, 1864
    John A. Logan

First Division, Peter J. Osterhaus, to July 15, 1864, sick
    Charles R. Woods, to August 15, 1864
    Peter J. Osterhaus
    First Brigade, Charles R. Woods, to July 15, 1864
        Milo Smith, to August 19, 1864
        Charles R. Woods, to August 22, 1864
        Milo Smith
    Second Brigade, James A. Williamson
    Third Brigade, Hugo Wangelin
    Artillery, Clemens Landgraeber
        Battery F, 2nd Missouri Light Artillery, Louis Voelkner
            Lewis A. Winn
        4th Battery, Ohio Light Artillery, George Froehlich
            Louis Zimmerer

Note 1. Charles R. Woods was assigned command of Third Division, Seventeenth Corps August 22, 1864.

Note 2. Third Brigade was organized December 1, 1863 from regiments of First Brigade and Second Brigade, and it was commanded by George A. Stone until March 8, 1864.

Second Division, Morgan L. Smith, to July 22, 1864
    Joseph A. J. Lightburn, to July 27, 1864
    Morgan L. Smith, to August 5, 1864
    Joseph A. J. Lightburn, to August 17, 1864
    William B. Hazen
    First Brigade, Giles A. Smith, to July 20, 1864
        James S. Martin, to August 4, 1864

        Theodore Jones
    Second Brigade, Joseph A. J. Lightburn, to July 22, 1864
        Wells S. Jones, to July 27, 1864
        Joseph A. J. Lightburn, to August 5, 1864
        Wells S. Jones, to August 17, 1864
        Joseph A. J. Lightburn, to August 24, 1864, wounded
        Wells S. Jones
    Artillery, Francis De Gress
        Battery A, 1st Illinois Light Artillery, Peter P. Wood, to May 10, 1864, sick
            George McCagg, Jr., to July 12, 1864
            Samuel S. Smyth, to July 22, 1864, captured
            George Echte
        Battery B, 1st Illinois Light Artillery, Israel P. Rumsey
        Battery H, 1st Illinois Light Artillery, Francis De Gress

Note 1. Giles A. Smith was assigned command of Fourth Division, Seventeenth Corps July 20, 1864.

Note 2. Battery B, 1st Illinois Light Artillery was consolidated with Battery A, 1st Illinois Light Artillery July 12, 1864.

Third Division, John E. Smith
    First Brigade, Jesse I. Alexander, to September 1, 1864, resigned
        Joseph B. McCown
    Second Brigade, Green B. Raum
    Third Brigade, Charles L. Matthies, to May 13, 1864
        Benjamin D. Dean, to May 31, 1864
        Jabez Banbury, to July 25, 1864
        Benjamin D. Dean, to August 1864
    Artillery, Henry Dillon
        6th Battery, Wisconsin Light Artillery, Samuel F. Clark
            James G. Simpson
        12th Battery, Wisconsin Light Artillery, William Zickerick

Note 1. Third Division was at Cartersville and other points in rear of the advancing army guarding the lines of communications and was not engaged in the battles of the campaign.

Note 2. Charles L. Matthies assumed command of the United States forces at Decatur, Alabama May 13, 1864.

Note 3. Third Brigade was discontinued in August 1864, and the regiments were assigned to First Brigade and Second Brigade.

Fourth Division, William Harrow
    First Brigade, Reuben Williams, to August 4, 1864
        John M. Oliver
    Second Brigade, Charles C. Walcutt

Third Brigade, John M. Oliver, to August 4, 1864
Artillery, Henry H. Griffiths, to May 20, 1864
  John T. Cheney
  Henry H. Griffiths, to August 11, 1864, muster out
  Josiah H. Burton
  Battery F, 1st Illinois Light Artillery, Josiah H.
    Burton
    Jefferson F. Whaley, to August 21, 1864, sick
    George P. Cunningham
  1st Battery, Iowa Light Artillery, William H. Gay
  Henry H. Griffiths
  William H. Gay

*Note. Third Brigade was discontinued August 4, 1864,
and the regiments were transferred to First Brigade,
Fourth Division.*

On September 14, 1864, Fourth Division was discontinued by consolidation with First Division and Second Division of Fifteenth Corps as follows: Second Brigade and one regiment of First Brigade were assigned to First Division, and the remainder of First Brigade was assigned to Second Division. On September 23, Second Division, Left Wing, Sixteenth Corps was transferred to Fifteenth Corps as a new Fourth Division, which was organized as follows:

Fourth Division, John M. Corse
  First Brigade, Roger Martin
  Second Brigade, Wheelock S. Merriman
  Third Brigade, Richard Rowett
  Artillery, Frederick Welker
    Battery B, 1st Michigan Light Artillery, Albert F.
      R. Arndt
    Battery H, 1st Missouri Light Artillery, John F.
      Brunner

In late September 1864, Hood marched north along the railroad with his army from Lovejoy's Station to destroy the railroad and interrupt Sherman's communications with the North, and also to threaten the invasion of Tennessee. Sherman followed with his army, including the Army of the Tennessee, as far as Gaylesville, Alabama and then, after sending two corps to reinforce George H. Thomas in Tennessee, he turned back toward Atlanta and began preparations for a march through Georgia to Savannah. Fifteenth Corps and Seventeenth Corps halted at Smyrna Camp Grounds, west of the Chattahoochee River. For details of the above movements, see Franklin and Nashville Campaign (Hood's Invasion of Tennessee).

Sherman established his headquarters at Kingston, and there on November 9, 1864 he announced the reorganization of his army into two wings as follows: the Left Wing, commanded by Henry W. Slocum, consisting of Fourteenth Corps and Twentieth Corps of the Army of the Cumberland; and the Right Wing, commanded by Oliver O. Howard, consisting of Fifteenth Corps and Seventeenth Corps of the Army of the Tennessee. The Right Wing was commonly called the Army of the Tennessee.

Sherman left Atlanta November 15, 1864 on his march across Georgia, with his two wings advancing by different routes so as to threaten both Augusta and Macon. Slocum's Left Wing marched eastward in the direction of Augusta, and Howard's Right Wing took roads to the south and east toward Gordon, which was about twenty miles east of Macon. Osterhaus' Fifteenth Corps marched down the Macon and Western Railroad, through Rough and Ready, to a point north of Jonesboro, and it then turned off to the southeast. It crossed the Ocmulgee River at Planter's (or Nutting's) Factory and marched through Hillsboro to Clinton. Seventeenth Corps marched generally by roads to the left in the same direction. Charles C. Walcutt's Second Brigade of Charles R. Woods' First Division, Fifteenth Corps advanced on a demonstration toward Macon, and was engaged in a sharp fight at Griswoldsville on November 22.

Fifteenth Corps then moved on to Gordon, and from there continued its march by a route south of the Ogeechee River and on the extreme right of Sherman's army. It passed through Irwinton, Irwin's Cross Roads, Swainsboro, Summerville, and Statesboro and approached Savannah during the first week in December 1864. It then moved into position on the right of Sherman's investing line in front of the city. William B. Hazen led his Second Division, Fifteenth Corps against Fort McAllister, which blocked traffic on the Ogeechee River, and captured the fort in an assault December 13. Federal troops occupied Savannah December 21, and Sherman then halted for a time for the troops to rest and refit.

For details of the organization and operations of Fifteenth Corps and of the Army of the Tennessee during November and December 1864, see Savannah Campaign (Sherman's March through Georgia), in Volume I.

While at Savannah, Sherman began preparations for continuing the march northward through the Carolinas to join Grant's forces in Virginia. The opening movement of this campaign was the transfer by sea of Howard's Right Wing (Army of the Tennessee) from Savannah to Beaufort, South Carolina to threaten Charleston, South Carolina. Frank P. Blair's Seventeenth Corps moved first, beginning January 3, 1865, and upon arrival at Beaufort took position at Pocotaligo, South Carolina on January 14. John A. Logan embarked January 14–16 with three divisions of Fifteenth Corps and followed Seventeenth Corps to Beaufort. By January 28, Logan's divisions were in position near Seventeenth Corps at Garden's Corners and Port Royal Ferry. John M. Corse had been ordered to march with his Fourth Division, Fifteenth Corps by land and join the rest of the corps near Beaufort, but because of floods and bad roads he was unable to move until January 27. He then moved along the south side of the Savannah River, following Slocum's Left Wing, and he reported to Slocum at Sister's Ferry January 30.

On February 1, 1865, Fifteenth Corps and Seventeenth Corps left the vicinity of Beaufort and marched by way of Bamberg and Orangeburg to Columbia, South Carolina, where they arrived February 17. While the rest of the Right Wing was marching toward Columbia, Corse's Fourth Division crossed the Savannah River at Sister's Ferry and rejoined Fifteenth Corps at Orangeburg February 11.

Fifteenth Corps occupied Columbia until February 20, 1865, and it then marched to Peay's Ferry on the Catawba River, where it was joined by Seventeenth Corps from Winnsboro February 22. Fifteenth Corps then moved on by way of Cheraw, South Carolina and arrived at Fayetteville, North Carolina on March 12.

On March 15, 1865, Sherman started his army in two columns toward Goldsboro, North Carolina. Slocum's Left Wing took the road through Averasboro and Bentonville, and Howard's Right Wing marched by roads to the right. Logan's Fifteenth Corps moved on the road by Beaman's Cross Roads toward Faison's Depot on the Wilmington and Weldon Railroad. Logan reached South River on March 15, and the next day, while Slocum was engaged at Averasboro, marched to the vicinity of the Goldsboro road. Fifteenth Corps reached Falling Creek Church, about three miles south of Cox's Bridge, on the evening of March 19, and there Sherman learned of Slocum's Battle of Bentonville that day. William B. Hazen's Second Division, Fifteenth Corps was immediately sent back to aid Slocum and, after marching all night, reached the battlefield early on the morning of March 20. Logan, with the rest of Fifteenth Corps, and followed by Seventeenth Corps, also marched back to Bentonville March 20. Both corps then formed on the right of Slocum's command. Fifteenth Corps was engaged in heavy skirmishing March 20–21 but was not otherwise engaged.

Logan's corps remained on the battlefield until March 23, caring for the wounded and burying the dead, and then resumed the march toward Goldsboro, where it arrived March 24.

After resting and refitting at Goldsboro, Fifteenth Corps advanced on April 10, 1865 with the rest of Sherman's army against Joseph E. Johnston's army, which was then encamped near Smithfield, North Carolina. Upon learning of Sherman's approach, Johnston retired toward Raleigh, closely followed by the Federal columns. Fifteenth Corps reached Raleigh April 13, then moved in the direction of Salisbury, North Carolina in an attempt to head off Johnston's army, which was believed to be moving in that direction. Fifteenth Corps was along the road toward Pittsboro April 15, when all troop movements were halted while Sherman and Johnston met near Durham's Station to discuss terms for ending hostilities. Johnston surrendered his army April 26, 1865, and this brought to an end the war in the East. The next day Fifteenth Corps was ordered to march to Washington, D.C.

For details of the organization and operations of Fifteenth Corps during the march through the Carolinas, see Carolinas Campaign, in Volume I.

While at Raleigh, on April 26, 1865, Fifteenth Corps was reorganized to consist of three divisions. First Division, Second Division, and Fourth Division were retained, but John E. Smith's Third Division was discontinued, and its regiments were assigned to the other three divisions. First Brigade, Third Division was consolidated with a part of Second Brigade, Fourth Division, and Fourth Division was then organized as follows:

Fourth Division, Fifteenth Corps, John M. Corse
  First Brigade, Elliott W. Rice
  Second Brigade, William T. Clark
  Third Brigade, Richard Rowett

Fifteenth Corps remained near Raleigh until April 29, 1865, and it then marched toward Washington. It moved out on the Louisburg road by way of Shocco Springs, to the right of Warrenton, and arrived on the Roanoke River at Robinson's Ferry on May 3. The corps crossed the river the next day and marched on by way of Pennington's Bridge on the Meherrin River, Lawrenceville, and Wyatt's Crossing on the Nottoway River, and was on the Boydton Plank Road, near Petersburg, Virginia, on May 6. From Petersburg, Fifteenth Corps marched to Manchester, opposite Richmond, May 9–10, and it remained there until May 13. It then moved through Richmond and Hanover Court House and arrived at Fredericksburg May 15. From there it marched on roads to the left of Seventeenth Corps by way of Stafford Court House, Dumfries, and Occoquan, arriving near Alexandria, Virginia May 19.

On May 12, 1865, Oliver O. Howard was assigned to duty in the War Department as commissioner of the Bureau of Refugees, Freedmen, and Abandoned Lands, and on May 19, John A. Logan was assigned command of the Army of the Tennessee. With his departure, William B. Hazen assumed command of Fifteenth Corps May 23, and John M. Oliver succeeded Hazen in command of Second Division, Fifteenth Corps.

Fifteenth Corps marched in the Grand Review in Washington May 24, 1865, and encamped near the city.

On May 29, 1865, the Army of the Tennessee was ordered to Louisville, Kentucky for muster out. Fifteenth Corps left Washington June 1–2 and traveled by rail to Parkersburg, West Virginia, and then by steamer to Louisville, where it arrived June 7–8 and went into camp near the city until the regiments were mustered out.

On June 16, 1865, John M. Oliver's Second Division was ordered to Little Rock, Arkansas to report to Joseph J. Reynolds, commander of the Department of Arkansas. The division left Louisville June 25, then served in the Department of Arkansas until the regiments were mustered out at the end of July. The corps was officially discontinued August 1, 1865.

COMMANDERS OF FIFTEENTH CORPS, ARMY OF THE TENNESSEE

William T. Sherman	January 5, 1863 to October 29, 1863
Frank P. Blair, Jr.	October 29, 1863 to December 11, 1863
John A. Logan	December 11, 1863 to July 22, 1864
Morgan L. Smith	July 22, 1864 to July 27, 1864
John A. Logan	July 27, 1864 to September 22, 1864
Peter J. Osterhaus	September 22, 1864 to January 8, 1865
John A. Logan	January 8, 1865 to May 23, 1865
William B. Hazen	May 23, 1865 to August 1, 1865

Note 1. Sherman was assigned command of Fifteenth Corps December 18, 1862.

Note 2. Logan was assigned command of Fifteenth Corps October 27, 1863, but he did not join the army and assume command until December 11, 1863.

SIXTEENTH CORPS, ARMY OF THE TENNESSEE

Sixteenth Corps was created in the Department of the Tennessee by a presidential order dated December 18, 1862. It was constituted December 22, 1862 to consist of John McArthur's Sixth Division, Isaac F. Quinby's Seventh Division, Leonard F. Ross' Eighth Division, Albert L. Lee's Second Brigade, Cavalry Division, and the forces in the districts of Columbus and Jackson. Stephen A. Hurlbut was assigned command.

At the end of December 1862, the organization of the divisions that were assigned to Sixteenth Corps was as follows:

Sixth Division, John McArthur
  First Brigade, George W. Deitzler
  Second Brigade, Thomas E. G. Ransom
  Third Brigade, Marcellus M. Crocker

Note. Joseph W. Mitchell's Battery F, Second Illinois Light Artillery was attached to First Brigade; Edward Brotzmann's Battery C, 1st Missouri Light Artillery was attached to Second Brigade; and Hamilton B. White's 10th Battery, Ohio Light Artillery was attached to Third Brigade.

Seventh Division, Isaac F. Quinby
  First Brigade, Jesse I. Alexander
  Second Brigade, Ephraim R. Eckley
  Third Brigade, George B. Boomer
  Artillery, Albert M. Powell
    Battery M, 1st Missouri Light Artillery, Junius W. MacMurray
    11th Battery, Ohio Light Artillery, Frank C. Sands
    6th Battery, Wisconsin Light Artillery, Henry Dillon
    12th Battery, Wisconsin Light Artillery, William Zickerick

Eighth Division, John E. Smith
  First Brigade, John W. Fuller
  Second Brigade, Joseph A. Mower
  Third Brigade, Ralph P. Buckland

Note 1. Buckland's Third Brigade was formerly Fifth Brigade, Third Division, District of Memphis, and it was transferred to Eighth Division at Oxford, Mississippi December 10, 1862.
Note 2. George Robinson's 3rd Battery, Michigan Light Artillery was attached to First Brigade; Joseph R. Reed's 2nd Battery, Iowa Light Artillery was attached to Second Brigade; and Albert J. S. Molinard's Battery F, 2nd United States Artillery was unassigned.

Because of Ulysses S. Grant's operations in northern Mississippi in late December 1862, Sixteenth Corps was not fully organized until January 10, 1863, when Charles S. Hamilton was assigned command during the temporary absence of Hurlbut. On January 15, the District of West Tennessee, Department of the Tennessee was organized to consist of the districts of Corinth, Columbus, Jackson, and Memphis, and Charles S. Hamilton was assigned command. This district consisted of all troops of Sixteenth Corps, but McArthur's Sixth Division, John Logan's Third Division, and Isaac F. Quinby's Seventh Division were detached from Hamilton's command.

On January 20, 1863, Sixth Division and Seventh Division were transferred to Seventeenth Corps, and James W. Denver's First Division and Jacob G. Lauman's Fourth Division were transferred from

Seventeenth Corps to Sixteenth Corps. At the same time, the District of Corinth was transferred from Seventeenth Corps to Sixteenth Corps.

The troops at Corinth under Hamilton's command in November and December 1862 were designated as Left Wing of the original Thirteenth Corps, but in the reorganization of December 22, 1862, they were assigned to Seventeenth Corps as Left Wing. Then, on January 20, 1863, they were designated as Left Wing, Sixteenth Corps, and this designation was continued until its divisions were transferred from Sixteenth Corps to Fifteenth Corps and Seventeenth Corps at the end of the Atlanta Campaign.

At the end of January 1863, Sixteenth Corps was organized as follows:

SIXTEENTH CORPS Charles S. Hamilton

First Division, John A. McDowell
  First Brigade, Charles C. Walcutt
  Second Brigade, Joseph R. Cockerill
  Artillery, William Cogswell
    Battery F, 1st Illinois Light Artillery, John T. Cheney
    Battery I, 1st Illinois Light Artillery, Edward Bouton
    Battery M, 1st Illinois Light Artillery, John B. Miller
    Battery D, 2nd Illinois Light Artillery, Harrison C. Barger
    4th Battery, Indiana Light Artillery, Asahel K. Bush

Note 1. Headquarters, First Division was at La Grange, Tennessee, and the troops were at Davis' Mills, Grand Junction, and La Grange.
Note 2. On February 17, 1863, First Division under James W. Denver was transferred to Charles S. Hamilton's command, which consisted of the districts of Corinth and Jackson.

Fourth Division, Jacob G. Lauman
  First Brigade, Isaac C. Pugh
  Second Brigade, Cyrus Hall
  Third Brigade, Amory K. Johnson
  Artillery
    Battery E, 2nd Illinois Light Artillery, Martin Mann
    Battery K, 2nd Illinois Light Artillery, Benjamin F. Rodgers
    9th Battery, Indiana Light Artillery, George R. Brown

5th Battery, Ohio Light Artillery, Anthony B. Burton

7th Battery, Ohio Light Artillery, Silas A. Burnap

15th Battery, Ohio Light Artillery, Edward Spear, Jr.

Note. Headquarters, Fourth Division was at Moscow, Tennessee.

Eighth Division, John E. Smith
  First Brigade, John W. Fuller
  Second Brigade, Joseph A. Mower
  Third Brigade, Ralph P. Buckland
  Artillery
    Battery E, 1st Illinois Light Artillery, Allen C. Waterhouse
    2nd Battery, Iowa Light Artillery, Joseph R. Reed

Note 1. The organization of Eighth Division is reported as of January 20, 1863.
Note 2. George Robinson's 3rd Battery, Michigan Light Artillery and Albert J. S. Molinard's Battery F, 2nd United States Artillery were attached to First Brigade.
Note 3. James M. Tuttle was assigned command of the division April 1, 1863, and two days later the designation was changed to Third Division, Fifteenth Corps, and Eighth Division was discontinued. The brigades of Eighth Division were reassigned as follows: First Brigade as Fourth Brigade, Second Division, Sixteenth Corps; Second Brigade as Second Brigade, Third Division, Fifteenth Corps; and Third Brigade as First Brigade, Third Division, Fifteenth Corps.

Cavalry Division
  First Brigade, Benjamin H. Grierson
  Second Brigade, Albert L. Lee

Note. First Brigade was at La Grange, Tennessee, and Second Brigade was at Germantown, Tennessee.

DISTRICT OF WEST TENNESSEE
Charles S. Hamilton

District of Columbus, Alexander Asboth
  Cairo, Illinois, James M. Tuttle
  Columbus, Kentucky, James S. Martin
  Fort Heiman, Kentucky, Matthewson T. Patrick
  Fort Pillow, Tennessee, Edward H. Wolfe
  Island No. 10, John A. Gordon
  Paducah, Kentucky, Henry Dougherty
  Union City, Tennessee, David Moore

District of Corinth, Grenville M. Dodge
  First Brigade, Thomas W. Sweeny
  Second Brigade, August Mersey
  Third Brigade, Moses M. Bane

Artillery at Corinth
  Battery G, 1st Illinois Light Artillery, Henry E. Jones
  Battery B, 2nd Illinois Light Artillery, Fletcher H. Chapman
  2nd Battery, Michigan Light Artillery, Albert F. R. Arndt
  2nd Battalion, 1st Missouri Light Artillery, Henry Richardson
  Glendale, Mississippi, John Morrill
  Tuscumbia, Alabama, Patrick E. Burke

District of Jackson, Jeremiah C. Sullivan
  First Brigade, Michael K. Lawler
  Second Brigade, Cyrus L. Dunham
  Third Brigade, Jonathan Richmond
  Fourth Brigade, Oliver Wood
  Artillery, Meredith H. Kidd
    14th Battery, Indiana Light Artillery, Francis W. Morse
    Battery K, 1st Missouri Light Artillery, Bazil D. Meek
    14th Battery, Ohio Light Artillery, Homer H. Stull
    7th Battery, Wisconsin Light Artillery, Galen E. Green
  Cavalry Brigade, John K. Mizner
  Bolivar, Tennessee, Mason Brayman
  Bethel, Tennessee, William W. Sanford

District of Memphis, James C. Veatch
Nine unbrigaded regiments of infantry and three regiments of cavalry

Stephen A. Hurlbut assumed command of Sixteenth Corps February 5, 1863, and two days later his command was extended to include the districts of Corinth, Jackson, Columbus, and Memphis. Hurlbut assumed command of these districts February 11, and their troops were attached to Sixteenth Corps. On February 17, Hamilton was assigned command of the troops in the districts of Corinth and Jackson, and James W. Denver's First Division was assigned to Hamilton's command. Hamilton was relieved from command in Sixteenth Corps on March 23, and the divisions and districts of the Left Wing, Sixteenth Corps reported directly to Headquarters, Sixteenth Corps, which was then commanded by Hurlbut. At that time the Left Wing consisted of the following:

Left Wing, Sixteenth Corps, Charles S. Hamilton
  District of Corinth, Grenville M. Dodge

District of Jackson, Jeremiah C. Sullivan
First Division, James W. Denver
Cavalry Brigade, Benjamin H. Grierson

Richard J. Oglesby reported to Sixteenth Corps April 6, 1863, and was assigned command of the Left Wing.

On April 16, 1863, Sixteenth Corps was reorganized into six divisions, with new numerical designations assigned. The organizaton at the end of April 1863 was as follows:

SIXTEENTH CORPS Stephen A. Hurlbut

First Division, William Sooy Smith
First Brigade, John M. Loomis
Second Brigade, Stephen G. Hicks
Third Brigade, Joseph R. Cockerill
Fourth Brigade, William W. Sanford
Artillery, William Cogswell
Battery F, 1st Illinois Light Artillery, John T. Cheney
Battery I, 1st Illinois Light Artillery, William N. Lansing
Battery M, 1st Illinois Light Artillery, Henry G. Eddy
Battery D, 2nd Illinois Light Artillery, Charles S. Cooper
6th Battery, Indiana Light Artillery, Michael Mueller
Battery K, 1st Missouri Light Artillery, Stillman O. Fish

Note 1. The number of First Division was unchanged in the reorganization.
Note 2. First Brigade was at Collierville, Second Brigade was at La Grange, Third Brigade was at Moscow, and Fourth Brigade was at Germantown, Tennessee.
Note 3. Third Brigade was organized March 22, 1863 from regiments of Second Brigade, First Division, Sixteenth Corps.
Note 4. Fourth Brigade was organized March 22, 1863 from the post of Bethel.
Note 5. First Division was transferred to Fifteenth Corps July 28, 1863 under Hugh Ewing, and was then reorganized December 20, 1863 from James M. Tuttle's Third Division, Fifteenth Corps.

Fourth Division, Jacob G. Lauman
First Brigade, Isaac C. Pugh
Second Brigade, Cyrus Hall
Third Brigade, George E. Bryant
Artillery, George C. Gumbart

Battery E, 2nd Illinois Light Artillery, George L. Nispel
Battery K, 2nd Illinois Light Artillery, Benjamin F. Rodgers
5th Battery, Ohio Light Artillery, Anthony B. Burton
7th Battery, Ohio Light Artillery, Silas A. Burnap
15th Battery, Ohio Light Artillery, James Burdick

Note. The number of Fourth Division was unchanged in the reorganization. Fourth Division was at Memphis, Tennessee.

First Cavalry Division, Cadwallader C. Washburn
First Brigade, Benjamin H. Grierson
Second Brigade, La Fayette McCrillis

Note 1. Washburn assumed command of the division April 9, 1863 (assigned April 3).
Note 2. Grierson departed April 17, 1863 with the 6th and 7th Illinois regiments of his brigade on a raid through Mississippi to Baton Rouge, Louisiana. The 2nd Iowa Regiment initially accompanied him but soon doubled back to La Grange, Tennessee.

District of Columbus (or Sixth Division, Sixteenth Corps), Alexander Asboth
Cairo, Illinois, Napoleon B. Buford
Clinton, Kentucky, David Moore
Columbus, Kentucky, George E. Waring, Jr.
Fort Heiman, Kentucky, Chauncey W. Griggs
Fort Pillow, Tennessee, Edward H. Wolfe
Hickman, Kentucky, detachment
Island No. 10, John A. Gordon
Paducah, Kentucky, James S. Martin

Note 1. Headquarters of the district was at Columbus, Kentucky.
Note 2. Almost all of the above commands were at least the equivalent of a brigade.
Note 3. Third Division, Sixteenth Corps was organized from the District of Columbus (or Sixth Division) January 24, 1864.

District of Memphis (Fifth Division, Sixteenth Corps), James C. Veatch
First Brigade, Charles D. Murray
Second Brigade, William H. Morgan
Third Brigade, Thomas Stephens
Fourth Brigade, John F. Ritter

Note 1. John W. Fuller's Fourth Brigade, District of Corinth was transferred to the District of Memphis as Third Brigade in May 1863.
Note 2. Third Brigade, commanded by John W. Fuller, was transferred to Second Division, Sixteenth Corps in November 1863 as Fuller's Brigade.

Note 3. James I. Gilbert's brigade (formerly James M. True's brigade) was assigned to the District of Memphis November 22, 1863 from First Brigade, Second Division, Army of Arkansas.

LEFT WING, SIXTEENTH CORPS
Richard J. Oglesby

District of Corinth (or Second Division, Sixteenth Corps), Grenville M. Dodge
  First Brigade, Thomas W. Sweeny
  Second Brigade, August Mersey
  Third Brigade, Moses M. Bane
  Fourth Brigade, John W. Fuller
  Cavalry Brigade, Florence M. Cornyn
  Bethel, Tennessee, Elliott W. Rice
  Danville, Mississippi, Patrick E. Burke
  Glendale, Mississippi, John Morrill
  Artillery, George H. Stone
    Battery G, 1st Illinois Light Artillery, Raphael G. Rombauer
    Battery B, 2nd Illinois Light Artillery, Fletcher H. Chapman
    12th Illinois Infantry, James N. McArthur
    52nd Illinois Infantry, Maurice J. McGrath
    57th Illinois Infantry, Peter M. Wickerstrum
    3rd Battery, Michigan Light Artillery, George Robinson
    Battery D, 1st Missouri Light Artillery, Henry Richardson
    Battery H, 1st Missouri Light Artillery, Frederick Welker
    Battery I, 1st Missouri Light Artillery, Benjamin Tannrath
    Battery F, 2nd United States Artillery, Charles Green

Note 1. Headquarters, Second Division was at Corinth, Mississippi.
Note 2. Fourth Brigade joined Second Division from First Brigade, Eighth Division in March 1863. It was then transferred to the District of Memphis (or Fifth Division), Sixteenth Corps in May 1863.
Note 3. The cavalry brigade was organized in March 1863.

District of Jackson (or Third Division, Sixteenth Corps), Nathan Kimball
  First Brigade, Mason Brayman
  Second Brigade, Michael K. Lawler
  Third Brigade, James M. True
  Cavalry Brigade, John K. Mizner
  Artillery, Meredith H. Kidd
    14th Battery, Indiana Light Artillery, Francis W. Morse

14th Battery, Ohio Light Artillery, Jerome B. Burrows
7th Battery, Wisconsin Light Artillery, Galen E. Green

Note 1. Headquarters, Third Division and headquarters of Third Brigade and Cavalry Brigade were at Jackson, Tennessee; headquarters of First Brigade was at Bolivar, Tennessee; and headquarters of Second Brigade, which was organized April 18, 1863, was at Corinth, Mississippi.
Note 2. The post of Bolivar, Tennessee was transferred to First Brigade, Third Division, Sixteenth Corps in March 1863.
Note 3. The post of Bethel, Tennessee was transferred to Fourth Brigade, First Division, Sixteenth Corps in March 1863.
Note 4. The Cavalry Brigade was organized in March 1863 from Cavalry Brigade, District of Jackson, and it was transferred to First Cavalry Division, Left Wing, Sixteenth Corps June 9, 1863.
Note 5. In May 1863, Third Division was broken up when First Brigade and Second Brigade were transferred to Kimball's Provisional Division, which was sent to Vicksburg to reinforce Ulysses S. Grant's army, and in August 1863 True's Third Brigade was sent to join Frederick Steele's Arkansas Expedition.
Note 6. Third Division was reorganized January 24, 1864 from the District of Columbus (or Sixth Division, Sixteenth Corps).

On June 9, 1863, the cavalry of the Left Wing, Sixteenth Corps was reorganized as follows:

First Cavalry Division, Left Wing, Sixteenth Corps, John K. Mizner
  First Brigade, La Fayette McCrillis
  Second Brigade, Edward Hatch
  Third Brigade, Florence M. Cornyn
  Fourth Brigade, Bazil D. Meek

Note. Third Brigade served in the District of Corinth, and it continued to report to Grenville M. Dodge, the district commander.

During May and early June 1863, William Sooy Smith's First Division, Jacob G. Lauman's Fourth Division, and a Provisional Division, Sixteenth Corps, which was organized largely from the District of Jackson (or Third Division) under the command of Nathan Kimball, were sent to reinforce Grant's army, which was then engaged in the siege of Vicksburg. This force was designated as Detachment Sixteenth Corps and was placed under the command of Cadwallader C. Washburn. When the Provisional Division was formed, the District of Jackson was discontinued.

The Detachment Sixteenth Corps serving with Grant at Vicksburg was organized as follows:

DETACHMENT SIXTEENTH CORPS, Cadwallader C. Washburn

First Division, William Sooy Smith
First Brigade, John M. Loomis
Second Brigade, Stephen G. Hicks
Third Brigade, Joseph R. Cockerill
Fourth Brigade, William W. Sanford
Artillery, William Cogswell
Battery F, 1st Illinois Light Artillery, John T. Cheney
Battery I, 1st Illinois Light Artillery, William N. Lansing
Cogswell's Battery, Illinois Light Artillery, Henry G. Eddy
6th Battery, Indiana Light Artillery, Michael Mueller

Note 1. First Division joined Grant's army from La Grange, Tennessee June 12, 1863.
Note 2. Fourth Brigade was discontinued July 28, 1863.
Note 3. First Division was transferred to Fifteenth Corps July 28, 1863.

Fourth Division, Jacob G. Lauman
First Brigade, Isaac C. Pugh
Second Brigade, Cyrus Hall
Third Brigade, George E. Bryant, to June 9, 1863
Amory K. Johnson
Artillery, George C. Gumbart
Battery E, 2nd Illinois Light Artillery, George L. Nispel
Battery K, 2nd Illinois Light Artillery, Benjamin F. Rodgers
5th Battery, Ohio Light Artillery, Anthony B. Burton
7th Battery, Ohio Light Artillery, Silas A. Burnap
15th Battery, Ohio Light Artillery, Edward Spear, Jr.

Note. Fourth Division joined Grant's army from Memphis, Tennessee during the period May 13–20, 1863. It was temporarily attached to Thirteenth Corps June 24, and was transferred to Thirteenth Corps July 28.

Provisional Division, Nathan Kimball
Engelmann's Brigade, Adolph Engelmann
Richmond's Brigade, Jonathan Richmond
Montgomery's Brigade, Milton Montgomery

Note 1. The Provisional Division was formed from First Brigade and Second Brigade of Third Division, Sixteenth Corps and four regiments of Sixth Division, Sixteenth Corps. It joined Grant's army from Memphis, Tennessee June 3, 1863.
Note 2. Kimball's Provisional Division was ordered to Helena, Arkansas at the end of July 1863 to join Frederick Steele's Arkansas Expedition, and after August 10, 1863 it operated in John M. Schofield's Department of the Missouri. For further information, see Little Rock, Arkansas Expedition (Steele).

For details of the operations of the troops of Sixteenth Corps with Grant's army at Vicksburg, see Operations against Vicksburg, Mississippi, 1861–1863, Grant's Operations against Vicksburg, Siege of Vicksburg, Mississippi.

During June and July 1863, the forces of Sixteenth Corps remaining in Kentucky, Tennessee, and northern Mississippi consisted of the following:

Fifth Division (or District of Memphis), James C. Veatch
Sixth Division (or District of Columbus), Alexander Asboth
Left Wing, Sixteenth Corps, Grenville M. Dodge
Second Division (or District of Corinth), Grenville M. Dodge
Third Brigade, Third Division, James M. True
Cavalry Division, John K. Mizner

Note. True's Third Brigade was at La Grange, Tennessee.

After the surrender of Vicksburg July 4, 1863, William T. Sherman led an expedition to Jackson, Mississippi to drive back an army assembled by Joseph E. Johnston and to destroy the town as a supply and rail center for Confederate forces. Two divisions of Sixteenth Corps participated in this operation. William Sooy Smith's First Division, Sixteenth Corps was temporarily attached to John G. Parke's Ninth Corps, and Jacob G. Lauman's Fourth Division, Sixteenth Corps was temporarily attached to Edward O. C. Ord's Thirteenth Corps June 24, 1863.

Alvin P. Hovey, commanding Twelfth Division, Thirteenth Corps, relieved Lauman in command of Fourth Division, Sixteenth Corps July 16, 1863, and he then attached Fourth Division, Sixteenth Corps to his own Twelfth Division, Thirteenth Corps. The brigades of Fourth Division were redesignated as Third Brigade, Fourth Brigade, and Fifth Brigade, respectively, of Twelfth Division, Thirteenth Corps. Marcellus M. Crocker relieved Hovey in command of Fourth Division July 23, and Fourth Division was then assigned to Thirteenth Corps on July 28.

On July 24, 1863, all territory in Arkansas as far south as the Arkansas River (District of Eastern Arkansas, Thirteenth Corps) was transferred to Sixteenth Corps as the District of Eastern Arkansas. Stephen A. Hurlbut was assigned command July 29.

On July 27, 1863, Frederick Steele was assigned command of an expedition that was to advance into the interior of Arkansas and capture Little Rock. This expedition, which was called the Arkansas Expedition (or Army of Arkansas), was organized at Helena, Arkansas in the Department of the Tennessee August 1–10. Third Division of the Arkansas Expedition, under the command of Samuel A. Rice, was organized from Thirteenth Division, District of Eastern Arkansas, Sixteenth Corps on August 1, and Second Division of the Arkansas Expedition, under the command of William E. McLean, was organized from Nathan Kimball's Provisional Division, Sixteenth Corps. First Division of the Arkansas Expedition was organized from John W. Davidson's Cavalry Division of the Department of the Missouri.

Steele's command left Helena August 10–11, 1863 and thereafter operated in the Department of the Missouri, where it reported to John M. Schofield, commander of the department. The troops of Sixteenth Corps were carried on the rolls of the corps as detached. True's Third Brigade, Third Division, Sixteenth Corps, which had been left at La Grange, Tennessee, was ordered to move about mid-August to join Steele's army in Arkansas. Upon arrival on September 18, it was redesignated as First Brigade, Second Division, Army of Arkansas. For details of Steele's operations, see Little Rock, Arkansas Expedition (Steele).

On August 20, 1863, Benjamin H. Grierson's Cavalry Division was reorganized as follows:

Cavalry Division, Benjamin H. Grierson
First Brigade, John K. Mizner
Second Brigade, La Fayette McCrillis
Third Brigade, Edward Hatch

Note. Headquarters of the division was at Memphis, Tennessee; of First Brigade at Corinth, Mississippi; of Second Brigade at La Grange, Tennessee; and of Third Brigade at Germantown, Tennessee.

The troops of Sixteenth Corps were further scattered in early November 1863 when Grenville M. Dodge, with the Left Wing, Sixteenth Corps (Second Division), followed William T. Sherman's Fifteenth Corps from Corinth, Mississippi as it moved eastward to the relief of William S. Rosecrans' Army of the Cumberland, which was besieged at Chattanooga, Tennessee. Dodge, however, moved only as far as Pulaski, Tennessee, where he remained to guard the Nashville and Decatur Railroad during Grant's battles around Chattanooga in late November.

The District of Corinth was again organized in December 1863, and John D. Stevenson, then commanding at Corinth, was assigned command. George B. Hoge assumed command of the post of Corinth, which consisted of a number of unassigned regiments. On January 27, 1864, troops from Corinth were organized into Second Brigade, District of Memphis, and the District of Corinth was discontinued.

January 24, 1864, the troops of Sixteenth Corps in the field were organized into four divisions, and at the end of the month the corps was organized as follows:

SIXTEENTH CORPS, Stephen A. Hurlbut

First Division, James M. Tuttle
First Brigade, William L. McMillen
Second Brigade, Joseph A. Mower
Third Brigade, James L. Geddes
Artillery, Nelson T. Spoor
Battery E, 1st Illinois Light Artillery, John A. Fitch
6th Battery, Indiana Light Artillery, Louis Kern
2nd Battery, Iowa Light Artillery, Joseph R. Reed

Note. First Division was organized December 20, 1863 from Tuttle's Third Division, Fifteenth Corps, and it was reorganized January 24, 1864.

LEFT WING
Grenville M. Dodge

Second Division, Thomas W. Sweeny
First Brigade, De Witt C. Anthony
Second Brigade, August Mersey
Third Brigade, Madison Miller
Fuller's Brigade (detachment), William Feeney
Artillery, Benjamin Tannrath
Battery B, 1st Michigan Light Artillery, Albert L. Pickett

Battery H, 1st Missouri Light Artillery, John H. Conant

Battery I, 1st Missouri Light Artillery, Benjamin Tannrath

14th Battery, Ohio Light Artillery, Seth M. Laird

Note 1. Second Division was at Pulaski, Tennessee.

Note 2. Fuller's Third Brigade, District of Memphis (or Fifth Division) was transferred from the District of Memphis to Second Division, Sixteenth Corps November 14, 1863.

Note 3. George H. Stone commanded the artillery of the Left Wing. Albert M. Murray's Battery F, 2nd United States Artillery was with Second Division but was not assigned to a brigade.

Third Division, Andrew J. Smith
First Brigade, David Moore
Second Brigade, William T. Shaw
Third Brigade, Edward H. Wolfe
Artillery
    3rd Battery, Indiana Light Artillery, James M. Cockefair
    9th Battery, Indiana Light Artillery, George R. Brown
    14th Battery, Indiana Light Artillery, Francis W. Morse

Note. Third Division was organized from the District of Columbus (or Sixth Division, Sixteenth Corps) January 24, 1864. The District of Columbus was discontinued as Sixth Division, Sixteenth Corps and became the District of Cairo under Hugh T. Reid.

Fourth Division, James C. Veatch

Note 1. No brigade organization was given in the original order, but on February 3, 1864 the following temporary organization was announced:
    First Brigade, Milton Montgomery
    Second Brigade, James H. Howe
Note 2. Fourth Division, Sixteenth Corps was transferred to Thirteenth Corps July 28, 1863. A new Fourth Division was organized from regiments of the corps January 24, 1864, under the command of Veatch, and was assigned January 25.
Note 3. Charles S. Cooper's Battery D, 2nd Illinois Light Artillery was assigned to Fourth Division.

Cavalry Division, Benjamin H. Grierson
First Brigade, John K. Mizner
Second Brigade, Albert G. Brackett
Third Brigade, La Fayette McCrillis
Waring's Brigade, George E. Waring, Jr.

Note. Isaac W. Curtis' Battery K, 1st Illinois Light Artillery was assigned to Second Brigade.

District of Cairo, Hugh T. Reid

Cairo, Illinois, Hugh T. Reid
Island No. 10, Robert M. Ekings
Columbus, Kentucky, William H. Lawrence
Paducah, Kentucky, Stephen G. Hicks
Union City, Tennessee, Isaac R. Hawkins

Note. The District of Columbus was discontinued as Sixth Division, Sixteenth Corps and was designated as the District of Cairo. Reid was assigned command January 25, 1864.

District of Memphis, Ralph P. Buckland
First Brigade, William L. McMillen
Second Brigade, George B. Hoge
First Colored Brigade, James M. Alexander
Fort Pickering, Ignatz G. Kappner

Note 1. Buckland was assigned command of the district January 25, 1864.
Note 2. Second Brigade was organized January 27, 1864 from troops of the District of Corinth, which was discontinued in the reorganization of January 24, 1864.

First Division, Third Division, and Fourth Division took part in William T. Sherman's expedition from Vicksburg to Meridian, Mississippi February 3–March 6, 1864, and upon their return they were immediately ordered away from the Vicksburg area. For details of the expedition, see Meridian, Mississippi Expedition.

On March 6, 1864, Veatch was ordered to take his Fourth Division, Sixteenth Corps to northern Alabama and join Grenville M. Dodge, who was guarding the Nashville and Decatur Railroad with his Second Division, Sixteenth Corps. Moving by way of Cairo, Illinois, Veatch had arrived at Decatur, Alabama by mid-April. Dodge's command, the Left Wing, Sixteenth Corps, then consisting of Second Division and Fourth Division, was concentrated at Huntsville, Alabama May 2; from there it moved into northern Georgia, and on May 9 it joined Sherman's army, then beginning its advance toward Atlanta.

March 10, 1864, Andrew J. Smith left Vicksburg in command of a force designated as Detachment Army of the Tennessee to take part in Nathaniel P. Banks' Red River, Louisiana Campaign of March 10–May 22. For this campaign, Smith's command was temporarily transferred to the Department of the Gulf, and it was organized as follows:

DETACHMENT ARMY OF THE TENNESSEE, Andrew J. Smith

First Division, Sixteenth Corps
    Second Brigade, Lucius F. Hubbard
    Third Brigade, Sylvester G. Hill

Note. First Brigade was left at Memphis, Tennessee.

Third Division, Sixteenth Corps
    First Brigade, William F. Lynch
    Second Brigade, William T. Shaw
    Third Brigade, Risdon M. Moore

Note. Joseph A. Mower was assigned command of both First Division and Third Division March 9, 1864. Prior to that date, Mower commanded First Division and Lynch commanded Third Division.

Provisional Division, Seventeenth Corps, T. Kilby Smith
    First Brigade, Jonathan B. Moore
    Second Brigade, Lyman M. Ward

For details of the operations of Detachment Army of the Tennessee during the Red River Campaign, see Red River, Louisiana Campaign.

Andrew J. Smith returned to Vicksburg with his command May 23, 1864 after the unsuccessful Red River Campaign, and on June 1 it was ordered to Memphis in the District of West Tennessee. It was then moved to La Grange, Tennessee on the Memphis and Charleston Railroad. From that time Smith's command was called Right Wing, Sixteenth Corps.

Meantime, on April 17, 1864, Cadwallader C. Washburn had been ordered to Memphis to relieve Stephen A. Hurlbut in command of the District of West Tennessee, and on May 2 Hurlbut was relieved of all command. No successor to the command of Sixteenth Corps was named. In June, Sixteenth Corps was divided into two widely separated parts: the troops of Andrew J. Smith's Right Wing, Sixteenth Corps were in West Tennessee; and the two divisions of Grenville M. Dodge's Left Wing were serving with William T. Sherman's army in Georgia. There was no commander of Sixteenth Corps at that time, but the Right Wing reported to Washburn, commander of the District of West Tennessee, and the Left Wing reported to James B. McPherson, commander of the Army of the Tennessee.

During the Atlanta Campaign, the Left Wing, Sixteenth Corps, commonly called Sixteenth Corps, consisted of the Second Division and Fourth Division. Sixteenth Corps was engaged at Rocky Face Ridge, Resaca, Lay's Ferry, Dallas, Kennesaw Mountain, the Battle of Atlanta on July 22, 1864, the siege of Atlanta, and Ezra Church. For details of these operations, see Atlanta, Georgia Campaign.

The organization of Left Wing, Sixteenth Corps during the Atlanta Campaign was as follows:

LEFT WING, SIXTEENTH CORPS, Grenville M.
    Dodge, to August 19, 1864, wounded
    Thomas E. G. Ransom

Second Division, Thomas W. Sweeny, to July 25, 1864
    Elliott W. Rice, to July 26, 1864
    John M. Corse
    First Brigade, Elliott W. Rice
    Second Brigade, Patrick E. Burke, to May 16, 1864,
        mortally wounded
        Robert N. Adams, to May 23, 1864
        August Mersey, to July 24, 1864
        Jesse J. Phillips
        Robert N. Adams
    Third Brigade, Moses M. Bane, to June 20, 1864
        William Vandever, to August 2, 1864
        Henry J. B. Cummings, to August 15, 1864
        Richard Rowett
    Artillery, Frederick Welker
        Battery B, 1st Michigan Light Artillery, Albert F.
           R. Arndt
        Battery H, 1st Missouri Light Artillery, Andrew T.
           Blodgett
        Battery I, 1st Missouri Light Artillery, John F.
           Brunner

Note 1. Third Brigade was at Rome, Georgia after May 22, 1864.
Note 2. Arndt's battery was at Rome, Georgia after May 22, 1864, and Brunner's battery was relieved for muster out May 22, 1864.

Fourth Division, James C. Veatch, to July 17, 1864, sick
    John W. Fuller, to August 4, 1864
    Thomas E. G. Ransom, to August 20, 1864
    John W. Fuller
    First Brigade, John W. Fuller, to July 17, 1864
        John Morrill, to July 22, 1864, wounded
        Henry T. McDowell, to August 4, 1864
        John W. Fuller, to August 20, 1864
        Henry T. McDowell
    Second Brigade, John W. Sprague
    Third Brigade, James H. Howe, to July 21, 1864
        William T. C. Grower, to August 20, 1864
        John Tillson
    Artillery, Jerome B. Burrows, to July 3, 1864
        George Robinson
        Battery C, 1st Michigan Light Artillery, George

Robinson
Henry Shier
14th Battery, Ohio Light Artillery, Jerome B. Burrows, to June 29, 1864
Seth M. Laird, to August 17, 1864
George Hurlbut
Battery F, 2nd United States Artillery, Albert M. Murray, to July 22, 1864
Joseph C. Breckinridge
Lemuel Smith
Rezin G. Howell

Note. Third Brigade was at Decatur, Alabama, and joined the army at Atlanta August 7, 1864.

On September 22, 1864, after the capture of Atlanta, Second Division, Sixteenth Corps was transferred to Fifteenth Corps as Fourth Division, Fifteenth Corps; Fourth Division, Sixteenth Corps was transferred to Seventeenth Corps as First Division, Seventeenth Corps; and Sixteenth Corps, Army of the Tennessee was discontinued.

During May, June, and July 1864, the only troops of Sixteenth Corps in western Tennessee and northern Mississippi belonged to Andrew J. Smith's Right Wing, Sixteenth Corps. At the end of May 1864, these troops were organized as follows:

RIGHT WING, SIXTEENTH CORPS, Andrew J. Smith

First Division, Joseph A. Mower
First Brigade, William L. McMillen
Second Brigade, Lucius F. Hubbard
Third Brigade, Sylvester G. Hill

Note. First Brigade was at Memphis after May 9, 1864, and it was reported as belonging to the District of Memphis, District of West Tennessee.

Third Division, David Moore
First Brigade, Charles D. Murray
Second Brigade, William T. Shaw
Third Brigade, Edward H. Wolfe

Note 1. William T. Shaw was assigned command of First Division July 31, 1864.
Note 2. Lyman M. Ward's brigade, Seventeenth Corps (from the Red River Expedition) was attached to the Right Wing, Sixteenth Corps in July 1864.
Note 3. Edward Bouton's First Brigade, United States Colored Troops was transferred to the Right Wing, Sixteenth Corps from the District of Memphis in June 1864.

After May 2, 1864 (ordered April 17), other forces that previously had been a part of Sixteenth Corps became a part of the District of West Tennessee under the command of Cadwallader C. Washburn. These were:

Cavalry Division, Benjamin H. Grierson
District of Columbus, Henry Prince
District of Memphis, Ralph P. Buckland

The Right Wing, Sixteenth Corps also reported to Washburn. For the organization of the troops in the District of West Tennessee, see Department of the Tennessee, Districts in the Department of the Tennessee, District of West Tennessee.

During the spring and summer of 1864, three expeditions were sent out from Memphis and La Grange, Tennessee into northern Mississippi in an attempt to destroy the Confederate cavalry commanded by Nathan B. Forrest. Forrest was a serious threat to the supply line for William T. Sherman's army, which was then advancing in Georgia toward Atlanta. The first was Samuel D. Sturgis' Expedition from Memphis into Mississippi June 1–13; the second was Andrew J. Smith's Tupelo, Mississippi Expedition July 5–21; and the third was Andrew J. Smith's Oxford, Mississippi Expedition August 1–30. The second and third expeditions were carried out by troops of the Right Wing, Sixteenth Corps. For the organization of the troops and the details of their operations, see Sturgis' Expedition from Memphis, Tennessee into Mississippi (Battle of Brice's Cross Roads); Tupelo, Mississippi Expedition (Andrew J. Smith); and Oxford, Mississippi Expedition (Andrew J. Smith).

On August 28, 1864, Sterling Price left Princeton, Arkansas with a Confederate army and, threatening Little Rock, moved northward toward Missouri. Late in the month, Third Division, Right Wing, Sixteenth Corps was detached from the District of West Tennessee and ordered to Tennessee to cooperate with William T. Sherman's army, which was then approaching Atlanta. At about the same time, Joseph A. Mower's First Division, Right Wing, Sixteenth Corps was sent up the White River to reinforce Frederick Steele, who was then commanding the Union forces in Arkansas.

On September 9, 1864, while Andrew J. Smith was at Cairo, Illinois with Third Division en route to Nashville, Tennessee, he was ordered to Missouri to reinforce the troops in the state in opposing the invasion of Price's army. Meantime, Mower's division, which had been following Price in Arkansas, was transferred by boat from Cape Girardeau to Jefferson City, Missouri, where it arrived October 17. There it joined Smith's Third Division, which had arrived in Missouri from Cairo.

Smith's two divisions joined other Union forces in pursuing Price across Missouri, and when he had been driven from the state, they returned to Saint Louis. The organization of Smith's command during Price's invasion of Missouri was as follows:

SIXTEENTH CORPS, Andrew J. Smith

First Division, Joseph J. Woods
    First Brigade, William L. McMillen
    Second Brigade, Lucius F. Hubbard
    Third Brigade, Sylvester G. Hill

Note. John A. Fitch's Battery E, 1st Illinois Light Artillery was attached to First Brigade; and John W. Coons' 2nd Battery, Iowa Light Artillery was attached to Second Brigade.

Third Division, David Moore
    First Brigade, Thomas J. Kinney
    Second Brigade, James I. Gilbert
    Third Brigade, Edward H. Wolfe
    Artillery
        Battery G, 2nd Illinois Light Artillery, John W. Lowell
        3rd Battery, Indiana Light Artillery, Thomas J. Ginn
        9th Battery, Indiana Light Artillery, Samuel G. Calfee

During the period November 1–30, 1864, Smith's command was transferred from Saint Louis to Nashville, Tennessee, which was then threatened by John B. Hood's Confederate Army of Tennessee.

Meantime, by an order of September 22, 1864, the following troops were transferred to Sixteenth Corps: First Division, Seventeenth Corps, together with all troops on the Mississippi River, except the cavalry and the regiments brigaded with Third Division, Seventeenth Corps, which was then in the field. By this order First Division, United States Colored Troops became Fourth Division, Sixteenth Corps. This division, which was near Vicksburg, was organized as follows:

Fourth Division, Sixteenth Corps, John P. Hawkins

First Brigade, Van E. Young
Second Brigade, Hiram Scofield
Goodrich's Landing, A. Watson Webber
Milliken's Bend, Julian E. Bryant

On September 27, 1864, Napoleon J. T. Dana was assigned command of Sixteenth Corps, including the combined districts of West Tennessee and Vicksburg. He assumed command October 15 and announced the following organization of Sixteenth Corps:

Right Wing, Andrew J. Smith
    First Division, John McArthur
    Second Division, Charles R. Woods

Left Wing, Grenville M. Dodge
    Third Division, Elias S. Dennis
    Fourth Division, John P. Hawkins

This organization, however, was not completed.

On October 18, 1864, four regiments commanded by Jonathan B. Moore were formed into a brigade, which was temporarily attached to First Division, Sixteenth Corps, then in Missouri.

On November 7, 1864, Sixteenth Corps was discontinued, and all troops on the east bank of the Mississippi River were detached from their several departments and corps and were ordered to report to Edward R. S. Canby, commander of the Military Division of West Mississippi.

December 5, 1864, the troops formerly belonging to the Right Wing, Sixteenth Corps, and which were then at Nashville, Tennessee in the Department of the Cumberland, were designated as Detachment Army of the Tennessee, and Andrew J. Smith was assigned command. This force was organized as follows:

DETACHMENT ARMY OF THE TENNESSEE, Andrew J. Smith

First Division, John McArthur
    First Brigade, William L. McMillen
    Second Brigade, Lucius F. Hubbard
    Third Brigade, Sylvester G. Hill, to December 15, 1864, killed
        William R. Marshall

Note. Cogswell's Battery, Illinois Light Artillery, commanded by S. Hamilton McClaury, was attached to

First Brigade; Joseph R. Reed's 2nd Battery, Iowa Light Artillery was attached to Second Brigade; and Stephen H. Julian's Battery I, 2nd Missouri Light Artillery was attached to Third Brigade.

Second Division, Kenner Garrard
   First Brigade, David Moore
   Second Brigade, James I. Gilbert
   Third Brigade, Edward H. Wolfe

Note 1. Second Division was formerly Third Division, Sixteenth Corps.
Note 2. Samuel G. Calfee's 9th Battery, Indiana Light Artillery was attached to First Brigade; Thomas J. Ginn's 3rd Battery, Indiana Light Artillery was attached to Second Brigade; and John W. Lowell's Battery G, 2nd Illinois Light Artillery was attached to Third Brigade.

Third Division, Jonathan B. Moore
   First Brigade, Lyman M. Ward
   Second Brigade, Leander Blanden
   Artillery
      14th Battery, Indiana Light Artillery, Francis W. Morse
      Battery A, 2nd Missouri Light Artillery, John Zepp

Note 1. Third Division was organized from regiments of Seventeenth Corps and other regiments at Nashville.
Note 2. T. Kilby Smith was assigned command of Third Division January 4, 1865.

Andrew J. Smith's Detachment Army of the Tennessee was engaged in the defense of Nashville and at the Battle of Nashville December 15–16, 1865. It advanced in pursuit of Hood's defeated army into northern Mississippi after the Battle of Nashville, and then February 5–8, 1865, it departed for New Orleans, Louisiana to reinforce the army that Edward R. S. Canby was organizing for a campaign against Mobile, Alabama. On February 18, it was reorganized as Sixteenth Corps, Military Division of West Mississippi. For further information, see Sixteenth Corps, Military Division of West Misissippi; and see also Land Operations against Mobile Bay and Mobile, Alabama.

COMMANDERS OF SIXTEENTH CORPS, ARMY OF THE TENNESSEE

Stephen A. Hurlbut   December 22, 1862 to January 10, 1863

Charles S. Hamilton	January 10, 1863 to February 5, 1863
Stephen A. Hurlbut	February 5, 1863 to April 17, 1864
No commander	April 17, 1864 to October 15, 1864
Napoleon J. T. Dana	October 15, 1864 to November 7, 1864

SIXTEENTH CORPS, MILITARY DIVISION OF WEST MISSISSIPPI

In June 1864, Sixteenth Corps, Army of the Tennessee was divided into two wings, and that part of the corps that was then in western Tennessee under the command of Andrew J. Smith was designated as Right Wing, Sixteenth Corps. This consisted of Joseph A. Mower's First Division and David Moore's Third Division.

In late August 1864, Sterling Price left Princeton, Arkansas with a Confederate force on an expedition into Missouri, and Smith's Right Wing was sent across the Mississippi River to reinforce the troops in Arkansas and Missouri. When Price was forced to turn back, Smith followed him across Missouri and then returned with his command to Saint Louis. Then John B. Hood threatened the invasion of Tennessee from Alabama with his Army of Tennessee, and November 1–30, Smith's Right Wing, Sixteenth Corps was sent to Nashville, Tennessee to reinforce the United States forces in that state commanded by George H. Thomas.

On December 5, 1864, Smith's command was reorganized as follows: John McArthur was assigned command of First Division; Third Division was redesignated as Second Division, and Kenner Garrard replaced David Moore in command; and a new Third Division was organized from regiments at Nashville and of Seventeenth Corps, and Jonathan B. Moore was assigned command.

On November 7, 1864, Sixteenth Corps was discontinued, and on December 8, the designation of Right Wing, Sixteenth Corps was changed to Detachment Army of the Tennessee.

Smith's command served in the defenses of

Nashville, aided in defeating Hood in the Battle of Nashville December 15–16, 1864, and then followed Hood's retreating army until it left the state. It remained in northern Mississippi until February 5–8, 1865, and then left Eastport, Mississippi for New Orleans to take part in Edward R. S. Canby's operations against Mobile.

On February 18, 1865, Smith's Detachment Army of the Tennessee was reorganized as Sixteenth Corps, Military Division of West Mississippi; Smith assumed command on February 22.

After its arrival at New Orleans, Sixteenth Corps was transferred to Mobile Bay, where it took part in Canby's operations that resulted in the occupation of Mobile and southern Alabama.

For details of the organization and operations of Sixteenth Corps, Military Division of West Mississippi, see Land Operations against Mobile Bay and Mobile, Alabama.

SEVENTEENTH CORPS, ARMY OF THE TENNESSEE

Seventeenth Corps was created in the Department of the Tennessee by a presidential order dated December 18, 1862. It was constituted December 22, 1862 to consist of James W. Denver's First Division, Thirteenth Corps; John A. Logan's Third Division, Thirteenth Corps; Jacob G. Lauman's Fourth Division, Thirteenth Corps; Benjamin H. Grierson's First Cavalry Brigade; and the forces in the District of Corinth commanded by Grenville M. Dodge. James B. McPherson was assigned command of the corps, but he did not assume command until January 11, 1863.

In late October 1862, Ulysses S. Grant, commanding the Department and Army of the Tennessee, planned a movement southward from West Tennessee into northern Mississippi, which, if successful, would force the evacuation of Vicksburg and Port Hudson and open the Mississippi River for Union traffic. For this purpose Grant organized an Army in the Field, and in December 1862 the divisions assigned to Seventeenth Corps were with Grant's army in northern Mississippi.

At the end of December 1862, the three infantry divisions mentioned above formed McPherson's Right Wing, Thirteenth Corps of Grant's Army in the Field, which was then at Abbeville, Mississippi. It was organized as follows:

RIGHT WING, THIRTEENTH CORPS, James B. McPherson

First Division, James W. Denver
  Second Brigade, John A. McDowell
  Third Brigade, Joseph R. Cockerill
  Artillery, William Cogswell
    Battery F, 1st Illinois Light Artillery, John T. Cheney
    Battery I, 1st Illinois Light Artillery, Edward Bouton
    Cogswell's Battery, Illinois Light Artillery, William Cogswell
    6th Battery, Indiana Light Artillery, Michael Mueller

Note. Cogswell's Battery was also known as Battery M, 1st Illinois Light Artillery.

Third Division, John A. Logan
  First Brigade, C. Carroll Marsh
  Second Brigade, Mortimer D. Leggett
  Fourth Brigade, John D. Stevenson
  Artillery, Charles J. Stolbrand
    Battery D, 1st Illinois Light Artillery, Henry A. Rogers
    Battery G, 2nd Illinois Light Artillery, Frederick Sparrestrom
    Battery L, 2nd Illinois Light Artillery, William H. Bolton
    8th Battery, Michigan Light Artillery, Samuel De Golyer
    3rd Battery, Ohio Light Artillery, William S. Williams

Fourth Division, Jacob G. Lauman
  First Brigade, Isaac C. Pugh
  Second Brigade, Cyrus Hall
  Third Brigade, Amory K. Johnson
  Artillery, George C. Gumbart
    Battery E, 2nd Illinois Light Artillery, Martin Mann
    Battery K, 2nd Illinois Light Artillery, Benjamin F. Rodgers
    9th Battery, Indiana Light Artillery, George R. Brown
    5th Battery, Ohio Light Artillery, Anthony B. Burton
    7th Battery, Ohio Light Artillery, Silas A. Burnap

15th Battery, Ohio Light Artillery, Edward Spear, Jr.

On January 5, 1863, McPherson fell back to Holly Springs with his command, and a short time later First Division moved to Davis' Mill, Grand Junction, and La Grange; Third Division to Memphis; and Fourth Division to Moscow, Tennessee.

During the campaign in northern Mississippi, McPherson used the designation Right Wing, Thirteenth Corps for his command until January 7, 1863, but then it was changed to Seventeenth Corps.

On January 20, 1863, First Division and Fourth Division were transferred from Seventeenth Corps to Sixteenth Corps, and they were left in the positions given above on the Memphis and Charleston Railroad. The District of Corinth was also transferred from Seventeenth Corps to Sixteenth Corps. At the same time, John McArthur's Sixth Division and Isaac F. Quinby's Seventh Division were transferred from Sixteenth Corps to Seventeenth Corps. All three divisions moved to Memphis, Tennessee, where McPherson established corps headquarters. On January 15, 1863, McArthur's Sixth Division was ordered to Lake Providence, Louisiana.

At the end of January 1863, Seventeenth Corps was organized as follows:

SEVENTEENTH CORPS, James B. McPherson

Third Division, John A. Logan
  First Brigade, Isham N. Haynie
  Second Brigade, Mortimer D. Leggett
  Third Brigade, John D. Stevenson
  Artillery, Charles J. Stolbrand
    Battery D, 1st Illinois Light Artillery, Henry A. Rogers
    Battery G, 2nd Illinois Light Artillery, Frederick Sparrestrom
    Battery L, 2nd Illinois Light Artillery, William H. Bolton
    8th Battery, Michigan Light Artillery, Samuel De Golyer
    3rd Battery, Ohio Light Artillery, William S. Williams

Sixth Division, John McArthur
  First Brigade, George W. Deitzler
  Second Brigade, Thomas E. G. Ransom
  Third Brigade, Marcellus M. Crocker

Note. Henry R. Henning's Battery F, 2nd Illinois Light Artillery was attached to First Brigade; William Z. Clayton's 1st Battery, Minnesota Light Artillery and Charles Mann's Battery C, 1st Missouri Light Artillery were attached to Second Brigade; and Hamilton B. White's 10th Battery, Ohio Light Artillery was attached to Third Brigade.

Seventh Division, Isaac F. Quinby
  First Brigade, Norman Eddy
  Second Brigade, Ephraim R. Eckley
  Third Brigade, Charles L. Matthies
  Artillery, Albert M. Powell
    Battery M, 1st Missouri Light Artillery, Junius W. MacMurray
    11th Battery, Ohio Light Artillery, Cyrus Sears
    6th Battery, Wisconsin Light Artillery, Henry Dillon
    12th Battery, Wisconsin Light Artillery, William Zickerick

Third Division and Seventh Division were near Memphis, Tennessee, and Sixth Division was at Lake Providence, Louisiana. Third Division followed Sixth Division to Lake Providence February 19, 1863, and was then ordered to Milliken's Bend on April 15.

Quinby's division left Memphis March 2, 1863 for Lake Providence. There, on March 5, it was ordered to join Leonard F. Ross, whose division from Helena, Arkansas was then in Mississippi on the Yazoo Pass Expedition. Quinby entered the Pass on March 14, and on March 21, on the Tallahatchie River, he met Ross, who was returning from his point of farthest advance near Greenwood, Mississippi. Quinby then moved on, accompanied by Ross, and made a second attempt against Fort Pemberton, near Greenwood. The combined force was unable to pass that point, however, and the expedition withdrew to the Mississippi River on April 5. Quinby proceeded on to Helena, Arkansas, and then downriver to join the other divisions of Seventeenth Corps at Milliken's Bend. For details of the Yazoo Pass Expedition, see Operations against Vicksburg, Mississippi, 1861–1863, Grant's Operations against Vicksburg, Bayou Expeditions, Yazoo Pass, Mississippi Expedition.

In preparation for Grant's movement to the rear of Vicksburg on the east side of the Mississippi River, McPherson was ordered to bring his Seventeenth Corps from Lake Providence to Milliken's Bend. Quinby's division, temporarily under the command of John B. Sanborn, arrived about April 15, 1863, and Logan's division arrived during the period April 16–19. McArthur left Hugh T. Reid's First Brigade at Lake Providence and followed the other two divisions to Milliken's Bend. For this campaign, Seventeenth Corps was designated as the Center of Grant's army.

John A. McClernand's Thirteenth Corps was the first to march downriver at the beginning of the campaign, and McPherson followed with the divisions of Sanborn and Logan. McArthur had not yet arrived from Lake Providence. Thirteenth Corps crossed the Mississippi River to Bruinsburg on April 30, and McPherson's two divisions crossed that day and the next.

The organization of Seventeenth Corps at the end of April 1863 was as follows:

SEVENTEENTH CORPS, James B. McPherson

Third Division, John A. Logan
  First Brigade, John E. Smith
  Second Brigade, Elias S. Dennis
  Third Brigade, John D. Stevenson
  Artillery, Charles J. Stolbrand
    Battery D, 1st Illinois Light Artillery, Henry A. Rogers
    Battery G, 2nd Illinois Light Artillery, Frederick Sparrestrom
    Battery L, 2nd Illinois Light Artillery, William H. Bolton
    8th Battery, Michigan Light Artillery, Samuel De Golyer
    3rd Battery, Ohio Light Artillery, William S. Williams

Note 1. Smith was assigned command of First Brigade April 23, 1863 upon the resignation of Isham N. Haynie.
Note 2. Dennis was assigned command of Second Brigade April 13, 1863.

Sixth Division, John McArthur
  First Brigade, Hugh T. Reid
  Second Brigade, Thomas E. G. Ransom
  Third Brigade, Marcellus M. Crocker
  Artillery, Thomas D. Maurice
    Battery F, 2nd Illinois Light Artillery, John W. Powell
    1st Battery, Minnesota Light Artillery, Henry Hurter
    Battery C, 1st Missouri Light Artillery, Charles Mann
    10th Battery, Ohio Light Artillery, Hamilton B. White

Note 1. Reid was assigned command of First Brigade April 22, 1863.
Note 2. The brigade return gives Crocker as commanding Third Brigade, but the division return reports William Hall commanding the brigade. It is important to note also that on April 30, 1863, Crocker was assigned command of Seventh Division, but he did not assume command until May 2.

Seventh Division, John B. Sanborn
  First Brigade, Jesse I. Alexander
  Second Brigade, Samuel A. Holmes
  Third Brigade, George B. Boomer
  Artillery, Frank C. Sands
    Battery M, 1st Missouri Light Artillery, Junius W. MacMurray
    11th Battery, Ohio Light Artillery, Fletcher E. Armstrong
    6th Battery, Wisconsin Light Artillery, Henry Dillon
    12th Battery, Wisconsin Light Artillery, William Zickerick

Note 1. Alexander commanded First Brigade after April 14, 1863, when Sanborn assumed temporary command of Seventh Division because of the absence of Isaac F. Quinby on sick leave.
Note 2. Holmes relieved Charles L. Matthies in command of Second Brigade April 24, 1863.

After crossing the Mississippi River, McClernand's Thirteenth Corps marched eastward from the river, and Logan's division followed. Both were engaged at the Battle of Port Gibson, Mississippi May 1, 1863. Seventeenth Corps then marched toward Jackson, Mississippi with Grant's army, and Logan's Third Division fought the Battle of Raymond on May 12. Crocker's Seventh Division came up during the fighting but was only slightly engaged. Crocker's division took part in the Battle of Jackson May 14, but Logan's division was in reserve and was not engaged.

Third Division and Seventh Division were engaged at the Battle of Champion Hill May 16, 1863, but troops of Seventeenth Corps were not present at the Battle of Big Black River Bridge. Seventh Division and Ransom's brigade of Sixth Division took part in the assault of May 19 at Vicksburg, and the entire corps was engaged in the second assault of May 22. Seventeenth Corps then took position on the right of Grant's line of investment during the siege of Vicksburg and remained there until the surrender on July 4. A Provisional Division of Seventeenth Corps was organized under McArthur, and it served on Sherman's Exterior Line at Vicksburg during the later stages of the siege.

The organization of Seventeenth Corps during the Vicksburg, Mississippi Campaign, May 1–July 4, 1863, was as follows:

SEVENTEENTH CORPS, James B. McPherson

Third Division, John A. Logan
  First Brigade, John E. Smith, to June 3, 1863
    Mortimer D. Leggett
  Second Brigade, Elias S. Dennis, to May 11, 1863
    Mortimer D. Leggett, to June 3, 1863
    Manning F. Force
  Third Brigade, John D. Stevenson
  Artillery, Charles J. Stolbrand
    Battery D, 1st Illinois Light Artillery, Henry A. Rogers
      George J. Wood
      Frederick Sparrestrom
    Battery G, 2nd Illinois Light Artillery, Frederick Sparrestrom
      John W. Lowell
    Battery L, 2nd Illinois Light Artillery, William H. Bolton
    8th Battery, Michigan Light Artillery, Samuel De Golyer
      Theodore W. Lockwood
    3rd Battery, Ohio Light Artillery, William S. Williams

Sixth Division, John McArthur
  First Brigade, Hugh T. Reid
  Second Brigade, Thomas E. G. Ransom
  Third Brigade, Marcellus M. Crocker, to April 30, 1863
    William Hall, to June 6, 1863
    Alexander Chambers
  Artillery, Thomas D. Maurice
    Battery F, 2nd Illinois Light Artillery, John W. Powell
    1st Battery, Minnesota Light Artillery, Henry Hurter
      William Z. Clayton
    Battery C, 1st Missouri Light Artillery, Charles Mann
    10th Battery, Ohio Light Artillery, Hamilton B. White
      William L. Newcomb

Note 1. Reid's First Brigade was at Lake Providence during the Vicksburg Campaign.
Note 2. August 4, 1863, Ransom was assigned to the command of the post and town of Natchez, Mississippi, and his Second Brigade was transferred as the garrison of that post.

Seventh Division, John B. Sanborn, to May 2, 1863
  Marcellus M. Crocker, to May 17, 1863
  Isaac F. Quinby, to June 3, 1863
  John E. Smith
  First Brigade, John B. Sanborn
  Second Brigade, Samuel A. Holmes, to June 3, 1863
    Green B. Raum
  Third Brigade, George B. Boomer, to May 22, 1863, killed
    Holden Putnam, to June 2, 1863
    Charles L. Matthies
  Artillery, Frank C. Sands
    Henry Dillon
    Battery M, 1st Missouri Light Artillery, Junius W. MacMurray
    11th Battery, Ohio Light Artillery, Fletcher E. Armstrong
    6th Battery, Wisconsin Light Artillery, Henry Dillon
      Samuel F. Clark
    12th Battery, Wisconsin Light Artillery, William Zickerick

At the end of July 1863, Seventeenth Corps was still at Vicksburg, with some changes in command. On July 22, John D. Stevenson assumed command of Third Division when Logan departed on leave because of ill health. McArthur also departed on leave July 30, and Chambers assumed command of Sixth Division. At that time, the brigades of Sixth Division were located as follows: First Brigade at Lake Providence, Second Brigade at Natchez, and Third Brigade at Vicksburg.

On August 7, 1863, Marcellus M. Crocker's Fourth Division, Thirteenth Corps (formerly of Sixteenth Corps) was transferred to Seventeenth Corps as Fourth Division, and by the same order Crocker was directed to move with the division to Natchez.

On September 11, 1863, John E. Smith left Vicksburg with his Seventh Division, Seventeenth Corps to reinforce Frederick Steele's army in Arkansas. He arrived at Helena on September 14, and at that time the designation of his division was changed to Second Division, Seventeenth Corps. Smith's division did not rejoin Seventeenth Corps. On September 22 it was ordered to join the Army of the Cumberland, which was then besieged by Braxton Bragg's Army of Tennessee at Chattanooga, and on

October 8, Smith's division joined Fifteenth Corps and marched with William T. Sherman's command to Chattanooga. It took part in the operations around Chattanooga in November 1863, and on December 20 was transferred to Fifteenth Corps as Third Division in place of James M. Tuttle's former Third Division, which had been left behind at Vicksburg. At the time of its transfer from Seventeenth Corps, the division was organized as follows:

Second Division, Seventeenth Corps, John E. Smith
    First Brigade, Jesse I. Alexander
    Second Brigade, Clark R. Wever
    Third Brigade, Jabez Banbury

For additional information, see Chattanooga-Ringgold Campaign (Battles of Missionary Ridge and Lookout Mountain, Tennessee).

On September 14, 1863, the designation of Sixth Division, Seventeenth Corps was changed to First Division, Seventeenth Corps, which then consisted of four divisions—First Division, Second Division, Third Division, and Fourth Division.

Seventeenth Corps was still at Vicksburg at the end of October 1863, and was organized as follows:

SEVENTEENTH CORPS, James B. McPherson

First Division, Elias S. Dennis
    First Brigade, Frederick A. Starring
    Second Brigade, Thomas W. Humphrey
    Third Brigade, Alexander Chambers
    Artillery, Thomas D. Maurice
        1st Battery, Minnesota Light Artillery, William Z. Clayton
        Battery C, 1st Missouri Light Artillery, Charles Mann
        Battery M, 1st Missouri Light Artillery, John H. Tiemeyer
        8th Battery, Ohio Light Artillery, James F. Putnam
        10th Battery, Ohio Light Artillery, Hamilton B. White

Second Division, John E. Smith
    First Brigade, Jesse I. Alexander
    Second Brigade, Green B. Raum
    Third Brigade, Charles L. Matthies
    Artillery, Henry Dillon
        Cogswell's Battery, Illinois Light Artillery, William Cogswell
        6th Battery, Wisconsin Light Artillery, Samuel F. Clark

        12th Battery, Wisconsin Light Artillery, William Zickerick

Third Division, John A. Logan
    First Brigade, Mortimer D. Leggett
    Second Brigade, Manning F. Force
    Third Brigade, Jasper A. Maltby
    Artillery, Charles J. Stolbrand
        Battery D, 1st Illinois Light Artillery, Theobold D. Yost
        Battery G, 2nd Illinois Light Artillery, John W. Lowell
        Battery L, 2nd Illinois LIght Artillery, William H. Bolton
        Battery H, 1st Michigan Light Artillery, Marcus D. Elliott
        3rd Battery, Ohio Light Artillery, John Sullivan

Fourth Division, Marcellus M. Crocker
    First Brigade, T. Kilby Smith
    Second Brigade, Cyrus Hall
    Third Brigade, Walter Q. Gresham
    Artillery, Benjamin F. Rodgers
        Battery F, 2nd Illinois Light Artillery, Walter H. Powell
        Battery K, 2nd Illinois Light Artillery, Francis M. Ross
        7th Battery, Ohio Light Artillery, Ellis Conant
        15th Battery, Ohio Light Artillery, Edwin F. Reeve

Edward F. Winslow's Cavalry Brigade, which had been attached to Fifteenth Corps since August 1863, was transferred to Seventeenth Corps when James M. Tuttle's Third Division, Fifteenth Corps returned to West Tennessee from Vicksburg. Winslow's cavalry remained attached to Seventeenth Corps until the District of Vicksburg was created March 12, 1864, and then the designation was changed to Cavalry Brigade, District of Vicksburg, Department of the Tennessee.

Seventeenth Corps remained more or less quietly at and near Vicksburg until early February 1864, and then a part of the corps and Winslow's cavalry accompanied Sherman on an expedition to Meridian, Mississippi. After Grant's victory at Missionary Ridge, Tennessee November 25, 1863, Sherman put his Fifteenth Corps in position along the Memphis and Charleston Railroad in northern Alabama and, after a visit in Ohio, started back to Vicksburg to prepare for the expedition. His plan, which had been approved by Grant, was to march out from Vicksburg as far as Meridian, which was 150 miles to the east, and upon arrival there he was to break up the Mobile and Ohio Railroad to the north and south of the town, and also the railroad running from Vicksburg to Selma, Alabama to the east and west of the town.

Sherman arrived at Vicksburg January 29, 1864, after stopping at Memphis to order Hurlbut to send three divisions of Sixteenth Corps to join the expedition. By February 1, McPherson was ready with Mortimer D. Leggett's Third Division, Marcellus M. Crocker's Fourth Division, Alexander Chambers' Third Brigade, First Division, and Edward F. Winslow's Cavalry Brigade of his Seventeenth Corps. On that date Stephen A. Hurlbut arrived with Andrew J. Smith's Third Division and James C. Veatch's Fourth Division of Sixteenth Corps. During the expedition, Winslow's cavalry was detached from Seventeenth Corps and served under Sherman's direct orders.

On February 3, 1864, Sherman left Vicksburg with his command in two columns, preceded by Winslow's cavalry, and marched toward Jackson. He arrived at Jackson February 6, then continued on through Brandon the next day and arrived at Morton on February 9. He was at Hillsboro February 10, Decatur February 12, and Meridian February 14. Sherman remained in Meridian five days and during that time destroyed the arsenal, storehouses and supplies of all kinds, and miles of the railroads. On February 20, Sherman started his command toward Canton, Mississippi, with Seventeenth Corps in the lead, and by February 27 the expedition had arrived there. Sherman then departed for Vicksburg and left Hurlbut in command, and on March 3 Hurlbut marched toward Vicksburg. For additional information about Sherman's expedition, see Meridian, Mississippi Expedition.

In March and April 1864, the troops of Seventeenth Corps were rather widely scattered. In fact, during most of this period Seventeenth Corps did not exist as an organized body. On March 12, James B. McPherson, the corps commander, was assigned command of the Department and Army of the Tennessee, and there was no corps commander from that date until May 4. On April 10, it was ordered that, until the reorganization of Seventeenth Corps, all troops on the Mississippi River that prior to that time had reported to the commander of Seventeenth Corps were to report through their brigade and division commanders to Headquarters, Sixteenth Corps, which was commanded by Stephen A. Hurlbut. On May 4, Frank P. Blair, Jr., who had been assigned command of Seventeenth Corps April 23, arrived at Cairo and assumed command.

Only First Division and a number of regiments of Seventeenth Corps remained in the Vicksburg area. A Provisional Division was organized from First Brigade, Fourth Division, and under the command of T. Kilby Smith left Vicksburg March 10, 1864 to become a part of Andrew J. Smith's Detachment Army of the Tennessee. With this detachment it took part in Nathaniel P. Banks' Red River Expedition in the Department of the Gulf. T. Kilby Smith's Provisional Division, which was sometimes called the Red River Division, was organized as follows:

Provisional Division, T. Kilby Smith
  First Brigade, Jonathan B. Moore
  Second Brigade, Lyman M. Ward

This division did not rejoin Seventeenth Corps. It did return to Vicksburg from the Red River, but it was sent to Memphis May 30, 1864. Then, commanded by Lyman M. Ward, it was attached to Andrew J. Smith's Right Wing, Sixteenth Corps in July 1864. The regiments of Seventeenth Corps, then commanded by Jonathan B. Moore, were formed into a brigade, which was temporarily attached to First Division, Sixteenth Corps. At that time Andrew J. Smith's command was in Missouri, where it served during Sterling Price's invasion of that state. Later, as a part of Sixteenth Corps, it was transferred to Nashville, Tennessee, where it participated in the Battle of Nashville December 15–16, 1864. For additional information, see Department of the Gulf, Operations in the Department of the Gulf, Red River, Louisiana Campaign; Price's Missouri Expedition; Franklin and Nashville Campaign (Hood's Invasion of Tennessee); and Sixteenth Corps, Army of the Tennessee.

Also during March and April 1864, many regiments of Third Division and Fourth Division were in the North on veterans' furlough, and were under orders to rendezvous at Cairo, Illinois. They were assembling there in late April. On April 18, Walter Q. Gresham was ordered to organize a detachment of regiments of Third Division and Fourth Division at Cairo, and move with it up the Tennessee River to intercept Nathan B. Forrest, who was then raiding in West Tennessee. This force was organized as follows:

Gresham's Detachment, Walter Q. Gresham
    First Brigade, Adam G. Malloy
    Second Brigade, Benjamin F. Potts

On April 25, 1864, this detachment was ordered to Clifton, Tennessee on the Tennessee River, where it arrived April 30. It later joined the column of Frank P. Blair's Seventeenth Corps that was en route from Cairo to Huntsville, Alabama, and proceeded with it to Huntsville (see below).

At the end of April 1864, Seventeenth Corps was organized as follows:

SEVENTEENTH CORPS Frank P. Blair, Jr.

Third Division, Mortimer D. Leggett
    First Brigade, Manning F. Force
    Second Brigade, Robert K. Scott
    Third Brigade (Maltby's Brigade), Jasper A. Maltby
    Artillery, Thomas D. Maurice
        Battery D, 1st Illinois Light Artillery, George P. Cunningham
        Battery H, 1st Michigan Light Artillery, William Justin
        Battery C, 1st Missouri Light Artillery, John L. Matthaei
        3rd Battery, Ohio Light Artillery, John Sullivan

Note 1. Maltby's Brigade was reported as the garrison of Vicksburg.
Note 2. Headquarters of Seventeenth Corps and headquarters of Third Division were at Cairo, Illinois.

Fourth Division, Marcellus M. Crocker
    First Brigade, T. Kilby Smith
    Third Brigade, Walter Q. Gresham
    Artillery, Edward Spear, Jr.
        Battery F, 2nd Illinois Light Artillery, Richard Osborne
        1st Battery, Minnesota Light Artillery, William Z. Clayton
        10th Battery, Ohio Light Artillery, William J. Mong
        15th Battery, Ohio Light Artillery, James Burdick

Note 1. First Brigade was absent in the Department of the Gulf with Nathaniel P. Banks' Red River Expedition.
Note 2. Second Brigade was attached to First Division in the District of Vicksburg.

Note 3. Headquarters of Fourth Division was at Cairo, Illinois.

DISTRICT OF VICKSBURG
Henry W. Slocum

First Division, Elias S. Dennis
    First Brigade, Frederick A. Starring
    Second Brigade, James H. Coates
    Artillery, William H. Bolton
        Battery L, 2nd Illinois Light Artillery, William H. Bolton
        Battery M, 1st Missouri Light Artillery, John H. Tiemeyer
        7th Battery, Ohio Light Artillery, Harlow P. McNaughton
    Second Brigade, Fourth Division, Benjamin Dornblaser
    Mississippi Marine Brigade, Alfred W. Ellet
    Maltby's Brigade, Jasper A. Maltby

Note 1. Second Brigade, Fourth Division was attached to First Division in April 1864 and was transferred to Second Brigade, First Division June 20, 1864.
Note 2. Third Brigade, First Division was discontinued April 20, 1864.

Cavalry Brigade, Horace P. Mumford

First Division Colored Troops, John P. Hawkins
    First Brigade, Isaac F. Shepard
    Second Brigade, Hiram Scofield
    Forces at Vicksburg
        3rd United States Colored Cavalry, Embury D. Osband
        Battery A, 2nd United States Colored Artillery, Robert Ranney
        4th United States Colored Heavy Artillery, Herman Lieb
    United States Forces Goodrich's Landing, A. Watson Webber

Note. Lieb's battery was designated as 4th United States Colored Heavy Artillery until April 26, 1864, when the designation was changed to 5th United States Colored Heavy Artillery.

Defenses and Post of Natchez, Mississippi, James M. Tuttle

After Blair had assumed command of Seventeenth Corps at Cairo May 4, 1864, he moved with the regiments assembled there to Huntsville, Alabama during the period May 11–23. On the way, Blair was joined by the detachment of regiments from Third Division and Fourth Division that Gresham had brought from Cairo to Clifton.

At Huntsville, Blair organized his command into two divisions commanded by Mortimer D. Leggett and Marcellus M. Crocker, and he then marched with these divisions by way of Rome to Acworth, Georgia, where on June 8 he joined William T. Sherman's army, which was then advancing toward Atlanta. These two divisions constituted the Seventeenth Corps that participated in the Atlanta Campaign as a part of the Army of the Tennessee. The organization of Seventeenth Corps during the Atlanta Campaign was as follows:

SEVENTEENTH CORPS, Frank P. Blair, Jr.

Third Division, Mortimer D. Leggett, to August 23, 1864, sick
Charles R. Woods
First Brigade, Manning F. Force, to July 22, 1864, wounded
George E. Bryant
Second Brigade, Robert K. Scott, to July 22, 1864, captured
Greenberry F. Wiles
Third Brigade, Adam G. Malloy
Artillery, William S. Williams
Battery D, 1st Illinois Light Artillery, Edgar H. Cooper
Battery H, 1st Michigan Light Artillery, Marcus D. Elliott
William Justin
3rd Battery, Ohio Light Artillery, John Sullivan

Fourth Division, Walter Q. Gresham, to July 20, 1864, wounded
William Hall, to July 21, 1864
Giles A. Smith
First Brigade, William L. Sanderson, to July 18, 1864
Benjamin F. Potts
Second Brigade, George C. Rogers, to July 5, 1864
Isaac C. Pugh, to July 19, 1864
John Logan
Third Brigade, William Hall, to July 21, 1864
John Shane, temporarily July 21, 1864
William Hall, to July 31, 1864
William W. Belknap
Artillery, Edward Spear, Jr., to August 25, 1864, to Third Division
William Z. Clayton
Battery F, 2nd Illinois Light Artillery, Walter H. Powell, to July 22, 1864, captured

George R. Richardson, to July 29, 1864
Wendolin Meyer
1st Battery, Minnesota Light Artillery, William Z. Clayton
Henry Hurter
Battery C, 1st Missouri Light Artillery, John L. Matthaei
10th Battery, Ohio Light Artillery, Francis Seaman
15th Battery, Ohio Light Artillery, James Burdick

Note. Second Brigade was at Allatoona June 8–13, 1864 and at Kennesaw and Acworth to the end of the campaign.

Seventeenth Corps was engaged at Dallas, Georgia and at Kennesaw Mountain, and it bore the brunt of John B. Hood's attack in the Battle of Atlanta July 22, 1864. It was also engaged at Ezra Chapel and was present at Jonesboro, but saw little action there. For details of the operations of Seventeenth Corps during the Atlanta Campaign, see Atlanta, Georgia Campaign.

On September 23, 1864, after the capture of Atlanta, John W. Fuller's Fourth Division, Sixteenth Corps was transferred to Seventeenth Corps as First Division, Seventeenth Corps. It was organized as follows:

First Division, Seventeenth Corps, John W. Fuller
First Brigade, Henry T. McDowell
Second Brigade, Wager Swayne
Third Brigade, John Tillson
Artillery, George Robinson
Battery C, 1st Michigan Light Artillery, Henry Shier
14th Battery, Ohio Light Artillery, George Hurlbut
Battery F, 2nd United States Artillery, Rezin G. Howell

Note. Joseph A. Mower was assigned command of First Division October 31, 1864.

The earlier First Division, Seventeenth Corps, which was commanded by Elias S. Dennis, remained at Vicksburg during the Atlanta Campaign. It was transferred to Morganza, Louisiana, in the Department of the Gulf, July 28, 1864, and it continued to use the designation First Division, Seventeenth Corps until August 18, 1864. On that date, Nineteenth Corps, Department of the Gulf was reorganized, and then First Division, Seventeenth Corps became Second Division, Nineteenth Corps, with Dennis in command. For further information, see Nineteenth Corps, Department of the Gulf, and see also Department of the Gulf, Troops in the Department of the Gulf.

Late in September 1864, Hood left Lovejoy's Station with his army and marched northward along the Nashville and Chattanooga Railroad to destroy the track and interrupt communications with the North, and also to threaten the invasion of Tennessee. Sherman followed with his army, including the Army of the Tennessee, as far as Gaylesville, Alabama, and then, after sending two corps to reinforce George H. Thomas' forces in Tennessee, he turned back toward Atlanta and began preparations for a march through Georgia to Savannah on the coast. Seventeenth Corps, with Fifteenth Corps, halted at Smyrna Camp Grounds, south of Marietta and about midway between that town and the Chattahoochee River. For details of the above movements, see Franklin and Nashville Campaign (Hood's Invasion of Tennessee).

Sherman established his headquarters at Kingston, Georgia, and there on November 9, 1864 he announced the reorganization of his army into two wings as follows: a Left Wing, commanded by Henry W. Slocum, consisting of Fourteenth Corps and Twentieth Corps of the Army of the Cumberland; and a Right Wing, commanded by Oliver O. Howard, consisting of Fifteenth Corps and Seventeenth Corps of the Army of the Tennessee. The Right Wing was commonly called the Army of the Tennessee.

Sherman left Atlanta November 15, 1864 on his march across Georgia, with his two wings advancing by different routes so as to threaten both Augusta and Macon. Slocum's Left Wing marched eastward in the direction of Augusta, and Howard's Right Wing took roads to the south and east toward Gordon, which was about twenty miles east of Macon. Seventeenth Corps marched to the southeast from Atlanta through McDonough, Monticello, and Hillsboro to Gordon, and then through Toomsboro to Ball's Ferry, where it crossed the Oconee River. From Ball's Ferry it marched eastward to Sebastopol (present-day Midville), near where it crossed the Ogeechee River, and then on to Millen, where it arrived on December 3. From there it marched to the southeast along the Georgia Central Railroad, to the left of Fifteenth Corps, and joined the rest of the army in front of Savannah, which was occupied by Federal troops on December 21. For details of Sherman's march through Georgia, see Savannah Campaign (Sherman's March through Georgia), in Volume I.

The organization of Seventeenth Corps during the march through Georgia was as follows:

SEVENTEENTH CORPS, Frank P. Blair, Jr.

First Division, Joseph A. Mower
    First Brigade, John W. Fuller
    Second Brigade, John W. Sprague
    Third Brigade, John Tillson

Third Division, Mortimer D. Leggett
    First Brigade, Manning F. Force
    Second Brigade, Robert K. Scott

Fourth Division, Giles A. Smith
    First Brigade, Benjamin F. Potts
    Third Brigade, William W. Belknap

Artillery, Allen C. Waterhouse
    Battery C, 1st Michigan Light Artillery, Henry Shier
    1st Battery, Minnesota Light Artillery, Henry Hurter
    15th Battery, Ohio Light Artillery, George R. Caspar

Sherman remained at Savannah a few weeks for the troops to rest and refit, and while there he began preparations for continuing the march northward through the Carolinas to join Grant's forces in Virginia. The opening movement of this campaign was the transfer by sea of Howard's Right Wing to Beaufort, South Carolina to threaten Charleston. Blair's Seventeenth Corps moved first, beginning January 3, 1864, and upon arrival at Beaufort took position at Pocotaligo, South Carolina on January 14. Fifteenth Corps followed and took position near Seventeenth Corps at Garden's Corners and Port Royal Ferry.

Seventeenth Corps and Fifteenth Corps left the vicinity of Pocotaligo February 1, 1865 and marched by way of Bamberg and Orangeburg to Columbia, South Carolina, where they arrived February 17. Seventeenth Corps then moved on to Winnsboro, destroying the railroad as it advanced, and there it turned eastward and marched by way of Cheraw, South Carolina to Fayetteville, North Carolina. It arrived on March 11. Fifteenth Corps marched to the right of Seventeenth Corps to the same destination.

On March 15, 1865, Sherman sent his army in two columns toward Goldsboro, North Carolina. Slocum's Left Wing took the road through Averasboro and Bentonville, and Howard's Right Wing moved by roads to the right of Slocum's line of advance. Seventeenth Corps moved out on the road to Clinton, North Carolina and halted a short distance beyond South River while Slocum was engaged at Averasboro on March 16. It then continued the march the next day and, on March 19, the day of Slocum's Battle at Bentonville, camped for the night at Smith's Chapel, about seven miles west of Mount Olive, North Carolina.

Early on the morning of March 20, 1865, Seventeenth Corps marched to Bentonville, following Fifteenth Corps, and formed in line of battle on the right of Slocum's command. Seventeenth Corps was engaged in skirmishing with the enemy March 20 and 21, and during the afternoon of March 21, Joseph A. Mower, with John W. Fuller's First Brigade and John Tillson's Third Brigade of his First Division, Seventeenth Corps, was seriously engaged while attempting to turn the Confederate left flank.

Seventeenth Corps remained on the battlefield of Bentonville until March 23, 1865 while caring for the wounded and burying the dead, and it then marched on to Goldsboro, where it arrived March 24.

After resting and refitting at Goldsboro, Seventeenth Corps advanced on April 10, 1865 with the rest of Sherman's army against Joseph E. Johnston's army, which at that time was encamped near Smithfield, North Carolina. Upon learning of Sherman's approach, Johnston retired toward Raleigh, closely followed by Sherman's columns. Seventeenth Corps reached Raleigh April 13, and was then sent on in the direction of Salisbury, North Carolina in an attempt to intercept Johnston's army, which was believed to be moving toward Charlotte. Seventeenth Corps was on the road toward Pittsboro April 15, when all troop movements were suspended while Sherman met with Johnston near Durham Station to discuss terms for ending hostilities. The war in the East was ended April 26, 1865 with the surrender of Johnston's army. The next day Seventeenth Corps was ordered to march to Washington, D.C. For details of the operations of Seventeenth Corps during the march through the Carolinas, see Carolinas Campaign, in Volume I.

The organization of Seventeenth Corps during Sherman's march through the Carolinas was as follows:

SEVENTEENTH CORPS, Frank P. Blair, Jr.

First Division, Joseph A. Mower, to April 3, 1865
  Manning F. Force
  First Brigade, Charles S. Sheldon, to January 25, 1865
    John W. Fuller
  Second Brigade, John W. Sprague, to January 29, 1865
    Milton Montgomery, to March 28, 1865
    John W. Sprague
  Third Brigade, John Tillson, to March 26, 1865
    Charles H. De Groat, to April 10, 1865
    James S. Wright
    John Tillson

Third Division, Mortimer D. Leggett
  Manning F. Force, to March 31, 1865
  Mortimer D. Leggett
  First Brigade, Manning F. Force, to January 15, 1865
    Cassius Fairchild, to March 31, 1865
    Manning F. Force, to April 3, 1865
    Cassius Fairchild, to April 4, 1865
    Manning F. Force
    Charles Ewing
  Second Brigade, Greenberry F. Wiles, to March 28, 1865
    Robert K. Scott

Fourth Division, Giles A. Smith
  First Brigade, Benjamin F. Potts
  Third Brigade, William W. Belknap

Note. A reorganization of Fourth Division was ordered April 28, 1865. The 14th and 15th Illinois regiments were detached from Potts' First Brigade, and the 23rd Illinois Regiment from Belknap's Third Brigade, and these three regiments were constituted as Second Brigade, Fourth Division under the command of Charles J. Stolbrand.

Artillery, Allen C. Waterhouse
  Frederick Welker
  Battery C, 1st Michigan Light Artillery, William W. Hyzer
  1st Battery, Minnesota Light Artillery, William Z. Clayton
  15th Battery, Ohio Light Artillery, Lyman Bailey
    James Burdick

On April 29, 1865, Seventeenth Corps began its

march toward Washington. It moved on a road just to the east of the Raleigh and Gaston Railroad, by way of Forestville, Jones' Springs, Warrenton, and Macon, and crossed the Roanoke River at Robinson's Ferry. From there, on May 4, it took the road toward Lawrenceville as far as White Plains, where it turned off to the left. It crossed the Meherrin River at Pennington's Bridge and continued on to the Boydton Plank Road, then followed that road to Petersburg, Virginia, where it arrived May 6. It then moved on and reached Manchester, Virginia, opposite Richmond, three days later.

It remained in camp at Manchester until May 12, 1865, and then resumed the march northward. It marched through the city of Richmond, passed through Hanover Court House and Bowling Green, and arrived at Fredericksburg on May 10. The corps crossed the Rappahannock River there May 17, then continued on by way of Stafford Court House, Dumfries, and Fairfax Court House and arrived near Alexandria, Virginia on May 19.

Seventeenth Corps marched in the Grand Review in Washington May 24, 1865, then went into camp near the city.

On May 29, 1865, the Army of the Tennessee was ordered to Louisville, Kentucky for muster out. Seventeenth Corps left Washington June 5–7 and traveled by rail to Parkersburg, West Virginia, and from there by steamer to Louisville, where it arrived June 10–12.

On June 12, 1865, Stolbrand's newly organized Second Brigade, Fourth Division was ordered to Saint Louis to report to John Pope, commander of the Military Division of the Missouri. The brigade embarked at Louisville June 21, arriving at Saint Louis four days later. It then reembarked and started up the Missouri River for Fort Leavenworth, Kansas.

All regiments of Seventeenth Corps were mustered out by July 28, 1865, and the corps was officially discontinued to date from August 1, 1865.

COMMANDERS OF SEVENTEENTH CORPS, ARMY OF THE TENNESSEE

James B. McPherson	January 11, 1863 to March 12, 1864
No commander	March 12, 1864 to May 4, 1864
Frank P. Blair, Jr.	May 4, 1864 to September 22, 1864
Thomas E. G. Ransom	September 22, 1864 to October 10, 1864
Mortimer D. Leggett	October 10, 1864 to October 24, 1864
Joseph A. Mower	October 24, 1864 to October 31, 1864
Frank P. Blair, Jr.	October 31, 1864 to June 24, 1865
Mortimer D. Leggett	June 24, 1865 to about July 1, 1865
Frank P. Blair, Jr	About July 1, 1865 to July 11, 1865

NINETEENTH CORPS, DEPARTMENT OF THE GULF

In November 1861, Federal authorities in Washington approved a plan for a joint army-navy operation to capture New Orleans and open the Mississippi River. David G. Farragut was assigned to command the entire operation, and Benjamin F. Butler to command the land force. Farragut arrived at Ship Island, off the Gulf Coast of Mississippi, February 20, 1862, and Butler followed with his command on March 20. That day Butler formally assumed command of the newly created Department of the Gulf.

When all preparations had been completed for the attempt on New Orleans, Farragut's fleet, followed by the land forces on transports, steamed up the Mississippi River toward Fort Jackson and Fort Saint Philip. The fleet passed the forts early on the morning of April 24 and proceeded on upriver to New Orleans, which was surrendered to the navy April 25.

On May 1, 1862, Butler occupied New Orleans with his land forces, and soon extended his control over the surrounding country.

For details of the organization of Butler's troops, see Department of the Gulf, Troops in the Department of the Gulf, and see also Department of New England, in Volume I.

On October 28, 1862, Nathaniel P. Banks established headquarters in New York for the purpose of organizing a force of New England and New York regiments, which he was to take to Louisiana to reinforce the troops in the Department of the Gulf. On November 8, Banks was assigned command of the Department of the Gulf, with orders to assume command when he arrived in Louisiana. The troops for Banks' expedition assembled in New York and at Fort Monroe, and finally consisted of thirty-nine infantry regiments, six batteries of artillery, and one battalion of cavalry. Twenty-one of the infantry regiments were in service for only nine months. Included in Banks' expedition were five regiments from the Defenses of Baltimore under William H. Emory. These regiments were the 38th Massachusetts and the 110th, 114th, 116th, and 128th New York, and they assembled at Fort Monroe, Virginia. Banks' expedition was transferred to Louisiana during December 1862, and on December 15, Banks relieved Butler in command of the Department of the Gulf at New Orleans.

At that time Butler's troops in the Department of the Gulf consisted of the following:

Grover's Division, Cuvier Grover (at Baton Rouge, Louisiana)

Sherman's Division, Thomas W. Sherman (at Carrollton, Louisiana)

Reserve Brigade, Godfrey Weitzel (in the District of La Fourche)

Defenses of New Orleans, Thomas W. Cahill

District of Pensacola, Florida, Neal Dow

In addition, there were some unassigned regiments and five regiments of Louisiana Native Guards (colored).

Organization of Nineteenth Corps, January 5, 1862.

When Banks' regiments had landed in Louisiana, he proceeded to reorganize the troops of the Department of the Gulf so as to form a field force, and also to provide a force for purposes of administration of the department. The main body of his command was organized into four divisions of three brigades each, and the garrison troops of the defenses and the permanent detachments for guard and provost duty were maintained as a separate force. The four divisions were organized as follows:

Grover's Division, Cuvier Grover
    First Brigade, William Dwight
    Second Brigade, Thomas W. Cahill
    Third Brigade, Oliver P. Gooding

Note. Grover's Division was organized December 30, 1862.

Emory's Division, William H. Emory
    First Brigade, George L. Andrews
    Second Brigade, Halbert E. Paine
    Third Brigade, Henry W. Birge

Note. Emory's Division was organized January 3, 1863.

Augur's Division, Christopher C. Augur
    First Brigade, Edward P. Chapin
    Second Brigade, Godfrey Weitzel
    Third Brigade, Nathan A. M. Dudley

Note 1. Augur's Division was organized January 12, 1863.
Note 2. Michael Corcoran's Brigade at Fort Monroe was assigned as First Brigade, Augur's Division in the order of January 12, 1863. However, Corcoran's Brigade was not sent to Louisiana, and First Brigade was organized February 9, 1863 from troops in the Department of the Gulf.
Note 3. Second Brigade, Augur's Division was formerly Weitzel's Reserve Brigade in the District of La Fourche.

Sherman's Division, Thomas W. Sherman
    First Brigade, Neal Dow
    Second Brigade, Alpha B. Farr
    Third Brigade, Frank S. Nickerson

Note 1. Sherman's Division was organized January 13, 1863.
Note 2. Neal Dow was assigned to First Brigade by the original order, but Thomas S. Clark was in command until February 26, 1863.

While this reorganization was in progress, Nineteenth Corps was constituted by an order of January 5, 1863, but which was retroactive to December 14, 1862, and Banks was assigned command. He assumed command of the corps January 16, 1863, with headquarters at New Orleans.

On January 14, 1863, the divisions of Nineteenth

Corps were given numerical designations as follows: Augur's Division was assigned as First Division, Nineteenth Corps; Sherman's Division as Second Division, Nineteenth Corps; Emory's Division as Third Division, Nineteenth Corps; and Grover's Division as Fourth Division, Nineteenth Corps.

Operations in West Louisiana, April 9, 1863–May 14, 1863. Early in 1863, Banks decided on an expedition to reach the rear of Port Hudson by way of the Atchafalaya River, and he began preparations for this undertaking. At his direction, Emory spent several weeks in February near the head of Bayou Plaquemine with his division while he attempted to find a navigable route into the Atchafalaya so that he could join a force under Weitzel, which was to move northward from Berwick Bay. Once joined, the combined force was to attempt to reach the Mississippi River above Port Hudson. While Emory was so engaged, David G. Farragut decided to move up with his fleet from the lower Mississippi and patrol the river between Vicksburg and the mouth of Red River. In order to do this, he asked Banks to make a demonstration against Port Hudson while he passed the enemy batteries there as he made his way upstream. Banks immediately complied, and on March 13, he started the divisions of Grover, Emory, and Augur toward Port Hudson. Farragut, however, succeeded in passing the batteries unaided on the night of March 24, and Banks was thus freed to return to his original plan of advancing along the Atchafalaya. For additional information, see Department of the Gulf, Operations in the Department of the Gulf, Operations against Port Hudson, Louisiana.

Grover's division left Baton Rouge March 26, 1863 and arrived at Brashear (or Brashear City), Louisiana April 9; Emory's division left Baton Rouge April 1 and arrived at Brashear April 8; and Godfrey Weitzel's Second Brigade, First Division, which was at Bayou Boeuf, left there April 2 and joined Grover and Emory. Banks, with this command, then crossed Berwick Bay and marched northward up the Atchafalaya and the Bayou Teche toward the Red River. He was engaged at Fort Bisland April 12–13, and again at Irish Bend April 14, and reached Opelousas on April 20. Banks then moved on from Opelousas, and his first troops ar-

rived at Alexandria on May 7. For details of this campaign, see Department of the Gulf, Operations in the Department of the Gulf, Operations in West Louisiana, April 9, 1863–May 14, 1863.

The organization of Nineteenth Corps at the end of April 1863 was as follows:

NINETEENTH CORPS, Nathaniel P. Banks

First Division, Christopher C. Augur
  First Brigade, Edward P. Chapin
  Second Brigade, Godfrey Weitzel
  Third Brigade, Nathan A. M. Dudley

  Unattached
    Louisiana Native Guards (three regiments)
    Companies C and E, 1st Louisiana Cavalry
    2nd Rhode Island Cavalry (battalion)
    1st Indiana Heavy Artillery, John A. Keith
    12th Battery, Massachusetts Light Artillery, Edwin M. Chamberlin

Note 1. First Division was at Baton Rouge, except Weitzel's Second Brigade, which was with Banks in western Louisiana.

Note 2. John E. Morton's 1st Battery, Maine Light Artillery, John F. Phelps' 6th Battery, Massachusetts Light Artillery, and Edmund C. Bainbridge's Battery A, 1st United States Artillery were attached to Second Brigade.

Second Division, Thomas W. Sherman
  First Brigade, Neal Dow
  Second Brigade, Alpha B. Farr
  Third Brigade, Frank S. Nickerson
  Artillery
    18th Battery, New York Light Artillery, Albert G. Mack
    Battery G, 5th United States Artillery, Jacob B. Rawles
    1st Battery, Vermont Light Artillery, George T. Hebard

Note. Second Division was at New Orleans.

Defenses of New Orleans, Thomas W. Sherman

Note 1. Sherman was assigned command of the Defenses of New Orleans January 10, 1863.

Note 2. The troops of the Defenses of New Orleans consisted of the following: Henry Rust's 13th Maine Infantry and Edmund J. Davis' 1st Texas Cavalry; detachments of 2nd Louisiana Native Guards, 31st Massachusetts Infantry, and 14th New York Cavalry; one company each of 12th Maine Infantry, 4th Wisconsin Infantry, 1st Louisiana Native Guards, and 2nd Massa-

chusetts Cavalry Battalion. In addition there were the
following batteries:
13th Battery, Massachusetts Light Artillery, Charles H.
J. Hamlen
21st Battery, New York Light Artillery, James Barnes
25th Battery, New York Light Artillery, John A. Grow
26th Battery, New York Light Artillery, George W. Fox

Third Division, William H. Emory
  First Brigade, Timothy Ingraham
  Second Brigade, Halbert E. Paine
  Third Brigade, Oliver P. Gooding
  Artillery, Richard C. Duryea
    4th Battery, Massachusetts Light Artillery, Joseph
     B. Briggs
    Battery F, 1st United States Artillery, Richard C.
     Duryea
    2nd Battery, Vermont Light Artillery, Pythagoras
     E. Holcomb

Note 1. Third Division was at Opelousas, Louisiana.
Note 2. Ingraham succeeded George L. Andrews in
command of First Brigade March 6, 1863. He was as-
signed command February 21, 1863, when Andrews was
appointed chief of staff at Headquarters, Department of
the Gulf.

Fourth Division, Cuvier Grover
  First Brigade, William Dwight
  Second Brigade, William K. Kimball
  Third Brigade, Henry W. Birge
  Artillery, Henry W. Closson
    2nd Battery, Massachusetts Light Artillery, Or-
     mand F. Nims
    Battery L, 1st United States Artillery, Henry W.
     Closson
    Battery C, 2nd United States Artillery, John I. Rod-
     gers

Note 1. Fourth Division was at Opelousas, Louisiana.
Note 2. Dwight was assigned command of First Bri-
gade February 12, 1863.

In addition to the above field force of Nineteenth
Corps, there were the following unassigned regi-
ments at various posts in the Department of the
Gulf:

Brashear, Louisiana, the 23rd Connecticut and the 176th
  New York

Ship Island, Mississippi, 2nd Louisiana Native Guards
  (detachment)

District of Key West and Tortugas, 90th New York and
  47th Pennsylvania

District of West Florida (or District of Pensacola), 15th
  Maine, 28th Connecticut, and 7th Vermont. Also in
  the district was Frank H. Larned's Battery H, 2nd
  United States Artillery, and Harvey A. Allen's Battery
  K, 2nd United States Artillery.

**Capture of Port Hudson, Louisiana, May 21,
1863–July 8, 1863.** Banks remained at Alexandria
until May 17, 1863, while he attempted to work out
some form of cooperation with Ulysses S. Grant at
Vicksburg for opening the Mississippi River, but
when this failed, he decided to move Nineteenth
Corps to Port Hudson. He marched with his Third
Division, Fourth Division, and Weitzel's Second
Brigade of First Division from Alexandria May
14–17, crossed the Atchafalaya River at Simsport
and the Mississippi River at Bayou Sara, and arrived before Port Hudson on May 24.

During this movement, Emory was too sick to
remain in the field. He returned to New Orleans,
where he relieved Thomas W. Sherman in command
of the Defenses of New Orleans. Sherman then
moved with his Second Division (less Second Brigade) to join Banks at Port Hudson. Halbert E. Paine
succeeded Emory in command of Third Division,
Nineteenth Corps. Augur moved with his First Division from Baton Rouge and, after an engagement
at Plains Store May 21, 1863, joined Banks' army
at Port Hudson May 25.

When all of Banks' troops had arrived, the investment of Port Hudson was complete. Banks made an
unsuccessful general assault on the strong enemy
works May 27, then began siege operations. He
once more attempted to take the works by storm on
June 14, and when this failed, he resumed siege
operations. This work was continued until Port
Hudson surrendered on July 8.

For the organization and operations of Banks'
forces at Port Hudson May 23–July 8, 1863, see Port
Hudson, Louisiana Campaign.

During the siege of Port Hudson, Richard Taylor,
commanding the Confederate forces in western
Louisiana, became active and threatened Banks'
communications with New Orleans. Immediately
after the surrender of Port Hudson, Banks sent
Augur's First Division and Grover's Fourth Division of Nineteenth Corps to Donaldsonville, Louisiana to deal with Taylor. Augur, however, was not
in command of First Division. He had been ill for

some time, and after the surrender of Port Hudson he departed for the North; he did not return to the Department of the Gulf. Godfrey Weitzel assumed command of First Division, Nineteenth Corps. For additional information about Taylor's campaign, see Department of the Gulf, Operations in the Department of the Gulf, Operations against Port Hudson, Louisiana, Operations in Louisiana, West of the Mississippi River.

From July 1863 to March 1864, with one exception, Nineteenth Corps was largely on post and garrison duty in the Department of the Gulf. The one campaign in which Nineteenth Corps was involved was an expedition up the Bayou Teche toward Texas (see below).

Command and Organizational Changes, July and August 1863. There were several changes in the organization and the higher officers of Nineteenth Corps during the rest of the summer of 1863. Largely in July and August 1863, the terms of enlistment of twenty-two nine-month regiments expired or were about to expire, and this reduced Nineteenth Corps to only thirty-seven regiments. As a result, Second Division was broken up and discontinued July 10, just after the surrender of Port Hudson. That day, First Brigade and Third Brigade were transferred to Third Division, to which William Dwight was assigned temporary command. On July 15, Second Brigade was also discontinued. Third Division was then reorganized under Dwight as follows:

Third Division, William Dwight
   First Brigade, Frank S. Nickerson
   Second Brigade, Hawkes Fearing, Jr.
   Third Brigade, Oliver P. Gooding

   Note 1. Dwight assumed command of the division July 12, 1863.
   Note 2. Fearing appears to have commanded Third Division from June 15 to July 6, 1863.
   Note 3. Third Brigade was ordered to Baton Rouge July 11, 1863.

First Brigade and Third Brigade of First Division were consolidated, and Weitzel's brigade resumed its original designation of Reserve Brigade. A new Second Brigade was organized from Gooding's brigade of Third Division. When two weeks later Weitzel's brigade was returned to First Division, it

was redesignated as Third Brigade, First Division. William B. Franklin, who had just arrived from the North, was assigned command of First Division. Emory was to retain command of Third Division, and Grover of Fourth Division.

In August 1863, Thirteenth Corps was sent down from Vicksburg to the Department of the Gulf, and Banks' command in the department then consisted of two corps. In addition, the organization of the Corps d'Afrique was nearing completion, and it thus became necessary to assign a new commander to Nineteenth Corps. Franklin was assigned on August 15, and he assumed command of the corps at Baton Rouge on August 20. Weitzel then assumed command of First Division. Weitzel's division, except for his old brigade, then commanded by Merritt, took post at Baton Rouge, where Emory's division, successively commanded by Nickerson and James W. McMillan, was also encamped.

Grover's division was assigned to the Defenses of New Orleans, but Birge's brigade occupied the La Fourche district, with headquarters at Thibodeaux, and Cahill's brigade served as the Garrison of New Orleans.

On August 15, 1863, orders were issued for the reorganization of Nineteenth Corps as follows:

NINETEENTH CORPS, William B. Franklin

First Division, Godfrey Weitzel
   First Brigade, Nathan A. M. Dudley
   Second Brigade, Oliver P. Gooding

Third Division
   First Brigade, Frank S. Nickerson
   Second Brigade, James W. McMillan

Fourth Division
   First Brigade, Henry W. Birge
   Second Brigade, Thomas W. Cahill

At the end of August 1863, when the above reorganization was completed, Nineteenth Corps was organized as follows:

NINETEENTH CORPS, William B. Franklin

First Division, Godfrey Weitzel
   First Brigade, George M. Love
   Second Brigade, James Smith

Third Brigade (or Reserve Brigade), Robert B. Merritt
Artillery, Edmund C. Bainbridge
   1st Battery, Maine Light Artillery, Albert W. Bradbury
   18th Battery, New York Light Artillery, George G. Curtiss
   Battery A, 1st United States Artillery, Edmund C. Bainbridge

Note 1. July 15, 1863, Augur went north on sick leave, and Weitzel assumed command of First Division. On August 15, Weitzel was assigned to the temporary command of the reorganized First Division, but Jacob Sharpe was reported in command as late as August 20, and Weitzel was not reported in command during the rest of the month.

Note 2. First Brigade was organized from regiments of First Brigade and Third Brigade, First Division.

Note 3. Second Brigade was organized from Third Brigade, Third Division. The former Second Brigade was designated by its former title of Reserve Brigade, and it was attached to the Defenses of New Orleans, District of La Fourche.

Note 4. First Brigade and Second Brigade were at Baton Rouge, and Third Brigade was at Thibodeaux (present-day Thibodaux).

Third Division, James W. McMillan
   First (Nickerson's) Brigade, Thomas W. Porter
   Second (McMillan's) Brigade, Alpha B. Farr
   Artillery
      4th Battery, Massachusetts Light Artillery, George G. Trull
      Battery F, 1st United States Artillery, Hardman P. Norris
      1st Battery, Vermont Light Artillery, Edward Rice

Note 1. Third Division was designated as Emory's Division, but Nickerson was assigned temporary command. McMillan assumed command August 29, 1863 and was relieved by William H. Emory on September 4.

Note 2. The troops of Third Division were at and about Baton Rouge.

Note 3. Porter was in temporary command of First Brigade while Nickerson was absent on detached service.

Fourth Division, Edward G. Beckwith
   First Brigade, Henry W. Birge
   Second Brigade, Thomas W. Cahill
   Artillery
      25th Battery, New York Light Artillery, John A. Grow
      26th Battery, New York Light Artillery, George W. Fox
      Battery C, 2nd United States Artillery, Theodore Bradley

Note 1. Fourth Division was designated as Grover's Division, with William H. Emory assigned temporary command. Grover was on leave of absence July 30–October 2, 1863, and when he reported for duty at the end of his leave, he was detached from Fourth Division and assigned command of Third Division.

Note 2. Fourth Division was transferred to the Defenses of New Orleans in August 1863.

Note 3. First Brigade was formerly Third Brigade, Fourth Division, and its troops were at Brashear, at Thibodeaux, and along the New Orleans, Opelousas, and Great Western Railroad.

Note 4. Second Brigade was formerly Second Brigade, Fourth Division, and it was at New Orleans.

Note 5. Third Brigade was discontinued August 15, 1863 by a change of designation to First Brigade.

Cavalry

Note. The cavalry of the corps consisted of ten companies of the 3rd Massachusetts Cavalry at Port Hudson, four companies of the 1st Texas Cavalry at New Orleans, and ten companies of the 4th Wisconsin Cavalry at Baton Rouge.

Reserve Artillery
   2nd Battery, Massachusetts Light Artillery, Ormand F. Nims
   6th Battery, Massachusetts Light Artillery, William W. Carruth
   Battery L, 1st United States Artillery, Franck E. Taylor

Expedition to Sabine Pass, Texas, September 4–11, 1863. In August 1863, William B. Franklin, commander of Nineteenth Corps, began organizing an expedition, which he was to lead into Texas. He was to proceed by sea to Sabine Pass, Texas, and then advance by land toward Houston and Galveston. Franklin's infantry force consisted of George M. Love's First Brigade and Robert B. Merritt's Third Brigade (or Reserve Brigade) of Godfrey Weitzel's First Division, and William H. Emory's Third Division of Nineteenth Corps; and William P. Benton's First Division and Francis J. Herron's Second Division of Thirteenth Corps. The expedition arrived at the Sabine River on the morning of September 8, but on attempting to move up the river, the gunboats ran into trouble. Franklin called off the attempt, and, without landing, his troops returned to New Orleans. For additional information, see Department of the Gulf, Operations in the Department of the Gulf, Sabine Pass, Texas Expedition.

Operation in the Bayou Teche Country, Louisiana, October 3, 1863–November 30, 1863. During October and November 1863, troops of Nineteenth Corps took part in an expedition along the Bayou Teche in another attempt to reach Texas. This expedition was led by William B. Franklin, commander of Nineteenth Corps, and his command consisted of Edward O. C. Ord's Thirteenth Corps, Department of the Gulf and two divisions of Nineteenth Corps. The organization of the troops of Nineteenth Corps that accompanied the expedition was as follows:

First Division, Godfrey Weitzel
    First Brigade, George M. Love
    Third Brigade, Robert B. Meritt

Third Division, Cuvier Grover
    First Brigade, Lewis Benedict
    Second Brigade, James W. McMillan

Franklin's column started from New Iberia and Berwick Bay October 3, 1863 and marched by the Bayou Teche to Opelousas, where it arrived on October 21. Banks then decided to go no farther, and Franklin returned with his command to New Iberia. For additional information, see Department of the Gulf, Operations in the Department of the Gulf, Texas Expeditions, Operations in the Teche Country, Louisiana.

At the end of December 1863, Nineteenth Corps was, with some exceptions, at and near New Iberia and was organized as follows:

NINETEENTH CORPS, William B. Franklin

First Division, William H. Emory
    First Brigade, George M. Love
    Second Brigade, Jacob Sharpe
    Third Brigade, Robert B. Merritt
    Artillery
        1st Battery, Maine Light Artillery, Albert W. Bradbury
        6th Battery, Massachusetts Light Artillery, Edward K. Russell

Note 1. Emory returned to the army from sick leave and relieved Weitzel in command of First Division December 13, 1863. Weitzel did not return to the Department of the Gulf, and the following spring he was assigned to the Army of the James.

Note 2. Sharpe assumed command of Second Brigade, which was at Baton Rouge, in November 1863.

Third Division, Cuvier Grover
    First Brigade, Lewis Benedict
    Second Brigade, James W. McMillan
    Artillery
        4th Battery, Massachusetts Light Artillery, George W. Taylor

Fourth Division, Edward G. Beckwith
    First Brigade, Henry W. Birge
    Second Brigade, Thomas W. Cahill
    Artillery Reserve, Henry W. Closson
        25th Battery, New York Light Artillery, John A. Grow
        Battery L, 1st United States Artillery, James A. Sanderson

Note 1. First Brigade was in the District of La Fourche, and Second Brigade was in the Defenses of New Orleans.
Note 2. The 25th Infantry, Corps d'Afrique was unattached in Fourth Division and was at New Iberia.

Reorganization of February 15, 1864. Nineteenth Corps was again reorganized by an order dated February 15, 1864, which was to take effect February 20. By this order First Division, Third Division, and Fourth Division were broken up and formed into two new divisions: a First Division to be commanded by William H. Emory, and a Second Division to be commanded by Cuvier Grover. New Orleans was selected as Headquarters, Nineteenth Corps on February 17, and the next day the organization of the brigades and their commanders was announced. In First Division, William Dwight was assigned command of First Brigade, James W. McMillan of Second Brigade, and the senior colonel of Third Brigade (Lewis Benedict) was to command that brigade. In Second Division, Frank S. Nickerson was assigned command of First Brigade, Henry W. Birge of Second Brigade, and Jacob Sharpe of Third Brigade.

The order of February 15, 1864 also included the organization of a new Third Division under the command of Joseph J. Reynolds. First Brigade was to be organized under Daniel P. Woodbury in the District of Key West and Tortugas; Second Brigade under Alexander Asboth in the District of West Florida; and Third Brigade under the senior colonel of the troops in the Defenses of New Orleans and the District of Baton Rouge. The reorganization of the new Third Division was not put into effect, however, and for all practical purposes, Third Division was discontinued February 15, 1864.

Red River, Louisiana Campaign, March 10, 1864–May 22, 1864. On March 15, 1864, Banks began his final effort to reach Texas by advancing up the Bayou Teche toward Alexandria, Louisiana at the beginning of his Red River Campaign. His army consisted of Emory's First Division and Grover's Second Division, the only divisions of Nineteenth Corps; Robert A. Cameron's Third Division and William J. Landram's Fourth Division of Thirteenth Corps; and Albert L. Lee's Cavalry Division, Department of the Gulf. Banks was joined at Alexandria by Andrew J. Smith's Detachment Army of the Tennessee and David D. Porter's fleet from the Mississippi.

Emory's division was the only division of Nineteenth Corps to accompany Banks' army when it marched up the Red River from Alexandria. Grover's division was left to occupy Alexandria, and the troops of Third Division, which was not yet organized, remained in the Defenses of New Orleans. Emory's division was engaged at Sabine Cross Roads and at Pleasant Hill, and retreated with Banks' army to Alexandria, where it arrived at the end of April 1864. There on May 2, Emory succeeded Franklin in command of Nineteenth Corps.

After remaining at Alexandria for a time, Nineteenth Corps and Detachment Thirteenth Corps moved on toward Morganza. During the march, on May 20, 1864, Emory assumed command of the combined forces and led them to Morganza, where they arrived May 22.

For details of the organization and operations of Nineteenth Corps during the Red River Campaign, see Red River, Louisiana Campaign.

Headquarters of Nineteenth Corps was established at Morganza May 23, 1864. and that day a new order was issued for the organization of Third Division. The division was to consist of two brigades, and these were to be formed from regiments sent to Morganza. This order was suspended June 11, and the regiments that had arrived at Morganza to form this division were ordered to report to Second Division.

Joseph J. Reynolds was assigned command of the

forces assembled at Morganza June 16, 1864, and he assumed command June 22.

Reorganization of June 27, 1864. On June 27, 1864, Nineteenth Corps was reorganized while at Morganza to consist of three divisions. The new Third Division was organized from troops of Thirteenth Corps. The organization of Nineteenth Corps at the end of June 1864 was as follows:

NINETEENTH CORPS, William H. Emory

First Division, Benjamin S. Roberts
    First Brigade, George L. Beal
    Second Brigade, James W. McMillan
    Third Brigade, Leonard D. H. Currie
    Artillery
        1st Battery, Delaware Light Artillery, Benjamin Nields

Note. Roberts assumed command of First Division June 18, 1864.

Second Division, Cuvier Grover
    First Brigade, Henry W. Birge
    Second Brigade, Edward L. Molineux
    Third Brigade, Jacob Sharpe
    Artillery, George W. Fox
        7th Battery, Massachusetts Light Artillery, Newman W. Storer
        26th Battery, New York Light Artillery, George W. Fox
        Battery C, 2nd United States Artillery, John I. Rodgers

Note 1. Birge was assigned command of First Brigade June 20, 1864.
Note 2. George F. McGinnis was assigned command of Second Division June 18, 1864, but he was unable to assume command because of ill health.
Note 3. On June 30, 1864, Alpha B. Farr was in command of First Brigade, and Robert B. Merritt was in command of Second Brigade.

Third Division, Michael K. Lawler
    First Brigade, Albert L. Lee
    Second Brigade, Robert A. Cameron
    Third Brigade, Frederick W. Moore

Note 1. Lee was assigned command of First Brigade and Cameron of Second Brigade June 18, 1864.
Note 2. Third Division was reorganized June 27, 1864 from troops of First Division and Fourth Division of Thirteenth Corps. First Brigade and Second Brigade were organized from First Division, and Third Brigade was organized from Fourth Division, Thirteenth Corps, which was serving in the District of Baton Rouge. Third Brigade, Third Division was carried on the rolls of the

District of Baton Rouge as Fourth Division, Thirteenth Corps.

Note 3. On June 30, 1864, Thomas W. Bennett was listed as the commander of Second Brigade, and David P. Grier as commander of Third Brigade.

Artillery Reserve, Henry W. Closson
   Company A, 1st Indiana Heavy Artillery, Abram W. Simmons

Note. Closson was chief of the corps artillery.

Shortly after the reorganization of Nineteenth Corps, First Division and Second Division were sent downriver to New Orleans, where they embarked during the first week in July 1864 and sailed for Virginia to reinforce the Union troops fighting in the East. These two divisions were under the command of William H. Emory. The leading troops arrived at Fort Monroe during Jubal A. Early's Washington Raid, and they were promptly sent to join the forces defending Washington. Emory's command was designated as Detachment Nineteenth Corps, and it later served with Philip H. Sheridan's Army of the Shenandoah. On November 7, 1864, Nineteenth Corps, Department of the Gulf was discontinued, and on that date the designation of Detachment Nineteenth Corps was officially changed to Nineteenth Corps. For details of the organization of Detachment Nineteenth Corps and Nineteenth Corps while with the armies in the East, see Volume I.

Joseph J. Reynolds was assigned command of Nineteenth Corps July 7, 1864, with headquarters to be established in New Orleans. Michael K. Lawler assumed command of all troops at Morganza, and Banks remained in command of the Department of the Gulf.

Reorganization of August 18, 1864. July 30, 1864, the troops in the Department of the Gulf were reinforced by the arrival at Morganza of Elias S. Dennis' First Division, Seventeenth Corps from Vicksburg. Nineteenth Corps was then reorganized on August 18, when First Division, Seventeenth Corps was redesignated as Second Division, Nineteenth Corps. At the end of August 1864, Nineteenth Corps was organized as follows:

NINETEENTH CORPS, Joseph J. Reynolds

Second Division, Elias S. Dennis

First Brigade, Benjamin Dornblaser
Second Brigade, James R. Slack
Artillery
   7th Battery (G), Massachusetts Light Artillery, Newman W. Storer
   26th Battery, New York Light Artillery, George W. Fox

Note 1. Second Division was formerly First Division, Seventeenth Corps.

Note 2. Joshua J. Guppey's Third Brigade, Second Division was with Gordon Granger's forces at Mobile Bay, Alabama.

Third Division, George F. McGinnis
   First Brigade, Lionel A. Sheldon
   Second Brigade, William T. Spicely
   Third Brigade, Frederick W. Moore
   Artillery
      1st Battery, Delaware Light Artillery, Charles G. Rumford

Unattached Artillery
   2nd Battery, Connecticut Light Artillery, Walter S. Hotchkiss
   2nd Battery (B), Massachusetts Light Artillery, William Marland
   17th Battery, Ohio Light Artillery, Charles S. Rice

Note. Rice's Ohio battery was at Mobile Bay, Alabama.

Cavalry Brigade, John M. Crebs

Reserve Artillery, Benjamin Nields
   1st Battery, Indiana Light Artillery, John W. Gerhardt
   Company A, 1st Indiana Heavy Artillery, Abram W. Simmons
   Company G, 1st Indiana Heavy Artillery, Benjamin S. Harrower
   15th Battery, Massachusetts Light Artillery, Timothy Pearson
   21st Battery, New York Light Artillery, James Barnes

Engineer Brigade, Peter C. Hains

Note. The Engineer Brigade consisted of four regiments of United States Colored Troops, two of which were at Mobile Bay, Alabama, one company of Kentucky Engineers and Mechanics, and the 1st Company of Pontoniers.

On August 29, 1864, Sterling Price assumed command of a Confederate force at Princeton, Arkansas. He then moved toward Little Rock, crossed the state, and entered Missouri on September 19.

When Edward R. S. Canby, commander of the Military Division of West Mississippi, learned of Price's advance in Arkansas, he immediately ordered reinforcements to report to Frederick Steele, commander of the Department of Arkansas. Elias S. Dennis' Second Division, Nineteenth Corps began embarkation at Morganza on the morning of September 3 for the trip upriver to the mouth of White River, where it was to report to Steele and go into camp. Third Brigade, Third Division, Nineteenth Corps also moved to the mouth of the White River, and on November 6, George F. McGinnis, commander of Third Division, Nineteenth Corps, was ordered to join Third Brigade at the mouth of the White River.

By an order of November 7, 1864, Nineteenth Corps was discontinued as an army corps in the Department of the Gulf. On November 25, the Reserve Corps, Military Division of West Mississippi was created to consist of troops that formerly belonged to Nineteenth Corps and which were within the limits of the Military Division of West Mississippi. For further information, see Reserve Corps, Military Division of West Mississippi.

COMMANDERS OF NINETEENTH CORPS, DEPARTMENT OF THE GULF

Nathaniel P. Banks	January 16, 1862 to August 20, 1863
William B. Franklin	August 20, 1863 to May 2, 1864
William H. Emory	May 2, 1864 to July 2, 1864
Benjamin S. Roberts	July 2, 1864 to July 5, 1864, on leave
Michael K. Lawler	July 5, 1864 to July 7, 1864
Joseph J. Reynolds	July 7, 1864 to November 7, 1864

TWENTIETH CORPS, ARMY OF THE CUMBERLAND JANUARY 9, 1863– SEPTEMBER 28, 1863

The Department of the Cumberland was re-created October 24, 1862, and William S. Rosecrans was assigned command. On the same date, the troops within the limits of the department were designated as Fourteenth Corps, but they were commonly called thereafter the Army of the Cumberland. Rosecrans assumed command of the Department of the Cumberland and of Fourteenth Corps October 30, 1862, and he then reorganized Fourteenth Corps to consist of three smaller units as follows: a Right Wing, commanded by Alexander McD. McCook; a Center, commanded by George H. Thomas; and a Left Wing, commanded by Thomas L. Crittenden. This was the organization of Rosecrans' army that fought at the Battle of Stones River (or Murfreesboro), Tennessee December 31, 1862–January 3, 1863. For additional information, see Stones River (or Murfreesboro), Tennessee Campaign.

On January 9, 1863, while at Murfreesboro, the Army of the Cumberland was reorganized to consist of three corps, which were formed from the two wings and the Center of the army. In this reorganization, the designation of the Right Wing was changed to Twentieth Corps, the Center to Fourteenth Corps, and the Left Wing to Twenty-First Corps. The organization of the new Twentieth Corps was the same as that of the Right Wing of the former Fourteenth Corps that fought at the Battle of Stones River. Alexander McD. McCook was assigned command.

On January 9, 1863, the organization of Twentieth Corps was as follows:

TWENTIETH CORPS, Alexander McD. McCook

First Division, Jefferson C. Davis
First Brigade, P. Sidney Post
Second Brigade, William P. Carlin
Third Brigade, William E. Woodruff

Note. Charles B. Humphrey's 5th Battery, Wisconsin Light Artillery was attached to First Brigade; William A. Hotchkiss' 2nd Battery, Minnesota Light Artillery was attached to Second Brigade; and Henry E. Stiles' 8th Battery, Wisconsin Light Artillery was attached to Third Brigade.

Second Division, Richard W. Johnson
First Brigade, William H. Gibson
Second Brigade, Joseph B. Dodge
Third Brigade, Philemon P. Baldwin

Note. Edmund B. Belding's Battery A, 1st Ohio Light

Artillery was attached to First Brigade; Warren P. Edgarton's Battery E, 1st Ohio Light Artillery was attached to Second Brigade; and Peter Simonson's 5th Battery, Indiana Light Artillery was attached to Third Brigade.

Third Division, Philip H. Sheridan
 First Brigade, Nicholas Greusel
 Second Brigade, Bernard Laiboldt
 Third Brigade, Luther P. Bradley

Note. Asahel K. Bush's 4th Battery, Indiana Light Artillery was attached to First Brigade; Henry Hescock's Battery G, 1st Missouri Light Artillery was attached to Second Brigade; and Charles Houghtaling's Battery C, 1st Illinois Light Artillery was attached to Third Brigade.

There was no significant change in the organization of Twentieth Corps until it was discontinued October 9, 1863. McCook remained in command of the corps during this period of its existence, but Richard W. Johnson assumed temporary command January 19, 1863 during the absence of McCook.

After the Battle of Stones River, the Army of the Cumberland occupied Murfreesboro and remained in the vicinity until June 1863. During this time there were many scouts, reconnaissances, and minor actions, but there were no major operations.

Late in June 1863, Twentieth Corps moved forward at the beginning of Rosecrans' Middle Tennessee (or Tullahoma) Campaign. On June 24, Twentieth Corps, under McCook, advanced from Murfreesboro to Liberty Gap. Johnson's Second Division occupied the Gap, and Philip H. Sheridan's Third Division and P. Sidney Post's First Brigade of Jefferson C. Davis' First Division halted for the night at Millersburg.

June 25, 1863, Johnson's division was engaged at Liberty Gap, and Post's First Brigade and William P. Carlin's Second Brigade of Davis' division moved up in support. Hans C. Heg's Third Brigade of Davis' division remained at Millersburg with the trains.

Post's and Carlin's brigades demonstrated at Liberty Gap June 26, 1863, while the rest of the corps moved to Hoover's Gap. On June 27, the corps was concentrated at Beech Grove, and it was then ordered to march to Manchester.

When Bragg learned that Rosecrans had occupied Manchester on the Confederate right flank, he abandoned his defensive lines and fell back to Tullahoma. Then, as the Army of the Cumberland advanced from Manchester toward Tullahoma, Bragg retired to Elk River June 30, 1863. Twentieth Corps then advanced and occupied Tullahoma. Early in July, Bragg withdrew from Middle Tennessee and fell back to Chattanooga. The army followed and occupied Shelbyville, Tullahoma, Manchester, and McMinnville, then halted to bring up supplies and wait for the roads to improve. In the early part of August, Jefferson C. Davis' First Division, Twentieth Corps was at Winchester, Richard W. Johnson's Second Division was at Tullahoma, and Philip H. Sheridan's Third Division was at Stevenson, Alabama.

The organization of Twentieth Corps during the Tullahoma Campaign was as follows:

TWENTIETH CORPS, Alexander McD. McCook

First Division, Jefferson C. Davis
 First Brigade, P. Sidney Post
 Second Brigade, William P. Carlin
 Third Brigade, Hans C. Heg
 Artillery
  2nd Battery, Minnesota Light Artillery, Albert Woodbury
  5th Battery, Wisconsin Light Artillery, George Q. Gardner
  8th Battery, Wisconsin Light Artillery, Henry E. Stiles

Second Division, Richard W. Johnson
 First Brigade, August Willich
 Second Brigade, Joseph B. Dodge
 Third Brigade, Philemon P. Baldwin
 Artillery, Peter Simonson
  5th Battery, Indiana Light Artillery, Alfred Morrison
  Battery A, 1st Ohio Light Artillery, Wilbur F. Goodspeed
  20th Battery, Ohio Light Artillery, Edward Grosskopff

Third Division, Philip H. Sheridan
 First Brigade, William H. Lytle
 Second Brigade, Bernard Laiboldt
 Third Brigade, Luther P. Bradley
 Artillery, Henry Hescock
  Battery C, 1st Illinois Light Artillery, Edward M. Wright
  11th Battery, Indiana Light Artillery, Arnold Sutermeister

Battery G, 1st Missouri Light Artillery, Henry Hescock

On August 16, 1863, Rosecrans' preparations were complete, and he began his long-delayed advance on Bragg's army at Chattanooga. At that time Sheridan's Third Division was at Stevenson, Alabama; Johnson's Second Division marched from Tullahoma to Caperton's Ferry; and Davis' First Division advanced from Winchester to a point near Stevenson. McCook's Twentieth Corps crossed the Tennessee River at Stevenson and Caperton's Ferry August 29–September 3, then moved over Sand Mountain and into Wills Valley. It then moved up the valley to Valley Head, crossed the mountain at Winston's Gap, and marched toward Alpine and Summerville, Georgia. Meantime, George H. Thomas' Fourteenth Corps had marched across Stevens' Gap into McLemore's Cove, and Crittenden's Twentieth Corps had occupied Chattanooga.

Rosecrans then discovered that Bragg was not retreating to the south as he had believed, and he immediately began the concentration of his army south of Chattanooga along Chickamauga Creek. McCook, by hard marching, was able to rejoin the other two corps of the army in time to take part in the Battle of Chickamauga September 19–20, 1863. During the battle of September 19, Twentieth Corps was on the right of the army along Chickamauga Creek near Crawfish Springs, but it was greatly reduced in strength when Johnson's and Davis' divisions were sent to the left to reinforce Thomas' Fourteenth Corps. When James Longstreet broke through the Union center on the second day of the battle, Davis' and Sheridan's divisions of Twentieth Corps (which were then between the Widow Glenn house and the Chattanooga La Fayette road) and Twenty-First Corps were cut off and driven from the field; they were reassembled at Chattanooga only after the battle. For details of the operations of Twentieth Corps during the Battle of Chickamauga, see Chickamauga, Georgia Campaign.

The organization of Twentieth Corps at the Battle of Chickamauga was as follows:

TWENTIETH CORPS, Alexander McD. McCook

First Division, Jefferson C. Davis
  First Brigade, P. Sidney Post

Second Brigade, William P. Carlin
Third Brigade, Hans C. Heg, to September 19, 1863, killed
  John A. Martin

Note 1. George Q. Gardner's 5th Battery, Wisconsin Light Artillery was attached to First Brigade; Albert Woodbury's 2nd Battery, Minnesota Light Artillery was attached to Second Brigade; and John D. McLean's 8th Battery, Wisconsin Light Artillery was attached to Third Brigade. Woodbury was wounded September 19, 1863, and was succeeded in command of the battery by Richard L. Dawley. William A. Hotchkiss was the division chief of artillery.

Note 2. First Brigade was guarding the trains and was not engaged.

Second Division, Richard W. Johnson
  First Brigade, August Willich
  Second Brigade, Joseph B. Dodge
  Third Brigade, Philemon P. Baldwin, to September 19, 1863, killed
  William W. Berry

Note. Wilbur F. Goodspeed's Battery A, 1st Ohio Light Artillery was attached to First Brigade; Edward Grosskopff's 20th Battery, Ohio Light Artillery was attached to Second Brigade; and Peter Simonson's 5th Battery, Indiana Light Artillery was attached to Third Brigade.

Third Division, Philip H. Sheridan
  First Brigade, William H. Lytle, to September 20, 1863, killed
  Silas Miller
  Second Brigade, Bernard Laiboldt
  Third Brigade, Luther P. Bradley, to September 19, 1863, wounded
  Nathan H. Walworth

Note. Arnold Sutermeister's 11th Battery, Indiana Light Artillery was attached to First Brigade; Gustavus Schueler's Battery G, 1st Missouri Light Artillery was attached to Second Brigade; and Mark H. Prescott's Battery C, 1st Illinois Light Artillery was attached to Third Brigade. Henry Hescock was chief of the division artillery.

By a presidential order of September 28, 1863, while the Army of the Cumberland was at Chattanooga, Twentieth Corps and Twenty-First Corps were discontinued by consolidation to form a new Fourth Corps, Army of the Cumberland under Gordon Granger. When the Army of the Cumberland was reorganized October 9, 1863, the organization of Fourth Corps was announced. McCook and

Crittenden were left without command. For details of the reorganization, see Fourth Corps, Army of the Cumberland.

TWENTIETH CORPS, ARMY OF THE CUMBERLAND APRIL 14, 1864– NOVEMBER 14, 1864

By a presidential order of April 4, 1864, Twentieth Corps, Army of the Cumberland was re-created by the consolidation of Eleventh Corps and Twelfth Corps of the Army of the Cumberland, and Joseph Hooker was assigned command. On the same day, the War Department issued an order designating the new corps as First Corps, but on April 6 Ulysses S. Grant directed that the designation be changed to Twentieth Corps, and Henry W. Halleck transmitted Grant's order the same day.

On April 14, 1864, the organization of Twentieth Corps was announced as follows:

A First Division under Alpheus S. Williams was to be formed by the consolidation of First Division, Twelfth Corps; First Brigade, Third Division, Eleventh Corps; and the 45th New York Infantry.

A Second Division under John W. Geary was to be formed by the consolidation of Second Division, Twelfth Corps; First Brigade, Second Division, Eleventh Corps; and the 119th New York Infantry.

A Third Division under Daniel Butterfield was to be formed by the consolidation of First Division, Eleventh Corps; Second Brigade, Second Division, Eleventh Corps; and the 26th Wisconsin Infantry.

A Fourth Division was also formed under Lovell H. Rousseau, but this was largely an administrative arrangement, and the division was detached on post and garrison duty and never joined the corps in the field.

The brigade and division commanders of the old Twelfth Corps retained their commands.

The announced organization of the new Twentieth Corps at the end of April 1864 was as follows:

TWENTIETH CORPS, Joseph Hooker

First Division, Alpheus S. Williams
First Brigade, Joseph F. Knipe
Second Brigade, Thomas H. Ruger
Third Brigade, James S. Robinson, to April 13, 1864
Hector Tyndale
Artillery, John D. Woodbury
Battery I, 1st New York Light Artillery, Christian Stock
Battery M, 1st New York Light Artillery, John D. Woodbury

Second Division, John W. Geary
First Brigade, Charles Candy
Second Brigade, Adolphus Buschbeck
Third Brigade, David Ireland
Artillery, William Wheeler
13th Battery, New York Light Artillery, William Wheeler
Battery E, Pennsylvania Light Artillery, James D. McGill

Third Division, Daniel Butterfield
First Brigade, William T. Ward
Second Brigade, Samuel Ross
Third Brigade, James Wood, Jr.
Artillery, Marco B. Gary
Battery I, 1st Michigan Light Artillery, Luther R. Smith
Battery C, 1st Ohio Light Artillery, Marco B. Gary

The organization of Fourth Division was not complete, but the 73rd Indiana, 18th Michigan, 102nd Ohio, 10th Tennessee, and 13th Wisconsin regiments of the post of Nashville, District of Nashville, Department of the Cumberland constituted the First Brigade, which was under the command of Robert S. Granger. The artillery and unassigned infantry were at the posts of Bridgeport, Alabama, Clarksville, Tennessee, Fort Donelson, Tennessee, and Gallatin, Tennessee, all in the District of Nashville.

Headquarters of the corps was in Lookout Valley, and the troops were distributed as follows:

Headquarters of Alpheus S. Williams' First Division was at Tullahoma, Tennessee, and the troops were on the Nashville and Chattanooga Railroad from Wartrace to Stevenson, Alabama.

The troops of John W. Geary's Second Division were at Bridgeport, Stevenson, Shellmound, and in Lookout Valley.

The troops of Daniel Butterfield's Third Division were in Lookout Valley.

The headquarters of Lovell H. Rousseau's Fourth Division was at Nashville, Tennessee, and the regiments were at Whiteside, Murfreesboro, Shellmound, Gallatin, Fort Donelson, and Clarksville.

On May 4, 1864, Twentieth Corps moved forward with the Army of the Cumberland at the beginning of William T. Sherman's campaign against Atlanta, Georgia, and it was engaged at the battles of Rocky Face Ridge, Resaca, Dallas (New Hope Church), Kennesaw Mountain, and Peach Tree Creek. For details of the operations of Twentieth Corps during the period May 3–September 8, 1864, see Atlanta, Georgia Campaign. The organization of Twentieth Corps during this period was as follows:

TWENTIETH CORPS, Joseph Hooker, to July 28, 1864
    Alpheus S. Williams, to August 27, 1864
    Henry W. Slocum

First Division, Alpheus S. Williams
    Joseph F. Knipe
    Alpheus S. Williams
    First Brigade, Joseph F. Knipe, to July 3, 1864
        Warren W. Packer, to July 17, 1864
        Joseph F. Knipe
    Second Brigade, Thomas H. Ruger
    Third Brigade, James S. Robinson
        Horace Boughton
    Artillery, John D. Woodbury
        Battery I, 1st New York Light Artillery, Charles E. Winegar
        Battery M, 1st New York Light Artillery, John D. Woodbury

Second Division, John W. Geary
    First Brigade, Charles Candy, to August 4, 1864
        Ario Pardee, Jr.
    Second Brigade, Adolphus Buschbeck, to May 22, 1864

        John T. Lockman, to June 7, 1864
        Patrick H. Jones, to August 8, 1864
        George W. Mindil
    Third Brigade, David Ireland, to May 15, 1864, wounded
        William Rickards, Jr., to May 16, 1864
        George A. Cobham, Jr., to July 20, 1864, killed
        David Ireland
    Artillery, William Wheeler, to June 22, 1864, killed
        Charles C. Aleshire
        13th Battery, New York Light Artillery, William Wheeler
        Henry Bundy
        Battery E, Pennsylvania Light Artillery, James D. McGill, to July 8, 1864
        Thomas S. Sloan

Third Division, Daniel Butterfield, to June 29, 1864
    William T. Ward
    First Brigade, William T. Ward, to May 15, 1864, wounded
        Benjamin Harrison
        William T. Ward
        Benjamin Harrison
    Second Brigade, Samuel Ross, to May 9, 1864
        John Coburn
    Third Brigade, James Wood, Jr.
    Artillery, Marco B. Gary
        Battery I, 1st Michigan Light Artillery, Luther R. Smith
        Battery C, 1st Ohio Light Artillery, Jerome B. Stephens

Artillery Brigade, John A. Reynolds
    Battery I, 1st Michigan Light Artillery, Luther R. Smith
    Battery I, 1st New York Light Artillery, Charles E. Winegar
    Battery M, 1st New York Light Artillery, John D. Woodbury
    13th Battery, New York Light Artillery, Henry Bundy
    Battery C, 1st Ohio Light Artillery, Jerome B. Stephens, to August 1, 1864
        Marco B. Gary
    Battery E, Pennsylvania Light Artillery, Thomas S. Sloan
    Battery K, 5th United States Artillery, Edmund C. Bainbridge

Note 1. The Artillery Brigade of the corps was organized July 27, 1864.

Note 2. Battery K, 5th United States Artillery joined the corps August 25, 1864.

For details of the operations of Twentieth Corps during the Atlanta Campaign, see Atlanta, Georgia Campaign.

Fourth Division, Twentieth Corps did not accompany the corps on the Atlanta Campaign, but remained in the District of Nashville, Department of the Cumberland. On May 8, 1864, Fourth Division was detached from Twentieth Corps, and thereafter it reported directly to Headquarters, Department of the Cumberland. At that time the troops of Fourth Division, Twentieth Corps in the District of Nashville consisted of the following:

District of Nashville, Lovell H. Rousseau
First Brigade, Fourth Division, Robert S. Granger
Unassigned troops of Fourth Division

Note. The unassigned troops of Fourth Division were at Murfreesboro, Duck River Bridge, McMinnville, Clarksville, Fort Donelson, and Elk River Bridge in Tennessee, and at Bridgeport, Alabama.

On May 30, 1864, the District of Nashville was merged into the District of Tennessee, Department of the Cumberland.

For additional information about Fourth Division, Twentieth Corps, see Department of the Cumberland, October 24, 1862–June 27, 1865, Districts in the Department of the Cumberland, District of Nashville and District of Tennessee.

After the capture of Atlanta by Sherman's army in September 1864, John B. Hood withdrew with his Confederate Army of Tennessee to Lovejoy's Station; he remained there until near the end of the month. He then moved northward along the Western and Atlantic Railroad to destroy Sherman's communications with the North, and also to threaten the invasion of Tennessee. Sherman left Twentieth Corps to occupy Atlanta, and with the rest of the army followed Hood.

The organization of Twentieth Corps, Army of the Cumberland at the end of September 1864 was as follows:

TWENTIETH CORPS, Henry W. Slocum

First Division, Alpheus S. Williams
First Brigade, Warren W. Packer
Second Brigade, Ezra A. Carman
Third Brigade, James S. Robinson

Second Division, John W. Geary
First Brigade, John Flynn
Second Brigade, Patrick H. Jones
Third Brigade, Henry A. Barnum

Third Division, Daniel Dustin
First Brigade, Franklin C. Smith
Second Brigade, Edward Bloodgood
Third Brigade, Philo B. Buckingham

Artillery Brigade, John A. Reynolds
Battery I, 1st Michigan Light Artillery, Henry J. Sawdy
Battery I, 1st New York Light Artillery, Charles E. Winegar
Battery M, 1st New York Light Artillery, David L. Smith
Battery C, 1st Ohio Light Artillery, Jerome B. Stephens
Battery E, Pennsylvania Light Artillery, Thomas S. Sloan
Battery K, 5th United States Artillery, Edmund C. Bainbridge

Hood marched northward as far as Dalton, Georgia, then turned to the west and continued on into northern Alabama. Sherman followed as far as Gaylesville, Alabama and halted there to await Hood's further movements. When Hood moved on to Decatur and Florence, Alabama, he sent the Fourth Corps and Twenty-Third Corps to reinforce George H. Thomas, who was then in command of the Union forces in Tennessee, and at the end of October 1864 moved back toward Atlanta and began preparations for a march through Georgia to Savannah. At that time he had under his immediate control only Fourteenth Corps and Twentieth Corps of the Army of the Cumberland and Fifteenth Corps and Seventeenth Corps of the Army of the Tennessee.

By an order of November 9, 1864, Sherman divided his army into two wings for his march through Georgia. The two corps of the Army of the Cumberland, the Fourteenth Corps and the Twentieth Corps, were assigned to the Left Wing, which was commanded by Henry W. Slocum, and the Fifteenth Corps and Seventeenth Corps of the Army of the Tennessee were assigned to the Right Wing, under Oliver O. Howard. Slocum's Left Wing was unofficially called the Army of Georgia.

On November 15, 1864, Sherman's army left Atlanta on its march toward Savannah, and Twentieth Corps was no longer reported in the Department of the Cumberland. Instead it was carried on the rolls of the Military Division of the Mississippi. At that time Twentieth Corps was organized as follows:

TWENTIETH CORPS, Alpheus S. Williams

First Division, Nathaniel J. Jackson
    First Brigade, James L. Selfridge
    Second Brigade, Ezra A. Carman
    Third Brigade, James S. Robinson

Second Division, John W. Geary
    First Brigade, Ario Pardee, Jr.
    Second Brigade, Patrick H. Jones
    Third Brigade, Henry A. Barnum

Third Division, William T. Ward
    First Brigade, Franklin C. Smith
    Second Brigade, Daniel Dustin
    Third Brigade, Samuel Ross

    Artillery, John A. Reynolds
        Battery I, 1st New York Light Artillery, Charles E. Winegar
        Battery M, 1st New York Light Artillery, Edward P. Newkirk
        Battery C, 1st Ohio Light Artillery, Marco B. Gary, to December 12, 1864, captured
            Jerome B. Stephens
        Battery E, Pennsylvania Light Artillery, Thomas S. Sloan

For further information about the organization and operations of Twentieth Corps, see Twentieth Corps, Army of Georgia.

In November 1864, Fourth Division, Twentieth Corps, which was not with the army in the field, was organized as follows:

Fourth Division, Twentieth Corps, Lovell H. Rousseau
    First Brigade, William P. Lyon
    Second Brigade, Edwin C. Mason

On November 26, 1864, the garrison of Nashville, Tennessee was organized as Second Brigade, Fourth Division, Twentieth Corps. Second Brigade was commanded by John F. Miller during the Battle of Nashville December 15–16, 1864.

Fourth Division, Twentieth Corps was discontinued February 28, 1865, and the troops became a part of First Division, Department of the Cumberland. For additional information, see Department of the Cumberland, October 24, 1862–June 27, 1865.

TWENTIETH CORPS, ARMY OF GEORGIA NOVEMBER 14, 1864– JULY 28, 1865

On November 15, 1864, William T. Sherman's army left Atlanta on its march across Georgia toward Savannah. Alpheus S. Williams' Twentieth Corps marched with Henry W. Slocum's Left Wing (or Army of Georgia) by way of Stone Mountain and arrived at Madison November 18. From there it moved on to Milledgeville November 22, and two days later it joined Jefferson C. Davis' Fourteenth Corps, also of the Left Wing, at Sandersville. The corps then marched by different routes, assembled at Lewisville November 30, and reached Springfield December 7. Twentieth Corps then joined the rest of the army on a line of investment formed in front of Savannah. When Hardee evacuated Savannah on December 20, John W. Geary's Second Division, Twentieth Corps moved in and occupied the city the next day.

For additional information, see Savannah Campaign (Sherman's March through Georgia), in Volume I.

At Savannah, Sherman began preparations for continuing his march northward through the Carolinas to join Grant's forces in Virginia. As a part of Henry W. Slocum's Left Wing, or Army of Georgia, Alpheus S. Williams' Twentieth Corps began leaving Savannah in January 1865 and marching toward Augusta, Georgia. William T. Ward's Third Division crossed the Savannah River to Screven's Ferry on January 2 and moved out to Hardeeville and Purysburg in South Carolina on January 17. Nathaniel J. Jackson's First Division left Savannah on January 17. John W. Geary's Second Division was delayed in starting because of heavy rains and bad roads and did not leave Savannah until January 26. It then marched along the south side of the Savannah River to Sister's Ferry, where it crossed the river February 5.

Meantime, First Division and Third Division had advanced to Robertsville on January 29, and on February 2 they had moved on toward Blackville, South Carolina. Geary's division followed, and the three divisions of the corps were united at Blackville on February 9. From Blackville, Twentieth Corps advanced to Lexington, South Carolina and then, passing to the west of Columbia, marched through Winnsboro and Cheraw, South Carolina, arriving at Fayetteville, North Carolina on March 11.

On March 15, 1865, Williams, with Jackson's First Division and Ward's Third Division, left Fayetteville and marched northward along the Cape Fear River toward Averasboro. Geary's Second Division marched with the trains toward Goldsboro, North Carolina by roads to the right of those used by the rest of the corps. Jefferson C. Davis' Fourteenth Corps, also of Slocum's Left Wing, followed Williams toward Averasboro.

On March 16, 1865, Jackson's and Ward's divisions, with Judson Kilpatrick's cavalry division, were engaged a short distance south of Averasboro with Hardee's Confederate corps, and Fourteenth Corps was moved up in support. Fighting continued through the afternoon, but that night Hardee withdrew. For details of the Battle of Averasboro, see Carolinas Campaign, Fayetteville to Goldsboro, North Carolina, in Volume I.

The next day Twentieth Corps followed Fourteenth Corps toward Bentonville on the Goldsboro road. On March 19, 1865, Fourteenth Corps was strongly attacked just south of Bentonville by Joseph E. Johnston's entire army, and Twentieth Corps was quickly moved up in support. James S. Robinson's Third Brigade, First Division, Twentieth Corps was sent up in support of William P. Carlin's First Division, Fourteenth Corps, and William Cogswell's Third Brigade, Third Division, Twentieth Corps was sent to aid James D. Morgan's Second Division, Fourteenth Corps. Fighting together, Fourteenth Corps and Twentieth Corps repulsed the final enemy attacks that afternoon.

Geary's division came up in support of the other two divisions of Twentieth Corps on the morning of March 20, 1865, and the rest of Sherman's army arrived during the day. Both armies remained on the field near Bentonville. with active skirmishing through March 21, and that night Johnston retired with his army toward Smithfield, North Carolina. The next day Fourteenth Corps and Twentieth Corps moved on toward Goldsboro, where they arrived March 23. For details of the Battle of Bentonville, see Carolinas Campaign, Fayetteville to Goldsboro, North Carolina, in Volume I.

While at Goldsboro, on April 2, 1865, Joseph A. Mower, formerly commander of First Division, Seventeenth Corps, assumed command of Twentieth Corps, and Williams then relieved Jackson in command of First Division.

After resting and refitting at Goldsboro, Twentieth Corps advanced on April 10, 1865 with the rest of Sherman's army toward Smithfield, where Johnston's army was then encamped. Upon learning of Sherman's approach, however, Johnston retired toward Raleigh, North Carolina, and was closely followed by Sherman's marching columns. Twentieth Corps arrived at Raleigh on April 13 and then moved on, following Fourteenth Corps, toward Charlotte, North Carolina in an attempt to intercept Johnston's army, which was believed to be moving in that direction.

Twentieth Corps was on the road east of Martha's Vineyard April 15, 1865 when all troop movements were suspended while Sherman and Johnston met near Durham Station to discuss terms for ending hostilities. Johnston surrendered his army April 26, 1865, and thus ended the war in the East. For additional information about the operations of Twentieth Corps after leaving Goldsboro, see Carolinas Campaign, Goldsboro to Raleigh, North Carolina (Surrender of Joseph E. Johnston's Army), in Volume I.

The organization of Twentieth Corps during the Carolinas Campaign was as follows:

TWENTIETH CORPS, Alpheus S. Williams, to April 2, 1865
  Joseph A. Mower

First Division, Nathaniel J. Jackson, to April 2, 1865
  Alpheus S. Williams
  First Brigade, James L. Selfridge
  Second Brigade, William Hawley
  Third Brigade, James S. Robinson

Second Division, John W. Geary
  First Brigade, Ario Pardee, Jr., to March 30, 1865

George W. Mindil
Second Brigade, George W. Mindil, to March 30, 1865
Patrick H. Jones
Third Brigade, Henry A. Barnum

Third Division, William T. Ward
First Brigade, Henry Case, to April 19, 1865
Benjamin Harrison
Second Brigade, Daniel Dustin
Third Brigade, Samuel Ross, to January 16, 1865
William Cogswell
Artillery, John A. Reynolds, to April 1, 1865
Charles E. Winegar
Battery I, 1st New York Light Artillery, Charles E. Winegar
Warren L. Scott
Battery M, 1st New York Light Artillery, Edward P. Newkirk
Battery C, 1st Ohio Light Artillery, Jerome B. Stephens
Battery E, Pennsylvania Light Artillery, Thomas S. Sloan

Twentieth Corps remained near Jones' Cross Roads, North Carolina until April 28, 1865, then moved back to Raleigh, with orders to march to Washington, D.C. The corps left Raleigh on April 30, marching through Williamsboro on a road to the east of that used by Fourteenth Corps, and arriving at Taylor's Ferry on the Roanoke River on May 4. It then continued on, crossed the Meherrin River at Saffold's Bridge, and moved by the Lewiston road to the Boydton Plank Road, where it turned to the north. It arrived May 5 at Blacks and Whites (present-day Blackstone), on the South Side Railroad, west of Petersburg. From there it marched by way of Bevil's Bridge, Clover Hill, and Falling Creek, arriving at Manchester, opposite Richmond, Virginia, on May 8.

Twentieth Corps remained at Manchester until May 11, 1865, and it then marched through Richmond, Hanover Court House, Ashland, and Anderson's Bridge on the North Anna River, arriving at Spotsylvania Court House on May 14. It then passed Chancellorsville, crossed the Rapidan River at United States Ford, continued on by way of Brentsville and Fairfax Station, and arrived near Alexandria, Virginia on May 19. The corps marched in the Grand Review in Washington May 24, then went into camp near Bladensburg, Maryland.

On June 4, 1865, the western regiments serving with Twentieth Corps, which consisted of six Ohio regiments, two Wisconsin regiments, and one regiment each from Indiana and Illinois, were transferred to Jefferson C. Davis' Fourteenth Corps, where they were organized into a temporary division. For additional information, see Fourteenth Corps, Army of Georgia. The next day, June 5, 1865, twelve eastern regiments of Twentieth Corps were transferred to Christopher C. Augur's Department of Washington. The remaining regiments of the corps were mustered out by June 13.

The organization of Twentieth Corps, Army of Georgia during the period April 27–June 1865 was as follows:

TWENTIETH CORPS, Joseph A. Mower, to June 9, 1865, on leave

First Division, Alpheus S. Williams, to June 4, 1865
First Brigade, James L. Selfridge, to June 5, 1865
Second Brigade, William Hawley, to June 4, 1865
Third Brigade, James S. Robinson, to June 7, 1865

Second Division, John W. Geary, to June 14, 1865
First Brigade, George W. Mindil, to May 10, 1865
Ario Pardee, Jr., to June 6, 1865
Second Brigade, Patrick H. Jones, to June 11, 1865
Third Brigade, Henry A. Barnum, to June 12, 1865

Third Division, William T. Ward, to June 14, 1865, on leave
First Brigade, Benjamin Harrison, to June 8, 1865
Second Brigade, Daniel Dustin, to June 7, 1865
Third Brigade, William Cogswell, to June 14, 1865

By an order of July 28, 1865, Twentieth Corps was officially discontinued, to date from June 1, 1865.

TWENTY-FIRST CORPS, ARMY OF THE CUMBERLAND

When the Department of the Cumberland was re-created October 24, 1862 after the Battle of Perryville, Kentucky, the troops in the department were designated as Fourteenth Corps, Department of the Cumberland, but they were commonly called the

Army of the Cumberland. When William S. Rose-crans assumed command of the Department of the Cumberland on October 30, he reorganized Fourteenth Corps into three separate commands as follows:

Right Wing, Fourteenth Corps, Alexander McD. McCook
Center, Fourteenth Corps, George H. Thomas
Left Wing, Fourteenth Corps, Thomas L. Crittenden

For details of the organization of Fourteenth Corps (or Army of the Cumberland) during the period October 30, 1862–January 9, 1863, see Army of the Cumberland, October 24, 1862–November 14, 1864.

On January 9, 1863, after the Battle of Stones River, Rosecrans reorganized the Army of the Cumberland with the formation of three new corps from the two wings and the center of the former Fourteenth Corps. In this reorganization, the designation of the former Left Wing, Fourteenth Corps was changed to Twenty-First Corps, Army of the Cumberland, and Thomas L. Crittenden was assigned command.

The organization of Twenty-First Corps at the time of its formation was as follows:

TWENTY-FIRST CORPS, Thomas L. Crittenden

First Division, Milo S. Hascall
    First Brigade, George P. Buell
    Second Brigade, George D. Wagner
    Third Brigade, Charles G. Harker
    Artillery, Seymour Race
        8th Battery, Indiana Light Artillery, George Estep
        10th Battery, Indiana Light Artillery, Jerome B. Cox
        6th Battery, Ohio Light Artillery, Cullen Bradley

Note. Estep's battery was attached to First Brigade; Cox's battery was attached to Second Brigade; and Bradley's battery was attached to Third Brigade.

Second Division, John M. Palmer
    First Brigade, Charles Cruft
    Second Brigade, William B. Hazen
    Third Brigade, William Grose
    Artillery, William E. Standart
        Battery B, 1st Ohio Light Artillery, William E. Standart
        Battery F, 1st Ohio Light Artillery, Norval Osburn

Batteries H and M, 4th United States Artillery, Charles C. Parsons

Third Division, Samuel Beatty, to March 13, 1863
    Horatio P. Van Cleve
    First Brigade, Benjamin C. Grider
    Second Brigade, James P. Fyffe
    Third Brigade, Samuel W. Price
    Artillery, George R. Swallow
        7th Battery, Indiana Light Artillery, George R. Swallow
        Battery B, Pennsylvania Light Artillery, Alanson J. Stevens
        3rd Battery, Wisconsin Light Artillery, Cortland Livingston

Note. Price was in temporary command of Third Brigade during the absence of Stanley Matthews.

After the Battle of Stones River, which was fought December 31, 1862–January 3, 1863, the Army of the Cumberland occupied Murfreesboro and remained in the vicinity until June 1863 while it prepared for further operations. Late in June 1863, the Army of the Cumberland, including Twenty-First Corps, moved forward at the beginning of the Tullahoma (or Middle Tennessee) Campaign, by which Rosecrans forced Braxton Bragg to withdraw his Confederate Army of Tennessee from Middle Tennessee to Chattanooga, beyond the Tennessee River.

During the Tullahoma Campaign, Twenty-First Corps was not engaged in the fighting for the gaps in the range of hills held by the enemy south of Murfreesboro, but instead it marched on the far left of the army and June 30, 1863 arrived at Manchester, Tennessee and rejoined the rest of the army. Van Cleve's Third Division was left at Murfreesboro at the beginning of the Tullahoma Campaign, but it moved forward to McMinnville during the period July 7–10 and rejoined the corps in the field.

For details of the operations of the Army of the Cumberland and of Twenty-First Corps during the Tullahoma Campaign, see Tullahoma (or Middle Tennessee) Campaign.

The organization of Twenty-First Corps during the Tullahoma Campaign was as follows:

TWENTY-FIRST CORPS, Thomas L. Crittenden

First Division, Thomas J. Wood

First Brigade, George P. Buell
Second Brigade, George D. Wagner
Third Brigade, Charles G. Harker
Artillery, Cullen Bradley
    8th Battery, Indiana Light Artillery, George Estep
    10th Battery, Indiana Light Artillery, William A. Naylor
    6th Battery, Ohio Light Artillery, Cullen Bradley

Second Division, John M. Palmer
First Brigade, Charles Cruft
Second Brigade, William B. Hazen
Third Brigade, William Grose
Artillery, William E. Standart
    Battery G, 1st Ohio Light Artillery, William E. Standart
    Battery F, 1st Ohio Light Artillery, Daniel T. Cockerill
    Battery H, 4th United States Artillery, Harry C. Cushing
    Battery M, 4th United States Artillery, Francis L. D. Russell

Note. In July 1863, during the temporary absence of Crittenden, John M. Palmer was in command of Twenty-First Corps, and Charles Cruft was in charge of Palmer's Second Division.

Third Division, Horatio P. Van Cleve
First Brigade, Samuel Beatty
Second Brigade, George F. Dick
Third Brigade, Sidney M. Barnes
Artillery, Lucius H. Drury
    7th Battery, Indiana Light Artillery, George R. Swallow
    Battery B, Pennsylvania Light Artillery, Alanson J. Stevens
    3rd Battery, Wisconsin Light Artillery, Cortland Livingston

When Bragg withdrew from Middle Tennessee to Chattanooga early in July 1863, Rosecrans halted the army to bring up supplies and to wait for the roads, which were in bad condition because of the recent rains, to improve. In mid-August, prior to the beginning of the Chickamauga Campaign, First Division, Twenty-First Corps was at Hillsboro, Tennessee; Second Division was at Manchester; and Third Division was at McMinnville.

During the later part of August 1863, when all preparations were complete, the Army of the Cumberland again advanced toward Chattanooga to engage Bragg's army. Twenty-First Corps, marching on the left of the army, crossed the Cumberland Mountains and moved into the Sequatchie Valley on August 19, then crossed the Tennessee River at Shellmound and Battle Creek September 3–4. The corps assembled at Shellmound, then advanced on the main road toward Chattanooga. Near Whiteside, Crittenden learned that the enemy had evacuated Chattanooga, and he then hurried forward and occupied the town September 9.

Crittenden then left George D. Wagner's Second Brigade of Thomas J. Wood's First Division to garrison Chattanooga, and with the rest of the corps he marched on the road toward Ringgold, Georgia. Twenty-First Corps then moved to the right and took position at Lee and Gordon's Mills, south of Chattanooga on Chickamauga Creek. It was joined there by Fourteenth Corps and Twentieth Corps just prior to and during the Battle of Chickamauga, which was fought September 19 and 20, 1863.

During the early part of the fighting on Chickamauga Creek, both Twenty-First Corps and Twentieth Corps were considerably reduced in numbers by sending reinforcements northward to support George H. Thomas, who was commanding on the left of Rosecrans' army. When James Longstreet's corps broke through the Union line at the Brotherton house during the fighting on September 20, both corps were cut off and driven in complete confusion from the field. Twenty-First Corps was not reassembled until after the battle, when the army was near Chattanooga. For details of the operations of Twenty-First Corps during the advance from Tennessee and the Battle of Chickamauga, see Chickamauga, Georgia Campaign.

The organization of Twenty-First Corps at the Battle of Chickamauga was as follows:

TWENTY-FIRST CORPS, Thomas L. Crittenden

First Division, Thomas J. Wood
    First Brigade, George P. Buell
    Second Brigade, George D. Wagner
    Third Brigade, Charles G. Harker
    Artillery
        8th Battery, Indiana Light Artillery, George Estep
        10th Battery, Indiana Light Artillery, William A. Naylor
        6th Battery, Ohio Light Artillery, Cullen Bradley

Note. Estep's battery was attached to First Brigade; Naylor's battery was attached to Second Brigade; and Bradley's brigade was attached to Third Brigade.

Naylor's battery was at Chattanooga during the battle and was not engaged.

Second Division, John M. Palmer
First Brigade, Charles Cruft
Second Brigade, William B. Hazen
Third Brigade, William Grose
Artillery, William E. Standart
Battery B, 1st Ohio Light Artillery, Norman A. Baldwin
Battery F, 1st Ohio Light Artillery, Giles J. Cockerill
Battery H, 4th United States Artillery, Harry C. Cushing
Battery M, 4th United States Artillery, Francis L. D. Russell

Note. Baldwin's battery was attached to First Brigade; Cockerill's battery was attached to Second Brigade; and Cushing's and Russell's batteries were attached to Third Brigade.

Third Division, Horatio P. Van Cleve
First Brigade, Samuel Beatty
Second Brigade, George F. Dick
Third Brigade, Sidney M. Barnes
Artillery
7th Battery, Indiana Light Artillery, George R. Swallow
Battery B, Pennsylvania Light Artillery, Alanson J. Stevens
Samuel M. McDowell
3rd Battery, Wisconsin Light Artillery, Cortland Livingston

Note. Battery B, Pennsylvania Light Artillery was also called 26th Battery, Pennsylvania Light Artillery.

By a presidential order dated September 28, 1863, Twentieth Corps and Twenty-First Corps were consolidated to form a new Fourth Corps, Army of the Cumberland, and Gordon Granger was assigned command. The organization of Fourth Corps was announced October 9, and Twenty-First Corps was discontinued. For further information, see Fourth Corps, Army of the Cumberland.

TWENTY-THIRD CORPS, ARMY OF THE OHIO

Twenty-Third Corps, Army of the Ohio was created by an order of April 27, 1863, and it was to consist of the troops in the Department of the Ohio, except those belonging to Ninth Corps. George L. Hartsuff was assigned command, but the corps was not announced by Ambrose E. Burnside, commanding the Department of the Ohio, until May 22. Hartsuff assumed command May 28.

In June 1863, the corps consisted of four divisions, and its complete organization was as follows:

TWENTY-THIRD CORPS, George L. Hartsuff

First Division, Samuel D. Sturgis
First Brigade, Samuel P. Carter
32nd Kentucky Infantry, Thomas Z. Morrow
103rd Ohio Infantry, John S. Casement
12th Rhode Island Infantry, George H. Browne
1st East Tennessee Mounted Infantry, Robert K. Byrd
2nd East Tennessee Mounted Infantry, James P. T. Carter
112th Illinois Mounted Infantry, Thomas J. Henderson
1st Kentucky Cavalry, Frank Wolford
1st Battery, East Tennessee Light Artillery, R. Clay Crawford
Second Brigade, Samuel A. Gilbert
24th Kentucky Infantry, John S. Hurt
100th Ohio Infantry, Patrick S. Slevin
104th Ohio Infantry, James W. Reilly
44th Ohio Mounted Infantry, Ackber O. Mitchell
45th Ohio Mounted Infantry, George E. Ross
9th Ohio Cavalry, 1st Battalion, William D. Hamilton
Battery D, 1st Ohio Light Artillery, Andrew J. Konkle
Wilder's Battery, Indiana Light Artillery, Casper W. McLaughlin
Third Brigade, August V. Kautz
9th Michigan Cavalry, James I. David
2nd Ohio Cavalry, George A. Purington
7th Ohio Cavalry, Israel Garrard
Mountain Howitzer Battery, Jesse S. Law of 2nd Ohio Cavalry
Unassigned
2nd Maryland Infantry, Thomas B. Allard
21st Massachusetts Infantry, George P. Hawkes
48th Pennsylvania Infantry, Daniel B. Kaufman
Battery D, 1st Rhode Island Light Artillery, William W. Buckley

Note. First Division consisted of troops in the District of Central Kentucky. First Brigade was at Somerset, Second Brigade was at Mount Vernon, and Third Brigade was at Jamestown. The unassigned units had be-

longed to the Ninth Corps but did not accompany it to Mississippi for the Siege of Vicksburg.

Second Division, Jeremiah T. Boyle
  First Brigade, James M. Shackelford
    91st Indiana Infantry, John Mehringer
    12th Kentucky Infantry, William A. Hoskins
    65th Indiana Mounted Infantry, Thomas Johnson
    3rd Kentucky Cavalry (two battalions), Eli H. Murray
    3rd Kentucky Cavalry (one battalion), Robert Boyle
    8th Kentucky Cavalry (one battalion), Benjamin H. Bristow
    15th Kentucky Cavalry, Company C, Jonathan Belt
    22nd Battery, Indiana Light Artillery, Benjamin F. Denning
    Twyman's Company Kentucky Scouts, Edward W. Ward
  Munfordville, Kentucky, Charles D. Pennebaker
    27th Kentucky Infantry, John H. Ward
    33rd Kentucky Infantry, James F. Lauck
    6th Battery (one section), Michigan Light Artillery, Luther F. Hale
  Bowling Green, Kentucky, Cicero Maxwell
    26th Kentucky Infantry, Thomas B. Fairleigh
    34th Kentucky Infantry, Selby Harney
    8th Kentucky Cavalry, Company D, Samuel F. Johnson
    6th Battery (one section), Michigan Light Artillery, Byron D. Paddock
    Artillery in Position, Norman S. Andrews
  Lebanon, Kentucky and other points
    63rd Indiana Infantry, James McManomy
    20th Kentucky Infantry, Charles S. Hanson
    34th Kentucky Infantry, Company C, Christopher C. Hare
    25th Michigan Infantry, Benjamin F. Orcutt
    50th Ohio Infantry, Silas A. Strickland
    East Tennessee Scouts (one battalion), Reuben A. Davis

Note. The troops of Second Division were in the District of Kentucky.

Third Division, Henry M. Judah
  First Brigade, Mahlon D. Manson
    107th Illinois Infantry, Joseph J. Kelly
    23rd Michigan Infantry, Marshal W. Chapin
    111th Ohio Infantry, John R. Bond
    14th Illinois Cavalry, Horace Capron
    5th Indiana Cavalry, Felix W. Graham
    Elgin (or Renwick's) Battery, Illinois Light Artillery, Andrew M. Wood

Henshaw's Battery, Illinois Light Artillery, Edward C. Henshaw
Second Brigade, Edward H. Hobson
    80th Indiana Infantry, Lewis Brooks
    13th Kentucky Infantry, William E. Hobson
    16th Kentucky Infantry, James W. Gault
    9th Kentucky Cavalry, Richard T. Jacob
    11th Kentucky Cavalry, William E. Riley
    12th Kentucky Cavalry, Eugene W. Crittenden
    24th Battery, Indiana Light Artillery, Joseph A. Sims
Third Brigade, Joseph A. Cooper
    3rd East Tennessee Infantry, William Cross
    5th East Tennessee Infantry, James T. Shelley
    6th East Tennessee Infantry, Edward Maynard
    11th Kentucky Mounted Infantry, John B. Tyler
    Detachment manning two pieces of artillery, Judge R. Clingan

Note. First Brigade was at Tompkinsville, Kentucky; Second Brigade was at Marrowbone, Kentucky; and Third Brigade was at Carthage, Tennessee.

Fourth Division, Julius White
  First Brigade, Daniel Cameron
    65th Illinois Infantry, William S. Stewart
    14th Kentucky Infantry (seven companies), George W. Gallup
    14th Kentucky Infantry (three companies), Drew J. Burchett
    10th Kentucky Cavalry (two battalions), John M. Brown
    39th Kentucky Mounted Infantry, John Dils, Jr.
    McLaughlin's Squadron, Ohio Cavalry, Richard Rice
    Battery M (2nd section), 2nd Illinois Light Artillery, John C. Phillips
    Battery M (1st section), 2nd Illinois Light Artillery, William C. G. L. Stevenson
  Second Brigade, Samuel R. Mott
    8th East Tennessee Infantry, Felix A. Reeve
    118th Ohio Infantry, Thomas L. Young
    5th East Tennessee Cavalry, Jesse H. Strickland
    10th Kentucky Cavalry (eight companies), Ralph R. Maltby
    14th Kentucky Cavalry, Henry C. Lilly
    8th Michigan Cavalry, Grover S. Wormer
    15th Battery, Indiana Light Artillery, John C. H. Von Sehlen
    19th Battery, Ohio Light Artillery, Joseph C. Shields

Note. Troops of First Brigade were at Louisville and Pikeville, Kentucky, and Second Brigade was at Camp Nelson, Kentucky.

When Burnside was assigned command of the Department of the Ohio, he was instructed to move into East Tennessee to occupy the country and protect the loyal citizens residing there. Burnside's first attempt was interrupted when the Ninth Corps, which was to accompany Twenty-Third Corps on the expedition to Knoxville, was sent from Kentucky to join Ulysses S. Grant's army at Vicksburg, Mississippi.

At the end of June 1863, Burnside was again preparing to move into East Tennessee with the available troops of Twenty-Third Corps. Then John H. Morgan, with his Confederate cavalry division, crossed the Cumberland River on July 2 and moved northward through Kentucky on his raid into Indiana and Ohio. From then until late in July, Burnside was occupied in directing the troops of his department in the pursuit of Morgan. All available cavalry of Twenty-Third Corps and some infantry were sent after Morgan, and they finally captured him and the remnant of his command near New Lisbon, Ohio on July 26. For details, see Morgan's Raid into Indiana and Ohio.

At the end of July 1863, the organization of Twenty-Third Corps was essentially the same as that given above, but there were some changes in position of the various units of the corps. Corps headquarters was at Lexington, Kentucky, and the divisions of the corps were located as follows: First Division headquarters and First Brigade and Third Brigade were at Danville, and Second Brigade was at Camp Nelson, Kentucky. Second Division headquarters was at Louisville, Kentucky; First Brigade was at Russellville; Detachment United States Forces was at Bowling Green; and Detachment United States Forces was at Munfordville, Kentucky. Third Division headquarters was at Glasgow, Kentucky; First Brigade was at Lebanon; Second Brigade was at Glasgow, Kentucky; and Third Brigade was at Carthage, Tennessee. Fourth Division headquarters and First Brigade were at Catlettsburg, Kentucky, and Second Brigade was at Camp Nelson, Kentucky.

With Morgan disposed of, Burnside once again turned his attention to the occupation of East Tennessee. One of his first steps was to reorganize Twenty-Third Corps, which was effected by an order of August 6, 1863. The new organization was as follows:

TWENTY-THIRD CORPS, George L. Hartsuff, to September 25, 1863
Mahlon D. Manson

First Division (or District of Kentucky), Jeremiah T. Boyle

Note 1. In the reorganization of August 6, 1863, First Brigade, Second Brigade, and Third Brigade were discontinued, and the troops of the division were distributed at various posts in the state of Kentucky.
Note 2. On November 6, 1863, First Division, or District of Kentucky, was sub-districted as follows:
   District of Southwestern Kentucky, Cicero Maxwell
   District of South Central Kentucky, Edward H. Hobson
   District of Eastern Kentucky, George W. Gallup
   District of North Central Kentucky, Speed S. Fry
   District of Somerset, Kentucky, Theophilus T. Garrard

Second Division, Mahlon D. Manson, to August 21, 1863
Julius White
First Brigade, Orlando H. Moore
Second Brigade, Marshal W. Chapin

Note 1. Second Division was near Lebanon, Kentucky.
Note 2. Second Brigade was organized August 6, 1863.

Third Division, Milo S. Hascall
   First Brigade, Samuel A. Gilbert
   Second Brigade, Daniel Cameron

Note. Third Division was near Danville, Kentucky.

Fourth Division, Samuel P. Carter
   First Brigade, Julius White, to August 21, 1863
      Robert K. Byrd
   Second Brigade, Edward H. Hobson
   Third Brigade, James M. Shackelford

Note 1. Fourth Division was near Stanford, Kentucky.
Note 2. Third Brigade was organized August 6, 1863 and was discontinued November 3, 1863.
Note 3. First Brigade, then commanded by Charles D. Pennebaker, was detached from the division in October 1863.

By August 16, 1863, Ambrose E. Burnside had assembled in Kentucky an army, consisting of three divisions of George L. Hartsuff's Twenty-Third Corps, for an advance into East Tennessee. The next day, Manson's Second Division marched from Lebanon, Hascall's Third Division from Danville, and Carter's Fourth Division from Sanford, and by the end of the month Hartsuff's columns were approaching Knoxville. Jeremiah T. Boyle's First Division of Twenty-Third Corps remained in Kentucky.

On September 2, 1863, the cavalry occupied Knoxville, and other troops of the army arrived at Kingston, Loudon, and Lenoir's Station. Burnside occupied Knoxville with his infantry, and then, about mid-September, sent out his cavalry and infantry to the east of Knoxville. He soon drove back into Virginia the Confederate force in East Tennessee and proceeded to occupy a number of positions in the eastern part of the state. The enemy, however, remained a constant threat to the troops of Twenty-Third Corps. Soon after arriving in East Tennessee, Burnside sent back orders for Ninth Corps, which had returned to Kentucky from Vicksburg, to hurry forward and join him and Hartsuff's Twenty-Third Corps. When Ninth Corps arrived, under the command of Robert B. Potter, it was used to guard the occupied country, and in late October was on the Tennessee River below Knoxville.

Toward the end of October 1863, troops of Twenty-Third Corps were engaged in guarding the Tennessee River between Loudon and Kingston, Tennessee. On October 28, White sent Samuel R. Mott's First Brigade of his Second Division to Kingston, and he remained with Marshal W. Chapin's Second Brigade on the north side of the river, opposite Loudon. At that time Hascall's Third Division was at Knoxville.

Some important command changes occurred in Twenty-Third Corps during August and September 1863. On August 21, Julius White relieved Manson in command of Second Division, and on September 25, Manson relieved Hartsuff in command of Twenty-Third Corps.

For details of Burnside's campaign in East Tennessee August 16–October 19, 1863, see East Tennessee Campaign (Burnside).

On August 31, 1863, during the East Tennessee Campaign, Twenty-Third Corps was organized as follows:

TWENTY-THIRD CORPS, George L. Hartsuff, to September 25, 1863
Mahlon D. Manson

First Division, Jeremiah T. Boyle
Bowling Green, Kentucky, commander not given

Munfordville, Kentucky, Charles D. Pennebaker
Louisa, Kentucky, George W. Gallup
Mount Sterling, Kentucky, Ralph R. Maltby
Camp Nelson, Kentucky, Charles W. Davis
Frankfort, Kentucky, Thomas B. Allard
Hopkinsville, Kentucky, Eli H. Murray
New Haven, Kentucky, James McManomy
Lexington, Kentucky, Joshua K. Sigfried
Russellville, Kentucky, Benjamin H. Bristow
Louisville, Kentucky, commander not given
Eminence, Kentucky, Richard T. Jacob
Glasgow, Kentucky, William Y. Dillard
Muldraugh's Hill, Kentucky, Silas A. Strickland
Smithland, Kentucky, Jonathan Belt

Second Division, Julius White
First Brigade, Orlando H. Moore
Second Brigade, Marshal W. Chapin

Note. Andrew M. Wood's Elgin Battery, Illinois Light Artillery was attached to First Brigade, and Edward C. Henshaw's Battery, Illinois Light Artillery was attached to Second Brigade.

Third Division, Milo S. Hascall
First Brigade, Samuel A. Gilbert
Second Brigade, Daniel Cameron

Note. William H. Pease's Battery D, 1st Ohio Light Artillery was attached to First Brigade, and Wilder's Battery, Indiana Light Artillery, then commanded by Hubbard T. Thomas, was attached to Second Brigade.

Fourth Division, Samuel P. Carter
First Brigade, Robert K. Byrd
Second Brigade, John W. Foster
Third Brigade, James M. Shackelford

Note 1. William H. Torr's 15th Battery, Indiana Light Artillery was attached to First Brigade; John H. Colvin's Battery M, 1st Illinois Light Artillery was attached to Second Brigade; and R. Clay Crawford's 1st East Tennessee Battery was attached to Third Brigade.
Note 2. A Fourth Brigade, commanded by John W. Foster, was organized in October 1863 and was transferred to the Cavalry Corps, Army of the Ohio November 3, 1863.
Note 3. Fourth Division was discontinued November 3, 1863 and was formed into the Cavalry Corps, Army of the Ohio.

Unattached
Cavalry Brigade, Frank Wolford
Reserve Artillery, Andrew J. Konkle
Battery M, 2nd Illinois Light Artillery, John C. Phillips

24th Battery, Indiana Light Artillery, Henry W. Shafer

19th Battery, Ohio Light Artillery, Joseph C. Shields

Battery D, 1st Rhode Island Light Artillery, William W. Buckley

On November 3, 1863, the cavalry of Twenty-Third Corps was organized into a Cavalry Corps, Army of the Ohio, as follows:

CAVALRY CORPS, James M. Shackelford

First Division, William P. Sanders
   First Brigade, Frank Wolford
   Second Brigade, Robert K. Byrd
   Third Brigade, Charles D. Pennebaker

Second Division, James P. T. Carter
   First Brigade, Israel Garrard
   Second Brigade, John W. Foster

When the reorganization was completed, however, John W. Foster was in command of Second Division, and Horace Capron was in command of Second Brigade, Second Division.

On November 4, 1863, James Longstreet's corps of two divisions and a part of Joseph Wheeler's cavalry were detached from Braxton Bragg's Army of Tennessee, which was then besieging Chattanooga, Tennessee, and Longstreet was ordered to advance into East Tennessee and drive Burnside's army from Knoxville and from the eastern part of the state. Longstreet arrived with his command at Sweetwater (Sweet Water), Tennessee, and on November 13 began his advance on Knoxville.

White, with Chapin's brigade, was active, together with Potter's Ninth Corps, in delaying Longstreet's advance, and it was engaged at Campbell's Station November 16, 1863. It then moved back with Burnside's army and took its place in the line of defenses in front of the city. Hascall's division was in reserve at Knoxville during the siege November 17–December 4, and during that time it was active on both sides of the Holston River.

On December 7, 1863, after Longstreet had abandoned the siege and moved off to the east with his army, Twenty-Third Corps joined in the pursuit and advanced to a point near Rutledge. Then when

Longstreet resumed the offensive, the corps was engaged in skirmishing with the enemy near Bean's Station on December 15. The next day, Hascall's division fell back to Blain's Cross Roads, and Mott's brigade from Kingston arrived there the same day. On December 17, White, with Chapin's brigade, arrived at Blain's Cross Roads, and the next day Mott's brigade rejoined the division.

On December 12, 1863, Jacob D. Cox, then commanding the District of Ohio, Department of the Ohio, was ordered to Kentucky to relieve Boyle in command of the troops in the state. Upon arriving there, however, Cox was ordered on to East Tennessee. When he arrived at Knoxville, he was assigned to the command of Twenty-Third Corps December 20, and the next day he assumed command, relieving Manson. Manson then assumed command of Second Division, relieving White.

December 25, 1863, Mott's brigade was moved up to support Samuel D. Sturgis' cavalry command near Talbott's Station, and a part of the brigade was engaged at Mossy Creek on December 29. At the end of December 1863, Twenty-Third Corps, except Mott's brigade, was at Strawberry Plains.

For details of the operations and organization of Twenty-Third Corps during November and December 1863, see Knoxville, Tennessee Campaign.

The organization of Twenty-Third Corps December 31, 1863 was as follows:

TWENTY-THIRD CORPS, Jacob D. Cox

First Division, Jeremiah T. Boyle
   District of Eastern Kentucky, George W. Gallup
   District of Northern Central Kentucky, Speed S. Fry
   District of Somerset, Theophilus T. Garrard
   District of Southern Central Kentucky, Edward H. Hobson
   District of Southwestern Kentucky, Cicero Maxwell

Note 1. Cox assumed command of Twenty-Third Corps December 21, 1863.

Note 2. Troops of the District of Eastern Kentucky were at Louisa and Catlettsburg.

Note 3. Troops of the District of Northern Central Kentucky were at Booneville, Camp Nelson, Flemingsburg, Lexington, Mount Sterling, and Paris.

Note 4. Troops of the District of Somerset were at Barboursville, London, Point Isabel, Somerset, and Stanford.

Note 5. Troops of the District of Southern Central

Kentucky were at Cave City, Columbia, Glasgow, Muldraugh Hill, Munfordville, New Haven, and Nolin.

Note 6. Troops of the District of Southwestern Kentucky were at Bowling Green, Hopkinsville, Russellville, and Smithland.

Note 7. First Division was discontinued January 10, 1864.

Second Division, Mahlon D. Manson, to January 26, 1864
  Henry M. Judah
  First Brigade, Samuel R. Mott
  Second Brigade, Marshal W. Chapin

Note 1. Second Division was at Strawberry Plains and Mossy Creek.

Note 2. Andrew M. Wood's Elgin Battery, Illinois Light Artillery was attached to First Brigade, and Edward C. Henshaw's Battery, Illinois Light Artillery was attached to Second Brigade.

Note 3. The First East Tennessee Brigade, commanded by James G. Spears, was attached to Twenty-Third Corps January 21, 1864, and was made a part of Second Division, Twenty-Third Corps January 27, 1864.

Third Division, Milo S. Hascall
  First Brigade, James W. Reilly
  Second Brigade, Daniel Cameron

Note 1. Third Division was at Strawberry Plains and Herrell's Ford.

Note 2. William H. Pease's Battery D, 1st Ohio Light Artillery was attached to First Brigade, and Wilder's Battery, Indiana Light Artillery, commanded by Hubbard T. Thomas, was attached to Second Brigade.

Reserve Artillery, Andrew J. Konkle
  24th Battery, Indiana Light Artillery, Joseph A. Sims
  19th Battery, Ohio Light Artillery, Joseph C. Shields

Note. The Reserve Artillery was at Knoxville, Tennessee.

Twenty-Third Corps, less First Division, which was in Kentucky, remained in East Tennessee until the end of April 1864, and then it departed to join William T. Sherman's army at the beginning of the Atlanta Campaign. The corps was not seriously engaged during the winter, but it was moved from place to place at various times in an attempt to find grain and forage, and also to counter threatening movements by Longstreet toward Knoxville.

About mid-January 1864, Second Division and Third Division marched from Strawberry Plains to Dandridge, along with Fourth Corps and the cavalry, but they then returned to Strawberry Plains a few days later. Mott's brigade, which had been at Mossy Creek until January 15, marched back to Strawberry Plains and rejoined Second Division. The corps then moved back slowly to Knoxville, where it arrived January 24.

Beginning on February 10, 1864, Jenkins' division of Longstreet's corps with some cavalry advanced to Strawberry Plains and threatened Knoxville, but on February 22 it began to fall back to the east. Second Division, Twenty-Third Corps advanced from Knoxville to Strawberry Plains February 24, and then on to New Market, but at the end of the month Second Division was back at Strawberry Plains, and Third Division and the cavalry were at Knoxville. Ninth Corps also advanced in pursuit of Jenkins' retiring column.

During March 1864, Twenty-Third Corps was at Mossy Creek, and from that point it made reconnaissances to Panther Creek and to Morristown. Second Division remained at Mossy Creek until April 26, and it then marched by way of Knoxville to Calhoun, where it arrived on April 30. Third Division spent most of the month in the vicinity of Bull's Gap, and then it moved, both by marching and by rail, to Charleston, Tennessee, where it arrived and went into camp.

For additional information about the operations of Twenty-Third Corps during the period January–April 1864, see Army of the Ohio (Burnside), Winter of 1863–1864; and see also Army of the Ohio (Schofield).

Meantime, on April 3, 1864, Alvin P. Hovey had left Nashville with six new Indiana regiments to join Twenty-Third Corps in East Tennessee. He passed through Chattanooga on April 20 and arrived at Charleston April 24. As noted above, on April 10, while on the march, Hovey's command was designated as First Division, Twenty-Third Corps, but it did not join the corps until the end of the month, when he arrived at Charleston.

On April 9, 1864, John M. Schofield assumed command of Twenty-Third Corps, and immediately began preparations for joining William T. Sherman for the campaign against Atlanta, Georgia. The next day he ordered the reorganization of the corps, which was completed April 11, as follows:

TWENTY-THIRD CORPS, John M. Schofield
First Division, Alvin P. Hovey

First Brigade, Richard F. Barter
Second Brigade, John C. McQuiston
Artillery
    23rd Battery, Indiana Light Artillery, James H. Myers
    24th Battery, Indiana Light Artillery, Henry W. Shafer

Second Division, Henry M. Judah
  First Brigade, Milo S. Hascall
  Second Brigade, Marshal W. Chapin
  Artillery
    Battery F, 1st Michigan Light Artillery, Byron D. Paddock
    19th Battery, Ohio Light Artillery, Joseph C. Shields

Third Division, Jacob D. Cox
  First Brigade, James W. Reilly
  Second Brigade, Mahlon D. Manson
  Artillery
    15th Battery, Indiana Light Artillery, Alonzo D. Harvey
    Battery D, 1st Ohio Light Artillery, Giles J. Cockerill

Fourth Division, Jacob Ammen
  First Brigade, Theophilus T. Garrard
  Second Brigade (Reserve Artillery), Davis Tillson
  Third Brigade, Silas A. Strickland

Note 1. Fourth Division was formerly a cavalry division, but was reorganized April 11, 1864 to consist of troops in East Tennessee. This organization was also called District of East Tennessee. Headquarters was at Knoxville. For additional information, see Department of the Ohio, August 19, 1862–January 17, 1865, District of East Tennessee.
Note 2. First Brigade was at Cumberland Gap; Second Brigade occupied the defenses of Knoxville; and Third Brigade held the line of the Tennessee River from Loudon to Hiawassee.

Fifth Division, Stephen G. Burbridge

Note. Fifth Division was organized during April 1864 from all troops in the District of Kentucky. Headquarters was at Lexington, Kentucky. For additional information, see Army of the Ohio, August 19, 1862–January 17, 1865, District of Kentucky.

Cavalry Corps, George Stoneman

Note. The Cavalry Corps, Army of the Ohio was much depleted because of its hard service in East Tennessee during the winter of 1863–1864, and it was brought to
Paris, Kentucky by Samuel D. Sturgis to remount and refit. George Stoneman was assigned command of the cavalry April 9, 1864, and he moved the corps to Nicholasville, Kentucky to continue the work of preparing it for the field.

In late April 1864, when Sherman began to assemble the corps of his armies in preparation for the advance into Georgia, Hovey's newly organized First Division, Judah's Second Division, and Cox's Third Division of Twenty-Third Corps were near Charleston, Tennessee. These three divisions of Twenty-Third Corps that were in the field and ready for service in the coming campaign were under the personal command of Schofield and were known as the Army of the Ohio, although the army consisted of only the one corps, and as such it took part in Sherman's Atlanta Campaign. It was also designated as the Left of Sherman's Army of Invasion of Georgia. Jacob Ammen's Fourth Division remained in East Tennessee, and Stephen G. Burbridge's Fifth Division remained in Kentucky. Stoneman's cavalry also remained in Kentucky for some time, but two brigades joined the Army of the Ohio near Dalton, Georgia at the beginning of the campaign.

On April 30, 1864, just before the beginning of Sherman's march toward Atlanta, the four infantry divisions of Twenty-Third Corps that were in East Tennessee were organized as follows:

TWENTY-THIRD CORPS, John M. Schofield

First Division, Alvin P. Hovey
  First Brigade, Richard F. Barter
  Second Brigade, John C. McQuiston
  Artillery
    23rd Battery, Indiana Light Artillery, Luther S. Houghton
    24th Battery, Indiana Light Artillery, Henry W. Shafer

Second Division, Henry M. Judah
  First Brigade, Joseph A. Cooper
  Second Brigade, Milo S. Hascall
  Artillery
    Battery F, 1st Michigan Light Artillery, Byron D. Paddock
    19th Battery, Ohio Light Artillery, Joseph C. Shields

Third Division, Jacob D. Cox
  First Brigade, James W. Reilly

Second Brigade, Mahlon D. Manson

Fourth Division, Jacob Ammen
  First Brigade, John Mehringer
  Second Brigade, Davis Tillson
  Third Brigade, Silas A. Strickland

Note 1. The following batteries were a part of First Brigade, Fourth Division: Thomas Gallagher's Battery L, 1st Michigan Light Artillery; Augustus H. Emery's Battery M, 1st Michigan Light Artillery; Peter Cornell's 22nd Battery, Ohio Light Artillery; and William O. Beebe's Battery B, 1st Tennessee Light Artillery.

Note 2. The following batteries were a part of Second Brigade: John E. McGowan's 1st United States Colored Heavy Artillery; John H. Colvin's Battery K, 1st Illinois Light Artillery; Andrew M. Wood's Elgin Battery (also called Renwick's Battery), Illinois Light Artillery; John S. White's section of Wilder's Battery, Indiana Light Artillery; and James H. Walley's 21st Battery, Ohio Light Artillery.

Note 3. Henshaw's Battery, Illinois Light Artillery, commanded by Azro C. Putnam, was attached to Third Brigade.

During the first few days of May 1864, the troops of William T. Sherman's Army of the Military Division of the Mississippi, which consisted of the Army of the Tennessee, the Army of the Cumberland, and the Army of the Ohio (Twenty-Third Corps), moved toward their assigned positions for an advance on Dalton, Georgia at the beginning of the Atlanta Campaign. This was scheduled to begin May 5, but it was delayed until May 7.

On May 3, 1864, as a part of Sherman's movement, Schofield's Twenty-Third Corps moved from Charleston, Tennessee to Cleveland, and the next day it moved on to Red Clay on the Tennessee and Georgia state line. It remained there until May 7, then advanced to a position north of Dalton, east of Rocky Face Ridge, on the left of the Army of the Cumberland.

Stoneman's cavalry was at Nicholasville, Kentucky preparing for field service when Twenty-Third Corps left Charleston for Red Clay, but James Biddle's Second Cavalry Brigade and Alexander W. Holeman's Independent Cavalry Brigade of Stoneman's command left Nicholasville for the front at the end of April 1864 and with Stoneman joined the Army of the Ohio north of Dalton on May 10.

Twenty-Third Corps was engaged with Joseph E. Johnston's Army of Tennessee during the operations at Rocky Face Ridge May 8–10, 1864. It then

marched with the rest of the army to Resaca, Georgia, where it was again engaged at the Battle of Resaca May 14–15.

When Johnston abandoned his lines at Resaca following the battle and marched southward, Sherman's army followed along the Western and Atlantic Railroad, with Twenty-Third Corps moving on the extreme left to Cartersville, Georgia. From there it was sent forward to the railroad bridge over the Etowah River.

Instead of attempting to force a crossing of the river to the southeast of Cartersville, Sherman moved to the right, crossed the river south of Kingston, and advanced to a line extending from Dallas, past New Hope Church, to the vicinity of Pickett's Mill. During this movement, Twenty-Third Corps moved forward on the left of the army and occupied a position on the left of the new line. It was engaged in the usual skirmishing while the army was in line there, but it was not engaged in any of the heavy fighting that occurred at Dallas, New Hope Church, and Pickett's Mill.

When Johnston was finally forced to fall back in the direction of Marietta, Georgia, Sherman began to move his army back toward the railroad at Allatoona and Acworth. While this movement was in progress, Twenty-Third Corps remained in position near the intersection of the Dallas and Acworth road and the Burnt Hickory and Marietta road to cover the passage of the troops and trains toward the railroad, and it then followed the rest of the army.

While near Acworth, on June 9, 1864, the number of divisions in Twenty-Third Corps was reduced from three to two. Alvin P. Hovey became dissatisfied with his treatment as commander of First Division and tendered his resignation. He was then given a thirty-day leave of absence; his division was temporarily broken up June 9, and the brigades were assigned to Second Division and Third Division. Hovey did not return to the army, however, but served as commander of the District of Indiana until the end of the war. When First Division was broken up, First Brigade was temporarily assigned to Third Division, but it retained is original designation until August 11, when the division was officially discontinued. Second Brigade was temporarily assigned to Second Division, but it also retained its original designation until August 11.

On June 10, 1864, after the necessary preparations had been completed, Sherman put the army in motion from the vicinity of Acworth toward Marietta. Twenty-Third Corps moved forward on the right of the army, on the Sandtown road, until the army was halted during the latter part of June 1864 by the new defensive line established by the enemy at Kennesaw Mountain, in front of Marietta.

Twenty-Third Corps was not engaged at the Battle of Kennesaw Mountain June 27, 1864, but it secured the right flank of the army from an enemy attack from the south.

On July 3, 1864, after Johnston had evacuated the lines in front of Marietta and fallen back toward the Chattahoochee River, Sherman resumed his flanking movements to the right by sending the Army of the Tennessee from the left of his line to a position beyond Twenty-Third Corps. Twenty-Third Corps held its position on the right until the Army of the Tennessee had passed, and it then remained massed in rear of the Army of the Tennessee July 4–5. On the latter date the corps began moving toward Soap Creek, on the left of the army, and during the period July 9–11, it crossed to the east bank of the Chattahoochee River.

When the rest of Sherman's army had crossed the river, Twenty-Third Corps marched eastward to the vicinity of Decatur, Georgia, east of Atlanta. At that point, the Army of the Tennessee came up on the left of Twenty-Third Corps, and together they moved up to the Confederate defenses on the east side of Atlanta. Twenty-Third Corps was not engaged at the Battle of Peach Tree Creek, July 20, 1864, or the Battle of Atlanta, July 22, 1864.

The corps remained on the lines northeast of Atlanta until after Sherman had begun the general movement of his troops to the west side of the city in an attempt to cut the railroads running out to the south and southwest. During this movement, the Army of the Tennessee was attacked unsuccessfully at Ezra Church July 28, 1864, and then Sherman resumed his advance southward toward the railroad running between Atlanta and East Point.

Finally, on August 1, 1864, Schofield marched out from his position east of Atlanta and, passing in rear of the rest of the army, moved to a new position on the right of the Army of the Tennessee, and on the right of the army. Twenty-Third Corps and troops of the Army of the Tennessee made some attempts to reach the railroad, but with only limited

success. After an unsuccessful attack by Twenty-Third Corps on August 6, the enemy withdrew to a new line. Schofield then advanced to a new position along the south bank of the South Branch of Utoy Creek and remained there, forming a pivot for the rest of the army as it moved forward, until August 28.

Then, while the rest of Sherman's army marched on the right toward Jonesboro, Georgia, Twenty-Third Corps moved southward along the Macon and Western Railroad, destroying the track as it advanced. It was not present at the Battle of Jonesboro August 31–September 1, 1864, but it did join in the pursuit of the enemy to Lovejoy's Station after the battle. When Sherman called off the pursuit, Twenty-Third Corps marched back to Jonesboro with the rest of the army, and then moved back to its former camps near Atlanta. It did not remain there very long, but moved on to Decatur, Georgia on September 7, and there Schofield established his headquarters and the corps went into camp for the rest of the month.

While at Decatur, there were some changes in command in the corps. On September 14, 1864, Schofield departed to look after affairs of his Department of the Ohio; Cox assumed temporary command of Twenty-Third Corps, and James W. Reilly assumed command of Cox's Third Division. Also on September 14, Henry M. Judah, commanding Second Division, was directed to report to Stephen G. Burbridge, commanding the District of Kentucky, for assignment to duty on a general court martial. Joseph A. Cooper assumed command of Second Division, and Charles S. Parrish assumed command of Cooper's First Brigade, Second Division.

The organization of Twenty Third Corps during the Atlanta Campaign May 3–September 8, 1864 was as follows:

TWENTY-THIRD CORPS, John M. Schofield, to May 26, 1864
    Jacob D. Cox, May 26–27, 1864
    John M. Schofield

First Division, Alvin P. Hovey
    First Brigade, Richard F. Barter
    Second Brigade, John C. McQuiston, to June 23, 1864
        Peter T. Swaine
    Artillery

23rd Battery, Indiana Light Artillery, Luther S. Houghton

Aaron A. Wilber

24th Battery, Indiana Light Artillery, Alexander Hardy

Note 1. First Brigade was temporarily assigned to Third Division June 9, 1864, but it retained its original designation of First Brigade, First Division until August 11, 1864, when First Division was discontinued. This brigade was sometimes called Fourth Brigade, Third Division.

Note 2. Second Brigade was temporarily assigned to Second Division June 9, 1864, but it retained its original designation of Second Brigade, First Division until First Division was discontinued August 11, 1864.

Note 3. 23rd Battery, Indiana Light Artillery was temporarily attached to Third Division June 10, 1864 and was permanently assigned thereto August 11, 1864. 24th Battery, Indiana Light Artillery was temporarily attached to Second Division June 10, 1864, and was then assigned to the Cavalry Division July 6, 1864.

Second Division, Henry M. Judah, to May 18, 1864, on leave

Milo S. Hascall

First Brigade, Nathaniel C. McLean, May 5, 1864– June 4, 1864

Joseph A. Cooper

Second Brigade, Milo S. Hascall, to May 16, 1864

John R. Bond, to June 18, 1864, sick

William E. Hobson, to August 15, 1864

John R. Bond

Third Brigade, Silas A. Strickland

Artillery, Joseph C. Shields

22nd Battery, Indiana Light Artillery, Benjamin F. Denning, to July 1, 1864, mortally wounded

Edward W. Nicholson

Battery F, 1st Michigan Light Artillery, Byron D. Paddock

Marshall M. Miller

19th Battery, Ohio Light Artillery, Joseph C. Shields

Note 1. Strickland's brigade joined the army May 28, 1864 near Pumpkin Vine Creek and was designated as Provisional Brigade until June 8, 1864, when the designation was changed to Third Brigade, Second Division.

Note 2. Second Brigade, First Division was attached to Second Division, without change of designation, June 9, 1864, and it was then broken up August 11, 1864. It was sometimes called Fourth Brigade, Second Division.

Note 3. The 22nd Battery, Indiana Light Artillery joined Second Division June 29, 1864.

Third Division, Jacob D. Cox, to May 26, 1864

James W. Reilly, May 26–27, 1864

Jacob D. Cox

First Brigade, James W. Reilly, to May 26, 1864

James W. Gault, May 26–27, 1864

James W. Reilly

Second Brigade, Mahlon D. Manson, to May 14, 1864, wounded

John S. Hurt, May 14–16, 1864

Milo S. Hascall, May 17–18, 1864

John S. Hurt, May 18–21, 1864

John S. Casement, to June 4, 1864

Daniel Cameron, to July 31, 1864

John S. Casement

Third Brigade, Nathaniel C. McLean, to June 17, 1864

Robert K. Byrd, to August 9, 1864

Israel N. Stiles

Dismounted Cavalry Brigade, Eugene W. Crittenden

Artillery, Henry W. Wells

15th Battery, Indiana Light Artillery, Alonzo D. Harvey

Battery D, 1st Ohio Light Artillery, Giles J. Cockerill

Note 1. Third Brigade was organized June 5, 1864, and was discontinued by the transfer of regiments August 11, 1864. The brigade was reorganized by an order of August 9, 1864, and that day Stiles assumed command.

Note 2. First Brigade, First Division was temporarily attached to Third Division, without change of designation, June 9, 1864, and it was broken up August 11, 1864. It was sometimes called Fourth Brigade, Third Division.

Note 3. Crittenden's Dismounted Cavalry Brigade was assigned to Third Division June 21, 1864, and it was transferred to the Cavalry Division August 22, 1864.

After the evacuation of Atlanta and the Battle of Jonesboro, John B. Hood's Confederate Army of Tennessee retired to Lovejoy's Station, where it remained until September 18, 1864. Hood realized that his position there was untenable if Sherman should advance again, and he also believed that because of the low morale of the army he would be less likely to sustain another attack. He therefore decided that an advance was essential to restore the morale of the men, and accordingly he set out to turn Sherman's right flank and attempt to destroy his communications with the North and in this way force him to retire from Atlanta.

On September 18, 1864, Hood moved from Lovejoy's Station to Palmetto, Georgia, and he remained there until September 29. He then marched to Lost Mountain October 3, and from there he sent Samuel G. French's division to attempt the capture of Allatoona on the Western and Atlantic Railroad.

French's attack on the Federal works at Allatoona on October 5 was repulsed, and he then rejoined Hood's army.

Meantime, Sherman had learned of rumors that Hood had left Lovejoy's Station with his army and was on the move, and, as a precaution, he sent troops to reinforce the garrisons at Rome and Chattanooga. Finally, on October 3, 1864, Sherman issued orders for his army to follow Hood.

That day, Cox, with the Army of the Ohio (Twenty-Third Corps), was directed to march by way of Buck Head to the bridge over the Chattahoochee River. The next day he crossed the river and marched by way of Marietta and Acworth to Allatoona, where he arrived October 8. On October 10, Cox left Allatoona; he marched by way of Cartersville and Kingston and arrived at Rome October 12.

The organization of Twenty-Third Corps September 30, 1864, while at Decatur, Georgia, was as follows:

TWENTY-THIRD CORPS, Jacob D. Cox

Second Division, Joseph A. Cooper
First Brigade, Charles S. Parrish
Second Brigade, John R. Bond
Third Brigade, John Mehringer
Artillery
22nd Battery, Indiana Light Artillery, Edward W. Nicholson
Battery F, 1st Michigan Light Artillery, George Holbrook
19th Battery, Ohio Light Artillery, Frank Wilson

Third Division, James W. Reilly
First Brigade, S. Palace Love
Second Brigade, John S. Casement
Third Brigade, Thomas J. Henderson
Artillery
15th Battery Indiana Light Artillery, Alonzo D. Harvey
23rd Battery, Indiana Light Artillery, Aaron A. Wilber
Battery D, 1st Ohio Light Artillery, Giles J. Cockerill

Fourth Division, Jacob Ammen
First Brigade, William Y. Dillard
Second Brigade, Davis Tillson
Third Brigade, Michael L. Patterson

Note. Ammen's division was in East Tennessee and was not with Cox in Georgia.

Cleveland, Tennessee
2nd Ohio Heavy Artillery, Horatio G. Gibson

After the failure of French's attack on Allatoona, Hood marched westward with his army by way of Dallas and Van Wert and struck the railroad north of Resaca October 12, 1864. He moved on to Dalton the next day, and there he turned west and marched by way of Villanow and Alpine, Georgia, reaching Gadsden, Alabama on October 20. He then marched to Decatur, Alabama and arrived there October 26. From Decatur he moved to Tuscumbia, Alabama, where he remained from October 30 to November 10. He finally moved on to Florence, where he arrived November 13.

From Rome, Cox moved on northward with the rest of Sherman's army, reaching Calhoun and Resaca October 15, 1864. From Resaca Cox marched northwest to Villanow on October 16, then passed through Gover's Gap (or Mattox's Gap) October 18, and arrived near Melville Post Office on the Gaylesville road October 19. The next day he established corps headquarters at Gaylesville, and the corps camped nearby.

Sherman halted his pursuit of Hood at Gaylesville, and while there he planned the future movements of his army. He decided to send sufficient reinforcements to George H. Thomas, then commanding the United States forces in Tennessee, to prevent Hood's occupation of the state, and to march back with the rest of his army toward Atlanta and prepare for a march across Georgia toward Savannah on the Atlantic Coast.

Schofield returned to the army at Gaylesville, and on October 22, 1864 he resumed command of Twenty-Third Corps (Army of the Ohio in the Field). Cox resumed command of his Third Division.

On October 27, 1864 (ordered October 26), David S. Stanley, with his Fourth Corps, Army of the Cumberland, marched to Chattanooga; he then moved on to Pulaski, Tennessee.

After the departure of Fourth Corps, Sherman marched back with the rest of the army to Rome, and there he decided to send Schofield with his Twenty-Third Corps to join Thomas as an additional reinforcement. From Rome Twenty-Third Corps marched to Dalton November 1, 1864, where it was to be moved by rail to Nashville as rapidly as transportation could be obtained.

On November 11, 1864, Thomas H. Ruger, formerly commander of Second Brigade, First Division, Twentieth Corps at Atlanta, arrived at Nashville. He then moved on to Johnsonville, Tennessee, where he relieved Joseph A. Cooper in command of Second Division, Twenty-Third Corps. Upon being relieved, Cooper resumed command of his First Brigade, Second Division.

On November 14, 1864, by Thomas' order, Schofield assumed command of all United States forces at Pulaski, Tennessee and those troops operating in front of the town.

By November 15, 1864, the troops of Twenty-Third Corps were in position in Tennessee as follows: Cox's Third Division was at Pulaski; Silas A. Strickland's Third Brigade of Ruger's Second Division was at Columbia; and Cooper's First Brigade and Orlando H. Moore's Second Brigade of Second Division were at Johnsonville. During the period November 21–23, Moore's brigade started by rail toward Columbia, and it had arrived there by November 24.

On November 24, 1864, Ruger was assigned command of a provisionally organized division that consisted of Moore's and Strickland's brigades.

Finally, after a pause at Decatur, Hood advanced on November 21–22, 1864 with his Army of Tennessee toward Columbia at the beginning of his invasion of Tennessee.

On November 24, 1864, when Schofield learned of Hood's approach, he ordered Cox to move back from Lynnville, where he had been encamped, toward Columbia and hold the town until the rest of Schofield's command arrived. Cox was soon engaged on the Mount Pleasant road and succeeded in holding up the enemy's advance until Schofield had occupied a defensive position in front of the town. Schofield then evacuated Columbia and withdrew during the night of November 27 to a new defensive position north of the Duck River.

Hood soon arrived in front of the lines at Columbia, and then, instead of attacking, he moved eastward on a wide flanking movement to gain the rear of Schofield's army at Columbia. He marched along the south bank of the Duck River, then crossed to the north bank, and moved to a position near Spring Hill, where he arrived on the night of November 29.

In response to this movement, Schofield moved a part of his command to Spring Hill. He then decided to move on with all of his army, including Cox's division and Ruger's division of Twenty-Third Corps, to Franklin, Tennessee. This movement was completed during the night of November 29, 1864, and the next morning Schofield put his army in position on a line along the south and west sides of Franklin with its flanks resting on the Harpeth River. On the morning of November 30, Cox was placed in temporary command of Twenty-Third Corps, and he put the corps in position on the left of the line, with his left on the Harpeth River. Stanley's Fourth Corps was formed on the right of Cox, with its right on the Harpeth.

Late in the afternoon of November 30, Hood launched a series of attacks on Schofield's line, and much of the heaviest fighting took place on the front of Twenty-Third Corps. Schofield's divisions, however, maintained their positions and inflicted terrible losses on the enemy. For details of the movement of Twenty-Third Corps from Decatur, Georgia to Franklin, Tennessee, see Franklin and Nashville Campaign (Hood's Invasion of Tennessee); and for details of the Battle of Franklin, see Franklin and Nashville Campaign (Hood's Invasion of Tennessee), Battle of Franklin, Tennessee.

The organization of Twenty-Third Corps at the Battle of Franklin November 30, 1864 was as follows:

TWENTY-THIRD CORPS, Jacob D. Cox

Second Division, Thomas H. Ruger
    First Brigade, Joseph A. Cooper
    Second Brigade, Orlando H. Moore
    Third Brigade, Silas A. Strickland
    Artillery
        22nd Battery, Indiana Light Artillery, Edward W. Nicholson
        Battery F, 1st Michigan Light Artillery, Byron D. Paddock
        19th Battery, Ohio Light Artillery, Frank Wilson

Note. Cox was in temporary command of Twenty-Third Corps while John M. Schofield was in command of the United States Forces at Franklin.

Third Division, Jacob D. Cox
    First Brigade, James W. Reilly

Second Brigade, John S. Casement
Third Brigade, Israel N. Stiles
Artillery
　15th Battery, Indiana Light Artillery, Alonzo D.
　　Harvey
　23rd Battery, Indiana Light Artillery, Aaron A.
　　Wilber
　Battery D, 1st Ohio Light Artillery, Giles J. Cock-
　　erill

Note. While Cox led the corps at Franklin, James W.
Reilly took charge of Third Division.

On the night of November 30, 1864, following the Battle of Franklin, Schofield's army, including Twenty-Third Corps, withdrew to Nashville, where it arrived on the morning of December 1 and joined the army that Thomas was assembling there. The troops that Schofield brought to Nashville then came under Thomas' control, and Schofield resumed command of Twenty-Third Corps. The corps took position on the left of Thomas' defensive line, between the Nashville and Chattanooga Railroad and the Hillsboro road. Hood followed Schofield from Franklin and entrenched his army on a line south of Nashville, facing Thomas' army.

By an order of December 8, 1864, Twenty-Third Corps was reorganized to consist of three divisions. On that date, Darius N. Couch relieved Thomas H. Ruger in command of Second Division, and Ruger was assigned command of First Division, which was to be organized as rapidly as possible, but this was not completed until after the Battle of Nashville.

On December 15, 1864, after a long delay caused by bad weather, Thomas launched an attack on Hood, and in a battle lasting that day and the next completely routed the Army of Tennessee and drove it south toward the Tennessee River. Twenty-Third Corps did not take part in the heaviest fighting at the Battle of Nashville December 15–16, but it was engaged both days. For details of the Battle of Nashville, see Franklin and Nashville Campaign (Hood's Invasion of Tennessee), Battle of Franklin, Tennessee.

The organization of Twenty-Third Corps at the Battle of Nashville was as follows:

TWENTY-THIRD CORPS, John M. Schofield

Second Division, Darius N. Couch

First Brigade, Joseph A. Cooper
Second Brigade, Orlando H. Moore
Third Brigade, John Mehringer
Artillery
　15th Battery, Indiana Light Artillery, Alonzo D.
　　Harvey
　19th Battery, Ohio Light Artillery, Frank Wilson

Third Division, Jacob D. Cox
　First Brigade, Charles C. Doolittle
　Second Brigade, John S. Casement
　Third Brigade, Israel N. Stiles
　Artillery
　　23rd Battery, Indiana Light Artillery, Aaron A.
　　　Wilber
　　Battery D, 1st Ohio Light Artillery, Giles J. Cock-
　　　erill

On December 29, 1864, while Twenty-Third Corps was at Columbia, Tennessee, the reorganization of First Division was announced, and on December 31 the corps was organized as follows:

TWENTY-THIRD CORPS, John M. Schofield

First Division, Thomas H. Ruger
　First Brigade, John M. Orr
　Second Brigade, John C. McQuiston
　Third Brigade, Minor T. Thomas
　Artillery
　　22nd Battery, Indiana Light Artillery, Edward W.
　　　Nicholson
　　Battery F, 1st Michigan Light Artillery, Byron D.
　　　Paddock

Note 1. First Brigade and Second Brigade had the
same composition as they did when the division was
discontinued August 11, 1864 during the Atlanta Cam-
paign.
Note 2. First Brigade consisted of the 120th, 124th,
and 128th Indiana regiments, which were taken from
Third Division.
Note 3. Second Brigade consisted of the 123rd, 129th,
and 130th Indiana regiments, which were taken from
Second Division.
Note 4. Third Brigade was organized from the 8th
Minnesota, 174th Ohio, and 178th Ohio regiments,
which were from Robert H. Milroy's Defenses of the
Nashville and Chattanooga Railroad at Murfreesboro.
Minor T. Thomas assumed command of Third Brigade
December 30, 1864.

On January 14, 1865, while Twenty-Third Corps was at Columbia, Tennessee, it was ordered to North Carolina to cooperate with William T.

Sherman's Army of the Military Division of the Mississippi as it arrived from its march northward through the Carolinas from Savannah, Georgia. The corps, commanded by John M. Schofield, embarked at Clifton, Tennessee, on the Tennessee River, January 15–19, moving eastward by way of Louisville, Kentucky, Cincinnati, Ohio, and Pittsburgh, Pennsylvania, and arriving at Washington, D.C. It then sailed from Alexandria and began to arrive in North Carolina at Fort Fisher on February 8. The last troops arrived February 23. The advance elements of Twenty-Third Corps were almost immediately assigned to aid Alfred H. Terry's United States Forces at Fort Fisher in its operations against Robert F. Hoke's Confederate troops that were guarding Wilmington, North Carolina. Jacob D. Cox's Third Division, to which Orlando H. Moore's Second Brigade of Darius N. Couch's Second Division was attached, advanced with Terry's command and was present at the occupation of Wilmington, North Carolina on February 22. For details of the campaign against Wilmington, see Department of North Carolina, January 31, 1865–May 19, 1866, Operations in the Department of North Carolina, Capture of Wilmington, North Carolina, in Volume I.

On February 9, 1865, Schofield assumed command of the Department of North Carolina, and thereafter his command was designated as Department of North Carolina, Army of the Ohio.

The other two brigades of Couch's division arrived February 22–23, 1865, and by February 26, Second Division and Third Division were assembled at Wilmington. Thomas H. Ruger's First Division arrived at Fort Fisher February 22–23, but it was ordered to New Berne, where it arrived during the period February 28–March 1.

February 25, 1865, Cox was assigned command of the newly constituted District of Beaufort, with his headquarters at New Berne. Upon Cox's departure from Wilmington to assume his new command, James W. Reilly assumed temporary command of Third Division, Twenty-Third Corps. On February 28, Couch assumed command of Second Division and Third Division, and Nathaniel C. McLean took temporary charge of Couch's Second Division.

At New Berne, on March 1, 1865, Cox organized a Provisional Corps for the purpose of advancing along the Atlantic and North Carolina Railroad toward Goldsboro and putting the road in running order to that point. Ruger's First Division was included in Cox's corps, and it was engaged at the Battle of Kinston (or Wise's Forks), North Carolina March 8–10. For additional information, see Department of North Carolina, January 31, 1865–May 19, 1866, Troops in the Department of North Carolina, Cox's Provisional Corps, Army of the Ohio; and see also Department of North Carolina, January 31, 1865–May 19, 1866, Operations in the Department of North Carolina, Advance of Schofield's Army to Goldsboro (Battle of Kinston or Wise's Forks), all in Volume I.

Couch left Wilmington with his own Second Division and Reilly's Third Division of Twenty-Third Corps on March 6 and joined Cox's command near Kinston March 13–14. Cox remained at Kinston until the railroad was repaired to that point, and on March 20 he marched with his Provisional Corps and Couch's two divisions toward Goldsboro, where he arrived the next day.

William T. Sherman's Army of the Military Division of the Mississippi arrived at Goldsboro from its march through the Carolinas March 23–24, 1865, and there he was joined by Schofield's army.

On March 24, 1865, Reilly's Third Division of Twenty-Third Corps was replaced by Ruger's First Division of Cox's Provisional Corps, and Reilly's division was assigned as the garrison of Goldsboro. Couch, with Ruger's First Division and his own Second Division, moved back on the railroad to a point about midway between Goldsboro and Kinston, and Couch established his headquarters at Moseley Hall.

March 31, 1865, Cox was assigned by the president to the permanent command of Twenty-Third Corps, and Cox's Provisional Corps was discontinued. Thus, for the first time since their arrival in North Carolina, the three divisions of Twenty-Third Corps were united under a single commander.

On April 1, 1865, in preparation for further operations against Joseph E. Johnston's army, Sherman designated Cox's Twenty-Third Corps and Alfred H. Terry's Tenth Corps as the Center of his army. Schofield, as commander of the Army of the Ohio, was assigned command of the Center. This organization was to be in effect while Twenty-Third Corps and Tenth Corps were operating with the Army of the Tennessee (Sherman's Right Wing) and the Army of Georgia (Sherman's Left Wing).

On April 7, 1865, Reilly resigned, and Samuel P. Carter was assigned command of Third Division, Twenty-Third Corps. Then, on April 9, Ruger's First Division and Couch's Second Division marched from Moseley Hall to Goldsboro, where they joined Carter's Third Division, and the next day Twenty-Third Corps, as a part of Sherman's army, advanced against the forces commanded by Johnston, which at that time were near Smithfield, North Carolina. When Sherman began his advance, Johnston retired toward Raleigh, North Carolina, and he was closely pursued by Sherman's command. Twenty-Third Corps arrived at Raleigh April 13–14 and went into camp.

All movements of the army were suspended April 15, while Sherman and Johnston met near Durham Station, North Carolina to discuss terms for ending hostilities. Johnston surrendered his army on April 26, 1865, and the war in the East was ended.

The organization of Twenty-Third Corps at the end of April 1865 was as follows:

TWENTY-THIRD CORPS, John M. Schofield, to
    March 31, 1865
    Jacob D. Cox

First Division, Thomas H. Ruger
    First Brigade, John M. Orr, to March 14, 1865
        Israel N. Stiles
    Second Brigade, John C. McQuiston
    Third Brigade, Minor T. Thomas
    Artillery
        Battery F, 1st Michigan Light Artillery, Byron D.
            Paddock
        Elgin Battery (also called Renwick's Battery),
            Illinois Light Artillery, Andrew M. Wood

Note. George W. Alexander's 22nd Battery, Indiana Light Artillery was transferred to First Division, Tenth Corps April 5, 1865.

Second Division, Darius N. Couch, to April 30, 1865
    Joseph A. Cooper
    First Brigade, Orlando H. Moore, to April 26, 1865
        Joseph A. Cooper
    Second Brigade, John Mehringer
    Third Brigade, Silas A. Strickland
    Artillery
        19th Battery, Ohio Light Artillery, Frank Wilson

Note. Alonzo D. Harvey's 15th Battery, Indiana Light Artillery was detached at Wilmington April 5, 1865.

Third Division, Silas A. Strickland, to April 7, 1865
    Samuel P. Carter
    First Brigade, Oscar W. Sterl
    Second Brigade, John S. Casement
    Third Brigade, Thomas J. Henderson
    Artillery
        Battery D, 1st Ohio Light Artillery, Cecil C. Reed

Note. James H. Myers' 23rd Battery, Indiana Light Artillery was detached at Wilmington April 5, 1865.

For additional information about the organization and operations of Twenty-Third Corps during the final days of the war in North Carolina, see Carolinas Campaign, Goldsboro to Raleigh, North Carolina (Surrender of Joseph E. Johnston's Army), in Volume I.

Sherman's Army of the Tennessee and Army of Georgia began their march toward their final rendezvous in Washington, D.C. April 27, 1865, but Cox's Twenty-Third Corps and Terry's Tenth Corps remained in the Department of North Carolina until they were discontinued.

Twenty-Third Corps remained in camp at Raleigh until May 4, 1865, and it then marched to Greensboro, North Carolina. Ruger's division continued on to Charlotte, North Carolina. It arrived there May 11–16 and remained in the vicinity until discontinued on August 1. Joseph A. Cooper's Second Division (commanded by Couch until April 30) moved to Salisbury, North Carolina, where it remained until discontinued July 4. Carter's Third Division advanced from Raleigh to Greensboro May 6, and it remained there until it was discontinued July 4. Carter was then assigned command of the District of Salisbury, Department of North Carolina on July 6.

Twenty-Third Corps was officially discontinued, to date from August 1, 1865.

COMMANDERS OF TWENTY-THIRD CORPS, ARMY OF THE OHIO

George L. Hartsuff	May 28, 1863 to September 25, 1863
Mahlon D. Manson	September 25, 1863 to December 21, 1863
Jacob D. Cox	December 21, 1863 to February 10, 1864

George Stoneman	February 10, 1864 to April 4, 1864
Jacob D. Cox	April 4, 1864 to April 9, 1864
John M. Schofield	April 9, 1864 to May 26, 1864
Jacob D. Cox	May 26, 1864 to May 27, 1864
John M. Schofield	May 28, 1864 to September 14, 1864
Jacob D. Cox	September 14, 1864 to October 22, 1864
John M. Schofield	October 22, 1864 to November 30, 1864
Jacob D. Cox	November 30, 1864 to December 1, 1864
John M. Schofield	December 1, 1864 to March 31, 1865
Jacob D. Cox	March 31, 1865 to June 19, 1865
Thomas H. Ruger	June 19, 1865 to June 27, 1865
Samuel P. Carter	June 27, 1865 to July 12, 1865

CAVALRY CORPS, ARMY OF THE CUMBERLAND

In the western armies there was no official corps organization composed of cavalry until October 29, 1864, when the Cavalry Corps, Military Division of the Mississippi was organized under James H. Wilson. In May 1863, however, David S. Stanley's cavalry command at Murfreesboro, Tennessee was called Cavalry Corps, Department (or Army) of the Cumberland, and this was the designation of the cavalry of the department until October 1864.

The first cavalry division of the western armies was formed as a part of Don Carlos Buell's Army of the Ohio September 5, 1862, when John Kennett assumed command of a division consisting of a First Brigade, commanded by Edward M. McCook, and a Second Brigade, commanded by Lewis Zahm. A Third Brigade, commanded by Ebenezer Gay, was soon added to the division.

When the Department of the Cumberland was re-created October 24, 1862, the designation of Kennett's command was changed to Cavalry Division, Department (or Army) of the Cumberland. On November 24, 1862, David S. Stanley was assigned chief of cavalry of the Department of the Cumberland, and was placed in charge of all cavalry of the department. During the Stones River (or Murfreesboro), Tennessee Campaign of December 26, 1862–

January 5, 1863, the cavalry was organized as follows:

CAVALRY, David S. Stanley

First Cavalry Division, John Kennett
    First Brigade, Robert H. G. Minty
    Second Brigade, Lewis Zahm

Reserve Brigade, David S. Stanley

Note. The Reserve Brigade was under the immediate direction of Stanley during the Stones River Campaign.

When the Army of the Cumberland advanced from Nashville toward Murfreesboro at the beginning of the Stones River Campaign, the cavalry moved out in three columns under the personal direction of Stanley. Kennett, commanding the Cavalry Division, marched with his First Brigade, then commanded by Robert H. G. Minty, in front of Thomas L. Crittenden's Left Wing on the Murfreesboro Pike. Lewis Zahm's Second Brigade marched south on the Franklin Pike to clear away enemy cavalry in that direction, and it then moved eastward by a road that ran parallel to the route of Alexander McD. McCook's Right Wing to protect its right flank. The Reserve Brigade, under Stanley's personal direction, moved ahead of McCook's wing on the Nolensville Pike.

On the night of December 30, 1862, Zahm's brigade camped on the right of Rosecrans' line near Murfreesboro. The next morning it covered the right of Johnson's division as it was driven back at the beginning of the Battle of Stones River, and it was almost continuously engaged with the enemy cavalry during that time. During the rest of the battle, the cavalry was on the extreme right flank of the army on or near Overall Creek. For additional information about the operations of the cavalry during the Stones River Campaign, see Stones River (or Murfreesboro), Tennessee Campaign.

The cavalry of the Army of the Cumberland remained in Middle Tennessee until June 1863, when the Army of the Cumberland moved forward at the beginning of the Tullahoma (or Middle Tennessee) Campaign. During the period April 9–12, 1863, the Cavalry Division was sent to aid Gordon Granger, who was contending with Earl Van Dorn near Franklin, Tennessee. The division was engaged April 10 and was organized as follows:

Cavalry Division, Army of the Cumberland, David S. Stanley
  First Brigade, William B. Sipes
  Second Brigade, Oliver P. Robie
  Third Brigade, Daniel M. Ray

Note. James W. Paramore commanded Second Brigade in March and April 1863, and Robie assumed command April 10, 1863.

The cavalry command consisted of three brigades until May 1863, and then it was reorganized into two divisions as the Cavalry Corps, Army of the Cumberland. At the end of the month the corps was organized as follows:

CAVALRY CORPS, ARMY OF THE CUMBERLAND, David S. Stanley

First Division, Robert B. Mitchell
  First Brigade, Archibald P. Campbell
  Second Brigade, Edward M. McCook

Note 1. Andrew J. Konkle's Battery D (one section), 1st Ohio Light Artillery was attached to Second Brigade.
Note 2. A Third Brigade was organized July 8, 1863 from the 4th, 6th, and 7th Kentucky Cavalry of Campbell's First Brigade and the 5th Kentucky Cavalry of McCook's brigade, and Louis D. Watkins was assigned command.

Second Division, John B. Turchin
  First Brigade, Robert H. G. Minty
  Second Brigade, Eli Long

Note. Nathaniel M. Newell's section of Battery D, 1st Ohio Light Artillery was attached to First Brigade, and James H. Stokes' Battery, Illinois Light Artillery was attached to Second Brigade.

The above was the organization of the cavalry of the Army of the Cumberland during the Tullahoma (or Middle Tennessee) Campaign June 23–July 7, 1863. At the beginning of the campaign, Robert B. Mitchell's First Cavalry Division accompanied Granger's Reserve Corps, which advanced on the right of the army. On June 24, John B. Turchin moved out from Murfreesboro with his Second Cavalry Division to Woodbury, Tennessee in preparation for moving by way of McMinnville and Pocahontas to Manchester. That day, however, Stanley detached Minty's Second Brigade and marched with it to join Mitchell's division. Stanley, with Minty's brigade and Mitchell's division, cooperated with Granger in the movements leading to

the capture of Guy's Gap and Shelbyville, Tennessee. Stanley's cavalry then moved to Manchester, Tennessee June 30. After the departure of Minty's brigade, Turchin, with Eli Long's Second Brigade, joined Thomas L. Crittenden, who was advancing with the divisions of John M. Palmer and Thomas J. Wood of his Twenty-First Corps by way of Bradyville toward Manchester. Turchin, with Long's brigade, arrived at Manchester June 28.

The cavalry then joined in the pursuit of Braxton Bragg's army toward Decherd, Tennessee, where it arrived July 3, 1863. Turchin's Second Cavalry Division then moved on to Salem, Tennessee, about twelve miles southwest of Winchester, July 10. Headquarters of the Cavalry Corps was at Winchester at the end of July 1863.

For details of the operations of the army during this period, see Tullahoma (or Middle Tennessee) Campaign.

There were some changes in the cavalry while it was in Middle Tennessee. A Third Brigade, First Cavalry Division was organized July 8, 1863 from regiments of Kentucky cavalry taken from First Brigade and Second Brigade, and Louis D. Watkins was assigned command. On July 29, George Crook succeeded Turchin in command of Second Cavalry Division. A Third Brigade, Second Cavalry Division was organized August 5, and William W. Lowe was placed in command.

The Army of the Cumberland remained on a line that extended from McMinnville to Winchester, Tennessee until mid-August 1863, and then it began its advance toward Chattanooga. For this movement, Minty's brigade of Crook's Cavalry Division was attached to Horatio P. Van Cleve's Third Division of Thomas L. Crittenden's Twenty-First Corps, which advanced on the left of the army. Minty's cavalry advanced on the left of Van Cleve's division through Sparta and Pikeville and into the Tennessee River Valley opposite Chattanooga. It then remained along the river above Chattanooga for a time, watching the fords and ferries.

Edward M. McCook's First Cavalry Division advanced and crossed the Tennessee River at Caperton's Ferry September 3, 1863, and Long's Second Brigade of Crook's division crossed at Bridgeport September 2; under the direction of Stanley, they marched up Wills Valley, ahead of McCook's Twentieth Corps, to Valley Head. Then on the night of September 8 and early morning of September 9, Stanley moved up onto Lookout Mountain at Winston's Gap, and during the next several days he conducted scouts and reconnaissances in the direction of Alpine and Summerville and toward La Fayette in Georgia.

On the evening of September 14, 1863, Robert B. Mitchell, the commander of First Cavalry Division, who had been absent from the army on sick leave, arrived at Valley Head on his return and relieved Stanley, who was ill, in command of the Cavalry Corps. Stanley then departed for Nashville.

On September 13, 1863, when William S. Rosecrans ordered Alexander McD. McCook to move back from near Alpine and join the army in McLemore's Cove, Mitchell's cavalry followed the infantry up to the top of Lookout Mountain. Then on September 15, Crook moved with Long's brigade to Dougherty's Gap, and Edward M. McCook moved with his division to Valley Head. From there he sent Louis D. Watkins' Third Brigade to Winston to take charge of the sick and the prisoners, and with Archibald P. Campbell's First Brigade and Daniel M. Ray's Second Brigade he marched to Dougherty's Gap. Edward M. McCook then moved down into McLemore's Cove with his command, and Watkins moved to Stevens' Gap.

On September 12, 1863, Minty crossed the Tennessee River with his brigade at Friar's Island. He camped that night at Chattanooga, and the next day he joined Crittenden at Lee and Gordon's Mills. On September 15, Minty was sent into Pea Vine Valley, east of Reed's Bridge on Chickamauga Creek, to watch the country in the direction of Ringgold.

On the morning of September 18, 1863, during the opening moves of the Battle of Chickamauga, Minty began skirmishing with Nathan B. Forrest's Confederate cavalry on Pea Vine Creek, about one mile east of Reed's Bridge on Chickamauga Creek, and he then fought a delaying action with Forrest's troopers and Bushrod R. Johnson's infantry at Reed's Bridge until forced to retire about noon. During this action he was aided by John T. Wilder's mounted brigade of Joseph J. Reynolds' Fourth Division, Fourteenth Corps. After Minty's withdrawal from Reed's Bridge, he reported to Gordon Granger, commander of the Reserve Corps, and was sent to Missionary Ridge to cover Granger's left flank. During the Battle of Chickamauga, Mitchell, with

the rest of the cavalry, was on the right of the army watching the fords on upper Chickamauga Creek.

At the time of the Battle of Chickamauga, the Cavalry Corps was organized as follows:

CAVALRY CORPS, Robert B. Mitchell

First Cavalry Division, Edward M. McCook
  First Brigade, Archibald P. Campbell
  Second Brigade, Daniel M. Ray
  Third Brigade, Louis D. Watkins

Note 1. Third Brigade was organized July 8, 1863.
Note 2. Washington L. Elliott was assigned command of First Cavalry Division October 12, 1863.
Note 3. Nathaniel M. Newell's Battery D (one section), 1st Ohio Light Artillery was attached to Second Brigade.

Second Cavalry Division, George Crook
  First Brigade, Robert H. G. Minty
  Second Brigade, Eli Long
  Third Brigade, William W. Lowe
  Artillery
    Chicago (Illinois) Board of Trade Battery, James H. Stokes

Note. Third Brigade was organized August 5, 1863; it was at Murfreesboro, Tennessee during the time of the Battle of Chickamauga and was not engaged.

On November 8, 1863, Crook's Second Cavalry Division was reorganized as follows:

Second Cavalry Division, George Crook
  First Brigade, William W. Lowe
  Second Brigade, Eli Long
  Third Brigade, John T. Wilder

Note. The former Third Brigade was discontinued November 8, 1863 and was reorganized the same day by the assignment of Wilder's Mounted Infantry Brigade. This brigade was assigned to the cavalry from Fourth Division, Fourteenth Corps October 16, 1863 and was assigned to Second Cavalry Division November 8, 1863

Washington L. Elliott assumed command of the Cavalry Corps, Army of the Cumberland November 20, 1863.

During the winter of 1863–1864, headquarters of the Cavalry Corps was at Chattanooga, Tennessee. First Cavalry Division was at Talbott Station, Tennessee in December 1863; in East Tennessee in January and February 1864; and at Cleveland, Tennessee during March and April 1864. Second Division was at Pulaski, Tennessee in December 1863, and headquarters of the division was at Huntsville, Alabama in February and March 1864. During that period, detachments of the division were at Bridgeport and Huntsville, Alabama; Rossville, Georgia; and Calhoun, Collierville, Columbus, Nashville, and Pulaski in Tennessee.

In preparation for William T. Sherman's campaign against Atlanta, Georgia in the spring of 1864, the Cavalry Corps was reorganized by an order of April 2, 1864 (to take effect April 1) to consist of four divisions. At the end of April 1864 it was organized as follows:

CAVALRY CORPS, Washington L. Elliott

First Division, Edward M. McCook
   First Brigade, Joseph B. Dorr
   Second Brigade, Oscar H. La Grange
   Third Brigade, Louis D. Watkins
   Artillery
      18th Battery, Indiana Light Artillery, William B. Rippetoe

Note. Third Brigade was opposite Chattanooga, and the remainder of the division was at Cleveland, Tennessee.

Second Division, Kenner Garrard
   First Brigade, Robert H. G. Minty
   Second Brigade, Eli Long
   Third Brigade, John T. Wilder
   Artillery
      Chicago (Illinois) Board of Trade Battery, George I. Robinson

Note. Third Brigade was composed of regiments of mounted infantry.

Third Division, Robert H. G. Minty, to April 17, 1864
   Eli H. Murray, to April 26, 1864
   Judson Kilpatrick
   First Brigade, William W. Lowe
   Second Brigade, Charles C. Smith
   Third Brigade, Eli H. Murray

Fourth Division, Alvan C. Gillem
   First Brigade, Duff G. Thornburgh
   Second Brigade, George Spalding
   Third Brigade, John K. Miller

The Fourth Cavalry Division remained in Middle Tennessee during the spring and summer of 1864, but the other three divisions accompanied Sherman on the Atlanta Campaign of May 3–September 8, 1864. Alvan C. Gillem, in addition to commanding the Fourth Cavalry Division, also commanded the Defenses of the Nashville and Northwestern Railroad, with headquarters at Nashville, Tennessee. In May 1864 the brigades of Fourth Division were stationed as follows: First Brigade at Camp Thomas, Second Brigade at Tullahoma, and Third Brigade at Gallatin, Tennessee.

Jacob M. Thornburgh was in temporary command of Fourth Division in July 1864, and he was succeeded by George Spalding. Gillem was transferred to East Tennessee in August 1864, and at that time Fourth Division consisted of only two brigades. The regiments of Third Brigade had been transferred to Andrew Johnson's Governor's Guard, leaving the division organized as follows:

Fourth Cavalry Division, George Spalding
   First Brigade, Jacob M. Thornburgh
   Second Brigade, William J. Clift

During Sherman's advance into Georgia, a special cavalry force of two brigades was formed in Nashville under the command of Lovell H. Rousseau, commander of the District of Tennessee. Thomas J. Harrison commanded the First Brigade, and William D. Hamilton commanded the Second Brigade until July 9, 1864, when he was succeeded by Matthewson T. Patrick. Rousseau left Nashville July 7, in personal command of this force, on a raid to the West Point and Montgomery Railroad. This has been known as Rousseau's Raid, or the Opelika Raid. Rousseau reached Marietta, Georgia July 22, but shortly thereafter he left his cavalry, under the command of Thomas J. Harrison, with Sherman's army and returned to Nashville. For additional information, see Rousseau's Opelika, Alabama Raid.

During the advance into Georgia, Sherman's cavalry generally marched on the flanks of the army until it reached Atlanta. Then, while the cavalry still protected the flanks, Sherman sent out some of the divisions of his cavalry, including the divisions of Kenner Garrard and Edward M. McCook of the Army of the Cumberland, in a number of attempts to destroy the vital railroad lines south of the city, but these were generally unsuccessful. For details of the operations of the Cavalry Corps of the Army of the Cumberland during the Atlanta Campaign, see Atlanta, Georgia Campaign.

During the Atlanta Campaign, the Cavalry Corps, Army of the Cumberland was organized as follows:

CAVALRY CORPS, Washington L. Elliott

First Cavalry Division, Edward M. McCook
  First Brigade, Joseph B. Dorr, to July 20, 1864
    John T. Croxton
    Joseph B. Dorr, to July 30, 1864, captured
    James P. Brownlow, to August 20, 1864
    John T. Croxton
  Second Brigade, Oscar H. La Grange, to May 9, 1864, captured
    James W. Stewart, to May 26, 1864, captured
    Horace P. Lamson, to July 21, 1864
    William H. Torrey, to July 30, 1864, wounded and captured
    Horace P. Lamson
  Third Brigade, Louis D. Watkins, to July 5, 1864
    John K. Faulkner, to August 10, 1864
    Louis D. Watkins
  Artillery
    18th Battery, Indiana Light Artillery, William B. Rippetoe, to September 7, 1864
    Moses M. Beck

Second Cavalry Division, Kenner Garrard
  First Brigade, Robert H. G. Minty
  Second Brigade, Eli Long, to August 20, 1864, wounded
    Beroth B. Eggleston
  Third Brigade (mounted infantry), John T. Wilder, to June 14, 1864, sick
    Abram O. Miller
  Artillery
    Chicago (Illinois) Board of Trade Battery, George I. Robinson

Third Cavalry Division, Judson Kilpatrick, to May 13, wounded
  Eli H. Murray, to May 21, 1864
  William W. Lowe, to July 23, 1864
  Judson Kilpatrick
  First Brigade, Robert Klein
    Matthewson T. Patrick
    J. Morris Young
  Second Brigade, Charles C. Smith, to July 2, 1864
    Thomas W. Sanderson, to August 6, 1864
    Fielder A. Jones
  Third Brigade, Eli H. Murray, to May 13, 1864
    Smith D. Atkins, to May 21, 1864

    Eli H. Murray
  Artillery
    10th Battery, Wisconsin Light Artillery, Yates V. Beebe

Note. Thomas J. Harrison, the commander of Second Brigade, was captured July 31, 1864 while in command of a Provisional Division composed of 8th Indiana, 2nd Kentucky, 5th Iowa, 9th Ohio, and 4th Tennessee cavalry regiments, and one section of Battery E, 1st Michigan Light Artillery. Fielder A. Jones assumed command of his division.

Fourth Cavalry Division, Alvan C. Gillem
  First Brigade, Jacob M. Thornburgh
  Second Brigade, George Spalding
  Third Brigade, John K. Miller

Note. Fourth Cavalry Division was formed from Tennessee regiments April 1, 1864.

On October 29, 1864, the separate cavalry commands of the departments of the Military Division of the Mississippi were organized into the Cavalry Corps of the Military Division of the Mississippi. James H. Wilson was assigned command October 24 and assumed command October 29. The Cavalry Corps, Army of the Cumberland was thus discontinued, and the designations of the cavalry divisions were changed as follows: Edward M. McCook's First Cavalry Division became First Cavalry Division, Military Division of the Mississippi; Eli Long's Second Cavalry Division became Second Cavalry Division, Military Division of the Mississippi; Judson Kilpatrick's Third Cavalry Division became Third Cavalry Division, Military Division of the Mississippi; and George Spalding's Fourth Cavalry Division became Seventh Cavalry Division, Military Division of the Mississippi.

There were, however, some cavalry organizations remaining in the Department of the Cumberland. On February 28, 1865, Alvan C. Gillem was assigned command of the cavalry forces in the District of East Tennessee, and on March 17 these forces were organized into a cavalry division designated as Cavalry Division, District of East Tennessee, Department of the Cumberland. Gillem was assigned command, and his division was organized as follows:

Cavalry Division, District of East Tennessee, Alvan C. Gillem
  First Brigade, William J. Palmer

Second Brigade, Simeon B. Brown
Third Brigade, John K. Miller

For additional information about Gillem's Cavalry Division, see Stoneman's Raid into Southwestern Virginia and Western North Carolina, in Volume I.

In April 1865, Embury D. Osband's Cavalry Division of the Department of the Mississippi was included in the District of West Tennessee, Department of the Cumberland. This division was organized as follows:

Cavalry Division, Embury D. Osband
    First Brigade, John E. Phelps
    Second Brigade, William Thompson
    Third Brigade, Otto Funke

COMMANDERS OF THE CAVALRY CORPS, ARMY OF THE CUMBERLAND

John Kennett	October 24, 1862 to November 24, 1862
David S. Stanley	November 24, 1862 to September 9, 1863
Robert B. Mitchell	September 9, 1863 to November 14, 1863
David S. Stanley	November 14, 1863 to November 20, 1863
Washington L. Elliott	November 20, 1863 to August 19, 1864
Richard W. Johnson	August 19, 1864 to October 29, 1864

Note. The designation of Cavalry Corps was not used until May 1863.

CAVALRY CORPS, ARMY OF THE OHIO

The cavalry forces of Don Carlos Buell's Army of the Ohio, District of the Ohio were organized into a Cavalry Division under the command of John Kennett September 5, 1862. At that time Buell's army was at Nashville and Murfreesboro while it was retiring northward as Braxton Bragg's Army of Tennessee advanced from Chattanooga on its way to Kentucky. The division was organized as follows:

Cavalry Division, Army of the Ohio, John Kennett
    First Brigade, Edward M. McCook
    Second Brigade, Lewis Zahm

On September 17, 1862, Ebenezer Gay was assigned as chief of cavalry to Charles C. Gilbert, then commanding at Louisville, Kentucky. Gay then organized a Third Brigade of the Cavalry Division.

On October 8, 1862, the day of the Battle of Perryville, the Cavalry Division was organized as follows:

Cavalry Division, John Kennett
    First Brigade, Edward M. McCook
        1st Indiana, Robert R. Stewart
        1st Kentucky, Frank Wolford
        3rd Kentucky, Eli H. Murray
        4th Kentucky, Jesse Bayles
    Second Brigade, Lewis Zahm
        5th Kentucky, John Q. Owsley
        3rd Ohio, Douglas A. Murray
        4th Ohio, John L. Pugh
    Third Brigade, Ebenezer Gay
        9th Kentucky (detachment), John Boyle
        2nd Michigan, Archibald P. Campbell
        9th Pennsylvania, Thomas C. James

Gay's brigade advanced with the Army of the Ohio to Perryville and was present during the battle. McCook's and Zahm's brigades were not at Perryville, but they came up later and joined the army in the pursuit of Bragg's and E. Kirby Smith's forces toward East Tennessee after the battle.

On October 24, 1862, the Department of the Cumberland was re-created. The designation of Buell's army was changed to Fourteenth Corps, Department of the Cumberland, and William S. Rosecrans was assigned command. Kennett's division then became a part of the Army of the Cumberland and was present during the Battle of Stones River.

When the Department of the Ohio was reorganized on August 19, 1862, the troops of the department were scattered among the many districts of the department, and the largest cavalry organizations were regiments.

The Twenty-Third Corps, Army of the Ohio was

created by an order of April 27, 1863, and when it was organized May 22, 1863 under George L. Hartsuff, there were two cavalry brigades in the department. August V. Kautz commanded the First Cavalry Brigade, District of Central Kentucky, and Frank Wolford commanded a cavalry brigade in the same district.

Kautz remained in command of First Brigade at Monticello, Kentucky until June 24, 1863, and he then commanded the Third Brigade (a cavalry brigade) of Samuel P. Carter's First Division, Twenty-Third Corps from June 24 to August 6. During this period, Kautz led his brigade in the pursuit of John Hunt Morgan through Ohio in July. In June 1863, Kautz's brigade was organized as follows:

Third Brigade, First Division, August V. Kautz
9th Michigan Cavalry, David I. James
2nd Ohio Cavalry, George A. Purington
7th Ohio Cavalry, Israel Garrard
Mountain Howitzer Battery, Jesse S. Law

Wolford's brigade was discontinued in June 1863.

During June 1863, Samuel R. Mott commanded Second Brigade, Fourth Division, Twenty-Third Corps, which was also a cavalry brigade, and it was organized as follows:

Second Brigade, Fourth Division, Samuel R. Mott
8th East Tennessee, Felix A. Reeve
118th Ohio, Thomas L. Young
5th Tennessee Cavalry, Jesse H. Strickland
10th Kentucky Cavalry, Ralph R. Maltby
14th Kentucky Cavalry, Henry C. Lilly
8th Michigan Cavalry, Grover S. Wormer
15th Battery, Indiana Light Artillery, John C. H. Von Sehlen
19th Battery, Ohio Light Artillery, Joseph C. Shields

Note. At that time the other brigades of Twenty-Third Corps were mixed brigades consisting of infantry and cavalry regiments and also artillery. For details, see Twenty-Third Corps, Army of the Ohio.

On August 6, 1863, Twenty-Third Corps was reorganized in preparation for Ambrose E. Burnside's East Tennessee Campaign, and Fourth Division was organized to consist of mounted troops as follows:

Fourth Division, Samuel P. Carter

First Brigade, Robert K. Byrd
112th Illinois Mounted Infantry, Thomas J. Henderson
8th Michigan Cavalry, Grover S. Wormer
45th Ohio Mounted Infantry, George E. Ross
1st Tennessee Mounted Infantry, John Ellis
15th Battery, Indiana Light Artillery, William H. Torr
Second Brigade, John W. Foster
14th Illinois Cavalry, Horace Capron
5th Indiana Cavalry, Felix W. Graham
65th Indiana Mounted Infantry, Thomas Johnson
9th Ohio Cavalry (four companies), William D. Hamilton
8th Tennessee Cavalry (four companies), John M. Sawyers
Battery M, 1st Illinois Light Artillery, John H. Colvin
Third Brigade, James M. Shackelford
9th Michigan Cavalry, James I. David
2nd Ohio Cavalry, George A. Purington
7th Ohio Cavalry, Israel Garrard
2nd Tennessee Mounted Infantry, Daniel A. Carpenter
Battery K, 1st Michigan Light Artillery, Charles J. Thompson
1st Battery, Tennessee Light Artillery, R. Clay Crawford

In addition to the mounted troops of Carter's Fourth Division, Twenty-Third Corps, Frank Wolford commanded an Independent Cavalry Brigade, which reported to corps headquarters. This brigade was organized as follows:

Wolford's Cavalry Brigade, Frank Wolford
1st Kentucky Cavalry, Silas Adams
11th Kentucky Cavalry, Milton Graham
12th Kentucky Cavalry, Eugene W. Crittenden
Howitzer Battery, Jesse S. Law

Wolford's brigade remained as an independent brigade until transferred to the Cavalry Corps, Army of the Ohio November 3, 1863.

The above was the organization of the mounted troops that Burnside led into East Tennessee in August 1863, but in October 1863 a Fourth Cavalry Brigade, Fourth Division was organized, largely from regiments of the other brigades of the division. John W. Foster was assigned command. The brigade was organized as follows:

Fourth Brigade, Fourth Division, John W. Foster
  14th Illinois Cavalry, Horace Capron
  5th Indiana Cavalry, Felix W. Graham
  65th Indiana Mounted Infantry, Thomas G. Brown
  9th Ohio Cavalry (four companies). William D. Hamilton
  8th Tennessee Cavalry, John M. Sawyers
  Battery M, 1st Illinois Light Artillery, John H. Colvin

On September 10, 1863, Samuel P. Carter was assigned as provost marshal of East Tennessee, and James M. Shackelford assumed command of Fourth Division, Twenty-Third Corps. On October 31, 1863, Fourth Division was organized as follows:

Fourth Division, Twenty-Third Corps, James M. Shackelford
  First Brigade, Charles D. Pennebaker
  Second Brigade, Emery S. Bond
  Third Brigade, James P. T. Carter
  Fourth Brigade, John W. Foster

In the western armies, there were no formal corps organizations composed of cavalry until October 24, 1864, when James H. Wilson was assigned command of the Cavalry Corps, Military Division of the Mississippi, which was to consist of the mounted troops of the armies of the Cumberland, the Ohio, and the Tennessee. On November 3, 1864, however, a temporary cavalry organization known as the Cavalry Corps, Army of the Ohio was formed from Fourth Division, Twenty-Third Corps, and James M. Shackelford was assigned command. The corps was organized as follows:

CAVALRY CORPS, James M. Shackelford

First Division, William P. Sanders, to November 18, 1863, killed
  Frank Wolford
  First Brigade, Frank Wolford, to November 18, 1863
    Silas Adams
  Second Brigade, Robert K. Byrd
    Emery S. Bond
  Third Brigade, Charles D. Pennebaker

Note. Byrd was in command of the post of Kingston, Tennessee during the Knoxville, Tennessee Campaign.

Second Division, James P. T. Carter
  First Brigade, Israel Garrard
  Second Brigade, John W. Foster

Orders for all military movements of the Cavalry Corps came from Headquarters, Army of the Ohio, and returns and reports were submitted to Headquarters, Twenty-Third Corps.

On December 12, 1863, all cavalry forces in the Department of the Ohio were consolidated into a separate corps, and on December 15, Samuel D. Sturgis assumed command of all the cavalry in the department except that commanded by Washington L. Elliott, who was at Kingston, Tennessee with Edward M. McCook's First Division, Cavalry Corps, Army of the Cumberland. At the end of December 1863, the cavalry corps, which was at Mossy Creek, with a detachment near Buffalo Creek, was organized as follows:

CAVALRY CORPS, Samuel D. Sturgis

First Division, Frank Wolford
  First Brigade, Silas Adams
  Second Brigade, Emery S. Bond, to January 1864
    Thomas J. Henderson
  Third Brigade, Charles D. Pennebaker, to January 1864
    S. Palace Love

Second Division, John W. Foster, to January 1864
  Israel Garrard
  First Brigade, Israel Garrard, to January 1864
    George G. Miner
  Second Brigade, Horace Capron, to January 1864
    Thomas H. Butler
  Artillery
    John H. Colvin's Battery, Illinois Light Artillery

Note. Two of the three regiments of Second Brigade, First Division were mounted infantry; all three regiments of Third Brigade, First Division were mounted infantry; and one regiment of Second Brigade, Second Division was mounted infantry.

The cavalry of the Army of the Ohio participated vigorously in Burnside's East Tennessee Campaign August 16–October 19, 1863; the Knoxville, Tennessee Campaign November 4–December 23, 1863; and the operations in East Tennessee during the rest of the winter of 1863–1864. For details of these operations, see East Tennessee Campaign (Burnside); Knoxville, Tennessee Campaign; and Army of the Ohio (Burnside).

The Cavalry Corps had been in the field almost continuously from August 1863 to January 1864, and by early February 1864 both men and animals had been so reduced in numbers, and were in such poor physical condition, that John G. Foster, then commanding the Department of the Ohio, ordered Sturgis to dismount one of his divisions and turn over the horses to the cavalry divisions of Edward M. McCook and Israel Garrard. This was done, and by February 11, Sturgis was on his way to Paris, Kentucky with the dismounted men of Wolford's First Cavalry Division, which was to be remounted, reorganized, and reequipped for field service.

Garrard's Second Cavalry Division remained in East Tennessee until March 22, 1864, when it was ordered to Knoxville, and was then sent on to Kentucky to join the rest of the corps.

On April 8, 1864, because of the withdrawal of the mounted infantry regiments, Sturgis ordered the reorganization of the Cavalry Corps as follows:

CAVALRY CORPS, Samuel D. Sturgis

First Division, Israel Garrard
    First Brigade, commander not given
    Second Brigade, Horace Capron

Second Division, James Biddle
    First Brigade, Eugene W. Crittenden
    Second Brigade, Alexander W. Holeman

Sturgis was relieved, however, before the reorganization could be carried out. George Stoneman was relieved from command of Twenty-Third Corps April 4, 1864; the next day he was ordered to Kentucky to assume command of all cavalry in the state except that belonging to the District of Kentucky, and he was directed to assemble his command at or near Lexington, Kentucky and to organize them for field service. Sturgis was then relieved as chief of cavalry of the Army of the Ohio, and on April 9, Stoneman was assigned command of a newly organized Cavalry Division, Army of the Ohio.

At the time of the reorganization of Twenty-Third Corps April 11 or 10, 1864, Stoneman's cavalry was organized as follows:

Cavalry Division, George Stoneman
    First Brigade, James Biddle
    Second Brigade, Thomas H. Butler
    Third Brigade, Horace Capron

During April 1864, Stoneman reorganized his

Cavalry Corps to consist of two divisions, and at the end of the month it was organized as follows:

First Division, Charles D. Pennebaker
    First Brigade, commander not given
        1st Kentucky Cavalry, Silas Adams
        11th Kentucky Cavalry, Alexander W. Holeman
    Second Brigade, commander not given
        6th Indiana Cavalry, Courtland C. Matson
        8th Michigan Cavalry, Elisha Mix
    Third Brigade, commander not given
        16th Illinois Cavalry, Christian Thielemann
        12th Kentucky Cavalry, Eugene W. Crittenden

Second Division, Israel Garrard
    First Brigade, Israel Garrard
        9th Michigan Cavalry, Solomon P. Brockway
        7th Ohio Cavalry, Solomon L. Green
    Second Brigade, no commander given
        5th Indiana Cavalry, Thomas H. Butler
        16th Kentucky Cavalry, George F. Barnes

Note. As of the end of April 1864, not all of the units of this organization were ready to take the field.

During April 1864, William T. Sherman, commanding the Military Division of the Mississippi, was making preparations for the movement of his army into Georgia for his campaign against Atlanta, and on April 26, Schofield ordered Stoneman, then at Nicholasville, Kentucky, to move forward at once with his available cavalry, and to leave that part of his force not yet ready for field service with orders to follow as soon as refitted.

On April 28–29, 1864, James Biddle's Second Brigade (consisting of three regiments) left Nicholasville, with orders to be at Kingston, Tennessee by May 5–6. Alexander Holeman's Independent Brigade of two regiments left Nicholasville on April 30 and followed one day's march behind Biddle. The 5th Indiana Cavalry left May 1 and marched in rear of Holeman. Stoneman did not join Schofield's Army of the Ohio in front of Dalton until May 10, three days after Sherman began his advance toward Atlanta. During the Atlanta Campaign, Stoneman's cavalry was generally called Stoneman's Cavalry Division or Stoneman's Command.

All the men of Biddle's and Holeman's brigades that were left behind were placed under Horace Capron, who was to complete their refitting and then send them forward to rejoin their regiments as rapidly as possible.

On May 30, 1864, when Sherman's army was on the line of Dallas New Hope Church Pickett's Mill in Georgia, the following cavalry of the Army of the Ohio was still reequipping at Nicholasville, Kentucky:

First Brigade, Israel Garrard
   16th Kentucky Cavalry, George F. Barnes
   9th Michigan Cavalry, George S. Acker
   7th Ohio Cavalry, George G. Miner
Third Brigade, Horace Capron
   8th Michigan Cavalry, Elisha Mix
   14th Illinois Cavalry (detachment), William W. Rowcliff
   6th Indiana Cavalry (detachment), Isaac M. Brown
   McLaughlin's (Ohio) Squadron, Richard Rice

Note. In addition to the above troops, detachments of the 16th Illinois, 5th Indiana, and 11th and 12th Kentucky cavalry regiments were attached to Capron's brigade, and were under the command of Friedrich Schambeck.

When ready for the field, Capron's brigade served for a time guarding Sherman's supply line, and it then joined the army on June 28, 1864, the day after the Battle of Kennesaw Mountain. Garrard's brigade remained in Kentucky until July, joining Stoneman's command in the field on July 27.

Stoneman's Cavalry Division operated on the flanks of Sherman's army during the advance toward Atlanta, and was on the left flank near Decatur, Georgia in late July 1864. On July 27, Stoneman left Decatur on a raid to Macon, Georgia with a command consisting of Biddle's First Brigade (designation changed to Second Brigade July 31), Capron's Third Brigade, and Adams' Independent Brigade (formerly Holeman's). On arriving near Macon, however, Stoneman believed himself to be confronted by a superior force, and he began to withdraw on the road along which he had advanced. On July 31, Stoneman and many of his men were captured, and his division was largely destroyed. On August 1, Horace Capron assumed command of remnants of the division.

In a reorganization of the cavalry of the Army of the Ohio August 11, 1864, Israel Garrard was assigned command of the Cavalry Division, which was organized as follows:

Cavalry Division, Israel Garrard
   First Brigade, Horace Capron
   Second Brigade, George S. Acker

Note 1. First Brigade consisted of dismounted men, and Second Brigade of mounted men.
Note 2. William D. Hamilton also commanded a Mounted Brigade August 16–23, 1864.

For details of the operations of Stoneman's cavalry during the Atlanta Campaign, see the following: Atlanta, Georgia Campaign; and see also Atlanta, Georgia Campaign, Cavalry Raids on the Railroads South of Atlanta, Georgia, Stoneman's Raid to Macon, Georgia.

The Cavalry Division retained the above organization during the remainder of the Atlanta Campaign and through September 1864, while Twenty-Third Corps (Army of the Ohio) was encamped near Decatur, Georgia. In October it marched back with the army in pursuit of John B. Hood's Army of Tennessee, and on November 1 it moved northward with Twenty-Third Corps to join George H. Thomas' forces in Tennessee.

On November 10, 1864, while the corps was in Middle Tennessee, the Cavalry Corps, Army of the Ohio was discontinued. The Cavalry Corps, Military Division of the Mississippi was created by an order of October 24, 1864, and James H. Wilson assumed command that day. On November 9, 1864, Wilson announced the organization of the new corps as consisting of eight divisions, and the cavalry of the Army of the Ohio was assigned as Sixth Division, Cavalry Corps, Military Division of the Mississippi. Richard W. Johnson assumed command of this division on November 24. For additional information, see Franklin and Nashville Campaign (Hood's Invasion of Tennessee).

CAVALRY CORPS, DISTRICT OF WEST TENNESSEE

For details of the organization and operations of the Cavalry Corps, District of West Tennessee, see Cavalry Forces of the Department of the Tennessee, Cavalry in the District of West Tennessee.

CAVALRY CORPS, MILITARY DIVISION OF THE MISSISSIPPI

The Cavalry Corps, Military Division of the Mississippi was created by an order dated October 24, 1864, to consist of the cavalry forces of the Military Division. James H. Wilson was assigned command, and he assumed command October 24. The cavalry forces of the division at that time consisted of seventy-two cavalry and mounted infantry regiments, and sixty-one of these were incorporated into the Cavalry Corps.

The cavalry forces in the Military Division of the Mississippi at the end of October 1864 were as follows:

CAVALRY OF THE DEPARTMENT OF THE CUMBERLAND, Washington L. Elliott

First Division, Edward M. McCook
First Brigade, John T. Croxton
Second Brigade, Horace P. Lamson
Third Brigade, Louis D. Watkins

Note 1. First Division was at Calhoun, Georgia.
Note 2. On November 9, 1864, the designation of First Division, Department of the Cumberland was changed to First Division, Cavalry Corps, Military Division of the Mississippi.

Second Division, Kenner Garrard
First Brigade, James F. Andress, to November 6, 1864
Abram O. Miller
Second Brigade, Beroth B. Eggleston, to November 16, 1864
Robert H. G. Minty
Third Brigade, Abram O. Miller

Note 1. Second Division was at Rome, Georgia.
Note 2. October 29, 1864, Garrard was ordered to reorganize his division into two brigades, and move with it to Nashville, Tennessee. Third Brigade was transferred to First Brigade November 6, 1864.
Note 3. On November 9, 1864, the designation of Second Division, Department of the Cumberland was changed to Second Cavalry Division, Cavalry Corps, Military Division of the Mississippi.
Note 4. On November 16, 1864, Second Division, Cavalry Corps was organized into brigades.

Third Division, Judson Kilpatrick
First Brigade, commander not given

Second Brigade, William Thayer
Third Brigade, Smith D. Atkins

Note 1. Third Division was at Stilesboro, Georgia.
Note 2. On November 9, 1864, the designation of Third Division, Army of the Cumberland was changed to Third Cavalry Division, Cavalry Corps, Military Division of the Mississippi.

Fourth Division, George Spalding
First Brigade, Jacob M. Thornburgh
Second Brigade, William J. Clift

Note. Fourth Division was composed of Tennessee cavalry regiments; First Brigade was at Decatur, Alabama, and Second Brigade was at Pulaski, Tennessee.

CAVALRY CORPS, DISTRICT OF WEST TENNESSEE, Benjamin H. Grierson

First Division, Edward Hatch
First Brigade, Oliver Wells
Second Brigade, Datus E. Coon

Note 1. First Division was at Pulaski, Tennessee.
Note 2. On November 9, 1864, the designation of First Division, Cavalry Corps, District of West Tennessee was changed to Fifth Division, Cavalry Corps, Military Division of the Mississippi.

Second Division, Edward F. Winslow
First Brigade, Joseph Karge
Second Brigade, John W. Noble

Note 1. Winslow, with a detachment of his Second Division, was in Missouri, and the remainder of the division was in West Tennessee.
Note 2. On November 9, 1864, the designation of Second Division, Cavalry Corps, District of West Tennessee was changed to Fourth Division, Cavalry Corps, Military Division of the Mississippi.

CAVALRY, ARMY OF THE OHIO
First Brigade, Horace Capron
Second Brigade, Israel Garrard

Note 1. First Brigade was at Pulaski, Tennessee, and the regiments under Garrard were at Atlanta, Georgia. Second Brigade was not carried on the rolls of the Cavalry Corps.
Note 2. First Brigade and Second Brigade of Sixth Division, Cavalry Corps, Military Division of the Mississippi were organized from the cavalry forces attached to the Army of the Ohio.

CAVALRY, DISTRICT OF TENNESSEE
Five cavalry regiments of the District of Tennessee, Department of the Cumberland were stationed

at Pulaski and Tullahoma in Tennessee and at Larkinsville in Alabama.

UNASSIGNED

Two unassigned cavalry regiments were at Wauhatchie, Tennessee and at Gaylesville, Alabama.

Wilson assumed command of the Cavalry Corps, Military Division of the Mississippi October 29, 1864, and he established his headquarters with Sherman's army, which was then at Gaylesville, Alabama, where it had halted after following John B. Hood's Army of Tennessee northward from Atlanta. The next day, however, Wilson was ordered to Nashville to organize his command to aid in opposing Hood, who was then threatening an invasion of Tennessee.

The appointment of Wilson to command the Cavalry Corps of the Military Division of the Mississippi presented a problem because George Stoneman, chief of cavalry of the Army of the Ohio; Washington L. Elliott, chief of cavalry of the Army of the Cumberland; Benjamin H. Grierson, chief of cavalry of the District of West Tennessee; and Kenner Garrard were all senior to Wilson, and they were all necessarily relieved of their commands.

On November 9, 1864, the office of chief of cavalry of the Military Division of the Mississippi was abolished, and on the same day the organization of the Cavalry Corps, Military Division of the Mississippi was announced as follows:

CAVALRY CORPS, James H. Wilson

First Division, Edward M. McCook
Second Division, Eli Long
Third Division, Judson Kilpatrick
Fourth Division, Benjamin H. Grierson
Fifth Division, Edward Hatch
Sixth Division, no commander named
Seventh Division, George Spalding
Eighth Division, no commander named

Note 1. First Division was formerly First Division, Cavalry Corps, Department of the Cumberland.
Note 2. Second Division was formerly Second Division, Cavalry Corps, Department of the Cumberland.
Note 3. Third Division was formerly Third Division, Cavalry Corps, Department of the Cumberland.
Note 4. Fourth Division was formerly Second Division, Cavalry Corps, District of West Tennessee.

Note 5. Fifth Division was formerly First Division, Cavalry Corps, District of West Tennessee.
Note 6. Sixth Division was organized from the cavalry division that was attached to the Army of the Ohio.
Note 7. Seventh Division was formerly Fourth Division, Cavalry Corps, Department of the Cumberland.
Note 8. Eight Division was not organized at the time, but was to consist of regiments to be assigned at a later date.

The cavalry divisions were to consist of two brigades of five regiments each in order to obtain better brigade commanders and to simplify administration.

Some time elapsed before the above reorganization was effected, and there were some changes ordered before the organization of the corps was completed.

Wilson arrived at Nashville November 6, 1864, and he found there Horace Capron's brigade of Sixth Division, then commanded by Thomas J. Harrison, and also John T. Croxton's brigade of First Division. Hatch's Fifth Division from West Tennessee was on the march from Clinton to join the Army of the Tennessee, but it was ordered instead to Pulaski, Tennessee.

Wilson took the field November 21, 1864 to organize and command the cavalry that was to operate with John M. Schofield's army that was being collected to oppose Hood's invasion of Tennessee. On November 24, the cavalry that was concentrated at Pulaski under the personal direction of Wilson consisted of the following:

Fifth Division, Cavalry Corps, Edward Hatch
 First Brigade, Sixth Division, Cavalry Corps, Thomas J. Harrison (formerly Capron's brigade)
 First Brigade, First Division, Cavalry Corps, John T. Croxton

Capron's and Croxton's brigades were formed into a Temporary Division for the Franklin and Nashville Campaign under the command of Richard W. Johnson.

November 24, 1864, Israel Garrard was assigned command of a Provisional Brigade that was formed to accompany a supply train from Nashville to Columbia, Tennessee. It arrived there November 28 and was then sent to engage the enemy along Duck

River. Garrard later assumed command of his regiment in Sixth Division.

November 29, 1864, John H. Hammond's First Brigade of Seventh Division joined Wilson's forces at Franklin.

After the Battle of Franklin, Wilson's cavalry retreated with Schofield's army to Nashville, and remained in the vicinity to take part in the Battle of Nashville December 15–16, 1864. For details of the operations of the Cavalry Corps, Military Division of the Mississippi, see Franklin and Nashville Campaign (Hood's Invasion of Tennessee).

The organization of the Cavalry Corps at the Battle of Nashville December 15–16, 1864 was as follows:

CAVALRY CORPS, MILITARY DIVISION OF THE MISSISSIPPI, James H. Wilson

First Division
    First Brigade, John T. Croxton

Note. Edward M. McCook, with the Second Brigade and Third Brigade of his First Division, was absent on an expedition against a Confederate force commanded by Hylan B. Lyon in western Kentucky.

Fifth Division, Edward Hatch
    First Brigade, Robert R. Stewart
    Second Brigade, Datus E. Coon

Note. Fifth Division was organized into two brigades November 28, 1864.

Sixth Division, Richard W. Johnson
    First Brigade, Thomas J. Harrison
    Second Brigade, James Biddle

Note. The two brigades of Sixth Division were organized December 1, 1864 after the Battle of Franklin. Harrison's brigade was mounted, but Biddle's brigade was dismounted.

Seventh Division, Joseph F. Knipe
    First Brigade, John H. Hammond
    Second Brigade, Gilbert M. L. Johnson

Eli Long's Second Division was near Elizabethtown, Kentucky in December 1864.

Note. The regiments of Third Division and Fourth Division were not assembled at that time.

Wilson's cavalry took an active part in the pursuit of Hood's defeated army after the Battle of Nash-

ville, and on January 13, 1865, after the pursuit had ended, the divisions were ordered to Gravelly Springs in northwestern Alabama, where they were to go into camp and refit and reorganize. On December 20, 1864, Wilson sent Johnson and Knipe with their dismounted brigades back to Nashville to remount, and he continued on with Hatch's division and the brigades of Croxton and Hammond to Gravelly Springs. They were followed later by the divisions of Eli Long, Emory Upton, and Edward M. McCook. Kilpatrick's Third Division was with Sherman's army near Savannah, Georgia, where it was then preparing for its march northward through the Carolinas. Within a few weeks' time, the entire corps of six divisions was assembled at Gravelly Springs.

Because, in general, Wilson's Cavalry Corps was in the process of organization during much of the period included in the above description, a brief history of the organization of each division is summarized here.

First Division, Cavalry Corps. First Division was organized November 9, 1864 from First Division, Cavalry Corps, Department of the Cumberland. The serviceable horses of McCook's First Division and Kenner Garrard's Second Division, Department of the Cumberland, and Israel Garrard's Cavalry Brigade of the Army of the Ohio were sent to Judson Kilpatrick's Third Division, Department of the Cumberland in preparation for Sherman's march through Georgia to Savannah. The dismounted men of First Division and Second Division were ordered to Louisville, Kentucky for remount and equipment. Only Croxton's First Brigade of First Division was with Wilson during the Franklin and Nashville Campaign.

The division was organized as follows:

First Division, Edward M. McCook
    First Brigade, John T. Croxton
    Second Brigade, Oscar H. La Grange
        Horace P. Lamson, temporarily
    Third Brigade, Louis D. Watkins

Note 1. Watkins commanded the division temporarily in January 1865, and Croxton, also temporarily, in February 1865.
Note 2. Third Brigade was discontinued January 23, 1865.

Second Division, Cavalry Corps. Second Division was organized from Second Division, Cavalry Corps, Department of the Cumberland, which was commanded by Kenner Garrard. On October 29, 1864, Garrard was ordered to organize his division into two brigades and to take it to Nashville, Tennessee. The serviceable horses of the division were turned over to Kilpatrick's Third Division, Department of the Cumberland, and the dismounted men of the division were sent to Louisville, Kentucky for remount and equipment.

Second Division, Cavalry Corps was organized November 16, 1864 under the command of Eli Long as follows:

Second Division, Cavalry Corps, Eli Long, to April 2, 1865
　Robert H. G. Minty
　First Brigade, Abram O. Miller, to April 2, 1865
　　Jacob G. Vail, to April 12, 1865
　　Frank White
　Second Brigade, Robert H. G. Minty, to April 2, 1865
　　Horace N. Howland

Second Division remained in Kentucky, near Elizabethtown, in December 1864, and then moved to Nashville early in January 1865.

Third Division, Cavalry Corps. Third Division was formed from Third Division, Department of the Cumberland by an order of November 9, 1864, and it was assigned to accompany Sherman's army on its march through Georgia to Savannah. The serviceable horses of First Division and Second Division were turned over to Kilpatrick to put his division in readiness for the campaign. Sherman's army, accompanied by Kilpatrick's division, left Atlanta on November 17 and arrived near Savannah December 10, occupying the city on December 21. Then in January 1865, Kilpatrick left Savannah and marched northward through the Carolinas. Third Division did not operate again under the personal direction of the corps commander, but it did retain its designation of Third Division, Military Division of the Mississippi during the march through Georgia and the Carolinas Campaign.

The organization of Third Division was as follows:

Third Division, Cavalry Corps, Judson Kilpatrick

First Brigade, Thomas J. Jordan, to November 10, 1864
　Eli H. Murray, to January 20, 1865
　Thomas J. Jordan
Second Brigade, William Thayer, to November 5, 1864
　Smith D. Atkins
Third Brigade, Eli H. Murray, to November 10, 1864
　George E. Spencer, from January 1865 to April 1865
　Michael Kerwin, to April 25, 1865
　Thomas T. Heath, to June 26, 1865

Fourth Division, Cavalry Corps. According to the order of November 9, 1864 which announced the organization of the Cavalry Corps, Military Division of the Mississippi, Fourth Division was to be formed from Edward F. Winslow's Second Division, Cavalry Corps, District of West Tennessee, and Benjamin H. Grierson was assigned command.

A detachment of Second Division under Winslow was in Missouri at that time because of Sterling Price's invasion of the state (see Price's Missouri Expedition). Troops of Winslow's command were widely scattered during their operations, and they were assembled for duty with Wilson only with considerable difficulty. Grierson was relieved from command of Fourth Division December 13, 1864, and Emory Upton was assigned command in his place. Upton was ordered to go to Louisville, Saint Louis, and Memphis for the purpose of collecting the men and horses of Winslow's command, and of bringing them to Nashville by way of Louisville. At the end of January 1865, the division was assembled at Nashville, and was under orders to join Wilson and the Cavalry Corps at Gravelly Springs, Alabama.

The organization of Fourth Division was as follows:

Fourth Division, Benjamin H. Grierson, to December 13, 1864
　Emory Upton
　First Brigade, Edward F. Winslow
　Second Brigade, Israel Garrard, to March 8, 1865
　　Andrew J. Alexander

Fifth Division, Cavalry Corps. Fifth Division was organized November 28, 1864 from First Division, District of West Tennessee, which was commanded by Edward Hatch. During the latter part of October 1864, First Division was at Clifton, Tennessee on the Tennessee River, but on October 29, Hatch was ordered by Oliver O. Howard, commanding the Army of the Tennessee, to join the Army of the Tennessee by marching by way of Pulaski, Tennessee and Stevenson, Alabama. The next day, however, Hatch was ordered by George H. Thomas, commanding the Department of the Cumberland, to halt at Pulaski and cooperate with John T. Croxton in resisting the advance of John B. Hood's Army of Tennessee from Florence, Alabama into Tennessee. At that time First Division, Cavalry Corps, District of West Tennessee was organized as follows:

First Division, Cavalry Corps, Edward Hatch
    First Brigade, Oliver Wells
    Second Brigade, Datus E. Coon

Hatch remained under Thomas' orders until November 9, 1864, when the Cavalry Corps, Military Division of the Mississippi was created. Thereafter, as Fifth Division, it was a part of James H. Wilson's command.

Fifth Division took part in the Franklin and Nashville Campaign, and in the pursuit of Hood's defeated army after the Battle of Nashville. For details, see Franklin and Nashville Campaign (Hood's Invasion of Tennessee). When the pursuit ended, Fifth Division accompanied Wilson to Gravelly Springs, Alabama, and in mid-January 1865 Wilson's command was in the Gravelly Springs–Waterloo area.

The organization of Fifth Division during the period of its existence was as follows:

Fifth Division, Cavalry Corps, Edward Hatch, to January 18, 1865, on leave
    Robert R. Stewart
    First Brigade, Robert R. Stewart, to January 18, 1865
        Abram Sharra, to February 3, 1865
        Richard H. Brown, to February 8, 1865
        Oliver Wells, to May 28, 1865
    Second Brigade, Datus E. Coon

Note. Fifth Division was broken up May 28, 1865.

Sixth Division, Cavalry Corps. The organization of Sixth Division from cavalry that was previously attached to the Army of the Ohio was announced November 17, 1864 as follows:

Sixth Division, Richard W. Johnson
    First Brigade, Horace Capron
    Second Brigade, William W. Lowe
    Third Brigade, William J. Palmer

This announced organization is misleading, however, because at the end of November 1864, only five regiments were with the division. Lowe was not with the division; Thomas J. Harrison was in command of First Brigade; and the Third Brigade, which consisted of the 5th Tennessee Cavalry and the 15th Pennsylvania Cavalry (commanded by Palmer), had no organization and the regiments were scattered.

Beginning at the end of December 1864, the division was organized as follows:

Sixth Division, Richard W. Johnson
    First Brigade, Thomas J. Harrison, to February 17, 1865
        Thomas H. Butler, June 27, 1865
        Elisha Mix, to July 1865
    Second Brigade, William W. Lowe, to December 9, 1864
        James Biddle, to January 1, 1865
        William W. Lowe, to February 1865
        James Biddle, to June 27, 1865
        Francis M. Davidson

Seventh Division, Cavalry Corps. It was announced November 9, 1864 that Seventh Division, Cavalry Corps, Military Division of the Mississippi was to be organized from Fourth Division, Cavalry Corps, Department of the Cumberland, then commanded by George Spalding. Seventh Division, however, was not actually formed at that time. On November 16, Fourth Division was broken up, and Joseph F. Knipe was assigned command of Seventh Division. On November 20, Knipe was sent to Memphis to bring to Nashville the detachments of Benjamin H. Grierson's cavalry command and also the trains of Hatch's division. John H. Hammond arrived at Nashville November 25 to assume command of a new brigade to be designated as First Brigade, Seventh Division. At that time Wilson reported that he was organizing Seventh Division in the field as the necessary troops came forward.

At the end of November 1864, the organization of only Hammond's First Brigade had been completed. The organization of Second Brigade (dismounted) was announced January 9, 1865, and it was assigned to Gilbert M. L. Johnson.

On February 3, 1865, Knipe was ordered with his Seventh Division to New Orleans, where he was to report to Edward R. S. Canby, commander of the Military Division of West Mississippi, for service in the Department of the Gulf in the campaign against Mobile, Alabama.

Eighth Division, Cavalry Corps. Eighth Division was announced in the organization orders of November 9, 1864, but it was never organized.

* * * * * * * * * *

At the end of February 1865, Wilson's headquarters was at Gravelly Springs, Alabama, and the divisions of the Cavalry Corps were located as follows: John T. Croxton's First Division was at Waterloo, Alabama; Eli Long's Second Division was at Gravelly Springs; Judson Kilpatrick's Third Division was with William T. Sherman's army in the Carolinas; Emory Upton's Fourth Division was at Gravelly Springs; Edward Hatch's Fifth Division was at Eastport, Mississippi; Richard W. Johnson's Sixth Division was at Pulaski, Tennessee; and Joseph F. Knipe's Seventh Division was on the Mississippi River en route to New Orleans.

The organization of the Cavalry Corps at the end of February 1865 was as follows:

CAVALRY CORPS, James H. Wilson

First Division, John T. Croxton
    First Brigade, John T. Croxton
    Second Brigade, Oscar H. La Grange

Note. Croxton was in temporary command of First Division during the absence of Edward M. McCook.

Second Division, Eli Long
    First Brigade, Abram O. Miller (mounted infantry)
    Second Brigade, Robert H. G. Minty

Fourth Division, Emory Upton
    First Brigade, Edward F. Winslow
    Second Brigade, Israel Garrard

Note. Andrew J. Alexander assumed command of Second Brigade March 8, 1865.

Fifth Division, Edward Hatch

First Brigade, Oliver Wells
Second Brigade, Datus E. Coon

Note. Hatch was on leave from January 17, 1865, and Robert R. Stewart was in temporary command of the division.

Sixth Division, Richard W. Johnson
    First Brigade, Thomas J. Harrison
    Second Brigade, James Biddle
    Fayetteville, Tennessee, 5th Tennessee Cavalry
    Wauhatchie, Tennessee, 15th Pennsylvania Cavalry

Note. The 5th Tennessee Cavalry and 15th Pennsylvania Cavalry had been designated in orders as Third Brigade.

Seventh Division, Joseph F. Knipe
    First Brigade, George W. Jackson
    Second Brigade, Gilbert M. L. Johnson

Wilson remained with four of his divisions near Gravelly Springs, Waterloo, and Chickasaw, all in the extreme northwest corner of Alabama, from March 1 to March 22, 1865, and he then started south on his raid to Selma, Alabama. He left Hatch's Fifth Division, which was dismounted, at Gravelly Springs, and took with him Edward M. McCook's First Division, Eli Long's Second Division, and Emory Upton's Fourth Division.

Selma was the most important military center in the area, with foundries, gun factories, and an armory. The town was taken by assault April 2, 1865 by the divisions of Long and Upton. Croxton's First Brigade of McCook's division was detached and sent from Elyton (present-day Birmingham) to Tuscaloosa, Alabama to destroy the bridge there over the Black Warrior River and also stores and public buildings.

Wilson remained at Selma until April 9, 1865, waiting for Croxton to return, and he then moved on through Montgomery, Alabama and Columbus and West Point, Georgia, arriving in Macon, Georgia on April 20. There Wilson learned that the war in the East had ended. Croxton had been unable to rejoin Wilson's column in Alabama, but he moved on eastward alone across the state and finally rejoined his command at Macon on April 30. For details of Wilson's raid, see Wilson's Raid to Selma, Alabama.

The organization of Wilson's command during the raid through Alabama was as follows:

CAVALRY CORPS, James H. Wilson

First Division, Edward M. McCook
    First Brigade, John T. Croxton
    Second Brigade, Oscar H. La Grange

Second Division, Eli Long, to April 2, 1865, wounded
    Robert H. G. Minty
    First Brigade, Abram O. Miller, to April 2, 1865
        wounded
        Jacob G. Vail
        Frank White
    Second Brigade, Robert H. G. Minty, to April 2, 1865
        Horace N. Howland

Fourth Division, Emory Upton
    First Brigade, Edward F. Winslow
    Second Brigade, Andrew J. Alexander

Wilson's cavalry was used to prevent the escape of Jefferson Davis as he fled south from Richmond, Virginia, and some of Wilson's troops captured Davis at Irwinville, Georgia May 10, 1865.

The Cavalry Corps, Military Division of the Mississippi was discontinued June 26, 1865, and the troops remaining in the Military Division were ordered to report to the commanders of the departments in which they were then serving.

CAVALRY CORPS, MILITARY DIVISION OF WEST MISSISSIPPI

During February and March 1865, while preparations were underway for operations against Mobile, Alabama, there were numerous changes in the distribution and organization of the cavalry forces in the Military Division of West Mississippi.

On March 1, 1865, Benjamin H. Grierson was assigned command of all cavalry in the Military Division of West Mississippi, and was also assigned to the special command of the cavalry forces assigned for service in the field against Mobile. His command was designated as Cavalry Forces, Military Division of West Mississippi.

As early as February 3, 1865, Joseph F. Knipe, with his Seventh Division, Cavalry Corps, Military Division of the Mississippi, had been ordered from the Department of the Cumberland to New Orleans. Knipe's division left Nashville, Tennessee on February 12 and arrived in New Orleans by March 10. It was then ordered to embark for Fort Gaines on Mobile Bay, Alabama March 18. Knipe's division was organized as follows:

Seventh Cavalry Division, Military Division of the Mississippi, Joseph F. Knipe
    First Brigade, George W. Jackson
    Second Brigade, Gilbert M. L. Johnson

In addition to Knipe's division, ten regiments of cavalry had been ordered to report to Grierson by early March 1865. Some of these were from the Department of the Gulf, and some were from outside the department. On March 5, Joseph Karge was ordered with his 2nd New Jersey Cavalry from the District of Natchez, Department of Mississippi to New Orleans, where he arrived March 10. His regiment was assigned to Knipe's division on March 10.

By an order of March 21, 1865, the cavalry forces of the Military Division of West Mississippi that were designated for service in the field were organized into three divisions of two brigades each. This organization was designated as Cavalry Corps, Military Division of West Mississippi, and Grierson was assigned command. Headquarters of the corps at that time was at New Orleans. The final organization of the cavalry based on the above order, however, was not immediately effected.

A Separate Cavalry Brigade, District of West Florida was organized February 8, 1865 under the command of Thomas J. Lucas, and another brigade, designated as Special Cavalry Expedition, was formed in West Florida in March. On March 29, the mounted troops operating from Pensacola, Florida with Frederick Steele's so-called Column from Pensacola were constituted as a division, designated as Cavalry Division Operating from Pensacola. Thomas J. Lucas was assigned command. The division was organized as follows:

Cavalry Division Operating from Pensacola, Thomas J. Lucas
    First Brigade, Morgan H. Chrysler
    Second Brigade, Andrew B. Spurling

Note. First Brigade was formerly Separate Cavalry Brigade, District of West Florida, and Second Brigade was formerly Special Cavalry Expedition, District of West Florida.

The organization of the cavalry during the operations against Mobile March 17–April 12, 1865 was as follows:

First Division, Joseph F. Knipe
 First Brigade, Joseph Karge
 Second Brigade, Gilbert M. L. Johnson

Lucas' Division, Thomas J. Lucas
 First Brigade, Morgan H. Chrysler
 Second Brigade, Andrew B. Spurling

April 14, 1865, Grierson, then at Blakely, Alabama, ordered that the cavalry designated for the field be organized as follows:

First Brigade, Joseph R. West
Second Brigade, Joseph F. Knipe
Third Brigade, Thomas J. Lucas

Note 1. West arrived in New Orleans from the Department of Arkansas March 27, 1865, and on April 2 was ordered to report to Grierson.

Note 2. Third Brigade was organized April 14, 1865 from First Brigade and Second Brigade, District of West Florida (Lucas' Division).

Note 3. Karge relieved Knipe in command of Second Brigade April 17, 1865. West did not arrive at Blakely with his regiments, and Karge's 2nd New Jersey Cavalry was transferred to Second Brigade.

Note 4. Lucas was ordered to join Grierson's division April 16, 1865.

May 2, 1865, Joseph R. West was in New Orleans organizing a cavalry force designated for special field service. On the same date, Joseph Bailey was assigned command of three regiments that were to form a part of West's command. On May 15, the cavalry assigned to West was constituted as Second Cavalry Division, Military Division of West Mississippi, and it was organized as follows:

Second Cavalry Division, Joseph R. West
 First Brigade, Joseph F. Knipe
 Second Brigade, Joseph Bailey

The Military Division of West Mississippi was discontinued May 17, 1865, and on May 23, Grierson announced the following organization of the cavalry of the newly organized Department of the Gulf:

Second Brigade, Joseph Karge
Third Brigade, Thomas J. Lucas

Note. Joseph R. West was assigned command of First Brigade, but he remained in New Orleans to complete the organization of the newly constituted Second Cavalry Division.

April 17, 1865, Grierson, with his cavalry division, left Blakely and marched northward to Montgomery, Alabama. Upon arrival there he reported for duty to Andrew J. Smith, commanding Sixteenth Corps, Military Division of West Mississippi.

May 27, 1865, Lucas was ordered to move with his brigade to Vicksburg, Mississippi, and he arrived there June 4. Karge was left with his brigade at Columbus, Mississippi, and Grierson with his staff returned to New Orleans.

June 12, 1865, the brigade organizations of West's Second Cavalry Division were terminated by the transfer of regiments to other commands.

CAVALRY FORCES OF THE DEPARTMENT OF THE TENNESSEE

Cavalry in the District of West Tennessee. When the Army of the Tennessee, District of West Tennessee was first organized, the cavalry of the army was not organized into brigades and divisions, but was distributed as regiments among the several divisions of the army.

The initial cavalry division in the District of West Tennessee was the Cavalry Division, Army of the Mississippi that John Pope brought to Tennessee from the Mississippi River after the Battle of Shiloh. This division served in the District of West Tennessee until the latter was merged into the Department of the Tennessee October 15, 1862. At that time the cavalry in the department was organized as follows:

Cavalry Division, Army of the Mississippi, John K. Mizner
 First Brigade, Edward Hatch
 Second Brigade, Albert L. Lee

The designation of Mizner's division was then

changed to Cavalry Division, Third Division, District of West Tennessee (Corinth, Mississippi).

In addition to the Cavalry Division, regiments of cavalry served with First Division, District of West Tennessee (Memphis, Tennessee); Second Division, District of West Tennessee (Jackson, Mississippi); and Fourth Division, District of West Tennessee (Columbus, Kentucky).

When the Department and Army of the Tennessee was organized October 25, 1862, the cavalry organizations became a part of the original Thirteenth Corps. The cavalry forces were not organized as a separate corps that reported to Headquarters, Thirteenth Corps, and they generally did not serve as a unit organization, but were instead assigned to the districts or divisions of the department as regiments or brigades.

On November 26, 1862, the cavalry of Ulysses S. Grant's Army in the Field (see Thirteenth Corps, Army of the Tennessee, October 24, 1862–January 14, 1863), which was then operating in northern Mississippi, was organized into the Cavalry Division, Thirteenth Corps, and T. Lyle Dickey was assigned command. The division was organized as follows:

Cavalry Division, Thirteenth Corps, T. Lyle Dickey
    First Brigade, Albert L. Lee
    Second Brigade, Edward Hatch
    Third Brigade, Benjamin H. Grierson

Note. First Brigade was assigned to Charles S. Hamilton's Left Wing of Grant's Army in the Field; Second Brigade was assigned to James B. McPherson's Center; and Third Brigade was assigned to William T. Sherman's Right Wing.

A cavalry brigade was organized in the District of Jackson in November 1862 under the command of John K. Mizner. On June 9, 1863, this brigade was transferred to First Cavalry Division, Left Wing, Sixteenth Corps.

Dickey's Cavalry Division was reorganized December 30, 1862 to consist of two brigades. The First Brigade, under the command of Benjamin H. Grierson, was with Seventeenth Corps at Corinth, Mississippi, and the Second Brigade, under Albert L. Lee, was with Sixteenth Corps. On January 20, 1863, the District of Corinth was transferred to Sixteenth Corps, and then the Cavalry Division served with Sixteenth Corps.

On April 9, 1863, Cadwallader C. Washburn assumed command of the Cavalry Division in the District of West Tennessee (assigned April 3). The division was organized as follows:

First Cavalry Division, Cadwallader C. Washburn
    First Brigade, Benjamin H. Grierson
    Second Brigade, La Fayette McCrillis

On April 17, 1863, during Grant's campaign at Vicksburg, Grierson left the district with his First Brigade on his celebrated raid through Mississippi to Baton Rouge, Louisiana.

On April 12, 1863, a cavalry brigade was organized in the District of Corinth under the command of Florence M. Cornyn, and in May this brigade was designated as Third Brigade, Cavalry Division, Sixteenth Corps.

The cavalry of the Left Wing, Sixteenth Corps was reorganized June 9, 1863 as follows:

First Cavalry Division, John K. Mizner
    First Brigade, La Fayette McCrillis
    Second Brigade, Edward Hatch
    Third Brigade, Florence M. Cornyn
    Fourth Brigade, Bazil D. Meek

Note 1. Third Brigade served in the District of Corinth and continued to report to Grenville M. Dodge, commander of the district.
Note 2. Fourth Brigade was organized in June 1863 and was discontinued in August 1863.

The cavalry of Sixteenth Corps was reorganized August 20, 1863 as follows:

Cavalry Division, Sixteenth Corps, Benjamin H. Grierson
    First Brigade, John K. Mizner
    Second Brigade, La Fayette McCrillis
    Third Brigade, Edward Hatch

Note 1. Headquarters, First Brigade was at Corinth, Mississippi; Headquarters, Second Brigade was at La Grange, Tennessee; and Headquarters, Third Brigade was at Germantown, Tennessee.
Note 2. Grierson returned to Memphis from the Department of the Gulf in late July 1863 and was appointed chief of cavalry July 24. He was injured when leaving Vicksburg on his return, and he had no field duty for several months.
Note 3. Second Brigade was discontinued March 14, 1864 and was reorganized in April 1864.
Note 4. Third Brigade was discontinued November

30, 1863 and was reorganized December 31, 1863 from Second Brigade, Fifth Division, Sixteenth Corps. It was again reorganized May 4, 1864.

Note 5. A fourth brigade was added to the Cavalry Division in December 1863. It was organized from Sixth Division, or District of Columbus, under the command of George Waring, Jr. It was designated as Detached Brigade, Cavalry Division in December 1863 and then as Waring's Brigade in January 1864. It was discontinued in January 1864.

On April 17, 1864, Cadwallader C. Washburn was ordered to Memphis to relieve Stephen A. Hurlbut in command of the District of West Tennessee, and on May 2 Hurlbut was relieved of command of Sixteenth Corps. No commander was named for Sixteenth Corps, and the designation of Grierson's Cavalry Division became Cavalry Division, District of West Tennessee, Department of the Tennessee, although the designation of Sixteenth Corps was used until June 1864. The division was organized as follows:

Cavalry Division, District of West Tennessee, Benjamin H. Grierson
First Brigade, George E. Waring, Jr.
Second Brigade, Edward F. Winslow
Third Brigade, Henry B. Burgh

Note. Datus E. Coon assumed command of Third Brigade in July 1864.

Late in July 1864, the cavalry in the District of West Tennessee was organized into a cavalry corps of two divisions. This command was designated as Cavalry Corps, District of West Tennessee, Department of the Tennessee, and was organized as follows:

CAVALRY CORPS, DISTRICT OF WEST TENNESSEE, Benjamin H. Grierson

First Division, Edward Hatch
First Brigade, Thomas P. Herrick
Oliver Wells
Second Brigade, Datus E. Coon

Second Division, Edward F. Winslow
Frederick W. Benteen
First Brigade, Joseph Karge
Second Brigade, John W. Noble

Note. Karge relieved Winslow in command of Second Division August 17, 1864, during Andrew J. Smith's Oxford, Mississippi Expedition, when Winslow became ill.

Winslow was sent into Arkansas September 2, 1864 with a detachment of Second Division to oppose Sterling Price at the beginning of his expedition into Missouri. John W. Noble was in command of Second Division in September 1864 during Winslow's absence. Winslow's command consisted of the following:

Second Division, Cavalry Corps (detachment), Edward F. Winslow
First Brigade (detachment), Joseph Karge
Second Brigade (detachment), George Duffield

Winslow's command marched through Arkansas to Cape Girardeau and then proceeded to Saint Louis, Missouri, where it arrived October 8–10, 1864. It remained in the Department of the Missouri during Price's Expedition, which ended early in December. For additional information, see Price's Missouri Expedition.

The Cavalry Corps of the Military Division of the Mississippi was created by an order dated October 24, 1864, and its organization was announced October 29. James H. Wilson was assigned command. The divisions of the Cavalry Corps, District of West Tennessee were then transferred to the Cavalry Corps, Military Division of the Mississippi. At that time the Cavalry Corps of the District of West Tennessee was organized as follows:

CAVALRY CORPS, DISTRICT OF WEST TENNESSEE, Benjamin H. Grierson

First Division, Edward Hatch
First Brigade, Oliver Wells
Second Brigade, Datus E. Coon

Second Division, Edward F. Winslow
First Brigade, Joseph Karge
Second Brigade, John W. Noble

Note. Detachments of Second Division were in Missouri operating against Sterling Price during his invasion of the state.

On October 24, 1864, the office of chief of cavalry of the Department of the Tennessee was abolished.

On November 9, 1864, the Cavalry Corps, Military Division of the Mississippi was organized into eight divisions, and the cavalry divisions of the Cavalry Corps, District of West Tennessee were assigned as follows: First Division became Fifth Division, and Second Division became Fourth Division of the Cavalry Corps, Military Division of the Mississippi. For further information, see Cavalry Corps, Military Division of the Mississippi.

Cavalry of the District of Eastern Arkansas. Cadwallader C. Washburn organized a cavalry division in the District of Eastern Arkansas and led it on an expedition from Helena, Arkansas toward Grenada, Mississippi November 27–December 6, 1862, in conjunction with Ulysses S. Grant's attempt to reach Vicksburg, Mississippi by marching southward through Mississippi. Washburn's division consisted of two brigades commanded by Hall Wilson and Thomas Stephens.

The District of Eastern Arkansas was transferred to the Department of the Tennessee January 21, 1863, and the next day it was attached to Thirteenth Corps. On February 8, the cavalry of Thirteenth Corps in the District of Eastern Arkansas was organized as follows:

Second Cavalry Division, Thirteenth Corps, Cadwallader C. Washburn
  First Brigade, Conrad Baker
  Second Brigade, Cyrus Bussey

Note. In the order announcing the organization of Washburn's division, the division was designated as Second Cavalry Division, Army of the Tennessee.

The Cavalry Division was reorganized in April 1863 as the Cavalry Division, District of Eastern Arkansas, Thirteenth Corps as follows:

Cavalry Division, District of Eastern Arkansas, Cyrus Bussey, to May 1863
  Cadwallader C. Washburn, to June 1863
  First Brigade, Benjamin L. Wiley
  Second Brigade, Powell Clayton, to May 1863
    Cyrus Bussey, to June 1863

In June 1863, the cavalry of the District of Eastern Arkansas was again reorganized. First Brigade was broken up, and a new brigade was formed under the command of Powell Clayton. This brigade was designated as Clayton's Independent Bri-

gade, District of Eastern Arkansas, and on July 7 it was temporarily attached to Thirteenth Division, Thirteenth Corps, District of Eastern Arkansas. On July 29, the District of Eastern Arkansas was transferred to Sixteenth Corps, and Clayton's brigade was then attached to Sixteenth Corps. On August 10, it was attached to Frederick Steele's Arkansas Expedition, and it left the Department of the Tennessee. Second Brigade was sent to Vicksburg, Mississippi.

Cavalry at Vicksburg, Mississippi. In June 1863, Second Brigade of the Cavalry Division, District of Eastern Arkansas was designated as Bussey's Brigade and was sent to Grant's army at Vicksburg, Mississippi. It was unattached until it participated in William T. Sherman's Jackson, Mississippi Campaign July 5–25; during that time it was attached to John G. Parke's Ninth Corps until July 19, and then to Fifteenth Corps. Thomas Stephens assumed command of the brigade July 31.

Francis J. Herron's division of Grant's army at Vicksburg was designated as Second Division, Thirteenth Corps July 28, 1863. Regimental records indicate that Bussey's command was attached as Cavalry Brigade, Second Division, Thirteenth Corps, but it does not so appear on the roster of the army at that time. Bussey's brigade, then commanded by Thomas Stephens, was broken up in August 1863.

Edward F. Winslow was assigned command of a cavalry brigade of Fifteenth Corps August 8, 1863. This brigade left the Big Black River near Vicksburg August 10 on a raid to the Mississippi Central Railroad. It moved northward through Grenada, Mississippi and arrived at Memphis, Tennessee on August 22. A short time later, the brigade returned to Vicksburg, where it was reorganized and attached to Fifteenth Corps as Winslow's Brigade.

In late September 1863, Sherman left Vicksburg with First Division and Second Division of Fifteenth Corps to aid in the relief of William S. Rosecrans' Army of the Cumberland, then besieged at Chattanooga, Tennessee. Upon Sherman's departure, Winslow's Brigade was attached to James M. Tuttle's Third Division, Fifteenth Corps, which was left at Vicksburg. When Tuttle's division returned to West Tennessee on November 8, Winslow's Brigade was transferred to Seventeenth Corps.

Winslow's Brigade took part with Seventeenth Corps in Sherman's Meridian, Mississippi Campaign February 3–March 6, 1864, and it then remained with Seventeenth Corps until April. John H. Peters commanded the brigade in March, and Horace P. Mumford in April. Winslow was transferred to West Tennessee in late April.

The District of Vicksburg was created April 12, 1864, and the cavalry of the district was designated as Cavalry Brigade, Seventeenth Corps, District of Vicksburg. Commanders of the brigade were Horace P. Mumford, Thomas Stephens, Lucien H. Kerr, and Embury D. Osband. In August the designation of the Cavalry Brigade was changed to Cavalry Forces, District of Vicksburg; Kerr was in command in September 1864, and Osband in October 1864.

There was no significant change in the organization of the cavalry at Vicksburg until the District of Vicksburg was merged into the Department of Mississippi November 28, 1864.

RESERVE CORPS, ARMY OF THE CUMBERLAND

In late January 1863, Gordon Granger, formerly commander of the Army of Kentucky, was assigned command of the troops that were assembling at Louisville, Kentucky for transfer to Nashville, Tennessee in the Department of the Cumberland. This command was organized into a division of four brigades, which was commanded by Absalom Baird. Granger's command was known as Baird's Division, but it was commonly called the Army of Kentucky because some of its troops formerly belonged to Granger's Army of Kentucky. The division was organized as follows:

Baird's Division (or Army of Kentucky), Absalom Baird
    First Brigade, John Coburn
    Second Brigade, Smith D. Atkins
    Reid's Brigade, William P. Reid
    Crook's Brigade, George Crook

Note. First and Second brigades were formed from regiments of the Third Division of the former Army of Kentucky; Reid's Brigade was from the District of Western Kentucky, Department of the Ohio; and Crook's Brigade was from Western Virginia.

Granger, with Baird's Division, arrived in Tennessee during February 1863 and took position at Nashville and in the vicinity. Granger's troops were organized into three divisions, commanded by Absalom Baird, George Crook, and Charles C. Gilbert. Crook's division consisted primarily of the regiments of his brigade and some unassigned regiments from western Kentucky. Gilbert's division consisted of Coburn's brigade and other regiments at the post of Franklin, Tennessee. Gilbert's command occupied Franklin, Tennessee on February 12, and later in the month Crook's command was sent to Carthage, Tennessee.

On March 4, 1863, John Coburn's First Brigade of Baird's Third Division, Army of Kentucky, with some cavalry, marched south out of Franklin on a reconnaissance toward Spring Hill, and the next day it was captured after a sharp fight by Earl Van Dorn's Confederate cavalry at Thompson's Station. For details, see Engagement at Thompson's Station, Tennessee.

On June 8, 1863, before the beginning of William S. Rosecrans' Middle Tennessee (or Tullahoma) Campaign, a new corps, designated as the Reserve Corps, was created in the Army of the Cumberland. Gordon Granger was assigned command, and the corps was organized as follows:

RESERVE CORPS, Gordon Granger

First Division, Absalom Baird
    First Brigade, Smith D. Atkins
    Second Brigade, William P. Reid
    Third Brigade, William L. Utley
    Artillery
        Battery M, 1st Illinois Light Artillery, George W. Spencer
        9th Battery, Ohio Light Artillery, Harrison B. York
        18th Battery, Ohio Light Artillery, Charles C. Aleshire

Note 1. First Division was formerly Baird's Division of Granger's Army of Kentucky. First Brigade was formerly Second Brigade, Baird's Division; Second Brigade was formerly Reid's Brigade, Baird's Division; and Third Brigade was formerly First Brigade, Baird's Division. Crook's Brigade of Baird's Division was transferred to Fourteenth Corps, and was designated as Third Brigade, Fourth Division.

Note 2. Third Brigade, formerly Coburn's First Brigade, was captured at Thompson's Station, Tennessee March 5, 1863 and was exchanged in May 1863. Coburn was then assigned to duty in Indianapolis for two months, and Utley commanded the brigade temporarily until June 24, 1863. Then Henry C. Gilbert commanded the brigade until Coburn returned in July.

Second Division, James D. Morgan
　First Brigade, Robert F. Smith
　Second Brigade, Daniel McCook
　Third Brigade, Charles C. Doolittle
　Artillery, James Thompson
　　Battery I, 2nd Illinois Light Artillery, Charles M. Barnett
　　Battery E, 1st Ohio Light Artillery, Stephen W. Dorsey
　　10th Battery, Wisconsin Light Artillery, Yates V. Beebe

Note. Second Division was organized from Robert B. Mitchell's Fourth Division of Fourteenth Corps.

Third Division, Robert S. Granger
　First Brigade, William P. Lyon
　Second Brigade, William T. Ward

Note 1. Headquarters, Third Division was at Nashville, Tennessee.
Note 2. First Brigade was organized from troops at Fort Henry and Fort Donelson, and was at Fort Donelson and Fort Heiman.
Note 3. Second Brigade was organized from troops of the Garrison of Gallatin, Tennessee, and the headquarters of the regiments were at Gallatin, Lavergne, and Stewart's Creek.
Note 4. A Third Brigade, commanded by James G. Spears, was organized in August 1863 from East Tennessee regiments belonging to Twenty-Third Corps.
Note 5. James P. Flood's Battery C, 2nd Illinois Light Artillery and Jonas Eckdall's Battery H, 2nd Illinois Light Artillery were attached to First Brigade; and John J. Ely's 5th Battery, Michigan Light Artillery was attached to Second Brigade.

Because the Reserve Corps was composed in part of troops of the former Army of Kentucky, it was frequently referred to as the Army of Kentucky, but this was not a proper designation.

The Reserve Corps played only a minor role in the Middle Tennessee (or Tullahoma) Campaign June 23–July 7, 1863. Morgan's Second Division remained at Nashville; Lyon's First Brigade, Third Division was at Fort Donelson; and Ward's Second Brigade, Third Division was posted at Gallatin, La Vergne, Stewart's Creek, and Murfreesboro. Granger, with Baird's First Division, took part in the operations during the period June 23–27, and also

during this period Granger exercised control over Robert B. Mitchell's First Division of David S. Stanley's Cavalry Corps, Army of the Cumberland. For further information, see Tullahoma (or Middle Tennessee) Campaign.

When Rosecrans' Army of the Cumberland advanced toward Chattanooga in mid-August 1863, at the beginning of the Chickamauga Campaign, the Reserve Corps remained in Middle Tennessee guarding the railroads and on garrison duty. First Division, then commanded by James B. Steedman, was at and near Shelbyville; James D. Morgan's Second Division was at Murfreesboro; and Robert S. Granger's Third Division was at Nashville.

On September 6, 1863, after the Army of the Cumberland had crossed the Tennessee River at the beginning of its advance, Rosecrans ordered Granger to concentrate his available troops at Bridgeport, Alabama and then move with them to join the army near Chattanooga. Granger, with Steedman's First Division and Daniel McCook's Second Brigade, Second Division, arrived at Rossville, Georgia September 17, on the evening of the day when the first movements of the Battle of Chickamauga occurred.

Granger's command remained near Rossville and along the road to Ringgold, Georgia until the late morning of September 20, 1863, and it was then heavily engaged on Horseshoe Ridge during the closing hours of the battle. It retreated with the Army of the Cumberland to Chattanooga. The organization of Granger's force of the Reserve Corps at the Battle of Chickamauga was as follows:

RESERVE CORPS. Gordon Granger

First Division, James B. Steedman
　First Brigade, Walter C. Whitaker
　Second Brigade, John G. Mitchell

Note. Charles C. Aleshire's 18th Battery, Ohio Light Artillery was attached to First Brigade; and Thomas Burton's Battery M, 1st Illinois Light Artillery was attached to Second Brigade.

Second Division
　Second Brigade, Daniel McCook

Note 1. Charles M. Barnett's Battery I, 2nd Illinois Light Artillery was attached to Second Brigade.
Note 2. First Brigade and Third Brigade were along the railroad near Bridgeport and Stevenson, Alabama.

Robert S. Granger's Third Division was at Nashville during the Battle of Chickamauga.

The Reserve Corps was discontinued October 9, 1863, and the troops were reassigned as follows:

First Division, Reserve Corps:
  First Brigade to Second Brigade, First Division, Fourteenth Corps
  Second Brigade to Second Brigade, Second Division, Fourteenth Corps
  Third Brigade to the post of Murfreesboro

Second Division, Reserve Corps:
  First Brigade to First Brigade, Second Division, Fourteenth Corps
  Second Brigade to Third Brigade, Second Division, Fourteenth Corps
  Third Brigade was broken up, and the regiments were assigned to the post of Nashville, the post of Gallatin, the Engineer Brigade, and Second Brigade, Second Division, Fourteenth Corps.

Third Division, Reserve Corps:
  First Brigade was broken up, and the regiments were assigned to Ward's Brigade, post of Nashville; the post of Chattanooga; and Clarksville, Tennessee.
  Second Brigade to Ward's Brigade, post of Nashville
  Third Brigade was assigned to the post of Chattanooga, but it served in East Tennessee.

Granger was assigned command of the new Fourth Corps, which was formed by the consolidation of Twentieth Corps and Twenty-First Corps of the Army of the Cumberland, as directed by the order of October 9, 1863.

RESERVE CORPS, MILITARY DIVISION OF WEST MISSISSIPPI

On November 25, 1864, Edward R. S. Canby, commander of the Military Division of West Mississippi, announced the formation of the Reserve Corps, Military Division of West Mississippi, which was to consist of the troops formerly belonging to Nineteenth Corps that were then within the limits of the Military Division of West Mississippi. The se-

nior officer present was to command the corps until a permanent commander was assigned.

At the time the order creating the Reserve Corps was issued, most of the troops of Second Division and Third Division, Nineteenth Corps were in Arkansas. They had been sent to reinforce Frederick Steele, commander of the Department of Arkansas, during Sterling Price's expedition into Missouri in September 1864. The units of these divisions had become widely scattered during the operations in Arkansas, but in November 1864 they were assembling at Memphis, Tennessee and at the mouth of the White River in Arkansas. George F. McGinnis was in command of the latter post. Third Brigade, Second Division, Nineteenth Corps was at Paducah, Kentucky, where Alexander Shaler was under orders to bring it to the mouth of the White River. On November 30, Michael K. Lawler was assigned command of the troops of Nineteenth Corps (at that time, designated as Reserve Corps) that were at Memphis.

On December 5, 1864, the Reserve Corps was reorganized to consist of four brigades as follows: First Brigade, Michael K. Lawler; Second Brigade, Elias S. Dennis; Third Brigade, Christopher C. Andrews; and Fourth Brigade, William McE. Dye. A permanent commander of the Reserve Corps had not yet been assigned, and the commanding officer of each brigade was ordered to report directly to, and receive orders from, Headquarters, Military Division of West Mississippi. First Brigade, Reserve Corps was formerly Second Brigade, Second Division, Nineteenth Corps; Lawler was assigned command December 1, 1864, while the brigade was at Memphis. Second Brigade, Reserve Corps was formerly First Brigade, Second Division, Nineteenth Corps; it was at Memphis until January 1, 1864, when it departed for Kennerville (Kenner), Louisiana. Third Brigade, Reserve Corps was formerly Second Brigade, Third Division, Nineteenth Corps; it was at Morganza during December 1864. Christopher C. Andrews was relieved from duty in the Department of Arkansas December 5, 1864, and was assigned command of Third Brigade, but he did not relieve William T. Spicely, who was in temporary command of the brigade, until January 3, 1865. Third Brigade was then ordered to Kennerville. William McE. Dye's Fourth Brigade, Reserve Corps was formerly First Brigade, Third Division,

Nineteenth Corps. It was at Devall's Bluff in November and December 1864, with Charles Black in temporary command, but on January 6, 1864 it was ordered to New Orleans. Two regiments of the Reserve Corps remained at the mouth of the White River under McGinnis and were later transferred to the Department of Arkansas. McGinnis and Shaler were relieved from duty in the Reserve Corps December 5, 1864, and were assigned to duty in the Department of Arkansas.

On December 31, 1864, the forces of the Reserve Corps had not yet been assembled, but they consisted of the following:

Reserve Corps
First Brigade, Michael K. Lawler
Second Brigade, Elias S. Dennis
Third Brigade, William T. Spicely
Fourth Brigade, Charles Black
United States Forces at the Mouth of White River, George F. McGinnis
Cavalry Forces, Edmund J. Davis
Artillery, Benjamin Nields
    2nd Battery, Connecticut Light Artillery, Walter S. Hotchkiss
    1st Battery, Delaware Light Artillery, Thomas A. Porter
    2nd Battery (B), Massachusetts Light Artillery, William Marland
    4th Battery (D), Massachusetts Light Artillery, George W. Taylor
    7th Battery (G), Massachusetts Light Artillery, Newman W. Storer
    26th Battery, New York Light Artillery, Adam Beattie
    17th Battery, Ohio Light Artillery, Charles S. Rice

Reserve Artillery
Company A, 1st Indiana Heavy Artillery, Abram W. Simmons
Company G, 1st Indiana Heavy Artillery, Benjamin S. Harrower
1st Battery, Indiana Light Artillery, Lawrence Jacoby
15th Battery, Massachusetts Light Artillery, Albert Rowse
21st Battery, New York Light Artillery, James Barnes

Note 1. In the Official Records of the War of the Rebellion, Joseph J. Reynolds is given as commander of the Reserve Corps, but he assumed command of the Department of Arkansas December 22, 1864.
Note 2. On December 14, 1864, the designation of

First Brigade, Third Division, Nineteenth Corps was changed to Fourth Brigade, Reserve Corps.
    Note 3. Christopher C. Andrews assumed command of Third Brigade January 3, 1865.
    Note 4. The cavalry was transferred to the Department of the Gulf January 3, 1865.

On January 6, 1865, Frederick Steele was assigned command of a camp that was to be established at Kennerville for the purpose of preparing troops assembling there for field service. Lawler's First Brigade, Dennis' Second Brigade, and Andrews' Third Brigade arrived at Kennerville early in January, and Black's Fourth Brigade arrived from Devall's Bluff in February.

One of Canby's first steps was to reorganize the Reserve Corps into three divisions of three brigades each. On February 3, 1865, he announced the organization of two brigades of First Division, Reserve Corps as follows: First Brigade, First Division, commanded by Michael K. Lawler, consisted of regiments of First Brigade, Reserve Corps; and Second Brigade, First Division, commanded by Elias S. Dennis, consisted of regiments of Second Brigade, Reserve Corps. The regiments that were to form Third Brigade, First Division had not yet arrived from Arkansas. A short time later, Third Brigade, commanded by Loren Kent, was organized to consist of one regiment each from First Brigade, Reserve Corps; Second Brigade, Reserve Corps; United States Forces Mouth of White River; and District of Eastern Arkansas, Department of Arkansas.

On February 3, 1865, Lawler departed on a twenty-day leave, and John A. McLaughlin, as senior officer, assumed temporary command of First Brigade, First Division, Reserve Corps. On February 8, James R. Slack was assigned command of First Brigade, First Division and was directed to report to Gordon Granger at Fort Gaines, Alabama.

On February 12, 1865, Canby announced the new organization of the Reserve Corps. First Division was organized as given above. First Brigade, Second Division consisted of three regiments from the District of South Alabama, and one regiment each from Fourth Brigade, Reserve Corps and the District of La Fourche, Department of the Gulf. Second Brigade, Second Division consisted of two regiments from the District of South Alabama, and one regiment each from Second Brigade, Reserve Corps and Third Brigade, Reserve Corps. Third Brigade, Second Division consisted of two regiments each from Third Brigade, Reserve Corps and Fourth Brigade, Reserve Corps, and also one regiment from Natchez, Mississippi. First Brigade, Third Division consisted of one regiment each from the following: First Brigade, Reserve Corps; Fourth Brigade, Reserve Corps; United States Forces Mouth of White River; and New Orleans. Second Brigade, Third Division consisted of two regiments from New Orleans, and two regiments from Frederick Salomon's First Division, District of Little Rock, Department of Arkansas. Third Brigade, Third Division consisted of four regiments from Salomon's First Division, District of Little Rock, Department of Arkansas.

During February 1865, the Reserve Corps was transferred from Kennerville to New Orleans. There the troops embarked for the Gulf Coast in preparation for Canby's movement against Mobile, Alabama in March and April. February 4–12, Dennis' Second Brigade, First Division was transferred to Dauphin Island (James H. Coates was assigned command of the brigade February 11); February 11–18, Loren Kent's Third Brigade, First Division was transferred to Dauphin Island; February 15, James R. Slack's First Brigade, First Division (originally commanded by Lawler) departed for Fort Gaines; February 17, Black's Fourth Brigade, Reserve Corps departed for Barrancas, Florida; and February 24–28, Third Brigade, Reserve Corps was transferred to Barrancas.

For details of the movements of the Reserve Corps, and of the reorganization of the corps February 3, 1865, see Land Operations against Mobile Bay and Mobile, Alabama.

Apparently the reorganization of the Reserve Corps, Military Division of West Mississippi was not fully completed when it was merged into the newly organized Thirteenth Corps, Military Division of West Mississippi February 18, 1865.

MISCELLANEOUS ORGANIZATIONS

☆ ☆ ☆ ☆

BANKS' EXPEDITION TO THE GULF OF MEXICO (OR BANKS' SOUTHERN EXPEDITION)

For the organization of Banks' Expedition to the Gulf of Mexico, see Department of the Gulf, Troops in the Department of the Gulf.

BANKS' SOUTHERN EXPEDITION

For details of the organization of this expedition, see Department of the Gulf, Troops in the Department of the Gulf, Banks' Expedition to the Gulf of Mexico (or Banks' Southern Expedition).

BUTLER'S EXPEDITIONARY CORPS

For details of the organization of Butler's Expeditionary Corps, see Department of the Gulf, Troops in the Department of the Gulf, Butler's Gulf Expedition (New Orleans).

BUTLER'S GULF EXPEDITION (NEW ORLEANS)

For details of the organization of Butler's Gulf Expedition, see Department of the Gulf, Troops in the Department of the Gulf, Butler's Gulf Expedition (New Orleans).

CALIFORNIA COLUMN

The California Column is a name sometimes used for the Column from California, which see below.

COLUMN FROM CALIFORNIA

On January 31, 1862, George Wright, commander of the Department of the Pacific, assigned James H. Carleton to command an expedition that was to move eastward from southeastern California, through southern Arizona Territory, and into New Mexico. The purpose of this expedition was to recapture the forts in New Mexico and Texas that had earlier been seized by Confederate forces, and to capture or drive from that area the enemy troops then operating there. Carleton was also to open the Southern Mail Route.

With the exception of a battery of United States Artillery, the troops assigned to this expedition consisted of California Volunteers. Carleton arrived at Fort Yuma on the Colorado River May 1, 1862, and there on May 15 he designated his command as the Column from California.

The leading troops of Carleton's command occupied Tucson, Arizona Territory May 20, 1862. Although some troops had gone on ahead toward New Mexico, the main body of the Column from California did not leave Tucson until July 20–23, and it began to arrive on the Rio Grande near Fort Thorn August 7.

Upon arrival, these troops occupied posts in southern New Mexico and northern Texas, and Carleton then organized the territory under his control as the District of Arizona.

For additional information, see Department of New Mexico, Troops and Operations in the Department of New Mexico, Expedition from California, through Arizona, to New Mexico and Northwestern Texas (Column from California); and see also Department of the Pacific, District of Southern California, Column from California.

COLUMN FROM PENSACOLA, FLORIDA (STEELE)

This was the designation used for the command that Frederick Steele led from Pensacola, Florida to Blakely, Alabama to cooperate with troops under Edward R. S. Canby in the capture of Mobile. For details of the organization and operations of the Column from Pensacola, see Land Operations against Mobile Bay and Mobile, Alabama.

DISTRICT OF THE OHIO

The description of the District of the Ohio requires special treatment because, like the District of West Tennessee, it was for a time not included in any department, but was subject only to the orders of the general in chief of the army, Henry W. Halleck.

The district was constituted March 19, 1862 as a district in the Department of the Mississippi, and it included all the territory of the Department of the Ohio that was transferred to the newly created Department of the Mississippi. The depots for prisoners of war at Indianapolis, Indiana and Columbus, Ohio were excepted, and their commanders reported directly to Headquarters, Department of the Ohio. Don Carlos Buell, commander of the Army of the Ohio, was assigned command of the district.

With this change in organization, Buell's army, which was operating in the district, was properly the Army of the District of the Ohio, but nevertheless it was known as the Army of the Ohio until it was discontinued after the Battle of Perryville in October 1862.

Buell's army fought at the Battle of Shiloh and later became a part of Halleck's Army of the Department of the Mississippi during its advance on Corinth, Mississippi in May 1862. Halleck organized his army into two wings, a center, and a reserve for the Corinth Campaign, and Buell's army was assigned as the Center. On June 10, 1862, after the Confederates evacuated Corinth, the wing organization of the army was discontinued, and Buell resumed command of the Army of the Ohio (temporarily less George H. Thomas' First Division). Buell was then ordered to march eastward along the Memphis and Charleston Railroad toward Chattanooga, Tennessee.

On June 12, 1862, the District of the Ohio was redefined to include that part of the states of Kentucky and Tennessee east of the Tennessee River, except Fort Henry and Fort Donelson, and also such parts of northern Alabama and Georgia that were occupied, or might be occupied, by United States troops. Buell was again assigned command of the district.

The District of the Ohio remained a part of the Department of the Mississippi, and was subject to the orders of Halleck, as department commander, until July 16, 1862. On that date, Halleck left his headquarters at Corinth for Washington, D.C. to become general in chief of the army. This left the Department of the Mississippi without an assigned commander, but Ulysses S. Grant, commander of the District of West Tennessee, and senior officer in the department, exercised control over affairs of the department. Grant, however, did not issue orders to Buell, and the District of the Ohio was no longer a part of the Department of the Mississippi. Buell remained in command of the army in the field and of the District of the Ohio; he received his orders directly from, and reported to, Halleck in Washington.

The Department of the Ohio was re-created August 19, 1862 under the command of Horatio G. Wright, but Buell continued to receive orders from Halleck and not the department commander.

The Department of the Mississippi was discontinued September 19, 1862, although the District of the Ohio had not been a part of that department for some time.

On September 27, 1862, when the Army of the Ohio arrived at Louisville during Braxton Bragg's invasion of the state, Buell, who was subject only to orders from Halleck, was assigned command of all troops at Louisville, which then included the Army of the Ohio and troops of Wright's Department of the Ohio. This caused a command problem, and Halleck clarified the status of Buell and Wright as follows: Buell was in command of only that part of the District of the Ohio that was not included in the Department of the Ohio, and was also in command of the army that was operating against the forces of Bragg and E. Kirby Smith in Kentucky and Tennessee. Buell's Army of the Ohio was independent of Wright, the department commander, and was subject only to orders from the general in chief.

The District of the Ohio was discontinued when it was merged into the re-created Department of the Cumberland October 24, 1862.

For details of the organization and operations of the troops in the District of the Ohio, see Army of the Ohio (Buell), and see also Invasion of Kentucky and Tennessee (E. Kirby Smith and Braxton Bragg).

DISTRICT OF WEST TENNESSEE

The District of West Tennessee was constituted February 14, 1862, during Ulysses S. Grant's operations at Fort Donelson, as a district in the Department of the Missouri, and Grant was assigned command. The limits of the district were not defined, but as organized it consisted of the troops operating with Grant on the Tennessee River. Grant assumed command February 17, the day after the surrender of Fort Donelson, with headquarters at Fort Donelson, and that same day announced the organization of the district. For the organization of the troops of Grant's command, see Army of the Tennessee, District of the Tennessee.

The Department of the Mississippi was created March 11, 1862, and the territory of the Department of the Missouri was included in the new department. The District of West Tennessee thus became a district in the Department of the Mississippi. Henry W. Halleck, formerly commander of the Department of the Missouri, was assigned command of the Department of the Mississippi.

Grant moved his army, which was properly the Army of the District of West Tennessee, to Savannah and Pittsburg Landing, Tennessee in March 1862, and at Savannah, shortly before the Battle of Shiloh, Grant began to call his army the Army of the Tennessee. This was the army commanded by Grant at the Battle of Shiloh April 6–7, 1862, and for details of its organization and operations, see Battle of Shiloh (or Pittsburg Landing), Tennessee, and see also Army of the Tennessee, District of West Tennessee.

After Shiloh, Halleck joined the army in the field and assumed personal command of Grant's Army of the Tennessee, Don Carlos Buell's Army of the Ohio, and John Pope's Army of the Mississippi, all of which were assembled near Pittsburg Landing. Halleck's army, which was formed by combining the three armies, became the Army of the Department of the Mississippi.

On April 30, 1862, in preparation for an advance on Corinth, Mississippi, Halleck reorganized his army to consist of a Right Wing, Center, Left Wing, and Reserve. Grant retained command of the District of West Tennessee, but was made second-in-command to Halleck and was virtually without command during the advance of the army toward Corinth.

When the reorganization was completed, Halleck advanced very slowly toward Corinth, and when he arrived in front of the town, the enemy withdrew to the south toward Tupelo, Mississippi on the night of May 30, 1862. Halleck's troops then occupied Corinth and the surrounding country. For information about the organization of Halleck's command and its movements, see Halleck's Advance on Corinth, Mississippi, and see also Army of the Ohio (Buell), Army of the Mississippi (Pope, Rosecrans), and Army of the Tennessee, District of West Tennessee.

The wing organization of the army was abolished June 10, 1862, and Grant resumed command of the Army of the Tennessee. On June 11, the Army of the Ohio began to leave the District of West Tennessee on its march along the Memphis and Charleston Railroad toward Chattanooga, Tennessee. George H. Thomas' First Division, Army of the Ohio was attached to the Army of the Tennessee as Seventh Division, and did not rejoin the Army of the Ohio until the end of July 1862.

June 12, 1862, the District of West Tennessee was defined as consisting of the state of Tennessee west of the Tennessee River, and also Fort Henry and Fort Donelson. The district was redefined July 16 to include the District of Cairo and the District of Mississippi of the Department of the Mississippi, and also that part of Mississippi occupied by United States troops, including the Army of the Mississippi. Grant was assigned command, with headquarters at Corinth, Mississippi.

On July 16, 1862, Halleck relinquished command of the Department of the Mississippi and left for Washington, D.C. to become general in chief of the army. The next day Grant assumed command of all troops of the Army of the Tennessee, the Army of the Mississippi, and the districts of Cairo and Mississippi. Although not officially assigned, Grant was, in effect, in command of the Department of the Mississippi after Halleck's departure. Grant, as commander of the District of West Tennessee, was not subject to the orders of any department commander, but received orders from, and reported to, Halleck in Washington until October 16, 1862.

The Department of the Mississippi was discontinued September 19, 1862, and the District of West Tennessee was then not in any department until it was assigned to the newly created Department of the Tennessee October 16. On that date, Grant was assigned command of the Department of the Tennessee.

When the Department of the Tennessee was organized, the District of the Tennessee was discontinued, but it was reconstituted as the District of West Tennessee, Department of the Tennessee January 15, 1863.

The Department of Mississippi (not to be confused with the Department of the Mississippi) was created November 28, 1864 to consist of the state of Mississippi and that part of the state of Tennessee west of the Tennessee River. Thus the District of West Tennessee, to which James C. Veatch was assigned command, became a district in the Department of Mississippi. For additional information, see

Department of Mississippi, November 28, 1864– May 17, 1865, Districts in the Department of Mississippi, District of West Tennessee.

February 10, 1865, that part of Tennessee west of the Tennessee River was transferred as the District of West Tennessee to the Department of the Cumberland. The transfer was completed March 1, and Benjamin S. Roberts was assigned command of the District of West Tennessee. For further information, see Department of the Cumberland, October 24, 1862–June 27, 1865, Districts in the Department of the Cumberland, District of West Tennessee.

Headquarters of the District of West Tennessee were as follows:

Fort Donelson, Tennessee	February 17, 1862 to March 17, 1862
Savannah, Tennessee	March 17, 1862 to March 31, 1862
Pittsburg Landing, Tennessee	March 31, 1862 to April 30, 1862
In the Field	April 30, 1862 to May 31, 1862
Corinth, Mississippi	May 31, 1862 to June 22, 1862
Memphis, Tennessee	June 23, 1862 to July 16, 1862
Corinth, Mississippi	July 16, 1862 to September 26, 1862
Jackson, Tennessee	September 26, 1862 to October 16, 1862

On October 16, 1862, the District of West Tennessee was discontinued as a separate organization when the Department of the Tennessee was created. Later, the district was reconstituted as a district in several departments.

The commanders of the District of West Tennessee up to October 16, 1862 were as follows:

Ulysses S. Grant	February 17, 1862 to March 4, 1862
Charles F. Smith	March 4, 1862 to March 17, 1862
Ulysses S. Grant	March 17, 1862 to October 16, 1862

Halleck relieved Grant from command of the Army of the District of West Tennessee March 4, 1862, and Smith led the army from Fort Henry up the Tennessee River to Savannah. Halleck relented, however, and restored Grant to command on March 17, before the Battle of Shiloh.

POSTS AND DISTRICTS IN THE DISTRICT OF WEST TENNESSEE

District of Cairo. The District of Cairo, Department of the Mississippi (which see) was included in the District of West Tennessee July 16, 1862, but when the Department of the Ohio was re-created on August 19, it included the state of Illinois, and Cairo was thus transferred to the Department of the Ohio. On September 10, however, the District of Mississippi, District of West Tennessee, and District of Cairo were combined to form a new district, designated as the District of Mississippi, District of West Tennessee (see below).

William K. Strong commanded the District of Cairo from March 21 to August 12, 1862, and James M. Tuttle from August 12 to September 10, 1862.

Corinth, Mississippi. After the evacuation of Corinth by Confederate forces during Halleck's advance on the town, George H. Thomas was assigned command of the post and garrison June 11, 1862. The troops under his command consisted of his own First Division, Army of the Ohio (then temporarily designated as Seventh Division, Army of the Tennessee); Thomas A. Davies' Second Division, Army of the Tennessee; and John B. S. Todd's Sixth Division, Army of the Tennessee. Todd was assigned command of Sixth Division June 2, 1862, relieving Thomas J. McKean.

On July 19, 1862, Thomas was ordered to move eastward with his division and rejoin Don Carlos Buell's Army of the Ohio, which was then in northern Alabama along the Memphis and Charleston Railroad, and he soon left the District of West Tennessee.

Thomas was succeeded in command of the United States Forces at Corinth by Edward O. C. Ord in June 1862. Ord's command consisted of Second Division, Army of the Tennessee, temporarily commanded by Richard J. Oglesby, and Sixth Division, Army of the Tennessee, temporarily commanded by John McArthur.

In the reorganization of the District of West Tennessee September 24, 1862 (see below), the troops of the post and garrison of Corinth became a part of Third Division, District of West Tennessee, which was commanded by William S. Rosecrans. Third Division, District of West Tennessee was transferred to the Department of the Tennessee on October 26 as the District of Corinth, Thirteenth Corps.

Commanders of the post and garrison of Corinth were as follows:

George H. Thomas	June 11, 1862 to July 19, 1862
Edward O. C. Ord	July 19, 1862 to August 5, 1862
George Cadwalader	August 5, 1862 to August 13, 1862
Edward O. C. Ord	August 13, 1862 to September 24, 1862

Note. Cadwalader was in temporary command of the post and garrison while Ord was absent on inspection duty.

District of Jackson. On June 2, 1862, just after the enemy evacuated Corinth, John A. McClernand, commanding the Reserve of Halleck's Army of the Department of the Mississippi, was ordered to proceed from near Corinth toward Jackson and Memphis, Tennessee. He was directed to move by way of Purdy and Bethel, and to repair and guard the railroads of that part of West Tennessee.

John A. Logan, commanding McClernand's First Division, Army of the Tennessee of the Reserve, arrived at Jackson June 21, 1862, and Lewis Wallace's Third Division, Army of the Tennessee of the Reserve had moved on toward Memphis (see below, Memphis, Tennessee).

The Reserve of the army was discontinued by an order of June 24, 1862, but McClernand was reporting from Headquarters, Reserve as late as July 5.

On June 24, 1862, McClernand was assigned command of all troops occupying the country south of Union City, Tennessee and north of the Memphis and Charleston Railroad, with troops on the following railroads: the Mississippi Central Railroad, with posts at Bolivar, Jackson, and Humboldt, Tennessee; the Memphis and Ohio Railroad, with posts at Brownsville and Humboldt, Tennessee; and the Mobile and Ohio Railroad, with posts at Bethel, Henderson, and Jackson, Tennessee. Although not officially so designated by the order of June 24, McClernand's command became known as the District of Jackson, District of West Tennessee.

In the reorganization of the District of West Tennessee September 24, 1862 (see below), the District of Jackson became a part of Second Division, District of West Tennessee. Edward O. C. Ord was assigned command of Second Division, with headquarters at Jackson or Bolivar. On October 26, Second Division, District of West Tennessee was transferred to the Department of the Tennessee as the District of Jackson, Thirteenth Corps.

As noted above, the first troops to occupy Jackson, Tennessee belonged to John A. Logan's First Division of McClernand's Reserve, Army of the Department of the Mississippi. On July 5, 1862, after the Reserve of the army had been discontinued, the designation of Logan's First Division (McClernand's) was changed to First Division, District of Jackson. The names of the brigade commanders and the dates of their command are not given, but a study of the records indicates the following:

First Brigade, John A. Logan
Second Brigade, Andrew J. Babcock
   Michael K. Lawler
   Lyndorf Ozburn
Third Brigade, Leonard F. Ross
   Elias S. Dennis
   C. Carroll Marsh
Fourth Brigade, Frank L. Rhoads

In September 1862, the organization of Logan's forces in the district was given as follows:

Post of Jackson, Michael K. Lawler
   Second Brigade, Lyndorf Ozburn
   Third Brigade, C. Carroll Marsh
   Third Sub-division, Isham N. Haynie (Haynie commanded the post of Bethel)
   Fourth Brigade, Frank L. Rhoads
   Cavalry, Lucien H. Kerr

In July 1862, Leonard F. Ross was assigned command of a division at Bolivar to protect the Mississippi Central Railroad. This division was designated as Second Division, District of Jackson, but there is little detailed information about its composition. Such information as can be found in the records indicates the following:

Marcellus M. Crocker commanded Second Division in August 1862, and was also in command of the post of Bolivar at that time. Earlier, Crocker (commander of Third Brigade, Sixth Division from Corinth) was in command of First Brigade, Second Division, and Mortimer D. Leggett was in command of First Brigade during August and September

1862. Alexander Chambers (commander of the 16th Iowa of Sixth Division from Corinth) commanded Fifth Brigade, Second Division.

Leonard F. Ross was in command at Bolivar in September 1862, and he was ordered to take his Second Division, District of Jackson to reinforce Edward O. C. Ord's command near Iuka, Mississippi. He was near Burnsville, Mississippi during the Battle of Iuka September 17, but returned to Bolivar on September 23.

Meantime, Stephen A. Hurlbut had arrived at Bolivar from Memphis September 13, 1862 with Fourth Division, Army of the Tennessee, and he then remained in the District of Jackson.

October 3, 1862, James B. McPherson was assigned command of the brigades of Michael K. Lawler and John D. Stevenson from the District of Jackson. He was ordered to take them to Corinth, Mississippi during the Battle of Corinth, October 3–4. For additional information, see Battle of Corinth, Mississippi.

On October 11, 1862, McPherson was directed to turn over the command of his two brigades at Corinth to Lawler, and to report in person to Grant's headquarters at Jackson, Tennessee. He was assigned command of the United States Forces at Bolivar on October 14. McPherson's command reported to Hurlbut, then commander of Second Division, District of West Tennessee.

The commanders of the District of Jackson were as follows:

John A. McClernand	June 24, 1862 to August 25, 1862
John A. Logan	August 25, 1862 to September 24, 1862
Edward O. C. Ord	September 24, 1862 to October 5, 1862
Stephen A. Hurlbut	October 5, 1862 to October 26, 1862

Note. Leonard F. Ross was in temporary command of the district during the first week in September 1862, while Logan was absent at Cairo, Illinois.

Memphis, Tennessee. Memphis was first occupied June 6, 1862 by the 43rd and 47th Indiana regiments of James R. Slack's First Brigade, Third Division of John Pope's Army of the Mississippi. These two regiments had been left at New Madrid, Missouri when Pope left for Fort Pillow before joining

Halleck's army near Hamburg, Tennessee. That day Lewis Wallace's Third Division of the Reserve, Army of the Department of the Mississippi marched westward from near Corinth, Mississippi; it arrived at Memphis June 18. Wallace remained at Memphis until July 22, then departed on leave. Alvin P. Hovey assumed command of Third Division.

William T. Sherman marched from Chewalla, Tennessee June 11, 1862 with his own Fifth Division and Stephen A. Hurlbut's Fourth Division of the Army of the Tennessee and, moving westward along the Memphis and Charleston Railroad, arrived in Memphis July 20. Sherman assumed command at Memphis the next day.

July 22, 1862, the infantry of Third Division under Hovey was ordered to Helena, Arkansas to join Samuel R. Curtis and the Army of the Southwest, which was moving toward Helena from northwestern Arkansas.

September 5, 1862, Hurlbut with his Fourth Division was ordered to Brownsville, Tennessee as a detached command, and he was then sent to Bolivar, where he arrived September 13. Hurlbut remained in the District of Jackson.

In the reorganization of the District of West Tennessee September 24, 1862, all territory south of the Hatchie River and west of Bolivar that was occupied by Federal troops was designated as First Division, District of West Tennessee. William T. Sherman was assigned command of the division.

First Division was transferred to the Department of the Tennessee October 26, 1862 as the District of Memphis, Thirteenth Corps.

Grant's headquarters of the District of West Tennessee was at Memphis from June 23 to July 16, 1862.

The commanders of the District of Memphis were as follows:

James R. Slack	June 6, 1862 to June 18, 1862
Lewis Wallace	June 18, 1862 to July 21, 1862
William T. Sherman	July 21, 1862 to October 26, 1862

Note. From September 21, 1862, Sherman's command was designated as First Division, District of West Tennessee.

District of Mississippi. The District of Mississippi, Department of the Mississippi was included in the District of West Tennessee July 16, 1862. Isaac F. Quinby was assigned command, with headquarters at Columbus, Kentucky.

The District of Mississippi and the District of Cairo were combined September 10, 1862 to form a single district, which was designated as the District of Mississippi. Quinby was assigned command of the new district.

In the reorganization of the District of West Tennessee September 24, 1862, the district became a part of Fourth Division, District of West Tennessee. Quinby was assigned command of Fourth Division.

Fourth Division was transferred to the Department of the Tennessee October 26, 1862 as the District of Columbus, Thirteenth Corps.

The principal organization of troops in the district was the Central Division of the Mississippi, commanded by Grenville M. Dodge, whose headquarters was at Trenton, Tennessee. For additional information, see Department of the Mississippi (Halleck), Districts in the Department of the Mississippi, District of Mississippi.

Army of the Mississippi. On July 16, 1862, the Army of the Mississippi, which John Pope had brought to Hamburg, Tennessee at the beginning of Halleck's advance on Corinth, became a part of the District of West Tennessee. For additional information, see Army of the Mississippi (Pope, Rosecrans).

DIVISIONS OF THE DISTRICT OF WEST TENNESSEE

On September 24, 1862, the District of West Tennessee was reorganized by the formation of four divisions as follows:

First Division. First Division consisted of all territory of the district south of the Hatchie River and west of Bolivar, Tennessee that was occupied by United States troops. William T. Sherman was assigned command, with headquarters at Memphis, Tennessee.

Second Division. Second Division consisted of all territory south of the Kentucky state line between the Hatchie River on the west and Bethel Station on the east, including Bolivar, south of the Hatchie River. Edward O. C. Ord was assigned command, with headquarters at Jackson.

Third Division. Third Division consisted of all territory occupied by the Army of the Mississippi, and the forces of the post and garrison of Corinth, Mississippi, at that time commanded by Ord. William S. Rosecrans was assigned command, with headquarters at Corinth. The troops at Corinth consisted of David S. Stanley's Second Division and Charles S. Hamilton's Third Division of the Army of the Mississippi, and John K. Mizner's cavalry.

Fourth Division. Fourth Division was composed of what was then known as the District of Cairo and the District of Mississippi, including Fort Henry and Fort Donelson, and exclusive of that territory lying in the state of Tennessee and along the railroads. The posts of the district were Big Muddy, Cairo, and Mound City in Illinois; Fort Heiman, Paducah, Columbus, Smithland, and Hickman in Kentucky; Bird's Point, Missouri; and Fort Henry, Fort Donelson, and Fort Pillow in Tennessee. Isaac F. Quinby was assigned command, with headquarters at Columbus, but Grenville M. Dodge was assigned temporarily during Quinby's absence on leave.

There were no further organizational changes in the district until it was discontinued when it was merged into the Department of the Tennessee October 16, 1862.

OPERATIONS IN THE DISTRICT OF WEST TENNESSEE

During March 1862, Grant's Army of the District of West Tennessee advanced from Fort Henry up the Tennessee River to Savannah and Pittsburg Landing in Tennessee, and on April 6–7 it was engaged at the Battle of Shiloh. Don Carlos Buell's Army of the Ohio joined Grant at Pittsburg Landing and, together with the Army of the Tennessee, succeeded in forcing the enemy to withdraw toward Corinth, Mississippi April 7. For details, see Battle of Shiloh (or Pittsburg Landing), Tennessee.

Henry W. Halleck, commanding the Department of the Mississippi, arrived at Pittsburg Landing from Saint Louis April 12, 1862 and assumed personal command of the Union troops assembled there, including John Pope's Army of the Mississippi, which arrived there from the Mississippi River on April 21. Then during the period April 29–May 30, Pope advanced with his combined armies against Corinth, which was evacuated by the enemy on the night of May 29–30. Halleck's troops occupied the town on May 30. For details, see Halleck's Advance on Corinth, Mississippi.

Sterling Price advanced with a Confederate army to Iuka, Mississippi in September 1862, and was engaged there on September 19 with William S. Rosecrans' Army of the Mississippi. For details, see Engagement at Iuka, Mississippi. Then two Confederate armies commanded by Price and Earl Van Dorn attempted to recapture Corinth, Mississippi in a battle of October 3–4, 1862, but they were defeated by Rosecrans' Army of the Mississippi and two divisions of Grant's Army of the Tennessee. For details, see Battle of Corinth, Mississippi.

There were no further major engagements before the District of West Tennessee was discontinued October 16, 1862.

INDIAN EXPEDITION (WEER, SALOMON)

Indian Expedition is the name sometimes used for the troops of the expedition to the Indian Territory June 28–July 1862 that was led by William Weer, and later by Frederick Salomon. For information about this command, see Department of Kansas, May 2, 1862–September 19, 1862, Troops and Operations in the Department of Kansas.

LEFT WING FORCES IN EAST TENNESSEE (WILLCOX)

In October 1863, during Ambrose E. Burnside's East Tennessee Campaign, a special organization known as Left Wing Forces in East Tennessee was organized under the command of Orlando B. Willcox. It was formed from four new Indiana regiments brought to East Tennessee by Willcox, and three regiments taken from Third Division, Twenty-Third Corps. At the end of October 1863, this force was near Greeneville, Tennessee and was organized as follows:

Left Wing Forces in East Tennessee, Orlando B. Willcox
First Brigade, John R. Mahan
115th Indiana, Alfred J. Hawn
116th Indiana, William C. Kise
117th Indiana, Thomas J. Brady
118th Indiana, George W. Jackson
Second Brigade, William A. Hoskins
12th Kentucky, Joseph M. Owens
103rd Ohio, John S. Casement
8th Tennessee, Felix A. Reeve
Not brigaded
Company L, 3rd Indiana Cavalry, Oliver M. Powers
Company M, 3rd Indiana Cavalry, Charles U. Patton
22nd Battery, Indiana Light Artillery, James H. Myers
Battery M, 1st Michigan Light Artillery, Edward G. Hillier
21st Battery, Ohio Light Artillery, James W. Patterson

Willcox then moved his command to Maynardville, Tennessee, and it was expanded to include Cumberland Gap and the troops in the vicinity. On December 31, 1863, it was organized as follows:

Left Wing Forces in East Tennessee, Orlando B. Willcox
First Brigade, John R. Mahan
115th Indiana, Alfred J. Hawn
2nd North Carolina (mounted), Andrew J. Bahney
23rd Battery, Indiana Light Artillery, James H. Myers
Second Brigade, George W. Jackson
116th Indiana, William C. Kise
118th Indiana, Henry C. Elliott
Cumberland Gap, Tennessee, Wilson C. Lemert
86th Ohio, Robert W. McFarland
129th Ohio (Company A), Frederick H. Stedman
16th Illinois Cavalry (two battalions), Friedrich Schambeck
4th Battalion, Ohio Cavalry, Joseph T. Wheeler
11th Tennessee Cavalry (five companies), Reuben A. Davis

Battery L, 1st Michigan Light Artillery, Thomas Gallagher
22nd Battery, Ohio Light Artillery, George W. Taylor
Battery B, 1st Tennessee Light Artillery, James A. Childress
Tazewell, Tennessee, Christian Thielemann
34th Kentucky, William Y. Dillard
129th Ohio (eight companies), Howard D. John
3rd Indiana Cavalry (Company L), George J. Langsdale
3rd Indiana Cavalry (Company M), Thomas G. Schaeffer
6th Indiana Cavalry (two battalions), Courtland C. Matson
Battery M, 1st Michigan Light Artillery, Edward G. Hillier

Early in January 1864, the designation of Willcox's command was changed to District of the Clinch, and on January 17, Theophilus T. Garrard was ordered to move with his 91st Indiana Infantry to Cumberland Gap and relieve Willcox in command of the district. On January 19, Willcox assumed command of Ninth Corps, then in East Tennessee.

On January 31, 1864, the troops of the district consisted of the following unbrigaded regiments and batteries:

District of the Clinch, Theophilus T. Garrard
91st Indiana, John Mehringer
117th Indiana, Thomas J. Brady
118th Indiana, Henry C. Elliott
34th Kentucky, William Y. Dillard
2nd North Carolina (mounted), James A. Smith
129th Ohio, Howard D. John
16th Illinois Cavalry, Christian Thielemann
6th Indiana Cavalry (two battalions), Courtland C. Matson
11th Tennessee Cavalry, Reuben A. Davis
Battery L, 1st Michigan Light Artillery, Thomas Gallagher
Battery M, 1st Michigan Light Artillery, Augustus H. Emery
22nd Battery, Ohio Light Artillery, George W. Taylor
Battery B, 1st Tennessee Light Artillery, Isaac P. Knight

Garrard remained in command of the District of the Clinch until April 12, 1864, at which time Twenty-Third Corps was reorganized. On that date Garrard's troops at Cumberland Gap were assigned to First Brigade of Jacob Ammen's Fourth Division, Twenty-Third Corps, with Garrard in command of the brigade.

SHIP ISLAND, MISSISSIPPI EXPEDITION

For details of the organization of the Ship Island, Mississippi Expedition, see Department of the Gulf, Troops in the Department of the Gulf.

SIBLEY'S SIOUX EXPEDITION

The troops commanded by Henry Hastings Sibley during a campaign against the Sioux Indians in the summer of 1863 was sometimes called Sibley's Sioux Expedition. For additional information, see Department of the Northwest, Troops and Operations in the Department of the Northwest, Sibley's and Sully's Sioux Expeditions, Summer of 1863.

STEELE'S COLUMN FROM PENSACOLA, FLORIDA

For details of the organization of Steele's Column from Pensacola, see Land Operations against Mobile Bay and Mobile, Alabama.

SULLY'S SIOUX EXPEDITION

Alfred Sully's Sioux Expedition in the summer of 1863 was part of a larger operation against the Indians in which Henry Hastings Sibley led a column from Fort Pope, near Mankato, Minnesota, up the Red River toward Devil's Lake, while Sully ascended the Missouri River from Fort Randall, Dakota Territory to intercept the Indians that were being driven westward by Sibley. Sully was late in starting, and failed to intercept the Indians, but he closed the campaign with a disastrous defeat of a band of Indians at White Stone Hill early in September 1863. For details of Sully's Sioux Expedition, see Department of the Northwest, Troops and Operations in the Department of the Northwest, Sibley's and Sully's Sioux Expeditions, Summer of 1863.

UNITED STATES COLORED TROOPS

Immediately after the fall of Fort Sumter, many blacks in the North asked that they be permitted to serve in the Union army, but the request was refused, and during the early stages of the war they were used only for labor in the construction of fortifications and other military installations.

In May 1861, Benjamin F. Butler established a precedent for the confiscation of runaway slaves when he refused to return three slaves who had been working on the construction of a Confederate battery, and who had run away and appeared at Fort Monroe. Butler's action was upheld when two months later Congress passed an act that authorized the confiscation of property belonging to persons who were in insurrection against the United States.

Early in the war, Union troops effected lodgments in various parts of the Confederacy, particularly along the Mississippi River and the Atlantic coast, and in time slaves in large numbers began to arrive within the Union lines. At first these were employed by the army as cooks and servants and in the quartermaster's department, but it was not long until the number of slaves arriving at the Union posts from the plantations was greater than could be given such employment. By this time, the sentiment favoring the use of blacks as soldiers was increasing, and finally Congress passed the Militia Act of July 17, 1862 that authorized the president to organize black men and use them for military purposes.

The first black troops to serve as soldiers in the army were not organized under Union authority. An organization known as Louisiana Native Guards was established April 23, 1861, when free colored men of New Orleans were legally enrolled as a part of the militia of the state of Louisiana. Its officers, who were black, were commissioned by Confederate Governor Thomas O. Moore. The Native Guards had not been enthusiastic about serving under Moore, and when Benjamin F. Butler occupied New Orleans May 1, 1862, they immediately offered their services to Butler.

As early as July 1862, John W. Phelps, commanding the Union forces at Carrollton, Louisiana, proposed that three regiments of colored troops be raised in the Department of the Gulf, and soon thereafter the organization of colored regiments began. The first regiment of Louisiana volunteers was organized July 30, 1862, and on August 22, Butler, believing that the Native Guards and all other free colored people were loyal to the United States, decided to enlist them in the volunteer forces of the United States and issued a proclamation to that effect. Four regiments, designated as regiments of Native Guard Infantry, were organized as follows: 1st Regiment Native Guard Infantry, September 27, 1862; 2nd Regiment, October 19, 1862; 3rd Regiment, November 24, 1862; and 4th Regiment, February 10, 1863. The 1st Regiment of Engineers was organized April 28, 1863.

On September 24, 1862, President Abraham Lincoln issued his Emancipation Proclamation, which stated that all slaves in those areas of the South that were in rebellion against the United States on January 1, 1863 would be free, and from that time large numbers of black soldiers, and white officers to command them, were accepted into the service of the United States.

Because of the immense amount of work required for the administration of the affairs of this new body of troops, the War Department created, by an order of May 22, 1863, the Bureau of Colored Troops to take over this task. This bureau was under the general supervision of the adjutant general's office, and Charles W. Foster was placed in charge. His responsibility was to process the raising of black troops and the securing of white officers to command them.

The total number of troops, commissioned and enlisted, that were enrolled in this branch of the service during the war was 186,000. Most of these men served on garrison and occupation duty, but a great many belonged to units that were in combat, where they fought well. Of the numerous colored regiments raised during the war, many were organized into brigades, and some of the brigades were organized into divisions. The Twenty-Fifth Corps, Army of the James, which was organized December 3, 1864, was composed entirely of United States Colored Troops in its infantry components, with only its artillery brigade consisting entirely of white batteries.

During the Civil War, with the exception of the artillery, regiments that were composed of black troops were specifically designated as "colored" regiments, or regiments of African descent, but for uniformity in this presentation, except for a special organization known as Corps d'Afrique, the word "colored" is used to refer to regiments of black troops.

The colored regiments that were first organized were generally designated as regiments of the states in which the troops had resided. After June 1863, however, when the designation of United States Colored Troops was adopted, the newly raised regiments were so designated, and all but a few of the regiments that had been organized earlier were assigned numerical designations of United States Colored Troops.

The regiments of colored troops organized during the war are listed below. The first list consists of those regiments with state designations, and the second list consists of the regiments with their numerical designations of United States Colored Troops (USCT).

Alabama Regiments

1st Alabama Colored Siege Artillery. Organized at Memphis and in western Tennessee June 20, 1863–April 2, 1864. Designation changed to 6th United States Colored Heavy Artillery March 11, 1864, and then to 7th United States Colored Heavy Artillery April 26, 1864.

1st Alabama Colored Infantry. Organized at Corinth, Mississippi May 21, 1863. Designation changed to 55th USCT March 11, 1864.

2nd Alabama Colored Infantry. Organized at Pulaski, Tennessee November 20, 1863–January 14, 1864. Designation changed to 110th USCT June 25, 1864.

3rd Alabama Colored Infantry. Organized at Pulaski, Prospect, and Lynnville in Tennessee and Sulfur Branch Trestle in Alabama January 13–April 5, 1864. Designation changed to 111th USCT June 25, 1864.

4th Alabama Colored Infantry. Organized at Decatur, Alabama March 31–August 10, 1864. Designation changed to 106th USCT May 16, 1864.

Arkansas Regiments

1st Arkansas Colored Light Battery. Organized at Pine Bluff, Arkansas June 4, 1864. Designation changed to Battery H, 2nd United States Colored Light Artillery December 13, 1864.

1st Arkansas Colored Infantry. Organized in Arkansas May 1, 1863. Designation changed to 46th USCT March 11, 1864.

2nd Arkansas Colored Infantry. Organized in Arkansas September 4–December 25, 1863. Designation changed to 54th USCT March 11, 1864.

3rd Arkansas Colored Infantry. Organized at Saint Louis, Missouri August 12–September 29, 1863. Designation changed to 56th USCT March 11, 1864.

4th Arkansas Colored Infantry. Organized at Duvall's Bluff, Little Rock, and Helena, Arkansas December 2, 1863–March 1, 1864. Designation changed to 57th USCT March 11, 1864.

5th Arkansas Colored Infantry. Organized in Little Rock, Arkansas April 23–November 8, 1864 and designated as 112th USCT. Consolidated with 11th USCT (old) and 113th USCT (old) April 1, 1865 to form 113th USCT (new).

6th Arkansas Colored Infantry. Organized at Little Rock, Arkansas March 1–June 20, 1864. Designation changed to 113th USCT June 25, 1864.

Connecticut Regiments

29th Connecticut Infantry (colored). Organized at New Haven, Connecticut March 8, 1864.

30th Connecticut Infantry (colored). Organized at New Haven, Connecticut March 1864. Consolidated with 31st USCT May 18, 1864.

Iowa Regiment

1st Iowa Colored Infantry. Organized at Keokuk, Iowa and Benton Barracks, Missouri October 15–December 4, 1863. Designation changed to 60th USCT March 11, 1864.

Kansas Regiments

1st Kansas Colored Infantry. Organized at Fort Scott, Kansas January 13–May 2, 1863. Designation changed to 79th USCT December 13, 1864.

2nd Kansas Colored Infantry. Organized at Fort Scott and Leavenworth, Kansas August 11–October 17, 1863. Designation changed to 83rd USCT December 13, 1864.

Louisiana Regiments

1st Louisiana Colored Heavy Artillery. Organized at New Orleans, Louisiana October 29–November 8, 1862. Designation changed to 1st Heavy Artillery, Corps d'Afrique November 19, 1864.

1st Battery, Louisiana Colored Light Artillery. Organized at Hebron's Plantation, Mississippi November 6, 1863. Designation changed to Battery A, 2nd United States Colored Light Artillery March 11, 1864, and then to Battery C April 26, 1864.

2nd Battery, Louisiana Colored Light Artillery. Organized at Big Black River Bridge, Mississippi December 21, 1863. Designation changed to Battery B, 2nd United States Colored Light Artillery March 11, 1864, and then to Battery D April 26, 1864.

3rd Battery, Louisiana Colored Light Artillery. Organized at Helena, Arkansas December 1, 1863. Designation changed to Battery C, 2nd United States Colored Light Artillery March 11, 1864, and then to Battery E April 26, 1864.

1st Regiment Louisiana Colored Engineers. Designation changed June 6, 1863 to 1st Regiment Engineers, Corps d'Afrique.

1st Louisiana Native Guards. Organized at New Orleans, Louisiana September 27, 1862. Designation changed to 1st Infantry, Corps d'Afrique June 6, 1863.

2nd Louisiana Native Guards. Organized at New Orleans, Louisiana September 27, 1862. Designation changed to 2nd Infantry, Corps d'Afrique June 6, 1863.

3rd Louisiana Native Guards. Organized at New Orleans, Louisiana November 24, 1862. Designation changed to 3rd Infantry, Corps d'Afrique June 6, 1863.

4th Louisiana Native Guards. Organized at New Orleans, Louisiana February 10–March 6, 1863. Designation changed to 4th Infantry, Corps d'Afrique June 6, 1863.

5th Louisiana Colored Infantry. Organization not completed.

6th Louisiana Colored Infantry. Organized at New Orleans July 4, 1863 for sixty days. Served at that place.

7th Louisiana Colored Infantry. Organized at Holly Springs and Memphis, Tennessee, and Island No. 10 December 1, 1863–February 1, 1864. Designation changed to 64th USCT March 11, 1864.

8th Louisiana Colored Infantry. Organized at Lake Providence, Louisiana May 5, 1863. Designation changed to 47th USCT March 11, 1864.

9th Louisiana Colored Infantry. Organized at Memphis, Tennessee; Island No. 10; and Vicksburg and Goodrich's Landing in Louisiana November 19–December 14, 1863. Designation changed to 1st Mississippi Colored Heavy Artillery September 26, 1863, and to 63rd USCT March 11, 1864.

10th Louisiana Colored Infantry. Organized at Lake Providence and Goodrich's Landing, Louisiana May 6–August 8, 1863. Designation changed to 48th USCT March 11, 1864.

11th Louisiana Colored Infantry. Organized at Milliken's Bend, Louisiana May 5, 1863. Designation changed to 49th USCT March 11, 1864.

12th Louisiana Colored Infantry. Organized at Vicksburg, Mississippi July 11–27, 1863. Designation changed to 50th USCT March 11, 1864.

13th Louisiana Colored Infantry. Organized at Milliken's Bend, Louisiana during Grant's Vicksburg Campaign.

By an order of June 6, 1863, the colored regiments in the Department of the Gulf were designated by number as regiments of the Corps d'Afrique as follows:

1st Cavalry, Corps d'Afrique. Organized at New Orleans September 1863–July 19, 1864. Designation changed April 4, 1864 to 4th United States Colored Cavalry.

1st Heavy Artillery, Corps d'Afrique. Designation changed to 7th United States Colored Heavy Artillery April 4, 1864.

1st Engineers, Corps d'Afrique. Organized at Camp Parapet, Louisiana April 28, 1863. Designation changed to 95th USCT April 4, 1864.

2nd Engineers, Corps d'Afrique. Organized at New Orleans August 15, 1863. Designation changed to 96th USCT April 4, 1864.

3rd Engineers, Corps d'Afrique. Organized at New Orleans August 26, 1863. Designation changed to 97th USCT April 4, 1864.

4th Engineers, Corps d'Afrique. Organized at New Orleans, Camp Parapet, and Berwick City, Louisiana September 3, 1863–March 3, 1864. Designation changed to 98th USCT April 4, 1864.

5th Engineers, Corps d'Afrique. Organized February 10, 1864 from 15th Infantry, Corps d'Afrique. Designation changed to 99th USCT April 4, 1864.

1st Infantry, Corps d'Afrique. Organized June 6, 1863 from 1st Louisiana Native Guards. Designation changed to 73rd USCT April 4, 1864.

2nd Infantry, Corps d'Afrique. Organized June 6, 1863 from 2nd Louisiana Native Guards. Designation changed to 74th USCT April 4, 1864.

3rd Infantry, Corps d'Afrique. Organized June 6, 1863 from 3rd Louisiana Native Guards. Designation changed to 75th USCT April 4, 1864.

4th Infantry, Corps d'Afrique. Organized June 6, 1863 from 4th Louisiana Native Guards. Designation changed to 76th USCT April 4, 1864.

5th Infantry, Corps d'Afrique. Organized in the District of Pensacola June 6, 1863. Designation changed to 77th USCT April 4, 1864.

6th Infantry, Corps d'Afrique. Organized June 6, 1863 from the 1st Regiment, Ullmann's Brigade, then being raised by Daniel Ullmann. The designation was changed to 78th USCT April 4, 1864.

7th Infantry, Corps d'Afrique. Organized June 6, 1863 from the 2nd Regiment, Ullmann's Brigade, then being raised by Daniel Ullmann. The designation was changed to 79th USCT April 4, 1864.

8th Infantry, Corps d'Afrique. Organized June

6, 1863 from the 3rd Regiment, Ullmann's Brigade, then being raised by Daniel Ullmann. The designation was changed to 80th USCT April 4, 1864.

9th Infantry, Corps d'Afrique. Organized June 6, 1863 from 4th Regiment, Ullmann's Brigade, then being raised by Daniel Ullmann. The designation was changed to 81st USCT April 4, 1864.

10th Infantry, Corps d'Afrique. Organized June 6, 1863 from 5th Regiment, Ullmann's Brigade, then being raised by Daniel Ullmann. The designation was changed to 82nd USCT April 4, 1864.

11th Infantry, Corps d'Afrique. Organized at Port Hudson August 17, 1863. Designation changed to 83rd USCT April 4, 1864.

12th Infantry, Corps d'Afrique. Organized at Port Hudson September 24–October 16, 1863. Designation changed to 84th USCT April 4, 1864.

13th Infantry, Corps d'Afrique. Organized at New Orleans March 11, 1863 as a part of Mardon W. Plumly's brigade. Designation changed to 85th USCT April 4, 1864.

14th Infantry, Corps d'Afrique. Organized at New Orleans August 12–September 3, 1863 as a part of Marsdon W. Plumly's brigade. Designation changed to 86th USCT April 4, 1864.

15th Infantry, Corps d'Afrique. Organized at New Orleans August 27, 1863 as a part of Marsdon W. Plumly's brigade. Designation changed to 5th Engineers, Corps d'Afrique February 10, 1864.

16th Infantry, Corps d'Afrique. Organized at New Orleans October 8–16, 1863 as a part of Marsdon W. Plumly's brigade. Designation changed to 87th USCT April 4, 1864.

17th Infantry, Corps d'Afrique. Organized at Port Hudson September 24, 1863. Designation changed to 88th USCT April 4, 1864.

18th Infantry, Corps d'Afrique. Organized at Port Hudson October 9–November 8, 1863. Designation changed to 89th USCT April 4, 1864.

19th Infantry, Corps d'Afrique. Organized at Madisonville, Louisiana February 11, 1864. Designation changed to 90th USCT April 4, 1864.

20th Infantry, Corps d'Afrique. Organized at Fort Pike, Louisiana September 1, 1863. Designation changed to 91st USCT April 4, 1864.

22nd Infantry, Corps d'Afrique. Organized at New Orleans September 30–October 24, 1863. Designation changed to 92nd USCT April 4, 1864.

25th Infantry, Corps d'Afrique. Organized at New Iberia, Louisiana November 21, 1863. Designation changed to 93rd USCT April 1864.

Massachusetts Regiments

5th Massachusetts Cavalry (colored). Organized at Readville, Massachusetts January 9, 1864–May 5, 1865.

54th Massachusetts Infantry (colored). Organized at Camp Meigs, Readville, Massachusetts March 30–May 13, 1863.

55th Massachusetts Infantry (colored). Organized at Readville, Massachusetts May 31–June 22, 1863.

Michigan Regiment

1st Michigan Colored Infantry. Organized at Detroit, Michigan February 17, 1864. Designation changed to 102nd USCT May 23, 1865.

Mississippi Regiments

1st Mississippi Colored Cavalry. Organized at Vicksburg and vicinity October 9, 1863–March 1, 1864. Designation changed to 3rd United States Colored Cavalry March 11, 1864.

1st Mississippi Colored Heavy Artillery. Organized at Vicksburg as 9th Louisiana Colored Infantry August 7, 1863–January 17, 1864. Designation changed to 1st Mississippi Colored Heavy Artillery September 26, 1863, then to 4th United States Colored Heavy Artillery March 11, 1864, and to 5th United States Colored Heavy Artillery April 26, 1864.

2nd Mississippi Colored Heavy Artillery. Organized at Natchez, Mississippi September 12, 1863–January 21, 1864. Designation changed to 5th United States Colored Heavy Artillery March 11, 1864, and to 6th United States Colored Heavy Artillery April 26, 1864.

1st Mississippi Colored Infantry. Organized at Milliken's Bend, Louisiana and Vicksburg, Mississippi May 16, 1863–March 7, 1864. Designation changed to 51st USCT March 11, 1864.

2nd Mississippi Colored Infantry. Organized at Vicksburg, Mississippi July 27–December 22, 1863. Designation changed to 52nd USCT March 11, 1864.

3rd Mississippi Colored Infantry. Organized at Warrenton, Mississippi May 19, 1863. Designation changed to 53rd USCT March 11, 1864.

4th Mississippi Colored Infantry. Organized at Vicksburg, Mississippi December 11, 1863–January 11, 1864. Designation changed to 66th USCT March 11, 1864.

5th Mississippi Colored Infantry. Organization not completed.

6th Mississippi Colored Infantry. Organized at Natchez, Mississippi August 27, 1863. Designation changed to 58th USCT March 11, 1864.

Missouri Regiments

1st Missouri Colored Infantry. Organized at Benton Barracks, Missouri December 7–14, 1863. Designation changed to 62nd USCT March 11, 1864.

2nd Missouri Colored Infantry. Organized at Benton Barracks December 18, 1863–January 16, 1864. Designation changed to 65th USCT March 11, 1864.

3rd Missouri Colored Infantry. Organized at Benton Barracks, Missouri January 19–February 13, 1864. Designation changed to 67th USCT March 11, 1864.

4th Missouri Colored Infantry. Organized at Benton Barracks, Missouri March 8–April 23, 1864. Designation changed to 68th USCT March 11, 1864.

North Carolina Regiments

1st North Carolina Colored Heavy Artillery. Organized at New Berne and Morehead City, North Carolina March 14, 1864–April 30, 1865. Designation changed to 14th United Stated Colored Heavy Artillery March 17, 1865.

1st North Carolina Colored Infantry. Organized at New Berne, North Carolina June 30, 1863.

Designation changed to 35th USCT February 8, 1864.

2nd North Carolina Colored Infantry. Organized at Portsmouth, Virginia October 28, 1863. Designation changed to 36th USCT February 8, 1864.

3rd North Carolina Colored Infantry. Organized at Norfolk, Virginia January 30, 1864. Designation changed to 37th USCT February 8, 1864.

Rhode Island Regiment

14th Rhode Island Colored Heavy Artillery. Organized at Providence, Rhode Island August 23, 1863–January 25, 1864. Designation changed to 8th United States Colored Heavy Artillery April 4, 1864, and to 11th United States Colored Heavy Artillery May 21, 1864.

15th Rhode Island Colored Infantry. Organization not completed.

South Carolina Regiments

1st South Carolina Colored Infantry. Organized at Beaufort, South Carolina January 31, 1863. Designation changed to 33rd USCT February 8, 1864.

2nd South Carolina Colored Infantry. Organized at Beaufort and Hilton Head, South Carolina May 22, 1863–December 32, 1864. Before its organization was completed, its designation changed to 34th USCT.

3rd South Carolina Colored Infantry. Organized at Hilton Head, South Carolina June 19, 1863.

4th South Carolina Colored Infantry. Organized at Fernandina, Florida June 19, 1863. Consolidated with the 3rd South Carolina Colored Infantry to form the 21st USCT March 14, 1864.

5th South Carolina Colored Infantry. The organization of this regiment was not completed, and the troops were transferred to the 3rd and 4th South Carolina regiments.

Tennessee Regiments

1st Tennessee Colored Heavy Artillery. Organized at Memphis and Fort Pickering, Tennessee

June 5–December 22, 1863. Designation changed to 2nd United States Colored Heavy Artillery March 11, 1864, and to 3rd United States Colored Heavy Artillery April 26, 1864.

2nd Tennessee Colored Heavy Artillery. Organized at Columbus, Kentucky June 16, 1863–April 19, 1864. Designation changed to 3rd United States Colored Heavy Artillery March 11, 1864, and to 4th United States Colored Heavy Artillery April 26, 1864.

Memphis Colored Light Battery. Organized at Memphis, Tennessee November 23, 1863. Designation changed to Battery D, 2nd United States Colored Light Artillery March 11, 1864, and to Battery F April 26, 1864.

1st Tennessee Colored Infantry. Organized at La Grange, Tennessee June 6–27, 1863. Designation changed to 59th USCT March 11, 1864.

2nd Tennessee Colored Infantry. Organized at La Grange, Tennessee June 30–August 8, 1863. Designation changed to 61st USCT May 11, 1864.

* * * * * * * * * *

United States Colored Troops (USCT)

1st United States Colored Cavalry. Organized at Camp Hamilton, Virginia December 22, 1863.

2nd United States Colored Cavalry. Organized at Fort Monroe, Virginia December 22, 1863.

3rd United States Colored Cavalry. Organized from the 1st Mississippi Colored Cavalry March 11, 1864.

4th United States Colored Cavalry. Organized from 1st Cavalry, Corps d'Afrique April 4, 1864.

5th United States Colored Cavalry. Organized at Camp Nelson, Kentucky October 24–30, 1864.

6th United States Colored Cavalry. Organized at Camp Nelson, Kentucky November 1, 1864–June 21, 1865.

1st United States Colored Heavy Artillery. Organized at Knoxville, Tennessee February 20–November 12, 1864.

2nd United States Colored Heavy Artillery. Organized from 1st Tennessee Colored Heavy Artillery March 11, 1864, and redesignated as 3rd United States Colored Heavy Artillery April 26, 1864.

3rd United States Colored Heavy Artillery. Organized from 2nd United States Colored Heavy Artillery and redesignated as 3rd United States Colored Heavy Artillery April 26, 1864.

4th United States Colored Heavy Artillery. Organized from 2nd Tennessee Colored Heavy Artillery March 11, 1864 as 3rd United States Colored Heavy Artillery, and redesignated as 4th United States Colored Heavy Artillery April 26, 1864.

5th United States Colored Heavy Artillery. Organized from 1st Mississippi Colored Heavy Artillery March 11, 1864 as 4th United States Colored Heavy Artillery, and redesignated as 5th United States Colored Heavy Artillery April 26, 1864.

6th United States Colored Heavy Artillery. Organized from 2nd Mississippi Colored Heavy Artillery March 11, 1864 as 5th United States Colored Heavy Artillery, and redesignated as 6th United States Colored Heavy Artillery April 26, 1864.

7th United States Colored Heavy Artillery. Organized from 1st Alabama Colored Siege Artillery March 11, 1864 as 6th United States Colored Heavy Artillery, and redesignated as 7th United States Colored Heavy Artillery April 26, 1864.

8th United States Colored Heavy Artillery. Organized at Paducah, Kentucky April 26–October 13, 1864.

9th United States Colored Heavy Artillery. Organized at Clarksville and Nashville, Tennessee October 8–November 1, 1864.

10th United States Colored Heavy Artillery. Organized from 1st Heavy Artillery, Corps d'Afrique November 19, 1863, and designated as 7th United States Colored Heavy Artillery April 4, 1864. It was redesignated as 10th United States Colored Heavy Artillery May 21, 1864.

11th United States Colored Heavy Artillery. Organized from 14th Rhode Island Colored Artillery as 8th United States Colored Heavy Artillery April 4, 1864, and redesignated as 11th United States Colored Heavy Artillery May 21, 1864.

12th United States Colored Heavy Artillery. Organized at Camp Nelson, Kentucky July 15, 1864.

13th United States Colored Heavy Artillery. Organized at Camp Nelson, Kentucky June 23, 1864.

14th United States Colored Heavy Artillery. Organized from the 1st North Carolina Colored Heavy Artillery at New Berne and Morehead City, North Carolina March 17, 1865.

Battery A, 2nd United States Colored Light Artillery. Organized from 1st Battery, Louisiana Colored Light Artillery March 11, 1864, and redesignated as Battery C, 2nd United States Colored Light Artillery April 26, 1864. A new Battery A was organized at Nashville, Tennessee April 30, 1864.

Battery B, 2nd United States Colored Light Artillery. Organized from 2nd Battery, Louisiana Colored Light Artillery March 11, 1864, and redesignated as Battery D, 2nd United States Colored Light Artillery April 26, 1864. A new Battery B was organized at Fort Monroe, Virginia January 8–February 27, 1864.

Battery C, 2nd United States Colored Light Artillery. Organized from the 3rd Battery, Louisiana Colored Light Artillery March 11, 1864, and redesignated as Battery E, 2nd United States Colored Light Artillery April 26, 1864.

Battery D, 2nd United States Colored Light Artillery. Organized from the 1st Battery, Memphis (Tennessee) Colored Light Artillery March 11, 1864, and redesignated as Battery F, 2nd United States Colored Light Artillery April 26, 1864.

Battery E, 2nd United States Colored Light Artillery. Organized from Battery C, 2nd United States Colored Light Artillery April 26, 1864.

Battery F, 2nd United States Colored Light Artillery. Organized from Battery D, 2nd United States Colored Light Artillery April 26, 1864.

Battery G, 2nd United States Colored Light Artillery. Organized at Hilton Head, South Carolina May 24, 1864.

Battery H, 2nd United States Colored Light Artillery. Organized from 1st Battery, Arkansas Colored Light Artillery December 13, 1864.

Battery I, 2nd United States Colored Light Artillery. Organized at Memphis, Tennessee April 19, 1865.

Independent Colored Battery. Organized at Leavenworth, Kansas December 23, 1864.

1st United States Colored Infantry. Organized in the District of Columbia May 19–June 30, 1863.

2nd United States Colored Infantry. Organized at Arlington, Virginia June 23–November 11, 1863.

3rd United States Colored Infantry. Organized at Camp William Penn, near Philadelphia, Pennsylvania, August 3–10, 1863.

4th United States Colored Infantry. Organized at Baltimore, Maryland July 15–September 1, 1863.

5th United States Colored Infantry. Organized at Camp Delaware, Ohio August 6, 1863–January 15, 1864.

6th United States Colored Infantry. Organized at Camp William Penn, near Philadelphia, Pennsylvania, July 28–September 12, 1863.

7th United States Colored Infantry. Organized at Baltimore, Maryland September 26–November 12, 1863.

8th United States Colored Infantry. Organized at Camp William Penn, near Philadelphia, Pennsylvania, September 22–December 4, 1863.

9th United States Colored Infantry. Organized at Camp Stanton, at Baltimore, Maryland, November 11–30, 1863.

10th United States Colored Infantry. Organized in the state of Virginia November 18, 1863.

11th United States Colored Infantry (old). Organized at Fort Smith, Arkansas December 19, 1863–March 3, 1864. Consolidated with 112th USCT (old) and 113th USCT (old) April 22, 1865 to form a new 113th USCT.

11th United States Colored Infantry (new). Organized from the 7th United States Colored Heavy Artillery January 23, 1865.

12th United States Colored Infantry. Organized in the state of Tennessee July 24–August 14, 1863.

13th United States Colored Infantry. Organized at Nashville, Tennessee November 19, 1863.

14th United States Colored Infantry. Organized at Gallatin, Tennessee November 16, 1863–January 8, 1864.

15th United States Colored Infantry. Organized at Nashville, Tennessee December 2, 1863–March 11, 1864.

16th United States Colored Infantry. Organized at Nashville, Tennessee December 4, 1863–February 13, 1864.

17th United States Colored Infantry. Organized at Nashville, Tennessee December 12–21, 1863.

18th United States Colored Infantry. Organized in the state of Missouri February 1–September 28, 1864.

19th United States Colored Infantry. Organized at Camp Stanton, Baltimore, Maryland, December 25, 1863–January 16, 1864.

20th United States Colored Infantry. Organized at Riker's Island, New York Harbor February 9, 1864.

21st United States Colored Infantry. Organized from the 3rd South Carolina Colored Infantry and 4th South Carolina Colored Infantry March 14, 1864.

22nd United States Colored Infantry. Organized at Philadelphia, Pennsylvania January 10–29, 1864.

23rd United States Colored Infantry. Organized at Camp Casey, Virginia November 23, 1863–June 30, 1864.

24th United States Colored Infantry. Organized at Camp William Penn, near Philadelphia, Pennsylvania, January 30–March 30, 1865.

25th United States Colored Infantry. Organized at Philadelphia, Pennsylvania January 13–February 12, 1864.

26th United States Colored Infantry. Organized at Riker's Island, New York Harbor February 27, 1864.

27th United States Colored Infantry. Organized at Camp Delaware, Ohio January 16–August 6, 1864.

28th United States Colored Infantry. Organized at Indianapolis, Indiana December 24, 1863–March 31, 1864.

29th United States Colored Infantry. Organized at Quincy, Illinois April 24, 1864.

30th United States Colored Infantry. Organized at Camp Stanton, Baltimore, Maryland, February 12–March 18, 1864.

31st United States Colored Infantry. Organization began at Hart's Island, New York Harbor April 29, 1864 and was completed in the field in Virginia November 14, 1864. The 30th Connecticut (colored), while in the process of organization, was consolidated with this regiment May 18, 1864.

32nd United States Colored Infantry. Organized at Camp William Penn, at Philadelphia, Pennsylvania, February 17–March 7, 1864.

33rd United States Colored Infantry. Organized from the 1st South Carolina Colored Infantry February 8, 1864.

34th United States Colored Infantry. Organized from the 2nd South Carolina Colored Infantry February 8, 1864.

35th United States Colored Infantry. Organized from the 1st North Carolina Colored Infantry February 8, 1864.

36th United States Colored Infantry. Organized from the 2nd North Carolina Colored Infantry February 8, 1864.

37th United States Colored Infantry. Organized from the 3rd North Carolina Colored Infantry February 8, 1864.

38th United States Colored Infantry. Organized in the state of Virginia January 23, 1864.

39th United States Colored Infantry. Organized at Baltimore, Maryland March 22–31, 1864.

40th United States Colored Infantry. Organized at Nashville and Greenville, Tennessee February 29, 1864.

41st United States Colored Infantry. Organized at Philadelphia, Pennsylvania September 30–December 7, 1864.

42nd United States Colored Infantry. Organized at Nashville and Chattanooga, Tennessee April 20, 1864.

43rd United States Colored Infantry. Organized at Philadelphia, Pennsylvania March 12–June 3, 1864.

44th United States Colored Infantry. Organized at Chattanooga, Tennessee and Rome and Dalton, Georgia April 7–September 16, 1864.

45th United States Colored Infantry. Organized at Philadelphia, Pennsylvania June 13–August 19, 1864.

46th United States Colored Infantry. Organized from the 1st Arkansas Colored Infantry March 11, 1864.

47th United States Colored Infantry. Organized from the 8th Louisiana Colored Infantry March 11, 1864.

48th United States Colored Infantry. Organized from the 10th Louisiana Colored Infantry March 11, 1864.

49th United States Colored Infantry. Organized from the 11th Louisiana Colored Infantry March 11, 1864.

50th United States Colored Infantry. Organized from the 12th Louisiana Colored Infantry March 11, 1864.

51st United States Colored Infantry. Organized from the 1st Mississippi Colored Infantry March 11, 1864.

52nd United States Colored Infantry. Organized from the 2nd Mississippi Colored Infantry March 11, 1864.

53rd United States Colored Infantry. Organized from the 3rd Mississippi Colored Infantry March 11, 1864.

54th United States Colored Infantry. Organized from the 2nd Arkansas Colored Infantry March 11, 1864.

55th United States Colored Infantry. Organized from the 1st Alabama Colored Infantry March 11, 1864.

56th United States Colored Infantry. Organized from the 3rd Alabama Colored Infantry March 11, 1864.

57th United States Colored Infantry. Organized from the 4th Arkansas Colored Infantry March 11, 1864.

58th United States Colored Infantry. Organized from the 6th Mississippi Colored Infantry March 11, 1864.

59th United States Colored Infantry. Organized from the 1st Tennessee Colored Infantry March 11, 1864.

60th United States Colored Infantry. Organized from the 1st Iowa Colored Infantry March 11, 1864.

61st United States Colored Infantry. Organized from the 2nd Tennessee Colored Infantry March 11, 1864.

62nd United States Colored Infantry. Organized from the 1st Missouri Colored Infantry March 11, 1864.

63rd United States Colored Infantry. Organized from the 9th Louisiana Colored Infantry March 11, 1864.

64th United States Colored Infantry. Organized from the 7th Louisiana Colored Infantry March 11, 1864.

65th United States Colored Infantry. Organized from the 2nd Missouri Colored Infantry March 11, 1864.

66th United States Colored Infantry. Organized from the 4th Mississippi Colored Infantry March 11, 1864.

67th United States Colored Infantry. Organized from the 3rd Missouri Colored Infantry March 11, 1864. Consolidated with the 65th USCT July 12, 1865.

68th United States Colored Infantry. Organized from the 4th Missouri Colored Infantry March 11, 1864.

69th United States Colored Infantry. Organized at Pine Bluff, Devall's Bluff, and Helena in Arkansas and Memphis, Tennessee December 14, 1864–March 17, 1865.

70th United States Colored Infantry. Four companies organized at Natchez, Mississippi April 23–October 1, 1864. The organization was completed November 8, 1864 by the consolidation of these four companies with the 71st USCT.

71st United States Colored Infantry. Organized at Big Black River Bridge and Natchez in Mississippi and at Alexandria, Louisiana March 3–August 13, 1864. Consolidated with the 70th USCT November 8, 1864.

72nd United States Colored Infantry. Organized at Covington, Kentucky April 18–22, 1865.

73rd United States Colored Infantry. Organized from the 1st Infantry, Corps d'Afrique April 4, 1864. Consolidated with the 96th USCT September 27, 1865.

74th United States Colored Infantry. Organized from the 2nd Infantry, Corps d'Afrique April 4, 1864. The 91st USCT was consolidated with this regiment July 7, 1864.

75th United States Colored Infantry. Organized from the 3rd Infantry, Corps d'Afrique April 4, 1864.

76th United States Colored Infantry. Organized from the 4th Infantry, Corps d'Afrique April 4, 1864.

77th United States Colored Infantry. Organized from the 5th Infantry, Corps d'Afrique April 4, 1864. Its organization was completed May 24, 1864 by its consolidation with the 85th USCT.

78th United States Colored Infantry. Organized from the 6th Infantry, Corps d'Afrique April 4, 1864. The 98th USCT was consolidated with this regiment August 1, 1865.

79th United States Colored Infantry (old). Organized from the 7th Infantry, Corps d'Afrique April 4, 1864. The regiment was broken up July 28,

1864. A new 79th USCT was to be organized by the consolidation of the 80th and 83rd USCT, but this reorganization was not completed.

79th United States Colored Infantry (new). Organized from the 1st Kansas Colored Infantry December 13, 1864.

80th United States Colored Infantry. Organized from the 8th Infantry, Corps d'Afrique April 4, 1864.

81st United States Colored Infantry. Organized from the 9th Infantry, Corps d'Afrique April 4, 1864.

82nd United States Colored Infantry. Organized from the 10th Infantry, Corps d'Afrique April 4, 1864.

83rd United States Colored Infantry (old). Organized from the 11th Infantry, Corps d'Afrique April 4, 1864. Regiment broken up July 28, 1864.

83rd United States Colored Infantry (new). Organized from the 2nd Kansas Colored Infantry December 13, 1864.

84th United States Colored Infantry. Organized from the 12th Infantry, Corps d'Afrique April 4, 1864. The 87th USCT was consolidated with the 84th USCT August 31, 1865.

85th United States Colored Infantry. Organized from the 13th Infantry, Corps d'Afrique April 4, 1864; having failed to complete its organization, it was consolidated with the 77th USCT May 24, 1864.

86th United States Colored Infantry. Organized from the 14th Infantry, Corps d'Afrique April 4, 1864.

87th United States Colored Infantry (old). Organized from the 16th Infantry, Corps d'Afrique April 4, 1864. Consolidated with the 95th USCT November 26, 1864 to form the 81st USCT (new). Designated as the 87th USCT (new) December 10, 1864.

87th United States Colored Infantry (new). Organized by the consolidation of the 87th USCT (old) and 95th USCT November 26, 1864.

88th United States Colored Infantry (old). Organized from the 17th Infantry, Corps d'Afrique April 4, 1864. Broken up July 28, 1864.

88th United States Colored Infantry (new). Organized at Memphis, Tennessee February 20–August 10, 1865.

89th United States Colored Infantry. Organized from the 18th Infantry, Corps d'Afrique April 4, 1864. Broken up July 28, 1864.

90th United States Colored Infantry. Organized from the 19th Infantry, Corps d'Afrique April 4, 1864. Broken up July 28, 1864.

91st United States Colored Infantry. Organized from the 20th Infantry, Corps d'Afrique April 4, 1864. Consolidated with the 74th USCT July 7, 1864.

92nd United States Colored Infantry. Organized from the 22nd Infantry, Corps d'Afrique April 4, 1864.

93rd United States Colored Infantry. Organized from the 25th Infantry, Corps d'Afrique April 4, 1864. Broken up June 23, 1865.

94th United States Colored Infantry. Organization not completed.

95th United States Colored Infantry. Organized from the 1st Engineers, Corps d'Afrique April 4, 1864. Consolidated with the 87th USCT November 26, 1864 to form the 81st USCT (new).

96th United States Colored Infantry. Organized from the 2nd Engineers, Corps d'Afrique April 4, 1864.

97th United States Colored Infantry. Organized from the 3rd Engineers, Corps d'Afrique April 4, 1864.

98th United States Colored Infantry. Organized from the 4th Engineers, Corps d'Afrique April 4, 1864. Consolidated with the 78th USCT August 26, 1865.

99th United States Colored Infantry. Organized from the 5th Engineers, Corps d'Afrique April 4, 1864.

100th United States Colored Infantry. Organized in the state of Kentucky May 3–June 1, 1864.

101st United States Colored Infantry. Organized in the state of Kentucky September 16, 1864–August 5, 1865.

102nd United States Colored Infantry. Organized from the 1st Michigan Colored Infantry May 23, 1864.

103rd United States Colored Infantry. Organized at Hilton Head, South Carolina March 10, 1865.

104th United States Colored Infantry. Organized at Beaufort, South Carolina April 28–June 25, 1865.

105th United States Colored Infantry. Organization not completed.

106th United States Colored Infantry. Organized from the 4th Alabama Colored Infantry May 16, 1864.

107th United States Colored Infantry. Organized at Louisville, Kentucky May 3, 1863–September 15, 1864.

108th United States Colored Infantry. Organized at Louisville, Kentucky June 20–August 22, 1864.

109th United States Colored Infantry. Organized at Louisville, Kentucky July 5, 1864.

110th United States Colored Infantry. Organized from the 2nd Alabama Colored Infantry June 25, 1864.

111th United States Colored Infantry. Organized from the 3rd Alabama Colored Infantry June 25, 1864.

112th United States Colored Infantry. Organized at Little Rock, Arkansas April 23–November 8, 1864. Consolidated with the 11th USCT (old) and 113th USCT (old) April 1, 1865 to form the 113th USCT (new).

113th United States Colored Infantry (old). Organized from the 6th Arkansas Colored Infantry in June 1864. Consolidated with the 11th USCT (old) and 112th USCT to form the 113th USCT (new) April 1, 1865.

113th United States Colored Infantry (new). Organized at Little Rock, Arkansas by the consolidation of the 11th USCT (old), 112th USCT, and 113th USCT (old) April 9, 1864.

114th United States Colored Infantry. Organized at Camp Nelson, Kentucky July 4, 1864.

115th United States Colored Infantry. Organized at Bowling Green, Kentucky July 15–October 21, 1864.

116th United States Colored Infantry. Organized at Camp Nelson, Kentucky June 6–July 12, 1864.

117th United States Colored Infantry. Organized at Covington, Kentucky July 18–September 27, 1864.

118th United States Colored Infantry. Organized at Baltimore, Maryland October 19, 1864 from men from Kentucky.

119th United States Colored Infantry. Organized at Camp Nelson, Kentucky January 18–May 16, 1865.

120th United States Colored Infantry. Organized at Henderson, Kentucky November 1864–June 1865.

121st United States Colored Infantry. Organized at Maysville, Kentucky October 8, 1864–May 31, 1865.

122nd United States Colored Infantry. Organized at Louisville, Kentucky December 31, 1864.

123rd United States Colored Infantry. Organized at Louisville, Kentucky December 2, 1864.

124th United States Colored Infantry. Organized at Camp Nelson, Kentucky January 1–April 27, 1865.

125th United States Colored Infantry. Organized at Louisville, Kentucky February 13–June 2, 1865.

126th United States Colored Infantry. Not organized.

127th United States Colored Infantry. Organized at Philadelphia, Pennsylvania August 23–September 10, 1864.

128th United States Colored Infantry. Organized at Hilton Head, South Carolina April 23–29, 1865.

135th United States Colored Infantry. Organized at Goldsboro, North Carolina March 28, 1865.

136th United States Colored Infantry. Organized at Atlanta, Georgia July 15, 1865.

137th United States Colored Infantry. Organized at Selma, Alabama April 8, 1865, and mustered into United States service at Macon, Georgia June 1, 1865.

138th United States Colored Infantry. Organized at Atlanta, Georgia July 15, 1865.

* * * * * * * * *

Many of the black regiments listed above were not assigned to larger black, or predominantly black, organizations, but they served during the war either in mixed black and white commands or as unassigned regiments on post and garrison duty and as occupation forces in the southern states. There were, however, many brigades, some divisions, and one army corps organized during the last three years of the war that were composed entirely of black regiments. Because of limitations of time and space, it is impossible to give a complete description of these larger units, but the more significant of these organizations are given below with a listing of the regiments of which they were composed. It must be emphasized, however, that there were frequent re-organizations and redesignations of these units, and the regiments of which they were composed changed from time to time by transfers from one organization to another. The following information is given here primarily for the purpose of providing a better understanding of the employment of black regiments in the larger organizations during the latter part of the war.

Western Theater

Department of Arkansas. In January 1864, there were present in the District of Eastern Arkansas the 2nd Arkansas Colored Infantry, the 3rd Arkansas Colored Infantry, the 4th Arkansas Colored Infantry (organizing), the 1st Iowa Colored Infantry, and the 3rd Battery, Louisiana Colored Artillery, together with a number of white regiments. The colored regiments, with their designations changed, respectively, to 54th, 56th, 57th, and 60th United States Colored Troops, remained in the district.

On February 1, 1865, the reorganization of Frederick Salomon's First Division, Seventh Corps at Little Rock was announced, and the Second Brigade, commanded by James M. Williams, consisted of the 11th, 54th, 57th, 79th, 83rd, 112th, and 113th United States Colored Troops.

Department of the Gulf. On July 10, 1863, Daniel Ullmann was ordered to organize a brigade in the District of Port Hudson to be known as Ullmann's Brigade. When organized, it consisted of the 6th, 7th, 8th, 9th, and 10th regiments, Corps d'Afrique.

On September 22, 1863, the regiments of the Corps d'Afrique in the District of Baton Rouge and Port Hudson were organized into two divisions as follows:

First Division
  First Brigade: 1st, 2nd, 3rd, 11th, and 12th regiments of Corps d'Afrique
  Second Brigade: 4th, 7th, 8th, 9th, and 10th regiments of Corps d'Afrique
Second Division
  First Brigade: 5th, 13th, 14th, 15th, and 16th regiments of Corps d'Afrique

Second Brigade: 6th, 17th, 18th, 19th, and 20th regiments of Corps d'Afrique

April 4, 1864, the designations of the Corps d'Afrique and the black regiments of the various states were changed to numbered regiments of United States Colored Troops. In June 1864, the larger organizations that were composed of the colored regiments in the Department of the Gulf were as follows:

Colored Brigade, United States Forces in Texas, commanded by Justin Hodge, consisted of the 87th and 95th USCT. In August 1864 these two regiments were joined, as unattached regiments, by the 81st USCT, and in September 1864 by the 64th and 67th USCT.

At Morganza, Louisiana there was a Provisional Brigade, commanded by Theodore H. Barrett, consisting of the 62nd, 65th, 67th, and 83rd USCT. The 90th and 99th USCT were at Morganza, but they were not brigaded.

At Port Hudson, the two divisions of the former Corps d'Afrique, commanded temporarily by John McNeil during the absence of Daniel Ullmann, were reorganized as follows:

First Division, Charles W. Drew
  First Brigade, William H. Dickey
    73rd, 75th, 84th, and 92nd USCT
  Second Brigade, John F. Appleton
    76th, 78th, 80th, 81st, and 82nd USCT

Second Division
  Second Brigade, James C. Clark
    79th, 88th, and 89th USCT

Note. First Brigade was broken up.

There was also an Engineer Brigade in the Department of the Gulf consisting of the 95th, 96th, 97th, 98th, and 99th USCT, but the regiments were scattered, with one each at Brazos Santiago, Texas, and Port Hudson and Morganza, Louisiana, and two regiments at Carrollton, Louisiana.

In the District of West Florida there was a brigade, commanded by William C. Holbrook, that consisted of the 25th, 82nd, and 86th USCT.

By an order of October 18, 1864, the colored

troops in the Department of the Gulf were reorganized into three divisions, and George L. Andrews was assigned command. The new organization was as follows:

First Division, Daniel Ullmann
    First Brigade, Henry N. Frisbie
        73rd, 75th, 84th, and 92nd USCT
    Second Brigade, Alonzo J. Edgerton
        65th, 67th, and 99th USCT

Second Division, Charles W. Drew
    First Brigade, Theodore H. Barrett
        62nd and 76th USCT, and 4th USC Cavalry
    Second Brigade, Samuel B. Jones
        2nd, 78th, 81st (old), and 81st (new)

Third Division, Cyrus Hamlin
    First Brigade, John C. Cobb
        25th, 82nd, 86th, 96th, and 97th USCT
    Second Brigade, Simon Jones
        20th, 93rd, and 98th USCT, and 10th USC Heavy
        Artillery
    Third Brigade, Charles A. Hartwell
        74th, 77th, and 80th USCT, and 11th USC Heavy
        Artillery

Note. First Brigade was in the District of West Florida.

A division of United States Colored Troops was organized at New Orleans by an order of February 23, 1865, and John P. Hawkins was assigned command. On February 26, Frederick Steele was assigned command of the United States Troops Operating from Pensacola Bay, which were to be a part of Edward R. S. Canby's forces operating against Mobile, Alabama, and Hawkins' division was assigned as a part of Steele's Column from Pensacola Bay, Florida. The division was organized as follows:

First Division, John P. Hawkins
    First Brigade, William A. Pile
        73rd, 82nd, and 86th USCT
    Second Brigade, Hiram Scofield
        47th, 50th, and 51st USCT
    Third Brigade, Charles W. Drew
        48th, 68th, and 76th USCT

Army of the Tennessee. In May 1863, an African Brigade was organized at Milliken's Bend, across the Mississippi River from Vicksburg, in the District of Northeastern Louisiana. This brigade, which was commanded by Isaac F. Shepard, consisted of the 8th, 9th, 11th, and 13th Louisiana Colored Infantry, and the 1st and 3rd Mississippi Colored Infantry. The 1st Arkansas Colored Infantry and the 10th Louisiana Colored Infantry were also at Goodrich's Landing, Louisiana.

In July 1863 the following regiments were present at John E. Smith's post of Vicksburg: 1st and 2nd Mississippi Colored Infantry; 6th, 9th, and 12th Louisiana Colored Infantry; and 1st Mississippi Colored Heavy Artillery.

In December 1863, John P. Hawkins was in command of the colored regiments at Goodrich's Landing and at Vicksburg, which consisted of the following:

At Goodrich's Landing
    1st Arkansas; 10th and 11th Louisiana; 3rd Mississippi; 1st Mississippi Cavalry; and 1st Battery, Louisiana Light Artillery

At Vicksburg
    1st and 2nd Mississippi; 8th and 12th Louisiana; and 1st Mississippi Heavy Artillery

On January 22, 1864, Hawkins was ordered to move his First Brigade, commanded by Hiram Scofield, from Goodrich's Landing to Haynes' Bluff. At the end of January 1864, the colored regiments at Vicksburg consisted of the following: the 7th, 8th, and 12th Louisiana Colored Infantry; the 1st, 2nd, 4th, and 6th Mississippi Colored Infantry; the 1st and 2nd Mississippi Heavy Artillery; and the 2nd Battery, Louisiana Colored Light Artillery.

In January 1864, Edward Bouton commanded a First Brigade in the District of Memphis, District of West Tennessee, Sixteenth Corps, which consisted of the 1st Alabama Colored Infantry and the 1st and 2nd Tennessee Colored Infantry. In April 1864, after the colored regiments were assigned numerical designations of the United States Colored Troops, the regiments of Bouton's brigade consisted of the 59th and 61st USCT and Battery D, 2nd United States Colored Light Artillery. In addition, the following colored regiments were at Fort Pickering, which was commanded by Ignatz G. Kappner: 55th USCT and the 3rd and 6th United States Colored Heavy Artillery.

On April 4, 1864, the colored regiments of Seventeenth Corps at Vicksburg were organized with their new designations as regiments of United States Colored Troops as follows:

First Division United States Colored Troops, John P. Hawkins
  First Brigade, Isaac F. Shepard
    46th, 48th, 49th, and 53rd USCT
  Second Brigade, Hiram Scofield
    47th, 50th, and 52nd USCT

Forces at Vicksburg
  3rd United States Colored Cavalry; Battery A, 2nd United States Colored Light Artillery; and 4th United States Colored Heavy Artillery

United States Forces at Goodrich's Landing and other points, A. Watson Webber
  51st and 66th USCT and Battery B, 2nd United States Colored Light Artillery

Eastern Theater

Department of North Carolina. During June and July 1863, Edward A. Wild was at New Berne, North Carolina, where he was engaged in recruiting and organizing the 1st, 2nd, and 3rd North Carolina colored regiments. These were organized as Wild's Colored Brigade, and on July 29 they were sent to report to Quincy A. Gillmore, commanding the Department of the South. The brigade was then assigned to Folly Island, where it arrived during the period August 2–9.

In January 1865, Alfred H. Terry was assigned command of a force taken from Benjamin F. Butler's Army of the James and was ordered to the coast of North Carolina to attempt the capture of Fort Fisher. Terry's command consisted of Adelbert Ames' Second Division, Twenty-Fourth Corps; Charles J. Paine's Third Division, Twenty-Fifth Corps; and Joseph C. Abbott's Second Brigade, First Division, Twenty-Fourth Corps. Paine's division was composed of colored regiments and was organized as follows:

Third Division, Twenty-Fifth Corps, Charles J. Paine

First Brigade, Delevan Bates
  1st, 27th, and 30th USCT
Second Brigade, John W. Ames
  4th, 6th, and 39th USCT
Third Brigade, Elias Wright
  5th, 10th, 37th, and 107th USCT

Terry captured Fort Fisher January 15, 1864, and then remained with his troops in the Department of North Carolina.

On April 2, 1865, when William T. Sherman's army was at and near Goldsboro, North Carolina, Tenth Corps was reorganized from troops in the Department of North Carolina. Paine's division was designated as Third Division, Tenth Corps and was organized as follows:

Third Division, Tenth Corps, Charles J. Paine
  First Brigade, Delevan Bates
    1st, 30th, and 107th USCT
  Second Brigade, Samuel A. Duncan
    4th, 5th, and 39th USCT
  Third Brigade, John H. Holman
    6th, 27th, and 37th USCT

Department of the South. During June and July 1863, Edward A. Wild organized a brigade of colored regiments at New Berne, North Carolina, and it was then sent to Folly Island in the Department of the South. Upon arrival there, it was assigned to Israel Vogdes' division on Folly Island as Third Brigade, or African Brigade, and it consisted of the 55th Massachusetts Regiment (colored) and the 1st, 2nd, and 3rd North Carolina (colored) regiments. In January 1864, Third Brigade was commanded by James C. Beecher and consisted of the 55th Massachusetts and the 1st North Carolina (colored) regiment.

Also in August 1863, James Montgomery commanded the Fourth Brigade of Alfred H. Terry's division on Morris Island, and this brigade consisted of the 54th Massachusetts (colored) and the 2nd and 3rd South Carolina colored regiments. Montgomery's brigade remained on Morris Island until January 31, 1864. It was then organized as Montgomery's Brigade and was ordered to Hilton Head.

Early in February 1864, Truman Seymour led an expedition to Florida, and among the troops of the expedition were some colored regiments. On February 25, the troops of Seymour's District of Florida, Department of the South were temporarily organized into two divisions, the First Division commanded by Adelbert Ames and the Second Division by Israel Vogdes. Ames' Third Brigade, commanded by Milton S. Littlefield, consisted of the 54th Massachusetts (colored) and 55th Massachusetts (colored) infantry. There were two colored brigades in Vogdes' division: Benjamin C. Tilghman's Second Brigade consisted of the 1st North Carolina (35th USCT) and 3rd United States Colored Troops; and James Montgomery's Third Brigade consisted of the 2nd South Carolina (34th USCT) and 3rd South Carolina (37th USCT). In April 1864, the 3rd, 7th, 8th, 21st, and 35th USCT were in the District of Florida, but they were scattered at the various posts in the district.

Elsewhere in the Department of the South in April 1864 were the following black regiments: At Hilton Head was Bayley's Brigade, commanded by Thomas Bayley, which consisted of the 1st Michigan Colored Infantry and the 9th and 32nd USCT; at Port Royal Island, under Rufus Saxton, were the 29th Connecticut (colored) and the 26th and 33rd USCT; and on Morris Island were the 21st and 34th USCT.

In November 1864, as William T. Sherman marched with his army through Georgia toward Savannah, John G. Foster, commanding the Department of the South, organized an expedition on Hilton Head Island for the purpose of cutting the Charleston and Savannah Railroad near Pocotaligo, South Carolina. This was done to prevent enemy reinforcements from reaching Savannah. The troops of the expedition were designated as the Coastal Division, and John P. Hatch was assigned command. Alfred S. Hartwell's Second Brigade was a colored brigade and consisted of the 54th Massachusetts (colored), the 55th Massachusetts (colored), and the 34th, 35th, and 102nd USCT. Edward E. Potter's First Brigade was largely a white brigade, but the 32nd USCT was one of the regiments of the brigade.

Department of Virginia and North Carolina. On October 10, 1863, Edward A. Wild was ordered to Norfolk, Virginia to organize the 3rd North Carolina (colored), and he was later assigned command

of the colored troops of the department. His command was known as the African Brigade, and on December 31, 1863 it consisted of detachments of the 55th Massachusetts (colored), the 1st, 2nd, and 3rd North Carolina (colored), and the 1st, 5th, and 10th USCT.

The Second Brigade, United States Forces at Yorktown, Virginia and vicinity was organized January 20, 1864 under the command of Samuel A. Duncan, and it consisted of the 4th, 5th, and 6th USCT. It was transferred April 23, 1864 as Second Brigade to Hinks' Colored Division, which was organized that day at Yorktown, Virginia as follows:

Hinks' Division, Edward W. Hinks
  First Brigade, Edward A. Wild
    10th, 22nd, and 37th USCT
  Second Brigade, Samuel A. Duncan
    4th, 5th, and 6th USCT

At the end of April 1864, the Army of the James was organized at Yorktown, Virginia in Benjamin F. Butler's Department of Virginia and North Carolina. It consisted of the reorganized Eighteenth Corps of that department and the reorganized Tenth Corps transferred from the Department of the South. The Army of the James was then moved to Bermuda Hundred. Hinks' division of Eighteenth Corps was designated as Third Division and was organized as follows:

Third Division, Eighteenth Corps, Edward W. Hinks
  First Brigade, Edward A. Wild
    1st, 10th, 22nd, and 37th USCT
  Second Brigade, Samuel A. Duncan
    4th, 5th, and 6th USCT

At the end of June 1864, Third Division was organized as follows:

Third Division, Eighteenth Corps, Edward W. Hinks
  First Brigade, John H. Holman
    1st and 10th USCT and 1st USC Cavalry (dismounted)
  Second Brigade, Samuel A. Duncan
    4th, 5th, 6th, and 22nd USCT and 2nd USC Cavalry (dismounted)

In August 1864, Third Division consisted of three brigades, but John H. Holman's First Brigade was also reported as Second Brigade, Third Division,

Tenth Corps. The division was organized as follows:

Third Division, Eighteenth Corps, Charles J. Paine
    First Brigade, John H. Holman
        1st, 22nd, and 37th USCT
    Second Brigade, Alonzo G. Draper
        5th, 36th, and 38th USCT
    Third Brigade, Samuel A. Duncan
        4th, 6th, and 10th USCT

The organization of Third Division was the same at the end of October 1864, but Alonzo G. Draper commanded the division, Abial G. Chamberlain commanded First Brigade, Dexter E. Clapp commanded Second Brigade, and John W. Ames commanded Third Brigade. In addition to Third Division, there was also a colored Provisional Brigade commanded by Edward Martindale, and it consisted of the 107th, 117th, and 118th USCT.

In August 1864, William Birney was transferred from the Department of the South with a brigade of colored regiments to Tenth Corps, Army of the James, and at the end of the month he was assigned command of Third Division, Tenth Corps, which was then organized as follows:

Third Division, Tenth Corps, William Birney
    First Brigade, James Shaw, Jr.
        29th Connecticut (colored), 7th, 8th, and 9th USCT
    Second Brigade, John H. Holman
        1st and 22nd USCT

Note 1. Second Brigade was also reported as First Brigade, Third Division, Eighteenth Corps.
Note 2. Birney's command was reduced to one brigade in September 1864, but it was reorganized as a division by an order of October 5, 1864.

On October 29, 1864, Elias Wright assumed command of Second Brigade, Third Division, which then consisted of the 29th Connecticut (colored) and the 8th and 45th USCT.

On November 2, 1864, Third Division was reorganized as follows:

Third Division, Tenth Corps, William Birney
    First Brigade, James Shaw, Jr.
        29th Connecticut (colored) and 7th, 9th, and 116th USCT
    Second Brigade, Elias Wright
        8th, 41st, 45th, and 127th USCT

On December 3, 1864, Tenth Corps and Eighteenth Corps were discontinued, and the white infantry troops of the two corps were assigned to a new corps, commanded by Edward O. C. Ord, and designated as Twenty-Fourth Corps, Army of the James. The colored troops of the Department of Virginia and North Carolina were organized into a new corps, commanded by Godfrey Weitzel, and designated as Twenty-Fifth Corps, Army of the James. Twenty-Fifth Corps was organized as follows:

TWENTY-FIFTH CORPS, Godfrey Weitzel

First Division, Charles J. Paine
    First Brigade, Delevan Bates
        1st, 27th, and 30th USCT
    Second Brigade, John W. Ames
        4th, 6th, and 39th USCT
    Third Brigade, Elias Wright
        5th, 10th, 37th, and 107th USCT

Second Division, William Birney
    First Brigade, Charles S. Russell
        7th, 109th, 116th, and 117th USCT
    Second Brigade, Ulysses Doubleday
        8th, 45th, and 127th USCT
    Third Brigade, Henry C. Ward
        28th, 29th, and 31st USCT

Third Division, Edward A. Wild
    First Brigade, Alonzo G. Draper
        22nd, 36th, 38th, and 118th USCT
    Second Brigade, Edward Martindale
        29th Connecticut (colored) and 9th and 41st USCT
    Third Brigade, Henry G. Thomas
        19th, 23rd, and 43rd USCT

During the period May 23–June 26, 1865, the troops of Twenty-Fifth Corps embarked at City Point, Virginia for Texas, and these were the last troops to be mustered out of the service. The corps was discontinued January 8, 1866.

Army of the Potomac. In the spring of 1864, when Ninth Corps was reorganized in preparation for Grant's spring campaign in Virginia, a new Fourth Division was formed under Edward Ferrero to consist of colored regiments. It was organized as follows:

Fourth Division, Ninth Corps, Edward Ferrero
 First Brigade, Joshua K. Sigfried
  27th, 30th, 39th, and 43rd USCT
 Second Brigade, Henry G. Thomas
  19th, 23rd, and 31st USCT

Note. The 28th and 29th USCT joined Second Brigade in June 1864.

Ferrero's division was generally used to guard the army's trains during the advance on Richmond.

UNITED STATES FORCES OPERATING FROM PENSACOLA, FLORIDA

For the organization of this command, see Land Operations against Mobile Bay and Mobile, Alabama.

UNITED STATES FORCES COMMANDED BY GEORGE H. THOMAS

The army that was assembled under the command of George H. Thomas at Nashville, Tennessee in November and December 1864 for the defense of the state against an invasion by John B. Hood's Confederate Army of Tennessee was known as United States Forces Commanded by George H. Thomas. For details of the organization of this command, and also of its operations, see Franklin and Nashville Campaign (Hood's Invasion of Tennessee).

UNITED STATES FORCES IN TEXAS

During the period October-December 1863, troops of Thirteenth Corps, Department of the Gulf embarked from New Orleans and Algiers, and landed on the coast of Texas. They soon established Federal control over the region and continued to occupy the country along the coast until the end of the war. Most of the troops were withdrawn before Thirteenth Corps was discontinued June 11, 1864, and those remaining were then designated as United States Forces in Texas. For more detailed information, see Department of the Gulf, Operations in the Department of the Gulf, Rio Grande Expedition and Operations on the Coast of Texas.

YAZOO RIVER EXPEDITION (WILLIAM T. SHERMAN), MISSISSIPPI

For the organization of Sherman's expedition, see Operations against Vicksburg, Mississippi, 1861–1863, Early Attempts to Capture Vicksburg, Yazoo River, Mississippi Expedition (William T. Sherman)—Battle of Chickasaw Bayou (or Walnut Hills).

BATTLES AND CAMPAIGNS

✰✰✰✰

PART I: LIST OF CAMPAIGNS, BATTLES, ENGAGEMENTS, AND EXPEDITIONS

Adairsville, Georgia, Engagement at, May 17, 1864. See Atlanta, Georgia Campaign, From Resaca, Georgia to the Etowah River.

Allatoona, Georgia, Engagement at, October 5, 1864. See Franklin and Nashville Campaign (Hood's Invasion of Tennessee), Movements of the Armies September 18, 1864–November 29, 1864, Engagement at Allatoona, Georgia.

Apache Canyon, New Mexico, Skirmish at, March 26, 1862. See Department of New Mexico, Troops and Operations in the Department of New Mexico, Sibley's Invasion of New Mexico, Skirmish at Apache Canyon, New Mexico.

Arkansas Expedition (Steele), August 1, 1863–September 14, 1863. See Little Rock, Arkansas Expedition (Steele).

Arkansas Post (or Fort Hindman), Arkansas, Engagement at, January 4–17, 1863. See Operations against Vicksburg, Mississippi, 1861–1863, Early Attempts to Capture Vicksburg, Engagement at Arkansas Post (or Fort Hindman), Arkansas.

Atlanta, Georgia, Battle of, July 22, 1864. See Atlanta, Georgia Campaign, Battles around Atlanta, Georgia, Battle of Atlanta, Georgia.

Atlanta, Georgia Campaign, May 3, 1864–September 8, 1864. See Part II, below.

Bald Hill (or Leggett's Hill), Georgia, Engagement at, July 21, 1864. See Atlanta, Georgia Campaign, Battles around Atlanta, Georgia, Battle of Atlanta, Georgia.

Banks' Expedition to the Gulf of Mexico (or Banks' Southern Expedition), November-December 1862. See Department of the Gulf, Troops in the Department of the Gulf.

Baton Rouge, Louisiana, Battle of, August 5, 1862. See Department of the Gulf, Operations in the Department of the Gulf, Battle of Baton Rouge, Louisiana.

Baylor's Invasion of Southern New Mexico, July 1861. See Department of New Mexico, Troops and Operations in the Department of New Mexico.

Bayou Boeuf (or Bayou Boeuf Crossing), Louisiana, Capture of Union Forces at, June 24, 1863. See Department of the Gulf, Operations in the Department of the Gulf, Operations against Port Hudson, Louisiana, Operations in Louisiana, West of the Mississippi River.

Bayou De Glaize (Yellow Bayou or Old Oaks), Louisiana, Engagement at, May 18, 1864. See Red River, Louisiana Campaign, Engagement at Yellow Bayou (Bayou De Glaize, or Old Oaks), Louisiana.

Bayou Fourche, Arkansas, Engagement at, September 10, 1863. See Little Rock, Arkansas Expedition (Steele).

Bayou Meto, Arkansas, Action at, August 27, 1863. See Little Rock, Arkansas Expedition (Steele).

Bean's Station, Tennessee, Engagement at, December 14, 1863. See Knoxville, Tennessee Campaign, Engagement at Bean's Station, Tennessee.

Beech Grove (Mill Springs, Logan's Cross Roads, or Fishing Creek), Kentucky, Engagement at, January 19, 1862. See Part II, below, Engagement at Mill Springs (Logan's Cross Roads, Fishing Creek, or Beech Grove), Kentucky.

Belle Prairie (Mansura, or Smith's Plantation), Louisiana, Engagement at, May 16, 1864. See Red River, Louisiana Campaign, Engagement at Mansura (Belle Prairie, or Smith's Plantation), Louisiana.

Belmont, Missouri, Engagement at, November 7, 1861. See Western Department, Operations in the Western Department, Engagement at Belmont, Missouri.

Big Black River Bridge, Mississippi, Engagement at, May 17, 1863. See Operations against Vicksburg, Mississippi, 1861–1863, Grant's Operations against Vicksburg, Movement of the Army to the Rear of Vicksburg, Engagement at the Big Black River Bridge, Mississippi.

Blair's Mechanicsburg Expedition, Mississippi, May 26, 1863–June 4, 1863. See Operations against Vicksburg, Mississippi, 1861–1863, Grant's Operations against Vicksburg, Siege of Vicksburg, Mississippi, Blair's Mechanicsburg, Mississippi Expedition.

Blakely (or Fort Blakely), Alabama, Siege and Capture of, April 1–9, 1865. See Land Operations against Mobile Bay and Mobile, Alabama, Siege and Capture of Spanish Fort and Fort Blakely, Alabama.

Blue Springs, Tennessee, Action at, October 10, 1863. See East Tennessee Campaign (Burnside).

Bluff Springs, Florida, Action at, March 25, 1865. See Land Operations against Mobile Bay and Mobile, Alabama, Siege and Capture of Spanish Fort and Fort Blakely, Alabama.

Booneville, Mississippi, Action at, July 1, 1862. See Army of the Mississippi (Pope, Rosecrans), Advance on Corinth, Mississippi, Action at Booneville, Mississippi.

Boonville, Missouri, Capture of, June 17, 1861. See Operations in Missouri in 1861, Capture of Jefferson City and Boonville, Missouri—Engagement at Boonville.

Bragg's Invasion of Kentucky and Tennessee, August 14, 1862–October 19, 1862. See Part II, below, Invasion of Kentucky and Tennessee (E. Kirby Smith and Braxton Bragg).

Brashear (or Brashear City), Louisiana, Capture of, June 23, 1863. See Department of the Gulf, Operations in the Department of the Gulf, Operations against Port Hudson, Louisiana, Operations in Louisiana, West of the Mississippi River.

Brice's Cross Roads (Tishomingo Creek, or Guntown), Mississippi, Battle of, June 10, 1864. See Sturgis' Expedition from Memphis, Tennessee into Mississippi (Battle of Brice's Cross Roads).

Brown's Ferry, Tennessee, Operations at, October 26–29, 1863. See Army of the Cumberland, October 24, 1862–November 14, 1864, Siege of Chattanooga, Tennessee, Reopening of the Tennessee River.

Brush Mountain, Georgia, Combat at, June 15, 1864. See Atlanta, Georgia Campaign, Advance of the Army from Acworth toward Marietta, Georgia.

Butler's Gulf Expedition (New Orleans), February-October 1862. See Department of the Gulf, Troops in the Department of the Gulf.

Buzzard's Roost Gap (or Mill Creek Gap), Geor-

gia, Combat at, May 8, 1864. See Atlanta, Georgia Campaign, Demonstration at Rocky Face Ridge, Georgia (Combats at Mill Creek Gap or Buzzard's Roost Gap and Dug Gap).

Byram's Ford, Missouri, Action at, October 22, 1864. See Price's Missouri Expedition, Action at Byram's Ford, Missouri.

California, Expedition from, through Arizona, to Northwestern Texas and New Mexico. See Department of New Mexico, Troops and Operations in the Department of New Mexico, Expedition from California, through Arizona, to New Mexico and Northwestern Texas (Column from California).

Camden, Arkansas Expedition (Steele), March 23, 1864–May 3, 1864. See Department of Arkansas, Operations in the Department of Arkansas.

Camp Jackson at Lindell's Grove, Saint Louis, Missouri, Capture of, May 10, 1861. See Operations in Missouri in 1861, Capture of Camp Jackson at Lindell's Grove, Saint Louis, Missouri.

Camp Wildcat (or Rock Castle Hills), Kentucky, Action at, October 21, 1861. See Engagement at Mill Springs (Logan's Cross Roads, Fishing Creek, or Beech Grove), Kentucky.

Campbell's Station, Tennessee, Engagement at, November 16, 1863. See Knoxville, Tennessee Campaign, Engagement at Campbell's Station, Tennessee.

Cane River Crossing (or Monett's Ferry), Louisiana, Engagement at, April 23, 1864. See Red River, Louisiana Campaign, Engagement at Monett's Ferry (or Cane River Crossing), Louisiana.

Carrion Crow Bayou (or Grand Coteau), Louisiana, Action at, November 3, 1863. See Department of the Gulf, Operations in the Department of the Gulf, Operations in the Teche Country, Louisiana.

Carthage, Missouri, Engagement near, July 5, 1861. See Operations in Missouri in 1861, Advance of the Southwestern Column—Engagement near Carthage, Missouri.

Champion Hill, Mississippi, Battle of, May 16, 1863. See Operations against Vicksburg, Mississippi, 1861–1863, Grant's Operations against Vicksburg, Movement of the Army to the Rear of Vicksburg, Battle of Champion Hill, Mississippi.

Chaplin Hills (or Perryville), Kentucky, Battle of, October 8, 1862. See Invasion of Kentucky and Tennessee (E. Kirby Smith and Braxton Bragg), Battle of Perryville (or Chaplin Hills), Kentucky.

Chattanooga-Ringgold Campaign (Battles of Lookout Mountain and Missionary Ridge, Tennessee), November 23, 1863–November 27, 1863. See Part II, below.

Chickamauga, Georgia, Battle of, September 19–20, 1863. See Chickamauga, Georgia Campaign.

Chickamauga, Georgia Campaign, August 16, 1863–September 22, 1863. See Part II, below.

Chickasaw Bayou (or Walnut Hills), Mississippi, Battle of, December 20–29, 1862. See Operations against Vicksburg, Mississippi, 1861–1863, Early Attempts to Capture Vicksburg, Yazoo River, Mississippi Expedition (William T. Sherman)—Battle of Chickasaw Bayou (or Walnut Hills).

Coates' Yazoo, Mississippi Expedition, January 31, 1864–March 6, 1864. See Meridian, Mississippi Expedition.

Corinth, Mississippi, Battle of, October 3–4, 1862. See Part II, below.

Corinth, Mississippi, Halleck's Advance on, April 29, 1862–May 30, 1862. See Part II, below.

Cox's Plantation (also Koch's or Kock's Plantation), Louisiana, Engagement at, July 13, 1863. See Department of the Gulf, Operations in the Department of the Gulf, Operations against Port Hudson, Louisiana, Operations in Louisiana, West of the Mississippi River.

Dallas, Georgia, Combats at, May 26, 1864–June 1, 1864. See Atlanta, Georgia Campaign, Dallas New Hope Church Pickett's Mill Line, Hardee's Demonstration at Dallas, Georgia.

Dalton, Georgia, Demonstration on, February 22–27, 1864. See Part II, below.

Dandridge, Tennessee, Operations about, January 16–17, 1864. See Army of the Ohio (Burnside), Operations about Dandridge, Tennessee.

Davis' Bridge (also Hatchie Bridge), Hatchie River, Tennessee, Engagement at, October 5, 1862. See Battle of Corinth, Mississippi.

Donaldsonville, Louisiana, Confederate Attack on, June 28, 1863. See Department of the Gulf, Operations in the Department of the Gulf, Operations against Port Hudson, Louisiana, Operations in Louisiana, West of the Mississippi River.

Dug Gap, Georgia, Combat at, May 8, 1864. See Atlanta, Georgia Campaign, Demonstration at Rocky Face Ridge, Georgia (Combats at Mill Creek Gap or Buzzard's Roost Gap and Dug Gap).

East Tennessee Campaign (Burnside), August 16, 1863–October 9, 1863. See Part II, below.

Egypt Station, Mississippi, Engagement at, December 28, 1864. See Department of Mississippi, November 28, 1864–May 17, 1865, Cavalry Forces in the Department of Mississippi.

Elkhorn Tavern (or Pea Ridge), Arkansas, Battle of, March 7–8, 1862. See Battle of Pea Ridge (or Elkhorn Tavern), Arkansas.

Ezra Church, Georgia, Battle of, July 28, 1864. See Atlanta, Georgia Campaign, Battles around Atlanta, Georgia, Battle of Ezra Church.

Fair Garden, Tennessee, Engagement near, January 26–27, 1864. See Army of the Ohio (Burnside), Engagement near Fair Garden, Tennessee.

Farmington, Mississippi, Engagement at, May 9, 1862. See Halleck's Advance on Corinth, Mississippi.

Farragut's Expeditions against Vicksburg, Mississippi, May 1862–June 1862. See Operations against Vicksburg, Mississippi, 1861–1863, Early Attempts to Capture Vicksburg.

Fishing Creek (Mill Springs, Logan's Cross Roads, or Beech Grove), Kentucky, Engagement at, January 19, 1862. See Engagement at Mill Springs (Logan's Cross Roads, Fishing Creek, or Beech Grove), Kentucky.

Forrest's Attack on Memphis, Tennessee, August 21, 1864. See Expedition from La Grange, Tennessee to Oxford, Mississippi.

Fort Bisland, Louisiana, Engagement at, April 12–13, 1863. See Department of the Gulf, Operations in the Department of the Gulf, Operations against Port Hudson, Louisiana, Operations in West Louisiana.

Fort Blakely (or Blakely), Alabama, Siege and Capture of, April 1–9, 1865. See Land Operations against Mobile Bay and Mobile, Alabama, Siege and Capture of Spanish Fort and Fort Blakely, Alabama.

Fort Davidson, Pilot Knob, Missouri, Attack on, September 27, 1864. See Price's Missouri Expedition, Attack on Fort Davidson, Pilot Knob, Missouri.

Fort De Russy, Louisiana, Capture of, March 14, 1864. See Red River, Louisiana Campaign, Capture of Fort De Russy, Louisiana.

Fort Donelson, Tennessee, Siege and Capture of, February 12–16, 1862. See Capture of Fort Henry and Fort Donelson, Tennessee.

Fort Gaines, Alabama, Capture of, August 8, 1864. See Land Operations against Mobile Bay and Mobile, Alabama, Capture of Fort Gaines, Alabama and Fort Morgan, Alabama.

Fort Henry, Tennessee, Capture of, February 6, 1862. See Capture of Fort Henry and Fort Donelson, Tennessee.

Fort Hindman (or Arkansas Post), Arkansas, Engagement at, January 4–17, 1863. See Operations against Vicksburg, Mississippi, 1861–1863, Early Attempts to Capture Vicksburg, Engagement at Arkansas Post (or Fort Hindman), Arkansas.

Fort Morgan, Alabama, Capture of, August 23, 1864. See Land Operations against Mobile Bay and Mobile, Alabama, Capture of Fort Gaines, Alabama and Fort Morgan, Alabama.

Fort Pillow, Tennessee, Capture of, April 12, 1864. See Part II, below.

Fort Sanders, Tennessee, Assault on, November 29, 1863. See Knoxville, Tennessee Campaign, Assault on Fort Sanders, Knoxville, Tennessee.

Franklin, Tennessee, Battle of, November 30, 1864. See Franklin and Nashville Campaign (Hood's Invasion of Tennessee), Battle of Franklin, Tennessee.

Franklin and Nashville Campaign (Hood's Invasion of Tennessee), September 18, 1864–December 27, 1864. See Part II, below.

Galveston, Texas, Attempt to Occupy, December 21, 1863–January 1, 1864. See Department of the Gulf, Operations in the Department of the Gulf, Texas Expeditions, Attempt to Occupy Galveston, Texas.

Gilgal Church (or Golgotha Church), Georgia, Combat at, June 15, 1864. See Atlanta, Georgia Campaign, Advance of the Army from Acworth toward Marietta, Georgia.

Glorieta (or Pigeon's Ranch), New Mexico, Engagement at, March 28, 1862. See Department of New Mexico, Troops and Operations in the Department of New Mexico, Sibley's Invasion of New Mexico, Engagement at Glorieta (or Pigeon's Ranch), New Mexico.

Golgotha Church (or Gilgal Church), Georgia, Combat at, June 15, 1864. See Atlanta, Georgia Campaign, Advance of the Army from Acworth toward Marietta, Georgia.

Grand Coteau (or Carrion Crow Bayou), Louisiana, Action at, November 3, 1863. See Department of the Gulf, Operations in the Department of the Gulf, Operations in the Teche Country, Louisiana.

Grant's Northern Mississippi Campaign (Operations on the Mississippi Central Railroad from Bolivar, Tennessee to Coffeeville, Mississippi), October 31, 1862–January 10, 1863. See Operations against Vicksburg, Mississippi, 1861–1863, Early Attempts to Capture Vicksburg.

Grierson's Raid, April 17, 1863–May 2, 1863. See Part II, below.

Guntown (Brice's Cross Roads, or Tishomingo Creek), Mississippi, Battle of, June 10, 1864. See Sturgis' Expedition from Memphis, Tennessee into Mississippi (Battle of Brice's Cross Roads).

Halleck's Advance on Corinth, Mississippi, April 29, 1862–May 30, 1862. See Part II, below.

Harrisburg (or Tupelo), Mississippi, Engagement at, July 14, 1864. See Tupelo, Mississippi Expedition (Andrew J. Smith).

Hartsville Road, near Gallatin, Tennessee, Action on the, August 21, 1862. See Army of the Ohio (Buell), Return of the Army of the Ohio from Corinth, Mississippi to Tennessee, Action on the Hartsville Road, near Gallatin, Tennessee.

Hatchie Bridge (or Davis' Bridge), Hatchie River, Tennessee, Engagement at, October 5, 1862. See Battle of Corinth, Mississippi.

Helena, Arkansas, Attack on, July 4, 1863. See Part II, below.

Henderson's Hill, Louisiana, Affair at, March 21, 1864. See Red River, Louisiana Campaign, Affair at Henderson's Hill, Louisiana.

Hood's Invasion of Tennessee (Battles of Franklin and Nashville), September 18, 1864–December 27, 1864. See Franklin and Nashville Campaign (Hood's Invasion of Tennessee).

Hoover's Gap, Tennessee, Skirmishes at, June 24–26, 1863. See Tullahoma (or Middle Tennessee) Campaign.

Indian Expedition to Indian Territory (Weer-Salomon), June 28, 1862–July 1862. See Department of Kansas, May 2, 1862–September 19, 1862, Troops and Operations in the Department of Kansas, Expedition to the Indian Territory (Weer-Salomon).

Indian Hill (or Orchard Knob), Tennessee, Skirmish at, November 23, 1863. See Chattanooga-Ringgold Campaign (Battles of Lookout Mountain and Missionary Ridge, Tennessee), Skirmish at Orchard Knob (or Indian Hill), Tennessee.

Indian Territory, Expedition to (Weer-Salomon), June 28, 1862–July 1862. See Department of Kansas, May 2, 1862–September 19, 1862, Troops and Operations in the Department of Kansas, Expedition to the Indian Territory (Weer-Salomon).

Irish Bend, Louisiana, Engagement at, April 14, 1863. See Department of the Gulf, Operations in the Department of the Gulf, Operations against Port Hudson, Louisiana, Operations in West Louisiana.

Island No. 10, Mississippi River, Capture of, April 7, 1862. See Capture of New Madrid, Missouri and Island No. 10, Mississippi River.

Iuka, Mississippi, Engagement at, September 19, 1862. See Engagement at Iuka, Mississippi.

Ivey Farm (Ivey Hill, or Ivey's Hill), Mississippi, Engagement at, February 22, 1864. See Meridian, Mississippi Expedition, William Sooy Smith's Expedition from Memphis, Tennessee toward Meridian, Mississippi.

Jackson, Mississippi, Engagement at, May 14, 1863. See Operations against Vicksburg, Mississippi, 1861–1863, Grant's Operations against Vicksburg, Movement of the Army to the Rear of Vicksburg, Engagement at Jackson, Mississippi.

Jackson, Mississippi Campaign (William T. Sherman), July 5–25, 1863. See Part II, below.

Jefferson City, Missouri, Capture of, June 15, 1861. See Operations in Missouri in 1861, Capture of Jefferson City and Boonville, Missouri—Engagement at Boonville.

Jenkins' Ferry, Arkansas, Engagement at, April 30, 1864. See Department of Arkansas, Operations in the Department of Arkansas, Camden, Arkansas Expedition (Steele), Engagement at Jenkins' Ferry, Arkansas.

Jonesboro, Georgia, Battle of, August 31, 1864–September 1, 1864. See Atlanta, Georgia Campaign, Battle of Jonesboro, Georgia.

Kennesaw Mountain, Georgia, Battle of, July 27, 1864. See Atlanta, Georgia Campaign, Advance of the Army from Acworth toward Marietta, Georgia, Battle of Kennesaw Mountain, Georgia.

Kentucky, Invasion of, by E. Kirby Smith and Braxton Bragg, August 14, 1862–October 19, 1862. See Invasion of Kentucky and Tennessee (E. Kirby Smith and Braxton Bragg).

Kilpatrick's Raid from Sandtown to Lovejoy's Station, Georgia, August 18–22, 1864. See Atlanta, Georgia Campaign, Cavalry Raids on the Railroads South of Atlanta, Georgia.

Knoxville, Tennessee, Relief of (William T. Sherman), November 27, 1863–December 6, 1863. See Part II, below.

Knoxville, Tennessee, Siege of, November 17, 1863–December 4, 1863. See Knoxville, Tennessee Campaign, Siege of Knoxville, Tennessee.

Knoxville, Tennessee Campaign, November 4, 1863–December 23, 1863. See Part II, below.

Koch's (Kock's, or Cox's) Plantation, Louisiana, Engagement at, July 13, 1863. See Department of the Gulf, Operations in the Department of the Gulf, Operations against Port Hudson, Louisiana, Operations in Louisiana, West of the Mississippi River.

Kolb's Farm, Georgia, Engagement at, June 22, 1864. See Atlanta, Georgia Campaign, Advance of the Army from Acworth toward Marietta, Georgia, Engagement at Kolb's Farm, Georgia.

La Fourche (or Cox's Plantation), near Donaldsonville, Louisiana, Engagement on, July 13, 1863. See Department of the Gulf, Operations in the Department of the Gulf, Operations against Port Hudson, Louisiana, Operations in Louisiana, West of the Mississippi River.

La Fourche Crossing, Louisiana, Engagement at, June 20–21, 1863. See Department of the Gulf, Operations in the Department of the Gulf, Operations against Port Hudson, Louisiana, Operations in Louisiana, West of the Mississippi River.

Lake Providence, Louisiana Expedition, February 1863–March 1863. See Operations against Vicksburg, Mississippi, 1861–1863, Grant's Operations against Vicksburg, Bayou Expeditions.

Leetown, Arkansas, Battle of, March 7, 1862. See Battle of Pea Ridge (or Elkhorn Tavern), Arkansas.

Leggett's Hill (or Bald Hill), Georgia, Engagement at, July 21, 1864. See Atlanta, Georgia Campaign, Battles around Atlanta, Georgia, Battle of Atlanta, Georgia.

Lexington, Missouri, Siege and Capture of, September 13–20, 1861. See Missouri, Operations in, in 1861, Siege and Capture of Lexington, Missouri.

Liberty Gap, Tennessee, Skirmishes at, June 24–27, 1863. See Tullahoma (or Middle Tennessee) Campaign.

Lindell's Grove, Saint Louis, Missouri, Capture of Camp Jackson at, May 10, 1861. See Missouri, Operations in, in 1861, Capture of Camp Jackson at Lindell's Grove, Saint Louis, Missouri.

Little Blue River, Missouri, Action at the, October 21, 1864. See Price's Missouri Expedition, Action at the Little Blue River, Missouri.

Little Rock, Arkansas, Capture of, September 10, 1863. See Little Rock, Arkansas Expedition (Steele).

Little Rock, Arkansas Expedition (Steele), August 1, 1863–September 14, 1863. See Part II, below.

Logan's Cross Roads (Mill Springs, Fishing Creek, or Beech Grove), Kentucky, Engagement at, January 19, 1862. See Engagement at Mill Springs (Logan's Cross Roads, Fishing Creek, or Beech Grove), Kentucky.

Lookout Mountain, Tennessee, Battle of, November 24, 1863. See Chattanooga-Ringgold Campaign (Battles of Lookout Mountain and Missionary Ridge, Tennessee).

Lost Mountain, Georgia, Actions at, June 10, 1864 and July 1, 1864. See Atlanta, Georgia Campaign, Advance of the Army from Acworth toward Marietta, Georgia.

Lovejoy's Station, Georgia, Action at, September 2–3, 1864. See Atlanta, Georgia Campaign, End of the Campaign.

Lovejoy's Station, Georgia, Kilpatrick's Raid to, August 18–22, 1864. See Atlanta, Georgia Campaign, Cavalry Raids on the Railroads South of Atlanta, Georgia, Kilpatrick's Raid from Sandtown to Lovejoy's Station, Georgia.

Lovejoy's Station, Georgia, McCook's Raid to, July 27–31, 1864. See Atlanta, Georgia Campaign, Cavalry Raids on the Railroads South of Atlanta, Georgia, McCook's Raid to Lovejoy's Station, Georgia.

McAfee's Cross Roads, Georgia, Action at, June 11, 1864. See Atlanta, Georgia Campaign, Advance of the Army from Acworth toward Marietta, Georgia.

McCook's Raid to Lovejoy's Station, Georgia, July 27–31, 1864. See Atlanta, Georgia Campaign, Cavalry Raids on the Railroads South of Atlanta, Georgia.

Macon, Georgia, Stoneman's Raid to, July 27, 1864–August 1864. See Atlanta, Georgia Campaign, Cavalry Raids on the Railroads South of Atlanta, Georgia, Stoneman's Raid to Macon, Georgia.

Mansfield (Sabine Cross Roads, or Pleasant Grove), Louisiana, Battle of, April 8, 1864. See Red River, Louisiana Campaign, Battle of Sabine Cross Roads (Mansfield, or Pleasant Grove), Louisiana.

Mansura (Belle Prairie, or Smith's Plantation), Louisiana, Engagement at, May 16, 1864. See Red River, Louisiana Campaign, Engagement at Mansura (Belle Prairie, or Smith's Plantation), Louisiana.

Mechanicsburg, Mississippi, Blair's Expedition to, May 26, 1863–June 4, 1863. See Operations against Vicksburg, Mississippi, 1861–1863, Grant's Operations against Vicksburg, Siege of Vicksburg, Mississippi, Blair's Mechanicsburg, Mississippi Expedition.

Mechanicsburg, Mississippi, Kimball's Expedition to, June 2–8, 1863. See Operations against Vicksburg, Mississippi, 1861–1863, Grant's Operations against Vicksburg, Siege of Vicksburg, Mississippi, Kimball's Expedition from Haynes' Bluff to Sartartia and Mechanicsburg, Mississippi.

Memphis, Tennessee, Forrest's Attack on, August 21, 1864. See Expedition from La Grange, Tennessee to Oxford, Mississippi, Forrest's Attack on Memphis, Tennessee.

Meridian, Mississippi Expedition, February 3, 1864–March 6, 1864. See Part II, below.

Middle Tennessee (or Tullahoma) Campaign, June 23, 1863–July 7, 1863. See Tullahoma (or Middle Tennessee) Campaign.

Mill Creek Gap (or Buzzard's Roost Gap), Georgia, Combat at, May 8, 1864. See Atlanta, Georgia Campaign, Demonstration at Rocky Face Ridge, Georgia (Combats at Mill Creek Gap or Buzzard's Roost Gap and Dug Gap).

Mill Springs (Logan's Cross Roads, Fishing Creek, or Beech Grove), Kentucky, Engagement at, January 19, 1862. See Engagement at Mill Springs (Logan's Cross Roads, Fishing Creek, or Beech Grove), Kentucky.

Milliken's Bend, Louisiana, Engagement at, June 7, 1863. See Operations against Vicksburg, Mississippi, 1861–1863, Grant's Operations against Vicksburg, Siege of Vicksburg, District of Northeastern Louisiana—Engagement at Milliken's Bend.

Missionary Ridge, Tennessee, Battle of, November 25, 1863. See Chattanooga-Ringgold Campaign (Battles of Lookout Mountain and Missionary Ridge, Tennessee).

Missouri, Operations in, in 1861. See Part II, below.

Mobile Bay and Mobile, Alabama, Land Operations against, July 29, 1864–April 12, 1865. See Part II, below.

Monett's Ferry (or Cane River Crossing), Louisiana, Engagement at, April 23, 1864. See Red River, Louisiana Campaign, Engagement at Monett's Ferry (or Cane River Crossing), Louisiana.

Morgan's Raid into Indiana and Ohio, July 2, 1863–July 26, 1863. See Part II, below.

Mossy Creek, Tennessee, Action at, December 29, 1863. See Knoxville, Tennessee Campaign, Action at Mossy Creek, Tennessee.

Munfordville, Kentucky, Siege and Capture of, September 14–17, 1862. See Invasion of Kentucky and Tennessee (E. Kirby Smith and Braxton Bragg), Siege and Capture of Munfordville, Kentucky.

Murfreesboro, Tennessee, Action at, and Surrender of, July 13, 1862. See Army of the Ohio (Buell), Return of the Army of the Ohio from Corinth, Mississippi to Tennessee, Action at, and Surrender of, Murfreesboro, Tennessee.

Murfreesboro (or Stones River), Tennessee, Battle of, December 31, 1862–January 2, 1863. See Stones River (or Murfreesboro), Tennessee Campaign.

Nashville, Tennessee, Battle of, December 15–16, 1864. See Franklin and Nashville Campaign (Hood's Invasion of Tennessee), Battle of Nashville, Tennessee.

New Hope Church, Georgia, Battle of, May 25, 1864. See Atlanta, Georgia Campaign, Dallas New Hope Church Pickett's Mill Line, Battle of New Hope Church, Georgia.

New Madrid, Missouri and Island No. 10, Mississippi River, Capture of, March 3, 1862–April 8, 1862. See Capture of New Madrid, Missouri and Island No. 10, Mississippi River.

New Mexico, Baylor's Invasion of, July 1861. See Department of New Mexico, Troops and Operations in the Department of New Mexico, Baylor's Invasion of Southern New Mexico.

New Mexico, Sibley's Invasion of, February 7, 1862–April 22, 1862. See Department of New Mexico, Troops and Operations in the Department of New Mexico, Sibley's Invasion of New Mexico.

Noonday Creek, Georgia, Combat at, June 20, 1864. See Atlanta, Georgia Campaign, Advance of the Army from Acworth toward Marietta, Georgia.

Northern Mississippi Campaign against Vicksburg (Grant), October 31, 1862–January 10, 1863. See Operations against Vicksburg, Mississippi, 1861–1863, Early Attempts to Capture Vicksburg, Grant's Northern Mississippi Campaign (Operations on the Mississippi Central Railroad from Bolivar, Tennessee to Coffeeville, Mississippi).

Noyes' Creek, Georgia, Combat at, June 19, 1864. See Atlanta. Georgia Campaign, Advance of the Army from Acworth toward Marietta, Georgia.

Oak Hills (or Wilson's Creek), Missouri, Battle of, August 10, 1861. See Operations in Missouri in 1861, Battle of Wilson's Creek (or Oak Hills), Missouri.

Old Oaks (Yellow Bayou, or Bayou De Glaize), Louisiana, Engagement at, May 18, 1864. See Red River, Louisiana Campaign, Engagement at Yellow Bayou (Bayou De Glaize, or Old Oaks), Louisiana.

Old Town Creek, Mississippi, Engagement at, July 15, 1864. See Tupelo, Mississippi Expedition (Andrew J. Smith).

Olley's Creek, Georgia, Combat at, June 26, 1864. See Atlanta, Georgia Campaign, Advance of the Army from Acworth toward Marietta, Georgia.

Opelika, Alabama Raid (Rousseau), July 10, 1864–July 22, 1864. See Rousseau's Opelika, Alabama Raid.

Orchard Knob (or Indian Hill), Tennessee, Skirmish at, November 23, 1863. See Chattanooga-Ringgold Campaign (Battles of Lookout Mountain and Missionary Ridge, Tennessee).

Oxford, Mississippi, Expedition from La Grange, Tennessee to, August 1–30, 1864. See Expedition from La Grange, Tennessee to Oxford, Mississippi.

Palmetto (or Palmito) Ranch, Texas, Battle of, May 12–13, 1865. See Part II, below.

Palmito (or Palmetto) Ranch, Texas, Battle of, May 12–13, 1865. See Battle of Palmetto (or Palmito) Ranch, Texas.

Peach Tree Creek, Georgia, Battle of, July 20, 1864. See Atlanta, Georgia Campaign, Battles around Atlanta, Georgia, Battle of Peach Tree Creek, Georgia.

Pea Ridge (or Elkhorn Tavern), Arkansas, Battle of, March 6–8, 1862. See Part II, below.

Perryville (or Chaplin Hills), Kentucky, Battle of, October 8, 1862. See Invasion of Kentucky and

Tennessee (E. Kirby Smith and Braxton Bragg), Battle of Perryville (or Chaplin Hills), Kentucky.

Picacho Pass, Arizona Territory, Skirmish at, April 15, 1862. See Part II, below.

Pickett's Mill, Georgia, Battle of, May 27, 1864. See Atlanta, Georgia Campaign, Dallas–New Hope Church–Pickett's Mill Line, Battle of Pickett's Mill, Georgia.

Pigeon's Ranch (or Glorieta), New Mexico, Engagement at, March 28, 1862. See Department of New Mexico, Troops and Operations in the Department of New Mexico, Sibley's Invasion of New Mexico, Engagement at Glorieta (or Pigeon's Ranch), New Mexico.

Pilot Knob, Missouri, Attack on Fort Davidson, September 27, 1864. See Price's Missouri Expedition, Attack on Fort Davidson, Pilot Knob, Missouri.

Pine Hill (or Pine Mountain), Georgia, Action at, June 10, 1864. See Atlanta, Georgia Campaign, Advance of the Army from Acworth toward Marietta, Georgia.

Pine Mountain (or Pine Hill), Georgia, Action at, June 10, 1864. See Atlanta, Georgia Campaign, Advance of the Army from Acworth toward Marietta, Georgia.

Pittsburg Landing (or Shiloh), Battle of, April 6–7, 1862. See Battle of Shiloh (or Pittsburg Landing), Tennessee.

Plains Store, Louisiana, Action at, May 21, 1863. See Port Hudson, Louisiana Campaign, Action at Plains Store.

Pleasant Grove (Sabine Cross Roads, or Mansfield), Louisiana, Battle of, April 8, 1864. See Red River, Louisiana Campaign, Battle of Sabine Cross Roads (Mansfield, or Pleasant Grove), Louisiana.

Pleasant Hill, Louisiana, Engagement at, April 9, 1864. See Red River, Louisiana Campaign, Engagement at Pleasant Hill, Louisiana.

Poison Spring, Arkansas, Engagement at, April 18, 1864. See Department of Arkansas, Operations in the Department of Arkansas, Camden, Arkansas Expedition (Steele).

Port Gibson, Mississippi, Battle of, April 30, 1863–May 1, 1863. See Operations against Vicksburg, Mississippi, 1861–1863, Grant's Operations against Vicksburg, Movement of the Army to the Rear of Vicksburg, Battle of Port Gibson, Mississippi.

Port Hudson, Louisiana, Operations against. See Department of the Gulf, Operations in the Department of the Gulf, Operations against Port Hudson, Louisiana; and see also Port Hudson, Louisiana Campaign.

Port Hudson, Louisiana Campaign, May 14, 1863–July 8, 1863. See Part II, below.

Powder Springs, Georgia, Combat at, June 30, 1864. See Atlanta, Georgia Campaign, Advance of the Army from Acworth toward Marietta, Georgia.

Prairie Grove, Arkansas, Battle of, December 7, 1862. See Part II, below.

Price's Missouri Expedition, August 29, 1864–December 2, 1864. See Part II, below.

Raymond, Mississippi, Engagement at, May 12, 1863. See Operations against Vicksburg, Mississippi, 1861–1863, Grant's Operations against Vicksburg, Movement of the Army to the Rear of Vicksburg, Engagement at Raymond, Mississippi.

Red River, Louisiana Campaign, March 10, 1864–May 22, 1864. See Part II, below.

Relief of Knoxville, Tennessee (William T. Sherman), November 27, 1863–December 6, 1863. See Part II, below.

Resaca, Georgia, Battle of, May 14–15, 1864. See Atlanta, Georgia Campaign, Battle of Resaca, Georgia.

Richmond, Kentucky, Battle of, August 30, 1862.

See Invasion of Kentucky and Tennessee (E. Kirby Smith and Braxton Bragg), Battle of Richmond, Kentucky.

Ringgold Gap, Taylor's Ridge, Georgia, Engagement at, November 27, 1863. See Chattanooga-Ringgold Campaign (Battles of Lookout Mountain and Missionary Ridge, Tennessee), Pursuit of Bragg's Army into Georgia.

Rio Grande Expedition, and Operations on the Coast of Texas, November 1863–December 1863. See Department of the Gulf, Operations in the Department of the Gulf, Texas Expeditions.

Rockcastle Hills (or Camp Wildcat), Kentucky, Action at, October 21, 1861. See Engagement at Mill Springs (Logan's Cross Roads, Fishing Creek, or Beech Grove), Kentucky.

Rocky Face Ridge, Georgia, Demonstration at (Combats at Mill Creek Gap or Buzzard's Roost Gap, and Dug Gap), May 8–11, 1864. See Atlanta, Georgia Campaign, Demonstration at Rocky Face Ridge, Georgia (Combats at Mill Creek Gap or Buzzard's Roost Gap and Dug Gap).

Rousseau's Opelika, Alabama Raid, July 10, 1864–July 22, 1864. See Part II, below.

Russell's House, Mississippi, Action at, May 17, 1862. See Halleck's Advance on Corinth, Mississippi.

Sabine Cross Roads (Mansfield, or Pleasant Grove), Louisiana, Battle of, April 8, 1864. See Red River, Louisiana Campaign, Battle of Sabine Cross Roads (Mansfield, or Pleasant Grove), Louisiana.

Sabine Pass, Texas Expedition, September 4–11, 1863. See Department of the Gulf, Operations in the Department of the Gulf, Texas Expeditions.

Saltville, Virginia, Action at, October 2, 1864. See Part II, below.

Selma, Alabama, Capture of, April 2, 1865. See Wilson's Raid to Selma, Alabama.

Selma, Alabama, Wilson's Raid to, March 22, 1865–April 24, 1865. See Part II, below.

Shiloh (or Pittsburg Landing), Tennessee, Battle of, April 6–7, 1862. See Part II, below.

Ship Island, Mississippi Expedition, November 1861–December 1861. See Department of the Gulf, Troops in the Department of the Gulf.

Sibley's and Sully's Sioux Expeditions, Summer of 1863. See Department of the Northwest, Troops and Operations in the Department of the Northwest.

Sibley's Expedition to Wood Lake, Minnesota after Little Crow, September 1862. See Department of the Northwest, Troops and Operations in the Department of the Northwest.

Sibley's Invasion of New Mexico, February 7, 1862–April 22, 1862. See Department of New Mexico, Troops and Operations in the Department of New Mexico.

Smith's Plantation (Mansura, or Belle Prairie), Louisiana, Engagement at, May 16, 1864. See Red River, Louisiana Campaign, Engagement at Mansura (Belle Prairie, or Smith's Plantation), Louisiana.

Smith's (William Sooy) Expedition from Memphis, Tennessee toward Meridian, Mississippi, February 11, 1864–February 26, 1864. See Meridian, Mississippi Expedition, William Sooy Smith's Expedition from Memphis, Tennessee toward Meridian, Mississippi.

Southern New Mexico, Baylor's Invasion of, July 1861. See Department of New Mexico, Troops and Operations in the Department of New Mexico, Baylor's Invasion of Southern New Mexico.

Spanish Fort, Alabama, Siege and Capture of, March 26, 1865–April 8, 1865. See Land Operations against Mobile Bay and Mobile, Alabama, Siege and Capture of Spanish Fort and Fort Blakely, Alabama.

**Spring Hill, Tennessee, Engagement at, Novem-

ber 29, 1864. See Franklin and Nashville Campaign (Hood's Invasion of Tennessee), Movements of the Armies September 18, 1864–November 29, 1864, Movements of the Armies to Spring Hill, Tennessee (Engagement at Spring Hill).

Steele's Bayou, Mississippi Expedition, March 14–27, 1863. See Operations against Vicksburg, Mississippi, 1861–1863, Grant's Operations against Vicksburg, Bayou Expeditions.

Steele's Little Rock, Arkansas Expedition, August 1, 1863–September 14, 1863, See Little Rock, Arkansas Expedition (Steele).

Stoneman's Raid to Macon, Georgia, July 27, 1864–August 6, 1864. See Atlanta, Georgia Campaign, Cavalry Raids on the Railroads South of Atlanta, Georgia.

Stones River, Tennessee, Battle of, December 31, 1862–January 2, 1863. See Stones River (or Murfreesboro), Tennessee Campaign.

Stones River (or Murfreesboro), Tennessee Campaign, December 26, 1862–January 5, 1863. See Part II, below.

Streight's Raid from Tuscumbia, Alabama toward Rome, Georgia, April 26, 1863–May 3, 1863. See Part II, below.

Sturgis' Expedition from Memphis, Tennessee into Mississippi (Battle of Brice's Cross Roads), June 2–13, 1864. See Part II, below.

Sturgis' Expedition from Memphis, Tennessee to Ripley, Mississippi, April 30, 1864–May 11, 1864. See Part II, below.

Sully's Northwestern Indian Expedition, July 1864–October 1864. See Department of the Northwest, Troops and Operations in the Department of the Northwest.

Teche Country, Louisiana, Operations in, October 3, 1863–November 30, 1863. See Department of the Gulf, Operations in the Department of the

Gulf, Texas Expeditions, Operations in the Teche Country, Louisiana.

Tennessee River, Reopening of the, October 23–30, 1863. See Army of the Cumberland, October 24, 1862–November 14, 1864, Siege of Chattanooga, Tennessee, Reopening of the Tennessee River.

Texas Expeditions. See Department of the Gulf, Operations in the Department of the Gulf.

Thompson's Station, Tennessee, Engagement at, March 5, 1863. See Part II, below.

Tishomingo Creek (Brice's Cross Roads, or Guntown), Mississippi, Battle of June 10, 1864. See Sturgis' Expedition from Memphis, Tennessee into Mississippi (Battle of Brice's Cross Roads).

Tullahoma (or Middle Tennessee) Campaign, June 23, 1863–July 7, 1863. See Part II, below.

Tupelo (or Harrisburg), Mississippi, Engagement at, July 14, 1864. See Tupelo, Mississippi Expedition (Andrew J. Smith).

Tupelo, Mississippi Expedition (Andrew J. Smith), July 5–21, 1864. See Part II, below.

Utoy Creek, Georgia, Operations near, August 5–7, 1864. See Atlanta, Georgia Campaign, Operations near Utoy Creek, Georgia.

Valverde, New Mexico, Engagement at, February 21, 1862. See Department of New Mexico, Troops and Operations in the Department of New Mexico, Sibley's Invasion of New Mexico, Engagement at Valverde, New Mexico.

Varnell's Station, Georgia, Combat at, May 9, 1864. See Atlanta, Georgia Campaign, Demonstration at Rocky Face Ridge, Georgia (Combats at Mill Creek Gap or Buzzard's Roost Gap and Dug Gap).

Verona, Mississippi, Engagement at, December 25, 1864. See Department of Mississippi, November 28, 1864–May 17, 1865, Cavalry Forces in the Department of Mississippi.

Vicksburg, Mississippi, Assault on, May 19, 1863. See Operations against Vicksburg, Mississippi, 1861–1863, Grant's Operations against Vicksburg, Investment of Vicksburg, Mississippi, Assault on Vicksburg, Mississippi, May 19, 1863.

Vicksburg, Mississippi, Assault on, May 22, 1863. See Operations against Vicksburg, Mississippi, 1861–1863, Grant's Operations against Vicksburg, Investment of Vicksburg, Mississippi, Assault on Vicksburg, Mississippi, May 22, 1863.

Vicksburg, Mississippi, Farragut's Expeditions against, May 1862–June 1862. See Operations against Vicksburg, Mississippi, 1861–1863, Early Attempts to Capture Vicksburg.

Vicksburg, Mississippi, Grant's Operations against, February 1863–July 4, 1863. See Operations against Vicksburg, Mississippi, 1861–1863, Grant's Operations against Vicksburg.

Vicksburg, Mississippi, Investment of. See Operations against Vicksburg, Mississippi, 1861–1863, Grant's Operations against Vicksburg, Investment of Vicksburg, Mississippi.

Vicksburg, Mississippi, Operations against, 1861–1863. See Part II, below.

Vicksburg, Mississippi, Siege of, May 23, 1863–July 4, 1863. See Operations against Vicksburg, Mississippi, 1861–1863, Grant's Operations against Vicksburg, Siege of Vicksburg, Mississippi.

Walnut Hills, Battle of, December 20–29, 1862. See Operations against Vicksburg, Mississippi, 1861–1863, Early Attempts to Capture Vicksburg, Yazoo River Expedition (William T. Sherman)—Battle of Chickasaw Bayou (or Walnut Hills).

Wauhatchie, Tennessee, Engagement at, October 29, 1863. See Army of the Cumberland, October 24, 1862–November 14, 1864, Siege of Chattanooga, Tennessee, Reopening of the Tennessee River, Engagement at Wauhatchie, Tennessee.

West Louisiana, Operations in, April 9, 1863–May 14, 1863. See Department of the Gulf, Oper-ations in the Department of the Gulf, Operations in West Louisiana.

Westport, Missouri, Engagement at, October 23, 1864. See Price's Missouri Expedition, Engage-ment at Westport, Missouri.

White Stone Hill, Dakota Territory, Action at, September 3, 1863. See Department of the North-west, Troops and Operations in the Department of the Northwest, Sibley's and Sully's Sioux Expedi-tions, Summer of 1863.

William Sooy Smith's Expedition from Mem-phis, Tennessee toward Meridian, Mississippi, February 11, 1864–February 26, 1864. See Me-ridian, Mississippi Expedition.

Wilson's Creek (or Oak Hills), Missouri, Battle of, August 10, 1861. See Operations in Missouri in 1861, Battle of Wilson's Creek (or Oak Hills), Mis-souri.

Wilson's Plantation (or Farm), Louisiana, Skir-mish at, April 7, 1864. See Red River, Louisiana Campaign, Skirmish at Wilson's Plantation (or Farm), Louisiana.

Wilson's Raid to Selma, Alabama, March 22, 1865–April 24, 1865. See Part II, below.

Wood Lake, Minnesota, Sibley's Expedition to, after Little Crow, September 1862. See Depart-ment of the Northwest, Troops and Operations in the Department of the Northwest, Sibley's Expedi-tion to Wood Lake, Minnesota after Little Crow.

Yazoo, Mississippi Expedition (Coates'), Janu-ary 31, 1864–March 6, 1864. See Meridian, Mis-sissippi Expedition, Coates' Yazoo, Mississippi Expedition.

Yazoo Pass, Mississippi Expedition, February 24, 1863–April 8, 1863. See Operations against Vicksburg, Mississippi, 1861–1863, Grant's Oper-ations against Vicksburg, Bayou Expeditions.

Yazoo River, Mississippi Expedition (William T. Sherman), December 20, 1862–January 2, 1863.

See Operations against Vicksburg, Mississippi, 1861–1863, Early Attempts to Capture Vicksburg, Yazoo River Expedition (William T. Sherman)—Battle of Chickasaw Bayou (or Walnut Hills).

Yellow Bayou (Bayou De Glaize, or Old Oaks), Louisiana, Engagement at, May 18, 1864. See Red River, Louisiana Campaign.

PART II: BATTLES AND CAMPAIGNS

ATLANTA, GEORGIA CAMPAIGN MAY 3, 1864–SEPTEMBER 8, 1864

On March 2, 1864, Ulysses S. Grant, commanding the Military Division of the Mississippi, was called to Washington, D.C., and on March 9 he received his commission as lieutenant general. Three days later he was placed in command of the Armies of the United States. Grant then returned to Tennessee to wind up his affairs there, and on March 18, William T. Sherman assumed command of the Military Division of the Mississippi, and James B. McPherson succeeded him in command of the Army of the Tennessee. Grant then returned to Washington to assume his new duties, and on March 26 he established his headquarters at Culpeper Court House and began preparations for the spring campaigns of 1864.

The plan that Grant formulated, unlike those of previous years, called for a simultaneous advance of the armies on all fronts so as to maintain a constant pressure on the Confederate armies and thus prevent them from transferring troops from an area that was not threatened to strengthen another that was under attack.

According to this plan, George G. Meade's Army of the Potomac, which Grant would accompany in person, was to move toward Richmond, Virginia against Robert E. Lee's Army of Northern Virginia. Sherman was to advance with his Army of the Military Division of the Mississippi southward from Chattanooga, along the Western and Atlantic Railroad, toward the important rail center of Atlanta, some 120 miles to the southeast. In conjunction with Sherman's advance, Nathaniel P. Banks was to advance from New Orleans with the available forces of his Department of the Gulf against Mobile, Alabama. The defeat of Banks' army along the Red River in Louisiana, however, forced a cancellation of projected movement against Mobile, and this left Sherman to make the major effort in the West that spring.

The troops under Sherman's command at the end of April 1864 consisted of George H. Thomas' Army of the Cumberland, James B. McPherson's Army of the Tennessee, and John M. Schofield's Army of the Ohio (Twenty-Third Corps). The Army of the Cumberland consisted of Oliver O. Howard's Fourth Corps, John M. Palmer's Fourteenth Corps, and Joseph Hooker's Twentieth Corps; the Army of the Tennessee consisted of John A. Logan's Fifteenth Corps, Grenville M. Dodge's Sixteenth Corps, and Frank P. Blair's Seventeenth Corps. The Army of the Ohio consisted of only one corps, the Twenty-Third Corps, to which George Stoneman's cavalry division was attached.

Of the Army of the Tennessee, only Fifteenth Corps was at full strength at the beginning of the Atlanta Campaign. Two divisions of Seventeenth Corps were on veterans' furlough in Illinois, Indiana, Iowa, and Ohio, but at that time were assembling at Cairo, Illinois under Mortimer D. Leggett and Marcellus M. Crocker to form a part of Seventeenth Corps, which was to be commanded by Frank P. Blair, Jr. Blair, with his two divisions, did not join Sherman's army until it had arrived at Acworth and Big Shanty in Georgia about June 9, 1864. The First and Third divisions of Sixteenth Corps were detached under Andrew J. Smith and were with Nathaniel P. Banks' expedition on the Red River in Louisiana. Dodge had with him in northern Alabama only the Left Wing of Sixteenth Corps, which consisted of the Second and Fourth divisions. Thus McPherson had with him at the beginning of May 1864 only five of the nine divisions of his army.

Sherman's first objective at the beginning of the campaign was Dalton, Georgia, about twenty-five miles southeast of Chattanooga, where Joseph E. Johnston's Confederate army was encamped. To reduce this stronghold, Sherman proposed to move Schofield's Twenty-Third Corps south from the vicinity of Cleveland, Tennessee to the front of Johnston's defensive position in Crow Valley north of Dalton, and then connect with Thomas' Army of the Cumberland on his right. Thomas was to advance with his Army of the Cumberland against the front of Rocky Face Ridge, which covered the approaches to Dalton from the west. Howard's Fourth Corps, advancing on the left of the Army of the Cumberland, was to threaten the northern end of Rocky Face Ridge; Palmer's Fourteenth Corps was to move up in front of Mill Creek Gap; and Hooker's Twentieth Corps was to advance on the right toward Dug Gap.

Originally it was intended that McPherson's Army of the Tennessee would march on the far right of Sherman's line in the direction of Rome, Georgia, but because it was so understrength at the beginning of the campaign, McPherson was directed to advance on the right of the Army of the Cumberland toward Snake Creek Gap and attempt to reach the Western and Atlantic Railroad at Resaca, Georgia.

Before proceeding with an account of the operations against Dalton, it will be helpful to give a brief description of the country to the north and west of Dalton through which Sherman's armies were to advance. South of Chattanooga, the branches of Chickamauga Creek, which have their origin nearly west of Dalton, flow northward through parallel valleys for about twenty miles before emptying into the Tennessee River a short distance east of Chattanooga. On the eastern side of the drainage basin of Chickamauga Creek, and west of Dalton, is a high north-south ridge called Rocky Face Ridge, which rises to a height of roughly 700 feet above the adjacent valleys. Near the summit of this ridge, on the western side, the rise is almost perpendicular, and this part of the ridge has been called the "palisades."

A short distance to the west of Rocky Face Ridge, and parallel to it, is a lower ridge through which the Western and Atlantic Railroad passes as it runs from Chattanooga to Dalton, and on to Atlanta. This ridge is called Tunnel Hill.

There are only three passes or gaps in Rocky Face Ridge through which roads pass toward Dalton, and toward Resaca farther south. The northernmost of these is Mill Creek Gap, which is about three and a half miles northwest of Dalton. The names Mill Creek Gap and Buzzard's (Buzzard) Roost are sometimes used synonymously, but Buzzard's Roost was the name given to the high walls on the sides of the gap.

Mill Creek, which flows northward along the western face of the ridge, turns and runs through this gap, and then flows in a southerly direction for five or six miles before emptying into a branch of the Connasauga River, which farther south joins the Coosawattee River to form the Oostanaula (also spelled Oostenaula) River.

After passing through Tunnel Hill, the Western and Atlantic Railroad ran through Mill Creek Gap to Dalton, and then on to the south for about fifteen miles to Resaca, where it crossed the Oostanaula River on its way toward Atlanta. A wagon road running from Chattanooga to Dalton also ran through Mill Creek Gap.

Rocky Face Ridge extends for about three miles to the north of Mill Creek Gap, to a point a short distance beyond Tunnel Hill, and it then breaks down into a number of separate hills. About four miles south of Mill Creek Gap is Dug Gap, which is a narrow opening near the top of Rocky Face Ridge, and about eleven or twelve miles south of Dug Gap is the third gap, called Snake Creek Gap. This gap is about five or six miles in length; its western end was near Villanow, and at its eastern end was Sugar Valley, west of Resaca. It should be noted here that in some reports the ridge south of Mill Creek Gap was called Chattoogata Ridge or Chattoogata Mountain, and it was through this ridge or mountain that Dug Gap and Snake Creek Gap ran.

The country at the northern end of Rocky Face Ridge was open to the north and east, and any Union force approaching Dalton from the direction of Cleveland, Tennessee could arrive in front of the town without crossing the ridge.

After his defeat at Missionary Ridge in November 1863, Braxton Bragg led his Army of Tennessee back to Dalton, where it went into winter quarters. On December 26, 1863, Joseph E. Johnston arrived at Dalton and assumed command of the army, relieving Bragg.

Johnston's command was organized into two corps, commanded by William J. Hardee and John B. Hood, and a cavalry corps under Joseph Wheeler. Soon after Sherman began his advance into Georgia, however, the Confederate authorities ordered Leonidas Polk to organize a field force in his Department of Alabama, Mississippi, and East Louisiana and join Johnston's army. Polk's command, which was called the Army of Mississippi, consisted of two infantry divisions commanded by William W. Loring and Samuel G. French, and a cavalry division commanded by William H. Jackson. James Cantey's brigade of Polk's command arrived at Resaca on the evening of May 7, 1864, and it was later joined by Daniel H. Reynolds' brigade, after which Cantey's command was called Cantey's Division. Polk arrived at Resaca with Loring's division on May 11. French's division arrived at Rome, Georgia on May 17 and joined Johnston's army at Kingston the next day.

The divisions of Hood's corps were placed to defend Mill Creek Gap and the northern end of Rocky Face Ridge, and also to defend the open country to the east of the ridge and north of Dalton. The Confederate defenses east of the ridge were about four miles north of Dalton, and they extended across Crow Creek Valley to the high ground commanding the East Tennessee and Dalton Railroad, where they turned back to the south so as to cover the ground east of Dalton. Alexander P. Stewart's division was placed in Mill Creek Gap; Benjamin F. Cheatham's division of Hardee's corps, which had reported to Hood, was on the crest of the ridge and extended for about one mile north of Stewart's position; Carter L. Stevenson's division of Hood's corps was in position across Crow Valley, east of the ridge, with its left connecting with the right of Cheatham's division; and Thomas C. Hindman's division, also of Hood's corps, was on the right of Stevenson.

William B. Bate's division of Hardee's corps was on the crest of the ridge and extended for about one mile south of Mill Creek Gap; Patrick R. Cleburne's division was in camp on Mill Creek, on the Spring Place road; and William H. T. Walker's division was in reserve near Dalton.

Two Arkansas regiments of Reynolds' brigade of Cantey's division were guarding Dug Gap, and J. Warren Grigsby's Kentucky cavalry brigade was nearby. The rest of Cantey's command was in position in front of Resaca.

OPENING MOVEMENTS OF THE ARMY

The day originally set for the beginning of Sherman's campaign was May 5, 1864, and accordingly the first few days in May were spent in moving the troops forward to their assigned positions for the advance toward Dalton. Schofield and McPherson, however, experienced some difficulty in getting their armies up in time, and the starting date was changed to May 7, 1864. On April 28, Sherman moved his Headquarters, Military Division of the Mississippi from Nashville to Chattanooga to be present with the army at the beginning of its movement toward Dalton.

In April 1864, the divisions of Schofield's Army of the Ohio (Twenty-Third Corps), which was in East Tennessee, were somewhat scattered. Alvin P. Hovey's First Division was at Charleston; Henry M. Judah's Second Division and Jacob D. Cox's Third Division were on the East Tennessee and Virginia Railroad from Knoxville to Bull's Gap; and Fourth Division and Fifth Division were distributed for the permanent occupation of East Tennessee and Kentucky, and they did not accompany Schofield on the march to Atlanta. On May 2, the First, Second, and Third divisions were assembled at Charleston, and the next day they moved to Cleveland, Tennessee. On May 4, Schofield moved to Red Clay on the Tennessee-Georgia state line, and he remained there and in the vicinity until May 7.

George Stoneman was to join Schofield's infantry with a cavalry force from the Department of the Ohio. Details of the composition of this force, however, are generally lacking in most accounts of the campaign, and a brief description is inserted here. In mid-April 1864, Stoneman's Cavalry Corps, Army of the Ohio was at Nicholasville, Kentucky, where it was being remounted and refitted for field service. On April 26, Schofield ordered Stoneman to move forward at once from Nicholasville with his available force and to leave that part of the corps not yet ready for field service to follow as soon possible.

James Biddle's Second Brigade of three regiments left Nicholasville April 28–29, 1864 and marched toward Kingston, Tennessee, where it was to arrive by May 6. Alexander W. Holeman's Independent Brigade of two regiments left April 30, with orders to move one day's march in rear of Biddle. The 5th Indiana Cavalry departed May 1 and marched in rear of Holeman. This was the organization of Stoneman's cavalry command at the beginning of the Atlanta Campaign. It was generally called Stoneman's Division, or sometimes Stoneman's Command. Because these troops had to march from Central Kentucky, they did not join the army in front of Dalton until May 10. Israel Garrard's First Brigade did not join Stoneman's division in the field until July 27, and Horace Capron's Third Brigade joined the next day, just before the beginning of Stoneman's raid to Macon, Georgia.

At the beginning of May 1864, Palmer's Fourteenth Corps, Army of the Cumberland was encamped to the south and east of Chattanooga. Absalom Baird's Third Division was in the vicinity of Ringgold, Georgia; Richard W. Johnson's First Division was at Graysville; and Jefferson C. Davis' Second Division was encamped south of Chattanooga, with James D. Morgan's First Brigade and John G. Mitchell's Second Brigade near McAfee's Church and Daniel McCook's Third Brigade at Lee and Gordon's Mills. On May 2–3, Davis' division and Johnson's division joined Baird's division near Ringgold. Palmer's corps remained near Ringgold until May 7.

On April 10, 1864, Oliver O. Howard relieved Gordon Granger in command of Fourth Corps, Army of the Cumberland, which was in East Tennessee, and at that time David S. Stanley's First Division was at Blue Springs and Ooltewah; John Newton's Second Division was at Loudon; and Thomas J. Wood's Third Division was at Knoxville. By April 25, Howard had concentrated his divisions near Cleveland, Tennessee.

On May 3, 1864, when Schofield arrived at Cleveland with his Army of the Ohio (Twenty-Third Corps), Howard left there, marching in two columns, one by way of Salem Church and the other by Red Clay, and arriving at Catoosa Springs, Georgia, about three miles east of Ringgold, on the morning of May 4. Howard then took position on the left of Palmer's Fourteenth Corps. Edward M. McCook's First Cavalry Division, Army of the Cumberland covered the left of Howard's columns on the march from Cleveland.

At the end of April 1864, Hooker's Twentieth Corps was along the Nashville and Chattanooga Railroad, with corps headquarters in Lookout Valley. Alpheus S. Williams' First Division was on the railroad from Wartrace to Anderson, Tennessee,

near the Tennessee-Alabama state line, but on May 1 it was concentrated at Bridgeport. From there the division moved eastward along the railroad through Shellmound and Whiteside, and on May 3 it arrived in Chattanooga Valley, at the eastern base of Lookout Mountain, where Williams reported to Hooker.

John W. Geary's Second Division was on the railroad, with Adolphus Buschbeck's Second Brigade near the base of Lookout Mountain in Lookout Valley; Charles Candy's First Brigade at Bridgeport and vicinity; and David Ireland's Third Brigade between Stevenson, Alabama and Anderson, Tennessee. On May 1, 1864, Geary was ordered to concentrate his First Brigade and Second Brigade at Bridgeport, and on May 3 he marched eastward with his two brigades to Shellmound, where he was joined by some detachments of his command. Then on May 4 he moved on through Whiteside, crossed Lookout Valley and Lookout Mountain, and arrived in Chattanooga Valley. He was joined there by Buschbeck's brigade, which arrived from Lookout Valley.

Daniel Butterfield's Third Division, which had been stationed in Lookout Valley, crossed Lookout Mountain into Chattanooga Valley and then moved south through Rossville and camped at Lee and Gordon's Mills May 2, 1864. Williams' division followed Geary and camped at Lee and Gordon's Mills on May 4, and Geary's division followed Williams the next day.

Butterfield moved on and reached Ringgold May 4, 1863, and two days later marched to Leet's Tanyard. On May 5, Williams' division marched to Pleasant Grove Church, three miles southwest of Ringgold; that night Geary's division bivouacked at Post Oak Church, and the next day it moved to Pea Vine Church.

When Thomas finally had his Army of the Cumberland in line for the general advance May 7, 1864, his left was at Catoosa Springs and his right was at Leet's Tanyard.

At the end of April 1864, John A. Logan's Fifteenth Corps and Grenville M. Dodge's Left Wing, Sixteenth Corps of the Army of the Tennessee were guarding the Tennessee and Alabama Railroad from Nashville, Tennessee to Decatur, Alabama, and the Memphis and Charleston Railroad from Decatur to Stevenson, Alabama. That part of Seventeenth Corps that was designated to take part in Sherman's

Georgia campaign was organizing at Cairo, Illinois, but was under orders to concentrate at Chattanooga as rapidly as possible.

Logan's Headquarters, Fifteenth Corps and John E. Smith's Third Division were at Huntsville, Alabama; Peter J. Osterhaus' First Division was at Woodville; Morgan L. Smith's Second Division was at Larkinsville; and William Harrow's Fourth Division was at Scottsboro. Dodge's headquarters and Thomas W. Sweeny's Second Division of Sixteenth Corps were in the field, and James C. Veatch's Fourth Division was at Decatur.

On April 29, 1864, Dodge moved eastward with his two divisions toward Chattanooga. Sweeny's division moved from Pulaski, Tennessee to Athens, Alabama, and Veatch's division from Decatur, with orders to assemble at Huntsville. Moses M. Bane's Third Brigade of Sweeny's division was left at Decatur to watch the railroad. On May 2, Dodge left Huntsville and marched along the road toward Stevenson, Alabama, and two days later Sweeny's division entrained at Larkinsville and Veatch's division at Woodville for Chattanooga. Dodge's divisions arrived at Chattanooga on the morning of May 5, and immediately marched out on the Rossville road, with Sweeny in the lead. Sweeny's division bivouacked that night at Lee and Gordon's Mills, and Veatch's division at Rossville.

On May 1, 1864, Logan left John E. Smith's division at Huntsville to guard the railroad, and marched with his other three divisions along the road toward Chattanooga. He passed through Stevenson and Bridgeport, arriving at Chattanooga during the night of May 5 and the morning of May 6, and he then set out on the road to join Dodge at Lee and Gordon's Mills.

Dodge remained at Lee and Gordon's Mills until the morning of May 7, 1864, the day set for the advance of Sherman's army toward Dalton. That day, Dodge, followed by Logan, marched south on the road past Rock Spring Church, and that night his division bivouacked near the western end of Gordon's Gap. Logan's corps camped on the road to his rear. Dodge sent John W. Sprague's Second Brigade of Veatch's division on to the south to seize and hold Ship's Gap, which passed through Taylor's Ridge east of La Fayette, Georgia. Sprague gained possession of the gap about 9:00 that night.

On May 8, 1864, Dodge marched through Ship's Gap and Villanow, halting that night in Snake Creek Gap. Logan followed during the day and bivouacked at the western end of the Gap.

DEMONSTRATION AT ROCKY FACE RIDGE, GEORGIA (COMBATS AT MILL CREEK GAP OR BUZZARD'S ROOST GAP AND DUG GAP), MAY 8–11, 1864

Meantime, while McPherson was marching on the right toward Snake Creek Gap, Thomas and Schofield were beginning their advance as ordered. At daybreak on May 7, 1864, Thomas advanced toward Tunnel Hill in three columns as follows: Palmer's Fourteenth Corps moved forward on the direct road from Ringgold; Howard's Fourth Corps from Catoosa Springs by way of Dr. Lee's house; and Hooker's corps crossed Taylor's Ridge and moved up to the vicinity of Trickum in Dogwood Valley. Williams' division crossed the ridge at Nickajack Gap and halted at Trickum; Geary crossed at Gordon's Gap, passed Gordon's Springs, and marched to the Thornton farm on the Rome road; and Butterfield crossed the ridge at Gordon's Gap and moved to Trickum. Hooker did not advance past Trickum, but remained there close to Rocky Face Ridge, where he covered the road south to Villanow.

Palmer encountered some resistance as he advanced toward Tunnel Hill, but when Howard came up on his left, the enemy abandoned the hill and fell back into Mill Creek Gap. Palmer then moved up and took position on the right of Howard on Tunnel Hill.

On May 7, 1864, Schofield moved forward from Red Clay and connected with the left of the Army of the Cumberland at Dr. Lee's farm, near Tunnel Hill. It also held the ground to the east and pushed forward a reconnaissance against the enemy's position at the north end of Rocky Face Ridge.

On the morning of May 8, 1864, Howard ordered Newton to move northward with his Second Division, Fourth Corps for about two miles to a point where it was comparatively easy to move up onto the northern end of Rocky Face Ridge. Charles G.

Harker's Third Brigade of Newton's division ascended the ridge and then moved southward along
the crest until stopped about one-half mile north of
Buzzard's Roost by a strong enemy force in a well-
fortified position. The rest of Newton's division
formed a line that ran diagonally down the ridge.

At 8:30 A.M. Stanley's First Division and Wood's
Third Division of Fourth Corps also moved up close
to the ridge, giving all possible support to Harker
by their fire from the valley.

Schofield also moved his corps closer to
Johnston's army May 8, 1864. His right division
under Judah connected with Newton's division at
the northern end of Rocky Face Ridge, and Cox's
division, on the left, moved to the east for about a
mile to Kincannon's Cross Roads. From there James
W. Reilly's First Brigade of Cox's division moved
on south for about a mile to Huffacre's, and Mahlon
D. Manson's Second Brigade remained at the crossroads. Hovey's division was in the center, and when
Schofield's line was completed, it covered the direct
road from Dalton to Varnell's Station.

On May 8, 1864, Johnson's First Division and
Davis' Second Division of Fourteenth Corps moved
up from Tunnel Hill to a position in front of Mill
Creek Gap, and Baird's Third Division marched
south on the road to Villanow for about a mile to
connect with the left of Hooker's Twentieth Corps
and cover the ground to the right of Johnson's division. In the afternoon Baird moved up to support
Johnson and Davis in front of Mill Creek Gap.

On May 8, 1864, Geary was ordered to advance
with two brigades of his division and seize Dug
Gap, which cut through the crest of Rocky Face
Ridge above the Babb farm. At 11:00 A.M. Geary
advanced with Candy's and Buschbeck's brigades
and James D. McGill's Battery E, Pennsylvania
Light Artillery to Mill Creek, near the Babb house,
at the foot of the ridge. Leaving three regiments to
guard the battery, which was firing from near the
Babb house, Geary crossed Mill Creek about 3:00
P.M. and started up the ridge, with Buschbeck's
brigade on the right and Candy's brigade on the left.

Guarding the gap above were two Arkansas regiments of Daniel H. Reynolds' brigade of Cantey's
division, and Grigsby's Kentucky cavalry brigade
was close by. Reynolds' infantry opened with a
heavy fire, and Geary halted briefly at the foot of
the palisades before charging on toward the top of

the ridge. Some men gained the crest, but they were
soon driven back. Grigsby's men then came up and,
fighting dismounted, added their fire to that of the
infantry. Geary tried again and still a third time to
drive the enemy from their works, but each time he
was driven back. Finally about dusk, Patrick R.
Cleburne came up with Hiram B. Granbury's brigade and Mark P. Lowrey's brigade of his division,
but by that time Geary had begun to withdraw down
the ridge. Geary remained at the foot of the mountain, however, until May 11, 1864.

It has been noted earlier that on the night of May
8, 1864, McPherson's Army of the Tennessee occupied Snake Creek Gap, with orders to advance to
Resaca and the Western and Atlantic Railroad the
following day.

At the eastern end of Snake Creek Gap was Sugar
Valley, where the country bordering on the
Oostanaula River became more open, and through
this valley ran the road to Resaca, which was
crossed by the road from Dalton to Rome.

In obedience to his orders, McPherson marched
out of Snake Creek Gap on the morning of May 9,
1864 and took the road toward Resaca and the
Western and Atlantic Railroad. Dodge's corps was
leading, and it was preceded by a portion of Judson
Kilpatrick's Third Cavalry Division of the Army of
the Cumberland, which had joined McPherson's
column at Villanow May 8. About three and a half
miles from the town, the cavalry encountered troops
of Cantey's command, and when these had been
driven back, they came up on a strong enemy works
on the road. McPherson then deployed his infantry,
with Sixteenth Corps on the left of the Resaca road
and Fifteenth Corps on the right of the road. Dodge
pushed forward and soon found a strong enemy
force in a well-fortified position. He skirmished
with the enemy until dark; McPherson, apprehend-
ing that he could not reach the railroad that day,
decided to withdraw his command to the crossroads
in Sugar Valley, in front of the entrance to Snake
Creek Gap, and took up a position to keep open the
way forward for the rest of Sherman's army. He then
reported the events of the day to Sherman.

Meantime, during the day, the Army of the Ohio
and the Army of the Cumberland demonstrated
strongly against Johnston's lines farther north in
front of Dalton as a diversion for McPherson's attack on Resaca. Early on the morning of May 9,

1864, Schofield formed his corps in line across Crow Valley to the east of Rocky Face Ridge, with Judah's division on the right next to the ridge, Cox's division on the left, and Hovey's division in reserve, covering Schofield's left flank. Edward M. McCook's cavalry division made strong demonstrations on the left of Schofield. Twenty-Third Corps advanced steadily during the day, driving back the enemy skirmishers, until at dark it had arrived in front of the enemy's main line north of Dalton.

There was a spirited cavalry action near Varnell's Station, Georgia on May 9, 1864, when Oscar H. La Grange's Second Brigade of McCook's cavalry division advanced from the station toward the enemy's position on a hill on Johnston's main line. As the brigade approached the hill, it was vigorously attacked by men of William H. Allen's and George G. Dibrell's brigades of John H. Kelly's cavalry division, fighting dismounted. La Grange's brigade was overwhelmed and routed, with the loss of its commander, who was captured with more than 100 of his men.

Thomas also maintained his pressure at Rocky Face Ridge. On the morning of May 9, 1864, Newton moved his other two brigades to the top of the ridge and formed them immediately in rear of Harker's brigade. Harker then again attacked along the crest and forced the enemy back to their main works, but he could go no farther. George D. Wagner's Second Brigade of Newton's division moved to the eastern slope of the ridge to attack the enemy works there, but it was soon stopped by an impassable ravine in front of the entrenched position.

In addition to Newton's attacks on the top of the ridge, there were two other efforts by Thomas' men to gain position closer to the enemy's lines. Stanley's First Division of Fourth Corps made a strong reconnaissance into the entrance of Mill Creek Gap, but it soon came under such heavy fire that it was forced to halt. To the right of Stanley, south of Mill Creek Gap, Palmer sent Morgan's First Brigade of Davis' First Division of Fourteenth Corps up a spur of the ridge, and it worked its way up the slope to a position very close to the enemy works.

On the night of May 9, 1864, after Johnston learned of McPherson's advance toward Resaca that day, he ordered Hood to move Hindman's division of his corps and Walker's and Cleburne's divisions of Hardee's corps to Resaca, but when Hood reported the next day that McPherson had withdrawn to Sugar Valley, Johnston directed him to leave Cleburne and Walker at Tilton, about six miles north of Resaca, and to return to Dalton with Hindman's division.

Also on May 9, 1864, the leading elements of Loring's division of Polk's Army of the Mississippi arrived at Resaca from northern Alabama, and on May 11, Polk arrived with the rest of the division and assumed command of the Confederate forces at Resaca.

On May 10, 1864, after Sherman had received McPherson's report from Sugar Valley informing him of his failure to reach the Western and Atlantic Railroad at Resaca the day before, Sherman decided to move with the rest of his army through Snake Creek Gap and join McPherson for another attempt to capture Resaca. In preparation for this movement, Sherman directed Schofield to pull back his Twenty-Third Corps and march past the rear of Howard's Fourth Corps, and then face to the left and take position on the right of Howard, facing east. Sherman also issued orders for Williams' division of Hooker's corps to move through Snake Creek Gap and support McPherson, and he ordered Geary and Butterfield to follow with their divisions of Twentieth Corps. Howard was to remain in his original position in front of Rocky Face Ridge and protect Sherman's line of communications back to Chattanooga.

Sherman did not begin his movement until George Stoneman arrived with his cavalry, which was to take the place of Twenty-Third Corps and watch the roads back to Chattanooga and Cleveland. Finally, at sunrise May 11, 1864, Palmer's Fourteenth Corps began the march south, and it was closely followed by Schofield's Army of the Ohio (Twenty-Third Corps). Later that day, all of Sherman's army, except Fourth Corps and Stoneman's cavalry, was assembled near McPherson's position at the eastern end of Snake Creek Gap.

Johnston remained with most of his army at Dalton until May 12, 1864, and then, when he learned from Wheeler that most of Sherman's army had left the area and moved south, he started his infantry southward through Tilton toward Resaca. Johnston left Wheeler behind with his cavalry to watch Howard and delay his movement when he too started for Resaca.

BATTLE OF RESACA, GEORGIA, MAY 14–15, 1864

Resaca, Georgia was a small village on the north bank of the Oostanaula River a short distance below its confluence with the Connasauga River, which flows southward to the east of Resaca on its way to the Oostanaula. About one-half mile west of Resaca, Camp Creek flows down from the north, crosses the road from Snake Creek Gap to Resaca (present-day La Fayette Road or Route 136), and empties into the Oostanaula River about one mile south and to the west of Resaca. On both the east and west sides of the valley of Camp Creek, the ground rises to a series of ridges and hills overlooking the valley, and about two miles north of Resaca there is an east-west range of rugged hills between Camp Creek and the Connasauga River.

Polk's Army of the Mississippi, commonly called Polk's corps while with Johnston's army, had been the first of the Confederate troops to arrive at Resaca, and it had been placed out to the west of town to watch the road running in from Snake Creek Gap. Polk's corps naturally formed the left of the Confederate line when Johnston's army arrived from Dalton and took position in front of Resaca. A part of Polk's corps was placed on the west side of Camp Creek, near its mouth, to occupy some high ground there that covered the railroad bridge at Resaca. The rest of the corps was farther to the right on the east side of Camp Creek.

When Hardee's corps arrived, it was placed on the hills east of Camp Creek, and it extended Polk's line northward to a point about two to two and one-half miles north of the Oostanaula River, where Camp Creek curves away to the northwest. That part of the line held by Polk and Hardee was essentially along the route of present-day U.S. 75 from its crossing of the Oostanaula to a point about three miles to the north of the river. At the latter point, beginning on the right of Hardee's line, Hood's corps held a line that curved to the east from the valley of Camp Creek and followed the series of high wooded hills to the Connasauga River. This part of Johnson's line faced to the north. Most of Wheeler's cavalry was on the far Confederate right, east of the Connasauga.

When Sherman's army had passed through Snake Creek Gap as it moved south, Sherman brought his trains into the gap and protected them by directing Schofield to leave Hovey with Richard F. Barter's First Brigade of his division at the mouth of the gap and John C. McQuiston with his Second Brigade in rear of the trains at the western end of the gap, about five miles southeast of Villanow. In addition, Kenner Garrard's Second Cavalry Division of the Army of the Cumberland, which had joined the army at Villanow from Columbia, Tennessee May 10, 1864, picketed the roads to the rear of the army.

On the morning of May 13, 1864, McPherson's Army of the Tennessee marched out on the road toward Resaca to cover the movements of the rest of the army. Logan's Fifteenth Corps was in front, and it was supported by Veatch's Fourth Division of Dodge's Sixteenth Corps. On May 12, Logan had sent Morgan L. Smith's Second Division out from Sugar Valley on the Resaca road to its intersection with the road from Dalton to Rome as a support for Kilpatrick's cavalry, which was attempting to advance against the enemy cavalry. Upon arriving there, about two miles from Resaca, Smith deployed his division on the right of the road, with Joseph A. J. Lightburn's Second Brigade on the right and Giles A. Smith's First Brigade on the left. The next day Logan, with Osterhaus' First Division and Harrow's Fourth Division, moved out of their works and advanced to join Smith at the crossroads. Osterhaus deployed his division on the left of Morgan L. Smith's division, with Charles R. Woods' First Brigade on the right, James A. Williamson's Second Brigade on the left, and Hugo Wangelin's Third Brigade in reserve. Harrow's Fourth Division was in reserve.

Logan completed his deployment by about 1:00 P.M., and about one-half hour later the corps, preceded by a strong line of skirmishers, advanced through rough and hilly country that was covered in most places by heavy timber and dense undergrowth toward Resaca, driving the enemy before him. Logan finally emerged from the woods onto open ground that extended about 700 yards to his front to the line of commanding hills west of Camp

Creek that were occupied by a part of Polk's corps and which covered the town of Resaca and the bridges there over the Oostanaula River. After an exchange of artillery and infantry fire, Logan again advanced and about 4:30 P.M. drove the enemy from the crest and back across Camp Creek.

The road to Resaca ran through a short gap between these hills, which were about 400 yards from the river, and at the eastern end of this gap the road crossed Camp Creek on a bridge. Logan did not attempt to cross the creek that evening, but Morgan L. Smith's division took position on the hills to the right of the Resaca road, and Osterhaus' division on the left, and they bivouacked there that night. At first Harrow's division remained in reserve, but later he deployed farther to the left to fill a gap in the line created by the withdrawal of Hooker's Twentieth Corps.

When Logan arrived at this position on the hills, there was a considerable gap between the right of his line and the Oostanaula River, and Veatch's division of Dodge's Sixteenth Corps was brought up on the right of Logan, with its right extending to the river. Sweeny's Second Division of Sixteenth Corps was in reserve.

At 8:00 A.M. May 13, 1864, Hooker's Twentieth Corps moved out on the Resaca road following Fifteenth Corps, and it halted at noon at the Isaac King house, about two and one-half miles from Resaca. Hooker then deployed Butterfield's division on the left of Fifteenth Corps on a narrow road that ran into the main road from Dalton to Rome, and he deployed Williams' division on the left of Butterfield, where it watched the roads from the direction of Dalton.

Geary's division was formed in column in rear of Butterfield, but at 7:00 P.M. it moved up into the front line to cover the road from Dalton to Rome. Candy's First Brigade was placed on the right of the road, and Ireland's Third Brigade and Buschbeck's Second Brigade were formed on the left of the road. Later, Butterfield's division was sent to the left to relieve a part of Johnson's First Division of Palmer's Fourteenth Corps, and then Harrow's reserve division of Logan's Fifteenth Corps was deployed to the left to fill the gap thus created.

About noon May 13, 1864, Palmer's Fourteenth Corps moved out from Snake Creek Gap and marched to the northeast, and it then advanced by country roads that ran roughly parallel to the main Resaca road until it came up to the hills on the west side of the Camp Creek Valley, where it took position on the left of Hooker's corps. Richard W. Johnson's First Division was on the right, with William P. Carlin's First Brigade on the right of the division, John H. King's Second Brigade was on the left, and Benjamin F. Scribner's Third Brigade was in reserve. Later in the evening, Butterfield's division came up to support the right of Palmer's corps, and William T. Ward's First Brigade relieved King's brigade of Johnson's division.

Baird's Third Division was delayed on the march, and it did not arrive on the hills and take position on the left of Johnson's division until dark. Ferdinand Van Derveer's Second Brigade was on the right of the division, and John B. Turchin's First Brigade was on the left. George P. Este's Third Brigade, which had been left to garrison Ringgold, Georgia, arrived on the extreme left of the army on the evening of May 13, 1864, and on the morning of May 14 it was moved up and formed on the left of the division.

Davis' Second Division was in reserve on the left of the corps during the night of May 13, 1864, and it connected with the pickets of Schofield's Twenty-Third Corps on its left.

When Palmer's corps was in line on the night of May 13, 1864, its left was nearly opposite the point where Camp Creek curved back to the northwest, and where, on the opposite side of the valley, that part of Johnston's line that was held by Hood's corps turned away from the creek and ran back toward the east.

On the morning of May 13, 1864, Schofield left Hovey's division of his Twenty-Third Corps at Snake Creek Gap with the trains and advanced with the divisions of Cox and Judah on the road toward Resaca. Upon arriving at the intersection of the Dalton and Rome road, Schofield marched northward on the latter road for two miles, then moved across country to come up on the left of Palmer's Fourteenth Corps.

Because of the difficult nature of the country through which it had to pass, progress was slow, but by noon the corps was in position, facing north toward Camp Creek. Cox's division was on the left, with the left of Reilly's First Brigade resting on the eastern slopes of Rocky Face Ridge, and with

Manson's Second Brigade on the right, where it extended Cox's line across the Dalton and Rome road. Later in the day, Manson's brigade connected with Judah's division on its right.

At dawn May 13, 1864, Howard, whose Fourth Corps was in position in front of Mill Creek Gap, found that the gap was open, and a short time later he had his men on the road marching toward Dalton. Howard arrived at Dalton at 9:00 A.M. and promptly moved out on the road toward Resaca, with Edward M. McCook's cavalry advancing along the base of Rocky Face Ridge on his right. Wheeler's cavalry delayed Howard's advance during the day, and when Confederate infantry at Tilton supported the cavalry, Howard was forced to halt for the night about eight miles from Dalton and about one mile from Schofield's left flank.

On the morning of May 14, 1863, the divisions of Howard's Fourth Corps continued their march southward toward Resaca, where they were to take position on the left of Schofield's Army of the Ohio and on the left of Sherman's army. In anticipation of the arrival of Fourth Corps, Sherman had ordered Palmer and Schofield to advance with four divisions of their corps and fully develop the enemy's positions on their fronts. The two corps, with Palmer's Fourteenth Corps on the right and Schofield's corps on the left, were formed about 9:00 A.M. to the west of Camp Creek, and they then advanced for about three-fourths to one mile, while swinging to the right, until they found the enemy in position on the hills east of Camp Creek. In Palmer's corps, Johnson's division was on the right, with Carlin's brigade on the right of the division, King's brigade on the left, and Scribner's brigade in reserve. Baird's division was on the left of Johnson, with Van Derveer's brigade on the right of the division and Turchin's division on the left. During the day, Este's Third Brigade, which had arrived from Ringgold, came up and was placed in reserve.

In Schofield's corps, Judah's division was on the right, with Milo S. Hascall's Second Brigade on the left. Cox's division was on the left, with Manson's brigade on the right and Reilly's brigade on the left. During the day Hovey came up from Snake Creek Gap with McQuiston's and Barter's brigades of his division, but they were not engaged.

Meantime, Newton's division of Howard's corps, followed by Wood's division, marched on the right of the corps toward the left of Schofield's line, while Stanley's division moved to the left on the main road from Tilton toward Resaca. When Howard arrived near Schofield's left, he found Schofield advancing with his command toward the front and right. He then placed Newton's division on the left of Twenty-Third Corps, and changed the direction of Wood's march by sending him down a road that ran south between the roads used by Stanley and Newton. As Fourth Corps advanced, the divisions converged and Howard's line was shortened, and by the time the corps arrived near the enemy's line, most of Newton's division had been squeezed out of line and had fallen back in reserve.

At about 11:30 A.M., Palmer's divisions had moved down into Camp Creek Valley and had moved forward to attack the enemy positions on the far side. They were soon stopped, however, by a destructive fire from the enemy works, and very few men had succeeded in getting beyond Camp Creek. The troops were then withdrawn with difficulty to the foot of the ridge on the west side of the valley, where they were re-formed. That evening Scribner's brigade was brought up into line to the left of King's brigade to relieve Turchin. Later that night, Daniel McCook's brigade of Davis' division relieved Carlin's brigade.

Schofield also attacked about 11:30 A.M., with Judah's division on the right and Cox's division on the left, and the axis of the attack was in a southeasterly direction along the line of present-day Highway I-75. When Judah's division came up on the left of Baird's division, its right passed through Turchin's line before it started, and Judah and Turchin, with their lines intermingled, advanced together.

Cox succeeded in carrying and holding the line of entrenchments on his front, but Judah's division, which attacked at the angle in the works where Hood's line turned back to the east, was unable to get sufficient men forward because of the difficult nature of the terrain and was driven back with severe losses. Cox's men were exposed to a heavy fire, and Newton's division was brought up to support them and to help in holding the ground that they had gained in the attack. The enemy later fell back and formed a new position several hundred yards to the rear.

Meantime, when Stanley's division of Howard's

corps arrived at the front, about two and a half miles north of Resaca, it halted until Wood's division came up on its right. Wood arrived at about 2:00 P.M., and together the two divisions advanced toward Hood's works until they were stopped by a heavy fire. Wood's division, which was then between Stanley's division on the left and Newton's division on the right, was formed with August Willich's First Brigade on the right, William B. Hazen's Second Brigade on the left, and Samuel Beatty's Third Brigade in reserve. When Wood advanced with Stanley, however, the division front contracted, and Willich's brigade was forced out of line, but it formed in rear and followed the movement forward. Hazen's brigade, then alone in the front line, captured the enemy's first line and pushed on for about 250 yards before it was stopped by a stronger second line. Wood's division remained in that position for the rest of that day and that night.

Stanley, to the left of Wood, was then ordered to hold the Dalton road, which ran northward past his left flank. At that time his left flank was completely exposed, and he sent Charles Cruft's First Brigade across the road to protect the left of the division. Walter C. Whitaker's Second Brigade was on the right of Cruft and to the right of the road, and William Grose's Third Brigade was on the right of Whitaker and to the left of Hazen's brigade of Wood's division.

At about the time that Howard's line was formed, Hood moved forward to strike the left of Stanley's division. Earlier, Hood had noted the weakness of the Federal left north of Resaca, and at about 4:00 P.M. he had advanced with the divisions of Alexander P. Stewart and Carter L. Stevenson to turn the essentially unprotected flank. The line from which Hood advanced was to the right of present-day U.S. 41, about four miles north of Resaca, and was along the line of present-day Chitwood Road.

When Cruft's brigade was threatened by Hood's preparations for the attack, Peter Simonson's 5th Battery, Indiana Light Artillery was brought up and placed to sweep the ground to the rear of Cruft. When Hood struck, Cruft's regiments were driven back in disorder, but that attack, and then a second attack, were repulsed by the fire of Simonson's battery.

Earlier, Sherman had become concerned about Howard's exposed left flank, and about 4:30 P.M.

he sent Williams' division of Hooker's corps, which at the time was massed in rear of Butterfield's division, and then Geary's division of the same corps, past the rear of Palmer's, Schofield's, and Howard's lines to the far left. With the departure of Hooker's two divisions, Palmer's line was extended to hold the front west of Camp Creek. Williams' division arrived on the left as Hood prepared to attack again, and Williams sent forward Robinson's brigade, which, together with Simonson's battery and some of the broken regiments of Cruft's brigade that had re-formed near the battery, finally brought Hood's attack to a halt. It was then dark, and the fighting on that part of the field ended for the day.

After the repulse of Hood, Howard's line was extended as a continuation of the line gained by Cox's troops earlier in the afternoon.

About mid-afternoon, Cox's men ran out of ammunition; Manson's brigade was relieved by Harker's Third Brigade of Newton's division, and at about 4:00 P.M. Reilly's brigade was relieved by Willich's brigade of Wood's division. As a result of thus pulling Cox's division out of the line, Willich's brigade was brought into line immediately on the right of Hazen's brigade of Wood's division, and Samuel Beatty's brigade of the division remained in reserve.

During the afternoon, Schofield's entire corps was pulled out of line, and the right of Newton's division then connected with the left of Palmer's corps.

Late in the afternoon of May 14, 1864, Francis T. Sherman's First Brigade of Newton's division relieved Harker, and the next day Wagner's Second Brigade of Newton's division relieved Sherman's brigade.

McPherson's Army of the Tennessee spent most of May 14, 1864 in making feints and demonstrations against Polk's line to prevent the transfer of enemy troops to the north where there was heavy fighting. That morning Harrow's division was withdrawn from the left of McPherson's line and placed in the rear of the divisions of Osterhaus and Morgan L. Smith as a reserve, but there still was no serious action until about 5:30 P.M. At that time, because of the heavy firing on the Federal left, Logan sent forward an assaulting column that crossed Camp Creek and captured and entrenched the hills on the far side of the creek. The attacking force consisted of Charles R. Woods' First Brigade of Osterhaus' division on the left and Giles A. Smith's First Brigade of Morgan L. Smith's division on the right. The enemy counterattacked at 7:30 P.M.; Joseph A. J. Lightburn's Second Brigade of Morgan L. Smith's division was sent forward across the creek, and the attack was repulsed. From the hills gained by McPherson's brigades, the railroad bridge and the wagon bridge over the Oostanaula River at Resaca came under Federal artillery fire, and that night the enemy laid a pontoon bridge over the river out of range upstream.

Early in the day, by Sherman's orders, McPherson sent Sweeny's division of Dodge's corps to Lay's Ferry on the Oostanaula, which was about 100 yards below the mouth of Snake Creek, with instructions to make a lodgment of the south bank and cover the laying of a pontoon bridge by the engineers. Two regiments of Patrick E. Burke's Second Brigade crossed the river that afternoon, but because of a false rumor of the approach of a strong enemy force, Burke's regiments recrossed to the right bank of the river, and Sweeny's command then withdrew to a less exposed position and camped that night about a mile and a half from the river.

When Johnston learned of Sweeny's crossing of the Oostanaula, he sent William H. T. Walker's division southward toward Calhoun that night, but when Walker reported that there were no Federal troops on the south bank of the river, he was recalled.

During the night of May 14, 1864 and the following morning, there were several changes in troop positions along Sherman's line that were made in preparation for an attack by Hooker's Twentieth Corps against the right of Johnston's entrenched line north of Resaca the next day. Butterfield's division of Hooker's corps, which had remained in its position on the hills west of Camp Creek during the night, moved off to the left on the morning of May 15 and rejoined the other divisions of the corps near the road from Dalton to Resaca. Also on the morning of May 15, Schofield's Twenty-Third Corps was sent to the extreme left of the army.

The departure of Hooker's corps and Schofield's corps from the center and left center of Sherman's line necessitated some changes in the dispositions of Palmer's Fourteenth Corps. During the night of May 14, 1864, Davis' division moved to the right

and relieved Butterfield's division of Hooker's corps, and the next morning Baird's division was withdrawn from the front line and sent to the extreme right of Palmer's corps to occupy the ground vacated by Williams' and Geary's divisions of Hooker's corps. When Baird arrived in his new position, he connected on his right with the left of Logan's Fifteenth Corps of the Army of the Tennessee. Johnson extended his division line to relieve Van Derveer's brigade, and Carlin's brigade, which had been relieved the evening before by Daniel McCook's brigade of Davis' division, was put in on the left to relieve Hovey's division of Twenty-Third Corps.

Hovey's division, which earlier had relieved Judah's division of Twenty-Third Corps, was sent to the left at 11:00 A.M. to join the other divisions of the corps on the extreme left. With Schofield's departure, Newton's division of Howard's corps connected on its right with the left of Palmer's corps. Wood's division remained on the left of Newton, and Stanley's division on the left of Wood.

When Cox arrived on the left of the line, he relieved Williams' division and a part of Geary's division and entrenched on a ridge that extended north and south for about a mile between the railroad and the Dalton road. In this position he covered the extreme left of the army, which was then facing south. Judah's and Hovey's divisions then came up in support. Cox's division remained on the ridge until 3:00 P.M., and it was then moved up and placed in reserve to the rest of the corps on ground gained by Twentieth Corps that afternoon.

Geary's division of Twentieth Corps, which had been ordered to the Federal left, along with Williams' division, during Hood's attack on the left of Stanley's division on the previous afternoon, did not arrive on the left of the army until after dark, and it was then formed in line on the left of Williams' division, covering the Dalton road. Ireland's brigade was placed on the extreme left of the line, and Candy's brigade on the right of Ireland. Buschbeck's brigade of Geary's division, which had been left behind for a time when the rest of the division moved, came up about 3:00 A.M. May 15, 1864 and was then placed on the left and rear of Ireland.

When Butterfield's division arrived on the left, it was placed on the right of Geary's division, with

John Coburn's Second Brigade on the right, William T. Ward's First Brigade in the center, and James Wood's Third Brigade on the left.

Hooker was ordered to attack at 11:00 A.M. Butterfield's attack was to be made by Ward's brigade, and it was to be supported on the right by Coburn's brigade and on the left by Wood's brigade. Geary's division was to attack on the left of Butterfield, with Ireland's brigade in front, Buschbeck's brigade in line behind Ireland, and Candy's brigade in rear of Buschbeck.

Williams' division was ordered to support Butterfield and Geary, and it marched out from its bivouac about noon, but while Williams was moving forward, Hooker learned that the enemy was threatening an attack on his left from the direction of the railroad, and he directed Williams to place his troops in position to cover and protect his left flank. Williams faced his division to the left and formed his division in line of battle facing east, with Joseph F. Knipe's First Brigade on the right, Thomas H. Ruger's Second Brigade in the center, and James S. Robinson's Third Brigade on the left. In this position, Williams' men repulsed all attempts by the enemy to advance from near the railroad.

Butterfield formed his line as directed about one mile from the enemy works about noon. Because of some confusion, James Wood's Third Brigade attacked first, and it was followed by Ward's First Brigade, but both attacks were beaten back. Ward's brigade advanced through the thick woods and succeeded in capturing a lunette and four guns, but under a heavy fire, the men fell back and were forced to leave the guns in the lunette. That night, however, Ward's men succeeded in bringing back the guns. This lunette, which was occupied by Max Van Den Corput's Georgia battery, was about 300 yards east of U.S. 41 and about the same distance north of Chitwood Road. Ward was wounded in the attack that afternoon, and Benjamin Harrison succeeded him in command of the brigade.

After making some progress, Twentieth Corps was in turn attacked. Hovey's division, which had arrived on the left at about 3:00 P.M., was placed in the advance of Twenty-Third Corps and sent forward to support Williams at 4:30 P.M., and it formed on the left of Twentieth Corps and aided in repelling the attack. That night Hovey entrenched on a prolongation of Hooker's line, and Cox's and Judah's divisions were brought up and placed on the left of Hovey's line when it was learned that it had reached the Connasauga River.

Johnston had planned to attack again on the Federal left on May 15, 1864, and had issued orders for Hood to attack, but when Johnston learned that Sweeny had again crossed the Oostanaula that morning, Hood's order was countermanded. Stewart, however, did not receive the countermanding order, and he attacked alone at 4:00 P.M.

Between 3:00 and 4:00 P.M., Geary was ordered to relieve Butterfield's leading brigade, and then all of Butterfield's division was withdrawn and placed in reserve. Thereafter, Geary, with Williams on his left, maintained a steady musketry fire during the evening and into the night.

Meantime, during May 15, 1864, the rest of Sherman's army skirmished and demonstrated all along the line to the right of Hooker's corps. Howard's corps, which was to the immediate right of Twentieth Corps, was directed to be ready to join in the attack if circumstances were favorable. Stanley was instructed to leave one brigade in reserve and to follow Hooker's movement with the other two brigades of his division. At the same time, Wood was ordered to follow up any advantage gained by Hooker, and Newton was ordered to demonstrate during Hooker's attack, and to follow any movement made by Wood.

At 1:00 P.M., as Hooker was making some progress on the left, all divisions of Fourth Corps were ordered to advance and demonstrate on their fronts. The brigades of Hazen and Willich of Wood's division advanced against the enemy works, but they were quickly driven back.

At 4:30 P.M. Stanley, Wood, and Newton were directed to push their skirmishers forward, which they did, and firing continued until dark.

Farther to the right, Palmer's Fourteenth Corps and McPherson's Army of the Tennessee demonstrated on their fronts to hold the attention of the enemy forces opposing them.

On the far right, Sweeny's division of Dodge's Sixteenth Corps made an important contribution by again crossing the Oostanaula River and threatening Johnston's line of retreat south of Resaca. At 8:00 A.M. Elliott W. Rice was ordered to cross the river with his First Brigade, which he did without difficulty. After the crossing was secured, a pontoon bridge was laid, and Patrick E. Burke's Second Brigade crossed the river and joined the First Brigade. Sweeny was not present on the south bank of the river at that time, and Rice assumed the direction of both brigades.

Also on May 15, 1864, Garrard was ordered to make a reconnaissance toward Rome, Georgia with his Second Cavalry Division, and he was operating in that direction during the fighting that day at Resaca.

Sherman was preparing to press the investment of Resaca May 16, 1864, but during the night Johnston withdrew from his defenses and, after destroying the bridges, marched southward toward Calhoun and Adairsville. Leonidas Polk's and William J. Hardee's corps crossed the river at the railroad bridge and the wagon road bridge and marched to Calhoun. Hood's corps crossed on the pontoon bridge that had been constructed the night before above Resaca, and it took the road to Adairsville by way of Spring Place.

FROM RESACA, GEORGIA TO THE ETOWAH RIVER

As Johnston marched southward toward Calhoun on the night of May 15, 1864, it was his intention to find a suitable place for a defensive line where he could block Sherman's pursuit and thus force him to make a frontal assault on a strongly fortified position. In this way he hoped to inflict such heavy losses on the Union army that Sherman would be forced to give up his attempt to reach Atlanta.

Before describing the movements of the armies as they marched southward from Resaca, it is necessary to describe briefly the country through which they were about to pass. From Resaca the Oostanaula River flows in a southwesterly direction to Rome, Georgia, where it is joined by the Etowah River, which flows in from the east. At Rome the two rivers join to form the Coosa River, which runs off to the west.

The distance from the Oostanaula River at Resaca due south to the Etowah River is about thirty miles, and the country between the two rivers was generally more open and less rugged than that through which Sherman's army had passed on its advance to the Oostanaula. After crossing the Oostanaula at Resaca, the Western and Atlantic Railroad ran south through Calhoun and Adairsville to Kingston, which is on the Etowah River, and there it turned to the east and ran north of the Etowah through Cassville Station, about two miles south of Cassville, then continued on to the southeast through Cartersville before crossing the Etowah River about four miles northwest of Allatoona. Beyond the river, the railroad ran through Allatoona Pass, a gap in a range of hills that extends along the south side of the river. A branch of the Western and Atlantic ran from Kingston westward to Rome.

Johnston had hoped to find a defensive position suitable for his purpose near Calhoun, and on May 16, 1864, he halted his army in the valley of Oothcaloga Creek a mile or so south of the town. At that point the roads on which Hood and Hardee were traveling were only about one mile apart. During the march that day, Cheatham's division of Hardee's corps and Wheeler's cavalry served as the rear guard.

Meantime, Sherman had entered Resaca on the morning of May 16, 1864 and had begun preparations for starting his troops across the river and southward in pursuit of Johnston. Sherman planned to move his army forward in four columns, covering a rather wide front, with George H. Thomas' Army of the Cumberland moving south in the center, along the railroad and wagon road toward Calhoun and Adairsville; John M. Schofield's Army of the Ohio (Twenty-Third Corps) was to cross the Connasauga River north of Resaca and then march south by roads on the left of Thomas; James B. McPherson's Army of the Tennessee was to cross the Oostanaula at Lay's Ferry and march due south between the Army of the Cumberland and the river; and Kenner Garrard's cavalry and Jefferson C. Davis' Second Division of John M. Palmer's Fourteenth Corps were to march down the west bank of the Oostanaula toward Rome.

Thomas' troops occupied Resaca at 9:00 A.M. May 16, 1864; they immediately began repairing the bridges, and they also constructed a pontoon bridge above the railroad bridge. When this work was completed, Oliver O. Howard's Fourth Corps began crossing the river, and by nightfall it was south of the river and was marching toward Calhoun, where it spent the night. Palmer's Fourteenth Corps, less Davis' division, camped at Resaca that night and did not follow Howard until the next morning.

Because of the congestion at the bridges at Resaca on May 16, 1864, Joseph Hooker was ordered to move with his Twentieth Corps on the road to Newtown, and to cross the Oostanaula at that point, which was about five miles southeast of Resaca and about three miles northeast of Calhoun. When Hooker began his march that day, John W. Geary's Second Division, the leading division, moved forward to within about one mile of Resaca, then turned off to the left toward Newtown. Geary waited for an hour at the crossing of the Newtown road, and then, upon learning that he could not cross on the ferry at Newtown, he marched eastward toward Fite's Ferry on the Connasauga River. He arrived there at 9:00 A.M. and crossed the river, and then, after George Stoneman's cavalry, proceeded on to McClure's Ferry on the Coosawattee River. Geary crossed the river there on two ferry boats and an improvised bridge, and the other divisions of the corps came up and crossed during the night. The corps camped on the morning of May 17 about one mile south of the river.

When Hooker changed his line of march from the Newtown crossing to Fite's Ferry, he moved onto the road on which Schofield was to advance, and this led to some difficulties. Schofield also crossed the Connasauga at Fite's Ferry, and upon reaching the Coosawattee he was forced to march farther upstream toward Field's Mill, but because of the delay caused by Hooker's column moving on the same road, Twenty-Third Corps got no closer than within about four miles of Field's Mill that day.

At daylight May 16, 1864, Sherman personally ordered Thomas W. Sweeny to cross the Oostanaula at Lay's Ferry with his Second Division of Grenville M. Dodge's Sixteenth Corps and to move out at once and secure the Rome and Calhoun crossroads, which was about three miles from Lay's Ferry. Dodge arrived at Lay's Ferry with the advance of James C. Veatch's Fourth Division at 9:00 A.M., and there he found that only Moses M. Bane's Third Brigade of Sweeny's division had been sent forward. Sweeny was not present at the time, and Dodge promptly sent forward the rest of Sweeny's division toward the crossroads. Dodge followed and

found Bane skirmishing with the enemy, and he then ordered Patrick E. Burke to take position on the right of Bane with his Second Brigade, and Elliott W. Rice with his First Brigade to move up on the left of Bane.

Burke moved forward with his brigade and seized the crossroads, and he was then directed to hold his ground until Veatch came up. After a time, Veatch arrived and was in the act of placing his division on the right of Sweeny's line when the enemy attacked. This was repulsed by Sweeny's brigades, and a short time later the enemy withdrew. That day, May 16, 1864, Burke was mortally wounded, and Robert N. Adams assumed temporary command of Second Brigade. Adams was replaced by August Mersey on May 23.

John A. Logan's Fifteenth Corps of the Army of the Tennessee arrived at the crossroads about dark, and Peter J. Osterhaus' First Division was sent up to support Sweeny. McPherson then ordered the two corps to bivouac for the night.

Also on May 16, 1864, Davis began his march toward Rome. He advanced fifteen miles along the west bank of the Oostanaula and camped at dark that night a few miles from the Armuchee Creek. During the night, Garrard's cavalry passed through Davis' camp en route to Lay's Ferry, and he reported that he had been unable to find a crossing of the Oostanaula north of Rome.

When Joseph E. Johnston arrived at Calhoun on May 16, 1864, he examined the ground and considered it not suitable for a good defensive position. When he learned from his engineers that there was a better position farther south at Adairsville, he withdrew from Calhoun on May 17 and fell back to a point a mile or two south of Adairsville.

When Howard found that Johnston had left his front, he started his corps in pursuit. With John Newton's Second Division leading, and David S. Stanley's First Division close behind, Howard left Calhoun at 5:30 A.M. May 17, 1864 and advanced on the wagon road toward Adairsville. Thomas J. Wood's Third Division moved forward along the railroad, on the right of the other two divisions, toward the same place. Howard was engaged in heavy skirmishing all day, and he was finally forced to halt at 4:00 P.M. because of determined resistance by the enemy.

Absalom Baird's Third Division of Palmer's

corps crossed the Oostanaula at 3:00 A.M. May 17, 1864 and followed closely behind Howard's corps. Richard W. Johnson's First Division also crossed the Oostanaula that morning and marched through Calhoun toward Adairsville. Johnson bivouacked at 11:30 that night on the left of Baird, and about two miles from Adairsville.

Hooker's corps also resumed its advance on the morning of May 17, 1864, to the east of the other corps of the Army of the Cumberland. Geary's division, which was the first division of the corps to cross the Coosawattee, rested south of the river that morning while the other divisions crossed. Then at 1:00 P.M. the entire corps marched south and then to the southwest through Red Bud to the direct road from Newtown to Adairsville. It moved south on the latter road until it came up in close support on the left of Howard's corps, and it then halted for the night about three or four miles from Calhoun.

On the far left, Schofield continued his advance, but it took all day to get his troops across the Coosawattee. Schofield was aware that Thomas was advancing on his right, and in order to be in position near Adairsville the next morning, he marched at 10:00 that night, reaching Big Spring, about three miles from Adairsville, at 2:00 A.M. May 18, 1864.

May 17, 1864, McPherson, with Dodge's and Logan's corps, marched to the southeast from the Rome and Calhoun crossroads, east of the Oostanaula River, to McGuire's Cross Roads. He spent the night there, about ten miles to the east and a little north of Rome.

After Garrard had left Davis on the Rome road and moved back to Lay's Ferry, Davis decided to continue on and attempt to capture Rome, and early on the morning of May 17, 1864, he resumed his march southward toward the town. About noon Davis encountered enemy pickets at Farmer's Bridge over Armuchee Creek, eight miles from Rome, and he halted his column for a rest. About 2:00 P.M. he resumed the advance, with John G. Mitchell's Second Brigade in the lead, and upon arriving near the enemy works that evening, Davis moved Daniel McCook's Third Brigade up to the front. At about that time the enemy attacked, but this was repulsed by Mitchell and McCook. Davis halted in front of the works that night. James D. Morgan's First Brigade was massed in reserve during the enemy attack.

Meantime, when Johnston arrived at Adairsville from Calhoun, he looked for a good position where he could oppose Sherman's advance, but again decided that he could not accept battle there. The valley across which he had hoped to form his defensive line was so wide that his army when deployed could not cover the entire width, and he could not secure his flanks on the adjoining hills. Therefore, on the night of May 17, 1864, he continued his retreat toward Cassville. For this movement Johnston divided his force into two columns at Adairsville, and he sent William J. Hardee's corps down the road to the south to Kingston and moved the corps of John B. Hood and Leonidas Polk down the direct road to the southeast toward Cassville. The distance from Adairsville to Kingston was about twenty-one miles, and the distance from Adairsville to Cassville was about the same. Hardee had been instructed that after reaching Kingston he was to turn to the left and follow the road east for about seven miles to Cassville and there rejoin the other two corps.

When Sherman learned that Johnston had left Adairsville during the night, he ordered Thomas to resume the pursuit on the morning of May 18, 1864. Sherman was aware that Johnston's army had taken two roads during his retreat, and accordingly Thomas sent Howard and Palmer along the direct road toward Kingston and ordered Hooker to take the road running out to the southeast from Adairsville toward Cassville. Howard and Palmer halted that night about three miles north of Kingston, and Hooker stopped near Cassville to await further orders.

Davis' division of Palmer's corps occupied Rome May 18, 1864. At that time Frank P. Blair was at Decatur, Alabama and moving toward the front with two divisions of his Seventeenth Corps. Blair was then ordered to move forward by way of Rome to join the army, and Davis was directed to hold the town until Blair arrived and relieved him.

On the left, Schofield continued his march southward from Big Spring during May 18, 1864. The road used by Schofield was roughly parallel to the road from Newtown to Adairsville and was about five miles to the east of it. It ran southward past Marsteller's Mill, near Sallacoa, which was almost due east of Adairsville, and then on to Cassville. Schofield halted near the McDow farm that night.

An important command change occurred in Twenty-Third Corps that day. Henry M. Judah was relieved from command of Second Division and was granted leave of absence because of physical disability. Milo S. Hascall was assigned command of the division.

On May 18, 1864 the Army of the Tennessee advanced from McGuire's Cross Roads to Adairsville, with Logan's Fifteenth Corps in the lead, and from there it marched to the southwest across Gravelly Plateau and halted that night at Woodland.

On the morning of May 18, 1864, Johnston's army continued its march until it had crossed Two Run Creek, a stream of considerable size that crossed the Adairsville road at a right angle about two miles north of Cassville and then ran on to the southwest before emptying into the Etowah River at Kingston. Just south of the creek, Johnston formed his corps in line of battle, and from this line he planned to attack the pursuing Federals the next morning. What followed is somewhat controversial, but the attack was not delivered, and Johnston then moved his command back to a curving ridge just south of Cassville, with a broad open valley on its front. The eastern end of this ridge is about one mile east of Cassville, and the southern end is near the railroad, a short distance west of Cassville Station. Johnston placed Hood's corps on the right, Polk's corps in the center, and half of Hardee's corps on the left. The remainder of Hardee's corps formed an extension of the line on the ridge to the southwest of the railroad.

On the morning of May 19, 1864, Howard marched with his Fourth Corps, with Stanley's division in front, and reached Kingston at 8:00 A.M. He halted there until 11:00 A.M., then turned to the east and marched along the railroad toward Cassville. About midway between Kingston and Cassville, he encountered an enemy force on the high ground beyond Two Run Creek, and when the Federal artillery had cleared the way, he pushed on, with constant skirmishing, to within two miles of Cassville. It was then dark, and Howard halted his command for the night.

Palmer followed Howard to Kingston, with Baird's division in front and Johnson's division following. Upon arrival at Kingston, Johnson was ordered to post his division on a range of hills south of the town, but during the afternoon he was ordered to move out to the east of town and take position on the right of Fourth Corps. Baird joined Fourth Corps about four miles from Kingston, and formed with the right of his division on the railroad and connecting with the right of Wood's division.

Johnson remained in Kingston until 2:30 P.M., and he was then directed by Palmer to move out rapidly to the south and seize Gillem's Bridge over the Etowah River. Upon arriving at the bridge, Johnson found some of Garrard's cavalry already there, but he disposed his troops so as to cover all approaches to the bridge, and he remained there until the morning of May 20, 1864. That morning Johnson moved out on the Cassville road about four miles and formed on the right of Baird.

Hooker, who had been advancing, with skirmishing, on the direct road from Adairsville to Cassville, connected with the left of Fourth Corps that evening near the crossing of Two Run Creek. Hooker continued on and occupied Cassville at about 10:00 that night.

On May 19, 1864, Schofield's Twenty-Third Corps advanced from McDow's, crossed the upper reaches of Two Run Creek, and about 4:00 P.M. formed in line of battle, with Twentieth Corps on his right, and then advanced to a point about one mile to the northeast of Cassville.

Also on May 19, 1864, the Army of the Tennessee advanced to the vicinity of Kingston and went into camp on the Etowah River. On May 22, Bane's Third Brigade of Sweeny's Second Division of Sixteenth Corps was sent to Rome to garrison the town, and it took no further part in the Atlanta Campaign.

When the Federal artillery arrived at Cassville, it opened fire on Hood's and Polk's forces on the ridge and continued firing until dark. That night Hood and Polk reported to Johnston that neither corps could hold its position the next day because parts of the line were enfiladed by the Federal artillery. Polk and Hood both urged the abandonment of the line at once, and finally Johnston yielded, and before daybreak May 20, 1864, the enemy had departed from the ridge. Johnston's army fell back from Cassville, through Cartersville, and then crossed the Etowah River near the railroad bridge.

On May 20, 1864, when Sherman discovered that Johnston had withdrawn from Cassville, he sent Schofield's corps, with Jacob D. Cox's division in the lead, in pursuit through Cartersville to the

Etowah bridge, where Cox drove the enemy rear guard across the river.

Sherman secured two good bridges across the Etowah near Kingston, and he then allowed the army to rest until May 23, 1864. During this period the railroad to the rear was repaired, and supplies were brought forward in preparation for further operations.

ADVANCE OF THE ARMY FROM THE ETOWAH RIVER TO DALLAS, GEORGIA

After crossing the Etowah River beyond Cartersville, Johnston occupied the hills in the vicinity of Allatoona Pass with a part of his army, and he held the rest in rear of the hills in readiness to move wherever it might be needed, depending on Sherman's next line of advance. Sherman was aware of the strength of Johnston's position beyond the Etowah, and, instead of attempting to force a passage of the river from the direction of Cartersville and continue his advance along the railroad, he decided to make a flanking movement to the right. His plan was to cross the Etowah to the west of Cartersville, where the hills on the south bank were farther from the river and the country was somewhat more open. Once across the river, the army was to march to Dallas, Georgia, a small village about twenty-five miles almost due south from Kingston and about fifteen miles west of Marietta. After reaching Dallas, it was Sherman's intention to shift his army to the left and return to the railroad at Acworth and Big Shanty, thus regaining his supply line with the North.

The entire region between the Etowah and Chattahoochee rivers was rugged and difficult to traverse. It was a desolate area in which there were only a few openings and very few farms, and the latter were generally small and unproductive. The rest of the country was covered with trees and dense underbrush, and in some places the pine forests were so thick as to be almost impenetrable. The country west of the railroad is generally very hilly, with occasional mountains rising to greater heights, but farther west the hills are lower and sandy and the country has a more rolling appearance. The march of an army across this region would have been difficult because of the many steep ridges and deep ravines that crossed the roads, and also because many of the streams that flowed through the area were bordered with quicksand and shallow marshy ponds.

There were two rather prominent, nearly parallel ridges that extended from northeast to southwest across this part of Georgia that were of significance during the battle. One of these was the so-called Allatoona Ridge, which ran along Allatoona Creek, and the other was a ridge that extended along Pumpkin Vine Creek.

For the advance toward Dallas, Sherman's army was to march in three columns, as it had since the beginning of the campaign, with Schofield's Army of the Ohio on the left, Thomas' Army of the Cumberland in the center, and McPherson's Army of the Tennessee on the right.

Sherman's general march orders were as follows:

Thomas was to march south from Kingston on parallel roads through Euharlee and Stilesboro toward Dallas. Davis' division of Palmer's corps, which was then at Rome, was to march on the direct road to Dallas by way of Van Wert.

McPherson was to march south to the right of Thomas to Van Wert, and from Van Wert to move eastward to Dallas. Blair's Seventeenth Corps had not yet joined the army, but it was on the road to Rome. Upon arrival there, Blair was under orders to relieve Davis, garrison the town, and then march with the rest of his corps to Kingston.

Schofield was to cross the Etowah above Euharlee and then march by roads to the east of Thomas to Burnt Hickory (also called Huntington), and from there to Dallas.

George Stoneman's cavalry of the Army of the Ohio was to cross the Etowah east of Schofield's crossing and cover the movements of the army on the left flank. Judson Kilpatrick's Third Cavalry Division, then commanded by William W. Lowe, was left on the north bank of the Etowah to cover the line of the river; Kenner Garrard's Second Cavalry Division was to cover the movement of the army on the right; and Edward M. McCook's First Cavalry Division was to cover the front of Thomas' advance.

McCook's cavalry division crossed the Etowah River at Island Ford on the morning of May 23, 1864, then marched by way of Euharlee toward Stilesboro. It was stopped short of the latter town by enemy cavalry that was supported by infantry, and it was unable to proceed farther that day.

On the morning of May 23, 1864, Howard's Fourth Corps of the Army of the Cumberland crossed the Etowah River at Gillem's Bridge, and Palmer's Fourteenth Corps crossed about a mile to the west at Island Ford. The roads from the two crossings joined north of Euharlee, and after reaching the junction, the two corps moved forward on the same road to Euharlee Creek, where they halted for the night near Barrett's Mill.

Hooker, whose corps was to have crossed the Etowah with the rest of the Army of the Cumberland, became impatient, and instead of awaiting his turn, he moved upstream and crossed at Milam's Bridge on two pontoon bridges that had been laid the night before for the passage of Schofield's troops that morning. After crossing the river, Hooker moved south, passing to the west of Stilesboro, and halted for the night near the other two corps of the Army of the Cumberland on Euharlee Creek.

On the morning of May 24, 1864, Geary's division of Hooker's corps was sent out on the Allatoona road to cross Raccoon Creek and cover the way leading up the creek until relieved by Schofield. The other two divisions of Hooker's corps marched toward Burnt Hickory. Howard's corps crossed Euharlee Creek at Barrett's Mill that morning and camped that night at Burnt Hickory, on the right of Hooker's Corps. Palmer's corps was unable to reach Burnt Hickory that day because the trains on the road delayed passage, and also because of the difficult nature of the ground. As a result, Palmer spent the night on Allatoona Ridge, about midway between Stilesboro and Burnt Hickory. McCook's cavalry division reached Burnt Hickory about 2:00 P.M. that day.

On the evening of May 22, 1864, Stoneman's cavalry marched to Milam's Bridge, where the roads from Cartersville and Cassville to Stilesboro crossed the Etowah River. The bridge there had been burned, but Stoneman crossed by a ford above the mouth of Raccoon Creek, then moved into position to cover the laying of two pontoon bridges the next morning for the crossing of Schofield's Army of the Ohio.

When Schofield arrived from Cartersville at Milam's Bridge on the morning of May 23, 1864, he was forced to wait all day while Hooker's corps crossed the river and moved on out of the way. Schofield camped north of the river that night. Early the next morning he crossed the river on the pontoon bridges, and Hascall's division marched eastward on the Allatoona road until it relieved Geary's division. Hascall then crossed Richland Creek and took position beyond the Rowland house to cover the road to Burnt Hickory and to protect the moving trains. Cox's division followed Hascall's division to Richland Creek, and it then moved up the creek and halted at Sligh's Mill, at the fork of the Acworth and Burnt Hickory roads. Hovey's division marched to the southeast on a road that ran to the east of and nearly parallel to the road from Euharlee that ran by way of Burnt Hickory to New Hope Church. Hovey camped that night beyond Burnt Hickory at the Widow Thompson (or Thomason) house. He remained there until May 29.

McPherson's Army of the Tennessee also began its advance on the far right early on the morning of May 23, 1864. Logan's Fifteenth Corps and Dodge's Sixteenth Corps crossed the Etowah at Wooley's Bridge, near the mouth of Conasene Creek, and marched southward on a road that ran to Swaintown, where it joined the road that ran from Rome through Van Wert and on to Dallas. After a march of eighteen miles, McPherson's corps camped on Euharlee Creek, and the next day it marched on for eight miles through Swaintown and Van Wert toward Dallas.

Davis' division of Palmer's corps left Rome on May 24, 1864 and marched to Euharlee Creek. Upon arriving there, it encountered McPherson's troops marching on the road, and Davis halted for the night.

DALLAS–NEW HOPE CHURCH–
PICKETT'S MILL LINE

On the morning of May 23, 1864, Johnston was aware that there was some activity of the Federal troops along the Etowah, but he made no new dispositions of his troops until that afternoon, when his cavalry under Joseph Wheeler and William H. Jackson reported that Sherman, with his entire army, was moving across the Etowah River south of Kingston and was advancing toward Dallas. Johnston then ordered Hardee to march with his corps by way of New Hope Church and take position on the road that ran from Stilesboro, through Dallas, and on to Atlanta. He also directed Polk to march with his corps in the same general direction, but to move a little farther to the south.

On May 24, 1864, Hardee and Polk reached the Stilesboro and Atlanta road a few miles south of Dallas, and Hood, who had been ordered to follow Hardee and Polk with his corps, was about four miles from New Hope Church, on the road from Allatoona. By May 25, Johnston's army was entrenched near and to the east of Dallas. Hood's corps was on the right, with its center at New Hope Church, which was about four miles northeast of Dallas at the intersection of the road from Dallas to Allatoona and the road from Van Wert to Marietta, and its line was in front of, and covering, the Dallas and Acworth road. Polk's corps was in the center, and was closed up on the left of Hood. Hardee's corps was on the left, with his left extending across the road from Dallas to Atlanta south of Dallas, and at a point where the road crossed a ridge that was the watershed between the Etowah and the Chattahoochee rivers.

Battle of New Hope Church, Georgia, May 25, 1864. During the day of May 25, 1864, Sherman's army continued to close in on Dallas. That morning Joseph Hooker's Twentieth Corps moved out from Burnt Hickory on three different roads toward Dallas. Alpheus S. Williams' First Division marched in the center on the direct road from Burnt Hickory to Dallas, which ran almost due south from Burnt Hickory; John W. Geary's Second Division took a road to the right that curved away to the southwest and then back to the southeast to rejoin the main Dallas road; and Daniel Butterfield's Third Division, preceded by Edward M. McCook's cavalry division, took a road that ran to the southeast from Burnt Hickory toward New Hope Church.

About 10:00 A.M., at about the same time that Hood was getting his corps in position at New Hope Church, Geary's division of Hooker's corps crossed Pumpkin Vine Creek at Owen's Mill, and it then marched to the southeast toward the church. At 11:00 A.M., after advancing about a mile and a half beyond the creek, Geary found enemy skirmishers about four and a half miles from Dallas.

Hooker and Thomas were with Geary at that time. They halted the division, and the men began to throw up temporary breastworks for cover. Charles Candy's First Brigade was deployed, and it was supported by John T. Lockman's Second Brigade (Buschbeck's brigade) and George A. Cobham's Third Brigade (Ireland's brigade). Also at that time, Hooker ordered the divisions of Williams and Butterfield of his corps to move up immediately and support Geary, and Thomas sent out orders for Howard and Palmer to bring up their corps and support Hooker. Sherman wanted to push Geary forward at once and attack, but he finally decided to wait until the other two divisions of Hooker's corps arrived. Williams and Butterfield were not far off, but because of the difficult nature of the country and the narrow, crowded roads on which they had to travel, it was not until mid-afternoon that Hooker's three divisions were assembled and ready to advance. Williams' division moved up to a position on the right of Geary, and Butterfield's division moved to the left and rear of Geary.

About 5:00 P.M., under threatening skies and with a thunderstorm developing, Hooker's corps began its advance toward New Hope Church. For the attack, each division was formed in a column of brigades. In Williams' division, which led the attack, James S. Robinson's Third Brigade was in front, Thomas H. Ruger's Second Brigade came next, and Joseph F. Knipe's First Brigade followed Ruger. As the division advanced and became engaged, Ruger's brigade passed lines with Robinson's brigade and relieved the latter. Later Robinson relieved Ruger when his men were nearly out of ammunition. Knipe's brigade relieved a part of Ruger's brigade and covered its right flank.

Butterfield's division, which followed Williams, was formed with James Wood's Third Brigade in front, John Coburn's Second Brigade behind Wood, and William T. Ward's First Brigade at the rear of the column.

Geary's division, which started forward with the corps, but which was in reserve, had Cobham's Third Brigade in front, Candy's First Brigade behind Cobham, and Lockman's Second Brigade in rear of Candy.

During the advance, before the attack was launched on the enemy works, Butterfield's brigades moved off to the flanks, leaving Geary's division supporting Williams. Also during the advance, Wood's brigade of Geary's division moved off to the left, and Coburn's brigade moved up into the front line. Ward's brigade, which was in the rear, was not engaged that evening.

As Williams' division advanced, it drove back the enemy skirmishers and then came up to a ridge fronting a valley. On the far side of the valley was another ridge that was nearly parallel to that occupied by Williams' division, and on that ridge Hood's corps was entrenched, with Thomas C. Hindman's division on the left, Alexander P. Stewart's division in the center, at New Hope Church, and Carter L. Stevenson's division on the right. To reach Hood's line, Williams' men had to pass through the thick woods that covered the slope of the ridge on which he was formed, then move across the valley, and finally climb through the dense woods on the far slope as they moved up the ridge. To add to the problems of the attackers as they advanced, most of the fighting that evening took place to the accompaniment of thunder and lightning and in a pouring rain that continued on through the night.

Several attempts were made to drive the enemy from their breastworks, and some of Hooker's men advanced as far as the works, but they could go no farther. During the attack, Coburn was ordered to relieve Robinson's brigade of Williams' division, but in the confusion of the fighting, Coburn was unable to find Robinson and instead relieved Knipe's brigade of Williams' division, whose ammunition was exhausted. Coburn's and Wood's brigades continued fighting until after dark, and they then fell back.

Butterfield's and Geary's divisions relieved Williams' division during the night, and Williams moved back into reserve.

The other corps of the Army of the Cumberland, in response to Thomas' orders, marched to the support of Hooker's corps. On the morning of May 25, 1864, Howard's Fourth Corps marched south on a road that ran to the right of the Burnt Hickory road to avoid the congestion on the latter road. Howard's march was to bring him to the road from Van Wert

to Dallas, and upon arriving there he was to turn to the left on that road and continue on into Dallas. About 2:00 P.M., however, when Howard was about six or seven miles from Dallas, he received an order from Thomas directing him to move across to the Burnt Hickory road by the first road that he found running in that direction, and then to move by that road to support Hooker.

The head of Howard's column reached Pumpkin Vine Creek just as Williams' division of Hooker's corps was passing on its way toward New Hope Church. A little after 5:00 P.M., the head of Newton's division arrived on the field and was placed in rear of Hooker, who was then preparing to attack Hood's line. The rest of Howard's corps came up later, but by that time it was dark, and the troops could not be formed in line. As they came up, they were halted to the right and to the left of the road to wait for morning. Howard's corps was not engaged at New Hope Church that evening.

* * * * * * * * * *

Troops of Palmer's Fourteenth Corps did not arrive at New Hope Church until Hooker's battle of May 25, 1864 had ended. Palmer, with Baird's and Johnson's divisions, had bivouacked on Raccoon Creek during the night of May 24, and the next day Johnson's men worked until midnight helping to get the wagons of Twentieth Corps over the hills and out of the way so that Palmer's corps could continue its march toward Burnt Hickory. Palmer finally resumed his march at 1:00 A.M. May 26, arriving at Burnt Hickory at daylight that morning. Palmer then left Baird's division at Burnt Hickory to protect the trains and the rear of the army, and with Johnson's division continued on for two miles on the road toward Dallas before halting at 7:00 A.M. to await orders from Thomas. Then at 11:30 A.M. May 26, Johnson resumed his march, crossed Pumpkin Vine Creek at Owen's Mill, and early in the afternoon moved up and formed in reserve in rear of Howard's Fourth Corps, about three miles east of Pumpkin Vine Creek.

While Thomas was concentrating his Army of the Cumberland in the vicinity of New Hope Church, Schofield's Right Wing and McPherson's Left Wing were also moving in the direction of Dallas. On May 25, 1864, after it had been learned that Hooker had found the enemy on his front, Schofield left Alvin P. Hovey's First Division to protect the trains; Milo S. Hascall's Second Division (commanded by Henry M. Judah until May 18) and Jacob D. Cox's Third Division took the road from Sligh's Mill at 5:00 P.M. and marched through Burnt Hickory toward Owen's Mill. Hooker's trains greatly impeded the progress of Schofield's column, as did the heavy rain that fell during the march, and when Schofield finally halted at midnight, his divisions were still west of Pumpkin Vine Creek. During the march that night, Schofield was injured by a fall from his horse, and Cox assumed temporary command of his own and Hascall's divisions during May 26 and May 27. Cox continued the march that night, and at 4:00 A.M. on May 26, he reported with his two divisions to Sherman on the Dallas road near New Hope Church. Hovey moved with his division to Burnt Hickory, and he remained there to hold the road until relieved by Nathaniel C. McLean's First Brigade of Hascall's Second Division May 30; he then rejoined the other two divisions of Twenty-Third Corps.

On May 25, 1864, Logan's Fifteenth Corps of the Army of the Tennessee, followed by Dodge's Sixteenth Corps, continued its march on the Van Wert and Dallas road until it reached Pumpkin Vine Creek west of Dallas, and both corps halted there for the night.

Davis, whose division of Fourteenth Corps had halted on Euharlee Creek the night before when he found McPherson's Army of the Tennessee on the road, continued his march toward Dallas May 25, following the Army of the Tennessee. When he arrived at Van Wert, however, he again came up with McPherson's columns, and at that point he decided to turn off to the east on a road that ran over the Allatoona Ridge between the Burnt Hickory and Dallas road on the left and the road on which McPherson was moving on the right. Moving without difficulty on this road, Davis camped that night within three miles of Dallas.

Sherman spent most of the day of May 26, 1864 getting his troops in line in front of the ridge occupied by Johnston's army, and probing ahead to determine the exact positions of the enemy's lines. On the right, McPherson's Army of the Tennessee and Davis' division of Palmer's corps advanced through Dallas and formed in line to the east and southeast of the town. The Army of the Tennessee, preceded by Garrard's cavalry division, advanced in two columns through Dallas, with Dodge's Sixteenth Corps on the left and Logan's Fifteenth Corps on the right. Dodge marched out of Dallas on the Powder Springs road for about two miles, and he then entrenched on a line that ran across the Powder Springs road and the Dallas and Marietta road. This line was in front of the range of hills occupied by Hardee's corps, and which at that point ran from north-northeast to south-southwest. Logan's corps was on the right of Dodge, with Peter J. Osterhaus' First Division on the left, connecting with Dodge; Morgan L. Smith's Second Division in the center, across the Dallas and Marietta road; and William Harrow's Fourth Division on the right, and extending across the Villa Rica road. Garrard's cavalry extended McPherson's line to the right.

That morning Davis' division also marched toward Dallas on the road from Burnt Hickory and, after crossing Pumpkin Vine Creek at Bishop's Bridge, two miles from Dallas, entered the town at about the same time as Dodge's corps. Davis then moved out to the east and formed on the Dallas and Marietta road, on the left of Dodge. When this line east of Dallas was formed, there was a gap of three or four miles between the left of Davis' line and the right of Hooker's corps.

On the morning of May 26, 1864, after the failure of Hooker's attempt to break through Hood's line at New Hope Church the evening before, Sherman began to extend his line farther to the left in an attempt to envelop the Confederate right flank. Hooker's corps remained in much the same positions that it had occupied the night before. Geary's division was on the front line, with his brigades in line from left to right as follows: Candy's brigade, Lockman's brigade, Coburn's brigade of Butterfield's division, and Cobham's brigade of Geary's division. The road to New Hope Church ran through Candy's brigade, which that morning was not connected on its left with any other Federal troops. Butterfield's other brigades were in the rear, and Williams' division was in reserve.

Howard's Fourth Corps, which had arrived in rear of Hooker during the late evening of May 25, 1864, was moved to the left and then advanced close to the enemy's lines. About noon May 26, William Grose's Third Brigade of Stanley's division came up and connected with Geary's division on his right. The rest of Stanley's division was held in reserve. Newton's division then came up on the left of Stanley, and Wood's division took position on the left of Newton.

When Cox reported to Sherman early on the morning of May 26, 1864 with the two divisions of Schofield's Army of the Ohio, he was directed to move to the left toward Brown's sawmill, which was on the Little Pumpkin Vine Creek (present-day Pickett's Mill Creek), and then move up in line on the left of Howard's corps. Passing through dense woods and undergrowth, Cox marched to the northeast and finally came up on the left of Howard. The two corps then advanced, while wheeling to the right, until the left of Cox's line crossed the Dallas and Allatoona road. The two corps then occupied a position along a line of hills that were separated from the right of Johnston's line by a narrow valley. In this position, the two corps covered the Dallas and Allatoona road.

There was almost constant fighting all along the line during May 26, 1864 as Sherman's army moved up into position and pressed closer to the enemy's lines, but there was no major engagement.

With his army then well in hand, and with Schofield's Army of the Ohio covering the road to Allatoona, Sherman decided to extend his line farther to the left and reestablish his connection with the Western and Atlantic Railroad south of the Etowah River. To begin this movement, Sherman ordered Thomas to withdraw Wood's division from the line held by the Army of the Cumberland, and to occupy the space thus formed by extending the fronts of the other divisions of the corps. Wood was then to march with his division and attempt to turn the right flank of Johnston's line. In this movement, Wood was to be supported by Johnson's division of Palmer's corps, which was already in reserve in rear of Howard, and also by McLean's First Brigade of Hascall's Second Division of Schofield's corps.

Battle of Pickett's Mill, Georgia, May 27, 1864. From reports sent in by McCook, whose cavalry division had been operating beyond the Federal left that day, Sherman believed that the only enemy force beyond the left of the Army of the Ohio was Wheeler's Confederate cavalry. On May 26, 1864, however, Johnston had learned of the Federal

movements that day, and had ordered a shift of his infantry to strengthen the right of his line. Johnston directed Hood to move Hindman's division from his (Hood's) left at New Hope Church to the right of the Confederate line, and he also ordered Patrick R. Cleburne's division of Hardee's corps, then near Dallas, to move to the right of Hindman. Cleburne arrived with his division in the vicinity of Pickett's Mill about 2:00 or 3:00 P.M. May 26, then placed Lucius E. Polk's brigade on the right of Hindman, and formed the brigades of Hiram B. Granbury, Daniel C. Govan, and Mark P. Lowrey en echelon to the right and rear of Polk. Cleburne then entrenched his position on the night of May 26 and the morning of May 27.

At 10:00 A.M. May 27, 1864, Wood's division was relieved on the Fourth Corps line, and it moved to the rear of Schofield's line. At 11:00 A.M. Howard, with Wood's division, and Johnson's division following in support, marched northward on the Allatoona road to a point beyond the lines of the Army of the Ohio, then marched to the east. After advancing about two miles, Wood turned south, but instead of being beyond the right of the enemy's line, his skirmishers soon found a strong line of entrenchments on their front. Howard withdrew Wood's division and marched on to the east for another mile, then again turned south. Johnson's division and McLean's brigade conformed to Wood's movements.

After an examination of the ground ahead, Howard concluded that his command overlapped the enemy's right, and he prepared for an attack. Wood formed his division in a column of brigades, with William B. Hazen's Second Brigade in front, William H. Gibson's First Brigade in rear of Hazen, and Frederick Knefler's Third Brigade in rear of Gibson.

Johnson's division was brought up en echelon to the left of Wood. John H. King's Second Brigade was formed in rear of Wood's line, and Benjamin F. Scribner's Third Brigade was on the left of King, but just before Johnson attacked, Scribner advanced to the left of Gibson's brigade and moved forward with Wood's column. William P. Carlin's First Brigade was in reserve during the evening and was not engaged.

McLean was directed to support Wood's attack on the right by moving forward out of the woods in which his brigade was concealed and onto the open ground of a wheatfield when the attack started. By this movement, he was to attract the attention of the enemy and draw his fire.

At 4:30 P.M. May 27, 1864, Wood gave the order to attack, and Hazen's brigade, formed in two lines, moved forward beyond what was believed to be the right flank of Johnston's line. Meantime, however, before the attack started, the Confederate positions in front of the Federal left had undergone some changes. Earlier, Cleburne had sent Govan's brigade out on a reconnaissance to observe any Federal movements, and Govan reported Howard's movement toward the Confederate right. Cleburne then ordered Govan to take position on the right of Lucius E. Polk's brigade, along the south side of the wheatfield, and he also placed Thomas J. Key, commanding Hotchkiss' artillery battalion, with Richard W. Goldthwaite's battery, to the right of Govan's new position, where it was able to enfilade a deep ravine that ran to the northeast from the right of Govan.

Then, about 4:00 P.M., a short time before Hazen began his advance, Cleburne ordered Granbury to move with his brigade and form on the right of Govan. Granbury took position along a ridge that extended to the northeast from a point near the right of Govan's brigade and formed on the southern crest of the ravine covered by Key's guns.

John H. Kelly's Confederate cavalry division, fighting dismounted, held the right of Johnston's line from the right of Granbury's brigade to Little Pumpkin Vine Creek (present-day Pickett's Mill Creek).

As Hazen's brigade advanced through dense woods and underbrush, the first line moved straight ahead toward the ravine, and its right soon came under a heavy fire from Granbury's brigade. The second line, however, instead of following the first, veered off to the left, coming on the left of the first line and moving to the southeast into a cornfield that was located just to the east of Granbury's line. This line of approach would have carried Hazen's left beyond the right of the enemy's line, but when Granbury realized his danger, he called on Govan for help.

For some reason, possibly because of a confusion of orders, McLean did not advance into the wheatfield in front of Govan as directed but remained concealed in the woods. Thus, when called

on for help, Govan was not threatened, and he promptly sent George F. Baucum with a part of his brigade to the right of Granbury to the cornfield to check the left of Hazen's advance. Baucum's line did not extend far enough to the right, however, and Cleburne then sent Lowrey's brigade to the right of Baucum in the cornfield.

Meantime, the right of Hazen's brigade had advanced across the ravine and moved up the slope on the far side almost to the enemy works, and the left of the line was moving into the cornfield. The left of Hazen's line was then assailed by the Confederates under Baucum and Lowrey; it was soon driven from the cornfield, and his men on the hillside beyond the ravine were under very heavy fire and were seriously threatened. Finally, with no support in sight, Hazen gave the order to withdraw.

For some reason, Gibson's brigade did not follow closely behind Hazen during the advance that afternoon, but it was coming up as Hazen's defeated brigade withdrew through the woods. Gibson was then ordered to attack, and he finally moved forward about 6:00 P.M. His brigade crossed the ravine and charged up the hill beyond; despite a heavy fire, some troops were able to get close to the enemy breastworks, but, like the men of Hazen's brigade earlier, they were forced to take cover on the slopes of the hill. Once again, the attacking line was not supported, and finally, being under attack on both flanks and in front, Gibson ordered his men to take cover in the ravine. From the ravine, Gibson's brigade, and some of Hazen's men who had not been able to retire when the brigade withdrew, kept up a steady fire on the enemy line.

By that time it was about 7:00 P.M. and almost dark, too late for another attack, but Wood ordered Frederick Knefler to lead his brigade forward and hold a line in front of the enemy entrenchments until the wounded on the hillside and in the ravine could be collected and brought back. This Knefler did without any serious trouble, and he remained there on the hill until the wounded were removed.

Earlier, before Hazen's attack was started, Kelly had formed his dismounted cavalry beyond the right of Cleburne's division so as to oppose a possible Federal advance along the Little Pumpkin Vine Creek. Kelly placed a part of his command on a hill to the southwest of Pickett's Mill, and the rest on a second hill across the creek.

A short time after Hazen began his advance, Scribner's brigade of Johnson's division moved forward on the left of Hazen, with the left of the brigade on Little Pumpkin Vine Creek. Scribner had not progressed very far when he was struck by a heavy fire from Kelly's dismounted troopers on the hill across the creek from the mill. Scribner then halted his brigade and sent three regiments across the creek, a short distance north of the mill, to drive the enemy from the hill. This was soon accomplished, but the loss of time seriously impaired any chances for the success of Howard's attack. Instead of being on the left of Hazen during his battle in the cornfield, Scribner was out of contact and was some distance away near Pickett's Mill.

Having finally cleared the east bank of Pumpkin Vine Creek, however, Scribner's brigade continued its advance along both sides of the creek until it finally arrived at the cornfield and joined on the left of Knefler. The enemy made several attempts to drive back Scribner's brigade, but all of these were repulsed. By that time it was dark, and the fighting had slackened, but both sides kept up a steady fire.

Around 10:00 or 11:00 P.M., Granbury launched an attack on Knefler's line, but it was quickly beaten back. A short time later, when the wounded had been removed, Knefler withdrew. This exposed the right of Scribner's line, but Scribner managed to hold the line vacated by Knefler with a regiment of skirmishers until midnight, and then he too withdrew.

Wood's defeated troops moved back about one-half mile to a line of breastworks that had been constructed by the brigades of Carlin and King of Johnson's division during the battle. This line had been prepared in order to enable Howard to hold the ground gained in his move to the left that day if his attack on the Confederate right was unsuccessful. Carlin's brigade was on the left of this line, and King's brigade was on the right. The depleted brigades of Wood's division were placed on the right of King, and Scribner's brigade was placed in reserve.

Hardee's Demonstration at Dallas, Georgia, May 27, 1864–June 1, 1864. On May 27, 1864, the day of the Battle of Pickett's Mill, McPherson's Army of the Tennessee was still on the line east of Dallas, but it was under orders from Sherman to move to the left as a part of the general movement of the army. Johnston was aware that a part of Sherman's army was extending toward the Confederate right, and that day he ordered Hardee to demonstrate against McPherson's line to determine whether it was still held in strength. At 5:00 that morning, Osterhaus became concerned about the left of his line; he ordered Hugo Wangelin to deploy his Third Brigade on the left of James A. Williamson's Second Brigade, but before Wangelin came up, the enemy struck the left of Williamson's line and forced him to fall back. Wangelin then attacked and recovered the lost ground.

That afternoon the enemy also made an attack on Harrow's division, which was on the left of McPherson's line, but this was easily repulsed.

On the afternoon of May 28, 1864, McPherson was preparing to withdraw from his position east of Dallas and move to the left when Johnston ordered Hardee to make a forced reconnaissance on his front. Hardee selected William B. Bate's division to make this attack, and Bate prepared to advance with his three brigades in separate columns against Harrow's division, which was on the right of Logan's line. As a part of this attack, Frank C. Armstrong's dismounted cavalry brigade was to move forward and attempt to force its way through the Federal line between the right of Harrow's division and the left of Garrard's cavalry.

The Villa Rica road, which ran south out of Dallas, passed through Harrow's line, and where it crossed the road, the line turned at a right angle from north-south to east-west. Reuben Williams' First Brigade was to the right of the road, facing south; Charles C. Walcutt's Second Brigade was on the left of the road and the left of Williams' brigade, facing east; and John M. Oliver's Third Brigade was on the left of Walcutt, also facing east. Morgan L. Smith's division was on the left of Harrow, and Osterhaus' division was on the left of Smith.

As Armstrong advanced, he came under such a heavy fire that Bate's brigade commanders became confused about the signal to start the attack. From the intensity of the fire, each believed that the others were engaged, and as a result they all ordered an attack on Logan's line. About 3:30 P.M., Bate advanced against Harrow's line, with his left brigade moving along the Villa Rica road, and struck the entire front of Walcutt's brigade, the right of

Oliver's brigade, and the left of Williams' brigade. The attack was pushed with great determination, but it was finally halted only a short distance in front of Harrow's breastworks. Attempts were also made later against the divisions of Morgan L. Smith and Osterhaus, but they were easily repulsed.

During the attack on the right of Logan's line that afternoon, Williamson's Second Brigade of Osterhaus' division, which was in reserve, was ordered to the right to support Harrow. Osterhaus placed Charles R. Woods in command of his own First Brigade and Wangelin's Third Brigade, and he then went with Williamson's brigade to the right, arriving in time to aid in repelling Bate's and Armstrong's attack. Williamson's brigade was placed on the right of Williams' brigade of Harrow's division, refused at a right angle to Williams' line, facing west. As soon as its position was secured, Osterhaus returned to his front, and there he found Woods and Wangelin engaged in repelling an attack. All attacks that day had been beaten back with serious enemy losses. As a result of Hardee's attacks, however, the withdrawal of the Army of the Tennessee from in front of Dallas was postponed until June 1, 1864.

On May 28, 1864, Sherman's army was in position on the Dallas–New Hope Church–Pickett's Mill line, from right to left, as follows; McPherson's Army of the Tennessee, near Dallas; Davis' division of Palmer's Fourteenth Corps; Hooker's Twentieth Corps, Army of the Cumberland; Howard's Fourth Corps (less Wood's division), Army of the Cumberland; Schofield's Twenty-Third Corps, Army of the Ohio; Wood's division of Fourth Corps; and Johnson's division of Fourteenth Corps was on the left near Pickett's Mill. Stoneman's cavalry was on a hill to the left of Johnson's division, and McCook's cavalry division was on the road that ran east from Burnt Hickory Church by way of Golgotha to Marietta. McCook's cavalry was guarding the left of the army.

Baird's division of Fourteenth Corps moved with the trains to Burnt Hickory and remained there until May 30, 1864. Baird then left John B. Turchin's First Brigade of his division in charge of the trains at Burnt Hickory and moved with his other two brigades to the front; on June 2, he took position in rear of Johnson's division.

On June 1, 1864, the movement of the army to the left, which had been interrupted by Hardee's attacks on the Army of the Tennessee at Dallas, was resumed. That morning Logan's Fifteenth Corps moved back, then marched to the left and relieved Hooker's corps near New Hope Church. Dodge's Sixteenth Corps moved to the vicinity of Owen's Mill on Pumpkin Vine Creek, where it covered the roads from Van Wert, Burnt Hickory, and Kingston. Davis' division of Palmer's corps also moved to the left and relieved Hovey's division of Schofield's corps. After a time, Dodge's corps moved up and took position on the left of Howard's corps, and when the movement was completed, the Army of the Tennessee and Davis' division occupied the entire line previously held by Hooker and Schofield.

When Schofield's corps was relieved, it moved to the extreme left on the Burnt Hickory and Dallas road to the vicinity of Burnt Hickory Church, which was located about two and a half miles north and a little east of Owen's Mill and near the head of Allatoona Creek at the crossing of the Burnt Hickory and Marietta road. Hooker's corps also moved to the left in support of Schofield, and it occupied the hills on the extreme left that had earlier been held by Stoneman. Stoneman had been sent to Allatoona June 1, 1864, and McCook's cavalry had moved to the left of Schofield on the Dallas and Acworth road.

When he arrived near Burnt Hickory Church, Schofield formed his corps in line, with Hovey's division on the right, Cox's division in the center, and Hascall's division on the left. Then, on June 2, 1864, he advanced with his left on the road to Marietta for a mile and a half and drove the enemy back across Allatoona Creek near the Dallas and Acworth road. Cox's division, which was somewhat in advance, crossed the creek and entrenched on a line facing to the southeast. The other two divisions of the corps then came up, and Hovey's division entrenched on the right of Cox, and Hascall's division on the left of Cox. Hooker's corps also advanced in support of Twenty-Third Corps, and Butterfield's division was placed en echelon on the left of Schofield.

While Schofield and Hooker were advancing on the left of Sherman's line, Thomas sent forward Baird's and Johnson's divisions of Palmer's corps, and they pushed forward to a point beyond Pickett's Mill.

By that evening, Sherman's right had moved from the vicinity of Dallas to New Hope Church, and his left had been extended for a distance of about three miles. The entire line was strongly entrenched.

MOVEMENT OF THE ARMY TO THE WESTERN AND ATLANTIC RAILROAD

Meantime, Johnston had been shifting his line to his right to conform to Sherman's movements. By the evening of June 2, 1864, that part of the Confederate line beyond Pickett's Mill, toward which Sherman was now advancing, ran due east from the mill for about a mile, then turned and ran northward to the point reached by Schofield in his advance that day. Federal artillery was then able to enfilade both legs of the enemy's line. The situation worsened for Johnston when on June 3 Hooker moved Geary's and Butterfield's divisions eastward along the road toward Acworth, with McCook's cavalry operating still farther to the east. Stoneman and McCook reached Acworth that day.

That same day, Schofield transferred Hovey's division from the right of his line to the left, and with Hooker moving still farther out on that flank, Johnston realized that he could not hold the New Hope Church Pickett's Mill line much longer. Therefore, on June 3, he pulled back the north-south part of his line that was in front of Schofield to a new position that was an extension of the Pickett's Mill line that ran eastward from the mill.

Then, on the night of June 4, 1864, Johnston evacuated the entire line and retreated to a new position that ran from Lost Mountain eastward to Brush Mountain, about two or three miles north of Marietta. Pine Mountain was a high and isolated hill that rose in front of the center of Johnston's new position, and when occupied by Confederate troops it formed a salient in the new line. The defenses of Pine Mountain were somewhat exposed on the west side; to protect that flank, an advanced line was constructed to the southwest of the mountain, and this line crossed the Burnt Hickory and Marietta road about a mile north of Gilgal Church (also

known locally as Hard Shell Church). The Sandtown road crossed the Burnt Hickory and Marietta road at the church and continued on to the south to Sandtown on the Chattahoochee River.

After Johnston had retired to his new line, Sherman moved his army toward the Western and Atlantic Railroad at Allatoona and Acworth without further opposition. During this movement, Schofield held his position near the intersection of the Dallas and Acworth and the Burnt Hickory and Marietta roads to cover the passage of the hospitals and trains, and Hooker's corps, followed by the rest of the Army of the Cumberland, moved toward Acworth. On June 6, 1864, Hooker moved to the vicinity of the McLean house, which was on the Sandtown road near its intersection with the Burnt Hickory and Marietta road, about three miles south of Acworth. Palmer's corps took position on the left of Hooker, with its left resting on Proctor's Creek. Howard's corps was in the vicinity of the Durham house.

On June 5, 1864, after Johnston's withdrawal, the corps of Logan and Dodge left the vicinity of New Hope Church and moved by roads in rear of the Federal lines to Burnt Hickory Church and from there to Acworth, where Logan arrived on the morning of June 6, and Dodge arrived that evening. Logan moved out on the road to Marietta about two miles and took position to cover the road. Harrow's division was on the right, Morgan L. Smith's division in the center, and Osterhaus' division on the left. Dodge bivouacked that evening southwest of Acworth.

All further movements were then halted until June 10, 1864 while the Etowah railroad bridge was rebuilt and supplies were brought forward to prepare the army for further operations. The main supply base of the army was moved forward from Kingston, and new depots for the armies were established as follows: for the Army of the Tennessee at Big Shanty, the Army of the Cumberland at Acworth, and the Army of the Ohio at Allatoona.

On June 8, 1864, Sherman's army was reinforced when Frank P. Blair's Seventeenth Corps arrived at Acworth from Kingston and joined McPherson's Army of the Tennessee. It then took position on the left of McPherson's line, on the extreme left of Sherman's army.

On June 9, 1864, there was a significant change

in the organization of Schofield's Twenty-Third Corps. Hovey, who had tendered his resignation, was granted a leave of absence for thirty days, and on June 9, Richard F. Barter's First Brigade of Hovey's First Division was temporarily attached to Cox's Third Division, and John C. McQuiston's Second Brigade, First Division was temporarily assigned to Hascall's Second Division. Both brigades were to retain their original designations in the new organization, but Barter's brigade was sometimes called Fourth Brigade, Third Division. Later, on August 11, First Division was officially discontinued, and the two brigades of the division were assigned to Second Division and Third Division.

When Johnston evacuated the line of New Hope Church and Pickett's Mill, it was the general belief that he would retire to a new position beyond the Chattahoochee River, but when Sherman learned that the enemy had halted on a line in front of Marietta, he realized that there would be more hard fighting before he reached the Chattahoochee.

In preparation for a further advance, Sherman ordered Garrard to report to McPherson, and to cover with his cavalry the movement of the Army of the Tennessee, which was to advance on the left of the army. He also sent Stoneman's cavalry to cover the right of the army, and assigned to McCook's cavalry the task of picketing the rear of the army and of protecting the bridges and fords of the Etowah River.

ADVANCE OF THE ARMY FROM ACWORTH TOWARD MARIETTA, GEORGIA

On June 10, 1864, when all preparations had been completed, Sherman's army resumed its advance from the vicinity of Acworth toward Marietta. At that time, Johnston's army was in position on a line of hills that ran westward from Brush Mountain and Kennesaw Mountain to Lost Mountain, with an advanced position on Pine Mountain, which was near the center of the line. William J. Hardee's corps was on the Confederate left, with its left at Lost Mountain and its right at Pine Mountain, where William B. Bate's division held the line. Leonidas

Polk's corps (officially Army of Mississippi) extended the line to the east from the right of Pine Mountain, across the Western and Atlantic Railroad, to the Acworth and Marietta wagon road. A part of Polk's front was covered by Noonday Creek. John B. Hood's corps was on the right of Johnston's line and was massed behind Noonday Creek, along the base of Brush Mountain. Joseph Wheeler's cavalry covered the Confederate right, and Jackson's cavalry the left.

The country in front of the lines held by Hardee and Polk was particularly difficult for troop movements because it was very hilly, in places mountainous, and it was generally covered by thick forests and dense undergrowth. It was even more difficult at the time of Sherman's advance because the incessant rains had rendered the roads and fields almost impassable, and the streams that traversed the region, which were normally small and insignificant, were then in flood and difficult to cross.

On June 10, 1864, James B. McPherson's Army of the Tennessee marched six miles from Acworth to Big Shanty, on the road toward Marietta. John A. Logan's Fifteenth Corps moved in advance, with Frank P. Blair's Seventeenth Corps on the left and Grenville M. Dodge's Sixteenth Corps following as rear guard. About one mile south of Big Shanty, Logan found some enemy troops blocking his way, but these were soon dislodged by artillery fire, and he then continued on until he found the enemy holding an entrenched line about two and a half miles beyond Big Shanty. He then halted for the night.

On June 11, 1864, Blair advanced to within range of Brush Mountain and entrenched, and Logan remained in the position that he had gained the day before. James C. Veatch's Fourth Division of Dodge's corps took position near Big Shanty, with its right resting on the railroad near Moon's Siding and its left connecting with Fifteenth Corps. Veatch held this position until June 18, and during this time he was almost constantly engaged in heavy skirmishing.

On June 10, 1864, George H. Thomas advanced with his Army of the Cumberland from his camps south of Acworth. John M. Palmer marched southward with his Fourteenth Corps toward the Burnt Hickory and Marietta road, and Oliver O. Howard followed with his Fourth Corps and took position on the right of Palmer near Pine Mountain. Joseph Hooker was to have followed with his Twentieth Corps on the same road, but because the road was occupied during the day, he was unable to move.

On June 11, 1864, Palmer and Howard moved to the left and advanced a short distance in front of their positions of the previous night. Palmer's left was then near the Western and Atlantic Railroad, where it connected with the right of the Army of the Tennessee. Alpheus S. Williams' First Division of Hooker's corps left its camps and moved out about a mile and a half to the left, connecting on its left with David S. Stanley's First Division of Howard's corps. Daniel Butterfield's Third Division of Hooker's corps, which had earlier moved forward on the Acworth and Sandtown road to Mount Olivet Church, near Kemp's sawmill, did not march with the army at first, but remained near the church until June 15.

On the right of Sherman's line, John M. Schofield's Twenty-Third Corps, then reduced to two divisions, also advanced June 10, 1864 and moved toward the left of Johnston's line near Lost Mountain. Milo S. Hascall, commanding Second Division, left John C. McQuiston's Second Brigade, First Division, which was temporarily attached to Second Division, at Allatoona Church to guard the trains, and with the rest of his division advanced on the Burnt Hickory and Marietta road toward the Sandtown road. He halted at the Davis house that day. Jacob D. Cox's Third Division marched past the right of Hooker's corps on the Acworth and Sandtown road and took position on the left of Hascall, about one-half mile north of Gilgal Church (also called locally Hard Shell Church). During the next few days, both divisions closed in slowly on the enemy's lines.

Because of steady rain during June 12 and 13, 1864, there were no major troop movements of the army, but during the period June 13–14, John W. Geary's Second Division of Twentieth Corps moved up and formed on the left of Williams' division, relieving a part of Fourth Corps that had been in position there.

On June 14, 1864, the rain slackened somewhat, and Palmer's corps and the left of Howard's corps advanced about three-fourths of a mile toward the enemy's works. Howard's right at the time was up close toward Pine Mountain.

An event of serious importance to the Confederacy occurred on June 14, 1864, when Leonidas Polk was killed by an artillery shell on the summit of Pine Mountain, where he and some other officers were studying the dispositions of the Federal troops near the base of the mountain. William W. Loring then assumed temporary command of Polk's corps.

During the night of June 14–15, 1864, the enemy abandoned the advanced position at Pine Mountain, which was then threatened with envelopment, and withdrew to the main line of works that extended from Lost Mountain to Kennesaw Mountain. Bate's division, which had held Pine Mountain, was placed in reserve.

After the evacuation of Pine Mountain, Howard's and Hooker's corps of the Army of the Cumberland and Schofield's corps of the Army of the Ohio moved forward toward the enemy's main line. The right of Palmer's corps also moved forward, keeping its connection with the left of Howard's corps. When the enemy withdrew from Pine Mountain, they still retained possession of the trenches that connected the main line with the mountain, and they also continued to hold some detached works that covered this line.

Early on the morning of June 15, 1864, Howard occupied Pine Mountain; Geary's division and Williams' division of Hooker's corps attacked and, after a sharp struggle, captured the connecting line and its outworks. Geary's division then moved on and at 4:00 P.M. attacked the enemy's main line, and Williams' division came up in support. The fighting continued until dark, but without significant result, except that the Federal lines approached closer to the enemy's works.

At daylight June 15, 1864, Butterfield's division broke camp at Mount Olivet Church on the Sandtown road and moved down the road toward Gilgal Church, which was about two and a half miles distant. Butterfield drove in the enemy pickets and moved up to the front of the entrenched line, which at that point was held by Patrick R. Cleburne's division of Hardee's corps. Cleburne resisted all efforts of Butterfield to advance farther, and the fighting ended there for the day.

Schofield's Twenty-Third Corps joined the general advance June 15, 1864. Hascall moved forward with his right extending beyond the left flank of the enemy's entrenched skirmish line, and when Cox also advanced, the enemy skirmishers fell back to their main line. As Schofield advanced, Cox's division was forced out of the line by Butterfield's division, which, as noted above, was moving down the Sandtown road toward Gilgal Church on the left of Cox. Cox then moved back into reserve.

Early on the morning of June 16, 1864, Butterfield's division moved up on the right of Geary, but there was little change in the positions of the rest of the Army of the Cumberland that day.

On June 16, 1864, Hascall advanced his division up close to the enemy's works between Gilgal Church and Lost Mountain; in this movement Hascall pulled away from the right of Hooker, and Cox's division was moved up to close this gap. About sunset, the artillery of Twentieth Corps and Twenty-Third Corps opened on the enemy lines at Gilgal Church and continued firing until dark.

At 10:00 on the night of June 16, 1864, Hardee began to withdraw his four divisions from the line between Lost Mountain and the rear of Pine Mountain, and during the night he fell back to a new position on the east side of Mud Creek, facing west. The corps of Loring and Hood remained on their lines of June 15, generally facing to the northwest. Johnston's new line of breastworks behind Mud Creek left the original line of works at the right of Hardee's former position near Pine Mountain and then bent back and followed the high ground east of Mud Creek to a point beyond the road from Lost Mountain to Marietta. In retiring to this line, Hardee pivoted on his right and swung back his left for a distance of about three miles.

Heavy rains that fell during June 17 and June 18, 1864 again made all movements of the army difficult, but nevertheless Thomas pushed his army forward in pursuit of Hardee's retiring columns. Early on the morning of June 17, Howard's and Hooker's corps crossed the abandoned trenches and advanced, while swinging to the southeast, until they reached Mud Creek, where they found Hardee in his new position on a line of hills on the far side of the creek. The right of Palmer's corps conformed to the movements of Howard's corps on its right, but Palmer's left remained on the railroad in front of Kennesaw Mountain, where it connected with the right of the Army of the Tennessee.

When Howard arrived in front of Mud Creek, he formed his divisions with Thomas J. Wood's Third Division on the right, John Newton's Second Division on the left, and David S. Stanley's First Division in reserve.

Hooker's corps advanced on the right of Howard's corps and halted in line in front of Mud Creek. Williams' division was on the left, with its left on the Marietta road, connecting with Howard's line. Geary's division marched to the southeast on the road from Gilgal Church to the Sandtown road, and then it continued on that road to the Darby house, which was about five miles due west of Marietta. From there it moved to the left and formed in line between the Darby house and Mud Creek. During the afternoon, Butterfield's division came up and formed on the right of Geary.

Schofield's Twenty-Third Corps also joined in the pursuit of Hardee's corps, with Cox's division marching on the Sandtown road and Hascall's division advancing on his right. Cox pushed back the enemy cavalry, with constant skirmishing, until he reached the intersection of the Sandtown road and the road from Lost Mountain Post Office to Acworth, at the Darby house. There Schofield found the enemy in a strong position behind Mud Creek, and he ordered Cox to advance on the road toward Marietta and attempt to find the left flank of the enemy's line. Cox soon reached the valley of Mud Creek, where he connected with the right of Hooker's corps. Hascall's division, which was following Cox, came up and was placed in reserve on the right of Cox's division. Schofield then prepared to cross the creek beyond the enemy's left flank, but the heavy rains had caused the water to rise to such a height that it was impossible to cross. It was thus necessary to suspend operations until June 19, 1864.

On June 17, 1864, Nathaniel C. McLean was relieved from command of Third Brigade of Cox's division, at his own request, and Robert K. Byrd, as the senior officer present, assumed command of the brigade.

Early on June 18, 1864, despite a heavy rain, Howard ordered Newton and Wood to advance strong skirmish lines against Hardee's position. Some of Newton's men succeeded in gaining a part of his advanced works, and then Newton moved up his entire division in support. Absalom Baird's Third Division of Palmer's division then came up on the left of Newton, and Wood's division moved up and occupied a ridge on the right of Newton.

Because of the weather, there was little other activity on Sherman's front that day.

On the night of June 18, 1864, Johnston withdrew his entire line to a position closer to Marietta. Kennesaw Mountain was the key to this new line, which ran from Brush Mountain on the north, along the summit of Kennesaw Mountain, and then along the hills to the south. Hood's corps was on the Confederate right, on the high ground east of the railroad and above Noonday Creek, which flowed northward past the western side of Brush Mountain toward the Etowah River.

Loring's corps (formerly Polk's) occupied Kennesaw Mountain, with Winfield S. Featherston's division on the right and extending down the southeastern slope of the mountain to the railroad; Edward C. Walthall's division was on the mountain to the left of Featherston; and Samuel G. French's division held a part of the crest to the left of Walthall, and it then ran down the southwestern slope of the mountain.

Hardee's corps was on the left of Johnston's line, with its divisions extending, in order to the left, from the left of Loring's corps, as follows: William H. T. Walker's, William B. Bate's, Patrick R. Cleburne's, and Benjamin F. Cheatham's. From Kennesaw Mountain southward, the front of Hardee's corps was covered by Noyes' Creek, which because of the heavy rains was a stream of considerable size. The road from Lost Mountain to Marietta passed through the right of Hardee's line.

Early on the morning of June 19, 1864, when Thomas learned that the enemy had withdrawn from the Mud Creek line, he started the Army of the Cumberland forward in pursuit. About 7:00 A.M. Howard's corps, advancing on the Burnt Hickory and Marietta road, came up in front of Hardee's main line, which was on the ridges west of Marietta. Stanley's division was in the lead, and it was followed by the other two divisions of the corps. Stanley encountered the enemy skirmishers near the Wallace house, on the Burnt Hickory and Marietta road, about three-fourths of a mile from Noyes' Creek, and drove them back across the creek. Stanley pushed his division up close to the enemy works and formed his line, with Isaac M. Kirby's First Brigade on the right, Walter C. Whitaker's Second Brigade in the center, and William Grose's Third Brigade on the left. Newton's and Wood's divisions

then came up, and Newton's division took position on the left of Stanley.

Palmer, who was on the left of Howard, swung his right forward and worked his way up close to the base of Kennesaw Mountain.

Hooker's corps, which had been moving forward on the right of Howard, crossed Mud Creek early on the morning of June 19, 1864 and moved up on the right of Howard. Williams' division crossed Mud Creek and Noyes' Creek and moved up close to the enemy's new works, some two or three miles beyond. Geary's division advanced on the Dallas and Marietta road, crossed Mud Creek, and came up to Noyes' Creek, where it was delayed for a time while the bridge was repaired. Geary then crossed the creek, advanced about a mile, and entrenched on a line in front of the enemy's works, connecting on his left with Williams' division. Toward evening, Butterfield's division arrived and formed on the right of Geary.

When Johnston's line was pulled back on the night of June 18, 1864, the troops in front of the Army of the Tennessee retired to a new position about two miles in rear of their former line. On June 19, Dodge advanced his Sixteenth Corps on the Burnt Hickory and Marietta road and soon found Johnston's new line on his front on the crest of Kennesaw Mountain. Dodge then placed James C. Veatch's Fourth Division close to the mountain, connecting on the right with Palmer's Fourteenth Corps and on the left with Logan's Fifteenth Corps. Thomas W. Sweeny's Second Division of Sixteenth Corps was left at Big Shanty in reserve. Logan's corps also followed the enemy until it was close to the base of Kennesaw Mountain, and it then entrenched on the left of Veatch. When Blair's Seventeenth Corps, which was on the left of the army, advanced, it found that the enemy had evacuated the position at Brush Mountain, and Blair then occupied the crest of the mountain. During the period June 20–22, Blair strengthened his position on Brush Mountain and sent out skirmishers toward Kennesaw Mountain.

On June 19, 1864, Schofield marched down the Sandtown road for about three miles from his positions on Mud Creek until his leading troops reached the crossing of Noyes' Creek. There he found that the planking had been removed from the bridge, and he made no serious attempt to cross the creek. He did demonstrate during the day as a diversion for George Stoneman, who was operating in the direction of Powder Springs.

About three or four miles north of the village of Powder Springs was Powder Springs Church, from which point a road ran eastward to Marietta. This road crossed the Sandtown road on a ridge that rose from the valley of Noyes' Creek just beyond the crossing where Schofield had been halted by the destroyed bridge. A road that ran from Powder Springs village to Marietta crossed the Sandtown road at the Andrew J. Cheney house, about a mile and a half south of Noyes' Creek, and it joined the Powder Springs Church and Marietta road near the Kolb house.

About 4:00 P.M. June 20, 1864, Stanley ordered a demonstration with a strong line of skirmishers all along his front. In front of the division line, and across Noyes' Creek, were two hills which were out in front of a salient in Hardee's line and which were held by the enemy. The hill on the right was bare, and was called Bald Hill (not to be confused with the Bald Hill at Atlanta), and this was held by the 9th Kentucky (Confederate) as an outpost. About sundown, Whitaker's brigade charged and captured the hill on the left, and Kirby's brigade captured Bald Hill. Because of some misunderstanding of orders, Kirby withdrew all but a party of skirmishers from the hill that evening, and at about 10:00 P.M. the 9th Kentucky drove off the skirmishers and recaptured the hill. The next morning, however, Kirby, with the help of artillery fire and troops of Richard H. Nodine's First Brigade of Wood's division, recaptured the hill.

Also on July 20, 1864, Sherman ordered Kenner Garrard to move out on a reconnaissance with his cavalry, cross Noonday Creek, and move up near Brush Mountain. About 1:00 P.M., by Garrard's orders, Robert H. G. Minty's First Brigade of his Second Cavalry Division crossed the creek, then moved southward along the Bell's Ferry road in the direction of Marietta. Near the Robert McAfee house, Minty was attacked by all of Joseph Wheeler's cavalry, and a violent and confused fight began that lasted for about two hours, during which there were several charges and countercharges. In the end, Minty was driven back almost to Noonday Creek, but then Abram O. Miller's Third Brigade of Mounted Infantry (formerly John T. Wilder's) came

up and, with the aid of artillery posted on the north bank of the creek, they finally halted Wheeler's advance.

There were some changes in position of the troops of Howard's and Hooker's corps on June 20, 1864, which were made in order to extend the right of Sherman's line farther to the right. At dark that day Frederick Knefler's Third Brigade of Wood's Third Division relieved Charles Candy's First Brigade and David Ireland's Third Brigade of Geary's division of Hooker's corps. Geary left Patrick H. Jones' Second Brigade in position on the left of Butterfield, and moved Candy's and Ireland's brigades to the right. He placed Candy's brigade on the right of Butterfield's division, and Ireland's brigade bivouacked in rear of the right of Butterfield's line. That night Newton's division relieved Williams' division of Hooker's corps, which then moved to the right of Butterfield. Early on the morning of June 21, Jones' brigade was relieved on the front line, and it moved back and joined Geary. Geary then moved with Jones' and Ireland's brigades to the right of Candy's brigade; when that was done, his division formed a continuous line, connecting on its left with Williams' division, which had moved there the night before. Hooker's divisions were then in line, with Butterfield on the left, Williams in the center, and Geary on the right.

On June 20, 1864, Daniel Cameron's Second Brigade of Cox's division forced a crossing of Noyes' Creek; by the next morning all of Cox's division was across the creek, and Hascall's division had moved up in close support. Hascall's pickets connected with the left of Hooker's corps.

As Sherman continued to extend his line to the right as he advanced toward Marietta, Johnston became concerned about the possibility of an attack on his left by way of the Powder Springs and Marietta road, and finally, on June 21, 1864, when Hooker's corps was near that road and Schofield's corps was moving toward it, Johnston decided to move Hood's entire corps from its position near Brush Mountain on the right to the Powder Springs and Marietta road on the left. Hood began his march on the night of June 21, and by the next morning he had arrived with his corps near Zion Church on the Powder Springs and Marietta road, about one mile east of the Kolb farm. During the morning of June 22, Hood deployed his troops on a wooded ridge that ran at a right angle to the road, with Thomas C. Hindman's division on the right, Carter L. Stevenson's division in the center, and Alexander P. Stewart's division serving as a reserve on the left.

On the morning of June 22, 1864, Hooker's Twentieth Corps and Schofield's Twenty-Third Corps continued their advance toward the left. At 3:00 that morning, Geary sent forward George A. Cobham with his own 111th Pennsylvania and the 137th New York of Ireland's Third Brigade to drive the enemy from a high hill about a mile in advance of his main line, and then early in the day Geary moved his entire division up to the hill and began entrenching a line to hold the position against a possible attack.

Also on June 22, 1864, Butterfield's division moved forward to attack a hill on its front and to the left of Geary. James Wood's Third Brigade was on the right, John Coburn's Second Brigade was on the left, and William T. Ward's First Brigade was in supporting distance in rear of Wood's brigade. Wood's brigade charged and took the hill, and it was then occupied by Wood, with a part of Ward's brigade on the right and Coburn's brigade on the left.

Williams' division moved up and formed on another ridge to the right of Geary, with his right on the Powder Spring and Marietta road near the Kolb house. Williams' division was separated from Geary's division by a swampy ravine, through which a stream flowed toward Noyes' Creek to the rear of the line.

On June 22, 1864, Schofield crossed Noyes' Creek with his corps, and Cox advanced with his division to the south and east on the Sandtown road until he reached the intersection with the Powder Springs and Marietta road at the Cheney farm. He then entrenched along a ridge overlooking Olley's Creek to the southeast. Hascall followed Cox to the Powder Springs and Marietta road, and he then turned left on that road and marched out about two miles toward Marietta. He then halted and took position on the right of Williams' division of Hooker's corps at the Kolb house. Hascall's line curved around to the right, and the right of the division faced the valley of Olley's Creek and covered the road from Cheney's to the Kolb farm. Silas A. Strickland's Third Brigade, McQuiston's Second Brigade, First Division, Twenty-Third Corps, and William E. Hobson's Second Brigade entrenched on this line. It should be noted that Hobson had relieved John R. Bond, who was ill, in command of Second Brigade on June 18, and also that Peter T. Swaine relieved McQuiston in command of First Brigade, First Division (attached to Hascall's division) on June 23.

Engagement at Kolb's Farm, Georgia, June 22, 1864. As the Federal troops advanced on the right of Sherman's army on the morning of June 22, 1864, they learned from prisoners taken by the skirmishers that Hood's corps had arrived on their front and that his troops were not far ahead. Aware of Hood's aggressive nature, Hooker and Schofield immediately began to prepare for an expected attack.

Their line crossed the Powder Springs and Marietta road near the house and farm buildings of Peter V. Kolb, and across the road from the Kolb house was a large field that was surrounded by woods.

Hooker's troops were deployed along the ridges, just outside the line of trees on the western side of the field, with Williams' division on the right next to the road. Thomas H. Ruger's Second Brigade was on the right of the division, next to the road; Joseph F. Knipe's First Brigade was in the center; and James S. Robinson's Third Brigade was on the left, about 200 yards to the left and rear of Knipe. While Williams' men entrenched, he brought up his artillery and placed Charles E. Winegar's Battery I, 1st New York Light Artillery in front of Robinson's brigade, and John D. Woodbury's Battery M, 1st New York Light Artillery in front of Knipe's brigade.

In front of Knipe's brigade was the open field mentioned above, which extended for about 1,000 yards to the trees on the far side. A deep gully ran along the front of the brigade some distance out in the field. Except for the two regiments on the left of Ruger's brigade, the front of the rest of the brigade was covered by thick woods.

Geary's division was on a hill to the left of Williams' line, and separated from it by the swampy ravine mentioned above. Jones' Second Brigade was on the right, Ireland's Third Brigade was in the center, and Candy's First Brigade was on the left. Geary brought up William Wheeler's 13th Battery, New York Light Artillery and James D. McGill's Battery E, Pennsylvania Light Artillery, and they were massed in front of the infantry line.

Farther to the left, and hidden in the woods, was Butterfield's division. Butterfield brought forward Luther R. Smith's Battery I, 1st Michigan Light Artillery and Jerome B. Stephens' Battery C, 1st Ohio Light Artillery, and they did good service later in the day when they aided in repelling Hood's attack. Butterfield's infantry, however, was not engaged.

Upon arriving at his position on the right of Williams, Hascall noted that a ridge just in front of the one that he then occupied would be very important for further operations, and he ordered his skirmish line, supported by George W. Gallup's 14th Kentucky (Union) of Strickland's brigade, to advance and seize the ridge and hold it.

When Schofield learned that Hood's corps was on his front, he brought up his artillery and placed Joseph C. Shields' 19th Battery, Ohio Light Artillery in an open field near his line and Byron D. Paddock's Battery F, 1st Michigan Light Artillery near the road. As a further precaution, at 4:30 P.M. Schofield directed Cox to leave one of his brigades at Cheney's and move with the other three brigades of his division to take position on the right of Hascall's line.

About 5:00 P.M. June 22, 1864, Hindman's and Stevenson's divisions of Hood's corps, which had been advancing through the wood that bordered the eastern side of the field in front of Williams' line, emerged onto the open ground, and all Union batteries, about forty guns, opened with a heavy fire. Hindman's division, on the Confederate right, advanced on the north side of the Powder Springs and Marietta road toward the center of Williams' division and the right of Geary's division, and Stevenson's division moved forward on the left of Hindman, south of the road, toward Hascall's division.

Knipe's brigade held its ground against Hindman's attack, but the enemy gained some ground in the swampy ravine between Williams' and Geary's divisions. The attack was finally repulsed with the help of the two left regiments of Ruger's brigade and Wheeler's battery of Geary's division, which was on a hill on the right of Geary's line, and Woodbury's battery of Williams' division, which was on the front and left of Williams' line.

Hindman's men fell back to the ravine in front of Knipe's line, where they re-formed and attacked again, but this attack was also repulsed.

On the Federal right, Gallup's 14th Kentucky (Union) had been on the ridge in front of Hascall's line for only a short time when a part of Stevenson's division approached the crest. Gallup's men fired only a single volley at close range, and then fell back, while resisting stubbornly for more than an hour, and moved into Hascall's main line. As soon as Gallup's men had moved clear of the field of fire of the artillery, Shields' and Paddock's batteries opened with canister and soon drove the enemy from their front. Although there was still some fighting for a time, the battle was essentially over.

That night John H. King's First Division (Richard W. Johnson's division) of Palmer's Fourteenth Corps relieved Stanley's division of Howard's Fourth Corps, and Stanley relieved Butterfield's division. Butterfield then moved to the right and camped that night in rear of the divisions of Geary and Williams. Also during the night, Cox arrived with three of his brigades (James W. Reilly's First Brigade was at Cheney's) and took position on the right of Hascall. Daniel Cameron's Second Brigade was on the left, next to Hascall's division; Richard F. Barter's attached brigade was on the right of Cameron; and Robert K. Byrd's Third Brigade was on the right of Barter.

Battle of Kennesaw Mountain, Georgia, June 27, 1864.

After the Engagement at Kolb's Farm June 22, 1864, Sherman carefully considered his next move, finally deciding on a direct assault on Johnston's line at Kennesaw Mountain. His only alternative was to continue the advance by the flanking movements that he had been using since the beginning of the campaign. There were, however, some problems associated with such a movement at that time. If he moved the army farther to the right, he would have to leave the railroad, which was his direct line of supply, and the accumulation of supplies that would be needed while away from the railroad and their transportation to the front could be accomplished only with considerable difficulty because of the weather and the condition of the roads. In addition, Sherman believed that there might be an element of surprise that could contribute to his success if he abandoned his usual method of advance and resorted to a direct assault on the enemy's works. Accordingly, on June 24, Sherman issued orders for a general assault on Johnston's lines in front of

Kennesaw Mountain and Marietta, and he directed that it begin at 8:00 A.M. June 27.

According to Sherman's orders, the principal attack was to be made by Thomas' Army of the Cumberland against the enemy center, at a point selected by Thomas as being most promising of success, and he further directed that if the attack was a success, Thomas was to advance troops and seize the Western and Atlantic Railroad somewhere south of Marietta.

McPherson was to threaten an attack on the right of the enemy line by sending Garrard's cavalry and an infantry division of his Army of the Tennessee to approach Marietta from the north. McPherson was also to deliver a real attack at a point south and west of Kennesaw Mountain. He was instructed to open fire on the mountain with his artillery, then advance a strong skirmish line and attempt to capture the works on the summit if they were only lightly held by the enemy, which Sherman thought was probable.

Schofield was also ordered to demonstrate on the far Federal right with his Army of the Ohio to threaten the enemy's left flank. He was authorized to attack the enemy line near the Powder Springs and Marietta road if, in his opinion, there was any prospect of success.

On June 25 and June 26, 1864, there were several changes in the positions of McPherson's and Thomas' troops that were made in preparation for the attack on June 27. On June 25, Logan was ordered to relieve Jefferson C. Davis' Second Division of Palmer's corps, and at 8:00 that evening William Harrow's Fourth Division of Fifteenth Corps moved to the right of Dodge's Sixteenth Corps and relieved Davis. Davis then marched with his division to the right and took position in reserve in rear of the right of Howard's line. This movement was completed by dawn June 26.

On June 26, 1864, Thomas W. Sweeny's Second Division of Dodge's corps came up from Big Shanty and relieved Peter J. Osterhaus' First Division of Logan's Fifteenth Corps, and then Osterhaus moved to the right and relieved Absalom Baird's Third Division of Palmer's corps. That night Baird moved with his division to a position in reserve, not far from that occupied by Davis' division. When this movement was completed, Davis' and Baird's divisions were on the right of Howard's Fourth Corps.

Also on June 26, Logan ordered Morgan L. Smith to move his Second Division of Fifteenth Corps to the right and relieve John H. King's (Richard W. Johnson's) First Division of Fourteenth Corps. Osterhaus and Smith began their movements at 8:00 P.M., and by daylight on June 27, Logan had relieved all of Palmer's divisions, and the divisions of Fifteenth Corps were again together in line, directly in front of Kennesaw Mountain, with Osterhaus' division on the right, Harrow's division on the left, and Morgan L. Smith's division in reserve.

On the night of June 26, 1864, Charles C. Walcutt was ordered to report with his Second Brigade of Harrow's Fourth Division, Fifteenth Corps to Morgan L. Smith. Smith's division was to assault the enemy works to the right of Kennesaw Mountain the next morning, and Walcutt's brigade was to join in the assault.

On June 26, 1864, Schofield was at his headquarters at the Cheney house with Reilly's First Brigade of Cox's division. About a mile south of the Cheney house, the Sandtown road ran down into the valley of Olley's Creek, crossed the creek, and ran up to the high ground on the far side, continuing on toward Sandtown. About two miles or more beyond Olley's Creek, the road crossed the road running from Salt Springs to Marietta. After the engagement at Kolb's farm, Hood had extended his line to the left to cover the Salt Springs and Marietta road, and William H. Jackson's Confederate cavalry was in position along Olley's Creek, where it held the principal crossings. Schofield decided not to attack along the road from Powder Springs toward Marietta, but instead he sent forward Reilly's brigade on the Sandtown road to Olley's Creek, where Lawrence S. Ross' cavalry brigade of Jackson's cavalry division was in a strong position on the far side. Reilly made no serious attempt to cross the creek, but Cox sent Byrd's brigade from his line near the Kolb house to outflank Ross' position. Byrd marched across country to Olley's Creek, which he reached at a point about one mile upstream from the crossing where Reilly had been halted at the bridge, and he then crossed the creek and entrenched a position on a small hill on the south bank.

On the morning of June 27, 1864, Sherman began his attack at Kennesaw Mountain as planned. Kennesaw Mountain is not a single peak, but instead is actually a high rocky ridge, about two miles in length, which extends from the northeast at the Western and Atlantic Railroad to the southwest, where it ends near Noyes' Creek. From this ridge rise two peaks or crests of unequal height. The higher of these two crests is at the northern end of the ridge; it is called Big Kennesaw Mountain, and it is separated by a shallow depression from the southern crest, which is about 200 feet lower than Big Kennesaw and is called Little Kennesaw. Extending southward is a spur of the mountain that is partially separated from Little Kennesaw by a deep ravine that cuts into the western side of the ridge near its southern end, and this latter elevation is today called Pigeon Hill.

At 8:00 on the morning of June 27, 1864, the troops of McPherson's Army of the Tennessee began the opening moves of the Battle of Kennesaw Mountain. Mortimer D. Leggett's Third Division of Blair's Seventeenth Corps, with Garrard's cavalry on his left, advanced as ordered on the left of McPherson's line along the Bell's Ferry road toward Marietta to carry out his feint on the Confederate right. Manning F. Force's First Brigade was on the right, Adam G. Malloy's Third Brigade was in the center, and Robert K. Scott's Second Brigade was on the left. Leggett drove the enemy skirmishers from their advanced works, but he soon came under a heavy cross fire and at about 10:00 A.M. was forced to withdraw for some distance, but he continued to threaten the enemy's right.

Following his orders, Dodge deployed as skirmishers the 9th Illinois and 66th Illinois of August Mersey's Second Brigade of Thomas W. Sweeny's Second Division and the 64th Illinois of Henry T. McDowell's (John W. Fuller's) First Brigade of James C. Veatch's Fourth Division and started them up the slopes of Kennesaw Mountain. They soon came under a heavy fire from above, but despite this and the difficult and exhausting climb, they finally reached the crest. There, contrary to their expectations, they found that the enemy works were strongly held, and that they could not be taken with the available force. The three regiments then secured a position as close up to the enemy's line as possible and continued to threaten an attack until the fighting ended.

McPherson decided to attempt to break the enemy line by capturing Pigeon Hill and thereby isolating Loring's corps on Kennesaw Mountain.

Morgan L. Smith's Second Division of Logan's Fifteenth Corps was selected for that purpose, and long before daylight June 27, 1864, Smith began moving forward toward his assigned position. After a march of several miles, he halted his division about one-half mile in front of Pigeon Hill and formed his troops for the attack. The Burnt Hickory and Marietta road, which ran in by way of Gilgal Church, passed through the position where Morgan L. Smith was to form his line. He placed Giles A. Smith's First Brigade on the north side of the road and Joseph A. J. Lightburn's Second Brigade on the south side of the road, where it was to advance on the right of Giles A. Smith's brigade. Morgan L. Smith also placed Charles C. Walcutt's Second Brigade of Harrow's Fourth Division of Fifteenth Corps, which was temporarily attached to Morgan L. Smith's command, on the left of Giles A. Smith's brigade, with instructions to move up into the ravine between Little Kennesaw Mountain and Pigeon Hill.

When the Federal artillery ceased firing about 8:15 A.M. June 27, 1864, Morgan L. Smith's line moved forward, preceded by a strong skirmish line. Progress was slow because of the difficult terrain, and also because of a swampy stream that flowed through dense thickets of saplings, tangled vines, and thick growth of briers and bushes. Despite these impediments, Lightburn's brigade continued to advance, and it then charged and drove the enemy skirmishers from their rifle pits and back to their main line. The brigade was soon halted, however, by a heavy fire, and the troops fell back, with some taking shelter in the captured rifle pits and some in the woods beyond.

The brigades of Giles A. Smith and Walcutt were much disorganized by crossing the tangled and swampy ground, but they were able to move on and pass through the enemy's skirmish line. Walcutt's brigade succeeded in pushing forward into the mouth of the ravine separating Little Kennesaw Mountain and Pigeon Hill, and Giles A. Smith's men reached the base of Pigeon Hill and began to climb the slope. Some moved up close to the enemy's main line, which was held by Francis M. Cockrell's brigade of Samuel G. French's division, and a few reached the parapet of the works, but those that were not killed or wounded were forced to fall back and seek cover.

Walcutt's brigade moved forward some distance into the ravine, and some of the men began to ascend the slopes of Little Kennesaw toward the works held by Claudius W. Sears' brigade of French's division. Walcutt's line was soon stopped when it encountered a very heavy fire and, in places, by impassable ledges of rock. Most of Walcutt's men took shelter behind rocks and trees and continued firing, but soon Giles A. Smith's brigade fell back to the base of Pigeon Hill, and Walcutt moved back to the mouth of the ravine. After dark that night, Morgan L. Smith's defeated troops returned to their lines.

Farther to the south, Thomas prepared to launch his main attack against the Confederate center, which was held by Hardee's corps. From Pigeon Hill, Hardee's line ran southward along a wooded ridge for some three miles to the creek previously mentioned as flowing toward Noyes' Creek between the divisions of Williams and Geary near the Kolb house (present-day John Ward Creek). Hardee's divisions were in line from right to left as follows: William H. T. Walker's division was on the right, facing northwest, between the Burnt Hickory and Marietta road and Noyes' Creek; William B. Bate's division was between Noyes' Creek and the Dallas and Marietta road, facing west; Patrick R. Cleburne's division was between the Dallas and Marietta road and a hill on the ridge that would soon bear the name of Cheatham Hill, also facing west; and Benjamin F. Cheatham's division was on the left, south of Cheatham Hill, and facing southwest.

The part of Hardee's line that was selected by Thomas for his attack was held by the divisions of Cleburne and Cheatham. Cleburne's brigades were in line from the right, at the Dallas and Marietta road, to the left at Cheatham Hill as follows: Hiram B. Granbury, Daniel C. Govan, Mark P. Lowrey, and Lucius E. Polk. Cheatham's divisions were in position as follows: Alfred J. Vaughan's brigade held the salient of the line at Cheatham Hill (later to be known as the "Dead Angle"); George Maney's brigade, commanded by Francis M. Walker, was on the left of Vaughan, on the southern face of the salient; Marcus J. Wright's brigade, commanded by John C. Carter, was to the left of Maney's brigade; and Otho F. Strahl's brigade was on the left of Cheatham's line.

Thomas experienced some difficulty in getting his troops forward during the early morning and in line for the attack, but by 9:00 A.M., one hour after the scheduled time, he was ready. Howard's Fourth Corps advanced on the Dallas and Marietta road, and Thomas J. Wood's Third Division took position north of the road, facing Bate's Confederate division; John Newton's Second Division, which was to lead the assault, was south of the road, on the right of Wood; and David S. Stanley's First Division was formed to support Newton. Newton's brigades were in line as follows: Charles G. Harker's Third Brigade was on the right, George D. Wagner's Second Brigade was in the center, and Nathan Kimball's First Brigade was on the left, where it was held in reserve. Walter C. Whitaker's Second Brigade of Stanley's division was ordered to support Harker's brigade in the attack.

Jefferson C. Davis' Second Division of Palmer's Fourteenth Corps was in position on the right of Newton's division. Davis placed Daniel McCook's Third Brigade on the left of the division line, next to Harker's brigade, and John G. Mitchell's Second Brigade on the right. James D. Morgan's First Brigade relieved Whitaker's brigade of Stanley's division in the entrenchments on the morning of June 27, 1864.

At 9:00 A.M. Newton, with Harker's and Wagner's brigades, advanced toward the enemy works. Wagner moved directly toward that part of Cleburne's line that was held by the brigades of Lowrey and Polk, and Harker attacked toward the northern face of the salient, where the line was held by Vaughan's brigade and the left of Polk's brigade. Newton's men suffered terrible losses as they advanced. Some men on the right of Harker's brigade managed to get inside the abatis in front of the works on Cheatham Hill, but they were unable to get inside the entrenchments. Harker's men fell back to a ravine, where they regrouped and attacked again, but once more they were beaten back. Harker was killed within a short distance of the enemy's line, and Luther P. Bradley assumed command of the brigade. Wagner's brigade was also beaten back.

Immediately to the south of Newton's division, Davis' Second Division of Palmer's corps attacked directly toward the so-called "Dead Angle" on Cheatham Hill and the south face of the salient. Daniel McCook's brigade was on the left, and Mitchell's brigade was on the right. Like the other attacks that morning, this one, too, ended in failure. McCook's leading regiment, the 125th Illinois, reached the parapet of the breastworks and for a short time engaged in hand-to-hand fighting, but was forced to fall back. The other regiments of the brigade came up successively, and each in turn was driven back. Mitchell's brigade also advanced under a very heavy fire toward the enemy works, and some men succeeded in getting inside, but they were quickly killed, wounded, or captured. The survivors of Davis' attack fell back about thirty yards to a somewhat sheltered position just under the crest of the hill and continued firing until the fighting ended later in the day. McCook was killed in the attack, and Oscar F. Harmon, the officer next in rank, was killed a few minutes later. Caleb J. Dilworth was then the senior officer present, and he took charge of the brigade.

John W. Geary's Second Division of Hooker's Twentieth Corps advanced on the right of Palmer's corps, but it did not join in the attack.

Sherman was disappointed by the failure of his attacks on the Kennesaw line that morning, but they may have contributed to Schofield's successes that day on the Sandtown road by preventing enemy troops from moving from the Kennesaw line to the left to support Hood's corps and Jackson's cavalry.

Before daylight on the morning of June 27, 1864, Daniel Cameron's Second Brigade of Cox's division of Schofield's corps moved from the vicinity of the Kolb farm to Olley's Creek, and then crossed the creek and moved up to the position established by Byrd's brigade the night before. Cameron then moved downstream to his right toward the Sandtown road, where Ross' Confederate cavalry brigade was holding the crossing against Reilly's brigade. Thus threatened on his flank, Ross withdrew to the south, and Reilly's brigade crossed the creek and joined Cameron.

That afternoon, Cox, with the brigades of Cameron and Reilly, crossed the valley of Olley's Creek, then crossed the ridge south of the valley along which the road ran from Salt Springs to Marietta, and finally took position on the hills north of Nickajack Creek. Byrd continued to hold the position south of Olley's Creek, about a mile above the Sandtown road crossing, and during the day Barter's brigade moved up from near the Kolb house to form a connection between Hascall's division and Byrd's brigade. Cox then held a line of about four miles.

In addition to Schofield's advance that day, Stoneman's cavalry division, which was then operating on the right of Schofield, arrived at a point within about five miles of the Chattahoochee River. These movements placed Sherman's right flank closer to the Chattahoochee than was Johnston's army.

ADVANCE OF THE ARMY ACROSS THE CHATTAHOOCHEE RIVER

After the repulse of Sherman's assaults at Kennesaw Mountain June 27, 1864, he decided to resume his flanking movements to the right toward the Chattahoochee River. The next few days were spent in making preparations and in bringing up supplies to sustain this movement, which was away from the railroad.

By July 1, 1864, Sherman was ready, and he issued orders for the Army of the Tennessee to leave its positions on the left of the army, assigning to Garrard the task of guarding that flank with his cavalry, and to march in rear of Thomas' Army of the Cumberland and Schofield's Army of the Ohio and take position on the extreme right flank of the army, beyond the Army of the Ohio.

On the night of June 30, 1864, Milo S. Hascall's Second Division of Twenty-Third Corps had been relieved by John W. Geary's Second Division of Hooker's Twentieth Corps, and at 6:00 A.M. July 1, Hascall marched to the right for about three and a half miles on the Old Tennessee road to a new position on the right of Jacob D. Cox's Third Division of Twenty-Third Corps. Joseph A. Cooper's First Brigade of Hascall's division marched in front, and it was followed by Silas A. Strickland's Third Brigade, and then by William E. Hobson's Second Brigade. When Hascall's division came up on the right of Cox's line, the division was formed with Hobson's brigade on the left, Cooper's brigade in the center, and Strickland's brigade on the right. Peter T. Swaine's Second Brigade, First Division of Twenty-Third Corps, which was attached to Hascall's division, also advanced with Hascall, apparently in reserve. When the division was thus formed, Hascall moved toward the enemy's left flank. That evening, July 1, he reached the Moss house, on the road from Powder Springs to Ruff's Station, and upon arrival there he took position with his right covering the Old Tennessee road and his left covering the Marietta road. The center of Hascall's line was on the road to Ruff's Station.

Cox also made some changes in the positions of his troops on July 1, 1864. He moved Daniel Cameron's Third Brigade forward to the left of his line on the Marietta and Sandtown road and moved Richard F. Barter's First Brigade, First Division, Twenty-Third Corps, which was attached to Cox's division, to the Cheney house.

At 4:00 A.M. July 2, 1864, Logan started Morgan L. Smith's Second Division of Fifteenth Corps down the Sandtown road toward the right of Schofield's corps. At 8:00 that evening, Blair's Seventeenth Corps set out to follow Smith on the Sandtown road.

During the morning of July 2, 1864, Smith's division came up and relieved the brigades of Cooper and Strickland on the right of Hascall's line. These two brigades moved to the left and took position between the other two brigades of Hascall's division on the right and Cox's division on the left. Smith's division was then in position on the right of Schofield's corps, and on the right of Sherman's army.

During the night of July 2, 1864, Johnston abandoned his lines at Kennesaw Mountain and in front of Marietta and withdrew with his army about four miles to the southeast of Marietta. He took up a strong position along a ridge that crossed the Western and Atlantic Railroad at Smyrna Station. This line extended for a distance of about six miles from Rottenwood Creek on the right to Nickajack Creek on the left.

When Federal pickets reported early on the morning of July 3, 1864 that Johnston's army had departed during the night, Sherman started his entire army in immediate pursuit, with the Army of the Cumberland advancing along the railroad, the Army of the Ohio to the right of the Army of the Cumberland, and the Army of the Tennessee on the far right.

During July 3, 1864, Blair's Seventeenth Corps continued its march down the Sandtown road until it came up with Morgan L. Smith's division of Fifteenth Corps, which had halted at a point where the road to Ruff's Mill branched off. Blair then moved on to the Widow Smith's house, but withdrew and camped that night on a branch of Nickajack Creek. Dodge's Sixteenth Corps followed Blair down the Sandtown road and about 3:00 P.M. passed by the flank of Schofield's Twenty-Third Corps. It bivouacked that night on Nickajack Creek near Ruff's Mill. Thomas W. Sweeny's Second Division of Sixteenth Corps crossed the creek and entrenched on the east side. On July 3, Logan marched with Peter J. Osterhaus' First Division and William Harrow's Fourth Division past Kennesaw Mountain to Marietta, where he bivouacked for the night.

On July 3, 1864, Thomas' Army of the Cumberland advanced through Marietta, with Palmer's Fourteenth Corps moving along the Western and Atlantic Railroad on the main Marietta and Atlanta road, Hooker's Twentieth Corps on the right of Palmer, and Howard's Fourth Corps on the left of Palmer.

On June 29, 1864, Daniel Butterfield had departed for the North on leave, and William T. Ward had assumed command of his Third Division, Twentieth Corps. He was in command when Hooker advanced on July 3 from his positions north of Kolb's farm and marched by different routes to Marietta.

Ward led his division toward Marietta on the Powder Springs and Marietta road and, although delayed by a sharp engagement near the town, he continued on to join the rest of the corps.

John W. Geary's Second Division marched across country on the right of Ward's division toward Neal Dow's Station, about four miles south of Marietta on the railroad. Geary encountered enemy skirmishers at Maloney's Church, and also at that point made connection with Palmer's corps, which was advancing on his left. Geary then proceeded on south for about two miles to the enemy's main line and formed his division on the left of the corps.

Alpheus S. Williams' First Division moved forward on the left of the corps by country paths, reaching the main road about one-half mile west of Marietta. From there it followed Ward's division on the Turner's Ferry road until it came up to Johnston's main line. The division camped at 4:00 that evening on the left of Geary's division.

Palmer's corps, consisting of Richard W.

Johnson's First Division (then commanded temporarily by John H. King), Jefferson C. Davis' Second Division, and Absalom Baird's Third Division, also passed through Marietta July 3, 1864, bivouacking for the night about four miles south of the town. Palmer arrived in rear of Ward's division of Twentieth Corps and relieved Ward, and Ward then moved to the right of Williams' and Geary's divisions and took position on the right of Geary. Palmer's corps took position on the left of Hooker's corps. Palmer's divisions remained in position July 4, but that day Newell Gleason's Second Brigade (commanded by Ferdinand Van Derveer until June 27) of Absalom Baird's Third Division was sent to garrison Marietta.

All three brigade commanders of King's division were changed during this period. On July 2, 1864, William P. Carlin departed on leave, and Anson G. McCook assumed temporary command of First Brigade until Carlin returned to the army on August 2. William L. Stoughton was wounded July 4, and Marshall F. Moore assumed command of his Second Brigade. Benjamin F. Scribner became ill and left the army July 5, and Josiah Given assumed command of his Third Brigade.

Howard's Fourth Corps left its lines near Kennesaw Mountain at 5:00 A.M. July 3, 1864 and marched to Marietta, with David S. Stanley's First Division in the lead, and Thomas J. Wood's Third Division and John Newton's Second Division following. The corps passed through Marietta and followed the Western and Atlantic Railroad southward. Stanley halted that night at Ruff's Station and deployed, and Wood and Newton halted in reserve at Neal Dow's Station, about four miles south of Marietta.

Kenner Garrard's cavalry division moved to Marietta July 3, 1864, then covered the left of Sherman's army as it moved south.

At 9:00 A.M. July 4, 1864, Logan left Marietta with the divisions of Osterhaus and Harrow of his Fifteenth Corps and moved by way of the Cheney house, with orders to report to McPherson on the far right of Sherman's army. While on the march down the Sandtown road that day, south of Cheney's, Morgan L. Smith's division joined Logan, and Fifteenth Corps was thus reunited. The corps camped that night on the Sandtown road.

Early on July 4, 1864, James C. Veatch's Fourth Division of Dodge's Sixteenth Corps moved out about two miles on the road to Ruff's Station and came up in front of the enemy's works held by Hood's corps. Sweeny's Second Division came up later and took position on the right of Veatch.

Blair's Seventeenth Corps also advanced on July 4, 1864, with Walter Q. Gresham's Fourth Division in the lead, and, after marching about three miles, took position about three-fourths of a mile from the enemy's works. Mortimer D. Leggett's Third Division was placed where it would be in position to advance on the right, down the Sandtown road toward Howell's Ferry, if so ordered. Stoneman's cavalry covered the right of Blair's corps during the day.

By its movements on July 4, 1864, the Army of the Tennessee came into position near Nickajack Creek, on the left of Johnston's line, with Blair's corps on the right, Dodge's corps in the center, and Logan's corps on the left.

On July 4 and 5, 1864, Schofield's corps remained in rear of McPherson's army, with the divisions massed.

Hooker did not advance his corps July 4, 1864, but he made some adjustments in his line by sending Williams' division about two miles to the right to a new position between Geary's division and Ward's division. About 2:00 P.M. Ward's division moved off toward Nickajack Creek and took position on the left of Twenty-Third Corps and near Sixteenth Corps.

The advance of the Army of the Tennessee on July 4, 1864 seriously threatened the left of Johnston's line near Nickajack Creek, and that night Johnston withdrew with his army about three miles to a previously prepared position in front of the Chattahoochee River crossing of the Western and Atlantic Railroad. This line was about six miles long, with its center about a mile from the river and both flanks resting on the river, one above the bridge and the other below the bridge. The right of Johnston's new line was near Howell's Ferry and Rottenwood Creek, and the left covered the mouth of Nickajack Creek and Mason and Turner's Ferry.

On the morning of July 5, 1864, after finding that Johnston had again fallen back, Sherman's army relentlessly moved forward in pursuit. The Army of the Cumberland advanced along the railroad, and the Army of the Tennessee advanced on the right toward Mason and Turner's Ferry. The Army of the Ohio remained at Smyrna in reserve.

July 5, 1864, George Stoneman's cavalry moved still farther to the right, reaching Sandtown on the Chattahoochee River. Also that day, Sherman ordered Garrard to move up the Chattahoochee River to Roswell, a mill town on the river, and seize the bridge over the river, and also to destroy the important textile factory that was located there.

Sherman did not expect Johnston to make a serious stand in his new position north of the Chattahoochee River, and he ordered a close investment of the works and began preparations for crossing the river and moving on Atlanta, about twelve miles to the southeast.

Early on the morning of July 5, 1864, Gresham's division of Blair's corps moved forward on the road to Turner's Ferry. At 6:00 P.M. it reached a position on Nickajack Creek about 500 yards from the enemy's works. Leggett marched with his division to Howell's Ferry on the Chattahoochee. He left a brigade there, then moved upriver to connect with the left of Gresham's division at the mouth of Nickajack Creek. Blair remained in this position until July 10.

On July 5, 1864, Dodge's corps moved to Widow Mitchell's house on the Sandtown road, and the next day August Mersey's Second Brigade of Sweeny's division was sent to the Sandtown Ferry. On July 7, Dodge moved Veatch's division to the forks of the Green and Howell's Ferry road, and from there he sent out skirmishers to the bank of the Chattahoochee River.

On July 7, 1864, Logan replaced Hooker's Twentieth Corps with his Fifteenth Corps. Logan then placed Harrow's division on the right, where it connected with the left of Blair's Seventeenth Corps; Osterhaus' division in the center; and Morgan L. Smith's division on the left, where it connected with the right of the Army of the Cumberland. Logan's corps remained in this position until July 12.

Thomas' Army of the Cumberland on the left also moved forward July 5, 1864. Hooker's corps moved forward, on the left of the Army of the Tennessee, with Geary's division in front, and Williams' and Ward's divisions following. Geary arrived on Nickajack Creek, formed a strong picket line in front of the enemy works, and massed his divisions in the woods on the Dodd farm. Palmer's corps was

across Nickajack Creek on the left of Geary's division, but did not connect with it.

On July 5, 1864, Williams' division moved across country to the Turner's Ferry road and took position on the high ground overlooking the Chattahoochee. Ward's division camped that night on the left of the road in rear of Geary's and Williams' divisions.

July 6, 1864, Williams moved his division across Nickajack Creek to the east side and took position on the right of Palmer's corps. That day Geary's division was relieved by Osterhaus' division of Fifteenth Corps, and he then moved it northward, following Williams' division, to the road running to Vining's Station. Upon arriving there, he turned eastward and camped that night east of Nickajack Creek.

On July 7, 1864, Geary's division moved two miles to the north and formed in line on the right of Ward's division. It then connected on the right with Osterhaus' division at Nickajack Creek. Geary remained in this position July 8, but the next day he moved forward about one mile to the west bank of the Chattahoochee. This brought Hooker's divisions in line, with Geary on the right, Ward in the center, and Williams on the left. Hooker remained in this position until July 17.

On July 5, 1864, Palmer's corps of the Army of the Cumberland advanced to a position in front of Hardee's corps, about a mile and a half from the Chattahoochee. Baird's division marched up on the road to Vining's Station, and then along the railroad until it encountered the head of King's division. King's division was moving in on the right of Baird and reached the railroad ahead of him. Both divisions then moved up in front of Johnston's new line. King's division took position to the right of the railroad, and Baird formed on the the left of King, with his line extending back along the railroad. Davis' division then came up and formed on the corps line. On July 10, Baird's division moved to Pace's Ferry, and King's and Davis' divisions moved up to the river bank, where they took positions guarding the line of the river. The corps remained in these positions until July 17. On July 15, John B. Turchin, commanding First Brigade of Baird's division, departed for the North on sick leave, and Moses B. Walker assumed command of his brigade.

On July 5, 1864, Howard's corps advanced along

the railroad to Vining's Station, and from there Howard marched out on a road that ran to the east, crossed the Chattahoochee River at Pace's Ferry, and continued on to Atlanta. Wood's Third Division was in the lead, Stanley's First Division followed Wood, and Newton's Second Division brought up the rear. Wood's division skirmished during the day with some enemy dismounted cavalry, but that evening the corps camped on high ground close to and facing the Chattahoochee River, with Stanley's division in position above Pace's Ferry.

Stanley's and Davis' divisions remained in this position until July 10, 1864, but on July 7, Newton's division was moved to a new position, with its left resting on Rottenwood Creek. Then on July 9, Howard sent Newton's division upriver to Roswell to support Garrard's cavalry in crossing the Chattahoochee River at that point. Garrard had moved to Roswell July 5, destroyed the factory the next day, and then crossed the river and secured the ford July 9. Newton crossed the river about dusk July 9 and relieved Garrard, who returned to the north bank. On July 10, Dodge arrived with the two divisions of his Sixteenth Corps and relieved Newton. The next day Newton recrossed to the north bank of the river and camped near Shallow Ford, and on July 12, he marched back with his division to his camp on Rottenwood Creek. On July 10, Stanley's and Wood's divisions moved to a point near the mouth of Soap Creek in support of Schofield's Twenty-Third Corps, which had crossed the Chattahoochee River there and was entrenched on the high ground beyond.

July 5, 1864, Hascall's division of Schofield's corps remained in camp, but Cox's division moved on the road to Ruff's Station to the Moss house at the junction of the Sandtown road and the road to Smyrna Station. The next day Hascall's division moved across Nickajack Creek toward Ruff's Station, and Cox's division moved to Smyrna Camp Ground on the railroad. On July 7, Hascall's division remained in camp near the railroad, but Cox's division moved out two miles toward Rottenwood Creek and went into camp.

On July 8, 1864, Cox marched on the road that ran to a paper mill on Soap Creek (Sope Creek), not far from the point where the creek flowed into the Chattahoochee River near Isham's Ford and Phillips' Ferry. This crossing was about six miles upstream from Powers' Ferry and Vining's Station, and was about the same distance from Cox's camp at Smyrna Camp Ground. Hascall followed Cox with a train of pontoon bridging materials for crossing the river.

When Cox arrived at the mill, which had been burned, he sent Daniel Cameron with the Second Brigade of his division northward across Soap Creek and up the Chattahoochee for about one-half mile to an old rock fish dam that had been built across the river. It was Sherman's intention that Cox cross the Chattahoochee at the mouth of Soap Creek at 4:00 that afternoon and that, as a diversion, Cameron was to cross the river at the fish dam, move down the east bank, and drive away any enemy forces that might be present to oppose Cox's crossing.

Cameron's brigade crossed the river as ordered, and at 4:00 P.M. Cox began crossing the rest of his division. The first troops of Cox's division to cross the river belonged to the 12th Kentucky (Union) Regiment of Robert K. Byrd's Third Brigade, and they were ferried across in pontoon boats under the cover of a heavy fire from the rest of Byrd's brigade. When the men of the 12th Kentucky (Union) had landed on the far side of the river, they moved up the bank against little opposition and established a defensive position on a ridge near the river to protect the crossing of the rest of the division. Meantime, the boats continued to ferry troops across the river while the engineers built a pontoon bridge. Byrd's brigade and a part of Richard F. Barter's attached brigade were ferried across, but when the engineers had completed their work, the rest of Barter's brigade crossed on the bridge. At 8:00 that night, James W. Reilly's First Brigade crossed on the bridge and camped in rear of Cameron's and Barter's brigades.

On July 9, 1864, Cox advanced his division to another ridge in front of the one occupied the night before, and there he formed his brigades in line, from left to right, as follows: Eugene W. Crittenden's dismounted cavalry brigade, which had been attached to the division June 21, 1864; Cameron's brigade; Byrd's brigade; Barter's brigade; and Reilly's brigade. Also on July 9, Joseph A. Cooper's First Brigade and William E. Hobson's Second Brigade of Hascall's division crossed the river; Hobson's brigade was placed on the right of

Cox's line, and Cooper's brigade was placed in reserve. On July 11, the rest of Hascall's division crossed the river and was formed on the right of Hobson to prolong Schofield's line to the right.

On July 9, 1864, McPherson began the movement of his Army of the Tennessee from its position on the right of Sherman's army to Roswell, on the extreme left of the army. That day Dodge moved back with his Sixteenth Corps on the Sandtown road, with orders to march by way of Marietta to Roswell. Dodge halted his command at 10:00 that night about a mile east of Marietta; he resumed the march at 3:00 A.M. July 10. He arrived at Roswell that day, forded the Chattahoochee River, and relieved John Newton's Second Division of Fourth Corps in the works that they had constructed to protect the crossing. The next day Newton recrossed to the north bank of the river and camped near Shallow Ford, and on July 12 he marched back with his division to his camps on Rottenwood Creek.

The time between noon July 10 and July 12 was spent in building a bridge across the Chattahoochee, but Sixteenth Corps remained in its position near Roswell until July 17, while waiting for supplies to be brought up and making the necessary preparations for a resumption of the advance toward Atlanta.

On the night of July 9, 1864, after Johnston had learned that Federal troops had crossed to the east bank of the Chattahoochee, he abandoned his defensive line in front of the railroad crossing of the river and withdrew his army to the east bank to a new position in front of Atlanta. On the morning of July 10, when Sherman learned of Johnston's departure, all divisions of the army that had remained in front of Johnston's line pushed forward, occupied the abandoned works, and moved up to the river bank in preparation for crossing.

On July 10, 1864, Sherman ordered Howard to move with the divisions of Stanley and Wood of his Fourth Corps to a position near the mouth of Soap Creek, where he would be in position to support Schofield's Twenty-Third Corps, which was on the high ground beyond the river. On July 12, Stanley's division crossed the Chattahoochee River on Schofield's bridge and moved down the east bank of the river to cover the building of a bridge at Powers' Ferry, about two miles below the mouth of Soap Creek.

Wood's division crossed the river at Powers' Ferry July 12, 1864 and went into camp, remaining there until July 17. Newton's division, having returned from Roswell after having been relieved by Sixteenth Corps, crossed the river at Powers' Ferry and took position on the left of Wood. Newton remained there until July 18. On July 17, Wood's division moved downstream to cover the laying of a pontoon bridge at Pace's Ferry for the passage of Fourteenth Corps, and late that afternoon Wood returned to his camp.

At 5:00 P.M. July 12, 1864, Logan started his Fifteenth Corps of the Army of the Tennessee on the road to follow Dodge's Sixteenth Corps toward Roswell. The corps passed through Marietta on the morning of July 13, and that evening Logan's leading division reached Roswell. The other two divisions camped a short distance from the town. On July 15, Logan crossed the Chattahoochee at Roswell and took position on the left of Dodge.

When the rest of McPherson's army departed for Roswell, Blair's Seventeenth Corps was detached and left behind near the Chattahoochee to await the return of Stoneman's cavalry, which had moved out on an expedition of four or five days in the direction of Campbelltown as a diversion, and also with instructions to destroy the Atlanta and West Point Railroad southwest of Atlanta if possible. Finally, on July 16, 1864, Blair marched toward Roswell, rejoining the rest of the Army of the Tennessee on the south side of the Chattahoochee on the morning of July 17.

BATTLES AROUND ATLANTA, GEORGIA

On the morning of July 17, 1864, Sherman began his final advance toward Atlanta. In the weeks to follow, there would be much hard fighting around the city, but in the end, on September 1, 1864, Sherman would achieve his goal of the campaign, the capture of Atlanta. For this advance, Sherman directed McPherson to move forward with the Army of the Tennessee on the left of the army toward Stone Mountain and the Georgia Railroad, which connected Atlanta with Augusta, Georgia and the Carolinas; Schofield, with the Army of the Ohio, was to advance in the center toward Decatur, Georgia, which was also on the Georgia Railroad; and Thomas, with the Army of the Cumberland, was to move forward on the right toward Atlanta.

On the morning of July 17, 1864, the Army of the Tennessee began its march from near Roswell toward Decatur. Logan moved first with his Fifteenth Corps, and at 5:30 A.M. marched down the road toward Cross Keys until he reached Providence Church. He then turned to the left onto a road (sometimes called the Decatur road), continuing on that road until he reached Nancy's Creek, where he camped for the night.

Dodge, with his Sixteenth Corps, followed Logan and marched southward on the road to Old Cross Keys, which was about three miles southwest of Cross Keys on Nancy's Creek. He then crossed the creek and camped on the far side that night. Dodge had been advancing that day between Blair's Seventeenth Corps on the left and Schofield's Twenty-Third Corps on the right, and during the night he established connections with both corps.

On July 17, 1864, the Army of the Ohio moved forward on the right of the Army of the Tennessee. Cox's division moved that day to Sandy Springs Church, and then on to Old Cross Keys, with Reilly's brigade in the lead, and the division camped that night on the north bank of Nancy's Creek, where it connected with Dodge's corps. Hascall's division marched on the right of Cox, on the Sandy Creek and Buck Head road, and halted on the road that night about two and one-half miles from Buck Head and about two miles from Cox's division.

On July 17, 1864, Hooker's Twentieth Corps moved forward from its camps to the Chattahoochee River, crossing to the east side during the day. That morning William T. Ward's Third Division crossed the river at Pace's Ferry, marching to the left on the main road and camping that night about a mile from Nancy's Creek. Alpheus S. Williams' division remained near Nickajack Creek until July 17, and that afternoon followed Ward's division across the river at Pace's Ferry. Williams then turned to the left, marched for a mile or so from the bridge, and camped that night on the Howell's Ferry road that ran south from Pace's Ferry along the Chattahoochee to Howell's Ferry, which was near the mouth of Nancy's Creek. At 5:00 P.M. John W. Geary's Second Division followed Ward to Pace's

Ferry, crossing the river just before dark. Geary then took the road that branched to the left from the Buck Head road, advanced about two miles, and camped that night west of Nancy's Creek.

On the morning of July 17, 1864, Palmer's Fourteenth Corps moved to Pace's Ferry, and during the day it crossed the river. Jefferson C. Davis arrived at Pace's Ferry at daylight that morning with James D. Morgan's First Brigade and John G. Mitchell's Second Brigade of his Second Division, and, after a delay while a bridge was being completed, he crossed the river and moved up to the high ground beyond. Morgan, whose brigade was in the lead, found the enemy about a mile from the river but pushed on, and that night Davis' entire division took position near Kyle's Bridge on Nancy's Creek. Richard W. Johnson, who had resumed command of First Division July 13, crossed next and moved up into position on the left of Davis. There he formed his division with Marshall F. Moore's Third Brigade on the left of Davis, Anson G. McCook's First Brigade on the left of Moore, and John H. King's Second Brigade in reserve with the artillery. At 4:00 P.M. Moore advanced to the southeast on the road to Buck Head as far as Nancy's Creek, where he bivouacked for the night. Absalom Baird's Third Division crossed last and joined the other two divisions near Nancy's Creek. Caleb J. Dilworth's Third Brigade of Davis' division remained in its camp of the day before, but on the morning of July 18, it crossed the river and rejoined the division.

Early on the morning of July 18, 1864, McPherson's Army of the Tennessee began its march toward Decatur and Stone Mountain. Logan's Fifteenth Corps left its camps at 5:00 A.M. and marched on the Roswell and Decatur road as far as the Widow Rainey's house, and there it turned off and moved toward Stone Mountain by way of Blake's Mill to Browning's Court House at the intersection of the Stone Mountain road and the Lawrenceburg and Decatur road. Logan halted there in support of Garrard's cavalry, which was engaged in destroying the track of the Georgia Railroad. Joseph A. J. Lightburn's Second Brigade of Morgan L. Smith's Second Division moved on about three miles to Stone Mountain Depot, where it arrived at 3:00 P.M. and destroyed about two miles of track. It then rejoined the corps, which camped that night at Henderson's Mill.

Blair's Seventeenth Corps followed Logan July 18, 1864 and camped that night near Cross Keys.

At 6:00 on the morning of July 18, 1864, Dodge moved across country with his Sixteenth Corps to Peach Tree Road, crossed that road, and continued on to the Roswell and Decatur road, which he reached at the Widow Rainey house. He then moved south on the latter road toward Decatur and bivouacked that night on the North Fork of Peach Tree Creek.

Schofield's Twenty-Third Corps resumed its march toward Decatur July 18, 1864, with Cox's division in the lead. Cox marched by way of Old Cross Keys to Johnson's Mill on the North Fork of Peach Tree Creek, and from there he moved to the House plantation on the old Peach Tree road, camping there that night. Hascall's division, which had been advancing on the right of Cox during the day, passed Cox's camp that evening and prepared to take the lead in the march the next day.

On July 18, 1864, Thomas' Army of the Cumberland crossed Nancy's Creek and advanced to a position in front of the old Peach Tree road that ran from Turner's Ferry to Decatur. At the end of the day, the right of Palmer's Fourteenth Corps rested near the junction of Nancy's Creek with Peach Tree Creek, Hooker's Twentieth Corps was on the left of Palmer, and Howard's Fourth Corps was on the left of Hooker at Buck Head.

Howard moved out at 4:30 that morning toward Buck Head. He encountered little opposition as he marched southward until he reached Nancy's Creek near Sardis Church, where he found enemy cavalry in position on the far side. There was some delay while a bridge was rebuilt, but then Howard crossed the creek, pushed on, and arrived at Buck Head about noon. He then took position to the left of the town along the road that ran from Turner's Ferry, through Buck Head, to Decatur. During the advance that day, David S. Stanley's First Division was in the lead, John Newton's Second Division followed, and Thomas J. Wood's Third Division brought up the rear.

During the afternoon, Hooker's corps advanced on the right of Howard toward Buck Head, but before arriving there it turned to the right, camping that night on the road to Howell's Mill, which was located on Peach Tree Creek. It should be noted here, to avoid confusion, that there was another "Howell's Mill," not far away, on Nancy's Creek about one-half mile above its junction with Peach Tree Creek.

On July 18, 1864, Palmer's Fourteenth Corps crossed Nancy's Creek at Kyle's Mill and took position below and to the right of Hooker's corps. During the afternoon, Jefferson C. Davis' Second Division, with Caleb J. Dilworth's Third Brigade in the lead, marched out to Peach Tree Creek, camping that night on the north side of the creek, a short distance below Howell's Mill. Davis picketed along the bank of the creek from in front of his position on down to the mouth of the creek. Baird and Johnson advanced with their divisions on the Buck Head and Howell's Ferry road, and they formed in line, with Baird in front of Johnson, and with the skirmishers extending out in front to Peach Tree Creek.

Sherman continued the advance of his army on July 19, 1864, with the Army of the Tennessee pressing forward on the left toward Decatur. That morning Dodge's corps continued its march on the Roswell and Decatur road, and about two and one-half miles south of the North Branch of Peach Tree Creek, it encountered Schofield's corps, which was coming into the road from the right. Dodge then cut a road parallel to the Decatur road, crossed the South Fork of Peach Tree Creek at Mason's Mill, and entered Decatur at about the same time as the advance units of Twenty-Third Corps.

Dodge was then ordered to occupy and hold Decatur. For this purpose, he placed his Fourth Division—commanded by John W. Fuller since Veatch had become ill July 17, 1864—south of the town, and he brought up Thomas W. Sweeny's Second Division and placed it on the right of Fuller, west of the town.

Logan's corps moved to the railroad near Decatur, about six miles from Atlanta. After destroying some track, it moved on and camped on the north side of Decatur that night. Blair's corps, which had been following Logan, camped that night nearby.

Early on the morning of July 19, 1864, Hascall's division of Twenty-Third Corps, which had passed Cox's division at the House plantation the evening before, crossed the forks of Peach Tree Creek and marched toward Decatur. Peter T. Swaine's Second Brigade, First Division of Twenty-Third Corps, which was attached to Hascall's division, was in the lead, and it was strongly opposed by the enemy cavalry. Swaine pushed on, however, and occupied Decatur, but he was soon relieved by a part of Dodge's corps that had just arrived.

Cox's division marched at 5:00 that morning, in rear of Hascall's division, on the road toward Decatur. About a mile and a half from the town, Cox turned off to the right on the Atlanta road and moved forward toward Pea Vine Creek. This stream rises not far from Decatur and flows to the northwest to empty into Peach Tree Creek at a point almost due south of Buck Head and about one mile west of the junction of the North Fork and the South Fork of Peach Tree Creek. That night Cox camped and entrenched on the north bank of Pea Vine Creek, about four miles from Atlanta. Cameron's brigade was on the left, Reilly's brigade was on the right, and Barter's and Byrd's brigades were in reserve. That evening, when troops of the Army of the Tennessee arrived at Decatur, Hascall withdrew from the town and moved into position, where he supported Cox.

Early on the morning of July 19, 1864, the Army of the Cumberland resumed its advance toward Peach Tree Creek and Atlanta. On the left, Howard sent Wood with William H. Gibson's First Brigade and Frederick Knefler's Third Brigade of his division down the Buck Head and Atlanta road on a reconnaissance, and at 6:30 A.M. Wood reached the crossing of Peach Tree Creek. There he found the enemy entrenched on the far side, and about noon he directed Knefler to force a crossing of the creek and secure a lodgment on the south side of the creek. Knefler found a crossing place a short distance below the destroyed bridge on the Buck Head and Atlanta road, and he soon gained the south bank. A short time later, Gibson crossed farther upstream and then joined Knefler, and the two brigades soon had a strongly entrenched position south of the creek.

Also that morning, Stanley moved out from Buck Head with his division on a reconnaissance along the road toward Decatur, and he soon reached the bridge over the North Fork of Peach Tree Creek, which had been destroyed. Stanley then rebuilt the bridge, crossed the creek, and encamped on the far side that night on a line facing Atlanta.

Newton's division also moved out from Buck Head on a road that ran southward between the roads used by Stanley and Wood.

During the afternoon of July 19, 1864, William B. Hazen's Second Brigade of Wood's division was ordered up from Buck Head, where it had remained that morning when Wood moved south, to join the other two brigades south of Peach Tree Creek. That night Wood left Hazen to hold the bridgehead, and with Gibson's and Knefler's brigades he returned to Buck Head to pick up the camp equipage that they had left there when they started out on their reconnaissance that morning. About 11:00 that night, Newton sent Nathan Kimball's First Brigade across Peach Tree Creek to reinforce Hazen's brigade.

On July 19, 1864, Palmer's corps began crossing Peach Tree Creek. During the afternoon, Dilworth's brigade of Davis' division forced a crossing of the creek at the mouth of Green Bone Creek near Howell's Mill, and a short time later he was strongly attacked by the enemy. This attack was repulsed, but during the action, John G. Mitchell's Second Brigade crossed the creek and supported Dilworth. James D. Morgan's First Brigade of Davis' division was held in reserve on the north bank of the creek.

Baird was in reserve with his Third Division July 19, 1864, but he sent Moses B. Walker's First Brigade to cross the creek with Davis, and Walker moved into position on the left of Davis' line about dark. During the night Baird, with Newell Gleason's Second Brigade and George P. Este's Third Brigade, crossed Peach Tree Creek at Howell's Mill, and by midnight Baird's two brigades were entrenched on the hills south of the creek on the left of Davis.

Johnson's division of Palmer's corps spent the day of July 19, 1864 constructing bridges over Peach Tree Creek.

On July 19, 1864, Hooker advanced his Twentieth Corps in preparation for crossing Peach Tree Creek. Williams moved his division to the front and camped on the north side of the creek above Howell's Mill. Ward's division spent the day building bridges across the creek.

Geary advanced his division about two miles to a hill overlooking Howell's Mill, where Davis' division of Palmer's corps had already arrived and was then skirmishing with the enemy across the creek. Hooker moved Geary to the left, past the Casey house, and Geary massed his division in the woods on the hills above Peach Tree Creek. In this position he was about three-fourths of a mile above Howell's Mill on Peach Tree Creek, and his skirmishers connected with Howard's skirmishers on his left. Geary then prepared to cross the creek, and at about 3:00 P.M. he opened fire with the twelve guns of William Wheeler's 13th Battery, New York Light Artillery and Thomas S. Sloan's Battery E, Pennsylvania Light Artillery (also called Knap's Battery) on the Confederate positions on the hills south of the creek. Under the cover of this fire, the engineers constructed a foot bridge, and David Ireland's Third Brigade crossed the creek on the bridge and drove the enemy from the hills beyond. Geary followed with Charles Candy's First Brigade and Patrick H. Jones' Second Brigade and placed them in position on the right of Ireland.

Battle of Peach Tree Creek, Georgia, July 20, 1864. On July 20, 1864, Sherman again moved forward with his entire army toward Atlanta. On the left, McPherson's Army of the Tennessee marched westward from Decatur, with Logan's Fifteenth Corps starting at 5:00 A.M. on the direct road to Atlanta, and with Dodge's Sixteenth Corps following at 1:00 P.M. on the same road. Also that day, Blair marched with his Seventeenth Corps through Decatur, then advanced toward Atlanta on the left of Logan and Dodge by using country roads to the south of the Georgia Railroad. At the same time, Schofield's Twenty-Third Corps was advancing on a road parallel to that used by Logan and Dodge and about a mile and a half to the north of it.

Joseph Wheeler, who had been opposing Thomas' advance toward Peach Tree Creek July 17–18, 1864 with John H. Kelly's division and the brigades of Alfred Iverson, John S. Williams, and Samuel W. Ferguson, moved on July 19 to the Confederate right to delay McPherson's advance from Decatur.

As Logan advanced July 20, 1864, he soon encountered Wheeler's cavalry on his front along present-day Whitefoord Avenue. Because he was not connected with any other Federal troops on his right, he asked for help in protecting that flank. Dodge sent forward Thomas W. Sweeny's Second Division of his Sixteenth Corps to fill the gap between the right of Logan's corps and the left of Schofield's line. That night John W. Sprague was sent back to Decatur with his Second Brigade of John W. Fuller's Fourth Division, Sixteenth Corps to relieve Garrard's cavalry and guard the trains of the army that had been left there.

Logan halted about two and one-half miles from Atlanta and formed his corps for defense by placing Morgan L. Smith's Second Division, his leading division, across the road, facing Atlanta, and holding most of Charles R. Woods' First Division and William Harrow's Fourth Division in reserve. Woods had assumed command of First Division July 15, 1864, when Peter J. Osterhaus departed because of illness.

About three miles east of Atlanta, Blair came upon Wheeler's cavalry entrenched on a hill about a mile south of the railroad, and he deployed Walter Q. Gresham's Fourth Division in line of battle. Benjamin F. Potts' First Brigade, which was in the lead, advanced to within about 400 yards of Wheeler's position, and Potts then halted while he established contact with Fifteenth Corps on his right and waited for William Hall's Third Brigade to come up on his left. Mortimer D. Leggett's Third Division, which had been marching in reserve, was then moved up to the left of Gresham's line.

The hill occupied by Wheeler, and which was the scene of severe fighting July 20, 21, and 22, 1864, was called "Bald Hill" in some accounts of the battle, and after the Battle of Atlanta July 22, it was called Leggett's Hill. Present-day Moreland Avenue, which runs north and south, crosses Bald Hill just south of present-day Memorial Drive.

When Gresham's preparations were completed, he moved forward with his division to Bald Hill and launched an attack against Wheeler's line. Ferguson's brigade, which was on the right of Wheeler's position, was forced to give way, but Wheeler was able to reestablish his line and to hold the hill until the fighting ended that night. About midnight, Patrick R. Cleburne's division of Hardee's corps came up from the left of Hood's line and reinforced the Confederate line south of the railroad.

During the attack that afternoon, Gresham was seriously wounded, and William Hall, the senior officer of the division, assumed temporary command. Later that day, Giles A. Smith, commander of the First Brigade, Second Division, Fifteenth Corps, was assigned command of Gresham's division, and James S. Martin was assigned command of Smith's brigade.

On July 20, 1864, Schofield advanced with his Twenty-Third Corps about one and a half miles on a road from Cross Keys that ran to the southwest by way of the Howard house and Lewis' Mill toward Atlanta. Jacob D. Cox's Third Division, which was in the lead, encountered the enemy in position about three miles from Atlanta. The enemy line at that point was nearly parallel to the road on which Cox was marching, and Cox swung his right forward until his line was in front of the enemy works, with Daniel Cameron's Second Brigade on the right, James W. Reilly's First Brigade in the center, Richard F. Barter's First Brigade, First Division on the left, and Robert K. Byrd's Third Brigade in reserve. Milo S. Hascall's Second Division followed Cox on the road that day, and when Cox had halted and formed in line, William E. Hobson's Second Brigade of Hascall's division was brought up and placed on the right of Cox.

David S. Stanley's First Division of Howard's Fourth Corps, which had been advancing about a mile to the right of Cox, then came up on the right of Hobson, and together they advanced and gained possession of an important ridge close to the enemy's works.

That evening Hascall left Hobson's brigade to fill the gap between Cox and Stanley, and with his remaining brigades he moved to the left of Cox's line. Joseph A. Cooper's First Brigade of Hascall's division moved forward on the Atlanta road; Silas A. Strickland's Third Brigade was placed on the left of Cox; and Peter T. Swaine's Second Brigade, First Division was moved to the left of Hascall's line. Hascall then attacked and drove the enemy into an entrenched line near the Howard house.

On the morning of July 20, 1864, Howard was ordered to move one of the divisions of his Fourth Corps on the direct road toward Atlanta, and to move with the other two divisions on the most direct road to support Schofield, who was advancing on his left. Howard then ordered Newton to relieve Wood's division, and directed Wood to close up on Stanley, who was on the Decatur road. At 7:00 that morning, Stanley marched out on the Decatur road to the match factory, and there he turned to the right and advanced to the South Fork of Peach Tree Creek, which he began crossing at about 10:00 A.M. At that time Schofield was advancing on a road about a mile to the left. Stanley soon came up to the enemy works near the Wright house, on the right of Schofield. Wood marched about four miles to his

left that day, following Stanley's division by a road that crossed both forks of Peach Tree Creek above their junction, and when it came up, it formed on the right of Stanley. Stanley was engaged in some severe skirmishing that afternoon and evening.

John Newton's division was left to advance toward Atlanta on the direct road, but because it was then separated by about two miles from the other two divisions of the corps, Howard directed Newton to report for orders to Thomas, who had arrived on the ground about noon that day. Thomas then instructed Newton to remain where he was until Twentieth Corps came up and joined him on the right, and then to advance with Twentieth Corps toward Atlanta.

Newton moved his Second Division forward that morning and relieved Wood, and he was then about one-half mile south of Peach Tree Creek, with his left flank toward Clear Creek, and his entire line covering the crossroad leading to Collier's Mill. Newton formed his division on a line that was nearly perpendicular to Peach Tree road, with Nathan Kimball's First Brigade on the right of the road, John W. Blake's Second Brigade on the left of the road, and Luther P. Bradley's Third Brigade in position along the road in rear of the other two brigades. Newton also placed Wilbur F. Goodspeed's Battery A, 1st Ohio Light Artillery between the two front-line brigades. Blake was in temporary command of the Second Brigade of Newton's division from July 10 to July 25, during the illness of George D. Wagner.

On the morning of July 20, 1864, Joseph Hooker's Twentieth Corps also moved forward. Early that morning, Alpheus S. Williams' First Division crossed Peach Tree Creek, passed through Geary's division, and followed a farm road along a wooded ridge that crossed the Howell's Mill road at the H. Embry house, which was at the intersection of the Howell's Mill road and present-day Collier Mill Road (in July 1864 this was only a path). Williams halted about 600 yards from the Embry house and placed James S. Robinson's Third Brigade on the left (the position was across present-day Northside Drive) and Joseph F. Knipe's First Brigade on the right of Robinson. Thomas H. Ruger's Second Brigade was in rear of Knipe's line, but it was later moved to the right to connect with Palmer's Fourteenth Corps. A deep hollow separated Williams' division from Palmer's corps on his right, and another, deeper ravine was on his left. The ground in front of Williams' line was covered by dense woods and thickets. Williams placed the guns of Charles E. Winegar's Battery I, 1st New York Light Artillery and John D. Woodbury's Battery M, 1st New York Light Artillery so that they swept the ravines on both flanks and also the wooded ridge in front of Knipe's brigade.

At 10:00 that morning, Geary's skirmishers moved forward, supported by Candy's brigade, and with Jones' brigade following Candy. Geary crossed two wooded ridges and finally drove the enemy from a third ridge, and by noon Candy's brigade was formed on this ridge, with Jones' brigade in support to its left and rear, and with Ireland's brigade on a ridge in rear of Jones. Geary's left was covered by a ravine that ran down the slope to Shoal Creek (Tanyard Branch of Peach Tree Creek), and his right was on high ground and somewhat in advance of the left. There was open ground in front of Geary's left, and there he placed Henry Bundy's 13th Battery, New York Light Artillery and Thomas S. Sloan's Battery E, Pennsylvania Light Artillery and Candy's brigade. He then placed Jones' brigade on the right of Candy and Ireland's brigade in rear of Jones. Geary's division was separated from Williams' division on the right by a deep wooded ravine.

Ward's division crossed Peach Tree Creek on a bridge in rear of Newton's line, and then advanced to a hill on the left of Geary's position. This hill overlooked Shoal Creek, which ran through a deep valley between Ward's position and Geary's division on the right. There was open country in the valley, especially around Collier's Mill, which was a short distance in front of Ward's right flank. Ward's skirmishers, aided by Bundy's battery, which was firing from across the valley, soon forced the enemy to withdraw from the hill. The skirmishers then occupied the hill, and Ward moved into a cornfield at the base of the hill, with Benjamin Harrison's First Brigade on the right, John Coburn's Second Brigade in the center, and James Wood's Third Brigade on the left. The division remained there until about 3:00 P.M., when Hood's attack began, and it then advanced to the high ground in its front. Ward was unable to take his artillery with him when he advanced that morning because of the

difficult nature of the country through which he moved; it was left near Newton's bridge and was used by Thomas later in the day. Newton's division was ahead and to the left of Ward's division.

At daylight July 20, 1864, Johnson's division of Palmer's Fourteenth Corps crossed Peach Tree Creek and took position on the left of Baird's division, connecting on the left with Williams' division of Twentieth Corps. Anson G. McCook's First Brigade was on the left of the division, and on the east side of the Howell's Mill road, and it was the only brigade of Palmer's division that was engaged that evening.

When Johnson advanced that morning, Baird moved forward George P. Este's Third Brigade and placed it on the left of Moses B. Walker's First Brigade, which had crossed Peach Tree Creek with Davis' Second Division the day before and had taken position on a range of wooded hills about one-half mile in front of Baird's first position. Baird's division was under artillery fire all day, but was not otherwise engaged. Baird posted Otho H. Morgan's 7th Battery, Indiana Light Artillery and William P. Stackhouse's 19th Battery, Indiana Light Artillery in front of Johnson's division, where they were in position to deliver a cross fire on the enemy farther to their left. The batteries had just gone into position when the enemy attacked on the front of Twentieth Corps and on the left of First Division, Fourteenth Corps. Davis' division remained in its former position on the right of Fourteenth Corps during July 20, 1864.

Meantime, on July 10, 1864, after Joseph E. Johnston had withdrawn his army to the east side of the Chattahoochee River, he occupied a new line along high ground about a mile or so south of Peach Tree Creek, where it covered Atlanta on the north and west. This line began on the left at the Western and Atlantic Railroad, about two miles from the Chattahoochee River, and extended eastward for about six miles. It crossed the high ground on which today the Crest Lawn Cemetery is located, then crossed the Howell's Mill road, the valley of Shoal Creek, Peach Tree road at present-day Spring Street, the valley of Clear Creek, and then on about one mile to the east to the intersection of present-day North Highland Avenue and Zimmer Drive. There the line turned back to the south, making a sharp salient, and ran nearly parallel to present-day Highland Avenue and Moreland Avenue to the Georgia Railroad. It then continued on to the south and southeast to the vicinity of present-day Glenwood Avenue and Flat Shoals Avenue.

In addition to the advanced line, the Confederate engineers had constructed an inner line of works around the city. These works were roughly in the shape of a square, with the east, south, and west sides about three miles in length, and the north side somewhat shorter. At their nearest points these works were about one and one-fourth miles from the center of Atlanta. There were nineteen positions for batteries along this line, and in addition there were positions for batteries on a number of commanding hills in front of the entrenched line.

President Jefferson Davis and Confederate authorities in Richmond had become dissatisfied with Johnston's handling of the Army of Tennessee during its retreat from Dalton, and on July 17, 1864, Davis issued an order relieving Johnston in command of the army and assigning John B. Hood to command in his place. Hood assumed command the next day and almost immediately began preparations for an attack on Thomas' Army of the Cumberland as it was crossing Peach Tree Creek. In addition to the change in command of the army, there were also some changes in the commanders of the corps of the army. Alexander P. Stewart was placed in command of Leonidas Polk's former Army of Mississippi, relieving William W. Loring; Benjamin F. Cheatham assumed command of Hood's corps; and George Maney assumed command of Cheatham's division. Stewart's corps was on the left of Hood's line, Hardee's corps was in the center, and Cheatham's division was on the right.

According to the plan devised by Hood, Cheatham's corps was to remain in its position on the right, and Hardee and Stewart were to attack, beginning on the right, en echelon by divisions at intervals of 200 yards, against the left of Thomas' line and drive the Army of the Cumberland to the north and west toward the Chattahoochee River, with Peach Tree Creek in its rear. Thus, William B. Bate, whose division was on the right, was to attack first, and he was to be followed, in order to the left, by William H. T. Walker, George Maney, William W. Loring, Edward C. Walthall, and Samuel G. French. This attack was to begin at 1:00 P.M. July 20, 1864.

James B. McPherson and Schofield on Sherman's left, however, had advanced more rapidly from the east toward Atlanta than Hood had expected, despite Wheeler's efforts to slow them down, and on the morning of July 20, 1864, they were threatening Hood's far right flank. When Hood learned of this, he delayed his attack until he could shift his command a division front to the right to strengthen that flank. It was not until about mid-afternoon that the necessary adjustments had been made in Hood's line, and he was ready to attack.

At that time Hood's divisions were in line from left to right as follows:

Stewart's Corps. Samuel G. French's division was on the extreme left, with Matthew D. Ector's brigade on the left, and Francis M. Cockrell's brigade, commanded by Elija Gates, was on the right. Claudius W. Sears' brigade, commanded by William S. Barry, was posted on the Chattahoochee River.

Edward C. Walthall's division was on the right of French, with Daniel H. Reynolds' brigade on the left, south of the Embry house, and on the left side of the Howell's Mill road; and James Cantey's brigade, commanded by Edward A. O'Neal, was on the right side of the road near Mount Zion Church. William A. Quarles' brigade was in line, but was not to advance with the other two brigades; it was to wait until they had passed its front and then follow in support.

William W. Loring's division was to the right and front of the right flank of Walthall's division, and was in position between present-day Northside Drive and present-day Walthall Drive. Winfield S. Featherston's brigade was on the left, and Thomas M. Scott's brigade was on the right of the division line. Loring's other brigade, under John Adams, was on the Chattahoochee River.

Hardee's Corps. Benjamin F. Cheatham's division, then commanded by George Maney, was on the right of Loring's division and was due south of Collier's Mill. Marcus J. Wright's brigade, commanded by John C. Carter, was on the left of the division; Maney's brigade, commanded by Francis M. Walker, was in the center; Alfred J. Vaughan's brigade, commanded by Michael Magevney, Jr., was on the right; and Otho F. Strahl's brigade was in reserve.

William H. T. Walker's division was on the right of Maney's brigade, with its right on Peach Tree road. States Rights Gist's brigade was on the left, next to Maney; Clement H. Stevens' brigade was in the center; and Hugh W. Mercer's brigade was on the right, next to Peach Tree road.

Patrick R. Cleburne's division was in reserve in rear of Walker's line.

William B. Bate's division was about one mile to the northwest of Walker's division and was formed along the west side of Clear Creek, near its junction with Peach Tree Creek, and it faced to the northwest. Jesse J. Finley's brigade was on the left of the division, Joseph H. Lewis' brigade was on the right, and Robert C. Tyler's was in reserve.

Cheatham's Corps. Benjamin F. Cheatham's corps was farther to the right, with Joseph Wheeler's cavalry, and it was not engaged at the Battle of Peach Tree Creek. Gustavus W. Smith's Georgia Militia was on the inner line of works around the city.

The Confederates had completed their changes in position by about 2:00 P.M. and were ready to advance, but even then Hood's attack did not take place as planned. About 2:00 P.M. Hardee informed Stewart, who was on his left, that he was ready to attack; Loring, whose division was on the right of Stewart's line, observed some movement of Maney's division of Hardee's corps to his right and assumed that it was time for his attack. Accordingly, at about 2:45 P.M. Loring ordered his division forward, although Bate, who was to have attacked first, had not yet moved.

Featherston, commanding Loring's right brigade, advanced toward the right of Collier's Mill and drove back Ward's skirmishers to their main line. Ward then counterattacked and drove the enemy back. Featherston continued his attacks for the next several hours, but without success.

Loring's left brigade, commanded by Thomas Scott, advanced across the Collier road and attacked in the direction of Collier's Mill on Shoal Creek. He soon came under a very heavy fire from Geary's artillery and also infantry fire from a detachment of about 100 men—taken from the 102nd Illinois and 79th Ohio of Harrison's First Brigade of Ward's division—who were armed with Spencer rifles. Geary's artillery was in line from the the left of

Candy's brigade to Collier's Mill, and Ward's division was about 300–400 yards to the north, a little east of the mill. Scott's line was soon stopped, and then Harrison, advancing along Shoal Creek, counterattacked and drove the enemy beyond the Collier road. Coburn's brigade and Wood's brigade of Ward's division then came up and aided in repelling the attack.

Bate, who was to have started the attack that afternoon, did not begin his advance until about 3:15 or 3:30 P.M., and he then moved to the northwest along Clear Creek for about a mile, through thick woods and dense undergrowth, expecting to strike Union troops. Instead, he moved into the gap between Newton's division and the divisions of Wood and Stanley, which were farther to the east, and for a time Bate found no Federal troops on his front.

While Bate was thus engaged, Walker's division advanced along the west side of Peach Tree road toward Nathan Kimball's First Brigade (formerly Francis T. Sherman's brigade) on the right of Newton's line. As Walker advanced, he received a heavy fire from Goodspeed's battery, but his men pressed the attack vigorously, and Clement Stevens captured a part of Kimball's works before being driven back.

After Walker's attack had started, Maney advanced and passed around Kimball's right flank, which was somewhat unprotected because Ward's division of Twentieth Corps, which was on the right of Kimball, was several hundred yards to his right and rear. Kimball quickly refused the right of his line to meet Maney's attack, and he was soon supported by Ward's division. At the time of the enemy attack, Ward's division was in position in rear of the hill mentioned above, which was to the right and rear of Kimball's brigade, and then, acting on their own initiative, the brigade commanders led their troops to the top of the hill and opened fire, forcing the enemy to fall back.

Meantime, at about 4:00 P.M., as Scott's attack was ending in failure, Walthall advanced with two of his brigades against the right of Geary's division and the front of Williams' division, which was about 500 yards to the rear of Geary. O'Neal's brigade, which was on the right of the division, charged across the Collier road against the right of Geary's line and had some initial success. Geary then changed front to the right under heavy fire to connect with the left of Williams' division. This was done by changing the front with all of Candy's brigade except the 147th Pennsylvania and deploying Ireland's and Jones' brigades in one line, with Ireland's left connecting with Candy's right and Jones' right with the left of Robinson's brigade, which was on the left of Williams' line. O'Neal pushed forward into the ravine that separated Geary's and Williams' divisions, and was soon driven back with very heavy losses by a deadly cross fire by the refused part of Geary's line and Robinson's brigade, and also by the Federal artillery firing canister.

Daniel H. Reynolds, advancing with his brigade to the left of O'Neal, attempted to move into the ravine that ran between the right of Williams' line and the left of Johnson's division of Palmer's Fourteenth Corps. Williams deployed a part of Ruger's brigade, which was in rear of Knipe's brigade, and Reynolds was soon stopped. Anson G. McCook's First Brigade of Johnson's division, which was on the left of Palmer's line, aided in repelling the attack on the right of Williams' line, but apparently McCook was not under attack.

With the failure of the attacks on the right of the Army of the Cumberland, the fighting at Peach Tree Creek ended. O'Neal was without support on his right, and no enemy troops came up to help Reynolds. Quarles' brigade of Walthall's division, which was to have followed O'Neal and Reynolds, was, for some reason, unable to move forward and attack. Further, French's division, which was on the left of Walthall, did not attempt to advance that afternoon. By 6:00 P.M. the Battle of Peach Tree Creek was over, and at dusk Stewart ordered his troops back to their entrenchments.

During the afternoon, while Bate was attempting to find the left of Newton's line, he ran into Bradley's reserve brigade, and Bradley, aided by a section of Goodspeed's battery and George W. Spencer's Battery M, 1st Illinois light Artillery, drove back Bate's troops.

Also during the afternoon attacks on Newton's left and front, Thomas directed Jerome B. Stephens' Battery C, 1st Ohio Light Artillery and Luther R. Smith's Battery I, 1st Michigan Light Artillery of Ward's Third Division, Twentieth Corps to move forward and take position, and they aided in repulsing the enemy attacks on Newton's line.

Battle of Atlanta, Georgia, July 22, 1864. On July 21, 1864, Sherman's army resumed, on a limited scale, its advance on Atlanta, which had been interrupted by Hood's attack at Peach Tree Creek the day before. George H. Thomas' Army of the Cumberland made some adjustments in its positions and pushed forward toward Hood's advanced line north of Atlanta. That day, Alpheus S. Williams' First Division, John W. Geary's Second Division, and William T. Ward's Third Division of Joseph Hooker's Twentieth Corps, and John Newton's Second Division of Oliver O. Howard's Fourth Corps spent the day burying the dead and caring for the wounded.

During the night of July 20, 1864, the enemy withdrew from the area between the left of Newton's division and the North Fork of Peach Tree Creek, and the next day Thomas J. Wood moved forward the right of his Third Division of Fourth Corps about a mile and a half to a point near the enemy works. David S. Stanley's First Division of Fourth Corps also moved up on the left of Wood near the enemy works. Newton's division, as already noted, did not move that day, but remained in position on the Buck Head and Atlanta road. On the far right, John M. Palmer's Fourteenth Corps moved up close to John B. Hood's advanced line.

John M. Schofield's Army of the Ohio spent the day of July 21, 1864 making reconnaissances, cutting roads, and opening connections with James B. McPherson's Army of the Tennessee on its left. Milo S. Hascall's Second Division made the connection with the Army of the Tennessee, and Jacob D. Cox's Third Division worked at strengthening its works along present-day Briarcliff Road.

On July 21, 1864, the Army of the Tennessee was more active than the rest of Sherman's army. Early that morning, McPherson ordered Frank P. Blair, commanding Seventeenth Corps, to capture Bald Hill, which he had failed to do the day before. Joseph Wheeler's cavalry still held the hill, but he was supported on the left by Patrick R. Cleburne's division, which had arrived during the night, and whose line extended northward from Bald Hill to the Georgia Railroad.

That morning Giles A. Smith's Fourth Division of Seventeenth Corps was on the right of the corps line, connecting with the left of John A. Logan's Fifteenth Corps, and Mortimer D. Leggett's Third

Division was on the left of the line, and on the left of Sherman's army. About 2:00 that morning, Giles A. Smith had arrived and relieved William Hall, who had been in temporary command of Fourth Division, Seventeenth Corps since Walter Q. Gresham was wounded in the attack on Bald Hill the day before.

Manning F. Force's Third Brigade of Leggett's division was selected to make the attack on Bald Hill, and it was to be supported on the right by Giles A. Smith's division. Force moved out with his brigade for the attack, and for a time he advanced under the cover of the hill, but he then moved out into the open and charged the works on the crest. This attack, like that of the day before, struck Samuel W. Ferguson's cavalry brigade, which gave way and left the right of William W. Allen's brigade exposed. Force then again charged, driving from the hill Wheeler's cavalry and Cleburne's right brigade, commanded by Joseph T. Smith. At the same time, Giles A. Smith launched a supporting attack to the right of Leggett against Cleburne's division between the Georgia Railroad and Bald Hill, but it was soon stopped by a heavy fire. Joseph T. Smith's men, however, held their ground for about a half-hour until Leggett had secured Bald Hill, and then they fell back to their main lines. The Confederates made several attempts to recapture the hill that day, but all were repulsed.

The Federal occupation of Bald Hill, which was a commanding position, forced the Confederates to fall back from their lines in front of Giles A. Smith's division, and also from in front of Fifteenth Corps to a position nearer Atlanta.

Later in the day of July 21, 1864, enemy troops were observed moving to the Federal left, and to counter this movement, Giles A. Smith's Fourth Division was sent to the left of Leggett's Third Division, where it took position on the Flat Shoals road (or old McDonough road) along a continuation of the same ridge on which Leggett's division was formed. The left flank of Giles A. Smith's division was refused to face toward the east.

On July 21, 1864, Logan's Fifteenth Corps remained in essentially the same position that it had occupied the day before, on the right of Seventeenth Corps, but Logan brought up William Harrow's Fourth Division and placed it on the left of Morgan L. Smith's Second Division and formed Charles R.

Woods' First Division (commanded by Peter J. Osterhaus until July 15) on the right of Morgan L. Smith's division.

Grenville M. Dodge's Sixteenth Corps was to the right of Fifteenth Corps, but it was not all in line. Late in the evening of July 21, 1864, John W. Fuller was ordered to move with the First Brigade of his Fourth Division, commanded by John Morrill, and place it in reserve in rear of Seventeenth Corps. It took position south of Bald Hill at present-day Langley Street. Fuller also took Albert M. Murray's Battery F, 2nd United States Artillery, which was attached to Fuller's division, and placed it in front of Giles A. Smith's division of Seventeenth Corps.

Very early on the morning of July 22, 1864, Federal pickets all along the line reported that the enemy had evacuated their main line of advanced works and had retired toward Atlanta, and soon Sherman's entire army was moving forward in pursuit. On the front of Howard's Fourth Corps, the skirmishers of Stanley's and Wood's divisions occupied the vacated works, and at 4:30 A.M. both divisions moved southward toward Atlanta in pursuit. About two miles from camp, and two miles from Atlanta, Stanley and Wood came up on the enemy on an exterior line of works.

At 7:00 A.M. Howard ordered Stanley to deploy and attempt to connect with Schofield's Twenty-Third Corps on his left, and by 8:20 A.M. Stanley had completed his deployment in front of the enemy works. An hour later Wood, who was marching on the direct road to Atlanta, was ordered to deploy on the right of Stanley and to connect with Stanley's division. About 9:00 A.M. the head of Newton's division, which was advancing on the Buck Head and Atlanta road, arrived at the Walker house and formed on the right of Wood's division.

On the evening of July 22, 1864, Howard's corps held a line about two miles in length, with its left connecting with Twenty-Third Corps on the road that ran into Atlanta by way of the August Hurt house, about one-half mile southeast of the Buck Head and Atlanta road, and its right connecting with Hooker's Twentieth Corps to the right of the Buck Head and Atlanta road.

On the morning of July 22, 1864, Hooker's Twentieth Corps advanced on the right of Howard's corps, and to the right of the Buck Head and Atlanta road, toward Atlanta. Ward's division moved south on the left of the corps line, and it connected on the left with the right of Newton's division of Fourth Corps. Geary's division moved forward on the right of Ward and marched across country for about a mile in the direction of Atlanta. It crossed the works abandoned by the enemy, then turned to the right and moved up to the road running from Howell's Mill to Atlanta. Williams' division of Twentieth Corps and Palmer's Fourteenth Corps were marching on this road, but Geary followed them to a point where the Marietta and Atlanta road joined, and he then took position about one-half mile east of the Howell's Mill road, where he connected with the right of Ward's division.

Williams' division moved forward toward Atlanta on the Pace's Ferry road, on the right of Geary, and took position about two miles from the city. It connected on the left with Geary's division and on the right with Fourteenth Corps. On July 23, 1864, Ward advanced his line somewhat, remaining in that position until July 27, when he was relieved by Geary, and he then moved back into reserve.

On July 22, 1864, Palmer's Fourteenth Corps also advanced toward Atlanta, with Richard W. Johnson's First Division on the left, next to Hooker's corps, Absalom Baird's Third Division in the center, and Jefferson C. Davis' Second Division on the right, and on the right of Sherman's army. Baird's division advanced to the Marietta and Atlanta road, following it until it reached the railroad about two miles from Atlanta, and there he came up with Williams' division, which had already moved up close to the enemy's works. Baird then moved southward along the west side of Atlanta to a point where the Atlanta and Turner's Ferry road intersected the road running from White Hall to Turner's Ferry, and he put his division in line at that place. Davis' division, keeping to the right of Baird, moved to the west side of the Marietta and Atlanta road and took position on the Turner's Ferry road, where it connected with the right of Baird's division. The right of Palmer's corps rested near the Western and Atlantic Railroad, about two and a half miles from Atlanta. Davis remained in position until July 28, and Baird's and Johnson's divisions did not move until August 3.

On the morning of July 22, 1864, Schofield's Army of the Ohio, or Twenty-Third Corps, was in position northeast of Atlanta, between the Army of the Cumberland on the right and the Army of the Tennessee on the left. When Schofield learned from his pickets at about 1:00 A.M. that the enemy had abandoned their line on his front, he advanced his corps, moving to the right of Fifteenth Corps of the Army of the Tennessee, to the front of the Howard house on the road running in from the South Fork of Peach Tree Creek to Atlanta. Upon arriving there, he entrenched his position and established his batteries, with Hascall's Second Division on the left, next to Fifteenth Corps, and Cox's Third Division on the right.

About noon Schofield sent James W. Reilly's First Brigade of Cox's division back to Pea Vine Creek to secure a position covering the trains at Decatur, and to protect the rear of Twenty-Third Corps. About an hour later, when the fighting began on the left of McPherson's line, Cox was directed to move with Daniel Cameron's Second Brigade, Richard F. Barter's First Brigade, First Division, Twenty-Third Corps, and Alonzo D. Harvey's 15th Battery, Indiana Light Artillery to a point on the Georgia Railroad about one and a half miles from Decatur, where it was to protect the left and rear of the Army of the Tennessee. Barter entrenched on the left of the railroad, Cameron's brigade on the right, and Harvey's battery was placed between the two brigades. Robert K. Byrd's Third Brigade remained in position to the right of Hascall's division, and during the day was engaged fortifying its line.

Very early on the morning of July 22, 1864, the Army of the Tennessee, which was to be engaged in heavy fighting that day, was generally in position along a north-south line facing west toward Atlanta. This line began on the right at a point north of the railroad near present-day Austin Avenue at Euclid Avenue, where it connected with Twenty-Third Corps, and ran southward along present-day Moreland Avenue, crossed the Georgia Railroad about one and a half miles east of Atlanta, then ran over Bald Hill, and continued down the Flat Shoals road (or old McDonough road) to a point in present-day East Atlanta.

Thomas W. Sweeny's Second Division of Dodge's Sixteenth Corps was on the right of the line of the Army of the Tennessee, next to Twenty-Third Corps. Logan's Fifteenth Corps was on the left of Sweeny's division, with Charles R. Woods' First Division on the right, Morgan L. Smith's Second

Division in the center, and William Harrow's Fourth Division on the left. The Georgia Railroad passed through Logan's line between Woods' division and Morgan L. Smith's division.

Blair's Seventeenth Corps was on the left of the Army of the Tennessee and on the extreme left of Sherman's army. Leggett's Third Division was on Bald Hill, on the right of the corps line, and next to Fifteenth Corps. Giles A. Smith's Fourth Division was on the left of Leggett's division and was posted on a ridge that extended along the Flat Shoals road. Benjamin F. Potts' First Brigade was on the right of the division line, next to Leggett's division, and William Hall's Third Brigade was on the left, and was partially refused to run back to the north across the Flat Shoals road.

Fuller, with Morrill's First Brigade, Fourth Division of Sixteenth Corps, was in reserve on the left of the army, in rear of the center of Seventeenth Corps; John W. Sprague's Second Brigade, Fourth Division was at Decatur guarding the trains; and James H. Howe's Third Brigade, Fourth Division, commanded by William T. C. Grower after July 21, was at Decatur, Alabama July 22, and it did not join the army at Atlanta until August 7.

At about 4:00 A.M. July 22, 1864, pickets of the Army of the Tennessee discovered that the enemy had evacuated their works on the front of the army and had fallen back to their main line of works near Atlanta. McPherson then advanced his lines, and the troops soon occupied the line that had been held by the enemy the evening before. Work was immediately begun on reversing the enemy's works to make them defensible.

Fifteenth Corps moved up to the new line in the same position, by divisions, as it had assumed the day before. Sweeny did not advance his entire division of Sixteenth Corps but sent forward a strong line of skirmishers. The rest of Sweeny's division was in reserve north of the railroad at present-day Candler Park. Blair, too, sent forward only a line of skirmishers, and continued to occupy Bald Hill and the ridge along Flat Shoals road with his main force.

Soon after McPherson had occupied his new position, he ordered Dodge to withdraw Sweeny's division from the right of the Army of the Tennessee, and to mass it in rear of a new position that was to be selected for Seventeenth Corps on the left of the army. Fuller was also instructed to move

Morrill's First Brigade of Fourth Division, Sixteenth Corps to the left of Blair's corps when it arrived at its new position. Sweeny moved promptly and had arrived at a point about one-half mile south of the Georgia Railroad and about three-fourths of a mile in rear of Blair's corps when he was informed that Blair would not move into his new position until that night. Sweeny was then ordered to bivouac where he was, which was near the intersection of present-day Memorial Drive with the Clay road (present-day Clay Street) and Clifton Street. Dodge also ordered Fuller to entrench the line that Morrill was to occupy, but at the time that Sweeny had halted, Fuller had not yet moved. The gap between the left of Twenty-Third Corps and the right of Fifteenth Corps that had been created by the withdrawal of Sweeny's division was filled by extending the flanks of the two corps.

Meantime, while Sherman was closing in on Atlanta, Hood was preparing for another attack. After his defeat at Peach Tree Creek July 20, 1864, Hood considered his situation and realized that his principal concern was McPherson's Army of the Tennessee, which was approaching Atlanta from the east and was threatening to pass around the Confederate right flank and move into the city. Accordingly, to counter this threat, Hood directed William J. Hardee to move back with his corps from his position south of Peach Tree Creek on the night of July 21 and march by a circuitous route, first to the south through Atlanta, then eastward to a point beyond the left flank of McPherson's line, and finally to turn back to the north and attack the rear of the Army of the Tennessee at daylight on the morning of July 22. At the same time, Benjamin F. Cheatham's corps, which was then in the defensive works east of Atlanta, was to attack to the left of Hardee. Alexander P. Stewart's corps, which was on the left of Hardee on the line south of Peach Tree Creek, was to move back into the main inner defense line near Atlanta.

Wheeler, with two divisions of his cavalry, was to move with Hardee until the latter was east of Atlanta, and he was then to move on to the east and attempt to destroy the Federal wagon train at Decatur.

Hardee left his lines about two and a half miles north of Atlanta at midnight and marched down the Buck Head and Atlanta road (present-day Peach Tree Road) to Atlanta. His column then passed through the city and moved out to the southeast on the McDonough road (present-day McDonough Boulevard) to a point a short distance north of South River, and there it turned back to the northeast on the Fayetteville road and marched toward Decatur. Sometime after midnight, early on the morning of July 22, Cleburne's division, which had withdrawn into Atlanta from its earlier position between the Georgia Railroad and Bald Hill, joined Hardee's column on the McDonough road.

The head of Hardee's column crossed Entrenchment Creek at Cobb's Mills on the Fayetteville road, about six miles southeast of Atlanta, and a short distance beyond reached a road that branched off to the left and ran toward the north. At that point Hardee ordered Cleburne to move up this road, which was along the line of present-day Bouldercrest Drive, and deploy his division for the attack in the area of present-day East Atlanta. According to Hood's orders, Hardee was to begin his attack at daylight on the morning of July 22, 1864, but the last of Hardee's corps did not leave Atlanta until about 3:00 that morning, and it was shortly after dawn when Cleburne's division turned off on the road that ran toward the left of Blair's Seventeenth Corps.

Hardee continued on along the Fayetteville road with the divisions of William H. T. Walker, William B. Bate, and George Maney for a mile or so as far as Sugar Creek, and then Hardee's column, with Walker's division in the lead, turned off to the left on a road that ran roughly parallel to that used by Cleburne. Walker soon came up to Mrs. Terry's mill pond, which was wide and deep and about one-half mile long and was directly across his line of march. Hardee ordered Walker and Bate to move around the western side of the pond, which required a considerable amount of time.

Maney's division also came up to the pond, but Hardee decided to shift his division to the extreme left of his corps instead of following Walker and Bate around this obstruction. Maney then marched back to the southwest to reinforce Cleburne and extend his line to the left. It was not until shortly before 5:00 P.M. that Maney arrived in rear of Cleburne's line and prepared to attack.

After passing Terry's pond, Walker, followed by Bate, turned back toward the northeast. Just after the head of Walker's column reached the eastern slope of the valley beyond Sugar Creek Bridge, at a point on present-day Glenwood Avenue near its intersection with Wilkinson Drive, Walker was killed by a Federal picket, and Hugh W. Mercer assumed command of his division.

Mercer and Bate quickly deployed, with Mercer's division in Sugar Creek Valley, facing to the northwest, and Bate's division on the right, facing west. When the deployment was completed, both divisions advanced. The first contact was made shortly after noon, when Walker's men encountered the pickets that were out in front of Dodge's Sixteenth Corps.

Meantime, Cleburne had completed the deployment of his division across the Flat Shoals road, just south of present-day Glenwood Avenue, with his right extending beyond the left of Blair's line and toward the left of Mercer's division. Daniel C. Govan's brigade was on the left, to the west of the Flat Shoals road; James A. Smith's brigade was on the right, east of the Flat Shoals road; and Mark P. Lowrey's brigade was in reserve about 500 yards in rear of the front line.

The last two miles of Hardee's advance were over unfamiliar and very difficult ground. The area traversed had never been cultivated and was covered with dense oak forests and thick and tangled undergrowth of bushes, briers, and vines, and in addition there were numerous swamps and ravines across which the men had to make their way. The nature of the country accounts in part for the lateness of the hour when Hardee began his attack, but also there was the long march of about fifteen miles all through the latter part of the night, during which the men had no sleep at all.

About noon July 22, 1864, Dodge and Sweeny heard firing on the left and rear of Blair's corps, and Sweeny immediately sent out skirmishers in that direction. They soon came upon the enemy in the woods in rear of Blair's line. Dodge ordered Sweeny to form in line of battle on the ground that he then occupied, facing to the east and south, and at the same time he ordered Fuller to post a regiment to cover the right flank of Sweeny's position.

Elliott W. Rice's First Brigade was on the left of Sweeny's division, along the Clay road (present-day Clay Street), facing to the east, with its right near present-day Memorial Drive, and August Mersey's Second Brigade was on the right, along Memorial

Drive, facing south, with its left extending across present-day Clifton Street. Jerome B. Burrows' 14th Battery, Ohio Light Artillery of Fuller's Fourth Division, Sixteenth Corps, commanded temporarily by Seth M. Laird, was placed between Rice and Mersey, and Andrew T. Blodgett's Battery H, 1st Missouri Light Artillery of Sweeny's division was placed on present-day Clifton Street, to the left and rear of Rice's brigade, facing east. Sweeny's division was scarcely in position when the enemy was discovered in heavy force on its front. When Fuller noted this, he ordered out the whole of Morrill's brigade instead of the one regiment, and it took position to the right of Sweeny's division.

Sometime after noon, Bate's Confederate division approached Rice's brigade from the east along present-day Memorial Drive, with Robert C. Tyler's brigade on the right, Joseph H. Lewis' brigade in the center, astride present-day Memorial Drive, and Jesse J. Finley's brigade on the left, attacking toward the left of Mersey's brigade. Mercer's division attacked from the southeast, on the left of Bate, with J. Cooper Nisbet's brigade on the right, advancing toward Mersey's brigade; Mercer's brigade, commanded temporarily by Cincinnatus S. Guyton, in the center, moving along the west side of Sugar Creek; and States Rights Gist's brigade on the left, advancing on Morrill's brigade of Fuller's division, which was in position just north of present-day McPherson Avenue. As Bate's and Mercer's men pushed forward toward Sweeny's line, they were struck by a destructive fire and were soon forced to halt. Sweeny then ordered a charge, and the enemy columns on the Federal left and front were driven back into the woods. After repulsing this first attack, Dodge retired his line somewhat and refused both flanks. During the afternoon, Mercer and Bate renewed their attempts to advance, but they were unable to do so.

There was a gap of about one-half mile between the left of Blair's corps and the right of Sweeny's division, and this had resulted from a delay in moving Blair's corps to a new position farther to its right. The direction of Hardee's attack was such that some of his troops moved forward into this gap, and when this was noted by Dodge, he sent out the 12th Illinois and the 81st Ohio of Mersey's brigade to protect his right flank. These regiments found a position from which they were able to deliver fire

that struck the enemy's flank and forced them to halt. Morrill's brigade also changed front to meet this threat and forced the enemy to fall back. Fuller advanced with Morrill's brigade but was soon struck by a heavy fire on his right flank. He then changed front to the rear and advanced on the enemy in the woods and drove them back.

McPherson was near Sweeny's division during its battle early that afternoon and, becoming concerned about the gap between Sixteenth Corps and Seventeenth Corps, he ordered Logan to send Hugo Wangelin's Third Brigade of Charles R. Woods' division of Fifteenth Corps, which was then in reserve north of the railroad, on the far right of the Army of the Tennessee, to move to the left of the army and support Fuller, who was with Morrill's brigade.

A short time after ordering Wangelin forward, McPherson rode off toward the line of Seventeenth Corps, which was then becoming engaged. He was crossing the gap between the two corps, accompanied by his staff, when he ran into some of Cleburne's skirmishers who were moving northward, and he was instantly killed about 2:00 P.M. John A. Logan was then assigned temporary command of the Army of the Tennessee, and Morgan L. Smith succeeded Logan in command of Fifteenth Corps. Joseph A. J. Lightburn assumed command of Smith's Second Division, Fifteenth Corps.

Meantime, about 1:00 P.M. Cleburne had begun his attack, advancing to the left of Mercer's division. James A. Smith's brigade, Cleburne's right brigade, drove back Morrill's brigade. Govan's brigade, advancing to the left of James A. Smith, moved into the gap and captured Albert M. Murray's Battery F, 2nd United States Artillery, while it was moving back to rejoin its proper command, which was Fuller's Fourth Division, Sixteenth Corps. Also captured with the guns were Murray and Joseph C. Breckinridge of the battery.

Govan's left regiments struck Hall's brigade, which was on the left of Giles A. Smith's division at the intersection of the Flat Shoals road and present-day Glenwood Avenue. Hall's line was driven back, but it then counterattacked and forced Govan's men to retire. Govan swung around the rest of his brigade until he overlapped the left of Hall's brigade, and he then charged and captured Hall's works, two guns of Walter H. Powell's Battery F,

2nd Illinois Light Artillery, and a number of prisoners.

Lowrey's brigade did not take part in this attack, but remained in position about 500 yards in rear of Cleburne's front line.

After their initial successes, Govan and James A. Smith continued their attacks. Govan pushed on and struck Potts' brigade of Giles A. Smith's division, which was on the right of Hall's brigade, and James A. Smith's brigade swung around to the left toward the eastern face of Bald Hill, which was held by Leggett's division. Force's First Brigade was on the right of Leggett's line at what is today the intersection of Moreland Avenue and Memorial Drive. Adam G. Malloy's Third Brigade was on Bald Hill, and Robert K. Scott's Second Brigade was on the left of the division, with its right on the hill and its left connecting with Potts' brigade of Giles A. Smith's division.

James A. Smith's brigade advanced against Bald Hill across the same ground over which Leggett's and Giles A. Smith's divisions had passed the day before to attack Wheeler's cavalry and Cleburne's division. Leggett's men quickly crossed to the reverse side of their entrenchments and succeeded in driving the attackers back. The enemy then reformed and attacked again, and there was savage fighting for possession of the works, but this too was repulsed. Force was seriously wounded during the fighting, and he was succeeded in command of the brigade by George E. Bryant. Scott was injured at the beginning of the attack, and he was replaced in command of the brigade by Greenberry F. Wiles.

John Sullivan's 3rd Battery, Ohio Light Artillery, Marcus D. Elliott's Battery H, 1st Michigan Light Artillery, and Edgar H. Cooper's Battery D, 1st Illinois Light Artillery, all of Leggett's division, were in action and aided in repelling the attack.

When James A. Smith's brigade attacked Bald Hill, Charles C. Walcutt's Second Brigade of Harrow's Fourth Division, Fifteenth Corps, which was to the right of Leggett's division, changed front to the left rear and, as the enemy moved up the hill, delivered a flanking fire that aided in repulsing the attack. Josiah H. Burton's Battery F, 1st Illinois Light Artillery and William H. Gay's 1st Battery, Iowa Light Artillery of Harrow's division also added their fire in defense of the hill.

At about 3:00 P.M., it appeared to Hood, from where he was observing the fighting, that the Federal left was being driven back by Hardee's attack, and he then ordered Cheatham to advance with his corps from the entrenched line on the east side of Atlanta against Leggett's division of Blair's corps and Morgan L. Smith's Fifteenth Corps (Logan's corps).

Carter L. Stevenson's division, which was on the right of Cheatham's corps, advanced against Leggett's division on Bald Hill and Walcutt's brigade of Harrow's division, which was immediately to the right of Leggett. Joseph B. Palmer's brigade, on the left of Stevenson's line, advanced against Walcutt's brigade; Edmund W. Pettus' brigade in the center advanced against the left of Walcutt's brigade and the right of Leggett's division; and Alexander W. Reynolds' brigade on the right moved toward Leggett's division on Bald Hill. Alfred Cumming's brigade advanced in rear of Pettus' brigade. As the enemy attacked at Bald Hill, the men of Leggett's division moved back to the east side of their works and soon drove the attackers back down the hill.

John C. Brown's division, attacking to the left of Stevenson, succeeded in breaking through the Fifteenth Corps line at the Georgia Railroad and driving back a part of the corps to the line that they had held before advancing that morning. Until an early hour on the morning of July 22, 1864, Arthur M. Manigault's brigade had occupied an entrenched line that crossed the railroad at a point between present-day Haralson Avenue and De Gress Avenue, and behind Manigault's line was an unfinished brick house belonging to George M. Troup. This house faced the railroad and the Decatur wagon road (present-day De Kalb Avenue), and was on the site of the present-day East Atlanta Primitive Baptist Church at 191 De Gress Avenue, NE.

When Brown's division abandoned this advanced line that morning and fell back closer to Atlanta, Morgan L. Smith's Second Division, Fifteenth Corps advanced with the rest of the Army of the Tennessee and occupied the vacated works on both sides of the railroad. James S. Martin's First Brigade was in front as the division advanced, and it was followed by Joseph A. J. Lightburn's Second Brigade. Upon arrival on the new line, Smith immediately put his men to work getting it in a defensible condition by reversing the works in some places and relocating them in others. At the Hurt plantation, the line was moved to the west of the unfinished house, where it crossed the railroad a short distance east of the Widow Pope's house, which was located near the junction of present-day Battery Place and De Kalb Avenue. At the point where the railroad passed through the Federal line, it ran through a deep cut.

Morgan L. Smith also sent out to the front a line of skirmishers, and he supported them with Wells S. Jones' 53rd Ohio of Lightburn's Second Brigade; the 111th Illinois of Martin's First Brigade, both regiments under the command of Jones; and a section of Samuel S. Smyth's Battery A, 1st Illinois Light Artillery. Jones took position in support of the skirmishers about one-half mile in advance of the main Federal line.

At about 3:00 P.M. there were a series of command changes in the Army of the Tennessee that were caused by the death of McPherson an hour earlier. Logan was assigned temporary command of the Army of the Tennessee, Morgan L. Smith assumed command of Fifteenth Corps, Joseph A. J. Lightburn was assigned command of Second Division, Fifteenth Corps, and Wells S. Jones was assigned command of Lightburn's Second Brigade.

About 3:00 or 3:30 P.M., when Benjamin F. Cheatham's line began to advance, the skirmishers of Morgan Smith's Second Division were driven in, and Jones fell back with his support to the main line. There he found his Second Brigade in the works on the north side of the railroad, with its left resting on the railroad, and a part of Martin's First Brigade on the left of Second Brigade, with its right on the railroad.

Earlier, at about 2:00 P.M., Martin had been ordered to take his reserve regiments, which consisted of the 116th Illinois, 127th Illinois, and 6th Missouri, and report with them to William Harrow, whose Fourth Division, Fifteenth Corps was to the immediate left of Lightburn's division. Samuel R. Mott was assigned command of the two regiments of Martin's brigade, the 57th Ohio and 55th Illinois, remaining in the works south of the Hurt house. Upon reporting to Harrow, Martin was assigned to a position in rear of Mortimer D. Leggett's Third Division of Seventeenth Corps, but almost immediately he received orders to move eastward on the Decatur road and report to Dodge. After Martin had reported to Dodge, his regiments were placed on the left of the line of Sixteenth Corps.

During the afternoon of July 22, 1864, in obedience to Cheatham's orders, Brown advanced his division astride the railroad, with Arthur M. Manigault's brigade on the left, just north of the railroad, and Zachariah C. Deas' brigade, commanded by John G. Coltart, on the right, just south of the railroad. Jacob H. Sharp's brigade followed Manigault, and Samuel Benton's brigade, commanded by William F. Brantly, followed Coltart. Manigault halted briefly in a ravine in present-day Springvale Park to wait until Coltart's brigade came up on his right, and he then advanced to the Widow Pope's house, under a heavy fire from Samuel S. Smyth's Battery A, 1st Illinois Light Artillery, which was posted at the railroad cut, and from Francis De Gress' Battery H, 1st Illinois Light Artillery, which was in position on the high ground at the northern end (the dead end) of present-day Battery Place. While some of Manigault's men opened fire on Lightburn's men from the Widow Pope's house, the main column pushed up the wagon road toward the Federal entrenchments. Under cover of the smoke from Smyth's guns, the enemy moved through the railroad cut and emerged about seventy-five yards in rear of the lines held by Jones' brigade and Mott's two regiments of Martin's brigade, and a short time later Manigault's men drove Jones' brigade and Martin's regiments in confusion from their positions to the north and south of the railroad. Some of Lightburn's men halted in the shelter of a ravine behind their front line, but the rest continued on to the line of works from which the division had advanced early that morning. Morgan L. Smith and Lightburn began the task of re-forming their men for a counterattack in the ravine.

On the Confederate right of Brown's division, Coltart's brigade advanced and struck the left flank of John M. Oliver's Third Brigade of Harrow's division, which was on the left of Mott's regiments, and drove it back. Brantly's brigade attacked farther to the Confederate right against Reuben Williams' First Brigade of Harrow's division, which was in position with its right on present-day Boulevard Drive and its left connecting with Charles C. Walcutt's Second Brigade, and forced it to fall back for some distance.

The position occupied by Charles R. Woods' First Division, Fifteenth Corps after it had advanced early that morning was on the left of Schofield's

Twenty-Third Corps, with its right resting at the Howard house, to the right of Lightburn's division. James A. Williamson's Second Brigade was on the right, Milo Smith's First Brigade was on the left, and Hugo Wangelin's Third Brigade was in reserve. At 11:00 that morning, Wangelin's brigade was detached and sent to the left to take position between Seventeenth Corps and Sixteenth Corps.

When the enemy broke through Lightburn's line at the railroad that afternoon, they halted on a line that was some 300–400 yards to the left and rear of Woods' division; its position became untenable, and Woods immediately formed a new line facing the enemy's left flank. He did this by swinging back the left of Williamson's brigade, while keeping its right in its original position at the Howard house, and changing the front of Milo Smith's brigade by refusing its left flank and taking position on the right of Williamson's brigade. Woods also advanced six guns belonging to George Froehlich's 4th Battery, Ohio Light Artillery and Louis Voelkner's Battery F, 2nd Missouri Light Artillery to aid in repelling the enemy attack.

At about 4:00 P.M., after Brown's division had begun its attack, Henry D. Clayton was ordered to close to the right with his division on the left of Brown and join in the attack against Fifteenth Corps. Clayton then formed his division with Alpheus Baker's brigade, commanded by John H. Higley, on the left of the first line; Marcellus A. Stovall's brigade, commanded by Abda Johnson, on the right of the first line; Randall L. Gibson's brigade was in rear of Baker's brigade; and James T. Holtzclaw's brigade, commanded by Bushrod Jones, was in rear of Johnson.

When the division was formed, Johnson's brigade attacked on the left of Brown's division, north of the railroad, and Jones was ordered to follow with his brigade. Clayton then observed some of Woods' men advancing toward his left, and he ordered Higley to advance with his brigade, then change front obliquely to the left and attack. Higley made some progress but was soon driven back. Gibson's brigade was moved to the right to support Brown, who by that time had been repulsed by Lightburn. Both Johnson and Gibson made some initial gains but were driven back.

When the enemy attacked Woods' position in front of the Howard house, Giles J. Cockerill's Bat-

tery D, 1st Ohio Light Artillery was moved from the line of Robert K. Byrd's Third Brigade of Jacob D. Cox's Third Division, Twenty-Third Corps and placed on a ridge about 100 yards in front of the Howard house, and it did good service in holding up the enemy's advance. Hascall also placed William E. Hobson's Second Brigade of his Second Division, which had been in reserve, near the Howard house.

When the enemy broke through Morgan L. Smith's line that afternoon, Logan went in person at 4:00 P.M. to Dodge to ask for help in driving back the enemy and recovering the position that Smith had occupied at the time of the attack. August Mersey's Second Brigade of Thomas W. Sweeny's Second Division was turned over to Logan, who led it back to the rear of the works held by Morgan L. Smith's division early that morning, and there it was deployed on the right of the railroad.

Logan also ordered Martin, who was then with Sweeny's division with his three regiments, to rejoin Lightburn's division. Martin marched back at the double-quick and, on arriving in front of the early morning line of works, formed his brigade in line of battle south of the railroad; Jones' brigade was placed in rear of Martin.

When Morgan L. Smith had completed his preparations, he ordered his line to move forward, with Woods' division on the right, Lightburn's division in the center, and Harrow's division on the left. Woods' men soon recaptured De Gress' battery and drove the enemy from the works they had captured north of the railroad. By 5:00 P.M. Lightburn and Harrow had reoccupied the works that they had lost that afternoon, and the entire front line east of Atlanta had been restored.

When Logan took Mersey's brigade from Sweeny's division to help Fifteenth Corps, he instructed Dodge to call on Schofield if he needed help, and at about 5:00 P.M., when the enemy made a demonstration on the left of Sixteenth Corps, Dodge asked Schofield for a brigade. Cox sent Barter's brigade, which was then on the railroad near Decatur, but the demonstration consisted only of artillery fire, and Barter was not engaged.

Meantime, at about 4:00 P.M. Lowrey's brigade had arrived at the front from its position in reserve and had renewed the attack against Giles A. Smith's division south of Bald Hill. The brigade charged right up to the Federal entrenchments, and the men engaged in vicious hand-to-hand fighting across the parapet, but finally Lowrey's brigade was forced to retire with the loss of about half of his command.

At about 5:00 P.M., as Lowrey's attack was ending, the final Confederate attack of the day was made by Maney's and Cleburne's divisions. Maney attacked from the southwest, on the left of Cleburne's division, with Francis M. Walker's brigade on the left, John C. Carter's brigade in the center, Michael Magevney's brigade on the right, and Otho F. Strahl's brigade in rear of the center of the line. Maney's division struck the front held by Scott's brigade of Leggett's division and Potts' brigade of Giles A. Smith's division, and Cleburne's division moved up on the right of Maney against the front and rear of Hall's brigade. Under a very heavy musketry and artillery fire, Giles A. Smith's division was forced to fall back on Bald Hill.

Leggett then moved out Wiles' Second Brigade to a line parallel to that which Giles A. Smith held. Wangelin's brigade of First Division, Fifteenth Corps moved forward, and a new line was formed that extended eastward from the crest of Bald Hill, facing south, with Wiles' brigade of Leggett's division on the right, Giles A. Smith's Fourth Division in the center, and Wangelin's brigade on the left. Fuller, with Morrill's brigade and Sweeny's division of Sixteenth Corps, was farther to the left.

Leggett also held the line to the right of Bald Hill with Malloy's brigade; the 11th Iowa of Hall's brigade of Giles A. Smith's Fourth Division and the 16th Wisconsin of Manning F. Force's First Brigade of Leggett's division held the angle of the works on the hill; and the rest of Leggett's Third Division held Bald Hill and extended down the east slope and into an open field.

The enemy made an attack on this line in heavy force. There was savage hand-to-hand fighting for possession of the breastworks, and this continued until dark, but then the enemy withdrew and the Battle of Atlanta was over.

Meantime, during the afternoon of July 22, 1864, while Hardee's and Cheatham's corps and the Army of the Tennessee were engaged just east of Atlanta, there was also fighting at Decatur, Georgia, farther to the east. Garrard's cavalry division, which had been covering the left flank of the army and the trains, was sent out that day to Covington, Georgia to continue the destruction of the Georgia Railroad. Wheeler's Confederate cavalry, which had accompanied Hardee's corps on its flanking movement that morning, moved on eastward about four miles, and shortly after noon advanced on John W. Sprague's Second Brigade of Fuller's Fourth Division, Sixteenth Corps, which was at Decatur guarding the trains. When Sprague learned of Wheeler's approach, he sent out four companies of Milton Montgomery's 25th Wisconsin, commanded by Jeremiah M. Rusk, and four companies of Charles E. Brown's 63rd Ohio, all commanded by Montgomery of the 25th Wisconsin, but they were quickly driven back into their works in front of the town. There, Sprague's brigade, supported by two sections of Trumbull D. Griffin's Chicago Board of Trade Battery, Illinois Light Artillery (also called Stokes' Battery) of Kenner Garrard's Second Cavalry Division and a section of Henry Shier's Battery C, 1st Michigan Light Artillery of Fuller's Fourth Division, Sixteenth Corps, resisted for a time an attack by Wheeler's dismounted cavalrymen; but when Wheeler attacked on his right flank and rear, Sprague fell back, first to a hill at the south line of the town, then to the courthouse square, and he finally withdrew from the town and moved northward on the road to Roswell, halting at the junction of the Pace's Ferry road, about a mile north of Decatur. There he was joined by Reilly's First Brigade of Twenty-Third Corps, which had been sent up from Pea Vine Creek. Wheeler did not pursue, however, but withdrew upon being recalled by Hardee. During Wheeler's attack on Sprague, the Northern teamsters hurried with their wagons to safety in rear of Twenty-Third Corps.

Battle of Ezra Church, Georgia, July 28, 1864. During the first few days following the Battle of Atlanta, Sherman's army remained generally in the positions that it had occupied at the close of the battle, while Sherman and Hood considered their next moves. Sherman, with Orlando M. Poe, his chief engineer, examined the enemy's inner line of works around Atlanta, and concluded that they were too strong for a successful attack. This, together with the fact that Sherman did not have a sufficient force to conduct regular siege operations, caused him to decide on a further effort to destroy the railroads that were bringing in the supplies needed for Hood's army at Atlanta.

At that time Federal forces held the Western and Atlantic Railroad running in from Chattanooga, and the Army of the Tennessee had effectively destroyed a part of the Georgia Railroad, which connected the city with Augusta, Georgia. Thus the only remaining railroads connecting Atlanta with the rest of the Confederacy were the Macon and Western Railroad, which ran to the northwest from Macon, Georgia through Lovejoy's Station, Jonesboro, and Rough and Ready to East Point, and the Atlanta and West Point Railroad, with which the Macon and Western shared a common track from there to Atlanta. The latter railroad ran in to East Point from West Point through La Grange, Newnan, Palmetto, and Fairburn.

Lovell H. Rousseau, moving south from Decatur, Alabama with a Provisional Cavalry Division of the Army of the Cumberland, had destroyed a part of the Montgomery and West Point Railroad at Opelika, Alabama July 17, 1864. This was a significant break in the enemy's communications because this railroad connected at West Point with the Atlanta and West Point Railroad, which ran on to Atlanta. The break was only temporary, however, because it could be repaired in a comparatively short time.

Sherman then decided that the best means of closing these last supply lines was to extend his right flank closer to the railroad by moving the Army of the Tennessee from its position on the left of the army to a new position on the right of the Army of the Cumberland, west of Atlanta. Simultaneously with this movement, Sherman planned to send his cavalry on raids to break up the railroads south of Atlanta.

By July 25, 1864, repairs on the Western and Atlantic Railroad had been completed, including the rebuilding of the bridge over the Chattahoochee River, to the camps of George H. Thomas' Army of the Cumberland. This enabled Sherman to abandon the Roswell road as a supply line for the army, and to bring up supplies closer to the right of the army as it extended southward toward the Macon and Western Railroad on the west side of Atlanta. Sherman then sent the trains and field hospitals of the Army of the Tennessee to a point near the mouth of Peach Tree Creek, and he issued orders for the Army of the Tennessee to begin its march on the night of July 26.

Just prior to and during the march of the Army of the Tennessee to the west of Atlanta, there were several significant changes in command in the army, and these are given here to prevent confusion in later descriptions of troop movements and positions. It has already been noted that John A. Logan was assigned temporary command of the Army of the Tennessee following the death of James B. McPherson July 22, 1864. On July 26, however, Sherman assigned Oliver O. Howard, commander of Fourth Corps, Army of the Cumberland, as the permanent commander of the Army of the Tennessee. Howard assumed command on the night of July 26, after the army had started its march.

Joseph Hooker, the senior corps commander of Sherman's army and a former army commander himself, was angered at being thus passed over for the command of the Army of the Tennessee. He asked to be relieved, and his request was granted. To replace Hooker in command of Twentieth Corps, Sherman selected Henry W. Slocum, who was at that time in command at Vicksburg, Mississippi. Until Slocum arrived, which was not until August 27, Alpheus S. Williams was in temporary command of Twentieth Corps.

As a result of the above changes, there were several other changes in command in Fourth Corps, Fifteenth Corps, and Twentieth Corps. When Howard assumed command of the Army of the Tennessee, Logan returned to the command of Fifteenth Corps, and Morgan L. Smith again took charge of Second Division, Fifteenth Corps. Then Joseph A. J. Lightburn resumed command of Second Brigade, Second Division, relieving Wells S. Jones, who returned to his regiment.

When Howard assumed command of the Army of the Tennessee, he was succeeded in command of Fourth Corps by David S. Stanley. William Grose took charge of Stanley's First Division, Fourth Corps, and P. Sidney Post assumed command of Grose's Third Brigade, First Division, Fourth Corps.

When Williams assumed command of Twentieth Corps, Joseph F. Knipe took charge of Williams' First Division, Twentieth Corps, and Warren W. Packer assumed command of Knipe's First Brigade, First Division, Twentieth Corps.

There were also several changes in command in Sixteenth Corps following the Battle of Atlanta July 22, 1864. John Morrill had been wounded that day, and Henry T. McDowell assumed command of his First Brigade of John W. Fuller's Fourth Division. August Mersey's term of service had expired, and, at his own request, he was relieved from command of Second Brigade, Second Division July 24. Jesse J. Phillips assumed command of the brigade.

On July 25, 1864, Thomas W. Sweeny, John W. Fuller, and Grenville M. Dodge engaged in a disgraceful argument, which ended in a fight; Sweeny was placed under arrest and sent to Nashville, Tennessee for court martial. Elliott W. Rice assumed temporary command of Sweeny's Second Division, and on July 26, John M. Corse, acting inspector general of the Army of the Tennessee, was assigned as permanent commander of the division. Sweeny was acquitted of the charges against him, but he did not return to the army.

Sixteenth Corps was the first corps of the Army of the Tennessee to start on its march to extend the Federal line on the right. When Corse assumed command of Second Division, Elliott W. Rice's First Brigade was in position on the extreme left of the army at a point about midway between Atlanta and Decatur and about 1,000 yards south of the Georgia Railroad. Jesse J. Phillips' Second Brigade was somewhat scattered, with two regiments on the line of Leggett's Third Division of Seventeenth Corps; one regiment was engaged in destroying track on the railroad; and one regiment of mounted infantry was on picket and scouting duty beyond Decatur. During the afternoon of July 26, the troops of Second Division marched to the north of the railroad, where the brigades of Rice and Phillips were united.

Fuller, with Henry T. McDowell's First Brigade, Fourth Division, remained in the position that he had occupied at the close of the battle of July 22 until July 26. John W. Sprague's Second Brigade, which had been at Decatur during the Battle of Atlanta, rejoined the division July 25.

About midnight July 26, 1864, Dodge's Sixteenth Corps began its march toward the west side of Atlanta. Corse's division, which moved first, followed a road made during the night to the Decatur and Buck Head road, and there it turned to the left and moved westward on a road that ran south of Peach Tree Creek. When the head of the column reached the Buck Head and Atlanta road near Sherman's headquarters, the corps bivouacked until daylight in rear of Fourth Corps. At that point Howard joined the Army of the Tennessee and assumed command.

When Dodge's column moved out on its march during the night of July 26, Sprague's brigade of Fourth Division was left behind to cover the rear of the corps. It occupied a line of works that was nearly parallel to the Decatur road until the withdrawal was completed, and it then followed the rest of the corps westward.

At daylight July 27, Dodge resumed his movement and marched past the rear of Alpheus S. Williams' Twentieth Corps and John M. Palmer's Fourteenth Corps until he reached the extreme right of the Army of the Cumberland, which was at that time some two or three miles from Atlanta and about four miles from the Chattahoochee River. Sixteenth Corps then advanced to Proctor's Creek at a point near where the Turner's Ferry road crossed the creek. Corse's division crossed the creek about 3:00 P.M. and passed by the flank of Jefferson C. Davis' Second Division of Fourteenth Corps, which at that time formed a refused right flank of Palmer's corps, and formed in line with Rice's brigade on the left and Phillips' brigade on the right. The division then moved forward, with its left on Proctor's Creek, to a ridge about 1,500 yards to the east, where it entrenched on a line facing due east toward Atlanta. When this line was completed, it connected on the left with Absalom Baird's Third Division of Palmer's corps and extended southward along a road that ran south from Elliott's Mill to Ezra Church, a Methodist meeting house, which was located in the southeast corner of what is today Mozley Park. During the evening, Fuller's division came up and formed on the right of Corse, and during the night both divisions entrenched. Dodge's line was just south of present-day North Avenue, NW, and at Chapel Road.

Frank P. Blair's Seventeenth Corps remained in position east of Atlanta until about 1:00 A.M. July 27, 1864, and it then withdrew from its lines, which at that time were on the extreme left of Sherman's army, and marched past the rear of Fifteenth Corps and followed Sixteenth Corps to the right. When Blair arrived in rear of Sixteenth Corps beyond

Proctor's Creek, it was too dark to proceed any farther, and the corps bivouacked for the night.

Early on the morning of July 28, 1864, Blair moved up on the right of Dodge's corps, with Mortimer D. Leggett's Third Division on the left, next to Sixteenth Corps, and Giles A. Smith's Fourth Division on the right, with its right extending down to Ezra Church. The position at Ezra Church was significant because the church was located near the intersection of the Lick Skillet road (or Bell's Ferry road) and the road from Elliott's Mill. The Lick Skillet road left Atlanta at the southwest suburb near the racecourse and ran westward to the village of Lick Skillet, near the Chattahoochee River.

John A. Logan's Fifteenth Corps, commanded by Morgan L. Smith until July 28, 1864, remained, with the exception of Charles R. Woods' First Division, on its lines east of Atlanta until early on the morning of July 27. At that time it was withdrawn from its entrenchments and started on its way to the west side of Atlanta, following Seventeenth Corps. Earlier, on the morning of July 23, Woods' two brigades had been relieved on the right of the Fifteenth Corps line by troops of John M. Schofield's Twenty-Third Corps, and they had marched back on the road to Decatur, where they took position about two miles from the town on the extreme left of Sherman's army. The men spent the day of July 24 destroying more of the track of the Georgia Railroad, and they then remained in camp until the night of July 26, when they rejoined the corps. Woods' division marched on July 27 with the rest of Fifteenth Corps, following Seventeenth Corps toward the right of Sherman's army. The division camped that night in rear of Seventeenth Corps.

William Harrow's Fourth Division, Fifteenth Corps reached a point on the Green's Ferry road that night, and Charles C. Walcutt's Second Brigade camped in rear of Corse's division of Sixteenth Corps; John M. Oliver's Third Brigade camped on the south side of the Marietta road; and Reuben Williams' First Brigade camped in rear of Sixteenth Corps. Morgan L. Smith's Second Division, commanded by Lightburn until the morning of July 28, 1864, went into camp west of the Western and Atlantic Railroad at 10:00 on the night of July 27.

There were also some significant changes in the positions of the troops of Schofield's Twenty-Third Corps following the Battle of Atlanta. At 2:00 A.M.

July 23, 1864, Richard F. Barter's First Brigade, First Division, Twenty-Third Corps and Daniel Cameron's Second Brigade of Cox's Third Division, which had moved to the left of the Army of the Tennessee near Decatur during the battle, were marched back to the front of the Howard house, and they were then placed in line between the right of Fifteenth Corps and the left of Milo S. Hascall's Second Division, Twenty-Third Corps.

Robert K. Byrd's Third Brigade of Cox's division, which had been in line on the right of Hascall's division during the battle, rejoined the division, and Cox's brigades were then in line with Byrd's brigade on the right, Barter's brigade in the center, and Cameron's brigade on the left, next to Fifteenth Corps. James W. Reilly's First Brigade of Cox's division remained on Pea Vine Creek.

Schofield's line was unchanged until July 26, 1864, and then, with the departure of the Army of the Tennessee from its left, the line was refused. The new line began at the left of Hascall's right brigade, ran back in rear of the former line, and was then refused so that the left of the new line faced east to protect the left of Sherman's army. On this part of the line, Schofield's troops occupied the old works that had been held by the enemy in front of Twenty-Third Corps on July 20. At 6:00 P.M. July 26, Reilly's brigade rejoined the division and was placed in position near the left of the new line.

Meantime, on the west side of Atlanta, the Army of the Tennessee resumed its advance early on the morning of July 28, 1864. Woods began forming his division of Fifteenth Corps in line on the right of Giles A. Smith's Fourth Division, Seventeenth Corps. This was completed about daylight, and then Smith advanced his division, while swinging around to the left, and Woods' division also moved forward, conforming with Smith's movements. When Woods' division was finally established in its assigned position about noon, its line was along a ridge that ran in a north-south direction, facing east, and its right was near Ezra Church. Milo Smith's First Brigade was on the left, connecting with the right of Giles A. Smith's division; James A. Williamson's Second Brigade was in the center; and Hugo Wangelin's Third Brigade was on the right, near the church.

In front of Milo Smith's brigade was a shallow valley where there were open fields, and on the high ground on the far side of the valley was a wooded area about one-half mile to the east. It was soon evident that the enemy was present in the woods in considerable force. The country in front of Wangelin's position was covered with a thick growth of small trees.

On July 28, 1864, Harrow's division of Fifteenth Corps advanced on the right of Woods' division, arriving about noon on the right of Woods' line. Harrow then placed Oliver's brigade in line on the right of and at nearly a right angle to Woods' line, facing south; he placed Reuben Williams' brigade on the right of Oliver, also facing south; and he held Walcutt's Second Brigade in reserve.

Morgan L. Smith's Second Division of Fifteenth Corps formed on the right of Harrow's overnight bivouac position about 3:00 A.M. July 28, 1864, with James S. Martin's First Brigade on the right and Joseph A. J. Lightburn's Second Brigade on the left. The division then advanced about two miles and took position on the right of Harrow's new line and on the extreme right of Sherman's army, facing south. The position occupied by Harrow and Morgan L. Smith was along a wooded ridge that extended westward from Ezra Church on a line that was nearly parallel to the Lick Skillet road. This ground was high and partly overlooked some open ground to the front. Logan's line ended on the extreme right in the area of present-day West Lake Avenue, just west of present-day Battle Hill Haven.

Early on the morning of July 27, 1864, John B. Hood's cavalry reported that Federal troops were apparently attempting to extend their right flank southward, and that afternoon Hood directed Alexander P. Stewart and Stephen D. Lee to prepare their corps for a movement to the west side of Atlanta to strengthen his left flank. Lee had arrived at Atlanta just the day before, and on the morning of July 28, he assumed command of Hood's old corps, relieving Benjamin F. Cheatham. Cheatham then resumed command of his division, and George Maney returned to his brigade.

Despite his defeat at Peach Tree Creek July 20, 1864, and again east of Atlanta on July 22, Hood decided to try once again to stop Sherman's advance by a flank attack. This time he planned to attack Howard's Army of the Tennessee while it was on the march, and before it had time to entrench in a good position.

According to Hood's plan, which was to be executed July 28, 1864, Lee was to move out from the defenses on the west side of Atlanta on the Lick Skillet road (present-day Gordon Road) with the divisions of John C. Brown and Henry D. Clayton and take up a defensive position near the road junction at Ezra Church, about three miles from the city. Stewart was to move from his positions in the works at Atlanta with the divisions of Edward C. Walthall and William W. Loring, and halt near the fortifications on the west side of the city until Lee was in position at Ezra Church. The next morning, July 29, Stewart was to move out on the Lick Skillet road to a point beyond Lee's divisions, and beyond the right of Howard's line, and then attack Howard's right flank and rear.

William J. Hardee's corps, Carter L. Stevenson's division of Lee's corps, Samuel G. French's division of Stewart's corps, and troops of Gustavus W. Smith's Georgia Militia were to remain in the works in front of Thomas' Army of the Cumberland and Schofield's Army of the Ohio.

Hood's attack, however, did not develop as planned, because at the time of Lee's advance, troops of Logan's Fifteenth Corps were already moving into position at Ezra Church. Lee was not aware of this, however, and at about 10:00 A.M. he ordered Brown and Clayton to move out on the Lick Skillet road and take up their assigned positions at Ezra Church. Brown advanced about a mile to the Poor House, which was located at a point near the junction of the Lick Skillet road and present-day West Lake Avenue, and there he learned from William H. Jackson, whose cavalry was out in front, that Federal troops were in force not far ahead. With the ground around Ezra Church already occupied by Logan's troops, it was clearly impossible for Lee to take up his assigned position there while Stewart marched on out beyond Logan's line for his flank attack. Lee then, on his own initiative, decided to attack at once.

Brown formed his division on the south side of the Lick Skillet road, with its center near the junction of that road and present-day Anderson Avenue. George D. Johnston's brigade (formerly Deas' brigade) was on the right, Jacob H. Sharp's brigade was in the center, William F. Brantly's brigade was on the left, and Arthur M. Manigault's brigade was in reserve.

About noon, Brown's division advanced about a half-mile through thick woods to the line held by Morgan L. Smith's division and the right of Harrow's division, and it then came under a very heavy fire from Martin's and Lightburn's brigade of Morgan L. Smith's division, and Reuben Williams' and Oliver's brigades of Harrow's division. Brown's attack exerted great pressure on Morgan L. Smith's division, and enemy troops were on the point of turning its right flank when Howard directed Blair to send all troops that he could spare to reinforce and extend the right of Logan's line. Blair immediately sent from Giles A. Smith's division the 15th Iowa of William Hall's Third Brigade and the 32nd Ohio of Benjamin F. Potts' First Brigade, both under the command of William W. Belknap. Blair also sent the 12th Wisconsin and the 31st Illinois of George E. Bryant's First Brigade of Leggett's Third Division to reinforce Morgan L. Smith's division. At 2:00 P.M., when Harrow was again under attack, Giles A. Smith sent the 13th Iowa of Hall's brigade and the 3rd Iowa of Potts' brigade, both under the command of John Shane, to reinforce Harrow. The timely arrival of the above regiments secured Logan's right flank and aided in repulsing the Confederate attacks. Dodge sent the 35th New Jersey of Sprague's Second Brigade of Fuller's Fourth Division and the 64th Ohio of McDowell's First Brigade of Fuller's Division, both under the command of John J. Cladek, and these regiments were put in line about 2:00 P.M. At 3:00 P.M. Dodge also sent Phillips with the 12th Illinois and 81st Ohio of his Second Brigade of Corse's Second Division to support Logan's line.

Walcutt's Second Brigade of Harrow's division was in reserve at the time of Brown's attack, but it did not fight in the Battle of Ezra Church as a unit. About 1:00 P.M., when Oliver's brigade was under attack, Harrow learned of a gap in the line between the left of Oliver's brigade and the right of Wangelin's brigade of Woods' division, and he sent the 103rd Illinois of Walcutt's brigade to occupy that space. A short time later Harrow sent the 46th Ohio and 97th Indiana of Walcutt's brigade to support the 103rd Illinois, and these regiments aided materially in driving the enemy from Oliver's front. The 6th Iowa and 40th Illinois of Walcutt's brigade were sent to the extreme right of Logan's corps, where they drove the enemy from a commanding elevation to the right of Morgan L. Smith's division and helped hold that flank.

After about an hour of severe fighting, Brantly's brigade, which was engaged on the left of Brown's division, began to break up under the heavy fire, and a Federal counterattack drove the enemy back with severe losses. Brown then attacked again with Manigault's brigade, which was supported by artillery, but this effort too was unsuccessful. George D. Johnston, commanding Deas' brigade of Brown's division, was wounded early in the attack, and he was succeeded in command of the brigade, in turn, by John G. Coltart and Benjamin R. Hart, both of whom were wounded, and finally by Harry T. Toulmin.

About noon, Clayton's division followed Brown westward on the Lick Skillet road for about a mile, and it then moved to the right and took position north of the road in front of Ezra Church, facing north. Clayton had placed Randall L. Gibson's brigade in position on the left of his line, had directed Alpheus Baker to form his brigade in reserve, and was in the process of putting James T. Holtzclaw's brigade in line on the right when, unknown to Clayton, Edward H. Cunningham of Lee's staff ordered Gibson to attack.

At about 1:00 P.M., Gibson's brigade struck Logan's line near Ezra Church at the salient formed where the right of Woods' division joined the left of Harrow's division at approximately a right angle. The Federal troops at the salient had been alerted by the sounds of Brown's attack to their right, and they greeted the advancing Confederates with a deadly fire. Gibson's brigade was strongly repulsed with heavy losses, largely by the fire of Wangelin's brigade of Woods' division and Oliver's brigade of Harrow's division.

Gibson then asked for support, and Clayton ordered up Baker's brigade from its position in the rear. Baker attacked on the right of Wangelin's brigade but was thrown back with crippling losses. During this attack, Milo Smith sent the 76th Ohio of his First Brigade of Woods' division as an additional reserve for Wangelin's line.

Following Gibson's repulse, Clayton ordered Holtzclaw to move by his left flank and take position where he was concealed from Logan's men but close enough to their works to cover the ground over which Gibson and Baker had attacked, and where he could check a Federal advance if one came. Clayton hastily formed the remains of Gibson's and Baker's brigades, both of which had lost about half of their numbers, in rear of Holtzclaw. Soon after dark, Clayton moved his division back through the Confederate breastworks west of Atlanta to a new position on the left of Hood's army.

Stewart's divisions arrived on the western side of Atlanta after Lee had begun his attack, and they soon moved out on the Lick Skillet road in support. Walthall's division, followed by Loring's division, marched out to a point near the Poor House, where he formed in line of battle. Walthall's left rested on the Lick Skillet road, with his right slightly in advance, not far from the Poor House. Daniel H. Reynolds' brigade was on the left, James Cantey's brigade was on the right, and William A. Quarles' brigade was held in reserve to watch Walthall's left flank.

A short time after 2:00 P.M., Walthall advanced over the same ground covered by Brown in his earlier attack. Walthall soon came under a devastating fire from Morgan L. Smith's line and the right of Harrow's line, and he was driven back with the loss of about one-third of his men. Quarles moved up to the left of Walthall's other two brigades, and he too suffered a bloody repulse. Stewart then ordered Walthall to hold his ground until Loring could come forward and cover his retreat. Stewart was wounded during the attack, and Walthall assumed command of the corps. Quarles assumed command of Walthall's division. Loring was wounded while deploying his troops to aid Walthall, and Winfield S. Featherston assumed command of his division.

Quarles was then ordered to withdraw his division (formerly Walthall's) to a position on the left of Featherston's division (formerly Loring's), and by 4:00 P.M. this movement had been completed. From that time on until dark there was only skirmishing on that part of the line, and at 10:00 P.M. Walthall's division withdrew into the line of works at Atlanta.

On July 27, 1864, as the Army of the Tennessee was moving into position on the right of the Army of the Cumberland, Sherman anticipated that Hood would take some countermeasures, and that evening he ordered Jefferson C. Davis to march the next morning with his Second Division of Palmer's Fourteenth Corps by a roundabout route so as to

come up on the right of Logan's corps, which was then advancing on the extreme right of the army. Davis would then be in position to strike any enemy force that might move against Logan's right flank. Davis' division was selected for this movement because at that time it was in rear of Baird's division, where it had been thrown out of line when Dodge's Sixteenth Corps connected on the right of Baird's line. Davis' orders were to move out on the morning of July 28 to Turner's Ferry on the Chattahoochee River, then on to White Hall or East Point, and finally to advance on the Lick Skillet road toward the right flank of Logan's new line.

On the morning of July 28, 1864, Davis was not well, and he turned over the active command of his division to James D. Morgan. Morgan assumed command at 9:00 A.M. and led his command out from Elliott's Mill on the road toward Turner's Ferry. Upon arriving there, Morgan halted for an hour to give his men some rest and let them have a midday meal, and he then resumed the march toward East Point. While on the road, Morgan received orders to march at once to the support of Logan, whose corps was under attack. Morgan then reversed his course and moved back to Turner's Ferry. His march from there to join Logan was very slow because of a lack of good maps and difficult country, and he did not arrive at his assigned position until after the fighting had ended, long after dark. Morgan then put his division in camp on the right of Logan's division.

CAVALRY RAIDS ON THE RAILROADS SOUTH OF ATLANTA, GEORGIA

After the Battle of Atlanta, Sherman decided to make an effort to drive Hood's army from Atlanta by closing his remaining supply lines by moving against the Macon and Western Railroad and the Atlanta and West Point Railroad. This was to be done by two simultaneous operations. One was to transfer the Army of the Tennessee to the west side of Atlanta to extend the right of Sherman's line to the right in the direction of East Point and the railroad, and the other was to move out his cavalry on expeditions to break up the Macon and Western

Railroad near Lovejoy's Station. The movement of the Army of the Tennessee has been described in the preceding section, and it remains to detail the operations of the cavalry in their attempts against the railroad.

On July 22, 1864, Lovell H. Rousseau arrived with his Cavalry Division, Army of the Cumberland at Marietta, Georgia after his successful raid on the Montgomery and West Point Railroad at Opelika, Alabama, and it was immediately sent to relieve George Stoneman's Cavalry Division, Army of the Ohio, which was on the Chattahoochee near Turner's Ferry. Immediately after being relieved, on July 24, Stoneman marched around the rear of the army to join Sherman east of Atlanta.

Sherman then ordered all of his cavalry to prepare for an expedition to destroy the Macon and Western Railroad. For this purpose he ordered Stoneman to assume command of his own division and Kenner Garrard's Second Cavalry Division of the Army of the Cumberland and directed him to move on the left of the army, around the east side of Atlanta, to McDonough, nearly thirty miles southeast of Atlanta. At the same time he assigned to Edward M. McCook the command of his own First Cavalry Division, Army of the Cumberland, and Rousseau's Cavalry Division, then organized as a brigade under the command of Thomas J. Harrison, and ordered him to move on the right to Fayetteville, some thirty miles south of Atlanta, and do all possible damage on the enemy's left and rear. Upon arriving at their assigned positions and carrying out such destruction as they could, Stoneman and McCook were to join at Lovejoy's Station on the Macon and Western Railroad and destroy the track and installations in the vicinity.

Just before starting on the expedition, Stoneman asked Sherman that, after fulfilling his orders and breaking up the railway, he be permitted to move on southward through Macon to Andersonville, Georgia and release the Federal prisoners that were confined there. Sherman assented to this request, but with the provisions that Stoneman first defeat Joseph Wheeler's cavalry and break up the railroad, and that he send back Garrard's cavalry to the left flank of the army and make the expedition with only his own cavalry division.

Stoneman's Raid to Macon, Georgia, July 27, 1864–August 6, 1864. Stoneman left his camps about four miles north of Decatur at 4:00 A.M. July 27, 1864 and entered Decatur at sunrise. There he found Garrard with his division ready to accompany the column. Stoneman's command was organized for the expedition as follows:

Cavalry Division, Army of the Ohio, George Stoneman
    First Brigade, James Biddle
        5th Indiana Cavalry and 6th Indiana Cavalry (mounted portion)
    Second Brigade, Silas Adams
        1st Kentucky Cavalry and 11th Kentucky Cavalry
    Third Brigade, Horace Capron
        14th Illinois Cavalry, 8th Michigan Cavalry, and a part of 1st Ohio Squadron

Second Cavalry Division, Army of the Cumberland, Kenner Garrard
First Brigade, Robert H. G. Minty
Second Brigade, Eli Long
Third Brigade, Abram O. Miller

Instead of following orders and moving toward McDonough with his entire command, Stoneman sent Garrard's division to Flat Rock to occupy the attention of Wheeler's cavalry while he headed with his division, by way of Covington, in the direction of Macon and Andersonville. Apparently he had decided to march to Andersonville and release the prisoners before defeating Wheeler and joining McCook.

After Garrard's departure for Flat Rock, Stoneman marched eastward with his division along the Georgia Railroad all that day and the following night, and he halted at 4:00 A.M. July 28, 1864 two miles from Covington. Stoneman rested his command until 8:00 A.M., then resumed his march and arrived at Covington about 9:00 A.M. He halted there about two hours to feed the horses, and while there he sent Silas Adams with the Second Brigade to Mechanicsburg on the Ocmulgee River to watch the enemy movements in that direction. Adams was ordered to rejoin the main column at Clinton.

At Covington Stoneman turned to the south, leaving the railroad behind him, crossed the Ulcohachee River, and marched through Starrsville (Stearnesville), halting for the night within a mile of Monticello.

Meantime, on the morning of July 27, 1864, Wheeler had been unaware of Stoneman's march toward Covington, but he did observe Garrard's march toward Flat Rock, and he hastened with his cavalry to get ahead of him on the road. There was some skirmishing during the day, and that night Garrard's pickets were attacked by William W. Allen's cavalry brigade of William T. Martin's division. Garrard's troopers then constructed barricades and lay in line of battle all night. At daybreak July 28, Garrard found that his command was surrounded. After an engagement of several hours, with no word from Stoneman, Robert H. G. Minty's First Brigade attacked and broke through the enemy's lines, and the rest of the division followed to Latimer's and Lithonia, which was on the Georgia Railroad between Decatur and Covington.

Wheeler soon learned of Stoneman's march, and he was preparing to follow him when he was informed that McCook's cavalry was moving on the left of Hood's army. Wheeler then ordered Alfred Iverson to take his own brigade, Allen's brigade of Martin's division, and John S. Williams' brigade, commanded by William C. P. Breckinridge, of William Y. C. Humes' division and follow and attack Stoneman wherever he might be found. Wheeler received orders to aid William H. Jackson, whose cavalry division was alone in front of McCook's column, with such troops as he could spare, and he immediately sent Henry M. Ashby's brigade of Humes' division. He also ordered John H. Kelly to remain with George G. Dibrell's brigade of his division to watch Garrard and to send Robert H. Anderson's brigade to reinforce Jackson. Wheeler then started toward Jonesboro and soon caught up with Ashby's brigade on the road.

Stoneman resumed his march southward early on July 29, 1864, arriving at Monticello at sunrise. He continued on and passed through Hillsboro, halting about noon within four miles of Clinton. He then sent out a detachment to destroy the Milledgeville and Eatonton Railroad near Milledgeville, marched on through Clinton, and halted within about ten miles of Macon. He remained in camp there until about dawn July 30.

July 30, 1864, Stoneman again sent Adams' brigade out to the left, with orders to move to the Ocmulgee above Macon and observe the crossings on the river, and then move downstream toward Macon.

When the main column arrived within about five miles of Macon, he sent out another detachment to destroy the Georgia Central Railroad near Gordon. Both this detachment and the one sent earlier destroyed track and bridges near Milledgeville and Gordon, and they also destroyed twenty-two cars loaded with commissary and quartermaster supplies.

Meantime, Stoneman's main column continued on toward Macon and ran into enemy pickets about three miles from the town. The enemy troops in Macon at that time were under the command of Howell Cobb, and they consisted of some Georgia Reserves, local defense companies, armed citizens, and some Georgia Militia that Governor Joseph E. Brown was organizing in the town.

Horace Capron was ordered to picket the Griswold (Griswoldville) road, and with the remainder of his Third Brigade he was to move to the left to the Georgia Central Railroad. He was then to follow the railroad toward Macon, destroying the public property as he advanced. Capron destroyed about five miles of track; cars, engines, and buildings on the road; and also a machine shop. James Biddle's First Brigade aided in this work of destruction.

Meantime, Adams, whose brigade had been moving down the Ocmulgee, arrived within about a mile of Macon and met some of Cobb's command. Adams attacked, drove them back, and continued skirmishing for some time.

At about the same time that Stoneman came up against Cobb's troops, scouts reported that Iverson's cavalry was moving down the west bank of the Ocmulgee toward Macon.

At about 3:00 P.M. July 30, 1864, Stoneman decided that he could not reach the railroad bridge with his available force, and he decided to withdraw all of his command and continue his march southward, probably toward Andersonville. He sent Adams' brigade ahead to cross the river about seven or eight miles south of Macon and continued his march in that direction.

Adams had advanced only about two miles, however, when a scout reported that a large column of Confederate cavalry was entering Macon. Stoneman then ordered his column to withdraw northward by the road on which he had marched to Macon. Capron's brigade, which was in the lead, arrived at Clinton just at dark, and there it was met by enemy pickets. These were driven back, and the march was continued, against some opposition, to a point about eight miles north of Clinton, near Hillsboro. There Capron was attacked, and skirmishing continued throughout the night.

At daybreak July 31, 1864, Capron advanced about a mile, and then, at Sunshine Church, south of Round Oak, he found the enemy in line of battle. Stoneman came up and placed his entire command in position, with Adams' brigade and the 8th Michigan of Capron's brigade on the left, the rest of Capron's brigade on the right, and Biddle's brigade in reserve.

Between 9:00 and 10:00 A.M., Stoneman's line moved forward, but it was soon charged by the enemy and brought to a halt. At about the same time, an enemy mounted force appeared on his rear and charged the right of Capron's line. Stoneman appears to have overestimated the strength of Iverson's command, and, finding himself between the Ocmulgee and Oconee rivers, which at that point were only about twenty miles apart, and with enemy forces on his front and rear, he considered his position desperate. He tried from sunrise July 31, 1864 until noon to break out from his encirclement, but without success. Stoneman then came to the conclusion that it was impossible for the entire force to escape. He granted permission for Adams and Capron to attempt to cut their way through, but he remained with Biddle's brigade to engage the enemy until the other two brigades were well on their way toward Athens, and he then surrendered. Stoneman and about 700 of his men were taken prisoner.

Capron escaped with a part of the 14th Illinois, the 8th Michigan, and a part of the 6th Indiana of Biddle's brigade. Adams' brigade came out fairly intact a little later. Altogether, some 1,200–1,300 men escaped from Stoneman's position.

Adams moved out to the northeast by way of Eatonton and halted some five miles beyond the town, and about thirty-five miles from the battlefield. Capron's brigade also moved for a time on the Eatonton road, but he moved off of the road, and to the left of Eatonton, and traveled all night, during which he passed to the left of Madison. When he halted, he had gone about as far as Adams.

Adams passed through Madison about 2:00 P.M. August 1, 1864, and about dark he was joined by Capron. At about the same time, Courtland C. Matson of the 6th Indiana arrived with the remnants of Biddle's brigade. The two brigades continued the march until midnight, then halted about twelve miles from the bridge across the Oconee River near Athens.

On the morning of August 2, 1864, Adams approached the Oconee River near Watkinsville, but when faced with stiff opposition there, he decided to move on upriver toward Jefferson. Adams and Capron decided to attempt a crossing of the river at Athens, but when Adams approached the river, he found that he could not get over because the crossing was protected by artillery. Adams then sent a courier to inform Capron of his problem and to instruct him to march to a ford about two and a half miles above the town where the two brigades could cross. Capron's guide, however, took the wrong road and led the column about six miles from the route agreed upon. Capron spent about six hours trying to communicate with Adams, and finally, when he learned that enemy cavalry was approaching on his right, he moved forward on the Hog Mountain road for about eighteen miles to Jug Tavern. He halted there briefly to feed the horses, then continued on along the same road until he passed the road running from Jefferson to Lawrenceville. By that time the men and horses were almost totally exhausted, having marched fifty-four miles in the twenty-four hours since the battle near Hillsboro, and Capron called a halt for a rest of a few hours. Meantime, Adams had continued his march from near Athens to a point about sixteen miles northeast of Lawrenceville, where he halted at midnight.

Just before daylight August 3, 1864, Breckinridge's cavalry brigade, which had been pursuing the retreating Federals, charged into Capron's camp, completely surprising and scattering the entire force. Some men were killed, some were captured, and some made their way back through the woods to Sherman's lines. Capron became separated from his command but escaped and made his way to Marietta, where he arrived August 7.

When Adams learned of the attack on Capron, he hurried to his assistance, but he arrived too late to be of any help. Adams pursued Breckinridge for a short distance and drove him back, but he then gave up the chase and marched toward the Chattahoochee River. He arrived on the river before dark, crossed at an old ford, and went into camp at 9:00

P.M. At daylight August 4, 1864, Adams resumed the march, arriving at Marietta at 11:00 that morning with about 500 of his men.

McCook's Raid to Lovejoy's Station, Georgia, July 27–31, 1864. On July 27, 1864, the same day that Stoneman set out from Decatur on his march toward Macon, Edward M. McCook moved out from Turner's Ferry with his cavalry and headed toward Fayetteville and the Macon and Western Railroad beyond. McCook's command consisted of his own First Division, Cavalry Corps of the Army of the Cumberland and Harrison's brigade, which consisted of cavalry that Rousseau had brought to Marietta from Opelika. The expedition commanded by McCook was organized as follows:

First Cavalry Division, Edward M. McCook
  First Brigade, John T. Croxton, to July 30, 1864
    James P. Brownlow
    8th Iowa Cavalry, 4th Kentucky Mounted Infantry, and 1st Tennessee Cavalry
  Second Brigade, William H. Torrey, to July 30, 1864, captured
    Horace P. Lamson
    2nd Indiana Cavalry, 4th Indiana Cavalry, 1st Wisconsin Cavalry

Harrison's Brigade, Thomas J. Harrison, captured July 31, 1864
  8th Indiana Cavalry, 2nd Kentucky Cavalry, 5th Iowa Cavalry, 9th Ohio Cavalry, and 4th Tennessee Cavalry.

July 27, 1864, McCook's command moved southward along the west bank of the Chattahoochee River to Campbellton, and it halted there at 3:00 P.M. to await the arrival of the pontoon train. The train arrived at 3:00 A.M. July 28, and the division immediately started for Smith's Ferry, about six miles south of Campbellton, where it arrived at daylight. John T. Croxton's First Brigade, which was in the lead, began crossing the river immediately by means of a small boat. At 3:00 P.M. the pontoon bridge was completed, and William H. Torrey's Second Brigade began crossing on the bridge. When across the river, Torrey moved out in advance of the division on the road to Palmetto. Croxton's horses were then brought over on the bridge, and his brigade took a road to the right of

that used by Torrey. Both brigades arrived at Palmetto at approximately the same time, about sundown. The men of Thomas Harrison's Cavalry Brigade were nearly exhausted by their long march through Alabama to Opelika and Marietta, and because of this the brigade was generally held in reserve.

After arriving at Palmetto, McCook's men spent two hours destroying about two and a half miles of the Atlanta and West Point Railroad, and the division then marched on toward Fayetteville, with Torrey's brigade in the lead. As the division marched along the road that night, it captured many wagons of Hood's army trains, and it finally arrived at Fayetteville at daylight July 29, 1864. McCook left Fayetteville a short time later, about sunrise, with Croxton's brigade in the lead, and marched on the road toward Lovejoy's Station.

When McCook reached the Flint River, about four miles from Fayetteville, he captured more of the enemy's trains, then moved on and reached the Macon and Western Railroad about one-half mile north of Lovejoy's Station. He proceeded to destroy more than two miles of track, and also about five miles of telegraph line, and he burned two trains, a large amount of cotton, and several hundred wagons. At 2:00 P.M. McCook had heard nothing from Stoneman, who was to have met him there, but he did learn that a part of Wheeler's cavalry was between Lovejoy's Station and McDonough. McCook decided that it was time to withdraw, and he began to return at once toward the Chattahoochee River by way of Newnan, which was on the Atlanta and West Point Railroad.

Meantime, when Hood had learned of McCook's advance toward his left flank, he had only Jackson's cavalry division in that area. Hood did not believe that Jackson alone was strong enough to stop McCook, and he directed Wheeler to send help. Wheeler immediately sent Henry M. Ashby, with his brigade of William Y. C. Humes' division, to move at once toward Jonesboro, and he directed John H. Kelly to send Robert H. Anderson's brigade of his division to follow Ashby's brigade. Wheeler also set out for Jonesboro and soon caught up with Ashby's brigade on the road.

McCook had moved only about two miles from the railroad on his return march when he was attacked by Lawrence S. Ross' cavalry brigade of

Jackson's division, which had moved onto the road between Croxton's brigade and Torrey's brigade, which was ahead on the road. Croxton drove the enemy from the road and moved on after Torrey. About two miles farther on, Croxton crossed the Flint River, then moved on very slowly during the night because of the congestion on the road, but he passed through Fayetteville and was approaching Newnan toward morning.

When Wheeler, with Ashby's brigade, reached Fayetteville during the night of July 29, 1864, he found that McCook had already passed through the town and was about an hour's march ahead on the road to Newnan. Anderson's brigade was on the road to the rear but had not yet come up. Wheeler followed McCook closely, with some skirmishing, and finally overtook him about two miles from Newnan.

When the head of McCook's column neared Newnan, McCook learned that Philip D. Roddey's dismounted cavalry brigade, which was on its way from Alabama to join Hood, was in the town. McCook then moved off to the right to take the road to La Grange. Torrey's brigade was in the lead, Croxton's brigade followed, and Harrison's brigade was in the rear.

Wheeler then ordered Ashby to move through Newnan and down the La Grange road to get in front of McCook, and Wheeler with the rest of the cavalry moved between the La Grange road and the railroad in an attempt to strike McCook's flank as he moved southward. Ashby struck the head of McCook's column as it was entering the main La Grange road, about three and a half miles below Newnan. McCook was then forced to form his division in line of battle at Brown's Mill, between Newnan and the Chattahoochee River.

From then on there was nothing but trouble for McCook. Wheeler and Ashby attacked and forced him into a disorderly retreat, and for more than two hours there was constant fighting, with charge and countercharge following one after the other. Anderson's brigade at last came up and joined Wheeler, and Roddey's brigade arrived from Newnan and formed on the left of Wheeler's line.

Finally, one column under McCook succeeded in breaking out, and it marched toward the Chattahoochee River, closely followed by Anderson's brigade. Fielder A. Jones, with his 8th Indiana Cavalry, the 5th Iowa Cavalry, and a part of the 4th Tennessee Cavalry of Harrison's brigade, and a part of the 2nd Indiana Cavalry of Torrey's brigade, remained with McCook and crossed the river. McCook moved with his command to Corinth, and there he turned to the right and marched to Philpot's Ferry, where he arrived at 11:00 P.M. and crossed the river. McCook, however, lost his prisoners and captured materials, and about 500 of his men. Torrey was captured July 30, 1864, and Horace P. Lamson assumed command of his Second Brigade.

Back near Brown's Mill, Harrison came up and relieved Croxton's brigade and tried to force his way out but failed. Croxton then attempted to break out, but shortly after starting, he was attacked in rear, and Croxton became separated from the rest of his brigade. Croxton, however, succeeded in making his way out and arrived at Sweet Water Town August 12, 1864.

James P. Brownlow assumed command of Croxton's brigade and moved on by-roads toward Franklin on the Chattahoochee River, and he was followed by Wheeler. Brownlow reached the river at Rotherwood at 1:00 A.M. July 31, 1864, and he had with him only about 250 men when he crossed the river. The 1st Tennessee Cavalry had with it about 600 men when it broke through the enemy's lines, but only about 150 of them crossed the river with Brownlow.

After finally crossing the river, McCook marched to Wedowee, Alabama, and from there to Marietta, where he arrived August 4, 1864.

Kilpatrick's Raid from Sandtown to Lovejoy's Station, Georgia, August 18–22, 1864. After the failure of Stoneman's and McCook's raids to Macon and Lovejoy's Station and Sherman's inability to extend his right far enough to reach the Macon and Western Railroad (for details, see the following section), Sherman decided that to reach the railroad and destroy it, he would have to move in that direction with his entire army. Accordingly, on August 16, 1864, he issued orders for this movement, which was to begin August 18. Before the army began its march, however, Sherman learned that on August 10, Joseph Wheeler had left his camps at Covington and had marched to the east and north of Atlanta with a large cavalry force, and that he was then at Adairsville and marching northward along the Western and Atlantic Railroad, destroying the track as he advanced.

When Wheeler departed, he left behind only Jackson's cavalry division, which consisted of the brigades of Frank C. Armstrong, Lawrence S. Ross, and Samuel W. Ferguson, to cover the left of Hood's army and the Macon and Western Railroad south of Atlanta. This meant that Sherman then had the larger cavalry command, and he decided to try once again to break up the railroad with a cavalry expedition.

Sherman suspended the proposed infantry movements for the time being. He directed Judson Kilpatrick to move with about 5,000 cavalry from his camp near Sandtown and break the Atlanta and West Point Railroad at Fairburn, and then to proceed on to the Macon and Western Railroad and destroy it thoroughly. Sherman also instructed Kilpatrick to avoid combat with any infantry that he might encounter, but to attack any cavalry force that he could find.

Kilpatrick had been wounded in the fighting near Resaca May 13, 1864 and had returned to his home to recover. During his absence, Eli H. Murray had commanded his Third Division of the Cavalry Corps until May 21, when he was relieved by William W. Lowe. The division had remained on the Western and Atlantic Railroad north of the Etowah River when Sherman advanced on Atlanta, and it was still on this duty when Kilpatrick returned to the army July 23 and resumed command. Kilpatrick's headquarters was at Cartersville, and his orders were to protect the railroad from the Etowah to Tunnel Hill.

Because of the losses suffered by the cavalry during Stoneman's and McCook's raids on the railroad, Kilpatrick was ordered to join the army with his division, and Sherman then reorganized his cavalry to consist of three divisions commanded by McCook, Garrard, and Kilpatrick. On August 11, 1864, Israel Garrard was assigned to command all cavalry of the Army of the Ohio in the field, formerly commanded by Stoneman, and to reorganize it and put it in condition for active service.

Kilpatrick left Cartersville with his division August 3, 1864 and moved to Sandtown, where he went into camp near the Chattahoochee River. He crossed the river August 15 and fortified a position on the far side.

In preparation for Kilpatrick's movement against the railroads, Sherman ordered Garrard to send two brigades of his division to join Kilpatrick's expedition. In response to this order, on the evening of August 17, 1864, Robert H. G. Minty's First Brigade and Eli Long's Second Brigade of Second Cavalry Division, both under the command of Minty, marched from their camps near Buck Head, and on the morning of August 18, Minty reported with his brigades to Kilpatrick at Sandtown.

That evening Kilpatrick left Sandtown with his Third Division, then commanded by Murray, and Minty with the two brigades of Garrard's Second Division, and his instructions were to destroy the enemy's communications south of Atlanta. Kilpatrick's command was organized for this expedition as follows:

Third Division, Cavalry Corps, Eli H. Murray
    First Brigade, Robert Klein
        3rd Indiana Cavalry (four companies) and 5th Iowa Cavalry
    Second Brigade, Fielder A. Jones
        8th Indiana Cavalry, 2nd Kentucky Cavalry, and 10th Ohio Cavalry
    Third Brigade, Robert H. King
        92nd Illinois Mounted Infantry, 3rd Kentucky Cavalry, and 5th Kentucky Cavalry
    10th Battery, Wisconsin Light Artillery, Yates V. Beebe

Second Division, Cavalry Corps, Robert H. G. Minty
    First Brigade, Robert H. G. Minty
        4th Michigan Cavalry, 7th Pennsylvania Cavalry, and 4th United States Cavalry
    Second Brigade, Eli Long
        1st Ohio Cavalry, 3rd Ohio Cavalry, and 4th Ohio Cavalry
    Chicago Board of Trade Battery, Illinois Light Artillery, George I. Robinson

Note. Minty was in temporary command of the two brigades of the division only during the period August 18–23, 1864.

Kilpatrick's command moved southward on the road past Owl Rock Church, and as Robert H. King's Third Brigade, Third Cavalry Division, which was at the head of the column, approached Camp Creek, it encountered enemy pickets. It quickly forced them back across the creek, and at about 10:00 P.M. drove the supporting regiment from its camp about a mile beyond and pursued it to Stevens' (Stephens') farm, about seven miles from the railroad at Fairburn.

Robert Klein, whose First Brigade, Third Division was under Kilpatrick's direct control, left the main column about 11:00 P.M. August 18, 1864, or a little later, reaching Fairburn on the Atlanta and West Point Railroad at 1:30 A.M. August 19. Klein's men destroyed some track and telegraph line, and the brigade marched on to Fayetteville, where it arrived at 7:00 A.M. Klein then moved on south to Mount Zion Church, where he turned to the left and crossed Flint River about eight miles from Fayetteville and about eight miles from Fayette Station, which was about midway between Griffin and Lovejoy's Station on the Macon and Western Railroad.

Klein finally reached the railroad at Bear Creek Station, about four miles north of Fayette Station, about 11:00 A.M., and his brigade destroyed several miles of track at intervals along the road toward Lovejoy's Station to the north. At Bear Creek he captured and burned a train of nine cars loaded with supplies. The enemy was aware of the presence of Federal cavalry on the railroad, and soon Klein was confronted by Ferguson's and Armstrong's cavalry brigades and by Daniel H. Reynolds' infantry brigade of Edward C. Walthall's division, which had been sent down by rail to help the cavalry. In the presence of this force, Klein turned around and led his brigade back along the road on which he had come. He recrossed the Flint River and became engaged with the enemy about two miles from Fayetteville. He continued on, however, passed through Fairburn about 7:30 P.M., and finally reached Sandtown at 11:00 A.M. the next day, August 20, 1864.

Meantime, Kilpatrick had continued on from Stevens' farm, and at about 12:30 A.M. August 19, 1864, he drove Ross' brigade from his front and in the direction of East Point. Fielder A. Jones, with his Second Brigade, Third Division, kept the enemy from the road until the rest of the division had passed, and it then fell in at the rear of the column.

Kilpatrick crossed the Atlanta and West Point Railroad at daylight, and there his rear brigade was attacked by Ross. This attack was repulsed, and Kilpatrick again moved forward on the Fayetteville road, where he soon found Ross again on his front. Ross slowly retired in the direction of Jonesboro, and about 2:00 P.M. he crossed the Flint River, destroying the bridge after he had passed. Minty and Long, commanding detachments of their brigades, crossed the river under the cover of artillery fire and drove the enemy from the crossing. After the bridge was repaired, the column crossed the river and proceeded on to Jonesboro, where it arrived at 5:00 P.M., after driving some enemy cavalry from the town. While there, Kilpatrick learned that Klein had destroyed the track at Bear Creek Station.

For the next six hours, Kilpatrick's men were engaged in destroying the railroad. At 11:00 that night, Murray's two brigades were attacked about a mile below Jonesboro, but the attack was repulsed. Kilpatrick then suspended the work on the railroad and drove the enemy back about a mile and a half.

At that time, Kilpatrick became concerned about a possible enemy attack from the direction of Atlanta, and before daylight July 20, 1864, he marched off in the direction of Covington. After traveling about five miles, he halted until the enemy came up, then continued his march. He left Long's brigade to cover the rear of his column as it moved forward on the road toward McDonough. Long was wounded in the fighting that day, and Beroth B. Eggleston assumed command of his Second Brigade.

After advancing on this road for about six miles, Kilpatrick moved across country to the Fayetteville road, and he finally reached the railroad about one mile above Lovejoy's Station at 11:00 A.M. July 20, 1864. He then advanced toward the station but was driven back by Reynolds' infantry brigade. Kilpatrick was in serious trouble for a time, but the enemy was finally checked and driven back, largely by the efforts of Minty and Long.

At about the same time, Murray reported that his rear had been attacked by a strong force of enemy cavalry, and a short time later Kilpatrick discovered that he was surrounded by enemy cavalry and infantry with artillery. Kilpatrick then decided to attack the line held by the cavalry, and Minty charged in three columns and ran over the left of their line. Murray broke through their center, and in a short time Jackson's cavalry was driven back in disorder. Kilpatrick quickly re-formed his command and engaged the infantry for almost two hours. He finally withdrew toward the east, crossed Cotton Indian Creek and South River on the morning of August 21, 1864, and, marching by way of Lithonia, he reached the Federal lines at Decatur at 2:00 P.M. August 22.

OPERATIONS NEAR UTOY CREEK, GEORGIA

When the Army of the Tennessee reached the vicinity of Ezra Church on its march to extend Sherman's line to the right, it was in position to threaten seriously the line of the railroad between Atlanta and East Point, and Confederate engineers immediately began to lay out a new defensive line to cover this vital supply route. This line began at the city's inner defenses at a point near where the Lick Skillet road left the city, and it ran to the southwest for about four miles, crossing the North Branch of Utoy Creek, and ending on some hills near the road from Atlanta to Sandtown. In terms of today's landmarks, the line started at West Fair and Ashby streets and from there ran to the southwest across Gordon Street (Lick Skillet road) near the point where it is joined by Cascade Street, then across the John A. White Park and Greenwood Cemetery, and ended on the Sandtown road.

During the night following the Battle of Ezra Church, John C. Brown's division (Hindman's division) of Stephen D. Lee's corps withdrew from its position near the Lick Skillet road and moved to a new position along the projected new line of entrenchments. The next day Brown's men began construction of defensive works along this line. Henry D. Clayton's division of Lee's corps then moved up on the left of Brown, and it continued the work of fortification down to the Sandtown road. Carter L. Stevenson's division of Lee's corps had been detached from the corps and was in position immediately in front of Atlanta. J. Patton Anderson arrived at Atlanta from Florida, and on July 30, 1864 assumed command of Hindman's division, relieving Brown. Anderson's division held the line from the Lick Skillet road to the North Branch of Utoy Creek, and Clayton's division from the right of Anderson to the Sandtown road.

Meantime, after the Battle of Ezra Church July 28, 1864, Sherman had resumed the movement that he had begun July 25 of extending his right flank southward toward the railroad between Atlanta and East Point.

On the morning of July 29, 1864, James D. Morgan's Second Division of John M. Palmer's Fourteenth Corps, which had spent the previous night near the left of the Army of the Tennessee, moved up about a mile and a half from its bivouac, crossed the Green's Ferry road, and entrenched on the right of John A. Logan's Fifteenth Corps. Also that morning, William T. Ward's Third Division of Alpheus S. Williams' Twentieth Corps moved from its position in the entrenchments facing Atlanta to the extreme right of the army to support Morgan's division on a reconnaissance. It halted in rear of Morgan's line and bivouacked for the night, but the next day it moved up and took position on the right of Morgan.

July 31, 1864, Sherman decided to send John M. Schofield's Twenty-Third Corps, which was then in position on the east side of Atlanta, on the left of the army, to the west side of the city to a new position on the right of the Army of the Tennessee. Kenner Garrard's Second Cavalry Division relieved the troops of Twenty-Third Corps in their entrenchments, and on August 1, Jacob D. Cox's Third Division broke camp and marched in rear of the army, bivouacking that night in rear of the Army of the Cumberland. That same evening, Milo S. Hascall's Second Division followed Cox toward the right. After Schofield's departure, William Grose's First Division of David S. Stanley's Fourth Corps and Nathan Kimball's First Brigade of John Newton's Second Division, Fourth Corps extended their lines to occupy all of the line previously held by Twenty-Third Corps. The infantry of Fourth Corps continued to hold this line until August 1, 1864.

At daybreak August 2, 1864, Cox continued his march. He took position on the north bank of the North Branch of Utoy Creek on the right of the Army of the Tennessee. Hascall followed Cox that day and formed his division on the right of Cox's line. Morgan's and Ward's divisions, which were then in reserve near the right of the line, were ordered to support Schofield in case of attack.

Later in the day, Ward moved back with his division and rejoined Twentieth Corps on the line of entrenchments in front of Atlanta, and that night he relieved Richard W. Johnson's First Division and Absalom Baird's Third Division of Palmer's Fourteenth Corps in the entrenchments. At 10:00 the next morning, August 3, 1864, Palmer moved out to the right with these two divisions to take position in support of Schofield's right flank for an attack that day by Twenty-Third Corps.

Johnson's division moved first and halted near Morgan's division, about two miles north of the North Branch of Utoy Creek. Baird followed Johnson but passed through both Johnson's and Morgan's divisions, and also Cox's division of Twenty-Third Corps, and arrived on the North Branch of Utoy Creek about 5:00 P.M. Baird then moved his division, on Sherman's orders, into line on the right of Hascall's division of Twenty-Third Corps, which was preparing to cross the creek. When Baird arrived on the right of Hascall, the latter had already crossed the creek at Herring's Mill and had established his division in line on the first range of hills to the left of the road on which he had moved. Baird crossed at the same place and at about 5:00 P.M moved up into position on the right of Hascall. Johnson's division crossed the creek about a mile below the mill and reached the old Decatur and Sandtown road that day on the right of Baird.

After spending the first few days of August 1864 getting his troops in position, Sherman decided to move forward with his right on August 4, 1864 and attempt to reach the railroad between Atlanta and East Point. To secure better cooperation among the troops on that flank, Sherman placed Palmer's Fourteenth Corps under Schofield's direction, and he ordered Schofield to advance with his own Twenty-Third Corps and Fourteenth Corps and gain possession of the railroad. This command arrangement contributed significantly to the failure of this undertaking.

Palmer was offended by the order placing him under Schofield, whom he regarded as his junior in rank, and he refused to take orders from him. Sherman was asked to decide the question of rank, and the rest of the day was spent in comparative inactivity while he attempted to resolve the problem. That night Sherman informed Palmer that Schofield was indeed the senior officer, and he attempted to persuade Palmer to serve under him. Palmer refused, however, and offered his resignation. This was accepted by Sherman.

Largely because of the confusion resulting from the controversy over rank, Fourteenth Corps and Twenty-Third Corps accomplished little August 4, 1864. About 1:00 P.M. Morgan moved to the right with his division from its position on the right of the Army of the Tennessee, with orders to cross the North Branch of Utoy Creek and take position on the right of Baird's division. Morgan crossed the creek but was unable to reach his assigned position that day, and he bivouacked that night about two miles in rear of Baird's line.

Baird had expected to advance on August 4, 1864, but when Hascall on his left did not move, and when Morgan did not come up on his right, where he was to support Baird's attack, Baird simply remained in his entrenchments. About 4:00 P.M. he sent Newell Gleason's Second Brigade out on a reconnaissance toward the enemy's line, but it was called back at dark. Johnson sent Marion C. Taylor's First Brigade of his division out about a mile to the extreme right, and it bivouacked that night on the north side of the North Branch of Utoy Creek. He also sent John H. King's Second Brigade on a reconnaissance to the right, but it returned that evening.

On August 5, 1864, Sherman and Schofield again attempted to get the movement toward the railroad started, but they had only limited success. At 4:30 A.M. Baird received orders from Schofield detailing the movements of Twenty-Third Corps and Fourteenth Corps for that day. Baird refused to move as ordered, however, because he claimed that he had no authority to take orders from Schofield, but he did refer the matter to Palmer, his corps commander. Baird's orders were to move forward toward the enemy's line at 6:00 A.M., and Morgan was to move up and form on the right of Baird's division and support it. Cox's Division of Twenty-Third Corps was directed to be prepared to move up between Hascall and Baird if a gap should develop between them. At 7:00 A.M. Palmer directed Baird to act under Schofield's orders that day. At about the same time, Baird found the head of Cox's column well closed up on his rear and left, but he was informed that Hascall would not advance that morning, because he was already fairly close up to the enemy's works.

Finally, at about 8:00 A.M. Baird sent forward a strong line of skirmishers, supported by heavy reserves; they moved under a heavy fire and gained all the ground up to within a short distance in front of the enemy's main line. Baird's men then en-trenched on this position.

At the time that Baird advanced, Morgan's division had not arrived at the front. Morgan did not begin his advance that morning until 10:00 A.M., and he then moved about a mile to the right and front and took position on the right of Baird, with his right across the road that ran from the Sandtown road to the village of Lick Skillet.

Johnson's division moved out to the Sandtown road, then turned to the left, and finally came up and formed on the right of Morgan's division. It then advanced to a ridge overlooking the Sandtown road. Later in the day, Cox's division was moved to the right of Fourteenth Corps, and was placed in reserve to Johnson's division.

It is important to note here, to avoid any confusion when reading accounts of the troop movements along Utoy Creek, that a number of officers refer in their reports to the road that ran from the Sandtown road to the village of Lick Skillet as the Lick Skillet road. This road is not to be confused with the Lick Skillet road frequently mentioned above in the accounts of the fighting about Ezra Church. The latter road ran out westward from Atlanta along the ridge between Proctor's Creek and the North Branch of Utoy Creek to Lick Skillet and followed the course of present-day Gordon Street at Atlanta.

At this point, Schofield decided to make no further attempt to get any cooperation from Palmer's Fourteenth Corps. He ordered Cox to relieve Johnson's division of that corps, and he directed Johnson to relieve Hascall's division, which was then on the left of Baird. When relieved, Hascall was to march to the right, in rear of Baird's division, and join Cox's division. In this way, Schofield would unite the two divisions of his corps on the extreme right of Sherman's line.

Johnson left his position on the line about 8:00 P.M. to relieve Hascall, and Cox moved up into position on the right of Morgan's division. There Cox fortified a position on a low wooded ridge north of the Sandtown road. In front of his line was an open valley through which a tributary of the South Branch of Utoy Creek flowed to the southwest into the creek. Beyond the creek, to the south, was another, and higher, ridge, which was held in some force by the enemy. Cox's line was along the north side of the Sandtown road between present-day

Tuckawanna Drive on the right and present-day Willis' Mill Road on the left. Robert K. Byrd's Third Brigade was on the left of Cox's line, John S. Casement's Second Brigade (commanded by Daniel Cameron until July 31) was in the center, Richard F. Barter's Fourth Brigade (designated until August 11 as First Brigade, First Division, Twenty-Third Corps) was on the right, and James W. Reilly's First Brigade was in reserve.

Early on the morning of August 6, 1864, Hascall's division was relieved by Johnson's division, and it then marched to a position to the right and rear of Cox's line.

That morning Cox strengthened the skirmish line of his division and prepared to advance against the ridge on the far side of the valley to develop the enemy's position. Reilly was to support the skirmishers with his brigade and attempt to gain the crest of the ridge. Casement's brigade was to move up and support Reilly.

Just that morning, William B. Bate's division of William J. Hardee's corps, which had been ordered to the left of Stephen D. Lee's corps, arrived and took an advanced position on the ridge that was about one-fourth mile south of and roughly parallel to the Sandtown road, facing north. Joseph H. Lewis' brigade was on the left, about one-fourth mile east of present-day Harbin Road; Robert C. Tyler's brigade was on the right of Lewis' brigade, and extending across present-day Dodson Drive; Henry R. Jackson's brigade was next to the right, and in line across present-day Willis' Mill Road; and Jesse J. Finley's brigade was on the right of the division, across present-day Venetian Drive. Finley's and Jackson's brigades were in front of Morgan's division, and Lewis' and Tyler's brigades were in front of Cox's division. Thus the delay occasioned by Palmer's refusal to serve under Schofield's orders gave the enemy time to extend their left flank and occupy ground that on August 4, 1864 was not defended.

At 10:00 A.M. the skirmishers, supported by the 104th Ohio of Reilly's brigade, advanced and drove the enemy back into their works on the ridge, except on the left of Cox's line. Reilly then attacked and succeeded in gaining a position close up to the enemy's breastworks, but he was halted there by a destructive fire from Bate's men. Reilly held his position for some time, however, but when he found that the works were too strong to carry, he was ordered back. A part of Casement's brigade moved out across the valley to cover Reilly's withdrawal.

Soon after reaching the road that ran from the Sandtown road to Lick Skillet, Schofield was ordered to attack and capture a battery that enfiladed Cox's line as it advanced. William E. Hobson's Second Brigade of Hascall's division was then sent to a point that was thought to be beyond the extreme left of the enemy's position, but on attempting to advance, Hobson found that there were enemy entrenchments on his front. Hascall, who was then on the right of Cox, attempted to move past the enemy's flank to capture the battery. Joseph A. Cooper, with his own First Brigade and Peter T. Swaine's Fourth Brigade (designated until August 11, 1864 as Second Brigade, First Division, Twenty-Third Corps), moved on beyond the Sandtown road and drove the enemy back through the woods in rear of their left flank. Cooper's brigades forced the battery to fall back, but they failed to capture it.

As Cooper advanced, Hascall moved Silas A. Strickland's Third Brigade forward and, with the help of Hobson's brigade, held the line between Cox's division and Cooper's two brigades. By that time, however, it was too late to continue the attack, and Cooper's command was ordered to withdraw. Hascall's division was then formed on the right of Cox's division, and nearly at a right angle to it, south of the Sandtown road. The division was in line along what is today Adams Drive, facing east toward the left flank of Bate's advanced line. Hascall's brigades were in line as follows: Hobson's brigade was on the left, next to the Sandtown road; Strickland's brigade was on the left center; Swaine's brigade was on the right center; and Cooper's brigade was on the right.

The movements of the divisions of Baird and Morgan on August 6, 1864 were to have depended upon the success of Cox and Hascall in turning the enemy's left flank, or in breaking through their line at the Sandtown road. When their attempts failed, both Baird's and Morgan's men remained in their works.

Although the attacks by Schofield on August 6 were not successful in their initial purpose, the position gained by Hascall enabled him to enfilade Bate's line, and during the night Bate abandoned his advanced position and withdrew to the main line that had been constructed to cover the railroad. The main line occupied by Bate crossed the Sandtown road just west of the junction of present-day Cascade Road, and from there it ran south and a little west to the junction of present-day Willis' Mill Road and the Campbellton road, near the Robert Baugh house.

On the morning of August 7, 1864, the men of Fourteenth Corps and Twenty-Third Corps found the works on their fronts deserted, and Schofield immediately pushed forward his entire line, from the center of Morgan's division, and entrenched on a position in front of the enemy's main line. Schofield then extended his front as much as possible in preparation for a further effort to turn the enemy's left flank. Twenty-Third Corps crossed to the south side of South Utoy Creek, and the line of Fourteenth Corps was extended to the creek at a point about two and one-half miles from East Point.

Schofield sent out a reconnaissance from Twenty-Third Corps toward the railroad between East Point and Red Oak and found the enemy strongly entrenched on a line that extended so far to the Federal right that his corps could not reach its flank unless detached from the rest of the army. Schofield then entrenched on a strong line along the south bank of the South Branch of Utoy Creek, where it formed a strong right flank of the army, and where it could serve as a pivot for a movement that was contemplated for the rest of the army. He remained in this position until August 28.

The strong force encountered by Schofield was Patrick R. Cleburne's division of Hardee's corps, which was sent on August 7 to take position on the left of Bate. Cleburne continued the fortification of the main Confederate line, which eventually passed to the west of East Point and then curved around until it reached the Macon and Western Railroad about a mile south of the town.

On August 7, 1864, the controversy over the relative ranks of John M. Palmer and John M. Schofield was finally resolved. That day Palmer was relieved of his command, and he left Sherman's army for departmental duty in Kentucky, where he spent the rest of the war. Richard W. Johnson assumed temporary command of Fourteenth Corps; John H. King assumed command of Johnson's First Division, Fourteenth Corps; and John R. Edie assumed command of King's Second Brigade, First Division, Fourteenth Corps.

BATTLE OF JONESBORO, GEORGIA, AUGUST 31, 1864– SEPTEMBER 1, 1864

After the fighting along Utoy Creek had ended, Sherman was finally convinced that infantry attacks against the entrenched Confederate lines were not likely to be successful, and he also realized that Hood's men were capable of constructing such lines at a rate equal to that of Sherman's advance. He therefore decided to make no more attempts against the railroad between Atlanta and East Point, but instead to carry out a plan that he had been considering for some time. Basically, this plan was to establish Twentieth Corps in a defensive position covering the crossings of the Chattahoochee River northwest of Atlanta, and to move with the rest of his army and destroy the Atlanta and West Point Railroad near Fairburn and Red Oak, then march eastward and destroy the Macon and Western Railroad at or near Jonesboro. For this expedition, the army was to move with wagons loaded with supplies for fifteen days.

Before starting this movement, however, Sherman decided to try using artillery to destroy factories, warehouses, and other installations of military value, in the hope that that would end the usefulness of Atlanta as a manufacturing center. Since July 20, 1864, when Francis De Gress' battery had first opened fire on Atlanta, Sherman had kept up a slow and intermittent fire on the city, primarily for its psychological effect on the defenders and the townspeople. However, although it caused considerable damage in some parts of the city, it had no effect in gaining possession of Atlanta.

Sherman then decided to increase the volume of the artillery fire, and he brought up by rail from Chattanooga eight 4 1/2–inch rifled guns. These were put in position on the front of the Army of the Cumberland by John M. Brannan, chief of artillery of the Department of the Cumberland, and on August 10, 1864 they were ordered to open fire and continue day and night on military targets in Atlanta. This bombardment caused much destruction

and many fires, and otherwise created some confusion, but there were no signs that the enemy had any intention of abandoning the city.

Finally Sherman decided that artillery alone would not solve his problems. On August 16 he issued orders describing the movements for the general advance of the army toward the railroads south of Atlanta, and he directed that these begin August 18.

At about the time of the issuance of these orders, however, Sherman learned that Joseph Wheeler had moved from Covington, to the east of Atlanta, with a large cavalry force and, marching to the east and north of Atlanta, had reached the Western and Atlantic Railroad near Adairsville on Sherman's line of communications.

With the departure of Wheeler, Sherman had the larger cavalry force, and he decided to try once again to use his cavalry to break up the railroads south of Atlanta. Accordingly, he suspended the execution of his orders for the movements of his army on August 18, ordering Judson Kilpatrick to take about 5,000 cavalry and move from his camps near Sandtown and destroy the Atlanta and West Point and the Macon and Western railroads. Kilpatrick left on his mission on the night of August 18, and, after inflicting considerable damage to both railroads, he continued on around Atlanta, reaching Decatur August 22. For details of this raid, see above, Cavalry Raids on the Railroads South of Atlanta, Georgia, Kilpatrick's Raid from Sandtown to Lovejoy's Station, Georgia.

According to the estimates received by Sherman, the damage done to the railroads by Kilpatrick would interrupt service to Atlanta for only about ten days. Sherman was then convinced that the cavalry alone was incapable of preventing the continued use of the railroads serving Atlanta, and he therefore reissued the orders for the advance of his entire army, excepting Twentieth Corps, to begin on August 26. In preparation for this movement, all sick and wounded men and all unnecessary wagons were sent back across the Chattahoochee River.

There were numerous changes in the higher command of Sherman's army during August 1864, and for a better understanding of the descriptions of the troop movements during his period, and the Battle of Jonesboro, the more important of these are summarized here by corps as follows:

In Fourth Corps: August 4, 1864, Nathan Kimball, commanding First Brigade of John Newton's Second Division, Fourth Corps, assumed command of First Division, Fourth Corps, relieving William Grose. Emerson Opdyke succeeded Kimball in command of First Brigade, Second Division.

William B. Hazen, commanding Second Brigade, Third Division, Fourth Corps, was transferred to the Army of the Tennessee August 17, 1864 and was assigned command of Second Division, Fifteenth Corps. Oliver H. Payne assumed command of Hazen's brigade in Fourth Corps.

In Fourteenth Corps: August 7, 1864, Richard W. Johnson relieved John M. Palmer in command of Fourteenth Corps by right of seniority, and John H. King assumed command of Johnson's First Division, Fourteenth Corps. On August 17, William P. Carlin relieved John H. King in command of First Division, Fourteenth Corps.

August 9, 1864, Jefferson C. Davis, who was absent from the army because of illness, was assigned as permanent commander of Fourteenth Corps. On August 22, Davis, who had recovered, returned to the army and assumed command of Fourteenth Corps, relieving Johnson.

James D. Morgan, who had been in temporary command of Jefferson C. Davis' Second Division, Fourteenth Corps since July 28, 1864, was assigned permanent command August 23, when Davis returned to duty and assumed command of Fourteenth Corps.

In Fifteenth Corps: On July 11, 1864, Peter J. Osterhaus had been granted a leave of absence because of disability, and on August 15 he returned to the army and resumed command of First Division, Fifteenth Corps. Charles R. Woods, who had been in command of First Division during his absence, resumed command of his First Brigade, First Division.

William B. Hazen, commanding Second Brigade, Third Division, Fourth Corps, was transferred to the Army of the Tennessee August 17, 1864 and was assigned command of Second Division, Fifteenth Corps. Morgan L. Smith, the former commander of

Second Division, Fifteenth Corps, was forced to leave the division because of an earlier wound.

On August 22, 1864, Charles R. Woods was relieved from command in Fifteenth Corps and was assigned command of Third Division, Seventeenth Corps, relieving Mortimer D. Leggett, who was sick. Milo Smith succeeded Woods in command of First Brigade, First Division, Fifteenth Corps.

Joseph A. J. Lightburn, commander of Second Brigade, Second Division, Fifteenth Corps, was wounded August 24, 1864 and left the army on leave of absence. Wells S. Jones assumed command of his brigade.

In Sixteenth Corps: On August 4, 1864, Thomas E. G. Ransom assumed command of Fourth Division, Sixteenth Corps, and John W. Fuller resumed command of his First Brigade, Fourth Division.

August 19, 1864, Grenville M. Dodge, commander of Sixteenth Corps, was wounded, and on August 20, Ransom assumed command of the corps. Fuller resumed command of Fourth Division, Sixteenth Corps. Except for the period August 4–20, Henry T. McDowell commanded First Brigade, Fourth Division.

In Seventeenth Corps: August 22, 1864, Charles R. Woods, commander of First Brigade, First Division, Fifteenth Corps, was relieved from command in Fifteenth Corps. He was assigned command of Third Division, Seventeenth Corps, replacing Mortimer D. Leggett, who was ill.

In Twentieth Corps: Henry W. Slocum arrived on the Chattahoochee River August 27, 1864 and assumed command of Twentieth Corps, which had moved back from in front of Atlanta to cover the crossings of the river. Upon being relieved in command of the corps by Slocum, Alpheus S. Williams resumed command of his First Division, replacing Joseph F. Knipe.

In Twenty-Third Corps: July 31, 1864, John S. Casement succeeded Daniel Cameron in command of Second Brigade of Jacob D. Cox's Third Division, Twenty-Third Corps.

August 9, 1864, Israel N. Stiles relieved Robert K. Byrd in command of Third Brigade, Third Division, Twenty-Third Corps.

Movement of the Army from Utoy Creek against the Railroads South of Atlanta. The first movements of Sherman's advance against the railroads south of Atlanta began on the night of August 25, 1864. That night David S. Stanley's Fourth Corps, which was at that time north of Atlanta on the left flank of Sherman's line, began its withdrawal. It marched westward in rear of Alpheus S. Williams' Twentieth Corps, and Kenner Garrard's dismounted cavalry moved into the lines vacated by Stanley's corps. Also, at 8:00 that night, the divisions of Twentieth Corps were withdrawn from their lines in front of Atlanta and were massed about 800 yards in rear of their former line, with orders to march to the Chattahoochee River as soon as the rear of Fourth Corps had passed by on its march to the right. Joseph F. Knipe's First Division and Benjamin Harrison's First Brigade of William T. Ward's Third Division were placed near the Montgomery Ferry road; John W. Geary's Second Division was near the Howell's Mill and Pace's Ferry road; and John Coburn's Second Brigade and James Wood's Third Brigade of Ward's division were near the Turner's Ferry road.

John Newton's Second Division, which brought up the rear of Stanley's Fourth Corps, reached Proctor's Creek at 3:00 A.M. August 26, 1864. Stanley halted there until 8:00 A.M., then resumed the march southward. He crossed Utoy Creek and took position that night in line of battle in the vicinity of Utoy Post Office, facing east.

On the morning of August 26, 1864, Williams' corps marched in three columns on the roads toward the Chattahoochee River. Upon arriving there, Knipe formed his division on a line south of Montgomery's Ferry, at the railroad crossing, to protect the bridges there. Knipe then sent Harrison's brigade to the north side of the river. Geary's division took position on the high ground in front of Pace's Ferry, and Ward's division occupied the hills on the south bank of the river at Turner's Ferry.

Henry W. Slocum arrived on the Chattahoochee River August 27, 1864 and assumed command of Twentieth Corps, relieving Williams. Williams then resumed command of his First Division, relieving Knipe.

Garrard's cavalry division covered the rear of Fourth Corps and Twentieth Corps as they pulled out of their lines of entrenchments, and it then crossed the Chattahoochee River to Vining's Station August 26, 1864. The next day Garrard moved to Sandtown. Robert H. G. Minty's First Brigade then camped near Sweet Water Creek, and the men spent the time from August 28 to September 10 in camp and picketing and scouting the country from Campbellton to Marietta. Beroth B. Eggleston's Second Brigade recrossed the Chattahoochee at Sandtown and moved on the left flank and rear of Sherman's army as it advanced toward Jonesboro.

During the night of August 26, 1864, Jefferson C. Davis' Fourteenth Corps withdrew from its positions on the line, moved to the right and rear, and went into bivouac on the south side of Utoy Creek. This movement was not completed until after daylight August 27. William P. Carlin's First Division was in position on the left of Twenty-Third Corps, James D. Morgan's Second Division was on the left of Carlin, and Absalom Baird's Third Division was on the left of Morgan.

John M. Schofield's Twenty-Third Corps did not join in the movements of the rest of the army August 26, but remained in position along the south bank of the South Branch of Utoy Creek in front of East Point, where it served as the pivot for the other corps of the army.

On August 25, 1864, new works were constructed for Thomas E. G. Ransom's Sixteenth Corps, which was in line on the left of Seventeenth Corps, facing Atlanta. The new line began at a point near the center of the Seventeenth Corps line, not far from Ezra Church, and ran westward along the ridge that had been occupied by John A. Logan's Fifteenth Corps during the Battle of Ezra Church. That night Sixteenth Corps was moved into the new line without incident, and it remained there during the night, where it served as a rear guard for the rest of the army as it advanced toward Camp Creek.

At 8:00 P.M. August 26, 1864, Logan began to withdraw his Fifteenth Corps from its entrenchments in front of Atlanta. Then, with Peter J. Osterhaus' First Division on the right, William B. Hazen's Second Division in the center, and William

Harrow's Fourth Division on the left, the corps moved southward across Utoy Creek to Judge Wilson's house, then south by a country road to Camp Creek, where it arrived early on the morning of August 27. Osterhaus' and Hazen's divisions were placed in position a mile south of the creek, and Harrow's division was held in reserve.

Frank P. Blair's Seventeenth Corps also left its entrenchments at 8:00 P.M. August 26, 1864. It marched westward on the Green's Ferry road, crossed Utoy Creek, and arrived at Dry Pond, about a mile southeast of Sandtown, at daylight August 27. From there it moved south, arriving on Camp Creek at 10:00 that morning.

At 3:00 A.M. August 27, 1864, Sixteenth Corps withdrew from its new line near Ezra Church and followed Seventeenth Corps to Dry Pond, where it arrived at 6:00 A.M. It remained there for three hours, then moved on to the Campbell house, a march of ten miles. John M. Corse then formed his Second Division on the right of Seventeenth Corps, with John W. Fuller's Fourth Division in reserve.

On August 27, 1864, Stanley's Fourth Corps marched from the vicinity of Utoy Post Office and took position at Mount Gilead Church on Camp Creek, about four miles southwest of East Point. There the corps was formed in line, facing south.

Fourteenth Corps spent the day of August 27, 1864 on the south side of Utoy Creek cutting roads and preparing for the march next day.

On the morning of August 28, 1864, Oliver O. Howard's Army of the Tennessee moved forward on the right of Sherman's army to the Atlanta and West Point Railroad. Blair's Seventeenth Corps moved out on the Jonesboro road and encamped near Shadna Church on the railroad, about two and one-half miles northeast of Fairburn. Ransom's Sixteenth Corps followed Seventeenth Corps to the railroad, where it formed in reserve to Seventeenth Corps.

Logan's Fifteenth Corps started forward from Camp Creek at 8:00 A.M. August 28, 1864, with Osterhaus' division in the lead, and marched toward Fairburn on a country road. On this march, Fifteenth Corps was the left column of Sherman's army, and the trains were following behind. About two miles from its bivouac of the night before, the corps crossed the Atlanta and Campbellton road and came

up to the Fairburn road two and a half miles from the railroad. Blair and Ransom were moving on this road, and Logan was forced to cut a new road through the woods, which was parallel to the Fairburn road, for about three miles to reach the railroad. The head of the column arrived on the railroad near Shadna Church about noon, and Osterhaus took position to cover the railroad. Hazen's division soon came up and took position on the left of Osterhaus, and both divisions entrenched. Harrow's division remained massed in the rear.

Immediately upon arriving on the railroad, the troops of the Army of the Tennessee began destroying the track near Fairburn, and this work was continued the next day.

George H. Thomas' Army of the Cumberland also advanced to the Atlanta and West Point Railroad August 28, 1864. Fourteenth Corps moved at 4:00 that morning on the Campbellton road to Mount Gilead Church on Camp Creek, about four miles west of East Point. There it passed to the rear of Fourth Corps and, taking the lead, marched on by way of the Redwine place and went into position at Red Oak Station during the afternoon. There Fourteenth Corps formed in line south of the railroad, with Morgan's division on the right, Baird's division in the center, and Carlin's division on the left. Fourth Corps then came up and prolonged the line to the left of Fourteenth Corps.

Schofield's Twenty-Third Corps finally moved from its line on the south bank of the South Branch of Utoy Creek at 3:00 P.M. August 28, 1864, following Fourth Corps and Fourteenth Corps on the road to Mount Gilead Church on Camp Creek. In its movement it was covering the left flank of Sherman's army, and also the trains of the army. Milo S. Hascall's Second Division reached Mount Gilead Church that day and occupied the works constructed earlier by Fourth Corps. Jacob D. Cox's Third Division halted for the night at Mrs. Holbrook's plantation, about two miles from the church.

During August 29, 1864 the Army of the Tennessee spent the day destroying track near Fairburn, and the Army of the Cumberland destroyed track near Red Oak and cut roads for the advance the next day.

On August 29, 1864 Schofield's Twenty-Third

Corps crossed Camp Creek near Mount Gilead Church and took position on the left of the Army of the Cumberland on the south side of the creek. Cox's division marched to Azariah Mimm's plantation, about a mile and a half northeast of Red Oak, near the railroad, and then closed up on the left of Fourth Corps near the Oliver house. Hascall's division also crossed Camp Creek and took position on the left of Cox, with his left near the creek.

On August 30, 1864, the entire army, except Twenty-Third Corps, again moved forward, while wheeling to the left, toward the Macon and Western Railroad. At 7:00 A.M. Logan's Fifteenth Corps advanced on the direct road to Jonesboro, crossing Pond Creek and Shoal Creek. Judson Kilpatrick's cavalry, which was out in advance, encountered some resistance at the crossings of both creeks but, with the help of skirmishers of Hazen's division, drove the enemy back and continued the march. About 3:30 P.M., Logan reached Renfroe's Cross Roads (on some maps, Renfrew's), about four miles northwest of Jonesboro on the road from Fairburn. This was the assigned stopping place for Logan that day, but there was no water there for the men and horses, and Howard ordered the corps to move on to the Flint River.

When the head of Logan's column arrived at the Flint River at about 5:00 P.M., the enemy was found to be in position on the far side, but Hazen, with the help of two regiments of Kilpatrick's cavalry, drove the enemy back from the river and secured the crossing. Logan then crossed over and put his corps in position about three-fourths of a mile east of the Flint River on the highest ground between the river and the railroad.

During the night, Logan formed his corps with Hazen's division on the left, with its right on the Jonesboro road (present-day Route 138), about one-half mile from the railroad, with its left bent back toward the river. Harrow's division was on the right of the Jonesboro road, connecting with the right of Hazen's line, and its right bent back toward the river on that flank. Wells S. Jones' Second Brigade was on the right of Hazen's line, next to the road, and Theodore Jones' First Brigade was on the left. John M. Oliver's First Brigade was on the left of Harrow's line, next to the road, and Charles C. Walcutt's Second Brigade was on the right.

Osterhaus' division was bringing up the rear that day. It crossed to the east side of the river about midnight, but it was not until near daylight August 31, 1864 that it had established a strong defensive line between the right of Harrow's division and the river. Except for the 25th Iowa and some pickets, the rest of Osterhaus' division was formed on an entrenched second line.

At 6:30 A.M. August 30, 1864, Ransom's Sixteenth Corps also advanced toward Jonesboro on a road to the right of the main Jonesboro road used by Logan. Kilpatrick's cavalry covered the front of the column, and it was supported by the 2nd and 7th Iowa Infantry of Elliott W. Rice's First Brigade of John M. Corse's Second Division. Sixteenth Corps made slow progress during the day, because it was necessary to cut new roads and build several bridges, and it was almost constantly engaged in skirmishing. Finally, about 10:00 P.M. the corps bivouacked on the west side of Flint River, about a mile and a half from Jonesboro, and to the right and rear of Fifteenth Corps. Blair's Seventeenth Corps followed Sixteenth Corps on the road toward Jonesboro that day, but it was delayed by the trains moving on its front, and it was finally compelled to bivouac near Renfroe's after having moved only six miles in fifteen hours.

Kilpatrick's cavalry division had moved ahead and crossed to the east side of the Flint River that evening. Shortly before dark, it attacked and attempted to reach the railroad, but it was driven back.

Thomas' Army of the Cumberland advanced on August 30, 1864 between Howard's Army of the Tennessee on the right and Schofield's Army of the Ohio on the left. Early that morning, Davis' Fourteenth Corps moved eastward on a country road to the left of the Army of the Tennessee, halting at Shoal Creek for a few hours. It then moved on to Couch's place, about six miles north of Jonesboro on the road from Rough and Ready to Jonesboro. Absalom Baird's Third Division was on the left of the corps, marching within supporting distance of Fourth Corps, which was advancing on its left. James D. Morgan's Second Division, followed by William P. Carlin's First Division, marched on a more direct road to the right, and kept within supporting distance of Baird. Fourteenth Corps encountered no resistance during the day and went into camp before dark. The corps connected with Fourth Corps on the left, and its right was about a mile from

Renfroe's Cross Roads, where the Army of the Tennessee was passing.

Fourth Corps advanced on the left of Fourteenth Corps August 30, 1864, halting at dark near Mrs. Long's house, in the vicinity of Flat Rock, on the Atlanta and Fayetteville road, with troops near Mud Creek and the Mann house.

On August 30, 1864, Schofield's Twenty-Third Corps moved up to the Atlanta and West Point Railroad at Red Oak. From there it moved out toward East Point about a mile and a half and entrenched on a position covering the movement of the army trains, while at the same time threatening an attack on East Point, which was still held by a strong enemy force. Jacob D. Cox's Third Division moved in rear of Fourth Corps to the railroad, and then up the railroad about a mile and a half to a road running to Morrow's Mill and Mount Zion Church, where it bivouacked for the night. In this position, Cox was on the extreme left of the army and separated from it by about three miles. Milo S. Hascall's Second Division marched in rear of Cox, crossed the railroad at Red Oak, and took position on the right of Cox near the East Point road.

After daylight August 31, 1864, Howard and Logan began to improve the position that Fifteenth Corps had established during the night near Jonesboro. Logan brought up from the second line almost all of James A. Williamson's Second Brigade and Hugo Wangelin's Third Brigade of Osterhaus' First Division, Fifteenth Corps and extended his line to the right to connect with the refused line, which had been formed during the night, in order to establish a permanent line. Osterhaus also sent the 76th Ohio and 30th Iowa regiments of Milo Smith's First Brigade to support the left of Logan's first line and to report to Hazen.

On the morning of August 31, 1864, Corse's Second Division of Sixteenth Corps was on the west side of the river, about two miles from Jonesboro, with Elliott W. Rice's brigade in line facing south and Robert N. Adams' Second Brigade (commanded by Jesse J. Phillips until August 2) in rear of Rice, facing north, to the rear and left of Logan's line.

At daylight August 31, 1864, Blair's Seventeenth Corps advanced from its bivouac of the night before to the west bank of Flint River. Upon arriving there, it relieved Adams' brigade of Corse's division, then took position on the left of Fifteenth Corps, remaining on the west side of the river, with its line refused and facing northeast. Charles R. Woods' Third Division was on the right, and Giles A. Smith's Fourth Division was on the left.

When Seventeenth Corps relieved Adams' brigade, which had been in position on the left of Logan, Adams moved across the river and relieved the 25th Iowa and 31st Iowa of Williamson's brigade, which had been covering Logan's right flank. These two regiments then joined Williamson's brigade on the front line. Adams' brigade was formed along a ridge on the right of Williamson's brigade, and at nearly a right angle to it, along present-day Magnolia Drive, facing south.

At 10:00 A.M., Andrew T. Blodgett's Battery H, 1st Missouri Light Artillery was placed on the right of Adams' brigade, and about 1:00 P.M. Rice's brigade of Corse's division was sent across the river and placed in reserve to Adams. When the enemy advanced that afternoon, Rice's brigade was brought up on the right of Blodgett's battery, and to the right of Adams' brigade. Rice's brigade was also on the ridge along present-day Magnolia Drive, facing south.

Osterhaus also ordered up two sections of the 4th Battery, Ohio Light Artillery, commanded by George H. Haug and George Hust, and put them in position on the right of Williamson's brigade, facing south. He sent the 9th Iowa of Williamson's brigade and the 29th Missouri of Wangelin's brigade to support the battery.

At 9:00 A.M. August 31, 1864, Woods, on Blair's order, sent George E. Bryant's First Brigade across the river to report to Logan, and it was then placed on the left of Hazen's division. Later in the day he also sent the other two brigades of the division, Greenberry F. Wiles' Second Brigade and Adam G. Malloy's Third Brigade, across the river to form on the left of Bryant.

On the morning of August 31, 1864, Kilpatrick's cavalry crossed back to the west bank of the Flint River and moved south about a mile and a half to Anthony's Bridge. Kilpatrick then rebuilt the bridge, which had been destroyed, crossed the river with five regiments of his division, and moved well up to the enemy's flank and rear in the direction of the railroad, where he fortified his position.

From the beginning, the enemy had been aware

of movements in Sherman's army, but they had been unopposed, except by Confederate cavalry, while John B. Hood pondered their meaning. As early as August 25, 1864, enemy troops in the trenches at Atlanta were aware that there was some activity on their front. The next day Hood learned that Thomas' Army of the Cumberland had disappeared from its positions north of Atlanta, but its whereabouts at that time were unknown. Soon, however, Hood became convinced that Joseph Wheeler's raid on Sherman's communications north of Marietta had been successful, and that Sherman was withdrawing his army across the Chattahoochee River at Sandtown.

On August 27, 1864, however, Lawrence S. Ross, commanding a brigade of William H. Jackson's cavalry division, reported that Federal infantry were marching toward Fairburn on the Atlanta and West Point Railroad. Suspecting that this was another raid on the railroad, on August 28 Hood ordered Joseph H. Lewis' brigade of John C. Brown's division (formerly William B. Bate's division), Daniel H. Reynolds' brigade of Edward C. Walthall's division of Alexander P. Stewart's corps, and Moses W. Hannon's cavalry brigade of John H. Kelly's division to Jonesboro to cooperate with Frank C. Armstrong's brigade of Jackson's cavalry division, which was then operating out to the west of the town. The rest of Brown's division was ordered to Rough and Ready.

By August 30, 1864, Hood was aware that Sherman was on the move with most of his army, but he was still uncertain as to its destination. Possible points were East Point, Rough and Ready, and Jonesboro, but it was still too early to decide which one. That day, Armstrong, who was then about eight miles west of Jonesboro, reported that a large force of Federal infantry was advancing on his front, but Hood did not believe that it was headed for Jonesboro.

On August 30, 1864 Hood directed Stephen D. Lee to move his headquarters to East Point and to keep his corps in readiness to move in support of William J. Hardee's corps if needed. Later that day, Hood ordered Patrick R. Cleburne's division and a part of Brown's division to extend their lines to a point three miles south of East Point toward Rough and Ready.

Finally, at 5:00 P.M. August 30, 1864, when the head of Logan's Fifteenth Corps reached the Flint River in front of Jonesboro, Armstrong sent a message to Hood informing him that a Federal attack on the Macon and Western Railroad that night was a possibility. Hood then ordered Hardee to move with his corps to Jonesboro and for Lee to follow with his corps. Hood placed Hardee in command of both corps, and Cleburne assumed command of Hardee's corps. He also ordered Lewis and Reynolds, who were already at Jonesboro with their brigades, to hold their positions until help arrived.

Cleburne, with Hardee's corps, began his movement to Jonesboro on the evening of August 30, 1864; he arrived the next morning, but was not in position until 9:00 A.M. Lee did not move with his corps until after midnight and did not arrive in position on the right of Cleburne until about 11:00 A.M. The last of Lee's brigades did not arrive until 1:30 P.M.

When Cleburne had established his corps on the left, his troops were in position as follows:

Cleburne's division, commanded by Mark P. Lowrey, was on the extreme left of the Confederate line between the Jonesboro and Fayetteville road and the Flint River, with the brigades in line as follows: Hiram B. Granbury's brigade was on the left; Lowrey's brigade, commanded by John Weir, was in the center; Hugh W. Mercer's brigade, commanded by Charles H. Olmstead, was on the right; and Daniel C. Govan's brigade was in reserve.

William B. Bate's division, commanded by John C. Brown, was on the right of Lowrey, with its right on present-day Tara Boulevard (Route 7, U.S. 41/19). Jesse J. Finley's brigade, commanded by Daniel L. Kenan, was on the right; Joseph H. Lewis' brigade was in the center; Henry R. Jackson's brigade was on the left; and Robert C. Tyler's brigade, commanded by Thomas B. Smith, was in reserve.

George Maney's division was in reserve in rear of Brown's division. Maney's brigades were in line from right to left as follows: Maney's own brigade, commanded by George C. Porter, was on the right, across present-day Tara Boulevard; Alfred J. Vaughan's brigade, commanded by George W. Gordon, was on the left of Porter; Marcus J. Wright's brigade, commanded by John C. Carter, was on the left of Gordon; and States Rights Gist's brigade, commanded by James McCullough, was on the left of the line. Otho F. Strahl's brigade, commanded by Andrew J. Kellar, was on a second line in rear of Porter's brigade.

When Lee's corps came up, it was placed on the right of Cleburne's corps on a line parallel with, and about 200 yards in front of, the Macon and Western Railroad, generally facing west. The corps was formed in two lines, with the first line along the west side of the Fayetteville road, with its right near the junction of that road with present-day Route 3 and its left resting on present-day Tara Boulevard, and on the right of Brown's division. There were six brigades on the first line. On the right, from right to left, were Jacob H. Sharp's brigade, Zachariah C. Deas' brigade, and William F. Brantly's brigade, all belonging to J. Patton Anderson's division; and on the left, also from right to left, were Joseph B. Palmer's brigade, Daniel H. Reynolds' brigade (commanded by Washington M. Hardy), and Edmund W. Pettus' brigade, all belonging to Carter L. Stevenson's division. Anderson was directed to exercise control of only his three brigades on the first line, and Henry D. Clayton would command the reserve line.

Arthur M. Manigault's brigade of Anderson's division was placed on the second line in rear of Brantly's brigade, astride present-day North Avenue (Route 138). Clayton sent Marcellus A. Stovall's brigade of his division to support Stevenson's division, and he then moved up with his two remaining brigades, Randall L. Gibson's and James T. Holtzclaw's, and placed them on the right of Manigault's brigade, with Gibson on the right and Holtzclaw next to Manigault. Alpheus Baker's brigade of Clayton's division had just been sent to Mobile, Alabama and was no longer with Hood's army. Alfred Cumming's brigade of Stevenson's division was placed on the second line to the left of Manigault's brigade, and Stovall's brigade of Clayton's division was placed on the left of Cumming.

According to Hood's orders, Hardee was to attack and drive the Federal troops back across the Flint River. Hardee's attack was to begin with Lowrey advancing on the extreme Confederate left against Howard's right flank, and then the rest of the Confederate line was to attack progressively from left to right, with Lee's divisions attacking after Cleburne's corps had become engaged.

Battle of Jonesboro, Georgia, August 31, 1864. The Battle of Jonesboro began about 3:00 P.M. August 31, 1864 when Granbury, commanding Lowrey's left brigade, advanced against the line held by Corse's division, which faced south on the right of Howard's line. As Granbury wheeled northward in his attack, he presented his left flank to the five dismounted regiments of Kilpatrick's cavalry division. Kilpatrick's men immediately opened fire, and they were supported by Yates V. Beebe's 10th Battery, Wisconsin Light Artillery and the troopers remaining on the west side of the Flint River. Lowrey's men then began to turn to the left to meet this threat, instead of to the right as ordered, and they were not again involved in the attack on Corse's line that afternoon. John Tillson's Third Brigade of John W. Fuller's Fourth Division, Sixteenth Corps was sent across the river to reinforce Corse's division, but the enemy attack had been repulsed before it arrived, and Tillson did not take part in the action that day.

Lowrey finally forced Kilpatrick to fall back and recross the river. Then, acting without orders, Granbury crossed the river in pursuit with his brigade, and he was followed by Weir's and Olmstead's brigades. Lowrey, however, soon ordered his brigades to withdraw across the river.

That afternoon, by Blair's orders, Giles A. Smith, with his Fourth Division, Seventeenth Corps, moved south about two and a half miles and relieved Kilpatrick's cavalry. Smith then moved across to the east side of Flint River and just before dark drove the enemy back. After being relieved, Kilpatrick's cavalry moved to Glass' Bridge below Lovejoy's Station.

Brown's division, according to plan, attacked next and moved up toward the front of Osterhaus' division and the left of Corse's division. It came under a very heavy infantry fire, aided greatly by artillery fire, and, being unsupported on the left because of Lowrey's change of direction, it was soon driven back. Cleburne then ordered Maney to move forward and attack, but upon arriving in front of the Federal position, Maney thought that Howard's position was too strong, and he decided not to attack. Maney was relieved from command that night, and John C. Carter assumed command of the division. Apparently Maney was not again assigned command in the armies of the Confederacy.

Lee's artillery opened fire about 2:00 P.M., and when he heard the sounds of Cleburne's battle on his left, he advanced his first line, consisting of the six brigades of Anderson's and Stevenson's divisions, up the slope of the ridge toward Logan's line. This attempt was no more successful than the earlier attacks, and Lee's men were soon stopped by a heavy fire, with many of the men taking cover on the ground and others fleeing to the rear. Attempts to rally the troops and continue the fight failed, and then Anderson brought up his reserves and launched another attack. This ended as the first attack had, with most of the men taking cover without reaching the Federal works. The attack was particularly severe on the front of Hazen's division on Logan's left, but Harrow on the right had no difficulty in stopping the enemy attacks. Anderson and Cumming were wounded during the fighting.

By 4:30 P.M. Hardee's troops were withdrawing from the front all along the line and returning to their original positions.

At about 10:00 P.M. that night, after Lowrey's division had recrossed the Flint River, William W. Belknap's Third Brigade (formerly commanded by William Hall) of Giles A. Smith's Fourth Division of Seventeenth Corps was sent back north and across the river to take position on the left of Charles R. Woods' Third Division, Seventeenth Corps. Early the next morning, September 1, 1864, Benjamin F. Potts' First Brigade of Fourth Division was also moved back to join Belknap on the left of Woods' division. Thus, on the morning of September 1, Blair's Seventeenth Corps was in line on the left of Logan's Fifteenth Corps east of the river.

* * * * * * * * * *

Meantime, while Howard's Army of the Tennessee was getting in position near Jonesboro and repelling Hardee's attack on August 31, 1864, Thomas' Army of the Cumberland and Schofield's Army of the Ohio (Twenty-Third Corps) were continuing their operations against the Macon and Western Railroad to the north. On the night of August 30, Sherman learned that Howard was near Jonesboro, and he issued orders for the movements of the rest of the army for the next day. Schofield's Twenty-Third Corps was to advance on the left of Thomas' Army of the Cumberland toward Rough and Ready on the Macon and Western Railroad, and Stanley's Fourth Corps was to move in connection with Twenty-Third Corps toward the railroad. In addition, Thomas was directed to send out a part of Davis' Fourteenth Corps on a reconnaissance toward the railroad to the right of Fourth Corps.

At daylight August 31, 1864, Schofield's corps moved out from Oliver's, marching on the Rough and Ready road to the position of Fourth Corps at Morrow's Mill on the Flint River. Then, passing to the left and front of Fourth Corps, Cox arrived on the Macon and Western Railroad about a mile below Rough and Ready at 3:00 P.M. Cox destroyed a considerable amount of track and drove the enemy back about a mile toward Rough and Ready that evening. Hascall's division moved to protect the flank of the army by crossing the river a mile above Morrow's Mill to cover the roads from Atlanta and East Point. Hascall halted his division near the East Point road for a time, then moved to a point near Rough and Ready Station.

Early on the morning of August 31, 1864, David S. Stanley's Fourth Corps moved out from its bivouac near Mrs. Long's and marched toward the railroad on a road to the right of that used by Twenty-Third Corps, by way of Thame's Mill. John Newton's Second Division was left to hold the position at Thame's Mill until Schofield came up, and then Newton followed the rest of the corps toward the railroad.

Upon arriving near the mills on Crooked Creek, on the Decatur road, Stanley's advance found the enemy entrenched on the far side of the creek. Stanley immediately deployed Nathan Kimball's First Division and Thomas J. Wood's Third Division, and when they advanced, the enemy cavalry that were holding the bridge abandoned their works and fled to the rear. Newton's division then came up and was placed in position covering the direct road to Jonesboro, and Kimball and Wood continued their advance toward the railroad.

As Stanley advanced, Schofield's Twenty-Third Corps was marching on the main road running to the railroad, and Stanley was forced to use roads parallel to the main road farther to the south. Stanley arrived on the railroad at 4:00 P.M., just a short time after Cox's division arrived, and he put his divisions on the right of Twenty-Third Corps. Stanley made a small break in the railroad, but devoted most of the rest of the day to preparing a secure line facing Jonesboro. He started the real work of destruction of the track at 3:00 A.M. September 1.

Also on the morning of August 31, 1864, Absalom Baird, with his own Third Division and John G. Mitchell's Second Brigade of James D. Morgan's Second Division of Fourteenth Corps, started out on the reconnaissance toward the Macon and Western Railroad. Baird's leading troops, belonging to Caleb H. Carlton's 89th Ohio Infantry of Moses B. Walker's First Brigade, reached the railroad about four miles from Jonesboro at 6:00 P.M. At that point Carlton was about two miles from his supports, and was preparing to withdraw, when he was directed by Baird to hold his position on the railroad. Baird then sent forward Newell Gleason's Second Brigade of his division to join Carlton, and entrenched his command on the Rough and Ready road near the Smith house.

During the morning of August 31, 1864, William P. Carlin's First Division of Fourteenth Corps moved to Renfroe's to serve as a guard for the trains that were assembling there. Late in the afternoon, however, Carlin was sent to support the Army of the Tennessee when it was attacked near Jonesboro by Hardee's command. Morgan's division was then ordered to Renfroe's to take the place of Carlin. Carlin joined Howard as directed, but he arrived after Hardee's attack had been repulsed, and he was not engaged. Carlin then returned to his camp of the previous night.

About 4:00 in the afternoon of August 31, 1864, Sherman learned that Howard had repulsed an attack on his lines near Jonesboro and was still holding his position west of the town. At about the same time, he learned that Schofield's Twenty-Third Corps was on the railroad below Rough and Ready, destroying the track as it advanced; that Stanley's Fourth Corps was on the railroad below Schofield, also destroying the track as it approached Jonesboro; and that Baird's division of Davis' Fourteenth Corps was on the railroad, still farther south, only four miles from Jonesboro.

Sherman also knew that two of Hood's corps were at Jonesboro, but he did not know whether Stewart's corps was still at Atlanta or had joined the other two corps. Sherman then decided to move his entire army on Jonesboro; if Stewart was not there, he would be able to divide Hood's army by placing his army between the two parts. Meantime Sherman ordered Howard to hold his position of the day before, facing Jonesboro, while the rest of the army moved up to join him. Also, on the night of August 31, Sherman directed Henry W. Slocum to send out troops of his Twentieth Corps to determine what was happening at Atlanta, and, if Stewart had departed, to move into the town if possible.

Sherman then issued the orders for the movements of September 1, 1864 for the Army of the Cumberland and the Army of the Ohio to join the Army of the Tennessee at Jonesboro. Davis' Fourteenth Corps was to move up and deploy, facing south, with its right connecting with Logan's Fifteenth Corps and its left extending to the railroad north of Jonesboro. When Davis came up to the left of Logan, Blair was to withdraw his Seventeenth Corps and move with it to the right of the army. Both Stanley's Fourth Corps and Schofield's Twenty-Third Corps were to continue their movements down the Rough and Ready road and the railroad, destroying the track as they advanced. Sherman had hoped that all troops would be in position near Jonesboro by noon September 1, but several more hours were required for Davis to come up and take position, and Stanley did not arrive until nearly dark. Howard was instructed to hold the line where he then was and keep Hardee occupied while the rest of the army concentrated on his left.

During the afternoon of August 31, 1864, Hood, at Atlanta, learned that Federal troops had cut the railroad between Atlanta and Jonesboro, and he had also received reports that led him to believe that Sherman was planning to attack East Point the next day. Fearing for the safety of Atlanta, Hood sent a message to Hardee at 6:00 P.M. directing him to send Lee's corps back to Atlanta. Lee received the order from Hardee at 1:00 A.M. September 1, and he immediately started his corps on the road. About six miles from Atlanta, however, Lee was directed to halt his column and take position to cover the evacuation of the city. Hardee remained with his corps at Jonesboro to cover the front of Macon.

After the departure of Lee, Hardee began the task of forming a new line for the defense of his position at Jonesboro. He first moved Lowrey from the left of his line to occupy the works vacated by Lee, and he moved up Maney's division, then commanded by John C. Carter, to hold Lowrey's former line. Lowrey received Hardee's order to relieve Lee at 1:30 A.M. September 1, 1864, and he promptly moved up to put his division in position. When the line was formed, Govan's brigade was on the right, Granbury's brigade was on the right center, Lowrey's brigade, commanded by Weir, was on the left center, and Mercer's brigade, commanded by Olmstead, was on the left. Brown's division was to the left of Lowrey. Lowrey's new line ran almost due north and south, and nearly parallel to the railroad, with the right of Govan's brigade refused on the right toward the railroad.

During the early afternoon, Hardee learned that Federal troops were moving to his right, and he sent Lewis, with his own brigade of Brown's division, and Gist's brigade, commanded by McCullough, of Carter's division to the right to report to Lowrey. Lewis' brigade was placed on the right of Govan, with its right near the railroad, and McCullough's brigade was formed on the right of Lewis, on the east side of the railroad. The right of McCullough's brigade curved back on a line that was almost parallel to the railroad. By this arrangement, a sharp salient was formed in the Confederate line, with Govan's brigade at the apex, which was just north of the Warren house. Lewis was placed in command of his own and McCullough's brigades. At about the time that this line was formed and entrenched, Davis' Fourteenth Corps moved forward to attack.

Battle of Jonesboro, Georgia, September 1, 1864. On the morning of September 1, 1864, Davis was ordered to march with Morgan's Second Division and two brigades of Carlin's First Division to join Baird's division, and together they were to move up and support the left of Howard's line. That morning Carlin sent Marion C. Taylor's First Brigade of his division, with William P. Stackhouse's 19th Battery, Indiana Light Artillery, to the right to protect the trains, and it moved about a mile south of the Renfroe house and entrenched. Carlin then marched rapidly from his camps near the Smith house to the Rough and Ready road with John R. Edie's Second Brigade and Marshall F. Moore's Third Brigade, halting a short distance in advance of Baird's field

works. His orders were to take position on the right of Baird's division, which was then on the Rough and Ready and Jonesboro road, east of Mrs. Evans' house. Before taking position, however, Carlin was ordered to move forward with his division toward Jonesboro.

Morgan, with Charles M. Lum's First Brigade and Caleb J. Dilworth's Third Brigade, marched back from Renfroe's that morning on the Fayetteville road to the Rough and Ready and Jonesboro road, then followed Carlin to Baird's position. John G. Mitchell's Second Brigade of Morgan's division, which had been serving with Baird on his reconnaissance toward the railroad, rejoined the division at that time. Morgan was directed to form in rear of the right of Baird's line, but before doing so he was ordered to follow Carlin toward Jonesboro.

Upon arriving at Baird's headquarters, Davis was informed by Thomas that Stanley's Fourth Corps was moving down the Macon and Western Railroad that morning, and that Thomas wanted the two corps to move within supporting distance toward Jonesboro. Davis immediately started his Fourteenth Corps forward, with Carlin's division in advance and Morgan's division following, and with Baird's division in reserve. After advancing to within about two miles of Jonesboro, the head of the column reached the Smith house, near Muncus Creek (Moker's Creek), and there it found the pickets of the Army of the Tennessee. Carlin's division then took position parallel to the road, facing the railroad about a mile and a half to the east.

Carlin then sent Moore's brigade and the 16th United States Infantry of Edie's brigade on a reconnaissance toward the railroad. After encountering some resistance, Moore's command soon drove the enemy back and occupied their position. Edie's brigade immediately moved up to the right of Moore and pushed his skirmishers out toward the railroad. Carlin then placed Mark H. Prescott's Battery C, 1st Illinois Light Artillery on a ridge, on the right flank of the enemy's line, which was then facing Morgan's division that was coming up on the right of Carlin. George Q. Gardner's 5th Battery, Wisconsin Light Artillery of Morgan's division was also brought up on the ridge. Carlin sent out the 21st Ohio Regiment of Moore's brigade to the left and front, and it soon established a connection with Stanley's Fourth Corps, which was arriving and taking position on the left of Carlin, with its right resting on the railroad.

Carlin again changed front to the right, with the left of Moore's brigade resting on the railroad in line of battle, and Edie's brigade on his right. Davis then ordered Carlin to advance toward Jonesboro until he came up to the enemy's works.

Meantime, when the head of Morgan's column, which had been following Carlin's division toward Jonesboro, reached the Toland house, about three and a half miles north of the town, it halted to allow Carlin to move into position. That done, Morgan was first ordered to take position on the left of Carlin, but this order was soon changed, and Morgan was directed to cross the Flint River and take position on a ridge east of the river and on the right of Carlin, facing south. The right of Morgan's line was to connect with the left of Logan's Fifteenth Corps of the Army of the Tennessee. It has been noted that Giles A. Smith's Fourth Division of Blair's Seventeenth Corps had joined Charles R. Woods' Third Division of the same corps on the right of Fifteenth Corps during the night of August 31 and the morning of September 1, but about 3:00 P.M. September 1, both were withdrawn to the west bank of the Flint River and then moved down to the bridge about two miles below. Blair did not reach the bridge until dark, but he then crossed the river and put his corps in line on the right of Ransom's Sixteenth Corps that night. Morgan's division was to occupy the position vacated by Blair's Seventeenth Corps that afternoon.

Morgan's division crossed the river, then crossed a swamp on the far side, and took position about 200 yards in front of the enemy's works, with Dilworth's brigade on the right and Mitchell's brigade on the left. In taking up its position, Carlin's division moved to the left, and in so doing created a gap between its right and the left of Morgan. Morgan then brought up Lum's brigade from its position in reserve and placed it on the left of Mitchell to close the gap.

Baird's division, which was to follow Morgan's division on the Jonesboro road, was unable to advance until about noon, when the road was finally clear, and when it arrived on Muncus Creek, it was massed in rear of Carlin's division in reserve. This was only shortly before Davis' attack began at 4:00 P.M. Later George P. Este's Third Brigade was sent up to relieve Edie's brigade of Carlin's division, but Moses B. Walker's First Brigade and Newell Gleason's Second Brigade remained in reserve to the right of the railroad.

By noon September 1, 1864, Davis had his First Division and Second Division in position north of Jonesboro, with his right on the left of Logan's line and his left on the railroad, generally facing south. At that time, Stanley's Fourth Corps was still four miles north of Jonesboro and tearing up the track as it moved southward, and Schofield's Twenty-Third Corps was still farther to the north, in rear of Stanley.

Davis then received permission from Thomas to attack the enemy works from the hill held by Edie's brigade. He brought up his troops in column and deployed into line, with Edie's brigade on the right and Moore's brigade on the left.

At 4:00 P.M. September 1, 1864, after a heavy bombardment of the Confederate line by the batteries of Prescott and Gardner, Carlin advanced his two brigades through a dense woods to an open field for an attack. This was to be directed against the salient held by Govan's brigade on the right of Hardee's line, just north of the Warren house. Carlin's troops lost their alignment in passing through the woods and underbrush, and about 300–400 yards from the enemy's works they halted to readjust their lines. This completed, they advanced under a heavy fire from the infantry and Charles Swett's battery, commanded by Henry N. Steele, and Thomas J. Key's battery, commanded by James G. Marshall, and were soon stopped. Edie's brigade got close to the breastworks, but the men were then forced to take cover and wait until help arrived.

Moore's brigade, advancing on the left of Edie, also ran into trouble. Stanley's Fourth Corps, which had been expected to come up on the left of Carlin's division, had not arrived, and Moore, compelled to attack without support on his left, was soon driven back.

Immediately after Carlin's repulse, Davis prepared for a second attack. He brought up Este's Third Brigade of Baird's division to replace Edie's brigade, which had suffered severely in its attack; he re-formed and reinforced Moore's brigade; and he ordered Morgan to attack simultaneously with Carlin with his entire division. Thus, for Davis' second attack, which began about 5:00 P.M., the brigades of his corps advanced in line from left to right as follows: Moore's brigade of Carlin's division; Este's brigade of Baird's division; and then Lum's brigade, Mitchell's brigade, and Dilworth's brigade of Morgan's division. This attack was also directed toward the salient held by Govan's brigade.

The 10th Kentucky and 74th Indiana on the right of Este's brigade quickly crossed the entrenchments on their front and drove back the enemy, but the 14th Ohio and 38th Ohio on the left of Este's line were stopped before reaching the works. These two regiments, however, managed to hold their positions under a constant fire. Este then asked for help, and William T. C. Grower brought up his 17th New York of Lum's brigade. Joined by Grower's regiment, Este's two left regiments then advanced and carried the works on their front. Grower was mortally wounded in the attack.

On the right of Govan's line, Lewis' brigade was also forced to fall back, largely by Federal troops moving into its rear after crossing Govan's works. Moore's brigade, attacking on the left of Este, was held in check for some time, but it finally broke through McCullough's line near the railroad.

On Morgan's front, Lum's brigade and Mitchell's brigade attacked with Carlin's brigades, and together they stormed over Govan's works and drove back the defenders on their front. Davis' men captured 600 prisoners, including Govan and the artillery. Dilworth's brigade, on the right of Morgan's line, also advanced, but it soon became hard-pressed. The outcome of Dilworth's attack was in some doubt until Mitchell's brigade succeeded in entering the works on its front, and then Dilworth charged and drove the enemy back toward the railroad. As Dilworth was attempting to re-form his line, he was wounded; he was succeeded in command of the brigade by James W. Langley.

Hardee and Cleburne made strenuous efforts to contain the break in their line and finally succeeded. The remnants of Govan's and Lewis' brigades were rallied, and Cleburne brought up from the left Gordon's brigade and put it in position near the Warren house. With the help of Granbury's brigade, which was on the left of Govan, this line stopped Davis' advance at that point. Farther to the right, the troops of McCullough counterattacked and stabilized their line. Finally, when the fighting had ended, the enemy had taken a new position about 150 yards in rear of their original line.

Nathan Kimball's and John Newton's divisions of Stanley's Fourth Corps were so delayed by enemy skirmishers and dense undergrowth that they did not arrive in front of Hardee's line until about 5:00 P.M. Only William Grose's Third Brigade and Isaac M. Kirby's First Brigade of Kimball's division succeeded in passing through the entanglements in front of the enemy's line, and by that time it was dark.

Newton's Second Division was forced to move farther to the left, beyond Kimball's brigades, and it was not until after dark that it got in position. George D. Wagner's Second Brigade was on the right, next to Kimball; Emerson Opdyke's First Brigade was in the center; and Luther P. Bradley's Third Brigade was on the left.

Thomas J. Wood's Third Division of Fourth Corps was in charge of the trains September 1, 1864, and did not arrive near the front until after dark. P. Sidney Post's Second Brigade camped with the trains that night, and Frederick Knefler's Third Brigade and Charles T. Hotchkiss' First Brigade were massed in rear of Newton's division. The term of service of William H. Gibson, former commander of First Brigade of Wood's division, had expired August 24, and Hotchkiss had succeeded him in command of the brigade.

On September 1, 1864, Schofield's Twenty-Third Corps also moved in the direction of Jonesboro. Cox pushed his advance as far as Rough and Ready, destroying the track as he went forward, while Hascall came in from the extreme left and followed in support of Stanley as he moved toward Jonesboro. Cox followed Hascall as soon as Garrard's cavalry arrived to cover the rear of Schofield's corps and also the trains. Schofield followed Stanley closely, destroying the track as he advanced, but at dark he halted in rear of Wood's division on the railroad.

EVACUATION OF ATLANTA, GEORGIA

Around midnight August 31, 1864, after he had learned of Hardee's defeat that day, and also that most of Sherman's army was between Atlanta and Jonesboro, Hood issued instructions for the evacuation of Atlanta the next day. On the morning of September 1, Stephen D. Lee marched southward with his corps toward Lovejoy's Station on the Macon and Western Railroad, and about 5:00 that afternoon Hood, with Alexander P. Stewart's corps and Gustavus W. Smith's Georgia Militia, began marching out of the city on the road toward Lovejoy's Station. All stores, supplies, and other items of military value were destroyed, in some cases causing considerable damage to the city. This was particularly true when a train loaded with ammunition was set afire. French's division was the last to leave the city, and it moved out about 11:00 P.M. Hood's column reached Lovejoy's Station on September 3.

On September 2, Garrard reported to Sherman that advanced elements of Slocum's Twentieth Corps, which had been ordered out on a reconnaissance toward Atlanta, had received the surrender of the city from Mayor James M. Calhoun, and that Federal troops had then moved on into the city.

END OF THE CAMPAIGN

On the night of September 1, 1864, Hardee withdrew with his corps from in front of Jonesboro and moved southward toward Lovejoy's Station. The next day, Sherman started his army in pursuit. Logan's Fifteenth Corps marched on the main road from Jonesboro to Lovejoy's Station, and Blair's Seventeenth Corps moved on a road to the right of and parallel to that used by Logan. Ransom's Sixteenth Corps advanced through woods and across fields between Logan's and Blair's columns. Upon arrival in front of the enemy's works near Lovejoy's Station, Blair took position on the right, and on the extreme right of Sherman's army, and Logan's corps took position on the left of Blair. Ransom massed his division in reserve on the right of Fifteenth Corps.

At 9:00 A.M. September 1, 1864, Stanley's Fourth Corps started in pursuit of Hardee's column, marching on the east side of the railroad, and on the left of the Army of the Tennessee. About noon, Stanley came up on the enemy about a mile north of Lovejoy's Station and deployed his corps, with Newton's division on the right, Wood's division in

the center, and Kimball's division on the left. Stanley started his corps forward about 3:30 P.M. and, after marching through very difficult country, came up in front of a defended line of works. He promptly attacked and drove the enemy back, but it was then nearly dark, and he entrenched the position that he had gained. Wood was wounded in the attack, and he was succeeded by P. Sidney Post in command of Third Division.

Davis' Fourteenth Corps was left behind at Jonesboro to bury the dead and to protect the right and rear of the rest of the army as it moved south. Marion C. Taylor's First Brigade of Carlin's division, which had been at Renfroe's guarding the trains during the battle of September 1, rejoined the division while it was at Jonesboro after the battle.

Schofield's Twenty-Third Corps came up and halted in rear of the right flank of Fourth Corps, but it did not take part in Stanley's engagement.

At that time Sherman decided to call off the pursuit of Hood, and he ordered the army to return to the vicinity of Atlanta and to give the men some much-needed rest. The army began its withdrawal from in front of Lovejoy's Station on the night of September 5, 1864.

Stanley's Fourth Corps returned to Jonesboro and remained in camp there September 6. The next day it marched back through Rough and Ready, then went into camp on the Decatur road and the Georgia Railroad east of Atlanta. Davis' Fourteenth Corps remained at Jonesboro until the morning of September 7, and then it too marched to Rough and Ready. The next day it moved to White Hall, where it went into permanent camp.

The Army of the Tennessee also returned to Jonesboro, arriving there September 6. The next day Logan's Fifteenth Corps marched to Morrow's Mill, and on September 8, it moved to East Point and went into camp. Blair's Seventeenth Corps also moved to the vicinity of East Point September 7, and the next day it moved to a new camp on the Macon and Western Railroad. Ransom's Sixteenth Corps marched toward East Point September 7 and camped that night on the Fayetteville and East Point road, about six miles north of Renfroe's. The next day it marched to East Point and occupied the old enemy breastworks that were west of the railroad and between the Newnan road and the Sandtown road.

Twenty-Third Corps marched back to Jonesboro with the rest of the army September 5, 1864, and the next day resumed the positions previously held on the railroad north of the town. On September 7, the corps marched toward Decatur, Georgia, and the next day it went into camp near that town.

ORGANIZATION OF SHERMAN'S ARMY DURING THE ATLANTA CAMPAIGN

The organization of the Union field forces of the Military Division of the Mississippi, commanded by William T. Sherman, during the Atlanta Campaign May 3–September 8, 1864 was as follows:

ARMY OF THE CUMBERLAND
George H. Thomas

FOURTH CORPS, Oliver O. Howard, to July 27, 1864
David S. Stanley

First Division, David S. Stanley, to July 27, 1864
William Grose, to August 4, 1864
Nathan Kimball
First Brigade, Charles Cruft, to June 10, 1864, sick
Isaac M. Kirby
Second Brigade, Walter C. Whitaker, to June 30, 1864, sick
Jacob E. Taylor
Third Brigade, William Grose, to July 27, 1864
P. Sidney Post, to August 4, 1864
William Grose, September 4, 1864
John E. Bennett
Artillery, Peter Simonson, to June 16, 1864, killed
Samuel M. McDowell, to June 27, 1864, killed
Theodore S. Thomasson
3rd Battery, Indiana Light Artillery, Alfred Morrison
Battery B, Pennsylvania Light Artillery, Samuel M. McDowell
Jacob Ziegler

Note. The artillery of First Division became a part of the corps' Artillery Brigade July 26, 1864.

Second Division, John Newton
First Brigade, Francis T. Sherman, to May 22, 1864
Nathan Kimball, to August 4, 1864
Emerson Opdyke

Second Brigade, George D. Wagner, to July 10, 1864, sick
John W. Blake, to July 25, 1864
George D. Wagner
Third Brigade, Charles G. Harker, to June 27, 1864, killed
Luther P. Bradley
Artillery, Charles C. Aleshire, to June 24, 1864
Wilbur F. Goodspeed
Battery M, 1st Illinois Light Artillery, George W. Spencer
Battery A, 1st Ohio Light Artillery, Wilbur F. Goodspeed
Charles W. Scovill

Note. The artillery of Second Division became a part of the corps' Artillery Brigade July 26, 1864.

Third Division, Thomas J. Wood, to September 2, 1864, wounded
P. Sidney Post, temporarily
Thomas J. Wood
First Brigade, August Willich, to May 15, 1864, wounded
William H. Gibson, to June 6, 1864
Richard H. Nodine, to August 1, 1864, muster out
William H. Gibson, to August 25, 1864, muster out
Charles T. Hotchkiss
Second Brigade, William B. Hazen, to August 17, 1864, to Army of the Tennessee
Oliver H. Payne, to August 19, 1864
P. Sidney Post
Third Brigade, Samuel Beatty, to May 23, 1864, sick
Frederick Knefler
Artillery, Cullen Bradley
Bridges' Battery, Illinois Light Artillery, Lyman Bridges, to May 23, 1864
Morris D. Temple, to June 8, 1864, muster out
Lyman A. White
6th Battery, Ohio Light Artillery, Oliver H. P. Ayres, to May 30, 1864
Lorenzo D. Immell, to June 28, 1864
Oliver H. P. Ayres, to July 6, 1864, wounded
Lorenzo D. Immell

Note. The artillery of Third Division became a part of the corps' Artillery Brigade July 26, 1864.

Artillery Brigade, Thomas W. Osborn, from July 26 to July 30, 1864
Lyman Bridges
Battery M, 1st Illinois Light Artillery, George W. Spencer
Bridges' Battery, Illinois Light Artillery, Lyman A. White

5th Battery, Indiana Light Artillery, Alfred Morrison
George H. Briggs
Battery A, 1st Ohio Light Artillery, Wilbur F. Goodspeed
Battery M, 1st Ohio Light Artillery, Frederick Schultz
6th Battery, Ohio Light Artillery, Lorenzo D. Immell, to August 1, 1864
Cullen Bradley
Battery B, Pennsylvania Light Artillery, Jacob Ziegler

Note. The Artillery Brigade was organized July 26, 1864 from the batteries previously assigned to the divisions of Fourth Corps.

FOURTEENTH CORPS, John M. Palmer, to August 7, 1864, relieved
Richard W. Johnson, to August 22, 1864
Jefferson C. Davis

First Division, Richard W. Johnson, to May 29, 1864, disabled
John H. King, to June 6, 1864
Richard W. Johnson, to June 13, 1864
John H. King, to July 13, 1864
Richard W. Johnson, to August 7, 1864
John H. King, to August 17, 1864
William P. Carlin
First Brigade, William P. Carlin, to July 2, 1864, on leave
Anson G. McCook, to July 27, 1864
Marion C. Taylor, to August 2, 1864
William P. Carlin, to August 17, 1864
Marion C. Taylor
Second Brigade, John H. King, to June 13, 1864
William L. Stoughton, to July 4, 1864, wounded
Marshall F. Moore, to July 13, 1864
John H. King, to August 16, 1864
John R. Edie
Third Brigade, Benjamin F. Scribner, to July 5, 1864, sick
Josiah Given, to July 15, 1864
Marshall F. Moore
Artillery, Lucius H. Drury
Battery C, 1st Illinois Light Artillery, Mark H. Prescott
Battery I, 1st Ohio Light Artillery, Hubert Dilger

Note. The artillery of First Division became a part of the corps' Artillery Brigade July 24, 1864.

Second Division, Jefferson C. Davis, to July 28, 1864, sick
James D. Morgan
First Brigade, James D. Morgan, to July 28, 1864
Robert F. Smith, temporarily

James D. Morgan, to August 24, 1864
Charles M. Lum
Second Brigade, John G. Mitchell
Third Brigade, Daniel McCook, to June 27, 1864, mortally wounded
Oscar F. Harmon, June 27, 1864, mortally wounded
Caleb J. Dilworth, to September 1, 1864, wounded
James W. Langley
Artillery, Charles M. Barnett
Battery I, 1st Illinois Light Artillery, Alonzo W. Coe
5th Battery, Wisconsin Light Artillery, George Q. Gardner

Note 1. James D. Morgan was in temporary command of Second Division from July 28, 1864 to August 23, 1864, and he was also in command of First Brigade. Morgan was assigned permanent command of Second Division August 23, 1864.
Note 2. The artillery of Second Division became a part of the corps' Artillery Brigade July 24, 1864.

Third Division, Absalom Baird
First Brigade, John B. Turchin, to July 15, 1864, sick
Moses B. Walker
Second Brigade, Ferdinand Van Derveer, to July 27, 1864, sick
Newell Gleason
Third Brigade, George P. Este
Artillery, George Estep
7th Battery, Indiana Light Artillery, Otho H. Morgan
19th Battery, Indiana Light Artillery, William P. Stackhouse

Note. The Artillery of Third Division became a part of the corps' Artillery Brigade July 24, 1864.

Artillery Brigade, Charles Houghtaling
Battery C, 1st Illinois Light Artillery, Mark H. Prescott
Battery I, 2nd Illinois Light Artillery, Charles M. Barnett
7th Battery, Indiana Light Artillery, Otho H. Morgan
19th Battery, Indiana Light Artillery, William P. Stackhouse
20th Battery, Indiana Light Artillery, Milton A. Osborne
Battery I, 1st Ohio Light Artillery, Hubert Dilger
5th Battery, Wisconsin Light Artillery, George Q. Gardner, to July 28, sick
Joseph McKnight

Note. The 20th Indiana Battery was assigned to the

brigade August 14, 1864, and Dilger's Ohio battery was relieved August 14, 1864.

TWENTIETH CORPS, Joseph Hooker, to July 28, 1864
 Alpheus S. Williams, to August 27, 1864
 Henry W. Slocum

First Division, Alpheus S. Williams, to July 28, 1864
 Joseph F. Knipe, to August 27, 1864
 Alpheus S. Williams
 First Brigade, Joseph F. Knipe, to July 3, 1864
  Warren W. Packer, to July 17, 1864
  Joseph F. Knipe, to July 28, 1864
  Warren W. Packer, to August 28, 1864
  Joseph F. Knipe
 Second Brigade, Thomas H. Ruger
 Third Brigade, James S. Robinson, to July 24, 1864
  Horace Boughton
 Artillery, John D. Woodbury
  Battery I, 1st New York Light Artillery, Charles E. Winegar
  Battery M, 1st New York Light Artillery, John D. Woodbury

Note. The artillery of First Division became a part of the corps' Artillery Brigade July 27, 1864.

Second Division, John W. Geary
 First Brigade, Charles Candy, to August 4, 1864
  Ario Pardee, Jr.
 Second Brigade, Adolphus Buschbeck, to May 22, 1864
  John T. Lockman, to June 7, 1864
  Patrick H. Jones, to August 8, 1864
  George W. Mindil
 Third Brigade, David Ireland, to May 15, 1864, wounded
  William Rickards, Jr., May 15–16, 1864
  George A. Cobham, Jr., to June 6, 1864
  David Ireland
 Artillery, William Wheeler, to June 22, 1864, killed
  Charles C. Aleshire
  13th Battery, New York Light Artillery, William Wheeler, to June 22, 1864
   Henry Bundy
  Battery E, Pennsylvania Light Artillery, James D. McGill, to July 8, 1864, resigned
   Thomas S. Sloan

Note. The artillery of Second Division became a part of the corps' Artillery Brigade July 27, 1864.

Third Division, Daniel Butterfield, to June 29, 1864, on leave
 William T. Ward

First Brigade, William T. Ward, to May 15, 1864, wounded
 Benjamin Harrison
 William T. Ward, to June 29, 1864
 Benjamin Harrison
Second Brigade, Samuel Ross, to May 9, 1864
 John Coburn
Third Brigade, James Wood, Jr.
Artillery, Marco B. Gary
 Battery I, 1st Michigan Light Artillery, Luther R. Smith
 Battery C, 1st Ohio Light Artillery, Jerome B. Stephens

Note 1. On August 27, 1864, First Brigade was relieved from duty with Third Division and reported to corps headquarters for orders. The brigade was placed north of the Chattahoochee River for the purpose of guarding the trains and commissary and ordnance depots of the army.
Note 2. The artillery of Third Division became a part of the corps' Artillery Brigade July 27, 1864.

Artillery Brigade, John A. Reynolds
 Battery I, 1st Michigan Light Artillery, Luther R. Smith
 Battery I, 1st New York Light Artillery, Charles E. Winegar
 Battery M, 1st New York Light Artillery, John D. Woodbury
 13th Battery, New York Light Artillery, Henry Bundy
 Battery C, 1st Ohio Light Artillery, Jerome B. Stephens, to August 1, 1864
  Marco B. Gary
 Battery E, Pennsylvania Light Artillery, Thomas S. Sloan
 Battery K, 5th United States Artillery, Edmund C. Bainbridge

Note. Bainbridge's regular battery joined the brigade August 25, 1864.

UNATTACHED TROOPS

Reserve Brigade, Joseph W. Burke, to May 27, 1864, muster out
 Heber Le Favour, assumed command May 31, 1864

Pontoniers, George P. Buell

Note. Buell commanded the Pioneer Brigade until June 17, 1864.

Siege Artillery
 11th Indiana Battery, Arnold Sutermeister

CAVALRY CORPS, Washington L. Elliott

First Cavalry Division, Edward M. McCook
    First Brigade, Joseph B. Dorr, to July 20, 1864
        John T. Croxton, to July 30, 1864
        Joseph B. Dorr, July 30, 1864, captured
        James P. Brownlow, to August 12, 1864
        Richard Root, commanded temporarily August 8, 1864
        John T. Croxton
    Second Brigade, Oscar H. La Grange, to May 9, 1864, captured
        James W. Stewart, to May 26, 1864, captured
        Horace P. Lamson, to July 21, 1864
        William H. Torrey, to July 30, 1864, wounded and captured
        Horace P. Lamson
    Third Brigade, Louis D. Watkins, to July 5, 1864
        John K. Faulkner, to August 10, 1864
        Louis D. Watkins
    Artillery
        18th Battery, Indiana Light Artillery, William B. Rippetoe

Note 1. Third Brigade was at Wauhatchie, La Fayette, Calhoun, Dalton, Resaca, and other points in rear of the army during the Atlanta Campaign.

Note 2. McCook was also in command of a Provisional Cavalry Division (reorganized as a brigade) under Thomas J. Harrison July 27–31, 1864 during Judson Kilpatrick's raid on the railroads south of Atlanta. Harrison was captured July 30, 1864.

Second Cavalry Division, Kenner Garrard
    First Brigade, Robert H. G. Minty
    Second Brigade, Eli Long, to August 20, 1864, wounded
        Beroth B. Eggleston
    Third Brigade (mounted infantry), John T. Wilder, to June 14, 1864, sick
        Abram O. Miller
    Artillery
        Chicago Board of Trade Battery, Illinois Light Artillery, George I. Robinson

Note 1. Second Brigade was operating in northern Alabama until June 6, 1864.

Note 2. Judson Kilpatrick, in addition to commanding his Third Cavalry Division, also commanded First Brigade and Second Brigade of Garrard's Second Division August 18–22, 1864 during his raid on the railroads south of Atlanta.

Third Cavalry Division, Judson Kilpatrick, to May 13, 1864, wounded
    Eli H. Murray, to May 21, 1864

William W. Lowe, to July 23, 1864
Judson Kilpatrick
First Brigade, William W. Lowe, to May 21, 1864
    Robert Klein, to August 23, 1864
    Matthewson T. Patrick, to August 26, 1864
    J. Morris Young, to September 5, 1864
    Thomas J. Jordan
Second Brigade, Charles C. Smith, to July 2, 1864
    Thomas W. Sanderson, to August 6, 1864
    Fielder A. Jones
Third Brigade, Eli H. Murray, to May 13, 1864
    Smith D. Atkins, to May 21, 1864
    Eli H. Murray
Artillery
    10th Battery, Wisconsin Light Artillery, Yates V. Beebe

ARMY OF THE TENNESSEE
James B. McPherson, to July 22, 1864, killed
John A. Logan, to July 27, 1864
Oliver O. Howard

FIFTEENTH CORPS, John A. Logan, to July 22, 1864
    Morgan L. Smith, to July 27, 1864
    John A. Logan

First Division, Peter J. Osterhaus, to July 15, 1864, sick
    Charles R. Woods, to August 15, 1864
    Peter J. Osterhaus
    First Brigade, Charles R. Woods, to July 15, 1864
        Milo Smith, to August 19, 1864
        Charles R. Woods, to August 22, 1864
        Milo Smith
    Second Brigade, James A. Williamson
    Third Brigade, Hugo Wangelin
    Artillery, Clemens Landgraeber
        Battery F, 2nd Missouri Light Artillery, Louis Voelkner
            Lewis A. Winn
        4th Battery, Ohio Light Artillery, George Froehlich
            Louis Zimmerer

Note 1. Charles R. Woods was assigned command of Third Division, Seventeenth Corps August 22, 1864.

Note 2. Third Brigade was organized December 1, 1863 from regiments of First Brigade and Second Brigade and was commanded by George A. Stone until March 8, 1864.

Second Division, Morgan L. Smith, to July 22, 1864
    Joseph A. J. Lightburn, to July 27, 1864
    Morgan L. Smith, to August 5, 1864
    Joseph A. J. Lightburn, to August 17, 1864
    William B. Hazen

First Brigade, Giles A. Smith, to July 20, 1864
    James S. Martin, to August 4, 1864
    Theodore Jones
Second Brigade, Joseph A. J. Lightburn, to July 22, 1864
    Wells S. Jones, to July 27, 1864
    Joseph A. J. Lightburn, to August 5, 1864
    Wells S. Jones, to August 17, 1864
    Joseph A. J. Lightburn, to August 24, 1864, wounded
    Wells S. Jones
Artillery, Francis De Gress
    Battery A, 1st Illinois Light Artillery, Peter P. Wood, to May 10, 1864, sick
        George McCagg, Jr., to July 12, 1864
        Samuel S. Smyth, to July 22, 1864, captured
        George Echte
    Battery B, 1st Illinois Light Artillery, Israel P. Rumsey
    Battery H, 1st Illinois Light Artillery, Francis De Gress

Note 1. Giles A. Smith was assigned command of Fourth Division, Seventeenth Corps July 20, 1864.

Note 2. Battery B was consolidated with Battery A July 12, 1864.

Third Division, John E. Smith
    First Brigade, Jesse I. Alexander, to September 1, 1864, resigned
        Joseph B. McCown
    Second Brigade, Green B. Raum
    Third Brigade, Charles L. Matthies, to May 15, 1864
        Benjamin D. Dean, to May 31, 1864
        Jabez Banbury, to July 25, 1864
        Benjamin D. Dean, to August 1864
    Artillery, Henry Dillon
        6th Battery, Wisconsin Light Artillery, Samuel F. Clark
        James G. Simpson
        12th Battery, Wisconsin Light Artillery, William Zickerick

Note 1. The troops of Third Division were at Cartersville and other points in rear of Sherman's advancing army guarding the lines of communications, and they were not engaged in the battles of the campaign.

Note 2. Third Brigade was discontinued in August 1864, and its regiments were transferred to First Brigade and Second Brigade.

Fourth Division, William Harrow
    First Brigade, Reuben Williams, to August 4, 1864
        John M. Oliver
    Second Brigade, Charles C. Walcutt
    Third Brigade, John M. Oliver

Artillery, Henry H. Griffiths, to May 20, 1864
    John T. Cheney
    Henry H. Griffiths, to August 11, 1864, muster out
    Josiah H. Burton
    Battery F, 1st Illinois Light Artillery, Josiah H. Burton
        Jefferson F. Whaley, to August 21, 1864, sick
        Josiah H. Burton
    1st Battery, Iowa Light Artillery, William H. Gay
        Henry H. Griffiths
        William H. Gay

Note 1. Third Brigade was discontinued August 4, 1864, and the regiments were assigned to First Brigade, Fourth Division.

Note 2. On September 14, 1864, Fourth Division was consolidated with First Division and Second Division of Fifteenth Corps as follows: Second Brigade and one regiment of First Brigade were assigned to First Division, and the remainder of First Brigade was assigned to Second Division.

LEFT WING, SIXTEENTH CORPS, Grenville M. Dodge, to August 19, 1864, wounded
    Thomas E. G. Ransom

Second Division, Thomas W. Sweeny, to July 25, 1864, in arrest
    Elliott W. Rice, to July 26, 1864
    John M. Corse
    First Brigade, Elliott W. Rice
    Second Brigade, Patrick E. Burke, to May 16, 1864, mortally wounded
        Robert N. Adams, to May 23, 1864
        August Mersey, to July 24, 1864
        Jesse J. Phillips, to August 2, 1864
        Robert N. Adams
    Third Brigade, Moses M. Bane, to June 20, 1864
        William Vandever, to August 2, 1864
        Henry J. B. Cummings, to August 25, 1864
        Richard Rowett
    Artillery, Frederick Welker
        Battery B, 1st Michigan Light Artillery, Albert F. R. Arndt
        Battery H, 1st Missouri Light Artillery, Andrew T. Blodgett
        Battery I, 1st Missouri Light Artillery, John F. Brunner

Note 1. Left Wing, Sixteenth Corps was commonly called simply Sixteenth Corps during the campaign.

Note 2. Second Division was transferred to Fifteenth Corps September 22, 1864 and designated as Fourth Division, Fifteenth Corps.

Note 3. Third Brigade was posted at Rome, Georgia May 22, 1864, and it remained there during the rest of the Atlanta Campaign. It was designated as a Separate Brigade September 22, 1864.

Note 4. Brunner's Missouri battery was relieved for muster out May 22, 1864.

Fourth Division, James C. Veatch, to July 17, 1864, sick
  John W. Fuller, to August 4, 1864
  Thomas E. G. Ransom, to August 20, 1864
  John W. Fuller
  First Brigade, John W. Fuller, to July 17, 1864
    John Morrill, to July 22, 1864, wounded
    Henry T. McDowell, to August 4, 1864
    John W. Fuller, to August 20, 1864
    Henry T. McDowell
  Second Brigade, John W. Sprague
  Third Brigade, James H. Howe, to July 21, 1864
    William T. C. Grower, to August 20, 1864
    John Tillson
  Artillery, Jerome B. Burrows, to July 3, 1864
    George Robinson
    Battery C, 1st Michigan Light Artillery, George Robinson
      Henry Shier
    14th Battery, Ohio Light Artillery, Jerome B. Burrows, to June 29, 1864
      Seth M. Laird, to August 17, 1864
      George Hurlbut
    Battery F, 2nd United States Artillery, Albert M. Murray
      Joseph C. Breckinridge, to July 22, 1864, captured
      Lemuel Smith
      Rezin G. Howell

Note 1. Fourth Division was transferred to Seventeenth Corps September 22, 1864 and was designated as First Division, Seventeenth Corps September 23, 1864.

Note 2. Fuller's Brigade from Fifth Division (or District of Memphis) November 11, 1863 was designated as First Brigade, Fourth Division, Sixteenth Corps March 10, 1864.

Note 3. Third Brigade, Fourth Division remained at Decatur, Alabama when Dodge's command left northern Alabama at the beginning of the Atlanta Campaign, but it advanced and joined the army August 7, 1864.

SEVENTEENTH CORPS, Frank P. Blair, Jr.

Third Division, Mortimer D. Leggett, to August 23, 1864, sick
  Charles R. Woods
  First Brigade, Manning F. Force, to July 22, 1864, wounded
    George E. Bryant

  Second Brigade, Robert K. Scott, to July 22, 1864, captured
    Greenberry F. Wiles
  Third Brigade, Adam G. Malloy
  Artillery, William S. Williams
    Battery D, 1st Illinois Light Artillery, Edgar H. Cooper
    Battery H, 1st Michigan Light Artillery, Marcus D. Elliott
      William Justin
    3rd Battery, Ohio Light Artillery, John Sullivan

Note 1. Blair was assigned command of Seventeenth Corps April 23, 1864.

Note 2. Seventeenth Corps joined the army in Georgia June 8, 1864.

Note 3. Third Brigade was discontinued November 2, 1864, and the regiments were assigned to First Brigade and Second Brigade.

Fourth Division, Walter Q. Gresham, to July 20, 1864, wounded
  William Hall, to July 21, 1864
  Giles A. Smith
  First Brigade, William L. Sanderson, to July 18, 1864
    Benjamin F. Potts
  Second Brigade, George C. Rogers, to July 5, 1864
    Isaac C. Pugh, to July 19, 1864
    John Logan (colonel)
  Third Brigade, William Hall, to July 20, 1864
    John Shane, to July 21, 1864
    William Hall, to July 31, 1864
    William W. Belknap
  Artillery, Edward Spear, Jr., to August 25, 1864
    William Z. Clayton
    Battery F, 2nd Illinois Light Artillery, Walter H. Powell, to August 22, 1864, captured
      George R. Richardson, to July 29, 1864
      Wendolin Meyer
    1st Battery, Minnesota Light Artillery, William Z. Clayton
      Henry Hurter
    Battery C, 1st Missouri Light Artillery, John L. Matthaei
    10th Battery, Ohio Light Artillery, Francis Seaman
    15th Battery, Ohio Light Artillery, James Burdick

Note 1. Gresham relieved Marcellus M. Crocker, who was sick, in command of Fourth Division at Decatur, Alabama May 27, 1864.

Note 2. First Brigade was reorganized May 26, 1864.

Note 3. Second Brigade was reorganized June 20, 1864, and it was discontinued November 6, 1864.

Note 4. Matthaei's Missouri battery was at Allatoona and Kennesaw, and Seaman's Ohio battery was at Kennesaw from July 11, 1864.

ARMY OF THE OHIO
John M. Schofield, to May 26, 1864
Jacob D. Cox, May 26–27, 1864
John M. Schofield

TWENTY-THIRD CORPS, John M. Schofield

First Division, Alvin P. Hovey
  First Brigade, Richard F. Barter
  Second Brigade, John C. McQuiston, to June 23, 1864
    Peter T. Swaine
  Artillery
      23rd Battery, Indiana Light Artillery, Luther S. Houghton
      Aaron A. Wilber
      24th Battery, Indiana Light Artillery, Alexander Hardy

Note 1. First Division was discontinued August 11, 1864, and the regiments were attached to Second Division and Third Division.
Note 2. Hovey departed on leave June 9, 1864, and his two brigades were temporarily assigned to Second Division and Third Division.
Note 3. First Brigade, First Division was temporarily attached to Third Division June 9, 1864, but retained its original designation until August 11, 1864, when it was permanently assigned as Fourth Brigade, Third Division. It was sometimes referred to as Fourth Brigade before August 11, 1864.
Note 4. Second Brigade, First Division was temporarily attached to Second Division June 9, 1864, but it retained its original designation until August 11, 1864 when it was permanently assigned to Fourth Brigade, Second Division. It was sometimes called Fourth Brigade, Second Division before August 11, 1864.

Second Division, Henry M. Judah, to May 18, 1864, on leave
  Milo S. Hascall
  First Brigade, Nathaniel C. McLean, to June 4, 1864
    Joseph A. Cooper
  Second Brigade, Milo S. Hascall, to May 16, 1864
    John R. Bond, to June 18, 1864, sick
    William E. Hobson, to August 15, 1864
    John R. Bond
  Third Brigade, Silas A. Strickland
  Artillery, Joseph C. Shields
      22nd Battery, Indiana Light Artillery, Benjamin F. Denning, to July 1, 1864, mortally wounded
      Edward W. Nicholson
      Battery F, 1st Michigan Light Artillery, Byron D. Paddock
      Marshall M. Miller
      19th Battery, Ohio Light Artillery, Joseph C. Shields

Note 1. Hascall was transferred to Second Brigade, Third Division May 16, 1864.
Note 2. Third Brigade joined the army May 28, 1864 and was designated as Provisional Brigade until June 8, 1864.

Third Division, Jacob D. Cox, to May 26, 1864
  James W. Reilly, to May 27, 1864
  Jacob D. Cox
  First Brigade, James W. Reilly, to May 26, 1864
    James W. Gault, to May 27, 1864
    James W. Reilly
  Second Brigade, Mahlon D. Manson, to May 14, 1864, wounded
    John S. Hurt, to May 16, 1864
    Milo S. Hascall, to May 18, 1864
    John S. Hurt, to May 21, 1864
    John S. Casement, to June 4, 1864
    Daniel Cameron, to July 31, 1864
    John S. Casement
  Third Brigade, Nathaniel C. McLean, June 5 to June 17, 1864
    Robert K. Byrd, to August 9, 1864
    Israel N. Stiles
  Dismounted Cavalry Brigade, Eugene W. Crittenden
  Artillery, Henry W. Wells
      15th Battery, Indiana Light Artillery, Alonzo D. Harvey
      Battery D, 1st Ohio Light Artillery, Giles J. Cockerill

Note 1. Hascall was assigned command of Second Division May 18, 1864.
Note 2. McLean was transferred to the District of Kentucky June 17, 1864.
Note 3. Third Brigade was organized June 5, 1864.
Note 4. The Dismounted Cavalry Brigade was assigned to the division June 21, 1864 and was transferred to the Cavalry Division August 22, 1864.

Cavalry Division, George Stoneman, to July 31, 1864, captured
  Horace Capron, from August 1, 1864
  First Brigade, Israel Garrard
  Second Brigade, James Biddle
    Thomas H. Butler
    James Biddle, to July 31, captured
  Third Brigade, Horace Capron
  Independent Brigade, Alexander W. Holeman
    Silas Adams
  Artillery
      24th Battery, Indiana Light Artillery, Alexander Hardy, to July 31, 1864, captured
      Hiram Allen

Note 1. First Brigade joined the army in the field July 27, 1864.

Note 2. Second Brigade was designated as First Brigade until July 31, 1864.

Note 3. Third Brigade joined the army in the field July 28, 1864.

Note 4. The artillery was assigned to the division July 6, 1864.

The Cavalry Division, Army of the Ohio was wrecked during Stoneman's raid to Macon, Georgia July 27–August 6, 1864, and Stoneman, Biddle, and Butler were captured. The division was reorganized August 11 under the command of Israel Garrard, as follows:

Cavalry Division, Israel Garrard
  First Brigade (dismounted), Horace Capron
  Second Brigade (mounted), George S. Acker, to August 16, 1864
    William D. Hamilton, to August 23, 1864
    George S. Acker

CHATTANOOGA-RINGGOLD CAMPAIGN (BATTLES OF LOOKOUT MOUNTAIN AND MISSIONARY RIDGE, TENNESSEE) NOVEMBER 23–27, 1863

After the Union defeat at the Battle of Chickamauga September 19–20, 1863, William S. Rosecrans' Army of the Cumberland retreated to Chattanooga and prepared a strong defensive position. After a short delay, Braxton Bragg's army followed, but it did not attack. Instead, Bragg entrenched on a line that extended from the Tennessee River on the right and back to the river on the left. It ran southward along Missionary Ridge, then across the Chattanooga Valley and Lookout Mountain and into Lookout Valley. William J. Hardee, who was then in command of Daniel H. Hill's former corps, was in command of the Confederate troops on the right; John C. Breckinridge was in command of the center of the line, on Missionary Ridge; and James Longstreet was in command on the left.

Rosecrans' army was not actually under siege because it was not completely surrounded, but in effect it was because the enemy held the railroad and the river, and prevented all communication by those routes through Bridgeport and Stevenson, Alabama to connections with the North.

October 27, 1863, the Tennessee River was reopened by forces assembled by Ulysses S. Grant, commander of the Military Division of the Mississippi, and preparations were then begun for the complete liberation of Chattanooga. For details of the events during the above period, see Army of the Cumberland, October 24, 1862–November 14, 1864, Siege of Chattanooga, Tennessee, Reopening of the Tennessee River.

On November 4, 1863, Longstreet's corps was sent toward Knoxville to attempt to drive Union forces under Ambrose E. Burnside from East Tennessee. After Longstreet's departure there were numerous changes along Bragg's line of investment. On November 12, Carter L. Stevenson's division was ordered to move from its position on the right at Tunnel Hill to the left of the line and report to Hardee, who on November 24 assumed command of all troops west of Chattanooga Creek. On November 14, William H. T. Walker's division (commanded by States Rights Gist) occupied that part of Hardee's line west of Chattanooga Creek to the Chattanooga road at the base of the mountain; Benjamin F. Cheatham's division (commanded by John K. Jackson) occupied the northern slope of Lookout Mountain at the Cravens farm, from the left of Gist's line to Smith's Trail on the western side of the mountain; and Stevenson's division occupied the top of the mountain. Breckinridge remained in command of the troops on Missionary Ridge.

On the night of November 22, 1863, Patrick R. Cleburne was ordered to move with his own division and Simon B. Buckner's division (then commanded by Bushrod R. Johnson) to East Tennessee to reinforce Longstreet, who was then besieging Knoxville. On the morning of November 23, Cleburne was at Chickamauga Station on the Western and Atlantic Railroad arranging for the transportation of his two divisions to Loudon, Tennessee when he was ordered to return to the lines at Chattanooga. All of Buckner's division had already departed except Alexander W. Reynolds' brigade, but Cleburne marched back with his division and Reynolds' brigade and camped that night in rear of Missionary Ridge. Reynolds' brigade did remain under

Cleburne's command but reported directly to Bragg.

On the night of November 23, 1863, Gist's division (Walker's) was moved to the extreme right of the enemy line on Missionary Ridge, and to fill the vacancy thus created, Jackson's brigade (commanded by John C. Wilkinson) of Jackson's division (Cheatham's) was moved from the Cravens house slope, and Alfred Cumming's brigade of Stevenson's division was brought down from the top of the mountain.

At 2:00 P.M. November 24, 1863, when Grant's troops were becoming quite active, Cleburne was ordered with his division to Tunnel Hill. That day Hardee was placed in command of the Confederate right, on Missionary Ridge, which was then threatened by William T. Sherman's divisions of the Army of the Tennessee. On November 25, the day of the Battle of Missionary Ridge, Hardee's command consisted of Cleburne's division, Gist's division (Walker's), Jackson's division (Cheatham's), and Stewart's division.

Preparations for the Attack. While awaiting reinforcements that William T. Sherman, commanding the Army of the Tennessee, was bringing to Chattanooga, Grant completed his plan for the campaign that was to drive Bragg's army from in front of Chattanooga and back into Georgia. This plan called for three coordinated attacks on the Confederate lines on Lookout Mountain and Missionary Ridge. Sherman was to assemble the four divisions of his Army of the Tennessee on the north bank of the Tennessee River, opposite the mouth of Chickamauga Creek, and then cross the river and deliver the main attack on the extreme right of the enemy line on Missionary Ridge. After Sherman began his movement southward along Missionary Ridge, George H. Thomas was to make a secondary attack on the Confederate center with that part of his Army of the Cumberland that was in position in front of Chattanooga. Joseph Hooker, commanding Eleventh Corps and Twelfth Corps, was to make an attack from Lookout Valley on the Confederate left at Lookout Mountain.

In preparation for these attacks, Grant began to move his troops into position. When the Army of the Cumberland was reorganized after the Battle of Chickamauga, the troops assigned to Jefferson C.

Davis' Second Division of John M. Palmer's Fourteenth Corps were widely scattered at posts along the Tennessee River from Stevenson, Alabama to Smith's Ferry, Tennessee, where they connected with the pickets of Burnside's forces in East Tennessee. On November 19, 1863, orders were issued for the division to concentrate on the Tennessee River at Caldwell's Crossing, about four miles above Chattanooga and opposite the northern end of Missionary Ridge. Davis' division was to remain in this position, with the necessary materials for crossing the river, until joined by Sherman's troops.

The head of Sherman's column arrived at Bridgeport, Alabama November 15, 1863, and it then continued the march toward Brown's Ferry on the Tennessee River. John E. Smith's Second Division, Seventeenth Corps crossed the river at Brown's Ferry November 20–21, then moved on behind Stringers Ridge, north of Chattanooga, to the vicinity of the place selected for Sherman's crossing, near Davis' division, at Caldwell's Crossing. Morgan L. Smith's Second Division of Frank P. Blair's Fifteenth Corps followed John E. Smith's division and crossed the river at Brown's Ferry November 21. Hugh Ewing's Fourth Division, Fifteenth Corps, which had been sent from Bridgeport to Trenton, Georgia to demonstrate against Lookout Mountain, crossed the river at Brown's Ferry November 22–23. Delays that occurred during Ewing's crossing, which were caused by breaks in the bridge, prevented Peter J. Osterhaus' First Division, Fifteenth Corps from joining Sherman in time for his movement to Missionary Ridge on the morning of November 24. Accordingly, this division was left behind, and it was attached to Hooker's command in Lookout Valley. Davis' division of Fourteenth Corps was then assigned to Sherman's command in place of Osterhaus' division.

On November 22, 1863, Oliver O. Howard's Eleventh Corps left Lookout Valley, crossed the Tennessee at Brown's Ferry, and marched directly to Chattanooga. It then recrossed the river to the south bank and went into camp near Fort Wood, a work on the exterior defenses of Chattanooga. This was located a short distance east of Chattanooga, just east of the East Tennessee and Georgia Railroad (also called the Chattanooga and Cleveland Railroad). Also on November 22, Charles Cruft was ordered to move from Shellmound with Walter C.

Whitaker's Second Brigade and William Grose's Third Brigade of David S. Stanley's First Division, Fourth Corps and report to Hooker in Lookout Valley. Cruft was delayed in starting because at that time Sherman's troops were passing by on the road to the front, but on the evening of November 23, he arrived near Hooker's headquarters and went into camp. Cruft's two brigades marched with only six regiments each, with two regiments of Second Brigade detached at Shellmound and two regiments of Third Brigade at Whiteside. First Brigade, First Division, Fourth Corps, then commanded by David A. Enyart, remained at Bridgeport, Alabama. Stanley, who had been assigned command of First Division, Fourth Corps November 12, was ordered to establish his headquarters at Bridgeport and assume command of the road from that point to Whiteside and also the front toward Trenton.

On November 17, 1863, Eli Long's Second Brigade of the Second Cavalry Division was ordered to move from Woodville, Alabama to Chattanooga, where it arrived on the evening of November 22. Two days later it was ordered to take position to the left of Sherman's divisions.

Thus, by the evening of November 23, 1863, all of Grant's troops were in position to take part in the attacks that were ordered to begin the next day. These consisted of the following:

ARMY OF THE CUMBERLAND, George H. Thomas

Fourth Corps, Gordon Granger
Fourteenth Corps, John M. Palmer
Eleventh and Twelfth Corps, Joseph Hooker
    Eleventh Corps, Oliver O. Howard
    Second Division, Twelfth Corps, John W. Geary
Engineer Troops, William F. Smith
Artillery Reserve, John M. Brannan
Cavalry Brigade, Eli Long
Post of Chattanooga, John G. Parkhurst

DETACHMENT ARMY OF THE TENNESSEE, William T. Sherman

Fifteenth Corps, Frank P. Blair, Jr.
Second Division, Seventeenth Corps, John E. Smith

As has been noted above, there were some reassignments of brigades and divisions in preparation for the battles at Chattanooga, and the troops participating in the attacks on November 24–25, 1863 were organized as follows:

SHERMAN'S COMMAND, William T. Sherman

Eleventh Corps, Oliver O. Howard
Second Division, Fifteenth Corps, Morgan L. Smith
Fourth Division, Fifteenth Corps, Hugh Ewing
Second Division, Fourteenth Corps, Jefferson C. Davis
Second Division, Seventeenth Corps, John E. Smith

Note 1. Howard reported to Sherman and came under his command November 25, 1863.
Note 2. Frank P. Blair, Jr. commanded the two divisions of Fifteenth Corps.
Note 3. Sherman generally called John E. Smith's division Third Division, Fifteenth Corps, although it belonged to Seventeenth Corps.

HOOKER'S COMMAND, Joseph Hooker

Second Brigade and Third Brigade, First Division, Fourth Corps, Charles Cruft
Second Division, Twelfth Corps, John W. Geary
First Division, Fifteenth Corps, Peter J. Osterhaus

Note 1. William P. Carlin's First Brigade, First Division, Fourteenth Corps was sent to Hooker on Lookout Mountain during the evening of November 24, 1863, but it returned to its division the next morning.
Note 2. Cruft was in command of six regiments each of Second Brigade and Third Brigade of First Division, Fourth Corps. David A. Enyart's First Brigade was opposite Bridgeport, Alabama, and David S. Stanley was in command of First Division, with headquarters at Bridgeport.

THOMAS' COMMAND, ARMY OF THE CUMBERLAND, George H. Thomas

Fourth Corps, Gordon Granger
    Second Division, Philip H. Sheridan
    Third Division, Thomas J. Wood

Fourteenth Corps, John M. Palmer
    First Division, Richard W. Johnson
    Third Division, Absalom Baird

Skirmish at Orchard Knob (or Indian Hill), Tennessee, November 23, 1863. A preliminary engagement, little more than a skirmish, opened the fighting at Chattanooga on November 23, 1863. In response to a rumor that Bragg was planning to withdraw from his lines about Chattanooga, Grant ordered a reconnaissance in force in the direction of

Orchard Knob, a hill about midway between the Union lines in front of Chattanooga and Missionary Ridge. At that time the first line of enemy pickets in front of Thomas was located a short distance east of the Western and Atlantic Railroad, and it passed in front of Fort Wood.

On November 23, 1863, Gordon Granger's two divisions of his Fourth Corps formed in line of battle between Fort Wood and the Western and Atlantic Railroad. Thomas J. Wood's Third Division was on the left, with its left extending nearly to Citico Creek, and Philip H. Sheridan's Second Division was on the right of Wood. Wood was ordered to advance toward Orchard Knob, and Sheridan was directed to follow on the right and rear of Wood. Absalom Baird's Third Division of Fourteenth Corps also moved out of its camps within the lines surrounding Chattanooga, and it formed on the right of Sheridan's division, between the Rossville road and Moore's Road, which ran due east from Fort Negley to Missionary Ridge. Baird was then in position to protect Granger's right. Howard's Eleventh Corps was massed in rear of Granger's line, where it was to watch the left of Wood's division. Richard W. Johnson's First Division of Fourteenth Corps remained in the entrenchments at Chattanooga under arms to render any necessary aid to the attacking forces.

About 2:00 P.M. Wood moved forward, with William B. Hazen's brigade on the right, August Willich's brigade on the left, and Samuel Beatty's brigade in reserve. The enemy pickets were soon driven back, and Willich's brigade captured Orchard Knob without much trouble. Hazen's brigade took an elevation to the right of Orchard Knob, and Sheridan moved his division up to a series of hills, where he extended the line of Fourth Corps to the southwest. Grant then decided to hold Orchard Knob, and he ordered Eleventh Corps to move up and form on the left of Wood. The troops fortified their advanced positions during the night and awaited the attack orders for the next day.

Battle of Lookout Mountain, Tennessee, November 24, 1863. About 3:00 A.M. November 24, 1863, Hooker issued orders for an attack on Lookout Mountain that was to begin later that morning.

At its northern end, where the battle was fought, Lookout Mountain rises steeply from the Tennessee River for a distance of about 400 yards, then falls off to form a bench or plateau, on which there were the cultivated fields and the farmhouse of Robert Cravens. Beyond this bench the mountain again rises sharply on a slope of about 45 degrees for another 300 or 400 yards to a line of nearly perpendicular cliffs of barren rock, which are from 30 to 100 feet in height, and extend upward to the summit of the mountain. These cliffs are commonly referred to as the Palisades. Generally the sides of the mountain are steep and rugged, are covered with boulders and trees, and are cut by numerous ravines. On the slope of the Cravens farm, the enemy had constructed a continuous line of earthworks, and farther down the mountain were rifle pits and redoubts that were designed to prevent any successful attack from along the river.

The enemy forces on the Confederate left, which included Lookout Mountain, were under the command of Carter L. Stevenson. Edward C. Walthall's brigade of Jackson's division (Cheatham's) held the line of defensive works on the slope below the Palisades, with its right extending to the vicinity of the Cravens house. To the right of Walthall, and somewhat below the Cravens house, was John C. Moore's brigade of Jackson's division, which extended around the northern base of the mountain to the eastern slope. On top of the mountain were Edmund W. Pettus' and John C. Brown's brigades of Stevenson's division. On a line extending eastward from the Chattanooga road, at the bottom of the mountain, toward Chattanooga Creek, were Alfred Cumming's brigade of Jackson's division (Cheatham's) and Jackson's brigade (commanded by Wilkinson) of Jackson's division.

At dawn November 24, 1863, Whitaker's brigade of Cruft's command was detached and ordered to report to Geary at Wauhatchie, Tennessee. Cruft's other brigade, commanded by Grose, was to advance to Lookout Creek and seize and repair the bridge just below the railroad bridge. Osterhaus' First Division, Fifteenth Corps was to march from Brown's Ferry to Lookout Creek in preparation for crossing.

When Hooker advanced that morning, he found the water in Lookout Creek so deep because of recent rains that he could not cross without building a temporary bridge at the main road. Accordingly, he ordered Geary's division to march to Wauhatchie

Station on the Nashville and Chattanooga Railroad preparatory to crossing the creek. Whitaker's brigade joined Geary at Wauhatchie, and together they crossed the railroad about 8:00 A.M., marching under the cover of some woods to a point on Chattanooga Creek about two and a half miles from its mouth. Geary then bridged the creek and, after crossing, formed his command in line of battle. George A. Cobham's Second Brigade was on the right, next to the mountain; David Ireland's Third Brigade was in the center; and Charles Candy's First Brigade was on the left, next to Lookout Creek. Whitaker's brigade was in reserve, about 300 yards in rear of the first line, with its right in rear of the center of Cobham's brigade. Geary then marched down the right bank of the creek, with his movements concealed from the enemy by a heavy mist that had settled over the mountain. He advanced about a mile and a half, while moving up the slope of the mountain, without opposition, and he then encountered enemy pickets about one mile from the Confederate main line on the mountain and drove them back.

Hooker also ordered Grose to advance with his brigade and cross Lookout Creek at a destroyed bridge near the railroad crossing of that creek. Grose was unable to repair the bridge because of enemy fire from across the creek, and Hooker then sent Charles R. Woods' brigade of Osterhaus' division about 800 yards upstream to construct another bridge. He also directed Grose to leave two regiments at the destroyed bridge and to move with the other four regiments of his brigade to join Woods and cross the creek with him.

Woods' bridge was completed about 11:00 A.M., and at about the same time Geary's command arrived abreast of the bridge. Woods and Grose then crossed the creek and formed on the left of Geary's line as it moved forward. When the line passed the destroyed bridge, Grose's two regiments that had been left there earlier joined the advance. They moved along the road on the left of Osterhaus and drove back Moore's brigade until they reached the mouth of Chattanooga Creek, and there they entrenched. The destroyed bridge was quickly rebuilt and used for communication with the troops fighting on the mountain.

Under the cover of a heavy artillery fire, Hooker's troops then advanced against the enemy forces on the mountain. Cobham's Second Brigade moved forward on the right, close under the cliffs at the top of the upper slope, and below were Ireland's Third Brigade and Candy's First Brigade. Whitaker's brigade followed in support on the right. Osterhaus' division and Grose's brigade advanced on the left of Geary's line.

A little before noon, Geary's brigades rounded the point of Lookout Mountain and moved out across the bench on the northern slope against Walthall's line. At about noon the fog that had covered the mountain lifted, and for the first time that day, everything on the slopes could be clearly seen. Cobham's brigade was held up for a time, but when Whitaker's brigade came up in support, the advance continued. Ireland's brigade became engaged in heavy fighting at the Cravens house, and with help from Whitaker drove the enemy from the Cravens house grounds to a new position several hundred yards beyond. Ireland followed Walthall, but Whitaker halted at the Cravens house. Moore, whose Confederate brigade was a little to the east of Walthall, attempted to get his men in position to stop the advancing Federals. He had just occupied the breastworks when at about 2:00 P.M. a heavy fog again blanketed the battlefield, and the troops were unable to see beyond their immediate front. This fog did not clear during the remainder of the day. This, and a shortage of ammunition, caused a lull in the battle.

Walthall finally halted his brigade in a previously prepared position about 400 yards beyond the Cravens house, and Moore moved back to join him. Walthall's line was then formed on the left, up the slope, and Moore connected with the right of Walthall, with his line crossing the bench and running down the lower slope.

Meantime, about 12:30 P.M., Pettus' brigade had been ordered down from the top of the mountain. It arrived at the scene of the fighting, probably about 1:30 P.M., and it then relieved Walthall's brigade and was almost immediately engaged. Later, Walthall, having replenished his ammunition, returned to the line and took position on the left of Pettus.

Woods' brigade of Osterhaus' division had moved along the lower slope of the mountain in line of battle, with its left on the Chattanooga road, and at about this time it had reached a position where it covered the ground between the Cravens house on the right and the Chattanooga road at a point where it ran around a projection of the mountain, about 250 feet above the Tennessee River. Williamson's brigade of Osterhaus' division was held in reserve for a time at the beginning of the advance, and during this period, five of its six regiments were detached and sent on various missions. Finally, Williamson, with his remaining regiment, and accompanied by Osterhaus, moved up near the Cravens house and joined Woods' brigade. Later, two of Williamson's regiments rejoined the brigade and were also placed on Osterhaus' line. Grose's brigade was on the lower slope of the mountain.

Candy's brigade was pulled out of the line for a time, and between 2:00 and 3:00 P.M., Candy was injured by a fall. A short time later he was ordered to relieve Ireland's brigade, which was in advance of the Cravens house. Then William R. Creighton assumed command of the brigade. When Ireland's brigade was relieved, it moved to some cleared ground at the end of the mountain to rest.

From about 2:30 P.M. until dusk, there was skirmishing, sometimes heavy, along the line, and then the fighting ended.

About 5:00 P.M., William P. Carlin's First Brigade, First Division, Fourteenth Corps crossed Chattanooga Creek near its mouth on a flatboat to aid Hooker. Hooker then ordered Carlin to move with his brigade to the Cravens house, where he arrived after dark. Carlin prepared a defensive position and at 7:00 P.M. reported to Geary, who was the senior officer on that part of the field. Geary then ordered Carlin to send two regiments to the extreme right of the line, where they relieved Cobham's brigade about 9:00 P.M. When relieved, Cobham's brigade moved down the slope and bivouacked at the base of the mountain. Carlin's other regiments remained near the Cravens house until 8:30 P.M., at which time three regiments were sent to fill a gap on the left of Williamson's brigade of Osterhaus' division. These regiments were attacked that night, but they were able to hold their position.

The troops spent a miserable night on the mountain, but when morning came, the Federal troops found that the enemy had departed. About 2:00 A.M. November 25, 1863, all enemy forces withdrew from Lookout Mountain and the Chattanooga Valley and moved to help defend Missionary Ridge.

That morning Carlin's brigade returned to its division at Chattanooga, and the rest of Hooker's command moved across Chattanooga Valley toward the southern end of Missionary Ridge.

Battle of Missionary Ridge (Sherman's Attack), November 25, 1863. Sherman began the movement of his divisions from their camps to the south side of the Tennessee River, near the mouth of Chickamauga Creek, about midnight November 23, 1863. Giles A. Smith's First Brigade of Morgan L. Smith's Second Division, Fifteenth Corps crossed the river first in pontoons, and during the remainder of the night and the next morning, the troops crossed in pontoons in the following order: the remainder of Morgan L. Smith's division, John E. Smith's division, Ewing's division, and Davis' division of Fourteenth Corps. When the troops had crossed, the pontoons were used to build a bridge across the river, and this was completed about noon November 24.

On the morning of November 24, 1863, Adolphus Buschbeck, with three regiments of his First Brigade, Second Division, Eleventh Corps, moved up the river from Chattanooga to Sherman's crossing place. He was temporarily detached from Eleventh Corps and was assigned to Ewing's division to watch the right of Sherman's advance.

About 1:00 P.M. November 24, 1863, Sherman marched toward the northern end of Missionary Ridge, with Morgan L. Smith's division on the left, moving along Chickamauga Creek, John E. Smith's division in the center, and Ewing's division on the right. All three divisions were under the direction of Frank P. Blair, Jr., commander of Fifteenth Corps. Davis' division followed in support. Sherman's troops occupied the northernmost hill on the ridge at 3:30 P.M. without opposition. Sherman then sent Joseph A. J. Lightburn's Second Brigade of Morgan L. Smith's division, Joseph R. Cockerill's Third Brigade of Ewing's division, and Jesse I. Alexander's First Brigade of John E. Smith's division to hold the hill.

Sherman had believed that Missionary Ridge was a continuous ridge, but he soon found that the hill that he had occupied was an isolated one and was separated by a deep depression from the hill over the railroad tunnel (Tunnel Hill), which was his immediate objective. He made no serious attempt to advance farther that evening. Sherman's position was about one and one-fourth miles from Tunnel Hill.

Late in the morning of November 24, 1863, Cleburne learned that Sherman had crossed the Tennessee River, and he was then directed to send a brigade and a battery to the East Tennessee and Georgia Railroad to guard the bridge over Chickamauga Creek. Cleburne sent Lucius E. Polk's brigade for this purpose, and it took position on a hill north of Chickamauga Creek near the railroad bridge.

Between 2:00 and 3:00 P.M. November 24, 1863, Cleburne was ordered to move with the rest of his division to the northern end of Missionary Ridge and occupy the high ground near the mouth of Chickamauga Creek. James A. Smith's brigade, which was leading Cleburne's division, found that Sherman already had possession of the hill at the northern end of Missionary Ridge. Smith then fell back and took position on the main ridge, with two regiments facing the hill held by Sherman and his right regiment refused, facing east, to protect his right flank.

When Mark P. Lowrey's brigade came up, it was placed on the left of Smith, along the west side of the ridge, south of the tunnel. St. John R. Liddell's brigade (commanded by Daniel C. Govan) was formed on a spur that extended out from Missionary Ridge at a point just north of the tunnel. This spur ran out for about 1,000 yards and ended on Chickamauga Creek. Polk's brigade remained in position on the hill north of the creek near the railroad bridge.

Later there were some changes made in Cleburne's positions. James A. Smith's brigade was moved back a short distance to a new line. The left of this line was on the crest of the main ridge, about 150 yards north of the tunnel, and it ran northward from that point for the distance of the front of one regiment, then bent back and ran in a direction a little north of east. The right of Smith's brigade ended about 200 yards from the left of Govan's brigade. Smith was wounded early in the fighting the next day, and Hiram B. Granbury assumed command of the brigade.

Still later, John C. Brown's and Alfred Cumming's brigades of Carter L. Stevenson's division came up and formed on the left of Lowrey's brigade, south of the tunnel, and Gist's division

(Walker's) arrived and took position on the left of Stevenson. In another change, two regiments of Lowrey's brigade were sent to another spur that extended out to the east from the northern end of the main ridge and ended at Chickamauga Creek.

During the night of November 24, 1863, Lightburn's, Cockerill's, and Alexander's brigades remained on the hill gained by Sherman that afternoon. Morgan L. Smith's division occupied the ground between the hill and Chickamauga Creek; Ewing's division was on the right of the hill; and John E. Smith's division was held in reserve near the base of the hill. Davis' division was placed in supporting distance of the other divisions, on the road leading from the river to the rear of Sherman's position. It remained in reserve the next day and was not engaged.

Sherman began the battle for Missionary Ridge soon after sunrise November 25, 1863, when John M. Corse's Second Brigade of Ewing's division marched toward the front of Tunnel Hill. At the same time, John M. Loomis' First Brigade, also of Ewing's division, advanced on the right of Corse along the western base of Missionary Ridge toward the tunnel, where the East Tennessee and Georgia Railroad (also called the Chattanooga and Cleveland Railroad) passed under the ridge. Ewing's attack was supported by Green B. Raum's Second Brigade and Charles L. Matthies' Third Brigade of John E. Smith's division. On the left of Sherman's line, Morgan L. Smith's division advanced along the eastern base of Missionary Ridge.

As Corse advanced, he encountered enemy pickets and drove them back about three-fourths of a mile to the base of Missionary Ridge. Then, under cover of a heavy artillery fire, he moved up the ridge. On arriving at the top, Corse's men advanced and occupied the works on a secondary ridge that had been vacated earlier by James A. Smith's Confederate brigade when it moved back to a new position. Corse then made a strong attack against the new position of Smith's brigade, but after violent hand-to-hand fighting, his men were driven back to the abandoned works that they had first occupied. During this attack Corse was wounded, and he was succeeded in command of the brigade by Charles C. Walcutt. James A. Smith was also wounded, and Hiram B. Granbury assumed command of his brigade. About one-half hour later, Walcutt led the brigade in another attack, but this too was repulsed. It was then about noon, and there was a lull in the fighting.

While Corse had been fighting on the ridge, Loomis had been moving forward on the right toward the tunnel, with John E. Smith's brigades in the rear, and he finally reached the embankment of the East Tennessee and Georgia Railroad not far from where the track entered the tunnel. There he became engaged with Cumming's brigade of Stevenson's division, and after some sharp fighting, Cumming's men withdrew up the hill. This also occurred about noon, just before the lull in the fighting.

About an hour later, the action was resumed. At that time Loomis' left flank was unprotected, and he ordered up two regiments of Buschbeck's brigade of Howard's Eleventh Corps that had been attached to Loomis' command. Buschbeck made a vigorous but misdirected attack up the hill to the left of Loomis' brigade, with the result that the left of the latter brigade was still exposed. Loomis then called on John E. Smith for help, and Matthies' Third Brigade of Smith's division advanced from its position in support and moved up the ridge. It reached the crest near the enemy's breastworks about 1:30 P.M., and two regiments of Raum's Second Brigade followed Matthies up the ridge. In the resulting fighting, Matthies was wounded, and Benjamin D. Dean succeeded him in command of the brigade.

Fighting on the ridge was deadly and persistent for about an hour and a half, with numerous charges and countercharges, until finally about 3:30 P.M. the enemy charged with the bayonet and drove the Federal troops down the hill. They soon re-formed, however, and moved back up the ridge. A second charge by the enemy was repulsed, but in a third charge Matthies' brigade, then commanded by Dean, was driven off the ridge to stay. Walcutt and Loomis attempted to continue the struggle, but they too were finally forced to quit. At 4:30 P.M. Loomis withdrew, and a short time later he bivouacked for the night. Walcutt fought on until dark, and then he too left the ridge.

Morgan L. Smith's division advanced along the eastern base of the hill and moved up to the enemy works, but it was unable to gain a permanent lodgment. In fact, he did not at any time seriously threaten Cleburne's right flank that day.

Sherman's three brigades that had been placed on the detached hill the evening before remained in position there during the fighting that day and were not engaged.

About 9:45 on the morning of November 25, 1863, Howard was ordered to report to Sherman with his Eleventh Corps. He arrived at the pontoon bridge about an hour later, and was then sent to occupy the ground vacated that morning by the troops that were moved to the right to support the attack along the ridge. Howard formed his line with the left on Chickamauga Creek, near Boyce's Station on the Western and Atlantic Railroad, and his right far up the ridge. Howard remained in this position during the rest of the battle.

Hooker's Advance to Missionary Ridge, November 25, 1863. Early on the morning of November 25, 1863, Hooker was ordered to advance his command from Lookout Mountain across Chattanooga Valley to Rossville, and upon arriving there he was to pass through the Rossville Gap and move on to the left and rear of Bragg's line on Missionary Ridge. Hooker advanced slowly that morning and at about 10:00 A.M. arrived at Chattanooga Creek, where he found the bridge destroyed. After a delay of about three hours, while the bridge was being rebuilt, Osterhaus' division crossed and moved on to Rossville. Osterhaus found the Rossville Gap occupied by enemy troops, and he sent Woods' First Brigade to take the ridge on the right and Williamson's Second Brigade to occupy the ridge on the left. The enemy then departed and left the gap under Hooker's control. Hooker then ordered his whole line to advance against Bragg's left flank along Missionary Ridge. Osterhaus' division was east of the ridge, Cruft's two brigades were on the crest, and Geary's division was in the valley to the west of the ridge. After the enemy was driven from two positions, the battle was ended by Thomas' attack against the Confederate center, and Hooker's troops encamped for the night.

Battle of Missionary Ridge (Thomas' Attack), November 25, 1863. After their defeat at Lookout Mountain, the troops of Stevenson's division and Jackson's division (Cheatham's) withdrew to Missionary Ridge to join the divisions under Hardee and Breckinridge which were holding the ridge.

Missionary Ridge is a long ridge, ranging from 400 to 600 feet in height, which begins at McFarland's on the south and runs in a northeasterly direction for about five miles to its northern end on Chickamauga Creek, about two miles from the point where it empties into the Tennessee river above Chattanooga. Between Chattanooga and Missionary Ridge, which at the time of the battle was from three to four miles distant, there was a level plain that was broken in places by low hills or knobs and some wooded areas. The Army of the Cumberland was encamped on this plain near the town.

It has already been noted that on November 23, 1863, Wood's Third Division and Sheridan's Second Division of Granger's Fourth Corps had advanced from the defenses of Chattanooga, captured Orchard Knob, and established an advanced line about midway between Chattanooga and Missionary Ridge. It has further been noted that Baird's Third Division of Palmer's Fourteenth Corps also moved forward to protect the right of Granger's advance. These divisions then remained in their forward positions during the rest of November 23 and November 24. Wood's division was on the left of this new line, Sheridan's division was in the center, and Baird's division was on the right. Howard's Eleventh Corps remained in its former position on the left of Wood.

A number of changes were made on Thomas' line, however, during the morning and early afternoon of November 25, 1863. About 9:00 A.M., Howard departed with his Eleventh Corps to aid Sherman in his attack on the northern end of Missionary Ridge. Also, about noon that day, Baird's division was moved from the right of the line to be within supporting distance of Sherman, but while the division was marching toward Tunnel Hill, Baird was ordered to the left of Granger's corps to occupy a part of the gap between Granger and Sherman. Baird was established in his new position by about 2:30 P.M.

During November 23–24, 1863, Johnson's First Division, Fourteenth Corps had occupied the rifle pits and entrenchments in front of the old encampments of the army at Chattanooga. On the afternoon of November 25, John C. Starkweather's Third Brigade was left to hold the entrenchments, and William P. Carlin's First Brigade and Marshall F.

Moore's Second Brigade advanced and formed on the right of Sheridan's division in the area vacated earlier by Baird. At about that time, William L. Stoughton arrived and joined the division, and as senior officer assumed command of Moore's brigade.

When Thomas had established his divisions in position for the attack on Missionary Ridge on the afternoon of November 25, 1863, his line was a little more than two miles in length and was about one mile from Missionary Ridge on the left and about one-half mile on the right. His troops were in position on this line as follows:

Absalom Baird's Third Division of Palmer's Fourteenth Corps was on the left of the line, with its right connecting with Wood's division at a point not far to the north of Orchard Knob, and its left extending well off toward the railroad tunnel. John B. Turchin's First Brigade was on the right, Ferdinand Van Derveer's Second Brigade was in the center, and Edward H. Phelps' Third Brigade was on the left.

Thomas J. Wood's Third Division of Granger's Fourth Corps was on the right of Baird, on the broad southern slope of the hill on which Fort Wood stood. This slope extended gradually down into the valley through which the Western and Atlantic Railroad ran. William B. Hazen's Second Brigade was on the right, August Willich's First Brigade was in the center, and Samuel Beatty's Third Brigade was on the left, next to Baird.

Philip H. Sheridan's Second Division of Granger's Fourth Corps was to the right of Wood's division, with its left to the west of Orchard Knob and its right extending across the Moore road. The center of Sheridan's line was opposite the Thurman house on Missionary Ridge, which was Bragg's headquarters. Francis T. Sherman's First Brigade was on the right, Charles G. Harker's Third Brigade was in the center, and George D. Wagner's Second Brigade was on the left.

Richard W. Johnson's First Division of Palmer's Fourteenth Corps was on the right of Sheridan, and on the right of Thomas' line, with William P.

Carlin's First Brigade on the right and William L. Stoughton's Second Brigade on the left.

Thus, at the time of the attack, Thomas' eleven brigades were in line, in order from left to right, as follows: Phelps, Van Derveer, and Turchin of Baird's division; Beatty, Willich, and Hazen of Wood's division; Wagner, Harker, and Francis T. Sherman of Sheridan's division; and Stoughton and Carlin of Johnson's division. Thomas was with Grant at the latter's headquarters on Orchard Knob.

On the afternoon of November 25, 1863, all of Bragg's army was in position on Missionary Ridge. William J. Hardee commanded on the Confederate right, where his troops were battling Sherman for possession of Tunnel Hill. Patrick R. Cleburne's division was at Tunnel Hill; Carter L. Stevenson's division was on the left of Cleburne, south of the tunnel; and States Rights Gist's division (Walker's) was on the left of Stevenson. Hardee's divisions were on the ridge north of that part of the line attacked by Thomas that afternoon.

John C. Breckinridge was in command on the left of the line on Missionary Ridge, with his troops in order from the left of Hardee's corps as follows: Thomas C. Hindman's division (commanded by J. Patton Anderson), Breckinridge's own division (commanded by William B. Bate), and Alexander P. Stewart's division. Alexander W. Reynolds' brigade of Simon B. Buckner's division was also on the left of Breckinridge's line. When the attack began, Anderson's division (Hindman's) and Bate's division (Breckinridge's) were directly in the path of Thomas' four divisions.

Grant did not intend to order a frontal assault by the troops on the center of his line until there had been some decisive results by Sherman and Hooker on the flanks, but when this failed to materialize by mid-afternoon, he finally decided to act. He ordered a limited attack by Thomas to relieve some of the pressure on Sherman, and the four division commanders were directed to advance and occupy the enemy rifle pits at the base of Missionary Ridge.

The time of the attack has variously been given as some point between 3:30 and 4:10 P.M., but the probable time was a little before 4:00 P.M. The path of the advance was wooded in front of the right of Baird's division and all of Wood's division, but the land was almost entirely cleared in front of Sheridan's and Johnson's divisions. Under a heavy enemy fire, Thomas' troops rushed forward. They soon captured the rifle pits at the base of the ridge and drove the enemy troops up the slope toward their main line on the crest. While in the captured rifle pits, however, the Federal troops were subjected to a very heavy fire from the enemy works on the crest and along the slopes, and their position soon became untenable. After suffering from this fire for some time, one regiment and then another, without orders from their officers, began to move up the hill. Finally, the entire line, cheered on by their officers, charged up the ridge toward the summit, 500 yards distant, and in a short time had broken Bragg's line in six places and had driven the enemy from the ridge and down the far side.

Turchin's brigade was probably the first to reach the top, and it broke through the line of J. Patton Anderson's brigade (commanded by William F. Tucker), then penetrated the line between the brigades of Zachariah C. Deas and Arthur M. Manigault to the Confederate right of Tucker. Beatty's brigade of Wood's division then came up on the right of Turchin, and both brigades moved along the ridge to their left. They soon met Van Derveer's brigade coming up, and it joined them in sweeping the ridge farther to the left.

Sheridan's troops, to the right of Wood's division, reached the crest and penetrated the enemy line a short time after Turchin (some say that he was the first at the top), and they then moved to both the right and the left along the ridge, forcing the enemy to retreat down the rear slope or surrender. Most, however, fled down the back of the ridge when their line was broken. Wagner's brigade, on the right of Sheridan's division, and Hazen's brigade of Wood's division to its left suffered about 40 percent of the total casualties of Thomas' eleven brigades that participated in the attack.

After the Federals had gained the crest in front of Bate's division (Breckinridge's), they began to work around its flanks. Soon the entire Confederate line began to crumble, and the troops were driven from the ridge and down the far side in complete disorder. Hardee's corps was not involved in Thomas' attack, but when the rest of Bragg's army had fled, Hardee also left the ridge and joined in the retreat toward Dalton, Georgia.

Pursuit of Bragg's Army into Georgia. Soon after the Confederates were driven from Missionary Ridge, late in the afternoon of November 25, 1863, Federal troops were started in pursuit. Sherman's command moved first from the left of the Union line. About midnight, Davis, with his Second Division, Fourteenth Corps was ordered to cross Chickamauga Creek and move along the east bank toward Chickamauga Station on the Western and Atlantic Railroad. Howard followed Davis with his Eleventh Corps at 4:00 A.M. November 26, and John E. Smith's Second Division, Seventeenth Corps followed Howard. Finally, at daybreak, Blair's two divisions of Fifteenth Corps set out on the same road. Sherman's column moved forward against considerable opposition past Chickamauga Station and arrived near Graysville, Georgia during the evening of November 26.

Meantime, John M. Palmer's Fourteenth Corps and Hooker's command had been marching toward Graysville from the right of the Union line. Palmer, with two brigades of Johnson's division (Starkweather's brigade had remained at Chattanooga) and Baird's division, led the way on the road to Graysville. He was followed at about 10:00 A.M. November 26, 1863 by Osterhaus' First Division, Fifteenth Corps, Geary's Second Division, Twelfth Corps, and Cruft's two brigades of First Division, Fourteenth Corps.

When Palmer reached the Chattanooga La Fayette road, he was ordered to continue on to Graysville, and Hooker's command was sent toward Ringgold. Palmer camped at Graysville that night and then, with all three of his divisions, joined Hooker near Ringgold the next day, November 27, 1863.

Hooker then advanced to Ringgold Gap, where the Western and Atlantic Railroad passed through Taylor's Ridge, and Peter J. Osterhaus' division was sent forward to capture the ridge. Osterhaus was soon heavily engaged, and William R. Creighton's First Brigade of John W. Geary's division of Twelfth Corps was ordered to advance and attack on his left. George A. Cobham's Second Brigade of Geary's division was then sent to aid Osterhaus, and it was soon followed by David Ireland's Third Brigade of Geary's division. After five hours of severe fighting, the ridge was finally carried. Creighton was killed near the end of the action, and he was succeeded in command of the brigade by Thomas J. Ahl.

While Hooker was engaged at Ringgold Gap November 27, 1863, Howard's Eleventh Corps was ordered to move toward the Dalton and Cleveland Railroad between Dalton, Georgia and Cleveland, Tennessee, and that evening it was at Parker's Gap, west of Red Clay, Georgia. Adolph Von Steinwehr, who was sick, was left at Graysville, and Adolphus Buschbeck assumed temporary command of his Second Division. Blair's Fifteenth Corps remained at Graysville that day and the next.

November 28, 1863, Davis' Second Division left Fourteenth Corps near Ringgold and moved to Parker's Gap, where it camped near Eleventh Corps. That day Grant ordered Sherman to take Eleventh Corps, Fifteenth Corps, and Davis' division of Fourteenth Corps and move to the Hiwassee River in the direction of Knoxville, Tennessee. He also ordered John E. Smith's division of Seventeenth Corps to move to Chattanooga November 28.

November 29, 1863, Sherman marched to Cleveland in three columns. For information about the further movements of Sherman's command, see Relief of Knoxville, Tennessee (William T. Sherman).

By this time the pursuit of Bragg had ended, and the various remaining units of the army then in Georgia were assigned to new positions. November 29, 1863, Johnson's and Baird's divisions of Fourteenth Corps marched back to Chattanooga. Cruft's brigades of First Division remained at Ringgold November 29, but the next day Grose's brigade was sent to the old battlefield of Chickamauga to bury the dead. When this task was completed, Grose was to move to Whiteside. Whitaker's brigade marched to Wauhatchie December 1, and the next day both Whitaker's and Grose's brigades resumed their former positions at Whiteside and Shellmound.

Geary's division and Osterhaus' division remained at Ringgold until December 1, 1863, and that day both returned to Chattanooga.

During the pursuit of Bragg, Granger, with the divisions of Sheridan and Wood, had remained at Chattanooga, but on November 27, 1863 Granger was ordered to march at once to the relief of Burnside's army, which was then besieged at Knoxville. For further information, see Relief of Knoxville, Tennessee (William T. Sherman).

The organization of the Union forces during the battles about Chattanooga November 23–November 27, 1863 was as follows:

ARMY OF THE CUMBERLAND
George H. Thomas

FOURTH CORPS, Gordon Granger

Second Brigade and Third Brigade, First Division,
Charles Cruft
Second Brigade, Walter C. Whitaker
Third Brigade, William Grose

*Note 1. First Division was under the immediate com-
mand of Joseph Hooker during the battles of November
24–25, 1863.*
*Note 2. David S. Stanley, commander of First Divi-
sion, was at Bridgeport, Alabama with his First Brigade
and Battery M, 4th United States Artillery. The 115th
Illinois and 84th Indiana of Second Brigade, and the 5th
Battery, Indiana Light Artillery were at Shellmound,
Tennessee; and the 30th Indiana and 77th Pennsylvania
of Third Brigade, and Battery H, 4th United States Artillery were at Whiteside, Tennessee.*

Second Division, Philip H. Sheridan
First Brigade, Francis T. Sherman
Demi-Brigade, Silas Miller, temporary
Demi-Brigade, Bernard Laiboldt, temporary
Second Brigade, George D. Wagner
Demi-Brigade, Gustavus A. Wood, temporary
Third Brigade, Charles G. Harker
Demi-Brigade, Nathan H. Walworth, temporary
Demi-Brigade, Emerson Opdyke, temporary
Artillery, Warren P. Edgarton
Battery M, 1st Illinois Light Artillery, George W.
Spencer
10th Battery, Indiana Light Artillery, William A.
Naylor
Battery G, 1st Missouri Light Artillery, Gustavus
Schueler
Battery I, 1st Ohio Light Artillery, Hubert Dilger
Battery G, 4th United States Artillery, Christopher
F. Merkle
Battery H, 5th United States Artillery, Francis L.
Guenther

*Note. The last three of the above batteries were tem-
porarily attached to the division.*

Third Division, Thomas J. Wood
First Brigade, August Willich
Second Brigade, William B. Hazen
Third Brigade, Samuel Beatty
Artillery, Cullen Bradley
Bridges' Battery, Illinois Light Artillery, Lyman
Bridges
6th Battery, Ohio Light Artillery, Oliver H. P.
Ayres

Battery B, Pennsylvania Light Artillery, Samuel
M. McDowell
20th Battery, Ohio Light Artillery, Edward
Grosskopff

*Note. Grosskopff's battery was temporarily attached
to the division from the Artillery Reserve.*

ELEVENTH AND TWELFTH CORPS, DETACH-
MENT ARMY OF THE POTOMAC, Joseph Hooker

ELEVENTH CORPS, Oliver O. Howard

Second Division, Adolph Von Steinwehr
First Brigade, Adolphus Buschbeck
Second Brigade, Orland Smith

*Note. First Brigade was assigned to Hugh Ewing,
commanding Fourth Division, Fifteenth Corps.*

Third Division, Carl Schurz
First Brigade, Hector Tyndale
Second Brigade, Wladimir Krzyzanowski
Third Brigade, Frederick Hecker

*Note. Eleventh Corps was under William T.
Sherman's direction during the battles of November 24–
25, 1863.*

Artillery, Thomas W. Osborn
Battery I, 1st New York Light Artillery, Michael
Wiedrich
13th Battery, New York Light Artillery, William
Wheeler
Battery K, 1st Ohio Light Artillery, Nicholas Sahm
Battery I, 1st Ohio Light Artillery, Hubert Dilger
Battery G, 4th United States Artillery, Christopher F.
Merkle

*Note. Dilger's and Merkle's batteries were temporar-
ily attached to Second Division, Fourth Corps.*

TWELFTH CORPS

Second Division, John W. Geary
First Brigade, Charles Candy, to November 24, 1863,
disabled
William R. Creighton, to November 27, 1863,
killed
Thomas J. Ahl
Second Brigade, George A. Cobham, Jr.
Third Brigade, David Ireland
Artillery, John A. Reynolds
Battery E, Pennsylvania Light Artillery, James D.
McGill
Battery K, 5th United States Artillery, Edmund C.
Bainbridge

Note 1. Henry W. Slocum commanded Twelfth Corps, but he was at corps headquarters at Tullahoma, Tennessee.

Note 2. First Division was engaged in guarding the Nashville and Chattanooga Railroad from Wartrace Bridge to Bridgeport, Alabama.

Note 3. Second Division was under the immediate command of Joseph Hooker during the battles of November 24–25, 1863.

FOURTEENTH CORPS, John M. Palmer

First Division, Richard W. Johnson
First Brigade, William P. Carlin
Second Brigade, Marshall F. Moore, to November 25, 1863
William L. Stoughton
Third Brigade, John C. Starkweather
Artillery
Battery C, 1st Illinois Light Artillery, Mark H. Prescott
Battery A, 1st Michigan Light Artillery, Francis E. Hale
Battery H, 5th United States Artillery, Francis L. Guenther

Note 1. First Brigade was sent to reinforce Joseph Hooker during the Battle of Lookout Mountain November 24, 1863. The brigade returned to the division the next day.

Note 2. Moore was in temporary command of Second Brigade during the absence of John H. King, who was sick. Stoughton arrived at Chattanooga on the morning of November 25, 1863 and assumed command of Second Brigade by seniority. He led the brigade in the assault on Missionary Ridge that afternoon.

Note 3. Third Brigade occupied the fort and breastworks at Chattanooga during the engagements of November 23–25, 1863.

Second Division, Jefferson C. Davis
First Brigade, James D. Morgan
Second Brigade, John Beatty
Third Brigade, Daniel McCook
Artillery, William A. Hotchkiss
Battery I, 2nd Illinois Light Artillery, Henry B. Plant
2nd Battery, Minnesota Light Artillery, Richard L. Dawley
5th Battery, Wisconsin Light Artillery, George Q. Gardner

Note 1. Second Division was under the immediate command of William T. Sherman during the battles of November 24–25, 1863.

Note 2. First Brigade and Second Brigade took part in the assault on Missionary Ridge November 25, 1863.

Third Division, Absalom Baird
First Brigade, John B. Turchin
Second Brigade, Ferdinand Van Derveer
Third Brigade, Edward H. Phelps, to November 25, 1863, killed
William H. Hays
Artillery, George R. Swallow
7th Battery, Indiana Light Artillery, Otho H. Morgan
19th Battery, Indiana Light Artillery, Robert G. Lackey
Battery I, 4th United States Artillery, Frank G. Smith

ENGINEER TROOPS, William F. Smith

Engineers: 1st Michigan Engineers (detachment); 13th, 21st, and 22nd Michigan Infantry; and 18th Ohio Infantry
Pioneer Brigade, George P. Buell

ARTILLERY RESERVE, John M. Brannan

First Division, James Barnett
First Brigade, Charles S. Cotter
Second Brigade, commander not given

Second Division, commander not given
First Brigade, Josiah W. Church
Second Brigade, Arnold Sutermeister

CAVALRY

Second Brigade, Second Cavalry Division, Eli Long

POST OF CHATTANOOGA, John G. Parkhurst

ARMY OF THE TENNESSEE
William T. Sherman

FIFTEENTH CORPS, Frank P. Blair, Jr.

First Division, Peter J. Osterhaus
First Brigade, Charles R. Woods
Second Brigade, James A. Williamson
Artillery, Henry H. Griffiths
1st Battery, Iowa Light Artillery, James M. Williams
Battery F, 2nd Missouri Light Artillery, Clemens Landgraeber
4th Battery, Ohio Light Artillery, George Froehlich

Note. First Division was under the immediate com-

mand of Joseph Hooker during the battles of November 24–25, 1863.

Second Division, Morgan L. Smith
First Brigade, Giles A. Smith, to November 24, 1863, wounded
Nathan W. Tupper
Second Brigade, Joseph A. J. Lightburn
Artillery
Battery A, 1st Illinois Light Artillery, Peter P. Wood
Battery B, 1st Illinois Light Artillery, Israel P. Rumsey
Battery H, 1st Illinois Light Artillery, Francis De Gress

Fourth Division, Hugh Ewing
First Brigade, John M. Loomis
Second Brigade, John M. Corse, to November 25, 1863, wounded
Charles C. Walcutt
Third Brigade, Joseph R. Cockerill
Artillery, Henry Richardson
Battery F, 1st Illinois Light Artillery, John T. Cheney
Battery I, 1st Illinois Light Artillery, Josiah H. Burton
Battery D, 1st Missouri Light Artillery, Byron M. Callender

Note. Third Division, Fifteenth Corps was left at Vicksburg when the corps left for Chattanooga, and it was later transferred to West Tennessee.

SEVENTEENTH CORPS

Second Division, John E. Smith
First Brigade, Jesse I. Alexander
Second Brigade, Green B. Raum, to November 25, 1863, wounded
Francis C. Deimling, temporarily November 25, 1863
Clark R. Wever
Third Brigade, Charles L. Matthies, to November 25, 1863, wounded
Benjamin D. Dean, temporarily November 25, 1863
Jabez Banbury
Artillery, Henry Dillon
Cogswell's Battery, Illinois Light Artillery, William Cogswell
6th Battery, Wisconsin Light Artillery, Samuel F. Clark
12th Battery, Wisconsin Light Artillery, William Zickerick

CHICKAMAUGA, GEORGIA CAMPAIGN AUGUST 16, 1863– SEPTEMBER 22, 1863

When Braxton Bragg's Confederate Army of Tennessee withdrew from Middle Tennessee, beginning June 30, 1863, it moved back to Chattanooga, and went into camp there and in the vicinity July 7. William S. Rosecrans' Army of the Cumberland followed as far as supplies and the condition of the roads would permit, and it then took up a position extending from McMinnville to Winchester, Tennessee.

Rosecrans' next objective was Chattanooga, which, because of its location, was one of the most important towns in the South. There the Tennessee River cuts through the ridges of the Appalachian Mountains and forms a natural gateway between the North and the South. In addition, Chattanooga was a very important rail center. It was connected by the Memphis and Charleston Railroad with Memphis on the west; by the Western and Atlantic Railroad with Atlanta to the south; by the East Tennessee and Georgia Railroad with Knoxville, and then by connecting lines with Richmond, Virginia to the east; and by the Nashville and Chattanooga Railroad and the Louisville and Nashville Railroad with Nashville and Louisville to the north.

An immediate offensive against Bragg's army, however, could not, in Rosecrans' opinion, be undertaken until necessary preparations were completed. He also felt compelled to wait until Ambrose E. Burnside could advance with an army from Kentucky to protect his left flank by occupying Cumberland Gap and Knoxville. In addition, he believed that an advance was not practicable until the railroad from Nashville had been repaired to the Tennessee River so that necessary supplies could be brought to the front. Rosecrans was also concerned with the problem of securing forage for the animals of the army, and the corn that was raised in the valleys of southern Tennessee and northern Alabama would not be ripe and available to the army until mid-August.

Advance of the Army to the Tennessee River. Finally, all preparations were completed, and on

August 16, 1863, the army left its camps and advanced toward the Tennessee River. The three corps moved as follows:

Crittenden's Twenty-First Corps. Thomas L. Crittenden's Twenty-First Corps marched on the left of the army, crossing the Cumberland Mountains at three different points and moving into the Sequatchie Valley. Horatio P. Van Cleve left George F. Dick's Second Brigade of his Third Division at McMinnville to guard the stores accumulated there, and with Samuel Beatty's First Brigade and Sidney M. Barnes' Third Brigade marched on the Harrison Trace road through Spencer and Pikeville, Tennessee and into the Sequatchie Valley, where he arrived August 19, 1863.

Robert H. G. Minty's First Brigade, Second Cavalry Division, which had been placed under Van Cleve's orders, moved on the left of Van Cleve's division through Sparta, Tennessee to Pikeville. Minty then moved on into the Tennessee River Valley opposite Chattanooga, and he remained in the vicinity of Smith's Cross Roads from September 1 until September 5, picketing the area and guarding the fords and ferries on the river. On September 6 he moved downstream about six miles, remaining there on the river until September 11.

John M. Palmer's Second Division also marched from McMinnville, but advanced on the road through Irvin College to Dunlap, Tennessee in the Sequatchie Valley, where it arrived August 19, 1863. From Dunlap, William B. Hazen's Second Brigade advanced to Poe's Tavern, Tennessee, about fifteen miles north of Chattanooga.

John T. Wilder's First Brigade of Mounted Infantry was detached from Joseph J. Reynolds' Fourth Division of Fourteenth Corps at University Place, or University (present-day Sewanee), Tennessee August 17, 1863, and it marched by way of Tracy City and Therman, arriving at Dunlap about an hour ahead of Palmer's infantry. Wilder then moved on to Poe's Tavern and took position on the north bank of the Tennessee River from Chattanooga to Harrison's Ferry, about twelve miles upstream.

George D. Wagner's Second Brigade of Thomas J. Wood's First Division, Twenty-First Corps marched from Pelham to Hillsboro, Tennessee, rejoining the other two brigades of the division that were stationed there. Then on August 16, 1863, Wood's division marched by way of Tracy City and Altamont to Therman in the Sequatchie Valley, where it arrived on August 20. Wagner's brigade was sent on to the eastern edge of Walden's Ridge to reconnoiter and threaten a crossing of the Tennessee River near Chattanooga. It also served as a support for Wilder's brigade of mounted infantry.

George P. Buell's First Brigade and Charles G. Harker's Third Brigade of Wood's division remained at Therman until September 1, 1863, and they then moved down the Sequatchie Valley to Jasper, Tennessee in preparation for crossing the Tennessee River. Also on September 1, Palmer's and Van Cleve's divisions followed Wood down the valley and prepared to cross the river.

At Poe's Tavern, on September 3, 1863, Hazen assumed command of all troops that were to be left north of the river, including his own brigade, Wagner's brigade, Wilder's brigade, and Minty's cavalry brigade. Hazen's line extended from Kingston to Williams' Island, Tennessee, a distance of seventy-five miles. His mission was to watch the fords and ferries on the Tennessee, and to threaten a crossing to the south bank above Chattanooga.

Thomas' Fourteenth Corps. August 16, 1863, George H. Thomas' Fourteenth Corps began its march toward the Tennessee River. Absalom Baird's First Division and James S. Negley's Second Division marched from near Decherd, Tennessee by way of Tantalon to Crow Creek, between Anderson's Station on the Nashville and Chattanooga Railroad and Stevenson, Alabama. On September 1, both divisions moved on to Cave Spring near Stevenson to be ready to cross the Tennessee River at Caperton's Ferry, the crossing for the town of Stevenson.

John M. Brannan, commanding Third Division, reported to Joseph J. Reynolds, commanding Fourth Division, and at the latter's direction advanced with his division from Winchester, Tennessee on the Pelham road by way of Decherd to University Place in the Cumberland Mountains. Brannan then moved on to the east about ten miles and camped August 19, 1863 in Sweeden's Cove. He remained there until August 22, then marched to Battle Creek, about five miles below Jasper, Tennessee and to the northwest of Shellmound, Tennessee. The division remained at Battle Creek until August 29.

Reynolds' division left Decherd August 16, 1863 and ascended the mountains to University Place. At that point Wilder's First Brigade was detached and sent to watch the north bank of the Tennessee River opposite Chattanooga. Reynolds, with Edward A. King's Second Brigade and John B. Turchin's Third Brigade, marched on to Jasper, where he arrived August 21. The next day King's brigade took possession of Shellmound Ferry, but Turchin's brigade remained at Jasper until September 1, at which time it advanced to cross the Tennessee River.

McCook's Twentieth Corps. When repairs on the Nashville and Chattanooga Railroad were completed from Nashville to Bridgeport, Alabama July 25, 1863, Philip H. Sheridan's Third Division advanced from Cowan and occupied Bridgeport. From there, Sheridan sent a detachment to Stevenson, Alabama. On August 16, the other two divisions of McCook's corps also advanced to the Tennessee River. Jefferson C. Davis' First Division marched south from Winchester, through Mountain Top, and camped on Big Crow Creek near Stevenson. It remained there until August 28. Richard W. Johnson's Second Division advanced from Tullahoma by way of Salem (Old Salem), about eleven miles to the southwest, to Larkinsville, Alabama (near present-day Hollywood, Alabama). From there it moved on to Bellefonte, Alabama, near Caperton's Ferry.

Stanley's Cavalry Corps. At the end of Rosecrans' Middle Tennessee (or Tullahoma) Campaign, David S. Stanley established headquarters of the Cavalry Corps at Winchester, Tennessee, where he arrived July 22, 1863. Robert B. Mitchell's First Division, then commanded by Edward M. McCook, was at Fayetteville, Tennessee; Eli Long's Second Brigade of John B. Turchin's Second Division was at Pulaski, Tennessee; and Turchin, with Robert H. G. Minty's First Brigade, was at Salem, Tennessee.

On August 11, Edward M. McCook, with Mitchell's division, was sent from Fayetteville to Huntsville, Alabama, and from there to positions along the Memphis and Charleston Railroad to pro-

tect the road and to guard the line of the Tennessee River from Whitesburg to Bridgeport, Alabama. On August 16, Minty's brigade was sent to Sparta, Tennessee.

Stanley remained at Winchester with Long's brigade until the Army of the Cumberland began its advance toward Chattanooga, and then he moved to Stevenson, Alabama, where he was to join McCook's division in preparation for crossing the Tennessee River.

Granger's Reserve Corps. Granger's Reserve Corps did not accompany the army on its march to the Tennessee River, but was left to guard the railroad from Murfreesboro to Cowan and from Wartrace to Shelbyville, Tennessee. It did, however, join the army at Rossville, Georgia on September 17, 1863 (see below).

Crossing of the Tennessee River. The Army of the Cumberland crossed the Tennessee River during the period August 29–September 4, 1863 as follows:

Twenty-First Corps. Wood, with George P. Buell's First Brigade and Charles G. Harker's Third Brigade, crossed at Shellmound September 2–3 (Wagner's Second Brigade was left north of the river under the command of Hazen); Palmer, with Charles Cruft's First Brigade and William Grose's Third Brigade, crossed at Battle Creek September 3–4 (William B. Hazen's Second Brigade remained north of the river); and Van Cleve, with Samuel Beatty's First Brigade and Sidney M. Barnes' Third Brigade, crossed at Shellmound September 4 (George F. Dick's Second Brigade was at McMinnville).

Fourteenth Corps. Negley's division crossed at Caperton's Ferry September 1; Baird's division crossed at Bridgeport September 4; Brannan's division crossed at Battle Creek August 31–September 2; and Reynolds' division crossed at Shellmound August 29–September 1.

Twentieth Corps. Davis' division crossed at Caperton's Ferry August 29–30; Johnson's division crossed at Caperton's Ferry August 31; and Sheridan's division crossed at Bridgeport September 2–3.

Cavalry Corps. Edward M. McCook's First Cavalry Division crossed at Caperton's Ferry September 3, and Eli Long's Second Brigade of George Crook's Second Cavalry Division crossed at Bridgeport September 2. Robert H. G. Minty's First Brigade of Second Cavalry Division remained north of the river.

Movement of the Army to Chickamauga Creek, Georgia. Once across the Tennessee River, it was necessary for the Army of the Cumberland to cross two parallel mountain ranges, which ran across its path from the northeast to the southwest, in order to reach Chattanooga and Bragg's army. The first mountain, only a short distance from the river, was called Raccoon Mountain at its northern end, but farther to the southwest it was called Sand Mountain. The second barrier was the Lookout Mountain Range, which was separated from Raccoon and Sand mountains by Wills' Valley (also called Lookout Valley). Lookout Creek flowed through this valley and emptied into the Tennessee River near Brown's Ferry.

There were only three usable gaps in the Lookout Mountain Range, and Rosecrans planned to send a corps through each of these. The first gap was at the north end of the range at the Tennessee River, and through this gap the Nashville and Chattanooga Railroad ran along the Tennessee River into Chattanooga.

The next gap to the southwest was Stevens' Gap, which was about twenty-six miles south of Chattanooga and six miles south of Trenton, Georgia. Through this gap a road ran eastward into McLemore's Cove. McLemore's Cove is a natural cul-de-sac some six miles wide which lies between Pigeon Mountain on the east and Lookout Mountain on the west. Pigeon Mountain branches off from the eastern side of Lookout Mountain about forty-five miles below Chattanooga, then curves around and runs to the northeast, roughly parallel to Lookout Mountain. The West Branch of Chickamauga Creek flows northward through this valley, between the two mountains toward the Tennessee River. The only practicable means of entry into McLemore's Cove from the west was at Stevens' Gap. On the east, there were roads running through three gaps in Pigeon Mountain into the cove. These were, from north to south, Catlett's Gap, Dug Gap, and Blue Bird Gap. At the extreme southern end of McLemore's Cove was Dougherty's Gap.

The third gap in Lookout Mountain was Winston's Gap at Valley Head, Georgia, forty-two miles south of Chattanooga. The road passing through this gap ran by way of Alpine and Summerville to Rome, Georgia.

According to Rosecrans' march orders for the advance of the army south of the Tennessee River, Crittenden's corps was to move on the direct road toward Chattanooga by way of the gap at the Tennessee River and threaten the town, while Thomas' and McCook's corps marched south against Bragg's left flank. Thomas was to move through Stevens' Gap into McLemore's Cove, and McCook was to move far to the south and pass through Winston's Gap toward Alpine and Summerville.

Crittenden's corps was assembled on the south side of the river near Shellmound September 5, 1863, and at 2:30 P.M. it advanced up the valley of Running Water Creek toward Whiteside, Tennessee. Wood's division moved first, and it was followed in turn by Palmer's division and then Van Cleve's division. The next day Crittenden's column was halted when it came up to strong enemy works.

At 5:45 A.M. September 9, 1863, Crittenden learned that Bragg had evacuated Chattanooga, and he promptly ordered Wood's division to move forward and occupy the town. Wood marched at once, but along the way, Smith D. Atkins, with his 92nd Illinois Mounted Infantry, passed Wood's division, entering Chattanooga at 9:30 A.M. Wood's division arrived at 12:30 P.M., and Wood was placed in command of the town. Wagner's Second Brigade crossed from the north side of the river during the afternoon and evening of September 9 and rejoined Wood's division.

Palmer's and Van Cleve's divisions, which were following Wood, came up about dark, but after passing the northern end of Lookout Mountain, they turned south and camped that night at Rossville, Georgia, five miles from Chattanooga. Dick's brigade of Van Cleve's division, which had been left at McMinnville when the army advanced in mid-August, arrived at Rossville about sunset and rejoined the division.

On the morning of September 10, 1863, Palmer and Van Cleve marched from Rossville toward Ringgold, Georgia in pursuit of Bragg, who was believed to be retreating toward Rome, Georgia. That same day, Wood left Wagner's brigade to garrison Chattanooga, and with Buell's and Harker's brigades followed Palmer and Van Cleve. On September 9, Wilder's brigade of mounted infantry crossed the Tennessee River at Friar's Island, eight miles above Chattanooga, and the next day it moved southward toward Ringgold. It passed Van Cleve's division coming up from Rossville, and it then moved on in front through Ringgold to Tunnel Hill.

On the night of September 10, 1863, Rosecrans learned that Bragg had not retreated very far, and that he was at that time with his army near La Fayette, Georgia. At 5:00 the next morning, Harker's brigade of Wood's division was ordered back, and it was sent out on a reconnaissance on the Chattanooga–La Fayette road as far as Lee and Gordon's Mills on Chickamauga Creek. At 11:00 P.M. September 11, Wood, with Buell's brigade, joined Harker. Also on September 11, Hazen's brigade, which had crossed the Tennessee River at Friar's Island the day before, rejoined Palmer's division at Graysville, Georgia, and then Crittenden, with Palmer's and Van Cleve's divisions, moved on to Ringgold. Upon arrival there, Crittenden was ordered to return with his divisions to the Chattanooga–La Fayette road (hereafter called the La Fayette road) and take position with Wood near Lee and Gordon's Mills, which he did September 12. Wilder was called back from Tunnel Hill to protect Crittenden's left while on the march, and he came in after dark that night. On September 13, Crittenden sent Wilder to rejoin Reynolds' division of Fourteenth Corps, which was then in McLemore's Cove.

Minty's cavalry brigade crossed the Tennessee at Friar's Island September 12, 1863 and camped that night at Chattanooga. The next day Minty joined Crittenden at Lee and Gordon's Mills and was assigned the duty of watching the front and left of Crittenden's line.

There were some changes in the positions of Crittenden's forces during September 13–14, 1863, but on September 16, Wood's division (less Wagner's brigade at Chattanooga) was at Lee and Gordon's Mills; Van Cleve's division was at Crawfish Springs; and Palmer's division was at Gower's Ford, about six miles southwest of Lee and Gordon's Mills on West Chickamauga Creek.

On September 15, 1863, Minty's cavalry was sent to the Pea Vine Valley, east of Reed's Bridge on Chickamauga Creek, with instructions to camp at or near Leet's Cross Roads and guard the country in that vicinity.

Wilder's brigade rejoined Reynolds' division of Fourteenth Corps at Cooper's Gap September 14, 1863, but three days later it was again detached and sent down Chickamauga Creek to guard Alexander's Bridge.

Meantime, Thomas and McCook were carrying out their march orders. After crossing the Tennessee River, Negley's division of Thomas' Fourteenth Corps moved over Sand Mountain and into Lookout Valley, and it then marched to Johnson's Crook, about five miles south of Trenton, Georgia. John Beatty's First Brigade then turned east, arriving at the base of Lookout Mountain September 6, 1863, and the next day it ascended the mountain and seized Stevens' Gap. William Sirwell's Third Brigade arrived September 7, and during September 7–9, it was engaged in repairing roads and assisting the artillery and wagons up the mountain. Timothy R. Stanley's Second Brigade joined Beatty's brigade on the mountain September 8, and that day Beatty moved to Cooper's Gap, about three miles north of Stevens' Gap. Stanley's and Sirwell's brigades then descended the mountain into McLemore's Cove at the foot of Stevens' Gap. September 9, Beatty's brigade moved southward along the base of the mountain to rejoin the other two brigades.

Baird's division of Fourteenth Corps followed Negley over Sand Mountain and into Lookout Valley, and it then camped on the night of September 8, 1863 at Johnson's Crook while it waited for Negley to get his division over Lookout Mountain. The next day Baird moved his division to the top of the mountain.

After Reynolds, with the two brigades of his division, had crossed the Tennessee at Shellmound, he marched over Raccoon Mountain, reaching Trenton September 7, 1863. Brannan's division followed from its crossing at Battle Creek, also arriving at Trenton September 7. Reynolds' division remained in camp at Trenton until September 10, and Brannan's division until September 11.

September 10, 1863, Negley's division moved out from the base of Lookout Mountain into

McLemore's Cove on the road toward La Fayette. Sirwell's brigade was in the lead, and it was followed by Stanley's brigade. Beatty's brigade guarded the wagon train during the advance. As Sirwell approached Dug Gap in Pigeon Mountain, he encountered Confederate skirmishers, and he drove these back across Chickamauga Creek. Federal skirmishers followed the enemy across the creek and reached a point near the Widow Davis house, called Davis' Cross Roads. At that point the road from Stevens' Gap to Dug Gap crossed a road running up the valley from Crawfish Springs. Upon arrival at the crossroads, Negley learned from a Union citizen that Confederate forces were present in force on his front and on both flanks. In fact, at that time, Thomas C. Hindman's division of Polk's corps was on Negley's left in McLemore's Cove, on the road from Crawfish Springs, and it was supported by Simon B. Buckner's corps. Daniel H. Hill was near La Fayette, with the forward elements of his corps in front of Negley at Dug Gap and on his right at Blue Bird Gap.

At sundown Negley made a strong demonstration in the direction of Dug Gap and drove in the enemy skirmishers, and then at 9:00 P.M. he moved to a defensive position about a mile from Dug Gap. He formed his line in a woods west of the Crawfish Springs road and adjoining the Widow Davis house.

Negley then informed Thomas of his situation, and Baird's division was ordered to his support. Baird moved down from Lookout Mountain late in the afternoon of September 10, 1863 and bivouacked in McLemore's Cove at the foot of Stevens' Gap. He then left John H. King's Third Brigade to guard the trains and depots, and at 3:00 A.M. September 11, he marched with Benjamin F. Scribner's First Brigade and John C. Starkweather's Second Brigade to join Negley at the Widow Davis house. Baird arrived there at 8:00 A.M. and reported to Negley, who was the senior officer present. Baird then relieved Negley's troops on a line extending from the Dug Gap road to the Chattanooga road, and Baird moved farther to the left.

Negley then learned that the enemy was advancing on his front and on both flanks, and he ordered the trains back to Bailey's Cross Roads and prepared to withdraw his infantry. By 2:00 P.M. the trains were on their way, and Beatty's and Scribner's brigades were with them for their protec-

tion. An hour later the enemy approached, and Stanley's and Starkweather's brigades became sharply engaged, but by that evening Baird's and Negley's divisions had withdrawn safely to Bailey's Cross Roads, where they occupied a good defensive position.

When Negley's division moved out into McLemore's Cove September 10, 1863, Reynolds' division was ordered up from Trenton at daylight to support the left of Baird's division on Lookout Mountain. At 8:00 the next morning, Brannan's division was directed to follow Reynolds and support him. Reynolds reached the top of Lookout Mountain September 11, then moved to the left on the road to Cooper's Gap. Brannan's division was delayed by Reynolds' troops and trains, and did not reach the eastern base of the mountain in McLemore's Cove until 11:00 A.M. September 12. That day Edward A. King's brigade of Reynolds' division was ordered to report to Negley, who had returned to the foot of Stevens' Gap from the Widow Davis', and it was placed in line on the left of John Beatty's brigade.

On the night of September 12, 1863, Thomas' divisions were in position as follows; Negley's division was on the right, on high ground running back toward Lookout Mountain; Baird's division was across the road running from Stevens' Gap to Dug Gap, facing east; Brannan's division was on the left of Baird; and Reynolds' division was on the left at Cooper's Gap with Turchin's brigade.

While Crittenden's and Thomas' corps were moving into position south of Chattanooga, McCook's corps was moving to the far right to seize Winston's Gap. After crossing the Tennessee River at Caperton's Ferry, forty miles below Chattanooga, Davis' division marched over Sand Mountain to the road leading to Rome, Georgia by way of Winston's Gap, camping on September 2, 1863 in Wills Valley, three and a half miles from Winston's Gap. Two days later, Davis crossed Valley Head to Winston's and seized the gap at Lookout Mountain. Johnson's division followed Davis and occupied the latter's former camp in Wills Valley. Both divisions remained in camp until September 8.

McCook's other division under Sheridan crossed Sand Mountain from Bridgeport, camping on September 5, 1863 near Trenton. The division then moved up the valley by way of Easley's to Stevens'

Mill, ten miles distant, and it remained there in camp until September 10.

During the night of September 8 and early morning of September 9, 1863, Stanley with his cavalry passed Davis' division and moved up onto Lookout Mountain on a reconnaissance toward Alpine and Summerville. Davis then left P. Sidney Post's First Brigade to hold Winston Gap and guard the trains, and with the other two brigades followed Stanley to support his movement. On September 9, Hans C. Heg's Third Brigade moved to Neal's Gap on the southeast side of the mountain; William P. Carlin's Second Brigade followed the cavalry and camped that night at the base of the mountain near Alpine

September 8, 1863, Johnson's division marched to Long Spring on the Trenton road, and on September 10 it marched to Winston's Gap and across Lookout Mountain to Alpine.

During the evening of September 9, 1863, McCook learned of Bragg's evacuation of Chattanooga, and he received orders to move forward through Summerville in pursuit. The next day, however, McCook learned from Stanley that Bragg's army was not retreating, but that it was then in position near La Fayette, and accordingly he suspended the movement toward Summerville.

On September 10, 1863, Sheridan's division advanced from Stevens' Mill to Valley Head and Winston's Gap, and the next day it joined the corps at Alpine.

September 10, 1863, Stanley sent scouts out toward Rome and La Fayette, and Louis D. Watkins' Third Brigade, First Cavalry Division drove the enemy cavalry through Summerville. The next day Edward M. McCook moved out with his two cavalry brigades on a scout toward Rome. Also on September 11, Watkins' brigade was sent to support the 39th Mounted Infantry that Alexander McD. McCook had sent toward La Fayette to communicate with Thomas. When it became certain that Bragg was at La Fayette, and was not retreating, both scouting expeditions were ordered back to Alpine.

By September 11, 1863, the three divisions of Twentieth Corps were assembled at Alpine, and they remained there in camp until September 13.

After the evacuation of Chattanooga by the enemy September 8–9, 1863, Rosecrans concluded that, from the available information, Bragg's army

was retreating toward Rome, Georgia, and he further believed that the main body of the army would move by Ringgold and Dalton. Accordingly, on September 10 he sent Crittenden's corps toward Ringgold and Dalton in pursuit, but upon arrival at Ringgold the next day, Crittenden reported that only some cavalry had retired toward Dalton. Other information coming into army headquarters September 11 indicated that Bragg was not retreating, but that he had halted in the vicinity of La Fayette, Georgia with the bulk of his army. This was essentially confirmed during that afternoon and night by a reconnaissance of Wood's division of Crittenden's corps toward Lee and Gordon's Mills. Acting on this information, Rosecrans sent a message at 10:00 P.M. September 11 to McCook at Alpine, suggesting that he, McCook, close up to the left on Thomas in McLemore's Cove.

At noon September 12, 1863, Rosecrans received a message from McCook, sent the day before, informing him that Bragg was not retreating on Rome but was at that time near La Fayette. Finally, at 4:00 P.M. that day, Thomas reported to Rosecrans the results of Negley's and Baird's advance on Dug Gap September 10–11. With this report the situation seemed clear, and Rosecrans immediately began the concentration of his army in McLemore's Cove.

September 12, 1863, Crittenden moved back with his two divisions from Ringgold to join Wood's division at Lee and Gordon's Mills, and in an order dated 11:15 A.M. September 12, Rosecrans directed McCook to march with two of his divisions to support Thomas in McLemore's Cove.

During September 13, 1863, the divisions of Negley, Baird, and Brannan remained in the same positions that they had occupied the day before, awaiting the arrival of McCook. Edward A. King's brigade was relieved from duty with Negley's division; it then moved to the foot of Cooper's Gap, and then Reynolds formed his Second Brigade and Third Brigade on the road from Cooper's Gap to Catlett's Gap.

September 14, 1863, Reynolds moved his two brigades to Pond Spring, which was near Chickamauga Creek, about five and one-half miles southwest of Crawfish Springs and about three miles west of Catlett's Gap in Pigeon Mountain. Wilder's First Brigade arrived at Pond Spring that day and rejoined the division. Also on September

14, Brannan advanced a brigade to Chickamauga Creek about a mile to the right and south of Reynolds' position at Pond Spring.

At 12:30 A.M. September 13, 1863, McCook received an order from Thomas, at Rosecrans' direction, instructing him to leave one division to guard the trains and move with the other two divisions of his corps to Stevens' Gap to support Fourteenth Corps. During the rest of that day and the next, McCook moved his corps back over Lookout Mountain to Valley Head. Post's First Brigade of Davis' division was with the corps trains, and William H. Lytle was assigned with his own First Brigade of Sheridan's division and Joseph B. Dodge's Second Brigade of Johnson's division as additional guards for the trains. Lytle was then sent with his two brigades to Dougherty's Gap at the head of McLemore's Cove, where he arrived at 11:00 A.M. September 16.

When McCook arrived at the western base of Lookout Mountain, he marched with the divisions of Davis and Johnson through Valley Head and then, by Long's Spring, on the direct road to Stevens' Gap. Sheridan took a less direct route down Lookout Valley to Johnson's Crook and then over Stevens' Gap. He camped on the night of September 16, 1863 at the base of Lookout Mountain in McLemore's Cove. That night Davis' division was at the head of Stevens' Gap, three miles behind Sheridan, and Johnson's division was on the mountain, twelve miles to the rear, on the road that ran toward Stevens' Gap. Post's brigade with the trains was following Johnson. Davis and Johnson came up during September 17 and rejoined the corps in McLemore's Cove.

Lytle with his two brigades arrived at Dougherty's Gap September 16, 1863, and there he was ordered on to Stevens' Gap. Lytle started immediately, and his brigades rejoined their divisions in McLemore's Cove September 18. When Post's brigade came up, it was ordered to hold Stevens' Gap. It was subsequently ordered to report to Robert B. Mitchell, then commanding the Cavalry Corps, and Post did not again report to Davis until he arrived at Chattanooga on the morning of September 22.

After crossing the Tennessee River, Stanley's cavalry moved over Sand Mountain, arriving in Wills Valley September 3, 1863. The next day

George Crook, with Eli Long's brigade, was sent to Winston's Gap at Valley Head. Edward M. McCook's cavalry division remained four miles down the valley, and during September 5–7 it was engaged in scouting and shoeing horses. On September 8, Crook ascended Lookout Mountain at Winston's Gap, and the next day Edward M. McCook's cavalry division followed Crook across Lookout Mountain into Broomtown Valley and camped near Alpine. Stanley's cavalry brigades were then engaged in scouting and in reconnaissances in front of Twentieth Corps toward Rome, Summerville, and La Fayette (see McCook's movements, above).

When the cavalry returned to Alpine September 14, 1863 from its scouts toward Rome and La Fayette, it found that Twentieth Corps had been ordered to Stevens' Gap to support Fourteenth Corps, and the division then followed McCook's infantry to the top of Lookout Mountain.

On the evening of September 14, 1863, Robert B. Mitchell, commander of First Cavalry Division, who had been absent on sick leave, arrived at Valley Head. The next morning he relieved Stanley, who was ill, in command of the Cavalry Corps, and Stanley then returned to Nashville.

On September 15, 1863, Crook moved to Dougherty's Gap to relieve Lytle's two brigades. The next day Edward M. McCook, who had moved his cavalry division to Valley Head, left Louis D. Watkins' Third Brigade at Winston's Gap to take charge of the sick and prisoners, and marched with Archibald P. Campbell's First Brigade and Daniel M. Ray's Second Brigade to Dougherty's Gap. Edward M. McCook then moved down into McLemore's Cove and camped. On September 19, Watkins was ordered to move with his brigade toward Stevens' Gap.

On September 6, 1863, Rosecrans ordered Gordon Granger to concentrate all available troops of his Reserve Corps at Bridgeport, Alabama in preparation for joining the army near Chattanooga. Daniel McCook's Second Brigade, Second Division arrived at Bridgeport from Columbia, Tennessee September 10, and Walter C. Whitaker's First Brigade and John G. Mitchell's Second Brigade of James B. Steedman's First Division arrived at Bridgeport the next day. These brigades had been relieved by other troops from duty along the railroad from Murfreesboro to Cowan and from Wartrace to Shelbyville, Tennessee. On September 12, Daniel McCook's brigade moved to Shellmound on its way to Rossville, Georgia, and Steedman's division followed the next day. All of Granger's troops had arrived at Rossville by September 17.

On the night of September 17, 1863, the corps of Thomas, Crittenden, and McCook were reassembled in McLemore's Cove within supporting distance of one another, and were in position as follows:

Thomas' Fourteenth Corps. The right of Baird's division was at Gower's Ford, three miles north of and a little west of Catlett's Gap, and his line extended northward along Chickamauga Creek to Bud's Mill; the right of Negley's division was at Bud's Mill, and his left connected with Van Cleve's division of Crittenden's corps at Owens' Ford; Brannan's division was on the right of Baird, and it covered the fords between Gower's Ford and Pond Spring; Turchin's brigade of Reynolds' division occupied Catlett's Gap until the evening of September 17, 1863 and was then relieved by Edward A. King's brigade and placed in reserve. On September 17, Wilder's brigade was again detached and sent down Chickamauga Creek to guard Alexander's Bridge, three miles below Lee and Gordon's Mills.

McCook's Twentieth Corps. Davis' division was in front of Brooks' house in front of Dug Gap; Johnson's division was at Pond Spring; and Sheridan's division was at the foot of Stevens' Gap.

Crittenden's Twenty-First Corps. Crittenden's corps, as already noted, had moved to the vicinity of Lee and Gordon's Mills September 11–12, 1863. Wood's division, with the exception of George D. Wagner's Second Brigade, which was at Chattanooga, was in position near the mill. Van Cleve's division was at Crawfish Springs. Palmer's division was on the right of the corps, along Chickamauga Creek, with Charles Cruft's First Brigade at Matthews' house, near Owens' Ford, and William B. Hazen's Second Brigade and William Grose's Third Brigade at Gower's Ford. On the evening of September 16, Cruft moved back about a mile and a half to Abercrombie's (Crummy's) house.

When Thomas' Fourteenth Corps advanced into McLemore's Cove September 17, Palmer's brigades moved to the left to make room for the divisions of Negley and Baird.

Mitchell's Cavalry Corps. On September 16, 1863, Edward M. McCook, with Campbell's brigade, moved down into McLemore's Cove and bivouacked at Cedar Grove Church, seven miles from Blue Bird Gap. Daniel M. Ray's Second Brigade of McCook's division and Crook with Long's brigade were at Dougherty's Gap, and Watkins' brigade of McCook's division was at Winston's Gap. Minty's brigade of Crook's division was east of Reed's Bridge in Pea Vine Valley.

Granger's Reserve Corps. Granger, with the brigades of Whitaker and Mitchell of Steedman's First Division and Daniel McCook's Second Brigade of James D. Morgan's Second Division, held Rossville Gap.

Army Headquarters. During the advance of the army to McLemore's Cove, army headquarters was established as follows: at Chattanooga September 10–14, at Stevens' Gap September 15, and at Crawfish Springs September 16–19. At 1:00 P.M. September 19, the first day of the Battle of Chickamauga, Rosecrans moved up and made his headquarters at Widow Glenn's house, on the Dry Valley road that ran from Crawfish Springs, by way of McFarland's Gap, to Chattanooga.

Bragg's Confederate Army. Bragg's army that faced the Army of the Cumberland on the evening of September 17, 1863 bore little resemblance to the army that had withdrawn from Middle Tennessee to Chattanooga in July. It had received heavy reinforcements and had been almost completely reorganized, and there had been a number of changes in the commanders of the larger units. A brief description of the organization of Bragg's army is given here to explain the origin of each of the new corps and divisions.

POLK'S CORPS, Leonidas Polk

Cheatham's Division, Benjamin F. Cheatham
   Jackson's Brigade, John K. Jackson
   Maney's Brigade, George Maney

Smith's Brigade, Preston Smith
Strahl's Brigade, Otho F. Strahl
Wright's Brigade, Marcus J. Wright

Note. Jackson's Independent Brigade of Bragg's army was assigned to Cheatham's Division August 23, 1863.

Hindman's Division, Thomas C. Hindman
    Anderson's Brigade, J. Patton Anderson
    Deas' Brigade, Zachariah C. Deas
    Manigault's Brigade, Arthur M. Manigault

Note. Jones M. Withers commanded the division until Hindman was assigned August 13, 1863, at which time Deas was in temporary command. Edward C. Walthall's brigade of this division was transferred July 31, 1863 to St. John R. Liddell's division of William H. T. Walker's newly organized Reserve Corps.

HILL'S CORPS, Daniel H. Hill

Cleburne's Division, Patrick R. Cleburne
    Wood's Brigade, Sterling A. M. Wood
    Polk's Brigade, Lucius E. Polk
    Deshler's Brigade, James Deshler

Note 1. Hill relieved William J. Hardee in command of the corps July 24, 1863, and Hardee was sent to Mississippi.
Note 2. Deschler's brigade was commanded by Thomas J. Churchill until August 31, 1863.
Note 3. St. John R. Liddell's brigade of this division was transferred to a newly created division of William H. T. Walker's Reserve Corps. Liddell was assigned command of the division, and Daniel C. Govan took charge of Liddell's brigade.

Breckinridge's Division, John C. Breckinridge
    Helm's Brigade, Benjamin H. Helm
    Adams' Brigade, Daniel W. Adams
    Stovall's Brigade, Marcellus A. Stovall

Note. Originally Hill's corps consisted of Cleburne's division and Alexander P. Stewart's division, but on September 3, 1863, Stewart's division was transferred to Simon B. Buckner's corps from East Tennessee.

WALKER'S RESERVE CORPS, William H. T. Walker

Walker's Division, States Rights Gist
    Gist's Brigade, Peyton H. Colquitt
    Ector's Brigade, Matthew D. Ector
    Wilson's Brigade, Claudius C. Wilson

Note. Walker's division was sent to Bragg from Joseph E. Johnston's Confederate Department of Mississippi August 23, 1863. John Gregg's brigade of this division was left in Mississippi for a time, but was later ordered to join Bragg and was assigned to Bushrod R. Johnson's newly created Provisional Division.

Liddell's Division, St. John R. Liddell
    Liddell's Brigade, Daniel C. Govan
    Walthall's Brigade, Edward C. Walthall

Note. This was a new division formed from Liddell's brigade of Cleburne's division, Hill's corps, and Walthall's brigade of Hindman's division, Polk's corps.

BUCKNER'S CORPS, Simon B. Buckner

Stewart's Division, Alexander P. Stewart
    Bate's Brigade, William B. Bate
    Clayton's Brigade, Henry D. Clayton
    Brown's Brigade, John C. Brown

Preston's Division, William Preston
    Gracie's Brigade, Archibald Gracie, Jr.
    Kelly's Brigade, John H. Kelly
    Trigg's Brigade, Robert C. Trigg

Buckner's Corps was constituted August 6, 1863 to consist of the troops of Buckner's former Department of East Tennessee, which on that date was included in Bragg's new Department of Tennessee. These troops were later organized as Preston's Division.

Late in August 1863, as an army under Ambrose E. Burnside approached Knoxville, Tennessee from Kentucky, Bragg, who was unable to reinforce Buckner, ordered the latter to fall back to the Hiwassee River, where he would be within supporting distance. Buckner withdrew along the East Tennessee and Georgia Railroad by way of Loudon, Tennessee to Charleston on the Hiwassee, and then on to Ooltewah, Tennessee. There, on September 3, Buckner's corps was reconstituted to consist of the corps as originally organized, and also Alexander P. Stewart's division of Hill's corps, which had joined Buckner. Bushrod R. Johnson's brigade of Stewart's Division was detached and assigned to a new Provisional Division commanded by Johnson. When Buckner's corps was organized, it moved on south from Ooltewah to Ringgold, Georgia, and from there it marched to La Fayette, Georgia to join Bragg.

JOHNSON'S PROVISIONAL DIVISION, Bushrod R. Johnson

Johnson's Brigade, John S. Fulton
Gregg's Brigade, John Gregg
McNair's Brigade, Evander McNair

Note. Johnson's division was a new division formed from Johnson's brigade of Stewart's division, Buckner's corps; Gregg's brigade of Walker's division, Department of Mississippi; and McNair's brigade of French's division, also from the Department of Mississippi.

WHEELER'S CAVALRY CORPS, Joseph Wheeler

Wharton's Division, John A. Wharton
Martin's Division, William T. Martin

FORREST'S CAVALRY CORPS, Nathan B. Forrest

Armstrong's Division, Frank C. Armstrong
  Armstrong's Brigade, James T. Wheeler
  Forrest's Brigade, George G. Dibrell

Pegram's Division, John Pegram
  Davidson's Brigade, Henry B. Davidson
  Scott's Brigade, John S. Scott

In addition to the troops listed above as present with the army as of September 17, 1863, two divisions that had been detached from Robert E. Lee's Army of Northern Virginia were en route to join Bragg's army. On September 9, the day Rosecrans' troops occupied Chattanooga, John B. Hood's division of Longstreet's corps began loading at Orange Court House, Virginia for the trip by rail to Georgia. Lafayette McLaws' division of the same corps followed Hood as rapidly as transportation became available. Only a total of five brigades, however, arrived on Chickamauga Creek in time for the battle, and on the morning of September 18, the three brigades of Hood's division, commanded by James L. Sheffield, Jerome B. Robertson, and Henry L. Benning, were at Catoosa Station and in the vicinity of Ringgold. These brigades were temporarily attached to Johnson's division, which was also near Ringgold.

On the night of September 17, 1863, Bragg's army was in position as follows: Wheeler's cavalry was on the extreme Confederate left in McLemore's Cove; Hill's corps was opposite La Fayette; and the corps of Polk, Buckner, and Walker extended, in that order, northeast from Rock Springs Church to a point southeast of Alexander's Bridge on

Chickamauga Creek. Forrest's cavalry was on the right front of the army. As just noted, Johnson's division and the three brigades of Hood's division were around Catoosa Station and Ringgold. Bragg's headquarters was at Leet's Tan Yard.

During the preceding week, the Confederate forces had failed to take advantage of several opportunities to strike the scattered forces of the Army of the Cumberland, but on the night of September 17, 1863, after the army had concentrated in McLemore's Cove, Bragg issued orders for a general attack the next day. His plan was to move his divisions up the east side of Chickamauga Creek, then cross the creek above Lee and Gordon's Mills, and move into position between the Army of the Cumberland and Chattanooga. Johnson's division was to advance from Ringgold, cross Chickamauga Creek at Reed's Bridge, and then turn to the left (south) and move up the west bank of the creek toward the Union left at Lee and Gordon's Mills. Walker's corps was to cross the creek at Alexander's Bridge, about one and one-fourth air miles above (south of) Reed's Bridge, and then to unite with Johnson's division in an attack on Rosecrans' left flank. Buckner's corps was to cross the Chickamauga at Thedford's Ford, about one air mile above Alexander's Bridge, and join in the attack. Polk's corps was to support the Confederate attack west of the creek by attempting to cross at Lee and Gordon's Mills. Hill's corps was to guard the Confederate left flank, on the left of Polk. Wheeler's cavalry was to watch the far Confederate left, and Forrest's cavalry was to support Johnson's movement on the Confederate right.

BATTLE OF CHICKAMAUGA, SEPTEMBER 19–20, 1863

Movements of September 18, 1863. The fighting that occurred September 18, 1863, as the Confederate troops moved into position along Chickamauga Creek, is not generally considered part of the Battle of Chickamauga, but the movements of that day are included here to provide a better understanding of the events of the next day.

Early on the morning of September 18, Johnson's Provisional Division, to which Robertson's brigade was temporarily attached, advanced from Ringgold toward Reed's Bridge. About 7:30 A.M. Forrest's cavalry, which was moving out in front, began skirmishing with Minty's troopers who were posted along Pea Vine Creek, about a mile east of Chickamauga Creek, and when Johnson's infantry arrived, they forced Minty back toward Reed's Bridge.

During the late morning, an enemy column was observed moving toward Dyer's Bridge, which was about one and one-fourth miles north of Reed's Bridge, and at noon a detachment of Wilder's brigade, consisting of a part of the 72nd Indiana, the 123rd Illinois, and a section of Eli Lilly's 18th Battery, Indiana Light Artillery, all under Abram O. Miller, was sent north from Alexander's Bridge to guard the left flank of Minty's cavalry, who were still fighting at Reed's Bridge.

Finally, at about 2:00 P.M. Minty was driven from the bridge, but he continued to resist until 3:30 P.M., and he then called in Miller's force at Dyer's Bridge and retired upstream toward Crittenden's position at Lee and Gordon's Mills. Johnson's division crossed to the west bank of Chickamauga Creek at 4:30 P.M. and then, according to orders, followed Minty toward Lee and Gordon's Mills.

Meantime, while Johnson and Forrest were engaged with Minty at Reed's Bridge, Walker arrived near Alexander's Bridge about noon with the divisions of Gist and Liddell. Posted near the Alexander house, where they were in position to guard the bridge, were Wilder's brigade of mounted infantry and four guns of Lilly's battery. Walthall's brigade of Liddell's division charged the bridge about noon, and then again about 2:30 P.M., but both attacks were repulsed. Finally, Liddell's division moved downstream to Byram's Ford, about midway between Alexander's Bridge and Reed's Bridge, and, finding it unguarded, began to cross at 3:30 P.M.

Wilder's left flank was threatened when Liddell crossed the creek, but Wilder continued to hold his position near Alexander's Bridge until 5:00 P.M., then withdrew to the west toward the Viniard field. Just before dark he took up a new position about one-half mile east of the La Fayette road. He was joined there by Minty's dismounted cavalry, and also by Miller's command when it arrived from Dyer's Bridge. Also that evening, George F. Dick came up with two regiments of his Second Brigade

of Van Cleve's division and took position on the right of the cavalry. This force held Johnson in check until the morning of September 19, despite a vigorous attack delivered about 9:00 P.M. September 18.

At 4:00 P.M. September 18, 1863, Granger sent Daniel McCook's Second Brigade, Second Division of his Reserve Corps from Rossville to aid Minty at Alexander's Bridge, and at the same time he ordered Whitaker's First Brigade of Steedman's First Division to move out in the direction of Ringgold Bridge (or Red House Bridge). McCook arrived too late to help Minty, but after dark he ran into Evander McNair's brigade of Johnson's division about one mile from Reed's Bridge. He then took position and waited for daylight. During the night he was joined by Mitchell's Second Brigade of Steedman's division.

Whitaker encountered Scott's Brigade of Forrest's cavalry division at the crossing of Spring Creek on the Ringgold road and, after some skirmishing, withdrew to McAfee Church. Scott fell back to Ringgold Bridge.

During the night of September 18, 1863, Bragg's forces continued to cross to the west side of Chickamauga Creek as follows: Gist's division of Walker's Reserve Corps crossed at Byram's Ford and bivouacked near the Alexander house; Law's brigade (commanded by Sheffield) and Benning's brigade of Hood's division (commanded by Law) arrived in the vicinity of Alexander's Bridge and camped for the night; Gracie's Brigade of Preston's Division crossed the creek at Dalton's Ford and bivouacked; Clayton's Brigade of Stewart's Division crossed at Thedford's Ford and halted for the rest of the night; and Cheatham's Division of Polk's Corps bivouacked in line of battle south of Preston's Division.

Meantime, on September 18, 1863, when Rosecrans learned of Bragg's movement down Chickamauga Creek, he began shifting troops to the Federal left to be in position to protect the line of communication of the army with Chattanooga. At 4:00 P.M. Thomas began moving his Fourteenth Corps northward from the vicinity of Pond Spring in McLemore's Cove with orders to form on the left of Crittenden's Twenty-First Corps, north of Lee and Gordon's Mills. Negley's division led the way as far as Crawfish Springs, and then it turned eastward to Glass' Mill, which was located on Chickamauga Creek about two miles east and a little south of Crawfish Springs, and two miles south of Lee and Gordon's Mills. When he arrived there about daylight September 19, Negley relieved Palmer's division of Crittenden's corps, and Palmer then moved to the left of Van Cleve's division, about one mile north of Lee and Gordon's Mills. Palmer in turn relieved Minty's and Wilder's brigades, which then withdrew across the La Fayette road to the west of the Viniard house.

Baird's division of Thomas' corps followed Negley to Crawfish Springs, continuing on past the Widow Glenn house and reaching the Kelly field at the crossroads south of the Kelly house at daylight September 19, 1863. The division first deployed across the La Fayette road, facing south, but it then changed front to the east, facing Chickamauga Creek.

Brannan's division followed Baird to the Kelly field and then, passing to the rear of Baird, marched on north to the McDonald house, on the present-day site of Chickamauga National Military Park Headquarters.

Reynolds, with the brigades of Edward A. King and Turchin, brought up the rear of Fourteenth Corps on its night march from Crawfish Springs, and it did not arrive on the battlefield at Poe's field until about 1:30 P.M. September 19.

Troops of Crittenden's corps also joined the movement toward the left, and they came up in support of Thomas. As noted above, when Palmer's division was relieved by Negley near Glass' Mill, it moved into position about one mile north of Lee and Gordon's Mills. Then about noon September 19, 1863, it was ordered to march north and join Thomas.

About 1:00 P.M. September 19, 1863, Van Cleve left Barnes' brigade of his division at Lee and Gordon's Mills, and with the brigades of Dick and Samuel Beatty moved up to support Palmer.

Wood's division remained near Lee and Gordon's Mills until 3:00 P.M., and it was then ordered to close up on the right of Van Cleve's division.

During the night of September 18, 1863, McCook's corps was finally assembled in McLemore's Cove when Lytle arrived from Dougherty's Gap with his own brigade of Sheridan's division and Dodge's brigade of

Johnson's division. Post's brigade of Davis' division was detached to hold Stevens' Gap. McCook was then ordered to march with the rest of his corps to Crawfish Springs as soon as Thomas had departed. Johnson's division started at dawn September 19, and it was followed by Davis' division and then Sheridan's division.

At 10:15 A.M., while at Crawfish Springs, McCook was assigned command of the troops remaining on the right of the army. At the same time McCook was directed to send Johnson's division to the Widow Glenn's house to report to Thomas. Immediately after Johnson had started, Davis was also ordered with his division to Widow Glenn's. At about that time the advance of Sheridan's column came up, and Sheridan was sent to support the right of Crittenden's corps at Lee and Gordon's Mills. Upon arriving there, Sheridan relieved Negley's division of Thomas' corps, which then withdrew from the fords of Chickamauga Creek and marched to the left to rejoin the corps.

On the morning of September 19, 1863, Gordon, with the three brigades of his Reserve Corps, was generally guarding the road from Rossville to Ringgold, about four miles north of the battlefield.

Mitchell's cavalry was watching the fords on upper Chickamauga Creek.

Battle of September 19, 1863. Early on the morning of September 19, 1863, Daniel McCook reported his encounter of the night before with McNair's Confederate brigade west of Chickamauga Creek, and at 7:30 A.M. Brannan's division was sent out to destroy this brigade, if possible, and to determine what was going on in that area. Van Derveer's brigade advanced on the left along the road running from the McDonald house to Reed's Bridge. Croxton's brigade moved on the right on a road running from the Kelly house to Jay's sawmill, which was located close to Chickamauga Creek, just off the Reed's Bridge road. Connell's brigade was left at McDonald's as a reserve, but it was soon ordered up, first to support Croxton and then to support Van Derveer.

As Croxton's brigade advanced, it met Forrest's dismounted cavalry at the edge of a woods west of Jay's sawmill and drove it back. Walker sent Gist's division, consisting of the brigades of Ector and Wilson, to aid Forrest, and soon Croxton was seriously engaged. Brannan then moved Van Derveer's brigade to the left to form on the left of Croxton. Then, as the fighting developed, the regiments of Connell's brigade were brought up to reinforce Brannan's front line.

As Brannan's division advanced, Baird's division moved forward on its right and rear to protect its right flank. John H. King's brigade was on the left, next to Croxton; Scribner's brigade was on the right; and Starkweather's brigade was held in column to the rear as a reserve. At 10:30 A.M. Starkweather's brigade was moved up to relieve Croxton, who was hard pressed and nearly out of ammunition. Croxton then moved to the rear to replenish his ammunition.

At about the same time, Baird's advance struck the flank of Gist's division, and then Ector and Wilson retired to Jay's sawmill, where they remained until late afternoon. At about 11:00 A.M. Baird learned that a large enemy force was on his right in the direction of Alexander's Bridge. This was Liddell's division of Walker's Reserve Corps. Baird then ordered John H. King's brigade to change front to the right, and while it was executing this order, it was assailed on its right flank by Liddell and was broken and driven back in disorder. Scribner's and Starkweather's brigades were also forced back, but Van Derveer and Connell held their ground.

Johnson's division of McCook's corps reached the Poe field, about a mile and a half south of Kelly's, about 12:00–12:30 P.M. It then advanced on the right of Baird to the D. C. Reed house east of the crossing of the Brotherton and Alexander's Bridge roads. Willich's brigade was on the right, Baldwin's brigade was on the left, and Dodge's brigade was in reserve. Then Johnson's division, with help from Brannan's and Baird's re-formed divisions, drove Liddell back about a half-mile to some high ground near Jay's sawmill.

Shortly after noon, almost immediately after he had driven Liddell back, Johnson became engaged with Cheatham's division of Polk's corps. This division had moved forward at 11:00 A.M. from the vicinity of Dalton's Ford, where it had crossed Chickamauga Creek early that morning and then formed in line of battle about a mile to the north and northwest of the Alexander house, directly in rear of Liddell's division. The brigades of Jackson, Pres-

ton Smith, and Wright were on the front line, in that order from left to right. The brigades of Maney and Strahl were in reserve.

Meantime, additional reinforcements were arriving to support Thomas' troops that were engaged on the Federal left. Palmer's and Van Cleve's divisions of Crittenden's corps were coming up and entering the line on the right of Johnson. Palmer's division had marched up the La Fayette road, and at about 12:30 P.M. had formed on the right of Johnson in the woods east of the Poe farm. The division then advanced with the brigades en echelon to the right, with Hazen's brigade on the left, Cruft's brigade to the right and rear of Hazen, and Grose's brigade to the right and rear of Cruft. Palmer's advance encountered Cheatham's division at 1:30 P.M. near the Brock house, south of the Brotherton road that ran to Reed's Bridge.

In response to an order of 1:00 P.M., Van Cleve left Barnes' brigade at Lee and Gordon's Mills and moved rapidly to the left with the brigades of Samuel Beatty and Dick to support Palmer. About 2:30 P.M. Van Cleve formed in line of battle east of Brotherton's, on the right of Palmer, with Samuel Beatty's brigade on the left, on the right of Grose, and Dick's brigade on the right of Beatty. Van Cleve arrived in time to aid Johnson and Palmer in repulsing Cheatham's attack.

Reynolds' division was the last of Fourteenth Corps to arrive, and Reynolds reached Poe's field with the brigades of Edward A. King and Turchin at 1:30 P.M. He then sent Turchin to support Hazen and Cruft, who were under attack by Cheatham. He also sent Edward A. King's brigade to aid Van Cleve. King then formed on the right of Dick's brigade to the southeast of Brotherton's. For a time, Turchin protected Hazen's left, but at 3:30 P.M. he relieved Hazen's brigade, which then retired to Poe's field for more ammunition.

Farther to the left Brannan's division, which had been fighting since early morning, withdrew about 2:00 P.M. to a ridge about one-half mile east of the La Fayette road, and an hour later it moved on back to that road.

Meantime, on the Confederate side, Stewart's division of Buckner's corps had crossed Chickamauga Creek at Thedford's Ford during the night of September 18 and the morning of September 19, 1863, and shortly after noon it followed

Cheatham's division down the creek for about three-fourths of a mile. It then turned to the left, and at 2:30 P.M. it formed in line of battle east of Poe's and Brotherton's, on the left of Cheatham's division. It then advanced in column of brigades, with Clayton's brigade in front, then Brown's brigade, and Bate's brigade in the rear.

At about the time of Stewart's attack, Van Cleve's division was advancing to support Palmer, and it soon became engaged with Stewart. There was savage fighting in the area for a time, and at about 3:15 P.M. Brown's brigade advanced and relieved Clayton. Dick and Samuel Beatty were forced back, but then the line was strengthened when Edward A. King's brigade of Reynolds' division came up and formed on the right of Dick.

Van Cleve's reinforced line charged and drove Stewart back for some distance through the woods. Bate's brigade then came into line on the left of Brown's brigade and immediately advanced, forcing Samuel Beatty's and Dick's brigades back across the La Fayette road, carrying Edward A. King's brigade with them.

Van Cleve formed a new line along a low ridge in the Brotherton fields, south of the Brotherton house, and west of the La Fayette road. Bate and Clayton, the latter followed by Brown, again advanced and, after a stubborn Federal resistance, broke through the center of Van Cleve's line, moving across the Glenn-Kelly road and onto the Dyer farm. Clayton's brigade penetrated as far as the Dyer tanyard, which was only about one-fourth mile from the Dry Valley road and three-fourths mile north of the Widow Glenn's house. Samuel Beatty's and Dick's brigades were forced back to and beyond the Dry Valley road. Bate crossed the La Fayette road farther north near the Brotherton house against opposition from the brigades of Grose and Hazen.

When Thomas learned that Stewart had broken through Van Cleve's line, he ordered Brannan to move down from the Federal left between the La Fayette road and the Glenn-Kelly road to reinforce the center.

When Hazen's brigade of Palmer's division had obtained more ammunition near the Poe house, it moved south, with its left on the La Fayette road, toward the Brotherton house and field to support Reynolds' line. By that time, Van Cleve had been driven from the Brotherton field, but Hazen, with help from Reynolds' troops, held his position for about one-half hour. Grose's brigade of Palmer's division was sent to support Hazen, and he had scarcely begun to move when the enemy attacked Turchin's brigade of Reynolds' division and Cruft's brigade of Palmer's division. These two brigades were in position east of Brotherton's and along the road running from Brotherton's to Reed's Bridge, facing southeast. As the pressure mounted, the brigades of Hazen, Grose, Cruft, and Turchin were driven back.

Hazen and Reynolds then collected all available guns from the batteries of Palmer's and Reynolds' divisions, and these opened with a heavy fire on Stewart's men. The batteries engaged were as follows: William E. Standart's Battery B, 1st Ohio Light Artillery (commanded by Norman A. Baldwin); Giles J. Cockerill's Battery F, 1st Ohio Light Artillery; Harry C. Cushing's Battery H, 4th United States Artillery; Francis L. D. Russell's Battery M, 4th United States Artillery; Samuel J. Harris' 19th Battery, Indiana Light Artillery; and George R. Swallow's 7th Battery, Indiana Light Artillery. In addition, Wilder's brigade of Reynolds' division, with its Spencer repeating rifles, and Eli Lilly's 18th Battery, Indiana Light Artillery, aided in repulsing the enemy attack and driving Stewart's troops back across the La Fayette road.

Another important factor in hastening Stewart's withdrawal from the Dyer farm was the approach of Brannan's and Negley's divisions toward his isolated position. While Brannan was marching southward, west of the La Fayette road, toward Brotherton's, which was in the rear of Stewart, Negley's division of Thomas' corps, which had been retained at Crawfish Springs during the morning, came up from the south to Widow Glenn's. It then moved across the Glenn and Dyer farms toward Clayton's brigade. With the appearance of Negley's division on his flank, Stewart withdrew his division past the Brotherton house to the east side of the La Fayette road.

On the morning of September 19, 1863, when the fighting began on Thomas' front, Davis was ordered forward from Crawfish Springs to the Widow Glenn's with the two brigades remaining with his division. Upon arriving there, Davis marched eastward to occupy the unguarded line that ran south from the right of Van Cleve's division to the left of Wood's division, near Lee and Gordon's Mills. At 2:00 P.M., at about the time that Van Cleve's division formed on the right of Palmer, Davis arrived at the front and took position a few hundred yards east of the La Fayette road, in front of the Viniard house. Heg's brigade was formed on the left of the division line, north of the Viniard house, and Carlin's brigade was placed on the right, in front of and to the south of the Viniard house.

Barnes' brigade of Van Cleve's division, which had been left at Lee and Gordon's Mills when the division moved north to support Thomas, had also been ordered to the Viniard farm, and it arrived at about the same time as Davis. Barnes was then placed on the right of Carlin, on the extreme right of the Union line.

When the above troops were in position, there still remained a gap of nearly one-half mile between the left of Heg's brigade and the right of Edward A. King's brigade of Reynolds' division, which had arrived and formed on the right of Van Cleve. This interval was unprotected except by Wilder's brigade, which was in position some distance to the rear, between the Widow Glenn's and the La Fayette road.

The arrival of Davis' division and Barnes' brigade was opportune, because at that time Hood was preparing his troops, then about one-half mile to the east, for an attack toward the La Fayette road. Hood was in command of a temporary corps consisting of his own division of Longstreet's corps and Bushrod R. Johnson's Provisional Division. As noted above, Johnson's division and Robertson's brigade of Hood's division had marched to their present position during the late evening of September 18, 1863, and they were joined later by Hood's other brigades, commanded by Sheffield and Benning, which had arrived from Ringgold. Law had been in command of Hood's division since the latter was wounded at Gettysburg, and he remained in command of the division at Chickamauga while Hood was in charge of the temporary corps.

At 2:30–3:00 P.M. Hood's line advanced, with Bushrod R. Johnson's division on the Confederate right and Law's division on the left and rear. Fulton's brigade of Johnson's division and Robertson's brigade of Law's division struck Carlin's brigade and forced it back across the La

Fayette road to a position west of the Viniard house. Then Carlin's right, with the help of Barnes, attacked and regained the La Fayette road. Farther to the Union left, Benning's brigade advanced on the front of Heg's brigade, and at the same time Gregg and McNair attacked Heg's left flank. Heg was killed, and John A. Martin assumed command of the brigade. Martin was pushed back across the road, but finally he reestablished his line and was able to hold his ground.

About 4:00 P.M. Wood's division, having been relieved at Lee and Gordon's Mills by Lytle's brigade of Sheridan's division, came up in support of Davis. Buell's brigade was placed in rear of Carlin and Heg (Martin), and it became engaged about 4:30 P.M. Harker's brigade moved to the north end of the Viniard farm, and it attacked Bushrod R. Johnson's exposed flank, south of Brotherton's, and drove the division back across the La Fayette road.

Earlier that day, September 19, 1863, Sheridan had moved from Crawfish Springs to Lee and Gordon's Mills to watch the fords of Chickamauga Creek, but then he was ordered to march with the brigades of Bradley and Laiboldt to support the troops fighting at the Viniard farm. Upon arrival there, Bradley was sent to reinforce Carlin and Barnes on the Federal right, and he immediately attacked and drove the enemy back. Bradley was wounded, and he was succeeded in command of the brigade by Nathan H. Walworth. Laiboldt's brigade then came up on the right of Bradley (Walworth) to secure that flank.

Wilder's brigade also aided in driving back the enemy attacks on Davis' left during the late afternoon.

About sunset, after the arrival of the brigades of Wood's and Sheridan's divisions, Davis' division was relieved, and it retired a few hundred yards west of Viniard's, where it bivouacked for the night.

Just before dark, Hindman's division of Polk's corps and Preston's division of Buckner's corps arrived and took position on the left of Hood. At that time the fighting on the southern end of the battlefield was subsiding. Trigg's brigade of Preston's division was sent to support Hood, but no other brigades of Preston and Hindman were engaged.

Meantime, during the afternoon of September 19, 1863, Cleburne's division of Hill's corps marched down the east side of Chickamauga Creek to

Thedford's Ford, and it crossed the creek there at 4:30 P.M. during Hood's battle at the Viniard farm. Cleburne turned to the right and at sunset arrived in front of Johnson's division on the Union left. Cleburne then formed in line of battle, with his right at Jay's sawmill and his left extending about a mile to the south and southwest. Lucius E. Polk's brigade was on the right, Sterling A. M. Wood's brigade was in the center, and Deshler's brigade was on the left.

Richard W. Johnson's division was in line about a mile east of Brotherton's, with Dodge's brigade on the right, Willich's brigade in the center, and Baldwin's brigade on the left. Johnson's division was unsupported, and the nearest Federal troops on that flank belonged to Turchin's brigade, which was about one-half mile distant. Baird's division was to the left of Johnson, and Scribner's and Starkweather's brigades were moved up to support Johnson. John H. King's brigade was left on the road from McDonald's to Reed's Bridge to hold the ground vacated by Brannan's division and the other two brigades of Baird's division.

Thomas was preparing to move his two divisions on the left back to new positions at the Kelly field, but before they could be withdrawn, Cleburne's division attacked from the D. C. Reed farm about dark. Cleburne's left overlapped the right of Dodge's brigade, and Dodge, having discovered a considerable gap between his brigade and Willich's brigade on his right, was in the process of adjusting his line when Cleburne struck. Dodge was forced to fall back, and Willich and Baldwin were ordered to retire abreast of Dodge. Willich fell back as ordered, but at that time Baldwin was under heavy attack in the Winfrey field, and he did not feel that he could successfully disengage. He decided to remain where he was and attempt to prevent the enemy from advancing farther. Baldwin was killed during the engagement, and he was succeeded in command of the brigade by William W. Berry.

Preston Smith's brigade of Cheatham's division came up to support Deshler's brigade, which was being pushed hard by Johnston. Smith attacked to the north and northwest of the Alexander house. Smith was killed at about the same time as Baldwin, and Alfred J. Vaughan, Jr. assumed command of the brigade. Scribner's and Starkweather's brigades of Baird's division, which were on the left of Johnson, were also attacked.

Fighting continued for about an hour in the darkness, and then Baird and Johnson retired to the new positions that had been assigned, where they spent the night.

Battle of September 20, 1863. During the night of September 19 and the early morning of September 20, both armies prepared for a resumption of the battle during the coming day.

On the Union left, Thomas moved his troops back a short distance to a new position east of the La Fayette road, and he strengthened this line with breastworks of rails, logs, and anything that would stop an enemy bullet. The line selected by Thomas ran to the southeast from the McDonald house, on the La Fayette road, along the Alexander's Bridge road to the northeast corner of the Kelly field; then along the eastern side of the Kelly field, which was about one-half mile east of the La Fayette road, to the southeast corner of the field; and from there it curved back along the south side of the field to the La Fayette road, a short distance north of the Poe house.

Early on the morning of September 20, 1863, this line was held, from left to right in the order named, by the divisions of Baird, Johnson, Palmer, and Reynolds.

Baird's division of Thomas' corps held the northeast corner of the Kelly field, about one-fourth mile east of the La Fayette road, with Scribner's brigade at the angle of the line, Starkweather's brigade on the right, facing east, and John H. King's brigade on the left, along the south side of the Alexander's Bridge road, facing to the northeast.

Johnson's division of McCook's corps was on the right of Baird, with Dodge's brigade on the left, Berry's brigade (formerly Baldwin's) on the right, and Willich's brigade in reserve. When Baird formed his division during the night, it did not reach to the McDonald house as intended, and early on the morning of September 20, Dodge's brigade was detached and sent to the left of Baird. At 9:00 A.M. Willich's brigade moved up to support Berry.

Palmer's division of Crittenden's corps occupied the line on the right of Johnson, facing southeast, with Cruft's brigade on the left, Hazen's brigade on the right, and Grose's brigade in reserve. Palmer's right was at the southeast corner of the Kelly field.

Reynolds' division of Thomas' corps was on the

right of Palmer, a short distance beyond the south edge of the Kelly field. Turchin's brigade was next to Palmer, facing southeast, and Edward A. King's brigade was to the right and rear of Turchin. King's line was slightly retired, facing south, with its right on the La Fayette road a short distance north of the Poe house.

Brannan's division of Thomas' corps bivouacked on the Dyer farm during the night of September 19, 1863, but before daylight the next morning it moved up and took position on the right of Reynolds' division, facing east. Croxton's brigade was on the left, with its left a short distance west of the right of Edward A. King's brigade; Connell's brigade was on the right of Croxton, along the southern edge of the Poe field; and Van Derveer's brigade was to the rear in reserve.

Negley's division of Thomas' corps, which had arrived on the field from Crawfish Springs during the evening of September 19, 1863, and which had aided in driving Stewart's division back across the La Fayette road, bivouacked that night along the west side of the Brotherton field, south of the Dyer road. Stanley's brigade was on the left of the division, west of the Brotherton house; Sirwell's brigade was on the right; and John Beatty's brigade was in reserve.

The remaining divisions of the army were not on the front line early on the morning of September 20, 1863, but were in position to the right and rear of Brannan and Negley. Wood's division of Crittenden's corps had moved back after midnight from the vicinity of the Viniard farm to the Widow Glenn's; early on the morning of September 20, it took position in reserve, west of the Dry Valley road, on the eastern slope of Missionary Ridge.

Van Cleve's division of Crittenden's corps, which had been driven back from Brotherton's during Stewart's attack the evening before, bivouacked that night west of the Dry Valley road.

The divisions of Davis and Sheridan of McCook's corps moved back from the Viniard farm during the night, and on the morning of September 20, 1863, they occupied the high ground near the Widow Glenn's. Lytle's brigade came up from Lee and Gordon's Mills and rejoined Sheridan's division. At 10:00 A.M. Davis moved to the left and connected with the right of Van Cleve's division near Lytle's Station.

On the morning of September 20, 1863, Wilder's brigade of Reynolds' division was ordered to take position on the right of McCook's line and to report to McCook for orders. Upon reporting, Wilder was directed to move his brigade to the crest of an eastern spur of Missionary Ridge, about one-fourth mile south of Widow Glenn's.

Mitchell's cavalry was on the far right of the army guarding the upper fords of Chickamauga Creek. Granger's three brigades of the Reserve Corps were at and near McAfee Church. Minty's cavalry, which reported to Granger at daylight September 20, 1863, was posted at Missionary Mills on Missionary Ridge to cover Granger's left flank.

Meantime, in the woods east of the La Fayette road, Bragg was completing his preparations for an attack on the left of Thomas' line, which was to begin early on the morning of September 20, 1863. Longstreet had arrived on the battlefield from Ringgold about 11:00 P.M. September 19 and reported to Bragg. Also arriving that night were Joseph B. Kershaw's brigade and Benjamin G. Humphreys' brigade of Lafayette McLaws' division of Longstreet's corps. McLaws personally was in Atlanta at that time, and Kershaw was in command of both his own brigade and Humphreys' brigade.

During the night, Bragg divided his army into a right wing under Polk and a left wing under Longstreet. Polk's command consisted of the divisions of Breckinridge and Cleburne of Hill's corps, Cheatham's division of Polk's corps, and Liddell's and Gist's divisions of Walker's Reserve Corps. Forrest's cavalry, which was operating on the Confederate right, was under Bragg's direct orders. Longstreet's command consisted of Law's division (Hood was commanding the corps) and Kershaw's two brigades of McLaws' division; Bushrod R. Johnson's division, which had been assigned to Hood's (Longstreet's) corps; Hindman's division of Polk's corps, which had been assigned to Longstreet; and Preston's and Stewart's divisions of Buckner's corps.

Bragg's plan for the attack that morning was similar to that of the day before, which was to turn the Federal left and cut off the Army of the Cumberland from Chattanooga, and then drive it back into McLemore's Cove. Bragg ordered Polk to make the initial attack on the Union left at daylight

September 20, 1863 with the divisions of Breckinridge and Cleburne of Hill's corps. The other divisions of the army were then to attack in succession from right to left.

Cleburne's division was already in its assigned position, but it was necessary to bring up Breckinridge's division from Lee and Gordon's Mills. During the night of September 19, 1863, Breckinridge crossed Chickamauga Creek at Alexander's Bridge and marched northward past the rear of Cleburne's division, and early on the morning of September 20 he was in position to attack on the right of Cleburne, on the extreme right of Bragg's infantry line.

Hill's corps was to advance first, and Cheatham's division of Polk's corps, which was on the left of Cleburne, was directed to follow on the left of Hill. Walker was ordered to hold his corps in reserve. All was ready for the Confederate advance by daylight September 20.

While Hill was getting his troops in position and was waiting for orders to advance, Rosecrans was making every effort to strengthen his line in anticipation of an attack that he was certain would come that day. At 2:00 A.M. September 20, 1863, Thomas learned that Baird's division was unable to cover the ground to the Reed's Bridge road, on which the McDonald house stood, and he requested that Negley's division be moved up in the rear of Baird's division to cover that flank. Rosecrans immediately ordered Negley to report to Thomas, and he also directed McCook to cover Negley's original position in the line after the latter had departed for the left flank. A short time later Rosecrans learned that neither Negley nor McCook had moved, and he then ordered Wood to move up from his position west of the Dry Valley road and relieve Negley so that the latter could carry out his earlier orders to move to the left. This order resulted in a sequence of events that were to have a profound influence on the outcome of the battle that day.

For some reason, Wood was slow in coming up to relieve Negley, and finally at 8:00 A.M. Rosecrans personally started John Beatty's reserve brigade of Negley's division northward to strengthen Thomas' left. Rosecrans later found Wood, and he severely castigated him in the presence of his staff for his tardiness in relieving Negley, and in doing so charged him with disobedience of orders. Fol-

lowing this encounter, Wood marched eastward with his division to relieve Negley. Wagner's brigade of Wood's division was in Chattanooga, and Wood thus had only two of his brigades under his immediate command. To bring the division to full strength, Barnes' brigade of Van Cleve's division was ordered at 11:00 A.M. to accompany Wood and act under his orders.

Negley's two brigades were not relieved until between 9:00 and 9:30 A.M., and then Sirwell's brigade was sent back to reestablish the former line of the division and guard the ammunition train. At 10:00 A.M. Negley left Sirwell and marched with Stanley's brigade to take position on the left of Baird. While on the march, Thomas ordered Negley to take charge of all available artillery and mass it on the elevated ground at the eastern end of what later became known as Horseshoe Ridge. Negley posted the guns in rear of Brannan and Reynolds so as to cover the ground to the left and rear of Baird's division. He also brought Sirwell's brigade up on the ridge to support the artillery. Stanley's brigade moved on to the north, following John Beatty, to hold the line to the left of Baird.

After Negley's departure to reinforce the left of Thomas' line, Wood formed his division on Negley's former line, which was in a fringe of woods behind the house and fields of the Brotherton farm. Wood's line extended southward from the right of Brannan's division for about one-fourth mile, with Barnes' brigade on the left next to Brannan, Harker's brigade in the center, and Buell's brigade on the right. McCook, who was personally present on the front line at that time, found that Wood's division did not have the battle strength of Negley's division, and that it did not occupy all of Negley's breastworks. The right of this line was thus unoccupied. McCook then directed Sheridan to send forward a brigade of his division to complete the line, and at about 11:00 A.M. Laiboldt's brigade was on its way.

Meantime, Davis had moved with his two brigades to the left from the Widow Glenn's house, and at 10:00 A.M. connected with the right of Van Cleve's division near Lytle's Station. Both Davis and Van Cleve then moved eastward toward the front line. Upon arrival there, Davis was ordered to take position on the right of Wood, Carlin's brigade was placed in the works on the right of Buell's brigade, and Martin's brigade (formerly Heg's) was formed in rear of Carlin. These changes were made just after McCook had asked Sheridan for a brigade, and when Laiboldt's brigade arrived, it was formed in column as a support on the right and rear of Carlin's brigade.

Van Cleve, with the brigades of Samuel Beatty and Dick, came up in rear of of the Poe farm, and then Dick was ordered to move with his brigade to the left of Thomas.

At 9:00 A.M. Barnes' brigade was relieved from serving with Wood's division, and it too was then ordered to the left. An hour later, at about the time that Hill began his attack on Thomas' line, Van Derveer's brigade of Brannan's division was also ordered to follow Negley's division, Dick's brigade, and Barnes' brigade to the vicinity of the Kelly field.

Although Polk had been ordered to begin his attack at daylight September 20, 1863, there was much confusion at the various Confederate headquarters that morning, and Hill's corps, which was to begin the attack, did not get under way until 9:45 A.M. Breckinridge's division then advanced on the Confederate right of the Alexander's Bridge road, with Adams' brigade on the right, Stovall's brigade in the center, and Helm's brigade on the left. The two right brigades passed beyond the left of Thomas' line to the vicinity of the Cloud house, which was on the La Fayette road, and Helm's brigade approached obliquely against Baird's breastworks north of the Kelly field at a point where it was held by Scribner's brigade and John H. King's brigade of Baird's division and Dodge's brigade of Johnson's division on their left.

John Beatty's brigade of Negley's division, which had been sent earlier to support Thomas, was arriving on the left of Baird as Breckinridge attacked, and it was quickly moved northward about one-fourth mile to the vicinity of the McDonald house, where it formed across the La Fayette road facing north.

As Adams and Stovall advanced, they swung around to the left until they faced south, and they then moved toward John Beatty's line and the Kelly field beyond. Stovall's brigade was on the east side of the La Fayette road, and Adams' brigade was on the west side of the road. Beatty's brigade resisted stubbornly but was slowly pushed back; during the fighting two of his regiments became separated, and they did not again appear on that part of the field.

Stovall's brigade was soon checked by the left of Baird's line, but Adams' brigade pushed on. Then Stanley's brigade of Negley's division arrived and joined in the fighting on the right of John Beatty. At 11:00 A.M. Van Derveer's brigade of Brannan's division arrived and went into action on the right of Stanley. Dick's brigade of Van Cleve's division also came up and went into position supporting Stanley. Together these brigades drove Adams back about one-half mile to the vicinity of the McDonald house. Adams was wounded and captured, and Randall L. Gibson assumed command of his brigade.

While Adams and Stovall were advancing on the right, Helm's brigade struck Baird's breastworks at the northeast corner of the Kelly field, but it was checked there by a devastating fire from infantry and artillery. Despite repeated efforts to advance, the attack was repulsed, and after suffering terrible losses, including Helm, who was killed, the brigade withdrew. Joseph H. Lewis assumed command of Helm's brigade.

About fifteen minutes after Breckinridge attacked, Cleburne's division on his left moved forward along the left of the Alexander's Bridge road toward the Union breastworks that ran along the east side of the Kelly field. Lucius E. Polk's brigade was on the right, Sterling A. M. Wood's brigade was in the center, and James Deshler's brigade was on the left. Polk's brigade advanced against the line held by Starkweather, commanding Baird's right brigade, and Berry's brigade of Johnson's division (formerly commanded by Baldwin). Polk's attack was repulsed with heavy losses. Wood's brigade advanced against the line held by Palmer's division and Turchin's brigade, which held the left of Reynolds' line. The left of Wood's line advanced almost to the Poe house, near the La Fayette road, but it was then driven back, and Polk's brigade was withdrawn from the line.

Because the two wings of Bragg's army were converging as they advanced, Deshler's brigade soon encountered Stewart's division, which was advancing on the right of Longstreet's Left Wing, and it was then thrown completely out of the line and into the rear of the Left Wing. Deshler was ordered to move to the right to fill the gap created by Wood's withdrawal, and to connect with the left of Polk's brigade. While executing this movement, Deschler was killed, and Roger Q. Mills assumed command of his brigade.

Cleburne's division was then withdrawn about 400 yards to shelter behind the crest of a hill.

At 11:00 A.M. Stewart's division moved forward under direct orders from Bragg and, with Wood's brigade of Cleburne's division on its right, attacked the line held by Brannan and Reynolds. Stewart's advance reached a point about 200–300 yards beyond the La Fayette road near the Poe house, but it could go no farther, and it was then driven back by heavy artillery and infantry fire.

As the attacks by Breckinridge, Cleburne, and Stewart were coming to an end, Leonidas Polk was preparing for a new attack on the Union left. John K. Jackson's brigade of Cheatham's division was sent to occupy the position vacated by Helm's brigade, and Walker was directed to move with his Reserve Corps and report to Hill for orders. Gist, commanding Walker's division, advanced with the brigades of Colquitt (Gist's brigade), Ector, and Wilson to a position between Breckinridge's division on the right and Cleburne's division on the left. Colquitt attacked the Union breastworks at the northeast corner of the Kelly field, where Helm had been so decisively repulsed earlier in the day, and his brigade was also driven back with heavy losses. Colquitt was killed, and Leroy Napier assumed command of the brigade.

Liddell's two brigades were then moved up to support the front line. Walthall moved his brigade to the left of Gist to support Cleburne. He failed to contact Polk's brigade, however, and soon came under the fire of Johnson's division and was driven back. Govan's brigade moved to the right, then advanced westward between the Kelly field and the McDonald house to the La Fayette road. It then turned to the south and moved forward to the north end of the Kelly field. There the left of Govan's line struck the right of John H. King's brigade and Barnes' brigade and was stopped. The right of the brigade continued on but was driven back when it ran into a terrible fire from the 15th Ohio and 49th Ohio and Wilbur F. Goodspeed's Battery A, 1st Ohio Light Artillery of Willich's brigade.

By noon September 20, 1863, all troops of Polk's Right Wing had retired out of range of Thomas' line, and they were not engaged again until late in the afternoon, when Rosecrans' army was withdrawing toward McFarland's Gap in Missionary Ridge.

During the morning, Longstreet formed the troops of his Left Wing for the attack that was to begin after the troops on the right had become engaged. Longstreet formed his command in a column of assault on the left of Stewart's division, with Bushrod R. Johnson's division in front, then Law's division (Hood's) behind Johnson, and Kershaw with two brigades of McLaws' division in rear of Law. Hindman's division of Leonidas Polk's corps, which had been assigned to Longstreet, was on the left of Johnson's division, and Preston's division of Buckner's corps was in reserve to the left and rear of Hindman.

Johnson prepared to attack on a front of two brigades, which were formed about 600 yards east of the La Fayette road, and their line extended from the Poe farm on the Confederate right to a point south of the Brotherton house on the left. McNair's brigade was on the right, Johnson's brigade (commanded by Fulton) was on the left, and Gregg's brigade was in reserve. Gregg had been wounded the day before, and his brigade was commanded by Cyrus A. Sugg.

While Longstreet was thus preparing to attack, trouble was developing opposite his front on the Union center and right. Shortly after 10:00 A.M. Sanford C. Kellogg of Thomas' staff passed along the Glenn-Kelly road on his way to Rosecrans' headquarters at the Widow Glenn's to ask for reinforcements. As he passed the rear of the Poe field, he did not see the men of Brannan's division because they were posted in a wooded area, and at 10:30 A.M. he reported to Rosecrans that a part of his line was unoccupied. Believing that a wide gap existed between the left of Thomas J. Wood's division and the right of Reynolds' division, Rosecrans directed Frank S. Bond, aide de camp, to issue an order to Wood that he believed would correct this situation. This is the now famous order to Wood directing him to "close up on Reynolds as fast as possible and support him." The intent of the order was for Wood to close to the left on Reynolds, but with Brannan's division actually intervening, this order was technically impossible to execute.

Wood received Bond's order about 11:00 A.M. and, possibly remembering Rosecrans' reprimand an hour or so earlier for disobedience of orders, he immediately ordered Harker and Buell to move their brigades at the double quick. Contrary to the spirit of the order, Wood pulled his two brigades out of the line, leaving a gap one-fourth mile wide at the Brotherton farm, and started them marching northward in column along the rear of Brannan's division to report to Reynolds. About ten minutes after Wood's brigades had pulled out of the breastworks at Brotherton's, Hood's three divisions advanced directly toward that part of the Union line.

McNair's and Fulton's leading brigades of Johnson's division crossed the La Fayette road and passed the Brotherton house, one brigade on each side, then entered the gap left by Wood. The only opposition that they encountered was from the flanking fire from Davis' division on their left and Brannan's division on their right. Johnson then simply marched straight ahead, across the Dyer fields, toward the Dyer house.

Johnson's reserve brigade under Sugg came up on the right of McNair, striking Brannan's right brigade under Connell and driving it back in confusion to the north and west. The enemy then moved on Croxton's brigade, which, with its flank unprotected, also broke and fled to the rear. Reynolds refused the right of his line, which then faced south near the Kelly house, and he continued to hold this position during the afternoon.

Brannan collected as many of his men as he could rally, and moved back with them to the soon-to-be-famous Horseshoe Ridge, where he began to establish a defensive position.

Samuel Beatty's brigade of Van Cleve's division, which had been ordered to the front that morning, arrived in rear of Brannan's division at about the same time that Connell's brigade gave way, and then it too was struck on the flank and driven back in disorder. Some regiments and parts of regiments of Beatty's brigade later joined Brannan on the ridge.

Harker's brigade of Wood's division, which was the leading brigade on the march to support Reynolds, was beyond the reach of Hood's attack, but Buell's brigade had scarcely moved the distance of a brigade front when it was struck on the right flank and driven in disorder from the field. Buell was able to rally only a part of one regiment, the 58th Indiana, but with this small fragment of his command, he fell back to Horseshoe Ridge, where he remained with Brannan during the rest of the afternoon.

After Harker's brigade had passed Reynolds' division on its way north, it halted to await orders, and was then directed to move back and help contain the Confederate advance. Harker advanced against Robertson's brigade of Law's division, which was following Johnson toward the Dyer fields. A sharp engagement then ensued near the Glenn-Kelly road, and Robertson was forced to fall back until Kershaw's brigade came up in support. Hood was wounded during the action and left the field. A short time later Kershaw advanced, and Harker's brigade, under the direction of Wood, withdrew to Horseshoe Ridge and formed on the left of Brannan.

About 1:00 P.M. Sirwell's brigade was sent to help check the enemy advance on the left and rear of Negley's artillery position on the eastern slope of the ridge, and it too was driven back in confusion.

Meantime, Johnson had pushed on to the Dyer house and then onto a ridge about one-fourth mile beyond. The Vittetoe house (also spelled Vidito and Viditoe) was to his right and front, and the Dry Valley was a short distance beyond. Horseshoe Ridge, on which the Federal troops were then assembling, was about one-half to three-fourths of a mile to the north of Johnson's position. During his advance, Johnson had moved ahead of all supporting troops, and about noon he halted and asked for reinforcements.

When Hood's divisions advanced shortly after 11:00 A.M., Hindman's division moved forward on their left on a front of about one-fourth mile, with Deas' brigade on the right, Manigault's brigade on the left, and J. Patton Anderson's brigade in reserve. Hindman crossed the La Fayette road and quickly overwhelmed Carlin's and John A. Martin's (formerly Heg's) brigades of Davis' division, driving them in complete rout from the field. Post's brigade of Davis' division was with the cavalry on the extreme Union right and was not engaged.

McCook quickly deployed Laiboldt's brigade of Sheridan's division and ordered it to advance through Davis' disorganized troops in an attempt to stop Hindman, but this brigade too was broken and driven to the rear. Sheridan's other two brigades, under William H. Lytle and Nathan H. Walworth, had earlier been ordered to support Thomas, and they were in column marching to the left as Hindman approached. They were struck by Anderson's brigade and were forced to fall back to the left, where they resisted for a time, but they were finally driven back toward McFarland's Gap. Lytle was killed in this engagement, and Silas Miller assumed command of his brigade. When Hindman approached the Widow Glenn's, Wilder's brigade, with the 39th Indiana Mounted Infantry of Willich's brigade, engaged Manigault's brigade and succeeded in driving it back to the La Fayette road. Trigg's brigade of Preston's division then came up, and Wilder withdrew. Manigault later rejoined his division.

Only a short time after the enemy breakthrough at the Brotherton farm, the entire Federal right had been overwhelmed, and the troops were streaming back to the north along the Dry Valley road toward McFarland's Gap, and Rossville on beyond. Rosecrans, McCook, and Crittenden were also cut off from Thomas' Left Wing by Longstreet's advance, and they fell back with the troops of the Right Wing and finally made their way to Chattanooga. This left Thomas, as the senior officer, in command of all Union troops remaining on the field. These consisted of the divisions of Baird, Johnson, Palmer, and Reynolds, which remained in position behind their breastworks east of the La Fayette road at the Kelly field, and also of those troops that were assembling under Wood and Brannan on Horseshoe Ridge. Early in the afternoon, Thomas arrived at the Snodgrass house and established his headquarters only a hundred yards in rear of the lines of Wood and Brannan.

The position on which the remnants of the right of the army began to assemble after the breakthrough at the Brotherton farm was on a curving ridge, concave to the south, which extended eastward for about one-half mile from the base of Missionary Ridge. It began at the Dry Valley road, a short distance north of the Vittetoe house, and terminated in an open field a short distance west of the La Fayette road. The summit of the ridge was cut by some shallow depressions, and because of these there were three slight elevations or hills on the ridge that were of significance during the fighting on the afternoon of September 20, 1863.

The first elevation was at the eastern end of the ridge, and from this crest the slopes descended gently toward the La Fayette road to the east and to the Snodgrass farmlands to the north. The crest was about 200 yards south of the Snodgrass house and almost due west of the Kelly house. For convenience in this discussion, this hill is designated as Hill No. 1. Hill No. 2 was about 200 yards to the west and a little north of Hill No. 1, and it was about twenty feet higher than the latter. An observation tower was later built on Hill No. 2. Hill No. 3 was about 175 yards west and a little south of Hill No. 2, and it was about ten feet lower than the latter. From Hill No. 3 the ridge extended to the southwest for about three-eighths of a mile to the Dry Valley road.

Various names have been used to designate this ridge, or parts of it, and these should be clarified before attempting to describe the troop positions and the fighting that occurred there during the afternoon of September 20, 1863. In Confederate accounts of the battle, the ridge has been called Horseshoe Ridge, although it does not have the shape of a horseshoe, and it probably did not have that appearance to the Confederate officers who used that name. Many writers refer to the Federal position as being on Snodgrass Hill, although, as noted above, the position was not on a single hill but rather on a long ridge along which there were slight elevations. Further, it should be noted that the ridge could not in its entirety realistically be called Snodgrass Hill because the Snodgrass house and farmlands were at the extreme eastern end of the ridge, and the house was about 200 yards north of the crest that has been described above as Hill No. 1. Still other accounts refer to the position occupied by Brannan and Wood as Snodgrass Hill, and the western part of the ridge, later occupied by Steedman's division, as Horseshoe Ridge. To simplify matters in this account of the battle, the entire ridge on which Federal forces fought on the afternoon and evening of September 20, 1863 is here referred to as Horseshoe Ridge, and the separate elevations are called Hill No. 1, Hill No. 2, and Hill No. 3.

At the time of Longstreet's attack, during the late afternoon of September 20, the only Union troops on the high ground west of the La Fayette road belonged to William Sirwell's brigade of Negley's division and the artillery that Negley had collected to protect the left and rear of Thomas' line. At 1:00 P.M. Sirwell's brigade was sent out to check the enemy troops that were then approaching the left and rear of Negley's position, but it quickly became involved in Longstreet's attack and was driven back.

Morton C. Hunter's 82nd Indiana Regiment of Connell's broken brigade of Brannan's division halted in its retreat near the crest of Hill No. 2, and about 1:00 P.M. Brannan arrived with fragments of the 4th Kentucky, 10th Kentucky, and 14th Ohio of Croxton's brigade. Croxton was wounded at the time of the enemy breakthrough; William H. Hays assumed command of what was left of the brigade and brought it back to Horseshoe Ridge. Hays' brigade was placed in line with its left in front of and just to the left of Hill No. 2, and its right extending toward the left of Hunter's 82nd Indiana.

Stanley, whose brigade of Negley's division had been scattered during the fighting on the left of Baird's breastworks that morning, withdrew to Horseshoe Ridge with detachments of the 11th Michigan and 19th Illinois and took position on the left of Hays (Croxton) and in front of, and to the right of, the crest of Hill No. 2. Later the 18th Ohio of the brigade arrived and took position on Stanley's line.

Fragments of the 9th Kentucky and 17th Kentucky of Samuel Beatty's brigade of Van Cleve's division also joined Brannan, and these were placed in rear of the 58th Indiana of Buell's brigade. The 13th Ohio of Dick's brigade of Van Cleve's division also came up and formed on the crest of Hill No. 2. A little before 2:00 P.M., in response to a request from Brannan, Negley sent the 21st Ohio of Sirwell's brigade to reinforce Brannan, and it was placed on the right of Brannan's line just south of the crest of Hill No. 3.

As noted earlier, during the enemy's advance, Harker's brigade of Wood's division had engaged Robertson's brigade of Law's division and had driven it back, but when Kershaw's division—which was following Law—came up, Wood, with Harker's brigade, retired to the eastern end of Horseshoe Ridge. There Wood formed the brigade on Hill No. 1 on the left of Brannan (Stanley's brigade), with a part of the 44th Indiana of Dick's brigade of Van Cleve's division in support.

Meantime, Negley had decided to save the artillery under his command, and with Sirwell's brigade (less the 21st Ohio), two regiments of John Beatty's brigade, and a part of Connell's brigade of Brannan's division as a guard, he marched back

through McFarland's Gap to Rossville with his guns.

Following their initial attack, Longstreet's divisions halted for a time, and then early in the afternoon they were re-formed and realigned to face north toward the new Union line on Horseshoe Ridge.

Kershaw's division advanced on the Confederate right, with Benjamin G. Humphreys' brigade on the right and Kershaw's own brigade on the left. Humphreys' brigade reached a point on the Glenn-Kelly road, about 650 yards to the southeast of the Snodgrass house, where it remained during the rest of the day, but Kershaw's brigade continued on and attacked Harker's brigade on Hill No. 1. Fighting was severe; the Confederates gained the crest of the hill at several points within a few yards of Harker's line, but they were finally forced to fall back to the base of the hill and wait for support to come up on their left.

Meantime, Johnson, who was in command of his own and Hindman's divisions, had been preparing for a resumption of his attack. He finally got his troops in line, with his brigades in order from the Confederate left to right as follows: Deas', Manigault's, Fulton's (Johnson's), Sugg's (Gregg's), and Anderson's. McNair's brigade was in reserve in rear of Sugg. At 2:00 P.M. Johnson advanced against the western part of Horseshoe Ridge, to the Federal right of Brannan's position, and upon arriving at the crest he encountered Steedman's division of Granger's Reserve Corps, which was just arriving on the field,

On the morning of September 20, 1863, Granger's command was concentrated around McAfee Church on the Rossville-Ringgold road, and from this position the sounds of Thomas' battle to the south could be clearly heard. After a time the sounds appeared to be shifting to the west, and at 11:00 A.M. Granger, who was that day under orders to support Thomas, directed Steedman to march with his two brigades in the direction of the firing. Whitaker's brigade marched first, and it was followed by Mitchell's brigade. Daniel McCook's brigade of Second Division was left at McAfee Church.

Steedman encountered Forrest's cavalry near the La Fayette road, but he continued on and at noon passed the Cloud house, which was on the road about one-half mile north of McDonald's. At Cloud's, Steedman's column left the road and marched across the cleared fields of the Mullis and Snodgrass farms toward the Snodgrass house, which was a mile and a half distant. The head of Steedman's column reached Thomas at the Snodgrass house at 1:00 P.M., and his entire command was on the field by 1:30 P.M.

Initially, it was intended that Steedman's troops be placed on the left of Harker's brigade, where they would connect with Reynolds' division, but as Whitaker was approaching, Johnson was beginning his advance on the ridge. To meet this emergency, Steedman's division was immediately sent to the Federal right instead of to the left, and it arrived at the northern base of the ridge just as Johnson moved up the other side. Steedman then charged with Whitaker's brigade on the left, and it was followed a short time later by Mitchell's brigade on the right. There was heavy fighting for possession of the crest of the ridge, but finally Johnson's brigades were forced to retire. Steedman's division then prolonged Brannan's line almost a half-mile to the Federal right. Johnson again advanced, but without success, and the action developed into a series of attacks that lasted the remainder of the afternoon.

At 2:00 P.M. Van Derveer, whose brigade was then in reserve in rear of the center of Reynolds' line, heard the firing on Horseshoe Ridge; he marched in that direction, and at 2:30 P.M. he reported to Brannan, who was his division commander. Van Derveer's brigade was then placed on the right of Brannan's line, between the 21st Ohio of Negley's division and Whitaker's brigade of Steedman's division. Van Derveer's brigade aided in repelling the attacks by Johnson's and Hindman's divisions.

Thomas received additional reinforcement before the final heavy enemy attack that evening. A little after 4:00 P.M., preparations for an attack in front of Harker's line were observed, and Hazen's brigade of Palmer's division was brought up and formed on the left of Harker. Hazen's line was then extended to the left by the 44th Indiana and 86th Indiana of Dick's brigade.

Finally, at 3:20 P.M. Longstreet prepared for an all-out attack on Horseshoe Ridge, and he ordered Preston's division of Buckner's corps to move up from its position in reserve, about 600 yards east of

the La Fayette road and about midway between the Brotherton house and Viniard house. The division advanced across the La Fayette road and the Dyer farm, with Archibald Gracie's brigade on the right and John H. Kelly's brigade on the left. Buckner, who supervised the advance, held Robert C. Trigg's brigade in reserve near Brotherton's, but later Trigg moved up and joined in the attack on the Federal right.

When Buckner arrived, Gracie's brigade relieved Kershaw's brigade and Kelly's brigade relieved Anderson's brigade, and at about 4:30 P.M. both brigades moved forward in a final effort to drive Thomas from Horseshoe Ridge. Gracie advanced against Hill No. 1, which was held by the brigades of Harker and Hazen, and Kelly advanced against the position held by Brannan. The fighting lasted for about an hour, with some Confederate successes, but the enemy suffered terrible losses. Finally, about sunset, Thomas began to withdraw from Horseshoe Ridge, through McFarland's Gap, toward Rossville.

About 5:00 P.M. Polk began an attack on the Kelly field line, and about a half-hour later the Federal troops began to retire from that part of the field. Reynolds' division moved first, with orders to fall back and cover the retirement of the divisions of Palmer, Johnson, and Baird on the La Fayette road. As Reynolds moved northward, Liddell's division on the extreme Confederate right advanced to make its third attack of the day on the left of the line near the McDonald house. Turchin's brigade was leading Reynolds' column, and it was followed by Edward A. King's brigade, which was then commanded by Milton S. Robinson, who had assumed command at 5:00 P.M. when King was killed. Turchin deployed his brigade to meet Liddell, driving him back across the La Fayette road. Reynolds' division was then posted to hold the road back to McFarland's Gap, and the remaining divisions of the left wing withdrew in good order under its protection.

The troops on Horseshoe Ridge also withdrew toward McFarland's Gap, and by midnight September 20, 1863, the entire Union army had arrived in the vicinity of Rossville on the west side of Missionary Ridge, about five miles from Chattanooga.

On the morning of September 21, 1863, the army, under the direction of Thomas, was placed as follows: Crittenden's Twenty-First Corps occupied

Missionary Ridge north of Rossville Gap; Thomas' Fourteenth Corps occupied Rossville Gap and the road south to McFarland's Gap; McCook's Twentieth Corps and the mounted infantry and cavalry extended across the Chattanooga Valley to the base of Lookout Mountain.

Palmer's division of Crittenden's corps held the point of Missionary Ridge immediately north of the Rossville Gap, facing east; Wood's division of Crittenden's corps was on the left of Palmer, along the ridge; and Steedman's division of Granger's corps was on the left of Wood. Van Cleve's division of Crittenden's corps had been sent to Chattanooga, and it arrived there early on the morning of September 21, 1863. Dick's brigade of Van Cleve's division and the 39th Indiana Mounted Infantry were sent on the afternoon of September 21 to hold the gaps in Missionary Ridge east of Chattanooga, and also the bridge on the Harrison road over Chickamauga Creek.

Baird's division of Thomas' corps held Rossville Gap, and Negley's division of Thomas' corps was sent forward to a point overlooking the road to Ringgold and the Chickamauga battlefield. Brannan's and Reynolds' divisions of Thomas' corps were in position to the north and south of the road at McFarland's Gap.

John Beatty's brigade of Negley's division and Daniel McCook's brigade of Granger's Reserve Corps held the road immediately south of Rossville Gap.

Johnson's, Sheridan's, and Davis' divisions of McCook's Twentieth Corps were formed in line to the west across the Chattanooga Valley.

Mitchell's cavalry was at McFarland's Gap opposing Wheeler, and Minty's cavalry was beyond Rossville near McAfee Church, on the road to Ringgold,

Bragg was inactive September 21, 1863, with only Wheeler's cavalry approaching the Union lines. That night the entire Union army withdrew to Chattanooga, where the last troops arrived after daylight September 22. Upon arrival, McCook's corps formed on the right, next to Lookout Mountain and the Tennessee River; Thomas' corps occupied the center of the line; and Crittenden's corps was on the left, with its left extending back to the river to the east and north of Chattanooga. By nightfall all Union forces were covered by entrenched lines.

Bragg then bestirred himself and advanced his forces to take position where they could cut off communications of the Army of the Cumberland at Chattanooga with the North. Bragg's line extended from Lookout Mountain on the left, across Chattanooga Valley to Missionary Ridge, and then along the base and summit of Missionary Ridge to the Tennessee River above Chattanooga on the right.

The Army of the Cumberland remained in Chattanooga in a state of siege until the end of October 1863, at which time its supply line was reopened by troops commanded by Ulysses S. Grant. The army continued to hold its position at Chattanooga, confronting Bragg, until late November; then, after being reinforced, it attacked and drove Bragg's army back to Dalton, Georgia. For further information see Chattanooga-Ringgold Campaign (Battles of Lookout Mountain and Missionary Ridge, Tennessee).

On October 16, 1863, the Military Division of the Mississippi, consisting of the departments of the Cumberland, Tennessee, and Ohio, was created, and Ulysses S. Grant was assigned command. Orders were issued October 16 and October 18 for George H. Thomas to relieve William S. Rosecrans in command of the Army of the Cumberland, and on October 19, Thomas assumed command.

The organization of the Army of the Cumberland at the Battle of Chickamauga September 19–20, 1863 was as follows:

ARMY OF THE CUMBERLAND
William S. Rosecrans

FOURTEENTH CORPS, George H. Thomas

First Division, Absalom Baird
First Brigade, Benjamin F. Scribner
Second Brigade, John C. Starkweather
Third Brigade, John H. King

Note. 4th Battery, Indiana Light Artillery, commanded by David Flansburg to September 19, 1863 (wounded), and then by Henry J. Willits, was attached to Second Brigade; Battery A, 1st Michigan Light Artillery, commanded by George W. Van Pelt to September 19, 1863 (killed), and then by Almerick W. Wilbur, was attached to First Brigade; and Battery H, 5th United States Artillery, commanded by Howard M. Burnham to September 19, 1863 (mortally wounded), and then by Joshua A. Fessenden, was attached to Third Brigade.

Second Division, James S. Negley
  First Brigade, John Beatty
  Second Brigade, Timothy R. Stanley, to September
    20, 1863, wounded
    William L. Stoughton
  Third Brigade, William Sirwell

Note. Bridges' Battery, Illinois Light Artillery, commanded by Lyman Bridges, was attached to First Brigade; Battery G, 1st Ohio Light Artillery, commanded by Alexander Marshall, was attached to Third Brigade; and Battery M, 1st Ohio Light Artillery, commanded by Frederick Schultz, was attached to Second Brigade. Schultz was chief of artillery of Second Division.

Third Division, John M. Brannan
  First Brigade, John M. Connell
  Second Brigade, John T. Croxton, to September 20,
    1863, wounded
    William H. Hays
  Third Brigade, Ferdinand Van Derveer

Note. Battery D, 1st Michigan Light Artillery, commanded by Josiah W. Church, was attached to First Brigade; Battery C, 1st Ohio Light Artillery, commanded by Marco B. Gary, was attached to Second Brigade; and Battery I, 4th United States Artillery, commanded by Frank G. Smith, was attached to Third Brigade. Josiah W. Church was chief of artillery of Third Division.

Fourth Division, Joseph J. Reynolds
  First Brigade, John T. Wilder
  Second Brigade, Edward A. King, to September 20,
    1863, killed
    Milton S. Robinson
  Third Brigade, John B. Turchin

Note 1. Wilder's brigade was detached from the division, and served as mounted infantry.
Note 2. 18th Battery, Indiana Light Artillery, commanded by Eli Lilly, was attached to First Brigade; 19th Battery, Indiana Light Artillery, commanded by Samuel J. Harris to September 19, 1863 (disabled), and then by Robert G. Lackey, was attached to Second Brigade; and 21st Battery, Indiana Light Artillery, commanded by William W. Andrew, was attached to Third Brigade. Samuel J. Harris was acting chief of artillery of Fourth Division.

TWENTIETH CORPS, Thomas L. Crittenden

First Division, Jefferson C. Davis
  First Brigade, P. Sidney Post
  Second Brigade, William P. Carlin
  Third Brigade, Hans Heg, to September 19, 1863,
    killed
    John A. Martin

Note 1. Post's brigade was guarding the trains during the Battle of Chickamauga and was not engaged.
Note 2. 5th Battery, Wisconsin Light Artillery, commanded by George Q. Gardner, was attached to First Brigade; 2nd Battery, Minnesota Light Artillery, commanded by Albert Woodbury (wounded), and then by Richard L. Dawley, was attached to Second Brigade; and 8th Battery, Wisconsin Light Artillery, commanded by John D. McLean, was attached to Third Brigade. William A. Hotchkiss was chief of artillery of First Division.

Second Division, Richard W. Johnson
  First Brigade, August Willich
  Second Brigade, Joseph B. Dodge
  Third Brigade, Philemon P. Baldwin, to September
    19, 1863, killed
    William W. Berry

Note. Battery A, 1st Ohio Light Artillery, commanded by Wilbur F. Goodspeed, was attached to First Brigade; 20th Battery, Ohio Light Artillery, commanded by Edward Grosskopff, was attached to Second Brigade; and 5th Battery, Indiana Light Artillery, commanded by Peter Simonson, was attached to Third Brigade. Simonson was chief of artillery of Second Division.

Third Division, Philip H. Sheridan
  First Brigade, William H. Lytle, to September 20,
    1863, killed
    Silas Miller
  Second Brigade, Bernard Laiboldt
  Third Brigade, Luther P. Bradley, to September 19,
    1863, wounded
    Nathan H. Walworth

Note. 11th Battery, Indiana Light Artillery, commanded by Arnold Sutermeister, was attached to First Brigade; Battery G, 1st Missouri Light Artillery, commanded by Gustavus Schueler, was attached to Second Brigade; and Battery C, 1st Illinois Light Artillery, commanded by Mark H. Prescott, was attached to Third Brigade. Henry Hescock was chief of artillery of Third Division.

TWENTY-FIRST CORPS, Thomas L. Crittenden

First Division, Thomas J. Wood
  First Brigade, George P. Buell
  Second Brigade, George D. Wagner
  Third Brigade, Charles G. Harker

Note 1. Wagner's brigade was at Chattanooga during the Battle of Chickamauga and was not engaged.
Note 2. 8th Battery, Indiana Light Artillery, commanded by George Estep, was attached to First Brigade; 10th Battery, Indiana Light Artillery, commanded by

William A. Naylor, was attached to Second Brigade; and 6th Battery, Ohio Light Artillery, commanded by Cullen Bradley, was attached to Third Brigade. Bradley was chief of artillery of First Division.

Second Division, John M. Palmer
  First Brigade, Charles Cruft
  Second Brigade, William B. Hazen
  Third Brigade, William Grose

Note. Battery B, 1st Ohio Light Artillery, commanded by Norman A. Baldwin, was attached to First Brigade; Battery F, 1st Ohio Light Artillery, commanded by Giles J. Cockerill, was attached to Second Brigade; and Battery H, 4th United States Light Artillery, commanded by Harry C. Cushing, and Battery M, 4th United States Artillery, commanded by Francis L. D. Russell, were attached to Third Brigade. William E. Standart was chief of artillery of Second Division.

Third Division, Horatio P. Van Cleve
  First Brigade, Samuel Beatty
  Second Brigade, George F. Dick
  Third Brigade, Sidney M. Barnes
  Artillery, George R. Swallow
    7th Battery, Indiana Light Artillery, George R. Swallow
    26th Battery, Pennsylvania Light Artillery, Alanson J. Stevens, killed
    Samuel M. McDowell
    3rd Battery, Wisconsin Light Artillery, Cortland Livingston

RESERVE CORPS, Gordon Granger

First Division, James B. Steedman
  First Brigade, Walter C. Whitaker
  Second Brigade, John G. Mitchell

Note. 18th Battery, Ohio Light Artillery, commanded by Charles C. Aleshire, was attached to First Brigade; and Battery M, 1st Illinois Light Artillery, commanded by Thomas Burton, was attached to Second Brigade.

Second Division
  Second Brigade, Daniel McCook

Note. Battery I, 2nd Illinois Light Artillery, commanded by Charles M. Barnett, was attached to Second Brigade.

CAVALRY CORPS, Robert B. Mitchell

First Division, Edward M. McCook
  First Brigade, Archibald P. Campbell
  Second Brigade, Daniel M. Ray

Third Brigade, Louis D. Watkins

Note. One section of Nathaniel M. Newell's Battery D, 1st Ohio Light Artillery was attached to Second Brigade.

Second Division, George Crook
  First Brigade, Robert H. G. Minty
  Second Brigade, Eli Long
  Artillery
    Chicago (Illinois) Board of Trade Battery, James H. Stokes

BATTLE OF CORINTH, MISSISSIPPI OCTOBER 3–4, 1862

After the Battle of Iuka, Mississippi, which was fought September 19, 1862, Sterling Price marched south with his Army of the West, consisting of the divisions of Dabney H. Maury and Louis Hebert, to Baldwyn, Mississippi, where he arrived September 23. At that time Earl Van Dorn, commander of the Confederate District of the Mississippi, was at Holly Springs with Mansfield Lovell's First Division of the district. Price was under orders to join Van Dorn for an attack on Corinth, Mississippi, and upon his arrival at Baldwyn, he so notified Van Dorn. The latter then ordered Price to move to Ripley, and he marched for the same point with Lovell's division. The two commands joined at Ripley September 28, and, as senior officer, Van Dorn assumed command of the combined forces.

The next day Van Dorn marched almost due north, reaching Pocahontas, Tennessee on the Memphis and Charleston Railroad October 1. By moving in that direction, he threatened Memphis, Jackson, Bolivar, and Corinth, all of which were garrisoned by Federal troops, and thus concealed during the first few days of his march his real objective. At Pocahontas, Van Dorn turned abruptly to the east toward Corinth; he crossed the Hatchie River at Davis' Bridge (or Hatchie Bridge) at 4:00 A.M. October 2, bivouacking that night at Chewalla, Tennessee, ten miles northwest of Corinth.

In command at Corinth was William S. Rosecrans, commander of the Army of the Mississippi, and the troops under his command consisted of David S. Stanley's Second Division and Charles S. Hamilton's Third Division of the Army of the Mississippi, and Thomas A. Davies' Second Division and Thomas J. McKean's Sixth Division of the Army of the Tennessee. As Van Dorn marched northward from Ripley, however, only the divisions of Davies and McKean were at Corinth. Stanley's and Hamilton's divisions, which had been engaged at Iuka, were watching the enemy's movements to the south and southwest of Corinth on a line extending from near Jacinto to Rienzi, Mississippi. Rosecrans was aware of Van Dorn's advance, but he was uncertain as to his objective, and as a precaution he ordered Stanley and Hamilton to move closer to Corinth, where they would be available if needed.

At the end of September 1862, Corinth, toward which Van Dorn was advancing, was protected in some degree by three systems of fortifications that had been built at different times. To the north and west of Corinth, and at a distance of about two miles from it, was a line of old earthworks that had been constructed by the Confederates under Pierre G. T. Beauregard during April and May 1862, when they occupied the town after their retreat after the Battle of Shiloh. This line is generally referred to as the Beauregard Line. It began on the west at the Chewalla road, ran to the northeast for a short distance, then generally eastward to a point beyond the Mobile and Ohio Railroad, and then on to the southeast and across the Purdy road. This old line extended on southward along Phillips Creek on the east side of town, but this part of it was not occupied during the Battle of Corinth.

When Henry W. Halleck occupied Corinth after its evacuation by the enemy at the end of May 1862, he constructed a line of six lettered batteries to protect the town on the south and west. These were erected as a continuation of the Beauregard Line. Three of these on the west were of significance during the Battle of Corinth. Battery D was about one mile west of Corinth, on the Kossuth road; Battery E was north and a little west of Battery D, on the Smith Bridge road; and Battery F was due north of Battery E, on high ground between the Smith Bridge road and the Memphis and Charleston Railroad.

In September 1862, while Grant was at Corinth,

an inner defensive line was constructed to protect the town and the large army supply depot at the intersection of the Memphis and Charleston and the Mobile and Ohio railroads at the southwestern edge of town. This line consisted of a series of redoubts or batteries that were later connected by breastworks. The southern part of this line curved around a hill upon which Corona College stood, and this part of the line was sometimes called the College Hill Line. The batteries on the inner line were, from left to right, as follows: Battery Lothrop was south of the town and to the west of the Mobile and Ohio Railroad; Battery Tannrath was just south of Corona College; Battery Phillips was northwest of the college and just north of the northern Kossuth road; Battery Williams was west of Corinth and just south of the Memphis and Charleston Railroad; Battery Robinett was just north of Battery Williams and between the Memphis and Charleston Railroad and the Chewalla road; and Battery Powell was north of Corinth on a ridge east of the Purdy road.

On the afternoon of October 1, 1862, Rosecrans sent out John M. Oliver's Second Brigade of McKean's division to Chewalla to scout the country to the west for the presence of the enemy.

At midnight on the night of October 2–3, 1862, Rosecrans ordered Stanley to move with his division from the Tuscumbia River to Corinth, and by 7:00 A.M. October 3, the division was formed in line of battle in front of the Whitfield house, Grant's former headquarters. This line faced west a short distance in rear of Battery D and Battery E on Halleck's old line, and it extended across the Kossuth road and the Smith Bridge road.

Also during the night of October 2, Rosecrans ordered his other divisions to take position in advance of the inner line of redoubts and about halfway out to the old Confederate line of breastworks, or Beauregard Line. By 9:00 A.M. October 3, these divisions were in line as follows:

Hamilton's division was north of Corinth covering the Purdy and Pittsburg Landing roads and the ground between them, with Napoleon B. Buford's First Brigade on the right and Jeremiah C. Sullivan's Second Brigade on the left. Later Hamilton's line was moved forward to the Beauregard Line near its intersection with the Purdy road, about two and one-half miles north of Corinth.

Davies' division was northwest of town between the Memphis and Charleston Railroad and the Mobile and Ohio Railroad. It was in a woods about a mile and a half from Corinth at the forks of the Chewalla road and the Columbus road, which ran off from the former road to the right. About 10:00 A.M. the right of Davies' line was extended to the Mobile and Ohio Railroad, where it connected with the left of Hamilton's division. Pleasant A. Hackleman's First Brigade was on the right, Richard J. Oglesby's Second Brigade was on the left of Hackleman, and Silas D. Baldwin's Third Brigade was in reserve on the left and rear of Oglesby.

McKean's division was on the left of Davies, with Marcellus M. Crocker's Third Brigade on the left, facing west, near Battery F, on Halleck's old line, and John McArthur's First Brigade was on the right, with its left on the Memphis and Charleston Railroad. Oliver's Second Brigade was out in front near the old line of breastworks.

As noted above, Stanley's division was on the left, essentially in reserve watching the road to Kossuth and the Smith Bridge road, but about 11:00 A.M. it changed front and established a connection with McKean on the right and with its left near Battery D.

Meantime, the enemy had been active that morning. At dawn October 3, 1862, Van Dorn resumed his march toward Corinth, with Oliver's brigade resisting stubbornly as it fell back along the Chewalla road. Oliver needed help, and early that morning McKean sent forward his First Brigade to reinforce him. John McArthur, who had been absent on special service, had just returned and was assigned temporary command of the brigade, relieving Benjamin Allen. When McArthur joined Oliver, he assumed command of both brigades. Under steady pressure by the enemy, McArthur was pushed back to the Beauregard Line of breastworks, where he asked for additional reinforcements.

Lovell's division, which led Van Dorn's column that morning, advanced along the right side of the Memphis and Charleston Railroad, and around 10:00 A.M. arrived within about three miles of Corinth. It formed in line of battle on the south side of the track and prepared to attack. Maury's division

then came up and deployed on the Confederate left of Lovell, with its right on the railroad, and Hebert's division formed on the left of Maury. William H. Jackson's cavalry brigade was on the right of Van Dorn's line, and Frank C. Armstrong's cavalry was on the left.

When Lovell advanced to attack that morning, he encountered Oliver's and McArthur's brigades near the old line of breastworks. Then, acting on McArthur's request for help, Davies sent forward Baldwin's brigade of his division. Baldwin found Oliver's brigade holding the Chewalla road on the left of the old line of breastworks, and he then formed his brigade on the right of Oliver's line. When Baldwin was in position, his line extended from the right of the Memphis and Charleston Railroad, across the Chewalla road, and into the old line of breastworks. McArthur then assumed control of Baldwin's brigade, in addition to his own and Oliver's brigades.

Lovell began the enemy attack on the Confederate right when he advanced against McArthur's position. Then, in an attempt to relieve the pressure on Baldwin's brigade, Davies moved the rest of his division out on the Columbus road, where he halted within about one-half mile of the old line of works. From there, on Rosecrans' orders, Davies sent Oglesby's brigade and Hackleman's brigade forward to the old line of works. There they took position with Hackleman on the left and Oglesby on the right of the division line. Baldwin's brigade was supporting Oliver farther to the left.

As Maury attacked on the left of Lovell, Hackleman's brigade became heavily engaged, and John D. Martin's brigade of Hebert's division struck Oglesby's brigade. Davies' left was driven back about a half-mile, and then Davies withdrew Hackleman and Oglesby on the Columbus road to a position about 1,000 yards in rear of the old line of works. He also ordered Baldwin to fall back to the junction of the Chewalla and Columbus roads. Thus, by 10:30 A.M. Federal troops had been driven from the entire line of the old breastworks.

Maury was finally able to penetrate the line between Davies and McArthur, and the entire Federal line fell back to a new position about one-half mile in front of the inner line of redoubts. At the same time, McArthur refused his right flank and Davies his left flank. Lovell also moved his division past the left of McKean's division and came up in front of the redoubts southwest of Corinth, thus forcing McArthur's brigades and Crocker's brigade of McKean's division to fall back to the redoubts. Oliver then withdrew to the rear of McKean's division.

Maury and Hebert launched another violent attack on Davies' battered division and forced it back on Battery Robinett. Mower's brigade of Stanley's division was sent to aid Davies in his retreat, and Stanley was preparing to send Fuller's brigade when the fighting ended for the day about 5:30 P.M. During the day, Davies lost his three brigade commanders. Hackleman was mortally wounded, and Thomas W. Sweeny assumed command of his First Brigade; Oglesby was severely wounded and was succeeded in command of Second Brigade by August Mersey; and Baldwin was also severely wounded and was succeeded in command of Third Brigade by John V. Du Bois.

While the enemy attacks on the Federal left were in progress, Rosecrans attempted to mount an attack by Hamilton's division on the far right against the left flank of Hebert's division as it advanced against Davies. Time was lost while Rosecrans attempted to clarify his orders to Hamilton, but finally Hamilton was able to change front with his division to the west, facing the Mobile and Ohio Railroad and the left flank of Hebert's division. In this movement, however, Buford's brigade marched too far to the right to get in position for an attack that evening, and Sullivan's brigade was too weak to attack alone. Thus the Federals lost a promising opportunity to win the battle that evening.

When the fighting ended a little before 6:00 P.M., Rosecrans' divisions had been forced back about two miles and had taken position along the redoubts west and southwest of town. The enemy followed and spent the night within a few hundred yards of the Federal line.

During the night of October 3, 1862, Rosecrans made preparations for a strong defense against the expected enemy attack the next morning. McKean was assigned to hold the left of the line in the vicinity of Battery Phillips, south of the Memphis and Charleston Railroad. The principal point on this line was College Hill. Stanley was ordered to support the line on either side of Battery Robinett; he formed his line across the Memphis and Charleston

Railroad and occupied Battery Williams on the left and Battery Robinett on the right. By so doing, he relieved Davies' division, which then moved to the east of the Mobile and Ohio Railroad, with its right near Battery Powell and its left near the railroad, just north of Corinth. In this position it faced northwest. Sweeny's First Brigade (formerly Hackleman's) was on the right, with its right near Battery Powell, and Du Bois' Third Brigade (formerly Baldwin's) was on the left. Mersey's Second Brigade (formerly Oglesby's) was in reserve in rear of Sweeny's line. Hamilton's division was on the extreme right, facing north, with Sullivan's Second Brigade on the left next to Davies' division. Buford's brigade was farther east behind a ridge, where it could not be seen from the west. John K. Mizner with his cavalry was to guard the flanks and rear of Rosecrans' line.

Van Dorn also made some changes in the positions of his command that night. He placed Lovell's division to the south of the Memphis and Charleston Railroad, facing east toward Corinth; Maury's division in front of Battery Robinett, with three batteries established to cover all the ground west of Corinth; and Hebert's division on the left of Maury.

Van Dorn's plan for the next morning was for Hebert to open the attack on the Confederate left by moving down the Mobile and Ohio Railroad against Battery Powell and Hamilton's division. At the same time, Maury's artillery was to open on Battery Robinett, and then the infantry was to advance straight toward Corinth between the two railroads. At the same time, Lovell was to attack vigorously from the southwest toward Corinth.

Hebert was to have attacked at daylight October 4, 1862, but he was delayed in getting into position. From his position of the night before, it was necessary for him to move his division by a flank march of about a mile to the east, and across the Mobile and Ohio Railroad, before arriving at his starting point beyond the Purdy road, and this required more time than expected. The attack was further delayed when Hebert reported sick, and it was nearly 9:00 A.M. when Martin E. Green led the division forward.

Green's four brigades pivoted on the right, swung around until they were in position in a woods, facing south, and then attacked along the east side of the Purdy road. Robert McClain's and W. Bruce

Colbert's Missouri brigades on the right moved against Battery Powell, and the other two brigades moved against Hamilton's line east of the battery. Henry Dillon's 6th Battery, Wisconsin Light Artillery, supported by the 80th Ohio and 10th Iowa of Sullivan's brigade, which were at and near Battery Powell, resisted for a time, but they were finally driven back and the battery was captured. Sweeny's First Brigade of Davies' division was also supporting Battery Powell on the left, but it was quickly driven back. A short time later, however, the 56th Illinois and 10th Missouri of Sullivan's brigade, supported by Lorenzo D. Immell's 12th Battery, Wisconsin Light Artillery, counterattacked, and with the help of the 52nd Illinois of Sweeny's brigade recaptured Battery Powell. William L. Cabell's brigade, which was then with Hebert, attempted to retake Battery Powell, but it was repulsed with heavy loss. Green's attack ended about 1:00 P.M., and then this division retired into the woods and did not advance again.

Soon after 10:00 A.M., after Green had become engaged, Maury moved forward with his division against the right of Stanley's line and the front of Davies' division, which was on the left of Hamilton. Davies' line was quickly broken and swept away, and many of the enemy troops pushed forward into the interval between the left of Hamilton and the right of Stanley and into the center of Corinth. There was violent fighting in the streets for a time between remnants of Davies' division, the 5th Minnesota of Mower's brigade, and the 22nd Ohio of Mersey's brigade of Davies' division, and when troops of Hamilton's division also began to move in from the north and east, the enemy quickly retired from the town.

About 11:00 A.M., John C. Moore's brigade advanced down the Chewalla road and launched a heavy attack against Battery Robinett and John W. Fuller's First Brigade of Stanley's division, which was supporting it. Fuller's regiments were in line as follows: the 43rd Ohio was to the left of Battery Robinett; the 63rd Ohio was to the right of the battery; and the 27th Ohio and 39th Ohio were, in that order, to the right of the 63rd Ohio. The 11th Missouri of Mower's Second Brigade was in position immediately behind Battery Robinett. The rest of Mower's brigade was across the Memphis and Charleston Railroad on the low ground between Battery Williams and Battery Phillips.

Moore's first attack, which was against Battery Robinett and the 63rd Ohio to its right, was repulsed, but the column was re-formed and again charged the works, with William P. Rogers' 2nd Texas in the lead. The leading troops reached the ditch, where Rogers was killed, and a few men got inside the battery, but they were soon killed or captured. The 63rd Ohio was forced back, and the left of the 27th Ohio, which was on the right of the 63rd Ohio, was also driven back. Then, as the situation was becoming critical, the 11th Missouri counterattacked, and it was soon joined by the 27th Ohio. The 43rd Ohio to the left and the 63rd Ohio to the right soon followed, and all combined to drive the enemy from their front in complete disorder. By 2:00 P.M. the fighting was over, and all along the line the enemy began to pull back when Van Dorn led his army in retreat up the road toward Chewalla.

During the battle of October 3, 1862, James B. McPherson, who had been engaged in the construction of railroads, but who held no command, arrived at Jackson, Tennessee from Columbus. He was ordered by Grant to take command of the unassigned brigades of Michael K. Lawler and John D. Stevenson, which were along the railroad between Jackson and Corinth, and which belonged to the District of Jackson, District of West Tennessee, and organize them into a division and proceed with it to Corinth. McPherson picked up his two brigades October 4, moved them by rail to within twelve miles of Corinth, and then marched with them to Corinth, where he arrived at 4:00 that evening.

On October 4, 1862, in obedience to an order from Grant, Stephen A. Hurlbut moved with his division from Bolivar to Pocahontas with instructions to intercept Van Dorn if he should retreat in that direction. Hurlbut bivouacked for the night on the west bank of the Hatchie River, just south of the railroad. The following morning Edward O. C. Ord, commanding Second Division, District of West Tennessee, who had been in Kentucky, arrived and assumed command of the division.

Rosecrans delayed the pursuit of Van Dorn's army until the next morning, and then he started McPherson's fresh division out on the road to Chewalla, where Van Dorn had spent the night. Stanley followed McPherson, and McKean and Hamilton pursued on parallel roads. By some mistake, the four divisions came into the road together about seven miles from Corinth, and because of the time lost in straightening this out, the army got no farther than Chewalla that day.

Van Dorn reached the Hatchie River at Davis' Bridge early in the morning of October 5, 1862, but Ord promptly attacked with James C. Veatch's Second Brigade, which was supported by Jacob G. Lauman's First Brigade, and secured the bridge. Ord was wounded during the attack, and Hurlbut resumed command of the division. Van Dorn then moved down the Boneyard road, to the east of the river, to Crum's Mill, and there his army crossed on the bridge that night. The next day Van Dorn continued on through Ripley to Holly Springs. Rosecrans and Hurlbut pursued as far as Ripley, and then they returned to Corinth and Bolivar.

The organization of the United States forces commanded by Rosecrans at the Battle of Corinth and during the pursuit was as follows:

ARMY OF THE MISSISSIPPI, William S. Rosecrans

Second Division, David S. Stanley
  First Brigade, John W. Fuller
  Second Brigade, Joseph A. Mower, wounded October 4, 1862

Note 1. Carl A. Lamberg's 3rd Battery, Michigan Light Artillery, John D. McLean's 8th Battery (one section), Wisconsin Light Artillery, and Thomas D. Maurice's Battery F, 2nd United States Artillery were attached to First Brigade.
Note 2. Nelson T. Spoor's 2nd Battery, Iowa Light Artillery was attached to Second Brigade.

Third Division, Charles S. Hamilton
  First Brigade, Napoleon B. Buford
  Second Brigade, Jeremiah C. Sullivan, temporarily disabled October 3, 1862
  Samuel A. Holmes

Note 1. Junius W. MacMurray's Battery M, 1st Missouri Light Artillery and Henry M. Neil's 11th Battery, Ohio Light Artillery were assigned to First Brigade.
Note 2. Henry Dillon's 6th Battery, Wisconsin Light Artillery and Lorenzo D. Immell's 12th Battery, Wisconsin Light Artillery were assigned to Second Brigade.
Note 3. Holmes commanded Second Brigade during the night of October 3, 1862 and during the battle the next day, but Sullivan was on the field and aided in the direction of his troops.

Cavalry Division, John K. Mizner
  First Brigade, Edward Hatch
  Second Brigade, Albert L. Lee

ARMY OF THE TENNESSEE (OR ARMY OF WEST TENNESSEE)

Second Division, Thomas A. Davies
  First Brigade, Pleasant A. Hackleman, to October 3, 1862, mortally wounded
  Thomas W. Sweeny
  Second Brigade, Richard J. Oglesby, to October 3, 1862, wounded
  August Mersey
  Third Brigade, Silas D. Baldwin, to October 3, 1862, wounded
  John V. Du Bois
  Artillery, George H. Stone
    Battery D, 1st Missouri Light Artillery, Henry Richardson
    Battery H, 1st Missouri Light Artillery, Frederick Welker
    Battery I, 1st Missouri Light Artillery, Charles H. Thurber
    Battery K, 1st Missouri Light Artillery, Charles Green

Sixth Division, Thomas J. McKean
  First Brigade, Benjamin Allen, to morning of October 3, 1862
  John McArthur
  Second Brigade, John M. Oliver
  Third Brigade, Marcellus M. Crocker
  Artillery, Andrew Hickenlooper
    Battery F, 2nd Illinois Light Artillery, Joseph W. Mitchell
    1st Battery, Minnesota Light Artillery, G. Frederick Cooke
    3rd Battery, Ohio Light Artillery, Emil Munch
    5th Battery, Ohio Light Artillery, Bellamy S. Matson
    10th Battery, Ohio Light Artillery, Hamilton B. White

The following forces were sent to reinforce Rosecrans, but were not engaged at the Battle of Corinth:

ARMY OF THE TENNESSEE (OR ARMY OF WEST TENNESSEE)

Provisional Division, James B. McPherson
  Lawler's Brigade, Michael K. Lawler
  Stevenson's Brigade, John D. Stevenson

Note. McPherson's division arrived at Corinth after the battle had ended October 4, 1862 and was not engaged, but it did join in the pursuit of Van Dorn the next morning.

Fourth Division, District of West Tennessee, Stephen A. Hurlbut
First Brigade, Jacob G. Lauman
Second Brigade, James C. Veatch
Provisional Brigade, Robert K. Scott

Note 1. Edward O. C. Ord assumed command of Fourth Division at Davis' Bridge at 8:00 A.M. October 5, 1862, but was wounded three hours later, and Hurlbut resumed command.

Note 2. Fourth Division was not at Corinth, but was engaged at Davis' Bridge on the Hatchie River October 5, 1862.

Note 3. Scott's Provisional Brigade was attached to the division from Leonard F. Ross' division of Ord's command at Jackson and Bolivar.

For additional information about the organization of the Union troops under Grant's command in western Tennessee and northern Mississippi, see Army of the Tennessee, District of West Tennessee, and also Army of the Mississippi (Pope, Rosecrans).

HALLECK'S ADVANCE ON CORINTH, MISSISSIPPI APRIL 29, 1862– MAY 30, 1862

After the Battle of Shiloh April 6–7, 1862, Pierre G. T. Beauregard led his defeated army back to Corinth, Mississippi and began preparations to put it in condition for further operations. Recognizing the importance of holding Corinth, which was located on the Mobile and Ohio Railroad and the Memphis and Charleston Railroad, Beauregard called for reinforcements and began construction of a strong defensive line about the town.

There was also activity at this time in the Union camps at Pittsburg Landing, on the Tennessee River. Henry W. Halleck, commander of the Department of the Mississippi, moved his headquarters to Pittsburg Landing, where he arrived April 12, 1862. He assumed personal command of Ulysses S. Grant's Army of the Tennessee and Don Carlos Buell's Army of the Ohio, both of which had fought at Shiloh.

Halleck then began preparations for an advance against Corinth. He ordered John Pope to bring his Army of the Mississippi, which had been operating on the Mississippi River at New Madrid, Missouri and Island No. 10, to the Tennessee River. Pope arrived at Pittsburg Landing April 21, and his army then disembarked at Hamburg, Tennessee, four miles above the landing, and took position there on the left of the Army of the Ohio.

Some preliminary movements for the advance on Corinth began on April 29, 1862, and the next day Halleck announced the reorganization of his command into a Right Wing, Center, Left Wing, and Reserve as follows:

Right Wing, George H. Thomas
Second Division, Army of the Tennessee, Thomas A. Davies
Fourth Division, Army of the Tennessee, Stephen A. Hurlbut
Fifth Division, Army of the Tennessee, William T. Sherman
Sixth Division, Army of the Tennessee, Thomas J. McKean
Seventh Division, Army of the Tennessee, Thomas W. Sherman

Note. Thomas W. Sherman's First Division, Army of the Ohio was temporarily attached to the Army of the Tennessee as Division.

Center, Don Carlos Buell
Second Division, Army of the Ohio, Alexander McD. McCook
Fourth Division, Army of the Ohio, William Nelson
Fifth Division, Army of the Ohio, Thomas L. Crittenden
Sixth Division, Army of the Ohio, Thomas J. Wood

Left Wing, John Pope
First Division, Army of the Mississippi, Eleazer A. Paine
Second Division, Army of the Mississippi, David S. Stanley
Third Division, Army of the Mississippi, Schuyler Hamilton
Cavalry Division, Army of the Mississippi, Gordon Granger

Reserve, John A. McClernand
First Division, Army of the Tennessee, Henry M. Judah
Third Division, Army of the Tennessee, Lewis Wallace

Note. Thomas L. Crittenden's Fifth Division, Army of the Ohio was nominally assigned to the Reserve, but it remained under Buell's command.

Ulysses S. Grant, commander of the District of West Tennessee (and formerly of the Army of the Tennessee), was assigned by Halleck as second in command of the army, and he played no significant role in the advance on Corinth.

For the complete organization of Halleck's army during its advance on Corinth, see Army of the Tennessee, District of West Tennessee; Army of the Ohio (Buell); and Army of the Mississippi (Pope, Rosecrans).

The general advance of the army toward Corinth began during the first few days of May 1862, and it proceeded very slowly during the rest of the month. Although the strength of Halleck's army was roughly 100,000 men, he advanced with great caution and entrenched at the end of each day's march. He did encounter some resistance, sometimes quite vigorous; there was daily skirmishing along the front, and numerous reconnaissances were sent out to examine the country and determine the enemy positions. Consequently, by May 25, nearly a month after the start of the march, as the army was approaching the enemy fortifications, it had advanced only about twenty miles. At that time Halleck's movements had developed more into siege operations than a general advance, but Corinth was never under siege in the sense that it was encircled.

Before the movements of the army during the advance on Corinth are described, it is necessary to describe briefly some of the principal features of the country through which it passed, the most significant of which are the roads and streams that traversed the region.

The principal roads, beginning on the Union left, were as follows: The Hamburg-Corinth road ran out of Hamburg to the southwest, crossed Chambers Creek (Chester Creek) and Seven-Mile Creek, and then continued on through Farmington to Corinth. The distance from Hamburg to Corinth was about seventeen miles. Next was the direct road from Pittsburg Landing to Corinth. This road began at Pittsburg Landing on the Tennessee River and ran to the southwest, across Lick Creek, to Monterey (or Pea Ridge), which was about ten miles from the landing. From there it continued on to the south-west, crossed the Old State Line road and Chambers Creek, and then ran on to Corinth, about nine miles from Monterey. Next, in order to the right, was the Purdy-Farmington road, which ran generally south from Purdy to Locust Grove, at the intersection with the Old State Line road. It then continued on to the south for several miles on a line about a mile west of and parallel to the direct Pittsburg Landing–Corinth road until the two roads converged near the Driver house, about three miles from Corinth and two and one-fourth miles northwest of Farmington. From Driver's the road continued on to Farmington. The last of the roads running into Corinth that is of interest in this campaign was the Purdy-Corinth road. This road ran generally south out of Purdy, through Gravel Hill, and then on into Corinth. For the last several miles before entering Corinth, this road ran roughly parallel to the Mobile and Ohio Railroad, and about one-half to three-fourths of a mile to the east of it.

There was also another important road that has already been mentioned that ran east and west across the above-mentioned roads north of Corinth. This was the Old State Line road, which began on the Tennessee River below Hamburg and ran westward toward Memphis, Tennessee. The course of this road through the region of Halleck's advance was generally about one-half to one mile north of the old Tennessee-Mississippi state line, and about three miles above the new state line (the 35th parallel). This road crossed the Hamburg-Corinth road about nine miles from the Tennessee River, and several miles farther on it crossed the Pittsburg Landing–Corinth road about two miles southwest of Monterey. Two miles farther on, it crossed the Purdy-Farmington road at Locust Grove.

There were also several creeks that flowed through the region covered by Halleck's advance. Chambers Creek flowed generally eastward through northern Mississippi, not far from the state line, before turning to the northeast to empty into the Tennessee River a short distance below Hamburg, Seven-Mile Creek flowed to the east, north of Farmington, and emptied into Chambers Creek east of the Hamburg-Corinth road. Near Corinth were two streams that flowed from north to south a short distance east of the town. The one closer to Corinth was Phillips' Creek, which flowed south about a mile to the east of the Mobile and Ohio Railroad until it joined Bridge Creek to the southeast of Corinth. Bridge Creek ran south about one-half to three-fourths of a mile east of Phillips Creek, with a high ridge between the two streams. After passing the mouth of Phillips Creek, Bridge Creek flowed on to the southwest, south of Corinth, and emptied into the Tuscumbia River. A part of the main Confederate defensive line was along the high ground west of Phillips Creek.

The Memphis and Charleston Railroad ran along the southern edge of Corinth on a line from the northwest to the southeast, and at the southwestern corner of the town, the Mobile and Ohio Railroad, running from south to north, crossed the Memphis and Charleston Railroad.

On April 26, 1862, before the army began its advance toward Corinth, Eleazer A. Paine's First Division and David S. Stanley's Second Division of Pope's Left Wing (Army of the Mississippi) were in line about six miles west of Hamburg, with their center on the Hamburg-Farmington road and their right extending across the Pittsburg Landing–Corinth road. Gordon Granger's Cavalry Division, Army of the Mississippi was covering the country out in front of these two divisions. Schuyler Hamilton was under orders to move his Third (or Reserve) Division forward the next day to a position about a mile in rear of the front line.

Pope's Left Wing advanced to Chambers Creek on April 30, remaining there until May 3. Pope then continued the advance on the Hamburg-Farmington road toward Corinth, and drove the enemy back across Seven-Mile Creek. He then placed his command in camp about a mile and a half north of the creek and remained in position there for about two weeks. On May 8, Pope made a reconnaissance to within a mile and a half of Corinth with the divisions of Paine and Stanley and then returned to camp. Stanley left Joseph B. Plummer's Second Brigade of his division (commanded that day by John M. Loomis because of the illness of Plummer) at Farmington as an advance guard. Early on the morning of May 9, John M. Palmer's First Brigade of Stanley's division arrived from the rear to relieve Loomis, and had just passed to the front when it was attacked by a strong force of the enemy. The two brigades resisted vigorously for about two hours, aided by Henry Hescock's Battery G, 1st Missouri Light Artillery and Nelson T. Spoor's 2nd Battery,

Iowa Light Artillery, then fell back across Seven-Mile Creek and returned to their camps.

Meantime, on May 2, 1862, Don Carlos Buell, commanding Halleck's Center (Army of the Ohio), had begun his advance toward Corinth. That day William Nelson's Fourth Division, Army of the Ohio crossed Lick Creek at the Greer house and moved on south to the Old State Line road. Upon arriving there, it turned to the west and halted on the road at Mount Olivet, about two miles from the intersection of that road with the Pittsburg Landing–Corinth road. Buell's other three divisions followed the next day, with Thomas J. Wood's Sixth Division and Thomas L. Crittenden's Fifth Division crossing at Greer's, and Alexander McD. McCook's Second Division crossing near Atkin's Mill. Heavy rains on May 4–5 prevented any further advance for a few days.

Finally, on May 7, 1862, when the roads had been repaired, Buell's divisions again advanced. They turned off the Old State Line road to the left, about three-fourths of a mile from the intersection with the Pittsburg Landing–Corinth road, and advanced on three different roads to the south and southwest to Chambers Creek. Wood's division was on the right, Nelson's division was on the left, and McCook's division was in the center. Crittenden's division followed McCook's division in reserve. The main body of Buell's cavalry remained about five miles to the rear, where forage was available.

On May 8, 1862, the divisions of Wood and McCook worked on the construction of roads. Nelson's division was sent across Chambers Creek, and then about two miles to the left to Nichols' Ford on Seven-Mile Creek to support Pope's reconnaissance through Farmington toward Corinth. Nelson then returned to his former position at 4:00 the next morning, but was again sent at 10:30 A.M. that same day to Nichols' Ford to support Pope, whose two advanced brigades at Farmington had been attacked. Crittenden's division, which had been in reserve, was also brought up and sent to the left to support Pope.

The interval between Pope's right and Buell's left was too great for a prompt support of Pope, who was somewhat isolated on Halleck's left, and on May 10, 1862, Buell moved his whole force to the left some three miles. Nelson remained in his position at Nichols' Ford; Wood crossed Chambers

Creek and closed in on the right of Nelson; and McCook also crossed Chambers Creek and took position in reserve. On May 12, Crittenden moved up on the left of Nelson's division.

On May 14, 1862, McCook's division advanced to the front on a reconnaissance toward the enemy lines, then moved back to its position in reserve.

It was not until May 4 that George H. Thomas' Right Wing (Army of the Tennessee) began its movement toward Corinth. That day William T. Sherman's Fifth Division advanced on the direct road from Pittsburg Landing to Corinth, through Monterey, to the Old State Line road. There it turned to the right and marched westward on that road. It halted that night about one mile from Locust Grove, which was at the intersection of the Old State Line road and the Purdy-Farmington road. Stephen A. Hurlbut's Fourth Division came up on the left of William T. Sherman, and Thomas W. Sherman's Seventh Division formed on the direct Pittsburg Landing–Corinth road, on the left of Hurlbut; Thomas A. Davies' Second Division and Thomas J. McKean's Sixth Division were in reserve.

May 7, 1862, the Right Wing again advanced. William T. Sherman's division then moved up and occupied a line running north and south along the Purdy-Farmington road through Locust Grove, facing west; Hurlbut's division was on the left of William T. Sherman; and the other divisions were farther to the left, toward the Pittsburg Landing–Corinth road.

May 11, 1862, William T. Sherman moved south about a mile from Locust Grove, with Hurlbut on his left, and Davies' division on the Pittsburg Landing–Corinth road to the left of Hurlbut. On May 13, 1862 these three divisions were in position on a line running from the Easel house on the right to the Pittsburg Landing–Corinth road on the left. William T. Sherman's division was on the right, facing west; Hurlbut's division was in the center, facing southwest; and Davies' division was on the left, facing south. The left of Davies' division rested on the Pittsburg Landing–Corinth road, and it was almost squarely along the new Tennessee-Mississippi state line.

May 14, 1862, Thomas ordered Thomas W. Sherman, Davies, and McKean to advance with their divisions to the vicinity of Seven-Mile Creek, with

the left of their line on the Pittsburg Landing–Corinth road.

May 16, 1862, the Right Wing again moved forward, against considerable resistance, and occupied the ground in front of the Purdy-Farmington road, and its line extended from the Pittsburg Landing–Corinth road to the Purdy-Corinth road.

Halleck then ordered a general advance along the entire line for May 17, 1862. That day Pope moved out of his camps in rear of Seven-Mile Creek and advanced to Farmington, where he again encamped. Paine's division was on the left of the road to Corinth, facing west; Stanley's division was on the left of Paine, facing southwest; and Hamilton's division was on the left of Stanley, facing south.

On May 20, 1862, Pope made a reconnaissance toward Corinth, but otherwise the Right Wing remained in camp until May 28.

On May 17, 1862, during the general advance, Buell also crossed Seven-Mile Creek, on the right of Pope, and moved up to the Purdy-Farmington road. Wood's division was on the right, with its right near the Driver house, on the Pittsburg Landing–Corinth road; Nelson's division was on the left of Wood; and Crittenden's division was on the left of Nelson, with its left on the road from Farmington to Corinth. McCook's division was in reserve. This line was not completed until after dark. Pope's Left Wing was in line on the left of Crittenden, and Thomas W. Sherman's division, the left division of Thomas' Right Wing, was on the right of Wood. In this position, Buell was about two miles from the main line of enemy entrenchments in front of Corinth.

May 18, 1862, Buell's divisions again advanced—Crittenden about 400 yards; Nelson about one-half mile, into some woods in front of his right; and Nelson to a wooded ridge in front of his right.

May 27, 1862, McCook's division was moved up from reserve to a position in front of Wood's division and Thomas W. Sherman's division of Thomas' Left Wing. McCook then advanced and, with some skirmishing, drove the enemy across Bridge Creek.

Thomas' Right Wing also joined in the general advance of May 17, 1862. That day, William T. Sherman advanced with a force consisting of James W. Denver's Third Brigade and Morgan L. Smith's First Brigade of his division against a commanding position at the Russell house, just two miles from the line of enemy works. Sherman was supported by two regiments and a battery from Hurlbut's division. Sherman soon encountered stiff opposition, but continued his advance and drove the enemy back to the area around Russell's. Sherman left a strong picket there, with a brigade in close support.

That same day, Thomas W. Sherman's division advanced along the Pittsburg Landing–Corinth road; it drove the enemy on its front back across Bridge Creek, then occupied the ground as far as the creek. Between Bridge Creek and Phillips' Creek, in front of Thomas W. Sherman's division, was a thickly wooded hill, called Serratt's Hill (also spelled Suratt), which overlooked the enemy works beyond. The Widow Serratt's house was located at the point where the Pittsburg Landing–Corinth road crossed Bridge Creek in front of Sherman's left.

By May 19, 1862, the left of Thomas' line had moved up to form on the left of the line held by William T. Sherman and Hurlbut. Davies' division was on the left of Hurlbut, McKean was to the left of Davies, and Thomas W. Sherman was to the left of McKean. The left of Thomas W. Sherman's division was at the junction of the Pittsburg Landing–Corinth road and the Purdy-Farmington road, near the Driver house.

May 21, 1862, William T. Sherman, supported by Hurlbut on the left, advanced his division to the Russell house, then entrenched on a line extending from the Purdy-Corinth road on the right to the Purdy-Farmington road on the left. Hurlbut's division connected with the left of William T. Sherman's and extended the line in a southerly direction along the main ridge between Bridge Creek and Phillips' Creek. Then in order to the south, along the same ridge, were the divisions of Davies and McKean. McKean's division connected with the center of Thomas W. Sherman's division, which was on the left of Thomas' line. Thomas' line faced the enemy's defensive works on the far side of Phillips' Creek.

While the rest of Halleck's army was closing in on Corinth, McClernand's Reserve had been assigned positions to the north guarding the rear of the army. McClernand began his advance May 4, 1862 by moving Lewis Wallace's Third Division, Army of the Tennessee from the vicinity of the bridge on the Purdy–Pittsburg Landing road over Owl Creek to Michie's (also spelled Mickey's) house, northeast of Monterey, and Henry M. Judah's First Division, Army of the Tennessee to the south of Lick Creek, near Monterey.

Following these initial movements, there was a period of heavy rains, and for a time the troops were engaged in repairing and constructing bridges, especially over Lick Creek. Finally, however, on May 11, 1862, Judah's division moved forward about two and one-half miles and camped near Locust Grove, at the intersection of the Old State Line road and the Purdy-Farmington road. This position was the same as that held earlier by William T. Sherman's division of the Right Wing.

May 14, 1862, Leonard F. Ross' Second Brigade of Judah's division was detached and ordered forward a mile and a half to the Easel house, which had recently been vacated by William T. Sherman's division.

McClernand had received reports that the enemy was using the Mobile and Ohio Railroad to move out troops to turn the Federal right flank, and he prepared to move out a part of his command to the railroad to meet this threat. As a preliminary, he ordered Wallace to send out Charles R. Woods' brigade to an intermediate point on the Old State Line road to fortify a strong position and hold the road. Then, to act in conjunction with Woods' advance, he ordered Judah to move out to the railroad with a strong force and destroy the track. Judah took with him Ross' brigade, a battalion of cavalry, and eight guns, and John A. Logan's First Brigade of Judah's division in support. Judah reached the railroad and destroyed some track, and the troops then returned to their camps.

On May 15, 1862, McClernand's troops were generally along the Old State Line road from the vicinity of Pittsburg Landing almost to the Mobile and Ohio Railroad. Wallace's division, which was encamped at Michie's farm, was guarding Owl Creek and Lick Creek from the road bridge over Owl Creek to a point near Monterey. Judah's division was at Locust Grove, with Ross' brigade at the Easel house. On May 21, Logan's brigade left its position at Locust Grove and moved to Easel's.

On May 27, 1862, Pope sent Washington L. Elliott, colonel of the 2nd Iowa Cavalry, to move with his own regiment (commanded by Edward Hatch) and the 2nd Michigan Cavalry, to which Philip H. Sheridan had been assigned command that day, on an expedition against the Mobile and Ohio Railroad. Elliott left Pope's position near Farmington that night with his brigade and marched to Iuka, and from there by a circuitous route to Boonville, Mississippi, twenty-two miles south of Corinth. There he destroyed the depot and some cars, some track both above and below the town, and large quantities of stores of military value, including cars loaded with ammunition. When this work was done, Elliott returned and rejoined the army May 31, after the evacuation of Corinth.

Halleck issued orders on May 27 for a general advance of the army the next day. He ordered Pope to advance along the left-hand (or southern) road and establish batteries for the bombardment of the enemy works, and he further instructed him to cross Bridge Creek and carry the enemy's works at the Widow Phillips' house if possible. On May 28, Pope advanced as ordered, and Stanley's division occupied the eastern bank of Bridge Creek, in front of the enemy works. Stanley's right extended to the north toward the Boxe house, on the right-hand (or northern) road, where Crittenden's division of Buell's Center was in line facing west. Stanley's left was bent back to the east along the road on which the division had advanced, facing south. Paine's division was en echelon on the left of Stanley, facing southwest, and Hamilton's division was on the left of Paine, facing south.

On the right of Pope, Buell's divisions also advanced May 28, 1862. McCook's division drove the enemy from Serratt's Hill, a commanding position within about 1,000 yards of the enemy's line of defenses. Nelson drove the enemy from Bridge Creek and gained a position about 1,300 yards from the enemy's works. Crittenden advanced about three-fourths of a mile to support Nelson, and Wood's division remained in its original position. Buell's left flank connected with the right of Pope's command, and his right flank, which then was entirely in front of Thomas W. Sherman's division, extended to within one-half mile of the Purdy-Corinth road.

On the night of May 27, 1862, William T. Sherman was ordered to advance from his camp at the Russell house and drive the enemy from a house (the so-called "double log house") that was situated on a high ridge on his front, on the Purdy-Corinth road. The next morning, Sherman formed the troops selected for the attack in line as follows: Morgan L. Smith's First Brigade of Sherman's division, with Samuel E. Barrett's Battery B, 1st Illinois Light Artillery and Allen C. Waterhouse's Battery E, 1st Illinois Light Artillery, were to attack along the Purdy-Corinth road; James W. Denver's Third Brigade of Sherman's division, with the Morton Battery, took position on the right of Smith; James C. Veatch's brigade of Hurlbut's division moved through the woods on the left and connected with the left of Smith's brigade; and John A. Logan's brigade of Judah's division, which had been placed under Sherman's orders, advanced from the Easel house and formed on the right of Denver's brigade. Judah also sent Ross' brigade of his division to the Bowie Cut on the Mobile and Ohio Railroad, to the right of Sherman's line, where he entrenched a position and watched the right flank. Axel Silfversparre's Battery H, 1st Illinois Light Artillery and Charles Mann's Battery C, 1st Missouri Light Artillery also took part in the engagement.

Sherman's advance started about 8:00 A.M., and a short time later the enemy was driven from the ridge. An attempt was made that afternoon to recapture the position, but it was soon repulsed.

May 29, 1862 was comparatively quiet, but Thomas W. Sherman advanced two of his brigades across Bridge Creek to fill a gap that existed between the left of McKean's division and the right of Buell's line, which had advanced the day before.

The enemy evacuated Corinth during the night of May 29–30, 1862 and retreated southward toward Tupelo, Mississippi. Federal troops occupied Corinth the next morning, and Halleck sent Pope with his Army of the Mississippi in pursuit of the enemy. Soon the divisions of Davies and Thomas W. Sherman were added to the pursuing column. Pope established headquarters at Boonville and pushed troops forward to Baldwyn and beyond. Then, on June 9, Halleck informed Pope that Buell's Army of the Ohio had been ordered east, and instructed him to abandon the pursuit and to select a good position for his army someplace between Corinth and Baldwyn. For further information, see Army of the Mississippi (Pope, Rosecrans); Army of the Ohio

(Buell); and Army of the Tennessee, District of West Tennessee.

DEMONSTRATION ON DALTON, GEORGIA
FEBRUARY 22–27, 1864

February 14, 1864, Ulysses S. Grant ordered George H. Thomas, commander of the Army of the Cumberland, to send out from the vicinity of Chattanooga a reconnaissance in force toward Dalton, Georgia. John M. Palmer was assigned command of the expedition, which consisted of his own Fourteenth Corps, which was near Chattanooga; Charles Cruft's First Division, Fourth Corps, which was at Blue Springs, Tennessee; and Eli Long's Second Brigade, Second Cavalry Division. Palmer was directed to occupy Dalton and to push on to the south beyond the town as far as possible.

Palmer began his advance on the morning of February 22, 1864. Cruft left his First Brigade at Ooltewah, Tennessee to guard the East Tennessee and Georgia Railroad, and at 8:00 A.M. marched with his Second Brigade and Third Brigade to Red Clay, Georgia. Long was ordered to establish communications with Cruft at Red Clay and then advance on the Spring Place road toward Dalton.

Richard W. Johnson's First Division and Absalom Baird's Third Division of Fourteenth Corps marched from Chattanooga to Rossville, and they then took the direct road to Ringgold, Georgia, which they occupied that day. At that time, the brigades of Jefferson C. Davis' Second Division, Fourteenth Corps were somewhat scattered, with Carter Van Vleck's Second Brigade guarding the railroad to Knoxville, James D. Morgan's First Brigade at McAfee Church, and Daniel McCook's Third Brigade at Chickamauga Station. February 23, 1864, Davis concentrated First Brigade and Third Brigade at Ringgold, and Second Brigade joined them there that night.

February 23, 1864, First Brigade of Charles L. Matthies' Detachment Fifteenth Corps, commanded by Willard A. Dickerman, reported to Cruft at Red Clay, and that day Cruft's division marched to the farm of Dr. Lee. This was located on the road that

ran from Catoosa Station to Varnell's Station, at the point where it intersected the road running from Cleveland to Tunnel Hill. Cruft arrived at Dr. Lee's farm about 9:00 P.M.

February 23, 1864, Johnson's division, led by Thomas J. Harrison's 8th Indiana Cavalry, moved through the gap in front of Ringgold to Catoosa Station, three miles to the south. Harrison drove back the enemy cavalry force that was stationed there and pursued it to Tunnel Hill, where it was reinforced. Johnson then sent forward William P. Carlin with his First Brigade to support Harrison, and together they drove the enemy from the town and to the hills beyond. By that time it was dark, and Harrison and Carlin returned to Catoosa Station.

On the morning of February 24, 1864, Palmer's command was in position as follows: Baird's division was south of Taylor's Ridge, near Ringgold; Cruft's division was at Dr. Lee's farm; Johnson's and Davis' divisions were in advance toward Tunnel Hill, with William P. Boone's 28th Kentucky (mounted infantry) and Harrison's 8th Indiana Cavalry; and Long's brigade was at Varnell's Station on the Cleveland and Dalton Railroad.

That morning, Johnson again advanced toward Tunnel Hill, with Carlin's brigade in the lead, and John H. King's Second Brigade and Henry A. Hambright's Third Brigade following, in that order. Davis left his Second Brigade to hold the gap at Ringgold, and with James D. Morgan's First Brigade and Daniel McCook's Third Brigade advanced in support of Johnson.

At Tunnel Hill Johnson came under artillery fire; he halted Carlin and sent the brigades of Hambright and King to occupy some high ground to the left. Then Davis, with Palmer's permission, sent Morgan's brigade to the left of King's brigade to occupy a hill some one-half to three-fourths of a mile north of the tunnel. Morgan's brigade then outflanked the enemy position, which was soon abandoned. The enemy retreated toward Buzzard's Roost Gap in front of Dalton. This gap, through which the Western and Atlantic Railroad runs through Rocky Face Ridge, was also called Mill Creek Gap, and the high crests on its sides were called Buzzard's Roost. Davis followed the enemy with his two brigades and was supported by King's brigade of Johnson's division. Johnson camped that night with the brigades of Carlin and Hambright near Tunnel Hill.

About noon February 24, 1864, Grose's brigade of Cruft's division moved out from Dr. Lee's on a reconnaissance on the road from Catoosa Station to Varnell's Station. It crossed Rocky Face Ridge three miles north of Tunnel Hill, then moved down the valley on the eastern side of the ridge toward Buzzard's Roost Gap and Dalton. The next day, Cruft joined Grose with the other two brigades.

February 25, 1864, Davis' division, supported by King's brigade, came up to Buzzard's Roost Gap in Rocky Face Ridge, where they found the enemy in strong force. There was skirmishing throughout the day, and Johnson's division moved up in support of Davis. Late that evening, Hambright and King relieved Davis in front of Buzzard's Roost Gap, and Carlin was held in reserve.

At 3:00 A.M. February 25, 1864, Baird's division started from Tunnel Hill to join Cruft's division and Long's cavalry brigade on the east side of Rocky Face Ridge for an advance toward Dalton. Upon arrival there, Baird formed on the right of Cruft, and together they advanced along the valley to uncover Buzzard's Roost Gap so that they could unite with Palmer's divisions south of the ridge.

February 26, 1864, Johnson and Davis skirmished with the enemy in front of Buzzard's Roost Gap, while awaiting the arrival of Cruft and Baird on the opposite side of the ridge. The latter two divisions, however, encountered strong resistance, and advanced only with difficulty. Finally, after Cruft and Baird had skirmished until dark, Palmer concluded that the enemy was too strong to force out of Dalton, and he ordered the withdrawal of his command. Johnson moved to Tyner's Station with two brigades, and sent one to Graysville; Davis retired to his old campground in front of Rossville; Baird's division moved to Ringgold; Cruft returned to his old positions at Ooltewah and Blue Springs; and Long's brigade went to Cleveland.

The organization of Palmer's forces during the demonstration on Dalton, February 22–27, 1864 was as follows:

FOURTH CORPS

First Division, Charles Cruft
First Brigade, Willard A. Dickerman

Second Brigade, Thomas E. Champion
Third Brigade, William Grose
Artillery, Peter Simonson
5th Battery, Indiana Light Artillery, Alfred Morrison
Battery H, 4th United States Artillery, William A. Heilman

Note. David A. Enyart's First Brigade of the division remained at Ooltewah, Tennessee, and was replaced for this expedition by Charles L. Matthies' brigade (commanded by Dickerman) of Fifteenth Corps. Matthies' brigade was ordered to rejoin Fifteenth Corps March 1, 1864.

Cavalry
4th Michigan (detachment), William W. Van Antwerp
4th Ohio (detachment), Philip H. Warner

FOURTEENTH CORPS, John M. Palmer

First Division, Richard W. Johnson
First Brigade, William P. Carlin
Second Brigade, John H. King
Third Brigade, Henry A. Hambright
Battery A (section), 1st Michigan Light Artillery, Clark M. Harris

Second Division, Jefferson C. Davis
First Brigade, James D. Morgan
Second Brigade, Carter Van Vleck, temporarily to February 26, 1864
John G. Mitchell
Third Brigade, Daniel McCook
2nd Battery (section), Minnesota Light Artillery, Henry W. Hardee

Third Division, Absalom Baird
First Brigade, John B. Turchin
Second Brigade, Ferdinand Van Derveer
Third Brigade, William H. Hays
19th Battery, Indiana Light Artillery, Samuel J. Harris, to February 25, 1864, wounded
William P. Stackhouse

CAVALRY

Second Brigade, Second Cavalry Division, Eli Long
Unassigned
8th Indiana Cavalry, Thomas J. Harrison
28th Kentucky (mounted infantry), William P. Boone
15th Pennsylvania Cavalry, William J. Palmer

EAST TENNESSEE CAMPAIGN (BURNSIDE) AUGUST 16, 1863– OCTOBER 19, 1863

From the beginning of hostilities, the administration in Washington wished to occupy East Tennessee with United States forces. Eastern Tennessee, like Western Virginia, was a mountainous country where slavery had never become established, and where the people had little interest in states' rights. When Tennessee seceded from the Union, the inhabitants of the eastern part of the state remained strongly pro-Union, and the Confederate authorities soon began to take strong repressive measures to keep that part of Tennessee in the Confederacy.

However, the use of United States troops to occupy and establish Union control in eastern Tennessee was virtually impossible during the early part of the war because of its isolation from the North. Kentucky remained neutral during the summer of 1861, and consequently provided a barrier against the passage of United States troops toward Tennessee. There were also additional difficulties, even after Confederate troops invaded Kentucky and put an end to its neutrality. The mountains of East Tennessee were covered by dense forests, and consisted of an almost impenetrable jumble of peaks and valleys, through which ran only a few very bad roads.

President Lincoln wished to occupy this region for several reasons. First it was a strong center of people who were loyal to the Union, and who would, Lincoln believed, strongly support a Union army if it could move into the upper Tennessee River valley. As an additional reason, he wished to protect the loyal citizens of the region from the severe treatment that they were suffering from Confederate authorities and Southern sympathizers. Finally, there was the very practical reason that the series of connecting railroads that ran westward from Richmond, Virginia to Memphis, Tennessee, connecting the eastern and western parts of the Confederacy, ran, in part, through East Tennessee. The East Tennessee and Virginia Railroad ran from Bristol, Tennessee to Knoxville, Tennessee, and the East Tennessee and Georgia Railroad ran on from Knoxville to Chattanooga.

The first effort to move an army into East Tennessee occurred in October 1861, when George H. Thomas set out for Cumberland Gap. He got only as far as London, Kentucky, however, when he was called back.

In 1863, the administration grew more insistent, and in March 1863 Ambrose E. Burnside was ordered to Kentucky with two divisions of his Ninth Corps. Upon arriving there, he was directed to assume command of the Department of the Ohio, and to move as soon as practicable against Knoxville. Burnside then began serious preparations for a movement toward East Tennessee.

On April 11, 1863, he designated the troops serving in the Department of the Ohio as the Army of the Ohio, and it was to consist of the two divisions of Ninth Corps and the various regiments then stationed in Kentucky. On April 27, Burnside ordered the organization of the troops in Kentucky into the Twenty-Third Corps, Army of the Ohio, and assigned George L. Hartsuff to the command of the corps.

Burnside then began to make the necessary dispositions of the troops of Ninth Corps and Twenty-Third Corps for an advance into Tennessee. He left his headquarters at Cincinnati June 3, 1863 to assume personal command of the expedition, which was to consist of the two divisions of Ninth Corps under Orlando B. Willcox and a part of Twenty-Third Corps under Hartsuff. On his arrival at Lexington, Kentucky, however, Burnside received an order from Henry W. Halleck to send John G. Parke with the two divisions of Ninth Corps to reinforce Ulysses S. Grant's army at Vicksburg, and they began to leave immediately for Mississippi.

Burnside, however, continued his preparations for the Knoxville expedition, hoping that he could spare sufficient troops from Twenty-Third Corps for that purpose. He was then interrupted a second time by the approach of John H. Morgan, who had crossed the Cumberland River near Burkesville, Kentucky and moved in the direction of Columbia with his cavalry division. Hartsuff immediately ordered all available forces in pursuit. Morgan approached Green River July 4, 1863, but was repulsed by a Federal force commanded by Orlando H. Moore. Morgan then moved on through Lebanon, Kentucky to the Ohio River, crossed into Indiana, and moved across the southern part of the state and into Ohio. A considerable part of Twenty-Third Corps was sent in pursuit, and many of these troops did not return to their commands until after Morgan and the remnants of his division were captured near New Lisbon, Ohio on July 26.

Before Morgan's appearance in Kentucky, Burnside had intended to advance on the left of William S. Rosecrans' Army of the Cumberland, which moved out late in June 1863 at the beginning of the Tullahoma (or Middle Tennessee) Campaign, but because of Morgan's raid, Burnside was unable to move at that time. Having driven Braxton Bragg's Confederate Army of Tennessee from Tennessee, Rosecrans prepared to continue his advance toward Chattanooga, Tennessee and northern Georgia. Once again, Burnside was asked to cooperate with Rosecrans by advancing into East Tennessee to connect with the Army of the Cumberland as it advanced against Bragg's army at Chattanooga.

In late April 1863, when Burnside was threatening an invasion of East Tennessee, Simon B. Buckner was ordered from Mobile, Alabama to assume command of the Department of East Tennessee. He arrived at Knoxville on May 11 and relieved Dabney H. Maury, who in turn assumed command of the Department of the Gulf. Buckner remained at Knoxville until the latter part of August, and then, as the Army of the Cumberland began crossing the Tennessee River, Buckner turned over the command of his department to Samuel Jones, who was in southwest Virginia, and moved with William Preston's infantry division of his corps to Loudon. Before leaving, he left John W. Frazer's brigade to hold Cumberland Gap, and he also left Alfred E. Jackson's brigade on the railroad east of Knoxville between Carter's Depot (or Station) and Bristol, Tennessee. Then, just before the Battle of Chickamauga, Bragg ordered Buckner to Chattanooga to join his Army of Tennessee. Thus, when Burnside finally approached Knoxville, he encountered little resistance.

While awaiting the return of Ninth Corps from Vicksburg, Burnside sent William P. Sanders with a mixed brigade of cavalry and mounted infantry on a raid into East Tennessee. Sanders left June 14, 1863 and returned June 23; during his raid he seriously disrupted Confederate communications and destroyed a number of railroad bridges, including the long bridge over the Holston River.

Burnside had hoped that he could delay his advance into East Tennessee until the divisions of Ninth Corps had returned from Vicksburg, but the necessity of his cooperating with the movements of Rosecrans' army toward Chattanooga compelled him to proceed without them.

Twenty-Third Corps was reorganized for the expedition by an order of August 6, 1863, and the three divisions that were to accompany Burnside were ordered to rendezvous as follows: Mahlon D. Manson's Second Division at or near Lebanon, Kentucky; Milo S. Hascall's Third Division at or near Danville, Kentucky; and Robert K. Byrd's First Brigade and James M. Shackelford's Third Brigade of Samuel P. Carter's Fourth Division at Stanford, Kentucky and Felix W. Graham's Second Brigade at Glasgow, Kentucky. Carter's Fourth Division consisted of regiments of cavalry and mounted infantry. Frank Wolford's Independent Cavalry Brigade was to assemble at Somerset, Kentucky, and Andrew J. Konkle's Reserve Artillery was at Camp Nelson.

Burnside left his headquarters at Cincinnati, Ohio August 10, 1863 to rejoin the reorganized Twenty-Third Corps, which was to be under the direction of Hartsuff on the march into East Tennessee. To ensure that the department would be properly supervised during his absence, he left Orlando B. Willcox in command of the District of Indiana (and Michigan), Jacob D. Cox in command of the District of Ohio, and Jeremiah T. Boyle in command of the District of Kentucky.

By August 16, 1863, Burnside had succeeded in organizing a force of about 15,000 men, and the next day he finally set out on the road toward Knoxville. The movements of the army are given here in some detail as follows:

August 17, 1863, Hascall's Third Division moved from Danville, Kentucky to Stanford; Byrd's First Brigade and Shackelford's Third Brigade of Carter's Fourth Division moved from Stanford to Crab Orchard, Kentucky; and Manson's Second Division left Lebanon for Columbia.

August 18, 1863, John W. Foster's Second Brigade, Fourth Division marched from Glasgow to Rose's Cross Roads.

August 19, 1863, Hascall's division moved on from Stanford to Crab Orchard, and Byrd's brigade from Crab Orchard to Mount Vernon, Kentucky.

August 20, 1863, Manson's division arrived at Columbia, and Byrd's brigade continued on from Mount Vernon toward Lebanon.

On August 20, 1863, Burnside's orders to Hartsuff for the future movements of Twenty-Third Corps were as follows: Hascall's division was to move to Kingston, Tennessee by way of Somerset, Chitwood's, Huntsville, and Montgomery; Manson's division was to march from Columbia, Kentucky to Montgomery, Tennessee by way of Creelsboro, Albany, and Jamestown; Graham's cavalry brigade, which was at Glasgow, was to join Manson's column by way of Burkesville and Albany, Kentucky and Jamestown, Tennessee; Wolford's cavalry brigade was to guard the supply and ammunition trains that were with Hascall's division; Carter's division was to move by way of Mount Vernon, London, and Williamsburg, all in Kentucky, then over the Jellico Mountains to Chitwood's in Tennessee, and from there to Kingston by way of Huntsville and Montgomery in Tennessee. Burnside accompanied Carter's column. The road south from Somerset, Kentucky to Kingston, Tennessee, which was used by Burnside's main column, followed closely the line of present-day U.S. Route 27.

August 20, 1863, Manson's division arrived at Columbia, and Byrd's brigade moved from Mount Vernon toward Lebanon.

August 21, 1863, Julius White relieved Manson in command of Second Division, and the division moved from Columbia toward Creelsboro. Hascall's division moved from Crab Orchard to Buck Creek; Shackelford's brigade advanced from Crab Orchard to Mount Vernon; Byrd's brigade moved from Mount Vernon to London; and Foster's brigade left Glasgow.

August 22, 1863, Hascall's division marched on from Buck Creek to Smith's Ferry on the Cumberland River.

August 23, 1863, White's division (formerly Manson's) arrived at Mud Camp on the Cumberland River; Samuel A. Gilbert's First Brigade of Hascall's Third Division marched to Sloan's Valley; and Foster's Second Brigade, Fourth Division crossed the Cumberland River.

August 24, 1863, Gilbert's brigade moved on to Indian Creek, and Daniel Cameron's Second Brigade of Hascall's division moved up to Sloan's Valley.

August 25, 1863, Gilbert's brigade moved to a point about three miles south of Pine Knot Tavern, and Cameron's brigade advanced to Indian Creek.

August 26, 1863, White's division advanced to Jamestown; Gilbert's brigade, with Konkle's Reserve Artillery, moved to Chitwood's; and Byrd's and Shackelford's brigades of Carter's division also marched to Chitwood's.

August 27, 1863, Cameron's brigade of Hascall's division arrived at Chitwood's.

August 28, 1863, Byrd's and Shackelford's brigades marched toward Montgomery.

August 30, 1863, Hascall's division and the Reserve Artillery advanced to the White Oak road, and White's division arrived at Montgomery.

August 31, 1863, Byrd and Shackelford passed through Montgomery and moved on to the Emery (Emory) Iron Works. Skirmishers then drove the enemy from Winter's Gap, and Foster's brigade moved up and occupied the gap. Cameron's brigade and the Reserve Artillery advanced to Schooler's (Schouler's), three miles south of Wartburg. White's division was in camp between Schooler's and the Emery Iron Works.

September 1, 1863, White's division and Byrd's brigade of Carter's division moved to Kingston, and Hascall's division and the Reserve Artillery marched to the Emery Iron Works. Shackelford's brigade advanced to Walker's Ferry on the Clinch River. At Indian Tavern, forty-five miles from Knoxville and eight miles from Montgomery,

Foster's brigade was detached from the column and sent through Winter's Gap to occupy Knoxville.

September 2, 1863, Foster's brigade occupied Knoxville; Hascall's division and the Reserve Artillery reached Poplar Creek; Byrd's brigade arrived at Kingston; and Shackelford's brigade marched to Lenoir's Station (present-day Lenoir City) on the East Tennessee and Georgia Railroad.

September 3, 1863, White's division and Hascall's division marched to Lackey's plantation, and Shackelford's brigade moved to Knoxville.

On September 4, 1863, there were some changes ordered in the command in Twenty-Third Corps. Samuel P. Carter was assigned as provost marshal general of the District of East Tennessee, and James M. Shackelford assumed command of the Fourth Division of mounted troops. James P. T. Carter assumed command of Shackelford's Third Brigade, Fourth Division.

Before leaving Kentucky, Burnside had organized a brigade of new troops under the command of John F. De Courcy, which he attached to Ninth Corps, and he had ordered that this brigade move from Pittman down on the north side of Cumberland Gap and, if possible, gain possession of the gap. Upon arriving in Knoxville, however, Burnside learned that the enemy still held the gap, and on September 4, 1863 he sent Shackelford's Third Brigade to move up to the gap from the south.

Also on September 4, Burnside moved White's division to Loudon, ordered Gilbert's brigade to Knoxville, and sent Cameron's brigade of Hascall's division to Lenoir's.

When Shackelford arrived on the south side of Cumberland Gap September 6, 1863, he moved up and took position to invest the enemy's line of works. Meantime, De Courcy had arrived on the north side of the gap, where he could cut off the escape of the garrison in that direction. In addition to these two brigades, Burnside ordered Gilbert, with a part of his brigade and a battery, to move up to the gap to support Shackelford, and Burnside accompanied Gilbert's column. Gilbert reached the gap September 9, and that day John W. Frazer, commanding the enemy forces at the gap, surren-

dered with about 2,500 men, 12 guns, and large quantities of stores.

After the surrender of Cumberland Gap, Shackelford's brigade, then commanded by James P. T. Carter, and Gilbert's brigade returned to Knoxville by way of Morristown; Carter arrived September 13, 1863, and Gilbert came up the next day. De Courcy's brigade, then commanded by Wilson C. Lemert, remained at Cumberland Gap to garrison the works. Burnside had placed De Courcy under arrest for alleged improper conduct during the siege. On September 10, Foster's brigade and the 103rd Ohio Infantry of Cameron's brigade occupied Greeneville, northeast of Knoxville, on the East Tennessee and Virginia Railroad.

Before leaving Cumberland Gap for Knoxville, Burnside received a communication from Thomas L. Crittenden, commanding Twenty-First Corps of Rosecrans' Army of the Cumberland, dated September 10, 1863, informing Burnside that he was in possession of Chattanooga. In the same dispatch he forwarded a request from Rosecrans that Burnside move his cavalry down the Tennessee River to occupy the country then held by Robert H. G. Minty's cavalry brigade of Rosecrans' army, which had been ordered to cross to the south side of the river.

This communication led Burnside to believe that he need have no apprehension about Rosecrans' army, and he then decided to occupy all important points in East Tennessee above Knoxville and, if possible, to push on and reach the important saltworks at Saltville, above Abingdon in Virginia.

On September 13, 1863, while at Knoxville, Burnside received an order from Halleck, dated September 11, directing him to occupy and hold the gaps in the mountains along the North Carolina border, and also to hold the line of the Holston River, or some point where he could prevent the enemy from advancing into East Tennessee from Virginia. Halleck also ordered Burnside to connect with Rosecrans' army, at least with his cavalry.

Burnside then ordered Byrd, who had been at Kingston with his cavalry brigade, to move to Athens, Tennessee and communicate with Minty, in compliance with Rosecrans' request. He then began to move the rest of his command eastward as follows: on September 15, White's Second Division left Loudon; passing through Knoxville, it arrived at New Market on September 17. Also on September 15, Cameron's brigade of Hascall's Third Division left Knoxville, arriving at Jonesboro September 19. September 16, James P. T. Carter's Third Brigade of Shackelford's cavalry division and Frank Wolford's Independent Brigade marched from Knoxville to Greeneville.

On September 17, 1863, Foster moved out from Greeneville in search of the enemy, and the next day drove some of John S. Williams' troops from the ford above Kingsport. Foster followed and September 19 pushed Williams back from Bristol, destroying the railroad bridge there, and also quantities of stores. He returned to Blountsville the next day.

On September 17, 1863, Burnside received a dispatch from Halleck, dated September 14, ordering him to reinforce Rosecrans as rapidly as possible because it was thought that Bragg was concentrating his forces in preparation for giving battle. Burnside then issued orders directing all troops not then in the presence of the enemy to turn about and march toward Knoxville. Also on September 17, Burnside left Knoxville and started up the Holston Valley to assume personal direction of the troops advancing against the enemy.

The Battle of Chickamauga was fought September 19–20, 1863, but the troops of Twenty-Third Corps were not engaged. The only part of Burnside's command that was between Knoxville and Chattanooga at the beginning of the battle was Byrd's cavalry brigade, which was at Athens, but White's Second Division and Wolford's cavalry brigade were marching in that direction. On September 19, Wolford's brigade returned from Greeneville to Knoxville, and the next day it moved on toward Athens to join Byrd. White also turned back from Morristown and moved toward Knoxville. White reached Knoxville September 20, and the next day moved on to Loudon.

Meantime, the rest of Burnside's command continued its advance up the valley as follows: September 20, Gilbert's brigade of Hascall's Third Division marched from Knoxville toward Morristown and Jonesboro to join Cameron's brigade of the same division. September 21, Hascall, with Cameron's brigade, moved from Jonesboro to a point near Carter's Depot (or Station) on the railroad, and he was joined there the next day by Gilbert's brigade.

On September 23, 1863, the enemy having evacuated Carter's Station, Hascall's division moved back to Jonesboro. The next day Gilbert's brigade continued on to Knoxville, and Cameron's brigade to Henderson. Foster's brigade, which had arrived at Carter's Station, also marched back to Jonesboro. On September 25, Cameron moved toward Morristown and Foster toward Knoxville. The next day Cameron moved by rail to Concord.

September 25, 1863, Byrd, who was then at Calhoun, was attacked, and he fell back to within about two miles of Athens. He was joined there by Wolford, and two days later the two brigades retired to Loudon. On September 29 they marched back to Sweetwater (Sweet Water), Tennessee, and the next day they continued on to Loudon.

Foster's brigade arrived at Knoxville September 28, 1863, and James P. T. Carter fell back from Carter's Depot to Henderson. Two days later Carter moved back to Greeneville.

Meantime, on September 9, 1863, Burnside sent orders by telegraph for Ninth Corps, which had arrived in Kentucky from Vicksburg, to join him at once in East Tennessee. In mid-August 1863, John G. Parke's Ninth Corps began to arrive in Kentucky from Vicksburg. Edward Ferrero's First Division arrived at Cincinnati on August 12 and camped at Covington, Kentucky. It then moved to Nicholasville on August 18. Robert B. Potter's Second Division arrived at Cincinnati August 20, and it too encamped at Covington.

On August 22, 1863, there was a reorganization of Ninth Corps, and Parke transferred Benjamin C. Christ's Third Brigade, Second Division to First Division as Second Brigade. He also attached John F. De Courcy's brigade to Second Division, and it later became Third Brigade of that division. There was also a change in command August 25, when Parke left because of illness, and Potter assumed command of the corps. Simon G. Griffin assumed command of Second Division, and Zenas R. Bliss succeeded Griffin in command of First Brigade, Second Division.

August 26, 1863, First Division marched to Crab Orchard, and Second Division moved up to

Nicholasville. Corps headquarters was established at Lexington September 1.

September 9, 1863, Edwin Schall's Second Brigade of Griffin's division moved up to Crab Orchard to garrison the town, and the next day Ferrero's division broke camp and marched toward Knoxville. On September 12, Zenas R. Bliss' First Brigade, Second Division joined Schall's brigade at Crab Orchard. Then, on September 16, Bliss' brigade and Second Division headquarters followed First Division toward Knoxville. Schall's brigade remained at Crab Orchard.

Ferrero's division marched over bad roads by way of Cumberland Gap and Morristown and arrived at Knoxville September 25, 1863. Bliss' brigade arrived at Knoxville September 28, and Ninth Corps headquarters arrived September 30.

At the time that Ninth Corps arrived in East Tennessee, the advance troops of Burnside's command consisted of James P. T. Carter's Third Brigade of Shackelford's Fourth Division, Twenty-Third Corps, which was at Bull's Gap, fifty-six miles east of Knoxville, and troops of Hascall's Third Division of Twenty-Third Corps, which were in support at Morristown.

On September 30, 1863, Samuel Jones ordered Robert Ransom, Jr., then commanding the Confederate troops in East Tennessee, to move down the valley and drive the Federal troops beyond Greeneville. John S. Williams, who had been assigned command of the troops in the vicinity of Bristol, occupied Greeneville October 2. In response to this movement, Burnside began sending reinforcements to join Carter's brigade at Bull's Gap.

On October 4, 1863, David Morrison's First Brigade, First Division and Zenas R. Bliss' First Brigade, Second Division, both under the command of Potter, were sent by rail to Bull's Gap.

October 5, 1863, Orlando B. Willcox, with four new Indiana regiments from Camp Nelson, Kentucky, reported to Burnside from Cumberland Gap, and he was directed to move to Bull's Gap by way of Morristown. Two days later, Benjamin C. Christ's Second Brigade and Daniel Leasure's Third Brigade of Ferrero's division were also sent to Bull's Gap. Early in October, William A. Hoskins was at Morristown in command of a mixed brigade consisting of infantry, cavalry, and artillery, and on

October 8 Burnside ordered this brigade to Bull's Gap, where Hoskins was to report to Willcox. Burnside also ordered Shackelford to move up the valley with all of his cavalry except Byrd's and Wolford's brigades. Burnside, in person, left Knoxville on the morning of October 9 and joined the forces at Bull's Gap that same day.

On October 10, 1863, Burnside advanced with his command, and at Blue Springs, about midway between Bull's Gap and Greeneville, he found Williams' command in a strong position between the wagon road and the railroad that ran to Greeneville. The cavalry skirmished with the enemy during most of the afternoon while John W. Foster moved with his brigade toward a point near Rheatown, which was in rear of the enemy, on his line of retreat.

At 3:30 P.M. Burnside ordered Potter to advance Ferrero's division and attempt to break through the center of the enemy's line. By 5:00 P.M. Ferrero had formed his three brigades for the assault, and the line then moved forward. They soon broke through Williams' position and drove him back, and during the night he retired toward Virginia. Although Foster was to have been in position to prevent the enemy's retreat, he was unable to prevent the enemy from passing by on the road and moving back toward Virginia.

Early on the morning of October 11, 1863, Burnside started in pursuit and drove the enemy beyond the Watauga River. Shackelford advanced through Blountsville, and on October 16 he was at Bristol, with his advanced troops ten miles out on the Abingdon road. On October 21 he was back at Jonesboro, and he then took position where he could prevent another enemy advance into East Tennessee.

Hoskins' brigade was left at Jonesboro to support the cavalry, and Willcox's division was left at Greeneville. Ninth Corps returned to Knoxville October 14–15, 1863. Toward the end of October, Hascall's division of Twenty-Third Corps returned from Carter's Station to Knoxville, and White's division of the same corps guarded the Tennessee River between Loudon and Kingston.

For information about the later operations of Burnside's command in East Tennessee, see Knoxville, Tennessee Campaign.

The organization of the troops in the field under Burnside's command during the East Tennessee Campaign was as follows:

ARMY OF THE OHIO
Ambrose E. Burnside

NINTH CORPS, John G. Parke, to August 25, 1863, sick
    Robert B. Potter

First Division, Edward Ferrero
    First Brigade, David Morrison
    Second Brigade, Ebenezer W. Peirce
      Benjamin C. Christ
    Third Brigade, Cornelius Byington
      Daniel Leasure
    Artillery
      Batteries L and M, 3rd United States Artillery, John
        Edwards, Jr.

Second Division, Robert B. Potter, to August 25, 1863
    Simon G. Griffin
    First Brigade, Zenas R. Bliss
    Second Brigade, Edwin Schall
    Artillery
      Battery L, 2nd New York Light Artillery, Jacob
        Roemer
      Battery D, Pennsylvania Light Artillery, George
        W. Durell

TWENTY-THIRD CORPS, George L. Hartsuff, September 24, 1863
    Mahlon D. Manson

Second Division, Mahlon D. Manson, to August 21, 1863
    Julius White
    First Brigade, Orlando H. Moore
    Second Brigade, Marshal W. Chapin

Note. The Elgin Battery, Illinois Light Artillery, commanded by Andrew M. Wood, was attached to First Brigade, and Henshaw's Battery, Illinois Light Artillery, commanded by Edward C. Henshaw, was attached to Second Brigade.

Third Division, Milo S. Hascall
    First Brigade, Samuel A. Gilbert, to October 14, 1863
      James W. Reilly
    Second Brigade, Daniel Cameron

Note. Battery D, 1st Ohio Light Artillery, commanded by William H. Pease, was attached to First Brigade, and

Wilder's Battery, Indiana Light Artillery, commanded by Hubbard T. Thomas, was attached to Second Brigade.

Fourth Division, Samuel P. Carter, to September 4, 1863
    James M. Shackelford
    First Brigade, Robert K. Byrd
    Second Brigade, Felix W. Graham, to August 28, 1863
      John W. Foster
    Third Brigade, James M. Shackelford, to September 4, 1863
      James P. T. Carter

Note 1. The 15th Battery, Indiana Light Artillery, commanded by William H. Torr, was attached to First Brigade; Battery M, 1st Illinois Light Artillery, commanded by John H. Colvin, was attached to Second Brigade; and Charles J. Thompson's Battery K, 1st Michigan Light Artillery and R. Clay Crawford's 1st Tennessee Battery were attached to Third Brigade.
Note 2. The brigades of Fourth Division were composed of cavalry and mounted infantry.

Independent Cavalry Brigade, Frank Wolford

Reserve Artillery, Andrew J. Konkle
    Battery M, 2nd Illinois Light Artillery, John C. Phillips
    24th Battery, Indiana Light Artillery, Henry W. Shafer
    19th Battery, Ohio Light Artillery, Joseph C. Shields
    Battery D, 1st Rhode Island Light Artillery, William W. Buckley

Willcox's Division, Orlando B. Willcox
    115th Indiana, Alfred J. Hawn
    116th Indiana, William C. Kise
    117th Indiana, Thomas J. Brady
    118th Indiana, George W. Jackson
    21st Battery, Ohio Light Artillery, James W. Patterson

Before leaving Kentucky for East Tennessee, Burnside organized an Independent Brigade of new troops under John F. De Courcy, which moved down to the north side of Cumberland Gap to prevent the escape of the Confederate garrison there when attacked. His command consisted of two infantry regiments, 800 mounted men, and a battery. After the surrender of the gap September 9, 1863, De Courcy's command was left as garrison of the post, but De Courcy was relieved for writing what was deemed an improper letter, and Wilson C. Lemert assumed command in his place.

CAPTURE OF FORT HENRY AND FORT DONELSON, TENNESSEE FEBRUARY 6, 1862– FEBRUARY 16, 1862

On September 3, 1861, the neutrality of Kentucky was ended when Leonidas Polk, with a Confederate force, occupied Columbus, Kentucky. On September 6, Ulysses S. Grant, commanding Federal forces at Cairo, Illinois, seized Paducah, Kentucky and placed Charles F. Smith in command of the United States Forces in Western Kentucky. Later, Smithland, at the mouth of the Cumberland River, was occupied by Smith's troops.

In September 1861, when Albert Sidney Johnston assumed command of the Confederate Department No. 2, which included the states of Kentucky and Tennessee, along with other territory to the south and west, he established a defensive line in Kentucky that extended from Columbus on the west, through Bowling Green, to Cumberland Ford on the east. In addition, there were skeleton garrisons at Fort Henry on the Tennessee River and Fort Donelson on the Cumberland River. Even before Grant began his movement toward Fort Henry around the first of February 1862, Johnston had moved a part of his forces into position to defend the Cumberland River. He stationed Gideon J. Pillow with his brigade at Clarksville, and sent John B. Floyd and Simon B. Buckner with their troops to Russellville.

By January 1862, several plans had been proposed for offensive operations by Federal troops against Johnston's Kentucky line, but there was no general agreement as to which of these plans should be adopted. There was, however, some strong support for a movement up the Tennessee and Cumberland rivers. The control of these important waterways would provide the means for advancing deep into Confederate territory as far south as northern Mississippi and Alabama.

There has been considerable controversy about who first proposed this line of advance, but the fact is that, from the beginning, it was an obvious route of considerable promise, and it had been considered for some time by a number of people, including George B. McClellan, general in chief of the army; Henry W. Halleck, commander of the Department of the Missouri; and Ulysses S. Grant, commander of the District of Cairo.

Grant, particularly, was strongly in favor of an advance against Fort Henry on the Tennessee River, and he asked for permission to visit Halleck to discuss the matter with him. Permission was granted January 22, 1862, but Grant was strongly rebuffed by Halleck when he brought up the subject of Fort Henry. Grant then returned to Cairo, but he was persistent, and on January 28 he informed Halleck that if given permission to do so, he could take and hold Fort Henry. That same day, Flag Officer Andrew H. Foote, commanding the United States Forces Western Waters, wrote to Halleck to say that he supported Grant's proposal. Finally, on February 1, Halleck authorized Grant to organize and lead an expedition up the Tennessee River against Fort Henry.

On February 1, 1862, in preparation for this movement, Grant reorganized his command of the District of Cairo into four brigades, assigning John A. McClernand to the command of a First Division, to consist of the First Brigade and the Second Brigade of the district. The division was organized as follows:

First Division, John A. McClernand
    First Brigade, Richard J. Oglesby
    Second Brigade, William H. L. Wallace

Eleazer A. Paine's Third Brigade and James D. Morgan's Fourth Brigade did not accompany Grant, but Paine remained in command at Cairo and Mound City, and Morgan at Bird's Point.

Grant also ordered Charles F. Smith to organize a Second Division from troops at Paducah, Smithland, and Fort Holt. Smith's division was organized as follows:

Second Division, Charles F. Smith
    First Brigade, John McArthur
    Second Brigade, Lewis Wallace
    Third Brigade, John Cook

In addition to the land forces, Flag Officer Andrew H. Foote, commanding United States Forces Western Waters, was ordered to move from Cairo with the ironclad gunboats *Essex, Carondelet, Cincinnati,* and *Saint Louis* to Paducah, where they were to rendezvous with the wooden gunboats *Con-*

estoga, Lexington, and *Tyler* at noon February 2, 1862.

Foote joined Grant at Paducah, and there they awaited the arrival of the transports carrying McClernand's division. McClernand finally arrived there late that night, and Grant immediately ordered him to move on up the Tennessee River with his command. Grant also ordered Charles F. Smith to follow, but only a part of his command accompanied McClernand because of a lack of boats.

The transports moved up the Tennessee River, escorted by the *Essex* and the *Saint Louis,* and the troops disembarked at 4:30 P.M. February 4, 1862 at Itra Landing, on the east bank of the river. This was opposite Pine Bluff, and was about sixty-five miles from Paducah and eight miles below Fort Henry. When the troops had landed, the transports returned for the rest of Charles F. Smith's division.

Grant then made a reconnaissance upstream to determine the range of the guns in Fort Henry. After coming under fire, he returned to Itra Landing, and ordered McClernand to reembark his troops and move them upriver to Bailey's Ferry, which was three miles below Fort Henry, and just out of range of its guns.

All of Grant's forces were finally ashore by the night of February 5, 1862. That night, Charles F. Smith was sent across the Tennessee River to take Fort Heiman, an uncompleted earthwork opposite Fort Henry, but the fort had been evacuated the day before. John McArthur's First Brigade of Smith's division was left at Fort Heiman, and the rest of the division returned to Bailey's Ferry.

Grant could scarcely have picked a worse time for his advance against Fort Henry. There had been heavy rains, and the Tennessee had overflowed its banks, with the result that much of the country near the river was underwater. This made all land movement slow and difficult, but at 11:00 A.M. February 6, 1862, Grant and Foote began their advance toward the fort.

Foote steamed upriver with his four ironclad gunboats in the lead, and Lieutenant Commander S. Ledyard Phelps with three wooden gunboats following. Lloyd Tilghman, commanding at Fort Henry, had doubted his ability to hold the fort against a determined attack, and that morning had ordered Adolphus Heiman, with his own and Joseph Drake's brigades, to march to Fort Donelson to

avoid capture. Personally he had remained with a small number of artillerists to gain time for the rest of the troops to move to safety.

At 12:30 Foote's gunboats opened fire at a distance of about 1,700 yards, and the guns of the fort promptly returned the fire. The gunboats continued to fire as they slowly advanced to within 600 yards of the fort. They suffered some damage, but finally at 1:50 P.M. a white flag appeared, and Tilghman surrendered to Foote before Grant's infantry arrived.

McClernand had marched out from Bailey's Ferry with his First Division at the same time that Foote started up the river, and he was followed by John Cook's Third Brigade of Charles F. Smith's Second Division. McClernand's orders were to get on the road from Fort Henry to Fort Donelson to the east of Fort Henry so as to prevent reinforcements from reaching Tilghman, and also to prevent the escape of the garrison. McClernand was also to be prepared to storm the fort if that became necessary. The distance from Bailey's Ferry to Fort Henry was only eight miles, but because of the heavy rains, the roads were soft and difficult, and McClernand did not arrive on the road until after Heiman had passed with his two brigades. McClernand learned of the surrender of Fort Henry at 3:00 P.M., and the head of his column arrived at the fort about a half-hour later.

Grant had intended to march immediately on Fort Donelson, but he was forced to wait for a time until the roads had dried. Meantime, Halleck had been attempting to send forward reinforcements for Grant's army, and on the evening of February 8, 1862, eight regiments arrived at Fort Henry. Included in the new arrivals was Charles Cruft's Thirteenth Brigade, Fifth Division of Don Carlos Buell's Army of the Ohio, which had been sent down the Ohio River from Owensboro, Kentucky.

On February 10, 1862, Grant organized a new Third Brigade, First Division, consisting of the 17th Illinois, 43rd Illinois, and 49th Illinois, and William R. Morrison was assigned command. Also that day, Grant organized a new Fourth Brigade, Second Division from the 14th Iowa, 25th Indiana, 52nd Indiana, and Birge's Sharpshooters, and Jacob G. Lauman was assigned command.

Finally, at about noon February 11, 1862, Grant

issued orders for the army to begin its march toward Fort Donelson, and directed McClernand to begin the movement of his division that afternoon. Accordingly, Richard J. Oglesby marched out with his First Brigade about five miles from Fort Henry on the Ridge Road and bivouacked for the night. William R. Morrison followed Oglesby with his Third Brigade and halted for the night about one-half mile to his rear. William H. L. Wallace's Second Brigade moved out five and one-half miles on the Telegraph Road and camped for the night. The Telegraph Road was the direct road between Fort Henry and Fort Donelson, and the Ridge Road ran out to the southeast from Fort Henry and then eastward past Peytoma Furnace on a course roughly parallel to the Telegraph Road and about two miles south of it. Both roads converged on Dover, Tennessee, near Fort Donelson on the Cumberland River.

Foote, who had returned to Cairo after the surrender of Fort Henry to prepare for the reduction of Fort Donelson, sailed with his fleet February 11, 1862 toward the Cumberland River to cooperate with Grant, and that same day Grant sent six regiments that had arrived at Fort Henry, but had not disembarked, to follow Foote toward Fort Donelson on the transports.

On the morning of February 12, 1862, Grant left Lewis Wallace with three regiments of his Second Brigade to occupy Fort Henry and Fort Heiman to protect them against a possible attack from Columbus, Kentucky, and he moved with the rest of his army toward Fort Donelson. McClernand's division, with T. Lyle Dickey's 4th Illinois Cavalry out in front, continued along the two roads that it had occupied the night before, and about noon the advance came within sight of Fort Donelson. Charles F. Smith's division followed McClernand. McArthur's First Brigade of Smith's division, which had been left at Fort Heiman, was the last of Grant's command to come up from Fort Henry, and it arrived within about three miles of Fort Donelson at 6:00 P.M. At 10:30 P.M. McArthur moved up about one-half mile closer to the enemy works and camped for the rest of the night.

The town of Dover, Tennessee, which the Confederate defenses enclosed, is situated on a bluff on the west side of the Cumberland River. Immediately below the town, Indian Creek flows into the river from the south, and about one-half mile below the mouth of Indian Creek, Hickman Creek flows into the river from the south and southwest.

A ridge extends toward the Cumberland between the two creeks and ends on a bluff, about 100 feet above the water. Fort Donelson, a bastioned earthwork, stood on this ridge near its eastern end. On the slope of this ridge that faced downstream were two water batteries. The one that was farther downstream was called the Lower Battery, and the other was the Upper Battery.

In addition to these defensive works, a line of entrenchments for infantry had been constructed about the fort and the town. The entire area was protected on the north by the valley of Hickman Creek, which at that time was inundated by backwater from the Cumberland River. The right of the line of the Confederate defensive works, which faced west, began on the north at Hickman Creek and followed the high ground southward to the valley of Indian Creek. This part of the line ran generally parallel to the river and from about one-fourth to three-fourths of a mile from it. About midway between the two creeks was a salient, where Porter's battery was established.

The left of the enemy line, which faced toward the south and southwest, began just above Dover on the end of a ridge that extended eastward toward the Cumberland River between two small streams that flowed into the river from the southwest. From a point near the river, the line ran westward along a ridge to its end, where it dropped off into the valley of a stream that ran northward to empty into Indian Creek. This valley was called Erin Hollow. The line crossed this valley and continued on up to the crest of a V-shaped elevation between the stream and Indian Creek. Between these two streams, and on the elevation, the line made a great salient, facing south, with its left near the small stream and its right on the valley of Indian Creek, near the Pinery Road. Maney's Confederate battery and Heiman's brigade held this salient.

There was a break in the enemy line at the valley of Indian Creek, but just to the north of the valley was the left of the Confederate defenses, facing west, that were described above. The entire line, which was about two and one-half miles in length, was constructed along the crests of ridges (except at the crossing of Indian Creek and Erin Hollow) that were from fifty to eighty feet high, and which faced valleys that were filled with underbrush and felled trees that made them difficult to cross.

Prior to Grant's movement against Fort Henry, Lloyd Tilghman was in command of Fort Henry, Fort Heiman, and Fort Donelson, and under his command were Heiman's and Drake's brigades at Fort Henry and four Tennessee regiments that served as the garrison of Fort Donelson. After the surrender of Fort Henry, however, the troops at Fort Donelson were strongly reinforced. Bushrod R. Johnson arrived at Fort Donelson late on the night of February 7, 1862, and he then assumed command of the post. His troops consisted of the brigades of Heiman and Drake, which had arrived safely from Fort Henry, and the regiments of the garrison.

On February 7–8, 1862, Gabriel C. Wharton's brigade of Floyd's Confederate division arrived from Cumberland City (Cumberland). On February 9, Pillow arrived from Clarksville, and at the same time Thomas J. Davidson's brigade (formerly Charles Clark's) arrived from Hopkinsville, Kentucky. Pillow, as the senior officer, relieved Johnson of command at Fort Donelson. On February 11, Buckner arrived from Russellville with the brigades of John C. Brown and William E. Baldwin of his division. Pillow then assigned Buckner to the command of the right of the line of defenses and Johnson to the command of the left.

Floyd arrived from Clarksville February 13, 1862 with John McCausland's brigade of his division from Cumberland City, and that day Floyd assumed command at Fort Donelson. Pillow was assigned as his second in command.

When all of Floyd's troops were in position, Buckner was in command on the right from Hickman Creek to the valley of Indian Creek, with Brown's brigade and a part of Baldwin's brigade holding this part of the line of entrenchments. Johnson was in command on the left, and his line extended from the valley of Indian Creek to a point south of Dover, not far from the river. Johnson's brigades were on this part of the line, in order from the Confederate right to left, as follows: Heiman's, Drake's, Wharton's, Davidson's, McCausland's, and then Baldwin with the rest of his brigade. Nathan B. Forrest's cavalry was between Baldwin and the river.

When William H. L. Wallace approached Fort Donelson on the Telegraph Road on February 12, 1862, he was unable to cross Hickman's Creek, so he turned to the right and moved up the creek to join Oglesby, who had arrived on the Ridge Road. Oglesby then moved on with his brigade to the Federal right, crossed Indian Creek, and moved by the Pinery Road to the Wynn's Ferry road. He was followed by Morrison's brigade, and William H. L. Wallace's brigade brought up the rear of the column. By dusk McClernand's division was in position facing the enemy works held by Heiman and Drake.

Charles F. Smith's division arrived within about a mile and a half of Fort Donelson about 3:00 P.M. February 12, 1862, and as his command came up on the road from Fort Henry, John Cook's Third Brigade and Jacob G. Lauman's Fourth Brigade turned off to the left and advanced past Mrs. Crisp's house, where Grant would later make his headquarters. The two brigades continued on and moved up to the top of a ridge about one mile in front of the extreme right of Buckner's entrenchments. They then bivouacked for the night behind the crest of the ridge, with Lauman's brigade on the left and Cook's brigade on the right. During the day, the weather had been pleasant, but that night it turned cold, and the troops were forced to spend an unpleasant night without fires.

On the morning of February 13, 1862, Charles F. Smith ordered a reconnaissance against the right of Buckner's line, and by 10:00 A.M. both brigades were formed near the Widow Crisp's house, with Lauman on the left and Cook on the right. They advanced with great difficulty through underbrush, climbed the steep slope of a ridge, and finally reached the crest, which was about three-fourths of a mile from Buckner's line. Between the ridge and the enemy's entrenchments was a deep valley, the floor of which was covered with tangled underbrush and felled trees.

Lauman and Cook moved down the hill and into the valley, where they came under a heavy fire. James C. Veatch's 25th Indiana Regiment of Lauman's brigade succeeded in crossing the valley and moving partway up the opposite slope before it halted. It remained in position there for about two hours, exposed to a steady fire, and was then withdrawn. The division then moved back to the ridge near Mrs. Crisp's farm, where it had camped the night before.

While Charles F. Smith was engaged on the Federal left February 13, 1862, McClernand continued his movement to the right. His objective was to reach the Cumberland River above Dover and thus complete the investment of Fort Donelson and the outer line of entrenchments. Troopers of Silas Noble's 2nd Illinois Cavalry and T. Lyle Dickey's 4th Illinois Cavalry moved out in front of the infantry and reached a point on some high ground above the flooded valley of Lick Creek. They reported back to McClernand that the way was clear, and McClernand ordered his brigade commanders to continue the march.

As the brigades advanced, Maney's battery, on the hill at Heiman's salient, opened fire, and McClernand directed Morrison to advance with his brigade and attempt to silence these troublesome guns. Morrison's brigade consisted of only the 17th and 49th Illinois regiments. Meantime, Isham N. Haynie's 48th Illinois Regiment had been detached from William H. L. Wallace's brigade to support a battery when the rest of the brigade moved on that morning. Haynie was then ordered to form his regiment on the left of Morrison's brigade and join in the attack on Maney's battery. Haynie, as senior officer, claimed command, but in the end it appears that no one commanded all three regiments, which were in line from left to right as follows: 48th Illinois, 17th Illinois, and 49th Illinois.

About 1:00 P.M., the Illinois regiments moved down the slope from the Wynn's Ferry road and into Erin Hollow, the valley of the stream mentioned earlier that flowed northward into Indian Creek. They advanced up the hill that was crowned by the works of Heiman's salient. Some troops reached a point within about fifty yards of the enemy entrenchments, but after about fifteen minutes they were driven back. The 45th regiment of William H. L. Wallace's brigade was sent to reinforce Morrison, and the attack was resumed, but it was unsuccessful. Morrison was wounded during the fighting, and Leonard F. Ross, colonel of the 17th Illinois, assumed command of Third Brigade.

In addition to the two infantry engagements on February 13, 1862, Commander Henry Walke, who had arrived near Fort Donelson the day before with the *Carondelet,* opened fire on the water battery about 9:00 A.M. as a diversion for Grant's troops. Walke fired at long range from the cover of a heavily wooded point, and did not approach closer to the

fort. After about two hours, Walke withdrew, but he resumed firing early in the afternoon and continued until about dusk.

On the morning of February 13, 1862, Grant ordered Lewis Wallace, who had been left in command at Fort Henry, to bring up the regiments that had been left with him and rejoin the army at Fort Donelson.

During the evening of February 13, 1862, Foote's gunboats, along with the transports carrying reinforcements for Grant, arrived below Fort Donelson.

There was also an adjustment of troops on the Federal lines that night. When McClernand had moved his division to the right earlier in the day, there was left a rather wide interval between the right of Smith's division and the left of McClernand's division. At McClernand's request, John McArthur detached two regiments of his First Brigade of Charles F. Smith's division and moved them out to the right to within one-fourth mile of the left of McClernand's line.

On the night of February 13, 1862, weather conditions worsened. A strong wind came up, snow began to fall, and it was so cold that the ground froze. No fires were permitted, and the soldiers suffered greatly from exposure.

Lewis Wallace arrived from Fort Henry about noon February 14, 1862. With him came the 8th Missouri and 11th Indiana regiments, formerly of his Second Brigade of Charles F. Smith's division, and these were organized into Fifth Brigade, Second Division under the command of Morgan L. Smith, commander of the 8th Missouri.

Lewis Wallace was then placed in command of a new Third Division of Grant's army that was organized from troops recently arrived on the transports. First Brigade, commanded by Charles Cruft, consisted of the four regiments that Cruft had brought to Fort Henry from the Department of the Ohio. Third Brigade was assigned to John M. Thayer, and it consisted of Thayer's 1st Nebraska from the Department of the Missouri and two new Ohio regiments. Second Brigade was not organized at that time, but the 46th, 57th, and 58th Illinois regiments, which had been assigned to Second Brigade, were attached to Thayer's command.

Lewis Wallace then moved his new division out to a position on the right of Charles F. Smith. This was on a ridge in front of the left of Buckner's line, and was separated from the left of McClernand by the valley of Indian Creek.

McClernand moved his division closer to the Cumberland River, with Oglesby advancing almost to the left flank of the Confederate line. The 8th, 18th, and 29th Illinois regiments of Oglesby's brigade were posted across the three roads that ran up from the Wynn's Ferry road, through the enemy entrenchments, and into Dover.

At 5:00 P.M. February 14, 1862, McArthur was ordered to move his brigade to the far right of McClernand's line as a reserve for Oglesby. McArthur reached his assigned position at 7:00, after dark, and went into camp.

The only offensive action during the day was Foote's attack on the water battery at Fort Donelson. About 3:00 P.M. Foote steamed up the Cumberland River with his ironclad gunboats *Saint Louis, Louisville, Pittsburgh,* and *Carondelet* in the lead, and these were followed by the wooden gunboats *Conestoga* and *Tyler.*

Foote opened fire when about a mile and a half from the fort, and then continued to fire, while advancing slowly, until the ironclads were within about 400 yards of the water battery. The battle lasted for about an hour and a half and then, when the *Saint Louis* and the *Louisville* were disabled, and the other two ironclads were damaged, Foote withdrew. He was wounded during the action, but he remained with the fleet.

During the night of February 14, 1862, the Confederate leaders met in a council of war at Dover to discuss plans for the next day. Present were Floyd, Pillow, Buckner, and Jeremy F. Gilmer, chief engineer of the Confederate Western Department. Their decision was to attack early the next morning, drive back the Federal right, and, when the way was clear on their left, march out with their entire force from Fort Donelson and escape in the direction of Charlotte and Nashville. Pillow was to begin the attack at 5:00 A.M. February 15 by advancing against the right of McClernand's line. Buckner was also to join in the attack, and was to cover the retreat if Pillow was successful in driving back the Federal right.

Pillow did not begin his advance until 7:00 A.M., and then Baldwin's brigade, which was on the left of Pillow's line, came up against Oglesby's brigade, and the battle began. When McArthur, who was in support of Oglesby, heard the firing, he moved his

brigade up on the right of Oglesby. Resistance was stubborn for a time, but finally enemy troops worked their way around McArthur's flank and forced him to retire. Oglesby's line was then seriously threatened.

By 8:00 A.M. McClernand was in trouble, and he sent to Lewis Wallace for help. According to Grant's orders, Wallace understood that he was to remain where he was with his division, and for that reason he felt that he could not comply with McClernand's request for help. He did send to headquarters at Mrs. Crisp's house for instructions, but Grant was absent from his headquarters that morning, conferring with Foote on his flagship about future operations.

Soon, McClernand repeated his request for aid, and at 8:45 A.M. Lewis Wallace, on his own responsibility, ordered Cruft to advance with his brigade, and he directed Thayer to cover the upper Indian Creek valley.

By 10:00 A.M. Oglesby was near the end of his resistance. His ammunition was nearly exhausted, and his right, after the departure of McArthur, was beginning to give way. Finally, after the enemy had moved to his right and rear, Oglesby was forced to withdraw.

When McArthur's and then Oglesby's brigades were driven back, Pillow's division advanced on a line parallel to the front of their entrenchments, and Baldwin's brigade, with McCausland's brigade on his right, arrived in front of William H. L. Wallace's brigade. Later Ross' brigade (formerly Morrison's), which was on the left of Wallace, was also engaged. Finally, when Wallace's ammunition was exhausted, he fell back about one-half mile, and then the brigades of McClernand's division re-formed in rear of Thayer's brigade.

Cruft's brigade of Lewis Wallace's division was left fighting alone, and it was soon forced to withdraw to the right and rear.

By noon, the entire position held at dawn by McClernand's division was in the hands of the enemy, and the road running out from Fort Donelson was clear. Pillow halted his pursuit of the retiring Federals at 1:00 P.M., and then, inexplicably, with the road to Charlotte open, he ordered his troops to return to the positions in the entrenchments that they had occupied the day before. Only Drake's brigade and an additional regiment remained out in front.

After his conference with Foote, Grant returned to his lines about 1:00 P.M., and not until then did he learn of Pillow's attack and McClernand's defeat. He ordered Charles F. Smith to assault the enemy works on his front, which he correctly assumed were then only lightly held. At 2:00 P.M. Smith ordered an attack by Lauman's brigade, to which the 52nd Indiana of Cook's brigade was attached. With the 2nd Iowa in front, and followed in order by the 52nd Indiana, 25th Indiana, 7th Iowa, and 14th Iowa, Lauman advanced and drove the enemy from their outer works and back to another ridge nearer Fort Donelson. Smith then sent up Cook's brigade and the artillery of his division, and together with Lauman's brigade, they occupied Buckner's former position on the Confederate right. Later in the day, Buckner came back with his command, but he was unable to drive Smith from the captured works. After McArthur was driven from his position on the right of Oglesby that morning, he retired to the rear of the Federal line, where he remained until 4:00 P.M. Then he was ordered to the left to support the other two brigades of Smith's division.

After ordering Charles F. Smith to attack Buckner's position, Grant moved on and ordered Lewis Wallace to regain the ground on the Federal right lost by McClernand that morning. Nearby was Morgan L. Smith's Fifth Brigade of Charles F. Smith's division, which earlier had been sent to aid McClernand during the attack on his position. Wallace directed Morgan L. Smith's brigade to take the lead in the attack and for Cruft's brigade to follow. Ross' brigade, with the 46th, 57th, and 58th Illinois regiments (the regiments intended for the Second Brigade of Lewis Wallace's division, but which were then attached to Thayer's brigade), was also sent forward to support the other two brigades on their left.

As the column approached the ridge then held by Drake, Wallace put his brigades in position as follows: Morgan L. Smith's brigade was across the Wynn's Ferry road, facing north; Cruft's brigade was on the right of Morgan L. Smith, with its right near the Forge Road; and Ross' brigade was on the left of Morgan L. Smith. This line was completed by about 2:00 P.M., and then the three brigades advanced. They soon came under fire but continued on up the hill. Smith's brigade reached the crest and became engaged in a sharp struggle for the enemy works, but this was soon ended when Cruft and Ross came up, and Drake fell back into the line of Confederate works. The way out from Fort Donelson, which earlier had been open to the enemy, was thus closed.

On the night of February 15, 1862, at another meeting of the Confederate generals at Dover, they decided that they had no choice but to surrender the fort and the army defending it. Neither Floyd nor Pillow wished to take part in the surrender, and in the end, Floyd turned over the command to Pillow, who in turn passed it on to Buckner. Buckner agreed to arrange for the surrender. Forrest refused to surrender his cavalry, and he led his command out along the river and escaped.

Soon after daybreak February 16, 1862, a Confederate officer appeared on Lauman's front with a white flag and a letter from Buckner to Grant asking for terms of surrender. It was then that Grant sent his well-known reply, "No terms except unconditional and immediate surrender can be accepted. I propose to move immediately upon your works." Buckner then surrendered Fort Donelson and his command to Grant.

The United States forces commanded by Ulysses S. Grant at Fort Donelson were as follows:

First Division, John A. McClernand
  First Brigade, Richard J. Oglesby
    8th Illinois, Frank L. Rhoads
    18th Illinois, Michael K. Lawler, wounded
      Daniel H. Brush, wounded
      Samuel B. Marks
    29th Illinois, James S. Rearden
    30th Illinois, Elias S. Dennis
    31st Illinois, John A. Logan, wounded
    Battery A, 1st Illinois Light Artillery, Jasper M. Dresser
    Battery E, 2nd Illinois Light Artillery, George C. Gumbart
  Second Brigade, William H. L. Wallace
    11th Illinois, Thomas E. G. Ransom, wounded
      Garrett Nevins (temporarily)
    20th Illinois, C. Carroll Marsh
    45th Illinois, John E. Smith
    48th Illinois, Isham N. Haynie
    Battery B, 1st Illinois Light Artillery, Ezra Taylor
    Battery D, 1st Illinois Light Artillery, Edward McAllister
    4th Illinois Cavalry, T. Lyle Dickey

Third Brigade, William R. Morrison, wounded
   Leonard F. Ross
   17th Illinois, Francis M. Smith
      Henry H. Bush
   49th Illinois, Phineas Pease

Second Division, Charles F. Smith
  First Brigade, John McArthur
    9th Illinois, Jesse J. Phillips
    12th Illinois, Augustus L. Chetlain
    41st Illinois, Isaac C. Pugh
  Third Brigade, John Cook
    7th Illinois, Andrew J. Babcock
    50th Illinois, Moses M. Bane
    52nd Indiana, James M. Smith
    12th Iowa, Joseph J. Wood
    13th Missouri, Crafts J. Wright
    Battery D, 1st Missouri Light Artillery, Henry Richardson
    Battery H, 1st Missouri Light Artillery, Frederick Welker
    Battery K, 1st Missouri Light Artillery, George H. Stone
  Fourth Brigade, Jacob G. Lauman
    25th Indiana, James C. Veatch
    2nd Iowa, James M. Tuttle
    7th Iowa, James C. Parrott
    14th Iowa, William T. Shaw
    Birge's Missouri Sharpshooters
  Fifth Brigade, Morgan L. Smith
    11th Indiana, George F. McGinnis
    8th Missouri, John McDonald

Third Division, Lewis Wallace
  First Brigade, Charles Cruft
    31st Indiana, John Osborn
      Frederick Arn
    44th Indiana, Hugh B. Reed
    17th Kentucky, John H. McHenry, Jr.
    25th Kentucky, James M. Shackelford
  Second Brigade
    46th Illinois, John A. Davis
    57th Illinois, Silas D. Baldwin
    58th Illinois, William F. Lynch
    20th Ohio, Charles Whittlesey

Note. Second Brigade was not organized, but the above regiments were attached to Thayer's Third Brigade.

  Third Brigade, John M. Thayer
    1st Nebraska, William D. McCord
    58th Ohio, Ferdinand F. Remple
    68th Ohio, Samuel H. Steedman

    76th Ohio, William B. Woods
  Unattached
    Battery A, 1st Illinois Light Artillery, Peter P. Wood
  32nd Illinois Infantry, Henry Davidson

CAPTURE OF FORT PILLOW, TENNESSEE
APRIL 12, 1864

On March 15, 1864, Nathan B. Forrest moved northward from Mississippi with his cavalry command on a raid into West Tennessee and Kentucky. He passed through Jackson, Tennessee, Union City, and Trenton and reached Paducah, Kentucky on the Ohio River. He remained there for a short time and then withdrew to Jackson, Tennessee in early April. From there, on April 10, he sent James R. Chalmers with his First Cavalry Division to capture Fort Pillow. The next day Chalmers, with the brigades of Tyree H. Bell and Robert McCulloch of his division, moved westward from Sharon's Ferry on Forked Deer Creek toward the fort.

Fort Pillow was a strong earthwork that had been built at the top of the bluffs on the east side of the Mississippi River, about forty-five miles above Memphis, Tennessee. Federal troops were sent there to protect the passage of Federal boats on the river from any interference by Forrest if he should move that way. The parapet of the fort was about 125 yards in length, and it extended out from the river in the form of a rough semicircle, facing to the east. The river side of the fort was open to the bluff, which fell off sharply from the crest to the river bank below. On the land side, the fort was surrounded by a ditch about eight feet deep. Along the front of the fort, on the northern and eastern sides, the ground sloped down into a ravine, through which flowed a stream called Coal Creek. On the slope of the hill on the south side of the fort, and below the level of the fort, were several barracks for the troops and a number of storerooms.

Lionel F. Booth, commander of the 6th United States Colored Heavy Artillery, commanded the garrison of the fort, which consisted of 295 white troops of the First Battalion of the 13th Tennessee

Cavalry, and 262 black troops of the 6th United States Colored Heavy Artillery (formerly the 1st Alabama Siege Artillery and later designated 11th United States Colored Troops) and one section of Battery D, 2nd United States Colored Light Artillery (later designated Battery F) . William F. Bradford was in command of the battalion of the 13th Tennessee Cavalry and was also second in command in the fort. The garrison was supported by the gunboat *New Era,* commanded by James Marshall, which was on the river below the fort.

Chalmers arrived in front of the fort at dawn May 12, 1864, and he then placed Bell's brigade on the northern and eastern sides of the fort and moved McCulloch's brigade into position south of the fort. Chalmers encountered only a slight resistance from the Federal pickets as he completed these movements, and by 8:00 A.M. he had completed the investment of the fort, and had opened with rifle and artillery fire. About 9:00 A.M. Booth was killed by a sharpshooter, and Bradford succeeded him in command of the garrison.

Forrest arrived on the field at 10:00 A.M. and assumed personal direction of Chalmers' division. He ordered McCulloch to gain possession of the buildings south of the fort, and directed Bell to move his men into the shelter of the ravine of Coal Creek, which ran along the northern and eastern sides of the the Federal works at a distance varying from 10 to 150 yards.

By 11:00 A.M. McCulloch's men were in position in and among the buildings south of the fort, and Forrest prepared for an attack. At 3:30 P.M., when he had replenished his ammunition, he demanded the surrender of the garrison, and Bradford asked for one hour to decide on the answer to that demand.

While awaiting a reply, Forrest observed three steamboats approaching in the direction of the fort, and to him it appeared that one boat was carrying a large number of Federal troops. Upon seeing this, Forrest informed Bradford that he had only twenty minutes to make known his decision. Forrest also took the precaution of sending two detachments of 200 men each down the bluffs to the river bank to prevent the troops carried by the steamer from landing, and also to prevent troops of the garrison from escaping by way of the river. One detachment, under the command of Charles W. Anderson, assis-

tant adjutant general on Forrest's staff, was sent to cover the landing immediately below the fort, and the other, commanded by Clark R. Barteau, moved down the ravine of Coal Creek and took position on the river bank, north of the fort.

In reply to Forrest's demand for the surrender of the fort, Bradford refused, and Forrest then ordered his troops to attack. They quickly moved forward into the ditch, then scaled the parapet and moved into the interior of the fort. Many of the defenders were killed or captured there, and the remainder fled down the bluffs to the river bank, where they met a similar fate, largely at the hands of Anderson's men. Bradford survived the capture of the fort but was killed later while on his way as a prisoner to Jackson.

The capture of Fort Pillow was of no great military significance, but it has received wide publicity because of the controversy that developed almost immediately after the fighting had ended, and which continued for many years after the war. There were numerous reports by Union survivors that many prisoners had been killed after they had surrendered, and that there were numerous atrocities committed by Forrest's men during the fighting and after it had ended. As a result, the affair came to be known in the North as the "Fort Pillow Massacre." In addition, it was claimed that the black troops had suffered especially because of the strong objections in the South to the use of black soldiers by the North. This feeling was based in part on the reports of losses sustained by the garrison during the action. Of the approximately 560 Union men of the garrison (295 black and 262 white), 231 were reported as killed and 100 as seriously wounded. It has also been estimated that about two-thirds of all black soldiers at the fort were killed, while only one-third of all white soldiers lost their lives. Further, the reports show that Forrest took 226 prisoners, and of these 168 were white and only 58 were black. Forrest's losses were said to be 14 killed and 58 wounded.

The Confederate officers present at Fort Pillow vigorously denied the allegations of improper conduct on the part of their soldiers, and in later years strong evidence was presented in the South to support the claim that Forrest's men were not guilty of the charges laid against them. Both sides of the controversy are given in detail in a careful study by

Albert Castel that was published in *Civil War History,* Volume 4, No. 1 (March 1958).

FRANKLIN AND NASHVILLE CAMPAIGN (HOOD'S INVASION OF TENNESSEE) SEPTEMBER 18, 1864– DECEMBER 27, 1864

MOVEMENTS OF THE ARMIES SEPTEMBER 18, 1864– NOVEMBER 29, 1864

After the evacuation of Atlanta, Georgia September 1, 1864, John B. Hood's Confederate Army of Tennessee withdrew to the south and halted at Lovejoy's Station. William T. Sherman's victorious Army of the Military Division of the Mississippi did not follow but encamped around the city. On September 18, Hood left Lovejoy's Station and marched to the north and west along the Western and Atlantic Railroad, which was Sherman's line of communication with the North. By gaining possession of the railroad and moving toward Tennessee, Hood hoped to draw Sherman's army northward out of Georgia.

Toward the end of September 1864, Joseph Wheeler's Confederate cavalry attempted to break the railroad in northern Georgia, and at the same time Nathan B. Forrest made a similar attempt in Middle Tennessee. Forrest crossed the Tennessee River September 20 and advanced along the Nashville and Decatur Railroad (Tennessee and Alabama Railroad) as far as Pulaski, Tennessee. He did not, however, attack the town, which was defended by Lovell H. Rousseau's command of the District of Tennessee, Department of the Cumberland. A part of Forrest's command under Abraham Buford moved off to the east, but was driven back across the Tennessee River October 3. Three days later, Forrest followed with the rest of his command and left Tennessee.

Meantime, Sherman had heard rumors that Hood's army was on the move. Because of this information, and also because of the activity of the enemy cavalry, Sherman, on September 25, 1864, ordered George D. Wagner's Second Division, Fourth Corps (commanded by John Newton until September 24, when he was ordered to Key West, Florida) to move back from Atlanta to Chattanooga. There, on September 28, Wagner relieved James B. Steedman's command of the District of the Etowah so that it could aid in driving the enemy cavalry from the Nashville and Chattanooga Railroad and the Nashville and Decatur Railroad.

September 26, 1864, Sherman ordered John M. Corse to move to Rome, Georgia with his Fourth Division, Fifteenth Corps to cover the railroad north of the Etowah River.

September 28, 1864, James D. Morgan's Second Division, Fourteenth Corps was also ordered from Atlanta to Chattanooga to reinforce the troops opposing Forrest in Tennessee. First Brigade left that evening, and Second Brigade and Third Brigade followed the next day; they arrived at Chattanooga on September 30. On September 29, George H. Thomas, commanding the Department and Army of the Cumberland, left Atlanta with Morgan's division with orders from Sherman to take charge of affairs in Tennessee. Thomas remained only a short time at Chattanooga, then moved on to Nashville, where he arrived October 3.

On October 1, 1864, as a precautionary measure, Sherman issued orders for the army to be prepared to march if Hood should attempt to strike the railroad south of the Etowah River. The next day it was clear to Sherman that Hood was moving toward Marietta, Georgia, and on October 3 he issued the march orders for the army. Henry W. Slocum's Twentieth Corps was to remain and hold Atlanta and the Chattahoochee River bridge, and the rest of the army was to assemble on the railroad at Smyrna Camp Grounds, between the Chattahoochee and Marietta. That day, October 3, the main body of Hood's army was near Lost Mountain, about nine miles west and a little south of Marietta. Alexander P. Stewart's corps had been detached and was moving toward the railroad north of Marietta in an attempt to capture Allatoona and destroy the bridge over the Etowah. Stewart captured Acworth and Big Shanty, then sent Samuel G. French's division to capture Allatoona. Stewart rejoined Hood with the rest of his command on the morning of October 5.

Engagement at Allatoona, Georgia, October 5, 1864. The Federal garrison at Allatoona was commanded by John E. Tourtellotte and consisted of the 93rd Illinois, 18th Wisconsin (seven companies), and Tourtellotte's own 4th Minnesota. These regiments belonged to Joseph B. McCown's First Brigade of John E. Smith's Third Division, Fifteenth Corps. Also present was Marcus Amsden's 12th Battery, Wisconsin Light Artillery. When French's division approached, however, Corse came up from Rome with Richard Rowett's Third Brigade of his Fourth Division, Fifteenth Corps. Corse then assumed command of the two brigades.

The defensive works held by Corse consisted of two field redoubts, one on each side of the railroad. The redoubts were located on the crests of hills that formed a part of an east-west ridge across the line of the tracks. Tourtellotte occupied the eastern redoubt with his infantry and a section of Amsden's Wisconsin battery. When Corse arrived, he moved into the western redoubt with a part of his infantry and part of Amsden's battery. Most of Rowett's brigade was placed in an advanced line of trenches that faced west. This line was supported by the 93rd Illinois Infantry of Tourtellotte's brigade.

During the night of October 4, 1864, French moved up with his division, and at daybreak the next morning he quickly advanced on Allatoona. He subjected the Federal works to artillery fire for about two hours, then demanded the surrender of the garrison. When this was refused by Corse, French sent Claudius W. Sears' brigade to the north, or rear, of the redoubts to begin the attack, and at the same time he directed Francis M. Cockrell's brigade, supported by William H. Young's brigade, to assault the works from the west.

Sears formed his brigade across the railroad, and charged against the flank and rear of Rowett's troops. Simultaneously, Cockrell and Young attacked on Rowett's front. The Federals resisted strongly, but after two hours of fighting, Corse was forced to withdraw his men to the trenches immediately around the redoubt. Because the troops in the west redoubt then bore the brunt of the attack, Tourtellotte sent reinforcements to Corse, who continued to resist. Finally, a little before 2:00 P.M., French recalled his brigades and marched away in the direction of New Hope Church. Losses were heavy on both sides, and among the wounded were Tourtellotte and Rowett.

* * * * * * * * * *

After the engagement at Allatoona had ended, Hood moved on by way of Dallas and Van Wert, and on October 12, 1864, he struck the railroad north of Resaca. He then proceeded to destroy the railroad as far north as Tunnel Hill and occupied Dalton. At that point he turned west and marched through Villanow toward La Fayette, Georgia. Meantime, Sherman's army had been moving up in pursuit. It left Smyrna Camp Ground October 5, marched north through Marietta, past Kennesaw Mountain, and continued on by way of Allatoona, Cartersville, Kingston, and Rome, reaching Resaca on October 14, two days after Hood struck the railroad there. The next day Sherman marched on to Dalton. At that time Hood was near La Fayette, but from there he moved on to the southwest toward Gadsden, Alabama.

When Sherman reached Dalton, he too turned west and marched by way of Villanow, Ship's Gap (near La Fayette), Chattooga Creek, and Summerville toward Gaylesville, Alabama. He arrived there October 20, 1864, and that same day Hood reached Gadsden. Hood then moved on through Summerville, Decatur, and Courtland, arriving at Tuscumbia, Alabama on October 30. The next day he crossed the Tennessee River and occupied Florence. Sherman did not pursue Hood beyond Gaylesville, but remained in the vicinity until the end of the month, while he awaited news of the enemy's movements and considered his future plans. He finally decided to send reinforcements to Thomas in Tennessee to take care of Hood and to march back with the rest of his army to Atlanta. There he would prepare for a march through Georgia to a point on the Atlantic coast near Savannah.

Transfer of Fourth Corps and Twenty-Third Corps to Middle Tennessee, October 26–27, 1864. October 26, 1864, Sherman ordered David S. Stanley to march the next day with his Fourth Corps to Chattanooga to reinforce Thomas. Stanley marched to Alpine, Georgia on October 27, and from there he continued on toward Chattanooga, arriving two days later. He then moved by rail to

Athens, Alabama, and from there marched toward Pulaski, Tennessee. Stanley, with Thomas J. Wood's Third Division, Fourth Corps, arrived at Pulaski November 1, and Walter C. Whitaker, with Second Brigade and Third Brigade of his First Division, Fourth Corps, arrived November 3. Isaac M. Kirby's First Brigade, First Division was guarding the trains, and did not arrive at Pulaski until the night of November 12. George D. Wagner's Second Division, Fourth Corps left Chattanooga at 9:00 A.M. November 1, arriving at Pulaski on the night of November 4. Prior to the arrival of Stanley at Pulaski, Robert S. Granger, commanding the District of Northern Alabama, held the posts of Decatur, Athens, Pulaski, and Columbia.

After the departure of Stanley from Gaylesville, Sherman marched back with the rest his army to Rome, Georgia, and then on to Kingston, where he arrived November 2, 1864. While at Rome, Sherman decided to send John M. Schofield's Twenty-Third Corps, Army of the Ohio north to Tennessee as an additional reinforcement for Thomas. While Sherman marched from Atlanta to Gaylesville, Schofield was absent from the army at Louisville, Kentucky and Knoxville, Tennessee, attending to business affairs of his Department of the Ohio, but he rejoined Twenty-Third Corps at Gaylesville on October 21 and resumed command of the corps the next day.

From Rome, Twenty-Third Corps marched to Resaca November 1, 1864, then proceeded on, part by rail and part by road, to Dalton, where it halted to await transportation to Nashville. On November 3, Schofield went forward by rail with Second Division, Twenty-Third Corps, which had been under the temporary command of Joseph A. Cooper since Milo S. Hascall had resigned on October 27. Jacob D. Cox remained at Dalton with his Third Division for several days until additional transportation arrived.

Schofield arrived at Nashville November 5, 1864 with the first troops of Cooper's Second Division, which belonged to Cooper's own First Brigade, temporarily commanded by George W. Gallup. Thomas had just learned that Forrest, who was then raiding in western Tennessee, had threatened Johnsonville, which was on the Tennessee River sixty miles to the west of Nashville, and that the Federal garrison of the post had destroyed the stores

that had been accumulated there and had fled eastward without offering any resistance. Thomas immediately sent Schofield with Gallup's brigade out on the Nashville and Northwestern Railroad by way of Gillem's Station to Johnsonville, where he arrived on the night of November 5, only to find that the enemy had departed. Orlando H. Moore's Second Brigade of Cooper's division arrived at Nashville during the afternoon of November 6, and it was also ordered to move on to Johnsonville the next day.

Upon learning that Forrest had left Johnsonville, Thomas ordered Schofield to leave sufficient troops at that place to ensure a strong defense of the post, then to proceed with the remainder of his troops to Pulaski. Upon arriving there, Schofield was to assume command of all troops in the vicinity. He left Cooper's and Moore's brigades at Johnsonville. The other brigade of the division, Silas A. Strickland's Third Brigade, arrived at Nashville November 9, 1864, and the next day was sent to Spring Hill. It remained there until November 13, then advanced to Columbia. While at Columbia, Strickland's brigade was completely reorganized. On November 14, the 20th Kentucky of the brigade, which had only a short time to serve, was ordered to the District of Kentucky, and the same day the 27th Kentucky was sent home for muster out. On November 23, 91st Illinois and 123rd Indiana were sent to Williamsport, Tennessee. Then, on November 24, 72nd Illinois and 44th Missouri of the Army of the Tennessee, which had been ordered from Memphis to report to Thomas, were assigned to Strickland's brigade. On November 27, the 183rd Ohio, a new regiment, was assigned to the brigade.

Thomas H. Ruger, formerly commander of Second Brigade, First Division, Twentieth Corps at Atlanta, arrived at Nashville, and November 11, 1864 he was ordered to Johnsonville to relieve Cooper in command of Second Division, Twenty-Third Corps. When Ruger assumed command of the division, Cooper resumed command of his own First Brigade of the division.

Schofield's other division, Cox's Third Division, left Dalton, Georgia November 5–7 and arrived at Nashville November 8–9. It then moved forward as follows: to Thompson's Station November 11, to Columbia November 12–13, to Lynnville November 14, and to Pulaski, where it halted, November 15.

Schofield returned to Nashville from Johnsonville November 8, 1864 and remained there until November 13. He then moved on to Pulaski, where he arrived that evening. He assumed command of the troops at Pulaski the next day. His command consisted of Stanley's Fourth Corps; Cox's Third Division, Twenty-Third Corps, which at that time was at Lynnville; and Strickland's Third Brigade, Second Division, Twenty-Third Corps, which was at Columbia. The cavalry near Pulaski belonged to James H. Wilson's Cavalry Corps, Military Division of the Mississippi, which was then only incompletely organized. Edward Hatch's Fifth Cavalry Division, consisting of Robert R. Stewart's First Brigade and Datus E. Coon's Second Brigade, and John T. Croxton's First Brigade of Edward M. McCook's First Cavalry Division were in front of Pulaski, along Shoal Creek. Horace Capron's brigade, which had recently arrived from Kentucky, was near Pulaski, but on November 14 it was sent out on the road to the west to Waynesboro. The organization of Richard W. Johnson's Sixth Cavalry Division was announced November 17, and Capron's brigade was assigned to that division as First Brigade.

November 20, 1864, Thomas ordered Ruger to leave Cooper's brigade at Johnsonville and to move with Moore's brigade to Columbia as soon as trains for its transportation arrived. Ruger left with one regiment at 8:30 A.M. November 22, and the other four regiments followed the next day. The brigade arrived at Columbia November 23, and the next day Ruger was assigned command of a provisionally organized division consisting of Moore's and Strickland's brigades. On November 23, Cooper's brigade was ordered to march from Johnsonville and take position at Centerville and Beard's Ferry on the Duck River. Cooper began his march November 25, and two days later arrived at Centerville, about midway between Johnsonville and Columbia. He left two regiments to guard the ford there and with the rest of his brigade marched on to Beard's Ferry, about fifteen miles farther upstream.

Pulaski was located on the Nashville and Decatur Railroad, thirty miles south of Columbia, and about midway between Columbia and Decatur. Columbia was at the crossing of the Duck River, and from there the railroad and a turnpike ran northward to Nashville, forty-five miles distant. About midway between Pulaski and Columbia, and on the railroad, was the village of Lynnville. About eighteen miles to the west of Pulaski was the town of Lawrenceburg, which was on the direct road from Florence, Alabama to Columbia, by way of Mount Pleasant. About twenty-nine miles beyond Lawrenceburg, and forty-three miles north of Decatur, was Waynesboro, which was on the road from Savannah to Columbia. This road joined the direct road that ran through Lawrenceburg at Mount Pleasant.

When Schofield learned from Stanley of the exposed position of his troops at Pulaski, he halted Cox, whose division was then approaching the town and was about four miles to the north, and directed him to cover the road running in from Lawrenceburg. Then, using his discretionary orders to withdraw if he thought it necessary, Schofield ordered Cox to move back to Lynnville on the morning of November 22, 1864. The next day, Stanley, with his Fourth Corps, also moved back from Pulaski, bivouacking at Lynnville late that night. Meantime, Cox had also fallen back, and had arrived within seven miles of Columbia before he halted for the night.

Movements of the Armies to Columbia, Tennessee, November 21–27, 1864. Finally, after a long delay, Hood moved his army out of the bridgehead at Florence on November 21–22, 1864, marching toward Columbia on three separate roads. Benjamin F. Cheatham's corps marched on the left, on the road to Waynesboro; Alexander P. Stewart's corps on the right, on the road to Lawrenceburg; and Stephen D. Lee's corps in the center, on country roads between those on which the other two corps were advancing.

Forrest's cavalry covered the front of the infantry. James R. Chalmers' division, accompanied by Forrest in person, advanced on the left, and during November 23, 1864 it steadily pushed back Capron's cavalry brigade toward Columbia. About midnight November 23, Schofield, who was then at Lynnville, received word from Ruger at Columbia that Capron had been engaged all day with Forrest's cavalry, and that it had been driven back about eight miles to Mount Pleasant. Schofield then realized the extent of his danger and issued orders for the withdrawal of his army. He ordered Croxton to withdraw his cavalry from Shoal Creek, and at 1:00 A.M.

November 24, he directed Cox to march at once to Columbia and secure the town until Fourth Corps could arrive from Pulaski. Cox received the order at 4:00 A.M., and had his column in motion before daylight.

About 7:30 A.M., when within about two miles of Columbia, Cox heard the firing from the Mount Pleasant Pike, about a mile distant, and he turned to the left and moved in that direction. He arrived on the pike, about three miles from Columbia, just after Capron had passed, and he promptly formed his infantry to check Forrest's advance. He was successful in this effort and took position behind Bigby Creek.

At 3:00 A.M. November 24, 1864, Stanley's Fourth Corps started for Columbia, with Wagner's Second Division, which was then in camp at Lynnville, in the lead. It was followed, in order, by Wood's Third Division, the Artillery Brigade, the trains, and Whitaker's First Division. Schofield, riding at the head of the column, reached Columbia about 10 A.M., and as fast as the divisions arrived, he put them in position to cover the approaches to the town from the south. The line that he occupied ran around the south side of Columbia, with both flanks resting on Duck River, and this was strengthened with barricades and earthworks. Cox's division was on the right, about one mile west of town, covering the Mount Pleasant Pike, with its right on the river; Wagner's division was on the right of Fourth Corps, connecting on its right with Cox; Wood's division was on the left of Wagner, facing south, and connecting with Wagner at the Pulaski Pike; and Whitaker's division was on the left of Wood, with its left near Duck River. Most of November 25 was spent in strengthening the position, but at 5:15 P.M. the divisions of Whitaker and Wagner moved back to a shorter interior line that was more easily defended with the force available, and Wood's division was extended to cover the entire outer line. The interior line was occupied by 10:00 P.M.

Meantime, Hood's infantry had been moving up from Mount Pleasant, while Forrest's cavalry invested Columbia on the south and kept up a steady fire on Schofield's lines. On the morning of November 27, 1864, the infantry arrived in front of the town and relieved the cavalry. When relieved, Forrest moved out on picket duty and to look for cross-

ings of Duck River. During the night, Schofield evacuated Columbia, then withdrew to the north side of the river. He burned the bridges and established a new defensive line behind the river.

Movements of the Armies to Spring Hill, Tennessee (Engagement at Spring Hill, Tennessee), November 28–29, 1864.

On the night of November 27, 1864, Hood decided on a plan to turn Schofield's left flank. Forrest was to move up Duck River the next day, and seize the fords east of Columbia. He was to push back the Federal cavalry and so enable Hood to lay a pontoon bridge at Davis' Ford. Then, on November 29, Hood was to cross Duck River with Cheatham's and Stewart's corps and Edward Johnson's division of Lee's corps, and march on the Davis Ford road toward Spring Hill. This was a small village at a road junction on the Columbia Turnpike (Franklin and Columbia Turnpike) about twelve miles north of Columbia. Upon arriving there, Hood would be squarely across Schofield's line of retreat to Franklin and Nashville. Lee, with the divisions of Carter L. Stevenson and Henry D. Clayton, was to remain at Columbia with the trains and the artillery of the army, and he was to demonstrate in front of Schofield and compel the latter to remain in position just north of Columbia.

After Schofield's command had retreated from Pulaski, Wilson concentrated his cavalry at Columbia November 24, 1864. He then moved to the north side of Duck River and took position east of the town, between Columbia and the Lewisburg Turnpike, to watch the enemy movements in that direction. Hatch's division and Croxton's brigade took position about six miles east of Columbia, on the road to Shelbyville, and Capron's brigade at Rally Hill, on the Lewisburg Turnpike, where it covered the Duck River crossing of that road. Croxton's and Capron's brigades were temporarily formed into a division under the command of Richard W. Johnson. A part of Robert R. Stewart's brigade of Hatch's division was sent west of Columbia to watch the fords between that place and Williamsport. On the evening of November 28, Stewart was ordered to march by way of Spring Hill and join Wilson.

November 28, 1864, Hood's movement began as planned. Forrest's cavalry moved out to the east to the crossings of Duck River. Abraham Buford's division marched to the point where the Lewisburg

Turnpike crossed Duck River; James R. Chalmers' division to Holland's Ford, seven miles east of Columbia; William H. Jackson's division to Huey's Mill, a mile farther on, and between Chalmers and Buford; and Forrest, with a part of Jacob B. Biffle's brigade (also referred to as a demi-brigade and as a regiment), was at Davis' Ford, about five miles east of Columbia and two miles west of Chalmers.

About noon November 28, 1864, pickets of Capron and Croxton reported the presence of the enemy in force at the various fords on the river between Columbia and the Lewisburg Turnpike. J. Morris Young, with four regiments of Capron's brigade, offered such strong resistance that Buford was unable to cross the river at the Lewisburg Turnpike, but Jackson and Chalmers succeeded in crossing at the other fords after some sharp skirmishing. Forrest, with Biffle's brigade, was not opposed. When finally across the river, Forrest advanced and drove the Federal cavalry beyond Rally Hill, then interposed his command between the main body of Wilson's cavalry and Young's detachment at the Duck River crossing of the Lewisburg Turnpike. Young was nearly surrounded but managed to cut his way through the enemy lines and escape. Wilson then ordered his scattered detachments to Hurt's Corners (or Cross Roads), and there he rallied his command and checked Forrest's further attempts to advance that evening. John H. Hammond's First Brigade of Joseph F. Knipe's Seventh Cavalry Division, which was then coming up from Nashville, was ordered to halt at Spring Hill and report to Wilson.

During the night of November 28, 1864, Buford's division joined Forrest, and early the next morning the Confederate cavalry again advanced and drove the Union troopers back. Croxton's brigade served as rear guard during the withdrawal and stubbornly contested every foot of the way. Capron's brigade, which had been severely punished the evening before, took the lead on the road toward Franklin, and Hatch's division marched between Capron and Croxton, supporting Croxton.

By mid-morning November 29, 1864, Forrest had reached Mount Carmel, where the road from Murfreesboro to Spring Hill crossed the Lewisburg Turnpike, on which Wilson was retiring. At that point, Coon's brigade of Hatch's division halted to occupy a barricade that had been constructed earlier by Capron, and the rest of the cavalry continued on to the north toward Franklin. Forrest made two determined attempts to clear the road but was repulsed by Coon. At that time, however, Forrest had gained possession of the direct road to Spring Hill, the Mount Comfort road, which covered the road on which Hood's infantry was then advancing, and he did not continue the pursuit of Wilson. Instead, he left behind a detachment to watch Wilson and moved with the rest of his command toward Spring Hill, which was then held by two Federal regiments. Forrest arrived in front of Spring Hill at about the same time that Stanley came up from Columbia with two divisions of his Fourth Corps.

After the engagement at Mount Carmel, Wilson continued on without molestation on the Lewisburg Turnpike to Franklin, where he was joined that night by Hammond's brigade from Spring Hill. Wilson then placed his brigades in position on the north bank of the Harpeth River, where he watched the river from Franklin as far east as Triune.

Meantime, Hood's infantry had begun crossing Duck River at daylight November 29, 1864 on a pontoon bridge that had been laid at Davis' Ford. Cheatham's corps crossed first, with Patrick Cleburne's division in the lead, and it was followed by the divisions of William B. Bate and John C. Brown. Stewart's corps came next, and Edward Johnson's division of Lee's corps, which was temporarily attached to Stewart's corps, brought up the rear. Cheatham's corps marched northward on the Davis Ford road, which ran roughly parallel to the Columbia Turnpike and about four miles to the east of it. It was not until 3:00 P.M., or later, that Cleburne reached the Rally Hill road where it crossed Rutherford Creek, about two and one-half miles from Spring Hill.

About sunrise that morning, Schofield learned from Wilson that Forrest's cavalry was north of Duck River and that bridges were being laid above Columbia for the infantry to cross. Schofield decided to send his trains and three divisions of infantry to Spring Hill, and to keep Wood's Third Division, Fourth Corps and Cox's Third Division, Twenty-Third Corps in position near Columbia. Schofield then ordered Stanley to leave Wood's division and two batteries at Columbia and to move with the rest of his command to Spring Hill. He also ordered Ruger to assemble his division of Twenty-Third Corps and move with it to Spring Hill.

That morning, Cox's division was in position on a ridge across a tongue of land in the bend of the river north of Columbia. He had been ordered to hold this position until dark and then follow the rest of the army to Spring Hill. He was directed, however, to keep his pickets out until midnight. Wood's division was en echelon to the left and rear of Cox. Shortly after issuing the above orders, however, Schofield received dispatches from Thomas at Nashville in which the latter expressed his desire that the position at Columbia be held until Andrew J. Smith arrived from Missouri with his three divisions of Right Wing, Sixteenth Corps, Department of the Tennessee.

At about that time, Lee opened fire on Cox's line, and Schofield then ordered a strong reconnaissance to learn more of the situation upriver before moving his troops to Spring Hill. Accordingly, he deployed his troops so as to meet an advance of the enemy on his rear, or from an enemy force moving downriver against his left flank. He countermanded Ruger's orders and directed him to obstruct the roads and fords on Duck River down toward Centerville. He also sent a message to Cooper directing him to move with his brigade, then at Beard's Ferry near Centerville, to Franklin. He ordered Nathan Kimball to halt his First Division, Fourth Corps at Rutherford Creek, three or four miles in rear of Wood's position, and about midway between Columbia and Spring Hill. Kimball had resumed command of First Division November 27, 1864, relieving Whitaker, who resumed command of Second Brigade, First Division.

About 11:00 A.M., Schofield learned from his reconnaissance upriver that enemy infantry was north of Duck River and was moving toward Spring Hill. About one hour later, Forrest arrived in front of Spring Hill after turning back from his pursuit of Wilson's cavalry.

When Stanley arrived within about two miles of Spring Hill with the head of Wagner's division, he learned that Forrest was approaching the town on the Mount Carmel road. Stanley immediately sent forward Emerson Opdyke's First Brigade, which was leading Wagner's division, and it arrived just in time to assist the two regiments that were garrisoning the place in repulsing an by attack Buford's cavalry brigade.

Stanley parked his wagon train west of Spring Hill, between the Nashville and Decatur Railroad and the Columbia Turnpike, then deployed Wagner's three brigades on a semicircular line east of the town, with the two flanks resting on the turnpike. Opdyke's brigade was on the left, where it protected the trains; Luther P. Bradley's Third Brigade was in the center, about one-third mile east of the turnpike; and John Q. Lane's Second Brigade was on the right, facing south. Forrest continued his attacks on this line until about 3:00 P.M., but without success. Bradley was wounded during the engagement and was succeeded in command of Third Brigade by Joseph Conrad.

At about 3:00 P.M., just as Forrest's attacks on Wagner's division were ending, the head of Hood's infantry column reached the Rally Hill road where it crossed Rutherford Creek, only two and one-half miles from Spring Hill. After crossing the creek, the Rally Hill road continued on to the west for a short distance, crossed McCutcheon Creek, and then ran almost due north along the west side of McCutcheon Creek to a point a short distance east of Spring Hill, where it turned to the west and into the village. Upon reaching the Rally Hill road, Hood ordered Cleburne, commanding his leading division, to hurry forward and assist Forrest in gaining possession of the turnpike. He ordered Cheatham to wait until Bate's division arrived, and then to move forward with it and support Cleburne. Brown's division, which was bringing up the rear of Cheatham's column, was to follow the other two divisions of the corps when it arrived. According to orders, Cleburne moved west from the Rally Hill road, and soon his right brigade struck Stanley's line southeast of Spring Hill. Cleburne then turned to the north toward Spring Hill, and at 4:00 P.M., about a half-hour before sunset, he launched the first infantry attack on the Federal line. Tyree H. Bell's cavalry brigade of Forrest's cavalry, fighting dismounted, supported Cleburne, but the attack was repulsed.

For some reason, Cheatham did not meet Bate's division and conduct it to Spring Hill as ordered. Instead, when it arrived at the Rally Hill road, it continued on to the north on that road until ordered by Hood to move to the west toward the Columbia Turnpike. About dark, Bate arrived on the Nat Cheairs farm near the turnpike, and about a mile and a half south of Spring Hill. Cheatham then ordered Bate to lead his division to the north and form on the right of Cleburne's division. Cheatham had been ordered to attack the Federal line at Spring Hill when his troops were in position. Brown was to begin the attack, and Bate and Cleburne were to follow. Brown was not in position, however, until about 5:30 P.M., and by that time it was quite dark. Bate then discovered that he was outflanked on his right, and he did not attack. Consequently, Cleburne and Bate, who were waiting for the signal from Brown, did not attack that evening.

Hood had ordered Stewart's corps, which was following Cheatham, to halt south of Rutherford Creek, but when he learned that Brown was outflanked, he ordered Stewart to move to the Columbia Turnpike at a point north of Spring Hill. Stewart started about 6:00 P.M., on a road east of the Rally Hill road, and soon became lost. When he finally arrived at the front, he formed on the right of Brown, but he did not reach the turnpike.

The last of Hood's infantry on the flanking march, Edward Johnson's division of Lee's corps, finally arrived behind Stewart and took position close to the Nat Cheairs house, near the left of Cheatham's line. After Hood's infantry had arrived in the positions described above, they made no further offensive movements that night.

Schofield's March to Franklin, Tennessee, Night of November 29–30, 1864. By 3:00 P.M. November 29, 1864, Schofield had decided that Hood did not intend to attack the divisions of Kimball and Wood, which were en echelon to the left and rear of Cox's line near Columbia, and he then marched rapidly toward Spring Hill with Orlando H. Moore's Second Brigade and Silas A. Strickland's Third Brigade of Ruger's division. By the time Schofield reached Rutherford Creek, he had heard the sounds of the engagement at Spring Hill, and he ordered Whitaker's Second Brigade of Kimball's division to follow him.

Schofield arrived at Spring Hill with Ruger's division about dark, and there he learned that Forrest's cavalry was on the turnpike at Thompson's Station, about three miles to the north. Schofield then continued on with Ruger's division, but he found that the road was clear and that there were no enemy troops on it. He then left Ruger's division at Thompson's Station and rode back to Spring Hill to direct further movements.

Whitaker's brigade, which had accompanied Ruger's division to Spring Hill, was ordered to extend Stanley's line to the right to give better cover to Cox's division when it withdrew from its position at Columbia that night and marched to Spring Hill. Cox, as noted above, had been directed to remain at Columbia until that night, and then to follow the rest of the army to Spring Hill. At 7:00 P.M., after dark, Cox withdrew from his position at Duck River, but he left his pickets out until midnight. The pickets were supported by the 12th Kentucky and 16th Kentucky of James W. Reilly's First Brigade of Cox's division, the whole commanded by Laurence H. Rousseau of the 12th Kentucky. When Schofield left Spring Hill for Thompson's Station with Ruger's division, he directed Stanley to halt Cox at Spring Hill until he received further information from him. Cox arrived at Spring Hill about midnight; he halted his division on the road and then reported to Stanley. When Schofield returned from Thompson's Station, he started Cox's division on the march toward Franklin, where he arrived the next morning. When Cox arrived at Spring Hill, Wood's division was already following, and Kimball was preparing to follow Wood. Later that night, Wood's division deployed north of Spring Hill, facing east, to cover the road north.

The trains followed Cox north about 1:00 A.M. November 30, 1864, and they were protected by Ruger's division, with the men marching on both sides of the wagons. Wood's division was also ordered to move on toward Franklin, keeping off the road, and marching on the right flank of the trains. Shortly after their departure, Schofield learned that the trains had been attacked at Thompson's Station, and he ordered Kimball to push on with his division and clear the road.

Wagner's division, which was detailed to bring up the rear of Schofield's column, was still at Spring Hill when Cox's pickets and their supports arrived there from Duck River at 4:00 A.M. The last wagons did not leave Spring Hill until an hour later, and it was not until 6:00 A.M. that the last of Wagner's troops finally left the town.

On the road north, Lane's brigade marched in column on the right of the trains, and Conrad's brigade in column on the left of the trains. Opdyke's brigade marched in line of battle in rear of Schofield's command, and was frequently engaged with the enemy cavalry during the march that morning.

The first troops of Schofield's army, Cox's Third Division, Twenty-Third Corps, arrived near the outskirts of Franklin about 4:30 on the morning of November 30, 1864, some two and one-half hours before dawn.

Cooper's First Brigade of Ruger's Second Division, Twenty-Third Corps, which had earlier been detached, remained at Centerville and Beard's Ferry on Duck River guarding the right flank of Schofield's army until November 30, 1864, and that day Cooper was directed to move back with his brigade to Clarksville, Tennessee. He reached Charlotte on December 3 and arrived at Clarksville two days later. He remained there until December 8, then left for Nashville. He arrived at Edgefield that day and rejoined the army.

BATTLE OF FRANKLIN, TENNESSEE, NOVEMBER 30, 1864

Franklin, Tennessee, near where a bloody battle was to be fought on the afternoon of November 30, 1864, was partially enclosed in a great loop of the Harpeth River, which flows past the eastern and northern sides of the town. The Harpeth flows toward Franklin from the southeast, on a course roughly parallel to the Lewisburg Turnpike, until it reaches the Nashville and Decatur Railroad (present-day Louisville and Nashville Railroad) at the southern edge of the town. There it turns back at almost a right angle and runs on to the northeast for about a half-mile before making another right-angled turn to the northwest. A little less than a mile farther on, it flows west for several hundred yards, then doubles back in almost a U-turn to run to the northeast and away from Franklin. The northern bank of the river is generally higher than the southern bank, and on the north side there are some commanding hills. One such elevation is east of the railroad, just above the northeastern bend of the river, and on this hill was Fort Granger.

There were three roads that ran out from Franklin to the south and southwest, and all of these figured prominently in the battle that afternoon. One was the Columbia Turnpike, which ran almost due south

from the public square and, after leaving the town, crossed a gently undulating plain before rising to the crest of Winstead Hill, about two miles from the southern edge of Franklin. The easternmost road was the Lewisburg Turnpike, which ran out of town to the southeast along the west bank of the Harpeth River to a point near the ford that was close to the Widow McGavock's house. From there it continued on almost due south for more than a mile before veering off to the east of south toward Lewisburg. The westernmost road was the Carter's Creek Turnpike, which began at the public square and ran out of town to the southwest for some distance before turning south toward Carter's Creek Station, on the railroad below Spring Hill. Near this road, and about one-half mile southwest of the Carter house, there was a low hill on which stood a house and orchard known as the Bostick place. Between the Bostick house and the Carter house was a shallow valley, through which flowed a small stream with marshy banks. This stream crossed the Carter's Creek Turnpike, then ran on northward along the west side of Franklin before emptying into the Harpeth River at the loop (or U-turn) mentioned above, at the northwestern edge of the town.

The last house on the Columbia Turnpike as it left Franklin was the home of Fountain Branch Carter, which stood on the west side of the road. The Carter house was about two miles from the gap through which the Columbia Turnpike crossed Winstead Hill, and a little less than three-fourths of a mile from the crossing of the Harpeth River to the north. It stood on a slight elevation, which was about forty feet above the town square and ten feet above the level of the ground surrounding it. The crest of this elevation was about 200 yards in length from east to west, and it extended about equal distances on both sides of the Columbia Turnpike. Beyond the Carter house to the south, the ground rose slightly to a low crest, about one-half mile distant, then fell away again to a somewhat lower level. About a half-mile beyond the crest just mentioned, or one mile from the Carter house, there was a rocky hill on the west side of the road, which was known locally as Privet Knob, but in some reports of the battle it was called Stone Hill, and also Merrill's Hill. This hill was about midway between the Carter house and the crest of Winstead Hill.

Schofield's Defensive Line. When Jacob D. Cox's division arrived near Franklin on the morning of November 30, 1864, it took position on the left of the line, between the Columbia Turnpike and the Harpeth River. Cox was placed in temporary command of Twenty-Third Corps that morning, while Schofield looked after the affairs of the army in preparation for the impending battle. James W. Reilly took charge of Cox's division. Reilly then took position on the left of Schofield's line, between the Columbia Turnpike and the Harpeth River, and immediately began to prepare a defensive line south of the town to protect the crossings of the Harpeth until the rest of the army came in and the trains and artillery had safely crossed to the north bank of the river.

The following is a brief description of the ground on which Reilly formed his division that morning. The low hill on which the Carter house stood extended southward on the east side of the Columbia Turnpike from the Carter house to form an advanced salient on what would soon become the Federal main defensive line. Near the apex of this salient was a cotton gin, a large barn-like structure, which was about 120 yards south of the Carter house and about 80 yards east of the Columbia Turnpike. To the east of the cotton gin, the ground sloped downward slightly, then rose gradually to the Lewisburg Turnpike, which was about one-half mile distant. Between the Lewisburg Turnpike and the Harpeth River was another low hill through which the railroad passed in a deep cut. The river, as it flowed northward just east of the town, was just beyond the railroad and the deep cut.

The line began on the left at the low elevation near the river bank just north of the railroad cut, then ran westward on a slight curve a short distance north of the present-day Confederate cemetery, then along the salient in front of the cotton gin, and ended at an earthwork that had been constructed for artillery on the eastern side of the Columbia Turnpike (present-day U.S. Highway 31). This line ran parallel to present-day Cleburne and Stewart streets to the Columbia Turnpike, and the site of the earthwork and battery was just north of the intersection of Cleburne Street and U.S. Highway 31, about 100 hundred yards south of the Carter house.

At a point just at the western side of the cotton gin, 80 yards from the Columbia Turnpike, Cox's line bent back at an angle, and when it reached the turnpike, it was some 50 yards north of the line at the point where it passed the cotton gin. By this arrangement, the infantry and artillery at the cotton gin could fire due west at any enemy troops advancing up the turnpike toward Franklin.

Reilly placed the brigades of his Third Division on the line as follows: Thomas J. Henderson's Third Brigade, then commanded by Israel N. Stiles because of the illness of Henderson, was on the extreme left between the Lewisburg Turnpike and the river; John S. Casement's Second Brigade was on the right of Stiles, with his line extending westward to a point near the base of the low hill on which the cotton gin stood; and Reilly's First Brigade was on the right of Casement, with its line passing in front of the cotton gin and ending on the Columbia Turnpike at the earthwork for artillery. Reilly's men had established a defensible position by noon.

Thomas H. Ruger's Second Division of Twenty-Third Corps, which had been following Cox's division during the night, began to arrive at Franklin about 7:00 A.M., soon after daylight, and it was ordered to report to Cox, who was in temporary command of the corps. Ruger was then directed to take position on the right of Third Division, between the Columbia Turnpike and the Carter's Creek Turnpike. Ruger had with him only two brigades. As noted earlier, Cooper's brigade had been detached at Centerville to guard the crossings of Duck River and was at that time withdrawing toward Clarksville. It was then marching toward a crossing of the Harpeth several miles downstream from Franklin. The line selected for Ruger to the right of the turnpike ran due west for about 50 yards across the top of the Carter House Hill, then bent back to the northwest, and then down along the southwest slope of the hill, which faced the Bostick place about one-half mile distant. The line ran on to the Carter's Creek Turnpike, near present-day Eleventh Avenue South. For some distance this line ran parallel to present-day Strahl Street.

Silas A. Strickland's Third Brigade was on the left of the division line, with its left on the Columbia Turnpike, and Orlando H. Moore's Second Brigade was on the right of Strickland, with its right extended to cover the Carter's Creek Turnpike. Ruger's breastworks were completed by 2:00 P.M.

When Giles J. Cockerill, chief of artillery of

Twenty-Third Corps, arrived at Franklin with the corps artillery, he was ordered to cross the Harpeth at once. When the artillery reached the north bank, Cockerill's own Battery D, 1st Ohio Light Artillery was placed in Fort Granger, and the rest of the guns were parked nearby. The trains of Twenty-Third Corps followed the artillery across the river.

When Ruger's men began the construction of their works on the west side of the turnpike, they left an opening through which the road passed so that the trains and artillery that were coming in could move on down the road through Franklin to the crossing of the Harpeth. When they finally had passed on to safety, however, the road was still left open so that George D. Wagner's Second Division of Fourth Corps, which had halted in an advanced position south of the line, would be able to pass through when it retired within the lines. Because of this weakness in his position, Cox constructed a second line of works, or a retrenchment, across the turnpike, about 70 yards in rear of the gap in the line. The retrenchment began about 50 feet east of the turnpike and ran due west for about 100 yards, then bent back and ran in a northwesterly direction for about 50 yards. This line was about 20 yards south of the Carter house and ran just behind the office and smokehouse of the Carter farm.

The artillery of Fourth Corps began to arrive at Franklin during the late morning of November 30, 1864, and at noon Lyman Bridges, chief of artillery, reported to Cox with four batteries. Cox placed Bridges' guns on his line as follows: Theodore S. Thomasson's 1st Battery, Kentucky Light Artillery in the earthwork on the left of the turnpike, in line with Reilly's brigade; two guns of Aaron P. Baldwin's 6th Battery, Ohio Light Artillery at the salient at the cotton gin, and two guns on the left of the Lewisburg Turnpike; John S. Burdick's 20th Battery, Ohio Light Artillery on the right of the Columbia Turnpike, on the retrenchment, just west of the Carter smokehouse where the line bent back to the northwest; and Jacob Ziegler's Battery B, Pennsylvania Light Artillery at the Carter Creek Turnpike, on the right of Ruger's line. Later, when it became known that the enemy was preparing to attack, Samuel Canby's Battery M, 4th United States Light Artillery and Alexander Marshall's Battery G, 1st Ohio Light Artillery were placed on the extreme left; Bridges' own battery, Bridges'

Battery, Illinois Light Artillery (commanded by Lyman A. White), and Charles W. Scovill's Battery A, 1st Ohio Light Artillery were placed in reserve near the center of the line.

Just before the battle began, Bridges placed his own battery on the right of the turnpike near the center of Strickland's line. He sent one section of Scovill's battery to reinforce the 20th Battery, Ohio Light Artillery just west of the Carter house (Scovill was directed to assume command of all six guns), and he placed the other section of Scovill's battery close to the turnpike, on the left, so that it would be in position to rake the road if the enemy should break through the line of works.

Stanley's Fourth Corps, which had been following Twenty-Third Corps on the Columbia Turnpike, began to arrive near Franklin late on the morning of November 30, 1864. Nathan Kimball's First Division, which was in the lead, arrived on Winstead Hill about 11:00 A.M. and reported to Cox. Kimball then left Walter C. Whitaker's Second Brigade in position on the hill, to the right of the turnpike, and moved on into the town with Isaac M. Kirby's First Brigade and William Grose's Third Brigade. Upon arriving there, Kimball was assigned position on the right of Ruger, on the extreme right of Schofield's line. Thomas J. Wood's Third Division, Fourth Corps, which was following Kimball, arrived next and was sent across the Harpeth to take position on the north bank of the river. There, with the artillery of Twenty-Third Corps, he could cover the final crossing of the army. Wagner's division of Fourth Corps, which was bringing up the rear of the army, finally arrived on Winstead Hill and relieved Whitaker's brigade, and at 1:00 P.M. Whitaker moved on into Franklin and rejoined Kimball's division.

About noon, Kimball took position on the right of Ruger, between the Carter's Creek Turnpike and the Harpeth River to the northwest of Franklin. Kimball formed his brigades en echelon on the flank and rear of Ruger to guard against an enemy attack from the west. The low ground along the stream that flowed through the area made it difficult to form a continuous line, and Kimball placed his division on the higher ground northward toward the river. The line extended from the Carter's Creek Turnpike, across present-day West Main Street, then curved back to the west and north along the Hillsboro road to the intersection of that road with the present-day Del Rio Pike. Grose's brigade was placed on the left of this line in immediate support of Ruger's right and Ziegler's Battery B, Pennsylvania Light Artillery. Kirby's brigade was in the center, and Whitaker's brigade was on the left, next to the river.

When Wagner arrived on Winstead Hill (called Stevens' Hill in the reports of Wagner and Opdyke), he placed a part of Emerson Opdyke's First Brigade to cover the gap in the hill through which the turnpike ran, and extended the rest of the brigade to the left to a high point east of the gap. He placed a section of Alexander Marshall's Battery G, 1st Ohio Light Artillery on this elevation, and the brigades of Lane and Conrad extended the line to the east toward the Lewisburg Turnpike. When Opdyke arrived, Whitaker's brigade and a section of Samuel Canby's Battery M, 4th United States Artillery were holding the high ground on Winstead Hill to the west of the gap. Then, as already noted, Whitaker withdrew into the town at 1:00 P.M. When he departed, Wagner followed with the brigades of John Q. Lane and Joseph Conrad, and Opdyke's brigade brought up the rear.

Wagner, with the head of his column, had arrived within about one-half mile of Cox's main line, and the rear of Opdyke's brigade was just leaving Winstead Hill, when the column was halted. Stanley then ordered Wagner to return to Winstead Hill. When Opdyke was again on the hill, he observed a column of enemy infantry approaching on the Columbia Turnpike, and another on the Lewisburg Turnpike to the east. The latter column was at the point of turning the left flank of Wagner's position on Winstead Hill, and because of this threat, Wagner again withdrew from the hill. He halted Lane's brigade and George H. Mitchell's section of Marshall's battery at Privet Knob, about one mile in front of the Federal main line, and placed Opdyke and Conrad in support on the first rise south of Cox's line, which was about one-half mile from the Carter house. Opdyke objected to this advanced position and, with Wagner's permission, withdrew his brigade to a position about 200 yards north of the Carter house, on the right of the turnpike, where he remained massed as a reserve. Conrad remained out in front of the main line on the rise of ground. Conrad's brigade was formed with its right on the turnpike and its left running back at an angle to the

road, and extending about two-thirds of the distance to the Nashville and Decatur Railroad.

At 2:00 P.M. Lane reported to Wagner that the enemy was about to envelop his flanks. His skirmish line on Privet Knob and the artillery slowed the enemy advance until about 2:30 P.M., and then Lane was ordered to withdraw. He moved back and formed on the right of Conrad, on the west side of the turnpike. His line ran back from the turnpike at an angle of about forty-five degrees, and extended to the northwest for about 400 yards. Wagner's line was thus in the shape of a wide inverted V, with the apex on the Columbia Turnpike. The section of artillery was at the apex of the line, to the left of the turnpike.

Hood's Advance to Franklin. Meantime, back at Spring Hill, Hood had learned at daylight that Schofield's army had passed during the night and was then on the road to Franklin. He immediately sent Nathan B. Forrest in pursuit with the divisions of Abraham Buford and William H. Jackson, and ordered James R. Chalmers out to the west to the Carter's Creek Turnpike, on which he turned to the right and advanced toward Franklin. Hood followed Forrest up the Columbia Turnpike with the corps of Alexander P. Stewart and Benjamin F. Cheatham and Edward Johnson's division of Stephen D. Lee's corps. By noon, Hood, with the van of Stewart's corps, had arrived within a few miles of Winstead Hill, which was then occupied by Wagner's division and Whitaker's brigade of Kimball's division. To drive Wagner from the hill and clear the road to Franklin, Hood directed Stewart to move eastward with his corps on present-day Henpeck Lane, just south of Winstead Hill, to the Lewisburg Turnpike, which was about a mile and a half distant. Stewart was then to turn northward, advance across country beyond Wagner's left flank, and force him to abandon Winstead Hill. At the same time, Hood ordered Cheatham to prepare for an attack along the Columbia Turnpike. It was the advance of Stewart that Opdyke had observed and which had caused Wagner to withdraw from the hill at 1:00 P.M.

Stewart formed his corps on a line that extended from the Lewisburg Turnpike on the right, to a point about one-half mile from the Nashville and Decatur Railroad on the left. The line began about three-fourths of a mile south of the point where the turnpike came up to the river, northwest of the Widow McGavock's house, and it ran somewhat south of west in the direction of Winstead Hill. The distance between the railroad and the Lewisburg Turnpike where Stewart formed his corps was about a mile and a half. William W. Loring's, Edward C. Walthall's, and Samuel G. French's divisions were in line, in that order, from the Confederate right to left. In each division, except French's, there were two brigades on the front line and one in reserve. In Loring's division, Thomas M. Scott's brigade was on the right and Winfield S. Featherston's brigade was on the left of the front line, and John Adams' brigade was in reserve; in Walthall's division, William A. Quarles' brigade was on the right and Charles M. Shelley's brigade was on the left of the front line, and Daniel H. Reynolds' brigade was in reserve; and in French's division, Claudius W. Sears' brigade was on the front line, and Francis M. Cockrell's brigade was in reserve. Matthew D. Ector's brigade of French's division was absent guarding the pontoon train. Abraham Buford's cavalry division was on the right of Stewart, between the Lewisburg Turnpike and the Harpeth River, and it was ordered to advance dismounted when the infantry moved forward.

Cheatham formed his corps about a half-mile in front of Privet Knob, with his right about three-fourths of a mile in front of Stewart's left. Patrick R. Cleburne's division was on the right, between the Columbia Turnpike and the railroad, with Hiram B. Granbury's brigade on the right, Daniel C. Govan in the center, and Mark P. Lowrey's brigade on the left. The front occupied by the division was a little less than a half-mile. John C. Brown's division was on the left of the Columbia Turnpike, with the brigades of George W. Gordon and States Rights Gist on the front line, and the brigades of Otho F. Strahl and John C. Carter on the second line. Gordon's brigade was next to the turnpike, and Gist's brigade was on the left of Gordon; Strahl's brigade was behind Gordon, and Carter's brigade was behind Gist. William B. Bate's division was ordered to move to the left of Brown's division, and to the left of Privet Knob until its left was on the Carter's Creek Turnpike. It was then to advance to the front of the Bostick house. When Hood's attack began, Bate was moving toward the Bostick house, and Chalmers' cavalry division was under orders to ad-

vance beyond Bate's division. Johnson's division of Lee's corps was held in reserve.

Confederate Attacks on the Evening of November 30, 1864. By 3:00 P.M. Hood's army was prepared to attack, even though the two divisions of Lee's corps from Columbia and most of the artillery had not arrived. A little before 4:00 P.M. the line moved forward, with Cheatham's corps advancing along the Columbia Turnpike, Cleburne's division on the right, and Brown's division on the left. The center of the line was slowed somewhat by the brigades of Lane and Conrad, which Wagner had unaccountably left out in front of the Federal main line, but they were quickly overrun and driven back in total disorder into Cox's works. They were closely followed by the enemy, and both the pursued and the pursuers entered the line with little semblance of organization at about the same time at and near the gap at the turnpike.

The break in the lines was rapidly widened when the 100th Ohio, Reilly's right regiment, was driven back just east of the turnpike, and Strickland's brigade, west of the road, was forced to withdraw. The 50th Ohio on the left of Strickland's front line was driven back on the Carter buildings, where it rallied on Opdyke's brigade. The right wing of the 72nd Illinois on the right of Strickland's line held firm, but the left wing of the regiment was swept away. It rallied on the 183rd Ohio, which was in reserve, and continued to fight on the retrenchment, or second line. The right wing of 72nd Illinois was then moved back to the second line. The gap in the line then extended from the cotton gin on the left to the left of Moore's brigade on the right.

At the time of Hood's attack, Opdyke's brigade of Wagner's division was massed in column on the west side of the turnpike, about 200 yards north of the Carter house, and when the enemy crossed the breastworks and advanced toward the Carter buildings, Opdyke deployed his brigade across the road and advanced to drive them back. Reilly's reserve regiments also joined in the counterattack. Before the breakthrough occurred, the 12th Kentucky Regiment had been brought forward from Reilly's second line and placed in position where it could deliver a raking fire on any enemy force that might advance on the turnpike within the line of works. The 16th Kentucky of Reilly's reserve and the 44th

Illinois, the left regiment of Opdyke's brigade, advanced on the left of the turnpike and occupied the ground that had been held by Thomasson's Kentucky battery. The 8th Tennessee of Reilly's brigade and 12th Kentucky doubled on the line of Reilly's 104th Ohio, the right wing of which had been driven back, and together they firmly solidified Reilly's line near the cotton gin.

When Opdyke advanced, he was soon engaged in furious hand-to-hand fighting around the Carter buildings and along the turnpike in rear of the front line, but finally, together with the reserves of Strickland's and Reilly's brigades and some of Wagner's men who had rallied and returned to the front, they drove Brown's troops back to the main line, where they remained on the outer face of the works until the fighting ended that night. Cleburne, who had attacked east of the turnpike, in front of the cotton gin, was driven back from the breastworks and was subjected to a devastating flank fire from Casement's brigade.

Opdyke's and Strickland's brigades, and other troops that had been driven back earlier but had returned, joined in the fighting, occupied the second line or retrenchment, and then constructed a barricade across the Carter garden to extend this line. Opdyke was west of the turnpike, with his left regiment on the left of the road, where it connected with Reilly's brigade.

For hours there was heavy firing across the Carter yard and gardens, but Brown's division did not attack again as a unit. The division suffered terrible losses, which included Brown, who was wounded, and his four brigade commanders. Gist and Strahl were killed, Carter was mortally wounded, and Gordon was captured.

In approaching Cox's line after passing Lane's position, Brown's division angled to the right, and Gordon's brigade crossed the Columbia Turnpike and joined Cleburne in his attack east of the road. During the Federal counterattack, Gordon and a part of Cleburne's division were driven back to the outer face of the works just to the south and west of the cotton gin. From then until the end of the battle, Gordon's men, the remnants of Granbury's brigade, and part of Govan's brigade, who were huddled on the outside of the works between the cotton gin and the turnpike, were subjected to a terrible cross fire. Farther to the east, where a part of Cleburne's divi-

sion was in front of Reilly's brigade and a part of Casement's brigade, all attacks were repulsed with heavy losses. Cleburne was killed, and fourteen of his brigade and regimental commanders were either killed, wounded, or missing.

So far, the account of the fighting at the center of Schofield's line makes it appear that only the divisions of Brown and Cleburne assaulted the lines held by Reilly's and Strickland's brigades. In fact, however, this was not the case. For a better understanding of what actually happened that evening, it is necessary to consider next the attacks on both the left and right of the Federal line.

When Stewart's divisions advanced that morning against the Federal left, they encountered difficulties almost from the start. Part of the trouble resulted from the fact that Loring's division on the right was guided by the Harpeth River, which, on the right of Stewart's advance, flowed to the northwest toward the outskirts of Franklin. Thus, the distance between the railroad and the river on the line where Stewart deployed was about a mile and a half, but to the north, where Loring struck Stiles' line at the railroad cut, this distance had been reduced to a matter of yards. As a result, during the advance, Loring and Walthall were forced to take ground to the left, and when Stewart came up to Cox's line, Walthall's and French's divisions were to the west of the railroad, and Loring's division was on the railroad and to the west of it. During this movement, Walthall, who was moving to the left, came up in front of Cleburne's division, which had been delayed somewhat by Conrad's brigade on the low ridge in front of the center of the Federal line. In fact, it appears that the left of Walthall's line passed over a part of Conrad's advanced position.

Walthall also had other difficulties. As he advanced, he came up to a field that had been surrounded by a hedge of Osage orange. When Stiles had entrenched his position behind the northern side of this field, he had thinned out the hedge on the northern side to give him a better field of fire but still provide some protection. He had cut the hedge on the east and west sides of the field, and used the cuttings to form an abatis on other parts of the line, but he had left the hedge on the south side of the field to impede the movements of the enemy as they advanced. When Walthall struck the latter hedge, Reynolds' brigade was forced to move around it to the left, and after passing it was unable to resume its place in the line. Shelley's brigade was then brought up to fill the gap thus created.

Meantime, Loring's division had come up and attacked Stiles' brigade in two lines, in an attempt to turn its position by way of the railroad cut. Loring's first attack was repulsed with heavy losses. His second attack, which closely followed the first, reached the works but was then thrown back. Featherston's brigade of Loring's division appears to have struck the works held by Casement's brigade. Walthall, in his advance, came up en echelon to the left of Loring and extended to the rear of Loring's division for the length of a brigade. As a result, Quarles' brigade, and possibly Reynolds' brigade, of Walthall's division were following Featherston, and they attacked Casement's line in succession. All of these attacks were repulsed with great losses.

Shelley's brigade of Walthall's division apparently struck the Federal line between the turnpike and the cotton gin on the front of Reilly's brigade. Probably, Cockrell's and Sears' brigades of French's division followed Shelley, and two brigades of Cleburne's division followed French. In addition, as has been noted, Gordon's brigade of Brown's division crossed to the east side of the turnpike and attacked on the front of Reilly's brigade. Thus it appears that on the front of Reilly and the Kentucky battery at the turnpike, six enemy brigades struck the line, one after the other. In addition to these attacks, many of the enemy troops rallied and then attacked again and again.

Earlier, when Hood formed his line of battle, he sent Bate's division of Cheatham's corps to the left of Brown. When Bate was ready to advance, Henry R. Jackson's brigade, which was on the right of the division, moved up to the east of the Bostick house. When Bate's troops approached the Bostick house, they encountered Federal pickets, and then Thomas Benton Smith (commanding Robert C. Tyler's brigade) changed direction and extended his brigade all the way to the Carter's Creek Turnpike. Then, as Smith's brigade moved forward past the Bostick house, it was struck by a heavy fire from the left, and Robert Bullock (commanding Jesse J. Finley's brigade) was ordered to bring his brigade up from reserve and form in line across the Carter's Creek Turnpike. Bate then attacked. Jackson passed over

a part of the former position of Lane's brigade, west of the Columbia Turnpike, and followed the brigades of Gist and Carter, on Brown's first and second lines, respectively, which had preceded him. Jackson struck the front of Moore's brigade and was driven back by the heavy fire from the entrenchments. Jackson's brigade was thus the third line to attack on the Federal right center. Smith's brigade also struck the front of Moore's brigade. Both Jackson and Smith made repeated attacks, but all were repulsed. Bullock finally attacked about 5:00 P.M. and was repulsed by a part of Grose's brigade of Kimball's division west of the Carter's Creek Turnpike.

Chalmers' cavalry division made a weak attack on the far Federal right against the brigades of Kirby and Whitaker of Kimball's division, but it was easily repulsed, and Chalmers did not press the attack.

Late in the evening, Johnson's division of Lee's corps was sent forward to aid Cheatham and attacked near the Carter house, but it accomplished little.

Because of the many casualties among the higher officers of Hood's army, there are comparatively few Confederate reports of the Battle of Franklin, and thus there is considerable uncertainty as to the exact movement of some of the units of Hood's army. After the war, Jacob D. Cox made a thorough study of the battle, and the information presented here has been taken largely from his book, *The Battle of Franklin,* published in 1897.

James H. Wilson's cavalry corps was also active November 30, 1864. During the night of November 29, Wilson assembled his cavalry on the Triune road, about two and one-half miles east of Franklin, and established his headquarters at the Matthews house. He sent John H. Hammond's brigade out to Triune to watch the country in that direction and covered the fords with pickets for a distance of several miles above Franklin. At that time, Hammond reported directly to Wilson, and John T. Croxton's and Thomas J. Harrison's brigade (formerly Horace Capron's) constituted a division commanded by Richard W. Johnson. The brigades of Datus E. Coon and Robert R. Stewart formed a division that was commanded by Edward Hatch.

Soon after daylight November 30, 1864, at Schofield's direction, Wilson sent Croxton out to the south on the Lewisburg Turnpike to Douglas

Church, where he was in position to cover the right flank of the infantry, which was then marching north on the Columbia Turnpike from Spring Hill. When Wagner's division of Fourth Corps, which was serving as rear guard of the army that day, had passed, Croxton moved back and formed on the left of Wagner, who was in position on Winstead Hill, facing south. Also that morning, Hammond marched from Triune by way of Petersburg to Wilson's Mill. There he took position on the Brentwood Turnpike, northeast of Matthews' Cross Roads (or Corners).

Forrest, who had been covering the advance of Hood's infantry, waited until Stewart's corps arrived near Winstead Hill, then marched with his two divisions to a point beyond the Lewisburg Turnpike. This movement placed him on the flank of Wagner's division, which was on Winstead Hill, and forced Croxton to fall back toward McGavock's Ford, which was about a mile and a half upstream from the center of Franklin. Croxton skirmished with the enemy for a time, then crossed to the north bank of the Harpeth at McGavock's Ford.

After Hood had deployed his infantry for the attack that afternoon, Forrest ordered Buford to dismount his division and take position on the left of Stewart's line, and to advance with Stewart when he attacked. Forrest also sent Jackson's division out on a reconnaissance toward Hughes' Ford, about three miles above Franklin, where a road ran to the north directly to Wilson's position at the Matthews place. When the Confederate infantry advanced, Forrest was to cross the Harpeth and drive away Schofield's troops that were holding the hill at Fort Granger.

At 3:00 P.M. Wilson learned that Forrest's cavalry was crossing the Harpeth at Hughes' Ford, and he promptly ordered Hatch to move south from the crossroads and strike the front of Forrest's advance. At the same time he directed Croxton to move from McGavock's Ford against Forrest's flank. He held Harrison's brigade in reserve. Jackson advanced from Hughes' Ford; he pushed back Wilson's picket and its supports and soon reached a position on some hills overlooking a valley, on the far side of which Hatch was approaching. Advancing dismounted, Hatch charged and finally drove the enemy back across the river. Croxton's brigade arrived too late to take part in the action, but it joined in the pursuit of Jackson.

By sunset November 30, 1864, the repulse of Hood's army was complete all along the line, and Schofield began to prepare for the withdrawal of the army from Franklin toward Nashville. Wood's division, which was then north of the Harpeth, was to cover the retreat. Samuel Beatty's Third Brigade was deployed on the north bank above Franklin; Abel D. Streight's First Brigade was along the bank, immediately across from the town; and P. Sidney Post's Second Brigade was along the river below the town.

The order for the withdrawal was issued between 6:00 and 7:00 P.M. and directed that the movement begin at midnight. This was to be done by drawing back the troops from the right and left of the position at the Carter house, with the troops from the left crossing the river at the railroad bridge, and those on the right by the foot bridge. Once across the river, all were to march to Brentwood by the Nashville Turnpike. Wood's division was to act as the rear guard. The trains of the army had been on the road to Nashville for some time.

On the right, Fourth Corps crossed first, with Lane's and Conrad's brigades of Wagner's division in the lead (Opdyke's brigade remained out on the line for some time and accompanied Ruger's division later) and Kimball's division following. Ruger's division, with Opdyke's brigade of Wagner's division, moved through town and crossed the river at a wagon bridge a little below the railroad crossing. Reilly's brigade was the last to leave the line, and when Ruger and Opdyke had passed, the brigade faced to the left and moved through the trenches to the railroad bridge, where it crossed. Schofield's skirmishers were kept out another hour.

Cox, with his division, took the lead on the road to Brentwood. Schofield had been directed to establish a defensive line at Brentwood, where he would be joined by Andrew J. Smith with his Right Wing, Sixteenth Corps from Missouri. The troops halted at Brentwood and prepared to take position on the hills, facing south, to stop Hood if he continued the pursuit. Thomas, however, decided to assemble the army within the lines at Nashville and ordered that the march be resumed. The advance of the army arrived near Nashville before noon December 1, 1864, and the rest of the troops arrived during the day.

The organization of the Union forces commanded by John M. Schofield at the Battle of Franklin November 30, 1864 was as follows:

FOURTH CORPS, David S. Stanley

First Division, Nathan Kimball
First Brigade, Isaac M. Kirby
Second Brigade, Walter C. Whitaker
Third Brigade, William Grose

Note. Kimball, who had been absent, rejoined the division and assumed command November 25, 1864.

Second Division, George D. Wagner
First Brigade, Emerson Opdyke
Second Brigade, John Q. Lane
Third Brigade, Luther P. Bradley, to November 29, 1864, wounded
Joseph Conrad

Third Division, Thomas J. Wood
First Brigade, Abel D. Streight
Second Brigade, P. Sidney Post
Third Brigade, Samuel Beatty

Note. Stanley was wounded November 30, 1864, and Thomas J. Wood relieved him in command of Fourth Corps December 2. Samuel Beatty assumed command of Third Division.

Artillery Brigade, Lyman Bridges
6th Battery, Ohio Light Artillery, Aaron P. Baldwin
Bridges' Battery, Illinois Light Artillery, Lyman A. White
Battery A, 1st Ohio Light Artillery, Charles W. Scovill
Battery G, 1st Ohio Light Artillery, Alexander Marshall
Battery B, Pennsylvania Light Artillery, Jacob Ziegler
Battery M, 4th United States Artillery, Samuel Canby
20th Battery, Ohio Light Artillery, John S. Burdick

Note. The artillery of this brigade was assigned November 23, 1864, at the beginning of the campaign.

TWENTY-THIRD CORPS, Jacob D. Cox, temporarily

Second Division, Thomas H. Ruger
First Brigade, Joseph A. Cooper
Second Brigade, Orlando H. Moore
Third Brigade, Silas A. Strickland

Note. Cooper's brigade was not present at the Battle

of Franklin, but was west of the town, on the march toward Clarksville from the Duck River.

Third Division, James W. Reilly, temporarily
First Brigade, James W. Reilly
Second Brigade, John S. Casement
Third Brigade, Israel N. Stiles

Note. Thomas J. Henderson, who was the commander of Third Brigade, was so ill on the morning of November 30, 1864 that he turned over the command of the brigade to Stiles, but he was present on the line during the battle, helping in any way that he could.

Artillery, Giles J. Cockerill
15th Battery, Indiana Light Artillery, Alonzo D. Harvey
23rd Battery, Indiana Light Artillery, Aaron A. Wilber
Battery D, 1st Ohio Light Artillery, Giles J. Cockerill

BATTLE OF NASHVILLE, TENNESSEE, DECEMBER 15–16, 1864

Union Lines before Nashville. When John M. Schofield arrived with his army near Nashville during the morning of December 1, 1864, he was ordered by George H. Thomas, commanding at Nashville, to move into the fortified lines in front of the city. Construction of these works had been started under the direction of James St. Clair Morton of the Corps of Engineers of the United States Army when Nashville was first occupied by Union forces in February 1862, but progress had been slow until November 1864. Then, because of the threat of invasion of the state by John B. Hood's Army of Tennessee, work was speeded up under the supervision of Zealous B. Tower of the army engineers.

Nashville is situated in a big bend of the Cumberland River, and the entrenched lines followed a roughly semicircular course from the river above the city around to the river below. The defenses began on the Federal left, at a hill where the city reservoir was then located and which later became the site of the city hospital. From there they ran through present-day South Nashville, across the grounds of what was later Howard School and

Children's Museum to Fort Negley, on Cloud's Hill, and from there on to Fort Casino, about one-half mile to the southwest. About one-fourth of a mile to the north and west of Fort Casino was Fort Morton, which was located on a high hill just south of present-day South Street. From Fort Morton, an interior line ran a little to the north of west across the Granny White Pike and the Hillsboro Pike. Immediately after crossing the latter road, the line turned to the south, curved around a hill, then ran back to the north, forming a salient around the Taylor house, which was located on what is now the highest point on the campus of Vanderbilt University. From the salient, the interior line continued on to the northwest, across the Harding Pike and the Nashville and Northwestern Railroad to Hill 210, near the corner of present-day Twenty-Third Avenue North and Hermosa Street. From Hill 210, the line ran northward to Fort Gillem, the present site of Fisk University, then northwest to Fort Garesche, which stood on a hill across which ran the old Hyde Ferry road (present-day Buchanan Street), and near the intersection of Buchanan with Twenty-Fifth and Twenty-Sixth avenues. Finally, the works ran north of, and parallel to, the Hyde Ferry road and ended on the river about one-fourth of a mile north of the ferry.

An exterior line was also constructed at some distance in front of the line of the interior works. This line of works began on the left of Fort Casino and ran to the southwest along the crests of some high hills, east of the Granny White Pike, then crossed the pike near the present-day intersection of Acklen Avenue. From that point, the line ran over a hill to the west of the pike, where the house of Mrs. Lawrence stood, and then to the southwest along high ground. It crossed present-day Belmont Boulevard near Blair Boulevard and continued on to the southwest to Lawrence Hill (also called Lauren's Hill and Lawrins' Hill), which was between present-day Belmont Boulevard and the Hillsboro Pike. At that point, the outer line formed a salient about one-half mile north of Montgomery Hill. From this salient, the line turned back to the northwest, crossed the Hillsboro Pike (now Twenty-First Avenue South) just north of present-day Blair Boulevard, the Harding Pike, and the Nashville and Northwestern Railroad, then ran on to the north across the Charlotte Pike and finally ended on a hill

on present-day Centennial Boulevard, overlooking the Cumberland River. The description of the fortified lines about Nashville, both Union and Confederate, especially with reference streets and locations in present-day Nashville, is derived almost in its entirety from Stanley F. Horn's excellent book *The Decisive Battle of Nashville,* published by the University of Tennessee Press at Knoxville.

The two lines of fortifications in front of Nashville completely covered the eight principal roads that radiated from the city and ran out to the east, south, and west. From east to west, these roads were as follows:

Lebanon Pike (present-day U.S. 70 North), east of Nashville
Murfreesboro Pike (U.S. 41)
Nolensville Pike (Alternate U.S. 31)
Franklin Pike (U.S. 31)
Granny White Pike
Hillsboro Pike (U.S. 431)
Harding Pike (or Hardin Pike) (U.S. 70)
Charlotte Pike (U.S. 70 North), west of Nashville

Schofield's Twenty-Third Corps was placed on the left of these works from Fort Casino to the Nolensville Pike on the left, including Fort Negley. Thomas J. Wood's Fourth Corps occupied the center of the line, and it extended westward from Fort Casino on the left, across the Granny White and Hillsboro pikes, to a point midway between the Hillsboro Pike and Harding Pike, where it connected with the left of Andrew J. Smith's Right Wing, Sixteenth Corps. (*Note. On December 6, 1864, Sixteenth Corps was discontinued, and Smith's command was designated as Detachment Army of the Tennessee.*) Smith's First Division and Third Division had arrived on transports from Saint Louis, debarking November 30. Second Division joined them on December 1. These divisions occupied the works on the Federal right, from the right of Wood's corps near the Hillsboro Pike, to the Cumberland River, about three miles, on a direct line, west of the city.

At first, James H. Wilson's Cavalry Corps, Military Division of the Mississippi was in position between the left of Schofield's line and the river above Nashville, but on December 3, 1864 it moved to Edgefield, north of the river, to train, refit, and remount. The space formerly held by the cavalry was then occupied by James B. Steedman's Provisional Detachment, District of the Etowah, which arrived near Nashville from Chattanooga during the evening of December 1. On December 3, Steedman's command was placed on the extreme Federal left, on the north side of Brown's Creek. Its line extended to the left from the Nolensville Pike, across the Murfreesboro Pike, and ended on the left near Major Lewis' house, a short distance from the Lebanon Pike.

On the river side to the north, Nashville was protected by the navy. Acting Rear Admiral S. Phillips Lee, commander of the Mississippi Squadron of inland war vessels, was the overall chief of naval operations in the area. Commander Le Roy Fitch was in command of the squadron at Nashville and vicinity, however, and he had the responsibility for patrolling the Cumberland River above and below Nashville to prevent Confederate forces from crossing the river.

Confederate Lines before Nashville. On the morning of December 2, 1864, Hood's Army of Tennessee, which had followed Schofield from Franklin, arrived in front of Nashville and deployed on the hills south of the city. Hood's original line extended westward from Rains' Hill, past Montgomery Hill, to the Hillsboro Pike, and then back along the pike for a short distance. At Montgomery Hill, Hood's line faced the main Federal salient, several hundred yards to the north. Hood then decided that this line was too close to the Federal works, and on December 10 he withdrew to a stronger position some distance to the rear. The abandoned works were then occupied by a strong skirmish line.

Stephen D. Lee's corps was formed on the center of the new line, with its center on the Franklin Pike, near its intersection with present-day Thompson's Lane. From the Franklin Pike the line extended to the west along the south side of what is now Woodmont Boulevard to a point about 1,500 yards east of the Granny White Pike. To the east of the Franklin Pike, it ran to the northeast across the Nashville and Decatur Railroad (Tennessee and Alabama Railroad) to a point about midway between the Franklin Pike and the Nolensville Pike.

Benjamin F. Cheatham's corps was on the right of Lee, and his line ran about two miles to the

northeast to Rains' Cut on the Nashville and Chattanooga Railroad.

Alexander P. Stewart's corps was on the Confederate left. Its line ran westward from the left of Lee's corps, across the Granny White Pike, and then, a short distance beyond the pike, it curved to the northwest and ran across present-day Woodmont Boulevard to a hill just east of the Hillsboro Pike. A work known as Redoubt No. 1 was constructed on this hill. The line curved around this hill, forming a strong salient, and then ran to the southwest along the Hillsboro Pike, past Redoubt No. 2 at present-day Woodmont Boulevard, and Redoubt No. 3, about 100 yards south of Redoubt No. 2. It ended at a point about midway between Woodmont Boulevard and present-day Harding Place. Redoubt No. 4 was constructed at some distance in front of the left of Stewart's line, and a detached work, Redoubt No. 5, was located on the extreme left, just west of the Hillsboro Pike and a short distance north of Harding Place. Hood's force was too small to envelop the Federal defenses, and for this reason his line did not extend to the Cumberland River. On the Confederate right, Cheatham's line ended a short distance beyond the Nolensville Pike, a mile from the river, and on the left Stewart's line ended near the Hillsboro Pike, four miles from the river.

December 3, 1864, Hood divided Nathan B. Forrest's cavalry command. He assigned James R. Chalmers' division to watch the line between Stewart's corps and the river and sent Forrest with the divisions of Abraham Buford and William H. Jackson to the Confederate right to destroy the Nashville and Chattanooga Railroad to Murfreesboro. On December 9, Buford's division was sent to the vicinity of the Hermitage, east of Nashville, to watch the Cumberland River and protect the Confederate right flank. Forrest, with Jackson's division, continued the work of destruction on the railroad near Murfreesboro. Chalmers attempted to cover the Confederate left with the brigades of Edmund W. Rucker and Jacob B. Biffle, but on December 10, Biffle was sent to support Buford, leaving only Rucker's brigade to watch the four-mile interval between the left of Stewart and the river.

Matthew D. Ector's brigade of Samuel G. French's division, then commanded by David Coleman, was sent to relieve Chalmers' cavalry on the

Harding Pike. Chalmers then moved to the left and took position between the Charlotte Pike and the river, and Ector's brigade formed behind Richland Creek, between the Harding Pike and the Charlotte Pike.

The First Day, December 15, 1864. Immediately after the Battle of Franklin, Thomas informed Henry W. Halleck in Washington that he would remain on the defensive within the works at Nashville until Wilson could reorganize, reequip, and remount his cavalry and put it in condition to contend with Forrest. Immediately after Hood arrived in front of Nashville, however, the authorities in Washington began to press Thomas to take the offensive without delay and drive the enemy out of Tennessee. At the urging of Secretary of War Edwin M. Stanton and President Abraham Lincoln, Ulysses S. Grant, commander of the Armies of the United States, also became concerned about affairs in Tennessee, and he repeatedly urged Thomas to move. Then, on December 7, 1864, he sent a peremptory order for Thomas to attack Hood at once.

From December 2 through December 8, 1864, the weather in Central Tennessee had been fair and mild, but on the night of December 8, a cold rain mixed with snow began to fall, and the temperature dropped. For a week there was rain, sleet, and freezing rain, and all the country around Nashville became covered with a sheet of ice. As a result, all troop movements of the armies were practically impossible. On December 3, Thomas had informed Halleck that he would probably be able to advance in about a week, but because of the weather, the movement planned for December 10 was necessarily postponed.

As early as December 8, 1864, Grant had thought of removing Thomas and replacing him with Schofield, and the next day he went so far as to prepare an order to that effect, but after considering the matter further, he suspended the order. Finally, on December 13, Grant sent John A. Logan (who was absent from the Army of the Tennessee and was then at City Point, Virginia) to Nashville with orders to relieve Thomas, and the next day Grant followed to assume general command in person. Logan had arrived at Louisville and Grant at Washington when they received the news of Thomas' victory at Nashville December 15, and both returned to City Point.

As the weather improved at Nashville, Thomas issued orders December 14, 1864 for an advance by his army against the enemy works. Thomas' plan was to advance the right of his line in a wide wheeling movement to the left against the left and rear of Hood's position on the Hillsboro Pike. Wilson's cavalry on the Federal right and Andrew J. Smith's Detachment Army of the Tennessee on the left of Wilson were to make the turning movement, and Wood's Fourth Corps was to serve as the pivot for their advance. Schofield's Twenty-Third Corps was to remain near the entrenchments to cooperate with Wood and to protect the left of Fourth Corps from an enemy attack. Later, Thomas modified his plan slightly. He ordered Steedman, who originally was to have remained in his works, to make a diversionary attack on Hood's right as a preliminary to the main attack.

The army began to move early on the morning of December 15, 1864, when the troops left the entrenchments and marched to their assigned positions for the advance. Charles Cruft's Provisional Division of Steedman's Provisional Detachment, District of the Etowah moved out at 4:00 A.M., relieved the troops of Fourth Corps and Twenty-Third Corps, and occupied their positions on the exterior line of works. Cruft then picketed the front of this line from the Acklen place, about midway between the Granny White Pike and the Hillsboro Pike, to Fort Negley and covered the approaches to the city by the Granny White Pike, the Franklin Pike, and the Nolensville Pike.

At 4:00 A.M., John F. Miller, commander of the post of Nashville, reported to Steedman with the garrison troops of Nashville. Miller was then assigned to the works between Fort Negley and the Lebanon Pike, where he covered the approaches to the city by the Murfreesboro Pike and the Lebanon Pike.

At 6:00 A.M., James L. Donaldson, chief quartermaster, Department of the Cumberland, reported to Steedman with his armed employees of the quartermaster's and commissary departments, and they were placed on the interior line from Fort Morton, near the right of Cruft's division, to the Cumberland River below Nashville.

At 6:30 A.M., Steedman advanced with Thomas J. Morgan's First Colored Brigade, Charles R. Thompson's Second Colored Brigade, Charles H.

Grosvenor's Third Brigade of white troops, and two batteries of artillery of his Provisional Detachment to make his demonstration on the right of Hood's line, about two miles to the south. There was some delay in getting into position because of a dense fog, but by 8:00 A.M. he was ready to begin his attack. Steedman drove back Cheatham's advance skirmish line into the main works, but all further attempts against that line were repulsed. Steedman then withdrew his command and, except for some firing along the line, made no further effort that day.

While the above-described movements were in progress, preparations were under way about five miles to the west for the main attack on the Confederate left. At 6:00 A.M., Kenner Garrard's Second Division of Smith's Detachment Army of the Tennessee marched out on the Harding Pike, then moved by the left flank until it connected with the right of Wood's Fourth Corps. This placed Garrard's division on the left of Smith's line, with James I. Gilbert's Second Brigade on the left, David Moore's First Brigade in the center, and Edward H. Wolfe's Third Brigade on the right, with its right on the Harding Pike.

At 7:00 A.M., John McArthur's First Division of Smith's detachment marched out to form on the right of Garrard's division. Sylvester G. Hill's Third Brigade advanced on the Harding Pike and took position on the right of Garrard. William L. McMillen's First Brigade and Lucius F. Hubbard's Second Brigade took the Charlotte Pike, and they reached Richland Creek without encountering any opposition. They then moved to the left, and Hubbard formed on the right of Hill and McMillen on the right of Hubbard.

Jonathan B. Moore's Third Division of Smith's detachment advanced on the Harding Pike and formed in rear of the center of Smith's line as a reserve.

Wood's Fourth Corps was ordered to move at 6:00 A.M., but because of the dense fog it did not start until 8:00 A.M. At that time, Washington L. Elliott's Second Division moved by its right and formed en echelon to the left and rear of Smith's line. Elliott had succeeded Wagner in command of Second Division December 2, 1864 because of the performance of the latter at the Battle of Franklin. Then, on December 9, Wagner was relieved from further duty with the Army of the Cumberland at his own request. Elliott deployed his division, with Emerson Opdyke's First Brigade on the right, John Q. Lane's Second Brigade on the left, and Joseph Conrad's Third Brigade in reserve. Elliott was ordered to advance with Smith.

Nathan Kimball's First Division, Fourth Corps moved over to the Hillsboro Pike inside the Federal works, then advanced on the pike, forming en echelon to the left and rear of Elliott's division. William Grose's Third Brigade was on the right, Isaac M. Kirby's First Brigade was on the left, with its left on the Hillsboro Pike, and Walter C. Whitaker's Second Brigade was in reserve, near the center of the line. Kimball's orders were to advance with Elliott.

Samuel Beatty, who had assumed command of Third Division, Fourth Corps December 2, 1864, moved his division out to the left and took position en echelon to the left and rear of Kimball. P. Sidney Post's Second Brigade was on the right, Abel D. Streight's First Brigade was on the left, and Frederick Knefler's Third Brigade was in reserve. Beatty was ordered to advance with Kimball.

Schofield's orders were to start at dawn and move his Twenty-Third Corps across the rear of Fourth Corps so as to be in position near the right of the corps to support the attack on the enemy left. At the appointed time, Darius N. Couch, who had been assigned command of Second Division, Twenty-Third Corps December 8, 1864, led his division out of the works on the Harding Pike and formed his troops in rear of the left of Smith's line. Joseph A. Cooper's First Brigade was in front, Orlando H. Moore's Second Brigade was behind Cooper, and John Mehringer's Third Brigade was in rear of Moore.

John S. Casement's Second Brigade of Jacob D. Cox's Third Division, Twenty-Third Corps remained temporarily in the old works to support Cruft's line during Steedman's demonstration on the enemy right, but Cox, with the other two brigades of the division, marched out by way of the Hillsboro Pike to take position in rear of the right of Wood's line as a reserve to the center of Thomas' attacking line.

Wilson's cavalry, which had been at Edgefield, north of the Cumberland River, since December 4, 1864, recrossed the river on December 12 and massed in rear of Smith's line between the Harding and Charlotte pikes. Wilson's orders for December 15 were to advance at 6:00 A.M. on the right of Smith's Detachment Army of the Tennessee and support him in the movement to the left and rear of Hood's line. Because of the heavy fog that morning, and a delay caused by McArthur's division moving across his front, Wilson was unable to start until about 10:00 A.M. Edward Hatch's Fifth Cavalry Division was on the left, with its left on the Harding Pike, connecting with the right of Smith's infantry. Robert R. Stewart's First Brigade was dismounted and was on the first line, and Datus E. Coon's Second Brigade, mounted, was in support.

At 4:00 A.M., Richard W. Johnson's Sixth Cavalry Division marched out on the Charlotte Pike to the exterior line of fortifications, and then was forced to wait until McArthur's division had moved.

John T. Croxton's First Brigade, First Cavalry Division left the defenses near the Nashville and Northwestern Railroad, taking position on the right of Hatch and on the left of Johnson, between the Charlotte and Harding pikes. The other two brigades of First Division were absent in western Kentucky, under the division commander, Edward M. McCook, in pursuit of Confederate raiders commanded by Hylan B. Lyon.

Joseph F. Knipe's Seventh Cavalry Division remained inside the works in readiness to support the other cavalry divisions when the general advance began.

Finally, at 10:00 A.M., after Wilson's divisions had reached their assigned positions on his right, Andrew J. Smith began his advance. Wheeling gradually to the left, he was soon in line south of the Harding Pike, and almost parallel to it, and moving toward Hood's left on the Hillsboro Pike. At 12:30 P.M., Smith's left had arrived at a point opposite the right of Fourth Corps, and then Wood ordered the corps to join in the advance.

Hatch's division advanced on the right of Smith's infantry and soon found Coleman's (Ector's) brigade entrenched on the high ground west of Richland Creek and north of the Harding Pike. Robert R. Stewart's First Brigade, fighting dismounted and supported by Coon's brigade, then advanced and forced Coleman to withdraw to the main Confederate defensive line on the Hillsboro Pike, where it arrived about 11:00 A.M. After Coleman withdrew, Hatch moved across country toward the Hillsboro

Pike, where he established a connection with the right of Smith's infantry and then advanced on its right flank.

Johnson's division marched westward on the Charlotte Pike and soon encountered Rucker's brigade of Chalmers' division posted on a ridge west of Richland Creek, near the pike, at a point near present-day Fifty-Fourth Avenue. James Biddle's Second Brigade then deployed and advanced against Rucker's line. He made slow progress, but Thomas J. Harrison's First Brigade moved to the front and soon drove the enemy from the ridge. Johnson pursued Rucker as far as the Davidson house, where he remained during the day and then bivouacked there that night. The next morning, Johnson found the enemy works abandoned, and he then marched with his division to rejoin the corps. He arrived on the Hillsboro Pike about 2:00 P.M. Croxton's brigade advanced on the left of Johnson and supported him until sundown, but he was then ordered to rejoin the corps on the Hillsboro Pike.

That part of Hood's line toward which Thomas' right wing was advancing was occupied by troops of Stewart's corps as follows: William W. Loring's division was on the right of the corps, facing north, and it extended from a point east of the Granny White Pike to Redoubt No. 1, which was on a high hill near the Hillsboro Pike. Winfield S. Featherston's brigade was on the right, Scott's brigade (commanded by John Snodgrass) was in the center, and Adams' brigade (commanded by Robert Lowry) was on the left. From Loring's left, the line curved around the hill to form a strong salient, then continued on to the southwest. Claudius W. Sears' brigade of Samuel G. French's division, which was attached to Edward C. Walthall's division that morning, was on the main line to the left of Loring, facing west, and holding the western face of the salient on which redoubts No. 1 and No. 2 were located.

Walthall's division of Stewart's corps was not in line when Thomas began his advance. Since December 10, 1864 it had been in bivouac near the Felix Compton house, about five and a half miles from Nashville. As Wilson and Smith approached west of the Hillsboro Pike at the beginning of the attack, Walthall manned redoubts No. 4 and No. 5, which were on his immediate front, and placed the remainder of his division in line behind a stone wall that ran along the east side of the pike, covering the ground between redoubts No. 3 and No. 4. When Walthall's division was in position along the Hillsboro Pike, his brigades were in line, in order from the right of Sears' brigade, as follows: Daniel H. Reynolds' brigade, Quarles' brigade (commanded by George D. Johnston), and Cantey's Brigade (commanded by Charles M. Shelley). Shelley's brigade was on the left of the line, opposite Redoubt No. 4.

As Wood's Fourth Corps advanced on the left of Smith's line, Samuel Beatty's Third Division came up in front of Montgomery Hill, the salient of Stewart's advance skirmish line, which was about one-half mile north of Redoubt No. 1. Wood promptly opened fire with his artillery on Montgomery Hill, and at 1:00 P.M. Post's brigade of Beatty's division advanced and captured the hill. Post was supported by Streight's brigade of the same division.

Up to that time, Schofield's two divisions of Twenty-Third Corps had remained idle in the positions to which they had moved early that morning, which was to the rear of the junction of Fourth Corps and Smith's Detachment Army of the Tennessee. As Smith's line advanced, it moved farther to the left than Thomas had intended, and about 1:00 P.M. Thomas ordered Schofield to march with his corps by the rear of Smith's line and form on its right. This movement would enable Hatch to operate farther to the right, and therefore more effectively, against the enemy's far left.

A little after 1:00 P.M., Wood learned that Schofield's troops had been moved from their position in reserve near Lawrence Hill to the right of Smith, and Wood was then ordered to move his reserves to the right. Accordingly, the reserve brigade of each division was shifted to the right.

Wood's entire line continued to move forward, with constant skirmishing, until it approached the main Confederate line. In swinging to the left, however, the right of Fourth Corps, which previously had been in line to the rear of Smith's left, passed to the front of Smith's line. The center of Wood's line, Kimball's First Division, arrived directly opposite the hill on which Redoubt No. 1 was located.

Meantime, Smith's infantry and Wilson's cavalry had been approaching the Confederate line on the Hillsboro Pike. About 11:00 A.M., McArthur's right brigade under McMillen and Coon's brigade of

Hatch's cavalry division, advancing on the right of McMillen, arrived in front of Redoubt No. 5, the detached earthwork on the extreme left of Alexander P. Stewart's line. After a preparatory artillery bombardment of about an hour, both brigades charged, entering the works at the same time and driving out the defenders. McMillen's brigade was supported on the left by Hubbard's brigade of McArthur's division. After the capture of Redoubt No. 5, both Hubbard and McMillen obliqued to the left and moved up in front of Redoubt No. 4. They then charged and captured the redoubt about 2:00 P.M. After McArthur's troops had gained possession of the two redoubts, Smith opened fire with his artillery on Walthall's line, but he did not attack at that time.

At 1:30 P.M., Lyman M. Ward, with his First Brigade of Jonathan B. Moore's Third Division of Smith's Detachment Army of the Tennessee, was ordered to report to McArthur as a support for his assaulting columns. Ward did not arrive until Redoubt No. 4 had fallen, however, and he was then directed to occupy the two captured redoubts and hold them if the enemy attempted their recapture.

During the attacks on redoubts No. 4 and No. 5, Schofield's divisions passed in rear of Smith's line; by the time the redoubts had been taken, Couch's division had formed on the right of Smith, and Cox's division was close behind. After Schofield arrived on the Hillsboro Pike, Wilson remounted his cavalry that had been holding that part of the line, crossed the pike, and advanced to the rear of Hood's left wing. He took position where he could command both the Hillsboro Pike and the Granny White Pike, but was not engaged again that evening.

About 2:45 P.M., Couch's division of Twenty-Third Corps crossed the Hillsboro Pike about one-half mile south of the right flank of Smith's line, and advanced toward the left and rear of Stewart's line. Coleman's (Ector's) brigade, which had arrived from its defeat at Richland Creek at about 11:00 A.M., was first placed behind the stone wall along the Hillsboro road, but it was then sent to the vicinity of the Compton house when the Federal threat developed on Stewart's left. As Couch advanced, he passed between Coleman's brigade and the left of Walthall's line. Coleman was thus cut off from the Confederate troops on his right, and he fell back toward the Granny White Pike.

Reynolds' brigade was detached from the right of Walthall's line and was sent to the left to form a line northeast of the Compton house, where it was to extend toward the left of Shelley's brigade. Reynolds was able to hold his new line for only a short time and was then driven back toward the east.

Early in the afternoon, Arthur M. Manigault's brigade (commanded by William L. Butler) of Edward Johnson's division arrived from the right of the enemy line, and it was placed opposite Redoubt No. 4. Later, Zachariah C. Deas' brigade of Johnson's division came up and took position between the right of Butler and the left of Walthall's line, but they offered little resistance to the Federal advance and were soon driven back.

Meantime, Hill's brigade of McArthur's division arrived in front of that part of Stewart's position that was defended by Redoubt No. 3, which was located to the northeast of Redoubt No. 4, and a short distance west of the Hillsboro Pike. After a strong artillery preparation, Hill's men charged and captured the redoubt. Hill was killed in the assault, and was succeeded in command of the brigade by William R. Marshall. Marshall then pushed on to the northeast and captured Redoubt No. 2, which was just south of the enemy salient and Redoubt No. 1, and then pushed on to the left and rear of Redoubt No. 1.

Shortly after 4:00 P.M., Jonathan B. Moore advanced his Third Division of Smith's detachment and occupied a gap that had developed in McArthur's line between Hubbard's brigade and Hill's brigade when the latter moved to the left to attack Redoubts No. 3 and No. 2. Moore then formed Ward's First Brigade and Leander Blanden's Second Brigade on a line facing Walthall's position along the stone wall east of the Hillsboro Pike. Sometime after 4:00 P.M., after an artillery preparation had ended, Moore's brigades advanced against the brigades of Quarles and Shelley, which were posted behind the stone wall. The enemy soon began to give way, and when Couch's division, with Hubbard's brigade of McArthur's division, moved to the east of the Hillsboro Pike and to the rear of the stone wall, the enemy broke and fled eastward toward the Granny White Pike.

By that time, Jacob H. Sharp's brigade and William F. Brantly's brigade of Johnson's division had come up from the right, but they were unable to halt the Federal advance, which had completely turned the enemy left flank and had gained the rear of both Walthall's and Loring's divisions. The commanders of these two divisions were then ordered to withdraw. Loring promptly complied, but Walthall's troops were already in retreat from the Hillsboro Pike.

Meantime, Garrard's division of Smith's detachment and Wood's Fourth Corps had been moving forward against Stewart's right and center. After the capture of Montgomery Hill, Wood's corps moved south toward the high hill at the salient of the enemy main line, and on which stood Redoubt No. 1. Wood placed two batteries of his artillery so as to deliver a converging fire on the crest of the hill, and he ordered his division commanders to move up as close to the enemy works as they could. This order was promptly obeyed, with Elliott's division taking position on the right, next to Smith, Kimball's division in the center, and Beatty's division on the left.

About a half-hour after the artillery opened fire, Wood ordered Kimball to capture the hill with his division. Around 4:30 P.M., Grose's brigade advanced along the Hillsboro Pike, then crossed the road and charged up the hill. At the same time, Kirby's brigade moved directly forward on the left of Grose. Grose captured the left end of the works on the hill, and Kirby entered the entrenchments on the left of Grose. Hill's brigade of McArthur's division (then commanded by Marshall), which, as noted earlier, had advanced on the right toward Redoubt No. 1, reached the enemy works at about the same time as Kimball's brigades. Whitaker's brigade did not take part in the attack. Elliott's division moved forward after Kimball's attack, and its troops entered the works farther to the right, but they arrived after the defenders had been withdrawn. Lane's brigade attacked on the left of Elliott's line and Opdyke's brigade on the right, and Conrad's brigade was in reserve in rear of Opdyke. Beatty's division, on the left of Kimball, also occupied the enemy works on its front.

Almost simultaneously with Wood's advance, Garrard's division attacked the fortifications at the angle of the enemy works. Wolfe's brigade was on the right, David Moore's brigade was in the center, and Gilbert's brigade was on the left. At the time of the attack, Garrard's division was advancing on a line that was at a right angle to that of Wood, and to avoid the confusion that would result if the lines crossed, Garrard ordered Moore's and Gilbert's brigades to take position in reserve. Wolfe's brigade moved on toward Redoubt No. 1. At 4:00 P.M., Gilbert's brigade marched to the rear of Moore's brigade to support Wolfe, but the enemy had fled before Gilbert was ready to attack. Gilbert then moved on about a half-mile to the right and formed on the right of Moore.

When Coleman's brigade was cut off by Couch's advance, it fell back and took position on a high hill a short distance west of the Granny White Pike, just a short distance south of present-day Harding Place. This hill was later called Shy's Hill, after Colonel William M. Shy of the 20th Tennessee Regiment, who was killed there during the fighting of December 16, 1864. On another hill, to the north of Shy's Hill, Bate's division of Cheatham's corps was forming, after having marched from the Nolensville Pike on the far right of the Confederate line.

As Couch's division advanced to the east of the Hillsboro Pike, Cooper's brigade arrived in front of the hill occupied by Bate. Cooper charged, with Orlando H. Moore's brigade on his left, and drove Bate from the hill. The enemy then advanced on Couch's right in an effort to recapture the position, and about 4:00 P.M. Mehringer's brigade was sent to the right to counter this threat. Cox's division of Twenty-Third Corps, which was following Couch, then came up and was ordered by Schofield to support Couch. Cox sent Stiles' brigade off to the right to occupy some high ground in that direction, and he sent Charles C. Doolittle's brigade to the right of Mehringer. He also sent Casement's brigade to the left of Mehringer. By dark the enemy's attack on Couch's right had been repulsed, and Mehringer's brigade then rejoined the division. Cox's two brigades remained in position on a line at nearly a right angle with Couch's line.

Smith's Detachment Army of the Tennessee halted for the night on a line between the Hillsboro Pike and the Granny White Pike and roughly parallel to them. Schofield's corps also spent the night east of the Hillsboro Pike, on the right of Smith. Couch's division remained on a line running east and west across the hill captured from Bate, facing Shy's Hill to the south. Cox's division was on a north-south line, at a right angle to Couch's line, facing east toward Shy's Hill and a portion of the refused Confederate line to the south. Stiles' brigade of Cox's division entrenched its position on the hill that he occupied farther to the south. Jonathan B. Moore's division of Smith's detachment was placed in the gap between Couch and Cox.

Wood's Fourth Corps, after capturing Stewart's salient and the line to the east, was ordered to move eastward to the Franklin Pike, but at dark it had reached only the Granny White Pike. It then bivouacked for the night about three-fourths of a mile west of the Granny White Pike, with its right connecting with Smith's left near the line of the abandoned Confederate works.

Steedman's command remained in the positions that it had occupied earlier in the day.

Knipe's cavalry division, which had followed in rear of Hatch during the day, arrived on the Hillsboro Pike soon after Redoubts No. 4 and No. 5 had been captured. Knipe moved by the rear right of Hatch, crossed the Hillsboro Pike near the six-mile post, then turned to the left and advanced toward the Granny White Pike. John H. Hammond's mounted First Brigade, which was in the lead, moved on by the Otter Creek road to the Granny White Pike to block the road at a gap just beyond the site of Granny White's Tavern, but Gilbert M. L. Johnson's Second Brigade, which was dismounted, bivouacked near the Hillsboro Pike.

Johnson's cavalry division, which had been occupied during the day on the far Federal right, bivouacked that night near the Charlotte Pike. Croxton's cavalry brigade had been in position to the right and rear of Johnson during the day, but at sundown it was ordered to rejoin the corps on the Hillsboro Pike.

During the night of December 15–16, 1864, Hood formed a new defensive line south of his original line. At the end of the fighting that day, the right of his line, which had been held at the beginning of the battle by Cheatham's corps, was occupied only by Mark P. Lowrey's (formerly Brown's) division, and it was then under orders to move to Hood's left. As noted above, Bate's division had already arrived on the Confederate left, where it had been engaged with Couch's division, and Cleburne's division (then commanded by James A. Smith) was on the way to join Bate.

After Cheatham's corps had departed for Hood's left, Lee's corps held the right of the enemy line.

During the night, Lee fell back about two miles along the Franklin Pike to a point about four miles from Brentwood and formed a new line, with Henry D. Clayton's division on the right, Carter L. Stevenson's division in the center, and Edward Johnson's division on the left. Clayton's division occupied a hill, known locally as Peach Orchard Hill, which formed a natural salient at the eastern end of Hood's line. Clayton's right was refused to the south along the eastern side of the hill, and his left extended westward a short distance beyond the Franklin Pike. In some battle reports, Peach Orchard Hill, which was located just south of the present-day Elysian Fields road and just east of the Franklin Pike, was referred to as Overton's Hill, probably because it was on the Overton farm. Stevenson's and Johnson's divisions extended Lee's line to the west along the south side of present-day Battery Lane Road, facing north. Both divisions were west of the Franklin Pike.

Stewart's corps was on the left of Lee's line and extended the line on to the west, also along the south side of Battery Lane Road to a point near the Granny White Pike, a short distance east of Shy's Hill. Loring's division was on the right, next to Johnson's division of Lee's corps, and Walthall's division was on the left, next to the Granny White Pike.

Cheatham's corps was on the left of Stewart, and it continued Hood's line on to the west and north, over and around Shy's Hill, then turned back to the south, where that part of the line faced west. Shy's Hill formed a strong natural salient on the western end of Hood's line. Bate's division was on the right of Cheatham's line, and extended from the left of Stewart to the crest of Shy's Hill. Coleman's brigade was on the crest of the hill, at a right angle to Bate's line; Mark P. Lowrey's division was on the left of Coleman's brigade, facing west, and running southward to a hill south of Shy's Hill; and James A. Smith's division was on the left, with its left refused to the east near present-day Tyne Boulevard. Coleman's brigade was withdrawn from Shy's Hill about noon and placed in reserve, and Bate's division was extended to occupy the vacated position. Later, when Peach Orchard Hill was threatened by Wood and Steedman, three brigades of Joseph A. Smith's division were sent to the Confederate right to support Lee, leaving only Daniel C. Govan's brigade on the left of Lowrey's division.

The air-line distance from Peach Orchard Hill to Shy's Hill was about two and one-half miles, but because the Confederate line followed ground that was adaptable for defense, and was refused at both ends, its total length was about three and one-half miles.

The Second Day, December 16, 1864. Early on the morning of December 16, 1864, the troops of Thomas' command, except Twenty-Third Corps, began to move forward to their assigned positions for an attack on Hood's new line. During most of the day, Schofield's Twenty-Third Corps remained on or near the positions occupied the night before. Couch's division was on the left, facing south toward Bate's line, with its left near the Granny White Pike. Orlando H. Moore's brigade was on the left, near the pike; Cooper's brigade was in the center; and Mehringer's brigade was on the right. Cox's division was on the right of Couch, facing southeast toward Hood's refused line south of Shy's Hill. Casement's brigade was on the left, Doolittle's brigade was on the right of Casement, and Stiles' brigade was to the right and rear of Doolittle.

Smith's Detachment Army of the Tennessee, which was on the left of Schofield, was in motion early that morning. At 4:00 A.M. Jonathan B. Moore's Third Division moved back to the Hillsboro Pike, then south on the pike for about a mile and a half, and took position on the right of Cox's division to guard its right flank. Third Division remained there in reserve during the day.

At daybreak, Smith moved out with his other two divisions and, after wheeling to the right, advanced to within 600 yards of the enemy's new line. McArthur's division was on the right, and Garrard's division was on the left. Marshall's brigade (formerly Hill's) of McArthur's division was east of the Granny White Pike, with its right on the pike; Hubbard's brigade was on the right of Marshall, west of the pike; and McMillen's brigade was on the right of Hubbard, connecting on the right with Couch's division near the base of Shy's Hill. Garrard's three brigades were in line, in order from right to left from the left of Marshall's brigade, as follows: Gilbert's brigade, David Moore's brigade, and Wolfe's brigade. Wolfe's brigade connected on the left with Wood's Fourth Corps. When Smith had completed his deployment, he opened fire on the enemy works with his artillery, but he did not advance his infantry at that time.

At 6:00 A.M., Wood's Fourth Corps moved forward from the left of Smith to the Franklin Pike, where it arrived at 8:00 A.M. and deployed in line of battle facing south. Elliott's division was on the right of the pike, with Opdyke's brigade on the left of the division, next to the pike; Lane's brigade was in the center; and Conrad's brigade was on the right. Beatty's division was on the left of Elliott, with Post's brigade on the right of the division next to the Franklin Pike; Streight's brigade was on the left; and Knefler's brigade was in reserve. Kimball's division was in rear of Elliott.

In the above order, the corps advanced about three-fourths of a mile to the enemy skirmish line, with Kimball's division marching near the pike in rear of Elliott. At that point it was discovered that Wood's line was not long enough to connect with Smith's command on the right, and Kimball's division was brought up on the right of Elliott to fill the gap. Grose's brigade of Kimball's division was formed on the left, next to Elliott, Whitaker's brigade was on the right next to Smith, and Kirby's brigade was in reserve. At 10:15 A.M., when Kimball's division was in line, Fourth Corps again advanced for about three-fourths of a mile, and drove the enemy skirmishers back into their works. Wood then halted about 400–600 yards from the enemy line and opened fire with his artillery.

On the Federal left, Steedman advanced at 6:00 A.M. and found the enemy works on his front abandoned. He hurried his troops out on the Nolensville Pike, driving back the enemy cavalry as he advanced, and took position between the Nashville and Decatur Railroad and the Nolensville Pike, on which he refused his left. As Steedman advanced, he uncovered the approaches to Nashville by way of the Murfreesboro and Nolensville pikes, and Cruft then pushed forward John G. Mitchell's brigade, which occupied Riddle Hill to protect Steedman's rear against enemy cavalry.

Then, about 1:00 P.M., Steedman moved to the right to join Wood in an attack on the enemy right flank and rear. When first deployed, Thompson's Second Colored Brigade was formed on the right of Steedman's line, next to Wood, and Morgan's First Colored Brigade was on the left of Thompson. Grosvenor's Third Brigade of Cruft's division was ordered to the left of Thompson, and it later took part in the attack. The rest of Cruft's troops remained near Nashville on the lines of defenses.

At 3:00 P.M., after a strong artillery preparation, Wood launched an attack on Clayton's division and Edmund W. Pettus' brigade of Stevenson's division at Peach Orchard Hill. The attack was made by Post's brigade of Beatty's division, and it was supported by Streight's brigade of the same division. At the same time, Thompson's brigade of Steedman's command advanced on the left of Post, and Grosvenor's brigade of Cruft's division attacked on the left of Thompson. The Federal troops advanced to a point near the enemy works, where they were subjected to a very heavy artillery and musketry fire and were forced to retire. Post was wounded in the attack and was succeeded in command of the brigade by Robert L. Kimberly.

Meantime, on the far right, Wilson's dismounted cavalry had advanced on a front of about a mile and a half. Hatch's division was on the left, next to Schofield, Hammond's brigade of Knipe's division was on the right, and Croxton's brigade was in reserve. The cavalry crossed the Granny White Pike, turned to the northeast toward the rear of Hood's left flank, and about noon reached a line of hills directly in rear of the position held by Bate and Walthall, facing toward the north. Coleman's (Ector's) brigade was then brought up from reserve near Shy's Hill and hurried to a hill east of the Granny White Pike, which was to the left and rear of Bate. There, with Reynolds' brigade of Walthall's division, they succeeded in holding up Wilson's advance until the collapse of the Confederate line later in the afternoon.

At about the same time as Wood's unsuccessful attempt at Peach Orchard Hill, Thomas was making preparations for an attack on the left of Hood's line. At 8:00 A.M. McArthur's division moved forward and, wheeling to the right of Twenty-Third Corps, formed on a line at a right angle to that of the night before, with the Granny White Pike running through the line between Second Brigade and Third Brigade. Then, at 9:00 A.M., McArthur moved up to within charging distance of the enemy line. At 3:00 P.M., McArthur informed Smith that he could take Shy's Hill, and when he received no reply, he ordered McMillen to storm the hill. He also ordered the other two brigades of the division, which were to the left of McMillen, to attack the positions on their respective fronts after McMillen had moved about halfway up the hill. McMillen promptly moved out by the right flank and took position in front of Couch's line, directly in front of Shy's Hill. Couch sent forward a brigade to occupy that part of McArthur's line vacated by McMillen. At 3:30 P.M. McMillen's artillery opened fire, and under the cover of this fire, the infantry advanced to the assault. In a short time they reached the top of the hill and stormed the enemy works, taking many prisoners. Hubbard's brigade, on the left of McMillen, followed and soon entered the works on its front. About 4:00 P.M., Marshall attacked on the left of Hubbard and also overran the enemy entrenchments. Garrard's division on the left of Marshall joined in the charge, and by 4:30 P.M. Smith's men had driven the enemy from Shy's Hill, and from the line to the east, and had forced them to flee in disorder toward the Franklin Pike.

At about the same time that McArthur attacked at Shy's Hill, Coon's brigade of Hatch's cavalry division carried a high wooded hill beyond the left of the enemy entrenched line, and at 4:30 P.M., immediately after the capture of Shy's Hill, Doolittle's brigade, supported by the brigades of Stiles and Casement of Cox's division, stormed and captured a hill on the extreme flank of Cheatham's line.

Bate's division was destroyed in the attacks that afternoon. Some of the troops fled eastward toward the Franklin Pike, and the rest were surrounded and taken prisoner. Among the captured were Bate's three brigade commanders. Following the capture of Shy's Hill, the entire Confederate left wing collapsed, and the troops fled from the field in complete disorder. As Smith's troops pursued Cheatham's fleeing troops eastward, they struck Stewart's exposed left flank and drove his disordered troops to the Franklin Pike.

When Wood learned of Smith's advance on his right, he immediately ordered his Fourth Corps forward to join in the assault. Beatty's division soon took Peach Orchard Hill, but by that time most of Clayton's men had joined in the retreat. Lee's corps held the Franklin Pike near the Overton house until most of Hood's defeated army had escaped to the south, and then it too retired. At 10:00 P.M. Lee formed a new rear guard line at Hollow Tree Gap, beyond Brentwood, seven miles north of Franklin.

Wood pursued for a time but then halted for the night several miles north of Lee's position. As Schofield moved eastward following the collapse of the enemy's defensive line, he met Smith's command moving south and at a right angle to his line of advance, and both commands halted. Wilson remounted his cavalry and moved down the Granny White Pike until he encountered Chalmers' cavalry just north of the road to Brentwood. Fighting there, on a cold and rainy night, Chalmers held the Federal cavalry in check until Hood's infantry were passing Brentwood on the Franklin Pike.

* * * * * * * * *

During the next ten days, both armies were engaged in an almost continuous running battle that extended from the battlefield at Franklin to the Tennessee River, and most of that time there was rain, sleet, snow, and below-freezing temperatures. The remnants of Hood's army fell back through Franklin December 17, 1864, closely followed by Thomas, and the next day they crossed Duck River at Columbia. There they were joined by Forrest, who had arrived from Murfreesboro. Forrest was placed in charge of a rear guard consisting of his cavalry and several thousand infantry from a number of Confederate brigades that had been assembled under the command of Walthall.

Hood left Columbia December 20, 1864 and moved on through Pulaski in the direction of Florence, Alabama. On Christmas morning, Hood's advance reached the Tennessee River at Bainbridge, Alabama, a few miles above Florence. He began crossing on a pontoon bridge the next morning, then marched toward Tupelo, Mississippi.

The last serious efforts to interrupt Hood's retreat were made by Wilson's cavalry. Wilson attacked Forrest's rear guard south of Pulaski on Christmas day, and again at Sugar Creek December 26, but he was delayed on both occasions, and finally, on December 27, Forrest, with the last of his rear guard, crossed the Tennessee River. Two days later, Thomas issued an order declaring that the pursuit was ended.

The organization of the United States forces commanded by George H. Thomas at the Battle of Nashville, Tennessee December 15–16, 1864 was as follows:

FOURTH CORPS, Thomas J. Wood

First Division, Nathan Kimball
    First Brigade, Isaac M. Kirby
    Second Brigade, Walter C. Whitaker
    Third Brigade, William Grose

Second Division, Washington L. Elliott
    First Brigade, Emerson Opdyke
    Second Brigade, John Q. Lane
    Third Brigade, Joseph Conrad

Note. George D. Wagner was relieved from command of Second Division December 2, 1864 and was succeeded by Elliott. December 9, 1864, Wagner was relieved from duty with the Army of the Cumberland, at his own request.

Third Division, Samuel Beatty
    First Brigade, Abel D. Streight
    Second Brigade, P. Sidney Post, to December 15, 1864, wounded
        Robert L. Kimberly
    Third Brigade, Frederick Knefler

Note 1. Beatty succeeded Wood in command of Third Division when the latter assumed command of Fourth Corps December 2, 1864.
Note 2. Knefler succeeded Beatty in command of Third Brigade when the latter assumed command of Third Division December 2, 1864.

Artillery, Wilbur F. Goodspeed
    25th Battery, Indiana Light Artillery, Frederick C. Sturm
    1st Battery, Kentucky Light Artillery, Theodore S. Thomasson
    Battery E, 1st Michigan Light Artillery, Peter De Vries
    Battery G, 1st Ohio Light Artillery, Alexander Marshall
    6th Battery Ohio Light Artillery, Aaron P. Baldwin
    Battery B, Pennsylvania Light Artillery, Jacob Ziegler
    Battery M, 4th United States Artillery, Samuel Canby

TWENTY-THIRD CORPS, John M. Schofield

Second Division, Darius N. Couch
    First Brigade, Joseph A. Cooper
    Second Brigade, Orlando H. Moore
    Third Brigade, John Mehringer
    Artillery
        15th Battery, Indiana Light Artillery, Alonzo D. Harvey
        19th Battery, Ohio Light Artillery, Frank Wilson

Note. Thomas H. Ruger was relieved from command of Second Division December 8, 1864 and was assigned command of First Division, which was to be organized as soon as practicable. Couch was assigned command of Second Division.

Third Division, Jacob D. Cox
    First Brigade, Charles C. Doolittle
    Second Brigade, John S. Casement
    Third Brigade, Israel N. Stiles
    Artillery
        23rd Battery, Indiana Light Artillery, Aaron A. Wilber
        Battery D, 1st Ohio Light Artillery, Giles J. Cockerill

Note. Doolittle was relieved from duty with John F. Miller, commander of the post of Nashville, December 7, 1864 and was assigned the command of James W. Reilly's First Brigade, Third Division.

DETACHMENT ARMY OF THE TENNESSEE, Andrew J. Smith

First Division, John McArthur
    First Brigade, William L. McMillen
    Second Brigade, Lucius F. Hubbard
    Third Brigade, Sylvester G. Hill, to December 15, 1864, killed
        William R. Marshall

Note. Cogswell's Battery, Illinois Light Artillery, commanded by S. Hamilton McClaury, was attached to First Brigade; Joseph R. Reed's 2nd Battery, Iowa Light Artillery was attached to Second Brigade; and Stephen H. Julian's Battery I, 2nd Missouri Light Artillery was attached to Third Brigade.

Second Division, Kenner Garrard
    First Brigade, David Moore
    Second Brigade, James I. Gilbert
    Third Brigade, Edward H. Wolfe

Note 1. December 7, 1864, Garrard was relieved from duty with Second Cavalry Division, Cavalry Corps, Military Division of the Mississippi, and the next day was assigned command of Second Division, Detachment Army of the Tennessee (former Third Division, Sixteenth Corps).
Note 2. Samuel G. Calfee's 9th Battery, Indiana Light Artillery was attached to First Brigade; Thomas J. Ginn's 3rd Battery, Indiana Light Artillery was attached to Second Brigade; and John W. Lowell's Battery G, 2nd Illinois Light Artillery was attached to Third Brigade.

Third Division, Jonathan B. Moore
    First Brigade, Lyman M. Ward

Second Brigade, Leander Blanden
Artillery
    14th Battery, Indiana Light Artillery, Francis W. Morse
    Battery A, 2nd Missouri Light Artillery, John Zepp

PROVISIONAL DETACHMENT, DISTRICT OF THE ETOWAH, James B. Steedman

Provisional Division, Charles Cruft
    First Brigade, Benjamin Harrison
    Second Brigade, John G. Mitchell
    Third Brigade, Charles H. Grosvenor
    Second Brigade, Army of the Tennessee, Adam G. Malloy
    First Colored Brigade, Thomas J. Morgan
    Second Colored Brigade, Charles R. Thompson
    Artillery
        20th Battery, Indiana Light Artillery, Milton A. Osborne
        18th Battery, Ohio Light Artillery, Charles C. Aleshire

Note. The Provisional Division was composed mainly of detachments of Fourteenth Corps, Fifteenth Corps, Seventeenth Corps, and Twentieth Corps, which had been unable to join their proper commands, then serving with William T. Sherman on his march through Georgia. Mitchell's Second Brigade consisted of troops of Fourteenth Corps; Harrison's First Brigade, of troops of Twentieth Corps; and Malloy's brigade, of troops of Fifteenth Corps and Seventeenth Corps. Grosvenor's brigade consisted of miscellaneous regiments.

POST OF NASHVILLE, John F. Miller

    Second Brigade, Fourth Division, Twentieth Corps, Edwin C. Mason
    Unattached regiments and detachments of regiments

GARRISON ARTILLERY, John J. Ely

QUARTERMASTER'S DIVISION, James L. Donaldson

Note. Donaldson's division consisted of quartermaster's employees.

CAVALRY CORPS, MILITARY DIVISION OF THE MISSISSIPPI, James H. Wilson

First Division
    First Brigade, John T. Croxton

Note 1. Second Brigade and Third Brigade of this

division were absent on an expedition in western Kentucky, under the division commander, Edward M. McCook.

Note 2. The Board of Trade Battery, Illinois Light Artillery, commanded by George I. Robinson, was attached to Croxton's brigade.

Fifth Division, Edward Hatch
    First Brigade, Robert R. Stewart
    Second Brigade, Datus E. Coon

Note. Joseph A. McCartney's Battery I, 1st Illinois Light Artillery was attached to Coon's brigade.

Sixth Division, Richard W. Johnson
    First Brigade, Thomas J. Harrison
    Second Brigade, James Biddle
    Battery I, 4th United States Artillery, Frank G. Smith

Seventh Division, Joseph F. Knipe
    First Brigade, John H. Hammond
    Second Brigade, Gilbert M. L. Johnson
    14th Battery, Ohio Light Artillery, William C. Myers

Note. Hammond was assigned command of First Brigade December 10, 1864.

GRIERSON'S RAID
APRIL 17, 1863–
MAY 2, 1863

As part of his plan to capture Vicksburg, Mississippi in the spring of 1863, Ulysses S. Grant ordered a number of raids, which he hoped would serve as diversions while he moved with his Army of the Tennessee against the city. Two of these raids were to be made by cavalry to destroy vital railroads and supplies and to do as much damage as possible as they passed through the country.

One of the raids was to be carried out by Abel D. Streight, with an infantry force from the Army of the Cumberland mounted on mules; he was to ride east and south across northern Alabama and northern Georgia and destroy the Western and Atlantic Railroad below Dalton, Georgia. Streight started April 22, 1863, five days after the scheduled departure date, and he was soon pursued by Nathan B. Forrest with four cavalry regiments from Tennessee. Although Streight lost his entire force not far from Rome, Georgia, the absence of Forrest while in pursuit of Streight greatly aided, if it did not make possible, the success of the Second Cavalry raid conducted by Benjamin H. Grierson in Mississippi.

Three other expeditions ordered by Grant were carried out by infantry. On April 18, 1863, a column consisting of three infantry regiments, a battery, and a small cavalry force marched southward from Memphis, Tennessee to engage James R. Chalmers, commanding the Confederate defenses south of Memphis, whose base was at Panola, Mississippi. William Sooy Smith moved by rail from La Grange, Tennessee to Coldwater, Mississippi against the right flank of Chalmers' position along the lower Tallahatchie River. The third column was commanded by Grenville M. Dodge, who marched eastward from Corinth, Mississippi with 5,000 men from the District of Corinth along the Tennessee River toward Tuscumbia, Alabama. Smith's expedition served as a diversion on the right of Grierson's line of march, and Dodge's column from Corinth served a similar purpose on the left of Grierson.

On April 17, 1863, Benjamin H. Grierson left La Grange, Tennessee on a raid against the Southern Railroad of Mississippi. He was in command of the First Brigade of Cadwallader C. Washburn's First Cavalry Division of Sixteenth Corps, which consisted of Grierson's own 6th Cavalry, commanded by Reuben Loomis, Edward Prince's 7th Illinois Cavalry, and Edward Hatch's 2nd Iowa Cavalry. He also took with him four guns of Jason B. Smith's Battery K, 1st Illinois Light Artillery.

There were several reasons why Grant thought this raid would be helpful in enabling the Army of the Tennessee, which was then in front of Vicksburg, to capture the city. The most important of these was that Grierson's activities would divert the attention of John C. Pemberton, who was in command of the Confederate Department of Mississippi and Eastern Louisiana at Jackson, Mississippi, from Grant's planned crossing of the Mississippi River below Vicksburg. In addition, the raid was expected to draw off troops from the Confederate army near Vicksburg, and also to divert reinforcements on their way to join the army. Finally, Grierson hoped to cut the railroad running from Meridian, Mississippi to Vicksburg and thereby interrupt the flow of supplies to that place.

At the time that Grierson left La Grange, John A. McClernand's Thirteenth Corps of Grant's command on the Mississippi River was already concentrated near New Carthage, Mississippi, and James B. McPherson's Seventeenth Corps was en route from Milliken's Bend to join him in preparation for crossing to the east bank of the river.

Enemy resistance to Grierson's early movements was to be seriously hampered by the confused military situation existing in northern Mississippi at that time. Clark R. Barteau, commanding the 2nd Tennessee Cavalry (Confederate), was a part of Daniel Ruggles' First Military District, whose headquarters was at Columbus, Mississippi. In addition to Barteau's command, Governor John Pettus, commanding the Mississippi state troops, had authorized Samuel J. Gholson to muster in three regiments of cavalry for state service, and at that time Gholson was in northern Mississippi completing the organization of these regiments. Two weeks before Grierson's departure from La Grange, Barteau was assigned command of all Confederate mounted troops in the northern part of Ruggles' district. By this order, Barteau was placed in command of a cavalry force that was actually under the command of two officers, Barteau and Gholson.

Just after 7:00 A.M. April 17, 1863, Grierson marched out of La Grange toward Ripley, Mississippi. He camped that night four miles northwest of the town. At 8:00 the next morning, the column arrived in Ripley, and from there Hatch was ordered to march on to the east of Ripley with the 2nd Iowa Cavalry on a feint toward the Mobile and Ohio Railroad, which was twenty miles distant. Four miles east of the town, however, Hatch turned to the south and marched on a road that ran parallel to the road from Ripley to New Albany, which was used by Grierson with Reuben Loomis' 6th Illinois Cavalry and Edward Prince's 7th Illinois Cavalry. The purpose of Hatch's demonstration was to occupy the attention of Barteau and Gholson's state troops until after dark to enable the rest of the column to move southward during the day unmolested.

During the afternoon, Barteau learned that Grierson was at New Albany, and he then marched to Chesterville, where Gholson's troops were organizing. Upon arriving there, he began preparations for an expected attack by Hatch, who, according to

Barteau's information, was only about five miles away.

When Grierson reached the Tallahatchie River, he did not use the bridge at New Albany but crossed at a ford about two miles upstream, where he paused to water and feed the horses. He then continued on and halted for the night about five miles south of New Albany at the Sloan plantation. Grierson did not hear from Hatch that night. Meantime, Hatch did not move on Centerville as Barteau had expected, but instead turned away toward Pontotoc to rejoin Grierson's main column.

Before continuing the march on the morning of April 19, 1864, Grierson sent out a detachment to communicate with Hatch and to threaten an attack on Centerville. He also sent out an expedition to New Albany, which he had by-passed, and another toward King's Bridge, where other Mississippi state troops were organizing. When these missions had been accomplished, the detached troopers rejoined Grierson, and the column moved on toward Pontotoc. It passed through the town sometime after 4:00 that afternoon and camped that night along Chiwapa Creek, about six miles south of Pontotoc. The 2nd Iowa Cavalry rejoined the main column that evening.

At 10:00 on the night of April 19, 1864, Barteau learned that Grierson had reached Pontotoc, and he immediately started in pursuit. From midnight until dawn April 20, Barteau marched to the southeast, and at 8:30 A.M. his advance had reached a point on the road from Pontotoc to Okolona, eight miles north of the latter place. He continued on toward Pontotoc and halted at noon about five miles from the town. He was then informed that Grierson had marched west from Pontotoc early that morning on the road to Oxford.

Actually, Grierson had not marched toward Oxford with his brigade, but he had arranged for a clear trail to be left on the road indicating that he had. The tracks were made by a column consisting of men and horses that were disabled or were not fit for further marching that were being sent back to La Grange under the command of Hiram Love of the 2nd Iowa. Accompanying Love were some prisoners and horses and mules that had been captured by the raiders. Love was under instructions to make it appear that a much larger force had used the road to Oxford.

About an hour after Love had departed with his command, Grierson marched toward Houston on a rainy day, with Hatch's cavalry in the lead. About mid-afternoon the advance arrived in Houston and created a diversion while the main column passed unobserved around the town. South of Houston, the three regiments moved back to the main road, which they followed southward until dusk. The column then halted at the Kilgore plantation, just outside the village of Clear Springs, about twelve miles from Houston.

When Barteau reached Pontotoc, he halted for a time to learn more about the force that had marched toward Oxford early that morning. He finally decided, however, that it was not Grierson's main column, and he then marched south toward Houston, ten hours behind Grierson.

During the night of April 20, 1863, Grierson decided to send Hatch and his 2nd Iowa on a raid to the Mobile and Ohio Railroad in the vicinity of West Point. The purpose of this movement was twofold—first, Hatch was to divert attention from Grierson and the two remaining regiments as they moved southward and, at the same time, to create the impression that the Mobile and Ohio Railroad was the main objective of the expedition; and second, he was to destroy the railroad as far south as Macon, then turn back to the north, capturing Columbus if possible and destroying more of the railroad south of Okolona. When this was accomplished, Hatch was to return to La Grange.

At 7:00 A.M. April 21, 1863, Grierson marched southward with his brigade to Clear Springs, and there Hatch turned off with his regiment to the east toward the railroad. Grierson, with his two remaining regiments, marched on to the south, reaching Starkeville at 4:00 P.M. He passed on through the town and halted at dark about five miles beyond in the midst of a violent rainstorm.

Meantime, Barteau, followed by Gholson's state troops, had been pursuing Grierson. Barteau reached the Kilgore plantation at 11:00 A.M., long after Grierson had departed. Hatch, however, upon leaving Grierson's column for the Mobile and Ohio Railroad, had arranged his tracks so well that Barteau concluded that the entire Federal column had started for the railroad. Then, instead of following Grierson, Barteau turned eastward and followed Hatch on the road toward Palo Alto.

Barteau caught up with Hatch at Palo Alto, and after skirmishing for about two hours, Hatch attacked and drove back the state troops about three miles. Skirmishing continued until dark, at which time Barteau was between Hatch and the Mobile and Ohio Railroad. That night Hatch withdrew northward and crossed the Houlka River.

At dawn April 22, 1863, the 6th Illinois Cavalry, followed by the 7th Illinois Cavalry, moved out through flooded country toward Louisville. The two regiments passed through the town after dark and finally halted at midnight ten miles south of Louisville at the Estes plantation. At this point, Grierson was only about forty miles from the Southern Railroad of Mississippi, which was the supply line for the garrison of Vicksburg.

Before leaving on his march that morning, Grierson had sent out a company of cavalry under Stephen A. Forbes on a feint toward Macon on the Mobile and Ohio Railroad. After marching all day, Forbes arrived near the railroad and attracted much attention, but with his small force, he did not attempt to capture the town. He then turned back to rejoin the command.

After marching north from Palo Alto, Hatch reached Okolona, which was undefended, and about sunset charged into the town. He burned a number of buildings filled with cotton, then moved on and halted at a plantation five miles to the north. Barteau had been following Hatch, but he arrived too late to save Okolona.

During the day of April 23, 1864, Grierson moved on south. He crossed the Pearl River, and a short time later arrived at Philadelphia. Shortly after 3:00 P.M. the column continued on toward Decatur, halting about 5:00 P.M. on a plantation seven miles south of Philadelphia.

At 10:00 that night, Grierson ordered William Blackburn to take the 1st Battalion of the 7th Illinois Cavalry and march rapidly to Newton Station on the Southern Railroad of Mississippi. Blackburn was informed that the rest of the column would follow an hour later. He promptly moved out on the road toward Decatur, and he drew near the town about 3:00 A.M. April 24, 1864.

Meantime, far to the north, Hatch was continuing his march northward toward La Grange, destroying bridges and capturing horses and mules as he advanced. He camped that night near Tupelo. Barteau

also moved northward during the day in rear of Hatch, but he was unable to catch up with him. Gholson, however, who had been absent from his command, arrived that day and joined Barteau, and he then proceeded to assume command of all cavalry in the area, including Barteau's regiment.

By sunup April 24, 1863, Blackburn has passed through Decatur and had arrived within six miles of Newton Station. He then moved on to the station in time to capture a train loaded with ordnance and commissary supplies for the enemy troops at Vicksburg. A short time later, a second train with cars loaded with ammunition, arms, and commissary and quartermaster stores was captured. The cars, locomotives, and supplies were destroyed, and the depot was burned. The rest of Grierson's column then came up, and the troops burned bridges and trestlework and destroyed track for some distance to both the east and west of the station.

By 2:00 P.M. Grierson was ready to move on, but he soon ordered a rest of about three hours a short distance south of the station. He resumed the march late in the afternoon and reached Garlandville just before dark. Grierson then turned his column to the southwest and moved slowly forward until nearly midnight, finally camping on the Bender plantation, about two miles west of Montrose. This was the first time in forty hours that the horses had been unsaddled, and none of the men had slept more than a few hours in the last seventy-two.

Back in northern Mississippi, Hatch was repeatedly attacked by Barteau and Gholson near Birmingham April 24, 1863, but he continued to move northward and finally crossed Camp Creek, where he burned the bridge. His part in Grierson's raid ended April 26, when he finally rode back into La Grange.

When Pemberton learned that Grierson was on the road at Newton's Station, he immediately began shifting regiments and brigades from one point to another in an attempt to capture or destroy the Federal raiders. He remained preoccupied with this task until Grant crossed the Mississippi River.

On the morning of April 25, 1863, Grierson left the Bender plantation, marching westward through pine forests to the Nichols plantation, where he halted until 2:00 P.M. He then moved south along the Leaf River and halted at dark on the Mackadore plantation, about twenty miles south of Forest Station on the railroad running from Vicksburg to Jackson.

At 6:00 A.M. April 26, 1863, the column marched west from the Mackadore plantation. It reached Raleigh at about 8:00 A.M. It then continued on, marching all afternoon through a heavy rain, passed through Westville after dark, and halted about two miles farther on at the Williams plantation. That night, Grierson was only twenty miles from the New Orleans and Jackson Railroad. After feeding the horses, he ordered Prince to move on with two battalions of his 7th Illinois Cavalry and secure the ferry at the Pearl River. Grierson, with the rest of his command, was to follow in two hours.

Prince advanced during the rest of the night and began crossing the river just before daylight. When Grierson came up, he directed Prince to move on immediately to the New Orleans and Jackson Railroad, and, as soon as he had crossed, Grierson would follow with Loomis' 6th Illinois Cavalry. Because of the small capacity of the ferry, the last companies of Loomis' command were not across the river until about 2:00 P.M.

Grierson's men entered Hazelhurst, which was on the railroad, about fourteen miles west of the Pearl River, early in the afternoon of April 27, 1863. They remained in the town until evening, and then, with the 6th Illinois Cavalry in the lead, the column passed through Gallatin, about four miles out, at sunset, finally halting about midnight at Thompson's plantation, near Hargraves.

When Pemberton learned during the afternoon of April 27, 1863 that Grierson's cavalry was at Hazelhurst, he immediately sent out orders for the movement of troops to protect the Big Black River Bridge, and for troops to move up from the surrounding area to aid in capturing the Federal raiders.

Grierson left Thompson's plantation at 6:00 A.M. April 28, 1863 and marched westward, with Grand Gulf as his possible destination. At that time he had received no news that Grant had crossed the Mississippi River, and in the absence of such information, he was uncertain about his next movements. As he marched westward on the Natchez road that morning, he believed that it was too early to turn northward toward Grand Gulf, and at 10:00 A.M. he halted his command on the road while he considered his situation.

He finally decided to send back, as a feint, a battalion of his cavalry to Bahala (later Breckinridge) on the New Orleans and Jackson Railroad to do as much damage as possible, and then rejoin the main column. He also decided that when the battalion returned, he would move north under cover of darkness. George W. Trafton, with four companies of the 7th Illinois Cavalry, moved back to the east at about 11:00 A.M, and Grierson with the rest of his command continued on along the Natchez road toward Union Church. Grierson halted at Snyder's plantation, about two miles northeast of the church.

Meantime, on April 27, 1863, Pemberton had ordered John S. Bowen, at Grand Gulf, to send Wirt Adams with his regiment of Mississippi cavalry to intercept Grierson's raiders. A short time after receiving the order, a detachment of Adams' command, commanded by S. B. Cleveland, left Natchez, about fifty miles downriver, and marched eastward toward Hazelhurst. At about the same time, Adams with the rest of his cavalry moved eastward from Grand Gulf toward Fayetteville to get in rear of Grierson's command. His advance troops arrived on the Natchez road several miles east of Grierson's position, but then halted to wait for the rest of his men to come up.

While feeding their horses at Snyder's plantation, Grierson's pickets observed Cleveland's detachment approaching along the Natchez road; they charged, and Grierson's men drove the enemy back beyond Union Church. There was skirmishing until dusk, and Grierson bivouacked for the night at the church.

While returning that night from his expedition to the railroad, Trafton captured a small party of Adams' command, and from these men he learned of plans to cut off and capture Grierson's raiders. Trafton reported to Grierson at Union Church about 3:00 A.M. April 29, 1863 and informed him of Adams' movements. At 6:00 that morning, Grierson turned back from his position at Union Church and marched for the New Orleans and Jackson Railroad at Brookhaven. There he destroyed the railroad, the telegraph line, and all government property, and about dark he moved southward and encamped at the Gill plantation, eight miles from Brookhaven.

The next morning he continued the march southward along the railroad, destroying all bridges and trestlework as he advanced, to Bogue Chitto Station. There he burned fifteen freight cars, then moved on along the railroad, destroying all bridges and water tanks. He arrived at Summit about noon.

Up to that time, Grierson had heard nothing of Grant's crossing the Mississippi River, and he thereupon decided to abandon any attempt to join Grant and to continue on to Baton Rouge, Louisiana. He rested the men and horses for two hours at Summit, then began his march to the southwest on the Liberty road. After marching fifteen miles, he halted until daylight on the Spurlark plantation.

At dawn May 1, 1863, the day Grant finally crossed the Mississippi at Bruinsburg, Grierson resumed his march. After threatening Magnolia and Osyka, he left the road and moved rapidly to the southwest through thick forests, following lanes and country roads that ran along the high ground between the Amite and Tickfaw rivers. At about 11:15 A.M., shortly after turning into the road that runs from Clinton to Osyka, an advance party of Grierson's command approached Wall's Bridge on the Tickfaw River. There it was fired on from across the river by an enemy force consisting of three companies of James De Baun's 9th Louisiana Partisan Rangers. At noon the advance party attempted to cross the river but was sharply repulsed. De Baun continued to hold his position until the rest of Grierson's command came up, and he then withdrew in the direction of Osyka.

At this time Grierson's danger was increasing as a number of enemy cavalry forces were closing in from various directions and threatening to cut him off as he attempted to escape to Baton Rouge. The more important of these forces were Wirt Adams' Mississippi Cavalry, Robert V. Richardson with three companies of the 20th Mississippi Mounted Infantry, William R. Miles with his Louisiana Legion, and Hughes' Battalion of Mississippi Cavalry, commanded by Christopher C. Wilbourn.

After crossing the Tickfaw River at Wall's Bridge, Grierson moved south of the Greensburg road. He recrossed the Tickfaw at Edward's Bridge and succeeded in crossing the Amite River at Williams' Bridge at midnight. At that time enemy forces were only about two hours behind him on the road. Grierson immediately moved on to Sandy Creek, where he arrived at daylight May 2, 1863. He drove away a Confederate force belonging to Wilbourn's command that was encamped there,

then continued on toward Baton Rouge. He crossed the Comite River and moved on, halting for a time on a plantation six miles from the town. Finally Grierson marched into Baton Rouge about 3:00 P.M. May 2, and later went into camp near the town. This was the day that Grant's troops occupied Port Gibson.

ATTACK ON HELENA, ARKANSAS
JULY 4, 1863

Helena, Arkansas was occupied by Union troops July 12, 1862, and from that time until the end of the war, the post was held by United States forces. There were several reasons why the Confederates would have liked to recapture the town, but they did not consider that they had the strength to do so. Most important of these reasons were the following: Federal occupation of Helena threatened at all times an invasion of Arkansas; from Helena as a base, the Federals controlled the trade and the sentiments of a large and important part of the state; and in 1863 the town became a very important depot for Federal troops taking part in the siege of Vicksburg.

During Ulysses S. Grant's operations at Vicksburg, James A. Seddon, Confederate secretary of war, suggested an attack on Helena as a diversion to aid John C. Pemberton in his defense of Vicksburg. At that time Theophilus H. Holmes was at Little Rock, in command of the Confederate District of Arkansas in E. Kirby Smith's Trans-Mississippi Department. In May 1863 Sterling Price was at Little Rock, in command of an infantry division consisting of four brigades that were commanded by Dandridge McRae, Mosby M. Parsons, James F. Fagan, and James C. Tappan. In addition, John S. Marmaduke commanded a cavalry division consisting of three brigades commanded by Joseph O. Shelby, Colton Greene, and L. Marsh Walker. Marmaduke's headquarters was at Jacksonport, Arkansas. At the end of May 1863, Price moved with the brigades of McRae and Parsons to Jacksonport. Upon arrival there, he assumed command of all Confederate forces in northeastern Arkansas.

When it was first suggested to him, Holmes was reluctant to attempt a movement against Helena, but finally, considering the possible benefits of such an undertaking, he decided on June 15, 1863 to lead an expedition to capture the town. According to Holmes' plan, which he worked out with Price, Price left Jacksonport June 22 with the brigades of McRae and Parsons and Marmaduke's cavalry division and moved with them toward Helena. At the same time, Fagan was ordered to move with his brigade, which earlier had been left at Little Rock, and join Price near Helena.

Fagan, accompanied by Holmes, advanced by way of Devall's Bluff and Clarendon to Trenton, where he arrived June 28, 1863. Price marched by way of Augusta, Oakland, and Moro toward Helena, but his march was greatly slowed by heavy rains, and he did not arrive at Moro until July 1. From there he moved on by the Spring Creek road. On the morning of July 3, Price and Fagan crossed Lick Creek and advanced toward Helena. When Holmes arrived from Little Rock, he assumed personal command of the army, and he then issued orders for an attack July 4.

Benjamin M. Prentiss, whose headquarters was at Helena, was in command of the Federal District of Arkansas. During June 1863 he received information that led him to believe that the enemy planned a movement to some point on the west bank of the Mississippi River, and, believing that Helena was the probable objective, he began preparations for the defense of the town. He ordered the construction of four outlying batteries on prominent hills that commanded the roads leading into Helena. In addition, he ordered the digging of rifle pits and the erection of breastworks for the infantry supports for the batteries. He also ordered that the roads be obstructed by felling trees. In addition to the four batteries, there was also a redoubt at the western edge of town called Fort Curtis. The batteries were designated as A, B, C, and D, and were located as follows: Beginning on the right, north of Helena, Battery A was located on Rightor's Hill, between the Sterling road and the old Saint Francis road; Battery B, which was on the left of Battery A, was on the Upper Saint Francis road that ran in toward Helena from the northwest; Battery C was next to the left and was on Graveyard Hill, north of the Upper Little Rock road, which entered Helena from the west; and on the left of the line was

Battery D, which was on Hindman's Hill between the Upper Little Rock road and the Lower Little Rock road.

The Federal troops at Helena belonged to Thirteenth Division, Thirteenth Corps of the Army of the Tennessee, which was commanded by Frederick Salomon during the temporary absence of Leonard F. Ross. Prentiss assigned Salomon to the special supervision of the defenses of Helena. William E. McLean, commanding First Brigade, was placed in charge of the left of the line of defenses, and Samuel A. Rice, with his Second Brigade and Powell Clayton's cavalry brigade, was assigned to hold the right flank. The 33rd Missouri Regiment, whose men had been trained as artillerists, manned the guns at batteries A, B, C, and D, and also at Fort Curtis.

Rice, who established his command post at Rightor's Hill, sent the 29th Iowa and the 36th Iowa to reinforce the detachment of 33rd Missouri that was manning the guns at Battery A, and he sent the 28th Wisconsin to support Battery B. McLean placed the 2nd Arkansas (African Descent), with a detachment of 35th Missouri, in the entrenchments about a half-mile south of town. Behind the levee, on the left of 2nd Arkansas, was a section of John O'Connell's Battery K, 1st Missouri Light Artillery, and the other section was on the left of 2nd Arkansas. The 43rd Indiana was behind the breastworks on Hindman's Hill, protecting Battery D, and a section of Melvil C. Wright's 3rd Battery, Iowa Light Artillery was on the left of the 43rd Indiana, where it covered the Upper Little Rock road.

At the beginning of the attack, the 33rd Iowa, the remainder of the 35th Missouri, and a section of the 3rd Battery, Iowa Light Artillery were held in reserve near Fort Curtis.

At about 4:00 A.M. July 4, 1863, Fagan's brigade approached Battery D by way of the Upper Little Rock road and prepared to attack. A part of the brigade also advanced on the Lower Little Rock road, but these troops were driven back, largely by the fire of the gunboat *Tyler* on the river.

At daylight Fagan deployed his brigade to the right and left of the Upper Little Rock road, then charged and drove the 43rd Indiana from its first line of works on Hindman's Hill. The regiment fell back to a second line, and there it was joined by six companies of the 33rd Iowa and a detachment of the 35th Missouri from the reserves.

The guns from Battery C and those in position along the Lower Little Rock road then opened fire, with a deadly effect on Fagan's brigade. Fagan, however, continued his advance up the slopes of Hindman's Hill, and by 7:00 A.M. had arrived in front of Battery D. Fagan then launched an attack on Battery D, but this was driven back.

Meantime Price, with the brigades of Parsons and McRae, had advanced toward Graveyard Hill and Battery C. Parsons' brigade, which was in the lead, came under a heavy fire from Battery C, and it then halted to await the arrival of McRae's brigade on its left. When McRae arrived, both brigades charged up Graveyard Hill toward Battery C. The first attack was repulsed, and a second attack also failed, but on the next attempt the defenders were driven from Battery C, and the battery was captured. The men driven from Battery C, however, re-formed at the bottom of the hill. All Federal artillery that could be brought to bear opened with a heavy fire on Graveyard Hill, and, as a precaution, Salomon ordered the 1st Indiana Cavalry to Fort Curtis.

Price then divided his force and sent a part of it as a feint to threaten Fort Curtis, while McRae's brigade crossed the ravine between Graveyard Hill and Hindman's Hill to attack Battery D. McRae was soon stopped by a heavy fire, and his men took shelter in the ravine. Seeing this, the Federal troops supporting the battery advanced and surrounded McRae's brigade, capturing many of its men.

The men who had been supporting Battery C, aided by a detachment of the 1st Indiana Cavalry, soon recaptured Battery C and took a number of prisoners. This was about 10:00 A.M.

Before daylight that morning, Marmaduke's cavalry approached the Union works from the northwest on the old Saint Francis road. At dawn, Shelby's brigade reached a point about 200 yards from the works on the crest of Rightor's Hill, but it was quickly brought to a halt by the fire of the 29th Iowa. The enemy succeeded in establishing a battery within about 400 yards of Battery A, but the fire from two guns served by a detachment of the 1st Indiana Cavalry and a section of Wright's 3rd Battery, Iowa Light Artillery soon forced the battery to withdraw.

At about the same time, L. Marsh Walker's brigade advanced from the north on the Sterling road, which ran roughly parallel to the river and 500 to 700 yards from it. Walker was prevented from making much progress by Clayton's cavalry brigade, which had taken position behind the levee a short distance to the east of the Sterling road. Wright's 3rd Battery, Iowa Light Artillery was on the left of Clayton.

All attacks north of the town were repulsed. At 10:30 A.M. Holmes decided to withdraw, and the fighting at Helena was over. Skirmishing with the enemy covering the retreat was continued for a time, but at 2:00 P.M. that too ended.

Prentiss expected the attack to be renewed the next day, and he kept his troops on the line of defenses overnight. It was not until July 6, 1863 that Clayton led a cavalry column out on a reconnaissance, and he found that Holmes' troops had left the area.

The organization of the Union forces engaged at Helena, Arkansas July 4, 1863 was as follows:

DISTRICT OF EASTERN ARKANSAS, Benjamin M. Prentiss

Thirteenth Division, Thirteenth Corps, Frederick Salomon
  First Brigade, William E. McLean
    43rd Indiana Infantry, John C. Major
    35th Missouri Infantry, Horace Fitch
    28th Wisconsin Infantry, Edmund B. Gray

  Second Brigade, Samuel A. Rice
    29th Iowa Infantry, Thomas H. Benton, Jr.
    33rd Iowa Infantry, Cyrus H. Mackey
    36th Iowa Infantry, Charles W. Kittredge
    33rd Missouri Infantry, William H. Heath

  Cavalry Brigade, Powell Clayton
    1st Indiana Cavalry, Thomas N. Pace
    5th Kansas Cavalry, Wilton A. Jenkins

  Artillery
    3rd Battery, Iowa Light Artillery, Melvil C. Wright
    Battery K, 1st Missouri Light Artillery, John O'Connell

  2nd Arkansas Infantry (African Descent), George W. Burchard

ENGAGEMENT AT IUKA, MISSISSIPPI SEPTEMBER 19, 1862

In July 1862, Braxton Bragg's Confederate Army of the Mississippi was in position near Tupelo, Mississippi, to which point it had retreated after the evacuation of Corinth on May 30, when Henry W. Halleck's Army of the Department of the Mississippi approached the town from Pittsburg Landing.

At the end of July 1862, Bragg's army was transferred to Chattanooga, Tennessee in preparation for a movement planned by Bragg and E. Kirby Smith for the invasion of Kentucky and Tennessee. For details, see Invasion of Kentucky and Tennessee (E. Kirby Smith and Braxton Bragg). When the army left Mississippi, Sterling Price was left at Tupelo with his Confederate Army of the West to occupy that part of the state. Price's army consisted of two infantry divisions, commanded by Henry Little and Dabney H. Maury, and a cavalry brigade, commanded by Frank C. Armstrong.

In addition to Price's army at Tupelo, Earl Van Dorn commanded another force in Mississippi. Van Dorn's command was designated as the District of Mississippi, which extended along the Mississippi River, and he was charged with defending Vicksburg, keeping communications open with the Trans-Mississippi, and preventing Federal forces from occupying the northern part of the state. At that time, Van Dorn's headquarters was at Jackson, Mississippi.

On August 2, 1862, Bragg informed Price that Ulysses S. Grant, commander of the District of West Tennessee, had been sending reinforcements to Don Carlos Buell, commander of the Army of the Ohio, who was then in Middle Tennessee, and he directed Price to use his force to prevent the further transfer of Federal troops to Tennessee. On August 11, Bragg directed Van Dorn to cooperate with Price in this effort. Finally, on September 11, President Jefferson Davis ordered Van Dorn to assume command of both his own and Price's armies.

Meantime, however, Price, conforming to his orders to hold Grant's forces in West Tennessee and northern Mississippi, had started his army northward from Tupelo toward Iuka, a town on the Memphis and Charleston Railroad, about twenty miles

southeast of Corinth. Price had been further instructed that if upon arriving at Iuka he found that William S. Rosecrans, commanding the Federal Army of the Mississippi, had gone with his army to Nashville, he, Price, was to move into Tennessee toward Nashville.

Also, as a part of the overall Confederate plan, Van Dorn had started his army northward from Jackson toward Holly Springs, Mississippi, where he arrived September 11, 1862.

Price's army, preceded by Armstrong's cavalry, marched northward through Saltillo, Baldwyn, and Booneville, and Armstrong entered Iuka September 13, 1862. He soon withdrew, however, when he was confronted by a strong Federal force. Price's infantry arrived the next day and moved into the town. There Price learned that Rosecrans had sent the divisions of Eleazer A. Paine, Jefferson C. Davis, and Gordon Granger to reinforce Buell, but that he still remained west of Iuka with two divisions of his Army of the Mississippi. For additional information, see Army of the Mississippi (Pope, Rosecrans).

When he received this information, Price decided not to go to Tennessee, but to move instead against Rosecrans, who was reported to have gone to Corinth. Price then informed Van Dorn that he was ready to cooperate with the latter in an attack on Corinth.

On September 15, 1862, Joseph A. Mower, commanding Second Brigade of David S. Stanley's Second Division of Rosecrans' army, led a reconnaissance on the Burnsville road to within about two miles of Iuka, reporting back that the enemy occupied the town in force. Grant then decided that it was time to act. He was concerned that Price might move into Tennessee to reinforce Bragg during his advance against Buell, and he began to concentrate his forces to prevent such a movement. He also wanted to attack Price at Iuka before the latter could be reinforced by Van Dorn from Holly Springs.

Grant decided on the following plan: Edward O. C. Ord, commanding the post and garrison of Corinth, was to advance with three infantry divisions along the Memphis and Charleston Railroad to the vicinity of Iuka, and to be in position to attack on September 19, 1862. Rosecrans was to concentrate his two divisions at Jacinto, Mississippi, about twelve miles southeast of Corinth, and from there march eastward by the Tuscumbia road to the Fulton road to a position in rear of Price, where he would be able to cut off the enemy retreat from Iuka. Grant also ordered Stephen A. Hurlbut, commanding at Bolivar, Tennessee, to demonstrate against Van Dorn at Holly Springs.

On September 18, 1862, Ord advanced with John McArthur's Sixth Division and Thomas A. Davies' Second Division of the Army of the Tennessee, and Leonard F. Ross' Second Division, District of Jackson to Burnsville, about eight miles from Iuka. Grant also established his headquarters at Burnsville. Ord was ordered to move up toward Iuka and be ready to attack the next morning. Later, however, when Grant learned that Rosecrans had been delayed on his march, he changed this order and directed Ord to begin his attack when he heard the sound of Rosecrans' guns on his right.

On September 18, 1862, Charles S. Hamilton's Third Division, Army of the Mississippi was in camp at Jacinto, and that morning Stanley's Second Division left its camps on Clear Creek, near Corinth, and moved to join him. Stanley marched out on the Burnsville road to Patrick's house and turned to the right, arriving that evening within about a mile of Jacinto.

On the night of September 18, 1862, Price at Iuka learned of President Davis' order of September 11 assigning Van Dorn to the command of both armies, and the next day he received Van Dorn's reply to his offer to cooperate in an attack on Corinth. He also received an order from Van Dorn directing him to move with his Army of the West toward Rienzi the next day to effect the junction of the two armies. Accordingly, Price issued orders for his army to be ready to move toward Rienzi on the morning of September 20.

At 5:00 A.M. September 19, 1862, Rosecrans' column, consisting of Hamilton's and Stanley's divisions, and preceded by John K. Mizner's 3rd Michigan Cavalry, moved out from Jacinto on the Tuscumbia road toward Barnett's house, which was about twelve miles distant. Driving enemy pickets ahead of him, Rosecrans reached Barnett's at noon. Then, instead of continuing on to the Fulton road as expected, Hamilton, whose division was leading the column, was instructed to take the direct road (the Jacinto road) to Iuka. John B. Sanborn's First Brigade marched first, and it was followed by Jeremiah

C. Sullivan's Second Brigade. Stanley's division followed Hamilton, with Joseph A. Mower's Second Brigade in front and John W. Fuller's First Brigade bringing up the rear of the column.

Hamilton's division advanced steadily during the afternoon, driving back the enemy skirmishers. Sometime before 5:00 P.M., the head of the column arrived within a mile and a half of Iuka. This was at a point near a crossroad that led from the Jacinto road to the Fulton road. The leading troops halted on the brow of a densely wooded hill that fell off abruptly both to the right and to the left of the road, and in consequence there was little room on the crest to form a battle line. The skirmishers continued to move forward, and about 300 yards farther on, they found a large force of the enemy occupying a strong position across the road and along a deep ravine.

Meantime, at 2:00 P.M. that day, while Price was preparing for the march of the army to Rienzi, he learned that his pickets on the Jacinto road were being driven in, and that Rosecrans was advancing in force along that road toward Iuka. At that time all of Maury's division was confronting Ord, who was expected to attack from the direction of Burnsville, and Little's division was along the southern edge of Iuka. Price quickly ordered Little to send Louis Hebert's brigade of his division out on the Jacinto road. Price, in person, took the brigade to the front. When he found that he was outnumbered, he ordered Little to send another brigade, and a short time later John D. Martin joined Hebert with his brigade.

When Martin's brigade first arrived at the front, it was formed in rear of Hebert, but a short time later Martin, with two regiments of his brigade, was sent to the left of Hebert's line, and two regiments were led by Little to the right of Hebert's line. It was this force that Hamilton found on his front.

Hamilton's skirmishers were soon driven back on the head of the column, and Sanborn, whose brigade was the first to come up, began to form his regiments in line of battle across the road. Frank C. Sands' 11th Battery, Ohio Light Artillery, then under the command of Cyrus Sears, was placed near the road, on the crest of the hill, where it commanded the road ahead. Charles L. Matthies' 5th Iowa Regiment was placed in the woods on the crest of the hill and on the right of the road, with its left near the battery. The next regiment to come up was George B. Boomer's 26th Missouri, and it was sent to the right and a little to the rear of the 5th Iowa. Then Norman Eddy's 48th Indiana arrived, and it was formed on the left of the road and a little in front of the battery.

At about 5:00 P.M., at which time only the above three regiments and the battery were in position, the enemy opened with a heavy artillery and infantry fire, then launched a determined attack on Sanborn's line. At the first fire by the enemy infantry, most of the horses of the battery were killed, and, although it continued to fire for some time, the fighting that ensued for the next three hours was largely an infantry battle.

As the other regiments of Sanborn's brigade came up, they were sent to protect the flanks of the line that he had already established on the hill. Ebenezer Le Gro's 4th Minnesota was formed on the left of the 48th Indiana, and Addison H. Sanders' 16th Iowa was placed en echelon on the right of the line.

When the head of Sullivan's brigade arrived on the road in rear of the front line, Sanborn was hard-pressed, and Sullivan sent Nicholas Perczel's 10th Iowa and a section of Lorenzo D. Immell's 12th Battery, Wisconsin Light Artillery out to the left on an old road that ran to the north from the Jacinto road. They then took position in a field on the extreme left of the army to protect the left and rear of Sanborn's brigade. Sullivan also ordered Samuel A. Holmes to take his 10th Missouri to the right of Sanborn's line. When Sullivan found that no more troops of his brigade could be brought into action at that time, he placed his other two regiments in rear of the center of Sanborn's line as a reserve and went forward to report to Hamilton for service. He was then sent to take charge of the right of Hamilton's line and to see that the flank was not turned.

The fighting grew in intensity, but for a time Sanborn's front line held its ground. The battery continued to do good service even though it had lost about half its men. Finally, however, the line began to give way slowly, and the men fell back to a position just below the crest of the hill, where they were halted by the exertions of Hamilton and Sanborn. This withdrawal exposed the battery, which was unable to move, and the enemy then moved into position. Hamilton's troops rallied, however, and

again advanced to the top of the hill and recaptured the battery. The enemy then charged again, and once more the Federal line fell back.

When the 48th Indiana, on the left of the battery, was driven back, the enemy occupied a position commanding the battery. A further attack also drove back the 16th Iowa, and then the enemy advanced toward the rear of Sanborn's line. The two reserve regiments of Sullivan's brigade were quickly formed to meet this threat. Matthias H. Bartilson's 80th Ohio formed near a log church, at the junction of the Jacinto road and the road along which Perczel and the artillery had taken position, and John W. Rankin's 17th Iowa took position on its right. They immediately opened fire, and the enemy fell back up the hill. The 17th Iowa, however, soon came under a heavy fire and retired in some confusion.

The enemy continued to attack Hamilton's right, and the position of the battery again changed hands. Boomer brought up four companies of his 26th Missouri and put them in line between the battery and the left of the 5th Iowa to strengthen the line.

The enemy also attempted to turn Hamilton's left, but this attack was beaten back by Perczel's 10th Iowa and Immell's guns. This attack ended the fighting on the Federal left, and then the 4th Minnesota moved to the right to support that part of the line.

At about this time, Stanley's division arrived on the road in rear of the line of battle, and Rosecrans ordered Mower's brigade, which was the leading brigade of the division, to move up to support the front line. For some reason, only Andrew J. Weber's 11th Missouri of Mower's brigade went forward, and Weber, hearing the heavy firing on the right, led his regiment in that direction. He formed in line of battle in an open field on the extreme right of the line, then moved forward into the woods beyond, on the right of the 5th Iowa and the 26th Missouri. He became engaged almost immediately, but held his position for about an hour until his ammunition was exhausted.

Boomer's 26th Missouri remained in line with the 5th Iowa and the 11th Missouri for about an hour until his ammunition was exhausted, and then the 26th Missouri, 5th Iowa, and 11th Missouri fell back together. On its way to the rear, the 5th Iowa passed through the 10th Missouri, which earlier had been ordered to support the right of Hamilton's line, and was then on its way to take position near the road.

The battle finally ended at dark. Hamilton's division was withdrawn to a field several hundred yards in rear of its original first line, and Stanley's division, which had been only slightly engaged, covered the front that night.

Little was killed during the fighting that evening, and his division, then commanded by Hebert, bivouacked on the ground from which Hamilton had been driven.

It is a curious fact that although there was heavy firing for several hours along the Jacinto road, only a few miles south of Ord's position near Iuka, neither Ord nor Grant heard any sound of Rosecrans' battle. Consequently, Ord did not attack, and his three divisions remained idle during the evening of September 19, 1862.

After the battle, Price decided to carry out his earlier orders to join Van Dorn, and that night he returned to Iuka to make preparations for the withdrawal of his army. He ordered Maury to move with his division to the south of Iuka to join Hebert's division, and he left Armstrong's cavalry to hold the ground in front of Ord. Price then withdrew during the night, and his army marched south on the Fulton road.

Preceded by cavalry under Mizner and Edward Hatch, Rosecrans' infantry followed the enemy column for about fifteen miles and then, being far behind, returned to Jacinto.

Price continued his march and arrived at Baldwyn September 23, 1862. He then started the next day for Rienzi. For further information, see Battle of Corinth, Mississippi.

The organization of the Union forces at the Battle of Iuka was as follows:

ARMY OF THE MISSISSIPPI, William S. Rosecrans

Second Division, David S. Stanley
First Brigade, John W. Fuller
27th Ohio, Zephaniah S. Spaulding
39th Ohio, Edward F. Noyes
43rd Ohio, J. L. Kirby Smith
Battery M, 1st Missouri Light Artillery, Albert M. Powell
8th Battery (one section), Wisconsin Light Artillery, John D. McLean
Battery F, 2nd United States Artillery, Thomas D. Maurice
Second Brigade, Joseph A. Mower

26th Illinois, Robert A. Gillmore
47th Illinois, William A. Thrush
11th Missouri, Andrew J. Weber
8th Wisconsin, George W. Robbins
2nd Battery, Iowa Light Artillery, Nelson T. Spoor
3rd Battery, Michigan Light Artillery, Alexander W. Dees

Third Division, Charles S. Hamilton
First Brigade, John B. Sanborn
48th Indiana, Norman Eddy
5th Iowa, Charles L. Matthies
16th Iowa, Addison H. Sanders
4th Minnesota, Ebenezer Le Gros

26th Missouri, George B. Boomer
11th Battery, Ohio Light Artillery, Cyrus Sears
Second Brigade, Jeremiah C. Sullivan
10th Iowa, Nicholas Perczel
17th Iowa, John W. Rankin
10th Missouri, Samuel A. Holmes
24th Missouri (Company F)
80th Ohio, Matthias H. Bartilson
12th Battery, Wisconsin Light Artillery, Lorenzo D. Immell

Cavalry Division, John K. Mizner
2nd Iowa Cavalry, Edward Hatch
7th Kansas Cavalry (Companies B and E), Frederick Swoyer
3rd Michigan Cavalry, Lyman G. Willcox

JACKSON, MISSISSIPPI CAMPAIGN (WILLIAM T. SHERMAN) JULY 5–25, 1863

In June 1863, during Ulysses S. Grant's investment of Vicksburg, Mississippi, Joseph E. Johnston assembled an army for the purpose of relieving John C. Pemberton's forces that were defending the city. Johnston's so-called Army of Relief consisted of four infantry divisions, commanded by John C. Breckinridge, Samuel G. French, William W. Loring, and William H. T. Walker, and a cavalry division commanded by William H. Jackson. On June 29, the army marched westward from Jackson, arriving on the east bank of the Big Black River July 1. French, Loring, and Walker bivouacked along the river between Brownsville and the railroad crossing of the river, and Breckinridge camped near Edwards Station. For the next three days, Jackson's cavalry searched vainly for a possible place where the army might cross. On July 5, Johnston learned that Vicksburg had been surrendered the day before. He immediately retreated toward Jackson, with orders to protect that vital rail center.

On the night of July 4, 1863, William T. Sherman, whose Army of Observation had been guarding the line of the Big Black River during the siege of Vicksburg, was ordered to march against Johnston's army. Sherman reached the Big Black River the next day, and on the evening of July 6, Edward O. C. Ord's Thirteenth Corps crossed the river at the railroad bridge and Frederick Steele's Fifteenth Corps crossed at Messinger's Ford. The two corps halted that night about four miles east of the river. John G. Parke's Ninth Corps arrived on the river at Birdsong Ferry July 5 and found the enemy forces still on the opposite bank. The next day, however, some troops gained a lodgment on the east bank, then built a bridge. The corps crossed July 7 and marched out from Birdsong Ferry that evening, bivouacking near Bolton at 10:00 that night.

On July 7, 1863, Ord marched east on the main road to Jackson and Steele on the Bridgeport road, and both halted that night at Bolton. Because of the intense heat, the army marched at night. Steele's advance arrived near Clinton at 3:00 A.M. July 9, and Ord's advance came up at daylight. On July 8, Parke also advanced on the Bridgeport road toward Jackson, but when he came up on the rear of Steele's corps, he turned off and advanced on a side road, bivouacking that night a few miles from Clinton. On July 9, Parke again came up in rear of Steele, and he then turned off to the left and succeeded in opening a road across the plantations. He marched until dark along a route nearly parallel to the main Jackson road.

During the afternoon of July 9, 1863, Ord's corps moved on to the east of Clinton, halting at the junction of the Bridgeport road and the Jackson (or Clinton) road. A short time later, Steele's corps came up on the Bridgeport road. To make room for Steele's corps, Ord was ordered to move south to the Raymond road and advance toward Jackson from the southwest.

On the morning of July 10, 1863, Parke resumed his march and turned into a plantation road that ran to the Livingston-Canton road, five miles north of Canton. He halted at dark and occupied a line north of Jackson, at a right angle to the Canton road, that extended from the Pearl River on the left, across the Mississippi Central Railroad, to the Livingston road on the right. The next day the corps moved up close to the enemy entrenchments, with William Sooy Smith's First Division, Sixteenth Corps, which was temporarily attached to Ninth Corps, advancing on the road to Jackson.

July 10, 1863, Sherman ordered Ord to operate along the Raymond road toward Jackson, Steele along the road from Clinton, and Parke along the Livingston road.

On July 11, 1863, the three corps moved up close to the enemy entrenchments and took positions in preparation for the investment of the town. Ord's divisions, which were on the right of the army, were in position to the south and west of Jackson as follows: Jacob G. Lauman's Fourth Division, Sixteenth Corps, which was temporarily attached to Thirteenth Corps, was on the extreme right between the Pearl River and New Orleans and Jackson and Great Northern Railroad; Alvin P. Hovey's Twelfth Division was on the left of Lauman, between the New Orleans and Jackson Railroad and the Raymond road; William P. Benton's Fourteenth Division was on the left of Hovey's division north of the Raymond road, facing east; and Peter J. Osterhaus' Ninth Division was on the left of the corps line, directly west of Jackson and facing east. Andrew J. Smith's Tenth Division was on the extreme right of the army.

John M. Thayer's First Division of Steele's corps was on the left of Osterhaus' division, with its left on the Jackson road; Frank P. Blair's Second Division was north of the Jackson road, on the left of Thayer and extending across the Southern Railroad of Mississippi; and James M. Tuttle's Third Division was in reserve on the Clinton road.

On July 12, 1863, in violation of orders and without adequate preparation, Lauman advanced on the enemy works with Isaac C. Pugh's First Brigade of his division. Pugh was driven back, with a loss of 465 of the 880 men of the brigade. A short time later, Ord relieved Lauman and placed Alvin P.

Hovey in charge of the division. Upon assuming command, Hovey attached Lauman's division to his own Twelfth Division and redesignated Lauman's brigades, respectively, as Third Brigade, Fourth Brigade, and Fifth Brigade of Twelfth Division.

On July 12, 1863, the supply trains of the army were ordered to report to John McArthur at the Big Black River Bridge, and the next day McArthur left with his division of Seventeenth Corps on the road to Jackson. His division was posted at Clinton and Champion Hill to guard the road.

While awaiting the arrival of the wagon train with the artillery ammunition before beginning the bombardment of the town, Sherman's army worked its way closer to the enemy entrenchments. Despite efforts by Jackson's cavalry to intercept the train, it finally arrived, and when Johnston learned of this, he decided to abandon the defense of Jackson. During the night of July 16, 1863, he evacuated the town, crossed the Pearl River, and marched through Brandon to Morton, thirty-five miles east of Jackson.

Blair's division occupied Jackson July 17, 1863, and that day Sherman sent Steele forward with three brigades of Fifteenth Corps toward Brandon, thirteen miles east of Jackson. He pushed back some enemy cavalry and destroyed a stretch of track. He camped there on the night of July 19, but returned to Jackson the next day.

On July 20, 1863, Parke started back with the two divisions of Ninth Corps to return to his old camps at Milldale, near Snyder's Bluff, and on July 21, Sherman sent Ord back to Vicksburg by way of Raymond. Parke arrived at Milldale on the evening of July 23.

While at Jackson, Sherman's cavalry destroyed the railroad as far north as Canton and as far south as Brookhaven. After the evacuation of the city, Sherman remained at Jackson with Fifteenth Corps until July 23, 1863 to complete the work of destruction on the railroads and everything of military value in the city, and that day he moved back to Clinton. He then continued on by way of Champion Hill and recrossed the Big Black River July 25 and went into camp.

The organization of Sherman's Expeditionary Army during the campaign against Jackson, Mississippi July 5–25, 1863 was as follows:

EXPEDITIONARY ARMY
William T. Sherman

NINTH CORPS, John G. Parke

First Division, Thomas Welch
   First Brigade, Henry Bowman
   Third Brigade, Daniel Leasure
   Artillery
      Battery D, Pennsylvania Light Artillery, George W. Durell
      Batteries L and M, 3rd United States Artillery, John Edwards, Jr.

Note. Second Brigade was transferred to Second Division as Third Brigade in June 1863.

Second Division, Robert B. Potter
   First Brigade, Simon G. Griffin
   Second Brigade, Edward Ferrero
   Third Brigade, Benjamin C. Christ
   Battery L, 2nd New York Light Artillery, Jacob Roemer
   Artillery Reserve
   Battery E, 2nd United States Artillery, Samuel N. Benjamin

First Division, Sixteenth Corps, William Sooy Smith
   First Brigade, John M. Loomis
   Second Brigade, Stephen G. Hicks
   Third Brigade, Joseph R. Cockerill
   Fourth Brigade, William W. Sanford
   Artillery
      Battery F, 1st Illinois Light Artillery, John T. Cheney
      Battery I, 1st Illinois Light Artillery, William N. Lansing
      Cogswell's Battery, Illinois Light Artillery, Henry G. Eddy
      6th Battery, Indiana Light Artillery, Michael Mueller

Cavalry, Cyrus Bussey

Note. First Division, Sixteenth Corps and Bussey's cavalry command were temporarily attached to Ninth Corps.

THIRTEENTH CORPS, Edward O. C. Ord

Ninth Division, Peter J. Osterhaus
   First Brigade, James Keigwin
   Second Brigade, Daniel W. Lindsay
   Cavalry Brigade, Hugh Fullerton

Mounted Infantry, John G. Fonda
Artillery, Charles H. Lanphere
    7th Battery, Michigan Light Artillery, Charles H. Lanphere
    1st Battery, Wisconsin Light Artillery, Oscar F. Nutting

Tenth Division, Andrew J. Smith
  First Brigade, Richard Owen
  Second Brigade, William J. Landram
  Artillery
    Chicago Mercantile Battery, Illinois Light Artillery, Patrick H. White
    17th Battery, Ohio Light Artillery, Charles S. Rice

Twelfth Division, Alvin P. Hovey
  First Brigade, William T. Spicely
  Second Brigade, James R. Slack
  Artillery
    Battery A, 1st Missouri Light Artillery, George W. Schofield
    2nd Battery, Ohio Light Artillery, Augustus Beach
    16th Battery, Ohio Light Artillery, Russell P. Twist

Fourteenth Division, William P. Benton
  First Brigade, David Shunk
  Second Brigade, Michael K. Lawler

Note. Martin Klauss' 1st Battery, Indiana Light Artillery was attached to First Brigade, and Peter Davidson's Battery A, 2nd Illinois Light Artillery was attached to Second Brigade.

Fourth Division, Sixteenth Corps, Jacob G. Lauman
  First Brigade, Isaac C. Pugh
  Second Brigade, Cyrus Hall
  Third Brigade, George E. Bryant
  Artillery
    Battery E, 2nd Illinois Light Artillery, George L. Nispel
    Battery K, 2nd Illinois Light Artillery, Benjamin F. Rodgers
    5th Battery, Ohio Light Artillery, Anthony B. Burton
    7th Battery, Ohio Light Artillery, Silas A. Burnap
    15th Battery, Ohio Light Artillery, Edward Spear, Jr.

Note. Fourth Division, Sixteenth Corps was temporarily attached to Thirteenth Corps. Lauman was superseded by Alvin P. Hovey July 12, 1863. Upon assuming command, Hovey attached Fourth Division, Sixteenth Corps to his own Twelfth Division, Thirteenth Corps and redesignated the brigades of Lauman's division as follows: First Brigade became Third Brigade, Twelfth Division; Second Brigade became Fourth Brigade, Twelfth Division; and Third Brigade became Fifth Brigade, Twelfth Division.

FIFTEENTH CORPS, Frederick Steele

First Division, John M. Thayer
  First Brigade, Bernard G. Farrar
  Second Brigade, Charles R. Woods
  Third Brigade, Milo Smith
  Artillery
    1st Battery, Iowa Light Artillery, Henry H. Griffiths
    Battery F, 2nd Missouri Light Artillery, Clemens Landgraeber
    4th Battery, Ohio Light Artillery, Louis Hoffmann

Second Division, Frank P. Blair, Jr.
  First Brigade, Giles A. Smith
  Second Brigade, Joseph A. J. Lightburn
  Third Brigade, Hugh Ewing
  Artillery
    Battery A, 1st Illinois Light Artillery, Peter P. Wood
    Battery B, 1st Illinois Light Artillery, Israel P. Rumsey
    Battery H, 1st Illinois Light Artillery, Levi W. Hart
    8th Battery, Ohio Light Artillery, James F. Putnam

Third Division, James M. Tuttle
  First Brigade, William L. McMillen
  Third Brigade, Joseph J. Woods
  Artillery, Nelson T. Spoor
    Battery E, 1st Illinois Light Artillery, Allen C. Waterhouse
    2nd Battery, Iowa Light Artillery, Joseph R. Reed

Note. Second Brigade had been detached earlier and sent to Young's Point, Louisiana.

INVASION OF KENTUCKY AND TENNESSEE (E. KIRBY SMITH AND BRAXTON BRAGG) AUGUST 14, 1862– OCTOBER 19, 1862

On April 12, 1862, following the Battle of Shiloh, Henry W. Halleck, commander of the Department of the Mississippi, arrived at Pittsburg Landing from Saint Louis and assumed personal command of Ulysses S. Grant's Army of the Tennessee, John Pope's Army of the Mississippi, and Don Carlos Buell's Army of the Ohio. Then, in preparation for an advance on Corinth, Mississippi, Halleck organized his combined command into a Right Wing, Center, Left Wing, and Reserve. During the month of May 1862, Halleck's forces advanced toward Corinth. On May 30, as they drew near, Pierre G. T. Beauregard, commanding the Confederate Army of the Mississippi, evacuated the town and retired southward toward Tupelo, Mississippi.

Pope's Union Army of the Mississippi followed Beauregard to and beyond Booneville, Mississippi, and when it appeared the Confederates were going to make a stand at Baldwyn, Halleck sent Buell, on June 4, 1862, with William Nelson's Fourth Division and Thomas L. Crittenden's Fifth Division of his Army of the Ohio to Booneville to support Pope. Beauregard, however, continued his retreat to Tupelo.

June 10, 1862, Halleck revoked the order issued at Pittsburg Landing, dividing the army into wings, and on that date Buell resumed command of the Army of the Ohio (except George H. Thomas' First Division, which was attached to the Army of the Tennessee); Pope resumed command of the Army of the Mississippi, and Grant of the Army of the Tennessee. For additional information about the organization and movements of Halleck's command during the advance on Corinth, see Halleck's Advance on Corinth, Mississippi.

Also on June 10, 1862, Halleck directed Buell to return with his army to Tennessee and occupy the eastern and southeastern parts of the state, including some important posts on the railroads in the area, such as Chattanooga and Knoxville in Tennessee and Dalton in Georgia. The route selected for the march east was through northern Alabama. At that time George H. Thomas' First Division, Alexander McD. McCook's Second Division, and Thomas J. Wood's Sixth Division were near Corinth, Nelson's division was near Booneville, and Crittenden's division was at Baldwyn, all in Mississippi.

June 11, 1862, Wood's division advanced from Corinth eastward toward Decatur, Alabama, with orders to repair the Memphis and Charleston Railroad. At the same time, Buell ordered Ormsby M. Mitchel, whose Third Division, Army of the Ohio

was on the railroad at Huntsville and Stevenson, Alabama, to put the Nashville and Chattanooga Railroad in running order as quickly as possible.

Also on June 11, McCook's division left Corinth and marched toward Florence, Alabama, where it arrived June 15. Crittenden's division followed closely in rear of McCook. Crittenden marched from Baldwyn, by way of Booneville, to Iuka, Mississippi, and there turned into the road behind McCook. Wood's division then advanced to Tuscumbia and beyond to repair the railroad, and Nelson's division moved up from Booneville to take Wood's place between Iuka and Tuscumbia.

At the time of Buell's advance, George H. Thomas' First Division, Army of the Ohio was attached to the Army of the Tennessee and was under Grant's orders. On June 22, 1862, Grant ordered Thomas to move forward and take position between Iuka and Tuscumbia and relieve Nelson, who was to advance and rejoin the rest of the Army of the Ohio.

The divisions of McCook and Crittenden began crossing the Tennessee River at Florence June 22, 1862, and Nelson's division followed them across as it came up to the river. The three divisions then moved on eastward on the north side of the river and began arriving at Athens, Alabama on June 27. Wood's division continued on along the railroad to Decatur, Alabama, and had finished crossing the river there by July 6.

On July 2, 1862, Mitchel was relieved from command of Third Division, Army of the Ohio and ordered to Washington, D.C., and William Sooy Smith assumed temporary command of the division. On July 11, Smith was assigned command of all guards on the Nashville and Decatur Railroad, the Nashville and Chattanooga Railroad, and the Memphis and Charleston Railroad, and Lovell H. Rousseau assumed command of Third Division.

McCook and Crittenden marched from Athens about July 4, 1862, arriving at Battle Mountain, near Jasper, Tennessee, on July 14. Nelson remained at Athens to repair the road, and Wood halted at Decatur to protect the crossing there.

In July 1862, Confederate cavalry became active, with John H. Morgan's men in Kentucky and Nathan B. Forrest along the Nashville and Chattanooga Railroad. On July 13, Forrest, advancing from McMinnville, captured Murfreesboro, with its garrison commanded by Thomas T. Crittenden, and large quantities of stores. Nelson's division was ordered to Murfreesboro to drive Forrest from the town and protect the railroad from further depredations. Nelson arrived there the next day. After the raid, two brigades of Wood's division were ordered from Decatur to Shelbyville, and later to Dechard, Tennessee. Wood's other brigade was sent to Stevenson, Alabama.

Thomas' division remained in rear of the army on the Memphis and Charleston Railroad from Iuka to Decatur, including Tuscumbia and Florence, until July 28, 1862. It then marched eastward to rejoin the Army of the Ohio, arriving at Athens and Huntsville at the end of July.

August 2, 1862, Nelson moved with two of his brigades from Murfreesboro to McMinnville and arrived there the next day. His other brigade joined them later when relieved at Murfreesboro by other troops. On August 16, Nelson was relieved from command of Fourth Division, which was then at McMinnville, and was ordered to Kentucky to take charge of and to organize the new troops arriving there for the defense of the state. Jacob Ammen was in temporary charge of the division until August 23, when William Sooy Smith assumed command. When Nelson departed, Thomas was relieved from command of First Division and was sent to McMinnville to direct affairs in that area. He assumed command there August 19. About August 21, Wood arrived at McMinnville from Dechard with his division, and Thomas was then in command of Fourth Division and Sixth Division. Albin Schoepf assumed temporary command of Thomas' division, which was then at Dechard.

Meantime, while Buell's army was marching eastward toward Tennessee, the enemy at Tupelo became active. On June 27, 1862, Braxton Bragg relieved Beauregard in command of the Confederate Army of the Mississippi. Bragg's command also included the Confederate Department No. 2 (Western Department), and on July 5 he assigned William J. Hardee to the temporary command of the army while he took care of department business.

July 21, 1862, Bragg ordered Hardee to move the army from Tupelo to Chattanooga. The infantry was to go by rail by way of Meridian, Mississippi; Mobile and Montgomery in Alabama; and West Point and Atlanta in Georgia. The artillery, cavalry, and trains were to move across country by way of Columbus, Mississippi, Tuscaloosa and Gadsden, Alabama, and Rome, Georgia. The infantry began its movement July 23, and by mid-August, all had arrived at Chattanooga. At that time, however, the trains and artillery had not arrived, and some units were still coming in. When Hardee departed from Corinth, he left the Confederate Army of the West, which Earl Van Dorn had brought from Arkansas, in Mississippi under the command of Sterling Price to look after the Union forces in northern Mississippi and western Tennessee.

Bragg arrived in person at Chattanooga July 30, 1862 and met with E. Kirby Smith, commander of the Confederate forces in East Tennessee, to plan an invasion of Kentucky and Tennessee. According to their arrangement, Smith was to advance from Knoxville against George W. Morgan's Seventh Division, Army of the Ohio at Cumberland Gap and then move on into Kentucky, and Bragg was to march northward from Chattanooga into Middle Tennessee. Smith left Knoxville on August 14, and Bragg's army began crossing the Tennessee River at Chattanooga August 19. On August 15, before beginning his advance, Bragg reorganized his army into a Right Wing, commanded by Leonidas Polk, and a left wing under William J. Hardee. Polk's wing consisted of the divisions of Benjamin F. Cheatham and Jones M. Withers, and Hardee's wing of the divisions of Samuel Jones and Sterling A. M. Wood. Simon B. Buckner joined the army and assumed command of Wood's division on August 19.

At that time, Nelson's division (then commanded by Ammen) was at McMinnville; the divisions of Crittenden and McCook were at Battle Creek, near Jasper, Tennessee; the divisions of Thomas and Wood were on or near the Nashville and Chattanooga Railroad; and Rousseau's division (formerly commanded by Mitchel) was on the railroad from Huntsville northward toward Nashville. Wood's division joined Thomas, who was in command at McMinnville, August 21, 1862.

On August 14, 1862, Smith left Knoxville with the divisions of Patrick R. Cleburne and Thomas J. Churchill (transferred to Smith's command from Bragg's army) and marched by way of Rogers' Pass to Barboursville, Kentucky, where he arrived August 18. Smith left Carter L. Stevenson's division to invest Morgan's position at Cumberland Gap, and with the rest of his command left Barboursville on August 25. He marched by way of London, Big Hill, and Kingston, arriving near Rogersville, a few miles south of Richmond, Kentucky, on August 29.

Battle of Richmond, Kentucky, August 30, 1862. Meantime, while Smith was advancing toward Kentucky, William Nelson, then at McMinnville, Tennessee, was ordered on August 16 to turn over the command of his Fourth Division, Army of the Ohio to Jacob Ammen, then return to Kentucky to organize the troops assembling there and drive back the enemy forces invading the state. Nelson assumed command at Lexington August 24, and the next day organized the regiments there into an infantry division, which he designated as First Division. He also called his command the Army of Kentucky. Nelson's division consisted of two infantry brigades and one cavalry brigade and was organized as follows:

Army of Kentucky (or First Division), William Nelson
   First Brigade, Mahlon D. Manson
   Second Brigade, Charles Cruft
   Cavalry Brigade, James S. Jackson

Cruft's brigade was encamped just south of Richmond, Kentucky, and Manson's brigade was two miles farther south on the road to Rogersville and Kingston. At the end of August 1862, Nelson in person was at Lexington, and the two brigades near Richmond were under the command of Manson. At that time Smith's column was approaching Richmond from Big Hill.

During the morning of August 29, 1862, Ruben Munday, who was in command of a small detachment of Federal cavalry about seven or eight miles south of Richmond, became engaged with Smith's cavalry, and by early afternoon he was forced to fall back to the north. At 2:00 P.M. Manson left his camp with his First Brigade and advanced along the road about three miles to Rogersville, driving the enemy cavalry before him. Then, sending his cavalry in pursuit, he bivouacked for the night. During the night, Smith brought up his two infantry divisions and prepared to attack the next morning.

Early on the morning of August 30, 1862, Manson advanced his brigade and formed a defensive line to the left of the road, on a wooded hill, about one and a half miles south of Rogersville, and at 6:00 that morning he ordered Cruft to bring his brigade to the front. Manson placed his leading regiment, the 55th Indiana, on the left of the road, and the 69th Indiana on the right of the road. He sent Edwin O. Lanphere's improvised battery to the left of the 55th Indiana, where it took position on some high ground, and the 71st Indiana formed in its rear in support of the battery and as a reserve. When the 16th Indiana of Manson's brigade came up, it took position on the left of the 55th Indiana in a woods.

Meantime, Cleburne's division, which was at the head of Smith's column, had arrived in front of Manson's line, and Cleburne formed his division, with Benjamin J. Hill's brigade in front and Preston Smith's brigade in reserve. Preston Smith's brigade later moved up on the left of Manson's line. Cleburne's troops then engaged in skirmishing and artillery fire while waiting for Churchill's division to come up. Churchill arrived, with Thomas H. McCray's brigade in front and Evander McNair's brigade in reserve, and took position on the left of Cleburne.

After a time, the enemy artillery ceased firing, and then both Confederate divisions attacked. The 16th Indiana held its ground for about an hour, and when the enemy attempted to turn its flank, the 71st Indiana was moved up to support it. Seven companies of the 69th Indiana were also transferred from the right to the left of the line to join the 71st Indiana. Finally, under the pressure of the attack, the Federal center and right gave way. The left held a short time longer, but it too was forced back in disorder, and then most of the troops fled in disorder toward Richmond. This happened about 10:30 A.M.

Cruft's brigade began to arrive just as the rout became general. The 95th Ohio was sent to occupy the ground previously held by the 69th Indiana to support Manson's right, but it too soon joined in the retreat. The 18th Kentucky of Cruft's brigade was sent to support the left, but after a desperate effort to stem the enemy advance, it was driven back with heavy loss. The two remaining regiments of Cruft's brigade, the 12th Indiana and 66th Indiana, with Luther F. Hale's 6th Battery, Michigan Light Artillery, were later placed in line across the road about one mile to the rear near Rogersville. Manson formed his retreating troops on these two regiments, but he then again retired about three-fourths of a mile and formed a new line, with Cruft's brigade on the right and Manson's brigade on the left. Sometime after noon, the enemy again attacked, and soon Manson's command was forced to fall back toward its camps near Richmond.

While Manson and Cruft were attempting to rally the fleeing men, Nelson arrived on the field and aided in forming a third line just south of Richmond. This last line extended from the left of the road, through the cemetery, and on through the woods on the right. Cruft's brigade was on the left of this line, and Manson's brigade was on the right.

The enemy, who had pursued the fleeing troops, again attacked, routing Nelson's troops and driving them from the field in complete disorder. Nelson was wounded and Manson was captured, and Cruft collected such remnants of the two brigades as he could and led them back to Louisville. E. Kirby Smith moved on to Lexington and then occupied Frankfort.

* * * * * * * * * *

When Smith thus gained control of Central Kentucky, Cumberland Gap was no longer tenable, and on September 17, 1862, Morgan evacuated the fortified position at the gap and retreated northward by way of Manchester to Greenup on the Ohio River.

Meantime, in Tennessee, Buell learned on August 20, 1862 that Bragg was crossing the Tennessee River at Chattanooga, and he ordered McCook to move from Battle Creek up the Sequatchie Valley with his own and Crittenden's divisions. McCook learned, however, that Bragg was at Dunlap, and he returned to Battle Creek. Buell then decided to concentrate his army at Altamont, and he ordered McCook with his two divisions to Pelham. Upon arriving there, McCook found Thomas' First Division, then commanded by Schoepf, and he assumed command of all three divisions.

By August 28, 1862, Bragg had completed the crossing of the Tennessee, and that day he began his march up the Sequatchie Valley toward Central Tennessee. Two days later, Buell ordered the concentration of his army at Murfreesboro. On August 30, the divisions of the Army of the Ohio were at the following places: Schoepf's First Division was at Pelham; Wood's Sixth Division and William Sooy Smith's Fourth Division, both under Thomas, were

at McMinnville; McCook's Second Division was at Altamont; and Crittenden's Fifth Division was at Hillsboro. Rousseau's Third Division, which had been guarding the Nashville and Decatur Railroad, had marched earlier directly to Nashville. On September 5, Buell's entire army had arrived at Murfreesboro. Buell did not remain long at Murfreesboro but continued on to Nashville.

In response to Buell's request for reinforcements, three divisions of William S. Rosecrans' (formerly John Pope's) Army of the Mississippi were sent to join the Army of the Ohio. Jefferson C. Davis' Fourth Division, under the command of Robert B. Mitchell, arrived at Murfreesboro September 1, 1862, and Eleazer A. Paine's First Division, under John M. Palmer, arrived at Nashville September 12. Philip H. Sheridan was given command of a part of Gordon Granger's Fifth Division, consisting of the four regiments of the so-called Pea Ridge Brigade and his own 2nd Michigan Cavalry, and arrived at Louisville on September 14. It did not join Buell's army, however, until the end of the month. For additional information, see Army of the Mississippi (Pope, Rosecrans).

Bragg, in the meantime, had continued his march up the Sequatchie Valley by way of Dunlap and Pikeville. He reached Sparta, Tennessee the same day that Buell arrived at Murfreesboro, fifty miles to the west.

From Bragg's movements, it became evident to Buell that Nashville was not the enemy's objective, but that instead Bragg's army was moving toward Kentucky. Buell then assigned George H. Thomas to command the forces at Nashville, which consisted of Thomas' own First Division, Army of the Ohio, John M. Palmer's First Division, Army of the Mississippi, and the United States Forces at Nashville, commanded by James S. Negley. On September 14, 1862, Negley's command at Nashville was organized into Eighth Division, Army of the Ohio, and Negley was assigned command. Then Buell, with the rest of the Army of the Ohio and Mitchell's Fourth Division, moved northward toward Bowling Green, Kentucky.

Bragg also moved north from Sparta toward Kentucky on a route to the east of that followed by Buell. His army crossed the Cumberland River at Carthage and Gainsboro, Tennessee, then passed through Tompkinsville, Kentucky, reaching Glasgow September 12, 1862. The vanguard of Buell's army entered Bowling Green two days later.

Siege and Capture of Munfordville, Kentucky, September 14–17, 1862. At Munfordville, Kentucky, which was about fifty miles to the east and north of Bowling Green, Federal troops had constructed strong fortifications on the south side of Green River, opposite the town, to protect the crossing of the Louisville and Nashville Railroad. These works extended from the vicinity of Woodsonville on the left around to the railroad crossing on the right. The principal work on this line was Fort Craig, which was on the left near Woodsonville. John T. Wilder commanded the garrison of the works at Munfordville, which was a part of the command of Charles C. Gilbert at Louisville. Wilder's command was designated as United States Forces at Green River.

Buell had hoped to join Wilder at Munfordville, but he was delayed north of Bowling Green by Joseph Wheeler's cavalry, and Bragg arrived there first. At Tompkinsville, on September 12, 1862, James R. Chalmers' brigade, Withers' division of Bragg's Right Wing was sent to Cave City on the Louisville and Nashville Railroad, south of Munfordville. The next day, John S. Scott's cavalry brigade of E. Kirby Smith's army arrived on the north side of the Green River, opposite Wilder's position, and demanded the surrender of the Federal garrison, but Wilder refused.

At daylight the next morning, Chalmers, who had arrived from Cave City, made a furious attack on Wilder's advanced line. It held out for about an hour, and then about 5:30 A.M., fighting became general along the whole line. An hour later, the enemy advanced against Fort Craig but was driven back by a destructive fire from the defenders. A short time later, a second attack was repulsed with heavy losses.

During the morning of September 14, 1862, Wilder was reinforced by six companies of the 50th Indiana under Cyrus L. Dunham, who had been sent down from Louisville by Gilbert. Dunham was the ranking officer, but he directed Wilder to continue in command during the fighting that day, and then he assumed command. There was continued firing along the line during September 14, and that night Chalmers withdrew to Cave City.

The fighting was not renewed September 15, 1862, but that day Bragg ordered his entire army to advance on Munfordville. That night Richard Owen, with the 60th Indiana, arrived from Lebanon Junction to further strengthen Dunham's command.

September 16, 1862, Polk's Right Wing crossed Green River about ten miles above Munfordville, then marched down the north bank of the river to a point on the hills overlooking Dunham's position. Hardee's Left Wing also came up and occupied the hills on the south side of the Federal entrenchments. Nathan B. Forrest's cavalry completed the investment by taking position north of Munfordville to prevent the escape of the garrison to Louisville.

Bragg demanded the surrender of the garrison, and when Dunham reported this to Gilbert, he was relieved from command because the latter feared that Dunham would surrender. Wilder again assumed command, but when he realized that his small force was completely surrounded by Bragg's entire army, he felt compelled to surrender. He did so the next day, September 17, 1862, and this left Bragg's army firmly holding the road between Buell's army and Louisville.

* * * * * * * * *

After Wilder's surrender, Bragg occupied the captured works and remained south of Munfordville for a few days to watch Buell. Buell's army advanced from Bowling Green, but as it approached Munfordville, Bragg began to withdraw September 19, 1862. He marched a short distance north on the road to Louisville, and then, instead of remaining between Buell and Louisville, he turned off to the right and moved by way of Hodgensville and New Haven toward Bardstown, where he arrived September 22.

Back on September 15, when Buell was aware that Bragg was in Kentucky, and not moving on Nashville, he had ordered Thomas at Nashville to move with his division and Palmer's division by way of Bowling Green and rejoin the Army of the Ohio. Later, however, Palmer's division was sent back to Nashville, and Thomas reported with his division to Buell near Munfordville on September 20. James S. Negley assumed command of the troops at Nashville when Thomas departed.

When Bragg turned off the main road to Louisville, he left the way open for Buell. The Army of the Ohio promptly moved northward and by September 29 had arrived safely in the city.

September 29, 1862, Buell announced the reorganization of his army into three army corps as follows: First Corps, Army of the Ohio, to be commanded by Alexander McD. McCook; Second Corps, Army of the Ohio, to be commanded by Thomas L. Crittenden; and Third Corps, Army of the Ohio, to be commanded by Charles C. Gilbert. These corps were organized from the Army of the Ohio, two of the divisions from the Army of the Mississippi, and many new regiments that had arrived at Louisville from the North. James S. Negley's Eighth Division at Nashville and Ebenezer Dumont's Twelfth Division were not attached to an army corps. George H. Thomas was assigned as second in command of the Army of the Ohio. For details of the reorganization, see Army of the Ohio (Buell), and see also below, Battle of Perryville (or Chaplin Hills), Kentucky.

Battle of Perryville (or Chaplin Hills), Kentucky, October 8, 1862. On October 1, 1862, when the reorganization was completed, the Army of the Ohio began its advance from Louisville toward Bardstown, where Bragg's army was resting after its long march northward from Chattanooga. Joshua W. Sill's Second Division of McCook's First Corps marched eastward on the Shelbyville road toward Frankfort to occupy the attention of E. Kirby Smith's forces, and Dumont's Independent Twelfth Division followed close behind.

McCook, with his other two divisions, Lovell H. Rousseau's Third Division and James S. Jackson's Tenth Division, marched out about six miles on the road to Bardstown, then turned off to the left on the Taylorsville road. He continued on this road through Jeffersontown and arrived at Taylorsville, on Salt River, the next day. McCook remained there until October 4, then moved on to Bloomfield, and camped there until October 6.

Crittenden's Second Corps marched on the direct road to Bardstown (present-day U.S. 150), and Gilbert's Third Corps moved on roads to the right through Shepherdsville toward the same place

Meantime, on September 28, 1862, Bragg left Bardstown for Lexington, Kentucky to confer with E. Kirby Smith. When he departed, he left Polk in command of the Confederate Army of the Mississippi at Bardstown, instructing him to fall back to the newly established depot at Bryantsville if confronted by a force too large to safely engage in battle. Each of Buell's columns began skirmishing with enemy cavalry and artillery a few miles outside of Louisville, and both Polk and Bragg were soon aware of the Federal advance. On October 2, Bragg, who did not correctly understand the situation, changed his orders to Polk and directed him to move toward Frankfort instead of Bryantsville. Polk, however, who had a clearer picture of what was happening, decided that such a move was impracticable, and on the afternoon of October 3, he moved out of Bardstown on the road by way of Springfield toward Perryville. The rear of Polk's column had departed from Bardstown only a few hours before Buell's troops began to arrive, but there was heavy skirmishing with the enemy cavalry before Crittenden's corps finally entered the town.

On the Federal left, McCook left Bloomfield October 6, 1862 and marched by way of Chaplin and Willisburg; he reached Mackville, about ten miles from Perryville, the next day. On the right, Crittenden moved out from Bardstown to Springfield and from there to Haysville, which was on the road from Lebanon to Danville. According to his instructions, Crittenden was to have camped at Haysville on the night of October 7, but because no water could be found there, he moved on to a stream about three and a half to four miles from the direct road from Haysville to Perryville. On October 6, Gilbert's corps followed Crittenden to Springfield.

During October 7, 1862, Gilbert's corps, accompanied by Buell, advanced on the road from Springfield, arriving that evening within about four miles of Perryville. Ebenezer Gay's Third Brigade of John Kennett's cavalry division moved ahead of the infantry throughout the day and was stubbornly opposed by enemy cavalry under Joseph Wheeler. Gay finally came up on enemy infantry in strong force on the far side of Doctor's Creek, a tributary of the Chaplin Fork of Salt River, commonly called Chaplin River. Robert B. Mitchell's Ninth Division led the corps during the day, but when the enemy was discovered ahead, Philip H. Sheridan's Eleventh Division passed to the front and halted for the night on the hills on the south side of road. Mitchell's division formed in line of battle across the road that evening, and Albin Schoepf's First Division was in reserve.

Buell then sent orders to McCook at Mackville and Crittenden beyond Haysville to march toward Perryville at 3:00 A.M. October 8, 1862 and take position on the left and right of Gilbert, respectively. The Confederate Army of the Mississippi, with which Polk had marched from Bardstown October 3, was still divided into two wings, but at the time of the battle, the two divisions of Hardee's Left Wing were commanded by Simon B. Buckner and J. Patton Anderson, and Polk's Right Wing consisted of the divisions of Benjamin F. Cheatham (temporarily commanded by Daniel S. Donelson) and Jones M. Withers. When Polk reached Perryville, he ordered Hardee to remain there, then marched on with the Right Wing to Harrodsburg, where he reported to Bragg. Hardee put his troops in position on the high ground east of the Chaplin River, with Buckner's division on the left near Perryville and Anderson's division on the right. It was Hardee's troops that Gilbert found in front of him on the evening of October 7.

Confronted by Gilbert's corps, Hardee asked Bragg for reinforcements, and late in the afternoon of October 7, 1862, Bragg directed Polk to move back to Perryville with Cheatham's division and to send Withers' division on toward Versailles. Bragg also instructed Polk to assume command of all Confederate troops at Perryville and to attack Buell early the next morning. Polk arrived at Perryville before midnight and put his troops in position along a ridge along the east side of the Chaplin River, with his left resting on Perryville, opposite the Federal center. Cheatham's division was on the left, Anderson's division was in the center, and Buckner's division was on the right.

Before proceeding with an account of the Battle of Perryville, it is necessary to describe briefly some of the principal features of the ground over which it was fought. At the time of the battle, as there are today, there were three roads running in from the west to Perryville. The middle of these was the Springfield Pike (or Road), which ran eastward from Springfield to Perryville, and was the road on which Gilbert's corps approached the battlefield on October 7, 1862. This is the route today of U.S. 150. About a mile and three-fourths east of the place where Gilbert halted for the night, the Springfield

Pike crossed a stream called Doctor's Creek a short distance east of the Peters house, then ran up the western slope of Peters Hill. It then continued on, past the Turpin house near the crest of the hill, and descended into the valley of a small stream called Bull Run Creek. It crossed that stream about one mile from Perryville and then ran on into the town. For some distance west of Perryville, the route of the Old Springfield Pike differed from that of present-day U.S. 150. The old road left Perryville one block south of U.S. 150, ran along the southern side of the cemetery, and a short distance beyond crossed to the north side of U.S. 150, not far from the base of Peters Hill. It then ran up the eastern slope of the hill, past the Turpin house near the crest, before descending to the valley of Doctor's Creek on the far side. U.S. 150 today runs along the south side of Peters Hill to Doctor's Creek, near where it rejoins the old route of the Springfield Pike.

The northernmost of the three roads was called the Mackville Pike, which ran in a generally southeasterly direction from the village of Mackville to Perryville. From Wilson's Creek, just west of the battlefield, the road ran a little south of east, crossed the Benton road, and continued on past the Russell house and along the high ground to the edge of the hills overlooking the valley of Doctor's Creek. Beside the road, at the foot of the hill, stood the home of Squire Henry P. Bottom. After crossing the creek, the road turned to the southeast and ran into Perryville. That part of the Old Mackville Pike that runs through the battlefield today is called the Hayes-Mayes Road. In the battlefield area, the present-day New Mackville Pike (Kentucky Road 1920) does not follow the same route as the Old Mackville Pike. It diverges from the latter some distance to the west and runs through the northern edge of the battlefield, just north of the present-day Perryville Battlefield State Shrine and not far from the Chaplin River.

The road farthest to the south, on which Crittenden approached the battlefield, was the Lebanon Pike (present-day Kentucky Route 52). It ran to the northeast from Lebanon to a point about a mile south of Perryville, then ran due north into Perryville on what is today U.S. 68.

Another road of considerable significance during the battle was the Benton road. This road left the Springfield Pike at a point about midway between the Dorsey house, where Buell had established his headquarters, and the crossing of Doctor's Creek, and ran off to the northeast. It crossed the Old Mackville Pike just west of the Russell house and continued on to the Chaplin River, which it crossed about four miles from the Springfield Pike. Buell established his headquarters at the Dorsey house because there he could communicate readily with his left flank by way of the Benton road, and the right flank by way of a nearby crossroad (present-day Short Line Road) that ran south to the Lebanon Pike.

A little more should be said about the Chaplin River and the two smaller streams, Bull Run Creek and Doctor's Creek, that have already been mentioned. Doctor's Creek flowed into the area from the south, then along the south side of the Springfield Pike for about three-fourths of a mile, before crossing to the north side of the pike near the Peters house. From there it flowed to the northeast for about a mile and a half, crossed the Mackville Pike near the Squire Bottom house, and continued on for a little more than a mile until it emptied into the Chaplin River at Walker's Bend.

Bull Run Creek was a smaller stream that also flowed into the area from the south. After crossing the Springfield Pike, it continued on north for about a mile and emptied into Doctor's Creek just south of the Mackville Pike.

The Chaplin River flowed northward through Perryville, then on to the north with some loops and bends for about two and a half miles to a point north of the Crawford house. There it made a great loop to the west and south, then immediately turned back to the west and north to form a second loop, giving the river course the shape of a great letter S. The second loop of the river was known as Walker's Bend, from the Walker farm located in its interior. The outlet road from the farm ran out to the north.

Between Bull Run Creek and the Chaplin River to the east was a range of hills. On the hill between the Springfield Pike and the Mackville Pike, and about midway between the two roads, was the home of Sam Bottom, which gave the hill the name of Sam Bottom Hill. On the morning of October 7, 1862, Hardee sent St. John R. Liddell with his brigade of Buckner's division across the Chaplin River to Sam Bottom Hill. Upon arrival there, Liddell formed his brigade along the top of the slope above

the valley of Bull Run Creek, with its right on the Mackville Pike and its left on the Springfield Pike. In this position it could watch both roads. That afternoon, Liddell sent the 7th Arkansas Regiment out to a position near the Turpin house on Peters Hill.

When Gilbert's corps halted for the night on the Springfield Pike on the evening of October 7, 1862, the troops were in desperate need of water, which was very scarce because of a long drought in that part of Kentucky. That night Buell ordered Sheridan to push on beyond Doctor's Creek early the next morning and gain possession of the pools of water remaining in the stream. At daylight the next morning, October 8, Daniel McCook's Thirty-Sixth Brigade of Sheridan's division, with Charles M. Barnet's Battery I, 2nd Illinois Light Artillery, crossed Doctor's Creek with slight opposition and secured the pools of water. McCook soon found, however, that he could not hold his position unless he could drive the enemy from the hill beyond. McCook's brigade then charged up Peters Hill and drove the 7th Arkansas back to Liddell's main line on Sam Bottom Hill. McCook was in possession of Peters Hill by about 5:00 A.M. For about an hour there was a spirited exchange of artillery fire between Barnet's battery and the enemy artillery on Sam Bottom Hill. At about the time that the firing ended, Sheridan arrived with Bernard Laiboldt's Thirty-Fifth Brigade, Nicholas Greusel's Thirty-Seventh Brigade, and Henry Hescock's Battery G, 1st Missouri Light Artillery.

Liddell reacted quickly to the loss of Peters Hill, and ordered forward the 5th and 7th Arkansas regiments to retake it. They were driven back, however, and by 6:00 A.M. the fighting on that part of the field was over for the morning. By 11:00 A.M. Liddell had withdrawn his brigade to a new position east of the Chaplin River.

Meantime, the other two corps of Buell's army had been marching toward Perryville. Alexander McD. McCook's corps left Mackville at 5:00 A.M. October 8, 1862 and by 9:00 A.M. had arrived within three miles of Perryville, where it halted west of the Benton road. Because of the greater distance that Crittenden's corps had to travel because of its search for water the evening before, it did not arrive on the Lebanon Pike to the south of the Dorsey house until sometime before noon.

At 10:00 A.M. October 8, 1862, Gilbert ordered Mitchell to move forward with his division and take position within supporting distance of Sheridan's division on Peters Hill. Mitchell advanced about two miles, and about noon sent William P. Carlin's Thirty-First Brigade and William W. Caldwell's Thirty-Second Brigade to the right and rear of Sheridan's line, where they formed under cover. Mitchell also sent Michael Gooding's Thirtieth Brigade into the valley north of Doctor's Creek, and close to the creek, where it covered the left of Sheridan's position and watched the interval between Gilbert and McCook.

McCook's corps finally began to arrive on the field about 10:30 A.M., near the close of Sheridan's action on the left. Lovell H. Rousseau's division, which was in the lead, was put in line along the Benton road near the Russell house, some distance to the left of Gilbert. This position was on a hill overlooking the ground toward Doctor's Creek and the Chaplin River. James S. Jackson's division was placed on high ground immediately to the right of the Mackville road, and it was held in column so that it could move promptly to wherever it might be needed.

Upon arriving on the field, McCook was summoned to Buell's headquarters on the Springfield Pike. Rousseau waited for about an hour for his return, then decided to resume the march to the Chaplin River to get water for his men. He advanced William H. Lytle's Seventeenth Brigade, which was on the right of the division line, about a half-mile to Doctor's Creek to obtain water. The 10th Ohio Regiment of Lytle's brigade was sent across to the east side of creek as skirmishers to cover the front of the brigade. Lytle's men soon came under enemy fire, and Leonard A. Harris' Ninth Brigade was sent forward to form on the left of Lytle. Cyrus O. Loomis' 1st Battery, Michigan Light Artillery of Lytle's brigade and Peter Simonson's 5th Battery, Indiana Light Artillery of Harris' brigade were placed on the slope above Doctor's Creek, on the left of the Mackville Pike, and near the center of Rousseau's line.

Only Lytle's and Harris' brigades were with McCook at that time. While McCook's corps was on the march toward Perryville that morning, Jackson's division moved into the road at Mackville behind Rousseau's two leading brigades, thus separating them from John C. Starkweather's 28th Brigade (Rousseau's other brigade, which was at the rear of the division), which was then forced to follow Jackson. As a result, Starkweather did not arrive on the field and take position until about 1:30 P.M., shortly before the battle began.

When Starkweather arrived on the Mackville Pike, he was sent up the Benton road about a half-mile to a point on a hill where the road turns abruptly to the west. There he formed his brigade in line along the road. David C. Stone's Battery A, Kentucky Light Artillery was posted at the bend of the road, and Asahel K. Bush's 4th Battery, Indiana Light Artillery was in position to the left of Stone. To the left of Starkweather's position was a deep ravine through which flowed Wilson's Creek, ahead was an open cornfield, and on the right was the line of Harris' brigade.

When McCook returned from Buell's headquarters, he ordered Jackson, with William R. Terrill's Thirty-Third Brigade and Charles C. Parsons' battery of Terrill's brigade, to take position on some high ground about 600 yards from the Chaplin River, and to send forward skirmishers to obtain water. McCook also placed George Webster's Thirty-Fourth Brigade, with Samuel J. Harris' 19th Battery, Indiana Light Artillery of the brigade, to the left of the Russell house, in rear of the center of Rousseau's line.

By about 1:30, only a short time before the enemy attack began, McCook had his troops in position as follows: Lytle's brigade was on the extreme right, across the Mackville Pike, on the slope of the hill a short distance above Doctor's Creek, and its right was near the so-called "Burnt Barn," which stood in a field on the right of the Mackville Pike on the slope above the Squire Bottom house. Lytle's brigade was separated from Sheridan's division on Peters Hill by a distance of about one-half mile. Harris' brigade extended McCook's line northward from the left of Lytle's brigade along a ridge toward Terrill's position. Terrill's brigade was on the left of the line, overlooking the Chaplin River at Walker's Bend, with its right on a wooded knoll, and its left bent back to hold the high ground to the left and rear.

The first of Crittenden's troops did not arrive near Perryville until about 11:00 A.M. October 8, 1862. At that time William Sooy Smith's Fourth Division arrived on the Lebanon Pike to the south of Sheridan's position and took position on the right of the pike and on the extreme right of Buell's line. Horatio P. Van Cleve's Fifth Division came up next and about 1:00 P.M. formed on the left of the road and on the left of Smith's division. Thomas J. Wood's Sixth Division, which had marched all the night before in order to reach camp, required some rest, and it was not until between 3:00 and 4:00 P.M. October 8 that it moved into line on the left of Van Cleve and to the right of Sheridan.

Meantime, back at Harrodsburg, Bragg had waited for the sounds of Polk's battle, which he had ordered for early that morning, and as the hours passed with no indication that a battle was in progress, he hurried forward to Perryville. He arrived there at 10:00 A.M. and, displeased with Polk's arrangements, immediately began the regrouping of his troops for an attack.

Cheatham's division, which consisted of the brigades of Donelson (commanded by John H. Savage), Alexander P. Stewart, and George Maney, was transferred from the Confederate left to the far right. The brigades marched north from Perryville along the Chaplin River to the Crawford house, then crossed the river, continuing the march northward to the vicinity of the Goodnight house. The division was then moved across the Chaplin River into Walker's Bend when it was learned the Buell's left extended still farther to the northwest.

Samuel Powell's and Daniel W. Adams' brigades of Anderson's division were on the Confederate left, with one brigade on each side of the Springfield Pike, facing Gilbert's corps. Adams' brigade took position on Sam Bottom Hill, where Liddell's brigade had been earlier in the day. Buckner, with the brigades of Bushrod R. Johnson and Patrick R. Cleburne, was on the hills on the Confederate right of the Mackville Pike and in front of its crossing of Doctor's Creek. Liddell's brigade was in reserve. Buckner's brigades were in front of Lytle's brigade of Rousseau's division.

John C. Brown's and Thomas M. Jones' brigades of Anderson's division, and Sterling A. M. Wood's brigade of Buckner's division were detached from their commands and occupied the interval between the right of Buckner's position and the left of Cheatham's division.

Finally, a little before 2:00 P.M. October 8, 1862,

hours after the expected time, Bragg launched a vigorous attack all along the front of McCook's corps. This was particularly severe on McCook's left, where Cheatham's division advanced from Walker's Bend. Donelson's brigade, which moved first, crossed the Chaplin River and climbed the steep bluff beyond, at the top of which there was a stretch of level ground. Beyond this bench or shelf there were several rises and depressions, and beyond these McCook was forming his left flank. Donelson halted briefly at the top of the bluff, then advanced in line of battle over the last rise and into the open ground in front of McCook's surprised troops. Donelson was surprised, too, because he had expected to outflank McCook's line, but instead he advanced straight into the left flank. Parsons' battery off to Donelson's right opened with a heavy fire that struck Donelson's right flank, while Harris' battery on the left fired into his left flank. This fire, combined with the infantry fire of the 2nd and 33rd Ohio of Harris' brigade and the 24th Illinois and 79th Pennsylvania of Starkweather's brigade, forced Donelson to fall back.

Stewart's brigade, which was following Donelson, moved up on his right. Maney's brigade, moving around through the woods, came up on the right of Stewart and quickly surprised Parsons' battery and the 123rd Illinois of Terrill's brigade of Jackson's division. Cheatham's entire division then advanced and, with furious fighting, slowly drove McCook's left back toward the Mackville Pike. Jackson was killed at the first onslaught, and by 2:30 P.M. Terrill's brigade was hard-pressed. A short time later it was driven back in confusion across a cornfield to its rear, losing Parsons' battery. About 3:30 P.M. Terrill was killed while attempting to rally his troops near the position of Starkweather's batteries at the bend of the Benton road.

The right of Cheatham's division then struck Starkweather's brigade, which, with the aid of the cross fire from Stone's and Bush's batteries, held its ground for some time. Finally, however, at about 4:00 P.M., it was forced to retire to the vicinity of the Russell house on the Mackville Pike. Maney's brigade gained the crest formerly occupied by Starkweather's brigade, but Stewart's brigade on his left was driven back by a heavy fire from regiments of George Webster's brigade of Jackson's division,

Leonard A. Harris' brigade of Rousseau's division, and Samuel J. Harris' battery of Webster's brigade. With the left of Maney's brigade thus exposed, it too was forced to fall back, and the fighting on that part of the field ended for the day.

According to Bragg's plan of attack, Jones' brigade of Anderson's division was to follow up Cheatham's attack by advancing on his left. Jones crossed Doctor's Creek near the Widow Bottom house, turned to the left, and soon encountered the 10th Wisconsin of Harris' brigade and the 42nd Indiana of Lytle's brigade posted on high ground beyond a feature of the battlefield known as the "sinkhole" (now filled in). With these brigades was Simonson's battery, and when Jones approached their line, all opened fire. Soon Jones was driven back with heavy losses and up the hill from which his attack started.

After Jones' brigade had crossed Doctor's Creek and started its attack, Buckner ordered Bushrod R. Johnson's brigade to move forward on its left. Johnson's brigade moved forward from the hill on which the Chatham house stood, crossed Doctor's Creek near Squire Bottom's house, and took position behind a stone wall above the creek. Buckner had also ordered Daniel Adams' brigade to move to its right from its position on Sam Bottom Hill and attack the right of McCook's corps, and it was waiting in position there when Bushrod R. Johnson arrived.

On the hill above the Squire Bottom house, Lytle's brigade was deployed with his regiments on both sides of the Mackville Pike. The 3rd Ohio was between the road and the "Burnt Barn" about 200 yards to the west, and the 15th Kentucky was in rear of the 3rd Ohio. The 10th Ohio was formed across the road from the 3rd Ohio, and the 42nd Indiana was on its left. The 88th Indiana was farther to the rear on the east side of the road.

There was severe fighting for some time as Johnson's and Adams' brigades attempted to drive back Lytle's brigade. Then at 3:15 P.M., Buckner ordered forward the brigades of Brown and Cleburne. Brown crossed Doctor's Creek and advanced to the hill where Jones had been repulsed a short time before. Cleburne's brigade advanced on the left of Brown in support of Johnson. Lytle, thus struck on his front and right flank, was slowly forced back to the east side of the Mackville Pike

and then northward along the road until at 4:00 P.M. he was on his original line near the Russell house. Harris' brigade on the left of Lytle repulsed several attacks, and then it too gave way. During its withdrawal, Webster's brigade changed front and moved to the right to aid Harris, but finally both brigades were driven back to a line near the Russell house. From their new position, the Federal troops delivered a terrible fire on the advancing enemy, and Adams' and Cleburne's brigades began to withdraw down the hill toward Doctor's Creek. Moments later, Wood's brigade struck Webster's brigade and drove it back. While attempting to rally his men, Webster was mortally wounded about 5:30 P.M., and he was succeeded in command of the brigade by William P. Reid.

During the afternoon, Loomis' battery was placed near the Russell house, and William A. Hotchkiss' battery and Gay's cavalry brigade a short distance farther west, and they did good service in repelling the enemy attacks during the evening.

Liddell's brigade had been held in reserve since its action at Sam Bottom Hill that morning, and at 5:00 P.M., when the Confederate attack on the left had been stalled, it was ordered forward from its position east of the Chatham Hill. It moved forward across the hill and then Doctor's Creek, and up the hill on the far side toward the Benton road.

Despite an urgent request from McCook for help, Gilbert refused to send troops, because at that time Sheridan's division on Peters Hill was under attack by Samuel Powell's Confederate brigade. Sometime after 4:30 that evening, when the enemy attack had been repulsed, Gilbert sent Michael Gooding's Thirtieth Brigade of Robert B. Mitchell's Ninth Division from its position on Doctor's Creek, to the left and rear of Sheridan's line, to support McCook. He also ordered Schoepf's division to move into the interval between Sheridan and McCook, and Schoepf ordered Moses B. Walker, commanding his leading brigade, to replace Gooding's departing brigade.

Gooding's brigade arrived on the left of McCook at about the same time that Starkweather's brigade withdrew. Gooding formed his line on the right of the Benton road a short distance east of its intersection with the Mackville Pike. Then, when he saw Harris' brigade engaged with Wood's brigade, Gooding ordered his brigade forward, and when it reached the top of the hill near the Mackville Pike it opened fire on Wood's men and brought them to a halt. Fierce fighting continued, however, and Oscar F. Pinney's 5th Battery, Wisconsin Light Artillery of Gooding's brigade was brought up to a small hill in rear of the brigade line to add its fire to that of the infantry.

When Gooding's brigade arrived on McCook's left, the brigades of Rousseau's and Jackson's divisions withdrew to a new position a short distance to the northeast of, and roughly parallel to, the Benton road. A short time later Liddell's brigade came up in rear of Wood's brigade, and then at 6:00 P.M. it moved to the right of Wood's brigade and resumed the attack. The contest continued without significant results until the fighting ended at dark. At about that time, Gooding was captured.

James B. Steedman's Third Brigade of Schoepf's division had been ordered to follow Gooding and support McCook, but it arrived too late to be engaged that evening.

At 3:30 P.M. Powell's brigade of Anderson's division arrived at its assigned position south of the Springfield Pike, about three-fourths of a mile from Sheridan's position on Peters Hill. Powell then deployed his brigade on a hill just south of Sam Bottom Hill, which had been occupied that morning by Liddell's brigade. For a time, Powell's artillery exchanged fire with Hescock's and Barnett's batteries on Peters Hill. This was followed by a lull, and then about 4:15 P.M. Powell's infantry emerged from the timber in which it had formed and moved obliquely down the hill toward Sheridan's position.

After reaching the bottom of the hill, the brigade crossed Bull Run Creek, crossed a cornfield south of the Springfield Pike, and moved up the slope on the far side. When the troops reached the crest of the hill, they came under a heavy fire from Hescock's and Barnett's guns. Powell's line then fell back, but the troops re-formed and again charged across the cornfield and up the hill. Again they were met by a murderous artillery fire, and once again they fell back. Powell's men charged across the cornfield a third time, but on the far side they were struck by a heavy infantry fire and forced to take cover behind a rail fence. Some troops of the 88th Illinois of Greusel's Thirty-Seventh Brigade moved forward to a new position, from which they opened with a deadly fire on the men behind the fence, preventing any further advance.

By this time, Mitchell had received a request from Sheridan for help, and he promptly moved up with William P. Carlin's Thirty-First Brigade and William W. Caldwell's Thirty-Second Brigade to the right of Sheridan. His other brigade, under Gooding, as has been noted, was sent from Doctor's Creek to reinforce McCook. Carlin's brigade was placed on the first line, and Caldwell's brigade to his rear. Mitchell then ordered Carlin to advance toward Powell's position.

Off to the right, about a half-mile from Sheridan's position, George D. Wagner's Twenty-First Brigade of Thomas J. Wood's Sixth Division had arrived and taken position on the extreme left of Crittenden's corps. Wagner had observed Powell's movement and had sent the 40th Indiana of his brigade and Jerome B. Cox's 10th Battery, Indiana Light Artillery to occupy a hill about 600 yards distant. Cox's battery arrived first and began to shell Powell's line.

When Carlin's brigade arrived at the crest of a hill above Powell's position, it opened fire, and soon thereafter the enemy began to give way and fall back toward Perryville.

It was at that time, when the threat on Gilbert's front was over, that Gilbert sent Gooding's brigade to report to McCook, as mentioned above.

Greusel's brigade was involved in some of the heaviest fighting that evening and sustained heavy losses. Carlin pursued Powell's retreating troops almost to Perryville. The 15th Wisconsin and 21st Illinois, which were in the lead of Carlin's brigade, finally reached a hill about 600 yards from the town. Shortly after sundown, these two regiments, being unsupported, fell back and rejoined Carlin's brigade. During the pursuit, Wagner's brigade had followed Carlin, but both brigades were prevented from advancing by a heavy enemy fire, and they bivouacked for the night in their forward position.

With the exception of Wagner's brigade, Crittenden's corps was not engaged during the day. Charles G. Harker's Twentieth Brigade of Wood's division moved up about dark to support Wagner, but it was not in action.

The Army of the Ohio was poorly handled at the Battle of Perryville. Buell, who had been injured during the march to Perryville, spent the entire day at his headquarters, some two to two and one-half miles in rear of the army, and until around 4:00 P.M. had little or no knowledge of affairs at the front.

Certainly, only at 4:00 P.M. did he learn of McCook's battle, which had been in progress for two hours. Although only nine of Buell's twenty-three brigades had been seriously engaged on October 8, he allowed Bragg to withdraw from the field that night without molestation.

The organization of the Army of the Ohio at the Battle of Perryville October 8, 1862 was as follows:

ARMY OF THE OHIO
Don Carlos Buell
George H. Thomas, Second in Command

FIRST CORPS, Alexander McD. McCook

Second Division, Joshua W. Sill
  Fourth Brigade, Harvey M. Buckley
  Fifth Brigade, Edward N. Kirk
  Sixth Brigade, William H. Gibson
  Artillery
    Battery A, 1st Ohio Light Artillery, Wilbur F. Goodspeed
    Battery E, 1st Ohio Light Artillery, Warren P. Edgarton
    Battery H, 5th United States Artillery, Francis L. Guenther

Note. Sill's division marched from Louisville toward Frankfort, Kentucky October 1, 1862 and did not rejoin the corps until October 11. It was not present at the Battle of Perryville.

Third Division, Lovell H. Rousseau
  Ninth Brigade, Leonard A. Harris
  Seventeenth Brigade, William H. Lytle, wounded and captured
    Curran Pope
  Twenty-Eighth Brigade, John C. Starkweather

Note. Peter Simonson's 5th Battery, Indiana Light Artillery was attached to Harris' brigade; Cyrus O. Loomis' 1st Battery, Michigan Light Artillery was attached to Lytle's brigade; and David C. Stone's Battery A, Kentucky Light Artillery was attached to Starkweather's brigade.

Tenth Division, James S. Jackson, killed
  Albert S. Hall
  Thirty-Third Brigade, William R. Terrill, killed
    Albert S. Hall
    Thomas G. Allen
  Thirty-Fourth Brigade, George Webster, killed
    William P. Reid

Note. Charles C. Parsons' Battery (improvised) was attached to Terrill's brigade, and Samuel J. Harris' 19th Battery, Indiana Light Artillery was attached to Webster's brigade.

SECOND CORPS, Thomas L. Crittenden

Fourth Division, William Sooy Smith
  Tenth Brigade, William Grose
  Nineteenth Brigade, William B. Hazen
  Twenty-Second Brigade, Charles Cruft

Note 1. Samuel Canby's Battery H, 4th United States Artillery and John Mendenhall's Battery M, 4th United States Artillery were attached to Grose's brigade; Daniel T. Cockerill's Battery F, 1st Ohio Light Artillery was attached to Hazen's brigade; and William E. Standart's Battery B, 1st Ohio Light Artillery was attached to Cruft's brigade.

Note 2. Fourth Division was on the field of Perryville but was not engaged.

Fifth Division, Horatio P. Van Cleve
  Eleventh Brigade, Samuel Beatty
  Fourteenth Brigade, Pierce B. Hawkins
  Twenty-Third Brigade, Stanley Matthews
  Artillery
    7th Battery, Indiana Light Artillery, George R. Swallow
    Battery B, Pennsylvania Light Artillery, Alanson J. Stevens
    3rd Battery, Wisconsin Light Artillery, Lucius H. Drury

Note. Fifth Division was on the field of Perryville but was not engaged.

Sixth Division, Thomas J. Wood
  Fifteenth Brigade, Milo S. Hascall
  Twentieth Brigade, Charles G. Harker
  Twenty-First Brigade, George D. Wagner

Note 1. George Estep's 8th Battery, Indiana Light Artillery was attached to Hascall's brigade; Cullen Bradley's 6th Battery, Ohio Light Artillery was attached to Harker's brigade; and Jerome B. Cox's 10th Battery, Indiana Light Artillery was attached to Wagner's brigade.

Note 2. Only Wagner's brigade of Wood's division was engaged at Perryville. It was briefly in action at the close of Sheridan's battle on the far Federal right, late in the evening.

THIRD CORPS, Charles C. Gilbert

First Division, Albin Schoepf
  First Brigade, Moses B. Walker
  Second Brigade, Speed S. Fry

Third Brigade, James B. Steedman
Artillery
  4th Battery, Michigan Light Artillery, Josiah W. Church
  Battery C, 1st Ohio Light Artillery, Daniel K. Southwick
  Battery I, 4th United States Artillery, Frank G. Smith

Note. Schoepf's division was on the field of Perryville and was under fire, but it was not seriously engaged.

Ninth Division, Robert B. Mitchell
  Thirtieth Brigade, Michael Gooding, captured
  Thirty-First Brigade, William P. Carlin
  Thirty-Second Brigade, William W. Caldwell

Note 1. P. Sidney Post later assumed command of Gooding's brigade.
Note 2. Gooding's brigade was heavily engaged late in the evening and suffered severe losses. Carlin's brigade also saw some action late in the day.
Note 3. Oscar F. Pinney's 5th Battery, Wisconsin Light Artillery was attached to Gooding's brigade; William A. Hotchkiss' 2nd Battery, Minnesota Light Artillery was attached to Carlin's brigade; and Stephen J. Carpenter's 8th Battery, Wisconsin Light Artillery was attached to Caldwell's brigade.

Eleventh Division, Philip H. Sheridan
  Thirty-Fifth Brigade, Bernard Laiboldt
  Thirty-Sixth Brigade, Daniel McCook
  Thirty-Seventh Brigade, Nicholas Greusel
Artillery
  Battery I, 2nd Illinois Light Artillery, Charles M. Barnett
  Battery G, 1st Missouri Light Artillery, Henry Hescock

UNATTACHED TO CORPS OF THE ARMY

Eighth Division, James S. Negley
  Seventh Brigade, John F. Miller
  Twenty-Ninth Brigade, Timothy R. Stanley
Artillery
  Battery B, Kentucky Light Artillery, George W. Nell
  Battery M, 1st Ohio Light Artillery, Frederick Schultz
  Battery G, 1st Ohio Light Artillery, Alexander Marshall

Note. Negley's division was at Nashville, Tennessee.

Twelfth Division, Ebenezer Dumont
  Thirty-Eighth Brigade, Marshal W. Chapin

Thirty-Ninth Brigade, George T. Limberg
Fortieth Brigade, Abram O. Miller
Ward's Brigade, William T. Ward
Artillery
  Stokes' Battery, Illinois Light Artillery, James H. Stokes
  13th Battery, Indiana Light Artillery, Benjamin S. Nicklin
  18th Battery, Indiana Light Artillery, Eli Lilly

Note. Dumont's division followed Sill's division toward Frankfort, Kentucky and was not present at the Battle of Perryville.

Cavalry Division, John Kennett
  First Brigade, Edward M. McCook
  Second Brigade, Lewis Zahm
  Third Brigade, Ebenezer Gay

Thirteenth Division, John M. Palmer
  First Brigade, George W. Roberts
  Second Brigade, James D. Morgan

Note 1. Thirteenth Division was organized from First Division, Army of the Mississippi, and was at Nashville, Tennessee.
Note 2. Yates V. Beebe's 10th Battery, Wisconsin Light Artillery was attached to Roberts' brigade, and Charles Houghtaling's Battery C, 1st Illinois Light Artillery was attached to Morgan's brigade.

Forces at the Post of Nashville
Artillery
  11th Battery, Indiana Light Artillery, Arnold Sutermeister
  12th Battery, Indiana Light Artillery, James E. White
  5th Battery, Michigan Light Artillery, John J. Ely
  Battery A, Tennessee Light Artillery, Ephraim P. Abbott
Infantry and Calvary
  10th Tennessee, Alvan C. Gillem
  Nashville Union Guard; Fry's Kentucky Scouts; and a detachment of 50th Indiana Infantry
  5th Kentucky Cavalry (five companies), William B. Stokes
  6th Kentucky Cavalry (seven companies), Dennis J. Halisy

End of the Campaign. At midnight October 8, 1862, Bragg began preparations to withdraw from Perryville, and early the next morning the army marched toward Harrodsburg. Bragg halted about eight miles from Perryville and took up a defensive position, but when Buell did not pursue, he moved on to Harrodsburg, where he was joined by E. Kirby Smith's army on October 10. That night the combined forces marched toward Bryantsville.

Meantime, Buell ordered his army across the Chaplin River, but he decided to delay any further advance until Sill's division arrived from Frankfort. He ordered Dumont's division to remain at Frankfort. While awaiting Sill, who did not arrive until October 11, Buell put the Army of the Ohio in position with its right four miles from Danville, its center on the Perryville-Harrodsburg road (present-day U.S. 68), and its left near Duckville, where it covered the roads converging on Harrodsburg.

October 11, 1862, a cavalry force, supported by infantry, sent out on a reconnaissance found Bragg's troops in position about two miles from Harrodsburg, but they withdrew during the day to Bryantsville. The next day Buell ordered McCook's corps to Harrodsburg, Crittenden's corps to the left and rear of Danville, and Gilbert's corps to a point about midway between the two towns.

Bragg remained at Bryantsville October 12, 1862, and the next day began the withdrawal of the army from Kentucky. The head of his column reached Cumberland Gap October 19, then moved on to Knoxville, Tennessee.

Buell learned of Bragg's departure from Bryantsville October 14, 1862, and immediately ordered his troops in pursuit. Wood's division of Crittenden's corps marched at 12:00 that night and engaged a force of enemy cavalry and artillery at Stanford the next morning. The rest of Crittenden's corps and McCook's corps followed Wood's division through Danville and Stanford to Crab Orchard, and Gilbert's corps marched by way of Lancaster to the same place. McCook and Gilbert halted at Crab Orchard, while Crittenden followed the retreating enemy to London on the direct road and to Manchester on a branch road.

The pursuit ended at London, and then the Army of the Ohio was ordered to turn back and march to Glasgow and Bowling Green. Buell returned to Louisville and left Thomas to direct the movements of the army. McCook marched back by way of Stanford, Lebanon, Somerville, and Cave City to Bowling Green; Gilbert followed the same route to Bowling Green, except that he marched by way of Campbellsville instead of Somerville. Crittenden marched back from London through Somerset, Co-

lumbia, and Edmonton to Glasgow. The cavalry was left at London to refit. For additional information, see First Corps, Second Corps, and Third Corps, Army of the Ohio.

On October 24, 1862, the Department of the Cumberland was re-created from a part of the territory of the discontinued Department of the Mississippi and such parts of northern Alabama and Georgia as might be occupied by Federal troops. This territory included that of the District of the Ohio, to which the Army of the Ohio technically belonged, and when William S. Rosecrans assumed command of the Department of the Cumberland October 30, he relieved Buell in command of the Army of the Ohio. Buell's Army of the Ohio, when Rosecrans assumed command, was designated as Fourteenth Corps, Department of the Cumberland, but it was commonly called the Army of the Cumberland.

KNOXVILLE, TENNESSEE CAMPAIGN NOVEMBER 4, 1863– DECEMBER 23, 1863

After Ambrose E. Burnside, with his Army of the Ohio, had driven forces under Samuel Jones from East Tennessee in October 1863, he repositioned his troops for a better defense and administration of the region, and he also made some changes in their organization. For details of the organization and operations of Burnside's forces in East Tennessee prior to October 20, 1863, see East Tennessee Campaign (Burnside).

The principal movements of the army in October and early November 1863 were as follows:

On October 21, 1863, James M. Shackelford's Fourth Division (cavalry), Twenty-Third Corps, which had advanced to Bristol, had moved back to Jonesboro, where William A. Hoskins' brigade was left to support the cavalry.

Orlando B. Willcox's division of Indiana troops remained at Greeneville, and in October 1863 it was designated as Left Wing Forces in East Tennessee. Its organization was as follows:

Left Wing Forces, Orlando B. Willcox
First Brigade, John R. Mahan
Second Brigade, William A. Hoskins
Troops not brigaded
    23rd Battery, Indiana Light Artillery, James H. Myers
    12th Battery, Michigan Light Artillery, Edward G. Hillier
    21st Battery, Ohio Light Artillery, James W. Patterson
    3rd Indiana Cavalry (two companies)

By October 20, 1863, Ninth Corps had returned to Knoxville, but on that date Edward Ferrero's First Division marched to Loudon Bridge on the Tennessee River, and two days later Simon G. Griffin's Second Division also arrived at Loudon Bridge. Upon its arrival, Ferrero's division crossed the river and occupied Loudon. While at Loudon in October 1863, Joshua K. Sigfried assumed command of Second Division during the temporary absence of Griffin, and Thomas B. Allard assumed command of Sigfried's First Brigade, Second Division.

Julius White's Second Division of Twenty-Third Corps had moved to Loudon September 21, 1863, and at the end of October it was on the Tennessee River between Loudon and Kingston.

Milo S. Hascall's Third Division, Twenty-Third Corps, which consisted of Samuel A. Gilbert's First Brigade (commanded by James W. Reilly after October 14, 1863) and Daniel Cameron's Second Brigade, was withdrawn from its position at Carter's Station and at the end of October was at Knoxville.

Shackelford's cavalry division of Twenty-Third Corps, except Robert K. Byrd's First Brigade, was in the field in East Tennessee at the end of October. Byrd's brigade was at Kingston, where Byrd was in command of the post.

On October 27, 1863, Burnside decided to abandon temporarily the valley of the Tennessee River below Loudon and withdraw to a stronger position along the northern bank of the river from Kingston to Lenoir's Station (present-day Lenoir City). The latter was about six miles northeast of Loudon and about twenty-five miles from Knoxville.

On October 28, 1863, all Federal troops at Loudon crossed to the north bank of the Tennessee River. The pontoon bridge there was taken up and moved to Knoxville, where it was laid across the Holston River near the mouth of First Creek to provide a ready communication between the two banks of the river. Burnside then sent Samuel R. Mott's First Brigade of Julius White's Second Division, Twenty-Third Corps to reinforce Byrd's troops at Kingston, and he left White, with Marshal W. Chapin's Second Brigade of his division, on the north side of the Tennessee River opposite Loudon.

Burnside also ordered Robert B. Potter's Ninth Corps to Lenoir's Station, where all of the corps had arrived by October 31, 1863, except Wilson C. Lemert's Third Brigade, Second Division, which was at Cumberland Gap.

The pontoon bridge across the Holston was completed November 1, 1863, and that day William P. Sanders crossed to the south side of the river with Frank Wolford's First Brigade and Charles D. Pennebaker's Third Brigade of the newly reorganized First Cavalry Division to guard the country down to the Little Tennessee River. Also on November 1, Cameron's brigade of Twenty-Third Corps crossed the river and occupied the heights on the south side opposite Knoxville.

On November 1, 1863, Israel Garrard was in command of a cavalry brigade at Rogersville, Tennessee, and on November 6 he was totally defeated by a Confederate force under William E. Jones and Henry L. Giltner, with the loss of a great part of his command, including four pieces of artillery. Following his defeat, Garrard returned with the remnants of his brigade to Morristown, and Willcox with his Left Wing was ordered to Bull's Gap. Thereafter, until November 17, operations in the area were confined to cavalry actions, skirmishing, and foraging.

On November 3, 1863, Burnside announced the temporary organization of the mounted forces with his army in East Tennessee into a Cavalry Corps, as follows:

CAVALRY CORPS, James M. Shackelford

First Division, William P. Sanders
    First Brigade, Frank Wolford
    Second Brigade, Robert K. Byrd

Third Brigade, Charles D. Pennebaker

Second Division, James P. T. Carter
  First Brigade, Israel Garrard
  Second Brigade, John W. Foster

When the reorganization was effected, however, it appears that John W. Foster assumed command of Second Division, and Horace Capron assumed command of Second Brigade.

On November 5, 1863, Felix W. Graham's cavalry command was ordered to fall back on Hoskins' brigade at Rheatown, Tennessee. Shackelford then moved up in support with the main body of his cavalry.

Advance of Longstreet toward Knoxville. On November 3, 1863, Braxton Bragg detached James Longstreet's corps from the Army of Tennessee, which was then besieging Chattanooga, and ordered him to move with his two divisions and Joseph Wheeler, with four brigades of his cavalry, to East Tennessee to capture or disperse the Union army commanded by Burnside. On November 4, Lafayette McLaws' division marched to Tyner's Station for movement by rail to Sweetwater (Sweet Water), Tennessee, and Hood's division, commanded by Micah Jenkins, marched to the railroad tunnel through Missionary Ridge, where it was to take the cars to the same destination. Longstreet's movement began very slowly, however, because of a lack of rail transportation. Trains for McLaws' division were not ready until November 5, and his brigades did not reach Sweetwater until November 6–8. When Jenkins arrived at the tunnel, there were no trains at all, and on November 6–8 the troops finally marched to Cleveland, Tennessee, hoping to find cars along the way. Longstreet finally reached Sweetwater, but his last brigade did not come up until November 12. Wheeler's cavalry arrived there November 11.

Before proceeding with a description of the movements of the armies as Longstreet advanced toward Knoxville, it will be helpful to note some of the more important features of the country through which he passed. A few miles east of Loudon, the Holston River, which flows past Knoxville, and the Little Tennessee River come together to form the Tennessee River, which flows westward to Kings-

ton before turning to the southwest toward Chattanooga. It is important to note that this description of the origin of the Tennessee River was accepted in the area at the time of the Civil War, but it should be emphasized that there is no way of stating exactly where the river begins. In 1889 the Tennessee legislature declared that Kingsport, in Sullivan County, was the upper limit of the Tennessee River, which in effect changed the name of the Holston River of Civil War times to the Tennessee River.

The East Tennessee and Georgia Railroad from Chattanooga to Knoxville crossed the Tennessee River at Loudon, about thirty-five miles from Knoxville, then ran along the north bank of the Tennessee and Holston rivers to that city.

West of the railroad and parallel to it is a spur of the Clinch Mountain range, through which several wagon roads run by way of gaps or passes. On the west side of this spur, and near its base, is the main road from Loudon to Knoxville, which ran about seventeen miles to Campbell's Station. There it joined the Kingston and Chattanooga road, which passed through a gap and joined the wagon road that ran along with the railroad east of the mountain spur at Campbell's Station.

Longstreet planned to advance on Knoxville from Sweetwater by crossing the Little Tennessee River above its confluence with the Holston River and march by way of Maryville to the hills on the east side of the Holston River, opposite Knoxville. The transportation for the pontoons, however, did not arrive at Sweetwater, and Longstreet decided to cross the Tennessee River with his infantry at a point near the railroad and march directly on Knoxville. He found, however, that the Little Tennessee was fordable by cavalry, and he decided to send Wheeler in that direction.

Wheeler had established pickets along the Tennessee River from Loudon to a point below Kingston, where a strong Federal force held the north bank of the river. On November 12, 1863, Wheeler was ordered to leave his pickets along the river, cross the Little Tennessee at the fords with the rest of his command, and advance to Maryville. He was to capture the Union outpost there, and ride up the east side of the Holston River and occupy the heights overlooking the city.

At dark on November 13, 1863, Wheeler, with most of his four brigades, moved out on a night march toward Maryville. He crossed the Little Tennessee at Motley's Ford, and upon reaching Maryville, George G. Dibrell's brigade scattered the 11th Kentucky Cavalry that was in position there. In a short time John T. Morgan's brigade was engaged with Wolford's cavalry brigade, which was the main Federal force in the area. At dawn November 14, Wheeler crossed Little River and marched north to carry out the rest of his order, which was to seize and hold the hills overlooking Knoxville on the southeast. As Wheeler advanced from Maryville, he soon encountered Wolford's and Pennebaker's brigades of Sanders' cavalry division, which fell back behind Stock Creek and burned the bridge. Wheeler dismounted half of his cavalry, advanced across the creek, pushed back Sanders' cavalry, and moved up to the heights opposite Knoxville. He then made an unsuccessful attack on the left flank of the Federal line, and a short time later he withdrew to the north bank of the Holston River at Louisville. He rejoined Longstreet's command on November 17.

On November 12, 1863, most of Longstreet's infantry had arrived at Sweetwater, and he then issued orders for an advance at daylight November 13 along the line of the railroad toward Knoxville. The troops at the rear moved up during the night, and they continued on to join Longstreet as soon as they had cooked their breakfast. The head of Jenkins' column halted near Loudon and remained concealed from the Federal pickets during the day of November 13. At dark a detachment of Jenkins' brigade, then commanded by John Bratton, was sent out to capture the Federal pickets at Huff's Ferry. A regiment then crossed the Tennessee River to cover the laying of a pontoon bridge, and as soon as it was completed, Jenkins' division crossed to the north bank of the river and constructed breastworks for the protection of the bridge. McLaws' division marched during the night of November 13 and arrived at Loudon at 5:00 A.M. November 14. It bivouacked about a mile and a half from the town and crossed the river on the morning of November 15.

On the evening of November 13, 1863, as Longstreet approached Huff's Ferry, Chapin's brigade of White's division, Twenty-Third Corps was encamped on the north side of the Tennessee River, opposite Loudon, where it was engaged in picketing the river from Huff's Ferry to Blair's Ford. Just before

daylight the next morning, however, White was ordered to march with Chapin's brigade to Lenoir's Station.

Early on the morning of November 14, 1863, Potter, who was then at Lenoir's Station with his Ninth Corps, learned that the enemy had crossed the river at Huff's Ferry, and he ordered his troops to be ready to move. A short time later he started his trains toward Knoxville under a strong guard. About 9:00 A.M., White came in from near Loudon with Chapin's brigade.

Also on the morning of November 14, Burnside, who was at Knoxville, received information that the enemy was crossing at Huff's Ferry, and he hurried forward to Lenoir's Station to assume personal command of the troops assembled there. Burnside left John G. Parke, his chief of staff, in charge at Knoxville with Hascall's division of Twenty-Third Corps.

Burnside arrived at Lenoir's Station about noon November 14, 1863. He ordered Chapin's brigade to move forward toward Huff's Ferry, and he ordered Ferrero's division of Ninth Corps to support Chapin. At 4:00 P.M. Chapin encountered Jenkins' skirmishers, and he advanced and drove them back about a mile and a half until he was halted about dark by artillery fire.

During the night of November 14, Potter moved Simon G. Griffin's Second Division, commanded by Joshua K. Sigfried during the temporary absence of Griffin, with Samuel N. Benjamin's Battery E, 2nd United States Artillery of his headquarters command, and three guns of John C. H. Von Sehlen's 15th Battery, Indiana Light Artillery to a point opposite Loudon.

At this point it was not Burnside's intention to fight a major battle to the southwest of Knoxville, but his movements during the next few days were designed to delay Longstreet's advance and get his troops back to Knoxville, where he would prepare a defensive position and make a stand.

Soon after daylight November 15, 1863, Ferrero's division began to fall back toward Lenoir's Station, and Chapin's brigade followed, covering its rear. When the column arrived near the Loudon road, Potter sent the artillery and Ferrero's division back to Lenoir's Station, with orders to cover the approaches to the station, and he also relieved Chapin's brigade as rear guard with

Allard's brigade of Sigfried's division of Ninth Corps. Allard was not attacked that day; he remained near Loudon until 2:00 P.M., then fell back to Lenoir's Station.

A strong force of enemy skirmishers appeared before Potter's line at Lenoir's Station about 4:00 P.M., but it was checked by the fire of Jacob Roemer's Battery L, 2nd New York Light Artillery.

During the evening of November 15, 1863, James Biddle arrived at Lenoir's Station with four companies of the 6th Indiana Cavalry of the Ninth Corps headquarters command, and Erskine Gittings' Batteries L and M, 3rd United States Artillery. Also that day, John F. Hartranft relieved Sigfried in command of Second Division, Ninth Corps. Sigfried resumed command of his First Brigade of the division, relieving Allard.

Engagement at Campbell's Station, Tennessee, November 16, 1863. Burnside believed that Longstreet would attempt to intercept the Federal line of march to Knoxville by seizing the junction of the Knoxville and Kingston road and the road from Lenoir's Station to Campbell's Station, which was about three-fourths of a mile west of the latter place. He ordered Hartranft to move with Second Division and Benjamin's and Von Sehlen's guns, and also Biddle's cavalry, to hold the road junction, and also to send out detachments on the roads from Campbell's Station to Clinton and Concord. William W. Buckley, with his Battery D, 1st Rhode Island Light Artillery, had already started for the junction.

Hartranft began his march about dusk November 15, 1863, and soon both he and Biddle reported difficulties. Because of recent heavy rains, the roads in the area were in terrible condition, and both Hartranft and Biddle were experiencing great difficulty in moving their artillery. Biddle dismounted some of his men and used their horses to move the guns. On the morning of November 16, White destroyed some of his wagons and their contents so that the teams could be used to move the artillery of both Ninth Corps and Twenty-Third Corps.

On the morning of November 15, 1863, Longstreet resumed his advance from Huff's Ferry. Jenkins' division, which was already north of the river, marched toward Lenoir's Station, and McLaws' division crossed the river that morning

and followed Jenkins. At the Burns house the road branched; the road to the right ran to Lenoir's Station, the road to the left led to the Knoxville and Kingston road, and the latter road ran on toward the east to Campbell's Station and then on to Knoxville. Jenkins' division turned off to the right on the road toward Lenoir's Station, which was several miles distant, and halted for the night not far from the station. McLaws arrived at the fork about 4:00 P.M. and halted there for the night.

At 8:00 A.M. November 16, 1863, McLaws moved out on the road to the left, as Burnside had anticipated, and marched for the road junction, west of Campbell's Station, in an effort to cut the Federal line of march to Knoxville.

At dawn November 16, 1863, Burnside's command at Lenoir's Station was on the road to Campbell's Station, following Hartranft and Biddle. The latter two commands arrived at the road junction that morning ahead of McLaws' division, and Hartranft immediately placed his and Biddle's troops in position to hold the road from Kingston, and also the roads from Clinton and Concord. His orders were to hold his position until that night to enable the trains to move past the junction on their way to Knoxville.

At 5:00 A.M. Sigfried's First Brigade of Hartranft's division was sent to occupy the road from Campbell's Station to Kingston. Edwin Schall's Second Brigade of Hartranft's division and Benjamin's battery did not arrive until 9:00 A.M., and they then joined Sigfried's brigade.

After securing the roads, Hartranft ordered Biddle to move out on the road to Kingston until he met the enemy and then to attack them. Biddle found McLaws' advance about two and a half miles west of the junction, and he immediately deployed his command as skirmishers and advanced. McLaws, however, made no immediate attempt to continue the march, but waited until more troops arrived to support his skirmishers.

Meantime, White, with Chapin's brigade, which had remained at Lenoir's Station during the night of November 15, 1863, marched early the next morning and arrived near Campbell's Station about 11:00 A.M. At 6:15 A.M., Ferrero's First Division of Ninth Corps, with its artillery, followed White, with William Humphrey's Third Brigade covering the rear of the column. Ferrero arrived at the road junction about 10:00 A.M., a short time after White, and he was followed closely all the way from Lenoir's Station by Jenkins' division. Both McLaws and Jenkins began to press the Federals strongly on both roads at 11:00 A.M.

By White's order, Chapin placed his brigade on some elevated ground on the south side of the road to Knoxville, just east of Campbell's Station, about three-fourths of a mile from the road junction. Henshaw's Battery, Illinois Light Artillery and Joseph A. Sims' 24th Battery, Indiana Light Artillery were on the center of Chapin's line on a small hill.

Ferrero's division took position on the road from Lenoir's Station on the left of Hartranft's division, which was on the road from Kingston. David Morrison's First Brigade was formed on the left of William Humphrey's Third Brigade, which was falling back on the road under heavy pressure from the enemy, and Benjamin C. Christ's Second Brigade was placed on the left of the road, supporting some batteries. Hartranft continued to hold McLaws' division at bay on the Kingston road while the rest of Burnside's column arrived and got into position, and Humphrey's brigade performed a similar service on the Lenoir's Station road.

After the trains and artillery had passed the road junction and moved on to the east, Potter, under Burnside's direction, prepared to move his command to a new line at Campbell's Station. Morrison's brigade was left for a time in front of the road junction, covering both roads, until the movement was completed. Potter sent Biddle with his cavalry and one section of Erskine Gittings' Batteries L and M, 3rd United States Artillery to the rear, and he also ordered the troops of Ferrero and Hartranft that were not then in position to fall back.

Humphrey's brigade fell back to a position on the extreme right of Potter's line, and Christ's brigade was moved to the rear of and in support of Humphrey's brigade. Morrison's brigade was withdrawn and was placed in support of Buckley's battery. About 1:30 P.M. Humphrey was relieved by Christ, and he moved back to the rear of Campbell's Station with his brigade. This left Christ's brigade on the extreme right of the line. White, with Chapin's brigade, held the center of the line, and Hartranft's division the left of the line. Benjamin's battery was placed on the right of the Knoxville road, with Gittings' battery on his right. Von

Sehlen's battery and Buckley's battery were in rear of the line, and Roemer's battery was on the left of the road.

Sometime after noon, the enemy attacked the new line at Campbell's Station, and at one time threatened Christ's brigade on the right. Christ changed the front of his brigade to the right and, aided by Buckley's guns, repelled the attack.

During the enemy's attacks, they threatened to occupy some high ground on the Federal left that commanded the Campbell's Station line, and Burnside decided to withdraw about three-fourths of a mile to a new position on a ridge. He ordered the withdrawal at 2:00 P.M. Under the cover of Benjamin and Gittings' batteries, and protected on the rear by Chapin's brigade, Ferrero's division and Hartranft's division fell back to the ridge. The new line was established by 4:00 P.M., with Ferrero's division on the right and Hartranft's division on the left. Roemer's guns and a regiment of Chapin's brigade were between the right of Hartranft's line and the road. The rest of Chapin's brigade was in rear of Hartranft's line. The enemy brought artillery and opened fire on Hartranft's line, but their infantry made no further aggressive movements that evening.

About dusk, Burnside issued orders for Potter and White to move back to Knoxville. Ferrero's division marched first and began to arrive at Knoxville about midnight; Hartranft followed, and arrived about daybreak November 17, 1863. White, with Chapin's brigade, brought up the rear and came into Knoxville after Hartranft.

On November 16, 1863, Orlando B. Willcox was ordered to fall back from Bull's Gap to Cumberland Gap with his Left Wing Forces in East Tennessee, which then consisted of his division of six-month Indiana regiments; Edward G. Hillier's Battery L, 1st Michigan Light Artillery; James W. Patterson's 21st Battery, Ohio Light Artillery; James H. Myers' 23rd Battery, Indiana Light Artillery; and Felix W. Graham's and Israel Garrard's cavalry brigades, which formed a division under John W. Foster.

Willcox arrived at Cumberland Gap November 20, 1863. He assumed command of Wilson C. Lemert's brigade, which held the gap, and he established a strong post at Tazewell, Tennessee. He remained there with his Left Wing during the rest of the year, holding the posts and watching the surrounding country. At the end of December 1863, his command was organized as follows:

Left Wing Forces in East Tennessee, Orlando B. Willcox
   First Brigade, John R. Mahan
   Second Brigade, George W. Jackson
   Cumberland Gap, Wilson C. Lemert
   Tazewell, Christian Thielemann

Siege of Knoxville, Tennessee, November 17, 1863–December 4, 1863. During the fighting at Campbell's Station November 16, 1863, Orlando M. Poe, chief engineer of the Department of the Ohio, was at Knoxville, where he was selecting the lines of defense of the city, and preparing to put Burnside's troops in position as they arrived from the front.

In order to describe the defenses of Knoxville, it is necessary to note briefly the principal features of the surrounding country. On the northern bank of the Holston River, there was a plateau or ridge about one-half mile in width, which began about two miles above Knoxville and ran along the river as far down as Lenoir's Station. The crest of the ridge was generally about 150 feet above the level of the river, but there were some hills along the ridge that rose to heights of 200 to 230 feet above the river.

There were three creeks that flowed in valleys through this ridge into the Holston River, and this gave the ridge the appearance of a series of separate hills. The easternmost creek was First Creek, which ran between the city of Knoxville and East Knoxville, or Temperance Hill; the next was Second Creek, about 1,000 yards west of First Creek, and it separated the city of Knoxville from College Hill; and the last was Third Creek, which ran into the Holston about one mile west of Second Creek.

To the north and west of Knoxville, the ridge sloped downward to a valley on the far side about one-half to three-fourths of a mile wide, and beyond this valley was another ridge that was somewhat lower than the one along the river. When Longstreet's divisions arrived from Campbell's Station, they took position along this second ridge and established their batteries on its higher points. The railroad from Virginia to Chattanooga ran along the southern edge of the valley, which was generally covered by open fields.

The Knoxville of 1863 was located on that part of the ridge between First Creek and Second Creek and between the river and the valley beyond the ridge.

The high ground east of First Creek was known as Temperance Hill, and to the east of this hill, and separated from it by a small valley, was Mabry's Hill. From Mabry's Hill the ground descends unevenly to the floor of the Holston valley. Immediately south of Temperance Hill, on the bank of the Holston River, was Flint Hill. That part of the ridge between Second Creek and Third Creek includes a hill that lies to the northwest of the Tennessee College.

South of the Holston River there are a series of hills, the highest of which is directly opposite Knoxville, where Gay Street runs down to the river. This range of hills runs almost parallel to the river and about one-half mile from it, and beyond it is a broad valley.

The line of defenses selected by Poe began on the river about one-fourth mile below the mouth of Second Creek and ran almost due west for about 900 yards to Battery Noble. It is important to note that the names of the batteries and forts on Poe's line that are given here were not assigned until after the siege of Knoxville had ended, but they are used here to simplify the description of the siege line.

From Battery Noble the line ran almost north for about 600 yards to Fort Sanders (formerly Confederate Fort Loudon), which was between the railroad and the Knoxville and Kingston road. At Fort Sanders the line turned back to the northeast on a course parallel to the river, and it ran along the top of a bluff, overlooking the valley to the north, for about 1,600 yards to Battery Wiltsie, opposite the railroad station. Included on that part of the line was Battery Zoellner, between Fort Sanders and Second Creek; Battery Galpin, just east of Second Creek; and Fort Comstock and Battery Wiltsie.

From Battery Wiltsie the line continued on along the crest of the bluffs for about 2,400 yards, passing over Temperance Hill, to Mabry's Hill. On this part of the line was Battery Billingsley, just west of First Creek; Fort Huntington Smith on Temperance Hill; Battery Clifton Lee and Battery Stearman in the depression between Temperance Hill and Mabry's Hill; and Fort Hill on the eastern end of Mabry's Hill. At this point the line turned back sharply to the south, forming a prominent salient near the Dandridge road, and from there it ran southward for about 1,300 yards before ending on the river at a ravine about 1,000 yards above the mouth of First Creek.

A short interior line was constructed that ran from Fort Sanders to a point near the mouth of Second Creek, and on this line Fort Byington was built around the college. Farther to the east, another interior line ran from Temperance Hill to the eastern end of Flint Hill, where Battery Fears was constructed.

To strengthen this line of fortifications, breastworks for infantry were constructed to connect the batteries and forts. In addition, dams were built on First Creek and Second Creek, where they were crossed by the Federal works, and the water thus backed up made an approach toward the works in those places difficult, especially in front of Temperance Hill.

Detached defensive works were also constructed on four of the hills south of the Holston River. Fort Stanley was built on a hill directly opposite the pontoon bridge, near the mouth of First Creek. Infantry trenches extended from this fort, across the Sevierville road, to the high ground beyond. Fort Dickerson occupied a hill opposite the mouth of Second Creek; Fort Higley was on the next hill to the west of Fort Dickerson; and the fourth hill was occupied only with trenches for infantry or dismounted cavalry.

During the night of November 16, 1863, as Burnside's troops were moving back from Campbell's Station to Knoxville, Sanders recrossed to the north side of the Holston River with Wolford's First Brigade and Pennebaker's Third Brigade of his First Cavalry Division. He was ordered to move out to the west and cover Potter's and White's troops until they could get into position and prepare a defensive line. Sanders fell back slowly as Longstreet advanced on November 17, then he finally made a stand with Wolford's brigade, under his personal direction, on a hill just north of the Kingston road, near the Armstrong house. This position was about one mile in front of Fort Sanders and about one-half mile west of the point where the Kingston road crossed Third Creek. Sanders' other brigade, under Pennebaker, also turned about to face the enemy at a point where the Clinton road passed over the ridge about one mile northwest of Fort Sanders.

Sanders' men constructed a breastworks of fence rails and held their ground against repeated attacks until dark that day. The enemy again unsuccessfully attacked Sanders' line on November 18, but finally, during the afternoon, Wolford's and Pennebaker's brigades were forced to withdraw into the lines at Knoxville. About 2:30 P.M. that day, while fighting in front of the works that would later be called Fort Sanders, Sanders was mortally wounded, and Wolford assumed command of his division. Silas Adams took charge of Wolford's brigade.

As the troops came in from Campbell's Station, they were placed on the line of defense as follows:

Morrison's First Brigade of Ferrero's First Division, Ninth Corps held the left of the line. Its left began on the river at a point to the left of the Powell house, and it extended to Fort Sanders, which was at the salient of the line, to the right of the Kingston road. Humphrey's Third Brigade of Ferrero's division was on the line from Fort Sanders to a point about midway between the fort and Second Creek. Christ's Second Brigade of Ferrero's division extended the line from the right of Humphrey's brigade to Second Creek, where the creek flowed under the railroad. At that point it connected with the left of Hartranft's Second Division, Ninth Corps.

Sigfried's First Brigade of Hartranft's division, with one regiment of Schall's Second Brigade of the division, held the line to the right of Christ's brigade, and it ran along the top of the bluff from Second Creek to Gay Street. The two remaining regiments of Schall's brigade were in a field on the north side of Gay Street, with their right extending to First Creek. At that point Schall's brigade connected with the left of Chapin's Second Brigade of White's Second Division of Twenty-Third Corps. The line of Chapin's brigade extended eastward from First Creek across Temperance Hill to the Bell house.

William A. Hoskins' Second Brigade of Willcox's Left Wing Forces continued the line from the Bell house across Mabry Hill to the Holston River at a point a little below the glass works. Flint Hill, covering the bridgehead, was manned largely by men from Union Tennessee regiments.

Daniel Cameron's Second Brigade of Milo S. Hascall's Third Division, Twenty-Third Corps was in position south of the river, and James W. Reilly's First Brigade of the same division was in reserve and served on both sides of the river.

Burnside's artillery was placed along the defensive line as follows:

Samuel N. Benjamin's Battery E, 2nd United States Artillery, two sections of William W. Buckley's Battery D, 1st Rhode Island Light Artillery, and one section of Jacob Roemer's Battery L, 2nd New York Light Artillery were in Fort Sanders, and they were supported by the 79th New York Infantry of Ninth Corps Headquarters command.

One section of Buckley's battery was near the Powell house, on the line of Morrison's brigade.

One section of Roemer's battery was on the grounds of the college (also referred to as seminary or university).

Erskine Gittings' Batteries L and M, 3rd United States Artillery were in position near the center of Hartranft's line, on the bluff overlooking the depot.

John C. H. Von Sehlen's 15th Battery, Indiana Light Artillery was in the field to the right of Gay Street, near the right of Hartranft's line.

Joseph A. Sims' 24th Battery, Indiana Light Artillery and Henshaw's Battery, Illinois Light Artillery (commanded by Edward C. Henshaw) were on Temperance Hill and the adjacent ridge.

Joseph C. Shields' 19th Battery, Ohio Light Artillery and one section of Wilder's Battery, Indiana Light Artillery (also known as 26th Battery, Indiana Light Artillery), commanded by Hubbard T. Thomas, were on Mabry's Hill.

Andrew J. Konkle's Battery D, 1st Ohio Light Artillery, commanded by William H. Pease, and two sections of Wilder's Battery were on the heights south of the Holston River.

By dark November 18, 1863, the fortifications on the line of defenses were nearing completion, and the line of infantry entrenchments was almost continuous. That day Longstreet's skirmishers appeared, and they moved up in front of the still-uncompleted works. The siege of Knoxville then began, and from that time until November 29, there was daily skirmishing and some more vigorous offensive operations.

On November 19, 1863, the enemy extended their skirmish line to the left, and the next day Longstreet's offensive line began to appear, with its right approaching the Holston River near the Armstrong house, just west of Third Creek.

At 8:00 P.M. November 23, 1863, enemy troops advanced on Hartranft's position near the Clinton road. The federal skirmishers fell back for some distance on the left, and small parties set fire to some houses, machine shops, and the roundhouse on the railroad. This brought a halt to the enemy advance. Later, after the fire had died down, Hartranft ordered an advance, but his troops failed to recover all the ground lost.

Hartranft was then ordered to attack again the next morning, November 24, 1863, and drive the enemy back. For this attempt, he detailed the 48th Pennsylvania and the 21st Massachusetts regiments of Sigfried's First Brigade, both under the command of George P. Hawkes of the 21st Massachusetts. A part of James W. Reilly's First Brigade of Milo S. Hascall's Third Division, Twenty-Third Corps, which was in reserve in the town, moved up to occupy that part of the line vacated by Hawkes' regiments. Hawkes' men advanced at daylight that morning; they soon recovered the ground lost the day before, and then reestablished their former skirmish line.

On November 24, 1863, the enemy began crossing to the south side of the Holston River, at a point about two miles below the pontoon bridge, and skirmished with Cameron's brigade of Hascall's division to the southwest of Knoxville. The enemy then occupied a position on a hill near the crossing, and the next day advanced in an attempt to gain the high ground opposite Knoxville, where Wheeler's cavalry had failed a short time before. The attack was strongly repulsed by Cameron's brigade; Pennebaker's cavalry brigade of Wolford's division, which had recrossed to the south side of the river on November 22; and Reilly's brigade, which had been sent across the river to reinforce Cameron. The enemy established a battery on the hill first occupied near the river, and this position was about a mile and a half from Fort Sanders. As a result, the fort was put in condition to sustain a fire from that direction.

Assault on Fort Sanders, Knoxville, Tennessee, November 29, 1863. After remaining in front of Knoxville for about a week, Longstreet finally decided to attack. His plan called for a major assault on Fort Sanders on November 29, 1863, with most of the rest of his command joining in the attack on adjacent parts of the line.

About 11:00 on the night of November 28, the enemy attacked the Federal picket lines, and after about two hours of fighting succeeded in occupying them, thus bringing Longstreet's advanced line on the crest of a ridge within about 100 yards of the northwest salient of Fort Sanders. Skirmishing continued during the rest of the night, while the artillery subjected the works to a slow fire, principally Fort Sanders. It was thus certain that Fort Sanders was to be the object of an enemy attack, and Hascall was directed to send Reilly's brigade up to reinforce Ferrero.

Longstreet's attack was to be made in two columns by troops of McLaws' division against the northwestern angle of Fort Sanders. The column on the right was to consist of Benjamin G. Humphreys' brigade in a column of regiments, led by the 13th Mississippi regiment, and it was to be followed closely by three regiments of Goode Bryan's brigade. The column on the left was to consist of William T. Wofford's brigade, also in column of regiments, with the 16th Georgia Regiment leading.

Following the main attack, George T. Anderson's brigade of Jenkins' division was to move against the works about 100 yards to the left of Fort Sanders. If the fort was captured, Henry L. Benning's brigade and Jenkins' brigade, commanded by John Bratton, both of Jenkins' division, were to follow Anderson. If, however, the attack failed, Anderson was to wheel to his right and attempt to take the fort from the rear, which was not enclosed.

In addition to the above attacking troops, Joseph B. Kershaw's brigade of McLaws' division was to advance on the right of the fort as soon as it was captured. Bushrod R. Johnson's brigade and Archibald Gracie's brigade, both attached to Longstreet's corps, were to be held in readiness to take advantage of any Confederate successes.

The garrison of Fort Sanders consisted of Benjamin's and Buckley's batteries, a section of Roemer's battery, and an infantry force consisting of men from the 79th New York of the Ninth Corps Headquarters command, the 29th Massachusetts of Christ's brigade, and the 2nd Michigan and 20th Michigan of Humphrey's brigade. Altogether there were about 500 men in the fort.

The weather on November 27–28 had been wet and foggy and generally disagreeable, and it had not improved on the morning of the attack. The enemy opened with a heavy artillery fire on Fort Sanders at about 6:00 on the morning of November 29, and about twenty minutes later, the enemy columns moved forward under the cover of a heavy fog against the northwest angle of the fort. The men advanced under a very heavy Federal fire, passed through a slight abatis and an entanglement of telegraph wire, and some reached the ditch in front of the fort. They attempted to climb the walls of the fort, and a few reached the crest, but they were all quickly killed or captured. The men remaining in the ditch were under a heavy flank fire of musketry and canister. Many were killed or wounded, and some surrendered; the rest fell back in a disorderly retreat. Anderson, on the left, made no progress, and because the attacks of the remaining brigades were contingent on the success of the main assault, Longstreet's attack was soon ended.

* * * * * * * * * *

Longstreet made no further serious attacks on the defensive lines at Knoxville, but remained more or less quietly in front of the city until he learned of the approach of Sherman's relief column. Then, on December 2, 1863, he decided to abandon the siege and withdraw eastward toward Virginia. After sending his wagons on ahead on December 3, Longstreet began the movement of his men from the west side of Knoxville, and on the afternoon of December 5 he reached Blain's Cross Roads. He continued on to Rutledge the next day and remained there until December 8. He then moved on and arrived at Rogersville the next day.

Shackelford, with Wolford's First Cavalry Division, which had been in position on the south side of the river at Knoxville, led the pursuit of Longstreet on the morning of December 5, 1863. Shackelford came up with the enemy on December 6 and skirmished with the rear guard until December 9, when he reached Bean's Station and went into camp. He remained there with the cavalry, covering the front of the army, until attacked by Longstreet December 14.

On December 7, 1863, Potter's Ninth Corps and Manson's Twenty-Third Corps broke camp at Knoxville and started in pursuit of Longstreet. Both corps were under the immediate direction of John G. Parke, formerly Burnside's chief of staff, who was assigned as commander of the United States Forces in the Field. Potter's corps advanced that day to Flat Creek, about four miles from Blain's Cross Roads. White, with Chapin's brigade of his Second Division, Twenty-Third Corps, also advanced to Flat Creek December 7, but Hascall's division of Twenty-Third Corps had, for some reason, turned off from the main road on a road to Armstrong's Ferry. Hascall crossed the Holston River at the ferry and then moved on to Strawberry Plains, where he recrossed to the north bank of the river.

On December 8, 1863, Potter moved on to a point about fifteen miles beyond Flat Creek, and the next day arrived at Rutledge, about thirty-five miles from Knoxville. He then took up position there and remained until December 13.

White, with Chapin's brigade, remained on Flat Creek December 8, 1863, then advanced to within about seven miles of Rutledge. He established camp there and remained until December 17. Hascall marched from Strawberry Plains to Blain's Cross Roads on December 8, and the next day advanced to within three miles of Rutledge, where he remained in camp until the evening of December 14.

On December 9, 1863, while at Rutledge, Parke informed Burnside that, because of the fatigued condition of his men, he would follow Longstreet no farther unless ordered to do so.

On December 12, 1863, John G. Foster, who had arrived the day before, relieved Burnside in command of the Department of the Ohio, and he immediately assumed the direction of the Union forces in East Tennessee. Also on December 12, Samuel D. Sturgis was assigned command of all cavalry forces in the Department of the Ohio. Sturgis did not assume command, however, until December 15, the day after the engagement at Bean's Station, and then Shackelford departed on leave.

Engagement at Bean's Station, Tennessee, December 14, 1863. On December 12, 1863, Longstreet learned that a part of the force sent by Grant to reinforce Burnside at Knoxville had returned to Chattanooga, and he was also informed that Burnside's main force was between Rutledge and Blain's Cross Roads, with three cavalry brigades and one infantry brigade in advance at Bean's Station. He issued orders for his command to advance on December 14 and attempt to surprise and capture the force at Bean's Station.

According to Longstreet's plan, his main force was to march on the direct road from Rogersville to Bean's Station; William T. Martin, with four brigades of cavalry, was to move down along the south side of the Holston River to a point opposite or below Bean's Station, then cross to the north bank and attack on the right or rear of the Federal line; and William E. Jones, with two cavalry brigades, was to march down on the north side of the Clinch Mountains and take position to block the Bean's Station Gap and prevent Shackelford's troops from escaping by that route.

Longstreet's advance was slowed by muddy roads, caused by rain during the night of December 13, 1863, but the infantry was able to get in position in front of the Federal line at Bean's Station in time to attack that afternoon. Martin's cavalry, however, did not arrive at the crossing of the Holston River until that night. Jones reached the gap during the day and captured some wagons, but then, for some reason, he withdrew. Thus Longstreet was forced to attack without the help of the cavalry.

Bushrod R. Johnson, commanding Buckner's division, advanced about 2:00 P.M. against Wolford's cavalry division, which consisted of Silas Adams' First Brigade, Emery S. Bond's Second Brigade, and Charles D. Pennebaker's Third Brigade, and drove it back to the buildings at the station. There, however, Wolford's troopers offered strong resistance.

Kershaw's brigade, advancing at the head of McLaws' division, was sent forward to the right of Johnson to cut off the Federal force holding the gap. That accomplished, Kershaw was to move against the left flank of Shackelford's line in the valley. Kershaw advanced as ordered, but before he could come up on Shackelford's line, the cavalry had withdrawn to a new position about four miles below Bean's Station. By that time it was dark, and Kershaw halted for the night.

On the morning of December 15, 1863, Longstreet sent Benjamin G. Humphreys with his brigade of McLaws' division to capture the Federal troops that had been cut off there, but when he arrived, he found that they had escaped. Also that morning, Longstreet ordered Jenkins' division and Martin's cavalry to pursue Shackelford, and they soon came up in front of his new line. Shackelford, however, had been reinforced. On the evening of December 14, Hascall's division of Twenty-Third Corps had been ordered up in support of the cavalry, and at daylight on the following morning, Hascall deployed his troops in line of battle with the cavalry. Hascall's men threw up some breastworks, which they occupied during the day, and skirmished with the enemy. Longstreet did not attack, however, and at dark Hascall marched back to his camp near Rutledge. That night the cavalry, then commanded by Sturgis, withdrew to Blain's Cross Roads.

At daylight December 16, 1863, Longstreet sent Martin and Jenkins in pursuit of the retiring Federals, but after a time Jenkins halted his infantry, while Martin continued the advance to near Blain's Cross Roads. Martin, however, made no further attack. By that time the weather had become too bad for effective operations, and Longstreet withdrew his infantry to Russellville to go into winter quarters.

When Parke learned of Longstreet's advance on December 14, 1863, he decided to move Ninth Corps back from Rutledge to Blain's Cross Roads, and Ferrero's First Division completed the movement that day. Hartranft's Second Division started back the next day, and on December 16 it halted and formed in line of battle about two miles from Blain's Cross Roads, facing Longstreet's approaching columns.

On December 16, Hascall's division also fell back to Blain's Cross Roads, and White, with Chapin's brigade, joined him there the next day. Thus, by December 17, Parke had the greater part of his command assembled in the vicinity of Blain's Cross Roads.

Meantime, when Longstreet threatened the cap-

ture of Knoxville, reinforcements were ordered to East Tennessee to reinforce Burnside's army. On November 27, 1863, shortly after the Union victory at Missionary Ridge, Ulysses S. Grant ordered Gordon Granger to move with Philip H. Sheridan's Second Division and Thomas J. Wood's Third Division of his Fourth Corps, Army of the Cumberland from Chattanooga to the relief of Burnside at Knoxville. The next day Grant also ordered William T. Sherman, who was then leading the forces pursuing Bragg's defeated army toward Dalton in Georgia, to march toward Knoxville with the following troops: Eleventh Corps, Army of the Cumberland; Second Division of Fourteenth Corps, Army of the Cumberland; a part of Fifteenth Corps, Army of the Tennessee; and Eli Long's Second Brigade, Second Cavalry Division of the Army of the Cumberland. Granger joined Sherman's column en route, and they arrived at Maryville, Tennessee December 5. There Sherman learned that Longstreet had abandoned the siege and moved off to the east of Knoxville. Sherman then ordered Granger to continue on with his two divisions and report to Burnside at Knoxville, and Sherman, with the rest of his command, marched back to Chattanooga. For details of Sherman's relief expedition, see Relief of Knoxville, Tennessee (William T. Sherman).

On November 30, 1863, James G. Spears, with his First East Tennessee Brigade, was placed under Granger's orders as the latter moved with his two divisions toward Knoxville. The proper designation of Spears' brigade was Second Brigade, Second Division, Fourteenth Corps, but at that time it was on detached duty near the mouth of Sale Creek, where it emptied into the Tennessee River from the north, about twenty miles northeast of Chattanooga.

On November 30, 1863, in obedience to Granger's orders, Spears marched with his brigade toward Kingston, where he arrived December 3. As senior officer present, Spears assumed command of all Federal troops at and near Kingston, which consisted of his own First East Tennessee Brigade; Samuel R. Mott's First Brigade of White's Second Division, Twenty-Third Corps; Robert K. Byrd's 1st Tennessee Mounted Infantry, commanded by John Ellis while Byrd commanded the post of Kingston; a battalion of 3rd Indiana Cavalry under Robert Klein; eight pieces of artillery attached to Spears' brigade; and nine guns attached to Mott's brigade.

Mott's brigade had been at Kingston since October 28.

Spears left Kingston with his command December 4, 1863 and marched toward Loudon, arriving there December 6. That day he was instructed by Granger, who had learned of Longstreet's withdrawal from in front of Knoxville, to remain at Loudon until further orders.

On December 7, 1863, Granger arrived at Knoxville with Sheridan's and Wood's divisions from their camps between Maryville and the Little Tennessee River, and he was ordered to remain there and hold the city. Granger then ordered Spears to march to Knoxville with his own and Mott's brigade. Spears arrived there December 9, then moved on to Strawberry Plains the next day. On December 15, as a result of Longstreet's advance from Rogersville, Granger moved up from Knoxville and joined Parke's command at Blain's Cross Roads. That same day, Spears' brigade left Strawberry Plains and advanced to Richland Creek between Blain's Cross Roads and Rutledge. Mott's brigade marched to Blain's Cross Roads on December 16 and rejoined White's division December 18.

Additional cavalry was also sent to East Tennessee. On November 27, 1863, Washington L. Elliott, then at Murfreesboro, Tennessee, was ordered to march to East Tennessee with Archibald P. Campbell's First Brigade and Oscar H. La Grange's Second Brigade of Edward M. McCook's First Cavalry Division of his Cavalry Corps, Army of the Cumberland. Included in the column was Eli Lilly's 18th Battery, Indiana Light Artillery, which had been transferred from John T. Wilder's Mounted Infantry Brigade, Army of the Cumberland to Elliott's Cavalry Corps on November 17. Elliott was directed to hamper Longstreet's movements as much as possible, and if he did not find Longstreet, he was to report for duty to Burnside.

By the end of the month, the head of Elliott's column had reached Sparta, Tennessee, and he halted there until December 7 for the rest of his command to come up. Elliott crossed the Cumberland Mountains on December 7 and reached Kingston December 11. On December 14, the day of the engagement at Bean's Station, Foster ordered Elliott to march to Knoxville to reinforce the cavalry of the Army of the Ohio in its operations against Longstreet. On December 16, Elliott, with McCook's division, moved to Armstrong's Ford on the Holston River, seven miles above Knoxville, where it was intended to cross to the west side of the river and move on to Morristown and engage Martin's cavalry.

Upon arriving at the river, Elliott found the water too deep for the artillery and wagons to cross, and he sent Campbell's First Brigade across with instructions to meet the rest of the column at Strawberry Plains. La Grange was unable to cross there, however, with the artillery and wagons, and Campbell recrossed to the east bank at McKinney's Ford on December 18. McCook's division, then united, advanced to Nance's Ford, eight miles upstream, which was reported to be held by the enemy. No enemy was found there, however, and McCook countermarched his command to McKinney's Ford. Then Campbell's brigade again crossed to the west side of the river. That night the water in the river rose four feet, and La Grange, again being unable to cross, returned to Strawberry Plains. Finally, on December 23, the water had subsided enough to permit La Grange to cross with his artillery and wagons and join Campbell, and together the two brigades pushed on to New Market.

Action at Mossy Creek, Tennessee, December 29, 1863. December 23, 1863 is the date generally accepted as the end of the Knoxville Campaign. At that time Longstreet's infantry was going into winter quarters on the south side of the Holston River at Russellville; Potter's Ninth Corps and Granger's Fourth Corps were in camp at Blain's Cross Roads; and Twenty-Third Corps, commanded by Jacob D. Cox since December 21, moved from Blain's Cross Roads to Strawberry Plains a short time later. The rainy and very cold weather prevailing in the mountains at that time of the year made further effective military operations almost impossible. The cavalry of both armies, however, remained in the field for some time, and for that reason its operations, including the Action at Mossy Creek, are described here.

On December 23, 1863, the day Elliott with McCook's cavalry division arrived at New Market, Wolford, with Adams' First Brigade and Bond's Second Brigade of his First Cavalry Division, and Israel Garrard with his brigade of John W. Foster's Second Division, both of the Army of the Ohio, were ordered to cross the Holston River at McKinney's Ford and march to New Market.

The next day Sturgis sent Campbell's brigade of McCook's division and Garrard's brigade of Foster's division, with two sections of Lilly's battery, from New Market to Dandridge, ten miles to the southeast, to drive back a brigade of Confederate cavalry reported to be there. Campbell engaged the enemy at Hays' Ferry, within four miles of Dandridge, and drove them back. Campbell soon became sharply engaged and called on Garrard for help, but when Garrard did not come up, Campbell began a fighting withdrawal. After proceeding about a mile, with the enemy pressing his rear, Campbell attacked and drove the enemy back, and he then continued on toward New Market, where he arrived that night.

On December 25, 1863, Sturgis, then at New Market, reported to Parke that all the enemy cavalry was on his right, on the roads from Morristown and Mossy Creek to Dandridge, and that he was reluctant to move out with his command because he feared an attack on his rear. He asked that an infantry brigade and a battery be sent to New Market to support him and cover his movements. Parke then ordered Mott to move with his brigade of Mahlon D. Manson's Second Division, Twenty-Third Corps to New Market to support Sturgis, and he directed Cox to send a brigade of his Twenty-Third Corps to take Mott's place at Strawberry Plains.

December 26, 1863, on a cold and rainy day, McCook formed his division in line of battle, then crossed Mossy Creek and established a line a short distance east of the creek. Mossy Creek was the name of a town and station on the East Tennessee and Virginia Railroad (present-day Jefferson City), and also of a small creek that flowed past the town. The next day McCook advanced both brigades about four miles, against little resistance, to Talbott's Station, where he placed Campbell's brigade and La Grange's brigade in position on the Morristown road.

The cavalry of the Army of the Ohio remained at New Market until December 27, 1863, then moved up to Mossy Creek and went into camp, four miles east of New Market. During the evening of December 28, Sturgis heard that there was a brigade of enemy cavalry at Dandridge, and he ordered Wolford's division and Foster's division to march during the night and attempt to capture this force.

At 2:00 A.M. December 29, 1863, Lilly was ordered to take position with his entire battery at daylight on a hill on the Morristown road about one-half mile northeast of the bridge over Mossy Creek.

At dawn that morning, Sturgis ordered La Grange to take his brigade out of line on the Morristown road near Talbott's Station and march with it on the road to Dandridge as far as the gap in Bay's Mountain. In this position, which was about halfway to Dandridge, La Grange would be able to support Wolford and Foster if they got into trouble, or he could return to Mossy Creek if needed there.

La Grange was ordered to take with him to Bay's Mountain two guns of Lilly's battery, and consequently, when Lilly took position on the hill as ordered, he had with him only three of his five guns. Campbell, at Talbott's Station, sent back Thomas J. Jordan's 9th Pennsylvania Cavalry to support the battery, and the 118th Ohio Infantry of Mott's brigade was also brought forward and sent into the dense woods on the left of Lilly's battery, where it was placed under Campbell's orders.

With the departure of the 9th Pennsylvania Regiment, Campbell had with him only Benjamin Smith's 2nd Michigan Cavalry and James P. Brownlow's 1st East Tennessee Cavalry to extend his brigade at Talbott's Station to cover the entire division line. This he did by placing one regiment on each side of the Morristown road. Sturgis did not intend that Campbell fight a battle in his advanced position, and he ordered Campbell to fall back to Mossy Creek if attacked.

At about 9:00 A.M. December 29, 1863, William T. Martin, commanding Longstreet's cavalry, advanced against Campbell's line with the divisions of Frank C. Armstrong and John T. Morgan, which had assembled the night before at Panther Creek. Campbell, in obedience to orders, formed his regiments in line of battle and retreated slowly toward Mossy Creek to delay the enemy advance while a defensive line was formed to his rear.

When Campbell arrived at a large brick house about a mile from Mossy Creek, he was forced to halt and fight. He placed the 2nd Michigan under cover until the enemy had approached to within about twenty yards, and then the regiment opened fire at close range and checked their advance. The 1st East Tennessee Cavalry then charged to the right of the brick house and drove back the center, forcing the entire line to halt for a time. Campbell's two regiments then pulled off the road into the thick woods, where they formed on the left of the 118th Ohio. This cleared the field in front of Lilly's battery, and it immediately opened with a heavy fire and checked the enemy's advance for some time.

A short time after Lilly's battery went into action, at about 11:00 A.M., the enemy opened fire from a battery on a hill about 1,000 yards distant on the south side of the Morristown road. After the two batteries had exchanged fire for about an hour, a second enemy battery opened from another hill to the left of the first, and a short distance north of the East Tennessee and Virginia Railroad. Through the area where the fighting took place, the railroad ran from Talbott's Station to Mossy Creek, and from near the position of the left of the second Confederate battery to the crossing of the Morristown road near Mossy Creek, the railroad ran through a deep cut.

Lilly did not reply to the fire of the enemy artillery after the second battery opened, except for an occasional shell, but continued to fire with canister at the advancing enemy line and held it in check for about an hour.

Martin's men advanced toward the left of Campbell's line, and Campbell placed Brownlow's 1st East Tennessee Cavalry on a hill on the extreme left, to the left of Mossy Creek, and formed Smith's 2nd Michigan on the left of the 118th Ohio of Mott's brigade. All but one battalion of Jordan's 9th Pennsylvania was moved from the front of Lilly's battery to the right to meet this threat. Campbell then ordered Brownlow to charge the enemy's line with the 1st East Tennessee, using sabers. The attackers quickly broke through the line, and when they returned, they brought with them twenty-six prisoners. This unexpected attack brought to a halt the enemy's flanking movement.

When the enemy advanced that morning, a section of the Elgin Battery (also called the 5th Battery, Illinois Light Artillery) of Mott's brigade, commanded by Andrew M. Wood, was brought up and placed on a hill near the Widow Mendenhall's barn, in front of Mossy Creek. This was near the junction of the Chunky Bend road and the Morristown road, about one-half mile to the right and to the rear of Lilly's battery. The Elgin Battery was supported by William J. Palmer with an unassigned command of about 250 men belonging to his 15th Pennsylvania Cavalry, the 10th Ohio Cavalry, and the 1st East Tennessee Mounted Infantry. Palmer was encamped that morning at Montcastle's place, about three miles from Mossy Creek, and his command was withdrawn and placed in rear of the Benjamin Branner and William Mann houses and outbuildings, which were on opposite sides of the Chunky Bend road, near its junction with the Morristown road. At that time Palmer's position was on the extreme right of Sturgis' line, and it covered the bridge and ford at Mossy Creek.

Having failed in their attacks on the Federal left, the enemy began assembling troops opposite the Federal right for an attack on the Elgin Battery and its supports. The battalion of the 9th Pennsylvania that was still supporting Lilly's battery was then moved to the right to aid in the protection of the battery, and the enemy attack was repulsed. The attack was then shifted to the hill held by Lilly's battery, but this was repulsed about 1:00 P.M. by the battery firing canister. When this attack failed, enemy sharpshooters moved up into the railroad cut and inflicted a number of casualties, seriously hampering the work of the gunners.

By that time the men of Lilly's battery were almost completely exhausted after three hours of working the guns. During the fighting that day, the three guns had fired 512 rounds, and of the fifty men of the battery, ten were killed or wounded. In addition, a number of the horses of the battery were killed. Sometime after 2:00 P.M., Lilly withdrew his battery about a mile and a half to a hill just north of Mossy Creek, and then Sturgis withdrew his entire line to a new position to the east and north of the creek.

Meantime, the 16th Kentucky Infantry of Mott's brigade had moved up, and it was placed under cover on the right of Sturgis' line to protect the Elgin Battery. The battalion of the 9th Pennsylvania Cavalry was then relieved in protecting the battery, and it moved to the left to support Lilly's battery in its new position.

When the enemy advanced against Campbell's line at Talbott's Station on the morning of December 29, 1863, Sturgis immediately ordered La Grange to return with his brigade and the artillery from Bay's Mountain to Mossy Creek, and he also ordered Wolford and Foster to return from Dandridge if they found no enemy troops there.

At about 2:00 P.M. La Grange arrived near Mossy Creek, and he was sent under cover to take position on the Federal right. He formed his brigade south of the Chunky Bend road, with his right resting on a bend of Mossy Creek about 300–400 yards north of present-day U.S. Route 11. The brigade faced to the east and northeast. The section of Lilly's Battery that had accompanied La Grange to Bay's Mountain unlimbered on the Chunky Bend road and opened fire. The enemy then began to fall back, and while La Grange and the other troops on the Federal right advanced against the enemy's left flank, Campbell's brigade and the 118th Ohio Infantry moved forward on their front. Sturgis' command pushed forward steadily, with little resistance, for about four miles to a point beyond the position held by Campbell's brigade on the Morristown road near Talbott's that morning. By that time it was dark, and the pursuit was ended.

That night the 118th Ohio Infantry, the 15th Kentucky Infantry, and the Elgin Battery of Mott's brigade returned to Mossy Creek to rejoin the brigade. During the day, the 25th Michigan of Mott's brigade was held in reserve on the Morristown road, and one battalion of the 80th Indiana of Mott's brigade was sent to guard the road from Dandridge to Dyer's Ferry.

The organization of the Union troops in East Tennessee during the Knoxville Campaign was as follows:

DEPARTMENT OF THE OHIO
Ambrose E. Burnside, to December 12, 1863
John G. Foster

NINTH CORPS, Robert B. Potter

Headquarters
6th Indiana Cavalry (four companies), James Biddle
79th New York Infantry, William S. Montgomery
Battery E, Second United States Artillery, Samuel N. Benjamin

First Division, Edward Ferrero
First Brigade, David Morrison
Second Brigade, Benjamin C. Christ
Third Brigade, Daniel Leasure, to November 5, 1863
William Humphrey
Artillery

Battery L, 2nd New York Light Artillery, Jacob Roemer
Battery D, 1st Rhode Island Light Artillery, William W. Buckley

Second Division, Joshua K. Sigfried, to November 15, 1863
John F. Hartranft
First Brigade, Thomas B. Allard, to November 15, 1863
Joshua K. Sigfried
Second Brigade, Edwin Schall, to December 12, 1863
Moses N. Collins

Third Brigade, Wilson C. Lemert
Artillery, Henry M. Neil
22nd Battery, Ohio Light Artillery, Amos B. Alger
Company K, 86th Ohio Infantry, James W. Owens
Company K, 129th Ohio Infantry, Allen D. S. McArthur

Note 1. Lemert's brigade became a part of Orlando B. Willcox's Left Wing Forces in East Tennessee in November 1863.
Note 2. The artillery of Second Division, Ninth Corps on December 31, 1863 was as follows: 15th Battery, Indiana Light Artillery and Batteries L and M, 3rd United States Artillery.

TWENTY-THIRD CORPS, Mahlon D. Manson, to December 21, 1863
Jacob D. Cox

Second Division, Julius White, to December 21, 1863
Mahlon D. Manson
First Brigade, Samuel R. Mott
Second Brigade, Marshal W. Chapin

Note. Andrew M. Wood's Elgin Battery, Illinois Light Artillery was attached to First Brigade; and Edward C. Henshaw's Battery, Illinois Light Artillery was attached to Second Brigade.

Third Division, Milo S. Hascall
First Brigade, James W. Reilly
Second Brigade, Daniel Cameron

Note. William H. Pease's Battery D, 1st Ohio Light Artillery was attached to First Brigade; and Wilder's Battery, commanded by Hubbard T. Thomas, was attached to Second Brigade.

Reserve Artillery, Andrew J. Konkle
24th Battery, Indiana Light Artillery, Joseph A. Sims
19th Battery, Ohio Light Artillery, Joseph C. Shields

CAVALRY CORPS, James M. Shackelford, to December 15, 1863, on leave
Samuel D. Sturgis

First Cavalry Division, Frank Wolford
First Brigade, Silas Adams
Second Brigade, Emery S. Bond
Third Brigade, Charles D. Pennebaker

Second Division, John W. Foster
First Brigade, Israel Garrard
Second Brigade, Horace Capron
Artillery
Battery K, 1st Illinois Light Artillery, John H. Colvin

LEFT WING FORCES IN EAST TENNESSEE, Orlando B. Willcox

First Brigade, John R. Mahan
Second Brigade, George W. Jackson
Cumberland Gap, Tennessee, Wilson C. Lemert
Tazewell, Tennessee, Christian Thielemann

TROOPS FROM THE ARMY OF THE CUMBERLAND

FOURTH CORPS, Gordon Granger

Second Division, Philip H. Sheridan
First Brigade, Francis T. Sherman
Second Brigade, George D. Wagner
Third Brigade, Charles G. Harker
Artillery, Warren P. Edgarton
Battery M, 1st Illinois Light Artillery, George W. Spencer
10th Battery, Indiana Light Artillery. William A. Naylor
Battery G, 1st Missouri Light Artillery, Lorenzo D. Immell

Third Division, Thomas J. Wood
First Brigade, August Willich
Second Brigade, William B. Hazen
Third Brigade, Samuel Beatty
Artillery
Bridges' Battery, Illinois Light Artillery, Lyman A. White
6th Battery, Ohio Light Artillery, Cullen Bradley
Battery B, Pennsylvania Light Artillery, Samuel M. McDowell

Note. David S. Stanley's First Division, Fourth Corps

was at Bridgeport, Alabama, but it joined the corps in East Tennessee in January 1864.

CAVALRY CORPS, Washington L. Elliott

First Division, Edward M. McCook
First Brigade, Archibald P. Campbell
Second Brigade, Oscar H. La Grange

Note 1. Elliott accompanied First Division to East Tennessee, but Louis D. Watkins' Third Brigade remained with the Army of the Cumberland. George Crook's Second Division of the Cavalry Corps remained at Pulaski, Tennessee.
Note 2. Eli Lilly's 18th Battery, Indiana Light Artillery accompanied Elliott's cavalry command when it moved into East Tennessee.

RELIEF OF KNOXVILLE, TENNESSEE (WILLIAM T. SHERMAN) NOVEMBER 27, 1863– DECEMBER 6, 1863

Union forces under Ambrose E. Burnside, advancing from Kentucky, occupied Knoxville, Tennessee September 2, 1863 and soon established control in that region. For details of these operations, see East Tennessee Campaign (Burnside).

On November 4, 1863, James Longstreet's Confederate Corps was detached from Braxton Bragg's Army of Tennessee, which was then investing Chattanooga, and sent to Knoxville in an effort to reoccupy the town and to drive Burnside from East Tennessee. Longstreet crossed the Tennessee River below Loudon November 12, then advanced slowly against steady opposition by Burnside's forces, who finally retired within the fortified lines at Knoxville on November 17. Longstreet then placed the town under siege from that date until December 4. See Knoxville, Tennessee Campaign.

The administration in Washington, fearful of losing control of East Tennessee, and concerned about the safety of Burnside's army, asked Ulysses S. Grant, commander of the Military Division of the Mississippi, to send help from his forces at Chattanooga. Accordingly, on November 27, 1863, shortly after the Union victory at Missionary Ridge, and while Grant's forces were pursuing Bragg's defeated army into Georgia, Gordon Granger was ordered to march with Philip H. Sheridan's Second Division and Thomas J. Wood's Third Division of his Fourth Corps, Army of the Cumberland from Chattanooga to the relief of Knoxville. Granger moved out immediately on the River Road, through Harrison and Georgetown, toward Decatur, Tennessee.

At that time, William T. Sherman was in Georgia following Bragg's retreating army toward Dalton. With him were two divisions of Frank P. Blair's Fifteenth Corps, Jefferson C. Davis' Second Division, Fourteenth Corps, and Oliver O. Howard's Eleventh Corps. On the night of November 27, 1863, Howard's Eleventh Corps and Davis' division were at Parker's Gap at White Oak Mountain, in the direction of Red Clay, Georgia, and Blair's Fifteenth Corps was at Graysville, Georgia. On November 28, Sherman was directed by Grant to march with his command to the Hiwassee River, toward Knoxville, before returning to Chattanooga. That day John E. Smith's Second Division of Seventeenth Corps, which was a part of Sherman's command, returned to Chattanooga.

November 29, 1863, Sherman's command moved to Cleveland, Tennessee, and the next day it arrived at Charleston, Tennessee, on the Hiwassee River. Upon arriving there, Sherman learned that Granger, with his two divisions of Fourth Corps, was moving on his left toward Decatur, and he then received orders to assume command of Granger's troops, in addition to his own, and with this combined force to move on rapidly to the relief of Burnside at Knoxville. Sherman's column continued its advance along the East Tennessee and Georgia Railroad through Athens, arriving at Loudon on the Tennessee River on December 2. That day Granger was at Decatur, and was under orders to report to Sherman near Loudon.

The bridge over the Tennessee River at Loudon had been destroyed, and Sherman was forced to turn east toward Maryville, where he arrived December 5, 1863. At Maryville he learned that Longstreet had departed with his army from in front of Knoxville. After an unsuccessful assault on the fortifications at Knoxville November 29, and learning of Sherman's approach, Longstreet had withdrawn toward Rogersville, Tennessee during the night of December 3 and the following day.

Sherman then halted all the troops of his command at Maryville except the two divisions of Granger's Fourth Corps, which had originally been ordered to reinforce Burnside's army. Granger then moved on with his divisions to Little River and reported in person to Burnside for orders. David S. Stanley's First Division, Fourth Corps joined the other two divisions in East Tennessee in January, and Granger remained with his corps in East Tennessee during the rest of the winter.

On December 6, 1863, the remaining troops of Sherman's force began their return toward Chattanooga. This movement was conducted in a rather leisurely manner because much time was spent in occupying the country and gathering supplies. Fifteenth Corps was along the Hiwassee River December 14, when Sherman received orders to leave Eli Long's cavalry brigade at Charleston and return to Chattanooga. Davis' division remained at Columbus, Tennessee from December 7 to December 14, and it then marched toward Chattanooga. It arrived at its former camps December 19.

Eleventh Corps returned by much the same route that it had taken during its advance, arriving at its former encampment in Lookout Valley December 17, 1863.

The organization of the troops under Sherman's command at the time of the march to the relief of Burnside's army at Knoxville, Tennessee was as follows:

FOURTH CORPS, Gordon Granger

Second Division, Philip H. Sheridan
    First Brigade, Francis T. Sherman
    Second Brigade, George D. Wagner
    Third Brigade, Charles G. Harker
    Artillery, Warren P. Edgarton
        Battery M, 1st Illinois Light Artillery, George W. Spencer
        10th Battery, Indiana Light Artillery, William A. Naylor
        Battery G, 1st Missouri Light Artillery, Gustavus Schueler
        Battery I, 1st Ohio Light Artillery, Hubert Dilger
        Battery G, 4th United States Artillery, Christopher F. Merkle

Battery H, 5th United States Artillery, Francis L. Guenther

Note 1. David S. Stanley commanded First Division, with headquarters at Bridgeport, Alabama. First Brigade of the division was also at Bridgeport. Charles Cruft, with parts of Walter C. Whitaker's Second Brigade and William Grose's Third Brigade, was with Joseph Hooker's command during the pursuit of Bragg into Georgia.

Note 2. The last three of the above batteries were temporarily attached to the division.

ELEVENTH CORPS, Oliver O. Howard

Second Division, Adolph von Steinwehr
First Brigade, Adolphus Buschbeck
Second Brigade, Orland Smith

Third Division, Carl Schurz
First Brigade, Hector Tyndale
Second Brigade, Wladimir Krzyzanowski
Third Brigade, Frederick Hecker

Artillery, Thomas W. Osborn
Battery I, 1st New York Light Artillery, Michael Wiedrich
13th Battery, New York Light Artillery, William Wheeler
Battery K, 1st Ohio Light Artillery, Nicholas Sahm

Note. There was no First Division in Eleventh Corps at that time.

FOURTEENTH CORPS

Second Division, Jefferson C. Davis
First Brigade, James D. Morgan
Second Brigade, John Beatty
Third Brigade, Daniel McCook
Artillery, William A. Hotchkiss
Battery I, 2nd Illinois Light Artillery, Henry B. Plant
2nd Battery, Minnesota Light Artillery, Richard L. Dawley
5th Battery, Wisconsin Light Artillery, George Q. Gardner

Note. Davis' Second Division was attached to Sherman's command during the battles at Chattanooga.

FIFTEENTH CORPS, Frank P. Blair, Jr.

Second Division, Morgan L. Smith
First Brigade, Nathan W. Tupper

Second Brigade, Joseph A. J. Lightburn
Artillery
Battery A, 1st Illinois Light Artillery, Peter P. Wood
Battery B, 1st Illinois Light Artillery, Israel P. Rumsey
Battery H, 1st Illinois Light Artillery, Francis De Gress

Fourth Division, Hugh Ewing
First Brigade, John M. Loomis
Second Brigade, Charles C. Walcutt
Third Brigade, Joseph R. Cockerill
Artillery, Henry Richardson
Battery F, 1st Illinois Light Artillery, John T. Cheney
Battery I, 1st Illinois Light Artillery, Josiah H. Burton
Battery D, 1st Missouri Light Artillery, Byron M. Callender

Peter J. Osterhaus' First Division, Fifteenth Corps was assigned to Joseph Hooker's command November 23, 1863 and was not with Blair on the march to the relief of Knoxville.

Eli Long's Second Brigade, Second Cavalry Division, Army of the Cumberland reported to Sherman at Cleveland, Tennessee November 29, 1863. Long then marched through Benton and Columbus and joined Sherman's column at Athens, Tennessee about 2:00 A.M. December 2.

LITTLE ROCK, ARKANSAS EXPEDITION (STEELE) AUGUST 1, 1863– SEPTEMBER 14, 1863

July 27, 1863, Frederick Steele was assigned by Ulysses S. Grant, commanding the Department of the Tennessee, to organize and command an army and advance with it from Helena, Arkansas toward Little Rock. Steele arrived at Helena July 31 and began the organization of a force from Stephen A. Hurlbut's Sixteenth Corps, Army of the Tennessee and John W. Davidson's First Cavalry Division, Department of the Missouri, which was then operating in Arkansas. Steele's command was known as the Army of Arkansas, Arkansas Expedition, and also Steele's Little Rock Expedition.

The troops then at Helena consisted of Nathan Kimball's Provisional Division of Sixteenth Corps, which had recently arrived from Vicksburg, Mississippi, and Frederick Salomon's Thirteenth Division, Thirteenth Corps. Kimball's Provisional Division, which had been sent from Memphis, Tennessee to Vicksburg June 3, 1863, consisted of three brigades of Sixteenth Corps: First Brigade, Third Division; Third Brigade, Third Division; and four regiments of Sixth Division.

On August 10, 1863, the troops at Helena (Thirteenth Division, Thirteenth Corps) were organized into a division, which was designated as Third Division, Army of Arkansas. Samuel A. Rice was assigned command of this division during the absence of Salomon, who was on leave. That day, Rice marched out of Helena toward Little Rock. Kimball's Provisional Division was redesignated as Second Division, Army of Arkansas under William E. McLean, who had relieved Kimball in command August 4, when the latter departed on leave. The next day, McLean's division followed Third Division toward Little Rock.

When the army advanced into Arkansas, it was operating in the Department of the Missouri, and after it left Helena, Steele reported to John M. Schofield, commander of the Department of the Missouri. The troops from Sixteenth Corps were noted on the books at corps headquarters as detached.

The Confederate troops in Arkansas at that time belonged to Sterling Price's District of Arkansas. They consisted of Price's Division (commanded by Daniel M. Frost), L. Marsh Walker's Division (commanded by Archibald S. Dobbin after Walker was mortally wounded in a duel), and John S. Marmaduke's cavalry division. Marmaduke's and Walker's divisions, both under the command of Walker, advanced to Clarendon, then fell back before Steele's advance. Frost's division remained at and near Little Rock. Dobbin's division (formerly Walker's) was engaged at Ashley's Mills and at Bayou Fourche.

At the end of July 1863, Davidson's cavalry division was at Wittsburg, Arkansas, on the Saint Francis River west of Memphis. Then, during the period August 1–8, it marched to Clarendon, where

it joined the other two divisions of the army. James M. True's Third Brigade, Third Division, Sixteenth Corps, which was on the march to join Steele's army, did not arrive at Clarendon until August 29.

Steele's entire force, except True's brigade, was assembled at Clarendon, and August 17, 1863 it marched toward Devall's Bluff on White River, where it arrived August 23. The next day, Davidson moved on toward Brownsville, which he occupied August 25. He drove back the enemy into their entrenchments at Bayou Meto on August 26, then returned to Brownsville. Steele established a defensible camp at Devall's Bluff, and on September 1 he marched toward Brownsville, arriving the next day.

The road along the south side of Bayou Meto was impassable for military operations, and Steele ordered Davidson to make a reconnaissance around the enemy's left toward Austin. He also ordered Rice to move forward and make a diversion to aid Davidson's movement. Rice drove in the enemy's pickets, shelled the woods on the south side of the the river, and then camped for the night.

When Davidson returned from his reconnaissance and reported that a movement toward Austin was not feasible, Steele decided to advance around the enemy's right on a road that ran by Shallow Ford on Bayou Meto, and Ashley's Mills to the Arkansas River. He left True's brigade and John F. Ritter's Reserve Brigade of the cavalry division to guard the sick and the trains, and on September 6, 1863, with the cavalry out in front, he resumed the march with the rest of his command. The next day, he reached the Arkansas River near Ashley's Mills, where Davidson had a sharp skirmish with the enemy.

Steele spent September 8–9, 1863 reconnoitering and bringing up the sick and the trains from Brownsville. He then decided to attack. Davidson was to cross the river on a pontoon bridge and move directly toward Little Rock to threaten the Confederate right and rear. At the same time, Steele, with the infantry, was to attack the right flank of the enemy's works on the north bank of the river.

In accordance with this plan, Davidson crossed the river near Bearskin Lake on the morning of September 10, 1863. He was aided in this movement by Second Division, which covered the crossing. He then advanced on the direct road to Little Rock, without interruption until he reached Bayou Fourche, where he found the enemy in a defensive position. A heavy artillery fire from across the river soon caused the enemy to give way, and Davidson pursued toward Little Rock. Steele's two columns advanced nearly abreast on both sides of the Arkansas River. Price then evacuated the city and retired by way of Benton and Rockport to Arkadelphia. Little Rock was surrendered on the evening of September 10.

During the night of September 10, 1863, Davidson assigned Lewis Merrill to the command of a temporary division consisting of cavalry and artillery and directed him to pursue Price's retreating column. The division was organized as follows:

Merrill's Division, Lewis Merrill
   First Brigade, Washington F. Geiger
   Second Brigade, Powell Clayton
   Artillery, Gustave Stange
      Battery M, 2nd Missouri Light Artillery, Gustave Stange
      Battery K, 2nd Missouri Light Artillery, Thaddeus S. Clarkson
      George F. Lovejoy's Howitzers of Merrill's Horse (2nd Missouri Cavalry)

Merrill did not continue the pursuit very long, and soon returned to Little Rock with his command.

The organization of the Army of Arkansas during August 1863 was as follows:

ARMY OF ARKANSAS, Frederick Steele

First Cavalry Division, John W. Davidson
   First Brigade, Washington F. Geiger
   Second Brigade, John M. Glover
   Reserve Brigade, John F. Ritter
   Artillery, Julius L. Hadley
      Battery K, 2nd Missouri Light Artillery, Thaddeus S. Clarkson
      Battery M, 2nd Missouri Light Artillery, Gustave Stange
      25th Battery, Ohio Light Artillery, Julius L. Hadley

Note. Lewis Merrill, who had been ill, resumed command of First Brigade early in September, and commanded the brigade at the engagement at Bayou Fourche September 10, 1863.

Second Division (Provisional Division), William E. McLean, to September 6, 1863
   Adolph Engelmann
   First Brigade, William H. Graves
   Second Brigade, Oliver Wood

Third Division, Samuel A. Rice
   First Brigade, Charles W. Kittredge
   Second Brigade, Thomas H. Benton, Jr.

Cavalry Brigade, Unattached, Powell Clayton

Artillery, Mortimer M. Hayden
   Battery K, 1st Missouri Light Artillery, Stillman O. Fish
   3rd Battery, Iowa Light Artillery, Melvil C. Wright

Steele occupied Little Rock September 10, 1863, and established Headquarters, Army of Arkansas there.

James M. True's Third Brigade, Third Division, Sixteenth Corps was en route from Helena to join the army during August 1863, and did not appear on the original returns until September 10.

Kimball returned to the army from leave, and September 13, 1863 was assigned command of Second Division. The division was then reorganized as follows: True's brigade was assigned to Second Division and on September 18 was designated as First Brigade, Second Division; Graves' former First Brigade became Third Brigade; and Engelmann's brigade (formerly commanded by Wood) was continued as Second Brigade.

September 14, 1863, John E. Smith was sent with Seventh Division, Seventeenth Corps from Vicksburg to reinforce Steele, but after arriving at Devall's Bluff, he was ordered back to Vicksburg when it was learned that Little Rock had been occupied.

Salomon also returned to the army and October 8, 1863 was assigned command of Third Division, relieving Rice. Rice was then assigned command of Second Brigade, Third Division.

In November 1863, Kimball was ordered to Indiana, and Eugene A. Carr was assigned command of Second Division.

The Department of Arkansas was created January 6, 1864, and on that date the troops in the department were designated as Seventh Corps. For further information, see Department of Arkansas.

When Steele occupied Little Rock, there were other United States troops in western Arkansas that belonged to James G. Blunt's District of the Frontier, Department of Missouri. These were William

F. Cloud's Second Brigade, District of the Frontier, which was at Fort Smith, and Thomas M. Bowen's Third Brigade, District of the Frontier, which was at Van Buren. In December 1863, a force under James M. Williams occupied Roseville, Arkansas. In January 1864, these forces were included in Seventh Corps, Department of Arkansas.

MERIDIAN, MISSISSIPPI EXPEDITION FEBRUARY 3, 1864– MARCH 6, 1864

During the latter part of 1863, after the capture of Vicksburg by Union forces under Ulysses S. Grant, there was some apprehension among the Federal high command that Confederate forces might become active and threaten West Tennessee and possibly attempt again to close the Mississippi River to Federal shipping. Other events, however, prevented Grant from undertaking any offensive action at that time to strengthen his hold on the river.

After the Battle of Chickamauga in September 1863, William S. Rosecrans' defeated Army of the Cumberland retreated within the defenses of Chattanooga, and it was soon under siege when Braxton Bragg's Confederate Army of Tennessee moved up and occupied Lookout Mountain and Missionary Ridge. Rosecrans' situation soon became critical because of a serious shortage of food and supplies, and in late September, William T. Sherman was ordered to move with his Fifteenth Corps, Army of the Tennessee, which was then at Vicksburg, Mississippi, to Chattanooga to aid in relieving the Army of the Cumberland. Sherman left James M. Tuttle's Third Division, Fifteenth Corps at Vicksburg, and with Peter J. Osterhaus' First Division, Morgan L. Smith's Second Division, and Hugh Ewing's Fourth Division moved up the Mississippi River to Memphis, Tennessee. There he was joined by John E. Smith's Second Division, Seventeenth Corps and with his four divisions marched eastward toward Chattanooga.

While Sherman's movement was in progress, on October 18, 1863, Grant assumed command of the Military Division of the Mississippi, and Sherman succeeded Grant in command of the Army of the Tennessee. Shortly after Sherman assumed command, he proposed a plan for the destruction of the important Confederate rail center of Meridian, Mississippi and the enemy resources in Central Mississippi as a means of strengthening the Federal position at Vicksburg. Sherman's plan also included an expedition up the Yazoo River to the vicinity of Chula, and from there a movement to destroy the Mississippi Central Railroad between Canton and Grenada, Mississippi.

Sherman had more pressing matters to attend to at that time, however, and the Meridian expedition was delayed until the affairs at Chattanooga were concluded. Finally, after Grant succeeded in driving Bragg's army from Lookout Mountain November 24 and Missionary Ridge November 25, Sherman left his Fifteenth Corps, then commanded by Frank P. Blair, to aid in repairing the Nashville and Chattanooga Railroad between Nashville and Stevenson, Alabama, and he departed on leave for his home at Lancaster, Ohio. He then began to consider seriously his proposed expedition to Meridian.

At that time, the Union troops under Sherman's command that were on the Mississippi River consisted of the following: James B. McPherson's Seventeenth Corps was at Vicksburg, with Walter Q. Gresham's Third Brigade, Fourth Division at Natchez, Mississippi; and Stephen A. Hurlbut's Sixteenth Corps was at Memphis and other points in western Tennessee and western Kentucky. In addition, there was a fleet of Union gunboats on the river commanded by Elias K. Owen.

By late January 1864, Sherman's plans were completed. He was to move from Vicksburg toward Meridian, about 120 miles to the east, with a force consisting of two divisions of Seventeenth Corps, which were then at Vicksburg under the command of McPherson, and two divisions of Sixteenth Corps, which Hurlbut was to bring downriver from Memphis to Vicksburg. At the same time, William Sooy Smith, chief of cavalry of the Military Division of the Mississippi, was to march from Memphis not later than February 1 with a cavalry force of about 7,000 men. He was to proceed by way of Pontotoc, Okolona, and Artesia Depot, not far from Columbus, Mississippi, and arrive at Meridian about February 10. As he advanced, he was to destroy the Mobile and Ohio Railroad and all Confederate supplies along the route.

As a diversion for the main column, a fleet of five gunboats and transports carrying two regiments of infantry was to move up the Yazoo River to draw the attention of the enemy to that area. Still another diversion was ordered to be carried out by troops not belonging to Sherman's command. Nathaniel P. Banks was directed to make a feint on Mobile, Alabama with troops from his Department of the Gulf, and he was to be supported in this operation by Admiral David G. Farragut with his Western Gulf Blockading Squadron.

As a part of the overall military plans in the West, it was intended that the Meridian Expedition be completed by the end of February 1864 so that Sherman could send a part of his troops to Louisiana to join Banks for his projected movement up the Red River toward Shreveport.

Sherman had selected Meridian as the objective of his expedition for two important reasons. Two major rail lines crossed there, one running north and south, and the other east and west. The Southern Railroad of Mississippi ran westward from Meridian to Vicksburg, and at Meridian it connected with a rail line running eastward to Selma, Alabama. The Mobile and Ohio Railroad, which ran northward from Mobile, Alabama to Columbus, Kentucky, also passed through Meridian. These two railroads carried supplies for the Confederate forces operating in northern Mississippi and western Tennessee. In addition to its importance as a rail center, there were also railroad shops, warehouses for supplies, hospitals, and other public properties at Meridian, and their destruction would seriously hamper future enemy operations in the area.

At the end of his leave, Sherman left Lancaster and traveled to Cincinnati. From there he moved on to Cairo, Illinois, arriving on the night of January 3, 1864. He then continued on downriver on a steamboat, in freezing weather, and reached Memphis on the night of January 10. Upon arrival there, Sherman discussed his plans with Hurlbut, then resumed his journey, reaching Vicksburg on January 15. He then conferred with McPherson, and directed him to make some necessary troop dispositions in preparation for the coming expedition.

As a result of his discussions with Grant, McPherson ordered John P. Hawkins to transfer his force of United States Colored Troops from Milliken's Bend and Goodrich's Landing to Vicksburg and occupy the defensive works about the city. Also, on January 19, 1864, McPherson ordered Embury D. Osband, then at Skipwith's Landing, Mississippi with his 1st Mississippi Cavalry (Colored), to move with his command by steamboats to Snyder's Bluff on the Yazoo River and take position to protect that post.

With these and other matters attended to, Sherman returned to Memphis January 20, 1864 to complete the arrangements for transferring the troops of Sixteenth Corps to Vicksburg. At that time he learned that Andrew J. Smith's troops of the District of Columbus were still at Columbus, Kentucky, and that he had not yet started for Memphis as expected. James M. Tuttle's First Division was then at La Grange, Tennessee, and Tuttle was ordered to bring it to Memphis at once. Sherman remained at Memphis until Hurlbut had embarked with his two divisions for Vicksburg, and then on January 27 he followed him down the river.

Meantime, at Vicksburg, McPherson had been active in assembling his troops and preparing for the advance toward Meridian, and when Sherman arrived at Vicksburg January 29, 1864, he found McPherson ready. Hurlbut's troops, however, were behind schedule.

At the time Sherman was preparing for his Meridian Expedition, Leonidas Polk was in command of the Confederate Department of Alabama, Mississippi, and East Louisiana, with headquarters at Meridian. Under his command in Mississippi were two infantry divisions and two divisions of cavalry. William W. Loring's infantry division was at Canton, and it consisted of three brigades commanded by John Adams, Abraham Buford, and Winfield S. Featherston. Samuel G. French's infantry division was at Brandon, east of Jackson, and it consisted of the brigades of Matthew D. Ector, Francis M. Cockrell, and Evander McNair.

The cavalry corps of Polk's department was commanded by Stephen D. Lee, and it consisted of two divisions. William H. Jackson's division consisted of four brigades: Peter B. Starke's brigade was at Brownsville; Lawrence S. Ross' brigade was along the Yazoo River and the Mississippi Central Railroad, with headquarters near Benton; Wirt Adams' brigade was near Raymond; and Samuel W.

Ferguson's brigade was at Aberdeen. On the night of January 26, 1864, however, Ferguson was ordered to Jackson. He left Aberdeen January 28 and reached Clinton February 5. Troops of Nathan B. Forrest's Cavalry Department were at Oxford, Mississippi.

In preparation for his advance on Meridian, Sherman divided his army into two wings. The Right Wing was commanded by McPherson, and it consisted of Mortimer D. Leggett's Third Division, Marcellus M. Crocker's Fourth Division, and Alexander Chambers' Third Brigade of First Division, all of Seventeenth Corps. James M. Tuttle's First Division of Sixteenth Corps did not arrive at Vicksburg from Memphis until February 3, and because of its late arrival, Sherman assigned Chambers' brigade to march with the expedition, and he directed Tuttle to remain near Vicksburg with his two brigades. Hurlbut commanded the Left Wing of the army, which consisted of Andrew J. Smith's Third Division and James C. Veatch's detachment of Fourth Division of Sixteenth Corps. Edward F. Winslow's cavalry brigade was to operate as a separate command and was to report directly to Sherman.

When Andrew J. Smith's Third Division of Sixteenth Corps disembarked at Vicksburg, it marched out on the road to Bridgeport, and on February 2, 1864 it advanced to Camp Creek. The first troops of Veatch's Fourth Division of Sixteenth Corps began landing at Vicksburg at 2:00 A.M. February 2, and they then marched out on the Bridgeport road and went into camp six miles east of the city. The rest of the division arrived during the day.

Sherman's army began its advance from Vicksburg February 3, 1864. Winslow's cavalry and McPherson's Right Wing marched by way of the Baldwin's Ferry road and the Jackson road to the Big Black River Bridge. About 8:00 A.M. Winslow arrived near the destroyed railroad bridge over the Big Black; he crossed the river about noon and moved on toward Edwards Station.

At noon February 3, 1864, McPherson's Right Wing began crossing the Big Black on the pontoon bridge. Winslow's cavalry advanced through Edwards Station and camped that night at the bridge over Baker's Creek. The infantry followed Winslow, and Leggett's division halted for the night near Amsterdam; Crocker's division camped near Ed-

wards Station, five miles from the river; and Chambers' brigade camped on the east bank of the Big Black River. The only Confederate troops present to oppose Sherman's advance that day were the cavalry brigades of Wirt Adams and Peter B. Starke, but, as noted above, early on the morning of February 5, Ferguson's brigade reached Clinton from Aberdeen and joined the other two brigades.

Hurlbut's divisions also began their advance on the morning of February 3, 1864. Andrew J. Smith's division started first and moved to Messinger's Ford on the Big Black River, camping there that night on the west bank. Veatch's division did not march until about 2:00 P.M. February 3, and it halted for the night on Clear Creek, ten miles from Vicksburg, where Smith's division had spent the previous night.

Tuttle, with James L. Geddes' Third Brigade and Joseph A. Mower's Second Brigade of his division, marched out to the Big Black River Bridge and remained there during the campaign to occupy the bridgehead after the rest of the army had departed.

Early on the morning of February 4, 1864, McPherson's column resumed its advance, with Crocker's division marching in front. The mounted troops that were ahead of Crocker's division encountered strong resistance from some of Adams' cavalry at Champion Hill, and Cyrus Hall's Second Brigade was sent forward to help clear the way. Crocker's division advanced only about ten miles that day, and Leggett's division followed. The corps halted for the night near the junction of the Clinton, Bolton, and Raymond roads. Chambers' brigade moved up from the Big Black to a position near the site of the Champion house.

At daybreak February 4, 1864, Andrew J. Smith's division crossed the Big Black River on a pontoon bridge and, with David Moore's First Brigade in front, marched toward Reynolds' Ponds. Moore's brigade was first engaged with Starke's cavalry near Queen's Hill Church, and then again near Reynolds' Ponds, but shortly before dark Starke withdrew, and Smith halted near Reynolds' Ponds. Queen's Hill Church was at a point where the road on which Hurlbut was traveling branched, with the left branch running to Canton, and the right branch to Clinton. Reynolds' Ponds was east of the Joseph Davis plantation on the Bridgeport road. Veatch's division marched at 5:30 that morning, with James H. Howe's Second Brigade in front, and Milton

Montgomery's First Brigade, which accompanied the trains, following Howe. The corps halted near the Cowan house, eighteen miles from the river, at 10:00 A.M.

At daylight February 5, 1864, Andrew J. Smith continued his march eastward, and a short time later he encountered Adams' cavalry about a half-mile east of Baker's Creek. Smith pushed on, however, and camped that night east of Clinton. Veatch remained at Queen's Hill Church until 1:00 P.M., then moved eastward and halted for the night at 5:00 P.M. about midway between the church and the Joseph E. Davis plantation, about eighteen miles from the river.

McPherson's Right Wing also began its march early on February 5, 1864. It moved eastward along the Jackson road with Leggett's division in the lead, pursuing the enemy through Clinton. Winslow, operating on the left flank of Seventeenth Corps, entered Clinton by the Raymond road just as the infantry was moving in on the main Jackson road and when the rear of the enemy column was marching out to the east.

At Clinton, by Sherman's orders, McPherson turned off from the road to the left to attempt to find a plantation road that entered Jackson between the roads that ran into the town from Clinton and Raymond. Hurlbut marched eastward that day on the main Clinton-Jackson road. After marching two and a half miles across fields, McPherson's advance came into a road and found Winslow's cavalry. Winslow moved out against the flank of the enemy cavalry that was falling back on the main road before Hurlbut, and McPherson followed Winslow. It was hoped by this movement that the cavalry would be able to pass to the left of Adams' and Starke's cavalry and regain the Jackson road in their rear. Winslow's cavalry crossed Lynch Creek, not far from Jackson, just after dark and rode into Jackson on the Raymond road just as the enemy was withdrawing from the town.

During the afternoon, McPherson's infantry continued its advance toward Jackson by way of the Robinson road. It became dark, however, before it reached Jackson, and Seventeenth Corps camped on the Robinson road near Lynch Creek, about two and a half miles west of the town. During the evening, McPherson became concerned that only cavalry held Jackson, and he sent forward Manning F.

Force's First Brigade of Leggett's division to support Winslow. At 10:30 P.M. Force came up and took position behind the enemy's old defensive line near the Clinton road.

On February 5, 1864, Hurlbut's corps moved southward from the Bridgeport road to the Jackson road and followed in rear of the army. Veatch's division, which followed Andrew J. Smith's division, did not leave Queen's Hill Church until 1:00 P.M., and both divisions camped that night east of Clinton.

French's Confederate division reached Jackson late in the afternoon of February 4, 1864. When Sherman's men entered the town, French, with his infantry and a part of Lee's cavalry, was east of the Pearl River on the way to Brandon. The rest of the enemy's cavalry was unable to cross the river and was forced to retreat northward toward Canton. Loring's division was also west of the Pearl River, and both Loring and the cavalry would have to find a crossing of the river before they could rejoin French's troops marching for Brandon.

On the morning of February 6, 1864, Winslow made a reconnaissance in the direction of Canton, but after advancing about five miles and finding no enemy troops, he returned toward Jackson and camped near the Insane Asylum.

At 5:00 A.M. Veatch moved from his camp, ten miles east of Queen's Hill Church. He halted at 10:00 A.M. four miles west of Jackson. Crocker's and Leggett's divisions remained in their camps until about 11:00 A.M. while the pioneers constructed a bridge over the Pearl River, and about noon the two divisions moved into Jackson. The bridge over the river was completed about 3:30 P.M., and then Chambers' brigade crossed and established a bridgehead near Conway Slough, about two miles east of the river.

The army resumed the march eastward on the morning of February 7, 1864. Leggett marched through Jackson at sunrise February 7, crossed the Pearl River, and marched to Conway's Slough, where Chambers was in camp, and he halted there until Crocker came up. Crocker crossed the river soon after Leggett and marched eastward along the Wire Road, north of the railroad. As soon as Crocker had passed Conway Slough, Leggett and Chambers resumed their march and followed Crocker.

Hurlbut's Sixteenth Corps broke camp at 7:00

A.M. February 7, 1864, and James H. Howe's Second Brigade of Veatch's division marched into Jackson, where it relieved McPherson's provost guard. Andrew J. Smith's division then began to cross the river, and it was followed by Milton Montgomery's First Brigade of Veatch's division. Winslow's cavalry brigade, which had spent the night near the Insane Asylum, marched to the river and crossed after Montgomery. Howe's brigade, which had been holding Jackson, then crossed the river after Winslow. Seventeenth Corps marched eastward on the Wire Road that day, passed through Brandon during the afternoon, and camped that night on a branch of Richland Creek, about two miles northeast of Brandon. Hurlbut's Sixteenth Corps, except Howe's brigade, camped that night around Brandon and on Terrapin Skin Creek, several miles west of Brandon. The town of Brandon was completely destroyed by Sherman's men.

At Brandon, Winslow's cavalry, which had been left behind at Jackson for a time, came up and was assigned to lead the column on the remainder of the march to Meridian.

On the morning of February 8, 1864, the march was resumed, with Winslow's cavalry out in front. Winslow skirmished with the cavalry of Adams and Starke almost continuously during the day, and he camped that night on Line Creek, about five miles from Morton. Seventeenth Corps marched from Brandon and followed the cavalry until late afternoon, then camped on Line Creek. Sixteenth Corps marched from Terrapin Skin Creek at 11:00 A.M., passed through Brandon, and finally halted at 10:00 P.M. at the point where the Wire Road crossed the Southern Railroad of Mississippi, near present-day Gulde.

Before daybreak on February 9, 1864, Seventeenth Corps resumed its march eastward from Line Creek toward Morton. Sixteenth Corps left its camps on the Wire Road at 5:30 that morning and followed Seventeenth Corps, marching several miles in its rear. Winslow's cavalry, which had been moving out in front of the column, had ridden back to report to Hurlbut on Line Creek, and it then moved out again, this time in front of Sixteenth Corps. In that order they passed through Morton at 4:00 P.M., and then the camps of Seventeenth Corps and Sixteenth Corps bivouacked at 9:00 that night on the west bank of Shockalooo Creek, after a march of twenty-five miles.

On February 10, 1864, Winslow again marched in front of the infantry and was engaged during the day with Ferguson's cavalry, which had been left to cover the enemy's retreat. Winslow camped that night about five miles in advance of the infantry on Hontokalo Creek. The advance units of Sixteenth Corps left their camps at 6:00 A.M. February 10 and entered Hillsboro about 9:00 A.M. Seventeenth Corps left Morton about 6:00 A.M., passed through Hillsboro about dark, and halted on Tallabogue Creek, three and a half miles east of Hillsboro. On passing through Hillsboro, some of Sherman's men were fired on from the houses of the town, and Federal troops promptly burned almost every house in the town.

On February 11, 1864, the army advanced toward Decatur, about fourteen miles distant. The march that day was exceedingly difficult because of narrow muddy roads, swampy ground, burned bridges, and constant enemy opposition, and progress was tiresome and slow. Sixteenth Corps left its camps on Tallabogue Creek and, with Winslow in advance, marched eastward, camping that evening on the east bank of Conehatta Creek. Seventeenth Corps, which followed Sixteenth Corps, finally halted late at night on Tuscalameta Creek.

The early part of the morning of February 12, 1863 was spent repairing roads through the Tuscalameta Swamp, and it was not until 8:00 A.M. that Sixteenth Corps began its march, with Winslow's cavalry leading the way. Ferguson's cavalry delayed the Federal march until about noon, and then it withdrew to a new position about two miles distant. At about that time, Stephen D. Lee arrived at Decatur with the brigades of Adams and Starke. Andrew J. Smith's division, which was leading Sixteenth Corps that morning, entered Decatur sometime after noon. Sherman then ordered Hurlbut to move on for about four miles and halt for the night. The head of McPherson's Seventeenth Corps was about four miles west of Decatur. Winslow halted about 5:00 P.M. on Tallasher Creek, east of Chunky Creek, after a march of about fifteen miles. Seventeenth Corps bivouacked that night in the destroyed town of Decatur. During the march of the army that day, most of the houses were burned, and most of the public property was destroyed.

Winslow marched out from his camps on

Tallasher Creek at daylight February 13, 1864 and almost immediately became engaged with Ferguson's cavalry. Winslow pushed ahead, however, and by late that evening he had arrived within fourteen miles of Meridian. Sherman ordered him to continue his advance and directed Hurlbut to move forward and support the cavalry. Winslow experienced considerable difficulty in advancing his brigade because of the difficult nature of the ground and the stubborn resistance offered by Ferguson, but he did not halt until after midnight, when he was within ten miles of Meridian.

Sixteenth Corps followed Winslow's cavalry that morning. It crossed Tallasher Creek and moved up to the bridge over Tallahatta Creek, which had been destroyed but was soon rebuilt. At this point, Force's brigade and Chambers' brigade were detached to guard the wagon trains of the two corps and also the sick and wounded, which were to be left there. The rest of Sixteenth Corps continued its march and camped that night on Bogue Filliah (also spelled Filiah) after a difficult march of only eight miles. Seventeenth Corps left Decatur on the morning of February 13, 1864 and followed Sixteenth Corps all day. It camped that night west of Tallahatta Creek.

At daybreak February 14, 1864, Force's brigade of Leggett's division was detached and sent to Chunky Station, eight miles to the south, to destroy the Southern Railroad of Mississippi at that point. Force encountered the enemy about one mile from Chunky Station and, after a sharp fight, drove them back across Chunky Creek (or River) about 9 A.M. Force then destroyed the depot, the railroad bridge, some extensive trestlework, water tanks, and track, and in addition burned many of the houses of the village. Force, with his brigade, returned to the wagon train the next day.

Leggett, with Benjamin F. Potts' Second Brigade and Jasper A. Maltby's Third Brigade of his division of Seventeenth Corps, began his march on the Meridian road at 9:00 A.M. February 14, 1864. Progress was slow because it was necessary to build a bridge across Tallahatta Creek and to corduroy some of the road, and McPherson was still about seven miles from Meridian at 4:00 P.M. He then ordered Leggett to march with his two brigades to Meridian and to send Force's brigade to Oktibbeha Creek (also spelled Okatibee), where Crocker's di-

vision was to camp that night. The two brigades sent to Meridian were instructed to report directly to Sherman for orders. Seventeenth Corps marched about thirteen miles that day and bivouacked near the Matthews plantation on the Oktibbeha. That night, McPherson ordered Crocker to move with his division into Meridian the next morning.

At 6:30 A.M. February 14, 1863, Sixteenth Corps moved out from Bogue Filliah, with Andrew J. Smith's division in the lead, and marched to Sukualena Creek. There the main column turned to the right and moved south to the Meridian road. It then followed that road to Oktibbeha Creek, two and a half miles west of Meridian. After a bridge was rebuilt across the creek, Winslow crossed and found that the enemy had withdrawn. He then moved forward toward Meridian, and quickly overran the Confederate rear guard that was covering the evacuation of the town. Winslow then moved into Meridian and on beyond the town. Polk, with the infantry and artillery of his command, had already left Meridian and had moved by rail to Demopolis, Alabama. When the Federal infantry arrived in Meridian, Winslow marched east on the Demopolis road and halted at 3:00 P.M. at McLemore's plantation. Sixteenth Corps reached Meridian at about 5:00 P.M. and went into camp near the railroad.

During the evening of February 14, 1864, Sherman assigned to Hurlbut the task of destroying the railroads running to the east and north of Meridian, and directed McPherson to do the same on the railroads running to the south and west of the town. He also ordered Winslow to remain in position east of Meridian to cover Hurlbut's troops while they worked at destroying the railroad.

Early on the morning of February 15, 1864, Leggett's and Crocker's divisions of Seventeenth Corps marched out from their positions of the night before to the south and west of town and went into camp. The divisions of Veatch and Andrew J. Smith of Sixteenth Corps moved to camps to the north and east of Meridian.

The army rested on February 15, 1864 and the next day began a systematic and complete destruction of the railroads running out of Meridian. During the next few days, the track, bridges, and trestlework were completely destroyed, as were the depots, storehouses, arsenal, hospitals, hotels, offices, and cantonments.

On February 16, 1864, Potts' and Maltby's brigades of Leggett's division destroyed seventeen miles of track west to Chunky's Station, and Force's brigade marched to Meridian. Crocker's division marched south to Enterprise to work on the track, and Walter Q. Gresham's Third Brigade moved on to Quitman, twenty-nine miles south of Meridian, to destroy a long bridge over the Chickasawhay River, and also a bridge and some extensive trestlework on the Mobile and Ohio Railroad between Enterprise and Quitman. Gresham completed his work and returned to Enterprise the next day.

On February 16, 1864, Veatch's brigade of Hurlbut's corps marched toward Marion, on the Mobile and Ohio Railroad, and destroyed the six miles of track between Meridian and Marion. Andrew J. Smith's division destroyed the track on the Selma railroad, east of Meridian. During the next two days this work was continued without interruption. On February 17, Maltby's brigade continued the destruction of the railroad, but Potts' brigade marched northward from Chunky Station to relieve Chambers in charge of the wagon trains. When relieved, Chambers marched to Meridian to aid in the destruction of the railroad.

It will be remembered that when William Sooy Smith's cavalry command was ordered to leave Memphis by February 1, 1864, it was to have joined Sherman at Meridian by February 10. On February 18, however, when Sherman's work of destruction on the railroads was nearly finished, he had received no information about Smith's progress. Because Smith was so far behind schedule, Sherman was concerned about his safety, and he decided to wait one more day before starting his return trip toward Vicksburg.

On February 18, 1864, Veatch's division was at Marion, and Andrew J. Smith's division, which had been destroying the railroad east of Meridian, was marching to join him there. Force's brigade of Leggett's division was at Meridian, Potts' brigade was with the trains on the Tallahatta, and Maltby's brigade was working on the railroad. On February 19, Crocker's division left Enterprise and moved back to the vicinity of Meridian. Leggett's division continued its destruction of the track west of Meridian.

At daybreak February 20, 1864, Sixteenth Corps broke camp at Marion and, with Veatch's division in front, marched on the road toward Louisville. Winslow's cavalry brigade covered the rear of the column that day. The corps camped that night at the confluence of Oktibbeha Creek and Pender Creek.

On February 20, 1864, troops of Seventeenth Corps burned the rest of the buildings in Meridian and prepared to depart. Force's and Chambers' brigades of Leggett's division left Meridian and marched back to the Tallahatta. Early that morning, Potts' brigade, with the wagon trains, marched out of the campground on the Tallahatta, camping that night a mile east of Decatur. Crocker's division, which had been encamped about four miles west of Meridian, followed Leggett's division and camped nearby that night.

February 21, 1864, Sixteenth Corps marched through Union and camped in and near Decatur. Winslow's cavalry, as it had the day before, covered the rear of Sixteenth Corps as it marched and camped that afternoon at Decatur.

Sherman was still concerned about William Sooy Smith, and at Union, on the morning of February 22, 1864, he directed Winslow to ride north with his cavalry and attempt to find Smith's column. Winslow started north early that morning and camped that night on the Atkins plantation. The next morning he rode on toward Louisville, twenty-six miles to the north, on the road used by Grierson on his raid during the Vicksburg Campaign. He passed through Philadelphia, crossed the Pearl River, and continued on to a point about ten miles south of Louisville. At that time he had received no word from Smith, and scouts sent out to determine his whereabouts returned without having discovered a trace of his cavalry. Winslow then decided to proceed no farther. He turned westward and marched across to the main road from Louisville to Kosciusko. From Kosciusko he turned south, passing through Thomastown and Sharon and arriving at Canton at 2:00 P.M. February 25.

Meantime, on February 22, 1864, Sixteenth Corps marched from Union and camped after dark near Tuscalameta Swamp. Seventeenth Corps, except Potts' brigade, marched from Decatur, crossed Tuscalameta Swamp, and camped on Hontokalo Creek. Potts' brigade with the trains halted at Hillsboro.

Early on the morning of February 23, 1864, Seventeenth Corps left Hontokalo Creek and marched through the charred ruins of Hillsboro, camping two miles west of the town on Shockaloo Creek. Sixteenth Corps resumed its march that morning, crossed Tuscalameta Swamp, and camped for the night one-half mile east of Hillsboro. That night all of Sherman's army, except Winslow's brigade, was encamped around Hillsboro.

From that point there were two roads leading to the Pearl River, and they converged near Ratliff's Ferry on the river. Sixteenth Corps left Hillsboro at 9:00 A.M. February 24, 1864, with Andrew J. Smith's division leading, and marched to the northwest on the northern road. It bivouacked that night two miles beyond Coffee Bogue Creek. Seventeenth Corps marched that day on the southern road and bivouacked near Pearl River.

Most of the day February 25, 1864 was spent building a bridge over the Pearl River. When this work was completed about 5:00 P.M., a part of Sixteenth Corps crossed the river, and the rest of Sixteenth Corps and all of Seventeenth Corps camped on the east bank that night. At 2:00 that afternoon, Winslow's cavalry arrived at Canton, ahead of the infantry.

Before daybreak February 26, 1864, Seventeenth Corps began crossing the river. During the day, Crocker's division remained to guard the bridge in the event Winslow might arrive there to cross the river, but Leggett's division marched into Canton. As soon as Seventeenth Corps had crossed the river, the rest of Sixteenth Corps followed, and it was on the west bank by 2:30 P.M. Crocker camped that night at Terry's plantation, about twelve miles east of Canton.

On the evening of February 26, 1864, Sherman's troops were in camp as follows: Winslow's brigade on Three-Mile Creek, east of Canton; Leggett's division about a mile and a half east of Canton; Crocker's division at Terry's plantation, a mile and a half west of the Pearl River; and Sixteenth Corps mostly north of Canton.

Sherman then ordered his troops to rest in their camps about Canton for a time, and he returned under escort to Vicksburg, where he arrived February 28, 1864. He then left for New Orleans to confer with Nathaniel P. Banks and Admiral David D. Porter about the planned expedition on the Red River in northern Louisiana.

On March 1, 1864, by Sherman's orders, Sixteenth Corps left Canton and marched toward Vicksburg. It camped that night at Livingston after a march of about twelve miles. Seventeenth Corps followed Sixteenth Corps during the afternoon and bivouacked about five miles west of Canton on the Livingston road.

On March 2, 1864, the trains passed Edwards Station about 2:00 P.M. and moved on to the Big Black River. Sixteenth and Seventeenth Corps continued their march that day toward the Big Black River.

On March 3, Sixteenth Corps marched from Bogue Chitto and passed through Brownsville and Queen's Hill Church, crossing the Big Black River at 4:30 P.M. Seventeenth Corps crossed the Bogue Chitto that day, marched through Edwards Station, crossed the Big Black River, and returned to Vicksburg. Thus ended Sherman's Meridian Expedition.

William Sooy Smith's Expedition from Memphis, Tennessee toward Meridian, Mississippi, February 11, 1864–February 26, 1864. On January 27, 1864, when Sherman prepared his plans for the Meridian Expedition, he assigned William Sooy Smith, chief of cavalry on Ulysses S. Grant's staff, to the command of the cavalry of the Department of the Tennessee, and directed him to cooperate with the main column under Sherman, which was to march from Vicksburg toward Meridian.

Smith was ordered to leave Collierville, a station on the Memphis and Charleston Railroad twenty-five miles east of Memphis, by February 1, 1864 and join Sherman at Meridian as near February 10 as possible. He was also ordered to destroy all enemy supplies, public property, and the Mobile and Ohio Railroad south of Okolona as he advanced. In addition, Smith was to engage any enemy cavalry that he might meet and drive them south, but his principal mission was to destroy the railroad. Benjamin H. Grierson, commander of the Cavalry Division of Sixteenth Corps, was to accompany the expedition as second in command.

Smith's command was to consist of George E. Waring's First Brigade, William P. Hepburn's Second Brigade, La Fayette McCrillis' Third Brigade, and Charles S. Bowman's 4th United States Cavalry, which was not assigned to a brigade. Isaac W. Curtis' Battery K, 1st Illinois Light Artillery was attached to Hepburn's brigade, and a mountain howitzer battery of four guns, commanded by Charles P. Knispel, was a part of the 4th Missouri Cavalry.

Smith, with the brigades of Hepburn and McCrillis, was ready to depart February 1, 1864 as ordered, but Waring's brigade had not yet arrived. Waring had left Union City, Tennessee January 22, but because of heavy rains the roads were muddy, and in some places under water, and most streams were difficult to cross. Consequently, the march was very slow. Instead of proceeding without Waring, Smith waited at Collierville until he arrived February 8, and then he delayed an additional three days while he organized a pack train.

When James M. Tuttle moved south from Memphis to Vicksburg with his First Division, Sixteenth Corps to join Sherman's expedition to Meridian, he left William L. McMillen's First Brigade at Memphis, and this brigade was assigned temporarily to William Sooy Smith's command. On February 8, 1864, while waiting for Waring, Smith ordered McMillen to move southward from Memphis along the Mississippi and Tennessee Railroad as a diversion for the main column. McMillen marched through Hernando and Senatobia toward Panola, and on February 10 he was directed to move toward Wyatt, where he arrived February 13. The purpose of McMillen's movement was to attract the attention of Nathan B. Forrest, whose Confederate cavalry was south of the Tallahatchie River, while Smith's cavalry force crossed the river farther east. McMillen moved to Waterford February 14, and there he learned that Smith had crossed the river at New Albany that day. With his mission thus accomplished, McMillen turned back toward Memphis, arriving there February 18.

Finally, Smith began to move. On February 10, McCrillis' brigade marched south out of Collierville, crossed the Coldwater River, and camped that night four miles east of Byhalia. His other two brigades began their march from Collierville February 11. Waring's brigade moved out on the road to Moscow eleven miles, and Hepburn's brigade marched to a point east of Byhalia, not far from where McCrillis' brigade had halted the night before. McCrillis had remained in camp that day.

February 12, 1864 Waring's brigade marched to Hudsonville; Hepburn's brigade to a point two miles beyond Waterford; and McCrillis' brigade passed through Holly Springs and halted on Tippah Creek. The next day, Waring marched to a point three miles east of Holly Springs, and Hepburn and McCrillis crossed Tippah Creek and marched toward New Albany.

February 14, 1864, Waring remained east of Holly Springs, while Hepburn and McCrillis crossed the Tallahatchie River at New Albany and camped five miles south of the town. Waring spent the day of February 15 crossing Tippah Creek, and his entire command was not over until daylight the next morning. As a result of this delay, Hepburn and McCrillis were separated by some distance from Waring, and they spent the day in camp. During February 16, Waring marched to New Albany, crossed the Tallahatchie River, and camped at a point near where Hepburn's and McCrillis' brigades had spent the night before. That day these two brigades moved on to within about eight miles of Pontotoc.

At the time that Smith began his advance from Collierville, Forrest's cavalry consisted of four brigades, commanded by Robert V. Richardson, Robert McCulloch, Tyree H. Bell, and Jeffrey E. Forrest, brother of the cavalry commander. McCulloch's and Jeffrey E. Forrest's brigades constituted a division under James R. Chalmers. When the Federal cavalry moved into Mississippi, detachments of Forrest's command were south of the Tallahatchie River watching the crossings, and the rest of his troops were ordered to move eastward through Houston in the direction of West Point and Columbus. Bell's brigade was posted along the Tombigbee River to prevent Smith from crossing to reach Columbus, and Jeffrey E. Forrest was sent to watch the road on which Smith was moving.

On February 17, 1864, Smith moved on south, and about ten miles from Houston he met and defeated a small force of Mississippi State Troops commanded by Samuel J. Gholson. He then moved on to the swamp of Houlka Creek, about three miles north of Houston, and there he decided not to continue on that road. On the morning of February 18, Smith sent Grierson with Hepburn's brigade to Aberdeen to threaten Columbus, and with the other two brigades marched to Okolona, then down the railroad to Egypt Station.

On February 19, 1864, Smith concentrated his division at Prairie Station, about fifteen miles north of West Point, and the next day marched toward West Point. He had proceeded only about five miles when he encountered Jeffrey E. Forrest's brigade, but after some sharp skirmishing, Forrest retired with his men in the direction of West Point. He then passed through the town and halted three miles to the south on Sakatonchee Creek at Ellis' Bridge. Smith's division entered West Point at 3:30 P.M. that afternoon, February 20.

On February 21, 1864, apparently because Smith believed that Stephen D. Lee's cavalry had arrived in the area to join Forrest, and thinking that Sherman had probably completed his mission at Meridian, he ordered his command to fall back on the road by which he had arrived. Then, while Datus E. Coon, with the 2nd Iowa Cavalry of Hepburn's brigade, demonstrated in front of Ellis Bridge, the rest of Smith's column withdrew from West Point and marched toward Okolona.

When Smith retired, Forrest ordered Richardson and Gholson to move toward Okolona, and he also ordered Clark R. Barteau, commanding Bell's brigade while the latter was sick, to march from the Tombigbee and attempt to intercept Smith at Okolona. Chalmers, with Jeffrey E. Forrest's brigade, followed Smith on the Okolona road.

About six miles north of West Point, the enemy advance came up with Smith's column. McCulloch's brigade then moved to the front and attacked, and Smith continued the retreat, halting that night about three miles south of Okolona.

Smith's column resumed the march on the morning of February 22, 1864 on the Pontotoc road, with Hepburn's brigade moving first, then Waring's brigade, and McCrillis' brigade bringing up the rear. As Waring's brigade was passing to the left of Okolona, the 7th Indiana, the rear regiment, was sent to support the 4th United States Cavalry, which had been placed at the edge of the town to watch the enemy's movements, and which was then under attack by Jeffrey E. Forrest, who was followed by McCulloch and Barteau. McCrillis' brigade was also sent to join the 4th United States and 7th Indiana, and for some inexplicable reason, McCrillis' brigade broke and fled northward in complete confusion, leaving five guns in the hands of the enemy. Upon learning of McCrillis' rout, Waring formed his brigade in line and held his position until McCrillis' disorganized troops passed through his line.

Smith's entire command then fell back rapidly to a stronger position about nine or ten miles to the north, where it halted at 5:00 P.M. February 22, 1864 on the Ivey Farm plantation, also called Ivey Hill or Ivey's Hill, seven miles northwest of Okolona near Tallaboncla. There on open sloping ground the cavalry was deployed to fight dismounted on a line that passed through the plantation buildings. Four regiments were placed in line, with a battery near the road. Just to the right of the battery, the 4th Missouri and six companies of the 7th Indiana of Waring's brigade were formed for a charge, and the 3rd Tennessee of McCrillis' brigade was sent to the extreme right to strike the enemy's flank while the other two regiments attacked on his front. While these dispositions were being made, Jeffrey E. Forrest and McCulloch attacked. Smith's rear guard became hard-pressed, and it was withdrawn, but when the enemy came under artillery fire, they were forced to halt. Jeffrey E. Forrest was killed in this attack, and McCulloch was wounded. The 4th Missouri, 7th Indiana, and 3rd Illinois then charged and drove the enemy back. Smith's men held their ground for about an hour while the pack train and the regiments that had become disorganized by the fighting had passed to the rear, and late that evening the entire division marched back to within about two miles of Pontotoc.

Smith continued the retreat to New Albany the next day, and on February 24 moved on to Hudsonville. Waring's brigade arrived at Collierville February 25, and at Memphis the next day. On February 26, Hepburn's and McCrillis' brigades halted at Germantown, between Collierville and Memphis.

Coates' Yazoo, Mississippi Expedition, January 31, 1864–March 6, 1864. As mentioned earlier, it was a part of Sherman's plan for his Meridian Expedition that a fleet of gunboats, accompanied by infantry on transports, move up the Yazoo River as far as Greenwood and Fort Pemberton and remain on the river for two or three weeks to draw attention from Sherman's main column and William Sooy Smith's cavalry expedition. The expedition was to be commanded by James H. Coates, colonel of the 11th Illinois Infantry, and consisted of his own regiment, commanded by George C. McKee; the 8th Louisiana (Colored), commanded by Ferdinand E. Peebles; and the 1st Mississippi Cavalry (Colored), commanded by Embury D. Osband. Elias K. Owen commanded the gunboats.

The 11th Illinois, the 8th Louisiana, and a detachment of the 1st Mississippi embarked on transports at Vicksburg January 31, 1864 and the next day moved up the Yazoo to Haynes' Bluff. On February 2, the expedition moved on upriver and anchored below Sartartia; early the next morning it passed Sartartia and then came under attack from Lawrence S. Ross' Confederate cavalry firing from the bank of the river at Liverpool. Coates then put his troops ashore, and they quickly became engaged. Ross repulsed two attacks, and at dark the troops were ordered back to the boats.

On February 4, 1864, the fleet moved on upriver to within six miles of Yazoo City, remaining there the next day. Then, uncertain of the enemy strength ashore, the boats dropped back down the river nearly to Liverpool. When Coates learned that the enemy had left for Benton, he returned on the evening of February 9 and took possession of Yazoo City. The next day Osband arrived from Haynes' Bluff with the rest of his 1st Mississippi regiment.

At daylight February 11, 1864, Coates moved up to a point near the head of Honey Island, where he sent Osband's regiment ashore to drive back some enemy cavalry. Then, after Osband had returned to the transports, the fleet moved on upriver, arriving at Greenwood at 9:00 P.M. February 14. Federal troops found Fort Pemberton, near Greenwood, evacuated.

On the morning of February 16, 1864, Osband's cavalry marched toward Grenada. Upon arriving within about five miles of the town, Osband learned that it was held by Nathan B. Forrest's cavalry. He then returned to Greenwood on February 17.

Coates remained at Greenwood until the morning of February 19, 1864, and he then received instructions to return to Yazoo City and to hold that place until further orders. He immediately moved downriver with his command and with cotton, corn, and stock that he had collected, and arrived within six miles of of Yazoo City on February 28. At that point Osband's cavalry was sent ashore, with orders to move to the rear of the town and gain possession of all roads running into it. Osband drove back Ross' cavalry.

The boats moved on down the river to Yazoo City, and the infantry disembarked. They then de-

ployed; the 11th Illinois occupied the works commanding the Benton road, and the 8th Louisiana took position on a road to the right commanding the bluffs. About noon February 29, the camp and garrison equipment arrived, and by March 1 each regiment was established in comfortable quarters.

On the night of March 4, Coates learned that Ross had been reinforced by Robert V. Richardson's cavalry brigade, and the next day the enemy attacked the pickets on the Benton road. The fighting soon extended along Coates' entire line. Richardson finally succeeded in entering the town, but at 2:00 P.M. Coates' men charged through the streets and drove back his troops, who retired out of range.

On the evening of March 6, 1864, Coates was ordered to begin embarking all of his force and his stores and move to Liverpool. He disembarked there and marched to Haynes' Bluff. After leaving Osband's regiment there, he marched with the rest of his command to Vicksburg.

* * * * * * * * *

The organization of Sherman's army during the Meridian Expedition was as follows:

MERIDIAN EXPEDITION
William T. Sherman

SIXTEENTH CORPS, Stephen A. Hurlbut

First Division, James M. Tuttle
  First Brigade, William L. McMillen
  Second Brigade, Joseph A. Mower
  Third Brigade, James L. Geddes
  Artillery, Nelson T. Spoor
    Battery E, 1st Illinois Light Artillery, John A. Fitch
    6th Battery, Indiana Light Artillery, Louis Kern
    2nd Battery, Iowa Light Artillery, Joseph R. Reed

Note 1. First Brigade and Fitch's battery cooperated with William Sooy Smith's column advancing from Memphis during the period February 6–15, 1864. It took no further part in the Meridian Expedition.
Note 2. Upon arrival at Vicksburg, Second Brigade went into camp at the Big Black River bridge February 4, 1864. On February 27 it departed for Canton as guard for a supply train for the army.
Note 3. Third Brigade went into camp at the Big Black River Bridge February 4, 1864.

Third Division, Andrew J. Smith
  First Brigade, David Moore

Second Brigade, William T. Shaw
Third Brigade, Edward H. Wolfe, to February 28, 1864
   Risdon M. Moore
Artillery, James M. Cockefair
   3rd Battery, Indiana Light Artillery, Thomas J. Ginn
   9th Battery, Indiana Light Artillery, George R. Brown
   14th Battery, Indiana Light Artillery, Francis W. Morse

Fourth Division (detachment), James C. Veatch
   First Brigade, Milton Montgomery
   Second Brigade, James H. Howe

Note. Montgomery's First Brigade was organized at Clear Creek, Mississippi from the 25th Wisconsin, 35th New Jersey, and 3rd Missouri regiments by an order dated February 3, 1864.

SEVENTEENTH CORPS, James B. McPherson

First Division
   Third Brigade, Alexander Chambers

Third Division, Mortimer D. Leggett
   First Brigade, Manning F. Force
   Second Brigade, Benjamin F. Potts
   Third Brigade, Jasper A. Maltby
   Artillery, William S. Williams
   Battery H, 1st Michigan Light Artillery, Marcus D. Elliott
      3rd Battery, Ohio Light Artillery, Thomas J. Blackburn

Note. A detachment of the 26th Battery, Ohio Light Artillery was attached to the 3rd Battery, Ohio Light Artillery.

Fourth Division, Marcellus M. Crocker
   First Brigade, T. Kilby Smith
   Second Brigade, Cyrus Hall
   Third Brigade, Walter Q. Gresham
   Artillery, John W. Powell
      Battery F, 2nd Illinois Light Artillery, Walter H. Powell
      7th Battery, Ohio Light Artillery, Harlow P. McNaughton
      15th Battery, Ohio Light Artillery, Edward Spear, Jr.

CAVALRY, Edward F. Winslow

   5th Illinois Cavalry, Abel H. Seley

   11th Illinois Cavalry, Lucien H. Kerr
   4th Iowa Cavalry, John H. Peters
   10th Missouri Cavalry, Frederick W. Benteen

SMITH'S COLUMN, William Sooy Smith

Cavalry Division, Benjamin H. Grierson
   First Brigade, George E. Waring, Jr.
   Second Brigade, William P. Hepburn
   Third Brigade, La Fayette McCrillis
   Unassigned
      4th United States Cavalry, Charles S. Bowman

YAZOO EXPEDITION, James H. Coates

   11th Illinois Infantry, George C. McKee
   8th Louisiana Infantry (Colored), Ferdinand E. Peebles
   1st Mississippi Cavalry (Colored), Embury D. Osband

ENGAGEMENT AT MILL SPRINGS (LOGAN'S CROSS ROADS, FISHING CREEK, OR BEECH GROVE), KENTUCKY JANUARY 19, 1862

During the early months of the war, Kentucky remained neutral, although there were many citizens who strongly supported the Rebellion, and many others who were staunchly loyal to the Union. There was intense feeling within the state between these two factions, and this seriously hampered the efforts of the pro-Union leaders to recruit and organize loyal Kentucky troops.

On July 6, 1861, William Nelson established Camp Dick Robinson just north of Bryantsville, Kentucky to receive the approximately 2,000 men who had previously been recruited. These men immediately moved into the camp, and were soon organized into three Kentucky infantry regiments under Thomas E. Bramlette, Speed S. Fry, and Theophilus T. Garrard. A cavalry regiment was also organized under Frank Wolford.

Neutrality in the state ended September 3, 1861 when, on orders from Leonidas Polk, Confederate troops entered Kentucky from Tennessee and occupied Columbus, on the Mississippi River. A short time later Felix K. Zollicoffer, commanding Confederate troops in eastern Tennessee, moved through Cumberland Gap into Kentucky and encamped at Cumberland Ford, about ten miles north of the gap. By September 19, Zollicoffer had secured the region in the vicinity of Cumberland Gap, and thus completed the eastern end of a Confederate defensive line that extended from Columbus, Kentucky, through Bowling Green, to Cumberland Gap.

Eastern Tennessee and southeastern Kentucky were opposed to secession and were strongly pro-Union, and for this reason there was considerable pressure in the North for a Federal advance into the region to protect the loyal citizens. George H. Thomas was assigned command at Camp Dick Robinson September 10, 1861, and he began preparations for an expedition for this purpose. The troops of his command, however, were all new and inexperienced, and there was no transportation available for moving his army, so the idea was necessarily soon abandoned. There was, nevertheless, an increase in military activity in southeastern Kentucky.

Action at Rockcastle Hills (or Camp Wildcat), Kentucky, October 21, 1861. While Thomas was attempting to get his command ready for active operations, Zollicoffer made several demonstrations from Cumberland Ford, and Garrard's 3rd Kentucky Infantry was moved forward to a strong position on Wildcat Mountain (called Camp Wildcat), just beyond the Rockcastle River, to guard the pass through the hills. When William T. Sherman, commander of the Department of the Cumberland, learned that Garrard's troops were menaced by Zollicoffer, he ordered Thomas to advance his command from Camp Dick Robinson to Crab Orchard so as to be nearer the forces at Rockcastle Hills.

October 17, 1861, Garrard reported that Zollicoffer was advancing in force, and Thomas sent John Coburn's 33rd Indiana and John M. Connell's 17th Ohio regiments to support Garrard. Two days later, he sent Albin Schoepf to the Rockcastle Hills, with orders to assume command of all Union troops there. He also sent with Schoepf Wolford's cavalry regiment, James B. Steedman's 14th Ohio regiment, and William E. Standart's Battery B, 1st Ohio Light Artillery. Samuel P. Carter followed the next day with his Tennessee Brigade, consisting of the 1st East Tennessee and 2nd East Tennessee regiments.

Zollicoffer arrived in front of the position held by Coburn's regiment east of Camp Wildcat on the morning of October 21, 1861 and promptly attacked. After severe fighting for about an hour, Coburn, aided by a part of Wolford's dismounted cavalry, succeeded in driving the enemy back. A part of Connell's regiment arrived near the close of the action and moved into line. The enemy advanced again about 2:00 P.M., and at about that time, Steedman's 14th Ohio came up and aided in repelling the second attack. Carter's brigade did not arrive to take part in the action. That night Zollicoffer withdrew and marched back to Cumberland Ford.

* * * * * * * * * *

Schoepf remained at Rockcastle Hills until November 12, 1861, and then he received orders to withdraw. While he was on the march, this order was revoked, and Carter's two regiments returned to London, Kentucky. Garrard's regiment remained with Carter at London, but Schoepf continued on with his other regiments and joined Thomas at Crab Orchard.

November 15, 1861, Don Carlos Buell assumed command of the Department of the Ohio, which had been expanded to include that part of Kentucky east of the Cumberland River. Thus, on that date, Buell relieved Sherman in command of the Department of the Cumberland, which was then discontinued. At that time Thomas was with his command, then called the Eastern Division, Department of the Ohio, at Crab Orchard.

November 17, 1861, Buell ordered Thomas to move with his division toward Columbia, Kentucky, which he believed to be threatened by an enemy force. Because of the bad condition of the roads, Thomas was compelled to march by way of Danville and Lebanon to reach Columbia.

November 27, 1861, Schoepf, who had arrived near Lebanon, was ordered to move with Connell's 17th Ohio, Edwin D. Bradley's 38th Ohio, and Standart's battery to Somerset, Kentucky. Schoepf arrived there December 1 and entrenched a position at Waitsboro, which was about six miles south of Somerset, at the Cumberland River crossing of the

Somerset-Monticello road. William A. Hoskins' 12th Kentucky regiment was already in camp there watching the river.

November 30, 1861, Buell announced the brigade organization of the Department of the Ohio (see Army of the Ohio [Buell]), and at that time the regiments constituting the Eastern Division were located as follows:

At Camp Dick Robinson: 31st Ohio Infantry and John M. Hewett's Battery B, Kentucky Light Artillery

Crab Orchard: 33rd Indiana Infantry

Columbia: 1st Kentucky Infantry and 1st Kentucky Cavalry

London: 1st East Tennessee Infantry, 2nd East Tennessee Infantry, and 3rd Kentucky Infantry

Somerset (or en route there): 12th Kentucky, 17th Ohio, 38th Ohio, and Standart's battery

Lebanon: 10th Indiana, 2nd Kentucky, 4th Kentucky, 10th Kentucky, 14th Ohio, all infantry regiments, and Dennis Kenny's Battery C, 1st Ohio Light Artillery

December 3, 1861, Thomas ordered Ferdinand Van Derveer's 35th Ohio Infantry, which had arrived at Camp Dick Robinson, to march to Somerset, and on December 11 he also ordered Moses B. Walker's 31st Ohio Infantry from Camp Dick Robinson to Somerset.

December 6, 1861, Thomas assumed command of the newly constituted First Division, Department of the Ohio, and announced its organization as follows:

First Division, Department of the Ohio, George H. Thomas
  First Brigade, Albin Schoepf
    33rd Indiana, John Coburn
    17th Ohio, John M. Connell
    12th Kentucky, William A. Hoskins
    38th Ohio, Edwin D. Bradley
  Second Brigade, Mahlon D. Manson
    4th Kentucky, Speed S. Fry
    14th Ohio, James B. Steedman
    10th Indiana, William C. Kise (Manson's regiment)
    10th Kentucky, John M. Harlan
  Third Brigade, Robert L. McCook
    18th United States Infantry, Henry B. Carrington
    2nd Minnesota, Horatio P. Van Cleve
    35th Ohio, Ferdinand Van Derveer
    9th Ohio, Gustave Kammerling (McCook's regiment)

Twelfth Brigade, Samuel P. Carter
  1st East Tennessee, Robert K. Byrd
  2nd East Tennessee, James P. T. Carter
  6th Kentucky, Theophilus T. Garrard
  31st Ohio, Moses B. Walker

1st Kentucky Cavalry, Frank Wolford
Squadron, 3rd Regiment Indiana Cavalry, Felix W. Graham
Artillery, Walker E. Lawrence
  Battery B, 1st Ohio Light Artillery, William E. Standart
  Battery C, 1st Ohio Light Artillery, Dennis Kenny, Jr.
  Battery B, Kentucky Light Artillery, John M. Hewett

When the brigade organization was announced, First Brigade was directed to take post at Somerset, Second Brigade and Third Brigade, with Thomas, at Lebanon, and Twelfth Brigade at London.

Engagement at Mill Springs (or Logan's Cross Roads, Fishing Creek, Beech Grove), January 19, 1862. After the action at Rockcastle Hills, Zollicoffer remained at Cumberland Ford until November 6, 1861, and then, in response to a rumored Union advance toward East Tennessee, he marched toward Jacksboro, Tennessee. He arrived at Jacksboro the next day and remained there until after November 15. He then marched by way of Huntsville and Jamestown, Tennessee toward Kentucky. He crossed into Kentucky near Albany November 24 and, marching by way of Monticello, arrived at Mill Springs on the Cumberland River November 29.

On December 2–3, 1861, Zollicoffer's artillery shelled the camp of Hoskins' 12th Kentucky, and some of the enemy cavalry crossed to the north bank of the Cumberland River. Then, during the period December 5–8, Zollicoffer crossed his entire command and established a fortified camp at Beech Grove. When Schoepf learned that the enemy was north of the river in force, he moved back through Somerset and occupied a strong position three miles north of the town, where he commanded the roads to Crab Orchard and Stanford. December 7, 1861, Carter, with his two East Tennessee regiments, left London and joined Schoepf at his new position north of Somerset.

December 18, 1861, Schoepf conducted a reconnaissance with his entire command and found Zollicoffer entrenched north of Mill Springs on a line that extended from a loop of the Cumberland River to White Oak Creek.

Buell, who had been reluctant to reinforce Schoepf, then learned that Zollicoffer's brigade was the only enemy force encamped in that part of Kentucky, and he decided to drive it from the state. On December 29, 1861, he ordered Thomas to advance on Zollicoffer's position from Columbia and strike his left flank, while Schoepf attacked on his front. Two days later, Thomas left Lebanon with Mahlon D. Manson's Second Brigade, Gustave Kammerling's 9th Ohio and Horatio P. Van Cleve's 2nd Minnesota of Robert L. McCook's Third Brigade, and a battalion of Wolford's cavalry and advanced by way of Campbellsville and Columbia.

Heavy rains, swollen streams, and almost impassable roads greatly hampered the march, and it was not until January 17, 1862 that Thomas, with William C. Kise's 10th Indiana of Manson's brigade, the two regiments of McCook's brigade, Wolford's battalion of 1st Kentucky, and Dennis Kenny's Battery C, 1st Ohio Light Artillery, arrived at Logan's Cross Roads, about ten miles from Zollicoffer's camp and about the same distance from Somerset. Thomas then halted until the 4th Kentucky, 10th Kentucky, 14th Ohio, and 18th United States Infantry, all of which had been detained by the bad roads, arrived.

Thomas then ordered Schoepf, who was north of Somerset, to send Carter's Tennessee brigade and Hoskins' 12th Kentucky across Fishing Creek to support the force at Logan's Cross Roads until the rest of his column arrived. Thomas also sent Steedman's 14th Ohio and John M. Harlan's 10th Kentucky to attempt the capture of the enemy's wagon train, which was out on a foraging expedition.

Carter's troops crossed Fishing Creek on the Columbia road and late that night moved to Logan's Cross Roads, where they bivouacked. The 12th Kentucky also joined Thomas that night and camped opposite the 9th Ohio on the Somerset-Columbia road.

Fry's 4th Kentucky arrived on the evening of January 18, 1862 and camped near the 10th Indiana. A battalion of Michigan engineers and Henry S. Wetmore's 9th Battery, Ohio Light Artillery also arrived that evening.

Meantime, there had been some changes in the enemy camp. On October 26, 1861, William H. Carroll's Confederate brigade had been ordered from Memphis to report to Zollicoffer in East Tennessee and, after a long delay, had arrived at Knoxville. From there it had moved on and joined Zollicoffer at Beech Grove early in January 1862. On November 11, 1861, George B. Crittenden had been assigned command of the Confederate forces in East Tennessee, and on November 24 he had arrived and established headquarters at Knoxville. Crittenden was not pleased when Zollicoffer moved his command to the north bank of the Cumberland River, and early in January 1862 he proceeded to Mill Creek and assumed personal command of Zollicoffer's and Carroll's brigades. Crittenden then decided that it was unsafe to attempt to recross the river in the presence of Thomas' strong force, and instead he prepared to take the offensive.

At midnight January 18, 1862, Crittenden marched northward toward Logan's Cross Roads. Zollicoffer's brigade was in the lead, Carroll's brigade followed, and one infantry regiment and two cavalry regiments brought up the rear as a reserve. About daylight the next morning, after a difficult march of nine miles, Crittenden's cavalry encountered Wolford's pickets about two miles from the Union camp. The pickets opened fire, but fell back on their reserve, which consisted of two companies of the 10th Indiana, and together they made a stand. Wolford then brought up the rest of his cavalry battalion, and Manson ordered up the remaining companies of Kise's 10th Indiana. Kise formed his regiment across the road to Mill Springs, and Wolford's dismounted cavalry joined him on this line.

Kise and Wolford were almost immediately engaged, and they resisted strongly for about an hour. Then, overwhelmed by superior numbers and almost surrounded, the 10th Indiana fell back, and Wolford followed. Meantime, Fry, with his 4th Kentucky, had been ordered forward from his camp to the rear, and he arrived at the front as the 10th Indiana was withdrawing. Fry formed his line on the left of the road and occupied the position formerly held by Wolford. Fry's line was near the road and parallel to it. Fry was soon engaged, and despite a series of severe attacks, he was able to hold his position for more than an hour.

Zollicoffer was killed early in the fighting, and two of his regiments gave way in some disorder, but then Carroll's brigade came up, and Crittenden ordered a general advance.

While Kise, Wolford, and Fry were engaged, Thomas ordered Robert L. McCook to move forward with the 2nd Minnesota and 9th Ohio, the only regiments of his brigade that were with him, and when the 10th Indiana was forced back, McCook moved to the front. The 2nd Minnesota was obstructed in its movement by the men of the 10th Indiana, who were scattered through the woods awaiting ammunition, and by the 4th Kentucky, which was ahead of the 10th Indiana and still resisting. Finally, however, the 2nd Minnesota passed through the 10th Indiana and 2nd Minnesota and deployed on the left of the road, on ground formerly occupied by these two regiments. There was desperate fighting for about a half-hour, and then Kammerling's 9th Ohio of McCook's brigade came up and charged the enemy left, which began to give way.

On the morning of January 19, 1862, Carter had formed his two regiments, the 1st and 2nd East Tennessee, on the left of Thomas' line to protect the road running from Somerset to Mill Springs. Hoskins' 12th Kentucky, which had camped near the 9th Ohio during the night, marched south on the road to Mill Springs as far as the Logan house, arriving there ahead of the 9th Ohio. At that point, however, Hoskins was ordered to report to Carter, and he took position on the left of the 1st East Tennessee, and on the extreme left of Thomas' line. Carter then advanced on the left of the 2nd Minnesota and 9th Ohio. The 1st East Tennessee deployed and attacked the enemy right flank, which began to give way, and soon the entire Confederate line broke and fled in confusion toward the Cumberland River.

Thomas followed to a point near the enemy camp at Beech Grove and then deployed and advanced to high ground that commanded the enemy entrenchments. From this position, Standart's and Wetmore's batteries fired in the direction of the Cumberland crossing until dark to prevent Crittenden's escape. Farther to the right, Kenny's battery added its fire to that of the other two batteries.

The 14th Ohio and 10th Kentucky arrived on the field during the pursuit, and were placed in advance of Thomas' line in preparation for an assault on the enemy works at daylight the next day. Schoepf's brigade arrived about dark and was also placed in position for the attack the next day. During the night, however, Crittenden's demoralized army recrossed to the south side of the Cumberland River, and the fleeing remnants did not halt until they reached Chestnut Mound, about eighty miles from Nashville, Tennessee. Crittenden left behind at Beech Grove his artillery, wagons, horses, and supplies, and as an organized force, his command virtually ceased to exist.

* * * * * * * * *

After the Battle of Mill Springs, Carter's brigade was sent toward Cumberland Gap, and the rest of Thomas' command was concentrated at Somerset. February 15, 1862, Thomas was ordered with his division to Munfordville, Kentucky to take part in a general advance toward Bowling Green. That town, however, was evacuated by the Confederates on February 14, and Thomas then marched to Bardstown. When he arrived there, he was ordered to Louisville, where his division was to embark on transports for a movement to Nashville, Tennessee. Thomas arrived at Nashville March 2–4.

OPERATIONS IN MISSOURI IN 1861

In the early part of 1861, Missouri was a large slaveholding state, whose government was sympathetic with the Southern cause, and who hoped to work out some plan for cooperation with the other Southern states. On the other hand, there was strong Union sentiment in the city of Saint Louis, and Frank P. Blair, Jr. and Nathaniel Lyon, commander of the United States Arsenal there, which was the strongpoint for the military defense of the state, planned to move against the secessionist movement headed by Governor Claiborne F. Jackson and ex-governor Sterling Price.

Capture of Camp Jackson at Lindell's Grove, Saint Louis, Missouri, May 10, 1861. As part of the plan of the pro-Southern faction to gain control of the state, the Missouri Militia was ordered to assemble for enrollment and drill at Lindell's Grove, at the western edge of Saint Louis, on May 3, 1861. Daniel M. Frost was placed in command of the camp, which he named Camp Jackson.

There were strong indications that Frost's command might be planning for some aggressive action, and Lyon was greatly concerned that this might be an attempt to capture the Saint Louis arsenal. Accordingly, on the afternoon of May 10, he marched out with the greater part of his troops and forced the surrender of Frost and his Missouri Militia. For the organization of Lyon's command at that time, see Department of the West, Troops in the Department of the West. Lyon then marched his prisoners back to the arsenal, where they were confined for a time. On the way, rioting broke out, and a number of people were killed. There was further rioting the next day, during which more people lost their lives.

On May 31, 1862, Lyon succeeded William S. Harney in command of the Department of the West, and immediately began to prepare for action.

At Governor Jackson's request, a conference was held on June 11 at the Planter's House in Saint Louis in an attempt to reconcile the differences between the two factions. Present were Jackson, Thomas Snead, his secretary, Price, Blair, and Lyon. After several hours of discussion, Lyon finally stated that he would not yield to the state of Missouri, and further declared, "This means war." Jackson, Price, and Snead then returned to Jefferson City and prepared for hostilities.

One of the first moves was to create nine military districts in the state, and to the command of these districts were assigned Alexander W. Doniphan, Monroe M. Parsons, James S. Rains, John B. Clark, N. W. Watkins, B. Randolph, William Y. Slack, and James H. McBride.

The organization of the troops in each district was called a division, but in reality it was a brigade and later was so called. Jackson named this new organization the Missouri State Guard, and assigned Price to its command.

Plans for Lyon's Campaign in Missouri, June 1861. On May 31, 1861, Lyon succeeded William S. Harney in command of the Department of the West, and he promptly began to consider how to deal with the pro-Southern forces in the state. In addition to the threat posed by Jackson's Missouri State Guard at Jefferson City against the loyal troops at Saint Louis, Nicholas B. (Bart) Pearce with a brigade of Arkansas troops and Ben McCulloch with a Confederate brigade had moved into northern Arkansas, near the Missouri state line. To meet this combined threat, Lyon decided to organize his command into two columns and move out and drive back the enemy forces. One column was to move into southwestern Missouri to occupy the country, and to prevent the enemy from moving from Arkansas into southwestern Missouri. The other column was to move along the Missouri River toward Kansas, and drive back troops of Price's Missouri State Guard from Jefferson City. It was also to prevent the passage of troops from the pro-Southern counties to the north to join the Southern forces south of the river, and to close all cross-river traffic and all navigation on the river. When these immediate objectives had been attained, the two columns were to join south of the Osage River and endeavor to trap Jackson's state forces between them.

The first-mentioned column, which was called the Southwestern Column (or Southwestern Expedition), was assigned to Thomas W. Sweeny, and consisted of the following:

Southwestern Column, Thomas W. Sweeny
   3rd Missouri Volunteers, Franz Sigel
   5th Missouri Volunteers, Charles E. Salomon
   3rd Regiment Home Guards, John McNeil
   4th Regiment Home Guards, B. Gratz Brown
   Battalion Missouri Light Artillery, Frank Backof
      Battery, Christian Essig
      Battery, Theodore Wilkins

Note. The Home Guards were also called the United States Reserve Corps.

The column that Lyon led westward along the Missouri River consisted of the following:

Lyon's Column, Nathaniel Lyon
   1st Missouri Volunteers, Frank P. Blair, Jr.
   2nd Missouri Volunteers, Henry Boernstein
   Regular recruits (two companies), Warren L. Lothrop
   Company B, 2nd United States Infantry (Lyon's company), William Griffin
   Company F, 2nd United States Artillery, James Totten

Capture of Jefferson City and Boonville, Missouri—Engagement at Boonville, June 17, 1861.
Lyon's column left Saint Louis on transports June 13, 1861, but the boats tied up that night only a few miles above Saint Charles. They continued on up the Missouri River the next morning toward Jefferson City, where they arrived during the afternoon of June 15. Lyon found the city evacuated, and the next day, after leaving Henry Boernstein with three companies of his 2nd Missouri Volunteers to occupy the town, he proceeded on toward Boonville, about fifty miles upstream. The rest of Boernstein's regiment, under the command of Peter J. Osterhaus, accompanied Lyon.

Lyon spent the night of June 16, 1861 just west of Rockport, about fifteen miles from Boonville, and the next morning continued on to a point about six miles from Boonville and two miles below a camp of enemy forces under Price. Price was forced to depart for home because of illness, and John S. Marmaduke assumed command of his troops. Lyon then disembarked his command and deployed them in line of battle on either side of a road that ran along the river toward Boonville.

After advancing about two miles, Lyon encountered enemy skirmishers, and about a mile farther on, at a point where the valley between the river and a line of bluffs to the south narrowed, he found Marmaduke's troops posted on a low ridge that extended from the bluffs to the river. The road on which Lyon was advancing ran up and over this ridge, and along the crest of this ridge a lane ran down toward the river. The enemy troops were posted along a fence that ran along this lane. The brick house of William M. Adams and a wooded area behind it provided shelter for some of Marmaduke's men.

As Lyon's troops advanced, both sides opened with a heavy fire, but when Totten's battery shelled the house with deadly accuracy, the enemy gave way. Under a heavy fire, Marmaduke attempted to make a stand at the top of the bluff, but when Lyon's men charged with fixed bayonets, his troops broke and fled toward Boonville. They made another brief stand at the fairgrounds, and Jackson's troops retired to the south toward Tipton, Missouri. Lyon then entered the town and received its surrender.

When Price recovered from his illness, he left Lexington with a small escort to seek aid from McCulloch, who was with his Confederate brigade at Cowskin Prairie, an area of grassland in the extreme southwest corner of Missouri. Many men joined Price along the road as he marched south, and by the time he reached Cowskin Prairie, he had with him about 1,200 new volunteers.

Jackson moved southward from Boonville with the troops of the Missouri State Guard belonging to the divisions of James S. Rains, John B. Clark, William Y. Slack, and Monroe M. Parsons. It should be remembered that at that time in Missouri, the militia brigades were called divisions, although they were only of brigade size. These divisions were moving toward a selected rendezvous near Lamar, Missouri, about fifty miles south of the Osage River. With Governor Jackson were Lieutenant Governor Thomas C. Reynolds, Senator David R. Atchison, and other members of the refugee state government. By July 3, 1861, Jackson's troops were in camp three miles south of Lamar and twenty miles north of Carthage.

Advance of the Southwestern Column—Engagement near Carthage, Missouri, July 5, 1861. On the afternoon of June 11, 1861, Francis Hassendeubel's 1st Battalion of Franz Sigel's 3rd Missouri Volunteers left Saint Louis by rail for Rolla, Missouri, about ninety miles to the southwest. Two days later, Henry Bischoff's 2nd Battalion, and also Frank Backof's artillery battalion, followed Hassendeubel to Rolla.

The last of Sweeny's troops, under the command of Charles E. Salomon, entrained at Saint Louis on the afternoon of June 15, 1861. Salomon's command consisted of his own 5th Missouri Volunteers, John McNeil's 3rd Regiment Home Guards, and B. Gratz Brown's 4th Regiment Home Guards. The Home Guards were to guard from guerrilla attacks the railroad from Saint Louis to Rolla and the wagon road from Rolla to Springfield.

Sweeny did not accompany the column when it departed, but remained for a time in Saint Louis to arrange for the forwarding of supplies for the army. Sigel, as the senior officer, was in command of the column until Sweeny arrived.

When Sigel left the cars with his regiment at Rolla, he marched immediately for Springfield, about 125 miles to the southwest. He arrived there June 23, 1861, then continued on to Neosho, which was about sixty miles southwest of Springfield and about twenty miles due south of Carthage. This was the place selected by Lyon for the Southwestern Column to take position and await the arrival of Jackson's Missouri State Guard, which were retreating southward toward southwestern Missouri. It was expected that these troops would be closely followed by Lyon's column from Boonville.

Salomon arrived at Springfield June 27, 1861 and then, without waiting for Sweeny, moved on to join Sigel at Neosho. Sigel was then in command of a brigade consisting of his own and Salomon's regiments and Backof's two batteries.

Sweeny left Saint Louis June 23 with 300 men. He arrived at Springfield July 1 and established his headquarters there. At Springfield he learned of Lyon's occupation of Boonville, and he also learned that enemy troops under Governor Jackson, Lieutenant Governor Thomas C. Reynolds, James S. Rains, and David R. Atchison were moving south in his direction.

Sweeny then ordered Sigel, whose headquarters was at Sarcoxie, to concentrate his command at Neosho and move in the direction of Carthage, where Sweeny believed the enemy forces to be. It was hoped that Sigel would be able to delay the enemy in their march until Lyon could come up and attack them from the rear.

Sigel marched through Neosho July 3, 1861, and Salomon, who was at Mount Vernon, was ordered to join him. On the night of July 4, Sigel encamped a mile to the southeast of Carthage, behind Spring River. There he learned that Jackson was marching south from Lamar and was only ten miles to the north of his camp. He moved on that evening and occupied Carthage.

At daybreak the next morning, Sigel and Salomon marched north out of Carthage to meet Jackson. About nine miles out on the road, the column entered a wooded area, about one-half mile in width, that bordered Coon Creek. Sigel found Jackson's Missouri troops in position on high ground about two miles north of the creek.

Sigel and Salomon considered the situation for a time and decided to attack. Their troops crossed Coon Creek at a ford, then deployed in column of companies to the right and left of the road, and under cover of the woods. Bischoff's 2nd Battalion, 3rd Missouri Volunteers was on the left of the line;

next to the right were four pieces of artillery under Backof; the 5th Missouri Volunteers were in the center in two separate battalions under Salomon and Christian D. Wolff; next to the right were three guns under Christian Essig; and on the right was Hassendeubel's 1st Battalion of the 3rd Missouri Volunteers.

When Lyon's troops emerged from the woods, they were about 1,200 yards from the enemy position. After they had advanced 300–400 yards, both sides opened fire, and this continued for one-half to one hour. Then Sigel observed the enemy cavalry moving out to the right and to the left; he believed that it was their intention to attack both of his flanks, and that his baggage train and his line of retreat were threatened. He then ordered his command to withdraw.

Sigel's troops were well across Coon Creek before Jackson left the ridge in pursuit. Sigel's artillery forced Jackson to halt about 400 yards from the ford, and held them there until the infantry had moved out some distance on the road to Carthage. Sigel retired in good order to Carthage, aided frequently by the artillery. Upon arrival there, he sent the baggage train toward Mount Vernon by way of Sarcoxie, and he then held up the enemy advance for several hours until the train was well on the road. After dark Sigel followed the train, which he joined at Sarcoxie the next morning.

The enemy abandoned the pursuit of Sigel at dark and, after pausing briefly at Carthage, moved on to Cowskin Prairie. There Price assumed command of all Missouri troops and began preparing them for field service.

Sigel continued the retreat from Sarcoxie to Mount Vernon, where he stopped for a day's rest, and then marched on to Springfield.

Lyon's Advance from Boonville to Springfield, July 3, 1861–July 13, 1861. When Lyon arrived at Boonville June 17, 1861, he ordered reinforcements to join him there before beginning his march toward Springfield. He also ordered Samuel D. Sturgis to march south from Fort Leavenworth with his available force and attempt to reach the Osage River in time to prevent Jackson's force from escaping to the southwest.

On June 27, 1861, John D. Stevenson arrived at Boonville from the arsenal at Saint Louis with four companies of his 7th Missouri Volunteers, and John F. Bates arrived from northern Missouri with his 1st Iowa Regiment. On that same day, John M. Schofield arrived at Boonville from Saint Louis and was assigned by Lyon as his adjutant general. Two days later Charles A. Stifel arrived with his 5th Missouri Volunteers. On June 29, Stevenson was assigned command of the Missouri River from Kansas City to its mouth, and also of the adjacent country.

Although Lyon had expected to leave Boonville by June 26, 1861, he had been delayed by heavy rains that began that day and continued for several days. Consequently, he did not begin his advance until July 3, the same day that Jackson's State Guards assembled south of Lamar, Missouri.

July 3, 1861, the Department of the West was discontinued by the creation of the Western Department. John C. Fremont was assigned command of the newly created Western Department, but he did not arrive from the East to assume command until July 25. Meantime, Lyon continued in command of the army in the field.

At 3:30 A.M. July 3, 1861, Lyon left Boonville, marching through Sedalia and Green Ridge toward Clinton, about 100 miles to the southwest. On July 7, he established contact with Sturgis' column, which had arrived from Fort Leavenworth and was encamped on the Grand River west of Clinton. When Lyon came up, he camped near Sturgis.

Sturgis' command consisted of the following:

1st Kansas Volunteers, George W. Deitzler
2nd Kansas Volunteers, Robert B. Mitchell
Three companies of the 1st United States Infantry
Two companies of the 2nd United States Infantry
Four companies of the 1st United States Cavalry
One company of Dragoons
One company of Kansas Mounted Rangers
Du Bois' Battery (improvised), John V. Du Bois

Gordon Granger was adjutant general on Sturgis' staff.

From Clinton, Lyon continued on, accompanied by Sturgis' command, and reached the Osage River about twelve miles above Osceola on July 9, 1861. There he learned from Sweeny at Springfield of Sigel's defeat at Carthage, and he then continued on by forced marches toward Springfield, about eighty miles to the southeast, to support Sweeny and Sigel.

He left the Osage at sunup July 11, arriving at Springfield on July 13. Lyon's strenuous efforts to reach the town were not necessary, however, because Sigel had arrived there safely from the battlefield.

When Lyon's column joined Sweeny's Southwestern Column at Springfield, Lyon was in immediate command of all of his forces in the field, and July 15, 1861 he called his army the Army of the West. All was not well with the army, however, because the Missouri Volunteers and Home Guards had enlisted for ninety days, and their periods of service would expire within the next week or two. By July 26, about 2,000 men had left for Saint Louis and discharge. Thus Lyon's force was considerably reduced in numbers.

On July 24, 1861, Lyon reorganized the Army of the West as follows:

Army of the West, Nathaniel Lyon
    First Brigade, Samuel D. Sturgis
    Second Brigade, Franz Sigel
    Third Brigade, George L. Andrews
    Fourth Brigade, George W. Deitzler

For the complete organization of the Army of the West, see the following section, Battle of Wilson's Creek (or Oak Hills).

Battle of Wilson's Creek (or Oak Hills), Missouri, August 10, 1862. Meantime, to the southwest, Price with his Missouri State Guard, McCulloch with his Confederate brigade, and Pearce with his Arkansas brigade were making plans to attack Lyon's Army of the West at Springfield. In late July 1861, the commanders of the southern forces in northern Arkansas and southwestern Missouri decided that it was time to combine their forces and move toward Lyon's Army of the West at Springfield. On July 25, Sterling Price, with his Missouri State Guard, left Cowskin Prairie for Cassville, where he arrived July 28. At the same time, McCulloch, with his Confederate Brigade, and Pearce, with his brigade of the secessionist Army of Arkansas, marched north and joined Price at Cassville July 29–30. Then on August 1, the combined force began its march toward Springfield.

At Springfield, meantime, Lyon had been making every effort to lead an advance against the enemy, but he had been prevented from doing so by an almost total lack of supplies. Then, when he learned that the Southern forces were advancing, he decided to move out and attack Price before he could join forces with McCulloch and Pearce.

Accordingly, on August 1, 1861, Lyon marched out on the Springfield-Fayetteville road (also called the Wire Road or Telegraph Road) and camped that night on Terrell (also spelled Tyrel) Creek, twelve miles from Springfield. That night, James S. Rains, with the enemy advance guard consisting of 400 Mounted Riflemen, was in camp on the road ahead five miles north of Crane Creek.

On the morning of August 2, 1861, when Rains learned that Lyon was advancing, he advanced his command and encountered Lyon's advance guard at Dug Springs. This consisted of Frederick Steele's battalion of four companies of regulars, James Totten's Battery F, 2nd United States Artillery, and David S. Stanley's troop of the 1st United States Cavalry. In the ensuing action, Rains' command was driven back in disorder. The next day Lyon continued his advance, camping that night at Curran Post Office and McCulla's farm, the latter about twenty-four miles from Springfield on the Springfield-Fayetteville road.

At that time the command situation in the southern forces was unusual. Each of the three generals—Price, McCulloch, and Pearce—had complete authority over his own troops, but no one of them was subject to the orders of the others. Price was determined to advance and attack Lyon, but McCulloch was not in favor of such action. Finally, on August 4, 1861, Price, although the senior officer, offered to serve under McCulloch if the latter would attack. McCulloch reluctantly agreed, and soon after midnight on the morning of August 5, the Southern army began its advance toward Curran Post Office.

Meantime, however, on August 4, Lyon, who was almost completely out of food, and in danger of being cut off by the advancing enemy, began to withdraw toward Springfield, where he arrived safely on the morning of August 6.

McCulloch continued his march northward on the Springfield road during August 5, halting that night at Moody's Spring near Terrell Creek. He then moved on to Wilson's Creek, where there was ripening corn and good grass, and went into camp.

Before proceeding with a detailed description of the Battle of Wilson's Creek, it is necessary to describe briefly the more important features of the area in which the battle was fought. Wilson's Creek rises about five miles southwest of Springfield and flows westward for about six miles, then turns to the south and runs in that direction for eight to ten miles between steep bluffs and high hills, cut by ravines, until it merges into James River.

The Springfield road (or Telegraph Road) ran out of Springfield to the southwest. About ten miles from the town, it dropped down through a heavily wooded defile, a short distance south of the J. O. Ray house, and into the valley of Wilson's Creek. After crossing the creek at a ford, the road curved to the south and ran along the west side of Wilson's Creek through a narrow valley to a stream called Skegg's Branch, which was a tributary of Wilson's Creek that flowed into the latter from the west. After crossing Skegg's Branch, the road left the valley and ran up a steep slope to the top of a bluff where the Sharp house stood. It then continued on across the prairie toward Fayetteville.

To the south of the Sharp house, and along the west side of Wilson's Creek, there was a large expanse of grassland known as Sharp's field, and just south of this field was the Dixon homestead, near Terrell (or Tyrel) Creek.

On the plateau to the north of the ford where the road coming in from Springfield crossed Wilson's Creek, and on the east side of the creek, was the Ray cornfield, and farther north was Gibson's Mill.

Below the ford, the valley of Wilson's Creek was bordered on the east by a line of bluffs, some rising to a height of eighty feet, and at the top they leveled off to a thickly overgrown plateau. Along the west side of the creek was a narrow grassy meadow, and beyond the meadow was a line of bluffs fifty to sixty feet high that ended at Skegg's Branch. Just west of these bluffs, the ground rose to form a hill that dominated the country around, and whose crest was about 150 feet above the valley floor. Because this hill was thickly covered by scrub oak, it was known locally as Oak Hill, and the surrounding area of high ground was known as Oak Hills. Much of the heaviest fighting during the Battle of Wilson's Creek took place on Oak Hill, and it soon became known as "Bloody Hill."

The top of Oak Hill was about one-fourth mile in length and only about half as wide, but extending out from the summit to the east and south were several rather broad ridges that were separated by deep ravines. The first of these ridges ran out to the east toward Wilson's Creek, and the others, which were about one-third mile in length, extended down toward the valley of Skegg's Branch. It was on the top of the hill and on the lower ridges that the greater part of the fighting at Wilson's Creek took place. For convenience in referring to the ridges later in the discussion of the battle, it is best to assign them numerical designations as follows: the eastern ridge running toward Wilson's Creek as Ridge No.1, and the other ridges running to the south as ridges No. 2, No. 3, etc., in order from east to west.

When McCulloch's army halted on Wilson's Creek on August 6, most of the cavalry camped in Sharp's field, south of the Sharp house. Price's Missouri State Guards camped in the meadow along the west side of Wilson's Creek and along Skegg's Branch. McCulloch's brigade was east of the creek on the bluff above the ravine through which the Springfield road descended into the valley of Wilson's Creek, southeast of the Ray house and field. Pearce's Arkansas brigade was on the bluff to the left of McCulloch, east of Wilson's Creek, between the ford of the Springfield road and the mouth of Skegg's Branch. William E. Woodruff's battery was between McCulloch and Pearce on the bluff above the ford. Richard H. Weightman's infantry brigade of James S. Rains' division was also on the plateau east of the creek. James Cawthorn's Mounted Brigade of Rains' division was on outpost duty, with a part of his command on Ridge No. 1 (see above) of Oak Hill, and the rest about two-thirds of a mile upstream in the vicinity of Gibson's Mill.

At Springfield, on the day after he had returned from Curran Post Office, Lyon learned that McCulloch was encamped on Wilson's Creek, only about ten miles distant. Lyon was then in desperate circumstances. He had received no supplies from Rolla and no reinforcements from Fremont, and he had no expectation of receiving any. In considering his situation, he realized that it would be impossible to entrench at Springfield and defend the town against an attack, and that it would be a dangerous undertaking to attempt to retreat with his army to Rolla. Finally he decided that his best course would

be to attack the enemy at Wilson's Creek before they could be further reinforced.

On the morning of August 9, 1861, in consultation with Sigel, Lyon decided on a plan of attack. According to this plan, the Army of the West was to move that night in two columns and attack the enemy camp at dawn the next morning. Sigel was to move with a brigade south out of Springfield to a point beyond Oak Hills and then attack the camp from the east, and Lyon, with the rest of the army, was to march westward to a point beyond the enemy camp and attack from the west.

Sigel moved out from his camp south of Springfield at 6:30 that evening. He marched down the Springfield road about four miles, then turned off to the left from the road and continued on over open country about twelve miles due south. Eugene A. Carr, with his own Company I, 1st United States Cavalry and Charles E. Farrand's Company C, 2nd Dragoons, was in the lead, and he was followed by Charles E. Salomon's 5th Missouri Volunteers and Anselm Albert's 3rd Missouri Volunteers. Six pieces of artillery under Gustavus A. Schaefer and Edward Schuetzenbach accompanied the column.

After a march of five hours, Sigel rested his men, and at 2:00 A.M. August 10, 1861 he resumed the march. He soon reached a wagon road that crossed Wilson's Creek a short distance to the west, near the Dixon homestead on Terrell Creek. At 4:30 A.M. the head of Sigel's column arrived near Sharp's field, where the enemy cavalry under Thomas J. Churchill, James P. Major, Benjamin Brown, and Elkanah Greer were camped. Sigel then left two guns under Schuetzenbach near the edge of the bluff overlooking the cavalry camp, with Carr and some infantry in support, and with the rest of his brigade crossed Wilson's Creek and Terrell Creek, then followed a rough trail into the shelter of a thick woods. There he waited for the sounds of Lyon's attack to the north.

Lyon left his camps at 7:00 P.M., with his command divided into three brigades. He marched westward on the Mount Vernon road, with Charles W. Canfield's Company B, 1st United States Cavalry out in front. Following the cavalry was Samuel D. Sturgis' First Brigade, with Joseph B. Plummer's battalion of regular infantry in front. Behind Sturgis was George L. Andrews' Second Brigade, and then George W. Deitzler's Third Brigade. Thomas W.

Sweeny, Lyon's acting inspector general, was with the column and, although not commanding a brigade, rendered valuable service later in the day by rallying broken units and leading them back into action.

The route selected for Lyon's march that night was as follows: He was to move out on the Mount Vernon road about six miles to the vicinity of Little York, and from there he was to march south on a narrow wagon road until he came to the big bend of Wilson's Creek where it turned south toward Gibson's Mill. Upon arriving there, he was to turn to the west and march across the valley, past the E. B. Short farm, to a point beyond the enemy's camp, and there he was to turn back to the southeast toward the northern slope of Oak Hill.

At about 1:00 A.M. August 10, 1861, when within a few miles of the enemy's camp, Lyon halted his column and waited for daylight before resuming his advance. At 4:15 A.M. he was near the Short farm.

Lyon discovered the enemy's camp shortly after sunrise, and he prepared to move forward. He sent Plummer to the east side of Wilson's Creek with his battalion of regulars and ordered Clark Wright's Mounted Home Guards to move forward on the left of the army and protect its flank. At the same time, he started his troops obliquely to the southeast across the land lying between Wilson's Creek on the left and Skegg's Branch on the right. He also ordered Andrews to bring up his 1st Missouri Volunteers to the head of the column on the west bank, with instructions to keep abreast of Plummer's command across the creek.

Having made these dispositions, Lyon advanced more rapidly, with each regiment in column of companies. His line passed to the west of the Short farm, crossed the valley of Spring Branch, which emptied into Wilson's Creek a short distance to the east, and arrived at the northern slope of Oak Hill. During this movement, James Totten's battery closely followed the 1st Missouri Regiment.

When the advance troops came up to Ridge No. 1, they found it occupied by a part of Cawthorn's brigade, and then Peter J. Osterhaus' battalion of 2nd Missouri Volunteers was deployed to the right and two companies of the 1st Missouri Volunteers to the left. The firing became heavy, but the skirmishers, aided by Totten's artillery, soon cleared

the ground ahead. On the east side of the creek, Plummer encountered the outpost of Cawthorn's brigade south of Gibson's Mill and drove it back. When Totten's guns opened fire on Cawthorn's camps on both sides of the creek, the men fled in complete disorder to the south, but they were re-formed under the bluffs at the foot of the hill between the ford of Wilson's Creek and Skegg's Branch.

Price then prepared to attack Lyon's position on Oak Hill. He formed Rains, with Cawthorn's men, below the end of Ridge No. 2, with his right extending toward Wilson's Creek, and placed William Y. Slack, with John T. Hughes' regiment, and John C. C. Thornton's battalion on the left of Price's line. The other troops of the Missouri State Guard were placed in line as follows: John B. Clark, with John Q. Burbridge's brigade, was on the left of Slack; Monroe M. Parsons, with Joseph Kelly's regiment, was on the left of Clark; and James H. McBride's brigade was on Price's extreme left. Weightman's brigade of Rains' command also came up and joined on the line.

As Lyon's troops moved up the hill, the 1st Missouri Volunteers, with Osterhaus' battalion of the 2nd Missouri Volunteers, was on the right to protect that flank; the 1st Kansas was on the left; and Totten's battery was between the two wings. The 2nd Kansas and the 1st Iowa brought up the rear.

Across Wilson's Creek, Plummer, moving south from Gibson's Mill, entered Ray's field, and there to the south he saw the smoke of Woodruff's battery firing from beyond the Springfield road. Plummer pushed forward with the intention of capturing or driving off the battery, and he soon entered the Ray cornfield. When James McIntosh learned of this, he led Louis Hebert's 3rd Louisiana up to the fence at the southern edge of the cornfield. Firing became heavy on both sides, and Hebert was soon driven back. He re-formed his regiment in rear of the Ray house, however, and moved up into the cornfield and renewed the fight. Plummer was then wounded, and his men were finally forced to withdraw slowly into the open field to the north, where they were exposed to a heavy fire.

Lyon then ordered John V. Du Bois' battery to take position on Ridge No. 1, almost opposite Ray's field, and he sent the 1st Iowa and Steele's regulars to protect the battery. Du Bois opened fire on

McIntosh's troops that were engaged with Plummer and drove them back. Frederick Steele's regulars then aided Plummer in withdrawing to the safety of the valley of Spring Creek on the west side of Wilson's Creek. Wright's Home Guards were not engaged in this action. Plummer's battle lasted about an hour.

When Lyon's men reached the plateau at the summit of Oak Hill, the line was about 1,000 yards in length, with the 1st Missouri and Osterhaus' battalion of the 2nd Missouri on the right, the 1st Kansas on the left, and the 2nd Kansas in reserve. A short time later, the 1st Iowa returned from supporting Du Bois' battery and was placed on the left of the 1st Kansas.

The enemy line, which was only a few hundred yards ahead, then advanced, and the battle for Oak Hill began. For an hour there was almost continuous and heavy firing, with neither side gaining any distinct advantage, and then Price withdrew his command down the bluff to the valley of Wilson's Creek. There he re-formed his troops and advanced for a second time up the hill. At that time, Lyon's units were in position as follows: partly on the crest and extending eastward down the lower Ridge No. 1 were, in order from west to east, Robert B. Mitchell's 2nd Kansas; Charles W. Canfield's Company B, 1st United States Cavalry; Steele's four companies of the 2nd United States Infantry; and Du Bois' battery. On the summit of the plateau was Totten's battery, with two guns covering the slope down toward Wilson's Creek between Ridge No. 1 and Ridge No. 2, and four guns directed toward the ravine between Ridge No. 2 and Ridge No 3. Below the level of the guns, George W. Deitzler's 1st Kansas was on Ridge No. 2, George L. Andrews' 1st Missouri Volunteers was on Ridge No. 3, and Peter J. Osterhaus' battalion of 2nd Missouri Volunteers was on Ridge No. 5.

Soon the two forces were again engaged in deadly fighting as Price's troops attempted to gain possession the hill. Lyon's line was driven back two or three times, but each time the troops rallied and moved forward again. The fighting continued with undiminished intensity for another hour, and then once more Price's line fell back to the bottom of the hill. Then Slack and Clark charged the line held by the 1st Missouri in an attempt to break through. Andrews and his men resisted strongly for a time,

and then Mitchell's 2nd Kansas came up in support, and the enemy was driven back.

About this time, Steele was sent with his battalion of regulars to support Totten's battery.

There was another lull, and then Price's State Guard advanced for the third time against Lyon's entire line. The 1st Missouri and 1st Kansas were soon in trouble, but they were strengthened by the 1st Iowa and held their positions. This effort was particularly violent, and in repeated attacks, Price's men came up to within 30–40 yards of Lyon's line. This attack, too, failed, and there was another lull of about a half-hour.

Major's Riflemen, fighting dismounted, made a limited attack on Steele's regulars, who had been supporting Du Bois' battery. Du Bois, who had been aiding Totten during the earlier fighting, had received orders to move his battery from the center of the line to the right, and he was preparing to move when Major attacked. Steele, who was greatly outnumbered, was being driven back when Du Bois opened with an enfilade fire and drove Major back with heavy losses.

It was then 7:00 A.M., two hours after the battle had begun, and during that time there had been no word from Sigel's column. At that time, however, Lyon heard the sounds of firing on Sigel's front to the south. When Sigel heard the sounds of Totten's guns that morning, he opened with his artillery on the enemy cavalry encampment along Wilson's Creek, below the Sharp house. The cavalrymen rapidly withdrew into the shelter of the valley of Skegg's Branch, and there they re-formed for an attack. When they charged against Sigel's position, however, they were quickly driven back. Instead of following the retiring cavalrymen, Sigel's men began to plunder the enemy's camp, but they were soon driven out of the camp and into the woods beyond by J. G. Reid's battery of Pearce's Arkansas brigade. Sigel then moved his brigade northward and at 8:30 A.M. took position at the top of the bluff, with his line across the Springfield road, just south of the Sharp house.

When Sigel was thus discovered on their rear, the enemy quickly brought up troops to meet him. McCulloch moved down Wilson's Creek with his battalion of 1st Arkansas Mounted Riflemen, Samuel M. Hyams' battalion of 3rd Louisiana, and James McIntosh's 2nd Arkansas Mounted Riflemen, and these were joined by several companies of Brown's and Major's cavalry.

As McCulloch's line advanced, Sigel at first believed it to be the 1st Iowa of Lyon's command because of the uniforms, and he withheld his fire. When he received a volley at close range, his command was completely shattered, and his scattered troops began to make their way back to Springfield, with no attempt to re-form. Five guns were lost during the retreat. Carr escaped with a portion of his cavalry in formation. Sigel, with a small escort, reached Springfield late that morning, then went to bed without communicating with Lyon. Salomon also returned to Springfield without his troops. Stragglers of Sigel's brigade came in during the afternoon and that night.

With Sigel thus disposed of, McCulloch moved with his command to join Price for another attack on Oak Hill, and at 9:00 A.M. made an all-out assault on the hill. For an hour there was deadly fighting on the southern slopes, during which the 1st Iowa was brought up from reserve, but finally the enemy once again withdrew into the brush along Wilson's Creek. Lyon was killed in this attack near the end of Ridge No. 3, and Sturgis assumed temporary command of the Army of the West.

The enemy then launched their fourth full-scale attack, but it too was repulsed, and they retired to the foot of the hill. By that time it was 11:30 A.M., and then, against the advice of Granger, Schofield, and Sweeny, Sturgis ordered the army to retire to Springfield.

The fighting at Wilson's Creek was unusually persistent and deadly, and this is reflected in the heavy losses on both sides. The Northern forces lost 1,317 men killed, wounded, and missing out of about 5,400 present, and the Southern forces lost 1,336 out of about 10,200 present.

Plummer's regulars, the van of Sturgis' column, entered Springfield from the battlefield about 5:00 P.M. August 10, 1861, and Steele's regulars, who brought up the rear, came in after dark. At 5:00 P.M. Sturgis turned over the command of the army to Sigel, who was the senior officer. Sigel then decided to withdraw to Rolla, and began the retreat the next morning. Because of Sigel's performance on the march, a number of officers, including Schofield, demanded a change of command, and after three days on the march, Sigel turned over the command to Sturgis.

On August 19, 1861, nine days after the Battle of Wilson's Creek, Sturgis' column reached Rolla, and the troops then traveled by rail to Saint Louis. They were then sent to reinforce John Pope's command in northern Missouri. At this point, the Army of the West was discontinued.

Back at Wilson's Creek, Price wanted to pursue and attack Sturgis' army, but McCulloch would not accompany him. In the end, McCulloch and Pearce returned to Arkansas. Price remained at Springfield until August 25, 1861, and then he marched northward toward Lexington, Missouri.

The organization of Lyon's army at the Battle of Wilson's Creek was as follows:

ARMY OF THE WEST
Nathaniel Lyon

SOUTH COLUMN (Sigel's Brigade), Franz Sigel
    3rd Missouri Volunteers, Anselm Albert
    5th Missouri Volunteers, Charles E. Salomon
    Backof's Battalion Missouri Artillery (detachment)
        Gustavus A. Schaefer's battery
        Edward Schuetzenbach's battery
    Cavalry, Eugene A. Carr
        Company I, 1st United States Artillery, Eugene A. Carr
        Company C, 2nd United States Dragoons, Charles E. Farrand

Note. Sigel's Brigade was Second Brigade, Missouri Volunteers.

NORTH COLUMN, Nathaniel Lyon

First Brigade, Samuel D. Sturgis
    Plummer's Battalion of Regulars, Joseph B. Plummer
    Battalion 2nd Missouri Infantry, Peter J. Osterhaus
        Battery F, 2nd United States Artillery, James Totten
        Kansas Rangers, Samuel N. Wood
        1st United States Cavalry (Company B), Charles W. Canfield

Note. Plummer's battalion consisted of companies B, C, D, and a company of recruits, 1st United States Infantry.

Second Brigade, George L. Andrews
    Steele's Battalion of Regulars, Frederick Steele

1st Missouri Volunteers, George L. Andrews
Du Bois' Battery (improvised), John V. Du Bois

Note. Steele's battalion consisted of companies B and E, 2nd United States Infantry; Warren L. Lothrop's company of General Service Recruits; and John Morine's company of Rifle Recruits.

Third Brigade, George W. Deitzler
    1st Kansas, George W. Deitzler, wounded
        John A. Halderman
    2nd Kansas, Robert B. Mitchell, wounded
        Charles W. Blair

Note. Deitzler commanded Third Brigade while Thomas W. Sweeny was serving as acting inspector general on Lyon's staff.

Unattached
    1st Iowa, William H. Merritt
    Clark Wright's and Theodore A. Switzler's Missouri
        Home Guard Cavalry
    Missouri Pioneers, John. D. Voerster

Note. Merritt commanded 1st Iowa in place of John F. Bates, who was sick.

Siege and Capture of Lexington, Missouri, September 13–20, 1861. While at Springfield, Price considered the problem of how he could best use his army to promote the Southern interests in Missouri, and finally concluded that he should attempt to gather up the thousands of pro-Southern men in various parts of Missouri who wanted to join in the effort to drive the Federal forces from the state. A great many of these men resided north of the Missouri River, but were unable to join Price's army because Federal troops controlled the river and occupied strong positions at all the principal river crossings. Price believed that if he could take Lexington, Missouri, he could open the crossing there and enable an estimated 5,000–6,000 men to move to the south side and join his army before Union forces had established a stronger control over the region.

Thus, on August 25, 1861, Price marched out of Springfield with his Army of the Missouri State Guard toward the Missouri River. First he moved to the northwest to Dry Wood Creek, near the Kansas state line between Fort Scott, Kansas and Nevada, Missouri. There he was observed by troops of James H. Lane's Kansas Brigade, and troops under James

Montgomery, who commanded at Fort Scott, skirmished for a time and then withdrew into Kansas. Price then marched northward from Nevada, by way of Papinsville, to Warrensburg, Missouri.

When Fremont learned of Price's advance, he ordered John Pope and Samuel D. Sturgis to concentrate their commands at Lexington, and directed Lane to withdraw to Fort Leavenworth.

On the night of August 30, 1861, James A. Mulligan was encamped with his 23rd Illinois Regiment outside Jefferson City, 125 miles from Lexington. He reported to Jefferson C. Davis, commanding in the town, and was ordered to march with his regiment to Tipton and join Thomas A. Marshall, who was there with his 1st Illinois Cavalry. Mulligan was then to assume command of both regiments. Upon arriving at Tipton, however, he did not find the cavalry, and he marched to Lexington, where he found Marshall with his regiment and about 350 men of the Missouri Home Guard.

Everett Peabody, who had arrived at Kansas City with his 13th Missouri Infantry from Saint Joseph, Missouri, had started toward Lexington, but was then ordered south to help Lane, who, as already noted, had encountered Price at Dry Wood Creek. On September 10, 1861, Mulligan received a communication from Peabody stating that he was retreating from Warrensburg, fifty-four miles distant, and that Price was following him toward Lexington. A short time later Peabody arrived with his regiment at Lexington. Mulligan was then near the town with his own, Marshall's, and Peabody's regiments, and artillery commanded by William Waldschmidt, Adams, and Gustave Pirner. As the senior officer, Mulligan assumed command of all troops at Lexington.

North of Lexington, on a hill overlooking the town and the Missouri River, was the campus of the Masonic College. Mulligan abandoned the town to the enemy and about noon September 11, 1861 began the construction of fortifications on College Hill. One of these was a rectangular earthwork, with bastions at the angles and embrasures for cannon, which was thrown up close to and surrounding the college building, and the other was an irregular earthwork, farther out at a distance of from 200 to 800 feet from the inner works, that was protected by traverses and some redoubts.

That evening, when the work had hardly started, Mulligan's pickets were driven in at the Garrison Fork of Tabo Creek, five miles south of the town, and Mulligan thus learned that the enemy was nearby. He ordered Peabody out to the south to meet the advance of Price's column, and at dawn May 12, 1861, Peabody moved out with three companies of his regiment and burned the bridge over which Price would have to pass to enter the town from that direction. Price then withdrew and marched around to the Independence road, which entered Lexington along the Missouri River from the west. Mulligan sent six companies from Peabody's and Marshall's regiments, under the command of Robert T. Van Horn, to make a stand near the Machpelah Cemetery at the southern edge of Lexington.

Leading Price's advance were elements of William Y. Slack's division, which was commanded by Benjamin A. Rives during the absence of Slack, who was wounded at Wilson's Creek. When John T. Hughes' regiment of Rives' brigade and some dismounted cavalry approached, Van Horn's men opened fire, and there was a sharp contest for about a half-hour before the Federals began to withdraw. James H. McBride's division came up and moved into the Machpelah Cemetery. There was some skirmishing there, and then McBride pushed on through the cemetery and to the outskirts of the town, where there was further skirmishing. Monroe M. Parsons' division was ordered up in support, and about 4:00 P.M. the fighting increased on the east side of the road running into town. Mulligan's forward troops then withdrew to the positions on College Hill. Parsons pursued, and there was an exchange of infantry and artillery fire for another hour and a half, and finally, soon after sunset, Price withdrew to the fairgrounds about two miles south of town to wait for the rest of his column to come up.

On September 13, 1861, in a pouring rain, the work on the entrenchments continued, and as Price's regiments arrived, they were placed around the college grounds. Price's ammunition trains arrived on September 17, and he then prepared to attack Mulligan's position on the hill. Rains posted his division to the east and southeast of the college, and Parsons deployed his command in line along Main (or North) Street, then moved forward through the town to within striking distance of the works on the hill. Rives was ordered to move

eastward along the river bank to the bluff at the north end of College Hill and thus complete the encirclement of Mulligan's position. When these troops were in position, the college grounds were completely surrounded, and Mulligan's men were cut off from water.

When Rives' column reached the river front, it was pinned down by the fire from Union snipers who had moved into the flour mill, the ruins of the Morrison foundry, and other buildings along the river. After a time the snipers were forced out of the buildings, and they retired up the hill toward the brick house of Oliver Anderson and toward the Union earthworks on College Hill, which were about 100 yards beyond the Anderson house. At that time the Anderson house was used as a Union hospital and flew a hospital flag. As the enemy pursued, they came under fire from the retreating Federals, who had taken cover on the lawn of the Anderson house and, as the enemy claimed, from the house itself. When Thomas A. Harris came up with his division to support Rives and McBride, he decided, according to his report, that the house "was invaluable to me as a point of annoyance and mask for my approach to the enemy." Then, with Rives' cooperation, Harris stormed and occupied the house, although it flew a hospital flag. This resulted in a vigorous controversy as to whether it was used by Union sharpshooters, as the enemy claimed, but the fact is that when the enemy entered the building, it was occupied by sick and wounded, and no armed soldier was found inside.

Mulligan then decided that the hospital should be retaken, and the Montgomery Guards, a company of his 23rd Illinois, and a company of Peabody's regiment advanced and recaptured the building. They remained in possession during the rest of the day, but were driven out at dark.

At the end of the day September 18, 1861, McBride's division was on the left of Rives, below the bluff north of College Hill, and Harris' division was on the left of McBride and on the right of Rains on the encircling enemy line.

Throughout the day of September 19, 1861, Mulligan was under fire, and his situation was becoming critical. The troops were suffering from lack of water and were low on ammunition, and there seemed little prospect of help from Fremont. There had been one effort to relieve the troops at Lexington. On September 16, Samuel D. Sturgis had been ordered by John Pope to move from Macon City, Missouri with about 1,100 men to the aid of Mulligan. Sturgis detrained his command at Utica on the Hannibal and Saint Joseph Railroad and marched toward the Missouri River. Price learned of this attempt to relieve Mulligan, and he sent Parsons and Congreve Jackson across the river with 3,000 men to intercept Sturgis, who was then about fifteen miles from Lexington. When Sturgis neared the Missouri River bottom, he was informed by a native that Parsons was waiting for him in the woods ahead. Sturgis then turned off to the west and marched for Kansas City.

On September 20, 1861, the enemy resorted to a novel means of advancing against the Union breastworks. They formed a line of hemp bales near the Anderson house, and as these were rolled forward, the infantry advanced under their cover. While this advance was in progress, unauthorized white flags appeared on the breastworks, and in the discussion which followed, Mulligan decided to surrender. Captured, along with his troops, were Marshall, Mulligan, and Peabody, the latter two being wounded.

Price remained at Lexington until the end of September, and then he began his march back toward Springfield, Missouri.

LAND OPERATIONS AGAINST MOBILE BAY AND MOBILE, ALABAMA
JULY 29, 1864– APRIL 12, 1865

Following the opening of the Mississippi River in July 1863 by the capture of Vicksburg and Port Hudson, Rear Admiral David G. Farragut, commanding the West Gulf Blockading Squadron, turned his attention to operations against Mobile Bay. He was ready to move against Mobile soon after the surrender of Port Hudson, but was delayed in taking any action until the next year. Nathaniel P. Banks, commanding the Department of the Gulf, became involved in some expeditions against Texas and could not spare the troops to help Farragut, and

the latter then decided to take some of his ships north for an overhaul before committing them to further action.

In January 1864, Farragut made a reconnaissance at Fort Morgan and Fort Gaines at the entrance to Mobile Bay, and he then sought help from the navy and from Banks for an effort to close Mobile Bay. Farragut could easily run through the main ship channel from the gulf into Mobile Bay, but once inside, his heavy ships would be unable to move beyond a comparatively small area of deep water that lay within range of the guns of the Confederate forts at the entrance to the bay. Because of this, Farragut asked Banks to send a force of about 5,000 men to land in rear of the forts and attack them under the cover of a heavy fire from the fleet.

Once again, however, operations against Mobile were delayed because land forces were not available. When troops were requested from Banks, he was preparing for his campaign up the Red River, and then later, at the end of the campaign, two divisions of Nineteenth Corps were sent to Virginia to reinforce Grant's forces operating against Lee.

Capture of Fort Gaines, Alabama, August 8, 1864, and Fort Morgan, Alabama, August 23, 1864. It was not until late July 1864 that Edward R. S. Canby, commander of the Military Division of West Mississippi, who was directed to assist the navy in the capture of the forts at the entrance to Mobile Bay, could complete the necessary arrangements. Then Canby sent Gordon Granger, with such forces as he could collect, to operate with Farragut against the defenses of Mobile Bay. Granger had relinquished command of Fourth Corps, Army of the Cumberland April 10, and on June 21 had been ordered to report to Canby.

On July 29, 1864, Granger embarked with about 1,800 men from New Orleans to cooperate with Farragut at Mobile Bay. These troops landed on the west side of Dauphin Island August 3, and then began preparations for the siege of Fort Gaines.

About sundown August 4, 1864, the last of four monitors that had been assigned to Farragut's fleet arrived, and just before dawn on August 5, the fleet steamed toward the main ship channel. Farragut passed the forts at the entrance to the bay, and once inside engaged the Confederate naval forces guarding the approaches to Mobile. The enemy was soon defeated, and Farragut was in control of the waters at the southern end of the bay.

Fort Gaines surrendered August 8, 1864, and Granger then left a small force to hold the fort and immediately crossed the bay with the rest of his command. He landed on Mobile Point, near Pilot Town, in rear of Fort Morgan, and began the investment of Fort Morgan on August 9.

Granger believed that his force was too small to force the surrender of Fort Morgan, and he asked Canby for reinforcements. The following troops were sent to Mobile Bay during August 1864:

On August 4, Henry Bertram arrived in New Orleans with the 94th Illinois, 20th Iowa, 38th Iowa, and 20th Wisconsin regiments from the United States Forces in Texas (formerly Second Division, Thirteenth Corps), and August 7, he was sent on to Dauphin Island to report to Granger. Bertram's brigade arrived off Fort Gaines August 8, and two days later landed on Mobile Point, Alabama. On August 12, it moved to South Beach and began operations against Fort Morgan. Bertram's brigade was designated as Second Brigade, United States Forces Mobile Bay.

By August 11, the 77th Illinois, 67th Indiana, 34th Iowa, 96th Ohio, and 3rd Maryland Cavalry (dismounted) regiments of Frederick W. Moore's Third Brigade, Third Division, Nineteenth Corps were with Granger under the command of George W. Clark.

On August 13, Joseph Bailey was ordered to Mobile Point to report to Granger for duty. On that same day, Richard Arnold, chief of artillery of the Department of the Gulf, was ordered to take charge of the siege materials that were being collected at that place. Jacob B. Rawles' Battery B, 5th United States Artillery was assigned to Arnold, and the latter was also directed to take such ordnance stores as might be needed at Mobile Bay from Fort Jackson and Fort Saint Philip.

On August 22, Joshua J. Guppey was ordered to Mobile Point with his Third Brigade, Second Division, Nineteenth Corps, which consisted of the 161th New York, the 23rd Wisconsin, the 2nd Battery, Connecticut Light Artillery (detachment), and the 17th Battery, Ohio Light Artillery (detachment). It should be noted here that Nineteenth Corps was reorganized August 18.

George H. Gordon arrived at Fort Gaines about August 21 and was assigned command of the western defenses of Mobile, which at that time consisted of only a few troops. When Fort Morgan surrendered on August 23, Granger turned over the command of the United States Forces at Mobile Bay to Gordon and returned to New Orleans.

At about that time, George D. Robinson, commanding the Engineer Brigade, Department of the Gulf, was also sent to Mobile Bay. He was later assigned command of a brigade consisting of the 96th and 97th United States Colored Troops of the Engineer Brigade.

Fort Morgan surrendered August 23, 1864, and after the surrender, United States forces continued to occupy Mobile Point, Dauphin Island, and the adjacent country during the fall and winter of 1864–1865.

United States Forces in South Alabama and West Florida, August 1864–March 1865. At the end of August 1864, the United States Forces, Mobile Bay, commanded by Gordon, were organized as follows:

United States Forces, Mobile Bay, George H. Gordon
  Troops at Mobile Point, Joseph Bailey
  Second Brigade, Henry Bertram
  Third Brigade, Second Division, Nineteenth Corps, Joshua J. Guppey
  Clark's Brigade, George W. Clark

Note 1. Guppey returned to Morganza, Louisiana, and in October 1864 was ordered with Second Division, Nineteenth Corps to Arkansas.
Note 2. The designation of Bertram's brigade was changed to Second Brigade, Provisional Division, Department of the Gulf, and it reported through the district commander to Thomas W. Sherman, commander of the Defenses of New Orleans.
Note 3. Clark's brigade consisted of four regiments of Frederick W. Moore's Third Brigade, Third Division, Nineteenth Corps.

September 12, 1864, the District of West Florida and South Alabama was created to secure better cooperation among the troops in West Florida and in the Mobile Bay area. Granger was assigned command of the district, which included the District of West Florida, the United States Forces on Dauphin Island, and United States Forces on Mobile Bay.

At the end of October 1864, the organization of Granger's command was as follows:

DISTRICT OF WEST FLORIDA AND SOUTH ALA-
BAMA, Gordon Granger

United States Forces, Mobile Bay, Henry Bertram
Mobile Point, Alabama, Henry Bertram
Dauphin Island, George D. Robinson

District of West Florida, Joseph Bailey
First Brigade, Ladislas L. Zulavsky
Second Brigade, Ephraim W. Woodman
Forces at Fort Barrancas, Camp Barrancas, and Fort
Pickens

In December 1864, United States Forces, Mobile
Bay was designated as the District of South Alabama, and Bertram was assigned command. At the
end of the month, Granger's command was organized as follows:

DISTRICT OF WEST FLORIDA AND SOUTH ALA-
BAMA, Gordon Granger

District of West Florida, Thomas J. McKean
First Brigade, George E. Yarrington
Second Brigade, Ephraim W. Woodman

*Note. First Brigade consisted of regiments of United
States Colored Troops, and Second Brigade of two cavalry regiments.*

District of South Alabama, Henry Bertram

*Note 1. Bertram's command consisted of eight infan-
try regiments, three cavalry regiments, and artillery.*
*Note 2. Elias S. Dennis assumed command of the
district February 9, 1865.*

On January 23, 1865, Granger announced the
reorganization of the troops of the District of West
Florida and South Alabama as follows: a First Brigade and a Second Brigade were to be formed in the
District of South Alabama, and a Third Brigade in
the District of West Florida. As a result of the
activities preparatory to the campaign against Mobile in March and April 1865, however, this organization appears to have been of short duration.

On January 18, 1865, Ulysses S. Grant ordered
Canby, commander of the Military Division of West
Mississippi, to move against Mobile, Montgomery,
and Selma, Alabama, and shortly thereafter the
forces in South Alabama and West Florida were
heavily reinforced for this movement.

Among the first troops to be sent from New

Orleans were those of the Reserve Corps, Military
Division of West Mississippi. On January 6, 1865,
Frederick Steele was assigned command of a camp
to be established at Kennerville (Kenner), Louisiana
for the purpose of preparing troops for transfer to
West Florida and South Alabama for field service
against Mobile. Three brigades of the Reserve
Corps, Military Division of West Mississippi assembled at Kennerville in January 1865, and the
Fourth Brigade in February 1865, and when ready
they were transferred to New Orleans for embarkation. Christopher C. Andrews' Third Brigade was
transferred to Barrancas, Florida January 24–28.

The Reserve Corps was reorganized February 3,
1865 (announced February 12) from the original
brigades of the Reserve Corps and additional regiments, and Granger was assigned command. The
corps was organized as follows:

RESERVE CORPS, MILITARY DIVISION OF WEST
MISSISSIPPI, Gordon Granger

First Division, Frederick Steele, to February 8, 1865
James C. Veatch, to February 18, 1865
First Brigade, Michael K. Lawler, to February 4, 1865
John A. McLaughlin, to February 18, 1865
Second Brigade, Elias S. Dennis
Third Brigade, Loren Kent

*Note. James H. Coates assumed command of Third
Brigade February 7, 1865, the same day that Kent was
assigned.*

Second Division, Christopher C. Andrews
First Brigade, Samuel L. Glasgow
Second Brigade, William T. Spicely
Third Brigade, John Charles Black

*Note. Apparently Second Division was organized by
March 4, 1865, at which time the designation was
changed to Second Division, Thirteenth Corps.*

Third Division, William P. Benton
First Brigade, David P. Grier
Second Brigade, Henry M. Day
Third Brigade, Conrad Krez

*Note. Day assumed command of Second Brigade Feb-
ruary 25, 1865; Grier was assigned command of First
Brigade February 25, 1865; and Krez was assigned
command of Third Brigade, Third Division, Thirteenth
Corps February 27, 1865. Thus, when fully organized,
the designation of Third Division was Third Division,
Thirteenth Corps.*

The reorganization ordered February 3, 1865 was not fully completed before Thirteenth Corps was re-created from troops of the Reserve Corps by an order of February 18, 1865. Meantime, the other brigades of the Reserve Corps, and some newly organized brigades, were sent to the Gulf Coast. Elias S. Dennis' Second Brigade, First Division moved to Dauphin Island February 4–12, and James H. Coates assumed command of the brigade February 11. James R. Slack was assigned command of First Brigade, First Division (originally Michael K. Lawler's brigade), and departed with it for Fort Gaines, Alabama February 15. Loren Kent's Third Brigade, First Division was transferred to Dauphin Island February 11–18, and John Charles Black's Fourth Brigade, Reserve Corps departed for Barrancas, Florida on February 17.

On February 10, 1865, the Department of the Gulf was redefined to include only the states of Louisiana and Texas, and thus the District of West Florida and South Alabama was no longer included in the Department of the Gulf. Thereafter the commander of the district reported directly to Headquarters, Military Division of West Mississippi.

On February 18, 1865, Thirteenth Corps, Military Division of West Mississippi was finally reorganized from Granger's Reserve Corps. Granger was assigned command (assumed command February 25) and established headquarters at Fort Gaines, Alabama. Thirteenth Corps was organized into three divisions as follows: First Division, James C. Veatch; Second Division, Christopher C. Andrews; Third Division, William P. Benton. First Division was at Dauphin Island; Second Division was in West Florida, except Bertram's brigade, which was at Mobile Point, Alabama; and Third Division was at Mobile Point. Benton was assigned command of United States Forces at Mobile Point on February 21. For a more detailed description of the organization of Thirteenth Corps, see Thirteenth Corps, Military Division of West Mississippi, and also see below, United States Forces Operating against Mobile, Alabama.

Additional reinforcements for Canby arrived in Louisiana in February and March 1865. Early in February, Andrew J. Smith's Detachment Army of the Tennessee was in camp at Eastport, Mississippi, where it had halted at the end of the pursuit of John B. Hood's army after its defeat at Nashville, Tennessee in December 1864. On February 7–8, Smith's command embarked at Eastport and traveled by way of the Tennessee and Mississippi rivers, past Cairo, Memphis, and Vicksburg, arriving at New Orleans on February 20–22. After disembarking there, it moved to Chalmette, about four miles below New Orleans, and went into camp. Meantime, on February 18, while it was en route downriver, the designation of Smith's command had been changed to Sixteenth Corps, Military Division of West Mississippi.

On February 28, 1865, First Brigade, First Division, Sixteenth Corps had been ordered to Dauphin Island to report to Granger, and Second Brigade and Third Brigade of the division followed March 4–5. By March 7, First Division, Sixteenth Corps was again united on Dauphin Island. Second Division embarked at Chalmette March 6 and arrived at Dauphin Island March 10–11. Third Division followed Second Division, embarking March 12, and arrived at Fort Gaines March 16.

For details of the organization of Smith's command, see Sixteenth Corps, Military Division of West Mississippi, and also see below, United States Forces Operating against Mobile, Alabama.

First Division, United States Colored Troops, Military Division of West Mississippi was organized under John P. Hawkins in New Orleans February 23, 1865 and was assigned to Steele's command at Pensacola. The division began embarkation at Algiers, Louisiana for Pensacola that same day. For additional information, see Department of the Gulf, Troops in the Department of the Gulf, United States Colored Troops (USCT) in the Department of the Gulf, and also see below, United States Forces Operating against Mobile, Alabama.

During the period February 12–March 10, 1865, Joseph F. Knipe's Seventh Division, Cavalry Corps, Military Division of the Mississippi was transferred from the Department of the Cumberland to New Orleans and then to Mobile Bay. It accompanied Canby's column from Navy Cove on its movement to Spanish Fort and Blakely, Alabama. Additional cavalry regiments were also sent to Canby from the Department of Arkansas, the Department of the Gulf, and the Department of Mississippi, and these were organized into a Cavalry Corps, Military Division of West Mississippi under the command of Benjamin H. Grierson. For additional information, see Cavalry Corps, Military Division of West Mississippi.

By mid-March 1865, Canby's force was assembled at the lower end of Mobile Bay and near Pensacola, Florida, and the weather conditions were suitable for the advance on Mobile. The movement was to be made in two columns, with one commanded by Canby and the other by Steele. The main part of the army under Canby was to establish itself on firm ground on the east side of Mobile Bay, and Steele was to move with a smaller force from Pensacola to threaten Montgomery and Selma, and to cover the operations of the cavalry while destroying the Alabama and Florida and Mobile and Great Northern railroads. Steele was then to turn west and join Canby for operations against Spanish Fort and Blakely.

Canby's command consisted of the following:

THIRTEENTH CORPS, Gordon Granger

First Division, James C. Veatch
Third Division, William P. Benton
First Brigade, Second Division, Henry Bertram

Note. The rest of Second Division was with Steele's Column at Pensacola, Florida.

SIXTEENTH CORPS, Andrew J. Smith

First Division, John McArthur
Second Division, Kenner Garrard
Third Division, Eugene A. Carr

SEVENTH CAVALRY DIVISION, MILITARY DIVISION OF THE MISSISSIPPI, Joseph F. Knipe

SIEGE TRAIN, Richard Arnold

Siege and Capture of Spanish Fort, Alabama, March 26, 1865–April 8, 1865, and Fort Blakely, Alabama, April 1, 1865–April 9, 1865. On March 17, 1865, Canby's command began its advance toward Mobile. That day, Benton's Third Division, Thirteenth Corps and Bertram's First Brigade of Andrews' Second Division, Thirteenth Corps, which were on Mobile Point, left from Navy Cove and marched by way of Shell Bank and Bayou Portage toward Dannelly's Mills (also spelled on one map as Dandy's Mills) on the North Branch of Fish River. Also on March 17, Veatch's First Division, Thirteenth Corps crossed on transports from Dauphin Island to Navy Cove, and the next day followed Benton and Bertram toward Dannelly's Mills. These troops arrived at Dannelly's Mills March 22–24.

John McArthur's First Division and Kenner Garrard's Second Division of Sixteenth Corps embarked on transports at Dauphin Island March 19, 1865, then moved up Mobile Bay to the mouth of Fish River. They moved up the river and disembarked at Dannelly's Mills March 20–21. Lyman M. Ward's Second Brigade and James L. Geddes' Third Brigade of Eugene A. Carr's Third Division, Sixteenth Corps embarked at Fort Gaines and arrived at Dannelly's Mills March 21–22. Jonathan B. Moore's First Brigade of Carr's division embarked at Cedar Point and joined the other two brigades at Dannelly's Mills.

Canby's column remained near Dannelly's Mills until March 25, 1865, then marched toward Spanish Fort. It arrived near the fort March 26–27, then moved up and began the investment of the Confederate works. When Canby's line was completed, the divisions were in position as follows: beginning on the right was Carr's division of Sixteenth Corps, with its right on Bay Minette; then in order to the left were McArthur's division of Sixteenth Corps, Benton's division of Thirteenth Corps, Veatch's division of Thirteenth Corps, and on the left was Bertram's brigade of Second Division, Thirteenth Corps, with its left on D'Olive's Creek. The brigades of these divisions were in line as follows:

Carr's division: James L. Geddes' Third Brigade was on the right, Jonathan B. Moore's First Brigade in the center, and Lyman M. Ward's Second Brigade on the left.

McArthur's division; William L. McMillen's First Brigade was on the right, Lucius F. Hubbard's Second Brigade in the center, and William R. Marshall's Third Brigade on the left.

Benton's division: Conrad Krez's Third Brigade was on the right, Henry M. Day's Second Brigade in the center, and David P. Grier's First Brigade on the left.

Veatch's division: Elias S. Dennis' Second Brigade

was on the right, James R. Slack's First Brigade in the center, and William B. Kinsey's Third Brigade on the left.

Garrard's division of Sixteenth Corps was placed in an entrenched camp covering the Blakely road at a point where it crossed Minette Creek. While there it covered the right and rear of the army.

On March 19, 1865, Frederick Steele started on the march toward Mobile with his Column from Pensacola. That day he sent Andrew B. Spurling with a detachment of cavalry by water to Creigler's Mills with orders to move northward to Milton and Evergreen on the Alabama and Florida Railroad and, after inflicting as much damage as possible, to join the main body near Pollard, Alabama. Steele concentrated the rest of his command at Pensacola as follows: Christopher C. Andrews with William T. Spicely's Second Brigade and Frederick W. Moore's Third Brigade of his Second Division, Thirteenth Corps; John P. Hawkins with his First Division, United States Colored Troops; and Thomas J. Lucas' Separate Cavalry Brigade.

March 20, 1865, Steele's column, with Lucas' cavalry in advance, marched northward along the Alabama and Florida Railroad toward Pollard. The march was very slow because of terrible roads and high water, and it was not until March 24–26 that they arrived near the town. About 11:00 A.M. March 25, Lucas came up to James H. Clanton's Confederate brigade, which was formed in line of battle along the north bank of Canoe Creek, near Bluff Springs, Florida. Algernon S. Badger's 1st Louisiana Cavalry, supported by a battalion of 2nd New York Veteran Cavalry under Edward Van Voast, immediately charged and completely routed Clanton's command. The enemy lost, in addition to the killed and wounded, more than 100 prisoners, including Clanton, who was wounded and captured. Lucas then moved on to Pollard.

On March 26, Andrews was sent into Pollard to take possession of government property there, to collect supplies, and to attempt to establish contact with Spurling. Spurling arrived that evening after destroying some track on the railroad and capturing and destroying two trains and much supplies.

Steele then turned west and marched along the Mobile and Great Northern Railroad. He was to have moved to Holyoke, but because of a lack of forage and food, he moved instead to Stockton, where he arrived March 31, 1865. He then marched to the front of Blakely April 1, and began siege operations the next day. Hawkins' division was on the right of Steele's line, between the Stockton road on the left and a swamp on the right. Charles W. Drew's Third Brigade was on the right of the division line, next to the swamp, Hiram Scofield's Second Brigade was on the center, and William A. Pile's First Brigade was on the left. Andrews' two brigades were on the left of the Stockton road, with William T. Spicely's Second Brigade on the right, next to the road, and Frederick W. Moore's Third Brigade on the left.

On March 30, 1865, Veatch's division of Thirteenth Corps was withdrawn from the line of entrenchments and was sent to Holyoke to convoy supplies for Steele's column and to hold that place until Steele arrived. Marshall's brigade of McArthur's division replaced Veatch's division on the line. On April 3, Veatch's division joined Steele's investing force at Blakely. It then took position on the line of investment between the left of Andrews' division and the Pensacola road. Dennis' brigade was on the right of the division, next to Andrews; Slack's brigade was on the center; and Kinsey's brigade was on the left, next to the Pensacola road.

March 27, 1865, Garrard's division of Sixteenth Corps was left as a rear guard for the corps' trains, and was placed in an entrenched camp to cover the Blakely road at a point where the road crossed Minette Creek. It remained there until April 3, and the next day joined Steele's force at Blakely. Garrard's division was then moved to the left of Veatch's division and to the left of Steele's line of investment. Its right was on the Pensacola road, and its left ended on a swamp. James I. Gilbert's Second Brigade was on the right, next to the road; Charles L. Harris' Third Brigade was on the center of the line; and John I. Rinaker's First Brigade was on the left, next to the swamp.

Thomas J. Lucas' cavalry brigade (commanded by Morgan H. Chrysler) of Steele's Column from Pensacola and Gilbert M. L. Johnson's Second Brigade of Knipe's First Cavalry Division of Canby's command were assigned the duty of covering the rear of the army.

The Confederate forces holding Spanish Fort and

Blakely (or Fort Blakely) belonged to Dabney H. Maury's District of the Gulf. St. John R. Liddell, commander of the East Division, had his headquarters at Blakely, and most of Maury's forces were ordered to report to him. Randall L. Gibson, who was in command of the Confederate forces on the eastern shore of Mobile Bay, was ordered with his brigade (commanded by Francis L. Campbell) and two regiments of James T. Holtzclaw's brigade (commanded by Bushrod Jones) to Spanish Fort, where Gibson assumed command. Bryan M. Thomas' brigade of Alabama Reserves and Isaac W. Patton's artillery were also sent to Spanish Fort. After three days of the siege, Holtzclaw's brigade and Matthew D. Ector's brigade (commanded by David Coleman) of Samuel G. French's division (commanded by Francis M. Cockrell) relieved Thomas.

When the Federal troops arrived in front of Spanish Fort, Canby realized the enemy position was too strong for a successful assault, and he immediately began regular siege operations. He steadily pushed his siege works forward toward the enemy entrenchments, and finally at 11:00 P.M. April 8, 1865, Gibson was forced to evacuate the fort. Bertram's brigade of Second Division, Thirteenth Corps then moved up and occupied the abandoned works.

Meantime, Steele had also been pressing forward with siege operations at Blakely. On the morning of April 9, after the evacuation of Spanish Fort, Andrew J. Smith was ordered to move McArthur's division and Carr's division of Sixteenth Corps to the left of Steele's line at Blakely and prepare for an assault on the enemy works. In addition, Granger left Bertram's brigade at Spanish Fort and sent Benton's division of Thirteenth Corps to report to Steele. Benton marched with his division to the rear of Blakely, but he was not in position to join in the assault on the evening of April 9. McArthur's division took position in reserve to Garrard's division, which was on the left of Steele's line at Blakely. Carr's division was also placed in reserve.

Canby ordered an assault on the enemy lines at Blakely for the evening of April 9. At that time the divisions on Steele's front line were, in order from right to left, Hawkins' division of United States Colored Troops, Andrews' division of Thirteenth Corps (Second Brigade and Third Brigade), Veatch's division of Thirteenth Corps, and Garrard's division of Sixteenth Corps. The divisions of Benton, McArthur, and Carr were in support of the front line. Canby launched a successful attack at about 5:00 P.M. and soon gained possession of the enemy works at Blakely. At this point, all enemy resistance in front of Mobile was at an end.

Federal Troop Movements after the Capture of Fort Blakely. On April 10, 1865, Veatch's and Garrard's divisions returned to Thirteenth and Sixteenth Corps, respectively, and then Canby began to move his troops forward to occupy Mobile and the surrounding country.

At sundown April 11, the divisions of Veatch and Benton of Thirteenth Corps marched from the rear of Blakely for Starke's Landing, and the next morning they crossed to the western shore of Mobile Bay. At 11:30 A.M. they landed about five miles below Mobile, and then they marched northward without opposition and occupied the city.

Benton's division remained in the defenses of Mobile until April 13, 1865, then moved by way of Whistler (or Whistler's Station) on the Mobile and Ohio Railroad, and Mount Vernon on the Tombigbee River, to McIntosh's Bluff on the Tombigbee. It arrived at the latter place April 26–27. On May 4, Richard Taylor surrendered the Confederate forces in the Department of Alabama, Mississippi, and East Louisiana, and four days later the paroles of Taylor's troops were accepted by Canby's commissioners. On May 9, Benton's division returned from McIntosh's Bluff to Mobile, where it remained during the rest of the month. Then, on May 30, Benton's division was ordered to report to Frederick Steele for service in Texas. On June 1, seven regiments of the division embarked for Brazos Santiago, and the rest remained near Mobile.

Veatch's division remained at Mobile until May 26–27, 1865, and then it embarked for New Orleans. On May 31, the division left New Orleans for the Red River, and First Brigade arrived at Shreveport June 7.

Andrews, with Second Brigade and Third Brigade of his Second Division, Thirteenth Corps, remained near Blakely until April 19, 1865, and then moved to Mobile the next day. On April 22, Andrews' brigades, forming a part of Steele's Column from Pensacola, moved up the Alabama River, arriving at Selma, Alabama on April 27. Andrews remained at Selma until May 11–12, then embarked and moved down the river to Mobile, where he arrived May 12–13. There Andrews was joined by First Brigade under Bertram, which had moved from Spanish Fort to Mobile on May 6. During June, Andrews' division embarked for Galveston, Texas, and by the end of the month all but three regiments of the division had left Mobile. Upon arrival in Texas, the troops were stationed at Galveston, Houston, Millican, and Columbus.

Meantime, on April 13, Smith, with the three divisions of his Sixteenth Corps, had marched from Blakely toward Montgomery, Alabama, where he arrived April 25–26. First Division remained in camp near Montgomery until May 10, then marched to Selma, Alabama, where it arrived May 14. Third Brigade remained at Selma, where it relieved Andrews' division of Thirteenth Corps and served on post and garrison duty. On May 16, First Brigade was sent by rail to Meridian, Mississippi, and Second Brigade by rail to Demopolis, Alabama. The troops of the brigade were encamped at Demopolis, Uniontown, and Marion, Alabama. On June 1, First Brigade, Second Division left Montgomery for Mobile, and upon arrival there June 9, it was assigned to provost duty. The other two brigades of the division remained at Montgomery. During May and June, Third Division, Sixteenth Corps remained at and near Montgomery, but on May 23, First Brigade occupied Tuskegee, Alabama. It remained there during June.

Hawkins' First Division, United States Colored Troops had left Blakely April 20, 1865 with Steele's column and arrived at Montgomery May 1. During the month, Hawkins' division returned to Mobile, and on June 11 left there on transports for New Orleans. Then on June 23, the division left New Orleans for Alexandria, Louisiana.

The United States forces commanded by Canby during the operations against Mobile, Alabama March 17–April 12, 1865 were known as the Army of West Mississippi, and were organized as follows:

UNITED STATES FORCES OPERATING AGAINST MOBILE, ALABAMA
Edward R. S. Canby

Engineer Brigade, Joseph Bailey
96th and 97th United States Colored Troops

1st Company of Pontoniers

Note. Bailey was assigned command of the Engineer Brigade March 15, 1865.

Siege Train, James Totten
Companies B, C, H, I, K, L, 1st Indiana Heavy Artillery, Benjamin F. Hays
18th Battery, New York Light Artillery, Albert G. Mack

THIRTEENTH CORPS, Gordon Granger

First Division, James C. Veatch
First Brigade, James R. Slack
Second Brigade, Elias S. Dennis
Third Brigade, William B. Kinsey
Artillery, George W. Fox
    4th Battery (D), Massachusetts Light Artillery, George W. Taylor
    7th Battery (G), Massachusetts Light Artillery, Newman W. Storer

Note 1. Veatch assumed command of First Division February 27, 1865.
Note 2. Kinsey assumed command of Third Brigade March 15, 1865.

Second Division, Christopher C. Andrews
First Brigade, Henry Bertram
Second Brigade, William T. Spicely
Third Brigade, Frederick W. Moore
Artillery
    2nd Battery, Connecticut Light Artillery, Walter S. Hotchkiss
    15th Battery, Massachusetts Light Artillery, Albert Rowse

Note 1. Andrews assumed command of Second Division March 4, 1865.
Note 2. First Brigade was organized February 12, 1865, and was detached and in camp at Mobile Point, Alabama. Bertram assumed command March 4, 1865.
Note 3. Andrews, with Second Brigade and Third Brigade of Second Division, was attached to Steele's Column from Pensacola.

Third Division, William P. Benton
First Brigade, David P. Grier
Second Brigade, Henry M. Day
Third Brigade, Conrad Krez
Artillery
    21st Battery, New York Light Artillery, James Barnes
    26th Battery, New York Light Artillery, Adam Beattie

Note. Krez was assigned command of Third Brigade February 27, 1865.

Mortar Batteries
Company A, 6th Michigan Heavy Artillery, Seldon F. Craig
Company K, 6th Michigan Heavy Artillery, Charles W. Wood

SIXTEENTH CORPS, Andrew J. Smith

First Division, John McArthur
First Brigade, William L. McMillen
Second Brigade, Lucius F. Hubbard
Third Brigade, William R. Marshall, wounded March 25, 1865
Artillery
3rd Battery, Indiana Light Artillery, Thomas J. Ginn
2nd Battery, Iowa Light Artillery, Joseph R. Reed

Second Division, Kenner Garrard
First Brigade, John I. Rinaker
Second Brigade, James I. Gilbert
Third Brigade, Charles L. Harris

Note. David Moore commanded First Brigade until February 11, 1865, and he was then succeeded by Rinaker.

Third Division, Eugene A. Carr
First Brigade, Jonathan B. Moore
Second Brigade, Lyman M. Ward
Third Brigade, James L. Geddes

Note 1. Carr assumed command of Third Division March 14, 1865.
Note 2. Second Brigade was organized under Ward at Fort Gaines March 15, 1865.
Note 3. Third Brigade was organized at Chalmette March 1, 1865, and Charles Turner assumed command. The brigade was reorganized March 15, 1865 under the command of Geddes.

Artillery Brigade, John W. Lowell
Cogswell's Battery, Illinois Light Artillery, William R. Elting
Battery G, 2nd Illinois Light Artillery, Perry Wilch
1st Battery, Indiana Light Artillery, Lawrence Jacoby
14th Battery, Indiana Light Artillery, Francis W. Morse
17th Battery, Ohio Light Artillery, Charles S. Rice

CAVALRY CORPS, MILITARY DIVISION OF THE MISSISSIPPI

Seventh Division, Joseph F. Knipe
First Brigade, Joseph Karge
Second Brigade, Gilbert M. L. Johnson

Note. This division was also known as Knipe's Division, and also First Cavalry Division of Canby's command. It accompanied Canby's column on its movement to Spanish Fort and Blakely, Alabama.

COLUMN FROM PENSACOLA, FLORIDA
Frederick Steele

First Division, John P. Hawkins
First Brigade, William A. Pile
Second Brigade, Hiram Scofield
Third Brigade, Charles W. Drew

Note. Hawkins' division consisted of nine regiments of United States Colored Troops.

Lucas' Cavalry Division, Thomas J. Lucas
First Brigade, Morgan H. Chrysler
Second Brigade, Andrew B. Spurling
Artillery
2nd Battery (B), Massachusetts Light Artillery, William Marland

Note. Lucas' division was organized March 29, 1865. Prior to that date, First Brigade, commanded by Lucas, was designated as Separate Cavalry Brigade; and Second Brigade was designated as Special Cavalry Expedition.

Thirteenth Corps
Second Division, Christopher C. Andrews
Second Brigade, William T. Spicely
Third Brigade, Frederick W. Moore

Note. Bertram's First Brigade was with Canby's column at Mobile Bay.

DISTRICT OF SOUTH ALABAMA
T. Kilby Smith

Dauphin Island, Byron Kirby

Mobile Point, Charles E. Clarke

Note. The troops on Dauphin Island consisted of six companies of the 3rd Maryland Cavalry and Companies C, E, F, H, and I of the 6th Michigan Heavy Artillery. At Mobile Point there were Battery G, 1st Michigan Light Artillery and Companies B, D, and G of the 6th Michigan Heavy Artillery.

MORGAN'S RAID INTO
INDIANA AND OHIO
JULY 2, 1863–JULY 26, 1863

After the Battle of Stones River, Tennessee December 31, 1862–January 3, 1863, Braxton Bragg withdrew with his Army of Tennessee to a defensive position in front of Tullahoma, Tennessee, and William S. Rosecrans remained with his Army of the Cumberland at Murfreesboro while he prepared for an advance that would drive Bragg's army out of Middle Tennessee.

During the spring of 1863, Bragg expected a Federal advance toward Chattanooga, and he was also concerned that Ambrose E. Burnside, commanding the Department of the Ohio, and also the Union troops in Kentucky, might cooperate with Rosecrans' advance southward from Murfreesboro by leading an army from Kentucky into East Tennessee.

In an attempt to prevent Burnside from joining Rosecrans in an offensive movement against the Confederate forces in Tennessee, and also to divert troops from the Army of the Cumberland at Murfreesboro and so weaken Rosecrans' advance, Bragg directed John H. Morgan to conduct a cavalry raid into Kentucky during the early part of June 1863. At that time Morgan was south of the Cumberland River in Tennessee with a cavalry division consisting of Basil W. Duke's First Brigade and Adam R. Johnson's Second Brigade.

Bragg authorized Morgan to move with his command anywhere in Kentucky that would enable him to accomplish his purpose, but he disapproved a proposal by Morgan that the latter cross the Ohio River and continue his raid into Indiana and Ohio. Morgan was delayed in starting his movement when William P. Sanders led a Federal cavalry force on a raid from Kentucky into East Tennessee June 14–24, 1863.

During the latter part of June 1863, while Morgan waited for matters to be resolved in East Tennessee, Henry M. Judah's Third Division of George L. Hartsuff's Twenty-Third Corps, Army of the Ohio was in South-Central Kentucky and northern Tennessee watching the crossings of the Cumberland River. On June 22, Judah learned that Morgan was moving toward Carthage, Tennessee, and he left Glasgow, Kentucky with Mahlon D. Manson's First Brigade and moved to Scottsville, Kentucky to prevent the enemy from entering the state by that route. Morgan, however, turned away from Carthage and moved toward Burkesville, Kentucky. When Judah learned of this, he moved Manson's brigade to Tompkinsville and Edward H. Hobson's Second Brigade to Marrowbone, Kentucky, about fourteen miles northeast of Tompkinsville. Joseph A. Cooper's Third Brigade of Judah's division was at Carthage.

On June 30, 1863, by Burnside's orders, James M. Shackelford's First Brigade of Jeremiah T. Boyle's Second Division, Twenty-Third Corps moved from Glasgow to Ray's Cross Roads. Then, at 5:00 P.M. on July 1, when Hobson reported that Morgan was moving in his direction, he ordered Shackelford to Marrowbone to join Hobson. When he arrived, Hobson, as senior officer, assumed command of both brigades.

Finally, on July 2, Morgan's division crossed the Cumberland River at Burkesville, Kentucky without opposition and moved on to the north. The next day Morgan attempted to force Hobson's position at Marrowbone, but after a short time he moved on toward Green River.

July 4, 1863, Morgan attacked Orlando H. Moore, whose 25th Michigan Infantry occupied a strong position guarding the Green River Bridge on the Columbia road at Tebb's Bend. Morgan was driven back with severe losses, and the next day he moved on to Lebanon, Kentucky, where he captured Charles S. Hanson's 20th Kentucky Infantry, which was garrisoning the town. Morgan then marched on by way of Springfield, Bardstown, and Garnettsville and on July 8 reached Brandenburg on the Ohio River. That day, despite orders to the contrary, Morgan crossed the river to Mauckport, Indiana with his command. They camped that night at Frakes' Mill, about five miles north of the river. When Morgan moved into Indiana, Orlando B. Willcox was in command of the District of Indiana, Department of the Ohio, and he immediately began the assembly and organization of the troops in the state to resist the invasion. These were ordered to Mitchell and Seymour on the Ohio and Mississippi Railroad, where they could readily be moved by rail to various points where they might be needed. At the request of Governor Oliver P. Morton, the War

Department detailed Lewis Wallace, who was then in the state, to help in the defense of Indiana. Wallace collected the troops and organized a brigade in Indianapolis. Willcox also had help from other officers in defending the state. Henry B. Carrington, a former commander of the District of Indiana, helped in organizing the Legion, and he later led a brigade in the pursuit of Morgan.

Meantime, as Morgan moved forward, Burnside was making every effort to assemble the available cavalry of his command for the pursuit of the enemy raiders. Judah, in person, went to Marrowbone July 4, 1863. That day he ordered Shackelford's brigade to march toward Columbia, and the next day he directed Hobson to follow Shackelford with his brigade. Before Judah left Marrowbone, he ordered Manson to march with his brigade from Tompkinsville to Glasgow, and Judah then went in person to Glasgow. Upon arriving there, he assumed command of the cavalry of Manson's brigade, which consisted of Horace Capron's 14th Illinois Cavalry; Felix W. Graham's 6th Indiana Cavalry, commanded by Thomas H. Butler; William E. Riley's 11th Kentucky Cavalry; and Edward C. Henshaw's Battery of Illinois Light Artillery. Judah then started in pursuit of Morgan, but was delayed for thirty-six hours at the crossing of Green River by high water, and he did not reach Elizabethtown, Kentucky until July 8, twenty-four hours behind Morgan. The next day he moved on to Litchfield (Leitchfield), Kentucky, about thirty miles to the west of Elizabethtown, to watch the crossings of Green River.

Meantime, Hobson's and Shackelford's brigades had moved northward through Columbia and Campbellsville, and on July 6 they were at Lebanon, Kentucky. They were joined there that day by Frank Wolford with five cavalry regiments from Somerset. The cavalry of the three commands consisted of the following regiments:

Hobson's brigade: Richard T. Jacob's 9th Kentucky Cavalry, Eugene W. Crittenden's 12th Kentucky Cavalry, and Joseph A. Sims' 24th Battery, Indiana Light Artillery.

Shackelford's brigade: Benjamin H. Bristow's 8th Kentucky Cavalry, Robert Boyle with one battalion of Eli H. Murray's 3rd Kentucky Cavalry, and Benjamin F. Denning's 22nd Battery, Indiana Light Artillery.

Wolford's command: Wolford brought with him to Lebanon, as his own brigade, his 1st Kentucky Cavalry and Robert K. Byrd's 2nd East Tennessee Mounted Infantry of Samuel P. Carter's First Brigade of Samuel D. Sturgis' First Division, Twenty-Third Corps; and also George A. Purington's 2nd Ohio Cavalry, Israel Garrard's 7th Ohio Mounted Infantry, and Jesse S. Law's four mountain howitzers. The latter three commands belonged to August V. Kautz's Third Brigade of Sturgis' division of Twenty-Third Corps, which Kautz commanded during the raid.

At Lebanon, Hobson turned over the command of his brigade to Shackelford and assumed command of the cavalry forces there, which totaled about 2,500 men, and consisted of his own brigade and the brigades of Shackelford, Wolford, and Kautz. With this force, he left Lebanon on July 7, 1863 in pursuit of Morgan. That day he marched by way of Springfield and Bardstown, reaching Bardstown Junction that evening about 5:00 P.M., and he halted there for the night. There Hobson learned from Boyle that Morgan had marched to Brandenburg.

On the morning of July 8, 1863, as soon as needed rations had been issued, Hobson moved out on the road to Brandenburg. He reached Garnettsville about 5:00 P.M. and two hours later learned that Morgan was crossing the Ohio River into Indiana. Hobson arrived within about twelve miles of Brandenburg, then halted while he went to Rock Haven, about three miles distant, to try to get the cooperation of some naval vessels, which were believed to be at Rock Haven, in an attack on the enemy at Brandenburg. The vessels had moved on, however, and Hobson decided not to attempt an attack that night. At 7:00 on the morning of July 9, he arrived at Brandenburg after Morgan had crossed. Hobson then sent to Louisville for transports to carry his troops across the river; they arrived that evening, and by 2:00 A.M. July 10, all of his command was safely in Indiana near Mauckport.

Meantime, Morgan had advanced from Frakes' Mill July 9, 1863 and that morning had encountered a force of about 400 Home Guards and citizens commanded by Lewis Jordan, colonel of the 6th Regiment of the Indiana Legion in Harrison County, which occupied some rough breastworks a short distance south of Corydon. After a brief engagement, following which Jordan surrendered his command, Morgan moved on through Corydon and Palmyra and arrived at Salem July 10. There he turned east, and that same day he marched through Canton, New Philadelphia, and Vienna, halting for the night at Lexington. Early on the morning of July 11, Morgan turned north and advanced through Paris (or Paris Crossing) until he came up to the Muscatatuck River, just south of Vernon. There, on the high ground just north of the river, Hugh T. Williams, commanding the 11th Indiana Legion of Ohio County, had posted his regiment and some other troops, and also two pieces of artillery, to guard the bridges on the Madison and Indianapolis Railroad near Vernon.

Morgan demanded the surrender of the town, and Williams refused. Meantime, help was on the way. John Love, commanding at Seymour, Indiana, arrived at Vernon with a part of his force and assumed command of the troops there, which then numbered about 1,000 men. Also that day, Wallace arrived at Vernon with the brigade that he had organized at Indianapolis. Later, when it was learned that Morgan was headed for Osgood, James Hughes started by rail with troops from Mitchell toward that place. Morgan had passed before he arrived, but both Wallace and Hughes followed Morgan toward Ohio.

After Williams' refusal to surrender, Morgan withdrew to Dupont, where he spent the night of July 11, 1863. At 4:00 A.M. July 12, Morgan marched toward Versailles, where he arrived about noon. He then continued on through Osgood and Milan and reached Sunman's Station late in the day. Early on the morning of July 13, Morgan marched eastward from Sunman's Station, crossing the state line into Ohio at Harrison about noon that day.

As Morgan moved eastward toward Ohio, Hobson followed in close pursuit, generally along the route used by Morgan. Hobson left Mauckport at daylight July 10, 1863 and, passing through Corydon and Palmyra, reached Salem the next day. From there he continued on eastward to Lexington, where he arrived about 8:00 that evening and halted for the night. On the morning of July 12, Hobson

turned north toward Vernon, but at Paris, south of Vernon, he turned off to the east toward Dupont, where he again took up Morgan's trail. Hobson's men rode on through Versailles, and the head of his column arrived at Harrison, on the state line, about dark that evening without having caught up with the enemy raiders. The rear of his command did not arrive until nearly morning July 13.

Meantime, as Morgan continued his raid across Indiana and into Ohio, Burnside was making vigorous efforts to move other troops into position to cooperate with Hobson's column and to prevent the return of Morgan to Kentucky.

On the evening of July 6, 1863, at Danville, Kentucky, William P. Sanders assumed command of a Provisional Cavalry Brigade, which consisted of Grover S. Wormer's 8th Michigan Cavalry, James I. David's 9th Michigan Cavalry, and the 11th Battery, Michigan Light Artillery. Sanders marched with his new command that evening for Lawrenceburg and Frankfort in Kentucky to prevent enemy forces from crossing the Kentucky River in that area.

Also on July 6, Burnside directed Carter to concentrate the forces of his brigade of Sturgis' division at Stanford, Kentucky, and to be ready for a rapid movement in any direction.

On July 9, however, when Burnside learned that Morgan had crossed the Ohio at Brandenburg, he ordered Sanders to march toward Eminence, on the railroad from Louisville to Lexington. Sanders arrived there at 8:00 A.M. July 10, and he marched on that day toward Westport, about twenty miles above Louisville on the Ohio River. He reached Westport before daylight July 11, then embarked his brigade on transports with orders to move upriver to Madison or Vevay, Indiana. Upon arriving there, he was to receive further orders.

On July 9, Manson, who was at Munfordville with the infantry of his First Brigade of Judah's division, was ordered to Louisville with three regiments of his brigade. He arrived there at 5:30 the next morning. On July 11 his command moved upriver on transports, arriving at Madison at 1:00 A.M. July 12. He moved on to Vevay that day.

Sanders reported to Manson near Vevay and was directed to proceed to Cincinnati. Upon arriving there, he was ordered to move on to Avondale, three miles east of the city, and that night, July 13, 1863, he was ordered to join Hobson's column, which was then pursuing Morgan in Ohio. Sanders reported to Hobson on the morning of July 14 near Batavia, and remained with the column until Morgan surrendered July 26.

On July 12, Manson was ordered to move with his entire force to Lawrenceburg, where he arrived at 7:00 the next morning. He moved on to Maysville, Kentucky July 15, and continued on upriver to Portsmouth the next day.

At Litchfield, Kentucky, Judah, who had arrived there July 9, 1863, learned that Morgan had crossed the Ohio River into Indiana, and at 2:00 P.M. July 11 he received an order to move with his command to Elizabethtown, and from there to move by rail the next day to Louisville. Judah arrived at Louisville July 13, and he then moved up the Ohio River on steamboats, reaching Cincinnati on July 14. He was delayed there while his regiments were supplied with horses, and he then left for Portsmouth, Ohio on the afternoon of July 15. Judah left behind the 11th Kentucky Cavalry, which had not received its horses, and with the rest of his command reached Portsmouth on the afternoon of July 16 and disembarked.

While the above-described movements were in progress, Morgan's cavalry reached Harrison, Ohio about 1:00 P.M. July 13, 1863. He remained there a few hours, then pushed on and arrived at the northern edge of Cincinnati after dark. He passed through the northern outskirts of the city that night, and the next morning he marched eastward, passing close to Camp Dennison and through Batavia, halting that night, July 14, at Williamsburg, twenty-eight miles beyond Batavia. The next morning Morgan continued on through Piketon, on the Scioto River north of Portsmouth, then through Jackson and Vinton, and reached Pomeroy on the Ohio River July 18. From there he moved by way of Chester toward Buffington Island in the Ohio River, arriving at Portland on the river sometime after dark.

Hobson left Harrison with his command on the morning of July 13, 1863 and, passing through Glendale, halted that night at Newberry to feed and rest. Early the next morning, Hobson marched on toward Batavia, entering the town about 9:00 A.M. At this point Sanders arrived with his Provisional Brigade from Cincinnati and joined Hobson's column on the morning of July 14.

On July 14, 1863, Burnside ordered Benjamin P. Runkle, then commanding a brigade in Kentucky, to go in person to Marietta, Ohio to organize and train the state militia troops ordered to assemble at that point. On July 16 Runkle was at Chillicothe, Ohio with a force of about 2,300 armed men and about 3,000 men without arms. He was then under the direction of Jacob D. Cox, commander of the District of Ohio, Department of the Ohio. As Morgan moved eastward, Runkle moved to Hamden July 17, then on to Scott's Landing on the Little Hocking River July 19. Then, on July 23, he moved to Marietta to intercept Morgan if he should turn in that direction in an attempt to cross the Ohio River.

Hobson had considerable difficulty in moving his artillery forward because of the poor condition of the horses, and he divided his command. On the morning of July 16, while at Winchester, Ohio, he ordered Kautz to hurry forward with his brigade and make every effort to overtake Morgan and force him to fight. He also directed Sanders to follow in support of Kautz. Hobson, with the brigades of Shackelford and Wolford, and the artillery were to follow as rapidly as possible.

Kautz reached Jasper, across the Scioto River from Piketon, at 11:00 A.M. July 16, 1863 and found the bridge over the Ohio Canal destroyed. He was forced to wait five or six hours until a new bridge was constructed and he could continue the pursuit. Consequently, he did not reach Jackson until the night of July 17. He rested his command until 3:00 A.M. July 18, and then, with Sanders' brigade, which had just come up, he moved on to Rutland. There Kautz received reliable information that Morgan intended to recross the Ohio River at Buffington Island, and after a brief halt, he marched on through Chester and followed Morgan on the road from Chester to Portland, near Buffington Island.

Soon after daylight July 18, 1863, Kautz encountered enemy pickets about two miles from Portland. At that time, he had with him only about 400 men of his 2nd and 7th Ohio Cavalry regiments, and Sanders, with his command, was about an hour's march behind. Shackelford, with Wolford following in his rear, was back somewhere beyond Chester. Despite his small numbers, and the fact that his supports were far behind, Kautz decided to attack.

Meantime, Judah's cavalry command, which had

disembarked at Portsmouth at 9:00 A.M. July 16, 1863, had marched that night to Centerville (about midway between present-day Oak Hill and Thurman), about thirty miles distant, and had arrived there July 17. The next morning, July 18, Judah continued on toward Pomeroy, moving between the line of Morgan's march and the Ohio River. Upon arriving at Pomeroy, Judah learned that Morgan was marching by way of Chester toward Buffington Island. At 10:00 P.M. July 18, Judah marched by way of Racine toward Buffington Island and, after traveling all night, arrived on the last hills above the river bottom at Buffington Island at 5:30 A.M. July 19.

About 5:00 A.M. July 19, Kautz, who was advancing to the left of Judah, drove in the enemy's pickets near Portland, and a short time later, Judah set out in a heavy fog with a small force on a reconnaissance along the road running toward the river. He was soon attacked by some of Duke's men who were attempting to capture a force of Ohio Home Guards which was entrenched near the river. Hobson was forced to fall back on his main force, and then opened fire with his dismounted troopers and two guns that were attached to the 5th Indiana Cavalry. In a short time, the enemy began to withdraw, and Judah drove them back on Hobson's forces.

It soon became evident to Hobson that Morgan did not intend to make a stand at Buffington Island. In fact, at that time, Morgan was retreating along the river bank, where there was no road, and when Hobson observed this, he sent orders to Shackelford, who was about five miles to the rear, to halt his own and Wolford's brigades at the forks of the road on which they were advancing, about three miles from the river, to intercept Morgan and prevent him from moving into the rear of Kautz and Judah. A short time after Shackelford was in position, Colonel William W. Ward and Colonel Richard C. Morgan, John H. Morgan's brother, surrendered their commands, totaling about 400 men, to Bristow's 8th Kentucky Cavalry of Shackelford's brigade.

Hobson then ordered Kautz and Sanders, with Silas Adams' 1st Kentucky Cavalry of Wolford's brigade, to push forward and drive Morgan's command toward the position of Shackelford and Wolford. A short time later Shackelford asked for help, and Hobson sent Kautz's brigade to join him that night.

At about that time Judah's column came up, and Judah immediately assumed command of the entire force pursuing Morgan.

Sometime before noon July 19, 1863, Duke surrendered his brigade to David's 9th Michigan Cavalry of Kautz's brigade, and later still other troops of Morgan's cavalry surrendered.

During the night of July 19, 1863, the remnant's of Morgan's command escaped by a path leading from the river and then marched northward to Athens on the Hocking River. From there it moved through Eagleport, on the Muskingum River, Campbell's Station, and Hammondsville to Salineville, near New Lisbon, where it was finally run down and captured.

On the morning of July 21, 1863, Shackelford resumed the chase with about 500 volunteers who had serviceable horses, consisting of men from Capron's 14th Illinois Cavalry of Judah's command, and Wolford with detachments of the 1st Kentucky Cavalry, 2nd East Tennessee Cavalry, 45th Ohio Mounted Infantry, and 2nd Ohio Cavalry. Traveling day and night, Shackelford came up with the enemy at Washington (present-day Old Washington, east of Cambridge) and skirmished the rest of the day as he pressed on. At daylight July 25, Shackelford again came up with the enemy, and there was further skirmishing.

Meantime, help had been sent forward by Burnside, and it would soon join Shackelford's command. On the evening of July 23, a detachment of the 9th Kentucky Cavalry under George W. Rue moved from Covington, Kentucky to Cincinnati, then moved by train through Columbus, Ohio to Bellaire on the Ohio River. It arrived there July 24 and patrolled the river until 1:00 P.M. the next day. At that time it moved north along the river by rail to Shanghai, beyond Steubenville, where it disembarked that evening. It then joined Shackelford at Hammondsville at 8:00 A.M. July 26. In addition to Rue's command, Burnside sent forward by rail from Cincinnati William B. Way, with detachments of his own 9th Michigan Cavalry and the 8th Michigan Cavalry, to Mingo (Mingo Junction), near Steubenville. Way arrived at Mingo on July 25 and then marched to join Shackelford.

At dark July 25, 1863, Shackelford's main column reached Richmond, and Way's command was about two and one-half miles in advance in the direction of Springfield. At 10:00 that night Way informed Shackelford that he had skirmished sharply with Morgan's men and that Morgan was moving from Springfield toward Hammondsville. Shackelford then put his column in motion on the Hammondsville road, about midway between Richmond and Hammondsville, and about midnight he came up on Rue's command, which was moving in the direction of Richmond. Rue halted for a time and then followed Shackelford to Hammondsville, where they arrived at daylight the next morning.

By that time Shackelford had lost Morgan. He sent out scouts on all roads in the vicinity and directed Rue, who had just come up, to take the advance with the detachment of his 9th Kentucky Cavalry, and also a part of the 1st Kentucky Cavalry and 3rd Kentucky Cavalry, and try to find Morgan. Shackelford had moved about five miles in the direction of Salineville when he learned that Morgan was also marching toward that town.

A short time later, Shackelford learned that Morgan was at Salineville, and he moved in that direction. Rue, with the advance, soon entered the town, and there he learned that Morgan, with about 400 men, had crossed the railroad and was moving in the direction of Smith's Ford on the Ohio River. Shackelford then ordered Rue to move back from his position in advance and attempt to head off Morgan on the New Lisbon road. Shackelford had gone about seven miles when he was informed that Morgan had turned into the New Lisbon road ahead of him. Rue soon came up with the enemy, who were pursued by Way, and Shackelford ordered his whole column to move forward. Morgan realized that any further attempt to escape was useless, and he surrendered his command, then numbering about 364 officers and men and 400 horses, to Rue on July 26, 1863. Rue held Morgan and his men until Shackelford came up and took charge of them as prisoners of war.

For details of the organization of Burnside's command during Morgan's raid, see Twenty-Third Corps, Army of the Ohio.

After Morgan and his men had been captured and the raid had ended, all the troops of the Army of the Ohio returned to their proper commands in Kentucky. After a reorganization of the army August 6,

1863, Burnside led it in a successful expedition to occupy East Tennessee. For further information, see East Tennessee Campaign (Burnside).

CAPTURE OF NEW MADRID, MISSOURI AND ISLAND NO. 10, MISSISSIPPI RIVER MARCH 3, 1862–APRIL 8, 1862

In April 1861, Confederate forces under Gideon J. Pillow began construction of defensive works at New Madrid, Missouri and on Island No. 10 in the Mississippi River opposite the Kentucky-Tennessee state line. Island No. 10 was so named because it was the tenth island in the Mississippi River below Cairo, Illinois. These works, which were about sixty miles below Columbus, Kentucky, were to be untested until March 1862.

When the Confederate first line of defense in Kentucky was broken by the fall of Fort Henry February 6, 1862 and Fort Donelson February 16, 1862, Fort Pillow, Tennessee was selected as the beginning of a new second line on the Mississippi River. The works at New Madrid and Island No. 10, however, were retained as an outpost of the second line.

When Columbus was evacuated by the Confederates during the period February 20–March 2, 1862, Leonidas Polk, commanding First Corps of the Confederate Army of the Mississippi, sent John P. McCown with his division to New Madrid and Island No. 10 to reinforce the troops already there. McCown's division consisted of four brigades, commanded by Edward W. Gantt, Rufus P. Neely, Samuel F. Marks, and Alexander P. Stewart.

New Madrid and Island No. 10 were selected as defensive positions by the enemy because of the curious course of the Mississippi River in that region. After passing Hickman, Kentucky, the river flows to the southwest and south to a point just below the Kentucky-Tennessee state line, and there it makes a great U-shaped bend and flows north for about six miles to a point above New Madrid. Island No. 10 lies in the river at the bottom of this bend. About three miles above New Madrid, the river turns to the west and then south, making another

U-shaped bend, and it then flows on to the south past Point Pleasant, Missouri and Tiptonville, Tennessee before turning to the southwest around Riddle's Point. Because of these bends, the river flows in the shape of an inverted S from a point about ten miles above Island No. 10 to Point Pleasant. The long neck of land lying between the northerly course of the river below Island No. 10 and the southerly course below New Madrid is called New Madrid Bend.

Beginning at Hickman, Kentucky, a great swamp, which later becomes Reelfoot Lake, extends along the left bank of the Mississippi and empties into the river about forty miles below Tiptonville, thus creating a long peninsula between it and the river.

A good road led south from opposite Island No. 10, along the west bank of Reelfoot Lake, to Tiptonville, and if the river was blocked, as it was later by Federal batteries, only this road could be used to supply the troops at Island No. 10 and New Madrid.

On February 18, 1862, Henry W. Halleck, commanding the Union Department of the Missouri, ordered John Pope to organize and command a force, with which he was to march down the Mississippi River and capture the Confederate fortifications at New Madrid and Island No. 10. Pope arrived at Commerce, Missouri on February 21, and immediately began the organization of his army, which he called the Army of the Mississippi. For additional information, see Army of the Mississippi (Pope, Rosecrans).

On February 28, 1862, Pope began his march, and on March 3 he arrived in front of New Madrid. There Pope found the town defended by five infantry regiments, several companies of artillery, and six gunboats on the river. The troops occupied a bastioned earthwork about one-half mile below the town, an irregular earthwork at the northern end of the town, and a line of entrenchments connecting the two. Pope examined the works and decided not to attack. He believed that the works could be carried, but he doubted that his troops could hold them because they would be exposed to the fire of the enemy gunboats, which had been raised sufficiently by high water in the river to fire directly into the line of fortifications. Instead, Pope decided to invest the town and requested that siege guns be sent down the river from Cairo.

While awaiting the arrival of the guns, he sent Joseph B. Plummer, commanding Fifth Division, Army of the Mississippi, with his division, less one regiment, to capture Point Pleasant, which was about twelve miles below New Madrid. Plummer's command consisted of John M. Loomis' Second Brigade (26th Illinois and 11th Missouri), John Bryner with the 47th Illinois of his First Brigade, a squadron of the 2nd Michigan Cavalry and 3rd Michigan Cavalry, Albert M. Powell's Battery M, 1st Missouri Light Artillery, and one company of engineer troops.

Plummer left New Madrid March 5, 1862 and occupied Point Pleasant the next day with a part of his command. He then emplaced his guns along the river bank and had his men construct a line of rifle pits for their protection. On the night of March 11, eight companies of the 7th Illinois Cavalry under William P. Kellogg joined Plummer, and the next day the 8th Wisconsin, Bryner's other regiment, also arrived at Point Pleasant. On March 17, Plummer brought up the rest of his division and placed them in the town.

The siege guns requested by Pope from Cairo arrived at New Madrid, by way of Sikeston, about sunset March 12, 1862. Josiah W. Bissell, who had been sent from Cairo with his Engineer Brigade, accompanied the guns downriver and placed them in position that night. The artillery opened on the works at New Madrid at daylight the next morning, and on the morning of March 14, Pope found that the enemy had evacuated the town, and had crossed the river to New Madrid Bend. His troops then advanced and occupied the town.

Immediately after his success at New Madrid, Pope began the construction of batteries along the west bank of the Mississippi at several prominent points to close the river between New Madrid and Tiptonville with his artillery. The lower battery was below Tiptonville, and it was supported by John M. Palmer's Third Division, which was in position about a mile and a half to the rear. Plummer's division was at Point Pleasant. The completion of the batteries required about a week, and they extended Pope's line seventeen miles along the river.

After the occupation of New Madrid, Pope turned his attention to the capture of Island No. 10 and the troops on New Madrid Bend. He decided to attempt this by crossing a part of his army to the east bank of the river and then attacking the enemy position from the rear. It was not possible to carry out this plan, however, until the enemy batteries opposite the crossings were silenced and the enemy gunboats on the river were driven off. This could not be accomplished without the aid of a naval force, which was then en route down the Mississippi from Cairo under the command of Flag Officer Andrew H. Foote. Foote arrived near Island No. 10 March 15, 1862 with six gunboats and ten mortarboats.

Arriving with Foote, on transports, was a mixed brigade of infantry and artillery from the District of Cairo under the command of Napoleon B. Buford. This brigade was known as the Flotilla Brigade, and it was placed under Pope's orders if it should be needed. It did not join Pope's army on the west side of the river, and it played only a minor role in the operations against Island No. 10. Buford did land his brigade at Hickman on March 30, 1862, and led it to Union City, Tennessee, where he destroyed an enemy camp. He then returned to Hickman the next day.

When the naval vessels arrived, Pope asked Foote to send two gunboats downriver, past the batteries on Island No. 10, to destroy the Confederate batteries along the east bank of the river and to aid in the crossing his army. Foote believed that the attempt would be too dangerous, and he refused Pope's request. Instead, Foote began to shell the upper part of the island in an attempt to destroy the batteries there, but with little success.

Halleck then directed Pope to build a road through the swamps from New Madrid to a point opposite Island No. 10 and establish a battery there to cooperate with the navy in the bombardment of the enemy works on the island. When the construction of this road was found to be impracticable, Schuyler Hamilton, commander of Second Division, suggested that a canal be dug from the Mississippi River above Island No. 10 to New Madrid to open a water route to the river below New Madrid that was not covered by enemy guns. This plan was approved, and Bissell, with his Engineer Brigade and an infantry regiment, started work on the project. The canal began on the river between Island No. 8 and Island No. 9 and ran westward into Wilson's Bayou, which emptied into the Mississippi just above New Madrid. The canal was completed in eight days, and then the bayou was cleared to provide a navigable channel. The work was finally

completed April 1, 1862, and on April 5, four steamboats and some barges were brought through the canal to a point near the mouth of the bayou, where they were tied up and kept out of sight of the enemy.

Meantime, Foote had decided to send a gunboat downriver, and on March 30, 1862 he ordered Commander Henry Walke, commanding the gunboat *Carondelet,* to run past the batteries on Island No. 10 the first foggy or rainy night and proceed on to New Madrid. Upon arriving there, he was to cover the crossing of Pope's army to the Tennessee side of the river. Walke successfully passed the batteries on the stormy night of April 4, and Lieutenant Commander Egbert Thompson followed on the night of April 6 with the *Pittsburg.*

On April 7, 1862, the *Carondelet* and *Pittsburg* steamed downriver and, with the aid of a land battery established on the west bank some time before, silenced the Confederate guns at Watson's Landing, where Pope planned to land his troops. Watson's Landing was on the western side of New Madrid Bend, about five miles below New Madrid.

On the morning of April 7, 1862, Eleazer A. Paine's Fourth Division and Charles Houghtaling's Battery C, 1st Illinois Light Artillery embarked on the steamboats concealed in Wilson's Bayou and, under the cover of the gunboats, crossed to Watson's Landing, where they arrived about noon. The troops then disembarked and immediately marched toward Tiptonville, which was about fourteen miles from the landing. James D. Morgan's First Brigade took the lead, and it was followed by Gilbert W. Cumming's Second Brigade. About nine miles from the landing, Morgan encountered a small Confederate force, which offered little resistance, and he then continued on to Tiptonville.

David S. Stanley's First Division crossed the river from the upper fort at New Madrid and followed Paine's division toward Tiptonville. Schuyler Hamilton's Second Division also crossed the river that day and joined the movement toward Tiptonville. These three were the only divisions of Pope's army to cross the river. Joseph B. Plummer's Fifth Division was still at Point Pleasant, and John M. Palmer's Third Division remained in support of the lower battery, which had been constructed to command the town of Tiptonville and the Tennessee shore for a distance of about a half-mile below to prevent the embarkation of enemy troops.

The Confederate troops that were retreating down New Madrid Bend before Paine's division, and from the river near Island No. 10, which surrendered to Foote April 7, 1862, met in great confusion at Tiptonville on the night of April 7, and they were soon driven back into the swamps by Paine's men. Finally, at 4:00 A.M. April 8, William W. Mackall, who had relieved McCown in command of the troops at New Madrid and Island No. 10 March 31, finding his troops cut off, and unable to resist, surrendered his command.

After the surrender of the Confederate forces at Tiptonville, Pope was ordered to move with his Army of the Mississippi down the river and attempt to capture Fort Pillow, which was about eighty miles below New Madrid, and about the same distance above Memphis. Leaving James R. Slack's First Brigade of Palmer's Third Division to garrison New Madrid, and a regiment of the Flotilla Brigade at Island No. 10, Pope embarked with the rest of his army on April 12, 1862. Two days later he arrived at a point about four miles above Fort Pillow and began preparations to move against the fort. He did not remain there long, however, because he was ordered to Pittsburg Landing on the Tennessee River to join Halleck's Army of the Department of the Mississippi for an advance on Corinth, Mississippi. For further information, see Army of the Mississippi (Pope, Rosecrans), and see also Halleck's Advance on Corinth, Mississippi.

The organization of Pope's army at New Madrid and Island No. 10 March 3–April 8, 1862 was as follows:

ARMY OF THE MISSISSIPPI, John Pope

First Division, David S. Stanley
First Brigade, John Groesbeck
Second Brigade, J. L. Kirby Smith

Second Division, Schuyler Hamilton
First Brigade, William H. Worthington
Second Brigade, Nicholas Perczel
Artillery
11th Battery, Ohio Light Artillery

Third Division, John M. Palmer
First Brigade, James R. Slack
Second Division, Graham N. Fitch
Cavalry

7th Illinois Cavalry, William P. Kellogg
Artillery
Battery G, 1st Missouri Light Artillery, Henry Hescock

Fourth Division, Eleazer A. Paine
First Brigade, James D. Morgan
Second Brigade, Gilbert W. Cumming
Cavalry
1st Illinois Cavalry (companies H and I), David P. Jenkins

Fifth Division, Joseph B. Plummer
First Brigade, John Bryner
Second Brigade, John M. Loomis
Artillery
Battery M, 1st Missouri Light Artillery, Albert M. Powell

Cavalry Division, Gordon Granger
2nd Michigan Cavalry, Selden H. Gorham
3rd Michigan Cavalry, Robert H. G. Minty
John K. Mizner

Artillery Division, Warren L. Lothrop
2nd Battery, Iowa Light Artillery, Nelson T. Spoor
5th Battery, Wisconsin Light Artillery, Oscar F. Pinney
6th Battery, Wisconsin Light Artillery, Henry Dillon
7th Battery, Wisconsin Light Artillery, Richard R. Griffith
3rd Battery, Michigan Light Artillery, Alexander W. Dees
8th Battery, Michigan Light Artillery, Samuel De Golyer
Battery C, 1st Illinois Light Artillery, Charles Houghtaling
Battery F, 2nd United States Artillery, John A. Darling
Daniel P. Walling
Unassigned Troops
Engineer Regiment of the West, Josiah W. Bissell
22nd Missouri Infantry, John D. Foster
2nd Iowa Cavalry, Washington L. Elliott
2nd Illinois Cavalry (four companies), Harvey Hogg
Companies B, C, and D, 4th United States Cavalry, Michael J. Kelly
Companies A, B, C, D, H, and L, 1st United States Infantry, George A. Williams

Flotilla Brigade, Napoleon B. Buford
27th Illinois Infantry, Fazilo A. Harrington
42nd Illinois Infantry, George W. Roberts

15th Wisconsin Infantry, Hans C. Heg
Battery G, 1st Illinois Light Artillery, Arthur O'Leary
Battery I, 2nd Illinois Light Artillery, Frederick Sparrestrom

EXPEDITION FROM LA GRANGE, TENNESSEE TO OXFORD, MISSISSIPPI AUGUST 1–30, 1864

During the advance of William T. Sherman's army toward Atlanta, Georgia in the spring and summer of 1864, Nathan B. Forrest, with cavalry in Mississippi, was in a position where he could easily move into Tennessee or northern Georgia and disrupt his long supply line that extended back through Chattanooga and Nashville to Louisville, Kentucky. From the beginning, Sherman was concerned about this possibility, and he repeatedly urged, first Stephen A. Hurlbut and then Cadwallader C. Washburn, commanders of the District of West Tennessee, to send out expeditions to defeat Forrest, or at least prevent him from leaving Mississippi.

In response to Sherman's orders, Samuel D. Sturgis led an expedition to Brice's Cross Roads June 2–13, 1864, and he not only failed to defeat Forrest but was himself badly defeated. Andrew J. Smith was partially successful in his expedition to Tupelo, Mississippi July 5–21, but the threat of Forrest was not eliminated. Then in late July, Washburn ordered Smith to make another effort to defeat Forrest by moving with a force to La Grange, Tennessee, and then southward through Holly Springs to Waterford, Mississippi. For details of Sturgis' expedition and Smith's first expedition, see Sturgis' Expedition from Memphis, Tennessee into Mississippi (Battle of Brice's Cross Roads); and see also Tupelo, Mississippi Expedition (Andrew J. Smith).

Smith began his advance from Memphis, Tennessee on August 1, 1864 with a force consisting of Joseph A. Mower's First Division and William T. Shaw's Third Division of Smith's Right Wing, Sixteenth Corps, and Benjamin H. Grierson's Cavalry Corps, District of West Tennessee, which consisted of Edward Hatch's First Division and Edward F. Winslow's Second Division.

Smith's infantry of Sixteenth Corps moved by rail from Memphis to La Grange during the period August 1–3, 1864, and the next day it began moving southward toward Holly Springs, Mississippi. Grierson's cavalry also began its march August 1. Hatch's division marched from Memphis with orders to concentrate at Holly Springs. Winslow's division marched in detachments from Memphis and White's Station, just east of Memphis, as guards for the wagon train and artillery, which took the direct road to Holly Springs.

At the beginning of Smith's advance into Mississippi, Forrest's cavalry was between Okolona and Pontotoc, and was under the immediate command of James R. Chalmers. Forrest had been wounded in the foot during an engagement at Old Town Creek July 15, 1864, the day after the Engagement of Tupelo (or Harrisburg), Mississippi, but he had remained with his men although unable to exercise complete control.

Aware that Smith was on the march, Chalmers left Okolona August 4, 1864 with his cavalry division and a battery and marched toward Oxford. He arrived there the next day with Robert McCulloch's brigade and the battery. Chalmers then moved northward to the Tallahatchie River and burned the trestle of the Mississippi Central Railroad that crossed the river there.

By the time Chalmers had reached Oxford, Smith's men had repaired the Mississippi Central Railroad as far Waterford, and on August 5, 1864, Joseph J. Woods' Third Brigade of Mower's division moved forward to that place. The rest of Smith's command was north of Waterford along the railroad.

On August 7, 1864, Smith sent forward from Waterford the 7th Minnesota and 35th Iowa regiments of Woods' brigade and the 12th Missouri Cavalry of Thomas P. Herrick's First Brigade of Hatch's cavalry division to protect the pioneers while they built a bridge over the Tallahatchie. This force drove back the enemy skirmishers and halted that night north of the river, with pickets established on the south bank.

By August 8, 1864, Forrest was again in command of his cavalry and had ordered James J. Neely's brigade of Chalmers' division and Abraham Buford's cavalry division to Pontotoc to be ready to take the field with Forrest on August 9.

Very early on the morning of August 8, 1864, Hatch's cavalry division and John W. Noble's Second Brigade of Winslow's cavalry division left Holly Springs and marched southward to the Tallahatchie River, where they arrived about 10:00 A.M. The 7th Indiana Cavalry of Joseph Karge's First Brigade of Winslow's division also moved to the Tallahatchie, and the next day it joined Noble's brigade. The rest of Karge's brigade remained at Holly Springs until August 17.

Upon arriving at the river, Hatch found the enemy in strong force on the far side, at the railroad bridge. The 35th Iowa opened fire on the enemy's sharpshooters, and the 3rd Iowa and 10th Missouri cavalry regiments of Noble's brigade advanced dismounted. After a brief skirmish, the enemy retired. The 35th Iowa of Woods' brigade then crossed the Tallahatchie on driftwood lodged against the railroad bridge, and Herrick's brigade of Hatch's division supported the 35th Iowa. Noble, with the 3rd Iowa Cavalry and the 4th Iowa Cavalry of his brigade, crossed at the railroad bridge. With the south bank thus secured, Mower's pioneers began constructing a bridge over the river, and this was completed that evening.

When Chalmers fell back from the Tallahatchie, he halted and took position on some high ground a mile or so from the river. Early on the morning of August 9, 1864, Hatch's division and Noble's brigade crossed the river on the bridge constructed by the engineers the day before and moved south. They soon came up to Chalmers' new line and formed for an attack. Hatch then opened with his artillery, and advanced so as to strike the Confederate position in front and on both flanks. Chalmers withdrew about 11:00 A.M. and fell back eight miles to Hurricane Creek. After a brief stand there, he again fell back to Oxford, eight miles distant.

August 8, 1864, the 33rd Missouri and 6th Battery, Indiana Light Artillery of Woods' brigade moved up to the Tallahatchie, and the next day the brigade moved into camp on the south side of the river. On August 10, the 12th Iowa joined the brigade. On August 9, Mower's division also moved up to the Tallahatchie.

There was little fighting August 10, 1864, but there were some changes in the positions of Smith's troops. Edward H. Wolfe's Third Brigade of Shaw's division was ordered up from Holly Springs to the

Tallahatchie and was directed to report to Mower. Hatch returned from his pursuit of Chalmers with his cavalry division and Noble's brigade of Winslow's cavalry division and went into camp at Abbeville.

After sunup August 11, 1864, Forrest arrived at Oxford and joined Chalmers with Neely's brigade of Chalmers' division and Tyree H. Bell's brigade of Buford's division. During the afternoon, Chalmers' division, then consisting of McCulloch's, Neely's, and Hinchie P. Mabry's brigades, and reinforced by Bell's brigade, moved up to the south bank of Hurricane Creek, a small stream that crossed the Oxford and Holly Springs road, about eight miles north of Oxford. By the afternoon of August 12, Forrest's men had formed a strongly entrenched line.

About noon August 13, 1864, Mower marched south from Abbeville, with three regiments of Wolfe's brigade, two regiments and a battery of the First Division, and Hatch's cavalry division and arrived in front of Forrest's line on Hurricane Creek. Hatch ordered Mathew H. Starr to move with his 6th Illinois Cavalry and the 9th Illinois Cavalry of Datus E. Coon's Second Brigade of Hatch's division on the enemy's left and cross the creek about two miles below the enemy's position at the road, while Herrick moved with his brigade to cross the creek about two miles above and attack the enemy's right flank. Mower's infantry, preceded by the 2nd Iowa Cavalry, moved up on the main road, which was held by the enemy.

Both Starr and Herrick met the enemy before crossing the creek, and after three or four hours of sharp skirmishing, Starr drove the force in front of him across the creek and captured the enemy works. In the meantime, the 2nd Iowa Cavalry had driven the enemy's skirmishers across the creek; a battery of Mower's division opened fire, and this was continued for about an hour. Herrick advanced to the creek with heavy skirmishing, but when the enemy artillery opened on his brigade, he could go no farther. Starr, on the other flank, continued his attack, and the enemy finally gave way and retreated to Oxford. The infantry was not engaged. That night Hatch moved back to the Tallahatchie River.

For the next five days after the engagement at Hurricane Creek, there was little activity except picket firing along the creek. On the morning of

August 17, 1864, Shaw moved with Charles D. Murray's First Brigade and James I. Gilbert's Second Brigade of his division to Waterford, and the next day crossed the Tallahatchie to Abbeville, where he joined Mower's division. Also on August 17, Winslow, who was suffering from an injury, was relieved from command of Second Cavalry Division by Karge, and he then returned to Memphis. The next day Karge moved toward Abbeville, arriving there August 19.

Meantime, Forrest had decided to strike at Memphis in an effort to force Smith to withdraw his column from Mississippi. About noon August 18, 1864, Forrest left Oxford with 2,000 men of his command and marched toward Panola. Chalmers was left at Oxford with the rest of the Confederate cavalry, with instructions to demonstrate strongly and attempt to conceal the fact that Forrest had departed with a part of his command. On the morning of August 19, Chalmers attacked the Federal position all along Hurricane Creek, but was forced to withdraw, largely because of wet ammunition. The next day Buford joined Chalmers with his brigade from Pontotoc.

On August 19, 1864, in a pouring rain, Wolfe moved forward with his Third Brigade of Shaw's division to Hurricane Creek and camped. Also that day, Grierson ordered Hatch to move toward Oxford, and he became engaged with Chalmers on Hurricane Creek.

August 20, 1864, Chalmers again attacked about four miles north of Oxford, but did little to delay the Federal advance.

On August 21, 1864, Smith's command began to advance toward Oxford. Wolfe's brigade moved forward from Hurricane Creek to within two miles of Oxford, and Mower's division advanced from Abbeville to Hurricane Creek. The cavalry moved up on the flanks of the infantry. Chalmers attacked again that day and was engaged until about 11:00 A.M. He then withdrew through Oxford and across the Yacona River and established his headquarters at Springdale.

At 6:00 A.M. August 22, 1864, Smith advanced his infantry, with Hatch's cavalry moving on the right and Karge's cavalry on the left, and at 8:00 A.M. his troops entered Oxford from the east, west, and north. All was relatively quiet in the town until about noon, and then the court house, many stores,

and some houses were burned. When Smith finally withdrew about 5:00 P.M., the town was a smoking ruin.

While at Oxford, Smith learned that Forrest had marched with a part of his command to Memphis and had made an attack on the city, and Smith then began to retire. He directed Grierson to send Hatch's cavalry division toward Panola, while Grierson with Karge's division moved back to Abbeville. The infantry withdrew to their camps of the day before near Hurricane Creek.

On August 23, 1864, when Chalmers learned that Smith had withdrawn from Oxford, Buford, with McCulloch's brigade, crossed the Yacona at Oliver's Bridge, and Chalmers, with Mabry's brigade, crossed at Carr's Bridge, and they marched northward through Oxford. About noon Chalmers' advance came up on the Federal rear guard at Abbeville and, against some resistance, pushed on to the Federal main line. There was skirmishing for about two hours as Smith's line advanced, pushing the enemy back to Hurricane Creek. This was the last fighting of the campaign.

Smith then continued his march northward, and by August 26, 1864 he was back in Holly Springs. On August 28 he moved his command to La Grange, and early in September his troops were back in Memphis.

Forrest's Attack on Memphis, Tennessee, August 21, 1864. Although Forrest's attack at Memphis was not a part of Smith's expedition to Oxford, a very brief description of Forrest's activities is given here because they were related to, and caused by, Smith's movement into northern Mississippi, and also because they had a decisive effect on Smith's Oxford Expedition. Forrest left Oxford on the evening of August 18, 1864 and marched westward to Panola. He crossed the Tallahatchie River there and continued on to the north, arriving in front of Memphis at 3:00 A.M. August 21.

A force consisting of about one-third of Forrest's command was detached and directed to ride over the Federal pickets and into the heart of the city. The rest of the command was to remain outside and engage any Federal troops that might move against them.

The detachment moved into Memphis on the Hernando road, and then it split up, with the different parties attempting to capture the Union commanders in the city. One party rode to the headquarters of Cadwallader C. Washburn, commander of the District of West Tennessee, on Union Street; another went to the Gayoso house, where Stephen A. Hurlbut was supposed to be staying; and still another moved to the headquarters of Ralph P. Buckland, commander of the District of Memphis. All these officers, however, escaped capture.

The detachment then moved to the Irving Prison, but it was repulsed by the prison guard. By this time the provost guard had rallied from its surprise and was moving against the enemy. The detachment then hurriedly left the city and rejoined the forces left outside. A sharp fight ensued, which lasted until 9:00 A.M., and then Forrest's entire force moved off on the Hernando road. Such cavalry as had been left with Washburn during Smith's expedition followed Forrest to Hernando, twenty-five miles from Memphis, and from that point Forrest retreated without molestation toward Panola. He then moved on to Grenada, and arrived there August 23, 1864.

* * * * * * * * *

The organization of the army that Andrew J. Smith led from Memphis into Mississippi to Oxford was as follows:

RIGHT WING, SIXTEENTH CORPS, Andrew J. Smith

First Division, Joseph A. Mower
  First Brigade, William L. McMillen
  Second Brigade, Lucius F. Hubbard
  Third Brigade, Joseph J. Woods
  Artillery
    Battery E, 1st Illinois Light Artillery, John A. Fitch
    6th Battery, Indiana Light Artillery, Michael Mueller
    2nd Battery, Iowa Light Artillery, Joseph R. Reed

Third Division, William T. Shaw
  First Brigade, Charles D. Murray
  Second Brigade, James I. Gilbert
  Third Brigade, Edward H. Wolfe
  Artillery
    Battery G, 2nd Illinois Light Artillery, John W. Lowell
    3rd Battery, Indiana Light Artillery, Thomas J. Ginn
    9th Battery, Indiana Light Artillery, Wallace Hight

14th Battery, Indiana Light Artillery, Francis W. Morse

Note. Shaw assumed command of Third Division July 31, 1864, relieving David Moore.

CAVALRY CORPS, DISTRICT OF WEST TENNESSEE, Benjamin H. Grierson

First Division, Edward Hatch
  First Brigade, Thomas P. Herrick
  Second Brigade, Datus E. Coon

Second Division, Edward F. Winslow, to August 17, 1864
Joseph Karge
First Brigade, Joseph Karge, to August 17, 1864
  Joseph C. Hess
Second Brigade, John W. Noble

Note. Winslow was forced to return to Memphis because of a physical disability.

BATTLE OF PALMETTO (OR PALMITO) RANCH, TEXAS
MAY 12–13, 1865

Although commonly called the Battle of Palmetto (or Palmito) Ranch, this was a minor engagement of no military significance that was fought on the bank of the Rio Grande in Texas about one month after Robert E. Lee had surrendered his army at Appomattox Court House, Virginia. It has, however, achieved considerable recognition because it was the last battle of the Civil War, and the last shot was fired there.

During February 1865, Lewis (Lew) Wallace came to Brazos Island, which was just off the Texas coast, a few miles north of the mouth of the Rio Grande, and which was held by Union forces. There he arranged a meeting with James E. Slaughter, commander of the West Sub-district of Texas, and John S. Ford, commander of the Cavalry of the West, which was near Brownsville. While there Wallace arranged to meet with Slaughter and Ford at Point Isabel, and at that meeting he explained to them that in his opinion, further fighting on the Rio

Grande was useless and could not in any way affect the outcome of the war. Both officers agreed with Wallace, and when they returned to Brownsville, the Confederate mounted troops of the sub-district were broken up into small groups, and these were scattered between the Rio Grande and the Arroyo Colorado and put in camps wherever they could find wood, food, and water. For the next several months there was no fighting, and it was the intention of all that there should be none.

Early on the morning of May 11, 1865, however, Theodore H. Barrett, then commanding the Federal garrison on Brazos Island, ordered David Branson, with a force consisting of his own 62nd United States Colored Troops and a detachment of the 2nd Texas (Union) Cavalry (which had not yet been mounted) under James W. Hancock, to proceed to the mainland, then move up the Rio Grande and pick up any units of Confederate soldiers that had not yet surrendered. He was then to occupy Brownsville.

The start of Branson's expedition was delayed by a storm and a breakdown of the engine of the steamer that was to be used for the crossing, but finally, with great difficulty, it was able to cross at Boca Chica by 9:30 P.M. that day.

At 2:00 A.M. May 12, 1865, after a long and circuitous march, Branson's men surrounded the buildings at White's Ranch, where a Confederate outpost had been reported, but they found that the men encamped there had departed a day or two earlier. Branson then continued his march, and at 8:30 A.M. arrived at Palmetto Ranch, which was on a slight elevation that commanded the road from Brazos Santiago to Brownsville. There he found the encampment of George H. Giddings' battalion of Texas cavalry, commanded by W. N. Robinson. Both parties were surprised by this confrontation because of the truce that had existed since the meeting of Slaughter and Ford with Wallace.

Robinson did not intend to be captured without a fight, however, and he immediately prepared for action. Branson also deployed his men, and after skirmishing during the morning, he advanced about noon and drove the enemy from their camp. Branson then destroyed Palmetto Ranch and halted on the hill there to rest and feed the horses and men.

After falling back from Palmetto Ranch, Robinson sent a messenger to Ford at Brownsville, twelve miles distant, informing him of the Federal attack and asking for help. Then at 3:00 P.M., without waiting for reinforcements, Robinson counterattacked. Branson, realizing that his position at Palmetto Ranch was untenable, moved back to White's Ranch, skirmishing a part of the way, and took position for the night. He then sent a messenger to Barrett on Brazos Island asking for reinforcements.

On the morning of May 13, 1865, Barrett joined Branson with 200 men of the 34th Indiana (Morton's Rifles) Regiment, commanded by Robert G. Morrison, and assumed command of the whole force at White's Ranch. Barrett immediately ordered an advance toward Palmetto Ranch, which had been reoccupied by the enemy. He soon encountered the enemy cavalry but pushed on and reached the ranch about 7:00 or 8:00 A.M. As the Federals approached, Giddings' battalion again fell back.

At about 11:00 that morning, while Ford was marching toward Palmetto Ranch, he learned that Robinson had again been attacked. Ford hurried forward and finally reached San Martin Ranch about 3:00 P.M., and there he found Robinson confronting Barrett's troops. Barrett was in position about one-half mile in front of Robinson, with skirmishers of the 34th Indiana out in front, supported by Hancock's dismounted company of the Second Texas (Union) Cavalry. In rear of the skirmishers was the Federal main line of battle, consisting of Branson's 62nd United States Colored Troops. This line was at a right angle to the road, with its left on the Rio Grande, and it extended northward for about three-fourths of a mile.

Ford studied the disposition of Barrett's forces and decided to attack. He placed Robinson in command of the main body of cavalry, which was deployed with Anderson's battalion, commanded by D. W. Wilson, on the right and Giddings' battalion on the left. Two companies of cavalry and a battery were sent to the extreme Confederate left to strike the Federal right flank.

About 4:00 P.M. the enemy skirmishers moved forward, and at the same time the enemy artillery opened fire. The flanking party then attacked the exposed right of the Federal skirmish line. Barrett was surprised by this attack and ordered a retreat, but when the main line fell back, the skirmish line was left unsupported. At Ford's order, Robinson's cavalry charged and completely overran the Federal skirmishers, capturing forty-eight men. Barrett's command retreated toward Brazos Island in near rout, and the enemy pursued past White's Ranch toward Boca Chica for a distance of eight miles.

Slaughter came up with additional troops and assumed command, and he then directed Ford to continue the pursuit. Ford remonstrated, however, because both his men and horses were exhausted and, being close to Brazos Island, he expected that Federal reinforcements would soon appear. Finally, when Barrett's men had returned to the safety of Brazos Island, Ford withdrew with his men about eight miles and went into camp. Ford's men learned from prisoners that Robert E. Lee and Joseph E. Johnston had surrendered their armies in the East, and about two weeks later, Ford's cavalry was disbanded to avoid formal surrender.

BATTLE OF PEA RIDGE (OR ELKHORN TAVERN), ARKANSAS MARCH 6–8, 1862

The principal objective of both Northern and Southern forces in Missouri during the first year of the war was the control of the state of Missouri. To this end, the Battle of Wilson's Creek was fought in southwest Missouri August 10, 1861, but this did not resolve the issue. Although the result was a Confederate victory, and the Southern forces were not driven out of Missouri, they were unable to follow up their success and gain control of the state.

On December 25, 1861, Samuel R. Curtis was assigned command of the Union District of Southwest Missouri, and was given the mission of driving the pro-Southern forces back into Arkansas. At that time Sterling Price, commanding the Missouri State Guard, was at Springfield, Missouri, and Ben McCulloch, commanding the Confederate forces in northwestern Arkansas, was at Fayetteville.

Curtis established his headquarters at Rolla, Missouri, where he assumed command December 28, 1861. He then advanced and established a forward supply base at Lebanon, Missouri, about sixty miles southwest of Rolla.

By February 7, 1862, Curtis had assembled his force there and organized it into divisions, and he then designated his command as the Army of the Southwest. Franz Sigel commanded First Division, and Alexander Asboth commanded Second Division. Sigel was given control of both First Division and Second Division, and Peter J. Osterhaus was put in charge of First Division. Third Division, which had been transferred from John Pope's District of Central Missouri, was commanded by Jefferson C. Davis, and Fourth Division was assigned to Eugene A. Carr.

On February 9, 1862, Curtis began his advance from Lebanon during a heavy snowstorm; Carr's division entered Springfield five days later. Price, confronted by a superior force and without adequate supplies, withdrew into Arkansas on February 16. By the last of February, Price and McCulloch had joined forces and had moved into the Boston Mountains, about midway between Fayetteville and Fort Smith, Arkansas.

Finally, on February 14, 1862, when all preparations had been completed, Curtis moved out of Springfield on the Telegraph Road (or Wire Road) toward Arkansas. Two days later at Potts' Hill, less than a mile south of the Arkansas state line, Curtis' advance encountered a small force of the enemy. Clark Wright's battalion of Missouri Cavalry, John McConnell's battalion of the 3rd Illinois Cavalry, and Calvin A. Ellis' 1st Missouri Cavalry, who were moving in advance of Carr's division, were engaged with Price's rear guard and after a brief action cleared the road.

The next day the same cavalry units were halted at the Telegraph Road crossing of Little Sugar Creek by enemy artillery on the hills across the creek. An attack by the cavalry was repulsed, and then for a time there was an exchange of artillery fire across the valley. The enemy artillery finally withdrew, but when the Federal cavalry arrived at the top of the slope on the far side of the creek in pursuit, they were again halted by the artillery, which had taken a new position about one-half mile south of the creek. The cavalry waited for William Vandever to come up with his Second Brigade of Carr's division and Mortimer M. Hayden's 3rd Battery, Iowa Light Artillery, and after a short engagement the enemy withdrew.

From Little Sugar Creek the Telegraph Road ran

on to the south through Cross Hollows, where the enemy was reported to hold a strong position. Further, Curtis received information that Missouri State Guard troops were at Bentonville, to the right of his position. When Curtis considered this information, he decided to change his line of march from the Telegraph Road to a route farther west. He sent a part of the cavalry south on the Telegraph Road to reconnoiter the area around Cross Hollows, and he also sent Asboth with a part of his cavalry and two pieces of artillery on the road to Bentonville with instructions to occupy the town if possible. Asboth moved into the town, after a brief skirmish, about noon.

During the next two days, the divisions of Osterhaus, Asboth, and Carr marched to Osage Springs, which was about five miles south of Bentonville and seven miles west of Cross Hollows. Davis' division remained on Little Sugar Creek for a time, then moved to a position near Cross Hollows. When the enemy learned of the presence of Curtis' army at Osage Springs, where it flanked their position at Cross Hollows, they abandoned Cross Hollows and also Fayetteville to the south. On February 22, 1862, Curtis, with Carr's division, occupied Cross Hollows. Also on February 22, Asboth was ordered to assume command of all cavalry that had been or might be ordered to report to him at Mud Town, south of Cross Hollows, and with them to proceed to Fayetteville. His cavalry command occupied Fayetteville February 23.

With these dispositions completed, Curtis realized that his forces were too widely scattered to be secure in the presence of the strong enemy forces that were reported to be close enough to be threatening. On the other hand, Curtis was reluctant to bring the various units close together, because by doing so he would give up much of the country that he had occupied and where forage could be found, and in addition such movement would leave open the way for enemy raids to the north into Missouri. Curtis finally decided to draw in his army somewhat, but to continue to hold the Bentonville–Little Sugar Creek–Cross Hollows area.

Curtis left Carr's division at Cross Hollows, but ordered Asboth's cavalry force, which was too far in advance, to move back to Osage Springs. Asboth, in retiring, left an outpost at Elm Springs. He then ordered Asboth's and Osterhaus' divisions, both

under Sigel, to march from Osage Springs to the McKisick farm, four and one-half miles southwest of Bentonville, where there was good water and grass for the horses. Some of the troops camped at the nearby Cooper farm. Sigel then sent out Frederick Schaefer with his 2nd Missouri Regiment and a detachment of cavalry to Osage Mills (Smith's Mills), seven miles east of McKisick's farm, as an outpost toward Elm Springs, and also as a guard for the mill. He sent out a detachment of cavalry to Osage Springs.

On March 1, 1862, Curtis ordered Davis to move back up the Telegraph Road with his division, which was then near Cross Hollows, to Little Sugar Creek to prepare and hold a strong defensive position on the bluffs north of the creek. There he would have his division across the Telegraph Road leading back to Missouri, and he would also hold a position upon which the rest of the army could withdraw if seriously threatened.

On February 28, 1862, Earl Van Dorn, who had recently been assigned command of the Confederate Trans-Mississippi District of Department No. 2, arrived at Van Buren, Arkansas. On March 1, he continued on to the north to join the Southern forces in the Boston Mountains. He reached Price's headquarters on Cove Creek during the evening of March 2, and the next day Price and Van Dorn rode to McCulloch's headquarters, where an attack on Curtis' Army of the Southwest was planned. The next morning Van Dorn marched with his army, which he called Army of the West, to meet Curtis. He reached Fayetteville March 4 and camped that night two miles north of the town on the road to Elm Springs and Bentonville.

The next day Van Dorn marched to Elm Springs, and there he learned that Sigel's two divisions were in an isolated position southwest of Bentonville. He decided to move against them before they could be supported or move out of reach and join the rest of the army on the Telegraph Road. That evening, March 5, 1862, Albert Pike, with about 800 men belonging to Stand Watie's and John Drew's Cherokee Indian regiments, approached Van Dorn's army at Elm Springs from the Indian Territory.

Van Dorn's Army of the West consisted of the following: McCulloch's Division, which consisted of an infantry brigade commanded by Louis Hebert and a cavalry brigade commanded by James McIntosh; Albert Pike's Indian Command; and Sterling Price's Missouri troops. The latter consisted of Henry Little's First Brigade, Missouri Volunteers; William Y. Slack's Second Brigade, Missouri Volunteers; Colton Greene's Third Brigade, Missouri Volunteers; Martin E. Green's Second Division, Missouri State Guard; John B. Clark, Jr.'s Third Division, Missouri State Guard; D. Herndon Lindsay's Fifth Division, Missouri State Guard; Daniel M. Frost's Seventh and Ninth divisions, Missouri State Guard; and James S. Rains' Eighth Division, Missouri State Guard. It should be noted that the designation of the Missouri State Guard units as divisions is misleading because they were actually only of brigade size, and some of them consisted only of detachments of smaller units.

Sigel was promptly informed of Van Dorn's approach, and he directed Schaefer to fall back to Bentonville with his 2nd Missouri. At 2:00 A.M. March 6, 1862, he started his divisions from McKisick's farm on the road to Bentonville. Asboth moved first, and he was followed by the trains of both divisions; Osterhaus followed the trains. The two divisions passed through Bentonville between 4:00 and 8:00 A.M., arriving at the camp on the bluffs north of Little Sugar Creek where the army was to assemble at about 2:00 P.M.

Sigel ordered Schaefer's 2nd Missouri, Hugo Wangelin's 12th Missouri, Gustavus M. Elbert's 1st Missouri Horse Battery (Missouri Flying Battery), and the available cavalry force under Joseph Nemett to remain at Bentonville as a rear guard under Sigel's control. By some error, the 2nd Missouri moved on toward Little Sugar Creek, and Sigel was left with eight companies of the 12th Missouri, five companies of Nemett's 5th Missouri cavalry (Benton Hussars), and five pieces of Elbert's battery, totaling about 600 men. Sigel remained with his rear guard at Bentonville to await the arrival of the outpost troops from Osage Springs.

Sigel was informed of Van Dorn's arrival near the town at 10:00 A.M., and a half-hour later marched eastward on the road toward Little Sugar Creek. From 10:30 A.M. until 3:30 P.M. Sigel was almost constantly in sight of the enemy and under fire as he moved along the road. There was an exchange of artillery fire about a mile and a half east of Bentonville, where the road turned north toward Little Sugar Creek, but when the firing ended, Sigel

moved on to the north. About three miles north of the bend in the road, and six miles from Curtis' position on the Telegraph Road north of Little Sugar Creek, the road ran down through a ravine into the valley of Little Sugar Creek. While traversing this ravine, Sigel's command was attacked by Price's Missourians, and he soon was in serious trouble. Asboth and Osterhaus, who had just arrived at their assigned position with Davis' division, immediately marched back down the valley of Little Sugar Creek to help Sigel's rear guard. Osterhaus took with him all of his regiments and Louis Hoffmann's 4th Battery, Ohio Light Artillery, and also the 15th Missouri of Asboth's division.

The first reinforcements to reach Sigel were the 2nd Missouri, the 25th Illinois, and a few companies of the 44th Illinois. One section of Hoffmann's battery unlimbered and opened fire on the enemy, and the other two sections were placed on the road about a mile east of the action. The 36th Illinois was deployed in line across the valley in support of the artillery. McIntosh's cavalry brigade attacked Osterhaus' line but was repulsed, and a short time later, Sigel with his divisions moved on to join Curtis on the line of defenses north of Little Sugar Creek.

On the morning of March 6, 1862, Davis deployed Thomas Pattison's First Brigade to the right of the Telegraph Road, on the edge of the bluffs, about 100 feet above the creek below, and Julius White's Second Brigade was formed on the left of the road. During the night of March 5, Carr's division came up from Cross Hollows, and it was placed on the left of Davis' division, and on the extreme left of Curtis' line. During the afternoon of March 6, Sigel's two divisions arrived from Bentonville; Osterhaus' division was placed on the right of Davis, and Asboth's division on the extreme right, where the Bentonville road entered the lines. Asboth's division faced to the west and southwest, and the other three divisions faced south.

The enemy bivouacked that evening along Little Sugar Creek, with McIntosh's cavalry at an old Confederate campsite called Camp Stephens, which was about four miles southwest of Curtis' position. At Camp Stephens, the road from Bentonville to Keetsville, Missouri (present-day Washburn, Missouri), commonly called the Bentonville Detour, branched off to the north from the Bentonville road and ran past the right of Curtis' defensive line, joining the Telegraph Road about three and a half miles north of Elkhorn Tavern, and well to the rear of Curtis' army. The Detour ran up a narrow valley from Camp Stephens to the high ground north of Little Sugar Creek, and then it veered off to the northeast to Twelve Corners Church, which was located just beyond the western end of Pea Ridge Mountain (or simply Pea Ridge), and from there it continued on to the east, north of Pea Ridge, until it joined the Telegraph Road at Cross Timber Hollow north of Elkhorn Tavern. Pea Ridge is a rugged plateau about two miles in length, from east to west, and it rises to a height of about 160 feet above the surrounding country. Elkhorn Tavern was at the eastern end of Pea Ridge and was located at the junction of the Telegraph Road and the Huntsville road, which ran in from the east.

Back on Little Sugar Creek, Van Dorn was aware of the difficulties of attempting to drive Curtis from his positions on the bluffs above the creek, and he decided to move up the Bentonville Detour and gain the rear of Curtis' army. At 8:00 that night, Price's Missouri troops moved up the Detour toward Cross Timber Hollow, south of Keetsville. This was a narrow defile about ten miles in length that extended across the Missouri-Arkansas state line and extended south toward Elkhorn Tavern. The Telegraph Road ran through Cross Timber Hollow. The distance from Camp Stephens to the Telegraph Road was about eight miles, and Van Dorn expected Price to be in position north of Elkhorn Tavern by daylight March 7, 1862. Price's march was delayed, however, by obstructions that Grenville M. Dodge had formed by felling trees across the road, and Price did not arrive on the Telegraph Road until about 7:00 A.M. March 7.

When Price started his march, the rest of Van Dorn's army was south of Little Sugar Creek, and there was no bridge on which to cross. McIntosh's cavalry crossed without difficulty and followed Price on the Detour about 10:00 P.M., but the water in the creek was almost freezing, too cold for the infantry to wade. Hebert finally constructed a rude bridge with poles on which men crossed slowly. In fact it was almost daylight when Pike's Indians, who were bringing up the rear, had completed their crossing. By 8:00 A.M. most of Price's men had reached the Telegraph Road, but McCulloch's infantry, McIntosh's cavalry, Pike's Indian Regi-ments, and five batteries were several miles away to the west and south on the Bentonville Detour.

Van Dorn then decided not to wait for the rest of his army to come up, but to attack at once with Price's command and move down the Telegraph Road toward the rear of Curtis' position on Little Sugar Creek. At the same time he directed McCulloch to move across country to the south with his division and Pike's regiments, past the hamlet of Leetown, and to attack the right and rear of Curtis' line. McCulloch then countermarched his command around the western end of Pea Ridge and headed toward Leetown.

The country north of Pea Ridge was broken up with high ridges, some 150 feet high, and deep hollows through which the Telegraph Road ran. At the southern end of this defile, called Tanyard Hollow, was an open space where a tanyard was located, about three-fourths of a mile north of Elkhorn Tavern. From the tanyard the road rose gradually to Elkhorn Tavern, and along the side of the road a deep hollow ran up to a spring near the tavern. At the head of this hollow, and crossing it, there was a terrace running along the foot of the mountain. From the tavern the road dropped off from the ridge and ran down the hill to the south. Another hollow, called Williams Hollow, ran out to the southeast from near the tanyard, and the head of this hollow was near the Clemens field, which was east of Elkhorn Tavern and north of the Huntsville road. Between Elkhorn Tavern and Leetown, which was about two miles to the west, was another hill called Round Top, which was just south of the western end of Pea Ridge.

Curtis spent the night at his headquarters near Pratt's store, which was about midway between Little Sugar Creek and Elkhorn Tavern, and almost due east of the hamlet of Leetown. At about 6:00 A.M. March 7, 1862, Curtis learned of the Confederate movement northward on the Bentonville Detour, but until about two hours later, he was unaware that the enemy had passed his right flank.

Between 8:00 and 9:00 that morning, Curtis sent Cyrus Bussey with his unattached 3rd Iowa Cavalry, eight companies of Missouri cavalry regiments, and three guns of Gustavus M. Elbert's 1st Missouri Horse Battery (Missouri Flying Battery) to break up the enemy movement on the Bentonville Detour.

Curtis then called a council of war at his head-quarters to determine whether the army should stay and fight or withdraw into Missouri. He finally decided to remain on the field and engage the enemy.

Leading Price's column that morning as it marched southward along the Telegraph Road toward Elkhorn Tavern was James T. Cerneal's Missouri Cavalry Battalion. The only Union troops ahead of Cerneal that were north of Curtis' headquarters were Eli W. Weston's 24th Missouri Infantry, which was posted at Elkhorn Tavern. When Weston learned of the enemy approach that morning, he sent a company under Robert W. Fyan to block the road in Tanyard Hollow, and just south of the tanyard it encountered Cerneal's troopers. About 8:00 A.M. Fyan was reinforced with two more companies, and in the narrow ravine he was able to stop the enemy advance. Cerneal then moved to his left through Williams Hollow and emerged north of the Huntsville road to the east of Elkhorn Tavern. Fyan, however, arrived near the mouth of Williams Hollow with his three companies of the 24th Missouri before Cerneal, and he was able to halt his further progress.

At about 10:00 A.M., Curtis learned from Weston that the enemy was advancing from the north on the Telegraph Road, but at that time Curtis could not be sure of the magnitude of this threat. He ordered Carr, however, to send a brigade of his division to Elkhorn Tavern, and by chance Carr's First Brigade, commanded by Grenville M. Dodge, was at Pratt's store awaiting orders. Dodge was immediately sent north to aid Weston.

Battle of Leetown, Arkansas, March 7, 1862. When Bussey moved out with his command toward the Bentonville Detour, he left the Telegraph Road near Pratt's store and traveled west past Winton Spring and Leetown and into the Oberson and Mayfield cornfields north of the village. Bussey was joined by Osterhaus, and under the latter's orders moved north across the fields and through a strip of woods to the Wiley Foster house. Beyond this house was an open prairie that lay just west of Round Top, and on the far side enemy troops were seen in the edge of the woods.

A short time before, McCulloch's division, followed by Pike's command, had left the Detour at the western end of Pea Ridge, and had marched south on a country road that led to the prairie mentioned above. It was McIntosh's cavalry that Osterhaus and Bussey saw across the prairie. Elbert's gunners soon scattered the enemy horsemen, and then Osterhaus ordered Bussey to charge with his cavalry. Bussey sent forward two companies of his 3rd Iowa Cavalry, and upon entering the woods on the far side of the prairie, they came upon McIntosh's dismounted brigade. After a quick exchange of fire, the Federal troopers turned and fled, and McIntosh immediately pursued. At about the same time, Pike led his men around to the northeast side of the prairie and deployed them along the Ford road that ran eastward to the north of the prairie. Pike then charged across the prairie, drove back the artillery supports, and captured Elbert's guns.

Martin Welfley's battery of Missouri Light Artillery (later designated as Battery B, 1st Missouri Light Artillery) was advancing toward the prairie at that time, and it was caught up in Bussey's panicky retreat. Welfley also fell back, losing one gun.

Meantime, Nicholas Greusel's Second Brigade of Osterhaus' division had advanced toward the front, and had just passed Leetown when it met Bussey's fleeing troopers. Greusel then moved on to the fields north of Leetown, where he met McIntosh's advancing skirmish line. Greusel deployed his brigade behind a line of fences that ran along the south side of the fields, and a short time later, McIntosh's dismounted men charged across the field. This attack was repulsed, and McIntosh fell back to the north of the field and prepared for a second attack. Before this could be launched, however, six guns belonging to Louis Hoffmann's 4th Battery, Ohio Light Artillery; Welfley's Battery, Missouri Light Artillery; and Peter Davidson's Battery A, 2nd Illinois Light Artillery (Peoria Battery) had been brought up and placed in position in Greusel's line. With the help of this artillery, McIntosh's second attack was repulsed.

McCulloch then came forward and personally began to organize the cavalry for still another charge. During the lull in the fighting that ensued, at about 1:30 P.M., Greusel sent forward two companies of the 36th Illinois to find out what the enemy was planning to do. When these troops reached the north end of the field, they observed what appeared to be an important man and opened fire. The man was McCulloch, and he was killed instantly by the fire.

When McIntosh learned of McCulloch's death, he assumed command of the division, and while preparing for another attack, he too was killed. Albert Pike was the next officer in seniority on that part of the field, but he was not present at the time and did not assume command until about 3:00 P.M. Hebert was next after Pike in seniority, but at that time he was leading his brigade eastward over a ridge that connected Pea Ridge with Round Top in order to reach the eastern side of Round Top, from which point he could advance on the left of McIntosh when he attacked. Hebert became lost in the rough country, however, and did not attack until sometime later.

While a part of the Confederate troops were inactive because of the lack of a commander, and while Hebert was trying to find his way around Round Top, Greusel and Osterhaus were reinforced. When Bussey's command was routed earlier in the day, Curtis, who had ordered Jefferson C. Davis' division to Elkhorn Tavern, changed his mind and sent Davis toward Leetown. Julius White's Second Brigade arrived first and was placed on the right of Greusel, behind the same line of fences occupied by the latter. Thomas Pattison's First Brigade was held for a time to the right and rear of White's brigade.

Hebert finally got his men in position east of Round Top and, moving southward, struck White's line. White withstood for a time numerous and persistent attacks, but finally he was forced to swing back his line, pivoting on the right of Greusel, until it was at a right angle to its original position. This withdrawal left the way open for Hebert's brigade. It moved forward and captured two guns of Davidson's battery, which was unsupported near the southeast corner of the Oberson cornfield, the easternmost of the Leetown fields, but these guns were later recovered.

When Hebert advanced against White's line, Davis ordered Pattison to move forward on the right, through the woods, and attack Hebert's brigade from the rear. Pattison misjudged his position, however, and when he attacked, he passed through the attacking column and cut off many of the leading troops, including Hebert, from the rear units. Evander McNair assumed command of what was left of the brigade; he attempted to re-form his command and, despite a heavy fire from Hoffmann's battery and counterattacks by Pattison and Greusel, managed to lead them from the field. Hebert was captured later, before he could rejoin his command.

After Hebert's defeat, the battle around Leetown ended. Without adequate leadership, most of the Confederate troops in the area did not know what to do, and consequently there was no further attack.

Battle of Elkhorn Tavern, Arkansas, March 7, 1862. It was noted earlier that when Curtis learned of Weston's engagement near Elkhorn Tavern, he sent Dodge's brigade of Carr's division north to support Weston. When Dodge arrived at the tavern, he moved out to the east on the Huntsville road to support the companies of the 24th Missouri that were attempting to prevent Cerneal from outflanking the Union position.

South of the Huntsville road, and about midway between the point where Cerneal emerged from Williams Hollow and Elkhorn Tavern, was the Clemens field, and directly across the road to the north was the Clemens house. To prevent Cerneal from advancing along the Huntsville road toward Elkhorn Tavern, Dodge placed two guns of Junius A. Jones' 1st Battery, Iowa Light Artillery in the northeast corner of the field to check Cerneal. This position was about 800 yards east of Elkhorn Tavern. Dodge then deployed his brigade along the north and east sides of the field. A short time later, Jones' two guns were withdrawn to Elkhorn Tavern, where they rejoined the rest of the battery.

Meantime, Price's main force, with Little's brigade in the lead, had been approaching on the Telegraph Road, and upon arriving at the tanyard, Little deployed his men across Tanyard Hollow. The 1st Battery, Iowa Light Artillery, however, prevented it from advancing farther.

At about this time, William Vandever brought up his Second Brigade, the other brigade of Carr's division, to Elkhorn Tavern, and it was advanced to the northeast slope of Pea Ridge, north of the tavern, where it faced Little's brigade.

The 1st Battery, Iowa Light Artillery, which had done good service in checking the enemy advance, was finally forced to withdraw, but it was replaced by Mortimer Hayden's 3rd Battery, Iowa Light Artillery (Dubuque Battery), which was attached to the 9th Iowa Infantry of Vandever's brigade. Hayden's battery was placed in an advanced position on the Telegraph Road, but a short time later it was forced back to the high ground at the tavern.

With both Little and Cerneal unable to advance, Price formed Slack's brigade on the right of Little, and ordered him to move forward to the west of Tanyard Hollow and onto the lower slopes of Pea Ridge. While advancing, Slack received a wound, from which he later died. Thomas H. Rosser assumed command of Slack's brigade.

By this time the rest of Price's command was moving into place. James P. Saunders' Fifth "Division," Missouri State Guard turned off from the Telegraph Road and moved through Williams Hollow to join Cerneal east of Elkhorn Tavern, near the Clemens field. Lindsay arrived at the tanyard with his Sixth "Division," Missouri State Guard, and then moved up and formed in the middle of Little's line.

When Little had his men in position, he attacked up the hill from Tanyard Hollow toward Elkhorn Tavern, but he was finally stopped by the 9th Iowa Infantry and Hayden's battery of Vandever's brigade within 300 yards of the tavern.

When Saunders' troops arrived on his front, Dodge expected an attack, and he withdrew his regiments some distance back across the field so that the enemy would have to advance against him over open ground. Dodge then held his position against severe artillery fire and infantry attacks until Vandever withdrew that evening.

Fighting on Vandever's front continued to be severe as the Confederate units to the right of Little joined in the attack. Rosser's brigade moved up the slopes of Pea Ridge with little opposition because the troops of the 24th Missouri had been pulled back. Daniel M. Frost's Ninth "Division" was brought up to strengthen Little's right. Then Little, Lindsay, and Frost advanced up the hill along the Telegraph Road, and Rosser passed around the left of Carr's line at Elkhorn Tavern. In this final advance, Vandever was forced to a new position about one-half mile south of the tavern. His new line was behind a fence running along the south side of the Ruddick field, on the east side of the Telegraph Road, and a short distance north of Pratt's store.

David Shunk's 8th Indiana Regiment of Pattison's brigade of Davis' division fought with Vandever during the day, and between 3:00 and 4:00 P.M. Curtis ordered Asboth to move forward and support Carr. Asboth in person arrived with William B. Chapman's 2nd Battery, Ohio Light Artillery and placed it in position just west of the Telegraph Road near the junction of the Ford road. He also deployed four companies of the 2nd Missouri Infantry, under Frederick Schaefer, on the right and left of the guns. This force, although small, aided in stopping Price's advance. By that time it was nearly dark, and the fighting ended for the day on that part of the field.

For some time Dodge was not aware that the enemy had occupied Elkhorn Tavern, and he continued to resist at the Clemens field, although he was then facing four enemy batteries and the infantry and cavalry that had been strengthened by the arrival of James S. Rains' Eighth "Division" of the Missouri State Guard. Then when the 35th Illinois of Dodge's brigade, which was holding the Huntsville road between Clemens' field and Elkhorn Tavern, was flanked and driven back with the loss of many prisoners, Dodge withdrew with the rest of his command through the woods to his rear and to the south. He then formed a new line on the right of Vandever's position on the south side of Ruddick's field. The men of Carr's division then bivouacked that night in the woods south of Ruddick's field.

About 2:00 that afternoon, while the fighting was going on near Leetown, Curtis directed Sigel to take the remainder of the troops of First Division and Second Division that had been held in reserve between Little Sugar Creek and Elkhorn Tavern and reinforce Osterhaus and Davis. When Sigel arrived with these troops on the battlefield north of Leetown, however, the enemy forces were retreating and the battle had ended. Davis' division was left on the battlefield to collect the dead and wounded, and Sigel, with Osterhaus' division, marched north to the Ford road and then eastward on that road toward Elkhorn Tavern. The battle at Elkhorn Tavern had ended before Sigel arrived, and his troops bivouacked on the Ford farm, west of the tavern.

During the night, Davis' division was called in from Leetown, and the next morning it relieved Carr's division on the Telegraph Road. Carr was then withdrawn and placed in reserve. Pattison's brigade of Davis' division was placed on the right of the road, with Martin Klauss' 1st Battery, Indiana Light Artillery near the center of the brigade line.

White's brigade did not take position until the next morning, and then it was formed on the left of Pattison's brigade, west of the road. It was supported by Davidson's battery.

Sometime after 1:00 A.M. March 8, 1862, Sigel marched with Osterhaus' division from the Ford farm to a position on the left of Davis' division, in the Ford and Cox cornfields, south of the Ford road. William N. Coler's First Brigade was on the right, behind the southern fence of the Cox cornfield, and Nicholas Greusel's Second Brigade was on the left, extending to the northwest from the left of Coler's line. Asboth's division was then brought up and placed in reserve in rear of Coler's line.

Battle of Elkhorn Tavern, Arkansas, March 8, 1862. The Battle of Pea Ridge was renewed on the morning of March 8, 1862 with heavy artillery fire. Under this fire, White's brigade and a part of Pattison's brigade were forced to fall back for some distance.

The action was particularly severe on Sigel's front and in a wooded area in the angle formed by the Ford road and the Telegraph Road and immediately west of their junction. This woods was occupied by enemy artillery and infantry and was subjected to a particularly heavy artillery fire. Sigel then advanced his skirmishers to within 400 yards of the woods, and Osterhaus' division was brought up behind the skirmish line. Asboth also advanced to the line just vacated by Osterhaus. Sigel then extended his line to the left until it crossed the Ford road to a point beyond the right flank of the enemy forces holding the road. At the same time, some of Asboth's regiments moved up to the woods.

Little realized that soon his position would no longer be tenable, and when this was reported to Van Dorn, the latter decided to withdraw. He directed Little to hold his position as long as possible to cover his retreat, and then began to withdraw eastward on the Huntsville road.

Sigel then began his attack, with his left moving up the southern side of Pea Ridge, and his right moving into the southern edge of the woods mentioned above. Sigel then advanced his guns so that they could fire eastward along the Ford road and into the woods, where they inflicted severe damage.

When Sigel advanced, Davis brought forward his brigades to the southern side of Ruddick's field, but White's brigade, which had earlier been on the west side of the Telegraph Road, was placed on the right with Pattison's brigade. Carr's division was also brought up and placed on the right of Davis. Both divisions then advanced across Ruddick's field toward the enemy's lines.

It was then time for Little to withdraw, which he did with considerable difficulty, fighting as he went and finally getting away safely on the Huntsville road.

The organization of Samuel R. Curtis' Army of the Southwest at the Battle of Pea Ridge March 6–8, 1862 was as follows:

FIRST DIVISION AND SECOND DIVISION, Franz Sigel

First Division, Peter J. Osterhaus
    First Brigade, William N. Coler
    Second Brigade, Nicholas Greusel
    Artillery
        Welfley's Battery, Missouri Light Artillery, Martin Welfley
        4th Battery, Ohio Light Artillery, Louis Hoffmann

Note. Franz Sigel commanded First Division and Second Division.

Second Division, Alexander Asboth
    First Brigade, Frederick Schaefer
    Not brigaded
        2nd Battery, Ohio Light Artillery, William B. Chapman
        1st Missouri Horse Artillery (Flying Battery), Gustavus M. Elbert
        Benton Hussars (5th Missouri Cavalry), Missouri Cavalry, Joseph Nemett
        Fremont Hussars, Missouri Cavalry, Emeric Meszaros

Note. Franz Sigel commanded First Division and Second Division.

Third Division, Jefferson C. Davis
    First Brigade, Thomas Pattison
    Second Brigade, Julius White

Note. Martin Klauss' 1st Battery, Indiana Light Artillery was attached to First Brigade, and Peter Davidson's Battery A, 2nd Illinois Light Artillery (Peoria Battery) was attached to Second Brigade.

Fourth Division, Eugene A. Carr
    First Brigade, Grenville M. Dodge
    Second Brigade, William Vandever

Note. Junius A. Jones' 1st Battery, Iowa Light Artillery was attached to First Brigade, and Mortimer M. Hayden's 3rd Battery, Iowa Light Artillery was attached to Second Brigade. Jones was wounded and was succeeded in command of the battery by Virgil J. David.

Unassigned
  Bowen's Battalion Missouri Cavalry, William D. Bowen
  3rd Iowa Cavalry, Cyrus Bussey
  3rd Missouri Infantry, Joseph Conrad
  24th Missouri Infantry, Eli W. Weston

SKIRMISH AT PICACHO PASS, ARIZONA TERRITORY
APRIL 15, 1862

The so-called Battle of Picacho Pass was in reality a very minor action of little or no lasting significance, but it is included here among the operations of the Civil War because it took place in the Arizona Territory, and has the distinction of being the farthest west of any engagement of the war. Because it is generally so little known, it is described here in some detail, although the numbers involved were very small.

On October 20, 1861, George Wright assumed command of the Department of the Pacific, with headquarters at San Francisco. Earlier, before the regular troops on the West Coast had been sent east, there had been some consideration of a plan to send troops through Mexico to invade Texas, but with their departure, this plan was necessarily abandoned. Wright, however, revived the idea and formulated a plan to march eastward from California to Texas. By so doing he could drive Confederate forces from New Mexico and thereby prevent an enemy invasion of southern California from that region.

Wright believed that the enemy did intend to invade California, a movement that he wished to prevent, and when he learned in December 1861 that Henry Hopkins Sibley had arrived in western Texas with troops for another advance into New Mexico, he had added incentive for his march across Arizona. George B. McClellan approved Wright's plan December 18, and he then began preparations for the expedition.

Wright selected Fort Yuma, on the Colorado River, for the assembly of his troops and as a base of operations, and he assigned James H. Carleton to command the expedition, which later became known as the Column from California.

In January 1862, Confederate General Sibley, who was then at Fort Thorn, New Mexico, sent Sherod Hunter, with about 100 mounted Texas troops, to occupy Tucson, Arizona Territory. Hunter arrived there February 28 and assumed command. Meantime, Wright and Carleton were making preparations for the movement eastward from Fort Yuma along the Southern, or Overland Mail, Road to the Rio Grande.

Earlier, Carleton had learned of Hunter's march and, believing his destination to be Tucson, on February 11, 1862 ordered William A. McCleave, who was then near San Bernardino, California, to move up the Gila River with thirty men of Company A, 1st California Cavalry to look for the enemy and to secure the government's store of wheat and flour at White's Mill near the Pima Villages. McCleave was unaware that Hunter had marched from Tucson a few days after assuming command, and had arrived at White's Mill before him. When McCleave and nine of his men rode to the Ami White house on the evening of March 6, they were all captured by Hunter.

Carleton soon learned of Hunter's arrival at Tucson, and, although his column was not yet ready to march, he ordered Edwin A. Rigg, commanding at Fort Yuma, to send a detachment of troops to drive Hunter from Tucson, and also to attempt the rescue of McCleave and his men. Rigg selected William P. Calloway to command the expedition, which consisted of Calloway's own Company I, 1st California Cavalry; Benjamin F. Harvey's Company A, 1st California Cavalry; Nathaniel J. Pishon's Company D, 1st California Cavalry; and two mountain howitzers.

The infantry began its march from Fort Yuma at 9:00 P.M. March 22, 1862 and arrived at Stanwix Station (or Grinnell's Ranch), eighty miles east of Fort Yuma, on March 28. Harvey's cavalry had arrived there twelve days before, and Pishon's cavalry was following the infantry about a day's march behind.

On March 29, 1862, some of Hunter's men fired on two of Calloway's pickets, who were about six miles north of Stanwix Station on the Gila River. Pishon's cavalry, who had just arrived, were sent in pursuit, but they soon returned. On April 4, the Confederate scouts who had fired on Calloway's pickets returned to Tucson and reported to Hunter the approach of a strong Union force.

When Calloway had assembled his three companies at Stanwix Station, he left there April 8, 1862 and arrived at the Pima Villages four days later. On April 14 he set out for Tucson. On the afternoon of April 15, as Calloway's column approached Picacho Pass, he learned from Indian scouts that a small force of the enemy was ahead. This was a party of nine Confederate scouts, led by Jack W. Swilling, who had been sent out to watch Calloway's movements.

Upon receiving this information, Calloway sent forward James Barrett with a small detachment of Company A, 1st California Cavalry with instructions to move down the main road until he was near Picacho Pass, then turn off and move in on Swilling's men from the east. Ephraim C. Baldwin, commanding a detachment from Company D, 1st California Cavalry, was to follow Barrett, then move off the road and approach the enemy from the west. In this way Calloway would cut off Swilling's pickets stationed in the pass when they were attacked by Calloway's main force.

Unfortunately for the success of this movement, Barrett did not follow instructions and moved out eight miles in advance of the main force. Then, without waiting for Baldwin, he charged on the enemy, who were concealed in some thickets, fired his pistol, and demanded the surrender of Swilling and his men. They responded with a volley that struck down four of Barrett's men. The firing then became general for a time, and three of the enemy surrendered. Barrett and two of his men were killed, and three were wounded. One of the enemy was killed, four were wounded, three surrendered, and one escaped.

Calloway finally came up with the rest of his command, but the fighting at Picacho Pass had ended. Calloway remained at the pass that night. At that point he was uncertain of the strength of the enemy forces at Tucson; he knew that on the road ahead there was serious danger of ambush; he was low on provisions; and he had also learned that McCleave and his men, whom he hoped to rescue,

had already been taken east to the Rio Grande. For these reasons, he ordered his men to turn back toward Fort Yuma. Upon arriving near Stanwix Station, he met the head of Carleton's Column from California, and his men returned to their proper commands and moved eastward with them.

When Hunter learned that a large Union force was soon to move into Arizona, he decided to leave and move back to the east. He left Tucson May 4, 1862 with his command and marched for the Rio Grande. He arrived in the Mesilla Valley on May 27 and left western Arizona to Carleton's men.

For additional information, see Department of the Pacific, Districts in the Department of the Pacific, District of Southern California; and see also Department of New Mexico, Troops and Operations in the Department of New Mexico, Expedition from California, through Arizona, to New Mexico and Northwestern Texas (Column from California).

PORT HUDSON, LOUISIANA CAMPAIGN MAY 14–JULY 8, 1863

One of the more important of the Northern military objectives during the early part of the Civil War was opening the Mississippi River, which was closed by the Confederate fortifications at Vicksburg, Mississippi and, after August 1862, at Port Hudson, Louisiana.

Port Hudson was of particular importance, because as long as it was held by Confederate forces, they could control the river from there as far north as Vicksburg, and thus supplies from western Louisiana, Texas, and Mexico could be transferred by way of the Red River to the garrisons of the fortifications on the Mississippi and to other parts of the Confederacy east of the river.

Nathaniel P. Banks, commander of the Department of the Gulf, did not believe that he had sufficient force to take Port Hudson by direct attack, and because of this he decided on an expedition up the Bayou Teche in western Louisiana in an attempt to reach the Red River and the Mississippi above Port Hudson and thus cut off supplies from the enemy troops that were stationed at that post.

On April 9, 1863, Banks left Berwick Bay with a detachment of Nineteenth Corps and marched up the Teche toward the Red River. He took with him William H. Emory's Third Division, Cuvier Grover's Fourth Division, and Godfrey Weitzel's Second Brigade, First Division of Nineteenth Corps. After two engagements and long marches, the first of Banks' troops reached Alexandria May 7, and the rest of his column arrived near the town soon after.

Banks remained at Alexandria for a week while attempting to work out some method of cooperation with Ulysses S. Grant in a campaign for opening the Mississippi River. He learned, however, that Grant had crossed his army to the east side of the Mississippi River and was then moving toward the rear of Vicksburg, and that he could expect no help from that quarter. Banks then had several options available to him—he could follow Richard Taylor's Confederate forces in western Louisiana toward Shreveport, in which direction they were then moving; he could proceed on to Vicksburg to aid Grant; he could return to his former positions; or he could move against the Confederate fortifications at Port Hudson. He decided on the latter course.

Movement of Nineteenth Corps to Port Hudson, Louisiana. On May 14, 1863, Banks began to move his army from Alexandria toward Port Hudson. That morning, Grover's division broke camp at Stafford's plantation and marched by way of Cheneyville, Enterprise, and the Bayou de Glaize, arriving at Simsport on May 17. Grover immediately began to cross the Atchafalaya River and put his division in camp near corps headquarters on the Sims plantation the next day.

On May 4, 1863, Emory, who was sick, left the army for New Orleans, and Halbert E. Paine assumed command of his division. On May 15, Paine's division followed Grover from Alexandria and marched by way of Lecompte, the Bayou Rouge, and the Bayou de Glaize at the crossing of the Marksville road to Simsport, where it arrived May 18. Paine's division crossed the Atchafalaya to the Sims plantation the next day.

On May 15, 1863, Banks left Alexandria for New Orleans to take care of department business.

Weitzel, with his own brigade and William Dwight's First Brigade of Grover's division, was ordered to remain at Alexandria until May 17, 1863. Dwight, in person, left Alexandria to carry dispatches from Banks to Grant at Vicksburg, and he did not rejoin the army until May 22, when it was in front of Port Hudson.

Weitzel left Alexandria as ordered May 17, 1863, camping that night at the Murdock plantation to guard the crossing of the Bayou Huffpower road and the road to Opelousas. Weitzel remained in camp there until May 22, then marched toward Simsport. He arrived there the next day and began to cross the Atchafalaya to join the rest of the army.

May 18, 1863, Banks ordered Christopher C. Augur, commanding First Division, Nineteenth Corps at Baton Rouge, to march with all of his available force to the rear of Port Hudson and take position there so as to prevent the escape of the garrison if forced to withdraw. Banks also assigned Emory, who was too sick to take the field, to the command of the Defenses of New Orleans, and directed Thomas W. Sherman to take Neal Dow's First Brigade and Frank S. Nickerson's Third Brigade of Second Division, Nineteenth Corps and join Augur near Port Hudson.

Banks left New Orleans May 20, 1863 and arrived at his headquarters on the Sims plantation the next day. He then issued orders for the troops of Nineteenth Corps that were encamped there to move toward Bayou Sara and Port Hudson.

At 8:30 A.M. May 21, 1863, Paine's division left its camp near the Atchafalaya River, opposite Simsport, and marched to Morganza on the Mississippi River. Grover's division followed on the river as rapidly as transports were available.

The wagon train of the army moved down the road along the river to the landing directly opposite Bayou Sara (Point Coupee). The train was escorted by the 110th New York and the 162nd New York regiments of Timothy Ingraham's First Brigade of Paine's division and a section of William W. Carruth's 6th Battery, Massachusetts Light Artillery. All were under the command of Lewis Benedict, colonel of the 162nd New York.

At 2:00 A.M. May 22, 1863, Banks and Grover went ashore at Bayou Sara with the advance troops of Grover's division. The rest of the division soon landed at Bayou Sara, and it was followed by Paine with Hawkes Fearing's Second Brigade and Oliver

P. Gooding's Third Brigade of his division from Morganza.

The above were not the first Federal troops to arrive near Port Hudson. Earlier, on May 13, 1863, Augur had sent Benjamin H. Grierson with the cavalry of his command and Nathan A. M. Dudley's Second Brigade, First Division, Nineteenth Corps from Baton Rouge up to the Merritt plantation, which was located at the junction of the Springfield Landing road and the Bayou Sara road. There these troops would be in position to threaten the enemy at Port Hudson, and also to observe their movements. Dudley took position near White's Bayou, a branch of the Comite River, where it covered the road to Clinton and also the road to Jackson, Louisiana.

On May 20, 1863, Augur arrived with the rest of his command from Baton Rouge and joined Dudley's brigade. Augur was then in position to link up with Banks' main column when it arrived from Simsport, and also to cover the landing of Sherman's two brigades from New Orleans at Springfield Landing, below Port Hudson.

When Augur arrived near Port Hudson, his command consisted of Dudley's brigade; Edward P. Chapin's First Brigade, First Division, Nineteenth Corps; John F. Godfrey's Squadron, consisting of two companies of Louisiana Cavalry; one section of Albert G. Mack's 18th Battery, New York Light Artillery, commanded by David W. McConnell; two sections of Jacob B. Rawles' Battery G, 5th United States Artillery; and Pythagoras E. Holcomb's 2nd Battery, Vermont Light Artillery.

Action at Plains Store, Louisiana, May 21, 1863.
At 6:30 A.M. May 21, 1863, Augur advanced with his command toward the crossing of the Plains Store road and the Bayou Sara road to clear the way for the approach of Banks' column. Grierson, who was in the lead, encountered an enemy force near Plains Store at the edge of a woods that extended along the southern side of the open plantation grounds (or Plains). This force consisted of Frank P. Powers' cavalry, a few companies of infantry, and George Abbay's Mississippi Battery. Grierson then skirmished with the enemy for a time while Augur's main force advanced toward the front. By 10:00 A.M. Augur had arrived at the open ground, but he was stopped there by Abbay's guns. Augur then

brought up some of Dudley's artillery, and for the next two hours there was a vigorous exchange of fire between the two batteries. When this ended, Dudley moved his brigade up to the right of the road to Port Hudson, where it supported Holcomb's battery and prepared to bivouac for the night. Chapin halted his brigade on the left of the road in support of Rawles' battery. The 48th Massachusetts of Chapin's brigade was sent out on the road to support some of the artillery. Augur's other regiments bivouacked below Plains Store on the Bayou Sara road.

About noon that day, May 21, 1863, William R. Miles, with about 400 men of his Louisiana Legion and R. M. Boone's Louisiana Light Battery, marched out of the works at Port Hudson to relieve Powers' command. Augur's troops had just begun to bivouac when Miles arrived at the front. Miles formed two companies of his command under James T. Coleman on his right and three companies under Frederick B. Brand on his left, and he then advanced toward Augur's position. Coleman's troops soon ran over some advanced Federal guns, and the 48th Massachusetts, which had been badly placed to support them, fled to the rear in confusion. It passed through the 49th Massachusetts, which was then advancing, and caused some disorder, but it was able to hold its ground and later advanced.

Meantime, Brand had led his three companies to a position on the flank of Chapin's brigade, and he then opened fire on the rear of the 116th New York. This regiment changed front to the rear, then charged, forcing Brand to fall back. Another charge by Augur's troops soon followed, and Miles' command withdrew to their entrenchments at Port Hudson.

* * * * * * * * *

When Banks arrived at Bayou Sara May 22, 1863, he learned that Augur had been engaged at Plains Store the day before. Despite a violent rain and wind storm, Banks immediately advanced Grover's division until it met Augur's outlying detachments. When Grover learned from them that Augur was in no trouble, he bivouacked near Thompson's Creek, northwest of Port Hudson. Paine followed Grover from Bayou Sara with his division and halted on the Perkins plantation, about a mile in rear of him. Banks set up his headquarters with Grover.

After the engagement at Plains Store, Augur put his troops in position in front of the works occupied after the fighting ended.

Also on May 22, Sherman's two brigades arrived from the trip upriver from New Orleans and came ashore at Springfield Landing. They then marched to a position on the Bayou Sara road and took position on the left of Augur's line. Thus, on the evening of May 22, 1863, the Confederate troops at Port Hudson were virtually surrounded.

Investment of Port Hudson. Weitzel's two brigades, which were the last to leave Simsport, finally arrived near Port Hudson on May 25, 1863, and then Banks began to establish his lines closer to Port Hudson, all along the front. Weitzel moved up the Telegraph Road from Bayou Sara to a place called the sugarhouse, which was near the bridge over Foster's Creek, and he then took position to the east of the great swamp north of Port Hudson.

Paine advanced his division into the thick woods on the left of Weitzel. Grover moved forward with his division to a ravine through which Sandy Creek flowed, north of the Clinton and Port Hudson Railroad. He then crossed the ravine and moved up to the crest of a steep hill on the other side. Augur formed his division across the Plains Store road, on the left of Paine's line, and under the cover of a thick woods some distance in front of the enemy entrenchments.

Sherman's division was on the extreme left of Banks' line, where it held the road to Baton Rouge. The right of Sherman's line was near the White House, the house of the Gibbon plantation; the center was at the Troth house, which was about three-fourths of a mile east of the Mississippi River from a point at the southern end of the enemy entrenchments; and the left was on the river.

When Augur left Baton Rouge for Port Hudson, he placed Charles W. Drew, with his 4th Louisiana Native Guards, in Fort Williams to hold the post, and directed John A. Nelson to have his 1st and 3rd Louisiana Native Guards ready to move to Port Hudson. When Nelson arrived at Port Hudson, his two regiments were placed at the sugarhouse near Foster's Creek on the extreme right of the Federal line.

In addition to the above troops, Banks placed Benedict, with his two regiments and a section of artillery, at the Hermitage Plantation, on the west bank of the Mississippi, to prevent the enemy from escaping from Port Hudson by water.

The presence of navy ships and gunboats on the river, both above and below Port Hudson, completed the investment.

When all troops had moved up, Banks placed Weitzel in command of the right wing of the army, which consisted of his own brigade, under Stephen Thomas; Dwight's brigade of Grover's division, under the command of Jacob Van Zandt; Paine's division; and Nelson's two regiments of Louisiana Native Guards. The brigades of Thomas and Van Zandt were assigned to a temporary division commanded by Dwight, who had rejoined the army May 22, 1863 from detached service at Vicksburg.

Before describing the assaults and the subsequent siege operations at Port Hudson, it is necessary to describe briefly the country about the town and the line of entrenchments constructed to defend it. The Mississippi River flowed generally southward from Bayou Sara, but at a point about two miles above Port Hudson it turned and flowed to the east until it struck a high bluff upon which Port Hudson stood. The river then turned to the south and for some distance ran along the foot of the bluffs. It was along the bluffs on this stretch of the river that the Confederates had constructed batteries to prevent Federal ships from passing up and down the river.

The bluff ended a short distance above Port Hudson, and the ground fell off into a ravine, on the far side of which was a narrow ridge. Sandy Creek was a short distance away, and it flowed through a large part of the enemy-held region to the north and east of Port Hudson. To the northwest of the town was a large swamp and thick canebrakes, and through this area Thompson's Creek flowed on its way to the Mississippi. To the north of Port Hudson the ground was very difficult and was crossed by a number of ravines or gullies, through which flowed Big Sandy Creek and its many branches. Much of this area was covered by thick woods, and the ravines were filled with felled trees and dense undergrowth.

About a mile and a half below Port Hudson, a valley about 300 yards wide cut through the line of bluffs from the river, then ran northward behind the bluffs and nearly parallel to the river. Ross Landing was about a half-mile south of this gap in the bluffs. To the east of Port Hudson, and beyond the ravine, a plateau extended away from the river to the open fields of the Gibbon and Slaughter plantations.

A number of roads radiated out from Port Hudson to the north, east, and south. Beginning on the Confederate left, the Telegraph Road ran out to the northwest along the river to Bayou Sara. Then, in order from left to right, there were the Bayou Sara road, the road to Jackson, the Plains Store road, and the road to Baton Rouge. The Clinton and Port Hudson Railroad, which began at Hickey's Landing on the river, about a half-mile south of Port Hudson, ran to the northeast to Clinton, Louisiana.

The line of works that the enemy had constructed for the defense of Port Hudson was about four and one-half miles in length; it began on the enemy right, on the high ground above the break in the line of bluffs about a mile and a half below Port Hudson. From there it extended to the northeast for about three-fourths of a mile, to an angle in the line about five-eighths of a mile west and a little to the north of the Gibbon plantation house. On this part of the line the entrenchments crossed a number of ridges, deep ravines, and narrow plateaus. From the angle, the line continued on, a little to the east of north, across the broad cottonfields of the Gibbon and Slaughter plantations, for about one and one-fourth miles, to a point on the Plains Store road, about a half-mile to the northwest of the Slaughter plantation house.

From the Plains Store road, the line ran to the northwest for about one-fourth of a mile, across a number of deep gullies and the Clinton and Port Hudson Railroad, to the Jackson road. From there it extended on a little west of north for about three-fourths of a mile, through fields and across hills, to the deep ravine of a branch of Sandy Creek. At the time of the investment of Port Hudson, the entrenchments ended on this ravine. The country between this point and the Mississippi River to the west was thought to be too difficult for a successful attack from the north. In this area Sandy Creek flows westward into the swampy valley of Foster's Creek. From the end of the entrenchments on Sandy Creek to the mouth of Foster's Creek was about one and one-half miles.

Prior to the arrival of Banks' army before Port Hudson, Franklin Gardner was in command of the Confederate troops of the garrison, and these were organized into five brigades, commanded by Wil-

liam N. R. Beall, Abraham Buford, John Gregg, S. B. Maxey, and Albert Rust. On May 4, 1863, however, after Grant had begun his movement to the rear of Vicksburg, Gardner's command was greatly reduced when he sent a large part of his force to reinforce John C. Pemberton at Vicksburg. That day, the brigades of Buford and Rust departed for Vicksburg; the next day Gregg's brigade followed. Then on May 8, Maxey's brigade also left the garrison. When Banks prepared for his first assault later in May, Isaiah G. W. Steedman, colonel of the 1st Alabama Regiment, was in command of the Confederate left wing, Beall's brigade was on the center of the line, and William R. Miles, commander of Miles' Legion, held the Confederate right.

Assault at Port Hudson, Louisiana, May 27, 1863. On the night of May 26, 1863, Banks decided to try for an early ending of the campaign by launching an attack on the enemy works early the next morning. According to Banks' plan, the artillery was to open fire at daylight all along the line, and the naval vessels on the river were to join in this bombardment. When the firing ended, Weitzel was to advance his right wing against the Confederate left flank.

Grover, who was on the left of Weitzel, was given conditional, and somewhat vague, orders for his participation in the battle. His actions were to be determined as the attack developed as follows: he was to support the left-center, to reinforce either the right or left of the line as needed, to support the artillery reserve, or to join in the attack against the enemy works on his front.

Augur's and Sherman's divisions, which held the center and left of Banks' line, respectively, were to begin their attacks by advancing their skirmishers during the artillery preparation.

The ground across which Banks' divisions were to pass in the attack that morning was the partially cleared land of the Gibbon and Slaughter plantations on the left and center and the rough and wooded areas farther to the right. In some places in the fields, especially on Augur's approach, the trees that had only recently been cut were still lying on the ground and were a serious obstacle to troops moving forward to attack.

The Federal artillery opened at dawn May 27, 1863 as scheduled, and at 6:00 A.M. Weitzel, believing that Augur and Sherman were moving forward on his left, began to advance his troops through the thick woods toward the front. His command was formed in a column of brigades, with Dwight's brigade under Van Zandt in front and Weitzel's brigade under Thomas following close behind and slightly to the left. On the immediate left of Van Zandt and Thomas, Paine advanced Fearing's Second Brigade and held Gooding's Third Brigade in reserve.

For about an hour, Weitzel's men advanced through the woods and across the ravines in front of the enemy works and slowly, with severe fighting, drove back the skirmishers and troops of Steedman's outposts into their main line of entrenchments. These forward enemy troops were under the command of M. B. Locke.

The ground traversed by Thomas' brigade was less difficult than that in front of Van Zandt, and Thomas gradually moved ahead. During the attack, Van Zandt's brigade shifted to the right because of the nature of the ground and the heavy fire to which it was subjected, and when this occurred, Paine advanced his troops to fill the gap thus created. Gooding's brigade arrived in front of the 10th Arkansas Regiment and then launched an attack but was driven back. Fearing's brigade reached the ditch on its front, but it too was soon forced to retire.

The ground on this part of the field was badly broken by numerous ravines and gullies and was covered with logs and trees, and the advance of Weitzel's troops was necessarily slow and disorganized. They finally reached and held a ridge just north of Sandy Creek and about 200 yards in front of the enemy main line, but they could go no farther. Thomas finally advanced across a small stream known as Little Sandy Creek and fortified a position on a hill to the right that later became known as Fort Babcock.

The position finally gained by Thomas' and Van Zandt's brigades was the same as that later occupied by the Federal siege batteries Nos. 3, 4, and 5. This was about one mile north and a little to the east of Port Hudson, and was about midway between the Jackson road and the Mississippi River. On some maps showing the works at Port Hudson, the Federal batteries are shown by arabic numerals and the Confederate batteries by roman numerals. With the help of the pioneers, the batteries of Richard C.

Duryea, Ormand F. Nims, Eben D. Haley, Edmund C. Bainbridge, and William W. Carruth were brought up to the ridge with the infantry and opened fire on Steedman's position.

Paine's division was about 600 yards to the left and slightly to the rear of Weitzel's line, and was to the right and rear of the position later occupied by siege battery No. 6.

To support the attack by Weitzel and Paine, Grover sent the 159th New York of Henry W. Birge's Third Brigade up to the left of Paine to attack the left of the position held by the 15th Arkansas. In advancing, however, it was hit by a destructive flank fire and driven back. Grover then ordered forward the 12th Maine of William K. Kimball's Second Brigade and the 13th and 25th Connecticut of Birge's brigade. They were to attack some troops of the 15th Arkansas who were in position on a hill that extended out from the right of the main Confederate line of defenses. These regiments were able to reach the outside of the parapet before being driven back. There was furious fighting for several hours around the entrenchments on this hill, which were later called "Fort Desperate." This position was later occupied by siege battery No. 6.

There was another attack that morning by troops on the far right of the Federal line. Earlier in the day, Dwight had assumed command of John A. Nelson's two colored regiments when he assumed command of a temporary division of the right wing. Dwight then ordered Nelson to attack the extreme Confederate left at the angle in the line where it turned back to the south toward the river. That portion of the line was along the crest of a steep bluff, where it overlooked the low ground near the sugarhouse, which was near the point where the Telegraph Road crossed Foster's Creek.

At 7:00 A.M. Nelson's 1st Louisiana Native Guards advanced toward the enemy position on the bluff, and it was followed by the 3rd Louisiana Native Guards. The leading regiment was met by a murderous musketry and artillery fire and driven back on the 3rd Louisiana Native Guards, which was just crossing the creek in support. After some confused fighting, Nelson's troops were driven back beyond the sugarhouse, where they remained during the rest of the day.

At 10:00 A.M., after the fighting on the Federal right had been going on for several hours, there had been no sounds of Augur's and Sherman's attacks on the left. Meantime, Augur had formed his division and had been waiting for orders to attack. Banks, however, whose headquarters was nearby, had been waiting to hear the sounds of Sherman's battle to the south before ordering Augur to advance. For reasons not clearly understood, Sherman did not attack that morning, and finally at noon Banks rode over to the left and found Sherman and his staff at lunch. There was an unpleasant situation when Banks expressed in vigorous terms his displeasure at Sherman's inactivity, and then Banks left.

When Banks returned to his headquarters, he decided to replace Sherman in command of Second Division with George L. Andrews, his chief of staff. Andrews did not arrive at Sherman's headquarters until 1:30 P.M., and then he found that Sherman had formed his division and was preparing to attack. Andrews did not relieve Sherman but permitted him to proceed with his attack.

Nickerson's brigade, which was on the right of Sherman's line, advanced with the 14th Maine out in front as skirmishers, and it was followed in column of regiments by the 24th Maine, 176th New York, and 165th New York. The right of the brigade was on the road that ran east from the Bayou Sara road past the Slaughter plantation house.

Dow's brigade advanced on the immediate left of Nickerson's brigade, with the 6th Michigan in front, and it was followed by the 15th New Hampshire, the 26th Connecticut, and the 128th New York. The left of Dow's brigade was at the Gibbon plantation house.

Sherman's division was formed under the cover of a woods, and beyond the woods were fields that extended several hundred yards to the front. When Dow's and Nickerson's brigades emerged from the woods and advanced onto the open ground, they came under an intense fire from Beall's artillery. As the line advanced, Sherman was wounded, and Dow, the senior officer after Sherman, was also wounded. This left the command of the division to Nickerson, but he was with his brigade and in the confusion of the attack was not notified. As a result, there was no one who exercised control of the division for some time, but Thomas S. Clark assumed command of Dow's brigade. Later Andrews assumed temporary command of the division.

Although Sherman's division became much disordered by the artillery fire, it continued to advance for a time, but finally it lost almost all semblance of order, and most of the men sought cover. There were some further attacks by small groups of men, but these were unsuccessful. Many of the men found shelter in a ravine to the right, and others behind logs and stumps or anything that afforded some protection. Dow's men, who were not far from the woods to their rear, began to fall back about 4:30 P.M., but the rest of the division remained out in front until after dark before coming in.

When Banks heard the sounds of Sherman's battle, he ordered Augur to attack. Augur's division was already formed, with Chapin's brigade deployed across the Plains Store road and Dudley's brigade in reserve. The 21st Maine was out in front of Chapin's brigade as skirmishers on the left side of the road, and immediately in rear of the skirmishers was a storming party of 200 volunteers under the command of James O'Brien. These troops were concealed in the woods at a point nearly opposite the site of siege battery No. 13, which was constructed later. The 116th New York was deployed on the right of the road, and the 49th Massachusetts was on its left. Deployed in close support were the 48th Massachusetts, the 2nd Louisiana of Dudley's brigade, and the remainder of the 21st Maine.

Augur's troops advanced under a heavy musketry and artillery fire and moved into the thick abatis in front of the enemy works. At that point, however, they could no longer withstand the enemy fire, and the men began to take cover wherever any protection could be found. About an hour later, O'Brien attempted to get his men to renew the attack, but he was killed, and the few men who had been willing to follow him sought cover. Augur's attack was the last attempt to storm the enemy works that day. Edward P. Chapin, commander of First Brigade of Augur's division, was killed in the attack of May 27, 1863, and he was succeeded in command of the brigade by Charles J. Paine.

* * * * * * * * *

After the failure of his attacks May 27, 1863, Banks decided that the only way he could reach the enemy works was by using regular siege operations. He directed Richard Arnold, his chief of artillery, and David C. Houston, chief engineer, to begin the preparation of batteries and other works necessary for the siege. He further directed Arnold to bring up the remainder of the siege train, which had been placed under his immediate command before the attack of May 27, and also ordered Houston to provide the entrenching tools and other necessary siege materials.

Arnold and Houston selected the sites for the batteries, and on May 30, 1863, details began constructing these works and the connecting lines of rifle pits. For the next two weeks, all regiments along the line labored day and night digging rifle pits and trenches, constructing covered ways and breastworks, and mounting guns in the batteries. Banks' siege artillery consisted of forty guns, and his field artillery was in excess of sixty guns. In addition, there were the many guns of David G. Farragut's fleet on the river.

The line of siege batteries began on the Federal right near the sugarhouse on the bank of Foster's Creek and extended around in front of the enemy works to the Mount Pleasant road on the far left. The distance from the batteries to the Confederate line of entrenchments varied from about one-third to two-thirds of a mile.

Banks needed reinforcements for his army and also laborers for conducting siege operations, and he ordered that all available regiments on the Bayou Teche and Atchafalaya River be sent to Port Hudson, and also that all armed colored troops at New Orleans be sent to Springfield Landing. Also on June 1, 1863, he further directed that all able-bodied Negroes and stragglers at Baton Rouge and all troops that had been raised, both armed and unarmed, be sent to Port Hudson.

The regiments from the Bayou Teche and Atchafalaya country moved by way of Brashear to Algiers, and then by transport upriver to Port Hudson. This movement was completed between May 28 and June 1, 1863. The regiments that were thus transferred to Port Hudson were the 41st Massachusetts (3rd Massachusetts Cavalry), 114th New York, 4th Massachusetts, 16th New Hampshire, 22nd Maine, 90th New York, 52nd Massachusetts, 26th Maine, and a detachment of 13th Connecticut.

There were several changes in command after the assaults of May 27, 1863, and also some changes in position of the troops on the line of investment.

When Sherman was wounded May 27, George L. Andrews, Banks' chief of staff, assumed temporary command of Second Division. Nickerson succeeded Andrews the next morning, and Dwight assumed command May 30 (assigned May 29), relieving Nickerson. Nickerson then resumed command of Third Brigade, Second Division.

Dow, who had been slightly wounded May 27, 1863, had hoped to be assigned command of Second Division, and when Dwight was assigned instead, Dow requested a transfer from the Department of the Gulf. Banks refused to grant this request, but on the night of June 30, Dow was captured by a small party of Confederates while he was convalescing from his wound at the Heath plantation, two miles from Port Hudson.

Samuel P. Ferris' 28th Connecticut Regiment, which had joined the army from western Louisiana, was assigned to First Brigade, Third Division June 2, 1863, and as senior officer, Ferris assumed command of the brigade. Joseph S. Morgan's 90th New York, which had also arrived from western Louisiana, was assigned to First Brigade, Fourth Division, and Morgan as the senior officer assumed command of that brigade. Charles J. Paine's 2nd Louisiana Regiment of Dudley's Third Brigade, First Division was transferred to Chapin's First Brigade, First Division, and as senior officer, Paine assumed command of the brigade in place of Chapin, who had been killed May 27.

On the afternoon of May 27, 1863, Grover was placed in command of the right wing of Banks' army, but Dwight's First Brigade of Grover's division, then temporarily commanded by Van Zandt (and later by Joseph S. Morgan), remained with Weitzel as a part of the temporary division consisting of Dwight's brigade and Weitzel's brigade, the latter commanded by Thomas.

Halbert E. Paine's division was taken from the right wing, originally commanded by Weitzel, and was placed on the left of Grover's division, where it covered the Jackson road. Augur was assigned command of the left wing of the army, which consisted of his own First Division and Dwight's (formerly Sherman's) Second Division.

All along the line, the Federal troops occupied essentially the advanced positions that they had gained in the fighting on May 27, 1863. From right to left the line was held by Weitzel, Grover, Paine,

Augur, and Dwight. Augur's division was shifted somewhat to the left and, with Charles J. Paine's First Brigade, occupied a part of the ground that had been on Sherman's front May 27.

Dwight closed up his division somewhat and moved closer to the river. By so doing, he covered the road that ran out toward the south from the right of the Confederate works, around the northern and eastern slopes of Mount Pleasant (just north of Ross Landing), and on past the Troth house.

Grierson's cavalry was massed behind the center of the Federal line to guard the rear of the army.

Assault at Port Hudson, June 14, 1864. During the investment of Port Hudson, John L. Logan, colonel of the 11th Arkansas Regiment, was in rear of Banks' lines with a small force of infantry, cavalry, and artillery. He was not a serious threat to the besiegers, but he was an annoyance, and finally Banks ordered Benjamin H. Grierson with his cavalry to dispose of him.

On the morning of June 3, 1863, Grierson learned that Logan was at Clinton, and at 5:00 A.M. he set out with 1,300 men and eight pieces of artillery toward the town. A short distance from Clinton, Grierson encountered a part of Logan's command under Thomas R. Stockdale, and a sharp fight ensued. Then Logan came up with the rest of his men, and together they drove Grierson back to a position beyond the Amite River. Upon learning of the failure of the cavalry, on June 5 Banks sent Halbert E. Paine with 4,000 men and a strong artillery support to join Grierson. Grierson moved out to Clinton, but upon arrival there he found that Logan had departed. Grierson then destroyed everything in the town that was of military value to the enemy, and then he and Paine returned to Port Hudson late on June 8.

After the failure of the two expeditions to Clinton, Banks decided to make another assault on the enemy lines at Port Hudson. By so doing he hoped to bring to an early end the fighting around the town.

Meantime, while Banks had been preparing for siege operations after the costly assaults of May 27, 1863, the enemy had also been busily preparing their defenses against further attacks. The Confederate line remained generally the same as before, but it had been greatly strengthened by the construc-

tion of new works and the improvement of the existing ones.

As noted earlier, a deep ravine cut through the line of bluffs along the river below Port Hudson and then ran back from the river toward the north. On the crest of the bluff, just north of this ravine, was a major Confederate earthwork known as the "Citadel." The enemy's main defensive line began on the south at the Citadel, then ran to the northeast along the northern crest of the above-mentioned ravine, and on to an angle in front of Augur's division. From this angle the line ran for about a mile, a little to the east of north, to the Plains Store road. At that point it turned back slightly to the left and continued on for about one-half mile to a strongly fortified position known as the "Priest Cap." This earthwork was at an angle of the Confederate line, which was about three-fourths of a mile north of the Clinton and Port Hudson Railroad, and was the site of Confederate batteries XIV and XV. From the Priest Cap, the works extended back to the northwest for about three-fourths of a mile, across the head of a ravine, to Fort Desperate. That part of the enemy line was in front of the positions held by Grover and Weitzel. From Fort Desperate to the river, the enemy defenses consisted only of rifle pits and dugouts.

On the morning of June 10, 1863, the Federal artillery on the siege lines, and from the gunboats on the river, opened with a heavy fire on the enemy works at Port Hudson, and this was continued throughout the day and into the night to give the impression that an attack was imminent. That night Banks ordered a strong reconnaissance all along the line. This was done for the purpose of locating the enemy batteries, and also of acquiring more information about the ground between the two lines.

At 1:00 A.M. June 11, 1863, the regiments assigned as skirmishers formed and moved forward into the darkness without any real understanding of what they were to do. As the skirmishers advanced, the enemy infantry opened with a heavy fire, and to add to their problems, at 3:00 A.M. it began to rain. All this, combined with the blackness of the night, created great confusion among the troops, and as a result they accomplished nothing. There were some losses, including many men who wandered into the enemy lines and were taken prisoner; these were particularly heavy in Weitzel's brigade and Morgan's brigade of Grover's division.

Just before noon June 13, 1863, the artillery, mortars, and gunboats again opened with an intense fire on Port Hudson, and at the end of an hour, Banks sent a formal request to Gardner for the surrender of the post. When this request was refused, the bombardment was resumed and was continued for the rest of the day. That evening Banks issued orders for an assault on the enemy works the next morning.

In anticipation of this attack, Banks had ordered Dudley to send the 50th Massachusetts of his Third Brigade and Charles J. Paine to send the 48th Massachusetts of his First Brigade of Augur's division to reinforce Dwight, and he directed Dudley, in person, to report to Grover with his 161st New York and 178th New York. When this transfer was completed, Augur was left with only five regiments of his division under his immediate command. These consisted of four regiments of Charles J. Paine's brigade and the 30th Massachusetts of Dudley's brigade.

The main attack was entrusted to Grover. who was then in command of the right wing, and it was to be directed against the fortification of the Priest Cap. This attack was to be made by Halbert E. Paine's Third Division, reinforced by the two regiments from Augur's division, and it was to be supported by Weitzel's brigade (commanded that day by Elisha B. Smith because of the illness of Stephen Thomas). Paine's approach to the enemy works was to be from the cover of a ravine at a point near Duryea's siege battery No. 12. The skirmishers were to begin the attack at 3:30 A.M. June 14, 1863.

At 2:45 A.M., Augur was to open with his artillery on the enemy works to his front, and a half-hour later he was to make a diversionary attack with his skirmishers. He was further instructed, however, that his diversion was to be changed to a full-scale attack if he felt that there was any promise of success.

A short time after 3:30 A.M., Dwight was to send out two regiments on the Federal far left and attempt to find a way into the enemy works near the river.

At the scheduled time of 3:00 A.M. June 14, all of Banks' artillery and that of the navy began their bombardment, and at 4:00 A.M. Halbert E. Paine,

leading his column in person, began his advance. Paine had formed his troops under cover of a woods in preparation for the attack. The 4th Wisconsin and 8th New Hampshire of Fearing's Second Brigade, deployed as skirmishers, led the way, and they were followed by two companies of the 4th Massachusetts, three companies of the 110th New York, and one company of the 38th Massachusetts, all carrying improvised grenades. Gooding's Third Brigade came next, immediately behind the grenade carriers, as follows: the 31st Massachusetts led the brigade and carried bags of cotton for filling the ditch in front of the parapet of the enemy works; the 38th Massachusetts and 53rd Massachusetts followed the 31st Massachusetts in line of battle; and the 156th New York brought up the rear. Fearing, with the 133rd New York and the 173rd New York, followed in rear of Gooding; and Ferris' First Brigade brought up the rear of Paine's division. Ormand F. Nims' battery, with a small detachment of engineers, was in rear of the division.

When all was ready, Paine led his column out of the woods and onto the open ground beyond. The fields ahead were gently rolling, traversed by deep ravines, and barren of trees, with only a few stumps and some underbrush to shelter the skirmishers.

When Paine's leading troops had advanced to within about 100 yards of the left (Union) face of the Priest Cap, the enemy opened fire. This caused the troops to halt, and most of them sought protection behind such shelter as was available. Some men of the 4th Wisconsin, 8th New Hampshire, 38th Massachusetts, and 53rd Massachusetts reached the ditch in front of the breastworks, and a few climbed over the parapet and into the interior of the works, but they were soon killed or taken prisoner. The rest of the advanced troops, however, were soon driven back to the cover of a low ridge, where they waited for the main body to advance. When the main column came up, it fared no better, and all attempts to advance failed.

Paine succeeded in rallying his men behind the ridge for a new charge, but at the very outset he was disabled by a severe wound, and the officers experienced difficulty in getting their men forward. There was no concerted charge by the division, but some regiments, and even smaller groups, attempted to advance. However, after suffering severe losses, they abandoned the effort. By 8:00 A.M. the fighting in this area had ended, with the complete failure of the attack, and throughout the rest of the day, the men of Paine's division remained scattered over the field in front of the left face of the Priest Cap, behind whatever cover they had been able to find.

Weitzel had been ordered to attack that morning against the right (or north) face of the Priest Cap. This attack was to have been made simultaneously with that of Paine on the left, but it was delayed by a fog that covered the ground. For this and other reasons, Weitzel was not able to advance until 7:00 A.M.

Weitzel formed his attacking column as follows: the 12th Connecticut and 75th New York of his own brigade (commanded that day by Elisha B. Smith) were deployed as skirmishers to cover the head of the column; then came the 91st New York of Morgan's First Brigade of Grover's division carrying grenades; and then the 24th Connecticut of William K. Kimball's Second Brigade of Grover's division carrying bags filled with cotton. In support of these advanced troops, and immediately to their rear, was the remainder of Weitzel's brigade, which was formed in column of regiments as follows: 8th Vermont, 114th New York, and 160th New York. Behind Weitzel was the main body of Morgan's brigade, and Birge's Third Brigade of Grover's division was in reserve.

According to Weitzel's plan for the attack, the skirmishers were to advance to the Priest Cap, with the 75th New York on the right and the 12th Connecticut on the left; the 91st New York was to advance to the ditch and throw their grenades over the parapet; the 24th Connecticut was to advance next and fill the ditch with cotton bags; and then the storming column, consisting of four brigades, was to cross the ditch and enter the enemy works. Weitzel's brigade (commanded by Smith) was to lead the storming column, and was to be followed by Morgan's brigade, Kimball's brigade, and then Birge's brigade, the latter three of Grover's division.

The only approaches to the right face of the Priest Cap were through the ravine of Big Sandy Creek and also the ravine of one of its branches. Because these streams flowed toward the Confederate entrenchments, their ravines became deeper, and the sides more difficult to climb, as they neared the Priest Cap. The two streams were separated by a ridge that in places was about 200 yards wide but generally was quite narrow.

The smaller of the two streams flowed to within a very short distance of the enemy breastworks, and then the stream, with its ravine, turned abruptly to the north, serving as an effective ditch until it joined the Big Sandy below the bastion. From the bastion on the Union right, the Priest Cap on the left, and the connecting works in front, the enemy was able to sweep with fire the larger ravine of Big Sandy Creek. The smaller ravine extended toward the south to the crest from which Paine's division had been driven, and behind which the survivors of the attack were attempting to re-form.

After considering both routes of approach, Weitzel decided to make his attack through the larger ravine. He moved out with his command to the right of the Jackson road, over rough ground and through woods, and entered the main ravine. He then made his way along the ravine to the front of the north face of the Priest Cap. When he reached this point, he was some distance in front of siege battery No. 6. Weitzel then advanced his troops up the ridge toward the enemy earthworks, which were only 20 to 50 yards distant. He succeeded in gaining the crest of the ridge under a heavy fire, but only a few men were able to advance farther.

The 75th New York, which attacked first, was soon stopped and forced to take cover. The 12th Connecticut, which had been delayed in making its approach, then came up and charged, but it too was repulsed. The 91st New York succeeded in advancing close to the works and, after tossing its grenades over the parapet, charged but was driven back.

Then Smith moved forward with the rest of Weitzel's brigade and went into action. The 114th New York rushed forward in a determined attack and was repulsed with heavy losses. Some troops of the regiment reached the ditch and remained there until they were finally withdrawn. The rest of the brigade then advanced, using the ravine as a cover, but it suffered the same fate as the troops that had gone before it. Smith was mortally wounded early in the attack and was succeeded in command of the brigade by John B. Van Petten. Van Petten led the brigade in another attack but with no success.

Weitzel then received orders from Banks to storm

the enemy works regardless of the cost, and he directed Richard E. Holcomb, then commanding Morgan's brigade, to advance with his brigade. Under a heavy fire, the brigade became somewhat disordered, and while Holcomb was attempting to rally his men, Birge came up with his brigade. Both brigades then charged. A short time later, Holcomb was killed, and then his troops, in some confusion because of a lack of leadership, the difficult terrain, and the heavy fire to which they were subjected, began to give way. Some men were able to find shelter in the ditch in front of the works, but the rest fell back. After the death of Holcomb, Simon G. Jerrard was in temporary command of Morgan's brigade.

Despite orders for further attacks on the Priest Cap, many officers objected, and the assault was not renewed. The troops remained under cover along the ridge until dark, and they then withdrew.

To divert attention from the attacks of Paine and Weitzel, Augur advanced his skirmishers at 3:45 A.M. to feign an attack against that part of the enemy line held by the 16th Arkansas. Two hours later, he sent a second line of skirmishers forward to add their fire to that of the troops already engaged. There was some sharp fighting along Augur's front that morning, but there was no serious attack. Augur's men remained out in front during the day, but they returned to their lines after dark.

Dwight, on the Federal right, did not receive his orders to attack until daylight, and he then sent the 6th Michigan and the 14th Maine of his division to the extreme Federal left to attack the Confederate works near the river and attempt to force their way past the Citadel along the waterfront. If successful, the two regiments were to move on and attack the enemy works from the rear.

The two regiments crossed a ravine and ascended a ridge close to the river at a point about one-fourth of a mile from the left of the Citadel. The 14th Maine, followed by the 6th Michigan, then advanced along the river toward the enemy works. There were, however, difficulties ahead. This route led them across the valley or ravine, mentioned earlier, that cut through the line of bluffs in front of the Citadel, and this valley was completely covered by enemy fire. Further, if Dwight's regiments could successfully cross this valley, they would still have to climb the steep bluffs beyond to reach the enemy

works. Soon after the two regiments had started their advance, they were forced to halt by the heavy enemy fire, and about an hour later they were forced to withdraw to the Mount Pleasant road.

Dwight sent the 14th Maine back to Nickerson's Third Brigade and the 6th Michigan back to Clark's First Brigade, and then ordered an advance toward the enemy works near the Citadel by the Mount Pleasant road. This was a narrow road that ran from Troth's Landing on the river, across the ravine, and along the side of Mount Pleasant to the Troth house.

Clark's brigade was selected for the attack, and it was formed for the advance along the road. Clark deployed his own 6th Michigan as skirmishers and supported them with the 128th New York. The 15th New Hampshire followed these regiments, and the 26th Connecticut brought up the rear. The 6th Michigan and 128th New York went forward in a column of companies on the Mount Pleasant road, but a short time later, the head of the column was hit by artillery fire, and the regiments were forced to deploy. Later, however, as the front narrowed, the regiments were again formed in column.

When the skirmishers reached the ravine mentioned above, about 300 yards from the Citadel, they could go no farther, and they sought shelter in the ravine, which was covered with felled trees, underbrush, vines, and briers. When Clark's main force came up, it joined the skirmishers in the ravine. Clark's troops continued to fire from the shelter of the ravine during the day, but they made no further attempts to advance. After dark, all men except the skirmishers were withdrawn to their former positions.

Nickerson's brigade, led by Lewis Benedict, attempted to move forward through a field on the right of Clark to support his attack, but it was driven back by artillery fire. Benedict then re-formed his brigade and again advanced, and a few men reached the abatis in front of the works before taking cover. The brigade remained on the field until after dark and was then withdrawn.

While all attacks on the enemy works that day ended in complete failure, Dwight did gain an advantageous position on a hill between Mount Pleasant and the river. Later, on the commanding northern slope of this hill, Joseph Bailey, Dwight's engineering officer, constructed a battery that overlooked the enemy batteries on the southern end of their defensive line. This was designated as siege battery No. 24.

Siege of Port Hudson Continued, June 15, 1863–July 8, 1863. After the repulse of June 14, 1863, Banks decided against any further assaults at Port Hudson and instead began to push forward with regular siege operations. From that time until the surrender of the garrison July 8, work continued without cessation, night and day, on the construction of approaches, parallels, and platforms for sharpshooters. While this work was going on, there was almost constant Federal artillery fire, sharpshooting by both sides, and some limited attacks at the head of the saps of zigzags.

A system of approaches was begun at four different places on the Union line, and these were extended out toward the enemy entrenchments. The main approach was started near Duryea's siege battery No. 12, which was on the front of Paine's division (then commanded by Fearing). It began several hundred yards north of the Jackson road, and from there it was pushed out through winding ravines and along the contours of a hill to the crest of a ridge overlooking the Priest Cap, which was only a few yards distant. This line was extended off to the left as a parallel in front of the enemy works and was only about 20–50 yards distant from them. A zigzag was also run forward into the ditch in front of the works.

On Grover's front, some 200 yards to the right of the main approach, a zigzag was started from a ravine near Bainbridge's siege battery No. 8, which was about one-fourth mile north and a little east of Fort Desperate. This zigzag was extended out toward the ditch of Fort Desperate. The digging on this approach had to be done behind barrels filled with dirt and behind cotton bales.

On June 17, 1863, David C. Houston, who had been directing siege operations, was forced to give up this work because of ill health, and he was succeeded as chief engineer of the army by John C. Palfrey.

On Dwight's southern front, a covered way was constructed that began at Roy's siege battery No. 20, just north of the Troth house, and ran along the side of Mount Pleasant to the hill near the river where Bailey's siege battery No. 24 was constructed by June 20, 1863. This trench connected siege batteries Nos. 20, 21, 22, 23, and 24. From a point near the river, close to battery No. 24, a zigzag was run out from the covered way, across the ravine, and to the foot of the hill below the Citadel. The zigzag approached to within 100 yards of the enemy works.

A secondary approach, which began in a ravine in front of siege battery No. 18, just south of the Gibbon house, ran out to a parallel facing Confederate battery XXVII, and about 350 yards distant from it. This battery occupied an outwork in front of the southeastern angle of the enemy works.

The fourth major approach began in a ravine near the Slaughter house and ran out about one-fourth mile to the southwest to siege battery No. 16, where the guns of Rawles' battery and one other gun were posted. This position was within 400 yards of the enemy line.

As the work on the siege lines continued, both sides suffered greatly from the terrible conditions prevailing at that time. These included a burning sun overhead, almost unbearable heat, high humidity, bad water, lack of proper food, exhausting work, the strain of constant vigilance, and physical disorders such as sunstroke, malaria, and diarrhea. As a result, there was a serious loss in the number of troops fit for duty, and also a general loss in effectiveness in those who were still in ranks.

During June 1863, in addition to the work of pushing forward the approaches, there was some local fighting along the entrenchments. At 6:00 P.M. June 29, Grover attempted to drive back some Confederate troops that occupied an outwork in front of the main line by attacking down the exterior ditch. He was unsuccessful, but later that night he attacked again. Some troops reached the ditch, but all were recalled before daylight.

Just before sundown June 29, 1863, Dwight ordered Nickerson to attack the Citadel with the 165th New York of his brigade and the 6th Michigan of Clark's brigade. These troops moved out through the approach mentioned above that ran from siege battery No. 24, across the ravine, to the base of the Citadel hill. On emerging from the approach, the troops charged up the hill, but under a heavy fire from above they were forced to take cover in depressions on the hillside. They remained on the slopes of the hill all night and returned to their lines the next morning. Late that afternoon, June 30, Dwight ordered the same two regiments to attack the Citadel again. This attack fared no better than the first, and the troops were withdrawn.

Following these failures, Joseph Bailey began to dig a tunnel under the Citadel in preparation for laying a mine. Grover also began tunneling under the Priest Cap for a similar purpose. On July 7, 1863, the Federal approaches, parallels, and mines were all completed, and the troops were made ready for a major assault, but this was postponed for two days because of bad weather.

Then, on July 7, 1863, Banks learned of the surrender of Vicksburg on July 4, and he immediately informed Gardner of this development. After Gardner was assured that Vicksburg had indeed surrendered, a cease-fire was arranged at 12:30 A.M. July 8. The agreement of surrender was reached at 2:00 that afternoon, but because of the lateness of the hour, the ceremony was postponed until the next morning. With the completion of the official surrender, which began at 7:00 A.M. July 9, the siege of Port Hudson ended.

The organization of Banks' forces during the operations about Port Hudson was as follows:

NINETEENTH CORPS, Nathaniel P. Banks

First Division, Christopher C. Augur
First Brigade, Edward P. Chapin, to May 27, 1863, killed
Charles J. Paine
Second Brigade, Godfrey Weitzel
Stephen Thomas, sick
Elisha B. Smith, June 14, 1863, mortally wounded
John B. Van Petten
Third Brigade, Nathan A. M. Dudley

Note. When the army arrived at Port Hudson, Weitzel was assigned command of the right wing, and Thomas assumed command of Second Brigade. Although Thomas was sick during the assaults of June 14, 1863, he joined the brigade and aided in its direction for a time. Weitzel also commanded a provisional division, consisting of his own Second Brigade, First Division and Jacob Van Zandt's First Brigade, Fourth Division.

Artillery
1st Indiana Heavy Artillery (seven companies), John A. Keith
1st Battery, Maine Light Artillery, John E. Morton
6th Battery, Massachusetts Light Artillery, John F. Phelps
12th Battery, Massachusetts Light Artillery (one section), Edwin M. Chamberlin

18th Battery, New York Light Artillery, Albert G. Mack
Battery A, 1st United States Artillery, Edmund C. Bainbridge
Battery G, 5th United States Artillery, Jacob B. Rawles

Unattached
1st Louisiana Engineers, Corps d'Afrique, Justin Hodge
1st Louisiana Native Guards, Chauncey J. Bassett
3rd Louisiana Native Guards, John A. Nelson
1st Louisiana Cavalry, Harai Robinson
2nd Rhode Island Cavalry, Augustus W. Corliss

Second Division, Thomas W. Sherman, to May 27, 1863, wounded
George L. Andrews, May 27, 1863
Frank S. Nickerson, May 28–30, 1863
William Dwight
First Brigade, Neal Dow, to May 27, 1863, wounded and later captured
David S. Cowles, May 27, 1863, killed
Thomas S. Clark
Third Brigade, Frank S. Nickerson
Lewis Benedict
Artillery, William Roy
1st Indiana Heavy Artillery (one company), William Roy
21st Battery, New York Light Artillery, James Barnes
1st Battery, Vermont Light Artillery, George T. Hebard

Note 1. Second Brigade was serving in the Defenses of New Orleans.
Note 2. Benedict was in command of Third Brigade June 14, 1863.

Third Division, Halbert E. Paine, to June 14, 1863, wounded
Hawkes Fearing, Jr.
First Brigade, Timothy Ingraham, to June 2, 1863
Samuel P. Ferris
Second Brigade, Hawkes Fearing, Jr., to June 14, 1863
John H. Allcot
Lewis M. Peck
Third Brigade, Oliver P. Gooding
Artillery, Richard C. Duryea
4th Battery, Massachusetts Light Artillery, Frederick W. Reinhard
Battery F, 1st United States Artillery, Richard C. Duryea

2nd Battery, Vermont Light Artillery, Pythagoras E. Holcomb

Fourth Division, Cuvier Grover
First Brigade, William Dwight
Jacob Van Zandt, to early June 1863
Joseph S. Morgan
Richard E. Holcomb, June 14, 1863, killed
Simon G. Jerrard, June 14, 1863
Joseph S. Morgan
Second Brigade, William K. Kimball
Third Brigade, Henry W. Birge
Artillery, Henry W. Closson
2nd Battery, Massachusetts Light Artillery, Ormand F. Nims
Battery L, 1st United States Artillery, Henry W. Closson
Battery C, 2nd United States Artillery, Theodore Bradley

Note. The command of First Brigade is somewhat confusing. Dwight did not command his brigade at Port Hudson. During his absence at Vicksburg, while the army advanced to Port Hudson, the brigade was commanded by Jacob Van Zandt. When Dwight returned to the army, he was assigned command of a temporary division consisting of his own brigade and Weitzel's brigade, and Van Zandt retained command of First Brigade. Further, during the assaults of June 14, 1863, Morgan, the brigade commander, was on the field, but Holcomb, and later Jerrard, were ordered to take the brigade into action.

Cavalry, Benjamin H. Grierson
6th Illinois Cavalry, Reuben Loomis
7th Illinois Cavalry, Edward Prince
1st Louisiana Cavalry (detachment)
2nd Massachusetts Cavalry Battalion
14th New York Cavalry (detachment)

Corps d'Afrique, Daniel Ullmann

Note. Ullmann's command consisted of the 6th, 7th, 8th, 9th, and 10th infantry regiments, but at the time of the Port Hudson campaign, they were not yet fully organized.

BATTLE OF PRAIRIE GROVE, ARKANSAS DECEMBER 7, 1862

At the end of November 1862, James G. Blunt, commanding the Union Army of the Frontier, was with his First Division on Cane Hill, about twelve miles southwest of Fayetteville, Arkansas, in the northwestern part of the state. Francis J. Herron, commanding James Totten's Second Division (then temporarily under Daniel Huston, Jr.) and his own Third Division of the Army of the Frontier, was in camp near Wilson's Creek, southwest of Springfield, Missouri. At about the same time, Thomas C. Hindman had assembled a Confederate army, which he called First Army Corps of the Trans-Mississippi Army, on the Arkansas River in the vicinity of Van Buren, Arkansas. For details of the organizations and movements of the two armies prior to the Battle of Prairie Grove, see Army of the Frontier.

Cane Hill was a ridge about eight miles long and five miles wide, which was located in the southwestern part of Washington County, Arkansas, just north of the base of the Boston Mountains. There were three villages on Cane Hill called Russellville, Boonsboro, and Newburg, and these extended rather close together for three or four miles along the road to Fayetteville. The main part of Blunt's division was in and around Newburg.

There were three roads running northward from Van Buren that were of significance in the troops' movements that led to the Battle of Prairie Grove. One of these was the Telegraph Road (sometimes called the Wire Road), which ran northward out of Van Buren and generally followed mountain ridges to Fayetteville. Another was the Cove Creek road. It turned off to the Federal left (north) from the Telegraph Road at a place called Oliver's, about nineteen miles from Van Buren, and ran up the valley of Cove Creek to the base of the mountains. It then crossed the mountains and the prairies beyond and entered Fayetteville from the southwest. At the Morrow house, fifteen miles north of Oliver's, a branch of the Cove Creek road turned off to the Federal left and ran on to Newburg, seven miles distant. The third road branched off to the left from the Telegraph Road twelve miles from Van Buren and generally followed the present-day Arkansas-Oklahoma state line to Evansville, Arkansas, and from there on to the north through Cincinnati, Arkansas and Maysville to Fort Scott, Kansas. From Evansville, a road ran eastward through the Cane Hill area and on to Fayetteville.

On December 3, 1862, Hindman began his march northward from Van Buren toward Cane Hill, where he expected to defeat Blunt's isolated force. John S. Marmaduke's cavalry division, which was posted well in advance at Dripping Springs, moved out ahead of the infantry, with Joseph O. Shelby's brigade on the Cove Creek road, Emmett McDonald's brigade on the Telegraph Road, and Charles A. Carroll's brigade on the road to the west that ran northward along the state line. Hindman, with the infantry divisions of Francis A. Shoup and Daniel M. Frost, marched up the Telegraph Road, then turned off on the Cove Creek road at Oliver's, arriving at Morrow's on December 6. Before dawn that morning, Shelby had attacked the 2nd Kansas of Blunt's command, which was on outpost duty, and had driven it back to within two miles of the main force at Newburg. Blunt held Cane Hill with William Weer's Second Brigade and William F. Cloud's Third Brigade, but Frederick Salomon's First Brigade was at Rhea's Mills, eight miles to the north, where a large supply train had just arrived from Fort Scott.

On the morning of December 3, 1862, Blunt informed Herron at Wilson's Creek of Hindman's advance, and he directed him to move forward with all possible speed to Cane Hill. Herron's cavalry that was at Cassville led the way, arriving within supporting distance of Blunt December 5. Herron's main column crossed the old Pea Ridge Battlefield that same day, and that evening Herron received an order from Blunt to send forward all of his cavalry to Cane Hill. Herron sent forward the 10th Illinois Cavalry, the 1st Iowa Cavalry, the 8th Missouri Cavalry, and the 1st Battalion of the 2nd Wisconsin Cavalry, all under the command of Dudley Wickersham, and they reached Blunt in safety.

At midnight December 6, 1862, Herron's first troops arrived at Fayetteville, which was only one day's march from Cane Hill. Huston's Second Division, which brought up the rear of the column, came into Fayetteville at sunrise December 7.

During the night of December 6, 1862, Hindman, having learned of the approach of Herron's divisions, decided to make a feint on Blunt's division at Cane Hill, and march to the right with his main force on the Cove Creek road to intercept Herron and destroy him, before turning to the west to attack Blunt. At 4:00 A.M. December 7, Hindman left Carroll's Arkansas Cavalry Brigade (then commanded by James C. Monroe) to occupy Blunt's

attention, and he sent Marmaduke with Shelby's and McDonald's cavalry brigades across the mountain to the junction of the Cove Creek road with the Fayetteville–Cane Hill road, which was between Blunt and Herron. Hindman followed the cavalry with the infantry divisions of Shoup and Frost, with Shoup's division in the lead.

On the morning of December 7, 1862, M. La Rue Harrison's 1st Arkansas Cavalry and Eliphalet Bredett's 7th Missouri Cavalry were advancing from Fayetteville on the road to Cane Hill to join Blunt, when about daylight they encountered Marmaduke's cavalry division at Walnut Grove. Marmaduke immediately charged and in a sharp engagement routed the two regiments, driving them back in disorder to within six miles of Fayetteville, where about 7:00 A.M. they met the head of Herron's main column, which was then about four miles from Illinois Creek. The pursuing Confederates were soon stopped by Union artillery and infantry, and they then fell back beyond Illinois Creek and joined Hindman's infantry divisions.

Shoup's division arrived near the designated road junction about 10:00 A.M., and when he learned that Marmaduke was falling back from his pursuit of the Federal cavalry, he placed his troops in position to meet an expected attack from the direction of Fayetteville. When Hindman came up, he decided to form his command on the defensive position selected by Shoup instead of pushing on to meet Herron as originally planned.

The position where Hindman formed his line was along the brow of a densely wooded hill that fell off sharply on the northern slope to a fairly level stretch of land called Crawford's Prairie (also called Rhea's Mills Valley), on which there were a number of large fields enclosed with fences, some of which had been planted in corn. The valley was about one-half mile in width, and rising from the northern side was another range of hills.

The road running from Fayetteville to Cane Hill, upon which Herron was approaching, entered the area where the battle was to be fought from the northeast and continued on to the southwest. It crossed Illinois Creek about three-fourths of a mile from the hill, then ran across the eastern end of Crawford's Prairie and passed over the midpoint of the hill where Hindman formed his line, still running in a southwesterly direction. Beside this road, on the crest of the hill, stood Prairie Grove Church, which was to give its name to the battle. The road from Cove Creek, on which Hindman was approaching, joined the Fayetteville–Cane Hill road near the church.

Hindman reached the hill about 10:00 A.M., but he was too late to attack Herron before help could arrive. He was between Herron and Blunt, but Blunt was only four or five miles to his left and rear, and Herron was only about a mile or so to his front and right and was still advancing. Hindman appears to have changed his mind about attacking, because he began to put his troops in position for defense. He placed Shoup's division across the Fayetteville–Cane Hill road, on the hill, and facing toward the ford at Illinois Creek. When Marmaduke returned from his pursuit of the Union cavalry, he placed Shelby's dismounted brigade on the hill to the right of Shoup, and sent McDonald's brigade, still mounted, around the eastern foot of the hill to watch the enemy's right flank. Lane's Texans, then commanded by R. P. Crump, were on the left flank.

Frost's division, to which had been added a Texas brigade and a Missouri regiment, both commanded by John S. Roane, was held in reserve until Blunt's movements had been determined.

Herron's column arrived on the hills above the ford at Illinois Creek before noon, and to feel the enemy's position, he sent Joseph Foust's Battery E, 1st Missouri Light Artillery, supported by the 94th Illinois of William W. Orme's Second Brigade of Herron's Third Division, across the creek on the Fayetteville–Cane Hill road. After opening fire, the battery and its supports were quickly driven back across the creek. Herron was thus convinced that he was facing Hindman's entire force, and he immediately prepared for an attack. He ordered Orme to cross at the ford with his brigade and take position there, and at the same time he directed Henry Bertram to follow with his brigade and form his infantry on the right of Orme.

He sent Huston, commanding Second Division, to cut a road through the woods to the creek at a point about one-half mile north of the road. When this task was completed, Huston crossed with David Murphy's Battery F, 1st Missouri Light Artillery and placed it in a commanding position on the hills north of Crawford's Prairie. The battery was supported by the 37th Illinois and the 20th Iowa of

William McE. Dye's Second Brigade and the 26th Indiana of John G. Clark's First Brigade of Second Division. Murphy's battery opened fire about noon and promptly drew a return fire from the enemy. Then Frank Backof's Battery L, 1st Missouri Light Artillery, Herman Borris' Battery A, 2nd Illinois Light Artillery, and Joseph Foust's Battery E, 1st Missouri Light Artillery were also sent across the creek, and these were supported by the 19th Iowa and 94th Illinois of William W. Orme's Second Brigade and the 20th Wisconsin of Henry Bertram's First Brigade of Herron's Third Division.

When Huston's division and Herron's division were formed in line of battle, the infantry and artillery advanced across Crawford's Prairie toward Hindman's position in front of Prairie Grove Church. When within about 100 yards of the hill, the 20th Wisconsin and 19th Iowa were ordered to charge William D. Blocher's enemy battery, which Shoup had placed near the William Morton house. They quickly overran the battery and moved on up to the crest of the hill. When they arrived within sixty or seventy yards of the enemy line, James F. Fagan's brigade and a part of Dandridge McRae's brigade of Shoup's division, and Shelby's brigade of Marmaduke's division charged and drove the Union regiments back down the hill and out onto the prairie, and they recaptured the battery.

Herron then ordered Huston to attack, and Huston led forward, in person, the 26th Indiana of his First Brigade and the 37th Illinois of Second Brigade. His regiments passed through the troops who were retiring from the first attack, then advanced up the hill against Shoup's brigades, which were supported by R. G. Shaver's brigade of Frost's division. Huston's attack was soon repulsed, and the troops retired to a position on the prairie beyond musket range of the enemy on the hill. They remained in that position until the close of the action.

Meantime, Blunt had been active since early that morning. At 7:00 A.M. Blunt's Second Brigade and Third Brigade exchanged fire with Monroe's cavalry south of his position at Cane Hill, and he then realized that Hindman with his main force had moved toward Fayetteville to interpose his command between Herron and Cane Hill. Then before 10:00 A.M., Blunt started with his division toward Fayetteville. Dudley Wickersham, with the cavalry, was in the lead, and by mistake he took the road to

Rhea's Mill instead of the direct road toward Fay-etteville. Not wishing to separate his command, Blunt followed the cavalry with his infantry to Rhea's Mill.

Blunt, with his First Division, was at Rhea's Mill, about five miles west of Prairie Grove Church, when he heard the sounds of Herron's and Hindman's artillery to the east. He then left Freder-ick Salomon's First Brigade to guard the trains and marched with William Weer's Second Brigade and William F. Cloud's Third Brigade to the sound of the guns.

Blunt arrived on the field about 2:00 P.M. and advanced onto the western end of Crawford's Prai-rie, about one mile from Hindman's position. He formed his command in line of battle, with his left connecting with Dye's Second Brigade, Second Di-vision, which was on the right of Herron's line. Blunt then posted John W. Rabb's 2nd Battery, In-diana Light Artillery, Marcus D. Tenney's 1st Bat-tery, Kansas Light Artillery, and Henry Hopkins' 2nd Battery, Kansas Light Artillery, and they were soon in action.

The 1st Iowa Cavalry, the 10th Illinois Cavalry, and a battalion of the 2nd Wisconsin Cavalry of Bertram's brigade, and the 8th Missouri Cavalry of Orme's brigade, all of Herron's Third Division; and the 3rd Wisconsin Cavalry of Salomon's brigade of Blunt's First Division were on the extreme right of the Union line, where they guarded the right flank and the road running back to the wagon train at Rhea's Mills.

When Blunt's troops appeared, Hindman sent Frost's division, which had been held in reserve, to the left of Shoup's line on the hill.

Under the cover of a heavy artillery fire, the Union infantry advanced all along the line. Blunt's division immediately attacked Frost's line, and Her-ron renewed his attack on Shoup and Marmaduke.

Weer's brigade attacked on the right of Blunt's line, and Cloud's brigade on the left. The 20th Iowa of Dye's brigade, led by Dye himself, attacked on the left of Cloud's brigade. Several attempts were made to reach the crest of the hill, but each of these was repulsed.

By 3:00 P.M. virtually all of Blunt's Army of the Frontier was engaged, and they continued the battle for another three hours, until the fighting ended at dark. A final attack on Shoup's position succeeded

in driving back the right of the enemy line out of the woods on the hill and onto the prairie to the south, but upon arriving on the open ground beyond the woods, the Union troops were struck by such a devastating fire that they were driven back, and they were not in action again that day.

At dark the Federal troops withdrew to a line that was beyond the range of the enemy on the hill, where they bivouacked for the night. Hindman had resisted all attempts to drive him from the ground around Prairie Grove Church during the afternoon, but realizing that he was in a difficult situation, he decided to withdraw that night, and when the Union troops awakened the next morning, they found that the enemy had departed.

The organization of the Union troops at the Battle of Prairie Grove December 7, 1862 was as follows:

ARMY OF THE FRONTIER, James G. Blunt

First Division, James G. Blunt
  First Brigade, Frederick Salomon
  Second Brigade, William Weer
  Third Brigade, William F. Cloud

Note. Marcus D. Tenney's 1st Battery, Kansas Light Artillery was attached to Second Brigade; and John W. Rabb's 2nd Battery, Indiana Light Artillery and Henry Hopkins' Battery, Kansas Light Artillery were attached to Third Brigade. Hopkins' Battery was manned by Company B, 2nd Kansas Cavalry, and was later designated as 3rd Battery, Kansas Light Artillery.

Second Division, Daniel Huston, Jr.
  First Brigade, John G. Clark
  Second Brigade, William McE. Dye

Note. Herman Borris' Battery A, 2nd Illinois Light Artillery (called the Peoria Battery) was attached to First Brigade, and David Murphy's Battery F, 1st Missouri Light Artillery was attached to Second Brigade.

Third Division, Francis J. Herron
  First Brigade, Henry Bertram
  Second Brigade, William W. Orme

Note. Frank Backof's Battery L, 1st Missouri Light Artillery was attached to First Brigade, and Joseph Foust's Battery E, 1st Missouri Light Artillery was at-tached to Second Brigade.

Cavalry Brigade (temporary), Dudley Wickersham

Note. Wickersham's cavalry brigade was organized temporarily from a battalion of the 2nd Wisconsin Cav-

alry of First Brigade and the 8th Missouri Cavalry of Second Brigade.

Unattached
    1st Arkansas Cavalry, M. La Rue Harrison
    14th Missouri State Militia Cavalry, John M. Richardson

PRICE'S MISSOURI EXPEDITION AUGUST 29, 1864– DECEMBER 2, 1864

As early as June 1864, E. Kirby Smith, commanding the Confederate Trans-Mississippi Department, had considered the possibility of an invasion of Missouri from Arkansas. In addition, Sterling Price, commanding the District of Arkansas at Camden, had hoped to bring relief to the Southern sympathizers in Missouri, and to organize the many guerrilla bands in the state for effective service there, and he had been urging that he be allowed to lead an army into Missouri. Finally, on August 4, 1864, Smith ordered Price to prepare to move with his entire cavalry force into Missouri. He was instructed to advance to Saint Louis and capture the supplies and military stores there and then, when it became necessary, to withdraw across the state and return through Kansas and the Indian Territory. He was to gather up all horses, mules, cattle, and military stores as he went, and return with them to Arkansas.

On August 27, 1864, Price turned over the command of his district to John B. Magruder, and two days later, at Princeton, Arkansas, he assumed command of the expeditionary force, which was composed exclusively of cavalry, and which he called the Army of Missouri.

At Princeton, Price assembled the divisions of James F. Fagan and John S. Marmaduke, and on August 30, 1864 he marched to the northwest to Dardenelle, where he crossed the Arkansas River September 6. He then marched on to the northeast, crossed White River, and arrived at Batesville, Arkansas September 13. From there Price moved to Powhatan, where the greater part of Joseph O. Shelby's division joined him on September 17.

Price then advanced to the state line in three columns and entered Missouri September 19, 1864. Fagan's division marched in the center by way of Martinsburg, Reeves' Station, and Greenville; Marmaduke to the right through Bloomfield; and Shelby to the left by Doniphan and Patterson. The three columns were to reunite at Fredericktown, Missouri, about twenty-one miles southeast of Pilot Knob, which they did September 24–25.

Early in September 1864, when William S. Rosecrans, then commanding the Department of the Missouri, learned of the impending invasion, he began preparations for the defense of the state. At that time Andrew J. Smith was aboard transports with his Third Division, Right Wing, Sixteenth Corps, on his way from Memphis, Tennessee to join William T. Sherman's Army in northern Georgia. Smith was stopped at Cairo, Illinois on September 6, and on September 9 he was ordered to Saint Louis. On September 13 he arrived at Jefferson Barracks, below the city, and reported to Rosecrans. At that time Third Division was commanded by William T. Shaw, but on October 29, while at Harrisonville, Missouri, he left for muster out and was succeeded in command of the division by David Moore.

Joseph A. Mower's First Division, Right Wing, Sixteenth Corps was also on its way to join Sherman when it was diverted by orders from Washington to reinforce Frederick Steele in Arkansas. Steele then directed Mower to pursue Price. Mower's troops marched to Cape Girardeau, but they did not arrive there until October 6, 1864, and by that time Price had arrived at a point between Franklin and Jefferson City. Mower then moved on to Saint Louis, where he arrived October 8. Price left Fredericktown September 26, 1864, and with the divisions of Marmaduke and Fagan marched toward Pilot Knob, the southern terminus of the Saint Louis and Iron Mountain Railroad, eighty-six miles from Saint Louis. Price advanced by way of Arcadia, where he spent the night. He sent Shelby by way of Farmington to destroy the railroad north of Pilot Knob.

Attack on Fort Davidson, Pilot Knob, Missouri, September 27, 1864. On the morning of September 27, 1864, Price resumed his advance, with Fagan's division in the lead, and during the morning forced his way through the gap between Pilot Knob Mountain and Shepherd's Mountain and into the lower end of the valley where Pilot Knob and nearby Fort

Davidson were situated. Fort Davidson was a small hexagonal earthwork that had been erected to guard the supplies that were stored in Pilot Knob. It mounted four siege guns and three howitzers, and it was located about 300 yards from the base of Pilot Knob and about 1,000 yards from the gap between Pilot Knob and Shepherd's Mountain.

September 24, 1864, Rosecrans, having learned that Price had entered Missouri, ordered Thomas Ewing, Jr., commander of the District of Saint Louis, which included Pilot Knob, to take James I. Gilbert's Second Brigade of Andrew J. Smith's Third Division, Sixteenth Corps, which was then at Jefferson Barracks, to patrol and garrison the Saint Louis and Iron Mountain Railroad. Ewing left most of the brigade at De Soto and proceeded on, arriving at Pilot Knob on the morning of September 26 with five companies of the 14th Iowa Infantry under William J. Campbell.

James Wilson, of the 3rd Missouri State Militia Cavalry, commanded the Third Sub-district of the District of Saint Louis, with his headquarters at Pilot Knob. Wilson had withdrawn his outposts from Patterson, Centerville, Fredericktown, and Farmington and assembled them at Pilot Knob. His force consisted of six companies of the 47th Missouri Infantry, one company of the 50th Missouri Infantry, six companies of the 3rd Missouri State Militia Cavalry, one company of the 2nd Missouri State Militia Cavalry, one company of the 1st Missouri State Militia Infantry, and William C. F. Montgomery's Battery H, 2nd Missouri Light Artillery. In addition there was the detachment of the 14th Iowa that came with Ewing.

At 2:00 P.M. September 27, 1864, the enemy launched a violent attack on the southern and eastern faces of Fort Davidson, with Marmaduke advancing on the Confederate left from Shepherd's Mountain and Fagan on the right from the slopes of Pilot Knob. This attack was repulsed with heavy losses, and the fighting finally ended at dark.

* * * * * * * * * *

Ewing, expecting the attack to be renewed the next morning and acting under orders to retire if attacked by Price's army, began to withdraw from the fort at 3:00 A.M. September 28, 1864. Before leaving, he arranged for the magazine to be blown up two hours after his withdrawal, and this was done. Ewing retreated by way of Harmony and Osage and arrived at Leasburg, on the railroad from Saint Louis to Rolla, at sundown September 29. There he prepared a fortified position.

Price did not begin the pursuit until noon September 28, 1864, and Marmaduke and Shelby did not arrive in front of Ewing's position at Leasburg until the morning of September 30. They did not attack, however, and the next morning Ewing was gone. Cavalry reinforcements from John McNeil's District of Rolla had reached Ewing, and he then withdrew toward Rolla.

Meantime, Price had taken Fagan's division and marched toward Saint Louis. He arrived at Richwood, about forty miles southwest of the city. At that time Andrew J. Smith, with Shaw's Third Division, was in position just across the Meramec River, supported by three brigades of the Enrolled Missouri Militia. Price then decided that the city was too strong to be taken by assault, and he did not approach any closer to Saint Louis during the campaign.

On October 1, 1864, Price met Marmaduke and Shelby, who were returning from their unsuccessful pursuit of Ewing from Pilot Knob, near Saint Clair, and the latter moved on that day to Union, sixteen miles west of Franklin. On October 2, Price and Fagan joined Marmaduke and Shelby at Union, and together they marched on through Mount Sterling and Moreau, arriving near Jefferson City on October 7.

Meantime, Rosecrans had called out the Missouri State Militia, and had ordered John McNeil, commanding the District of Rolla; John B. Sanborn, commanding the District of Southwest Missouri; Egbert B. Brown, commanding the District of Central Missouri; and Clinton B. Fisk, commanding the District of North Missouri, to move with all haste the available cavalry from their districts to Jefferson City. Brown had hurriedly collected about 2,500 from the country west of Sedalia and was then engaged in preparing the defenses of the capital. The concentration of these troops had been completed by October 6, 1864, and Fisk, as the senior officer present, assumed command. Fisk immediately organized his command into four brigades, which were commanded by Brown, McNeil, Sanborn, and Franklin W. Hickox of the Enrolled

Missouri Militia. The first three of these brigades were assigned to the fortified line about Jefferson City, with McNeil's brigade on the right, Sanborn's brigade on the center, and Brown's brigade on the left. Hickox's brigade was held in reserve.

After examining Fisk's position at Jefferson City, Price decided that it was too strong to attack, and he then moved on west toward Boonville. When the enemy retired from before the town, Fisk followed along the California road with the cavalry of the garrison and was soon engaged with the rear guard.

At 10:30 A.M. October 8, 1864, a short time after Price's withdrawal, Alfred Pleasonton arrived at Jefferson City and assumed command of the troops there. Pleasonton had been on leave of absence in the East at the time that Price entered Missouri, and had been ordered to return to the army. Pleasonton then assigned to Sanborn the available cavalry at Jefferson City, and also Charles H. Thurber's Battery H, 2nd Missouri Light Artillery, to which a section of Battery L, 2nd Missouri Light Artillery was attached. Sanborn then organized the 4,100 cavalrymen of his command into three provisional brigades as follows:

First Brigade, John F. Philips
Second Brigade, John L. Beveridge
Third Brigade, Joseph J. Gravely

Sanborn was directed to follow Price and attempt to delay his march as much as possible until other Federal troops could be brought up. Philips' First Brigade moved out on the Springfield road toward Versailles and Warsaw, and Beveridge's Second Brigade and Gravely's Third Brigade marched along the railroad toward California and Tipton.

Rosecrans ordered Andrew J. Smith, who was moving west on the road from Saint Louis, to move as rapidly as possible to Jefferson City. Mower's division, which had arrived at Saint Louis from Cape Girardeau, left Saint Louis on river transports for Jefferson City October 7–8 and arrived there October 15–18. En route, at Saint Charles on October 11, Mower left the division (ordered September 27) to report to William T. Sherman, commander of the Military Division of the Mississippi. That same day Joseph J. Woods assumed command of Mower's First Division, Right Wing, Sixteenth Corps. After arriving at Jefferson City, Woods pro-

ceeded on by rail with his division to a point near Sedalia; he joined Smith and Shaw's division at Sedalia October 20.

Edward F. Winslow, with a part of his Second Division, Cavalry Corps of the District of West Tennessee, had earlier been sent to Arkansas, where it joined Mower's division. He was also ordered to take his command to Saint Louis, and he arrived there October 8–10, 1864. Winslow was then ordered to move west and join the forces pursuing Price. The detachment of First Brigade (then commanded by Samuel E. W. Simonson in place of Joseph Karge, who was sick) embarked for Jefferson City on October 11. Winslow, with George Duffield's Second Brigade, left Saint Louis that same day; he marched westward by way of Washington, Russellville, and California, reaching Jefferson, twenty miles beyond California, on October 16. There he was ordered to join Pleasonton without delay. Only a part of Winslow's Second Brigade ever joined him, the rest having been diverted by Pleasonton's orders.

Edward C. Pike, commander of the First Military District, Enrolled Missouri Militia, was given the responsibility of guarding the Federal line of communications between Saint Louis and Jefferson City with his three brigades of Enrolled Missouri Militia.

Sanborn pursued Price's column through Versailles to Boonville, which Price had occupied October 10, 1864. Sanborn was too weak to attack, and he withdrew to California, where he was joined by Winslow's brigade, then temporarily commanded by Edwin C. Catherwood, October 14.

On the night of October 12, 1864, Price left Boonville and moved on west toward Lexington. Sanborn kept pace on a parallel route to the south.

While Price's main column moved on, Shelby, with a part of his division and John B. Clark's brigade of Marmaduke's division, crossed the Missouri River at Arrow Rock and on October 15, 1864 captured Glasgow, where it was reported that about 5,000 guns had been stored. After about seven hours of fighting, Chester Harding, Jr., with about 550 men, was forced to surrender. Also on October 15, M. Jeff. Thompson, with another detachment of Shelby's division, captured Sedalia.

While Shelby, Clark, and Thompson were thus engaged, Price marched on through Marshall and Waverly to Lexington without encountering many

Union troops. Most of the forces in western Missouri and eastern Kansas had been assembled in and near Kansas City.

In September 1864, when Price invaded Missouri, Samuel R. Curtis, commanding the Department of Kansas, had under his command only a few thousand United States Volunteers, and most of these were widely scattered over western Kansas and eastern Colorado Territory, where they were engaged in protecting the roads and the scattered posts from Indians.

On September 17, 1864, Curtis, who was then at Fort Leavenworth, learned of Price's invasion, and he immediately began preparations to defend Kansas if that should become necessary. He ordered as many men as could be spared from the posts on the frontier to assemble at Kansas City, and he ordered James G. Blunt, who was then on an Indian expedition, to bring his command to Fort Leavenworth.

The only volunteer troops that were then along the Kansas-Missouri border were the 5th, 11th, and 16th Kansas Cavalry, the 2nd Colorado Cavalry, and a part of the 3rd Wisconsin Cavalry.

On October 9, 1864, Governor Thomas Carney, after a considerable delay, called out the Kansas State Militia to support Curtis' force. George W. Deitzler, commander of the Kansas State Militia, established his headquarters at Olathe, Kansas on October 10 and began to move the militia regiments toward the border, where they were assembled near Shawneetown.

Blunt, with his command, was at Fort Larned when he received Curtis' order to march to Fort Leavenworth. Blunt arrived there October 8, 1864, and two days later moved to Olathe. Upon arrival there, he was ordered by Curtis to relieve George Sykes in command of the District of South Kansas. Blunt immediately assumed command of the district and established his headquarters at Paola, and in the field.

On October 11, 1864, Curtis took the field in person, and on October 13 he designated his command as the Army of the Border. He assigned Blunt to command the right wing, which was to assemble at Hickman Mills, and assigned Deitzler to command the left wing, which consisted of Kansas State Militia, and which was to concentrate at Shawneetown on the Kansas state line.

At daylight October 13, 1864, on orders from Curtis, Blunt marched toward Hickman Mills, Missouri with the 11th Kansas Volunteer Cavalry, detachments of the 5th and 16th Kansas Volunteer Cavalry, William D. McLain's Independent Battery, Colorado Artillery, and a part of the 5th and 10th Regiments of Kansas State Militia (mounted). He arrived at Hickman Mills with his command at 11:00 A.M. October 14, 1864, and the next day Charles R. Jennison and Charles W. Blair arrived with the 15th Kansas, a battalion of the 3rd Wisconsin Cavalry, detachments of the 14th Kansas, the 6th Regiment Kansas State Militia, and a section of the 2nd Battery, Kansas Light Artillery.

On October 15, 1864, Blunt organized his command as the First Division, Army of the Border as follows:

First Division, Army of the Border, James G. Blunt
   First Brigade, Charles R. Jennison
   Second Brigade, Thomas Moonlight
   Third Brigade, Charles W. Blair

William H. M. Fishback was assigned immediate command of the State Militia, with orders to report to Blair, but this arrangement did not last long.

At 7:00 P.M. October 16, 1864, Blunt marched with his First Brigade and Second Brigade to Pleasant Hill, where he arrived at 1:00 A.M. October 17. At daylight that morning, he moved eastward on the Warrensburg road, but upon learning that Shelby had captured the town, Blunt sent back the militia and proceeded on to Holden, where he arrived at 11:00 A.M. There he learned that Price was near the Missouri River, below Waverly, that Sanborn's cavalry was at or near Dunksburg, twelve miles northwest of Sedalia, and that Andrew J. Smith's infantry was at California, within supporting distance. At Holden, Blunt asked that his Third Brigade and the 2nd Colorado Cavalry and 16th Kansas Cavalry be sent up to support him. Then he marched toward Lexington at 7:00 that evening; Moonlight's brigade arrived there at 10:00 on the morning of October 18. Enemy troops approaching from the east arrived before the town the next morning.

Earlier, on October 17, 1864, James H. Ford, who was in command of his own 2nd Colorado Cavalry and the 16th Kansas Cavalry at Independence, Missouri, had sent J. Nelson Smith with a detachment of the two regiments to Lexington, Missouri. He occupied the town that day but withdrew at daylight the next morning to Independence before Blunt arrived.

Meantime, Curtis, with the assistance of Deitzler, had completed the organization of the State Militia, and had concentrated the main body of these troops at Shawneetown and farther south along Turkey Creek. Curtis wished to move this command to Lexington, but most of the Kansas Militia refused to leave the state, although some did move up to Independence, and to the Big Blue River.

Curtis decided to form his first defensive line along the Big Blue, and he sent Blair's Third Brigade of Blunt's division to fortify a position along the left bank of the river.

At about 11:00 A.M. October 19, 1864, Blunt's pickets in front of Lexington were attacked. While they resisted, Blunt formed his two brigades in line of battle to the southeast of the town where there was extensive open ground on his front, and the road to Independence was to his rear. He was able to hold his position until about 3:00 P.M.; then, faced by what he believed to be the greater part of Price's army, he assigned Moonlight to cover the retreat with his Second Brigade, and he withdrew toward Independence. With frequent stands to cover the retreat, Moonlight fell back about six miles to a ridge, where he held on until dark. Blunt then continued the march toward Independence, and at 9:00 A.M. October 20, he halted at the crossing of the Little Blue River, nine miles east of Independence. Then, under orders from Curtis, Blunt left Moonlight with his Second Brigade and two howitzers at the crossing of the Little Blue, and in the afternoon he continued on to Independence with the rest of his command.

Action at the Little Blue River, Missouri, October 21, 1864. After Blunt had departed for Independence, Moonlight spent the remainder of the day fortifying a position at the river crossing of the Independence road. He also sent out some of his companies to watch the fords in the vicinity.

The enemy did not appear that day, but early on the morning of October 21, 1864, Price resumed the march toward Independence, with Marmaduke in the lead. At daybreak Marmaduke's troopers encountered Moonlight's pickets about a mile east of the Little Blue and drove them back toward the

river. As the enemy moved down the slope on the east side of the valley of the Little Blue, they came under a heavy fire from Moonlight's men posted beyond the river. Fighting was violent for a time as the enemy attempted to cross the stream, but finally Moonlight was forced to fall back about two miles, where he formed a new line on the left of the Independence road. Then, a short time later, he advanced and drove the enemy back toward the river.

At about this time, Blunt, who had been ordered up from Independence, arrived with all the volunteer force and formed on the right of Moonlight. Before leaving Independence for the Little Blue, Blunt acquired a Fourth Brigade, commanded by James H. Ford, which consisted of the 2nd Colorado and a part of the 16th Kansas regiments.

When the deployment was completed, Blunt's troops were in line as follows: on the left, and on the left of the Independence road, was a battery of four howitzers manned by Company E, 11th Kansas Cavalry, and on the road was the 11th Kansas Cavalry of Moonlight's brigade; next in order to the right were the 16th Kansas Cavalry, McLain's Independent Colorado Battery, and the 2nd Colorado Cavalry (commanded by J. Nelson Smith) of Ford's brigade; and to the right of Ford, in order, were the 3rd Wisconsin Cavalry, the 15th Kansas Cavalry, and Henry L. Barker's howitzers (manned by Company G, 15th Kansas Cavalry), all of Jennison's brigade. Blunt advanced his line about a mile, but then, being greatly outnumbered and threatened on both flanks, he was forced to retire to Independence. There he formed in line of battle on the eastern side of the town, and at 5:00 P.M. he fell back to the main camp of the Kansas Militia, and to the prepared positions on the Big Blue River.

The defensive line that Curtis had prepared on the Big Blue extended southward from the Missouri River for about fifteen miles to Russell's Ford, near Hickman Mills. Deitzler was assigned command of the left of this line, which extended northward from the Independence road to the Missouri River, and was held by the Kansas State Militia. Blunt was assigned command of the right of the line, which ran southward from the Independence road to Hickman Mills.

About two miles south of the Independence road, on the Big Blue, was Simmons' Ford, and three miles beyond was Byram's Ford. These two fords were on secondary roads that ran in from Independence to Westport. Moonlight was at Simmons' Ford with his 11th Kansas Regiment, the 10th Kansas State Militia, and a section of artillery; W. D. McCain, with a battalion of the 4th Kansas State Militia, guarded Byram's Ford. On October 22, 1864, Jennison arrived with his First Brigade and assumed command at the ford. Farther upstream, Russell's Ford was held by the 2nd Kansas State Militia and part of the 3rd Kansas State Militia, and these were joined later by the 21st Kansas State Militia.

Meantime, as Price's divisions had been moving westward toward Independence, Sanborn's cavalry force and Andrew J. Smith's infantry had been following closely on his left.

On October 19, 1864, Sanborn received orders from Pleasonton, who was then moving in person to the front, to reorganize the cavalry force, and he also received information that Winslow's cavalry brigade was at Sedalia. That day, at Brownsville, Egbert B. Brown relieved Philips in command of First Brigade; and John McNeil relieved Beveridge in command of Second Brigade at Kilpatrick's Mill. Pleasonton came up and assumed command of the Cavalry Division October 20, relieving Sanborn, who in turn relieved Gravely in command of Third Brigade. Winslow's brigade was assigned to the division as Fourth Brigade. Pleasonton's cavalry was then organized as follows:

Cavalry Division, Alfred Pleasonton
  First Brigade, John B. Sanborn
  Second Brigade, Egbert B. Brown
  Third Brigade, John McNeil
  Fourth Brigade, Edward F. Winslow, to October 23,
    1864, wounded
    Frederick W. Benteen

Pleasonton left Dunksburg October 19, 1864 with his command and arrived in Lexington at midnight October 20. He then moved on to the west, and at 5:00 A.M. October 22, the day after Blunt's battle, he arrived at the crossing of the Little Blue River.

On October 19, 1864, Andrew J. Smith's Sixteenth Corps was on the road in the area of Sedalia and Georgetown. Instead of continuing on to the west, it turned to the northwest and arrived at Lexington on October 21.

Action at Byram's Ford, Missouri, October 22, 1864. On the morning of October 22, 1864, Price ordered Shelby and Fagan to force a crossing of the Big Blue and attack Curtis' Army of the Border before Pleasonton, and Andrew J. Smith could come up in support. Marmaduke was assigned the task of delaying Pleasonton until Curtis was defeated.

Price began his attack at 9:00 A.M. October 22, 1864 with a feint at the Independence road crossing of the Big Blue. Toward noon, Shelby decided to force a crossing at Byram's Ford, which was then held by Jennison's brigade, a part of Blair's brigade of Kansas State Militia, and Barker's battery. A number of frontal attacks at the ford failed, but at about 2:00 P.M. the enemy crossed the Big Blue at Hinkle's Ford, which had been left unguarded, and soon Jennison was driven back from the ford toward Westport. He was pursued by M. Jeff. Thompson's cavalry brigade, but offered such resistance that Moonlight's brigade was able to join him near the state line, a few miles south of Westport. Jennison and Moonlight then deployed and attacked, forcing Thompson to fall back about two miles. It was then nearly dark, and Jennison withdrew to Westport and bivouacked north of the town. Moonlight camped that night just east of Shawnee Mission. Ford's Fourth Brigade also moved to Westport.

M. S. Grant, commanding a cavalry force of Kansas State Militia, was at Russell's Ford watching the Big Blue when Shelby crossed the river. He fell back rapidly to the west in an attempt to join Jennison, but he was overtaken at the Mockabee farm on the Harrisonville road, which ran north from near Hickman Mills to the road from Westport to Independence. When Grant attempted to make a stand at the Mockabee farm, he was overwhelmed by a violent attack by troopers of Shelby's division under Sidney D. Jackman and B. Frank Gordon and was virtually destroyed, with the remnants retreating into Kansas.

During the day of October 22, 1864, Pleasonton arrived in rear of the Confederate army and found Fagan's pickets on the Little Blue River. He then drove the enemy back through Independence. At dark Winslow's brigade pursued the rear guard on the Byram's Ford road, and that night it arrived within three miles of the ford. About midnight, Pleasonton sent McNeil's brigade south on the Independence road to Little Santa Fe, then ordered Brown out with his brigade on the Byram's Ford road to relieve Winslow. Brown was ordered to attack at the ford at daylight, and Sanborn's and Winslow's brigades were ordered to support him.

Engagement at Westport, Missouri, October 23, 1864. When Curtis, who had expected Price's attack to be made on his left wing along the Independence road, learned that his right had been driven back and the enemy troops had crossed the Big Blue at Byram's Ford, he decided to abandon his entrenched line on the Big Blue and fall back to Kansas City. Deitzler had completed the withdrawal of his Kansas State Militia before sundown, and he then took position in the works around Kansas City. This movement completed, Curtis began to form his troops in line facing south instead of east. Blunt's division was already at and near Westport, and early the next morning, Deitzler was ordered to move all the Kansas State Militia units out of the entrenchments at Kansas City and assemble them at Westport.

At 3:00 A.M. October 23, 1864, Curtis issued orders for the concentration of Blunt's division along Brush Creek. This creek runs east and west about two miles south of Westport and is bordered on both sides by a thick forest some two miles in width. Jennison's First Brigade moved forward and took position in the woods north of Brush Creek, between Wornall's Lane and the State Line road. Wornall's Lane ran out to the south from Westport, crossed Brush Creek, and ran up to the crest on the far side, then on south past the Wornall house. Jennison's line was formed as follows: McLain's Independent Colorado Battery was on the left, next to Wornall's Lane; the 3rd Wisconsin Cavalry was on the right of the battery; and the 15th Kansas was on the right of the brigade, with its right near the State Line road. Barker's battery was in rear of Jennison's line.

Ford's Fourth Brigade took position on the left of Jennison's brigade, with the 16th Kansas on the right, next to Wornall's Lane, and the 2nd Colorado on the left.

Moonlight's Second Brigade was formed along the west side of the State Line road, perpendicular to Jennison's line, with 11th Kansas on the left, 15th Kansas in the center, and 5th Kansas on the right.

At dawn October 23, 1864, Blunt advanced his division, crossed Brush Creek, and pushed out his skirmishers into a cornfield beyond the woods on a line extending from the Bent house, near the State Line road, to the right of Wornall's Lane.

Meantime, Shelby and Fagan had been ordered to attack at daylight in an attempt to keep open the road to the south for the wagon train, and as Blunt moved forward, the two Confederate divisions were advancing and were then one mile to the south, beyond the Wornall house. Shelby's division was in advance, and Fagan's division was following in support. Contact was soon made, the Federal skirmishers were driven back, and then the main line opened fire. The fighting continued for about an hour, during which Blunt's brigades were slowly pushed back through the woods to the high ground above Brush Creek. Jennison's and Ford's brigades then recrossed the creek, and Moonlight's brigade returned to Shawnee Mission.

Following this first setback, Curtis spent the next two hours preparing for a second attack. During the morning, Blair had brought up his Third Brigade, which consisted of the 4th, 5th, 6th, 10th, and 19th regiments of the Kansas State Militia; James H. Dodge's 9th Battery, Wisconsin Light Artillery; and a section of the United States Colored Battery, commanded by Lieutenant Patrick H. Minor. Blair then formed his brigade along Brush Creek, on the right of Curtis' line. Part of the brigade formed on the left of Ford's brigade and the rest on the right of Moonlight's brigade in time for the first attack that morning.

It was almost 11:00 A.M. before Curtis was ready to attack, and he then sent Blair's brigade across Brush Creek and into the woods on the other side. Blair's brigade was then on the right of Curtis' line because Moonlight had been ordered south to keep between the enemy and the Kansas state line. Curtis ordered forward the rest of his line, but it was forced to fall back to Brush Creek before it reached the high ground on the south side.

Curtis then re-formed his troops and again advanced. At about that time, Curtis learned from a local Union man about a narrow gully that ran from Brush Creek in a southwesterly direction up to the plain beyond the crest above the creek. The man then led Curtis with his escort, which consisted of Company G, 11th Kansas Cavalry and Dodge's 9th

Wisconsin Battery, up this gully to a position just west of the Bent house, and there the battery opened fire on the left and rear of Shelby's line, forcing him to fall back.

Meantime, Blunt, with his First Brigade and Fourth Brigade, had been attempting to gain the crest south of Brush Creek, but with little success. When the 9th Wisconsin Battery opened on the surprised Confederates, Blunt's men charged and occupied the line of stone fences that had been held by Shelby's troopers. Then McLain's Colorado battery, Barker's battery, Daniel C. Knowles' 2nd Battery, Kansas Light Artillery, and some guns of other Kansas State Militia units added their fire to that of Dodge's guns.

The artillery fire continued for about an hour, and then Curtis' line again moved slowly forward. By noon it had reached a position along a lane just south of the Bent house. By that time Shelby's two brigades and Archibald S. Dobbin's brigade of Fagan's division had moved back to a new position a short distance north of the Wornall house. Fagan, with the brigades of William F. Slemons and Thomas H. McCray, had moved east toward the Harrisonville road to support Marmaduke, who was then engaged with Pleasonton near Byram's Ford.

After a brief pause, Blair's brigade on the extreme right and Jennison's brigade in the center again advanced against Shelby's weakened line. At about this time, Shelby learned that Pleasonton had forced a crossing at Byram's Ford, and Curtis, who had heard the sounds of Pleasonton's battle to the right and rear of Shelby's position, ordered a charge all along the line. Jennison, with his brigade and the 2nd Colorado Cavalry, charged down Wornall's Lane and struck Thompson's brigade just south of the Wornall house, and at the same time Thompson was struck by the fire of Battery H, 2nd Missouri Light Artillery of Pleasonton's division that had been placed in Hinkle's Grove to the southeast of the Wornall house. Thompson's men then broke and fled to the rear, but they soon took position again behind a line of stone fences that stretched away from the road to the east and west.

It is now necessary to describe the operations of Pleasonton's cavalry during the morning and early afternoon. It has already been noted that Pleasonton had ordered Brown to relieve Winslow's brigade on the Byram's Ferry road, and to attack at Byram's Ferry at daybreak October 23, 1864. Brown was slow in starting, however, and when Pleasonton heard no sounds of the attack that he had ordered, he hastened to the front. Upon arriving there, he found that no preparations for the attack had been made. He immediately placed Brown under arrest, placed John F. Philips in command of First Brigade, and then ordered Philips and Winslow to attack.

Winslow then placed Philip Smiley's Battery H, 2nd Missouri Light Artillery near the top of the hill on the east side of the Big Blue River, near the road that ran down to the ford. Philips dismounted his men, formed them on the left of the road, and then ordered them down the slope toward the river. At the same time, Edward W. Dee, with a battalion of the 4th Iowa of Winslow's brigade, moved toward the river through a wooded ravine, about 300 yards to the right of the ford.

Philips' brigade soon came under a heavy fire from the enemy and was forced to halt a short distance from the ford. The troopers of the 4th Iowa, however, managed to cross before they were observed by Marmaduke's pickets, and after they had secured a foothold on the west bank of the river, they opened fire on the enemy guarding the ford. Meantime, Philips had also crossed the river and had advanced his brigade up to the top of the bank beyond, driving back Marmaduke's advanced line.

From the top of the river bank, an open field extended westward for about 900 yards, and at the western edge of the field was a line of outcroppings of rock that formed a rough and irregular wall about twelve to fifteen feet high. Marmaduke's main line was formed along the crest of a tree-covered hill that rose some distance behind the rock wall.

While Philips and Dee were forcing a passage of the river, Pleasonton and Winslow brought up the rest of the division. Winslow then led his brigade across the Big Blue and took position between Philips and Dee. Winslow, as the senior colonel, assumed command of the troops west of the river while Pleasonton attempted to get Sanborn's brigade up to the ford.

Philips then resumed the attack by leading his mounted brigade forward in column along the road from the ford to Little Santa Fe. He was unable to pass the rock ledge, however, and he then halted his command on the left of the road. It was about 1:00 A.M. when Winslow formed his brigade in the field in front of the rock ledge, and for the next hour there was severe fighting, during which both Philips' and Winslow's brigades became fully engaged. For a time all attempts to scale the rock wall and press on toward Marmaduke's main line failed, but in a final charge, both brigades scrambled to the top of the rocks, re-formed, and charged toward the crest of the hill. Winslow was wounded in this attack, and Frederick W. Benteen assumed command of his brigade. Marmaduke was driven from his position, but he continued to resist as he was slowly driven back through the trees and onto the prairie beyond. There the enemy resistance ended, as Marmaduke's men fled westward to join the rest of Price's army.

Pleasonton then came up with Sanborn's brigade, and Sanborn took over the pursuit. He pushed Marmaduke back to the Harrisonville road, but at that point Fagan joined Marmaduke and opened with artillery fire on Sanborn. Then Jackman, who had been sent by Shelby to help Marmaduke, arrived, and together with Fagan he charged and drove Sanborn back. Finally, when Benteen came up, the enemy was driven back. Pleasonton then arrived with Philips' brigade, and he ordered Philips to continue the pursuit.

Pleasonton sent Battery H, 2nd Missouri Light Artillery to Hinkle's Grove to the right of Shelby's line just as Curtis began to advance his entire line in a general charge. Shelby was forced to fall back to a line of stone fences south of the Wornall house. Finally, when Marmaduke, Fagan, and the wagon train had passed and were on their way south, Shelby withdrew, and the Engagement at Westport was over.

* * * * * * * * * *

Pleasonton and Curtis followed Price's army to Little Santa Fe, where they halted for the night. That evening Curtis relieved from duty the members of the Kansas State Militia who lived north of the Kansas River.

At Little Santa Fe, Curtis ordered a temporary reorganization of his army, designating Blunt's command of Kansas troops as First Division and Pleasonton's division as Second Division of the Army of the Border.

The next morning, Blunt took the advance and Pleasonton followed as they marched south. When they reached West Point and learned that Price was at Trading Post, on the Osage River, Curtis ordered Pleasonton to take the lead. At 1:00 A.M. October 25, 1864, Sanborn, whose brigade was leading Pleasonton's division, came up on Price's army in camp along the Marais des Cygnes, near Trading Post. Before dawn on October 25, Sanborn charged suddenly and unexpectedly, driving the enemy out of their camp and capturing a large amount of camp equipage.

Price continued the retreat south and was followed by Benteen and Philips, who overtook the retreating column at Mine Creek, a tributary of the Little Osage River. The enemy wagon train held up the retreat while it crossed the Little Osage a few miles to the south, and Marmaduke and Fagan took position to hold up Pleasonton's pursuit. Phillips then charged against the center of the enemy line, while Benteen moved around and attacked the enemy right flank. The enemy force was routed, losing eight guns and 600 men, including Marmaduke, William L. Cabell, and six colonels. Shelby, who had the Confederate advance that day, then rode back past the wagon train and was able to delay Curtis as the retreat continued on slowly until dark.

Curtis was engaged with Price again that day, October 25, 1864, at Charlot, near Fort Scott, and that night Curtis moved into Fort Scott. He left there the next morning and reached Carthage early on October 28. He was engaged at Newtonia, Missouri that day, then continued the pursuit into Arkansas. He reached Fayetteville November 4, in time to prevent its capture by Price.

From Fayetteville Curtis moved into the Indian Territory, crossing the Arkansas River November 7, 1864, about thirty miles west of Fort Smith. There the pursuit ended.

Rosecrans reached Warrensburg on the evening of October 26, 1864, then decided against any further personal participation in the pursuit. On October 29, he ordered the recall of his troops. The Missouri troops were directed to return to the posts where they had previously been stationed, and on November 1, Andrew J. Smith's Right Wing, Sixteenth Corps and Winslow's cavalry brigade (then commanded by Benteen) were ordered to return to Saint Louis for transfer to Nashville, Tennessee, which was threatened by the advance of John B.

Hood's Confederate Army of Tennessee into the state.

When Curtis ended the pursuit of Price on the Arkansas River, he ordered the return of the troops of his Army of the Border to Kansas. Blunt, with Moonlight's brigade, was to march by way of Fort Smith; Jennison was to return by the route of the army through Missouri and Arkansas; and Ford was to accompany Curtis by way of Fort Gibson and Fort Scott to Fort Leavenworth.

Organization of the Troops in Missouri and Kansas during Price's Invasion of Missouri.

There were three principal forces that were assembled in Missouri and Kansas in September and October 1864 for the purpose of capturing or driving from Missouri the army led by Sterling Price during his invasion of the state. These were Samuel R. Curtis' Army of the Border, Alfred Pleasonton's Provisional Cavalry Division, and Andrew J. Smith's Right Wing, Sixteenth Corps. In addition, the state militia was called out in Kansas, and troops of the Enrolled Missouri Militia formed a part of Rosecrans' army. These troops were organized as follows:

ARMY OF THE BORDER
Samuel R. Curtis

First Division, Army of the Border, James G. Blunt
First Brigade, Charles R. Jennison
Second Brigade, Thomas Moonlight
Third Brigade, Charles W. Blair
Fourth Brigade, James H. Ford

Note. A battery of howitzers commanded by Henry L. Barker and manned by Company G, 15th Kansas Cavalry was attached to Jennison's brigade; a battery of howitzers manned by Company E, 11th Kansas Cavalry was attached to Moonlight's brigade; and the following were attached to Blair's brigade: James H. Dodge's 9th Battery, Wisconsin Light Artillery, William D. McLain's Independent Colorado Battery, and a two-gun battery of the 2nd Kansas State Artillery.

Unassigned Kansas State Militia, George W. Deitzler

Note. These troops consisted of the 2nd, 7th, 9th, 12th, 13th, 14th, 18th, 20th, 21st, and 23rd Kansas State Militia, and the 2nd Colored Kansas State Militia.

Unattached
Kansas City Home Guards, Kersey Coates

ARMY OF THE DEPARTMENT OF THE MISSOURI
William S. Rosecrans

Provisional Cavalry Division, John B. Sanborn, to October 20, 1864
Alfred Pleasonton
First Brigade, John F. Philips, to October 19, 1864
   Egbert B. Brown, to October 22, 1864
   John F. Philips
Second Brigade, John L. Beveridge, to October 19, 1864
   John McNeil
Third Brigade, Joseph J. Gravely, to October 20, 1864
   John B. Sanborn
Fourth Brigade, Edward F. Winslow, to October 22, 1864, wounded
   Frederick W. Benteen

Note 1. Winslow's brigade joined Pleasonton October 20, 1864 and was assigned to the division as Fourth Brigade.

Note 2. John J. Sutter's Battery B, 2nd Missouri Light Artillery and a battery of howitzers were attached to Second Brigade, and William C. F. Montgomery's Battery H, 2nd Missouri Light Artillery and a section of Charles H. Thurber's Battery L, 2nd Missouri Light Artillery were with the Cavalry Division.

Enrolled Missouri Militia, Edward C. Pike

On September 25, 1864, Edward C. Pike, commander of the 1st Military District, ordered all Enrolled Militia of the district to report for active service. These he organized as follows:

First Division, Enrolled Missouri Militia, Edward C. Pike
First Brigade, Madison Miller
Second Brigade, C. D. Wolfe
Third Brigade, George F. Meyers

Note. Pike reported for orders to Thomas Ewing, Jr., commander of the District of Saint Louis, Department of the Missouri.

RIGHT WING, SIXTEENTH CORPS
Andrew J. Smith

First Division, Joseph A. Mower, to October 11, 1864
   Joseph J. Woods
Second Brigade, Lucius F. Hubbard
Third Brigade, Sylvester G. Hill
Artillery

Battery E, 1st Illinois Light Artillery, John A. Fitch

Third Division, William T. Shaw, to October 29, 1864
David Moore
First Brigade, Thomas J. Kinney
Second Brigade, James I. Gilbert
Third Brigade, Edward H. Wolfe
Artillery
3rd Battery, Indiana Light Artillery, Thomas J. Ginn
9th Battery, Indiana Light Artillery, Wallace Hight

RED RIVER, LOUISIANA CAMPAIGN MARCH 10, 1864– MAY 22, 1864

When Federal troops were first sent to Louisiana, it was a part of the administration's plan that they establish posts in eastern Texas. Although they had made several attempts to do so, all had failed except for the occupation of some territory on the Gulf Coast of Texas.

In a letter of January 4, 1864 to Nathaniel P. Banks, commander of the Department of the Gulf, General-in-Chief Henry W. Halleck repeated his instructions of the previous summer for a combined army and navy operation on the Red River toward Shreveport, Louisiana in an effort to open the way into eastern Texas. According to this plan, Banks was to move northward by way of the Bayou Teche to Alexandria, where he was to be joined by a force sent downriver from Vicksburg by William T. Sherman and a fleet of gunboats from the Mississippi Squadron under the command of Rear Admiral David D. Porter. Banks' instructions were to lead his army up the Red River, then turn westward and march into Texas. A large cavalry force was also included in Banks' expedition for the purpose of operating on the plains of eastern Texas against a large body of Confederate cavalry reported to be in that area.

In addition to Banks' column, Frederick Steele was to march southward from the line of the Arkansas River and cooperate with Banks in an effort to capture Shreveport.

As a part of the arrangement between Banks and Sherman, Porter was to have his fleet at the mouth of the Red River in time for the expected spring rise of the water in the river. Sherman was to send with Porter 10,000 men of the Army of the Tennessee, and they were to be at Alexandria on March 17, 1864. The troops sent were First Division and Third Division of Sixteenth Corps, both under the command of Joseph A. Mower, and T. Kilby Smith's Provisional Division of Seventeenth Corps. All three divisions were under Andrew J. Smith, whose command was known as Detachment Army of the Tennessee.

It is important to note that Ulysses S. Grant, then commanding the Military Division of the Mississippi, opposed the Red River Campaign, and on sending Smith's command to Alexandria, he imposed a definite restriction on its use. On March 4, 1864, in agreeing to send troops to Banks, Sherman informed Banks that these troops should be back on the Mississippi River within thirty days of their entry into the Red River because they were needed in the upcoming spring campaign. In a letter dated March 15, this arrangement was confirmed by Grant three days after he had assumed command of the Armies of the United States. In that letter he stated that if Banks could not take Shreveport within ten to fifteen days longer than the thirty days that Sherman had allowed his troops to be absent from his command, they should be returned immediately. This order was to have an important effect on the termination of the campaign.

By March 2, 1864, Porter had assembled thirteen ironclads and nine other warships at the mouth of the Red River. Smith embarked his command at Vicksburg on March 10 and joined Porter about noon the next day.

The only obstacle to an uninterrupted passage up the Red River to Alexandria was an earthwork on the south bank of the river known as Fort De Russy, which was near Marksville, Louisiana, about midway between the mouth of the Red River and Alexandria. Smith and Porter then devised a plan to capture the fort.

Capture of Fort De Russy, Louisiana, March 14, 1864. About noon March 12, 1864, Porter's fleet and the transports entered the Red River, proceeding upstream until they reached the head of the

Atchafalaya River. At that point, Porter with nine gunboats turned off and steamed down the Atchafalaya toward Simsport (sometimes spelled Simmsport), and these were followed by the transports carrying Smith's infantry. The rest of Porter's fleet continued on up the Red River to threaten Fort De Russy, while Smith landed his troops and marched overland to attack the fort.

About 5:30 that same evening, the transports arrived at Simsport, which was on the right bank of the Atchafalaya near the Bayou De Glaize, about thirty miles by land from Fort De Russy. On the morning of March 13, 1864, Smith sent Mower out on the road toward Fort De Russy and instructed T. Kilby Smith to have his division of Seventeenth Corps ready to support Mower if needed. About three miles from the landing, at the fork of the Yellow Bayou and the Bayou De Glaize, Mower found William R. Scurry's brigade of John G. Walker's Confederate division occupying an unfinished earthwork. Scurry quickly withdrew when the Federal troops appeared. Mower pursued for about two miles, then withdrew to the landing. Smith disembarked his land transportation and directed the transports to rejoin Porter's main fleet and proceed with it to Fort De Russy.

Smith left the landing about 9:00 P.M. March 13, 1864 and bivouacked for the night four miles from Simsport. He resumed the march toward Fort De Russy at 3:00 the next morning, arriving at Mansura early in the afternoon. There Smith learned that the bridges across the Bayou De Glaize had been destroyed, and that Walker had concentrated his division about five miles west of Mansura, at the point where the army was to cross the bayou. Smith bridged the bayou at Mansura and, with the aid of a ferryboat, crossed his command. He then marched toward Fort De Russy, leaving Walker's division on his left. T. Kilby Smith's division brought up the rear and watched the left flank and rear of the column. On the afternoon of March 14, Mower passed through Marksville, two and a half miles from Fort De Russy, and at 4:00 P.M. arrived in front of the fort.

Mower ordered William T. Shaw to advance with his Third Brigade, Third Division, Sixteenth Corps to a position on the road from Marksville to the fort and about 800 yards from the fort. The 24th Mis-

souri of Shaw's brigade was formed on the left of the road, and the 14th Iowa on the right of the road. James M. Cockefair's 3rd Battery, Indiana Light Artillery was placed on the right of the 24th Missouri, next to the road. Two companies of the 14th Iowa were sent forward as skirmishers, and they occupied some rifle pits about 300 yards from the fort. When the 22nd Iowa of the brigade arrived, it was sent to the right to support the 14th Iowa, and then the 37th Iowa came up and relieved the 14th Iowa. William F. Lynch's First Brigade, Third Division, Sixteenth Corps was formed on the left of Shaw. Just before dark, the brigades of Lynch and Shaw charged over the parapet and captured the fort.

The naval vessels did not arrive in time to aid in the capture of the fort, but a short time later they steamed on toward Alexandria, where the advance arrived March 15, 1864. Mower with his two divisions embarked at Fort De Russy on the night of March 15 and arrived at Alexandria the next day. T. Kilby Smith's division remained at Fort De Russy a few days to destroy the works, and on March 18 moved on to Alexandria.

* * * * * * * * * *

With the fall of Alexandria, Walker fell back with his division to Natchitoches, and he was accompanied by Henry Gray's brigade of Alfred Mouton's division. Richard Taylor, commanding the Confederate District of West Louisiana, called in Camille J. Polignac's brigade from the line of the Tensas River, and he then assembled his forces at the Carroll Jones plantation, which was on the road between Opelousas and Fort Jessup, and about 20 miles southwest of Alexandria.

In the meantime, Banks had been busy preparing for his expedition. He had brought back from Texas Robert A. Cameron's Third Division and Thomas E. G. Ransom's Fourth Division of Thirteenth Corps, and he had ordered them to join William B. Franklin, commander of Nineteenth Corps, who was on the lower Teche. Ransom assumed command of the two divisions of Detachment Thirteenth Corps March 15, 1864, and William J. Landram assumed command of Fourth Division, Thirteenth Corps.

The two divisions disembarked at Algiers, Louisiana and marched to Berwick. Landram then marched on and joined Franklin's command, but Cameron remained at Berwick until his trains arrived.

Albert L. Lee's cavalry division, except John G. Fonda's Second Brigade, was also ordered to join Franklin. Fonda was directed to remain with his brigade at Port Hudson. By March 10, 1864, the four brigades of the cavalry division were concentrated at the cavalry camp near Franklin, Louisiana. Thomas J. Lucas' First Brigade and Harai Robinson's Third Brigade were already at Franklin, and they were joined there by Nathan A. M. Dudley's Fourth Brigade and Oliver P. Gooding's Fifth Brigade. The latter two brigades arrived from New Orleans by way of Donaldsonville and Thibodeaux.

On March 12, 1864, the wagons of Cameron's brigade, Detachment Thirteenth Corps reached him at Berwick, and the next morning he marched with his division to join Franklin. At the time Banks was detained in New Orleans on department business, and he placed Franklin in command of the troops that were assembled for the march to Alexandria. These consisted of William H. Emory's First Division, Nineteenth Corps, Ransom's Detachment Thirteenth Corps, and Lee's cavalry.

During the evening of March 13, 1864, the cavalry began the advance of the army from Franklin toward Alexandria. When on the road, Lee's column was nine miles long, and the last troopers did not leave Franklin until the next morning. As soon as the departing cavalry had left the road clear, Emory's division of Nineteenth Corps began its march, and it was followed by Ransom's Detachment Thirteenth Corps. Emory was in command of Nineteenth Corps while Franklin commanded the army during the absence of Banks. Lee's cavalry arrived at Alexandria on March 19, Emory's Nineteenth Corps on March 25, and Ransom's Detachment Thirteenth Corps on March 26. Banks, in person, left his headquarters in New Orleans March 23 and arrived at Alexandria the next day. He then assumed command of the combined forces of Franklin and Smith, which were called the Army of the Gulf.

While the army was at Alexandria, it was joined by William H. Dickey with his First Brigade, First Division, Corps d'Afrique from the garrison of Port Hudson.

In the initial planning, Cuvier Grover's Second Division, Nineteenth Corps was to have marched with Franklin up the Teche, but Grover was not ordered to concentrate his division at Thibodeaux until March 10, 1864. Then the plan was changed, and Grover was ordered to move his division to Alexandria on transports by way of the Mississippi and Red rivers. Jacob Sharpe's Third Brigade, which had been at Baton Rouge, finally disembarked at Alexandria March 26. Edward L. Molineux's Second Brigade embarked at Algiers about March 25 and arrived at Alexandria March 28. Frank S. Nickerson's First Brigade remained at Carrollton in the Defenses of New Orleans until April 25, and it then moved to Alexandria, where it arrived April 18.

Affair at Henderson's Hill, Louisiana, March 21, 1864. When Federal troops arrived at Alexandria, Taylor sent William G. Vincent with his 2nd Louisiana Cavalry to the crossing of Bayou Jean de Jean to hold the road on which he expected Banks to move toward Shreveport. At 6:30 on the morning of March 21, 1864, Mower marched out of Alexandria with a force to drive the enemy from their position on the road. Mower's command consisted of Lucius F. Hubbard's Second Brigade and Sylvester G. Hill's Third Brigade of First Division, Sixteenth Corps; the 89th Indiana Infantry of Lynch's First Brigade, Third Division, Sixteenth Corps; George R. Brown's 9th Battery, Indiana Light Artillery; and Lucas' First Brigade of the Cavalry Division.

After marching out about twenty-two miles, with the cavalry in the lead, Mower found the enemy entrenched on Henderson's Hill, near the crossing of the bayou. He halted about 1:00 P.M. to wait until it was dark. That night, he crossed the Bayou Rapides and made a flanking march of about eight miles, in a drenching rain and cold wind, to the rear of the enemy position on the hill. The 16th Indiana Mounted Infantry led the march, and about midnight, when the column finally reached the enemy camp, the infantry advanced and in a sharp attack surprised and captured Vincent's command. Mower then destroyed the enemy camp and returned to Alexandria.

* * * * * * * * * *

When Banks arrived at Alexandria, the water in the river was too low for the gunboats to pass. The transports could not be sent above the rapids until gunboats had cleared the way, and consequently it was necessary to haul supplies for the army from a depot established at Alexandria to another above the rapids. Then, when Banks finally began his movement upriver, he left Grover's division to protect the depots and carry supplies from one to the other. In addition, Grover's division was to serve as the garrison of Alexandria.

Finally, on March 26, 1864, after the first of the gunboats was able to pass the rapids, the army began its advance toward Shreveport. Andrew J. Smith marched with his Detachment Army of the Tennessee to Cotile Landing on the Red River above Alexandria, and there he was to await the arrival of the transports for the trip upriver. This arrangement was necessary because the transports would have been unable to pass the rapids with troops aboard. Smith reached Cotile Landing on March 28, and he embarked his troops as the transports arrived.

Before describing the further movements of the army, it will be helpful to digress briefly and note some of the characteristics of the Red River, along which Banks' army was to advance. At Grand Ecore the river divided into two channels of unequal size, and for the next sixty miles they flowed in a southeasterly direction until they rejoined about twenty miles above Cotile Landing. Between the two channels was a long, narrow island. The right-hand, or more southerly, channel, along which the road ran, was known as Cane River or Old Red River, and was formerly the main channel of the river. The left-hand, or more northerly, channel followed a less winding course, and it was the only one that was navigable. It was known as the Rigolets du Bon Dieu, or more commonly as the Bon Dieu.

On March 27, 1864, Franklin was ordered to march as rapidly as possible with Detachment Thirteenth Corps and Emory's division of Nineteenth Corps to Natchitoches, which was about four miles from Grand Ecore. Lee's cavalry, which was already out in front in that direction, was also ordered to Natchitoches. Lee crossed Cane River at Monett's Ferry, marched up the island, and, after recrossing the river above Cloutierville, arrived at Natchitoches on March 31. Franklin's divisions marched on the same road used by the cavalry and encamped at Natchitoches on April 2.

April 2, 1864, Andrew J. Smith's troops, which finally were all on the transports, left Cotile Landing and, accompanied by Porter's fleet, moved up to Grand Ecore, where they arrived the next day.

Porter remained at Grand Ecore until the river, which was rising slowly, was deep enough to permit the passage of his boats, and then on April 7, 1864 he started upriver with six gunboats. A fleet of twenty transports carrying T. Kilby Smith's division and supplies for the army followed closely behind. Porter's destination was Springfield Landing, about 110 miles above Grand Ecore, and he expected to be there by April 9.

When Banks arrived at Grand Ecore, he had to decide which road to take as he continued his advance toward Shreveport. A short distance above Natchitoches, the main road turned off from the river road toward the west and ran across a barren wilderness through Pleasant Hill and Mansfield to Shreveport. There was another and longer road east of the river, an old military road, that ran from Campti to Fort Towson. According to Porter, there was another road that ran on along the river and from which the army could be supplied from the fleet. Banks, however, had no definite information about the latter road, and not having the time to make a reconnaissance, he decided to take the road through Mansfield. This road was little more than a sunken path through the forest that ran around and over hills of red clay and sand. When it rained, as it did on April 7, 1864, the road was turned into mud. There were only a few rough buildings along this road and virtually no water. In addition, trees and thickets grew right up to the road on both sides and limited almost all organized movement to the road itself.

On April 6, 1864, the army once again began the march toward Shreveport. That morning, Lee left Natchitoches with Lucas' First Brigade, Robinson's Third Brigade, and Dudley's Fourth Brigade, and that night they camped at Crump's Corners, twenty-three miles out on the road toward Pleasant Hill.

The cavalry train followed a short distance behind Lee's troopers. From that time, Lee's movements were under the direction of Franklin. Ransom, with Cameron's Third Division and Landram's Fourth Division of Thirteenth Corps, followed Lee and camped that night about seven miles in rear of the cavalry. Emory's First Division of Nineteenth Corps followed Ransom, and the trains of the army followed Emory.

Andrew J. Smith remained at Grand Ecore until the next day and then, when Porter had departed with the fleet, marched out on the road toward Pleasant Hill behind the rest of the army. When all of Banks' troops were on the march, they were strung out for about twenty miles along the narrow road. Dudley's brigade of the Corps d'Afrique was assigned to guard the main wagon train, and Gooding's cavalry brigade covered the left and rear of the marching column.

Meantime, Confederate forces had been assembling to resist the Federal advance. Under the command of Thomas Green, cavalry regiments were hastening from Texas to reinforce Taylor. These were commanded by Xavier B. Debray, Alexander W. Terrell, James B. Likens, James P. Major, Arthur P. Bagby, William P. Hardeman, Peter C. Woods, and August Buchel. In addition to the cavalry, E. Kirby Smith, commander of the Confederate Trans-Mississippi Department, directed Sterling Price to send the infantry divisions of Mosby M. Parsons and Thomas J. Churchill from his District of Arkansas to Shreveport.

The Confederate forces had not completed their concentration when Franklin's divisions marched out of Natchitoches April 6, 1864. Taylor's two infantry divisions, commanded by Alfred Mouton and John G. Walker, had reached Pleasant Hill April 1, and two days later Taylor established headquarters at Mansfield. On April 4–5, Mouton and Walker moved on to Mansfield. At that time, the greater part of Green's cavalry was with Taylor, and Parsons' and Churchill's divisions were at Keatchie, between Shreveport and Mansfield, and about twenty miles from the latter place.

Skirmish at Wilson's Plantation (or Farm), Louisiana, April 7, 1864. On the morning of April 7, 1864, Lee resumed the march toward Pleasant Hill, with Robinson's brigade in the lead and supported by Lucas' brigade. Robinson easily pushed back the enemy cavalry until about 2:00 P.M. and then, about three miles beyond Pleasant Hill, he found the enemy in a strong position at Wilson's plantation (or farm). This force consisted of Major's brigade of Green's division, then commanded by Walter P. Lane. Robinson dismounted his brigade and attempted to drive the enemy back, but he was unable to do so. Soon Robinson was hard-pressed, and Lucas' brigade was sent forward in support. Lucas arrived just in time to help in repulsing a determined enemy attack, and then the two brigades, fighting dismounted, forced Major to fall back to Carroll's Mill, seven miles beyond Pleasant Hill.

At 5:30 A.M. April 7, 1864, Ransom resumed his march, and at 2:00 P.M., after advancing nineteen miles, the head of his column reached Pleasant Hill. He then put his troops in camp. During the day, Ransom had overtaken Dudley's brigade and the cavalry train. Emory's division of Nineteenth Corps, which was following Ransom, arrived at Pleasant Hill about 5:00 P.M. The army trains were far behind on the road. Andrew J. Smith's Detachment Army of the Tennessee, which had left Grand Ecore only that morning, was a day's march behind Ransom and Emory.

At the front, Lee became concerned because of the strong resistance he had encountered at Wilson's farm. As his mounted men advanced, they were confined to the single narrow road, and behind them the wagons of the cavalry train filled the road back for a distance of two or three miles. Accordingly, Lee asked Franklin to send forward a brigade of infantry, but Franklin, without orders to do so, refused. Later that evening, Banks joined Franklin and, an hour or two before midnight, directed him to send a brigade forward to report to Lee at dawn. Franklin then directed Ransom to send either a brigade or a division, as he thought best, and Ransom in turn ordered Landram to take Frank Emerson's First Brigade of his Fourth Division and join Lee. Landram marched at 3:00 A.M. April 8, 1864 and reported to Lee two hours later.

On the evening of April 7, 1864, Franklin ordered Lee to move forward as far as possible, taking his train with him, so as to clear the road for the advance of the infantry the next morning. At that time the cavalry was about six miles beyond Pleasant Hill and, upon receiving Franklin's orders, moved forward four miles to Carroll's Mill on Ten Mile Bayou, where it arrived at nightfall. There Lee was stopped by the enemy cavalry.

Battle of Sabine Cross Roads (Mansfield, or Pleasant Grove), Louisiana, April 8, 1864. April 8, 1864, Franklin, with Banks' approval, marched out about ten miles to the west of Pleasant Hill with the infantry and the trains of Thirteenth Corps and Nineteenth Corps and bivouacked for the day. This was done for several reasons: to give the men and animals a much-needed rest, to enable Banks' long column to close up, and to clear the ground so that Smith's troops could camp at Pleasant Hill.

Soon after sunrise, Lee's cavalry, with Emerson's infantry brigade attached, was on the road. Lucas' brigade was in the lead, with one regiment out as skirmishers. It was supported by two regiments of Emerson's brigade. Lee steadily drove back the enemy cavalry with almost constant skirmishing. About noon, after advancing six miles, and arriving within about three miles of Mansfield, Lee's line emerged from the woods that bordered the road and moved into a large clearing. This extended for about 600 yards on each side of the road, which crossed the clearing, and was about 800 yards wide. A large hill, called Honeycutt Hill, occupied the center of the clearing, and among the scattered growth of trees on the crest of that hill was a line of Confederate skirmishers.

Lee ordered Landram to move forward with Emerson's brigade, and he soon gained possession of the hill. The 19th Kentucky was sent forward as skirmishers, and after advancing about a half-mile to the thick woods on the far side of the clearing, they found both infantry and cavalry in a strong line of battle.

Meantime, Ransom had marched from Pleasant Hill at 5:00 that morning, and at 10:30 A.M. had reached a point ten miles distant on the north branch of the Bayou St. Patrice, which was the place designated for his camp that day. A short time before 3:00 P.M., Emory, who had also been advancing, went into camp on the south branch of Bayou St. Patrice, where he was within supporting distance of Ransom. Smith continued his march that day toward Pleasant Hill and, after covering twenty-one miles, bivouacked about two miles east of the village.

About 11:00 A.M. April 8, 1864, as Ransom was preparing to bivouac, Franklin received a request from Lee for additional infantry to relieve Emerson's men, who were exhausted by marching and fighting during the past twelve hours. Franklin directed Ransom to go in person with Joseph W. Vance's Second Brigade of Landram's division to make certain that Emerson's brigade was relieved and that it did return to Franklin's command instead of remaining with Lee.

Banks joined Franklin at Carroll's Mill about 11:00 A.M. April 8, 1864, and remained there for about a half-hour before leaving for the front. On the way he passed Ransom moving up with Vance's brigade, and about 1:00 P.M. arrived at the clearing. There he found troops of Lee's command skirmishing with the enemy. After discussing the situation with Lee, Banks sent back orders for Franklin to bring forward the rest of the infantry as rapidly as possible.

Meantime, on April 7, 1864, Taylor had ridden out on the road to Pleasant Hill, where Green's cavalry was engaged with Lee's troopers. Late in the day, after Lee had been forced to halt at Carroll's Mill, Taylor decided that it was time to make a stand the next day. On his way back to Mansfield, he selected the clearing with the hill as the place where he would meet Banks.

Taylor immediately began preparations for this encounter. He sent orders for Price's two divisions to march from Keatchie at dawn the next morning to join him at Mansfield, a distance of about twenty miles. He also ordered Mouton and Walker to start early on the morning of April 8 and bring their divisions of his command from their camps just north of Mansfield to Sabine Cross Roads.

The position selected by Taylor was along the road from the Sabine River to Bayou Pierre, which at that point ran through the woods along the northwest side of the clearing just described. There Taylor formed his line as follows: Hamilton P. Bee with two regiments of cavalry was on the extreme Confederate right; John G. Walker's division was on the left of Bee, with William R. Scurry's brigade on the right of the division, Thomas N. Waul's brigade on the center, and Horace Randal's brigade on the left; Xavier B. Debray's cavalry regiment was formed across the Mansfield road in front of Walker's left; Alfred Mouton's division was on the left of Walker, with its right flank not far from the road, and with Henry Gray's brigade on the right of the division and Camille J. Polignac's on the left; and James P. Major's cavalry division, consisting of his own and Arthur P. Bagby's brigades, on the extreme left. The divisions of Churchill and Parsons were on the way to the front, but they did not arrive on the field in time to take part in the battle that day.

In obedience to Franklin's orders, Ransom started forward with Vance's brigade about 11:00 A.M. April 8, 1864 on his march of five and a half miles to relieve Emerson's brigade. Ransom arrived in person at the clearing about 1:30 P.M. and found Emerson's brigade on the hill supporting the 19th Kentucky of his brigade, which was out in front skirmishing with the enemy. Emerson's brigade was in position just to the right of the Mansfield road, and Ormand F. Nims, who had brought up his 2nd Battery (B), Massachusetts Light Artillery of Lee's cavalry division, placed his guns near the left of Emerson's line. Dudley's cavalry brigade was covering the ground to the left of Nims and Emerson. When Vance's brigade arrived about 3:30 P.M., it was put in position to cover the right of Emerson's brigade. Lucas' cavalry brigade was on the right of Vance, and with Lucas were a section of Jacob B. Rawles' Battery G, 5th United States Artillery of the cavalry division and a section of Herbert H. Rottaken's Howitzer Battery of the 6th Missouri Cavalry. Pinckney S. Cone's Chicago Mercantile Battery, Illinois Light Artillery was in rear of Emerson's brigade. Robinson's cavalry brigade was with the cavalry train and was on the road about a half-mile to the rear.

There was little activity along the front for about two hours, and then at 4:00 P.M. Mouton's division advanced against the right of Banks' line. Ransom observed this movement and advanced his five right regiments to meet it. After a sharp engagement, Mouton was checked and driven back some 200 yards from the right of Ransom's position. The enemy rallied, however, and opened with a heavy fire. Mouton's attack was supported on the right by Randal's brigade and on the left by Major's cavalry.

After Mouton's attack had started, Taylor ordered Walker to advance and turn the Federal left, while the cavalry of Bee and Debray moved into the rear of the line. Walker advanced against some opposition by the 3rd Massachusetts Cavalry of Dudley's

brigade, which was skirmishing out in front, and then he came under an accurate fire from Nims' battery on the hill. The two batteries of Landram's division, the Mercantile Battery and Martin Klauss' 1st Battery, Indiana Light Artillery, were brought up to the hill to add their fire to that of Nims' battery.

Walker's men continued to advance, however, and they finally charged up the hill. They struck the flank of the 23rd Wisconsin and the 67th Indiana of Emerson's brigade, drove them back, and captured three of Nims' guns. Ransom's left was crushed in the attack, and soon his entire line was threatened with envelopment. He then issued orders for his troops to withdraw to the woods at the southeastern edge of the clearing. Some of Ransom's right regiments did not receive the order because of the death of the bearer, and many of their men were taken prisoner. The 48th Ohio and the 130th Illinois were almost completely destroyed.

Emerson, commanding the First Brigade of Landram's division, and Vance, commanding the Second Brigade, were wounded and captured while at the head of their brigades. Francis A. Sears assumed command of First Brigade, and Albert H. Brown of Second Brigade. Ransom was wounded while assisting Landram in organizing his troops in the edge of the woods, and he was succeeded in command of Detachment Thirteenth Corps by Robert A. Cameron. William H. Raynor assumed command of Cameron's division.

Meantime, shortly after 3:00 P.M., Franklin had received Banks' order to bring forward the rest of his infantry. He then sent back word to Emory that he was leaving and started with Cameron's First Division, Detachment Thirteenth Corps for the front. Cameron arrived just as Landram was attempting to rally his men at the edge of the woods and prevent the enemy from advancing across the clearing from the hill. Cameron then deployed his division, with Aaron M. Flory's First Brigade on the right of the road and William H. Raynor's Second Brigade on the left of the road, and he moved forward to occupy the edge of the woods. Some of Dudley's men rallied and formed on the left of Cameron.

The enemy continued to move around the flanks of the Federal line, however, and Cameron's weak division (about 1,300 men), the remnants of Landram's division, and the troopers of Dudley's brigade were not sufficient to stop the attack. They did hold for about an hour, and then their line began to break up. Soon the entire force was in full flight to the rear, and all attempts to halt them failed. The pursuit was not vigorous, and it was slowed somewhat as Dudley and Lucas successively formed lines to cover the retreat. Flory was wounded in the attack and was succeeded in command of First Brigade by Bradford Hancock.

When the teamsters of the cavalry train learned of the defeat of the troops at the front, they abandoned the wagons and left them standing on the narrow road about a mile from the battlefield. This blockage of the road forced the fleeing infantry to pass by through the woods on the sides of the road, and also prevented the artillery from escaping to the rear. Altogether, the army lost twenty guns that evening. Harai Robinson, commanding the Third Brigade of the cavalry division, which was guarding the cavalry trains, was wounded near the trains as the enemy advanced, and he was succeeded in command of the brigade by John M. Crebs.

Earlier that evening, Franklin had realized that the army might be in trouble, and he sent back word to Emory to hurry forward with his First Division of Nineteenth Corps. He also instructed Emory to form a defensive line at the first suitable place that he found on the road. At 4:00 P.M., a short time after receiving Franklin's order, Emory started forward from his position on Ten Mile Bayou, finally arriving at a place about two miles from the battlefield called Pleasant Grove. At that point there was a small clearing with a fenced farm, and across this clearing there was a ravine through which a small stream flowed. Emory proceeded to form his division in line along the eastern side of the ravine. He ordered William Dwight to deploy First Brigade across the road and to hold his position at all costs. He then directed James W. McMillan to form his Second Brigade on the right of Dwight, and Lewis Benedict to take position with his Third Brigade on the left of Dwight. Lucas' cavalry brigade was placed on the right of Emory's line. When these orders had been issued, Emory accompanied William B. Kinsey, with his 161st New York Infantry of Dwight's brigade, to the front to hold the enemy until the division was in position. Kinsey succeeded in this mission and then rejoined the brigade.

The enemy followed the 161st New York as it came in, but it was soon halted by a heavy fire from Dwight's brigade and driven back with severe losses. Taylor next attempted to turn the right of Emory's line, but Emory moved McMillan's brigade, which had been placed to the right and rear of Dwight, to a line at a right angle to the main line and easily checked the enemy advance. On the left, Benedict repulsed all attacks. The attacks at Pleasant Grove lasted only about a half-hour, but by that time it was dark, and the fighting ended for the day.

Engagement at Pleasant Hill, Louisiana, April 9, 1864. After his defeat that evening at Sabine Cross Roads, Banks' first concern was to re-form his disorganized troops at some place to the rear, and sometime before 10:00 P.M. he issued orders for the withdrawal of the army. By midnight the movement was under way. The remnants of Detachment Thirteenth Corps, then commanded by Cameron, marched first, and Dwight's brigade, which was the last to leave the field, brought up the rear. The march of the army was slow because of the presence of stragglers and wagons on the road, and it did not arrive at Pleasant Hill until 8:30 A.M. April 9, 1864.

Meantime, Andrew J. Smith's command had arrived near Pleasant Hill the previous evening and had camped in the vicinity of the Old Cemetery. Oliver P. Gooding's Fifth Brigade of the cavalry division had arrived with Smith.

Early on the morning of April 9, 1864, Lee's cavalry, with what was left of Cameron's Detachment Thirteenth Corps, arrived at Pleasant Hill. In a short time Cameron's command was re-formed in comparatively good order, and it was then sent out on the Fort Jessup road to watch the extreme left flank of the army. At 11:00 A.M., however, Cameron received an order from Franklin, which he understood as directing him to move toward Crump's Hill to follow and protect the right flank and rear of the trains. Whether he was mistaken in this belief or not, he left the Fort Jessup road at noon, and at 5:00 P.M. he was about four and a half miles from the battlefield.

Emory's division of Nineteenth Corps reached the village at about 8:00 that morning, and each of the brigades was directed to take the position on the campground that it had occupied April 7, 1864.

While the army was re-forming at Pleasant Hill, Banks considered his next move. He could make another attempt to reach Shreveport, but at that time only a few days remained before the Detachment Army of the Tennessee was, according to Grant's orders, to be sent back to Vicksburg. In addition, Banks was under orders to have his entire force back on the Mississippi River by May 1, 1864 in readiness to join in a movement on Mobile, Alabama. He could remain at Pleasant Hill, but not for long because of a lack of water and the difficulty in obtaining supplies. His remaining option was to abandon the campaign and withdraw with his army to the Red River at Grand Ecore. Banks decided on the latter course, and on April 9 he ordered the wagon train to start back toward the Red River. To guard the train, he sent Dickey's brigade of the Corps d'Afrique and most of Lee's cavalry division. Lucas, with about 1,000 men, half from his own brigade and half from Gooding's brigade, was detached from the cavalry division and ordered to remain with the army under the immediate orders of Franklin. After putting the trains in motion, Banks placed his army in position to cover the movement.

Pleasant Hill, a small village of about a dozen buildings, was situated in a clearing on a slight elevation or plateau. The village, which was on the main road from Natchitoches to Shreveport, was the center for roads running out to Fort Jessup and Many (Manny) to the south, to the crossings of the Sabine River to the west, and toward the Red River to the north and east. Later in the day, the Battle of Pleasant Hill was to be fought in this area.

At 9:00 A.M. April 9, 1864, just as Franklin's retreating troops began to come in from Sabine Cross Roads and Pleasant Grove, William T. Shaw's Second Brigade, Third Division, Sixteenth Corps was ordered out from its campground near the cemetery to take position on the Mansfield road north of Pleasant Hill. Shaw experienced some difficulty in moving forward because of the teams and wagons on the road, but he eventually reported to Emory and was directed to relieve McMillan's Second Brigade of Emory's division. The latter was in position south of and perpendicular to the Mansfield road, about one-half mile north of the village. Irving D. Southworth's 25th Battery, New York Light Artillery was on the right of McMillan's brigade.

Shaw relieved McMillan with three of his regiments and sent the fourth, the 24th Missouri Infan-

try, to hold some high ground to the north of the Mansfield road, where it commanded the former position of McMillan's brigade. Shaw's other regiments were, from right to left, the 14th Iowa, 27th Iowa, and 32nd Iowa. The 14th Iowa was on the Mansfield road, and the other two regiments were south of the road.

Benedict's Third Brigade of Emory's division was in position to the left of Shaw's brigade and was on the south side of the road that ran out from Pleasant Hill to Logansport on the Sabine River (commonly called the Sabine road). About mid-afternoon, Benedict was moved back about 300 yards from a woods that he had occupied to the dry bed of a stream that ran through a shallow valley about 400 yards in front of Pleasant Hill. In this new position, Benedict's line was nearly perpendicular to the road, with his right resting near the road. Franck E. Taylor's Battery L, 1st United States Artillery was placed on high ground to the rear so that it could fire over the heads of Benedict's men. There was an interval of about 700 yards between the right of Benedict's brigade and the left of Shaw's brigade to the north.

Dwight's First Brigade of Emory's division was on the extreme right of the Federal line, and as the result of a shift of Shaw's brigade to the right, the left of Dwight's line was to the rear of Shaw's right regiment. Dwight's line was on a ravine north of and nearly parallel to the Mansfield road, and it was nearly at a right angle to Shaw's line, which ran through a fringe of woods. Southworth's 25th Battery, New York Light Artillery was in position on some high ground between Shaw and Dwight.

McMillan's brigade, after being relieved by Shaw, was placed in reserve to the right and rear of Dwight's brigade.

When Emory's division was finally in position, it was generally a short distance north of Pleasant Hill, and it was in front of the junction of the Mansfield road and the Sabine road.

About a mile to the rear of Shaw's brigade, and about 400 yards behind Benedict's line, the troops of Mower's divisions of Sixteenth Corps (except Shaw's brigade) were in position. They were strongly posted in a woods to cover the crossing of the roads to Many (Manny) and Fort Jessup, Natchitoches, and Blair's Landing on the Red River. Lucius F. Hubbard's Second Brigade, First Division was at the southern edge of Pleasant Hill, on the north side of the Mansfield road. The rest of the troops of Sixteenth Corps were on the south side of the road and in position in front of the road to Many. Risdon M. Moore's Third Brigade, Third Division was on the left of Hubbard, next to the Mansfield road; Sylvester G. Hill's Third Brigade, First Division was along the Many road, to the left of Moore's brigade; and William F. Lynch's First Brigade, Third Division was on the left of Hill, with his 58th Illinois Regiment advanced to a position on the left of Benedict's brigade of Emory's division. George T. Hebard's 1st Battery, Vermont Light Artillery was in position near the right of Mower's line.

While Banks was getting his army in position at Pleasant Hill, Taylor had also been active. During April 8, 1864, Churchill, with his own division (under the command of James C. Tappan) and Parsons' division, had marched from Keatchie to Mansfield, but had arrived too late to take part in the Battle of Sabine Cross Roads. About 12:00 that night, Taylor ordered Churchill to move his two divisions forward to the battlefield of the evening before and be in position to attack at dawn April 9. Churchill started toward Sabine Cross Roads at 2:00 A.M.

At dawn, however, Taylor found that Banks had departed, and he immediately started in pursuit with his entire force. Green moved out first with his cavalry, and he was followed, in order, by Churchill's two divisions, Parsons' division, Walker's division, and finally Mouton's division, then commanded by Polignac. Green's cavalry arrived near Pleasant Hill at 9:00 A.M. as Banks was forming his troops around the village. At 1:00 P.M. the head of Churchill's column arrived at a point about two miles northwest of Pleasant Hill where a road to the south branched off the Mansfield road. When the rest of the army came up, Taylor halted for two hours to permit his infantry to rest.

At 3:00 P.M. the movement was resumed, and Churchill marched south through the woods for about two miles to the Sabine road. He then faced toward Pleasant Hill and formed his command in line of battle, with Parsons' division on the right and Tappan's division on the left. Three regiments of cavalry covered Churchill's right.

Walker's division was deployed on a line between the Mansfield road and the Sabine road, fac-

ing toward the road junction at Pleasant Hill. Scurry's brigade was on the right, and the brigades of Waul and Randal were en echelon to the left of Scurry. The right of Scurry's line was about one-fourth mile to the rear of the prolongation of Tappan's line.

Bee, with the cavalry brigades of Debray and Buchel, was placed on the Mansfield road, to the left of Randal's brigade, and he was supported by Polignac's infantry division. On the left of Bee, and north of the road, were the dismounted brigades of Major and Bagby.

At 4:30 P.M., Taylor began the Battle of Pleasant Hill on the Mansfield road when he opened fire with his artillery on the 25th Battery, New York Light Artillery and on the front of the 24th Missouri of Shaw's brigade. About a half-hour later, Churchill began his battle on the Sabine road by advancing against the front of Benedict's line. At that time, Parsons' division was on the Confederate right of the road, with Simon P. Burns' brigade on the left, next to the road, and John B. Clark's brigade on the right. Tappan's brigade was on the left of the road, with H. L. Grinsted's brigade on the right, on and to the left of the road, and Lucian C. Gause's brigade on the left of Grinsted. Benedict's brigade was heavily outnumbered, and it was soon driven out of the dry stream bed in which it was posted and up the hill to the rear. The men did not halt in their retreat until they had reached the comparative safety of the woods in which Mower's divisions were posted. Benedict was killed during the attack, and Francis Fessenden assumed command of his brigade.

When Walker heard the sounds of Churchill's battle, he started his brigades forward, and at about the same time Green ordered Bee to charge the line held by Shaw. When Bee arrived within about 200 yards of Shaw's position, he was struck by a heavy flank fire from the 24th Missouri and a frontal fire from the right regiments of Shaw's brigade and was quickly repulsed. Major then advanced against the right of Shaw's line with his dismounted cavalry.

The retreat of Benedict's brigade had left the right of Shaw's line completely exposed to a flank attack. While Shaw was engaged on the front and right, Walker's division was advancing toward his unprotected left flank, and soon Scurry's brigade began to move around the flank of the 32nd Iowa, Shaw's left regiment. Shaw was then in imminent danger of being cut off. When Andrew J. Smith saw that Shaw was almost surrounded, he ordered him to withdraw. The 32nd Iowa was cut off; the other three regiments were able to retire to safety, but only with difficulty.

When Shaw fell back, Walker struck the front of Dwight's brigade, and Major advanced on its flank and rear. When Dwight saw the enemy moving past his rear, he moved the 153rd New York and 114th New York across to the other side of the Mansfield road. He left the 116th New York on the north side of the road, and to protect his flanks, he moved the 29th Maine and the 161st New York to the left of his new line. By making these changes in his position, Dwight was able to hold his ground.

Back on the Federal left, Emory ordered McMillan to move from his position in reserve and attempt to halt Churchill's advance toward Pleasant Hill. McMillan advanced to a point near the junction of the Sabine road and the Mansfield road, but three of his four regiments became disorganized when struck by a heavy enemy fire. At this point the Federal left and center, except for Mower's divisions, were completely broken, and enemy troops were in the village of Pleasant Hill. At this juncture, however, Thomas Newlan's 58th Illinois of Lynch's First Brigade of Mower's Third Division, Sixteenth Corps moved out of the woods on the extreme left of the Federal line and struck the right of Churchill's division, which was unprotected. The 89th Indiana and 119th Illinois of Lynch's brigade soon followed the 58th Illinois, and together they drove the enemy back into the shallow valley that Benedict's brigade had occupied earlier in the day. When Smith observed Lynch's success, he ordered his whole line forward. He was joined on the right in this attack by some men of Benedict's and McMillan's brigades.

Under the pressure of Smith's attack, first Parsons and Tappan and then Walker were forced to fall back. The victorious Federals, advancing on a great wheel to the right, and pivoting on the village of Pleasant Hill, soon drove the enemy back into the woods to the north. As darkness fell, the Confederate withdrawal almost became a rout as Taylor's divisions left the field. During the evening, Polignac and Green continued their unsuccessful attacks north of the Mansfield road, but they too ceased in their efforts as it grew dark, and they finally left the field.

About midnight, Banks decided not to remain at Pleasant Hill any longer, and at 2:00 A.M. April 10, 1864, the army began the march back to Grand Ecore. Emory's division marched first and was followed by Mower's two divisions. The army arrived at Grand Ecore on the evening of April 11.

At that time, Porter's fleet was in some danger farther up the river. It had reached Loggy (or Boggy) Bottom on the afternoon of April 10, 1864, and there Porter learned of the battles at Sabine Cross Roads and Pleasant Hill. Porter then turned about and began the return to Grand Ecore as rapidly as possible. On the way down the river, he was engaged a number of times with enemy forces that were attempting to intercept his fleet, but on the morning of April 14 he reached Campti, where he met Andrew J. Smith, who was coming to his aid. By midnight April 15, the fleet had arrived at Grand Ecore. Porter did not remain there, however, but continued on downriver toward Alexandria.

When Banks reached Grand Ecore, he asked for reinforcements for the army. April 12, 1864, Henry W. Birge embarked at Alexandria with his own Second Brigade of Grover's division and the 38th Massachusetts and the 128th New York regiments of Jacob Sharpe's Third Brigade of Grover's division; he joined Emory at Grand Ecore the next day. Frank S. Nickerson's First Brigade of Grover's division embarked at New Orleans to join Grover's division at Alexandria, and it arrived there April 18.

There were several changes in command and some organizational changes in the army while it was at Grand Ecore. April 16, 1864, Charles P. Stone, Banks' chief of staff, was relieved from duty in the Department of the Gulf and ordered to Cairo, Illinois. The next day, William Dwight was assigned as chief of staff, and George L. Beal assumed command of Dwight's First Brigade of Emory's division.

April 18, 1864, Albert L. Lee was relieved from command of the cavalry division and was assigned to the cavalry depot at New Orleans for the purpose of reorganizing the cavalry of the department. Dudley was relieved from command of Fourth Brigade, Cavalry Division and was ordered to report to Lee at New Orleans. Edmund J. Davis was assigned command of Dwight's brigade. Richard Arnold was assigned temporary command of all cavalry with the army in the field and was ordered to report to

Franklin, who commanded Nineteenth Corps and Detachment Thirteenth Corps.

After arriving at Grand Ecore, Birge was assigned command of a temporary division consisting of the 13th Connecticut and 1st Louisiana of his own brigade, both under the command of William O. Fiske; the 38th Massachusetts and 128th New York of Sharpe's brigade, both under the command of James Smith; and Francis Fessenden's Third Brigade of Emory's division (formerly Benedict's brigade).

On April 19, 1864, Banks issued the order for the return of the army to Alexandria. That day he sent Andrew J. Smith with his Detachment Army of the Tennessee to Natchitoches to cover the retreat, and Smith arrived there the next day. At 5:00 P.M. April 21, Banks started his army on its march down the Red River, and at the same time he turned over the direction of the marching column to Franklin. Birge's temporary division was in the lead, and it was followed, in order, by the trains, Emory with the brigades of Beal and McMillan, Cameron with Detachment Thirteenth Corps, T. Kilby Smith's division of Seventeenth Corps, and Mower with his two divisions of Sixteenth Corps.

Arnold's cavalry did not serve as a unit during the march down the river. Gooding's brigade was out in front of the army; John M. Crebs (commanding Robinson's brigade) accompanied Birge's division; Edmund J. Davis (commanding Dwight's brigade) covered the right flank of the column; and Lucas reported to Andrew J. Smith with his brigade, which then served as the rear guard.

The army crossed Cane River about two miles below Grand Ecore, then followed the road along the river, which ran down the entire length of the island between the two channels of the Red River to Monett's Ferry. There it recrossed the Cane River about forty miles from Grand Ecore and from there ran on to Alexandria.

The crossing of the trains near Grand Ecore was completed by 1:30 A.M. April 22, 1864, and the rear of the column that marched from Grand Ecore crossed a little after 2:30 A.M. The last of the troops of Smith's command, which brought up the rear, did not cross the river from Natchitoches until 5:00 A.M. April 22.

While Banks was marching south from Grand Ecore, Taylor had with him only Polignac's infantry division and a reorganized cavalry corps under John A. Wharton that consisted of the divisions of Hamilton P. Bee, James P. Major, and William Steele, and with this small force he attempted to harass the retreating Federal column. The infantry divisions of Churchill, Parsons, and Walker had departed for Arkansas to join Price April 14, 1864.

Engagement at Monett's Ferry (or Cane River Crossing), Louisiana, April 23, 1864. At 2:30 on the morning of April 22, 1864, the van of Banks' army halted on the banks of Cane River about twenty miles below Grand Ecore, and by 11:00 A.M. the rest of the column had closed up. It then resumed the march, and Wharton with William Steele's cavalry followed close behind. At 3:00 P.M., Steele's cavalry, supported by Polignac, attacked Lucas' brigade at the rear of the column and forced Smith to deploy his command to aid Lucas. This forced the army to halt for an hour, but it then resumed the march. At 7:00 that evening, Birge halted about two miles below Cloutierville, and two hours later, Emory and Cameron closed up on Birge. Smith's Detachment Army of the Tennessee did not come in until 3:00 A.M. April 23. Gooding's cavalry brigade, which was out in front, had already discovered that the enemy was in possession of the crossing, and had camped for the night about three miles in front of Birge.

At 4:30 on the morning of April 23, 1864, the cavalry, followed by Emory's division, advanced toward Monett's Ferry and was soon engaged with the enemy skirmishers. When the cavalry moved into the open ground near the crossing, it came under the fire of the enemy guns across the river. Emory then withdrew all but the dismounted men and sent out a line of infantry skirmishers. Meantime, Birge and Cameron had come up in rear of Emory and halted.

Across the river on a high bluff, enemy troops were in a strong position obstructing the crossing. On the bluff were Bee, with the cavalry brigades of Terrell and Debray, and Major, with the cavalry brigades of Bagby and George W. Baylor, and with them they had twenty-four guns.

An examination of this position revealed that the crossing could not be forced by a direct attack, and Davis was sent out with his cavalry brigade to find a ford farther down the river. Davis reported back that there was no place to cross in that direction, and Banks then decided on a flanking movement to the right. Birge was ordered to march back with his division and the remnants of Cameron's Detachment Thirteenth Corps to a ford about two miles above the enemy position on the bluff, cross the river there, and march against the Confederate left flank. At the same time, Emory ordered McMillan, who was in temporary command of Emory's division while the latter was in command of all troops attempting to dislodge the enemy at the crossing, to deploy Beal's First Brigade and McMillan's Second Brigade (then commanded by Henry Rust, Jr.) and threaten a crossing of the river at Monett's Ferry. Henry W. Closson, commanding the artillery reserve of Nineteenth Corps, was directed to advance his guns and open fire on the enemy position on the bluff.

Birge began his turning movement at 9:00 A.M. April 23, 1864, but because of the nature of the ground and the ford, progress was slow. The island was low and flat, and near the river it was swampy and covered with nearly impenetrable brakes. Birge finally crossed the river, then marched on a long detour to the south and southeast. Late in the afternoon he found the enemy in position on a sandy hill that was covered with trees, thickets, and fallen logs. The right flank of this line was protected by a deep ravine, and the left flank by a swamp and small lake. Troops of Bee's division were on the hill.

William O. Fiske, who was at the head of Birge's column, emerged from the thickets through which he had been advancing in front of the center of Bee's line. Fessenden, who was following Fiske, brought his brigade up in front of the enemy left. Birge then assigned to Fessenden the task of taking the hill. Fiske deployed in two lines, with the 13th Connecticut and the 1st Louisiana in front, and this line was supported by James Smith with the 38th Massachusetts and the 128th New York. Fessenden deployed his brigade behind a hedge, with his regiments in line, from right to left, as follows: 165th New York, 173rd New York, 30th Maine, and 162nd New York. Cameron's troops of Thirteenth Corps were placed in reserve.

In front of Fessenden's line was an open field, and on the far side was the hill held by Bee. When all was ready, Fessenden advanced across the field, re-formed his line, and then charged up the hill. He was wounded early in the fighting, and Justus W. Blanchard assumed command of the brigade. Fessenden's troops soon gained the crest and opened fire on the retreating enemy. Blanchard then re-formed his men, descended the hill, and moved on to a second ridge, from which the enemy withdrew. The troops on that part of the enemy line, commanded by George W. Baylor, fell back to a second position.

Birge's troops, which had become disordered by the advance, halted to re-form, then advanced into a field in front of Baylor's position. They were met by a heavy and unexpected fire and were forced to take cover. Despite this temporary success, Bee believed that both of his flanks had been turned and that his center was threatened, and he ordered his division to retire. Baylor then pulled back his regiments and joined Bee's troops in retreat. When Birge's troops again advanced, they found that the enemy had departed and that the ford was open.

* * * * * * * * *

Bee retreated to the Beasley place, thirty miles distant, on the road to Fort Jessup, and by so doing left the road to Alexandria open. A pontoon bridge was completed a short time after dark, and the army resumed its march toward Alexandria. By 2:00 P.M. April 24, 1864, the last troops had crossed Cane River, and they then marched without incident past Cotile Landing and Henderson's Hill. That night the leading troops bivouacked near Bayou Rapides. The head of Banks' column finally marched into Alexandria at 2:00 P.M. April 25, and the next day Andrew J. Smith's command arrived.

At Alexandria, Banks found that Porter's fleet had arrived safely, but during the month that it had been on the river above Alexandria, the water level had fallen more than six feet, and it was then impossible for the vessels to pass the rapids and reach the Mississippi River. Thus, Banks was forced to remain at Alexandria with his army to protect the fleet until such time that it could continue on down the Red River. Fortunately, Joseph Bailey, acting chief engineer on Franklin's staff, devised a plan for raising the water level at the rapids by constructing a dam across the river. Banks approved the plan, and work was started April 30, 1864. The dam was completed May 8, and some boats succeeded in passing the rapids that day, but the next morning a part of the dam gave way and the water level dropped. Bailey then constructed another dam at the upper rapids, which was completed in three days and three nights, and the rest of the fleet passed to safety below the rapids. The troops of the army that were engaged in constructing the dams consisted of details taken from about thirty regiments.

There were some changes in command of the army during its stay at Alexandria. On April 26, 1864, John A. McClernand arrived from Texas to take command of Detachment Thirteenth Corps. He brought with him Michael K. Lawler's Second Brigade, First Division, Thirteenth Corps, which arrived at Alexandria April 18–26. At that time McClernand was ill, and on May 1, Lawler assumed temporary command of Detachment Thirteenth Corps. On May 10 he officially assumed command of Detachment Thirteenth Corps.

April 30, 1864, Birge was relieved from duty with Second Division, Nineteenth Corps and ordered to Baton Rouge to assume command of the post.

On May 2, 1864, Franklin was finally disabled by a wound that he had received April 8 at Sabine Cross Roads, and he left for New Orleans. Emory then assumed command of Nineteenth Corps, and McMillan assumed command of Emory's First Division. Rust took charge of McMillan's Second Brigade, First Division.

May 13, 1864, Banks' army left Alexandria and marched toward Simsport on the Atchafalaya River. Lawler led the column with his Detachment Thirteenth Corps; Emory came next with Nineteenth Corps, and Andrew J. Smith brought up the rear with the Detachment Army of the Tennessee. The army marched along the south bank of the Red River as far as Fort De Russy to cover the withdrawal of Porter's gunboats and transports. It was harassed along the way by the enemy cavalry under Steele, Major, and Bagby, and Polignac's infantry, and at the same time Isaac F. Harrison's Confederate cavalry brigade marched along the north bank of the river.

Engagement at Mansura (Belle Prairie, or Smith's Plantation), Louisiana, May 16, 1864. On the morning of May 16, 1864, on the prairie of Avoyelles beyond Marksville, Banks found Taylor's forces in position across his line of retreat near Mansura. Banks promptly deployed his army to the right of the road, with Smith's command on the right, Cameron's Third Division, Detachment Thirteenth Corps in the center, and Emory's Nineteenth Corps on the left, next to the road. Then, pivoting on the road near the village of Cocoville, the line wheeled to the left and approached Mansura from the west. Finally, as Banks' line passed Mansura and approached Taylor's position, Emory's Nineteenth Corps was on the left of the road, Dickey's colored brigade was on the right of Emory and on the right of the road, James Keigwin's brigade of Thirteenth Corps (formerly Lawler's) was on the right of Dickey, and Smith's command was on the right of the line. Arnold's cavalry was on the flanks. The engagement that followed consisted largely of artillery fire and lasted about four hours, but as the Federal line advanced, Taylor withdrew. Banks then moved on and bivouacked that night eight miles from the Atchafalaya River. The next morning the army moved on to Simsport, where the gunboats and transports had arrived two days earlier.

Engagement at Yellow Bayou (Bayou De Glaize, or Old Oaks), Louisiana, May 18, 1864. On May 18, 1864, troops of Andrew J. Smith's command, which formed the rear guard of the army, were in position near Yellow Bayou to cover the army as it crossed the Atchafalaya. At the time, Smith was at the landing and Mower was in command of the troops along the bayou. Mower had with him Sylvester G. Hill's Third Brigade, First Division, Sixteenth Corps, which consisted of the 33rd Missouri and the 35th Iowa; William F. Lynch's First Brigade, Third Division, Sixteenth Corps; and William T. Shaw's Second Brigade, Third Division, Sixteenth Corps. Edmund J. Davis' cavalry brigade was also with the infantry. With Mower was John H. Tiemeyer's Battery M, 1st Missouri Light Artillery of Seventeenth Corps; George R. Brown's 9th Battery, Indiana Light Artillery of Sixteenth Corps; and James M. Cockefair's 3rd Battery, Indiana Light Artillery of Sixteenth Corps.

On the retreat toward Simsport May 17, 1864, Mower's command had crossed, and taken position along, Yellow Bayou. When Mower learned the next morning that his skirmishers were engaged on the road running along Yellow Bayou, he ordered his three brigades to recross the bayou and drive the enemy back. Hill's brigade crossed first, Lynch's brigade followed, and Shaw's brigade crossed last.

Mower skirmished with the enemy for about two miles and then, after passing through a dense thicket, found the enemy in strong force on the far side of a field. When the Federal troops appeared, the enemy opened fire with twelve guns. Mower then formed a line, with Hill's brigade on the right and Lynch's brigade on the left. Thomas J. Kinney was in command of Lynch's brigade while Lynch was absent at the Atchafalaya River. Tiemeyer's battery was on the right of the line, and Brown's battery was near the left of the line (there were two regiments to its left). Shaw's brigade was halted in reserve, but two regiments were detached to support the batteries. Cockefair's battery was also in rear of Mower's line.

After a time, the enemy advanced in force against the front and left flank of Mower's line, and Kinney immediately changed the front of 119th Illinois to the left to protect that flank. The Federal cavalry that was on the left of Mower's line soon gave way, and the enemy infantry moved toward the rear of the line. The two regiments remaining with Shaw, the 27th Iowa and the 32nd Iowa, and two guns of Cockefair's battery were sent to the left, where they formed a line at a right angle to the left of Mower's line. The 14th Iowa of Shaw's brigade, which was supporting Brown's battery, also faced to the left. The combined fire of the infantry on that flank and the guns of Brown's and Cockefair's batteries soon drove the enemy back.

At 4:00 P.M., Mower ordered a second advance and soon found the enemy in the thicket previously mentioned. After a sharp fight, they were driven from the thicket and back across the open field. Mower then returned to his original line. Lynch, who was on the Atchafalaya when the battle started, hurriedly rejoined his brigade, but a short time later he was wounded, and Kinney resumed command. Kinney was injured when his horse was killed, and Hervey Craven assumed command of the brigade. Craven led the brigade during the last charge. Hill was wounded during the last attack and turned over the command of the brigade to William B. Keeler.

The enemy did not renew the attack, and at dark Mower's brigades moved back to their positions of the night before.

* * * * * * * * * *

Meantime, back at Simsport, Bailey had constructed a bridge of steamboats across the Atchafalaya River, and on May 19, 1864 the troops at Simsport crossed on this bridge. Smith's command then came in and crossed over on the evening of May 20. The whole army then marched toward the Mississippi River and arrived at Red River (or Red River Landing) May 21. From there the troops of the Army of the Tennessee returned to Vicksburg. Thirteenth Corps, Nineteenth Corps, and the cavalry, all under the command of Emory, marched on to Morganza, Louisiana and went into camp May 22.

The organization of the forces commanded by Nathaniel P. Banks during the Red River, Louisiana Campaign March 10–May 22, 1864 was as follows:

DETACHMENT THIRTEENTH CORPS, Thomas E. G.
    Ransom, to April 8, 1864, wounded
    Robert A. Cameron, to April 27, 1864
    John A. McClernand, to May 1, 1864, sick
    Michael K. Lawler

First Division
    Second Brigade, Michael K. Lawler, to May 1, 1864
        James Keigwin

Note. At the beginning of the campaign, First Division and Second Division were in Texas. Lawler's brigade was later transferred from Texas to Alexandria, where it arrived April 18–26, 1864. April 17, 1864, Fitz Henry Warren was ordered to bring the First Brigade of the division to the Red River as soon as practicable, and he arrived near Fort De Russy in May 1864.

Third Division, Robert A. Cameron, to April 8, 1864
    William H. Raynor, to April 27, 1864
    Thomas H. Bringhurst, April 27, 1864
    Robert A. Cameron
    First Brigade, Aaron M. Flory, to April 8, 1864, wounded and captured
        Bradford Hancock, to April 27, 1864
        Thomas H. Bringhurst
    Second Brigade, William H. Raynor, to April 8, 1864
        James R. Slack

Fourth Division, William J. Landram
  First Brigade, Frank Emerson, to April 8, 1864, wounded and captured
    Francis A. Sears, to April 28, 1864
    Frederick W. Moore
  Second Brigade, Joseph W. Vance, wounded and captured
    Albert H. Brown, to April 19, 1864
    Job R. Parker

Artillery, Adolph Schwartz
  1st Battery, Indiana Light Artillery, Martin Klauss
    Lawrence Jacoby
  Chicago Mercantile Battery, Illinois Light Artillery, Pinckney S. Cone
    Henry Roe
  Battery A, 1st Missouri Light Artillery, Elisha Cole
  2nd Battery, Ohio Light Artillery, William H. Harper
  1st Battery, Wisconsin Light Artillery, Jacob T. Foster

NINETEENTH CORPS, William B. Franklin, to May 2, 1864, disabled by a wound
  William H. Emory

First Division, William H. Emory, to April 23, 1864
  James W. McMillan, to April 24, 1864
  William H. Emory, to May 2, 1864
  James W. McMillan
  First Brigade, William Dwight, to April 18, 1864
    George L. Beal
  Second Brigade, James W. McMillan, to April 23, 1864
    Henry Rust, Jr., April 23, 1864
    James W. McMillan, to May 2, 1864
    Henry Rust, Jr.
  Third Brigade, Lewis Benedict, to April 9, 1864, killed
    Francis Fessenden, to April 23, 1864, wounded
    Justus W. Blanchard
  Artillery, George T. Hebard
    Benjamin Nields
    25th Battery, New York Light Artillery, Irving D. Southworth
    Battery L, 1st United States Artillery, Franck E. Taylor
    1st Battery, Vermont Light Artillery, George T. Hebard
    1st Battery, Delaware Light Artillery, Thomas A. Porter

Note. The 1st Battery, Vermont Light Artillery was with First Division until the army reached Grand Ecore on its return to Alexandria, and then it was transferred to the corps' Artillery Reserve. The 1st Battery, Dela-

ware Light Artillery was transferred from the Artillery Reserve to First Division.

Second Division, Cuvier Grover
  First Brigade, Frank S. Nickerson
  Second Brigade, Edward L. Molineux, to early April 1864
    Henry W. Birge, to about April 21, 1864
    Henry W. Birge, from April 25, 1864
  Third Brigade, Jacob Sharpe
  Artillery, George W. Fox
    7th Battery (G), Massachusetts Light Artillery, Newman W. Storer
    26th Battery, New York Light Artillery, George W. Fox
    Battery F, 1st United States Artillery, Hardman P. Norris
    Battery C, 2nd United States Artillery, John I. Rodgers

Note 1. First Brigade was at Carrollton, Louisiana until transferred to Alexandria April 15–18, 1864.
Note 2. At Grand Ecore, Second Brigade was incorporated into a temporary division under Birge for the march to Alexandria. The temporary division was broken up April 25, 1864, and the brigade returned to Second Division.

Artillery Reserve, Henry W. Closson
  1st Indiana Heavy Artillery (two companies), William S. Hinkle
  1st Battery, Vermont Light Artillery, Edward Rice
  1st Battery, Delaware Light Artillery, Benjamin Nields

CORPS D'AFRIQUE
  First Brigade, First Division, William H. Dickey

Note. Dickey's brigade consisted of four regiments of United States Colored Troops.

CAVALRY, Albert L. Lee

  First Brigade, Thomas J. Lucas
  Third Brigade, Harai Robinson, to April 8, 1864, wounded
    John M. Crebs
  Fourth Brigade, Nathan A. M. Dudley, to April 18, 1864
    Edmund J. Davis
  Fifth Brigade, Oliver P. Gooding
  Artillery
    2nd Battery (B), Massachusetts Light Artillery, Ormand F. Nims
    Battery G, 5th United States Artillery, Jacob B. Rawles

Note. John G. Fonda's Second Brigade was at Port Hudson.

DETACHMENT ARMY OF THE TENNESSEE, Andrew J. Smith

First Division and Third Division, Sixteenth Corps, Joseph A. Mower

First Division
    Second Brigade, Lucius F. Hubbard
    Third Brigade, Sylvester G. Hill, to May 18, wounded
        William B. Keeler

Note. First Brigade, First Division was at Memphis, Tennessee.

Third Division
    First Brigade, William F. Lynch, to May 18, 1864
        Thomas J. Kinney, May 18, 1864
        William F. Lynch, afternoon of May 18, 1864, wounded
        Thomas J. Kinney, disabled
        Hervey Craven
    Second Brigade, William T. Shaw
    Third Brigade, Risdon M. Moore

Artillery, James M. Cockefair
    3rd Battery, Indiana Light Artillery, James M. Cockefair
    9th Battery, Indiana Light Artillery, George R. Brown

Note. Mower was assigned command of both First Division and Third Division of Sixteenth Corps at the beginning of the campaign, April 9, 1864.

Provisional Division, Seventeenth Corps, T. Kilby Smith
    First Brigade, Jonathan B. Moore
    Second Brigade, Lyman M. Ward
    Artillery
        Battery M, 1st Missouri Light Artillery, John H. Tiemeyer

ROUSSEAU'S OPELIKA, ALABAMA RAID
JULY 10, 1864–
JULY 22, 1864

In late June 1864, when William T. Sherman's Army of the Military Division of the Mississippi was near Kennesaw Mountain and Marietta in Georgia during the Atlanta Campaign, Lovell H. Rousseau, commander of the District of Nashville, Department of the Cumberland, asked permission to lead an expedition to destroy the Montgomery and West Point Railroad, over which supplies were sent from Alabama to Joseph E. Johnston's Army of Tennessee in Georgia. The Montgomery and West Point Railroad connected at West Point with the Atlanta and West Point Railroad, which carried the supplies on to Atlanta.

On June 29, 1864, Sherman granted permission for Rousseau to make preparations for the expedition, but directed him to make no move until it could be determined that Nathan B. Forrest's cavalry would not be in a position to interfere. Rousseau proceeded to organize a Provisional Division, which consisted of the following regiments: the 8th Indiana Cavalry and 2nd Kentucky Cavalry from the Second Brigade of Judson Kilpatrick's Third Cavalry Division, Army of the Cumberland, then commanded by William W. Lowe; the 5th Iowa Cavalry from First Brigade of Third Cavalry Division; the 9th Ohio Cavalry from the District of Northern Alabama; and the 4th Tennessee Cavalry of the District of Nashville. One section of Battery E, 1st Michigan Light Artillery, commanded by Leonard Wightman, was also attached to the division. Rousseau divided his command into two brigades, assigning Thomas J. Harrison to command First Brigade and William D. Hamilton to command Second Brigade. Hamilton was needed to command his own regiment, however, and a couple of days later Matthewson T. Patrick was assigned to command Second Brigade.

On June 30, 1864, Sherman informed Rousseau that the expedition should start from Decatur, Alabama and move to the railroad between Tuskegee and Opelika, and when the railroad had been destroyed, he was to join Sherman's army with his command.

Rousseau left Decatur July 10, 1864 with a mounted force of about 2,500 men and marched to the southeast to Somerville, where he halted for the night. He crossed Sand Mountain July 11, then passed through Blountsville the next day, crossed Strait Mountain, and halted that night about five miles from Ashville. On the evening of July 13, Rousseau's column reached the Coosa River at

Greensport Ferry. On the morning of July 14, it moved downstream about four miles to a ford at Ten Islands, where it prepared to cross. The crossing was opposed by a Confederate force under James H. Clanton, which consisted of the 6th and 8th Alabama Cavalry and some state militia, but they were driven back, and on the evening of July 15, the column reached Talladega. There the troopers captured large quantities of food and other commissary stores and destroyed what they could not use. They also destroyed two gun factories, several railroad cars, and the depot, which also contained supplies.

To confuse the enemy as to his real intentions, Rousseau then marched south toward Montgomery, Alabama. On the evening of July 16, 1864, he arrived on the Tallapoosa River at Stowe's Ferry. He spent the night getting his command across the river, and then, without rest, pushed on toward Montgomery. After a time, however, he turned off to the left and marched through Dadeville, arriving at Loachapoka on the Montgomery and West Point Railroad, twelve miles southwest of Opelika, about sunset July 17. At 10:00 that night, after a short rest, Rousseau's men began destroying track, bridges, stations, and other structures on the railroad. They continued this work with little interruption until about 10:00 A.M. July 19.

On July 18, 1864, about six miles of track were destroyed on the road at Chehaw Station, about twelve miles southwest of Loachapoka, and also at Notasulga, six miles west of Loachapoka. On July 19, Rousseau's command pushed eastward along the railroad to Opelika, destroying the track as they advanced. This also included the burning of large quantities of stores of all kinds, bridges and trestle-work, water tanks, and station buildings and their contents. At Auburn the track was destroyed, and a large amount of lumber and other stores were burned. Some track was also destroyed on the Columbus branch of the railroad, south from its junction at Opelika for about two miles. The total length of the railroad destroyed by the raiders was about thirty miles. There was little interference with this work, but there was some skirmishing with Clanton's cavalry near Chehaw Station.

Rousseau halted work about a mile east of Opelika. He allowed the men to rest for a few hours on the afternoon of July 19, then took up the march toward Marietta, Georgia to join Sherman's army.

He marched northward through Rough and Ready, Alabama and La Fayette to Roanoake and halted at midnight twenty-five miles from Opelika. On July 20 he marched about thirty-five miles, passing through Wedowee, Carrollton, and Villa Rica; he reached Marietta July 22.

Rousseau then returned to Nashville, Tennessee, but he left his cavalry with Sherman under the command of Thomas J. Harrison. Almost immediately, Sherman ordered Harrison to move with his command to Sandtown on the Chattahoochee River. Upon arriving there, Harrison relieved George Stoneman's Cavalry Division, which immediately moved to the east of Atlanta in preparation for its raid toward Macon, Georgia. Harrison's cavalry, then organized as a brigade, was assigned to Edward M. McCook's command, and with McCook's division took part in his raid on the Macon and Western Railroad. For details of McCook's expedition, see Atlanta, Georgia Campaign, Cavalry Raids on the Railroads South of Atlanta, Georgia, Kilpatrick's Raid from Sandtown to Lovejoy's Station, Georgia.

ACTION AT SALTVILLE, VIRGINIA OCTOBER 2, 1864

On September 11, 1864, Stephen G. Burbridge, commander of the District of Kentucky, proposed to John M. Schofield, commanding the Department of the Ohio, that he lead an expedition to capture Saltville in southwestern Virginia. This town and the surrounding area were of great importance to the Confederacy because of the large salt works located there and the lead mines near Wytheville to the east, and also because the Virginia and Tennessee Railroad, an important east-west line of communication, ran through the region.

Schofield was not enthusiastic about the proposal, but when Henry W. Halleck, the army chief of staff, approved the idea, Schofield authorized Burbridge on September 19, 1864 to proceed with his plan. Also on that date, Burbridge directed Nathaniel C. McLean, commander of First Division, District of Kentucky at Mount Sterling, to march toward Saltville the next day.

On September 20, 1864, McLean left Mount Sterling with his division of three brigades, which consisted of regiments of Kentucky Cavalry, Kentucky Mounted Infantry, the 11th Michigan Cavalry, and the 12th Ohio Cavalry. A section of mountain howitzers was attached to James W. Weatherford's 13th Kentucky Cavalry of Edward H. Hobson's First Brigade.

McLean was to be joined en route by the 26th Kentucky Mounted Infantry and the 11th Kentucky Cavalry of Hugh Ewing's Second Division, District of Kentucky, and also by about 600 men of the 5th United States Colored Cavalry, which was then being organized at Camp Nelson under James S. Brisbin. This detachment of the 5th United States Colored Cavalry consisted of the troops of the regiment that had been organized by that time, and it was to join McLean under the command of James F. Wade.

To create a diversion as Burbridge advanced toward Saltville and Abingdon, Schofield ordered Jacob Ammen to march from Knoxville, Tennessee with 800 men and Alvan C. Gillem with 1,650 men toward Bull's Gap, Tennessee. Ammen was to hold Bull's Gap while Gillem moved on and attacked Jonesboro, Tennessee, about thirty-eight miles to the east.

Marching eastward from Mount Sterling, Burbridge's column passed through Saylersville and arrived at Prestonburg, Kentucky September 24, 1864. There he was joined by Wade's detachment of the 5th United States Colored Cavalry from Camp Nelson. Wade's command was temporarily assigned to Robert W. Ratliff's Fourth Brigade.

Burbridge's column was soon observed by the enemy, and this was promptly reported to John Echols, who was in command of the Confederate forces in southwestern Virginia. These troops were a part of John C. Breckinridge's Department of Western Virginia and East Tennessee. Echols' only available troops in southwestern Virginia at the time of Burbridge's advance were Henry L. Giltner's cavalry brigade and Robert Smith's battalion, the 13th Virginia Reserves. John C. Vaughn's cavalry division of Breckinridge's department was in East Tennessee, and Echols ordered it to Bull's Gap to delay the advance of Ammen and Gillem. Echols then began assembling troops to oppose Burbridge's advance.

Burbridge left Prestonburg September 26, 1864 and marched by way of Pikeville to the Louisa Fork of the Big Sandy River, reaching the summit of Laurel Mountain on the night of September 29. The march across the mountain was continued during the night in a violent storm, and Burbridge halted on the evening of September 30 on the farm of Reese T. Bowen in the Clinch River valley. At that point Burbridge encountered a part of Giltner's cavalry, which retired after a brief skirmish.

Meantime, at Ulysses S. Grant's suggestion, William T. Sherman, commanding the Military Division of the Mississippi, sent an order to Burbridge directing him to return from his expedition and report at Nashville, Tennessee for operations against Nathan B. Forrest's cavalry. This order, however, was not received by Burbridge, because as he advanced beyond Prestonburg, he lost all connection with headquarters at Lexington, and also with Ammen and Gillem in East Tennessee. The country to the rear of Burbridge's column was, at that time, infested with guerrillas and bushwhackers who prevented the Federal messengers from getting through. Consequently, Burbridge continued his march toward Saltville.

Gillem and Ammen moved with their commands, as ordered, to Bull's Gap, where they had arrived by September 25, 1864. Gillem then was informed that John S. Williams, with a cavalry division, had joined Vaughn in East Tennessee; believing that he had not sufficient force to meet the enemy on his front, Gillem requested that Ammen accompany him on the march eastward. On September 27, both commands left Bull's Gap and marched to Greeneville, then on to Rheatown the next day. On September 29 they moved on to Jonesboro, where they met a small enemy force, and from there they continued on the next day, against some opposition, to Carter's Station, about forty miles from Saltville. There they drove the enemy across the Holston River, but then they received their copy of the order directing Burbridge to withdraw to Kentucky, and they proceeded no farther. As a result, Vaughn was able to move with his command to Saltville.

At mid-morning October 1, 1864, Burbridge left the Bowen farm and advanced toward Saltville. About two miles out, he encountered the main body of Giltner's brigade, which was in position on the western slope of Clinch Mountain. After a brief resistance, Giltner retired to the top of the mountain. Burbridge again came up with his division about noon, and by moving against Giltner's flank forced him to fall back to Laurel Gap, only five miles from Saltville. Burbridge then forced his way through the gap, and the last obstruction on the way to Saltville was cleared. By that time, however, it was nearly dark, and instead of moving on and occupying the town, he went into camp in front of the gap. This delay was to prove costly to Burbridge. Late that day, Alfred E. Jackson arrived at Saltville and assumed command of the Confederate forces there, and that night Robert T. Preston arrived from Dublin, Virginia, east of Wytheville, with his regiment of Virginia Reserves to reinforce Jackson.

At the time of Burbridge's advance, Joseph Wheeler was in East Tennessee conducting a raid against the Federal communications around Knoxville. While near Knoxville, he yielded reluctantly to John S. Williams' request that he move with his own brigade and George G. Dibrell's brigade, both of John H. Kelly's division of Wheeler's cavalry corps, and some artillery on a raid to Strawberry Plains. Upon arriving at Strawberry Plains, Williams found the place too strong to attack, and when he attempted to rejoin Wheeler, he was unable to do so. He then moved off to the northeast, and by late September 1864 he had arrived at Bristol, Tennessee. Williams was then assigned to Echols' command, and he promptly marched toward Saltville to join the Confederate forces assembling there. Williams, as the senior officer present, assumed command of the Confederate forces at Saltville.

Early on the morning of October 2, 1864, Burbridge advanced and attacked Jackson's pickets about three miles from Saltville. These were men of Giltner's brigade who were out watching the roads on both sides of the North Fork of the Holston River. Giltner then withdrew slowly along the south side of the river, and Burbridge sent Robert W. Ratliff's Fourth Brigade across the river in pursuit of him. Ratliff followed Giltner for more than a mile toward Saltville until checked briefly at Sanders' Hill, just in front of Jackson's breastworks. While Giltner delayed Ratliff, the van of Williams' division, commanded by Felix H. Robertson, arrived and took position on a high ridge on the right of Giltner.

The enemy line was then formed with Williams' own brigade, which consisted only of the 9th Kentucky Cavalry and a battalion of the 1st Kentucky Cavalry, on the left, on a bluff along the river, and Giltner's brigade was on the right of Williams. On the right of Giltner's brigade was Robert Smith's battalion of Virginia Reserves, which was in advance of a small branch called Cedar Creek on Sanders' Hill. Robertson's brigade was on an elevation in advance of Cedar Creek, on the right of Smith's battalion, and Dibrell's brigade was on the right of Robertson's brigade and on the extreme right of the enemy line. Preston's regiment was in reserve in rear of the junction of Giltner's brigade and Robert Smith's battalion. Williams' brigade on the left faced to the northwest; the left of Giltner's line faced west; and Giltner's right and Robertson's and Dibrell's brigades faced to the northeast.

Burbridge's attack began about 11:00 A.M. October 2, 1864, with the heaviest fighting taking place on the Confederate right, where Ratliff's brigade began to press forward against Dibrell's and Robertson's brigades and Smith's battalion of Virginia Reserves. Ratliff advanced with the 11th Michigan Cavalry on the right, the 12th Ohio Cavalry in the center, and the 5th United States Colored Cavalry on the left. He soon forced Robertson and Dibrell to withdraw to the west side of Cedar Creek, and he then halted to re-form his brigade. When this was completed, Ratliff advanced to Cedar Creek, and then, after some severe hand-to-hand fighting, the enemy fell back to some breastworks about halfway up the slope of Chestnut Ridge. Ratliff charged and drove Robertson and Dibrell back to the top of the ridge.

By that time both sides were nearly out of ammunition, and finally the enemy retired to a position in front of Saltville. Ratliff followed to the top of the ridge, but he was forced to halt there when he ran out of ammunition.

Charles S. Hanson's Third Brigade, on the Federal right, arrived on the river bank about noon, and on the far side of the river, the left of Giltner's line and the 9th Kentucky of Williams' brigade held a strong position at the top of a bluff about 100 feet high. Hanson managed to get his men across the river, and, supported by two regiments of Edward H. Hobson's First Brigade, he started them up the bluff. Hanson was wounded in the attack, and his troops were soon withdrawn.

About 1:00 P.M., after the Federal attacks on both

the left and the right of their line had been stopped, Burbridge ordered Hobson to charge across the river at the ford east of Saltville with his remaining two regiments and some additional troops. Hobson, supported by James W. Weatherford's battery on some hills to the rear, crossed the river under a heavy fire and moved up the bluff at a point where the enemy line was held by the 10th Kentucky Mounted Infantry of Giltner's brigade. This regiment resisted until reinforcements came up, and then Hobson withdrew across the river.

About 5:00 P.M. the firing ceased all along the line, and at about that time, Vaughn arrived with the brigades of Basil W. Duke and George Cosby from Carter's Station.

Late in the day, just before the fighting ended, Burbridge finally received a copy of Sherman's order directing him to return from his expedition. Burbridge then left Hobson to bring back his command, and he departed immediately for Kentucky. McLean's division arrived at Lexington, Kentucky October 17, 1864.

The organization of Stephen G. Burbridge's command from the District of Kentucky during the Saltville, Virginia Expedition was as follows:

First Division, Nathaniel C. McLean
    First Brigade, Edward H. Hobson
        35th Kentucky Mounted Infantry, Edmund A. Starling
        40th Kentucky Mounted Infantry, Clinton J. True
        13th Kentucky Cavalry, James W. Weatherford

Note. A section of mountain howitzers was attached to Weatherford's regiment.

    Second Brigade, Francis N. Alexander
        30th Kentucky Mounted Infantry, Milton P. Hodges
        45th Kentucky Mounted Infantry, Lewis M. Clark
    Third Brigade, Charles S. Hanson
        37th Kentucky Mounted Infantry, Samuel Martin
        39th Kentucky Mounted Infantry, Stephen M. Ferguson
        109th United States Colored Troops, Orion A. Bartholomew
        1st Kentucky Cavalry, Alderson T. Keen
        Battery C, Kentucky Light Artillery, John W. Neville
    Fourth Brigade, Robert W. Ratliff
        26th Kentucky Mounted Infantry, Francis M. Page
        11th Kentucky Cavalry, Milton Graham

        11th Michigan Cavalry, Simeon B. Brown
        5th United States Colored Cavalry, James F. Wade
        12th Ohio Cavalry, Robert H. Bentley

WILSON'S RAID TO SELMA, ALABAMA MARCH 22, 1864– APRIL 24, 1865

In January 1865, as Ulysses S. Grant began to prepare for the spring campaigns of the armies of the United States, there was, in the South, a diminishing hope for the survival of the Confederacy. During the latter part of 1864, William T. Sherman, commander of the Military Division of the Mississippi, had marched across Georgia to Savannah, and he was then beginning his march northward through the Carolinas toward Virginia. By his victories at Franklin and Nashville in late November and December 1864, George H. Thomas, commander of the Department of the Cumberland, had destroyed John B. Hood's Confederate Army of Tennessee and was solidly in control of Central Tennessee. In Virginia, George G. Meade's Army of the Potomac was still besieging Petersburg, and within a few months it would drive Robert E. Lee's Army of Northern Virginia from the city toward Appomattox Court House.

Grant's plans for the spring of 1865 called for a continuation of the movements of Meade and Sherman against the Confederate forces in the East, and in the West he directed Edward R. S. Canby, commanding the Military Division of West Mississippi, to organize an expedition and move on Mobile and into Central Alabama. As a support for Canby's expedition, Grant ordered Thomas to send James H. Wilson, commander of the Cavalry Corps, Military Division of the Mississippi, with a force of about 5,000 men to make a demonstration toward Tuscaloosa and Selma, Alabama to divert attention from affairs at Mobile.

Upon receipt of this order, Wilson believed that he could accomplish nothing of importance with such a small force, and he suggested to Thomas that if permitted to march with his entire available force into Central Alabama, he would defeat Nathan B.

Forrest's cavalry command, capture Tuscaloosa, Selma, Montgomery, and Columbus, destroy everything of military value in those cities, and also break up rail communications in that part of the state. Thomas agreed with Wilson's proposal and so notified Grant.

Grant approved of Wilson's proposed movement, and on February 13, 1865 he directed Thomas to prepare an expedition, to be commanded by Wilson, consisting of about 10,000 cavalry to move into Central Alabama in conjunction with Canby's expedition to Mobile. Grant informed Wilson that he should have all the latitude of an independent commander, and this order relieved Wilson of any direct responsibility to either Thomas or Sherman. Wilson's orders were to move on Tuscaloosa, Selma, and Montgomery and to capture these towns if possible. This being accomplished, Wilson was then directed to move in the direction of Macon, Georgia, Mobile, Alabama, or westward toward the Mississippi River, as circumstances might dictate.

After the defeat of Hood's army at Nashville in December 1864, Wilson's Cavalry Corps had followed in pursuit as far as the Tennessee River, and it had then, except for Richard W. Johnson's Sixth Division, gone into winter quarters along the Tennessee River at Eastport, Mississippi and Waterloo and Gravelly Springs in Tennessee. Edward M. McCook's First Division was at Waterloo, Eli Long's Second Division and Emory Upton's Fourth Division were at Gravelly Springs, and Edward Hatch's Fifth Division was at Eastport. On January 5, 1865, Johnson's Sixth Division was ordered to Pulaski, Tennessee to watch the country north of the Tennessee River. On February 3, Joseph F. Knipe was ordered to move with his Seventh Division to New Orleans, in the Department of the Gulf, and report to Canby. Many of Knipe's men were without horses, and it was necessary to dismount Hatch's division to secure enough serviceable mounts for Knipe's command. Thus, upon moving out at the beginning of his expedition to Selma, Wilson had with him only McCook's First Division, Long's Second Division, and Upton's Fourth Division. For the complete organization of Wilson's command, see end of this section.

Wilson had planned to begin his movement on March 3, 1865, but heavy rains set in, causing the rivers and streams to rise and making the roads impassable, and the crossing of the Tennessee River was delayed until March 18. On that day, Wilson's divisions began crossing from Waterloo to Chickasaw, Alabama, a short distance east of Eastport. By March 21, all troops were across and ready to begin their march.

Finally, on the morning of March 22, 1865, Wilson's men broke camp and began their march toward Selma, almost 200 miles to the south. In an attempt to conceal from the enemy his true destination for as long as possible, Wilson planned to move his divisions by three different routes while passing through the mountainous country of northern Alabama, and then to bring them together for the final advance on Selma. According to Wilson's march orders, Upton's division was to march by roads to the east of the rest of the corps to Barton's Station on the Memphis and Charleston Railroad, and then past Russellville and Mount Hope to Jasper. Long's division was to march to Cherokee Station on the Memphis and Charleston Railroad, and then by way of Frankfort and Russellville to Bear Creek. There he was to cross the creek and move by way of Thorn Hill to Jasper. McCook's division was to follow Long to Bear Creek, but from there it was to move to the right on the road to Tuscaloosa as far as Eldridge, then eastward to Jasper. From Jasper the divisions of the corps were to move on the same road to Selma.

Upton reached Jasper first, on March 26, 1864, then pushed on toward Elyton (present-day Birmingham). He arrived at Saunders' Ferry on the Mulberry Fork of the Black Warrior River that day, and by noon March 27, his division was across the river and moving toward the crossing of the Locust Fork. McCook arrived next at Jasper, on March 27, then followed Upton to Saunders' Ferry, crossed the river the next day, and followed him toward the Locust Fork. Long halted at Jasper on the night of March 27, and the next day followed the other divisions across the forks of the Black Warrior River. Upton arrived at Elyton on the evening of March 28, McCook on March 29, and Long on March 30. At and near Elyton, Upton destroyed the Red Mountain Iron Works, the Cahaba Valley Mills, the Bibb Iron Works, the Columbia Works, and much public property. On March 30, Upton marched south with his division, camping at

Montevallo that night. Long's division followed Upton and arrived at Montevallo March 31.

At Elyton, John T. Croxton's First Brigade of McCook's division was detached, and Croxton was ordered to Tuscaloosa to destroy the bridge over the Black Warrior River, the factories and mills that were located there, and the University of Alabama, which was then used as a military training school. Croxton left Elyton at 4:00 P.M. March 30, 1865 and marched to the southwest on the road to Trion. He halted that night about eight miles from Elyton. McCook, with Oscar H. La Grange's Second Brigade and Moses M. Beck's 18th Battery, Indiana Light Artillery of his division, marched to Montevallo on March 31.

During the early part of Wilson's march, he encountered no opposition, but a few days after he had started, Forrest began to assemble his cavalry near Selma to prevent Wilson from reaching the city. On January 24, 1865, Forrest had assumed command of the Confederate District of Mississippi, East Louisiana, and West Tennessee, and on March 1, after reorganizing his cavalry, he moved his headquarters to West Point, Mississippi on the Mobile and Ohio Railroad.

When Wilson began his march, Philip D. Roddey's cavalry brigade was at Tuscaloosa (it later moved to Selma); Daniel W. Adams, commanding the Confederate District of Alabama, was at Montevallo, north of Selma, with a detachment of militia; Abraham Buford's cavalry division was at Montgomery; James R. Chalmers' cavalry division was at Pickensville, Alabama; and William H. Jackson's cavalry division and Edward Crossland's cavalry brigade were with Forrest at West Point.

On March 23, 1865, Forrest ordered Buford to move his division to Selma, and on March 25, two days before Wilson reached Jasper, Forrest directed Chalmers to move his division to Selma. Frank C. Armstrong's brigade was to move that day, Peter B. Starke's brigade was to follow the next day, and Wirt Adams' brigade was to follow Starke on March 27.

On March 24, 1865, Forrest ordered Crossland's brigade to move from West Point by way of Tuscaloosa and report to Daniel W. Adams at Montevallo, and on March 26 he ordered Jackson to move with his division and follow Crossland by way of Tuscaloosa toward Selma. With these dispositions made,

Forrest left West Point and moved with his escort to join his command near Selma; he arrived near Montevallo on the evening of March 31.

On March 31, 1865, after the corps had arrived at Montevallo, Upton marched from the town at 1:30 P.M. About two miles to the south, he met a Confederate force consisting of some men of Crossland's brigade and Roddey's brigade, and the detachment of militia under Daniel W. Adams. Andrew J. Alexander's Second Brigade of Upton's division quickly charged and drove the enemy back to their main position behind a small creek. Upton then prepared to flank this position while George B. Rodney's Battery I, 4th United States Artillery took position and opened fire. After some skirmishing, the enemy withdrew. Edward F. Winslow's First Brigade pursued until dark, and then the division camped for the night three miles north of Randolph. Long's division and McCook with La Grange's brigade camped that night south of Montevallo.

March 31, 1865, Croxton started at daylight and marched through Jonesboro toward Trion, which was nineteen miles east of Tuscaloosa. He arrived there about sunset, just as the rear of Jackson's division was moving out on its way eastward to join Forrest. About midnight Croxton learned that he had encountered a strong enemy force and that it was preparing for an attack the next morning. Croxton did not wish to become engaged, and on the morning of April 1 he marched west in an attempt to reach the road that ran from Jonesboro to Tuscaloosa. When he learned that the enemy was moving to cut him off, he marched to the northeast about ten miles on the Elyton road as far as Bucksville, and from that point he moved west to Johnson's Ferry on the Black Warrior River, some forty miles above Tuscaloosa. Croxton began crossing at sundown, and by the next day, April 2, his brigade was on the west bank of the river. Croxton did not rejoin the corps again until he arrived at Macon, Georgia on May 1. To avoid interrupting the description of Wilson's operations against Selma, Croxton's movements from April 3 to May 1, 1865 are given at the end of this section.

On the morning of April 1, 1865, Wilson learned from captured couriers that Jackson's division had camped the night before at Scottsville, on the Tuscaloosa and Centerville road, and that Chalmers' division was at Marion and had been ordered to cross the Cahaba River (spelled Cahawba in many reports) and move to a position between Wilson and Selma.

Wilson then ordered McCook to march with La Grange's brigade as rapidly as possible and seize the bridge over the Cahaba River at Centerville. That done, McCook was to push on and join Croxton in an attempt to defeat Jackson. McCook captured the bridge with little difficulty, left a force to guard it, and moved on, with skirmishing, to Scottsville, about seven miles north of Centerville on the road to Trion. He arrived there at 5:00 P.M., but failed to find Croxton, who had moved on toward Tuscaloosa about twenty-four hours earlier.

At daylight April 2, 1865, McCook sent out two regiments from Scottsville on the Trion road, and they soon found the enemy in a strong position. They skirmished for a time, and then McCook withdrew with his brigade toward the Cahaba River and the enemy followed. He recrossed the river and burned the bridge, and he also destroyed all boats that he found along the banks. By this action, he delayed a large part of Forrest's command from joining him in time for the defense of Selma. La Grange's brigade then marched from Centerville to Plantersville, and there it received an order to return and bring in the wagon train. It met the train near Randolph and served as its escort to Selma, where it arrived on the evening of April 6.

At daylight April 1, 1865, all of Wilson's corps, except Croxton's brigade, marched southward toward Randolph, with Upton's division in the lead. At Randolph, Upton turned to the left onto a road running to the southeast and marched to Maplesville. There he turned back to the right and moved forward on the old Selma road, which joined the main Selma road near Ebenezer Church, about six miles north of Plantersville.

When Long's division came up to Randolph, it continued on along the main road, to the right of Upton, toward Selma. Near Randolph, the head of Long's column met the enemy's skirmishers, and four companies of the 17th Indiana Cavalry of Abram O. Miller's First Brigade moved up and drove them back to Ebenezer Church, where the enemy was preparing to make a stand. Forrest was on the field in person at Ebenezer Church that day, having arrived with his escort and about 200 men of Armstrong's brigade. There was some heavy skir-

mishing, and then the rest of the 17th Indiana Cavalry moved up and formed on the left of the road. At about that time Upton's division, coming up from Maplesville, moved against the enemy's flank and rear. Upton struck that part of the enemy's line held by the militia, who fled, and then the entire line fell back in some disorder, leaving three guns and about 200 prisoners. Long and Upton followed the enemy to a point near Plantersville, where they camped for the night.

Capture of Selma, Alabama, April 2, 1865. At 6:00 A.M. April 2, 1865, Long's division of Wilson's corps left Plantersville, about twenty miles from Selma, and marched without opposition toward Selma. When Long arrived within about six miles of the city, he turned off to the right and moved across to the Summerville and Selma road, where he arrived about 3:00 P.M. He turned to the left on that road and marched southward until he arrived near the defensive line the Confederates had constructed around the city. This line was very strong, and it completely encircled the city on the north side of the Alabama River. It began on the Confederate left at the river, just below Selma, and ran northward along the east side of Valley Creek, just west of Selma; after crossing the Marion road and the railroad running from Selma to Meridian, it continued on in that direction for about one-half mile. It then curved to the northeast and ran along the northern side of the Plattenburg plantation for nearly a mile before turning back to the southeast. It then ran on for about two miles to the Alabama and Tennessee Rivers Railroad. The Range Line road passed through this part of the line a little over a mile northwest of the point where it crossed the railroad. From the railroad the line continued on to the south and southwest to the river east of Selma.

At about 4:00 P.M., Long dismounted his men and formed his division on both sides of the road in a position that was concealed from the enemy by an intervening ridge. Originally he placed Robert H. G. Minty's Second Brigade on the right and Abram O. Miller's First Brigade on the left, but before the attack, Miller led his brigade by the right flank, past Minty's brigade, and formed it on the right of the division. On the west side of the road were, in order from right to left, the 17th Indiana, 123rd Illinois, and 98th Illinois of Miller's brigade and the 4th

Ohio of Minty's brigade. George I. Robinson's Chicago Board of Trade Battery, Illinois Light Artillery was placed on the east side of the road, next to the road, and the 4th Michigan of Minty's brigade was formed on the left of the battery.

Upton's division left Plantersville about 10:00 A.M. April 2, 1865 and followed Long's division until the latter turned off toward the Summerville and Selma road. Upton continued on, however, and approached Selma on the Range Line road, arriving in front of the fortifications, on the left of Long's division, about 4:00 P.M. At this point the roads on which Long and Upton were advancing were about one and one-fourth miles apart. Upton then began to form his division for the attack. Alexander's brigade was halted, but remained mounted, about two miles from the enemy's works, and Winslow's brigade was formed dismounted on the road in front of the defensive line. The 3rd Iowa was placed on the right of the road, and the 10th Missouri on the left. Rodney's Battery I, 4th United States Artillery was put in position on the right of the road and in rear of the 3rd Iowa, and the 4th Iowa was on the left of the road in rear of the 10th Missouri.

Forrest arrived at Selma early on the morning of April 2, 1865 and reported to Richard Taylor, commander of the Confederate Department of Alabama, Mississippi, and East Louisiana, who was in the city at that time. Taylor left that afternoon by train for Demopolis, leaving Forrest in command of all Confederate troops in Selma. Forrest then placed Armstrong's brigade on the left of the enemy's works, Roddey's brigade on the right of the works, and Daniel W. Adams' militia on the center of the line. Forrest with his escort remained in rear of the works. Chalmers' division had not yet arrived, and Jackson's division was north of Selma.

Wilson's plan for the capture of Selma called for Upton's division to move around through a swamp and strike the enemy's right flank, while Long's division delivered the main assault on the Confederate left along the Summerville road. The attack was to be made late that evening and was to begin when a signal gun was fired. While waiting for the signal, however, a part of Chalmers' division, which was just then approaching Selma, began skirmishing with the 72nd Indiana, Long's rear guard. This was a serious development, and Long believed that to have any chance for success, he should attack at

once. He immediately dispatched the 3rd Ohio of Minty's brigade to support the rear guard and, without waiting for Wilson's signal gun, began his assault.

Long's men advanced at 5:00 P.M. and soon reached the crest of the ridge behind which they had been concealed, about 600 yards from the works held by Armstrong's brigade. There they came under a heavy fire, but they continued to advance until within about 150 yards of the works; then they charged and drove the enemy back to a second defensive line. Long's fight lasted only a little less than half an hour. Long was wounded during the attack, and Minty assumed command of his Second Division. Horace N. Howland took charge of Minty's Second Brigade. Miller was also wounded, and Jacob G. Vail assumed command of First Brigade.

Upton was getting his division in position for the attack when Long carried the works on the right. Upton then sent Winslow forward, with skirmishing, toward that part of the line held by Adams' militia, and the latter quickly gave way and fled toward the river. This left a gap in the line into which Winslow's men advanced toward the second line. Forrest, seeing that further resistance was useless, ordered his men to withdraw and escape as best they could. Wilson's troops then moved in and occupied Selma. By that time it was completely dark. Wilson captured that evening 31 field guns, 2,700 prisoners, and immense quantities of stores.

* * * * * * * * *

Forrest and his escort arrived at Plantersville on the morning of April 3, 1865, then moved on to Marion, arriving there the next morning. Jackson's division, Starke's brigade of Chalmers' division, and the artillery were already there when Forrest arrived.

Wilson assigned Winslow to the command of the city and directed Upton to march with his division at daylight April 3, 1865, drive back any enemy forces to the west side of the Cahaba, and open communications with McCook, who was bringing in the wagon train with La Grange's brigade. McCook and the train arrived at Selma on April 6. Wilson also began the construction of a pontoon bridge to enable him to cross the Alabama River.

While at Selma, Wilson learned that Croxton had been successful in his attack on Tuscaloosa, and he also learned that Canby had a sufficient force to capture Mobile and move into Central Alabama. With this information, Wilson was free to move as he thought best, and he immediately ordered his corps to cross to the south bank of the Alabama River. The crossing was completed by April 10, and the corps then marched toward Montgomery.

The advance of Wilson's column reached Montgomery at 7:00 A.M. April 12, 1865, and the rest of the column came up later. All public stores in the city were destroyed, and early on the morning of April 14, Wilson resumed his march eastward toward Tuskegee. Upon arriving there, he ordered La Grange to move with his brigade by way of Opelika and West Point to Macon, Georgia, and he also ordered Upton, with Minty's division following, to move directly toward Columbus.

On April 16, 1865, Upton arrived in front of Columbus, assaulted the works, and captured the town. He then destroyed all military stores, the ironclad *Jackson,* the arsenal, navy yard, foundry, paper mills, 15 locomotives, 200 railroad cars, 100,000 bales of cotton, and large quantities of artillery ammunition. Also on April 16, La Grange arrived at West Point and attacked and captured Fort Tyler and the town.

Early on the morning of April 17, 1865, Wilson's command resumed the march toward Macon. La Grange's brigade of McCook's division marched by way of La Grange, Griffin, and Forsyth to Macon, and Minty's division, followed by Upton's division, moved by way of the Double Bridges over the Flint River and Thomaston to Macon. Minty arrived at Macon on April 20, and Upton and La Grange came in the next day.

Movements of Croxton's Brigade after April 2, 1865. It will be remembered that Croxton's brigade was detached from the Cavalry Corps at Elyton March 30, 1865 and sent on a raid to Tuscaloosa, and that on the morning of April 3 it had arrived on the west bank of the Black Warrior River at Johnson's Ferry, north of Tuscaloosa. On April 3, Croxton began his march down the river from Johnson's Ferry toward Tuscaloosa, about forty miles to the southwest. His plan was to move that

day to Northwood, a town on the west bank of the river opposite Tuscaloosa, and then to force a crossing of the river the next day.

Croxton reached the outskirts of Northwood at 9:00 that night, and when it was learned that the enemy was taking up the planking on the bridge, the 2nd Michigan Cavalry moved forward and captured the bridge. The men then replaced the flooring of the bridge and rode into Tuscaloosa. There was some opposition and great disorder in the city during the night, but by the morning of April 4, 1864, Croxton's troops were firmly in control. They then proceeded to destroy the University of Alabama, a foundry, a factory, two niter works, and a large quantity of stores.

While at Tuscaloosa, Croxton attempted to find some safe way to move eastward and rejoin the corps, but he was unable to do so. He then decided to recross the Black Warrior and attempt to destroy the railroad between Demopolis and Meridian. On April 5, 1865, Croxton recrossed the Black Warrior River, destroyed the bridge, marched out to the west twenty-five miles, and camped that night at King's Store. The next morning, he moved out twelve miles on the road toward Pleasant Ridge, camping that night at Lanier's Mills on the Sipsey River, eight miles from Vienna. There he received information that caused him to change his plans. He learned that a large enemy force had left West Point, Mississippi and was moving down the Tombigbee River in his direction. He also learned that Forrest was at Marion, that Jackson was near Tuscaloosa, and that Wilson had captured Selma.

Croxton concluded that, based on this information, he would be unable to execute his plans to destroy the railroad, and he decided to turn back. He sent his men across the Sipsey to burn the mills, then marched eastward toward Tuscaloosa. He camped that night at Romulus, and on the morning of April 7, 1865 he arrived at Northport. There was still no word from Wilson, and, finding little forage in the area, he marched northward with his column twelve miles out on the Byler road and went into camp. He remained there until April 11, while he attempted to communicate with Wilson or learn of his movements since the capture of Selma. He was unable to learn anything whatsoever about Wilson, and he decided to recross the Black Warrior River and move into the Elyton Valley, where he hoped to learn whether Wilson had marched toward Mobile or Montgomery.

On April 11, 1865, Croxton moved his brigade to Wyndham's Springs, but he was unable to cross the river there. The next day he marched by the Jasper road to Wolf Creek, but again high water prevented him from crossing. On April 13 he moved around the head of Wolf Creek, and the next day he crossed Lost Creek at Holly Grove. On April 15 he marched to Comack's Mills on the Black Water Creek, about four miles north of Jasper. He rebuilt the bridge there and moved on to the east, camping that night about four miles from the Sipsey Fork of the Black Warrior.

He crossed the Sipsey Fork April April 16, 1865 and the next day marched by way of Arkadelphia to Hanley's Mills on the Mulberry Fork of the Black Warrior. He crossed the river there and marched to the southeast, passing through Mount Pinson, fourteen miles north of Elyton, on April 19 and Trussville on April 20, and arrived at Talladega on April 22. There Croxton turned to the east and passed through Munford's Station, Oxford, and Daviston, arriving on the Tallapoosa River on April 24. On April 25, he marched on by way of Arbacoochee to Hebron, Alabama, then crossed the state line to Bowdon, Georgia, camping that night at Carrollton. There the column turned to the southeast, crossed the Chattahoochee River on April 26, and the next day passed through Newnan, halting for the night at Flat Shoals on the Flint River. On April 28, Croxton marched toward Barnsville; he passed through Barnsville the next day, and camped that night at Forsyth. He arrived near Crawford's Station on April 30, then rejoined the corps at Macon on May 1.

For further information about Wilson's Selma Raid and the period following, see Cavalry Corps, Military Division of the Mississippi.

The organization of James H. Wilson's Cavalry Corps, Military Division of the Mississippi during the Selma Expedition March 22–April 24, 1865 was as follows:

CAVALRY CORPS, James H. Wilson

First Division, Edward M. McCook
    First Brigade, John T. Croxton
    Second Brigade, Oscar H. La Grange
    Artillery

        18th Battery, Indiana Light Artillery, Moses M. Beck

Second Division, Eli Long, to April 2, 1865, wounded
    Robert H. G. Minty
    First Brigade, Abram O. Miller, to April 2, 1865, wounded
        Jacob G. Vail, to April 20, 1865
        Frank White
    Second Brigade, Robert H. G. Minty, to April 2, 1865
        Horace N. Howland
    Artillery
        Chicago, Illinois Board of Trade Battery, Illinois Light Artillery, George I. Robinson

Fourth Division, Emory Upton
    First Brigade, Edward F. Winslow
    Second Brigade, Andrew J. Alexander
    Artillery
        Battery I, 4th United States Artillery, George B. Rodney

BATTLE OF SHILOH (OR PITTSBURG LANDING), TENNESSEE APRIL 6–7, 1862

On January 30, 1862, Henry W. Halleck, commanding the Department of the Missouri, authorized Ulysses S. Grant to organize an army in his District of Cairo for the purpose of capturing Fort Henry on the Tennessee River and Fort Donelson on the Cumberland River. Grant's army, known as the Army of the District of Cairo, with the aid of the navy's gunboats, captured Fort Henry on February 6 and Fort Donelson on February 16, and thus made possible the use of the Tennessee River for a deep penetration of the Confederacy by the army and navy. In fact, a short time later, Union gunboats steamed up the river as far as Florence, Alabama and returned, doing considerable damage to bridges and shore installations as they passed.

At the time of the capture of the forts, the Confederate forces remaining to oppose an invasion of Tennessee were Albert Sidney Johnston's Central Army of Kentucky (also called Army of Central Kentucky and Central Army), then at Edgefield, opposite Nashville, Tennessee, and Pierre G. T. Beauregard's command, consisting of troops guarding the Mississippi River and holding West Tennessee. Beauregard's headquarters was at Corinth, Mississippi, and his troops were stationed at Columbus, Kentucky, Island No. 10 in the Mississippi River, Corinth, Mississippi, New Madrid, Missouri, and Jackson, Humboldt, and Union City in Tennessee.

With the fall of Fort Donelson, Johnston was forced to withdraw from Nashville, and he moved south through Tennessee and then west to join Beauregard at Corinth.

On February 17, 1862, Grant assumed command of the newly created District of West Tennessee, and his army then became known as the Army of the District of West Tennessee, and later as the Army of the Tennessee.

Advance of the Army to Pittsburg Landing. On March 1, 1862, following the occupation of Nashville by Don Carlos Buell's Army of the Ohio, Halleck ordered Grant to lead an expedition up the Tennessee River to destroy the Bear Creek Bidge on the Memphis and Charleston Railroad, near Eastport, Mississippi. The purpose of this expedition was to interrupt communications between northern Alabama and Corinth, and thus delay or prevent Johnston from joining Beauregard with his army.

On March 7, 1862, Grant was relieved from command of the expedition up the Tennessee River because of alleged irregularities, and Charles F. Smith was assigned command in his place. Smith embarked his troops on transports at Fort Henry and then steamed upriver, arriving at Savannah, Tennessee, on the east bank of the river, March 11. The next day Smith sent Lewis Wallace with his Third Division to Crump's Landing on the west bank of the river, six miles above Savannah, for the purpose of destroying a bridge on the Mobile and Ohio Railroad that ran south from Columbus, Kentucky to Corinth. Wallace was unable to accomplish his mission, but he remained with his division near Crump's Landing.

Smith also sent William T. Sherman with his Fifth Division to destroy the Bear Creek Bridge in northern Mississippi, but because of heavy rains that flooded the area, he was unable to reach the Memphis and Charleston Railroad. He then reembarked his division and moved downriver to find a suitable place to land and renew his attempt on the railroad. The water in the Tennessee River had risen rapidly because of the rains, and the first suitable place to go ashore was at Pittsburg Landing, a landing place for boats engaged in river traffic. This was about nine miles above Savannah, on the west bank of the river.

Upon his arrival at Pittsburg Landing, Sherman found Stephen A. Hurlbut with his Fourth Division, which had been sent upriver to support Sherman's movement against the railroad. On March 16, 1862, Sherman and Hurlbut disembarked their troops and moved up to the top of the bluffs, which rose to a height of 80–100 feet above the level of the water in the river.

After an inspection of the area, Sherman concluded that another attempt on the Memphis and Charleston Railroad from that point was not feasible. He did, however, suggest to Grant, who had been restored to command, and had arrived at Savannah March 17, 1862, that Pittsburg Landing would be an excellent place to establish a base for the army. Grant accepted Sherman's suggestion, and ordered all troops then at Savannah to move up to Pittsburg Landing. John A. McClernand's First Division did not arrive at Savannah until March 20, and it too was later sent to join the other divisions. By the end of March, all of Grant's army, except Wallace's division at Crump's Landing, was at Pittsburg Landing. It was at about that time that Grant's army was first called the Army of the Tennessee.

Meantime, on March 11, 1862, Halleck was ordered to assume command of the newly created Department of the Mississippi, which was formed in order to secure better coordination among the Union forces operating in the West. Included in the new department was Buell's Army of the Ohio. Immediately upon receipt of this order, Halleck directed Buell to march with his army, then at Nashville, Tennessee, to Savannah. Buell began his march March 16, and during the afternoon of April 5, the day before the Battle of Shiloh, Jacob Ammen's Tenth Brigade of William Nelson's Fourth Division, the advance brigade of Buell's column, arrived near Savannah.

Battleground of Shiloh. Before proceeding with an account of the Battle of Shiloh, it is necessary to describe briefly the more important features of the region where the camps of the army were located and where the battle was fought. Beyond the bluffs along the river, rolling tableland stretched away to the west for a distance of two and a half to three miles, and in April 1862 this was covered with open forest, and in many areas with dense undergrowth. There were many farm houses in the area, and most of these were surrounded by a substantial area of cleared land. These fields were commonly known by the names of the farmers who worked the land. At the eastern end of this elevated ground, next to the river, the front was cut by deep ravines and sloughs, which at the time of the battle were overflowing because of the high water in the river.

This high ground west of the river was bordered on the south by Lick Creek, which emptied into the Tennessee River about two miles above (south of) Pittsburg Landing. On the north was Snake Creek, which emptied into the river about three-fourths of a mile below the landing. Flowing into Snake Creek, about one mile from its mouth, near the crossing of the Hamburg-Savannah road, was a major tributary called Owl Creek, which flowed through the area from southwest to northeast. All three streams flowed through muddy bottom lands, and at the time of the battle, because of the spring rains, they were wide and deep and virtually impassable. The distance between Lick Creek and Owl Creek–Snake Creek varied from about three to five miles.

There were several roads that traversed this region that were of considerable significance during the battle. From Pittsburg Landing a good road ran out to the west and then to the southwest to Corinth, about twenty-two miles distant. This was called the Corinth road, or the main Corinth road. About one mile out from the river, this road crossed another road called the Hamburg-Savannah road (also the River Road). The latter road ran northward from Hamburg, which was about four miles south of Pittsburg Landing, crossed Lick Creek, and ran on to the north on a course roughly parallel to the river, and back far enough from it to pass by the heads of the ravines running in from the river. The road crossed Snake Creek near the junction with Owl Creek and then continued on toward Savannah.

About one-fourth mile beyond the crossing of the Hamburg-Savannah road, the road to Corinth branched. The road to the left, which was called the eastern Corinth road, ran nearly south, crossed the Hamburg-Purdy road west of the Peach Orchard, and continued on to the south to the Bark Road, which it joined about three miles west of Hamburg. The right-hand branch, or the main Corinth road, ran to the west from the forks of the road for about a mile and crossed the Hamburg-Purdy road. There it turned toward the south and passed Shiloh Church about one-fourth mile beyond the Hamburg-Purdy road. At a point about five miles out from Pittsburg Landing, the main Corinth road intersected the Bark Road at a point that is today at the southwest corner of the Shiloh National Military Park. Lick Creek, which rises near Monterey, flows along the south side of the Bark Road ridge.

North of the main Corinth road, and at an average of about one mile from it, Owl Creek flows in a northeasterly direction until it empties into Snake Creek near the crossing of the Hamburg-Savannah road.

The general elevation of the land along the main Corinth road does not vary much, but on both sides of the road the surface is badly cut up by deep ravines, and in many of these there are flowing streams.

The Hamburg-Purdy road branched off from the Hamburg-Savannah road north of Lick Creek, and a short distance southeast of the Peach Orchard, then ran on to the northwest toward Purdy. It crossed the eastern Corinth road west of the Peach Orchard and the main Corinth road about one-fourth mile northeast of Shiloh Church, and then ran on across Owl Creek.

Camps of Grant's Army. A short time after going ashore, Sherman marched out with his division about two and a half miles on the main Corinth road to Shiloh Church. There on a ridge behind Shiloh Branch (or Oak Creek), Sherman established his camps where he was in position to guard the road from Corinth. Shiloh Branch flowed from southeast to northwest, passing about 300–400 yards south of Shiloh Church, and emptying into Owl Creek near the crossing of the Hamburg-Purdy road. Sherman detached David Stuart's Second Brigade and sent it to the far left, near the Tennessee River, to cover the Hamburg-Savannah road. Stuart took position at the junction of the Hamburg-Savannah road and the

Hamburg-Purdy road, not far from where the former crossed Lick Creek. At that point he was two miles south of Pittsburg Landing and well over one mile to the left of the other brigades of the division. Sherman placed his other three brigades as follows: Jesse Hildebrand's Third Brigade was to the left of Shiloh Church; Ralph P. Buckland's Fourth Brigade was to the right of Hildebrand, with its left at Shiloh Church; and John A. McDowell's First Brigade was on the right of Sherman's line, with its right on Owl Creek at the bridge where the Hamburg-Purdy road crossed the creek.

Hurlbut's Fourth Division camped along the Hamburg-Savannah road, about a mile from the river and a mile in rear of Sherman's camps. The center of the division was at the crossing of the main Corinth road and the Hamburg-Savannah road. Nelson G. Williams' First Brigade was to the right of the Corinth road; Jacob G. Lauman's Third Brigade was to the left of the road; and James C. Veatch's Second Brigade, which arrived later, camped to the right and rear of Williams' brigade.

Charles F. Smith's Second Division, then commanded by William H. L. Wallace, was encamped to the right and rear of Hurlbut, between the Hamburg-Savannah road and the Tennessee River and north of the Corinth road. John McArthur's Second Brigade was next to the Hamburg-Savannah road; Thomas W. Sweeny's Third Brigade was east of McArthur; and James M. Tuttle's First Brigade was between Sweeny's brigade and the river.

McClernand's First Division was encamped near the junction of the Hamburg-Purdy road and the main Corinth road, with C. Carroll Marsh's Second Brigade on the left of the Hamburg-Purdy road and Leonard F. Ross' Third Brigade on the left of the road. Abraham M. Hare's First Brigade was farther to the right in the direction of Owl Creek.

Benjamin M. Prentiss' Sixth Division was just then in the process of formation, and as the regiments assigned to the division arrived, they were placed in camp between Stuart's brigade of Sherman's division on the left and Sherman's other brigades on the right. Everett Peabody's First Brigade was on the right of the eastern Corinth road, and Madison Miller's Second Brigade was on the left of the road. Their camps were about one mile south of the junction of the eastern Corinth road and the main Corinth road, and about one-fourth mile

south of the Hamburg-Purdy road. Prentiss' division did not connect with Sherman's troops on the right or left, but was separated from them on both flanks by several hundred yards.

Lewis Wallace's Third Division was in camp to the north, across Snake Creek, near Crump's Landing. Morgan L. Smith's First Brigade was camped near the river; John M. Thayer's Second Brigade was at Stony Lonesome, about two miles out on the Purdy road; and Charles Whittlesey's Third Brigade was just beyond Adamsville on the same road.

Assembly of the Confederate Forces. While Grant's army was investing Fort Donelson, Albert Sidney Johnston, with his Central Army of Kentucky, was encamped at Edgefield, Tennessee, opposite Nashville. Immediately after receiving the news of the surrender of Fort Donelson, Johnston began preparations for the abandonment of Nashville and Central Tennessee. At that time Pierre G. T. Beauregard commanded an independent force in western Tennessee and northern Mississippi, which was guarding the Mobile and Ohio Railroad and the Memphis and Charleston Railroad, which crossed at Corinth, Mississippi. Johnston regarded it as imperative that he join Beauregard with his command before either force could be attacked separately.

Johnston moved first to Murfreesboro, where he was joined by the survivors of Fort Donelson, and also the remnants of the command that George B. Crittenden had brought back from the Confederate defeat at the Battle of Mill Springs or Logan's Cross Roads. Johnston then moved on to Huntsville, Alabama and, after a movement that lasted three weeks, arrived at Corinth March 24, 1862.

Also arriving at Corinth to join the Confederate army assembling there were Braxton Bragg with 10,000 men from Pensacola, Florida, Leonidas Polk with Benjamin F. Cheatham's division from Columbus, Kentucky, Daniel Ruggles with a brigade from New Orleans, troops that had escaped from Island No. 10 when it was evacuated, and troops from outlying garrisons that were under Beauregard's command.

By an order of March 29, 1862, Johnston organized a new Confederate Army of the Mississippi by the consolidation of his army from Kentucky and Beauregard's command. Johnston assumed command of the combined forces and assigned Beauregard as second in command. Later Johnston organized the army into four corps as follows:

First Corps, commanded by Leonidas Polk, which consisted of Charles Clark's First Division and Benjamin F. Cheatham's Second Division.

Second Corps, commanded by Braxton Bragg, which consisted of Daniel Ruggles' First Division and Jones M. Withers' Second Division.

Third Corps, commanded by William J. Hardee, which consisted of Thomas C. Hindman's First Brigade, Patrick R. Cleburne's Second Brigade, and Sterling A. M. Wood's Third Brigade.

Reserve Corps, commanded by John C. Breckinridge, which consisted of Robert P. Trabue's First Brigade, John S. Bowen's Second Brigade, and Winfield S. Statham's Third Brigade.

After the organization of the army was completed, Johnston and Beauregard decided to attack Grant's army at Pittsburg Landing before Buell's Army of the Ohio, which was then en route from Nashville to Savannah, could arrive there.

Johnston's army left Corinth about mid-afternoon April 3, 1862, and then heavy rains the next day and night rendered the roads almost impassable. Progress was very slow, but by 10:00 A.M. April 5, Hardee's corps, which was in the lead, was deployed across the road to Pittsburg Landing and about two miles from Shiloh Church. The other corps were to the rear, still struggling forward, but by late afternoon they too were in position for an attack the next morning. Bragg's corps was in line behind Hardee, Polk's corps was behind Bragg, and Breckinridge's corps, in column, was on the road behind Polk.

Battle of Shiloh, Sunday, April 6, 1862. Neither Grant nor his division commanders expected any attack on the army at Pittsburg Landing, but along the front of Prentiss' division, enemy cavalry had been observed at various times, and Everett Peabody, commanding Prentiss' First Brigade, had become uneasy. At about 3:00 A.M. April 6, 1862, Peabody sent out James E. Powell of the 25th Missouri with three companies of that regiment and two companies of the 12th Michigan Regiment on a reconnaissance in front of Prentiss' camps. Powell followed a trail through the woods (present-day Reconnoitering Road) about a mile to the southwest to the edge of the Fraley field. There, in the faint light, just at dawn, he observed enemy troops at the southwest corner of the field. These belonged to Aaron B. Hardcastle's infantry battalion of Sterling A. M. Wood's Third Brigade of Hardee's corps.

Powell formed his small command in a skirmish line, and a little before 5:00 A.M. advanced across the field. Upon reaching the center of the field, the enemy opened fire, and then both sides exchanged fire for about a half-hour without a change in position. At 6:15 A.M. Peabody sent forward David Moore with five companies of his 21st Missouri to reinforce Powell. Powell noted that Wood's brigade, which had arrived about 6:30 A.M., was replacing Hardcastle's troops on his front, and he then moved back and withdrew from Fraley's field and moved back toward his camps. Actually, at this point Johnston's entire line was advancing with Hardee's three brigades in the front line. Thomas C. Hindman, commanding the First Brigade of Hardee's corps, was disabled, and R. G. Shaver assumed command. Adley H. Gladden's brigade of Withers' division of Bragg's corps was also added to the front line to occupy a gap between Hardee's line and Lick Creek.

Powell was retiring along the trail on which he had advanced earlier in the morning when he met Moore coming forward with his five companies. This was about one-half mile from Fraley's field, or about halfway back to camp. Moore then sent back for the rest of his regiment, which joined him a few minutes after 7:00 A.M. He prepared to advance and soon met Company A of the 16th Wisconsin of Peabody's brigade, which had been out on picket, and it joined Moore's command. Shortly after advancing, Moore's line was struck by a heavy fire from Shaver's skirmishers, which were advancing along the east side of the main Corinth road. Moore then moved his troops into Seay field, just east of the road. He was wounded, and Humphrey M. Woodyard took command of the regiment. Woodyard's (Moore's) men then began to fall back, and Powell ordered his 25th Missouri to move back. Woodyard halted his command at the eastern edge of Seay field, and held this position until about 7:15 A.M.

Shaver's brigade, moving to the northeast, entered Seay field from the southern edge, and Woodyard withdrew to the northeastern corner of the field, where he was joined by three other companies of the 16th Wisconsin. Shaver's skirmishers then moved forward in a direction a little north of east and forced Woodyard to fall back.

About 7:00 A.M. Peabody heard the firing at Seay field, and he realized that the fighting was spreading. Peabody had only two regiments left in camp, and one of these, the 16th Wisconsin, was about 600 yards distant. He then assembled the 12th Michigan and the remaining companies of the 25th Missouri, and about 7:30 A.M. led them forward. On the way he met Powell coming back, and learned that the enemy had occupied Seay field. Taking the able-bodied men of Powell's command, he moved on and joined Woodyard. Peabody then formed a line on a ridge on the south side of present-day Reconnoitering Road, and Woodyard formed on his left. He had scarcely taken position when Shaver's brigade advanced, three lines deep. Shaver was momentarily halted, and for a time both sides exchanged a heavy fire across a ravine. Wood's brigade then came up on the left of Shaver, and about 8:15 A.M. both brigades charged Peabody's line, compelling Woodyard and Peabody to fall back in confusion through their camps.

Early on the morning of April 6, 1862, Prentiss ordered Miller, commanding the Second Brigade of his Sixth Division, to form his brigade in line of battle. Miller's brigade, which consisted of the 18th Missouri, the 61st Illinois, and temporarily the 18th Wisconsin of Peabody's brigade, took position along the northern edge of Spain field, which was just east of the eastern Corinth road. At 8:00 A.M. Miller moved his brigade to the south line of the field. Andrew Hickenlooper's 5th Battery, Ohio Light Artillery was placed in Spain field on the east side of the road, and Emil Munch's 1st Battery, Minnesota Light Artillery across the road to the right.

That morning Gladden's brigade had moved eastward on the Bark Road, then turned onto the eastern Corinth road, and a little after 8:00 A.M. approached Spain field. James R. Chalmers' brigade of Withers' division, which had been following Gladden, moved up on his right. Gladden was halted briefly by Miller's fire, and Miller pulled back to

the north side of the field when the troops on his right fell back. Gladden then charged into Spain field, but the attack was repulsed, and Gladden was mortally wounded about 8:15 A.M. Daniel W. Adams then assumed command of the brigade and ordered another advance, but his men were driven back across Spain field by the fire of Hickenlooper's and Munch's artillery.

This was only a brief respite, however, because by this time Peabody's brigade had been driven back by the attacks of Shaver and Wood, and Miller's men also began to move to the rear. Prentiss rallied the remnants of his command on the crest of a ridge not far to the rear of his camps. The troops remaining with him at that time consisted of what was left of the 18th Missouri, the 12th Michigan, and the 18th Wisconsin. The 23rd Missouri Regiment, which had arrived at the landing by boat shortly after the battle began, moved out and took position on Prentiss' new line.

At about daylight April 6, 1862, Jesse J. Appler, whose 53rd Ohio was on the left of Hildebrand's brigade and on the extreme left of Sherman's line, heard the sounds of the firing at the Fraley field, and he formed his regiment in line of battle a short distance south of his camp. When enemy troops approached on the right of Appler's line a little before 7:00 A.M., Appler withdrew his regiment to the rear of his camp. By that time Sherman was preparing his division to meet a possible attack on his front.

Hildebrand formed his 57th Ohio and 77th Ohio at their camps in front of Rhea's field. The 77th Ohio was on the right, next to the Corinth road, and Allen C. Waterhouse's Battery F, 1st Illinois Light Artillery was on the left of the 77th Ohio, overlooking Rhea's field. Appler's 53rd Ohio had moved out in front, and was in Rhea's field, and the 57th Ohio was about 400 yards in rear of Appler's line. Hildebrand then moved his other regiments forward to support Appler, but when he observed the regiments of Cleburne's brigade advancing to the right of Rhea's field, he proceeded no farther down the slope toward Shiloh Branch.

Between 6:00 and 7:00 A.M., Buckland learned that his pickets were engaged, and he formed his brigade on the left of the Corinth road. Then about 7:45 A.M. he ordered his brigade to advance into the woods on his front and form in line of battle.

The 10th Ohio was on the left of the line, next to the road; the 48th Ohio was on the center of the line; and the 72nd Ohio was on the right. The four left regiments of Cleburne's brigade approached to within 100 yards of Buckland's line and opened fire. Soon a heavy fire developed all along Buckland's line, and this was continued for about forty-five minutes. The infantry was supported by Ezra Taylor's Battery B, 1st Illinois Light Artillery, commanded by Samuel E. Barrett, which was posted to the right and a little in advance of Shiloh Church on the Corinth road. Despite strenuous efforts, Cleburne's men were unable to advance against the heavy Federal fire, and by 8:30 A.M. the enemy attack west of Shiloh Church had bogged down.

About 7:30 A.M. McDowell formed his brigade, which was on the left of Sherman's line, so as to hold the Hamburg-Purdy road, and also to protect the right front of Buckland's line. About 8:00 A.M. McDowell moved his line forward about fifty yards and then advanced to a ridge overlooking Shiloh Branch. At that time, it was noted that there was a gap of about 200 yards between the right of Buckland and the left of McDowell, and the latter then sent his 40th Illinois to occupy this gap and support Buckland.

At about 7:00 A.M., as Sherman prepared to meet the enemy attack, he sent to McClernand for help. McClernand's headquarters was about one-half mile northeast of Shiloh Church, and was just north of the main Corinth road, about 300 yards east of Water Oaks Pond. When McClernand became aware of the firing at the Fraley field that morning, he ordered James S. Rearden to hold his Third Brigade, which was on the left of the division and about one-fourth mile from Hildebrand's camps, in readiness for any emergency. Leonard F. Ross, the proper commander of Third Brigade, was sick, and Reardon was in temporary command of the brigade. Reardon, however, also became ill that morning, and Julius Raith assumed command of the brigade. By 8:00 A.M. Raith had formed his brigade in front of its camps, and he then moved forward about 100 yards to a better position in front of Sherman's review field. Raith's brigade was then about 100 yards to the left and rear of Waterhouse's battery and was too far to the rear of Hildebrand's line to protect it from an enemy flanking attack from the left.

As Hardee's corps advanced that morning, the brigades became somewhat separated. The two brigades commanded by Hindman advanced more rapidly than Cleburne's brigade, and Hindman's own brigade, then commanded by Shaver, inclined to the right and, as has already been noted, struck the right of Prentiss' division. Hindman, in person, with Wood's brigade, came up in front of Appler's 53rd Ohio Regiment, which was the left regiment of Hildebrand's brigade. Hindman then ordered Cleburne to move his brigade to the front of Buckland's line.

Cleburne continued his advance along the Pittsburg Landing–Corinth road, but was soon stopped by an almost impassable swamp that bordered the Shiloh Branch in front of the position held by Sherman's division. Cleburne then advanced two of his regiments to the right of the swamp and four regiments to the left of the swamp, and when the brigade approached Sherman's line, the regiments on the right were separated from those on the left by a distance of about one-fourth mile. Cleburne's two right regiments started up the slope from the Shiloh Branch toward Appler's regiment about 7:45 A.M., but they were driven back by the fire of the infantry and Waterhouse's battery. They rallied after retiring about 100 yards, but they were not strong enough to renew the attack, and they waited for reinforcements.

Cleburne's four left regiments approached to within about 100 yards of Buckland's line and opened fire. Soon there was heavy fighting all along the line; this was continued for about forty-five minutes, but Cleburne's left was unable to advance against heavy Federal fire. By 8:30 A.M. the enemy attack west of Shiloh Church had been brought to a halt.

J. Patton Anderson's brigade of Bragg's second line then came up and moved over a ridge west of Rhea's field toward Hildebrand's line. Anderson's brigade had been assigned as a reserve for the brigades of Gibson and Preston Pond, which were advancing on the Pittsburg Landing–Corinth road, but they were delayed on the march, and when Anderson reached the field, he was unsupported and was forced to wait until help arrived.

Robert M. Russell's brigade of Clark's division, from Polk's third line, which was also advancing on the main Corinth road, arrived at the front about 8:30 A.M. and halted at the south end of Rhea's field to await orders. Alexander P. Stewart's brigade of Polk's corps then came up and was placed on the right of Russell. A short time later, Bushrod R. Johnson's brigade, also of Polk's corps, came up, moving to the right and taking position to the left of Wood's brigade. Pond's brigade of Bragg's second line, which had been ordered up to protect the extreme Confederate left, did not follow the other brigades across the valley of Shiloh Branch, but moved on down the creek to a position beyond McDowell's brigade.

Anderson's and Russell's brigades then attacked on the front of Hildebrand's brigade, but they were driven back. Then Johnson's brigade came up, and his two right regiments, supported on the left by Russell's brigade and some of Anderson's men, advanced on the position of Waterhouse's battery and the regiments supporting it. The 57th Ohio began to break up and fall back through its camps, and what was left of the 53rd Ohio after its retreat from the Rhea field soon departed for Pittsburg Landing. A short time later Waterhouse was wounded, and his guns were withdrawn about 100 yards, but they then halted and resumed firing. Although the 57th Ohio had gone to the rear, the battery, aided by the 77th Ohio, was able to hold up the enemy advance temporarily. Finally, about 9:30 A.M., the battery was forced to leave the field and march toward Pittsburg Landing, leaving behind three guns in possession of the enemy. This was about an hour after Raith's brigade had taken position on the left and rear of Sherman. A short time later, the 77th Ohio began to break up. Hildebrand's brigade had then virtually disappeared, but Hildebrand remained on the field and offered his services to McClernand.

After the departure of Waterhouse and the 77th Ohio, Raith was able to hold up the enemy advance for a time, but then the pressure became too great. Stewart's brigade, which had at first been directed toward the camps of Peabody's brigade, moved to the left when the camps were found abandoned, and it then advanced toward Raith's brigade. On the right of Stewart, the brigades of Wood and Shaver, which had been pursuing Prentiss' routed division, were ordered to their left to join Stewart in the attack on Raith. This, together with an attack on his front by Russell, Johnson, and Anderson, was more than Raith could stand, and at about 10:00 A.M. he was forced to fall back.

Meantime, shortly after Raith had advanced, McClernand ordered his other two brigades to advance from their camps and form in line of battle. Marsh moved first and took position along a ridge in front of McClernand's headquarters, just south of the main Corinth road. To the left and front of Marsh was a clearing of about twenty acres, which was used by Sherman as a review field. Hare's brigade then came up and passed Marsh's brigade, taking position on its left. At about that time Raith's brigade gave way and retired to the northwest, but it then rallied and took position along the Hamburg-Purdy road, just west of Water Oaks Pond.

Edward McAllister's Battery D, 1st Illinois Light Artillery was placed between Marsh and Hare, at the northwestern corner of Sherman's review field; Jerome B. Burrows' 14th Battery, Ohio Light Artillery was placed in rear of the center of Marsh's line; and James P. Timony, commanding Dresser's Battery D, 2nd Illinois Light Artillery, was on the right of Marsh, near Water Oaks Pond. Farther to the right, in front of the left of Raith's re-formed brigade, was George L. Nispel, commanding Schwartz's Battery E, 2nd Illinois Light Artillery, which was supporting Sherman's line.

Wood's Confederate brigade, moving up after the defeat of Raith, struck the 45th Illinois and 48th Illinois, which were supporting McAllister's battery on the left of Marsh's line, and as more of the enemy moved up, both regiments and McAllister's battery were soon driven back. When the regiments on the left had departed, the 11th Illinois, Marsh's last regiment, soon followed. Burrows' battery was captured, and Timony's battery, which for a time did good service, was finally overrun and captured.

At about the same time as the attack on Marsh, Hindman, who was advancing on the Confederate right, led Shaver's brigade and a regiment of Anderson's brigade in an attack on Hare's brigade, which soon began to break up. Fortunately, at about 9:00 A.M. James C. Veatch's Second Brigade of Fourth Division, which earlier that morning had been sent by Stephen A. Hurlbut to support Sherman on the right, was approaching the review field on the main Corinth road, and it was then moved into the woods in rear of Marsh's brigade, near McClernand's headquarters. Thus, when Marsh's line collapsed, the enemy struck the right of Veatch's brigade and drove the 15th Illinois and

46th Illinois from the field, and they did not rejoin the brigade that day. Veatch, however, remained in command of his 14th Illinois and 25th Indiana, and they continued to do good service during the rest of the afternoon. Veatch with his two regiments moved off to the northeast and was followed by Wood's and Shaver's brigades. Finally, however, at about 11:00 A.M., a little less than an hour after the attack on McClernand had begun, the enemy advance was halted.

Meantime, on Sherman's line, Buckland had been able for a time to hold his position to the right of Shiloh Church against Cleburne, and Barrett's guns continued to fire into Rhea's field from near the church. A little before 10:00 A.M., however, Buckland and McDowell were ordered to fall back to the Hamburg-Purdy road and form a new line. The two brigades then abandoned their camps and their original lines and started back. Barrett's battery moved back by the main Corinth road and joined McClernand.

Sherman, however, had some difficulty in forming a new line. McDowell's brigade, which had been only slightly engaged that morning, moved to the left along the Hamburg-Purdy road to a point just east of McDowell's headquarters, and then, encountering some opposition, it turned off to the left, marched to the northeast, and took position at the northeast corner of the Crescent Field. Buckland also had his troubles. His brigade moved back in good order, and about 10:30 A.M. attempted to form along the road on the right of McClernand, but he was so closely pursued by the enemy as he retired that he was unable to form a solid line along the Hamburg-Purdy road. Sherman had still another problem. Morton's 6th Battery, Indiana Light Artillery, commanded by Frederick Behr, which had been in rear of McDowell's brigade that morning, moved along the Hamburg-Purdy road as it retired toward the left of Sherman's line. As Behr was again getting his battery in position near the junction of the Hamburg-Purdy road and the main Corinth road, he was killed, and the men of the battery fled in disorder, abandoning their guns and taking the caissons with them.

When Raith retired from his advanced position to the vicinity of the junction of the Hamburg-Purdy road and the main Corinth road, he did not connect with the right of McClernand's line but joined on the left of Sherman. Shortly after Raith arrived there he was attacked by Johnson's brigade, with Anderson's brigade on its left. Anderson then attacked Sherman's unsteady line and about 11:00 A.M drove the men back into the thickets north of the Hamburg-Purdy road. Raith, with Nispel's (Schwartz's) battery, held for a time, and during the fighting Raith was mortally wounded. Finally, the remnants of Raith's brigade and Nispel's battery were driven back to Hare's camps. Then, with the troops on both sides exhausted and disorganized, the fighting slackened for a time.

Sherman rallied his men at the Jones field and began to organize a new battle line. He placed Barrett's battery at the southern end of the field, and it was soon in action. He also sent orders for McDowell to move with his brigade, which was the only remaining organized brigade of his division, to the left and form on the new defensive line at the camps of Hare's brigade. McDowell, who had just beaten off an attack by Pond's brigade at the Crescent Field, moved off to the northeast and took position along the edge of the Sowell field, facing nearly south. On the left of McDowell, Sherman had succeeded in forming a line consisting of men from a number of regiments, including the 70th Ohio of Buckland's brigade, and Barrett's battery. McClernand had collected men from the brigades of Raith, Marsh, and Veatch, and with them had formed a strong line on the left of Sherman. This line was strengthened by the 13th Missouri of McArthur's brigade of William H. L. Wallace's Second Division, which had been sent earlier in the day to join Sherman.

When the new defensive line had been formed, Sherman and McClernand decided to advance and attempt the capture of Marsh's camps, which were along a north-south line about one-fourth mile east of the Crescent Field. Sherman, with Marsh on his left, and soon joined by McDowell on his right, advanced about noon. They moved past the camp of the 20th Illinois of Marsh's brigade but were able to proceed only a short distance beyond that point.

At that time, Robert P. Trabue's brigade of Breckinridge's Reserve Corps, which was advancing on the Confederate left with Pond's brigade, met McDowell advancing near the camps of the 20th Illinois, about midway between the Jones field and the Woolf field, and drove him back under the cover of a ridge. There McDowell re-formed his brigade and continued to resist Trabue for about an hour and fifteen minutes.

At 1:00 P.M. McDowell was still fighting, but Marsh was beginning to fall back. Two fresh unbrigaded regiments, the 15th Iowa and 16th Iowa, which had been at the landing and had been assigned to Prentiss' division, joined McClernand at about this time. These two regiments, with a part of Hare's First Brigade of McClernand's division, then extended McClernand's line to the southeast. The two Iowa regiments formed in line, crossed Jones' field, and moved into the woods beyond, and there they held their position for one-half hour. McClernand then ordered his troops to fall back, but the enemy launched an attack on his line, and both McClernand and Sherman gave way and fell back. About 4:00 P.M. they took position to cover the Hamburg-Savannah road, on which Lewis Wallace's division was expected from Crump's Landing.

Sherman remained along the road behind McArthur's drill field for the rest of the day. At 4:00 P.M. Veatch with his two regiments retired to the east side of Tilghman's Creek, where they took position along the eastern side of the Cavalry Field.

When the Battle of Shiloh began on the morning of April 6, 1862, Grant was at his headquarters at Savannah, about nine miles downriver from Pittsburg Landing. When he heard the sounds of firing off to the south, he immediately prepared to move upriver by boat to determine its source.

Meantime, on April 5, 1862, William Nelson had arrived at Savannah from Nashville with his Fourth Division of Buell's Army of the Ohio, and Grant had ordered him to move with his division up the east bank of the river so that he would be in position to be ferried across the river to Crump's Landing or Pittsburg Landing, wherever he might be needed. Unknown to Grant, Buell had arrived at Savannah in person during the evening of April 5, but before leaving Savannah on the morning of April 6, Grant informed him by letter of the orders that he had given Nelson the evening before and the reasons for them. Then Grant left aboard the steamer *Tigress* for Pittsburg Landing.

On his way upriver, Grant stopped at Crump's Landing, where he met Lewis Wallace, whose First Division, Army of the Tennessee was posted in the vicinity. In a brief conversation with Wallace, Grant instructed him to have his division in readiness to execute any orders that he might receive.

Grant then proceeded on upriver and arrived at Pittsburg Landing sometime around 8:30 A.M. After learning that a battle was in progress, he moved out toward the front to find out what was happening. About one-half mile from the river he met William H. L. Wallace, and there he received his first information about the battle and learned that the camps of Prentiss and Sherman were under heavy attack. Grant then sent Algernon S. Baxter, assistant quartermaster, back to the landing with orders for Lewis Wallace to move to Pittsburg Landing with his division. Baxter did not arrive at the landing until about 11:00 A.M., and did not deliver the order to Wallace at Stoney Lonesome until around 11:30 A.M. He then returned to the landing.

During the rest of the day, Grant was engaged in visiting all parts of the battlefield, observing conditions on the battle line, conferring with his division commanders, and issuing necessary orders. According to Grant, he visited all of his division commanders several times during the day. Grant first met Sherman about 10:00 A.M. near the Jones field, but he seemed satisfied that Sherman was doing well and did not remain long with him. He did learn that Sherman's and McClernand's men were about out of ammunition, and he sent an aide back to the landing to have more sent forward. From there Grant went to the Union left, where the situation was more in doubt. When he met Prentiss, he informed him that Lewis Wallace was on the way, and that he could expect help during the afternoon.

While near the landing, Grant organized the ammunition trains for movement to the front, and he also made some dispositions of the regiments that he found there. He sent forward the 23rd Missouri, which had just arrived by boat to reinforce Prentiss, and he ordered the 15th Iowa and the 16th Iowa to form in line and halt the large numbers of stragglers that were arriving at the landing, and to organize them for a return to the front. Later Grant sent these two regiments to reinforce McClernand on the Federal right.

Also, during the day Grant attempted to hasten Lewis Wallace's march to Pittsburg Landing. About 10:30 he dispatched a courier with a verbal order to hurry, but when the courier returned, he reported to

Grant that Wallace had refused to move without a written order. Grant was angered by this development, but he sent an aide with written orders, who delivered the message about noon. Despite Grant's efforts, Wallace did not arrive near the landing until after the fighting had ended for the day.

Grant returned to the landing between 1:00 and 2:00 P.M. and met Buell, then returned to the front. He rode back to the landing later in the day and was present on the left of the line during the final attacks of the day. He then sent orders at nightfall to the division commanders instructing them to be ready to attack early the next morning.

While Sherman's and McClernand's divisions were falling back on the Union right, efforts were being made to reinforce the line on the left. Prentiss had been driven from his camps about 8:30 A.M., and his disorganized regiments had fallen back about one-half mile to the north, where about 9:00 A.M. he met Stephen A. Hurlbut with two brigades of his Fourth Division approaching from the direction of Pittsburg Landing. Prentiss was able to halt and assemble a fairly large number of his men.

Early that morning, Hurlbut's men heard the firing on the front of Prentiss' division, and his brigades were formed in front of their camps. At 7:30 A.M. Hurlbut learned that the left of Sherman's division was under attack, and he ordered Veatch to move with his Second Brigade and support Sherman. Hurlbut kept his other two brigades in line until 8:00 A.M., at which time he received word from Prentiss that he was in trouble and needed help. Hurlbut then formed his brigades in column and marched south on the Hamburg-Savannah road, with Nelson G. Williams' First Brigade in the lead and Jacob G. Lauman's Third Brigade following close behind. Just north of what was later to be known as the "Bloody Pond," Hurlbut turned off onto the Wheatfield Road, which ran out to the southwest to join the eastern Corinth road a short distance south of the Hamburg-Purdy road.

About 8:30 A.M., Hurlbut's marching columns began to encounter Prentiss' fleeing troops, which increased in numbers as they continued on, and Hurlbut learned that the enemy was not far ahead. When Hurlbut finally arrived at an old cottonfield, about one-half mile in rear of Prentiss' abandoned camps, he deployed his two brigades. He placed Lauman's brigade along the western edge of the field on a line nearly perpendicular to the Wheatfield Road, facing to the southwest. Lauman's line was protected in front by dense thickets and undergrowth. Williams' brigade was formed on the left of Lauman's line, facing south, with its left extending almost to the Hamburg-Savannah road, in the direction of Stuart's camps. In rear of Williams' line was a large peach orchard, which soon to become well known. A short time after Hurlbut's line was formed, Williams was disabled, and Isaac C. Pugh assumed command of his brigade.

Hurlbut placed Edward Brotzmann's Battery C, 1st Missouri Light Artillery (Mann's battery) at the angle of his line, between Lauman's and Williams' brigades; he placed Cuthbert W. Laing's 2nd Battery, Michigan Light Artillery (Ross' Battery) in support of Pugh's Second Brigade; and he placed John B. Myers' 13th Battery, Ohio Light Artillery on the right in front of Lauman's brigade.

While the Federals were attempting to establish a strong line on their center and left, Albert Sidney Johnston had been preparing to attack farther to the right against David Stuart's brigade of Sherman's division, which was posted on the extreme left of the Union line. About 9:30 A.M., after their earlier fighting that morning, the brigades of Adams, Jackson, and Chalmers were in line in that order from left to right, preparing for another attack toward the front of Hurlbut's division. At that time Johnston directed Withers to move back with the brigades of Chalmers and Jackson of his division and then march eastward with them and attack the Federal left. Chalmers, whose brigade was in the lead, was delayed for about a half-hour while he waited for a guide, and he then marched to the left of Lick Creek and along the right side of a ravine through which Locust Grove Branch flowed eastward into Lick Creek near the Federal left. Chalmers' brigade reached the Hamburg-Savannah road south of the Locust Grove Branch, and south of Stuart's camps, about 11:00 A.M.

A short time after Withers' departure, Gladden's brigade, then commanded by Adams, which was advancing from the direction of Prentiss' former headquarters, approached the angle in Hurlbut's line. At that time Adams' brigade was alone on that part of the field, because, as noted above, the brigades of Chalmers and Jackson had been sent to the

Confederate right against Stuart, and the brigades of Wood and Shaver, which had captured Peabody's camps, had moved off to the left to join in the attack on Sherman and McClernand.

Adams advanced to within 100 yards of Hurlbut's line and charged, but he was driven back. He rallied his brigade and again attacked unsuccessfully, then tried two more times before withdrawing. Adams was wounded, and Zachariah C. Deas succeeded him in command of the brigade. Additional troops were needed in order to renew the attack, and at 9:30 A.M. Johnston ordered Breckinridge to bring up his Reserve Corps.

During the early morning of April 6, 1862, Breckinridge had remained inactive with his reserve brigades near the junction of the main Corinth road and the Bark Road until 8:30. A short time before that hour, Beauregard had received information that the Confederate left was threatened by a large Federal force, and he then directed Breckinridge to march with his brigades and reinforce that part of the line. Upon receipt of this order, at 8:30 A.M., Breckinridge promptly marched northward on the main Corinth road, but he had not gone far when his orders were changed. Beauregard had learned that his earlier information was not correct, and he then directed Breckinridge to send only one brigade to the left, and to march back with his other two brigades and move to the right along Lick Creek. Shortly after 9:00 A.M., Breckinridge ordered Robert P. Trabue to continue his advance on the main Corinth road with his brigade, and with the brigades of John S. Bowen and Winfield S. Statham, Breckinridge marched back to the Bark Road, then eastward along that road toward the Confederate right.

When Johnston sent his 9:30 order to Breckinridge instructing him to bring up his Reserve Corps to renew the attacks on Hurlbut's division, he was unaware of Beauregard's earlier order and could scarcely have expected that Breckinridge would arrive in under two hours. Actually, however, Breckinridge had been marching in that direction with his two brigades for some time, and the staff officer carrying Johnston's order found Bowen's brigade, followed by Statham's brigade, advancing on the Bark Road. The officer then instructed them to hurry on their way to the right.

Bowen's brigade began to arrive in rear of the Confederate line about 11:00 A.M., and he then moved up to within one-half mile of the area where Jackson and Chalmers were confronting Stuart's brigade and troops under McArthur, which had just arrived and taken position on the right of Stuart and the left of Hurlbut. Bowen then advanced on the left of Jackson's brigade, which was meeting with strong opposition from McArthur. Statham, following Bowen, deployed about a half-mile to the left and rear of Bowen. Statham then moved forward through Prentiss' abandoned camps and, after resting for a time, advanced toward the front of Hurlbut's division in the Peach Orchard.

Meantime, during the quiet period following Adams' repulse, Hurlbut had reorganized his line. Pugh, commanding Williams' brigade, was directed to fall back to a new line in the Peach Orchard, and Lauman to withdraw to a position behind an old split-rail fence. Both brigades were formed with open ground to their front.

After Prentiss had retired with his fleeing troops behind Hurlbut's division, he succeeded in rallying a substantial part of his division, and about 10:00 A.M. brought them forward and placed them in position on the right of Hurlbut's line. His line was formed along an old wagon road that, because of many years of usage and erosion, ran along a shallow depression. This road, which later became the scene of some of the most desperate fighting of Shiloh, ran for about one-half mile from the main Corinth road on the right, along the northeastern side of the Duncan field, across the eastern Corinth road and the Wheatfield Road, and then along the north side of the Peach Orchard to the Hamburg-Savannah road on the left. This road later became known as the "Sunken Road," but this name implies a greater depth than it actually had. Actually, the road was depressed for only a part of its length.

The troops assembled by Prentiss and placed along the Sunken Road belonged to the 18th Missouri and 18th Michigan of Miller's brigade and the 12th Michigan and 25th Missouri of Peabody's brigade. In addition, the 23rd Missouri, which had just arrived by boat at Pittsburg Landing that morning, was sent out at 7:00 A.M. to join Prentiss' division, and when it arrived that morning, it was placed on the left of Prentiss' line.

Hickenlooper, who had lost two guns of his battery that morning, placed the remaining four guns on a low hill in rear of Prentiss' line between the eastern Corinth road and the Wheatfield Road. Munch's battery was also placed on the Sunken Road, just to the left of the eastern Corinth road, and opposite the southeast corner of the Duncan field.

To the right of Prentiss' division, along an extension of the Sunken Road line, were two brigades of William H. L. Wallace's division. Early that morning, Wallace, like the other division commanders, had been alerted by the firing to his front, and by about 8:00 A.M. he had formed his division in line at his camps. About an hour later he sent the 13th Missouri of John McArthur's brigade to reinforce Sherman, who was then seriously threatened, and the 14th Missouri and the 81st Ohio of McArthur's brigade to guard the bridge on the Hamburg-Savannah road over Snake Creek. Then he sent McArthur with the two remaining regiments of his brigade, the 9th Illinois and the 12th Illinois, to support David Stuart's brigade of Sherman's division on the far Union left.

When the above dispositions had been made, William H. L. Wallace marched with his other two brigades to support Prentiss' division. Upon joining Prentiss, Wallace placed James M. Tuttle's First Brigade on the right of Prentiss' line in the Sunken Road and Thomas W. Sweeny's Third Brigade on the right of Tuttle. At that time, Sweeny had with him only two regiments, the 7th Illinois and the 57th Illinois. The 8th Iowa was attached to Prentiss' command and was on the right of Prentiss' line; the 50th Illinois had been sent to support McArthur on the Federal left; and the 52nd Illinois and the 57th Illinois had not yet reported. The right of Sweeny's line rested on a wide and deep ravine that was filled with dense thickets, a short distance north of the main Corinth road. The line extended to the southeast along the northeastern side of the Duncan field and ended a short distance south of the main Corinth road. Tuttle's brigade extended the line along the edge of the Duncan field to a point just beyond the eastern Corinth road. The left of Tuttle's line rested on the 8th Iowa of Sweeny's brigade, which was attached to Prentiss' command.

Meantime, on the far Federal left, Stuart had been informed by Prentiss about 7:30 that morning that the enemy was advancing in force, and a short time later enemy pickets were observed on the Bark Road in front of Stuart's brigade. Stuart then sent to Hurlbut for help, but Hurlbut was unable to comply. About 9:00 A.M., however, William H. L. Wallace sent John McArthur with the 9th Illinois and 12th Illinois of his Second Brigade to reinforce Stuart. The 50th Illinois of Sweeny's brigade was also sent to reinforce McArthur. The camps of Stuart's brigade were located as follows: the camp of the 71st Ohio was along the south side of the Hamburg-Purdy road, just west of its junction with the Hamburg-Savannah road, and the camps of the 54th Ohio and 55th Ohio extended along the south side of the Hamburg-Savannah road to the southeast of the junction for a distance of about one-fourth mile. Stuart's headquarters was on the Hamburg-Savannah road about 400 yards southeast of the junction.

About 10:00 A.M. Stuart formed his brigade in rear of his camps. Hurlbut had sent Brotzmann's Battery (Mann's Battery), supported by the 41st Illinois of Williams' brigade, to aid Stuart, and it took position near the headquarters of Stuart's 71st Ohio. The 71st Ohio and 55th Illinois of Stuart's brigade formed to the left of the battery, facing west, and the 54th Ohio formed to their left, facing south.

McArthur left his camps about 9:00 A.M. with his 9th Illinois and 12th Illinois regiments, with Peter P. Wood's Battery A, 1st Illinois Light Artillery (Willard's Battery) of William H. L. Wallace's division in advance, and marched down the Hamburg-Savannah road toward Stuart's camps. McArthur arrived about 11:00 A.M. and placed the battery in position on the road in rear of the camp of the 71st Ohio, near the southeast corner of the Peach Orchard, and moved the infantry into a ravine to the east of the road, where it was protected from artillery fire. It was soon driven from the ravine by infantry fire, however, and then took position on the high ground to the rear. Its right was opposite the Peach Orchard and on the left of Hurlbut's division. The 50th Illinois of Sweeny's brigade of William H. L. Wallace's division then came up in support of McArthur, and about 11:30 A.M. it took position on the left of McArthur's line, extending it toward the east.

The line occupied by Wallace, Prentiss, Hurlbut, McArthur, and Stuart had scarcely been formed when it was attacked all along its front. The first attacks were directed against the line along the Sunken Road.

When Bragg, who was then commanding all

troops on the center of the Confederate line, found the troops of Wallace's, Prentiss', and Hurlbut's divisions barring his way to Pittsburg Landing, and the consequent destruction of Grant's army, he decided to break the line by direct frontal assaults. At that time, Benjamin F. Cheatham was leading forward from Polk's third line William H. Stephens' brigade of his division, and about 11:00 A.M. Stephens' brigade arrived at the southeast corner of the Duncan field, in front of the left of Tuttle's brigade. Stephens, who was sick at the time, and was then thrown from his wounded horse near the edge of the Duncan field, left the field, and Cheatham personally took charge of the brigade. Then, without support, it advanced straight ahead toward Tuttle's line at the Sunken Road. Stephens' men struggled forward through dense brush and thickets, but were driven back by destructive fire of the Federal infantry and artillery, and they suffered terrible losses. Cheatham then withdrew Stephens' brigade, and later moved it to the right and placed it on the left of Statham's brigade, south of the cottonfield.

Bragg was determined to try again. Randall L. Gibson's brigade was then in the Barnes field, which was on the west side of the eastern Corinth road, awaiting orders, and shortly after Stephens' defeat, Bragg personally directed Gibson to move up and make a second attempt. About noon Gibson crossed the eastern Corinth road and moved forward to the northern edge of a wheatfield, which was immediately to the left of the Wheatfield Road. Gibson then advanced through thick brush directly toward that part of the Sunken Road held by Prentiss' troops and Lauman's brigade of Hurlbut's division. Like Stephens' brigade, it was struck by a deadly fire, and after suffering heavy losses, it fell back to the wheatfield. Angered because he believed that Gibson should have done better, Bragg ordered a second attack. This was delivered without sufficient artillery preparation and suffered the same fate as the first. Bragg was determined to break through and, still displeased at what he believed was a poor performance by the brigade, ordered a third attack. This too was driven back by Prentiss, supported by a fresh regiment from Wallace's division and the artillery. Gibson then retired from the field by the eastern Corinth road. It was after Gibson's attack that the survivors of the

brigade called this part of the Federal line the "Hornet's Nest," because of the intensity of the fire that they encountered there. The name "Hornet's Nest" generally referred to that part of the Sunken Road line that extended from the eastern Corinth road on the right to and across the Wheatfield Road on the left.

Meantime, all had been quiet on the Federal left flank until about 11:00 that morning. About one-half hour earlier, Chalmers' brigade, which had been marching eastward toward the Federal left that morning, reached the Hamburg-Savannah road. Chalmers waited about a half-hour while James H. Clanton's Alabama cavalry regiment scouted ahead along the Tennessee River before its advance. Meantime, about 10:00 A.M. or a little later, Stuart had moved his regiments to the left 300–400 yards and formed them in line of battle on a heavily wooded ridge along the northern side of the Hamburg-Savannah road, and nearly parallel to the road, facing to the south and southwest. This line was north of the McCullar field, and its right was due east of and across the road from the camp of the 55th Ohio.

Chalmers placed Charles P. Gage's Alabama battery and Isadore P. Girardey's Georgia battery on the bluffs along the south side of the Locust Grove Branch, and they soon began firing on Stuart's line. When the enemy artillery opened, the men of the 71st Ohio became demoralized and fled to the north, and, except for one company, the regiment did not rejoin the brigade that day.

Chalmers' brigade then advanced across the Locust Grove Branch and drove back Stuart's skirmishers, and at 11:00 A.M. it was deployed across the Hamburg-Savannah road, with its right extending into the McCullar field. In that position it faced Stuart's line to the north of the field. Chalmers and Stuart maintained a random fire across the McCullar field until noon, and then Chalmers attacked, but he was unable to drive Stuart from the ridge.

Jackson's brigade of Withers' division, which had been following Chalmers to the right during the morning, finally came up and formed on the left of Chalmers' brigade. Jackson advanced against only slight opposition to the camps of Stuart's brigade, and he then moved on and attacked McArthur's line, but without success.

About noon, the left of the Confederate line was

strengthened by the arrival of Breckinridge with the brigades of Bowen and Statham. Then about 2:00 P.M. Bowen, aided by several regiments of Jackson's brigade, advanced against the left flank of McArthur's line, which was separated from the 54th Ohio and 55th Ohio of Stuart's brigade, and was therefore unprotected. Bypassing Stuart's regiments, Bowen and Jackson struck the 50th Illinois, which was on the left of McArthur's line, and it was soon overwhelmed and driven back in confusion. Then, in turn, the 12th Illinois and the 9th Illinois came under attack, and they followed the 50th Illinois to the rear. McArthur's regiments were driven back about one-fourth mile, but they were finally re-formed on the east side of the Hamburg-Savannah road, opposite the Wicker field.

After the departure of McArthur, Stuart's two regiments were separated from the nearest Union troops to their right, which belonged to Hurlbut's division at the Peach Orchard, by a distance of about one-half mile. At around 2:15 P.M., when he became aware of his danger, Stuart ordered his 54th and 55th Ohio regiments to fall back through a ravine to his rear and take position on a hill to his right. In passing through the ravine, the men came under a heavy fire, which threw them into some disorder and caused serious losses, but the remnants of Stuart's brigade finally reached the top of the hill and halted. Stuart realized, however, that his depleted command could accomplish little or nothing, and he then led his men northward toward Pittsburg Landing. With the withdrawal of both McArthur and Stuart from the left of the Union line, all the ground immediately east of Hurlbut's line at the Peach Orchard was undefended, and Hurlbut's left was in danger of envelopment.

Statham's brigade of Breckinridge's Reserve Corps arrived about noon in front of the left of Hurlbut's line in the Peach Orchard. It took position to the southeast of the cabin and clearing of the Sarah Bell place, which was about midway between the Peach Orchard and the Hamburg-Purdy road. The right of Statham's brigade was near the Hamburg-Savannah road. Stephens' brigade of Cheatham's division, after its repulse at the Hornet's Nest, moved to the right, and about 12:30 P.M. took position on the left of Statham, along the southern edge of the cottonfield, and in front of the right of Hurlbut's line.

Statham and Stephens' men then engaged in long-range firing with Hurlbut's men in the Peach Orchard. Johnston, who was directing affairs in person, ordered a charge against Hurlbut's line, but a part of Statham's line was in some confusion and refused to attack. Finally, however, about 2:00 P.M., after much persuasion, Statham and Stephens moved forward. At that time, Wood's battery (Willard's Battery) of William H. L. Wallace's division, which had been brought forward by McArthur that morning, was posted opposite the left of Hurlbut's line, just across the Hamburg-Savannah road to the east of the Peach Orchard. Pugh's brigade was to the right of the battery in the Peach Orchard. The 41st Ohio was on the left of the brigade, next to the road, and the 28th Illinois was on its right; both regiments were facing south. The 3rd Iowa and 32nd Illinois, the other two regiments of Pugh's brigade, extended the line diagonally to the northwest, and their right rested at the northwest corner of the cottonfield. Lauman's brigade was to the right of Pugh.

At 2:00 P.M. Johnston's line advanced directly toward Hurlbut's position, with Statham's brigade on the right and Stephens' brigade on the left in the cottonfield. On Pugh's left, the 41st Illinois and 28th Illinois were soon forced to fall back to the northern edge of the Peach Orchard, where they continued to fire, and Wood's battery was withdrawn up the Hamburg-Savannah road. On his right, however, the 32nd Illinois and 3rd Iowa, aided by Laing's battery (Ross' Battery), held their ground. On the right of the 3rd Iowa, three regiments of Lauman's brigade moved forward and took position along the northwestern side of the cottonfield and along the Wheatfield Road, and they then opened with a devastating fire on the flank of Stephens' brigade as it advanced across their front. The brigade suffered staggering losses, and the survivors soon broke and fled into the woods along the south side of the cottonfield.

As Hurlbut struggled to hold his position against Statham's attack, a serious threat was developing on his left. After McArthur and Stuart had been driven back east of the Hamburg-Savannah road about 2:15 P.M., Bowen, Jackson, and Chalmers did not move ahead directly toward Pittsburg Landing, but instead they began to swing to their left toward the sounds of the heavy firing at the Peach Orchard and along the Sunken Road. Their line of advance was directed toward the left and rear of Hurlbut's and Prentiss' embattled lines.

When Hurlbut finally learned that McArthur and Stuart had been defeated on his left, he withdrew Lauman's brigade from that part of the line adjacent to Prentiss' position, west of the cottonfield, and about 2:30 P.M. sent it to the Wicker field, a cleared space of about ten acres a short distance north of the "Bloody Pond." There it took position, facing to the southeast, on the extreme left of what was left of the Union line on that part of the field. It joined with the remnants of McArthur's command in halting the advance of the enemy toward the rear of Prentiss and William H. L. Wallace. Lauman was soon joined by the 28th Illinois and 32nd Illinois of Pugh's brigade, which took position near the Bloody Pond. Just as Lauman arrived at the Wicker field, he was confronted by Chalmers' brigade, which was following McArthur as he fell back toward the north. Together Lauman and McArthur succeeded in halting Chalmers' advance for a time.

At about this time, the weary Federal infantry fighting on the Federal left received some support from the navy. At about 3:00 P.M. the gunboats *Tyler,* commanded by William Gwin, and *Lexington,* commanded by James W. Shirk, which were anchored off the mouth of Dill Branch, opened fire on the Confederate troops advancing toward the rear of the Sunken Road line. This firing was continued for a time, but was not very effective in halting the enemy's advance, except perhaps psychologically. It did, however, cause Chalmers' men to seek shelter for a time in a ravine.

About 2:30 P.M. Johnston was mortally wounded while directing the attack against the Peach Orchard line, and for a time there was no one to exercise control of the general course of the battle. Beauregard, then at Shiloh Church, was notified that he was in command of the army, and Bragg went to the right to begin the assembly of the troops for a general advance. This line was ready to advance at 3:30–4:00 P.M.

At about 3:30 P.M., Hurlbut finally realized that the enemy was moving around his left flank and would soon be in his rear, and then, after notifying Prentiss of his intentions, he ordered his division to retire toward Pittsburg Landing. The 3rd Iowa was left in the vicinity of the cottonfield to cover the retreat, and it later fell back and joined Prentiss' command and continued fighting. When the encirclement of the troops defending the Sunken Road line was almost complete, the 3rd Iowa succeeded in cutting its way through the enemy lines and escaping to Pittsburg Landing.

Meantime, while Hurlbut was having his troubles at the Peach Orchard, the enemy persisted in their efforts to break through the line held by William H. L. Wallace and Prentiss. As Sherman and McClernand were pushed back to the north by the enemy attacks, some of the Confederate brigades that had been fighting on that part of the field were detached and sent to the right to join in the attacks on the Sunken Road line.

R. G. Shaver arrived by the eastern Corinth road about 3:00 P.M., shortly after the repulse of Gibson's third attack, and then moved up the road against Tuttle's brigade. This attack fared no better than those preceding it, and the men soon fled to the rear for about 400–500 yards, leaving many dead and wounded behind, before they could be rallied. Then, having been engaged since early morning, the brigade withdrew and took no further part in the fighting.

J. Patton Anderson's brigade, which had been fighting on the Confederate left, moved over to the eastern Corinth road, and about 4:00 P.M. it received orders to attack the Hornet's Nest at a point just south of the Duncan field. This attack was also repulsed with heavy losses.

Meantime, about 3:00 P.M., during a brief lull in the fighting, Sweeny moved forward with the two regiments of his brigade remaining with him from the edge of the Duncan field to an advanced position around the Duncan farmhouse. At about the same time, Daniel Ruggles arrived at the Duncan field from the vicinity of McClernand's captured camps, and he soon realized that the Union line at the Sunken Road could not be broken without the aid of artillery. About 4:00 P.M. he began to assemble all available batteries in the area, and to form them on a line that ran south from the main Corinth road and then southeast along the southwestern side of the Duncan field. These guns were formed in two groups, with one group in front of the Hornet's Nest and the other in front of the Duncan farmhouse. When Ruggles' artillery line was completed, it consisted of eleven batteries with sixty-two guns. Firing began at 4:00 P.M., and by 5:00 P.M. all guns were in action. Then two regiments of Preston Pond's brigade came up from near Owl Creek on the far Confederate left and drove Sweeny's regiments from the Duncan farmyard and back to the edge of the Duncan field.

Earlier in the afternoon, Sweeny, who was on the left of Wallace's line, had observed the enemy troops who were pursuing McClernand moving to the northeast beyond his right flank, and about 4:00 P.M. Wallace learned that McClernand was engaged about one-half mile to the right and rear of his line. A short time later, Sweeny was attacked from the north by regiments of Russell's and Pond's brigades, and his brigade began to break up. Soon it was in full flight to the northeast, and with its departure, the rest of Wallace's line began to break up. Sweeny was wounded at that time, and Silas D. Baldwin led back the 7th Illinois and 57th Illinois. The 8th Iowa, which was then with Prentiss, and the 58th Illinois were surrounded when the enemy came up on their rear, and they were captured.

Wallace finally realized that he was surrounded, and he ordered his division and Munch's battery to withdraw, but by that time it was almost too late. Tuttle faced his brigade to the rear to confront the enemy who were closing in from behind. The 2nd Iowa and 7th Iowa, led by Tuttle, charged and cut their way through, then continued on toward Pittsburg Landing. Wallace was mortally wounded during the retreat, and Tuttle assumed command of what was left of the division. The 8th Iowa, 12th Iowa, and 14th Iowa of Tuttle's brigade remained behind with Prentiss and were captured later.

Prentiss' men had been under almost constant attack since noon, and at 4:00 P.M., in expectation of another attack, Prentiss asked William H. L. Wallace for help. The 8th Iowa had already been sent to him, but then Tuttle sent the 14th Iowa. Also about 4:00 P.M., Prentiss withdrew his command to a new line that faced the approaching troops of Withers and Breckinridge. His new line began on the right, next to the 12th Iowa of Tuttle's brigade, and it then curved around to the left and ran almost due north to the eastern Corinth road at a point south of the junction of that road with the main Corinth road. Beginning on the right, the regiments were in line in order from right to left as follows: the 8th Iowa of Sweeny's brigade, facing generally south

toward the Wheatfield Road; the 18th Missouri of Miller's brigade, facing southwest; and facing east, in order, were the 21st Missouri of Peabody's brigade, the 12th Michigan of Peabody's brigade, the 18th Wisconsin of Miller's brigade, the 14th Iowa of Tuttle's brigade, and the 23rd Missouri, which was not assigned to a brigade. Later the 3rd Iowa of Pugh's brigade joined on the left of the 23rd Missouri.

Sometime after 4:00 P.M., Zachariah C. Deas' brigade (commanded earlier by Gladden and Adams), with Nathan B. Forrest's regiment of Tennessee cavalry on its left, advanced across the cottonfield against the 3rd Iowa, which was in position near the Manse George cabin. The 3rd Iowa fell back about 300 yards to a new position in the woods, then delivered a deadly fire that caused Deas' men to fall back in disorder into the cottonfield. The 3rd Iowa withdrew and joined Prentiss on the left of his new line. At that time Prentiss had under his command about 2,000 men, but only about 300 of them were with his division that morning. The rest belonged to William H. L. Wallace's and Hurlbut's divisions.

About 4:30 P.M., while Deas and Forrest were fighting at the front, George Maney arrived at the cottonfield with his 1st Tennessee Regiment from Lick Creek, where he had been watching the country toward Hamburg. At Cheatham's direction, he assumed command of Stephens' brigade, which was then without a commander because Stephens had left the field on account of illness. With the 1st, 9th, and 19th Tennessee regiments of the brigade, Maney followed Deas' brigade in the direction of Prentiss' line. As he was advancing, Deas' fleeing men passed through his lines and on to the rear, but Maney continued his attack. At that time, he was approaching Prentiss' new position from the southeast, Anderson's brigade from the southwest, Chalmers' brigade from the east, and Trabue's brigade and part of Russell's brigade from the north. Trabue and Russell met Chalmers near the junction of the main Corinth road and the eastern Corinth road, and the encirclement was complete.

Prentiss knew that he was about to be surrounded, but he refused to give up because he believed that he could hold out until the promised arrival of Lewis Wallace, who was expected to reach the field at any moment. Finally, however, Prentiss realized that his position was hopeless; at 5:00 P.M. he gave orders for his command to retreat, but at that time the way was no longer open. Some small parties made their way out, but other troops fought on until forced to surrender at about 5:45 P.M. By that time all of Grant's army that had survived that day had made its way back toward Pittsburg Landing.

As Grant's troops were steadily falling back all along the front, Joseph D. Webster, Grant's chief of staff, gathered all artillery within reach, some thirty-five to fifty guns, and placed them in position from about one-fourth to one-half mile from the river on commanding ground along the north side of Dill Branch, a wide and deep ravine that extended eastward and ended on the river a short distance above Pittsburg Landing. Included on Webster's line of guns were the heavy siege guns of Relly Madison's Battery B, 2nd Illinois Light Artillery, which had arrived from Saint Louis to be used at the expected siege of Corinth. During the afternoon, this battery had been posted one-fourth mile west of the log cabin at the top of the bluff to protect the vital main Corinth road, and about 5:30 P.M. it opened on Jackson's and Chalmers' advancing brigades south of Dill Branch.

When Hurlbut finally withdrew his troops from the Peach Orchard, he moved back to Pittsburg Landing, where he was joined by Veatch and his two regiments, which had been serving with McClernand during the day. Hurlbut then re-formed his division to support Webster's artillery. In addition to his own division, Grant directed Hurlbut to assume command of all regiments or parts of regiments that were near the landing or were later to arrive there. These included the 48th Ohio of Buckland's brigade and some of Wallace's regiments that later succeeded in breaking out of the Sunken Road line. That evening Hurlbut had under his command a force of about 4,000 men.

Bragg, who was commanding on the Confederate right that evening, decided to push on against Grant's final line and attempt to reach the landing, and he ordered Ruggles and Withers to organize their forces for the attack. Ruggles' brigades were somewhat scattered at the time, but he began to assemble such troops as were available. Only Chalmers' and Jackson's brigades of Withers' division were nearby, and Withers moved these two brigades up to the southern crest above Dill Branch,

opposite Webster's artillery. When Bragg's line was completed, Ruggles' command was on the left, with its left on the Hamburg-Savannah road, Jackson's brigade was in the center, and Chalmers' brigade was on the right, not far from the Tennessee River.

At about 5:00 P.M., or perhaps a little later, Beauregard sent orders for the divisions of the army to fall back and bivouac for the night. Ruggles and Jackson complied, but at that time Chalmers had already begun his attack, and he did not receive the order to withdraw. He therefore continued his futile attack and was still fighting when the first brigade of Buell's Army of the Ohio arrived on the high ground above the landing. This was Jacob Ammen's Tenth Brigade of William Nelson's Fourth Division, which had left Savannah at 1:00 P.M. and marched to the river bank opposite Pittsburg Landing at 5:00 P.M. It was then ferried across the river at 5:30 P.M. to join Grant's army.

William Grose's 36th Indiana of the brigade was the first regiment to cross. It arrived on the bluff above the landing a little after 5:00 P.M. and took position on the road. Then about 6:30 P.M. it was sent forward and to the left about 200 yards to support George H. Stone's Battery K, 1st Missouri Light Artillery of William H. L. Wallace's division. When the 6th Ohio of the brigade arrived, it moved up in support. The 24th Ohio was sent inland about one-half mile to the right of the batteries, and it then moved out another half-mile to see if there were any enemy forces in the area. It found none, however, and spent the rest of the night under arms.

Nelson crossed the river with the 36th Indiana on the first boat, and all of his infantry was on the west bank by 9:00 P.M. He then put his brigades in line just north of Dill Branch, about one-fourth mile south of the main Corinth road and between the Hamburg-Savannah road and the river. Ammen's brigade was on the left, Sanders D. Bruce's Twenty-Second Brigade was in the center, and William B. Hazen's Nineteenth Brigade was on the right.

That night, the troops of Grant's army that had retained their organization were in position to protect Pittsburg Landing. The troops under Hurlbut's command were on the right of the artillery, and their line ran slightly to the north of west. Tuttle, with the remains of William H. L. Wallace's division, was on the right of Hurlbut. At the close of the fighting that day on the Union right, McClernand's division was in position along the Hamburg-Savannah road, facing generally to the west. Marsh's brigade was on the right, Enos P. Wood's brigade (Raith's brigade) was in the center, and Hare's brigade was on the left. Veatch's brigade of Hurlbut's division was on the left of Hare. When Grant formed his line that evening, Veatch and Hare swung back, pivoting on the left of Wood, and formed on the right of Tuttle, with Hare's brigade next to Wood. These two brigades then faced toward the south, and Wood's and Marsh's brigades on right of Hare remained along the Hamburg-Savannah road, facing west. The troops of Sherman's division were also along the road to the right of Marsh's brigade.

The 13th Missouri of McArthur's brigade of William H. L. Wallace's division, which had been sent to join Sherman's division that morning, had become separated from Sherman, and it spent the night on the right of Wood's brigade. The 53rd Ohio of Hildebrand's brigade and the 81st Ohio of McArthur's brigade, which had been detached to guard the bridge over Snake Creek, bivouacked for the night in front of the camp of the 2nd Iowa of Tuttle's brigade. The 57th and 77th Ohio regiments of Hildebrand's brigade rejoined Sherman's division and formed on the left of his line.

During the fighting on the Federal right on the afternoon of April 6, 1862, McDowell was disabled by a fall, and at 2:30 P.M. his brigade of Sherman's division had retired to Pittsburg Landing, where it later took position behind Hurlbut's line. The next day the 6th Iowa and 40th Illinois of the brigade were attached to James A. Garfield's 20th Brigade of Thomas J. Wood's Sixth Division, but they were not engaged. Prentiss' division no longer existed as an organized force.

By the time that Grant had organized an effective defensive position in front of Pittsburg Landing, Lewis Wallace's Third Division, which had been expected all afternoon, was approaching the battlefield on the right of Sherman. At about 6:00 that morning, Wallace, who was at Crump's Landing, heard the sounds of firing from upriver, and he decided to concentrate his division at Stoney Lonesome, which was about two and one-half miles from Crump's Landing on the road to Adamsville. There he would be in position to march to Pittsburg Landing or to meet an advance of the enemy from the direction of Purdy. Accordingly, Wallace sent orders

to this effect to Morgan L. Smith, whose First Brigade was at Crump's Landing; to John M. Thayer, whose Second Brigade was at Stoney Lonesome; and to Charles R. Woods, whose Third Brigade was at Adamsville, about five miles west of Crump's Landing on the Purdy road.

After Wallace met Grant at 8:30 that morning, while the latter was on his way to Pittsburg Landing, he proceeded with his staff to Adamsville, where he arrived about mid-morning. Charles Whittlesey had just arrived there that morning, after being absent for a time, and had resumed command of his Third Brigade, relieving Woods. Leaving Whittlesey with his brigade at Adamsville to await further orders, Wallace moved to Stoney Lonesome to join Thayer and Smith, whose brigade had moved to that place. Wallace then waited there for further orders from Grant.

It was about 11:30 A.M. when Algernon S. Baxter, whom Grant had sent with the message for Wallace to bring his division to Pittsburg Landing, delivered the order to Wallace. Baxter then returned to Pittsburg Landing. Although Grant's instructions indicated that Wallace should hurry forward, he waited for a half-hour while the men ate their noon meal. Meantime, about 10:30 A.M., Grant had sent another courier to Wallace with a verbal order to hurry to Pittsburg Landing, and he found Wallace still at Stoney Lonesome before he had begun his march. According to the courier, who returned to the landing and reported to Grant, Wallace refused to march without written orders. Nevertheless, Wallace did move forward about noon with the cavalry out in front, then Smith's brigade, and Thayer's brigade bringing up the rear. Whittlesey's brigade had not yet arrived from Adamsville. The artillery of the division also accompanied the column.

For reasons that are not clearly understood, Wallace did not march by the direct Hamburg-Savannah road (or River Road), on which Grant had expected him to move to Pittsburg Landing, but instead he took a road to the right called the Shunpike Road that ran out to the southwest to Shiloh Church. Not only was this a longer route, but as matters had developed, it could not lead him to Pittsburg Landing as directed. About two hours before Wallace began his march, the divisions of Prentiss and Sherman had been driven northward from their camps, and for Wallace to continue his march on the Shunpike Road, and across Snake Creek and Owl Creek, would bring him onto the battlefield well in rear of the enemy's front line.

When Grant received the courier's report that Wallace would not move without a written order, he immediately sent such an order by William R. Rowley, an aide, and again directed Wallace to hurry. Rowley, accompanied by several orderlies, rode up the Hamburg-Savannah road to Crump's Landing, which at that time was almost deserted. He then continued on and finally came up to the rear of Wallace's column on the Shunpike Road near a place called Overshot Mill, which was a short distance north of Snake Creek. At that time the head of the column, which was about three miles long, was within about one-half mile of Clear Creek.

Rowley moved on along the column until he found Wallace, and then delivered his order. In the brief and somewhat unpleasant exchange that followed, Rowley informed Wallace that Grant's army had been driven back to within a half-mile of the river, and that it was in imminent danger of destruction. Wallace was surprised at this information, but he still refused to move until his cavalry had confirmed the information. When finally convinced that what Rowley had told him was true, Wallace ordered the two brigades that were with him to move back on the road toward Stoney Lonesome. Even then, Wallace caused a further delay when he decided to countermarch his command instead of simply reversing the column. Therefore, Smith's brigade, which was at that time in the lead, was forced to move back through Thayer's brigade so that it would continue the march to Pittsburg Landing in the lead. When Smith's men had passed through, Thayer's brigade also countermarched and followed in rear of Smith.

There was soon to be another problem. When Smith's brigade reached the vicinity of the Overshot Mill about 3:30 P.M., it turned off on a crossroad that ran from the mill toward the Hamburg-Savannah road. At about that time, the leading troops of Whittlesey's brigade, which had not left Adamsville until 2:00 P.M., arrived at the junction of the road from Adamsville with the Shunpike Road near Overshot Mill. Smith was then passing the junction, and Whittlesey was forced to wait until both Smith

and Thayer had passed before he could move into the road in rear of Thayer.

There were other delays during the rest of the afternoon and evening, but finally Wallace turned into the Hamburg-Savannah road, and at last, about 7:15 P.M., the head of his column began crossing Snake Creek. By that time the fighting on the first day of the Battle of Shiloh had ended. Then, as his regiments arrived, Wallace placed them in position along the road north of Pittsburg Landing, with his right not far from the junction of Owl Creek with Snake Creek. Wallace's division was in position by about 1:00 A.M. April 7, 1862: Whittlesey's brigade was on the right, Thayer's brigade was in the center, and Smith's brigade was on the left, all facing west toward Tilghman's Creek. In this position Wallace's troops bivouacked for the rest of the night. Sherman's battered division was to the left of Smith's brigade.

The night was passed in misery by the men of both armies in a drenching rain. The enemy occupied the camps of Prentiss, McClernand, and Sherman, and the Union troops sought shelter in the camp of William H. L. Wallace and the adjacent part of Hurlbut's camp.

Battle of Shiloh, Monday, April 7, 1862. During the night of April 6, 1862, Grant and Buell prepared for an attack the next morning. Buell's Army of the Ohio was to advance on the Federal left, down the Hamburg-Savannah road, and Grant's Army of the Tennessee was to move out on the right from its positions of the night before along the Hamburg-Savannah road and attack north of the main Corinth road.

At 4:00 A.M. William Nelson formed his Fourth Division of the Army of the Ohio along the crest of the ravine north of Dill Branch, with William B. Hazen's Nineteenth Brigade on the right, Sanders D. Bruce's Twenty-Second Brigade in the center, and Jacob Ammen's Tenth Brigade on the left. The division then crossed Dill Branch and marched obliquely to the southwest through difficult country, with its right near the Hamburg-Savannah road.

Thomas L. Crittenden's Fifth Division, Army of the Ohio, which had begun to arrive at Pittsburg Landing on boats at 9:00 the night before, had marched out on the main Corinth road, with William Sooy Smith's Fourteenth Brigade in the lead, and

Jeremiah T. Boyle's Eleventh Brigade following as its regiments arrived. The division halted for the night to the right and rear of Nelson's line. Crittenden aroused his men at 4:00 A.M. April 7, 1862, but he delayed in putting the division in motion until daylight. Smith's brigade, which was leading the division, started forward at 6:00 A.M.

During the night of April 6–7, 1862, Lovell H. Rousseau's Fourth Brigade of Alexander McD. McCook's Second Division, Army of the Ohio arrived on transports and disembarked at Pittsburg Landing. Edward N. Kirk's Fifth Brigade followed Rousseau toward morning, April 7. Rousseau moved out from the landing at 6:30 A.M. and followed in rear of Crittenden on the main Corinth road. Kirk's brigade followed a short time later.

When Beauregard learned of the activity of the Union forces that morning, he was aware that Grant had been reinforced during the night, and he immediately began the difficult task of forming his troops in line of battle to prevent the loss of the ground that his army had gained the day before. The Confederate forces had been badly disorganized by the fighting of the day before, and following their withdrawal from the front line at the end of the first day's battle, they had spent the night at various places all over the battlefield, in units of all sizes, generally in rear of the positions where they had been engaged that day.

Beauregard assigned William J. Hardee to assume the direction of the troops on the Confederate right; John C. Breckinridge was to take charge on the right center; Leonidas Polk was to command the troops on the left center; and Braxton Bragg was to assume command on the left. These officers were ordered to assume command of whatever troops were available and place them in position without regard for their original organization. When Beauregard's line was completed, it was occupied as follows:

Hardee's troops were in line from right to left as follows: James R. Chalmers' command, which was in David Stuart's camps; John K. Jackson's brigade, then commanded by Joseph Wheeler; Bushrod R. Johnson's brigade, then commanded by Preston Smith; and William H. Stephens' brigade, commanded by George Maney.

The troops of Breckinridge's command, on the left of Hardee, consisted of the following, from right to left: Alexander P. Stewart's brigade, Patrick R. Cleburne's brigade, Winfield S. Statham's brigade, and John S. Bowen's brigade, then commanded by John D. Martin.

Polk's troops were in position from right to left as follows: Robert P. Trabue's brigade, in line, extending across the main Corinth road, just west of the Duncan field; J. Patton Anderson's brigade; and Randall L. Gibson's brigade.

Bragg's command, which was on the left of the Confederate line, consisted of Sterling A. M. Wood's brigade, which was on the left of Polk's line; Robert M. Russell's brigade, which was on the left of Wood; and Preston Pond's brigade, which was on the extreme Confederate left, next to Owl Creek.

Very few of the above-mentioned brigades that were present at the beginning of the battle the day before were intact. Instead, they were more or less improvised by an order from Beauregard to the effect that as the regiments of the army moved up to the line, they were to be placed under the command of the first brigade officer that they met, and they were to serve that day with his brigade. There was another reason why the brigades did not have the same composition as the day before. Many regiments had been detached from their brigades and had been sent to various parts of the field, wherever they might be needed, and they did not rejoin their proper commands that night.

Ammen's and Bruce's brigades of Nelson's division generally faced Hardee's command. The divisions of Crittenden and McCook and Hazen's brigade of Nelson's division were generally opposed by the enemy forces under Polk and Breckinridge, and they fought over the same ground where Benjamin M. Prentiss' Sixth Division and William H. L. Wallace's Second Division had fought the day before. Grant's Army of the Tennessee advanced against Bragg's forces on the Confederate left.

At 5:20 A.M., Nelson's division approached the Cloud field, where Stephen A. Hurlbut's headquarters stood in the northwest corner near the Hamburg-Savannah road. There Hazen encountered a few enemy troops, but Nelson continued his advance until 6:00 A.M., at which time he was ordered to halt and wait until Crittenden's division came up and formed on his right.

When Nelson had advanced that morning, he had been forced to leave his artillery behind at Pittsburg Landing because of problems with transportation, and during the period while he waited for Crittenden, John Mendenhall's Batteries H and M, 4th United States Artillery of Crittenden's division arrived from Pittsburg Landing to support Nelson.

Sometime after 7:00 A.M., Crittenden arrived and formed his division on the right of Nelson, and in front of the camps of the 32nd Illinois and 41st Illinois of Hurlbut's Fourth Division, which were just west of the Cloud field. William Sooy Smith's brigade was in line of battle, and Boyle's brigade was in reserve near Hurlbut's headquarters in the Cloud field. The 14th Wisconsin, which had been assigned to Prentiss' division, did not arrive at Pittsburg Landing until the morning of April 7, 1862, and it then reported to Crittenden and served with William Sooy Smith's brigade during the rest of the day.

At about this time, McCook came up and took position on the right of Crittenden. Rousseau formed his brigade on the front line, in front of the camp of the 3rd Iowa of Hurlbut's division, which was about 300 yards west of the Cloud field, and north of the main Corinth road. Kirk's brigade followed in rear of Rousseau's brigade.

When Crittenden's division was finally in line, Nelson again moved forward to a position about one-half mile beyond Hurlbut's headquarters, and about one mile from Pittsburg Landing. At 8:00 A.M., Hazen's brigade arrived about 300 yards north of the Wicker field, which was a short distance north of the Bloody Pond. The 9th Indiana of Hazen's brigade was pushed forward to the northern edge of the field, where it was checked by the fire of Chalmers' brigade, which had moved up and taken position along the south side of the Wicker field.

For about an hour and a half, Chalmers and Hazen exchanged fire across the field, and about 9:00 A.M. Chalmers withdrew to a new position at Stuart's camps along the Hamburg-Purdy road. About an hour later, Withers moved his troops to the vicinity of Stuart's camps, where they formed along

the Hamburg-Purdy road on the left of Chalmers' line. At that time, Bowen's brigade of Breckinridge's corps, then commanded by John D. Martin, was to the left at the south end of the cottonfield.

At 9:00 P.M., after Chalmers had withdrawn from south of the Wicker field, Nelson moved forward to a new position at the Peach Orchard. Ammen's brigade was east of the Hamburg-Savannah road, facing south toward the Sarah Bell cabins; Bruce's brigade was in line along the low ridge at the north side of the Peach Orchard, also facing south; and Hazen's brigade was on the right of Bruce. Hazen, who had been ordered to protect the exposed right flank of Nelson's division, changed front to face toward the west, and took position along the Sunken Road at the Hornet's Nest. The 9th Indiana of Hazen's brigade, however, formed on the right of Bruce's line near the Manse George cabin, facing south.

A short time after 9:00 A.M., William R. Terrill's Battery H, 5th United States Artillery of McCook's division was sent to support Nelson, and about noon the 19th Ohio of Boyle's brigade was also sent to reinforce Nelson.

At 9:00 A.M. Crittenden, then in line on the right of Nelson, advanced on the main Corinth road to the junction of the eastern Corinth road, and he then turned off to the left and moved along the latter road. Boyle's brigade was on the right, with his right across the eastern Corinth road, and Smith's brigade was on the left, with his left near Hazen's brigade. Joseph Bartlett's Battery G, 1st Ohio Light Artillery was placed on the right of Boyle between the eastern Corinth road and the main Corinth road.

McCook's division advanced on the main Corinth road, and on the right of Crittenden, with Rousseau's brigade in front, and Kirk's brigade moving up in the rear. About 10:00 A.M. Rousseau was in position north of the main Corinth road, near the northeast corner of the Duncan field, facing toward the southwest. Kirk's brigade was in reserve, and William H. Gibson's Sixth Brigade had not yet arrived.

Meantime, on the morning of April 7, 1862, Grant's Army of the Tennessee had begun its advance against the left of the Confederate line north of the main Corinth road. Early that morning, James M. Tuttle collected as many of the men of William

H. L. Wallace's Second Division as he could find, and formed them in a column as a reserve to the Army of the Ohio, and he followed Crittenden's line up to the position at the Sunken Road. Tuttle then deployed his men in rear of Crittenden's line, and soon his regiments were sent to other parts of the line—the 2nd Iowa was sent to Nelson's division, the 7th Iowa to Crittenden's division, and the 13th Iowa to McCook's division. His 12th Illinois was engaged later that day. The regiments of John McArthur's Second Brigade, commanded by Thomas Morton on April 7, were also scattered, and they served with John A. McClernand's division, Lewis Wallace's division, and William T. Sherman's division.

The rest of Grant's army was generally in line along the Hamburg-Savannah road to the right of the Army of the Ohio. On the right of McCook's division were the units of Grant's army that had been engaged the day before, but they had been so depleted in numbers that they occupied a front of only about one-fourth mile. In order to the right, from the right of McCook's division, were Hurlbut's division, McClernand's division, and Sherman's division, all of which were at only a fraction of their former strengths. Completing Grant's line on the right was Lewis Wallace's Third Division, which had arrived on the field only the night before. The right of Lewis Wallace's division rested on the swamps of Owl Creek. Wallace's brigades were in line from right to left as follows: Charles Whittlesey's Third Brigade, with Charles H. Thurber's Battery I (Buell's Independent Battery), 1st Missouri Light Artillery on its line; John M. Thayer's Second Brigade, with George R. Brown's 9th Battery, Indiana Light Artillery (Thompson's Battery) on its left; and Morgan L. Smith's First Brigade.

As noted above, the remnants of William H. L. Wallace's division, then commanded by Tuttle, were in rear of Crittenden's line in reserve, and Prentiss' division had ceased to exist as an organized body.

The fighting on the Federal right began at daylight April 7, 1862 when Lewis Wallace's batteries became engaged with the enemy artillery. Then at 6:30 A.M. the division advanced, with the brigades en echelon, left in front, and with its right near Owl Creek. It crossed Tilghman's Creek and advanced against Pond's Confederate brigade, which was in position at the north end of the Jones field, in the camps of Abraham M. Hare's brigade of McClernand's division. At about 8:00 A.M. Morgan L. Smith's brigade arrived at Hare's camp and forced Pond's brigade to withdraw to the south side of the Jones field. Pond's brigade was then ordered from one part of the field to another, and was not again in action until about mid-afternoon. After Pond had departed, only Daniel Ruggles' division and Sterling A. M. Wood's brigade of Hardee's corps were left to face Lewis Wallace. After crossing Tilghman's Creek, Wallace halted along the northern edge of the Jones field to wait for Sherman to come up on his left.

David Stuart's Second Brigade of Sherman's division had remained at Pittsburg Landing during the night of April 6, 1862, but the next morning T. Kilby Smith, with the 54th Ohio and the 55th Illinois regiments of the brigade, joined Sherman's command along the Hamburg-Savannah road and fought during the day on the right of the division, next to Lewis Wallace's division. Ralph P. Buckland's Fourth Brigade, which had been scattered the day before, was reunited on the morning of April 7 and joined T. Kilby Smith's brigade on the front line. The 13th Missouri of John McArthur's Second Brigade of William H. L. Wallace's division, which had served with Sherman's brigade on the morning of April 6, and later in the day with McClernand's division, rejoined Sherman's division during its advance on the morning of April 7.

Sherman advanced slowly that morning and was stopped east of the Jones field about 9:00 A.M. by the fire of William H. Ketchum's Alabama battery, which was posted in the woods on the opposite side of the field. Also at the southern edge of the field were Gibson's brigade of Ruggles' division and Wood's brigade of Hardee's corps. Sherman waited there until 10:00 A.M. and then, when he was satisfied that Buell's troops were advancing on his left, he resumed his advance.

While waiting for Sherman to come up, Lewis Wallace decided to make a wide turning movement to his left so as to reach the enemy's exposed left flank. For this purpose he ordered Thayer to move to the right with his brigade, and then change front to a line facing south.

While Thayer was moving toward the right, the enemy prepared for an attack on the rest of Wallace's division and also Sherman's troops, who continued to hold a line along the eastern side of the Jones field. Ruggles, with Randall L. Gibson's brigade of his division, who had earlier been sent to help Pond, arrived about 9:00 A.M. and was then ordered to attack Brown's (Thompson's) battery, which was posted at the north end of the Jones field. Just as Gibson's brigade started forward, Wood's brigade came up and formed on its right.

Meantime, Brown's battery had been replaced by Thurber's battery, and the latter opened fire on Gibson and Wood as they began their advance from a line about one-fourth mile distant. Gibson continued on toward the battery, but Wood attacked in the direction of Sherman's line. Wood was quickly driven back in disorder, but Gibson's men succeeded in penetrating into the battery. There was furious fighting for a short time, but Gibson was finally driven back by the heavy fire of Wallace's two brigades and was forced to leave the guns behind.

While Gibson and Wood were thus engaged, McClernand and Hurlbut, with what was left of their divisions, had moved forward to positions on the left of Sherman, and Federal artillery then opened on Gibson's line from the east.

Thayer's brigade soon arrived at the Sowell field from the northeast. By 10:00 A.M. it had driven back John A. Wharton's regiment of Texas cavalry, which was the only Confederate force in that area.

Meantime, Wallace had ordered Whittlesey's brigade to move to the right and join Thayer's brigade, and when it arrived, the two brigades advanced and forced Ketchum's battery, which had been supporting Gibson and Wood, to withdraw from its position at the south end of the Jones field. Gibson, Wood, and Wharton were outflanked by the movement of Wallace's two brigades, and they were ordered to fall back in the direction of Shiloh Church.

On the morning of April 7, 1862, McClernand's division also moved forward from near the Hamburg-Savannah road. That morning Marcellus M. Crocker was in command of First Brigade in place of Hare, who had been wounded the evening before, and the brigade was attached to Tuttle's division, which was advancing in rear of Crittenden's division in reserve to the Army of the Ohio. Crocker's

brigade followed in rear of Tuttle as a reserve, and also to serve as a support for some of the batteries.

The 17th, 43rd, and 49th Illinois regiments of Julius Raith's Third Brigade, then commanded by Francis M. Smith, were attached to C. Carroll Marsh's Second Brigade, and they served with Marsh during the day.

McClernand, with Marsh's brigade, then advanced, and at 10:00 A.M. occupied a position to the east of the southern end of the Jones field and to the left of Sherman's division, which was along the east side of the Jones field. From there McClernand moved forward, while swinging to the left, until about 11:00 A.M. he had arrived on a line facing south toward the review field, about 400 yards north of the main Corinth road. At the same time, Sherman advanced across the Jones field and, swinging to the left, came up on the right of McClernand, about the same distance north of the Water Oaks Pond. Buckland's brigade was on the left and T. Kilby Smith's brigade (Stuart's brigade) was on the right of Sherman's line. Lewis Wallace's division moved south from the Sowell field, crossed the Crescent Field, and took position on the right of Sherman, with its right extending into the Crescent Field.

Hurlbut's division had bivouacked in front of Webster's guns during the night of April 6, 1862, and at 9:00 the next morning it was ordered forward to support McClernand, who was then engaged near the Jones field. Hurlbut moved out with Pugh's First Brigade and Edward Brotzmann's Battery C, 1st Missouri Light Artillery (Mann's Battery) and formed on the left of McClernand's line, and the brigade remained with McClernand during the rest of the day. At 10:00 A.M. Hurlbut ordered James C. Veatch to move forward with his Second Brigade and hold his brigade in reserve until needed.

During the advance of the Army of the Ohio that morning, Crittenden and McCook had moved out from Pittsburg Landing on the main Corinth road to the junction of the eastern Corinth road, just east of the Duncan field. There Crittenden turned off to the left and advanced on the eastern Corinth road, while McCook continued on along the main Corinth road. A gap thus developed between the two divisions, and about noon Veatch's brigade was sent to close it. Later Veatch moved to the camps of Raith's brigade along the southern side of the review field.

During the afternoon he advanced to the front, and, by Grant's personal order, the brigade made the final charge during the enemy's withdrawal.

Jacob G. Lauman's Third Brigade of Hurlbut's division remained where it had bivouacked the night before until 11:00 A.M., and it was then ordered to support McClernand's division, which was engaged near its old camps. Lauman formed his brigade on the right of McClernand's line, and to the left of Sherman, and he aided in driving the enemy back. The brigade held its position on the right of McClernand until the fighting ended that evening.

Meantime, there had been some severe fighting on the front of the Army of the Ohio on the left of the Federal line. When Bruce took position at the north end of the Peach Orchard, he came under a destructive fire from Irving Hodgson's Washington Artillery, which was posted at the northwest corner of the cottonfield, and when the infantry of Martin's and Statham's brigades added their fire, Bruce withdrew his brigade to the edge of the woods near the Bloody Pond.

At 10:00 A.M. Hardee ordered an attack by Martin's brigade, which was near Hodgson's guns, and a short time later Martin crossed a corner of the cottonfield and moved into the underbrush directly toward the position held by Hazen's brigade of Nelson's division and William Sooy Smith's brigade of Crittenden's division along the Sunken Road. As Martin approached, Hazen counterattacked; Bruce's men, who had rallied, changed front to meet this attack and were soon engaged. Hazen and Bruce were aided greatly by Mendenhall's battery, which was firing canister at point-blank range. With the 41st Ohio leading the attack, Hazen's and Smith's men advanced against Martin's brigade and drove it back. Hazen and Smith then pressed on and captured Hodgson's guns. Also present with the 41st Ohio at this point were the 6th Kentucky of Hazen's brigade and the 13th Ohio of William Sooy Smith's brigade. The enemy then attacked again and soon drove Hazen's brigade back in disorder, and Hazen and most of his men were out of action for the rest of the day. Smith's men returned to their former positions near the Sunken Road.

After ordering the attack on Hazen's and Bruce's brigades, Hardee went to the right to prepare for an attack on Nelson's unprotected left flank. He first ordered John C. Moore with his 2nd Texas Regiment to attack across the cottonfield toward the Peach Orchard, but this effort ended in a sharp repulse.

About one-fourth mile to the east of Moore's position, in the vicinity of Stuart's camps along the Hamburg-Purdy road, Chalmers was organizing an attacking force that consisted of some regiments of Jones M. Withers' division, which he placed in the front line, and Chalmers' own reorganized brigade, which he formed in the rear. When these troops were in position, the entire force under the direction of Chalmers advanced toward the front of Ammen's brigade to the north.

At 11:00 A.M. Ammen advanced his brigade from its position east of the Peach Orchard to the Sarah Bell cabins, which stood about midway between the Peach Orchard and the Hamburg-Purdy road. There Ammen met Chalmers and, after a severe fight, drove him back. Terrill's battery of McCook's division, which had just arrived at the front and taken position on the right of Ammen's brigade, opened with an effective fire on the enemy. About noon, Withers ordered Preston Smith, with the 154th Tennessee and a part of the 2nd Tennessee, to move up to the Hamburg-Purdy road and support Chalmers, and George Maney, with the remnants of his brigade, came up and joined on the left of Preston Smith. Chalmers then led these troops forward against Ammen's brigade and forced it to fall back. Terrill's battery, however, with the help of the 6th Ohio, which had been in reserve, held its ground and succeeded in halting the enemy advance.

On the front of the brigades of Hazen and Bruce, the fighting was gradually slowing down to an exchange of artillery fire, and at about 2:00 P.M. the fighting on the front of Nelson's division ended. A short time later, Withers' division began to withdraw westward along the Hamburg-Purdy road, past the Peach Orchard and the old cottonfield, and then it moved south on the eastern Corinth road to a point near Prentiss' former camps, to the south of the Barnes field.

Thomas J. Wood's Sixth Division, Army of the Ohio arrived on the field about 2:00 P.M., just as the enemy was beginning its withdrawal from the Confederate right, and it was ordered to move in the direction of the heaviest firing. Except for George

D. Wagner's Twenty-First Brigade, however, Wood's division did not get into line until the fighting had ended. Wagner's brigade did arrive at the front, and it took position along the Hamburg-Purdy road, just west of its intersection with the eastern Corinth road, north of the Barnes field.

At about that time, Martin's brigade made a final unsuccessful attack from the junction of the eastern Corinth road and the Wheatfield Road toward the 2nd Kentucky Regiment, which was supporting Terrill's battery in the Wheatfield. To the west of the line of Martin's attack, some enemy troops in the Barnes field advanced, under the immediate direction of Breckinridge, against Wagner's brigade, but they were driven back.

After the enemy had retired and moved off toward Corinth, Buell's divisions advanced to the Hamburg-Purdy road and remained there until they were ordered to bivouac for the night.

While Buell was thus engaged on the Federal left, there was also heavy fighting to the right of the Army of the Ohio as Grant's divisions advanced in the direction of Shiloh Church. In attempting to halt this advance, Bragg ordered Patrick R. Cleburne to attack with his brigade. Cleburne at first refused because he was without support, but when the order was repeated, he reluctantly ordered his men forward. He soon halted and remained under cover for a half-hour until an intense Federal artillery fire had ended, and then at 11:00 A.M. he charged from a point north of Sherman's review field against McClernand's line. Cleburne's brigade was quickly repulsed, and it fell back toward the review field in almost complete disorder.

McClernand followed but soon ran into a new Confederate line that had been reinforced by troops brought up from the rear by Benjamin F. Cheatham. Many of Cheatham's men belonged to Bushrod R. Johnson's brigade (then commanded by Preston Smith), but troops of many other units were also present. Anderson's brigade was on the right of the line, to the left of the northern corner of the review field; Cheatham's men were in the center, in the Woolf field, just north of the Water Oaks Pond; Wood's brigade was in front of the Water Oaks Pond; and Randall L. Gibson's Brigade was on the left of Wood. Cheatham, Wood, and Gibson were largely facing Sherman's line and the left of Lewis Wallace's division.

Cheatham's entire line advanced about noon and drove McClernand's troops back in some disorder, also causing some confusion in Sherman's line to its right. The fighting near the Water Oaks Pond was especially violent, and McClernand's condition rapidly became critical.

Meantime, about noon, Lovell H. Rousseau's brigade of McCook's division had arrived at the Woolf field, to the east of the Water Oaks Pond, and at that time the right of his line was exposed. When Edward N. Kirk's brigade, which was marching in rear of Rousseau, came up, it was placed in the front line to the right of Rousseau, and in rear of the Water Oaks Pond. William H. Gibson's Sixth Brigade of McCook's division did not arrive on the field until about noon, and it then moved forward and joined the division at the Woolf field at 2:00 P.M.

In an attempt to slow the enemy attack against McClernand, August Willich's 32nd Indiana regiment was detached from William H. Gibson's brigade and ordered by McCook to charge the enemy line with the bayonet. Willich advanced through Kirk's brigade, which had been withdrawn from the right of Rousseau when Sherman came up, and advanced under heavy fire, entering the woods on his front. He soon became heavily engaged, but maintained his position for about fifteen minutes before being driven back. His engagement in the woods, however, had gained some valuable time for the Federal troops fighting in that area. Willich's regiment did not rejoin Gibson's brigade that day.

Rousseau then attacked, and for forty minutes there was deadly fighting in McClernand's camps, but finally, aided by Edward McAllister's Battery D, 1st Illinois Light Artillery of McClernand's division and other batteries along the front, the troops of McClernand, Hurlbut, Rousseau, and Sherman forced the enemy to fall back to the east of the Water Oaks Pond and from McClernand's camps. At about 2:00 P.M., as Rousseau advanced, Sherman ordered T. Kilby Smith's Second Brigade (Stuart's brigade) to form on the right of Rousseau, and Buckland's Fourth Brigade on the right of Smith's brigade and to advance with Rousseau. Sterling A. M. Wood's brigade was scattered by this attack, and Cheatham's men fell back. Anderson's brigade had already moved to the south to help Robert P. Trabue, who was then engaged, and Randall L. Gibson's brigade joined in the general retreat past the Water Oaks Pond in the direction of Shiloh Church.

Lewis Wallace had become concerned about his left flank when Sherman's line had become somewhat disordered during the noon attack, and he had ordered Whittlesey to move with his brigade from his right flank to the left of his division to support T. Kilby Smith's brigade (Stuart's brigade) of Sherman's division. He also posted Thurber's battery so as to cover a possible retreat. Later, however, when Wallace heard firing to the west, and when the threat on his left had ended, he moved most of Whittlesey's brigade back to the right of his line.

Crittenden's division had generally been inactive on the right of Nelson's division until the attack made by Martin's brigade on the brigades of Hazen, William Sooy Smith, and Bruce about mid-morning. This was followed a short time later by an attack by a part of Trabue's brigade. When Trabue led his brigade forward at the beginning of the battle on the morning of April 7, 1863, he halted about three-fourths of a mile northeast of Shiloh Church and formed on a line north of and perpendicular to the main Corinth road. When it became clear from the sounds of Nelson's battle that troops of Buell's army were approaching on the Confederate right, Trabue was ordered to move his brigade to the west side of the Duncan field and support the line on that part of the field. As Trabue was moving to his new position, however, the 4th Kentucky Regiment and the 4th Alabama Battalion were detached by Bragg's orders and directed to join Robert M. Russell's brigade in an attack on Rousseau's brigade of McCook's division, which was at that time just north of the main Corinth road near the farm buildings in the Duncan field.

When the troops of Trabue's and Russell's brigades, and also some troops of Stewart's brigade, approached within about 100 yards of Rousseau's line, both sides opened fire, and after a struggle of about twenty minutes, the enemy was forced to fall back. They withdrew 400–500 yards to a line held by Anderson's brigade, and then Trabue and Russell, reinforced by Anderson's brigade, again advanced about 1:00 P.M., but they were once again forced to retire.

While part of Trabue's brigade and Russell's brigade were engaged with Rousseau north of the main Corinth road, Trabue with the 5th Kentucky, the 6th

Kentucky, and part of the 3rd Kentucky arrived on the west side of the Duncan field and attacked Crittenden's line at the Sunken Road. After an hour's fighting, the brigades of William Sooy Smith and Boyle, aided by Joseph Bartlett's Battery G, 1st Ohio Light Artillery, which was posted to the right of Smith's line near the forks of the main Corinth road and the eastern Corinth road, drove Trabue back toward the review field. Bartlett's battery was engaged until noon, and it then returned to Pittsburg Landing to replenish its ammunition. When it returned, the fighting had ended.

Crittenden then moved forward in pursuit of Trabue, with Boyle's brigade on the right, with its right near the main Corinth road, and Smith's brigade on the left. Advancing through the woods east of the review field, the troops of Smith and Boyle surprised Robert Cobb's Confederate Kentucky battery, which was near the northern corner of the field near the road, and captured one section of it. Smith and Boyle continued the advance for a time, but the brigades soon became disorganized by the fire of Thomas J. Stanford's Mississippi battery, which was in position at the edge of the review field on the Hamburg-Purdy road. When Bragg ordered a counterattack, Crittenden's line fell back. The enemy pursued, but were soon halted by the heavy fire of Rousseau's brigade, which had arrived in rear of Crittenden's brigades about 1:00 P.M. There was severe fighting for forty minutes, and then the enemy again retired.

Rousseau waited for reinforcements before resuming the advance, and during the lull that followed the end of the attack, the Federal troops suffered from the fire of Stanford's guns. Buell had no artillery with which to engage this battery, and at 1:00 P.M. he had ordered Mendenhall, who had been engaged on the right of Nelson's division, to move up and support Crittenden and McCook. The fire of Mendenhall's guns forced Anderson to pull back and seek cover for his brigade, and when the men of Smith's and Boyle's brigades again advanced, Trabue and Russell also fell back. Crittenden's men again passed through Cobb's battery and finally forced Stanford to retire, with the loss of four guns.

Beyond Cobb's battery, Smith and Boyle met Anderson, who had been joined by Russell and by some of Cheatham's men who had retired from the vicinity of McClernand's camps, and these combined forces finally halted the Federal advance. Mendenhall then brought up his guns to a position near Cobb's abandoned guns and opened fire with canister.

By this time Smith's and Boyle's troops had become scattered, and Rousseau's men had exhausted their ammunition. Rousseau left the 6th Indiana regiment of his brigade to support Mendenhall's battery and withdrew his brigade to replenish its ammunition. McCook then moved up Kirk's brigade to take Rousseau's place in the line, and William H. Gibson's brigade moved up on the left of Kirk. Kirk and Gibson had no sooner taken position than they encountered Anderson, Cheatham, Russell, and Pond, whose men had advanced after Rousseau had withdrawn. The fighting that followed was especially heavy along the southern edge of the review field. The fighting on the left of William H. Gibson was severe as Trabue attempted to turn that flank, and during the fighting the 77th Pennsylvania of Kirk's brigade was sent to support Gibson. Mendenhall was forced to withdraw his battery, but the 6th Indiana, which was supporting it, held its ground and forced the enemy to retire.

It was then about 3:00 P.M., and the brigades of Kirk and William H. Gibson, who were holding the front of the line, were in position along the Hamburg-Purdy road, south of the review field. About this time, the enemy in front of Gibson's brigade gradually began to fall back about one-fourth mile to Sherman's former headquarters, and they then moved on to the vicinity of Shiloh Church.

During the fighting near the review field, McCook had asked for help, and Jacob G. Lauman's brigade of Hurlbut's division was sent forward to attack to the right of McCook's line. When Lauman appeared, the enemy immediately withdrew. By that time Rousseau had resupplied his men with ammunition and was leading them back to the front. The appearance of what seemed to be two fresh brigades unnerved the enemy forces facing them, and at about 3:30 P.M. they left their lines and started for the rear. Earlier, about 2:00 P.M., Beauregard had finally decided that he would have to withdraw his army to avoid its complete destruction, and he had sent out orders to that effect. Finally he decided that the time had come. He organized a mixed command consisting of men of Wood's and Trabue's brigades

and posted them along the ridge near Shiloh Church to cover his retreat. By 4:00 P.M. what was left of his army was on the road toward Corinth.

The exhausted men of Grant's and Buell's armies did not attempt a pursuit that evening, but they bivouacked on the field near where the fighting had ended. At 4:00 P.M., after the enemy had retired from the field, the Army of the Ohio bivouacked on a line that extended from Stuart's camps on the left to near Shiloh Church on the right. Nelson's division was on the left on a line from Stuart's camps to near Prentiss' headquarters; Crittenden's division was in front of Prentiss' camps; and McCook's division was between Crittenden and the left of Shiloh Church.

McClernand's troops bivouacked in their former camps, and the brigades of Buckland and Hildebrand of Sherman's division spent the night in their former camps. Lewis Wallace's brigades slept in the former camps of McDowell's brigade of Sherman's division.

After Beauregard withdrew from the field on the evening of April 7, 1862, there was no pursuit, but the next morning Sherman moved out toward Corinth with T. Lyle Dickey's 4th Illinois Cavalry and the brigades of Hildebrand and Buckland. This column was supported by Thomas J. Wood's division of the Army of the Ohio, which happened to be near. About six miles out, at a place called Fallen Timbers, Sherman found Nathan B. Forrest with a cavalry force in position along a ridge to protect the rear of Beauregard's retreating army. There was some skirmishing, but no serious fighting; Sherman then returned to his camps, and the Battle of Shiloh was over.

It should be noted here, in concluding this account of the Battle of Shiloh, that the classic work of Wiley Sword, the book *Shiloh: Bloody April* (Morningside Bookshop, 1983), was an indispensable source of information about this extremely confusing struggle.

Organization of the Union Forces at Shiloh, Tennessee, April 6, 1862–April 7, 1862. In giving the organization of the Union forces engaged at the Battle of Shiloh, it seems necessary to list the regiments belonging to each brigade in order that the description of the battle may be more clearly understood. This is done because so many of the regiments engaged were detached or otherwise separated from their brigades during the fighting, and so often fought alone or with brigades other than their own or left the field and did not fight again.

The organization of the Union forces at Shiloh was as follows:

ARMY OF THE TENNESSEE
Ulysses S. Grant

First Division, John A. McClernand
  First Brigade, Abraham M. Hare, April 6, 1862, wounded
    Marcellus M. Crocker
    8th Illinois, James M. Ashmore, wounded
      William H. Harvey, killed
      Roger H. Sturgess
    18th Illinois, Samuel Eaton, wounded
      Daniel H. Brush, wounded
      William J. Dillon, killed
      Jabez J. Anderson
    11th Iowa, William Hall, wounded
    13th Iowa, Marcellus M. Crocker
  Second Brigade, C. Carroll Marsh
    11th Illinois, Thomas E. G. Ransom, wounded
      Garrett Nevins, wounded
      Lloyd D. Waddell
      Garrett Nevins
    20th Illinois, Evan Richards, wounded
      Orton Frisbie
    45th Illinois, John E. Smith
    48th Illinois, Isham N. Haynie, wounded
      Manning Mayfield
  Third Brigade, Julius Raith, mortally wounded
    Enos P. Wood
    17th Illinois, Enos P. Wood
      Francis M. Smith
    29th Illinois, Charles M. Ferrell
    43rd Illinois, Adolph Engelmann
    49th Illinois, Phineas Pease, wounded
  Artillery
    Battery D, 2nd Illinois Light Artillery (Dresser's Battery), James P. Timony
    Battery D, 1st Illinois Light Artillery, Edward McAllister, wounded
    Battery E, 2nd Illinois Light Artillery (Schwartz's Battery), George L. Nispel
    14th Battery, Ohio Light Artillery, Jerome B. Burrows, wounded

Second Division, William H. L. Wallace, April 6, 1862, mortally wounded

James M. Tuttle
  First Brigade, James M. Tuttle
    2nd Iowa, James Baker
    7th Iowa, James C. Parrott
    12th Iowa, Joseph J. Woods, wounded and captured
      Samuel R. Edgington
    14th Iowa, William T. Shaw, captured
  Second Brigade, John McArthur, wounded
    Thomas Morton
    9th Illinois, August Mersey
    12th Illinois, Augustus L. Chetlain
      James R. Hugunin
    13th Missouri, Crafts J. Wright
    14th Missouri, Benjamin S. Compton
    81st Ohio, Thomas Morton
  Third Brigade, Thomas W. Sweeny, wounded
    Silas D. Baldwin
    7th Illinois, Richard Rowett
    50th Illinois, Moses M. Bane, wounded
    52nd Illinois, Henry Stark
      Edwin A. Bowen
    57th Illinois, Silas D. Baldwin
      Gustav A. Busse
    58th Illinois, William F. Lynch, captured
    8th Iowa, James L. Geddes, wounded and captured
  Artillery
    Battery A, 1st Illinois Light Artillery (Willard's Battery), Peter P. Wood
    Battery D, 1st Missouri Light Artillery, Henry Richardson
    Battery H, 1st Missouri Light Artillery, Frederick Welker
    Battery K, 1st Missouri Light Artillery, George H. Stone

Note. The three Missouri batteries belonged to John S. Cavender's Battalion, Missouri Light Artillery.

Third Division, Lewis Wallace
  First Brigade, Morgan L. Smith
    11th Indiana, George F. McGinnis
    24th Indiana, Alvin P. Hovey
    8th Missouri, James Peckham
  Second Brigade, John M. Thayer
    23rd Indiana, William L. Sanderson
    1st Nebraska, William D. McCord
    58th Ohio, Valentine Bausenwein
    68th Ohio, Samuel H. Steedman

Note. The 68th Ohio was at Crump's Landing and was not engaged.

Third Brigade, Charles Whittlesey
    20th Ohio, Manning F. Force

56th Ohio, Peter Kinney
76th Ohio, Charles R. Woods
78th Ohio, Mortimer D. Leggett

Note. The 56th Ohio was at Crump's Landing and was not engaged.

Artillery
9th Battery, Indiana Light Artillery (Thompson's Battery), George R. Brown
Battery I, 1st Missouri Light Artillery (Buel's Battery), Charles H. Thurber

Fourth Division, Stephen A. Hurlbut
First Brigade, Nelson G. Williams, April 6, 1862, wounded
Isaac C. Pugh
28th Illinois, Amory K. Johnson
32nd Illinois, John Logan, wounded
41st Illinois, Isaac C. Pugh
Ansel Tupper, killed
John Warner
John H. Nale
3rd Iowa, William M. Stone, captured
George W. Crosley
Second Brigade, James C. Veatch
14th Illinois, Cyrus Hall
15th Illinois, Edward F. W. Ellis, killed
Louis D. Kelly
William Cam
46th Illinois, John A. Davis, wounded
John J. Jones
25th Indiana, William H. Morgan, wounded
John W. Foster
Third Brigade, Jacob G. Lauman
31st Indiana, Charles Cruft, wounded
John Osborn
44th Indiana, Hugh B. Reed
17th Kentucky, John H. McHenry, Jr.
25th Kentucky, Benjamin H. Bristow
William B. Wall, wounded
Benjamin T. Underwood
John McHenry, Jr.
Artillery
2nd Battery, Michigan Light Artillery (Ross' Battery), Cuthbert W. Laing
Battery C, 1st Missouri Light Artillery (Mann's Battery), Edward Brotzmann
13th Battery, Ohio Light Artillery, John B. Myers

Fifth Division, William T. Sherman, wounded
First Brigade, John A. McDowell, disabled
40th Illinois, Stephen G. Hicks, wounded
James W. Boothe

6th Iowa, John Williams, wounded
Madison M. Walden
46th Ohio, Thomas Worthington
Second Brigade, David Stuart, April 6, 1862, wounded
Oscar Malmborg, temporarily
T. Kilby Smith
55th Illinois, Oscar Malmborg
54th Ohio, T. Kilby Smith
James A. Farden
71st Ohio, Rodney Mason
Third Brigade, Jesse Hildebrand
53rd Ohio, Jesse J. Appler
Robert A. Fulton
57th Ohio, Americus V. Rice
77th Ohio, Wills De Hass
Benjamin D. Fearing
Fourth Brigade, Ralph P. Buckland
48th Ohio, Peter J. Sullivan, wounded
Job R. Parker
70th Ohio, Joseph R. Cockerill
72nd Ohio, Herman Canfield, killed
Ralph P. Buckland
Artillery, Ezra Taylor
Battery B, 1st Illinois Light Artillery (Taylor's Battery), Samuel E. Barrett
Battery E, 1st Illinois Light Artillery, Allen C. Waterhouse, wounded
Abial R. Abbott, wounded
John A. Fitch
6th Battery, Indiana Light Artillery (Morton Battery), Frederick Behr, killed

Sixth Division, Benjamin M. Prentiss, captured
First Brigade, Everett Peabody, April 6, 1862, killed
12th Michigan, Francis Quinn
21st Missouri, David Moore, wounded
Humphrey M. Woodyard
25th Missouri, Robert T. Van Horn
16th Wisconsin, Benjamin Allen, wounded
Second Brigade, Madison Miller, captured
61st Illinois, Jacob Fry
18th Missouri, Isaac V. Pratt, captured
18th Wisconsin, James S. Alban, killed
Not Brigaded
15th Iowa, Hugh T. Reid, wounded
16th Iowa, Alexander Chambers, wounded
Addison H. Sanders
23rd Missouri, Jacob T. Tindall, killed
Quin Morton, captured
Artillery
5th Battery, Ohio Light Artillery, Andrew Hickenlooper
1st Battery, Minnesota Light Artillery, Emil

Munch, wounded
William Pfaender

Unassigned Infantry
15th Wisconsin, John M. Oliver
14th Michigan, David E. Wood

Unassigned Artillery
Battery H, 1st Illinois Light Artillery, Axel Silfversparre
Battery I, 1st Illinois Light Artillery, Edward Bouton
Battery B, 2nd Illinois Light Artillery (siege guns), Relly Madison
Battery F, 2nd Illinois Light Artillery, John W. Powell, wounded
8th Battery, Ohio Light Artillery, Louis Markgraf

ARMY OF THE OHIO
Don Carlos Buell

Second Division, Alexander McD. McCook
Fourth Brigade, Lovell H. Rousseau
6th Indiana, Thomas T. Crittenden
5th Kentucky, Harvey M. Buckley
1st Ohio, Benjamin F. Smith
Regular Infantry, John H. King

Note. The regular troops consisted of Peter T. Swaine's 1st Battalion, 15th United States Infantry; Edwin F. Townsend's 1st Battalion, 16th United States Infantry; and Stephen D. Carpenter's 1st Battalion, 19th United States Infantry.

Fifth Brigade, Edward N. Kirk, wounded
34th Illinois, Charles N. Levanway, killed
Hiram W. Bristol
29th Indiana, David M. Dunn
30th Indiana, Sion S. Bass, mortally wounded
Joseph B. Dodge
77th Pennsylvania, Frederick S. Stumbaugh
Sixth Brigade, William H. Gibson
32nd Indiana, August Willich
39th Indiana, Thomas J. Harrison
15th Ohio, William Wallace
49th Ohio, Albert M. Blackman
Artillery
Battery H, 5th United States Artillery, William R. Terrill

Fourth Division, William Nelson
Tenth Brigade, Jacob Ammen
36th Indiana, William Grose
6th Ohio, Nicholas L. Anderson
24th Ohio, Frederick C. Jones

Nineteenth Brigade, William B. Hazen
9th Indiana, Gideon C. Moody
6th Kentucky, Walter C. Whitaker
41st Ohio, George S. Mygatt
Twenty-Second Brigade, Sanders D. Bruce
1st Kentucky, David A. Enyart
2nd Kentucky, Thomas D. Sedgwick
20th Kentucky, Charles S. Hanson

Fifth Division, Thomas L. Crittenden
Eleventh Brigade, Jeremiah T. Boyle
9th Kentucky, Benjamin C. Grider
13th Kentucky, Edward H. Hobson
19th Ohio, Samuel Beatty
59th Ohio, James P. Fyffe
Fourteenth Brigade, William Sooy Smith
11th Kentucky, Pierce B. Hawkins
26th Kentucky, Cicero Maxwell
13th Ohio, Joseph G. Hawkins
Artillery
Battery G, 1st Ohio Light Artillery, Joseph Bartlett
Batteries H and M, 4th United States Artillery, John Mendenhall

Sixth Division, Thomas J. Wood
Twentieth Brigade, James A. Garfield
13th Michigan, Michael Shoemaker
64th Ohio, John Ferguson
65th Ohio, Charles G. Harker
Twenty-First Brigade, George D. Wagner
15th Indiana, Gustavus A. Wood
40th Indiana, John W. Blake
57th Indiana, Cyrus C. Hines
24th Kentucky, Lewis B. Grigsby

Note. Sixth Division did not arrive on the battlefield until about 2:00 P.M. April 7, 1862, just as the fighting was ending. Wagner's brigade did reach the front and was engaged, but only the 57th Indiana suffered any losses, and these were slight.

STONES RIVER (OR MURFREESBORO), TENNESSEE CAMPAIGN DECEMBER 26, 1862– JANUARY 3, 1863

On October 24, 1862, as Confederate forces under Braxton Bragg and E. Kirby Smith were arriving in East Tennessee after the Battle of Perryville, President Abraham Lincoln ordered the reorganization of the Union forces in Kentucky and Tennessee. On that date William S. Rosecrans was assigned command of the newly re-created Department of the Cumberland and the troops formerly under Buell's command. On October 30, Rosecrans, then at Louisville, Kentucky, assumed command of the Department of the Cumberland, and Don Carlos Buell was relieved from the command of the District of the Ohio and the Army of the Ohio. The troops of Buell's former command were officially designated as Fourteenth Corps, Department of the Cumberland, but thereafter they were commonly known as the Army of the Cumberland. For information about the Army of the Ohio, see Army of the Ohio (Buell); and see also District of the Ohio in section on Miscellaneous Organizations.

Just before his removal from command, Buell had ordered the Army of the Ohio to abandon its pursuit of Bragg and Smith toward Knoxville and to concentrate at Bowling Green, Kentucky. This movement was in progress when Rosecrans assumed command of the army at Louisville, and it was almost completed when he arrived at Bowling Green November 1, 1862. The commands of Charles C. Gilbert and Alexander McD. McCook were at Bowling Green, and Thomas L. Crittenden's corps had halted at Glasgow, Kentucky. John Kennett's cavalry command had also reached Bowling Green.

In addition to the above troops, there were two divisions at Nashville, Tennessee. One of these was James S. Negley's Eighth Division, Army of the Ohio, which had been left at Nashville in September 1862 during the Confederate invasion of Tennessee and Kentucky (see Invasion of Tennessee and Kentucky [E. Kirby Smith and Braxton Bragg]). The other was Eleazer A. Paine's First Division of Rosecrans' Army of the Mississippi (commanded by John M. Palmer during the illness of Paine), which had arrived at Nashville from Tuscumbia, Alabama September 12, 1862 in response to a request from Buell for help. For additional information, see Army of the Mississippi (Pope, Rosecrans).

Rosecrans' first concern upon assuming command of the Army of the Cumberland was for the safety of Nashville and the troops garrisoning the post, which were then threatened by a Confederate force commanded by John C. Breckinridge at Murfreesboro, Tennessee. When Rosecrans arrived at Bowling Green, he immediately began preparations to reinforce the troops at Nashville and to open and protect the Louisville and Nashville Railroad, which was the important supply line for the army with the North.

One of the first steps taken by Rosecrans was the reorganization of Fourteenth Corps, which, because it constituted an entire army, was too large to be handled efficiently. Accordingly, by an order of November 5, 1862, he divided the army into three parts: a Right Wing, Center, and Left Wing. These were commonly referred to as army corps, although they were not officially so designated.

The Center, Fourteenth Corps was assigned to George H. Thomas, and it consisted of the following divisions: Lovell H. Rousseau's Third Division, Army of the Ohio; Ebenezer Dumont's Twelfth Division, Army of the Ohio; Speed S. Fry's First Division, Army of the Ohio; James S. Negley's Eighth Division, Army of the Ohio; and John M. Palmer's First Division, Army of the Mississippi. The divisions of Negley and Palmer were at Nashville and were regarded as temporarily detached, and they reported directly to Headquarters, Fourteenth Corps. On December 10, 1862, Palmer assumed command of William Sooy Smith's Fourth Division, Left Wing (see below), and Robert B. Mitchell assumed command of Palmer's division of the Center. On December 11, Joseph J. Reynolds assumed command of Twelfth Division in place of Dumont, who was sick.

The Right Wing, Fourteenth Corps was assigned to Alexander McD. McCook, and it consisted of the following divisions: Philip H. Sheridan's Eleventh Division, Army of the Ohio; William E. Woodruff's Ninth Division, Army of the Ohio; and Joshua W. Sill's Second Division, Army of the Ohio. On December 5, 1862, Jefferson C. Davis, who had been absent, resumed command of Ninth Division, relieving Woodruff, and on December 9, Richard W. Johnson relieved Sill in command of Second Division.

The Left Wing, Fourteenth Corps was assigned to Thomas L. Crittenden, and it consisted of the following divisions: Thomas J. Wood's Sixth Division, Army of the Ohio; William Sooy Smith's Fourth Division, Army of the Ohio; and Horatio P. Van Cleve's Fifth Division, Army of the Ohio. John

M. Palmer relieved Smith in command of Fourth Division December 10, 1862.

On November 4, 1862, McCook's corps marched from Bowling Green toward Nashville. Passing through Franklin, Mitchellville, and Tyree Springs, it arrived at Nashville November 7–9. Also on November 4, Crittenden left William Sooy Smith's division temporarily at Glasgow and marched with the divisions of Wood and Van Cleve of his corps by way of Scottsville toward Gallatin, Tennessee, where he arrived November 8. Crittenden was joined by Kennett's cavalry at Gallatin.

The Louisville and Nashville Railroad had been seriously damaged by enemy cavalry, especially at the railroad tunnels near Mitchellville, and Thomas was assigned the responsibility for completing repairs on the road, protecting it from further damage, and transporting supplies to Nashville. For this purpose, he established his headquarters at Gallatin, and disposed his troops as follows: he relieved William Sooy Smith's division at Glasgow with Scott's brigade of Dumont's division, sent Dumont with the brigades of William T. Ward and Abram O. Miller to Scottsville, occupied Gallatin with Fry's division, and used Rousseau's division to forward supplies and maintain communications with Nashville. Palmer's and Negley's divisions remained at Nashville.

When Thomas had completed the above dispositions, Crittenden crossed the Cumberland River with the divisions of Wood and Van Cleve and marched to Silver Springs, northeast of Nashville. There he was joined by William Sooy Smith's division from Glasgow.

November 22, 1862, Eleazer A. Paine was assigned command of the troops guarding the Louisville and Nashville Railroad, with headquarters at Gallatin, and Dumont was ordered to move with his two brigades from Scottsville to Gallatin.

On November 9, 1862, Rosecrans established his headquarters at Nashville, where he began preparations for offensive operations. He proceeded to resupply the army with clothing, ammunition, and other necessary supplies, and to accumulate stores at the depot at Nashville so that operations of the army would not be interrupted by enemy raids on the railroad.

When Rosecrans assumed command of the Army of the Cumberland, he retained for a time the numbers of the brigades and divisions that had been assigned in the Army of the Ohio. These were not systematic, however, and at times tended to be confusing. To remedy this situation, Rosecrans ordered on December 19, 1862 the following changes: the brigades in the divisions and the divisions in the wings of the army were to be numbered from right to left as First Brigade (or Division), Second Brigade (or Division), etc. For details of the relationships between the old and the new numerical designations, see Army of the Cumberland, October 24, 1862–November 14, 1864. For the new numerical designations, see below, Organization of Fourteenth Corps, or Army of the Cumberland, during the Period December 26, 1862–January 5, 1863.

While the Army of the Cumberland was assembling at Nashville, Bragg was moving his Army of the Mississippi toward Murfreesboro with the intention of holding Middle Tennessee in force during the coming winter. On September 30, 1862, Nathan B. Forrest had been sent back from Kentucky during Bragg's invasion of that state with orders to organize a new cavalry brigade at Murfreesboro. Forrest was joined there by John C. Breckinridge with a Confederate division from East Tennessee, and on November 7 Breckinridge was assigned command of all Confederate forces in Middle Tennessee.

November 13, 1862, Joseph Wheeler was assigned as chief of cavalry, and as commander of the Confederate cavalry in Middle Tennessee. He relieved Forrest, who then moved with his brigade to Columbia, Tennessee.

Bragg's army, then known as the Army of the Mississippi, remained near Knoxville after its retreat from Kentucky until early November 1862, then moved by rail by way of Chattanooga to Tullahoma. Bragg established his headquarters there November 14. While it was at Tullahoma, the name of the army was changed to the Army of Tennessee, the name by which it later became famous.

On November 21, 1862, after all of Bragg's troops had arrived, the army began its advance to the positions that it would hold until the beginning of Rosecrans' advance from Nashville toward Murfreesboro on December 26. Leonidas Polk's corps moved to Murfreesboro; William J. Hardee's corps moved to Shelbyville and then to Eagleville, with a brigade advanced to Triune; and E. Kirby Smith's command was ordered to take position in front of Manchester, Tennessee. On December 18, Carter L. Stevenson's division of Smith's command was detached and sent west to Mississippi, and the remaining division under John P. McCown was sent to Readyville, twelve miles east of Murfreesboro, on the road to McMinnville.

During December 1862, the strength of Bragg's army was seriously reduced by detachments for other service. On December 11, Forrest left Columbia with his brigade on a raid into West Tennessee. The purpose of this raid was to destroy the railroad between Ulysses S. Grant's base at Columbus, Kentucky and his Army of the Tennessee, which was then advancing into northern Mississippi. On December 18, Stevenson's division was sent to Mississippi to reinforce John C. Pemberton, commander of the Confederate Department of Mississippi and East Louisiana. On December 21, John H. Morgan departed with his cavalry brigade on a raid into Kentucky to destroy Rosecrans' communications with Louisville. Morgan struck the Louisville and Nashville Railroad north of Munfordville and followed it to Elizabethtown, which he captured, and then destroyed the railroad trestles at Muldraugh Hill.

Rosecrans was aware of the departure of these enemy forces, and this probably strongly influenced his decision to advance against Bragg's army at Murfreesboro. He ordered that the advance begin December 25, 1862, but later delayed the march by one day.

Rosecrans' plan for the advance of the Army of the Cumberland was as follows: McCook's Right Wing was to move on the Nolensville Pike to Triune; Thomas' Center was to march on the right of McCook by way of the Franklin Pike and the Wilson Pike so as to threaten the left of Hardee's corps at Triune and Eagleville, and if Hardee fell back, Thomas was to cross over to the left on country roads and occupy Nolensville; and Crittenden's Left Wing was to move on the left of the army on the Nashville-Murfreesboro Pike, directly toward Murfreesboro.

At Nolensville, Thomas would be in position to support McCook, who was under orders to attack Hardee at Triune. If Hardee fell back to Stewart's Creek, south of La Vergne, and made a stand there, Crittenden was to attack the front of this line while

Thomas moved against its left flank. McCook was to march to the support of Crittenden and Thomas if needed.

Advance of the Army to Murfreesboro. On the morning of December 26, 1862, the Army of the Cumberland marched out of Nashville toward Murfreesboro as ordered. Crittenden's Left Wing moved out on the Murfreesboro Pike (generally the route of present-day U.S. 41) toward La Vergne. McCook's Right Wing left its camps five miles south of Nashville and marched to the right of Crittenden on the Nolensville Pike (the route of present-day Alternate U.S. 31 and Alternate U.S. 41). Thomas' Center advanced on the right of the army on the Franklin road (the route of present-day U.S. 31) toward Brentwood.

Jefferson C. Davis' First Division of McCook's command marched at 6:00 A.M. on the Edmondson Pike, which ran south to the west of the Nolensville Pike, then moved across country toward Nolensville. Philip H. Sheridan's Third Division also marched at 6:00 A.M., but it took the direct road to Nolensville. Richard W. Johnson's Second Division, the reserve division of the Right Wing, followed Sheridan. Davis encountered some opposition about a mile south of Nolensville, but after a short engagement drove the enemy back. McCook then camped for the night.

During the day Thomas marched southward with James S. Negley's Second Division, Lovell H. Rousseau's First Division, and Moses B. Walker's First Brigade of Speed S. Fry's Third Division as ordered. Negley's leading brigade reached Brentwood, then took the Wilson Pike, which ran a little east of south from Brentwood to the Franklin-Murfreesboro Pike. When Negley reached Owens' Store, where he was to have camped for the night, he heard the sounds of Davis' engagement, and he then continued the march to the east that night to Nolensville to support Davis. Rousseau's division camped at Owens' Store, and Walker's brigade halted at Brentwood.

That day, December 26, 1862, Crittenden advanced with the Left Wing on the road to Murfreesboro, camping that night about one mile north of La Vergne.

The cavalry of the army advanced in three columns under the personal direction of David S. Stanley, chief of cavalry. John Kennett, commander of the Cavalry Division, marched with Robert H. G. Minty's First Brigade, which preceded Crittenden's corps on the Murfreesboro Pike; Lewis Zahm's Second Brigade marched south on the Franklin road to clear out any enemy cavalry in the area, and then moved by a road parallel to Thomas' column to protect its right flank; and the Reserve Brigade, which consisted of new regiments and was commanded by Stanley in person, preceded McCook on the Nolensville Pike.

The advance was resumed on December 27, 1862. McCook was delayed in starting until 1:00 P.M. because of a heavy fog, and he then moved on toward Triune to attack the troops of Hardee's corps reported to be near the town. When he neared Triune, however, McCook learned that the enemy had retired, and because it was then raining and snowing, he bivouacked for the night.

Negley's division of Thomas' corps remained at Nolensville until 10:00 A.M., then marched eastward on a country road, across the rear of McCook's corps, to the right of Crittenden's corps, which had arrived that day at Stewartsburg (or Stewartsboro), about five miles south of La Vergne on the Murfreesboro Pike. Rousseau's division reached Nolensville that night. Because of the condition of the roads, which had been caused by heavy rains, Walker's brigade moved back to Brentwood, and from there crossed over to the Nolensville Pike.

December 28, 1862, Crittenden remained in camp while waiting for the troops of the Right Wing and Center to get into position. Negley's division of Thomas' corps also remained in camp near Stewartsburg, and Rousseau's division joined him there that night.

During the morning of December 28, 1862, August Willich's First Brigade of Johnson's Second Division of McCook's corps moved out on a reconnaissance south of Triune to determine whether Hardee had retired toward Shelbyville or Murfreesboro. About seven miles out on the Shelbyville Pike, Willich learned that the enemy had marched east to the Salem Pike and then on to Murfreesboro. The rest of McCook's troops remained in camp during the day.

December 29, 1862, Crittenden advanced toward Murfreesboro, and within about two and a half miles of the town, he discovered the enemy in force on his front. McCook and Thomas were not yet up, and, it then being late in the afternoon, Crittenden halted and formed in line of battle. Wood's First Division was on the left, facing east, with its right on the Murfreesboro Pike and its left near Stones River. George D. Wagner's Second Brigade was on the right, across the Nashville and Chattanooga Railroad; Charles G. Harker's Third Brigade was on the center of the line; and Milo S. Hascall's First Brigade was on the left, next to the river.

Palmer's Second Division was on the right of Wood, facing to the southeast, about two miles from Murfreesboro. William Grose's Third Brigade was on the left, next to the Murfreesboro Pike, and Charles Cruft's First Brigade was on the right. William B. Hazen's Second Brigade had been sent out from La Vergne on December 27, 1862 on the Jefferson Pike to seize and hold the bridge over Stewart's Creek, and it did not rejoin the division until December 30. It was then placed in reserve.

Van Cleve's Third Division formed in reserve to the left and rear of Crittenden's line.

On December 29, 1862, Negley's division advanced to the right of Crittenden's corps to protect its right flank, and it halted that night in rear of Palmer's division. Rousseau remained with two of his brigades in camp at Stewartsburg, but John C. Starkweather's Third Brigade was detached and sent to the Jefferson Pike crossing of Stones River to watch the enemy movements in that direction. Walker's brigade of Fry's division arrived at Stewartsburg from Nolensville about dark that evening.

On December 29, 1862, McCook left Philemon P. Baldwin's Third Brigade of Johnson's division at Triune and marched with the rest of the corps on the Bole Jack's road toward Murfreesboro. This road ran eastward from the Nolensville Pike toward Murfreesboro, and was roughly parallel to, and about two to three miles north of, the Murfreesboro-Franklin road. McCook reached Wilkinson's Cross Roads, about five miles from Murfreesboro, late that evening and camped in line of battle. Sheridan's division was on the left of the Wilkinson Pike, and Davis' division was on the right. William E. Woodruff's Third Brigade of Davis' division was posted to watch the bridge over Overall's Creek. That evening Baldwin's brigade was ordered up from Triune, and it rejoined the division the next day.

The day of December 30, 1862 was spent getting

the army into position facing the enemy's lines in front of Murfreesboro. That morning Negley's division moved forward and to the right, and it formed on the right of Palmer's division, with John F. Miller's Third Brigade on the right of Palmer and Timothy R. Stanley's Second Brigade on the right of Miller. The two brigades then advanced several hundred yards to the Wilkinson Pike and took position facing southeast.

Rousseau's division (less Starkweather's brigade at Jefferson) left Stewartsburg on the morning of December 30, 1862 and marched on the pike toward Murfreesboro. At 10:30 A.M. the division arrived at a point about three miles from the town, in rear of Palmer's division, and halted with its left on the pike. It remained in position there during the rest of the day, and bivouacked that night. Starkweather's brigade left Jefferson the next morning and rejoined the division at 5:00 that same evening.

McCook's corps advanced at 9:30 A.M. December 30, 1862, and about noon Sheridan's division, which was in the lead, formed in line, with its left on the Wilkinson Pike, on the right of Negley's division. George W. Roberts' Third Brigade was on the left, facing east, and Joshua W. Sill's First Brigade was on the right, facing southeast. Frederick Schaefer's Second Brigade was in reserve.

Davis' division moved up on the right of Sheridan and took position about 300 yards south of and roughly parallel to the Wilkinson Pike. Davis then advanced, against some opposition, and that evening his line extended to the southwest from the right of Sheridan's division almost to the Murfreesboro-Franklin road. William E. Woodruff's Third Brigade was on the left, next to Sheridan, William P. Carlin's Second Brigade was in the center, and P. Sidney Post's First Brigade was on the right.

Johnson's division remained in reserve during most of the day, but late that afternoon Edward N. Kirk's Second Brigade moved up to the right of Davis' division. It then took position, facing east, in advance of a lane running south from the Griscom (Gresham) house to the Franklin road. The right of the brigade rested on the road. About dark, Willich's brigade advanced to the right of Kirk's line and formed along the Franklin Pike, west of the lane, with its right refused. Baldwin's brigade was held in reserve some distance to the rear, near Johnson's headquarters.

Crittenden's Left Wing remained in the same general position as of the day before, but early on the morning of December 31, 1862, Hazen's brigade relieved Grose's brigade on Palmer's first line, and Grose moved back in reserve.

When the Army of the Cumberland began its advance December 26, 1862, it was opposed by Joseph Wheeler's cavalry while Bragg called in his scattered detachments and formed them in line of battle about two miles north and west of Murfreesboro, where it covered the roads leading into the town. Leonidas Polk's corps was on the left, with Jones M. Withers' division in front and Benjamin F. Cheatham's division about 500 yards to the rear. William J. Hardee's corps was on the right, with John C. Breckinridge's division in front and Patrick R. Cleburne's division 800 yards to the rear. John K. Jackson's brigade, temporarily assigned to Breckinridge's division, was in reserve.

John P. McCown's division of E. Kirby Smith's command in East Tennessee, temporarily serving with Hardee, was in reserve near the center of the line, and was south of Stones River. Wheeler's cavalry was on the right of Bragg's line, and John A. Wharton's cavalry was on the left.

When Rosecrans' line was completed on December 30, 1862, Bragg made plans to attack the next morning. He decided to leave Breckinridge's division in position on the right to hold the east bank of Stones River, mass the rest of Hardee's corps on the west side of the river, and at daylight December 31 make a heavy attack on the right of the Federal line. Accordingly, during the night of December 29, Bragg sent McCown's division to the left to extend the Confederate line to the left of Withers' division, and on December 30 he also moved Cleburne's division from the rear of Breckinridge to the Confederate left to support McCown's division.

According to Bragg's attack order, the brigades were to advance in succession from left to right, with the pivot of this movement on James R. Chalmers' brigade, which was on the right of Polk's corps near the Nashville-Murfreesboro Pike.

By an interesting coincidence, Rosecrans also planned to attack at 7:00 A.M. December 31, 1862 and, like Bragg, he decided to make his main attack against the right of the enemy's line. He directed McCook to take a good position on the Union right and prevent, if possible, the enemy from advancing.

If attacked in greatly superior numbers, he was to resist stubbornly and fall back slowly. If not attacked, he was to engage and hold the enemy on his front. Thomas and Palmer were to advance skirmishers and engage the enemy's center and left as far as Stones River. Crittenden was to cross Van Cleve's division at the lower ford and advance on Breckinridge's Confederate division. Wood's division was to follow by brigades, crossing at the upper ford and moving forward on the right of Van Cleve toward Murfreesboro. James St. Clair Morton's Pioneer Brigade had prepared three fords for crossing and covered one of the fords, and Wood's division held the other two.

Battle of Stones River, Tennessee, December 31, 1862. At 6:30 A.M. December 31, 1862, the divisions of McCown and Cleburne of Hardee's Confederate corps advanced against the right of the Union line. McCown's division, consisting of the brigades of Matthew D. Ector, James E. Rains, and Evander McNair, formed the front line, and it was followed by Cleburne's division, consisting of the brigades of Lucius E. Polk, St. John R. Liddell, Bushrod R. Johnson, and Sterling A. M. Wood. McCown's division moved farther to the left than had been intended, and in so doing left a wide gap between his right and the left of Withers' division. As Cleburne advanced, he moved into this gap and in consequence became a part of the Confederate first line. The two divisions then advanced toward the right flank of McCook's corps.

At the time of the attack, Johnson was not on the front line in person, but was at division headquarters, where he was too far to the rear to give direct orders. To complicate matters further, Willich, commanding Johnson's right brigade, was absent from his command on a visit to division headquarters. Baldwin's brigade of the division was in reserve about one-fourth to one-half mile to the rear of the front line, not far from Johnson's headquarters.

The enemy struck Kirk's brigade first and then Willich's, and after a brief contest, both brigades were broken and driven to the rear. Kirk was mortally wounded, and Willich was captured as he attempted to rejoin his brigade. Joseph B. Dodge assumed command of Kirk's brigade and led it off the field. William H. Gibson was the senior officer present of Willich's brigade after Willich was cap-

tured, but he was cut off with a part of the brigade by the Confederate advance and was unable to assume command until later in the day. Meantime, William Wallace assumed temporary command and brought the remainder of the brigade back to the Nashville-Murfreesboro Pike.

The artillery of Johnson's division, which was camped near division headquarters, consisted of Edmund B. Belding's Battery A, 1st Ohio Light Artillery; Warren P. Edgarton's Battery E, 1st Ohio Light Artillery; and Peter Simonson's 5th Battery, Indiana Light Artillery. These batteries had barely time to get into action before they were overrun by the enemy, and Edgarton and most of his guns were captured.

Zahm's Second Cavalry Brigade covered the right of Johnson's division as it withdrew to the north along the east side of Overall Creek, and during the day it was almost constantly engaged with Wharton's Confederate cavalry as the latter attempted to gain the Nashville Pike and the rear of the army. Zahm was then ordered to form a line to protect McCook's ammunition train, but his brigade, together with the 2nd Tennessee (also called the 2nd Middle Tennessee) Cavalry of Stanley's Reserve Brigade, was driven back in disorder across Overall Creek and, except for skirmishing, did no more fighting that day.

When Johnson's brigades were driven back, the right of Davis' division of McCook's corps was exposed to the enveloping attack by McCown's division. Davis immediately ordered Post's brigade, which was facing south toward the Franklin road, to change front to the right. It then formed a new line at nearly a right angle to its former position, and in this way covered the right of Carlin's brigade.

When Baldwin learned of the defeat of Kirk and Willich, he quickly posted his brigade about one-fourth of a mile to the right of Post and formed a defensive line facing south in the direction of Hardee's approaching troops.

The above changes in position had scarcely been completed when the enemy struck Baldwin's and Post's brigades on the Union right flank, the brigades of Carlin and Woodruff of Davis' division, and Sill's brigade of Sheridan's division, all of which were on the front of the main Union line. The forces of McCown and Cleburne attacked Post and Baldwin, while the brigades of Sterling A. M. Wood of Cleburne's division and John Q. Loomis (Deas' brigade) of Withers' division and Alfred J. Vaughan, Jr.'s brigade of Cheatham's division attacked to their right. Later George Maney's brigade of Cheatham's division joined in the attacks on Carlin, Woodruff, and Sill. Baldwin held his ground for a time, but he was soon flanked and driven back, while fighting stubbornly, through the cedar thickets to the Nashville and Chattanooga Railroad, where the shattered division was re-forming.

Post continued to hold his ground against repeated attacks by McCown's division, but finally, when the enemy had passed to his right and rear, he was forced to withdraw.

The brigades of Carlin, Woodruff, and Sill, the latter reinforced by two regiments of Schaefer's brigade, repulsed two attacks on their front, but when Post withdrew, the right of Carlin's brigade was exposed, and it too was compelled to retire. Woodruff held fast for a time, but then the right of Sill's line, which protected the left of his line, was driven back, and Woodruff was almost surrounded. He finally extricated his command and fell back across some open fields to his rear to the edge of a woods where Davis was attempting to re-form his division. Davis, with the troops remaining with him, finally fell back to the railroad, where his division was re-formed. Sill was killed during the fighting on this part of the field, and Nicholas Greusel assumed command of his brigade.

During the fighting that morning, the infantry of Davis and Sheridan was strongly supported in repelling the enemy attacks by William A. Hotchkiss' 2nd Battery, Wisconsin Light Artillery; Oscar F. Pinney's 5th Battery, Wisconsin Light Artillery; Stephen J. Carpenter's 8th Battery, Wisconsin Light Artillery of Davis' division; Henry Hescock's Battery G, 1st Missouri Light Artillery; Asahel K. Bush's 4th Battery, Indiana Light Artillery; and Charles Houghtaling's Battery C, 1st Illinois Light Artillery of Sheridan's division.

At the beginning of the enemy attack on the morning of December 31, 1862, Sheridan's line ran north and south, facing east, on the south side of the Wilkinson Pike. Roberts' brigade was on the left, between the Wilkinson Pike and the Harding house, and Sill's brigade was on the right, south of a brick kiln, which was about three-fourths of a mile east and south of the Griscom house, and about one-

fourth mile south of the Wilkinson Pike. Schaefer's brigade was in reserve, but when Sill was attacked, Schaefer sent two of his regiments to support him. When Sheridan's right flank was exposed by Woodruff's retreat, Sheridan immediately began to withdraw Sill's brigade (then commanded by Greusel), together with Schaefer's regiments, to a new position facing the enemy attack. Schaefer's regiments then rejoined their brigade.

As Greusel's brigade and Schaefer's regiments began to withdraw, Roberts' brigade changed front, charged into the woods just vacated, and covered the withdrawal. After retiring, Greusel's and Schaefer's brigades formed on a new line at a right angle to the original line, facing south. Roberts was then ordered to return from his position in the woods and form on the new line.

The enemy turning column continued to move forward, with Cheatham's division keeping abreast on its right, with its left directed toward the Griscom house and its right toward the Blanton house. This movement threatened to envelop Sheridan's new line, and he was again forced to change position. He moved his left flank forward to connect with the right of Negley's division, which still occupied almost the same position that it had taken the night before. He then formed Roberts' brigade on the right of Negley and the brigades of Greusel and Schaefer on the right of Roberts, but the latter two brigades were formed at nearly a right angle to Roberts' brigade, facing west, so as to protect the left of Negley's line. Sheridan's division was then north of the Wilkinson Pike and west of present-day Van Cleve Lane, which at the time of the battle was a farm road.

Sheridan was scarcely established on his new line when Roberts' brigade and Negley's division came under heavy attack by the brigades of Alexander P. Stewart and J. Patton Anderson, and at the same time Hardee's troops struck the front of Greusel's and Schaefer's brigades. A heavy infantry and artillery fire from the Federal lines repulsed this attack.

At this time Rosecrans was vigorously engaged in attempting to form a strong defensive line along the Nashville Pike where he would halt the enemy advance, and he ordered Sheridan to hold his ground until the dispositions that he was then making were completed. Sheridan repulsed two more attacks, during which Roberts was killed. Fazilo A.

Harrington assumed command of the brigade, but he was mortally wounded, and then Luther P. Bradley took charge of the brigade. After the third attack, there was a lull in the fighting and Sheridan, with his ammunition almost exhausted, prepared to withdraw as soon as Rousseau, who had been ordered up, came into position with his division on Sheridan's right.

Early that morning, December 31, 1862, Rosecrans had established his headquarters in rear of the left of the army to direct the movements of the divisions of Wood and Van Cleve as they crossed Stones River to attack Breckinridge's division on the east side of the river. Van Cleve had begun crossing when Rosecrans heard the sounds of the battle on his far right, but he believed that this was caused by the demonstration that he had ordered for that morning. About an hour after the enemy attacked, however, he learned that McCook was hard-pressed, but he was not informed of the rout of Johnson's division or of the withdrawal of Davis' division. Consequently, Rosecrans simply ordered McCook to make a stubborn defense, and allowed Van Cleve to continue his crossing of the river.

Rosecrans was then informed that his right wing had been driven back, and finally he realized the extent of McCook's disaster. Rosecrans was then certain that the objective of Bragg's attack was to gain possession of the Nashville-Murfreesboro Pike in rear of the army, and he took immediate steps to prevent the loss of his line of communication and the defeat of his army. He canceled the plans for his own attack on the Confederate right and ordered Van Cleve to recall Samuel Beatty's First Brigade and Samuel W. Price's Third Brigade, which had already crossed the river. Van Cleve then left Price's brigade to hold the crossing, and with Beatty's brigade and James P. Fyffe's Second Brigade moved westward along the railroad to a position in reserve.

Rosecrans also ordered Wood to suspend his preparations for crossing the river, and to send Hascall's First Brigade and Harker's Third Brigade, which were then en route to the ford, to move to the right of the line and reinforce the troops fighting there. Hascall was unable to move because of the large number of fugitives arriving from the front, and he halted to await orders. He was then left in reserve, and Harker's brigade proceeded on to the right. Wood's other brigade, Wagner's Third Bri-gade, and Palmer's division of Crittenden's corps were ordered to hold the line between the left of Negley's division and Stones River.

When Thomas learned of Sheridan's change of position to the right of Negley, he sent Rousseau's division, which had been held in reserve, to the right and rear of Sheridan to support what was left of McCook's line. Later Van Cleve was ordered to the right of Rousseau, and Harker's brigade was sent farther down the Nashville Pike, where it was to advance on the right of Van Cleve.

Morton's Pioneer Brigade was posted on a knoll west of the pike and 400–500 yards in rear of the center of Palmer's line, where it supported James H. Stokes' Chicago Board of Trade Battery.

Rousseau advanced as ordered to a position in the cedar brakes, which covered much of the field, to the right and rear of Sheridan's line. The division faced west, with John Beatty's Second Brigade on the left, and Oliver L. Shepherd's Fourth Brigade of Regulars on the right. Benjamin F. Scribner's First Brigade was in reserve about 100 yards to the rear, opposite the center of the first line. Rousseau's artillery, commanded by Cyrus O. Loomis and consisting of David C. Stone's Battery A, Kentucky Light Artillery, George W. Van Pelt's 1st Battery, Michigan Light Artillery, and Francis L. Guenther's Battery H, 5th United States Artillery, was posted to cover the front of the division.

Shortly after taking position, Rousseau was attacked by Cleburne and McCown, and Shepherd's and Scribner's brigades were forced back. John Beatty's brigade held for some time longer, but when Sheridan's division withdrew about 11:00 A.M. to replenish its ammunition, Beatty was also forced to fall back.

Sheridan withdrew to a position in rear of the right of Palmer near the Nashville Pike. Then Roberts' brigade, commanded at that time by Bradley, was sent a short distance to the rear of the pike to aid in protecting the army's communications. Greusel's brigade was ordered to the extreme right to support Zahm's cavalry brigade, which was then threatened by Wharton's cavalry, and it remained in position there during the rest of the day. Schaefer's brigade was sent to a position on the railroad, and it later aided in repelling enemy attacks on Palmer's and Wood's divisions.

As the enemy attack extended to the right, it

finally reached the front of Negley's division, which was in position on the left of Sheridan. Timothy R. Stanley's Second Brigade was on the right, and Miller's Third Brigade was on the left. The infantry was supported by Alban A. Ellsworth's Battery B, Kentucky Light Artillery (Hewett's Battery), Alexander Marshall's Battery G, 1st Ohio Light Artillery, and Frederick Schultz's Battery M, 1st Ohio Light Artillery.

Negley held his position against attacks by the brigades of J. Patton Anderson (Walthall's brigade) and Alexander P. Stewart from 10:00 to 11:00 A.M. When Sheridan withdrew on his right, the division was almost surrounded, and it was only with difficulty that it succeeded in falling back.

Negley joined Rousseau, who was also retiring, and together the two divisions, under the direction of Thomas, formed a new temporary line in a shallow depression in open ground about 400–500 yards from the edge of a woods through which the enemy was advancing. Rousseau was soon attacked, but with the aid of Morton's Pioneers and Stokes' battery, he succeeded in holding his position until the artillery was posted on high ground to the rear near the pike.

Van Cleve, with Samuel Beatty's brigade of his division, arrived on the right of Rousseau as the latter was forming his line, and with the aid of George R. Swallow's 7th Battery, Indiana Light Artillery and Alanson J. Stevens' Battery B, Pennsylvania Light Artillery of Van Cleve's division, he repelled the enemy attack. James P. Fyffe's Second Brigade of Van Cleve's division arrived and formed on the right of Samuel Beatty, and Harker's brigade of Wood's division came up and formed on the right of Fyffe. Fyffe's brigade was quickly outflanked and forced back, and Beatty and Harker soon followed. Van Cleve's two brigades then took position on the left of Davis' and Johnson's re-formed divisions, and on the right of the Pioneer Brigade. There was no further fighting on that part of the field during the rest of the day.

As the Confederate attack developed toward the right, it reached the front of Negley's and Palmer's divisions about 9:00 A.M. At that time Chalmers' brigade of Withers' division advanced along the Nashville-Murfreesboro Pike. Palmer's division was in position on the right of the pike, with Hazen's brigade on the left, next to the pike, and Cruft's brigade on the right. Their line was at the Cowan cottonfield. Grose's brigade was in reserve about 100 yards in rear of the first line. Wagner's brigade of Wood's division was on the left of Palmer, with its left near Stones River, and Negley's division was on the right of Palmer.

The Federals repulsed all attacks until Negley finally withdrew about 11:00 A.M., but Palmer still continued to resist. About noon, Daniel S. Donelson's brigade of Cheatham's division advanced over the same ground as had Chalmers in his earlier attack and vigorously attacked Palmer's line. Cruft's brigade was almost enveloped by Donelson's troops on its front and by the enemy forces that were following Negley as he retired from Cruft's right. Grose's brigade quickly changed front to the rear to face the latter, and in a spirited attack drove them back. Cruft's brigade, with William E. Standart's Battery B, 1st Ohio Light Artillery, was finally driven back to the Nashville Pike, where it arrived about noon.

At this time, Rosecrans' line made a sharp angle at a point north of the Cowan house, with Wood's division on the left extending northward toward the river, Palmer's division holding the apex of the angle, and the rest of the army in line on the right and extending to the northwest along the Nashville-Murfreesboro Pike. Within this salient, a little to the northeast of the pike and on both sides of the railroad, was a low, rocky elevation of about four acres in extent that was covered with trees. This was called the Round Forest, and it became a key defensive point in the fighting on the afternoon of December 31, 1862. It was held by Palmer's division and by the brigades of Hascall and Wagner of Wood's division.

About 11:00 A.M., while the brigades of Grose and Cruft were still engaged, Hazen was ordered to fall back to the crest of the small hill in the Round Forest, between the pike and the railroad, and to hold that ground. He then retired his right flank and placed his troops behind the railroad embankment. Grose again changed front and moved to his left and reported to Hazen. He then occupied the same position that he had taken that morning. Daniel T. Cockerill's Battery F, 1st Ohio Light Artillery and Charles C. Parsons' Batteries H and M, 4th United States Artillery were posted to support Hazen and Grose.

About noon, when Donelson attacked, Palmer asked for help, and Hascall's brigade of Wood's division moved up and took position between Wagner and Sheridan on a part of the original line, immediately to the right of the railroad. Hascall remained there and aided in repulsing the enemy attacks on the Round Forest during the afternoon. Schaefer's brigade of Sheridan's division was also moved to the the right and front of Wood's division, on the left of the railroad. Schaefer was killed, and Bernard Laiboldt assumed command of the brigade.

At 2:00 P.M. the enemy again attacked the lines of Palmer and Wood with the brigades of Daniel W. Adams and John K. Jackson of Breckinridge's division, which had been brought across to the west bank of Stones River to support Polk. This attack was repulsed with heavy losses.

At about this time, Breckinridge arrived on the field with the brigades of William Preston and Joseph B. Palmer of his division, and at 4:00 P.M. advanced for the final attack of the day against the Federal left. Preston's brigade was on the right, next to the river, and Palmer's brigade was on the left and extended across the Nashville-Murfreesboro Pike. Like the previous attacks, this too was repulsed, and it then being almost dark, the fighting ended for the day. In addition to Palmer's batteries, George Estep's 8th Battery, Indiana Light Artillery, Jerome B. Cox's 10th Battery, Indiana Light Artillery, and Cullen Bradley's 6th Battery, Ohio Light Artillery, all of Wood's division, rendered great service in repelling the enemy attacks on the Round Forest.

During the night of December 30, 1862, Stanley was ordered, with his cavalry, to Stewart's Creek to protect one of the trains of the army, but when he arrived there at 5:00 the next morning, he found that all was secure and that the train was not threatened. As he started back, Stanley heard the firing at the beginning of the Battle of Stones River, and he marched in that direction. He was then ordered to the right of the army to protect the flank of McCook's corps, which was being driven back toward the railroad.

Stanley's command consisted of Minty's First Brigade of Kennett's First Cavalry Division and the 15th Pennsylvania Cavalry and 1st Tennessee Cavalry (also called 1st Middle Tennessee Cavalry) of Stanley's Reserve Brigade. Stanley took position on the right of McCook, with his right extending toward Wilkinson's Cross Roads. Minty's brigade crossed Overall Creek and took position parallel to and about three-fourths of a mile from the Nashville and Murfreesboro road. The 4th Michigan Cavalry was formed as a line of skirmishers and was supported by a part of the 1st Tennessee Cavalry, fighting dismounted. A battalion of the 7th Pennsylvania Cavalry and two companies of the 3rd Kentucky Cavalry were posted to the right and rear of the 4th Michigan, with the 15th Pennsylvania in their rear.

About 4:00 P.M. Wheeler advanced rapidly with his cavalry and drove back the 4th Michigan to the line of skirmishers of the 1st Tennessee, and he then charged against the 7th Pennsylvania. Minty attempted to move his dismounted skirmishers to the right to aid the 7th Pennsylvania, but he was prevented from doing so by the heavy enemy fire. At that time the 15th Pennsylvania gave way and retreated rapidly, and soon the 7th Pennsylvania and the dismounted men were forced to follow. Stanley then re-formed his men in a defensive position in rear of a low ridge, which protected them from enemy artillery fire.

Wheeler followed the retreating Federals toward their new position in three lines. At that point, Stanley ordered his men to charge, and he personally led companies K and H of the 4th Michigan Cavalry and about fifty men of the 15th Pennsylvania Cavalry against the line that was advancing toward his front and left. At the same time, Minty charged against the line that was approaching the front of his position with the 4th Michigan and 1st Tennessee, and they were supported on the right by the fire of the 15th Pennsylvania. The attacks by both Stanley and Minty were successful, and the enemy were driven back. Wheeler's other line held its ground for a time, but then Minty charged again, and it too was forced to retire. Kennett, commanding the cavalry division, arrived with reinforcements, and the fighting ended for the day. Minty held his ground that night with the 1st Tennessee, the 15th Pennsylvania, and the 4th Michigan.

Late on the evening of December 31, 1862, the Army of the Cumberland still held the line of the Nashville-Murfreesboro Pike. Beginning on the left at Stones River, and in order to the right, the troops were in position as follows: Wagner's brigade and Hascall's brigade of Wood's division; Hazen's brigade and Grose's brigade of Palmer's division (Cruft's brigade was supporting a battery on the railroad); Negley's division and Rousseau's division of Thomas' corps; Morton's Pioneer Brigade; Samuel Beatty's brigade and Fyffe's brigade of Van Cleve's division; Harker's brigade of Wood's division; Johnson's re-formed division; Sheridan's division; Davis' division; and Stanley's cavalry, which was on the extreme right on and near Overall's Creek.

Late in the afternoon, John C. Starkweather's Third Brigade of Rousseau's division and Moses B. Walker's First Brigade of Fry's division, which had been on duty in the rear, arrived and were posted in reserve in rear of the line of battle. Walker's brigade was in rear of the left of Sheridan's division, near the pike, and Starkweather was in rear of McCook's left.

At nightfall neither Rosecrans nor Bragg had accomplished what he had set out to do that morning. Rosecrans' attack had been called off before it actually started because Bragg attacked first, and Bragg, although his left had driven back the Federal right two or three miles, had failed to gain possession of the all-important road running back to Nashville. At both headquarters there was uncertainty that night as to what the other commanding general intended to do the following day. Bragg believed that Rosecrans would retreat to Nashville, and there is no doubt that the latter considered this possibility, but in the end he decided to remain where he was and await a further attack by Bragg. Bragg, however, ordered no attack for January 1, 1863, and simply waited to see what Rosecrans would do.

There were some changes in command in the Army of the Cumberland during the night of December 31, 1862. Thomas J. Wood had been slightly wounded during the morning, but had been able to remain with his command until 7:00 P.M. He then turned over the command of his First Division of Crittenden's corps to Milo S. Hascall, and George P. Buell took charge of Hascall's First Brigade, First Division. Van Cleve had also been wounded slightly during the day, but had continued to lead his Third Division of Crittenden's corps until the morning of January 1, 1863. Then Samuel Beatty assumed command of the division, and Benjamin C. Grider took over Beatty's First Brigade, Third Division.

During the night and the early morning of January 1, 1863, Rosecrans made some changes in troop positions and some readjustments in his defensive line. On the left he withdrew Palmer's and Hascall's divisions about 600–700 yards to a more favorable position, with the new left flank resting on Stones River at McFadden's Ford. He moved Hascall's division back and formed a new line across, and perpendicular to, the Nashville-Murfreesboro Pike, facing to the southeast, with its left connecting with the right of Palmer's division and its right on the position occupied by Stokes' Battery of the Pioneer Brigade. Buell's brigade was on the right; Harker's brigade, which had rejoined the division from the right of the line about 11:00 P.M., was in the center; and Wagner's brigade was on the left. Hazen's brigade of Palmer's division held the Round Forest until about dawn January 1, and it then fell back to the left of Hascall's division. Cruft's brigade was on the left of Hazen, and Grose's brigade was in reserve. A short time after Hazen withdrew, Chalmers' Confederate brigade, commanded by Thomas W. White, advanced and occupied the Round Forest. Later Palmer's division was relieved on the first line and placed in reserve near the river.

At 3:00 A.M. the brigades of Walker and Starkweather moved up from their positions in reserve on the right and relieved Samuel Beatty's division, which then rejoined Crittenden's corps near McFadden's Ford. Beatty was ordered to cross the river and form in line of battle on the high ground near the ford, facing Breckinridge's division, which had returned to its former position after its unsuccessful attacks on the Round Forest. When in position, Beatty's line extended to the northeast from a point near the ford, and it was almost perpendicular to the river. Price's brigade was on the right, and Fyffe's brigade was on the left. Grider's brigade was in reserve, near the ford, in rear of Price.

Grose's brigade of Palmer's division also crossed the river that day to support Beatty, but it returned to the west bank that evening. Then, on January 2, 1863, Grose rejoined Beatty and took position to the left and rear of Fyffe.

January 1, 1863 was relatively quiet, although Bragg demonstrated strongly against the Union right and center with artillery and with a show of infantry. About noon Rosecrans moved Negley to support McCook when he believed that the enemy attack on his right flank might be renewed, but Bragg did not attack.

Battle of Stones River, Tennessee, January 2, 1863. Nothing of significance happened on the morning of January 2, 1863, but about noon Breckinridge advanced patrols and skirmishers on the front of Beatty's division to determine the strength of the Union troops holding the high ground east of McFadden's Ford. Rosecrans realized that this activity might be a preliminary to a strong attack, and at about 1:00 P.M. he ordered Negley to move with his division from its position on the Federal right to support Crittenden. When Negley arrived, he took position in rear of the batteries on the west bank of Stones River. Rosecrans also sent Morton's Pioneer Brigade to reinforce Negley.

At about this time, Bragg became convinced that it was essential for the security of his position to hold the high ground east of Stones River near McFadden's Ford, and at 2:00 P.M. he ordered Breckinridge to attack and drive Beatty from the hills. At 3:00 P.M. Breckinridge advanced his skirmishers, and an hour later he attacked with the brigades of Gideon J. Pillow and Roger W. Hanson in the first line and the brigades of William Preston and Daniel W. Adams in the second line. Pillow had just arrived and relieved Joseph B. Palmer in command of his brigade.

Pillow and Hanson first struck Price's brigade and drove it back on Grider. Grider resisted briefly, and then both brigades were forced to retire across the river. Fyffe's brigade was not on the direct line of Breckinridge's attack, but it was in position to deliver a flanking fire into the enemy brigades as they passed. When Grider's brigade gave way, Fyffe withdrew to the north, but with Grose's brigade and Cortland Livingston's 3rd Battery, Wisconsin Light Artillery of Beatty's division, he continued to resist.

Meantime, on the west bank of the river, John Mendenhall, Crittenden's chief of artillery, had collected fifty-seven guns belonging to Crittenden's corps, Negley's division of Thomas' corps, and also Stokes' battery of the Pioneer Brigade, and had posted them so as to bear on the ground over which Breckinridge was attacking. Forty-five of these guns were massed on a ridge overlooking McFadden's Ford, and the other twelve were in

position about a mile to the southwest, where they could fire across the river into the enemy's flank. When Price's and Grider's troops had all recrossed the river and the field was clear, Mendenhall opened fire with all of his guns with deadly effect. This, combined with a heavy infantry fire from Fyffe's and Grose's men north of the ford, and from Negley's division and other troops west of the river, brought to a halt Breckinridge's men at the river bank. Then, as they began to give way, the Federals launched a vigorous counterattack. John F. Miller of Negley's division, without orders from his division commander, crossed the river with his Third Brigade and rapidly moved against the enemy. Timothy R. Stanley with his Second Brigade then joined Miller, and together they pressed forward as they drove Breckinridge's brigades back to their original positions. Davis' division of McCook's corps, which had been sent over from the Federal right that afternoon to support Samuel Beatty, quickly advanced on the right of Miller, along the river.

Many other troops joined in the pursuit. These included Morton's Pioneer Brigade, which had been sent earlier to support Negley; Hazen's brigade of Palmer's division; Grose's brigade of Palmer's division; and the re-formed brigades of Beatty's division.

That evening Davis was the ranking officer east of Stones River, and he assumed command of all troops that were pursuing Breckinridge. He then relieved the brigades of Miller and Stanley, and they passed to the rear and recrossed the river. He also relieved the troops of Beatty and Palmer, and by that time it was nearly dark. Davis then sent out skirmishers and bivouacked his troops for the night. Morton recrossed his brigade to the west bank that night.

At 5:00 P.M. January 2, 1863, James G. Spears was assigned command of a new brigade composed of East Tennessee regiments at Nashville. He marched with his brigade that night and reported to Rosecrans near Murfreesboro early the next morning. Spears' brigade was attached to Thomas' corps on January 3, and the next day it was assigned to Negley's division as First Brigade.

January 3, 1863, the weather was not favorable for active operations, and the two armies remained generally in the positions that they had occupied the night before. At 6:00 P.M. Thomas sent forward a part of John Beatty's brigade of Rousseau's division and a part of Spears' brigade to drive enemy skirmishers from a woods along the front of the line. They drove the enemy not only from the woods but also from their entrenchments beyond. This brief action ended the fighting at Stones River.

During the night of January 3, 1863, Bragg withdrew from his lines at Murfreesboro and retreated toward Shelbyville and Tullahoma. The Army of the Cumberland spent the next day burying the dead and caring for the wounded, and on January 5 Rosecrans occupied Murfreesboro.

For further information about the Army of the Cumberland after the Battle of Stones River, see Tullahoma (or Middle Tennessee) Campaign.

The organization of Fourteenth Corps, or Army of the Cumberland, during the period December 26, 1862–January 5, 1863 was as follows:

RIGHT WING, Alexander McD. McCook

First Division, Jefferson C. Davis
    First Brigade, P. Sidney Post
    Second Brigade, William P. Carlin
    Third Brigade, William E. Woodruff

Note. Oscar F. Pinney's 5th Battery, Wisconsin Light Artillery was attached to First Brigade; William A. Hotchkiss' 2nd Battery, Wisconsin Light Artillery was attached to Second Brigade; and Stephen J. Carpenter's 8th Battery, Wisconsin Light Artillery was attached to Third Brigade.

Second Division, Richard W. Johnson
    First Brigade, August Willich, to December 31, 1862
        captured
        William Wallace, December 31, 1862
        William H. Gibson
    Second Brigade, Edward N. Kirk, to December 31, 1862, mortally wounded
        Joseph B. Dodge
    Third Brigade, Philemon P. Baldwin

Note. Edmund B. Belding's Battery A, 1st Ohio Light Artillery was attached to First Brigade; Warren P. Edgarton's Battery E, 1st Ohio Light Artillery was attached to Second Brigade; and Peter Simonson's 5th Battery, Indiana Light Artillery was attached to Third Brigade.

Third Division, Philip H. Sheridan
    First Brigade, Joshua W. Sill, to December 31, 1862, killed
        Nicholas Greusel

Second Brigade, Frederick Schaefer, to December 31, 1862, killed
    Bernard Laiboldt
Third Brigade, George W. Roberts, to December 31, 1863, killed
    Fazilo A. Harrington, December 31, 1862, mortally wounded
    Luther P. Bradley

Note. Henry Hescock was chief of artillery of Third Division. Asahel K. Bush's 4th Battery, Indiana Light Artillery was attached to First Brigade; Henry Hescock's Battery G, 1st Missouri Light Artillery was attached to Second Brigade; and Charles Houghtaling's Battery C, 1st Illinois Light Artillery was attached to Third Brigade.

CENTER, George H. Thomas

First Division, Lovell H. Rousseau
    First Brigade, Benjamin F. Scribner
    Second Brigade, John Beatty
    Third Brigade, John C. Starkweather
    Fourth Brigade, Oliver L. Shepherd

Note. Cyrus O. Loomis was chief of artillery of First Division. George W. Van Pelt's 1st Battery, Michigan Light Artillery was attached to Second Brigade; David C. Stone's Battery A, Kentucky Light Artillery was attached to Third Brigade; and Francis L. Guenther's Battery H, 5th United States Artillery was attached to Fourth Brigade.

Second Division, James S. Negley
    First Brigade, James G. Spears
    Second Brigade, Timothy R. Stanley
    Third Brigade, John F. Miller

Note 1. First Brigade was organized January 2, 1863 and joined the Army of the Cumberland at Murfreesboro the next day. It was assigned to Second Division as First Brigade January 4, 1863.

Note 2. Frederick Schultz's Battery M, 1st Ohio Light Artillery was attached to Second Brigade; and Alban A. Ellsworth's Battery B, Kentucky Light Artillery and Alexander Marshall's Battery G, 1st Ohio Light Artillery were attached to Third Brigade.

Third Division, Speed S. Fry
    First Brigade, Moses B. Walker
    Second Brigade, John M. Harlan
    Third Brigade, James B. Steedman

Note. Only Walker's First Brigade was present with the army at Stones River. The other two brigades were near Gallatin, Tennessee and along the Louisville and Nashville Railroad. Josiah W. Church's 4th Battery, Michigan Light Artillery was attached to First Brigade.

Fourth Division, Robert B. Mitchell
　First Brigade, James D. Morgan
　Second Brigade, Daniel McCook
　Cavalry, artillery, and unattached troops

Note. Fourth Division was at Nashville, Tennessee and was not engaged at Stones River.

Fifth Division, Joseph J. Reynolds
　First Brigade, Albert S. Hall
　Second Brigade, Abram O. Miller

Note. Fifth Division was near Gallatin, Tennessee and along the Louisville and Nashville Railroad, and was not with the army at Stones River.

LEFT WING, Thomas L. Crittenden

First Division, Thomas J. Wood, to evening of December 31, 1862, wounded
　Milo S. Hascall
　First Brigade, Milo S. Hascall, to evening of December 31, 1862
　　George P. Buell
　Second Brigade, George D. Wagner
　Third Brigade, Charles G. Harker

Note. Seymour Race was chief of artillery of First Division. George Estep's 8th Battery, Indiana Light Artillery was assigned to First Brigade; Jerome B. Cox's 10th Battery, Indiana Light Artillery was assigned to Second Brigade; and Cullen Bradley's 6th Battery, Ohio Light Artillery was assigned to Third Brigade.

Second Division, John M. Palmer
　First Brigade, Charles Cruft
　Second Brigade, William B. Hazen
　Third Brigade, William Grose
　Artillery, William E. Standart
　　Battery B, 1st Ohio Light Artillery, William E. Standart
　　Battery F, 1st Ohio Light Artillery, Daniel T. Cockerill
　　Batteries H and M, 4th United States Artillery, Charles C. Parsons

Third Division, Horatio P. Van Cleve, to morning of January 1, 1863, wounded December 31, 1862
　Samuel Beatty
　First Brigade, Samuel Beatty, to morning of January 1, 1863
　　Benjamin C. Grider
　Second Brigade, James P. Fyffe
　Third Brigade, Samuel W. Price
　Artillery, George R. Swallow
　　7th Battery, Indiana Light Artillery, George R. Swallow

　　Battery B, Pennsylvania Light Artillery, Alanson J. Stevens
　　3rd Battery, Wisconsin Light Artillery, Cortland Livingston

CAVALRY, David S. Stanley

Cavalry Division, John Kennett
　First Brigade, Robert H. G. Minty
　Second Brigade, Lewis Zahm

Reserve Cavalry, under the immediate command of Stanley

MISCELLANEOUS COMMANDS

Pioneer Brigade, James St. Clair Morton

Note. James H. Stokes' Battery, Illinois Light Artillery was a part of the Pioneer Brigade.

Post of Gallatin, Tennessee, Eleazer A. Paine
　Ward's Brigade, William T. Ward
　Cavalry

STREIGHT'S RAID FROM TUSCUMBIA, ALABAMA TOWARD ROME, GEORGIA APRIL 26, 1863–MAY 3, 1863

On April 7, 1863, William S. Rosecrans, commander of the Army and Department of the Cumberland, assigned Abel D. Streight to the command of an Independent Provisional Brigade and ordered him to lead this force on an expedition to cut the Western and Atlantic Railroad south of Dalton, Georgia. The object of this expedition was to destroy the railroad and thereby prevent troops and supplies from being sent to Braxton Bragg's Confederate Army of Tennessee, which was at that time in position along the Duck River at Shelbyville and Tullahoma in Tennessee. It was Rosecrans' intention to move south with his army from Murfreesboro, Tennessee and drive Bragg out of the state and into Georgia, and he hoped that any serious interruption of Bragg's supply line would contribute materially to the success of his campaign.

The plan for Streight's expedition was as follows: He was to assemble his command at Nashville, Tennessee and then proceed on transports down the Cumberland River to Palmyra, below Clarksville, and disembark. Then, after collecting mules on which to mount his troops, he was to march to Fort Henry on the Tennessee River. There he was to reembark his command on the transports, which had been sent around by way of the Cumberland and Ohio rivers to the Tennessee. From Fort Henry the expedition was to proceed upriver to Eastport, Mississippi, where the troops were to disembark.

To draw attention from Streight's raid, and at the same time to engage and delay any pursuing column, a force of about 5,000 infantry and cavalry from Corinth, Mississippi, under the command of Grenville M. Dodge, was to move ahead of the expedition from Eastport, attack Tuscumbia, and drive any enemy force that it might encounter up the valley toward Decatur. Meantime, Streight was to move by roads to the right toward Rome, Georgia. Dodge was to hold any enemy force in check until Streight was well on his way.

Conforming to plan, Streight's brigade left Nashville April 10, 1863, and the next day the troops landed at Palmyra. Streight was delayed there because of problems with the poor quality of the mules that had been brought there for him, and he did not reach Fort Henry until April 15. He was again delayed until the transports arrived, but he finally reached Eastport on the afternoon of April 19.

Dodge had arrived at Eastport two days ahead of Streight, and had pushed on toward Tuscumbia. Near that city, however, Dodge was attacked by a cavalry brigade of the Confederate District of Northern Alabama, commanded by Philip D. Roddey, and he withdrew and encamped his command on Bear Creek, about twelve miles from Eastport, on the road to Tuscumbia. Streight joined Dodge on the morning of April 22 and followed him to Tuscumbia, where both commands arrived April 24.

At that time the only Confederate troops opposing Dodge and Streight belonged to Roddey's brigade, but help was on the way. On April 23, 1863, Nathan B. Forrest, who was commanding a brigade in Earl Van Dorn's First Confederate Cavalry Corps at Columbia, Tennessee, was ordered with one of his brigades to Decatur, Alabama to join

Roddey. Upon arriving there, he was to assume command of all Confederate forces opposing Dodge and Streight. Forrest crossed the Tennessee River at Brown's Ferry, below Decatur, on April 26 and joined Roddey on Town Creek, eighteen miles east of Tuscumbia, on present-day U.S. Alternate 72.

According to Rosecrans' original plan, Dodge was to advance no farther than Tuscumbia in support of Streight, but upon arriving there, Streight learned that Forrest was at Town Creek, and he insisted that Dodge advance and drive the enemy as far as Courtland or Decatur and hold them there. On April 27, Dodge drove the enemy across Town Creek. He crossed the creek the next day, but then returned to Town Creek and camped. He remained on Town Creek for a time and then retired to Tuscumbia.

Meantime, during the night of April 26, 1863, Streight left Tuscumbia with his brigade and marched south to Russell, Alabama. There he turned east and moved to Mount Hope, where he bivouacked on the night of April 27. The next day he pushed on toward Moulton, which was almost due south of Courtland, and he arrived on the evening of April 28.

That day Forrest learned that Streight was moving east toward Moulton, and on the morning of April 29 he left a part of his command to watch Dodge, and with two regiments of his brigade and six guns, and Roddey with one regiment and one battalion of his brigade started in pursuit. On April 29, Streight marched fifty-five miles, camping that night at the foot of Day's Gap on Sand Mountain. Forrest passed through Moulton that day, and at midnight arrived within about four miles of Streight's camp.

On April 30, 1863, the Federal rear guard was engaged as the rest of the column moved up to the summit of the pass. Streight moved on about six miles to a ridge called Hog Mountain, where he was again forced to fight a delaying action. He continued on during the night, and about 2:00 on the morning of May 1, he was once more engaged with Forrest's leading troops. About 10:00 A.M. May 1, Streight reached Blountsville, about forty-three miles from Day's Gap. He allowed his command to rest for two hours, and then pushed on toward Gadsden. Beyond Blountsville, the Federals attempted to slow the enemy's pursuit by obstructing the road, burning bridges, and fighting with the advance troops.

Late on the afternoon of May 1, 1863, Streight's brigade forded the East Branch of the Black Warrior River while the rear guard skirmished, and a short time later Forrest caught up with the raiders as they crossed Big Will's Creek, just south of Lookout Mountain.

The column arrived at Gadsden May 2, 1863, and with scarcely any rest marched on toward Rome. About twelve miles northeast of Gadsden, at Blount's plantation, Forrest attacked and scattered the 73rd Indiana and killed its commander, but Streight moved on after dark to the vicinity of Centre on the Coosa River. From there he marched northward, crossed Little River, and then marched eastward to Cedar Bluff, about twenty-eight miles from Gadsden and about ten miles from the Georgia state line. He arrived there about sunup May 3 and then continued on toward Rome.

About 9:00 A.M. Streight halted four miles east of Cedar Bluff, at the village of Lawrence, to rest and feed. There he learned that Rome was heavily guarded by the enemy, and he also learned that an enemy column was moving on a road that ran parallel to the one he was following and was at that time closer to Rome than he was. While Streight was pondering this information, his rear guard became engaged with Forrest's troopers, who had again caught up with the raiders. About noon May 3, 1863, Streight decided to surrender to Forrest.

Although Streight's raid failed in its principal purpose, it did contribute materially to the success of Union operations in Mississippi. The raid was carried out at the same time that Benjamin H. Grierson moved southward from La Grange in West Tennessee, on a raid through Mississippi, to Baton Rouge, Louisiana. By drawing Forrest's cavalry away into Alabama, Streight perhaps helped Grierson to make a successful march through Mississippi and, in so doing, to distract the attention of John C. Pemberton, commanding the Confederate forces at Vicksburg, at the critical time that Ulysses S. Grant's Army of the Tennessee was crossing the Mississippi River on its way to the rear of Vicksburg.

The organization of the Federal troops participating in Streight's raid in Alabama was as follows:

Streight's Provisional Brigade, Army of the Cumberland, Abel D. Streight
51st Indiana, James W. Sheets
73rd Indiana, Gilbert Hathaway
3rd Ohio, Orris A. Lawson
80th Illinois, Andrew F. Rodgers
1st Middle Tennessee Cavalry (two companies), D. D. Smith

Note. The regiments of the brigade were taken from Fourteenth Corps as follows: 51st Indiana (Streight's own regiment) and 73rd Indiana from Third Brigade, First Division; 3rd Ohio from Second Brigade, First Division; and 80th Illinois from First Brigade, Fifth Division.

Second Division (or District of Corinth), Grenville M. Dodge
Third Brigade, Moses M. Bane
Fourth Brigade, John W. Fuller
Cavalry Brigade, Florence M. Cornyn

Note 1. Second Division, or District of Corinth, Mississippi, was a part of Sixteenth Corps, Department of the Tennessee.
Note 2. Fuller's brigade joined Dodge from Corinth April 21, 1863.

STURGIS' EXPEDITION FROM MEMPHIS, TENNESSEE INTO MISSISSIPPI (BATTLE OF BRICE'S CROSS ROADS) JUNE 2–13, 1864

As William T. Sherman advanced more deeply into Georgia toward Atlanta in May 1864, he became increasingly concerned about the safety of his ever-lengthening line of communication that ran back through Chattanooga and Nashville to Louisville, Kentucky. His main cause for concern was Nathan B. Forrest, who was then at Tupelo, Mississippi with his Confederate cavalry and was in position to ride into northern Georgia and Tennessee and destroy the railroads that were carrying Sherman's supplies to the front.

On May 19, 1864, Sherman directed Cadwallader C. Washburn, commander of the District of West Tennessee, to move with a cavalry force commanded by Samuel D. Sturgis to destroy the Mobile and Ohio Railroad and also to attempt to defeat or disperse Forrest's cavalry. About a month earlier, Sturgis had led a column from Memphis against Forrest's command, which was then at Jackson, Tennessee, but Forrest was able to move south past Sturgis and arrived at Tupelo, Mississippi with little interference. Sturgis then returned to Memphis without having inflicted any damage on Forrest's cavalry. For additional information, see Sturgis' Expedition from Memphis, Tennessee to Ripley, Mississippi.

Upon arriving at Memphis from his unsuccessful expedition, Sturgis reported to Washburn, who ordered him to report to Sherman. A short time later, however, Sherman directed Washburn to attempt again to defeat Forrest, and he ordered Sturgis to return to Memphis and assume command of the new expedition. Sturgis arrived at Memphis and reported to Washburn only three days before the expedition was to start, and was assigned command by an order dated May 31, 1864. Sturgis received this order on June 1, the day that Washburn's troops began to move out of Memphis, and he assumed command the next day near La Fayette, Tennessee.

Sturgis' orders were to proceed to Corinth, Mississippi by way of Salem and Ruckersville, and capture any Confederate force that might be there. He was then to move south and destroy the Mobile and Ohio Railroad as far south as Tupelo and Okolona, and with a part of his force he was to continue the destruction as far as possible in the direction of Macon and Columbus. He was then to move to Grenada, Mississippi, and from there back to Memphis.

Washburn's troops began their movement on June 1, 1864. George E. Waring's First Brigade of Benjamin H. Grierson's Cavalry Division, Sixteenth Corps marched that day twenty-three miles from White's Station to La Fayette, where it camped for the night. Edward F. Winslow's Second Brigade of Grierson's division moved with the artillery and the wagon train from Memphis to Collierville and camped there that night in a heavy rain. Henry B. Burgh's Third Brigade of Grierson's division was left behind to guard Memphis.

On June 1, 1864, the following troops moved by rail on the Memphis and Charleston Railroad from Memphis to La Fayette, where they bivouacked for the night: William L. McMillen's First Brigade,

First Division, Sixteenth Corps, which was then serving in the District of Memphis; Edward Bouton's First Brigade, United States Colored Troops of the District of Memphis; and Alexander Wilkin's 9th Minnesota Infantry, which had just arrived at Memphis.

George B. Hoge's Second Brigade of the District of Memphis arrived at the depot at Memphis at 2:00 P.M. June 1, 1864, and there it was reinforced by the 81st Illinois and the 95th Illinois of T. Kilby Smith's Provisional Division, Seventeenth Corps, which had just arrived at Memphis from Nathaniel P. Banks' Red River Expedition on May 30. Hoge's brigade did not leave Memphis until 6:30 that evening because of a lack of transportation, but then it too moved eastward by rail toward La Fayette. About 9:00 P.M., when the train was between Collierville and La Fayette, it became dark, and the men left the cars and bivouacked along the track. The train returned to Memphis.

Hoge marched at 6:00 A.M. June 2, 1864 and arrived at La Fayette at 11:00 that morning. There he found McMillen's and Bouton's brigades already in camp, and he moved on and went into camp about a mile east of the town. Winslow's cavalry continued its march with the artillery and supply train to La Fayette that day, and there he turned over the artillery and train to the care of the infantry.

Sturgis left Memphis by train at 5:00 on the morning of June 2, 1864, and when he arrived at La Fayette, he assumed command of the expedition. He then proceeded to organize his three infantry brigades into a Provisional Division, placing McMillen, the senior officer, in command. Alexander Wilkin commanded the First Brigade, George B. Hoge the Second Brigade, and Edward Bouton the Third Brigade. For complete details of the organization of Sturgis' Expedition, see end of this section.

During June 2, 1864, while Sturgis completed the organization of his infantry, Grierson's cavalry moved out to the east at 5:00 A.M. and camped in the rain that night about two miles west of Moscow. It was still raining on the morning of June 3, when Grierson resumed his march and moved in a southeasterly direction. He passed through Early Grove, near the Mississippi state line on Clear Creek, then crossed the Mississippi Central Railroad near Lamar, halting for the night about a mile east of

Salem on the road to Ruckersville. Sturgis directed Grierson to remain near Salem until the infantry came up.

At 3:30 A.M. June 3, 1864, McMillen's infantry left La Fayette and marched out on the road to Lamar, following the cavalry. Wilkin's brigade was in the lead, Hoge's brigade followed Wilkin, and Bouton's brigade, which was then guarding the trains, brought up the rear. Because of the almost constant rain that had fallen since the column had left Memphis, the roads were nearly impassable, and many of the streams were very difficult to cross; therefore progress that day was slow. Wilkin's and Hoge's brigades camped near Lamar that night, but Bouton's brigade and the trains were only then crossing the swamp of Clear Creek, and they did not halt until 11:00 P.M., about four miles from Lamar.

June 4, 1864, Grierson, following his instructions to wait until the infantry came up, remained with his cavalry near Salem. Wilkin's and Hoge's infantry brigades spent the morning of June 4 at Lamar, waiting for Bouton and the wagon train to arrive, but that afternoon McMillen's division marched to the Robinson plantation, four miles from Salem.

Early on the morning of June 5, McMillen and the train moved on, joining the cavalry two miles east of Salem at 11:00 A.M. Upon their arrival there, rations were issued, and the infantry spent the rest of the day in camp. At 4:00 P.M., however, Grierson moved out with the cavalry toward Ruckersville, halting that night at Dunbar's Mill, which was at the intersection of the Saulsbury and Ripley road and the Salem and Ruckersville road.

While at Salem, Sturgis ordered Grierson to send out a detachment of his cavalry to Rienzi, Mississippi to destroy the track of the Mobile and Ohio Railroad that ran through the town. Joseph Karge was selected for this mission, and on June 5, 1864 he started out with his 2nd New Jersey Cavalry for Ripley. He arrived there about midnight, then moved out on the Rienzi road, finally camping for the rest of the night about three miles east of Ripley.

Very early on the morning of June 6, 1864, Karge rode on toward Rienzi. He arrived there about noon and drove some Confederate troops from the town, then destroyed several miles of track. He then moved north toward Corinth, but after traveling a short distance in that direction, he turned back and marched to the southwest on the road toward Ellis-

town, where he expected to find Grierson's cavalry division.

Grierson left Dunbar's Mill at 7:00 A.M. June 6, 1864 and marched to Ruckersville, but he then halted for twenty-four hours to await the arrival of the infantry and the train. At 4:00 that morning, McMillen resumed his march on another rainy day and followed the cavalry toward Ruckersville. About dark McMillen's command went into camp at the Widow Childers' place, at the junction of the Saulsbury and Ripley road and the Salem and Ruckersville road.

On the morning of June 7, 1864, Grierson learned from Karge that there were no enemy troops at Corinth, and that those that had been there had moved off to the south. Grierson passed this information on to Sturgis, and he also suggested that the line of march be shifted more to the south because he had heard that more fodder for the horses could be found in that direction. Sturgis then directed Grierson to move from Ruckersville on the direct road to Ripley toward Ellistown, and he ordered Karge to rejoin the army at Ellistown by way of Blackland or Carrollville. He also ordered McMillen to continue his march southward on the Ripley and Saulsbury road.

Grierson left Ruckersville during the early afternoon of June 7, 1864 and marched toward Ripley. Upon arriving there, he drove a small party of the enemy cavalry from the town and pursued them for about three miles on the New Albany road. Grierson sent forward a part of Winslow's brigade and the 7th Indiana Cavalry of Waring's brigade, and they skirmished with the enemy as they advanced for about two hours. The fighting ended at dark, and then Grierson pulled back until he found a good position and camped for the night.

On June 7, 1864, McMillen's infantry marched from the Widow Childers' crossroads, with Wilkin's brigade in front, Hoge's brigade following Wilkin, and Bouton's brigade with the train bringing up the rear. Hoge and Bouton camped at 4:00 that evening at the Crowder plantation, four miles north of Ripley, but Wilkin's brigade moved on and occupied the town.

At Ripley, on the night of June 7, 1864, Sturgis called a meeting with his division and brigade commanders to discuss the possibility of abandoning the expedition and returning to Memphis. Sturgis was concerned that because of the terrible conditions of the roads and the starved and exhausted condition of the animals, he might be unable to move the artillery and wagons. Only Grierson favored turning back, but finally he reluctantly agreed with McMillen, who wished to continue. Sturgis, too, was hesitant to return to Memphis a second time without engaging the enemy, and he ordered that the march be resumed.

On June 8, 1864, Sturgis directed that the army move to the southeast on the Fulton road instead of to the south on the road to Ellistown. That day Winslow's brigade marched out on the Fulton road about six miles, but Waring's brigade remained at Ripley to await the return of Karge, who arrived there that night.

Hoge and Bouton began their march at 4:00 on the morning of June 8, 1864. After passing through Ripley, they moved out five miles on the Fulton road and halted in rear of Winslow. Wilkin's brigade remained in camp at Ripley that day.

On June 9, 1864, Sturgis' troops remained in camp until noon while rations were issued, and then they advanced on the Fulton road and camped that night at Stubbs' plantation, about fourteen miles to the southeast of Ripley.

On his march from Memphis to Stubbs' plantation, Sturgis had encountered only slight opposition, but this was about to change. At the end of May 1864, Stephen D. Lee, commanding the Confederate Department of Alabama, Mississippi, and East Louisiana, ordered Forrest to march with 2,000 men of his own command and 1,000 men from Philip D. Roddey's cavalry command in north Alabama into Middle Tennessee for the purpose of destroying the Nashville and Chattanooga Railroad, which carried supplies to Sherman's army in Georgia. By an interesting coincidence, on June 1 Forrest left Tupelo for Tennessee with Abraham Buford's cavalry division and two batteries, on the same day that Sturgis' command started from Memphis.

Forrest had reached Russellville, in Franklin County, Alabama, when on the morning of June 3, 1864 he received a dispatch from Lee informing him that a large force of Union troops was moving from Memphis in the direction of Tupelo, and ordering him to return immediately. Forrest arrived ahead of his command at Tupelo on June 5, and there he learned of the general direction of Sturgis'

march, and also of Karge's movement toward Rienzi. Forrest then ordered Edmund W. Rucker to move to Rienzi, and from there to scout toward New Albany. Buford sent Tyree H. Bell's brigade to Rienzi but kept Hylan B. Lyon's brigade with him to await developments.

On June 7, 1864, scouts reported that Sturgis was moving in the direction of Ruckersville, and Forrest then moved with Buford's division to Baldwin, and the next day to Booneville. Rucker joined Forrest at Booneville on the evening of June 9, at about the same time that Sturgis' army was moving onto the Stubbs plantation. Meantime, Roddey had sent William A. Johnson's cavalry brigade of his command to join Forrest. Johnson reached Baldwyn June 9, and was then ordered to report to Forrest at Booneville. Also on June 9, Forrest learned that Sturgis was encamped on the Stubbs' plantation.

Battle of Brice's Cross Roads, Mississippi, June 10, 1864. At 5:30 A.M. June 10, 1864, Grierson moved out from Stubbs' plantation with his cavalry on the road toward Fulton, but McMillen's infantry did not leave their camps and follow him until 7:00 A.M. Thus, as the army marched to the southeast that morning, there was a considerable interval between the cavalry and the infantry, and this was to have serious consequences later in the day. On the road that morning, Grierson's cavalry was leading the way, with Waring's brigade in front and Winslow's brigade following; behind them came Hoge's brigade, the leading infantry brigade, and then Wilkin's brigade. Bouton's brigade, with the trains, brought up the rear.

About 9:00 A.M. Waring's brigade came up on a small group of enemy pickets that were attempting to destroy the bridge over Tishomingo Creek. Waring quickly drove them back, crossed the creek, and moved up to the high ground around Brice's Cross Roads, which was about one-half mile from the bridge. Brice's Cross Roads was the name given to the intersection of the Wire Road (which ran from Carrollton, where it was joined by the road from Baldwyn, to Pontotoc) and the Ripley and Fulton road. The crossroads was about six miles from Baldwyn, ten miles from Stubbs' plantation, and six miles from Guntown, a station and small village on the Mobile and Ohio Railroad. At the road intersection were the house and store of William Brice.

About 500 yards to the northeast of the crossroads, on the road to Baldwyn, was Bethany Church. There was a clearing of six acres around the Brice house, but beyond the borders of the field, the country was generally densely wooded and covered with an undergrowth of blackjack and scrub oak.

Thus, from Brice's Cross Roads, in addition to the Ripley road on which the army was advancing, a road ran to the northeast to Baldwyn, another to the southeast to Guntown and on to Fulton, and still another to the southwest to Pontotoc. When Waring halted at the crossroads that morning, he sent out a squadron of cavalry on each of the three roads to find out what was ahead. Grierson, expecting that the enemy might attempt to regain the bridge over Tishomingo Creek, ordered Winslow to mass his brigade in a field lying northwest of the point where the road running in from New Albany to the southwest joined the Ripley and Fulton road just north of the bridge.

Robert N. Hanson, commanding a squadron of the 4th Missouri Cavalry, had been sent out on the Baldwyn road by Waring that morning, and at a cornfield lying west of the Blackland road, he was attacked by two companies of the 12th Kentucky Cavalry of Lyon's brigade that had just arrived on the field. After the initial attack, the enemy retired into the woods on the east side of the field, which was surrounded by a rail fence, and fortified its position.

When Waring learned that Hanson had found the enemy on the Baldwyn road, he marched out with the detachment of 3rd Illinois and 9th Illinois, the 2nd New Jersey, and two mountain howitzers to reinforce Hanson. These troops took position with Hanson along the eastern side of the cornfield. The rest of Waring's brigade, the 7th Indiana and the 19th Pennsylvania, was formed in line of battle across the road, about one-half mile from the crossroads.

As the rest of Lyon's brigade came up, it advanced and forced Hanson's squadron, and the troops that had come up to support it, to fall back to Waring's main line.

A short time after 10:00 A.M. June 10, 1864, Grierson ordered Winslow to cross Tishomingo Creek with his brigade and take position on the Fulton road, on the left of Waring. The head of Winslow's column arrived at the crossroads about 10:30, and by 11:00 A.M. all of Grierson's troops were dismounted and in position covering the approaches to the crossroads.

The troops of Waring's brigade, which was on the left of the division, were in line along the rail fence at the western edge of the cornfield as follows: Frederick Graessle's mountain howitzers of the 4th Missouri Cavalry were on the Baldwyn road; the 4th Missouri Cavalry was on the left of the howitzers, north of the road; a squadron of the 7th Indiana Cavalry was on the extreme left, on the left of the 4th Missouri; and the detachment of 3rd Illinois and 9th Illinois was on the low ground in front of the howitzers. South of the road, and on the right of the howitzers, were two squadrons of the 7th Indiana; the rest of the regiment was held in reserve. On the right of the 7th Indiana, and on the right of Waring's line, was the 2nd New Jersey, and the right of this regiment was almost due east of Brice's Cross Roads. Winslow's brigade was on the right of Grierson's line, with a battalion of the 3rd Iowa Cavalry on the right of the 2nd New Jersey and the 4th Iowa Cavalry between the 3rd Iowa and the Fulton road. A battalion of the 3rd Iowa was on the right, south of the road, and the 7th Illinois and 10th Missouri cavalry, both mounted, were to the southwest on the Pontotoc road watching the road and the country between it and Tishomingo Creek.

Rucker's brigade of Buford's division then came up from Booneville and was placed on the left of Lyon to extend the Confederate line toward the Fulton road. Johnson's brigade of Roddey's cavalry came up next and was placed on the right of Lyon. It was nearly noon when Forrest had completed his line, and he then decided to attack.

The enemy first appeared in front of Waring's brigade, and the four mountain howitzers and a section of Francis W. Morse's 14th Battery, Indiana Light Artillery opened fire on Lyon's and Rucker's men as they moved out of the woods and started across the cornfield. Then Waring's troopers began firing from behind the rail fence on the west side of the field.

The 7th Indiana received the full impact of Rucker's charge, and it was soon in serious danger of being overwhelmed as the enemy threatened to turn its right flank. The 2nd New Jersey had been in position on the right of the 7th Indiana, but only a short time before Rucker began his attack, it was pulled out of the line and sent north of the Baldwyn road to protect Waring's left flank. The front of the 7th Indiana was extended to the right to fill a part of the gap left by the departure of the 2nd New Jersey, and soon the enemy broke through the right of the regiment's attenuated line and forced it to retreat.

To the Federal right of the position formerly held by the 7th Indiana, Rucker pushed forward against the men of the 3rd Iowa and 4th Iowa of Winslow's brigade. The 3rd Iowa was forced to withdraw to avoid being flanked on its left. Because of this movement, the 4th Iowa also fell back, but both regiments were able to readjust their lines and continue fighting.

On the Federal left of the former position of the 7th Indiana, fierce attacks by Lyon's and Johnson's brigades forced all of Waring's men that were north of the Baldwyn road to fall back. This included the artillery; the detachment of the 3rd Illinois and 9th Illinois; the 4th Missouri; the battalion of the 7th Indiana, which had been on the right of the line; the reserves of the 7th Indiana; and the 2nd New Jersey. It was then about noon, and for some time the fighting ceased while the men on both sides, who had been marching and fighting since early morning, got some much-needed rest.

Sometime after 1:00 P.M., Buford arrived with Bell's brigade, and Forrest then placed Buford in command of Lyon's and Johnson's brigades, and with Bell's brigade moved southward to the Fulton road. Forrest then moved to the northwest on that road and deployed Bell's brigade across the road, about 700 yards from Brice's Cross Roads.

Meantime, when Grierson learned that Waring had met the enemy on the Baldwyn road, he sent a message to Sturgis, who was riding at the head of the infantry column, informing him that he was at Brice's Cross Roads, and that his advance was skirmishing with the enemy on the Baldwyn road. He further stated that he had a good position and could hold it if the infantry was brought up without delay. Grierson then sent a second message to Sturgis asking for help, and Sturgis responded by directing McMillen to make a forced march with Hoge's brigade, his leading brigade, to support Grierson. He also ordered Wilkin's brigade and Bouton's brigade, with the trains, to follow as rapidly as possible. Because of the intense heat and high humidity

that day, the infantry suffered greatly as they hurried forward; most of the men were exhausted when they arrived at the front and were unable to fight effectively.

McMillen went forward with Hoge, and while on the road he received orders to hurry with the infantry because the cavalry was being driven back. The 113th Illinois Infantry, Hoge's leading regiment, arrived at Brice's Cross Roads between 1:00 and 2:00 P.M., and it immediately moved into action on the right of the Baldwyn road, not far from the Brice house, where it relieved Waring's cavalry brigade. As rapidly as Hoge's other regiments arrived, they were deployed to the right of the 113th Illinois to extend Hoge's line toward the Fulton road. These regiments relieved the regiments of Winslow's brigade as they went into position. When the line was completed, the 113th Illinois was in position across the Baldwyn road, a short distance southwest of Bethany Church, and the other regiments of the brigade were in line, in order from left to right, as follows: 120th Illinois, 108th Illinois, 95th Illinois, and 81st Illinois. The 81st Illinois was almost due east of the Brice house. Fletcher H. Chapman's Battery B, 2nd Illinois Light Artillery of the brigade was placed on the open ground about the Brice house, where it could fire over Hoge's men in the front line.

A short time after Hoge had completed his deployment, Wilkin's brigade came up, with the 95th Ohio marching in front. McMillen and Wilkin immediately moved out with this regiment about one-fourth mile beyond the Brice house and formed it on the left of Hoge's brigade to help the 113th Illinois hold the Baldwyn road. Wilkin then returned to the crossroads and took Michael Mueller's section of the 6th Battery, Indiana Light Artillery and the 72nd Ohio of his brigade to a position about 800 yards northwest of the Brice house, and northeast of the Ripley and Fulton road, to prevent the enemy from reaching the Tishomingo Bridge and blocking the road back to Ripley. He placed Mueller's guns near a log cabin that stood on a knoll overlooking the bridge and formed the 72nd Ohio with its right near the artillery and its left extending to within a short distance of the creek. John A. Fitch's Battery E, 1st Illinois Light Artillery and the 9th Minnesota were halted at the crossroads to await the arrival of Bouton's brigade with the wagon train.

When Buford passed through Old Carrollton that morning, he detached Clark R. Barteau's 2nd Tennessee Cavalry and sent it to move against Sturgis' left flank. Barteau marched westward along country roads until he was some distance to the north of Brice's Cross Roads, and then he turned to the south and moved along a lane that ran into the Ripley and Fulton road near the Tishomingo Bridge. He came up in front of Mueller's artillery and the 72nd Ohio on the knoll near the bridge, and when he heard the sounds of fighting to his left, he attacked this vital position then held by Mueller's artillery and the 72nd Ohio.

Sturgis then ordered Wilkin to relieve the remainder of Winslow's cavalry that were fighting on the Fulton road. The 114th Illinois and 93rd Indiana were moved out to the Fulton road, and the 114th Illinois was formed in line of battle on the right of Hoge's brigade, with its right extending to a point near the Fulton road. This regiment relieved Winslow's cavalry that was holding the Fulton road. The 93rd moved to the southwest of the Fulton road, and deployed on the right of the 114th Illinois. When Wilkin's troops were in position, the 3rd Iowa and 4th Iowa of Winslow's brigade withdrew and passed to the rear, crossed the creek, and assembled in the field where they had stopped earlier at the junction of the Ripley and New Albany roads, north of Tishomingo Creek. Winslow's horseholders were ordered to picket the country between the 93rd Indiana and Tishomingo Creek.

At about 2:30 P.M. Bouton arrived with his brigade at the Ames house, about one-half mile from Tishomingo Creek. Bouton, however, had received no orders to halt his long train of about 300 wagons at some safe place north of the creek; it continued on across the creek and parked in a field within range of the enemy artillery, and with the creek, which was crossed only by a narrow bridge, in its rear.

Bouton then sent forward from the Ames house two companies of the 55th United States Colored Troops, which, after crossing the creek, reported to Wilkin. They were ordered to take position on the knoll at the log cabin and help the artillery and 72nd Ohio stop Barteau's regiment, which was threatening to turn the left flank of the 72nd Ohio. The 4th Iowa Cavalry of Winslow's brigade was also sent dismounted to the knoll to support the troops already there.

McMillen had not yet completed the formation of his infantry line when Forrest attacked all along the front and on both flanks. Bell's brigade, which had completed its deployment at 2:00 P.M., advanced at 3:00 P.M and struck the 114th Illinois and the 93rd Indiana on the Fulton road. The 93rd Indiana was outflanked and driven back to the Pontotoc road, but it was soon rallied and was again ready to fight. The 9th Minnesota was then hurried up from the crossroads, and it took position on the right of the 93rd Indiana. Together they withstood all attacks south of the Fulton road while the 114th Illinois and the 81st Illinois held their positions north of the road. Rucker and Bell, however, continued to press forward; the 95th Illinois was forced to fall back, and in so doing uncovered the left flank of the 81st Illinois. Bell's attack then drove back the 114th Illinois, and the 81st Illinois was left fighting alone. It continued to hold its position until the men were nearly out of ammunition, and then it too fell back to the crossroads.

On the Confederate right, Forrest, with Buford and the brigades of Lyon and Johnson, attacked Hoge's line, and Hoge ordered up Chapman's battery to help repel the attack. Hoge's brigade held its ground for a time, but as Forrest's attack continued, the line collapsed. Lyon's men broke through south of the Baldwyn road on the front held by the 120th Illinois and the 108th Illinois, and the 113th Illinois, which was on the left of the 120th Illinois, was thus outflanked and forced back toward the crossroads. The 95th Ohio, on the left of the 113th Illinois, was in turn driven back, but it was rallied and held on north of the Baldwyn road.

McMillen, with the help of Hoge and Wilkin, attempted to rally their men, and they finally succeeded in forming a new line between the crossroads and Bethany Church. This line ran in a semicircle from north of the Brice house, across the Baldwyn road and the Fulton road, to a point south of the crossroads. The 95th Ohio was still in position north of the Baldwyn road, with its line refused in an effort to connect with the skirmishers of the 72nd Ohio. The line between the Baldwyn road and the Fulton road was held, from left to right, by the 113th Illinois, 120th Illinois, 95th Illinois, 81st Illinois, and 114th Illinois. The 93rd Indiana and the 9th Minnesota were in position south of the Fulton road, facing to the southeast, with the 93rd Indiana on the left, next to the 114th Illinois, and the 9th Minnesota on the right.

Forrest then pushed forward with his entire force. On the Confederate left, Bell's troops moved against the Federal right and reached the Pontotoc road, where they struck the 7th Illinois Cavalry and the 10th Missouri Cavalry of Winslow's brigade, who were guarding that road, and drove them back. The 93rd Indiana and 9th Minnesota fell back, fighting stubbornly, toward the crossroads. At the same time, Barteau's 2nd Tennessee Cavalry continued its attacks on the 72nd Ohio, on the knoll northeast of the Tishomingo Bridge.

As Forrest continued to press his attacks against the Federal flanks and drive them back, he threatened to capture the men still fighting at the crossroads. McMillen, realizing this, directed Chapman and Fitch to cover the withdrawal of his infantry with their artillery, and he then abandoned his line and fell back toward Tishomingo Creek. Before reaching the creek, he formed a final line to cover the retreat of the army across the bridge. This line began on the creek, a short distance north of the bridge, and extended back toward Brice's Cross Roads and across the Ripley road a short distance northwest of the Brice house. This line was only about seventy-five yards in advance of the road back to Ripley. On the left, at the knoll, the position was held by the 72nd Ohio, Mueller's section of artillery, the 4th Iowa dismounted cavalry, and the two companies of the 55th United States Colored Troops. Extending to the right from the knoll, in order, were the 95th Ohio, the 93rd Indiana, and the 9th Minnesota. The right of the 9th Minnesota rested on the Ripley road, and to its right were the troops of the 10th Missouri Cavalry and the 7th Illinois Cavalry. The 4th Iowa Cavalry of Winslow's brigade, fighting dismounted, was also fighting on the knoll for about one-half hour while the bridge, which had been blocked by the wagons of the train, was cleared, and then it moved on across the creek.

At this time the road from Brice's Cross Roads to the bridge and beyond the road to Ripley was filled with a confused mass of artillery, caissons, limbers, ambulances, wagons, and broken and disorganized troops. When the wagons of the supply train began to move back across the bridge, it soon became blocked, and the artillery and troops began crossing at fords, both above and below the bridge.

Meantime, back at the Ames house, Bouton, after sending the two companies of the 55th United States Colored Troops to report to Wilkin, advanced with seven companies of that regiment and placed them on the north side of the Fulton and Ripley road to cover the retreat of Sturgis' defeated army. Bouton then placed Carl A. Lamberg's battery on the ridge at the Ames house and formed the 59th United States Colored Troops on the right of the battery and the remaining company of the 55th United States Colored Troops on its left. This done, Bouton recalled the seven companies of the 55th Regiment that had been covering the retreat from the bridge.

Finally, when all the disorganized troops, artillery, and wagons had crossed the creek, the regiments on McMillen's final line began to fall back toward the bridge. Starting on the right, the 7th Illinois Cavalry and the 10th Missouri Cavalry crossed first, and they were followed in succession by the 9th Minnesota, the 93rd Indiana, and the 95th Ohio. The 72nd Ohio, the 4th Iowa Cavalry, and the two companies of black troops held their position at the knoll until all were safely over, and then they forded the Tishomingo above the bridge and rejoined the army. The 4th Iowa Cavalry remained to cover this withdrawal, and then it too retired, crossing the creek and following the retreating column.

As Sturgis' column moved back on the road toward Stubbs' plantation, Forrest followed, but the seven companies of the 55th United States Colored Troops that were formed on the road north of the creek were able to hold up the pursuit for a half-hour until the army had moved on and climbed out of the valley of Tishomingo Creek. The troops of the 55th Regiment then fell back about 400 yards to the high ground at the Ames house, and there they formed on the left of the 59th United States Colored Troops.

Meantime, McMillen, with what troops remained of his First and Second brigades, moved on to the Agnew house (called the "White House" in some reports), which stood on the ridge between Dry Creek and Little Dry Creek, and there he formed a line with troops of the 72nd Ohio, 9th Minnesota, 114th Illinois, 93rd Indiana, 95th Ohio, and 81st Illinois. He placed Wilkin in command of this line.

Bouton's brigade stubbornly contested the advance of Forrest, while being slowly forced back until it finally reached Wilkin's line. There was violent fighting in front of the Agnew house that evening, but after a time, McMillen's First Brigade and Second Brigade moved on in the direction of Stubbs' plantation. Bouton continued to cover the retreat, and while on this duty he became separated from the main column, but he rejoined it about 10:00 P.M. while it was crossing the Hatchie bottom, just south of Stubbs' plantation. The road crossing the swamp there was in terrible condition because of the recent rains, and this greatly delayed the movement of the army.

Sturgis reached Stubbs' plantation about 11:00 P.M. June 10, 1864, and there he found Winslow's brigade, which had been ordered there to stop the retreating column. Sturgis then instructed Winslow to allow all troops to pass on, and further directed him to destroy anything that would interfere with the passage of the troops. This order resulted in the loss of about 200 wagons and fourteen guns, and many of the caissons and limbers as they struggled to cross the Hatchie bottom in the mud. At that time Waring's brigade was on beyond Stubbs' plantation en route to occupy and hold Ripley. Winslow remained at Stubbs' plantation until the last of the army had passed by, and then at 2:50 A.M. June 11, he started for Ripley. After going a short distance, however, he learned that there were some troops still behind on the road, and he then halted until they had passed. It was not until daylight that he resumed the march toward Ripley.

Sturgis and McMillen reached Ripley about 5:00 A.M. June 11, 1864, and there McMillen halted to reorganize his infantry as the troops came in. By 7:30 A.M. he had his command in fairly good shape, and then, preceded by Waring's cavalry, he left Ripley and marched toward Salem. At about that time, Winslow arrived at Ripley, and he followed McMillen toward Salem. That night Sturgis' column halted about five miles south of Saulsbury. Sturgis continued the march, and at 8:00 A.M. June 12 he arrived at Collierville. At 9:00 P.M. the army resumed the march toward White's Station, and it arrived there on the morning of June 13.

* * * * * * * * * *

The organization of Sturgis' Expedition during the period June 2–13, 1864, including the Battle of Brice's Cross Roads, was as follows:

STURGIS' EXPEDITION, Samuel D. Sturgis

Infantry Division (Provisional), William L. McMillen
First Brigade, Alexander Wilkin
   114th Illinois, John F. King
   93rd Indiana, De Witt C. Thomas
   9th Minnesota, Josiah F. Marsh
   72nd Ohio, Charles G. Eaton
   95th Ohio, Jefferson Brumback
   Battery E, 1st Illinois Light Artillery, John A. Fitch

Second Brigade, George B. Hoge
   81st Illinois, Franklin Campbell
     Andrew W. Rogers
   95th Illinois, Thomas W. Humphrey, killed
     William H. Stewart, wounded
     Elliot N. Bush, killed
     Almon Schellenger
   108th Illinois, Reuben L. Sidwell
   113th Illinois, George R. Clarke
   120th Illinois, George W. McKeaig, wounded and captured
     Spencer B. Floyd
   Battery B, 2nd Illinois Light Artillery, Fletcher H. Chapman

Third Brigade, Edward Bouton
   55th United States Colored Troops, Edgar M. Lowe, wounded
     Arthur T. Reeve
   59th United States Colored Troops, Robert Cowden
   Battery F, 2nd United States Colored Artillery, Carl A. Lamberg

Cavalry Division, Benjamin H. Grierson
First Brigade, George E. Waring, Jr.
   7th Indiana, Thomas M. Browne
   Detachment 3rd and 9th Illinois, Anthony R. Mock
   4th Missouri, Gustav Von Helmrich
   2nd New Jersey, Joseph Karge
   19th Pennsylvania, Joseph C. Hess

Note. Four mountain howitzers commanded by Frederick Graessle were with the 4th Missouri Cavalry.

Second Brigade, Edward F. Winslow
   7th Illinois (detachment)
   3rd Iowa, John W. Noble
   4th Iowa, Abial R. Pierce
   10th Missouri (detachment), Martin H. Williams
   7th Battery, Wisconsin Light Artillery, Henry S. Lee

Note. Henry S. Lee was in charge of the artillery of the Cavalry Division, which consisted of one section of his own 7th Battery, Wisconsin Light Artillery; one section of Francis W. Morse's 14th Battery, Indiana Light Artillery; and one section of artillery of the 10th Mis-

souri Cavalry. *On June 10, 1864, the day of the Battle of Brice's Cross Roads, the section of Indiana battery was attached to Waring's brigade, and sections of the Wisconsin battery and of the 10th Missouri Cavalry were assigned to Winslow's brigade.*

STURGIS' EXPEDITION FROM MEMPHIS, TENNESSEE TO RIPLEY, MISSISSIPPI APRIL 30, 1864–MAY 11, 1864

In the early spring of 1864, Nathan B. Forrest led a cavalry command, consisting of two divisions, northward from Mississippi on a raid into West Tennessee and western Kentucky, and on April 12 he captured Fort Pillow after a brutal assault. Forrest then withdrew, with little interference, to Jackson, Tennessee to rest and recruit.

At that time, William T. Sherman, commanding the Military Division of the Mississippi, with headquarters at Nashville, was soon to begin his spring campaign by advancing into Georgia toward Atlanta, and he decided that it was necessary for the success of his plans to keep Forrest busy in northern Mississippi so that he would be unable to interrupt Sherman's preparations by moving on his communications in Tennessee.

Sherman was not pleased with Stephen A. Hurlbut, commander of the District of West Tennessee, because of his performance during the Meridian Campaign and his handling of affairs in West Tennessee during Forrest's raid, and on April 16, 1864 he assigned Cadwallader C. Washburn to relieve Hurlbut. Washburn assumed command of the District of West Tennessee on April 23.

On April 18, 1864, Samuel D. Sturgis, on orders from Sherman, left Nashville, Tennessee by boat to go to Memphis to assume command of all cavalry in and around the city. Sturgis' instructions were to march out and find Forrest and attack him, wherever he might be. Benjamin H. Grierson was assigned with his cavalry division to the area around Memphis, with orders to be ready to take the field when Sturgis arrived. Ralph P. Buckland, commander of the District of Memphis, with an infantry brigade from his district, was also ordered to be ready to move with the cavalry.

Sturgis arrived at Memphis April 24, 1864, and on April 29 he organized his command to consist of a cavalry division, which was to be commanded by George E. Waring, Jr. during the absence of Benjamin H. Grierson, who was ill, and two infantry brigades. One of these, First Brigade, First Division, Sixteenth Corps, was commanded by William L. McMillen; the other, a brigade from the District of Memphis, was commanded by Thomas H. Harris, assistant adjutant general on the staff of Sixteenth Corps.

Early on the morning of April 30, 1864, Sturgis left Memphis with Waring's cavalry division and the 113th Illinois Infantry, who were riding in wagons, and moved in a pouring rain to the northeast on the road toward Randolph, Tennessee. Because of the muddy roads, Sturgis was able to march only fifteen miles that day, and he camped for the night at Raleigh. The rest of McMillen's infantry moved by rail, on the Memphis and Charleston Railroad, as far as Grissom's Station, four miles west of Moscow, and they camped there that night while a bridge was built across the the Wolf River.

On the morning of May 1, 1864, Sturgis started Waring's cavalry and the 113th Illinois Infantry toward Oakland, six miles west of Somerville, Tennessee, where they bivouacked on another rainy night. Sturgis moved on to Somerville the next day and halted there to wait until the infantry arrived. He then sent out Joseph Karge, with his own 2nd New Jersey Cavalry, the 10th Missouri Cavalry, and a section of artillery, on a reconnaissance to Bolivar to get possession of the bridge over the Hatchie River at that point, and to learn what he could of Forrest's movements.

Meantime, Forrest had left Jackson earlier that day, May 2, 1864, and marched southward toward Bolivar on his way toward Mississippi. The head of his column reached Bolivar that afternoon and was soon engaged with Karge's cavalry west of the town. At dark, the enemy retired through the town, crossed the Hatchie River, and destroyed the bridge. The next day Forrest continued his march to the south. He passed through Ruckersville and Ripley without further molestation, and arrived at Tupelo, Mississippi on May 5.

During the night of May 2, 1864, Karge informed Sturgis of the fight with Forrest at Bolivar that afternoon. Sturgis, with Waring's cavalry, rode toward Bolivar at daylight the next morning and entered the town that afternoon. During the day, McMillen's and Harris' brigades, which had finally crossed Wolf River, marched to within eight miles of Bolivar. On May 4, the two infantry brigades and the supply train joined the cavalry about noon, and during the rest of the day the infantry rested and rations were issued.

Although Forrest was then forty-eight hours ahead of Sturgis, the latter decided to continue the pursuit at least as far as Ripley, Mississippi. On May 5, 1864, Waring's cavalry crossed the Hatchie River, marched through Pocahontas, and bivouacked that night on Muddy Creek, eight miles north of Ripley. Waring remained in camp on Muddy Creek May 6 while detachments were sent out to Salem, Ripley, and Hatchietown. From these cavalrymen, Sturgis learned that Forrest had passed through Ripley on May 4 and had joined Abraham Buford's division at Tupelo.

The infantry, which had followed Waring's column south from Bolivar, arrived on Muddy Creek on the afternoon of May 6, 1864 and went into camp with the cavalry.

Upon learning that Forrest was at Tupelo, Sturgis decided to return to Memphis. He left Muddy Creek May 7, 1864 and, marching west through Salem, camped that night beyond Lamar. He remained in camp there the next day to permit the men to get some much-needed rest. On May 9, Sturgis' command marched to Grissom's Bridge on the Memphis and Charleston Railroad, and from there the infantry moved by rail to Memphis. Waring's cavalry division marched to Germantown, between Collierville and Memphis, on May 10, and on to White's Station the next day. Sturgis had failed in his principal objective, but he consoled himself with the fact that Forrest had left Tennessee and was in Mississippi where Sherman wanted him to be.

ENGAGEMENT AT THOMPSON'S STATION, TENNESSEE MARCH 5, 1863

On March 3, 1863, William S. Rosecrans, commanding the Army of the Cumberland, ordered Charles C. Gilbert, commanding the post at Franklin, Tennessee, to send out a brigade on a reconnaissance toward Spring Hill and beyond to determine what enemy forces were on his front. This movement was to be made in conjunction with an expedition carried out by Philip H. Sheridan's Third Division, Twentieth Corps and Robert H. G. Minty's cavalry brigade from Murfreesboro. Sheridan's command was to advance by way of Eagleville toward Columbia, Tennessee.

John Coburn's First Brigade, which belonged to Absalom Baird's Third Division of Gordon Granger's Army of Kentucky, was selected for this expedition. This brigade had been encamped near Brentwood, Tennessee, but on March 2, 1863 it had been ordered to Franklin, which at that time was threatened by an enemy force.

On the morning of March 4, 1863, Coburn marched south from Franklin on the Columbia Pike. He took with him his First Brigade, to which Oliver H. Payne's 124th Ohio Regiment was attached; 600 cavalry under Thomas J. Jordan, which consisted of detachments from the 9th Pennsylvania Cavalry, the 2nd Michigan Cavalry, and the 4th Kentucky Cavalry of Archibald P. Campbell's Cavalry Brigade; and Charles C. Aleshire's 18th Battery, Ohio Light Artillery. Coburn's brigade consisted of James M. Henderson's 33rd Indiana, John P. Baird's 85th Indiana, Henry C. Gilbert's 19th Michigan, and William L. Utley's 22nd Wisconsin.

About four miles south of Franklin, Coburn ran into some pickets belonging to William H. Jackson's division of Earl Van Dorn's Confederate First Cavalry Corps. Coburn continued his advance for about two miles, then fell back for a short distance and camped for the night.

At 8:00 the next morning, Coburn moved on, with the cavalry in advance, and about two miles from his camp, and one mile from Thompson's Station on the Tennessee and Alabama Railroad, he encountered a strong enemy outpost. This was soon driven back on the enemy main line, which was a short distance beyond the station. Holding this line were Nathan B. Forrest's cavalry brigade and Jackson's cavalry division, which consisted of Frank C. Armstrong's brigade and John W. Whitfield's brigade.

Coburn's men pushed back the enemy skirmishers and advanced under fire past the station and up the ridge beyond. The enemy cavalry, fighting dismounted, then charged and drove the Federals back to a hill beyond the station. A short time later Coburn counterattacked, pushed Jackson back, and then attempted to make a stand behind the depot and other buildings at Thompson's Station. Soon, however, he was driven back to the hill to the north, and there he repulsed another enemy attack. By this time Forrest had arrived from a point beyond the Federal left, and had moved into the rear of Coburn's position. At about the same time, William T. Martin arrived with George B. Cosby's brigade of his, Martin's, division, then moved to the right and rear of Coburn's position. Coburn realized that he was surrounded and that further resistance was useless, and he surrendered his infantry, which consisted of about 1,500 officers and men. Meantime, the cavalry and the wagon train had withdrawn toward Franklin and thus escaped capture.

Coburn and his men were confined in Libby Prison in Richmond, Virginia until they were exchanged May 8, 1863.

TULLAHOMA (OR MIDDLE TENNESSEE) CAMPAIGN JUNE 23, 1863–JULY 7, 1863

For a short time after the Battle of Stones River (or Murfreesboro), Tennessee, Braxton Bragg's Confederate Army of Tennessee remained in position on the battlefield. Then on the night of January 3–4, 1863, it began to withdraw southward. Leonidas Polk's corps moved to Shelbyville, and William J. Hardee's corps to Tullahoma. When Bragg learned that William S. Rosecrans, commander of the Army of the Cumberland, did not intend to pursue, he ordered Polk to remain at Shelbyville and directed Hardee to move his corps back to Wartrace on the Nashville and Chattanooga Railroad.

Bragg made his headquarters at Wartrace and then proceeded to establish his troops on a line north of Duck River that extended to the northeast from Shelbyville on the left, through Wartrace, to the vicinity of Fairfield on the right. The front of this position was covered by a range of hills through which the roads from Murfreesboro to Tullahoma

passed by way of three depressions or gaps. These were, from east to west, as follows: Hoover's Gap, through which ran the road from Murfreesboro to Manchester (route of present-day U.S. 41 and Interstate 24); Liberty Gap, about four miles west of Hoover's Gap, through which passed the road from Millersburg to Wartrace; and Guy's Gap, which was on the direct road from Murfreesboro, by way of Old Fosterville, to Shelbyville. In addition to these three, the Nashville and Chattanooga Railroad ran through the Railroad Gap (or Bellbuckle Gap), a short distance west of Liberty Gap, near Fosterville.

Bragg's army remained in this position, virtually unmolested, during the first six months of 1863. Despite frequent urgings by Henry W. Halleck, general in chief of the army, to advance against Bragg, Rosecrans remained at Murfreesboro while he labored to prepare his army for the next campaign. During this period, however, he did send frequent reconnaissances and some limited expeditions against Confederate forces on his front. Finally, late in June 1863, Rosecrans was ready, and he began to move his troops out from Triune and Murfreesboro at the beginning of a campaign that was eventually to culminate in the Battle of Chickamauga, Georgia September 19–20, 1863. The operations of the first two weeks of this period are commonly called the Tullahoma or Middle Tennessee Campaign.

At the time of Rosecrans' advance, Polk's corps, which consisted of the divisions of Benjamin F. Cheatham and Jones M. Withers, held a strongly fortified line about five miles in length that covered the front of Shelbyville, with advanced troops at Guy's Gap to the north. Hardee's corps held the right of Bragg's line, and the troops were at or near the Railroad Gap, Liberty Gap, and Hoover's Gap. Alexander P. Stewart's division was on the right near Fairfield, where it supported a cavalry force of John A. Wharton's division of Joseph Wheeler's Cavalry Corps that was at Hoover's Gap. Patrick R. Cleburne's division was on the left of Stewart, with headquarters at Wartrace. St. John R. Liddell's brigade was posted at Bellbuckle, about five miles north of Wartrace, with advanced troops at the Railroad Gap and at Liberty Gap; Sterling A. M. Wood's brigade and Thomas J. Churchill's brigade were at Wartrace; and Lucius E. Polk's brigade was at Tullahoma. William T. Martin's division of Wheeler's Cavalry Corps covered the front of

Polk's corps from Liberty Gap westward, and Wharton's division was on Hardee's front, on the right of Martin.

When Rosecrans prepared his plans for the Middle Tennessee Campaign, which he hoped would force Bragg's army out of the state, he decided to avoid what would almost certainly prove to be costly attacks on Polk's strong position in front of Shelbyville. Instead, he planned to feint in that direction and then advance by way of Hoover's Gap to Manchester. By this movement he would turn Bragg's right flank and thereby force his withdrawal to the south.

The opening moves began June 23, 1863, and by the next day the entire army was on the march. All movements, from the beginning, were seriously hampered by heavy rains that began June 24. They continued almost without interruption for the next two weeks and rendered all except a few macadamized roads almost impassable.

At 8:30 A.M. June 23, 1863, Gordon Granger, commanding the Union forces at Triune, sent Robert B. Mitchell's First Division of David S. Stanley's Cavalry Corps south from Triune to threaten an advance on Shelbyville. Mitchell's division, consisting of Archibald P. Campbell's First Brigade and Edward M. McCook's Second Brigade, marched south along the route of present-day Alternate U.S. 41 through Eagleville to Rover, where the enemy attempted to block the way. After a sharp skirmish, Mitchell drove the Southerners back to Unionville, then returned to Rover, where he camped for the night.

At 9:00 A.M. June 23, 1863, Granger left Triune with Absalom Baird's First Division of his Reserve Corps and John M. Brannan's Third Division of George H. Thomas' Fourteenth Corps and marched southward to Salem, about five miles southwest of Murfreesboro on the road to Versailles. He camped at Versailles for the night. Brannan's division had been at Triune since early May and was under orders to rejoin Fourteenth Corps on the Manchester Pike (route of present-day U.S. 41) on June 25.

Early on the morning of June 24, 1863, Alexander McD. McCook's Twentieth Corps and George H. Thomas' Fourteenth Corps left Murfreesboro by different roads to occupy the gaps in the hills to the south. At daylight that morning, Philip H. Sheridan's Third Division of Twentieth Corps

marched out on the Shelbyville road (along the general route of present-day U.S. 231) to Christiana. Sheridan halted there until Brannan's division arrived from Salem on its way to rejoin Thomas, and he then moved on to Millersburg, where he bivouacked for the night.

Richard W. Johnson's Second Division of Twentieth Corps left Murfreesboro at 8:00 A.M. June 24, 1863. It followed Sheridan on the Shelbyville Pike for about six miles, then turned off to the left and marched directly to Millersburg. Johnson's orders were to occupy Liberty Gap, which was located a short distance south of the village. Jefferson C. Davis' First Division, Twentieth Corps followed Johnson's division to Millersburg and camped there that night with Sheridan's division.

After reaching Millersburg, Johnson's division, preceded by Thomas J. Harrison's 39th Indiana Mounted Infantry of August Willich's First Brigade, advanced toward Liberty Gap, which was held by two Arkansas regiments of Liddell's brigade under the command of L. Featherston. Harrison's mounted troops soon became engaged with enemy skirmishers, who resisted until the rest of Willich's brigade came up, and then they were driven back on their reserves, which were posted on the hills forming the northern entrance to the gap. Johnson brought up two regiments of John F. Miller's Second Brigade in preparation for an attack on the left of the enemy's position. About 5:15 P.M. Willich moved forward with his entire line and pushed through the gap. He halted about dark, and then Philemon P. Baldwin brought up his Third Brigade and cleared the enemy from the hills ahead. Baldwin picketed the front during the night, and Miller's two regiments picketed the flanks.

While McCook's columns were moving toward Millersburg and Liberty Gap, Thomas, with the three divisions of his corps remaining with him, marched from Murfreesboro on the Manchester road toward Hoover's Gap. Joseph J. Reynolds led off at 4:00 A.M. with his Fourth Division with orders to seize and hold Hoover's Gap. Lovell H. Rousseau's First Division followed at 7:00 A.M. to support Reynolds, and James S. Negley's Second Division marched at 10:00 A.M. in reserve.

About seven miles out of Murfreesboro, at Big Spring Branch, John T. Wilder's First Brigade of Reynolds' division encountered enemy cavalry pickets and drove them back to Hoover's Gap, sixteen miles from Murfreesboro. Wilder then attacked and drove the 3rd Kentucky of Wheeler's cavalry through the gap for about a mile and across McBride's Creek, a stream that flowed into the Garrison Fork of Duck River. At 3:00 P.M. William B. Bate's brigade, followed by Bushrod R. Johnson's brigade, and still later by Henry D. Clayton's brigade, came up from Fairfield and Beech Grove and attempted to recapture the gap. Wilder's brigade, with Eli Lilly's 18th Battery, Indiana Light Artillery, took positions on the hills at the southern end of the gap and repulsed all attacks with heavy fire from their Spencer repeaters.

Shortly after 4:00 P.M., Reynolds arrived with Albert S. Hall's Second Brigade (commanded by Milton S. Robinson while Hall was absent sick) and George Crook's Third Brigade of his division and placed these troops on both sides of the road to extend Wilder's line.

About dark, Rousseau's leading brigade, John H. King's brigade of regulars (commanded by Sidney Coolidge), came up to support Reynolds. Benjamin F. Scribner's First Brigade and Henry A. Hambright's Second Brigade of Rousseau's division camped that night near the Widow Hoover's house, within supporting distance of Reynolds, and Negley's division camped at Big Spring, in rear of Rousseau.

The rest of Rosecrans' army was also in motion June 24, 1863. As a part of the Union flanking movement, Thomas L. Crittenden's Twenty-First Corps was advancing by roads to the left of Thomas' corps toward Manchester, which was beyond the right flank of Bragg's line. That morning Crittenden, leaving Horatio P. Van Cleve's Third Division to garrison Murfreesboro, marched east on the Woodbury Pike with John M. Palmer's Second Division and Thomas J. Wood's First Division, in that order. He then turned off to the right toward Bradyville, where Palmer's division halted that night. Wood's division halted in rear of Palmer at Donald's Church.

John B. Turchin also moved eastward from Murfreesboro that morning with his Second Division of David S. Stanley's cavalry of the Army of the Cumberland toward Woodbury. His orders were to march by way of McMinnville and Pocahontas and approach Manchester from the northeast. When Turchin reached Cripple Creek, about eight miles out, he received orders to send Robert H. G. Minty's First Brigade back to Murfreesboro to report to Stanley. Turchin was then ordered to cooperate with Crittenden in his movement to Manchester, and with Eli Long's Second Brigade he marched by way of Readyville to Bradyville, where he joined Palmer and camped for the night.

The troops on the right of Rosecrans' army also continued their movements of the day before. On the morning of June 24, 1863, Mitchell's cavalry turned east at Rover and marched to Versailles, about eleven miles southwest of Murfreesboro, and from there moved to the southeast to Middleton (present-day Midland), which was west of Fosterville. Mitchell drove enemy skirmishers from the town, then moved back about five miles toward Salem and camped for the night.

After Minty's cavalry brigade had returned to Murfreesboro from Cripple Creek that morning, Stanley marched with it by way of Salem toward Middleton and joined Mitchell on the road that night.

On June 24, 1863, Granger marched with Baird's division from Salem to a point near Christiana on the Shelbyville-Murfreesboro road (roughly on the route of present-day U.S. 231), and upon arriving there went into camp.

At 7:00 that morning, Brannan moved from Salem to Christiana and relieved Sheridan's division of McCook's corps, which then advanced to Millersburg. Brannan remained at Christiana until relieved by Baird's division of Granger's corps, and he then advanced about two miles in the direction of Middleburg and camped that night on the Ross farm at Henry's Creek.

June 25, 1863 was another day of activity for the army. That morning Reynolds' division continued to hold Hoover's Gap, and during the morning, Scribner's brigade of Rousseau's division was brought up from the Widow Hoover's house to support the Federal batteries in front, and also to form a picket line on the extreme left.

During the day, Thomas received orders to attack the next morning and drive back Stewart's troops toward Fairfield, and if he was successful, he was then to move at once toward Manchester. At 4:00

that afternoon Hambright's Second Brigade of Rousseau's division was moved up into the gap in preparation for the attack.

Brannan's division remained on the Ross farm, not far from Millersburg, until 11:00 A.M. and then marched to join Fourteenth Corps on the Manchester Pike, where it encamped at Hoover's Mill.

Early on the morning of June 25, 1863, William P. Carlin reported to Johnson at Liberty Gap with his own Second Brigade and P. Sidney Post's First Brigade of Davis' First Division of McCook's corps. Davis was sick, but he arrived during the morning and took charge of his division. Hans C. Heg's Third Brigade of Davis' division remained in the rear at Millersburg in charge of the trains.

At about 8:00 A.M., Willich was ordered to relieve the advance pickets with his brigade, and a short time later, firing broke out between the contending forces. This continued during the day, sometimes becoming quite heavy. At 5:00 P.M. Willich's brigade was strongly attacked by Liddell's troops. Willich resisted, however, and the enemy was eventually driven back. Miller's brigade was then ordered up to relieve Willich, whose ammunition was nearly exhausted. During the advance, Miller was wounded, and Thomas E. Rose assumed command of the brigade. Rose then attacked and occupied a hill on his front and held this position until relieved by Carlin's brigade. McCook's troops then bivouacked for the night.

During June 25, 1863, Heg's brigade, with the Twentieth Corps trains, marched from Millersburg toward the Manchester Pike, arriving near Hoover's Gap the next day.

On the Federal left, Crittenden with his two divisions of Twenty-First Corps and Turchin with Long's cavalry brigade continued their advance toward Manchester, but progress was very slow because of the rain and the bad roads. Long's brigade camped that night at Lumley's Stand, about six miles east of Beech Grove; Palmer's division halted at Hollow Springs, four miles from Lumley's Stand; and Wood's division was on the road in rear of Palmer.

June 25, 1863, Granger, with Baird's division, remained in camp near Christiana, where he was joined by Mitchell's cavalry division and Stanley with Minty's cavalry brigade.

On the morning of June 26, 1863, Thomas continued with his preparations for the attack on Stewart's troops south of Hoover's Gap. He sent Hambright's brigade up to relieve Scribner's brigade, which was out in front, and Scribner was then ordered to the right to support Rousseau's attack. At 4:00 A.M. Brannan's division, which had recently arrived, moved up to the gap from its camps, and at 8 A.M. Negley's division also came up in support. All movements were slow because of the weather, but by 10:30 A.M. all troops were in their assigned positions.

The divisions of Rousseau and Brannan were posted so as to operate on the enemy's left flank from the hills north of the Fairfield road, while Reynolds' division advanced on the enemy's front and right. According to Thomas' attack orders, when Beech Grove, which was at the junction of the Manchester and Fairfield roads at the southern end of Hoover's Gap, was carried, Brannan and Rousseau were to push forward toward Fairfield, and Reynolds was to move along the Manchester Pike and seize and hold Matt's Hollow, a narrow defile through which the road passed, and then to move on to Manchester that night if possible.

At the appointed time, Thomas' line moved forward, and shortly after the attack began, Coolidge's brigade struck Stewart's left flank north of Garrison's Fork and forced him to retire to a new position south of the creek. James B. Steedman's Second Brigade of Brannan's division and Hambright's Second Brigade of Rousseau's division then advanced and drove Stewart from this new line. As the Federal troops advanced, the enemy began to threaten the right of their line, and Moses B. Walker's First Brigade of Brannan's division charged and forced them to fall back. Thereafter, Rousseau and Brannan advanced steadily toward Fairfield.

When Reynolds' division advanced on the left of Thomas' line, it encountered no resistance because the enemy had fallen back toward Fairfield, and after a time it moved toward the Manchester road as ordered. Late in the afternoon, Wilder's brigade seized Matt's Hollow and thus secured the passage to Manchester.

Carlin's and Post's brigades of Davis' division and Rose's brigade of Johnson's division remained at Liberty Gap during June 26, 1863, and Davis was ordered to demonstrate as if to advance on Shelbyville by way of Liberty Gap. Carlin advanced on the Wartrace road, supported by Post, and after moving forward a short distance, he met a strong enemy force. There was skirmishing during the rest of the day, but Carlin made no serious attack.

During the earlier operations of Davis and Johnson at Liberty Gap, Sheridan's division of McCook's corps remained in the rear at Millersburg. Then on the morning of June 26, 1863, Sheridan, with William H. Lytle's First Brigade and Bernard Laiboldt's Second Brigade, marched from Millersburg for Hoover's Gap. Laiboldt's brigade arrived there at dark that night, but Lytle's brigade, which was marching in rear of the wagon train, found the roads nearly impassable and marched only three or four miles that day. Luther P. Bradley's Third Brigade of Sheridan's division did not leave Millersburg June 26, but at 4:00 the next morning it left Millersburg with orders to join the other two brigades of the division at Hoover's Gap. Bradley overtook Lytle's brigade on the road and marched with it to Hoover's Gap.

Throughout the day of June 26, 1863, Crittenden's division and Turchin's cavalry struggled along over bad roads from Lumley's Stand toward Manchester. On the western end of the Union line, Stanley's cavalry and Granger with Baird's division remained at Christiana.

Wilder's brigade took possession of Manchester early on the morning of June 27, 1863, and the other two brigades of Reynolds' division, Robinson's and Crook's, arrived there later in the morning. Rosecrans' headquarters also moved to Manchester that morning.

Negley's division, which had been following Brannan and Rousseau in support toward Fairfield, turned off into the road running from Fairfield to Manchester, and it reached Manchester at 8:00 P.M. June 26, 1863. Brannan and Rousseau pursued Stewart's forces as far as Fairfield, and there they found that the enemy had departed. They then turned back and marched toward Manchester. Brannan arrived there at 10:00 P.M. June 27, and Rousseau came in two hours later.

Carlin's brigade and Post's brigade of Davis' division and Rose's brigade of Johnson's division, all under the command of Davis, remained at Liberty Gap until daylight June 27, 1863, and they then marched to rejoin the rest of McCook's corps at Hoover's Gap. Twentieth Corps was concentrated at Beech Grove early on June 27, and was then ordered to Manchester. Sheridan's division first marched to Fairfield, where it arrived at 4:00 P.M., then marched back to Manchester, arriving there at 8:00 the next morning. Johnson's and Davis' divisions marched directly from Beech Grove to Manchester, but because of the poor condition of the roads and the heavy army traffic, they did not arrive there until 3:00 A.M. June 29.

There was some action on the Federal right on June 27, 1863. At 6:00 A.M. Granger, with Stanley's cavalry and Baird's infantry division of his Reserve Corps, marched from Christiana toward Old Fosterville, with orders to drive Wheeler's cavalry from Guy's Gap. Stanley's cavalry moved in front, with Baird's infantry in close support.

At Old Fosterville, Mitchell's cavalry division turned off to the right to turn the gap, and Minty's brigade moved to the front and skirmished with the enemy for about two hours. Mitchell's division was then brought up and in the ensuing fighting drove the enemy back toward Shelbyville. Granger left Baird to hold the gap and with the cavalry pushed ahead, arriving at 6:00 P.M. in front of the enemy works, about three miles from Shelbyville. Minty's brigade, supported by Mitchell's division, charged and drove Wheeler's cavalry from the town and across Duck River. As Granger approached Shelbyville, he found that the defenses had been vacated, and he occupied the town about 6:30 P.M.

Late on June 26, 1863, Bragg learned that Federal troops had turned his right flank at Hoover's Gap, and that they were then in position to advance on his rear, and at 11:00 that night he issued orders for Polk and Hardee to fall back and concentrate their forces at Tullahoma. The movement began the next morning, and the last of the troops arrived at Tullahoma late on the afternoon of June 28.

Crittenden and his staff arrived at Manchester on the morning of June 28, 1863, but because of the weather and bad roads, Palmer's division camped that night about one mile from town, and Wood's division halted about three miles to its rear. The next day Palmer marched through Manchester and took position at Hillsboro. Wood remained in camp June 29, but the next day moved to Manchester.

After the occupation of Shelbyville, Granger ordered Stanley to move with his cavalry to Manchester, and he then returned with Baird's division to his camp at Christiana. Stanley spent the day of June 28, 1863 supplying his command with ammunition and rations, and the next day marched by way of Shelbyville and Wartrace to Fairfield and Beech Grove. He arrived at Manchester June 30, but he then moved that day and the next to Walker's Mill to obtain forage.

While the army was assembling at Manchester, Rosecrans sent Wilder with his brigade to cut the Nashville and Chattanooga Railroad in rear of Bragg's position at Tullahoma. Wilder left Manchester on the morning of June 28, 1863 and marched by way of Hillsboro to attempt to burn the Elk River Bridge and destroy the railroad between Decherd and Cowan. John Beatty's First Brigade of Negley's Second Division, Fourteenth Corps moved to Hillsboro to support Wilder's movement.

Upon reaching Decherd, Wilder destroyed some track and railroad installations and blew up the trestlework on the Winchester branch of the railroad, but he was unable to destroy the Elk River Bridge. He then began his return, pursued by Nathan B. Forrest's cavalry. He crossed the mountains by the Tracy City road and, marching by way of Pelham, reached Manchester safely at 1:00 P.M. June 30, 1863. Beatty's brigade remained at Hillsboro until noon June 29, and it then rejoined the division at Bobo's Cross Roads.

Upon reaching Manchester, Rosecrans correctly assumed that with the Confederate right flank thus turned, Bragg would be compelled to leave his entrenched position at Shelbyville and withdraw to Tullahoma, twelve miles to the southeast. Rosecrans quickly began the concentration of the army at Manchester and started preparations for an advance on Tullahoma.

At 2:00 P.M. June 28, 1863, Rousseau's and Brannan's divisions of Thomas' Fourteenth Corps moved forward toward Tullahoma and camped on Crumpton's Creek, six miles from Manchester. The next day Negley's and Reynolds' divisions of Fourteenth Corps followed Rousseau and Brannan toward Crumpton's Creek. Reynolds' division camped at Concord Church, where the road to Tullahoma left the Winchester road. Negley's division camped one mile south of Reynolds' division

at Bobo's Cross Roads, where the road from Tullahoma to Hillsboro crossed the Manchester and Winchester road. Brannan's division was placed three-fourths of a mile to the right of Reynolds, and Rousseau's division camped on Arnold's farm, near the railroad from Tullahoma to McMinnville, and in rear of Brannan.

On June 29, 1863, Sheridan's division of McCook's Twentieth Corps marched out seven miles from Manchester on the Lynchburg road to Crumpton's Creek and took position on the right of Brannan. The divisions of Johnson and Davis of Twentieth Corps remained at Manchester until July 1.

June 30, 1863, Thomas sent James B. Steedman's Second Brigade of Brannan's division out to reconnoiter the enemy's position at Tullahoma. He sent two regiments of William Sirwell's Third Brigade of Negley's division under James S. Hull on another road for the same purpose. Sheridan also sent Luther P. Bradley's Third Brigade of his division on still another road toward Tullahoma. All reported that the enemy was in force on the roads ahead.

During the day of June 30, 1863, however, Bragg had learned that the Federals were in strong force at Manchester, and that night he fell back from Tullahoma to the south side of Elk River near Decherd and Winchester. He then withdrew to Cowan, where he formed a defensive position at the foot of the mountain. He crossed the mountains by way of University Place, or University (present-day Sewanee), and moved on to Chattanooga. Forrest's cavalry covered the retreat.

July 1, 1863 was a day of considerable activity in the Army of the Cumberland. That morning Thomas learned from several sources that Bragg had evacuated Tullahoma, and he ordered Steedman's brigade of Brannan's division and two regiments of Milton S. Robinson's Second Brigade of Reynolds' division to advance and determine if these reports were true. Steedman's troops entered the town about noon, and they were joined later in the day by the rest of Brannan's division, Reynolds' division, and McCook's corps. That morning Johnson's and Davis' divisions of McCook's corps had marched out of Manchester toward Tullahoma on a reconnaissance, and when they learned that Federal troops were in possession of the town, they continued on and joined Sheridan's division, which had arrived earlier.

At Manchester that morning, Crittenden received orders to move out with the two divisions of his Twenty-First Corps and take position on the left of Thomas' line along Crumpton's Creek. While Crittenden was attempting to get his troops in position, Tullahoma was found to be evacuated. Palmer's division was halted at Hill's Chapel, and Wood was directed to await orders at Manchester. Later that day, July 1, 1863, Crittenden was directed to march by way of Hillsboro to Pelham. Wood reached Hillsboro that night, but Palmer was unable to march from Hill's Chapel as directed. Then during the night Palmer's orders were changed, and he was directed to move to Hart's tanyard instead of Pelham for the purpose of examining the crossing of Elk River at Stamper's Ferry.

At 10:00 P.M. July 1, 1863, Eli Long's Second Brigade of John B. Turchin's Second Cavalry Division moved from Manchester, where it had been on picket duty, to Hillsboro.

During the afternoon of July 1, 1863, after Rosecrans had issued orders for the pursuit of Bragg, Negley's division of Thomas' corps, with Rousseau's division in support, marched to Heffner's Mill (or Hale's Mill), about five and a half miles southeast of Tullahoma and three miles north of Bethpage Bridge on Elk River. Negley camped that night at Heffner's Mill, and Rousseau's division bivouacked at the Petty farm, a short distance to the north. Brannan and Reynolds were under orders to join them with their divisions the next morning.

July 2, 1863, Negley advanced to Bethpage Bridge, and there he found that the bridge had been burned and the water at the ford was too deep to cross. He was then ordered to attract the attention of the enemy while the divisions of Rousseau, Brannan, and Reynolds, which were following Negley, were sent to the left to cross Elk River at Jones' Ford, which was upstream. The three divisions arrived at the ford, but only Henry A. Hambright's Second Brigade of Rousseau's division crossed the river that evening. The rest of Fourteenth Corps camped on the north bank that night. On July 2, McCook left Johnson's division to garrison Tullahoma, and with the divisions of Sheridan and Davis marched south on roads to the west of the Nashville and Chattanooga Railroad. Sheridan left Tullahoma on the Winchester road at 3:00 A.M. and arrived at the ford on Elk River, about

three and a half miles from Winchester, at 8:00 A.M. The ford was impassable, and Sheridan, followed by Davis, marched to the left toward Allisona, then crossed Elk River near the mouth of Rock Creek. He reached Winchester at 4:00 A.M. July 3.

On Rosecrans' left, Crittenden accompanied Wood's division to Pelham July 2, 1863, but at 6:00 P.M. the division was ordered back to Hillsboro. Palmer's division moved to Hart's tanyard as directed.

July 2, 1863, Mitchell's cavalry division and Minty's brigade arrived at Manchester from their encampment, and they then marched toward Decherd. Long's brigade moved from Hillsboro toward the same point.

On the morning of July 3, 1863, Rousseau's and Brannan's divisions crossed Elk River at Jones' Ford, and Negley's division at Bethpage Ford. The three divisions then took position on the Winchester and Hillsboro road. Reynolds' division marched back from Jones' Ford to Bethpage Ford, but there Reynolds found Negley's division crossing, and he camped that night on the north bank of the river.

At daylight July 3, 1863, Sheridan entered Winchester with his division and then marched on to Cowan, where he went into camp. That day Louis D. Watkins, with four cavalry regiments, arrived from Shelbyville, by way of Tullahoma, and reported to Sheridan for duty. Watkins' command consisted of his own 6th Kentucky Cavalry and the 4th, 5th, and 7th Kentucky Cavalry regiments, all of which had been detached from Mitchell's cavalry division. On July 4, Sheridan sent Watkins on a reconnaissance to the top of the Cumberland Mountains beyond Cowan to determine whether Confederate forces were in position there. Watkins advanced, against some opposition, to a point near University Place, and then, finding that the enemy were there, he returned to camp. The next day, another reconnaissance by Watkins found that the last of Bragg's troops had departed. On July 8, Watkins' command was officially designated as the Third Brigade of Mitchell's division.

Davis' division marched from the Elk River crossing to Winchester, and there it was assigned to garrison the town.

July 3, 1863, Wood's division returned from Hillsboro to Pelham. Palmer's division moved back from Hart's tanyard to a point on the road from

Hillsboro to Winchester, and he remained there until July 8.

Stanley's cavalry command marched to Decherd, where it went into camp to rest and refit.

July 4, 1863, Thomas' corps advanced and took position generally along a road (an old Confederate military road) that ran southeast from Jones' Ford to University Place. The road ascended a spur of the Cumberland Mountains at Brakefield Point, northwest of University Place, and Negley's division took position on the road at the foot of the mountain. Rousseau's division camped a short distance in rear of Negley's division at Featherstone's, which was on the road near its intersection with the road from Pelham to Decherd. Brannan's division was still farther to the rear at Tate's (or Tait's), a short distance southeast of Jones' Ford, which was at the crossing of the road from Hillsboro to Winchester. Reynolds' division camped at Pennington's Cross Roads, about two and a half miles from Bethpage Ford.

At this time major movements were discontinued, and Rosecrans ordered the army into camp to await the arrival of supplies from the depot at Murfreesboro, and to prepare for a further advance against Bragg's army, which had retired toward Chattanooga.

When the army advanced from Manchester in pursuit of Bragg, Samuel Beatty's First Brigade of Van Cleve's Third Division, Twenty-First Corps moved from Murfreesboro to Manchester to garrison the town. On July 5, 1863, Van Cleve marched from Murfreesboro with his other two brigades, Sidney M. Barnes' Third Brigade and George F. Dick's Second Brigade; he arrived at McMinnville two days later. On July 8, Palmer's division of Crittenden's corps relieved Beatty's brigade at Manchester, and Beatty then rejoined Van Cleve's division at McMinnville on July 10.

There were some changes in the positions of the troops during July 1863, but at the end of the month the divisions of the army were encamped as follows:

Fourteenth Corps. Headquarters was at Decherd; First Division and Second Division were at Cowan; Third Division was near Winchester; and Fourth Division was at Decherd.

Twentieth Corps. Headquarters was at Winchester;

First Division was at Winchester; Second Division was at Tullahoma; and Third Division was at Cowan and Bridgeport, Alabama.

Twenty-First Corps. Headquarters was at Manchester; First Division was at Hillsboro; Second Division was at Manchester; and Third Division was at McMinnville.

Reserve Corps. The staff was at Nashville; First Division was at Shelbyville; Second Division was at Murfreesboro; and Third Division was at Nashville.

Cavalry Corps. Headquarters and the two divisions were at Winchester.

Bragg reached Chattanooga during the first week of July 1863, and he established his headquarters there and began fortifying the town. Polk's corps remained in and around Chattanooga, except J. Patton Anderson's brigade of Jones M. Withers' division, which was sent to Bridgeport, Alabama, where the Nashville and Chattanooga Railroad crossed the Tennessee River. Hardee's corps was distributed along the railroad from Chattanooga to Knoxville, with the center of his line at Tyner's Station. Forrest's cavalry was sent to Kingston on the north bank of the Tennessee River to picket the approaches from the Sequatchie Valley, and to watch the movements of Ambrose E. Burnside, who commanded the Federal troops in East Tennessee.

The organization of the Army of the Cumberland during the Tullahoma Campaign June 23–July 7, 1863 was as follows. The changes in command that occurred during the period July 7–August 16 are also included in order to better understand the organization of the army at the time of its advance on Chattanooga.

ARMY OF THE CUMBERLAND
William S. Rosecrans

FOURTEENTH CORPS, George H. Thomas

First Division, Lovell H. Rousseau
  First Brigade, Benjamin F. Scribner
  Second Brigade, Henry A. Hambright
  Third Brigade, John H. King

Artillery, Cyrus O. Loomis

    4th Battery, Indiana Light Artillery, David Flansburg

    1st Battery, Michigan Light Artillery, George W. Van Pelt

    Battery H, 5th United States Artillery, George A. Kensel

Note 1. About July 26, 1863, Rousseau was ordered to Washington, D.C., and John H. King assumed temporary command of First Division. Samuel K. Dawson assumed command of King's brigade. John C. Starkweather then relieved King in command of First Division, and King resumed command of his brigade.

Note 2. Absalom Baird, who was then absent from the army, was relieved from command of First Division, Reserve Corps, and was assigned command of First Division, Fourteenth Corps. Baird then relieved Starkweather, and Starkweather resumed command of Hambright's Second Brigade.

Second Division, James S. Negley

    First Brigade, John Beatty

    Second Brigade, William L. Stoughton

    Third Brigade, William Sirwell

    Artillery, Frederick Schultz

        Battery B, Kentucky Light Artillery, John M. Hewett

        Battery G, 1st Ohio Light Artillery, Alexander Marshall

        Battery M, 1st Ohio Light Artillery, Frederick Schultz

Note. Timothy R. Stanley resumed command of Second Brigade, temporarily commanded by Stoughton.

Third Division, John M. Brannan

    First Brigade, Moses B. Walker

    Second Brigade, James B. Steedman

    Third Brigade, Ferdinand Van Derveer

    Artillery

        4th Battery, Michigan Light Artillery, Josiah W. Church

        Battery C, 1st Ohio Light Artillery, Daniel K. Southwick

        Battery I, 4th United States Artillery, Frank G. Smith

Note 1. John M. Connell relieved Walker in command of First Brigade.

Note 2. On August 11, 1863, Steedman was relieved from command of Second Brigade and was assigned command of First Division of Granger's Reserve Corps. John T. Croxton was assigned command of Second Brigade.

Fourth Division, Joseph J. Reynolds

First Brigade, John T. Wilder

Second Brigade, Milton S. Robinson

Third Brigade, George Crook

Artillery

    18th Battery, Indiana Light Artillery, Eli Lilly

    19th Battery, Indiana Light Artillery, Samuel J. Harris

    21st Battery, Indiana Light Artillery, William W. Andrew

Note 1. Albert S. Hall was absent sick, and Robinson commanded Second Brigade during the Tullahoma Campaign. Later, Edward A. King relieved Robinson in command of the brigade.

Note 2. July 29, 1863, Crook was assigned command of Second Cavalry Division, relieving John B. Turchin, and Turchin assumed command of Crook's Third Brigade.

TWENTIETH CORPS, Alexander McD. McCook

First Division, Jefferson C. Davis

    First Brigade, P. Sidney Post

    Second Brigade, William P. Carlin

    Third Brigade, Hans C. Heg

    Artillery

        2nd Battery, Minnesota Light Artillery, Albert Woodbury

        5th Battery, Wisconsin Light Artillery, George Q. Gardner

        8th Battery, Wisconsin Light Artillery, Henry E. Stiles

Second Division, Richard W. Johnson

    First Brigade, August Willich

    Second Brigade, John F. Miller, to June 25, 1863, wounded

        Thomas E. Rose

    Third Brigade, Philemon P. Baldwin

    Artillery, Peter Simonson

        5th Battery, Indiana Light Artillery, Alfred Morrison

        Battery A, 1st Ohio Light Artillery, Wilbur F. Goodspeed

        20th Battery, Ohio Light Artillery, Edward Grosskopff

Note. Joseph B. Dodge, commander of Second Brigade, resumed command of the brigade, relieving Rose.

Third Division, Philip H. Sheridan

    First Brigade, William H. Lytle

    Second Brigade, Bernard Laiboldt

    Third Brigade, Luther P. Bradley

    Artillery, Henry Hescock

Battery C, 1st Illinois Light Artillery, Edward M. Wright

11th Battery, Indiana Light Artillery, Arnold Sutermeister

Battery G, 1st Missouri Light Artillery, Henry Hescock

TWENTY-FIRST CORPS, Thomas L. Crittenden

First Division, Thomas J. Wood
  First Brigade, George P. Buell
  Second Brigade, George D. Wagner
  Third Brigade, Charles G. Harker
  Artillery, Cullen Bradley
    8th Battery, Indiana Light Artillery, George Estep
    10th Battery, Indiana Light Artillery, William A. Naylor
    6th Battery, Ohio Light Artillery, Cullen Bradley

Second Division, John M. Palmer
  First Brigade, Charles Cruft
  Second Brigade, William B. Hazen
  Third Brigade, William Grose
  Artillery, William E. Standart
    Battery B, 1st Ohio Light Artillery, William E. Standart
    Battery F, 1st Ohio Light Artillery, Daniel T. Cockerill
    Battery H, 4th United States Artillery, Harry C. Cushing
    Battery M, 4th United States Artillery, Francis L. D. Russell

Third Division, Horatio P. Van Cleve
  First Brigade, Samuel Beatty
  Second Brigade, George F. Dick
  Third Brigade, Sidney M. Barnes
  Artillery, Lucius H. Drury
    7th Battery, Indiana Light Artillery, George R. Swallow
    Independent Battery B, Pennsylvania Light Artillery, Alanson J. Stevens
    3rd Battery, Wisconsin Light Artillery, Cortland Livingston

RESERVE CORPS, Gordon Granger

First Division, Absalom Baird
  First Brigade, Smith D. Atkins
  Second Brigade, William P. Reid
  Third Brigade, Henry C. Gilbert
  Artillery
    Battery M, 1st Illinois Light Artillery, George W. Spencer

9th Battery, Ohio Light Artillery, Harrison B. York

18th Battery, Ohio Light Artillery, Charles C. Aleshire

Note 1. The Reserve Corps was organized June 8, 1863.

Note 2. After the Tullahoma Campaign had ended, Walter C. Whitaker commanded First Division during the temporary absence of Baird. On August 11, 1863, Baird, who was still absent from the army, was assigned command of First Division, Fourteenth Corps, and James B. Steedman was relieved from command of Second Brigade, Third Division, Fourteenth Corps and was assigned to the command of First Division, Reserve Corps, relieving Whitaker.

Note 3. Thomas E. Champion replaced Atkins in command of First Brigade, and he in turn was succeeded by Whitaker when the latter was relieved in command of First Division by Steedman.

Note 4. John G. Mitchell succeeded Reid in command of Second Brigade, and John Coburn succeeded Gilbert in command of Third Brigade.

Second Division, James D. Morgan
  First Brigade, Robert F. Smith
  Second Brigade, Daniel McCook
  Third Brigade, Charles C. Doolittle
  Artillery
    Battery I, 2nd Illinois Light Artillery, Charles M. Barnett
    Battery E, 1st Ohio Light Artillery, Stephen W. Dorsey
    10th Battery, Wisconsin Light Artillery, Yates V. Beebe

Note. Second Division was at Nashville, Tennessee during the Tullahoma Campaign.

Third Division, Robert S. Granger
  First Brigade, William P. Lyon
  Second Brigade, William T. Ward

Note 1. James P. Flood's Battery C, 2nd Illinois Light Artillery and Jonas Eckdall's Battery H, 2nd Illinois Light Artillery were assigned to First Brigade; and John J. Ely's 5th Battery, Michigan Light Artillery was assigned to Second Brigade.

Note 2. Sanders D. Bruce relieved Lyon in command of First Brigade.

Note 3. Headquarters of Third Division was at Nashville; First Brigade was at Fort Donelson; and the regiments of Second Brigade were at La Vergne, Stewart's Creek, and Gallatin, Tennessee.

CAVALRY CORPS, David S. Stanley

First Cavalry Division, Robert B. Mitchell
  First Brigade, Archibald P. Campbell

Second Brigade, Edward M. McCook
Third Brigade, Louis D. Watkins

Note 1. One section of Andrew J. Konkle's Battery D, 1st Ohio Light Artillery was attached to Second Brigade.

Note 2. Watkins' brigade was at Franklin, Tennessee June 23, 1863, and it then moved by way of Triune to Murfreesboro, where it remained until the end of June. It advanced to Shelbyville on June 30 and joined Sheridan's division at Cowan on July 3. It was not formally designated as the "Third Brigade" until July 8.

Second Cavalry Division, John B. Turchin
First Brigade, Robert H. G. Minty
Second Brigade, Eli Long

Note 1. One section of Nathaniel M. Newell's Battery D, 1st Ohio Light Artillery was attached to First Brigade; and James H. Stokes' Illinois Battery was attached to Second Brigade.

Note 2. George Crook relieved Turchin in command of the division July 29, 1863, and Turchin was assigned command of Crook's Third Brigade, Fourth Division, Fourteenth Corps.

TUPELO, MISSISSIPPI EXPEDITION (ANDREW J. SMITH) JULY 5–21, 1864

On June 12, 1864, Cadwallader C. Washburn, commander of the District of West Tennessee at Memphis, learned of the defeat of Samuel D. Sturgis' expedition at Brice's Cross Roads two days before, and that his shattered command had arrived at Collierville, Tennessee, twenty-four miles east of Memphis on the Memphis and Charleston Railroad. Washburn immediately made preparations to move troops out in support of Sturgis, and ordered Andrew J. Smith to assemble a force at Memphis and have it prepared to move out as soon as possible. Smith had just arrived at Memphis from Vicksburg, Mississippi, to which place he had moved after taking part in Nathaniel P. Banks' unsuccessful Red River Campaign in Louisiana.

Sturgis arrived at Memphis from Collierville June 13, 1864, and then Washburn learned that Union losses at Brice's Cross Roads were not as great as had originally been reported. He then proposed that, with the approval of William T. Sher-

man, commander of the Military Division of the Mississippi, he move out with Smith's Sixteenth Corps and Benjamin H. Grierson's cavalry thirty or forty miles on a demonstration. Such movement would, he believed, cause Nathan B. Forrest to remain in northern Mississippi with his cavalry corps instead of moving into Middle Tennessee to destroy the railroad over which supplies were being sent to Sherman's army in Georgia.

On June 14, 1864, Washburn ordered Smith to have his corps ready to begin this movement on June 16. On June 16, Sherman directed Washburn to organize a force at Memphis, send it out to devastate the country through which he passed, and find and defeat Forrest.

On June 18, 1864, before Smith began his movement, Washburn sent Edward Bouton's First Brigade of United States Colored Troops out to guard the working parties that were repairing the Memphis and Charleston Railroad east of Collierville, and Bouton took position between Collierville and La Fayette.

On June 22, 1864, Joseph A. Mower's First Division, Sixteenth Corps moved by rail to Grissom's Bridge, which was as far east as the track had been repaired, and the division halted there for the night. The next day, Mower moved on to Moscow. David Moore's Third Division moved to Moscow June 24–25, and Smith then established his headquarters there.

Edward F. Winslow's First Brigade of Grierson's cavalry division left Memphis with the army's supply trains June 24, 1864 and arrived at Moscow the next day. Datus E. Coon's Second Brigade of the cavalry division also helped escort trains, then joined Winslow's brigade at Moscow. On June 27, Grierson moved his cavalry to La Grange.

Smith's infantry left its camps June 27, 1864, crossed Wolf River, and marched the fourteen miles to La Grange. Bouton's brigade was assigned to Smith's command, and it left La Fayette and moved to La Grange June 28–29.

On June 27, 1864, Washburn informed Smith that there was no reason to hurry in leaving the railroad, because by his presence there he was preventing Forrest from moving out of northern Mississippi. This was not what Sherman had in mind, however, and on July 2 Washburn ordered Smith to leave La Grange and the railroad as soon as his preparations could be completed and move against the Mobile and Ohio Railroad and Forrest's cavalry.

On June 28, 1864, Winslow's brigade left La Grange and moved on to Saulsbury, but Coon's brigade remained at La Grange.

Finally, late in the afternoon of July 5, 1864, Smith left La Grange and marched in the direction of Ripley. Coon's cavalry brigade took the lead, and it was followed, in order, by Mower's division, Moore's division, and Bouton's brigade. The column halted that night at Davis' Mills and camped on the Woodson plantation, five miles southeast of La Grange.

July 6, 1864, Smith's infantry, preceded by Coon's cavalry, marched on toward Ripley, halting that night within fifteen miles of the town. Winslow's cavalry brigade left Saulsbury at noon that day and joined Coon's brigade on the road to Ripley. Winslow then reported to Grierson.

On July 7, 1864, Smith resumed the march, and Coon, who was still leading the column, encountered some Confederate scouts. After a few shots were fired, however, the enemy withdrew, and Coon moved on until 3:00 P.M., when he had arrived within three and one-half miles of Ripley. There he found a strong force of enemy cavalry in position on a hillside overlooking the road. Coon was delayed for about an hour while getting his troops in position, and he then charged and forced the enemy to withdraw. Smith came up with Mower's leading brigade, and the army camped that night on North Tippah Creek, three miles northwest of Ripley.

July 8, 1864, Smith's column passed through Ripley, then on southward on the New Albany road, with Winslow's brigade in advance, and camped that night about one mile south of Orizaba. The next day, with Coon's brigade out in front, Smith moved on, crossing the Tallahatchie River at Williamson's Mill, and bivouacking that night south of the river in and around New Albany.

Meantime, the enemy had not been idle. On July 6, 1864, Forrest, who was then at Tupelo, learned that Smith had left La Grange and was advancing toward Ripley. From the direction of his march, Forrest concluded that Smith was moving toward Tupelo by way of Ellistown, and he ordered Abraham Buford to send Tyree H. Bell's brigade of his division to watch the Ripley and Ellistown road.

On July 7, 1864, Stephen D. Lee, commanding the Confederate Department of Alabama, Mississippi, and East Tennessee, arrived at Tupelo from Meridian, and he brought with him 600 foot soldiers commanded by Daniel Beltzhoover.

On July 8, 1864, Bell moved to Ellistown, and the next morning he marched northward on the road toward New Albany. Also on July 8, Forrest ordered James R. Chalmers, Abraham Buford, and Philip D. Roddey to have their divisions in readiness to move immediately upon receiving orders to do so.

July 9, 1864, Clark R. Barteau moved westward from Ellistown with his 2nd Tennessee Cavalry of Bell's brigade to the New Albany and Pontotoc road, and he then took position on that road about six miles south of New Albany. Also that day, Buford, with Hylan B. Lyon's brigade of his division, left Tupelo and marched to Ellistown, where he was joined by Hinchie P. Mabry's brigade, which had arrived from Saltillo.

On the night of July 9, 1864, Forrest learned that Smith was at New Albany, and he ordered Roddey's division to march at once from Corinth and join him. He also directed Chalmers to send Edmund W. Rucker's brigade from Verona to Tupelo, and for Robert McCulloch's brigade to move to Pontotoc. McCulloch reported to Buford at 9:00 A.M.

Smith was aware on July 10, 1864 that enemy forces were gathering in his front. Expecting increasing resistance, he ordered his command to march from New Albany on two roads that converged at Cherry Creek, about seven miles north of Pontotoc. Grierson's cavalry marched on the direct road toward Pontotoc, and the infantry took a road to the left that ran through Plentytude and rejoined the main road at Cherry Creek. Both columns were within supporting distance during the march. The infantry encountered no resistance that day, but Grierson ran into Barteau's men on the main road and drove them back to Cherry Creek. Upon arriving there, Smith found the enemy in line of battle, and he placed his men in camp that night on the north bank of the creek.

Early on the morning of July 11, 1864, Smith crossed Cherry Creek and resumed the march toward Pontotoc, with Coon's brigade out in front. McCulloch's brigade, which was on the road ahead, fell back slowly to Pontotoc, and when Smith's column came up, McCulloch evacuated the town and withdrew on the Okolona road. Smith's cavalry followed for about seven miles and then halted the pursuit. Smith's army camped that night on the hills south of Pontotoc. That morning, Roddey's division arrived at Okolona from Corinth. Late that night, Lyon's brigade of Chalmers' division relieved McCulloch's brigade on the Okolona road.

On July 12, Smith remained at Pontotoc while Grierson sent out patrols to learn what he could of the enemy on his front and flank. Grierson reported to Smith that the enemy was in a strong position on a hill that rose on the far side of a densely wooded swampy bottom that was about a mile and a half in width and was bordered on both sides by branches of Chiwapa Creek. Smith was reluctant to make a frontal attack on the strong position held by the enemy, and when he learned that the road from Pontotoc to Tupelo was practically unprotected, he decided to turn to the east at Pontotoc and march with his army toward Tupelo instead of Okolona.

On the morning of July 13, 1864, all of Grierson's cavalry, except the unassigned 7th Kansas Cavalry, moved out on the road to Tupelo, which was eighteen miles distant. The infantry followed the cavalry, with Moore's division in the lead and Mower's division following. Bouton's brigade, which had been sent out to the south of Pontotoc to protect the rear of the infantry as it left the town, and the 7th Kansas, which had been left in the town, then followed Mower's division with the wagon train. Lyman M. Ward's Fourth Brigade of Mower's division marched on both sides of the road to protect the train.

Winslow's cavalry skirmished with a small force of the enemy on the Tupelo road for about ten miles, until the latter turned off on the Verona road at Burrow's Shop. The cavalry then moved on toward Tupelo with no further opposition, and about noon it entered the town. Winslow immediately began the work of destroying the track and trestles of the Mobile and Ohio Railroad.

The enemy had believed that Smith was considering a withdrawal because of his pause at Pontotoc, and they were surprised when they learned that he was marching toward Tupelo. Forrest reacted quickly, however, to Smith's change of direction. Mabry's brigade was sent out on the Tupelo road and made a number of attacks on Bouton's rear guard during the day. Lee, with Chalmers' and Buford's divisions, moved across from the Okolona road to attack Smith's marching column. Rucker's brigade of Chalmers' division was then sent northward; it attacked Smith's wagon train as it was passing Burrow's Shop but was driven off by Ward's men. Buford's division was ordered to Verona.

At about this time, Lyon was assigned command of an infantry division consisting of dismounted cavalry and Beltzhoover's infantry, and Edward Crossland, as the senior officer, assumed command of Lyon's cavalry brigade.

After Rucker's attack on the wagon train at Burrow's Shop, Smith learned that Grierson's cavalry had occupied Tupelo; he then ordered the trains to pass to the front of Mower's division for better protection, and the column moved on. Moore's division was in the lead, ahead of the trains; Mower's division followed the trains; and Bouton's brigade brought up the rear.

As Buford approached the Pontotoc and Tupelo road at Coonewah Creek, he came up on the wagon train moving eastward, and he sent Bell's brigade ahead to attack and destroy it. Mower's division, which was then guarding the train, was marching in its rear, with its brigades in order from front to rear as follows: William L. McMillen's First Brigade, Alexander Wilkin's Second Brigade, Joseph J. Woods' Third Brigade, and Lyman M. Ward's Fourth Brigade. Bell's attack struck McMillen's brigade, but with help from Wilkin's and Woods' brigades and Joseph R. Reed's 2nd Battery, Iowa Light Artillery and Orrin W. Cram's section of the 6th Battery, Indiana Light Artillery, McMillen drove back Bell's men with severe losses to the Tennesseans.

As soon as the enemy had withdrawn, Mower's division resumed its march and was not attacked again that day. Bouton's brigade, however, was engaged in rear guard action during the afternoon.

Late in the day, Smith learned that Grierson was at Tupelo, and he ordered the trains to halt and park about two miles west of the town. He also began to form his troops in line of battle as they came up. He directed Moore to form his division south of the Pontotoc and Tupelo road, where it would be in position to cover the rest of the army as it arrived. Moore placed his troops in line of battle on the high ground east of the hamlet of Harrisburg, about two miles west of Tupelo. Charles D. Murray's First Brigade was on the right, with its right resting on the road; Edward H. Wolfe's Third Brigade was on the left of Murray's brigade; and James I. Gilbert's Second Brigade was in position to the rear, on high ground overlooking King's Creek, on the left flank of the wagon train park. Its assignment was to guard the train.

Mower's division arrived near Moore's position about 8:00 P.M., then went into camp north of the road. Bouton's brigade camped that night near the wagon train, and Grierson's cavalry remained at Tupelo.

Meantime, Forrest had assembled his cavalry that evening about four miles west of Tupelo. Buford, with Bell's and Crossland's brigades of his division, reported to Forrest at Coonewah Cross Roads that evening, and Chalmers' division also joined Forrest near the crossroads. Lyon's Infantry Division was delayed by the excessively hot weather and did not arrive until later that night.

It should be noted here that during the march from La Grange to Tupelo, and during the battle that was fought near there the next day, the weather played an important role. There had been no rain in the area for about a month, and all wet-weather streams were completely dry. It was only with difficulty that enough water for the men and animals could be found. Marching was especially trying because the roads were covered with a thick layer of dust. The weather was excessively hot, and because of a cloudless sky, there was no relief from the blazing mid-July sun. Because of the heat, the troops suffered terribly while on the march and also during the fighting, and many of the men were disabled by the heat and exhaustion.

Engagement at Tupelo (or Harrisburg), Mississippi, July 14, 1864. Early on the morning of July 14, 1864, Grierson's cavalry moved out of Tupelo on the road toward Pontotoc and at daylight was engaged in picketing the approaches to Smith's camps. Winslow's brigade rode out on the road to the west, beyond the hamlet of Harrisburg, and soon found the enemy in strong force on the road. Coon's brigade watched the approaches to Smith's position from the south.

Early that morning, Buford, with Bell's and Mabry's brigades, advanced to a crossroads about a mile and a half west of Harrisburg, where he joined Crossland's brigade, which had been sent forward earlier. Chalmers then came up and joined Buford at the crossroads.

That morning Smith began to form his troops in line of battle along the crest of a low ridge that rose to the east of Harrisburg. South of the Pontotoc and Tupelo road, this ridge ran to the southeast from a point a short distance east of Harrisburg, and the troops on this part of Smith's line faced to the southwest. About 100 yards north of the road, the ridge turned back to the right at nearly a right angle and ran on a line nearly parallel to the road.

That morning Mower formed his division on the ridge north of the road, with Woods' Third Brigade on the left, next to the road, Ward's Fourth Brigade in the center, and McMillen's Third Brigade on the right. These brigades faced to the north and northeast. Wilkin's Second Brigade was in reserve.

Murray's brigade of Moore's division moved forward that morning to a position south of the road and on the left of Mower's division. Richard Burns' 3rd Battery, Indiana Light Artillery of Gilbert's brigade was placed to cover the front of Murray's line. Wolfe's Third Brigade moved up to the ridge on the left of Murray, and the guns of John W. Lowell's Battery G, 2nd Illinois Light Artillery were placed on the line of the brigade. Gilbert's brigade was assigned to guard the train, and was also to serve as Smith's reserve.

Bouton's brigade was in position about 1,200 yards south of the parked train, facing south. Louis B. Smith's Battery I, 2nd United States Colored Artillery was placed on the line of Bouton's brigade. Winslow's brigade was still out in front of the line on the road to Pontotoc, and Coon's brigade was near Tupelo, watching the road to Harrisburg and the left of Smith's line.

When completed, Smith's line was about a mile and a half in length. The ground in front of this line sloped down to a shallow valley, beyond which, to the west and north, the ground was covered by a dense but fairly open woods. In front of Murray's brigade there was open ground that extended for about 300 yards to the line of trees on the far side of the valley. To the right of Murray's line, on the front of Mower's division, and to the left of Murray's line, in front of the rest of Moore's division and Bouton's brigade, the open fields between the crest of the ridge to the woods varied from 500 to 1,000 yards in width.

Stephen D. Lee was with Forrest's cavalry that morning, and despite the strength of Smith's position, he was apparently influenced by the state of affairs in his department generally and ordered an immediate attack. He assigned Forrest to the command of the right wing of his force, and directed him to swing Roddey's division around and attack the left flank of Smith's position. Lee assumed the personal direction of the center and left of his command for an advance on the front of Mower's division and the right of Moore's division.

Lee brought up his brigades and formed them in line of battle. Mabry's brigade was on the Confederate left, north of the Pontotoc and Tupelo road; Bell's brigade was to the left and rear of Mabry; Crossland's brigade was on the right of Mabry, and south of the road. Roddey's division was on the far right of the line, with its right refused. Chalmers' division was in reserve about 400 yards in rear of Crossland's brigade, with Rucker's brigade on the left and McCulloch's brigade on the right. Still farther back, near the road junction, Lyon was posted with his Infantry Division.

Lee's line was completed about 7:00 A.M., and then, with his front covered by a strong force of skirmishers, he began his advance through the woods toward Smith's position on the ridge. At that time Winslow withdrew his cavalry and passed through the infantry line, and he then took position, along with the 7th Kansas Cavalry, to picket the army's right and rear.

When Buford's division, which was on the left and center of Lee's line, reached the edge of the woods, the enemy artillery opened fire and shelled Smith's line on the ridge for about an hour. When the artillery ceased firing, Buford moved his division out of the woods and into the fields beyond, and he then ordered the attack. As Crossland advanced, he shifted his brigade to the right to make contact with Roddey's division, while at the same time Mabry's brigade veered off to the left. Buford then ordered Bell's brigade to move up between Crossland's and Mabry's brigades and fill the gap created by their divergent movements.

Crossland's brigade crossed the field in advance of the brigades of Bell and Mabry and charged that part of Smith's line that was held by Murray's brigade of Moore's division. Murray's infantry opened with a very heavy small-arms fire, and to this was added the fire from the right of Wolfe's brigade. Burns' Indiana battery of Gilbert's brigade opened with canister, and Lowell's Illinois battery of Wolfe's brigade also fired into the flank of Crossland's advancing line. Despite this deadly fire, the enemy advanced to within 50–100 yards of Murray's line, and then Murray ordered a charge. The survivors of Crossland's brigade were driven back in disorder across the field and into the woods. Murray's men then returned to their position on the ridge. Crossland succeeded in re-forming his men, and after a short rest, he was ordered back to cover the Verona road.

Meantime, Forrest had gone to the Confederate right to join Roddey's division, which was about one mile to the south of Buford's division, and while there he saw Crossland's defeated troops fleeing back from the ridge and across the creek. Forrest then went forward to examine the Union position on his front, and, finding it to be very strong, and held by a force greatly superior to his own, he decided not to send Roddey forward to attack. Instead, he ordered him to move back and form in line of battle covering the Tupelo and Verona road, and engaged the Union artillery on the left of Smith's line with his own artillery.

After Crossland's brigade had been driven back, Buford ordered Mabry and Bell to attack on the front held by Woods' and Ward's brigades of Mower's division. Mabry's brigade advanced at once, without waiting for Bell's brigade to come up. As soon as Mabry's men emerged from the woods, Reed's Iowa battery of Wilkin's brigade and Mueller's Indiana battery of Ward's brigade opened with a heavy fire. When Mabry arrived within about 300 yards of Mower's line, his brigade was struck by a terrific small-arms fire from the brigades of Woods and Ward. Mabry continued on, but when he arrived close to the Union position, his brigade was so reduced in numbers that it was forced to take cover in a depression in the ground.

Bell's brigade finally came up on the right and rear of Mabry's line, but when they again attempted to advance, they too were forced to take cover. Wilkin was killed during this attack, and John D. McClure assumed command of his brigade.

Bell's brigade remained on the slope of the ridge to cover the withdrawal of Mabry's brigade. As Mabry fell back, he met Rucker's brigade advancing to renew the attack. After the fighting had begun that morning, Chalmers had ordered Rucker to move to the left from his position at the crossroads and attack Mower's position north of the road, but he ordered McCulloch to remain at the crossroads. Then Chalmers, with Rucker's brigade, crossed to the north side of the Pontotoc and Tupelo road; he was moving forward to the attack when he met Mabry's retiring brigade. Rucker passed through Mabry's disorganized troops and started up the ridge. He was soon wounded, and William L. Duckworth assumed command of the brigade. Duckworth continued to move forward until he came up on the left of Bell's brigade, which then withdrew from its position near Woods' line. Rucker's brigade suffered very heavy losses, and it was quickly disorganized. Duckworth attempted to rally his men for an attack on Ward's position, but they soon fell back and took cover.

The fighting on his front had been going on for about two and a half hours when Mower, seeing Duckworth beginning to fall back, ordered Woods, Ward, and McClure to attack. As they swept forward, they drove Buford's men back down the slope and into the woods. After the enemy had departed, Mower's brigades returned to their positions on the ridge.

At the time of Rucker's attack, McCulloch's brigade moved forward and relieved Crossland's broken brigade. Lee then ordered McCulloch to cover the withdrawal of Crossland, Mabry, Bell, and Duckworth.

There was no further attack on Smith's front that day, except on Bouton's brigade on the far Federal left. During the afternoon, Bouton's men exchanged fire with some sharpshooters of Roddey's division, and Louis B. Smith's battery of United States Colored Artillery of Bouton's brigade shelled Roddey's position in the woods. About 5:30 P.M. Gilbert's brigade moved across country to take position on the left of Bouton when it appeared that the enemy was preparing to attack. There was no attack, however, and Smith recalled both Gilbert and Bouton from their advanced positions. Then about dark, Forrest led Duckworth's brigade forward from the Tupelo and Verona road and drove in the pickets in front of Bouton and Gilbert, but when these brigades opened with a heavy fire, the enemy retired.

Engagement at Old Town Creek, Mississippi, July 15, 1864. Despite its victory of the day before, Smith became aware on the morning of July 15, 1864 that his army was in serious difficulty. He learned that most of the remaining hardtack had spoiled, and that the ammunition for the artillery was running low. Smith concluded that he could not, without serious risk, pursue and attack Forrest, and that his only alternative was to return to Memphis.

At noon that day, Smith ordered Moore to withdraw with his division, move to Tupelo, and then march to the northwest on the road toward Ellistown. He also ordered the wagon train, with the sick and wounded, to follow Moore. Coon's cavalry brigade was to protect the flanks of the train, and Bouton's brigade was to guard its rear. Moore's division arrived at Old Town Creek, about five miles northwest of Tupelo, crossed the creek, and took position on a ridge beyond.

With Moore's departure, Mower shifted his brigades to the left to protect the rear of the marching column until it had moved on to safety. An attack by Forrest was repulsed, and Mower's division moved out of line and followed Moore and the wagon train. When Mower's division reached Old Town Creek, it crossed to the north bank, then passed through Moore's division before camping so as to be in position to lead the column on the march the next day.

Buford and Chalmers moved out in pursuit of the retreating Federals and soon overtook them at Old Town Creek. Buford then dismounted his cavalry and, with Bell's brigade on the right of the road and Crossland's brigade on the left, advanced and attacked Grierson's cavalry. Bell's attack struck Winslow's brigade, and Smith ordered McMillen's brigade, the rear brigade of Mower's division, which had just crossed the creek, to recross and go to the assistance of Winslow. Moore sent Gilbert's brigade and then Wolfe's brigade to join Winslow. McMillen formed his brigade on the left of the road and Gilbert's brigade on the right of the road.

Winslow's brigade was driven back, and Crossland's brigade, advancing on the left, came up against Gilbert's line. Crossland was wounded in the attack, and Absalom R. Shacklett assumed command of the brigade. The attackers were driven back with considerable loss, and then Chalmers, with

McCulloch's brigade, moved up to check Gilbert's pursuit. Forrest came forward during the engagement and was painfully wounded in the foot. Chalmers then assumed command of Forrest's cavalry. McCulloch was also wounded in the attack.

Chalmers then directed Buford to re-form his division, but Buford was unable to do so because by that time he was left with only a few men. The enemy then withdrew to a ridge about 400 yards distant. Later Buford withdrew his shattered command about two miles and went into camp. This left only McCulloch's brigade confronting Smith.

Smith had no intention of resuming the offensive, and he ordered McMillen and Gilbert to halt their pursuit. Because Mower's division was to lead the column the next day, McMillen's brigade was ordered to rejoin the division, and Wolfe's brigade of Moore's division was sent to take its place and aid in guarding the rear of the army.

* * * * * * * * *

At sunup July 16, 1864, Mower's division was on the road marching toward Ellistown. Wolfe's and Gilbert's brigades crossed to the north bank of Old Town Creek and joined Murray's brigade, and, with his division thus reunited, Moore moved out on the Ellistown road, following Mower. Winslow's brigade, reinforced by the 7th Kansas Cavalry, marched at the rear of Smith's column.

Smith halted his army at Ellistown that evening, but he was not yet free of the enemy cavalry. Chalmers came up that evening with Rucker's brigade, commanded by Duckworth, of his division and Roddey's division and ran into the 7th Kansas Cavalry, which was covering the rear of Smith's army. Aware that he was approaching a greatly superior force, Chalmers did not attack, and he finally withdrew.

On the morning of July 17, 1864, the army continued the march on the road to New Albany. It crossed the Tallahatchie River there, and camped that night near the town. At that point Chalmers gave up the pursuit and withdrew.

Smith camped at Vaughan's Ford on Tippah Creek on the night of July 18, 1864 and the next day moved on to Salem. About noon July 20, the advance of Smith's column arrived at La Grange, and Moore's and Mower's divisions camped at Davis'

Mills. They marched into La Grange the next day. At that point Smith broke up his army, and by July 23, the infantry had returned to its former camps near Memphis. Grierson's cavalry also returned to Memphis.

The organization of the forces commanded by Andrew J. Smith during the Tupelo Campaign was as follows:

RIGHT WING, SIXTEENTH CORPS, Andrew J. Smith

First Division, Joseph A. Mower
First Brigade, William L. McMillen
Second Brigade, Alexander Wilkin, to July 14, 1864, killed
John D. McClure
Third Brigade, Joseph J. Woods
Fourth Brigade, Lyman M. Ward

Note. One section of Battery E, 1st Illinois Light Artillery, commanded by Orrin W. Cram, was attached to First Brigade; Joseph R. Reed's 2nd Battery, Iowa Light Artillery was attached to Second Brigade; and Michael Mueller's 6th Battery, Indiana Light Artillery was attached to Fourth Brigade.

Third Division, David Moore
First Brigade, Charles D. Murray
Second Brigade, James I. Gilbert
Third Brigade, Edward H. Wolfe

Note. Wallace Hight's 9th Battery, Indiana Light Artillery was attached to First Brigade; Richard Burns' 3rd Battery, Indiana Light Artillery was attached to Second Brigade; and John W. Lowell's Battery G, 2nd Illinois Light Artillery and Francis W. Morse's 14th Battery, Indiana Light Artillery were attached to Third Brigade.

First Brigade, United States Colored Troops, Edward Bouton

Note. Bouton's brigade consisted of the 59th United States Colored Infantry, 61st United States Colored Infantry, 68th United States Colored Infantry, and Louis B. Smith's Battery I, 2nd United States Colored Artillery.

Cavalry Division, Benjamin H. Grierson
Second Brigade, Edward F. Winslow
Third Brigade, Datus E. Coon
Unattached
7th Kansas Cavalry, Thomas P. Herrick

Note. One section of Battery K, 1st Missouri Light Artillery was attached to Second Brigade.

OPERATIONS AGAINST VICKSBURG, MISSISSIPPI 1861–1863

From the earliest days of the war, Federal authorities were aware of the military, economic, and political importance of the Mississippi River. When President Abraham Lincoln declared the blockade of the South April 19, 1861, Winfield Scott, general in chief of the army, realized that to make this effective, it would be necessary to hold the line of the Ohio River and to gain control of the Mississippi River.

By the first of May 1861 he had formulated a basic plan for a Mississippi River expedition to start early in November of that year. This plan called for a combined land and naval force that would move down the river and capture and occupy the fortified enemy positions along its course. The advance was to continue until finally the southernmost points, New Orleans and the forts below, were in Union possession. Although this plan was never carried out, preparations were begun at Cincinnati, Cairo, and Saint Louis, and later in the year the same result was achieved by moving against the enemy strongholds from both the north and south. According to the revised plan, the army, supported by gunboats on the river, was to move down the Mississippi from the north, and a naval force, supported by the army, was to enter the Mississippi River from the Gulf of Mexico and proceed upstream.

The following is a brief summary of the earlier activities of Union forces along the Mississippi River.

The first significant engagement along the river was Ulysses S. Grant's attempt to capture Belmont, Missouri, opposite the Confederate stronghold of Columbus, Kentucky, on November 7, 1861. Although Grant occupied the enemy camp for some time, he was soon driven out and then returned with his command to Cairo, Illinois. For details, see Western Department, Operations in the Western Department, Engagement at Belmont, Missouri.

Columbus, Kentucky, which was the western anchor of the first Confederate defensive line in Kentucky, was evacuated February 20, 1862 after the surrender of Fort Henry on the Tennessee River to Andrew H. Foote of the navy and Fort Donelson on the Cumberland River to Grant's Army of the District of Cairo. See Capture of Fort Henry and Fort Donelson, Tennessee.

Federal control of the river was extended farther to the south when John Pope's Army of the Mississippi, aided by Foote's gunboats, occupied New Madrid, Missouri March 14, 1862 and then captured Island No. 10 on April 7. See Capture of New Madrid, Missouri and Island No. 10, Mississippi River.

The occupation of Corinth, Mississippi by Henry W. Halleck's Army of the Department of the Mississippi May 30, 1862 made the Confederate positions at Fort Pillow, Fort Randolph, and Memphis, Tennessee untenable, and the forts were evacuated on June 4. On June 6, a Union fleet under Charles H. Davis destroyed an enemy fleet commanded by James E. Montgomery on the river at Memphis, and the city was surrendered to Davis that day. Memphis was then occupied by Graham N. Fitch's Indiana Brigade, which was composed of regiments formerly belonging to John M. Palmer's Third Division of Pope's Army of the Mississippi. Thus, by the end of the first week in June 1862, the Mississippi River was under Union control down to Memphis and beyond.

Early in April 1862, David G. Farragut, with a fleet of ocean-going vessels, entered the mouth of the Mississippi River from the Gulf of Mexico. He ran past Forts Saint Philip and Jackson during the early morning hours of April 24, and the next day captured New Orleans. A Union army under Benjamin F. Butler occupied New Orleans on May 1, and an advance flotilla moved on up the Mississippi and captured Baton Rouge, Louisiana May 8 and Natchez, Mississippi May 12. Thus in May 1862, Vicksburg was the only important Confederate stronghold remaining on the river. Its capture therefore became of the utmost importance to the Federal authorities.

The various attempts to gain possession of the fortress of Vicksburg, including Grant's final and successful effort in 1863, are described in the following sections. Before proceeding with the description of the many attempts to capture Vicksburg, I wish to acknowledge the enormous contribution to our knowledge of these operations provided by Edwin C. Bearss' monumental three volumes of *The Vicksburg Campaign* (Morningside House, Inc.,

1985), which served as a valuable source of information in the preparation of this section.

EARLY ATTEMPTS TO CAPTURE VICKSBURG

Farragut's Expeditions against Vicksburg, Mississippi, May 1862–June 1862. The first attempt to capture Vicksburg was made in the spring of 1862 by David G. Farragut of the navy, with the aid of a brigade of infantry from Butler's Department of the Gulf. On May 7, a part of Farragut's fleet, accompanied by two regiments and a battery of Thomas Williams' Second Brigade, Department of the Gulf, moved up the river to Baton Rouge, which was captured the next day. S. Phillips Lee, with five gunboats, then proceeded on up the river and captured Natchez on May 12. Continuing on, Lee arrived before Vicksburg May 18 and demanded the surrender of the town, but this was refused.

Farragut arrived a short time later with additional vessels and transports carrying about 1,500 men of Williams' brigade. On May 24, 1862, Williams and Lee conducted a joint reconnaissance of the enemy's position, and the results were discouraging. Because of the strength of the defenses, Williams was unwilling to attack without reinforcements.

A few days later, Farragut left six gunboats to watch Vicksburg, and he started down the river with the rest of the fleet and Williams' brigade. Williams arrived at Baton Rouge early on the morning of May 29, 1862, and Farragut continued on downriver to New Orleans, where he arrived June 1.

When Farragut arrived there, he received an order, dated May 16, 1862, directing him to return to Vicksburg at once. David D. Porter's mortar flotilla was sent first, and upon arrival there on June 20, it subjected the town to a bombardment. That same day, Farragut left Baton Rouge with the large vessels of his fleet, which were accompanied by transports carrying a reinforced infantry brigade of four regiments and two batteries under the command of Williams. The fleet reached Vicksburg June 25 after stopping en route at Natchez and Grand Gulf to attack some recently constructed enemy batteries.

On June 27, 1862, Williams' troops, aided by 1,200–1,500 blacks, began the excavation of a canal across the De Soto Peninsula opposite Vicksburg. This was done to enable the fleet to move up and down the river without passing the strong enemy batteries at Vicksburg. The work was continued until the fall of the water in the river forced the abandonment of the project.

After a preliminary bombardment, Farragut, obeying his orders to pass upstream, steamed toward Vicksburg at 2:00 on the morning of June 28, 1862 and engaged the enemy batteries. By 6:00 A.M. most of the fleet had moved above the town and around the point of the De Soto Peninsula into the protected waters of the river beyond. There on July 1, Farragut was joined by the Mississippi River Squadron of Charles H. Davis, which had come down from Memphis.

An embarrassing interruption occurred July 15, 1862 when the Confederate ram *Arkansas* steamed out of the Yazoo River and engaged the combined Union fleets. After inflicting considerable damage, it finally reached Vicksburg. That evening Farragut made an unsuccessful attempt to destroy the ram by again passing the batteries and subjecting it to a heavy fire. A second attempt on the ram, which also failed, was made on July 22.

Two days later, realizing the futility of remaining longer in his present position, and concerned about the falling water in the river, Farragut weighed anchor and departed from Vicksburg with his fleet and transports. Williams arrived at Baton Rouge July 26, 1862 and disembarked, and Farragut continued on downriver to New Orleans. On July 28, Davis, with his River Squadron, also left Vicksburg for Helena, Arkansas. For additional information, see Department of the Gulf, Troops in the Department of the Gulf, Butler's Gulf Expedition (New Orleans).

During August 1862, Union forces yielded control of a long stretch of the Mississippi River between New Orleans and Vicksburg. On August 5, a large Confederate force under John C. Breckinridge attacked Williams' command at Baton Rouge. This attack was repulsed, but Breckinridge then marched to the north and west and a few days later occupied Port Hudson on the Mississippi. Then on August 15, Breckinridge began the construction of batteries along the bluffs of the river there, and in a short time this became the second important Confederate stronghold on the river. This gave the enemy virtual control of the Mississippi between Vicksburg and Port Hudson. For details, see Department of the Gulf, Operations in the Department of the Gulf, Battle of Baton Rouge, Louisiana.

On August 21, 1862, Federal forces abandoned Baton Rouge and withdrew to New Orleans. Baton Rouge was not reoccupied until December 17, 1862.

Grant's Northern Mississippi Campaign (Operations on the Mississippi Central Railroad from Bolivar, Tennessee to Coffeeville, Mississippi), October 31, 1862–January 10, 1863. The naval battle at Memphis, Tennessee June 6, 1862 gave the Union gunboats control of the upper Mississippi, and Ulysses S. Grant's victory at Corinth, Mississippi October 3–4, 1862 resulted in the control of western Tennessee and northern Mississippi by the army. With these two immediate objectives attained, there arose the question of how best the Union forces in this region could be employed.

On October 25, 1862, Grant assumed command of Thirteenth Corps of the newly created Department of the Tennessee, and the next day he proposed to Henry W. Halleck, general in chief of the army, that he move southward with a strong force along the Mississippi Central Railroad and attempt to gain the rear of Vicksburg and thus force the enemy to abandon the town.

Anticipating Halleck's approval, which was received November 3, 1862, Grant began the concentration of his army in the vicinity of Grand Junction, Tennessee during the period October 31–November 2. James B. McPherson, commanding the Right Wing of the Department of the Tennessee, marched from Bolivar, Tennessee with John A. Logan's Third Division and Thomas J. McKean's Fourth Division to La Grange, and Charles S. Hamilton, commanding the Left Wing, marched from Corinth with the divisions of David S. Stanley, Isaac F. Quinby, and John McArthur to Grand Junction. These troops arrived November 4.

Albert L. Lee was sent with his cavalry division to Holly Springs and occupied the town November 13, 1862.

The army finally began its advance into northern Mississippi on October 26, 1862 in two columns.

Grant, with McPherson's and Hamilton's wings, marched from Grand Junction and La Grange November 26, and William T. Sherman, with the divisions of James W. Denver, Morgan L. Smith, and Jacob G. Lauman from the District of Memphis, moved out from Memphis, Tennessee. The two columns were to meet at the end of the month south of Holly Springs.

Grant reached Holly Springs, sixty miles south of Grand Junction, on November 29, 1862. After establishing a large supply base for the army, he crossed the Tallahatchie River and entered Oxford, Mississippi on December 5. That same day, Sherman's command was at College Hill, a few miles to the north on the railroad. At that time, the cavalry was operating farther to the front at Water Valley and Coffeeville.

When Sherman joined McPherson and Hamilton, Grant reorganized his command as follows: Sherman's command was designated as the Right Wing of the Army, McPherson's command as the Center, and Hamilton's command as the Left Wing.

On December 4, 1862, Grant suggested to Halleck a modification to his original plan. He proposed to hold the enemy forces south of the Yalobusha River in the vicinity of Grenada, and to move a force from Memphis and Helena, Arkansas against Vicksburg. He selected Sherman to lead this expedition down the Mississippi River. Halleck approved Grant's proposal on December 5, and four days later, Sherman started for Memphis with Morgan L. Smith's division. The other two divisions of Sherman's wing that remained with Grant were assigned to McPherson's command.

On December 11, 1862, McPherson moved south from Oxford, reached the Yocona River (formerly the Yocknapatalfa River), and went into camp to guard the crossings. Hamilton's wing was in the Oxford-Waterford area.

Sherman reached Memphis December 12, 1862, and on December 20 he left there on transports at the beginning of his expedition to the Yazoo River. For details, see below, Yazoo River, Mississippi Expedition (William T. Sherman)—Battle of Chickasaw Bayou (or Walnut Hills).

Capture of Holly Springs, Mississippi, December 20, 1862. In December 1862, Earl Van Dorn assumed command of a cavalry division formed from three cavalry brigades, then in northern Mississippi, with orders to move against Grant's supply base at Holly Springs. As a diversion, Nathan B. Forrest led a cavalry force westward from Braxton Bragg's army in Middle Tennessee to destroy the Mobile and Ohio Railroad, which was Grant's supply line that ran south from Columbus, Kentucky through Jackson, Tennessee.

Van Dorn left Grenada, Mississippi on the evening of December 17, 1862 and marched to the east of Grant's army through Pontotoc and New Albany to Ripley, where he turned west toward Holly Springs. Grant learned of Van Dorn's movement, and on December 19 he warned Robert C. Murphy, commanding at Holly Springs, and also commanders of other posts up the line, to be on the lookout.

That night, when Van Dorn had arrived within a few miles of Holly Springs, he divided his command, sending one column toward the town on the Ripley road and the other on a side road to strike from another direction. Murphy's command was surprised, and although the troops attempted to form a defensive position, they were quickly routed and captured, along with immense quantities of supplies. The track and railroad buildings were destroyed, as were all supplies that could not be carried away. Van Dorn then returned to Grenada, where he arrived December 28, 1862.

* * * * * * * * * *

The destruction of Grant's supply base made it impossible to support the army in its advanced position, and on December 21, 1862, Grant began to withdraw to the north of the Tallahatchie River. Shortly thereafter he began the break-up of his army. On December 21, in response to a rumor that Braxton Bragg was advancing with an army on Corinth, Grant ordered the divisions of McArthur and Ross to that place, but the order was suspended when the rumor proved to be false. On December 11, Leonard F. Ross had relieved Stanley in command of his division of Hamilton's Left Wing, Department of the Tennessee. On December 26, Grant ordered Quinby's division to Memphis, where it arrived on December 29. Then during the last few days of December 1862 and the early part of January 1863, the divisions of McArthur, Denver, Logan, Lauman, and Ross were posted at La Grange, Moscow, Lafayette, and Collierville, where they were engaged in putting the Memphis and Charleston Railroad in working order. On January 4, Ross' division was sent to Corinth. Grant remained at Holly Springs, to which he had withdrawn, until January 8.

The work on the railroad was completed by January 10, 1863, and Grant then moved his headquarters to Memphis. There he began preparations for an expedition down the Mississippi River to join McClernand's command for another attempt to capture Vicksburg. On January 15, he began embarking the divisions of McArthur and Logan for the trip downriver, and he left Quinby's division at Memphis with orders to be prepared to move at any time. All three of these divisions were ordered to report to McPherson. Grant accompanied the expedition, and at Young's Point on January 30, he assumed command of all Union troops in front of Vicksburg.

Lauman's division was ordered to remain on duty along the railroad. To avoid confusion, it is necessary to give here a brief description of Lauman's command. When Sherman left Mississippi with Morgan L. Smith's division for Memphis on December 9, 1862, Denver's and Lauman's divisions of the District of West Tennessee remained with Grant's army. Denver's division was then designated as First Division and assigned to McPherson's command. On December 9, Lauman's division was broken up when Ralph P. Buckland's former Fifth Brigade of the District of West Tennessee was sent to the south of Abbeville to guard the railroad. On December 10, Buckland's brigade was assigned to Ross' division. Lauman's other brigade, the Sixth Brigade of the District of West Tennessee, was sent to Waterford, where it reported to Colonel John V. Du Bois. When Lauman had completed these dispositions, he relieved McKean in command of Fourth Division of McPherson's Right Wing, Thirteenth Corps, and he moved with this division to Oxford. On December 22, when the Army of the Tennessee was reorganized into four corps, Lauman's division was assigned to Seventeenth Corps as Fourth Division.

For additional information, and for the organization of Grant's army during the Northern Mississippi Campaign, see Thirteenth Corps, Army of the Tennessee, October 24, 1862–January 14, 1863.

Yazoo River, Mississippi Expedition (William T. Sherman)—Battle of Chickasaw Bayou (or Walnut Hills), December 20, 1862–January 2, 1863. In late November 1862, Sherman left Memphis, Tennessee with three divisions to join Grant in northern Mississippi for his movement southward along the Mississippi Central Railroad toward the rear of Vicksburg (see above). Sherman had just arrived near Oxford, Mississippi when Grant announced a modification of his original plan. He had decided to send Sherman back to Memphis to organize a force, and then, in cooperation with the navy, to move with it down the Mississippi River to the Yazoo River, and from there attempt to move into Vicksburg from the north.

Sherman returned to Memphis December 13, 1862 with Morgan L. Smith's Second Division, Right Wing, Thirteenth Corps, and there he found two divisions that had just arrived from the North. One was Ninth Division, Thirteenth Corps under George W. Morgan, which was formerly Seventh Division of Don Carlos Buell's Army of the Ohio. It had been ordered to Memphis in November 1862, and had arrived there in early December. When assigned to Sherman, it was redesignated as Third Division, Right Wing, Thirteenth Corps in Sherman's Yazoo Expedition. For additional information, see Army of the Ohio (Buell). The other division was Tenth Division, Right Wing, Thirteenth Corps under Andrew J. Smith. This division was formerly First Division, Army of Kentucky. When assigned to Sherman, it was redesignated as First Division, Right Wing, Thirteenth Corps in Sherman's Yazoo Expedition. For additional information, see Army of Kentucky (Granger). Morgan's division was largely depleted and in poor condition, but it was brought up to strength with new regiments that had been sent down from Indiana, Illinois, and Iowa by John A. McClernand, who had expected to command the expedition. Smith's division was also reinforced by four Indiana, two Illinois, and one Ohio regiments.

On December 12, 1862, Willis A. Gorman, commander of the District of Eastern Arkansas, was ordered to organize the troops at Helena into a Fourth Division under Frederick Steele, which was to join Sherman's expedition.

The three divisions at Memphis, whose organization was announced December 13, 1862, and Steele's division at Helena constituted Sherman's Yazoo Expedition, Department of the Tennessee. Sherman left Memphis with his three divisions December 20, 1862 and picked up Steele's division at Helena the next day. He moved on downriver, arriving at Milliken's Bend on Christmas Day, and then moved on to Young's Point.

At 8:00 A.M. December 26, 1862, Sherman's transports left Young's Point and moved up the Yazoo River, supported by the gunboats and the ram fleet of Acting Rear Admiral David D. Porter's Mississippi Squadron. George W. Morgan's Third Division moved first and disembarked at the eastern end of Johnson's plantation. Morgan then sent John F. De Courcy's Third Brigade out on the road to Mrs. Lake's house to protect the landing. De Courcy was engaged at Mrs. Lake's, but the enemy withdrew. Lionel A. Sheldon's First Brigade and Daniel W. Lindsey's Second Brigade camped that night south of the Yazoo and east of Boat Slough.

Frederick Steele's Fourth Division, which came up next, went ashore near where the Johnson house had formerly stood, but which was in ruins at that time. Steele sent out Frank P. Blair's First Brigade on the road to Vicksburg, which ran between Long Lake and Alligator Lake. Blair camped that night about two miles from the river, and Charles E. Hovey's Second Brigade and John M. Thayer's Third Brigade camped near the ruins of the Johnson house.

Morgan L. Smith's Second Division landed west of Steele's division, and Smith ordered David Stuart with his Fourth Brigade to move out on the Vicksburg road and follow Blair. When Stuart came up, he formed his brigade in line of battle on the right of Blair and camped for the night. Giles A. Smith's First Brigade camped near the river.

Andrew J. Smith's First Division did not arrive until about 1:00 P.M. the next day, December 27, 1862, and it then disembarked at Bunch's sawmill.

At the time of Sherman's advance up the Yazoo River, John C. Pemberton was in command of the Confederate Department of Mississippi and East Louisiana, and Martin L. Smith commanded the Second Military District, which included Vicksburg. Stephen D. Lee commanded a Provisional Division at Vicksburg, and William T. Withers commanded a Provisional Brigade of the division. On December 26, when Sherman's movement up the

Yazoo River became known, Lee placed Withers in command of the Confederate defenses covering Chickasaw Bayou. During the afternoon and evening of December 27, Withers was reinforced by two brigades from Grenada, Mississippi, commanded by John Gregg and John C. Vaughn, and Seth M. Barton's brigade from Middle Tennessee.

Sherman's plan for the attack December 27 was as follows: Morgan's division was to advance on the road past Mrs. Lake's house, force a crossing of Chickasaw Bayou, and then cross the River Road and attack Walnut Hills; Steele's division was to advance on the right of Morgan and join him in the attack on Walnut Hills; Morgan L. Smith's division was to advance, while moving to its left, then cross Chickasaw Bayou and take position on the River Road; Andrew J. Smith, when he arrived, was to advance on the road running south from the Johnson plantation and move toward Vicksburg from the Race Track, which was due north of Vicksburg, near the Mississippi River.

When Andrew J. Smith did not arrive in time for the attack that morning, Sherman changed his orders to Steele. He directed Steele to reembark the brigades of Thayer and Hovey and move with them up the Yazoo to Blake's Levee, on the east side of Thompson's Lake, which was mistakenly called Chickasaw Bayou in Sherman's orders. After going ashore there, Steele was to advance along the top of the levee toward Walnut Hills. When this movement was completed, Steele's division was to be on the left of Sherman's line, and Steele was to coordinate his movements with those of Morgan's division on his right. Blair's brigade of Steele's division, which had been left behind in its original position, was ordered to advance on the right of Morgan.

Steele changed positions as ordered, and then advanced along the levee, with Hovey's brigade in the lead. The march on the road atop the levee was difficult, and Steele was forced to camp that night near the head of Thompson's Lake.

About 7:00 A.M. December 27, 1862, Morgan began to move forward on the road that ran along the west side of Chickasaw Bayou, with De Courcy's brigade in the lead. It was followed, in order, by Lindsey and Sheldon. When De Courcy reached Mrs. Lake's field, he halted his column and sent out scouts to find out what was ahead. There was some skirmishing, but Morgan advanced no farther and bivouacked that night near Mrs. Lake's house.

Blair also advanced with his brigade, as ordered, on the right of Morgan. He then turned off from the road to Vicksburg, on which he had been marching, and continued on along a country lane that ran eastward toward Mrs. Lake's to join Morgan. Withers was at Mrs. Lake's house at 10:00 A.M., but after a brief engagement with Blair and Morgan he withdrew, and Morgan followed.

Morgan L. Smith's division followed Blair on the Vicksburg road, with Stuart's brigade in front and Giles A. Smith's brigade close behind. When Morgan L. Smith reached the point where Blair turned off, he continued on, with skirmishing, along the Vicksburg road until he reached Chickasaw Bayou. Progress was slow that day, and Morgan L. Smith halted for the night at the bayou. He then proceeded to look for a crossing.

As noted above, Andrew J. Smith's division arrived at Bunch's sawmill at about 1:00 P.M. December 27, 1862, but the last troops were not ashore until sunset. Stephen G. Burbridge's First Brigade marched that night on the road that ran along the Yazoo River to Johnson's plantation. There he turned south on the Vicksburg road and followed the route taken earlier by Blair and Morgan L. Smith. Burbridge halted about midnight, camping near the point where the lane used by Blair turned off toward Mrs. Lake's. William J. Landram's Second Brigade camped near the sawmill.

On the morning of December 28, 1862, Sherman's divisions resumed their attempts to cross Chickasaw Bayou and occupy Walnut Hills. Steele began his advance on Blake's Levee, with Hovey's brigade in front and Thayer's brigade in support. He soon came under a heavy fire and was unable to advance farther. When Sherman learned of this, he ordered Steele to move back to the Yazoo, reembark his command, and return to Johnson's plantation and support Morgan. Steele did not receive Sherman's order until 4:00 P.M., and he did not begin his withdrawal until after dark. Thayer's brigade, which was the first to return to the river, reembarked on the transports, but did not move downriver until the next morning, December 29. Hovey's brigade followed later that morning.

The activity on Morgan's front on the morning of December 28, 1862 began with an artillery exchange while Morgan prepared to attack. De Courcy formed his brigade in the field south of Mrs. Lake's house, and Lindsey massed his brigade within easy supporting distance. De Courcy advanced and by 12:30 P.M. had driven the enemy across Chickasaw Bayou. He then halted and prepared to resume the advance. He asked Lindsey to send up a regiment to protect his left flank as he moved forward. Lindsey responded by sending James Keigwin, with his 49th Indiana, to cross Chickasaw Bayou to his left and take position opposite the left of De Courcy.

Meantime, Sheldon had arrived at the front with the 69th Indiana and the 120th Ohio of his brigade. The Ohio regiment was sent across the bayou to support Keigwin, and the 69th Indiana was moved up to the left of De Courcy, between him and the bayou. Sheldon was sent across the bayou to command the two regiments on the east bank. The other two regiments of Lindsey's brigade, the 7th Kentucky and 114th Ohio, were massed in rear of De Courcy's line as a reserve. When all was ready, Morgan's division pushed steadily forward and drove the enemy from their advanced rifle pits, but it was stopped by artillery fire short of the enemy main line.

On the morning of December 28, 1862, Blair's brigade was in reserve, but sometime after 10:00 A.M. it was ordered to move up to the left of Morgan L. Smith's division, near Chickasaw Bayou. It was engaged there for a time and was then ordered to support Morgan's division, which was severely engaged to the southeast of Mrs. Lake's house. Blair was directed to support De Courcy, but a short time later he was ordered to cross Chickasaw Bayou and support Sheldon's regiments. It was late in the evening when Blair arrived on the east bank of the bayou, and it was then too late to attack that day. Sheldon was relieved by Blair, and he then recrossed Chickasaw Bayou with his troops and took position on the right of Lindsey.

Stuart arrived in front of Chickasaw Bayou late on December 27, 1862, and that night he sent out a reconnaissance to a ford at the Indian Mound (also called Mound and Sand Bar), which was not far from the Mississippi River, north of Vicksburg. He learned that the approaches to the ford were obstructed by felled trees, and he spent the rest of the night and the following morning attempting to clear

the path leading to the ford in preparation for an attack. Morgan L. Smith also ordered Giles A. Smith to move his brigade up close to the ford.

Morgan L. Smith was wounded on the morning of December 28, 1862, and at 8:00 A.M. Stuart assumed command of Second Division. T. Kilby Smith then assumed command of Stuart's brigade and was assigned the task of clearing the way to the ford.

Under Sherman's orders, Stuart directed T. Kilby Smith to force a crossing of the bayou, and preparations were begun for the attack. Then Andrew J. Smith, who had been assigned by Sherman to command the Right Wing of the army at about 3:00 P.M., came up and assumed command of Morgan L. Smith's division as well as his own division. T. Kilby Smith's attack was suspended for the time being, and the work of clearing the approaches to the ford was continued. Finally, as it was growing dark, Andrew J. Smith ordered the troops to bivouac for the night.

Early that morning, Andrew J. Smith, with Landram's brigade, had marched out from Bunch's sawmill, and by 8:00 A.M. had joined Burbridge's brigade, which had camped the night before near the point where the lane to Mrs. Lake's branched off from the Vicksburg road. Landram's brigade remained near the road junction, but Burbridge's brigade moved up to the right of Giles A. Smith's brigade of Morgan L. Smith's division, at the northern end of McNutt Lake.

On the morning of December 29, 1862, Sherman was determined to break through the Confederate center, and his plan was relatively simple. Morgan, with Blair's brigade on his left, was to advance along the road past Mrs. Lake's, cross Chickasaw Bayou, and occupy the crest of Walnut Hills beyond. Steele was to follow Morgan across the bayou, then take position to hold the River Road. Andrew J. Smith, with his own and Morgan L. Smith's divisions, was to cross the bayou at the Indian Mound and drive the enemy from their rifle pits covering the River Road.

When Sherman ordered the attack that morning, Morgan directed Blair and De Courcy to form their brigades for the advance. De Courcy's orders, which he did not receive until 11:00 A.M., were to cross Chickasaw Bayou at the bridge on Mrs. Lake's road. The brigades of Lindsey and Sheldon were to protect the working parties that were engaged in bridging the bayou at a point about midway between De Courcy's crossing and the Indian Mound. When the bridge was completed, Lindsey and Sheldon were to cross and join in the attack. Early that morning, Steele had advanced from Johnson's plantation with Thayer's brigade to Mrs. Lake's house, where he was to support Morgan's attack.

It was about noon when Morgan completed his preparations and began his attack. Blair, advancing on the left of Morgan, drove the enemy from their advanced rifle pits and moved up close to their main line, but in a very short time he was driven back. De Courcy advanced on Mrs. Lake's road, crossed Chickasaw Bayou on the bridge, and moved up to the open ground in front of the enemy's main line. The brigade was struck by a heavy fire and was shattered in the charge. Both Blair's brigade and De Courcy's brigade recrossed the bayou at the bridge south of Mrs. Lake's.

The 4th Iowa of Thayer's brigade crossed the bayou after De Courcy's brigade and formed on the right of De Courcy. It remained in position there until all other Union troops had recrossed the bayou.

Lindsey and Sheldon advanced to the southwest of De Courcy's crossing, but the bridge was not completed. When Lindsey learned of the repulse of the troops on his left, he recalled the two brigades. By that time it was dark.

That morning, on the Federal right, Andrew J. Smith prepared for his attack at the Indian Mound. Shortly after daylight he ordered Giles A. Smith to relieve Kilby Smith's brigade and prepare for the attack on Walnut Hills, and he then placed Kilby Smith's brigade in reserve. He also massed Burbridge's brigade in rear of Kilby Smith. That morning, Landram's brigade of Andrew J. Smith's division advanced from its position at the road junction, and formed in line of battle as it approached the Race Track.

When Giles A. Smith began his attack that morning, he crossed the bayou, but he was unable to cut a path up the bank on the other side. Small groups of the 6th Missouri of his brigade made unsuccessful attempts to carry the works at the Indian Mound, but the rest of the brigade made no significant advance.

Four regiments of Thayer's brigade passed by the right flank of Morgan's division as they advanced, and they arrived in front of the Race Track. There they formed in line of battle in rear of the 13th United States Infantry of Giles A. Smith's brigade, and of Lindsey's command, and they remained there until 3:00 P.M. They then retired and rejoined Thayer and the other two regiments of the brigade near Mrs. Lake's house.

When darkness finally brought an end to the fighting that day, Sherman's divisions had made no significant progress.

When Sherman examined the Confederate positions on December 30, 1862, he decided against any further assaults at Chickasaw Bayou, and then began to study other possible points of attack. He finally decided on Snyder's Bluff. After careful preparations, the troops assigned for the undertaking embarked on the transports about 9:00 on the night of December 31. About midnight, however, a thick fog covered the area, and this so delayed the movement of the vessels on the river that it was necessary to call off the attack. Sherman then decided to withdraw from the Yazoo and return to Milliken's Bend.

The organization of the troops commanded by William T. Sherman at Chickasaw Bayou December 27–29, 1862 was as follows:

SHERMAN'S YAZOO EXPEDITION, William T. Sherman

First Division, Andrew J. Smith
First Brigade, Stephen G. Burbridge
Second Brigade, William J. Landram
Artillery
  Chicago Mercantile Battery, Illinois Light Artillery, Charles G. Cooley
  17th Battery, Ohio Light Artillery, Ambrose A. Blount

Note. On December 29, 1862, Andrew J. Smith commanded both First Division and Second Division.

Second Division, Morgan L. Smith, to December 28, 1862, wounded
David Stuart
First Brigade, Giles A. Smith
Fourth Brigade, David Stuart, to December 28, 1862
  T. Kilby Smith
Artillery
  Battery A, 1st Illinois Light Artillery, Peter P. Wood

Battery B, 1st Illinois Light Artillery, Samuel E. Barrett

Battery H, 1st Illinois Light Artillery (one section), Levi W. Hart

Note. On December 29, 1862, Andrew J. Smith commanded both First Division and Second Division.

Third Division, George W. Morgan
First Brigade, Lionel A. Sheldon
Second Brigade, Daniel W. Lindsey
Third Brigade, John F. De Courcy
Artillery
  1st Battery, Wisconsin Light Artillery, Jacob T. Foster
  7th Battery, Michigan Light Artillery, Charles H. Lanphere

Fourth Division, Frederick Steele
First Brigade, Frank P. Blair, Jr.
Second Brigade, Charles E. Hovey
Third Brigade, John M. Thayer

Note. Louis Hoffmann's 4th Battery, Ohio Light Artillery was attached to First Brigade; Clemens Landgraeber's Battery F, 2nd Missouri Light Artillery was attached to Second Brigade; and Henry H. Griffiths' 1st Battery, Iowa Light Artillery was attached to Third Brigade.

Cavalry
  3rd Illinois Cavalry, La Fayette McCrillis
  6th Missouri Cavalry, Clark Wright
  Thielemann's Battalion (Companies A and B), Illinois Cavalry, Christian Thielemann

Engagement at Arkansas Post (or Fort Hindman), Arkansas, January 4–17, 1863. Although only indirectly related to Grant's efforts to capture Vicksburg, John A. McClernand's expedition against Arkansas Post is included here so as to preserve the continuity in the description of the movements and organization of the forces that later became a part of Grant's successful expedition against the city.

After Sherman's unsuccessful effort to capture Vicksburg by way of the Yazoo River and Chickasaw Bayou (see above), he withdrew from Johnson's plantation and proceeded down the river January 2, 1863. That day, at the mouth of the Yazoo, Sherman was met by McClernand, who had arrived the day before from Memphis with orders from the War Department to assume command of the expedition.

McClernand's arrangement with Lincoln and Edwin M. Stanton and his relationship with Grant at that time were, at best, quite unusual. In October 1862 McClernand had been given confidential orders by Stanton to organize troops in Indiana, Illinois, and Iowa, and to send them to Cairo, Memphis, or some other point for assembly. He was then to organize and command an army formed from these troops for an expedition down the Mississippi River to capture Vicksburg. McClernand apparently understood that this was to be an independent command, although it would be operating from Grant's Department of the Tennessee.

Sherman, however, had left Memphis with his expedition for the Yazoo in December 1862 while McClernand was still in the North, but the latter arrived at Memphis soon after, and then hurried down the Mississippi to assume command of the troops with Sherman. After meeting McClernand at the mouth of the Yazoo, Sherman proceeded on with his expedition to Milliken's Bend, and there, on January 4, 1863, McClernand assumed command of Sherman's Yazoo Expedition by the authority of an order from the general in chief of the army. He changed the designation of the command to Army of the Mississippi (not to be confused with John Pope's Army of the Mississippi). This, in effect, declared McClernand's independence of Grant. McClernand then reorganized his Army of the Mississippi as follows:

FIRST CORPS, George W. Morgan

First Division, Andrew J. Smith
First Brigade, Stephen G. Burbridge
Second Brigade, William J. Landram
Artillery
  Chicago Mercantile Battery, Illinois Light Artillery, Charles G. Cooley
  17th Battery, Ohio Light Artillery, Ambrose A. Blount

Note 1. First Corps was designated as the Left Wing for the Arkansas Expedition.
Note 2. First Corps was designated as Thirteenth Corps, Army of the Tennessee on December 18, 1862, but was not organized as such until January 12, 1863.
Note 3. First Division was formerly First Division of Sherman's Yazoo Expedition.

Second Division, Peter J. Osterhaus
First Brigade, Lionel A. Sheldon

Second Brigade, Daniel W. Lindsey
Third Brigade, John F. De Courcy
Artillery
  7th Battery, Michigan Light Artillery, Charles H.
    Lanphere
  1st Battery, Wisconsin Light Artillery, Jacob T.
    Foster

Note. Second Division was formerly Third Division of Sherman's Yazoo Expedition, which was commanded by George W. Morgan.

SECOND CORPS, William T. Sherman

First Division, Frederick Steele
  First Brigade, Frank P. Blair, Jr.
  Second Brigade, Charles E. Hovey
  Third Brigade, John M. Thayer

Note 1. Second Corps was designated as the Right Wing for the operations against Arkansas Post.
Note 2. Second Corps was designated as Fifteenth Corps, Army of the Tennessee December 18, 1862, but it was not organized as such until January 12, 1863.
Note 3. First Division was formerly Fourth Division of Sherman's Yazoo Expedition.
Note 4. Louis Hoffmann's 4th Battery, Ohio Light Artillery was attached to First Brigade; Clemens Landgraeber's 1st Missouri Horse Battery was attached to Second Brigade; and Henry H. Griffiths' 1st Battery, Iowa Light Artillery was attached to Third Brigade.

Second Division, David Stuart
  First Brigade, Giles A. Smith
  Second Brigade, T. Kilby Smith
  Artillery
    Battery A, 1st Illinois Light Artillery, Peter P.
      Wood
    Battery B, 1st Illinois Light Artillery, Samuel E.
      Barrett
    Battery H, 1st Illinois Light Artillery, Levi W. Hart

Note 1. Second Division was formerly Second Division of Sherman's Yazoo Expedition, and it was commanded by Morgan L. Smith until December 28, 1862.

On January 4, 1863, the Army of the Mississippi, accompanied by David D. Porter with a portion of his Mississippi Squadron, began its movement up the Mississippi River. It reached the mouth of White River on January 8. From there, William T. Sherman's Second Corps (or Right Wing) moved first, and George W. Morgan's First Corps (or Left Wing) followed. The transports carrying Sherman's corps began to arrive at Notrebe's (also spelled Notrib's) farm, three miles below Fort Hindman, at

5:00 P.M. January 9. Most of Sherman's transports did not arrive until after dark, and the troops did not begin to disembark until the next morning. The transports carrying Morgan's corps tied up that same day at Fletcher's Landing on the opposite bank of the Arkansas River, nine miles below Notrebe's farm. There, on the night of January 9, Daniel W. Lindsey's Second Brigade of Peter J. Osterhaus' Second Division was put ashore. Lindsey moved up the narrow tongue of land formed by a great bend in the river, and placed his artillery on Stillwell Point, nearly opposite Fort Hindman. There he could prevent the enemy from receiving reinforcements or from retreating by way of the river. Morgan's corps remained at Fletcher's Landing overnight, then crossed the river, and the troops disembarked below Notrebe's the next morning.

By 11:00 A.M. January 10, 1863, Sherman's troops were ashore. With Frederick Steele's First Division leading, McClernand's army began its advance on Arkansas Post. Steele was to attempt to march by a wide detour to the right and attempt to reach the Arkansas River above Arkansas Post. His column experienced great difficulties in crossing the swamps encountered on its march, and finally Steele learned that he was on the far side of a bayou that greatly increased the distance he would have to march to reach his objective. McClernand then ordered Sherman to countermarch Steele's division, which did not rejoin the main body of the army until early on January 11. Meantime, McClernand directed Sherman to send David Stuart's Second Division on the direct river road toward Arkansas Post.

The Confederate troops at Arkansas Post were commanded by Thomas J. Churchill, and they consisted of Robert R. Garland's First Brigade, James Deshler's Second Brigade, and John W. Dunnington's Third Brigade. The Confederate defenses began at Fort Hindman, on the Arkansas River, and consisted of a line of rifle pits and trenches that extended westward from the fort for a distance of less than a half-mile, where it ended on a swamp. Dunnington was on the right of the enemy line, and was in charge of the river defenses, including Fort Hindman; Garland's brigade was on the left of Dunnington; and Deshler's brigade was on the left of Garland and on the left of the line.

By 1:00 P.M. January 10, 1863, Morgan's corps had disembarked below Notrebe's farm. Andrew J.

Smith's First Division, with Stephen G. Burbridge's First Brigade in the lead, advanced on the river road toward Arkansas Post, and it was followed by Osterhaus' Second Division.

Steele's division arrived at Notrebe's farm just as Morgan's column was approaching, and Steele was directed to halt to permit Andrew J. Smith's division to pass. Burbridge's brigade halted on the left of Stuart's division, and William J. Landram's Second Brigade halted in rear of Burbridge. Osterhaus' division camped that night in a field south of the Crockett's Ferry road. Later that night, Steele's troops were started on the road and, after a march of eight hours, took position on the right of Stuart.

By the morning of January 11, 1863, McClernand had brought up all of his command except two brigades. Lindsey's Second Brigade of Osterhaus' Second Division, First Corps had been left in position across the river, and John F. De Courcy's Third Brigade of the same division, which had suffered severely in the assault at Chickasaw Bayou, was left in reserve to guard the boats at the landing.

The rest of the army was put in position in front of the enemy line as follows: Sherman's two divisions of his Second Corps were placed on the right, with Steele's First Division on the right, next to the swamp, and Stuart's Second Division on his left. Charles E. Hovey's Second Brigade of Steele's division was on the right; John M. Thayer's Third Brigade was on the left; and Frank P. Blair's First Brigade was in reserve, in rear of Thayer's brigade. Giles A. Smith's First Brigade of Stuart's division was on the right of the division line next to Steele, about 1,000 yards from the Confederate line, and T. Kilby Smith's Second Brigade was on the left and rear of Giles A. Smith's brigade.

Early that morning, Andrew J. Smith's First Division of Morgan's First Corps moved into position in front of Arkansas Post in rear of an open field, and formed in line, with Burbridge's brigade on the right, next to Giles A. Smith, and Landram's brigade to the left and rear of Burbridge's brigade. Osterhaus' division was on the extreme left, between the left of Andrew J. Smith's division and the river. Only Lionel A. Sheldon's First Brigade was with Osterhaus on the line, and it was on the extreme left of McClernand's line, next to the river, and directly in front of Fort Hindman.

At 1:00 P.M., Porter's gunboats on the river and the field artillery posted along his infantry line opened fire, and a little after 1:30 P.M. the infantry advanced. In the order to attack, Steele's division was to attempt to turn the enemy's left flank, and Hovey's and Thayer's brigades were to advance successively from right to left. Steele's brigades advanced on the front of Deshler's line, but they were repulsed. Then Giles A. Smith's brigade, on the left of Steele's division, advanced, and it was followed by T. Kilby Smith's brigade, which moved up on the left of Giles A. Smith. Both brigades halted in front of the enemy line, and the men took cover. Burbridge's brigade moved forward on the left of Stuart's division, and it was checked within about 200 yards of the enemy. Burbridge suffered severe losses, and Landram's brigade was ordered up to his support. About 3:00 P.M. Sheldon's brigade advanced, but it was unable to reach the fort.

By 4:00 P.M. the gunboats had silenced the guns in Fort Hindman. By 4:30 P.M. the infantry had worked its way up close to the enemy entrenchments and was ready for a final assault when Dunnington surrendered Fort Hindman to Porter. White flags then appeared along the works, and the enemy surrendered.

On January 12, 1863, immediately after the surrender of Arkansas Post, McClernand completed the reorganization of the troops of his command that had been ordered December 22, 1862. On that date an order was issued reorganizing the Army of the Tennessee into four army corps, to be designated as Thirteenth Corps, Fifteenth Corps, Sixteenth Corps, and Seventeenth Corps. Thirteenth Corps and Fifteenth Corps were not organized at that time because the troops from which they were to be formed were with Sherman's Yazoo Expedition. They then accompanied McClernand as the Army of the Mississippi on his expedition against Arkansas Post.

The Army of the Mississippi was discontinued by an order of January 12, 1863, and that day Sherman's Second Corps, Army of the Mississippi was redesignated as Fifteenth Corps, Army of the Tennessee. Morgan's First Corps, Army of the Mississippi was redesignated as Thirteenth Corps, Army of the Tennessee on January 14. McClernand remained in command of the expedition, which then consisted of Morgan's Thirteenth Corps and Sherman's Fifteenth Corps.

McClernand remained at Arkansas Post until January 16, 1863, then moved his command down to Napoleon, Arkansas, at the mouth of the Arkansas River. Two days later, Grant arrived to confer with McClernand, Sherman, and Porter regarding future plans. Before leaving, Grant directed McClernand to take the army to Young's Point, Louisiana, opposite Vicksburg, and await his arrival. On January 12, Grant had been authorized by Halleck to relieve McClernand if he deemed it necessary, and on January 30, Grant assumed immediate command of the Vicksburg Expedition at Young's Point, announcing thereafter that headquarters of the Department of the Tennessee would be in the field with the expedition. On January 31, McClernand relieved Morgan in command of Thirteenth Corps.

GRANT'S OPERATIONS AGAINST VICKSBURG

After Sherman's defeat at Chickasaw Bayou in December 1862 and the abandonment of the Northern Mississippi Expedition along the Mississippi Central Railroad early in January 1863, Grant decided to move his army down the Mississippi River and launch a full-scale attempt to capture Vicksburg from that direction.

January 19, 1863, Grant ordered John A. McClernand to move his Thirteenth Corps, then commanded by George W. Morgan, and William T. Sherman's Fifteenth Corps from the mouth of the Arkansas River, to which point they had moved after the capture of Arkansas Post (see above), to Young's Point, Louisiana, opposite Vicksburg.

James B. McPherson's Seventeenth Corps was also under orders to proceed to Vicksburg, but on January 25, 1863, McPherson was instructed to remain near Memphis because it was not certain that a suitable landing place could be found as a result of high water. John A. Logan's Third Division, Seventeenth Corps did not embark at Memphis until February 19 because of a lack of transports, and then, after that date, Seventeenth Corps was sent to Lake Providence, Louisiana.

Grant arrived at Young's Point from Memphis, and January 30, 1863 he assumed personal command of the Expedition against Vicksburg, which consisted of Thirteenth Corps, Fifteenth Corps, and Seventeenth Corps.

A frontal assault on Vicksburg was clearly not practicable, and during January and February 1863 it was not possible to reach the right flank of the Confederate positions above Snyder's Bluff and Haynes' Bluff because of high water.

A possible way to reach the enemy left flank below Vicksburg in safety was to reopen the old canal across the De Soto Peninsula, which Thomas Williams and troops of the Department of the Gulf had begun during June and July of the preceding year. If this canal could be completed, the Confederate batteries on the river at Vicksburg could be avoided, and troops could be safely landed below the town. Troops of Sherman's Fifteenth Corps worked on the canal from January 22 until March 7, when it was flooded by high water, and the project was abandoned.

While Sherman was working on the canal, Grant ordered the exploration of other routes by which the Confederate positions at Vicksburg could be outflanked. One of these, which would be another attempt to reach the enemy left flank, was by way of Lake Providence, and work was carried out on this project through February and March 1864. Two attempts were made to reach the Yazoo River above Snyder's Bluff and Haynes' Bluff, to the rear of Vicksburg and beyond the right flank of the Confederate defenses at the bluffs. One was the Yazoo Pass Expedition, which was continued from February 24 to April 8, 1863, and the other was the Steele's Bayou Expedition, which began on March 14 and ended one week later.

All of the above attempts were unsuccessful, and then Grant decided to open a way along the bayous on the west side of the Mississippi River from Milliken's Bend and Young's Point, past Richmond, Louisiana, to New Carthage, about thirty miles below Vicksburg. This was the route finally used by Grant in his successful movement to the rear of Vicksburg.

For details of the above-mentioned expeditions, see the following sections.

Bayou Expeditions

Lake Providence, Louisiana Expedition, February 1863–March 1863. At Young's Point, Louisiana, Grant had learned of a possible waterway connecting the Mississippi River at Lake Providence with the Red River to the south, and on January 30, 1863, the day he assumed personal command of the Expedition against Vicksburg, he ordered a brigade of infantry to be sent out to attempt to open this route, and he also asked David D. Porter to provide a gunboat to accompany the expedition. The route began on the Louisiana shore of the Mississippi at Lake Providence, about forty miles above Vicksburg, and it extended on through Bayou Baxter, Bayou Macon, and then by way of the Tensas River, Black River, and Red River to the Mississippi River below Vicksburg. it was a long and tedious route of about 400 miles, but it did offer some promise of success.

The principal work required was to cut a channel through Bayou Baxter and a swamp into Bayou Macon and, when this was completed, to cut the levee at Lake Providence. George W. Deitzler's First Brigade of John McArthur's Sixth Division, Seventeenth Corps was selected to explore the route, and it was to be accompanied by William L. Duff, chief of artillery, Department of the Tennessee. A favorable report was submitted, and February 5, 1863 Grant sent orders to McPherson at Memphis, Tennessee to take his corps to Lake Providence and begin the necessary work on the channel.

The other brigades of McArthur's division were also ordered to Lake Providence, but McArthur did not arrive there until February 24, 1863. John A. Logan's Third Division, Seventeenth Corps was unable to embark at Memphis until February 19 because of a lack of transports. McPherson arrived at Lake Providence on February 26. Isaac F. Quinby's Seventh Division, Seventeenth Corps did not arrive at Lake Providence until March 2, and it was then ordered to Grand Lake, where it arrived the next day.

McPherson pushed the work of opening the waterway during March 1863, and on March 18 the levee was cut. There were still obstacles to remove at the end of the month, but by that time Grant had decided to move south by land from Milliken's Bend, and the Lake Providence route was abandoned. Later, McPherson was ordered to move with his corps to Milliken's Bend to join the rest of Grant's army for the movement to the rear of Vicksburg.

Yazoo Pass, Mississippi Expedition, February

24, 1863–April 8, 1863. The most promising water route to the rear of Vicksburg began on the Mississippi River at a point opposite Helena, Arkansas, then ran through Moon Lake, Yazoo Pass, and the Coldwater River, and finally into the Tallahatchie River, which joined the Yalobusha River to form the Yazoo River near Greenwood, Mississippi. By utilizing this route, Grant hoped to land troops above the Confederate defenses at Snyder's Bluff and Haynes' Bluff on the Yazoo and then approach Vicksburg from the east.

The forces selected for this expedition consisted of Leonard F. Ross' Thirteenth Division, Thirteenth Corps of Benjamin M. Prentiss' District of Eastern Arkansas, and a naval force under Watson Smith. James H. Wilson accompanied the expedition as the engineer in charge, and Cadwallader C. Washburn, commander of the Cavalry Division of the District of Eastern Arkansas, was in command of the troops engaged in opening the pass, which work continued through most of February 1863.

Yazoo Pass was separated from the Mississippi River by a levee, which was cut by exploding a mine February 3, 1863. On February 23, Ross left Helena on transports and, accompanied by Watson Smith's gunboats, entered the pass. He reached the Tallahatchie River during the night of March 6, and five days later arrived before the Confederate Fort Pemberton (called by Ross Fort Greenwood) at Greenwood, Mississippi. On March 11, Ross sent two regiments ashore to attempt to find a practicable approach to the fort. They were engaged in some skirmishing, but were unable to move up close to the fort because of high water.

The gunboats were engaged at the fort March 13, and again on March 16, and a second reconnaissance was sent out March 14, but none of these actions produced any significant results.

Watson Smith became incapacitated and, after turning over command of the naval forces to James P. Foster, departed March 18, 1863.

When Ross found that he could not place his troops near the fort, he began to withdraw his command upriver on March 20, 1863. Meantime, on March 5, Quinby was ordered with his Seventh Division, then at Lake Providence, to follow Ross toward Greenwood. On March 14, Quinby, with John B. Sanborn's First Brigade, left his encampment below Helena and entered Yazoo Pass. The rest of the division was under orders to follow as rapidly as transportation was available.

On March 20, 1863, the same day that Ross began his withdrawal, George B. Boomer, in command of his own Third Brigade and Charles L. Matthies' Second Brigade of Seventh Division, started out to join Quinby, but these brigades did not arrive before Greenwood until April 3, two days before the final withdrawal of the Union forces.

About noon March 21, 1863, Quinby met Ross withdrawing up the Tallahatchie River and, as senior officer, assumed command of the combined force. Then, accompanied by Ross, he continued on down the river, arriving near Greenwood on March 23. Quinby made unsuccessful attempts against Fort Pemberton on April 2 and April 4, and he then received orders to withdraw. He departed on his return to the Mississippi River April 5.

The land forces of the Yazoo Pass Expedition were as follows:

YAZOO PASS EXPEDITION, Leonard F. Ross, to March 21, 1863
Isaac F. Quinby

Thirteenth Division, Leonard F. Ross
    First Brigade, Frederick Salomon
    Second Brigade, Clinton B. Fisk
    Artillery
        Battery A, 1st Missouri Light Artillery, George W. Schofield
        3rd Battery, Iowa Light Artillery, Mortimer M. Hayden

Note. Thirteenth Division, Thirteenth Corps was from Helena, Arkansas in Benjamin M. Prentiss' District of Eastern Arkansas, Thirteenth Corps.

Seventh Division, Seventeenth Corps, Isaac F. Quinby
    First Brigade, John B. Sanborn
    Second Brigade, Charles L. Matthies
    Third Brigade, George B. Boomer
    Artillery, Frank C. Sands
        Battery M, 1st Missouri Light Artillery, Junius W. MacMurray
        11th Battery, Ohio Light Artillery, Fletcher E. Armstrong
        6th Battery, Wisconsin Light Artillery, Henry Dillon
        12th Battery, Wisconsin Light Artillery, William Zickerick

Note. Second Brigade and Third Brigade did not arrive near Fort Pemberton until April 3, 1863, only two days before the withdrawal of the Union forces.

Steele's Bayou, Mississippi Expedition, March 14–27, 1863. On March 14, 1863, during the Yazoo Pass Expedition (see above), Rear Admiral David D. Porter, commanding the Mississippi Squadron, started up Steele's Bayou with a fleet of eleven vessels to explore what was thought to be a feasible water route to the Yazoo River at some point above Snyder's Bluff and Haynes' Bluff in rear of Vicksburg. On March 16, Grant ordered William T. Sherman to move with such force of his Fifteenth Corps as might be needed to clear out channels of the bayous to be traversed and to hold such points on the route as might be needed for the success of the expedition. The advance of this combined naval and land force was also intended to relieve Leonard F. Ross, who was at that time near Fort Pemberton at Greenwood, Mississippi with his division (see above, Yazoo Pass, Mississippi Expedition).

The route to be followed extended northward up Steele's Bayou from near the mouth of the Yazoo River to Black Bayou; then along Black Bayou eastward to Deer Creek; then again northward up Deer Creek to Rolling Fork. The latter connected Deer Creek with the Sunflower River, which flowed southward into the Yazoo River between Sartartia and Haynes' Bluff.

On March 16, 1863, Sherman overtook Porter as he was entering Deer Creek. That night Sherman sent ashore the 8th Missouri Regiment of Giles A. Smith's First Brigade of David Stuart's Second Division as a guard, and to clear the way for the rest of Stuart's division, which had been ordered to accompany the expedition. Stuart embarked his division at Young's Point on March 17 and moved up Muddy Bayou. He then crossed to Steele's Bayou and advanced toward Black Bayou with considerable difficulty.

By the evening of March 18, 1863, Stuart was within a few miles of Rolling Fork, and he arrived there the next day. About midnight on the night of March 19, Sherman received a message from Porter on Deer Creek stating that he was under attack and that the enemy were obstructing his passage at the mouth of Rolling Fork. Giles A. Smith's First Brigade of Stuart's division arrived at 4:00 P.M. March 20 at Hill's Plantation, which was located at the junction of Black Bayou and Deer Creek, and from there started forward at daylight the next morning to aid Porter. Smith came up with Porter about 4:00 P.M. and found the latter attempting to withdraw.

On the morning of March 22, 1863, T. Kilby Smith was also sent with his Second Brigade of Stuart's division to help Porter. This brigade was under the temporary command of Americus V. Rice while T. Kilby Smith was with Sherman and Stuart, who were preparing the way ahead. Hugh Ewing's Third Brigade of Stuart's division arrived at Hill's Plantation on March 23, but at that time the other two brigades and the fleet were returning from the mouth of the Rolling Fork.

Porter backed his boats down Deer Creek, protected by the infantry, during March 22 and 23, 1863, and all arrived at Hill's Plantation on March 24. The expedition remained there until March 26, and then Stuart's division returned to Young's Point the next day. Porter's fleet returned to the mouth of the Yazoo River March 28.

The Duckport Canal, Louisiana. When Grant decided to move his army to a point below Vicksburg at the opening of his final campaign to capture that city, he planned to open a series of bayous through which boats could pass with supplies for the army as it advanced. This route was to run from the Mississippi River at Milliken's Bend, past Richmond, Louisiana to New Carthage. Water was to be let into this system of bayous via a canal cut from Duckport, near Young's Point, to Walnut Bayou. Colonel George G. Pride was placed in charge of this project. He was authorized to call on McClernand to furnish a daily work detail of 2,000 men from his Thirteenth Corps and for Sherman to provide 1,000 men from his Fifteenth Corps. On March 29, 1863, work was started on the canal, which was forty feet wide and seven feet deep, and it was half completed by April 6. Water was let into the canal at Duckport April 13, but a short time later, a drop in the level of the river rendered the route through the bayous useless.

Movement of the Army to the Rear of Vicksburg

Grant's March Downriver, and the Crossing of the Mississippi. In March 1863, while efforts to

gain the rear of Vicksburg by the various bayou expeditions were continuing with little success, Grant, in cooperation with David D. Porter of the navy, developed a plan, which, as finally executed, was as follows: While Sherman's Fifteenth Corps demonstrated above Vicksburg, the other two corps were to move below Vicksburg along the west bank of the Mississippi, then cross to the east side of the river, and finally move inland and attack the city from the rear.

The success of this plan would depend on the discovery of a suitable land route through the Louisiana swamps from Milliken's Bend to the Mississippi in the vicinity of New Carthage, and also on the ability of the navy to transfer gunboats and transports downriver past the batteries at Vicksburg.

Exploration of a suitable route began at the end of March 1863. At that time, Grant had with him near Vicksburg only McClernand's Thirteenth Corps of four divisions and Sherman's Fifteenth Corps of two divisions. John E. Smith's Eighth Division of Sixteenth Corps, which had been brought downriver from Memphis to join the Yazoo Pass Expedition, was instead assigned March 22 to McPherson's Seventeenth Corps at Lake Providence. Then, on March 31, Eighth Division was ordered to join Sherman's Fifteenth Corps at Young's Point. James M. Tuttle was assigned command of the division April 1, and two days later it was designated as Third Division, Fifteenth Corps. John A. Logan's Third Division and John McArthur's Sixth Division of Seventeenth Corps were at Lake Providence, and Isaac F. Quinby's Seventh Division was absent from the corps on the Yazoo Pass Expedition until April 10.

March 29, 1863, McClernand was ordered to start his Thirteenth Corps from Milliken's Bend toward New Carthage, Louisiana, about thirty miles below Vicksburg, on the river. Peter J. Osterhaus' Ninth Division marched first to establish the route. Osterhaus occupied Richmond, Louisiana two days later, and he then moved on along Roundaway Bayou, arriving at New Carthage April 6.

Meantime, McPherson had been ordered to bring his Seventeenth Corps from Lake Providence to Milliken's Bend. Quinby's division, under the temporary command of John B. Sanborn since April 14 because of the illness of Quinby, arrived about April 15; Logan's division arrived April 16–19; and

McArthur with two of his brigades arrived about April 24. McArthur had left Hugh T. Reid's First Brigade (formerly George W. Deitzler's) at Lake Providence to guard the area.

In order to reduce the Confederate fortifications at Grand Gulf, and to ferry the army to the east bank of the Mississippi, it was necessary for the gunboats and transports to pass the batteries at Vicksburg and move on downriver. On the night of April 16, 1863, eight gunboats and two transports made a successful passage of the batteries; six more transports followed on April 22, although one transport was lost.

When this feat had been accomplished, Grant ordered Fifteenth Corps and Seventeenth Corps to follow McClernand to New Carthage. McPherson's corps moved first. Jesse I. Alexander's First Brigade and Charles L. Matthies' Second Brigade of Sanborn's division moved from Milliken's Bend to Richmond April 21–23, 1863, and George B. Boomer's Third Brigade followed two days later. Sanborn then marched along Roundaway Bayou, past Holmes' plantation, and arrived at Smith's plantation near New Carthage on April 26. Logan's division followed about one day's march behind. McArthur's division had not yet arrived from Lake Providence, but it was under orders to follow Logan the next day.

When McArthur did arrive, he was assigned to keep open the road from Richmond south to Smith's plantation, which was at the junction of Bayou Vidal and Roundaway Bayou, a few miles north of New Carthage. Thomas E. G. Ransom's Second Brigade was posted at Smith's plantation and William Hall's Third Brigade at Holmes' plantation, about midway between Richmond and Smith's plantation. Hall had been in command of Marcellus M. Crocker's brigade since April 30, 1863. On April 20, Jeremiah C. Sullivan was assigned command of all Union forces detached for the protection of the road from Milliken's Bend to New Carthage.

New Carthage proved to be an unsuitable place for the concentration of the army, and a new site was selected at Perkins' plantation, eight miles downriver at the south end of Bayou Vidal. This too was unsatisfactory, and the army finally assembled at Hard Times, opposite Grand Gulf. On April 27, 1863, McClernand collected his Thirteenth Corps at Perkins' plantation, and the next day two divisions moved by water to Hard Times, with the other two divisions to follow. McPherson's two divisions, with Logan's division in the lead, marched toward Hard Times by way of Lake Saint Joseph. Logan's division arrived at Hard Times April 29, with Sanborn's division close behind.

An attempt was made to cross the Mississippi at Grand Gulf April 29, 1863. The Ninth, Tenth, and Twelfth divisions of McClernand's corps, about 10,000 men, embarked on transports and barges in readiness to land after the gunboats had silenced the enemy batteries. The bombardment began at 8:00 A.M. and lasted until 1:30 P.M., but the enemy batteries continued to fire, and the crossing was not attempted.

Grant then moved his two corps downriver about three miles to Disharoon's (De Shroon's) plantation, and under cover of darkness, the gunboats ran down past the batteries at Grand Gulf. Then, during the day of April 30, 1863, McClernand's Thirteenth Corps crossed the river to Bruinsburg, Mississippi, and it was followed by Logan with John E. Smith's First Brigade and John D. Stevenson's Third Brigade of his Third Division, Seventeenth Corps. Once ashore, these troops marched rapidly eastward to gain the hills along the river before enemy forces could be brought up to oppose them. Elias S. Dennis' Second Brigade of Logan's division and Sanborn's division (formerly Quinby's) of Seventeenth Corps crossed the river May 1 and followed McClernand and Logan toward the hills.

The successful transfer of Thirteenth Corps and Seventeenth Corps to the east bank of the Mississippi without serious opposition was materially aided by a diversionary cavalry raid through eastern and Central Mississippi by Benjamin H. Grierson. Grierson left La Grange, Tennessee with a cavalry brigade April 17, 1863 and marched southward through eastern Mississippi. He arrived on the Southern Railroad of Mississippi at Newman's Station, east of Jackson, on April 24, and proceeded to destroy trains, track, and buildings in the area. He then continued on to the southwest through Hazelhurst and Brookhaven, arriving safely at Baton Rouge, Louisiana on May 2.

When John C. Pemberton, commanding the Confederate Department of Mississippi and East Louisiana, then at Jackson, learned that a Federal cavalry force was in the area, he promptly turned his attention to shifting troops to various points in an effort to capture or destroy it. He was thus preoccupied while Grant was engaged in crossing the Mississippi. For additional information, see Grierson's Raid.

Sherman's Fifteenth Corps was the last of the corps to leave the river bank across from Vicksburg and march south. On April 1, 1863, Steele's First Division of Fifteenth Corps was sent to Greenville, Mississippi, about 150 miles up the Mississippi River from Vicksburg, on an expedition to Deer Creek. After disembarking at Greenville, Steele moved inland to Deer Creek, then down Deer Creek as far as Rolling Fork, destroying supplies and diverting attention from Grant's movements opposite Vicksburg. Steele returned to Greenville April 10 and remained there until recalled April 22. He returned to Milliken's Bend on April 26.

On April 25, 1863, Grant ordered Sherman to start his Fifteenth Corps toward New Carthage, but because of the condition of the roads, this movement was suspended the next day. Then on April 27, Grant proposed that Sherman make a demonstration against the enemy positions at Snyder's Bluff, and two days later he embarked with Frank P. Blair's Second Division and proceeded up the Yazoo River. During April 30 and May 1, the Federal gunboats engaged the enemy batteries at Snyder's Bluff and Drumgould's Bluff, while the infantry landed as if to attack. When this action was completed, Sherman's mission was fulfilled, and he then returned to Young's Point.

On the morning of May 2, 1863, Steele's First Division moved out from Milliken's Bend and Tuttle's Third Division from Duckport, and both divisions marched toward Richmond on their way to Hard Times and Grand Gulf, which was evacuated by the Confederates that day. Blair's Second Division moved to Milliken's Bend, and it was left there to occupy the line from that point to Richmond, and to aid in hastening forward supplies for the army.

Steele's and Tuttle's divisions arrived at Hard Times, four miles above Grand Gulf, about noon May 6, 1863. During that night and the next day they crossed the river to Grand Gulf, and on May 8 they marched to Hankinson's Ferry on the Big Black River, where they relieved Marcellus M. Crocker's Seventh Division, Seventeenth Corps. Crocker had arrived at Port Gibson from the North

and relieved Sanborn in command of Quinby's Seventh Division.

May 5, 1863, Blair was ordered to leave Hugh Ewing's brigade of his division at Milliken's Bend and Richmond and to turn over the command of Milliken's Bend to Jeremiah C. Sullivan. Blair was then to follow the rest of Fifteenth Corps and join Grant's army. Blair, with Giles A. Smith's First Brigade and T. Kilby Smith's Second Brigade, arrived at Hard Times on the night of May 9, and he then crossed the river to Grand Gulf. He remained there until May 12, then accompanied a wagon train that was moving forward to join the army. Blair's division arrived near Raymond, Mississippi May 16.

Ewing's brigade was relieved May 13, 1863 by four regiments sent by James C. Veatch from his Fifth Division (or District of Memphis), Sixteenth Corps, and Ewing then marched to rejoin Blair's division. He arrived at Grand Gulf on the evening of May 15, then continued on and rejoined the division near Edwards Station May 18.

Ransom's Second Brigade of McArthur's Sixth Division, Seventeenth Corps remained near Smith's plantation, and Hall's Third Brigade of the same division stayed at Holmes' plantation guarding Grant's supply line until May 10, 1863. Then, after a new road had been opened to Hard Times, the old one was abandoned, and McArthur took his two brigades to Grand Gulf. Ransom's brigade marched on by way of Raymond, reaching Champion Hill on the evening of May 16, after the battle there that day. It continued on and arrived at the Big Black River at noon the next day. Hall's brigade remained as garrison of Grand Gulf until May 19, then left to join Seventeenth Corps at Vicksburg.

Battle of Port Gibson, Mississippi, April 30, 1863–May 1, 1863. Grant's first step after his troops had landed at Bruinsburg April 30, 1863 was to secure a firm bridgehead and then, after completing the necessary preparations, to start McClernand's Thirteenth Corps on a night march toward Port Gibson, where he was to seize the bridges over the Bayou Pierre. Eugene A. Carr's Fourteenth Division took the lead, and it was followed in turn by Peter J. Osterhaus' Ninth Division, Alvin P. Hovey's Twelfth Division, and Andrew J. Smith's Tenth Division. The leading brigade in

McClernand's advance was Charles L. Harris' Second Brigade of Carr's division, and it was followed by William P. Benton's First Brigade of the same division. Harris, who was ill, was relieved by William M. Stone at 10:00 that night, but Harris remained with the brigade. Michael K. Lawler relieved Stone at Port Gibson May 2 and remained in command of the brigade during the campaign for Vicksburg.

McClernand's column marched past Windsor Plantation to Bethel Church, and there it turned into the Rodney–Port Gibson road. Stone's brigade advanced along this road, crossed Widow's Creek at midnight, and moved up the hill toward the Shaifer house, about a mile distant. There, at about 1:00 A.M. May 1, 1863, it encountered enemy outposts, and when Benton heard the sounds of Stone's engagement, he hurried forward to his support. There was sharp fighting near Magnolia Church for a few hours, and then Carr came up and ordered the two brigades to bivouac and wait for daybreak.

When the Union fleet passed Grand Gulf on its way downriver, John S. Bowen, who was in charge of the Confederate defenses there, ordered Martin E. Green to move with a small force to cover the roads running into Port Gibson from the Mississippi River. Green arrived at Port Gibson early on the morning of April 30, 1863 and placed his command west of the town near the junction of the Rodney and Bruinsburg roads. It was Green's troops that Stone encountered near Magnolia Church. On the evening of April 29, the Confederate brigades of William E. Baldwin and Edward D. Tracy were sent down from Vicksburg to support Bowen.

In the area where the developing battle was to be fought, there were two roads that ran in from the Mississippi toward Port Gibson. These two roads followed roughly parallel ridges that were separated by an almost impassable ravine until they joined just outside Port Gibson. The two roads were separated at their greatest distance by about one mile. The northern road was the Bruinsburg road, and the road to the south, on which McClernand's corps was moving, was the Rodney road.

At the Shaifer house, a country road branched off to the left and ran north for about a mile to the Bruinsburg road. When Tracy arrived from Vicksburg with his Confederate brigade, he placed it in position across this country road a short distance south of the Bruinsburg road and roughly parallel to it, facing south.

At daybreak May 1, 1863, McClernand discovered Tracy's troops on the country road to his left, and to prevent this force from moving up on his rear as he advanced, he sent out four companies of Benton's brigade to hold the road. Osterhaus arrived from the river with his division at 5:30 A.M., and McClernand ordered him to deploy and advance toward Tracy's position so that Carr's division could move on toward the Confederate line near Magnolia Church. Theophilus T. Garrard's First Brigade, Osterhaus' leading brigade, formed in line of battle about one-half mile north of the Shaifer house, with Charles H. Lanphere's 7th Battery, Michigan Light Artillery on the right of the road. Garrard advanced and was soon engaged with Tracy's brigade and forced to halt. Lionel A. Sheldon's Second Brigade then came up and formed in rear of Lanphere's battery. Charles B. Kimball's 1st Battery, Wisconsin Light Artillery also arrived and was placed on the left of the Michigan battery.

Osterhaus decided to turn the enemy left flank, and at 8:15 he ordered an attack. The two brigades advanced and succeeded in driving the enemy back about 400 yards to Tracy's main line, and there they were stopped. Tracy was killed and was succeeded in command of the brigade by Isham W. Garrott. By 10:00 A.M. the Federal artillery had silenced the enemy's guns, and by 11:00 A.M. Osterhaus had extended his front until Garrott's entire line was engaged. By noon Osterhaus had reorganized his line for an attack, but he refused to advance until reinforced.

Meantime there was activity on the Rodney road to the south. This road ran off to the southeast from the Shaifer house, where McClernand had his headquarters, along a narrow ridge, and on the road, about 600 yards beyond the Shaifer house, was Magnolia Church. At 6:15 A.M., when the country road had been secured, Carr's division advanced toward Magnolia Church. Stone's brigade was deployed on the left of the Rodney road, and Benton's brigade was on the road to the rear. Benton's brigade was then ordered up to form on the right of Stone. Henry H. Griffiths' 1st Battery, Iowa Light Artillery was east of the Shaifer house, north of the road, and Martin Klauss' 1st Battery, Indiana Light Artillery was south of the road.

At 6:30 A.M., when he heard the sounds of Osterhaus' battle, McClernand ordered Carr to attack. Carr ordered Stone to hold his position and directed Benton to move forward on the right and gain possession of the ridge on which Magnolia Church stood. Benton advanced through a ravine and arrived on the ridge at about 7:30. He then discovered the enemy's main line on a ridge to the east, on the far side of another ravine, and about 200 yards distant.

Bowen arrived near Port Gibson early on the morning of May 1, 1863 and immediately sent for Baldwin and Francis M. Cockrell to bring up their brigades. He then met with Green and ordered him to advance his brigade to the ridge east of Magnolia Church. It was Green's troops that confronted Carr's brigades that morning. At 8:30 A.M. Green attempted to drive back Benton's brigade, but he was repulsed with heavy losses. Baldwin's brigade, which was approaching from Bayou Pierre, was ordered to support Green, but it had not yet arrived.

Meantime, Hovey's division of McClernand's corps had arrived at Widow's Creek at daylight that morning and had remained there until 6:30 A.M., when it was ordered forward to take position south of the Shaifer house. George F. McGinnis' First Brigade was deployed along a ridge, and James R. Slack's Second Brigade was formed on the next ridge to the west. Hovey was then directed not to become engaged until Andrew J. Smith's division arrived.

Stephen G. Burbridge's First Brigade of Smith's division arrived at 8:00 A.M. and was placed on a ridge south of the Rodney road, and at 8:30 William J. Landram's Second Brigade came up and formed on the left of Burbridge.

When Benton advanced that morning, a gap developed between the two brigades of Carr's division, and when Benton asked for help when he was attacked by Green, Hovey's division moved up into this gap, with Slack's brigade on the left next to Stone, and McGinnis' brigade on the right next to Benton. By this time it was 10:00 A.M. Hovey then attacked with the 34th Indiana of McGinnis' brigade and the 56th Ohio of Slack's brigade, but they were repulsed. Then Stone's brigade and the 97th Illinois of Landram's brigade moved up on the left and extended the Federal line to a point beyond Green's right flank.

Hovey then ordered an attack, and his brigades advanced against the enemy center. At the same time Stone's brigade, supported by the 97th Illinois of Landram's brigade, advanced north of the road, and Benton's brigade on the Federal right stormed the ridge on its front, south of the road. Green's troops were driven back along the Rodney road for about a mile, and then passed through Baldwin's brigade, which was deploying across the road on the ridge above Willow Creek, about 1,000 yards west of the junction of the Rodney and Bruinsburg roads. Green's disorganized brigade was sent out on the Bruinsburg road to reinforce Garrott, and arrived in rear of his line about 2:30 P.M.

It should be noted here that south of the Rodney road, two branches of Willow Creek flowed north, about 600 yards apart, through valleys on both sides of a ridge, and they joined to form Willow Creek just before it crossed the Rodney road. The western branch, which flowed nearly parallel to the Rodney road, was called the White Branch, and the branch on the eastern side of the ridge was the Irwin Branch.

Meantime, Cockrell had received his orders to reinforce Bowen's troops at 10:00 A.M., and an hour later he left Grand Gulf with his brigade for Port Gibson. He reached the road junction behind Baldwin's brigade by 12:30 P.M. The 6th Missouri of Cockrell's brigade was then sent to reinforce Garrott on the Bruinsburg road, and the 3rd Missouri and 5th Missouri were moved out rapidly on the Rodney road to reinforce Baldwin. Cockrell was sent through the hollow of the Irwin Branch, to the left of Baldwin's line, to turn the Federal right flank.

Both Carr and Hovey were ordered to follow Green when he was driven back, and they moved on toward Port Gibson about noon. McGinnis advanced on the road; Benton was on the right for a time and then followed McGinnis in column on the road; Slack moved up on the left of McGinnis; and Stone, on the extreme left, moved up through the ravine of Arnold's Creek. McClernand's leading brigades then formed in line along a ridge overlooking Willow Creek, with Stone's brigade on the left, Slack's brigade in the center, and McGinnis' brigade on the right. Ambrose A. Blount's 17th Battery, Ohio Light Artillery of Andrew J. Smith's division then came up and opened fire across the valley, and McClernand's line advanced, but it soon came under a very heavy fire and was stopped.

McClernand then rearranged his line. He took two of Slack's regiments out of the line and sent them, with two regiments of Landram's brigade, to protect his right flank, and when Slack arrived on the right, he relieved Burbridge's brigade. Burbridge then moved to the center of the line to relieve Landram, who moved back into reserve; Stevenson's brigade of Seventeenth Corps, which had arrived from the Shaifer house, was sent forward to strengthen the center of the line. Stone's brigade was still on the left of the line, but had moved out farther to the left.

Samuel De Golyer's 8th Battery, Michigan Light Artillery of Logan's division was then brought up, and Hovey posted Frank B. Fenton's Battery A, 2nd Illinois Light Artillery, George W. Schofield's Battery A, 1st Missouri Light Artillery, Augustus Beach's 2nd Ohio Light Artillery, and James A. Mitchell's 16th Battery, Ohio Light Artillery on the ridges overlooking the White Branch of Willow Creek.

During the afternoon, Burbridge's brigade of Andrew J. Smith's division followed Carr and Hovey on the road in rear of Benton's brigade, and Landram's brigade of Smith's division, and then Stevenson's brigade of Logan's division came up on the road in rear of Slack and Stone. Burbridge's brigade was then brought up to form a refused flank on the right of McClernand's line.

It will be remembered that about noon May 1, 1863, Osterhaus, back on the country road near the Bruinsburg road, had formed his division for an attack on Garrott's (formerly Tracy's) line, but that he refused to advance until reinforced. The reinforcements were to come from Logan's division, which was then some distance to the rear. John D. Stevenson's Third Brigade and John E. Smith's First Brigade had crossed the Mississippi the night before, but Logan himself did not cross until the morning of May 1, and he then started his two brigades toward the battlefield. Elias S. Dennis' Second Brigade was still on the west bank of the river, but was under orders to follow when it crossed.

McPherson and Logan arrived with the head of the column at the Shaifer house at 2:00 P.M., and then Grant sent Stevenson's brigade to join McClernand on the Rodney road, and McPherson, with Logan, accompanied John E. Smith's brigade to reinforce Osterhaus. By 3:00 P.M. Smith's brigade was in position on the left of Osterhaus, who then gave the order for the long-delayed attack. In fierce fighting, Garrott's troops were forced to give way. On the left, John E. Smith's brigade advanced through ravines between the Bruinsburg road and the Bayou Pierre, and pushed Garrott's troops back along the Bruinsburg road. Green's troops, which had formed on the left of Garrott, were only slightly engaged. There was no general attack during the afternoon, but the pressure on Garrott's right steadily increased.

Late in the afternoon, Dennis' brigade of Logan's division came up from Bruinsburg, and began to deploy in rear of John E. Smith's brigade on the Federal left, but by that time the enemy had withdrawn from Osterhaus' front. At 5:00 P.M., Green, who was the senior officer of the Confederate right, assumed command and directed Garrott to retire. Green and Garrott retreated on the road to Andrew's Ferry, where they crossed the Bayou Pierre, and bivouacked for the night on the far side.

Shortly after McClernand's preparations were completed, Cockrell's regiments, which had moved up the valley of the Irwin Branch, advanced across the ridge in front of McClernand's right and struck the flank of Slack's line. Hovey's guns immediately opened fire in an attempt to halt this attack. Slack's two regiments were driven back in disorder, but the 29th Wisconsin of McGinnis' brigade changed front to the right and slowed the attack until the 8th Indiana of Benton's brigade came up in support. McGinnis also sent the 24th Indiana to help, then posted the 34th Indiana and a section of the 16th Battery, Ohio Light Artillery on an elevation on the extreme right of the line. Benton put his 99th Illinois and 18th Indiana regiments along the slope of the ridge in front of the guns, and Burbridge brought up the 67th Indiana from reserve to support Slack. Benton's 8th Indiana then relieved McGinnis' 29th Wisconsin when it ran out of ammunition, and the 19th Kentucky of Landram's brigade relieved Slack's 47th Indiana. The fighting on the federal right lasted for more than an hour, and finally Cockrell's regiments were driven back over the ridge. Benton then advanced to the ridge between the White Branch and Irwin Branch of Willow Creek and extended the Federal line to the south.

At 3:30 P.M., when McClernand had made no further move, Bowen ordered Baldwin to attack. Baldwin advanced at 4:00 P.M. but was quickly stopped. Then the Federal troops in front of Cockrell advanced and forced the enemy to give ground. Burbridge and Stevenson moved up to the ridge occupied by Benton, and these brigades, with the aid of De Golyer's battery, drove the enemy back. Finally, at 6:00 P.M., Bowen ordered Baldwin to retire. Stevenson's brigade followed for a time, but it was then near dark, and Grant's army camped near the battlefield during the night of May 1, 1863.

The Union troops of Grant's Army of the Tennessee that were engaged at Port Gibson May 1, 1863 were organized as follows:

THIRTEENTH CORPS, John A. McClernand

Ninth Division, Peter J. Osterhaus
First Brigade, Theophilus T. Garrard
Second Brigade, Lionel A. Sheldon
Artillery
  7th Battery, Michigan Light Artillery, Charles H. Lanphere
  1st Battery, Wisconsin Light Artillery, Charles B. Kimball

Note. Daniel W. Lindsey relieved Sheldon in command of Second Brigade May 1, 1863.

Tenth Division, Andrew J. Smith
First Brigade, Stephen G. Burbridge
Second Brigade, William J. Landram
Artillery
  17th Battery, Ohio Light Artillery, Ambrose A. Blount

Twelfth Division, Alvin P. Hovey
First Brigade, George F. McGinnis
Second Brigade, James R. Slack
Artillery
  Battery A, 2nd Illinois Light Artillery, Frank B. Fenton
  Battery A, 1st Missouri Light Artillery, George W. Schofield
  2nd Battery, Ohio Light Artillery, Augustus Beach
  16th Battery, Ohio Light Artillery, James A. Mitchell

Fourteenth Division, Eugene A. Carr
First Brigade, William P. Benton
Second Brigade, William M. Stone

Artillery
  1st Battery, Indiana Light Artillery, Martin Klauss
  1st Battery, Iowa Light Artillery, Henry H. Griffiths

Note. Charles L. Harris was sick and was relieved in command of Second Brigade by Stone at 10:00 on the night of April 30, 1863. Stone, in turn, was succeeded by Michael K. Lawler on May 2.

SEVENTEENTH CORPS, James B. McPherson

Third Division, John A. Logan
First Brigade, John E. Smith
Second Brigade, Elias S. Dennis
Third Brigade, John D. Stevenson
Artillery
  8th Battery, Michigan Light Artillery, Samuel De Golyer
Cavalry
  Company A, 2nd Illinois Cavalry, John R. Hotaling

Note. Third Division was only lightly engaged, and Smith's was the only brigade that suffered significant casualties.

Advance from Port Gibson to Fourteen-Mile Creek, Mississippi, May 2–12, 1863. At 10:00 A.M. May 2, 1863, the leading troops of McClernand's Thirteenth Corps entered Port Gibson, and McPherson's Seventeenth Corps soon followed. Sanborn's Seventh Division of Seventeenth Corps, which had crossed the Mississippi at Bruinsburg the day before, arrived at Port Gibson and rejoined the corps about 11:00 A.M. Marcellus M. Crocker, who had just arrived from the North, relieved Sanborn in command of the division at Port Gibson, and Sanborn resumed command of his First Brigade, relieving Jesse I. Alexander.

When Federal troops entered Port Gibson, they found that the bridge over the Little Bayou Pierre had been destroyed, and work was immediately started to rebuild it. While this work was going on, John E. Smith's brigade of Logan's division, Seventeenth Corps, accompanied by Dennis' brigade of the same division, crossed at a ford about three miles above the town and marched northward to Humphrey's plantation on the road to Vicksburg. The brigades halted there until the rest of the corps came up.

When the bridge over the Little Bayou Pierre was completed, Crocker's division, followed by

Stevenson's brigade of Logan's division, crossed and moved northward toward the Big Bayou Pierre. Logan's other two brigades joined the column as it passed Humphrey's plantation. Crocker's leading troops arrived at Grindstone Ford on the Big Bayou Pierre at 7:30 P.M., and found the bridge there had been destroyed. McPherson's two divisions camped south of the bayou while men worked through the night to rebuild the bridge.

McClernand's Thirteenth Corps spent the day of May 2, 1863 and the following night at Port Gibson.

On the morning of May 3, 1863, after the bridge at Grindstone Ford had been completed, Logan's division, with John E. Smith's brigade in the lead, crossed the Big Bayou Pierre and marched northward to Willow Springs, a short distance north of Big Bayou Pierre. Crocker's division followed in support. Logan had been opposed during his advance but had driven the enemy back and pushed on. From Willow Springs, McPherson sent Logan to pursue the enemy that had retreated on the Ingleside road in the direction of Grand Gulf, and directed Crocker to follow those who had withdrawn on the road to Hankinson's Ferry on the Big Black River.

Crocker was opposed on his march by Cockrell's brigade, and his progress was slowed. Logan, who had turned into the Hankinson's Ferry road at a crossroads east of Grand Gulf, arrived at Hankinson's Ferry ahead of Crocker. Logan captured the bridge over the Big Black, and then Logan and Crocker bivouacked in the fields south of the river.

Back in Port Gibson, on the morning of May 3, 1863, McClernand left Carr's division to occupy the town and to protect the army's line of communications, and then moved with the divisions of Osterhaus, Andrew J. Smith, and Hovey to Willow Springs, where he arrived about dark and camped for the night. Lawler's brigade of Carr's division was left in the town of Port Gibson, and Benton's brigade was posted along the road from Port Gibson to Grindstone Ford.

May 3, 1863, Confederate forces began evacuating the area between the Big Black River and Big Bayou Pierre, including Grand Gulf, and Grant was thus left without serious opposition south of the Big Black River.

Grant established his headquarters at Hankinson's Ferry on the morning of May 4, 1864.

He directed McPherson and McClernand to remain where they were until the army trains and Sherman's Fifteenth Corps, which was then en route down the west side of the Mississippi River from Milliken's Bend, arrived and joined the army.

According to Grant's plan, his next objective was Edwards Station on the Southern Railroad of Mississippi, and he issued orders for some preliminary movements of the army in that direction. On the morning of May 5, 1863, Osterhaus' division of Thirteenth Corps left Willow Springs and marched eastward on a road between the Big Black River and Big Bayou Pierre. It camped that night at Rocky Springs, with an advanced force at Big Sand Creek. Also that day, Carr moved up from Port Gibson and the road to Grindstone Ford and joined Hovey and Andrew J. Smith at Willow Springs.

On May 6, 1863, McClernand marched with Hovey's division to Rocky Springs and joined Osterhaus' division, which had remained there during the day. Other than these movements, there was little activity in Thirteenth Corps and Seventeenth Corps.

On the evening of May 6, 1863, Frederick Steele's First Division of Sherman's corps reached Hard Times, on the west bank of the Mississippi, and James M. Tuttle's Third Division camped that night about seven miles to the rear. During the night, Steele's division crossed to Grand Gulf, and Tuttle joined Steele with his division at Grand Gulf after dark on May 7. That morning, May 7, Blair, with Giles A. Smith's First Brigade and T. Kilby Smith's Second Brigade of his division of Fifteenth Corps, left Milliken's Bend for Hard Times on his way to rejoin the corps. Hugh Ewing's Third Brigade of Blair's division was to remain at Milliken's Bend until relieved by four regiments from Memphis, and then it was to rejoin the division.

Also on the evening of May 6, 1863, Grant, believing that Sherman was across the river, issued orders for Thirteenth Corps and Seventeenth Corps to resume the advance toward Edwards Station. McClernand was to advance from Rocky Springs to Old Auburn, and Sherman's corps was to follow McClernand. At some point beyond Cayuga, McClernand was to halt and allow Sherman to pass. McPherson's corps was to move east through Utica to Raymond. When these movements had been completed, Grant's army would be on a line extending from Old Auburn to Raymond, and from this line it was to move north and strike the Southern Railroad of Mississippi on a front that extended from Bolton on the east to Edwards Station on the west. Upon arriving there, the army was to destroy the railroad, then move on Vicksburg from the east.

On schedule, Grant's army began to move eastward May 7, 1863. McClernand's divisions marched that day as follows: Osterhaus from Rocky Springs to Big Sand Creek; Carr from Willow Springs to Big Sand Creek, where he passed beyond Osterhaus; Hovey from Rocky Springs to Big Sand Creek, where he formed on the left of Osterhaus; and Andrew J. Smith from Willow Springs to Little Sand Creek. That day Grant moved his headquarters to Rocky Springs.

On May 7, 1863, Grant learned that Sherman had not completed the crossing of the river, and in fact would not march from Grand Gulf until dawn the next morning, and he then changed the planned march for Seventeenth Corps. Logan's division marched from Hankinson's Ferry to Rocky Springs as scheduled, but Crocker's division was ordered to remain at Hankinson's Ferry until relieved by troops of Sherman's Fifteenth Corps.

On the morning of May 8, 1863, Fifteenth Corps began the march eastward from Grand Gulf. Tuttle's division marched first and passed through Ingleside, camping that night at Willow Springs. Steele's division followed Tuttle to Ingleside, and there turned off on the road to Hankinson's Ferry. Upon arriving at Hankinson's Ferry, Steele relieved Crocker's division, which was guarding the bridge across the Big Black River.

The army continued its march eastward May 9, 1863. At dawn that morning, Crocker's division left Hankinson's Ferry and marched to Rocky Springs. It then continued on several miles before turning off on the Utica road, and halted that night at Utica Cross Roads, seven miles northwest of Utica. About noon May 9, Logan's division of Seventeenth Corps left Rocky Springs; it camped that evening near Crocker's division.

May 9, 1863, Andrew J. Smith's division of Thirteenth Corps moved up from Little Sand Creek to Big Sand Creek and joined the other three divisions of the corps, which had remained in camp there that day.

At 4:00 P.M. May 9, 1863, after Seventeenth Corps had departed from Rocky Springs for Utica, Tuttle's division of Fifteenth Corps marched from Willow Springs to Rocky Springs.

May 10, 1863, McClernand advanced from Big Sand Creek. By dark, the divisions of Osterhaus, Carr, and Hovey were in position along Five-Mile Creek, and Andrew J. Smith's division was to the rear at Cayuga. That day Grant transferred his headquarters to Cayuga.

On May 10, 1863, Tuttle's division remained at Rocky Springs, but late that afternoon, Steele's division, accompanied by Sherman, left Hankinson's Ferry. It camped that night on Big Sandy Creek. That day, Blair's division arrived at Hard Times and began crossing the river to Grand Gulf with the army trains. The crossing was completed the next day.

On the morning of May 10, 1863, Seventeenth Corps left its camps of the night before and, with Crocker's division in the lead, arrived at Utica about noon. It then continued on and that afternoon turned off on the road to Raymond. It followed that road for about four miles, then camped on the A. B. Wells plantation.

At dawn May 11, 1863, Steele's and Tuttle's divisions of Fifteenth Corps were on the march, and they halted that evening at Old Auburn. Also on May 11, Logan, followed by Crocker, advanced on the Raymond road about five miles to the J. Roach plantation, at the crossing of the Gallatin road, where they bivouacked for the night. McPherson was to march to Raymond the next day.

On May 12, 1863, Sherman's two divisions continued the march eastward, bivouacking that night at Dillon's plantation, seven miles west of Raymond. Also that morning, Blair's division and the trains moved out of Grand Gulf to join the army; they bivouacked that night at Willow Springs.

On May 12, 1863, McClernand moved out from his position at Five-Mile Creek, with Hovey in the lead, followed by Carr, and then Osterhaus. On reaching Old Auburn, McClernand turned north on the Telegraph Road toward Fourteen-Mile Creek. On reaching the creek, he secured Whitaker's Ford, then bivouacked south of the creek. Andrew J. Smith's division left Cayuga at dawn and marched to the northeast on a road to the west of the Telegraph Road. He then established a bridgehead at Montgomery Bridge on Fourteen-Mile Creek, three miles below Hovey's division, and bivouacked south of the creek. McClernand found enemy outposts along Fourteen-Mile Creek.

As Thirteenth Corps advanced northward in line to the east of Big Black River, detachments were left at Hall's Ferry and Baldwin's Ferry to protect the army's left flank.

Engagement at Raymond, Mississippi, May 12, 1863. On May 11, 1863, as McPherson's Seventeenth Corps marched along the road toward Raymond, John Gregg arrived at Raymond from Jackson with a Confederate force which included his own brigade, then under Cyrus A. Sugg, Hiram M. Bledsoe's battery, and other miscellaneous troops.

At 3:30 on the morning of May 12, 1863, Seventeenth Corps, which had camped at Roach's plantation the night before, resumed its march on the road toward Raymond. A cavalry battalion under John S. Foster covered the advance, and Logan's division, with Elias S. Dennis' Second Brigade in the lead, followed the cavalry. Crocker's division followed Logan one-half hour later.

Shortly after Foster had moved out on the road, he became engaged with Wirt Adams' Confederate cavalry, and by 9:00 A.M. the action had become so brisk that the Federal cavalry was ordered out to guard the flanks. Dennis deployed his 20th Ohio on the right and 78th Ohio on the left and took the lead. The rest of Logan's division followed in column on the road.

At about 9:00 A.M., Gregg deployed his troops about a mile to a mile and a half south of Raymond to cover the Utica road running in from the south and the Gallatin road farther to the east. He placed Bledsoe's battery on an elevation about 800 yards north of the point where the Utica road crossed Fourteen-Mile Creek.

Fourteen-Mile Creek, along which most of the fighting was to take place later in the day, crossed the Utica road at a right angle about two miles southwest of Raymond. A belt of thick and tangled woods extended along both sides of the stream, and was about 100 yards in width on the south side and 200 yards wide on the north side. From the edge of the woods on the south side of the creek, there was a large field that sloped up gently to the crest of a ridge 400 yards from Fourteen-Mile Creek.

Shortly before 10:00 A.M., Dennis' skirmishers crossed this ridge and moved down the slope toward Fourteen-Mile Creek. At 10:00 A.M. they came under fire from Bledsoe's battery and from enemy infantry in the woods. Samuel De Golyer's 8th Battery, Michigan Light Artillery came up and formed on both sides of the road and returned the fire. Dennis then deployed his brigade along the ridge to the left of the road, and moved down the slope and into the woods along the creek, with his skirmishers out to the edge of the woods to the north of the creek. John E. Smith's First Brigade of Logan's division came up and formed on the ridge to the right of the road, and it too advanced down the slope and into the woods. The regiments quickly became confused in the thick undergrowth, and all but the 23rd Indiana halted before reaching the creek. The latter regiment continued on to the northern edge of the woods.

John D. Stevenson's Third Brigade of Logan's division arrived on the ridge shortly after Smith's brigade had advanced, and had just been formed in line on the right of the road when the battle began.

Gregg attacked about noon and soon came under a heavy fire from Dennis' infantry in the creek bed and from the 23rd Indiana on the right. The 23rd Indiana, which was unsupported, was quickly driven back and across the creek, where it rallied on the right of the 20th Illinois of Smith's brigade, but Dennis' brigade held its position, with the exception of the 68th Ohio, the right regiment of the brigade, which fled to the rear. This exposed the flank of the 20th Ohio to its left, but in the presence of Logan in person, that regiment rallied and held its position in the creek bed.

The left regiments of Gregg's line reached Fourteen-Mile Creek to the east of Smith's brigade, and moved to the right through the woods along the creek bottom toward the rear of Smith's brigade. Stevenson's brigade then moved forward to the northeast to extend the right of Logan's line.

At 1:30 P.M. John B. Sanborn's First Brigade of Crocker's division came up and was sent forward into the woods on the left of Dennis. By that time the 7th Texas on the right of Gregg's line had been driven back, and then Sanborn sent the 48th and 59th Indiana to the right to reinforce Smith and Stevenson.

Samuel A. Holmes' Second Brigade of Crocker's

division arrived soon after Sanborn had advanced and was formed along the ridge west of the road. A short time later, the 10th Missouri and 80th Ohio of Holmes' brigade were sent to the right of Stevenson's brigade.

By the time that Holmes had arrived, Henry A. Rogers' Battery D, 1st Illinois Light Artillery was in position on the road, on the forward slope of the ridge, on the right of De Golyer's battery, and William S. Williams' 3rd Battery, Ohio Light Artillery was on the left of De Golyer. Fletcher E. Armstrong's 11th Battery, Ohio Light Artillery of Crocker's division came up and took position between De Golyer's battery and Rogers' battery. The Federal artillery was singularly ineffective during the battle that day.

There was stubborn fighting for several hours on the center and right of McPherson's line, and shortly after Holmes' brigade arrived, the enemy began to withdraw. Gregg marched back through Raymond toward Mississippi Springs, camping that night on the Jackson road, about three miles east of Raymond. Gregg was joined that night by William H. T. Walker's brigade, which had just arrived at Jackson from Savannah, Georgia. McPherson's corps bivouacked that night at Raymond, about seven miles east of Sherman's corps at Dillon's plantation. The organization of the troops present at the engagement of Raymond, Mississippi May 12, 1863 was as follows:

SEVENTEENTH CORPS, James B. McPherson

Third Division, John A. Logan
First Brigade, John E. Smith
Second Brigade, Elias S. Dennis
Third Brigade, John D. Stevenson
Artillery, Charles J. Stolbrand
Battery D, 1st Illinois Light Artillery, Henry A. Rogers
8th Battery, Michigan Light Artillery, Samuel De Golyer
3rd Battery, Ohio Light Artillery, William S. Williams

Note. The Battle of Raymond was fought largely by Logan's division, and First Brigade and Third Brigade suffered the heaviest losses.

Seventh Division, Marcellus M. Crocker
First Brigade, John B. Sanborn

Second Brigade, Samuel A. Holmes
Third Brigade, George B. Boomer
Artillery
11th Battery, Ohio Light Artillery, Fletcher E. Armstrong

Note. Seventh Division was held in reserve and was only lightly engaged.

Engagement at Jackson, Mississippi, May 14, 1863. The strong resistance by the Confederate forces at Raymond May 12, 1863 caused Grant to modify his original plan of operations. He decided that before marching against the railroad at Edwards Station, he would attempt to break up the enemy forces at Jackson, which he then believed to be stronger than he had originally thought. Believing that McPherson's corps, which was at Raymond, and nearest to Jackson, might not be sufficiently strong to capture the city, Grant ordered the entire army to move toward Jackson.

The corps were ordered to move at daylight May 13, 1863 as follows: McPherson was to march to Clinton and then toward Jackson; Sherman was to advance to Raymond, then move to Jackson by way of Mississippi Springs; and McClernand was to follow Sherman, with three of his divisions marching by the road on the north side of Fourteen-Mile Creek, and Andrew J. Smith's division going to Old Auburn to escort the trains of the army, which were then coming up. Blair's division of Sherman's corps arrived there with a wagon train on May 14. Thomas E. G. Ransom, with his Second Brigade of John McArthur's Sixth Division, Seventeenth Corps, arrived with a train at Willow Springs May 14, and reached Raymond at 8:00 A.M. May 16. Ewing's brigade of Blair's division was relieved at Milliken's Bend May 14, and it then escorted a wagon train eastward from Grand Gulf. It camped on the night of May 16 five miles west of Old Auburn, then rejoined the other two brigades of Blair's division in front of Vicksburg on May 18.

Conforming to the above orders, McPherson marched out from Raymond at dawn May 13, 1863, with Crocker's division in the lead and Logan's division following, and he occupied Clinton without opposition by mid-afternoon. Crocker then moved out on the Clinton-Jackson road and bivouacked a mile east of Clinton. Logan's division halted in the town. Sherman's corps left Dillon's plantation before daybreak that morning, with Tuttle's division in the lead, and reached Raymond about noon. Sherman then pushed on. Tuttle camped that night near Mississippi Springs, and Steele halted several miles east of Raymond. McClernand moved his corps to Raymond May 13, and the next day he sent Hovey's division to Clinton.

Gregg was at Mississippi Springs during the morning of May 13, 1863, but, believing that Grant's main attack would be made along the road from Clinton to Jackson, he then withdrew with his command to Jackson that evening so that all Confederate forces could be concentrated to oppose the expected attack on the Clinton-Jackson road. Later, when Gregg learned of Sherman's approach, he sent back Albert P. Thompson with a small force, including artillery, to delay Sherman's advance.

On the evening of May 13, 1863, Joseph E. Johnston arrived in Jackson from Tullahoma, Tennessee, where he had been ordered to assume command of the Confederate forces in Mississippi. At the same time, States Rights Gist's brigade, then under the command of Peyton H. Colquitt, arrived from Charleston, South Carolina. John Gregg was then assigned command of the Confederate forces at Jackson, and Robert Farquharson assumed command of Gregg's brigade.

Johnston had decided to withdraw from Jackson early on the morning of May 14, 1863, and he had made preparations to cover the withdrawal and gain time for the removal of stores from the city. At 3:00 that morning, Colquitt, at Gregg's direction, moved out about three miles on the Clinton road, and formed his brigade in line of battle across the road. This was at a point near the intersection of present-day Delaware and Capitol streets. William H. T. Walker's brigade followed Colquitt and halted about a mile to his rear in support. Later Gregg ordered Farquharson to move out of Jackson with his brigade about two and a half miles, then move to the north and northwest and take position on a ridge north of and parallel to Town Creek, where he would threaten McPherson's left flank.

At 5:00 A.M. May 14, 1863, McPherson's Seventeenth Corps moved out of Clinton on the road toward Jackson. Crocker's Seventh Division marched first, with Holmes' Second Brigade of the division in the lead, Sanborn's First Brigade following, and Boomer's Third Brigade in the rear. Logan's division followed Crocker. It had started raining the night before and was still raining that morning, and progress was slow because of the muddy roads.

About two miles east of Clinton, Holmes crossed to the south side of the Southern Railroad of Mississippi, arriving at 9:00 A.M. within a little more than a mile of Colquitt's position. Holmes then deployed his brigade with his left regiment between the railroad and the Clinton-Jackson road and two regiments on the right, south of the road. At that time the enemy artillery opened fire, and the Union batteries replied.

Meantime, Crocker had come up with his other two brigades. He placed Boomer's brigade on the left of the road, and Sanborn formed two of his regiments on the right of Holmes to lengthen the front line, and he placed two regiments in support of Holmes. John A. Logan's Third Division, which was following Crocker, then arrived and was formed in support of Crocker's division. John E. Smith's First Brigade was 400 yards in rear of Boomer, and John D. Stevenson's Third Brigade was on the left of Boomer, with orders to advance and gain the Livingston road. Elias S. Dennis' Second Brigade remained in the rear guarding the trains.

Sherman's Fifteenth Corps on the right also started early on the morning of May 14, 1863. It marched out from Mississippi Springs at 5:00 A.M., with James M. Tuttle's Third Division in the lead. Joseph A. Mower's Second Brigade of the division led the column, with Charles L. Matthies' Third Brigade following, and Ralph P. Buckland's First Brigade bringing up the rear. As noted earlier, Gregg's brigade, which had been in front of Sherman, had withdrawn to Jackson and had thus left the way open for Sherman's advance. About five miles beyond Mississippi Springs, however, Mower found Thompson's command in position beyond Lynch Creek, which was unfordable because of high water. Robert Martin's Georgia Battery, which was with Thompson, opened fire, and at 11:00 A.M. Tuttle prepared to attack. Nelson T. Spoor brought up the 2nd Battery, Iowa Light Artillery and Battery E, 1st Illinois Light Artillery of Tuttle's division; Mower's brigade supported the Iowa battery, and Matthies' brigade was placed in rear of the Illinois battery. Buckland's brigade was held in rear of the other two brigades.

Spoor's guns then opened, and in less than half an hour, Thompson's force was overwhelmed and forced to fall back to a new line in the edge of a woods. Tuttle crossed Lynch Creek on the bridge, which had not been destroyed, and redeployed his division, with Mower's brigade on the left of the road, Matthies' brigade on the right of the road, and Buckland's brigade in reserve, in rear of Matthies. Tuttle then advanced and the enemy fell back to the entrenchments near Jackson. When McPherson's attack developed on the Clinton road, Thompson's force was sent north, leaving only artillery to hold the entrenchments. Those cannons were effective enough to stop attacks by Mower and Matthies, and when Buckland moved up on the right of Matthies, he was forced to fall back under a heavy fire.

By 1:30 P.M. Sherman's advance had been halted, and then William L. McMillen was sent out to the right with his 95th Ohio of Buckland's brigade to examine the ground for a suitable point of attack. When he reached the New Orleans, Jackson, and Great Northern Railroad, he turned northward and advanced along the tracks toward the city, and soon arrived in rear of the Confederate artillery defending the earthworks in front of Tuttle. McMillen then advanced and captured the guns and the men manning them, and Mower and Matthies moved up into the empty works. Tuttle and Steele, whose division was following, halted for the night in the fields southwest of Jackson.

Meantime, the rain had stopped about 11:00 that morning, and McPherson, who had been waiting for it to end, finally ordered Crocker's division to attack on the Jackson-Clinton road. Crocker's line advanced to within about 500 yards of Colquitt's line, then halted to re-form for a final charge. With fixed bayonets, Crocker's men attacked, and after bitter fighting, Colquitt's brigade slowly gave way and fell back behind the earthworks near Jackson. Walker's brigade, which was supporting Colquitt, also retired behind the earthworks. Farquharson, who was on the Confederate right, marched cross-country toward the Canton road north of Jackson.

McPherson halted briefly when the enemy fell back, and then continued on toward Jackson. He deployed his division in front of the enemy defenses northwest of the city, but patrols soon reported that the works had been abandoned, and the enemy was in full retreat. About 3:00 P.M. McPherson ordered Crocker's division to occupy the city.

Stevenson's brigade of Logan's division was ordered to march cross-country to the Canton road and cut off the enemy retreat, but it did not arrive on the road until Gregg's command had passed on its way toward Canton.

The organization of the Union troops present at Jackson, Mississippi May 14, 1863 was as follows:

FIFTEENTH CORPS, William T. Sherman

First Division, Frederick Steele
  First Brigade, Francis H. Manter
  Second Brigade, Charles E. Hovey
  Third Brigade, John M. Thayer
  Artillery
    1st Battery, Iowa Light Artillery, Henry H. Griffiths
    Battery F, 2nd Missouri Light Artillery, Clemens Landgraeber
    4th Battery, Ohio Light Artillery, Louis Hoffmann

Note. First Division was in reserve and was not engaged.

Third Division, James M. Tuttle
  First Brigade, Ralph P. Buckland
  Second Brigade, Joseph A. Mower
  Third Brigade, Charles L. Matthies
  Artillery, Nelson T. Spoor
    2nd Battery, Iowa Light Artillery, Joseph R. Reed
    Battery E, 1st Illinois Light Artillery, Allen C. Waterhouse

SEVENTEENTH CORPS, James B. McPherson

Third Division, John A. Logan
  First Brigade, John E. Smith
  Second Brigade, Elias S. Dennis
  Third Brigade, John D. Stevenson
  Artillery, Charles J. Stolbrand
    Battery D, 1st Illinois Light Artillery, Henry A. Rogers
    Battery G, 2nd Illinois Light Artillery, Frederick Sparrestrom
    Battery L, 2nd Illinois Light Artillery, William H. Bolton
    8th Battery, Michigan Light Artillery, Samuel De Golyer
    3rd Battery, Ohio Light Artillery, William S. Williams

Note 1. Third Division was in reserve and was not engaged.

Note 2. Mortimer D. Leggett returned from leave on the morning of May 16, 1863, the day of the Battle of Champion Hill, and resumed command of Second Brigade, relieving Dennis.

Seventh Division, Marcellus M. Crocker
  First Brigade, John B. Sanborn
  Second Brigade, Samuel A. Holmes
  Third Brigade, George B. Boomer
  Artillery, Frank C. Sands
    Battery M, 1st Missouri Light Artillery, Junius W. MacMurray
    11th Battery, Ohio Light Artillery, Fletcher E. Armstrong
    6th Battery, Wisconsin Light Artillery, Henry Dillon
    12th Battery, Wisconsin Light Artillery, William Zickerick

Battle of Champion Hill, Mississippi, May 16, 1863. For some time after Grant's army had crossed the Mississippi River, Pemberton was uncertain about its destination. On May 11, 1863, he decided that Grant's immediate objective was the Big Black River Bridge on the Jackson road, and the next day he ordered Carter L. Stevenson's division from south of Vicksburg to join William W. Loring's and Bowen's divisions at the bridge. Pemberton moved his headquarters to Bovina, west of the Big Black, on the evening of May 12. The next day, his three divisions, under the general direction of Loring, moved east to Edwards Station, then took position to the south of the Jackson road, where they could cover all approaches to the bridge from the south and east. John S. Bowen's division was on the right, Loring's division was in the center, and Stevenson's division was on the left.

On the morning of May 14, 1863, Pemberton received a dispatch from Joseph E. Johnston at Jackson (written the night before), ordering him to attack what the latter believed to be four divisions of Grant's army that were at Clinton. Actually, there were only two divisions at Clinton; the other two were at Mississippi Springs.

On May 14, 1863, Grant received a copy of this order, and at 4:00 P.M., after Johnston's evacuation of Jackson, he ordered McPherson to move back with his corps to Bolton, twenty miles west of Jackson. This was done to prevent Johnston from joining Pemberton's army and moving with it into Vicks-

burg before Grant could arrive. Grant also directed McClernand to move immediately with his entire force to Bolton by the most direct roads. In a further order, he directed Blair to move with his division and the trains from Old Auburn to Bolton.

On the evening of May 14, 1863, Grant's forces were disposed as follows: McClernand's Thirteenth Corps was somewhat scattered, with Eugene A. Carr's Fourteenth Division and Peter J. Osterhaus' Ninth Division at Raymond, Alvin P. Hovey's Twelfth Division at Clinton, and Andrew J. Smith's Tenth Division between Old Auburn and Raymond with the trains. Sherman was at Jackson with two divisions of Fifteenth Corps, and McPherson was also at Jackson with two divisions of Seventeenth Corps. Frank P. Blair's Second Division of Fifteenth Corps was at Old Auburn, and Thomas E. G. Ransom's Second Brigade of John McArthur's Sixth Division, Seventeenth Corps was with a supply train at Willow Springs.

On May 15, 1863, the divisions of McClernand's Thirteenth Corps moved toward Bolton as follows: Hovey's division marched from its camp of the night before about four miles southwest of Clinton toward Bolton; Osterhaus' division and Carr's division moved out on the road that ran to the northwest from Raymond; and Andrew J. Smith's division marched from Auburn to Raymond. Blair's division of Sherman's corps followed Andrew J. Smith from Old Auburn to Raymond. Osterhaus' division arrived at Bolton at 8:00 A.M., but when McClernand learned that Hovey's division had been ordered to halt there, he ordered Osterhaus to march back to the Middle Road, about three miles south of Bolton, and then move west on that road. A short distance west of the road junction, Osterhaus bivouacked in line of battle. Carr's division had spent the night of May 14, 1863 at Forest Hill Church, which was beyond Mississippi Springs and about six miles from Jackson. The next morning it marched back through Raymond and encamped in rear of Osterhaus' division near the junction of the Bolton road and the Middle Road. Early on the morning of May 15, Andrew J. Smith's division of McClernand's corps and Blair's division of Sherman's corps marched from near New Auburn, with the wagon train, toward Raymond. Blair halted for the night near Raymond, but Smith moved on beyond Blair and camped at the point where the

Edwards Station road branched off from the Raymond-Bolton road.

McPherson, with John A. Logan's Third Division, left Jackson at 7:00 A.M. May 15, 1863 on the road to Clinton, and Marcellus M. Crocker's Seventh Division followed. Logan reached Bolton a little after 4:00 P.M. and formed in line of battle on the right of Hovey's division. George B. Boomer's Third Brigade and John B. Sanborn's First Brigade of Crocker's division halted on the road about three miles east of Bolton, and Samuel A. Holmes' Second Brigade camped near Clinton.

Sherman remained with his two divisions in Jackson to complete the destruction of roads, bridges, all railroad facilities, military supplies, and all factories producing military supplies.

Grant, who had ridden out from Jackson to Clinton that day, issued orders from his headquarters there for McClernand to advance toward Edwards Station the next morning.

Meantime, Pemberton had decided that to move his army farther from Vicksburg and attack a superior force, as ordered by Johnston May 13, 1863, was too hazardous. Instead, he issued orders for the army to move south on May 15 to the Dillon plantation and there cut Grant's supply line, which in fact had been abandoned some time before.

Pemberton's march was delayed until 1:00 P.M., and then, a short time after starting, the leading troops found Baker's Creek too deep to ford. Pemberton waited until 4:00 P.M. for the water to fall and then, when the creek was still unfordable, he marched his three divisions northward along the west side of Baker's Creek, crossed the creek at the Jackson road bridge, and marched east on the Jackson road to a place called the Crossroads. At that point the Jackson road turned to the left and ran northward over Champion Hill, the Middle Road came into the Jackson road from the east, and a plantation road (also called the Ratliff road) ran off to the southwest to the Ratliff house.

When the head of Pemberton's column arrived at the Crossroads, Loring's division turned to the right and marched out on the plantation road. It continued on that road, past the Ratliff house, to the Raymond road, which the plantation road joined a short distance beyond the Ratliff house. Loring then marched east on that road. A little before dark, Wirt Adams, whose cavalry was out in front, reported

that a strong Federal force was ahead near the Bolton road. Loring then halted his division for the night at Mrs. Ellison's house, which was about three-fourths of a mile east of Ratliff's. Bowen's division, which was following Loring, continued its march until about 10:00 P.M., and it then halted for the night on the plantation road north of the Ratliff house. Stevenson's division, which brought up the rear of Pemberton's column, arrived near Bowen's position about 3:00 A.M. May 16, 1863.

At 5:00 A.M. May 16, 1863, Grant, who had spent the night at Clinton, learned from some former railroad employees, who had observed Pemberton's movements the night before, that the enemy was still moving east. Grant then issued orders for the march of the army that day. He directed Sherman to move his divisions from Jackson to Bolton, and Frederick Steele's First Division left Jackson at 10:00 A.M and marched toward Bolton. James M. Tuttle's Third Division followed about noon. Grant also ordered Andrew J. Smith and Blair to march toward Edwards Station by way of the Raymond road, and at the same time he placed Blair's division temporarily under McClernand's orders. Osterhaus' and Carr's divisions of McClernand's corps were to advance toward Edwards Station on the Middle Road, and Hovey's division was to march toward the same place on the Jackson road. McPherson was to follow Hovey on the Jackson road. With the enemy not far ahead, all division commanders were instructed to advance with caution.

Andrew J. Smith, with Stephen G. Burbridge's First Brigade in the lead, began his march at daylight May 16, and Blair followed close behind. Osterhaus and Carr moved out on the Middle Road at 6:00 A.M., with Osterhaus' division in the lead. Hovey's division left Bolton at 6:00 A.M. and moved westward on the Jackson road. McPherson followed Hovey, with Logan's division in the lead.

As Andrew J. Smith advanced, a detachment of the 4th Indiana Cavalry encountered a small cavalry force near the Gillespie plantation, and then Smith ordered Burbridge to deploy his brigade and continue the march. Although there was brisk fighting along the Raymond road for about an hour and a half. Smith did not attempt a serious attack until William J. Landram's Second Brigade had arrived at the front.

A short time before Smith became engaged on the Raymond road, Pemberton received Johnston's order dated 8:30 A.M. May 15, 1863 directing him to move toward Clinton and join forces with Johnston north of the Southern Mississippi Railroad. Pemberton had just begun to reverse his column for the march north when Loring, then at Mrs. Ellison's, learned about the action on the Raymond road to the southeast with Smith's advance troops. Loring then suggested that Pemberton form his troops in line of battle, and Pemberton concurred. Loring's division was withdrawn to a ridge about three-fourths of a mile west of Mrs. Ellison's, where it was deployed on a line overlooking the valley of Jackson Creek. Abraham Buford's brigade was on the left of the division, Winfield S. Featherston's brigade was in the center, and Lloyd Tilghman's brigade was on the right, extending down into the valley. Martin E. Green's brigade of Bowen's division was massed near the Ratliff house, and Francis M. Cockrell's brigade was formed on the left of Green. On the left, Carter L. Stevenson directed Alexander W. Reynolds to form his brigade so as to cover the Crossroads, then sent the army trains to Brownsville. The trains had cleared the Jackson road by 9:30 A.M., and then Reynolds' brigade followed the trains on the road to Brownsville. After Reynolds' departure, Stephen D. Lee's brigade of Stevenson's division moved to the left and took position at the Crossroads. To the right of Lee's brigade, along the plantation road, were Alfred Cumming's brigade and then Seth M. Barton's brigade, the latter being the right brigade of the division.

For a time, the advance of Osterhaus' and Carr's divisions on the Middle Road was made without opposition, but about two miles west of Chapel Hill Church, the 3rd Illinois Cavalry, which was moving in front of the column, was fired upon by an enemy force posted in a woods along the road. Osterhaus ordered Theophilus T. Garrard's First Brigade forward and directed Lindsey to form his brigade in line of battle across the road. Carr halted his division in rear of Lindsey, placing Benton's brigade on the right of the road and Michael K. Lawler's Second Brigade on the left. Osterhaus' cavalry, followed by Garrard's infantry, then moved on until it was stopped by Alexander W. Reynolds' brigade, which was about one-third of a mile east of the Crossroads. Osterhaus attempted to advance with Garrard's brigade and Charles H. Lanphere's 7th Battery, Michigan Light Artillery, but without success.

Loring, who was under considerable pressure on the Raymond road, decided to retire about one-half mile to a strong position on a ridge near the Coker house, which was not far from the junction of the plantation road and the Raymond road.

Andrew J. Smith then moved up to Jackson Creek and halted until the bridge, which had been destroyed, was rebuilt. Finally, at 11:00 A.M. Burbridge crossed the creek and moved up onto the ridge that had just been vacated by Loring. William J. Landram's Second Brigade and Blair's division of Fifteenth Corps were ordered up in preparation for an attack.

During the morning, Pemberton had been expecting the main Federal attack to be made by Andrew J. Smith and Blair on the Raymond road, and Osterhaus and Carr on the Middle Road, but McClernand, acting on orders, was proceeding with caution. In response to a request from McClernand for instructions, Grant, who had arrived on the field from Clinton during the morning, sent an order at 12:35 P.M. directing him to attack if he thought there was a suitable opportunity. McClernand did not receive this order until 2:00 P.M., and, because of his instructions to move cautiously, his four divisions on the Middle and Raymond roads did not attack until later in the afternoon.

Strangely, it was not until 9:00 A.M. that Lee, at the Crossroads, learned of the approach of Hovey's division from Bolton on the Jackson road. To meet this threat, Lee moved his brigade to the left and occupied the summit of Champion Hill, about 400 yards north of the Crossroads. When Carter L. Stevenson became aware of the large Federal force that was assembling on the left flank of the Confederate line, he formed his division in line of battle facing to the northeast. Lee's brigade moved farther to the left along a ridge, and three regiments of Alfred Cumming's brigade moved up to occupy the crest of Champion Hill. Their line formed a salient atop the hill, with the faces at nearly a right angle to one another.

The leading troops of Hovey's division arrived at the Champion house about 9:45 A.M., and from there they could see Carter L. Stevenson's troops in line across the top of Champion Hill, about one-half mile to the southwest. George F. McGinnis, whose First Brigade was leading Hovey's division, halted and deployed his brigade in two lines on both sides of the Champion house, with one regiment of the first line on the left of the Jackson road, and two regiments on the right of the road. Two regiments were on the second line. When James R. Slack arrived, he moved his Second Brigade into a field on the left of McGinnis, southwest of the Champion house. George W. Schofield's Battery A, 1st Missouri Light Artillery was placed in rear of the infantry.

Logan arrived at the Champion house at 10:00 A.M., and was ordered by Grant to move his division into a field on the right of McGinnis' brigade. Logan then deployed his division on a line that was at nearly a right angle to McGinnis' line. Mortimer D. Leggett's Second Brigade was on the right of McGinnis, and John E. Smith's First Brigade was on the right and rear of Leggett. Samuel De Golyer's 8th Battery, Michigan Light Artillery was posted in rear of Leggett's line, and John D. Stevenson's brigade was placed in reserve in rear of De Golyer's battery. William S. Williams' 3rd Battery, Ohio Light Artillery was posted on high ground in rear of Logan's division.

Grant assigned to McPherson the general direction of the attack against the left of Pemberton's line, and at 10:30 Hovey and Logan moved out toward the positions held by Lee's and Cumming's brigades of Carter L. Stevenson's division. Logan was soon stopped by a heavy enemy fire, and he ordered John D. Stevenson to bring up his brigade and form on the right of John E. Smith's brigade and attempt to turn Lee's left flank. Seth M. Barton's brigade, which was on the right of Carter L. Stevenson's line, was then hurried cross-country to the left of Lee's brigade to check the advance of John D. Stevenson.

By 11:30 A.M., both Hovey and Logan had driven in the enemy outposts and had arrived near Carter L. Stevenson's main line. Then McPherson ordered both divisions to attack. Hovey's division approached in the direction of the salient of Cumming's brigade. Protected by the numerous ravines on the hill as it advanced, McGinnis' brigade soon came up abreast of Logan's division on its right, finally reaching a position about seventy-five yards from the summit. Then, with bayonets fixed, McGinnis' men struck the west face of the salient

and, after a brief but desperate struggle, drove Cumming's regiments from the hill.

The right of Lee's brigade, which had been holding out against the attacks of Leggett and John E. Smith, then came under attack from Hovey's brigades, and Lee was forced to withdraw his brigade about 500 yards to a new position covering the Jackson road.

John D. Stevenson's brigade, which had been moving up to the Federal right, then advanced from the northwest against Barton's brigade, and it, in turn, was driven back. John D. Stevenson followed and drove across the Jackson road; by so doing he cut off Barton's brigade from the rest of the army, and it escaped westward across the Baker's Creek Bridge. Upon reaching the far side of the creek, Barton rallied his command and took position to cover the bridge. Carter L. Stevenson's new line extended from the Crossroads on the right to the Baker's Creek Bridge on the left.

When John D. Stevenson's brigade reached the Jackson road east of Baker's Creek, it effectively blocked this important escape route to Vicksburg for Pemberton's army.

Slack, whose brigade was advancing on the left of McGinnis, then struck the 56th and 57th Georgia regiments of Cumming's brigade, which were guarding the Crossroads, and drove them back along the plantation road, and then Carter L. Stevenson's entire original line was gone.

Earlier, when Barton's brigade was in trouble, Pemberton had ordered Cockrell's brigade of Bowen's division to go to its aid, but while on the way to the left, Cockrell was ordered to the Crossroads, which was then threatened by Slack. Green's brigade, accompanied by Bowen, moved up and formed on the right of Cockrell. At 2:30 P.M. Bowen's two brigades advanced against the victorious brigades of Slack and McGinnis. Slack's men resisted stubbornly for some time, but they were finally driven back from the Crossroads, so recently gained, by Green's brigade, and Cockrell's brigade also drove McGinnis' brigade from Champion Hill. In less than an hour, Bowen had driven Hovey's division back about three-fourths of a mile and recaptured both the Crossroads and Champion Hill.

A short time before the defeat of Hovey's division, the advance troops of Crocker's division arrived near the Champion house. To provide support for the attacks by Leggett and John E. Smith on Lee's Confederate brigade, McPherson ordered Crocker to deploy Sanborn's brigade in a field to the right of De Golyer's battery, which was in rear of Leggett's line. Boomer formed his brigade in line of battle south of the Champion house, then moved it up with the intention of forming it on the left of Leggett. At about that time, however, Hovey's division was under heavy attack, and Boomer was ordered to help Hovey. He then faced his brigade about and marched up Champion Hill. As Boomer climbed the slope, McGinnis' broken brigade appeared above, retreating across the crest of the hill, closely followed by Cockrell's advancing brigade. Quickly, Boomer formed his men in line of battle, and in a short time they were able to check Cockrell's brigade.

Meantime, Hovey had succeeded in massing sixteen guns belonging to Battery A, 1st Missouri Light Artillery and the 16th Battery, Ohio Light Artillery of his division, and the 6th Battery, Wisconsin Light Artillery of Crocker's division in a field southeast of the Champion house, and from there the fire of these guns enfiladed the line of Green's advance.

Samuel A. Holmes' Second Brigade of Crocker's division, which had spent the night near Clinton and had marched that morning toward Edwards Station, arrived on the field during Bowen's attack. Holmes had with him only two of his regiments (the third was with the trains), and these he formed on the left of Boomer's line, preventing Green from turning Boomer's left flank.

Sanborn, commanding the First Brigade of Crocker's division, placed the 59th Indiana on the left of De Golyer's battery and the 4th Minnesota on the right of the battery, and sent the 48th Indiana and the 18th Wisconsin to the right of Boomer, on the northwestern slope of Champion Hill.

Strong resistance by the troops of Holmes, Boomer, and Sanborn, aided by the fire of Hovey's sixteen guns, finally succeeded in bringing Bowen's advance to a halt.

Meantime, Hovey's defeated troops had been reformed, and at about this time they were brought back and joined in the action. Then Logan's troops, which were on the right of Hovey, began to advance on the front of Cumming's and Lee's brigades, which were on the left of Bowen.

While the fighting was in progress on the Federal right, McClernand had made some changes in the disposition of his troops on the Federal left and center. Blair had deployed Giles A. Smith's First Brigade on the left of Osterhaus' division, and had ordered his Second Brigade, under T. Kilby Smith, to advance slowly in rear of Andrew J. Smith's division. Then, at 2:00 P.M., McClernand received Grant's dispatch of 12:35 directing him to attack if the opportunity arose. McClernand ordered Andrew J. Smith and Osterhaus to attack and Blair and Carr to support them.

Osterhaus then ordered Garrard to push ahead on the Middle Road. Reinforced by the 42nd Ohio of Lindsey's brigade, Garrard drove back a small Confederate force that was holding the road and advanced to within 600 yards of the Crossroads. Osterhaus then brought up the rest of Lindsey's brigade to form on the left of Garrard.

The approach of Osterhaus' troops on the Middle Road was reported to Bowen at about 4:00 P.M., and he realized that if Osterhaus reached the Crossroads before he could withdraw his troops beyond that point, his division might be destroyed. Accordingly, he hastened his retreat and called for help.

When Bowen's division left its position on the plantation road to aid Carter L. Stevenson, Loring's troops moved to the left to cover the line. Buford's brigade occupied the ground vacated by Bowen; Featherston also moved to the left to hold that part of the line formerly held by Buford; and Tilghman's brigade took position on both sides of the Raymond road, about one-third of a mile west of the Coker house.

When conditions on the Confederate left became critical, Pemberton ordered Loring to move his division up to support Carter L. Stevenson and Bowen. Loring, however, was confronted by McClernand's Thirteenth Corps, and he delayed in obeying Pemberton's order. Finally, he sent Buford's brigade northward on the plantation road. Then a part of the brigade was sent to aid Green, who was having difficulty in holding the Crossroads, and the rest of the brigade took position north of the Crossroads.

By that time, however, it was too late. Bowen's men were being forced to fall back by Federal troops converging on the Crossroads, and they were also driven from the crest of Champion Hill. Bowen then ordered a retreat, and his troops fell back in considerable confusion before the advance of Hovey and Crocker, who reached and held the Crossroads. Bowen finally succeeded in re-forming his troops behind Buford's brigade, which was then in position along a ridge several hundred yards south of the Crossroads. At this juncture, Pemberton issued the orders for his army to retire across Baker's Creek, and soon all Confederate forces were in full retreat.

A part of Carr's division advanced on the Federal right and crossed Baker's Creek at the bridge on the Jackson road. Carr then moved south on the west side of the creek to block the crossing on the Raymond road. Loring was thus cut off from the rest of the army, and he marched away to the south and did not again rejoin Pemberton at Vicksburg. Carter L. Stevenson and John S. Bowen succeeded in withdrawing their divisions through Edwards Station and into the defenses at the crossing of the Big Black River.

The organization of Grant's forces at the Battle of Champion Hill May 16, 1863 was as follows:

THIRTEENTH CORPS, John A. McClernand

Ninth Division, Peter J. Osterhaus
    First Brigade, Theophilus T. Garrard
    Second Brigade, Daniel W. Lindsey
    Artillery
        7th Battery, Michigan Light Artillery, Charles H. Lanphere
        1st Battery, Wisconsin Light Artillery, Jacob T. Foster

Tenth Division, Andrew J. Smith
    First Brigade, Stephen G. Burbridge
    Second Brigade, William J. Landram
    Artillery
        Chicago Mercantile Battery, Illinois Light Artillery, Patrick H. White
        7th Battery, Ohio Light Artillery, Ambrose A. Blount

Twelfth Division, Alvin P. Hovey
    First Brigade, George F. McGinnis
    Second Brigade, James R. Slack
    Artillery
        2nd Battery, Ohio Light Artillery, Augustus Beach
        16th Battery, Ohio Light Artillery, James A. Mitchell, killed
            Russell P. Twist

Battery A, 1st Missouri Light Artillery, George W. Schofield

Fourteenth Division, Eugene A. Carr
    First Brigade, William P. Benton
    Second Brigade, Michael K. Lawler
    Artillery
        Battery A, 2nd Illinois Light Artillery, Frank B. Fenton
        1st Battery, Indiana Light Artillery, Martin Klauss

FIFTEENTH CORPS, William T. Sherman

Second Division, Frank P. Blair, Jr.
    First Brigade, Giles A. Smith
    Second Brigade, T. Kilby Smith
    Third Brigade, Hugh Ewing
    Artillery
        Battery A, 1st Illinois Light Artillery, Peter P. Wood
        Battery B, 1st Illinois Light Artillery, Samuel E. Barrett

Note 1. Blair's division was near the field of battle but was not engaged. It was attached to McClernand's Thirteenth Corps at Champion Hill.

Note 2. Frederick Steele's First Division and James M. Tuttle's Third Division were not present at the Battle of Champion Hill. They marched from Jackson to Bolton May 16, 1863, and then on to Bridgeport on the Big Black River the next morning.

SEVENTEENTH CORPS, James B. McPherson

Third Division, John A. Logan
    First Brigade, John E. Smith
    Second Brigade, Mortimer D. Leggett
    Third Brigade, John D. Stevenson
    Artillery, Charles J. Stolbrand
        Battery D, 1st Illinois Light Artillery, Henry A. Rogers
        Battery L, 2nd Illinois Light Artillery, William H. Bolton
        8th Battery, Michigan Light Artillery, Samuel De Golyer
        3rd Battery, Ohio Light Artillery, William S. Williams

Seventh Division, Marcellus M. Crocker
    First Brigade, John B. Sanborn
    Second Brigade, Samuel A. Holmes
    Third Brigade, George B. Boomer
    Artillery, Frank C. Sands
        Battery M, 1st Missouri Light Artillery, Junius W. MacMurray

11th Battery, Ohio Light Artillery, Fletcher E. Armstrong

6th Battery, Wisconsin Light Artillery, Henry Dillon

12th Battery, Wisconsin Light Artillery, William Zickerick

Note. Thomas E. G. Ransom's Second Brigade of John McArthur's Sixth Division, Seventeenth Corps was at Raymond early on the morning of May 16, 1863 but did not arrive on the battlefield until after the fighting had ended.

Engagement at the Big Black River Bridge, Mississippi, May 17, 1863. When Pemberton's army withdrew after the Battle of Champion Hill, Carr's division of McClernand's Thirteenth Corps followed as far as Edwards Station, where it arrived at 8:00 P.M. and halted for the night. Most of the rest of Grant's army bivouacked between the battlefield and Edwards Station. Holmes' brigade of Quinby's Seventh Division of McPherson's Seventeenth Corps remained at the Crossroads watching the area, and Hovey's division of McClernand's corps remained at Champion Hill to bury the dead and care for the wounded. Quinby returned from sick leave May 16, 1863 and resumed command of his Seventh Division the next morning, relieving Crocker.

Sherman, with Frederick Steele's First Division and James M. Tuttle's Third Division of his Fifteenth Corps, spent the night at Bolton after marching that day from Jackson. Sherman's other division, under Blair, with the pontoon bridge of the army, camped that night near the Coker house.

When Pemberton reached the Big Black River on the evening of May 16, 1863, he decided to hold a fortified bridgehead east of the river to secure the crossing until Loring's division arrived. He then ordered John C. Vaughn to put his brigade on a part of the line of fortifications erected in front of the bridge that extended to the north of the railroad for about 500 yards. Then when Bowen's division arrived, he placed Green's brigade on the left of the line, between Vaughn's brigade and the river, and Cockrell's brigade on the right of Vaughn, south of the railroad. Pemberton also placed Bowen in command of the bridgehead and directed him to hold the position until Loring arrived. Loring, however, as has already been noted, was at that time marching away to the southeast, and he did not again join the army at Vicksburg.

About 1,000 yards north of the railroad, the Big Black River flowed westward to a line of bluffs, and there it turned to the south and ran along the foot of the bluffs toward the Mississippi River. The ground to the south and east side of the river in that area was low bottom land that had been cleared and was under cultivation. A bayou, which began about three-fourths of a mile east of the river from the bridge, flowed irregularly across this low ground and emptied into the Big Black about 1,000 yards north of the bridge. The bayou was filled with trees, which the enemy cut to form an abatis, and at the time of the battle the water was only a foot or two deep.

The Confederate breastworks extended along the west bank of this bayou, and they were constructed of cotton bales that had been covered with earth. These works were about one mile in length, and both ends were near the Big Black River.

Carr's division resumed the pursuit of Pemberton by 5:00 the next morning, May 17, 1863, and was closely followed by Osterhaus' division. Andrew J. Smith's division came next, and it was followed by Blair's division. Having only a short distance to travel, Carr arrived in front of the enemy works at an early hour, with William P. Benton's First Brigade in the lead. Carr posted the 33rd Illinois of Benton's brigade, which was leading the brigade, in a field to the north of the Jackson road; Martin Klauss' 1st Battery, Indiana Light Artillery on the road; and the 99th Illinois, 8th Indiana, and 18th Indiana of Benton's brigade north of the road in support of the battery.

Michael K. Lawler first formed his Second Brigade about 100 yards in rear of Benton, then moved up and to the right of Benton, with his right near the river.

When Osterhaus arrived with his division, he formed Daniel W. Lindsey's First Brigade in line of battle astride the Jackson road about one-half mile from the enemy works. Lindsey advanced about 300 yards, and Benton moved up on his right. Garrard, who was following Lindsey, then sent the 49th and 69th Indiana regiments of his brigade to support Lawler on the left, and the 7th Kentucky and 118th Illinois to the left of Lindsey.

Lawler advanced his brigade through a woods on his front to its western edge, where he was less than 400 yards from the enemy works. These woods did not extend all the way to the river, and there was a strip of open ground along the river. Lawler then moved his 11th Wisconsin, 21st Iowa, and 23rd Iowa forward and to the right from the edge of the woods to the shelter of a long depression formed by an old channel of the river that ran roughly parallel to the river and was close to the enemy works. There he re-formed his line facing to the southwest. Lawler also placed a section of Frank B. Fenton's Battery A, 2nd Illinois Light Artillery in the open space near the river, and moved the 22nd Iowa into the woods on the left to support the battery.

Meantime, Burbridge, accompanied by Andrew J. Smith, arrived at McClernand's line and formed his brigade on the left of the 7th Kentucky and 118th Illinois of Garrard's brigade, south of the railroad.

Patrick H. White's Chicago Mercantile Battery, Illinois Light Artillery was placed on the left of the 1st Battery, Indiana Light Artillery, between the Jackson road and the railroad; Jacob T. Foster's 1st Battery, Wisconsin Light Artillery was on the left of the Chicago Mercantile Battery, just to the south of the railroad; and Charles H. Lanphere's 7th Battery, Michigan Light Artillery was on the left of the Wisconsin battery. When posted, all batteries began firing to soften up the enemy works for an attack. Osterhaus was wounded during the artillery exchange, and Albert L. Lee was placed in temporary command of his division.

When Burbridge's brigade was in position, the 22nd Iowa rejoined Lawler's other three regiments in the depression, and the 49th and 69th Indiana regiments of Garrard's brigade took the place of the 22nd Iowa. These two regiments then formed on the left of Lawler, facing west.

With bayonets fixed, Lawler's regiments charged up out of the depression where they had been concealed, and they were supported on the left by the 69th and 49th Indiana regiments. The 33rd and 99th Illinois of Benton's brigade also charged on the left of the 49th Indiana. Lawler's men moved obliquely across the face of the enemy breastworks, past Green's brigade, and drove Vaughn's brigade in complete disorder toward the bridges to their rear.

With the departure of Vaughn's brigade, Cockrell's troops south of the railroad also broke and fled across the bridges. Then Burbridge's brigade and Albert L. Lee's division joined in the attack.

At about this time, Stephen D. Lee's and William E. Baldwin's brigades arrived from Bovina and formed on the bluffs on the west bank of the river, north of the railroad. They held this position until Pemberton's fleeing soldiers had crossed the Big Black and the bridges had been burned. Pemberton then ordered his army to retire within the defenses of Vicksburg.

The battle was ended before noon May 17, 1863, and McClernand's corps spent the rest of the day building bridges over the Big Black River and preparing for a continuation of the advance. By 8:00 A.M. May 18, three bridges had been completed, and the troops were crossing the river on their way toward Vicksburg.

McPherson's Seventeenth Corps left its bivouac at Baker's Creek at 10:00 A.M. May 17, 1863 and marched to Amsterdam, on the Big Black River, about three miles to the right of McClernand's position in front of Pemberton's bridgehead. McPherson arrived there about 2:00 P.M. and began building bridges in preparation for crossing the river.

Sherman's Fifteenth Corps had also advanced during May 17, 1863 in an attempt to turn the left flank of Pemberton's line at the Big Black River Bridge. During the night before, Sherman, then at Bolton with the divisions of Steele and Tuttle, had received orders to march with his command to Bridgeport, on the Big Black River, about seven miles above the railroad bridge. Sherman was to cross the river there and march westward toward Vicksburg. Blair's division of Sherman's corps, which had been serving with McClernand, followed Andrew J. Smith's division to Edwards Station on the morning of May 17, but upon arriving there, it was ordered on to Bridgeport with the pontoon bridge to rejoin Fifteenth Corps.

Sherman, with his two divisions, left Bolton at 4:30 A.M. May 17, 1863, with Steele in the lead and Tuttle close behind. Marching by a road north of Baker's Creek, the head of Steele's column arrived on the river at Bridgeport about noon. Blair had already arrived there shortly after 10:00 A.M. and had found a small enemy force guarding the crossing. After a few shells from Peter P. Wood's Battery A, 1st Illinois Light Artillery had forced their surrender, Blair's men began laying the pontoon bridge. When it was completed, Blair's division crossed the river before dark and bivouacked that night about two miles out to the west.

Steele followed Blair across, and the last of his troops were over by midnight. Steele camped that night near Blair. Tuttle halted on the east bank of the river that night, and at dawn May 18, 1863 started across the bridge, joining the rest of the corps west of the river.

The Federal forces engaged at the Big Black River Bridge May 17, 1863 belonged to McClernand's Thirteenth Corps, and were organized as follows:

THIRTEENTH CORPS, John A. McClernand

Ninth Division, Peter J. Osterhaus, wounded
    Albert L. Lee
    First Brigade, Theophilus T. Garrard
    Second Brigade, Daniel W. Lindsey
    Artillery
        7th Battery, Michigan Light Artillery, Charles H. Lanphere
        1st Battery, Wisconsin Light Artillery, Jacob T. Foster

Tenth Division, Andrew J. Smith
    First Brigade, Stephen G. Burbridge
    Chicago Mercantile Battery, Illinois Light Artillery, Patrick H. White

Fourteenth Division, Eugene A. Carr
    First Brigade, William P. Benton
    Second Brigade, Michael K. Lawler
    Artillery
        Battery A, 2nd Illinois Light Artillery, Frank B. Fenton
        1st Battery, Indiana Light Artillery, Martin Klauss

Investment of Vicksburg, Mississippi

After his defeat at Big Black River Bridge May 17, 1863, Pemberton retired with his army into the previously prepared fortifications covering Vicksburg. At daylight May 18, the divisions of Blair and Steele of Sherman's Fifteenth Corps, which had crossed the Big Black River at Bridgeport the day before, started toward Vicksburg on the Bridgeport road, with Blair's division in the lead and Steele's division following. After Tuttle's division had crossed the Big Black River, it followed the other two divisions.

By about 10:00 A.M. May 18, 1863, the head of Blair's column had marched nine miles and had reached the junction of the Bridgeport road and the Benton road (present-day Oak Ridge Road), which ran out to the northeast to Benton, Mississippi, a town east of Yazoo City. Blair halted there and waited for Steele and Tuttle to come up.

Early in the afternoon, Blair advanced to the Jackson road, and then on that road to a point where the Graveyard Road (so-named because it entered Vicksburg near the cemetery) branched off to the right. This was about two miles from the enemy defenses and four miles from Vicksburg.

Grant's first priority after arriving near Vicksburg was to establish a base on the Yazoo River from which the army could be supplied. He assigned Sherman to take position on the right of the army, and Blair's division was sent down the Graveyard Road to the right toward the Mississippi River to gain control of the area along the Yazoo. McClernand's corps was to move up on the left of the army, and McPherson's corps was to occupy the center of the line.

The rest of Sherman's corps followed Blair along the Graveyard Road, and by 8:00 A.M. May 19, 1863, Sherman had his corps in position about 400 yards from the enemy works along a ridge beyond Fort Hill that extended from the Mississippi River to the Graveyard Road. Steele's division was on the right, next to the river; Blair's division was on the left; and Tuttle's division was in reserve.

McPherson's Seventeenth Corps, which had been joined by Thomas E. G. Ransom's Second Brigade of John McArthur's Sixth Division, Seventeenth Corps on the evening of May 16, 1863 at Champion Hill, crossed the Big Black River at Amsterdam on the morning of May 18. It then marched by a plantation road to the northwest to the Bridgeport road, which it joined about three miles from the river. Ransom's brigade was in the lead, and it was followed by Logan's division and then Isaac F. Quinby's division. McPherson waited for Sherman's corps to pass and then moved onto the Bridgeport road and followed Sherman toward Vicksburg. The head of Ransom's brigade reached the point where the Graveyard Road branched off from the Jackson road about dark, and then Ransom took position on the left of Sherman's troops. Logan and Quinby camped on the road where there was water.

A short time before noon May 19, 1863, Logan and Quinby came up. Logan's division was placed on the left of Ransom, with Leggett's brigade in reserve, and Boomer's brigade of Quinby's division was placed on the left of Logan. Only Boomer's brigade of Quinby's division had arrived at the time, but the other two brigades came up from the Big Black River on May 21; Sanborn's brigade was placed on the left of Boomer, and Holmes' brigade was placed in reserve. During the morning of May 19, Ransom was ordered to move his brigade to the southwest from the Jackson road, and by 1:00 P.M. he had arrived on a ridge overlooking the North Fork of Glass Bayou, and only about 450 yards from the enemy works across the bayou.

On the morning of May 18, 1863, McClernand's Thirteenth Corps crossed the river near the Jackson road and the railroad bridge, and marched on the Jackson road toward Vicksburg, which was twelve miles distant. Andrew J. Smith's division was in the lead, and it was followed by Osterhaus' division and then Carr's division. Hovey's division was left for a time at Edwards Station and at the Big Black River.

On May 18, 1863, after Thirteenth Corps had crossed the river, Osterhaus, who had been wounded during the battle the day before, resumed command of Ninth Division. Albert L. Lee, who had commanded the division temporarily, was assigned command of First Brigade, Ninth Division during the absence of Theophilus T. Garrard, who had been ordered to report to Benjamin M. Prentiss at Helena, Arkansas.

At Mount Alban, about midway between the Big Black River and Vicksburg, McClernand's column turned off to the left and crossed over on a plantation road to the Baldwin's Ferry road. It turned to the right onto that road and about sunset arrived at Four-Mile Creek, four miles from Vicksburg. At 6:30 A.M. May 19, 1863, Thirteenth Corps arrived on a hill overlooking Two-Mile Creek, two miles from Vicksburg. Then McClernand placed Andrew J. Smith's division on the right of the Baldwin's Ferry road, Osterhaus' division on the left of the road, and Benton's brigade of Carr's division in reserve at the foot of the hill. The other brigades of

Carr's division and Hovey's division had not yet arrived from the Big Black River.

When Grant's troops were in position in front of the enemy defenses May 19, 1863, the investment of Vicksburg was not complete because there was a gap of about four miles between the left of McClernand's corps and the Mississippi River below the town.

Before proceeding further with a description of operations in front of Vicksburg, it is necessary to describe briefly the country to the east of the city, the line of enemy fortifications, and the troops occupying this line. The city of Vicksburg is situated at the top of a line of bluffs that run along the east side of the Mississippi River. This high ground extended eastward from the river for some distance, but it was uneven and difficult to traverse because erosion had cut numerous deep ravines into the surface, with very steep sides, separated by narrow ridges. The main roads running into Vicksburg from the east ran along the crests of these ridges.

The ridge followed by the Jackson road ran out from the northeast corner of Vicksburg for a distance of about two miles, and it then joined another ridge, which ran off to the west of south on an irregular line for several miles from the Jackson road. The crest of this ridge was unbroken and nearly level for its entire length. Between these two ridges, the country was broken up by numerous ravines through which flowed small streams that emptied into Stout's Bayou, which flowed southward along the line of the Yazoo and Mississippi Valley Railroad to empty into the Mississippi River south of Vicksburg. The Warrenton road ran into Vicksburg along a ridge between the bayou and the Mississippi.

The Confederate line began on the right at the Warrenton road, about three miles south of Vicksburg, crossed Stout's Bayou, and then ran to the northeast without interruption along the above-mentioned ridge to the Jackson road. From there it continued northward to a deep ravine, filled with a dense growth of cane and vines, called Glass Bayou. The line crossed the bayou and ran on along a ridge to the Graveyard Road, where it turned to the west and ran along another ridge for about two miles, ending on the Mississippi River at Fort Hill.

At the commanding points and salients on this line, the enemy had constructed earthworks for artillery, on an average of about 200 yards apart. Between these works there were lines of entrenchments that ran unbroken for a distance of about eight miles, except at Glass Bayou and Stout's Bayou.

Pemberton's army defending these works consisted of four divisions, commanded by Martin L. Smith, John H. Forney, Carter L. Stevenson, and John S. Bowen, and also Thomas N. Waul's Texas Legion. Stevenson's division was on the line between the Warrenton road and the Southern Railroad of Mississippi. Seth M. Barton's brigade extended from the Warrenton road to a point about one mile to the north; Alexander W. Reynolds' brigade ran from the left of Bowen to the Hall's Ferry road; Alfred Cumming's brigade ran from the Hall's Ferry road to the Square Fort (later named Fort Garrott), about three-fourths of a mile south of the railroad; and Stephen D. Lee's brigade held the line from the Square Fort north to the Railroad Redoubt, just south of the railroad.

Forney's division of two brigades was on the left of Stevenson's division. John C. Moore's brigade was formed on both sides of the Jackson road, and Louis Hebert's brigade extended the line on to the north from the left of Moore to the Graveyard Road.

Martin L. Smith's division was on the left of the line of works, facing north. Francis A. Shoup's brigade was in line westward from the Graveyard Road for about a mile; William E. Baldwin's brigade was on the left of Shoup; and John C. Vaughn's brigade was on the extreme left, and its line extended to the Mississippi River at Fort Hill.

Bowen's division was in reserve on the right of the line. Francis M. Cockrell's brigade was in rear of the right of Baldwin's brigade, and Martin E. Green's brigade (commanded by Thomas P. Dockery after the death of Green on June 27), most of which had been captured at the Big Black River Bridge, was in rear of Moore's brigade.

Assault on Vicksburg, Mississippi, May 19, 1863. During the early part of the day May 19, 1863, there was skirmishing along the line as the Federal troops were getting into position in front of the enemy works, but there were no serious engagements. It was Grant's opinion, however, that Pemberton's forces were demoralized by their defeats at Champion Hill and the Big Black River Bridge, and that

an assault on the Vicksburg fortifications would be successful. Accordingly, he ordered an attack for 2:00 that afternoon. At that time, only Sherman's Fifteenth Corps was in position near the enemy entrenchments. McPherson's Seventeenth Corps was almost three-fourths of a mile distant, and McClernand's Thirteenth Corps was about one-half mile from the works.

Sherman assigned to Frank P. Blair, commanding Second Division, Fifteenth Corps, the task of carrying the works at the Stockade Redan. At 2:00 P.M. T. Kilby Smith's brigade, on the left of Blair's line, advanced on both sides of the Graveyard Road; it reached a point about 150 yards from the Stockade Redan before being stopped by a heavy fire. Giles A. Smith's First Brigade attacked on the right of T. Kilby Smith's Second Brigade, and a few men reached the exterior slope of the redan, but they could go no farther. Hugh Ewing's Third Brigade, which had just joined the corps from Milliken's Bend, attacked to the west of the Stockade Redan, but it too failed. Because of the heavy fire, the attacking troops remained under cover in their advanced positions until dark, and they then returned to their lines.

During the afternoon, Frederick Steele's First Division advanced cautiously, and by mid-afternoon, Charles R. Woods' Second Brigade and Francis H. Manter's First Brigade began to entrench on the western end of the ridge above Mint Spring Bayou. At 2:00 P.M. John M. Thayer's Third Brigade moved out of a hollow, crossed Mint Spring Bayou, and moved up in front of the 26th Louisiana Redoubt. It remained in position there without attacking, then withdrew after dark.

At the time scheduled for the attack that afternoon, only Thomas E. G. Ransom's brigade of McPherson's command was in a favorable position for an advance. Because of some confusion, however, only the 17th Wisconsin and 95th Illinois regiments attacked, and they moved forward and down into the bottom of the North Fork of Glass Bayou. The 17th Wisconsin was unable to pass through the felled timber that covered the low ground, but the 95th Illinois pushed on to within 100 yards of the enemy works before being forced to take cover. The regiment remained in this advanced position until 4:00 the next morning, and then it withdrew.

John A. Logan's Third Division, on the left of Ransom, advanced slowly along the Jackson road, and by nightfall some of the troops had arrived within 100 yards of the enemy entrenchments. The skirmishers of John E. Smith's First Brigade occupied the Shirley house. George B. Boomer's Third Brigade of Quinby's division, on the left of Logan, made some progress but was still almost one-half mile from the earthworks at nightfall.

At 2:00 P.M. McClernand advanced his infantry from the ridge in front of Two-Mile Creek and moved across the creek toward the hills on the far side. Andrew J. Smith then deployed Stephen G. Burbridge's First Brigade to the left and William J. Landram's Second Brigade to the right, with its right resting on the railroad. Peter J. Osterhaus formed Lee's First Brigade in a single line south of the Baldwin's Ferry road, and massed Lindsey's brigade in rear of Lee. At the top of the ridge on the far side of the creek, McClernand's men came under a heavy fire; they also encountered serious difficulty in advancing through the difficult terrain. Lee's brigade lost all semblance of order as it moved forward into a ravine about 400 yards east of the Square Fort on enemy lines. Lee was wounded while attempting to restore order, and James Keigwin assumed command of his brigade. By dark McClernand had reached a line about 400 yards from the enemy works that extended from the Square Fort northward to the railroad. He occupied this position with a line of outposts, and withdrew the rest of his corps to the valley of Two-Mile Creek.

The organization of the troops that took part in the assault at Vicksburg May 19, 1863 was as follows:

ARMY OF THE TENNESSEE
Ulysses S. Grant

THIRTEENTH CORPS, John A. McClernand

Ninth Division, Peter J. Osterhaus
  First Brigade, Albert L. Lee, wounded
    James Keigwin
  Second Brigade, Daniel W. Lindsey
  Artillery, Jacob T. Foster
    7th Battery, Michigan Light Artillery, Charles H. Lanphere

1st Battery, Wisconsin Light Artillery, Oscar F. Nutting

Tenth Division, Andrew J. Smith
  First Brigade, Stephen G. Burbridge
  Second Brigade, William J. Landram
  Artillery
    17th Battery, Ohio Light Artillery, Ambrose A. Blount

Note. Alvin P. Hovey's Twelfth Division and Eugene A. Carr's Fourteenth Division were not engaged.

FIFTEENTH CORPS, William T. Sherman

First Division, Frederick Steele
  First Brigade, Francis H. Manter
  Second Brigade, Charles R. Woods
  Third Brigade, John M. Thayer
  Artillery
    1st Battery, Iowa Light Artillery, Henry H. Griffiths
    Battery F, 2nd Missouri Light Artillery, Clemens Landgraeber
    4th Battery, Ohio Light Artillery, Louis Hoffmann

Second Division, Frank P. Blair, Jr.
  First Brigade, Giles A. Smith
  Second Brigade, T. Kilby Smith
  Third Brigade, Hugh Ewing
  Artillery
    Battery A, 1st Illinois Light Artillery, Peter P. Wood
    Battery B, 1st Illinois Light Artillery, Samuel E. Barrett
    Battery H, 1st Illinois Light Artillery, Levi W. Hart

Third Division, James M. Tuttle
  First Brigade, Ralph P. Buckland
  Third Brigade, Charles L. Matthies

Note. Joseph A. Mower's Second Brigade was not engaged.

SEVENTEENTH CORPS, James B. McPherson

Sixth Division, John McArthur
  Second Brigade, Thomas E. G. Ransom

Note. McArthur, with William Hall's Third Brigade, was at Grand Gulf, and Hugh T. Reid's First Brigade was at Lake Providence.

Seventh Division, Isaac F. Quinby

Third Brigade, George B. Boomer
Artillery, Frank C. Sands
   11th Battery, Ohio Light Artillery, Fletcher E. Armstrong
   Battery M, 1st Missouri Light Artillery, Junius W. MacMurray
   6th Battery, Wisconsin Light Artillery, Henry Dillon

Note. Only Boomer's brigade of the division was engaged.

Assault on Vicksburg, Mississippi, May 22, 1863. After the failure of the assault on May 19, 1863, Grant spent the next two days opening communications with the Yazoo River near Chickasaw Bayou, where he established a base between Johnson's and Lake's plantations. This was on the same ground where Sherman had disembarked his army and made his assault the preceding December.

The gap between the left of McClernand's corps and the river below Vicksburg was still unoccupied by Federal troops, but William Hall's Third Brigade of McArthur's Sixth Division, Seventeenth Corps, which had been at Grand Gulf during the early part of the campaign in rear of Vicksburg, arrived at Warrenton on the night of May 21, 1863, and was to move forward on the Warrenton road the next day. In addition, George F. McGinnis' First Brigade of Hovey's Twelfth Division, Thirteenth Corps arrived near Vicksburg May 20, and two days later was ordered to support Osterhaus' division on the extreme left of the army.

On May 21, 1863, Grant decided to make a second general assault on the enemy works at 10:00 the next morning, and the main efforts were to be made along the Graveyard Road, the Jackson road, and the Baldwin's Ferry road.

Attacks on the Morning of May 22, 1863. For his attack on the Federal right, Sherman had ordered Frank P. Blair's Second Division to take position near the Graveyard Road, and James M. Tuttle's Third Division to move up in support of Blair. He also ordered Steele to advance his division and attack between Blair and the river.

On the morning of May 22, 1863, Blair massed his brigades on the Graveyard Road behind a ridge, with Hugh Ewing's brigade in front, then Giles A. Smith's brigade, and T. Kilby Smith's brigade in the rear. Tuttle's division was massed on the road in rear of Blair. Promptly at 10:00 A.M., Ewing's brigade charged along the road toward the Stockade Redan in rear of a storming party of 150 volunteers. When the storming party emerged from a cut through which the road passed, it was struck by a heavy fire from the enemy works, but despite heavy losses, the survivors moved on and sought cover in the ditch. Some of the men succeeded in reaching the exterior slope of the redan. Ewing's men were held up by the dead and wounded in the cut, but some pushed on, although they too soon took cover in the cut and in the ditch in front of the redan. They refused to attempt a further advance, and the attack on the Graveyard Road was stalled shortly after it began. The brigades of Giles A. Smith and T. Kilby Smith moved off into a hollow to the south of the road in search of a suitable place to attack, but felled timber in the hollow made it almost impossible to advance. They were not engaged again that morning.

Tuttle's advance was dependent upon Blair's success, and when Blair's attack failed, Tuttle simply waited for orders.

Steele ordered the brigades of his division to assemble at the point reached by Thayer in his attack of May 19, 1863, but because they had some distance to travel, Woods' and Manter's brigades were not close to the assembly point at 10:00 A.M. It was mid-afternoon before the division was assembled in a hollow north of Mint Spring Bayou, not far from Fort Hill. Sherman's Fifteenth Corps accomplished nothing on the morning of May 22.

On the left of Fifteenth Corps, McPherson's Seventeenth Corps prepared to move forward. Ransom's brigade of McArthur's division was on the right, in the ravines south of the Graveyard Road. Logan's division was in the center on the Jackson road, and Quinby's division was on the left, between the Jackson road and the Baldwin's Ferry road. Neither Ransom's division nor Quinby's division was in a position to attempt a serious attack that morning, because both were in front of re-entrants in the Confederate line and would be subjected to a deadly cross fire from the salients if they advanced very far. Logan was in front of the salient on the Jackson road, with John E. Smith's First Brigade on the road; John D. Stevenson's Third Brigade was a short distance to the left of Smith, and Mortimer D. Leggett's Second Brigade was in reserve.

By 11:00 A.M., Ransom had arrived behind a ridge 100 yards from the enemy works, but there he found that his right was covered by the fire from Green's Redan, and he could not advance. He waited until 2:00 P.M. for help to arrive, and then Giles A. Smith's brigade came up on his right.

Early on the morning of May 22, 1863, the Seventeenth Corps artillery opened on the enemy works both north and south of the Jackson road. At 10:00 A.M. John E. Smith moved up out of the ravine in rear of the Shirley house and advanced along the Jackson road toward the 3rd Louisiana Redan, which was just north of the road. Some troops reached the exterior slope of the redan, but they could go no farther.

Stevenson moved his men forward to a ravine about 200 yards southeast of the Great Redoubt, which extended south from the Jackson road for about 100 yards, and they then charged up the steep slope that was capped by the redoubt. As was true in the other attacks along the line, some men reached the ditch in front of the works before being forced to take cover, and they then fell back to re-form.

During the morning of May 22, 1863, Quinby massed his division about 500 yards from the enemy line to the right of the Great Redoubt, with Boomer's brigade on the right, Sanborn's brigade on the left, and Holmes' brigade in reserve. At 10:00 A.M. the brigades moved forward in columns of regiments about 200 yards to a ridge, where they came under a very heavy fire from the enemy works. Boomer and Sanborn then deployed under cover of the ridge in preparation for an attack by Boomer, which was to be supported by Sanborn. For some reason, Boomer did not advance, and because Sanborn was to support Boomer, neither did he. That was the only effort by Quinby's division that morning.

At daybreak May 22, 1863, the artillery of McClernand's Thirteenth Corps opened fire on the enemy works on their front. This continued until 10:00 A.M. in preparation for the attack that was to follow. Eugene A. Carr's Fourteenth Division was on the right, with William P. Benton's First Brigade on the Baldwin's Ferry road and Michael K. Lawler's Second Brigade just south of the railroad. Carr was to attack the Railroad Redoubt and the 2nd Texas Lunette, which was just south of the

Baldwin's Ferry road and several hundred yards northwest of the present-day Visitor's Center of the Vicksburg National Military Park. Andrew J. Smith's Tenth Division was to move up in rear of Carr and support his attack. Peter J. Osterhaus' Ninth Division was on the left of Carr, opposite a salient about midway between the railroad and the Square Fort. Daniel W. Lindsey's Second Brigade was on the right of the division, and James Keigwin's First Brigade was on the left. George F. McGinnis' brigade of Alvin P. Hovey's Twelfth Division, temporarily commanded by William T. Spicely, was formed in rear of Osterhaus.

At about 10:00 A.M., Benton's and Lawler's brigades moved forward. Benton attacked on the Baldwin's Ferry road toward the 2nd Texas Lunette, but was brought to a halt before reaching the work. Three regiments of the brigade moved off to the left to attack the entrenchments southwest of the lunette, but this attack too was repulsed. Stephen G. Burbridge's First Brigade of Andrew J. Smith's division, which was to support Benton, then moved forward, and by 10:30 A.M. its skirmishers were established within a few yards of the lunette.

A confusing situation then developed. Andrew J. Smith ordered Burbridge to send two of his four regiments to support Benton's three regiments near the Baldwin's Ferry road. When Burbridge protested, the order was suspended, but it was repeated a short time later, and Burbridge sent the 67th Indiana and four companies of the 23rd Wisconsin. Another attempt was made to take the lunette, and some troops nearly entered the work, but they were driven back. Burbridge's troops were then returned from service with Benton's brigade. There was fighting at the lunette during the afternoon, but without significant results.

Lawler's brigade, on the left of Benton, moved forward against the Railroad Redoubt, which was located on a hill just south of the railroad. The 21st and 22nd Iowa regiments charged up the hill and reached the ditch in front of the fort, where most of the men were halted. A small party entered the fort through a breach caused by Federal artillery, and were engaged in violent hand-to-hand fighting before withdrawing. The enemy left the fort for a time, but a heavy fire from other works prevented Lawler's Iowans from retaining possession of the interior.

William J. Landram's Second Brigade of Andrew J. Smith's division followed close behind Lawler's brigade. It suffered heavy losses, but succeeded in advancing into the ditch and to positions on the slope in front of the works. For the next several hours there was fighting around the fort, but little change in position.

At 10:00 A.M. Osterhaus' division on the left of Grant's line advanced between the Square Fort and the Railroad Redoubt, with Keigwin's brigade on the left, Lindsey's brigade on the right, and Spicely's brigade in reserve. When Keigwin's men crossed an exposed ridge about 250 yards from the Square Fort, they were stopped by a murderous fire from the fort, and they then sought cover. On the right, Lindsey's brigade was stopped about 200 yards from the enemy works. Spicely was not called up and was not engaged.

Attacks on the Afternoon of May 22, 1863. A short time after the morning assaults had started, all of Grant's forces were pinned down in the ditches in front of the enemy works, and by 11:30 A.M. Grant had correctly concluded that the attack was a failure. Unfortunately, however, at 11:00 A.M. McClernand had sent to Grant a request for help, and had erroneously stated that he had gained possession of two of the enemy's forts. Grant sent no reinforcements at the time, and McClernand repeated his request for help at noon. Grant still delayed, but finally decided to continue with his attacks, and at 2:00 P.M. he sent Quinby's division to report to McClernand. He also directed McPherson to renew his attack.

About 2:00 P.M. Sherman learned from Blair that Giles A. Smith's brigade had joined Ransom's brigade of McPherson's corps, and that they were in position to attack between the salient at the Graveyard Road and Glass Bayou. Sherman also sent Tuttle's division forward to support Blair's division, which was still in position on the line that it had gained that morning, and he further directed that they renew the attack.

At 2:15 P.M. Ransom and Giles A. Smith began their attacks. Smith's brigade was struck by a devastating enfilade fire from the southwest face of the Stockade Redan and driven back to a point about 100 yards from the redan. By dark the men had thrown up strong earthworks, which they continued to hold.

On the left of Giles A. Smith, Ransom's brigade advanced against the enemy works. Despite heavy losses, it moved to within a few yards of the rifle pits before being forced to fall back.

At about 3:00 P.M. Tuttle's division, except Ralph P. Buckland's First Brigade, which was supporting the corps artillery, was on the Graveyard Road, with Mower's brigade in front and Matthies' brigade in support. Mower then advanced to within 150 yards of the Stockade Redan. As he emerged from the protection of the cut through which the road ran, he was struck by a heavy fire, as his predecessors had been that morning, and his attack failed, although some of his men reached the ditch. Sherman then called off the attack.

Steele's division on the right had been working its way forward during the day; it finally arrived near the enemy works at 2:00 P.M. May 22, 1863, and it too was ordered to attack. That morning Thayer had assembled his brigade of Steele's division on the south side of Mint Spring Bayou, and he then waited until about mid-afternoon for the arrival of Steele with the rest of his division. At that time Woods' brigade arrived north of Mint Spring Bayou, and when Manter's brigade arrived, it was held north of the bayou as a reserve. Steele then joined Thayer and Woods.

Thayer deployed his brigade in line of battle, and Woods formed his brigade in column in rear of Thayer. At 4:00 P.M. the two brigades started up the steep slope south of Mint Spring Bayou, and some of the leading troops gained the exterior slope of the 26th Louisiana Redoubt. Woods then came up on the right of Thayer, and some of his men reached the vicinity of the works, but Steele's attack was soon halted.

Sherman ordered Ewing and Giles A. Smith to entrench the positions they then held, and for the rest of his troops to withdraw to less exposed positions as follows: T. Kilby Smith's brigade bivouacked in rear of Ewing and Giles A. Smith; Matthies' and Buckland's brigades of Tuttle's division bivouacked in rear of the corps artillery; Mower's brigade was at the junction of the Benton road and the Bridgeport road; and Steele's three brigades moved back to the positions that they had occupied before the attack.

On the left, Quinby's division, after an arduous advance through difficult terrain, did not reach

McClernand's position until nearly dark, and it was then immediately ordered to attack the entrenchments between the salient at the railroad and the salient at the Baldwin's Ferry road. The attack was a total failure. Boomer was killed during the advance, and Holden Putnam assumed temporary command of the brigade. Charles L. Matthies assumed command June 2, 1863.

Just at dark, Confederates occupying the 2nd Texas Lunette on the Baldwin's Ferry road, having been reinforced by men of Bowen's division, made a sortie and drove off the Federals remaining in the ditch. At about the same time, McClernand's troops retired from the ditch of the Railroad Redoubt, where they had been since morning.

Although it did not occur until about a month later, there was to be an unpleasant aftermath of the assaults of May 22, 1863. At the time, Grant had been dissatisfied with McClernand for his erroneous claim that he had gained a foothold in the enemy's works during the morning attack, which had led to a series of costly attacks that afternoon. Later, when Grant learned that McClernand, in violation of War Department regulations, had sent to the newspapers in Illinois copies of his congratulatory order to the men of his Thirteenth Corps, in which he spoke unfavorably of the conduct of troops of the other corps, Grant issued an order, dated June 18, 1863, for his removal. This order was delivered to McClernand at 2:00 A.M. June 19. At the same time, Grant assigned Edward O. C. Ord, who had arrived at Vicksburg from West Point, Virginia June 17, to the command of Thirteenth Corps.

The organization of Grant's Army of the Tennessee during the assault of May 22, 1863 was as follows:

THIRTEENTH CORPS, John A. McClernand

Ninth Division, Peter J. Osterhaus
    First Brigade, James Keigwin
    Second Brigade, Daniel W. Lindsey
    Artillery, Jacob T. Foster
        7th Battery, Michigan Light Artillery, Charles H. Lanphere
        1st Battery, Wisconsin Light Artillery, Oscar F. Nutting

Tenth Division, Andrew J. Smith

First Brigade, Stephen G. Burbridge
Second Brigade, William J. Landram
Artillery
    Chicago Mercantile Battery, Illinois Light Artillery, Patrick H. White
    17th Battery, Ohio Light Artillery, Ambrose A. Blount

Twelfth Division, Alvin P. Hovey
    First Brigade, William T. Spicely
    Artillery
        2nd Battery, Ohio Light Artillery, Augustus Beach
        18th Battery, Ohio Light Artillery, Russell P. Twist

Fourteenth Division, Eugene A. Carr
    First Brigade, William P. Benton
    Second Brigade, Michael K. Lawler
    Artillery
        Battery A, 2nd Illinois Light Artillery, Frank B. Fenton
        1st Battery, Indiana Light Artillery, Martin Klauss

FIFTEENTH CORPS, William T. Sherman

First Division, Frederick Steele
    First Brigade, Francis H. Manter
    Second Brigade, Charles R. Woods
    Third Brigade, John M. Thayer
    Artillery
        1st Battery, Iowa Light Artillery, Henry H. Griffiths
        Battery F, 2nd Missouri Light Artillery, Clemens Landgraeber
        4th Battery, Ohio Light Artillery, Louis Hoffmann

Second Division, Frank P. Blair, Jr.
    First Brigade, Giles A. Smith
    Second Brigade, T. Kilby Smith
    Third Brigade, Hugh Ewing
    Artillery
        Battery A, 1st Illinois Light Artillery, Peter P. Wood
        Battery B, 1st Illinois Light Artillery, Samuel E. Barrett
        Battery H, 1st Illinois Light Artillery, Levi W. Hart

Third Division, James M. Tuttle
    First Brigade, Ralph P. Buckland
    Second Brigade, Joseph A. Mower
    Third Brigade, Charles L. Matthies
    Artillery, Nelson T. Spoor
        Battery E, 1st Illinois Light Artillery, Allen C. Waterhouse

2nd Battery, Iowa Light Artillery, Joseph R. Reed

SEVENTEENTH CORPS, James B. McPherson

Third Division, John A. Logan
First Brigade, John E. Smith
Second Brigade, Mortimer D. Leggett
Third Brigade, John D. Stevenson
Artillery, Charles J. Stolbrand
Battery D, 1st Illinois Light Artillery, Henry A. Rogers
8th Battery, Michigan Light Artillery, Samuel De Golyer
3rd Battery, Ohio Light Artillery, William S. Williams
Battery L, 2nd Illinois Light Artillery, William H. Bolton

Sixth Division, John McArthur
Second Brigade, Thomas E. G. Ransom
Third Brigade, William Hall

Seventh Division, Isaac F. Quinby
First Brigade, John B. Sanborn
Second Brigade, Samuel A. Holmes
Third Brigade, George B. Boomer, killed
Holden Putnam
Artillery, Frank C. Sands
Battery M, 1st Missouri Light Artillery, Junius W. MacMurray
11th Battery, Ohio Light Artillery, Fletcher E. Armstrong
6th Battery, Wisconsin Light Artillery, Henry Dillon

Siege of Vicksburg, Mississippi, May 23, 1863–July 4, 1863

After the failure of the two assaults at Vicksburg, Grant decided to reduce the works by regular siege operations. To accomplish this, it was necessary to do two things: to occupy the gap that then existed between the left of McClernand's Thirteenth Corps and the Mississippi River near Warrenton, and to provide suitable protection for the rear of his investment line against the Confederate force that was forming under Joseph E. Johnston at Canton and Jackson, Mississippi. Grant's army was too small to complete the investment and at the same time protect his rear without reinforcements, but the neces-

sary troops were immediately ordered forward from Grant's own Department of the Tennessee, and also from the Department of the Missouri and the Department of the Ohio.

As one of the first steps in preparation for the siege, Grant ordered William Hall's Third Brigade, Sixth Division of Seventeenth Corps to move temporarily to the vicinity of Warrenton. This brigade had been stationed at Grand Gulf during the operations in rear of Vicksburg, but it had left there May 19, 1863 and gone to Young's Point. Two days later, however, it moved to Warrenton, and on May 23 it was ordered to take position on the extreme left of Grant's line at the Big Bayou crossing of the Warrenton road. Hall's brigade remained there until May 26.

Grant then increased the strength of the force guarding the Big Black River. James R. Slack's Second Brigade of Alvin P. Hovey's Twelfth Division, Thirteenth Corps had been left at the Big Black River Bridge to guard the crossing there when the army moved on to Vicksburg, and on May 24, 1863, Peter J. Osterhaus marched back to the Big Black River with James Keigwin's First Brigade of his Ninth Division and relieved Slack. Slack then rejoined Hovey's division. Daniel W. Lindsey's Second Brigade of Osterhaus' division was assigned to Hovey's command. When this arrangement was completed, Hovey's division was on the extreme left of the siege line, with Lindsey's brigade on the right, Slack's brigade in the center, and McGinnis' brigade on the left.

The first of the reinforcements to arrive were Jacob G. Lauman's Fourth Division, Sixteenth Corps from Memphis, Tennessee. It had been ordered to join Grant May 5, 1863, but because of a shortage of transportation, it did not arrive at Young's Point until May 13–20. Isaac C. Pugh's First Brigade and Cyrus Hall's Second Brigade were then ordered to Snyder's Bluff, where they arrived May 20. Then these two brigades, under the command of Lauman, marched to the far left of Grant's line and took position there May 24, relieving William Hall's brigade on the afternoon of May 25. On May 28, Lauman moved his division to the right to connect with the left of McClernand's corps, with his left on the Hall's Ferry road. When McArthur, with William Hall's brigade, was relieved by Lauman, he rejoined Seventeenth Corps.

George E. Bryant's Third Brigade of Lauman's division was ordered to Grand Gulf, and it remained there from May 18 to June 11, 1863, at which time Grand Gulf was abandoned (the abandonment was ordered May 31). Amory K. Johnson, whose cavalry command had been broken up, arrived at Grand Gulf June 9 and assumed command of Third Brigade, relieving Bryant, who resumed command of his 12th Wisconsin Regiment of the brigade. On June 11, Johnson, with his Third Brigade reported to Lauman.

On June 11, 1863, Francis J. Herron's Division, which consisted of troops formerly belonging to Second Division and Third Division of Herron's Army of the Frontier (formerly commanded by John M. Schofield) in Missouri, arrived at Young's Point from Missouri. Two days later, Herron crossed the river to Warrenton and moved his division into position on the left of Lauman, who closed up on McClernand. William Vandever's First Brigade of Herron's Division was placed on the left of the division line, and William W. Orme's Second Brigade was formed on the right, next to Lauman. When Herron's Division was in place, the investment of Vicksburg was complete.

On May 28, 1863, two brigades and four regiments of Sixteenth Corps were ordered to join Grant at Vicksburg. These were to be organized as a Provisional Division under the command of Nathan Kimball, formerly commander of Third Division, Sixteenth Corps. On May 30, Jonathan Richmond's Second Brigade of Third Division (or District of Jackson) left Jackson, Tennessee, arriving at Memphis late that evening. Richmond's brigade left Memphis on transports on the morning of May 31 and arrived at Snyder's Bluff June 2. Adolph Engelmann's First Brigade of Third Division (or District of Jackson) left Bolivar, Tennessee and arrived at Memphis May 31. Engelmann's brigade left Memphis June 1 and arrived at Snyder's Bluff June 3. The four unbrigaded regiments were taken from Sixth Division (or District of Columbus). The 25th and 27th Wisconsin left from Columbus, Kentucky, and the 40th Iowa from Paducah, Kentucky, and they reached Snyder's Bluff June 4. The 3rd Minnesota left Fort Heiman, Kentucky and arrived at Snyder's Bluff on June 9. At Snyder's Bluff, these four regiments were organized into a brigade under the command of Milton Montgomery. The organization of Kimball's command was then as follows:

Provisional Division, Nathan Kimball
  Engelmann's Brigade, Adolph Engelmann
  Richmond's Brigade, Jonathan Richmond
  Montgomery's Brigade, Milton Montgomery

On June 8, 1863, Cadwallader C. Washburn, who had been in command of the Cavalry Division, Sixteenth Corps, was assigned command of all troops of Sixteenth Corps then at Vicksburg, and also of those to arrive later. His command was designated as Detachment Sixteenth Corps, and his headquarters was at Snyder's Bluff.

William Sooy Smith's First Division, Sixteenth Corps, which had been at La Grange, Tennessee, arrived at Snyder's Bluff June 12, 1863 (ordered June 5).

June 2, 1863, Ambrose E. Burnside, commander of the Department of the Ohio, was directed to send reinforcements to Grant at Vicksburg. Thomas Welch's First Division and Robert B. Potter's Second Division of Ninth Corps, which were then in the Department of the Ohio, embarked promptly, and under the command of John G. Parke they steamed down the Ohio and Mississippi rivers toward Vicksburg. On the evening of June 14, transports with nearly 9,000 men aboard arrived at Young's Point.

Prior to their arrival, Grant had decided to send the troops of Ninth Corps to the south of Vicksburg and place them on the left of the investment line. After Parke's men had disembarked on the morning of June 15, 1863, they started on their march across De Soto Point to the Mississippi River below the town. Some of the men had been ferried across to the east bank when Parke received orders from Grant to return to Young's Point and then move up the Yazoo River to Snyder's Bluff. This change in plan was caused by a report that a large enemy force was approaching from the direction of Mechanicsburg and would probably attack Snyder's Bluff first.

By the afternoon of June 16, 1863, Parke's troops had reembarked at Young's Point and were on their way up the Yazoo River. They arrived at Snyder's Bluff that night, but they did not disembark until the next morning. Parke then put his troops in position, with those on the left of the corps in camp near

Snyder's Bluff and those on the right near Templeton's plantation. Parke's headquarters was established at Milldale, near the center of his line.

The Army of the Tennessee was reinforced by two cavalry regiments during the early part of June 1863. Cyrus Bussey's 3rd Iowa Cavalry from Helena, in the District of Eastern Arkansas, arrived at Snyder's Bluff on June 8, and the 2nd Wisconsin Cavalry arrived there from Memphis, Tennessee on June 13. These two regiments, together with the 5th Illinois Cavalry, which had arrived from Helena June 2, were formed as a cavalry brigade under the command of Bussey. This brigade served as unattached cavalry, and was engaged primarily on outpost duty and on reconnaissance in the territory between the Yazoo River and the Big Black River, where it covered the northeastern approaches to Snyder's Bluff. It assembled at Bear Creek on June 29 to watch the Benton road and the ford on the Big Black River below Birdsong Ferry.

Blair's Mechanicsburg, Mississippi Expedition, May 26, 1863–June 4, 1863. Grant became increasingly concerned about enemy activity in his rear, and on May 26, 1863 he ordered the organization of an expedition under Frank P. Blair, which was to move up the Yazoo River and drive out an enemy force reported to be in the area. Blair was also directed to lay waste to the country between the Yazoo and Big Black rivers.

Blair's command consisted of the following: a cavalry force under Amory K. Johnson that was composed of all cavalry units attached to Fifteenth Corps and Seventeenth Corps; and six brigades of infantry taken from Fifteenth Corps and Seventeenth Corps. The infantry was organized into two divisions as follows:

Mower's Division, Joseph A. Mower
Mower's Brigade, Lucius F. Hubbard
Manter's Brigade, Francis H. Manter
Lightburn's Brigade, Joseph A. J. Lightburn

Note 1. These three brigades were from Fifteenth Corps as follows: Mower's Brigade was Second Brigade, Third Division; Manter's Brigade was First Brigade, First Division; and Lightburn's Brigade was Second Brigade, Second Division.
Note 2. Lightburn succeeded T. Kilby Smith in command of Second Brigade, Second Division May 23, 1863.

McArthur's Division, John McArthur

Hall's Brigade, William Hall
Sanborn's Brigade, John B. Sanborn
Leggett's Brigade, Mortimer D. Leggett

Note. These three brigades were taken from Seventeenth Corps as follows: Hall's Brigade was Third Brigade, Sixth Division; Sanborn's Brigade was First Brigade, Seventh Division; and Leggett's Brigade was Second Brigade, Third Division.

All brigades except Hall's moved out a little before midnight May 26, 1863. Hall followed early the next morning. McArthur's division marched on the Benton road to Sulfur Springs, where it arrived on the night of May 27. Mower's division marched on a road near the river, past Drumgould's Bluff, Haynes' Bluff, and Snyder's Bluff, and joined McArthur at Sulfur Springs before noon May 28. Both divisions then moved on and camped at the Hart plantation that night. The expedition arrived near Mechanicsburg May 29 and drove off a small enemy force found there. Blair learned that Joseph E. Johnston was collecting a large force at Canton, Mississippi and, upon reporting this to Grant, was ordered to return to Haynes' Bluff if confronted by a greatly superior force. Blair left Mechanicsburg on May 30 and marched to Sartartia. He then returned to Haynes' Bluff by way of the Yazoo River Valley, and on the way obstructed roads, destroyed bridges and forage, and confiscated all livestock. Blair arrived at Haynes' Bluff June 1, 1863. Mower then moved to Snyder's Bluff by Grant's orders, and the other brigades of the expedition rejoined their respective commands on the lines of investment June 4.

Kimball's Expedition from Haynes' Bluff to Sartartia and Mechanicsburg, Mississippi, June 2–8, 1863. On June 2, 1863, Grant ordered Mower's brigade and Amory K. Johnson's cavalry command to return to Mechanicsburg, to watch the enemy movements, and to destroy the bridges in the area. Johnson's cavalry had been reinforced by the 5th Illinois Cavalry, which had just arrived from Helena, Arkansas. On June 3, Grant learned that Adolph Engelmann's brigade of Kimball's division had arrived from Memphis, and he assigned Engelmann to support Mower and the cavalry. On the evening of June 3, Mower's brigade left Haynes' Bluff and moved up the Yazoo on transports to

Sartartia. Kimball, with Engelmann's Brigade, remained that night at Johnson's plantation on the Yazoo on the transports that had just brought the brigade from Memphis, and the next he day joined Mower at Sartartia. Amory K. Johnson's cavalry also joined the expedition that day. Upon arriving at Sartartia, Kimball, who held higher rank than Mower and Johnson, assumed command of the expedition. Richmond's Brigade of Kimball's Division was assigned as garrison of the defenses at Snyder's Bluff.

Mower moved out from Sartartia toward Mechanicsburg, which he occupied after a brief skirmish June 5, 1863, and he was joined there by Kimball with Engelmann's brigade. Like Blair before him, Kimball was concerned about the threat posed by Johnston's force, and in addition he was concerned that falling water in the Yazoo River might jeopardize the withdrawal of the expedition from Sartartia if it was delayed too long. At daybreak June 6, Kimball's command evacuated Mechanicsburg, and Mower's and Engelmann's brigades took the road to Sartartia. Johnson's troopers burned the village and returned to Snyder's Bluff by way of the Benton road. By mid-afternoon of June 7, the column had reached Haynes' Bluff. Milton Montgomery had arrived at Sartartia with three regiments from Columbus and Fort Heiman, Kentucky; these returned to Haynes' Bluff, and his command was attached to Kimball's Division as Montgomery's Brigade.

On June 7, 1863, Elias S. Dennis, commanding the District of Northeastern Louisiana, was attacked by troops of the Confederate Trans-Mississippi Department at Milliken's Bend and Young's Point. The next day Mower was ordered with his brigade and Battery B, 1st Illinois Light Artillery to Young's Point to reinforce Dennis (see below).

Kimball's Division remained at Haynes' Bluff until June 15, 1863, then moved to Snyder's Bluff, where it remained during the rest of the siege.

District of Northeastern Louisiana—Engagement at Milliken's Bend, June 7, 1863. In late May 1863, with Grant's Army of the Tennessee on the east side of the Mississippi River, it became necessary to provide a better arrangement for the defense of the territory in Louisiana across the river from Vicksburg. Accordingly, on May 28, Grant

constituted the District of Northeastern Louisiana to consist of that part of the state occupied by troops of the Army of the Tennessee. This generally included the territory around Richmond, Milliken's Bend, Young's Point, and Lake Providence. Jeremiah C. Sullivan was assigned command, but he was relieved by Elias S. Dennis, who established his headquarters at Young's Point on June 3.

The troops in the district consisted of a detached brigade under George W. Neeley, which was composed of regiments that had been sent earlier from James C. Veatch's Fifth Division (or District of Memphis), Sixteenth Corps to relieve Hugh Ewing's Third Brigade, Second Division of Fifteenth Corps, which had been left to protect Grant's supply line between Milliken's Bend and Richmond when Grant crossed the Mississippi. In addition, there were five regiments of United States Colored Troops, which were designated as African Brigade. John P. Hawkins was assigned command of this brigade, but Isaac F. Shepard was in command during his absence.

As Grant's army closed in on Vicksburg from the east, E. Kirby Smith, commanding the Confederate Trans-Mississippi Department, finally decided to move to the support of Pemberton's army, which was then under heavy pressure. For this purpose, on May 20, 1863, he ordered Richard Taylor to move from near Alexandria, Louisiana with troops of his District of Western Louisiana, which had been reinforced by John G. Walker's Texas division from Arkansas, to attack Grant's bases and communications west of the Mississippi River. On June 5, Taylor, with Walker's division, occupied Richmond, Louisiana, about ten miles to the southwest of Milliken's Bend.

On the evening of June 5, 1863, Dennis learned that Isaac F. Harrison's Confederate cavalry battalion had occupied Richmond, and he ordered Herman Lieb, commanding at Milliken's Bend in place of Shepard, who was in arrest at that time, to move out on the morning of June 6 on a reconnaissance toward Richmond to find out what was happening in that direction.

Preceded by a part of Christopher H. Anderson's 10th Illinois Cavalry, Lieb left Milliken's Bend with his 9th Louisiana Colored Infantry at 2:00 A.M. June 6, 1863 and advanced to within about three miles of Richmond, where he encountered pickets of Harrison's cavalry. He returned to Milliken's Bend shortly after noon and reported to Dennis that he had found the enemy in some force near Richmond. Dennis then sent Samuel L. Glasgow's 23rd Iowa Regiment of Michael K. Lawler's Second Brigade of Eugene A. Carr's Fourteenth Division, Thirteenth Corps, which was then just returning from Memphis after having accompanied Confederate prisoners from Vicksburg to that point. He also reported to David D. Porter, commanding the United States Mississippi Squadron, the appearance of the enemy at Richmond, and Porter immediately sent the gunboat *Choctaw* to Milliken's Bend.

Back at Richmond, Taylor decided to attack Milliken's Bend and Young's Point immediately with Henry E. McCulloch's brigade and James M. Hawes' brigade, and he left Richmond on the evening of June 6, 1863, with Harrison's cavalry out in front, so as to be in position to attack at daylight June 7. McCulloch's brigade arrived within a mile and a half of Milliken's Bend at 6:00 A.M., while Hawes' brigade moved toward Young's Point. Hawes arrived before Young's Point that day, but he did not attack.

Lieb's men occupied a line of breastworks made with bales of cotton along the crest of the second from the river of two cross levees that had been constructed at that point. The 9th Louisiana Colored Infantry was on the left of this line; the 1st Mississippi Colored Infantry, the 13th Louisiana Colored Infantry, and the 23rd Iowa Infantry were in the center; and the 11th Louisiana Colored Infantry was on the right.

When Harrison's cavalry appeared in front of the works, it came under a heavy fire and withdrew to make way for the infantry. McCulloch's brigade then advanced through thick hedgerows that bordered the fields in front of Lieb's line. McCulloch's men suffered from a heavy Federal fire, but they continued to advance until they reached a point within about twenty-five yards of the levee. They then charged and after severe hand-to-hand fighting drove back the defenders to the line of the first levee near the river bank. When the enemy attempted to pursue, they came under a destructive fire from the *Choctaw,* and they fell back and sought cover behind the second levee. At 9:00 A.M. the gunboat *Lexington* arrived, and upon seeing this, Taylor withdrew about noon.

The next day, June 8, 1863, Joseph A. Mower's Second Brigade, Third Division, Fifteenth Corps, which had just returned to Haynes' Bluff from Mechanicsburg, was sent to Young's Point to reinforce Dennis' troops in the District of Northeastern Louisiana.

Sherman's Exterior Line at Vicksburg— Sherman's Army of Observation. June 22, 1863, a detachment of Federal cavalry that was engaged in obstructing the Birdsong Ferry road near the Hill plantation was overwhelmed by enemy cavalry sent out from Mechanicsburg. This seemed to confirm reports that Grant had received that Johnston intended to cross the Big Black River at Birdsong Ferry and march on the rear of the army investing Vicksburg. Sherman was immediately ordered to march with two brigades of his Fifteenth Corps and three brigades of Seventeenth Corps to Bear Creek, a tributary of the Big Black River, and to take position to oppose this expected advance.

Sherman's force consisted of the following:

Third Division, Fifteenth Corps, James M. Tuttle
    First Brigade, William L. McMillen
    Third Brigade, Joseph J. Woods

Note 1. Joseph A. Mower's Second Brigade was detached and was serving in the District of Northeastern Louisiana.
Note 2. Woods relieved Charles L. Matthies in command of Third Brigade June 1, 1863, and McMillen relieved Ralph P. Buckland in command of First Brigade June 22.

Provisional Division, John McArthur
    Force's Brigade, Manning F. Force
    Matthies' Brigade, Charles L. Matthies
    Chambers' Brigade, Alexander Chambers

Note. The three brigades of this division were taken from Seventeenth Corps. Force's Brigade was Second Brigade, Third Division; Matthies' Brigade was Third Brigade, Seventh Division; and Chambers' Brigade was Third Brigade, Sixth Division.

Tuttle's division started at sundown June 22, 1863, and the next morning was assigned to guard the Birdsong Ferry road. Tuttle camped at the George Trible (Tribble) plantation and established an outpost at the George Markham plantation.

McArthur's Provisional Division left after midnight and the next day was assigned to guard the

Messinger's Ferry road. It camped at Strauss' (Straus'), with an outpost at the Parson Fox place.

On June 19, 1863, John G. Parke's Ninth Corps and Cadwallader C. Washburn's Detachment Sixteenth Corps were near Snyder's Bluff and were at some distance from the main army. Because of this, Parke, as the senior officer, officially assumed command of both Ninth Corps and Detachment Sixteenth Corps that day. The day before, Parke had sent William Sooy Smith's First Division, Detachment Sixteenth Corps and Simon G. Griffin's First Brigade of Robert B. Potter's Second Division, Ninth Corps to occupy a line that extended from A. Green's on the Benton road, by way of McCall's plantation, to Tiffin (Tiffintown) on the Bridgeport road. On June 23, 1863, Parke moved his command to a new line that ran from Neily's (Neeley's) plantation to Oak Ridge Post Office, and he fortified both positions.

Farther to the south, Osterhaus had been guarding the Big Black River crossing near the railroad bridge, and also at the Bridgeport bridge, with James Keigwin's First Brigade of his division of Thirteenth Corps, and he was reinforced June 22, 1863 with Daniel W. Lindsey's Second Brigade. Thus Osterhaus' entire division was on the river on the right of Sherman's line, and on June 22 he was placed under Sherman's orders.

Although not a commonly used designation, the troops under Sherman's rear line along the west side of the Big Black River were called Sherman's Army of Observation.

Sherman's line as finally established was occupied as follows:

Osterhaus' division of Thirteenth Corps was guarding the Big Black River crossing near the railroad, and also at the Bridgeport bridge. Osterhaus, who had been on the river with James Keigwin's First Brigade, was reinforced by Daniel W. Lindsey's Second Brigade June 22, 1863.

McArthur's Provisional Division was near Tiffin (Tiffintown), about six miles west of Bridgeport, on the Bridgeport road, and four miles north of the Big Black River Bridge. It was in position there to guard the Messinger's Ferry road.

Parke had a small guard at Milldale and at the Templeton plantation on the Middle Road south of Snyder's Bluff. The rest of his Ninth Corps was on the east side of Clear Creek, connecting on the right with McArthur's division at Bryant's plantation, a short distance northwest of Tiffin, and on the left with William Sooy Smith's division near Neily's (Neeley's) plantation on the Benton road.

Tuttle's division was in advance of the main line, on a ridge that extended from McCall's plantation along the road to Birdsong Ferry. It was in position on the Trible (Tribble) plantation, just west of the crossing of Bear Creek. Troops of Tuttle's division were also on the road to Messinger's Ford.

William Sooy Smith's division was camped near Oak Ridge Post Office on the Benton road, about six miles east of Snyder's Bluff. It connected with Parke on the right, and was in position to guard the Benton road and also the lower Benton road, which crossed the Big Black River at Bush's Ferry.

Cadwallader C. Washburn, with Nathan Kimball's division, occupied the fortifications at Snyder's Bluff, and Cyrus Bussey's cavalry brigade was out in front scouting the country along the Big Black River.

There was no significant change in the positions of the troops of Sherman's command until Pemberton surrendered Vicksburg July 4, 1863. On that day, Sherman's Army of Observation, reinforced by Thirteenth Corps and Fifteenth Corps, started toward Jackson, Mississippi and Joseph E. Johnston's army. For further information, see Jackson, Mississippi Campaign (William T. Sherman).

Union Approaches during the Siege of Vicksburg. The principal activity along the siege lines at Vicksburg during May and June 1863 consisted of pushing forward parallels, erecting batteries, and digging approaches toward various strong points along the line of enemy works. There was frequent skirmishing and artillery fire as the work progressed, but there were no major attacks.

The approaches required a great deal of work and time, and most of them had been completed only to points close to the enemy works when Vicksburg was surrendered July 4, 1863. These approaches were designated by the name of the brigade or division commander who furnished the guards and working parties. The most important of these were as follows:

Thayer's Approach. This approach was constructed toward that part of the enemy works that was the object of Steele's attack May 22, 1863, and ran out across Mint Spring Bayou and up the hill toward the 26th Louisiana Redoubt. By June 26, the approach had reached a point within about sixty yards of the redoubt, and it was still closer when Vicksburg was surrendered July 4.

Ewing's, Buckland's, and Lightburn's Approaches. In the vicinity of the Graveyard Road, three approaches were pushed forward toward the Stockade Redan, to the 27th Louisiana Lunette to the Confederate left of the Stockade Redan, and Green's Redan to the Confederate right of the Stockade Redan. Ewing's approach was started May 23, 1863; it ran along and parallel to the Graveyard Road toward the Stockade Redan, and by June 3 had been driven to within 150 yards of the redan. By June 20, the head of Ewing's Approach was within a few feet of the counterscarp in front of the stockade, and then the men began digging lateral trenches to the right and left. On June 26, the enemy exploded a mine, but it had little effect. The Federals then began work on a tunnel under the Stockade Redan, and were preparing to explode a mine when Vicksburg was surrendered July 4.

Buckland's Approach, which was of little significance, was started on the night of May 30, 1863 by men of Tuttle's division. It began north of the Graveyard Road, crossed a branch of Mint Spring Bayou, and then ran up the slope toward the 27th Louisiana Lunette. Work was halted June 22 when Tuttle's division was sent to join Sherman's force on the Federal line in rear of Vicksburg. At that time the approach had opened a parallel only sixty yards from the 27th Louisiana Redoubt.

About June 28, 1863, men of T. Kilby Smith's Second Brigade of Blair's division, then commanded by Joseph A. J. Lightburn, began an approach that ran up the ridge toward the Confederate stockade west of the Graveyard Road. By July 2, the head of the sap was within 25 feet of the stockade, and there it was halted. Mining operations were

then started, but the work ceased with the surrender on July 4.

Giles A. Smith's Approach. During the last week of May 1863, men of Giles A. Smith's brigade began work on an approach toward Green's Redan, which was on the Confederate right of the Stockade Redan. This approach was started in a ravine about 200 yards south of Ewing's Approach and ran up to the high ground in front of Green's Redan. Work was not pushed vigorously until June 26, and then the pace quickened. By July 2, the two trenches that constituted the approach were close to the redan, and the next day Smith started mining operations. Work was stopped when Vicksburg was surrendered July 4.

Ransom's Approach. Men of Ransom's brigade started an approach in the ravine of the North Fork of Glass Bayou and pushed it toward the enemy works at a point about 200 yards north of Glass Bayou. By June 28, 1863, the head of the sap was only a few yards from the ditch in front of the works, and there work was stopped.

Logan's Approach. On May 26, 1863, work was started on an approach along the Jackson road toward the 3rd Louisiana Redan. The digging began about fifty yards southeast of the Shirley house and about 400 yards east of the redan. By June 3, the head of the sap was only about 125 yards from the redan. The Federals then constructed an earthwork called Battery Hickenlooper, after Andrew Hickenlooper, who was in charge of the work, and emplaced three guns in the battery. At the same time, a working party under the personal direction of Mortimer D. Leggett continued work on the approach. On June 8, the head of the sap was within seventy-five yards of the redan, and on June 16 it was only twenty-five yards away. Then mining operations were begun in preparation for exploding a mine. The mine was exploded at the redan on the afternoon of June 25, and the 45th Illinois of Leggett's brigade charged and entered the crater. It was relieved about 6:00 P.M. by the 20th Illinois of the same brigade. Then, in succession, the 31st Illinois of Leggett's brigade, the 56th Illinois of Green B. Raum's brigade, and the 23rd Indiana of Leggett's brigade occupied the crater. Leggett's brigade belonged to Logan's division, and Raum's brigade to John E. Smith's division of Seventeenth Corps. Although Federal troops held the crater until the morning of June 28, they were unable to penetrate the enemy lines. A second mine was exploded July 1, but this was not followed by an attack.

Andrew J. Smith's Approach. On June 11, 1863, troops of Andrew J. Smith's division of Thirteenth Corps began the construction of an approach along the Baldwin's Ferry road toward the 2nd Texas Lunette, which was about 100 yards distant. Two days later they started a second approach that ran from the same hollow about fifty yards south of and parallel to the first approach. Later these two approaches were connected by a trench that was converted into a parallel. The enemy began mining operations June 25, then exploded a mine that did no damage. The left approach reached the crater July 1, and that same day the right approach reached a point across the Baldwin road from the lunette. A mine was then started from the left approach, and had reached a point within a few feet of the lunette when Vicksburg was surrendered.

Carr's Approach. On the front of Eugene A. Carr's division, two approaches were run out toward the Railroad Redoubt. The right approach was started June 2, 1863 in a cut on the Southern Railroad of Mississippi, about 350 yards east of the redoubt, and ran west along the railroad. The left approach began at a point about 300 yards to the southeast of the redoubt. By mid-June, the heads of both approaches were within about eighty yards of the redoubt. At that point, the two approaches were connected by a trench, which was called the Second Parallel. Work was resumed on the approaches June 25, and by July 2 they were within ten yards of the counterscarp of the Railroad Redoubt. Work was ended with the surrender of Vicksburg July 4.

Hovey's Approach. On the night of June 24, 1863, Hovey completed a second parallel on his front, which was about 200 yards from the Square Fort (later named Fort Garrott), and he then began work on two approaches toward the fort. The right approach began near the left of Hovey's Second Parallel in a ravine about 180 yards southeast of the Square Fort, and the right approach was started in a hollow 160 yards from the fort. The two approaches joined about thirty yards southeast of the fort, and the head of the approach was within twenty yards of the ditch when the work ended July 3.

Slack's Approach. Men of Slack's brigade began work on an approach on the night of June 30, 1863, and it was directed toward a part of the enemy line held by the 23rd Alabama of Stephen D. Lee's brigade. Work was started near the right of Hovey's Second Parallel, about 275 yards northeast of the Square Fort, and the head of the approach was within ten yards of the enemy position when work was halted July 3.

Lauman's Approach. An approach was constructed by men of Lauman's division on the right of the Hall's Ferry road, and it was pushed out toward an earthwork called the Salient Work, which was about one mile south of the Square Fort where the Hall's Ferry road entered Vicksburg. The work on this approach involved a great deal of labor in construction of parallels and batteries and the emplacement of guns, and also was attended by considerable fighting, especially with artillery fire. Lauman completed a second parallel, and started work on a third parallel on the evening of June 21, 1863. The uncompleted work was captured by the enemy, but was restarted June 24 and was then opened and extended. On the night of June 25, an approach was started from the Third Parallel toward the Salient Work, which was only eighty-five yards distant. The head of the sap was within twenty-five yards of the Salient Work at the end of June, and was near the counterscarp when work ended July 3.

Herron's Approach. Herron's Division was on the extreme left of the Federal line at Vicksburg, where approach operations were difficult because of the nature of the ground. Nevertheless, Herron's men moved out on the night of June 16, 1863 and opened a line of rifle pits west of Stout's Bayou, about 800 yards from the enemy's fortifications. Artillery was then brought up to support the troops holding this line. There was no significant change in the position of Herron's troops until they opened and occupied a new parallel 200–300 yards from the enemy works. From then until the end of the siege, fighting on Herron's front was limited to artillery fire.

Surrender of Vicksburg, Mississippi, July 4, 1863. By July 1, 1863, Grant's approaches had reached the ditch in front of the enemy's works at several places, and at many others it was possible to move troops forward under cover to points within 100 to 500 yards of the works, and orders were then issued for an assault to be made July 6. At that time Pemberton was convinced that he could expect no help from Johnston, whose army was between Brownsville and the Big Black River, and he asked his four division commanders whether, in their opinion, they would be able to break through Grant's lines and evacuate their positions in front of Vicksburg. In reply, two suggested surrender, and the other two expressed their belief that an attempt at evacuation would fail.

At 10:00 A.M. July 3, 1863, white flags appeared above a part of the Confederate works, and all firing stopped immediately on that part of the line. Then General John S. Bowen, a division commander, and Louis M. Montgomery, Pemberton's aide-de-camp, approached the Union lines under a flag of truce, bearing a letter for Grant. In this letter, Pemberton proposed an armistice for the purpose of arranging terms for the surrender of Vicksburg. Bowen was received by Andrew J. Smith, commanding Tenth Division, Thirteenth Corps, and he asked Smith if he might see Grant. This request was refused, but then Bowen suggested that Grant meet with Pemberton. Grant agreed, and proposed that they meet at 3:00 that afternoon at a point in front of McPherson's corps.

At 3:00 P.M., as Grant had suggested, Pemberton, accompanied by Bowen and Montgomery, appeared at the appointed place between the lines. Grant was there, accompanied by corps commanders Edward O. C. Ord and James B. McPherson, division commanders John A. Logan and Andrew J. Smith, and several officers of Grant's staff. The meeting was held near an oak tree, on a hillside, within a few hundred feet of the enemy's works. When informed by Grant that the terms were unconditional surrender, Pemberton turned as if to leave, but Bowen, who wanted the surrender to take place, proposed that he and one of Grant's generals discuss the matter. Grant agreed, and then Bowen and Andrew J. Smith had a conference while Grant and Pemberton moved some distance away.

Bowen suggested that the Confederate army be permitted to march out, with the honors of war, taking with them their small arms and field artillery. This proposal was immediately rejected, and the meeting ended. Grant, however, agreed to send a message stating his final terms by 10:00 that night.

Upon returning to his headquarters, Grant sent for all of his corps and division commanders who were near the front at that time. When they had assembled, he informed them of the contents of Pemberton's letter, and of his reply, and he also described what had transpired at their meeting that afternoon. He then invited their suggestions. As a result of this meeting, Grant sent a letter to Pemberton stating that when the terms that he had proposed had been accepted, he would send in one division as a guard and take possession of the city at 8:00 A.M. July 4, 1863. Then, when rolls had been prepared and paroles signed by the officers and men, Pemberton would be allowed to march with his men out of the Union lines. The officers were to take with them side arms and clothing; the field, staff, and cavalry officers one horse each; and the rank and file only their clothing. Grant had departed from his original demand for unconditional surrender, explaining later that there were several practical reasons for doing so. These were based largely on the problems associated with handling such a large number of prisoners if they were not granted parole.

Late that night, Pemberton replied that he would accept Grant's terms, and at 10:00 A.M. July 4, 1863, he proposed to evacuate the works in and around Vicksburg and surrender the city and garrison by marching out and stacking colors and arms in front of his present lines. After this was done, the Union army could move in and take possession of the city. Pemberton's reply did not express full compliance with Grant's terms, and Grant then sent a message stating that if those terms were not fully accepted by 9:00 A.M. July 4, he would resume hostilities at once.

Pemberton finally capitulated and accepted the terms of surrender, and at the time agreed upon, the garrison of Vicksburg marched out and stacked their arms in front of their works. It was a solemn moment, and there was no cheering by the Union soldiers. After the arms were stacked, the men of the garrison marched back into their lines to wait until paroles could be prepared and signed.

Logan's Third Division, Seventeenth Corps,

which was nearest to the Confederate works, was the first to march into the city. There was almost immediate fraternization of the men of the two armies, and many of the Northern soldiers shared their rations with their erstwhile, and nearly starved, enemies.

By July 11, 1863, the paroles had been completed, and Pemberton's men marched out of the lines that they had held so valiantly and so long and began their long journey home. Pemberton surrendered a reported 29,500 men, 172 cannon, 60,000 muskets, and large quantities of ammunition.

The organization of Grant's Army of the Tennessee at the Siege of Vicksburg May 18–July 4, 1863 was as follows:

NINTH CORPS, John G. Parke

First Division, Thomas Welch
    First Brigade, Henry Bowman
    Second Brigade, Daniel Leasure
    Artillery
        Battery D, Pennsylvania Light Artillery, George W. Durell

Note 1. Parke's Ninth Corps joined from the Department of the Ohio June 14–17, 1863.
Note 2. Durell's battery was transferred from Second Division June 25, 1863.

Second Division, Robert B. Potter
    First Brigade, Simon G. Griffin
    Second Brigade, Edward Ferrero
    Third Brigade, Benjamin C. Christ
    Artillery
        Battery L, 2nd New York Light Artillery, Jacob Roemer

Artillery Reserve
    Battery E, 2nd United States Artillery, Samuel N. Benjamin

THIRTEENTH CORPS, John A. McClernand, to June 19, 1863
    Edward O. C. Ord

Ninth Division, Peter J. Osterhaus
    First Brigade, Albert L. Lee, to May 19, 1863, wounded
        James Keigwin
    Second Brigade, Daniel W. Lindsey
    Artillery, Jacob T. Foster
        7th Battery, Michigan Light Artillery, Charles H. Lanphere

1st Battery, Wisconsin Light Artillery, Oscar F. Nutting

Tenth Division, Andrew J. Smith
    First Brigade, Stephen G. Burbridge
    Second Brigade, William J. Landram
    Artillery
        Chicago Mercantile Battery, Illinois Light Artillery, Patrick H. White
        17th Battery, Ohio Light Artillery, Ambrose A. Blount
        Charles S. Rice

Twelfth Division, Alvin P. Hovey
    First Brigade, George F. McGinnis
    Second Brigade, James R. Slack
    Artillery
        Battery A, 1st Missouri Light Artillery, George W. Schofield
        2nd Battery, Ohio Light Artillery, Augustus Beach
        16th Battery, Ohio Light Artillery, Russell P. Twist

Fourteenth Division, Eugene A. Carr
    First Brigade, William P. Benton, to May 31, 1863, sick
        Henry D. Washburn, to June 27, 1863, sick
        David Shunk
    Second Brigade, Michael K. Lawler
    Artillery
        Battery A, 2nd Illinois Light Artillery, Frank B. Fenton
            Peter Davidson
        1st Battery, Indiana Light Artillery, Martin Klauss

FIFTEENTH CORPS, William T. Sherman

First Division, Frederick Steele
    First Brigade, Francis H. Manter, to June 13, 1863
        Bernard G. Farrar
    Second Brigade, Charles R. Woods
    Third Brigade, John M. Thayer
    Artillery
        1st Battery, Iowa Light Artillery, Henry H. Griffiths
        Battery F, 2nd Missouri Light Artillery, Clemens Landgraeber
        4th Battery, Ohio Light Artillery, Louis Hoffmann

Note. Farrar arrived from Missouri and, because of seniority, assumed command of First Brigade. Manter was assigned to duty at Steele's headquarters.

Second Division, Frank P. Blair, Jr.
    First Brigade, Giles A. Smith

Second Brigade, T. Kilby Smith, to May 24, 1863
  Joseph A. J. Lightburn, by seniority
Third Brigade, Hugh Ewing
Artillery
  Battery A, 1st Illinois Light Artillery, Peter P.
    Wood
  Battery B, 1st Illinois Light Artillery, Samuel E.
    Barrett
    Israel P. Rumsey
  Battery H, 1st Illinois Light Artillery, Levi W. Hart
  8th Battery, Ohio Light Artillery, James F. Putnam

Third Division, James M. Tuttle
  First Brigade, Ralph P. Buckland, to June 22, 1863,
    on furlough
    William L. McMillen
  Second Brigade, Joseph A. Mower
  Third Brigade, Charles L. Matthies, to June 1, 1863
    Joseph J. Woods
  Artillery, Nelson T. Spoor
    Battery E, 1st Illinois Light Artillery, Allen C.
      Waterhouse
    2nd Battery, Iowa Light Artillery, Joseph R. Reed

Unattached Cavalry
  4th Iowa Cavalry, Simeon D. Swan

SIXTEENTH CORPS (DETACHMENT), Cadwallader
  C. Washburn

First Division, William Sooy Smith
  First Brigade, John M. Loomis
  Second Brigade, Stephen G. Hicks
  Third Brigade, Joseph R. Cockerill
  Fourth Brigade, William W. Sanford
  Artillery, William Cogswell
    Battery F, 1st Illinois Light Artillery, John T.
      Cheney
    Battery I, 1st Illinois Light Artillery, William N.
      Lansing
    Cogswell's Battery, Illinois Light Artillery, Henry
      G. Eddy
    6th Battery, Indiana Light Artillery, Michael
      Mueller

Note. First Division joined from La Grange, Tennessee June 12, 1863.

Fourth Division, Jacob G. Lauman
  First Brigade, Isaac C. Pugh
  Second Division, Cyrus Hall
  Third Brigade, George E. Bryant, to June 9, 1863
    Amory K. Johnson
  Artillery, George C. Gumbart

Battery E, 2nd Illinois Light Artillery, George L.
  Nispel
Battery K, 2nd Illinois Light Artillery, Benjamin F.
  Rodgers
5th Battery, Ohio Light Artillery, Anthony B. Burton
7th Battery, Ohio Light Artillery, Silas A. Burnap
15th Battery, Ohio Light Artillery, Edward Spear,
  Jr.

Note. Fourth Division joined from Memphis, Tennessee May 13–20, 1863. It was assigned to Thirteenth Corps on June 24, and was permanently transferred July 28.

Provisional Division, Nathan Kimball
  Engelmann's Brigade, Adolph Engelmann
  Richmond's Brigade, Jonathan Richmond
  Montgomery's Brigade, Milton Montgomery

Note 1. Kimball's division joined from Memphis, Tennessee June 3, 1863.
Note 2. Engelmann's Brigade was formerly First Brigade, Third Division (or District of Jackson), Sixteenth Corps; Richmond's Brigade was Second Brigade, Third Division (or District of Jackson), Sixteenth Corps; and Montgomery's Brigade was composed of four regiments from Sixth Division (or District of Columbus), Sixteenth Corps.

SEVENTEENTH CORPS, James B. McPherson

Third Division, John A. Logan
  First Brigade, John E. Smith, to June 3, 1863
    Mortimer D. Leggett
  Second Brigade, Mortimer D. Leggett, to June 3, 1863
    Manning F. Force
  Third Brigade, John D. Stevenson
  Artillery, Charles J. Stolbrand
    Battery D, 1st Illinois Light Artillery, Henry A.
      Rogers
      George J. Wood
      Frederick Sparrestrom
    Battery G, 2nd Illinois Light Artillery, Frederick
      Sparrestrom
      John W. Lowell
    Battery L, 2nd Illinois Light Artillery, William H.
      Bolton
    8th Battery, Michigan Light Artillery, Samuel De
      Golyer
      Theodore W. Lockwood
    3rd Battery, Ohio Light Artillery, William S. Williams

Note. Battery G, 2nd Illinois Light Artillery rejoined the army at Vicksburg from Memphis, where it had been sent to refit, June 30, 1863. Meantime, on June 16, Sparrestrom had been assigned to Battery D, 1st Illinois Light Artillery.

Sixth Division, John McArthur
   First Brigade, Hugh T. Reid
   Second Brigade, Thomas E. G. Ransom
   Third Brigade, William Hall, to June 6, 1863
     Alexander Chambers
   Artillery, Thomas D. Maurice
     Battery F, 2nd Illinois Light Artillery, John W. Powell
     1st Battery, Minnesota Light Artillery, Henry Hurter
     William Z. Clayton
     Battery C, 1st Missouri Light Artillery, Charles Mann
     10th Battery, Ohio Light Artillery, Hamilton B. White
     William L. Newcomb

Note 1. Reid's First Brigade was at Lake Providence.
Note 2. Chambers, who had been wounded at the Engagement at Iuka, Mississippi September 19, 1862, returned to the army from leave June 6, 1863 and as senior officer assumed command of Third Brigade. Hall resumed command of his 11th Iowa Regiment.

Seventh Division, Isaac F. Quinby, to June 3, 1863, sick
   John E. Smith
   First Brigade, John B. Sanborn
   Second Brigade, Samuel A. Holmes, to June 10, 1863
     Green B. Raum
   Third Brigade, George B. Boomer, to May 22, 1863, killed
     Holden Putnam, to June 2, 1863

     Charles L. Matthies
   Artillery, Frank C. Sands, to June 6, 1863
     Henry Dillon
     Battery M, 1st Missouri Light Artillery, Junius W. MacMurray
     11th Battery, Ohio Light Artillery, Fletcher E. Armstrong
     6th Battery, Wisconsin Light Artillery, Henry Dillon, to June 6, 1863
     Samuel F. Clark
     12th Battery, Wisconsin Light Artillery, William Zickerick

Note. Holmes resigned June 10, 1863 for medical reasons.

HERRON'S DIVISION, Francis J. Herron
   First Brigade, William Vandever
   Second Brigade, William W. Orme

Note. Nelson Cole's Battery E, 1st Missouri Light Artillery and Joseph Foust's Battery F, 1st Missouri Light Artillery were attached to First Brigade; and Martin Welfley's Battery B, 1st Missouri Light Artillery was attached to Second Brigade.

UNATTACHED CAVALRY, Cyrus Bussey

DISTRICT OF NORTHEAST LOUISIANA, Elias S. Dennis

Detached Brigade, George W. Neeley
   African Brigade, Isaac F. Shepard
     Post of Milliken's Bend, Louisiana, Hiram Scofield
     Post of Goodrich's Landing, Louisiana, William F. Wood

INDEX OF CAMPAIGNS, BATTLES, ENGAGEMENTS, AND EXPEDITIONS

Note: Page numbers for Volume I are in lightface; page numbers for Volume II are in **bold.**

INDEX OF NAMES

Note: Page numbers for Volume I are in lightface; page numbers for Volume II are in **bold.**

INDEX OF UNION BATTERIES, REGIMENTS, AND OTHER ORGANIZATIONS

Note: Page numbers for Volume I are in lightface; page numbers for Volume II are in **bold.**

FRANK J. WELCHER is Professor Emeritus of Chemistry at Indiana University and at Purdue University. At the age of eleven, he visited the battlefield of Chickamauga with his father, and that event was the beginning of a lifelong interest in Civil War military history.